THE NEW
ANNUAL ARMY LIST,

AND

MILITIA LIST,

FOR

1860

(BEING THE TWENTY FIRST ANNUAL VOLUME),

CONTAINING

DATES OF COMMISSIONS, AND A STATEMENT OF THE WAR
SERVICES AND WOUNDS OF NEARLY EVERY OFFICER
IN THE ARMY, ORDNANCE, AND MARINES.

Corrected to the 29th December, 1859.

WITH AN INDEX.

BY

H. G. HART,

LIEUT.-COLONEL, H. P. DEPOT BATTALION.

LONDON:
JOHN MURRAY, ALBEMARLE STREET.
1860.

NOTICE.

It is particularly requested that ALL Communications be addressed ONLY to

LIEUT.COLONEL HART,

50, Albemarle Street,

London.

CONTENTS.

	PAGE
Actions or Battles	545
Adjutants of Recruiting Districts	369
Aides-de-Camp to the Queen	125
Artillery, Royal	370
Barrack-Masters	465
Canadian Rifles	356
Cape Mounted Riflemen	354
Cavalry Depôts	359
Ceylon Rifle Regiment	353
Chaplain Department	455
Chatham Garrison	359
Chelsea Hospital	463
Colonels	26
Commissariat Department	435
Depôt Battalions	359
Dragoon Guards	129
Dragoons	136
Engineers, Royal	390
Field Marshals	3
Fixed Establishment of General Officers	4
Foot Guards	159
Foot (Numbered Regiments)	169
Garrisons	463
General Officers	6
General Officers of the Indian Army	120
Gentlemen at Arms, the Honourable Corps of	123
Gold Coast Corps	358
Half-pay List	470
Hibernian Military School	463
Horse Guards, Royal Regiment of	128
Inspecting Field Officers	369
Invalid Depôt at Chatham	359
Kilmainham Hospital	463

	PAGE
Lieutenant-Colonels	40
Life Guards	126, 127
Local Rank	119
Majors	74
Malta Fencibles	368
Marines, Royal	411
Medals, &c. (Gold)	545
Medical Department	439
Military College	462
Military Asylum	463
Military Knights of Windsor	124
Military Prisons	463
Military Store Department	464
Military Train	156
Military and Civil Departments	462
Militia	615
Newfoundland Companies	357
Order of the Garter	548
——— Thistle	548
——— St. Patrick	548
——— Bath	549
——— St. Michael and St. George	555
Paymasters of Recruiting Districts	369
Retired Officers	103
Rewards for Distinguished Services	124
Rifle Brigade	343
St. Helena Regiment	357
School of Musketry at Hythe	358
Staff at Head Quarters	125
Staff of Great Britain	456
Staff on Foreign Stations	458
Staff Officers of Pensioners	452
West India Regiments	349
Yeomen of the Guard	122

EXPLANATIONS.

K.G.   Knight of the Order of the Garter.
K.T.   Knight of the Order of the Thistle.
K.P.   Knight of the Order of St. Patrick.
G.C.B. Knight *Grand Cross* of the Order of the Bath.
K.C.B. Knight *Commander* of the Order of the Bath.
C.B.   *Companion* of the Order of the Bath.
G.C.M.G. Knight *Grand Cross* of the Order of St. Michael and St. George.
K.C.M.G. Knight *Commander* of   ditto   ditto
C.M.G. *Companion* of   ditto   ditto
G.C.H. Knight *Grand Cross* of the Royal Hanoverian Guelphic Order.
K.C.H. Knight *Commander* of   ditto   ditto
K.H.   Knight of   ditto   ditto
K.C.   Knight of the Crescent.
 ☩   Before the Name, denotes that the Officer was at the battle of *Trafalgar*.
 ₽   Before the Name, denotes that the Officer served in the *Peninsula*, or the South of France.
 ⚜   Waterloo Medal. { Officers actually present in either of the actions of the 16th, 17th, or 18th June, 1815. Such Officers are allowed two years' additional service.
 V.C.   Victoria Cross.

The Figures prefixed to the Names denote the Battalions to which the Officers are *actually attached;* the Letters *s.* and *r.* after the name distinguish Officers employed on the *Staff*, or on the *Recruiting Service.* The Letters *R. M.* in the Cavalry Regiments allude to the Riding Masters; The * *before* the Name or Date of Commission denotes Temporary Rank only. The Letter ᴾ *before* the Date indicates that the Commission was *purchased.* General Officers, with the prefix of a †, are on the half pay of their last Regimental Commissions.

The words subscribed to the titles of Regiments, as " Peninsula," " Waterloo," &c., denote the Honorary Distinctions permitted to be borne by such Regiments on their colours and appointments, in commemoration of their Services.

NEW ANNUAL ARMY LIST.

1860.

FIELD-MARSHALS.

His Majesty the KING *of the* BELGIANS, KG. GCB. GCH., *General*, 2 May 1816 *Field Marshal*, 24 May 1816.

His Royal Highness FRANCIS ALBERT AUGUSTUS CHARLES EMANUEL, THE PRINCE CONSORT, *Duke of* SAXONY, *Prince of* SAXE COBURG AND GOTHA, KG. KT. KP. GCB. GCMG., 8 Feb. 1840. Colonel of the Grenadier Guards, 23 Sept. 1852; Governor and Constable of Windsor Castle, 18 May 1843; and Colonel-in-Chief of the Rifle Brigade, 23 Sept. 1852.

STAPLETON, *Viscount* COMBERMERE, GCB. GCH., *Second Lieutenant*, 26 Feb. 90; *Lieutenant*, 16 March 91; *Captain*, 28 Feb. 93; *Major*, March 94; *Lieut. Colonel*, 9 March 94; *Colonel*, 1 Jan. 00; *Major General*, 30 Oct. 05; *Lieut.General*, 1 Jan. 12; *General*, 27 May 25; *Field Marshal*, 2 Oct. 55; Constable of the Tower 11 Oct. 52; Colonel 1 Life Guards, 16 Sept. 29.

JOHN, *Earl of* STRAFFORD, GCB. GCH. *Ensign*, 30 Sept. 93; *Lieutenant* 1 Dec. 93; *Captain*, 24 May 94; *Lieut.Colonel*, 14 March 00; *Colonel*, 25 July 10; *Major General*, 4 June 13; *Lieut.General*, 27 May 25; *General*, 23 Nov. 41; *Field Marshal*, 2 Oct. 55; Governor of Londonderry and Culmore, 15 June 22; Colonel Coldstream Guards, 15 August 50.

B

FIXED ESTABLISHMENT OF GENERAL OFFICERS.

GENERALS.

1830. 22 July.
Francis Moore

1837. 10 January.
P John M'Kenzie

1841. 23 Nov.
P Richard Blunt, 66 F.
P Sir T. Makdougall Brisbane, Bart. GCB. GCH. 34 F.

1851. 11 Nov.
P Sir John Wright Guise, Bt. KCB. 85 F.
Richard Pigot, d Dr. Gds.
Sir Jas. Watson, KCB. 14 F.
P Sir H. Douglas, Bt. GCB. & GCMG. 15 F.

1854. 20 June.
Dennis Herbert
P Rt. Hon. Sir E. Blakeney, GCB. & GCH. 1 F. Gov. of Chelsea Hospital
P Sir John, Lord Seaton, GCB. GCMG. GCH. 2 Life Guards, Commanding the Troops in Ireland
P Sir Thomas M'Mahon, Bt. GCB. 10 F.
P Sir Alex. Woodford, GCB. GCMG. 40 F. Lt.-Gov. of Chelsea Hospital
Cosmo Gordon

P Hugh, Visc. Gough, KP. GCB. R. Horse Gds., Col. in-Chief of the 60th Rifles
P Sir James W. Sleigh, KCB. 9 Lancers
P Sir J.F. FitzGerald, KCB. 18 F.
P Sir Arthur B. Clifton, KCB. & KCH. 1 Drs.
P Hon. Hugh Arbuthnott, CB. 38 F.
P Sir J. Douglas, KCB. 42F.
P Sir Willoughby Cotton, GCB. KCH. 32 F.
P Sir J. Hanbury, KCH. 99 F.
P H. R. Earl Beauchamp, 10 Hussars
P Hon. E. P. Lygon, CB. 13 Drs.
Sir Geo. Whitmore, KCH. Royal Engineers
Henry Shadforth
P Sir Wm. Tuyll, KCH. 7 Hussars
Sackville H. Berkeley, 16 F.
Heller Touzel
P Sir George Scovell, KCB. 4 Lt. Drs.
P Ulysses, Lord Downes, KCB. 20 F.
P G. Marq. of Tweeddale, KT. CB. 30 F.

P Sir Henry Wyndham, KCB. 11 Hussars
P Fred. Ren. Thackeray, CB. R. Eng.
Gustavus Nicolls, R. Eng.
P Henry Evelegh, R. Art.
P Sir Edward Bowater, KCH. 49 F.
Joseph W. Tobin, R. Art.
P Sir W. M. Gomm, GCB. 13 F.

1854. 28 Nov.
P Sir H. D. Ross, GCB. R. Art.
P Sir Rob. Wm. Gardiner, GCB. KCH. R. Art.

1855.
P Hon. Henry Murray, CB. 14 Drs. 6 Feb.
T. Evans, CB. 81 F. 18 May
P Sir A. Maclaine, KCB. 52 F. 5 June
P Wm. Wood, CB. KH. 3 West India Regt. 31 Aug.
P Sir J. F. Burgoyne, Bt. GCB. R. Eng. Insp.Gen. of Fortifications 5 Sept.
P Sir Geo. Brown, GCB. KH. Rifle Brig. 7 Sept.
P Sir James Simpson, GCB. 87 F. 8 Sept.

1856. 20 Feb.
P C. Ashe a'Court-Repington, CB. KH. 41 F.

1856. 15 July.
His Royal Highness George W. F. C. Duke of Cambridge, KG. KP. GCB. GCMG. Scots Fusilier Guards, Comm. in Chief

1857.
P Wm. G. Power, CB. KH. R. Art. 4 Feb.
P H. J. Riddell, KH. 6 F. 26 Sept.

1858. 14 May.
P Colin, Lord Clyde, GCB. 93 F. Comm. in Chief E. Indies

1859.
P H. C. E. Vernon, CB. 2 Apr.
P Sir J. A. Hope, KCB. 9F. 12 June
P Sir Robert J. Harvey, CB. 2 West India Regt. 17 July
P Sir Frederick Stovin, KCB. KCMG. 83 F. 14 Aug.
F. Campbell, R. Art. 25 Sept.
P Sir Wm. F. P. Napier, KCB. 22 F. 17 Oct.
P J. Reeve, 61 F. 7 Dec.

LIEUTENANT-GENERALS.

1851. 11 Nov.
P Sir Charles Wm. Pasley, KCB. R. Eng.
P C.G. Ellicombe, CB. R. Eng.
P Thomas Kenan, CB. 63 F.
E. B. Wynyard, CB. 58 F.
P Sir James Ferguson, KCB. 43 F.
P Sir Tho. W. Brotherton KCB. 1 Dr. Gds.
P Sir A. J. Dalrymple, Bt.
P Sir James Hy. Reynett, KCH. 48 F.
P Sir John Bell, KCB. 4 F.
P Sir S. B. Auchmuty, KCB. 7 F.
P Sir J. Aitchison, KCB. 72F.

1854. 20 June.
P Wm. Jervois, KH. 76 F.
P Sir F. Cockburn, 95 F.
P R. Llewllyn, CB. 30 F.
P P. A. Lautour, 3 Drs. CB. KH.
P Sir Wm. Chalmers, CB. KCH. 78 F.
P Sir Harry George W. Smith, Bt. GCB. Rifle Br.
P Sir De Lacy Evans, GCB. 21 F.
P Wm. Hen. Scott, 36 F.
P Sir Tho. Willshire, Bart., KCB. 51 F.
P Edw. Fleming, CB. 27 F.
P P. Dainbrigge, CB. 20 F.
P Thos. E. Napier, CB. 71 F.
P W. H. Sewell, CB. 70 F.
P W. L. Darling, 98 F.
P Sir John M'Donald, KCB. 62 F.
P Geo. Wm. Paty, CB. KH. 70 F.

P Lord Jas. Hay, 86 F.
P Tho. J. Wemyss, CB. 17 F.
P Sir William Rowan, KCB. 19 F.
P Jas. Shaw Kennedy, CB. 47 F.
P A. W. M. Lord Sandys, 2 Drs.
P G. L. Goldie, CB. 77 F.
P Geo. P. Higginson, 94 F.
P Sir George Bowles, KCB. 1 W. I. R., Lieut. of the Tower of London
P Hon. H. F. C. Cavendish, 2 Dr. Gds.
P T. W. Robbins, 80 F.
P Roderick Macneil, 8 F.
Wm. Sutherland, CB. 54 F.
P H. Rainey, CB. KH. 93 F.
P Hon. Charles Gore, CB. KH. 91 F.
P W. L. Walton, 5 F.
Thomas J. Forbes, R. Art.
Charles Richard Fox
P Charles Aug. Shawe, 74 F.

1854. Nov. 28.
P Geo. Turner, CB. R. Art.
P. M. Wallace, R. Art.
Richard Jones, R. Art.
P John Michell, CB. R. Art.

1855.
P M. Fano, 96 F. 30 Jan.
P Sir J. M. Wallace, KH. 17 Lancers 6 Feb.
P Hon. John Finch, CB. 24 F. 20 Feb.
P Sir Wm. G. Moore, KCB. 60 F. 5 June

1856.
P F. C. Whinyates, CB. KH. R. Art. 1 June

Sir Richard England, GCB. KH. 50 F. 4 June
Sir Wm. John Codrington, KCB. 54 F. Governor and Comm. in Chief of Gibraltar 6 June
P Thomas Dyneley, CB. R. Art. 16 Dec.

1857.
P Sir Henry Somerset, KCB. KH., 25 F. Comm. in Chief at Bombay 20 Jan.
Geo. Cobbe, R. Art. 4 Feb.
P Alex. C. Mercer, from R. Art. 28 Aug.
Sir Geo. Aug. Wetherall, KCB. KH. 84 F. Adj.-General 8 Sept.
P Sir J. F. Love, KCB. KH. 57F. Inspector Gen. of Infantry 26 Sept.
P Sir D. M'Gregor, KCB. 12 Dec.

1858.
P Nicholas Hamilton, KH. 82 F. 11 Jan.
P Cha. Anth. Ferdinand Bentinck, 12 F. 15 Jan.
Cha. Geo. Jas. Arbuthnot, 89 F. 13 Mar.
C. G. Falconar, KH. 73 F. 20 July
P Alex. Fisher Macintosh, KH. 90 F. 2 Aug.
P Jos. Paterson, 60F. Gds. John H. Home, 56 F. 22 Sept.
J. Spink, KH. 2 F. 22 Oct.
P Sir James Jackson, KCB. KH. 6 Drs.

P Robert C. Mansel, KH. 68 F. Commanding the Eastern District 22 Oct.
P John Drummond do.
P Jas. Freeth, KH. 64 F. do.
Sir Charles R. O'Donnell do.
John Leslie, KH. 35 F. do.
P Robert B. Coles, 65 F. do.
P E. P. Buckley do.
Sir Rich. Doherty, 11 F. do.
P Edw. Byam, 18 Drs. 16 Nov.
P G. J. Harding, CB. R. Eng. 23 Nov.
Geo. Cha. Earl of Lucan, KCB. 8 Hussars 24 Dec.

1859.
Sir W. M. G. Colebrooke, CB. KH. R. Art. 10 Jan.
P Sir Cha. Yorke, KCB. 33 F. Mil. Sec. to H.R.H. Comm. in Chief 13 Feb.
P Sir John R. Eustace, KH. 2 Apr.
P B. Drummond, 3F. 9 Apr.
P J. Oldfield, KH. R. Eng. 10 May
P Hon. Sir E. Cust, KCH. 16 Drs. 14 May.
Dennis Daly 12 June
P Jer. Taylor, 50 F. 17 June
P F. J. Davies, 67 F. 14 Aug.
P Wm. Cator, CB. from R. Art. 25 Sept.
P John Fraser, 87 F. 17 Oct.
Sir J. M. Fred. Smith, KH. from R. Eng. 25 Oct.
Marcus Beresford, 20 F. 7 Dec.
P Sir James C. Chatterton, Bt. KH. 5 Drs. 13 Dec.

MAJOR-GENERALS.

1854. 20 June.
J. A. Earl of Rosslyn
P Wm. Thomas Knollys, Lt. Gen. Commanding at Aldershot
Sir H. R. Ferguson Davie, Bt.
P E. F. Gascoigne, 69 F. Commanding Dublin District
P Sir L. B. Lovell, KCB. KH. 12 Lancers

P St. J. A. Clerke, KH. 75F.
P Sir James H. Schoedde, KCB. 55 F.
Sir Henry J. W. Bentinck, KCB. 28 F.
P Thos. Reed, CB. 44 F.
Henry Visc. Melville, KCB. 100 F. Commanding the Troops in Scotland
P A. K. Clarke Kennedy, CB. KH. 6 Dr. Gds.
P Horatio George Broke, 98 F.

P. E. Craigie, CB. 31 F. Commanding a Div. of the Madras Army
Edmund F. Morris, CB. 97 F.
Henry Colvile
P E. Wm. Bouverie, 15 Hussars
Hon. Thomas Ashburnham, CB. from 29 F.
P Wm. CB. 7 Dr. Gds.
John Scott, CB. from 9 Lancers
Sir J. L. Pennefather, KCB.

46 F. Lt. Gen. Commanding Northern District
P E. W. Bell, Lt. Governor Commanding the Troops at Jamaica
P Thomas Burke
Jas. Tho. Earl of Cardigan, KCB. 5 Dr. Gds., Inspecting General of Cavalry
Sir Michael Creagh, KH.
John Eden, CB. Commanding the Cork District
Hon. Charles Grey

Fixed Establishment of General Officers.

W. Lord de Ros, Deputy Lieut. of the Tower
♀ John Geddes, KH.
P. S. Stanhope, from Gr. Gds.
♀ A. Maclachlan, from R. Art.
C. M. Hay, from Cold. Gds.
♛ Henry, Lord Rokeby, KCB, from Sco. Fus. Gds. Inspecting General of Foot Guards
Henry Edward Porter
John Dawson Rawdon
♛ Wm. Beckwith, KH.
♀ Henry Edw. Robinson
Henry E. Breton, from 53 F. Commanding the Troops at the Mauritius
♛ A. T. Maclean, from 13 Drs.
J. J. W. Angerstein, fr. Gr. Gds.
♛ Tho. Marten, KH.
♀ Thomas Gerrard Ball
♛ Eaton Monins
Geo. M. Eden, from Sco. Fus. Gds.
Geo. Dixon, fr. Sco. Fus. Gds.
♛ Fred. Maunsell, from Insp. Field Officer
Henry A. Scott, from R. Art.
Wm. Wylde, CB, from do.
Wm. Fludyer, from Gr. Gds.
John Winston Frith, from Insp. Field Officer
Henry Charles Russel, from R. Art.
John Hall, from 1 Life Gds.

1854. 28 Nov,
H. W. Gordon, from R. Art.
Geo. Henry Lockwood, CB.

1854. 12 Dec.
Sir Richard Airey, KCB. Quarter Master General
Sir Hugh H. Rose, GCB. 45 F. on the Staff in India
Hon. Sir Jas. Yorke Scarlett, KCB, from 5 Dr. Gds. Commanding South Western District
♀ Sir Harry D. Jones, KCB, from R. Eng. Governor Royal Military College
Sir George Buller, KCB.

from Rifle Br. Commanding the Troops in the Ionian Islands
1854. 16 Dec.
♛♛ William Brereton, CB. KH. from R. Art.

1855.
Francis Rawdon Chesney, from R. Art. 6 Jan.
John B. Gough, CB. Commanding a Brigade in Dublin 30 Jan.
Hon. Arthur Upton, from Coldst. Gds. 20 Feb.
Sir A. Josiah Cloete, CB. KH. Unatt. Commanding the Troops in the Windward and Leeward Isles 31 Aug.
♛♛ G. Macdonald 7 Sept.
♛♛ John Cox, KH. 18 Dec.

1856.
James Robertson Craufurd, from Gr. Gds. 19 June
Wm. S. Balfour 22 Aug.
William Booth 23 Sept.
Richard Greaves 9 Nov.

1857.
Thomas Gordon Higgins, from R. Art. Jan. 24
♛♛ Wm. Henry Elliott, KH. 29 Jan.
♀ Wm. Freke Williams, KH. Commanding a Brigade at Shorncliffe 14 April
Pringle Taylor, KH. 16 May
Tho. Henry Johnston 4 June
Henry A. Hankey 6 July
♛♛ John Campbell 9 July
Plomer Young, KH. 17 July
♛♛ William Bell, from R. Art. 20 Aug.
Henry Dive Townshend, from Depot Batt. 5 Sept.
Thomas Wright, CB. 8 Sept.

1858.
Thomas Wood, fr. Gr. Gds. 11 Jan.
Wm. H. Eden 15 Jan.
Joseph Clarke 16 Mar.
Sir J. Gaspard Le Merchant, Governor and Com-

mander-in-Chief at Malta 22 Mar.
Charles Gascoyne 3 Apr.
George Moncrieff, from Scots Fus. Gds. 14 June
♀ P. V. England, from R. Art. 9 Aug.
♀ Wm. Cuthbert Ward, from R. Eng. 2 Aug.
Marcus John Slade 26 Aug.
G. H. MacKinnon, CB. 22 Sept.
B. F. D. Wilson 10 Oct.
S. B. Boileau 26 Oct.
Hon. G. F. Upton, CB. from Coldst. Gds. do.
Hon. A. A. Dalzell do.
T. S. Pratt, CB. do.
♛♛ Orlando Felix do.
W. N. Hutchinson do.
♀ H. T. Lockyer, CB. KH. from 97 F. Commanding the Troops at Ceylon do.
Simeon Baynes do.
M. C. Johnstone, from 87 F. do.
♀ Wm. F. Forster, KH. Dep. Adj. General do.
F. Johnston do.
♀ Edw. Macarthur, CB. 26 Oct.
Day Hort Macdowall do.
♀ Sir Robert Garrett, KCB. KH. on the Staff in India do.
♛♛ A. H. Trevor, KH. do.
R. R. Wilford Brett do.
G. T. Colomb do.
Sir Sidney John Cotton, KCB, from 10 F., On the Staff, East Indies 26 Oct.
Man. Barlow do.
♀ J. N. Jackson, from 99 F. do.
Botet Trydell, from 83 F. do.
♀ J. Clark, KH. do.
R. W. Brough do.
E. H. D. E. Napier do.
Edward Harvey do.
Jus. Robt. Young do.
Sir John Michel, KCB., On the Staff, East Indies do.
R. P. Douglas do.
Chas. Craufurd Hay do.

W. L. Dames, from 37 F. 26 Oct.
C. Warren, CB., On the Staff at Malta do.
G. A. Malcolm, CB. do.
R. H. Wynyard, CB., from 58 F. Lt.Gen. Comm. the Forces at the C. of Good Hope, and Lieut.Gov. do.
♀ ♛♛ Richard Hardinge, KH., from R. Art. do.
Browne Willis, from R. Art. do.
♛♛ W. C. Anderson, from R. Art. do.
♀ W. R. Ord, from R. Eng. 1 Nov.
Henry Eyre 16 Nov.
♀ H. J. Savage, from R. Eng. 23 Nov.
Lord Wm. Paulet, Com a Brigade at Aldershot
♀ P. M'Pherson, CB. 34 Dec.

1859.
R. S. Armstrong, from R. Art. 16 Jan.
C. W. Ridley, CB. from Gr. Gds. 13 Feb.
John Patton 20 Feb.
D. A. Cameron, CB 25 Mar.
T. Matheson 2 Apr.
♀ George Bell, CB. 9 Apr.
H. N. Vigors, from St. Helena Regt. 1 May
L. A. Hall, from R. Eng. 10 May
R. Richardson-Robertson, CB. 14 May
S. Braybrooke, from Ceylon Rifles 12 June
♀ ♛♛ R. Law, KH. from R. Newfound. Comp. 17 July
Sir Chn. T. Van Strubenzee, KCB. 14 Aug.
Sir A. M. Tulloch, KCB. 9 Sept.
♀ ♛♛ J. Bloomfield, from R. Art. Insp. Gen. of Artillery 25 Sept.
W. G. Gold 17 Oct.
T. Foster, from R. Eng. 26 Oct.
Hon. R. Bruce 7 Dec.

GENERAL OFFICERS, Supernumerary to the Fixed Establishment, who were promoted, "FOR DISTINGUISHED SERVICE," out of their regular turn.

MAJOR GENERALS.
Sir Richard James Dacres, KCB., from Royal Artillery 29 June 55
Sir William Fenwick Williams, Bart. KCB. from Royal Artillery 2 Nov. 55
John Edward Dupuis, CB. from Royal Artillery 2 Nov. 55

Charles Ash Windham, CB. On Staff in India 8 Sept. 55
Sir John Eardley Wilmot Inglis, KCB, from 32 F. On the Staff in India 26 Nov. 57
Sir James Hope Grant, KCB, from 9 Lancers 26 Feb. 58
Sir William Rose Mansfield, KCB. 18 May 58
Sir Thomas Harte Franks, KCB, from 10 F. 20 July 58
Sir Edward Lugard, KCB, from 29 F., Secretary for Military Correspondence, War Office 20 July 58

GENERAL OFFICERS on the HALF-PAY of their former Regimental Commissions.

LIEUTENANT GENERALS.
Henry Duke of Cleveland, KG. Unattached 8 Sept. 57
♀ ♛♛ B. Lord Hotham, Unattached 26 Aug. 58
♀ ♛♛ Sir W. R. Clayton, Bt., Unatt. 26 Oct. 58
J. H. Richardson, Unatt. 2 Apr. 59
William Chamberlayne 17 July
Rt. Hon. Jonathan Peel, Unatt. 7 Dec.

MAJOR GENERALS.
J. H. Lord Howden, GCB. KH. Unatt. 29 June 54
♀ Thomas P. Thompson, do.
Fred. Thomas Buller, do.

Geo. Saunders Thwaites, h. p. 57 F. 20 June 54
♀ William Cowper Coles, Unatt. do.
Arthur Duke of Wellington, KG. Unattached do.
Jas. M. Haffie, h.p. 60 F. 31 Aug. 55
♀ Robert Blake Lynch, Unatt. do.
♛♛ Charles Diggle, KH. do. do.
♀ John Murray Belshes, do. do.
William Crokat, do. do.
♀ Norcliffe Norcliffe, KH. h.p. 18 Drs. do.
Robert Martin Leake, Unatt. do.
Alex. Maclean Fraser, do. 8 Dec 56
Peter Edwards, do. 14 Apr. 57
♀ ♛♛ William Cartwright, Unatt. 10 May 57
♛♛ Arthur Gore, do. do.

♀ David Goodsman, 10 May 57
♀ ♛♛ Thomas Robert Swinburne, Unattached 4 June 57
♛♛ George Whichcote, Unatt. do.
♛♛ James Arthur Butler, do. do.
♀ Fred. Meade, Unatt. 26 Oct. 58
♛♛ Albert Goldsmid, do. do.
♀ James Price Hely, KH., do. do.
♛♛ Chas. Rob. Bowers, do. do.
♀ John Arnaud, KH., do. do.
Richard Connop, do. do.
Thomas Molyneux Williams, KH., do. do.
♛♛ William Nepean, do. do.
W. Holmes Dutton, do. do.
♛♛ G. T. Earl of Albemarle, do. do.
Fra. Marq. of Conyngham, KP., GCH., do. do.

GENERALS.

	CORNET, 2d LIEUT. or ENSIGN.	LIEUT.	CAPTAIN.	MAJOR.	LIEUT.-COLONEL.	COLONEL.	MAJOR-GENERAL.	LIEUT.-GENERAL.	GENERAL.
Francis Moore	30 Sept. 87	31 Aug. 91	22 June 91	20 July 93	20 Dec. 94	1 Jan. 01	25 April 08	4 June 13	22 July 30
30 John M'Kenzie[1]	never	1 Jan. 87	13 Feb. 82	1 Mar. 94	15 July 95	29 April 02	25 Oct. 09	4 June 14	10 Jan. 37
30 Richard Blunt, 66 Foot	31 Jan. 87	23 Feb. 91	12 July 93	17 May 96	23 Aug. 99	25 Oct. 09	1 Jan. 12	27 May 25	23 Nov. 41
30 Sir T. Makdougall Brisbane, Bt., GCB. GCH., 34 Foot	10 Jan. 82	30 July 91	12 April 93	5 Aug. 95	4 April 00	25 July 10	4 June 13	do	do
30 Sir John Wright Guise, Bt., KCB, 85 Foot	4 Nov. 94	never	25 Oct. 98	never	25 July 05	4 June 13	12 Aug. 19	10 Jan. 37	11 Nov. 51
Richard Pigot, 4 Dragoon Guards	4 Sept. 93	16 Sept. 93	21 Dec. 98	29 April 02	1 May 06	4 June 14	19 July 21	do	do
Sir James Watson, KCB, 14 Foot	24 June 83	18 April 92	11 Mar. 95	3 Dec. 02	15 May 06	do	do	do	do
30 Sir Howard Douglas, Bt., GCB. GCMG., 15 Foot	1 Jan. 94	30 May 94	2 Oct. 99	20 Oct. 04	31 Dec. 06	do	do	do	do
Dennis Herbert[4]	Jan. 94	4 Sept. 94	21 Feb. 99	30 Jan. 00	28 Jan. 08	do	27 May	25 28 June	38 20 June 54
Alex. Armstrong,[5] Major on ret. full pay, late R. Irish Art.	7 July 83	31 Oct. 92	16 Dec. 98	24 July 00	25 April 08	do	do	do	do
Rt. Hon. Sir Edward Blakeney, GCB., GCH., 1 Foot, Governor of Chelsea Hospital	28 Feb. 94	24 Sept. 94	24 Dec. 94	17 Sept. 01	25 April 08	do	do	do	do
30 John, Lord Seaton, GCB. GCMG. GCH., 2 Life Guards, Commanding the Troops in Ireland	10 July 94	4 Sept. 94	12 Jan. 00	21 Jan. 08	2 Feb. 03	do	do	do	do
30 Sir Thomas M'Mahon, Bt., GCB., 10 Foot	2 Feb. 97	24 Oct. 99	8 Oct. 03	6 Nov. 06	4 May 09	do	do	do	do
30 Sir Alexander Woodford, GCB. GCMG., 40 Foot, Lieut. Governor of Chelsea Hospital	6 Dec. 94	15 July 95	11 Dec. 99	never	8 Mar. 10	do	do	do	do
Cosmo Gordon[6]	6 Dec. 92	28 Oct. 94	23 Oct. 00	12 Feb. 07	20 July 09	12 Aug. 19	22 July 30	23 Nov. 41	do
30 Hugh, Visct. Gough, KP., GCB., Royal Horse Guards, Colonel-in-Chief of 60 Rifles	7 Aug. 94	11 Oct. 94	25 June 03	8 Aug. 05	29 July 09	do	do	do	do
30 Sir James Wallace Sleigh, KCB., 9 Lancers	Feb. 95	29 April 95	25 Oct. 98	14 June 05	14 Dec. 09	do	do	do	do
Sir John Forster Fitzgerald, KCB., 18 Foot	29 Oct. 93	31 Jan. 94	9 May 94	25 Sept. 03	25 July 10	do	do	do	do
30 Sir Arthur Benj. Clifton, KCB. KCH., 1 Dragoons	6 June 94	7 Aug. 94	27 Feb. 99	17 Dec. 03	do	19 July 21	do	do	do
Hon. Hugh Arbuthnott, CB., 38 Foot	18 May 96	15 Sept. 96	20 Mar. 99	23 Nov. 04	9 May 11	do	do	do	do
Sir James Douglas, KCB, 42 Foot	10 July 99	19 June 00	16 Sept. 02	16 Feb. 09	30 May 11	do	do	do	do
Sir Willoughby Cotton, GCB. KCH., 32 Foot	31 Oct. 98	never	25 Nov. 99	never	12 June 12	25 July 21	do	do	do
Sir John Hanbury, KCH., 99 Foot	20 July 99	26 Sept. 99	3 June 02	never	20 Dec. 12	do	do	do	do
Henry Beauchamp, Earl Beauchamp, 10 Hussars	9 July 03	24 May 04	15 Jan. 07	14 May 12	18 June 15	24 Mar. 22	10 Jan. 37	9 Nov. 46	do
Hon. Edw. Pyndar Lygon, CB., 13 Lt. Dragoons	1 June 93	7 Nov. 05	15 Feb. 08	never	27 April 15	27 April 22	do	do	do
Sir George Whitmore, KCH., Royal Engineers	18 Sept. 93	5 Feb. 96	28 Feb. 01	4 June 13	21 July 13	23 Mar. 25	do	do	do
Henry Shadforth	23 May 97	26 Aug. 99	21 Mar. 00	25 Feb. 04	4 June 13	27 May 25	do	do	do
Sir William Tuyll, KCH., 7 Hussars	22 Oct. 99	18 July 01	7 April 04	20 Nov. 06	13 June 11	do	do	do	do
Sackville Hamilton Berkeley, 16 Foot	1 May 00	5 Nov. 00	25 Dec. 04	18 Feb. 08	20 June 11	do	do	do	do
Helier Touzel	20 Feb. 95	9 Dec. 95	4 Aug. 00	14 July 06	11 July 11	do	do	do	do
30 Sir George Scovell, KCB., 4 Light Dragoons	5 April 98	4 May 00	10 Mar. 04	30 May 11	17 Aug. 12	do	do	do	do
30 Ulysses, Lord Downes, KCB., 29 Foot	31 Mar. 04	12 Nov. 04	4 Sept. 06	31 Mar. 11	5 Sept. 12	do	do	do	do
30 George, Marquis of Tweeddale, KT. CB., 30 Foot	June 04	12 Oct. 04	14 May 07	14 May 12	21 June 13	27 May 25	do	do	do
30 Sir Henry Wyndham, KCB. 11 Hussars	27 Mar. 06	never	8 June 09	9 Aug. 13	20 Jan. 14	do	do	do	do
30 Frederick Rennell Thackeray, CB., Royal Engineers	18 Sept. 93	18 June 56	18 April 01	19 May 10	21 July 13	2 June 25	do	do	do

Generals.

	CORNET, 2d LIEUT. or ENSIGN.	LIEUT.	CAPTAIN.	MAJOR.	LIEUT.-COLONEL.	COLONEL.	MAJOR-GENERAL.	LIEUT.-GENERAL.	GENERAL.
Gustavus Nicolls, Royal Engineers	6 Mar. 94	3 Mar. 97	30 Mar. 02	4 June 13	1 Sept. 13	29 July 25	10 Jan. 37	9 Nov. 46	20 June 54
❦ ☒ Sir Edward Bowater, KCH, 49 Foot, Groom in *Waiting to the Queen*	31 Mar. 04	never	23 Aug. 09	never	25 July 14	12 Oct. 26	do	do	do
Joseph Webbe Tobin, Royal Artillery	1 Jan. 94	14 Aug. 94	4 Feb. 00	1 Jan. 12	19 July 21	31 Dec. 27	do	do	do
❦ ☒ Sir Wm. Maynard Gomm, GCB, 13 Foot	24 May 94	16 Nov. 94	25 June 96	1 Sept. 03	17 Aug. 12	16 May 29	do	do	do
❦ ☒ Sir Hew Dalrymple Ross, GCB, Royal Artillery	6 Mar. 95	10 May 96	1 Sept. 03	31 Dec. 11	21 June 13	22 July 30	28 June 38	11 Nov. 51	28 Nov. 54
❦ ☒ Sir Robert Wm. Gardiner, GCB, KCH, R. Art.	7 April 97	16 July 09	12 Oct. 09	3 Mar. 12	14 do	23 Nov. 30	23 Nov. 41	do	do
Sir Edward Nicolls, KCB, 8 *Major*, Royal Marines, on retired full pay	24 Mar. 95	27 Jan. 96	25 July 05	8 Aug. 10	12 Aug. 19	10 Jan. 37	9 Nov. 46	20 June 54	do
❦ ☒ Hon. Henry Murray, CB, 14 Light Dragoons	16 May 00	11 June 01	24 Aug. 02	26 Mar. 07	2 Jan. 12	22 July 30	28 June 38	11 Nov. 51	6 Feb. 55
Thomas Evans, CB, 81 Foot	3 Dec. 94	1 Oct. 95	19 Nov. 03	6 Feb. 03	13 Oct. 12	do	do	do	18 May 55
❦ Sir Archibald Maclaine, KCB, 52 Foot	16 April 94	29 April 95	22 Dec. 04	4 Oct. 10	25 Jan. 13	do	23 Nov. 41	do	5 June 55
Wm. Hallett Connolly, 9 *Col. Com.*, R. Mar. on ret. full pay	8 May 95	7 April 96	15 Aug. 05	12 Aug. 19	16 April 19	32 10 July 37	9 Nov. 46	20 June 54	20 June 55
Wm. Wood, CB, KH, 3 West India Regt.	27 Jan. 97	27 Dec. 97	3 Dec. 00	14 May 07	8 April 13	22 July 30	23 Nov. 41	11 Nov. 51	31 Aug. 55
❦ Sir John Fox Burgoyne, Bart., GCB, Royal Engineers, *Inspector General of Fortifications*	29 Aug. 98	1 July 00	1 Mar. 05	6 Feb. 12	27 April 12	do	28 June 38	do	5 Sept. 55
❦ Sir George Brown, GCB, KH, Rifle Brigade	23 Jan. 06	18 Sept. 06	20 June 11	26 May 14	29 Sept. 14	6 May 25	23 Nov. 41	do	7 Sept. 55
❦ ☒ Sir James Simpson, GCB, 87 Foot	3 April 11	never	25 Dec. 13	never	28 April 25	28 June 38	11 Nov. 51	29 June 55	8 Sept. 55
Charles Ashe a'Court-Repington, CB, KH, 41 Foot	17 Dec. 01	2 Sept. 02	25 July 04	26 Feb. 11	19 May 13	22 July 30	23 Nov. 41	11 Nov. 51	20 Feb. 56
His Royal Highness George W. F. C. *Duke of Cambridge, Commanding in Chief*. KG. KP. GCB. GCMG., Scots Fusilier Guards, *Commanding in Chief*	never	never	never	never	never	3 Nov. 37	7 May 45	19 June 54	15 July 56
Richard Uniacke, 10 *Capt.* on ret. full pay, late R. Irish Art.	16 Dec. 93	16 Dec. 93	1 July 94	1 Jan. 05	1 Jan. do	22 July 30	28 June 38	11 Nov. 51	16 Dec. 56
George Irving, *Captain*. do. do	never	3 Aug. 94	25 July 94	do 08	4 June 14	10 Jan. 37	do	do	do
James Irving, *Capt.*, retired full pay, late R. Irish Artillery	16 Dec. 93	00 11 Feb. 00	21 June 07	25 April 13	21 June 13	do	9 Nov. 46	20 June 54	4 Feb. 57
Wm. Greenshields Power, CB, KH, Royal Artillery	31 May 98	21 Dec. 98	13 June 02	21 Sept. 10	10 July 37	10 July 37	11 Nov. 51	20 June 55	1 July 57
Charles Menzies, KH, Royal Marines	17 Feb. 98	19 April 98	13 April 03	10 Jan. 13	4 June 12	13 22 July	23 Nov. 41	11 Nov. 51	26 Sept. 57
Henry James Riddell, KH, 6 Foot	Mar. 98	24 Dec. 98	9 Nov. 02	10 Dec. 12	4 June 12	13 22 do	20 June 41	do	do
Colin, *Lord* Clyde, GCB, 93 Foot, *Commander in Chief, East Indies*	26 May 08	28 June 09	9 Nov. 13	26 Nov. 25	26 Oct. 32	23 Dec. 42	20 June 54	4 June 56	14 May 58
☒ John Rawlins Coryton, Royal Marines	8 July 03	15 Aug. 05	31 July 08	23 Nov. 41	6 May 44	25 May 49	20 June 55	6 Feb. 57	8 Sept. 58
Thomas John Forbes, Royal Artillery	6 Mar. 95	13 April 95	9 Sept. 02	4 June 18	29 July 25	10 Jan. 37	9 Nov. 46	20 June 54	16 Jan. 59
Henry Charles Edward Vernon, CB, 11	8 Nov. 00	26 Sept. 99	17 July 02	13 June 13	21 June 13	do	11 Nov. 51	2 April 59
❦ Sir James Archibald Hope, KCB, 9 Foot	12 Jan. 00	3 June 03	18 Feb. 06	6 Mar. 11	21 June 13	22 July 30	23 Nov. 41	11 Nov. 51	12 June 59
Sir Robert John Harvey, CB., 2 West India Regt.	8 Oct. 03	24 Mar. 04	2 Jan. 06	25 July 13	do	22 July 30	23 Nov. 41	11 Nov. 51	17 July 59
❦ Sir Frederick Stovin, KCB. KCMG., 83 Foot	22 Mar. 00	7 Jan. 00	24 June 02	27 April 07	26 Aug. 13	22 July 30	11 Nov. 51	28 Nov. 54	14 Aug. 59
Frederick Campbell, Royal Artillery	12 Jan. 00	16 July 99	29 July 02	4 June 04	23 Nov. 13	11 June 38	11 June 38	11 June 54	25 Sept. 59
Robert Douglas, 23 CB., *Lt.Col.*, ret. full pay, Roy. Art.	1 Nov. 96	1 Sept. 98	20 July 04	4 June 13	31 Dec. 14	27 23 Nov.	20 June 41	28 Nov. 54	25 Sept. 59
Sir William Fra. Pat. Napier, KCB., 22 Foot	14 June 00	18 April 01	2 June 04	30 May 11	22 Nov. 13	22 July 30	23 Nov. 41	11 Nov. 51	17 Oct. 59
❦ ☒ John Reeve, 61 Foot	23 Oct. 00	never	11 April 05	25 Dec. 11	13 22 do	30 23 July	30 23 Nov.	11 Nov. 51	7 Dec. 59

LIEUTENANT-GENERALS.

	CORNET, 2d LIEUT. or ENSIGN.	LIEUT.	CAPTAIN.	MAJOR.	LIEUT.-COLONEL.	COLONEL.	MAJOR-GENERAL.	LIEUT.-GENERAL.
Sir Charles William Pasley, KCB, Royal Engineers	1 Dec. 97	28 Aug. 99	1 Mar. 05	5 Feb. 12	27 May 25	22 July 30	23 Nov. 41	11 Nov. 51
Charles Grene Ellicombe, CB., Royal Engineers	never	1 July 01	1 July 06	27 April 12	21 Sept. 18	do	do	do
Thomas Kenah, CB., 63 Foot	14 Aug. 99	9 May 00	3 Mar. 04	5 Nov. 12	27 Dec. 13	do	do	do
Edward Buckley Wynyard, CB., 58 Foot	17 Dec. 08	never	7 Jan. 08	25 Mar. 18	28 April 14	do	do	do
Sir James Ferguson, KCB., 43 Foot	30 Aug. 01	9 Feb. 04	1 Dec. 06	2 Dec. 12	16 May 14	do	do	do
Sir Thomas William Brotherton, KCB, 1 Dragoon Guards	24 Jan. 00	never	27 July 00	28 Nov. 01	19 May 14	do	do	do
Sir Adolphus John Dalrymple, 12 Bart.	25 Oct. 98	12 June 00	7 Jan. 03	15 Sept. 08	1 June 14	do	do	do
Sir James Henry Reynett, KCH., 48 Foot	25 Nov. 99	14 Mar. 00	24 Mar. 04	8 April 13	do	do	do	do
Sir John Beil, KCB, 4 Foot	15 Aug. 05	1 Oct. 07	12 Mar. 00	21 June 13	12 April 14	31 do	do	do
Sir Samuel Benjamin Auchmuty, KCB, 7 Foot	15 Oct. 97	13 Mar. 00	14 Nov. 05	21 June 13	do	do	do	do
Sir John Aitchison, KCB., 72 Foot	25 Oct.	never	22 Nov.	10	15 Dec.	6 May	36 do	do
William Jervois, KH. 76 Foot	7 April 04	8 Aug.	14 July	08	19 Dec. 13	22 Sept.	37 do	do
Sir Francis Cockburn, 95 Foot	16 Oct. 00	6 April 03	3 Mar.	04 27 June	11 27 Oct.	14 20 May	9 Nov. 46	20 June 54
Sir Richard Lluellyn, CB., 39 Foot	24 July 02	7 April 04	28 Feb.	05 28 April	13 18 June	14 10 Jan.	do	do
Peter Aug. Lantour, CB. KH., 3 Light Dragoons	31 Mar. 04	4 July	06 8 May	06 20 May	13 do	15 do	do	do
Sir William Chalmers, CB. KCH., 78 Foot	9 July 03	25 Oct.	05 27 Aug.	07 26 Aug.	13 do	do	do	do
Sir Harry Geo. W. Smith, Bart. GCB., Rifle Brigade	8 May 05	15 Aug.	05 28 Feb.	12 29 Sept.	14 do	do	do	do
Sir De Lacy Evans, GCB, 21 Foot	1 Feb. 07	1 Dec.	08 12 Jan.	15 11 May	15 do	do	do	do
William Henry Scott, 36 Foot	27 Oct. 05	never	28 Mar.	11 never	5 July 15	do	do	do
Sir Thomas Willshire, Bart., KCB., 51 Foot	June 05	5 Sept.	25 28 Aug.	04 21 Sept.	13 4 Dec.	15 do	do	do
Edward Fleming, CB, 27 Foot	24 June 02	6 July 04	30 May	07 1 April	13 18 July	16 do	do	do
Philip Bainbrigge, CB., 36 Foot	30 June 00	13 Nov. 05	17 Oct.	05 15 Oct.	12 21 June	17 do	do	do
Thomas Erskine Napier, CB., 71 Foot	3 July 05	1 May 06	27 Oct.	08 36 Dec.	13 do	do	do	do
William Henry Sewell, CB., 79 Foot	27 Mar. 06	26 Feb. 07	12 Mar.	12 3 Mar.	14 do	do	do	do
William Lindsay Darling, 98 Foot	13 Dec. 01	23 June 05	12 June 08	14 April 14	4 Sept. 17	do	do	do
Sir John M'Donald, KCB, 93 Foot	17 Dec. 08	21 Mar. 05	7 Sept.	09 26 Aug.	13 do	do	do	do
George William Paty, CB. KH., 70 Foot	28 April 04	7 May 05	28 April	08 2 June	14 do	do	do	do
Lord James Hay, 86 Foot	23 Jan. 06	6 Aug. 07	8 Feb.	10 never	26 Mar. 18	do	do	do
Sir James Wemyss, CB., 17 Foot	14 Oct. 00	1 Mar. 04	30 Nov.	06 21 June	13 21 Jan.	19 do	do	do
Sir William Rowan, KCB, 19 Foot	4 Nov. 03	15 June 04	19 Oct.	08 3 Mar.	14 do	do	do	do
James Shaw Kennedy, CB., 47 Foot	27 April 05	23 Jan. 06	16 July	12 18 June	15 do	do	do	do
Arthur W. M. Lord Sandys, 2 Dragoons	19 July 09	19 July 10	25 Aug.	13 27 July	15 do	do	do	do
George Leigh Goldie, CB., 77 Foot	3 Sept. 03	14 Mar. 05	4 Dec.	06 20 June	17 12 Aug.	19 do	do	do
George Powell Higginson, 94 Foot	6 Nov. 05	never	3 April	11 never	26 Oct.	20 do	do	do
Sir George Bowles, KCB., 1 West India Regt., Lieutenant of the Tower of London	20 Dec. 04	never	1 Feb.	10 18 June	15 14 June	21 do	do	do
Hon. Henry Fred. Compton Cavendish, 2 Dragoon Guards	never	26 May 05	6 June	11 2 April	18 12 July	21 do	do	do
Thomas Wm. Robbins, 80 Foot	26 Sept. 05	5 May 08	25 May	09 24 Dec.	18 24 Oct.	21 do	do	do
Roderick Macneil, 8 Foot	17 Mar. 08	9 May 09	1 Dec.	14 9 Aug.	21 25 Jan.	22 do	do	do

8

Lieutenant-Generals.

Name	CORNET, 2d LIEUT. or ENSIGN.	LIEUT.	CAPTAIN.	MAJOR.	LIEUT.-COLONEL.	COLONEL.	MAJOR-GENERAL.	LIEUT.-GENERAL.
William Sutherland, CB., 53 Foot	15 Dec. 04	1 July 06	18 Aug. 14	25 Sept. 17	16 May 22	10 Jan. 37	9 Nov. 46	20 June 54
Henry Rainey, CB., KH., 23 Foot	24 Aug. 04	1 Nov. 04	13 April 09	21 June 17	15 Aug. 22	do	do	do
Hon. Charles Gore, CB., KH., 91 Foot	21 Oct. 08	4 Jan. 10	13 Mar. 15	21 Jan. 19	19 Sept. 23	do	do	do
Wm. Lovelace Walton, 5 Foot	8 May 06	never	7 Mar. 11	never	20 Feb. 27	do	do	do
Charles Richard Fox	29 June 15	5 Nov. 18	9 Aug. 20	6 Nov. 24	14 Aug. 25	8 Aug. 37	do	do
Charles Augustus Shawe, 74 Foot	26 May 08	never	23 April 12	never	28 April 25	8 June 38	11 Nov. 51	28 Nov. 54
George Turner, CB., Royal Artillery	14 Jan. 97	16 July 99	29 July 04	4 June 14	25 Nov. 28	23 Nov. 38	20 June 54	28 Nov. 54
Peter Margetson Wallace, Royal Artillery	10 May 97	16 July 99	15 Nov. 04	4 June 14	30 Dec. 28	do	do	do
Richard Jones, Royal Artillery	12 Mar. 98	16 July 99	5 Dec. 04	4 June 14	31 Dec. 30	do	do	do
John Michell, CB., Royal Artillery	1 Mar. 98	2 Oct. 99	20 Feb. 05	29 Sept. 14	22 July 23	28 June 38	11 Nov. 51	30 Jan. 55
Millin ray Fane, 96 Foot	11 June 12	25 Sept. 13	28 July 14	2 Mar. 23	17 Sept. 25	do	do	6 Feb. 55
Sir James Maxwell Wallace, KH., 17 Lancers	14 Aug. 05	5 June 06	22 Oct. 07	1 Jan. 25	25 Sept. 23	do	do	20 Feb. 55
Hon. John Finch, CB., 24 Foot	5 Oct. 09	20 Dec. 11	10 17 Feb. 14	5 Mar. 24	25 Oct. 23	do	do	5 June 55
Sir Wm. George Moore, KCB., 60 Rifles	18 April 11	10 Sept. 12	14 April 14	21 Jan. 24	12 Feb. 37	26 Aug. 39	do	20 June 56
John Wright, KH., Col. Comm., retired full pay, R. Marines	21 April 96	10 June 99	27 July 08	16 Jan. 30	23 July 30	23 Nov. 41	do	1 June 56
Edw. Chas. Whinyates, CB., KH., Royal Artillery	1 Mar. 98	2 Oct. 99	8 July 05	18 June 15	22 July 25	28 June 38	do	4 June 56
Sir Richard England, GCB., KH., 50 Foot	25 Feb. 08	1 June 09	11 June 11	4 Sept. 23	29 Oct. 38	do	do	do
Sir William John Codrington, KCB., 54 Foot, *Governor and Commander in Chief at Gibraltar*	22 Feb. 21	24 April 23	20 July 26	never	8 July 36	9 Nov. 46	20 June 54	6 June 56
Thomas Dyneley, CB., Royal Artillery	1 Dec. 01	1 July 03	28 May 08	18 June 15	10 Jan. 37	28 June 38	11 Nov. 51	16 Dec. 56
Sir Henry Somerset, KCB. KH., 25 Foot, *Commander in Chief of Bombay Army*	5 Dec. 11	30 Dec. 12	6 Oct. 15	25 Mar. 23	17 July 24	28 June 38	11 Nov. 51	29 Jan. 57
George Cobbe, Royal Artillery	9 Oct. 99	7 Sept. 01	2 June 06	12 Aug. 19	20 Nov. 34	1 April 46	20 June 54	4 Feb. 57
Wm. Fergusson, KC., Col. Comm., ret. full pay, Royal Marines	10 Sept. 98	29 April 04	23 Feb. 14	10 July 37	9 Nov. 41	do	do	6 Feb. 57
S. Bardon Ellis, CB., Royal Marines	1 Jan. 04	29 Jan. 06	15 Nov. 26	6 May 41	26 May 41	3 Nov. 51	20 Nov. 55	20 Feb. 57
Thomas Wearing, do	5 May 04	24 Apr. 07	20 Dec. 27	23 Nov. 18	Dec. 46	20 Nov. 35	do	1 July 57
Alexander Cavalie Mercer, Royal Artillery	20 Dec. 99	1 Dec. 01	3 Dec. 06	12 Aug. 19	5 June 35	1 April 46	20 June 54	29 Aug. 57
Henry, Duke of Cleveland, KG., Lt. Col. Unatt. Colonel of Durham Militia	6 July 15	22 May 17	22 Oct. 18	3 July 23	25 Sept. 23	do	11 Nov. 38	8 Sept. 57
Sir Geo. Aug. Wetherall, KCB. KH., 84 F., Adjutant General	never	29 July 95	13 May 05	12 Aug. 19	11 Dec. 24	do	do	do
Sir Jas. Frdl. Love, KCB. KH., 57 F., Insp. Gen. of Inf.	26 Oct. 04	5 June 05	11 July 11	16 Mar. 15	5 May 25	do	do	26 Sept. 57
Sir Duncan M'Gregor, KCB.	12 July 00	31 Aug. 01	17 April 04	25 Nov. 13	26 May 25	do	do	12 Dec. 57
Nicholas Hamilton, KH., 82 Foot	15 June 96	9 Dec. 96	25 June 03	18 June 12	27 May 25	do	do	11 Jan. 58
Charles George James Arbuthnot, 89 Foot	16 Nov. 08	never	16 Mar. 16	18 June 20	3 July 23	1 Oct. 25	do	15 Jan. 58
Chesborough Grant Falconar, KH., 73 Foot	never	26 Dec. 95	29 Dec. 05	12 Aug. 19	22 Nov. 23	do	do	13 Mar. 58
Alexander Fisher Macintosh, KH., 90 Foot	1 Sept. 11	1 Nov. 12	9 June 16	18 Sept. 28	15 Dec. 25	do	do	20 July 58
Joseph Paterson, 60 Foot, Lt. Col. Unatt.	31 Oct. 10	11 June 12	9 June 16	18 Sept. 28	15 Dec. 25	do	do	2 Aug. 58
Alexander Fisher Macintosh, KH., 90 Foot, Lt. Col. Unatt.	27 June 99	never	25 Dec. 01	21 Jan. 13	24 Dec. 25	do	do	do
James Irvin Willes, Royal Marines	17 May 99	7 Feb. 99	1 23 Oct. 01	29 Nov. 06	4 Jan. 42	18 Oct. 48	20 June 55	8 Sept. 58
	12 Nov. 04	27 July 08	15 Oct. 29	6 May 42				

Lieutenant-Generals.

	CORNET, 2d LIEUT. or ENSIGN.	LIEUT.	CAPTAIN.	MAJOR.	LIEUT.-COLONEL.	COLONEL.	MAJOR-GENERAL.	LIEUT.-GENERAL.
John Home Home, 56 Foot	19 Jan. 13	never	30 June 15	never	10 May 27	11 Sept. 40	11 Nov. 51	22 Sept. 58
†ᴬᴰᴄ Sir Wm. Robert Clayton,¹⁶ Bart., Lt. Col. Unatt.	28 Sept. 04	14 Nov. 05	27 April 09	21 Dec. 15	8 April 26	23 Nov. 41	do	26 Oct. 58
John Spink, KH., 2 Foot	2 Sept. 06	9 Mar. 07	13 Oct. 12	13 May 24	20 May 26	do	do	do
ᴬᴅᴄ Sir Jas. Jackson, KCB. KH., 6 Dragoons	9 Oct. 06	25 Jan. 08	25 June 13	18 June 15	25 May 26	do	do	do
Robert Christopher Mansel, KH., 68 Foot, Com. East. Dist.	29 Jan. 07	27 Jan. 08	4 Feb. 13	5 July 21	10 June 26	do	do	do
John Drummond¹⁷	22 Nov. 10	never	26 May 14	never	22 June 26	do	do	do
James Freeth, KH., 64 Foot	25 Dec. 06	30 May 09	21 April 14	21 Jan. 19	11 July 26	do	do	do
Sir Charles Routledge O'Donnell	9 Sept. 13	7 Sept. 15	11 July 22	14 Jan. 26	15 Aug. 26	do	do	do
John Leslie, KH., 35 Foot	7 Aug. 06	2 June 08	30 Nov. 09	1 Jan. 19	29 Aug. 26	do	do	do
ᴬᴅᴄ Sir Robert Bartlett Coles, 65 Foot	20 Aug. 03	1 May 05	8 Sept. 08	24 Oct. 21	19 Sept. 26	do	do	do
ᴬᴅᴄ Sir Edward Pery Buckley,¹⁸ Equerry to the Queen	24 June 12	never	23 Mar. 14	19 July 21	26 Sept. 26	do	do	do
Sir Richard Doherty, 11 Foot	10 Sept. 03	22 Nov. 04	21 May 12	16 Sept. 24	do	do	do	do
ᴬᴅᴄ Edward Byam, 18 Foot	14 Nov. 11	29 April 13	26 Aug. 19	16 June 25	23 Mar. 25	do	do	16 Nov. 58
William Douglas, Lieut.-Col., ret. full pay, Royal Engineers	1 July 02	1 Oct. 02	1 July 06	12 Aug. 19	23 Mar. 25	38 June	do	23 Nov. 58
George Judd Harding, CB., Royal Engineers	1 Oct. 02	1 Dec. 02	1 Nov. 07	19 July 25	25	do	do	do
George Charles, Earl of Lucan, KCB., 8 Hussars	29 Aug. 16	24 Dec. 18	16 May 22	23 June 25	9 Nov. 26	41 Nov. 11	do	24 Dec. 58
Sir William M. George Colebrooke, CB. KH., Royal Artillery	17 Aug. 03	12 Sept. 03	27 Sept. 10	1 June 13	22 July 26	9 Nov. 41	46 June 20	16 Jan. 59
ᴬᴅᴄ Sir Charles Yorke, KCB., 33 Foot, Military Secretary to H.R.H. Commanding in Chief	22 Jan. 07	18 Feb. 08	24 Dec. 13	9 June 25	30 Nov. 26	23 Nov. 41	11 Nov. 51	13 Feb. 59
†John Henry Richardson, Lt. Col. Unatt.	16 Jan. 09	5 Sept. 11	4 Dec. 17	14 July 25	12 Dec. 26	do	do	2 April 59
Sir John Rowland Eustace, KH.¹⁹	June 08	3 Nov. 08	17 Mar. 14	9 Nov. 25	19 Dec. 26	do	do	2 April 59
ᴬᴅᴄ Berkeley Drummond, 3 F., Extra Groom in Waiting to the Queen	5 Mar. 12	never	4 July 15	never	21 Dec. 26	do	do	9 April 59
ᴬᴅᴄ John Oldfield, KH., Royal Engineers	2 April 06	1 July 06	1 May 11	22 July 30	12 Nov. 31	do	do	10 May 59
Hon. Sir Edw. Cust, KCH., 16 Lancers, Master of Ceremonies to the Queen	15 Mar. 10	27 Dec. 10	9 Dec. 13	24 Oct. 21	26 Dec. 26	do	do	14 May 59
Dennis Daly²¹	28 Aug. 00	15 Jan. 01	3 May 07	19 July 13	30 Dec. 21	do	do	12 June 59
†William Chamberlayne, Lt. Col. Unatt.	19 Aug. 06	18 Dec. 06	9 May 11	1 July 17	do 24	do	do	17 July 59
†Jeremiah Taylor, 59 Foot	28 Feb. 05	1 Oct. 07	2 Oct. 17	1 April 24	22 Mar. 27	do	20 June	14 Aug. 59
Francis John Davies, 67 Foot	3 Feb. 08	26 Jan. 09	12 Aug. 13	never	30 April 27	do	do	25 Sept. 59
William Cator, CB., from Royal Artillery	7 May 03	12 Sept. 03	1 May 09	12 April 14	22 July 30	9 Nov. 46	do	17 Oct. 59
John Fraser, 37 Foot	19 April 09	12 Sept. 11	28 Jan. 13	31 Oct. 18	24 May 27	23 Nov. 41	do	25 Oct. 59
Sir John Mark Fred. Smith, KH., from R. Engineers, Gentleman Usher of the Privy Chamber	1 Dec. 05	1 Mar. 06	1 May 11	never	16 Mar. 30	9 Nov. 46	do	
†Jonathan Peel, Lt. Col. Unatt.*	15 June 15	3 Dec. 18	13 Dec. 21	19 May 25	7 June 27	23 Nov. 41	11 Nov. 51	7 Dec. 59
Marcus Beresford, 20 Foot	4 Sept. 17	1 Feb. 21	16 Sept. 24	26 Sept. 26	6 Nov. 27	do	do	7 Dec. 59
ᴬᴅᴄ Sir James C. Chatterton, Bt., KH., 5 Lancers, Gentleman of the Privy Chamber	23 Nov. 09	6 June 11	26 Mar. 18	22 July 24	18 Dec. 27	do	do	13 Dec. 59

MAJOR-GENERALS.

Name	CORNET, 2d LIEUT. or ENSIGN.	LIEUT.	CAPTAIN.	MAJOR.	LIEUT.-COLONEL.	COLONEL.	MAJOR-GENERAL.
†John Hobart, *Lord* Howden, GCB. KH.,[1] [2] *Maj.*Unatt. *Equerry to H.R.H. the Duchess of Kent*	never	13 July	15 22 Oct.	18 9 June	25 25 Dec.	27 28 Nov.	41 11 Nov. 51
James Alex. *Earl of* Rosslyn	25 Feb. 19	9 July	20 25 Mar.	28 12 Dec.	26 31 Dec.	27 do	do
‡ Wm. Tho. Knollys, 62 F. *Lt. Gen. Commanding at Aldershot*	9 Dec. 13	never	25 Sept.	17 never	do	do	do
Sir Henry Robert Ferguson Davie, *Bart.*	18 Mar. 18	25 Feb.	19 26 Sept.	22 19 Dec.	26 8 May	do	do
‡ Ernest Fred. Gascoigne, 69 Foot, *Commanding Dublin District*	2 May 11	13 May	13 5 July	15 19 May	25 3 June	do	do
Sir Lovell Benjamin Lovell, KCB. KH., 12 Lancers	18 Dec. 05	19 May	08 12 Dec.	11 21 Jan.	19 21 Nov.	28 do	do
‡ *Sir* John Augustus Clerke, KH., 75 Foot	13 Oct. 08	6 June	11 11 Mar.	19 26 May	25 30 Dec.	28 do	do
‡ *Sir* James Holmes Schoedde, KCB, 55 Foot	May 00	8 Oct.	01 19 Sept.	05 21 June	13 20 Mar.	29 do	do
Sir Henry John Wm. Bentinck, KCB., 28 Foot, *Groom in Waiting to the Queen*	25 Aug. 13	never	18 Jan.	20 never	16 May	29 do	do
‡ Thomas Reed, CB., 44 Foot	26 Aug. 13	2 May	15 19 Feb.	24 15 June	26 11 Aug.	29 do	do
Henry, *Visc.* Melville, KCB., 100 Foot, *Commanding the Troops in Scotland*	never	18 Nov.	19 1 April	24 11 July	26 3 Dec.	29 do	do
‡‡‡ Alex. Kennedy Clarke Kennedy, CB. KH., 6 Dr. Gds.	8 Sept. 09	15 Dec.	04 13 Dec.	10 26 May	25 11 June	30 do	do
‡ Horatio George Broke, 88 Foot	29 May 06	15 Feb.	08 18 Mar.	15 28 July	14 20 July	30 do	do
Peter E. Craigie, CB., 31 Foot, *Commanding a Division of the Madras Army*	3 June 13	29 Sept.	14 24 Oct.	21 10 Aug.	26 21 Nov.	34 23 Dec.	42 do
Edmund Finucane Morris, CB., 97 Foot	21 June 10	21 April	13 1 Dec.	25 13 Sept.	33 22 Nov.	36 23 Dec.	42 do
Henry Colvile	never	29 Dec.	18 6 Dec.	17 never	6 July	30 31 Dec.	44 do
‡‡‡ Everard Wm. Bouverie, 15 Hussars, *Equerry to the Queen*	2 April 12	15 Oct.	12 9 Sept.	19 6 May	31 4 Dec.	32 16 Sept.	45 do
Hon. Thomas Ashburnham, CB.,[29] *from* 29 Foot	never	30 Jan.	23 22 June	26 never	27 Mar.	35 1 April	46 do
Michael White, CB., 7 Dragoon Guards	15 Aug. 04	14 May	05 7 Nov.	15 10 Jan.	37 13 Dec.	39 3 April	46 20 June 54
John Scott, CB., 3 Dragoon Guards	4 May 15	26 Oct.	15 28 June	21 9 Nov.	26 31 Aug.	30 19 June	46 do
Sir John Lysaght Pennefather, KCB., 46 Foot, *Lt.-Gen. Commanding the Northern District*	14 Jan.	18 20 Feb.	23 5 Nov.	25 22 Mar.	31 18 Oct.	39 do	46 do
‡ Thomas Perronet Thompson,[31] *Lt. Col. Unattached*	23 Jan. 06	21 Jan.	08 7 July	14 9 June	25 24 Feb.	29 9 Nov.	46 do
†Frederick Thomas Buller, *Lt. Col. Unattached*	never	30 Dec.	13 6 Sept.	21 never	4 June	29 do	do
‡ Edward Wells Bell,[33] *Lt. Gov. Comm. the Troops in Jamaica*	1 Oct. 94	16 May	11 20 June	22 19 Dec.	26 29 June	30 do	do
‡ Thomas Burke[35]	12 Sept. 95	23 Oct.	99 12 Aug.	04 22 July	13 22 July	30 do	do
‡‡ George Saunders Thwaites,[36] *Capt. h. p.* 57 Foot	6 May 24	23 Dec.	25 2 July	03 4 June	14 22 July	30 do	do
‡‡ James Thomas, *Earl of* Cardigan, KCB., 5 Dragoon Guards, *Inspecting General of Cavalry*		13 Jan.	25 9 June	26 3 Aug.	30 3 Dec.	30 do	do
‡‡ William Cowper Coles, *Lt. Col. Unattached*	31 Oct. 05	8 Feb.	07 19 Nov.	12 9 June	25 10 Dec.	30 do	do
Sir Michael Creagh, KH.[40]	9 May 02	28 Feb.	04 25 Nov.	09 24 Oct.	21 31 Dec.	30 do	do
John Eden, CB.,[41] *Commanding Cork District*	14 Feb. 07	14 Aug.	07 26 Nov.	18 9 June	25 do	do	do
Hon. Charles Grey, *Equerry to the Queen*	16 Nov. 20	10 April	28 16 June	25 19 Feb.	28 12 July	31 do	do
Wm. *Lord* de Ros, *Deputy Lieut. of the Tower of London*	29 Mar. 19	24 Aug.	21 23 Oct.	24 5 June	27 8 Sept.	31 do	do
‡ John Geddes, KH.[42]	Aug. 08	24 Oct.	05 1 Dec.	08 24 Feb.	25 11 Nov.	31 do	do

Major-Generals.

	CORNET, 2d LIEUT. or ENSIGN.	LIEUT.	CAPTAIN.	MAJOR.	LIEUT.-COLONEL.	COLONEL.	MAJOR-GENERAL.
Philip Spencer Stanhope, from Grenadier Guards	30 Mar. 15	never	17 July 23	never	16 Mar. 32	9 Nov. 46	20 June 54
‡ Alexander Maclachlan, from Royal Artillery	3 Dec. 03	6 Dec. 08	17 June 12	22 July 30	1 June 32	do	do
Charles Murray Hay, from Coldstream Guards	20 April 20	1 Nov. 21	24 Dec. 25	never	22 June 32	do	do
‡ Henry Lord Rokeby, KCB,[43] from Scots Fusilier Guards, *Inspecting General of Foot Guards*	21 April 14	never	12 June 23	never	21 Sept. 32	do	do
Henry Edward Porter	3 July	17 Dec.	14 July 25	4 Oct. 31	1 Feb. 33	do	do
John Dawson Rawdon	12 Dec.	22 30 Jan.	10 June 26	never	15 Nov. 33	do	do
‡ ▨ William Beckwith, KH,[45]	7 Jan.	13 12 Dec.	15 9 May	22 14 Feb. 28	6 Dec. 33	do	do
‡ Henry Edward Robinson[46]	28 May 06	9 Feb. 08	26 July 22	20 Sept. 27	1 Jan. 34	do	do
‡ ▨ Allen Thomas Maclean,[47] from 13 Dragoons	16 Mar.	15 27 July	20 21 July 22	25 31 Dec. 28	11 July 34	do	do
† Arthur, *Duke of Wellington*, KG., *Lt. Col. Unatt., Lt. Col. Commandant Royal Victoria Rifles*	4 Jan.	10 11 July	11 23 Dec. 18	29 Oct. 30	do	do	do
John Julius Wm. Angerstein, from Grenadier Guards	20 Mar. 23	1 July 27	8 May 28	2 Nov. 30	12 Aug. 34	do	do
‡ ▨ Thomas Marten, KH.[48]	never	9 April	2 April 25	never	12 Sept. 34	do	do
Matthew Charles Dixon,[49] *Maj. Gen.* ret. full pay, R. Engineers	22 Nov.	13 23 June	17 4 May	22 12 Dec. 26	29 May 35	do	do
‡ Thomas Gerrard Ball[50]	2 April 07	1 July 06	1 May	11 22 July 30	25 June 35	do	do
▨ Eaton Monins[51]	17 Sept.	1 Dec.	08 27 April	14 24 June 24	2 Oct. 35	do	do
James Stokes Bastard, *Maj. Gen.* retired full pay, Royal Artillery	1 Dec.	14 9 Sept.	19 23 June	25 19 Nov. 30	do	do	do
George Morton Eden, from Scots Fusilier Guards	15 Nov.	00 12 May	02 1 Feb.	08 27 May	25 27 April 36	do	do
George Dixon, from Scots Fusilier Guards	18 July	22 10 Sept.	26 9 May	26 11 Oct.	31 20 May 36	do	do
‡ Frederick Maunsell,[52] from *Inspecting Field Officer*	nevcr	20 Jan.	20 8 April	26 never	do	do	do
Duncan Grant,[53] *Colonel*, retired full pay, Royal Artillery	16 Mar.	12 28 Jan.	13 24 June	19 14 Aug.	27 23 May 36	do	do
Henry Alexander Scott, from Royal Artillery	23 Nov.	01 23 Nov.	17 1 May	08 27 May	12 July 36	do	do
William Wylde, CB., from Royal Artillery, *Groom of the Bed-chamber to H.R.H. the Prince Consort*	28 April	01 20 April 03	1 Feb.	08 27 May	25 10 Aug. 36	do	do
William Fludyer, from Grenadier Guards	8 Sept.	03 8 Sept. 03	16 Mar.	12 16 July	30 19 Aug. 36	do	do
‡ John Wharton Frith,[54] from *Inspecting Field Officer*	30 Dec.	19 25 Dec.	21 7 July	25 never	2 Dec. 36	do	do
Henry Charles Russel, from Royal Artillery	17 July	04 27 Feb.	05 29 Jan.	12 22 July	30 16 Dec. 36	do	do
John Hall, from 1 Life Guards	1 Apr.	12 12 Sept.	08 15 July	08 27 May	25 10 Jan. 37	do	do
‡ Adam Fife Crawford,[56] *Colonel* retired full pay, R. Artillery	12 June	17 24 July	17 2 Aug.	22 8 Sept.	31 27 Dec. 37	do	do
Henry William Gordon, from Royal Artillery	17 Aug.	08 12 Aug.	08 3 Aug.	10 22 July	30 10 Jan. 37	20 July 47	28 Nov. 54
‡ Joseph Darby,[57] *Lt.-Col.* retired full pay, Royal Artillery	17 Aug.	02 do	3 Aug.	10 22 July	30 do	1 Nov. 48	do
George Henry Lockwood, CB.[58]	1 July	02 do	22 Mar.	09 do	do	11 Nov. 51	do
Sir Richard Airey, KCB.,[59] *Quarter Master General*	10 Mar.	25 10 Aug.	26 7 Sept.	32 6 Mar.	39 23 May.	42 2 Aug. 50	do
Sir Hugh Henry Rose, GCB., KCB.,[60] *On the Staff in India*	15 Mar.	21 4 Dec.	25 22 Dec.	25 9 May	34 10 Feb.	38 11 Nov. 51	12 Dec. 54
Hon. Sir James Yorke Scarlett, KCB., from 5 Dragoon Gds., *Commanding the South Western District*	8 June	20 24 Oct.	21 22 July	25 11 June	26 17 Sept.	39 do	do
‡ Sir Harry David Jones, KCB., from R. Engineers, *Governor of the Royal Military College*	26 Mar.	18 24 June	18 24 June	18 10 Jan.	37 3 July	36 do	do
	17 Sept.	08 24 June	13 9 June 29	13 10 Jan.	37 7 Sept. 40	do	do

Major-Generals.

Name	2D LIEUT. ETC.	LIEUT.	CAPTAIN.	MAJOR.	LIEUT.-COLONEL.	COLONEL.	MAJOR-GENERAL.
Sir George Buller, KCB,⁶¹ from Rifle Brigade, Commanding the Troops in the Ionian Islands	2 Mar. 20	28 Mar.	25 Aug.	28 31 Dec.	39 27 Aug.	51 11 Nov.	54 12 Dec.
William Henry Slade,⁶³ Colonel, ret. full pay, R. Engineers	1 Nov. 06	1 May	07 4 Mar.	12 22 July	30 10 Jan.	37 5 Sept.	54 13 Dec.
Richard Thomas King,⁶⁴ Lt.Col. do. R. Artillery	8 Sept. 03	12 Sept.	03 8 May	11 do	do	11 Nov.	51 do
Charles Dixon, Lt.Col. do. R. Engineers	7 Oct.	06 1 Dec.	06 22 July	11 do	do	do	do
Thomas Grantham,⁶⁵ Colonel, do. R. Engineers	14 Dec.	04 29 Dec.	05 28 Oct.	15 10 Jan.	37 4 April	43 22 July	53 54 do
James Conway Victor,⁶⁶ Colonel, do. R. Artillery	1 June	10 1 May	11 19 June	21 10 Jan.	37 1 April	46 20 June	54 do
William Brereton, CB. KH., from R. Artillery	10 May	05 1 June	06 30 Sept.	16 21 Jan.	19 10 Jan.	37 11 Nov.	51 54 16 Dec.
Sherbourne Williams,⁶⁷ Lt.Col. ret. full pay, R. Engineers	25 July	07 1 May	08 17 Aug.	15 never	do	do	55 do
Francis Rawdon Chesney, from Royal Artillery	9 Nov.	04 20 Sept.	05 20 June	15 2 Dec.	36 27 April	38 do	6 Jan.
Charles Dalton,⁶⁸ Colonel, ret. full pay, Royal Artillery	1 Mar.	06 1 June	06 30 Dec.	22 10 Jan.	37 15 April	44 17 Mar.	54 do
Richard Burne Rawnsley, Colonel, do.	21 Mar.	06 22 Sept.	06 12 June	23 28 June	38 6 Jan.	45 20 June	54 do
John Heneage Grubbe, Lt.Col., ret. full pay, 66 Foot	20 Aug.	18 24 Feb.	25 3 May	26 19 Jan.	39 3 Sept.	47 28 June	54 9 Jan.
Philip Barry,⁶⁹ Colonel, ret. full pay, Royal Engineers	10 Feb.	09 1 Mar.	10 1 Oct.	14 10 Jan.	37 23 Nov.	41 17 Feb.	54 13 Jan.
Fred. William Whinyates,⁷⁰ Col. do.	14 Dec.	11 1 July	12 29 July	25 28 June	38 9 Nov.	46 20 April	54 do
John Bloomfield Gough, CB.,⁷¹ Commanding a Brigade at the Curragh	24 Feb.	20 1 Oct.	25 1 Aug.	26 26 May	41 23 Dec.	42 2 Aug.	55 30 Jan.
William Furneaux,⁷² Colonel, ret. full pay, Royal Artillery	26 Nov.	08 18 Nov.	11 6 Nov.	27 23 Nov.	41 19 Mar.	47 20 Nov.	54 55 7 Feb.
Rich. Goodwin Bowen Wilson,⁷³ Col. ret. full pay, Royal Artillery	17 Dec.	12 20 June	15 8 July	34 9 Nov.	46 1 Dec.	48 28 Nov.	55 20 Feb.
Hon. Arthur Upton, from Coldstream Guards	never	16 Feb.	25 16 May	29 never	31 Dec.	39 22 Aug.	51 55 do
Anthony Emmett,⁷¹ Colonel, ret. full pay, Royal Engineers	16 Feb.	08 24 June	09 21 July	13 5 July	21 10 Jan.	37 11 May	54 55 21 May
Marcus Antonius Waters,⁷³ Col. do.	30 Sept.	09 1 May	11 11 Nov.	16 10 Jan.	37 12 July	45 20 Aug.	55 do
Abraham Henry Gordon, Colonel Comm., ret. full pay, Royal Marines	5 Jan.	01 18 July	05 18 Dec.	24 28 June	38 26 Aug.	39 4 Jan.	55 20 June
John Montresor Pilcher,⁷⁶ do.	15 Jan.	01 15 Aug.	05 11 Feb.	26 never	11 May	41 17 Aug.	48 do
do.	do.	do.	11 Mar.	26 never	14 May	41 25 April	49 do
Thomas Stevens,⁷⁷ Col. 2nd Commandant	15 April	01	03 18 Oct.	31 July	26 25 Nov.	41 25 May	49 do
David Anderson Gibsone,⁷⁵ Col. Comm.	11 July	03 18 Oct.	05 do	do	do	46 23 May	51 do
Robert Mercer,⁷⁹ Col. Commandant	5 July	03 15 Aug.	05 do	do	9 Nov.	46 30 June	54 do
Donald Campbell,⁸⁰ Lt.Col.	do.	do.	do.	do.	4 Jan.	43 20 June	51 do
James Whylock,⁸¹ Col. 2nd Commandant	25 April	04 24 Mar.	07 31 Aug.	27 28 Sept.	40 7 Dec.	46 11 Nov.	51 do
George Butt Bary,⁸² Col. Commandant	10 Nov.	04 27 July	08 30 June	29 10 Nov.	40 27 Dec.	47 10 Jan.	52 do
Charles Compton Pratt,⁸⁴ Col. Commandant	14 Oct.	05 14 May	09 12 Oct.	32 9 Nov.	46 1 May	49 19 April	54 do
Henry James Gillespie,⁸³ Lt.Col.	11 Jan.	05 27 July	08 27 July	30 do	17 May	48 28 Nov.	54 do
Samuel Garnston,⁸⁶ Lt.Col.	27 Sept.	05 24 Aug.	09 16 April	32 do	17 Aug.	48 do	do
John Harvey Stevens,⁸⁷ Lt.Col.	28 Sept.	09 2 Sept.	09 do	do	do	do	do
Thomas Scott Reignolds,⁸⁸ CB. Lt.Col., ret. full pay, 18 Foot	23 June	25 25 April	28 26 April	31 30 July	42 30 Mar.	44 20 June	54 22 June
Sir Ricñard James Dacres, KCB., from Royal Art., Commanding at Woolwich	15 Dec.	17 29 Aug.	25 18 Dec.	37 11 Nov.	51 23 Feb.	52 25 Feb.	55 29 June
John Joseph Hollis, Lt.Col. ret. full pay, 25 Foot	9 July	08 1 Dec.	04 30 Mar.	09 22 July	30 9 Nov.	46 20 June	54 6 July
Hugh Evans,⁸⁹ Col. 2nd Comm., ret. full pay, Royal Marines	14 June	09 24 Nov.	09 24 Nov.	37 11 Nov.	51 23 Nov.	52 23 May	55 10 July
Henry Iyatt Delacombe, Royal Marines	21 Oct.	05 30 June	09 12 Oct.	32 9 Nov.	46 25 May	49 9 June	55 14 July
James M'Haffie, Captain, h. p. 60 Foot	7 Aug.	97 1 Feb.	98 24 Aug.	04 4 June	14 10 Jan.	37 11 Nov.	51 31 Aug.
Robert Blake Lynch,⁹⁰ Major, Unattached	1 Nov.	96 1 April	97 23 Nov.	04 do	do	do	do

Major-Generals. 14

	ENSIGN, ETC.	LIEUT.	CAPTAIN.	MAJOR.	LIEUT.-COLONEL.	COLONEL.	MAJOR GENERAL.
†⊕ Charles Diggle, KH,[91] *Major*, Unattached	31 Aug. 04	14 Feb. 05	24 May 10	18 June 15	10 Jan. 37	11 Nov. 51	31 Aug. 55
†⊕ John Murray Belshes,[92] *Major*, do.	14 Nov. 04	29 Aug. 05	4 Sept. 12	20 Mar. 17	do	do	do
⊕ Benjamin Orlando Jones[93]	29 May 05	23 Oct. 06	9 Sept. 12	4 Sept. 17	do	do	do
†⊕ William Croker,[94] *Major*, Unattached	9 April 07	30 June 08	31 Mar. 14	5 July 21	do	do	do
†⊕ Norcliffe Norcliffe, KH,[95] *Major*, h.p. 18 Hussars	5 Feb. 07	25 April 08	29 Feb. 16	9 Aug. 21	do	do	do
†⊕ Robert Martin Leake, *Colonel,* CB. KH.[96] *Commanding the Troops in the Wind-*	2 Oct. 05	11 Dec. 06	14 Feb. 11	18 July 22	do	do	do
ward and Leeward Islands }	29 June 09	17 May 10	5 Nov. 12	21 Nov. 22	do	do	do
⊕ George Macdonald[97]	5 Sept. 05	25 July 06	17 Aug. 15	13 Aug. 30	26 Feb. 33	do	7 Sept. 55
⊕ Bart. Vigors Derinzy, KH.[98] *Lt.Col.*, ret. full pay, *Insp. Field Officer*	26 May 06	16 Mar. 08	25 Oct. 14	4 Jan. 31	26 Feb. 33	do	do
Charles Ash Windham,[99] *CB. on the Staff in India*	never	30 Dec.	31 May 26	9 Nov. 33	29 Dec. 46	20 June 54	8 Sept. 55
Patrick Yule,[100] *Colonel,* ret. full pay, Royal Engineers	1 May	11 May 08	23 Mar. 25	28 June 38	1 April 46	do	9 Oct. 55
James Gordon,[101] *Colonel,* do.	11 July	24 June 09	1 Sept. 18	31 Mar. 38	31 Nov. 38	11 Nov. 51	27 Oct. 55
⊕ John Ashmore,[102] *Col. Comm.*, ret. full pay, Royal Marines	19 Nov.	5 Dec. 09	12 Oct. 32	9 Nov. 46	16 Nov. 49	21 June 54	4 Oct. 55
Charles Otway, *Colonel,* ret. full pay, Royal Artillery	1 July	5 Mar. 07	9 Nov. 08	9 Nov. 27	23 Nov. 41	9 Nov. 46	20 Nov. 54	2 Nov. 55
Sir William Fenwick Williams, *Bart.,* KCB,[96] *from Royal Artillery, Lt. General* }	14 July 14	25 July 25	16 Nov. 27	13 Aug. 40	22 May 46	31 Mar. 48	28 Nov. 54	do
Commanding the Division in North America							
John Edward Dupuis, CB, from Royal Artillery	13 Feb.	25 Mar. 08	8 Nov. 27	15 June 40	8 Jan. 47	22 April 52	17 Aug. 55	
⊕⊕ Join Cox, KH.[103]	16 Mar.	8 June 08	8 June 09	23 Dec. 27	19 June 40	28 Dec. 48	17 Feb. 53	11 Nov. 51	18 Dec. 55
⊕ William Henry Law,[104] *Lt.Col.,* retired full pay, 83 Foot	29 April 13	28 Nov. 16	14 July 25	28 June 38	22 Dec. 48	28 Nov. 54	16 May 56
⊕ Anthony Marshall,[105] *Lt.Col.,* do.	1 Oct.	1 Aug. 09	28 Feb. 14	10 Jan. 37	19 Feb. 41	11 Nov. 51	30 May 56
⊕ Robert Sloper Piper,[106] *Lt.Col.;* do.	10 Jan. 09	21 Dec. 09	16 Mar. 14	do	23 Nov. 41	20 June 54	23 May 56
Robert Andrews, *Colonel,* retired full pay, Royal Artillery	1 July	15 Oct. 06	26 Nov. 07	24 June 28	3 Sept. 45	20 June 54	7 June 56
Frederick Henry Baddeley, *Colonel,* retired full pay, Royal Engineers	1 Jan.	1 Aug. 14	25 June 25	9 Nov. 35	6 Sept. 46	28 Nov. 54	10 June 56
Peter Faddy,[107] *Lt.Col.,* retired full pay, Royal Artillery	8 Sept. 03	1 Nov. 03	5 Sept. 08	22 July 11	1 April 39	10 Aug. 50	11 Nov. 51	14 June 56
Hassel Richard Moor,[108] *Lt.Col.* do.	22 Dec. 03	1 May 04	1 Dec. 12	do	22 July 39	40		
Edward Sabine, from Royal Artillery	do	20 July	24 Jan. 13	10 Jan. 37	25 Jan. 41	28 Nov. 54	do
Francis Ringler Thomson,[109] *Colonel,* retired full pay, R. Engineers	1 June 12	21 July 13	29 July 25	28 June 38	1 Mar. 47	28 Nov. 54	7 June 56
James Robertson Craufurd, from Gr. Gds., *Commanding a Brigade at Shorncliffe*	14 June	21 Aug. 14	19 Sept. 26	never	18 Feb. 37	11 Nov. 51	19 June 56
Robert Clarke, *Colonel,* retired full pay, Royal Artillery	26 Nov.	8 Aug. 12	6 Nov. 23	23 Nov. 41	28 Nov. 46	20 June 54	7 July 56
Charles Brownlow Cumberland, *Lt.Col.,* retired full pay, 96 Foot	21 Dec.	15 Oct. 25	10 June 26	19 Sept. 34	22 July 41	do	8 July 56
Robert George Hughes,[110] *Lt.Col.,* retired full pay, 52 Foot	29 June	6 July 30	3 Dec. 32	19 Sept. 41	28 Feb. 50	31 Oct. 52	55	11 July 56
Thomas Budgen, *Colonel,* retired full pay, Royal Engineers	1 Jan.	1 Aug. 14	13 May 25	9 Nov. 35	21 Sept. 46	28 Nov. 54	1 Aug. 56
Pennel Cole,[111] *Colonel,* do.	1 Feb. 10	1 May 11	7 Feb. 17	10 Jan. 37	1 April 46	20 June 54	11 Aug. 56
William Stewart Balfour	8 Feb.	21 12 May	25 17 June 26	never	37	1 April 46	20 June 54	1 Feb. 37	22 Aug. 56
William Yorke Moore,[112] *Lt.Col.,* retired full pay, 54 Foot	15 Dec.	25 12 Dec.	26 19 July 33	30 Dec. 38	11 Nov. 51	28 Nov. 54	5 Sept. 56
Edward Matson,[113] *Colonel,* retired full pay, Royal Engineers	7 May 10	9 June 11	2 10 Jan. 21	37 1 April 46	20 June 54	10 Sept. 56
William Booth[114]	8 May 06	25 Mar. 09	3 May 24	28 June 27	11 July 37	11 Nov. 51	23 Sept. 56
Richard Greaves[115]	25 June	12 16 July 12	28 Oct. 24	8 May 28	29 Sept. 37	do	9 Nov. 56
⊕ John Alves,[116] *Lt.Col.* ret.f p. Dep. Bat. Serjt.-at-Arms to the Queen	5 Nov.	07 25 Dec.	10 13 Mar. 27	17 May 41	14 Mar. 51	9 Nov. 56	5 Dec. 56

Major-Generals.

	CORNET, ETC.	LIEUT.	CAPTAIN	MAJOR.	LIEUT.-COLONEL.	COLONEL.	MAJOR-GENERAL.
†Alexander Maclean Fraser,[117] *Lt.Col.*, Unattached	8 Nov. 04	17 July 05	25 June 24	29 July 36	27 Nov. 37	11 Nov. 51	8 Dec. 56
Thomas Gordon Higgins, from Royal Artillery	4 Oct. 06	1 Feb. 08	29 July 25	28 June 38	2 April 41	do	24 Jan. 57
⊕ Wm. Henry Elliott, *KH*,[118]	6 Dec. 09	13 Aug. 12	9 Nov. 20	12 July 31	27 June 38	do	29 Jan. 57
Samuel Hawkins,[119] *Col. 2nd Comm.*, ret. full pay, Royal Marines	28 Feb. 14	12 Oct. 32	21 Dec. 41	6 July 49	14 Mar. 54	30 Oct. 55	2 Feb. 57
ℂ ⊕ John Alexander Philips, Royal Marines	26 Aug. 06	17 July 13	27 May 34	9 Nov. 46	4 Sept. 51	1 Aug. 54	6 Feb. 57
⊕ Fortescue Graham, CB., Royal Marines	17 Nov. 08	6 May 25	10 July 37	11 Nov. 51	26 Nov. 51	20 June 54	20 Feb. 57
James Clarke,[120] *Lt.Col.*, ret. full pay, Royal Marines	19 Sept. 10	14 Nov. 23	10 Jan. 37	do	12 Nov. 51	28 Nov. 54	do
⊕ John Eyre,[122] *Colonel*, retired full pay, Royal Artillery	10 June 07	11 Feb. 08	6 Nov. 27	23 Nov. 41	8 July 46	20 June 54	23 Feb. 57
Joseph Childs,[123] *Col. Comm.*, retired full pay, Royal Marines	21 April 09	25 Sept. 27	10 July 37	9 May 43	18 Oct. 52	22 June 55	31 Mar. 57
†Peter Edwards, *Major*, Unattached	1 Oct. 07	3 June 09	17 Mar. 11	13 May 24	28 June 38	11 Nov. 51	14 April 57
⊕ Wm. Freke Williams, *KH*,[124] *Commanding a Brig. at Shorncliffe*	30 Aug. 10	10 June 11	31 Oct. 14	9 April 25	do	do	16 May 57
†⊕ ℂⓂ William Cartwright,[125] *Major*, Unattached	2 July 12	6 Jan. 14	16 Nov. 20	19 May 25	do	do	do
†ℂⓂ Arthur Gore,[126] *Major*, Unattached	22 Dec. 09	10 Oct. 14	5 July 08	27 May 25	do	do	do
⊕ⓂDavid Goodsman,[127] *Major*, do.	12 Aug. 14	23 Mar. 09	do	do	25	do	do	do
Pringle Taylor, *KH*.[128]	15 Aug. 11	2 July 12	2 Jan. 13	16 June 25	46 28 May	47 28 Nov.	54 26 May 57
†⊕ ℂⓂ Thomas Orlando Cater,[129] *Colonel*, ret.f. pay, Royal Artillery	1 April 09	16 Apr. 12	22 July 30	9 Nov. 25	28 June	11 Nov. 51	4 June 57
†⊕ ℂⓂ Thomas Robert Swinburne,[130] *Major*, Unattached	24 June 11	never	26 Dec. 12	10 Sept. 29	38 do	do	do
⊕ⓂGeorge Whincote,[131] *Major*, do.	10 Jan. 11	8 July 12	22 Jan. 18	29 Oct. 25	do	do	do
†ⓂJames Arthur Butler,[132] *Major*,	23 June 13	never	18 April 19	19 Nov. 26	do	do	do
Thomas Henry Johnston	21 Feb.	1 Oct. 25	24 Oct. 26	20 May 36	28 Dec. 38	do	1 July 57
John M'Arthur, *Lt.Col.*, retired full pay, Royal Marines	14 Apr. 09	25 Sept. 27	10 Jan. 37	11 Nov. 51	25 Feb. 52	13 Dec.	do
⊕ Samuel Robert Wesley, *Deputy Adjutant General*, R. Marines	26 June 10	24 Nov. 16	Nov. 27	do	1 Mar. 39	11 Nov. 51	6 July 57
Henry Aitchison Hankey	26 June 10	23 Mar. 10	15 Aug. 26	27 Sept. 33	29 Mar. 26	do	9 July 57
ℂⓂ John Campbell[133]	23 Jan. 12	28 Mar. 14	2 April 18	22 April 37	28	do	17 July 57
Plomer Young, *KH*,[134]	8 May 05	3 Sept. 06	20 April 13	10 Jan. 37	1 April 41	do	29 Aug. 57
⊕ William Dunn,[135] *Lt.Col.*, retired full pay, R. Artillery	22 Dec.	20 July 08	22 July 15	do	13 April 42	18 Mar. 52	do
⊕ ℂⓂ William Bell, from Royal Artillery	23 Nov. 04	2 Dec. 05	3 July 14	do	25 Nov. 41	20 June 54	do
James Fogo,[136] *Lt.Col.*, retired full pay, Royal Artillery	18 June 04	21 Dec. 04	4 Oct. 14	do	do	do	do
⊕ *Hon.* William Arbuthnott,[137] *Lt.Col.*, ret. full pay, R. Artillery	16 July 04	do	do	20 Dec.	do	do	do
⊕ Henry Blachley,[138] *Lt.Col.*,	10 Aug. 04	18 Feb. 05	do	15 May 05	23 Dec.	41 do	do
⊕ George John Belson,[139] *Lt.Col.*, do. do.	29 Sept.	16 July 04	21 May 05	23 May 15	1 Sept. 46	28 Nov. 47	2 Sept. 57
Robert Franck Romer, *Lt.Col.*, do. do. *Barrack Master at Winchester*	9 Nov.	21 July 04	13 June 21	30 June 13	29 Mar. 35	11 Nov. 39	5 Sept. 57
Charles Ogle Streatfeild, *Colonel*, retired full pay, Royal Engineers	20 Mar.	14 Dec. 13	21 Nov. 21	10 Oct. 21	24 April 37	do 39	8 Sept. 57
Henry Dive Townshend[141]	16 July	12 Sept. 14	14 April 14	12 Mar. 25			
Thomas Wright,[142] CB.	18 Dec.		do	30		28 Nov. 47	28 Nov. 57
Joseph Ellison Portlock,[143] *Col.*, retired full pay, Royal Engineers, *Member of the Council of Education*	20 July	13 Dec.	15 June 22	9 Nov. 46	13 Mar. 47		25 Nov. 54
Sir John Eardley Wilmot Inglis,[144] KCB., fr. 32 F., *On Staff in India*	2 Aug.	19 Jan. 33	29 Sept. 39	25 Feb. 43	7 June 48	5 June 49	26 Nov. 55
John Hungerford Griffin,[145] *Colonel*, ret. full pay, Royal Artillery	5 July	13 Oct. 28	21 Nov. 15	21 Nov. 34	5 Sept. 46	28 Nov. 49	22 Dec. 57
Thomas Wood, from Grenadier Guards	26 Nov.	20 June 12	25 June 23	28 June 38	28 June 38	11 Nov. 54	11 Jan. 58

15

Major-Generals.

	CORNET, ETC.	LIEUT.	CAPTAIN.	MAJOR.	LIEUT.-COLONEL.	COLONEL.	MAJOR-GENERAL.
William Hassall Eden	31 Mar. 14	22 June 20	13 July 23	29 Aug. 26	10 Aug. 39	11 Nov. 51	15 Jan. 58
Edward Augustus Parker, *Colonel Comm.* ret. full pay, R. Marines	23 Sept. 11	23 Feb. 30	26 Aug. 39	11 Nov. 51	13 Dec. 52	22 June 55	24 Feb. 58
Sir James Hope Grant,[146] K.C.B., from 9 Lancers, *Lt. General Commanding in China*	29 Aug. 26	26 Feb. 28	29 May 35	22 April 42	7 June 49	28 Nov. 51	26 Feb. 58
Joseph Clarke	22 Mar. 10	10 June 13	24 Feb. 25	26 June 33	17 Sept. 39	11 Nov. 51	16 Mar. 58
Sir John Gaspard Le Marchant,[147] *Governor, Lt. General and Commander in Chief at Malta*	26 Oct. 20	24 Oct. 21	30 June 25	14 Dec. 32	18 Oct. 39	do	22 Mar. 58
Hale Young Wortham,[148] *Colonel*, ret. full pay, R. Engineers	1 July 12	21 July 13	24 Sept. 25	28 June 38	16 April 47	28 Nov. 54	1 April 58
Thomas Aiskew Larcom, CB., *Lt. Col.* r.f.p.R. Engineers, *Under Secretary in Ireland*	1 June 20	9 Feb. 26	19 Mar. 40	11 Nov. 51	17 Feb. 54	28 Nov. 54	1 April 58
Charles Gascoyne	7 Dec. 20	30 Jan. 23	23 Aug. 25	31 Jan. 31	22 Oct. 39	11 Nov. 51	3 April 58
Sir William Rose Mansfield,[149] K.C.B., *Lt. Gen. on the Staff in China*	27 Nov. 35	31 Aug. 38	10 Feb. 43	3 Dec. 47	9 May 51	28 Nov. 54	18 May 58
William Fraser, *Colonel*, ret. full pay, Royal Artillery	1 May 15	5 Mar. 20	18 Mar. 36	9 Nov. 46	11 June 50	do	5 June 58
George Moncrieff, from Scots Fusilier Guards	never	8 April 26	6 July 30	never	24 Jan. 40	11 Nov. 51	14 June 58
John Casemir Harold,[150] *Lt. Col.*, ret. full pay, 11 Foot	25 Sept. 06	28 May 07	16 Feb. 15	10 Jan. 37	11 Nov. 51	14 April 57	1 July 58
Sir Thomas Harte Franks,[151] K.C.B., from 10 Foot	7 July 25	26 Sept. 26	1 Mar. 30	29 Dec. 43	28 Mar. 45	20 June 54	20 July 58
Sir Edward Lugard,[157] K.C.B., from 29 Foot, *Secretary for Military Correspondence, War Office*	31 July 28	31 Oct. 31	30 Dec. 43	3 April 46	7 June 49	do	do
Thomas James Valiant, *Lt. Col.*, ret. full pay, 40 Foot	29 May 28	17 Dec. 29	1 May 35	10 Jan. 46	25 June 52	25 June 55	6 Aug. 58
Poole Valiancey England, from Royal Artillery	10 May 05	1 June 06	11 Mar. 17	10 Jan. 37	17 Aug. 43	17 Feb. 55	9 Aug. 58
John Gordon,[152] *Lt. Col.*, retired full pay, Royal Artillery	10 May 05	1 June 06	5 Aug. 16	10 Jan. 37	6 April 43	20 June 54	do.
William Cuthbert Ward, from Royal Engineers	10 May 08	24 June 09	21 July 18	10 Jan. 37	9 Dec. 37	11 Nov. 51	12 Aug. 58
George Elliot,[153] *Lt. Col.*, ret. full pay, Royal Marines	1 Nov. 27	6 April 35	16 Aug. 44	......	22 June 55	22 June 55	24 Aug. 58
Marcus John Slade,[155] *Lt. Governor of Guernsey*	22 Jan. 28	22 Mar. 36	21 Jan. 45	7 July 46	20 June 54	14 July 55	do.
John Tatton Brown, Royal Marines	15 July 19	12 Nov. 29	22 April 26	27 Sept. 31	7 Feb. 40	11 Nov. 51	26 Aug. 58
George Henry MacKinnon, CB.[156]	21 May 11	14 Nov. 20	8 Feb. 39	11 Nov. 51	13 Dec. 52	22 June 55	8 Sept. 58
Benjamin Brandram Boileau	29 June 24	4 Nov. 24	21 Feb. 28	never 32	17 June 36	15 Dec. 40	22 Sept. 58
Samuel Brandram Boileau	25 Aug. 25	10 June 26	20 April 32	17 June 36	15 Dec. 40	do	10 Oct. 58
Hon. George Fred. Upton,[158] CB., from Coldstream Guards	4 Oct. 21	1 Aug. 26	25 Nov. 28	9 Dec. 36	18 Dec. 40	do	26 Oct. 58
Hon. Arthur Alexander Dalzell	24 Apr. 23	29 Oct. 23	12 Dec. 26	16 June 37	16 April 41	do	do
Thomas Simson Pratt, CB.,[159] *Commanding the Troops in Australia*	29 April 19	5 Feb. 24	26 June 27	5 Jan. 41	23 April 41	do	do
Orlando Felix[160]	2 Feb. 14	29 April 20	17 Sept. 25	25 Dec. 35	6 May 41	do	do
William Nelson Hutchinson, *Commanding Western District*	14 Aug. 10	10 Nov. 14	20 May 24	31 Oct. 26	18 June 41	do	do
Henry Frederick Lockyer,[161] CB., KH, from 97 Foot, *Commanding at Ceylon*	24 Feb. 20	25 Mar. 23	17 June 26	4 Dec. 32	7 Sept. 41	do	do
Simcoe Baynes[162]	24 June 12	28 Dec. 15	24 June 24	2 Oct. 35	26 Dec. 41	do	do
Montague Cholmeley Johnstone[163]	27 Feb. 23	16 Dec. 24	19 Sept. 26	27 July 38	16 Nov. 41	do	do
Frederick Meade,[164] *Major*, Unattached	26 Mar. 05	30 Mar. 09	7 April 25	19 Jan. 26	23 Nov. 41	20 June 54	do
William Frederick Forster,[165] KH, *Deputy Adjutant General*	10 June 13	26 Nov. 13	26 June 17	18 Feb. 26	do	do	do
Frederick Johnston	4 April 10	18 Feb. 13	21 Aug. 17	8 April 26	do	do	do
Albert Goldsmid,[166] *Major*, Unattached	30 May 11	20 Feb. 12	22 Feb. 16	10 June 26	do	do	do
Edward Macarthur,[167] CB.	27 Oct. 08	6 July 09	8 Feb. 21	10 June 26	do	do	do

16

Major-Generals.

	CORNET, ETC.	LIEUT.	CAPTAIN.	MAJOR.	LIEUT.-COLONEL.	COLONEL.	MAJOR-GENERAL.
Day Hort Macdowall[166]	15 April 13	10 Mar. 14	11 Sept. 17	18 July 26	23 Nov. 41	20 June 54	26 Oct. 58
† James Price Hely, KH.[169] *Major, Unattached*	4 April 95	9 July 03	15 Feb. 10	1 Aug. 26	do	do	do
† Charles Robert Bowers,[170] *Major, Unattached*	18 Jan. 10	18 Oct. 10	8 Dec. 18	15 Aug. 26	do	do	do
† John Arnaud, KH.[171] *Major,* do.	2 July 07	13 Sept. 08	13 Jan. 14	29 Aug. 26	do	do	do
Sir Robert Garrett,[173] KCB, *On the Staff in India*	6 Mar. 11	3 Sept. 14	2 July 17	14 Sept. 26	do	do	do
† Richard Connop, *Major, Unattached*	30 Dec. 13	15 Sept. 14	25 Sept. 17	do 26	do	do	do
† Thomas Molyneux Williams, KH.[174] *Major, Unattached*	14 Feb. 11	28 Feb. 12	16 Sept. 19	19 Sept. 26	do	do	do
† William Nepean,[175] *Major, Unattached*	11 July 09	2 April 12	4 Oct. 19	14 Nov. 26	do	do	do
Arthur Hill Trevor,[176] KH.	1 April 03	1 Jan. 10	27 July 15	12 Dec. 26	do	do	do
Richard Rich Wilford Brett	23 Dec. 13	24 July 14	24 May 16	30 Dec. 26	do	do	do
† William Holmes Dutton, *Major, Unattached*	never	4 May 15	15 Aug. 20	22 Mar. 27	do	do	do
† G. T. K., *Earl of* Albemarle,[177] *Major, Unattached*	4 April 15	25 May 20	17 Feb. 25	do 27	do	do	do
George Thomas Colomb	8 Dec. 08	18 Oct. 10	23 June 14	27 April 27	do	do	do
† *Fra. Marquis of* Conyngham, KP. GCH. *Major, Unattached*	21 Sept. 20	24 Oct. 21	12 June 23	2 Oct. 27	do	do	do
Sir Sidney J. Cotton, KCB., from 10 Foot, *On the Staff in India*	19 April 21	13 Feb. 12	1 Jan. 20	18 Jan. 28	do	do	do
Maurice Barlow[178]	21 July 14	23 Mar. 15	20 Dec. 21	12 June 28	do	do	do
† John Napper Jackson,[179] from 99 Foot	1 July 05	1 Jan. 06	28 Feb. 12	11 June 29	do	do	do
Botet Trydell,[180] from 83 Foot	19 Oct. 04	30 Oct. 06	28 Feb. 18	3 Dec. 29	do	do	do
† John Clark, KH.[181]	2 June 14	27 Nov. 21	29 Aug. 26	25 Dec. 29	do	do	do
Redmond William Brough	10 Mar. 07	15 July 08	10 Jan. 22	29 May 35	26 Nov. 41	do	do
Edw. Hungerford Delaval Elers Napier[182]	11 Aug. 25	11 Oct. 26	21 June 31	11 Oct. 39	31 Dec. 41	do	do
Edward Harvey[183]	24 Mar. 25	4 May 26	12 Oct. 30	30 April 41	do	do	do
James Robert Young	27 July 15	14 Dec. 18	13 May 26	31 Dec. 38	8 April 42	do	do
Sir John Michel, KCB.[184] *On the Staff in India*	3 April 23	28 April 25	12 Dec. 26	6 Mar. 40	15 Mar. 42	do	do
Robert Percy Douglas, *Inspector of Militia*	16 Mar. 20	19 Feb. 24	11 June 28	26 Oct. 41	30 Aug. 42	do	do
Charles Craufurd Hay, *Inspector General, School of Musketry*	27 June 24	24 Dec. 25	19 Sept. 26	16 June 41	1 Nov. 42	do	do
William Longworth Dames, from 37 Foot	26 July 28	24 Nov. 28	27 June 34	12 June 41	23 Dec. 42	do	do
Charles Warren, CB.[185] *On the Staff at Malta*	24 Nov. 14	13 Nov. 18	1 Aug. 22	21 Nov. 34	39	do	do
George Alexander Malcolm, CB.[186]	31 Dec. 25	7 June 27	30 Dec. 31	13 Dec. 39	do	do	do
Robert Henry Wynyard,[187] CB., from 58 Foot, *Lt. General Commanding at the* } *Cape of Good Hope*	25 Feb. 19	17 July 23	20 May 26	25 July 41	30 Dec. 42	do	do
George Durnford, *Lt. Col.,* retired full pay, Royal Artillery	1 Nov. 05	1 June 06	6 Aug. 21	10 Jan. 37	1 April 44	do	do
† Richard Hardinge, KH., from Royal Artillery	23 May 06	19 Dec. 06	17 July 23	28 June 38	5 April 45	do	do
† Joseph Hanwell, *Lt. Col.,* retired full pay, Royal Artillery	23 May 06	14 Jan. 07	17 July 23	do	10 April 45	do	do
Philip Sandilands,[188] *Lt. Col.,* retired full pay, R. Artillery	4 Oct. 06	1 Feb. 08	29 July 25	do	1 April 46	do	do
Browne Willis, from Royal Artillery	do	do	do	do	do	do	do
Benj. Hutcheson Vaughan-Arbuckle, *Lt. Col.,* ret. full pay, do.	4 April 07	do	1 April 27	28 Nov. 41	4 May 46	do	do
John Harbridge Freer, *Lt. Col.,* retired full pay, R. Artillery	do	do	5 July 27	do	do	do	do
Archibald White Hope, *Lt. Col.,* retired full pay, Royal Artillery	do	do	do	do	do	do	do
John Lewis Smith, *Lt. Col.,* retired full pay, Royal Artillery	10 June 07	do	6 Nov. 27	do	23 June 46	do	do

Major-Generals.

Name	ENSIGN, ETC.	LIEUT.	CAPTAIN.	MAJOR.	LIEUT.-COLONEL.	COLONEL.	MAJOR-GENERAL.
William Cochrane Anderson, from Royal Artillery	3 Nov. 07	1 Aug. 08	6 Nov. 27	23 Nov. 41	9 Nov. 46	20 June 54	26 Oct. 58
William Redman Ord, from Royal Engineers	25 April 09	29 May 10	20 Dec. 14	10 Jan. 37	18 Mar. 45	17 Feb. 54	1 Nov. 58
Henry Eyre, *Commanding at Chatham*	28 Aug. 17	20 April 26	3 April 28	17 Feb. 37	17 Mar. 43	20 June 54	16 Nov. 58
Henry John Savage, from Royal Engineers	30 Sept. 09	1 May 11	1 Dec. 15	10 Jan. 37	22 May 45	21 Mar. 54	23 Nov. 58
Lord William Paulet, CB.,[189] *Commanding a Brigade at Aldershot, Equerry to H.R.H. the Duke of Cambridge*	1 Feb. 21	23 Aug. 22	12 Feb. 25	10 Sept. 30	21 April 45	20 June 54	13 Dec. 58
Philip McPherson, CB.[190]	2 Nov. 09	13 June 11	13 Mar. 27	23 Nov. 41	4 July 43	20 June 54	24 Dec. 58
Nathaniel Massey Stack, *Lt. Col., retired full pay, Depot Battalion*	25 Nov. 28	29 Dec. 35	6 July 38	22 Dec. 48	8 June 52	28 Nov. 54	24 Dec. 58
Richard Say Armstrong, from Royal Artillery	17 Dec. 07	22 Mar. 09	6 Nov. 27	23 Nov. 41	9 Nov.	46 20 June 54	6 Jan. 59
Chas. Wm. Ridley, CB.,[191] from Gr. Guards, *Gentleman Usher to the Prince Consort*	never	21 Feb.	28 14 June 31	never	14 July 43	do	13 Feb. 59
John Patton	18 Sept. 17	1 Mar. 21	10 Sept. 25	31 Oct. 34	18 Aug.	do	20 Feb. 59
Hugh Manley Tuite, *Lt. Col., ret. full pay, Royal Artillery*	9 Nov.	30 26 Aug. 31	23 Nov. 41	never	20 June 54	20 June 57	2 Mar. 59
Duncan Alexander Cameron, CB.,[192] *Vice President of the Council of Army Education*	8 April 25	15 Aug. 26	21 June 33	23 Aug. 39	5 Sept. 43	20 June 54	25 Mar. 59
Thomas Matheson	17 Aug.	15 30 Oct. 23	2 Aug. 26	20 Oct. 37	17 Nov. 43	do	2 April 59
George Bell, CB.,[193]	14 Mar.	11 17 Feb. 14	7 Aug. 28	29 Mar. 39	5 Dec. 43	do	9 April 59
Horatio Nelson Vigors,[194] from St. Helena Regt.	12 April	27 11 Aug. 29	27 Mar. 35	20 Nov. 42	15 Dec. 43	do	1 May 59
Creighton Grierson,[195] *Lt. Col., ret. full pay, R. Engineers*	1 June	10 1 May 11	1 July 21	10 Jan. 37	1 April 46	do	10 May 59
Lewis Alexander Hall, from Royal Engineers	21 July	10 1 May 11	12 Jan. 25	28 June 38	1 April 46	do	10 May 59
Robert Richardson-Robertson, CB.[196]	8 June	26 9 April 29	16 Aug. 33	18 June 41	22 Dec. 43	do	14 May 59
Samuel Braybrooke,[197] from Ceylon Rifle Regt.	17 Dec.	12 29 April 18	6 Mar. 25	27 Feb. 35	26 Jan. 44	do	12 June 59
Daniel Bolton, from Royal Engineers	14 Dec.	11 1 July 12	7 June 25	28 June 38	9 Nov. 46	do	20 June 59
Augustus Flemyng, *Lt. Col., ret. full pay, Royal Marines*	7 Jan.	28 28 Jan. 36	21 Jan. 45	never	10 July 55	10 July 58	8 July 59
Robert Law, KH.,[198] from R. Newfoundland Companies	8 June	09 27 May 11	18 Oct. 30	9 Nov. 46	2 Feb.	44 20 June 54	17 July 59
Edward L'Estrange,[199] *Captain, retired full pay, 70 Foot*	10 Nov.	08 19 April 10	9 Nov. 30	18 Aug. 48	26 May	54 26 Oct. 58	19 July 59
Usher Williamson,[200] *Lt. Col., retired full pay, 27 Foot*	29 Aug.	26 11 Nov. 31	28 Feb. 37	27 Aug. 43	30 April	44 20 April 54	5 Aug. 59
Sir Charles Thomas Van Straubenzee, KCB.,[201] *On the Staff in China*	26 Nov.	28 22 Feb. 33	10 Mar. 42	never	19 Apr.	54 28 Nov. 54	14 Aug. 59
Henry William Parke,[202] *Colonel Commandant, ret. full pay, R. Marines*	9 April	22 12 Oct. 27	12 Feb. 32	never	31 May	54 28 Nov. 54	23 Aug. 59
Sir Alexander Murray Tulloch, KCB.,[202] *Military Superintendent of Out Pensioners*	20 Mar.	26 30 Nov. 27	12 Mar. 38	29 Mar. 39	20 June	54 20 June 54	9 Sept. 59
Edward Hely Hutchinson, *Lt. Col., retired full pay, 35 Foot*	28 April	27 10 Sept. 29	8 June 38	17 May 50	20 June 54	57 16 Sept. 59
Alexander Jardine,[203] *Lt. Col., retired full pay, 27 Foot*	22 April	26 10 17 Dec. 13	7 Feb. 32	9 Nov. 46	1 Nov. 48	20 June 54	25 Sept. 59
William George Gold[204]	25 April	25 26 June 28	11 Mar. 36	1 June 46	1 June 49	28 Nov. 54	7 Oct. 59
Thomas Foster, from Royal Engineers	1 Sept.	15 7 Sept. 19	29 June 32	10 Feb. 43	26 July 44	20 Nov. 54	17 Oct. 59
Thomas Hurdle, CB.,[205] *Colonel Commandant, retired full pay, Royal Marines*	28 April	12 16 Apr. 13	10 Jan. 37	29 Mar. 39	11 Nov. 48	20 June 51	20 June 54	25 Oct. 59
Thomas Peard Dwyer,[206] *Colonel Commandant, r. r. f. p. Royal Marines*	24 April	09 9 Nov. 13	26 Mar. 40	20 Mar. 46	15 Aug.	53 28 Nov. 54	2 Dec. 59
John Hamilton Stewart, *Lt. Col. retired full pay, 29 Foot*	19 Oct.	12 2 July 34	2 July 41	never	53 25 Jan.	41 27 May	54 2 Dec. 59
Hon. Robert Bruce, *Governor to H.R.H. the Prince of Wales*	23 July	27 18 Dec. 30	22 Feb. 33	never	2 Aug. 54	20 June 54	7 Dec. 59
Arthur Cunliffe Van Notten Pole	never	7 Nov.	26 5 June 30	18 Oct. 33	1 Dec. 37	2 Sept. 44	20 June 54	13 Dec. 59

War Services of the General Officers who are not Colonels of Regiments. 19

1 General M'Kenzie served the campaign of 1794 on the Continent, including the several actions between the Waal and Rhine, forcing the enemy from St. André, sortie from Nimeguen, and the actions at Thuyl and Geldermalsen. Served also on the eastern coast of Spain under Sir Wm. Henry Clinton.

4 General Herbert served on the Continent with the army under Lord Moira and the Duke of York. Engaged during the Carib war in St. Vincent's; at Port-au-Prince, in St. Domingo; and at Fort Irois during the three months' siege. Served also at the siege of Copenhagen, 1807.

5 General Armstrong went out to Flanders with Lord Moira, in 1794; joined the Duke of York at Antwerp, and was in that disastrous retreat through Holland in the winter of 1794-95, and embarked at Bremen. Served in Ireland during the Rebellion in 1798, and was Assistant-Adjutant-General of the Centre District under General R. Dundas, until the peace of 1802.

6 General Gordon served at the siege of Pondicherry, battle of Argaum, sieges of Asseerghur, Gawilghur, and various other hill forts. Served also at Walcheren in 1809.

8 Sir Edward Nicolls, with thirteen volunteers in a boat of the *Blanche* frigate, boarded and captured, on the 3rd Nov. 1803, the French armed cutter *Albion* from under the guns of Monte Christie, St. Domingo,—in this action he was severely wounded by a musket-ball, which entering the abdomen, and coming out at his right side, lodged in the arm. On board the *Standard* at the passage of the Dardanelles on the 19th Feb. 1807. On the 26th June 1808, with a boat's crew, he boarded and captured the Italian gun-boat *Volpe* near Corfu. Present at the reduction of the Island of Anholt in May 1809. Severely wounded at the attack on Fort Bowyer 15th Sept. 1814. Was frequently employed in boat and battery actions. In 1808 was, in a boat at the capture of a French brig; in 1804 he commanded the Royal Marines during the siege of Curagoa, and for 28 consecutive days was exposed to several attacks of the enemy. At the passage of the Dardanelles he captured the Turkish flag, and was honourably mentioned. In 1807 he was at the blockade of Corfu, and the expedition to Egypt. In North America he raised and commanded a regiment of Indians, and was senior Major of all the troops engaged in the attack on New Orleans in 1815. Was also governor of the islands of Anholt and Ascension. During the above service he had his left leg broken, and right leg severely wounded, was shot through the body and right arm, received a severe sabre cut in the head, was bayonnetted in the chest, and lost the sight of an eye in his 107th action with the enemies of his country. He was frequently mentioned in Dispatches, and received a sword of honor from the Patriotic Fund.

9 General Connolly served in Lord Bridport's action, 23rd June 1795. In 1796 served in the Mediterranean, including the evacuation of Bastia, capture of Porto Ferrajo, and destruction of Martello Tower in St. Fiorenzo Bay. On board H. M. S. *Excellent* in the battle off Cape St. Vincent, 14th Feb. 1797. Capture of Admiral Perrie's squadron off Toulon in 1798, consisting of three frigates and two brigs. On board the *Hannibal*, in the battle of Algesiras, 6th July 1801, wounded and taken prisoner. On board H. M. S. *Penelope*, in the action off Flushing and Ostend, under Sir Sydney Smith, 16th May 1804. Present at the siege of Copenhagen, and capture of Danish fleet in 1807, and at Nyebourgh in 1808. In 1812, on board H.M.S. *Hamadryad*, when attacked by French privateers; debarked with detachments at Scheveling, and took possession of the Hague in 1814. During the above periods he has been very frequently engaged with the enemy in affairs of gun-boats and batteries, &c. &c. He has received a reward from the Patriotic Fund. Has received the War Medal with two Clasps.

10 General Uniacke served in Ireland throughout the rebellion of 1798-99 and during the preceding and subsequent disturbances, part of the time as Aide-de-Camp to Sir James Duff.

11 Lieut.General Vernon served the campaign of 1808-9 in the Peninsula, as a Deputy-Assistant-Adjutant-General. Subsequently in the same capacity with the Duke of Wellington's army until June 1811, and was present at the battle of Talavera. Served with the 2nd battalion 66th, at the surprise of a French division at Arroyo de Molino, and other operations, until the capture of Badajoz. With the Queen's at the reduction of the Forts and battle of Salamanca—slightly wounded early in the day, and very severely at the close of the action, a ball having entered his breast and lodged near the heart, after tearing along two ribs. Followed the army again at the expiration of three weeks, and resumed the command of his regiment, with which he served in the various operations preceding, during, and subsequent to the siege of Burgos. He has received the Gold Medal for Salamanca, and the Silver War Medal with one Clasp for Talavera.

12 Sir Adolphus John Dalrymple served as Aide-de-Camp to Sir James Craig in the Eastern District, Malta, Naples, and Sicily, from July 1803 to May 1806, and as Military Secretary to Sir Hew Dalrymple in Portugal in 1808.

13 Lieut.General Wright's services:—Engaged in most of Lord Nelson's attacks on Rota and Cadiz in 1797; battle of the Nile; campaign of Naples in 1799; surrender of Ovo and Novo, Fort St. Elmo, Capua, and Guata; cutting out of the *Guiep* at Vigo; Egypt in 1801; and battle of Algiers in 1816. Has the Gold Medal for Egypt and the Silver War Medal with four Clasps.

14 Sir Duncan M'Gregor was actively employed in Sicily and Italy in 1806, including the skirmishes at St. Euphemie, battle of Maida, attack on Scylla Castle, and capture of Catrone. Campaign of 1807 in Egypt, including the attacks in the Desert, and siege of Rosetta. Campaign in Holland in 1809, including the attacks and captures of Ter Vere and Flushing. Campaigns in the Peninsula during part of 1813 and 14. Capture of Corsica in May 1814.

Wounded through the right shoulder by a musket-shot at Maida, for which battle he has received the War Medal with one Clasp.

15 Lord Hotham served in the Peninsula with the Coldstream Guards from April 1812 to Feb. 1814, with the exception of a short absence in consequence of a wound received at the battle of Salamanca. Served also the campaign of 1815, and was present at the battle of Waterloo. He has received the War Medal with four Clasps for Salamanca, Vittoria, Nivelle, and Nive.

16 Sir Wm. Robert Clayton accompanied his regiment, the Royal Horse Guards, to the Peninsula in Oct. 1812, and commanded a squadron at the battles of Vittoria, the Pyrenees, and at the period when Marshal Soult attempted to relieve Pampeluna. In 1815 again accompanied his regiment to the Netherlands, and was at the battles of Quatre Bras, Genappe, and Waterloo. He has received the War Medal with one Clasp for Vittoria.

17 Lieut.General John Drummond served in the Peninsula with the Coldstream Guards from January 1813 to the end of that war in 1814, and was present at the battle of Vittoria, the crossing of the Bidassoa, capture of St. Jean de Luz, battles of Nivelle and Nive, the investment of Bayonne and repulse of the sortie, and has received the War Medal with three Clasps; served also with the army of occupation in France.

18 Lieut.General Buckley served in the Peninsula with the Grenadier Guards, from March 1813 to the end of that war in 1814, including the passage of the Bidassoa, battle of the Nivelle and investment of Bayonne. Served also the campaign of 1815, and was present at the battles of Quatre Bras and Waterloo, and taking of Peronne. He has received the War Medal with two Clasps for Nivelle and Nive.

19 Sir John Rowland Eustace served in Upper Canada the campaigns of 1813 and 1814, in command of a troop of the 19th Light Dragoons attached to the division of the army under the immediate command of General Sir Gordon Drummond, and was engaged in the battle of Lundy's Lane near the Falls of Niagara on the 23d of July 1814, and commanded the whole of the cavalry outposts and piquets during the siege, was present at the storming of Fort Erie, and had the honour to be personally mentioned in the general orders of 1814 upon three different occasions. Accompanied the 1st battalion of the Grenadier Guards to Lower Canada in 1838, and was present with his regiment in the advance upon Napierville, and in the subsequent pursuit of the insurgents.

21 Major General Daly served with the 24th on the expedition to Egypt in 1801. In April 1805 he embarked with the 56th Regt. for Bombay, and he commanded four companies of the 2nd battalion employed in 1809, with a division in the field under Colonel Walker, at the storming of Mallia, and at the reduction of other Forts in the Kattiwar District.

22 Lord Howden served as Aide-de-camp to his Grace the Duke of Wellington during the years 1817 and 18, to the close of the occupation in France. Employed by Government on a special mission, and was present at the battle of Navarin in 1827 (wounded, and mentioned in Commander-in-chief's despatch); siege of Antwerp in 1832 (wounded); campaign in Spain, in Navarre and Basque Provinces, in 1834. Is a Knight of the Legion of Honor, Second Class of St. Anne of Russia, Knight of Charles the Third of Spain, Third Class of Leopold of Belgium, and Commander of the Saviour of Greece.

23 Lieut.General Douglas served at the capture of the Danish and Swedish West India Islands in 1801. On the expedition to the north of Germany in 1805 and 6. Peninsular campaigns from Feb. 1812 to March 1814, including the battles of Salamanca, Vittoria, and the Pyrenees (27th to 31st July); siege of San Sebastian from 24th Aug. to the 8th Sept., and battle of Nivelle. He has the Gold Cross for Salamanca, Vittoria, Pyrenees, and Nivelle, having commanded a field battery; and the Silver War Medal with one Clasp for St. Sebastian.

29 Major General Hon. T. Ashburnham commanded a brigade of the Army of the Sutlej at the battles of Ferozeshah and Sobraon, for which he has received a Medal with one Clasp.

31 Major General T. P. Thompson, prior to entering the Army, was several years in the Royal Navy. He served in the Rifle Brigade at the attack on Buenos Ayres, and was among the captured under General Crauford in the church of St. Domingo. Served in the Peninsula with the 14th Light Dragoons, and was present at the battles of Nivelle, Nive, Orthes, and Toulouse, for which he has received the War Medal with four Clasps. As Captain in the 17th Light Dragoons, was in the Pindarree and other campaigns in India from 1815 to 1819. In 1819 was in the expedition under Sir Wm. Grant Keir to the Persian Gulf, as Secretary and Arabic Interpreter, and being left there as Political Agent, he commanded a detachment of Native Troops ordered to act against the tribe of Beni-Boo-Ali, which detachment being defeated by the Arabs, necessitated the expedition under Sir Lionel Smith in the following year.

33 Major General Bell joined the Royal Fusiliers in the Peninsula in 1811, and served there until the end of the war, and was present at the actions of Fuentes Guinaldo and Aldea de Ponte, advance on Salamanca, affairs of St. Christoval and Rueda, battle of Salamanca, advance to and retreat from Madrid, advance from Portugal, battles of Vittoria, the Nivelle, and the Nive. In 1814 embarked with the Royal Fusiliers to join the force before New Orleans, and present at the assault. Joined the army at Paris, and remained until its withdrawal. He has received the War Medal with four Clasps.

34 Major General John Reed served at the siege of Flushing in 1809; and in the Peninsula from June 1811 to March 1814, including the actions at, and heights above, Moresco, battle of Salamanca, capture of Madrid and the Retiro, action at Olmas, and battle of Vittoria, where he was severely wounded in the right shoulder. He has the War Medal with two Clasps.

35 Major General Burke served in Jamaica and St. Domingo in 1796 and 97; in Holland in

1809. Volunteered at the taking of the Island of Schouwen. Served in the Peninsula in 1810-11-12, with the 5th Division of the Army; was present at the battle of Fuentes d'Onor; was slightly wounded at the affair of Barba del Puerco, in intercepting the retreat of the French garrison of Almeida; volunteered the Forlorn Hope of Sir James Leith's Division at the taking of Badajoz, where he received several severe wounds which have rendered him incapable of following his profession. He has received the War Medal with one Clasp for Badajoz.

36 Major General Thwaites was actively employed from 1795 to 1817. He served in the expedition to the coast of Holland in 1796; in the East Indies from 1796; then on marine duty on board H. M. S. *La Forte*, till wrecked in the Red Sea. The campaign of 1801 in Egypt, having volunteered, crossing the Desert of Suez with Colonel Lloyd's Detachment, with which he joined the Grand Vizier's Army on the advance to and surrender of Cairo. He served in the Peninsula as Captain of Light Infantry, 48th Regiment, from 1811 to 1813, including the siege and storming of Badajoz in 1812, the battle of Salamanca (wounded), advance to and occupation of Madrid, battles of Vittoria, and the Pyrenees (wounded in command of the Light Companies of the Brigade), besides minor affairs. He has received the Sultan's Gold Medal of the Order of the Crescent, and the War Medal with five Clasps.

39 Major General Coles served in South America with the 14th in 1807, including the operations previous to, and storming of, Monte Video. Served afterwards in the Peninsula from Aug. 1808 to Nov. 1811, and again from April 1813 to the end of that war in 1814; present with the 40th at the battles of Rolcia, Vimiera, and Talavera; with the 4th Dragoons at Busaco, Albuhera, and Usagre; and with the 12th Light Dragoons at the passage of the Bidassoa, the Nive and the Adour. He has received the War Medal with seven Clasps.

40 Sir Michael Creagh served in the expedition under Sir David Baird against the Cape of Good Hope; was wounded in the action of the Blue Bourg. In 1810 accompanied the expedition (as Brigade Major) which sailed from Madras against the French Islands: desperately wounded by a cannon shot (which carried away a part of his left shoulder, and killed six of his men), at the attack of the batteries before St. Dennis, Isle of Bourbon; thanked in general orders, and favourably mentioned in the despatches. In 1817 and 18 served (in command of the 86th flank companies) during the Mahratta and the Pindarree wars in India. In 1818 served in the Kandyan country (interior of Ceylon) during that harassing war, in command of the flank companies of the 86th and other detachments, receiving the repeated thanks of General Sir Robert Brownrigg for his services in the enemy's country.

41 Major General Eden served the campaign in Java in 1811 with the 22nd Light Dragoons, including the actions of the 10th and 26th Aug. Aide-de-camp to Sir Thomas Hislop at the battle of Maheidpore, and during the Mahratta war in 1817 and 18. He has received the War Medal with one Clasp for Java.

42 Major General Geddes served with the 27th in Calabria in 1806; at the capture of the island of Procida in 1809; in Sicily in 1810; and subsequently in the Peninsula, including the battles of the Nivelle, the Nive, Orthes, and Toulouse, at which last he received a severe wound, which broke the left thigh-bone near the hip-joint. He has the War Medal with four Clasps.

43 Lord Rokeby served the campaign of 1815 with the 3rd Guards, and was present at the battles of Quatre-Bras and Waterloo. Served the Eastern campaign of 1855 in command of a Brigade, including the siege and fall of Sebastopol (Medal and Clasp, KCB., Commander of the Legion of Honor, Sardinian Medal, and 3rd Class of the Medjidie).

45 Major General Beckwith served in the Peninsula with the 16th Light Dragoons, from July 1813 to the end of that war in 1814, including the battle of the Nivelle, and battles of the Nive on the 9th and 10th Dec., for which he has the War Medal with two Clasps. Served also the campaign of 1815, and was present at the retreat on 17th June and at the battle of Waterloo.

46 Major General Robinson served with the 48th in the Peninsula from June 1809 to October 1813, including the battles of Taluvera and Busaco, Lines at Torres Vedras, pursuit of Massena, action at Campo Mayor, siege of Ciudad Rodrigo, siege and storming of Badajoz (shot through the left arm at the assault, 6th April 1812); battle of Salamanca, capture of Madrid and retreat therefrom, battles of Vittoria, Roncesvalles, and the Pyrenees (severely wounded, left leg fractured 28th July 1813), besides various minor engagements and skirmishes. He subsequently served in the 30th Regiment, which he commanded for ten years, and retired on half-pay in 1843, having commanded the troops in Bermuda two years, and having served on full pay thirty-seven years in all quarters of the world. He has the War Medal with seven Clasps.

47 Major General Maclean served with the 13th Light Dragoons in every action and affair in which it was engaged in the Peninsula, from Dec. 1810 until wounded and taken prisoner at Couches, 13th March 1814. Was present with his regiment during the Waterloo campaign; engaged in command of the rear-guard for the brigade on the 7th June, and throughout the action on the 18th. Accompanied the 13th Dragoons to India in Feb. 1819; was employed in command of a cavalry brigade with the field force at the reduction of Kurnool, and served uninterruptedly with his regiment for twenty-two years, when he returned with it to England, and was placed on half-pay as 2nd Lieut.Colonel. He has received the War Medal with six Clasps for Albuhera, Vittoria, Pyrenees, Nivelle, Nive, and Orthes.

48 Major General Marten served the campaign of 1814 in the Peninsula with the Household Brigade. Also the campaign of 1815, including the battle of Waterloo.

49 Major General Dixon served in Canada during the war from 1812 to 1815; was wounded at the storming of Sandusky, and has received the Gold Medal for Detroit.

50 Major General Ball served in the Peninsula with the 34th, from June 1809 to Nov. 1813, including the siege of Badajoz in May 1811, battles of Busaco and Albuhera, siege of Badajoz in

War Services of the General Officers.

May 1811, actions at Arroyo de Molino and Almaraz, battle of Vittoria (wounded in the head), and affairs at the Pass of Maya (severely wounded in the left leg). He has received the War Medal with three Clasps.

51 Major General Monins served the campaign of 1815 with the 52nd Light Infantry, and was present at the battle of Waterloo. Served afterwards with the Army of Occupation in France.

52 Major General Maunsell served in the Peninsula from Aug. 1813 to the end of that war in 1814, including the siege of San Sebastian, passage of the Bidassoa, battles of Nivelle, 10th Nov. and Nive 9th, 10th, and 11th Dec. Served also in the American war, and was slightly wounded at Bladensburg, 24th Aug., and severely at New Orleans, 23rd Dec. 1814. He has received the War Medal with three Clasps.

53 Major General Grant served in Hanover in 1805, under Lord Cathcart.

54 Major General Frith was present in several affairs consequent upon the operations carried on by the division of the army under Colonel Chalmers in the Travancore war, particularly on the 15th January 1809, and the storming of the enemy's lines on the 21st Feb. following. Served also at the capture of the Isle of Bourbon, and of the Isle of France in 1810.

55 Lieut. General Fergusson served at the capture of Rear Admiral Perrée's squadron from Egypt when in pursuit of the French and Spanish fleets in June, 1799. Blockade of Malta and capture of Admiral Perrée's squadron *Le Généreux* 74, *Ville de Marseilles*, &c., with a reinforcement and supplies for the relief of the garrison. Was wrecked and severely injured on board H. M. S. *Queen Charlotte* when *burnt* off Leghorn in 1800, only *four* saved out of a detachment of nearly 200 marines, including supernumeraries, in all upwards of 700 persons perished. Served at the siege of Genoa and Savona. Destruction of the fort of Port Espezie, and guns carried off by H. M. S. *Santa Dorothea* in 1800, to which ship he then belonged. Served in Egypt under the command of Sir Ralph Abercromby in 1801 (*Medal*). In 1806 at Maida. Defence of Gaeta and surrender of Tropea; took possession of the latter town with his detachment. Served again in Egypt with the expedition under Major-General Fraser in 1807. He has been repeatedly engaged in severe boat actions, and against batteries, and debarked with detachments aiding in capturing and destroying ships and convoys on the enemy's coast. Has received the War Medal with one Clasp.

56 Major General Crawford served in a bomb vessel on the coast of France in 1804 and 5; in the lines in front of Sobral in Portugal, in 1809; with the army in Sicily in 1811, 12, and 13; at the capture of Genoa in 1814; and subsequently in the American war, including the battle of Bladensburg, and capture of Washington, and engagements before New Orleans, on 1st and 3rd Jan. 1815.

57 Major General Darby served in Hanover in 1805; at the siege of Copenhagen in 1807; and the Corunna campaign in 1808-9. Has the War Medal with one Clasp for Corunna.

58 Major General Lockwood commanded the 3rd Light Dragoons throughout the campaign of 1842 in Affghanistan under Gen. Pollock (Medal and CB.), and was present at forcing the Khyber Pass, storming the heights of Jugdulluck, action of Tezeen and Huftkotul, occupation of Cabool, siege and capture of Istaliff. He served also in the Punjaub campaign of 1848-9, and commanded a brigade at the battle of Goojerat (Medal and one Clasp).

59 Sir Richard Airey served throughout the Eastern campaign of 1854-55—first in command of a Brigade, and afterwards from the disembarkation in the Crimea as Quarter-Master-General, and was present at the battles of the Alma, Balaklava, and Inkerman, the siege and fall of Sebastopol (Medal and Clasps, KCB., Commander of the Legion of Honor, Commander of 1st Class of the Military Order of Savoy, and 2nd Class of the Medjidie).

60 The Hon. Sir James Scarlett served the Eastern campaign of 1854-55 in command of the Heavy Cavalry Brigade and afterwards of the Cavalry Division, including the battles of the Alma, Balaklava, and Inkerman, and siege of Sebastopol (Medal and Clasps, KCB., Commander of the Legion of Honor, Sardinian Medal, and 2nd Class of the Medjidie).

61 Sir George Buller served in the Rifle Brigade and commanded its 1st Battalion from 1841 to 1854. He served on the eastern frontier of the Cape of Good Hope in 1847-48-49; commanded one of the columns which entered the Amatola Mountains in the campaign of 1847 against the Gaika chief Sandilla, who surrendered himself to him. He commanded the troops, under Sir Harry Smith, which crossed the Orange River in 1848 to suppress the insurrection of the Dutch Boers—was severely wounded, and had his horse killed under him in the action of the 29th August at Boem Plaats, for which he was nominated a CB. Within a few months after the return of his Battalion to England he re-embarked with it in January 1852 for special service at the Cape; was engaged in all the operations in the Waterkloof in 1852-3, and commanded the 1st Division of the Army until the close of the Kaffir war (Medal). Returned to England in January 1854, and in April following embarked as a Brigadier-General of the Army of the East—commanded a Brigade of the Light Division in the Eastern campaign of 1854-55, including the battles of Alma and Inkerman, and siege of Sebastopol: had two horses shot under him at Inkerman, and suffered a severe contusion of the leg (Medal and Clasps, KCB., Commander of the Legion of Honor, and 2nd Class of the Medjidie). In August 1856, appointed to the command of the troops in the Ionian Islands.

63 Major General W. H. Slade was present at St. Sebastian in July and August 1813; blockade of Bayonne and repulse of the sortie. He was one of the officers selected to accompany the boats from Socoa to the mouth of the river Adour, and to assist in laying the bridge across. He has received the Silver War Medal with one Clasp for St. Sebastian.

64 Major General King served in a mortar-boat in the Faro of Messina for two months

in 1810. Advanced into the United States with Sir George Prevost's army, and commanded a battery against Plattsburg.

65 Major General Grantham served at the defence of Cadiz.

66 Major General Victor served in the Peninsula from December 1812 to the end of the war, including the battles of the Nive, Orthes, and Toulouse, for which he has the War Medal with three Clasps.

67 Major General Sherbourne Williams served at the capture of Guadaloupe in 1815.

68 Major General Dalton served at Walcheren and at the siege of Flushing in 1809.

69 Major General Barry served in the Peninsula from August 1812 to October 1813, and was severely wounded by a grape shot, 31st August 1813, when leading a party to the breach at the storming of St. Sebastian. He has received the Silver War Medal with one Clasp.

70 Major General Whinyates was present at the attack on Algiers by Lord Exmouth on 27th August 1816. Served with the army in France in 1817 and 1818. In February 1839 was commanding officer of Engineers with the Field Force in New Brunswick when the disputed territory was invaded by the state of Maine. Has the Medal for the battle of Algiers.

71 Major General Gough served as Deputy Quarter-Master-General of the army during the war in China, and received the brevet rank of Major and Lieut.-Colonel, together with the Companionship of the Bath, for his conduct in action; he having been present in almost every engagement during the expedition. He was afterwards present in the battle of Maharajpore, as Military Secretary to the Commander-in-Chief in India; and he commanded a Brigade of cavalry at the battles of Moodkee and Ferozeshah, and officiated as Quarter-Master-General in the battle of Sobraon, and was very severely wounded. Served the Punjaub campaign of 1848-9 as Quarter-Master-General Queen's Troops, and was present at the battles of Chillianwallah and Goojerat.

72 Major General Furneaux served in the Peninsula from October 1810 to April 1813, and was with the covering army at the siege of Badajoz.

73 Major General R. G. B. Wilson served in Holland, Belgium, and France, from December 1813 to January 1816, including the battles of Quatre Bras and Waterloo.

74 Major General Emmett's services :—sieges of Badajoz in 1811 and 12; passage of the Nive, battles before Bayonne, Orthes, and Toulouse. Attack on the American lines at New Orleans, every affair on that expedition, and the siege of Fort Bowyer. Slightly wounded at Badajoz in 1811; again on the advance towards Orthes; and very severely wounded at the assault of Badajoz in 1812. He has received the Silver War Medal with four Clasps.

75 Major General Waters served in the Peninsula from April 1812 to September 1814. Was at Cadiz when the siege was raised in the former year. In 1815 he was present in the actions of Quatre Bras and Waterloo. He led one of the columns to the assault of Peronne on the 26th June 1815, and was at the capture of Paris.

76 Major General Pilcher served with the boats of the British fleet in 1801 in their occasional attacks on the Spanish gunboats and vessels off Cadiz. In 1803 he served in the North Sea. In 1804 at the attack on the gun-boats and batteries at Boulogne. On 22nd July 1805 in the general action and defeat of the combined fleets of France and Spain; and on 16th Aug. in action with *La Topaze* French frigate. In Jan. 1806 he landed with the R. M. Battalion at the attack and capture of the Cape of Good Hope; in June following with the same Battalion at the attack and defeat of the Spanish troops on the road to Buenos Ayres, and at the capture of that city; also at its defence in August, and after three days' action was taken prisoner with the rest of the British. In 1811 he served in the North Sea in several actions with Danish gun-boats. In 1813-14 off the coast of France and America. Appointed to the 2nd Battalion R. M., and as Adjutant was at the attack of the American Army and its defeat on the road to Baltimore : at the attack on the American troops at Farnham Church he commanded the advance. In 1815 he was at the attack of the American Rifle force near Point à Petie, and at the capture of that fort in West Florida. From 1819 to 1821 he served at St. Helena—during the last nine months of Napoleon's life, and assisted with the Royal Marines at his interment.

77 Major General Thomas Stevens was present blockading Brest, the Helder, and Cadiz, and was engaged with batteries. In 1809 he was engaged with gun-boats in passing convoys through the Sound and Categat; in H. M. S. *Cerberus*, with convoy of armed transports and gun-boats in the Gulf of Friedland; in the boats of the squadron in the successful attack upon the Russian Flotilla of heavy armed gun-boats and armed Transports; and at the capture of a Russian schooner. From 1836 to 1840 he served in the Royal Marine Battalion on the north coast of Spain; was detached in command of a company for the defence of the Eastern Heights of Passages attacked by the Carlists, and in the Carlist attack of the Lines on the 6th June 1836; and he was also present at Fuentarabia, 11th July 1836. Has received the War Medal with one Clasp.

78 Major General Gibsone landed from the *Thunderer* and served on shore for eight days in Bearhaven Bay in 1804. He was on board the *Safeguard* mortar brig in a severe action with a division of Danish gun-boats off Anholt in June 1811, on which occasion the vessel was engaged for three and a half hours, and 19 were killed or wounded out of a complement of 29. The following year he was engaged at Cateria on the north coast of Spain, and accompanied Captain Parke with two heavy guns intended for the army besieging Burgos. In 1813 and 14 he served in the American war, and was present at the attack on Craney Island, taking of Hampton, defence of the Lines of Chippewa, and on other occasions on the Niagara Frontier, where he sustained a severe fracture of the left arm, and a violent contusion on the right breast.

79 Major General Mercer assisted at the destruction of the French squadron in Basque Roads. He was repeatedly landed on the north coast of Spain in 1810, co-operating with the Patriots. In 1812, while embarked on board H.M.S. *Java*, he was engaged with and captured by the United States frigate *Constitution*. Has received the War Medal with one Clasp.

80 Major General Donald Campbell served at Walcheren in 1809. Has received the War Medal with one Clasp.

81 Major General Whylock served in Sir Robert Calder's action off Ferrol; in boats cutting out from under batteries at Rota, 7th April 1808; commanded the Royal Marines landed from the Anglo-Sicilian Squadron to assist in the defence of the island of Capri when besieged by Gen. la Marque; at the capture of *Leda* from the harbour of Rovigno, 1st April 1809; at the attack and capture of a convoy under protection of a battery at Pesaro, 23rd April; on 15th May at the attack on the town of Rota and destruction of seven vessels; on 8th September at the cutting out of *La Pugliesse* from the harbour of Barletta. On 1st June 1812, commanded a storming party in Isle Verte, near Toulon—enemy routed and a demi-lune battery destroyed. At the capture of the Island of Powza, 27th February 1813; at the cutting out of an armed vessel from under the batteries of Orbetello, 9th May; and 14th Oct. following, at the capture of seventeen vessels at Marinello, after destroying a battery which protected them; at the siege and capture of St. Maria in March, and the siege and capture of Gerona in April, 1814; commanded the Royal Marines at the storming and capture of Sidon, 26th Sept. 1840 (made Brevet-Major), and was slightly wounded in the left arm; on 10th Oct. was in command of a supernumerary battalion when the city and garrison (2,000 men) of Beyrout surrendered; was senior officer of Marines at the bombardment and capture of St. Jean d'Acre (Medal). He has received the War Medal with two Clasps.

82 Major General Bury served with the Royal Marine Battalion on the north coast of Spain in 1836-38 (Knight 1st Class St. Fernando).

84 Major General C. C. Pratt was at the taking of Capri in the Bay of Naples, under Sir Sidney Smith, 11th May 1806. At the cutting out of six armed vessels from under the batteries of Lamica, in the Island of Cyprus, in January 1808. Belonged to the Battalion of Royal Marines commanded by Sir James Malcolm, which served in Spain, the coast of America, and Canada, for four years, and was present at all the services performed by it, including the battle of Frampton in the *Chesapeake*, and the storming and taking of the enemy's fort and post of Oswego on Lake Ontario. Served also in the Battalion of Royal Marines in Spain and was present at the battles of the 16th June 1836, and Hernani 16th March following, together with all the services performed there for nearly four years (Knight 1st Class St. Fernando).

85 Major General Gillespie was landed with a detachment of Royal Marines at Rosas on 7th Nov. 1808, and occupied the citadel. Present at the sortie on the 8th, when the British were forced by the superior number of the enemy to retire. Served on the China expedition (Medal), and was present at the attack and capture of the forts and works at Chuenpee, and the capture of Annunghoy and North Wantong.

86 Major General Garmston was at the taking of Fort Koupan, Isle of Timor, in 1814; capture of Java in 1812; attack of Palambang, Isle of Sumatra, and Sambass, Isle of Borneo; Algiers in 1816. Present at the Sortie from Bilboa 15th May; the advance on the 28th May; and was wounded at the defence of the lines of San Sebastian 6th June, 1836. He has received the Military War Medal with one Clasp for Java; the Naval War Medal with one Clasp for Algiers; and the Order of San Fernando for service in Spain.

87 Major General John Harvey Stevens served in the West Indies, &c. in 1806 and 1807, during the expedition to Walcheren in 1809, and was engaged in several flotilla affairs on the Scheldt. Served also at the successful defence of Cadiz and of Tarifa in 1810 and 1811; was engaged in several detached operations, particularly in one of a severe character on the river Guadalquiver. In 1813 was employed on the coast of America, where he was engaged in an attack on Craney Island, and at the taking of Hampton and Ocracoke under Sir George Cockburn. Served in Canada at the taking of Oswego, on which occasion he was mentioned in Sir Gordon Drummond's despatches. Engaged during a six weeks' siege of Fort Erie, and was intrusted with the construction of a field-work for the defence of the right of the position on Chippewa Creek, which was menaced by a very superior force. In 1816 he was on board the *Queen Charlotte* at the attack on Algiers under Lord Exmouth by whom he was detached to fire carcases at the enemy's vessels within the Mole. He was also present at the demonstrations before Algiers under Admiral Sir H. B. Neale. Has received the War Medal with one Clasp.

88 Major General Reignolds served with the 49th on the China expedition (Medal), and was present at the storming of the heights and forts above Canton, taking of Amoy, second capture of Chusan, storming of the fortified heights of Chinhae, taking of Ningpo, attack and capture of the enemy's entrenched camp on the heights of Segoan (severely wounded), capture of Chapoo (wounded), Woosung, and Chin Kiang Foo, and landing before Nankin. Served throughout the Burmese war of 1852-53 (Medal), nearly the entire period as a Brigadier. On the 4th April 1852 embarked with a force of 1,400 men from Maulmein for the attack on Martaban. Commanded at the attack on shore. Was on board H. M. S. *Rattler* during the ship's engagement with and destruction of the stockades on the river side in front of Rangoon, 11th April; the following morning landed at Rangoon in command of the 18th Royal Irish. On 13th April succeeded to the command of the 1st Bengal Brigade, which he commanded throughout the war, and was present at the storm and capture of Rangoon, capture of Prome, and repulse of the enemy on the night of 8th December 1852. For his services, was several times recommended by General Godwin to the Governor-General of India in Council. Returned from India with the 18th Royal Irish in May 1854; embarked December following for the Crimea, and was at the siege of Sebastopol until April 1855 (Medal and Clasp).

89 Major General Hugh Evans served in *Ulysses* and *Barossa* from 1810 to 1815 on the West India and North America station, and was engaged in the whole of the operations of the squadron up the Chesapeake in 1813.

90 Major General Lynch has the War Medal with two Clasps for Egypt and Fuentes d'Onor.

91 Major General Diggle served with the 52nd Regt. in Sicily, under Sir John Moore, and on the expedition to Gottenburgh. Subsequently he served in the Peninsula, and was present during the retreat and at the battle of Corunna, as also in the action of the Coa, battle of Busaco, and affairs when the Army fell back upon the Lines of Torres Vedras. He served also the campaign of 1813, 14, and 15, including the two attacks on the fortified village of Merxem,—in the latter of which he commanded the 2nd Battalion in the advance upon Antwerp for the bombardment of the French Fleet. He was also present at the battle of Waterloo, where during the repulse of the French Imperial Guard he was severely wounded, and received the Brevet of Major. He has received the War Medal with two Clasps for Corunna and Busaco.

92 Major General Belshes served with the 2nd Battalion 4th Regt. in the expedition to Walcheren in 1809. On the 1st Battalion arriving in Portugal, he resigned his staff appointment as Military Secretary at Gibraltar, and joined that Battalion then stationed at Torres Vedras, and served with it during the whole advance from Santarem and the Lines, and was present during several affairs; also at the battle of Fuentes d'Onor. In Dec. 1811 was appointed Aide-de-Camp to Sir James Leith, and was present at the storming of Badajoz, battle of Salamanca, and storming of St. Sebastian (mentioned in Despatches). Served under Lord Lynedoch at the passage of the Bidassoa, and was attached to Lord Hopetown at the passage of the Adour and the blockade of Bayonne : he has the War Medal with four Clasps.

93 Major General B. Orlando Jones accompanied the 36th to Hanover, and served the campaign of 1805-6. Embarked for the Peninsula in 1808, and served throughout the whole of that and 'the following campaigns without having been absent from his duty for a single day, and was present at the battles of Roleia and Vimiera. Attached to the Portuguese service in April 1809, and served at the battle of Busaco, occupation of the Lines at Lisbon, actions of Pombal, Redinha, and Condeixa, Puente de Murcella, Casal Nova, Ceira, Guarda, Foz d'Arouce, Sabugal, and Fuentes d'Onor, storming the forts at Salamanca (wounded), battle of Vittoria, actions of Tolosa and Villa Franca (severely wounded), passage of the Bidassoa, battles of the Nivelle, Bayonne (9th Dec.), St. Jean de Luz (11th, 12th, and 13th Dec.), passage of the Adour, blockade of Bayonne and repulse of the sortie. He has received the Silver War Medal with seven Clasps; and is a Knight of Charles the Third of Spain.

94 Major General Crokat served in Sicily in 1807; in Portugal in 1808, under Sir Arthur Wellesley; in Spain and at Corunna under Sir John Moore; on the Walcheren expedition in 1809; subsequently in the Peninsula. He had charge of Napoleon at St. Helena when he died, and he brought home the despatches of his death. Served afterwards in the East Indies. He has received the War Medal with four Clasps for Vimiera, Corunna, Vittoria, and Pyrenees (severely wounded).

95 Major General Norcliffe served in the Peninsula with the 4th Dragoons, and was present at the battles of Talavera, Busaco, and Albuhera; cavalry action of Usagre, and battle of Salamanca, in which last he was severely wounded and taken prisoner. He has received the War Medal with four Clasps.

96 Sir Josias Cloeté served in the 15th Hussars from 1809 to 1813, as Aide-de-Camp to Lord Charles Somerset, the Governor and Commander-in-Chief at the Cape of Good Hope, from 1813 to the end of 1816, when he was sent in command of an expedition to take possession of the islands of Tristan d'Acunha. Served in India during the Pindarree and Mahratta War from 1817 to 1819. Appointed to act as Deputy Quarter-Master-General at the Cape in 1820, and conducted the landing and settlement of a large body of emigrants sent out by Government. In 1822 was sent home with important despatches, and received the brevet rank of Major. In 1835 nominated a *KH*. In 1840 became Deputy Quarter-Master-General at the Cape. In 1842 commanded a body of troops sent to Natal to relieve a detachment besieged by Insurgent Boers, for which service was named a *CB*. Served during the Kaffir wars of 1846, and of 1851-53, (Medal), including the campaign in the Basoota country, and the battle of Berea. In acknowledgment of his services, received the honour of Knighthood.

97 Major General George Macdonald accompanied the expedition to Hanover in 1805; joined the army in Sicily in 1806, and was employed with it in its various operations until 1810 ; in the latter year he went with the expedition to Naples, and was present at the capture of Ischia and Procida; returned to Sicily and employed against the French army in 1811; in 1812 was employed in Spain, including the battle of Castalla, and siege of Tarragona; embarked for Canada in 1814, and was present at the operations before Plattsburg. He served also the campaign of 1815, and received three wounds at Waterloo, viz. in the leg, in the neck, and through the body, wounding the lungs.

98 Major General Dorinzy's services:—Campaign and battle of Corunna (severely wounded in both knees); expedition to Walcheren, including the siege and capture of Flushing (wounded in left arm). In the Peninsula campaigns, from December 1810 to the end of that war in 1814, including the affairs of Pombal and Redinha, re-capture of Campo Mayor, capture of Olivença, 1st siege of Badajoz, battle of Albuhera, siege and capture of Ciudad Rodrigo, siege and capture of Badajoz, battle of Salamanca, affair of Aldea de Ponte, retreat from Madrid, affairs of Osma and Jocauna, battle of Vittoria, blockade of Pampeluna, affairs of Roncesvalles, Zubisi, &c., battles of Pampeluna, 28th July, and of the Pyrenees, 30th July, affairs of Echalar, St. Estevan, &c., capture of San Sebastian, passage of the Bidassoa, battle of the Nivelle (dangerously wounded through the body, reported killed); battle of Orthes, affairs of Bastide de la Clarence, and Gave d'Oleron. Twice wounded, musket-ball in left arm, and by a splinter of a shell in the chest at the battle of Toulouse, but did not quit the field. He has received the Gold Medal for Toulouse, and the Silver War Medal and nine Clasps.

99 Major General Windham served the Eastern campaign of 1854-55, as an Assistant

Quartermaster General up to the fall of Sebastopol, and was promoted Major General " for his distinguished conduct in having with the greatest intrepidity and coolness headed the column of attack which assaulted the enemy's defences on the 8th September 1855" (Medal and Clasps, CB., Commander of the Legion of Honor, Commander 1st Class of the Military Order of Savoy, and 2nd Class of the Medjidie). Served in the Indian campaign of 1857-58, and commanded a Division throughout the operations at Cawnpore in Nov. and Dec. 1857 (Medal).

100 Major General Yule served in Canada during the greater part of the war of 1812-1814; was present at the affair of Street's Creek, and dismantled under fire the bridge there, by which the advance of a superior force of the enemy was retarded; was also in the actions of Chippewa (horse mortally wounded) and Lundy's Lane.

101 Major General James Gordon's services:—attack on the Castle of Scylla, June 1809; siege and capture of Santa Maura, March 1810.

102 Major General Ashmore was in the *Monarch* in Sir Samuel Hood's action with the French frigates in 1806. From November 1807 till August 1809 in the *Grampus*, employed at the Cape of Good Hope, Madagascar, and blockade of the Mauritius. From February 1810 to January 1812 in the *Poictiers* blockading Brest, Basque Roads, and in the Tagus: whilst in Basque Roads, was frequently in the boats sent to annoy the coasting trade, a service that brought them continually under fire of the batteries, or into action with the gun-boats. When in the Tagus, was with the detachment of Marines sent with a small force of Portuguese under General Trant to destroy the Pontoons preparing by Marshal Massena at Santarem to cross the Tagus; was on piquet under that town the night of the Marshal's retreat from the Lines. In 1812 he was attached to the 2nd Battalion at Santander, north coast of Spain. On the return of the battalions to England he joined the 1st Battalion; was at the attack on Norfolk, taking of the town of Hampton, &c. When the battalion was broken up at Isle Aux Noix he was left for Lake service till 1817. From August 1826 to August 1829 was serving on the South American station in the *Ganges*: was landed at Rio, on the occasion of the German and Irish troops revolting in 1828, to protect the Imperial family and palace of San Christoph, and co-operate with the French and other forces landed to quell the mutiny.

103 Major General John Cox, with the exception of a few months, served throughout the whole of the Peninsular war with the 95th (Rifle Brigade), commencing with the first affair, at Obidos, 15th Aug. 1808. He was also engaged with the enemy in the following battles, sieges, actions and affairs:—Battles of Rolcia and Vimiera, and surrender of Lisbon; subsequent campaign in Spain with Sir John Moore's Army, including its retreat—outpost affairs at Talavera, night defence of the post of Barba del Puerco against very superior numbers, affairs of Gallegos and Barquilla; action at Almeida, and defence of the bridge against every effort to force it; affairs at Mora Morta and Jula; battle of Busaco; affairs at Alenquer, Aruda, and Santarem; defence of the Lines of Torres Vedras; actions with Marshal Massena's Rear-guard at Pombal, Redinha, Condeixa, Caza Nova, Foz d'Arouce, Ponte de Marcella, Froixadas and Sabugal; at Almeida five successive days; at Marialva Bridge; battles of the 3rd and 5th May 1811 at Fuentes d'Onor; affairs at Naves d'Aver and Forcaylos; siege and storming of Ciudad Rodrigo; action at San Milan; battle of Vittoria; actions with the French Rear-guard at Echarrianos, Pampeluna, and forcing the heights of Santa Barbara and Pass of Echalar; at Vera, and carrying the entrenchments in its Pass; battles of the Pyrenees; several affairs at outposts; battles of Nivelle and Nive; action at Tarbes; victory of the 18th June at Waterloo, and capture of Paris. He was wounded at Vimeira by a musket-ball; received a contusion in the head at Redinha, a compound fracture of the left arm at the storming of Ciudad Rodrigo while clearing the left breach, and left leg badly fractured (ball lodged) in driving the enemy from the heights of Tarbes. Joined the army in Belgium, under the Prince of Orange, in the autumn of 1814; served the Waterloo campaigns in that country, and with the Army of Occupation in France, until its embarkation for England in 1818. He has received the War Medal with ten Clasps.

104 Major General W. H. Law served in the Peninsula from Sept. 1813 to the end of the war, including the battles of Nivelle and Nive, for which he has the War Medal with two Clasps.

105 Major General Marshall served in the Peninsula from January 1811 to October 1813, including the first siege of Badajoz, siege and storm of Ciudad Rodrigo, siege and storm of San Sebastian. Slightly wounded at Ciudad Rodrigo 16th Jan. 1812; severely wounded twice by musket-shots at San Sebastian 31st August 1813, when leading the advance of the column of attack up the great breach. He has received the War Medal with three Clasps.

106 Major General Piper served six campaigns in the Peninsula, France, and Flanders, from March 1810 to the 27th Jan. 16. From 1810 to 12 was employed in the Lines of Lisbon and Almeida; and from Jan. 1812 to the conclusion of hostilities in 1815, held the command of a Division of a Pontoon Train (having been entrusted during that period with the organization and equipment of four several bridges); threw the bridges of the Guadiana, Tagus, Bidassoa, Gave d'Oleron, Garronne, and Seine; served in the trenches at the last siege of Badajoz, from the morning of the 18th to the 23rd of March, when the bridges of communication below the town being destroyed and sunk, was despatched (by order of the Commander of the Forces) to re-establish and remain with them--passing shot, shell, and ammunition during the nights, and provisions during the daytime—for the remainder of the operations; received the thanks of Sir Rowland Hill at the passage of the Tagus in August same year, on the advance of his column to Madrid; and subsequently, when *en route* to Salamanca (in consequence of the enemy's cavalry intercepting the communication through the Sierra-do-Gato) was commanded by written instructions from the Commander of the Forces to retire with the bridges on Alcantra de la Reina and Badajoz, to Elvas, and finally to Abrantes; where, equipping a fresh train of boats for the operations of the ensuing year, advanced with the army from Sabugal and Frey-

nada to the Ebro and Vittoria; passage of the Bidassoa in Oct. and latter part of the blockade of Pampeluna; actions of the 9th and 11th Dec. 1813 at Bayonne; do. Toulouse in 1814; passed and repassed His Grace the Commander of the Forces and Staff during the operations of the day, from the right to the left bank of the river, on a fly-raft of three boats; and subsequently, advancing to Mongiscard on the Canal Royal du Midi, proceeded thence to Bordeaux. Proceeded to Ceylon, East Indies, 16th June 1816. Served as commanding engineer in the Kandian Provinces, during the insurrections of 1817 and 18. He has received the War Medal with three Clasps.

107 Major General Faddy, prior to entering the Royal Artillery, was a Midshipman on board the *Asia*, at the capture of the Dutch Fleet in Saldanha Bay in 1795: present at the attack on Fort Jerome, St. Domingo, and at the siege and capture of the city of Santo Domingo in 1809; served in the Peninsula and France from July 1810 to June 1814, including the siege of San Sebastian, passage of the Adour, investment of Bayonne and repulse of the sortie, besides various minor affairs.

108 Major General H. R. Moor served in the Peninsula from June 1809 to June 1813, including the battles of Busaco, Fuentes d'Onor, and Salamanca; sieges of Ciudad Rodrigo and Badajoz, action at Castrajon, and twelve other affairs with the enemy. Has the War Medal with five Clasps.

109 Major General F. R. Thomson was attached to the Prussian army in 1815, and served at Maubeuge, Landrecy, Phillipville, and Rocroi.

110 Major General Hughes served in the 80th Regt. with the army in Burmah in 1852-53; was present at the capture and occupation of Prome, and at the night attack of the enemy on the camp at Prome, 8 Dec. 1852. Commanded the expedition sent into the Poungdey district in Feb. and March 1853; succeeded in capturing arms and ammunition, and in bringing to Prome a large quantity of grain (Medal).

111 Major General Cole has received the Medal for the Kaffir war of 1851-53, during which he commanded the Royal Engineers in South Africa.

112 Major General W. Yorke Moore served as a Captain in the 39th Regt. throughout the campaign against the Rajah of Coorg in April 1834.

113 Major General Matson served in the Peninsula from Nov. 1812 to the end of the war, including the affair of San Milan, advance of the army and crossing the Ebro, battle of Vittoria, blockade of Pampeluna, sieges and storm of San Sebastian, passage of the Bidassoa, battle of the Nivelle, blockade of Bayonne and repulse of the sortie. In 1815 on the expedition to America; and with the army in the Netherlands from June 1815 to Nov. 1818. He has received the Silver War Medal with three Clasps.

114 Major General Booth's services:—Siege of Callinger (wounded at the assault). Nepaul war in 1814, including the sieges of Kolunga, Nahu, and Jetuck. Mahratta war in 1817-18, including the sieges of Singhur, Latarak, Pourunder, and Wursetta. Burmese war in 1824-5, wounded at the storming of Martaban.

115 Major General Greaves served with the 7th Fusiliers in America, in the campaign of 1814, and was also present in the attack on New Orleans, on the 8th Jan. 1815.

116 Major General Alves served the whole of the campaigns in Spain, Portugal, and France, of 1810, 11, 12, 13, and 14, with the 74th in Picton's division, without having ever been absent from it for a single day, including the battle of Busaco, retreat to the lines of Torres Vedras, occupation of them, and subsequent advance in pursuit of Massena, actions at Pombal, Redinha, Foz d'Arouce, Guarda, and Sabugal, battle of Fuentes d'Onor, siege of Badajoz in June 1811, actions at El Bodon and Aldea de Ponte, siege and storm of Ciudad Rodrigo, siege, storm, and escalade of the Castle of Badajoz in March and April 1812, battle of Salamanca, capture of Madrid and the Retiro, affairs on the retreat from Madrid to Salamanca and Portugal in Nov. 1812, subsequent advance and passage of the Ebro, battle of Vittoria, blockade of Pampeluna, the battles in the Pyrenees on the 27th, 28th, and 30th July, battles of the Nivelle, the Nive, and Orthes, actions of Vic Bigorre and Tarbes, and battle of Toulouse. He has the War Medal with eleven Clasps for Busaco, Fuentes d'Onor, Ciudad Rodrigo, Badajoz, Salamanca, Vittoria, Pyrenees, Nivelle, Nive, Orthes, and Toulouse.

117 Major General Alex. M. Fraser was employed in the expedition against Sambas in the Island of Borneo.

118 Major General W. H. Elliott embarked with the Regt. for Lisbon, 26th Jan. 1811, and was present at the battle of Fuentes d'Onor, covering the siege of Ciudad Rodrigo, second siege of Badajoz, affair near Val Moresco, battle of Salamanca, capture of Madrid and the Retiro, covering the siege of Burgos, retreat into Portugal, during which operation he served as Aide-de-Camp to Colonel Mitchell, 51st Regiment, commanding the Brigade, and received a contusion on the shoulder when in the act of delivering an order to an officer in advance. In June 1813, he was appointed an Aide-de-Camp to Major-General Inglis, and was present at the battles of the Pyrenees, 30th and 31st July—received a flesh wound, and had a horse killed; action at Lesaca, passage of the Adour, battle of Nivelle, attack of the heights of St. Pé, and battle of Orthes. Appointed Major of Brigade to the 1st Brigade, 7th Division, and served as such until the end of that war. He has received the War Medal and five Clasps. Served also the campaign of 1815, including the battle of Waterloo, capture of Cambray, and capitulation of Paris. Served in command of the Madras Brigade throughout the Burmese war of 1852-53; was on board the steam frigate *Ferooz* during the Naval action and destruction of the enemy's stockades on the Rangoon River, and served as Brigadier commanding the Madras Force during the succeeding three days' operations in the vicinity, and at the storm and capture of Rangoon.

119 Major General Hawkins commanded the Royal Marines, about 200 strong, at the attack and destruction of Malloodoo, in Borneo.

120 Major General James Clarke served in the attack on the Russian gun-boats and bat-

teries on Percola Point in 1809. At the capture of Guadaloupe in 1810, and at the battle of Algiers. War Medal with two Clasps.

122 Major General Eyre's services:—Expedition to Portugal and occupation of Lisbon in 1808; advance upon Madrid and retreat to Corunna in 1808-9; affair at Lugo and battle of Corunna, for which he has received the Silver War Medal with one Clasp. Eighteen years continued service in the West Indies, from Oct. 1810 to April 1828; and in command of the Royal Artillery in China, at Hong Kong, from August 1847 to May 1851.

123 Major General Childs served in H. M. S. *Gibraltar*, blockading Cherbourg, L'Orient, and Basque Roads, and frequently in boats cutting out French coasters. Early in 1813 he volunteered to serve in the 1st Battalion under Colonel Sir Richard Williams in the *Chesapeake*, and was at the attack of Craney Island, taking of the enemy's camp at Hampton, and capture of Kent Island, and in many minor engagements on the enemy's coast; after which he accompanied the battalion to Canada, and was actively employed on the Frontiers, and frequently in command of gun-boats on Lake Champlain. On the 11th Sept. 1814 he was engaged on board the *Confiance*, in one of the most severe actions fought during the war, in which Commodore Downie (the captain of the ship), Captain Anderson, R.M., and 41 men were killed, and upwards of 100 wounded, out of a complement of 260. He also served the Syrian campaign (Medal) of 1840, including the attack and capture of Sidon, capture of Beyrout, bombardment of Acre, and other desultory services. Has received the War Medal with one Clasp.

124 Major General W. F. Williams served in Senegal, Goree, and Sierra Leone during 1811 and 12; and in the Peninsula from August 1813 to the end of that war, including San Sebastian, the passage of the Bidassoa, battles of Nivelle and Nive (11th, 12th, and 13th Dec.), and the investment of Bayonne. He embarked for Bordeaux in 1814 with the expedition to the Chesapeak under General Ross, and was wounded at the battle of Bladensburg, first slightly in the left arm, and again severely by a musket-ball through the left shoulder. He served subsequently for several years in the West Indies; and he was sent on a particular service to Canada during the insurrection in that country in 1838 and 1839, whence he returned in June 1843, and was, the month following, again sent on a special service to Ireland. He has received the War Medal with three Clasps for St. Sebastian, Nivelle, and Nive.

125 Major General Cartwright served the campaigns of 1813 and 14 with the 61st, including the battles of the Pyrenees, Nivelle, Nive, Orthes, and Toulouse, for which he has received the Silver War Medal with five Clasps. Served the campaign of 1815 with the 10th Hussars, and was present at the battle of Waterloo.

126 Major General Gore served the campaign of 1815 with the 30th, and was slightly wounded at Waterloo.

127 Major General Goodsman served in the Peninsula with the 61st, and was wounded at Talavera, for which battle he has received the War Medal with one Clasp.

128 Major General Pringle Taylor proceeded in 1811 to join the 22nd Dragoons in the East Indies, where he served until their return to Europe and disbandment, 25th October 1820. He was in the field in 1815 and 16, and during the whole of the Mahratta war in 1817, 18, and 19; the published official records show that his conduct was conspicuous in the Brigade Cavalry actions of Bucktowlie and of Nagnoro, and of Ashta (20th Feb. 1818), when he incurred, as Brigade Major, the responsibility of countermanding the retreat and ordering measures which terminated in the entire defeat of the Peishwa, the death of the gallant Gokla, and the rescue of the Rajah of Satarrah, the most influential events in terminating the war. At the siege of Capaul-droog, he commanded a battery at the storm (13th May 1819), he blew open the first gate with a galloper gun of the 22nd Dragoons, and heading the Forlorn Hope, he stormed in succession the five distinct circles of fortifications, every man and officer of his party being either killed or wounded; he received at the summit of that strong hill fort, at the moment of success in its capture, a shot through his lungs and body that killed the Grenadier behind him. The Governor-General of India specially recommended him to favourable consideration for his services in India. In 1823 and 24 he was employed in the Cape Cavalry against the Caffres. In Jan. 1841 he was relieved from a bullet which had been in his body since 1819. In Aug. 1846 his life was imperilled from a surgical operation consequent upon the passage of some cloth driven into him by a shot. In Nov. 1848 he was relieved from a piece of bone broken in his body by a shot. From April 1854 to Dec. 1857 he was a Colonel on the Staff at the Cape of Good Hope, where at a period of peculiar difficulty and imminently threatened war he commanded in Kaffraria then under martial law. In 1827 he was sent to England from Malta to establish discipline in a corps that had fired at and nearly killed their Adjutant, their insubordination sustained by a turbulent mob at a period of popular excitement. He took command and the battalion shot at him three times on the public parade, they fired into his windows and shot through the cheek a field aide who stood behind him. Without calling in other troops he suppressed the mutiny, and alone he overawed the fury of the mob. The approbation of his Major General was submitted by his Lt. General to the Horse Guards, and elicited through the Adjutant General the Sovereign's record that "the decided and necessary measures to which he had resorted had effectually repressed the spirit that prevailed when he assumed the command."

129 Major General Cater served in the Peninsula from April 1810 to January 1814, including the defence of Cadiz, battle of Barrosa, and siege of Tarragona. Served also the campaign of 1815, including the battle of Waterloo, and taking of Cambray and Paris. He has received the Silver War Medal with one Clasp for Barrosa.

130 Major General Swinburne served with the 1st Guards in Holland under Lord Lynedoch, and subsequently in the Peninsula and South of France. Also the campaign of 1815, including the battles of Quatre Bras and Waterloo, storming of Peronne, capture of Paris: at Peronne he commanded a storming party. He served afterwards with the Army of Occupation in France.

131 Major General Whichcote joined the 52nd as a volunteer in December 1810, and served with it in the Peninsula, France, and Flanders, and was present in the actions of Sabugal, El Bodon, and Alfayates, siege and storm of Ciudad Rodrigo, and of Badajoz, battle of Salamanca, retreat from Burgos, battle of Vittoria, action at Vera, battles of the Pyrenees, Nivelle, the Nive, Orthes, Tarbes, Toulouse, and Waterloo. He has received the War Medal with nine Clasps.

132 Major General Butler served the campaign of 1815 with the 3rd Battalion of the Grenadier Guards, and was present in the battles of Quatre Bras and Waterloo (where he carried the colours), storming of Peronne, and capture of Paris.

133 Major General John Campbell served the Waterloo campaign with the 44th Foot.

134 Major General Plomer Young served as Adjutant of the 89th at the capture of the Isle of France in 1810, and at the capture of Java in 1811 (for which he has received the War Medal with one Clasp), on which last service he was wounded in the action of Weltevreden, and also at the storming of Fort Cornelis; and was, for his conduct on those occasions, appointed, by Major-General Sir Robert Gillespie, Major of Brigade to the Batavia Division of the Force. Accompanied Sir Robert as such in the arduous operations against Djocjocarta in 1812, which terminated by the storm of that capital (severely wounded), and capture of the Sultan. Served as Major of Brigade on the expedition to Ava from June 1824 until the close of the Burmese war in 1826, and was present at the principal affairs during that period, including operations in the vicinity of Rangoon, defeat of Bandoola's army at the Sheevedageen Pagoda, Tavoy, Mergui, Kokein, Denobiu, Prome, Melloon, and Pagahm Mew. He served in Canada in command of the Johnstown District during the insurrection of 1838, and commanded the Troops in the attack and defeat of the Brigands under Van Scoultz at the Windmill Point near Prescott, on the 13th Nov. of that year, and was promoted to Lieut.-Colonel by brevet in consequence.

135 Major General Dunn served the campaign of 1805 in Italy; battle of Maida and capture of Scylla Castle in 1806; expedition to Egypt in 1807, including the attack on Alexandria and Rosetta, and battle of El Hamet (taken prisoner). Defence of Scylla Castle in 1808; Peninsular campaigns of 1810 and 11, including operations before Ciudad Rodrigo, operations between the Aguada and Almeida, battles of the Coa, Busaco, and Albuhera; actions at Usagre and Aldea de Ponte, at which last he was severely wounded in the groin by a musket-ball, which remains unextracted. Served also in the American war in 1814, including the taking of Moose Island, and occupation of Castine. Has the War Medal with three Clasps for Maida, Busaco, and Albuhera.

136 Major General Fogo served in America during the whole war, including the battle of Plattsburg.

137 Major General the Honourable William Arbuthnott served in the Peninsula, and was present at the passage of the Douro, and the battles of Oporto, Talavera, and Busaco: for the two last he has received the War Medal with two Clasps.

138 Major General Blachley served in the Peninsula and France from Feb. 1812 to Aug. 1814, including the siege and capture of Badajoz, affair of Castrajon, battle of Salamanca, capture of Madrid and the Retiro, siege of Burgos, and retreat from thence, affair of Osma, battle of Vittoria, siege and capture of San Sebastian (both operations), passage of the Bidassoa and the Nivelle, actions of the 9th, 10th, 11th, and 12th Dec. 1813, in front of Bayonne, passage of the Adour, investment of Bayonne and repulse of the sortie, on which occasion he was wounded in the head by a musket-ball. He has received the Silver War Medal with five Clasps.

139 Major General Belson served in the Peninsula and South of France from July 1809 to the end of the war in 1814, including the retreat from Talavera, action in front of Almeida, action of the Coa, battle of Busaco, actions at Pombal, Redinha, Cazal Nova, Foz d'Arouce, and Sabugal; battle of Fuentes d'Onor, actions on the heights of the Agueda, sieges of Ciudad Rodrigo and Badajoz, actions at Castrajon (severely wounded), San Munos, San Milan, and Osma; battle of Vittoria, action with the French, 28th June 1813, in the morning before they entered Pampelana, in which he captured their last gun from Vittoria ; actions in the Pyrenees, passage of the Nivelle, Nive, and Gave d'Oleron; and battle of Orthes, besides various minor affairs and skirmishes. He has received the War Medal with nine Clasps.

141 Major General Townshend served with the 41st Regt. in the American war, and was present at the taking of Fort Niagara, Blackrock, and Buffalo, battle of Lundy's Lane, and assault on Fort Erie 14th August 1814, where he was severely wounded through the left shoulder. He was promoted to the Brevet rank of Lieut.-Colonel for services during the Canadian Rebellion in 1837-38.

142 Major General Wright served the campaign against the Rajah of Coorg in 1834, and received a very severe injury in the right leg in leading the advanced attack at the taking of the stockade of Periapatam, the frontier stockade of the Coorg territory. In 1839 he was employed in the operations against Kurnool, and was severely and dangerously wounded at the affair of Zorapore on the 18th of October. He commanded a Brigade in the battle of Maharajpore (Medal) on the 29th Dec. 1843, in which action his horse was shot under him in taking the battery at Chounda.

143 Major General Portlock served in the last American War.

144 Sir John Inglis served with the 32nd in Canada during the Rebellion in 1837, and was present in the actions of St. Denis and St. Eustache. He served also the Punjaub campaign of 1848-9, and was present at the first and second siege operations before Mooltan, including the attack on the enemy's position in front of the advanced trenches on the 12th Sept., where, after the death of Lieut.-Col. Pattoun, he succeeded to the command of the right column of attack; commanded the 32nd at the action of Soorjkoond; and also present at the storm and capture of the city and surrender of the fortress of Mooltan, surrender of the fort and garrison of Cheniote, and battle of Goojerat, for which services he received the brevet rank of Lieut.

Colonel (Medal and Clasps). Was promoted to the rank of Major General and nominated a KCB. " for his enduring fortitude and persevering gallantry in the defence of the Residency of Lucknow, for eighty-seven days, against an overwhelming force of the Enemy."

145 Major General Griffin served before Genoa in 1814.

146 Sir James Hope Grant served in China (Medal) as Brigade-Major to Lord Saltoun, and was present at the assault and capture of Chin Kiang Foo, and at the landing before Nankin. He served with the 9th Lancers at Sobraon (Medal) in 1846; and he commanded the Regiment during the greater part of the campaign in the Punjaub in 1848-9, including the passage of the Chenab at Ramnuggur, and battle of Chillianwallah: he was also present at the battle of Goojerat (Medal and Clasps). Commanded the Cavalry Brigade as Brigadier-General during the siege and at the assault of Delhi in 1857, and had his horse shot under him during the operations of the 19th June. Was promoted to the rank of Major General and nominated a KCB. " for his eminent services in command of the Cavalry Division at the siege of Delhi, and in that of a Division at the relief of Lucknow under Sir Colin Campbell, as also in the subsequent operations at Cawnpore when the rebel army sustained a total defeat."

147 Sir Gaspard Le Marchant served as Adjutant-General to the Anglo-Spanish Legion, and Brigadier-General in the Spanish service during the years 1835, 6, and 7: was present at the relief of Bilboa and affair before that town in Sept. 1835, engaged on the heights of Arlaban, in Alava, on the 16th, 17th, and 18th Jan.; in raising the siege of San Sebastian, and storming the Lines 5th May; passage of the Urmea, and taking of Passages 28th May; in the general action before Alza Oct. 1836, besides several affairs in Guipuzcoa, as also in the general actions of the 10th, 13th, 15th, and 16th March before Hernani : for these services he received a Medal, also 3rd Class St. Fernando, and Knight of Charles the Third.

148 Major General Wortham served the campaigns of 1813 and 14 in Spain and France, including the siege of St. Sebastian, from 20th Aug. to 9th Sept. 1813; battles of Orthes and Toulouse. Served afterwards with the army in America, from 14th Sept. 1814, to 24th May 1815, including the attack on the American Lines before New Orleans, 8th Jan. 1815, and the siege and capture of Fort Bowyer from 8th to 11th Feb. 1815. He has received the Silver War Medal with three Clasps.

149 Sir William Mansfield served with the 53rd in the campaign on the Sutlej in 1846, and was present at Buddiwal, Aliwal, and Sobraon, at which last he acted as Aide-de-Camp to the Commander-in-Chief (Medal and Clasps). He commanded the Regiment in the Punjaub campaign in 1849, and was present at the battle of Goojerat (Medal and Clasp). He was also constantly employed in the operations on the Peshawur frontier in 1851-52, whether his Regiment was in the field or not, and was present at the affairs of Nawadund, Pranghur, and Skarkote (horse wounded). Was promoted to the rank of Major General " in recognition of his valuable services as Chief of the Staff in the East Indies " having been present at the relief of Lucknow under Lord Clyde and subsequent operations, and commanded a Division at the battle of Cawnpore.

150 Major General Harold served the campaign and battle of Corunna, for which he has received the War Medal with one Clasp. Expedition to Walcheren and siege of Flushing.

151 Sir Thomas Franks commanded the 10th Regt. in the Sutlej campaign of 1845-6, including the battle of Sobraon (Medal), where he had a horse shot under him, and was slightly wounded: nominated a CB. Commanded the 10th in the Punjaub campaign of 1848-9, including the whole of the siege operations before Mooltan: 17th Aug. 1848 commanded the troops which repulsed the enemy's night-attack upon the British camp at Muttee Thol: 12th Sept. commanded the left column of attack at the defeat of the enemy in their stronglyentrenched position before Mooltan; and after the action succeeded to the command of the whole of the troops which were engaged, and held the position until relieved the following morning, although wounded and exposed to the repeated attempts of the enemy to retake it: 7th Nov. in the action of Soorjkoond commanded the right Brigade, and with it led the attack, capturing the whole of the enemy's guns at the point of the bayonet without firing a shot: 27th Nov. in the carrying of the heights before Mooltan, commanded the reserve on the extreme right, and directed the attack of its leading column. On the 18th Feb. 1849 he joined with the Mooltan force the army under Lord Gough, and commanded the 10th at the battle of Goojerat, and was specially named for his conduct both by the Commander in Chief and the Governor General (Medal and Clasps). Was promoted to the rank of Major General and nominated a KCB. " for his distinguished services in the command of a Column during the operations in India prior to and at the capture of Lucknow."

152 Major General Gordon was at the capture of Martinique in 1809, and of Guadaloupe in 1810, for which he has received the War Medal with two Clasps.

153 Major General George Elliot served with the Royal Marine Battalion in co-operation with the Spanish troops against the Carlists in 1837, and received the Cross of San Fernando, 1st Class. Served on the China expedition (Medal), and was wounded in the attack on the intrenched camps on the heights of Segoan, 15th March 1842. Was present at the bombardment of Odessa, 22nd April 1854; landed with the Royal Marines for the defence of Eupatoria ; was at the siege of Sebastopol (Medal and Clasp, and 5th Class of the Medjidie).

154 Major General Langford served with the Battalion in Spain from June 1836 to Sept. 1840, and was present in the actions of Fuenterabia and Hernani, besides various minor affairs. While serving in H. M. S. *North Star*, from Sept. 1841 to Sept. 1846, he participated in the operations of the Expeditionary Force in China, including the blockade of the Woosung River (Medal). On the termination of hostilities with China he proceeded in the *North Star* to New Zealand ; and was landed with all the detachments of Royal Marines from H.M. ships present, and appointed to command that force, together with a detachment of the 96th Regt.,

with which he was actively employed in the field against the insurgent chiefs, whose strongly-stockaded Pahs, or Villages, were successfully attacked and destroyed: for these services he obtained the Brevet rank of Major. Accompanied the expedition to the Baltic in 1854.

155 Major General Marcus J. Slade commanded the 90th Light Infantry throughout the Kaffir War of 1846-47 (Medal).

156 Major General MacKinnon served as Assistant Quarter-Master-General at the Cape of Good Hope during the Kaffir war of 1846-7 (Medal). Served as Colonel on the Staff and in command of the 2nd Division from the outbreak of the Kaffir war in December 1850 until April 1852, and received the thanks of the Commander of the Forces, Sir Harry Smith, in General Orders on fifteen different occasions on which he commanded in operations against the enemy.

157 Sir Edward Lugard served as a Major of Brigade throughout the campaign of 1842 in Affghanistan under Gen. Pollock, and was present in the actions of Mazeenu, Tezeen, and Jugdulluck, the occupation of Cabool, and the different engagements leading to it (Medal). He served throughout the campaign on the Sutlej (Medal);—as Dep. Assist. Adj. Gen. to Sir Harry Smith at the battles of Moodkee (wounded), Ferozeshah (wounded), and Sobraon;—as Adj. Gen. of the whole Force commanded by Sir Harry at the affair of Buddiwal, and in the battle of Aliwal; and he officiated as Adj.Gen. of Her Majesty's Forces in India, from the battle of Sobraon to the end of the campaign, when he was appointed Asst. Adj. Gen. to H.M.'s Forces in India. He again officiated as Adjt.Gen. throughout the Punjaub campaign in 1848-49, and was present at the passage of the Chenab, and battles of Chillianwallah and Goojerat (Medal and Clasps). Served as chief of the Staff on the Persian expedition in 1857. Was promoted to the rank of Major General and nominated a KCB. "for his services in the command of a Division at the capture of Lucknow, and subsequently in the command of the Azimghur Field Force."

158 Major General Hon. George Upton served in the 1st Battalion of Coldstream Guards throughout the Eastern campaign of 1854, including the battles of the Alma, Balaklava, and Inkerman (wounded and horse killed), and siege of Sebastopol (Medal and Clasps, CB., Officer of the Legion of Honor, and 3rd Class of the Medjidie).

159 Major General T. Simson Pratt served the campaign of 1814 in Holland, as a volunteer with the 56th Regt., and was present at the attack on Merxem, 2nd Feb, and the subsequent bombardment of Antwerp. He served with the 26th on the China expedition (Medal), and commanded the land forces at the assault and capture of the Forts of Chuenpee on the 7th January 1841, and again at the assault and capture of the Bogue Forts on the 26th February following. Commanded the 26th at the attacks on Canton from 24th May to 1st June; also at the night attack on Ningpo, at Segoan, Chapoo, Woosung, Shanghai, and at Chin Kiang Foo.

160 Major Gen. Felix served the campaign of 1815, and was slightly wounded at Quatre Bras.

161 Major General Lockyer served in the Peninsula with the 71st Regt. from Aug. 1813 to the end of the war, including the battles of Nivelle, Nive, Orthes, Aire (severely wounded on left wrist and elbow joint) and Toulouse, besides all the minor affairs after the army entered France. On the 20th May 1854 he sailed for the Pireus in command of the British contingent directed in conjunction with a French force for the occupation of Greece. November following he joined the army in the Crimea, and was placed in command of the 2nd Brigade, 2nd Division, and remained with the army the whole of the winter and spring of 1854-55, never missing a tour of duty in the trenches. Left the Crimea in Aug. 1855 to take up his appointment as commander of the Forces in the Island of Ceylon. He has received the War Medal with three Clasps, the Crimean Medal with Clasp for Sebastopol, is a CB. and KH., Officer of the Legion of Honor, and 3rd Class of the Medjidie.

162 Major General Baynes served as Midshipman in the Royal Navy for three years, and in 1809 was present at the capture of Ischia, Zante, Cephalonica, and Cerigo; and was in the action of the *Spartan* frigate in the Bay of Naples, 3 May 1810 (War Medal). Served in the Ionian Islands from 1812 to 1817, including the capture of Paxo in 1813, and occupation of Corfu on the evacuation by the French in 1814. Was with a detachment at Zante on 21st Oct. 1821, defending a Turkish man-of-war in an attack made by the Greeks, and was specially selected and actively employed in the disarmament of the inhabitants which followed. Served in the West Indies during the emancipation of the slaves in 1834. Served in North America during the boundary question in 1839-40.

163 Major General M. C. Johnstone served with the 27th Regt. in the Kaffir wars of 1834-35 and 1846-47 (Medal).

164 Major General Meade served with the 88th in the Peninsula in the campaigns of 1811, 12, 13, and 14, including the battle of Fuentes d'Onor, siege of Badajoz in 1811, battle of Salamanca (wounded), siege and storming of Badajoz, passage of the Nivelle and the Nive, battles of Orthes and Toulouse. In 1814 he accompanied his Regiment to America, and the following year joined the Army of Occupation in France. In 1821 he embarked for India on the Staff of Sir Thomas Reynell, and was at the siege and storming of Bhurtpore, for the capture of which fortress he received the rank of Major. He has received the War Medal with six Clasps.

165 Major General Forster served with the Scots Fusilier Guards before Bayonne in 1814. Joined the Brigade of Guards in Paris in 1815.

166 Major General Goldsmid served in the Peninsula with the 12th Light Dragoons, from 1812 to the end of that war in 1814, including the cavalry affairs at Castrajon, Quintare de Puerta, and Monasterio; battles of Salamanca, Vittoria, Nivelle, and Nive (for which he has received the War Medal with four Clasps); and siege of San Sebastian. Served also during the campaign of 1815, and was present at the battle of Waterloo.

167 Major General Macarthur was present as an Ensign in the 60th at the battle of Corunna. He afterwards served with the 39th in Sicily, and again in Spain, where he was engaged with

the enemy at Vittoria, in the Pyrenees, at the Nivelle and the Nive, at Bayonne, Orthes, and Toulouse, and where he also served on the personal staff of the late Lt.Gen. Sir Robert O'Callaghan. He accompanied his regiment from Bourdeaux to Canada, and afterwards served with it in the Army of Occupation in France. He has received the War Medal with seven Clasps.

168 Major General Macdowall served the campaign of 1814 in Holland with the 52nd, including the actions at Merxem and bombardment of Antwerp.

169 Major General Hely served in the West Indies with the 69th Regiment in 1801 and 1802, and subsequently with the 57th Regiment on the Coast of Africa, and in Gibraltar during the Plague, joined Lord Hill's division in the Peninsula in 1809, and was present at the battle of Busaco, in the actions of Pombal and Redinha, the first siege of Badajoz, battle of Albuhera— where he was twice wounded, and held the command of the Regiment after that action; battles of the Pyrenees, Nivelle, Nive, that before Bayonne on the 13th Dec. 1813, and Orthes; affairs of Peracbe, Aire, and Tarbes, and battle of Toulouse. Sailed for Canada at the conclusion of this war; returned after the peace with America, landing at Ostend; marched to Paris, and served with the Army of Occupation until the breaking up of that force. He has received the War Medal with six Clasps.

170 Major General Bowers was slightly wounded at Waterloo.

171 Major General Arnaud served in the Peninsula with the 11th, and was present at the battles of Busaco and Toulouse, for which he has received the War Medal with two Clasps.

173 Sir Robert Garrett served in the Peninsula with the 6th Division in 1811, and with the 4th Division in 1812 and 13, and was present in all the actions, sieges, and smaller affairs in which those two Divisions were respectively engaged, from Fuentes d'Onor in May 1811, until the end of 1813, when he was sent to England for recovery from his wounds. He received two wounds at the attack of the Forts at Salamanca, on which occasion the command of the Light Company of the Queen's and some Artillery devolved upon him, he being the only surviving officer of the column he attacked with; and he was again severely wounded in the Pyrenees. He has received the War Medal with four Clasps for Fuentes d'Onor, Salamanca, Vittoria, and Pyrenees. Served at the siege of Sebastopol in 1854-55 (Medal and Clasp, *KCB.*, Officer of the Legion of Honor, Sardinian Medal, and 3rd Class of the Medjidie).

174 Major General T. M. Williams previously to entering the Army served five years as Midshipman in the Navy, and was engaged in the attack of the French Fleet by Admiral Cornwallis on the 21st Aug. 1805. Assisted in the disembarkation of the British Army in Portugal in Aug. 1808, and at its embarkation during and after the battle of Corunna in 1809. Accompanied the expedition to Walcheren the same year, and served in the squadron of gun-boats in the Scheldt covering the disembarkation of the army, and at the bombardment and capture of the fortresses of Ter Vere, Ramakins, and Flushing. Landed with a division of sailors on the Island of South Beveland, and was present at the taking of Fort Batz, and at the subsequent defence and repulse of the enemy in their repeated efforts to repossess themselves of that important post; also in frequent gun-boat actions co-operating with the army during their evacuation of those islands in 1810. He quitted the Navy and entered the Army in Feb. 1811, and joined the 4th Regt. in Portugal in August of the same year, and served in that corps and the 77th, into which he was promoted from that period, to the termination of that war in 1814, without being a day absent from his Regt. He was present at the siege and storming of Badajoz, at the operations on the Bidassoa and Adour, and affairs at St. Jean de Luz, and at the Mayor's House in front of Bidart in Dec. 1813, and at the investment of Bayonne and repulse of the sortie. He has received the War Medal with one Clasp for Badajoz.

175 Major General Nepean served in the Peninsula with the 16th Light Dragoons and was present at the battle of the Nive on the 9th Dec. 1813, for which action he has received the War Medal with one Clasp. He served also the Waterloo campaign.

176 Major General Trevor served with the 33rd in Germany and Holland in 1813 and 14, including both attacks on Merxem, operations in front of Antwerp, and the storming of Bergen-op-Zoom. Served also the campaign of 1815, including the action at Quatre Bras, retreat on the following day, battle of Waterloo, advance to and capture of Paris. Also in Jamaica with the 33rd, and in China with the 59th.

177 Lord Albemarle served the Waterloo campaign with the 14th Foot.

178 Major General Barlow served as a General in the trenches during the siege of Sebastopol, and commanded a Brigade at its fall (Medal and Clasp, Sardinian Medal, and 3rd Class of the Medjidie).

179 Major General J. N. Jackson served in the Peninsula from 1810 to the end of the war in 1814, including the siege of Cadiz, Lines at Torres Vedras, Massena's retreat from Portugal, actions and affairs at Pombal, Redinha, Leira, Condeixa, Fleur-de-Lis, Guarda, Foz d'Arouce, and Sabugal; battle of Fuentes d'Onor, 3rd and 5th May, siege of Badajoz in June and July, 1811, actions at El Bodon and Guinaldo, siege and storm of Ciudad Rodrigo, third siege of Badajoz and storm of the Castle by escalade, 6th April 1812; battle of Salamanca, capture of Madrid, the Retiro, and Fort La China, and in command of an escort of the third Division in charge of the garrison of Fort La China *en route* to Ciudad Rodrigo. Retreat to Portugal, Oct. and Nov. 1812, battles of Vittoria, Pyrenees, Nivelle, Nive, and Orthes; actions at Vic Bigorre and Tarbes, battle of Toulouse, and all the various minor affairs during that period. He has received the War Medal and ten Clasps.

180 Major General Trydell served at the capture of the Cape of Good Hope in 1806, and was present at the battle of Blueberg. He served also in the Kandian Insurrection of 1817 and 18, in Ceylon.

181 Major General John Clark served the campaign of 1815, including the battle of Waterloo and storming of Cambray. Served also the campaigns of 1824 and 25 in Ava, including the taking

of Rangoon, Kimendine, Kamaroot, and Mahattee. Led the attack upon the fortified heights at Aracan, and was severely wounded in the neck, arm, and left side.

182 Major General Elers Napier was present with the Nizam's Subsidiary Force at the investment of Hyderabad in 1830. Served on the British Staff in the Syrian campaign of 1840-41, with the local rank of Lt.Colonel and Assistant Adjutant General ; held a responsible and independent command of an Irregular Force in the Naplouse mountains ; afterwards employed as Commissioner with a portion of the Turkish army (Brevet of Lt.Colonel, Syrian Medal and Gold Medal from the Sultan). Was subsequently employed on Diplomatic Missions by Lord Aberdeen and Lord Palmerston,—first, to bring back from the interior of Africa the chiefs of Mount Lebanon, who had been seized by Ibrahim Pasha and sent by Mehemet Ali to work in the mines of Sennaar ; and, secondly, to convey back to Beyrout several thousand Syrian Soldiers, who, contrary to the terms of the convention, had been retained in Egypt —was successful in the accomplishment of both these Missions. Was employed on the staff, with rank of Assist. Adjutant General, in the Kaffir war of 1846-47 (Medal), during which was in charge of Native Levies and Irregular troops attached to the 1st division, and organized a body of Irregular Horse, the nucleus of what subsequently became the Kaffir Mounted Police.

183 Major General Harvey served at the investment of Kolapore in the East Indies, in Sept. 1827. Employed on the Staff in the late operations against Ibrahim Pacha, in Syria, and was present at the skirmish with the Egyptian troops near Askelon, 15th Jan. 1841. Commanded the third Brigade of the Field Force at the capture of the Mahratta fortresses of Panulla and Pownughur on the 1st Dec. 1844, and received the thanks of the Bombay Government.

184 Sir John Michel was nominated a CB. after the termination of the Kaffir war in 1853, in consideration of his distinguished services in the Kaffir wars of 1846-47 and of 1851-3 (Medal). Was nominated to the 2nd Class of the Medjidie for service with the late Turkish Contingent. Served in the Indian Campaign in 1858-59 in command of the Mhow field force, and defeated the rebels under Tantia Topee at Beorora taking 27 guns, subsequently actively engaged in pursuing the fugitive bands (KCB. and Medal).

185 Major General Warren served under the Duke of Wellington in 1815. Commanded the 55th Regt. in an expedition against the Rajah of Coorg in April 1834 (Colonel Mill being in command of the column until a few days before he was killed) : led a successful assault on and captured the stockade of Kissenhally; and was severely wounded in an attack on the stockade of Soamwarpettah. Served in China from 1841 to 1844 (Medal): commanded the 55th in the expedition up the Yang-tse-kiang, and was severely wounded at the storming and capture of Chinkiangfoo, where he was personally engaged with three Tartars, whom he killed. Served the Eastern campaign of 1854-55, commanded the Regt. at the battle of Alma (received two contused wounds), siege of Sebastopol, and repulse of the sortie on the 26th October; commanded the 1st Brigade, 2nd Division, at the battle of Inkerman, and was severely and also slightly wounded; again slightly wounded at the attack on the Redan on the 8th Sept. (Medal and Clasps, Officer of the Legion of Honor, Sardinian Medal, and 3rd Class of the Medjidie).

186 Major General Malcolm served on the China expedition (Medal).

187 Major General R. H. Wynyard served with the force in New Zealand from Oct. 1845 until Jan. 1847, in command of the 58th Regt.; commanded the advance Division up the Kowa Kowa River, and on through the interior from the landing up to the position before Ruapekapeka, and entered the breach with the stormers in the assault on Kawiti's Pah on 11 Jan. 1846. Appointed to the command of the Forces in New Zealand in Jan. 1851, held Her Majesty's Commission as Lieut.-Governor of New Ulster from 1851 to 1853, and administered the government of the whole Colony from Dec. 1853 to Sept. 1855.

188 Major General Sandilands served with the expedition to Walcheren; also the campaign of 1815, and was engaged on the 17th June with the Horse Artillery in covering the retiring movement from Quatre Bras, and on the 18th of June he was present at the battle of Waterloo.

189 Lord William Paulet served the Eastern campaign of 1854, as Assistant Adjutant General to the Cavalry Division, including the battles of the Alma, Balaklava, and Inkerman, and siege of Sebastopol (Medal and Clasps, CB., Officer of the Legion of Honor, Commander 1st Class St. Maurice and St. Lazarus, and 3rd Class of the Medjidie).

190 Major General M'Pherson embarked for the Peninsula in May 1809 as a volunteer in the 52nd, and served as such in the advance up to Talavera and the retreat from thence, to 2nd Nov. 1809, when he was promoted to an Ensigncy in the 43rd, from which time he served with the Light Division until the end of that war in 1814, including the following battles, sieges, &c., viz. Coa, Mortiagoa, skirmish near and battle of Busaco, Coimbra, Alenquer, Pombal, Redinha, Miranda do Corvo, Foz d'Arouce, Sabugal. Fuentes d'Onor, Espejo, Soita, Ciudad Rodrigo, Badajoz, March and April 1812, Carvellejo, Petiegua, Salamanca, Nivelle, Bayonne, Nive, Tarbes, Tournefeuille and Toulouse. Contused on the head in the trenches at Badajoz by the bursting of a shell. Served as Aide-de-Camp to Sir Charles Napier throughout the operations in Scinde, including the battles of Meeanee and Hyderabad (Medal and CB.). He has received the War Medal with eight Clasps for Busaco, Fuentes d'Onor, Ciudad Rodrigo, Badajoz, Salamanca, Nivelle, Nive, and Toulouse. He also served in the Crimea, in command of the 1st Brigade 4th Division, on the heights and siege before Sebastopol, from 18th December 1854 to 15th June 1855, when he was obliged to leave from ill health, brought on by over-fatigue in the trenches (Medal and Clasp, Knight of the Legion of Honor, and 4th Class of the Medjidie).

191 Major General Ridley commanded the Grenadier Guards and afterwards a Brigade in the 1st Division at the siege and fall of Sebastopol from 1st Dec. 1854 (Medal and Clasp, Officer of the Legion of Honor, Sardinian and Turkish Medals, and 3rd Class of the Medjidie).

192 Major General Cameron served the Eastern campaign of 1854-55; commanded the 42nd Regiment at the battle of Alma, and the Highland Brigade at the battle of Balaklava on the expedition to Kertch, siege and fall of Sebastopol, and assault on the outworks 18th June (Medal and Clasps, *CB.*, Officer of the Legion of Honor, Sardinian Medal, and 3rd Class of the Medjidie).

193 Major General Bell served in the Peninsula from July 1811 to the end of that war in 1814, and was engaged in the Action of Arroyo de Molino, battle of Vittoria, battles in the Pyrenees, on the 7th, 25th, 30th, and 31st July 1813, battles of the Nivelle, the Nive, Bayonne, Orthes, Tarbes, and Toulouse, besides a great many affairs and skirmishes. He afterwards served in the East Indies, in the Burmese war, and in the West Indies. He was actively employed during the rebellion in Canada, particularly in the capture of St. Charles and St. Eustache; he afterwards commanded the small Fort and garrison of Coteau-du-Lac, an important position on the river St. Lawrence, and received the thanks of the Commander of the Forces for his exertions in recovering the guns and shots from the bottom of the river, and mounting them in position when it was reported impracticable; the guns were 24-pounders, sixteen of which and 4,000 round shot he recovered in the depth of a Canadian winter. He has received the War Medal with six Clasps for Vittoria, the Pyrenees, Nivelle, Nive, Orthes, and Toulouse; and the Indian Medal for Ava. Served the Eastern campaign of 1854-55, and commanded the Royals in the battles of Alma and Inkerman, and siege of Sebastopol, where he was wounded, and subsequently commanded a Brigade (Medal and three Clasps, *CB.*, Knight of the Legion of Honor, and 4th Class of the Medjidie).

194 Major General Vigors served throughout the campaigns of 1838 and 39 in Affghanistan. Commanded the two Flank Companies of the 13th Light Infantry, which formed a part of the force under Sir Robert Sale sent in pursuit of the ruler of Candahar, brother of the king of Cabool; crossed the rapid Helmond with eighteen men (the advance) on a small raft, landed close to the Fort of Girishk, which was found just vacated by the enemy. He commanded the left Flank Company of the 13th, with the forlorn hope, under Col. Dennie, at the storm and capture of the fort of Ghuznee (Medal), and was also present at the capture of Cabool, and in other minor affairs.

195 Major General Grierson served at Cadiz during parts of 1812 and 1813, and afterwards on the eastern coast of Spain.

196 Major General Richardson-Robertson served in South Africa, in command of the successful expedition against the insurgent Emigrant Boers, beyond the Orange River, in 1845. Also as Brigadier, and in command of the 7th Dragoon Guards in the Kaffir campaign of 1846-7 (Medal and *CB.*).

197 Major General Braybrooke served at the capture of the Kandian territories in 1815, and in the Kandian rebellion in 1817-18.

198 Major General Robert Law served with the 71st Regt. on Sir J. Moore's retreat at Lugo and Corunna in 1808-9; at the siege of Flushing in 1809; subsequently in the Peninsula, including the affair at Sobral, Massena's retreat, battle of Fuentes D'Onor, 3rd and 5th May 1811 (wounded in two places); covering first and second sieges of Badajoz, actions at Arroyo de Molino and Almaraz, defence of Alba de Tormes, battles of the Pyrenees and capture of enemy's convoy at Elisonda, in July 1813; battle of the Nive, affair at Cambo, employed in an armed boat at Urt on the river Adour, battle near Bayonne 13th Dec. 1813, affairs at Hellette, Arrivarette, St. Palais, and Aire; battle of Orthes, and affair at Tarbes, where he was severely wounded. Served also the campaign of 1815, including the battle of Waterloo—severely wounded, and horse killed by a cannon shot. Served afterwards with the Army of Occupation in France. He has received the War Medal with six Clasps.

199 Major General L'Estrange served the campaign of 1808-9 in Spain with the 14th, and was present at the battle of Corunna. Capture of the Isle of France in 1810. Capture of Java in 1811, and engaged with a Dutch brigade at St. Nicholas. At the storming of a strong Dutch Fort on the coast of Bantam. On board H.M.S. *Roscius* at the boarding and capture of eleven French gun-boats. Present at the siege and storm of Cornelis, and storm and capture of the heights of Serandole. At the capture of the town and fortress of Sambas, Isle of Borneo, in March 1813. Nepaul war in 1815; siege and capture of Hattras in March 1817; Mahratta campaign in 1817 and 18: siege and storm of Bhurtpore under Lord Combermere. He has received the War Medal and two Clasps for Corunna and Java.

200 Major General Williamson served with the 27th Regt. in the Kaffir war of 1834-35 (Medal).

201 Sir Charles Straubenzee served the campaign against the Rajah of Coorg in 1834. In the action of Maharajpore (Medal) on 29th Dec. 1843, he succeeded to the command of the 39th Regt. Served at the siege of Sebastopol in 1855, and commanded the 1st Brigade Light Division at the assault of the Redan on the 8th Sept.—wounded (Medal and Clasp, *CB.*, Officer of the Legion of Honor, Sardinian Medal, and 3rd Class of the Medjidie). Commanded the Troops throughout the operations in China in 1857 (*KCB.*).

202 Major General Parke's services :—Co-operation with the Spanish forces and Legion near San Sebastian, and under Espartero in raising the siege of Bilboa (Knight 1st Class St. Fernando).

203 Major General Jardine served during the Indian campaign of 1858, including the occupation, after the relief of Lucknow, of the fortified outposts and camp with Outram's force and repulse of the enemy's attacks (Medal).

204 Major General W. G. Gold served in the campaign on the Sutlej with the 53rd, including the battles of Buddiwal, Aliwal, and Sobraon (wounded), in the first of which he commanded the Regiment; Medal and one Clasp.

205 Major General Hurdle was at the attack on the forts and harbour of Courageaux in 1815; and battle of Navarino in 1827 (War Medal with one Clasp). He served during the revolutionary war in Greece in 1828, and received the Cross of the Redeemer of Greece. Was present in the engagement at Punta Obligada in the river Parana on the 20th Nov. 1845, for which he received the Brevet rank of Major. Commanded the Brigade of Royal Marines serving with the army in the Crimea, including the battle of Balaklava, siege and fall of Sebastopol in 1854-55; commanded the 2nd Brigade of the Army at the surrender of Kinbourn (Medal and Clasps, CB., Aide-de-Camp to the Queen, Officer of the Legion of Honor, Sardinian Medal, and 3rd Class of the Medjidie).

206 Major General Dwyer served in the blockading squadrons off Flushing, the Texel, and off Brest. Since the peace he has served in the East and West Indies, and the Mediterranean.

COLONELS.

	CORNET, 2d LIEUT. or ENSIGN.	LIEUT.	CAPTAIN.	MAJOR.	LIEUT.-COLONEL.	COLONEL.	WHEN PLACED ON HALF PAY.
Leicester, *Earl of Harrington*, CB.,[1] *Lieut.Col.*, Unattached	25 Sept. 99	20 Oct. 02	31 Mar. 03	4 June 14	29 Jan. 15	10 Jan. 37	20 July 26
Sir John Morillyon Wilson, CB. KH.[2] *Maj.* Unatt. *Major of Chelsea Hospital*	1 Sept. 04	28 Feb. 05	1 Jan. 07	5 July 14	27 Nov. 15	do	25 July 22
Hon. Fred. Macadam Cathcart,[3] *Capt.* h.p. 92 F., *Colonel Ayrshire Militia*	12 Jan. 05	1 May 06	17 Sept. 07	28 July 14	24 Feb. 20	do	18 May 20
Sir George Henry Hewett, Bart., *Lt.Col.*, Unattached	12 June 06	18 Dec. 06	12 April 10	18 June 12	26 Nov. 23	28 June 38	28 June 27
Wm. Henry Stopford-Blair,[3] *Lt.Col.*, h. p., Royal Artillery	15 Sept. 04	2 July 05	1 April 15	10 Jan. 37	23 Nov. 41	20 June 54	20 Dec. 41
Edw. Walter Forestier Walker, CB., *Lt.Col.*, Scots Fusilier Guards	never	8 Mar.	27 18 Oct. 31	never	6 Dec. 44	do	
Thomas Armstrong Drought, *Lt.Col.*, *Insp. Field Officer at Cork*	11 Nov.	13 16 Oct. 17	10 Oct. 22	31 Dec. 30	21 Mar. 45	do	
Charles Stuart, *Lt.-Col.*, h. p. Ceylon Regt.	30 Dec.	26 31 Dec. 28	26 July 32	never	15 April 45	do	22 Dec. 54
Hon. Augustus Almeric Spencer,[10] CB., *Lt.Col.*, h.p. 44 Foot, *Major General Commanding a Brigade at Aldershot*	8 April 25	5 July 27	6 April 31	21 July 43	17 May 45	do	15 May 57
Charles Ashmore, *Lt.Col.*, h.p. 4 Foot	25 Dec.	13 13 April 20	19 Aug. 28	15 Dec. 40	22 May 45	do	
Henry Keane Bloomfield,[11] *Lt.Col.*, 11 Foot, *Commanding at Colchester*	30 Sept.	13 7 Aug. 17	1 April 24	28 June 38	27 June 45	do	
John Lawrenson,[12] *Lieut.Col.*, h. p. 6 F., *Major General Commanding Cavalry Brigade at Aldershot*	12 Nov. 18	6 Dec. 21	27 Aug. 25	28 June 38	27 June 45	do	30 Sept. 56
Studholme John Hodgson,[13] *Lt.Col.*, Unattached	12 Dec.	19 3 Feb. 26	30 Dec. 26	28 Dec. 38	8 Aug. 45	do	8 Aug. 45
Charles Franklyn, CB., *Lt.Col.*, *Insp. Field Officer at York*	17 July	23 8 April 26	10 July 28	28 Dec. 38	16 Sept. 45	do	
Godfrey Charles Mundy,[14] *Lt.Col.*, Unatt., *Major General Commanding the Troops and Lt. Governor at Jersey*	25 Nov. 21	28 Aug. 23	13 May 26	31 Dec. 39	28 Nov. 45	do	
Francis Hugh George Seymour, *Lt.Col.* Unatt. *Equerry to The Queen*	never	12 July 27	24 Aug. 32	never	28 Nov. 45	do	10 Dec. 47
William A. M'Cleverty,[15] *Lt.Col.*, Unatt., *Assist. Adj. Gen. in Scotland*	26 Mar.	24 26 Aug. 25	21 May 29	23 April 41	19 Dec. 45	do	
Lewis Duncan Williams, *Lt.Col.*, Unattached	21 June	20 23 July 25	15 July 28	23 Nov. 41	30 Dec. 45	do	27 Nov. 57
Robert Blucher Wood,[16] CB., *Lt.Col.*, h. p. 97 Foot	34 12 Feb.	36 31 Feb. 36	5 Feb. 36	4 Oct. 41	17 May 44	do	2 April 52
Charles Emilius Gold, *Lt.Col.*, 65 Foot	20 Mar.	28 28 Oct. 31	5 Feb. 36	4 Oct. 44	do	do	
Charles Algernon Lewis, *Lt.Col.*, Grenadier Guards	18 Oct.	25 15 Aug. 26	12 April 33	never	never	do	
Richard French, *Lt.Col.*, Unattached	9 June	25 30 Dec. 26	2 Mar. 32	11 May 39	16 Jan. 46	do	21 May 50
William Parlby,[17] *Lieut.Col.*, h.p. 10 Hussars, *Major General Commanding Cavalry Brigade at Dublin*	3 Oct. 16	6 May 24	19 Sept. 26	23 Nov. 41	30 Jan. 46	do	
George Congreve,[18] CB., *Lt.Col.*, h.p. 29 Foot, *Quarter Master General, East Indies*	8 April 25	12 Jan. 26	12 June 28	do	11 Feb. 46	do	
John Thomas Hill, *Lt.Col.*, h.p. 80 Foot	13 Mar. 27	16 April 29	13 Feb. 35	12 Mar. 41	3 April 46	do	25 Aug. 57
John Longfield, CB., *Lt.Col.*, h. p. 8 Foot	23 June 23	26 Sept. 25	30 Jan. 35	19 Nov. 44	do	do	
Charles William Morley Balders,[19] CB., *Lt.Col.*, 12 Lancers, *Commandant, Cavalry Depot at Maidstone*	10 Nov. 25	25 Nov. 28	15 July 36	16 May 45	do	do	
Fred. William Hamilton, CB., *Major*, Grenadier Guards	never	12 July 31	1 Dec. 36	never	do	do	
Charles Hastings Doyle, *Lt.Col.*, *Inspector General of Militia in Ireland*	23 Dec. 19	27 Sept. 22	16 June 25	28 Sept. 38	14 April 46	do	15 April 47
Fred. Horn,[20] CB. *Lieut.Col.* h.p. 20 F. *Major General on the Staff at Malta*	26 Jan.	26 17 April 28	16 June 37	9 Aug. 39	do	do	
John Francis Glencairn Campbell, CB., *Lt.Col.*, 91 Foot	25 Oct.	27 27 Aug. 29	23 Nov. 32	8 July 43	8 May 46	do	
Lord Fred. Paulet, CB., *Lt.Col.*, Coldstream Guards	never	27 July 30	never	never	do	do	
John Rowland Smyth, CB., *Lt.-Col.*, *Insp. Field Officer at Liverpool*	5 July 21	26 May 25	22 April 26	17 Aug. 41	19 June 46	do	19 April 47

Colonels.

	CORNET, ETC.	LIEUT.	CAPTAIN.	MAJOR.	LIEUT.-COLONEL.	COLONEL.	WHEN PLACED ON HALF PAY.
Wm. James D'Urban, *Lt. Col. Unatt. Colonel on the Staff, Cape of Good Hope* ..	7 Oct. 19	25 Sept. 23	8 April 26	16 Oct. 35	31 July 46	20 June 54	2 April 52
ʙ Henry John French,²² *Lt. Col., Unattached*	27 Aug. 12	21 July 13	25 Sept. 23	23 May 36	do	do	
Terence O'Brien, *Lt.-Col. Unatt., Assistant Quarter Master General*	22 April 13	19 Jan. 15	20 Mar. 28	23 Nov. 41	do	do	
John ffollintt Crofton,²³ *Lt.Col., Unatt., Assistant Military Superintendent of Pensioners* }	18 Dec. 24	29 Aug.	17 July 26	15 April 42	7 Aug. 46	do	1 Oct. 56
John Grattan,²¹ *CB, Lt.Col., h.p. 18 Foot*	8 July 13	4 Sept. 23	4 Mar. 36	26 May 41	14 Aug. 46	do	
Hon. James Lindsay, *Major, Grenadier Guards*	never	16 Mar. 32	2 Dec. 36	never	do	do	
Hon. George Aug. Fred. Liddell, *Lt. Col., Unattached*	never	27 Nov. 28	24 April 35	never	8 Sept. 46	do	6 July 49
William Sullivan, *CB, Lt. Col., Insp. Field Officer at Belfast*	14 Oct. 24	8 April 28	21 June 36	27 Aug. 41	11 Sept. 46	do	
Arthur Aug. Thurlow Cumynghame, ²⁵ *CB, Lt. Col., Fort Major and Adj. of Guernsey* }	25 Mar. 29	9 Mar. 09	9 Dec. 13	10 Jan. 37	20 Oct. 46	do	25 Dec. 14
John Hankey Bainbrigge, *Major, Unatt. Fort Major, h.p. 51 Foot, *Major General Commanding a Brigade in Dublin* }	2 Nov. 30	22 May 35	17 Aug. 41	8 Aug. 45	3 Nov. 46	do	
St. Vincent William Ricketts, *Lt. Col., Unattached*	13 July 26	5 April 31	6 Nov. 35	7 April 43	6 Nov. 46	do	27 Aug. 52
ʙ William James King, *Major, h. p. Royal Staff Corps*	16 May 05	29 May 09	17 Feb. 14	25 June 30	9 Nov. 46	do	25 June 30
ʙ ᴄʙ James Henderson,²⁷ *KH., Major, Unattached*	9 Feb. 94	1 Oct. 94	19 Oct. 09	22 July 30		do	28 Nov. 34
ʙ Wm. Abraham Le Mesurier, ²⁶ *Capt., h. p. 95 Foot, Town Major of Alderney*	6 July 04	7 May 05	15 Mar. 10	do		do	19 Nov. 29
ʙ John Swinburn, ²⁹ *Major, Unattached*	28 Aug. 04	16 May 05	15 Aug. 10	do		do	22 Sept. 43
George Stuart, *Captain, h. p. 42 Foot*	1 Mar. 03	1 Sept. 04	21 Feb. 11	do		do	11 Nov. 42
Thomas Kelly,³⁰ *KC. do., h. p. Cheshire Fencibles, Fort Major of Tilbury Fort*	10 Mar. 95	25 June 03	28 Feb. 11	do		do	
ʙ ᴄʙ James Kerr Ross,³¹ *KH., Major, Unattached*	19 Mar. 07	4 May 08	22 Oct. 18	7 June 31		do	7 June 31
Eardley Wilmot, *Major, Unattached*	19 Mar. 11	19 July 11	22 May 25	21 June 31		do	21 June 31
Edward Basil Brooke, *Lt. Col., Insp. Field Officer in Dublin*	15 Dec. 17	9 April 25	11 July 25	5 July 31		do	
ʙ ᴄʙ John FitzMaurice, *KH., Major, Unattached, Clerk of the Cheque to Yeomen of the Guard* }	25 April 11	14 Jan. 13	16 June 25	30 Mar. 32		do	30 Mar. 32
John Campbell, *Lt. Col. Unatt., Lt. Col. Commandant Argyl and Bute Militia*	30 Mar. 15	11 Jan. 21	26 May 25	15 June 32		do	6 July 52
Frederick Hope, *Major, Unattached*	11 July 16	24 Oct. 21	9 June 25	4 Oct. 33		do	27 Sept. 42
Lewis Alexander During,³² *Major, Unattached*	25 Nov. 95	5 May 04	15 April 13	8 Nov. 33		do	13 Dec. 33
Joshua Simmons Smith, *Major, Unattached*	14 Aug. 17	17 May 22	19 April 27	31 Dec. 33		do	8 Mar. 50
Henry Arthur O'Neill, *Major, Unattached*	14 Oct. 21	10 Sept. 24	4 Feb. 26	28 Aug. 35		do	25 Oct. 42
ʙ Anthony R. Harrison,³³ *Colonel, retired full pay, Royal Artillery*	1 June 08	27 Oct. 10	6 Nov. 27	23 Nov. 41		do	
Richard Parker, *Lt.-Col. & Colonel, 1 Life Guards*	2 Aug. 22	31 July 25	30 June 28	do	42	do	
ʙ Henry Richard Wright,³⁴ *Lt. Col., ret. full pay, R. Art.*	6 July 08	29 Dec. 11	10 July 29	1 Nov. 43		do	
Charles Trollope,³⁵ *CB, Lt. Col. h.p. 62 F. *Maj.Gen. on the Staff in Nova Scotia*	19 Nov. 25	10 Oct. 26	23 Aug. 39	16 June 43	20 Nov. 46	do	
Andrew T. Hemphill, *Lt. Col., 26 Foot*	7 April 25	16 April 29	3 July 39	11 Feb. 46	8 Dec. 46	do	
ᴅ *Lord* George Aug. Fred. Paget,³⁶ *CB., Lt. Col., Unattached*	25 July 34	1 Dec. 37	17 Aug. 41	30 Jan. 46	20 Dec. 46	do	1 May 57
ʙ Brook Taylor, *Lt. Col., Unatt., Assistant Adjutant General of Militia*	15 May 27	15 June 30	28 Nov. 34	31 July 46	29 Dec. 46	do	
ʙ² Geo. Thos. Conolly Napier,³⁷ *CB. Lt. Col., Unat., Aide-de-Camp to the Queen, Deputy Quarter Master General in Canada* }	23 Mar 32	25 Aug. 37	16 Feb. 41	5 Nov. 47	15 Sept. 48	do	

Colonels.

	CORNET, ETC.	LIEUT.	CAPTAIN.	MAJOR.	LIEUT.-COLONEL.	COLONEL.	WHEN PLACED ON HALF PAY.
⚔ Francis Warde, *Colonel*, Royal Artillery	4 Mar. 09	8 Mar. 12	3 July 30	9 Nov. 46	7 May 47	13 Sept. 54	
⚔ William Bates Ingilby, *Colonel*, Royal Artillery	1 April 09	9 Apr. 12	22 July 30	do	7 May 47	6 Nov. 54	
Thomas Fyamore,[35] *Lt.Col.*, ret. full pay, R. Marines	6 April 11	23 April 29	3 Oct. 38	do	23 Nov. 52	20 Nov. 54	
James Buchanan,[39] *Lt.Col.*, ret. full pay, R. Marines	22 Feb.	24 Aug. 23	4 Nov. 41	9 Nov. 46	24 Feb. 54	20 Nov. 54	
William Sall,[3] KH. *Capt.* r. f. p. R. Newf. Cos. *Military Knight of Windsor*	30 Oct.	26 Nov. 94	9 July 00	14 June 22	14 June 22	30 28 Nov. 54	
Robert Terry,[41] *Captain*, retired full pay, 31 Foot	6 Aug. 99	7 Mar. 00	8 Oct. 03	4 June	14 22 July 30	do	
James W. Fairtlough,[42] *Lt.Col.*, retired full pay, 63 Foot	20 Aug.	22 24 May 04	4 Mar. 05	12 Aug.	19 17 Sept. 33	do	
Henry C. Streatfeild,[43] *Lt.Col.* retired full pay, 87 Foot	Oct.	01 13 Nov. 01	7 Nov. 05	12 Aug.	19 4 Oct. 33	do	
Henry Senior,[44] *Lt.Col.*, retired full pay, 65 Foot	6 May	13 28 Dec. 13	15 24 April 23	12 Mar.	29 19 Sept. 34	do	
Charles Hughes,[45] *Lt.Col.*, retired full pay, 24 Foot	25 May	96 11 May 97	28 Aug. 04	2 June	14 10 Oct. 35	do	
Joseph Kelsall, *Lt.Col.*, retired full pay, 70 F.	17 Dec.	03 21 Feb. 05	11 Nov. 13	23 Nov.	32 28 June 38	do	
William Blois, *Lt.Col.*, retired full pay, 52 Foot	3 May	15 30 Aug. 21	14 July 25	12 Aug.	34 11 May 39	do	
Edward T. Tronson,[46] *Lt.Col.*, retired full pay, 13 Foot	23 Nov.	06 26 Jan. 08	2 Sept. 19	27 Mar.	35 23 July 39	do	
⚔ Joseph Mark Harry, KH.,[49] *Major*, do, Cape Mounted Riflemen	23 April	07 11 Mar. 13	20 Dec. 27	22 July	27 22 July 41	do	
Gerald Rochfort,[50] *Major*, retired full pay, 3 Foot	28 April	06 1 May 10	2 June 14	6 Sept.	28 23 Nov. 41	do	
Philip Dundas,[51] *Lt.Col.*, retired full pay, 47 Foot	28 Feb.	05 25 Sept. 05	1 July 12	1 May	28 do	do	
Richard Willington,[52] *Lt.Col.*, retired full pay, 84 Foot	22 Aug.	05 25 Aug. 07	16 Nov. 20	28 June	31 do	do	
⚔ Richard Westmore,[53] *Lt.Col.*, retired full pay, 38 Foot	1 Oct.	12 2 Oct. 14	3 Dec. 25	28 June	38 8 April 42	do	
John H. Poole, CB.,[54] *Major*, retired full pay, 22 Foot	28 May	12 1 April 13	23 June 25	28 June	38 14 June 42	do	
Edward James White,[55] *Lt.Col.*, ret. full pay, 70 Foot	24 Mar.	14 30 Dec. 19	1 Nov. 30	18 Oct.	39 4 July 43	do	
Edward Wm. Bray, CB.,[36] *Major*, retired full pay, 39 Foot	30 Mar.	09 5 April 10	14 July 25	14 Dec.	32 23 Feb. 44	do	
Aralnuder Tennant,[57] *Lt.Col.*, retired full pay, 35 Foot	12 Jan.	05 20 April 08	6 April 19	10 Jan.	37 30 April 44	do	
⚔ Edward Rowley Hill,[58] *Lt.Col.* h. p. 63 F., *Dep. Adj. Gen. at Barbados*	20 Oct.	08 10 June 13	10 June 26	1 Aug.	34 9 Nov. 46	do	
Charles Wright, *Colonel*, Royal Engineers	23 Feb.	13 24 Feb. 14	26 Sept. 26	23 Nov.	41 1 Jan. 47	do	
George William Key, *Lt.Col.*, h. p. 44 Foot	2 July	13 1 Mar. 14	29 July 29	25 28 June	38 4 Feb. 47	do	
Edward Pole, *Lt.Col.*, 12 Lancers	5 July	13 25 Aug. 14	16 Sept. 33	14 June	42 9 Feb. 47	do	
Sir Joshua Jebb,[59] KCB., *Lt.Col.* r.f.p., R. Eng. *Insp. General of Military Prisons.*	1 July	25 19 Sept. 26	18 Nov. 31	30 July	44 30 Mar. 47	do	
Arthur Shirley,[60] *Lt.Col.*, Unattached	1 July	12 21 July 13	26 Feb. 28	23 Nov.	41 16 April 47	do	
Frederick Holt Robe, CB., *Lt.Col.*, Unattached	31 Aug.	30 1 Feb. 33	15 July 36	28 Aug.	46 16 April 47	do	
Sir Robert Walpole, KCB., *Lt.Col.* Rifle Brigade	22 Oct.	17 8 Apr. 25	22 Oct. 33	31 Dec.	41 28 May 47	do	
⚔ Henry Pester, *Colonel*, Royal Artillery	1 May	09 16 June 12	22 July 30	34 31 May	44 2 July 47	do	
Arthur Johnstone Lawrence,[61] CB., *Lt.Col.*, h. p. Rifle Brigade, *Major General Commanding a Brigade at Aldershot*	4 April	27 12 Feb. 30	24 Feb. 37	9 Nov.	46 20 July 47	do	23 Sept. 50
Hon. George Cadogan,[62] CB., *Lt.Col.*, h. p. Depot Battalion, Her Majesty's *Military Commissioner at Turin*	never	22 Feb. 33	9 Jan. 38	11 Sept.	46 1 Aug.	do	31 Oct. 51
John Charles Hope Gibsone,[63] *Lt.Col.*, Unatt., *Commandant of Cavalry Depot at Canterbury*	8 Oct.	30 16 Aug. 33	24 July 35	25 Feb.	45 6 Aug.	do	2 Aug. 53
Charles Philip Ainslie, *Lt. Col.*, 14 Light Dragoons	10 April	25 28 Jan. 26	16 Mar. 30	14 Oct.	42 3 Sept.	do	17 July 57
Freeman Murray, *Lt.Col.* h. p. 63 F., *Gov. & Com. in Chief at Bermuda*	24 Feb.	25 8 Apr. 26	21 Dec. 32	20 Aug.	44 5 Nov.	do	5 May 54

29

Colonels.

	ENSIGN, ETC.	LIEUT.	CAPTAIN.	MAJOR.	LIEUT.-COLONEL.	COLONEL.	WHEN PLACED ON HALF PAY.
Hon. Alex. Nelson Hood, *Lt.Col.*, h. p. 13 *Foot, Equerry to the Queen, and Clerk Marshal to the Prince Consort*	never	30 Aug. 31	1 July 36	9 Nov. 46	5 Nov. 47	28 Nov. 54	3 Mar. 54
David Russell, *CB., Lt. Col., Inspecting Field Officer in London*	10 Jan. 28	1 Oct. 29	5 April 33	7 July 45	10 Dec.	do	
Robert Wm. Story,[61] *Lt.Col., ret. full pay, Royal Artillery*	6 Nov. 09	18 Mar. 13	27 May 30	9 Nov. 46	21 Dec.	do	10 Nov. 56
Richard William Huey,[65] *Lt.Col.*, h. p. 1 *Foot*	26 Mar. 25	19 Dec. 26	11 June 30	13 Oct. 38	31 Dec.	do	
Horatio Shirley,[65] *CB., Lt.Col.*, h. p. 88 *Foot,* *Major General Commanding a Brigade at the Curragh*	12 May 25	31 Oct. 26	5 July 33	31 Dec. 41	18 Jan. 48		
William Samuel Newton, *Major, Coldstream Guards*	never	5 Dec. 34	31 Dec. 39	25 Feb. 45	27 Mar.	do	
Nicholas R. Brown, *Lt.Col., ret.* on full *pay,* 34 *Foot*	22 Mar. 21	2 June 25	2 May 37	23 Mar. 45	7 April	do	
Egerton Charles Wm. Milman, *Lt.-Col.*, 37 *Foot*	never	24 April 13	5 Feb. 35	10 Sept. 45	23 June	do	
Spencer Perceval, *Major, Coldstream Guards*	26 Feb.	5 April 29	13 Nov. 35	10 Sept. 45	19 July	do	
Henry Cooper, *Lt.Col.*, 45 *Foot*	30 Dec. 24	8 Oct. 27	14 Aug. 25	23 Nov. 41	21 July	do	
Randal Rumley, *Lt.Col. Unatt.,* *Major General on the Staff at Gibraltar*	30 July 13	15 Dec. 13	1 May 27	9 Nov. 46	9 Aug.	do	
Sir Henry Knight Storks,[67] *KCB., Lt.-Col., Unattached, Lord High Commissioner of the Ionian Islands*	10 Jan. 28	2 Mar. 32	30 Oct. 35	7 Aug. 40	15 Sept.	do	13 July 55
Thomas Charlton Smith,[68] *Major, Unatt*	24 June 13	5 Aug. 13	27 Mar. 19	30 Sept. 42	15 Oct.	do	25 Aug. 46
William Sutton, *Lt.Col.*, 31 *Foot*	5 June 27	16 Mar. 26	30 July 30	9 Nov. 46	15 Sept.	do	
Hon. George Cecil Weld Forester, *CB.,[64] Lt.Col., Royal Horse Guards*	27 May 24	1 Aug. 26	6 July 32	9 Nov. 46	19 Sept.	do	
Edward Cooper Hodge, *CB.,[64] Lt.Col., Unattached*	3 Aug. 26	3 July 28	19 Dec. 34	3 Dec. 41	3 Oct. 48	do	5 Aug. 59
Charles Cooke Yarborough,[69] *CB., Lt.Col.*, h. p., 91 *Foot*	9 June 25	19 Sept. 26	4 Jan. 33	19 May 45	13 Oct.	do	29 Jan. 56
Thomas Crombie,[70] *Lt.Col., Unattached*	13 Dec. 24	8 April 26	8 May 32	16 Nov. 41	20 Oct.	do	9 Feb. 55
Archibald Macbean,[71] *Lt.Col.,* R. *Artillery,* on ret. full *pay*	13 Dec.	23 July 14	28 Dec. 32	23 Nov. 41	1 Nov. 48	do	
George James,[72] *Lt.Col.,* do.	5 Mar. 10	25 Oct. 13	3 Sept. 31	9 Nov. 46	do	do	
Henry Palliser, *Colonel, Royal Artillery*	4 June 12	18 Feb. 14	27 Sept. 32	do	do	do	
Robert Longmore Garstin, *Lt.Col.*, do., on retired full *pay*	12 Dec.	20 Dec. 11	1 Aug. 33	do	do	do	
Henry Edward Doherty,[73] *CB., Lt.Col.*, h. p 9 *Foot*	31 Dec. 33	15 July 36	17 May 39	22 Oct. 47	23 Nov. 48	do	25 Aug. 57
Augustus Halifax Ferryman, *CB., Lt.Col.*, 89 *Foot*	27 June 34	30 June 37	16 April 41	22 Dec. 43	24 Nov.	do	
William John Ridley, *Major, Scots Fusilier Guards*	never	19 June 35	24 May 39	never	Dec.	do	
William Raikes Faber,[74] *Lt.Col., Unattached*	10 April 26	28 Aug. 28	22 Aug. 35	23 Dec. 42	15 Dec.	do	13 July 58
Thomas James Galloway, *Lt.Col.*, 70 *Foot*	13 Sept. 21	2 June 25	27 Dec. 27	23 Nov. 41	22 Dec.	do	
John Garrock,[74] *Major, Unatt., Assist.Qr.Master General at Ceylon*	4 Sept. 35	31 Dec. 39	25 Nov. 42	3 April 46	22 Dec.	do	
William Jones, *CB., Lt.Col.*, 61 *Foot*	10 April 25	12 Dec. 26	24 Nov. 35	26 July 44	29 Dec.	do	
Burke Cuppage, *Colonel, Royal Artillery*	17 Dec.	20 June 15	20 July 34	do	8 Jan. 46	49	
Robert Burn, *Colonel,* R. *Artillery*	17 Dec.	20 June	14 Aug. 34	do	29 Mar.	do	
Richard Beaumont Burnaby,[75] *Lt.Col.,* ret. full *pay* R. *Artillery, Lt. Col.,* Commandant Hampshire Artillery Militia	17 Dec.	28 June	9 Sept. 34	do	9 April	do	
Hon. Alexander Gordon,[76] *CB., Lt.Col. Unatt.,* *Deputy Quarter Master General, Extra Equerry to The Prince Consort*	never	2 May 34	15 May 40	never	10 April	do	
Corbet Cotton, *Lt.Col., Unattached*	9 April 25	29 Mar. 27	4 May 32	5 June 44	20 April 49	28 Nov. 54	20 April 49

Colonels.

	ENSIGN, ETC.	LIEUT.	CAPTAIN.	MAJOR.	LIEUT.-COLONEL.	COLONEL.	WHEN PLACED ON HALF PAY.
Matthew Smith, *Lt.-Col.*, 81 Foot	16 Sept. 42	31 Dec. 23	8 Feb. 34	23 Dec. 42	7 June 49	28 Nov. 54	
Maurice Griffin Dennis, *C.B., Lt.-Col.*, 60 Foot	9 May 26	5 July 27	15 Dec. 37	2 May 45	7 June do	do	
Henry Bates, *Lt.Col.*, 98 Foot	9 June 29	28 Nov. 33	8 Aug. 45	19 June 46	7 June do	do	
Augustus George Blachford, *Lt.-Col.*, 24 Foot	2 Nov. 25	12 Dec. 26	17 Aug. 41	14 Jan. 49	7 June do	do	
John MacDuff, *Lt.Col.*, 74 Foot	10 Feb. 14	26 June 27	13 April 39	13 Nov. 47	8 June do	do	
Thomas Maitland Wilson, *Lt.-Col.*, 8 Foot	15 April 24	13 May 26	23 Dec. 31	9 Nov. 46	15 June do	do	
Thomas Coryndon Luxmoore, *Lt.Col., ret. full pay, Royal Engineers*	1 Jan. 14	1 Aug. 14	6 Nov. 34	do	1 July do	do	
Charles Tyrwhitt,[77] *Lt.-Col., Unatt., Equerry and Aide de Camp to H.R.H. the Duke of Cambridge*	1 Aug. 34	26 Feb. 36	15 Nov. 39	never	6 July do	do	22 June 55
George Staunton, *Lt.-Col., Cape Mounted Riflemen*	5 Oct. 26	15 Feb. 31	8 June 39	28 Mar. 45	20 July do	do	
Charles Crutchley, *Lt.-Col., Commandant R. Military Asylum*	8 April 26	22 July 30	11 Dec. 35	22 Oct. 44	24 July do	do	
William Paris, *Lt.Col., ret. full pay, Royal Engineers*	1 Jan. 14	1 May 14	1 Mar. 35	9 Nov. 46	6 Aug. do	do	
Walter Hamilton, *CB., Lt.Col., Insp. Field Officer at Bristol*	28 Jan. 19	15 April 24	15 Mar. 33	9 Nov. 46	2 Oct. do	do	
Edward Vicars; *Lt.-Col., ret. full pay, Royal Engineers*	28 Mar. 22	8 April 26	23 July 40	10 Nov. 46	19 Oct. do	do	
Charles Rochfort Scott,[78] *Capt., h. p. Royal Staff Corps, Lieut. Governor, Royal Military College*	2 Jan. 12	20 July 15	25 June 30	31 Dec. 41	do	do	
Mark Kerr Atherley, *Lt.-Col.*, 92 Foot	28 Aug. 23	13 Aug. 25	25 Nov. 28	23 Nov. 41	23 Nov. 46	do	
Trevor Chute, *Lt.-Col.* 70 Foot	10 Aug. 32	28 Oct. 36	2 Aug. 39	23 April 47	14 Dec. do	do	
William Gustavus Brown, *Lt.-Col.*, 24 Foot	7 July 25	11 May 30	10 May 44	15 Jan. 49	21 Dec. do	do	
Henry Jervis, *Lt. Col., Depot Battalion*	11 Dec. 29	29 Dec. 14	19 Sept. 26	23 Nov. 41	8 Mar. 50	do	
Michael William Smith, *C.B., Lt.-Col.*, 3 Dragoon Guards	19 Nov. 30	21 Feb. 39	23 April 39	9 Feb. 47	8 Mar. do	do	
John Maxwell Perceval, *C.B., Lt.Col.*, 12 Foot	4 Dec. 33	18 Mar. 36	18 May 38	14 April 46	2 April do	do	
Henry William Stisted, *C.B., Lt.Col.*, 93 Foot	25 May 35	29 Sept. 38	29 April 42	26 May 48	19 April do	do	
Thomas James Adair,[74] *Lt.Col., Unattached*	23 Sept. 24	27 Feb. 11	27 Mar. 23	28 June 38	21 May do	do	1 July 58
Philip Melmoth Nelson Guy, *CB., Lt.-Col.*, 5 Foot	13 Dec. 24	12 June 28	29 Dec. 37	20 July 47	21 May do	do	
William How Hennis,[73] *Lt.Col., ret. full pay, R. Art*	1 May 15	1 Aug. 16	5 June 35	20 Oct. 46	23 May do	do	
Daniel Thorndike, *Colonel, Royal Artillery*	1 May 15	8 May 19	28 Dec. 35	9 Nov. 46	27 May do	do	
Harry Stow, *Lt.Col., ret. full pay, Royal Artillery*	1 May 15	26 Dec. 19	4 Feb. 36	do	27 May do	do	
Charles Gosling, *Colonel, Royal Artillery*	1 May 15	22 April 20	19 April 36	9 Nov. 46	20 June do	do	
Francis Seymour, *C.B., Major, Scots Fusilier Guards, Groom in Waiting to the Prince Consort*	2 May 34	16 June 37	4 Sept. 40	never	28 June do	do	
Charles Steuart, *C.B., Lt.-Col.*, 14 Light Dragoons	10 Dec. 25	5 Feb. 29	9 Nov. 38	25 April 48	7 July do	do	
Charles Henry Mee, *Lt.Col., Royal Artillery, on ret. full pay*	1 May 15	11 May 20	27 April 36	9 Nov. 46	16 July do	do	
John Leslie Dennis, *Lt.Col.*, 52 Foot	25 April 28	22 Sept. 30	17 May 41	29 Nov. 44	2 Aug. do	do	
C. R. Sackville, *Lord West*,[80] *CB., Lt. Col., h. p. Depot Battalion*	30 Aug. 33	5 June 35	15 April 42	3 April do	2 Aug. do	do	
Fred. Paul Haines, *Lt.Col.*, 8 Foot, *Military Secretary at Madras*	21 June 39	10 July 40	16 May 46	7 June 49	2 Aug. do	do	
John Arthur Lambert, *Major*, Grenadier Guards	never	21 July 35	11 Sept. 40	never	15 Nov. do	do	
Charles Bertie Symons, *Colonel, Royal Artillery*	10 July 21	2 Dec. 21	1 July 36	9 Nov. 46	22 Dec. 50	do	15 Aug. 56
William O'Grady Haly, *C.B., Lt.Col.*, 38 Foot	17 June 28	19 July 31	25 April 34	19 May 46	27 Dec. 50	do	
Henry Phipps Raymond, *Lt.-Col., Depot Battalion*	9 April 25	17 Mar. 27	21 Mar. 34	9 Nov. 46	17 Jan. 51	do	

Colonels.

	CORNET, ETC.	LIEUT.	CAPTAIN.	MAJOR.	LIEUT.-COLONEL.	COLONEL.	WHEN PLACED ON HALF PAY.
VC *Hon.* Henry Hugh Manvers Percy, *Capt. & Lt.Col.*, Grenadier Guards, *Aide de Camp to the Queen*	never	1 July 36	29 Dec. 40	never	7 Mar. 51	28 Nov. 54	
William Wallace d'Arley, *Lt.Col.*, ret. full pay, Royal Artillery	16 Dec. 16	10 Dec. 24	10 Jan. 37	never	4 April	do	
William Craig Emilius Napier, [82] *Major, Unatt., Major and Superintendent of Studies, Royal Military College*	28 Aug. 35	17 Nov. 37	29 April 42	18 Feb. 48	30 May	do	
Edmund Neal Wilford, *Colonel*, Royal Artillery	16 Dec. 16	3 Jan. 25	10 Jan. 37	never	6 June	do	
Henry Powell Wulff, *Colonel*, Royal Engineers	1 Aug. 14	1 July 25	15 Sept. 36	9 Nov. 46	5 July	do	
Montgomery Williams, *Lt.Col.*, Royal Engineers	24 Mar. 15	1 May 25	16 Jan. 37	never	14 July	do	
John Hawkshaw, *Lt.Col.*, ret. full pay, R. Engineers	24 Mar. 15	1 May 25	10 Jan. 37	never	4 July	do	18 July 51
Charles Augustus Arney, [83] *Lt.Col.*, Unattached	5 Nov. 25	9 Aug. 31	1 July 37	12 May 43	18 July	do	
Charles Henry Ellice, CB., *Lt.Col.*, 24 Foot		10 May 33	8 Aug. 45	21 Dec. 49	8 Aug.	do	
Thomas Hore, *Lt.Col.*, ret. full pay, Royal Engineers	24 Mar. 15	7 Feb. 17	10 Jan. 37	never	31 Aug.	do	
Henry Richmond Jones, CB., *Lt.Col.*, 6 Dragoon Guards	9 June 25	14 Nov. 12	12 June 30	9 Nov. 46	16 Sept.	do	
John Tylden, *Lt.Col.*, ret. full pay, Royal Artillery	16 Dec. 16	13 Feb. 26	10 Jan. 37	never	25 Sept.	do	
Thomas Myddelton Biddulph, *Lt.Col., Unatt., Master of the Queen's Household and Extra Equerry to Her Majesty*	7 Oct. 26	23 Feb. 29	16 May 34	9 Nov. 46	31 Oct.	do	31 Oct. 51
Charles Hagart, CB., [84] *Lt.Col.*, Unattached	15 June 32	12 Aug. 34	21 Oct. 37	10 Dec. 47	31 Oct. 51	do	13 May 59
Thomas Montagu Steele, CB., *Capt. & Lt.Col.*, Coldstream Guards, *Aide de Camp to the Queen*	12 Jan. 38	20 July 38	29 Mar. 44	never	31 Oct.	do	
Vance Young Donaldson, [85] *Major*, Unattached	14 Sept. 04	25 Dec. 05	24 June 13	10 Jan. 37	11 Nov.	do	6 Mar. 40
William Chambré, *Major*, Unattached	9 July 11	27 May 12	10 Jan. 22	do	do	do	30 July 44
Hon. Arthur Charles Legge, *Captain*, Unattached	23 May 13	16 Feb. 17	17 Jan. 22	do	do	do	23 June 37
Melville Dalyell, [86] *Captain*, h. p. 9 Foot	6 Oct. 08	14 June 10	31 Oct. 22	do	do	do	23 Mar. 38
William Long, [86] *Captain*, h. p. 9 Foot	9 Dec. 13	19 May 19	19 Sept. 25	do	do	do	23 Mar. 38
John Birtwhistle, [87] *Major*, Unattached	1 April 14	10 Jan. 16	19 May 24	17 Feb. 37	do	do	12 Mar. 41
James Creagh, *Lieut.Col.*, retired full pay, 86 Foot	1 Jan. 15	10 4 Mar. 20	12 7 April 25	24 28 June 38	do	do	
Nicholas Palmer, [88] *Major*, retired full pay, 56 Foot	11 Nov. 13	8 May 14	21 26 May 25	do	do	do	26 Oct. 41
Henry Sykes Stephens, KH., *Capt.*, Unattached	14 June 15	9 Nov. 18	9 June 25	do	do	do	12 Oct. 41
Charles Barry, *Captain*, Unattached	23 Mar. 14	8 Feb. 15	15 21 July 25	do	do	do	1 Oct. 56
James M'Queen, *Major*, Unattached	31 Mar. 14	11 Feb. 20	19 21 July 25	do	do	do	
Joseph Swinburne, [89] *Major*, retired full pay, 83 Foot	16 Aug. 09	4 June 12	6 Oct. 25	do	do	do	26 Jan. 41
Samuel Waynmouth, [90] *Major*, Unattached	18 May 12	28 Mar. 13	13 Oct. 25	do	do	do	
Daniel Frazer, *Major*, retired full pay, 42 Foot	31 Oct. 11	13 June 22	16 5 Nov. 25	do	do	do	9 June 44
Charles Smith, *Major*, Unattached	20 Oct. 21	13 April 14	31 Dec. 25	28 June 38	11 Nov. 51	do	
Charles Highmore Potts, *Captain*, retired full pay, 19 Foot	8 Feb. 16	13 Nov. 17	31 Dec. 25	do	do	do	14 Mar. 45
Francis Westenra, *Major*, Unattached	31 July 17	24 Oct. 21	do	20 Sept. 39	do	do	
Edgar Gibson, [91] *Major*, Unattached	5 Dec. 12	26 Mar. 14	24 May 24	22 May 29	18 Oct. 39	do	13 Dec. 39
Edward Last, [92] *Lt.Col.*, retired full pay, 21 Foot	13 Oct. 13	14 23 Jan. 23	25 Feb. 31	10 Jan. 40	do	do	10 Jan. 40
Leonard Morse-Cooper, [93] *Major*, Unattached	26 May 13	22 April 25	23 April 29	17 April 40	do	do	
Charles Wise *Major*, Unattached, 1st Warwick Militia	7 July	25	29			do	23 Sept. 45

Colonels.

	CORNET, ETC.	LIEUT.	CAPTAIN.	MAJOR.	LIEUT.-COLONEL.	COLONEL.	WHEN PLACED ON HALF PAY.
Francis Plunkett Dunne, *Major*, Unatt., *Lt.Col.*, Queen's County Militia	29 May 23	23 June 23	30 Dec. 25	18 Sept. 40	11 Nov. 51	28 Nov. 54	18 Sept. 40
Gilbert William Francklyn, *Lt.Col.*, 17 Foot	30 April 27	23 Nov. 27	9 Dec. 30	27 Aug. 41	do	do	
John Knight Jauncey,[34] *Major*, Unattached	12 Mar. 12	07 Feb. 13	5 June 22	17 Sept. 41	do	do	17 Sept. 41
George Hankey Smith, *Lt. Col.*, 73 Foot	7 April 18	7 Feb. 22	8 Apr. 25	21 Nov. 41	do	do	
Guy Clarke, *Major*, Unattached	17 Feb. 20	17 July 23	do	23 Nov. 41	do	do	
Robert Shaito Vicars, *Captain*, Unattached	10 Dec. 13	9 Aug. 23	21 April 26		do	do	19 July 50
Rawdon J. Popham Vassall, *Major*, Unattached	6 June 24	22 Oct. 25	22 May 26		do	do	12 May 43
Wm. Henry Adams, *Capt.*, Unatt., *Prof. of Fortification, R. Military College*	1 Feb. 21	11 Mar. 25	18 July 26		do	do	23 May 48
James Pattoun Sparks, CB., *Lt.Col.*, 38 Foot	27 July 27	30 July 27	5 Sept. 26		do	do	7 June 44
Alex. Houstoun, *Capt.*, h. p. 4 F., *Staff Officer of Pensioners*	4 Dec. 22	19 Nov. 23	12 Dec. 26		do	do	
John De Lacy,[35] *Major*, Unattached	30 May 23	15 June 24	13 Feb. 27		do	do	1 July 42
Richard Chetwode, *Captain*, h. p. 3 Dragoon Guards	24 May 20	15 Aug. 22	20 Mar. 27		do	do	3 Jan. 45
John Parson Westropp, *Captain*, Unattached	1 Jan. 22	23 June 22	27 April 27		do	do	25 Feb. 45
George Marmaduke Reeves, *Lt. Col.*, 99 Foot	24 8 April 22		27 April 27		do	do	18 Feb. 42
Robert Henry Lowth, CB., *Lt.Col.*, 36 Foot	4 Feb. 19	1 April 24	15 May 27		do	do	
Edward Charles Fletcher, *Captain*, h. p. 3 Dragoon Guards	30 Nov. 20	4 April 23	21 May 27		do	do	18 Mar. 42
Burton Daveney, *Major*, 1 Foot	27 April 27	2 July 27	8 Nov. 27		do	do	
Edward Bagot, *Major*, Unattached	23 Oct. 23	10 Dec. 25	8 Nov. 27		do	do	11 Mar. 42
James Patience, *Major*, 65 Foot	5 April 27	24 Oct. 27	13 Nov. 27		do	do	
James Scargill,[36] *Major*, Unattached	12 April 10	21 Oct. 12	17 Jan. 28		do	do	9 Nov. 49
Robert Lewis,[37] *Major*, Unattached	7 April 25	2 Mar. 26	12 Feb. 28		do	do	5 Dec. 51
Samuel Tryon, *Major*, Unattached	23 Jan. 23	10 Sept. 25	19 Feb. 28		do	do	27 Dec. 42
Thomas Williams, CB., *Lt.Col.*, 4 Foot	22 Sept. 7	2 July 22	17 June 28		do	do	
Oliver D. Ainsworth,[58] *Major*, Unattached	11 April 9	26 July 09	14 Aug. 28		do	do	16 June 43
Thomas Ogilvy, *Captain*, 2 Life Guards	9 Mar. 32	29 April 36	8 May 40		do	do	
George de Rottenburg, CB., *Lt.Col.*, 100 Foot	7 April 25	27 April 25	13 July 32	31 Dec. 41	do	do	
Graves Channey Swan, *Major*, Unattached	14 July 28	25 Oct. 31	11 Oct. 33	31 Dec. 41	do	do	23 Nov. 55
Richard Wilbraham, CB.,[39] *Lt.Col. Unatt. Assist. Adjutant General at Manchester*	25 Mar. 25	25 May 28	22 July 33	31 Dec. 41	do	do	
John Isaac Hope, *Colonel*, Royal Artillery	1 Sept. 15	1 July 21	10 Jan. 37	never	do	do	
William Henry Pickering, *Colonel*, Royal Engineers	16 Dec. 16	9 April 24	do	never	do	do	
Richard John Stothert, *Colonel*, Royal Engineers	1 Sept. 15	13 Mar. 24	19 Jan. 37	11 Nov. 51	24 Nov. 52	do	
George Hooton Hyde, *Lt.Col.*, ret. full pay, Royal Artillery	7 July 17	29 July 25	19 Jan. 37	11 Nov. 51	30 Nov. 52	do	
Alexander Gordon, *Colonel*, Royal Engineers	1 Sept. 15	2 Dec. 24	10 Jan. 37	11 Nov. 51	6 Dec. 52	do	
William Irwin, *Lt.Col.*, Depot Battalion	15 Nov. 27	19 Nov. 30	26 April 39	18 Jan. 48	26 Dec. 52	do	
Thomas Peters Flude, *Colonel*, Royal Artillery	7 July 17	29 July 25	29 Jan. 37	11 Nov. 51	30 Dec. 52	do	
Cowper Rose, *Colonel*, Royal Engineers	1 Sept. 15	12 Jan. 25	10 Jan. 37	11 Nov. 51	28 Jan. 52	do	
Charles William Wingfield, *Colonel*, Royal Artillery	8 July 18	1 April 26	30 Dec. 37	11 Nov. 51	18 Mar. 52	do	
William Biddlecomb Marlow, *Colonel*, Royal Engineers	1 Sept. 15	23 Mar. 25	28 Mar. 37	7 July 46	1 April 52	do	
Alexander Tulloh, *Colonel*, Royal Artillery	8 July 18	10 July 25	20 April 37	11 Nov. 51	do	do	
Henry Poole, *Colonel*, do.	5 Oct. 18	1 Feb. 25	13 Nov. 38	do	do	do	

Colonels.

	ENSIGN, ETC.	LIEUT.	CAPTAIN.	MAJOR.	LIEUT.-COLONEL.	COLONEL.	WHEN PLACED ON HALF PAY.
Henry Geo. Teesdale, *Colonel*, Royal Artillery	8 Dec. 19	26 May 27	23 Mar. 39	11 Nov. 51	1 Apr. 52	28 Nov. 54	
Noel Thomas Lake, CB., *Colonel*, Royal Artillery	5 July 20	5 July 27	10 Aug. 39	do	do	do	
Edmund de Burgh Sidley, *Lt.Col.*, retired full pay, 50 Foot	4 May 22	21 Feb. 22	11 June 30	8 Apr. 42	28 May 52	do	2 Feb. 55
Frank Adams, CB., *Lt.Col.*, 28 Foot	30 Dec. 23	23 Mar. 32	31 Dec. 33	29 Oct. 43	16 July 52	do	
James Robert Brunker, *Lt.Col.* Unattached	9 April 25	9 Sept. 28	14 Sept. 32	9 Nov. 46	24 Aug.	do	
Henry Darby Griffith, CB. *Lt.Col.*, 2 Dragoons, *Aide-de-Camp to the Queen*	25 Nov. 28	25 Nov. 31	1 Aug. 34	6 Nov. 46	27 Aug.	do	
Piercy Benn, *Colonel*, Royal Artillery	3 Feb. 21	13 Oct. 27	14 Aug. 39	11 Nov. 51	31 Aug.	do	
Thomas Akers Shone, *Lt.Col.*, ret. full pay, R. Artillery	11 July 22	6 Nov. 27	24 Nov. 39	11 Nov. 51	11 Nov. 52	do	
Andrew Spottiswoode,[100] *Lt.Col.* Unattached	10 May 33	29 April 36	11 Oct. 39	29 April 50	12 Nov. 52	do	21 Oct. 59
Ashton Ashton Shuttleworth, *Colonel*, R. Artillery	10 Dec. 24	8 Nov. 27	21 April 40	11 Nov. 51	7 Dec. 52	do	
James Webber Smith, CB.[101] *Lt.Col.*, Unatt., *Aide-de-Camp to the Queen*	11 July 26	25 Dec. 35	7 Sept. 38	11 Dec. 49	24 Dec. 52	do	5 June 55
Charles Henry Somerset, CB., *Lt.Col.*, 72 Foot, *Deputy Adjutant General at Bombay*	30 July 30	20 Sept. 39	8 Jan. 47	17 May 50	28 Jan. 53	do	
Luke Smyth O'Connor, CB., *Lt.Col.*, 1 West India Regt.	27 April 27	22 Mar. 31	17 Jan. 34	9 Nov. 46	3 Feb. 53	do	
Fred. Darley George,[102] CB., *Lt.Col.*, Unatt., *Inspector of Army Clothing*	24 Mar. 25	30 April 27	30 Aug. 43	4 July 49	4 Feb.	do	
John Yorke,[103] CB., *Lt.Col.*, Unatt., *Inspector of Army Clothing*	21 Dec. 32	5 Dec. 34	14 Dec. 41	4 Sept. 49	4 Feb.	do	
Henry Dunn O'Halloran, *Lt.Col.* 1 West India Regt.	1 Nov. 18	28 June 27	1 Sept. 38	11 Nov. 51	4 Feb.	do	10 Sept. 58
Herbert Mends,[111] *Lt.-Col.*, retired full pay, 2 West India Regt.	1 April 22	19 Feb. 24	19 Jan. 34	26 May 29	14 Feb. 53	do	10 Mar. 57
John H. Elphinstone Dalrymple, *Capt. & Lt.Col.*, Scots. Fus. Guards		10 Nov. 37	31 Dec. 44		25 Mar.	do	
Robert Kearsley Dawson, CB., *Lt. Col.* retired full pay, R. Engineers	1 Mar. 16	23 Mar. 25	18 Aug. 37	11 Nov. 51	29 Mar.	do	
Daniel Rainier, *Lt.Col.*, 98 Foot	4 Mar. 36	11 May 38	27 May 42	3 Sept. 50	1 April	do	
Henry Hope Graham, *Lt.Col.*, 50 Foot	15 Oct. 29	7 Sept. 32	7 Nov. 34	14 April 46	29 April	do	
Henry Renny, *Lt.-Col.*, 81 Foot	27 Dec. 33	7 Aug. 35	29 May 41	17 Nov. 48	27 May 53	do	
George Campbell, CB., *Lt.Col.*, 52 Foot	35 21 Dec.	26 Jan. 41	21 May 50		6 do		
Arthur Horne, *Lt.Col.*, 13 Foot	19 Nov. 25	27 Nov. 28	21 Feb. 34	9 Nov. 46	28 May	do	
Charles Herrick Burnaby,[104] *Lt.-Col.*, ret. full pay, R. Artillery	9 June 25	14 Nov. 27	12 Aug. 40	15 Sept. 48	28 May 53	do	
John Jarvis Bisset, *Captain*, Cape Mounted Riflemen, *Assist. Adjutant-General, Cape of Good Hope*	7 Feb. 40	16 Feb. 44	1 April 47	15 Sept. 48	do	do	
John Armstrong, *Captain*, Cape Mounted Riflemen	29 Oct. 37	7 Feb. 40	8 Jan. 47	22 Dec. 48	do	do	
William Fanshawe Bedford, *Lt.Col.*, 60 Foot	18 Dec. 28	28 June 33	23 July 41	12 Oct. 49	do	do	
Edward Alan Holdich, CB., *Major*, 20 Foot	2 July 41	26 July 44	22 Feb. 50	2 Aug. 50	do	do	
Robert Newton Phillips, *Lt.Col.*, Depot Battalion	27 May 36	2 Oct. 40	12 Jan. 44	17 Oct. 51	do	do	
Alfred H. Horsford, CB., *Lt.Col.*, Rifle Brigade	12 July 33	23 April 39	5 Aug. 42	26 Dec. 51	do	do	
Walter Douglas Phillipps Patton, *Major*, 74 Foot	28 Sept. 38	3 Nov. 40	19 May 46	27 Feb. 52	do	do	
George Jackson Carey, *Major*, Cape Mounted Riflemen	22 July 45	1 April 47	6 Oct. 48	28 Jan. 53	do	do	
Hon. Percy E. Herbert, CB., *Lt.Col.*, 82 Foot, *Aide de Camp to the Queen*	17 Jan. 40	7 Sept. 41	19 June 46	27 May 53	do	do	
Arthur Borton, CB., *Lieut.Col.*, Depot Battalion	13 July 32	8 April 35	30 July 41	3 April 46	10 June 53	do	
John Hill, *Colonel*, Royal Artillery	10 April 25	12 Nov. 27	22 July 40	11 Nov. 51	21 June 53	do	
Stanhope William Jephson, *Lt.Col.*, 2 Foot	26 Nov. 30	19 Feb. 36	28 Dec. 41	4 Aug. 48	1 July 53	do	

Colonels.

	CORNET, ETC.	LIEUT.	CAPTAIN.	MAJOR.	LIEUT.-COLONEL.	COLONEL.	WHEN PLACED ON HALF PAY.
George Monkland,[104] *Lt.Col.*, Unattached	11 July 34	25 May 38	10 July 46	7 Nov. 51	29 July 53	28 Nov. 54	4 Nov. 59
William Clendon, *Lt.Col.*, retired full pay, Royal Marines	9 Nov. 12	19 Jan. 32	11 May 41	never	15 Aug. 53	do	
David Elliot Mackirdy, *Lt.Col.*, 69 Foot	5 Apr. 33	30 Dec. 36	26 June 41	22 Feb. 50	25 Aug.	do	
John Studholme Brownrigg,[105] CB., *Lt.Col.*, Unatt., *Deputy Adjutant General in Ireland*	20 July 32	6 May 35	29 Dec. 40	11 Nov. 51	13 Sept.	do	
Benjamin Spicer Stehelin, *Colonel*, Royal Engineers	1 Aug. 16	2 June 25	31 Mar. 38	11 Nov. 51	19 Sept.	do	
John Geddes Walker, *Lt.Col.*, ret. full pay, R. Artillery	29 July 25	16 Nov. 27	13 Aug. 40	11 Nov. 51	22 Sept.	do	
William Montagu Scott M'Murdo, CB., *Colonel Commandant Military Train*, *Aide-de-Camp to the Queen*	1 July 37	5 Jan. 41	7 July 43	18 Feb. 48	21 Oct.	do	
William Bernard Ainslie, CB.,[106] *Lt.Col.*, Unattached	28 Sept. 30	24 Nov. 35	29 Sept. 37	1 Oct. 50	21 Oct.	do	25 Jan. 56
William Munro, CB., *Lt.Col.*, 39 Foot	20 June 34	1 April 36	2 July 44	7 May 52	11 Nov.	do	
Arnold Charles Errington, *Lt.Col.*, 51 Foot	4 Feb. 26	13 Sept. 31	14 July 37	25 July 45	9 Dec.	do	
Clement Alex. Edwards, CB., *Lieut.Col.*, 18 Foot	11 June 29	28 Nov. 34	13 Mar. 40	11 Nov. 51	9 Dec.	do	
Samuel Tolfrey Christie, CB., *Lt.Col.*, 80 Foot	22 Jan. 36	13 July 39	28 Aug. 45	31 Oct. 52	9 Dec.	do	
Benjamin Riky, *Lt.Col.*, 48 Foot	9 Nov. 30	30 May 34	8 Sept. 38	11 Nov. 51	13 Dec.	do	
William Mark Wood, *Capt. & Lt.Col.*, Coldstream Guards	22 July 38	24 May 44	20 Aug.	....	13 Dec.	do	
Henry Smyth, CB., *Lt.Col.*, 76 Foot	28 June 33	8 Oct. 36	2 Dec. 42	12 May 48	30 Dec.	do	
Lord Mark Kerr, CB., *Lt.Col.*, 13 Foot	19 June 35	14 Sept. 38	26 June 40	25 July 51	30 Dec.	do	
Stephen John Hill,[107] *Lt.Col.*, h. p. 2 West India Regt., *Governor and Commander-in-Chief of Sierra Leone*	10 Nov. 25	13 Feb. 28	15 April 42	15 Feb. 50	6 Jan. 54	do	28 Oct. 57
Henry Joseph Morris, *Colonel*, Royal Artillery	29 July 25	1 Jan. 28	27 Sept. 40	11 Nov. 51	12 Jan. 54	do	
John McCoy, *Colonel*, Royal Artillery	29 July 25	3 Jan. 28	25 Jan. 41	....	24 Jan.	do	
John Hamilton Stewart, *Lt.Col.*, 29 Foot	23 July 27	2 Aug. 34	2 July 41	27 May 53	25 Jan.	do	
Henry Wase Whitfeild, *Lt.Col.*, 2 West India Regt.	13 Feb. 28	28 Oct. 31	15 Apr. 42	14 Feb. 53	3 Feb.	do	
John Wilkie, *Lt.Col.*, 10 Hussars	11 May 38	29 May 40	17 May 44	27 Feb. 52	10 Feb.	do	
John Walpole, *Colonel*, Royal Engineers	1 Aug. 16	24 Sept. 25	28 Nov. 39	15 Sept. 48	17 Feb.	do	54
Henry Servante, *Colonel*, Royal Engineers	1 Aug. 16	29 July 25	27 May 39	11 Nov. 51	do	do	
Henry Owen Crawley, *Colonel*, Royal Engineers	do	do	17 Aug.	do	do	do	
John Twiss, *Colonel*, Royal Engineers	do	do	20 Sept. 40	do	do	do	
Edward Frome, *Colonel*, Royal Engineers	11 May 25	6 Dec. 26	7 Sept. 41	do	do	do	
Charles Edmund Wilkinson, *Lt.Col.*, Royal Engineers	6 Aug.	26 Feb. 28	19 Feb. 41	....	do	do	
John Wray Mitchell, *Colonel*, Royal Artillery	18 Oct.	3 Jan. 28	1 April 41	....	do	do	
Robert Fitzgerald Crawford, *Colonel*, Royal Artillery	19 May	12 May 29	1 April 41	....	do	do	
John St. George, CB., *Colonel*, Royal Artillery	19 May	11 July 29	1 April 41	....	do	do	
William Robert Nedham, *Lt.Col.*, Royal Artillery	19 May	12 July 29	1 April 41	....	do	do	
Edward Charles Warde, CB., *Colonel*, Royal Artillery	19 May	30 June 30	5 June 45	....	do	do	
Henry Percival de Bathe, *Capt. & Lt.Col.*, Scots Fus. Guards	....	do	14 Feb.	....	do	do	
Richard Waddy, CB., *Lt.Col.*, 50 Foot	17 Aug. 32	4 May 36	18 Nov. 41	14 Feb. 52	3 Mar. 54	do	
John William Ormsby, *Colonel*, Royal Artillery	6 Aug.	28 July 30	16 Sept. 41	....	17 Mar.	do	
William Turnbull Renwick, *Lt.Col.*, Royal Engineers	6 Aug.	7 Nov. 28	9 Mar. 41	....	21 Mar.	do	

Colonels.

	ENSIGN, ETC.	LIEUT.	CAPTAIN.	MAJOR.	LIEUT.-COLONEL.	COLONEL.	WHEN PLACED ON HALF PAY.
Thomas Holmes Tidy,[103] *Lt.Col.*, Unattached	14 Apr. 25	28 Sept. 26	2 Oct. 35	9 Nov. 46	28 Mar. 54	28 Nov. 54	1 Oct. 59
Robert Sanders,[109] CB., *Lt.Col.*, h.p. 19 Foot	26 May 37	26 Jan. 41	3 Feb. 43	6 Aug. 47	14 April do	do	10 Nov. 56
Richard Henry R. Howard Vyse, *Lt.Col.* Royal Horse Guards	30 Nov. 30	31 May 33	27 Sept. 42		21 April do	do	1 July 59
Thomas Weston Eastbrook Holdsworth,[110] *Lt.Col.*, Unattached	15 Jan. 36	14 Dec. 38	16 Aug. 44	17 June 51	5 May do	do	
Edmund Haythorne, *Lt.Col.*, 1 Foot	12 May 37	1 Sept. 39	11 Sept. 44	7 June 49	12 May do	do	
Thomas Brooke, *Lt.Col.*, 12 Foot	31 Oct. 34	29 July 36	15 May 45	2 April 50	19 May do	do	
Arthur Joseph Taylor, *Lt.Col.*, Royal Artillery	6 Aug. 28	22 July 30	25 Sept. 41		30 May 54		
George Maclean, *Lt.Col.* Royal Artillery	do	do	1 Oct. 30		do	do	19 Feb. 58
Henry Dalrymple White,[104] CB., *Lt.Col.*, Unattached	11 May 38	8 Feb. 39	17 May 44	22 Apr. 48	1 June 54	do	
Anthony Blaxland Stransham, *Colonel Commandant*, Royal Marines	1 Jan. 23	12 Oct. 32	12 Feb. 44	15 Apr. 49	9 June do	do	
Oliver Robinson,[112] *Major*, ret. full pay, 2 Foot	5 Oct. 25	24 Jan. 32	19 Feb. 36	13 Nov. 39	11 Nov. 51	1 Dec. 54	
Francis Wigston,[113] *Major*, do. 18 Foot	16 Mar. 26	1 June 32	18 Jan. 39	23 Dec. 42	9 Dec. 53	do	
Augustus Thomas Rice,[114] *Major*, do. 51 Foot	1 Oct. 31	10 Mar. 37	15 Oct. 41	23 June 52	do	do	
Wm. Henry Gillman, *Captain*, do. 68 Foot, *Capt.* 6 Lancashire Militia	1 July 33	14 May 36	13 May 41	9 Nov. 46	20 June 54	13 Dec. 54	
Edw. Fitzherbert Grant, *Lt.Col.* ret. full pay, Royal Artillery	29 July 25	30 April 28	19 Feb. 41	never	17 Feb. do	do	
George John Beresford, *Lt.Col.*, do.	18 Oct. 26	31 Dec. 28	1 April 41	never	14 22 May 44	do	
Hon. Robert Chas. Henry Spencer,[115] *Captain* do. do.	18 Dec. 35	30 Dec. 37	1 April 44	never	20 June 54	16 Dec. 54	
Henry Coope Stace, *Lt.Col.*, retired full pay, Royal Artillery	4 Aug. 30	4 July 37	17 Aug. do	46	17 Feb. do	5 Jan. 55	
⁑ Wm. Harloe Phibbs,[116] *Captain*, ret. f.p., *Staff Officer of Pensioners*	30 Oct. 25	24 June 28	3 June 36	1 April 41	31 Mar. 54	13 Jan. do	
Thomas Hosmer Rimington, *Lt.Col.*, ret. full pay, R. Engineers	6 Aug. 28	24 Jan. 29	27 Sept. 26	9 Nov. 46	22 Dec. 48	19 Jan. do	
Frederick Eld,[117] *Lt.Col.*, retired full pay, 90 Foot	23 Dec. 29	26 Sept. 31	5 April 31	9 Nov. 46	20 June do	19 Jan. do	
Henry Francis Ainslie, *Major*, retired full pay, 83 Foot	29 Jan. 24	7 Nov. 26	25 Nov. 28	3 June 48	11 Nov. 51	26 Jan. do	
William Slater, *Major*, retired full pay, Depot Battalion	9 Jan. 12	20 Jan. 14		never	15 Aug. 53	19 Feb. 55	
John Land,[118] *Lt.Col.*, retired full pay, Royal Marines	22 Dec. 22	11 July 32	30 Oct. 41		24 Feb. do	do	
Henry George Mitford,[119] *Lt.Col.* do.	25 Feb. 33	29 Aug. 32	4 Nov. 41	never	20 June 54	8 Mar. 55	
Alfred Tylee, *Lt.Col.*, retired full pay, Royal Artillery	26 Dec. 29	1 April 31	23 Nov. 41	20 June 54	18 Sept. do	do	
Francis Seymour Hamilton, *Lt.Col.*, ret. full pay, R. Artillery	25 July 32	17 Aug. 35	27 April do	27 April 42	20 June 46	20 Mar. do	
William Calder, *Captain*, ret. full pay, *Staff Officer of Pensioners*	14 July 14	24 June 24	6 July 35	9 Nov. 40	1 Aug. 54	30 Mar. do	
James Watson,[120] *Lieut.Col.*, retired full pay, 14 Foot	22 Mar. 21	25 Dec. 22	14 Dec. 41	12 Jan. 32	10 Jan. do	11 Nov. 54	15 May do
Sir Thos. St. Vincent H. C. Troubridge, Bt., CB.[121] *Lt.Col.*, h. p. 22 F., *Aide de Camp to the Queen*, *Deputy Adj.-Gen. Army Clothing*	24 Jan. 34	30 Dec. 36	14 Dec. 41	9 Aug. 50	12 Dec. 54	18 May do	
David Forbes,[122] *Major*, retired full pay, 91 Foot	29 Nov. 23	23 Nov. 32	24 July 35	14 April 46	28 May 53	5 June 55	
⁑ⱩCollingwood Dickson, CB., *Lt.Col.*, R. Art., *Aide de Camp to the Queen*	18 Dec. 35	29 Nov. 37	1 April 46	22 May 46	20 June 54	29 June do	
Wm. S. R. Norcott, CB., *Lt.Col.*, Depot Batt., *Aide de Camp to the Queen*	13 June 22	16 June 25	21 Feb. 40	1 Aug. 47	12 June 54	do	
John Wm. Gordon, CB., *Lt.Col.*, R. Engineers, *Aide de Camp to the Queen*, *Deputy Adjutant General*	1 Dec. 33	10 Jan. 37	12 July 45	12 Dec. 54	24 April 55	do	
Daniel Lyons,[123] CB., *Lieut.Col.*, Unatt., *Assist. Adjutant General to the Inspector General of Infantry*	26 Dec. 34	23 Aug. 37	29 Dec. 43	3 Aug. 49	21 Sept. 54	17 July 55	
Hon. Wm. Lygon Pakenham, CB.[124] *Lt.Col.*, Unatt., *Adj. General, East Indies*	25 Aug. 37	31 Aug. 38	26 Jan. 44	6 July 52	12 Dec. 54	do	
William Langley Tudor,[125] *Lt.Col.*, retired full pay, 86 Foot	9 April 25	26 Nov. 29	1 April 41	30 April 44	20 June 51	10 Aug. 55	

Colonels.

	ENSIGN, ETC.	LIEUT.	CAPTAIN.	MAJOR.	LIEUT.-COLONEL.	COLONEL.	WHEN PLACED ON HALF PAY.
Maximilian James Western, *Major*, retired full pay, 64 Foot	10 June 26	8 June 29	30 Dec. 35	11 April 45	20 June 54	17 Aug. 55	
James Graham,[127] *Lt.-Col.*, retired full pay, 89 Foot	22 April 25	19 April 31	27 April 33	9 Nov. 46	20 June 54	7 Sept. 55	
H. S. H. *Prince* W. A. Edward of Saxe Weimar, CB., *Capt. & Lt.Col., Gr.* Guards, *Aide de Camp to the Queen*	1 June 41	8 June 41	19 May 46	20 June 54	12 Dec. 54	5 Oct. 55	
Sir David Edward Wood, KCB., *Lt.-Col.*, Royal Artillery	18 Dec. 29	30 June 30	31 23 Nov. 41	never	20 June 54	2 Nov. 55	
James William Fitzmayer, CB., *Lt.-Col.*, do.	6 Nov. 30	26 Oct.	31 12 April 42	never	do	do	
Fred. Edward Chapman, CB., *Lt.-Col.*, Royal Engineers	18 June 35	28 Mar. 37	1 April 46	12 Dec. 54	24 April 55	do	
Sir George Robert Barker, KCB., *Lieut.Col.*, Royal Artillery	21 June 34	10 Jan. 37	21 May 45	12 Dec. 54	1 June 55	do	
Edward Robert Wetherall,[128] CB., *Lt.-Col.*, Unatt., *Deputy Quarter Master General in Ireland, Aide de Camp to the Queen*	27 June 34	22 Aug. 37	19 Dec. 45	12 Dec. 54	17 July 55	11 Dec. 55	
William Sadlier,[129] *Lt.-Col.*, retired full pay, 4 Foot	2 April 07	4 May 09	25 Aug. 25	4 Feb. 38	11 Nov. 51	1 Feb. 56	
Robert Alexander Cuthbert, *Major*, retired full pay, 15 Foot	25 Sept. 23	7 July 29	21 Mar. 45	20 June 54	25 Mar.		
Henry Francis Strange,[130] *Lt.-Col.*, ret. full pay, 25 Foot	23 May 15	7 April 25	29 June 26	23 Nov. 41	11 Nov. 51	9 May	
Henry Atwell Lake,[131] CB., *Lt Col.* Unatt., *Aide de Camp to the Queen*	1826	4 Mar. 31	15 Dec. 41	20 June 54	9 Feb. 55	24 June 56	12 Sept. 56
Peter Trant Murray Payne,[131A] *Lt.-Col.*, ret. full pay, Royal Marines	22 Oct. 27	30 Mar. 35	12 July 44	never	22 June 55	27 June 56	
William Joshua Crompton, *Captain*, ret. f.p., *Staff Officer of Pensioners*	10 Sept. 25	12 Dec. 26	11 April 34	9 Nov. 46	20 June 54	1 July	
John Charles Grey Courtis, *Lt.-Col.*, ret. full pay, Royal Marines	30 May 25	28 Dec. 33	4 Jan. 43	20 June 54	20 Nov. 54	2 July	
John Watson,[132] *Lt.-Col.*, retired full pay, 14 Foot	20 July 25	26 17 May 37	11 Aug. 36	11 Nov. 51	15 May 55	21 July	
George Pinder, *Lt.-Col.*, retired full pay, 15 Foot	24 Aug. 26	31 Dec. 30	21 Dec. 36	24 May 54	29 June 54	25 Aug.	
Peter Bennet Reyne, *Major*, ret. full pay, Ceylon Regiment	28 Sept. 18	15 Dec. 22	21 Dec. 26	23 Nov. 41	11 Nov. 51	29 Aug.	
Richard Going,[133] *Lieut.-Col.*, retired full pay, 1 Foot	9 April 26	2 Feb. 27	19 June 35	9 Nov. 46	20 June 54	6 Jan. 57	
Peter Brames Nolloth, *Lt.-Col.*, ret. full pay, Royal Marines	28 Jan. 26	19 Mar. 34	10 Aug. 43	20 June 54	8 Sept. 54	2 Feb.	
Edward Rea, *Colonel Commandant*, Royal Marines	3 Feb. 23	12 Oct. 32	5 May 42	20 June 54	21 June 54	6 Feb.	
Alexander Anderson, *Colonel Commandant*, Royal Marines	13 May 25	9 Dec. 33	5 May 42	do	7 July 54	20 Feb.	
Thos. Holloway, CB., *Col. Comm.*, R. Marines, *Aide de Camp to the Queen*	17 Mar. 25	9 Dec. 33	5 Nov. 42	do	20 Nov. 54	13 Mar.	
John Fraser, *Colonel Commandant*, Royal Marines	8 May 24	23 April 33	29 Sept. 42	28 Jan. 41	21 Oct. 54	1 April 57	
William Harrison Askwith, *Colonel*, Royal Artillery	29 Dec. 29	6 Nov. 30	23 Nov. 41	9 Nov. 46	20 June 54	20 June	
James Kennard Pipon, *Major*, Unattached, *Assistant Adjutant General*	3 Aug. 26	9 Dec. 28	6 Mar. 35	7 June 49	do	do	
Walter Unett, *Lt.-Col.*, 3 Light Dragoons	33 Aug. 33	31 Mar. 37	1 Nov. 42	5 April 50	do	do	
Archibald Little, CB., *Lt.-Col.*, 9 Lancers	4 Oct. 31	31 Aug. 32	24 Feb. 37	11 Nov. 51	do	do	
John Douglas,[134] CB., *Lt.-Col.*, h. p. Depot Batt. *Assist. Gen. of Cavalry*	18 June 29	25 Oct. 33	11 May 39		do	do	
William E. Delves Broughton, *Lt.-Col.*, Royal Engineers	6 Aug. 25	24 Feb. 29	1 April 41		do	do	
Richard John Nelson, *Lt.-Col.*, Royal Engineers	7 Jan. 26	22 May 29	1 Sept. 41		do	do	
George Burgmann, *Lt.-Col.*, Royal Engineers	15 Mar. 26	27 Oct. 29	30 Sept. 41		do	do	
Franklin Dunlop, CB., *Colonel*, Royal Artillery	18 Dec. 29	25 Nov. 30	23 Nov. 41		do	do	
Francis Dick, *Colonel*, Royal Artillery	do	26 Nov. 30	do		do	do	
Charles James Dalton, *Colonel*, Royal Artillery	do	29 April 31	do		do	do	
Fred. Marow Eardley Wilmot, *Lt.-Col.*, Royal Artillery	6 Nov. 30	27 Sept. 31	7 April 42		do	do	
John Henry Francklyn, CB., *Lt.-Col.*, Royal Artillery	26 July 31	23 June 32	13 April 42	20 June 54	28 June	28 June 57	

37

Colonels.

	ENSIGN, ETC.	LIEUT.	CAPTAIN.	MAJOR.	LIEUT.-COLONEL.	COLONEL.	WHEN PLACED ON HALF PAY.
Gloucester Gambier, CB., *Lt.Col.*, Royal Artillery	26 July	31 31 July	32 13 April	42 20 June	54 6 July	57 6 July	
George Thurles Finucane,[133] *Major*, ret. full pay, Unattached	22 Sept.	08 15 Mar.	10 17 June	28 23 Nov.	41 11 Nov.	51 14 July	
Sir John Douglas, KCB., *Lt.Col.*, 79 Foot	6 Sept.	33 8 July	36 8 June	41 1 Nov.	42 20 June	1 Aug.	
George Robert Harry Kennedy, *Lt. Col.*, Royal Artillery	6 Nov.	30 27 Oct.	31 13 April	42 do	do	20 Aug.	
*Carlo Cutajar, *Major*, retired full pay, R. Malta Fencibles	24 Feb.	22 23 Jan.	25 17 Feb.	37 20 April	47 28 Nov.	28 Aug.	
George Sandham, *Lt.Col.*, ret. full pay, Royal Artillery	9 Nov.	30 28 Oct.	31 13 April	42	20 June	20 Sept.	
Charles Vansittart Cockburn, *Lt.Col.*, Royal Artillery	9 Nov.	30 2 Feb.	32 13 April	42	do	20 Sept.	
Charles Barnston Daubeney,[135] CB., *Lt.Col.*, h. p. 71 Foot, *Inspector of Army Clothing*	12 Mar.	29 9 Aug.	31 28 Oct.	36 23 Dec.	42 do	30 Sept.	57 8 Oct. 58
James Thomas Mauleverer, CB., *Lt.Col.*, 30 Foot	18 April	34 19 Aug.	36 28 July	43 21 May	52 30 Sept.	do	
Henry Sebastian Rowan, CB., *Lt.Col.*, Royal Artillery	20 June	32 14 Aug.	34 18 Aug.	43 22 May	46 30 June	54 14 Oct.	57
Edward R. King, *Major*, retired full pay, 36 Foot	16 Feb.	26 31 July	28 4 Dec.	32 22 May	45 20 June	54 16 Oct.	57
Anthony Coningham Sterling, CB.[136] *Lt. Col.*, Unatt., *Military Secretary to the Commander in Chief, East Indies*	29 Jan.	26 14 April	29 11 Oct.	38 9 Nov.	46 do	17 Oct.	
John Chaytor, *Lt.Col.*, Royal Engineers	15 Mar.	26 16 Feb.	30 23 Nov.	41 20 June	54 20 Oct.	20 Oct.	
Charles Seagram,[137] *Captain*, retired full pay, 17 Foot	22 June	26 5 Mar.	31 15 April	42 15 Sept.	48 7 Sept.	30 Oct.	
Edward Walter Crofton, *Lt.Col.*, Royal Artillery	26 July	14 July	32 2 Aug.	42 20 June	54 6 Nov.	6 Nov.	
Hon. Richard W. Penn Curzon, CB., *Capt. & Lt.Col.*, Gren. Guards.	16 Dec.	31 1 Aug.	38 5 April	44 28 May	53 20 June	54 17 Nov.	
Gilbert John Lane Buchanan, *Lt.Col.*, Royal Artillery	11 Jan.	21 19 July	33 4 Apr.	43 20 June	46 20 June	54 4 Dec.	
James Clarke, *Major*, ret. full pay, 1 West India Regt.	24 Dec.	29 2 Dec.	31 9 June	38 13 July	47 12 Dec.	54 12 Dec.	
Thomas Westropp McMahon, CB., *Lt.Col.*, 5 Dragoon Guards	19 June	35 28 Dec.	38 27 Sept.	42 19 Sept.	48 do	do	57
Alexander Maxwell, CB., *Lt.Col.*, 46 Foot	30 May	34 31 Jan.	40 3 Jan.	45 27 Dec.	50 do	do	
Richard T. Farren, CB., *Lt.Col.*, Depot Battalion	5 June	35 28 July	38 27 Sept.	42 4 Feb.	53 do	do	
Robert Wardlaw, *Lt.Col.*, 1 Dragoons	28 April	28 12 Nov.	30 30 July	43 42 20 June	54 do	do	
John Thornton Grant, CB., *Lt.Col.*, 49 Foot	12 April	31 21 Aug.	35 30 June	43 do	do	do	
John Stewart Wood, CB.,[138] *Lt.Col.*, Unatt. Assist. Adj. Gen. at Aldershot	2 Oct.	35 6 July	38 14 July	43 do	do	do	
Alexander Low, *Lt.Col.*, 4 Dragoons	14 Dec.	37 15 Oct.	39 9 Nov.	46 14 July	54 do	do	
John Lintorn Arabin Simmons, CB. *Capt. R. Eng.*, *Consul General at Warsaw*	20 June	32 11 July	34 18 May	43 15 Sept.	48 13 Dec.	54 13 Dec.	57
St. John Thomas Browne, *Lt.Col.*, Royal Artillery							
Sir William Thomas Denison, KCB., *Lt.Col.* Royal Engineers, *Governor General of New South Wales*	15 Mar.	26 23 June	30 23 Nov.	41 20 June	54 13 Dec.	54 13 Dec.	57
Edward William Durnford, *Lt. Col.*, Royal Engineers	22 Sept.	26 5 Feb.	31 23 Nov.	41 20 June	54 do	do	
Edward Thomas Lloyd, *Lt. Col.*, Royal Engineers	do	24 June	31 do	33 do	do	do	
Henry Aylmer, *Lt.-Col.*, Royal Artillery	16 Dec.	31 21 Nov.	33 4 April	43 do	do	do	
Alexander Irving, CB., *Lt.Col.*, Royal Artillery	do	10 Mar.	34 4 May	43 do	do	do	
George Colt Langley, *Lt.Col.*, Royal Marines, *Assist. Adj.General*	30 June	29 10 July	37 4 May	47 13 Dec.	54 14 Dec.	57	
Henry James, *Lt. Col.*, Royal Engineers	22 Sept.	26 22 July	31 28 June	42 20 June	54 16 Dec.	16 Dec.	57
Charles Bingham, *Lt.Col.*, Royal Artillery, *Deputy Adjutant General*	20 June	32 20 July	34 17 Aug.	43 do	do	do	
William Robinson, *Lt.Col.*, Royal Engineers	22 Sept.	26 6 Oct.	31 24 Oct.	42 19 Feb.	47 22 Dec.	22 Dec.	
Percy Hill, CB., *Lt.Col.*, Rifle Brigade	24 April	35 5 Oct.	38 23 Jan.	46 22 Oct.	50 29 Dec.	29 Dec.	

Colonels.

	ENSIGN, ETC.	LIEUT.	CAPTAIN.	MAJOR.	LIEUT.-COLONEL.	COLONEL.	WHEN PLACED ON HALF PAY.
Thomas Rawlings Mould, *Lt.Col.*, Royal Engineers	22 Sept. 26	7 Oct. 31	16 Mar. 43	20 June 54	3 Jan. 55	3 Jan. 58	
John Noble Arbuthnot Freese, CB., *Lt.Col.*, Royal Artillery	20 June 32	9 Sept. 34	22 Aug. 43	20 June 54	6 Jan. 55	6 Jan. 58	
Fred. Darby Cleveland, *Lt.Col.*, do.	do.	do.	1 Sept. 43	20 June 54	do.	do.	
Henry Austin Turner, *Lt.Col.*, do.	do.	25 Nov. 34	14 Jan. 44	28 Nov. 54	do.	do.	
Thomas Beckett Fielding Marriott, *Lt.Col.*, do.	do.	20 Nov. 34	30 Mar. 44	never	do.	do.	
Alexander Barry Montgomery, CB., *Lt.Col.*, 1 Foot	25 Nov. 24	30 Oct. 26	16 Aug. 33	5 Dec. 43	20 June 54	13 Jan. 58	
George Wynne, *Lt.Col.*, Royal Engineers	22 Sept. 26	12 Nov. 31	4 April 43	20 June 54	13 Jan. 55	13 Jan. 58	
William Stace, *Lt.Col.*, Royal Engineers	4 May 27	18 Mar. 32	27 May 43	20 June 54	13 Jan. 55	do.	
Henry Drury Harness, CB., *Lt.Col.*, Royal Engineers	24 May 27	20 Sept. 32	30 June 43	do.	do.	do.	
Edmund Twiss Ford, *Lt.Col.*, Royal Engineers	30 Aug. 27	5 Feb. 33	15 Nov. 43	do.	do.	do.	
William Yolland, *Lt.Col.*, Royal Engineers	12 April 28	4 Sept. 33	19 Sept. 43	do.	do.	do.	
Thomas Elwyn, *Lt.Col.*, Royal Artillery	20 Dec. 28	29 Dec. 34	1 April 44	29 Sept. 54	do.	do.	
Charles Erskine Ford, *Lt.Col.*, Royal Engineers	29 April 29	1 May 34	10 Jan. 44	28 Nov. 54	do.	do.	
George Fred. Cooper Scott, *Major*, retired full pay, 76 Foot	25 Oct. 27	3 May 31	1 July 36	9 Nov. 46	20 June 54	15 Jan. 58	
Edward Harris Greathed, CB., 138*, *Lt.Col.*, Unattached	22 June 28	10 May 33	27 April 38	3 April 46	20 June 54	19 Jan. 58	28 Oct. 59
Sir John Jones, KCB., *Lt.Col.*, 60 Foot	12 June 28	2 Dec. 31	16 July 41	20 July 49	do.	do.	
Arthur Cavendish Bentinck, *Lt.Col.*, 4 Dragoon Guards	2 Nov. 38	31 Oct. 40	2 Mar. 47	27 June 51	8 Dec. 54	30 Jan. 58	
Richard D. Kelly, CB., *Lt.Col.*, 34 Foot	7 Mar. 32	30 July 36	24 Sept. 41	17 Mar. 48	12 Dec. 54	do.	
Charles James Wright, *Lt.Col.*, Royal Artillery	20 Dec. 32	20 Dec. 34	1 April 44	never	7 Feb. 55	7 Feb. 58	
George Aug. Fred. De Rinzy, *Lt.Col.*, do.	do.	28 Jan. 35	do.	never	7 Feb. 55	do.	
John Ramsay Stuart, CB., *Lt.Col.*, 21 Foot	20 Jan. 32	9 Feb. 35	10 Jan. 40	9 Feb. 49	15 Nov. 54	15 Feb. 58	
George Talbot, *Lt.Col.*, 43 F., *Deputy Qr.Master General at Madras*	2 Feb. 26	9 Sept. 28	3 April 35	9 Nov. 46	20 June 54	18 Feb. 58	
Fielding Alex. Campbell, *Colonel*, 2nd *Commandant*, Royal Marines	23 Sept. 26	27 May 34	21 Sept. 43	20 June 54	21 Feb. 55	21 Feb. 58	
George Evans Hunt, *Colonel*, 2nd *Commandant*, do.	16 Dec. 26	do.	3 May 44	never	do.	do.	
Hon. Robert Rollo, 139 *Lt.Col.*, Unatt., *Assist. Adjutant General in Canada*	10 Aug. 32	25 Sept. 35	5 Nov. 41	20 June 54	12 Dec. 54	23 Feb. 58	
William Hamilton Elliot, *Lt.Col.*, Royal Artillery	20 Dec. 32	4 April 35	1 April 44	never	25 Feb. 55	25 Feb. 58	
Evelyn Henry Fred. Pocklington, *Captain*, Unatt.	10 Feb. 29	30 Aug. 33	24 May 39	11 Nov. 51	8 Mar. 55	6 Mar. 58	13 July 47
Peter Maclean, *Lt.Col.*, do.	20 Dec. 32	2 Sept. 35	14 April 44	......	8 Mar. 55	8 Mar. 58	
Anthony Benn, *Lt.Col.*, do.	20 Dec. 32	6 May 35	15 April 44	......	8 Mar. 55	do.	
Charles William Dunbar Staveley, CB., *Lt.Col.*, 44 Foot	6 Mar. 35	4 Dec. 39	6 Sept. 44	7 Dec. 50	9 Mar. 55	9 Mar. 58	
John Douglas Johnstone, CB., *Lt.Col.*, 33 Foot	15 Aug. 27	16 Mar. 30	19 Oct. 38	3 Oct. 48	do.	do.	
Arthur Lowry Cole, CB., *Lt.Col.*, 17 Foot	22 Aug. 34	20 Nov. 38	7 Sept. 44	14 June 50	do.	do.	
Henry James Warre, CB., *Lt.Col.*, 57 Foot	3 Feb. 37	1 June 41	8 Jan. 47	7 Nov. 54	do.	do.	
George Edward Thorold, 139* *Lt.Col.*, retired full pay, 42 Foot	24 June 24	9 June 25	19 Sept. 26	23 Nov. 41	11 Nov. 54	16 Mar. 58	
James Draper, *Lt.Col.*, retired full pay, 64 Foot	18 Dec. 23	19 Nov. 25	24 Dec. 29	9 Nov. 46	20 June 54	do.	
Julius Edmund Goodwyn, CB., *Lt.Col.*, 41 Foot	5 Jan. 25	4 June 28	6 May 35	15 Sept. 50	12 Dec. 54	19 Mar. 58	
Rodolph de Salis, *Lt.Col.*, 8 Hussars	17 Dec. 30	28 June 33	13 July 38	19 Feb. 47	28 Nov. 54	20 Mar. 58	
Alfred Thomas Heyland, CB., *Lt.Col.*, 56 Foot	4 April 33	8 July 36	13 Dec. 41	22 June 54	12 Dec. 54	do.	
George Vaughan Maxwell, CB., *Lt.Col.*, 88 Foot	2 Feb. 38	26 April 39	6 Dec. 44	28 July 54	do.	23 Mar. 58	
Edward Selby Smyth, *Capt.* 2 F., *Deputy Qr.Master General, Cape of Good Hope*	26 Jan. 41	29 May 43	4 Aug. 48	28 May 53	23 Mar. 55	do.	

40-41

Colonels.

	ENSIGN, ETC.	LIEUT.	CAPTAIN.	MAJOR.	LIEUT.-COLONEL.	COLONEL.	WHEN PLACED ON HALF PAY.
William P. Purnell, CB., *Lt.Col.*, 90 Foot	24 Mar. 38	25 June 16	14 June 48	19 Jan. 55	9 Oct. 55	24 Mar. 58	
Edmund Richard Jeffreys, CB., *Lt.Col.*, Depot Battalion	16 June 25	11 Oct. 27	2 Feb. 38	12 May 43	20 June 54	1 April 58	
Fred. Aug. Yorke, *Lt.Col.*, R. Engineers, *Assist. Adjutant General*	5 Oct. 31	12 Aug. 35	20 June 44		1 April 55	do	
Charles Francis Skyring, *Lt.Col.*, R. Engineers	do	19 Aug. 35	16 Aug. 44		do	do	
Robert Gorges Hamilton, *Lt.Col.*, do.	29 May 32	5 Dec. 35	18 Dec. 44		do	do	
William Thomas Crawford, CB., *Lt.Col.*, Royal Artillery	21 June 33	1 July 36	5 April 45		do	do	
Pierrpont Henry Mundy, *Lt.Col.*, do.	20 Dec. 33	2 July 36	do		do	do	
William Henderson, *Lt.Col.*, do.	do	13 July 37	10 April 45		do	do	
William James Smythe, *Lt.Col.*	1 Oct. 36	10 Jan. 37	6 May 45		do	do	
Hon. Francis Colborne, CB., *Major*, 6 Foot	1 Oct. 36	18 Jan. 39	24 May 44	21 Oct. 53	12 Dec. 54	2 April 58	
Hon. St. George Gerald Foley,140 CB., *Major, Unatt., Military Secretary in China*	29 June 32	27 May 36	3 Aug. 41	9 Oct. 49		13 April 58	22 Aug. 56
Thomas Lemon, CB., *Colonel, 2nd Commandant*, Royal Marines	8 Oct. 27	5 Feb. 35	10 July 41		22 June 54	13 April 58	
John Kelsall,141 *Lt.Col.*, retired full pay, 83 Foot	14 July 25	30 April 27	4 Oct. 41	7 May 54	16 May 56	do	
Alex. Sebastian Leith Hay, CB., *Lt.Col.*, 93 Foot	25 Dec. 35	26 April 39	31 Mar. 48	21 Oct. 53	12 Dec. 54	16 April 58	
Caledon Richard Egerton, *Lt.Col.*, Depot Battalion	15 June 35	28 Mar. 39	15 Mar. 48	11 Nov. 51	9 Mar. 55	18 April 58	
Ernest Christian Wilford, *Major and Chief Instructor of Musketry at Hythe*	2 Sept. 31	14 Mar. 34	19 April 39	9 Nov. 46	20 Mar. 55	25 April 58	
Richard Clement Moody, *Lt.Col.*, Royal Engineers	5 Nov. 30	25 June 35	6 Mar. 44	never	13 Jan. 55	28 April 58	
Philip Reginald Cocks, *Lt.Col.*, h. p. Royal Artillery	21 June 33	18 Mar. 36	9 June 45	12 Dec. 54	1 April 55	1 May 58	26 May 58
David William Paynter, CB., *Lt.Col.*, Royal Artillery	30 Dec. 33	10 Jan. 37	9 May 45	27 Dec. 50	15 May 55	15 May 58	
George Dixon, CB., *Lt.Col.*, Depot Battalion	30 Dec. 28	26 Dec. 36	29 Nov. 39	8 Dec. 52	12 Mar. 55	20 May 58	
Charles Elmhirst, *Lt.Col.*, 9 Foot	14 Aug. 35	17 Oct. 37	22 Dec. 45	8 Aug. 54	9 Mar. 55	21 May 58	
Richard Chambre Hays Taylor, CB., *Lt.Col.*, 79 Foot	11 Dec. 35	29 Mar. 39	23 Aug. 44	never	12 Dec. 55	do	
William Charles Hadden, *Lt.Col.*, Royal Engineers	29 May 32	8 Feb. 36	26 Dec. 44		21 May 55	do	
Hon. Arthur Edward Harding, CB., *Capt. & Lt.Col.*, Coldstream Guards, *Equerry to the Prince Consort*	7 June 44	22 Dec. 45	1 June 49	12 Dec. 54	20 Feb. 55	25 May 58	
Robert Newport Tinely, *Lt.Col.*, Cape Mounted Rifles	4 April 32	19 July 33	15 Dec. 40	11 Nov. 51	9 Mar. 55	28 May 58	
Edward Arthur Somerset,144 CB., *Lt.Col., Unattached, Assistant Quarter Master General at Portsmouth*	29 Jan. 36	9 July 40	31 Jan. 45	12 Nov. 54	23 Mar. 55	29 May 58	
Matthew Benjamin George Reed, *Major*, ret. full pay, 84 Foot	26 Feb. 26	18 Nov. 19	26 Feb. 36	16 Sept. 45	20 June 54	4 June 58	
John Clark Kennedy,142 CB. *Lt.Col.* h.p. 18 F. *Assist. Qr.-Mas. Gen. at Aldershot*	25 Oct. 27	3 Dec. 37	7 June 41	49	22 June 55	do	
John Mitchell, *Colonel, 2nd Commandant*, Royal Marines	5 Oct. 27	29 Nov. 34	6 May 44		do	do	
Thomas Charles Cotton Moore, *Lt.Col.*, Depot Battalion	4 Dec. 27	26 Oct. 35	31 Oct. 44	48	6 Jan. 55	24 June 58	
Arthur Cyril Goodenough, CB., *Lt.Col.*, Royal Artillery	8 April 34	25 Nov. 36	26 Oct. 41	27 Mar. 53	29 June 55	29 June 58	
Peter Pickmore Faddy, *Lt.Col.*, Royal Artillery	31 June 29	10 Jan. 34	14 June 37	28 May 53	11 Nov. 54	1 July 58	
Henry William Bunbury,143 CB. *Lt.Col.* h.p. 23 F. *Assist. Adjutant Gen. at Dover*	29 June 30	30 Aug. 33	18 Aug. 38	11 Nov. 51	2 Dec. 54	12 July 58	
Charles Edmund Law, *Lt.Col.*, 66 Foot	2 Feb. 44	8 May 46	26 Dec. 51	7 July 54	5 Jan. 55	17 July 58	
Patrick Leonard MacDougall, *Major*, h. p. R. Canadian Rifles, *Commandant of the Staff College*	13 Feb. 36	11 May 39	7 June 44	9 Feb. 49	17 July 55	do	
Alexander Macdonald, CB., *Lt.Col.*, Rifle Brigade	23 June 37	11 May 41	24 Oct. 45	12 Dec. 54	do	20 July 58	
Charles Lawrence D'Aguilar, CB., *Lt.Col.*, Royal Artillery	6 June 38	22 July 40	22 April 47	do	26 Dec. 56	do	

Colonels.

Colonels.	ENSIGN, ETC.	LIEUT.	CAPTAIN.	MAJOR.	LIEUT.-COLONEL.	COLONEL.	WHEN PLACED ON HALF PAY.
Julius Augustus Robert Raines, CB., *Lt. Col.*, 95 Foot	28 Jan. 42	5 April 44	13 April 52	24 April 55	17 Nov. 57	20 July 58	
William Fenwick, CB., *Lt. Col.*, 10 Foot	26 Dec. 34	8 June 38	15 April 42	13 Sept. 48	18 May 55	26 July 58	
John Alfred Street, CB., *Lt. Col.*, Depot Battalion	29 Nov. 39	5 Oct. 41	7 Jan. 48	12 Dec. 54	19 June 55	11 Aug.	
Arthur Thomas Phillpotts, *Lt. Col.*, Royal Artillery	21 June 34	10 Jan. 37	3 Sept. 45	never	13 Aug. 55	19 Aug.	
Arthur John Reynell-Pack,[145] CB., *Lt. Col.*, h. p. 7 Foot, *Assist. Adjutant General at Cork*	9 Aug. 33	5 May 37	23 June 45	20 April 54	19 June 55	16 Aug.	
Charles Herbert, CB., *Lt. Col.*, 54 Foot	19 Nov. 25	10 Oct. 26	27 April 33	25 April 45	20 June 54	19 Aug. 58	
Mountjoy Francis Martyn, *Lieut. Col.*, 2 Life Guards	27 Dec. 27	22 Mar. 31	22 April 36	9 Nov. 46	20 June 54	29 Aug.	
William Bethel Gardner, *Lt. Col.*, Royal Artillery	21 June 34	10 Jan. 37	29 Oct. 45	never	1 Sept. 55	1 Sept.	
John Wm. Sidney Smith, CB., *Lt. Col.*, Depot Battalion	3 Feb. 29	4 Aug. 37	7 Aug. 40	11 Nov. 51	29 July 55	2 Sept.	
Francis Prym Harding, CB., *Lt. Col.*, 22 Foot	16 Mar. 38	18 Dec. 40	20 Jan. 47	27 Oct. 54	12 Dec. 54	9 Sept.	
Edward Stopford Claremont,[146] CB., *Major*, Unatt., *Her Majesty's Military Commissioner at Paris*	9 Feb.	16 July 38	14 Nov. 41	12 Dec. 45	14 Sept. 54	14 Sept. 55	10 Aug. 55
Charles Cameron Shute, *Lt. Col.*, 6 Dragoons	19 July 34	13 May 37	5 Mar. 39	1 June 47	12 Dec. 54	21 Sept.	
John Henry Lefroy, *Lt. Col.*, Royal Artillery	19 Dec. 34	10 Jan. 37	30 Nov. 45	never	24 Sept. 55	24 Sept. 58	
Charles James Buchanan Riddell, CB., *Lt. Col.*, Royal Artillery	19 Dec. 34	12 Dec. 37	12 Dec. 45	never	24 Sept. 55	do	
James Wells Armstrong, CB., *Lt. Col.*, Depot Battalion	18 Aug. 43	29 Nov. 44	20 Jan. 51	12 Dec. 54	17 July 55	1 Oct. 58	
John Fraser,[147] *Major*, Unattached, *Fort Major of Jersey*	29 May 09	12 Feb. 12	17 Aug. 32	15 April 42	20 June 54	10 Oct. 58	15 April 42
Joshua Allen Vigors, *Major*, retired full pay, 52 Foot	19 Sept. 29	17 Sept. 29	19 Oct. 38	11 Nov. 51	19 Jan. 55	15 Oct.	
Hamlet Coote Wade,[148] CB., *Captain*, h. p. 1 Dr. Guards, *Lt. Col. Commandant, North York Militia*	22 Feb. 27	9 Aug. 30	22 April 40	4 Oct. 42	20 June 54	26 Oct. 58	21 July 46
Ferdinand Whittingham, CB., *Lt. Col.* 4 Foot	2 Nov. 29	19 Feb. 32	30 April 41	23 Dec. 42	20 June do	do	
Cyprian Bridge, *Lt. Col.*, 58 Foot	8 April 25	31 Jan. 28	16 Dec. 36	30 Dec. 42	do	do	
Thomas Sydenham Conway, CB., *Capt.* & *Lt. Col.*, Gr. Gds.	14 Feb. 28	26 April 31	9 Dec. 36	4 July 43	do	do	
Thomas Le Marchant, *Major*, Unattached	14 June 27	11 June 30	17 Oct. 34	22 Dec. 43	20 June 54	26 Oct. 58	24 Nov. 54
Lord Alfred Paget, *Major*, Unattached, *Chief Equerry and Clerk Marshal to Her Majesty*	6 July	14 Mar. 34	20 Oct. 34	16 May 45	do	16 May 45	
John Singleton, *Lt. Col.*, 11 Foot	17 June 26	31 Dec. 27	15 Feb. 39	27 June do	do	do	
Alfred Francis W. Wyatt, *Major*, 65 Foot	12 Dec. 26	23 April 29	19 Sept. 34	23 Sept. 45	do	do	
Richard Gardiner, *Major*, 76 Foot	12 May 14	29 Sept. 25	5 April 33	11 Nov. 45	do	do	
Hugh Dennis Crofton, *Lt. Col.*, Depot Battalion	13 Mar. 35	29 Dec. 37	9 Aug. 37	30 Nov. do	do	do	
John Richard Blagden Hale,[149] *Captain*, Unattached	17 June 31	16 May 34	10 July 37	3 April 46	20 June 54	26 Oct. 58	10 Jan. 51
Arthur St. George H. Stepney, CB., *Capt.* & *Lt. Col.*, Coldst. Gds.	16 May 34	10 Nov. 37	15 April 42	do	do	do	
Charles Hind, *Major*, Unatt., *Lt. Col. Com.* 6 West York Militia	8 Oct. 29	7 Feb. 34	22 Feb. 39	14 April 46	20 June 54	26 Oct. 58	7 April 48
Augustus Francis Ansell, *Major*, Unatt., *Town Major at Halifax, Nova Scotia*	13 Jan. 20	19 Sept. 26	14 Dec. 32	1 May 46	do	do	24 May 50
Thomas Hook Pearson,[150] *Major*, Unattached	14 Mar. 25	1 Aug. 26	16 Aug. 31	19 June 46	do	do	7 April 48
Lawrence Fyler, *Lt. Col.*, 12 Lancers	7 Sept. 26	10 July 28	7 Feb. 34	do	do	do	
Archibald Campbell, *Captain*, h. p. 2 Ceylon Regt. *Staff Officer of Pensioners*	26 April 10	29 July 13	11 June 26	9 Nov. 29	20 June 46	26 Oct. 58	11 Aug. 29
James John Graham, *Major*, Unatt., *Staff Officer of Pensioners*	28 Oct. 24	8 April 25	26 Feb. 30	do	do	do	27 Sept. 42
Sir James Edward Alexander, *Lt. Col.*, 14 Foot	20 Jan. 25	26 Nov. 25	18 June 30	do	do	do	

Colonels.

	ENSIGN, ETC.	LIEUT.	CAPTAIN.	MAJOR.	LIEUT.-COLONEL.	COLONEL.	WHEN PLACED ON HALF PAY.
Percival Brown,[131] *Captain*, h. p. 62 Foot	25 Jan. 15	31 Mar. 22	18 Aug. 30	9 Nov. 46	20 June 54	26 Oct. 58	24 May 44
Richard Henry John Beaumont, *Captain*, Unattached	16 Dec. 24	6 Oct. 25	26 Nov. 30	do	do	do	28 June 50
George F. Mylius,[132] *Capt.*, Unatt., *Commandant, Royal Hibernian Military School*	17 Oct. 24	28 Jan. 26	30 Aug. 31	do	do	do	
Thomas Josephus Deverell, *Lt.-Col.*, 77 Foot	7 Nov. 22	25 June 29	do 32	do	do	do	17 April 45
🕮 Edward Trevor, *Captain*, h. p. Royal Artillery, *Staff Officer of Pensioners*	4 June 10	17 Dec. 13	23 June 32	do	do	do	
Alexander Henry Louis Wyatt, *Major*, 11 Foot	17 Sept. 25	24 Feb. 29	29 June 32	do	do	do	27 May 42
🕮 Geo. Herbert Fred. Campbell, *Captain*, h.-p. R. Staff Corps, *Staff Officer of Pens.*	never	11 June 30	27 July 32	do	do	do	15 April 56
Jasper Byng Creagh,[133] *Capt.*, h. p., 48 Foot	9 April 25	12 June 28	5 Oct. 32	do	do	do	24 Oct. 45
Edward A. G. Muller, *Major*, Depot Battalion	3 Feb. 20	11 Aug. 25	11 Jan. 33	do	do	do	20 June 34
Charles Frederick Parkinson, *Captain*, Unattached	10 Nov. 25	4 Sept. 28	22 Feb. 33	do	do	do	25 Feb. 45
Augustus Fred. Blyth, *Capt.*, h.p. 6 West India Regt.	19 Jan. 26	29 Aug. 26	5 April 33	do	do	do	12 May 48
Fred. Thomas Maitland, *Captain*, h.p. R. Staff Corps	9 April 25	12 Feb. 28	12 April 33	do	do	do	6 Feb. 46
Richard Leckonby Phipps, *Major*, Unatt., *Lt.-Col.* 1st *Somerset Militia*	10 April 25	1 Dec. 28	3 May 33	do	do	1 Nov. 58	
🕮 Richard Blacklin,[133] *Captain*, Unatt.	18 July 15	13 July 20	8 Aug. 33	do	do	9 Nov. 58	
His Royal Highness Albert Edward Prince of Wales and Duke of Cornwall, KG.						16 Nov. 58	5 April 39
Walter Campbell, *Captain*, Unatt., *Staff Officer of Pensioners*	23 June 25	5 June 26	20 Sept. 33	9 Nov. 46	20 June 54	23 Nov. 58	26 May 44
Edward Sterling Farmar, *Capt.*, Unatt., *Staff Officer of Pens*	2 Jan. 27	17 Jan. 30	18 Oct. 33	do	do	7 Dec. 58	
Archibald Inglis Lockhart, CB., *Lt.-Col.*, 92 Foot	31 Dec. 28	11 June 30	19 Auz. 36	do	do	10 Dec. 58	
Walter Craufurd Kennedy, *Lt.-Col.*, retired full pay, 5 Foot	27 Oct. 31	10 Nov. 34	21 Feb. 40	21 May 50	29 Aug. 57	13 Dec. 58	30 July 44
John Edward Orange, *Capt.* h. p. 34 F., *Staff Officer of Pensioners*	10 Apr. 25	15 Oct. 27	27 Dec. 33	9 Nov. 46	20 June 54	24 Dec. 58	
Thomas Edward Lacy, *Captain*, Unatt., *Assistant Adjutant General at Gibraltar*	8 April 25	3 Oct. 26	11 July 34	do	do	16 Jan. 59	
Philip Smyly, *Lt.-Col.*, 99 Foot	27 Mar. 28	18 June 30	18 July 34	17 May 50	17 July 57	1 Feb. 59	
Thomas Faunce,[136] *Major*, retired full pay, 13 Foot	5 April 27	02 Nov. 29	23 June 35	9 Nov. 46	20 June 54	20 Feb. 59	25 Oct. 50
🕮 Thomas Murray Prior,[137] *Captain*, h.-p. 5 Foot	6 Aug. 28	00 Feb. 32	20 Nov. 35	do	do	25 Mar. 59	
John Impett, *Captain*, 74 Foot	14 April 25	4 Oct. 29	30 Jan. 35	do	do	2 April 59	
George Wynell Mayow,[138] *Major*, Unatt., *Assist. Adjutant General at the Curragh*	9 June 25	12 Feb. 30	6 Mar. 35	do	do	9 April 59	4 April 45
John Francis Du Vernet, *Captain*, h.-p. R. African Corps, *Staff Officer of Pens.*	27 Mar. 08	8 April 24	24 April 35	21 Nov. 41	7 Sept. 55	26 Apr. 59	
Edward Blagden Hale, CB., *Lt.-Col.*, 82 Foot	2 Aug. 33	29 Jan. 35	5 Feb. 41	12 Dec. 48	2 Nov. 55	26 April 59	
John Alexander Ewart, CB., *Lt.-Col.*, 78 Foot	27 July 38	15 April 42	12 May 43	17 May 53	23 Nov. 55	26 April 59	
William West Turner, CB., *Lt.-Col.*, 97 Foot	19 Feb. 40	27 Dec. 42	27 May 49	1 Dec. 54	8 Dec. 56	26 April 59	
William Parke, CB., *Lt.-Col.*, 72 Foot	15 Dec. 40	7 Aug. 43	26 Mar. 49	7 June 54	20 June 54	1 May 59	3
Henry Errington Longden, CB., *Lt.-Col.*, 10 Foot	16 Sept. 16	25 Oct. 20	10 June 35	9 Nov. 46			1 Jan. 47
🕮 Wm. Thomas Blewett Mounsteven, *Capt.* h.-p. 79 Foot, *Staff Officer of Pensioners*	25 Nov. 25	14 Aug. 29	7 Aug. 35	do	do	10 May 59	6 Dec. 39
Hugh Plunkett Bourchier,[139] *Capt.*, h.-p. 19 Drs., *Town Major of Kingston, Canada*	12 May 25	20 Nov. 25	15 Sept. 35	do	do	14 May 59	26 May 48
🕮 Mountford Stoughton Heyliger Lloyd,[140] *Major*, Unattached	16 Dec. 25	13 Mar. 28	13 Nov. 35	do	do	12 June 59	31 Dec. 44
James Stuart, *Captain*, h.p. 84 Foot, *Staff Officer of Pensioners*	20 April 25	14 Dec. 25	1 April 46	12 Dec. 54	2 Nov. 55	14 June 59	
Edwin Wodehouse, CB., *Lt.-Col.*, R. Art., *Assist. Adj.-Gen., Aide de Camp to the Queen*	19 Dec. 34	22 Feb. 37	12 Feb. 37				
🕮 Henry Anderson, *Major*, Superintendent of the Invalid Depot at Chatham	22 July 13	15 June 15	12 Feb. 36	9 Nov. 46	20 June 54	20 June 59	

Colonels.

	ENSIGN, ETC.	LIEUT.	CAPTAIN.	MAJOR.	LIEUT.-COLONEL.	COLONEL.	WHEN PLACED ON HALF PAY.
Robert Pitcairn, *Captain*, retired full pay, *Staff Officer of Pensioners*	19 Jan. 26	26 Oct. 30	6 Sept. 39	11 Nov. 51	26 Oct. 58	1 July 59	
John Roche, *Captain*, Unattached	27 Oct. 26	29 Jan. 30	25 Mar. 36	9 Nov. 46	20 June 54	17 July 59	
Hamilton Fleming, *Lt.Col.*, retired full pay, Royal Marines	10 Mar. 28	15 April 36	16 Aug. 45	never	30 Oct. 55	22 July 59	
John West, *Major*, h. p. 42 Foot	18 Dec. 28	10 Mar. 33	20 May 36	9 Nov. 46	20 June 54	14 Aug. 59	7 Feb. 51
Robert Clifford Lloyd, *Lt.Col.*, 68 Foot	30 Dec. 26	8 June 30	3 June 36	9 Nov. 46	20 June 54	9 Sept. 59	
Henry Roxby Benson, *Lt.Col.*, 17 Lancers	31 Jan. 40	15 April 42	27 June 45	28 Oct. 54	20 Sept. 56	23 Sept. 59	
Mitchell George Sparks, *Lt.Col.*, 10 Foot	4 Nov. 19	26 Dec. 23	28 June 36	9 Nov. 46	20 June 54	25 Sept. 59	
William M'Pherson, *Captain*, Unattached, *Staff Officer of Pensioners*	29 Nov. 21	22 Sept. 25	17 Sept. 36	9 Nov. 46	20 June 54	17 Oct. 59	8 April 42
John Forbes, *Captain*, Unattached, *Staff Officer of Pensioners*	21 Nov. 11	21 Oct. 13	13 Oct. 36	9 Nov. 46	20 June 54	25 Oct. 59	20 Dec. 44
George Bent, CB., *Captain*, Royal Engineers, *Aide de Camp to the Queen*	16 Sept. 38	1 April 41	16 April 47	1 Sept. 54	2 Nov. 55	25 Oct. 59	
George Durnford, *Major*, retired full pay, 70 Foot	17 Oct. 26	8 Feb. 31	28 Nov. 37	26 May 50	29 Aug. 57	18 Nov. 59	
Henry Blankley Harrington Rogers, *Capt.*, Unatt., *Staff Officer of Pensioners*	17 Jan. 28	12 April 33	14 Oct. 36	9 Nov. 46	20 June 54	7 Dec. 59	22 Nov. 42
William Robert Haliday, *Major*, 36 Foot	12 Feb. 30	3 Mar. 33	11 Nov. 47	12 Dec. 54	6 June 56	13 Dec. 59	
Wm. Friend Hopkins, CB. *Lt.Col.* R. Marines, *Aide de Camp to the Queen*	27 Apr. 29	10 July 37	20 Apr. 47	never	20 Feb. 56	20 Dec. 59	
George Walkup Congdon, [161] *Lt.Col.*, retired full pay, R. Marines	4 Dec. 29	10 July 37	27 July 47			D v. 59	

1 Lord Harrington was employed in South America in 1807, and was present at the attack on Buenos Ayres. Served also in the Mahratta war of 1817 and 18, including the battle of Maheidpore, and storming of Talneir. Is a Commander of the Saviour of Greece.

2 Sir John Morillyon Wilson served as Midshipman in the Navy for nearly six years. He was employed on the coast of Ireland during the rebellion in 1798 ; in the expedition to the Helder in 1799, and Egypt in 1801, where he received a medal from the Capitan Pasha for having saved the lives of a boat's crew belonging to a Turkish man-of-war. He received three wounds while a Midshipman ; and the last was a severe wound on the head, which produced total deafness, in consequence of which he was invalided, and quitted the Navy in 1803. His health being restored, he entered the Army in 1804; and served in the third Battalion Royals at Walcheren in 1809, where he was twice wounded during the siege of Flushing. He afterwards served in the Peninsula, and was in the battles of Busaco, the retreat to the lines of Torres Vedras, and at the actions of Pombal, Redinha, Condeixa, Casal Nova, Foz d'Arouce, and Sabugal, the blockade of Almeida, and battle of Fuentes d'Onor. In 1812 he joined the 2nd Battalion Royals in Canada, and was in the attack made on Sackett's Harbour, and Great Sodus (where he received a severe bayonet wound). He was also in the actions at Black Rock, Buffalo, and the battle of Chippewa, in which he received seven wounds, and being left on the field of battle, he fell into the hands of the enemy. During his career in the two professions he received thirteen wounds, and has two balls still lodged. The brevet rank of Major, and that of Lieutenant-Colonel was conferred upon him for his conduct at Buffalo and Chippewa. Sir John has received the War Medal with two Clasps for Busaco and Fuentes d'Onor.

3 Colonel the Honourable Frederick M. Cathcart served as Aide-de-Camp to the Commander of the Forces in the expedition sent to the North of Germany in 1805-6 under General Lord Cathcart; and on the expedition sent to the Island of Rugen in the Baltic, to co-operate with the King of Sweden in 1807; and subsequently in the same year at the siege and capture of Copenhagen, on which occasion, being sent home with the despatches, he was promoted to a Troop in the 25th Light Dragoons. He continued to serve as Aide-de-camp to Lord Cathcart during the campaigns of 1813 and 1814 in Germany and France, and was present at the battles of Lutzen 3rd May, Bautzen 20th and 21st May, Dresden 28th Aug., Leipzic 16th, 18th, and 19th Oct. 1813, Brienne 1st Feb., Fère Champenoise 25th March, and capture of Paris 31st March 1814. In 1815 he was also employed in the same capacity at the head-quarters of the Allied Army under Marshal Prince Schwartzenberg. Is a Knight 2nd Class of St. Anne of Russia.

5 Colonel Stopford-Blair served on the expedition to South America in 1807. The campaign of 1815, including the battles of Quatre Bras and Waterloo (received a contusion), and capture of Paris.

10 Major-General Hon. A. A. Spencer served throughout the Eastern campaign of 1854-55, and commanded the 44th Regt. at the battles of Alma and Inkerman, siege of Sebastopol, and attack and occupation of the Cemetery and Suburbs on the 18th June—wounded. Served as Brigadier-General, and commanded the 1st Brigade, 4th Division, in support in the right attack on the assault of the Redan, and fall of Sebastopol on 8th Sept., and subsequently commanded the British land forces in the expedition to Kinbourn, resulting in the capture of those forts and the garrison of 1400 men (Medal and Clasps, *CB.*, Officer of the Legion of Honor, Sardinian Medal, and 3rd Class of the Medjidie).

11 Colonel Bloomfield served with the 59th Regt. the campaign of 1815, including the battle of Waterloo, storming of Cambray, and capture of Paris.

12 Major-General Lawrenson commanded the 17th Lancers in the Eastern campaign of 1854-55, including the cavalry affair of Bulganac and battle of Alma (Medal and Clasp, Sardinian Medal, and 4th Class of the Medjidie).

13 Colonel Hodgson served with the 45th in the Burmese war (Medal).

14 Major-General Mundy served at the siege and storming of Bhurtpore in 1825-6, as Aide-de-Camp to Lord Combermere (Medal).

15 Colonel M'Cleverty served the campaign against the Rajah of Coorg, in April 1834, with the 48th Regiment.

16 Colonel Robert B. Wood served as Aide-de-Camp and Military Secretary to Lord Hardinge throughout the campaign on the Sutlej (Medal), including the battles of Moodkee, Ferozeshah (severely wounded), and Sobraon (Medal and two Clasps, and *CB.*).

17 Major-General Parlby served in the Crimean campaign from 17th April to 2nd Sept. 1855, and commanded a Cavalry Brigade, and for a time also the Cavalry Division (Medal and Clasp for Sebastopol, Sardinian Medal, and 4th Class of the Medjidie).

18 Colonel Congreve commanded the 29th Regt. in the Sutlej campaign in 1845, and was severely wounded at the battle of Ferozeshah (Medal and *CB*). Also throughout the Punjaub campaign in 1848-49, including the passage of the Chenab, battles of Chillianwallah and Goojerat, and pursuit of the Seik army across the Jelum (Medal and two Clasps), officiated as Adjutant General H. M.'s Forces in India in 1857, and was present with the force which proceeded under the Commander in Chief against the Mutineers at Delhi ;—at the battle of Budlee-ke-Serai and the heights at Delhi on the 8th June, and subsequent siege operations until the end of July 1857.

19 Colonel Balders served the campaign on the Sutlej in 1845-6, and commanded the 3rd Light Dragoons in the battles of Moodkee and Ferozeshah (Medal and one Clasp). He was wounded in the groin whilst charging the enemy's batteries at Ferozeshah, on the evening of the 21st Dec. 1845. Received the Brevet of Lieut.-Colonel and *CB*.

20 Major-General Horn served the Eastern campaign of 1854-55 ; commanded the right Brigade 4th Division at the battle of Alma; and the 20th Regt. at the battles of Balaklava (and recapture of the redoubts and guns from the Russians, who had driven the Turkish force

therefrom the same morning) and Inkerman (twice wounded and horse shot under him): present throughout the siege operations against Sebastopol, and in the trenches at the two assaults and fall of the town (Medal and Clasps): at Inkerman he succeeded to the command of the 4th Division (Medal and Clasps, *CB.*, Officer of the Legion of Honor, Sardinian Medal, and 3rd Class of the Medjidie).

22 Colonel French served in the Peninsula from Aug. 1813 to the end of the war, including siege of San Sebastian, passage of the Bidassoa, battles of the Nivelle and Nive and investment of Bayonne. Served also in the American war, including the actions of Bladensburg, Baltimore, New Orleans, and Fort Bowyer. He has received the War Medal with two Clasps for Nivelle and Nive.

23 Colonel Crofton was appointed Persian interpreter to the force under Brigadier General Litchfield, in August 1832, and served with it throughout the arduous operations in Parkur, and against the tribes in the N. W. Desert, which ended in the taking of Balmeer.

24 Colonel Grattan was actively employed on the frontiers during the rebellion in Canada in 1838. He served in China with the 18th (Medal), and was present at the storming of the heights above Canton, and led the advance against the enemy's entrenched camp, for which he was selected by Sir Hugh Gough as the bearer of his despatches, promoted to the rank of Major, and appointed Brigade-Major of Fort St. George by Lord Hill. On his return to China—on board the *Madagascar*—in charge of Lord Auckland's despatches; the ship having caught fire during a gale of wind, he with a few others narrowly escaped the fate of fifty-seven souls who perished upon that occasion; he fell into the hands of the Chinese, and was detained 108 days in captivity; after which he was at the attack of Segoan, and commanded the 18th (after the fall of Lt.-Col. Tomlinson), at Chapoo, Woosung, and Changhai; and he was present at the storming of Chin Kiang Foo and the landing before Nankin. Served with the 18th Royal Irish in the last campaign in Burmah (Medal).

25 Colonel Bainbrigge served with the 20th in the Peninsula, in 1808 and 9, and again in 1812 and 13, and was present at the battles of Vimiera, Corunna, Vittoria, and the Pyrenees, (where he was twice wounded and lost an arm), for which he has received the War Medal with four Clasps. Served also in the Walcheren expedition.

26 Major-General Cunynghame served as Aide-de-Camp to Lord Saltoun during the latter part of the war in China (Medal), and was present at the storm and capture of Chinkiang-foo, and at the investment of Nankin. Served the Eastern campaign of 1854 as Assistant Quarter-Master General to the 1st Division, including the affair of Bulganack, battle of the Alma, taking of Balaklava, affair of 23rd Oct. on the heights of the Tchernaya, battles of Balaklava and Inkerman, and siege of Sebastopol (Medal and Clasps, *CB.*, Officer of the Legion of Honor, and 3rd Class of the Medjidie).

27 Colonel James Henderson served with the 92nd at the siege of Copenhagen and action at Kioge in 1807; with the expedition to Sweden, and afterwards to Portugal and Spain, under Sir John Moore in 1808-9, including the action at Lugo, and battle of Corunna. On the expedition to Walcheren in 1809. Served the campaigns of 1814 and 15 in France and Flanders with the 71st, including the affair of Tarbes, and battles of Toulouse and Waterloo, at which last he was severely wounded in the thigh by a grape-shot. He has received the War Medal with two Clasps for Corunna and Toulouse.

28 Colonel Le Mesurier served in the 24th at the capture of the Cape of Good Hope in 1806. In 1811, he joined the 2nd Battalion in the Peninsula, where he served until the end of that war in 1814, and was present at the sieges of Ciudad Rodrigo, Badajoz, battles of Salamanca, Vittoria, Pyrenees, Echalar, Nivelle, and Orthes (severely contused); and in the several affairs on the banks of the Dourdogne in front of Bordeaux, being on continual advance guard when that part of the army was moving forward on Angoulême. He has received the War Medal, with four Clasps.

29 Colonel John Swinburn served with the 43rd at the siege of Copenhagen in 1807; the campaign of 1808 in Portugal,—wounded in the head on the retreat to Vigo. Subsequent campaigns in the Peninsula until 1812, including the action of the Coa, battle of Fuentes d'Onor, action of Sabugal, battle of Busaco, retreat to and occupation of the Lines of Torres Vedras, subsequent advance in pursuit of Massena, and actions of Pombal and Redinha— wounded in the hip. Joined the army at Toulouse in April 1814. Present at New Orleans in Jan. 1815. Subsequently joined the Duke of Wellington's army at Brussels, was present at the capture of Paris, and remained with the Army of Occupation until the end of 1818. He has received the War Medal with two Clasps for Busaco and Fuentes d'Onor.

30 Colonel Thomas Kelly served with the late 26th Lt. Dragoons during the latter part of the Carib war in St. Vincent. He afterwards accompanied his Regt. to Portugal and from thence to Egypt—the Transport in which he embarked was attacked by a Spanish gunboat, which, after a sharp conflict, was beaten off. He served at the siege of Aboukir Castle, with the dismounted part of his Regt. He was also present in the action of the 21st March 1801, and in the affair of the advance of the army to the westward of Alexandria under Sir Eyre Coote. He was wounded in a night attack on the enemy's outposts on the 25th Aug. when, with a small detachment, he drove in the cavalry piquet, and captured the whole of the infantry piquets opposed to him, which were much more numerous than his own party. He has received the Gold Medal from the Grand Seignior for the Egyptian campaign, and also the Silver War Medal with one Clasp.

31 Colonel Ross served with the 92nd Highlanders the campaigns of 1811, 12, 13, and 14, including the actions of Arroyo de Molino, taking of Almaraz, in the affairs with the covering army during last siege of Badajoz, advance to and retreat from Madrid, defence of Alba de Tormes, battle of Vittoria, affairs in the valley of Bastan, affair at the pass of Maya, battles

of the Pyrenees, wounded in the left leg by a musket-ball ; as Aide-de-Camp to Sir John Buchan at the battles of the Nivelle and the Nive, taking the Heights of La Costa, battle of Orthes, action at Aire, battles of Toulouse, served the campaign of 1815 with the 92nd Highlanders, including the battle of Quatre Bras,—wounded in the left foot by a musket-ball; and battle of Waterloo,—wounded in the right arm by a musket-ball, and capture of Paris. He has received the War Medal with six Clasps.

32 Colonel During served in the Peninsula during the Corunna campaign, and subsequently from the latter part of 1812 to the end of that war in 1814, including the battles of Corunna, Vittoria, Pyrenees, the Nivelle, the Nive, Orthes, and Toulouse, for which he has received the War Medal with seven Clasps.

33 Colonel Harrison served in the Peninsula from Jan. 1810 to Sept. 1814, and was present at Cadiz, Isla, and Tarifa.

34 Colonel Wright served in Spain from 1st Jan. 1810, to the 31st Dec. 1812, including the defence of Cadiz, Fort Matagorda, and Tarifa.

35 Major-General Trollope commanded the troops in the Island of Cephalonia in 1848, 1849, and 1850. In August, 1848, the towns of Argostoli and Lixuri were attacked by armed Banditti, who were repulsed by the troops with loss on both sides. In 1849 the Island was disturbed by armed Insurgents,—martial law was proclaimed, which remained in force for six weeks, and was carried into effect by him: received the thanks of the Queen, and of the Legislature of the Ionian Islands, and was voted a sword by the inhabitants of Cephalonia. Served the Eastern campaign from 10th Nov. 1854,—from the 12th Nov. until July, 1855, as Colonel on the staff, he commanded the 1st Brigade 2nd Division; on 31st July he was Gazetted Brigadier-General, and commanded 2nd Brigade 3rd Division from that date until the army was broken up. Commanded in the trenches as General of the Day, Right attack, on three separate occasions when sorties were made upon them and repulsed, and was present on all other occasions when the 2nd Division was employed, including the 8th and 18th June,—on the former in command of the Old Guard, and on the latter in command of five Regiments; on the 8th Sept. he was in command of 2nd Brigade in reserve with the 3rd Division (Medal and Clasps, CB., Officer of the Legion of Honor, Sardinian Medal, and 3rd Class of the Medjidie).

36 Lord George Paget served the Eastern campaign of 1854-55 in command of the 4th Lt. Drs., including the battles of Alma, Balaklava, and Inkerman, and siege of Sebastopol (Medal and Clasps, Officer of the Legion of Honor, Sardinian Medal, and 3rd Class of the Medjidie): at Inkerman he commanded the Brigade of Light Cavalry.

37 Colonel George T. C. Napier commanded the Cape Mounted Riflemen at the battle of the Gwanga, and throughout the Kaffir war of 1846-47, for which services he received the Brevet rank of Lieut-Colonel. He also commanded the Regiment throughout the Kaffir war of 1850-52 (Medal), and commanded the Cavalry Brigade at the action of the Berea, for which he was nominated a CB.

38 Colonel Fynmore was at the capture of a French privateer schooner of 16 guns and 96 men, besides other boat service in 1811. In the partial action with the French fleet off Toulon in 1814. Was landed at Mahon in command of a guard to protect the person of the Spanish governor from the threatened violence of the Walloon guards. Sent to the city of Florence in 1815, to place himself under the directions of General Count Nugent, commander-in-chief of the Austrian army, as extra Aide-de-Camp, and was at the taking of the city of Naples. In 1823 he was sent up to the city of Lima to protect English merchants' property against the attacks of the Negro slaves during the civil war. The 20th Oct. 1827 was at the battle of Navarino, for which service he was promoted by His Royal Highness the Duke of Clarence, but in consequence of belonging to a gradation corps the appointment was afterwards cancelled. Served with the French army at the reduction of the town and fortress of Patras and the Morea castle; served afterwards in the West Indies, North Sea, and off Oporto during the civil war between Don Pedro and Don Miguel. In 1833 joined the Royal Marine Battalion at Lisbon, commanded by Colonel Adair, CB. In April, 1837, embarked on board H.M.S. Castor (36), on the 10th Oct. was landed in command of his detachment on the Albanian coast to attack pirates. Served on the S. E. coast of Spain from 4th Jan. 38 to 30 Jan. 39. Has the War Medal and Clasp for Navarino.

39 Colonel Buchanan served as Quarter-Master of the Royal Marine Battalion at D'Jouni, and on the coast of Syria during the Campaign in 1840-41 (Medal and Clasp, and Turkish Medal). Served also in the East Indies and Burmah during the war of 1852-53 (Medal).

40 Colonel Sall served at the taking of Maldonado and Monte Video in 1807. Also in the Peninsula from 1813 to the end of that war in 1814, and was present at the repulse of the sortie from Bayonne.

41 Colonel Terry served the campaign of 1799 in Holland with the 25th, including the battle of Egmont-op-Zee. Expedition to Egypt and surrender of Alexandria in 1801 ; capture of Madeira in 1807 ; capture of Guadaloupe and St. Martin's in 1810 ; re-capture of Guadaloupe in 1815. He has received the War Medal with two Clasps for Egypt and Guadaloupe.

42 Colonel Fairtlough served at the bombardment of Ter Vere, and siege and capture of Flushing in 1809. Also the capture of Guadaloupe in 1815.

43 Colonel H. C. Streatfeild served the Mahratta campaign of 1804, 5, and 6, including the assault of Bhurtpore, with the Grenadiers of the 65th, when out of 17 officers and 300 men who marched to the assault, 14 officers and 190 men were either killed or wounded. At the capture of the Isle of France in 1810. Served the Mahratta campaign of 1817 and 18, including the capture of Hattras.

44 Colonel Senior was severely wounded in the action between H. M. packet *Lapwing* and the American privateer *Fox*, off Barbadoes, 30th Sept. 1813.

War Services of the Colonels.

45 Colonel Hughes served the Egyptian campaign of 1801 with the 24th. Engaged with a French squadron in the Mosambique Channel, 3rd July 1810. Served the Nepaul campaigns of 1814, 15, and 16, and was wounded at Harriapore. Served also during the Mahratta war of 1816, 17, and 18. Gold Medal from the Grand Seignior for services in Egypt; and also the Silver War Medal with one Clasp.

46 Colonel Tronson served in the West Indies from 1808 to 1812, including the capture of Martinique and siege of Fort Bourbon in 1809, and capture of Guadaloupe in 1810. The campaigns of 1813, 14, and 15, in Canada, including the operations against Plattsburg. Throughout the Burmese war, and commanded a detachment of the 13th, which took possession of the city of Bassein previous to the arrival of Sir Robert Sale's Brigade destined for its capture; also present at Kokein, 15th Dec. 1826, Pagoda Point, Napadie, Mehadie, Melloon, where the command of the 13th devolved upon him, and on the 9th Feb. 1826, at the storming of Pagamue, where he was wounded in the right leg, but continued to lead the left wing until most severely wounded in the left leg, where the ball still remains. Served the campaign in Affghanistan under Lord Keane, and commanded the 13th at the assault and capture of the Fortress and Citadel of Ghuznee, for which he obtained the brevet rank of Lieut.-Colonel and Order of the Doranee Empire. Commanded the Regiment throughout the campaign in Kohistan, and at the sieges of Tootumdarrah, Jhoolghur (led and commanded the storming party), night attack at Baboo Koosh Ghur, Kardurrah, and Perwandurrah, when Dost Mahomed surrendered, and the force returned to Cabul. He has received the War Medal with two Clasps for Martinique and Guadaloupe; the Medal for Ava; and Medal for Ghuznee.

47 Colonel Harty served with the 33rd at the capture of Bourbon and the Isle of France in 1810; the campaigns of 1813 and 14 in Germany and Holland, including both the attacks on Merxem, and the assault on Bergen-op-Zoom. Also the campaign of 1815, including the battle of Quatre Bras, the retreat on the following day, and battle of Waterloo,—slightly wounded.

49 Colonel Burney served at the capture of Ischia and Procida, in 1809; defence of Cadiz in 1810; action of the Coa and Sabugal, battle of Fuentes d'Onor, retreat from Burgos. Served the campaign of 1814 in Holland, including the action at Merxem, bombardment of Antwerp, and storming of Bergen-op-Zoom. Engaged in the Burmese war at the attack of Padowa Pass and the fortified positions of Mahatee; storming the stockades and hills near, and taking the town and works of Arracan. Wounded on the 16th June 1815, at Quatre Bras, by a musket-shot in the left shin, and dangerously by a ball which entered the back part of the head. He has received the War Medal with one Clasp for Fuentes d'Onor.

50 Colonel Rochfort was at the capture of the Isle of France in 1810; and of Java in 1811, including capture of Cornelis, storming of Serandola and Fort Djocjocarta. Storming of redoubts at the island of Borneo; Nepaul campaign in 1814; siege and storm of Hattras; Mahratta campaigns of 1817 and 18; siege and storm of Bhurtpore 1825-6. He has received the War Medal with one Clasp for Java.

51 Colonel Dundas served in the 47th Regt. on the expedition to South America in 1806-7, and was present at the taking of Maldonado, in several skirmishes, and at the attack and storming of Monte Video. He served afterwards in the East Indies, and was present in 1814 at the capture of the Fort of New Nuggur, and in several skirmishes. He served also in the Burmese Territory from Jan. 1826 till peace was proclaimed.

52 Colonel Willington served in the East Indies from May 1813 to May 1823, including the campaigns of 1815 and 16 in Kattywar and Kutch; taking of Anjar; Deccan campaigns of 1817 and 18; campaign of 1819 in Candeish; and in Kutch in 1820.

53 Colonel Westmore served the campaigns of 1813 and 14 in Germany and Holland, including both attacks on Merxem, and the assault on Bergen-op-Zoom; served at Waterloo on the 16th, 17th, and 18th June, and was severely wounded.

54 Colonel Poole served throughout the operations in Scinde (Medal) under Sir Charles Napier, and commanded the 22nd at the battle of Meeanee, and a brigade at the battle of Hyderabad. He was also previously at the destruction of the Fort of Imaumghur in the Desert. He served the campaign in the Southern Mahratta country in 1844-5, including the investment and capture of the Forts Panulla and Pownghur.

55 Colonel White's services:—Campaign in Spain, under Sir John Moore, including the retreat to and battle of Corunna, where he was wounded. Siege of Flushing, and capture of Walcheren; campaigns in Canada, from Nov. 1813, to the end of the war. He has received the War Medal with one Clasp for Corunna.

56 Colonel Bray served the Mahratta campaigns of 1817, 18, and 19, and was present at the sieges and captures of Ryghur, Amulnier, and Asseerghur. He was on board the unfortunate ship *Kent*, which was burned in the Bay of Biscay, 1st March 1825. Commanded the 39th in the action of Maharajpore (Medal), and was severely wounded.

57 Colonel Tennant served at the siege of Flushing in 1809.

58 Colonel E. R. Hill served in the Peninsula from Sept. 1812 to the end of that war in 1814, including the affair of San Munos and retreat from Burgos, as a volunteer; battle of Vittoria, passage of the Bidassoa, battles of Nivelle and Toulouse: he has the War Medal with four Clasps.

59 Sir Joshua Jebb served in the last American war.

60 Colonel Arthur Shirley was nominated to the 2nd Class of the Medjidie, for service with the late Turkish Contingent.

61 Major-General Lawrence commanded the 2nd Batt. Rifle Brigade throughout the Eastern campaign of 1854, including the battles of the Alma (horse killed) and Inkerman, and siege of Sebastopol (Medal and Clasps, CB., Officer of the Legion of Honor, and 3rd Class of the Medjidie).

War Services of the Colonels.

62 Colonel Hon. George Cadogan served the Eastern campaign of 1854, including the battles of Alma, Balaklava, and Inkerman, and siege of Sebastopol (Medal and Clasps, *CB.*, Commander 2nd Class of St. Maurice and St. Lazurus, and 3rd Class of the Medjidie). He was employed as the Queen's Commissioner to the Sardinian Army in the Crimea.

63 Colonel J. C. Hope Gibsone served throughout the Kaffir war of 1846-7, and was present on almost every occasion in which the troops were engaged with the enemy; and he had the command of and led the charge of Cavalry in the decisive affair of the Gwanga, on the 8th June 1846, when a large body of the enemy was encountered and utterly broken, leaving upwards of 400 dead on the field, on which occasion his services were warmly acknowledged in the public dispatches, and his name particularly mentioned in General Orders.

64 Colonel Story served in the Peninsula and France from Nov. 1812 to May 1814 including the siege of San Sebastian, and passages of the Bidassoa and Adour. He has received the Silver War Medal and one Clasp for San Sebastian.

65 Colonel Huey served the Eastern campaign from April 1855 in command of the 2nd Battalion Royal Regiment, including the siege and fall of Sebastopol (Medal and Clasp, and 4th Class of the Medjidie).

66 Major-General Horatio Shirley served the Eastern campaign of 1854-55 ; commanded the 88th in the battles of Alma and Inkerman, and siege of Sebastopol ; was General Officer of the trenches in the attack on the Quarries on the 7th June, and at the attack on the 18th June, and commanded a Brigade at the attack on the Redan on the 8th Sept.—wounded (Medal and Clasps, *CB.*, Officer of the Legion of Honor, Sardinian Medal, and 3rd Class of the Medjidie).

67 Sir Henry Storks served as Assistant Adjutant-General at the Cape of Good Hope during the Kaffir war of 1846-47 (Medal).

68 Colonel T. C. Smith, prior to entering the Army, served for a short period in the Navy, and was three times wounded. He served in the Peninsula from June 1813 to the end of that war in 1814, and was present at the affair of Ordal. He served also the campaign of 1815, and was wounded at the battle of Waterloo.

68† Colonel Hodge commanded the 4th Dragoon Guards in the Eastern campaign of 1854-55 ; was on board H. M. S. *Sanspareil* in the naval attack on Sebastopol, 17th Oct. 1854 ; also present at the battles of Balaklava and Inkerman, siege of Sebastopol, night-attack on Russian outposts, 19th Feb. and battle of Tchernaya, 16 Aug. 1855 (Medal and Clasps, *CB.*, Officer of the Legion of Honor, and 3rd Class of the Medjidie).

69 Colonel Yarborough served with the 91st Regt. in the Kaffir war (Medal and *CB.*).

70 Colonel Crombie embarked in Feb. 1854 with the Coldstream Guards for Turkey, and served in Bulgaria.

71 Colonel Macbean served in the Peninsula and France, from July 1812 to August 1814, including the affair at Osma, battle of Vittoria, both sieges of San Sebastian and capture of it; passage of the Nivelle, 10th November, and actions of the Nive, 9th, 10th, 11th, and 12th December, 1813. Served also the campaign of 1815, including the capture of Paris. Served afterwards with the Army of Occupation until 1818. He has received the Silver War Medal with four Clasps.

72 Colonel James served in the Peninsula and France, from Oct. 1812 to April 1814, including the battles of Vittoria, the Pyrenees, Nivelle, and Orthes, for which he has received the Silver War Medal with four Clasps. Served subsequently in the American war.

73 Colonel Doherty served with the 14th Lt. Dragoons throughout the Punjaub campaign of 1848-9, including the action of Ramnuggur, passage of the Chenab, battles of Chillianwallah and Goojerat, pursuit of the enemy across the Jhelum, and of the Affghans over the Indus through the Khyber Pass (Medal and Clasps). At Ramnuggur he brought the charging squadrons, under Col. Havelock who was killed, across the nullah and out of the enemy's entrenchments; and at Goojerat he commanded a body of H. M. Dragoons and Native Light Cavalry.

73† Colonel Faber served with the 49th Regt. throughout the war with China (Medal), and was present at the first and second captures of Chusan, storm and capture of the heights above Canton, attack and capture of Amoy and of Chinhae, occupation of Ningpo and repulse of the night-attack, attack and capture of the enemy's entrenched camp on the heights of Segoan, of Chapoo, and of Woosung, and investment of Nankin.

74 Colonel Garvock served as a Major of Brigade in Sir Harry Smith's Division throughout the Sikh campaign (Medal and three Clasps), and was present at the battles of Moodkee, Ferozeshah (horse shot under him), Buddiwal, Aliwal, and Sobraon, where he was himself severely wounded, and his horse struck in three places. He also acted as Adjutant-General and Quarter-Master-General to Sir Harry Smith in the action with and defeat of the rebel Boers at Bloem Plaats (South Africa), 29th August 1848.

75 Colonel R. B. Burnaby served the campaign of 1815, including the battle of Waterloo.

76 Colonel Hon. Alex. Gordon served on the Quarter Master General's Staff throughout the Eastern campaign of 1854-55, including the battles of Alma, Balaklava, and Inkerman, and siege of Sebastopol (Medal and Clasps, *CB.*, Officer of the Legion of Honor, and 3rd Class of the Medjidie).

77 Colonel Tyrwhitt served the Eastern campaign of 1854, as Aide-de-Camp to the Duke of Cambridge, and was present at the battles of Alma and Inkerman, and siege of Sebastopol (Medal and Clasps, Knight of the Legion of Honor, and 5th Class of the Medjidie).

78 Colonel Rochfort Scott served with the expedition against New Orleans, and was present at the attack on the American Lines on the 8th Jan. 1815, and at the capture of Fort Boyer. Served afterwards in France with the Army of Occupation, from July 1815 to Dec. 1818 ; and with the allied Anglo-Turkish force in Syria, from Dec. 1840 to Nov. 1841 (Medal and Clasp).

78† Colonel Adair served in Spain from July 1810 to the end of the war, including the defence of Cadiz, battle of Barrosa, Fort San Philip, Balaguere, Villa Franca, Tarragona and Barcelona. Served also the Pindarree campaigns of 1817 and 18, and subsequently in the Deccan, including the siege and reduction of Rhyghur, Amulner, and Asseerghur. Twice severely wounded by matchlock balls, in the left arm and right side, at the siege of Asseerghur on the evening of the 19th March 1818, in repulsing a sortie made by the garrison of the fort into the town. He has received the War Medal and one Clasp for Barrosa.

79 Colonel Hennis served the campaign of 1815, and was present at the battle of Waterloo.

80 Lord West served on Sir Hugh Gough's Staff throughout the Sutlej campaign of 1845-46, as Aide-de-Camp in the battles of Moodkee and Ferozeshah, and as Officiating Military Secretary during the remainder of the campaign, and in the battle of Sobraon (Medal and Clasps). Landed with the 21st Fusiliers in the Crimea and was present at the battles fought there: commanded a detached wing in the battle of Inkerman and subsequently the regiment during the siege from 17th Nov. 1854 to 6 Aug. 1855, including a special command of two Regiments in support of the storming party of the left column against the Redan on the 18th June. Had command of the Regiment again on the 8th Sept., and during the assault was ordered to move to the point of attack in support. In the expedition to Kinbourn he held command of a Brigade (Medal and Clasps, *CB.*, Officer of the Legion of Honor, Sardinian Medal, and 3rd Class of the Medjidie).

82 Colonel William Napier served as Aide-de-Camp to Sir Charles Napier during his campaign of 1845 against the Desert and Mountain Tribes on the right bank of the Indus. Served also at the siege of Sebastopol as Assistant Director General Land Transport Corps (Medal and Clasp, and 5th Class of the Medjidie).

83 Colonel Arney commanded three companies of the 58th during the operations against the hostile natives in the Southern District of New Zealand in 1846. He commanded the troops encamped in the valley of the Hutt and Porirua; and the 58th at the affair of the Horokeivi, when the enemy were driven back and dispersed.

84 Colonel Hagart commanded the 7th Hussars in the Indian campaign from Dec. 1857, including the repulse of the attack on the Alumbagh till promoted Brigadier in March 1858. Commanded the 1st Cavalry Brigade in the operations beyond the Goomtee, at the siege of Lucknow (*CB.*, Medal and Clasp), and during the Rohilcund campaign, including the affair of Alleegunge, and the captures of Ruynghur, Shahjehanpore, Bareilly, and Mohumdee. In the autumn of the same year was attached to the Oude field force, and commanded the Cavalry of that Division at the occupation of Fyzabad, passage of the Gogra, and during the whole of the Trans-Gogra campaign till the conclusion of the war in 1859 (nine times mentioned in despatches).

85 Colonel Donaldson served in the Peninsula with the 57th, from June 1809 to the end of that war in 1814, including the siege of Badajoz in April 1811, battles of Albuhera, Vittoria, and the Pyrenees.

86 Colonel Long served with the 71st in the Peninsula, from Sept. 1813 to the end of that war in 1814, including the action at Cambo, battles of the Nive, before Bayonne (wounded), Orthes, Aire, Tarbes, and Toulouse. Also the campaign of 1815, including the battle of Waterloo. He has received the War Medal with four Clasps for Nivelle, Nive, Orthes, and Toulouse.

87 Colonel Birtwhistle served the campaign of 1814 in the south of France with the 32nd. Also the campaign of 1815, including the battle of Quatre Bras (slightly wounded), retreat on the 17th June, and battle of Waterloo (severely wounded).

88 Colonel Palmer served the campaign of 1814 in Holland, including the attack upon the village of Merxem, 13th Jan.; also second attack and capture 2nd Feb., when his Regiment captured two guns; bombardment of the French fleet in the Scheldt, from 3rd to 6th February. Actively engaged at Fort Frederick on the Scheldt, 22nd March, in impeding the passage of French line of battle ships to Fort Lillo, for the purpose of throwing provisions and assistance into the garrison. Again employed on the same duty 25th March following.

89 Colonel Jos. Swinburne served in the Peninsula from 1809 to the end of the war, including the battles of Oporto, Talavera (wounded in the right arm and foot), and Busaco ; actions at Pombal, Leria, Condeixa, Fleur-de-lis, Guarda, and Sabugal ; battle of Fuentes d'Onor, first siege of Badajoz, action at El Bodon, sieges of Ciudad Rodrigo and Badajoz, battles of Salamanca, Vittoria, Pyrenees, and Nivelle ; action at Salvaterre, battle of Orthes (wounded in the neck), action at Vic Bigorre, and battle of Toulouse. He has the War Medal with ten Clasps.

90 Colonel Waymouth served in the Peninsula with the 2nd Life Guards from Nov. 1812 to the end of that war in 1814, including the battle of Vittoria, investment of Pampeluna, and the battles of the Pyrenees. Also the campaign of 1815, including the action of Quatre Bras, covering the retreat on the 17th June, and battle of Waterloo. Severely wounded and taken prisoner, when charging the French cuirassiers at Waterloo. He has received the War Medal with two Clasps for Vittoria and Toulouse.

91 Colonel Edgar Gibson served in the Peninsula with the 1st Light Infantry Battalion of the King's German Legion, from Aug. 1813 to the end of that war in 1814, including the siege of San Sebastian, an action in the Pyrenees at the passage of the Bidassoa (wounded), and the subsequent actions in which the left wing of the army was engaged. Served also the campaign of 1815, and was present at the battle of Waterloo. He has received the War Medal with two Clasps.

92 Colonel Last commanded the troops in the southern district of New Zealand during the greater part of the operations against the hostile natives in 1846. He assisted in driving back the rebels who attacked the detachment posted under Lieut. Page (58th Regt.) at Boulcott's farm in the valley of the Hutt on the 16th May 1846 ; commanded at the capture of Te Rauparaha and several other influential chiefs, as well as disarming part of the tribe on the 23rd July ; and also commanded the combined force at the affair of the Horokiwi, on the 6th Aug.,

War Services of the Colonels. 47d

compelling the rebels to retreat and ultimately to disperse; was particularly mentioned in the Government Gazette of New Zealand, and also in the Dispatches of Lieut.-Governor Grey.

93 Colonel Morse-Cooper served the campaign of 1814 as a Volunteer from the R. M. College with the Royals, and was present at the investment of Bayonne and repulse of the sortie. Also the campaign of 1815, including the battles of Quatre Bras and Waterloo. Also served with the 11th Light Dragoons at the siege and capture of Bhurtpore in 1825-6, under Lord Combermere, where he volunteered for the dismounted Cavalry storming party. Slightly wounded at Bayonne, and severely at Waterloo, having received five wounds. Has received the Waterloo Medal, and a Medal for Bhurtpore.

94 Colonel Jauncey served on the expedition to Walcheren in 1809. Subsequently in the Peninsula from July 1812 to June 1814, including the battle of Castalla, siege of Tarragona, retreat from thence, its second siege, retreat from Villa Franca after the battle of the Pass of Ordall, and investment of Barcelona in 1814. Expedition to Naples in 1815.

95 Colonel de Lacy served with the 48th Regt. in the Peninsular war in the battle of Busaco, lines at Torres Vedras, pursuit of Marshal Massena, action of Campo Mayor, first siege of Badajoz, battles of Albuhera, Vittoria (wounded), Roncesvalles, and the Pyrenees (28th July to 2nd Aug. 1813), besides minor actions and skirmishes. He served seven years in Jamaica and the West Indies, and has received the War Medal with four Clasps.

96 Colonel Seargill served with the 9th at the defence of Tarifa, from May to Dec. 1811. Also in the south of France from March to May 1814, including the blockade of Bayonne and repulse of the sortie.

97 Colonel Robert Lewis served in the Burmese war.

98 Colonel Ainsworth served at the siege of Flushing in 1809, and subsequently in the Peninsula, including the battle of Fuentes d'Onor, and 2nd siege of Badajoz, and battle of Nivelle. Served also the campaign of 1815, and was present at the battle of Waterloo. He has received the War Medal with three Clasps.

99 Colonel Wilbraham served the Syrian campaign of 1840-41 (Medal), including the advance on Gaza and affair near Askelon. Served the Eastern campaign of 1854-55, as an Assistant Adjutant-General, including the battles in the Crimea and siege of Sebastopol (Medal and Clasps, CB., Officer of the Legion of Honor, and 3rd Class of the Medjidie).

100 Colonel Spottiswoode served as Brigade-Major of Cavalry with the left wing of the Army of Gwalior in 1843, and was present at the battle of Punniar (Medal). He served also in the like capacity in the Sutlej campaign in 1846, and was present at the battle of Sobraon (Medal). Commanded the 1st Dragoon Guards in the Crimean campaign from 16 Aug. 1855, including the siege of Sebastopol (Medal and Clasp, and 5th Class of the Medjidie).

101 Colonel Webber Smith served with the 48th Regt. the campaign against the Rajah of Coorg, in April 1834, and was wounded. Commanded the 95th Regt. in the Eastern campaign of 1854, and was severely wounded at the battle of Alma (Medal and Clasp, CB., and 5th Class of the Medjidie).

102 Colonel George served throughout the campaign in Scinde (Medal) under Sir Charles Napier, including the destruction of Imaumghur in the Desert, and the battles of Meeanee and Hyderabad, 1843, at which last he commanded the 22nd Regt. He served also the campaign in the Southern Mahratta country in 1844-5; and Brigadier Hicks being mortally wounded, Major George took command of detachments at the storm of the Petahs and northern front of Panulla and Powaghur, Nov. 27, and was present at the investment and capture of both those forts, being in command of the left flank post; and during the operations against the Forts Munnahur and Munsuntosh in the Southern Concan, commanded left wing 22nd Regt., and afterwards commanded the Field Brigade (temporarily) at Kolapore.

103 Colonel Yorke commanded the Royal Dragoons in the Eastern campaign of 1854, and was severely wounded at the battle of Balaklava, his horse also was severely wounded with grape shot in supporting the Light Cavalry charge prior to his own leg being shattered by a Rifle ball (Medal and Clasps, CB., Sardinian Medal, and 4th Class of the Medjidie). He commanded the Regt. during a violent gale in the Black Sea between Varna and the Crimea and this great disaster resulted in the loss of 250 horses of the Regt. including the greater part of the officers' chargers and detachments of other Regts. under his command.

104 Colonel C. H. Burnaby commanded the Royal Artillery on the Eastern Frontier, Cape of Good Hope, during the Kaffir war of 1846-7, and for this received the Brevet rank of Major. He also commanded the Royal Artillery on the Eastern Frontier from the breaking out of the war in Dec. 1850 until July 1852, and was appointed commandant of Grahaim's Town, with the District of Lower Albany; for services in this war he got the Brevet rank of Lieut.-Colonel (Medal).

104† Colonel Monkland served with the 74th Highlanders in the Kaffir war in 1851 (Medal).

105 Colonel Brownrigg served the Eastern campaign of 1854-55, as Assist. Adjutant-General, including the battles of Alma and Inkerman, and siege of Sebastopol, and was Chief of the Staff to Sir George Brown in the expedition to Kertch (Medal and Clasps, CB., Officer of the Legion of Honor, and 4th Class of the Medjidie).

106 Colonel W. B. Ainslie commanded the 93rd Highlanders throughout the Eastern campaign of 1854-55, including the battles of Alma and Balaklava, and siege of Sebastopol (Medal and three Clasps, CB., Sardinian Medal, and 4th Class of the Medjidie).

107 Colonel S. J. Hill commanded an expedition 80 miles up the Gambia in 1849; stormed and destroyed the fortified town of Bambacoo, 6th May; attacked and partially destroyed the fortified town of Keenung, 7th May; action and defeat of the enemy on the plains of Quenella. He also commanded a detachment of the 2nd and 3rd West India Regts. in the combined attack of the British and French naval and land force under Commodore Fanshawe in the

War Services of the Colonels.

attack and total defeat of pirates at the Island of Basis, Jeba River, Western Africa, 12th Dec. 1849. The thanks of the Lords of the Admiralty were conveyed to himself and detachment, and he received the brevet rank of Major.

108 Colonel Tidy served with the 14th Regt. at the siege and capture of Bhurtpore in 1825-26 (Medal).

109 Colonel Sanders commanded the 19th Regt. in the Eastern campaign of 1854 and was severely wounded at the battle of Alma (Medal and Clasp, CB., and 5th Class of the Medjidie).

110 Colonel Holdsworth served with the Queen's Royals the campaign in Affghanistan and Beloochistan, including the storm and capture of Ghuznee (Medal) and of Khelat (severely wounded). Also the campaign in the Southern Mahratta country in 1844 (including the storm of the Fortress of Punella); that in the Concan in 1845. Served in the Kaffir war of 1851-52, and commanded four companies of the Regiment with the expedition North of the Orange River, in 1852-53.

110† Colonel H. D. White served the Eastern campaign of 1854-55 in command of the Inniskilling Dragoons, including the battles of Balaklava, Inkerman, and Tchernaya, and siege and fall of Sebastopol (Medal and Clasps, Knight of the Legion of Honor, and 4th Class of the Medjidie).

111 Colonel Mends served as a Midshipman, Royal Navy, during the years 1812, 13, and 14, in North and South America. Served at every British possession in Western Africa, for fourteen years, and was present at the first attack made upon the Ashantees near the village of Donguah, 26th September 1823, under Sir Charles M'Carthy. Present also at the destruction of the native Dutch town of Succondee, 17th February 1824, and employed in the boats of H. M.'s ships of war skirmishing with the natives of that town and the Ashantees on the following morning. In action against the Ashantees, 21st May 1824; and at the defeat of their army on the heights in rear of Cape Coast Castle, 11th July following. On the 4th February 1826, whilst in command of Dixcove Fort, he was attacked by about 6,000 natives, the garrison consisting of only one corporal and nineteen privates (natives), Royal African corps; with these he defended the post, and forced the enemy to retreat with much loss in the killed and wounded. Besides the above he has been in various skirmishes with the natives.

112 Colonel Robinson served the campaign in Affghanistan and Beloochistan, including the storm and capture of Ghuznee (severely wounded) and of Khelat : Medal for Ghuznee. He also served in the Kaffir war of 1851-52-53, as Assistant-Quarter-Master General of the 2nd Division.

113 Colonel Wigston served with the 18th Royal Irish on the China expedition (Medal), at Canton, Amoy, Chusan, Chinhae, Ningpo, Segoan, Chapoo, and Chin Kiang Foo. Served also in Burmah from July 1852 to the end of the war in 1853 ; was present at the capture of Prome; and commanded the infantry, and subsequently, on the force being increased, the Right Wing of the troops employed under Sir John Cheape in the Donabew district against Meah Toon, and was severely wounded at the assault and capture of that chief's last position on the 19th March 1853. Received the brevet of Major for the China service, and that of Lieut.-Colonel for the Burmese service.

114 Colonel Rice served with the 51st during the war in Burmah from April to August 1852; was on board the E. I. C. steam sloop *Sesostris* during the Naval action and destruction of the enemy's stockades on the Rangoon River; served during the succeeding three days operations in the vicinity, and at the storm and capture of Rangoon; also at the assault and capture of Bassein, 19th May (severely wounded). Colonel Rice was mentioned in General Godwin's dispatches as " deserving the best consideration of Government" for capturing by storm with his company and a sub-division of the 9th Madras Native Infantry the enemy's stronghold, and entrenched position south of Bassein, armed with sixteen guns and twenty gingalls; honoured with the best thanks of the Governor-General in Council.

115 Colonel the Hon. R. C. H. Spencer served throughout the whole of the operations in China, and was present at the destruction of the batteries of Amoy, in H. M. S. *Blonde*, in 1840 ; at the capture of the forts of the Bocca Tigris, and subsequent operations in the Canton River ; at the storm and capture of the heights of Canton ; attack and captures of Amoy, Chusan (second operation), Chinhae, Chapoo, Woosung, Shanghae, and Chin Kiang Foo, and demonstration before Nankin (Medal).

116 Colonel Phibbs served in the Peninsula, with the 27th, from Nov. 1813 to the end of that war in 1814, including the battles of the Nivelle, Orthes, and Toulouse, for which he has received the War Medal with three Clasps. Served afterwards in the American war, and was present at the taking of Plattsburgh. Lost his left arm, and was shot through both legs at the battle of the Nivelle.

117 Colonel Eld served with the 90th Regiment during the Kaffir war of 1846-47 (Medal).

118 Colonel Land served as Adjutant to the Royal Marine Battalion at D'Jouni, and was present at the Bombardment of St. Jean d'Acre (Medal and Clasp for Syria, and Turkish Medal).

119 Colonel Mitford was employed on the coast of Syria during the whole of the operations against the Egyptians ; he landed and served with the Battalion at the Camp d'Jouni, and was present at the bombardment of St. Jean d'Acre. He has been presented with a Medal from the Sultan, and has the War Medal with one Clasp.

120 Colonel James Watson served with the 14th Regt. at the siege and storming of Bhurtpore in 1825-26 (Medal). Also at the siege of Sebastopol (Medal and Clasp).

121 Sir Thomas Troubridge served the Eastern campaign of 1854 with the 7th Fusiliers, and was very severely wounded at the battle of Inkerman—both legs amputated (Medal and Clasps, and 4th Class of the Medjidie).

122 Colonel Forbes served with the 91st Regiment in the last Kaffir war (Medal).

123 Colonel Lysons served in Canada during the rebellion in 1838-39, including the actions

of St. Denis and St. Eustache. Was honourably mentioned in Dispatches and General Orders on the occasion of the wreck of the transport *Premier* on 4th November 1843 and promoted in consequence. Served the Eastern campaign of 1854-55; was present at the battles of Alma and Inkerman, the minor affairs of Bulganac and Mackenzie's Farm, capture of Balaklava, and throughout the whole siege of Sebastopol; led the main column of the attack on the Redan by the Light Division on the 18th June, and commanded a Brigade in the latter part of the action (slightly wounded); was engaged in the final assault of the Redan on the 8th September (severely wounded); commanded the 2nd Brigade Light Division from October 1855 to the end of the war (Medal and Clasps, Brevet of Colonel, *CB.*, Officer of the Legion of Honor, Sardinian Medal, and 3rd Class of the Medjidie).

124 Colonel the Honourable W. L. Pakenham served the Eastern campaign of 1854-55, as Assistant Adjutant-General, up to the 24th June 1855, after which as Adjutant-General, including the battles of Alma, Balaklava, and Inkerman, and siege and fall of Sebastopol (Medal and Clasps, *CB.*, Officer of the Legion of Honor, Commander 2nd Class St. Maurice and St. Lazarus, and 3rd Class of the Medjidie).

125 Colonel Tudor served as Aide-de-Camp to General Grey, commanding the left wing of the army of Gwalior, in the action of Punniar, 29 Dec. 1843 (Medal). Also served the Sutlej campaign of 1845-6, as Aide de Camp to the same General, commanding 5th Division of the Army.

127 Colonel James Graham joined the 54th Regt. in Burmah, as a volunteer, in Dec. 1824, and was present at the carrying of the entrenched Fords of the Mahattee River, 27th March, and at the attack on the fortified heights of Arracan, 29th March 1825; at the latter he was wounded in the side and face: has received the Medal and Clasp for Ava. In July 1855 a Medical Board pronounced him as "totally unfit for service in the field;" but in consideration of the nature of his past services he was specially promoted to a Lieut.-Colonelcy, and allowed to retire upon the full pay of that rank.

128 Colonel Wetherall served in Canada during the rebellions of 1837-38, 1838-39, and was present in the actions of St. Charles, St. Eustache, and Pointe Oliviere. Was shipwrecked with the Royal Regt. in the transport "Premier." Served in the Crimea as Assistant Quarter Master General and was present at the battles of Alma, Balaklava, and Inkerman, the siege and fall of Sebastopol. Served at Kertch as Deputy Quarter Master General of the Turkish Contingent. Was subsequently Director General of Land Transport in the Crimea, and was charged with the reorganization of that force (Medal and four Clasps, *CB.*, Knight of the Legion of Honor, 3rd Class of the Medjidie, and Turkish Medal). Served as Deputy Q. M. General to the forces in China in 1857. Served in India in the Mutiny of 1857-58; was Chief of the Staff of the Central India field force and present at Koonch, Muttra, Golowlee (20th and 22nd May), and Calpee. Commanded South Oude field force in the campaign of 1858; and commanded the force at the attack and capture of the intrenched camp of Ramporc Rupea on 3rd Nov., and the subsequent operations of the campaign (Medal and Clasp).

129 Colonel Sadlier served in Sicily from July 1808 to June 1812, and was present at the capture of the islands of Ischia and Procida. Served subsequently in the Peninsula, including the battle of Castalla and siege of Tarragona, action at Villa Franca, besides various minor affairs: also in the American war, including the attack on Plattsburg; and subsequently with the Army of Occupation in France; served in the Eastern campaign of 1854-55, including the actions in the Crimea and siege of Sebastopol (Medal and two Clasps).

130 Colonel Strange served with the 26th Regt. on the China expedition (Medal), and was present at the defence of Ningpo, at Tseke, Chapoo, Woosung, Shanghae, Chinkiangfoo, and Nankin.

131 Colonel Lake was transferred from the Madras Engineers to the Royal Army as a Lieut.-Colonel Unattached for his services at the defence of Kars (*CB.* and 2nd Class of the Medjidie).

131† Colonel Payne served with the Royal Marine Brigade in the Crimea and at the surrender of Kinbourn in 1855 (Medal).

132 Colonel John Watson served with the 14th Regt. in the trenches at the siege of Sebastopol and assault of the 18th June (Medal and Clasp).

133 Colonel Going landed in the Crimea with the 2nd Battalion Royal Regiment on the 22nd April 1855, and was at the siege and fall of Sebastopol (Medal and Clasp, and 5th Class of the Medjidie).

133† Colonel Douglas served the Eastern campaign of 1854-55 in command of the 11th Hussars, including the affair of Bulganak, battles of Alma, Balaklava, and Inkerman, and siege of Sebastopol (Medal and Clasps, *CB.*, Knight of the Legion of Honor, and 4th Class of the Medjidie).

134 Colonel Finucane has served in Spain, France, Italy, the Mediterranean, Jamaica, and India. In 1814 he was with the Austrian Army in Italy and at the surrender of Genoa. He was in several affairs in Ava during the Burmese War: also at the storming of Bhurtpore. In the Spanish service in 1835, 36, as Lieut.-Colonel on the Staff, and has received the Cross of St. Fernando; also the War Medal for India with two Clasps.

135 Colonel Daubeney served with the 55th Regt. in the Coorg campaign, East Indies, in 1834, and was present at the assault and capture of the stockade of Kissenhully, and at the attack on the stockade of Soamwarpettah, where he had charge of one of the two guns attached to the Column, which by his perseverance and exertions he saved from capture during the retreat, served during the Chinese war of 1841-42, commanded the Light Company at the repulse of the enemy's night-attack at Chinhae, and at the storm and capture of Chapoo; served on the staff as Major of Brigade to Sir James Schoedde at Woosung, Shanghai, and Chinkiangfoo—twice mentioned in Dispatches (Medal, Brevet Major, and *CB.*). Served the Eastern

campaign of 1854, including the battles of Alma and Inkerman (wounded and horse shot), siege of Sebastopol, and repulse of the sortie of 26th October. Commanded the 55th Regt. at the battle of Inkerman, and succeeded to the command of the 1st Brigade, 2nd Division, after Colonel Warren was wounded, and brought it out of action—mentioned in Division Orders for the Alma and in the Dispatches for Inkerman (Medal and three Clasps, Knight of the Legion of Honor, and 4th Class of the Medjidie).

136 Colonel Sterling served the Eastern campaign of 1854-55, first as a Brigade-Major and afterwards as Assistant Adjutant-General to the Highland Division, including the battles of the Alma, Balaklava, and Inkerman, and siege of Sebastopol (Medal and Clasps, CB., Officer of the Legion of Honor, and 4th Class of the Medjidie).

137 Colonel Seagram served with the 45th Regt. in the Kaffir war of 1846-47 (Medal, and Brevet Major).

138 Colonel J. Stewart Wood served the Coorg campaign in 1834, in the Light Company of the 48th Regt.; he was on the storming parties of the Stoney River and the several stockades leading to the capture of the Huggal Pass, and at the taking of the hill fort of Nucknaud. He was throughout the campaigns in Affghanistan:—in 1838 and 39 as Aide-de-Camp to Sir Robert Sale; in 1840, 41, and 42 as Adjutant to the 13th Regt., and was on the storming party of the fortress of Ghuznee (Medal); on the storming party of the town and fort of Tootumdurrah; had charge of and planted the ladders at the storm of Joolghur (wounded); was in the night attack at Baboo Koosh Ghur, the destruction of Kardurrah, battle of Perwandurrah; at the storming of the Khoord Cabool Pass; in the skirmish of Tezeen; the forcing of the Jugdulluck Pass, reduction of the fort of Mamoo Khail, in the heroic defence of Jellalabad (wounded 17th March 1842), and in the sorties on the 14th Nov. and 1st Dec. 1841, 11th March, 24th March, and 1st April 1842; the battle of Jellalabad and defeat of the besieging force under Akbar Khan on the 7th April 1842—horse sabred under him (Medal). Was on the storming party of the Jugdulluck Pass, in the battle of Tezeen, and at the re-capture of Cabool (Medal). Served the Eastern campaign of 1854-55, as Assist. Adjutant-General to the 3rd Division and subsequently to Head Quarters, including the battle of Alma, capture of Balaklava, battle of Inkerman, and siege operations before Sebastopol, with the exception of the last attack (Medal and three Clasps, CB., Knight of the Legion of Honor, and 4th Class of the Medjidie).

138† Colonel Greathed served with the 8th Regt. at the siege of Delhi in 1857 (in command from 30th June to the end of the siege), present at the repulse of Sorties on the 9th, 14th, and 18th July, and commanded the 3d Brigade during the repulse of the enemy's attack on 23d July; commanded the Column sent to occupy the Khoodsiabagh and Ludlow Castle on 7th Sept. by which operation the batteries were advanced to within 180 yards of the walls; led the Regt. to the assault and served with it in the City; on the 24th Sept. left Delhi in command of a Movable Column and defeated the enemy at Bolundshur, Allyghur, and Agra; commanded the 3d Brigade of the Army under Lord Clyde from 10th Nov. 57 to 9th Jan. 58 and present at the action of Dilkoosha in Lucknow during the operations resulting in the relief of the garrison; commanded advanced pickets at Cawnpore from 30th Nov. to 7th Dec., including the affair of the 2d action of the 6th Dec., also present in the action of Khudagunj and occupation of Futtehghur (CB., and promoted Colonel for distinguished service in the field).

139 Colonel the Hon. Robert Rollo was one of two officers sent from Malta on a special mission to Tripoli in 1846 and received the thanks of the Secretaries for Foreign Affairs and Colonies conveyed through the Commander-in-Chief for his services upon that occasion. He embarked with the 42nd for the East and served with the Regt. in the campaign of 1854-55; was Brigade-Major from the battle of Balaklava and throughout the winter until he took command of his Regt.; commanded it upon the expedition to Kertch and surrender of Yenikale, and afterwards in the siege of Sebastopol and assault of the outworks on the 18th June (Medal and Clasps, Brevet Lieut.-Colonel, and 5th Class of the Medjidie).

139† Colonel Thorold served in the Indian campaign in 1857, and commanded the 42d Highlanders in the action at Cawnpore on 6th Dec. (horse shot) and at Seriaghat (Medal).

140 Colonel Hon. St. George G. Foley served the Eastern campaign of 1854-55, as Assistant Commissioner at the Head-Quarters of the French Army, and was present at various affairs connected with the siege and fall of Sebastopol (Medal and Clasps, CB., Officer of the Legion of Honor, and 4th Class of the Medjidie).

141 Colonel Kelsall served in Canada during the insurrection in 1837-38, and was named in General Orders, for dislodging a number of Brigands from two islands on the Detroit River and Lake Erie in the winter of 1838.

141† Colonel E. A. Somerset served with the Rifle Brigade in the Kaffir war of 1852-53 (Medal). Also the Eastern campaign of 1854-55, including the battles of Alma, Balaklava, and Inkerman, and siege of Sebastopol (Medal and Clasps, Knight of the Legion of Honor, and 5th Class of the Medjidie).

142 Colonel Clark Kennedy served with the 18th on the China expedition in 1842 (Medal), and was present at the investment of Nankin. Was Assist. Qr. Mas. Gen. to the force under Major-General D'Aguilar throughout the combined naval and military operations in the Canton River in April 1847, when the forts of the Bocca Tigris, the Staked Barrier, and of the city of Canton were taken. Served the whole of the Punjaub campaign of 1848-49 (Medal and two Clasps), and was present as Aide-de-Camp to Sir W. Whish at the first siege of Mooltan,—storming the Seikh intrenched position Sept. 12th, raising the siege, operations previous to and action of Soorjkoond Nov. 7th (attached to Brigadier Markham): second siege of Mooltan,—action of Dec. 27th, storm of the city Jan. 2nd. surrender of the citadel Jan. 22nd: surrender of the Fort and Garrison of Cheniote, battle of Goojerat. Appointed Aide-de-Camp to Brigadier-Gen. Mountain, and was present at the pursuit of the Seiks and the passage of the

Jhelum. Was then attached to the Staff of Sir Walter Gilbert, and present at the surrender of the Seikh army and guns; and the forced march upon Attock, which drove the Affghans across the Indus. Appointed Aide-de-Camp to Brigadier-Gen. Sir Colin Campbell, and was present at the advance upon and occupation of Peshawur 21st March 1849. Served in the Crimea from Dec. 1854 at the siege of Sebastopol: commanded the advanced wing of the 18th Royal Irish, the leading regiment of Eyre's Brigade in the assault of the 18th of June, and was wounded in the neck; appointed Assist.-Adj.-General at Hd.-Qrs. 10th Aug.; present at the assault on 8th Sept. (Medal and Clasp, CB., Sardinian Medal, and 5th Class of the Medjidie).

143 Colonel Bunbury served with the expedition through the Kohat Pass in 1850, as Aide-de-Camp to Sir Charles Napier. Served also the Eastern campaign of 1854-55, including the battle of Inkerman and siege of Sebastopol (Medal and Clasps, CB., Knight of the Legion of Honor, and 5th Class of the Medjidie).

145 Colonel Reynell-Pack served the Eastern campaign from Feb. 1855 at the siege of Sebastopol with the 7th Fusiliers, and was severely wounded when commanding the Regiment at the assault of the Redan on the 18th June (Medal and Clasp, CB., Knight of the Legion of Honor, and 5th Class of the Medjidie).

146 Colonel Claremont has received the Medal and Clasps, the Brevets of Major and Lieut.-Colonel, CB., Knight of the Legion of Honor, and 4th Class of the Medjidie, for his services in the late war with Russia.

147 Colonel John Fraser served in the Peninsula with the 53rd from Aug. 1811 to the end of that war in 1814, including the siege and capture of the fortified convents at Salamanca, battle of Salamanca, siege of the castle of Burgos, battles of Vittoria, the Pyrenees, the Nivelle, and Toulouse. Severely wounded at Pampeluna on the 26th July 1813. He has received the War Medal with five Clasps.

148 Colonel Wade served throughout the campaigns in Affghanistan from 1838 to 1842 inclusive,—he was Adjutant of the 13th at the storm and capture of Ghuznee (Medal), and Major of Brigade at the assault and capture of the town and forts of Tootumdurrah, storm of Jhoolghur, night attack at Baboo Koosh Ghur, destruction of Khardurrah, and assault of Perwandurrah. Present with the 13th at the storming of the Koord Cabool Pass (wounded), affair of Tezeen, forcing the Jugdulluck Pass, reduction of the fort of Mamoo Khail, heroic defence of Jellalabad and sorties on the 14th Nov. and 1st Dec. 1841, 11th March, 24th March, and 1st April, 1842; general action and defeat of Akbar Khan before Jellalabad (Medal), storming the heights of Jugdulluck, general action of Tezeen, and recapture of Cabool (Medal). Has the Order of the Dooranée Empire of the 3rd Class.

149 Colonel Hale served the Sutlej campaign of 1845-6 with the 3rd Light Dragoons and was present at the battles of Moodkee, Ferozeshah, and Sobraon (Medal and Clasps).

150 Colonel Pearson served at the siege of Bhurtpore, and was a volunteer for the dismounted cavalry storming party. He served also in the action at Maharajpore, 29th Dec. 1843 (Medal), and in the campaign on the Sutlej in 1846, including the battles of Buddiwal, Aliwal, and Sobraon: at Aliwal he commanded the right wing of the 16th Lancers, and subsequently the Regiment, as also at Sobraon.

151 Colonel Percival Brown served with the 41st in the Burmese war in 1824-25 (Medal).

152 Colonel Mylius served with the 26th throughout the China expedition (Medal), and was present at the first capture of Chusan, the operations before Canton from the 24th to the 31st May 1841, at Woosung, Shanghae, Chin Kiang Foo, and Nanking.

153 Colonel Creagh served in the Anglo-Spanish Legion, and was engaged on the heights of Arlaban in Alava, on the 16th, 17th, and 18th January 1836, besides several other affairs. He was also employed on a Particular service in Canada at the outbreak of the rebellion in 1837. Has received a Gold Medal from the Sultan for his services on the Danube.

155 Colonel Blacklin served with the 3rd Battalion Royals at Quatre Bras 16th June, the retreat on the 17th, and carried the King's Colour at Waterloo on the 18th (at which last he was wounded), capture of Paris, and with the army of occupation in France in 1815 and 1816. Embarked to join the 2nd battalion in the East Indies, and served with the army in the Deccan the campaigns of 1817, 18, and 19; the pursuit of the Nagpore Rajah; battle of Nagpore, and other minor actions and skirmishes. Served with Sir John Doveton's force in pursuit of the Peishwa; the siege of Asseerghur in 1819, and commanded the leading company at the assault; served afterwards in the West Indies and Turkey.

156 Colonel Faunce commanded the Light Company of the 4th Regt. at the recapture of the Fort of Nepaunce on the 21st Feb. 1841.

157 Colonel Prior served in the Peninsula with the 11th Dragoons, and was present at the battle of Salamanca, and various outpost affairs. Served also the campaign of 1815; commanded the skirmishes of the 18th Hussars on the 17th June, and received the first fire of the French army on that day; present also at the battle of Waterloo and capture of Paris. He has received the War Medal with one Clasp for Salamanca.

158 Colonel Mayow served the Eastern Campaign of 1854-55, first as a Brigade-Major and afterwards as Assistant Quartermaster-General to the Cavalry Division, including the battles of the Alma, Balaklava, and Inkerman, and siege of Sebastopol (Medal and Clasps, Knight of the Legion of Honor, Sardinian Medal, and 4th Class of the Medjidie).

159 Colonel Bourchier served in France with the army under the Duke of Wellington from 1815 to 1818; and in Canada during the insurrection in 1838 and 39, and was employed at Prescot, under Colonel Young, in organizing the Militia of that section of the Province.

160 Colonel Lloyd served the campaign of 1815 and was present at the battle of Waterloo, taking of Cambray, and capture of Paris. Served one campaign latter part of 1826 against the Rajah of Kolapore. Also the campaign in the Southern Mahratta Country in 1844 (including the storming of Punella), and that in the Concan in 1845.

161 Colonel Congdon served with the R. M. Battalion on the north coast of Spain during the Carlist War. Served with the expedition to the Baltic in 1855 (Medal).

LIEUTENANT-COLONELS.

	CORNET, 2d LIEUT. or ENSIGN.	LIEUT.	CAPTAIN.	MAJOR.	LIEUT.-COLONEL.	WHEN PLACED ON HALF PAY.
Rodolphe de May, *Lieut. Col.*, h. p. Watteville's Regiment	never	never	1 May 01	13 Nov. 06	21 May 12	24 Oct. 16
¶ Gabriel Burer, *Lieut. Col.*, Unattached	....	30 Dec. 97	24 Nov. 03	1 July 13	3 July 17	22 Mar. 27
¶ Benjamin Graves, *Major*, h. p. 12 Foot	April 95	19 Sept. 95	26 Aug. 04	24 Sept. 12	27 May 25	25 Jan. 18
William Leader Maberly, *Lt. Col.*, Unattached. *A Commissioner of the Audit Board.*	....	23 Mar. 97	14 May 18	19 May 25	30 Dec. 26	9 Mar. 32
Charles Hamilton Smith, KH., *Captain*, h. p. 15 Foot	....	30 Dec. 97	18 Jan. 06	13 Dec. 13	22 July 30	25 Oct. 21
¶ James Poole Oates, KH.,[3] *Captain*, h. p. 88 Foot	3 Mar. 97	12 May 97	19 Oct. 04	3 Mar. 14	do 26	6 Mar. 18
James Horton,[4] *Major*, h. p. Meuron's Regt.	5 Aug. 99	16 May 99	1 23 July 07	18 May 14	do 30	Sept. 19
John Thomas Whelan,[5] *Captain*, h. p. R. Newfoundland Fencibles	....	31 May 99	24 Nov. 03	4 June 14	do 25	June 16
¶ Henry Nooth,[7] *Captain*, h. p. 14 Foot	never	27 July 99	22 Aug. 04	do	10 Jan. 37	26 Mar. 18
¶ Carlisle Spedding,[8] *Captain*, h. p. 32 Foot	12 June 99	7 Aug. 00	17 July 06	12 Aug. 19	do 25	Aug. 21
Sir William Davison, KH., *Captain*, h. p. 2 Foot, *Equerry to H.R.H. the Duke of Cambridge*	never	never	25 Dec. 13	20 Oct. 21	do 25	Sept. 14
Marq. Guiseppe de Piro, CMG. *Lt. Col.* r. f. p. Royal Malta Fencibles	never	never	never	25 April 25	29 Dec. 37	
George Hunt Coryton,[9] *Lt. Col.*, h. p. Royal Marines	9 Nov. 05	22 Sept. 09	12 Oct. 32	9 Nov. 46	25 May 49	4 Sept. 51
Wm. Robert Brudenell Smith, *Major*, Unattached	29 July 24	28 Jan. 26	20 Mar. 27	21 June 39	11 Nov. 51	1 Mar. 44
Edward G. Wynyard, *Capt. & Lt. Col.*, Grenadier Guards	12 May 37	9 Jan. 38	25 Oct. 42		do	
Fred. C. Arthur Stephenson, CB., *Capt. § Lt. Col.*, Scots Fus. Guards		25 July 43	13 Jan. 46		do	
Charles Lygon Cocks, *Capt. § Lt. Col.*, Coldstream Guards	28 July 38	24 Jan. 40	7 Aug. 46		do	
Henry Poole Hepburn, *Capt. § Lt. Col.*, Scots Fus. Guards		19 Feb. 41	2 Oct. 46		do	
James Halkett, *Capt. § Lt. Col.*, Coldstream Guards	7 June 39	23 April 41	1 July 45		14 July 54	
Ralph Bradford, *Capt. § Lt. Col.*, Grenadier Guards		30 Oct. 40	19 Dec. 45		do	
Michael Bruce, *Capt. § Lt. Col.*, Coldstream Guards	2 Oct. 40	15 Dec. 40	30 Dec. 45		do	
Hon. Richard Charteris, *Capt. § Lt. Col.*, Scots Fusilier Guards		7 Oct. 40	14 May 47		do	
Dudley Wilmot Carleton, *Capt. § Lt. Col.*, Coldstream Guards	10 April 41	11 June 41	13 July 47		do	
Lord Augustus Charles Lennox FitzRoy,[15] *Lt. Col.*, Unatt., *Equerry to the Queen*	17 May 39	27 Aug. 41	30 July 47		do	
Francis Haygarth, *Capt. § Lt. Col.*, Scots Fusilier Guards	14 Feb. 40	21 May 41	30 Sept. 47		do	
James Talbot Airey, CB., *Capt. § Lt. Col.*, Coldstream Guards, *Aide-de-Camp to H.R.H. the Commander in Chief*	11 Feb. 30	3 May 33	22 July 42	11 Nov. 51	15 July 54	28 Nov. 55
F. W. H. Earl of Westmorland, *Capt. § Lt. Col.*, Coldstream Guards	24 Feb. 43	26 July 44	1 Aug. 48	7 June 49	20 Sept. 54	
Charles L. Brownlow Maitland, *Capt. § Lt. Col.*, Gren. Gds.		9 April 41	27 Mar. 46	15 Sept. 48	28 Sept. 54	
Lord Arthur Hay, *Capt. § Lt. Col.*, Grenadier Guards, *Assist. Adj. Gen. to Inspector-General of Foot Guards*		30 April 41	3 April 46		19 Oct. 54	
Henry Green Wilkinson, *Capt. § Lt. Col.*, Scots Fusilier Guards		13 Jan. 43	10 Dec. 47		3 Nov. 54	
Ullick Canning, *Lord Dunkellin*, *Capt. & Lt. Col.*, Coldstream Guards		27 Mar. 46	27 April 49		do	
Henry Edward Montresor, *Capt. & Lt. Col.*, Grenadier Guards	15 Dec. 40	14 May 41	31 Mar. 48		6 Nov. 54	
Hon. John Strange Jocelyn, *Capt. & Lt. Col.*, Coldstream Guards	7 Oct. 42	14 April 43	25 April 48		do	
William Gregory Dawkins, *Capt. & Lt. Col.*, Coldstream Guards	2 Aug. 44	6 Sept. 44	1 Sept. 48		do	
Clement William Strong, *Capt. & Lt. Col.* do.	18 Jan. 39	6 May 42			do	

Lieutenant-Colonels.

	ENSIGN, ETC.	LIEUT.	CAPTAIN.	MAJOR.	LIEUT.-COLONEL.	WHEN PLACED ON HALF PAY.
George Esdaile Elrington,[17] *Captain*, ret. f p.,[5] R. Veteran Battalion	28 Aug. 99	never	14 May 01	4 June 13	28 Nov. 54	
John Field Oldham, *Captain*, retired full pay, 8 R. Veteran Battalion	26 April 96	10 Feb. 97	4 Aug. 04	do	do	
Edward Goate,[15] *Captain*, retired full pay, 35 Foot	9 May 05	8 Jan. 07	27 June 11	22 July 30	do	
Joseph Williams,[16] *Captain*, retired full pay, Royal Marines	2 July 97	28 July 03	27 Aug. 11	do	do	
Philip Aubin,[18] *Major*, retired full pay, 57 Foot	14 Feb. 11	29 April 13	22 June 26	12 April 31	do	
Henry Clemens,[19] *Major*, retired full pay, 16 Foot	7 April 05	26 Aug. 07	1 Sept. 13	10 Jan. 37	do	
Julius Fleming, *Capt.*, do. R. Marines	22 Sept. 98	8 Mar. 04	27 July 14	do	do	
Peter John Willats,[20] *Major*, 48 Foot	31 Aug. 09	2 June 11	22 Dec. 14	do	do	
⚔ Richard Handcock,[22] *Capt.*, do. 46 Foot	10 Sept. 05	5 Nov. 06	30 July 18	do	do	
Frederick Wright,[23] *Captain*, do. R. Artillery	13 Sept. 05	1 June 06	29 April 20	do	do	
James Robert Colebrooke,[25] *Capt.*, do. R. Engrs.	1 June 10	1 May 11	20 Dec. 20	do	do	
John Bonamy,[26] *Captain*, do. R. Artillery	21 Mar. 06	3 June 06	31 Dec. 22	do	do	
Richard Manners,[27] *Captain*, do. 6 Foot	19 Dec. 11	10 Feb. 13	24 Jan. 23	28 June 38	do	
Ambrose Spong, *Captain*, do. 59 Foot	13 April 09	8 Feb. 10	22 May 23	do	do	
Isaac Richardson,[29] *Captain*, do. 60 Foot	15 Aug. 13	26 April 14	18 Nov. 24	do	do	
Robert Brown, *Captain*, do. 11 Foot	5 Dec. 05	1 Oct. 08	7 April 25	do	do	
James Jackson,[30] *Captain*, do. 16 Foot	2 May 08	8 June 09	do	do	do	
Lewis Shuldham Barrington Robertson,[31] *Capt.*, ret. f p. R. Artillery	2 Mar. 09	19 June 11	do	do	do	
William Raban, *Major*, retired full pay, 22 Foot	1 July 06	1 Feb. 08	29 July 25	do	do	
Thomas Hinton Hemmans, *Captain*, retired full pay, 78 Foot	3 Jan. 11	2 June 13	14 Feb. 28	18 Dec. 40	do	
William White Warburton,[32] *Capt.*, do. 67 Foot	15 May 11	2 Dec. 13	8 April 26	23 Nov. 41	do	
Martin Crean Lynch,[33] *Captain*, do. 14 Foot	17 Aug. 09	2 April 12	5 May 26	do	do	
Edward Boyd,[34] *Captain*, retired full pay, 29 Foot	11 Feb. 08	31 May 09	22 June 26	do	do	
Ewan M'Pherson,[35] *Captain*, do. 99 Foot	16 July 11	1 July 12	17 Aug. 26	do	do	
James Smith Law, *Captain*, do. do.	21 Jan. 13	5 Feb. 14	26 April 27	do	do	
John Pascoe,[37] *Captain*, do. do.	3 Nov. 07	16 July 08	6 Nov. 27	do	do	
George Spiller,[38] *Captain*, do. R. Artillery	4 April 08	29 July 08	do	do	do	
William Dempster, *Captain*, do. do.	2 May 08	7 Nov. 08	do	do	do	
Charles Rayner Newman,[29] *Major*, do. 41 Foot	9 Feb. 09	11 April 11	26 Feb. 28	do	do	
John Joseph Grier, *Captain*, do. 14 Foot	28 Sept. 09	15 Aug. 11	1 May 28	do	do	
Alexander Campbell,[40] *Captain*, do. 93 Foot	11 Sept. 17	9 April 25	31 July 28	do	do	
Henry Dixon, *Captain*, do. 38 Foot	17 Dec. 13	26 Nov. 21	25 Sept. 28	do	do	
James Poyntz,[41] *Captain*, do. 81 Foot	20 Aug. 12	21 Dec. 15	21 Nov. 28	do	do	
William Greenwood,[42] CB., *Capt.*, do. 30 Foot	14 April 14	19 July 15	28 Dec. 28	do	do	
Francis Smith Hamilton,[43] *Capt.*, do. R. Artillery	17 Dec. 12	22 May 15	22 Jan. 34	23 Dec. 42	do	
James Lynn,[44] *Captain*, do. R. Marines	2 May 11	2 Oct. 29	7 Nov. 38	do	do	
Edward Kenny,[45] *Major*, do. R. Engrs.	22 Sept. 26	13 Nov. 31	1 May 43	28 July 43	do	
John O'Grady,[46] *Major*, do. 89 Foot	17 June 13	1 Nov. 19	4 Dec. 32	26 Feb. 45	do	
⚔ Anthony Robt. L'Estrange,[47] *Maj.* do. 71 Foot	20 Sept. 10	22 Sept. 13	26 May 31	27 June 45	do	
	7 Dec. 14	20 Dec. 21	7 Jan. 30	14 April 46	do	

50

Lieutenant-Colonels.

Name	Ensign, etc.	Lieut.	Captain.	Major.	Lieut.-Colonel.	When placed on half pay.
John Thomas Griffiths, *Major*, retired full pay, 25 Foot	6 Sept. 14	17 May 21	1 Sept. 31	7 Aug. 46	28 Nov. 54	
Robert Alex. Andrews, *Captain*, ret. full pay, 30 Foot	18 Aug. 14	27 Mar. 24	20 Aug. 29	9 Nov. 46	do	
Benoit Bender,[48] *Captain*, do. 82 Foot	29 Dec. 14	4 April 24	26 Nov. 30	do	do	
D William Atkin,[49] *Captain*, do. R. Canadian Rifles	9 Mar. 10	2 July 11	31 Dec. 30	do	do	
Abraham Splaine, *Captain*, do. 81 Foot	28 Oct. 24	22 April 26	16 Mar. 32	do	do	
James Ward, *Captain*, do. do.	25 May 15	23 June 25	6 July 32	do	do	
D John Norman,[50] *Major*, do. 54 Foot	2 July 12	9 Nov. 15	9 July 32	do	do	
Angus William Mackay,[51] *Captain*, do. 21 Foot	24 July 02	30 June 08	27 July 32	do	do	
John Bolton,[52] *Captain*, do. 75 Foot	5 Nov. 13	26 Mar. 19	4 Sept. 35	do	do	
William Barnes,[53] *Captain*, do. 17 Foot	4 Feb. 13	23 July 14	14 Sept. 35	do	do	
Daniel Riley,[54] *Captain*, do. 24 Foot	13 Jan. 25	15 Dec. 25	25 Oct. 35	do	do	
Henry Alexander Kerr, *Capt.*, do. 1 Foot	17 Aug. 26	22 Mar. 32	18 Mar. 36	do	do	
William Beales, *Captain*, do. Unattached	24 June 13	12 Aug. 22	12 Aug. 36	do	do	
E James Fyumore,[55] *Captain*, do. R. Marines	1 Sept. 22	15 Nov. 36	do	do		
William Devonish Devcrell, *Lt. Col.*, Depôt Battalion	4 May 08	4 May 15	16 Nov. 20	7 April 37	5 Mar. 47	
Charles Edward Michel, *Lt. Col.*, 54 Foot	25 Nov. 28	23 Nov. 33	2 Feb. 38	25 June 47	do	
William Twisleton Layard, *Lt. Col.* Ceylon Rifle Regt.	22 Feb. 15	22 Nov. 23	16 Aug. 38	28 Sept. 47	do	
William Newhouse,[56] *Captain*, retired full pay, 5 Foot	14 Sept. 17	Sept. 18	13 Jan. 39	11 Nov. 51	do	
William M'Kinnon, *Captain*, do. 38 Foot	13 Mar. 03	18 Apr. 26	8 June 38	do	do	
Charles Irvine, *Captain*, do. R. Marines	9 Apr. 25	17 May 26	4 May 39	do	do	
Chas. Cartwright Williamson, *Capt.* do. do.	25 May 11	18 Dec. 26	26 Aug. 39	do	do	
John Gage Lecky, *Captain*, do. 38 Foot	22 April 26	26 Mar. 29	10 April 40	do	do	
George Markland, *Captain*, ret. full pay, Royal Artillery	9 April 20	12 Nov. 27	20 July 40	do	do	
Richard Howorth,[58] *Captain*, ret. full pay, Royal Engineers	6 Aug. 25	11 April 27	7 Sept. 40	do	do	
Frederick Tudor,[59] *Captain*, ret. full pay, 38 Foot	25 Nov. 24	29 Sept. 24	29 Sept. 40	do	do	
George Adams Barnes, *Captain*, ret. full pay, St. Helena Regt.	12 Dec. 22	23 Sept. 22	30 Oct. 40	do	do	
Charles Wm. Pearce, *Captain*, retired full pay, Royal Marines	26 Mar. 34	1 Dec. 31	6 Nov. 40	do	do	
Joseph Henry Laye, *Major*, Depot Battalion	2 May 34	1 Dec. 37	6 Mar. 41	20 June 54	do	
Powrie Ellis, *Lt.-Col.*, h. p., Royal Artillery	31 July 31	28 Dec. 32	26 Nov. 42	20 Nov. 54	4 Oct. 56	
George Grattan Biscoe, *Capt.*, retired full pay, 66 Foot	7 April 8	12 Feb. 36	27 Sept. 39	11 Nov. 54	1 Dec. 51	
Hugh Thomas Bowen, *Capt.*, retired full pay, 72 Foot	18 May 32	6 June 34	12 Feb. 42	20 June 54	do	
William Charles Forrest, *Lt.-Col.*, 7 Dragoon Guards	11 Mar. 36	5 Jan. 39	7 Sept. 41	3 Oct. 48	12 Dec. 54	
Hon. James William Bosville Macdonald, CB., [60] *Major*, Unatt., *Equerry and Aide de Camp* to H.R.H. the Duke of Cambridge	1 Oct. 29	24 Jan. 34	24 June 37	19 Oct. 49	do	
Robert Julian Baumgartner, CB.,[61] *Lt.-Col.*, 27 Foot	27 Sept. 33	30 June 37	23 April 41	23 Sept. 51	do	12 Dec. 54
Robert Blane,[61] CB. *Major*, Unatt. *Assist. Adjutant General, Dublin*	1 Nov. 31	25 Mar. 36	8 June 38	11 Nov. 51	do	
George Calvert Clarke, *Major*, 2 Dragoons	30 May 24	7 Oct. 31	20 Sept. 39	do	do	
George Valentine Edward Mundy, CB., *Lt. Col.*, 19 Foot	never	27 Feb. 35	1 May 45	do	do	
John Lucas Wilton,[62] CB., *Lt.-Col.*, Unattached	13 Mar. 27	16 Mar. 32	15 July 45	28 May 52	do	12 Dec. 54
Charles F. Fordyce,[63] CB. *Lt.-Col.*, Unatt., *Assist. Qr.-Mr. Gen. in Nova Scotia*	17 Feb. 38	3 July 40	30 Jan. 46	12 Oct. 52	do	28 Aug. 57

Lieutenant-Colonels.

	ENSIGN, ETC.		LIEUT.		CAPTAIN.		MAJOR.		LIEUT.-COLONEL.		WHEN PLACED ON HALF PAY.	
Henry Hume, CB. *Capt. and Lt.Col.*, Grenadier Guards	9 May	35	1 Dec.	37	19 Jan.	44	24 Dec.	52	12 Dec.	54		
Frederick Aurelius Wiltimper, [64] *Lt. Col.*, Unatt., *Major of the Tower of London*	23 Jan.	33	31 Mar.	38	5 Oct.	41	24 June	53	do		19 Sept.	54
George Aug. Filmer Salivar, *Lt. Col.*, 5 Lancers	29 July	36	26 Feb.	40	5 April	44	17 Feb.	54	do			
Henry Edward McGee, *Lt. Col.*, 3 West India Regt.	4 Sept.	40	3 Feb.	43	8 Aug.	45	14 April	54	do		10 July	55
Hon. James Pierce Maxwell, [65] *Lt. Col.*, Unattached	6 June	34	5 May	40	25 Aug.	41	20 June	54	do			
George Erskine, *Lt. Col.*, Military Train	17 Aug.	32	3 June	36	14 April	43	do		do		15 June	55
Thomas Scott Hawkins, [67] *Major*, Unattached	20 Mar.	32	17 Sept.	36	23 June	46	do		do		22 June	58
Edmund Yates Peel, [68] *Major*, Unattached	18 Mar.	38	3 Mar.	46	3 Nov.	46	do		do			
John Miller Adye, C.B., *Lt. Col.*, Royal Artillery	13 Dec.	36	7 July	38	29 July	46	22 Sept.	54	do			
Walter Raleigh Gilbert, *Lt. Col.*, h. p, Royal Artillery	16 Dec.	31	17 Oct.	33	4 April	43	20 June	54	13 Dec.	54	13 Jan.	55
Alexander Graham Wilkinson Hamilton, *Capt.*, ret. f. p., R. Artillery	16 Dec.	31	17 Dec.	33	1 May	43	20 June	54	27 Dec.	54		
Wilmot Henry Bradford, *Lt. Col.* Royal Canadian Rifles	24 May	33	26 Aug.	36	27 Aug.	41	8 Aug.	51	20 Dec.	54		
Hector Harvest, *Major*, Unattached	20 April	15	7 April	25	28 June	25	18 July	48	30 Jan.	55	18 July	48
James Dundas Gregory Tulloch, *Capt.*, h. p., 84 Foot, *Staff Officer of Pensioners*	18 July	30	14 Feb.	34	22 Aug.	34	20 June	54	9 Feb.	55	16 Feb.	44
William R. Preston, *Major*, 45 Foot	24 Sept.	21	22 Feb.	33	18 Oct.	39	19 July	48	20 Feb.	55		
Benjamin Beaufoy, [69] *Capt.*, ret. f. p., *Staff Officer of Pensioners*	8 Mar.	10	8 Oct.	12	14 Aug.	40	11 Nov.	51	30 Mar.	55		
John Cameron Macpherson, [70] *Major*, ret. full pay, 42 Foot	10 Sept.	30	21 June	33	6 Mar.	40	11 Nov.	51	24 April	55		
Hon. William Fred. Scarlett, *Capt. & Lt. Col.*, Scots Fus. Guards	14 April	46	12 June	46	23 Nov.	49	12 Dec.	54	do			
John Lardner, [72] *Major*, ret. full pay, 47 Foot	2 Sept.	22	2 July	25	2 Jan.	40	11 May	51	4 May	55		
Charles Clement Deacon, CB., *Lt. Col.*, 61 Foot	28 Aug.	35	2 Dec.	37	26 July	44	19 Aug.	49	11 May	55		
Joseph Wilkinson, *Major*, retir.d full pay, Rifle Brigade	30 Dec.	39	15 April	42	12 Jan.	47	29 Dec.	54	1 June	55		
Thomas Conyngham Kelly, CB., *Capt. & Lt. Col.*, Grenadier Guards	8 April	28	31 Aug.	30	6 May	43	20 July	49	15 June	55		
James Fred. D. C. Stuart, *Capt. & Lt. Col.*, Grenadier Guards	never		25 Oct.		12 Feb.	47	never		19 June			
Lord Fred. John FitzRoy, *Capt. & Lt. Col.*, Grenadier Guards	18 Sept.	40	14 July	43	31 Mar.	48	...		22 June	55		
Aug. Wm. Henry Meyrick, do., Scots Fus. Guards	never		8 Sept.	46	22 Feb.	50	...		do			
Alexander Essex F. Holcombe, *Lt. Col.*, 1 Foot	3 Dec.	30	12 Sept.	34	22 July	42	9 Aug.	50	26 June	55		
Joseph Samuel Adamson, [71] *Major*, ret. full pay, 38 Foot	15 Mar.	31	27 Sept.	33	1 Dec.	37	11 Nov.	51	29 June	55		
Arthur James Herbert, [74] *Lt. Col.*, Unatt., *Deputy Quarter Master General Ionian Islands*	5 April	39	15 April	42	8 Aug.	46	21 Sept.	54	17 July	55		
James Villiers, *Lt. Col.*, 74 Foot	31 Mar.	39	24 Sept.	41	24 Dec.	44	12 Dec.	54	do			
John Simpson, CB., *Lt. Col.*, 34 Foot	13 Mar.	35	3 Nov.	37	26 Jan.	44	29 Dec.	54	do			
James Ramsay, [75] *Major*, Unattached	18 May	32	19 May	34	30 Mar.	44	2 Aug.	50	20 July	55	29 April	56
Henry Furey Wakefield, [76] *Captain*, retired full pay, 28 Foot	17 Dec.		29 May	32	30 Dec.	43	20 June	51	do			
Charles Robert Shuckburgh, [77] *Captain*, ret. f. pay, *Staff Officer of Pensioners*	5 July	11	5 Aug.	13	21 June	39	11 Nov.	51	17 Aug.	55		
James Richardson, [78] *Captain*, retired full pay, *Staff Off. of Pensioners*	7 April	20	3 Nov.	25	2 April	41	20 June	54	do			
Thomas Donovan, *Major*, Cape Mounted Riflemen	15 Mar.	27	16 May	33	19 Nov.	41	15 Sept.	48	31 Aug.	55		
Henry Fred. Ponsonby, *Capt. & Lt. Col.*, Grenadier Guards, *Equerry to H.R.H. the Prince*	27 Dec.	42	16 Feb.	44	18 July	4.	19 Oct.	49	do			
William Wild Joseph Cockcraft, [79] *Capt.*, ret. full pay, 58 Foot	8 April	25	22 April	26	20 July	39	11 Nov.	51	do			
Peter Redmond Jennings, [80] *Major*, ret. full pay, 13 Foot	5 Aug.	30	13 Jan.	32	13 Jan.	42	20 June	54	do			
Oliver Pacet Bourke, [81] *Lt.Col.* h. p., 17 Foot	11 Dec.	35	27 Oct.	37	7 Nov.	44	3 Dec.	52	7 Sept.	55		
Richard Saunders, *Capt.*, ret. f. p., R. Newfoundland Companies	4 Nov.	09	25 Oct.	10	26 Oct.	41	20 June	54	do		10 Nov.	50

Lieutenant-Colonels.

	ENSIGN, ETC.	LIEUT.	CAPTAIN.	MAJOR.	LIEUT.-COLONEL.	WHEN PLACED ON HALF PAY.
Hon. Leicester Curzon, *Captain, Rifle Brigade, Assistant Military Secretary, Ionian Islands*	29 Nov. 45	12 Nov. 47	22 Dec. 54	17 July 55	8 Sept. 55	
Charles Sillery, *Lt.Col. h. p., 30 Foot, Deputy Quarter Master General in New Zealand*	24 Nov. 2	20 July 30	15 Mar. 38	11 Nov. 51	9 Sept. 55	
Robert Pratt, CB., *Lt.Col., 23 Foot*	16 June	27 June 37	23 Sept. 39	29 Dec. 54	do	
Bertie Edward Murray Gordon, *Lt.Col., 91 Foot*	26 Oct.	24 July 32	23 April 35	13 Oct. 48	30 Sept. 55	
Mottram Andrews, [83] *Major, retired full pay, 28 Foot*	9 April	24 July 2	24 Aug. 28	20 June 54	9 Oct. 55	
Henry Crawley, [84] *Major, retired full pay, 20 Foot, Major, South Gloucester Militia*	11 Oct.	11 June 30	9 Oct. 43	20 June 54	16 Oct.	
Arthur George Burrows, *Lt.Col., Royal Artillery*	19 Dec.	10 Jan. 34	26 Feb. 46	never	18 Oct.	
Charles Albert Denison, *Major, 52 Foot, Deputy Adjutant General at Madras*	22 Sept.	11 May 37	26 Oct. 41	20 June 54	23 Oct.	
William Lennox Ingall, CB., *Lt.Col., 62 Foot*	27 Dec.	23 July 42	7 Feb. 51	8 June 55	25 Oct.	
Roger Stuart Beatson, *Lt.Col., Royal Engineers*	29 May	3 May 32	26 Mar. 45	never	27 Oct.	
Thomas Pattle, *Lt.Col., 1 Drag. on Guards*	13 June	23 Dec. 34	18 Mar. 36	7 May 47	2 Nov. 55	
Francis Gregor Urquhart, *Major, 1 Foot*	18 Nov.	16 Aug. 31	7 May 36	13 Dec. 50	do	
Frederick Charles Aylmer, [85] *Lt.Col., Unattached*	4 Dec.	25 July 32	12 April 37	11 Nov. 51	do	
Alexander Murray, *Lt.Col., 87 Foot*	24 April	23 Oct. 30	20 May 34	30 Dec. 53	do	
Henry Augustus Strachan, [86] *Major, Unattached*	21 Sept.	2 June 32	20 Aug. 44	30 Dec. 53	do	
Hon. Charles Dawson Plunkett, *Major, 1 Foot*	1 Oct.	10 Mar. 35	5 June 39	20 June 54	do	
Kenneth Douglas Mackenzie, *Major, 32 Foot, Assistant Adjutant General, East Indies*	25 Nov.	9 Aug. 38	29 Dec. 43	do	12 Dec. 54	
William MacMahon, *Lt.Col., 44 Foot*	6 Nov.	28 Feb. 36	27 Sept. 44	12 Dec. 54	do	
William M'Call, [87] *Lt.Col., Unattached*	20 Nov.	8 June 38	14 Nov. 45	do	do	
John Josiah Hort, *Lt.Col., 36 Foot*	2 Oct.	30 Sept. 41	29 Dec. 46	do	do	
Robert Warden, *Lt.Col., 19 Foot*	8 Jan.	4 April 41	6 Aug. 47	do	do	
Hugh Smith, [88] *Major, Unatt., Assist. Adj.General, Cork*	6 June	1 Nov. 34	10 Dec. 47	do	do	9 Sept. 56
Joseph Edwin Thackwell, [89] *Major, Unattached*	19 June	7 April 41	26 May 48	do	do	
John Charles Wm. Fortescue, [90] *Major, Unatt.*	do	13 April 42	30 June 48	do	do	25 Jan. 56
Charles Henry Morris, CB. [91] *Major, h. p., Royal Artillery*	1 Jan.	12 Nov. 39	do 41	do	do	
Edmund Gilling Hallewell, [92] *Major, Unattached, Deputy Quarter Master General, Malta*	31 Dec.	15 April 43	1 Nov. 48	do	do	
Cuthbert George Ellison, *Capt. & Lt. Col., Grenadier Guards*	3 Nov.	5 April 44	29 Dec. 48	do	do	5 Aug. 57
William Sankey, *Major, 9 Foot*	9 April	8 Aug. 45	10 April 49	do	do	
William Inglis, *Lt.Col., 57 Foot*	7 Feb.	31 Dec. 40	27 April 49	do	do	
Edward Bruce Hamley, *Captain, Royal Artillery*	1 Jan.	15 Sept. 43	26 Oct. 49	do	do	8 July 56
George W. Alex. Higginson, *Capt. & Lt. Col., Grenadier Guards*	never	14 Feb. 45	14 May 50	do	do	
Lawrence Shadwell, [93] *Major, Unattached, Assistant Quarter Master General at Manchester*	6 April	17 Mar. 41	12 July 50	do	do	
John Hynde King, *Capt. & Lt. Col., Grenadier Guards*	25 June	7 July 44	7 Feb. 51	do	do	
George Gardiner Alexander, CB., *Lt.Col., Royal Marines*	4 Aug.	19 Jan. 38	10 Oct. 51	do	do	25 Sept. 57
Samuel Enderby Gordon, *Captain, Royal Artillery*	4 Aug.	19 Jan. 42	19 Jan. 52	do	do	24 May 59
Hon. Edward Thomas Gage, *Captain, Royal Artillery*	9 June	28 July 46	28 July 52	do	do	15 Jan. 56
Edward Stayton, CB., *Captain, Royal Engineers, Assist.Adjutant General*	9 Dec.	do	1 Sept. 52	do	do	
Eustace Fane Bonrchier, CB., *Captain, Royal Engineers*	do	do	20 June 54	do	do	
Horace William Montagu, *Captain, Royal Engineers*	1 Jan.	26 Dec. 42	9 Aug. 52	24 April 55	do	
		1 May 43	17 Feb. 54	do	do	

Lieutenant-Colonels.

Name	ENSIGN, ETC.	LIEUT.	CAPTAIN.	MAJOR.	LIEUT.-COLONEL.	WHEN PLACED ON HALF PAY
Colin Fred. Campbell, *Major*, 46 Foot	1 May 40	10 Mar. 42	13 Aug. 47	11 May 55	2 Nov. 55	
V℃ Fred. Francis Maude, CB., *Lt.Col.*, 3 Foot	13 Mar. 40	27 Aug. 41	10 Dec. 47	15 May 55	do	
Alfred Capel Cure, *Capt. & Lt.Col.*, Grenadier Guards	30 July 44	9 April 47	17 Aug. 52	25 May 55	do	
Edward Herbert Maxwell, *Lt.Col.*, 88 Foot	26 April 39	16 Nov. 41	8 Oct. 47	8 June 55	do	
James Daubeny, CB., *Major*, 62 Foot	4 July 45	28 April 46	6 July 52	8 June 55	do	
V℃ Matthew Charles Dixon, *Captain*, Royal Artillery	19 Mar. 39	11 April 41	30 June 48	17 July 55	do	
Charles Stuart Henry, *Captain*, Royal Artillery	18 June 42	18 May 43	28 June 49	do	do	
William James Loftus, *Major*, 38 Foot	9 Nov. 38	8 Nov. 42	19 July 50	29 July 55	do	6 Feb. 57
Robert Grove, 94 *Lt.Col.* Unattached	7 Feb. 40	7 Mar. 45	24 Nov. 48	9 Oct. 55	do	
Edward Price, CB., *Lt.Col.* Royal Artillery	19 Dec. 34	28 Feb. 37	1 April 46	never		
James William Domville, *Lt.Col.* Royal Artillery	do	6 Feb. 37	do	never		
Charles Pyndar Beauchamp Walker, *Lt.Col.*, 2 Dragoon Guards	27 Feb. 36	21 June 39	22 Dec. 46	8 Dec. 54	9 Nov. 55	
Hon. Percy Rob. Basil Feilding, *Capt. & Lt.Col.*, Coldstream Guards, *Assist. Quarter Master General, Dublin Division*	8 Aug. 45	7 Aug. 46	21 Aug. 51	12 Dec. 54	23 Nov. 55	
Isaac Moore, *Lt.Col.* Depot Battalion	20 Feb. 35	29 June 38	20 Feb. 44	do	30 Nov. 55	
William Henry Reeve, *Capt. & Lt.Col.*, Coldstream Guards	never	29 Dec. 46	29 Aug. 51	never	do	
William Clarke, *Major*, Unattached (*Qr.-Master* 15 Sept. 37)	24 April 38	4 Jan. 41	25 Nov. 49	23 Nov. 48	18 Dec. 55	1 Oct. 56
Charles Bariner, *Capt. & Lt.Col.*, Coldstream Guards	never	2 July 47	29 April 53	12 Dec. 54	21 Dec. 55	
Henry F. F. Johnson, *Major*, h.-p. 5 Foot, *Deputy Quarter Master General in the Mauritius*	23 Nov. 36	23 April 39	20 Jan. 43	5 Oct. 49	31 Dec. 55	
James Dodington Carmichael, CB. *Lt.Col.*, 32 Foot	12 July 38	11 May 41	18 April 45	20 Feb. 55	1 Feb. 56	
Edmund Augustus Whitmore, *Lt.Col.*, Depot Battalion	6 Aug. 41	10 July 46	1 June 49	12 Dec. 54	15 Feb. 56	
Nathan Smith Gardiner, 95 *Major*, Unattached	23 June 32	18 Jan. 34	36 Jan. 41	24 Nov. 48	20 Feb. 56	25 Mar. 53
Sampson Freeth, *Lt.Col.*, Royal Engineers	26 Sept. 32	13 May 36	18 Mar. 45	never	23 Feb. 56	
George Ashley Maude, CB., *Lt.Col.*, R. Art. Crown Equerry; *Extra Aide-de-Camp to H.R.H. The Commander in Chief*	19 Dec. 34	27 Mar. 37	1 April 46	12 Dec. 54	do	
Evan Maberly, CB., *Lt.Col.*, Royal Artillery	18 June 35	24 June 37	do	never	do	
William Manley Hall Dixon, *Lt.Col.* do.	do	30 Oct. 37	do	never	do	
Henry John Thomas, 95 *Lt.Col.*, h.-p., do., *Major*, *Kent Art. Militia*	18 Dec. 35	1 Feb. 38	do	never	do	15 Sept. 57
Charles Higginbotham, 97 *Major*, retired full pay, 63 Foot	29 June 29	20 Sept. 33	30 June 44	29 Dec. 54	26 Feb. 56	
Charles Edward Fairlough, *Lt.Col.* Depot Battalion	12 May 37	31 Dec. 39	25 Aug. 46	17 July 55	7 Mar. 56	
Edmund Robert Wm. Wingfield Yates, *Lt.Col.* Unatt.	24 Mar. 37	27 Oct. 39	27 Oct. 48	7 Sept. 55	14 Mar. 56	
William Aitchison, *Capt. & Lt.Col.*, Scots Fusilier Guards	21 Mr. 45	2 Oct. 46	24 May 50	never	25 Mar. 56	
John Cassidy Stock, 98 *Captain*, retired full pay, 10 Foot	23 Mar. 26	1 Feb. 29	12 July 42	20 June 54	4 April 56	
Alexander Munro, *Major*, retired full pay, 16 Foot	6 Oct. 15	26 June 28	1 July 41	21 April 54	18 April 56	
Thomas Gibbings, *Lt.Col.*, 2 West India Regt.	15 Jan. 47	27 April 49	22 Oct. 52	9 June 54	29 April 56	
Hon. Henry Wm. John B'ng, *Capt. & Lt.Col.*, Coldstream Guards	never	27 Aug. 47	3 Mar. 54	never	2 May 56	13 Mar. 57
Samuel Wells, CB., *Lt.Col.*, 23 Foot	9 April 25	23 15 Sept. 37	16 Sept. 51	16 May 56		
James Tedlie, *Major*, retired full pay, 35 Foot	19 May 25	5 June 27	23 July 38	8 July 51	16 May 56	
Richard Walter Lacy, *Lt.Col.*, 56 Foot	19 Mar. 32	15 Sept. 37	1 May 46	13 July 55	16 May 56	
Reginald Yorge Shipley, *Lt.Col.*, 7 Foot	15 Dec. 43	11 Dec. 46	30 April 52	12 Dec. 55	27 May 56	

Lieutenant-Colonels.

	ENSIGN, ETC.	LIEUT.	CAPTAIN.	MAJOR.	LIEUT.-COLONEL.	WHEN PLACED ON HALF PAY.
Henry George Hart, 39 *Major*, h. p., Depot Battalion	1 April 29	19 July 32	1 Dec. 42	15 Dec. 48	30 May 55	1 Dec. 56
John Williams Reynolds, *Capt.*, Unatt., *Dep. Adj.Gen. in Jamaica*	18 Sept. 35	2 Nov. 38	10 Jan. 40	11 Nov. 51	6 June 54	
Edward W. C. Wright, *Major*, Depot Battalion	21 Dec. 32	13 Nov. 35	2 July 41	26 Feb. 52	do	
Lord Alexander G. Russell, *Lt. Col*, Rifle Brigade	11 July 39	15 April 42	7 Aug. 46	28 May 53	do	
James Henry Craig Robertson, *Major*, 100 Foot	2 July 35	30 Dec. 35	27 Feb. 35	20 June 54	do	
Charles Henry Gordon, CB., *Major*, Depot Battalion	24 Nov. 33	28 July 38	13 May 42	do	do	
George Fred. Stevenson Call, *Lt. Col.*, 18 Foot	7 April 37	20 Sept. 35	30 Dec. 42	do	do	
Thomas Harrie, *Lt. Col.*, 63 Foot	19 July 32	2 May 34	26 Jan. 44	6 Nov. 54	do	
Percy Archer Butler, *Lt. Col.*, 28 Foot	1 Mar. 39	2 May 42	4 April 45	12 Dec. 54	do	
Andrew Browne, *Major*, 44 Foot	30 April 41	14 Oct. 42	8 Sept. 46	do	do	
Henry Edwin Weare, *Major*, 50 Foot	22 Oct. 41	22 Dec. 43	26 May 48	do	do	
Julius Richard Glyn, CB., *Major*, Rifle Brigade	16 July 41	13 Oct. 43	9 June 48	do	do	
Henry Meade Hamilton, *Major*, 12 Foot	9 Aug. 39	26 Oct. 41	11 May 49	do	do	
Thomas Henry Pakenham, *Major*, 30 Foot	12 July 41	19 Mar. 27	24 Sept. 50	do	do	
Michael Anthony Shrapnel Biddulph, *Captain*, Royal Artillery	17 June 43	26 April 44	4 Oct. 50	do	do	
George Harry Smith Willis, 100 *Major*, Unatt., *Assist. Adj.Gen. at Malta*	23 April 41	30 Aug. 44	27 Dec. 50	do	do	
Cadwallader Adams, *Major*, 49 Foot	25 Sept. 45	28 Mar. 47	5 Dec. 53	do	do	
Hon. Augustus Murray Cathcart, *Major*, 96 Foot	25 Sept. 46	21 July 48	21 Oct. 53	do	do	
Lumley Graham, *Major*, 19 Foot	13 Aug. 47	28 Feb. 51	7 June 54	do	do	
Joseph Edward Addison, *Captain*, h. p. 97 F. *Member of the Council of Army Education*	31 Jan. 40	15 July 43	9 Aug. 50	16 Feb. 55	do	24 Jan. 51
John Gwilt, *Major*, 34 Foot	25 Nov. 36	10 Aug. 38	14 Feb. 45	17 July 55	do	
Henry Charles Cunliffe Owen, CB. *Capt.* R. Eng., *Deputy Insp.Gen.of Fortifications*	19 Mar. 39	30 Sept. 41	28 Oct. 47	do	do	
William Gordon, *Major*, 17 Foot	20 July 38	3 April 40	2 Feb. 49	do	do	
John E. Collings, *Lt. Col.*, 33 Foot	21 June 39	22 Jan. 42	3 Oct. 48	19 Sept. 55	do	
Thomas Smith, CB., *Lt. Col.*, 90 Foot	16 July 41	16 Sept. 45	20 April 49	2 Nov. 55	do	
George Graydon, *Lt. Col.* Royal Artillery	18 Dec. 35	23 Mar. 38	1 April 46	never	7 June 56	
John Graham M'Kerlie, *Lt. Col.* Royal Engineers	27 Feb. 33	23 Sept. 36	1 April 45	never	10 June 56	
William George Hamley, *Lt. Col.*, do	5 Aug. 33	25 Sept. 36	1 May 45	never	do	
*Lewis Charles Augustus Meyer, *late Riding Master, Cavalry Depot, Maidstone*	......	......	26 May 45	28 Nov. 41	13 June 56	
Andrew Beatty, *Lt. Col.*, Royal Engineers	5 Aug. 33	6 Nov. 36	22 May 46	never	14 June 56	
Henry Paget Christie, *Lt. Col.*, Royal Artillery	18 Dec. 35	11 June 38	1 April 46	never	do	
George Anthony Leaton Blenkinsopp, *Captain*, 45 Foot	4 Sept. 35	31 May 38	29 Mar. 44	22 Dec. 48	19 June 56	
Arthur Sandys Stawell Walsh, CB., *Lt. Col.*, Royal Marines	12 April 28	6 Dec. 36	26 Aug. 46	never	28 June 56	
John George Augustus Ayles, *Lt. Col.*, do	13 May 28	10 Jan. 37	10 Oct. 46	never	5 July 56	
Edward W. Scovell, *Lt. Col.*, 96 Foot	29 Dec. 35	2 Oct. 38	13 Dec. 46	20 June 54	8 July 56	
Charles James Conway Mills, *Lt. Col.*, 94 Foot	26 Dec. 34	28 Aug. 38	25 June 41	22 Aug. 51	11 July 56	
William Neville Custance, CB., *Lt. Col.*, 6 Dragoon Guards	26 Dec. 34	26 June 38	16 Mar. 38	16 Sept. 51	1 Aug. 56	
Marcus Dill, *Lt. Col.*, Royal Engineers	1 Dec. 38	10 Jan. 37	16 April 46	never	11 Aug. 56	
Henry Garner Rainey, *Major*, 61 Foot	12 April 31	8 June 33	27 Dec. 42	20 April 49	22 Aug. 56	

Lieutenant-Colonels.

Name	ENSIGN, ETC.	LIEUT.	CAPTAIN.	MAJOR.	LIEUT.-COLONEL.	WHEN PLACED ON HALF PAY.
John A. Cole, *Lt.Col.*, 15 Foot	14 Jan. 31	26 May 33	14 Dec. 38	11 Nov. 51	25 Aug. 56	
Rowland Moffat, *Lt.Col.*, Unattached	22 June 32	7 Aug. 35	27 Aug. 41	4 Mar. 53	5 Sept.	7 Dec. 58
Philip John Bainbrigge, *Lt.Col.*, Royal Engineers	1 Dec. 33	10 Jan. 37	1 April 46	never	10 Sept.	
John Francis Cust, *Capt. & Lt.Col.*, Grenadier Guards	26 July 33	2 Aug. 44	1 June 49	never	16 Sept.	
Edw. d'Alton,[101] *Capt.*, retired f. p., R. Newfoundland Company	13 June 34	2 Aug. 36	23 Sept. 39	11 Nov. 51	19 Sept.	
Paris Wm. Aug. Bradshaw, *Maj.* Unatt., Assist. Adj. Gen. in Tasmania	26 Dec. 22	24 Feb. 25	30 Oct. 40	18 May 49	23 Sept.	
Archibald P. M'Neill Walter, CB. *Lt.Col.*, 35 Foot	31 July 35	3 July 32	29 Sept. 47	2 Dec. 53	17 Oct.	
Archibald Patrick G. Ross. *Lt.Col.*, Royal Engineers	1 Dec. 32	10 Jan. 37	1 April 46	never	29 Oct.	
John Halkett Le Couteur, *Capt. & Lt.Col.*, C.-ld-tream Guards	3 May 44	27 Mar. 46	15 Mar. 53	29 Sept. 55	18 Nov.	
Edward N-ville, *Capt. & Lt.Col.* Scots Fusilier Guards	1 June 41	29 Sept. 43	30 Sept. 50	12 Dec. 54	28 Nov.	
John Geo. Riwstorne, *Major*, 91 Foot	22 July 33	18 Aug. 14	10 Oct. 38	11 Nov. 51	26 Dec.	56
David Watson, *Major*, 82 Foot	12 July 35	24 Oct. 35	3 June 41	20 June 54	do	
George King, *Lt.Col.*, 13 Foot	13 April 31	16 Jan. 35	2 Aug. 42	do	do	25 Sept. 57
Tyrrell Matthias Byrne, [102] *Major*, Unattached	30 June 29	23 Mar. 32	16 June 43	do	do	
John Agmondisham Vesey Kirkland, *Lt.Col.*, 5 Foot	22 Aug. 37	27 July 38	6 Sept. 44	12 Dec. 54	do	
James Conolly, [103] *Major*, Unatt., Brigade Major at Portsmouth	17 June 36	14 June 37	14 June 45	do	do	
Fred. Robert Elrington, *Lt.Col.*, Rifle Brigade	7 June 33	23 Nov. 38	22 May 46	do	do	
Thomas Henry Clifton, [104] *Major*, Unatt., Equerry and Aide-de-Camp to H.R.H. The Duke of Cambridge, Commander in Chief	26 April 38	2 July 41	30 Mar. 47	do	do	16 June 57
John Edward Lewis, [105] *Major*, Unattached	12 Jan. 30	23 Jan. 35	13 July 47	do	do	27 Nov. 57
John Turner, CB., *Captain*, Royal Artillery	19 Mar. 35	7 May 41	30 June 48	do	do	
VÆ Edward Wm. Deddington Bell, *Lt.Col.*, 23 Foot	15 April 42	17 Nov. 43	18 Dec. 48	do	do	
Robert Lockhart Ross, *Major*, 93 Foot, Assistant Adjutant General at Bombay	15 Dec. 40	27 June 42	11 June 52	do	do	
Frederick Spence, *Lt.Col.*, 31 Foot	29 Dec. 29	1 Nov. 31	28 June 44	15 June 55	do	
Robert William Lowry, *Major*, 47 Foot	24 Dec. 40	12 May 43	18 Feb. 48	do	do	
Edward Westby Donovan, *Major*, 33 Foot	10 Jan. 40	14 June 42	22 Dec. 48	17 July 55	do	
James Frankford Manners Browne, CB., *Capt.*, Royal Engineers	1 Jan. 42	1 April 45	7 Feb. 54	do	do	
Robert Onesiphorus Bright, *Lt.Col.*, 19 Foot	9 June 43	2 April 47	23 Jan. 52	15 Sept. 55	do	
Spencer Delves Broughton, *Lt.Col.*, Royal Artillery	18 June 36	23 May 39	23 June 46	2 Nov. 55	do	
Richard Francis Waldo Sibthorp, [106] *Major*, Unattached	20 Sept. 39	10 Sept. 41	5 Mar. 47	do	do	31 July 57
William Augustus Fyers, CB., *Major*, Rifle Brigade	17 Oct. 34	20 May 36	7 May 47	do	do	
Hugh Arch. Beauchamp Campbell, CB., *Lt.Col.*, Royal Artillery	16 June 38	31 July 40	7 May 47	do	do	
William Pretyman, *Lt.Col.*, 60 Foot	30 Aug. 40	5 Aug. 42	11 Sept. 49	do	do	
Fowler Burton, *Lt.Col.*, 97 Foot	11 Nov. 42	14 June 50	25 April 51	do	do	4 Nov. 59
Henry Robert Carden, [104] *Major*, Unattached	27 July 38	7 Feb. 42	25 July 52	do	do	
George Latham Thomson, *Major*, 4 Foot	18 June 36	9 April 41	9 July 52	never	1 Jan. 57	
James Benjamin Dennis, *Lt.Col.*, Royal Artillery	18 June 36	28 June 38	1 April 46	never	24 Jan. 57	
John Travers, *Lt.Col.*, Royal Artillery	18 June 36	6 Oct. 38	6 April 46	20 June 54	27 Jan.	
Ralph Budd, *Lt.Col.*, 14 Foot	10 Mar. 25	16 Mar. 26	1 June 41	1 June 49	4 Feb.	20 July 49
Edmund Roche, [107] *Captain*, Unattached	11 July 37	29 April 42	20 July 49	21 July	57	

Lieutenant-Colonels.

	ENSIGN, ETC.	LIEUT.	CAPTAIN.	MAJOR.	LIEUT.-COLONEL.	WHEN PLACED ON HALF PAY.
Frederick Douglas Lumley,[108] *Major*, Unattached	22 Oct. 33	8 Jan. 38	25 Oct. 42	4 Aug. 49	5 Feb. 57	21 Dec. 55
John Hawkins Gascoigne, *Lt.Col.*, Royal Marines	4 June 28	23 May 37	9 Nov. 46	never	6 Feb. 51	
Robert John M'Killop, *Lt.Col.*, do.	3 Mar. 29	10 July 37	9 Dec. 46	never	do	
Henry Carr Tate, *Lt.Col.*	30 June 29	do	4 May 47	never	do	
Charles John Foster, *Lt.Col.*, 16 Lancers	8 April 36	21 Dec. 38	10 Dec. 47	21 Sept. 52	17 Feb. 57	
Hon. George Talbot Devereux, *Lt.Col.*, Royal Artillery	18 June 36	13 Nov. 38	13 April 46	28 May 53	23 Feb. 57	
Wm. Henry Beaumont de Horsey, *Capt. & Lt.Col.*, Grenadier Guards	never	22 Nov. 44	22 Mar. 50	12 Dec. 54	13 Mar. 57	
James Maurice Primrose, *Lt.Col.*, 43 Foot	6 Jan. 37	7 May 41	11 April 48	9 Feb. 55	20 Mar. 57	
Richard William Aldworth, *Lt.Col.*, 7 Foot	19 Aug. 44	22 Oct. 47	7 June 54	27 May 56	do	
William Cartan, *Captain*, ret. f. p., *Staff Officer of Pensioners*	17 July 15	12 Dec. 22	31 Aug. 38	11 Nov. 51	1 April 57	
Anthony Donelan,[109] *Capt.*, retired f. p., do.	9 April 25	7 Nov. 27	6 May 42	20 June 54	do	
Edward Hocker, CB., *Lt.Col.*, Royal Marines	30 Jan. 30	10 July 37	27 July 47	never	do	
George Holt, *Major*, retired full pay, 25 Foot	22 Feb. 12	25 May 25	30 Oct. 40	11 Nov. 51	3 April 57	
James Croft Brooke, *Major*, 8 Foot	31 Oct. 31	9 Sept. 33	31 Mar. 46	2 Oct. 49	14 April 57	
John William Grey, *Lt.Col.*, 85 Foot	16 May 34	1 June 38	31 Mar. 43	17 Dec. 52	28 April 57	
Robert Bruce, *Lt.Col.*, 2 Foot	9 June 38	22 May 40	21 July 45	28 May 53	2 May 57	
Aug. Henry Lane Fox, *Capt. & Lt.Col.*, Grenadier Guards		16 May 45	2 Aug. 50	12 Dec. 54	15 May 57	22 Feb. 50
Hon. Wellington Henry Stapleton Cotton, *Major*, Unattached	21 Oct. 37	18 May 41	29 Dec. 46	22 Feb. 50	6 May 57	
Richard Blackwood-Price, *Lt.Col.*, h. p., Royal Artillery	18 June 36	11 Dec. 38	13 April 46	never	26 May 57	21 Aug. 57
Cha. Higginson Tench-Hecker, *Lt.Col.*, Unatt., *Assist. Command. of Cav. Depot at Maidstone*	29 Aug. 26	28 Jan. 28	2 June 39	8 Mar. 50	4 June 57	
Henry Bingham, *Lt.Col.*, 60 Foot	30 April 27	28 Sept. 32	25 July 41	19 Oct. 51	19 June 57	
Henry Hamilton, CB., *Major*, 78 Foot	13 Aug. 29	29 Nov. 33	29 April 42	19 April 50	9 July 57	
Charles Wilson Randolph, *Capt. & Lt.Col.*, Grenadier Guards	10 Feb. 43	23 Mar. 45	15 Feb. 50	never	17 July 57	
Thomas Addison, *Major*, 2 Foot	15 Sept. 27	31 Jan. 30	16 Dec. 45	28 May 53	24 July 57	
George Maxwell, *Lt.Col.*, 63 Foot	23 Feb. 27	29 May 29	21 Oct. 43	20 June 54	14 Aug. 57	
Allan Hamilton Graham, *Lt.Col.*, Royal Artillery	18 June 36	3 July 39	8 July 46	never	21 Aug. 57	
Hon. Fred. Aug. Thesiger, *Lt.Col.*, 95 Foot	31 Dec. 44	23 Nov. 45	27 Dec. 50	55	28 Aug. 57	
Edmund Ogle, *Lt.Col.*, Royal Engineers	30 Jan. 34	10 Jan. 37	1 April 46	never	2 Sept. 57	
Colin Campbell M'Intyre, CB., *Major*, 78 Foot	9 April 25	17 July 28	28 April 57	19 June 50	5 Sept. 57	
Hon. James Colborne, *Major*, Unatt., *Military Secretary in Ireland*	21 Mar. 34	26 June 38	23 July 41	21 Aug. 50	8 Sept. 57	21 June 50
Fred. Alexander Campbell, *Lt.Col.*, Royal Artillery	30 Dec. 36	10 Aug. 39	14 Oct. 46	never	14 Sept. 57	
Henry Philip Goodenough, *Lt.Col.*, Royal Artillery	do	13 Aug. 39	9 Nov. 46	never	do	
Charles William Thompson, *Lt.Col.*, 7 Dragoon Guards	26 Feb. 36	17 Jan. 40	1 Dec. 48	9 Nov. 55	17 Sept. 57	
Henry George Buller, *L.Col.*, 94 Foot	26 June 35	8 June 38	5 June 44	1 July 54	18 Sept. 57	
Augustus Henry Irby, *Lt.Col.*, 51 Foot	15 July 37	5 Oct. 41	9 Aug. 50	6 June 56	do	
Sir Frederick Leopold Arthur, *Bart.*, *Major*, Unattached	6 Dec. 33	3 July 35	8 June 47	13 Dec. 50	28 Sept. 57	21 June 50
Thomas Ffrench,[110] *Captain*, retired full pay, 53 Foot	4 Dec. 12	26 April 28	31 Oct. 40	11 Nov. 51	30 Oct. 57	
Frederick English, CB., *Lt.Col.*, 53 Foot	22 Mar. 33	17 June 36	15 Dec. 40	11 Nov. 51	2 Nov. 57	13 Dec. 50

58

Lieutenant-Colonels.

	ENSIGN, ETC.	LIEUT.	CAPTAIN.	MAJOR.	LIEUT.-COLONEL.	WHEN PLACED ON HALF PAY.
William Freeland Brett, *Major*, 54 Foot	1 April 42	6 Dec. 44	25 June 51	14 Aug. 57	11 Nov. 57	
William Henry Hardy Forbes Clarke, *Major*, ret. full pay, 53 Foot	25 Nov. 24	1 May 26	29 Sept. 43	20 June 54	17 Nov.	
Edward Henry Cooper, *Capt. & Lt.Col.*, Grenadier Guards	16 May 45	11 Sept. 46	15 Aug. 48	never	17 Nov.	
Samuel B. Hamilton, *Lt.Col.*, 25 Foot	20 Sept. 33	14 July 37	12 Jan. 39	28 Nov. 41	24 Nov.	
Conolly M'Causland, *Lt.Col.*, Royal Engineers	9 Jun. 34	10 Jun.	1 April 40		25 Nov.	
Robert W. M'Leod Fraser, *Lt.Col.*, 6 Foot					25 Nov.	
Charles Lavallin Nugent, *Major*, Depot Battalion	21 Aug. 35	4 Feb.	16 Nov. 41	18 July	26 Nov.	
George Howard Vyse, *Major & Lt.Col.*, 2 Life Guards, *Gentleman Usher in Waiting to the Queen*	26 Nov. 30	17 April 35	1 Sept.	11 Nov. 51	27 Nov.	
James Alexander West, *Major*, retired full pay, 84 Foot	6 July	28 Feb.	8 April 42	29 June 54	do	
George Wm. Powlett Bingham, *CB., Lt.Col.*, 64 Foot	16 Feb.	8 April	29 Sept. 48	10 Dec. 56	29 Nov.	
John Cameron, *Lt.Col.*, Royal Engineers	12 Dec.	10 Jan.	1 April	46	2 Dec.	
Edmund Wodehouse, *Major*, 24 Foot	24 Mar.	15 Jan.	28 April 41	8 Aug. 46	12 Dec.	
Charles Lavallin Nugent — Edwyn Sherard Barnaby, *Capt. & Lt.Col.*, Grenadier Guards		3 Nov.	27 May 46	2 Nov. 53	18 Dec. 55	
George Bucknall Stakespear, *Lt.Col.*, Royal Artillery	30 Dec.	11 Sept.	9 Nov. 39	46	22 Dec.	
William Hope, *CB., Lt.Col.*, 71 Foot	4 Sept.	24 Mar.	30 May 38	31 Oct. 45	26 Dec.	
George James Ambrose, *Lt.Col.*, 3 Foot	4 July	5 Nov.	12 Oct. 40	17 July 52	31 Dec.	
Edward Knollys, *Major*, 75 Foot	18 Oct.	2 Nov.	7 Feb. 30	11 Jan. 37	11 Nov. 58	
Alfred Tipping, *Capt. & Lt.Col.*, Grenadier Guards	22 June	30 May 43	7 May 47	12 Dec.	do	
Richard Jenkins, *Captain*, Unatt., *Staff Officer of Pensioners*	1 Feb.	4 June 27	28 June 37	11 Nov. 54	15 Jan. 58	19 May 46
John Heatly, *Major*, 83 Foot	20 Sept. 31	28 Mar.	31 Mar. 34	20 June 46	19 Jan. 58	
Henry Aime Ouvry,[112] CB., *Lt.Col.* h. p. 9 Lancers, *Assist. Quarter Master General at Shorncliffe*	17 Oct. 33	4 Sept. 35	2 May 45	22 Sept. 54	do	
Charles E. P. Gordon, *Captain*, 75 Foot	13 Dec. 33	17 Feb. 37	25 April 45	29 Aug. 57	do	
John Hinde, *Major*, 8 Foot	28 Feb. 35	30 June 37	4 July 45	21 Oct. 57	do	
Reginald Gipps, *Capt. & Lt.Col.*, Scots Fusilier Guards	never	10 April 49	20 June 54	6 June 56	2 Feb. 58	
Poulet George Henry Somerset, *CB., Lt.Col.*, 7 Foot					do	
John Hope Winfield, *Lt.Col.*, 15 Foot	17 May 31	4 Oct. 33	18 Jan. 39	11 Nov. 51	19 Feb. 58	
Richard Knox, *Lt.Col.*, 18 Hussars	28 June 28	20 April 34	9 Mar. 42	20 June 54	do	
William John Chamberlayne, *Lt.Col.*, 3 West India Regt.	25 Nov. 42	6 Dec. 44	31 Aug. 47	27 Jan. 57	do	
Simon Fraser. *Lt.Col.*, Royal Marines	23 Feb. 30	10 July 37	27 July 43	12 Dec. 51	25 Feb. 58	
Robert Daly,[113] *Captain*, retired full pay, 3 Foot	8 Aug. 22	6 Jan. 26	15 Jan. 40	11 Nov. 54	23 Feb. 58	
James Elphinstone Robertson, *Lt.Col.*, 6 Foot	8 April 37	21 June 38	27 Oct. 43	20 June 56	5 Mar. 58	
David Anderson, *Lt.Col.*, 22 Foot	28 Dec. 38	15 May 41	2 Feb. 49	8 July 56	do	
Archibald Neil Campbell, *Lt.Col.*, 48 Foot	14 Aug.	8 April 31	1 Nov. 42	9 Dec. 53	do	
Archibald Campbell, *Major*, 29 Foot	7 Mar. 11	5 Mar. 12	27 Oct. 37	11 Nov. 51	16 Mar.	
Fred. Green Wilkinson, *Lt.Col.*, 42 Foot	27 Dec. 42	13 Aug.	17 Oct. 51	9 Oct. 55	do	
Mortimer R. S. Whitmore, *Captain*, h. p., 19 Drs., *Staff Officer of Pens.*	26 June 27	5 Aug. 28	16 Feb. 38	11 Nov. 54	22 Mar. 58	23 June 46
Giles Keane, *Major*, 86 Foot	21 June	2 July	23 Oct. 31	29 Oct. 42	24 Mar. 58	
William Wigram Barry, *Captain*, Royal Artillery	1 May 45	9 Nov. 46	17 Feb. 54	2 Nov. 55	do	
William Payn, *CB., Lt.Col.*, 53 Foot	27 May 42	12 Jan. 44	14 Mar. 51	6 June 56	do	

Lieutenant-Colonels.

	ENSIGN, ETC.	LIEUT.	CAPTAIN.	MAJOR.	LIEUT.-COLONEL.	WHEN PLACED ON HALF PAY.
Archibald Alison, [1st] *Lt.Col.*, Unattached	3 Nov. 46	11 Sept. 49	11 Nov. 53	6 June 58	24 Mar. 58	4 June 58
James Peter Robertson, CB., *Lt.Col.*, Military Train	29 Oct. 41	30 Sept. 42	21 Jan. 48	20 Feb. 57	do	do
Edward W. D. Lowe, CB., *Lt.Col.*, 21 Foot	20 May 37	12 Mar. 41	23 May 45	1 July 57	do	do
William Chester Master, CB., *Lt.Col.*, 5 Foot	28 April 39	26 Oct. 41	29 Dec. 46	4 Sept. 57	do	do
Richard Herbert Gall, CB., *Major*, 14 Light Dragoons	3 July 35	7 Dec. 38	31 Mar. 47	30 Sept. 57	do	do
George Bryan Milman, *Major*, 5 Foot	24 May 39	20 Sept. 42	29 Jan. 48	18 Sept. 57	do	do
V℃ John Christopher Guise, *Lt.Col.*, 90 Foot	6 June 45	13 Oct. 48	6 June 54	13 Nov. 57	do	do
Neville Hill Shute, *Lt.Col.*, 64 Foot	12 Mar. 41	2 Aug. 44	25 Sept. 50	20 Nov. 57	do	do
William Poilexfen Radcliff, *Lt.Col.*, 20 Foot	22 Mar. 41	25 Dec. 42	25 July 51	12 Dec. 54	26 Mar. 58	8 Oct. 47
Edward Adams, *Capt.*, Unatt. *Secretary & Adjutant R. Military Asylum*	9 April 25	31 Dec. 28	24 Feb. 38	11 Nov. 51	3 April 55	do
Arnold E. Burmester, *Major*, 53 Foot	31 Aug. 39	7 Mar. 34	15 Mar. 38	do	13 April 55	do
Edward Stele, CB., *Lt.Col.*, 83 Foot	18 April 34	15 Mar. 38	19 Mar. 47	19 Jan. 55	do	19 Dec. 56
V℃ *Hon.* Henry Hugh Clifford, [3rd] *Major*, Unattached	7 Aug. 46	13 April 49	29 Dec. 54	17 July 55	do	do
William Wood, [16th] *Captain*, retired full pay, Royal Marines	10 May 13	16 April 32	11 May 41	20 June 54	16 April 58	
V℃ Sir Charles Russell, *Bart.*, *Capt. & Lt.Col.*, Grenadier Guards	25 Aug. 32	9 June 43	16 Sept. 53	2 Nov. 55	23 April 58	
William Albert Stratton, *Lt.Col.*, 6 Foot	27 May 42	19 Nov. 44	30 Mar. 49	15 April 56	6 May 58	
Henry Copinger, *Major*, retired full pay, 16 Foot	28 April 25	6 Mar. 28	8 July 34	26 Dec. 42	7 May 58	
John Lewis, [17th] *Lt.Col.* Unattached	14 May 47	6 Dec. 50	20 Sept. 54	2 Nov. 55	do	25 Mar. 59
Richard Henry Crofton, *Lt.Col.* Royal Artillery	5 May 37	20 Nov. 39	9 Nov. 46		26 May 58	29 Dec. 43
John Sampson, *Capt.*, h. p., S Gar. Bn., *Staff Officer of Pensioners*	20 Nov. 10	9 Dec. 12	23 May 25	11 Nov. 51	27 May 58	
Murray Octavius Nixon, *Lt.Col.*, Royal Artillery	14 Dec. 37	25 Feb. 40	9 Nov. 46		5 June 58	24 Dec. 52
John Blaquiere Miani, *Capt.*, Unatt., *Town Major at Exeter*	10 Feb. 25	17 Nov. 25	2 June 25	11 Mar. 51	14 June 58	
Hon. Wenman Clarence Walpole Coke, *Capt. & Lt.Col.*, Scots Fus. Gds.	31 July 46	7 April 48	25 Mar. 53	2 Nov. 55	15 June 58	
John Owen Lewis, *Major*, retired full pay, 37 Foot	11 July 35	9 July 41	29 Oct. 41	20 June 54	do	
Henry Ralph Browne, *Lt.Col.*, 87 Foot	3 April 40	19 Sept. 43	25 Dec. 49	6 July 55	16 June 58	
Hon. Aug. Geo. Charles Chichester, *Lt.Col.*, 77 Foot	19 Feb. 41	22 Nov. 44	3 Aug. 49	20 June 54	22 June 58	
Francis Roger Palmer, CB., *Lt.Col.*, 60 Foot	15 Mar. 38	24 April 41	11 Mar. 45	5 Sept. 55	do	
*Guglielmo Petit, *Captain*, retired full pay, R. Malta Fencibles	25 Jan. 16	17 Feb. 27	10 May 30	29 Mar. 44	23 Mar. 58	
William Justin MacCarthy, [18th] *Major*, retired full pay, 84 Foot	29 May 35	30 June 38	29 Dec. 52	13 May 58	7 July 58	
William Henry Seymour, CB., *Lt.Col.*, 2 Dragoon Guards	7 May 47	10 June 52	11 Aug. 54	12 Dec. 57	do	
William Henry March, *Lt.Col.*, Royal Marines	30 Nov. 30	10 July 37	11 June 38	11 Nov. 51	20 July 58	
James Cockburn, *Captain*, Unatt., *Staff Officer of Pensioners*	12 Apr. 27	23 Aug. 33	2 June 47	1 June 54	do	21 Feb. 40
Arthur Scudamore, CB., *Major*, 14 Dragoons	29 May 35	18 Feb. 38	29 Oct. 42	20 June 54	do	
William Kier Stuart, *Major*, 86 Foot	6 Mar. 28	28 Sept. 30	8 April 41	do	do	
William Campbell Molian, CB., *Capt.*, 75 Foot	10 Jan. 40	2 April 41	13 Oct. 48	12 Dec. 54	do	
John Richard Anderson, CB., *Lt.Col.*, Royal Artillery	18 Dec. 40	23 Nov. 48	17 May 48	15 Dec. 55	do	
John William Cox, CB., *Major*, 13 Foot	25 June 38	22 April 40	9 April 45	9 May 51	21 Sept. 55	do
Robert Bruce, [48th] *Major*, Unattached	31 Mar. 43	28 Mar. 45	23 Nov. 52	2 Nov. 55	do	2 Dec. 59
Richard George Amherst Luard, [19th] *Major*, Unattached	6 July 45	14 May 47	23 May 51	2 Nov. 55	do	30 Oct. 54
Hon. Eyre Challoner Henry Massey, *Major*, 95 Foot	8 Oct. 47	21 Nov. 51	14 Jan. 53	2 Nov. 55	do	

Lieutenant-Colonels.

	ENSIGN, ETC.	LIEUT.	CAPTAIN.	MAJOR.	LIEUT.-COLONEL.	WHEN PLACED ON HALF PAY.
Lothian Nicholson, CB., *Captain*, Royal Engineers	6 Aug. 46	26 Jan. 47	1 April 55	2 Nov. 55	20 July 58	
William George Le Mesurier, CB., *Captain*, Royal Artillery	20 June 49	6 Aug. 49	28 Sept. 50	do 55	do	
Alexander Dalton Theilusson, *Major*, 72 Foot	12 Oct. 41	8 Oct. 44	28 Dec. 44	23 Nov. 49	do	
George Whitworth Talbot Rich, *Lt. Col.* 71 Foot	12 June 40	15 Apr. 42	12 Nov. 47	6 June 52	do 56	
Edward Thomas Gloster, *Captain*, 38 Foot	13 May 42	3 Jan. 45	30 July 45	do	do	
George Courtenay Viall, *Major*, 95 Foot	20 Jan. 43	22 May 46	25 Mar. 53	do	do	
John Ross, *Captain*, Rifle Brigade		14 Apr. 46	29 Dec. 48	do	do	
Charles Sawyer, *Major*, 6 Dragoon Guards	6 Sept. 33	8 April 36	8 Aug. 45	1 Aug. 56	do 56	
Thomas George Alex. Oakes, *Major*, 12 Lancers	16 Jan. 46	3 Sept. 47	22 Feb. 50	1 Aug. 56	do	
Henry Hope Crealock, *Captain*, 90 Foot	13 Oct. 48	24 Dec. 52	29 Dec. 54	26 Dec. 56	do	
Charles Napier North, *Major*, 60 Foot	20 May 36	28 Dec. 38	28 Dec. 48	19 June 57	do 57	
Sir William Russell, *Bart.*, CB., *Lt. Col.*, 7 Hussars	2 July 41	27 Feb. 46	16 April 47	18 Aug. 57	do	
Robert Bickerstaff, *Major*, 6 Dragoon Guards	8 Nov. 44	29 Dec. 46	10 Feb. 52	6 Nov. 57	do	
Alexander Cunningham Robertson, *Major*, 8 Foot	15 Sept. 37	20 Aug. 41	11 Nov. 45	19 Jan. 58	do 58	
William Drysdale, CB., *Major*, 9 Lancers	23 Sept. 35	31 Aug. 28	29 Oct. 47	19 Jan. 58	do	
Dunbar Douglas Muter, *Captain*, 60 Foot	14 Apr. 43	17 Jan. 45	31 May 54	19 Jan. 58	do	
VC Francis Cornwallis Maude, CB., *Captain*, Royal Artillery	1 Oct. 47	30 June 48	13 Dec. 54	do	do	
Laurence Pleydell Bouverie, *Captain*, 78 Foot	7 Sept. 41	28 Dec. 42	22 Dec. 54	19 Jan. 58	20 July 58	
John Butler Wheatstone, *Major*, retired full pay, 8 Foot	1 May 21	31 Mar. 26	16 Nov. 41	28 May 53	23 July 58	
Frederick Wellington John FitzWygram, *Lt. Col.*, 6 Dragoons	28 July 43	17 May 44	22 Dec. 48	19 Feb. 58	26 July 58	
John Home Purves, *Captain*, Unatt., *Equerry to H.R.H. the Duchess of Cambridge.*	never	29 Nov. 33	13 July 38	11 Nov. 58	2 Aug. 58	14 May 47
Arthur Leslie, *Lt. Col.*, 40 Foot	20 Nov. 38	6 May 42	3 April 46	25 June 52	6 Aug. 58	
Henry Law Maydwell, 12st *Maj.*, h. p., Depot Batt., *Dep. Adj. Gen. at Ceylon.*	21 Aug. 35	28 Sept. 36	15 April 41	28 May 53	do	
Legendre Charles Bourchier, *Lt. Col.*, 75 Foot	5 Apr. 33	12 Feb. 36	20 July 38	11 Nov. 55	9 Aug. 58	
Edward Lyneloch Gardiner, *Lt. Col.*, Royal Artillery	14 Dec. 37	16 Mar. 40	9 Nov. 46	20 July 55	do	
Henry Ramsden Priesiley, *Lt. Col.*, 42 Foot	27 Nov. 35	13 Jan. 38	20 Oct. 43	20 June 54	10 Aug. 58	
Galway Byng Payne, *Lt. Col.*, Royal Marines	17 May 31	10 July 37	4 Dec. 47	12 Dec. 54	11 Aug. 58	
Thomas White, *Major*, 49 Foot	7 Dec. 15	25 Aug. 24	5 Oct. 38	11 Nov. 51	12 Aug. 58	
John Summerfield Hawkins, *Lt. Col.*, Royal Engineers	20 April 34	10 Jan. 37	1 Apr. 46	14 June 58	do	
James Palmer, *Captain*, retired full pay, 3 West India Regiment	15	6 June 16	25 Aug. 39	11 Nov. 55	13 Aug. 58	
Francis Baring, *Capt. & Lt. Col.*, Scots Fusilier Guards		6 July 32	12 Oct. 32	2 Nov. 54	do	
Adolphus Fred. Bond, *Capt.* h. p. Staff Corps, *Staff Officer of Pensioners*	never	29 June 28	12 Oct. 38	11 Nov. 51	26 Aug. 58	28 July 43
Arthur George Vesey, *Captain*, *Lt. Col.*, 46 Foot	3 Apr. 29	25 Aug. 35	23 July 37	20 June 42	31 Aug. 58	
William Spring, *Captain*, retired full pay, 44 Foot	30 Dec. 26	1 June 32	16 Nov. 37	26 Dec. 45	7 Sept. 58	
Joseph Oates Travers, *Lt. Col.*, Royal Marines, *Assistant Adjutant General*	19 Sept. 31	10 July 34	27 Dec. 37	13 Apr. 47	8 Sept. 58	
Webbe Butler, *Lt. Col.*, 60 Foot	19 Sept. 34	15 Dec. 40	26 July 40	23 Mar. 44	9 Sept. 58	
George Aug. Schomberg, *Captain*, Royal Marines	16 Mar. 41	21 Sept. 43	1 July 53	2 Nov. 55	15 Sept. 58	
Thomas Edmond Knox, *Lt. Col.*, 67 Foot		24 June 38	31 July 43	17 Aug. 52	17 Sept. 58	
Alfred Augustus Chapman, *Lt. Col.*, 18 Foot	26 Jan. 38	17 Jan. 42	31 April 49	15 May 55	do	
Fred. Geddes Bull, *Captain*, h. P., 60 Foot, *Staff Officer of Pensioners*	20 May 42					
	25 Oct. 27	8 Feb. 31	23 Nov. 38	11 Nov. 51	22 Sept. 58	18 Aug. 43

Lieutenant-Colonels.

	ENSIGN, ETC.	LIEUT.	CAPTAIN.	MAJOR.	LIEUT.-COLONEL.	WHEN PLACED ON HALF PAY.
Robert Hume, *Lt. Col.*, 55 Foot	9 April 47	30 Nov. 49	21 Sept. 54	2 Nov. 55	8 Oct. 58	
William Boyle, *Lt. Col.*, 89 Foot	6 Dec. 38	21 May 41	4 Jan. 50	2 Nov. 55	13 Oct. 58	
Michael Gould Adams, *Captain*, Unattached	21 July 25	30 July 29	28 Dec. 38	11 Nov. 51	26 Oct. 58	31 Dec. 44
George Freeman Murray, *Captain*, 65 Foot	26 Apr. 28	29 June 32	5 Jan. 39	do	do	
Thomas Byrne, *Major*, 10 Foot	4 Nov. 19	5 Mar. 23	22 Jan. 39	do	do	
Edward Moore, *Lt. Col.*, 11 Foot	21 May 18	7 Apr. 25	7 Feb. 39	do	do	
Richard Mordesley Be-t, *Major*, 10 Foot	20 Apr. 32	16 Jan. 35	7 June 39	do	do	
Fitzwilliam Walker, *Major*, R. Canadian Rifles	31 Dec. 30	17 June 36	21 June 39	do	do	
George Ponsonby Hume, *Major*, 15 Foot	28 June 33	16 Dec. 36	20 Sept. 39	do	do	25 Feb. 42
Edward Osborne Broadley, *Capt.*, Unatt., *Staff Officer of Pensioners*	15 Aug. 26	29 Sept. 29	28 Sept. 39	do	do	29 Dec. 43
Owen Lloyd Ormsby, *Captain*, Unatt., *Staff Officer of Pensioners*	21 Dec. 32	2 Feb. 38	1 Nov. 39	do	do	
Henry Craigie Brewster, *Major*, 76 Foot	18 Oct. 33	19 Aug. 36	9 Nov. 39	do	do	
Charles Beamish, *Lt. Col.*, 35 Foot	26 April 31	20 Mar. 35	31 Dec. 39	do	do	
Henry Gahan, *Major*, St. Helena Regiment	13 June 30	15 June 32	6 Mar. 40	do	do	
Collingwood Fenwick, *Captain*, 76 Foot	4 Sept. 35	7 April 37	3 April 40	do	do	10 July 40
George Munro, *Captain*, Unatt., *Staff Officer of Pensioners*	20 Jan. 14	29 Mar. 21	10 July 40	do	do	25 April 45
Robert Russell Harris, *Capt.*, h. p., 60 Foot, *Staff Officer of Pensioners*	19 Oct. 20	18 Aug. 24	31 Oct. 40	do	do	29 Mar. 44
Francis Percy Nott, *Capt.*, h. p., 1 Gar. Bn., *Staff Officer of Pensioners*	23 June 26	10 May 29	1 Nov. 40	do	do	
John Ross Wheeler, *Lt. Col.* 29 Foot	30 July 28	25 Dec. 29	15 Dec. 40	do	do	
Andrew Timbrell Allan, *Lt. Col.* 25 Foot	23 Sept. 30	23 Dec. 32	31 Dec. 41	26 Dec. 51	do	
Thomas Ross, *Major*, 73 Foot	23 Mar. 38	18 May 31	4 June 47	22 Oct. 52	do	
Broadley Harrison, *Lt. Col.*, 11 Hussars	1 Oct. 39	7 Sept. 41	7 June 44	5 Nov. 52	do	
Charles Duesbery Robertson, *Lt.-Col.*, Royal Engineers	19 Dec. 34	31 Jan. 37	1 April 46	28 May 53	do	
Wyndham Edmund Bewes, *Captain*, 73 Foot	19 June 40	22 July 42	3 Aug. 49	4 Nov. 53	do	
Henry John Shaw, *Major*, 45 Foot	23 Mar. 38	1 June 39	1 July 46	11 Nov. 53	do	30 Oct. 57
William Clargys Wolfe, 12? *Major*, Unattached	30 Oct. 35	10 Mar. 37	7 Aug. 46	6 Jan. 54	do	17 April 57
John Miller, 113 *Major*, Unattached	29 Dec. 35	25 Jan. 39	15 Mar. 46	13 Jan. 54	do	13 Jan. 54
Jonas Pasley Harly, 12? *Major*, Unattached	29 Sept. 25	3 Nov. 26	25 June 41	3 Mar. 54	do	1 May 55
John Johnston, 115 *Major*, Unattached	24 May 27	9 Mar. 32	2 April 47	7 April 54	do	22 May 57
Charles William Green, *Major*, Unattached	7 April 38	13 Mar. 40	14 May 47	21 April 54	do	
Henry, Duke of Beaufort, *Major*, Unatt., *Lt. Col. Commandant R. Gloucestershire Hussars, Master of the Horse to the Queen*	17 Aug. 41	7 July 43	13 Aug. 47	12 May 54	do	21 April 54
Francis Peyton, *Major*, 98 Foot	29 Jan. 41	27 May 42	3 Sept. 50	19 May 54	do	
John Francis Kempt, *Major*, 12 Foot	16 June 30	19 May 37	29 April 51	do	do	
William Thomas Dickson, *Major*, 16 Lancers	23 April 47	25 Feb. 48	25 April 53	7 June 54	do	
George Butler Triscott Colman, *Lt. Col.*, *Major*, Unattached	31 Dec. 39	7 Jan. 42	24 July 50	12 Dec. 54	do	26 Mar. 58
Bartholomew O'Brien, *Lt. Col.*, Military Train	15 April 36	13 July 38	2 Aug. 53	13 Dec. 53	do	
Henry Armytage, *Capt. & Lt. Col.*, Coldstream Guards	never	30 July 47	13 Dec. 53	18 Dec. 55	do	
William Radcliffe, *Lt. Col.*, 75 Foot	27 Sept. 31	24 April 35	7 June 44	16 May 56	do	
Charles Wilson Austen, *Lt. Col.*, 83 Foot	14 Dec. 38	15 Dec. 40	1 Dec. 48		do	

Lieutenant-Colonels.

	ENSIGN, ETC.	LIEUT.	CAPTAIN.	MAJOR.	LIEUT.-COLONEL.	WHEN PLACED ON HALFPAY.
Thomas Knox, *Lt. Col.*, Royal Artillery	14 Dec. 37	15 June 40	9 Nov. 46	13 April 58	26 Oct. 58	
Robert Parker Radcliffe, *Lt. Col.*, Royal Artillery	14 Dec. 37	13 May 44	do		do	
Charles Wright Younghusband, *Lt. Col.*, Royal Artillery	14 Dec. 37	19 June 44	28 Nov. 46		do	
William Wynne Loider, *Major*, 59 Foot	7 Mar. 34	5 June 35	6 Feb. 41	20 June 54	1 Nov. 58	
*Antonio Maltei, *Lt. Col.*, Royal Malta Fencibles	24 Jan. 25	15 Jan. 27	11 April 45	28 Aug. 57	12 Nov. 58	
Bertram Charles Mitford, *Captain*, Unatt., *Town Major at Malta*	27 April 27	2 May 31	6 Feb. 41	20 June 54	16 Nov. 58	5 April 44
William Child, *Captain*, Unatt., *Staff Officer of Pensioners*	13 Nov. 22	11 Aug. 26	22 April 41	do	23 Nov. 58	12 Oct. 52
James Holt Freeth, *Lt. Col.*, Royal Engineers	12 Dec. 34	10 Jan. 37	1 Apr. 46	20 July 58	23 Nov. 58	
Edward D. Atkinson, *Lt. Col..*, 37 Foot	6 Oct. 27	28 July 40	20 Feb. 46	3 April 58	26 Nov. 58	
John Henry Ford Elkington, *Captain*, 6 Foot	28 Aug. 46	30 Mar. 49	2 Oct. 54		7 Dec. 58	
Cameron Neville Hogge, *Capt. & Lt.-Col.*, Grenadier Guards	1 Dec. 45	6 Aug. 47	24 Feb. 54		do	
Henry Buckley Jenner Wynyard, *Capt. Unatt., Town Major in Dublin*	9 Apr. 25	21 May 26	21 May 41	20 June 54	13 Dec. 58	23 Jan. 46
Bernard Granville Layard, *Captain*, h. p. 67 Foot	13 Aug. 26	12 Jan. 33	17 June 41	20 June 54	24 Dec. 58	15 Mar. 50
Duncan Munro Bethune, *Lt. Col.*, 9 Foot	17 Apr. 35	21 Mar. 38	22 Dec. 45	29 Dec. 54	24 Dec. 58	
John Cornick, *Lt. Col.*, 20 Foot	27 Aug. 41	25 Oct. 50	17 July 55		31 Dec. 58	
John Wellesley Thomas, *Major*, 67 Foot	7 June 38	7 Sept. 41	14 May 47	3 Dec. 54	31 Dec. 58	
Oliver Langley, *Lt. Col.* 16 Foot	19 Mar. 40	22 Mar. 44	22 Dec. 48	12 Oct. 57	11 Jan. 59	
William Bell, *Major*, 32 Foot	30 Nov. 15	26 April 28	2 July 41	29 June 54	16 Jan. 59	
Robert Corcyra Romer, *Lt. Col.* Royal Artillery	6 June 39	20 July 41	15 Mar. 47	26 Oct. 54	16 Jan. 59	
Henry Bird, *Major*, Gold Coast Artillery Corps	17 Sept. 27	18 April 42	9 Sept. 45	6 June 51	28 Jan. 59	
Henry James Day, *Major*, 99 Foot	25 Feb. 42	11 June 45	16 July 52	20 June 54	13 Feb. 59	
Sidney Burrard, *Capt. & Lt. Col.* Grenadier Guards	never	3 April 46	2 May 51	never	13 Feb. 59	
William Willby, *Lt. Col.* 4 Foot	27 May 36	7 Oct. 37	10 Dec. 47	7 Aug. 55	15 Feb. 59	
Henry Harpur Greer, *Lt. Col.* 68 Foot	10 Sept. 41	20 Aug. 44	31 Dec. 47	29 Dec. 55	18 Feb. 59	
John Cox Gawler, *Captain*, 73 Foot	9 Feb. 40	12 July 44	14 April 54	20 July 55	18 Feb. 59	
Henshaw Russell, *Captain*, h. p. 60 Foot, *Staff Officer of Pensioners*	16 May 34	24 Mar. 37	10 Sept. 41	20 June 54	20 Feb. 59	25 June 44
Thomas Francis Hobbs, *Lt. Col.* Depot Battalion	15 Jan. 47	21 May 50	2 April 52	11 May 55	8 Mar. 59	
Thomas Bythesea Mortimer, *Captain*, 7G Foot	16 Nov. 32	2 July 37	24 Sept. 41	20 June 54	25 Mar. 59	
Fenwick Boyce Barron, *Lt. Col.* 3 Dragoon Guards	8 May 40	26 Sept. 45	29 Dec. 46	15 June 57	1 April 59	
Charles Fanshawe, *Lt. Col.* Royal Engineers	19 Dec. 34	23 Feb. 37	1 Apr. 46	2 Aug. 58	1 April 59	
Robert Macleod Sutherland, *Major*, 92 Foot	25 Dec. 41	7 Aug. 43	5 Oct. 54	20 Mar. 54	2 April 59	
Thomas Lightfoot, CB. *Lt. Col.* 84 Foot	1 June 38	30 Oct. 40	20 June 51	24 Mar. 58	4 April 59	
William Henry Kenny, *Captain*, h.p. 61 Foot, *Staff Officer of Pensioners*	3 April 45	24 Dec. 32	15 Mar. 46	9 April 54	9 April 59	5 April 44
Percival Fenwick, *Lt. Col.* 69 Foot	28 Sept. 38	1 Nov. 46	14 May 47	19 June 57	22 April 59	
Henry Peel Yates, *Captain*, Royal Artillery	2 May 47	30 June 48	6 July 54	12 Dec. 54	26 April 59	
William Henry Kirby, *Major*, 94 Foot	14 Oct. 36	28 June 38	7 Dec. 45	29 Dec. 54	do	
Hon. David M'Dowall Fraser, *Captain*, Royal Artillery	11 Jan. 43	14 Jan. 44	27 May 50	2 Nov. 55	do	
John Edward Michell, *Captain*, Royal Engineers	31 Dec. 46	27 Sept. 47	20 June 54	2 Nov. 55	do	
Edmund Gilling Maynard, *Major*, 88 Foot	31 Dec. 41	23 Jan. 46	14 July 54	2 Nov. 55	do	
Hon. John Jocelyn Bourke, *Major*, 88 Foot	21 May 41	22 July 42	1 June 49	27 May 56	do	

Lieutenant-Colonels.

	ENSIGN, ETC.	LIEUT.	CAPTAIN.	MAJOR.	LIEUT.-COLONEL.	WHEN PLACED ON HALF PAY.
James Mitchell Macdonald, *Major*, Ceylon Rifles	26 Oct. 38	29 July 36	9 May 45	6 June 56	26 April 59	
Charles Hodgkinson Smith, *Captain*, Royal Artillery	16 Dec. 40	13 April 46	17 Feb. 54	do	do	
Charles Vernon Oxenden, *Major*, Rifle Brigade	23 Aug. 44	13 July 47	6 June 54	do	do	
William Pattison Tinling, *Major*, 90 Foot	4 June 47	20 April 49	8 Sept. 54	do	do	
Henry D'Oyley Torrens, *Major*, 23 Foot	18 Sept. 46	8 May 51	21 Sept. 54	do	do	
Nathaniel Octavius Simpson Turner, *Captain*, Royal Artillery	2 May 47	30 June 48	6 Nov. 54	do	do	
Thomas Bromhead Batt, *Major*, 79 Foot	3 April 40	2 Aug. 42	2 April 47	17 July 57	do	
George Henry Tyler, *Major*, 13 Foot	23 July 42	14 Apr. 46	8 Nov. 50	17 Nov. 57	do	
John Hamilton Cox, *Captain*, 75 Foot	10 Oct. 37	31 July 37	31 Mar. 48	19 Jan. 58	do	
VC Sir Henry Marshman Havelock, *Bart. Captain*, 18 Foot	31 Mar. 46	23 June 48	9 Oct. 57	19 Jan. 58	do	
Edward Gascoigne Bulwer, CB., *Major*, 23 Foot	23 Aug. 41	13 Dec. 50	21 Sept. 54	26 Jan. 58	do	
William Alexander Middleton, CB., *Captain*, Royal Artillery	20 Dec. 39	23 Nov. 41	30 June 48	24 Mar. 58	do	
Frederic Arthur Willis, CB., *Captain*, 90 Foot	27 Sept. 44	8 May 46	16 Jan. 52	24 Mar. 58	26 April 59	
Garnet Joseph Wolseley, CB., *Captain*, Royal Engineers	12 Mar. 52	16 May 53	26 Jan. 55	24 Mar. 58	do	
VC Wilbraham Oates Lennox, *Captain*, Royal Engineers	27 June 48	7 Feb. 54	25 Nov. 57	24 Mar. 58	do	
Augustus Frederick Steele, *Major*, 9 Lancers	18 Nov. 41	17 Mar. 48	24 May 50	22 June 58	do	
Coote Synge Hutchinson, *Major*, 2 Dragoon Guards	14 June 56	1 Aug. 51	30 Nov. 55	7 July 58	do	
Henry Radford Norman, *Major*, 10 Foot	31 Dec. 38	8 Apr. 42	4 Oct. 51	20 July 58	do	
John De Montmorency Murray Prior, *Captain*, 12 Lancers	25 Feb. 46	30 Apr. 46	8 July 52	20 July 58	do	
William Dascon Bushe, *Major*, 7 Hussars	4 Nov. 46	17 Apr. 47	8 June 52	20 July 58	do	
Eugene James Vaughan, *Capt., h.p. 57 Foot, Adjutant of Carmarthen Militia*	7 July 25	9 Nov. 26	24 Oct. 41	20 June 54	1 May 59	6 June 45
William Forbes Macbean, *Lt. Col. St. Helena Regiment*	2 Dec. 37	7 Jan. 42	8 June 49	15 Jan. 58	1 May 59	
Robert Hawkes, *Lt. Col.* 80 Foot	6 Sept. 31	8 July 37	11 Oct. 44	16 Dec. 56	4 May 59	18 Feb. 59
Malcolm MacGregor, h.p. *Captain*, Unattached	11 Nov. 38	12 Dec. 45	20 Nov. 41	20 June 50	10 May 59	
William Babington, *Lt. Col.* 7 Hussars	6 June 45	9 Oct. 46	14 June 50	12 Nov. 58	13 May 59	
William O'Neill, *Captain*, Unattached, *Staff Officer of Pensioners*	1 Oct. 38	12 May 18	28 Dec. 41	20 June 51	14 May 59	28 Dec. 41
Robert Talbot, *Lt. Col.* Royal Artillery	25 April 19	13 Aug. 40	28 May 47	26 Oct. 58	23 May 59	
Francis Lucas, *Lt. Major*, retired full pay, 16 Foot	42	30 Dec. 27	19 Nov. 44	5 Feb. 57	24 May 59	
Henry Holden, *Lt. Col.* 13 Light Dragoons	19 Dec. 37	30 Oct. 41	6 Oct. 45	19 Mar. 47	25 Sept. 55	31 May 59
John Maurice Wemyss, CB., *Captain*, Royal Marines	22 May 29	12 1 Dec. 37	1 Jan. 42	2 Oct. 55	31 May 59	
William Carruthers,[13] Unatt., *Brigade Major, Cape Town*	28 July 28	13 27 Mar. 43	15 Mar. 52	26 Dec. 58	12 June 50	22 July 42
Robert Stuart Baynes,[129] *Major*, Unattached	15 Oct. 32	16 12 Oct. 32	7 Feb. 46	20 June 54	17 June 58	
James Kennett Willson, *Captain*, h. p. R. Marines, *Staff Officer of Pensioners*	18 June 36	31 Mar. 38	1 Apr. 46	13 Apr. 58	20 June 59	21 Sept. 43
Gother Frederick Mann, *Lt. Col.* Royal Engineers	6 July 38	17 Aug. 41	22 Oct. 47	20 July 58	24 June 59	
Stephen Francis Charles Annesley, *Major*, 10 Foot	13 Mar. 40	31 Dec. 44	11 June 47	26 Oct. 58	24 June 59	
William Knox Orme, *Captain*, 10 Foot	never	8 Nov. 50	3 Nov. 54	never	24 June 59	
Henry Charles Fletcher, *Capt. & Lt.Col.* Scots Fusilier Guards	21 Aug. 49	23 Aug. 56	23 Oct. 54	30 Sept. 56	1 July 59	
Alexander Learmonth, *Lt. Col.* 17 Lancers	22 Feb. 32	10 July 48	27 1 Jan. 48	never	7 July 59	
Robert Murray Curry, *Lt. Col.* Royal Marines	19 Mar. 32	28 Sept. 37	4 May 48	never	12 July 59	
Edward Stanley Browne, *Lt.Col.* Royal Marines						

Lieutenant-Colonels.

	ENSIGN, ETC.	LIEUT.	CAPTAIN.	MAJOR.	LIEUT.-COLONEL.	WHEN PLACED ON HALF PAY.
Henry Charingbold Powell, *Captain*, Unatt., *Staff Officer of Pensioners*	9 April 25	17 July 26	8 April 42	20 June 54	17 July 59	
John Neptune Sargent, *Lt.Col.* 3 Foot	19 Jan. 44	11 Sept. 46	18 Nov. 53	2 Nov. 55	20 July 59	
Sir William Thomas Francis Agnew Wallace, *Bart.*, *Capt. & Lt. Col.* Grenadier Guards	20 July 47	3 Mar. 48	20 June 54	never	29 July 59	
Herman Stapylton, *Lt.Col.* 27 Foot	4 Aug. 37	19 Mar. 41	1 Dec. 46	9 Oct. 54	5 Aug. 59	
Edward Seager, *Lt.Col.* 8 Hussars	17 Sept. 41	29 June 43	26 Oct. 54	31 Jan. 57	5 Aug. 59	
Frederick Charles Keppel, *Capt. & Lt.Col.* Grenadier Guards	never	31 Mar. 46	20 June 54	never	5 Aug. 59	
William Robert Maxwell, *Lt.Col.* Royal Marines	11 July 32	15 Dec. 37	17 May 48	never	11 Aug. 59	
William M'Donald, *Captain*, 26 Foot	5 April 27	31 Jan. 42	30 8 April 42	20 June 54	14 Aug. 59	
Robert Boyle, *Captain*, Royal Marines	15 June 41	21 Jan. 45	24 Feb. 54	28 Aug. 57	16 Aug. 59	
James Ross Farquharson, *Capt. & Lt.Col.* Scots Fusilier Guards	never	25 Mar. 53	26 Dec. 54	never	16 Aug. 59	
Hon. Dudley Charles FitzGerald de Ros, *Major & Lt.Col.* 1 Life Guards, Equerry to H.R.H. the Prince Consort	7 Feb. 45	5 May 48	31 Oct. 51	30 Aug. 54	30 Aug. 59	
George Waller Meehan, *Captain*, Unatt., *Staff Officer of Pensioners*	17 April 28	14 April 36	15 April 42	20 June 54	9 Sept. 59	
Josiah Rogers John Coles, *Captain*, 9 Lancers	2 Sept. 36	22 Mar. 39	19 Mar. 47	20 July 58	9 Sept. 59	
Raymond Herbert White, *Capt. & Lt.Col.* Scots Fusilier Guards	10 April 49	13 April 52	29 Dec. 54	never	16 Sept. 59	
Thomas R. Crawley, *Lt.Col.* 15 Hussars	19 Dec. 34	9 Mar. 42	13 Oct. 54	26 Feb. 58	23 Sept. 59	
James Travers, *Captain*. 3 West India Regt.	28 Nov. 41	29 July 45	15 April 52	20 July 58	25 Sept. 59	
Arnold Thompson, *Lt.Col.* Royal Artillery	19 Mar. 39	13 Aug. 40	20 July 47	26 Oct. 58	25 Sept. 59	
Hugh Smith Baillie, *Major*, Royal Horse Guards	3 April 40	24 Mar. 43	7 Aug. 46	26 Oct. 58	30 Sept. 59	
Spencer Westmacott, *Lt.Col.* Royal Engineers	18 June 36	5 May 38	1 April 46	12 Aug. 58	13 Oct. 59	
James FitzHerbert de Teissier, *Capt.* Invalid Depot, Chatham	13 Sept. 33	1 April 36	6 May 42	20 June 51	17 Oct. 59	
Henry Grierson, *Major*, 15 Foot	9 Aug. 33	24 Feb. 37	6 May 42	20 June 50	18 Oct. 59	
William James Yonge,[130] *Major*, retired full pay, 60 Foot	27 July 26	17 May 27	10 July 46	25 Jan. 50	18 Oct. 59	
George John Peacocke, *Lt.Col.* 16 Foot	8 July 42	24 Oct. 45	21 June 50	7 May 57	18 Oct. 59	
James Robert Stedman Sayer, *Lt.Col.* 1 Dragoon Guards	23 May 45	31 Mar. 48	22 Nov. 50	6 Feb. 57	21 Oct. 59	
Hew Dalrymple Fanshawe, *Major*, Depot Battalion	4 July 34	25 Mar. 38	13 May 42	20 Aug. 54	25 Oct. 59	
William Collier Menzies, *Lt.Col.* Royal Engineers	5 May 37	1 Aug. 38	1 Apr. 46	26 Aug. 58	25 Oct. 59	
Robert Carey, *Major*, h. p. 40 F., *Deputy Adjutant General in Australia*	15 Nov. 39	19 Nov. 41	14 May 47	6 June 58	28 Oct. 59	
George Bennett, *Lt.Col.* 20 Foot	20 Dec. 46	8 Mar. 50	23 Dec. 54	20 July 58	28 Oct. 59	
Francis Lambton, *Capt. & Lt.Col.* Scots Fusilier Guards	22 April 53	28 Oct. 55	22 June 55	never	4 Nov. 59	
Thomas Dudley Fosbroke, *Lt.Col.* Coldstream Guards	30 Nov. 32	1 Jan. 38	17 May 48	17 Oct. 56	21 Nov. 59	
W. Gerald Littlehales Goodlake, *Capt. & Lt.Col.* Coldstream Guards	14 June 50	27 June 51	14 July 54	14 June 59	29 Nov. 59	
John Willett Payne Audain, *Major*, 16th Foot	14 Dec. 26	2 Oct. 35	27 May 42	20 June 51	7 Dec. 59	
Charles Joseph Hadfield, *Lt.Col.* Royal Marines	15 Feb. 33	26 April 38	17 May 48	17 Oct. 59	10 Dec. 59	
Hon. Fenton John Evans Freke, *Capt.* Unattached	24 Nov. 35	14 Mar. 37	28 May 42	20 June 54	13 Dec. 59	
Graeme Alexander Lockhart, *Capt.* 78 Foot	8 Dec. 37	8 April 42	19 April 50	24 Mar. 48	13 Dec. 59	
William Mure, *Capt. & Lt.Col.* Scots Fusilier Guards	22 Oct. 47	11 July 51	29 Dec. 54	never	16 Dec. 49	
George Lord Bingham, *Capt. & Lt.Col.* Coldstream Guards	29 Dec. 48	14 Oct. 51	22 Aug. 54	17 July 57	20 Dec. 59	
John Augustus Todd, *Capt.* 14th Light Dragoons	28 April 37	14 June 41	27 Nov. 46	28 July 58	do.	
Richard Carr Spalding, *Lt.Col.* Royal Marines	7 May 33	4 May 38	17 May 48	7 Dec. 59	do.	

War Services of the Lieutenant-Colonels.

1 Lieut.Colonel Burer was employed in 1800 with an Austrian Corps d'Armée, and frequently engaged before the enemy, especially at Kloster Eberach. In 1801 he served the Egyptian campaign, and was engaged on the 17th and 21st Aug. in driving the enemy into Alexandria. In 1807 he accompanied Sir Harry Burrard as Aide-de-Camp on the expedition to the Baltic, and was frequently engaged before Copenhagen on outpost duties, and present at its siege and capture. In 1808 he served in Portugal, and was present with the 71st at the battles of Roleia and Vimiera. In 1809 he was employed as Deputy-Assistant-Adjutant-General with the Walcheren expedition, and was present at the siege and taking of Flushing and Ter Vere. In March 1811 he embarked with two companies of the 71st for Portugal, and remained with the Regiment in the Peninsula until Jan. 1813, and was present with the covering Division before Badajoz in 1811, and in April 1812; also at Arroyo de Molino and Almaraz. He has received the War Medal with three Clasps for Egypt, Roleia, and Vimiera.

3 Lieut.Colonel Oates, during eight years' active service in the West Indies, was frequently engaged with the enemy, and twice severely wounded, viz. in the right side by a musket-ball at Cote de Fer, and in the left ankle in an attack near Port au Prince. Served also five years in the East Indies and in Egypt, and crossed the Desert under Sir David Baird. With the expedition to South America in 1807. Subsequently throughout the whole of the Peninsular war, including the battles of Talavera (severely wounded on the head by the bursting of a shell), Busaco, and Fuentes d'Onor; 2nd and 3rd sieges of Badajoz,—severely wounded at the storming of Fort Picurina; battles of Vittoria, Nivelle, and Orthes,—severely wounded through the right thigh. He has a Gold Medal for services in Egypt; and the Silver War Medal with ten Clasps.

4 Lieut.Colonel Horton served the campaign in Calabria under Sir John Stuart with the flank companies of the 61st and was present at the battle of Maida. He served also in the Peninsula and was severely wounded at the battle of the Nivelle. He has received the War Medal with two Clasps.

5 Lieut.Colonel Whelan served in the American war with the Royal Newfoundland Fencibles.

7 Lieut.Colonel Nooth served with the 7th Fusiliers, on the expedition against Copenhagen, in 1807. With the 2nd Battalion of the 14th, on the expedition under Sir David Baird, and was in the retreat of Sir John Moore's army, and at the battle of Corunna, for which he has received the War Medal with one Clasp. Accompanied the Battalion to Walcheren, and was present at the siege of Flushing.

8 Lieut.Colonel Spedding served in the Peninsula with the 4th Dragoons, and was present at the battles of Talavera, Busaco, Albuhera, and Salamanca (for which he has received the War Medal with four Clasps); actions of Campo Mayor, Los Santos, and Usagre, besides other affairs.

9 Lieut.Colonel Coryton served at the passage of the Dardanelles in 1807, and has received the War Medal with one Clasp.

15 Lord A. C. FitzRoy served in the Eastern campaign of 1854, with the Coldstream Guards, including the siege of Sebastopol, and battles of Balaklava and Inkerman—severely wounded (Medal and Clasps, Sardinian Medal, and 5th Class of the Medjidie).

16 Lieut.Colonel Goate's services:—Expedition to Germany in 1805 under Lord Cathcart; storming the heights of Soril, siege of Fort Bourbon and capture of Martinique in 1809; Nepaul war in 1815, and was engaged on the heights of Muckwanpore 15th Dec.; capture of Hattrass in 1816; Mahratta and Pindaree campaigns of 1817 and 18; Burmese war in 1825 and 26.

17 Lt.Colonel Elrington served in the Peninsula in 1811 and 1812.

18 Lieut.Colonel Aubin served in the Peninsula from Nov. 1811 to the end of the war, including battles of Vittoria, the Pyrenees, 25th, 28th, 30th, and 31st July; Nivelle, Nive, 9th, 11th, and 13th Dec. 1813, besides many other minor actions and skirmishes. Severely wounded through the left side, in action at Couchez, 18th March 1814. Served subsequently in the American war. He has received the War Medal with five Clasps.

19 Lieut.Colonel Clements served at the capture of the Cape of Good Hope in 1806; subsequently on the expedition to South America; the campaign of 1808-9 in Spain, and extra Aide-de-Camp to Sir John Moore at the battle of Corunna. On the expedition to Walcheren in 1809; the Peninsular campaigns from 1810 to 1814, including Cavares and Merina, Salamanca, Begar, Vittoria, Valley of Bastan, and the Pyrenees. He has received the War Medal with three Clasps for Corunna, Vittoria, and Pyrenees.

20 Lieut.Colonel Willats served in the Peninsula from 1812 to the end of the war, including the siege and storming of Ciudad Rodrigo, siege and storming of Badajoz from 19th Jan. to 6th April 1812; operations near and blockade of Bayonne. He has the War Medal with two Clasps.

22 Lieut.Colonel Handcock accompanied the expedition to Hanover in 1805; joined the army in Sicily in 1806, and was employed with its various operations from 1806 to 1810; went with the expedition to Naples, and was present at the capture of Ischia and Procida; returned to Sicily and employed against the French army in 1811. Served in Spain during 1812 and 13, including the battle of Castalla, siege of Tarragona, and affair of Villa Franca. Also the campaign of 1815, and was severely wounded at Waterloo.

23 Lt.Colonel Fred. Wright served at the capture of Madeira in 1808; and the campaign in the Peninsula, under Sir John Moore in 1808-9, and has the War Medal with one Clasp for Corunna.

24 Lieut.Colonel Baron served in the Peninsula from Jan. 1813 to the end of that war in 1814.

25 Lieut.Colonel Colebrooke served on the expedition to Walcheren in 1809.

26 Lieut.Colonel Bonamy served in the Peninsula with the 6th from Sept. 1813 to June 1814, including the battles of Nivelle, Nive, 9th, 10th, and 11th Dec., and Orthes. He has received the War Medal with two Clasps.

27 Lt.Col. Manners served in the Peninsula with the 59th from Aug. 1812 to May 1814, including the battle of Vittoria, siege and storming of San Sebastian in Aug. 1813, battle of the

War Services of the Lieutenant-Colonels.

Nive on the 9th, 10th, and 11th December 1813. Wounded at the storming of Bhurtpore on the 18th January 1826. He has received the War Medal with three Clasps.

29 Lt.Colonel Isaac Richardson served in the Peninsula with the 11th from Aug. 1809 to Oct. 1814, including the battle of Busaco, the subsequent retreat of the army to the lines before Lisbon, the advance and pursuit of the enemy when they broke up from Santarem, blockade of Almeida, and battle of Fuentes d'Onor. He has received the War Medal with one Clasp for Busaco.

30 Lieut.Colonel Jackson served in the Peninsula from Dec. 1809 to 1814, and was severely wounded through the left breast and in both arms at the battle of Albuhera. Served subsequently in the American war. He has received the War Medal with one Clasp.

31 Lieut.Colonel Robertson served with the expedition to Walcheren in 1809, and was present at the siege of Flushing. Also at the taking of the Kandian country, in Ceylon, under Sir Robert Brownrigg.

32 Lieut.Colonel Warburton served the Nepaul campaigns of 1817 and 18, and subsequently in the Deccan, including the capture of the Forts of Rhyghur and Asscerghur.

33 Lieut.Colonel Lynch served at the siege of Flushing. At Malta and the Ionian Islands under Lord Wm. Bentinck. At Genoa and in the south of France in 1814. At the siege and capture of Bhurtpore, and was wounded at the assault 18th Jan. 1826 (Medal).

34 Lieut.Colonel Boyd was employed in the Peninsula and south of France from March 1812 to the end of that war in 1814, and was present at the siege and storming of Badajoz, siege of Burgos, battles of the Nivelle and Nive, passage of the Adour, where he was actively employed in laying down the bridge of boats; investment of Bayonne, affairs of Vic Bigorre and Tarbes, and battle of Toulouse, at which last he was wounded on the hip by a 12-pound shot; and he was wounded in the thigh at the storming of Badajoz. He has received the Silver War Medal with four Clasps.

36 Lt.Colonel Ewan M'Pherson served the campaign of 1813 in Holland, including the actions at Merxem and bombardment of Antwerp. He served with the 99th in operations against the Natives in New Zealand, and was severely wounded.

37 Lieut.Colonel Pascoe served in the Peninsula and France from Aug. 1809 to Feb. 1814, including the battles of Salamanca, Vittoria, Nivelle, and Nive, passage of the Bidassoa, and other operations; sieges of Badajoz (first siege), Forts of Salamanca, Burgos, and San Sebastian. Army of Occupation from 1815 to 1818. He has received the War Medal with seven Clasps.

38 Lieut.Colonel Spiller served at Walcheren, and was present at the siege of Flushing, and the attack and capture of Ter Vere.

39 Lt.Colonel Newman served with the 14th at the siege and storming of Bhurtpore in 1825-6.

40 Lieut.Colonel Alex. Campbell served the campaign of 1814, in the south of France, including the investment of Bayonne. Served also throughout the Burmese war (Medal).

41 Lieut Colonel Poyntz served in the Peninsula as a volunteer with the 30th, from February to November 1811, including the occupation of the Lines at Torres Vedras, pursuit of Massena, actions of Sabugal, Almeida, and Barba del Puerco, and battle of Fuentes d'Onor, for which he has received the War Medal with one Clasp.

42 Lieut.Colonel Greenwood served on the China expedition (Medal).

43 Lieut.Colonel F. Smith Hamilton served in the China expedition in 1842 (Medal), and was present at the assault at the camp at Sagahon.

44 Lieut.Colonel Lynn is a Knight of Charles the Third, First Class of St. Fernando, and Commander of Isabella the Catholic, of Spain.

45 Lieut.Colonel Kenny served in the Peninsula, from June 1813, to the end of the war, including the action at Osma, battle of Vittoria, siege and capture of San Sebastian, passage of the Bidassoa (severely wounded above the left hip); St. Jean de Luz, and the series of actions between the 9th and 13th Dec. 1813 in front of the intrenched camp near Bayonne. Served also in Ava, and was present in most of the operations throughout the war. He has received the War Medal and three Clasps for Vittoria, San Sebastian, and Nivelle.

46 Lieut.Colonel O'Grady was present with the 62nd in the operations in 1814 against the French in retreat from Leghorn, including the affairs of Savona and Spezzia, forcing their positions on the heights of Neroi, and capture of Genoa. In the same year he served in the American war, and was present at the capture of Castine. He served with the 48th at the capture of Coorg in the East Indies in 1834; in command of the left wing of the Queen's Royals, during the campaign of 1844-5, in the Southern Concan and Sawant Warree country, including the investment and capture of the Forts of Monohur and Munsuntosh; and on particular service in the Kaffir war (South of Africa) during part of 1846-7 (Medal).

47 Lieut.Colonel L'Estrange served the campaign of 1815 with the 71st Regiment, and was present at the battle of Waterloo.

48 Lieut.Colonel Bender served in Canada from Dec. 1808, to Jan. 1815, and was present in the action of Maguaga, taking of Detroit, taking several Block-houses on the Miamic River, actions at the river Raisin and Miamic, storming of Sanduskey and Fort Niagara, engagement of 2nd Jan. 1814, actions at Black Rock and at Buffalo. He has received the War Medal and one Clasp for Fort Detroit.

49 Lieut.Colonel Atkin served with the 2nd Light Infantry of the King's German Legion at Walcheren in 1809, and in the Peninsula, from Dec. 1810 to the end of that war in 1814, including the attack on Guarda Heights, battle of Albuhera, sieges of Olivenca, Ciudad Rodrigo, Badajoz, and forts at Salamanca, battle of Salamanca, capture of Madrid and the Retiro, siege of Burgos and covering the retreat from thence, when the two Light Infantry Battalions of the German Legion repulsed a large body of French cavalry; battle of Vittoria, action at Tolosa, siege of San Sebastian, actions in the Pyrenees, passage of the Bidassoa (wounded), battles of Nivelle and Nive, investment of Bayonne (wounded) and repulse of the sortie, besides various minor affairs. Present also at the capture of Paris in 1815. He has the War Medal and six Clasps.

50 Lieut.Colonel Norman served in the Peninsula, and has received the War Medal with two Clasps for the battles of Vittoria and the Pyrenees; and he was severely wounded and taken prisoner in the Maya Pass.

51 Lieut.Colonel Mackay served with the 21st Fusiliers the campaign of 1807 in Egypt. Made prisoner of war in an engagement with the enemy in Calabria 16th June 1809, and detained as such until 14th May 1814. Present at New Orleans, 8th Jan. 1815.

52 Lieut.Colonel John Bolton served the Mahratta campaigns of 1817 and 18, and was present at the siege of Rhyghur.

53 Lieut.Colonel Barnes served at the capture of Fort Anjar in Cutch 25th Dec. 1815; the Mahratta campaigns of 1817-18; escalade of the Fort of Bhooj in Cutch, March 1819; siege of Ras-el-Kymah and Zyah in Arabia, Dec. 1819; escalade of Dwarka Ohamandel, Dec. 1820; action of Beni-Boo-Ally in Arabia, March 1821.

54 Lieut.Colonel Riley was in an engagement with a French squadron in the Mozambique channel 3rd July 1810; served the Nepaul campaign of 1814 and 15.

55 Lieut.Colonel Fynmore, previously to entering the Royal Marines, served several years as Midshipman in the Navy, and was at the battle of Trafalgar and at Buenos Ayres in 1807. In 1809-10 he served in the Great Belt in command of a gun-boat employed in the protection of our convoys, and was engaged with the enemy's gun and row-boats. On the night of the 1st of Aug. 1810 cut out three merchant vessels under a heavy fire of field-pieces and musketry. Six weeks detached from H. M. S. *Vanguard* the same year, to intercept the communication between the Port of Rostock and Wismar; assisted at the capture of a convoy of five sail, and drove on shore and destroyed an armed row-boat. In 1816 he served at Algiers; and in 1821, 22, and 23, in the West Indies, and was engaged with piratical vessels on the coast of Cuba, five of which were captured. Has received the War Medal with two Clasps for Trafalgar and Algiers.

56 Lieut.Colonel Newhouse served in the Light Division of the Deccan Army in the Mahratta war of 1817 and 1818, as extra Aide-de-Camp to Sir Lionel Smith, and commanded a Russela of the Poona Auxiliary Cavalry, and was wounded at the action of the 31st Jan. 1818. Served also in two expeditions to Cutch, the first in 1819, under Sir William Kier Grant, in which he volunteered with the Grenadier Company of the 65th in the storming of the Hill Fort of Bhooj, which was taken by escalade: in the second in 1820 with the right wing of the 65th, with the force under Colonel the Honourable Lincoln Stanhope. He served likewise on two expeditions to the Gulf of Persia—the first in 1819 under Sir W. K. Grant, and the second in 1821, under Sir Lionel Smith; and he was present at the battle and taking of Poonah in 1817, for which he has a Medal.

58 Lieut.Colonel Howorth was actively employed in Canada during the Rebellion in 1837-8-9; he served also in the Kaffir campaign in 1846 (Medal).

59 Lieut.Colonel Tudor served with the 38th Regt. throughout the Burmese war (Medal).

60 Lieut.Colonel the Hon. J. W. B. Macdonald served the Eastern campaign of 1854 as Aidede-Camp to the Duke of Cambridge, including the battles of Alma (horse shot), Balaklava, and Inkerman (horse shot), siege of Sebastopol and sortie of 26th October (Medal and Clasps, *CB*., Knight of the Legion of Honor, and 5th Class of the Medjidie).

61 Lieut.Colonel Blane served the Eastern campaign of 1854-55 as Assistant Adjutant-General, and subsequently as Military Secretary, including the battles of Alma, Balaklava, and Inkerman, and siege and fall of Sebastopol (Medal and Clasps, Knight of the Legion of Honor, Commander 2nd Class of St. Maurice and St. Lazarus, and 5th Class of the Medjidie).

62 Lieut.Colonel Wilton commanded the Fort of Loodianah during the early part of the Sutlej campaign, and was subsequently present with the 50th Regt. in the battle of Aliwal, where he was severely burnt by an explosion of one of the enemy's tumbrils; and battle of Sobraon, where he was very severely wounded, having received a shot in the hip, and three severe sabre wounds in the left shoulder, right arm broken: Medal and one Clasp. Served the Eastern campaign of 1854-55, including the battles of Alma and Inkerman, at the latter in command of the right wing of the 50th throughout that day, being detached to support the 1st Division, and commanded the Regt. at the fall of Sebastopol (Medal and three Clasps, *CB.*, Knight of the Legion of Honor, Sardinian Medal, and 4th Class of the Medjidie).

63 Lieut.Colonel Charles F. Fordyce served the Eastern campaign of 1854-55 with the 47th Regt., including the battles of Alma (contusion of left foot) and Inkerman, capture of Balaklava, siege of Sebastopol, and sortie of 26th Oct. 54 (Medal and Clasps, Brevet Lt. Colonel, *CB.*, and 5th Class of the Medjidie).

64 Lieut.Colonel Whimper served with the 98th Regt. on the China expedition (Medal) and was present at the capture of Chinkiangfoo. Served with the 55th Regt. in the Eastern campaign of 1854, including the battle of Alma—severely wounded and horse killed (Medal and Clasp, Brevet Lt.Colonel, and 5th Class of the Medjidie).

66 Lt.Colonel Hon. J. P. Maxwell served the Eastern campaign of 1854, including the battle of Alma and siege of Sebastopol,—severely injured in the head by a round shot in the trenches in October (Medal and two Clasps, Brevet Lt.Colonel, and 5th Class of the Medjidie).

67 Lieut.Colonel Hawkins served with the 1st Battalion Royals the Eastern campaign of 1854 and up to 3rd July 1855, including the battles of Alma and Inkerman, and siege of Sebastopol (Medal and Clasps, Brevet Lieut.Colonel, and 5th Class of the Medjidie).

68 Lieut.Colonel Peel served the Eastern campaign of 1854-55, including the affair of Bulganak, battle of Alma and Tchernaya, and siege of Sebastopol (Medal and Clasps, Brevet Lieut.Colonel, and 5th Class of the Medjidie).

69 Lieut.Colonel Beaufoy served with the 1st Battalion 27th Regt. in Sicily in 1810; afterwards on the eastern coast of Spain from 1812 to 1814, and was present at the battle of Castalla (contused), taking of Alcoy, battle of Villa Franca, and siege of Tarragona. After the con-

War Services of the Lieutenant-Colonels.

clusion of the Peninsular War he embarked with the Army for North America, and was present at the battle of Plattsburg. In 1819 he embarked for the East Indies, and served afterwards as an acting engineer at Sholapore. He served also in Canada during the rebellion.

70 Lieut.Colonel J. C. Macpherson served the Eastern campaign of 1854 with the 42nd Highlanders, including the battle of Alma and siege of Sebastopol (Medal and two Clasps).

72 Lieut.Colonel Lardner served with the 47th Regt. in the Burmese war from Dec. 1824 until peace was proclaimed (Medal); also in the Eastern campaign of 1854-55, including the battles of Alma and Inkerman, and siege of Sebastopol (Medal and three Clasps).

73 Lieut.Colonel Adamson served with the 38th Regt. throughout the Eastern campaign of 1854 and up to the 25th Jan. 1855, including the battle of Alma and siege of Sebastopol, and commanded in the 2nd parallel cf the Left Attack during its construction when a Russian party attacked it and were repulsed—acted as Major of his Regiment, during ten months of the Eastern expedition (Medal and Clasps for Alma, Inkerman, and Sebastopol).

74 Lieut.Colonel Herbert served the Eastern campaign of 1854-55, including the battles in the Crimea and siege of Sebastopol (Medal and Clasps, Knight of the Legion of Honor, and 5th Class of the Medjidie).

75 Lieut.Colonel Ramsay served with the 49th Regt. in China (Medal) and was present at Amoy, Chusan, Chinhae, Ningpo, Segoan, Woosung, Chinkiangfoo, and Nankin.

76 Lieut.Colonel Wakefield served with the 40th Regt. in Lower and Upper Scinde in 1839 and 40. He commanded the Grenadier Company during the whole of the operations in Candahar and in Affghanistan in 1841 and 42, and has received the Medal for Candahar, Ghuznee, and Cabool. He was also present in the action of Maharajpore, and has received the Bronze Star. Served also the Eastern campaign of 1854, including the battle of the Alma and siege of Sebastopol (Medal and Clasps).

77 Lieut.Colonel Shuckburgh served with the 40th Regt. in the Peninsula, from 1811 to the end of that war in 1814, and was present at the battle of Vittoria, the blockade of Pampeluna from 3rd to 15th July; skirmishes from Roncesvalles to Pampeluna on the 25th and 26th July; attacks on the heights of Sorauren on the 28th and 30th July; action of Irun, action of Vera on the 7th Oct., battles of the Nivelle, Orthes, and Toulouse, besides various minor actions and skirmishes. He has received the War Medal with six Clasps.

78 Lt.Colonel Jas. Richardson served as Adjt. of the Royals in the first Burmese war (Medal).

79 Lieut.Colonel Cockcraft served with the 58th Regt. in the expedition against Kawiti's Pah at Ruapekapeka in New Zealand.

80 Lieut.Colonel Jennings served with the 13th Regt. throughout the campaigns in Affghanistan from 1838 to 1842 inclusive, and was present at the storm and capture of Ghuznee (Medal), assault and capture of the town and forts of Tootumdurrah, storm of Jhoolghur, night attack at Baboo Koosh Ghur, destruction of Khardurrah, assault of Perwandurrah, storming of the Khoord Cabool Pass, affair of Tezeen, forcing the Jugdulluck Pass, reduction of the fort of Mamoo Khail, heroic defence of Jellalabad and sorties on the 14th Nov. and 1st Dec. 1841, 11th March, 24th March, and 1st April 1842; general action and defeat of Akbar Khan before Jellalabad (Medal), storming the heights of Jugdulluck, general action of Tezeen, and recapture of Cabool (Medal). Was severely wounded retiring into Jugdulluck with the rear-guard, 26th Oct. 1841, and slightly wounded in the general action before Jellalabad, 7th April 1842.

81 Lieut.Colonel Bourke served with the 17th Regt. the campaign in Affghanistan of 1838-39, under Lord Keane, including the storm and capture of Ghuznee (Medal) and of Khelat. Served also at the siege of Sebastopol from Dec. 1854 to Feb. 1855 (Medal and Clasp, and 5th Class of the Medjidie).

83 Lieut.Colonel Andrews served with the 28th Regt. at the siege of Sebastopol in 1854 (Medal and Clasp).

84 Lt.Colonel Crawley served with the 20th Regt. at the siege of Sebastopol (Medal and Clasp).

85 Lieut.Colonel Aylmer served with the 89th Regt. at the siege and fall of Sebastopol from 15th Dec. 1855, including the attacks on the 18th June and 8th Sept. (Medal and Clasp, Brevet Lieut.Colonel, Knight of the Legion of Honor, and 5th Class of the Medjidie).

86 Lieut.Colonel Strachan served with the 39th Regt. the campaign against the Rajah of Coorg in April 1834; also at the siege and fall of Sebastopol, including attacks on the 18th June and 8th Sept. (Medal and Clasp, Brevet Lieut.-Colonel, and 5th Class of the Medjidie).

87 Lieut.Colonel M'Call served the Eastern campaign of 1854-55, including the battles of Alma and Balaklava, expedition to Kertch and Yenikale, siege and fall of Sebastopol, and assaults of the 18th June and 8th Sept. (Medal and three Clasps, Brevet of Lt.Colonel, Knight of the Legion of Honor, and 5th Class of the Medjidie).

88 Lieut.Colonel Hugh Smith was present with the Buffs at the battle of Punniar (Medal). Served the Kaffir war of 1850-53 as Aide de Camp to Sir Harry Smith, and subsequently to Major-Gen. Yorke, and was present with various patrols and expeditions (Medal). Was selected by Sir George Cathcart as one of his Divisional Staff Officers when proceeding to the East, and served as D.A.Q.M.G. to the 4th Division at the battles of Alma, Balaklava, and Inkerman; was then appointed Assist. Adjutant General to the Division, and served as such at the siege and fall of Sebastopol and at the attacks of the Redan on the 18th June and 8th Sept. (Medal and Clasps, Brevet of Major and of Lieut.Colonel, Knight of the Legion of Honor, Sardinian Medal, and 5th Class of the Medjidie). Was senior staff officer at the capture of Kinbourn.

89 Lieut.Colonel Thackwell served with the 22nd in the campaign in Scinde and was present at the battle of Hyderabad (Medal). Also the campaign of 1844-45 in the Southern Mahratta country, including the investment and capture of forts Panulla and Pownghur. Served the Eastern campaign of 1854-55 as Brigade Major to 1st Brigade 2nd Division—in-

cluding the battles of Alma and Inkerman (horse shot), siege of Sebastopol and repulse of the sortie on 26th October. On 4th August 1855 he was appointed Assist. Adjutant-General to the 3rd Division and served with it until broken up in April 1856. He has received the Medal and three Clasps, the brevet rank of Major and of Lieut.Colonel, is a Knight of the Legion of Honor, has the Sardinian Medal, and 5th Class of the Medjidie.

90 Lieut.Colonel Fortescue served the Eastern campaign of 1854-55, including the affairs of Bulganac and M'Kenzie's Farm, battles of Alma, (horse killed), Balaklava, and Inkerman, capture of Balaklava, siege and fall of Sebastopol (Medal and Clasps, Brevets of Major and Lt.Col., Sardinian Medal, and 5th Class of the Medjidie).

91 Lt.Colonel Morris served the Eastern campaign of 1854-55, commanded a Field Battery at the battles of Balaklava and Inkerman (wounded), and repulse of the sortie on the 26th October 1854. Was attached from April to Nov. 1855 as Military Commissioner to the 2nd Corps of the French Army, and assisted at the carrying of the Lines of Tchernaya 25th May, the assault and capture of the Mamelon, and of the Malakoff; on the personal Staff of General Bosquet who commanded on these occasions, and was especially named by the General in official Dispatches. Was appointed an Assist.Adj.General in Nov. 1855, and attached to General Windham, Chief of the Staff (Medal and Clasps, C.B., Brevets of Major and Lt.Col., Sardinian Medal, and 5th Class of the Medjidie).

92 Lieut.Colonel Hallewell served the Eastern campaign of 1854-55 as D. A. Q. M. G. to the Light Division, including the battles of Alma and Inkerman, and siege of Sebastopol (Medal and Clasps, Brevets of Major and Lt.Colonel, Knight of the Legion of Honor, and 5th Class of the Medjidie).

93 Lieut.Colonel Shadwell served with the 98th on the China expedition in 1842 (Medal), and was present at the attack and capture of Chin Kiang Foo, and at the investment of Nankin. He served as extra Aide-de-Camp to Sir Colin Campbell at the battles of Chillianwallah and Goojerat (Medal and two Clasps). Served the Eastern campaign of 1854-55 as Aide-de-Camp to Sir Colin, including the battles of the Alma, Balaklava, and Inkerman, and siege of Sebastopol (Medal and Clasps, Brevets of Major and Lt.Colonel, Knight of the Legion of Honor, Sardinian Medal, and 5th Class of the Medjidie).

94 Lieut.Colonel Grove served throughout the Kaffir war of 1846-47 (Medal). Served also in the Crimea at the siege and fall of Sebastopol, and was severely wounded at the assault of the Redan on the 8th Sept. (Medal and Clasp, Brevet Lt.Col., and Knight of the Legion of Honor).

95 Lieut.Colonel Gardiner served with the 22nd Regiment throughout the operations in Scinde under Sir Charles Napier, including the destruction of the Fort of Imaumghur, and battles of Meeanee and Hyderabad (Medal).

96 Lieut.Colonel Thomas served in the Eastern campaign of 1854-55, including the siege and fall of Sebastopol (Medal and Clasp, Sardinian Medal, and 5th Class of the Medjidie).

97 Lieut.Colonel Higginbotham served with the 63rd Regt. at the siege of Sebastopol in 1855, and was severely wounded in the trenches (Medal and Clasp).

98 Lieut.Colonel Stock served with the 10th in the Sutlej campaign of 1845-6, and was present in the battle of Sobraon (Medal). He served also in the Punjaub campaign of 1848-9, and was present during the whole of the siege operations before Mooltan, including the affair of the 9th Sept., storming the enemy's strongly-entrenched position before Mooltan on 12th Sept. (in the latter part of which he commanded the Regt.), action of Soorjkoond, carrying the heights before Mooltan, and surrender of the fortress; was afterwards present at the battle of Goojerat (Medal and Clasps).

99 Lieut.Colonel Hart when commanding at Templemore received on the 8th July 1856 a despatch from the magistrates at Nenagh reporting that a serious outbreak had taken place on the part of the men of the North Tipperary Militia, who, being in a high state of mutiny, had overpowered their officers, seized upon the ammunition magazine, stormed the police barracks, taken possession and control of the town, in which they were firing shots and committing other outrages. Without a moment's hesitation—time not admitting of a reference to head quarters for instructions—he assembled his available force to the number of 574 of all ranks, and with these made a forced march of 23 miles in less than five hours—reaching Nenagh about six hours before the arrival of any other succour—and thus saved the town from being sacked. For his services in quelling this mutiny Major-General Eden commanding Kilkenny District expressed " approbation of the promptness with which he proceeded to Nenagh and of his judgment in taking so good a force;" Lord Seaton commanding the forces in Ireland requested that "his thanks may be conveyed to Lieut.-Colonel Hart for the promptitude with which he moved the Depots under his command to Nenagh, and further judicious control and forbearance with which he acted while in presence of the armed and infuriated insurgents;" and Major-General Sir James Chatterton recorded his "thanks and approbation of the steadiness, zeal, and good conduct of the officers and men evinced when employed at the late unfortunate conflict at Nenagh under the command of Lieut.-Colonel Hart, to whom Sir James Chatterton especially feels much indebted for the ability, activity, and intelligence there manifested."

100 Lieut.Colonel Willis served throughout the Eastern campaign of 1854-55, with the 77th Regt. until April 1855, after which as D. A. Q. M. Gen. at Head Quarters, was present at the battle of Alma, surrender of Balaklava Castle, battle of Inkerman, assault of the Quarries, attack of the Redan on 18th June, battle of Tchernaya, final assault of the Redan on 8th Sept., and during seven months in the trenches, including the repulse of three night sorties (Medal with three Clasps, Brevets of Major and Lieut.Colonel, Knight of the Legion of Honor, Sardinian Medal, and 5th Class of the Medjidie).

101 Lieut.Colonel d'Alton served in the 83rd during the suppression of the Insurrection in

War Services of the Lieutenant-Colonels.

Lower Canada in 1837; also in repelling the attacks of the American Brigands who landed near Prescott, Upper Canada, in 1838.

102 Lieut.Colonel Byrne served with the 2nd Battalion of the Royals at the siege of Sebastopol from 22nd April to 29th May 1855, and was wounded in the trenches (Medal and Clasp, Brevet Lt.Colonel, and 5th Class of the Medjidie).

103 Lieut.Colonel Conolly served the Eastern campaign of 1854 as Brigade-Major to the Heavy Cavalry Brigade, including the battle of Balaklava and siege of Sebastopol (Medal and Clasps, Knight of the Legion of Honor, and 5th Class of the Medjidie).

104 Lieut.Colonel Clifton served the Eastern campaign of 1854 as Aide de Camp to the Duke of Cambridge, including the battles of Alma,'Balaklava, and Inkerman (wounded and horse shot), siege of Sebastopol, and sortie of 26th October (Medal and Clasps, and 5th Class of the Medjidie).

105 Lieut.Colonel J. E. Lewis served with the 68th Light Infantry throughout the Eastern campaign of 1854-55, including the battles of Alma and Inkerman, siege and fall of Sebastopol (Medal and four Clasps, Brevets of Major and Lt.Colonel, and 5th Class of the Medjidie).

106 Lieut.Colonel Sibthorp served with the 1st Battalion 60th Rifles during the Punjaub campaign of 1848-9 (Medal and two Clasps); and was present at the second siege operations at Mooltan, including the siege and storm of the town (covering the advance of the storming parties), and capture of the citadel. Afterwards at the battle of Goojerat, the pursuit of the Seikh army, and the expulsion of the Affghan force beyond the Khyber Pass. Succeeded to the command of the Companies of the 60th Rifles that were engaged against the Hill Tribes in the expedition to the Euzofzye country on the 11th Dec., and also on the 14th Dec. 1849. Served with the 97th Regt. at the siege of Sebastopol from 20th May 1855, and was with the ladder party at the assault on the Redan on the 1th Sept.—severely wounded (Medal and Clasp, Brevet of Major and Lt.Colonel, Knight of the Legion of Honor, and 5th Class of the Medjidie).

106† Colonel Carden served with the 77th Regt., the Eastern campaign of 1854-55, including the battles of Alma and Inkerman, siege and fall of Sebastopol (Medal and Clasps, Brevets of Major and Lt.Colonel, Knight of the Legion of Honor, and 5th Class of the Medjidie).

107 Lieut.Colonel Edmund Roche served the campaign of 1838-39 in Beloochistan and Affghanistan as Aide de Camp, and at periods as Assist. Adjutant-General to Sir Joseph Thackwell, and was present at the storm and capture of Ghuznee, the occupation of Candahar and Cabool, and in several skirmishes. He served the campaign of 1842 with Sir George Pollock's force in Affghanistan, including the forcing of the Khyber Pass, relief of Jellalabad, and was Staff Officer to Colonel Taylor in the expedition against Lolpoora. Served as Assist. Quarter-Master-General of the Cavalry Division of the Army of the Sutlej in 1846, including the battle of Sobraon (charger wounded). For these services he has received three Medals and the Brevet rank of Major.

108 Lieut.Colonel Lumley served with the 31st Regt. in the Crimea from 22nd May to the end of June 1855, including the attack of the 18th June (Medal and Clasp for Sebastopol).

109 Lieut.Colonel Donelan commanded the Grenadiers of the 48th Regt. in the advance on the stockades and capture of the Coorg territory in the East Indies in April 1834, and was particularly mentioned in the dispatches for gallantry on that service.

110 Lieut.Colonel Ffrench served with the 26th Regt. in China (Medal), and was at Chusan, Ningpo, Chapoo, Shanghai, Woosung, Chin Kiang Foo, and Nankin. Served as a Brigade Major in the Punjaub campaign in 1849, and was present at the battle of Goojerat (Medal and Clasp).

111 Lieut.Colonel W. H. F. Clarke served with the 47th Regt. in the first Burmese war with the 53rd on the Sutlej (Medal), and was present at Buddiwal, Aliwal, and Sobraon. He has also the Punjaub Medal.

112 Lt.Colonel Ouvry served the Punjaub campaign of 1848-9 with the 3rd Light Dragoons, and commanded a squadron at the affair of Ramnuggur (horse shot under him); the passage of the Chenab at Wuzeerabad on the 1st Dec. 1848, with the force under Sir Joseph Thackwell; and at the action of Sadoolapore, and battles of Cnillianwallah and Goojerat (Medal and two Clasps). Commanded 9th Lancers before Delhi in 1857 until appointed as Aide de Camp to Sir A. Wilson, whom he attended during the assault (received thanks of Governor General in Council, Brevet Lt.Col., and CB.). After the fall of Delhi commanded the Cavalry Brigade of the Moveable Column, including actions at Bolundshur, Allighur, and battle of Agra. Commanded the Force at the action of Kanoj, and the Cavalry at the relief of Lucknow under Sir Colin Campbell (thanks of Governor-General in Council).

113 Lieut.Colonel Daly served with the 14th Regt. at the siege and capture of Bhurtpore in 1825-6, and was severely wounded at the assault—left leg amputated.

114 Lieut.Colonel Alison served with the 72nd Highlanders the Eastern campaign of 1855, including the expedition to Kertch, siege and fall of Sebastopol, and attack of the 18th June (Medal and Clasp, and Brevet Major).

115 Lieut.Colonel Hon. H. Clifford was at the battle of Boem Plaats in 1848, and served in the Kaffir war of 1852-53 (Medal). Also the Eastern campaign of 1854-55 as Aide-de-Camp to Major General Buller (Medal and Clasps, Brevet Major, Victoria Cross, Knight of the Legion of Honor, and 5th Class of the Medjidie).

116 Lieut.Colonel William Wood served in H.M.S. *Niger* of 30 guns at the capture of the French frigate *La Ceres* of 40 guns; also, of the American privateer *Dart*, and the recapture of the English ship *Adventure*.

117 Lt.Colonel Lewes served with "The Buffs" at the siege of Sebastopol in 1855, and commanded the covering party of the Buffs at the assault of the Redan on the 8th Sept. (Medal and Clasp, Brevet Major, Knight of the Legion of Honor, and 5th Class of the Medjidie).

118 Lieut.Colonel MacCarthy commanded the 84th Regt. with Havelock's Column on its first advance on Lucknow, including the actions of Oonao and Buseerutgunge.

118† Lt.Colonel Bruce served with the 23d Fusiliers at the siege and fall of Sebastopol from 10th Aug. 1855 (Medal and Clasp). Also in the Indian campaign in 1857-58, including the relief of Lucknow by Lord Clyde, defeat of the Gwalior Contingent at Cawnpore on 6th Dec., capture of Lucknow with attack on and occupation of the Iron Bridge from 11th to 14th March 1858 (Brevet of Lt.Colonel, Medal and Clasp).

119 Lieut.Colonel Luard served in the Crimea in the 77th Regt. from March 1855, and on the Staff as Brigade Major to General Straubenzee and D. A. A. G. at Head Quarters from June 1855 (Medal and Clasp, Brevet Major, Sardinian Medal, and 5th Class of the Medjidie). Served in China as Brigade Major 2nd Brigade in 1857-58, and mentioned in despatches as being the first person on the walls of Canton (Brevet Lt.Colonel).

120 Lieut.Colonel Wheatstone served with the 45th Regt. in the Kaffir war of 1851-53 (Medal, and Brevet Major).

121 Lieut.Colonel Maydwell served as Military Secretary to Sir Harry Smith in the Kaffir war of 1850-53 (Medal, and Brevet Major).

122 Lieut.Colonel Wolfe served with the 30th Regt. at the siege of Sebastopol in 1855, and at the assault of the Redan on the 18th June (Medal and Clasp, and 5th Class of the Medjidie).

123 Lieut.Colonel Miller volunteered and commanded the combined force (English and Danish) during the insurrection at Tortola, W. I., in August 1853. On his arrival martial law was proclaimed, and enforced for a period of six weeks, the natives, amounting to 7000, having completely destroyed the town, and threatened the lives of the European inhabitants, who fled for refuge to St. Thomas. He suppressed the rebellion, and restored the island to a state of order and tranquillity, and after re-establishing civil authority received the thanks of the President and Council, and was most favorably reported to the Colonial Office.

124 Lieut.Colonel Hardy served with the 58th Regiment in New Zealand, and was present at the attack and repulse of the hostile natives on the settlement and stockades of Wanganui, 19th May, and action of the 19th July 1847.

125 Lieut.Colonel Johnston served with the 66th Regiment in Canada, during the rebellion in 1837-38, and was in the action of St. Charles.

126 Lt.Colonel MacGregor commanded the Light Company of the 10th in the early part of the siege operations before Mooltan in 1848, including the repulse of the enemy's night attack upon the British camp at Muttee Thol, 17th August, and storming their strongly entrenched position before Mooltan, 12th September: severely wounded—left hand shattered by a musket shot (Medal and Clasp).

127 Lt.Colonel Lucas, with the effective men of the wing of the 6th Regt. stationed at Aden, formed part of an expedition of 500 men under the command of Lt.Colonel Pennycuick, which destroyed the Arab posts of Sheik Medi and Sheik Othman, and skirmished between those places on the 6th Oct. 1841.

128 Lt.Colonel Carruthers served in the Peninsula with the 43rd Regiment during the campaigns of 1813 and 1814, and was present at the Nivelle, Bayonne, Nive, Tarbes, Tournefeuille, and Toulouse, and has received the War Medal with three Clasps.

129 Lt.Colonel Baynes has the 5th Class of the Medjidie. Served with the 8th Regt. in the Indian campaign and was severely wounded at the assault of Delhi (Medal and Clasp).

130 Lt.Colonel Yonge served the Punjaub campaign of 1849, and was present during the second siege operations at Mooltan (including the siege and storm of the town and capture of the citadel), battle of Goojerat, pursuit of the Sikh army until its final surrender at Rawul Pindee, occupation of Attock and Peshawur, and expulsion of the Affghan force beyond the Khyber Pass (Medal and two Clasps).

MAJORS.

	CORNET, 2d LIEUT. or ENSIGN.	LIEUT.	CAPTAIN.	MAJOR.	WHEN PLACED ON HALF PAY.
ⓑ Nicholas Philibert de Brem,[1] *Captain*, h. p. Chasseurs Britanniques.........	never	*1 May 01	25 Nov. 03	4 June 14	1814
Bennet Holgate, *Major*, h. p. 40 Foot	12 May 04	23 Nov. 04	23 June 08	13 Nov. 17	9 Feb. 26
William Macdonald, *Capt.*, h. p. R. Marines	13 May 95	3 Oct. 90	15 Aug. 05	12 Aug. 19	4 Feb. 23
ⓑ Thomas Wilson,[2] *Captain*, h. p. 60 Foot..	Oct. 06	7 Jan. 01	14 Nov. 05	do	10 May 21
Christopher Wilkinson,[3] *Capt.*, h. p. R. Art.	27 Oct. 98	1 Aug. 00	24 April 06	do	1 July 25
ⓑ ⓠⓠ Charles Freeman Sandham,[4] *do. do.*.	27 Oct. 98	7 Nov. 00	1 June 06	do	7 June 22
ⓑ Richard Staunton Sitwell, *Major*, Unatt.	8 Oct. 02	3 April 05	22 Aug. 08	10 July 23	2 Aug. 26
ⓑ Hon. Sir Fra. Cha. Stanhope,[5] *Major*, do.	24 April 05	28 Aug. 06	18 Aug. 08	27 May 25	4 May 26
ⓟⓠⓠ Sir Trevor Wheler, *Bt.*,[6] *Maj.*, do. *Lt. Col. Comm. R. N. Devon Mounted Rifles*	17 Nov. 08	11 July 11	10 April 17	5 Feb. 29	30 Nov. 33
ⓑ Moyle Sherer,[7] *Captain*, Unattached	Jan. 07	4 June 07	26 Mar. 11	22 July 30	6 July 32
ⓟ William Henry Hartman,[8] *Captain*, Unatt.	9 July 03	28 Mar. 05	30 Oct. 12	do	16 Feb. 44
ⓑ Honeyman Mackay,[9] *Major*, Unattached	5 Aug. 07	30 June 08	30 May 16	do	29 May 35
Samuel Charters,[10] *Captain*, h.p. R. Artillery	14 Dec. 04	13 Feb. 06	15 Jan. 16	10 Jan. 37	2 Feb. 28
Charles Boyd, *Captain*, Unattached	15 Aug. 04	19 Dec. 05	12 July 16	do	3 May 39
George Montagu, *Captain*, Unattached	8 Dec. 14	31 Oct. 22	22 Oct. 25	28 June 38	3 June 42
John Buckley Castieau,[13] *Capt.*, h.p. R. Mar.	22 Sept. 08	13 April 24	10 July 37	10 Nov. 40	
William Elliott, *Captain*, Unattached......	6 Aug. 12	2 Sept. 13	6 July 27	23 Nov. 41	27 Jan. 43
ⓠⓠ Willoughby Montagu,[14] *do.*, h.p. R. Art.	26 Nov. 08	11 Aug. 11	6 Nov. 27	do	6 Nov. 27
George M'Leod Tew,[16] *Major*, Unattached..	19 Aug. 13	30 Sept. 19	12 Jan. 34	10 April 46	25 Aug. 48
Robert Miller Mundy,[17] *Capt.*, h. p. R. Art.	21 June 33	28 Dec. 35	28 April 44	20 Oct. 46	27 Sept. 47
Charles Hugh Lyle Tinling,[18] *Captain*, Unatt.	20 Nov. 17	3 May 21	30 Dec. 34	9 Nov. 46	9 Feb. 49
*Moderico de Marchesi Alessi, *Captain*, ret. full pay, Malta Fencibles	23 Jan. 25	15 Jan. 27	10 July 40	11 Nov. 51	
John Kenneth Mackenzie, *Captain*, Unatt., *Adjutant, Antrim Militia*	16 Dec. 31	16 Sept. 36	23 April 42	20 June 54	12 Jan. 55
G. B. C. Crespigny, *Capt.*, Paymas. at Hythe	29 Jan. 36	30 July 39	17 June	do	
W. Mauleverer, *Capt.*, h.p. 58 F., *S. O. of Pen.*	31 Aug. 30	13 Jan. 37	22 July	do	23 Aug. 44
William Garstin, *Captain*, h. p. 24 Drs., *do.*	28 Oct. 24	29 May 28	2 Aug.	do	9 Mar. 49
William Fred. Harvey, *Captain*, Unatt. *do.*	11 April 26	13 Aug. 29	5 Aug.	do	24 Jan. 51
John Bruce, *Captain*, h. p. 56 Foot, *do.*	31 July 28	12 April 31	19 Aug.	do	19 July 50
Fred. Brown Russell, *Capt.*,h.p.3 Dr. Gds., *do.*	2 Nov. 26	18 Feb. 30	13 Sept.	do	28 Dec. 49
Walter Warde, *Capt.* Unatt. *Staff O. of Pen.*	29 June 32	7 Aug. 35	25 Oct.	do	25 Oct. 42
Aug. Wm. Murray, *Major*, 1 West India Regt.	28 Dec. 32	28 Nov. 37	25 Nov.	do	
Charles S. S. Evans Gordon, *Captain*, 23 Foot, *Brigade Major at Chatham*..	12 Oct. 32	3 June 36	20 Dec.	do	
Henry Jackson, *Captain*, Depot Batt.	5 April 31	20 Sept. 33	27 Dec.	do	
Henry Dalton Smart, *Captain*, Unattached	31 Dec. 33	25 Aug. 37	8 Jan. 43	do	4 April 56
John Perkins Mayers, *Captain*, 86 Foot ..	20 July 30	23 April 39	27 Jan.	do	
John Richard Heaton, *Captain*, 37 Foot....	19 Dec. 34	22 Aug. 37	24 Feb.	do	
Charles William Thompson, *Captain*, 58 F.	23 Dec. 36	3 May 39	12 May	do	
Cha. S. Teale, *Capt.*, Unatt., *S. O. of Pens.*	7 April 25	10 Dec. 27	22 May	do	11 Oct. 44
Charles Parke Ibbetson, *Capt.*, h. p. 89 Foot	24 April 35	30 June 37	2 June	do	24 Sept. 47
Henry Chas. Capel Somerset, *Capt.*, h. p. 27 F., *Staff Officer of Pensioners*.....	4 Oct. 33	14 July 37	23 June	do	27 Sept. 44
Francis Carey, *Major*, 26 Foot	22 May 35	2 Sept. 37	7 July	do	
Henry J. Savage, *Major*, 91 Foot	5 June 35	11 May 38	8 July	do	
Wm. Little Stewart, *Major*, Depot Batt	12 April 33	13 Jan. 37	28 July	do	
Arthur Pigott, *Capt.*,h.p.20F. *S. O.of Pens.*	24 April 35	2 July 38	25 Aug.	do	5 Nov. 50
Abraham Collis Anderson, *Major*, Unatt. *Fort Major, Edinburgh Castle*	12 June 32	9 July 29	27 Aug.	do	22 June 58
Charles Murray,[19] *Major*, Unattached	21 June 33	30 Mar. 38	5 Sept.	do	12 Sept. 56
Edward Lynch Blosse, *Major*, Unattached..	15 Nov. 33	25 Jan. 39	5 Sept.	do	7 Sept. 58
William Pym Young, *Captain*, 65 Foot....	26 Oct. 30	27 Nov. 35	12 Sept.	do	
James Nugent, *Major*, 36 Foot	15 April 36	11 Jan. 39	22 Sept. 43	do	
John Porter, *Major*, 67 Foot	28 Mar. 34	29 Dec. 37	6 Oct.	do	
Henry Down Griffith, *Captain*, 45 Foot ..	13 June 30	6 April 36	20 Oct.	do	
Francis Gilbert Hamley, *Major*, 50 Foot ..	7 Aug. 35	25 July 37	2 Nov.	do	
John Henderson, *Major*, 16 Foot	20 Jan. 32	28 Nov. 34	10 Nov. 43	do	
Morley S. Tynte Dennis, *Captain*, 76 Foot..	18 Sept. 35	28 Nov. 37	do	do	
Henry Draper Nevill, *Major*, 22 Foot	16 Aug. 33	20 Jan. 37	5 Dec. 43	do	
Charles Barnard Hague, *Major*, 67 Foot ..	5 Sept. 35	30 Dec. 37	do	do	
Thomas Mathias Luz Weguelin, *Capt.*, 100 F.	23 Dec. 36	28 June 39	20 Dec. 43	do	
John James Bull, *Major*, 56 Foot	8 June 39	16 Nov. 41	do	do	
George Mein, *Major*, Depot Battalion	19 June 35	21 April 39	3 Nov. 46	30 June 54	
Geo. E. Hillier, *Captain*, 5 Lancers........	14 Dec. 38	16 April 41	10 Mar. 47	do	
Anthony Ormsby,[20] *Major*, Unatt.	13 July 38	2 July 41	25 Dec. 45	28 July 54	26 Aug. 50

Majors. 75

Name	ENSIGN, ETC.	LIEUT.	CAPTAIN.	MAJOR.	WHEN PLACED ON HALF PAY.
Henry St. George Ord, *Capt.*, R. Eng. *Lt.Gov. of Dominica*	14 Dec. 37	27 May 39	29 Oct. 46	8 Sept. 54	
Wm. C. Parkin Elliott, *Captain*, R. Marines	8 May 38	12 Feb. 42	19 Nov. 51	do	
Chas. Nasmyth, *Major,*[22] Unatt., *Brigade Major at Sydney, N.S.Wales*	14 Dec. 45	16 April 50	15 Sept. 54	15 Sept. 54	
Wm. Fra. Drummond Jervois,*Capt.*R.Eng. *Assist. Inspec. General of Fortifications*	19 Mar. 39	8 Oct. 41	13 Dec. 47	29 Sept. 54	
Marcus Louis,[23] *Capt.*, r. f. p., 5 R. Vet. Batt.	Jan. 95	8 Sept. 95	23 May 00	28 Nov. 54	
Oliver Fry, *Capt.* do. R. Artillery	....	17 Oct. 94	14 Oct. 01	do	
Geo. St. John Gifford, *do.* do. 11 R. Vet. Batt.	20 Feb. 96	25 April 97	3 Sept. 04	do	
Thos. Levet Metcalfe,[24] *do.*do. 6 do.	5 Aug. 96	23 May 00	25 April 05	do	
Arthur Fleming, *do.* do., Royal Artillery	17 Aug. 99	27 May 01	1 June 06	do	
Hen. Clinton Martin,[25] *do.* do. do.	20 Dec. 99	25 Dec. 01	13 Jan. 07	do	
Judge Thos. D'Arcy, *do.* do. 4 R. Vet. Batt.	31 Dec. 94	26 Sept. 95	11 May 08	do	
₪ Archib. Fullarton,[27] *do.* do. 6 do.	19 Mar. 01	15 Oct. 03	2 April 12	do	
₪ Richard Woods,[28] *do.*do. 8 do.	2 Dec. 06	28 Dec. 09	13 Aug. 12	do	
Thomas Hurdle, *do.* do., Royal Marines	15 Jan. 98	1 Dec. 03	18 Mar. 13	do	
Henry Augus. Colby,[29] *do.* do. R. Engineers	12 July 08	24 June 09	2 Sept. 13	do	
₪ Alexander Skene,[30] *do.* do. 4 R. Vet. Batt.	28 May 07	25 July 09	11 Nov. 13	do	
₪ John Lyon Hulme,[31] *do.* do. R. Engineers	24 June 09	10 July 10	20 Dec. 14	do	
₪ Thos. Ramsden Agnew,[32] *Capt.*, r. f. p. 2 R. Vet. Batt.*Dep.Storekeep. at Tipner*	19 Dec. 07	12 Oct. 09	22 June 15	do	
₪₪₪ John W. Pringle,[33] *Capt.* do. R. Eng.	23 Aug. 09	1 May 11	21 July 15	do	
Richard J. F. Crowther, *do.* do. R. Marines	2 Dec. 08	18 Aug. 04	19 July 21	do	
Ives Stocker, *do.*do. R. Engineers	14 Dec. 11	1 July 12	29 July 25	do	
Jasper Farmar, *do.* do. R. Marines	1 July 03	15 Aug. 05	31 July 26	do	
Wm. Steph. Knapman,[34] *do.*do. do.	1 Nov. 03	17 Jan. 06	do	do	
₪ Geo. Vaughan Tinling,[35]*do.* do. R. Engineers	1 July 12	21 July 13	10 Oct. 26	do	
John Wilson,[36] *do.* do. R. Marines	22 June 04	10 June 07	31 Aug. 27	do	
John Humby,[37] *do.*do. do.	30 July 04	10 June 07	31 Aug. 27	do	
₪₪₪ William Lemoine, *do.* do. R. Artillery	3 Oct. 07	5 June 08	6 Nov. 27	do	
₪ Charles Manners,[38] *do.* do. do.	3 Oct. 07	24 Sept. 08	do	do	
And. Archer Wm. Schalch,[39] *do.* do. do.	17 Dec. 07	10 Mar. 09	do	do	
Charles Gordon,[40] *do.* do. 93 Foot	22 June 09	15 Oct. 12	28 Feb. 28	do	
₪ ₪₪ Robt. Cochrane,[41] *do.* do. Rifle Brig. *Military Knight of Windsor*	9 Nov. 09	8 May 12	22 May 28	do	
Aylmer Dowdall,[42] *Captain*, do. 54 Foot	20 May 13	2 Mar. 17	2 May 29	do	
Richard Fry, *do.* do. 63 Foot	26 April 10	18 June 12	5 June 30	do	
₪ Hugh Morgan,[43] *do.* do. R. Artillery	21 Dec. 08	7 Feb. 12	30 June 30	do	
Thomas Waters, *do.* do. R. Marines	30 Nov. 04	27 July 08	22 July 30	do	
Geo. Thos. Welchman,[44] *do.*do. do.	31 Aug. 05	do	17 Mar. 31	do	
John Geo. Richardson,[45] *do.*do. do.	18 Sept. 05	14 Feb. 09	do	do	
Jas. Hunter Rutherford, *do.* do. Roy.Eng., *Gov. of Dublin Military Prison*	20 July 13	15 Dec. 13	12 Nov. 31	do	
Robert Webb,[46] *Captain*, do. R. Marines	24 Sept. 05	10 May 09	7 Mar. 32	do	
₪ John Hewett,[48] *do.* do. do.	12 Nov. 05	24 Sept. 10	12 Oct. 32	do	
George Bownell Pepyat, *do.* do. do.	31 Jan. 06	3 Sept. 11	do	do	
Peter Eason, *do.* do. 61 Foot	5 Oct. 09	8 Oct. 10	21 June 33	do	
William Henry Devon,[49] *do.* do. R. Marines	11 Feb. 06	15 Jan. 12	23 Dec. 33	do	
Hugh Brown, *do.*do. do.	12 Feb. 06	16 Jan. 12	10 Feb. 34	do	
₪ Evan Morgan,[50] *do.* do. R. Art., *Lt. Col. Glamorgan Militia Artillery*	17 Dec. 12	23 May 15	do	do	
David Galloway, *Capt.* do. R. Marines	4 Mar. 06	10 April 12	21 May 34	do	
Jervis Cook,[52] *do.*do. do.	26 May 06	28 Oct. 12	27 May 34	do	
James Shute,[53] *do.*do. do.	21 June 06	30 Jan. 13	do	do	
William Davis,[54] *do.*do. do.	26 Feb. 07	23 Feb. 14	do	do	
Colin Mackenzie,[55] *do.*do. R. Engineers	20 July 13	15 Dec. 13	26 Oct. 34	do	
John Milliquet Hewson,[56] *do.*do. 89 Foot	2 Sept. 12	22 May 15	13 Mar. 35	do	
Lewis Edw. Walsh, *do.* do. R. Marines	5 July 13	13 May 16	6 May 35	do	
Fred. Augustus Griffiths,*do.* do. do.	13 Dec. 13	8 Oct. 16	19 Aug. 35	do	
James Thos. Cracknell,[57] *do.*do. R. Marines	17 Aug. 07	19 June 21	26 Oct. 35	do	
Geo. Chas. Degen Lewis, *do.*do. R. Engineers	1 Aug. 14	1 July 15	5 Dec. 35	do	
Francis Holcombe, *do.* do. R. Artillery	1 May 15	9 Nov. 19	6 Jan. 36	do	
₪ Henry James,[58] *do.* do. R. Marines	7 Dec. 07	19 July 21	18 Mar. 36	do	
Adam Von Beverhoudt,[59]*do.*do. do.	21 Oct. 13	9 April 16	29 April 36	do	
John Kelly,[60] *do.* do. 6 Foot	8 Nov. 13	20 Dec. 24	27 May 36	do	
William John Stokes, *do.* do. R. Artillery	10 July 15	2 April 21	29 June 36	do	
Robert Shepherd, *do.* do. 76 Foot	10 July 23	13 May 26	5 Jan. 37	do	
John Richard Mascall,[62] *do.* do. R. Marines	7 Sept. 08	19 Dec. 22	10 Jan. 37	do	
John Dyson, *do.* do. R. Artillery	11 Dec. 15	11 Aug. 23	10 Jan. 37	do	
Rich. Wm. Pascoe,[63] *do.*do. R. Marines	12 Sept. 08	10 May 23	20 May 37	do	

Majors.

	ENSIGN, ETC.	LIEUT.	CAPTAIN.	MAJOR.	WHEN PLACED ON HALF PAY.
Wm. Young Fenwick, *Capt.* r. f. p. R. Art.	15 Dec. 17	29 July 25	23 June 37	28 Nov. 54	
Richard Searle,[61] *do. do.* R. Mar.	30 Sept. 08	13 April 24	10 July 37	do	
Henry Smith,[65] *do. do. do.*	18 Feb. 00	13 Aug. 25	do	do	
Peter Jno. Jas. Dusautoy,[66] *do. do. do.*	14 Mar. 00	16 May 26	do	do	
Robert Stuart Ridge,[67] *do. do.* 36 Foot	8 Sept. 14	28 Dec. 21	29 Sept. 37	do	
John Harvey, *do. do.* 37 Foot	14 April 14	10 April 25	9 Oct. 37	do	
Francis Wm. Pettingal, *do. do.* R. Eng.	1 Mar. 16	23 Mar. 25	20 Nov. 37	do	
Thomas Park,[68] *do. do.* R. Mar.	30 Aug. 09	28 Feb. 28	7 Dec. 37	do	
George Griffin, *do. do. do.*	18 Sept. 00	6 Mar. 28	9 Dec. 37	do	
John Campbell, *do. do.* 74 Foot	16 Sept. 13	28 Sept. 20	15 Dec. 37	do	
James Dowman,[69] *do. do.* R. Mar.	28 Nov. 09	8 Mar. 27	1 Jan. 38	do	
David Dickson, *do. do.* 95 Foot	9 Sept. 13	9 Nov. 20	26 Jan. 38	do	
Henry Nicholls, *do. do.* 04 Foot	25 July 11	15 Sept. 14	9 Feb. 38	do	
John Law,[70] *do. do.* R. Mar.	14 Mar. 10	6 June 28	26 April 38	do	
William Lancey, *do. do.* R. Eng.	1 Aug. 16	7 June 25	25 May 38	do	
John Blackall, *do. do.* 39 F., *Captain Londonderry Militia*	14 Oct. 12	4 May 14	1 June 38	do	
Edmund Nepean,[71] *Capt.*, ret. f.p. R. Mar.	27 Nov. 10	2 Oct. 28	do	do	
Valentine Beadon,[72] *do. do.* R. Mar.	14 Feb. 11	6 Feb. 29	8 June 38	do	
John Sidney Farrell, *do. do.* R. Art.	8 July 18	10 July 26	11 June 38	do	
Charles Oldershaw, *do. do.* R. Eng.	1 Aug. 16	29 July 25	13 June 38	do	
Hender Mounsteven,[73] *do. do.* 48 Foot	30 Dec. 12	6 Jan. 14	30 Nov. 38	do	
Hy. Higgins Donatus O'Brien, *do. do.* R. Art.	5 Oct. 18	2 Feb. 27	11 Dec. 38	do	
Arthur Gosset, *do. do. do.*	do	2 Mar. 27	1 May 39	do	
Samuel James Skinner, *do. do. do.*	23 Oct. 18	1 Apr. 27	16 May 39	do	
Robert Luard, *do. do. do.*	8 Dec. 19	12 May 27	20 May 39	do	
Geo. Gardine Shaw,[74] *do. do.* 63 Foot	30 May 11	21 Dec. 13	31 May 39	do	
John Gore, *do. do.* R. Art., *Professor, R. Military Academy, Woolwich*	8 Dec. 19	8 June 27	3 July 39	do	
James Turner, *Capt.*, ret. full pay, R. Art.	15 Nov. 24	17 Nov. 17	11 April 40	do	
George Mainwaring,[75] *do. do.* 22 Foot	3 May 15	17 Sept. 17	5 June 40	do	
John Low, *do. do.* R. Art.	28 Feb. 25	8 Nov. 27	19 June 40	do	
Joshua Edleston,[76] *do. do.* R. Mar.	19 Nov. 11	22 July 30	10 Aug. 40	do	
William John King,[77] *do. do.* 21 Foot	1 Mar. 17	20 Jan. 20	3 Oct. 40	do	
Rd. Matthews Poulden, *do. do.* R. Art.	29 July 25	3 Jan. 28	22 Oct. 40	do	
Robert Wright,[78] *do. do.* R. Mar.	6 May 12	4 June 31	13 Nov. 40	do	
Edward Appleton,[79] *do. do. do.*	26 Aug. 12	7 Oct. 31	5 Mar. 41	do	
Patrick Scott Campbell, *do. do.* R. Art.	19 May 28	19 Jan. 30	14 April 41	do	
Caleb Barnes, *do. do.* R. Mar.	10 Nov. 12	22 Feb. 32	11 May 41	do	
Peter Martin M'Kellar, *do. do.* R. Mar.	17 April 12	4 Apr. 32	11 May 41	do	
William Knowles,[80] *do. do.* 50 Foot	9 Aug. 33	20 July 38	25 June 41	do	
Henry Stephen Tireman, *do. do.* R. Art.	6 Aug. 28	4 July 30	21 July 41	do	
Richard Thompson, *do. do.* 51 Foot	1 Jan. 19	8 Nov. 27	28 Aug. 41	do	
Robert Roe Fisher, *do. do.* R. Art., *Lt. Col. Commandant Donegal Art.* ..	6 Aug. 28	22 July 30	2 Sept. 41	do	
John M'Caskill, *Capt.*, ret. f.p. 97 Foot	25 Jan. 25	27 June 28	26 Oct. 41	do	
William Baird Young, *do. do.* R. Art.	6 Aug. 28	1 Oct. 30	23 Nov. 41	do	
Rodney Mylius, *do. do.* Ceylon Regt.	16 May 22	30 May 24	9 Oct. 42	do	
Charles Cheetham, *do. do.* R. Art.	16 Dec. 31	16 July 33	4 April 43	do	
Alex. Fred. Wm. Papillon, *do. do. do.*	do	23 Oct. 33	do	do	
John Miller,[82] *do. do.* R. Mar.	18 July 25	7 May 34	12 April 43	do	
William Fulford, *do. do.* R. Art.	16 Dec. 31	22 Jan. 34	3 May 43	do	
Jas. Wm. Graves, *do.* Unatt., *S. O. of Pens.*	24 Oct. 34	31 May 39	26 Jan. 44	do	30 Jan. 52
Chas. Robert Wynne, *do.* ret. f. p., R. Art., *Lt. Col. Commandant Fife Artillery* ..	20 Dec. 32	5 June 35	15 April 44	do	
Kenneth Murchison,[83] *Capt.* ret. f.p. 29 Foot	1 Feb. 39	29 May 41	22 Dec. 45	do	
Charles Miller, *do. do.* R. Mar.	19 Mar. 28	20 July 36	7 April 46	do	
Philip Bolton, *do. do.* 77 Foot	6 July 09	25 July 11	10 Sept. 47	do	
William Macdonald, *do. do.* 93 Foot	23 Aug. 27	13 Jan. 34	3 Dec. 47	do	
Charles Stuart Miller, *do. do.* R. Eng.	19 Mar. 39	23 Nov. 41	12 Feb. 48	do	
Pitcairn Onslow,[84] *do. do.* R. Mar.	13 Nov. 33	6 April 39	14 July 48	do	
Dennis Dunn, *Capt.*, ret. f. p., 69 F.	23 May 45	18 Sept. 46	3 Dec. 52	do	
Lancelot Edward Wood, *Capt.* ret. f. p. 54 F.	21 May 29	22 June 32	24 May 46	1 Dec. 54	
Demetrius W. Grevis James, *Major*, 2 Foot	31 Jan. 40	15 Dec. 40	9 June 46	do	
John Oldright, *Capt.*, ret. full pay, 81 Foot	21 Sept. 38	28 Mar. 41	2 May 51	do	
Charles Duperier,[85] *Capt.*, do. 80 Foot	29 Dec. 40	26 July 44	7 May 52	do	
Henry Mackay, *do. do.* 79 F. *Adj. Forfar Art.*	18 June 41	11 April 44	6 June 54	do	
John James Grant, *Major*, R. Newf. Comp.	9 Mar. 26	12 Feb. 28	22 Mar. 44	12 Dec. 54	
George John Brown, *Major*, 4 Lt. Dragoons	17 April 40	14 July 43	30 Jan. 46	do	
Andrew Hunt,[86] *Major*, Unattached	22 Feb. 40	15 June 42	25 Aug. 46	do	7 Sept. 55
Fra. Rowland Forster, *Captain*, 4 Dr. Gds.	7 Feb. 40	11 Mar. 42	29 Jan. 47	do	

Majors. 77

	ENSIGN, ETC.	LIEUT.	CAPTAIN.	MAJOR.	WHEN PLACED ON HALF PAY.
Henry Hardinge, *Major*, Rifle Brigade	19 June 40	5 Aug. 42	7 May 47	12 Dec. 54	
Wm. Harry, *Earl of* Erroll,[57] *Major*, Unatt.	never	18 May 41	2 July 47	do	5 June 57
James S. Hawker Farrer, *Major*, 38 Foot ..	2 April 41	2 June 43	28 April 48	do	
Richard Thompson,[58] *Major*, Unatt.	25 Feb. 42	17 Nov. 43	23 May 48	do	2 Dec. 59
John James Brandling, C.B., *Captain*, R. Art.	19 Mar. 39	25 Jan. 41	1 May 48	do	
Hayes Marriott, *Captain*, Royal Marines ..	11 Oct. 33	16 June 38	17 May 48	do	
Cha. Trigance Franklin, C.B., *Capt.* R. Art.	1 Jan. 42	14 July 42	14 Oct. 48	do	
Philip Gosset Pipon, *Captain*, R. Artillery	18 June 42	18 Aug. 43	5 Sept. 49	do	
Wm. Stratton Aslett, *Captain*, R. Marines	26 July 37	5 Mar. 41	3 Oct. 49	do	
James Rose, *Major*, 2 Foot	16 Nov. 41	28 Dec. 46	5 Oct. 49	do	
John Davenport Shakespear, *Capt.*, R. Art.	18 June 42	9 Sept. 43	6 Mar. 50	do	
Hon. Wm. Charles Yelverton, *Capt.* R. Art.	11 Jan. 43	14 April 44	16 July 50	do	
John Cowell Bartley, *Major*, 5 Foot	26 April 39	20 Oct. 40	22 Aug. 50	do	
Edward Fellowes,[69] *Major*, Unattached ...	23 April 39	29 Apr. 42	6 Dec. 50	do	5 Mar. 58
Soame G. Jenyns, C.B., *Major*, 18 Hussars..	30 Dec. 45	24 Sept. 47	20 Dec. 50	do	
John Fraser L. Baddeley, *Captain*, R. Art.	17 June 43	17 Jan. 45	22 Feb. 51	do	
Arthur Tremayne, *Major*, 13 Dragoons.....	11 Sept. 46	20 Oct. 47	4 April 51	do	
Edward Tomkinson,[90] *Major*, Unattached, *Cavalry Depot at Canterbury* ....}	12 May 43	12 April 44	27 June 51	do	
John Hackett, *Major*, 44 Foot	17 Nov. 37	28 Aug. 39	25 July 51	do	
John W. Lovell, C.B., *Capt.*, R. Eng.	19 June 41	16 Aug. 44	6 Dec. 51	do	
Robert White, *Major*, 17 Lancers	15 Oct. 47	22 Dec. 48	26 Mar. 52	do	
Henry Lowther Chermside, *Capt.*, R. Art.	19 June 44	1 April 46	1 April 52	do	
John Thomas Dalyell, *Major*, 21 Foot	14 May 47	21 June 50	23 April 52	do	
George Neeld Boldero, *Major*, 21 Foot ...	8 Oct. 47	3 April 49	7 May 52	do	
Arch. Henry P. Stuart Wortley,[91] *Maj.* Unatt.	....	18 Aug. 48	14 May 52	do	12 Sept. 56
Edward George Hibbert, *Major*, 12 Foot ..	29 April 46	6 Oct. 48	28 May 52	do	
Henry Warter Meredith, *Major*, 41 Foot ..	6 June 45	3 Nov. 46	25 June 52	do	
John George Boothby, *Captain*, R. Artillery	19 June 44	1 April 46	5 Aug. 52	do	
William Hardy, *Major*, Depot Battalion ..	27 Sept. 42	8 May 46	12 Oct. 52	do	
Hon. Gilbert Elliot, *Major*, Rifle Brigade..	7 July 43	11 Sept. 46	12 Oct. 52	do	
John Wycliffe Thompson,[92] *Major*, Unatt., *Cavalry Depot, Canterbury* ....}	22 Nov. 44	3 Apr. 46	5 Nov. 52	do	
George Barstow, *Captain*, Royal Artillery..	19 Dec. 44	1 April 46	11 Nov. 52	do	
Cha. Carew de Morel, *Major*, Depot Batt...	24 Oct. 45	29 May 49	23 Nov. 52	do	
A. Wm. D. Burton, C.B., *Maj.*, 7 Dr. Gds...	8 Aug. 45	10 Apr. 49	2 Dec. 52	do	
Graham Le Fevre Dickson,[93] *Major*, Unatt.	5 Mar. 47	1 Aug. 48	7 Jan. 53	do	29 Feb. 56
James Gubbins, *Major*, 23 Foot	19 Dec. 44	13 Apr. 49	18 Feb. 53	do	
Cha. Fred. Torrens Daniell,[94] *Maj.*, Unatt., *Brigade Major in Dublin Division* ..}	3 Jan. 45	7 Mar. 49	20 May 53	do	16 Mar. 58
Gaspard Le Marchant Tupper, *Capt.* R. Art.	18 June 45	1 April 46	26 Sept. 53	do	
Hon. Wm. Geo. Boyle, *Lt. & Capt.*, Coldst. Gds.	9 Feb. 49	16 Sept. 51	13 Jan. 54	do	
Dixon Edward Hoste, C.B., *Capt.*, R. Art.	18 June 45	1 April 46	24 Dec. 54	do	
Paget Bayly,[95] *Major*, Unatt............	8 Mar. 39	26 Jan. 41	3 Feb. 54	do	10 Aug. 55
John Singleton, *Captain*, Royal Artillery ..	18 June 45	1 April 46	17 Feb. 54	do	
John Hardman Burke, *Major*, 3 Foot......	1 Nov. 39	3 Mar. 43	6 June 54	do	
Alastair M'Ian M'Donald, *Maj.*, Depot Batt.	27 Mar. 46	12 Nov. 47	do	do	
Charles Henry Ingilby, *Captain*, R. Artillery	16 Dec. 46	30 June 48	20 June 54	do	
Arthur Charles Greville,[96] *Major*, Unatt. ..	4 April 45	26 Aug. 49	7 July 54	do	15 Jan. 56
Philip S. Crawley, *Lt. & Capt.*, Coldst. Gds.	2 Mar. 47	23 June 48	14 July 54	do	
James Farrell Pennycuick, *Capt.* R. Art. ..	2 May 47	30 June 48	21 Sept. 54	do	
William John Chads, *Captain*, 64 Foot	19 Nov. 47	12 Sept. 48	20 June 54	15 Dec. 54	
Lachlan Hector Gilbert Maclean,[97] *Maj.* Unatt.	26 Dec. 34	31 Aug. 38	25 Feb. 48	22 Dec. 54	1 June 55
William Forbes, *Major*, Unattached	2 Dec. 31	11 Nov. 35	7 Feb. 45	29 Sept. 54	18 Jan. 56
Thomas Ormsby Ruttledge,[97]† *Maj.*, h.p. 32 F.	20 April 36	23 April 38	9 Sept. 45	do	20 July 59
John Fitz Thomas Dennis,[98] *Major*, Unatt.	4 Aug. 37	30 Oct. 38	25 Nov. 45	do	1 May 57
Duncan Campbell, *Major*,[99] Unattached ..	8 April 34	1 Feb. 39	3 Oct. 46	do	30 Nov. 55
Henry Collette, *Captain*, 67 Foot	26 Aug. 36	22 Jan. 39	23 Feb. 44	6 Jan. 55	
John Harpur, *Capt.* ret. f. p. 2 W. I. Regt. (Q.M. 5 March 38)}	15 Dec. 40	18 Aug. 42	6 Jan. 54	26 Jan. 55	
Matthew Cassan, *Capt.* Unatt., *S. O. of Pens.*	13 Dec. 33	19 May 38	13 Mar. 44	6 Feb. 55	1 Feb. 52
Robert Watson,[160] *Capt.*, r.f.p., Ceylon Regt.	7 July 37	29 Jan. 42	2 Mar. 47	16 Mar. 55	
Richard William Meheux,[101] do. do. R. Mar.	26 Dec. 29	10 July 37	27 July 47	29 Mar. 55	
George William Paty, *Major*, 56 Foot	6 Sept. 39	18 Feb. 42	6 Feb. 46	23 April 55	
Wm. Gordon Cameron, *Major*, 4 Foot	24 May 44	12 Feb. 45	17 July 53	24 April 55	
William Rickman, *Major*, Depot Battalion	12 Sept. 48	31 Oct. 51	24 Mar. 54	do	
John Patrick Redmond, *Major*, 61 Foot ..	7 Jan. 42	29 Sept. 43	20 May 48	11 May 55	
Edw. Conran, *Maj.* 3 W. I. Regt. (Q.M. 2 Dec. 42)	17 Oct. 45	5 Nov. 47	4 Feb. 53	15 May 55	
Edm. John Cruice, *Capt.* Unatt. *S. O. of Pens.*	29 April 25	13 June 30	5 April 44	18 May 55	26 Nov. 52
Augustus Fred. Jenner, *Major*, 11 Foot....	9 Oct. 35	21 June 39	5 April 44	5 June 55	
Robert Abraham Logan, *Major*, 57 Foot ..	26 Oct. 41	3 Mar. 43	7 Mar. 51	19 June 55	

Majors.

Name	ENSIGN, ETC.	LIEUT.	CAPTAIN.	MAJOR.	WHEN PLACED ON HALF PAY.
Henry Webb, *Capt.*, ret. full pay, 28 Foot..	18 June 41	14 Oct. 42	6 June 54	13 July 55	
John Guise Rogers Aplin, *Major*, 48 Foot..	7 Oct. 37	23 April 41	20 Nov. 45	17 July 55	
William Faussett, *Captain*, 44 Foot	7 July 43	23 Aug. 44	23 Mar. 49	do	
Gustavus Hume,[102] *Major*, Unattached	30 May 43	9 June 46	21 Sept. 52	do	22 Jan. 58
John Peel,[103] *Major*, h. p. Depot Battalion	22 June 47	19 Oct. 49	25 Nov. 53	do	
Francis Topping Atcherley, *Capt.*, 30 Foot	4 June 47	4 Aug. 48	16 Dec. 53	do	
John Nason, *Major*, Depot Battalion......	9 May 46	4 Sept. 49	20 Oct. 54	do	
Hon. James Stuart, *Captain*, Rifle Brigade	24 Oct. 45	15 Oct. 47	6 Nov. 54	do	
Alex. James Hardy Elliot,[104] *Maj.*, Unatt., *Brig. Maj. of Cavalry, Dublin Division*	18 July 48	14 June 50	22 Dec. 54	do	29 July 56
VC John A. Conolly, *Lt. & Capt.* Coldst. Gds.	25 Feb. 48	26 Aug. 50	29 Dec. 54	do	
Henry F. Berkeley Maxse,[105] *Maj.*, Unatt...	never	1 June 49	do	do	16 Mar. 58
Montagu Hamilton Dowbiggin, *Maj.*, 99 F.	30 June 48	16 Sept. 51	do	do	
Archibald Campbell Snodgrass, *Capt.*, 39 F.	6 Oct. 48	7 Nov. 51	do	do	
Patrick Robertson, *Major*, Depot Battalion	7 April 48	5 Dec. 51	do	do	
VC Claud Tho. Bourchier, *Capt.* Rifle Br..	10 April 49	6 June 54	do	do	
Louis Herries Hamilton, *Captain*, 87 Foot	6 April 38	17 Jan. 40	22 Dec. 46	20 July 55	
Charles Edward Conyers, *Captain*, h. p. 97 F.	18 Dec. 40	25 Nov. 42	9 Nov. 49	do	26 Feb. 56
George Hyde Page, *Captain*, 41 Foot	23 April 41	12 May 43	26 Jan. 55	do	
Bernard Edward Ward, *Captain*, 60 Foot..	1 Aug. 44	5 May 48	23 Mar. 55	do	
Frederick West, *Major*, Depot Battalion ..	12 Aug. 43	29 Jan. 47	3 Aug. 49	27 July 55	
Henry Friend Kennedy, *Major*, 60 Foot....	11 Sept. 40	7 April 42	20 Oct. 48	17 Aug.	
William Fulton, *Major*, 15 Foot.........	10 April 35	11 Oct. 39	12 April 44	31 Aug.	
Hugh Kennedy,[106] *Capt.*, ret. f. p. R. Marines	21 Mar. 34	10 Aug. 40	26 Oct. 48	4 Sept.	
Frederick R. Mein, *Major*, 1 Foot	22 Oct. 33	14 April 37	3 May 44	7 Sept.	
Hon. Wm. James Colville, *Capt.* Rifle Br..	22 Nov. 43	14 May 47	11 Oct. 53	8 Sept.	
Richard Oliver Fra. Steward,[107] *Maj.* Unatt.	20 Sept. 42	26 Sept. 45	7 June 50	9 Sept.	6 Jan. 57
Wm. Mayne, *Maj.* h.p. Land Transport Corps	17 Aug. 41	28 Sept. 43	9 Sept. 51	21 Sept.	1 April 57
Fra. Aug. Halliday, *Capt.* r. f. p. R. Marines	23 Feb. 30	10 July 37	27 July 47	27 Sept.	
V. Fred. Story, *Capt.* Unatt., *S. O. of Pens.*	25 Nov. 36	30 Oct. 40	26 May 44	30 Sept.	27 July 47
William Williamson, *Major*, 85 Foot......	16 Nov. 41	22 Nov. 44	1 Aug. 51	16 Oct.	
M'Kay Rynd, *Major*, 62 Foot	16 Dec. 45	5 Mar. 47	2 Sept. 53	25 Oct.	
Robert John Eagar, *Major*, 31 Foot	11 June 30	25 Jan. 33	8 Oct. 44	2 Nov. 55	
Thomas Wright Hudson, *Major*, 39 Foot ..	16 June 37	30 Oct. 40	7 Dec. 45	do	
John Dwyer, *Major*, 14 Foot	19 July 31	21 Nov. 34	22 Jan. 46	do	
Arthur Wombwell, *Major*, Depot Battalion	5 April 30	20 Oct. 41	8 May	do	
William Douglas, *Major*, 14 Foot	23 May 34	1 Aug. 38	18 Sept.	do	
William Fred. Carter, *Major*, 63 Foot	1 Dec. 37	2 April 41	4 June 47	do	
William Chauval Hodgson, *Major*, 79 Foot	18 Sept. 40	10 Feb. 43	11 June	do	
James Maxwell, *Major*, 34 Foot	24 Sept. 41	13 Oct. 43	22 June	do	
Francis Locker Whitmore,[108] *Major*, Unatt.	7 Aug. 35	10 May 39	3 Sept.	do	30 Mar. 58
Fran. Beckford Ward, *Captain*, R. Artillery	19 Mar. 39	31 Dec. 40	21 Dec.		
Algernon Robert Garrett, *Major*, 16 Foot..	1 June 41	27 Sept. 42	28 April 48	do	
Samuel Netterville Lowder, *Capt.* R. Marines	1 Nov. 33	7 Nov. 38	17 May	do	
Henry Rogers,[109] *Captain*, h. p. R. Artillery	19 Mar. 39	29 April 41	30 June	do	7 Dec. 58
Miller Clifford, *Captain*, Royal Artillery ..	19 June 41	13 April 42	30 June	do	
Alexander Hugh Cobbe, *Major*, 87 Foot ..	16 June 43	10 Jan. 45	21 July	do	
George Harrington Hawes, *Major*, 9 Foot..	24 Nov. 43	4 Jan. 46	19 Sept.	do	
Mortimer Adye, *Captain*, Royal Artillery ..	19 June 41	28 April 42	9 Oct.	do	
Alex. Cæsar Hawkins, *Capt.*, R. Artillery..	1 Jan. 42	2 Aug. 42	1 Nov. .48	do	
Wm. James Esten Grant, *Captain*, do. ...	1 Jan. 42	1 Dec. 42	1 Nov.	do	
George Shaw, *Captain*, Royal Artillery ..	18 June 42	3 May 43	9 April 49	do	
Aug. Fred. Francis Lennox, *Captain*, do. ..	18 June 42	4 May 43	7 May	do	
Hon. Hussey Fane Keane, *Captain*, R. Eng.	10 Mar. 39	28 June 42	14 Aug.	do	
Fred. Geo. Tho. Deshon, *Major*, Depot Batt.	29 Dec. 37	5 Jan. 41	30 Nov.	do	
Dawson Cornelius Greene, *Maj.* Depot Batt.	3 July 40	14 Jan. 42	11 Dec.	do	
Charles John Gibb, *Captain*, R. Engineers	20 Dec. 39	16 Mar. 43	16 April 50	do	
Geo. Thomas Field, *Captain*, Royal Artillery	11 Jan. 43	30 Oct. 43	23 May	do	
Charles John Strange, *Captain*, do.	11 Jan. 43	30 Mar. 44	11 June	do	
Horace Parker Newton, *Captain*, do.	11 Jan. 43	1 April 44	8 July	do	
Thomas Maunsell, *Major*, 28 Foot	27 May 42	23 May 45	8 Oct.	do	
Gust. H. Lockwood Milman, *Capt.* R. Art.	17 June 43	15 May 44	11 Nov.	do	
Charles Courtenay Villiers, *Captain*, 47 Foot	12 May 43	30 Jan. 46	27 Dec.	do	
Robert B. Hawley, *Major*, 60 Foot	28 Aug. 38	31 Dec. 39	10 Jan. 51	do	
John Robinson, *Captain*, 44 Foot	26 Oct. 42	22 Nov. 43	30 Jan.	do	
Charles Geo. Arbuthnot, *Capt.* R. Artillery	17 June 43	1 Feb. 45	4 April	do	
Fairfax Charles Hassard, *Capt.* R. Engineers	20 June 40	23 Sept. 43	14 July	do	
Francis Wm. Hastings, *Captain*, R. Artillery	17 June 43	5 April 45	24 July	do	
Thomas W. White, *Major*, 16 Lancers	7 May 47	7 Apr. 48	23 Sept. 51	do	
Edward Moubray, *Captain*, Royal Artillery	20 Dec. 43	10 April 45	25 Sept.	do	

Majors.

	ENSIGN, ETC.	LIEUT.	CAPTAIN.	MAJOR.	WHEN PLACED ON HALF PAY.
Geo. Brydges Rodney, *Captain*, R. Marines	19 Dec. 37	14 Aug. 41	6 Oct. 51	2 Nov. 55	
Charles Hood, *Major*, 58 Foot	26 June 44	20 Nov. 46	7 Nov.	do	
Hans Robert White,[110] *Major*, Unattached..	22 Dec. 43	19 Dec. 45	5 Dec.	do	12 Sept. 56
Edward Newdigate, *Major*, Rifle Brigade ..	29 May 42	14 April 46	30 April 52	do	
William Warry, *Major*, Depot Battalion	26 Jan. 44	12 Feb. 47	14 May	do	
Andrew Pitcairn, *Major*, 25 Foot	15 May 40	15 April 42	8 June	do	
William Roberts, *Major*, 28 Foot	1 Nov. 39	10 July 43	17 Aug.	do	
Henry Disney Ellis, *Major*, Depot Battalion	14 June 42	31 Jan. 45	21 Sept.	do	
Joseph Jordan, *Captain*, 34 Foot	14 Feb. 45	27 Mar. 48	29 Oct.	do	
Joseph Edw. W. Lawrence, *Capt.* h. p. R. Marines, *Paymaster Artillery Division*	27 Dec. 38	5 Nov. 42	13 Nov.	do	
William A. Armstrong, *Major*, Depot Batt.	1 Nov. 40	28 July 43	3 Dec.	do	
John Lawrie, *Major*, Depot Battalion	22 Dec. 43	7 Nov. 47	3 Dec.	do	
Anthony Wm. S. F. Armstrong, *Maj.* 18 F.	21 June 39	26 Jan. 41	12 Dec.	do	
Samuel Hackett,[111] *Major*, Unattached	20 Oct. 43	3 Dec. 47	31 Dec.	do	15 Jan. 56
Andrew Campbell Knox Lock, *Capt.* 50 F.	28 Sept. 47	8 June 49	12 Aug. 53	do	
George Skipwith, *Major*, Depot Battalion..	3 Nov. 40	15 Oct. 47	11 Nov.	do	
Edward Chippindall, *Major*, 19 Foot	10 Dec. 47	9 Jan. 49	23 Dec.	do	
Hon. Daniel Greville Finch, *Major*, 24 F...	2 May 45	22 Dec. 46	30 Dec.	do	
Anthony Charles Cooke, *Capt.* R. Engineers	17 June 43	1 April 46	17 Feb. 54	do	
Wm. Edm. Moyses Reilly, CB., *Capt* R. Art.	18 Dec. 45	3 April 46	do	do	
Wm. Hen. Dominic Fitzgerald,[112] *Maj*. Unatt.	8 Oct. 44	27 Mar. 46	24 Feb. 54	do	10 Dec. 56
Charles Edward Watson, *Major*, 7 Foot....	13 Oct. 43	8 Aug. 45	24 Feb.	do	
Edmund John Carthew, *Capt.* Royal Artillery	6 Aug. 46	1 Feb. 47	24 Feb.	do	
George Tito Brice, *Captain*, 17 Foot	22 Dec. 48	30 Nov. 49	7 April	do	
Matthew Jones Hayman,[113] *Major*, Unatt...	14 July 41	20 Aug. 42	6 June	do	2 Oct. 57
Jason Hassard, *Captain*, 57 Foot	3 Oct. 44	18 May 48	6 June	do	
George Cecil Henry, *Captain*, R. Artillery..	16 Dec. 40	23 Oct. 47	20 June	do	
Cha. Henry Spencer Churchill, *Capt.* 60. F.	10 Oct. 45	24 Sept. 47	4 Aug.	do	
Geo. Francis Coventry Pocock,[114] *Maj.* Unatt.	15 Dec. 45	5 Oct. 49	4 Aug.	do	26 Feb. 56
Frederic Percy Lea,[115] *Major*, Unattached, *Barrack Master at Barbados*	24 Sept. 41	19 Aug. 43	7 Aug.	do	8 Feb. 56
Henry Reynolds Werge, *Major*, 2 Foot	31 Dec. 39	8 April 42	19 Aug.	do	
William John Williams, *Capt.*, R. Artillery	2 May 47	30 June 48	24 Aug.	do	
VC Hugh Rowlands,[116] *Major*, Unattached	25 Sept. 40	21 April 51	25 Aug.	do	26 Aug. 59
William Bellairs,[117] *Major*, Unatt., *Dep. Assist. Adj. Gen. in Ireland*	8 May 46	6 July 49	15 Sept.	do	5 Mar. 58
Charles Mingaye Green, *Captain*, 30 Foot..	20 April 49	17 May 50	30 Sept.	do	
Nathaniel Steevens,[118] *Major*, Unattached, *Brigade Major, Curragh*	10 Dec. 45	29 Dec. 48	27 Oct.	do	
Cha. Edward Oldershaw, *Capt.* R. Artillery	2 May 47	30 June 48	29 Oct.	do	
Frederick Wells, *Captain*, 1 Foot	12 Oct. 41	2 Aug. 44	6 Nov. 54	do	
James William Dewar, *Major*, 97 F.	7 July 46	12 April 50	do	do	
Louis John Amadée Armit, *Captain*, R. Eng.	18 June 45	1 April 46	15 Nov. 54	do	
Charles Brisbane Ewart, *Capt.* R. Engineers	18 June 45	do	13 Dec. 54	do	
C. Butler Pet. Nugent Hodges Nugent, *do. do.*	18 Dec. 45	do	do	do	
Edward Charles Acheson Gordon, *do. do.*	18 Dec. 45	do	16 Dec. 54	do	
Phillip Dickson, *Captain*, Royal Artillery..	1 Oct. 47	30 June 48	20 Dec.	do	
Hugh Robert Hibbert, *Major*, 7 Foot	28 Sept. 47	16 Aug. 50	22 Dec.	do	
Daniel William Tupper, *Captain*, 50 Foot	2 Feb. 49	19 Mar. 52	22 Dec.	do	
Geo. Stephen Digby, CB., *Capt.*, R. Marines	16 Aug. 42	27 July 47	27 Dec.	do	
Charles Elgee, *Major*, Depot Battalion	14 April 46	18 Feb. 48	20 Dec. 54	do	
James William Hay,[120] *Major*, Unattached .	31 Dec. 47	1 Sept. 48	do	do	30 July 57
Henry George Woods,[121] *Major*, Unatt., *Assist. Military Sec. at Ceylon*	13 Oct. 43	20 Oct. 48	do	do	21 Dec. 55
Richard Preston, *Captain*, 44 Foot........	27 Feb. 46	24 Nov. 48	do	do	
Geo. E. Brown Westhead, *Maj*. Depot Batt.	7 April 48	25 Jan. 50	do	do	
Fitzwilliam Fred. Hunter,[122] *Major*, Unatt.	21 July 48	14 June 50	do	do	19 Feb. 58
Richard Lyons Otway Pearson, *Lt. & Capt.* Gr. Gds., *Deputy Assist. Adj. Gen.*	3 Dec. 47	4 April 51	do	do	
VC Fred. Cockayne Elton, *Maj*. Depot Batt.	19 Jan. 49	30 April 52	do	do	
Charles Cooch,[123] *Major*, Unatt., *Brigade Major at Colchester*	21 Aug. 49	25 June 52	do	do	16 Jan. 57
Arthur Frederick Warren, *Capt.* Rifle Brigade	23 July 47	11 Oct. 53	do	do	
Whitworth Porter, *Captain*, Royal Engineers	18 Dec. 47	1 April 46	3 Jun. 55	do	
John Edward Hope, *Captain*, Royal Artillery	1 Oct. 47	30 June 48	6 Jan.	do	
Wm. Windham Aug. Lukin, *Capt. do.*...	1 Oct. 47	do	7 Feb.	do	
Charles Edmund Walcott, *Captain*, do....	18 Dec. 47	do	7 Feb.	do	
William John Bolton, *Captain*, do....	18 Dec. 47	do	8 Mar.	do	
Philip Ravenhill, *Captain*, Royal Engineers	1 May 46	9 Nov. 46	1 April 55	do	
James Sinclair, *Captain*, Royal Artillery ..	18 Dec. 47	30 June 48	do	do	

Majors.

	ENSIGN, ETC.	LIEUT.	CAPTAIN.	MAJOR.	WHEN PLACED ON HALF PAY.
Lewis William Penn, *Capt.*, R. Artillery	18 Dec. 47	30 June 48	1 April 55	2 Nov. 55	
Edward Taddy, *Captain,* do...........	27 June 48	1 Nov. 48	do	do	
Frederick Miller, *Captain,* do.........	19 Dec. 48	19 Dec. 48	13 April 55	do	
Charles Herbert Sedley, *Capt.*, R. Engineers	17 Dec. 46	16 April 47	16 April	do	
Charles Henry Owen, *Capt.*, Royal Artillery	19 Dec. 48	19 Dec. 48	15 May	do	
William S. Philips, *Capt.* ret. full pay, 62 F.	25 Oct. 22	16 Feb. 26	15 June	do	
George Byng Harman,[124] *Major*, Unattached	18 Sept. 49	21 June 50	19 June	do	4 June 58
Paget Walter L'Estrange, *Capt.* R. Artillery	19 Dec. 48	19 May 49	29 June	do	
Reginald Henry Champion, *Captain,* do....	19 Dec. 48	6 Mar. 50	18 Aug.	do	
William Gilly Andrews, *Captain,* do....	20 June 49	27 May 50	7 Sept.	do	
Hon. S. J. G. Calthorpe, *Major,* 5 Dr. Gds.	23 May 48	23 May 51	14 Sept.	do	
Roderick Mackenzie, *Capt.* Royal Artillery	20 June 40	9 July 50	24 Sept.	do	
Fra. Horatio De Vere, *Capt.* Royal Engineers	1 Oct. 47	16 April 50	27 Oct. 55	do	
Alex. Dalton Thellusson, *Major,* 72 Foot ..	12 Oct. 41	8 Oct. 44	28 Dec. 40	23 Nov. 55	
Henry Wm. Dennie, *Capt.* ret. full pay, 28 F., *Barrackmaster at Maidstone* .. }	18 Dec. 41	30 Dec. 42	29 Dec. 54	30 Nov. 55	
Wm. Thomas Laird Patterson, *Major,* 91 F.	10 Dec. 34	12 July 39	19 May 45	14 Dec. 55	
Robert Hockings,[127] *Capt.* r. f. p. R. Marines	4 July 34	19 Sept. 40	1 Mar. 49	17 Dec. 55	
Herbert Russell Manners, *Maj.* Depot Batt.	28 Aug. 38	7 Jan. 42	13 Nov. 46	8 Jan. 56	
Gus. N. K. Anker Yonge, *Maj.* Depot Batt.	22 Aug. 34	29 June 37	1 Jan. 47	15 Jan. 56	
Thomas L. K. Nelson, *Major,* 40 Foot ..	25 Nov. 31	29 Jan. 36	10 July 46	15 Feb. 56	
Robert Dillon, *Major,* 30 Foot	8 June 38	29 Nov. 39	30 Nov. 49	15 Feb. 56	
Charles Henry Leslie, *Major,* 9 Foot	20 July 38	16 July 41	14 April 46	29 Feb. 56	
Edward John Holworthy, *Major,* 14 Foot..	12 Feb. 36	25 Jan. 39	17 Oct. 45	7 Mar. 56	
Edw. P. H.Ussher,[128] *Capt.* r. f. p., R. Mar.	27 Dec. 36	13 Jan. 41	10 Aug. 49	20 Mar. 56	
John Pelling Pigott, *do.* Unatt. *S. O. of Pen.*	15 Feb. 39	28 Jan. 42	19 Dec. 45	31 Mar. 56	1 Apr. 56
John Arthur Gildea, *Major,* 81 Foot	23 Aug. 39	30 April 42	14 April 46	0 April 56	
Richard Roundell Currer, *Major,* 96 Foot ..	16 Sept. 36	27 Sept. 39	20 Oct. 46	15 April 56	
James Owen Bovill, *Major,* 2 W. India Regt.	23 Mar. 47	20 Oct. 48	16 Dec. 53	29 April 56	
Garnet Man, *Capt. of a Company of Gentlemen Cadets, Royal Military College* .. }	13 Jan. 25	15 Mar. 27	5 July 44	30 May 56	
Robert Bates, *Major,* 19 Foot	6 June 34	25 Dec. 38	15 Oct. 45	6 June 56	
Henry Woodbine Parish, *Capt.,* 45 Foot, *Assist. Military Secretary at Barbados* }	9 Mar. 39	15 Apr. 42	6 Feb. 46	do	
Robert Portal, *Major,* 5 Lancers	17 Jan. 40	8 May 45	9 June 46	do	
Alex. Abercromby Nelson,[129] *Capt.* Unatt., *Assist. Mil. Sec. at the Mauritius* .... }	6 Mar. 35	15 Mar. 39	31 July 46	do	9 Feb. 55
Edward James Blanckley, *Major,* 6 Foot ..	22 May 35	17 Jan. 38	7 Aug. 40	do	
Stonehouse George Bunbury, *Staff Capt., Medical Staff Corps* .... }	28 June 33	25 Dec. 38	30 Dec. 46	do	
James Pollock Gore, *Captain,* 1 Foot......	6 Feb. 36	20 Dec. 39	20 Oct. 47	do	
Geo. Whitworth Talbot Rich, *Major,* 71 F.	12 June 40	15 Apr. 42	12 Nov. 47	do	
Alexander M'Kinstry, *Major,* 17 Foot	22 Feb. 39	25 Sept. 40	21 Aug. 49	do	
Humphrey Gray, *Major,* 21 Foot	25 Mar. 36	1 July 38	15 Feb. 50	do	
William Cosmo Trevor, *Major,* 14 Foot....	11 Mar. 42	22 Jan. 46	29 Nov. 50	do	
Cha. Raleigh Chichester, *Major,* Depot Batt.	31 Mar. 46	1 Sept. 48	6 Dec. 50	do	
Frederick Hammersley, *Captain,* 14 Foot ..	1 July 42	21 April 40	25 April 51	do	
Hercules Walker, *Major,* Rifle Brigade	22 May 42	30 Dec. 45	8 Aug. 51	do	
Robert Hamilton Currie, *Major,* 30 Foot ..	28 Dec. 38	14 Feb. 40	10 Feb. 52	do	
William Leckie, *Captain,* 39 Foot	10 Nov. 43	16 April 45	2 April 52	do	
Robert Blakeney, *Major,* 48 Foot	3 Nov. 46	10 Sept. 47	2 April 52	do	
Godfrey W. Hugh Massy,[130] *Major,* Unatt...	24 Oct. 45	2 Feb. 49	21 May 52	do	24 June 56
Dominic Jacotin Gamble, *Major,* 4 Foot ..	19 April 44	25 Feb. 45	16 July 52	do	
Edward Thomas Gloster, *Captain,* 38 Foot..	13 May 42	3 Jan. 45	30 July 52	do	
Rob. E. Fazakerley Craufurd, *Capt.* R. Art.	19 June 44	1 April 46	22 Mar. 53	do	
George Courtenay Vialls, *Major,* 95 Foot ..	20 Jan. 43	22 May 46	25 Mar. 53	do	
Thomas Wickham, *Captain,* 33 Foot	25 Oct. 42	22 Dec. 46	25 Mar. 53	do	
Thomas Beckwick Speedy,[131] *Capt.* Unatt., *Sec. & Adj. Royal Hibernian School* .. }	15 Mar. 39	23 Oct. 41	17 Feb. 54	do	17 Feb. 54
John Stokes, *Captain,* Royal Engineers	20 Dec. 43	1 April 46	do	do	
Francis Du Cane, *Captain,* do	19 June 44	do	do	do	
Henry Terrick FitzHugh, *Captain,* R. Art..	18 Dec. 45	13 April	do	do	
France James Soady, *Captain,* Royal Art...	1 May 46	29 July 46	do	do	
Joseph Godby, *Captain,* do ..	do	20 Oct. 46	do	do	
Henry Robert Crewe Godley, *Captain,* 28 F.	25 Sept. 40	21 July 48	do	do	
George Chetwode, *Major,* 8 Hussars	8 May 40	10 Mar. 43	24 Feb. 54	do	
Fred. Stuckley Savage, *Major,* 68 Foot....	30 Jan. 46	31 Dec. 47	10 Mar.	do	
John Spurway, *Captain,* Royal Artillery ..	6 Aug. 46	28 May 47	30 May	do	
Charles Alex. Boswell Gordon, *Capt.* 60 F.	21 April 43	13 Dec. 45	6 June 54	do	
George Stoddart Whitmore, *Captain,* 62 F.	23 Jan. 47	21 May 50	7 July	do	
Benjamin Bunbury Mauleverer, *Capt.* 88 F.	30 Aug. 44	8 Oct. 47	28 July	do	

Majors. 81

	ENSIGN, ETC.		LIEUT.		CAPTAIN.		MAJOR.		WHEN PLACED ON HALF PAY.
Thomas Tryon, *Major*, 7 Foot	12 May	48	1 Feb.	50	21 Sept.	54	6 June	56	
Francis Edw. Drewe, *Major*, Depot Battalion	17 May	50	23 Sept.	51	do		do		
Charles Robert Shervinton,[131] *Maj.* Unatt. *Brigade Major, Military Train*......	20 May	42	6 July	45	22 Sept.	54	do		
George Fred. Dallas, *Captain*, 46 Foot	16 May	45	28 April	48	do		do		
Henry Butler, *Major*, 57 Foot	2 Mar.	47	23 Mar.	49	6 Nov.	54	do		
Charles Le Mesurier Carey, *Captain*, 63 F..	13 Aug.	47	18 Jan.	50	do		do		
Charles William St. Clair, *Captain*, 57 Foot	18 July	48	24 Jan.	51	7 Nov.	54	do		
Edwin Ashley Tucker Steward, *Major*, 21 F.	15 Mar.	50	2 April	52	15 Nov.		do		
Arthur Vandeleur, *Captain*, Royal Artillery	1 Oct.	47	30 June	48	28 Nov.		do		
Frederick Miller, *Captain*, 80 Foot	16 May	45	4 April	46	1 Dec.		do		
Reginald Curtis, *Captain*, Royal Artillery..	1 Oct.	47	30 June	48	13 Dec.		do		
John Macdonald Cuppage, *Captain*, 89 Foot	10 Nov.	43	8 Aug.	45	29 Dec.	54	do		
Thomas Gore, *Captain*, 88 Foot	3 Mar.	43	19 Feb.	47	do		do		
William James Gillum,[132] *Major*, Unatt. ...	14 Feb.	45	2 July	47	do		do		19 Aug. 56
Frederic Smith Vacher, *Captain*, 33 Foot ..	8 Dec.	46	20 Oct.	48	do		do		
John Ross, *Captain*, Rifle Brigade...	14 April	46	29 Dec.	48	do		do		
Charles Pelgue Bertram, *Captain*, 41 Foot .	6 Feb.	47	22 Feb.	50	do		do		
John Aldridge, *Captain*, 21 Foot	12 April	50	23 April	52	do		do		
Arthur Maxwell Earle, *Captain*, 57 Foot ..	18 Jan.	50	15 Feb.	53	do		do		
William Powell Richards, *Captain*, R. Art.	1 Oct.	47	30 June	48	6 Jan.	55	do		
Algernon Brendon, *Captain*, do	do		do		do		do		
William Fletcher, *Captain*, 44 Foot	6 Nov.	46	21 Mar.	51	12 Jan.	55	do		
James do Havilland, *Captain*, R. Artillery..	1 Oct.	47	30 June	48	13 Jan.		do		
Edgar Grantham Bredin, *Captain*, do ..	18 Mar.	47	do		25 Feb.		do		
Cha. Harland Bell, *Capt.* Cape M. Riflemen	24 Mar.	43	2 Sept.	44	2 Mar.		do		
Wm. Henry Randolph Simpson, *Capt.* R. Art.	18 Dec.	47	30 June	48	1 April		do		
VC. Mark Walker, *Captain*, 3 Foot ...	25 Sept.	46	3 Feb.	54	15 May	55	do		
George Alderson Milman, *Capt.* R. Art. ...	19 Dec.	48	8 Jan.	49	29 May		do		
Charles Edward Burt, *Captain*, do	do		28 June	49	29 June		do		
Hazlitt Irvine, *Captain*, do	do		4 Sept.	49	6 July		do		
Shadwell Morley Grylls, *Captain*, do	do		3 Nov.	49	13 Aug.		do		
Wm. Follows, *Capt.* h.p. 18 Drs. *S.O.of Pens.*	13 Sept.	32	28 May	30	26 July	44	19 June	50	16 June 48
James Henley,[133] *Capt.* ret. full pay, 95 F.	6 Jan.	25	28 May	45	25 Aug.	54	24 June		
Nicholas Moore, *Capt.* ret. f.p. R. Marines..	15 July	30	13 Nov.	40	25 May	49	9 July		
Sydney Aug. Capel, *Captain*, h.p. 51 F. *Staff Officer of Pensioners* (Q.M.,11 Oct. 33)	7 July	37	25 May	39	30 July	44	22 Aug.		1 May 46
John Charles Hill Jones, *Major*, 54 Foot ..	16 Dec.	40	30 Dec.	42	9 Nov.	49	5 Sept.		
Thomas Southwell Brown, *Major*, 55 Foot .	14 Nov.	45	26 May	48	4 Aug.	54	19 Sept.		
Edward Charles Butler, *Captain*, 36 Foot ..	13 Jan.	37	5 Mar.	41	23 Aug.	44	23 Sept.		
Oliver Barker D'Arcey, *Major*, 18 Foot	8 April	26	9 Dec.	31	19 Dec.	45	30 Sept.		
George Bingham Jenings, *Major*, 19 Foot..	21 July	43	4 April	45	1 July	53	do		
Patrick Wm. Sydenham Ross, *Major*, 35 F.	9 Nov.	38	2 Sept.	42	16 Jan.	49	17 Oct.	56	
Griffin Nicholas, *Capt.* ret. full pay, 5 Foot	8 April	34	26 May	36	22 Feb.	45	24 Oct.		
Wm. Griffin Sutton, *Capt.* Unatt., *Riding Master Cavalry Depot at Maidstone* ..	19 Aug.	42	15 Jan.	47	13 April	55	31 Oct.		13 April 55
Henry Stratton Bush, *Major*, 41 Foot	16 Mar.	50	26 Nov.	52	24 Nov.	54	7 Nov.		
Geo. Rob. Pole, *Capt.* Unatt. *S.O. of Pens.*	11 Aug.	25	24 April	28	27 Sept.	14	9 Nov.		27 Sept. 44
Donald Wm. Tench, *Capt.* h. p. 55 Dr. do.	31 July	28	2 Dec.	31	1 Oct.	44	8 Dec.		23 May 51
John Thompson Aslett,[134] *Capt.* r.f.p. R.Mar.	16 April	32	16 Nov.	37	17 May	48	11 Dec.		
Edward Eldridge Haines, *Captain*, 92 Foot.	26 June	35	1 Feb.	39	3 April	46	26 Dec.	56	
Richard Anderson, *Captain*, 56 Foot	8 Jan.	41	7 April	43	29 Dec.	46	do		
Henry Loftus, *Major*, 71 Foot	26 Oct.	41	4 Aug.	43	22 Dec.	48	do		
Richard John Ross O'Conor, *Major*, 17 F..	12 April	39	1 Feb.	42	30 Nov.	49	do		
Richard Rocke, *Major*, 72 Foot	20 May	42	8 Nov.	44	8 Mar.	50	do		
William Francis Ring, *Captain*, 87 Foot ..	28 Oct.	31	8 May	35	15 Mar.	50	do		
Edw. Burgoyne Cureton, *Capt.* 12 Lancers..	21 June	39	19 Dec.	43	31 Jan.	51	do		
Hon. Edward S. Plunkett, *Captain*, 95 Foot	17 June	36	11 May	41	7 Mar.	51	do		
Henry Charles Fitzgerald, *Major*, 33 Foot .	25 Sept.	40	9 Oct.	42	2 Jan.	52	do		
Horatio Harbord Morant, *Major*, 68 Foot ..	20 Aug.	44	3 Nov.	46	21 Oct.	53	do		
Wm. Pole Collingwood, *Captain*, 21 Foot..	23 Mar.	47	15 Nov.	50	28 July	54	do		
Hopton Bassett Scott, *Captain*, 9 Foot	24 Dec.	47	28 Mar.	51	4 Aug.	54	do		
Joshua Grant Crosse, *Captain*, 88 Foot ...	25 Sept.	40	30 Aug.	44	30 Aug.	54	do		
Fred. Cherburgh Bligh, *Captain*, 41 Foot ..	15 Mar.	50	25 June	52	15 Sept.	54	do		
Wm. Donald Macdonald, *Captain*, 93 Foot	4 June	47	1 Oct.	50	10 Oct.	54	do		
Alexander J. J. Macdonald,[135] *Capt.* Unatt...	23 April	47	11 Nov.	51	29 Dec.		do		26 Nov. 58
Coote Buller,[136] *Capt.* Unatt.	13 July	47	12 Oct.	52	do		do		3 June 59
Fred. Ernest Appleyard, *Major*, Depot Batt.	14 June	50	12 Oct.	52	do		do		
Wm. L. Snyer,[137] *Capt.* r. f. p. R. Marines...	17 Nov.	34	6 Nov.	40	9 Mar.	49	2 Feb.	57	
P. Day Stokes, *Capt.* h.p. 4 F., *S.O. of Pens.*	22 Oct.	33	13 Jan.	38	8 Nov.	44	4 Feb.		6 Dec. 44
Hon. Horace M. Monckton, *Major*, 3 Dr...	23 April	41	29 April	42	4 May	49	17 Feb.	57	

82 Majors.

	ENSIGN, ETC.		LIEUT.		CAPTAIN.		MAJOR.		WHEN PLACED ON HALF PAY.	
Joseph Salis, *Major*, Military Train	10 May	44	8 Jan.	47	7 Aug.	51	20 Feb.	57		
V℃ Thomas De Courcy Hamilton,[138] *Maj.* Unatt. *Brigade Major, Ionian Islands*	30 Sept.	42	10 April	47	29 Dec.	54	10 Mar.		27 Nov.	57
Charles Thomas Vesey Bunbury, *Major*, 82 F.	30 Oct.	38	26 Dec.	40	16 Feb.	49	13 Mar.			
Peter John Macdonald,[139] *Major*, Unatt.	25 Oct.	39	18 June	41	26 Mar.	52	1 April	57	8 April	59
Henry Prim Hutton,[140] *Major*, Unatt.	9 Nov.	43	25 Dec.	45	6 June	54	do		8 April	59
Robert Daunt,[141] *Major*, Unatt.	28 July		40	16 Aug.	42	20 Dec.	54	do	8 April	59
John Simeon Fra. Dick,[142] *Major*, Unatt.	11 Dec.	47	19 April	50	25 Jan.	55	do		8 April	59
Henry James Buchanan,[143] *Major*, Unatt.	14 June	50	15 July	53	15 June	55	do		8 April	59
Henry Jackson Parkin Booth, *Major*, 43 F.	11 June	47	9 Aug.	50	29 July	53	3 April			
William Lacy, *Capt.* Unatt., *S. O. of Pens.*	20 April	26	30 Aug.	27	6 Dec.	44	14 April		6 Dec.	44
Robert Maunsell, *Major*, 85 Foot	24 June	42	28 Mar.	45	7 Nov.	51	28 April			
Thomas Martin, *Major*, 4 Foot	27 May	36	27 Oct.	39	5 Dec.	51	12 May			
Henry Joseph Coote,[144] *Capt.* h.p. 18 F.	23 Sept.	30	17 Sept.	39	7 Dec.	44	16 May		1 July	53
G. B. Stoney, *Capt.* h.p. 20 F., *S.O.of Pens.*	13 May	36	11 Jan.	39	19 Dec.	44	4 June		17 Sept.	50
Tho. Baker Pleydell,[145] *Capt.* r.f.p.R. Mar.	1 Nov.	33	3 Oct.	38	17 May	48	16 June			
Charles Napier North, *Major*, 60 Foot	29 May	36	28 Dec.	38	28 Dec.	48	19 June			
Wm. Ready, *Capt.* Unatt., *S. O. of Pens.*	19 May	25	28 June	27	24 Jan.	45	6 July		24 Jan.	45
Charles Fred. Hervey, *Captain*, Unatt.	2 Nov.	32	30 Dec.	34	23 Mar.	45	9 July		26 Oct.	49
R.S. O'Brien, *Capt.* h.p. 36 F., *S.O. of Pens.*	25 Nov.	31	19 Aug.	36	13 April	45	17 July		19 April	50
Henry Marsh, *Major*, 3 Dragoon Guards	5 Aug.	42	12 May	43	7 June	50	24 July			
Francis Hutchinson Synge, *Major*, 43 Foot	7 Sept.	41	9 June	46	17 Oct.	51	24 July			
Tom Benson, *Major*, 66 Foot	8 Nov.	42	8 Aug.	45	30 Mar.	49	25 Aug.			
Richard Barrett,[146] *Captain*, ret. full pay, Depôt Batt. (*Q.M.* 30 Oct. 35)	13 June	45	14 Aug.	48	6 June	54	28 Aug.			
V℃ Gronow Davis, *Captain*, Royal Artillery	18 Dec.	47	30 June	48	25 Feb.	55	28 Aug.			
Rt. F. Middlemore, *Capt.* Unat. *S.O. of Pens.*	19 Dec.	34	12 July	39	19 May	45	5 Sept.		9 Nov.	55
John Borrow, *Major*, 18 Foot	16 Feb.	41	23 Feb.	44	1 April	47	18 Sept.			
Granville Geo. C. Stapylton, *Major*, 98 Foot	15 June	39	13 Jan.	42	28 April	48	do			
Septimus Lyster, *Major*, 94 Foot	28 Dec.	38	18 Aug.	41	6 Oct.	48	do			
John Henry Dickson, *Major*, 51 Foot	15 Nov.	39	20 May	42	15 Mar.	53	do			
Sir Geo. Abercr. Robinson, *Bt.*, *Maj.*, 22 F.	26 July	44	14 Aug.	46	11 Dec.	49	25 Sept.	57		
Hon. Emelius J. Weld Forester,[147] *Capt.* Unat.	28 Dec.	32	9 April	38	23 May	45	26 Sept.		5 Mar.	58
Alexander Tayler, *Major*, 9 Foot	21 June	39	30 July	41	23 May	48	21 Oct.			
Michael Stocks, *Major*, 1 Dragoons	11 Dec.	46	20 July	49	25 Feb.	53	23 Oct.			
W. And. M. Barnard, *Lt. & Capt.* Gr. Gds.			23 Feb.	49	14 July	54	23 Oct.			
Prideaux William Gillum, *Captain*, 54 Foot	28 Oct.	43	31 Dec.	47	4 Aug.	54	11 Nov.			
James Handasyde Edgar, *Major*, 69 Foot	9 Oct.	35	28 June	39	29 Jan.	47	17 Nov.			
Annesley Paul Gore, *Major*, 53 Foot	7 Apr.	43	8 Jan.	47	1 Sept.	49	19 Nov.			
Stanhope Mason Gildea, *Major*, Unattached	29 April	37	11 May	38	19 May	46	24 Nov.	57	7 Oct.	59
H. M. Smyth, *Capt.*,h.p.44 F., *S. O. of Pens.*	7 June	31	20 Mar.	35	24 May	45	26 Nov.		19 April	50
Fred. Gordon Christie, *Capt.* Unatt. do.	8 Apr.	34	20 July	38	30 May	45	12 Dec.		9 Apr.	47
William Lyons, *Major*, 5 Foot	15 Jan.	41	12 Sept.	43	8 May.	52	26 Dec.	57		
V℃ Thomas Esmonde,[148] *Capt.* h. p. 18 Foot	22 Nov.	51	7 June	53	6 Apr.	55	29 Dec.		9 Oct.	57
Henry John King, *Major*, 3 Foot	8 Aug.	45	23 April	47	12 Nov.	52	31 Dec.			
William James Hutchins, *Major*, 12 Foot	2 Dec.	36	2 Dec.	40	20 Dec.	46	8 Jan.	58		
Richard Wollaston Clerke, *Major*, 26 Foot	12 Apr.	44	22 Dec.	46	7 Apr.	54	do			
Alfred Knight,[149] *Captain*, Unatt., *Town Major at Quebec*	18 June	12	14 Feb.	14	16 Sept.	45	11 Jan.		16 Sept.	45
William Temple Parratt, *Captain*, 14 Foot	5 Sept.	40	9 June	43	24 Oct.	45	15 Jan.	58		
V℃ Christopher Charles Teesdale, CB., *Captain*, Royal Artillery	18 June	51	22 Apr.	53	14 Jan.	58	do			
Edwin Gream Daniell, *Captain*, 8 Foot	2 Oct.	35	7 Sept.	38	25 Nov.	45	19 Jan.	58		
William Drysdale, CB., *Major*, 9 Lancers	29 Dec.	35	31 Aug.	38	29 Oct.	47	do			
William Brookes, *Captain*, 75 Foot	11 Jan.	33	16 Sept.	36	28 Jan.	48	do			
George Edward Baynes, *Captain*, 8 Foot	2 July	41	12 Dec.	43	17 Oct.	48	do			
Tho. Robert Drummond Hay, *Capt.* 78 Foot	2 Aug.	39	5 Nov.	41	17 Nov.	48	do			
Alexander William Gordon, *Captain*, 61 Foot	11 Mar.	42	3 April	44	29 Dec.	48	do			
Andrew John Macpherson, *Captain*, 24 Foot	19 April	42	26 July	44	14 Jan.	49	do			
Wm. Edw. Durand Deacon, *Capt.* 61 Foot	3 June	42	26 Jan.	44	28 July	49	do			
Sir Edw. FitzGerald Campbell, *Bt.Maj.* 60 F.	2 July	41	26 July	44	27 Dec.	50	do			
Thomas Clement Dunbar, *Captain*, 75 Foot	1 April	42	31 Mar.	45	23 Apr.	51	do			
Henry Edw. Hillman Burnside, *Capt.* 61 F.	27 Dec.	42	26 July	44	2 Sept.	51	do			
Charles Doyle Patterson, *Captain*, 10 Foot	21 June	39	4 Oct.	41	15 Mar.	53	do			
John Millar Bannatyne, *Captain*, 8 Foot	17 Dec.	47	10 Jan.	51	22 Apr.	53	do			
George Charles Synge, *Captain*, 52 Foot	16 Jan.	46	14 Apr.	48	27 May	53	do			
Henry Francis Williams, *Captain*, 60 Foot	19 May	43	20 Nov.	44	3 Mar.	54	do			
John Robert Wilton, *Captain*, 60 Foot	20 Dec.	38	3 Dec.	41	14 July	54	do			
Seymour John Blane, *Captain*, 52 Foot			28 June	50	9 Oct.	54	do			
Richard Freer, *Major*, 27 Foot	22 May	46	13 Dec.	49	23 Mar.	55	do			
Richard Dawson,[160] *Capt.* h. p. Staff Corps	21 May	41	14 Apr.	43	22 Dec.	54	do		18 Oct.	59

Majors.

	ENSIGN, ETC.	LIEUT.	CAPTAIN.	MAJOR.	WHEN PLACED ON HALF PAY.
Charles Potts Rosser, *Captain*, 6 Dr. Gds..	8 Jan. 41	3 Apr. 46	26 June 55	19 Jan. 58	
Charles Kenrick Crosse, *Captain*, 52 Foot..	12 July 50	15 Oct. 52	15 Apr. 56	do	
R. H. C. Drury Lowe, *Lt. & Capt.* Gr. Gds.	17 Sept. 50	27 Feb. 52	8 Jan. 58	do	
John Robertson Turnbull, *Captain*, 13 Foot	14 Jan. 48	4 May 49	11 Jan. 58	do	
William Kelty M'Leod, *Major*, 74 Foot....	6 June 45	31 July 46	24 Sept. 50	27 Jan.	
John Higgin Graham, *Major*, 22 Foot	6 May 42	7 Mar. 45	7 May 52	5 Mar.	
Herbert George Bowden, *Major*, 22 Foot ..	30 Apr. 41	30 May 43	22 Feb. 53	do	
Edmond William Sargent, *Major*, 18 Foot..	18 May 41	26 July 42	25 May 53	9 Mar.	
John B. Flanagan, *Major*, 81 Foot	8 Feb. 31	28 Aug. 35	11 Nov. 45	13 Mar.	
Charles Durie, *Captain*, Unattached	1 Aug. 34	6 July 38	9 Jan. 46	16 Mar.	22 Oct. 52
Thomas Anderson, *Major*, 64 Foot........	16 May 34	29 Dec. 37	22 Aug. 48	do	
John Chetham M'Leod, *Major*, 42 Foot....	21 Apr. 46	17 Nov. 48	29 Dec. 54	do	
Harvey Wellesley Pole Welman, *Capt.* 86 F.	2 Apr. 36	28 Dec. 38	9 Jan. 46	22 Mar.	
George Cornwall, *Major*, 93 Foot	8 July 36	9 Mar. 38	9 June 48	24 Mar.	
Fred. John Travers, *Captain*, Royal Artillery	19 Mar. 39	1 Apr. 41	30 June 48	do	
Cha. Scudamore Longden, *Capt.* do	20 Dec. 39	23 Nov. 41	30 June 48	do	
Graeme Alexander Lockhart, *Captain*, 78 Ft.	8 Dec. 37	18 Apr. 42	10 Apr. 50	do	
Henry F. Saunders, *Capt.* 3 W. India Regt.	30 July 30	27 Dec. 37	18 Apr. 51	do	
Robert Mockler, *Major*, 64 Foot..........	12 Sept. 43	12 Jan. 48	9 May 51	do	
Winter Goode, *Captain*, 64 Foot	26 Apr. 44	28 Aug. 46	25 June 52	do	
Joseph Maycock, *Captain*, 53 Foot........	20 Oct. 40	29 Apr. 42	4 Feb. 53	do	
Henry Francis, *Captain*, 64 Foot	23 June 43	14 Sept. 45	15 Mar. 53	do	
Alfred Picton Bowlby, *Captain*, 64 Foot. ..	31 Oct. 45	12 Mar. 48	15 Mar. 53	do	
George Robert Hopkins, *Captain*, 53 Foot..	28 Aug. 39	26 July 44	7 Nov. 53	do	
Dominick Sarsfield Greene, *Captain*, R. Art.	1 May 40	9 Nov. 46	17 Feb. 54	do	
Charles Edward Mansfield,[151] *Major*, Unatt.	1 Sept. 48	8 Aug. 51	29 Dec. 54	do	15 June 58
Erskine Scott F. G. Dawson, *Captain*, 93 Ft.	25 Nov. 45	11 June 52	29 Dec. 54	do	
Cornelius Cha. Rolleston, *Captain*, 84 Foot	20 May 42	7 July 45	2 Feb. 55	do	
Bendyshe Walton, *Captain*, 38 Foot	16 June 48	8 Feb. 50	8 Jan. 56	do	
Alfred Bassano, *Captain*, 32 Foot	3 Apr. 46	24 May 48	15 Oct. 56	do	
George Newton Fendall, *Captain*, 53 Foot..	11 Dec. 46	4 May 49	7 Nov. 56	do	
William Rudman, *Captain*, 32 Foot	22 Dec. 45	11 Feb. 48	15 May 57	do	
Browning Drew, *Captain*, 75 Foot........	7 Mar. 45	8 Jan. 47	13 June 57	do	
V.C. Samuel Hill Lawrence, *Captain*, 25 F.	12 Dec. 47	22 Feb. 50	1 July 57	do	
David O'Brien, *Captain*, 84 Foot	22 Nov. 44	20 May 46	21 July 57	do	
William Henry Petty Meara, *Captain*, 6 Foot	24 Dec. 46	5 Dec. 51	4 Sept. 57	do	
Henry Andrew Sarel, *Captain*, 17 Lancers .	13 July 47	15 Dec. 48	18 Sept. 57	do	
John Edmonstoune, *Captain*, 32 Foot......	15 Oct. 50	5 Jan. 55	2 Oct. 57	do	
Charles Marshall Foster, *Captain*, 32 Foot.	18 Apr. 51	14 Apr. 55	26 Nov. 57	do	
Wm. B. Robinson, *Maj.*, 3 West India Regt.	27 Apr. 49	26 Aug. 51	24 Mar. 54	26 Mar.	
Louis Howe Bazalgette, *Major*, 24 Foot ..	26 June 38	24 Sept. 41	7 Apr. 48	30 Mar.	
John M'Court, *Major*, Military Train	1 Jan. 43	1 July 45	9 Sept. 51	do	
Robert William Romer, *Captain*, 59 Foot..	30 Sept. 36	15 Jan. 40	2 Feb. 49	13 April 58	
Charles Kendal Bushe, *Captain*, 59 Foot ..	14 April 43	14 April 46	11 May 49	do	
William Francis Foote, *Captain*, R. Marines	1 Aug. 37	29 Mar. 41	16 Nov. 49	do	
Guy Rotton, *Captain*, Royal Artillery	17 June 43	5 April 45	2 July 51	do	
Richard Parke, *Captain*, Royal Marines ..	15 Feb. 42	26 Nov. 46	7 July 54	do	
Geo. Edwd. Owen Jackson, *Capt.*, do ..	27 Dec. 42	27 July 47	1 Mar. 55	do	
John Henry Lutman, *Major*, 24 Foot.....	8 Jan. 41	16 June 43	14 Jan. 49	17 Apr.	
George Waldegrave Bligh, *Major*, 60 Foot..	12 Mar. 41	26 July 44	12 Oct. 49	24 Apr.	
George King, *Major*, Depot Battalion	19 Oct. 38	7 Feb. 40	5 Nov. 47	30 Apr.	
Henry Pratt Gore, *Major*, 6 Foot	21 July 43	10 June 46	26 Nov. 52	6 May	
Tho. H. Smith, *Major*, 2 West India Regt.	9 Feb. 49	10 Dec. 52	19 Aug. 56	7 May	
Edward Buller Thorp, *Major*, 89 Foot	12 June 46	2 Feb. 49	11 Mar. 53	9 May	
William Lawes Peto, *Major*, 13 Foot	10 May 44	26 June 46	8 Feb. 50	21 May	
Herbert Vaughan Mundell, *Major*, 13 Foot .	2 Nov. 40	30 Dec. 45	15 Mar. 53	do	
Fred. Fletcher Vane, *Captain*, 23 Foot	17 Oct. 51	23 June 54	23 Mar. 55	4 June	
George Richard Browne, *Captain*, 88 Foot.	17 June 51	11 Aug. 54	24 Apr. 55	do	
Rob. Follett Synge, *Maj.*, 1 West India Regt.	20 Oct. 40	26 Sept. 42	6 June 54	15 June	
Godfrey Cooper, *Major*, Military Train	27 June 45	2 Apr. 47	4 Aug. 54	do	
Gibbes Rigaud, *Major*, 60 Foot	11 June 41	26 July 44	16 Aug. 50	22 June	
Henry Call Lodder, *Major*, 47 Foot	15 Jan. 41	19 Apr. 44	19 Sept. 48	25 June	
James Johnston, *Major*, 8 Foot	7 June 39	13 May 42	21 Apr. 46	26 June	
V.C. Alexander Roberts Dunn, *Maj.*, 100 F.	......	......	......	29 June	
W. Lee,[152] *Capt.* r. f. p. 6 F. (Q.M. 28 June 44)	28 July 40	26 Dec. 51	10 May 55	2 July	
John Walpole D'Oyly, *Major*, 11 Foot	17 Sept. 41	5 Sept. 43	15 June 49	13 July 58	
Edw. Henry Westropp, *Major*, 29 Foot....	2 Nov. 38	8 April 42	5 Aug. 47	do	
Pearson Scott Thompson, *Capt.* 14 Lt. Drgs.	5 Aug. 42	7 June 44	3 Sept. 47	20 July 58	
James Robert Gibbon, CB., *Capt.* R. Art...	18 Dec. 40	23 Nov. 41	30 June 48	do	
Francis P. Cassidy, *Captain*, 34 Foot	25 Nov. 28	13 Dec. 31	10 Nov. 48	do	

Majors.

Name	ENSIGN, ETC.	LIEUT.	CAPTAIN.	MAJOR.	WHEN PLACED ON HALF PAY.
Chardin Philip Johnson, *Captain*, 9 Lancers	14 Mar. 45	14 Apr. 46	19 Apr. 50	20 July 50	
Rich. Buckley Prettyjohn, *Capt.* 14 Dragoons	23 Feb. 38	18 Oct. 39	17 Sept. 50	do	
John Forster,[153] *Major*, Unatt	25 Aug. 43	3 Sept. 47	22 Nov. 50	do	18 Feb. 59
Mawdistly Gaussen Best, *Major*, 25 F.	12 Dec. 43	21 July 46	7 Mar. 51	do	
Thomas Hugh Cockburn, *Captain*, 43 Foot	6 Mar. 40	15 Apr. 42	9 Sept. 51	do	
Charles John William Norman, *Capt.* 72 F.	8 Nov. 44	8 Oct. 47	7 Oct. 51	do	
F. Montague M. Ommanney, *Capt.* R. Art.	20 Dec. 43	3 Sept. 45	2 Jan. 52	do	
Edmund Palmer, *Captain*, Royal Artillery	20 Dec. 43	4 Sept. 45	14 Jan. 52	do	
Fred. Dobson Middleton, *Captain*, 29 Foot	30 Dec. 42	18 Aug. 48	6 July 52	do	
Keith Ramsay Maitland, *Captain*, 79 Foot	4 July 45	25 July 46	24 Dec. 52	do	
Alexander Mackenzie, *Captain*, 78 Foot	7 Feb. 40	8 Apr. 42	15 Mar. 53	do	
John Everett Thring, *Captain*, R. Artillery	19 Dec. 44	1 Apr. 46	19 May 53	do	
William M'Mahon, *Captain*, 14 Light Drgs.	26 Nov. 42	6 Nov. 46	27 May 53	do	
Hugh Maurice Jones, *Major*, 73 Foot	22 Apr. 40	9 Aug. 50	1 July 53	do	
Septimus Moore Hawkins, *Major*, 97 Foot	2 June 43	30 Aug. 44	23 Dec. 53	do	
William Henry Kerr, *Captain*, 13 Foot	31 July 43	24 Jan. 51	13 Jan. 54	do	
Alexander Cockburn M'Barnet, *Capt.* 79 F.	19 Aug. 42	28 Nov. 45	10 Mar. 54	do	
Charles Craufurd Fraser, *Major*, 11 Hussars	3 Dec. 47	14 June 50	21 Apr. 54	do	
Arthur Need, *Captain*, 14 Light Dragoons	13 Oct. 39	17 June 42	1 June 54	do	
Archibald Richard Harenc, *Captain*, 97 F.	15 Apr. 42	25 Apr. 45	6 June 54	do	
Charles Edward Johns, *Captain*, 17 Foot	26 June 46	27 July 49	6 June 54	do	
Wm. Gustavus Alex. Middleton, *Capt.* 93 F.	24 July 46	3 Aug. 49	6 June 54	do	
John Maguire, *Captain*, 60 Foot	7 Feb. 40	4 July 43	20 June 54	do	
Horatio Page Vance, *Captain*, 38 Foot	3 Dec. 47	20 Dec. 50	4 Aug. 54	do	
Henry Foster, *Captain*, 95 Foot	25 Nov. 45	9 June 48	21 Sept. 54	do	
Jervoise Clarke Jervoise, *Major*, 23 Foot	13 June 50	9 May 51	21 Sept. 54	do	
Fred. William Burroughs, *Captain*, 93 Foot	31 Mar. 48	23 Sept. 51	10 Nov. 54	do	
Charles Darby, *Captain*, 86 Foot	6 Sept. 39	30 July 42	19 Dec. 54	do	
Arthur James Nixon, *Captain*, Rifle Brigade	30 Apr. 47	31 Oct. 51	20 Dec. 54	do	
Hon. Charles John Addington, *Capt.* 38 F.	16 Aug. 50	30 July 52	29 Dec. 54	do	
Henry Holford Stevenson, *Captain*, 79 Foot	29 June 49	24 Dec. 52	29 Dec. 54	do	
John Drysdale, *Captain*, 42 Foot	22 June 47	12 Oct. 52	12 Jan. 55	do	
James Herne Wade, *Captain*, 90 Foot	2 Feb. 49	24 Feb. 54	2 Feb. 55	do	
Robert Crosse Stewart, *Captain*, 35 Foot	25 Oct. 42	16 Sept. 45	7 Feb. 55	do	
Wm. Drummond Scrase Dickins, *Maj.* 20 F.	19 Aug. 51	7 June 54	20 Feb. 55	do	
Richard Henry Magenis, *Captain*, 32 Foot	10 April 49	5 May 54	25 Feb. 55	do	
William Hicks Slade, *Captain*, 5 Lancers	19 Mar. 47	23 May 48	9 Mar. 55	do	
Hon. Rich. Legge Newdigate, *Capt.* Rifle Br.	16 Sept. 51	6 June 54	23 Mar. 55	do	
Henry Lynch Talbot, *Captain*, R. Artillery	18 Dec. 47	30 June 48	1 Apr. 55	do	
Hon. Lewis Watson Milles, *Capt.* Rifle Br.	28 April 48	20 June 51	10 April 55	do	
VC Henry Wilmot, *Captain*, Rifle Brigade	29 May 49	17 Oct. 51	1 May 55	do	
Riversdale R. Glyn, *Captain*, Rifle Brigade	16 April 52	26 Oct. 54	10 Aug. 55	do	
Maxwell Lepper, *Captain*, 86 Foot	13 Aug. 47	23 Feb. 49	25 Aug. 55	do	
Martin Dillon, *Captain*, Rifle Brigade	18 Mar. 43	14 Nov. 44	2 Nov. 55	do	
William Tedlie, *Captain*, 60 Foot	5 May 48	13 April 52	25 Jan. 56	do	
Wm. Howley Goodenough, *Capt.* R. Artillery	19 Dec. 49	1 April 51	23 Feb. 56	do	
Thomas Bott, *Captain*, 6 Dragoon Guards	18 April 51	9 Mar. 55	22 Aug. 56	do	
Hon. Ivo De Vesci Twisleton Wykeham Fiennes, *Captain*, 7 Hussars	22 Nov. 50	8 June 52	3 Mar. 57	do	
VC C. Walker Heneage, *Capt.* 8 Hussars	19 Aug. 51	3 Sept. 54	12 May 57	do	
Robert Poore, *Captain*, 8 Hussars	5 Dec. 51	19 Jun. 55	17 Sept. 57	do	
Henry Buck, *Captain*, 53 Foot	28 July 42	14 Feb. 46	29 Sept. 57	do	
VC Herbert Taylor Macpherson, *Capt.* 82 F.	28 Feb. 45	13 July 48	6 Oct. 57	do	
VC James Leith, *Captain*, 2 Dragoons	4 May 49	27 May 53	27 July 58	do	
James D. Cowell, *Major*, 6 Dragoons	18 July 34	17 May 37	9 June 48	26 July	
Edmund D'Arcy Hunt, *Major*, 6 Dragoons	29 Oct. 47	19 Oct. 49	15 Sept. 54	do	
Charles Parker Catty, *Major*, 6 Foot	2 May 45	29 Jan. 47	26 Aug. 53	30 July	
Thomas Moubray, *Major*, 53 Foot	5 June 40	25 Feb. 42	15 Mar. 53	6 Aug.	
Taylor Lambard Mayne,[155] *Major*, Unatt.	6 Aug. 41	20 Dec. 42	2 Oct. 55	do	6 Aug. 58
Walter Welsford Lillicrap,[156] *Capt.* retired full pay, R. Marines	1 Nov. 33	16 June 38	17 May 48	24 Aug.	
Fred. Biscoe Tritton, *Major*, Depôt Battalion	22 Mar. 44	8 May 46	23 Sept. 51	do	
Henry Kent, *Major*, 77 Foot	8 Aug. 45	23 Aug. 50	27 Sept. 54	do	
Spier Hughes, *Major*, 84 Foot	31 Dec. 39	8 Apr. 42	15 Mar. 53	10 Sept.	
Penrose Charles Penrose, *Capt.* R. Marines	19 Dec. 37	3 July 47	22 Sept. 51	15 Sept.	
Thomas Valentine Cooke, *Capt.* do.	7 July 42	27 July 47	19 Dec. 54	do	
John Charles Downie Morrison, *Capt.* do.	18 Oct. 42	27 July 47	21 Feb. 55	do	
Charles John Ellis, *Captain*, Royal Marines	16 Mar. 47	25 Oct. 54	17 July 55	do	
Godfrey Clerk, *Captain*, Rifle Brigade	5 Dec. 51	25 Mar. 53	29 June 56	do	
Walter Pownall, *Major*, 3 Foot	6 Dec. 44	18 Oct. 45	6 Dec. 50	17 Sept.	
Francis Douglas Grey, *Major*, 63 Foot	9 May 46	13 Aug. 47	4 Nov. 53	do	

Majors. 85

Name	Ensign, etc.	Lieut.	Captain.	Major.	When placed on half pay.
William Agg, *Major*, 51 Foot	15 Oct. 50	19 May 53	13 Feb. 55	17 Sept. 58	
Henry Miles Stapylton, *Major*, 2 Dr. Guards	6 Dec. 50	11 Mar. 53	11 July 56	do	
F. T. Meik, *Captain*, Unatt., *S. O. of Pens.*	1 Nov. 28	4 May 32	3 April 46	22 Sept. 58	12 Nov. 52
Arthur A'C. Fisher, *Captain*, R. Engineers	1 Oct. 47	5 July 51	23 Feb. 56	do	
Geo. Montagu Stopford, do do	1 Oct. 47	14 July 51	23 Feb. 56	do	
V℃HowardCranfurdElphinstone do do	18 Dec. 47	11 Nov. 51	20 April 56	do	
Arthur Leahy, do do	27 June 48	17 Feb. 54	2 Dec. 57	23 Sept. 58	
John Clayton Cowell, *Captain*, Royal Eng.	19 June 50	17 Feb. 54	22 Sept. 58	23 Sept.	
Kenneth M. Moffatt, *Maj*. Canadian Rifles	5 Nov. 47	2 April 50	29 Dec. 54	24 Sept.	
Charles Clapcott, *Major*, 32 Foot	18 April 45	12 June 46	23 July 52	26 Sept.	
James Grime, *Captain*, retired full pay, 99 F.	15 Jan. 47	8 June 49	24 Nov. 57	5 Oct.	
James Waddell-Boyd, *Captain*, h. p. 14 Foot, *Staff Officer of Pensioners*	5 Feb. 36	2 May 38	1 May 40	10 Oct.	30 June 57
John Atkinson, *Major*, 89 Foot	22 Oct. 47	17 Jan. 51	4 Aug. 54	13 Oct.	
William Corbett, *Major*, 52 Foot	23 Nov. 38	31 Jan. 40	19 June 46	15 Oct.	
Cha. Wm. Meadowes Payne, *Capt*. Unatt.	1 Aug. 26	21 June 31	20 Dec. 35	26 Oct. 58	24 Sept. 41
Robert Michael Laffan, *Capt*. R. Engineers	5 May 37	1 April 39	1 May 46	do	
Geo. Bayly, *Capt*. Unatt., *S. O. of Pens.*	10 Feb. 25	17 April 30	8 May 46	do	25 June 52
Thomas Edmonds Mulock, *Major*, 70 Foot	18 Mar. 36	29 Nov. 39	8 May 46	do	
Arthur Henry Freeling, *Capt*. R. Engineers	14 Dec. 37	27 May 39	27 July 46	do	
William Percy Lea, *Major*, 87 Foot	22 Feb. 33	21 April 37	31 July 46	do	
Charles Fred. Campbell, *Major*, 87 Foot	15 Sept. 37	28 Aug. 40	2 Oct. 46	do	
Digby St. Vincent Hamilton, *Captain*, Unatt., *Staff Officer of Pensioners*	30 Aug. 33	30 Nov. 37	9 Nov. 46	do	30 Nov. 55
William Pilsworth, *Captain*, Unatt., *Staff Officer of Pensioners*	24 May 33	18 Mar. 38	9 Nov. 46	do	30 Nov. 55
Hampden C. B. Moody, *Capt*. R. Engineers	14 Dec. 37	22 Sept. 39	9 Nov. 46	do	
George Archibald Leach, *Captain*, R. Eng.	14 Dec. 37	28 Nov. 39	9 Nov. 46	do	
Philip John Stapleton Barry, *Capt*., R. Eng.	14 Dec. 37	3 April 40	17 Nov. 46	do	
G. W. Raikes, *Capt*. h.p. 76 F., *S.O. of Pens.*	14 Dec. 37	32 23 Oct. 35	22 Dec. 46	do	27 Dec. 50
James Montagu Brown, *Captain*, 93 Foot	17 April 28	14 Oct. 36	1 Jan. 47	do	
B. B. Keane, *Capt*. Unatt., *S. O. of Pens.*	8 May 35	11 Jan. 39	8 Jan. 47	do	10 Aug. 55
Henry Arthur White, *Captain*, Royal Eng.	14 Dec. 37	28 April 40	26 Jan. 47	do	
Hercules Atkin Welman, Depot Battalion.	17 Jan. 40	16 Mar. 43	3 Feb. 47	do	
Paul Bernard Whittingham, *Capt*., R. Eng.	14 Dec. 37	28 July 40	4 Feb. 47	do	
Lord Geo. J. Manners, *Capt*. N. Horse Gds.	20 Oct. 40	4 Aug. 43	5 Feb. 47	do	
Thomas Andrews Rawlins, *Staff Captain*, Invalid Depot at Chatham	7 Nov. 41	29 Dec. 43	5 Feb. 47	do	
*Salverio Gatt, *Major*, Roy. Malta Fencibles	26 Jan. 25	31 July 37	12 Feb. 47	do	
James William Gossett, *Capt*. R. Engineers.	16 June 38	7 Sept. 40	1 Mar. 47	do	
George Clement Baillie, *Capt*. R. Engineers.	16 June 38	19 Feb. 41	22 Mar. 47	do	
Tho. Hare, *Capt*., Cape Mounted Riflemen.	27 Mar. 35	6 Nov. 38	1 Apr. 47	do	
Fred. Campbell, *Capt*., Cape M. Riflemen	2 Mar. 39	16 Feb. 41	1 Apr. 47	do	
Rich. D'Oyly Fletcher, *Capt*. 1 W. India Regt.	21 Apr. 43	19 Apr. 44	9 Apr. 47	do	
Thomas Bernard Collinson, *Capt*. R. Eng.	16 June 38	9 Mar. 41	16 Apr. 47	do	
Edm. Y. Walcott Henderson, *Capt*. do	16 June 38	1 Apr. 41	22 Apr. 47	do	
G. F. Moore, *Capt*. Unatt., *S. O. of Pens.*	25 Oct. 39	9 Nov. 41	21 May 47	do	9 Oct. 55
Balcarres Dalrymple Wardlaw Ramsay, *Capt*. Unatt., *Dep. Assist. Qr. Mas. Gen.*	15 Dec. 40	5 Aug. 42	25 June 47	do	
*Felice Rizzo, *Capt*. Royal Malta Fencibles	15 Jan. 27	27 Oct. 39	20 July 47	do	
Jas. Delamain Meuds, *Capt*. 2 W. India Regt	3 Nov. 37	26 Oct. 39	29 July 47	do	
George Hughes Messiter, *Captain*, 69 Foot	15 June 30	29 Sept. 34	3 Sept. 47	do	
Thomas Tydd, *Captain*, 76 Foot	3 June 36	19 Oct. 38	3 Sept. 47	do	
James Florence Murray, *Major*, 83 Foot	28 Nov. 37	7 Jan. 42	14 Nov. 47	do	
Henry Macmanus Sall, *Captain*, 37 Foot	8 Dec. 37	1 Sept. 40	12 Sept. 48	do	
Rupert Barber Deering, *Major*, Depot Batt.	3 Mar. 37	17 Oct. 39	8 June 49	do	
John Bayly, *Captain*, Royal Engineers	19 Mar. 39	16 Sept. 41	3 Sept. 47	1 Nov.	
Algernon Robinson Sewell, *Major*, 15 Foot.	16 Feb. 38	18 Sept. 40	28 June 50	12 Nov.	
Henry Clerk, *Captain*, Royal Artillery	19 Mar. 39	13 Aug. 40	27 Sept. 49	16 Nov.	
Godfrey Rhodes,[157] *Major*, Unattached	19 Mar. 41	25 June 44	20 July 49	19 Nov.	19 Nov. 58
Wm. Charles Vanderspar, *Capt*. Ceylon Rifles	16 Aug. 39	9 Oct. 42	28 Sept. 47	23 Nov.	
Robert Prescott Harrison, *Captain*, 37 Foot	28 July 40	1 April 42	8 Feb. 50	26 Nov.	
Charles James Orton Swaffield, *Major*, 31 F.	27 Feb. 46	21 Jan. 48	19 Apr. 50	7 Dec.	
Arthur Charles Parker, *Captain*, 71 Foot	4 Mar. 42	16 Feb. 44	26 Dec. 51	do	
Sir William Gordon, *Bart*., *Capt*. 17 Lancers	14 June 50	18 July 51	26 Oct. 54	do	
John Henry St. John, *Captain*, 92 Foot	20 Nov. 46	23 Nov. 49	26 July 55	do	
Daniel Hen. Mackinnon, *Captain*, Unatt., *Staff Officer of Pensioners*	1 July 36	23 Mar. 38	15 Oct. 47	13 Dec.	11 Feb. 54
John Swaine Hogge, *Major*, 5 Foot	4 June 43	9 Nov. 46	3 June 53	17 Dec.	
Edm. Manningham Buller, *Maj*. Rifle Brig.	11 Oct. 45	24 Sept. 47	26 Sept. 54	do	

H

Majors.

Name	ENSIGN, ETC.	LIEUT.	CAPTAIN.	MAJOR.	WHEN PLACED ON HALF PAY.
Webster Thomas Gordon, *Major*, 66 Foot..	1 Dec. 46	12 Sept. 48	14 May 52	1 Jan. 59	
Geo. Rand,[156] *Captain*, r. f. p. Invalid Depot	8 Mar. 30	17 May 41	25 May 55	11 Jan. 59	
Chris. Monteith Hamilton, *Captain*, 92 Foot	3 Feb. 43	27 Sept. 44	12 Nov. 47	16 Jan. 59	
Chas. Penrose Coode, *Capt.*, r. f. p. R. Mar.	1 Aug. 37	11 May 41	24 Nov. 49	18 Jan.	
Barclay Thomas, *Major*, 27 Foot	31 Dec. 44	10 Nov. 47	8 Nov. 50	25 Jan.	
Hon. Wm. Leopold Talbot,[159] *Major*, Unatt.	20 May 42	26 Jan. 44	14 April 48	28 Jan. 50	28 Jan. 59
T. Cochrane, *Capt.*, Gold Coast Art. Corps	25 April 45	9 Jan. 47	25 Jan. 55	28 Jan.	
T. Smith, *Captain*, Unatt. *S. O. of Pens...*	13 Sept. 31	4 July 34	19 Nov. 47	13 Feb. 59	19 Nov. 47
Francis Fane, *Major*, 25 Foot	27 Aug. 41	12 Dec. 43	10 Jan. 51	18 Feb.	
J. Chester, *Captain*, h.p. Yk. Chass. *S. O. of Pens.*	2 Oct. 40	1 July 42	3 Dec. 47	20 Feb. 59	4 May 55
Thomas Nisbet, *Major*, 1 Dr. Gds.	29 May 49	8 Nov. 50	12 Nov. 52	25 Feb.	
James Arthur Gore, *Major*, 71 Foot	17 April 42	16 Dec. 45	8 June 52	4 Mar.	
E. J. Charter, *Major*, Depot Batt........	25 Oct. 42	16 Dec. 45	15 Mar. 53	8 Mar.	
H. A. Trevelyan, *Major*, 7 Hussars	17 Oct. 51	15 Feb. 53	8 Dec. 54	8 Mar.	
Wm. B. Tho. Rider,[160] *Capt.*, r. f. p. R. Mar.	10 Sept. 39	4 Jan. 43	13 Dec. 52	18 Mar.	
C. Pattison, *Capt.*, h.p. 56 F., *S. O. of Pens.*	7 Oct. 36	30 Aug. 39	10 Dec. 47	25 Mar. 59	16 Aug. 50
Thomas Peebles, *Major*, 11 Foot	17 Mar. 37	6 Feb. 41	6 June 51	1 April	
Frank Chaplin, *Major*, 3 Dr. Gds.	8 May 46	31 Oct. 58	8 April 53	1 April	
J. E. Sharp, *Capt.*, h.p. 1 F. *S. O. of Pens.*	24 April 35	9 Feb. 38	17 Dec. 47	2 April 59	5 June 57
Robert B. M'Crea, *Capt.*, R. Artillery ...	18 June 42	4 April 43	28 Nov. 48	8 April	
Thomas Teulon, *Major*, 35 Foot	29 Dec. 37	15 Dec. 40	31 Dec. 47	9 April	
Fitzroy Geo. Smith, *Major*, 7 Dr. Gds. ...	31 Dec. 47	11 Sept. 49	30 July 52	19 April	
Aug. Barnard Hankey, *Major*, 69 Foot ...	30 Oct. 40	20 June 45	20 May 49	22 April	
Henry C. Marriott, *Captain*, 82 Foot	5 Sept. 43	19 June 46	2 Feb. 49	26 April 59	
Geo. Edm. Halliday, *Captain*, 82 Foot ...	23 Aug. 39	15 April 42	10 Aug. 49	do	
John B. Thelwall, CB. *Captain*, 24 Foot ..	4 Aug. 43	3 April 46	21 Dec. 49	do	
Samuel Peters Jarvis, *Captain*, 82 Foot ...	14 June 45	15 Jan. 47	21 Sept. 52	do	
Geo. Samuel Young, *Captain*, 80 Foot	16 July 41	26 July 44	31 Oct. 52	do	
Wm. Roberts Farmar, *Captain*, 82 Foot ..	25 Feb. 45	11 April 46	13 May 53	do	
F. Van Straubenzee, *Captain*, 13 Foot ...	17 Aug. 38	30 April 41	6 June 49	do	
Geo. Murray Miller, *Captain*, 70 Foot	30 Jan. 46	2 April 47	4 Aug. 54	do	
Cha. F. Young, *Captain*, R. Artillery	2 May 47	30 June 48	13 Sept. 54	do	
W. H. *Visc.* Dangan, *Lt. and Capt.* Coldst. Gds.	never	23 July 52	21 Sept. 54	do	
Robert Stacy Colls, *Captain*, 32 Foot.....	14 Feb. 40	24 April 43	20 Feb. 55	do	
Bevil Granville, *Captain*, 23 Foot	16 May 51	6 June 54	16 Mar. 55	do	
Fra. Edw. Cox, *Captain*, R. Engineers	6 Aug. 40	20 Feb. 47	1 April 55	do	
John M'C. Campbell, *Captain*, R. Art. ...	27 June 48	1 Nov. 48	1 April 55	do	
E. C. D. Radcliffe, *Captain*, 88 Foot	9 July 52	18 Aug. 54	8 June 55	do	
Geo. Henry J. Heigham, *Captain*, 23 Foot	22 June 47	10 Feb. 54	6 July 55	do	
Thomas Casey Lyons, *Captain*, 20 Foot...	31 Aug. 45	2 Nov. 49	27 July 55	do	
J. H. Wyatt, *Captain*, Military Train	20 Sept. 44	26 June 46	3 Aug. 55	do	
Conyngham Jones, *Captain*, 60 Foot......	25 Feb. 48	21 Oct. 52	6 May 56	do	
A. Clarke Johnson, *Captain*, Roy. Artillery	19 June 50	17 Jan. 54	1 Jan. 57	do	
Sir C. F. Wheeler Cuffe, *Bart. Capt.* 66 Ft.	16 May 51	21 April 54	20 Mar. 57	do	
Thomas H. Stisted, *Captain*, 7 Hussars ..	3 April 46	10 Dec. 47	9 Oct. 57	do	
John Alexander Dalzell, *Captain*, 53 Foot..	30 Jan. 47	14 Mar. 51	19 Nov. 57	do	
John Terrence N. O'Brien, *Captain*, 20 Foot	11 Sept. 47	5 May 50	2 Feb. 58	do	
Fred. Montagu Alison, *Captain*, 19 Foot..	17 Oct. 51	1 Sept. 54	13 April 58	do	
Peter Burton Roe, *Captain*, 60 Foot	23 July 41	26 July 44	17 June 51	29 April 59	
Cha. W. Grange, *Captain*, Canadian Rifles	3 Nov. 43	2 May 45	31 Dec. 47	1 May 59	
Edward Hardinge, *Major*, 80 Foot........	11 Jan. 40	31 Dec. 41	22 Dec. 48	4 May 59	
William Ross King,[161] *Major*, Unattached..	11 July 45	5 Nov. 47	30 July 52	6 May 59	6 May 59
V℃ Wm. Geo. D. Stewart,[162] *Major*, Unatt.	2 June 42	21 Feb. 52	20 Dec. 54	6 May 59	6 May 59
Douglas Jones, *Captain*, Unattached.....	30 Dec. 36	26 Nov. 41	28 Jan. 48	10 May 59	7 Jan. 53
H. E. Delacombe,[163] *Captain*, r. f. p. R. Mar.	1 Aug. 37	11 May 41	23 Jan. 51	13 May 59	
George Wm. W. Carpenter, *Major*, 7 Foot	17 June 51	27 Jan. 54	12 Jan. 55	13 May 59	
T. L. J. Gallwey, *Captain*, Royal Engineers	19 Mar. 39	23 Nov. 41	2 Feb. 48	14 May	
Charles L. de Winton, *Major*, 16 Foot ...	15 Feb. 39	2 July 41	10 Mar. 48	24 May	
V℃ Hon. Aug. H. A. Anson, *Captain*, 7 Drs.	27 May 53	8 Dec. 54	6 July 55	28 May	
Edw. N. Molesworth, *Captain*, 27 Foot....	1 Dec. 37	2 April 41	2 Dec. 51	3 June	
T. Bourke, *Captain*, h.p. 27 F. *S. O. of Pens.*	9 May 34	2 May 37	27 Mar. 48	2 June 59	31 Aug. 55
Hon. Fred. B. Pakenham, *Major*, Unatt. ..	8 Feb. 42	20 Oct. 46	8 Oct. 50	14 June 59	14 June 59
George Henry Wynyard, *Major*, 58 Foot ..	3 May 44	10 Sept. 48	9 Oct. 55	do	
Valentine Baker, *Major*, 10 Hussars	1 Aug. 48	29 July 53	1 Aug. 56	do	
Hon. James C. Dormer, *Captain*, 13 Foot...	12 May 53	18 Aug. 54	11 Mar. 59	do	
Arch. A. Douglas, *Captain*, Royal Marines	12 May 48	25 May 49	7 May 59	17 June 59	
J. G. Cavendish Disbrowe, *Captain*, 43 Foot	never	2 Feb. 44	31 Mar. 48	20 June	
William Henry Orme, *Captain*, 85 Foot....	24 Jan. 45	3 April 46	13 Jan. 54	1 July	
V℃ Henry Edw. Jerome, *Captain*, 19 Foot	21 Jan. 48	30 April 52	23 July 58	1 July	

Majors.

	ENSIGN, ETC.	LIEUT.	CAPTAIN.	MAJOR.	WHEN PLACED ON HALF PAY.
James Dupre Brabazon,[164] *Major*, Unatt.	29 April 36	29 Jan. 41	20 Oct. 48	8 July 59	8 July 59
Rob. Hughes, *Captain*, 1 West India Regt.	2 June 39	18 June 41	6 April 48	17 July	
Fred. Wm. Lambton, *Captain*, 71 Foot	16 Sept. 51	22 Sept. 54	23 Oct. 57	19 July	
Richard England, *Major*, 55 Foot	18 Sept. 49	17 Aug. 52	29 Dec. 54	22 July	
Fred. William Gore, *Major*, 3 Foot	9 June 46	7 April 48	7 June 54	29 July	
Thomas Jones, *Major*, 4 Dragoon Guards	23 July 41	19 May 43	30 June 48	5 Aug.	
Fra. E. Macnaghten, *Major*, 8 Hussars	27 Oct. 46	23 May 48	8 Dec. 54	5 Aug.	
E. M. *Earl of* Longford, *Captain*, 2 Life Gds.	9 July 36	9 May 40	14 April 48	14 Aug.	
James Boyd, *Captain*, r. f. p. 86 Foot	8 April 42	13 Nov. 43	23 Jan. 55	16 Aug.	
Arthur Scott, *Captain*, 5 Foot	15 July 53	15 Dec. 54	31 Aug. 55	16 Aug. 59	
Richard Burnaby, *Captain*, Royal Engineers	19 Mar. 39	7 Dec. 41	14 April 48	9 Sept.	
Henry Lee, *Major*, 15 Hussars	12 Oct. 39	20 July 44	8 Dec. 54	23 Sept.	
Samuel Wm. Henry Hawker, *Captain*, 21 F.	19 Jan. 44	21 April 46	14 April 48	25 Sept.	
Cecil Rice, *Captain*, 72 Foot	1 Dec. 48	2 Aug. 50	1 Dec. 54	7 Oct.	
George Gooch Clowes, *Captain*, 8 Hussars	11 Mar. 53	19 Jan. 55	17 Sept. 57	7 Oct.	
Charles Rowley Platt, *Major*, 46 Foot	30 Sept. 42	26 July 44	17 Oct. 51	18 Oct. 59	
James Fraser, *Major*, 60 Foot	10 Sept. 41	26 July 44	7 Jan. 53	do	
Hamilton Charles Smith, *Major*, 80 Foot	8 Oct. 44	24 Dec. 45	1 May 53	do	
Herbert Dawson Slade, *Major*, 1 Dr. Gds.	25 Oct. 42	9 June 46	28 Aug. 49	21 Oct. 59	
Hans Thomas Fell White, *Major*, 40 Foot	12 May 43	14 May 47	13 Dec. 50	28 Oct.	
James M. Hill, *Major*, Military Train	1 Jan. 42	10 Aug. 42	1 Nov. 48	4 Nov. 59	
Henry Alfred Macdonald, *Major*, 77 Foot	30 Dec. 40	10 Nov. 43	26 Jan. 55	do	
Thomas S. Poer Field, *Captain*, R. Artillery	27 June 48	1 Nov. 48	1 April 55	do	
James Campbell, *Major*, Coast Artillery	1 July 47		10 May 55	do	
Geo. Lynedoch Carmichael, *Capt*. 95 Foot	15 Dec. 48	22 Oct. 52	20 Dec. 54	15 Nov. 59	
St. George Mervyn Nugent,[165] *Major*, Unatt., *Assist. Adj. Gen. at Aldershot*	25 Oct. 42	31 Dec. 44	15 Mar. 53	18 Nov. 59	
Wm. Jenny Pengelley,[166] *Capt*. r.f.p. R. Mar.	19 June 38	13 June 42	19 Jan. 52	20 Nov.	
Henry Torrens Walker, *Major*, 25 Foot	28 Oct. 36	4 July 39	16 Sept. 51	12 Dec. 59	
William Bayly, *Captain*, 8 Foot	26 Jan. 39	23 June 42	29 May 48	13 Dec. 59	
Lindsay Farrington, *Major*, 29 Foot	23 June 43	27 Sept. 44	9 July 50	13 Dec. 59	
Aug. Riversdale Warren, *Major*, 20 Foot	12 Dec. 52	16 June 54	1 May 55	13 Dec. 59	
George A. Ryan, *Major*, 70 Foot	31 May 44	31 Dec. 45	15 Nov. 50	16 Dec. 59	
𝓥𝓒 Joseph P. H. Crowe, *Captain*, 10 Foot	27 Oct. 46	17 Sept. 50	8 Jan. 58	20 Dec. 59	

War Services of the Majors.

1 Major de Brem served the campaigns in Germany from 1792 to 1800 ; in Egypt in 1801 ; in Naples in 1805 ; in Calabria in 1806 ; in Egypt in 1807 ; at the taking of Ischia in 1809 ; at the siege of Santa Maura in 1810 ; at the defeat of the French in Sicily in the same year ; in the campaigns of 1811, 12, 13, 14 in the Peninsula and south of France. Severely wounded in Germany on the 30th September 1796 ; and again at the battle of the Pyrenees on the 30th July 1813.

2 Major Thomas Wilson served in the 28th Regiment the Egyptian campaign of 1801 (Gold Medal). Expedition to Hanover in 1805-6. In the Peninsula, and was present at the battles of Busaco, in the Lines of Torres Vedras, affair of Campo Mayor, investment of Olivença, first siege of Badajoz, battle of Albuhera, surprise of Girard's Corps at Arroyo Molinos and Las Navas, affairs of Fuentes del Maestro, Miravete, and Bridge of Almaraz, retreat from Salamanca, and battle of Vittoria (severely wounded). He has the War Medal with four Clasps.

3 Major Christopher Wilkinson served the campaign of 1799 in Holland, under the Duke of York. Accompanied the expedition to the north of Germany in 1805, under Lord Cathcart.

4 Major Sandham served the campaign of 1799 in Holland, including the actions of the 27th Aug., 10th and 19th Sept., and 2nd Oct. Expedition to Copenhagen in 1807 ; to Sweden, and afterwards to Portugal and Spain, under Sir John Moore in 1808-9 ; subsequently to Walcheren, in 1809 ; the campaign in Holland, in 1814 ; and in Flanders and France in 1815, including the battle of Waterloo.

5 Major the Honourable Sir Francis Stanhope served in the 11th Foot at the siege of Flushing in 1809 ; and with the 1st Life Guards in the Peninsula and south of France, and was on the Staff at the battle of Toulouse, for which battle he has received the War Medal with one Clasp.

6 Sir Trevor Wheler served in the Peninsula with the 16th Light Dragoons from June 1810 to the end of that war in 1814, including the pursuit of Massena from the lines, actions of Pombal, Redinha, Foz d'Arouce, and Sabugal ; battle of Fuentes d'Onor, actions of Llerena and Castrejon, battle of Salamanca, retreat from Burgos, battles of Vittoria, the Nivelle, and the Nive, 9th to 12th Dec. Served also the campaign of 1815, including the battle of Waterloo. Sir Trevor has received the War Medal with four Clasps for Fuentes d'Onor, Salamanca, Vittoria, and Nivelle.

7 Major Sherer served in the Peninsula with the 34th Regt. from July 1809 to Dec. 1811, and from August 1812 to July 1813, including the battles of Busaco, Albuhera, Arroyo de Molino, Vittoria and Maya in the Pyrenees. He has received the War Medal with three Clasps for Busaco, Albuhera, and Vittoria.

8 Major Hartman served in the expedition to Hanover in 1805-6 ; at the siege of Copenhagen in 1807 ; in Sweden, Portugal, and Spain in 1808-9, including the advance and retreat of the army, and in the battle of Corunna. Expedition to Walcheren 1809 ; subsequent campaigns in the Peninsula and France, including the defence of Tarifa and affair of Casus Viejas, battle of Barrosa, actions of Arroyo del Molino and Almaraz, battles of Vittoria, the Pyrenees (25th, 30th and 31st July), Pass of Maya, Nivelle, Nive, Bayonne, and Orthes ; affair at St. Palais, and battle of Toulouse. He has received the War Medal with eight Clasps.

9 Major Mackay served with the 68th Regt. on the expedition to Walcheren, and at the capture of Flushing in 1809. Also in the Peninsula from June 1811 to the end of that war in 1814, including the battle of Salamanca, retreat from Burgos, and battles of Vittoria (wounded in the head), the Pyrenees, the Nivelle, and Orthes, for which he has received the War Medal with five Clasps.

10 Major Charters served with the expedition to Hanover, under Lord Cathcart, in 1805 ; the Walcheren expedition, in 1809 ; and campaign in Holland, under Lord Lynedoch, in 1814.

13 Major Casteau served with the R. M. Battalion on the North Coast of Spain co-operating with the troops of the Queen of Spain during the Carlist war in 1836-37 (Brevet Major and Cross of San Fernando).

14 Major Willoughby Montagu served at the siege of Dantzic, in 1813 ; also the campaign of 1815, including the battle of Waterloo and capture of Cambray. Is a Knight of 4th Class of St. Wladimir of Russia.

16 Major Tew served with the 50th Regt. in the battle of Punniar (Medal). Also the campaign of 1845-6 on the Sutlej (Medal and three Clasps), including the battles of Moodkee, Ferozeshah, Aliwal, and Sobraon (dangerously wounded).

17 Major Mundy was nominated to the 4th Class of the Medjidie for service with the Osmanli Horse Artillery as Lieutenant General, second in command.

18 Major C. H. L. Tinling served with the 13th Regt. at the capture of Rangoon, 11th May 1824 (Medal).

19 Major Murray served with the 42nd Highlanders at the siege and fall of Sebastopol from June 1855, and assault of the outworks on the 18th June (Medal and Clasp, and 5th Class of the Medjidie).

20 Major Ormsby served with the 80th Regiment during the Sutlej campaign of 1846, and was present at the affair of Buddiwal, and in the battles of Aliwal and Sobraon (Medal and one Clasp). Served during the Burmese war of 1852-3, and was present at the assault and capture of Pegu on 4th June 1852, where he commanded the storming party ; commanded at the Pagoda Hill stockade at Martaban on the night of the 18th July 1852, when attacked by the enemy ; and was also at the capture of Prome (Medal).

22 Major Nasmyth served at the defence of Silistria in May and June 1854 ; and afterwards in the Crimean campaign of the same year, including the battle of Alma and siege of Sebastopol (Medal and Clasps) ; he has also a Gold Medal awarded him by the Turkish Government, for his services with the Turkish Army in the campaign on the Danube in 1854.

23 Major Louis served the Egyptian campaign of 1801, for which he has received the Silver War Medal with one Clasp.

24 Major Metcalfe served the Egyptian campaign of 1801 with the 79th Highlanders, for which he has received the Silver War Medal with one Clasp.

25 Major H. C. Martin served on the expedition against the Danish and Swedish West India Islands in 1801 ; likewise on the expedition against the French Islands in 1803.

27 Major Fullarton served in the Peninsula with the 38th Regt., and was present at the battles of Roleia, Vimiera, Talavera, and Salamanca, for which he has received the War Medal with four Clasps.

28 Major Woods served with the Buffs in the Peninsula in 1808, 9, 10, and 11, was present at the passage of the Douro and capture of Oporto, battles of Talavera and Busaco, lines at Torres Vedras, action at Campo Mayor, and battle of Albuhera, where he was severely wounded, having lost his right leg. He has received the War Medal with three Clasps for Talavera, Busaco, and Albuhera.

29 Major Colby served at Walcheren in 1809.

30 Major Skene served in the Peninsula with the 24th Regt., and was present at the battle of Talavera (severely wounded), for which he has received the War Medal with one Clasp.

31 Major Hulme served in the Peninsula from March 1810 to the end of that war in 1814, including the 2nd siege of Badajoz, battles of Nivelle and Nive (10th to 13th Dec.), passage of the Adour, investment of Bayonne and repulse of the sortie. In March 1815 he joined the army in the Netherlands, and assisted in the organization of the Pontoon train at Antwerp :— Early in May, in order to secure a shorter and more direct communication between Brussels and Antwerp, he was entrusted with the construction of a bridge of vessels at Boom, across the Rupel, a large navigable branch of the Scheldt, which having completed and maintained until the victory at Waterloo rendered it no longer requisite, he followed the army to Paris in command of a division of the Pontoon train, where he remained until 1816. He has received the War Medal with two Clasps for Nivelle and Nive.

32 Major Agnew served with the 82nd Regt. during the Peninsular campaigns of 1808, 9, 12, and 13, and was present at the capture of Oporto, battle of Talavera, and subsequent affairs; also at the battle of Vittoria, where his leg was so severely fractured as to require three separate amputations of the thigh. He has received the War Medal with two Clasps.

33 Major Pringle served in the Peninsula from Jan. 1810 to the end of that War in 1814, including the battles of Nivelle and Nive (wounded), and investment of Bayonne. Served also the campaign of 1815, and was severely wounded at Waterloo. He has received the War Medal with three Clasps for Nivelle, Nive, and Orthes.

34 Major Knapman served at Lissa, in 1811 (wounded); and in boats cutting out an Algerine brig at Bona, in 1825 (War Medal with one Clasp).

35 Major G. V. Tinling served in the Peninsula from Nov. 1813 to the end of that war in 1814.

36 Major John Wilson served in the Artillery Companies of the 2nd Battalion Royal Marine during the war in North America in 1813. Has received the War Medal with one Clasp.

37 Major Humby has received the War Medal with one Clasp for the battle of Algiers.

38 Major Manners served in the Peninsula from Feb. 1810 to Dec. 1810, and was present at the battle of Barrosa (wounded), and the defence of Tarifa and Cadiz. He has received the Silver War Medal with one Clasp for Barrosa.

39 Major Schalch served at the capture of Guadaloupe in 1815.

40 Major Charles Gordon served in the American war in 1814 and 15 with the 93rd Regt., and was severely wounded in the left cheek at New Orleans, 8th Jan. 1815.

41 Major Robert Cochrane served in the Peninsula with the Rifle Brigade from August 1811 to the end of that war in 1814, including the defence of Cadiz, actions of the Aranjuaz, San Munos, and San Milan; battle of Vittoria, and action at the bridge of Vera. Served also the campaign of 1815, and was present at the battle of Waterloo and capture of Paris. Severely wounded in the left arm at Vera, and slightly in the left breast at Waterloo. He has received the War Medal with two Clasps.

42 Major Dowdall served the Mahratta campaigns of 1818 and 19, including the taking of Loghur, Isapoor, Kooaree, Rhygur, Raree, besides several other small forts, and he was severely wounded at the storming of Raree, having sustained the total loss of the right eye, and a portion of the nose and jaw-bone. Served also in the Burmese war under Sir Archibald Campbell, and was severely wounded in storming the Dalla stockades near Rangoon on the 9th Dec. 1824. Captain Dowdall commanded and led the Light Company of the 89th Regt. to five different storms.

43 Major Hugh Morgan served on the expedition to Walcheren in 1809, and was present at the bombardment of Flushing; served afterwards in the Peninsula from 1812 to the end of the war in 1814, including the defence of Cadiz, battles of the Pyrenees, siege of San Sebastian (severely wounded) and battle of Toulouse : he has received the War Medal with three Clasps.

44 Major Welchman served at Copenhagen in 1807; at Walcheren and forcing the Scheldt in 1809. Commanded 180 Marines at Cheribon and took possession of the fort, 4th Sept. 1811; also at the surrender of Panca, when a Regiment of Infantry laid down their arms. In the Royal Marine Battalion at the capture of Java in 1811. At the capture of the American frigate *President*, and expedition up the Penobscot, and commanded the detachment of Royal Marines at Manchias, where he captured three field-pieces, and was honourably mentioned. Was at the battle of Algiers, 1816 (War Medal and Clasps).

45 Major J. G. Richardson served in the Channel Fleet, under Lords Gardiner and St. Vincent; the Belleisle squadron, under Sir Richard Keates, when endeavouring to intercept Jerôme Bonaparte; and at the capture of *La Rhin* by *Mars* 74. With Admiral Murray and Brigadier-General Crauford's expedition of 5,000 men originally intended for Lima, but on arrival at the Cape of Good

War Services of the Majors.

Hope ordered to join General Whitelocke's army in Rio Plata; landed with Marines at Monte Video, and brigaded with detachments under command of the Hon. Lieut.-Col. Deane, 88th Regt. Served in the Baltic, and while passing the Sound, partially engaged the castle of Cronenberg; joined the squadron under Sir James Saumarez in pursuit of Russian fleet, to Rogerswick Bay. Severely wounded in several places on board *Africa* 64, in action with Danish flotilla consisting of 26 heavy gun and mortar boats, in Kioge Bay, near Copenhagen, 20 Oct. 1808—*Africa* seven killed, fifty-six wounded. Blockade of Texel, under Sir Samuel Hood; and Scheldt under Sir Richard Strachan and Sir Edward Pellew. Served with the Walcheren expedition in the *Theseus* 74, and dismantled and brought away its last gun-boat. Toulon fleet. Landed in company with other detachments of marines and seamen, and some Spanish troops, on an island in the Bay of Rosas; dislodged French garrison, and blew up the castle. Landed in company with other detachments of marines and seamen, 1812, at Sagona Bay, Island of Corsica,—destroyed and brought off a great quantity of valuable ship timber. Affairs of coasts, &c. Served in the West Indies and North America; and has received a reward from the Patriotic Fund.

46 Major Robert Webb served in H. M. S. *Superb* at the battle off St. Domingo, 6th Feb. 1806; at Copenhagen in 1807; at Walcheren in 1809. Wounded in an attack on an armed convoy in the Adriatic, 22nd May 1812. Has received the War Medal with one Clasp.

48 Major Hewett served blockading the French fleet off Brest, Rochefort, and Ferrol, and was severely wounded in the action with the combined fleets of France and Spain 22nd July 1805. In the 1st Battalion Royal Marines under Sir Arthur Wellesley, in Portugal, and at Lawris, and Galenga. In the 2nd Battalion, under Sir Sidney Beckwith, during the war in North America,—at the attack on Craney Island, the storming of Hampton, taking of Queentown, and Kent Island; frequently employed as an engineer officer, in command of outposts, and of gun-boats whilst attached to the Corps of observation, led the forlorn hope at the capture of Fort Oswego where he climbed the flagstaff and tore down the American Colors (severely wounded);—officially thanked by Colonel de Watteville for his conduct on this occasion.

49 Major Devon was Adjutant of the Artillery Companies of the Royal Marines serving in North America during the war in 1813-14.

50 Major Evan Morgan served in the Peninsula and France from October 1813, to June 1814, including the passage of the Adour, and battle of Toulouse, for which he has received the War Medal with one Clasp. He served also the campaign of 1814 in Canada, under Sir George Prevost.

52 Major Jervis Cook served at the capture of Martinique in 1809 and cutting out the French brig *Nisus*. At the destruction of *Loire* and *Seine* at Ance la Barque, and the capture of Guadaloupe in 1810. On the north-coast of Spain and in the Gironde, and attached to the Artillery in Flanders (War Medal with three Clasps).

53 Major Shute served with the Royal Marine Battalion in co-operation with the troops of the Queen of Spain against the Carlists in 1838.

54 Major William Davis was landed in 1809 at Mahon, in Minorca, in command of a detachment of Marines, to prevent the prisoners of war in the Lazaretto from rising and effecting their escape during a Mutiny of the Spanish Walloon Guards. At the capture and destruction of a fort on Isle Verte, near La Civitat, 1st June 1812, he received a severe wound by a rifle-ball, in the right thigh. On the 8th May 1813, as a volunteer, at the cutting out of an armed Xybec from under the fort and tower of Orbitello. At the capture of the island of Pouza, under Sir Charles Napier, where, as a volunteer, with a detachment of Marines, he landed, and stormed and captured one of the batteries. On the 4th Oct. 1813, as a volunteer in the storming of the fort protecting the anchorage at Marinello, when one gun-boat and thirteen of the enemy's vessels deeply laden were captured, and one gun-boat sunk. At the landing of the Italian Levy at Via Reggio in 1813. At the landing near Leghorn, in Dec. 1813, when 270 Marines charged and defeated between 600 and 700 French Infantry, supported by 30 Cavalry (received a sabre wound from the charge of Cavalry). At the capture of a castle near Spizzia, 25th March 1814. Present at the siege and capture of fort Santa Maria, 29th March following. Also at the capture of Genoa, under Lord William Bentinck.

55 Major Colin Mackenzie joined the army of the Netherlands on the 4th July 1814, and served under Lord Lynedoch, the Prince of Orange, and the Duke of Wellington, continuously from the above date, in Flanders and France, till the evacuation of Paris by the Allied Armies in the spring of 1816, and was present at the capture of Paris. Embarked in command of a Company of Royal Sappers and Miners for Canada, on the first outbreak, and served as Senior Royal Engineer on the Niagara Frontier during 1838-9.

56 Major Hewson served in the American war, and was engaged at the battle of Niagara and siege of Fort Erie. Served also in the Burmese war (Medal).

57 Major Cracknell assisted at the capture of eight armed vessels and twelve vessels laden with stores for the Russian Army at Percola Point on 7th July 1809 (War Medal with one Clasp).

58 Major Henry James was present at the capture of Fort San Philippo (Balageur), and siege of Tarragona in 1813. Also at the bombardment of Algiers in 1816 (War Medal with one Clasp).

59 Major Beverhoudt served at the capture of Guadaloupe in 1815.

60 Major John Kelly accompanied the effective men of the wing of the 6th Regt. stationed at Aden, which formed part of an expedition of 500 men under the command of Lieut.-Col. Pennycuick, which destroyed the Arab posts of Sheik Medi and Sheik Othman, and skirmishes between those places on the 6th Oct. 1841.

62 Major Mascall served in co-operation with the army at Corunna and during the defence of Cadiz. Was in a general Boat action near Port St. Mary's for which he has a Medal.

63 Major Pascoe has received the Silver War Medal with one Clasp for Java; also the Naval War Medal with one Clasp for the action with the French frigates off Madagascar and the surren-

der of the Isle de la Passe in Feb. 1811. Served in the 3rd Battalion R. M. in North America, participating in various important services during the war in 1814-15.

64 Major Searle served at Walcheren in 1809. Also throughout the Syrian campaign (War Medal with one Clasp and Turkish Medal).

65 Major Henry Smith served with the Royal Marine Battalion at d'Jouni in Syria in 1840, and was present at the bombardment of St. Jean d'Acre (Turkish Medal and War Medal with one Clasp).

66 Major Dusautoy served at Walcheren; at the capture of Genoa; and in two partial actions with French Fleets off Toulon and Marseilles.

67 Major R. S. Ridge served the Mahratta and Pindaree campaigns of 1817 and 18, and afterwards with the expedition to the Persian Gulf, including the siege of Ras-el-Kyma.

68 Major Thomas Park was actively employed in the Baltic during 1810, 11, and 12. From 1813 until the peace, served on the coast of America and the West Indies, including the attack on Cranie Island, and landed at the taking of Hampton, in the *Chesapeake*.

69 Major James Dowman served at the defence of Cadiz, 1810, 11, and 12, during which period he was repeatedly engaged in action against the enemy both on land and in boats, cutting out, &c. At the blockading of the French fleet off Brest in 1813. During the late campaign on the coast of Syria in 1840 and 41, including the storming and capture of Sidon, surrender of Beyrout, bombardment and fall of St. Jean d'Acre; served also with the Royal Marine Battalion at the camp at D'Jouni (War Medal and Clasp and Turkish Medal). Served in the Kaffir war of 1846-47 (Medal).

70 Major John Law was in the action with, and capture of, the *Chesapeake* by the *Shannon*, on the 1st June 1813. He was also at the capture of Fort St. Elmo, and the batteries at Naples on the 21st May 1815. Has received the War Medal with one Clasp.

71 Major Nepean served with the Royal Marines at the capture of a convoy and destruction of batteries at Fiuone, and in co-operation with the Austrian army at the reduction of Trieste in 1813.

72 Major Valentine Beadon served off the coast of France from 1811 to 1814, and was present in various boat actions. In 1815 he was at the capture of Naples and Gaeta; and in 1824 severely engaged with pirates in the West Indies.

73 Major Hender Mounsteven served at the attack of various posts, &c., on the Frontiers of Canada, and within the United States in 1813, 14, and 15. Served also with the 48th in the operations against the Rajah of Coorg, in April 1834.

74 Major Gardine Shaw served at the siege and capture of Hattrass, and throughout the Mahratta campaigns of 1817 and 1818. He served also at the siege and capture of the Forts of Punella and Pownghur in the Southern Mahratta Country in 1844-5.

75 Major George Mainwaring served with the 87th Regt. in the Burmese war, in 1825 and 26, He served with the 22nd throughout the operations in Scinde (Medal), under Sir Charles Napier, including the destruction of the Fort of Imaumghur, and the battles of Meeanee and Hyderabad.

76 Major Edleston served with the Royal Marines at the attack on New Orleans, 8th Jan. 1815.

77 Major W. J. King served the campaigns of 1818 and 19 in Concan, in India. Served in the Burmese war in 1824 and 25 (Medal with one Clasp), and received a severe contusion when leading the attack on the White Pagoda, an outwork of the stockade of Donabew.

78 Major Robert Wright served with the R. Marine battalion co-operating with the troops of the Queen of Spain against the Carlists in 1837-38 (Cross of San Fernando, 1st Class).

79 Major Appleton served in the Battalion of Marines in co-operation with the allied forces in Syria, and was present at the attack and surrender of the fortress of St. Jean d'Acre on the 3rd November 1840 (War Medal with one Clasp and Turkish Medal).

80 Major Knowles served with the 50th Regt. in the battle of Punniar 29 Dec. 1843 (Medal); and also the campaign on the Sutlej in 1845-6, including the battles of Moodkee, Ferozeshah, and Aliwal, for which he has received a Medal and two Clasps. He was slightly wounded at Ferozeshah, and dangerously wounded (right leg amputated) at Aliwal.

82 Major John Miller served at the battle of Navarino in 1827. Also with the R. M. battalion in Portugal in 1835. Commanded a Company during the operations on the coast of Syria in 1840 (Medal) and was with the battalion at D'Jouni. Sustained a severe fracture of the right leg in the service (War Medal with two Clasps).

83 Major Murchison served in the 29th Regt. in the Sutlej campaign of 1845-6, including the battles of Ferozeshah and Sobraon, in the last of which he was wounded (Medal and Clasp). Also in the Punjaub campaign in 1840, including the passage of the Chenab, and battles of Chillianwallah and Goojerat (Medal and Clasps).

84 Major Onslow was at the storming of Sidon in Syria (War Medal with one Clasp and Turkish Medal).

85 Major Duperier while in the 4th Light Dragoons was employed in Persia from 1833 to 1839 organizing the army of the Shah, who conferred on him the Gold Medal of the "Lion and Sun." He served with the 26th Regt. in China (Medal), at Ningpo, Chapoo, Shanghae, Woosung, and Chin Kiang Foo (wounded) and Nankin. Served with the 80th Regt. in the Burmese war in 1852-53 (Medal), including the operations in Donabew against Nameatoon.

86 Major Hunt served in the Eastern campaign of 1854-55, including the battle of Alma and siege of Sebastopol (Medal and Clasps, and 5th Class of the Medjidie).

87 Lord Erroll served with the Rifle Brigade in the Eastern campaign of 1854, and was severely wounded at the battle of Alma (Medal and Clasp, Brevet Major, and 5th Class of the Medjidie).

88 Major R. Thompson served in the Eastern campaign of 1854-55, and commanded the 5th Dragoon Guards during the winter and spring: present at the battle of Tchernaya, and siege of Sebastopol (Medal and Clasp, and 5th Class of the Medjidie).

War Services of the Majors.

89 Major Fellowes served the Eastern campaign of 1854-55 as D.A.Q.M.G., Cavalry Division, including the affairs of Bulganak and Mackenzie's Farm, battles of Alma, Balaklava, Inkerman, and Tchernaya, and siege of Sebastopol (Medal and Clasps, Brevet Major, Sardinian Medal, and 5th Class of the Medjidie).

90 Major Tomkinson served the Eastern campaign of 1854-55 with the 8th Hussars, including the battles of Alma, Balaklava (horse killed), and Inkerman, and siege of Sebastopol (Medal and four Clasps, Brevet Major, Sardinian Medal, and 5th Class of the Medjidie).

91 Major Stuart Wortley served with the Cape Mounted Riflemen throughout the Kaffir war of 1850-53 (Medal); and was present in all the principal engagements with the enemy: during the operations against the Waterkloof he commanded the cavalry attached to General Buller's division; on one occasion, while out with a patrol, he attacked and defeated a far superior force of the enemy; and on another, while in command of the advanced guard of General Buller's column, he surprised and drove back the enemy, inflicting severe loss. In March 1854 he was appointed D.A.Q.M. General Eastern Army, and served the campaign of 1854-55 (Medal and Clasps, Brevet Major, Sardinian Medal, and 5th Class of the Medjidie).

92 Major J. W. Thompson served the Eastern campaign of 1854-55 as D.A.Q.M.G. to the Second Division, including the battle of the Alma (severe contusion from the splinter of a shell), repulse of the Russian attack by the 2nd Division on the 26th Oct., battle of Inkerman (for which he received brevet rank as Major, and had his horse wounded), siege and fall of Sebastopol, and attack of the Redan on the 8th Sept. (Medal and Clasps, and 5th Class of the Medjidie).

93 Major Dickson served the Eastern campaign of 1854 with the 30th Regt., including the battles of Alma (severely wounded) and Inkerman (wounded), siege of Sebastopol, and repulse of the sortie of 26th Oct. (Medal and three Clasps, and 5th Class of the Medjidie).

94 Major C. F. T. Daniell served the Eastern campaign of 1854-55 as Brigade Major in the 3rd Division, including the battles of Alma and Inkerman, siege and fall of Sebastopol, and attack of the 18th June (Medal and Clasps, Brevet Major, Knight of the Legion of Honor, and 5th Class of the Medjidie).

95 Major Bayly served in the Eastern campaign of 1854 with the 30th Regt., including the siege of Sebastopol, repulse of the sortie on 26th Oct. (wounded in the cheek), and battle of Inkerman (severely wounded in the face and leg) (Medal and Clasps, and 5th Class of the Medjidie).

96 Major Greville served as Aide-de-Camp to Sir Harry Smith and to Sir George Cathcart in the Kaffir war of 1851-53 (Medal), and was present at the battle of Berea. Served again as Aide-de-Camp to Sir George Cathcart in the Eastern campaign of 1854, including the battles of Alma, Balaklava, and Inkerman (where Sir George was killed), and siege of Sebastopol (Medal and four Clasps, and 5th Class of the Medjidie).

97 Major Maclean served with the 49th Regt. throughout the war with China (Medal), and was present at the first taking of Chusan, storm and capture of the heights above Canton, attack and capture of Amoy, second capture of Chusan, attack and capture of the heights of Chinhae, occupation of Ningpo and repulse of the night-attack, attack and capture of Chapoo, Woosung, and Chin Kiang Foo.

97† Major Ruttledge served the campaign in Affghanistan under Lord Keane, including the storm and capture of Ghuznee (Medal), and storm and capture of Khelat. Served at the siege of Sebastopol from Dec. 1854 to 31 Aug. 1855, including the assault on the Redan on the 18th June (Medal and Clasp, and 5th Class of the Medjidie).

98 Major Dennis served with the 95th Regt. at the siege and fall of Sebastopol from 21st Feb. 1855 (Medal and Clasp, and 5th Class of the Medjidie).

99 Major Duncan Campbell served in the 83rd Regt. during the suppression of the insurrection in Lower Canada in 1837; also in repulsing the attacks of the American brigands who landed at Prescott, Upper Canada, in 1838. Served with the 90th Light Infantry at the siege of Sebastopo (Medal and Clasp).

100 Major Robert Watson served the campaigns of 1814 and 15 in Holland and the Netherlands, including the actions at Merxem and bombardment of Antwerp.

101 Major Meheux served the Eastern campaign with the Brigade of Royal Marines during the siege of Sebastopol from 1854 to April 1855, including the battle of Balaklava (Medal and two Clasps).

102 Major Hume served with the 38th Regt. the Eastern campaign of 1854-55, and was present at the battle of Alma, siege and fall of Sebastopol, was Aide de Camp to Sir John Campbell on the expedition to Kertch, and assault of the Redan on the 18th June, in which the Major General was killed; was D.A.A.G. 3rd Division from July 1855 (Medal and three Clasps, Brevet Major, Knight of the Legion of Honor, and 5th Class of the Medjidie). Served in India with the 38th from 12th Nov. 1857, to 9th August 1858; was present at the siege and capture of Lucknow, and with Grant's division during the summer campaign in Oude, including several minor affairs.

103 Major Peel served with the 34th Regt. in the Crimea in 1854-55, including the siege of Sebastopol and capture of the Quarries—severely wounded (Medal and Clasp, Brevet Major, and 5th Class of the Medjidie).

104 Major Elliot served five years in India, the last two on Lord Hardinge's staff, prior to entering the Royal Army, and was present with his regiment, the 8th Bengal Cavalry, at the battle of Punniar (Medal), as also in the Sutlej campaign, including the battle of Ferozeshah (Medal), Served the Eastern campaign of 1854-55 as Aide-de-Camp to General Scarlett, including the battle of Balaklava (severely wounded) and siege of Sebastopol (Medal and Clasps, Brevet Major, and Knight of the Legion of Honor).

105 Major Maxse served the Eastern campaign of 1854 as Aide-de-Camp to Lord Cardigan,

including the battles of Alma and Balaklava (wounded), and siege of Sebastopol (Medal and Clasps, and 5th Class of the Medjidie).

106 Major Hugh Kennedy served with the R. M. Battalion in Spain during the Carlist war; with the Baltic Expedition in 1854 (Medal); and with the Brigade in the Crimea during the siege of Sebastopol from Feb. 1855 (Medal and Clasp).

107 Major Steward served with the 41st Regt. in the Eastern campaign up to 19th Oct. 1854, including the battle of Alma, and siege of Sebastopol (Medal and two Clasps, and 5th Class of the Medjidie).

108 Major Whitmore landed in the Crimea with the 2nd Batt. on 22nd April 1855, and was at the siege and fall of Sebastopol (Medal and Clasp, Brevet Major, and 5th Class of the Medjidie).

109 Major Rogers served in the Eastern campaign in 1855, in the trenches with the Siege train before Sebastopol, and at the bombardments of April and 6th and 17th June (Medal and Clasp, and 5th Class of the Medjidie).

110 Major Hans R. White served with the 89th Regt. at the siege and fall of Sebastopol from 5th Jan. 1855, and attacks on the 18th June and 8th Sept. (Medal and Clasp, Brevet Major, and 5th Class of the Medjidie).

111 Major Hackett served with the 38th Regt. at the siege and fall of Sebastopol from 27th Jan. 1855 (Medal and Clasp, Brevet Major, and 5th Class of the Medjidie).

112 Major Fitzgerald served with the 7th Fusiliers in the Eastern campaign of 1854, up to Alma, in which battle he was severely wounded. Shot through both legs (Medal and Clasp, Brevet Major, and 5th Class of the Medjidie).

113 Major Hayman served with the 18th Royal Irish on the China expedition in 1842 (Medal). Accompanied the subsequent expedition under General D'Aguilar, which assaulted and took the Forts of the Bocca Tigris in the Canton River, those of the Staked Barrier, and of the city of Canton. Served also in the Burmese war of 1852-53, including the operations before Rangoon and capture of Prome (Medal). Served at the siege of Sebastopol from Dec. 1854, and was wounded 18th June 1855 (Medal and Clasp, Brevet Major, Knight of the Legion of Honor, and 5th Class of the Medjidie).

114 Major Pocock served with the 30th Regt. at the siege of Sebastopol, and was severely wounded at the assault of the Redan on the 8th Sept. (Medal and Clasp, Brevet Major, and 5th Class of the Medjidie).

115 Major F. P. Lea served with the 57th Regt. in the Crimea from 15th Nov. 1854 to 3rd July 1855, including the siege of Sebastopol and assault of the Redan on the 18th June—severely wounded in the right leg and foot by grape shot, also previously wounded in the head and face in the Trenches (Medal and Clasp, and 5th Class of the Medjidie).

116 Major Rowlands served with the 41st Regt. the Eastern campaign of 1854-55, including the battles of Alma and Inkerman (severely wounded), siege of Sebastopol, sortie of 26th Oct., and assault of the Redan on 8th Sept.—wounded (Medal and Clasps, Brevet Major, Victoria Cross, Knight of the Legion of Honor, and 5th Class of the Medjidie).

117 Major Bellairs served throughout the Eastern campaign of 1854-55 (from Dec. 1854 as D. A. Adjutant General to the 2nd Division), including the Battles of Alma (as Adjutant of the 49th Regt.) and Inkerman (where he was detached in command of the right wing of the 49th to operate to the right), siege and fall of Sebastopol, sortie of 26th October, attack of the Quarries on 7th June, and of the Redan on the 18th June and 8th September (Medal and three Clasps, Brevet Major, Knight of the Legion of Honor, and 5th Class of the Medjidie).

118 Major Steevens served with the 88th Regt. throughout the Eastern campaign of 1854-55, including the battles of Alma and Inkerman, siege of Sebastopol (contused wound in the trenches 28th July), and attack on the Redan on the 18th June and 8th Sept.; and was employed as Assistant Engineer in the trenches. Right attack at the commencement of the Siege (Medal and Clasps, Brevet Major, Knight of the Legion of Honor, and 5th Class of the Medjidie, and Turkish Medal).

120 Major Hay served the Eastern campaign of 1854-55, including the battles of Alma, Balaklava, and Inkerman, siege and fall of Sebastopol, affair of 18th June, and capture of Kinbourn (Medal and Clasps, Brevet Major, and 5th Class of the Medjidie).

121 Major Woods served as Adjutant 97th Regt. in the army of occupation in Greece from June to Nov. 1854 ; then joined the army in the Crimea, and served at the siege and fall of Sebastopol, and commanded the Grenadiers of the 97th with the storming party of the Redan on the 8th Sept.—wounded (Medal and Clasp, Brevet Major, and 5th Class of the Medjidie).

122 Major Hunter served in the 47th Regt. throughout the Eastern campaign of 1854-55, including the battles of Alma and Inkerman, capture of Balaklava, siege and fall of Sebastopol, sortie of 26th Oct., and storming of the Quarries—wounded (Medal and Clasps, Brevet Major, Knight of the Legion of Honor, and 5th Class of the Medjidie).

123 Major Cooch served with the 62nd Regt. at the siege of Sebastopol in 1854-55, including the sorties of 5th, 9th, and 10th May, attack of the Quarries on 8th June, and of the Redan on 18th June and 8th Sept. (Medal and Clasp, Brevet Major, Knight of the Legion of Honor, Sardinian Medal, and 5th Class of the Medjidie).

124 Major Harman served in the 34th Regt. in the Crimea from 9th Dec. 1854 to 11th July 1855, including the siege of Sebastopol, capture of the Rifle Pits on 19th April, and commanded the Grenadiers of the 34th Regt. at the assault of the Redan on the 18th June, when he received seven severe wounds (Medal and Clasp, and Brevet Major).

127 Major Hockings served in Spain with the Royal Marine Battalion (Cross of San Fernando) ; also with the R. M. Brigade in the Crimea during the siege of Sebastopol in 1854-55, including the battle of Balaklava (Medal and two Clasps).

War Services of the Majors.

128 Major Ussher served in China in 1841-42 (Medal), at the first capture of Chusan, attack on Chuenpee, and capture of Amoy. Served also with the Baltic Expeditions in 1854 and in 1855 (Medal).

129 Major Nelson served as Sub-Assistant Commissary-General, Bombay Army, throughout the operations under Sir Wm. Nott, in Candahar and Affghanistan during 1841-42; and as such under Sir Charles Napier at the battle of Hyderabad. Served as Aide-de-Camp to Sir Thomas Valiant in the action of Mahurajpore 29th Dec. 1843, and had a horse shot under him. He has a Medal for Affghanistan, another for Scinde, and a bronze star for Maharajpore.

130 Major Godfrey Massy served with the 19th Regt. the Eastern campaign of 1854-55, including the battles of Alma and Inkerman, and siege of Sebastopol (Medal and Clasps, and Brevet Major).

131 Major Speedy served the campaigns of 1841 and 42, in the 13th Light Infantry, and was present at the storming of the Khoord Cabool Pass, affair of Tezeen, forcing the Jugdulluck Pass, reduction of the fort of Mamoo Khail, defence of Jellalabad and sorties on the 14th Nov. and 1st Dec. 1841, 11th March, 24th March, and 1st April 1842, and general action and defeat of Akbar Khan. Medals for Jellalabad and Cabool.

131† Major Shervinton served in the 46th Regt. throughout the Eastern campaign of 1854-55, including the battles of Alma, Balaklava, and Inkerman, sortie of 26th Oct., siege and fall of Sebastopol. Having served uninterruptedly throughout the siege he was appointed to the Staff at Balaklava, and subsequently to the command of the 1st Battalion Land Transport Corps (Medal and Clasps, Brevet of Major, and 5th Class of the Medjidic).

132 Major Gillum served with the 2nd Battalion Royals at the siege of Sebastopol from 22nd April 1855, and was severely wounded at the attack of the 8th Sept.,—leg amputated (Medal and Clasp, Brevet Major, and Sardinian Medal).

133 Major Henley served the campaign of 1814 in the Peninsula, including the battle of Toulouse, for which he has received the War Medal with one Clasp.

134 Major J. T. Aslett served the Syrian campaign including the storm and capture of Sidon, D'Jounie, surrender of Beyrout, bombardment of Acre—slightly wounded by the explosion of a magazine (War Medal with one Clasp and Turkish Medal).

135 Major W. D. Macdonald served in the 95th Regt. in the Eastern campaign up to 6th Nov. 1854, including the battle of Alma (wounded), siege of Sebastopol, sortie of 26th October, and battle of Inkerman where he was dangerously wounded having received seventeen bayonet stabs (Medal and three Clasps, Brevet Major, and Sardinian Medal).

136 Major Buller served with the Rifle Brigade in the Eastern campaign of 1854, including the battle of Alma, siege of Sebastopol, and battle of Inkerman—severely wounded (Medal and three Clasps, and Brevet of Major).

137 Major Sayer served the Syrian campaign of 1840-41 (Medal with one Clasp and Turkish Medal). Also with the expeditions to the Baltic in 1854 and 1855, and with the R.M. Battalion serving in cooperation with the French army at the siege and capture of Bomarsund (Medal).

138 Major T. De C. Hamilton served with the 90th Regt. in Kaffirland during the whole of the war of 1846-47 (Medal). Served with the 68th Light Infantry the Eastern campaign of 1854-55, including the battles of Alma and Inkerman, siege and fall of Sebastopol (Medal and Clasps, Victoria Cross, and Knight of the Legion of Honor).

139 Major J. P. Macdonald served in the Crimea from June 1855 as D.A.Q.M.General attached to the Land Transport Corps (Medal and Clasp). Served in the Indian campaign of 1857-58, including the relief of Lucknow by Lord Clyde, occupation of the Alumbagh under Outram with the several engagements there, fall of Lucknow, relief of Azimghur, capture of Jugdispore, and subsequent operations, and was dangerously wounded on the 4th June when charging at the head of his troop a body of rebels near Jugdispore.

140 Major Hutton served with the 31st Regt. throughout the Sutlej campaign of 1845-46, including the battles of Moodkee, Ferozeshah (wounded), Buddiwal, Aliwal, and Sobraon (Medal and three Clasps). Served in the Crimea in 1855 during the siege and at the fall of Sebastopol (Medal and Clasp).

141 Major Daunt served with the 9th Regt. the campaign of 1842 in Affghanistan (Medal); also the Sutlej campaign of 1845-46, including the battles of Moodkee, Ferozeshah, and Sobraon (wounded): Medal and Clasps. Served in the Crimea from 15th Feb. 1855, including the siege and fall of Sebastopol, and assault on the batteries on the 18th June (Medal and Clasp).

142 Major Dick served in the Crimea from the 11th March 1855, as D.A.Q.M.G. attached to the Land Transport Corps, including the siege and fall of Sebastopol, and attacks of the 18th of June and 8th Sept., and accompanied the expedition to Kertch and Yenikale (Medal and Clasp).

143 Major Buchanan served as Adjutant with the 47th Regt. the Eastern campaign of 1854-55, including the battles of Alma and Inkerman, sortie of 26th Oct., siege and fall of Sebastopol —appointed Town Major (Medal and Clasps, Sardinian Medal, and 5th Class of the Medjidie).

144 Major Henry J. Coote served with the 22nd throughout the operations in Scinde (Medal) under Sir Charles Napier, and was present at the destruction of Imaumghur, and in the battles of Meeanee and Hyderabad (severely wounded). He was mentioned in orders as being the first man who entered the enemy's entrenched position, and also as having taken the first color from the enemy at the battle of Hyderabad. He served with the 36th in the Ionian Islands from 1849 until 1851, and commanded the troops at Sisi during the insurrection of 1849, and on three occasions defeated the insurgents, including their night attack on the village of Aggupader.

145 Major Pleydell served the Syrian campaign of 1840 — at D'Jouni, the storming of Sidon, and bombardment of Acre (War Medal with Clasp and Turkish Medal). Served also with the Baltic expeditions in 1854 and 1855 (Medal).

War Services of the Majors. 95—102

146 Major Barrett served in the Kandian Territories, Ceylon, during the whole of the Rebellion of 1817 and 18, and commanded an outpost during part of the above period.

147 Major Hon. E. J. W. Forester served throughout the campaigns in Affghanistan from 1838 to 1842 inclusive, including the storm and capture of Ghuznee (Medal), storming the Khoord Cabool Pass, affair of Tezeen, forcing the Jugdulluck Pass, reduction of the Fort of Mamoo Khail, defence of Jellalabad, and sorties on the 14th November and 1st December 1841, 11th March, 24th March, and 1st April 1842, general action and defeat of Akbar Khan before Jellalabad (Medal), storming the heights of Jugdulluck, general action of Tezeen, and recapture of Cabool (Medal). Served as an Aide-de-Camp to Sir Willoughby Cotton in 1838, 39, and 40, and at Ghuznee.

148 Major Esmonde served with the 18th Royal Irish in the Burmese war of 1852-53 (Medal). Also in the Crimea from 30th Dec. 1854 to 27th July 1855, including the siege of Sebastopol, assault and capture of the Cemetery on the 18th June (Medal and Clasp, Victoria Cross, and Brevet Major).

149 Major Kuight served with the 62nd at the capture of Genoa in 1814, and subsequently at the taking of Castine and Hamiltown in the United States of N. America.

150 Major Dawson was attached to the 22nd Regt. at the battle of Hyderabad (Medal), and he was present with the 40th Regt. in the action of Maharajpore, at which he was wounded (Medal). Served with the 75th Regt. at the siege of Delhi in 1857 and was severely wounded in right leg by a round shot on the 8th June (Medal and Clasp, and Brevet of Major).

151 Major Mansfield served as Aide de Camp to Sir Colin Campbell throughout the Eastern campaign of 1854-55, including the battles of Alma and Balaklava (Medal and Clasps, and Sardinian Medal).

152 Major Wm. Lee served with the Royal Marines at the capture of the Island of Carabusa together with several piratical vessels in its harbour, in 1828-29 (Medal). Served as Adjutant of the 6th Regt. in the Kaffir war of 1850-53 (Medal).

153 Major Forster served with the 6th Dr. Guards at the siege and fall of Sebastopol from 26 July 1859 (Medal and Clasp). Was second in command of the Wing of the Carabineers before Delhi; thence he accompanied General Showers' column and was at the affair of Kuttwalee when General Penny was killed,—on this occasion he led a charge against a band of fanatic Ghazees and was wounded in seven places, losing a portion of one hand (Medal and Clasp and Brevet of Major).

155 Major T. L. Mayne served the Punjaub campaign of 1848-49 with the 14th Light Dragoons, including the action of Ramnuggur (with the charging squadrons), passage of the Chenab, battles of Chillianwallah and Goojerat, pursuit of the enemy across the Jhelum, and of the Affghans over the Indus, to the Khyber Pass (Medal and two Clasps).

156 Major Lillicrap served with the R. M. Battalion at D'Jouni in Syria in 1840 (War Medal and Clasp, and Turkish Medal).

157 Major Rhodes served the campaign of 1853 and the spring campaign of 1854 on the Danube as Aide de Camp to the Spanish General Prim, was present at the battle of Oltenitza. Subsequently was attached to Selim Pacha's staff and accompanied the Turkish Irregular Cavalry in three successful sorties from the Quarantine Station; present in the Tete de Pont when the Russians unsuccessfully attacked and bombarded that position, retiring with loss; was also at the retreat of the Russians from Giergevo and Slobodsia in 1854. For the abovementioned services he has received the Spanish Order of Isabel the Catholic, also the Turkish Order of the Medjidie 4th Class, with a sword of Honor from the Sultan. Served the campaign of 1854 on the staff of the army in the Crimea, and was present at the battles of Balaklava and Inkerman and siege of Sebastopol (Medal and Clasps).

158 Major Rand served with the 49th Regt. throughout the operations in China (Medal).

159 Major Hon. W. L. Talbot served as Aide de Camp to General Airey at the siege and fall of Sebastopol from 6th Sept. 1855 (Medal and Clasp).

160 Major Rider served in Syria in 1840 and has the Medal and Clasp and Turkish Medal. Served also with the Baltic expedition in 1855 (Medal).

161 Major Ross King served with the 74th Highlanders throughout the Kaffir war of 1851-53 (Medal), and was present in the engagements of the Amalolas, Kroomie, Walerkloof, &c.—thrice mentioned in dispatches, also in General Orders 20th Sept. 1852.

162 Major Stewart served with the 93rd Highlanders the Eastern campaign of 1854-55 including the battles of Alma and Balaklava, siege and fall of Sebastopol (Medal and three Clasps, and 5th Class of the Medjidie).

163 Major Delacombe served with the R. M. Battalion in conjunction with the French troops at the operations prior to and at the surrender of the forts of Bomarsund in Aug. 1854. Served with the Baltic expedition in 1855, including the bombardment of Swenborg (Medal).

164 Major Brabazon was present at the storm and destruction of the fortified native Mandingo town of Sabajee on the Gambia, on the 1st June 1853.

165 Major Nugent served with the 29th Regt. in the Sutlej campaign in 1846 (Medal and Clasp), and was present at the battles of Ferozeshah and Sobraon (severely wounded).

166 Major Pengelley served with the expedition to the Baltic in 1855 (Medal). He has also the Silver Medal from the Royal Humane Society.

GENERAL AND FIELD OFFICERS
WHO HAVE RETIRED FROM THE SERVICE.

LIEUTENANT-GENERALS.

Bunbury, *Sir* Henry Edward, *Bart.*[1] *KCB.*	...	22 July 30
ʊ Johnson, William Augustus[2]	...	23 Nov. 41

MAJOR-GENERALS.

ʊ Bateman, Robert,[2] Unatt ...	...	31 Aug. 55
ʊ ʊʊ Beckwith, Charles,[3] *CB.* ...	...	9 Nov. 46
ʊ Bristow, Henry,[4] 38 F.	...	20 June 54
Charretie, Thomas[5]	...	9 Nov. 46
ʊ De Chabot, Louis William, *Visc.*[6] 50 F.	...	19 July 21
ʊ Dudgeon, Peter,[12] Unatt.	...	31 Aug. 54
Dwyer, Henry,[7] Unatt.	...	20 June 54
Farrer, James[8]	...	23 Nov. 41
ʊ ʊʊ Floyd, *Sir* Henry, *Bart.*[9] ...	...	11 Nov. 51
ʊ Owen Loftus,[14] Unatt.	...	16 May 57
Prinsle, John, Unatt.	...	10 Jan. 37
ʊʊʊ Rooke, *Sir Hon.* Willoughby,[10] *CB., KCH.*		22 July 30
ʊ Stewart, William,[11] 3 F.	...	22 July 30
Studd, Edward, Unatt	...	20 June 54
ʊ ʊʊ Woodford, *Sir* John George,[13] *KCB.*, *KCH.* Gr. Gds.	...	10 Jan. 37

COLONELS.

ʊ ʊʊ Allix, Charles,[1] Gr. Gds. ...	...	10 Jan. 37
ʊ Angelo, Edward Anthony,[2] *KH., Military Knight of Windsor*, 30 F.	...	9 Nov. 46
Anglesoy, Henry, *Marquis of*, 42 F.	...	28 June 38
ʊ Armytage, Henry,[3] Gr. Gds. ...	...	23 Nov. 41
Astell, Richard William, Gr. Gds.	...	11 Nov. 51
Austen, John,[4] *KH.* Cape M. R. ...	...	11 Nov. 51
Bagot, Chu., Gren. Gds., *Col.*[5] *Stafford Militia*		11 Nov. 51
Baillie, Hugh, Surrey Rangers ...	...	26 July 10
Barlow, George Edward Pratt,[6] 22 F.	...	28 June 38
Bazalgette, John,[7] 2 W. I. Regt. ...	...	11 Nov. 51
ʊ Beebie, Thomas Stirling,[8] 44 F. ...	...	20 June 54
Blackburne, William, 60 F. ...	...	28 Nov. 54
Blake, Matthew Gregory, Canadian Regt.	...	28 June 38
ʊ Blake, Wm. Williams.[9] *CB.* 11 Drs.	...	22 July 30
Blanc, Charles Collins, Gr. Gds. ...	...	9 Nov. 46
ʊ ʊʊ Boldero, Lonsdale,[10] Gr. Gds. ...	...	15 April 45
Boswell, *Sir* Geo. A. F. Houstoun, *Bt.* Cold. Gds.		11 Nov. 51
ʊ Boys, Edmund French,[11] 45 F. ...	...	20 June 54
ʊ Brugge, William,[12] 37 F.	...	20 June 54
Brinckman, Brinckman, Coldst. Gds.	...	9 Nov. 46
ʊ Brooke, Thomas,[13] Gren. Gds. ...	...	10 Jan. 37
ʊ ʊʊ Browne, Fielding,[14] *CB.* 66 F. *Barrack Master, Regent's Park*		10 Jan. 37
ʊ Browne, Robt. Fra. Melville,[15] Sco. Fus. Gds.		23 Nov. 41
Browne, Thomas Gore,[16] *CB.* 44 F. *Governor and Com. in Chief, New Zealand* ...		20 June 54
Burdett, *Sir* Robert, *Bart.* 68 F. ...	...	9 Nov. 46
Burrowes, Robert Edward,[15] *KH.* 66 F.	...	20 June 54
Campbell, James, 87 F.	...	28 Nov. 54
Cane, Stopford, 30 F.	...	11 Nov. 51
Cartwright, Henry, Gr. Gds. ...	...	20 June 54
Cecil, *Lord*, Thomas, Coldst. Gds. ...	...	9 Nov. 46
ʊ Chaplin, Thomas, Coldst. Gds. ...	...	23 Nov. 41
Clavering, Henry Mordaunt, 98 F.	...	29 April 02
Clifford, Robert Cavendish Spencer, Gr. Gds.	...	7 Sept. 55
Clinton, Frederick, Gr. Gds. ...	...	9 Nov. 46
Clinton, Henry, 1 Drs.	...	20 June 54
Close, Maxwell,[20] 79 F.	...	9 Nov. 46
Cockell, William,[21] 16 Foot ...	...	28 Nov. 54
Conroy, Henry George, Gr. Gds. ...	...	28 Nov. 54
ʊ Couper, *Sir* George, *Bt.*[22] *CB. KH.* 10 F. *Controller of the Household & Equerry to H.R.H. the Duchess of Kent*		10 Jan. 37
ʊ Cox, *Sir* William,[23] *Port. Serv.* ...	...	12 Aug. 19
Creagh, Giles Vandeleur, *Depot Batt.*	...	20 June 54
Daniell, Henry,[21] Coldst. Gds. ...	...	28 Nov. 54
d'Arcy, George A. K.[25] 3 West India Regt.		7 July 57
ʊʊʊ Dawkins, Henry,[26] Coldst. Gds. ...		10 Jan. 37
Denny, William,[27] 71 F.	...	20 June 54
Dobbin, Thomas,[28] 3 Drs.	...	23 Nov. 41
Doherty, Charles Edmund,[29] 13 Dragoons	...	28 Nov. 54
ʊ Drummond, William,[30] Sco. Fus. Gds.	...	10 Jan. 37
Dundas, Philip, 6 F.	...	9 Nov. 46
Dyson, John Daniel, 3 Dragoon Guards...	...	28 Nov. 54
Evelegh, Fred. Charles,[31] *CB.* 20 F.	...	12 May 58
ʊ Fairfax, *Sir* Henry, *Bart.*[32] 2 Life Gds.	...	23 Nov. 41
Farquharson, Peter,[33] 14 F.	...	20 June 54
Foley, *Hon.* Aug. Fred., Gren. Gds. ...	...	20 June 54
Fordyce-Buchan, George William,[34] 74 F.		28 Nov. 54
Fraser, James, 72 F.	...	28 Nov. 54
ʊ Fraser, William,[35] 43 F.	...	10 July 21
Gauntlett, George,[36] 62 F.	...	10 July 21
ʊʊʊ Gawler, George,[37] *KH.* 69 F. ...	...	9 Nov. 46
Gibbes, John George Nathaniel,[38] 60 F.		11 Nov. 51
ʊ Gloster, Thomas,[37] 68 F.	...	20 June 54
ʊ Gordon, Arthur Helsham,[10] Gr. Gds.	...	10 Jan. 37
Goulburn, Edward, Grenadier Guards	...	28 Nov. 54

Graham, William, Scots Fus. Gds. ...	...	9 Nov. 46
ʊ Graham, William,[42] 9 F.	...	8 Sept. 57
Greenwood, George, 2 Life Gds. ...	...	12 Jan. 38
Gregory, *Hon.* Jas. Michell,[43] 3 W. I. Regt.	...	15 May 57
Hall, Thomas,[44] Grenadier Guards ...	...	11 Nov. 51
Hamilton, *Sir* Chu. J. J.[45] *Bt. CB.* Scots Fus. Gds.		20 June 54
ʊ Hamilton, John Potter,[46] *KH.* Scots Fus. Gds.		12 Aug. 10
Hammond, Fred. 75 F.	...	20 June 54
Harcourt, Francis Venables, Coldst. Gds.	...	9 Nov. 46
ʊ Harris, Harry Buiteel,[48] *KH.* 93 F.	...	10 Jan. 37
Hay, *Lord* Edward, 7 Hussars ...	...	9 Nov. 46
Hill, Philip, 1 W. I. Regt.	...	20 June 54
ʊʊʊ Hill, *Sir* Robert Chambre,[50] *CB. R. H.* Gds.		
Lt. Col. N. Salop Yeomanry ...	...	1 Jan. 19
Hill, *Hon.* William Noel,[51] 13 F. ...	...	20 June 54
ʊ Hogge, John,[52] *KH.* 11 F.	...	23 Nov. 41
Holland, Launcelot, 34 F.	...	4 June 14
Honyman, *Sir* Ord,[53] *Bart.* Gr. Gds.	...	2 Oct. 46
Hopwood, Hervey, Grenadier Guards	...	22 Aug. 56
ʊ ʊʊ Horton, George William,[55] 7 Dr. Gds.	...	23 Nov. 41
ʊ ʊʊ Hughes, Robert,[56] W. I. Regt. ...	...	28 Nov. 54
ʊ ʊʊ Hutchinson, *Hon.* Henry Hely,[57] 6 Drs.	...	12 June 38
ʊ Irwin, Fred. Chidley,[58] *KH.* Unatt. ...	...	20 June 54
ʊ Joddrell, Henry Edmund,[59] Gr. Gds. ...	...	10 Jan. 37
ʊ ʊʊ Keane, Edward,[60] Gr. Gds. ...	...	28 June 38
ʊ Kyle, Alexander,[61] 26 F.	...	20 June 54
ʊ ʊʊ Lane, Henry,[62] Gr. Gds. ...	...	28 June 38
ʊ ʊʊ Lascelles, Charles P. R.[63] Gr. Gds.	...	23 Nov. 41
ʊ ʊʊ Le Blanc, Francis,[64] 46 F. ...	...	23 Nov. 41
ʊ Leconfield, George, *Lord*, 27 F. ...	...	22 July 30
ʊ Leslie, Charles,[65] *KH.* Gren. Gds. ...	...	9 Nov. 46
ʊʊʊ Linton, John,[66] Coldst. Gds. ...	...	9 Nov. 46
Lowe, Arthur Charles,[67] 11 F. ...	...	15 Mar. 58
M'Douall, James, *late of* 2 Life Guards	...	10 April 47
ʊ Macadam, William,[93] *KH.* 8 Foot ...	...	23 Nov. 41
Maclean, *Sir* Charles Fitzroy, *Bt.* 13 Drs.	...	9 Nov. 46
ʊ Macpherson, John,[70] 11 F.	...	20 June 54
ʊ Mudox, Henry,[71] *KH.* 12 Lancers ...	...	28 June 38
Massey, *Hon.* Nathaniel Henry Cha., 70 F. *Lt. Col. Comn.* 4 W. York Militia ...		20 June 54
Maxwell, *Sir* William Alex. *Bart.* 1 Drs.	...	11 Nov. 51
Meyrick, Wm. Henry, Gr. Gds. ...	...	10 Jan. 37
Murray, *Lord* James Chas. F.[73] Scots Fus. Gds. *Equerry to H.R.H. the Duchess of Kent*		20 Feb. 56
Myers, William James, R. Staff Corps	...	26 Oct. 58
Owen, Robert,[74] 72 F.	...	11 Nov. 51
Paget, Frederick, Coldst. Gds. ...	...	11 Nov. 51
Passy, Edmund Wm. Wilton, 56 F. ...	...	28 Nov. 54
Penleaze, Henry, Gr. Gds.	...	20 June 54
Pennant, *Hon.* Edw. Gordon Douglas, Scots Fus. Gds. *Lt. Col. Carnarvon Militia* ...		9 Nov. 46
Phipps, *Hon. Sir* Chu. B. *KCB.* Scots Fus. Gds.		11 Nov. 51
ʊ Pratt, Charles,[76] 11 F.	...	9 Nov. 46
Pringle, John Henry, Scots Fus. Guards, *Lt. Col. Com.* 6 Lancashire Militia ...		20 June 54
Raitt, Charles Robert, Unattached ...	...	28 Nov. 54
Reynardson, Edward Birch,[77] *CB.* Gr. Gds.		20 June 54
ʊ ʊʊ Richardson, William,[78] Royal Horse Gds.		10 Jan. 37
ʊ ʊʊ Riddlesden, John Buck,[79] 27 F. ...	...	1 Aug. 26
Robertson, James Alexander, 82 F. ...	...	16 Sept. 57
Robertson, James Macdonald,[80] 4 Dr. Gds.	...	9 Nov. 46
ʊ Salwey, Henry,[61] 2 Drs.	...	23 Nov. 41
Saumarez, *Hon.* John St. Vincent, 16 Drs.	...	20 June 54
Savage, John Morris, R. Art. ...	...	14 Jan. 55
ʊ Saunderson, Hardress Robert,[82] 73 F.	...	11 Nov. 51
Scott, *Hon.* Charles Grantham, Scots Fus. Gds.	...	30 Jan. 55
Skelly, Francis, 37 F.	...	28 Nov. 54
St. Quintin, Matthew C. D. 17 Drs. ...	...	11 Nov. 51
Skipwith, Henry,[81] 43 F.	...	9 Nov. 46
Taylor, Phillpotts Wright, Canadian Rifles	...	28 Nov. 54
Tempest, Thomas Richard Plumbe, 23 F.	...	20 June 54
Teulon, George, 16 F.	...	9 Nov. 46
Thornton, William, Gr. Gds. ...	...	11 Nov. 51
Todd, George, Coldst. Gds.	...	9 Nov. 46
Tulloch, Thomas,[85] 42 F.	...	26 Oct. 58
Turner, Fred. Henry, Scots Fus. Gds.	...	20 June 54
ʊ ʊʊ Vandeleur, John,[86] 4 Drs. ...	...	23 Nov. 41
Vicars, William Henry,[87] 61 F. ...	...	28 Nov. 54
Walpole, Horatio,[89] 79 F.	...	11 Nov. 51
ʊ Ward, John Richard,[90] *CB.* 2 Drs. ...	...	22 July 30
Wellesley, William Henry Charles, 7 F.	...	28 Nov. 54
Whyte, John James, 1 Dr. Gds. ...	...	11 Nov. 51
Wigram, Ely Docedeemus, Scots Fus. Gds.	...	11 Nov. 51
Wilbraham, *Hon.* Edw. Bootle, Coldst. Gds. *Col.* 6 Lancashire Militia ...		11 Nov. 51
ʊʊʊ Wildman, John,[91] 1 Dr. Gds. ...	...	20 June 54
ʊʊʊ Wood, John Manley,[92] 5 F. ...	...	28 Nov. 54
ʊ Woodgate, William,[93] *CB.* 60 F. ...	...	10 July 21
ʊ Wyatt, *Sir* Henry Robartes,[94] 29 F.	...	23 Nov. 41
ʊ Wyndham, Charles,[95] 36 F. ...	...	28 June 38
Yorke, Philip James, Scots Fus. Gds.	...	9 Nov. 46

Field Officers who have retired.

LIEUTENANT-COLONELS.

Name	Date
Addams, James, R. Art.	6 Nov. 27
ℙ Alexander, Henry,[1] 96 F.	11 Nov. 51
Allen, James, 2 W. I. Regt.	9 Nov. 46
ℙ Anderson, Joseph,[2] CB. KH. 50 F.	1 April 41
Andrews, Charles, 46 F.	11 Nov. 51
Andros, William,[3] 55 F.	11 Nov. 51
Armstrong, Alex. Boswell,[4] Cape M. Rifles	5 Nov. 47
Arthur, Thomas, 3 Dr. Gds.	12 May 43
Astley, John Dugdale,[6] Scots Fus. Gds.	16 June 57
Austen, Henry Edmund, 51 F.	20 June 54
Baddeley, Wm. Henry Clinton,[7] 49 F.	23 Mar. 55
Baines, Cuthbert A. 16 F.	28 Oct. 58
ℙ Barney, George,[8] R. Engineers	15 Aug. 40
Barrett, Knox, 56 F.	11 Nov. 51
Barrington, Henry, Gr. Gds.	1 Oct. 20
Barrow, Thomas, 68 F.	2 June 14
ℙ 𝔊𝔐 Barton, Alexander,[10] KH. 12 Drs.	10 Jan. 37
Barton, Hugh William, 69 F.	30 Dec. 58
Bathurst, Henry, Scots Fus. Gds.	13 Jan. 43
ℙ Bayly, Sir Henry,[12] KH. 77 F.	23 Nov. 41
ℙ Beckham, Thomas,[13] Unattached	20 June 54
Bell, Wm., 12 F. Barrack Master, Newport	30 Mar. 49
ℙ Bell, Thomas,[14] CB. 48 F.	20 Sept. 27
Bennett, William, 48 F.	10 Jan. 37
ℙ Bernard, Hon. Wm. Smyth,[15] 17 Drs.	11 Nov. 51
Bigge, William Matthew, 70 F. Lt.Col. Com. Northumberland Militia	23 April 47
Blachford, Owald Samuel, 15 Drs.	20 June 54
Black, George, 75 F.	13 Feb. 50
𝔊𝔐 Blanc, Sir Hugh S., Bt. Scots Fus. Gds.	31 Aug. 31
𝔊𝔐 Blathwayt, George Wm. 1 F.	11 Nov. 51
Blennerhasset, Barry,[17] 71 F.	7 Dec. 58
Blomefield, George, 7 Drs.	23 Nov. 41
Blount, Robert,[19] 68 F.	2 Nov. 55
Boldero, Henry George, 38 F.	11 Nov. 51
Bond, Edward,[20] Dep. Batt.	20 June 54
Bond, Henry,[21] 15 Hussars	11 Nov. 51
Bonham, John Brathwaite,[22] 50 F.	14 Feb. 52
𝔊𝔐 Bowen, Robert, Coldst. Gds.	27 Jan. 32
ℙ Brackenbury, Sir Edward,[23] 69 F.	10 Jan. 37
Brandreth, Fred., Scots Fus. Gds.	2 Oct. 46
Brisco, Hylton, 2 Dr. Gds.	16 June 57
Brown, Edward John Vesey,[25] 60 F.	27 May 56
ℙ Brown, Gustavus,[26] CB. 95 F.	17 Aug. 12
Browne, Brotherton, 94 F.	11 Nov. 51
𝔊𝔐 Browne, Barton Parker,[27] 11 Drs.	11 Nov. 51
ℙ Browne, George,[28] CB. 23 F.	23 Nov. 41
Browne, Hon. James Lyon,[29] 21 F.	24 April 55
ℙ 𝔊𝔐 Bruce, William,[30] KH. 48 F.	23 Nov. 41
ℙ Bunbury, Thomas,[31] CB. 80 F.	26 July 44
Burdett, Charles Sedley,[32] Coldst. Gds.	22 Aug. 59
Burdett, Francis, 17 Drs.	10 Oct. 48
Burton, Fran. Aug. Plunkett,[23] Coldst. Gds.	25 May 55
Butler Charles Richard,[92] 20 F.	26 Apr. 59.
Butler, Edward Kent S., 35 F.	17 June 30
Butt, John Wells, 95 F.	20 Oct. 58
ℙ 𝔊𝔐 Cadell, Charles,[35] KH. 94 F.	27 Sept. 33
Caine, William,[34] 26 F.	11 Nov. 51
Caldwell, William Bletterman, 76 F.	20 June 54
Cameron, Nathaniel, 79 F.	24 June 13
Campbell, Henry Dundas, Unatt.	28 June 38
Campbell, James, 61 F.	19 Aug. 40
Campbell, P. Wm. FitzRoy, Scots Fus. Gds.	9 Nov. 38
Carruthers, Richard,[37] CB. 2 F.	23 July 30
Cavan, Philip Charles, 30 F.	21 May 52
Charleton, Henry Wilmot, 2 Dr. Gds.	11 June 41
Church, Sir Richard,[39] GB. GCH. Greek L.I.	10 Nov. 12
Cleather, Edward John, 49 F.	20 June 54
Clephane, Robert Douglas,[40] 79 F.	6 June 56
Clerke, Sir Wm. Henry,[41] Bart., 47 F.	11 Nov. 51
Clitherow, John Christie, Coldst. Gds.	30 May 43
Cochrane, George, Ceylon Regt.	28 Sept. 47
Cocker, Barnard William, 38 F.	11 Nov. 51
Cole, Robert, 30 F.	31 Dec. 47
ℙ Colthurst, James Robert,[43] 18 F.	20 June 54
Colman, Thomas, 9 F.	11 Nov. 51
Connop, Henry, 55 F.	11 Nov. 51
ℙ Cooke, John Henry, 21 F. Sub. Officer Gent. at Arms	11 Nov. 51
Coote, Chidley, 31 F.	11 Nov. 51
ℙ 𝔊𝔐 Cowell-Stepney, J. Stepney,[44] KH. Cold. Gds.	15 June 30
Cox, Charles, 72 F.	11 Nov. 51
Cox, Samuel Symes, 56 F.	13 July 55
ℙ Crowe, John,[46] KH. 8 F.	10 Jan. 27
Cumberland, Bentinck Harry, 18 F.	11 Nov. 51
Cumming, Henry Wedderburne, Coldst. Gds.	27 May 53
ℙ Cust, Hon. Peregrine Francis,[48] 22 F.	9 Nov. 46
Dalgety, James W., 74 F.	20 July 5
Dalzell, Hon. Robert Alex. George,[49] CB. 63 F.	6 Nov. 54
Dashwood, Alexander Wilton, 74 F.	11 Nov. 51
Deare, Geo., 21 F. Lt.Col. Com. W. Suffolk Mil.	28 Dec. 38
De Bathe, Sir Wm. Plunkett, Bart.[50] 53 F.	9 April 25
De Lancey, John, 1 W. I. Regt.	11 Nov. 51
De Lancey, Peter, 75 F.	3 April 49
𝔊𝔐 Des Vœux B., Scots Fus. Gd.	3 July 29
ℙ De Visme Francis,[52] 80 F.	11 Nov. 51
ℙ Digby, Henry Robert [51] Scots Fus. Gds.	20 July 30
Digby, John Almerus,[53] Gren. Gds.	7 Dec. 58
Dillon, Francis William,[54] 69 F.	7 Dec. 47
ℙ 𝔊𝔐 Disbrowe, George, KH. Gr. Gds.	17 Aug. 21
Dixon, John, Gr. Gds.	18 May 41
Dixon, John, 73 F.	11 Nov. 51
ℙ Doyle, Michael Taylor,[56] Rifle Br.	10 Jan. 37
Drought, John Head,[57] 15 F.	11 Nov. 51
Duberley, George, 77 F.	22 Dec. 48
Dundas, Thomas, 32 F.	10 Jan. 37
Dunsmure, Charles, 42 F.	15 Feb. 50
ℙ Edmonds, Hamilton, 7 F. Barrack Mast. at Hounslow	11 Nov. 51
Edwards, Hugh Gore, 10 F.	10 Jan. 37
Egerton, Hon. Arthur Fred., Gr. Gds.	11 Sept. 57
Eyres, George William, Gr. Gds.	1 July 36
ℙ Falkiner, Samuel,[59] 23 F.	11 Nov. 51
Fane, Henry, 15 Drs.	17 Oct. 37
Farquharson, Henry Hubert, 1 F.	10 Mar. 37
Feilden, Robert,[61] 44 F.	29 June 55
ℙ 𝔊𝔐 Fendell, William,[62] 4 Drs.	24 Dec. 32
Ferguson, Robert, 70 F.	13 Mar. 35
Ficklin, Robert, 47 F.	11 Nov. 51
Findlay, Alexander, 3 W. I. R.	13 Feb. 52
FitzGerald, Charles Lionel, R. Art.	1 April 55
FitzGerald, Edward, KH. 98 F.	16 June 25
ℙ 𝔊𝔐 Fitz Roy, Lord Charles,[64] 26 F.	21 Jan. 19
Fitz Roy, Hugh, Gr. Gds.	20 Dec. 40
𝔊𝔐 Flamank, John,[65] 35 F.	9 Nov. 40
Fletcher, R., Gr. Gds.	26 Nov. 30
Forbes, John, Coldst. Gds.	7 Aug. 46
Forbes, Jonathan,[66] 78 F.	9 Nov. 46
Forbes, John Alexander, 92 F.	9 Nov. 46
Forester, Cecil William, 52 F.	22 Aug. 51
Forester, Hon. Henry Townsend, Gr. Gds.	24 Aug. 52
𝔊𝔐 Forlong, James, KH. 63 F.	7 May 41
Fraser, Hon. Alex. Edw.,[69] Scots Fus. Gds.	2 Feb. 58
Freeman, Thomas Inigo Wickham, 13 F.	11 Nov. 51
ℙ 𝔊𝔐 Fuller, Francis, CB.[70] 59 F.	27 May 25
ℙ Fuller, Frederick Hervey,[71] 91 F.	11 Nov. 51
Gaisford, John William, 72 F.	22 June 55
Gale, Alex. Robinson, 80 F.	11 Nov. 51
Gardner, James, Military Train	11 Nov. 51
ℙ Garner, John Hutchinson,[72] 93 F.	11 Nov. 51
Gilpin, Rich. Tho., Rifle Br. Col. Beds. Militia	11 Nov. 51
ℙ Girardot, Charles A.,[78] Coldst. Gds.	11 July 26
Glover, Sterling Freeman, 12 F.	14 Apr. 46
𝔊𝔐 Gooch, Henry,[74] Coldst. Gds.	26 Nov. 32
Gordon, John,[75] 47 F.	15 Dec. 50
Gordon, Sir William, Bart. 3 W. I. Regt.	20 June 54
ℙ Gore, George, KH. 9 Drs.	4 Dec. 17
Gould, Francis Augustus, 48 F.	11 Nov. 51
ℙ Graham, Henry,[77] 69 F.	11 Nov. 51
Grant, Alex. G., 85 F.	31 Aug. 55
Gunning, Matthew,[79] 6 F.	9 Nov. 46
Hagart, James M'Caul, CB. 7 Hussars	14 Aug. 57
ℙ 𝔊𝔐 Hulkett, Hugh,[81] CB. GCH. Ger. Legn.	1 Jan. 12
Hall, Charles, Scots Fus. Gds.	13 Aug. 25
ℙ 𝔊𝔐 Hall, George,[82] 54 F.	28 June 38
Hall, Jasper Taylor, 53 F.	23 Nov. 51
Hamilton, Sir James John, Bart., 39 F.	9 Nov. 46
Hammill, Thomas Cochrane,[84] Ceylon Regt.	11 Nov. 51
Hanmer, Henry, KH. R. H. Gds.	18 May 26
Harding, Benjamin, 2 Dr. Gds.	14 July 25
Harding, William,[85] 2 F.	23 Nov. 41
Hare, Hon. Richard, 90 F.	11 Nov. 51
ℙ 𝔊𝔐 Harris, Sir Thomas Noel,[86] Unatt.	13 Feb. 23
ℙ Harrison, John Bacon,[87] CB. 50 F.	19 June 12
ℙ Harrison, J. Christopher,[88] KH. 23 F.	22 July 30
Harvey, Henry B., 21 F. Major London Mil.	20 June 54
Hatton, Villiers La Touche, Gr. Gds.	29 June 55
𝔊𝔐 Hawkins, Henry, Scots Fus. Gds.	22 July 30
ℙ Hay, Sir Andrew Leith,[90] KH. 1 W. I. R.	21 June 31
Hay, David, 6 Dr. Gds.	1 Nov. 42
𝔊𝔐 Hewett, William, 53 F.	19 Aug. 28
Heyland, John Rowley, 7 F. Barrack Master at Birmingham	20 June 54
Hickey, Edward, 69 F.	9 Nov. 56
Hill, Charles John, 7 Drs.	5 April 33
Hill, George Staveley, Rifle Br.	20 June 54
Hill, Rich. Fred. 53 F. Col. Shropshire Mil.	13 May 36
Hogg, James Macnaghten, 1 Life Gds.	22 June 55
Holder, Charles,[94] Scots Fus. Gds.	17 Aug. 55
Holmes, Christopher Francis,[95] 6 F.	20 June 54
ℙ 𝔊𝔐 Home, Francis, Scots Fus. Gds.	15 Mar. 14
Hudson, Joseph Henry, Gr. Gds.	16 May 45
ℙ Humfrey, Benjamin Genle,[97] 97 F.	11 Nov. 51
Hunt, Wm. Thos. 3 W. I. Regt	5 Aug. 42
Hunter, James, 16 F.	11 Nov. 51
ℙ Hutton, Thomas,[98] 32 F.	28 June 38
Inge, William, 8 F.	11 Nov. 51

Field Officers who have retired.

Jackson, Basil, R. Staff Corps ... 9 Nov. 40
James, Charles, 12 F. ... 20 June 54
Johnston, James,[100] 99 F. ... 11 June 29
Johnston, William Fred.,[101] Gr. Gds. ... 10 Jan. 37
Johnstone, George, 15 F. ... 23 Aug. 39
Jones, Ebenezer, 66 F. ... 11 Nov. 51
Jones, Inigo Williams, 11 Hussars ... 24 Dec. 52
Jones, Thomas, 14 Drs. ... 10 Jan. 37
Kaye, George Lister Lister, Unatt. *Lt. Col. Com.*
5 W. York Militia ... 11 Nov. 51
Kearney, Charles, 2 Dr. Gds. ... 28 Oct. 37
Keating, James Singer, Rifle Br. ... 11 Nov. 51
Kelson, Charles,[103] Ceylon Regt. ... 20 June 54
Kelsall, Roger, R. Eng. ... 22 Apr. 45
Kidd, John M'Mahon, 87 F. ... 22 June 54
King, A. S., 10 F. ... 12 Aug. 10
Kingscote, R. N. F.,[104] *CB.* Scots Fus. Gds. ... 17 July 55
Kirwan, Andrew Hyacinth, 95 F. ... 11 Nov. 51
Kitchener, Henry Horatio, 9 F. ... 5 Nov. 47
Knox, Brownlow William, Scots Fus. Gds. *Major*
Bucks Yeomanry ... 15 Nov. 30
Knox, George, Coldst. Gds. ... 27 July 38
Knox, William, 13 Drs. ... 23 June 48
Leake, W. M., Royal Artillery ... 4 June 13
Leatham, James,[106] 4 F. ... 11 Nov. 51
Le Couteur, John,[107] 20 F. ... 11 Nov. 51
Leitrim, W., *Earl of*, 51 F. *Col. Leitrim Mil.* 20 June 54
Lennox, *Lord* Arthur, 68 F. *Sussex Militia* ... 22 Nov. 42
Lennox, *Lord* George, 6 Drs. *Lord in*
Waiting to H.R.H. The Prince Consort ... 12 June 23
Lillie, *Sir* John Scott,[109] *CB.* Gr. Gds. ... 10 Jan. 37
Lillie, Thomas,[110] Ceylon Rifles ...
Lindesay, Patrick,[111] 63 F. ... 9 Mar. 55
Lindsay, *Hon.* Charles Hugh,[112] Gr. Gds. ... 14 July 54
Lindsay, Martin George Thomas,[113] 91 F. ... 8 April 42
Lindsell, Robert Henry,[114] 28 F. ... 26 Dec. 56
Lister, Fred. D.[115] 6 Drs. ... 2 Nov. 55
Loftus, Ferrars, Gr. Gds. *Col. 3 W. York Mil.*
Long, Samuel, Gr. Gds. ... 13 Sept. 27
Lowndes, John Henry,[116] 9 F. ... 6 June 50
Lowther, *Hon. Hen.* Cecil, 12 F. *Col. Cumber-*
land Militia ... 20 April 17
Loyd-Lindsay, Rob. Jas.,[117] Scots Fus. Gds. ... 22 July 59
Luard, John,[118] 30 F. ... 28 June 38
Lushington, Franklin,[119] *CB.* Scots Fus. Gds. ... 20 June 54
Lys, George Mowbray,[120] *CB.* 20 F. ... 15 May 55
M'Alester, C. Arch.,[121] *KH.* Ceylon Rgt. ... 8 June 20
M'Call, James, 8 Drs. ... 17 Sept. 41
M'Niven, Thomas William Ogilvy,[122] 70 F. ... 31 Dec. 41
MacBean, Frederick,[123] *KH.* 84 F. ... 2 Nov. 38
Macbeath, George,[124] *CB.* Depot Batt. ... 20 June 54
Macdonald, Alexander, 68 F. ... 20 June 54
Macdonald, Robert,[125] *CB.* 35 F. ... 25 Aug. 29
Macdonald, John,[126] 5 F. *Lt. Col. Commandant*
Carnarvon Militia ... 11 Nov. 51
Macdonell, George,[127] *CB.* 70 F. ... 24 Feb. 14
MacDougall, *Sir* Duncan,[128] 70 F. ... 21 April 25
Macdougall, James,[129] 42 F. ... 1 Nov. 42
M'Dowell, Geo. James Muat,[130] *CB.* 16 Drs. ... 23 July 39
Mackey, John Alex, 57 F. ... 20 June 55
Maclean, Henry Dundas, 92 F. ... 9 Nov. 46
M'Pherson, Duncan,[132] 27 F. ... 28 Feb. 40
MacPherson, Duncan, 42 F. ... 10 Jan. 37
Mair, Cornelius Cuyler Philip, 34 F. ... 23 Nov. 41
Malet, Charles St. Lo, 8 F. ... 25 Oct. 42
Mansel, John,[134] *CB.* 53 F. ... 1 Jan. 12
Marryat, George, 23 F. ... 11 Nov. 51
Marshall, Wm.,[135] Insp. Field Officer. ... 16 July 30
Mathias, Wm. 62 F. 3 *Lancashire Militia* ... 20 June 54
Maxwell, Charles Francis, 82 F. ... 27 Oct. 48
Mayne, William, 1 F. ... 11 Nov. 51
Messiter, John, 28 F. ... 24 Aug. 42
Mill, James, 50 F. ... 23 Nov. 41
Miller, Fiennes S.,[137] *CD.* ... 4 June 14
Miller, James,[138] 11 Hussars ... 8 Mar. 50
Miller, Thomas, 9 81 F. ... 3 Sept. 50
Mills, William Maxwell,[140] 7 Dr. Gds. ... 23 Nov. 41
Mol y, John,[141] 9 F. ... 11 Nov. 51
Montgomery Lamb. Lyons,[142] Scots Fus. Gds. ... 15 July 54
Moore, Henry, 21 F. ... 11 Nov. 51
Moorsom, Robert,[144] Scots Fus. Gds. ... 20 June 54
Morris, *Sir* (—orge, 40 F. ... 4 June 14
Murray, *Sir* Arch. J., *Bart.* Scots Fus. Gds. ... 28 Dec. 20
Murray, John Digby, 5 Dr. Gds. ... 11 Nov. 51
Murray, Samuel Hood, 3 W. I. R. ... 7 June 54
Muter, Robert,[146] R. Canadian Rifles ... 9 Feb. 49
Naylor, James Sadler,[147] 8 Drs. ... 31 Jan. 58
Nesham, Thomas W. 60 F. ... 20 June 54
Nevill, Park Percy,[118] 63 F. ... 11 Nov. 51
Newdigate, Francis Wm., Coldst. Gds. ... 4 Sept. 54
Newton, Wm. Henry,[149] *KH.* Canadian Rifles ... 28 June 38
Neynoe, Charles Fitzroy, 62. F. ... 20 June 54
Nicholson, Thomas William,[150] *KH.* 55 F. ... 28 June 39
Nicoll, Samuel John Luke, 30 F. ... 4 Aug. 46

Nicolls, George Green, 1 Dr. Gds. ... 23 Nov. 41
Northey, William Brook, 1 F. ... 11 Nov. 51
Nugent, *Sir* George Edmund, *Bt.* Gr. Gds. ... 0 Jun. 38
Olivier, Henry Stephen, 65 F. ... 23 Nov. 41
Onslow, Arthur Edward, Scots Fus. Gds. ... 10 Dec. 47
O'Reilly, Anthony Alex.,[152] Unatt. ... 9 Nov. 46
Page, George Curry, R. Engineers ... 14 April 48
Paget, Patrick L. O., Scots Fus. Gds. ... 6 Nov. 54
Palmer, John, 34 F. ... 28 Nov. 54
Parker, Edward, 60 F. ... 20 June 54
Parlby, George, 4 F. ... 11 Nov. 51
Paschal, George Fred.,[154] Depot Batt. ... 11 Nov. 51
Paterson, James,[155] 3 F. ... 20 June 54
Pearce, William, *KH.* Coldst. Gds. ... 29 Aug. 26
Pearson, Charles, 9 F. ... 11 Nov. 51
Phillipps, Henry, 6 F. ... 11 Nov. 51
Phillott, Frederick J., Unattached ... 26 Oct. 58
Pitt, *Hon.* Horace, R. Horse Gds. ... 2 Sept. 53
Pottinger, William, 6 F. ... 2 May 46
Raines, Joseph Robert,[157] 95 F. ... 11 Nov. 51
Rainforth, William, 63 F. ... 20 June 54
Randolph, John Weech, 57 F. ... 11 Nov. 51
Ready, Charles,[158] 71 F. ... 0 Mar. 55
Reed, Thomas,[159] 70 F. ... 30 Dec. 47
Reeve, John,[160] Gr. Gds. ... 20 June 54
Richardson, Fred., 30 F. ... 20 June 54
Roberts, F. Thomas, Gr. Gds. ... 31 Dec. 14
Roberts, John Cramer, 95 F. ... 11 Nov. 51
Robertson, Archibald, 25 F. ... 11 Nov. 51
Robeson, George, Military Train ... 16 Jun. 57
Robinson, John George, Scots Fus. Gds. ... 12 Aug. 37
Romilly, Frederick, Scots Fus. Gds. ... 22 Jan. 47
Rose, John Rose Holden,[162] 17 Drs. ... 17 Sept. 57
Rothe, Lorenzo, 93 F. ... 21 Feb. 52
Rous, George Grey, Gr. Gds. ... 15 July 53
Rowley, *Sir* Charles, *Bart.* 9 Drs. ... 31 Aug. 30
Rudsdell, *Sir* Joseph, Gr. Gds. *KCMG.* ... 15 Aug. 26
Russell, Andrew Hamilton,[164] 58 F. ... 6 June 56
Russell, *Lord* Chas. Jas. Fox, 60 F., *Serjeant at*
Arms to the House of Commons ... 9 Nov. 40
Sampson, William Henry, Rifle Br. ... 20 June 54
Schreiber, George,[165] 38 F. ... 11 Nov. 51
Scott, Richard Andrew, 60 F. ... 20 June 54
Scott, Wm. Glendonvyn, 91 F. ... 31 Aug. 55
Sedley, Anthony Gardiner,[166] 3 W. I. R. ... 16 Sept. 45
Sharp, Richard Palmer,[16] 72 F. ... 1 Dec. 54
Shearman, John, 48 F. ...
Simmonds, Henry,[168] Ceylon Regt. ... 11 Nov. 51
Simmons, Joseph,[169] *CB.* 41 F. ... 7 Jan. 42
Slater, John James,[170] 82 F. ... 1 Nov. 42
Smith, David Rae,[171] 22 F. ... 10 July 47
Smith, George,[172] R. Horse Gds. ... 20 June 54
Somerville, Thomas Henry,[173] 8 F. ... 28 June 38
Sowerby, T., Coldst. Gds. ... 17 Sept. 58
Spence, James,[175] *CB.* 81 F. ... 14 May 17
Spencer, *Hon.* George Augustus, Coldst. Gds. ... 5 Jan. 46
Spicer, William Fred., 78 F. ... 20 Dec. 44
Stanley, *Hon.* Cha. Jas. Fox, Gr. Gds. *Col. 7* ... 4 June 11
Lancashire Militia ... 30 Dec. 40
Steevens, Charles, 20 F. ... 26 Aug. 13
Stevenson, George Milne, Coldst. Gds. ... 10 June 40
Stevenson, Thomas, 30 F. *Paymaster N. Glou-*
cester Militia ... 11 Nov. 51
Stewart, Donald, Unattached ... 26 Oct. 58
Stewart, Peter Desbrisay,[177] R. Art. ... 20 Dec. 41
St. Maur, Edward,[170] 51 F. ... 4 July 45
Stretton, Severus William Lynam,[179] 40 F.
Lt. Co. Hampshire Militia ... 6 May 42
Stracey, John Edward,[180] Scots Fus. Gds ... 24 May 50
Temple, John, 60 F. ... 11 Nov. 51
Thynne, *Lord* William, Gren. Gds. ... 31 Aug. 88
Tierney, *Sir* Matthew Edw., *Bt.* Coldst. Gds. ... 27 Apr. 49
Toole, William,[182] 82 F. ... 11 Nov. 51
Touzel, Thomas Percival, 27 F. ... 12 Oct. 57
Trench, Power Le Poer, 2 Dr. Gds. ... 11 Nov. 51
Trevelyan, James Harington, Unatt. ... 28 Nov. 44
Trotter, Robert Knox, 26 F. ... 11 Nov. 51
Turbervill, Gervas, *KH.* 12 F. ... 8 Oct. 30
Twopeny, Edward, 78 F. ... 10 Dec. 47
Tylden, *Sir* John Maxwell,[184] 52 F. ... 12 Aug. 19
Ussher, John,[185] 65 F. ... 20 June 54
Van Cortlandt, Henry Clinton,[186] 31 F. ... 30 Dec. 43
Vander Meulen, Charles James,[187] 73 F. ... 8 Apr. 42
Vane-Tempest, *Lord* Adolphus F. C. W.,[188] *Scots*
Fus. Gds. ... 15 Dec. 54
Vandeleur, Robert, 89 F. ... 23 Nov. 41
Vansittart, Robert, Coldst. Gds. ... 9 Nov. 51
Vaughan, Herbert, 90 F. ... 23 Nov. 41
Verner, *Sir* William, *Bart.* 12 F. ... 24 Dec. 18
Vincent, George Augustus, Coldst. Gds. ... 25 Apr. 48
Vincent, Thomas, 80 F. ... 11 Nov. 51
Wallington, J. C., 10 Drs. ... 3 April 40
Walpole, *Hon.* John, Coldst. Gds. ... 25 July 14
Ward, John,[190] 27 F. ... 6 July 57

Field Officers who have retired. 106

Watson, Albert,[191] Unattached ... ... 26 Oct. 58
Watson, William,[192] 3 Drs. ... ... 11 Nov. 51
Waugh, William Petrie,[193] 10 Drs. ... 20 June 54
꜀꜀ Webster, James Carnegie,[194] 18 F. ... 11 Nov. 51
꜀꜀ Wedgwood, Thomas, Scots Fus. Gds. ... 31 Dec. 30
West, John Temple, Gr. Gds. ... ... 6 July 52
Whannell, George,[196] 33 F ... ... 14 Apr. 43
Whentley, William, Scots. Fus. Gds. ... 18 Mar. 59
White, George Francis,[197] 31 F. ... ... 12 Dec. 54
ɓ Wightman, George, 48 F. ... ... 11 Nov. 51
ɓ Wilkie, Fletcher,[199] Unatt. ... ... 19 July 21
ɓ ꜀꜀ Wilkins, Geo.[200] CB., KH. Rifle Br. ... 4 June 14
ɓ ꜀꜀ Wilson, George Davis,[201] CB. Gr. Gds. ... 18 June 15
Wilson, Charles Townshend,[202] Coldst. Gds. ... 8 Dec. 54
Winchester, John, Marq. of, 10 Hussars, Col.
  Hampshire Militia ... ... 30 Dec. 26
ɓ Woodford, John, 93 F. ... ... 11 Nov. 51
ɓ Wrench, E. Ommanney, 0 Drs. ... ... 28 June 38
Wrottesley, Hon. Charles Alexander,[203] 7 F. ... 3 July 30
꜀꜀ Wyndham, Charles,[204] 2 Drs. Keeper of the
  Regalia, Tower ... ... 30 Dec. 37
Wynn, Herbert Watkin Wms., 2 W. I. Regt. ... 9 June 54
ɓ Yale, William Parry,[205] 32 F. ... ... 28 June 38
Young, James, 15 Drs. ... ... 11 Nov. 51

MAJORS.

ɓ Adair, James,[1] Unatt. ... ... 12 Dec. 26
Agnew, Charles, 11 F. ... ... 23 Nov. 41
Alcock, Thomas St. Leger, 95 F. Lt.Col. 1st
  Middlesex Militia ... ...
Amsinck, William,[2] 53 F. ... ... 23 Nov. 41
Anderson, Wm. H. H.,[3] 51 F. ... ... 1 Dec. 54
ɓ Andrews, Francis, 52 F. ... ... 10 Jan. 37
Archer, William Henry, 10 Drs. ... ... 16 May 45
Armstrong, Thomas, 46 F. ... ... 23 Nov. 41
Ashmore, William, 16 F. ... ... 21 Aug. 49
ɓ Austin, William,[5] 50 F. ... ... 4 July 45
Aylmer, George Edward, 40 F. ... ... 9 Nov. 46
ɓ ꜀꜀ Bacon, Anthony,[7] 17 Drs. ... ... 31 Dec. 25
ɓ ꜀꜀ Bacon, Cæsar, 28 Drs. ... ... 10 Jan. 37
Bagot, George, 17 F. ... ... 19 Oct. 49
Baird, Sir David, Bart.,[9] 98 F. ... ... 24 Mar. 58
Baker, Thomas Richard, 7 F. ... ... 31 Aug. 38
Balfour, Francis Walter,[9] Rifle Br. ... 6 June 56
Balfour, Robert William, 88 F. ... ... 11 Nov. 51
Barbor, Robert Douglas, 40 F., Barrack Master
  at Glasgow ... ... 11 Nov. 51
Baring, Henry Bingham, 1 Life Gds. ... 18 Nov. 30
Barnard, Robert Cary, 41 F. ... ... 9 Mar. 55
Barnston, William,[11] 55 F. ... ... 8 Oct. 58
Battley, D'Oyley W. 77 F. Carlow Militia ... 11 Nov. 51
Bayley, John Arthur,[13] 52 F. ... ... 19 Jan. 58
Beale, Wm. Gabbett, 1 F. ... ... 9 Nov. 46
Beamish, N. L., Unatt. ... ... 30 Dec. 26
Beare, William Gabbett, 1 F. ... ... 9 Nov. 46
Beauclerk, Lord George Aug.[15] 6 Dr. Gds. ... 10 Feb. 54
Beete, John Picton, 21 F. ... ... 26 June 38
Bell, Robert, 5 Dr. Gds. Captain Northumber-
  land Yeomanry ... ... 11 Nov. 51
Bent, John, 5 F. ... ... 22 July 30
Bere, Edward Baker,[16] 10 Drs. ... ... 19 June 06
Bethune, Robert,[17] 92 F. ... ... 7 Dec. 58
Bird, Edward M., 1 F. ... ... 4 June 54
Bird, Henry Charles, 47 F. ... ... 10 Jan. 58
ɓ Blackiston, John, 51 F. Gent. at Arms ... ...
Boileau, Charles Lestock, Rifle Br. ... 4 Dec. 35
Bonnor, Thomas, Ceylon Rifles ... ... 28 June 38
Boys, Henry, 75 F. ... ... 9 Nov. 46
Bowness, John, 67 F. ... ... 9 Nov. 46
Blackburn, John, 85 F. ... ... 29 Dec. 46
Bowler, John, 80 F. ... ... 4 Mar. 57
Brabazon, Hugh, Military Train ... ... 20 June 54
ɓ ꜀꜀ Brady, William S. Richardson,[19] 36 F. ... 28 June 38
Brand, James, 16 F. ... ... 23 Nov. 41
Brett, John Davy, 17 Drs. ... ... 28 May 52
Briggs, George,[21] 1 Dr. Gds. ... ... 3 June 53
Bringhurst, John Henry, 90 F. ... ... 22 Dec. 48
Browne, Hon. George Aug., 64 F. ... ... 1 Dec. 37
Bruce, Wm. Tyrrell, 18 F. Adjutant King's
  County Militia ... ... 9 Dec. 53
Bulkeley, Charles, 2 Life Gds. ... ... 28 June 38
Burke, William, Unatt. ... ... 21 July 30
Burslem, Rollo Gillespie,[23] 13 F. ... ... 8 Nov. 50
Bush, Robert, 60 F. ... ... 9 Nov. 46
Butler, Lord Walter, Scots Fus. Gds. Capt.
  Kilkenny Militia ... ... 11 July 37
ɓ Cairnes, Geo.,[24] 30 F. 4 West York Militia ... 4 Dec. 32
ɓ Calcott, Geo. Berkeley,[25] 30 F. ... ... 10 Jan. 37
꜀꜀ Caldecot, Henry,[26] Gr. Gds. ... ... 28 June 38
Calley, Henry, 10 F. Lt. Wilts Yeomanry ... 7 Aug. 46
Campbell, Renton Arch. Colin, 42 F. ... 12 Dec. 54
Campbell, Colin, 31 F. ... ... 20 June 54
Campbell, Colin Alexander, 74 F. ... ... 23 Nov. 41
Campbell, E. S. Norman, 90 F. ... ... 9 Nov. 46

Campbell, Henry Wotton,[28] 79 F., Governor of
  Military Prison at Montreal ... ... 26 Dec. 56
Campbell, John Cameron,[30] 9 Drs. Governor of
  Military Prison at Greenlaw ... ... 7 June 49
Campbell, Robert,[32] 46 F. ... ... 16 May 45
Campbell, Thomas Edmund, Unatt. ... 4 Nov. 40
Campsie, Geo. Richard, 31 Ceylon Rifles ... 26 Oct. 58
Carlyon, Thomas T. Spry, 3 Dr. Gds. ... 27 June 54
Chalmer, F. D., 7 Dr. Gds. ... ... 30 Dec. 26
Charlewood, John, 62 F. ... ... 11 Nov. 51
ɓ Caulfield, John, 6 Dr. Gds. Lt.Col. Com. Ros-
  common Militia ... ... 10 Jan. 37
Christie, Wm. Harvie, 80 F. ... ... 9 Nov. 88
Clerke, William Jonathan, 77 F. ... ... 9 Nov. 46
Coats, John,[37] 55 F. ... ... 11 Nov. 51
Cochran, James,[33] 41 F. ... ... 23 Nov. 41
ɓ Cochrane, Hon. Wm. Erskine,[34] 15 Drs. ... 16 Dec. 51
ɓ Cockburn, Wm. Horace,[35] 95 F. ... ... 28 June 38
Codd, William,[36] 48 F. ... ... 6 May 42
Cook, Edwin Adolphus,[37] 11 Hussars, Lt. West
  Kent Yeomanry ... ... 12 Dec. 54
Croker, Edward,[38] 96 F. ... ... 8 July 59
Cumberland, Geo. Burrell,[39] 42 F. ... 15 Feb. 50
Currie, George Alfred, 75 F. ... ... 20 June 54
꜀꜀ Daniell, John, 66 F. Barrack Master, Corfu 9 Mar. 32
Darell, Henry James,[40] 60 F. ... ... 28 Nov. 54
Darroch, Donald Geo. Angus,[41] 51 F. ... 20 June 54
Davenport, Trevor, 12 F. Adj. Cheshire Mil. ... 11 Nov. 51
Davenport, William Davenport, 94 F. Lt.Col.
  2 Cheshire Militia ... ... 9 Nov. 46
Davies, Joseph, 83 F. ... ... 20 June 54
Dawe, Charles, 8 F. ... ... 10 Jan. 37
ɓ De Renzy, George Webb, 4 Drs. Barrack
  Master, Exeter ... ... 10 Jan. 37
ɓ Dillon, Robert,[43] 32 F. ... ... 5 Nov. 18
Donaldson, Robert, 41 F. ... ... 5 Feb. 47
ɓ Drake, Sir Thos. T. F. E.,[44] Bart. 52 F. ... 26 May 14
ɓ Drewe, Edward Ward, 88 Foot ... ... 9 June 37
Driberg, William,[45] Unatt. ... ... 1 Mar. 50
Duckett, Sir George Floyd, Bart. 3 W. I. R. 11 Nov. 51
Duff, James,[46] 23 F. ... ... 20 July 58
Dyson, Edward, 3 Dr. Gds. ... ... 8 April 53
ɓ Edwards, Bidwell, KH. Unatt. ... ... 2 May 34
Elliott, Richard, 2 W. I. R. Paymaster Water-
  ford Militia ... ... 1 July 51
Elmsall, Wm. De Cardonnel,[48] 1 Drs. ... 12 Dec. 54
Elton, Isaac, Capt. 45 F. 1 Somerset Militia ... 9 Nov. 46
Erskine, Hon. David, 21 F. Col. Sec. at Natal ... 2 Apr. 55
Fane, Henry,[49] 4 Drs. Lt.Col. Com. S. Lincoln
  Militia ... ... 29 Dec. 46
Fawkes, Richard, 27 F. ... ... 16 Nov. 41
Fenwick, Horatio, Unatt ... ... 20 June 54
Ffrench, Edward, 74 F. ... ... 10 Jan. 37
FitzHerbert, Richard Henry, Rifle Br. ... 2 July 47
Forbes, George, 3 Drs. ... ... 20 June 54
Ford, Geo. 36 F. ... ... 13 May 26
Forsyth, Gerrard John,[51] 57 F. ... ... 26 Dec. 56
Fothergill, William, 50 F. ... ... 23 Nov. 41
ɓ Fox, Barry,[52] 64 F. ... ... 10 June 37
Frampton, Heathfield James,[53] 50 F. ... 29 Dec. 54
ɓ ꜀꜀ Fraser, James, 34 F. ... ... 10 Jan. 37
Fraser, Robert W. Macleod,[55] 6 F. ... 20 Dec. 51
Freer, Daniel Gardiner, 17 F. ... ... 12 Nov. 47
Frend, Geo. 26 F. N. Tipperary Militia ... 20 June 54
Fyffe, David, 44 F. ... ... 4 June 18
Fyffe, David, 46 F. ... ... 10 Dec. 6
Gage, Edward, Scots Fus. Gds. ... ... 28 June 38
Gavin, George O'Hulloran,[56] 16 Drs. ... 10 Dec. 47
ɓ Gell, Thomas,[57] 29 F. ... ... 22 June 15
Gerard, Sir Robert Tolver, 68 F. ... ... 11 Nov. 51
Gibson, Charles Frederick, 24 F. ... ... 20 June 54
Giffard, Edward Carter, 60 F. ... ... 20 Dec. 54
Gilley, Thomas, 7 F. ... ... 26 Dec. 56
Gillman, Bennett Watkins, 12 F. ... ... 20 June 54
Gordon, Duncan,[59] 59 F. ... ... 4 July 34
Gore, William Richard Ormsby, 13 Drs. ... 12 Oct. 52
ɓ Gosset, John N., Rifle Brigade, Barrack Mas-
  ter, Cork ... ... 25 May 35
Graham, Charles Campbell,[62] 42 F. ... 9 Nov. 55
Graham, George, 1 W. I. R. ... ... 7 June 31
꜀꜀ Graham, James Reg. Tovin, 2 Drs. ... 10 Jan. 37
Grant, James,[61] 3 Drs. ... ... 9 Nov. 46
Granville, Fred. 23 F. 2 Warwick Militia ... 10 May 46
Green, Andrew, 48 F. ... ... 13 Dec. 53
Greene, William, 61 F. ... ... 3 Mar. 14
Greenwood, J., 9 Drs. ... ... 31 Dec. 27
Grehan, Peter,[63] 78 F. ... ... 11 Nov. 51
Greig, John James, 24 F. Chief Constable, Liver-
  pool ... ... 20 June 54
ɓ Grubbe, Thomas Hunt,[64] 16 F. ... ... 23 Nov. 41
Hall, Samuel Madden Francis, 75 F. ... 11 July 37
Hamilton, William Digby, 13 Drs. ... ... 14 Feb. 46
ɓ Hammersley, Fred.[65] 18 F. ... ... 11 Nov. 51
ɓ ꜀꜀ Hare, William Henry,[66] 51 F. ... ... 19 July 21
Hawkes, Abraham, 39 F. ... ...

Field Officers who have retired.

Head, Sir Francis Bond, *Bart.*, *KCH*. ... 23 Dec. 28
Hepburn, Francis John Swayne, 00 F. ... 11 Nov. 51
Herbert, Arthur,[03] 39 F. ... 20 June 54
Hill, Edward, 90 F. ... 11 Nov. 51
Hill, *Lord* George Augusta, Unatt. ... 6 July 30
Holmes, James Nicol, *Canadian Rifles* ... 20 Dec. 54
Home, James Murray,[60] 16 F. ... 11 Nov. 51
Hopkins, John Paul,[70] *KH.*, 98 F. *Military Knight of Windsor* ... 5 Nov. 25
Hopper, Edward, 38 F. ... 28 Nov. 33
Hopson, William Hopson, 26 F. ... 5 Sept. 56
Hutton, Thomas,[72] 4 Drs... ... 6 June 56
Ince, Ralph Piggott, Rifle Br. ... 11 Nov. 51
Ingall, Fred. Lennox, 45 F. ... 20 June 54
Inglis, Raymond[73] 7 F. ... 6 June 56
Inglis, William,[74] 5 Dragoon Guards ... 12 Dec. 54
Jacks, Walter,[75] 7 Dr. Gds. ... 10 Jan. 37
Jackson, George Wm. Collins,[76] 7 Drs. ... 20 Feb. 56
Jeffery, John Morton, 98 F. ... 28 May 52
Jelf-Sharp, Henry, 86 F. ... 23 Nov. 41
Jocelyn, *Hon.* Aug. George Fred., 6 Dr. Gds ... 20 June 54
Jones, William Prime, 65 F. ... 11 Nov. 51
Judge, Arthur,[77] 1 W. I. R. ... 10 Jan. 37
Julius, William Mavor, 6 Drs. ... 11 Nov. 51
Kean, Henry,[78] 97 F. ... 23 Nov. 41
Keane, Edward A. W.,[79] *Lord*, 37 F. ... 5 Mar. 41
Keene, Edmund Ruck, 2 Dr. Gds... ... 16 June 57
Killeen, Arthur James, *Lord*,[81] 8 Drs. ... 2 Oct. 56
Knox, *Hon.* William Stuart, 51 F. ... 10 Nov. 55
Lachlan, Robert, 17 F. ... 13 Aug. 29
Law, Charles Fred., 69 F. ... 25 Aug. 53
Lawrell, Digby Henry, 64 F. ... 6 May 42
Leighton, Forrester Owen, 56 F. ... 20 May 36
Leslie, Lewis Xavier,[03] 99 F. ... 11 Nov. 51
Littledale, Edward, 1 Drs... ... 9 Nov. 46
Lockyer, Edmund, 57 F. ... 12 Aug. 19
Longmore, George, R. Staff Corps ... 24 Aug. 32
Lovett, Thomas Heaton,[84] 98 F. ... 4 April 40
Lucas, Richard, 29 F. ... 3 July 39
Lyon, William, 67 F. ... 23 Nov. 41
M'Leroy, William, 60 F. ... 9 Nov. 46
M'Murdo, Alured Charles,[86] 10 Drs. ... 9 Nov. 46
Macartney, James Nixon, 7 Dr. Gds. *Adj. North Devon Yeomanry*... ... 20 June 54
Maclean, William, 27 F. ... 11 Nov. 30
Macpherson, Evan, 80 F. ... 20 June 54
MacQueen, Donald J., *KH.*, 74 F. *Barrack Master, Dundee*... ... 22 July 30
Mair, Arthur, 62 F. ... 13 Nov. 35
Mairis, Valentine Hale, 7 F. ... 23 Nov. 41
Manley, Robert George,[37] 6 Drs... ... 12 Dec. 54
Margary, Alfred Robert, 54 F. ... 20 June 54
Marindin, Henry Richard, 1 F. ... 20 June 54
Marsh, Aug. Leacock,[88] 55 F. ... 12 Dec. 54
Marsh, Robert,[89] 2½ F. ... 3 April 46
Marston, Daniel, 86 F. ... 18 Nov. 13
Martin, Alexander, 45 F. ... 19 Dec. 16
Martin, Samuel Yorke, 52 F. ... 9 Nov. 46
Massy, Hugh, 85 F. *Major Longford Mil.* ... 31 Aug. 55
Massy, John,[91] Unattached ... 26 Oct. 58
Matson, Henry,[92] 58 F. ... 7 July 46
Maule, John, 62 F. ... 11 Nov. 51
Maunsell, Geo. 1 W. I. R. *Adj. E. York. Militia* 20 June 54
Mayne, John, 1 F. ... 9 Nov. 46
Mercer, Arthur Hill Hasted,[93] 39 F. ... 6 June 56
Meredith, Richard Martin,[94] 13 F. ... 15 Dec. 43
Methold, Edward, 3 Dr. Gds... ... 10 Jan. 37
Mildmay, Sir Henry St. John, *Bt.*, 2 Dr. Gds. ... 11 Nov. 51
Miller, George Cumming, 54 F. ... 19 Jan. 55
Milligan, William, 68 F. ... 23 Nov. 41
Minter, George,[96] 20 F. ... 29 Nov. 41
Mitchell, Parry, 53 F. ... 28 June 38
Mitford, John Philip,[97] 2 W. I. R. ... 20 June 54
Monro, David Arthur,[99] 12 Lancers ... 29 July 53
Montgomery, Francis Octavius, 45 F. *Lt. Col. North Down Militia* ... 6 Sept. 39
Moore, *Charles,* 32 F. *Governor of Military Knights of Windsor* ... 22 July 30
Moore, William, 74 F. ... 21 June 13
Munro, David, 94 F. ... 9 Dec. 28
Munro, John St. John, 60 F. ... 14 Aug. 46
Murray, *Hon.* David Henry, Scots Fus. Gds. ... 9 Nov. 46
Murray, Charles,[101] 16 F. ... 9 Nov. 46
Murray, William,[102] 10 Drs... ... 26 Dec. 56
Napier, *Hon.* Charles, 71 F. ... 17 June 26
Nash, Charles Widenham,[103] Canadian Rifles ... 23 Nov. 41
Northey, Aug. J. W., 41 F. ... 27 Dec. 50
Nugent, Andrew, 36 F. ... 9 Nov. 46
Nugent, George, 7 Dr. Gds ... 11 Jan. 33
O'Connell, Daniel, 40 F. ... 20 June 54
O'Grady, *Hon.* Thomas, 74 F. ... 10 July 46
O'Leary, Arthur,[105] 55 F... ... 23 Dec. 42
Ogle, Arthur,[106] 9 F. ... 23 Dec. 42
Orr, John,[107] 7 F.... ... 16 Mar. 15

Owen, Edward Barry, 17 F.... ... 5 Nov. 47
Owen, Hugh, 7 Drs... ... 4 Sept. 17
Parke, Charles, 3 F. ... 12 Aug. 19
Paul, Gregory, 57 F. ... 22 July 30
Payne, Wm. Aug. Townsend, 76 F. ... 11 Nov. 51
Paynter, George,[109] 1 Dragoon Guards ... 30 April 58
Peach, James Peach, 1 Dr. Gds. ... 12 Nov. 62
Peacocke, Stephen Ponsonby, 59 F. ... 11 Nov. 51
Petley, Patrick M'Leod, 38 F. ... 20 June 54
Philipps, Courtenay, 15 Drs. ... 5 April 33
Pole, Mundy, 46 F. ... 9 Nov. 46
Pole, Samuel, 12 Drs. ... 23 Nov. 41
Pollock, Samuel,[111] Rifle Br. ... 10 Jan. 37
Powys, *Hon.* Henry L. 60 F. *Leicester Militia* ... 2 Oct. 53
Prideaux, Sir Edm. Saunderson, *Bt.* 33 F. ... 5 Apr. 31
Pringle, Norman, 21 F. *Consul at Dunkirk* ... 23 June 14
Quentin, George Aug. Frederick, 10 Drs. ... 28 Apr. 46
Rawlinson, George,[114] 1 W. I. R. ... 10 Jan. 37
Reid, Henry,[115] 51 F. ... 10 Jan. 37
Richmond, Matthew, 96 F... ... 23 Nov. 41
Robertson, Charles,[116] 96 F. ... 10 Jan. 37
Robinson, Joseph, 60 F. *Paymaster N. Tipperary Militia* ... 28 Dec. 48
Rocke, Herbert,[117] 49 F. ... 6 June 56
Rose, H. M. St. Vincent, 25 F. ... 28 June 38
Russell, *Lord* Cosmo George, 93 F. ... 19 Oct. 49
Rutherfoord, Archibald,[119] 4 F. ... 1 Feb. 56
Ruxton, George, 34 F. ... 4 Aug. 37
Saltoun, Alex., *Lord*, 28 F. ... 16 July 52
Sawrey, Henry Beckwith, 88 F. *Adjutant Fermanagh Militia* ... 20 June 54
Scott, Edward, 8 Drs. ... 11 Nov. 51
Semple, H., 35 F. ... 12 Apr. 31
Semple, John, 19 F... ... 30 Aug. 42
Seton, George, R. Canadian Rifles ... 14 Dec. 55
Seton, William Carden, 41 F. ... 15 Oct. 47
Snuckburgh, Geo. Thos. Fra.,[121] Scots Fus. Gds. ... 12 Dec. 54
Skynner, Aug. Charles, 16 Drs. ... 23 Nov. 41
Smith, Seton Lionel, 54 F. ... 20 June 54
Smyth, Robert Carmichael, 93 F. ... 18 May 41
Speedy, James, 8 F... ... 28 Nov. 54
Spooner, Samuel, 46 F. ... 28 June 38
Stephenson, William Walter, Rifle Brigade ... 10 Jan. 37
Stevenson, Edward R., 76 F. ... 17 June 26
Stewart, William, 30 F. ... 13 Mar. 17
St. John, George Frederick Berkeley, 52 F. ... 3 Aug. 30
Straith, Hector, St. Helena Regt.... ... 28 June 38
Stuart, Donald,[123] 46 F. ... 9 Nov. 46
Studdert, Charles FitzGerald,[124] 80 F. ... 26 Aug. 59
Sutherland, Edward, *Barrack Master at Woolwich Gent.-at-Arms* ... 11 Nov. 51
Sutherland, William James, 21 F ... 10 Jan. 37
Sutton, John, 47 F. ... 15 Oct. 50
Sykes, Cam,[125] 48 F... ... 2 Nov. 55
Tattersall, Geo. Bulkeley, Ceylon Regt.... ... 18 May 40
Taylor, William, 70 F. ... 23 Feb. 44
Tennant, George, 85 F. ... 10 May 40
Thellusson,[128] Arthur John Bethell, Coldst. Gds. ... 2 Nov. 55
Thomson, Robert Thomas, 1 Dr. Gds. ... 14 Aug. 57
Townshend, Lee Porcher, 49 F. *Major Cheshire Yeomanry* ... 23 Dec. 31
Turner, Michael, 1 Dr. Gds. ... 18 June 15
Vane, Charles Birch, 9 F. ... 11 Nov. 51
Verney, Sir Harry, *Bart.* Unattached ... 13 Nov. 27
Vialls, Henry Thomas, 46 F. ... 28 May 53
Vivian, Chas. C., *Lord*, 10 Drs. .... 12 Aug. 34
Walker, Sam. G5 F. *Lt.-Col. Queen's own Militia* 19 Sept. 34
Waller, James W. S., *KH.* 10 F... ... 23 Mar. 32
Warburton, Henry William Egerton, 47 F. *Barrack Master, Mullingar* ... 17 Mar. 43
Waring, Henry, 59 F. ... 16 April 29
Warrant, Robert, 6 Drs. ... 24 April 28
Warren, William, Rifle Br. ... 23 Nov. 41
Way, Gregory Lowe,[130] 29 F. ... 8 Dec. 40
Webb, Vere,[131] 3 W. I. Regt. ... 9 Nov. 46
Weyland, John Thorne,[132] Unatt. ... 23 Nov. 41
Whitney, Benjamin,[133] 14 F. ... 25 Nov. 36
Wentworth, D'Arcy, Unattached ... 3 Nov. 37
Wilkinson, Arthur Philip Savage,[134] *C.B.* 13 F. ... 4 Oct. 42
Williams, Sir James Hamlyn, *Bt.* 7 Drs. ... 24 Oct. 21
Williams, Robert, 22 F. ... 23 Nov. 41
Wilson, Henry, 14 F. ... 19 July 21
Wing, Vincent,[135] Depot Batt. ... 12 Dec. 54
Wolfe, Edward, 28 F. ... 10 Jan. 37
Wollaston, Fred., 6 Drs. ... 1 Nov. 42
Wood, *Hon.* Henry Owen,[133] 37 F. ... 10 Jan. 37
Woodhouse, *Hon.* Berkeley, 8 Drs. *Col. East Norfolk Militia* ... 2 Mar. 39
Wood, John Joseph[137] *Military Train* ... 26 Dec. 56
Woollard, Gilbert, St. Helena Regt ... 11 Sept. 40
Wrixon, Nicholas, 21 F. *Paymaster, Notts' Militia* ... 11 Nov. 51
Yard, Frederick,[138] 32 F. ... 26 Nov. 57

War Services of General Officers who have retired from the Service.

1 Sir Henry Edw. Bunbury served in Holland in 1799, including the battles of the 19th Sept., 2nd and 7th October. Served also on the expedition to Naples and Calabria in 1805 and 6, and was present at the battle of Maida, for which he has received the Gold Medal. He is a Knight of the Tower and Sword of Portugal.

2 Lieut.-General Johnson served the campaign of 1808-9 in the Peninsula as a Major in the 32nd, and was present at the battles of Roleia, Vimiera, and Corunna, for which he has received the War Medal with three Clasps.

2† Major-General Bateman sailed with the 5th on the expedition for Hanover in 1805; was shipwrecked off the Texel and made prisoner of war. Having been exchanged in March 1806, he sailed in June following with the expedition under Major-General Craufurd, which landed in South America, and he was present at the attack of Buenos Ayres. Served also in the Peninsula in 1810, 11, and 13, and was severely wounded at Vittoria, for which battle he has the War Medal with one Clasp. Accompanied the regiment to America in 1814, and was present at Plattsburg.

3 Major-General Beckwith served in Hanover in 1805-6; at Copenhagen in 1807, including the action at Kioge. On the expedition to Sweden in 1808; and that to Portugal in 1808-9, including the action at Calcavellas on the retreat, and battle of Corunna. Proceeded to Walcheren in 1809; subsequently to the Peninsula, and was present in the actions of Pombal, Redinha, Condeixa, Foz d'Arouce, and Sabugal, battle of Fuentes d'Onor, sieges of Ciudad Rodrigo and Badajoz, battle of Salamanca, siege of Burgos, action at San Milan, battles of Vittoria, the Pyrenees, Vera, Nivelle, near Bayonne, Orthes, and Toulouse (Gold Medal). Served also the campaign of 1815, including the battles of Quatre Bras and Waterloo (lost left leg). During the great portion of the above service he was employed on the Staff. He is a Knight 2nd Class of St. Anne of Russia.

4 Major-General Bristow served in the Walcheren expedition in 1809 as a Captain in the 2nd Battalion 11th Regt., and was present at the siege of Flushing. He was in Garrison at Gibraltar in 1811 when the Spanish army of General Ballasteros took refuge under the guns of that Fortress. In Oct. and Nov. of the same year he was in Cadiz, part of the period during which the place was blockaded by the French. In Dec. he joined the army in Portugal, and was immediately placed on the Quarter-Master-General's Staff, on which he continued to the end of the war; and attached to Head Quarters the 7th or the 1st Division, was present at most of the operations carried on in the north of Spain under the Duke of Wellington. He has received the War Medal with three Clasps for the battles of Salamanca, Vittoria, and the Pyrenees. In 1823 he was at Cadiz during its bombardment by the French fleet.

5 Major-General Charretie served three years in the East Indies, and was present at the mutiny at Vellore in 1806, when nearly the whole of the 69th Regt. were massacred in their barracks. He served in the Peninsula with the 2nd Life Guards, from 1812 to the end of that war in 1814, including the battles of Vittoria, Pampeluna, and Toulouse. He has received the War Medal with two Clasps.

6 Viscount de Chabot served in Holland in 1799 ; in Spain, under Sir John Moore; with the expedition to Walcheren 1809; and subsequently in the Peninsula until 1810.

7 Major-General Dwyer served on the Staff of the late Marquis of Hastings, Commander-in-Chief in India, and was present during the Nepaul war, at the reduction of the Province of Kimaoon, and the storming of Almorah. He served also throughout the Pindarree war on the Staff, when he had charge of the communications of the combined armies.

8 Major-General Farrer has received the Silver War Medal with two Clasps for the Egyptian campaign of 1801, and for the battle of Maida.

9 Sir Henry Floyd accompanied General Sir William H. Clinton to Sicily in 1811, and to Spain in 1813, as his Aide-de-Camp, and was present at the battles of Biar and Castalla, siege and blockade of Tarragona, in conveying orders to Ordal, and subsequent blockade of Barcelona. Served also the campaign of 1815, with the 10th Hussars, and was present at the battles of Quatre Bras and Waterloo, and at the capture of Paris.

10 Sir Henry W. Rooke embarked with the 3rd Guards for Holland, in Aug. 1799, and was present in the actions of the 27th Aug., 10th and 19th Sept., 2nd and 6th October. Embarked again for Holland Nov. 1813, in command of the 2nd Battalion of that Regt., and was present at the advance to Antwerp, bombardment of the French fleet at Antwerp, and attack on Bergen-op-Zoom. Also the campaign of 1815, including the battles of Quatre Bras and Waterloo.

11 Major-General Stewart served in the Peninsula, and has received the Gold Medal for the battle of Albuhera.

12 Major-General Dudgeon served with the 58th in Egypt in 1801, and was present at the surrender of Grand Cairo and Alexandria. He served in Italy in 1805 and 6 ; and in the Peninsula from 1809 to 1813, including the Lines at Torres Vedras, covering the siege of Badajoz, battle of Salamanca, capture of Madrid, and siege of Burgos, at which last he was twice wounded, the second time most severely. He has the War Medal with two Clasps for Egypt and Salamanca.

13 Sir John Geo. Woodford served as Deputy-Assistant-Adjutant-General on the Expedition to Stralsund, and afterwards to Copenhagen, in 1807; and as Deputy-Assistant-Quarter-Master-General on the Expedition under Sir David Baird, which joined Sir John Moore's army in Galicia, and was present at the battle of Corunna, for which he has received the Silver War Medal with one Clasp. Served afterwards in the Peninsula as an Assistant-Quarter-Master-General, and has received the Gold Cross for the battles of Nivelle, Nive, Orthes, and Toulouse. Also the campaign of 1815, including the battle of Waterloo and the taking of Cambray.

14 Major-General Owen served on the Quartermaster-General's Staff with the Walcheren

Expedition in 1809; thence to Sicily, the Ionian Islands, and the eastern coast of Spain, where he was present at the affairs of Biar and Castella, siege and blockade of Tarragona. In 1814 he went in charge as a Quartermaster-General with the troops to America, where he served on the expedition up the Penobscott and at Castine. Commanded the 2nd Battalion, 73rd Regiment, at the taking of Paris in 1815. In 1816 was employed in the Candian War in Ceylon.

War Services of the Colonels who have retired from the Service.

1 Colonel Allix served in the Peninsula with the 1st Guards (part of the time as Adjutant and as Brigade-Major), and was present at the battles of Corunna, Salamanca, Pyrenees, and Nivelle (severely wounded), and at the sieges of Ciudad Rodrigo and Badajoz, for which he has received the War Medal with six Clasps. He served also the Waterloo campaign.

2 Colonel Angelo served with the expedition to Egypt in 1807; on the coast of Calabria in 1808; with the expedition to Walcheren in 1809; with the army to Catalonia in 1812 and 13, as an Assistant-Adjutant-General. Attached to the Austrian army, and acted as Aide-de-Camp to Major-General Count Nugent in the campaign against the Viceroy of Italy; present at the siege and capture of Trieste, Cattaro, and Ragusa, and in various services in the Adriatic.

3 Colonel Armytage served in the south of France with the Coldstream Guards from March to July 1814.

4 Colonel Austen served with the 25th Regt. at the landing at the Helder in August 1799, and was severely wounded at the battle of Egmont-op-Zee on the 2nd Oct. following. Served in Egypt in 1801, including the surrender of Alexandria. Also at the capture of Guadaloupe in 1810, and again in 1815. He has received the War Medal with two Clasps.

6 Colonel Barlow served in India under Lord Lake, during the campaigns of 1803, 4, and 5, and was present at the siege of Deig, battle of Futtyghur, siege of Bhurtpore, and battle of Afzalghur. Served also at the captures of Bourbon and the Isle of France in 1810.

7 Colonel Bazalgette sailed with the expedition from India to Egypt, under Sir David Baird, in 1801. Returned to India, and served two campaigns in the Dooab and Ceded Districts, under General Campbell. Served also on the expedition to the Penobscot, in the United States of North America. He has received the Silver War Medal with one Clasp for Egypt.

8 Colonel Begbie served in the Peninsula with the 82nd Regt. from Aug. 1808 to Nov. 1809, including the capture of Oporto and battle of Talavera, for which he has received the War Medal with one Clasp.

9 Colonel Blake served with the 20th Dragoons at the capture of the Cape of Good Hope in 1806; proceeded from thence to South America, and was in the action at Maldonado and siege of Monte Video. Served in Portugal in 1808 and 9, including the battles of Roleia and Vimiera (Gold Medal); also at the passage of the Douro. In Sicily in 1810 and 11; subsequently on the eastern coast of Spain, including the battle of Castalla, and action at Villa Franca.

10 Colonel Boldero served with the Grenadier Guards at Cadiz in 1810 and 11; in the Peninsula in 1812 and 13; in Holland in 1814; and the campaign of 1815, in which he served as Adjutant at the battles of Quatre Bras and Waterloo, and at the taking of Peronne. He has received the War Medal with one Clasp for Barrosa.

11 Colonel Boys served in the Peninsula from 1809 to 1811, and again from 1813 to the end of that war in 1814, including the action at Sabugal, and battles of Fuentes d'Onor, Orthes, and Toulouse, for which he has received the War Medal with three Clasps. Served also in the Burmese war (Medal).

12 Colonel Bragge served in the Peninsula with the 3rd Dragoons from 1811 to the end of that war in 1814, and was present in the battles of Salamanca and Vittoria, for which he has received the War Medal with two Clasps.

13 Colonel Brooke served in the Peninsula with the 1st Guards, and was present at the battles of Corunna, Nivelle, and Nive, for which he has the War Medal with three Clasps.

14 Colonel Fielding Browne accompanied the 40th Regt. to the Peninsula in July 1808, and was present at the battles of Roleia, Vimiera, Talavera, and Busaco; on the retreat to, and at the occupation of, the Lines of Torres Vedras, siege of Badajoz, in May 1811, and repulse of the sortie from Fort San Christoval; actions of El Bodon and Aldea de Ponte, siege and storming of Ciudad Rodrigo, siege and storming of Badajoz, action at Canizal, battle of Salamanca, capture of Madrid, and subsequent retreat therefrom. Served also on the expedition against New Orleans. Commanded the Regiment at the battle of Waterloo. He has received the Gold Medal for Badajoz (having commanded the Regiment at the assault); and the Silver War Medal with seven Clasps for the other battles and siege.

15 Colonel Melville Browne served as Aide-de-Camp to Sir Brent Spencer in the battles of Roleia, Vimiera, Busaco, Fuentes d'Onor (for which he has received the War Medal with four Clasps), and the different affairs during the retreat of Massena from Portugal. Served also at the siege of Flushing in 1809, as Aide-de-Camp to General Gore Browne.

16 Colonel Gore Browne commanded the 41st during the whole of the campaign of 1842 in Affghanistan, and was present in the engagements with the enemy on 28th March and 28th April in the Pisheen Valley; in that of the 29th May near Candahar, 30th Aug. at Goaine, 5th Sept. before Ghuznee, occupation and destruction of that fortress and of Cabool, expedition into Kohistan, storm, capture, and destruction of Istaliff, and in the various minor affairs in and between the Bolan and the Khyber Passes.

18 Colonel Burrowes served with the 12th at the capture of the Isle of France, in 1810, and commanded a detachment of that Regt. In boarding and capturing two French Privateers off the Isle de la Passe. Commanded a Battalion of details with a force under Colonel the

Honourable Leicester Stanhope in Kattywar, and was in advance at the storm and capture of the strong hill fortress of Meetialla.

20 Colonel Close served the Egyptian campaign of 1801, for which he has received the Silver War Medal with one Clasp.

21 Colonel Cockell served with the 14th Regt. at the siege and capture of Bhurtpore in 1825-26 (Medal).

22 Sir George Couper was Assistant-engineer at Copenhagen; Captain in the 92nd with Sir John Moore's army in Sweden and Portugal; Aide-de-Camp to Lord Dalhousie in Walcheren; 1st Aide-de-Camp to Sir H. Clinton in the Peninsula in 1811 and 12, to Lord Dalhousie from 1812 to the end of the war, and was present in all the actions in which they commanded Divisions during those periods. He was Assistant Quarter-Master-General with the army in the Gulf of Mexico in 1814-15. Sir George has received the War Medal with four Clasps for Badajoz, Salamanca, Vittoria, and Pyrenees.

23 Sir William Cox served at the re-taking of Grenada in 1796; in Egypt in 1801; employed on a particular service in Spain in 1808-9, and was present in the action at Lugo, and battle of Corunna. Commanded the fortress of Almeida, from April 1809 to the 27th August 1810, when, by the unfortunate explosion of its magazines, he was obliged to surrender it to the army under Marshal Massena. He has the War Medal with one Clasp for Corunna; and is a Knight of the Tower and Sword of Portugal.

24 Colonel Daniell accompanied the 2nd Battalion Coldstream Guards to North America in 1838 on the occasion of the insurrection in Canada, and returned from thence in 1842. Joined the 1st Battalion in the Crimea and served with it during the siege in 1855, and was in command of the Battalion at the period of the attack on the Redan the 8th Sept., and subsequent fall of Sebastopol, on which night he was in Orders as General of the Trenches (Medal and Clasp, and 4th Class of the Medjidie).

25 Colonel d'Arcy was present on the Staff during the operations of a field-force in the Southern Mahratta Country in 1844-45, under Major-General De la Motte.

26 Colonel Henry Dawkins served in the Peninsula with the Guards, from Feb. 1810 to the end of that war in 1814 : Major of Brigade from June 1810, including the battle of Fuentes d'Onor, siege of Ciudad Rodrigo, battle of Salamanca, siege of Burgos, battles of Vittoria, Nivelle, and Nive; passage of the Adour, blockade of Bayonne and repulse of the sortie, on which last occasion he was severely wounded. Served also the campaign of 1815, including the battle of Waterloo. He has received the War Medal with five Clasps.

27 Colonel Denny served in the Crimea in February 1855 (Medal and Clasp, and 5th Class of the Medjidie).

28 Colonel Dobbin served with the 19th in the Travancore war in 1809; at the capture of the Kandian territories in Ceylon in 1815. Also actively employed at the head of the Grenadier Company throughout the Kandian campaign of 1818, and received the thanks of Sir Robert Brownrigge on three occasions in General Orders, for a series of services against the insurgents.

29 Colonel Doherty commanded the 13th Lt. Drs. in the Eastern campaign of 1854-55, including the affairs of Bulganak and M'Kenzie's Farm, battles of Alma, Balaklava, Inkerman, and Tchernaya, and siege of Sebastopol; also present with the Light Brigade at Eupatoria (Medal and four Clasps, and 5th Class of the Medjidie).

30 Colonel William Drummond's services :—Peninsular campaigns from 1809 to 1812, including the battles of Busaco and Fuentes d'Onor, the retreat to the lines of Torres Vedras, and subsequent advance from thence. Campaign of 1811 in Holland, including the bombardment of Antwerp and storming of Bergen-op-Zoom. Campaign of 1815, including the battles of Quatre Bras and Waterloo. Received the rank of Brevet Major for his conduct at Waterloo. He has received the Silver War Medal with three Clasps.

31 Colonel Evelegh served with the 20th Regt. the Eastern campaign of 1854-55, and was present at the battles of Alma, Balaklava, and Inkerman, both attacks on the Redan, and through the whole of the siege operations before Sebastopol without being absent from a single tour of duty in the Trenches; also at the capture of Kinbourn. Embarked for India with the 20th Regiment, was made a Brigadier, and was present at the following actions and affairs,— Chanda, Ameerpore, Sultanpore, siege of Lucknow. Also commanded an independent force at Mohan, Hussengunge, Meeangunge, Poorwah, Murrowmow, capture of fort Simree, Berah, Buxarghat, and the fort of Oomero. Was mentioned about fifteen times in despatches; thanked twice by the Governor General in Council; has the Crimean Medal with four Clasps, order of CB., Legion of Honor, 4th Class of the Medjidie, Turkish Medal, and Indian Medal with Clasp.

32 Sir Henry Fairfax served in the Peninsula with the Rifle Brigade in 1812, on the retreat from Madrid, and in the affair of San Munos.

33 Colonel Farquharson served with the 65th Regiment at the capture of the Isle of France in 1810; at the capture of the fort of Now Nuggur in India, Feb. 1814; on the borders of Scindia's country in 1814 and 15 against the Pindarees; in Kattywar on the Brigade Staff in 1815; at the capture of Joorin, Bunder, Anjar, and Khuncoote in 1816, Dhingee and Dwarka. Action and capture of Poona, 17th March 1817 (Medal). At Ashtee, 21st Feb. 1818, the Mahratta General Gokla killed, and Satteria Reya captured. Storm and capture of Boojee Fort in Cutch, March 1819. Capture of the forts of Rass-el-Kyma and Zama, 8th and 22nd Dec. 1819. Served also in Arabia in 1812, and was present in the action of Beni-Boo-Ali, 2nd March.

34 Colonel Fordyce-Buchan served with the 74th Highlanders in the Kaffir war in 1851 (Medal). Served also with the Scots Fusilier Guards at the siege of Sebastopol (Medal and Clasp, and 5th Class of the Medjidie).

War Services of Retired Colonels.

35 Colonel William Fraser served in the Peninsula and south of France with the 92nd, from October 1813 to the end of that war in 1814, and has received the War Medal with one Clasp for the Nive, in which battle he was severely wounded.

36 Colonel Gauntlett was actively employed against the Maroons in the West Indies. Served also the campaign in Egypt.

37 Colonel Gawler served in the Peninsula with the 52nd Regt. from Nov. 1811 to the end of that war in 1814, including the siege and assault of Badajoz, battles of Vittoria, Pass of Vera, the Nivelle, the Nive, Orthes, and Toulouse, besides various minor affairs. Served also the campaign of 1815, and was present at the battle of Waterloo. Wounded below the right knee by a musket-shot at the storming of Badajoz, and in the neck by a musket-shot at San Munos. He has received the War Medal with seven Clasps.

38 Colonel Gibbes served with the 40th Regiment in South America in 1806-07, and was at the storming of Monte Video, at Sacramento de Colonna, and attack on Buenos Ayres. Served as Deputy Assistant-General to the 4th Division at Walcheren in 1809, and was at the attack on Ter Vere and siege of Flushing.

39 Colonel Gloster served in the Peninsula with the 61st from Oct. 1809 to the end of that war in 1814, including the battles of Busaco and Fuentes d'Onor, siege of the forts at Salamanca, battles of Salamanca, the Pyrenees (28th July to 2nd Aug.), the Nivelle, the Nive (9th to 13th Dec.), Orthes, and Toulouse. Wounded in the left arm at the battle of Salamanca, and through the right breast at Toulouse, the ball passing through the right lobe of the lungs and out at the back. He has received the War Medal with seven Clasps.

40 Colonel Gordon served in the Peninsula with the 5th Dragoon Guards and was present at the battle of Salamanca, for which he has received the War Medal with one Clasp.

42 Colonel William Graham (9 F.) served at the siege of Flushing in 1809, and afterwards in the Peninsula, including the blockade of Bayonne. Subsequently in the American war, including the action at Bladensburg and capture of Washington, action near Baltimore, and those in front of New Orleans on the 20th Dec. 1814; and 8th Jan. 1815; also at the taking of Fort Bowyer.

43 Colonel Gregory served in the American war in 1814 and 15, and commanded a gunboat belonging to the Flotilla under Commander Owen, on Lake Ontario, for which he received the thanks of the Naval Commander-in-Chief.

44 Colonel Hall served at the capture of the Isle of France in 1810; on the expedition to Java in 1811, including the actions at Batavia and Weltevreiden, storming the entrenched lines at Fort Cornelis, storming the heights of Serandole, and capture of the fort of Samarang. Present also at the siege and storming of Bhurtpore in 1825-6. He has received the War Medal with one Clasp for Java.

45 Sir Charles Hamilton commanded the 1st Battalion Scots Fusileer Guards at the battle of Alma, and had his horse shot under him (Medal and Clasps).

46 Colonel J. P. Hamilton served as a Cornet in the Scotch Greys in the army commanded by the Duke of York in Flanders and Holland during the campaign of 1794, and was present in the action near Cateau, and subsequently at the siege of Nimeguen—having previously to the latter been promoted to a Lieutenancy in the Greys by the Duke, for conveying very important despatches, under difficult and perilous circumstances, to the Prince of Orange, then commanding the Dutch Army. In May 1813 he commanded a Battalion at the battle of Castalla, and in the same year was second in command in the attack and capture of the fortress of Balaguer in Catalonia. In the spring of 1814 he joined the Duke of Wellington's army as Lieut.-Colonel of the 83rd Regiment.

48 Colonel Harris served the campaign of 1808-9 as a Deputy-Assistant-Quarter-Master-General to Sir David Baird's Division, and was present at the principal operations of the army, and at the battle of Corunna, for which he has received the War Medal with one Clasp.

50 Sir Robert Chambre Hill served on the Continent in 1794 and 95. Embarked with the Blues for the Peninsula in Oct. 1812. Soon after his arrival in Lisbon, was ordered to take command of the Household Brigade of Cavalry, which he commanded at and for some time after the battle of Vittoria, for which he has received the Gold Medal. Present also at the actions in the Pyrenees; and subsequently with Lord Hill's Division until after the battle of the 13th Dec. 1813 near Bayonne. Served also the campaign of 1815, in command of the Regiment, including the action on the 17th June, and battle of Waterloo, where he was severely wounded. He has the War Medal with one Clasp; and is a Knight of Maria Theresa of Austria, and 4th Class of St. Anne of Russia.

51 Colonel the Honourable Wm. Noel Hill served in the Burmese war, in 1825 and 26 (Medal), and was present in the actions of Prome and Tandwayn.

52 Colonel Hogge served the campaign in Calabria under Sir John Stuart and was present with the 20th at the battle of Maida. He served afterwards in the Peninsula with the 20th Regt., and was present at the battles of Vimiera (wounded), Corunna, Vittoria, Pyrenees, Nivelle, Nive, Orthes, and Toulouse. He has received the War Medal with nine Clasps.

53 Sir Ord Honyman served with the Grenadier Guards in the campaign of 1814 in Holland, and was present at the Bombardment of Antwerp and Storming of Bergen-op-Zoom where he commanded the leading sub-division of the storming party of the Grenadier Guards.

55 Colonel Horton served in the Peninsula with the 71st Regt. and was present at the battles of Nivelle, Nive, Orthes, and Toulouse, for which he has received the War Medal with four Clasps. He served also the Waterloo campaign.

56 Colonel Hughes served in the Peninsula from 1809 to 1814, including the first siege of Badajoz, and the battles of Busaco, Vittoria (wounded), Salamanca, and the Pyrenees, besides various minor actions and skirmishes. Present at Waterloo on the 16th, 17th and 18th June, and was wounded on the 18th. He has received the War Medal with four Clasps.

57 Colonel the Honourable H. Hely Hutchinson joined the Army in the Peninsula on the 12th July 1811, and was shortly afterwards appointed to a Troop in the 4th Portuguese Cavalry, but was employed principally on the Staff until the conclusion of the war in 1814. He was present in most of the affairs in which Lord Hill's Division was engaged, particularly at the surprise of the Bridge of Almaraz; and he was one of the first who gave information that the French had passed the Tormes. He served also the Waterloo campaign.

58 Colonel Irwin served in the Peninsula from April 1809 to Feb. 1814, including the capture of Oporto, battles of Talavera and Fuentes d'Onor, siege of Badajoz, siege and storm of Ciudad Rodrigo, siege of Badajoz and capture of the castle by escalade (7th April 1812), battle of Salamanca, capture of Madrid and the Retiro, battles of Vittoria and the Pyrenees, besides various affairs and Skirmishes on the advance and retreat of the army. Served also the Kandyan campaign of 1817 and 18 in Ceylon. He has received the War Medal with nine Clasps.

59 Colonel Jodrell served in Sicily in 1806 and 1807. He went to Cadiz in March 1810, and remained there till April 1811, having been present at the battle of Barrosa. In Sept. 1812 he joined the Duke of Wellington's army in the Peninsula, and served there until the end of that war in 1816. He has received the War Medal with three Clasps for Barrosa, Nivelle, and Nive.

60 Colonel Keane served with the 23rd Regt. on the expedition to the north of Germany in 1805; in Portugal and Spain under Sir John Moore, including the retreat to, and the battle of, Corunna. Served afterwards in the Peninsula with the 7th Hussars, and as Aide-de-Camp to Sir Hussey Vivian, from November 1813 to the end of the war in 1814, including the battles of the Nive, Orthes, and Toulouse. Also the campaign of 1815 in the same capacity, and was present at the battle of Waterloo and capture of Paris. He has received the War Medal with four Clasps for Corunna, Nive, Orthes, and Toulouse.

61 Colonel Kyle served in the Peninsula with the old 94th, from Jan. 1810 to the end of the war in 1814, including the defence of Cadiz, lines at Torres Vedras, actions at Redinha, Casal Novo, Foz d'Arouce, and Sabugal; battle of Fuentes d'Onor, second siege of Badajoz, action at El Bodon, siege and storm of Ciudad Rodrigo (slightly wounded), third siege of Badajoz, and storming of Fort Picurina, where he was severely wounded in leading the 94th party 3rd Division to one of the most desperate assaults that took place during the war; retreat to Portugal, battles of Vittoria, the Pyrenees, Nivelle, and Orthes; action at Vic Bigorre, and battle of Toulouse. He has received the Gold Medal for Vittoria, (having succeeded to the command of the Regiment); and the Silver War Medal with eight Clasps.

62 Colonel Lane served with the 15th Hussars during the campaigns of 1813, 14, and 15, in the Peninsula, France, and Flanders, and was present at the battle of Waterloo, also at the battles of Orthes and Toulouse, for which he has received the War Medal with two Clasps.

63 Colonel Lascelles served with the 1st Regt. of Guards in the Peninsula in 1813 and 1814, and has received the War Medal with two Clasps for the battles of the Nivelle and the Nive. He served also the campaign of 1815, including the battles of Quatre Bras and Waterloo, and taking of Peronne.

64 Colonel Le Blanc served in the Peninsula with the 4th Regt. and was present at the battles of Corunna, Fuentes d'Onor, Salamanca, and Vittoria, and at the sieges of Badajoz, and St. Sebastian (severely wounded at the assault and capture), for which he has received the War Medal with six Clasps. He served also the Waterloo campaign.

65 Colonel Leslie served with the 29th Regt. on the secret expedition under Sir Brent Spencer, and subsequently in the Peninsula from Aug. 1808 to Dec. 1811, and again from Feb. 1813, including the battles of Roleia and Vimiera, capture of Oporto, battle of Talavera, first siege of Badajoz, and battle of Albuhera, besides skirmishes and affrays at outposts. At the battle of Talavera he was severely wounded in the right leg, where the ball still remains. He has received the War Medal with four Clasps.

66 Colonel Linton served the campaign of 1815 with the 6th Dragoons, and was present at the battle of Waterloo.

67 Colonel Lowe served with the 16th Lancers at the siege of Bhurtpore in 1825-6, and was wounded.

68 Colonel Macadam landed in Portugal 1st Aug. 1808 with the 9th Regt., and served throughout the whole of the Peninsular war, including the battles of Roleia and Vimiera, passage of the Douro, defence of Tarifa, affairs on the retreat from Burgos in 1812, siege and storming of San Sebastian (twice wounded, and commanded the false attack on the breach on the night of the 29th of Aug.), passages of the Bidassoa (shot through the body) and Adour, several affairs connected with the investment of Bayonne, and also the repulse of the sortie, besides a variety of minor affairs, and other desultory services during the Peninsular war. Proceeded to Canada with his Regiment, and served the campaign of 1814. He has received the War Medal with four Clasps for Roleia, Vimiera, Vittoria, and St. Sebastian.

69 Colonel Macpherson served in Hanover in 1805 and 6; at Buenos Ayres in 1807; in Portugal and Spain from July 1808 to Jan. 1809, including the battles of Roleia and Vimiera; action at Lugo, and battle of Corunna. With the expedition to Walcheren, and siege of Flushing, where he was wounded; the Peninsular campaigns from May to Dec. 1812, including the battle of Salamanca, where he was severely wounded. He has received the War Medal with four Clasps.

71 Colonel Madox served the campaign of 1815 with the 5th Dragoons, and was present at the battle of Waterloo.

73 Lord James Murray served with the Scots Fusilier Guards the Eastern campaign from 18th ct. 1854 to the 28th Jan. 1855, including the battles of Balaklava and Inkerman, siege of Sebastopol, and sortie of 26th October (Medal and Clasps, and 5th Class of the Medjidie).

74 Colonel Robert Owen served with the 72nd Regt. at the capture of the Cape of Good Hope and battle of Blauberg in 1806.

76 Colonel Pratt served with the 82nd at the siege and capture of Copenhagen in 1807; in Portugal and Spain in 1808-9, including the battles of Roleia and Vimiera, retreat to, and battle of, Corunna, for which he has received the War Medal with three Clasps. At Walcheren in 1809, and was severely wounded at the investment of Flushing. In 1813 he was appointed to the Quarter-Master-General's staff of the army on the eastern coast of Spain, and served with a portion of that army in Italy and in the South of France until the close of the war in 1814.

77 Colonel Reynardson served with the Grenadier Guards the Eastern campaign of 1854, including the battles of Alma and Inkerman, and siege of Sebastopol (Medal and Clasps, and *CB*).

78 Colonel Richardson served with the Royal Horse Guards in Spain and France from Dec. 1813 to the end of the war in 1814, and has received the War Medal with one Clasp for Toulouse.

79 Colonel Riddlesden served in the Peninsula with the Royal Horse Guards and was present at the battles of Vittoria and Toulouse, for which he has received the War Medal with two Clasps. He served also the Waterloo campaign.

80 Colonel J. M. Robertson served with the 25th Regt. at the taking of Madeira in 1807; at the capture of Guadaloupe in 1810, and again in 1815.

81 Colonel Salwey served the campaigns of 1813 and 14, with the Coldstream Guards, and was present at nearly all the actions in the Pyrenees, the crossing of the Bidassoa, capture of St. Jean de Luz, battle of the Nivelle, heights of Bidart, crossing the Adour, investment of Bayonne, and repulse of the sortie. He has received the War Medal with two Clasps.

82 Colonel Saunderson served at Malta and in Sicily. In the Light Battalion under Sir James Kempt on the expedition to Naples in 1806. Accompanied the 2nd Battalion of the 39th Regt. to the Peninsula in 1809, and was present at the battle of Busaco, in the retreat to the Lines at Torres Vedras, and the advance from thence; re-capture of Campo Mayor, investment and opening of the trenches before Badajoz, battle of Albuhera (slightly wounded), capture of a strong Division of the French army under General Gerard at Arroyo de Molino, where he was severely wounded by a musket-shot, which fractured his skull, and was sent to England for recovery. Rejoined the army in the Peninsula, and acted as Deputy-Judge-Advocate. After the battle of Toulouse embarked with a Division of the army for Canada, where he was appointed to the Quarter-Master-General's Department, and was present at the affair of Plattsburg. He has received the War Medal with two Clasps for Busaco and Albuhera.

84 Colonel Skipwith commanded the 43d Lt.Inf. in the Kaffir war of 1851-53 (Medal).

85 Colonel Tulloch served the Eastern campaign of 1854-55, with the 42nd Regiment, including the battles of Alma and Balaklava (commanded the Regiment), and siege of Sebastopol (Medal and Clasps, and 5th Class of the Medjidie).

86 Colonel Vandeleur served in the Peninsula with the 71st Light Infantry, and afterwards with the 12th Light Dragoons, and was present at the battles of Fuentes d'Onor (severely wounded), Vittoria, Pyrenees, Nivelle, and Nive, for which he has received the War Medal with five Clasps. He served also the Waterloo campaign.

87 Colonel Vicars served with the 61st Regt. in the Punjaub campaign of 1848-49, including the passage of the Chenab, and battles of Sadoolapore, Chillianwallah, and Goojerat, and pursuit of the enemy to the Khyber Pass (Medal and two Clasps).

88 Colonel Robert Wallace served the campaign of 1815 in the King's Dragoon Guards, and was present at the battle of Waterloo.

89 Colonel Walpole served the campaign against the Rajah of Coorg in 1834, with the 39th Regiment.

90 Colonel Ward served in the Peninsula, and has received the Gold Medal and two Clasps for Salamanca, Badajoz (severely wounded at the assault), and the Pyrenees; and the Silver War Medal with one Clasp for Busaco.

91 Colonel John Wildman served in the Peninsula, France, and Flanders, with the 7th Hussars, and was present at the battle of Waterloo. He has received the War Medal with one Clasp for Orthes.

92 Colonel Wood served the Waterloo campaign with the 14th Foot.

93 Colonel Woodgate embarked with the 5th Battalion of the 60th Regt. on the expedition to Portugal in 1808 under Sir Arthur Wellesley, and was present at the battles of Roleia, Vimiera, Talavera, and Busaco; action at Sabugal, battle of Fuentes d'Onor (wounded), siege of Badajoz in 1811; action at El Bodon, siege and capture of Ciudad Rodrigo. He has received the Gold Medal for Fuentes d'Onor, and the Silver War Medal with five Clasps for Roleia, Vimiera, Talavera, Busaco, and Ciudad Rodrigo.

94 Sir Henry Wyatt served the campaigns of 1814 and 15, with the 1st Life Guards, and was present at the battle of Toulouse, and capture of Paris. He has received the War Medal with one Clasp.

95 Colonel Charles Wyndham served in the Peninsula with the 10th Hussars, and was present at the battles of Vittoria, Orthes, and Toulouse, for which he has received the War Medal with three Clasps.

War Services of the Lieutenant Colonels who have retired from the Service.

1 Lieut.Colonel Alexander, served in the Peninsula and South of France from 1812 to the end of that war in 1814, including the battles of Vittoria (wounded), Maya Pass, the Pyrenees 28th, 29th, 30th, and 31st July 1813), Nivelle, St. Palais, Nive, Bayonne, Orthes Aire, Tarbes, and Toulouse. He has received the War Medal with six Clasps.

2 Lieut.Colonel Anderson's services:— Expedition to Calabria, including the battle of Maida and subsequent operations, and capture of the fortress of Catrone; expedition to Egypt in 1807; Peninsula from April 1809 to Jan. 1812, including the battles of Talavera (wounded)

War Services of Retired Lieutenant Colonels. 114

and Busaco, retreat to the lines of Torres Vedras, and various affairs there; with the advance at Espinhal, battle of Fuentes d'Onor, and many other affairs and skirmishes. Served at the capture of Guadaloupe in 1815. Commanded a Brigade at the battle of Punniar (Medal), and was severely wounded at its head when in the act of charging the enemy's guns. He has received the War Medal with four Clasps for Maida, Talavera, Busaco, and Fuentes d'Onor.

3 Lieut.Col. Andros served with the 65th Regt. during the campaigns of 1814 and 1815 in Guzerat and Kutch, and was present at the capture of the Forts of Joosin, Anjar Khuncoote, Dhingee, and Dwarka. Served also throughout the Mahratta campaigns of 1816, 17, and 18, including the battle before and subsequent capture of Poonah, and the affair of Ashtee. Has received the Medal for Poonah.

4 Lieut.Colonel Armstrong served at the capture of Genoa in 1814, and subsequently in the American war, including the capture of Washington, attack before Baltimore 13th Sept. 1814; and on New Orleans, 8th Jan. 1815, where he was wounded and taken prisoner. Present when Graham's Town was attacked by about ten thousand Kaffirs, 22nd April 1819, and who were repulsed with great slaughter by three hundred men under the command of Colonel Wiltshire. Commanded in the Kat River Settlement during the Kaffir war of 1834-5, and w $\frac{a}{2}$ thanked in General Orders for his defence of that locality against an attack of Kaffirs on the 19th Feb. 1835. Served also throughout the whole of the Kaffir war of 1846-7, and was present at the attack on the Amatola, 16th April 1846, and two subsequent days' engagement.

6 Lt.Colonel Astley served with the Scots Fusilier Guards in the Eastern campaign of 1854 until severely wounded at the battle of Alma. Served at the siege and fall of Sebastopol, from 2 May 1855 (Medal and two clasps, Brevet of Major, and 5th Class of the Medjidie).

7 Lieut.Colonel Baddeley served with the 49th Regt. in China (Medal), and was present at Amoy, Chusan (2nd capture), Ningpo, Segoan, Chapoo, Woosung, and Chin Kiang Foo, at which last he was twice wounded—once dangerously by a ball which fractured the thigh-bone.

8 Lt.Colonel Barney served at the defence of Tarifa in 1811-12; also at the capture Guadaloupe and the Saintes in 1815.

10 Lieut.Colonel Barton's services:—Expedition to Walcheren; Peninsula from April, 1812, to the end of the war, including the cavalry affairs at Castrajon, Quintana de Puenta, and Monastero; battles of Salamanca and Vittoria, and siege of San Sebastian. Served also at Waterloo.

12 Sir Henry Bayly served the campaign of 1808-9, including the battle of Corunna; on the Walcheren Expedition also, and was present at the siege of Flushing. Embarked with the 51st Light Infantry for Lisbon in 1811, and was present at the battle of Fuentes d'Onor, covering the siege of Ciudad Rodrigo, second siege of Badajoz, storming the Fort of St. Christoval, affair near Val Moresco, battle of Salamanca, capture of Madrid and the Retiro, covering the siege of Burgos, retreat into Portugal, battles of Vittoria, the three days in the Pyrenees, and on the heights of Lasaca in front of Sebastian, where he lost his left arm and was shot in his right arm. Has received the War Medal with five Clasps. Served three years in the Ionian Islands.

13 Lieut.Colonel Beckham served the Peninsular campaigns of 1812, 13, and 14.

14 Lt.Col. Thos. Bell served with the 48th at the blockade of Malta, and siege of La Valetta. Also in the Peninsula from 1809 to the end of that war in 1814, including the passage of the Douro, battle of Albuhera (wounded), actions at Aldea de Ponte and Fuente Guinaldo, siege of Ciudad Rodrigo, siege and assault of Badajoz (severely wounded), battles of Salamanca, the Pyrenees, Nivelle, Orthes, and Toulouse. He has received the Gold Cross for Salamanca, Pyrenees, Nivelle, and Orthes, having on those occasions commanded the regiment; and the Silver War Medal with four Clasps for Albuhera, Ciudad Rodrigo, Badajoz, and Toulouse.

15 Lieut.Colonel Hon. W. S. Bernard served in the Peninsula in the 67th Regt.—at the siege of Cadiz and battle of Barrosa; and in the 4th Dragoons on the retreat from Burgos War Medal with one Clasp for Barrosa.

17 Lt.Colonel Blennerhasset served with the 71st Lt.Infantry at the siege and fall of Sebastopol, from 20 Dec. 1854 to 13 Feb. 55 (Medal and Clasp). Served also in the Indian campaign.

19 Lt.Colonel Blount served with the 68th Light Infantry the Eastern campaign of 1854-55, including the battles of Alma and Inkerman, siege and fall of Sebastopol (Medal and Clasps, Brevet of Lt.Colonel, Knight of the Legion of Honor, and 5th Class of the Medjidie).

20 Lt.Colonel Edward Bond served with the 53rd Regt. in the Sutlej campaign in 1846, and was present at the affair of Buddiwal, and actions of Aliwal and Sobraon (Medal and Clasp).

21 Lt.Colonel Henry Bond served in the 17th Light Dragoons at the taking of Anjar in Cutch in 1816: also throughout the Mahratta campaign of 1817 and 18. He was present with the 11th Light Dragoons at the siege and capture of Bhurtpore in 1825-6 (Medal). Accompanied the 3rd Light Dragoons into Affghanistan with the force under Sir George Pollock, and was present at the forcing of the Khyber Pass, and in every engagement in the advance of the army on Cabool: also commanded the Rear Guard on three different occasions,—engaged the enemy at Tezeen and Jugdulluck, and safely covered and protected the whole of the baggage of the army, notwithstanding the repeated attacks of the enemy (Medal).

22 Lieut.Colonel Bonham was present with the 50th Regiment in the battle of Punniar (Medal). He served also the campaign on the Sutlej (Medal and three Clasps), in 1845-6, including the battles of Moodkee, Ferozeshah, Aliwal, and Sobraon (dangerously wounded). In all these actions he commanded the Light Company.

23 Sir Edward Brackenbury served with the 61st Regiment in Sicily, in Calabria, at Scylla Castle, and at Gibraltar, in 1807-8. In the Peninsula from 1809 to the end of that war in 1814, including the battles of Talavera and Busaco, Lines at Torres Vedras, pursuit of the French from Portugal, battle of Fuentes d'Onor, storming and capture of Badajoz—horse shot in ad-

War Services of Retired Lieutenant-Colonels.

vancing to the attack; battle of Salamanca—took a piece of artillery from the enemy, guarded by four soldiers close to their retiring column, without any near or immediate support; retreat from Burgos, actions at Villa Muriel and Osma (horse shot), battle of Vittoria, siege, two assaults and capture of San Sebastian, passage of the Bidassoa, battles of the Nivelle and the Nive, actions in front of Bayonne near the Mayor's house, on the 10th, 11th, and 12th Dec. (slightly wounded and horse shot), blockade of Bayonne and repulse of the sortie. Has received the War Medal with nine Clasps; is a Knight of St. Fernando of Spain; a Knight of the Tower and Sword, and a Commander of St. Bento d'Avis of Portugal.

25 Lt.Colonel E. J. V. Brown served with the 88th Regt. the Eastern campaign of 1854-55, including the battles of Alma and Inkerman, and siege of Sebastopol (Medal and Clasps, Brevet Major, Sardinian Medal, and 5th Class of the Medjidie).

26 Lt.Colonel Gustavus Brown served in Holland in 1794, and was taken prisoner at the surrender of Grave. Served afterwards in the West Indies with the 60th from the commencement of 1796 to June 1809, and was present at the captures of St. Lucia and Grenada, the attack on Porto Rico, and surrender of Surinam. Proceeded to the Peninsula in 1810, and was attached to the Portuguese service; present at the battle of Busaco and attack on the forts of Salamanca; commanded the 9th Caçadores at the battle of Salamanca, siege of Burgos (from 19th Sept. to 21st Oct.), blockade of Pampeluna, actions in the Pyrenees near Pampeluna from 28th to 30th July; actions near Ordax on the 31st Aug. and 7th Oct., battles of the Nivelle and Nive, and action near Bayonne on the 13th Dec. During the above service he was three times wounded. He has received the Gold Cross for Salamanca, Pyrenees, Nivelle, and Nive.

27 Lieut.Colonel B. P. Browne served the campaign of 1815 with the 11th Dragoons, and was present at the battle of Waterloo. Also at the siege and capture of Bhurtpore, under Lord Combermere, in 1825-6; and was a volunteer for the dismounted cavalry storming party.

28 Lieut.Colonel George Browne served with the 23rd Regiment in Portugal and Spain, in 1808-9, including the retreat to, and battle of Corunna. On the expedition to Walcheren in 1809; the Peninsula campaigns of 1810, 11, 12, and 13, including the siege of Olivenca, first investment of Badajoz, battle of Albuhera, affairs of Fuente Guinaldo and Aldea de Ponte, siege of Ciudad Rodrigo, siege and assault of Badajoz, battle of Salamanca, retreat from Madrid, affair at Osma, and battles of Vittoria and the Pyrenees. Very severely wounded at the assault of Badajoz, slightly at Salamanca, and wounded at the Pass of Roncesvalles in the Pyrenees.

29 Lt.Colonel the Hon. J. L. Browne served the Eastern campaign of 1854-55 with the 21st Regt., including the battles in the Crimea and siege of Sebastopol (Medal and Clasps, and 5th Class of the Medjidie).

30 Lieut.Colonel Bruce served in the Peninsula with the 79th Regt. from 1812 to the end of that war in 1814, including the battles of the Pyrenees on the 28th, 29th, and 30th July, the blockade of Pampeluna, battles of the Nivelle and the Nive (10th to 13th Dec.), investment of Bayonne, and battle of Toulouse. Served also the campaign of 1815, and was severely wounded at Waterloo.

31 Lt.Colonel Bunbury served in the Peninsula from 1808 to the end of the war, including the capture of Oporto, battles of Talavera and Barrosa. He was Major of Brigade to the force which defended Tarifa (at the investment of which he had his horse shot under him), at the capture of Seville, defence of the bridge of Puente Largo near Aranjues. He was present at the battles of the Nivelle and of the Nive (severely wounded), investment of Bayonne, and commanded the 6th Cassadores at the battle of Toulouse. He commanded the troops, and was employed on various services for four years in New Zealand, from the establishment of the settlement until 1844,—towards the close of which year he was wrecked on one of the Andaman Islands,—and he commanded the troops and crews of the transports *Briton* and *Runnymede*, for fifty-one days, where, under the most trying yet providential circumstances, the lives of about 500 troops and seamen, and 104 women and children, were preserved. He commanded the 80th throughout the campaign on the Sutlej (Medal), including the battles of Moodkee (wounded), Ferozeshah (horse shot under him), and Sobraon. He has the War Medal and five Clasps.

32 Lt.Colonel C. S. Burdett served with the Coldst. Guards at the siege and fall of Sebastopol from Dec. 1854 (Medal and Clasp, and 5th Class of the Medjidie).

33 Lieut.Colonel Francis Alex. Burton served at the siege of Sebastopol (Medal and Clasp).

34 Lieut.Colonel Caine served in the Nepaul campaign of 1815, and was present in action at Jeetghur. In the Deccan war of 1817 and 18, including the action at Jhubbulpore, where he carried the regimental colour of the 17th in the attack of the heights defended by the Arabs. He was Major of Brigade at the assault and capture of Bhurtpore, and was present during the whole of the siege: wounded by a grape shot in the left foot whilst charging the enemy's guns on the day of the capture. He commanded the Grenadiers of the 26th at the capture of Chusan (Medal) 5th July 1840, and was British Commissioner, and Military Magistrate of that island until its evacuation in Feb. 1841. He has been in Asia from the commencement of his service to the present period, having left India in 1840 with the China expedition; and he is now employed as Lieut.-Governor of Hong-Kong. Has received the Indian War Medal with two Clasps for Nepaul and Bhurtpore.

35 Lieut.Colonel Cadell served at the siege of Copenhagen, in 1807; with the expedition to Sweden, and afterward to the Peninsula, including the battle of Corunna; with the expedition to Walcheren, in 1809; the Peninsula campaigns from 1811 to the end of that war in 1814, including the following battles, sieges, &c., viz. :—Barrosa (slightly wounded), Cadiz, Arroya de Molino, Almaraz (reduction of forts), Vittoria, Pyrenees (25th to 31st July), Nivelle, Nive, St. Palais, Orthes, and Toulouse. Served also the campaign of 1815, and was present at the battle of Waterloo.

War Services of Retired Lieutenant-Colonels.

37 Lieut.Colonel Carruthers served the campaign in Affghanistan and Beloochistan (3rd Class of the Dooranee Empire), and commanded the Regt. at the assault and capture of the fortress of Ghuznee (Medal), and at the assault and capture of the fortress and citadel of Khelat, He commanded the Forces, as a Brigadier, in the Southern Concan and Sawant Warree Country during the campaign of 1844 and 45.

39 Sir Richard Church served at the Ferrol in 1800; the Egyptian campaign of 1801, including the actions of the 8th, 13th, and 21st March, and taking of Alexandria. Served afterwards in Naples, Sicily, and Calabria, and was present at the battle of Maida, and defence of Capri, at which last he was wounded in the head. At the capture of Ischia in 1809; on the expedition to the Ionian Isles, and at the taking of Zante and Cephalonia. Severely wounded in an attack on Stellaura,—left arm shattered by a musket-shot. Sir Richard has received the War Medal with one Clasp for Maida; Grand Cross of St. George and Reunion, and Commander of St. Ferdinand and Merit, of Naples.

40 Lieut.Colonel Clephane served the Eastern campaign of 1854-55, including the battles of Alma and Balaklava, siege of Sebastopol, assault on 18th June, expedition to Kertch and Yenikale (Medal and three Clasps and Brevet of Lt.-Colonel, and Sardinian Medal).

41 Sir William Clerke served with the 52d Light Infantry in the Peninsula, and was present at the battles of the Nivelle, Nive (9th, 10th, and 11th Dec. 1813), Orthes, Tarbes, and Toulouse. Served also in the campaign of 1815, and was present at Waterloo, and subsequently with the Army of Occupation. Sir William has received the War Medal with four Clasps.

43 Lieut.Colonel James R. Colthurst served in the Peninsula, and was present at the battles of Corunna and Salamanca, for which he has received the War Medal with two Clasps. He served also the campaign of 1815, and was slightly wounded at Waterloo.

44 Lieut.Colonel Cowell Stepney served with the Coldstream Guards in the campaigns of 1810-11-12-13 in Portugal and Spain. Was present with his Regt. in the retreat from Busaco, Lines at Torres Vedras, advance after Massena to Santarem, and the French army's subsequent retreat to Portugal, affairs of Redinha and Foz d'Arouce, battle of Fuentes d'Onor, siege of Ciudad Rodrigo, covering army of Badajoz, battle of Salamanca, affair of Larena, siege of Burgos (led a storming party, 18th Oct.) retreat into Portugal, advance into Spain, affair of Osma, battle of Vittoria, affair of Tolosa, siege of St. Sebastian, and affair on the Bidassoa, after which he left the army for England in command of a detachment in charge of the garrison of St. Sebastian as prisoners of War. In 1814 he was at the bombardment of the French fleet at Antwerp. In 1815, Waterloo campaign and capture of Paris. In 1816-18, with army of Occupation in France. Has the War Medal with four Clasps and the Waterloo Medal and is a *KH*.

46 Lieut.Colonel Crowe served in the Peninsula with the 32nd Regt., from July 1811 to the end of that war in 1814, including the support of the siege of Ciudad Rodrigo, and covering the siege of Badajoz, action at Usagre, siege and storming the forts and battle of Salamanca, siege of Burgos, actions before Bayonne, and battle of Orthes. Served also the campaign of 1815, and was severely wounded at Quatre Bras.

48 Lieut.Colonel Hon. P. F. Cust served with the 3rd Dragoon Guards in the Peninsula from April 1809 to the end of that war in 1814, except the year 1812; and he was present at the battles of Talavera and Busaco, in all the affairs with his Regiment on the Retreat to the Lines of Lisbon, and lastly at the battle of Toulouse. He has received the War Medal with three Clasps.

49 Lieut.Colonel Hon. R. A. G. Dalzell served the Eastern campaign of 1854-55, with the 63rd Regiment, including the actions in the Crimea and siege of Sebastopol (Medal and Clasps and Sardinian Medal).

50 Sir William de Bathe served as Aide-de-Camp to Sir John Stuart in the different operations in the Mediterranean and defence of Sicily (wounded) when attacked by Murat, also in the expedition to the Bay of Naples and reduction of Ischia and Procida, and received the Order of St. Ferdinand of Merit. Subsequently he served in the Peninsula, and was present during the retreat from Burgos, and in the battles of Nivelle and Nive, for which he has the War Medal with two Clasps. In 1813 he embarked for America, was present at the attacks upon Washington, Baltimore, and New Orleans, and was mentioned in the despatches for personal bravery in the field, for which he was promoted Brevet Major.

51 Lieut.Colonel H. R. Digby served with the 52nd Regt. with the Walcheren Expedition in 1809, and subsequently in the Peninsula in the Light Division, including the siege of Ciudad Rodrigo, retreat from Burgos, battle of Vittoria, advance in the Pyrenees, affair of Tarbes and D'Oleron, and battle of Orthes and Toulouse on the staff of Sir Andrew Barnard (War Medal with four Clasps).

52 Lieut.Colonel De Visme has the War Medal with one Clasp for the battle of Fuentes d'Onor.

53 Lt.Colonel J. A. Digby served with the 12th Lancers in the Kaffir war of 1851-53 (Medal). Served with the Grenadier Guards before Sebastopol (Medal and Clasp).

54 Lieut.Colonel Dillon served in the expedition to St. Domingo in 1809. Served also in China (Medal), and was present at the first capture of Chusan, storm and capture of the heights above Canton, and of the sea-batteries on Amoy, and subsequent capture of the city.

56 Lt.Colonel M. T. Doyle sailed in 1805 with Lord Cathcart's expedition to Hanover, and being shipwrecked became a prisoner of war to the Dutch. In 1808 he went with Sir Arthur Wellesley's expedition to Portugal and was shot through the body at Roleia. In 1809 he was at the siege, sortie, and capture of Flushing, and storming of Fort Ramakins. In 1810, 11, and 12 he served in the Peninsula in Picton's Division,—in pursuit of Massena from Santarem, actions at Pombal, Redinha, Roblida, Condeixa, Sabugal, and Fuentes d' Onor; siege of Badajoz in 1811, cavalry affair at El Bodon, siege and storm of Ciudad Rodrigo, siege and storm of Badajoz (a ball lodged in the cavity of the chest, unextracted—a ball through the right arm, which was splintered—neck and head wounded); battle of Salamanca, capture of Madrid and the Retiro. In 1814 embarked for Canada in command of a detachment of the 5th—repelled two

attacks on the Transport by Privateers. Present with the Army at Plattsburg. He has received the War Medal with seven Clasps.

57 Lt.Colonel Drought served in the Peninsula, France, and Flanders with the 13th Dragoons, and has received the War Medal with five Clasps for Albuhera, Vittoria, Nivelle, Orthes, and Toulouse.

59 Lieut.Colonel Falkiner served in the Peninsula with the 61st Regt., and was present at the battles of Talavera, Busaco, and Salamanca, for which he has the War Medal with three Clasps.

61 Lieut.Colonel Feilden served the Eastern campaign of 1854-55, with the 44th Regt., including the battles of Alma and Inkerman, and siege of Sebastopol (Medal and Clasps).

62 Lieut.Colonel Fendell served in the Peninsula from 1809 to the end of the war, including the battles of Albuhera, Usagre, Vittoria, and Toulouse.

64 Lord Charles FitzRoy was at the battle of Corunna, and served on the Walcheren Expedition with the Guards. In 1811, he joined Lord Hill's staff, and was present at the siege and capture of Badajoz, battles of Vittoria, Pyrenees, Nivelle, Nive, Orthes, Toulouse, and Waterloo, and has received the War Medal with eight Clasps. He also served two years with the Army of Occupation in France.

65 Lieut.Colonel Flamank served in the Peninsula with the 51st Regt. from Jan. 1811, to the end of that war in 1814, including the battle of Fuentes d'Onor, second siege of Badajoz, covering the sieges of Ciudad Rodrigo and third siege of Badajoz, affair in front of Moresco, battle of Salamanca, retreat from Burgos, battles of Vittoria and the Pyrenees (30th and 31st July), passage of the Bidassoa, battles of Nivelle and St. Pé, and battle of Orthes. Served also the campaign of 1815, including the battle of Waterloo and capture of Cambray.

66 Lieut.Colonel Jonathan Forbes accompanied the 78th Regiment to Holland as a volunteer, and was present in action at Merxem 13th January, also on the 2nd February 1814, and at the bombardment of Antwerp. Served also the campaign of 1814 and 1815 in Flanders.

68 Lieut.Colonel Forlong served the campaigns of 1813 and 1814, in Germany and Holland, including the actions at Merxem, bombardment of Antwerp, and storming of Bergen-op-Zoom. Served also the campaign of 1815, and was severely wounded at Quatre Bras—right collar bone fractured and ball lodged in the right breast.

69 Lt.Colonel the Hon. A. E. Fraser served the Eastern campaign of 1854 with the Scots Fusilier Guards, including the battles of Alma, Balaklava, and Inkerman, siege of Sebastopol and sortie on the 26th Oct. (Medal and Clasps, Brevet Major, Sardinian Medal, and 5th Class of the Medjidie).

70 Lt.Colonel Francis Fuller served with the 59th at the capture of the Cape of Good Hope in 1806; the Peninsular campaigns from Dec. 1812 to Feb. 1814, including the battle of Vittoria, siege of San Sebastian, and battle of the Nive, where he was wounded in the shoulder and thigh. Campaign of 1815, including the battle of Waterloo, storming of Cambray, and capture of Paris. Commanded the regiment at the siege and capture of Bhurtpore, in 1825-6, under Lord Combermere, and was slightly wounded in the arm. He has received the Gold Medal for San Sebastian, having commanded the regiment there; and the Silver War Medal with three Clasps for Vittoria, Nivelle, and Nive.

71 Lieut.Colonel F. H. Fuller proceeded to the Peninsula in 1808, and was present with the 53rd Regt. at the capture of Oporto, battles of Talavera, Busaco, and Fuentes d'Onor, besides various skirmishes. He has received the War Medal with two Clasps for Talavera and Busaco.

72 Lieut.Colonel Garner joined the 1st Battalion of the 40th Regt. in the Pyrenees in 1813, and he served in the campaign of that and the following year. He has received the War Medal with one Clasp for Nivelle.

73 Lieut.Colonel Girardot served in the Peninsula with the Coldstream Guards from Jan. 1813 to the end of the War in 1814, and was present at the battle of Vittoria, the passage of the Bidassoa, capture of St. Jean de Luz, battles of Nivelle and Nive, and investment of Bayonne, and has received the War Medal with three Clasps. Served also with the Army of Occupation in France.

74 Lieut.Colonel Gooch served in Holland in 1814, and commanded an advanced party in protection of the ladders at the attack on Bergen-op-Zoom. Present with the Light Companies of the second Brigade of Guards at the battle of Quatre Bras, and assisted in the defence of Hougoumont at the battle of Waterloo.

75 Lieut.Colonel Gordon served the campaigns of 1816, 17, and 18, in Malwa; in the Persian Gulf in 1819 and 20, and in Ava in 1825 and 26. Wounded at Donabew 26th March, and on the Heights near Prome, 2nd Dec. 1825.

77 Lieut.Colonel Henry Graham joined the Peninsular army in 1810, and was present at the sieges of Ciudad Rodrigo and Badajoz, defence of Alba de Tormes, attack on the Pass of Maya, battles of Vittoria, Nivelle, Nive, and St. Pierre, Orthes, and Toulouse, besides various minor affairs. He has received the War Medal with six Clasps.

79 Lieut.Colonel Gunning served with the 79th Regt. at Ferrol in 1800; in Egypt in 1801, under Sir Ralph Abercromby, and was present at the actions of the 13th and 21st March, and with the Division that took Grand Cairo. Proceeded to India in 1805, and was at Vellore, with the 69th Regt. during the mutiny in the following year. Served with the Regt. at the capture of the Lines and Country of Travancore, in 1809. Also at the captures of the islands of Bourbon, Mauritius, and Java; at the storming of one of the Forts of the latter island with six Companies of the 69th Regt. under Lieut.-Colonel Macleod (who was killed); he was the first man that entered the Fort. Medal for services in Egypt.

81 Lieut.Colonel Halkett served with the 2nd Light Infantry Battalion of the King's German Legion on the expedition to the North of Germany in 1805-6. Landed on the Island of Rugen in July 1807; was employed at the siege of Stralsund, and in August re-embarked at Rugen for

Copenhagen, where the battalion formed part of the besieging corps. In April 1808 embarked with Sir John Moore's army for Gottenburg, and from thence to Portugal; belonged to the army which entered Spain with Sir John, and afterwards retired through Gallicia. Accompanied the expedition to Walcheren, and was present at the siege of Flushing. In Jan. 1811 embarked for Portugal; commanded the battalion at the battle of Albuhera, and was at the siege of Badajoz in 1811; commanded the battalion during the campaign of 1812, including the siege of the forts at Salamanca, action of the heights of Moresco, battle of Salamanca, and retreat from Burgos when the Light Brigade K. G. L. formed the rear-guard with the cavalry, and repulsed the repeated charges of the enemy's cavalry. In April 1813 embarked for the North of Germany, and was employed in organizing the Hanoverian troops; commanded a brigade of the same in Count Walmoden's army, and was engaged at the battle of Goerde, as also on several other occasions. In Jan. 1814 commanded the centre of the corps which besieged and captured Gluckstadt. Commanded the right of the corps which was employed at the blockade of Harburg. Served also the campaign of 1815, and was present at the battle of Waterloo. He has received the Gold Medal and one Clasp for the battles of Albuhera and Salamanca.

82 Lieut.Colonel George Hall served in the Peninsula from January 1811 to June 1812, and again from October 1813 to the end of that war in 1814, including the battle of Fuentes d'Onor, sieges of Ciudad Rodrigo and Badajoz (severely wounded), battle of the Nive, Orthes, and Toulouse. Served also the campaign of 1815, and was present at the battle of Waterloo.

84 Lieut.Colonel Hammill served the campaign of 1814 in Upper Canada.

85 Lieut.Colonel Harding served in the Peninsula with the 5th Regt. from August 1812, to the end of that war in 1814, including the retreat from Burgos and Madrid, battle of Vittoria, blockade of Pampeluna, battles of the Pyrenees from the 26th to the 29th July, the Nivelle and the Nive (from 9th to 13th Dec.); passage of the Gâve d'Oleron, battle of Orthes, actions of Vic Bigorre and Tarbes, and battle of Toulouse.

86 Sir T. Noel Harris served the campaigns of 1811, 1812, and 1813 in the Peninsula. Served with the Allied armies in Germany and France from the autumn of 1813 to the surrender of Paris in 1814, and was present in the battles of Grossbergen and Dennewitz, and battles at Leipsic of the 16th, 18th, and 19th October 1813. Passed the Rhine with Marshal Blucher's army in January 1814, and was present in all its battles and engagements up to the capitulation of Paris. Served the campaign of 1815, and was present at the battles of Quatre Bras and Waterloo, at which last he lost his right arm and was otherwise very severely wounded, and had also two horses killed under him. He has received the War Medal with four Clasps for the Peninsula; also the Order of Military Merit of Prussia, the Orders of St. Anne and of St. Vladimir of Russia, for services before the enemy.

87 Lt.Colonel Q. B. Harrison served with the 5th Regt. in Corsica in 1795, and was present in several skirmishes near Ajaccio. Egyptian campaign of 1801, including the actions of the 8th and 21st March. Capture of Copenhagen in 1807. Campaign of 1808-9, including the battles of Roleia, Vimiera, and Corunna. At the capture of Walcheren in 1800. Served afterwards in the Peninsula, and was present at the battle of Fuentes d'Onor, storming of Fort Napoleon near Almaraz,—commanded the right wing of the regt. while escalading the above fort, for which he obtained the brevet rank of Lieut.-Colonel. Present at the affair with the enemy at Alba de Tormes on the retreat of the army from Madrid; commanded the regt. at the repulse of an attack at Bejar, present at the battle of Vittoria; commanded the regt. in the actions in the Pyrenees on the 26th, 27th, 28th, 29th, 30th, and 31st July 1813; also at the battle of St. Pierre near Bayonne, action at Aire, battles of Orthes and Toulouse. He has received the Gold Medal and two Clasps for Pyrenees, Nive, and Orthes.

88 Lieut.Colonel John Christopher Harrison served at the siege of Copenhagen and capture of the Danish fleet in 1807; the campaign of Martinique, siege and capture of Fort Bourbon in 1809. Served afterwards in the Peninsula and was present at the actions of Redinha and Campo Mayor, siege and capture of Olivenca, siege of Badajoz in 1811, battle of Albuhera (severely wounded), siege and capture of Ciudad Rodrigo, siege and storming of Badajoz (received three severe wounds on the grand breach of San Trinidad). He has received the War Medal with four Clasps, and also the Waterloo Medal.

90 Sir Andrew Leith Hay went to Spain in 1808 as Aide-de-Camp to Major-General Leith, on a mission to the Spanish Armies, and was present in several affairs with them: afterwards joined the Army of Sir John Moore, and was present at the battle of Corunna; was with the 29th Regt. at Talavera; on the Staff at the battle of Busaco, and at Salamanca, where he was severely wounded and had two horses killed under him; was present at the battle of Vittoria, and taking of the Castle of San Sebastian; was Military Secretary and first Aide-de-Camp to Sir James Leith at the capture of Guadaloupe in 1815: has received the War Medal with six Clasps.

92 Lt.Colonel C. R. Butler served with the 20th Regt. the Eastern campaign of 1854-55, including the battles of Alma, Balaklava, and Inkerman (severely wounded), siege and fall of Sebastopol, sortie of 23rd March, and affair of 18th June (Medal and Clasps, Brevet Major, Knight of the Legion of Honour, and 5th Class of the Medjidie).

94 Lt.Colonel Holder served with the Scots Fusilier Guards at the siege and fall of Sebastopol from Nov. 1854 (Medal and Clasp, and 5th Class of the Medjidie).

95 Lt.Colonel Holmes served with the 2nd Battalion of the 14th, on the expedition under Lord William Bentinck in the Genoese territory, in 1814; and also served in the South of France, in 1815. Served with the 20th, with the Madras and Bombay Force, against the Rajah of Kolapore in 1827.

97 Lieut.Colonel Humfrey joined the 45th Regt. in the Peninsula in 1811, and served there until the end of that war in 1814, including the siege and storm of Ciudad Rodrigo—severely wounded, siege and storm of Badajox—in both of these attacks he served in the storming party

composed of the Flank Companies; storm of Fort Picurina under General Kempt, battle of Salamanca, capture of Madrid, retreat therefrom into Portugal, battle of Vittoria, blockade of Pampeluna, battle of the Pyrenees (severely wounded), battles of the Nivelle, Orthes, and Toulouse, besides numerous minor affairs and skirmishes. He has received the War Medal with nine Clasps.

98 Lieut.Colonel Hutton served in the Peninsula with the 4th Dragoons, from August 1811 to May 1813.

100 Lieut.Colonel James Johnston served in the 40th Regiment on the expedition to South America under Sir Samuel Achmuty in 1806, and was present at the landing near Monte Video, the advance to invest that town, and repelling the sortie made by its garrison, also at the whole operations of the siege, and was severely wounded at the storming of the breach on the 3rd Feb. 1807. Served throughout the Peninsular war from the landing at Mondego Bay in 1808, and including the battles of Roleia, Vimiera, Talavera, recapture of Campo Mayor and Olivenca, first siege of Badajoz, battle of Albuhera (severely wounded), capture of Badajoz, battle of Salamanca, advance to Madrid and subsequent retreat to Portugal, advance in 1813, battles of Vittoria, the Pyrenees, and Nivelle, besides numerous minor actions and skirmishes: he has received the War Medal with nine Clasps; the Portuguese Command Medal for Vittoria, Pyrenees, and Nivelle; and the Portuguese Cross for three campaigns, as also the Order of the Tower and Sword.

101 Lieut.Colonel Wm. Fred. Johnston served in the Peninsula in 1814. Was present at the battles of Quatre Bras and Waterloo, and taking of Peronne.

103 Lt.Colonel Kelson served with the late 103rd in the American war, and was present in the action of Lundy's Lane at the storming of Fort Erie, on the morning of the 15th August 1814, and at the repulse of the sortie on the 9th September following.

104 Lieut.Colonel Kingscote served the Eastern campaign of 1854-55, as Aide-de-Camp to Lord Raglan, including the battles of Alma, Balaklava, and Inkerman, and siege of Sebastopol (Medal and Clasps and CB.).

106 Lieut.Colonel Leatham served the campaign of 1815 with the 1st Dragoon Guards, and was present at the battle of Waterloo.

107 Lt.Colonel Le Couteur served during the whole of the last war in America. He was Adjutant to Colonel De Harem, who commanded the Light Division and seven hundred Indians, under Generals Vincent and De Rottenburg on the Niagara frontier; was engaged at Sackett's Harbour, the battle of Niagara, and was in the storming division at Fort Erie, where he was blown up by the springing of a mine; present also at the action of the Cross Roads and many skirmishes with the Light Division.

109 Sir John Scott Lillie served in the 6th Regt. with the first expedition to Portugal in 1808, and was present at the battle of Vimiera, and capture of Lisbon. In 1809, as Captain in the Lusitanian Legion, in various engagements for the defence of Portugal during the important interval between the embarkation at Corunna and the return of the second expedition to Lisbon. Campaign of 1810—Battle of Busaco, and retreat to the Lines at Torres Vedras. 1811—Actions of Pombal and Redinha, capture of Campo Mayor, sieges of Olivença and Badajoz. 1812—Battle of Salamanca, capture of Madrid, and retreat from Burgos. 1813—Actions at Ardea do Ponte, Osma, and Bridge of Subijana de Morellas (wounded), battle of Vittoria, blockade of Pampeluna, actions in the Pyrenees on the 24th, 25th, 26th, 28th, and 30th July, actions of Irun and St. Martial, capture of San Sebastian, passage of the Bidassoa, battles of the Nivelle (wounded) and the Nive. 1814—Battles of Orthes and Toulouse, at which last he was severely wounded and left for forty-eight hours on the field of battle, supposed to have been killed. Sir John has received the Gold Cross for the battles of the Pyrenees, Nivelle, Orthes, and Toulouse; and the Silver War Medal with seven Clasps for the others.

110 Lt.Colonel T. Lillie served in the Peninsula from Dec. 1812 to the end of the war, including the crossing of the Zadino; battle of Vittoria; blockade of Pampeluna from 5th to 18th July; pass of Roncesvalles, 28th July, battle of Pampeluna, 28th July, Nivelle, Nive (9th to 13th Dec.) Orthes (severely wounded), and Toulouse. Present at Waterloo on the 18th June, and at the storming of Cambray. He has received the War Medal and six Clasps. He commanded a detachment, consisting of 200 of the 15th Regiment and Ceylon Rifles, in defeating the insurgents at Matalé on the 29th July, during the suppression of the Rebellion in the Kandian Provinces in 1848.

111 Lieut.Colonel P. Lindesay served in the Crimea during 1855, and commanded the 63rd Regt. at the assault on the Redan on the 18th June, and on the 8th Sept. (severely wounded); also at the bombardment and capture of Kinbourn (Medal and Clasps).

112 Lieut.Colonel Hon. C. H. Lindsay served with the 43rd Light Infantry in Canada during the insurrection of 1837-38. Served in the Grenadier Guards in the Crimean campaign during the winter of 1854-55, including the flank march from Alma to Balaklava, taking of Balaklava, battle of Balaklava, repulse of the powerful sortie on the 26th Oct. 1854, battle of Inkerman, and siege of Sebastopol (Medal and three Clasps). In the Eastern campaign in 1854, including the battles of Balaklava and Inkerman, and siege of Sebastopol (Medal and Clasps).

113 Lieut.Colonel M. G. T. Lindsay served in Holland in 1814 and 15, and was present at the bombardment of Antwerp.

114 Lieut.Colonel Lindsell served with the 28th Regt. in the Eastern campaign of 1854, and up to the 15th Feb. 1855, including the battles of Alma and Inkerman, and siege of Sebastopol (Medal and three Clasps).

115 Lt.Colonel Lister served with the 9th Regt. the campaign of 1842 in Affghanistan and was wounded at Istaliff (Medal). Served also in the Crimea from 27th Nov. 1854, including the siege and fall of Sebastopol and assault of the enemy's batteries on the 18th June (Medal and Clasp, Brevet Lt.Colonel, and Sardinian Medal).

War Services of Retired Lieutenant-Colonels.

116 Lt.Colonel Lowndes served with the 47th Regt. throughout the Eastern campaign of 1854-55, including the battles of Alma and Inkerman, capture of Balaklava, siege and fall of Sebastopol, sortie of 26th Oct., and storming the Quarries on 7th June—severely wounded (Medal and Clasps, Brevets of Major and Lt.Colonel, Knight of the Legion of Honor, Sardinian Medal and 5th Class of the Medjidie).

117 Lt.Colonel Loyd Lindsay served with the Scots Fusilier Guards in the Eastern campaign of 1854-55, including the battles of Alma, Balaklava, and Inkerman, siege and fall of Sebastopol, and sortie of the 26th October (Medal and four Clasps, Victoria Cross, Knight of the Legion of Honor, and 5th Class of the Medjidie).

118 Lieut.Colonel Luard served in the Peninsula, from Jan. 1811 until the end of the war, including the actions of Pombal, Redinha, Condeixa, Campo Mayor, Los Santos, and Usagre, sieges of Ciudad Rodrigo, Burgos, and Salamanca, battle of Salamanca, blockade of Pampeluna and battle of Toulouse. Present at Waterloo 18th June 1815. Siege of Bhurtpore 1825-6.

119 Lt.Colonel Lushington served the campaign of 1842 in Affghanistan, and was severely wounded (Medal and CB.).

120 Lt.Colonel Lys was at the capture of Coorg in the East Indies in April 1834. Served in the Crimea from 10th June 1855, at the siege and fall of Sebastopol (Medal and Clasp, and 5th Class of the Medjidie).

121 Lieut.Colonel M'Alester served with the 35th Regt. in Holland in 1799; at the siege and capture of Malta in 1800; battle of Maida (War Medal with one Clasp); siege and capture of the Fort of Scylla in 1806; Egyptian campaign of 1807, including assault of the Western Lines, capture of Alexandria, and battle of El Hamet, in which he was wounded and taken prisoner. In 1811, at the capture of the Ionian Islands. In 1813, commanded the 2nd Battalion 35th Regt. during the campaign in the Netherlands, including assault of the village of Merxem and bombardment of Antwerp. In 1815, campaign in the Netherlands and France, including battle of Waterloo, assault and capture of Cambray, and capture of Paris.

122 Lieut.Colonel M'Niven served the campaigns of 1813 and 14, including the investment of Bayonne in 1813, battle of Orthes, action at Aire, and battle of Toulouse, where he was severely wounded near the groin by a musket-ball, while carrying the regimental colour of the 42nd Highlanders. In 1840 he was appointed on a particular service as Assistant-Adjutant-General in Syria.

123 Lieut.Colonel MacBean's services:—Battles of Roleia, Vimiera, and Corunna; expedition to Walcheren; Peninsula from Oct. 1812 to Nov. 1813, including the battle of Vittoria, Maya Pass, Pyrenees, 28th, 30th, and 31st July; and Pass of Echalar. Served also the campaign of 1815 in Upper Canada.

124 Lieut.Colonel Macbeath served with the 68th Light Infantry the Eastern campaign of 1854-55, including the battles of Alma and Inkerman, and siege of Sebastopol (Medal and Clasps and Sardinian Medal).

125 Lieut.Colonel Robert Macdonald, late of 35th Regiment, served at the siege of Fort Bourbon and capture of Martinique in 1808-9. Present with the 3rd Battalion of the Royals in the retreat from Burgos in 1812, and in the subsequent campaigns of 1813 and 14, including the action at Osma, battle of Vittoria, assault on the convent of San Sebastian 17th July, assault on the town 25th of July (severely wounded); and on the 31st Aug., although suffering from the effects of his wound, was present and engaged at the successful assault on San Sebastian, where he commanded two companies ordered to the breach in advance of the 1st Brigade of the 5th Division, and was at the surrender of the castle on the 8th of Sept. Engaged at the passage of the Bidassoa, battle of the Nivelle, battles of the Nive on the 10th, 11th, and 12th Dec., and repulse of the sortie from Bayonne. Served also the campaign of 1815, including the battles of Quatre Bras and Waterloo, where he was severely wounded. He has received the War Medal with five Clasps; and is a Knight 2d Class of St. Anne of Russia.

126 Lieut.Colonel John Macdonald served with the 93rd Regt. during the campaigns of 1811 and 12 against the Kaffirs on the frontier of the Cape of Good Hope. Also the campaign of 1814 in Louisiana, and battle before New Orleans on the 8th Jan. 1815—severely wounded in the head and leg.

127 Lieut.Colonel Macdonell served in the American war, and has received the Gold Medal for the action at Chateauguay.

128 Sir Duncan MacDougall served at the Cape of Good Hope, where he commanded on the Frontier for a short time; in Portugal, Spain, France, United States of America, and Canada; was at the siege of Badajoz, siege of the Forts at Salamanca, battle of Salamanca (severely wounded, and Medal), siege of Burgos, and retreat therefrom, storming of St. Sebastian (Medal), Passage of the Bidassoa, battles of the Nivelle (Medal), and the Nive (Medal), investment of Bayonne, battle of Bladensburg and capture of Washington, action near Baltimore, where General Ross, commanding-in-chief, to whom he was Aide-de-Camp, was mortally wounded; operations and battle before New Orleans, where Lieut.General Sir Edward Pakenham, commanding-in-chief, to whom he was Aide-de-Camp, was killed; siege of Fort Bowyer in Florida. Served as second in command and Quartermaster General in the British Auxiliary Legion of Spain.

129 Lieut.Colonel Macdougall served the campaigns, of 1813 and 14 in the Peninsula, including the affair of San Marcial; battles of Nivelle, Nive, 9th, 10th, 11th, 12th, and 13th Dec., Orthes, and Toulouse.

130 Lieut.Colonel M'Dowell served with the Army of India, under Lord Combermere in 1825-6, and was present at the siege and capture of Bhurtpore (Medal and Clasp). Served with the Army of the Indus under Lord Keane, throughout the campaign in Affghanistan, in 1838-9, and commanded the 16th Lancers at the storm and capture of Ghuznee (Medal and Cross Dooranée Order). Commanded a Brigade of Cavalry in the Army of Reserve, as-

117d   War Services of Retired Lieutenant-Colonels.

sembled on the Sutlej in 1842. Served with the Army of Gwalior in 1843, and commanded the 16th Lancers in the action of Maharajpore (Medal and CB.). Served throughout he Sutlej campaign under Lord Gough in 1846. Commanded the 16th Lancers at the battle of Buddiwal; a Brigade of Cavalry at Aliwal, and subsequently a Brigade of Cavalry, with a Troop of Horse Artillery attached, from Sobraon to the occupation of Lahore, and termination of the campaign (Medal for Aliwal and Clasp for Sobraon).

132 Lieut.Colonel M'Pherson served in Calabria in 1806. Present at the capture of Ischia in 1809. Served the campaigns of 1813 and 14 in the Peninsula, including the battles of Alcoy, Biar, and Castalla; siege of Tarragona in June 1813, and blockade of do. in Aug. following; action at Ordell (severely wounded through the body and left arm), and blockade of Barcelona. Served also in the American war, including the action in crossing the Sarenac, and battle of Plattsburg. Present at the capture of Paris in 1815. Served in the Kaffir War of 1834-35 (Medal).

134 Lieut.Colonel Mansel served with the 53rd Regt. in the attack at More Chabot and the siege of Morne Fortunée in St. Lucia in 1796; the whole of the Carib war in St. Vincent; at the reduction of Trinidad; and at the siege of Moro Castle in the island of Porto Rico in 1797. Returned from India in the spring of 1811, and joined the 2nd Battalion of the 53rd Regt. in the Peninsula; commanded the Light Companies of the 6th Division throughout the campaigns of 1811 and 12, including the skirmish with the enemy's cavalry near Carpio, sieges of Ciudad Rodrigo, Badajoz, and the forts at Salamanca, battle of Salamanca (horse shot under him), and siege of Burgos. Commanded a Provisional Battalion, consisting of four companies of the Queen's, and a like number of the 53rd Regt., at the battle of Toulouse. He has received the Gold Medal and one Clasp for Salamanca and Toulouse.

135 Lieut.Colonel Marshall served the Egyptian campaign of 1801; at the siege and capture of Copenhagen in 1807; the campaign of 1808-9 in Portugal and Spain, including the battle of Corunna; Walcheren Expedition in 1809, and subsequent campaigns in the Peninsula until the end of that war in 1814, including the battles of Busaco, Fuentes d'Onor, and Salamanca, siege of Burgos, wounded at the capture of the hornwork of the Castle when in command of two companies, and mentioned in dispatches, battles of Nivelle, Nive, Orthes, and Toulouse (severely wounded), besides various minor engagements and skirmishes. Served also the campaign of 1815, and was severely wounded at the battle of Quatre Bras—once in the leg, with loss of an arm. Served with local rank of Colonel in Canada from 1838 to termination of the Rebellion in 1839. He has received the Turkish Gold Medal for Egypt, the War Medal with eight Clasps, and the Waterloo Medal.

137 Lieut.Colonel Fiennes Miller served the campaign of 1815 with the 6th Dragoons, and was severely wonded at Waterloo.

138 Lt.Colonel James Miller served with the 11th Hussars in the Crimea from 29th July to 19th August 1855, and has the Medal and Clasp for Sebastopol.

139 Lieut.Colonel Thomas Miller served in the 40th Regt. at the capture of Manora and surrender of Kurrachee, Lower Scinde, in Feb. 1839. He served with the 10th Regt. in the Punjaub campaign of 1848-9, including the whole of the siege operations before Mooltan: was Major of Brigade at the repulse of the enemy's night-attack on the British camp at Muttee Thol on 17th Aug.: commanded the reserve of the Regt. at the storming of the heights before Mooltan on 27th Dec. 1848. He was afterwards present at the battle of Goojerat (Medal).

140 Lt.Colonel Mills served at the capture of Martinique in 1809, and of Guadaloupe in 1810.

141 Lt.Colonel Molloy served in the Peninsula with the Rifle Brigade, and was present at the battles of Roleia, Vimiera, Salamanca, Vittoria, Pyrenees, Nivelle, Nive, and Toulouse, for which he has received the War Medal with eight Clasps. He served also the campaign of 1815, and was severely wounded at Waterloo.

142 Lt.Colonel Montgomery, when on passage to India in the transport *Briton*, with troops was wrecked on the lesser Andaman, in Nov. 1844, and remained on that island 51 days suffering very severe privations. He served in the 80th Regt. throughout the Sutlej campaign of 1845-6, including the battles of Moodkee, Ferozeshah, and Sobraon (Medal and two Clasps). Also in the Burmese war of 1852 (Medal) including the capture of Martaban (wounded); the operations before Rangoon on the 12th, 13th, and 14th April, and the capture of the Great Dagon Pagoda (with the storming party), and capture of Prome.

144 Lt.Colonel Moorsom served in the Crimea from Nov. 1854, and was present at the siege and fall of Sebastopol (Medal and Clasp, and 5th Class of the Medjidie).

146 Lieut.Colonel Muter served in the Peninsula with the 7th Fusiliers, and was present at the passage of the Douro, capture of Oporto. The subsequent operations against Marshal Soult in the North of Portugal, and battle of Talavera, where, being dangerously wounded on the evening of the 28th July 1809, and taken prisoner while in hospital, he was detained in France until the Peace of 1814. He served at the assault upon New Orleans in Jan. 1815, and commanded the right advanced picquet on the night the army retired from its position—the picquets were exposed at intervals during the night to a heavy cannonade. He has the War Medal with one Clasp.

147 Lt.Colonel Naylor served with the 8th Hussars in the Crimea from 29th April 1855; including the siege and fall of Sebastopol, and battle of the Tchernaya (Medal and Clasp).

148 Lt.Colonel Neville served in the Peninsula with the 2nd Battalion of the 30th, from July 1810 to May 1813; also the campaign of 1814 in Holland, and that of 1815 in the Netherlands; he was present at the defence of Cadiz, occupation of the lines of Torres Vedras, various minor actions when in pursuit of Massena, battle of Fuentes d'Onor, siege of Ciudad Rodrigo, siege and storm of Badajoz (severely wounded in the head and leg when leading the ladder party in the Escalade of the St. Vincent Bastion), battle of Salamanca, capture of Madrid, siege of Burgos (severely wounded through the left shoulder in the storm of the first line of the castle, 4th Oct. 1812) bombardment of Antwerp, assault on Bergen-op-Zoom, battle of Water-

War Services of Retired Lieutenant-Colonels. 117c

loo, and capture of Paris: throughout all the above-mentioned sieges he acted as an Assistant Engineer. In 1817, 18, and 19 he served in the Mahratta war, from the battle of Mahidpore (as a volunteer) to the siege of Asseerghur ; and in 1820 he was attached to the Nizam's Troops at the capture of a Predatory Force. After serving 22 years in India with the 30th and 13th Dragoons, and 26th and 63rd Regts., his health failed when in command of the left wing of the 63rd, in a very unhealthy climate. He has received the War Medal with four Clasps ; the India War Medal and Clasps ; and the Cross of the Legion of Honor for services rendered on board the French ship *Bengalie* on passage from India to Europe in Aug. 1831.

149 Lieut.Colonel Newton received a commission at the early age of twelve, in consequence of the services of his father, then commanding a regt. of Light Dragoons. Served in the West Indies in the campaign of 1810, under Sir Geo. Beckwith, as a Regimental Officer ; was afterwards appointed Assistant Quarter Master General and Major of Brigade in St. Thomas and Grenada. Joined his regt. on their being ordered on service to the coast of America in 1814, where he served with the division under Sir John Sherbrooke. Joined the army under the Duke of Wellington in June 1815, was appointed one of the Staff Commandants in Belgium, and was present at the taking of Landrecy by the Prussians.

150 Lieut.Colonel Nicholson served the campaign of 1814 in Holland, including the bombardment of Antwerp, and storming of Bergen-op-Zoom, where he was severely wounded.

152 Lieut.Colonel O'Reilly served in the Peninsula with the 4th Dragoon Guards.

154 Lieut.Colonel Paschal served in the Peninsula with the 2nd Line Battalion of the King's German Legion, from Oct. 1813 to the end of that war in 1814, including the battles of the Nivelle and Nive, investment of Bayonne on the 27th Feb. 1814, and subsequent operations before that fortress. Served also the campaign of 1815, and was at Quatre Bras, attached to Sir Henry Clinton on the 17th June, and at the battle of Waterloo. He has received the War Medal and two Clasps, as also the Hanoverian War Medal.

155 Lt.Colonel Paterson commanded the Grenadiers of the Cameronians on the China expedition (Medal), and was present at the operations before Canton from the 24th to the 31st May 1841, defence of Ningpo, at Segoan, Chapoo, Woosung, Shanghae, Chin Kiang Foo, and Nanking. Commanded the Buffs at the Siege of Sebastopol from May to August 1855 (including the attack on the 18th June), and also from December until the close of the war (Medal and Clasp).

157 Lieut.Colonel Raines served at the battles of Rolcia, Vimiera, and Corunna, besides minor affairs during the retreat ; served also at Walcheren. He has the War Medal and two Clasps.

158 Lt.Colonel Ready landed in the Crimea in 1854, and commanded the 71st Highlanders at the siege of Sebastopol and expedition to Kertch: he held the rank of Brigadier in the Kertch District during its occupation by the Allies (Medal and Clasp, and Knight of the Legion of Honor.

159 Lieut.Colonel Reed served in the American war, including the action at Baltimore, Bladensburg, and capture of Washington.

160 Lieut.Colonel Reeve served the Eastern campaign of 1854 with the Grenadier Guards, including the battles of Alma, Balaklava, and Inkerman, and siege of Sebastopol (Medal and Clasps).

162 Lt.Colonel Rose served with the 3rd Light Dragoons throughout the campaign of 1842 in Affghanistan (Medal), including the forcing of the Khyber Pass, storming the heights of Jugdulluck, action at Tezeen and Huftkotul, relief of Jellalabad, and re-capture of Cabool. At the battle of Punniar, near Gwalior, commanded the left squadron of the 9th Lancers (Medal). He served in the Sutlej campaign in 1846, including the battle of Sobraon (Medal). Also in the Punjaub campaign of 1848-9, including the passage of the Chenab at Ramnuggur (where he commanded the 9th Lancers), and battles of Chillianwallah and Goojerat (Medal and Clasps).

164 Lt.Colonel A. H. Russell served with the 22nd Regt. in Scinde during its conquest. Served with the 58th in the south of New Zealand from 9th April 1845.

165 Lieut.Colonel Schreiber served the campaign of 1815 with the 11th Light Dragoons, including the battles of Quatre Bras and Waterloo (horse shot).

166 Lieut.Colonel Sedley served in the Peninsula from March 1812 to Dec. 1813, including the taking of the forts and the affair of the Guarena, battle of Salamanca, actions at Osma, Sabuganna de Morrilla (severely wounded through the lungs), and Pyrenees, 31st Aug. Wounded on the 18th June at Waterloo. Served also in the Burmese war, during the latter part of which he was detached with the command of two companies to keep open the communication on the Irrawaddy between Rangoon and the army under Sir Archibald Campbell. He has received the War Medal with three Clasps for Salamanca, Vittoria, and Pyrenees.

167 Lieut.Colonel Sharp served with the 26th Regiment in the first China expedition, (Medal). Commanded the 72nd Highlanders in the Crimea from the arrival of the regiment on the 13th June to the 31st July, 1855, including the expedition to Kertch, and siege of Sebastopol (Medal and Clasp).

168 Lieut.Colonel Simmonds served in the Peninsula from Feb. 1808 to Feb. 1813, including the affairs of Talavera and Alberche, battles of Talavera, Busaco, and Albuhera; covering the siege of Badajoz in 1812, engaged every day during the retreat from Madrid and Salamanca; the retreat to Portugal, and subsequent pursuit of Massena from the Lines, besides several minor affairs. He has received the War Medal and three Clasps.

169 Lt.Col. Simmons served in the Peninsula, as a volunteer with the 34th Regt., and afterwards as an officer in the 23rd, and in the Rifle Brigade, from Sept. 1811 to the end of that war in 1814, including the storming of the forts at Almaraz, affairs of San Munos and San Milan, battle of Vittoria, actions at Yanzi Bridge and Echalar, storming Vera Heights, crossing the Bidassoa, battle of Nivelle, battles of the Nive, on the 10th, 11th, and 12th Dec. 1813. Served with the 41st Regt. throughout the Burmese war, and was present at the storming of Rangoon and Syrian Pagoda ; led the head of the left column storming the trenches in front of the Dagon Pagoda,

storming a strong stockade in front of the Dagon Pagoda. Commanded the left wing of the 41st Regiment in the field against the Kolapore Rajah. Served with the regiment during the campaign of 1842 in Affghanistan, and commanded a column of attack in the action of the 28th April in the Pisheen Valley; present also in the actions near Candahar, at Goaine, and before Ghuznee; occupation and destruction of that fortress and of Cabool; expedition into Kohistan; storm, capture, and destruction of Istaliff, and in the various minor affairs in and between the Bolan and the Kyber Passes. Has the War Medal with three Clasps for Vittoria, Nivelle, and Nive.

170 Lieut.Colonel J. J. Slater served in the Peninsula and also in America, in 1814.

171 Lieut.Col. David Rae Smith served the campaign in the Southern Mahratta country in 1844-45 with the 22nd Regiment, and was present at the investment and capture of the forts of Panulla and Pownghur.

172 Lieut.Colonel George Smith served the campaigns of 1814 and 15, in Spain, France, and Flanders, and was present at the battle of Waterloo.

173 Lt.Colonel Somerville served with the 6th Regt. during the Kaffir war of 1846-47 (Medal); and with the 68th in the Eastern campaign of 1854-55, including the battles of Alma, Balaklava, and Inkerman, and siege of Sebastopol (Medal and Clasps, and 5th Class of the Medjidie).

175 Lieut.Colonel Spence was present with the 31st Regt. in the action of Stuola, near Genoa, on the 13th April 1814, and in the subsequent attacks upon the city of Genoa until its surrender, as also at the surrender of Corsica in the same year. In 1815 he served with the army in Naples. On the 1st March 1825, he was present at that lamentable catastrophe, the burning of the *Kent*, in the Bay of Biscay. He commanded the 31st Regt. throughout the campaign on the Sutlej (Medal and three Clasps), at the battles of Moodkee (soon after its commencement), Ferozeshah (for which he was appointed a CB.), Buddiwal, and Aliwal, and the 1st Brigade of Sir Harry Smith's division at the battle of Sobraon; and was one of only five officers out of thirty who escaped being wounded in all the actions. Had his horse shot under him at Ferozeshah and at Sobraon.

177 Lt.Colonel P.D. Stewart served in Hanover in 1805; and at the siege of Copenhagen in 1807.

178 Lieut.Colonel St. Maur accompanied the 51st Regt. on the expedition to Burmah in 1852, and was on board the E. I. C. steam frigate *Ferooz* during the naval action and destruction of the enemy's stockades on the Rangoon River, landed in command of the regiment, and was compelled to leave the field from a sun-stroke on the 13th April, during the operations in the vicinity of Rangoon.

179 Lieut.Colonel Stretton served the campaigns of 1812 and 13 in the Peninsula, with the 68th Light Infantry, and was severely wounded at the battle of Vittoria by two gun-shots lodged in the body, one of which has not been extracted. He has received the Silver War Medal with one Clasp for Vittoria.

180 Lieut.Colonel Stracey served with the Scots Fusilier Guards in the Eastern campaign in 1854, including the battle of Alma (Medal and Clasp).

182 Lieut.Colonel Toole joined the 40th Regt. in the Peninsula [early in Jan. 1810, and was present at the battle of Busaco, retreat to and occupation of the lines at Torres Vedras, pursuit of Massena, action of Redinha, capture of Campo Mayor, siege of Badajoz in May 1811 and repulse of the sortie from Fort San Christoval, siege and storming of Ciudad Rodrigo, siege and storming of Badajoz, in the breach of which fortress he was severely wounded. In October 1813 he rejoined the army at Vera, and was present at the battle of Nivelle, and in several minor affairs. Subsequently he served nearly one year and a half with the Army of Occupation in France. He has received the War Medal with four Clasps.

184 Sir John M. Tylden served as Brigade Major to Sir Samuel Auchmuty during the operations in South America in 1806-7, including the capture of Monte Video and the attack on Buenos Ayres. Served with the 43rd Light Infantry during Sir John Moore's campaign in Spain in 1808-9, and accompanied it again to the Peninsula in 1809. Accompanied Sir Samuel Auchmuty to India in 1810, and in 1811 served as the General's Military Secretary on the expedition to Java, and was present at the assault and capture of Cornelius. Served with the 52nd Light Infantry in the Peninsula during the campaigns of 1813 and 1814, including the battles of the Nive, Orthes, and Toulouse. In 1814 he accompanied Sir John Lambert's expedition to America as Assistant-Adjutant-General, and was present during the operations against New Orleans. He has received the War Medal with four Clasps.

185 Lieut.Colonel Ussher served the Nepaul campaigns of 1816 and 17 with the 66th Regt.

186 Lieut.Colonel Van Cortlandt was engaged at the following battles, sieges, &c. in the East Indies, viz. Sarsni, Bijighur, Kutchowra, Agra, Deig, Bhurtpore, Allyghur, Delhi, Laswarrie, and Futtehghur. Also several skirmishes during the campaigns of 1803, 4, 5, and 6. Present at the sieges of Komona and Gunowrie in 1808, and at Kalunga in 1814. Served the campaigns against the Pindarrees in 1817 and 18.

187 Lieut.Colonel Van der Meulen served in the Peninsula from May 1809 to Aug. 1811, and again from Sept. 1812 to the end of the war, including the battles of Talavera (severely wounded), Busaco, Albuhera (severely wounded), Vittoria, Pyrenees (severely wounded 28th July), Nivelle, Orthes, and Toulouse, besides various minor engagements and skirmishes.

188 Lord Adolphus Vane Tempest served with the Scots Fusilier Guards at the siege and fall of Sebastopol from Nov. 1854 (Medal and Clasp, and 5th Class of the Medjidie).

190 Lieut.Colonel Ward served with the 91st Regt. in the Kaffir war of 1846-47 (Medal).

191 Lt.Colonel A. Watson served during the suppression of the Rebellion in the Kandian Provinces, Island of Ceylon, in 1848, and was present when the insurgents were defeated at Matole on the 29th July.

192 Lieut.Colonel W. Watson served in the American war with the 41st Regt., and has received the War Medal with one Clasp for Fort Detroit.

193 Lieut.Colonel Waugh served the Mahratta campaign with the 16th Lancers, including the

War Services of Retired Lieutenant-Colonels.

battle of Maharajpore (Medal), 29th Dec. 1843; also as Assist.-Quarter-Master-General to Sir Harry Smith during the campaign of the Sutlej (Medal and one Clasp), including the battles of Buddiwal, Aliwal, and Sobraon (wounded).

194 Lt.Colonel Webster served the campaign of 1815 with the 44th Regt. and was severely wounded at Quatre Bras.

196 Lieut.Colonel Whannell served the campaigns of 1813 and 14 in Germany and Holland, including the attacks on Merxem, bombardment of the French fleet at Antwerp, and the attack on Bergen-op-Zoom.

197 Lieut.Colonel White served the campaign on the Sutlej in 1845-6, with the 31st Regt., including the battles of Moodkee and Ferozeshah, for which he has received the Medal and one Clasp. He was afterwards present at Buddiwal.

199 Lt.Colonel Wilkie served the campaign of 1799 in Holland; at the blockade and surrender of Malta in 1800; capture of the Cape of Good Hope in 1806; siege and storming Monte Video, and attack on Buenos Ayres. Landed in Portugal with Sir Arthur Wellesley, and served the subsequent campaign with Sir John Moore. Operations against Flushing in 1809 Campaign of 1815. He has the War Medal with three Clasps for Roleia, Vimiera, and Corunna.

200 Lieut.Colonel Wilkins served in Ireland during the Rebellion in 1798, and was wounded at New Ross. Landed with the force that occupied Madeira in 1801. From thence proceeded to the West Indies, where he was employed on the Staff. In 1809 joined the 95th Regt., now the Rifle Brigade, and embarked with the corps on the Scheldt expedition. In 1810 commanded a detachment of the regiment in the defence of Cadiz, and a battalion in 1812 at the battle of Salamanca. Accompanied the army to Madrid, and aided in covering the retreat into Portugal. In 1813 advanced with the army to within range of the guns of Burgos, when the enemy abandoned the fortress. Was present at the battle of Vittoria, and in several minor affairs in following the retreating army to Pampeluna and San Sebastian. Volunteered his services at the storming of the latter, but the honour being subsequently claimed by a senior officer, he resumed the command of the 2nd Battalion, and was sharply engaged with the enemy at the Bridge of Vera. Served in the campaign of 1815, including the advance on the 10th June, retreat on the 17th, and was in the command of the before-named battalion on the field of Waterloo, when, by a discharge of grape-shot from the enemy's artillery, both himself and horse were felled to the ground. In 1817 he joined the Army of Occupation in France, but, from the serious effects of his wound, was compelled to return to England. He has received the Gold Medal for Salamanca, and the Silver War Medal with two Clasps for Vittoria and the Pyrenees.

201 Lt.Colonel G. D. Wilson served with the 4th Regt. on the expedition to the Helder in 1799, and was present in the actions of the 2nd and 6th October. Siege of Copenhagen in 1807. Expedition, first to Sweden and afterwards to the Peninsula, under Sir John Moore, including the retreat through Spain, and battle of Corunna (wounded). Accompanied to Walcheren in 1809. Joined the army at the Lines of Torres Vedras in 1810, and was afterwards present in the pursuit of Massena, action of Sabugal, battle of Fuentes d'Onor, action at Barba del Puerco, storming of Badajoz (severely wounded), Aide-de-Camp to Major-General Pringle at the battle of Salamanca, capture of Madrid and the Retiro, siege of Burgos and retreat therefrom, affair of Villa Muriel, battles of the Nivelle, the Nive, and St. Pierre, Orthes, and St. Palais. Served also the campaign of 1815; commanded the 4th Regt. at the battle of Waterloo, and was wounded. He has received the Gold Medal for Badajoz, and the Silver War Medal with six Clasps for Corunna, Fuentes d'Onor, Salamanca, Pyrenees, Nivelle, and Nive.

202 Lieut.Colonel Charles T. Wilson served the Eastern campaign of 1854 with the Coldstream Guards, including the battles of Alma, Balaklava, and Inkerman, and siege of Sebastopol (Medal and Clasps).

203 Lieut.Colonel the Honourable C. A. Wrottesley served with the 16th Lancers at the siege of Bhurtpore in 1825-6.

204 Lieut.Colonel Wyndham received two severe wounds at Waterloo, on the 18th June.

205 Lieut.Colonel Yale has received a Medal for the battle of Albuhera.

War Services of the Majors who have Retired from the Service.

1 Major Adair served with the 27th Regt. in Sicily in 1810 and 11; in the Peninsula and France from 1812 to the close of that war in 1814, including the taking of Alcoy, covering the retreat from Biar, battle of Castalla, siege and subsequent blockade of Tarragona, and actions at Villa Franca. Subsequently in Flanders and France, including the occupation of Paris in 1815.

2 Major Amsinck served with the 27th Regt. in the Kaffir war of 1834-35 (Medal).

3 Major Anderson served with the 51st throughout the Burmese war of 1852-53; on board the E. I. C. steam frigate *Ferooz* during the naval action and destruction of the enemy's stockades on the Rangoon River; during the succeeding three days' operations in the vicinity, and at the storm and capture of Rangoon (Medal and Clasp); commanded the Regiment from Dec. 1852, until its embarkation for England in April 1854.

5 Major Austin served in the Peninsula from Oct. 1811 to April 1812, including the siege and storm of Ciudad Rodrigo, for which he has received the War Medal with one Clasp. Campaign of 1814 in Holland, including the taking of the fortified village of Merxem. Campaign of 1815, including the battle of Waterloo.

7 General Bacon served in the Peninsula with the 10th Lancers from February 1813 to the end of that war in 1814, and was present at the battle of the Pyrenees on the 28th July, with the covering party during the siege of San Sebastian, the different affairs on the Bidassoa and passage of that river, battle of the Nivelle, actions of the 9th, 10th, 11th, 12th, and 13th Dec. consequent on the passage of the Nive, passage of the Adour, besides various minor affairs (War

Medal with two Clasps). Served the campaign of 1815 with the 10th Hussars, including the battle of Quatre Bras, retreat on the 17th June, and battle of Waterloo, at which he was severely wounded in the last charge, and had two horses shot. In 1832 he was appointed Colonel-Commandant of the Portuguese Cavalry: during the siege of Oporto, overcoming many difficulties and daily exposed to fire, he formed that Regiment of Lancers which rendered so many important services; was promoted General on the field of battle at Loures 12th Oct. 1833, by the Emperor Dom Pedro in person, and he retained command of the Cavalry until the termination of the war, having taken part in nearly all the battles, sorties, and other operations. For special services was created at different periods a Knight, an Officer, and a Knight Commander of the Tower and Sword, and has the Portuguese Cross.

8 Sir David Baird served with the 74th Highlanders throughout the Kaffir war of 1851-53 (Medal).

9 Major F. W. Balfour served with the 2nd Battalion Rifle Brigade in the Eastern campaign of 1854-55, including the assault of the Redan on the 8th Sept., and siege and fall of Sebastopol (Medal and Clasp and Brevet Major).

11 Major Barnston served with the 55th Regt. in the Eastern campaign of 1854-55, including the battles of Alma and Inkerman (severely wounded), siege of Sebastopol and sortie of 26th October (Medal and Clasps, and Knight of the Legion of Honor).

13 Major Bayley served with the 52nd Lt. Inf. at the defeat of the Sealkote mutineers on the banks of the Ravee on the 12th and 10th July 1857; also at the siege of Delhi, and commanded and led the storming party of the 3rd Column at the assault of the Cashmere Gate on 14th Sept., where he was severely wounded (Brevet of Major, Medal and Clasp).

15 Lord George Beauclerk served with the 10th Hussars in the Crimea from 7th July 1855, including the battle of the Tchernaya, siege and fall of Sebastopol (Medal and Clasp).

16 Major Bere served with the 16th Lancers during the campaign in Affghanistan, under Lord Keane, and was present at the siege and capture of Ghuznee (Medal); and he commanded the party of the 16th Lancers, under Brigadier Cureton, sent to seize the guns and secure the possession of the citadel of Cabool, and was appointed at Cabool Assistant-Adjutant-General of Cavalry, and continued so until the reduction of Lord Keane's army in the Provinces. Also the campaign on the Sutlej in 1846 (Medal), including the battles of Buddiwal, Aliwal (wounded), and Sobraon.

17 Major Bethune served with the 92nd Highlanders in the Indian campaign of 1857-58, and was present at the actions of Rajghur, Mungrowlie, and Sindwaho, and affairs of Kurai and Burode (twice mentioned in despatches, Medal, and Brevet of Major).

19 Major Brady served the campaigns of 1813, 14, and 15, in the Peninsula, France, and Flanders, with the Royal Horse Guards, and was present at the battles of the Nivelle, Nive, Bayonne, Orthes, Toulouse, and Waterloo, at which last he was severely wounded, and had a horse shot under him.

21 Major Briggs served with the 1st Dragoon Guards in the Crimea from 10th August 1855, including the battle of the Tchernaya and siege of Sebastopol (Medal and Clasp).

23 Major Burslem served the campaigns of 1838, 39, and 40 in Affghanistan, with the 13th, and was present at the storm and capture of Ghuznee (Medal), assault and capture of the town and fortress of Tootumdurrah, storm of Joolghur, night attack at Baboo Koosh Ghur, destruction of Khardurrah, and assault of Perwandurrah.

24 Major Cairnes served at the siege of Flushing in 1809, and at different periods in the Peninsula.

25 Major Berkeley Calcott served the campaign of 1808-9 with the 43rd Regt., including the battle of Vimiera, the retreat under Sir John Moore, and the battle of Corunna. Expedition to Walcheren in 1809. Subsequently in the Peninsula, including the sieges and captures of Ciudad Rodrigo and Badajoz, battles of Salamanca, Vittoria, Nivelle, Nive, and Toulouse. Expedition to New Orleans. Campaign of 1815, and was present at the capture of Paris.

26 Major Caldecot served with the 39th Regt. in Malta and Sicily. Subsequently in the Peninsular campaigns of 1813 and 14, including the battles of Vittoria, the Pyrenees, Nivelle, and Nive, action at Garris, battles of Orthes and Toulouse. Served afterwards in Canada during the American war.

28 Major Henry W. Campbell served with the 79th Highlanders throughout the Eastern campaign of 1854-55, including the battles of Alma and Balaklava, siege and fall of Sebastopol, assault of the 18th Jan. and 8th Sept., expedition to Kertch and Yenikale (Medal and three Clasps, Brevet Major, and Knight of the Legion of Honor).

29 Major Robert Campbell was employed on field service in India from August 1820 to March 1825, including the siege of Kittoor.

30 Major John C. Campbell served with a wing of the 13th Light Dragoons in the Kurnoul campaign in 1839; served in the 9th Lancers in the Gwalior campaign in 1843, and was present at the battle of Punniar (Medal); in the Sutlej campaign in 1846 and present at the battle of Sobraon (Medal); and in the Punjaub campaign of 1848-49, including the passage of the Chenab at Ramnugger, and battles of Chillianwallah and Goojerat—in the latter battle he commanded the left squadron 9th Lancers which successfully charged the Sikh and Affghan cavalry (Medal and Clasps).

31 Major Campsie commanded two Companies of the Ceylon Rifles at Borilla in suppressing the Rebellion of 1848 in Ceylon.

32 Major Coats served with the 55th Regt. on the China Expedition in 1841-42 (Medal), including the attack and capture of Amoy, second capture of Chusan, and storming of Chin Kiang Foo. Served in the Eastern campaign of 1854, and was severely wounded at the battle of Alma (Medal and Clasp, and mentioned in orders by Sir De Lacy Evans).

33 Major Cochran served the campaigns of 1813 and 14 in Canada, including the action at Moravian Town. Also the campaign of 1824-5 in Ava, including the capture of Rangoon and Martaban, siege and capture of Denobia, battles of Prome and Pagahm Mew. Served the

War Services of Retired Majors.

campaign of 1842 in Affghanistan, and commanded a column of attack in the action of the 28th April in the Pisheen Valley; present also in the actions near Candahar, at Goaine, and before Ghuznee; occupation and destruction of that fortress and of Cabool. Expedition into Kohistan, storm, capture, and destruction of Istaliff, and in the numerous minor affairs in and between the Bolan and the Khyber Passes.

34 Major Hon. Wm. Erskine Cochrane served with the 15th Hussars the campaign of 1803-9 under Sir John Moore, and commanded a troop which attacked and defeated the French cavalry at Sahagun. In 1812 he accompanied his Regiment to Lisbon, and in the following year commanded a squadron in the battle of Vittoria: he has received the War Medal with two Clasps.

35 Major Wm. H. Cockburn was detached from Gibraltar for the defence of Tarifa in 1811 and 12, when the French were defeated, leaving their guns behind; served subsequently in the Peninsula to the end of that war in 1814, and was present at the investment of Bayonne and repulse of the sortie. Embarked afterwards for America, where he served until the termination of the war with the United States.

36 Major Codd served with the 48th Regt. in the operations against the Rajah of Coorg in 1834.

37 Major Cook served with the 11th Hussars in the Eastern campaign of 1854 and up to 20th Aug. 1855, including the affair of Bulganak, battles of Alma, Balaklava (wounded), and Inkerman, and siege of Sebastopol (Medal and Clasps).

38 Major Croker was detached as Assist. Quarter-Master-General in the action at Zoraporc near Kurnool on the 18th October 1839; and also in a like capacity in the action at Maharajpore, 29th December 1843 (Medal).

39 Major Cumberland served with the 42nd Highlanders the Eastern campaign up to 1st Feb. 1855, including the battles of Alma and Balaklava, and siege of Sebastopol; he succeeded to the command of the regiment a few days after Alma and continued in the command until the 1st Feb. 1855 (Medal and three Clasps).

40 Major Darell served with the 1st Batt. 60th Rifles during the second siege operations at Mooltan, including the siege and storm of the town and capture of the citadel of Mooltan. Afterwards at the battle of Goojerat (Medal), pursuit of the Sikh army under Rajah Shere Sing until its final surrender at Rawul Pindee, occupation of Attock and Peshawur, and expulsion of the Affghan force under the Ameer Dost Mahomed beyond the Khyber Pass.

41 Major Darroch served with the Royals in Canada during the Rebellion of 1837-8. He served also with the 62nd in the campaign on the Sutlej (Medal), and was wounded at Ferozeshah. Served with the 51st throughout the Burmese war of 1852-53; was on board the E. I. C. steam frigate *Ferooz* during the naval action and destruction of the enemy's stockades on the Rangoon River; served during the succeeding three days' operations in the vicinity (including the storming of the White House Redoubt), and at the storm and capture of Rangoon; also at the assault and capture of Bassein 19th May (wounded); and served as Deputy Assistant Qr. Master General at the taking of Pegu 21st November.

43 Major Dillon served with the 32nd Regiment at Copenhagen in 1807; the campaign of 1808-9 in Spain, including the battles of Roleia and Vimiera, retreat to and battle of Corunna; in 1809, Walcheren expedition, and siege and capture of Flushing; in 1812 was in support at the siege of Ciudad Rodrigo, and in the covering army at the siege and capture of Badajoz: he has received the War Medal with three Clasps.

44 Sir Thomas Drake served with the 52nd Regt. in 1808, on the expedition to Sweden under Sir John Moore and on the retreat to Corunna; in 1809, on the Walcheren expedition; from 1809 to 1812 inclusive, in the Peninsula, and was present in the action at Sabugal, battle of Fuentes d'Onor, siege and assault of Ciudad Rodrigo, and affair of San Munos—severely wounded (War Medal with two Clasps).

45 Major Driberg, prior to entering the army, served five years and a half as midshipman in the Royal Navy; in 1808, 9, and 10, on the East India station; in 1812 and 13 in the blockading squadrons off Flushing, Cherbourg, and Texel, and in the Baltic. In 1815 he served as a volunteer in the Kandian campaign in Ceylon.

46 Major Duff served with the 23rd Fusiliers in the Eastern campaign of 1854, including the siege of Sebastopol and battle of Inkerman where he was taken prisoner (Medal and Clasps, and 5th Class of the Medjidie).

48 Major Elmsall served with the 1st Dragoons. Served the Eastern campaign of 1854, including the battle of Balaklava (severely wounded), and siege of Sebastopol (Medal and Clasps, Brevet Major, and Knight of the Legion of Honor).

49 Major Fane served the campaign in Affghanistan, and was present at the storm and capture of Ghuznee (Medal).

51 Major Forsyth served the Eastern campaign of 1854-55, including the battles of Balaklava and Inkerman, siege of Sebastopol, capture of the Quarries, attack on the Redan on the 18th June (with the storming column), and on the 8th Sept.; also at Kinbourn (Medal and Clasps, Brevet Major, Knight of the Legion of Honour, and Sardinian Medal).

52 Major Fox served in the Peninsula with the Royals, and was present at the battles of Corunna and Fuentes d'Onor, for which he has received the War Medal with two Clasps.

53 Major Frampton was present with the 50th Regt. in the battle of Punniar (Medal). Served the campaign on the Sutlej (Medal and two Clasps), including the battles of Moodkee, Ferozeshah, and Aliwal, in which last he was dangerously wounded, and had his arm amputated. Served the Eastern campaign until taken prisoner in the trenches before Sebastopol on the 22nd Dec. 1854, having been present at the battles of Alma and Inkerman (wounded),—Medal and Clasps, and Knight of the Legion of Honor).

55 Major Fraser acted as staff officer to a detachment sent from Bombay in 1837, against the rebels in Canara. He served also in the Kaffir war of 1846-47 (Medal).

War Services of Retired Majors.

56 Major Gavin served with the 16th Lancers during the campaign in Affghanistan under Lord Keane, including the siege and capture of Ghuznee (Medal). He was also present at the battle of Maharajpore, 9th Dec. 1843 (Medal).

57 Major Gell served in the Peninsula in the 20th, and succeeded to the command of the Regt. at the battle of Albuhera, for which he has received the Gold Medal.

59 Major Gordon served at the capture of the Isle of France in 1810, and of Java in 1811, and was wounded at the assault of Fort Cornelius. Served also at the siege and capture of Bhurtpore.

60 Major Graham served with the 42nd Highlanders. Served the Eastern campaign from Dec. 1854, including the expedition to Kertch, siege and fall of Sebastopol, and assault upon the outworks 18th June (Medal and Clasp, and Brevet-Major).

61 Major Grant served with the 14th Regiment in the Nepaul war in 1815; at the siege and capture of the Fortress of Hattras in March 1817; in the Deccan and Pindurree campaigns in 1817 and 1818 under Lord Hastings, and commanded the Light Company when it was attached to a Flank Battalion in 1818. Was present with the 14th Regiment, at the siege and capture of Bhurtpore, and commanded the Grenadier Company when it led the right storming column on the day of the assault, 18th January 1826 (Medal and Clasp).

63 Major Grehan served with the Queen's Royals throughout the campaign in Affghanistan and Beloochistan under Lord Keane, and was present at the storm and capture of Ghuznee (Medal) and of Khelat.

64 Major Grubbe served with the 43rd Lt. Inf. in the Peninsula during the latter part of 1812, and was in action on the 16th Nov. on retreat from Burgos. Was also at New Orleans.

65 Major Hammersley served in the Peninsula from Aug. 1812 to the end of that war in 1814, and was present at the battles of Vittoria and Toulouse, and the investment of, and the Heights before Pampeluna. Shot through the shoulder whilst protecting a house in the neighbourhood of Dublin, on duty in 1806, when in the Militia. He has received the War Medal with two Clasps.

66 Major Wm. Henry Hare accompanied the expedition under Sir David Baird to Corunna, and was present throughout the retreat, and at the battle of Corunna. In Aug. 1809 embarked with the expedition to Walcheren, and was at the siege and capture of Flushing. Served in the Peninsular campaigns of 1811, 12, 13, and 14; and finally at the battle of Waterloo and capture of Cambray.

68 Major Herbert served with the 39th Regt. at the action of Maharajpore on the 29th Dec. 1843 (slightly wounded).

69 Major J. M. Home served the campaign of 1814 in Upper Canada with the 104th Regt.

70 Major Hopkins served with the 43rd Light Infantry during the campaign in Denmark in 1807, including the siege and surrender of Copenhagen, and battle of Kioge. In 1808 landed at Corunna with Sir David Baird's expedition, and joining the army of Sir John Moore was in the various operations until the retreat. In 1809, landed in Portugal with the Light Division, and was at the defending of the passage of the Tagus at Almaraz; in 1810 was engaged in several affairs between Almeida and Ciudad Rodrigo, action of the Coa (severely wounded), battle of Busaco, and various skirmishes; in 1811 engaged at Pombal, Redinha, Condeixa, Miranda de Coorg, Sabugal, and battle of Fuentes d'Onor; in 1812, was present during both the sieges and storming of Ciudad Rodrigo and Badajoz, commanding a Company at the assault of the breaches of each; present at the reduction of the forts of Salamanca, action at Castrajon, battle of Salamanca, and surrender of the Retiro in Madrid; in 1813, action of San Millan, battle of Vittoria, action with the enemy's rearguard on entering the Pyrenees, operations therein, action at the bridge of Yanzi, and attack of the heights of Santa Barbara; present also at the storm and capture of Saint Sebastian. Served in the campaign of 1815 and was at the capture of Paris. Has the War Medal with seven Clasps, and was twice severely wounded.

72 Major Hutton served with the 4th Light Dragoons. Served the Eastern campaign of 1854, including the battles of Alma and Balaklava (severely wounded in both thighs), and siege of Sebastopol (Medal and Clasps).

73 Major R. Inglis served with the 18th Royal Irish in the Crimea in 1854-55, including the siege and fall of Sebastopol, assault and capture of the Cemetry on the 18th June (Medal and Clasp and Brevet Major).

74 Major W. Inglis served in the Eastern campaign of 1854-55, including the battles of Balaklava and Inkerman, and siege of Sebastopol, for which he obtained Brevet rank as Major (Medal and Clasps).

75 Colonel Jacks served the campaign in Naples under Sir James Craig in 1805, and that in Sicily and Calabria under Sir John Stuart in 1806; in 1809 he was at the taking of the Islands of Ischia and Procida in the Bay of Naples. Subsequently he served on the Eastern Coast of Spain, and was present at the actions of Alcoy, Biar, Castalla, Villafranca, and various other affairs. In 1814 he was at the capture of Genoa. In 1835 he raised the 2nd Lancers of the British Legion under Sir De Lacy Evans, and was present in the various actions and other desultory operations of the Legion in Spain. For his services there he has received from the Spanish Government the Cross of Knight of the Military Order of St. Ferdinand (one conferred on the field of battle), and the Commandership of Isabel the Catholic; also the rank of Colonel in the Spanish Army.

76 Major Jackson served in the Sutlej campaign in 1846 with the 16th Lancers, and was present at the affair of Buddiwal, and in the actions of Aliwal and Sobraon (Medal and Clasp).

77 Major Judge accompanied the 27th Regt. on the expedition to Hanover in 1805. Joined the army in Sicily in 1806, and was employed with it, in a Grenadier battalion, during its various

operations, in 1810. Sailed with the force for Naples, and was present at the capture of Ischia and Procida in 1809. Returned to Sicily, and appointed Deputy-Assistant-Quarter-Master-General; employed against the French army in 1811. Served with that department during 1812 and 13 at the battle of Castalla, twice in active siege before Tarragona, in the affair at Villa Franca, and the pass of Balaguer. Rejoined the 27th Regiment, and sailed from Bourdeaux for Canada; present at the battle of Plattsburg, and the severely-contested passage of the Saranac.

78 Major Henry Kean served with the 25th Regiment at the capture of Madeira in 1807; after which he proceeded to the West Indies, where he was employed on the staff for upwards of ten years. He was at the taking of nearly all the West India Islands which were captured from 1809 to 1815, and was frequently mentioned in Dispatches: he has received the War Medal with two Clasps).

79 Lord Keane served on the late General Lord Keane's staff during the campaign in Affghanistan and Beloochistan, and was present at the assault and capture of Ghuznee, for which he has received a Medal.

81 Lord Killeen served with the 8th Hussars in the Crimea, from 19th November 1854, including the expedition to Kertch, siege and fall of Sebastopol (Medal and Clasp).

83 Major Leslie served the campaign of 1814 in Canada; also, with the 72nd Highlanders, the Kaffir campaign of 1834-35 (Medal).

84 Major Lovett served in the 98th Regt. with the expedition to the North of Chin in 1842 (Medal), and was present at the attack and capture of Chin Kiang Foo, and at the landing before Nankin.

86 Major M'Murdo served with the 8th Hussars at the siege of Hattras in 1817, and afterwards in the Pindaree war.

87 Major Manley served with the 6th Dragoons the Eastern campaign of 1854-55, including the battles of Balaklava, Inkerman, and Tchernaya, siege and fall of Sebastopol (Medal and Clasps, and Brevet Major).

88 Major A. L. Marsh served the Eastern campaign of 1854-5, with the 55th Regt., including the battles of Alma and Inkerman (succeeded to the command of the Regt.) and siege of Sebastopol (Medal and Clasps).

89 Major Robert Marsh served with the 24th Regt. in the Peninsula from Aug. 1812 to the end of that war in 1814, and was present at the battles of Vittoria, the Pyrenees, Nivelle (wounded), and Orthes, for which he has the War Medal with four Clasps. Served also the Nepaul campaign of 1815-16, and the Mahratta campaign of 1817-18.

91 Major John Mussy served with the 48th Regt. the campaign against the Rajah of Coorg in April 1834.

92 Major Matson joined the force in New Zealand under Colonel Despard in August 1845, and served as Acting Deputy Quartermaster-General, and was present at the assault and capture of Kawiti's Pah, at Ruapekapeka on the 11th Jan. 1846.

93 Major Mercer served in the 89th Regiment at the siege of Sebastopol, from the 15th December 1854 to the 7th July 1855, including the attack of the 18th June. Was severely contused in the head on the night of the 13th April when in command of a working party, in the trenches (Medal and Clasp and Brevet-Major).

94 Major Meredith served in the Peninsula from Nov. 1813 to June 1814, and was actively employed from the Pyrenees to the battle of Toulouse, at which he was present. Served in Canada in 1814 and 15; present at capture of Rangoon, May 1824. He has received the War Medal with one Clasp for Toulouse.

96 Major Minter served in the Kandian campaigns of 1817 and 18 under Sir Robert Brownrigg, and in the Burman Empire under Sir Archibald Campbell.

98 Major J. P. Mitford served on the Staff throughout the war in China (Medal), and was present at the operations before Canton, and at the investment of Nankin.

99 Major D. A. Monro served with the 12th Lancers in the Kaffir war of 1851-53 (Medal).

101 Major Charles Murray served in the Kandian War in Ceylon in 1817-18.

102 Major William Murray served with the 10th Hussars in the Crimea, from the 30th June 1855, including the battle of the Tchernaya, siege and fall of Sebastopol (Medal and Clasp and Brevet Major).

103 Major Nash served in the American war with the 103rd Regt., and was present at the action of Lundy's Lane, storming of Fort Erie, 15th Aug. 1814,—severely wounded in the leg by a musket-ball, and afterwards blown up by the explosion of a powder-magazine; present also in the action at Chippewa.

105 Major O'Leary served in 1811, 12, and 13, in the Peninsula, including the siege of Ciudad Rodrigo, battle of Salamanca, capture of Madrid, siege of Burgos, and retreat from thence. Served in the Nepaul war, and was severely wounded in taking the heights of Harriapore, 1st March 1816. Served in the Mahratta war in 1817 and 18; and also in China, at Amoy, Chusan, and Chinhae, including the repulse of the night-attack; and was Brigade Major to Colonel P. Craigie at these places, and afterwards Brigade Major to the Chusan Field-force from its formation in Nov. 1842, under the command of Sir James Schoedde, until the return of the 55th Regt. to England in 1844. He has received the Silver War Medal with two Clasps for Ciudad Rodrigo and Salamanca; the Medal for service in India; and also the one for China.

106 Major Ogle served the campaign in Affghanistan under General Pollock, and was wounded in forcing the Khyber Pass, 5th April 1842. He has the Medal for the re-capture of Cabool.

107 Major Orr served with the 7th Fusiliers at the siege and capture of Copenhagen in 1807; at the siege of Martinique in 1809; and in the Peninsula from 1810, including the battle of Albuhera (severely wounded by a musket-ball in the leg), passage of the Eslar and the Ebro, action of Osma, battle of Vittoria, investment of Pampeluna (wounded in the breast by a musket-

ball), action at the Pass of Roncesvalles, battle of the Pyrenees, passage of the Bidassoa, battles of the Nivelle, Nive, and Orthes, besides various minor actions and skirmishes : he has received the War Medal with eight Clasps.

109 Major Paynter served with the 1st Dragoon Guards in the Crimea from Aug. 1855, including the siege and fall of Sebastopol, and battle of the Tchernaya (Medal and Clasp).

111 Major Pollock served with the Light Brigade of Sir John Moore's army in the North of Spain and on the retreat to Corunna. Accompanied his Regiment (the 43rd) to Lisbon, and joined Sir Arthur Wellesley's army at Talavera the day after the battle, and was present in the action near Almeida on the Coa, battle of Busaco, actions of Pombal, Redinha, Miranda de Corvo, Foz d'Arouce, and Sabugal; battle of Fuentes d'Onor, siege and storming of Ciudad Rodrigo, siege and storming of Badajoz, and was severely wounded at the assault.

112 Major the Hon. Charles Powis, prior to entering the army, served five years and three months in the Royal Navy, and was present in H.M.S. *Blonde* at the taking of the Morea Castle, in the Gulf of Lepanto, in 1828. He served with the 9th Lancers in the campaign of 1848-9 in the Punjaub, including the passage of the Chenab at Ramnuggur, and battles of Chillianwallah and Goojerat (Medal and Clasps).

114 Major Rawlinson served with the expedition to Egypt in 1807; at the taking of the island of Zante, 1809; and at the siege of Santa Maura, 1810.

115 Major Henry Reid served at Cadiz from March 1813 to the end of the war. Served also in the American war, including the affair at Hampden.

116 Major Robertson served the campaign of Java, including the investment and storming of Fort Cornelis, storming the heights of Serendole, investment and storming of Djocjocarta, where he was severely wounded through the thigh. Present at the quelling of the insurrection at Proholingo, where his brother officers, Lieut. Colonel Fraser and Captain M'Pherson, were killed Served also in Flanders in 1815.

117 Major Rocke served with the 49th Regt. the Eastern campaign of 1854-55, including the battles of Alma and Inkerman, siege and fall of Sebastopol and sortie of 26th October (Medal and Clasps and Brevet of Major).

119 Major Rutherfoord served with the 4th Regiment, the Eastern campaign of 1854-55, including the battles in the Crimea, siege and fall of Sebastopol (Medal and Clasps).

121 Major Shuckburgh served with the Scots Fusilier Guards the Eastern campaign to November 1854, including the battles of Alma, Balaklava, and Inkerman (severely wounded), and siege of Sebastopol (Medal and Clasp).

123 Major Stuart served at the siege and capture of Kittoor in the East Indies in Dec. 1824.

124 Major Studdert served with the 9th Lancers at the battle of Punniar on 29th Dec. 1843 (Medal).

126 Major Sykes served with the 48th Regt. at the siege and fall of Sebastopol from 21st April 1855 (Medal and Clasp, Brevet of Major, and 5th Class of the Medjidie).

128 Major Thellusson served with the Coldstream Guards at the siege and fall of Sebastopol from 2nd May 1855 (Medal and Clasp, Brevet of Major, and 5th Class of the Medjidie).

130 Major Way served with the 29th Regiment throughout the Punjaub campaign in 1848-9 (Medal), including the passage of the Chenab, and battles of Chillianwallah and Goojerat.

131 Major Webb served with the Rifle Brigade during the campaigns of 1814 and 15 in Holland, the Netherlands, and France, including both the actions at Merxem, bombardment of Antwerp, and battle of Waterloo, at which last he was slightly wounded.

132 Major Weyland served the campaigns in Upper Canada from 1812 to 1815, including the actions at Fort George and Stoney Creek, at which last he was severely wounded.

133 Major Whitney served with the 2nd Battalion 44th Regt. in the Peninsula, and was severely wounded on crossing the Mondego (Medal). Went with the expedition to Holland in 1814, and was at the action of Merxem, bombardment of the French Fleet at Antwerp, and storming of Bergen-op-Zoom, where he was severely wounded and taken prisoner, leading the storming party, when planting the colors on the ramparts. Served the campaign of 1815, and was dangerously wounded while carrying the colors at the battle of Quatre Bras, and severely by a bayonet at Waterloo; was also at the capture of Paris. Served during the Burmese war, including storm and capture of stockades at Ramoo, Ramree, the intrenched positions on the Padway mountains and at Mahatty, led the storming party at the stockades on the heights of Aracan and at the siege and capture of Aracan (Medal).

134 Major Wilkinson served with the 13th Regt. throughout the Burmese war, including the landing at Cheduba, storming the stockade, and capture of the island; affair at Kumaroot, storming seven stockades at Kumaroot, attack and capture of Syriam, actions near Rangoon, on the 1st, 5th, and 7th Dec. 1824; storming of Kokien (wounded); expedition to Bassein, and capture Negrais, Bassein, and Lamina; actions at Sembike and Nadadee, storming of Melloon, and battle of Pagahm Mew. He also served throughout the campaigns in Affghanistan from 1838 to 1842 inclusive, including the expedition to Girishk, storm and capture of Ghuznee (Medal), storming of the Khoord Cabool Pass, affair of Tezeen, forcing the Jugdulluck Pass, reduction of the fort of Mamoo Khail, heroic defence of Jellalabad, and sorties on the 14th Nov. and 1st Dec. 1841, 11th March, 24th March, and 1st April 1842; general action and defeat of Akbar Khan before Jellalabad on the 7th April 1842 (Medal), in which action he commanded the centre column after the fall of Colonel Dennie. Commanded the 13th Regt. in storming the heights of Jugdulluck, in the general action of Tezeen, and at the recapture of Cabool (Medal), for which he has received the Companionship of the Bath.

135 Major Wing served with the 95th Regt. the Eastern campaign of 1854-55, including the battle of Alma (severely wounded) and siege of Sebastopol (Medal and Clasps, Brevet Major, and Sardinian Medal).

Officers Serving with Superior Local Rank, and Temporary Rank. 119

136 Major H. O. Wood served the Peninsular campaign of 1814, including the investment of Bayonne.
137 Major J. J. Wood served with the 18th Royal Irish in the Burmese war of 1852 (Medal. Served with the 82nd Regiment at the siege and fall of Sebastopol from 2nd Sept. 1855 (Medal and Clasp).
138 Major Yard served in the 32nd Regt. at the first and second siege operations before Mooltan, including the attack on the enemy's position in front of the advanced trenches on 12th Sept. 1848, the action of Soorjkoond, storm and capture of the city, and surrender of the fortress; also present at the surrender of the fort and garrison of Cheniote, and at the battle of Goojerat (Medal and Clasps).

OFFICERS SERVING WITH SUPERIOR LOCAL RANK, AND TEMPORARY RANK.

GENERALS.

₰ Colin, Lord Clyde, *GCB. Commander-in-Chief, East Indies*................ 11 July 57

LIEUTENANT-GENERALS.

₰ ₰₰₰ Sir Henry Somerset, *KCB. KH. Commander-in-Chief, Bombay* .... 26 Jan. 55
₰ W. T. Knollys, *Commanding at Aldershot* 15 Jan. 56
Sir Patrick Grant, *KCB. Commander in-Chief at Madras* .... 25 Jan. 56
Sir James Outram, *Bart. GCB. Particular Service in the East Indies* .... 14 Nov. 56
₰ ₰₰₰ Sir James Fred. Love, *KCB. Inspector General of Infantry* .... 14 Aug. 57
Marcus Beresford, *East Indies*............ 11 Sept. 57
Robert H. Wynyard, *CB, Commanding the Forces and Lt.Governor, Cape of Good Hope*................................... 8 Apr. 59
Sir William Fenwick Williams, *Bart. KCB. Commanding the Division in North America* .... May 59
Sir John L. Pennyfather, *KCB. Commanding the Northern District*........ 1 Oct. 59
Sir J. Gaspard Le Marchant, *Governor and Commander-in-Chief at Malta* .... do
Sir James Hope Grant, *KCB. China*...... 18 Oct. 59
Sir Wm. R. Mansfield, *KCB. China* .... 20 Dec. 59

MAJOR-GENERALS.

₰ Henry Frederick Lockyer, *CB. KH. Commanding the Troops at Ceylon* .... 31 Aug. 55

₰₰₰ John Bloomfield, *Inspector General of Artillery*....................... 18 May 59
₰ Edward Macarthur, *CB. Commanding the Troops in Australia* .... 25 Sept. 55
Godfrey Charles Mundy, Unatt., *Commanding the Troops in Jersey*......... 24 Feb. 57
Duncan Alexander Cameron, *CB*.......... 1 June 57
₰ Sir Robt. Garrett, *KCB. KH.East Indies* 7 Aug. 57
Sir Sydney John Cotton, *KCB.* do .. do
Sir John Michel, *KCB.* do .. do
Sir Wm. R. Mansfield, *KCB.* do .. do
Sir Henry Creswicke Rawlinson, *KCB. Envoy Extraordinary and Minister Plenipotentiary in Persia*............. 22 Apr. 59

COLONEL.

* Henry Charles Van Cortlandt, *CB. Commanding a Corps of Irregular Levies, East Indies*........................... 30 Oct. 57

LIEUTENANT-COLONELS.

J. D. G. Tulloch, *Military Superintendent of Pensioners in North America* ...... 20 July 53
John Bruce, *Staff Officer of Pensioners, Western Australia*.................... 26 Sept. 54

MAJOR.

William H. Kenny, *Staff Officer of Pensioners, New Zealand* .... 23 Mar. 49

The following Officers to have the temporary rank of Major-General while in command of Brigades, dated 24 *July,* 1856:—

₰ Wm. Froke Williams, *KH.*
₰ Sir Robert Garrett, *KCB. KH.*
Charles Warren, *CB.*
Lord William Paulet, *CB.*
Sir Charles T. van Straubenzee, *KCB.*
Hon. A. A. Spencer, *CB.* h. p. 44 F,
John Lawrenson, h. p. 6 F.

William Parlby, h. p. 10 Hussars.
Frederick Horn, *CB.* h. p. 20 F.
A. A. T. Cunynghame, *CB,* h. p. 51 F.
Charles Trollope, *CB.* h.p. 62 F.
Arthur J. Lawrence, *CB.* h. p. Rifle Br.
Horatio Shirley, *CB.* h. p. 88 F.
Randal Rumley, Unatt.

GENERAL OFFICERS OF HER MAJESTY'S INDIAN FORCES.

GENERALS.

Sir Hopton Stratford Scott, *KCB.* Mad. Inf.... 20 June 54
Sir James Lilyman Caldwell, *GCB.* Mad, Eng. do
Sir David Leighton, *KCB.* Madras Infantry ... do
James Welsh, do. do
Richard Podmore, Madras Infantry do
Sir Robert Houstoun, *KCB.* Bengal Cavalry... do
George Rees Kemp, Bombay Infantry do
John Alex. Paul Macgregor, Bengal Inf. do
Sir Wm. Richards, *KCB.* Bengal Inf. do
Jerry Francis Dyson, Bombay Infantry do
Alexander Fair, *CB.* Madras Infantry do
William Gilbert, Bombay Infantry do
James Ahmuty, Bengal Artillery 15 Sept. 55
Mossom Boyd, Bengal Infantry 9 April 56
Henry George Andrew Taylor, *CB.* Mad. Inf. 28 Sept. 57
Brook Bridges Parlby, *CB.* Madras Infantry 13 Oct. 57
John Truscott, Bengal Infantry 27 Jan. 58
Edw. Melian Gullifer Showers, Madras Art. 4 Mar.
Patrick Cameron, Madras Cavalry 24 Oct.
John Carfrae, Madras Infantry 5 Mar. 59
George Jackson, do. 13 Mar.
George Swiney, Bengal Artillery 15 May
Sir George Pollock, *GCB.* do. 17 May
Samuel Goodfellow, Bombay Engineers 30 May
Alexander Lindsay, *CB.* Bengal Artillery 11 Sept. 59

LIEUTENANT-GENERALS.

James Stewart Fraser, Madras Infantry 11 Nov. 51
Peter De la Motte, *CB.* Bombay Cavalry do
Edward Frederick, *CB.* Bombay Infantry ... do
George Benjamin Brooks, do. do
Peter Lodwick, do. do
Suetonius Henry Todd, Bengal Infantry do
John Briggs, Madras Infantry do
Henry Thomson, Bengal Cavalry do
Charles William Hamilton, Bengal Infantry... do
Edmund Frederick Waters, *CB.* do. do
Richard Collyer Andrée, do. do
George Mackenzie Stewart, Madras Infantry do
Sir Mark Cubbon, *KCB.* Madras Infantry ... do
Thomas Shubrick, Bengal Cavalry do
Thomas King, Madras Infantry do
William Cullen, Madras Artillery do
David Barr, Bombay Infantry do
Thomas Murrett, Madras Infantry do
Thomas Henry Paul, Bengal Infantry do
Francis Farquharson, Bombay Infantry do
John Henry, Madras Infantry 3 Aug. 55
Samuel Swinhoe, Bengal Infantry 15 Sept.
John Anderson, do. 5 Dec.
Frederick Young, do. 18 Feb. 56
Thomas Monteath Douglas, *CB.* Beng. Inf. 18 Mar.
William R. C. Costley, do. 2 April
Charles Herbert, *CB.*, Madras Infantry 9 April
Sir George Petre Wymer, *KCB.*, Bengal Inf. 8 June
Alexander Dick, Bengal Infantry 4 July
William Pattle, *CB.*, Bengal Cavalry 18 July
Thomas Fiddes, Bengal Infantry 15 Sept.
James Perry, Madras Infantry 6 Dec.
Hugh Ross, do. 29 May 57
James Ketchen, Madras Artillery 13 Oct.
Abraham Roberts, *CB.*, Bengal Infantry 13 Oct.
John Morgan, *CB.*, Madras Infantry 27 Jan. 58
Chas. Arthur G. Wallington, Bengal Inf. 4 Mar.
Thomas Oliver, do 4 May
Sir James Outram, Bart. *GCB.* Bombay Inf. 16 July
Duncan Gordon Scott, Bengal Infantry 23 July
Henry Hall, *CB.* Bengal Infantry 24 Oct.
Julius George Griffith, Bombay Artillery 4 Feb. 59
Samuel Shaw, Bengal Artillery 5
Charles Butler James, Bombay Infantry 15 May
Matthew Coombs Paul, Bengal Infantry 17 May
Sir John Cheape, *KCB.* Bengal Engineers ... 26 May
John Low, *CB.* Madras Infantry 30 May
Joseph Harris, Bengal Infantry 20 Aug.
John Tulloch, *CB.* Bengal Infantry 11
Richard Powney, Bengal Artillery 21
George Edward Gowan, *CB.* Bengal Art. 27 Sept.

MAJOR-GENERALS.

Patrick Montgomerie, *CB.* Madras Artillery... 26 June 54
Wm. Henry Hewitt, Bengal Infantry do
John Home, do. do
Geo. Wm. Aylmer Lloyd, *CB.* Bengal Inf. ... do
Alexander Tulloch, *CB.* Madras Infantry do

Arch. Brown Dyce, Madras Infantry 26 June 54
J. Wheeler Cleveland, do. do
Robert Blackall, Bengal Infantry do
David Capon, *CB.* Bombay Infantry do
Wm. Donald Robertson, do. do
Duncan Sim, Madras Engineers do
George Saudys, Madras Cavalry 28 Nov. 54
James Eckford, *CB.* Bengal Infantry do
Mathew Soppitt, Bombay Infantry do
Andrew Hervey, *CB.* Bengal Infantry do
Sir Scudamore Winde Steel, *KCB.* Mad. Inf. do
Fred. Schuler, Bombay Artillery do
George Moore, Bombay Infantry do
Maurice Tweedie, Madras Infantry do
Charles Montauban Carmichael, *CB.* Ben. Cav. do
Henry Lechmere Worrall, do..... do
Sir John Bennett Hearsey, *KCB.* do...... do
George Richard Pemberton, Bengal Infantry do
Donald Macleod, Madras Cavalry do
Stephen Davis Riley, Bengal Infantry do
Christopher Godley, *CB.* Bengal Infantry ... do
David Cuninghame, Bombay Cavalry do
Charles Dennis Dun, Madras Infantry do
James Parsons, *CB.* Bengal Infantry do
George Warren, do. do
Henry Fisher Salter, *CB.* Bengal Cavalry do
Thomas Mathew Taylor, do. do
Howard Dowker, Madras Infantry do
Henry Sargent, do do
George James Wilson, Bombay Infantry do
Joseph Garnault, Madras Infantry do
Robert Hawkes, Bengal Cavalry do
Arch. Fullerton Richmond, *CB.* Bengal Inf. do
James Bell, Madras Infantry do
George Conran, Madras Artillery do
Sir Patrick Grant, *KCB.* Bengal Infantry, Commander-in-Chief at Madras do
Christopher Dixon Wilkinson, *CB.* Ben. Inf. do
William Taylor, Madras Infantry do
Westrop Watkins, do. do
John Laurie, do. do
James Edwin Williams, Madras Infantry do
Francis Turnley Farrell, Bombay Infantry ... do
William Henry Marshall, Bengal Infantry do
Robert Alexander, Madras Infantry do
John Day Stokes, do. do
Francis Spencer Hawkins, *CB.* Ben. Inf. do
John Kynaston Luard, *CB.* Madras Infantry do
Edward Garstin, Bengal Engineers do
Adolphus Derville, Madras Infantry do
Richard Home, Bengal Infantry do
Sir Rob. John Hussey Vivian, *KCB.*, Mad. Inf. do
Thomas Littleton Green, do. do
Alexander Carnegy, *CB.* Bengal Infantry ... do
George Tomkyns, do. do
Sir Henry Gee Roberts, *KCB.*, Bombay Inf.... do
William Cavaye, Bombay Inf. do
David Forbes, do. do
Francis Straton, Madras Cavalry do
Charles Richard William Lane, *CB.* Ben. Inf. do
William John Gairdner, *CB.* Bengal Infantry do
George Brooke, *CB.* Bengal Artillery do
John Yaldwyn, Madras Infantry do
Benjamin Robertson Hitchins, do. do
Watkin Lewis Williams, Madras Infantry do
Eyre Evans Bruce, Madras Infantry do
Henry Coningham, Madras Cavalry do
William Justice, Madras Infantry do
Henry Chambers Murray Cox, Bengal Inf. ... do
John Hoggan, *CB.* Bengal Infantry ... do
George Huish, *CB.* do. do
Frederick Blundell, *CB.* Madras Artillery...... do
John Campbell, *CB.* Madras Infantry do
Thomas Bowes Forster, do. do
Fra. Frankland Whinyates, Madras Art. do
James Adam Howden, Madras Infantry do
Augustus Clarke, do. do
Charles Hamilton, *CB.* Bengal Infantry do
Edward Armstrong, Madras Infantry do
Maurice Stack, *CB.* Bombay Cavalry do
William Wyllie, *CB.* Bombay Infantry do
Walter Jno. Browne, *CB.* do. do
Philip Francis Story, *CB.* Bengal Cavalry 13 April 55
Alexander Woodburn *CB.* Bombay Inf. 1 May
George Grantham, Madras Infantry 3 Aug.
Henry Cracklow, Bombay Infantry 22 Aug.
William Prescott, Madras Infantry 15 Sept. 55
Henry Lawrence, Bengal Infantry 5 Dec.
Richard Budd, Madras Infantry 10 Feb. 56
George Hicks, *CB.* Bengal Infantry 18 Feb.

General Officers of Her Majesty's Indian Forces.

Henry Francis Caley, Bengal Infantry .... 18 Mar. 56
Hope Dick, do. .... 2 April
Joseph Nash, *CB.*, Bengal Infantry .... 9 April
James Alexander, *CB.*, Bengal Artillery ...... 18 May
John Theophilus Lane, *CB.* Bengal Artillery 8 June
George Hutton, Madras Infantry .... 4 July
Robert Stewart, Bengal Infantry .... 15 Sept.
Edward Pentingall, do. .... 4 Nov.
Henry Hancock, Bombay Infantry .... 28 Nov.
Edward Huthwaite, *CB.* Bengal Artillery...... 14 Mar. 57
Isaac Campbell Coffin, Madras Infantry ...... 29 May
Sir George Cornish Whitlock, *KCB.* do. .... 27 June
Fred. George Lister, Bengal Infantry ....22 Aug.
Sir Archdale Wilson, *Bart. KCB.* Bengal Art. 14 Sept.
David Downing, Bengal Infantry .... 15 Sept.
Thomas Macknight Cameron, Madras Infantry 3 Oct.
Walter Nugent Thos. Smee, do. 8 Oct.
Thomas Chase Parr, do. 13 Oct.
Fred. Hervey Sandys, Bengal Infantry .... 15 Oct.
Henry Prior, Madras Infantry.................... 2 Dec. 57
Nicholas Johnson, do. .... 3 Dec.
John Moule, Bengal Infantry..................... 27 Jan. 58
Louis Saunders Bird, Bengal Infantry......... 4 Mar.
David Birrell, do. .... 1 May
Thomas Polwhele, do. .... 4 May
Richard James Holwell Birch. *CB.* Beng. Inf. 1 May
George Campbell, Bengal Artillery .... 4 July

Peter Innes, Bengal Infantry .... 13 July 58
Alex. William Lawrence, Madras Cavalry...... 20 July
Sir Fred. Abbott, *CB.* late of Beng. Engineers,
 *Lieut. Governor of the Military College at
 Addiscombe* .... 23 July
John Fowler Bradford, *CB.* Bengal Cavalry ... do
Harry Meggs Graves, Bengal Infantry .... 27 Aug.
Charles Grant, *CB.* Bengal Artillery............ 14 Oct.
Archibald Spiers Logan, Madras Infantry ... 24 Nov.
Charles Æneas Shirreff, Madras Artillery...... 14 Nov.
Edward Messiter, Madras Infantry .... 23 Nov.
Stuart Corbett, *CB.* Bengal Infantry .... 4 Feb. 59
Henry Macan, Bombay Infantry .... 5 Mar.
William Sage, Bengal Infantry .... 13 Mar.
Sir Justin Sheil, *KCB.* do. .... 26 Apr.
Charles Wahab, Madras Infantry .... 6 May
James Manson, Bengal Infantry............... 15 May
George Twemlow, Bengal Artillery .... 17 May
Thomas Assheton Duke, Madras Infantry . 26 May
Nathaniel Jones, Bengal Infantry .... 30 May
James Clarke Charnock Gray, do .... 20 July
Thomas David Carpenter, Madras Infantry... 29 Aug.
Thomas Alex. Aug. Munsey, Madras Cavalry 11 Sept.
Robert Thorpe, Madras Infantry .... 21 Sept.
James Scott, Bombay Infantry .... 27 Sept.
Charlton Holl, Madras Infantry .... 25 Oct.
Charles Hewetson, Madras Infantry............ 28 Nov.

YEOMEN OF THE GUARD.
Her Majesty's Body Guard.
(INSTITUTED BY HENRY VII., IN THE YEAR 1485.)

Captain.—Henry John, *Earl of* Ducie, 28 June 59.
Lieutenant.—Sir Benjamin Travell Philipps, *Major-General late of Bengal Army*, 23 July 57.
Ensign.—𝔅 Sir George Houlton,¹ *Capt.* h.p. 43rd Foot, 25 Sept. 35.
Clerk of the Cheque and Adjutant.—𝔅 𝔚 John FitzMaurice,² KH., *Colonel* h.p. Unatt , 22 Apr. 47.

Exons.

𝔅 𝔚 Sir John Kincaid,³ *late a Captain in the Rifle Brigade*, 25 Oct. 44.
Thomas Parker Rickford, *late a Captain in the 23rd Fusiliers*, 24 May 51.
George Varnham Macdonald, *late Captain* 19*th Foot*, 6 Feb. 55.
Magnus Forbes Morton Herbert, *late Captain* 48*th Foot*, 6 Mar. 56.

140 Yeomen.

Agents.—Messrs. Cox & Co.

1 Sir George Houlton served in the Peninsula with the 43rd Light Infantry, through the whole of the retreat to Corunna under Sir John Moore in 1808. Served also in the Walcheren expedition in 1809. Subsequently in the Peninsula, including the retreat to the Lines of Torres Vedras in 1810, pursuit of Massena, actions of Pombal, Redinha, Casal Nova, Miranda de Corvo, Foz d'Arouce, Sabugal, Castrejon, San Christoval, San Munos, and San Milan; battles of Fuentes d'Onor, Salamanca, Vittoria (severely wounded), Pyrenees, Nivelle, Nive (9th, 10th, 11th, 12th, and 13th Dec. 1813), and Toulouse; siege and storming of Ciudad Rodrigo, and taking of the outwork of that place, Fort Reynard; and siege and storming of Badajoz. Has received the Silver War Medal with ten Clasps. Served in the storming of the Lines of New Orleans, and afterwards with the Army of Occupation in France.

2 Colonel FitzMaurice joined the Rifle Brigade in the Peninsula as a volunteer, in 1811, and served to the end of the war, including the affair at the Mill at Freixadas, action of Sabugal, battle of Fuentes d'Onor, sieges and assaults of Ciudad Rodrigo and Badajoz, action at San Milan, and battle of Vittoria—skirmishing in advance, he there with two Riflemen, took the *first* gun captured that day, and secured seven prisoners; pursued the enemy to Pampeluna, under the walls of which their *last* gun was taken; battles of the Pyrenees, carrying the heights of Echalar, and the fortified pass of Bera; defended an orchard in front of Arcangues for a whole day with one sub-division; battles of the Nivelle and the Nive, together with those near Bayonne on the 10th, 11th and 13th Dec, 1813; the brilliant action with Soult's rear-guard at Tarbes, and battle of Toulouse, besides numerous minor affairs. He served also the campaign of 1815, led the advanced guard at the battle of Quatre Bras, where he had the honor of firing the first shot. Leg broken at the storming of Badajoz, and severely wounded in the thigh at Quatre Bras. Received the Hanoverian Order, the Waterloo Medal, and the Silver War Medal with eight Clasps.

3 Sir John Kincaid joined the Rifle Brigade in 1809, and retired from it as a Captain in 1831. He served on the Walcheren expedition in 1809; and subsequently in the Peninsula, including the retreat to the lines of Torres Vedras in 1810, occupation of them, pursuit of Massena, actions at Santarem, Pombal, Redinha, Casal Nova, Foz d'Arouce (wounded), and Sabugal, battle of Fuentes d'Onor, actions near Fuente Guinaldo and Aldea de Ponte, siege and storming of Ciudad Rodrigo,—was one of the leaders of the storming party of the Light Division; siege and storming of Badajoz, actions on the heights of San Christoval and at Castrejon, battle of Salamanca, capture of Madrid, retreat from Salamanca, in which he was acting Brigade-Major to the 1st Brigade of the Light Division; actions at San Munos and San Milan, battle of Vittoria, and three days' severe skirmishing in following the enemy to Pampeluna, which ended in the capture of their last gun by the Rifle Brigade; battles of the Pyrenees, storming the heights of Echalar, storming the fortified heights of Bera, battles of the Nivelle and the Nive, together with those near Bayonne on the 9th, 10th, 11th, 12th, and 13th Dec. 1813; action at Tarbes, and battle of Toulouse, besides numerous minor affairs. Served also the campaign of 1815, was present at the battle of Quatre Bras, the retreat on the following day, battle of Waterloo, and capture of Paris: at Waterloo his horse was wounded in five places and killed under him. He has received the Silver War Medal with nine Clasps.

HONORARY PHYSICIANS TO HER MAJESTY.

𝔅 Sir John Mac Andrew, *MD. KCB.*, h.p. Inspector General of Hospitals .... 16 Aug. 59
Andrew Ferguson, M.D., h.p. Inspector General of Hospitals .... do
William Linton, *MD. CB.*, Inspector General of Hospitals .... do
John Forrest, *MD. CB.*, Inspector General of Hospitals .... do
James B. Brown Gibson, *MD. CB.*, Inspector General of Hospitals .... do
Thomas Galbraith Logan, *MD. CB.*, Inspector General of Hospitals .... do

HONORARY SURGEONS TO HER MAJESTY.

Thomas Alexander, *CB.*, Director General of the Army Medical Department ...... 16 Aug. 59
Alexander Melvin, h.p. Inspector General of Hospitals .... do
John Robert Taylor, *CB.*, Inspector General of Hospitals........................ do
Edward Bradford, h.p. Deputy Inspector General of Hospitals .... do
𝔅 𝔚 Thomas Mostyn, h. p. Deputy Inspector General of Hospitals .... do
John Ashton Bostock, *MD.*, Surgeon Major, Scots Fusilier Guards............... do

THE HONOURABLE CORPS OF GENTLEMEN-AT-ARMS,
The Body Guard of the Sovereign on all Public and State occasions.
(ESTABLISHED IN THE YEAR 1509.)

Captain.	Lieutenant.
Thomas Henry, Lord Foley.... 28 June 59	Sir William Topham..........P 18 Mar. 53

Standard Bearer.—David James Harmar, P 31 Jan. 48.

Gentlemen-at-Arms.

George Winchester ....P 30 Jan. 38	Charles Richard John Sawyer .. 6 Mar. 56
ⓑ John Blakiston[1] (*late Bt.Maj.*) 8 Dec. 43	Harwick Doncaster ....P 6 Mar. 56
ⓑ John Henry Cooke[2] .... 2 Oct. 44	Fred. John Robinson ....P 16 April 56
(*Brevet Lt.-Col. late of* 21 *F.*)	*Lt.-Col.* Francis Wheatley ....P 3 June 56
Francis Vanderlure Mills ......P 16 Nov. 48	Stephen Ryder Dampier ......P 19 July 56
Edward Goodwin, *Captain*	(*Capt. Aberdeen Militia*)
Cambridge Militia ....P 22 June 49	John Dutton Hunt ....P 13 June 57
Stapleton Charles Cotton ......P 16 Oct. 49	Sir Henry Orlando Robert Cham-
Charles Tyler ....P 12 Feb. 50	berlain, *Bart.* (*late Lt.* 23 *F.*) P 24 Oct. 57
Henry Shephard Smyth ......P 24 Aug. 50	Arthur Palliser ....P 22 Apr. 58
Thomas Howard ....P 20 Nov. 50	John Robin Harris ....P 11 June 58
Adolphus Geo. Finch Cotton ..P 21 Jan. 51	Nathaniel George Philips[6] ....P 9 July 58
Charles James Cox ....P 25 Feb. 51	(*late Capt.* 47 *F.*)
Markland Barnard ....P 14 May 51	James Lowndes, *Capt. Renfrew*
E. Sutherland (*late Brevet-Maj.*) 26 Feb. 52	*Militia*....................P 4 Nov. 58
Wm.Domvile(*late Capt.*2nd *F.*) P 6 Apr. 52	Frederic Stocks Bentley........P 15 Nov. 58
Francis John Helyar........,'..P 26 Apr. 52	Edward Pope Deane ....P 18 Feb. 59
Wm. Handcock Middleton ....P 6 May 54	James Hanning ....P 23 Feb. 59
Charles James Lindam,[3] *late of*	Sir Charles Henry John Rich,*Bt.*P 4 Mar.59
Rifle Brigade .... 19 May 54	Fred. Sykes Daubeney[7] ......P 5 Mar.59
Robert Grange ....P 3 Aug. 54	(*late Captain* 44 *F.*)
(*late Capt. Bengal Army*)	John W. Cheney Ewart ......P 26 May 59
Geo. Bridge, (*Capt. h.p.*)...... 1 Nov. 54	Rich. Hen. Stackhouse Vyvyan,
James W. Cookney ....P 5 July 55	*Lt. Cornwall Rangers*...... P 22 July 59
Arthur Hinton Moore ....P 1 Jan. 56	James Peters ....P 8 Aug. 59
Aug. Sam. Bolton[4](*late Capt.*31*F.*) 7 Feb. 56	

Adjutant.—William Walter Cargill, P 10 April 56.
Harbinger.—Samuel Wilson, P 24 Feb. 31.
Sub-Officers.—ⓑ Lt.-Col. Cooke, 24 June 48.
Scarlet—*Facing Blue Velvet.*   *Agents*—Messrs. Cox and Co.

1 Major Blakiston having passed through the Royal Military Academy at Woolwich in 1802, he proceeded to India as a Cadet in the East India Company's Service, and was appointed to the Corps of Engineers on the Madras Establishment, being then on half-pay as a Lieutenant in H.M. Service. In 1803 he served in the campaign against the Mahrattas, and was engaged in the battles of Assaye and Argaum, and at the sieges and assaults of Ahmednuggur and Gawilghur. At the suppression of the mutiny at Vellore in 1805 he directed the guns by which the gate was blown open. In 1810 he acted as Chief Engineer at the capture of the Island of Bourbon. Having been employed in reconnoitring the coast of the Isle of France previous to the arrival of the expedition, he was instrumental in discovering the spot where the descent was made; and, having been appointed to the charge of the Guides, he led the advance of the Army until the surrender of that Island. For his services on the above occasion he was nominated Extra Aide-de-Camp to the Commander-in-Chief, Sir Samuel Auchmuty, on the expedition to Java in 1811; and having been sent in advance with the Chief Engineer to fix on the point of landing, he was engaged in a serious affair on the coast in the boats of H. M. ships *Barracouta* and *Leda.* On the landing of the Army he was engaged in the affairs of Wellevrieden and Samarang, and at the siege and assault of the fortified position of Cornelis. In 1812, having attained the rank of Captain in the corps of Madras Engineers, he returned on furlough to England. Shortly afterwards, having been placed on full pay in H. M. 87th Regt., he was appointed to a Company in the 17th Portuguese Regt., with which he served in the Light Division of the Peninsular Army until the conclusion of the war; having been present at the battles of Vittoria, Nivelle, Nive, Orthes, and Toulouse, and in all the affairs in which the Light Division was engaged. At the siege of San Sebastian he volunteered as an Engineer, and while so engaged was severely wounded. For his services on this occasion he was promoted to a Company in the 27th Regt.; in 1816 was placed on half-pay; and on the 23rd June 1843 he was brought on full pay of the 51st Regt., and retired by the sale of his commissions. He has received the War Medal with six Clasps; also the Indian War Medal and Clasps.

2 Lt.-Col. Cooke served with the 43rd Regt. at Walcheren, in 1809. In June 1811 he joined the Light Division in the Peninsula, and was present at the siege and storming of Ciudad Rodrigo, and of Badajoz (wounded at the assault), actions of Castrejon and San Christoval, battle of Salamanca, actions of San Munoz and San Milan, battle of Vittoria (wounded), actions in the Pyrenees, siege of San Sebastian, the attack on the heights of Vera, battle of the Nivelle, battles of the Nive on the 9th, 10th, 11th, 12th, and 13th Dec., actions at Tarbes and Arcangues, battle of Toulouse, besides various affairs of less importance. On the 8th Jan. 1815, he was present at the attack on the American Lines before New Orleans. He served afterwards with the Army during the Occupation in France. He has received the War Medal with eight Clasps.

3 Captain Lindam served in the 10th Foot in the Sutlej campaign of 1845-46, and was severely wounded (lost a leg) at the battle of Sobraon (Medal). He served also four years as Paymaster in the Rifle Brigade in British Caffraria, including the Kaffir war of 1846-47.

4 Captain Augustus S. Bolton served the campaign on the Sutlej (Medal and three Clasps). He acted as Aide-de-Camp to Sir Harry Smith at Moodkee and Ferozeshah, and was Adjutant of the 31st at Buddiwal, Aliwal, and Sobraon (severely wounded).

6 Captain Philips served with the 47th Regt. in the Eastern campaign of 1854, and was severely wounded at the battle of Alma (Medal and Clasp).

7 Captain Daubeney served with the 55th Regt. on the China expedition in 1842 (Medal), and was present at the escalade and capture of Chin Kiang Foo, where he carried the Regimental Colour, which was shot in two places.

OFFICERS RECEIVING REWARDS
FOR DISTINGUISHED OR MERITORIOUS SERVICES.

Generals.
ȹ John M'Kenzie
Dennis Herbert
Cosmo Gordon
Helier Touzel
ȹ H. C. E. Vernon, *CB.*

Lieutenant General.
ȹ John Drummond

Major Generals.
Hon. T. Ashburnham, *CB.*
Sir Michael Creagh, *KH.*
ȹ⚔ W. Beckwith, *KH.*
ȹ⚔ A. T. Maclean
Sir George Buller, *KCB.*
ȹ Henry E. Robinson
ȹ Benjamin Orlando Jones
Sir A. Josias Clocté, *CB. KH.*
G. H. Lockwood, *CB.*
Sir Richard Airey, *KCB.*
Hon. Sir J. Y. Scarlett, *KCB.*
ȹ B. V. Derinzy, *KH.* ret. full pay
ȹ⚔ Charles Diggle, *KH.*
John Eden, *CB.*
ȹ John Geddes, *KH.*
ȹ Thomas G. Ball
ȹ Fred. Maunsell
John W. Frith
ȹ⚔ John Cox, *KH.*
⚔ Eaton Monins
ȹ⚔ George Macdonald
Charles Ash Windham, *CB.*
ȹ John Alves, ret. f. p. Depôt Batt.
ȹ⚔ Wm. Henry Elliott, *KH.*
Pringle Taylor, *KH.*
ȹ W. F. Williams, *KH.*
Plomer Young, *KH.*
H. D. Townshend
Thomas Wright, *CB.*
Sir John Eardley Wilmot Inglis, *KCB.*
Sir James Hope Grant, *KCB.*
Sir T. H. Franks, *KCB,* 10 F.
Sir Edward Lugard, *KCB.*
M. J. Slade
Lord William Paulet, *CB.*
George H. MacKinnon, *CB.*
C. Warren, *CB.*
John N. Jackson
Hon. Geo. F. Upton, *CB.*
⚔ Arthur Hill Trevor, *KH.*
Sir S. J. Cotton, *KCB.*
R. H. Wynyard, *CB.*
T. S. Pratt, *CB.*
J. R. Young
R. W. Brough
ȹ H. F. Lockyer, *CB. KH.*
M. C. Johnstone
ȹ Sir Robert Garrett, *KCB. KH.*
Sir John Michel, *KCB.*
ȹ Geo. Bell, *CB.*
ȹ P. M'Pherson, *CB.*

Charles William Ridley, *CB.*
D. A. Cameron, *CB.*
ȹ⚔ Rob. Law, *KH.*
Sir C. T. Van Straubenzee, *KCB.*

Colonels.
F. Horn, *CB.*, h. p. 20 F.
John R. Smyth, *CB.* I. F. O.
ȹ Sir John M. Wilson, *CB. KH.*
ȹ ⚔ J. Fitzmaurice, Unatt.
John Grattan, *CB.*, h. p. 18 F.
H. Shirley, *CB.*, h. p. 88 F.
W. O'Grady Haly, *CB.*, 88 F.
Lord George Paget, *CB.*, Unatt.
Hon. A. A. Spencer, *CB.*, h. p. 44 F.
A J. Lawrence, *CB.*, h.p. Rifle Brigade
David Russell, *CB.* Insp. Field Officer
Frank Adams, *CB.*, 28 F.
William Sullivan, *CB.*, Insp. Field Off.
L. S. O'Connor, *CB.*, 1 W.India Regt.
William Parlby, h. p. 10 Drs.
Sir H. K. Storks, *KCB.* Unatt.
ȹ ⚔ Thomas C. Smith, Unatt.
William Jones, *CB.* 61 F.
Edw. C. Hodge, *CB.*, Unatt.
W. S. Norcott, *CB.*, Depôt Batt.
ȹ Henry John French, Unatt.
Terence O'Brien, Unatt.
H. F. Robe, *CB.* Unatt.
E. W. F. Walker, *CB.* Scots Fus. Gds.
ȹ E. R. Hill, h. p. 63 F.
C. Trollope, *CB.*, h. p. 62 F.
T. A. Drought, Insp. Field Officer
W. Hamilton, *CB.* I. F. Officer
Arthur Borton, *CB.* Depôt Batt.
Daniel Lysons, *CB.* Unatt.
G. T. Finucane, ret. full pay
Walter Unett, 3 Drs.
H. C. B. Daubeney, *CB.*, h. p. 71 F.
John Thornton Grant, *CB.*, 40 F.
J. T. Mauleverer, *CB.*, 30 F.
James Creagh, ret. f. p. 86 F.
J. P. Sparks, *CB.* 38 F.
G. Campbell, *CB.* 52 F.
Charles Steuart, *CB.*, 14 Drs.
Sir John Jones, *KCB.* 60 F.
ȹ T. J. Adair, Unatt.
William Sutton, 31 F.
R. H. Lowth, *CB.* 86 F.
Charles Franklyn, *CB.* I. F. Officer
Sir Robert Walpole, *KCB.* Rifle Brigade
Thomas Hooke Pearson, Unatt.
L. Fyler, 12 Drs.
A. A. T. Cunynghame, *CB.*, h. p. 51 F.
A. H. Horsford, *CB.* Rifle Brigade
E. H. Greathed, *CB.* Unatt.

Lieutenant Colonels.
Edward W. C. Wright, Depôt Batt.
T. M. Byrne, Unatt.

Ensign.
Colin Macdonald, h. p. 50 F.

Quarter Masters.
James Murray, h. p. 24 F.
T. W. Edwards, h. p. 84 F.
ȹ⚔ John Payne, late of Gr. Gds.
ȹ ⚔ Wm. Kerr, h. p. 28 F.

ROYAL ARTILLERY.
Generals.
F. W. Tobin
ȹ ⚔ Sir Hew D. Ross, *GCB.*
ȹ ⚔ Sir R. Gardiner, *GCB. KCH.*
ȹ Robert Douglas, *CB.*

Lieutenant General.
⚔ W. A. Mercer
ȹ William Cator, *CB.*

Major Generals.
Henry William Gordon
ȹ⚔ William Brereton, *CB. KH.*
John E. Dupuis, *CB.*
Sir Richard James Dacres, *KCB.*
ȹ⚔ William Bell
ȹ P. V. England
ȹ⚔ R. Harding, *KH.*
⚔ W. C. Anderson

Colonel.
⚔ Collingwood Dickson, *CB.*

Lieutenant Colonel.
J. M. Adye, *CB.*

Lieutenant.
J. G. Burslem

Quarter Master.
S. Barnes

ROYAL ENGINEERS.
Generals.
ȹ Sir John F. Burgoyne, Bart. *GCB.*

Lieutenant Generals.
⚔ John Oldfield, *KH.*
Sir J. M. Fred. Smith, *KH.*

Major Generals.
ȹ Sir Harry D. Jones, *KCB.*
ȹ W. C. Ward.
ȹ W. R. Ord.
T. Foster.

Colonel.
F. E. Chapman, *CB.*

MEDICAL DEPARTMENT.
Inspectors General of Hospitals.
Sir John Hall, *M.D. KCB.* h. p.
ȹ Sir John MacAndrew, *M.D. KCB.* h. p.
James Henderson, *M.D.* h. p.

ROYAL MARINES.
General.
John Rawlins Coryton

Colonels.
A. B. Stransham
Alexander Anderson

MILITARY KNIGHTS OF WINDSOR.

Major Charles Moore, formerly of 32 F. (*Governor*)
ȹ ⚔ Quarter Master A. Heartley, h.p. R.Horse Gds.
ȹ Lieut. Tho. M'Dermott, late 7 R. Vet. Bn.
ȹ ⚔ Major Robert Cochrane, late of Rifle Br.
Captain A. W. Cassan, formerly of 65 F.
ȹ Lieut. Richard Nantes, h.p. 55 F.
ȹ Colonel William Sall, *KH.* late of R. Newf. Cos.
Colonel James Fitzgibbons, late of Canadian Militia
Captain Andrew Ellison, formerly of 60 F.

ȹ Captain John Duncan King, h. p. Unatt.
ȹ Captain James Scott, h. p. 9 F.
ȹ Captain Henry Hollinsworth, Unatt.
ȹ Colonel E. A. Angelo, *KH.* late of 80 F.
ȹ Captain George Loggan, late of 7 F.
ȹ Captain Joseph Douglas, Unatt.
ȹ Major John Paul Hopkins, *KH.* late of 98 F.
⚔ Captain S. Goddard, h. p. 14. F.
ȹ Lieut. Rowland Pennington, late R. Vet. Bn.

STAFF AT HEAD QUARTERS.

COMMANDING IN CHIEF.

General *His Royal Highness* George W. F. C. *Duke of* Cambridge, KG., KP., GCB., GCMG.
Colonel of the Scots Fusilier Guards.

Military Secretary ...... 𝔙 𝔐 Lieut.General *Sir* Charles Yorke, KCB., 33rd Foot.

Aides de Camp ..
- Lt.Colonel *Hon.* James Wm. B. Macdonald, CB., Unatt.
- Lieut.Colonel Thomas Henry Clifton, Unatt.
- Colonel Charles Tyrwhitt, Unatt.
- Lt.Colonel F. W. H. *Earl of* Westmorland, CB., Coldst. Guards.
- Lieut.Colonel G. A. Maude, CB. Royal Artillery (*Extra*).

ADJUTANT-GENERAL'S DEPARTMENT.

Adjutant General ...... Lieut.General *Sir* George Aug. Wetherall, KCB. KH., 84th Foot.
Deputy Adjutants General { Major General William Frederick Forster, KH.
{ Colonel *Sir* Thos. St. Vincent H. C. Troubridge, *Bt.* CB., h.p., 22 F. .
Assistant Adjutants General { Colonel James Kennard Pipon, Unattached.
{ Colonel Brook Taylor, Unatt.
Deputy Assist. Adjutant General ..... Major Richard L. Otway Pearson, Gr. Gds.
Superintendent of the Recruiting Department .. Colonel David Russell, CB.

Deputy Adjutant General to the Royal Artillery .... Colonel Charles Bingham.
Assistant Adjutant General do. .... Colonel Edwin Wodehouse, CB.
Deputy Assistant Adjutant General do. .... Capta'n Wm. Lambert Yonge.

Deputy Adjutant-General to the Royal Engineers .... Colonel John Wm. Gordon, CB.

QUARTER-MASTER GENERAL'S DEPARTMENT.

Quarter-Master General .... Major General *Sir* Richard Airey, KCB.
Deputy Quarter Master General .... Colonel *Hon.* Alexander Gordon, CB. Unattached.
Assistant Quarter Master General ... Colonel Terence O'Brien, Unattached.
Deputy Assistant Quarter Master General .. Major B. D. W. Ramsay, Unatt.

INSPECTOR GEN. OF INFANTRY .. 𝔙 𝔐 Lt.Gen. *Sir* Jas. Fred. Love, KCB. KH., 57 F.

Aides de Camp .... { Major G. H. Page, 41 F.
{ Major Taylor L. Mayne, Unatt.
Assistant Adjutant General .... Colonel Daniel Lysons, CB. Unatt.

Inspecting General attached to the Foot Guards ..... 𝔐 Major General *Lord* Rokeby, KCB.
Aide de Camp .... Captain Charles Napier Sturt, Gren. Guards.
Assistant Adjutant General .... Lieut.Colonel *Lord* Arthur Hay, Gr. Gds.

INSPECTING GENERAL OF CAVALRY .. Major-General *The Earl of* Cardigan, KCB.
Aide de Camp .... Lieut. W. D. N. Lowe, 3 Drs.
Assistant Adjutant General .... Colonel John Douglas, CB., h.p.

AIDES-DE-CAMP TO THE QUEEN.

Colonel T. Wood, Royal East Middlesex Militia.
———— John Le Couteur, Jersey Militia.
𝔙 𝔐 ———— Cha. *D. of* Richmond, *KG.* Sussex Mil.
———— James Priaulx, Guernsey Militia.
———— *Marquis of* Donegall, *G CH.* Antrim Mil.
———— *Lord* Dynevor, R. Carmarthen Militia.
———— George Thos. Conolly Napier, *CB.* Unatt.
———— *Sir* Thos. St. Vincent H. C. Troubridge, *Bt. CB.*, h. p. 22 F.
———— *Hon.* H. H. M. Percy, *CB.* Gr. Gds.
———— T. M. Steele, *CB.* Coldst. Gds.
———— Henry Darby Griffith, *CB.* 2 Drs.
———— James Webber Smith, *CB.* Unatt.
———— *Hon.* Percy E. Herbert, *CB.* 62 F.
———— Collingwood Dickson, *CB.* R. Art.
———— William S. R. Norcott, *CB.* Depot Batt.
———— John William Gordon, *CB.* R. Eng.
———— *H.S.H. Prince* W. A. Edward of Saxe Weimar, *CB.* Gr. Gds.
———— Wm. M. S. M'Murdo, *CB.* Military Train.
———— Edward Robert Wetherall, *CB.* Unatt.

Colonel John Christie, Bengal Cavalry.
———— Henry Atwell Lake, *CB.* Unatt.
———— Thomas Holloway, *CB.* R. Marines.
———— W. F. *Duke of* Buccleuch, *KG.* Edinburgh Militia.
———— John Wilson Patten, 3 R. Lancashire Mil.
———— Robert Alex. Shafto Adair, Suffolk Artillery Militia.
———— G. W. F. *Marquis of* Ailesbury, R. Wilts Yeomanry Cavalry.
———— Neville Bowles Chamberlain, *CB.* Beng.InA
———— John Alex. Ewart, *CB.* 78 F.
———— William Parke, *CB.*, 72 F.
———— Charles Reid, *CB.* Bengal Army.
———— Richard Baird Smith, *CB.* Bengal Army.
———— Thomas Tapp, *CB.* Bombay Army.
———— C. H. Robertson, *CB.* Bombay Army.
———— Edwin Wodehouse, *CB.* R. Artillery.
———— George Bent, *CB.* Royal Engineers.
———— Wm. Friend Hopkins, *CB.* R. Marines.

† B

1st Regiment of Life Guards.

"PENINSULA" "WATERLOO."

Colonel.

Years' Serv.		
Full Pay	Half Pay	
70		ῼ Stapleton, *Viscount* Combermere,[1] GCB. GCH. 2nd *Lieut.* 26 Feb. 1790; *Lieut.* 16 March 91; *Capt.* 28 Feb. 93; *Major*, March 94; *Lieut.-Col.* 9 March 94; *Col.* 1 Jan. 1800; *Maj.-Gen.* 30 Oct. 05; *Lt.-Gen.* 1 Jan. 12; *Gen.* 27 May 25; *Field-Marshal,*[2] Oct. 55; *Col.* 1st Life Guards, 16 Sept. 29.

Lieut.-Colonel and Colonel.

38	0	Richard Parker, *Cornet*, p 2 Aug. 22; *Lieut.* p 31 July 25; *Capt.* p 30 June 28; *Brevet-Major,* 23 Nov. 41; *Major & Lt.-Col.* 9 Nov. 46; *Col.* 20 June 54; *Lt.-Col. & Col.* 20 June 54.

Major and Lieut.Colonel.

15	0	Hon. Dudley Charles FitzGerald de Ros, *Cornet & Sub.Lieut.* p 7 Feb. 45; *Lieut.* p 5 May 48; *Capt.* p 31 Oct. 51; *Major & Lt.Col.* p 30 Aug. 59.

		CAPTAINS.	COR. AND SUB-LIEUT.	LIEUT.	CAPTAIN.	BREVET-MAJOR.
16	0	G.H. *Earl of* MountCharles	p 31 Dec. 44	19 Oct. 50	p 4 Aug. 54	
12	0	Henry, *Visct.* Elmley	p 5 May 48	p 13 Dec. 50	p 1 Dec. 54	
11	0	Richard Bateson	p 10 Mar. 49	p 31 Oct. 51	p 15 May 55	
11	0	Henry Wyndham	p 27 April 49	p 16 Jan. 52	p 22 June 55	
9	0	Algernon William Peyton	p 19 Aug. 51	p 4 Aug. 54	p 26 Feb. 56	
8	0	James Keith Fraser	p 16 April 52	p 23 Mar. 55	p 17 Nov. 57	
7	0	*Hon.* Robert W. Grosvenor	p 5 Aug. 53	p 22 June 55	p 8 Apr. 59	
6	0	*Lord* Charles W. B. Bruce	p 18 Aug. 54	p 26 Feb. 56	p 30 Aug. 59	
		LIEUTENANTS.				
6	0	*Hon.* Cecil Duncombe	p 3 Nov. 54	p 29 Feb. 56		
6	0	M. W. *Visct.* Powerscourt	p 1 Dec. 54	p 30 Sept. 56		
5	0	Eustace J. Wilson Patton	p 12 July 55	p 1 May 57		
5	0	*Hon.* Seym. J. G. Egerton	p 13 July 55	p 28 Aug. 57		
5	0	Rd. Myddelton Biddulph	p 21 Dec. 55	p 17 Nov. 57		
4	0	*Hon.* Wm. H. John North	p 8 Feb. 56	p 8 Apr. 59		
4	0	Chas. Wilmer Duncombe	p 22 July 56	p 26 Aug. 59		
3	0	J. H. R. *Lord* Earlsfort	p 26 Mar. 57	p 30 Aug. 59		
		CORNETS AND SUB-LIEUTENANTS.				
10	0	William Hessey, R.M.	13 Dec. 50			
6	0	John Limbert, *Adj.*	7 July 54			
3	0	Herbert Hay Langham	p 27 Mar. 57			
3	0	Edward Heneage	p 28 Aug. 57			
2	0	George Lewis Watson	p 31 Dec. 58			
1	0	Thos. Rumbold Richardson	p 11 Mar. 59			
1	0	*Hon.* Reginald A. J. Talbot	p 13 May 59			
1	0	Algernon Wm. F. Greville	p 26 Aug. 59			
1	0	Henry John Robert Osborn	p 30 Aug. 59			
6	0	*Adjutant.*—Cornet & *Sub-Lt.* John Limbert, 7 July 54.				
6	0	*Quarter Master.*—Hugh Hanly, 3 Feb. 54. [*Surgeon Major,* 1 Oct. 58.				
24	0	*Surgeon.*—James Cockburn, *Assist.-Surg.* 15 April 36; *Surgeon,* 12 Sept. 48;				
9	0	*Assistant Surgeon.*—Owen William George, M.D. 6 June 51.				
21	0	*Veterinary Surgeon.*—Thomas Jex, 4 Oct. 39; *1st Class* 1 July 59.				

Scarlet.—*Facings* Blue.—*Agents,* Messrs. Cox and Co.

[*Returned from France, January* 1816.]

1 Lord Combermere accompanied his Regt. (the 6th Dr. Gds.) to Flanders in Aug. 1793, and served to the end of that campaign, and until June of the following one. In 1796 he embarked in command of the 25th Lt. Drs. for the Cape of Good Hope, and served a short but active campaign under Sir Thomas Craig, when he accompanied his Regt. to India, where he served in the memorable campaigns of 1798 and 99, against Tippoo Sultaun, including the battle of Mallavelly, and siege of Seringapatam. Proceeded to the Peninsula in 1808, in command of a brigade of cavalry, consisting of the 14th and 16th Lt. Drs., at the head of which he distinguished himself, during the campaign in the north of Portugal, including the operations at Oporto, and afterwards at the battle of Talavera. In Aug. 1809, the local rank of Lieut.-Gen. was conferred upon him; and, early in 1810, he was appointed to the command of the whole allied cavalry under the Duke of Wellington, and remained in that command until the termination of the war in 1814, and distinguished himself at the head of the cavalry upon every occasion that presented itself, including the various actions in covering the retreat from Almeida to Torres Vedras, battle of Busaco, actions at Villa Garcia and Castrajon, battles of Fuentes d'Onor and Salamanca (severely wounded), action at El Bodon, battles of the Pyrenees, Orthes, and Toulouse. Served also at the siege and capture of Bhurtpore, in 1825 and 26, as Commander-in-Chief. His Lordship has received a Medal for Seringapatam; the Gold Cross and one Clasp for the battles of Talavera, Fuentes d'Onor, Salamanca, Orthes, and Toulouse; and the Silver War Medal with three Clasps for Busaco, Ciudad Rodrigo, and Pyrenees; he is a Grand Cross of the Tower and Sword of Portugal, and of Charles the Third, and St. Ferdinand of Spain.

2nd Regiment of Life Guards. 127

"PENINSULA" "WATERLOO."

Years' Serv.		
Full Pay	Half Pay	
66		Colonel.—⊕ ⊕⊕ John, Lord Seaton,¹ GCB. GCMG. GCH., Ens. 10 July 1794; Lieut. 4 Sept. 95; Capt. 12 Jan. 00; Major, 21 Jun. 08; Lt.Col. 2 Feb. 09; Col. 4 June 14; Major-Gen. 27 May 25; Lieut.Gen. 28 June 38; Gen. 20 June 54; Col. 2nd Life Guards, 24 March 54.
33	0	Lieut.Colonel.—Mountjoy Francis Martyn, Cor. P 27 Dec. 27; Lieut. P 22 Mar. 31; Capt. P 22 April 36; Bt.-Maj. 9 Nov. 46; Bt. Lt.Col. 20 June 54; Maj. & Lt.Col. P 14 July 54; Lt.Col. P 27 Nov. 57; Col. 29 Aug. 58.
30	0	Major and Lt.Col.—Geo. Howard Vyse, Cor. P26 Nov. 30; Lt. P 17 April 35; Capt. P 1 Sept. 37; Brev.Major, 11 Nov. 51; Maj. & Lt.Col. P 27 Nov. 57.

		CAPTAINS.	COR. AND SUB-LIEUT.	LIEUT.	CAPTAIN.	BREVET-MAJOR.
28	0	Thos. Ogilvy, c. 28 Nov. 54	P 9 Mar. 32	P 29 April 36	P 8 May 40	23 Nov. 41
24	0	E. M. Earl of Longford	P 9 July 36	P 9 May 40	P 14 Apr. 48	14 Aug. 59
17	0	Edw. Ffolliott Wingfield	P 12 May 43	P 29 June 48	P 28 Mar. 54	
13	0	John G. Carter Hamilton	P 22 Jan. 47	P 30 Nov. 49	P 14 July 54	
15	0	Henry Dalton Wittit Lyon	P 18 April 45	P 24 Sept. 47	20 Oct. 57	
11	0	Frederick Marshall³	P 18 Sept. 49	P 16 Sept. 51	P 4 Feb. 59	
7	0	Roger Palmer²	P 22 Jan. 53	4 Sept. 54	P 22 July 59	
7	0	Henry John Lloyd Wynne	P 13 May 53	P 17 July 57	P 28 Oct. 59	
		LIEUTENANTS.				
7	0	E. S. Fitzhard. Berkeley	P 18 Nov. 53	P 17 Nov. 57		
6	0	John Henniker Lovett	P 9 June 54	P 27 Nov. 57		
6	0	Francis Woodgate	P 15 Sept. 54	P 16 Apr. 58		
6	0	Jn. Wm. H. Cunninghame	P 15 Dec. 54	P 16 Apr. 58		
4	0	Alex. Chas. H. Stewart	P 14 Oct. 56	P 8 Oct. 58		
3	0	Robert Reid, Adj.	17 Nov. 57	3 June 59		
2	0	Thomas Leyland	P 15 Jan. 58	P 3 June 59		
2	0	Henry P. Ewart	P 26 Feb. 58	P 22 July 59		
2	0	Hamil. Sandf. Pakenham	P 30 July 58	P 28 Oct. 59		
		CORNETS AND SUB-LIEUTENANTS.				
4	0	Rd. D. Barré Cunninghame, Lieut. 30 Apr. 58	P 19 Aug. 56			
2	0	William Entwisle	P 31 Dec. 58			
1	0	Chas.BruceKnightAlleyne	P 18 Jan. 59			

1 Lord Seaton served with the army in North Holland in the campaign of 1799; in Egypt in 1801; and with the British and Russian troops employed on the Neapolitan frontier in 1805. Served in Sicily and Calabria in the campaign of 1806, and was at the battle of Maida. Was Military Secretary to General Fox, Commander of the Forces in Sicily and the Mediterranean in 1806 and 1807, and to Sir John Moore—in Sicily, Sweden, and Portugal, and in Spain in the campaign of 1808-9, and at the battle of Corunna. Joined the army of Lord Wellington in 1809 in Spain at Jaracejo and was sent to La Manche to report on the operations of the Spanish armies,—was at the battle of Ocana. Commanded a Brigade in Sir Rowland Hill's Division in the campaigns of 1810 and 1811, and was detached in command of the Brigade to Castel Branco to observe the movements of General Reynier's Corps d'Armée on the frontier of Portugal. Commanded a Brigade at the battle
[Continued below.

3	0	Adjutant.—Lieut. Robert Reid, 17 Nov. 57.
8	0	Quarter Master.—William Walker, 15 Oct. 52.
5	0	Riding Master.—John Reid, 9 Feb. 55.
16	0	Surgeon.—Thomas Tardrew, 23 May 51; Assist.-Surg. 12 July 44.
6	0	Assist.Surgeon.—Francis Trevelyan Buckland, 15 Aug. 54.
30	0	Veterinary Surgeon.—John Legrew, 9 July 30; 1st Class, 1 July 59.

Scarlet—Facings Blue.—Agents, Messrs. Cox & Co.
[Returned from France, February 1816.]

of Busaco and on the retreat to the Lines of Torres Vedras, and occupied with this Brigade—outside the Lines—the town of Alhandra and the advanced posts near Villa Franca during the time the army was in this position, and afterwards when Massena retired from the front of the Lines. Crossed the Tagus and had charge of the posts on that river opposite the French Corps at the confluence of the Zezere till the evacuation of Portugal by Massena. Commanded the advanced guard of Infantry and Cavalry at the combat of Campo Mayor in Portugal, and was detached in command of a Brigade and force of Artillery and Cavalry with orders to drive back the French outposts during the siege of Badajoz in 1811. Commanded a Brigade at the battle of Albuhera. In 1812 on the investment of Ciudad Rodrigo, commanded the force of the Light Division which stormed the Redoubt of San Francisco on the greater Teson, and the 52nd Light Infantry on the assault of the fortress and town. In 1813 commanded the 2nd Brigade of the Light Division at the attack of the French position and intrenched camp on the heights of Vera, at the battles of the Nivelle and the Nive, and during the operations of the campaign in the Basque Pyrenees. Led the attack of the 52nd Light Infantry on Marshal Soult's position at the battle of Orthes in 1814. Commanded the 2nd Brigade of the Light Division at the combats of Vic Bigorre and Tarbes, and the 52nd at the battle of Toulouse. Was appointed Prince Regent's Aide de Camp in 1814 and Military Secretary to the Prince of Orange, Commander in Chief of the British Forces in the Netherlands. In 1815, commanded the 52nd Light Infantry at the battle of Waterloo, and a Brigade on the march to Paris. Has held the following appointments,—Lieut.Governor of Guernsey; Lieut.Governor of Upper Canada, Commander of the Forces in Canada; Governor General of British North America; Lord High Commissioner in the Ionian Islands; and is now Commander of the Forces in Ireland. Has received the Grand Cross of the Bath, and of Hanover, and of St. Michael and St. George; the Order of Maria Theresa of Austria, of the Tower and Sword of Portugal, and of St. George of Russia; the Waterloo Medal; the Gold Cross and three Clasps; the Silver War Medal with five Clasps. Was severely wounded at Ciudad Rodrigo.

2 Captain Palmer served the Eastern campaign of 1854-55 with the 11th Hussars, including the affair of Bulganak, battles of Alma, Balaklava, and Inkerman, and siege of Sebastopol (Medal and Clasps).

3 Captain Marshall served in the Crimea during Sept. 1855 as Aide de Camp to Sir James Scarlett (Medal and Clasp for Sebastopol).

† B 2

Royal Regiment of Horse Guards.
"PENINSULA" "WATERLOO."

Years' Serv.		
Full Pay	Half Pay	
66		*Colonel.*—ẞ Hugh, *Viscount* Gough,[1] KP. GCB. *Ens.* 7 Aug. 94; *Lieut.* 11 Oct. 94; *Capt.* 25 June 03; *Maj.* 8 Aug. 05; *Lt.-Col.* 29 July 09; *Col.* 12 Aug. 19; *Maj.-Gen.* 22 July 30; *Lieut.Gen.* 23 Nov. 41; *Gen.* 20 June 54; *Colonel* of Royal Horse Guards, 29 June 55.
30	0	*Lieut.Colonel.*—Richard Henry R. Howard Vyse, *Cornet,* P 30 Nov. 30; *Lt.* P 31 May 33; *Capt.* P 27 Sept. 42; *Maj. & Lt.Col.* P 21 April 54; *Col.* 28 Nov. 54; *Lt.Col.* P 30 Sept. 59.
20	0	*Major.*—Hugh Smith Baillie, *Cornet,* P 3 April 40; *Lt.* P 24 Mar. 43; *Capt.* P 7 Aug. 46; *Brev.Maj.* 26 Oct. 58; *Maj. & Lt.Col.* P 30 Sept. 59.

		CAPTAINS.	CORNET.	LIEUT.	CAPTAIN.	BREV.-MAJ.
20	0	Lord Geo. John Manners	P 20 Oct. 40	P 4 Aug. 43	P 5 Feb. 47	26 Oct. 58
18	0	Robert Sheffield........	P 22 July 42	P 28 Feb. 45	P 13 July 49	
15	0	Duncan James Baillie ..	P 28 Feb. 45	P 28 Sept. 47	P 21 April 54	
13	0	Thomas Leslie[3]	P 5 Feb. 47	P 4 Mar. 53	P 28 Dec. 55	
7	0	R.M.L.WilliamsBulkeley	P 27 May 53	P 28 Dec. 55	P 18 Dec. 57	
6	0	Owen Lewis C. Williams	P 12 May 54	P 25 Jan. 56	P 7 May 58	
7	0	William Wray Hartopp[4]	P 11 Mar. 53	8 Dec. 54	P 1 Apr. 59	
6	0	Henry P. Keighly Peach	P 9 June 54	P 30 Sept. 56	P 30 Sept. 59	
		LIEUTENANTS.				
6	0	*Hon.* Geoffrey R.Clegg Hill	P 15 Dec. 54	P 27 Mar. 57		
5	0	Alan P., *Lord* Garlies ..	P 15 June 55	P 16 June 57	5 Cornet Martyn served as a Midshipman in the Royal Navy in the Black Sea, including the bombardment of Odessa and that of Sebastopol on the 17th Oct. 1854, served also in the Crimea with the Naval Brigade from 18th July to 15th Sept. 1855 (Turkish and Crimean Medals with one Clasp).	
5	0	Edward Hayward	10 April 55	13 Aug. 57		
5	0	Walter Palk Carew......	P 28 Dec. 55	P 18 Dec. 57		
4	0	Philip Bennet	P 25 Mar. 56	P 2 Feb. 58		
3	0	Fras. George Aug. Fuller	P 24 Feb. 57	P 15 June 58		
3	0	MyllesB.Bowyer Adderley	P 10 Mar. 57	P 1 Apr. 59		
3	0	Rich. G. Bomford Bolton[6]	P 22 May 57	P 30 Sept. 59		
		CORNETS.				
3	0	Cecil Edward Martyn[5] ..	P 19 June 57			
3	0	John Albert Craven	P 18 Dec. 57			
2	0	Cecil Robt. St. John Ives	P 15 Jan. 58			
2	0	Thos. Chas. D. Whitmore	14 May 58			
2	0	Digby H. Rich. Wingfield	P 26 Oct. 58			
2	0	Robert M'Alpine, *Adj.*..	24 Dec. 58			
2	0	John Alex. Burn Callander	P 31 Dec. 58			
1	0	Fred. Gustavus Burnaby	P 30 Sept. 59			

2	0	*Adjutant.*—Cornet Robert M'Alpine, 24 Dec. 58.
29	0	*Quarter Master.*—Herbert Turner, 1 Jan. 31.
4	0	*Riding Master.*—John Boswell, 25 March 56.
19	0	*Surgeon.*—Cosmo Gordon Logie, M.D. 26 Nov. 52; *Assist.-Surg.* 5 Oct. 41.
12	0	*Assistant Surgeon.*—Frederick George Kerin, 18 Aug. 48.
22	0	*Veterinary Surgeon.*—John Byrne,[7] 14 Dec. 38; *1st Class,* 1 July 59.

Blue—*Facings* Scarlet.
Agents, Sir Charles R. M'Grigor, *Bt.,* and Walter M'Grigor, Esq.
[*Returned from France,* 2 *February* 1816.]

1 Lord Gough served at the capture of the Cape of Good Hope, and the Dutch Fleet in Saldanha Bay, 1795. Served afterwards in the West Indies, including the attack on Porto Rico, the brigand war in St. Lucia, and capture of Surinam. Proceeded to the Peninsula in 1809, and commanded the 87th at the battles of Talavera, Barrosa, Vittoria, and Nivelle, for which engagements he has received a Gold Cross. He also commanded the Regiment at the defence of Cadiz and of Tarifa (slightly wounded in the head). At the battle of Talavera his horse was shot under him, and he himself was afterwards severely wounded in the side by a shell,—for his conduct in this action the Duke of Wellington subsequently recommended that his Lieut.-Colonelcy should be ante-dated to the date of his Dispatch, thus making him the first officer who ever received Brevet rank for services performed in the field at the head of a regiment. At Barrosa his Regiment captured the Eagle of the 8th French Regiment; and at Vittoria they captured the Baton of Marshal Jourdan. At the Nivelle he was again severely wounded. Commanded the Land Force at Canton—for which he was made a GCB.—and during nearly the whole of the operations in China,—for which service he was created a Baronet. On the 29th Dec. 1843, with the right wing of the army of Gwalior, he defeated a Mahratta force at Maharajpore, and captured 56 guns, &c. In 1845 and 46 the Army under his Lordship's personal command defeated the Seik Army at Moodkee, Ferozeshah, and Sobraon, for which and previous services he was raised to the Peerage; and, in 1849, he was created a Viscount after his crowning victory over the Seiks at Goojerat (Medal and Clasps). His Lordship is also a Knight of Charles the 3rd of Spain.

3 Captain Leslie served in the Eastern campaign of 1854, and was severely wounded at the battle of the Alma, while serving as orderly officer to Lord Raglan (Medal and Clasps).

4 Captain Hartopp served the Eastern campaign of 1854-55, including the battles of Balaklava (shot through the leg) and Tchernaya, and siege of Sebastopol (Medal and Clasps).

6 Lieut. Bolton served with the 5th Dragoon Guards in the Crimea in 1855 (Medal with Clasp for Sebastopol).

7 Veterinary-Surgeon Byrne served the Eastern campaign of 1854-55 with the 4th Light Dragoons, including the battles of Alma, Balaklava, Inkerman, and Tchernaya, siege and fall of Sebastopol; also present with the Light Cavalry Brigade at Eupatoria (Medal and four Clasps, and Turkish Medal).

1st (The King's) Regiment of Dragoon Guards. 129

Bangalore.
Depot, Canterbury.

The King's Cypher within the Garter.—"WATERLOO" "SEVASTOPOL."

Colonel.—⑭ Sir Thomas Wm. Brotherton,[1] KCB. *Ens.* 24 Jan. 1800; *Lt. & Capt.* 27 July 01; *Maj.* 28 Nov. 11; *Lt.Col.* 19 May 14; *Col.* 22 July 30; *Maj. Gen.* 23 Nov. 41; *Lt.Gen.* 11 Nov. 51; *Colonel* 1st Dragoon Guards, 17 July 59.

Years' Serv.		
Full Pay	Half Pay	
60		
26	0	**Lieut. Colonels.**—Thomas Pattle,[2] *Cornet,* ᴾ 13 June 34; *Lt.* ᴾ 23 Dec. 36; *Capt.* ᴾ 7 May 47; *Major,* ᴾ 13 Dec. 50; *Lieut.Col.* ᴾ 2 Nov. 55.
15	0	James Robert Steadman Sayer,[6] *Cornet,* ᴾ 23 May 45; *Lt.* ᴾ 31 Mar. 48; *Capt.* ᴾ 22 Nov. 50; *Major,* ᴾ 6 Feb. 57; *Lt.Col.* ᴾ 21 Oct. 59
11	0	**Majors.**—Thomas Nisbet,[6] *Cornet,* ᴾ 29 May 49; *Lieut.* ᴾ 8 Nov. 50; *Capt.* ᴾ 12 Nov. 52; *Major,* ᴾ 25 Feb. 59.
18	0	Herbert Dawson Slade,[3] *Cornet,* ᴾ 25 Oct. 42; *Lieut.* ᴾ 9 June 46; *Capt.* ᴾ 28 Aug. 49; *Major,* ᴾ 21 Oct. 59.

		CAPTAINS.	CORNET.	LIEUT.	CAPTAIN.	BREV.-MAJ.
14	0	Emanuel Bradbury	8 Dec. 46	25 May 48	26 June 55	
10	0	Thomas John Mitchell[3]..	ᴾ 12 July 50	ᴾ 4 April 51	ᴾ 6 Feb. 57	
10	0	Joseph Henry Anderson[6]	ᴾ 22 Nov. 50	ᴾ 22 Aug. 51	ᴾ 14 Aug. 57	
12	1¾	Henry Alexander[7]	ᴾ 3 Sept. 47	ᴾ 6 Dec. 50	ᴾ 1 Feb. 56	
10	0	Thomas Walter Still	ᴾ 15 Oct. 50	ᴾ 12 Oct. 52	ᴾ 9 Oct. 57	
9	0	Evelyn Harpur Crewe ..	ᴾ 14 Mar. 51	ᴾ 3 June 53	ᴾ 30 April 58	
9	0	Walter Clopton Wingfield	ᴾ 18 April 51	26 June 55	ᴾ 6 Aug. 58	
9	0	Joseph Ernest Edlmann..	ᴾ 19 April 51	26 June 55	ᴾ 10 Dec. 58	
8	0	Arthur Jas. P. Wadman[3]	23 Nov. 52	ᴾ 9 Oct. 55	ᴾ 25 Feb. 59	
7	0	James Gunter[6]	ᴾ 18 Feb. 53	ᴾ 21 Nov. 56	ᴾ 21 Oct. 59	
		LIEUTENANTS.				
9	0	R. Jas. Combe Marter ..	ᴾ 18 Jan. 51	ᴾ 29 Apr. 53		
7	0	John Cuningham[6]	ᴾ 11 Mar. 53	ᴾ 10 Mar. 57		
7	0	Henry Marlow Sidney ..	ᴾ 13 May 53	14 Aug. 57		
7	0	Robt. Alf. Loraine Grews[3]	ᴾ 10 June 53	ᴾ 14 Aug. 57		
5	0	David Wale,[6] *Adj*......	11 May 55	24 Aug. 57		
4	0	Charles Levett	15 Feb. 56	ᴾ 25 Aug. 57		
4	0	Chas. Rob. Kerr Hubback	7 Mar. 56	ᴾ 30 April 58		
4	0	Richard Harpur Crowe..	ᴾ 21 Nov. 56	ᴾ 6 Aug. 58		
3	0	William Edw. Marsland..	ᴾ 17 Feb. 57	ᴾ 10 Dec. 58		
3	0	Guy Webster	ᴾ 25 Aug. 57	ᴾ 25 Feb. 59		
		CORNETS.				
3	0	George Henry Bowyer ..	27 Aug. 57			
3	0	Henry Barker..........	28 Aug. 57			
3	0	James William Baillie[10]..	23 Oct. 57			
3	0	Frederick Sedley	24 Oct. 57			
3	0	Riversdale Elliot	25 Oct. 57			
3	0	Herbert H. Forbes Gifford	23 Oct. 57			
1	0	W. Lawrence Twentyman	11 Mar. 59			
1	0	Thos. Armstrong Gough..	31 May 59			
1	0	James Greatorex	ᴾ 18 Oct. 59			

6 Lt.-Col. Sayer, Major Nisbet, Captains Anderson and Gunter, Lieuts. Cuningham and Wale, Paymaster Smith, and Qr. M. Bradbury, served in the Crimean campaign from 16th August 1855, including the siege of Sebastopol (Medal and Clasp).

8 Doctor Jephson served in charge of the 61st the Punjaub campaign of 1848-9, and was present at the passage of the Chenab, and at the battles of Sadoolapore, Chillianwallah, and Goojerat (Medal and Clasps). He served also in medical charge of part of the 60th and 61st Regts. in the Euzofzye country under Lieut.-Col. Bradshaw. Served on the Staff and with the 1st Dr. Gds. in the Crimean campaign in 1855, including the siege of Sebastopol (Medal and Clasp, and 5th Class of the Medjidie).

7 Captain Alexander served with the 10th Hussars in the Crimea from 7th July 1855, including the battle of the Tchernaya and siege of Sebastopol (Medal and Clasp).

8	0	**Paymaster.**—William Smith,[6] 13 July 55; *Qr.-Master,* 23 April 52.
5	0	**Adjutant.**—*Lieut.* David Wale,[6] 6 July 55.
5	0	**Quarter Master.**—John Bradbury,[6] 20 July 55.
4	0	**Riding Master.**—George Rayment, 14 March 56.
10	0	**Surgeon.**—William Holmes Jephson,[8] M.D. 12 Jan. 55; *Assist.-Surg.* 12 July 44.
16	0	**Assistant Surgeons.**—William Alexander Davidson, M.D. 28 March 54.
3	0	Edward Louis M'Shechy, M.D. 27 May 57.
16	0	**Veterinary Surgeon.**—F. Delany, 25 Sept. 44; *1st Class V. S.* 1 July 59.

Scarlet—*Facings* Blue.—*Agents,* Messrs. Cox & Co.

[*Returned from the Crimea, July 1856. Embarked for India, 24 Aug. 1857.*]

1 Sir Thomas Brotherton served in Egypt under Sir Ralph Abercromby in 1801; in Germany under Lord Cathcart in 1805; in Portugal, Spain, and France during the whole of the Peninsular war from 1808 to 1814, and has received the War Medal with eight Clasps for the battles of Busaco, Fuentes d'Onor, Salamanca (wounded), Vittoria, Pyrenees, Nivelle, and Nive, in which last battle he was wounded and taken prisoner. Besides these he was present at all the cavalry affairs and skirmishes in which his Regt. the 14th Light Dragoons was engaged, and was at the action on the Coa: he was wounded several times in these skirmishes.

2 Lt.-Col. Pattle served with the 16th Lancers during the campaign in Affghanistan under Lord Keane, and was present at the siege and capture of Ghuznee (Medal). Also the campaign on the Sutlej in 1846, including the battles of Buddiwal, Aliwal (wounded), and Sobraon (Medal and Clasps).

3 Major Slade, Captains Mitchell, and Wadman, and Lieut. Grews, served in the Crimean campaign from Aug. 1855, including the battle of the Tchernaya and siege of Sebastopol (Medal and Clasp).

10 Cornet Baillie served at the siege of Sebastopol from 30th Jan. to 2nd Sept. 1855 as Aide de Camp to Lord Rokeby (Medal and Clasp).

2nd (The Queen's) Regiment of Dragoon Guards. [Lucknow. Depot, Canterbury.

The Royal Cypher within the Garter.

Years' Serv.			
Full Pay	Half Pay		
52		*Colonel.*—³⁄₄ Hon. Henry F. Compton Cavendish,¹ *Lieut.* P 26 May 08; *Capt.* P 6 June 11; *Major*, P 2 April 18; *Lt.Col.* P 12 July 21; *Col.* 10 Jan. 37; *Maj.Gen.* 9 Nov. 46; *Lt.Gen.* 20 June 54; *Col.* 2nd Dr. Gds. 2 June 53.	
13	0	*Lieut. Colonels.*—William Henry Seymour,² CB. *Ens.* P 7 May 47; *Lieut.* 10 June 52; *Capt.* 29 Dec. 54; *Major*, 13 May 58; *Lt.Col.* 7 July 58.	
24	0	Charles Pyndar Beauchamp Walker,⁵ *Ens.* P 27 Feb. 36; *Lieut.* 21 June 39; *Capt.* P 22 Dec. 36; *Major*, P 8 Dec. 54; *Lt.Col.* P 9 Nov. 55.	
9	7⁄12	*Majors.*—Coote Synge Hutchinson,⁴ *Cornet*, P 14 June 50; *Lieut.* P 1 Aug. 51; *Capt.* P 30 Nov. 55; *Major*, 7 July 58; *Bt.Lt.Col.* 26 April 59.	
9	7⁄12	Henry Miles Stapylton,⁵ *Cornet*, 6 Dec. 50; *Lieut.* P 11 Mar. 53; *Capt.* P 11 July 56; *Major*, P 17 Sept. 58.	

		CAPTAINS.	CORNET.	LIEUT.	CAPTAIN.	BREV.-MAJ.	BT.LT.COL.
19	0	George Bushman	30 Apr. 41	P 25 Nov. 53	16 June 57		
9	0	M. James Bradley Dyne	P 12 Dec. 51	P 27 May 53	P 16 June 57		
7	0	Francis Graham Powell⁶	P 20 Sept. 53	14 Sept. 55	P 24 July 57		
10	0	Henry Holden Steward⁷	P 12 Apr. 50	P 11 June 52	P 11 July 56		
7	0	Goodrich H. Allfrey⁸	P 21 Sept. 53	P 30 Nov. 55	7 Mar. 58		
14	0	John Theodore Ling⁹	P 4 Apr. 46	P 9 Apr. 47	P 16 Oct. 55		
5	0	S. Calvert¹⁰ (Q.M. 5 Jan. 55)	9 Oct. 55	16 June 57	20 Dec. 58		
5	0	Walter Colquhoun Grant¹¹	30 Nov. 55	16 June 57	29 Mar. 59		
14	0	George Thomas Gough¹²	4 Apr. 46	P 9 June 48	7 July 57		
8	0	William Henry Horne	P 27 Aug. 52	14 Sept. 55	P 31 Aug. 58		
		LIEUTENANTS.					
4	0	George Eugene Logan¹³	15 Apr. 56	16 June 57			
8	0	Henry Lavington Payne¹⁴	P 9 July 52	P 14 Sept. 55			
4	0	Thomas Wm. Sneyd¹⁵	P 2 May 56	P 24 July 57			
5	0	George Fred. Ormsby¹⁶	P 28 Dec. 55	P 7 Aug. 57			
3	0	William Thomas Foster¹⁷	P 19 June 57	5 Mar. 58			
3	0	H. John de Montmorency¹⁸	20 June 57	7 Mar. 58			
3	0	William Jones Thomas¹⁹	24 July 57	13 May 58			
3	0	Francis O'Beirne²⁰	P 7 Aug. 57	7 July 58			
3	0	Jno. Wm. Zorapore Wright	18 Dec. 57	P 5 Oct. 58			
4	0	Charles G. Alfred Barnes²¹	8 Jan. 56	29 Mar. 59			
		CORNETS.					
3	0	Charles Lever²⁸	17 Aug. 57				
3	0	Robert Henry Torrens²⁹	28 Aug. 57				
2	0	Rowland Veitch Betty	12 Feb. 58				
2	0	Edward Vandeleur	23 July 58				
2	0	John Taylor Marshall	6 Aug. 58				
2	0	Frederick Greatorex²⁹	P 26 Mar. 58				
2	0	Howard James Barton	26 Oct. 58				
2	0	George Batley	P 26 Nov. 58				
1	0	Westropp M'Mahon Weir	11 Feb. 59				
1	0	Allen Deane,³⁰ *Adj.*	24 May 59				
1	0	Arthur Brett	16 Aug. 59				
0	0	*Paymaster.*—Fred. Windham Lukin,²² 10 Aug. 55; *Ens.* P 16 May 51; *Lt.* P 18 Nov. 53.					
1	0	*Adjutant.*—Cornet Allen Deane,³⁰ 24 May 59.					
2	0	*Instructor of Musketry.*—Cornet J. T. Marshall, 4 March 59.					
5	0	*Quarter Master.*—William Rae,³³ 9 Oct. 55.					
2	0	*Riding Master*—James Russell, 24 Sept. 58.					
16	0	*Surgeon.*—Hampden Hugh Massy,²⁴ M.D., 28 Mar. 54; *Assist.Surg.* 22 Nov. 44.					
5	0	*Assistant Surgeons.*—John Harrison Robotham,²⁵ 23 April 55.					
7	0	Robert Fleetwood Andrews,²⁶ 30 Sept. 53.					
6	0	*Veterinary Surgeon.*—Tom Parinder Gudgin,²⁷ 13 Oct. 54.					

Scarlet. — Facings Buff.—*Agents*, Messrs. Cox & Co.

[*Returned from France*, 8 November 1818. *Embarked for India*, 24 July 1857.]

1 Lieut.General the Hon. Henry Cavendish served in the Peninsula from July 1808 to January 1809 and was wounded through the wrist at the battle of Corunna, where he served as Aide-de-Camp to Lord William Bentinck. He has the War Medal with two Clasps for Sahagun and Benevente, and Corunna.

2 Lt.Col. Seymour served with the 68th Light Infantry during the Crimean campaign of 1854-55, including the battles of Alma, Balaklava, and Inkerman, and siege of Sebastopol (Medal and four Clasps). Served with the 2nd Dragoon Guards in the Indian campaign in 1858-59, including the action of Nusserutpore, siege and capture of Lucknow (charger wounded), subsequent operations, action of Nawabgunge (in command of three squadrons and reoccupation of Fyzabad). Commanded the Regiment throughout the Oude campaign, including the action of Jamo (wounded), siege and capture of Birwah and Trans-Gogra affairs at Bungaon (frequently mentioned in despatches, Medal and Clasp, and CB.).

3 Lt.Col. Walker served the Eastern campaign of 1854, as Aide de Camp to the Earl of Lucan, including the battles of the Alma, Balaklava, and Inkerman, and siege of Sebastopol: was also at the Cavalry affair the day previous to Alma; at the surprise of the Russian rear-guard at Mackenzie's Farm; and served as a volunteer on board H.M.S. *Bellerophon* at the bombardment of Sebastopol on the 17th October (Medal and Clasps). Served in the field in India in 1859, first in command of a field force at Secrora in Oude, near which place he defeated the rebels on 27th April, and afterwards in command of the column which accompanied Sir Hope Grant to the Nepaul frontier including the action at the Jerwah Pass (Medal).

4 Lt.Colonel Hutchinson served in the Indian campaign in 1858-59, including the siege and capture of Lucknow and subsequent operations, and commanded a detached squadron in the action of Barre, and Trans-Gogra affairs at Bungaon and Newabghur (mentioned in despatches, Medal and Clasp, and Brevet of Lt.Colonel).

2nd (The Queen's) Regiment of Dragoon Guards. 130a

5 Major Stapylton served in the Indian campaign in 1858-59, including the action of Nusserutpore, siege and capture of Lucknow (charger wounded), subsequent operations, actions of Koorsee and Nawabgunge, the Oude campaign, action of Jamo, siege and capture of Birwah, and Trans-Gogra affairs at Bungaon (mentioned in despatches, Medal and Clasp).

6 Captain Powell served in the Indian campaign in 1858-59, including the action of Nusserutpore, siege and capture of Lucknow, subsequent operations, action of Koorsee, the Oude campaign, and commanded a detached squadron at the affair of Selimpore, and Trans-Gogra affairs at Bungaon and Newabghur (mentioned in despatches, Medal and Clasp).

7 Captain Steward served in the Indian campaign, and was present at the affair of Dawah, and Trans-Gogra affairs at Bungaon (Medal).

8 Captain Allfrey served in the Indian campaign in 1858-59, including the siege and capture of Lucknow, subsequent operations, action of Koorsee, the Oude campaign, and Trans-Gogra affairs at Bungaon and Newabghur (Medal and Clasp).

10 Captain Calvert served as Adjutant of the 2nd Dragoon Guards in the Indian campaign in 1858-59, including the siege and capture of Lucknow, subsequent operations, action of Koorsee, the Oude campaign, action of Jamo (charger wounded), siege and capture of Birwah (mentioned in despatches, Medal and Clasp).

11 Captain Grant (formerly a Captain in the 2nd Dragoons) served with the Eastern Army from Nov. 1854 as Captain Commandant of the Mounted Staff Corps, with local rank of Major (Medal and Clasp for Sebastopol). Served also from Oct. 1855 to the conclusion of the war as Assist.Qr.Mast.Gen. to the Cavalry Division Turkish Contingent, with the local rank of Lt.Colonel (4th Class of the Medjidie). Served with the 2nd Dragoon Guards in the Indian campaign in 1858-59, including the action of Nusserutpore, siege and capture of Lucknow, subsequent operations, and action of Koorsee (Medal and Clasp).

12 Captain Gough served with the 3rd Light Dragoons throughout the Punjaub campaign of 1848-9, including the action of Ramnuggur, passage of the Chenab, battles of Sadoolapore, Chillianwallah, and Goojerat (Medal and two Clasps). Served with the 12th Lancers throughout the Kaffir war of 1851-3 (Medal), and was present with every expedition, including the action of Berea, where he commanded the detachments of cavalry with Sir George Cathcart's column (mentioned in General Orders and despatches), and for one year commanded Sir George's escort until peace was established. Served in the Crimea with the 12th Lancers from their landing on the 8th May 1855, including the siege and fall of Sebastopol, battle of Tchernaya, and operations near Eupatoria under General D'Allonville (Medal and Clasp).

13 Lieut. Logan served in the Indian campaign in 1858-59, including the siege and capture of Lucknow, subsequent operations, action of Koorsee, the Oude campaign, action of Jamo, siege and capture of Birwah, and Trans-Gogra affairs in Bungaon and Newabghur (Medal and Clasp).

14 Lieut. Payne served in the Indian campaign in 1858-59, including the siege and capture of Lucknow, subsequent operations, actions of Koorsee and Barree, the Oude campaign, and commanded a detached squadron at crossing of the Gogra at Fyzabad (Medal and Clasp).

15 Lieut. Sneyd served in the Indian campaign in 1858-59, including the action of Nusserutpore, siege and capture of Lucknow, subsequent operations, and action of Koorsee (Medal and Clasp).

16 Lieut. Ormsby served in the Indian campaign in 1858-59, was present with the Regt. at the action of Nusserutpore, commanded a detachment at the relief of Azimghur, and served the Oude campaign, latterly as Orderly Officer to Brigadier Barker, including the action of Jamo, siege and capture of Birwah, and Trans-Gogra affairs at Bungaon and Newabghur (Medal).

17 Lieut. Foster served in the Indian campaign in 1858-59, including the siege and capture of Lucknow, subsequent operations, action of Koorsee and affairs at Bungaon (Medal and Clasp).

18 Lieut. de Montmorency served the Oude campaign of 1858-59, including the affair of Gooree, and Trans-Gogra affairs at Bungaon (Medal).

19 Lieut. Thomas served the Oude campaign of 1858-59, including the siege and capture of Birwah, and Trans-Gogra affairs at Bungaon (Medal).

20 Lieut. O'Beirne served the Oude campaign of 1858-59, including the crossing of the Gogra at Fyzabad, and affairs at Bungaon (Medal).

21 Lieut. Barnes served the Oude campaign of 1858-59, including the affair of Dawah, and Trans-Gogra affairs at Bungaon and Newabghur (Medal).

22 Paymaster Lukin served with the 17th Foot at the siege of Sebastopol from Dec. 1854 to June 1855 (Medal and Clasp). Served with the 2nd Dr. Guards in the Indian campaign of 1858-59, including the siege and capture of Lucknow and Trans-Gogra affairs at Bungaon (Medal and Clasp).

23 Qr.Master Rae served in the Indian campaign in 1858, including the siege and capture of Lucknow, and action of Koorsee (Medal and Clasp).

24 Doctor Massy served with the 31st Regt. towards the close of the Sutlej campaign in 1846. Served the Eastern campaign of 1854-55 with the 17th Lancers, including the affair of Bulganak, battles of Alma, Balaklava, and Inkerman, and siege of Sebastopol (Medal and Clasps, and 5th Class of the Medjidie). Served with the 2nd Dr. Guards in the Indian campaign of 1858-59, including the siege and capture of Lucknow, action of Koorsee, and Trans-Gogra affairs at Bungaon (Medal and Clasp).

25 Assist.Surgeon Robotham served in the Indian campaign in 1858-59, including the action of Nusserutpore, siege and capture of Lucknow, subsequent operations, action of Koorsee, the Oude campaign, action of Jamo, siege and capture of Birwah, Trans-Gogra affairs at Bungaon (mentioned in despatches, Medal and Clasp).

26 Assist.Surgeon Andrews served with the 1st Dr. Gds. in the Crimea from Aug. 1855, including the battle of the Tchernaya and siege of Sebastopol (Medal and Clasp). Served with the 2nd Dr. Guards in the Indian campaign in 1858-59 including the siege and capture of Lucknow, and actions of Koorsee and Nawabgunge, Trans-Gogra affairs at Bungaon (Medal and Clasp).

27 Veterinary Surgeon Gudgin served the Eastern campaign of 1854-55, including the affair of McKenzie's Farm, battles of Balaklava, Inkerman, and Tchernaya, siege and fall of Sebastopol (Medal and Clasps). Served in the Indian campaign in 1858-59, including the siege and capture of Lucknow, the Oude campaign, action of Jamo, siege and capture of Birwah, and Trans-Gogra affairs at Bungaon (Medal and Clasp).

28 Cornet Lever served in the Indian campaign in 1859 including the Trans-Gogra affairs at Bungaon (Medal).

29 Cornets Torrens and Greatorex served in the Indian campaign in 1859, including the Trans-Gogra affairs at Bungaon and Newabghur (Medal).

30 Cornet Deane served in the Indian campaign of 1857-59 and was present at the battle of Budlekeserai, and at Delhi throughout the siege operations, the assault, and capture of the city; also actions of Bolundshuhur and Allyghur, battle of Agra (wounded), affair of Maraigunge, relief of Lucknow by Lord Clyde, attack on the Gwalior mutineers at Cawnpore and Seraighat, action of Khodagunge, operations against Lucknow from 2nd to 19th March, attack on Rooyah, action of Allygunge, capture of Bareilly, action near Shahjehanpore and advance on Mahomdee, passage of the Gogra, and affairs at Muchleagon and Memdakote (Medal and Clasp).

131 3rd (*The Prince of Wales's*) *Regt. of Dragoon Guards.* [Gwalior. Depot, Canterbury.

"TALAVERA" "ALBUHERA" "VITTORIA" "PENINSULA."

Years' Serv.			
Full Pay	Half Pay		
45	—	**Colonel.**—John Scott,[1] CB., *Cornet*, P 4 May 15; *Lt*. P 26 Oct. 15; *Capt.* P 28 June 21; *Maj.* P 9 Nov. 26; *Lt.Col.* 31 Aug. 30; *Col.* 19 June 46; *Maj. Gen.* 20 June 54; *Col.* 3rd Dr. Gds., 13 Feb. 59.	
27	2 7/12	**Lieut. Colonels.**—Michael William Smith,[2] CB., *Ens.* P 10 Nov. 30; *Lt.* P 21 Feb. 34; *Capt.* P 23 April 39; *Maj.* 9 Feb. 47; *Lt.Col.* P 8 Mar. 50; *Col.* 28 Nov. 54.	
20	0	Fenwick Boyce Barron, *Cor.* P 8 May 40; *Lieut.* P 26 Sept. 45; *Capt.* P 29 Dec. 46; *Major*, 16 June 57; *Lt.Col.* P 1 Apr. 59.	
18	0	**Majors.**—Henry Marsh, *Cor.* P 5 Aug. 42; *Lieut.* P 12 May 43; *Capt.* P 7 June 50; *Maj.* P 24 July 57.	
14	0	Frank Chaplin,[2]† *Cor.* P 8 May 46; *Lieut.* 31 Oct. 48; *Capt.* P 8 Apr. 53; *Major*, P 1 Apr. 59.	

		CAPTAINS.	CORNET.	LIEUT.	CAPTAIN.	BREV.-MAJ.
16	0	Conyers Tower[3]	P 7 June 44	P 6 June 45	P 18 Jan. 50	
17	7/12	John Miller[4]	8 Nov. 42	4 June 45	2 Oct. 55	
9	7/12	James Swinburne	P 17 Sept. 50	P 8 Apr. 53	P 1 Feb. 56	
8	0	Arundell Neave	P 9 July 52	P 19 May 54	16 June 57	
17	7/12	Francis John MacFarlane[5]	P 6 Jan. 43	P 24 Oct. 45	6 July 55	
20	7/12	Thomas John Francis[6]	P 14 June 39	P 1 July 42	14 Sept. 55	
7	0	John Joseph Corrigan[7]	P 18 Feb. 53	P 20 June 55	P 25 Sept. 57	
7	0	Henry W. Berkeley	P 13 May 53	9 Oct. 55	P 29 Oct. 58	
6	0	Robert Norwood	P 14 July 54	18 June 57	P 29 Apr. 59	
5	0	John Charles Boucher	P 28 Dec. 55	18 June 57	P 18 Nov. 59	

		LIEUTENANTS.			
7	0	Hy. Fullerton Richmond[8]	P 21 Jan. 53	P 24 Mar. 54	
7	0	William Blenkinsop, R.M.	23 Dec. 53	P 29 Feb. 56	
7	0	Alfred Henderson White[9]	P 15 July 53	P 29 Dec. 54	
4	0	Geo. Romney Rawlinson	P 29 Aug. 56	P 31 July 57	
4	0	James Don, *Adj.*	12 Dec. 56	9 Oct. 57	
5	0	Nathaniel Gould	15 May 55	P 9 Oct. 57	
3	0	Edward Maunder	P 30 June 57	P 23 July 58	
3	0	Arthur C. Van Courtlandt	24 July 57	P 11 Jan. 59	
3	0	Clermont Hugh Costobadie	P 5 June 57	12 Nov. 58	
3	0	Philip Herbert Elliot	P 31 July 57	P 20 Apr. 59	
3	0	Henry Mapleton Hockin	11 Sept. 57	P 18 Nov. 59	

		CORNETS.		
3	0	Joseph Wm. Fitzgerald	14 July 57	
3	0	Thomas Dawson	16 Oct. 57	
3	0	Fra. Anthony S. Mannock	17 Oct. 57	
2	0	Robert George Smith	8 Jan. 58	
2	0	Winship Percival Roche	6 Aug. 58	
2	0	Edwin Brett	13 Aug. 58	
1	0	John Lloyd Egginton	P 31 May 59	

4	0	**Paymaster.**—Thomas Marshall Cockerill, 16 May 56.	
4	0	**Adjutant.**—Lieut. James Don, 12 Dec. 56.	
2	0	**Instructor of Musketry.**—Cornet Edwin Brett, 7 Sept. 59.	
7	0	**Quarter Master.**—Otho Vialls, 22 April 53.	
17	0	**Surgeon.**—Robert Marshall Allen,[10] 28 March 54; *Assist. Surg.* 3 June 43.	
6	0	**Assistant Surgeons.**—Charles John White,[11] 28 March 54.	
6	0	St. John Stanley,[13] 24 Feb. 54.	[1 July 59.
25	0	**Veterinary Surgeon.**—Richard John Gedaliah Hurford,[12] 17 July 35; *1st Class*,	

Scarlet—*Facings* Yellow.—*Agents*, Messrs. Hopkinson and Co.

[Returned from France, 25 January 1816. Embarked for India, Aug. 1857.]

1 Major General Scott was present with the French army under Marshal Gerard, at the siege of Antwerp, in Dec. 1832; and, by permission of the Marshal, he accompanied the troops upon every occasion during the siege. In Oct. 1838, he was appointed to the command of the cavalry of the Bombay division of the army of the Indus, as Brigadier; served in that rank during the campaigns of 1838 and 39, in Scinde and Affghanistan, and was present at the attack and capture of Ghuznee (Medal). During the latter part of 1839, he commanded a detached column, consisting of the whole of the artillery (excepting 4 guns), the cavalry, and one battalion of infantry; this column was destined to secure the subjugation of Upper Scinde, and to co-operate with the main column under Sir Thos. Willshire, directed against Khelat (2nd Class Doorance Empire). In the action at Maharajpore (Medal) on the 29th Dec. 1843, he commanded a Brigade of Cavalry, as also at the battle of Sobraon (Medal).

2 Colonel Smith has received the Order of the Medjidie, 2nd Class, for commanding the late Osmanli Cavalry.

2† Major Chaplin served the Punjaub campaign of 1848-9 with the 3rd Light Dragoons, and was present in the affair of Ramnuggur, passage of the Chenab at Wuzeerabad on the 1st Dec. 1848 with the force under Sir Joseph Thackwell, and battles of Sadoolapore, Chillianwallah, and Goojerat (Medal and two Clasps).

3 Captain Tower served with the 6th Dragoons in the Eastern campaign of 1854, including the battle of Balaklava, and siege of Sebastopol (Medal and Clasps).

7 Capt. Corrigan served as a Lieutenant in the 74th in the Kaffir war of 1851-52 (slightly wounded), and was afterwards attached to, and served with, the Cape Mounted Rifles as a Volunteer (Medal).

8 Lieut. Richmond served with the 10th Hussars in the Crimean campaign from 17th April 1855, and was present at the capture of Tchergaun, battle of the Tchernaya, siege and fall of Sebastopol (Medal and Clasp).

9 Lieut. White served with the 47th Regt. at the siege of Sebastopol from 14 Nov. 1854 to 18 Jan. 1855 Medal and Clasp).

Head Quarters at Brighton.] **4th (*Royal Irish*) Regt. of Dragoon Guards.** 132

Years' Serv.		On the Standards and Appointments the HARP AND CROWN, *and the Star of* ST. PATRICK, with the motto "*Quis separabit?*"—"PENINSULA." "BALAKLAVA." "SEVASTOPOL."				
Full Pay.	Half Pay.	*Colonel.*—Richard Pigot,[1] *Ens.* 4 Sept. 93; *Lieut.* 16 Sept. 93; *Capt.* 21 Dec. 93; *Major*, 29 April 02; *Lieut.Col.* 1 May 06; *Col.* 4 June 14; *Maj.Gen.* 19 July 21; *Lieut.Gen.* 10 Jan. 37; *Gen.* 11 Nov. 51; *Col.* 4th Dragoon Guards, 26 Nov. 49.				
67						
22	0	*Lt.Colonel.*—Arthur Cavendish Bentinck,[2] *Ens.* P 2 Nov. 38; *Lt.* P 31 Oct. 40; *Capt.* P 2 Mar. 47; *Maj.* P 27 June 51; *Lt.Col.* P 8 Dec. 54; *Col.* 30 Jan. 58.				
19	0	*Major.*—Thomas Jones,[3] *Cor.* P 23 July 41; *Lt.* P 19 May 43; *Capt.* P 30 June 48; *Major*, P 5 Aug. 59.				

		CAPTAINS.	CORNET.	LIEUT.	CAPTAIN.	BREV.-MAJ.
20	0	Fra. Rowland Forster,[4] *s.*	P 7 Feb. 40	P 11 Mar. 42	P 29 Jan. 47	12 Dec. 54
16	0	Michael M'Creagh[5]	26 July 44	P 10 Mar. 47	P 18 July 51	
14	0	Art. Masterson Robertson[8]	P 18 May 46	P 8 Oct. 47	P 25 June 52	
9	0	Robert Gunter[6]	P 16 May 51	P 25 June 52	P 7 Sept. 55	
7	1½	Christopher M'Donnel[7] ..	P 12 Mar. 52	P 17 June 53	P 14 Mar. 56	
8	0	Daniel Peploe Webb[3]	P 14 May 52	8 Dec. 54	P 11 Dec. 57	
11	0	John Edward Brodhurst	P 17 Sept. 49	P 24 Jan. 51	25 Apr. 55	
7	0	John Arthur Bragge[3]	P 13 May 53	29 Dec. 54	P 5 Aug. 59	
		LIEUTENANTS.				
7	0	Edward Rowe Fisher[13] ..	P 17 June 53	29 Dec. 54		8 Captain Robertson served in the Eastern campaign up to Nov. 1854, including the siege of Sebastopol, and battles of Balaklava and Inkerman (Medal and three Clasps).
7	0	George Alex. Muttlebury[9]	P 25 Nov. 53	P 7 Sept. 55		
6	0	Henry Ponsford	P 27 Jan. 54	P 14 Mar. 56		
5	0	Thomas Clark Gillespie .	10 April 55	P 4 Apr. 56		
5	0	Edward Harran,[10] *Adj.*...	23 Feb. 55	20 Mar. 57		
4	0	Robert Rintoul	25 Jan. 56	P 29 July 56		13 Lieut. Fisher and Qr. Master Drake served the Eastern campaign of 1854-55, including the battles of Balaklava and Tchernaya, and siege of Sebastopol (Medal and Clasps).
3	0	Henry Haskett Chilton..	P 17 Feb. 57	P 22 June 58		
3	0	Robert James Wright ..	17 Nov. 57	P 17 Sept. 58		
3	0	Henry Edward Bridges..	P 11 Dec. 57	P 5 Aug. 59		
		CORNETS.				
3	0	William Joice	31 Dec. 57			14 Paymaster Biggs served with the 4th Dr. Gds. the Eastern campaign of 1854-55, including the battles of Balaklava, Inkerman, and the Tchernaya, and siege of Sebastopol (Medal and Clasps, and Turkish Medal), and was acting Chief Paymaster of the Osmanli Irregular Cavalry in the spring of 1856.
2	0	Clement Rob. N. Royds ..	P 21 May 58			
2	0	John B. Smith Marriott .	P 24 Aug. 58			
2	0	Aug. G. Churchill Inge ..	26 Oct. 58			
2	0	Edw. A. F., *Lord* Seymour	P 29 Oct. 58			
1	0	Randolph R. Luscombe..	13 May 59			
1	0	Smith Hill Child	P 5 Aug. 59			
15	0	*Paymaster.*—John Biggs,[14] 16 Sept. 51; *Ens.* P 2 Sept. 45; *Lieut.* 17 Oct. 48.				
5	0	*Adjutant.*—*Lieut.* Edward Harran,[10] 7 Sept. 55.				
6	0	*Quarter Master.*—John George Drake,[13] 6 June 54.				
6	0	*Riding Master.*—George Price,[7] 13 April 55; *Cornet*, 5 Nov. 54.				
17	0	*Surgeon.*—Robert Cooper,[12] 18 March 53; *Assist.Surg.* 21 July 43.				
6	0	*Assist. Surgeon.*—William Macnamara, 6 Oct. 54.				
6	0	*Veterinary Surgeon.*—Luke Byrne, 3 Feb. 54.				

Scarlet—*Facings* Blue.—*Agent*, Andrew Lawrie, Esq.

[*Returned from the Crimea, July* 1856.]

1 General Pigot was actively employed in the West Indies in 1794 during the Maroon war, in the Mediterranean and capture of Minorca in 1798; at the capture of the Cape of Good Hope in 1806, and in the East Indies in 1818.

2 Colonel Bentinck served with the 7th Dr. Gds. in the Kaffir War in 1847 (Medal).

3 Major Jones, Captains Webb and Bragge served in the Eastern campaign of 1855, including the battle of the Tchernaya, and siege of Sebastopol (Medal and Clasp).

4 Major Forster served the Eastern campaign of 1854-55, including the battles of Balaklava and Inkerman, and siege of Sebastopol (Medal and Clasps, Brevet Major, Sardinian Medal, and 5th Class of the Medjidie).

5 Captain M'Creagh served the Eastern campaign of 1854-55, including the battle of Balaklava, siege of Sebastopol, and battle of Tchernaya (Medal and Clasps, Knight of the Legion of Honor, and 5th Class of the Medjidie).

6 Captain Gunter served during the Eastern campaign of 1854 and early part of the siege of Sebastopol (Medal and Clasp).

7 Captain M'Donnel and Riding Master Price served the Eastern campaign of 1854-55, including the battles of Balaklava and Inkerman, siege of Sebastopol, night-attack on Russian outposts 19th Feb. 1855, and battle of Tchernaya (Medal and Clasps).

9 Lieut. Muttlebury served the Eastern campaign of 1854-55, including the battles of Balaklava, Inkerman, and Tchernaya, and siege of Sebastopol (Medal and Clasps).

10 Lieut. Harran served the Eastern campaign of 1854-55, including the battle of Balaklava, siege of Sebastopol, night-attack on Russian outposts 10th Feb. 1855, and battle of Tchernaya (Medal and Clasps).

12 Surgeon Cooper served the Eastern campaign of 1854-55, including the battles of Alma, Balaklava, Inkerman, and Tchernaya, and siege of Sebastopol (Medal and Clasps); had charge of a general hospital which he established at Balaklava until he appeared in orders as surgeon of the 4th Dragoon Guards.

188 5th *(Princess Charlotte of Wales's) Reg. of Dr. Gds.* [Head Quarters at Aldershot.

The motto "*Vestigia nulla retrorsum.*"—"SALAMANCA" "VITTORIA" "TOULOUSE"
"PENINSULA" "BALAKLAVA" "SEVASTOPOL."

Years' Serv.		
36	Colonel.—James Thomas, *Earl of* Cardigan[1], KCB., *Cornet*, P 6 May 24; *Lt.* P 13 Jan. 25; *Capt.* P 9 June 26; *Major*, P 3 Aug. 30; *Lt.Col.* 3 Dec. 30; *Col.* 9 Nov. 46; *Major Gen.* 20 June 54; *Col.* 5th Dragoon Guards, 14 Aug. 59.	
Full Pay. / Half Pay.	Lt.Colonel.—Thomas Westropp M'Mahon,[2] CB., *Cornet*, 24 Dec. 29; *Lt.* P 2 Dec. 31; *Capt.* P 9 June 38; *Maj.* P 13 July 47; *Lt.Col.* 12 Dec. 54; *Col.* 12 Dec. 57.	
24 / 7		
9 / 3½	Major.—Hon. Somerset John Gough Calthorpe,[3] *Cor.* P 23 May 48; *Lt.* P 23 May 51; *Capt.* P 14 Sept. 55; *Bt.Major*, 2 Nov. 55; *Major*, 22 July 56.	

Full	Half		CORNET.	LIEUT.	CAPTAIN.	BREV.-MAJ.	BT.LT.COL.
		CAPTAINS.					
11	0	Fred. Hay Swinfen[4]	P 10 April 49	P 19 April 50	15 Dec. 54		
10	0	George Sapte Burnand[5]	P 12 April 50	P 28 Feb. 53	24 Dec. 54		
10	0	Richard T. Godman[6]....	P 17 May 50	P 3 Mar. 54	21 July 55		
8	0	Robert Garrard[7]	P 14 May 52	18 Nov. 53	P 13 Feb. 55		
9	½	Robt. Jas. Montgomery[8]	P 14 June 50	25 Aug. 54	29 July 56		
7	½	J. Stephenson Ferguson[8]	P 11 June 52	8 Dec. 54	5 Sept. 56		
7	0	Thomas Lewis Hampton[8]	P 21 Jan. 53	24 Dec. 54	P 7 Sept. 58		
6	0	Henry Hird Hay[5]	P 17 Mar. 54	20 Dec. 54	P 16 Aug. 59		
		LIEUTENANTS.					
5	0	Aug. William Travers ..	19 Feb. 55	P 8 Jan. 56			
5	0	L. Andrews Richardson..	P 20 Feb. 55	18 June 57			
6	0	James Hayes,[5] *Adj.*	10 Nov. 54	9 Oct. 57			
5	0	Henry Ellis White	1 May 55	9 Oct. 57			
5	0	Charles Morley Balders .	25 May 55	9 Oct. 57			
4	0	George Fred. Heyworth	P 8 Feb. 56	P 25 June 58			
4	0	Thomas Duffield........	P 28 Nov. 56	P 7 Sept. 58			
3	0	Wm. Butterworth Colvin	17 Nov. 57	P 16 Aug. 59			
3	0	Joseph H. P. FitzPatrick	27 Nov. 57	P 26 Aug. 59			
		CORNETS.					
3	0	William James Scarlett..	11 Dec. 57				
2	0	Wm. Miles Nairn Kington	26 Feb. 58				
2	0	Thomas Yate Benyon ...	14 May 58				
1	0	St. John Claud Paulet ..	6 Aug. 58				
1	0	Henry Darley..........	P 22 July 59				
2	0	*Paymaster.*—William George Proctor, 30 April 58.					
6	0	*Adjutant.*—Lieut. James Hayes,[5] 2 March 55.					
7	0	*Quarter Master.*—George William Bewley,[9] 8 July 53.					
5	0	*Riding Master.*—Maurice Day, 11 May 55.					
12	0	*Surgeon.*—Wm. Johnstone Fyffe,[10] M.D. 1 May 55; *Assist.Surg.* 8 Dec. 48.					
6	0	*Assistant Surgeon.*—William Cattell,[8] 28 March 54.					
8	0	*Veterinary Surgeon.*—Stephen Price Constant,[11] 15 Oct. 52.					

Notes in right-hand column:
7 Captain Garrard served in the Eastern campaign of 1854, including the battle of Alma — severely wounded (Medal and Clasp).
8 Captains Montgomery, Ferguson, and Hampton, and Assist.Surg. Cattell, served the Eastern campaign of 1854-55, including the battles of Balaklava and Inkerman, and siege of Sebastopol, and battle of the Tchernaya (Medal and Clasps). Capt. Hampton has the 5th Class of the Medjidie. Assist. Surgeon Cattell has also the Sardinian Medal.
9 Quarter Master Bewley served the Eastern campaign of 1854-55, including the battles of Balaklava and Inkerman, and siege of Sebastopol (Medal and Clasp).
10 Doctor Fyffe served the Eastern campaign of 1854-55, including the battles of Alma and Inkerman, and siege of Sebastopol (Medal and Clasps).
11 Veterinary Surgeon Constant served the Eastern campaign of 1854-55, including the battles of Alma, Balaklava, and Inkerman, and siege of Sebastopol (Medal and Clasps).

Scarlet—*Facings* Green.—*Agents*, Messrs. Cox & Co.
[*Returned from the Crimea*, 28 May 1850.]

1 Lord Cardigan commanded the Light Cavalry Brigade throughout the Eastern Campaign of 1854, including the battles of the Alma, Balaklava, and Inkerman, and siege of Sebastopol (Medal and Clasps), KCB., Commander of the Legion of Honor, and 2nd Class of the Medjidie).
2 Colonel M'Mahon served with the 9th Lancers in the Sutlej campaign in 1848, and was present at the battle of Sobraon (Medal). Served the Eastern campaign of 1854 as A. Q. M. G. to the Cavalry Division, including the battles of the Alma, Balaklava, and Tchernaya, and siege of Sebastopol; served also the campaign of 1855 in command of the 5th Dragoon Guards (Medal and Clasps, CB., Sardinian Medal, and 5th Class of the Medjidie).
3 Major *Hon.* S. J. G. Calthorpe served the Eastern campaign of 1854-55 as Aide de Camp to Lord Raglan, including the battles of Alma, Balaklava, and Inkerman, and siege of Sebastopol (Medal and four Clasps, Brevet Major, and 5th Class of the Medjidie).
4 Captain Swinfen served the Eastern campaign of 1854-55, including the battle of Balaklava (wounded) and siege of Sebastopol (Medal and Clasps).
5 Captains Burnand and Hay and Lieut. Hayes served the Eastern campaign of 1855, including the siege of Sebastopol (Medal and Clasps). Captain Hay and Lieut. Hayes were at the battle of Tchernaya.
6 Captain Godman served the Eastern campaign of 1854-55 as Adjutant of the 5th Dragoon Guards, including the battles of Balaklava, Inkerman, and Tchernaya, and siege of Sebastopol (Medal and Clasps).

Meerut. Depot, Maidstone.] **6th Regiment of Dragoon Guards (Carabineers).** 134

"SEVASTOPOL."

Years' Serv.			
Full Pay	Half Pay		
58		Colonel.—Alex. Kennedy Clark Kennedy,[1] CB. KH. *Cor.*, P 8 Sept. 02 ; *Lt.* 15 Dec. 04 ; *Capt.* P 13 Dec. 10 ; *Major*, P 26 May 25 ; *Lt.Col.* P 11 June 30 ; *Col.* 23 Nov. 41 ; *Maj.Gen.* 20 June 54 ; *Col.* 6 Dr. Gds. 14 June 58.	
35	0	Lieut.Colonels.—Henry Richmond Jones,[2] CB. *Cornet*, P 9 June 25 ; *Lieut.* P 14 Nov. 26 ; *Capt.* P 12 June 30 ; *Brevet Major*, 9 Nov. 46 ; *Major*, P 21 May 50 ; *Lieut.Col.* P 16 Sept. 51 ; *Col.* 28 Nov. 54.	
28	9/12	William Neville Custance,[3] CB. *Ensign*, P 11 Oct. 31 ; *Lieut.* P 26 June 35 ; *Capt.* P 16 Mar. 38 ; *Major*, P 16 Sept. 51 ; *Lt.Col.* 1 Aug. 56.	
27	0	Majors.—Charles Sawyer,[4] *Ensign*, P 6 Sept. 33 ; *Lieut.* P 8 April 36 ; *Capt.* P 8 Aug. 45 ; *Major*, 1 Aug. 56 ; *Bt.Lt.Col.* 20 July 58.	
16	0	Robert Bickerstaff, *Ens.* P 8 Nov. 44 ; *Lieut.* P 29 Dec. 46 ; *Capt.* P 10 Feb. 52 ; *Major*, P 6 Nov. 57 ; *Bt.Lt.Col.* 20 July 58.	

		CAPTAINS.	CORNET.	LIEUT.	CAPTAIN.	BREV.-MAJ.	BT.LT.COL.
7	0	Alex. George Dickson[6] ..	P 18 Feb. 53	6 June 54	P 1 June 55		
19	0	Charles Potts Rosser[7] ..	P 8 Jan. 41	3 Apr. 46	26 June 55	19 Jan. 58	
9	0	Thomas Bott[4]	P 18 Apr. 51	P 9 Mar. 55	P 22 Aug. 56	20 July 58	
5	0	Courtenay Wm. Bruce ..	15 May 55	P 26 Oct. 55	P 2 Oct. 57		
5	0	Fra. Nathaniel Astley ..	12 May 55	26 Nov. 55	P 6 Nov. 57		
8	0	William Thomas Betty ..	P 14 May 52	15 June 55	15 Dec. 57		
6	0	Fra. Geo. Savage Curtis	P 15 Dec. 54	24 Sept. 55	5 Mar. 58		
12	0	William Oliver Bird	P 15 Dec. 48	P 27 Aug. 52	P 4 Feb. 59		
12	0	Arthur Cooper	P 27 May 48	P 14 Dec. 49	P 12 Dec. 56		
9	0	Robert Scott Hunter[8] ..	P 17 June 51	17 Feb. 54	13 Sept. 55		
		LIEUTENANTS.					
7	0	Jas.JohnNeil Buchanan[14]	P 10 June 53	P 8 Sept. 54			
7	0	George Silvester Davies	P 18 Oct. 53	26 June 55			
6	0	Aug. Alfred de Bourbel ..	P 17 Mar. 54	23 Oct. 55			
4	0	John William Doering ..	P 16 May 56	P 22 Aug. 56			
5	0	Walter Blachford Gifford[9]	2 Oct. 55	P 19 Dec. 56			
5	0	Fred.A.Weatherley,[15] *adj.*	30 Mar. 55	P 26 June 55			
5	0	Geo.S.LeGriceStoddart[13]	28 Dec. 55	21 July 57			
4	0	Wm. Wallace Graham ..	2 May 56	15 Nov. 57			
4	0	Henry Reginald Forster	P 8 Aug. 56	P 4 Dec. 57			
5	0	William Howley Burder	P 21 Sept. 55	15 Dec. 57			
4	0	William Greaves Blake..	27 Feb. 56	P 26 Feb. 58			
3	0	William Duff Pereira ..	P 5 Dec. 57	P 19 July 59			
2	0	Tho. Macnaghten Turner	2 Feb. 58	P 19 July 59			
4	1 3/12	Wm. Gair,[10] *Dep. Ass. Commis.* 29 Sept. 54	18 Dec. 57	P 28 Oct. 59			
		CORNETS.					
3	0	John Buchan Hepburn..	P 4 Dec. 57				
2	0	Arthur George Smith ..	19 Feb. 58				
2	0	George Selwyn Marryat	16 Mar. 58				
1	0	Robert Stewart Blackett	P 4 Mar. 59				

2 Colonel Jones commanded the Carabineers in the Crimea from 14 Aug. 1855, including the battle of the Tchernaya, siege and fall of Sebastopol (Medal and Clasp, and 5th Class of the Medjidie).

4 Lt.Col. Sawyer and Major Bott served in the Crimea from 26th May 1855, including the battle of the Tchernaya, siege and fall of Sebastopol (Medal and Clasp).

7 Major Rosser served the campaign in the Southern Mahratta country in 1844. Also at the siege of Sebastopol in 1855, latterly as Aide de Camp to General Scarlett, and was at the battle of the Tchernaya (Medal and Clasp, and 5th Class of the Medjidie).

11 Qr. Master Fraser served at the siege and fall of Sebastopol from 14 Aug. 1855 (Medal and Clasp).

9	0	*Paymaster.*—Charles Sewell, 5 Jan. 55 ; *Cornet*, P 17 Oct. 51.	
5	0	*Adjutant.*—Lieut. Fred. Aug. Weatherley,[15] 5 Aug. 58.	
9	0	*Quarter Master.*—George Fraser,[11] 7 Nov. 51.	
2	0	*Riding Master.*—William James Hessey, 7 Dec. 58.	
8	0	*Surgeon.*—Donald Sinclair Smith, 28 Jan. 59 ; *Assist. Surg.* 27 Feb. 52.	
6	0	*Assistant Surgeons.*—Charles James Davenport, 15 Aug. 54.	
5	0	Stewart Aaron Lithgow, 3 Feb. 55.	
9	0	*Veterinary Surgeon.*—Alfred Job Owles,[16] 19 Dec. 51.	

Blue—*Facings* White.—*Agents*, Messrs. Cox & Co.

[*Returned from the Crimea, May* 1856. *Embarked for India,* 16*th Aug.* 1856.]

1 Major General Clark Kennedy served in the Peninsula with the Royal Dragoons from Sept. 1809 to Oct. 1813, including the battle of Busaco, covering the retreat to Torres Vedras, affair at Quinta de Torre, battle of Fuentes d'Onor (horse struck down by a shell), blockade of Almeida, actions at Navo d'Aver, Fuente Guinaldo, and Aldea de Ponte (appointed Brigade-Major to General Slade); covering the Siege of Ciudad Rodrigo, selected to command a party of Cavalry advanced to watch and report the enemy's movements during the siege of Badajoz, for which he was thanked by Lord Lynedoch ; engaged with a body of French Infantry under General Clausel, near Salamanca, battle of Vittoria, blockade of Pampeluna, besides various skirmishes and affairs of outposts. Campaign of 1815,—covering the retreat on the 17th June and battle of Waterloo (received two wounds and had two horses killed under him). Whilst leading his squadron in a successful charge against Count D'Erlon's corps at Waterloo, perceiving an Eagle to the left, he changed the direction of his squadron, ran the officer through the body who carried it, and captured the Eagle, which belonged to the 105th French Regiment of Infantry, and is now deposited in Chelsea Hospital. Has received the War Medal with two Clasps.

3 Lt.Colonel Custance served in the Crimean campaign from 14 Aug. 1855, including the battle of the Tchernaya, siege and fall of Sebastopol (Medal and Clasp, and Order of the Medjidie, 5th Class). Commanded the Carabineers at the outbreak of the Sepoy Mutineers at Meerut on 10th May 1857, as also during the campaign of that year, including the battles of the Hindun, 30th and 31st May (horse killed), battle of Budlekaserai, 8th June (horse wounded), affair of 9th June, and siege of Delhi; and commanded the Irregular Cavalry under Brigadier Grant, at the storming of the City 14th Sept. ; as also in the subsequent operations under Brigadier Showers. Commanded a Wing of the Regiment at the action of Bunkagaon on 8th Oct. 1858, also three squadrons in the subsequent campaign, including the actions of Mahoudispore, Bupoolpore, advance on and capture of Mitoudee, the affairs of Allygung, Bishwa, and pursuit of the rebels for three months through Rajpootana and Central India (Medal and Clasp and CB.).

6th Regiment of Dragoon Guards (Carabineers).

6 Captain Dickson served with the 62nd Regt. at the siege of Sebastopol in 1855, including the attack on the Quarries 8th June, and on the Redan 18th June (Medal and Clasp).

8 Captain Hunter served in the Eastern campaign of 1854-55, including the affair of M'Kenzie's Farm, battles of Balaklava and Inkerman, and siege of Sebastopol (Medal and three Clasps, and 5th Class of the Medjidie).

9 Lieut. Gifford was present with the Carabineers at the outbreak of the Sepoy mutiny at Meerut on 10 May 1857, and throughout the campaign of that year, including the battle of the Hindun, battle of Budiekaserai, affair of 9th June, siege and capture of Delhi.

10 Lieut. Gair served with the Field Train, R. Artillery, as Deputy Assist. Commissary during the Eastern campaign of 1854-55, including the affairs of Bulganac and McKenzie's Farm, battles of Alma, Balaklava, and Inkerman, siege and fall of Sebastopol (Medal and Clasps).

13 Lieut. Stoddart served with the Carabineers from the outbreak at Meerut to the pacification of Oude;—in 1857, being with Seaton's Column, he led the advanced guard in the attack upon Mynpoorie; in 1858 he served under Walpole near Futtehghur, afterwards with Troup's Column and its flying detachment under Col. Brind, was present in the actions of the 8th Oct. at Bunkagong, of the 18th Oct. at the Jungle, on 25th Oct. against 8000 rebels, at Metowlie on 8th Nov. (horse killed), and at Mehndie on 18th Nov.—mentioned in Col. Brind's despatch (Medal).

14 Lieut. Buchanan served with the 10th Hussars in the Crimean campaign from 17th April 1855, including the siege and fall of Sebastopol, battle of the Tchernaya, and affair of 21st Sept. near Kertch (Medal and Clasp). Served with the 6th Dr. Guards throughout the Indian campaign of 1857-59, including operations in Rohilcund and action of Nugeena, relief of Bareilly, relief of Shahjehanpore, capture of the fort of Remai and pursuit with destruction of the fort of Mahundee, action of Runkagaon, operations in Oude and actions of Mohndipore and Rusoolpore, attack and capture of fort Mitoulee, actions of Alligunj and Biswa. Also served as officiating D.Q.M.G. to the Agra field force under Brigadier Showers in Central India in pursuit of Tantia Topee, Feroze Shah, and others (Medal).

15 Lieut. Weatherley served with the 4th Lt. Drs. in the Crimean campaign from 13th Aug. 1855, including the battle of the Tchernaya, siege and fall of Sebastopol, and operations at Eupatoria (Medal and Clasp). Served with the 6th Dr. Guards in the Indian campaign including operations in Rohilcund and affair of Kukrowlie, taking of Bareilly, relief of Shahjehanpore and the two subsequent attacks, affairs of Mohumdee and Shahabad, operations in Oude and action of Buxarghat, Trans-Gogra actions of Majedia, Churdal, and Bankee (Medal).

16 Vet.Surgeon Owles served from 21st July 1855 at the siege and fall of Sebastopol (Medal and Clasp). Served the Indian campaign of 1857-58, including the actions of the Hindun on 30th and 31st May 1857, siege and capture of Delhi, taking of Bareilly, and operations in Oude (Medal and Clasp).

Depot, Canterbury. Senlkote.] *7th (The Princess Royal's) Regt. of Dragoon Guards.* 135

Years' Serv.			
Full Pay	Half Pay		
55		**Colonel.**—Michael White,[1] CB. *Cor.* p 15 Aug. 04; *Lt.* p 14 May 05; *Capt.* 7 Nov. 15; *Bt. Maj.* 10 Jan. 37; *Maj.* 4 Jan. 39; *Lt. Col.* p 13 Dec. 39; *Col.* 3 Apr. 46; *Maj. Gen.* 20 June 54; *Col.* 7 D. G. 26 Aug. 58.	
24	0	**Lt.Colonels.**—Charles Wm. Thompson,[3] *Ensign*, p 26 Feb. 36; *Lieut.* p 17 Jan. 40; *Capt.* p 1 Dec. 48; *Major*, p 9 Nov. 55; *Lt.Col.* 17 Sept. 57.	
24	0	Wm. Charles Forrest,[2] *Cor.* p 11 Mar. 36; *Lt.* p 5 Jan. 39; *Capt.* p 7 Sept. 41; *Major*, p 3 Oct. 48; *Bt.Lt.Col.* 12 Dec. 54; *Lt.Col.* p 5 Aug. 59.	
14	1	**Majors.**—Adolphus Wm. Desart Burton,[4] CB. *Ens.* p 8 Aug. 45; *Lt.* p 10 April 49; *Capt.* p 24 Dec. 52; *Bt.-Major*, 12 Dec. 54; *Major*, 5 Sept. 56.	
13	0	Fitzroy George Smith, *Cornet*, p 31 Dec. 47; *Lt.* p 11 Sept. 49; *Capt.* p 30 July 52; *Major*, 19 Apr. 59.	

		CAPTAINS.	CORNET.	LIEUT.	CAPTAIN.	BREV.-MAJ.
11	0	Wm. Wentworth Lamb..	p 30 Mar. 49	p 21 May 50	p 8 Dec. 54	
11	0	Tho. Edw. Dowbiggen ..	p 18 May 49	p 27 June 51	14 Sept. 55	
8	0	Peter Withington	p 9 July 52	p 13 Feb. 55	16 Sept. 57	
11	0	Henry Blinkhorn[5]	16 Feb. 49	14 Sept. 55	16 Sept. 57	
8	0	W. Fourbelle Dowdeswell	p 17 Aug. 52	14 Sept. 55	p 16 Sept. 57	
14	½	George E. F. Kauntze[5]†...	19 Dec. 45	p 28 Jan. 48	14 Sept. 55	
10	0	Newton Chas. Chichester	p 16 Aug. 50	p 22 Sept. 54	p 13 July 57	
6	0	James Vance Cleland ..	p 15 Dec. 54	p 9 May 56	p 26 Nov. 58	
5	0	John Richards Welstead	p 27 July 55	p 5 June 57	p 8 Apr. 59	
5	0	Robert Clarke	30 Nov. 55	p 3 Mar. 57	p 6 May 59	
		LIEUTENANTS.				
7	0	D. Scotland (Q.M.16 Dec.53)		17 Nov. 54	8 May 56	
4	0	Christopher Barton		16 May 56	15 Sept. 57	
4	0	Wm. Digby Wentworth..		p 22 Aug. 56	15 Sept. 57	
3	0	George Ross Caldwell[10]..		....	20 Feb. 57	
5	0	Edm. Prideaux Chichester[9]		20 Feb. 55	3 Aug. 55	
5	0	Edw. Hy. Ernest Kauntze		11 May 55	p 29 Feb. 56	
5	0	Wm. Bruce Armstrong[6]		22 June 55	18 Sept. 57	
4	0	William Chaine		p 12 Dec. 56	p 9 Oct. 57	
3	0	Edmund Molyneux		p 16 June 57	p 26 Nov. 58	
3	0	Robert Stewart Cleland..		p 7 July 57	p 8 Apr. 59	
3	0	Jas.Jno. London M'Adam		p 22 May 57	19 Apr. 59	
		CORNETS.				
3	0	Wm. Macnaghton Erskine		p 16 Oct. 57		
3	0	John M'Bryan		17 Oct. 57		
3	0	Clavering Redman		6 Nov. 57		
3	0	Edward Henry O'Dowd		27 Nov. 57		
3	0	Arthur Hare Vincent....		29 Dec. 57		
1	0	John Alex. Drake		p 11 Jan. 59		
1	0	Henry Bulkeley........		3 June 59		
2	0	Edward Goldsmith......		16 Aug. 58		

4	1/2	**Paymaster.**—John Smith, 17 Nov. 57; *Lieut.* 21 Sept. 55; *Capt.* 1 Feb. 56.
7	0	**Adjutant.**—*Lieut.* David Scotland, 17 Nov. 54.
3	0	**Instructor of Musketry.**—*Cornet* A. H. Vincent, 12 March 59.
6	0	**Quarter Master.**—George Gillam,[7] 17 Nov. 54.
3	0	**Riding Master.**—Henry Pearce Phillips, 2 Oct. 57.
11	0	**Surgeon.**—Edward James Franklyn,[11] M.D. 15 May 55; *Assist.Surg.* 19 Oct. 49.
7	0	**Assist. Surgeons.**—Opie Smith, 4 Feb. 53.
5	0	Edward M'Gill, M.D., 8 Jan. 55.
5	0	**Veterinary Surgeon.**—William Varley, 15 Aug. 55.

Scarlet—*Facings* Black.—*Agents,* Messrs. COX & CO.

[*Returned from Cape of Good Hope,* 7 *June* 1848. *Embarked for India,* 27 *Oct.* 1857.]

1 Major-General White was in the field in 1809, on the banks of the Sutlej; served at the capture of Hatras in 1817, and during the Mahratta campaign of 1817-18; was present at the siege and capture of Bhurtpore in 1825-6 (Medal and one Clasp). Commanded the cavalry throughout the campaign of 1842 in Affghanistan, and was present at the forcing of the Khyber Pass, storming the heights of Jugdulluck, action of Tezeen and Huft Kotul, and occupation of Caboul (Medal, and nominated a CB.). Served with the army of the Sutlej in 1845-6; commanded the whole of the cavalry at the battle of Moodkee (charger wounded); a brigade at the battle of Ferozeshah (wounded, charger killed by a round shot); and the 3rd Lt. Drs. at the battle of Sobraon (charger wounded); Medal and two Clasps, and appointed Aide de-Camp to the Queen. Served in the Punjaub campaign of 1848-9, in command of the 1st Brigade of Cavalry; was present in the affair of Ramnuggur, action of Sadoolapore, and battles of Chillianwallah and Goojerat (Medal and two Clasps).

2 Lt. Colonel Forrest served with the 4th Dr. Gds. the Eastern campaign of 1854-55, including the battles of Balaklava and Inkerman, siege of Sebastopol, night attack on Russian outposts 19th Feb. 1855, and battle of Tchernaya (Medal and Clasps, Brevet Lt.-Colonel, Sardinian Medal, and 5th Class of the Medjidie).

3 Lt.-Colonel Thompson served as a Captain in the British Legion, and was engaged at Hernani 30th Aug. 1835; at Arlaban, 16th, 17th, and 18th Jan.; and the action before San Sebastian, 5th May 1836, when he was severely wounded in the hip and the hand (K. S. F. and Medal). Served the campaign of the Punjaub in the 14th Light Dragoons; was engaged at Ramnuggur (horse wounded), 22nd Nov. 1848, at Chillianwallah, 13th Jan., and at Goojerat, 21st Feb. 1849 (Medal and two Clasps). Present also at the crossing of the Chenab, Jhelum, and Indus; at the surrender of the Seik army at Rawul Pindee, the capture of the Bridge of Boats at Attock, and pursuit of the Affghans to Peshawur.

4 Major Burton served in the Eastern campaign of 1854-55, and commanded the 5th Dragoon Guards at the battles of Balaklava, Inkerman, and Tchernaya, and siege of Sebastopol (Medal and three Clasps, Brevet Major, CB., and 5th Class of the Medjidie).

5 Capt. Blinkhorn served with the 16th Lancers in the battle of Maharajpore, 29th Dec. 1843 (Medal), also in the campaign on the Sutlej in 1846, including the battle of Sobraon, for which he has received a Medal and one Clasp.

6 Lieut. Armstrong served with the 7th Dragoon Guards at the Cape of Good Hope, and was with the expedition against the insurgent Boers beyond the Orange River in 1845; and he

7 Quartermaster Gillam served with a detachment of the 24th Regt. at the defeat of the Jhelum Mutineers on 7th July 1857, and was shot through the left arm.

9 Lieut. Chichester served with the 21st Fusiliers during the latter part of 1855 at the siege and fall of Sebastopol, and expedition to Kinbourn (Medal and Clasp).

10 Lieut. Caldwell served throughout the Kaffir war of 1846-7 (Medal).

11 Doctor Franklyn served throughout the siege and fall of Sebastopol in 1855 (Medal), was at Balaklava attending on the wounded during the cavalry action there; and was placed in charge of the Russian wounded after the battle of Inkerman; and served with the 77th Regt. before Sebastopol (Medal and Clasps, and 5th Class of the Medjidie).

5† Capt. Kauntze was present with the 11th Lt. Drs. at the siege and capture of Bhurtpore in 1825-6 (Medal and one Clasp); served with the 3rd Lt. Drs. throughout the campaign of 1842 in Affghanistan (Medal), and was present at the forcing of the Khyber Pass, capture of Mamoo Khail, storming the heights of Jugdulluck, actions of Tezeen and Huftkotul, and occupation of Caboul. He served also the Sutlej campaign of 1845-6, and was present at the battles of Moodkee (wounded), Ferozeshah (wounded), and Sobraon (severely wounded), Medal and two Clasps. Served in the Punjaub campaign of 1848-9, and was present at the affair of Ramnuggur, the passage of the Chenab at Wuzeerabad on the 1st December 1848, with a force under Sir Joseph Thackwell, action of Sadoolapore, and battles of Chillianwallah and Goojerat (Medal and two Clasps).

1st (Royal) Regiment of Dragoons.

[Head Quarters, Dublin.

The Crest of England within the Garter. The Eagle. "*Spectemur agendo*." "PENINSULA" "WATERLOO" "BALAKLAVA" "SEVASTOPOL."

Years' Serv.			
Full Pay	Half Pay		
66		Colonel.—💂 🎖️ Sir Arthur Benjamin Clifton,[1] KCB. KCH. *Cornet*, 6 June 94; *Lieut.* 7 Aug. 04; *Capt.* 27 Feb. 99; *Major*, 17 Dec. 03; *Lieut. Col.* 25 July 10; *Col.* 12 Aug. 19; *Major Gen.* 22 July 30; *Lieut.Gen.* 23 Nov. 41; *Gen.* 20 June 54; *Col.* 1st Dragoons, 30 Aug. 42.	
25	0	*Lieut.Colonel.*—Robert Wardlaw,[3] *Cornet*, p 5 June 35; *Lieut.* p 28 July 40; *Capt.* p 14 Oct. 42; *Major*, p 4 Feb. 53; *Brev. Lt.Col.* 12 Dec. 54; *Lt.Col.* p 10 March 57; *Col.* 12 Dec. 57.	
14	0	*Major.*—Michael Stocks,[5] *Cor.* p 11 Dec. 46; *Lt.* p 20 July 49; *Capt.* p 25 Feb. 53; *Major*, p 23 Oct. 57.	

		CAPTAINS.	CORNET.	LIEUT.	CAPTAIN.	BREV.-MAJ.
12	0	James Ainslie[7]	p 13 Oct. 48	p 21 Dec. 49	p 11 Oct. 53	
10	0	Walter John Coney[5]	p 18 Jan. 50	p 25 Feb. 53	22 Dec. 54	
7	0	G. Metcalfe Robertson[10]	p 12 May 53	29 Dec. 54	p 10 Mar. 57	
11	0	Henry F. Geo. Coleman	p 29 June 49	p 31 Jan. 51	p 11 Dec. 57	
5	0	John Gordon Graham	19 June 55	p 15 Feb. 56	p 19 Feb. 58	
8	0	Hume Nicholl	p 18 Aug. 52	9 Oct. 55	10 Apr. 59	
5	0	Cecil Frederic Holder	p 15 May 55	p 9 Oct. 55	p 23 Aug. 59	
4	0	Frederic Radford	p 20 Aug. 56	p 11 Dec. 57	p 23 Aug. 59	
		LIEUTENANTS.				
6	0	John Lee,[5] *Adj.*	5 Nov. 54	14 Feb. 56		
4	0	John Uppleby Graburn	7 Mar. 56	p 10 Mar. 57		
4	0	Daniel Finucane	p 19 Aug. 56	p 23 Oct. 57		
3	0	Walter Balfe	p 27 Jan. 57	p 19 Feb. 58		
3	0	John W. Simmons Smith	p 20 Mar. 57	2 July 58		
5	0	Edmund Wald. Park-Yates	p 27 July 55	18 June 57		
3	0	Henry St. George Osborne	p 31 Dec. 57	p 24 May 59		
2	0	Charles Hall	26 Feb. 58	p 23 Aug. 59		
2	0	Ralph William Caldwell	p 13 July 58	p 23 Aug. 59		
		CORNETS.				
2	0	Carr Stuart Glyn	p 16 July 58			
2	0	George Lake Harvey	30 July 58			
1	0	Charles Downes Manning	p 30 Sept. 59			

12 Doctor Forteath served with the troops engaged in suppressing the rebellion in Ceylon in 1848. Served the Eastern campaign of 1854-55, and was present at the affair of Bulganak, and battles of Alma, Balaklava, Inkerman, and Tchernaya, and siege of Sebastopol (Medal and Clasps).

13	0	*Paymaster.*—Henry Dixon,[13] 29 Oct. 52; *Ens.* p 6 Feb. 47; *Lt.* p 29 Dec. 48.
6	0	*Adjutant.*—*Lieut.* John Lee,[5] 24 April 55.
11	0	*Quarter Master.*—William Scott,[14] 26 Oct. 49.
5	0	*Riding Master.*—George Cruse,[8] 16 March 55.
17	0	*Surgeon.*—Alexander Forteath,[12] M.D. 28 March 54; *Assist.Surg.* 10 Feb. 43.
5	0	*Assist.Surgeon.*—Spencer Boyd Gibb, M.D. 17 May 55.
4	0	*Veterinary Surgeon.*—Evander Chambers, 8 March 56.

Scarlet—Facings Blue.—*Agents*, Messrs. Cox & Co. *Irish Agents*, Messrs. Cane & Sons.

[*Returned from the Crimea*, 27 May 1856.]

1 Sir Arthur Clifton's services:—Campaigns of 1809, 10, 11, 12, 13, 14, and 15. Commanded a squadron in covering and supporting four Spanish guns at the battle of Talavera, and employed in different subsequent operations; battle of Busaco, pursuit of Massena from Santarem, taking from him prisoners and baggage; battle of Fuentes d'Onor, actions at Navé d'Aver, El Bodon, Fuentes Guinaldo, and Alden de Ponte; several affairs during the retreat of the army from Salamanca to Ciudad Rodrigo; charged with a squadron a body of French Infantry under General Clausel, near Salamanca, killing or taking nearly a hundred of the enemy; battle of Vittoria, blockade of Pampeluna, several affairs in the Pyrenees, battle of Toulouse, skirmishing with the enemy and covering the retreat on the 17th of June, and battle of Waterloo. Sir Arthur has received the Gold Medal and one Clasp for Fuentes d'Onor and Vittoria; and the Silver War Medal with three Clasps for Talavera, Busaco, and Toulouse; is a Knight 2nd Class St. Anne of Russia, and 4th Class Wilhelm of Holland.

3 Colonel Wardlaw served the Eastern campaign of 1854-55, including the battles of Balaklava, Inkerman, and Tchernaya (commanded the Regt.), and siege of Sebastopol (Medal and Clasps, Knight of the Legion of Honor, and 5th Class of the Medjidie).

5 Major Stocks, Captain Coney, and Lieut. Lee, served the Eastern campaign of 1854-55, including the battles of Balaklava, Inkerman, and Tchernaya, and siege of Sebastopol (Medal and Clasps). Major Stocks has the 5th Class of the Medjidie.

7 Captain Ainslie served the Eastern campaign of 1855, including the battle of Tchernaya and siege of Sebastopol (Medal and Clasp).

8 Riding-Master Cruse served the Eastern campaign, including the battles of Balaklava and Inkerman, and siege of Sebastopol (Medal and Clasps).

10 Captain Robertson served the Eastern campaign of 1854-55, including the battles of Balaklava (horse shot under him), Inkerman, and Tchernaya, and siege of Sebastopol (Medal and Clasps).

13 Paymaster Dixon served the Eastern campaign of 1854-55 with the 7th Fusiliers, including the battles of Alma and Inkerman, and siege of Sebastopol (Medal and Clasps).

14 Qr.Master Scott served the Eastern campaign of 1854-55, including the battle of Inkerman and siege of Sebastopol (Medal and Clasps).

Head Quarters, Newbridge.] 2nd (*Royal North British*) *Regt. of Dragoons.* 137

On the Standards an Eagle.—"WATERLOO" "BALAKLAVA" "SEVASTOPOL."

Years' Serv.		
Full Pay	Half Pay	
51		Colonel.—翼 鯛 Arthur W. M. *Lord Sandys*,¹ *Cornet*, 27 July 09; *Lt.* 19 July 10; *Capt.* 25 Aug. 13; *Major*, 27 July 15; *Lt.Col.* 21 Jan. 19; *Col.* 10 Jan. 37; *MajorGen.* 9 Nov. 46; *Lt.Gen.* 20 June 54; *Col.* 2 Drs. 26 Aug. 58.
31	5/12	*Lieut. Colonel.*—Henry Darby Griffith,² CB. *Cor.* P 25 Nov. 28; *Lt.* P 25 Nov. 31; *Capt.* P 1 Aug. 34; *Maj.* P 6 Nov. 46; *Lt.Col.* P 27 Aug. 52; *Col.* 28 Nov. 54.
26	0	*Major.*—George Calvert Clarke,³ *Ensign*, P 30 May 34; *Lieut.* P 7 Oct. 36; *Capt.* P 20 Sept. 39; *Brevet Major*, 11 Nov. 51; *Brev. Lt.Col.* 12 Dec. 54; *Major*, 26 Feb. 58.

		CAPTAINS.	CORNET.	LIEUT.	CAPTAIN.	BREV.-MAJ.
11	0	George Buchanan⁴	P 16 Mar. 49	P 27 Aug. 52	8 Dec. 54	
8	0	Andrew Nugent⁵	P 17 Dec. 52	24 Nov. 54	P 8 Feb. 56	
7	0	Duncan McNeill⁶	P 20 Sept. 53	15 Dec. 54	P 17 July 57	
6	1½	Lenox Prendergast⁷	P 11 Mar. 53	8 Dec. 54	P 13 June 56	
9	1 5/12	Geo. Barrington Price⁸	P 17 May 50	15 Mar. 53	P 1 Aug. 56	
7	0	A. S. Montague Browne⁶	18 Nov. 53	P 16 Mar. 55	P 24 Dec. 58	
11	0	*V℃* James Leith⁹	4 May 49	P 27 May 53	27 July 58	20 July 58
6	0	Charles Hill Uniacke¹⁰	P 27 Jan. 54	23 Oct. 55	P 25 Feb. 59	
		LIEUTENANTS.				
5	0	James Brander Dunbar	12 Jan. 55	P 25 May 55		
6	0	Daniel Moodie¹⁴	30 Sept. 54	7 Feb. 56		
5	0	John Lorn Stewart	P 20 Feb. 55	P 8 Feb. 56		
5	0	Thomas Philip Parr	P 30 Mar. 55	P 19 June 57		
5	0	George Cleghorn	P 4 May 55	17 Sept. 57		
5	0	Samuel Seggie	19 Feb. 55	17 Nov. 57		
4	0	Hugh Edmond Browning	26 Feb. 56	27 Nov. 57		
3	0	Francis Lamb Philp	P 17 July 57	P 24 Dec. 58		
3	0	George Paulet	P 19 June 57	31 Jan. 58		
		CORNETS.				
3	0	Charles Hill	P 11 Sept. 57			
3	0	*V℃* John Grieve, *Adj.*	4 Dec. 57			
2	0	Percy Charles DuCane	2 July 58			
2	0	Thomas Hunt	26 Oct. 58			
2	0	John Wallace Hozier	P 17 Dec. 58			
1	0	William Connel Black	P 18 Mar. 59			

14	0	*Paymaster.*—John Henry King,¹³ 10 April 55; *Cornet*, P 23 Jan. 46; *Lieut.* [31 Dec. 47.]
3	0	*Adjutant.—V℃ Cornet* John Grieve, 18 Feb. 59.
10	0	*Quarter Master.*—Thomas Hamilton M'Bean,¹⁴ 16 Aug. 50.
3	0	*Riding Master.*—Nicholas Mills, 11 Sept. 57.
10	0	*Surgeon.*—Aug. Purefoy Lockwood,¹⁵ 21 Sept. 52; *Assist. Surg.* 17 Sept. 41.
3	0	*Assistant Surgeon.*—Thomas Rudd, MD., 1 Aug. 57.
5	0	*Veterinary Surgeon.*—Thornton Hart, 4 July 55.

Scarlet—*Facings* Blue.—*Agents*, Messrs. Cox & Co.

[*Returned from the Crimea*, 4 *July* 1856.]

1 Lord Sandys accompanied the 10th Hussars to the Peninsula in 1812, and was present in the action a Morales, and battles of Vittoria and Pampeluna. Served also the campaign of 1815, as an Aide-de-Camp to the Duke of Wellington, and was present at the battle of Waterloo. Has received the Silver War Medal with one Clasp for Vittoria.

2 Colonel Griffith served the Eastern campaign of 1854-55, in command of the Scots Greys, including the affair of M'Kenzie's Farm, battles of Balaklava (wounded in the head by a pistol-ball), Inkerman, and Tchernaya, siege and fall of Sebastopol (Medal and three Clasps, CB., Sardinian Medal, and 4th Class of the Medjidie).

3 Lt.-Colonel Clarke served the Eastern campaign of 1854-55, including the affair of M'Kenzie's Farm, battles of Balaklava (sabre cut on the neck), Inkerman, and Tchernaya, siege and fall of Sebastopol (Medal and three Clasps, Brevet Lt.-Col., Knight of the Legion of Honor, and 5th Class of the Medjidie).

4 Captain Buchanan served the Eastern campaign of 1854-55, including the battles of Balaklava and Inkerman, and siege of Sebastopol (Medal and Clasps: also Sardinian Medal).

6 Captains McNeill and Browne were at the battle of the Tchernaya, and the siege and fall of Sebastopol (Medal and Clasps).

9 Major Leith served with the 14th Lt.Drs. in the Persian expedition of 1857 (Medal). Also at the suppression of the mutiny at Aurungabad; with the Malwa field force at the siege and capture of Dhar, actions before Mundesore (wounded), battle of Gooravia, and relief of Neemuch; with the Central India field force under Sir Hugh Rose at the siege and capture of Rahutghur, relief of Saugor, capture of Gurrakota and pursuit across the Beas, forcing the Muddenpore pass, siege and capture of Jhansi, battles of the Betwa and Koonch, and all the affairs during the advance on Calpee (twice mentioned in despatches, Brevet of Major, Victoria Cross, and Medal).

10 Captain Uniacke served with the 10th Hussars in the Crimea from 17 April 1855, including the capture of Tchorgoun, siege and fall of Sebastopol (Medal and Clasp). Served with the Carabineers in India, and was present at the battles of the Hindun, battle of Budickaserai, affair of 9th June 1857, siege and fall of Delhi, and subsequent operations with Showers' Moveable Column.

14 Lieut. Moodie and Qr.-Master M'Bean served the Eastern campaign of 1854-55, including the affair of M'Kenzie's Farm, battles of Balaklava, Inkerman, and Tchernaya, siege and fall of Sebastopol (Medal and three Clasps, and 5th Class of the Medjidie).

138   3rd (*The King's Own*) *Regt. of Lt. Dragoons.*   [Head Quarters, Dublin.

The White Horse, within the Garter on the 2nd and 3rd Standards, with the Motto, *"Nec aspera terrent."* "SALAMANCA" "VITTORIA" "TOULOUSE" "PENINSULA" "CABOOL, 1842" "MOODKEE" "FEROZESHAH" "SOBRAON" " PUNJAUB" " CHILLIANWALLAH" " GOOJERAT."

Years' Serv.	Half Pay.		CORNET.	LIEUT.	CAPTAIN.	BREV.–MAJ.
Full Pay. 56	0	*Colonel.*—⚜ ⚜⚜ Peter Aug. Lautour,[1] CB. KH. *Cornet*, 31 Mar. 04; *Lt.* 4 July 05; *Capt.* 8 May 06; *Maj.* 20 May 13; *Lt.Col.* 18 June 15; *Col.* 10 Jan. 37; *Major Gen.* 9 Nov. 46; *Lt.Gen.* 20 June 54; *Col.* 3rd Drs. 26 May 55.				
27	0	*Lieut.Colonel.*—Walter Unett,[2] *Cornet*, ᴾ 23 Aug. 33; *Lt.* ᴾ 31 Mar. 37; *Capt.* ᴾ 1 Nov. 42; *Brev. Maj.* 7 June 49; *Maj.* ᴾ 3 Feb. 54; *Lt.Col.* 20 June 54; *Col.* 20 June 57.				
19	0	*Major.*—*Hon.* Horace Manners Monckton,[3] *Ens.* ᴾ 23 April 41; *Lt.* ᴾ 29 April 42; *Capt.* ᴾ 4 May 49; *Major*, ᴾ 17 Feb. 57.				
		CAPTAINS.	CORNET.	LIEUT.	CAPTAIN.	BREV.–MAJ.
9	0	Richard Michael Williams	ᴾ 16 May 51	ᴾ 29 Apr. 53	ᴾ 22 Sept. 54	
11	0	Edward Howard Vyse ..	ᴾ 21 Aug. 49	ᴾ 3 Feb. 54	ᴾ 17 Feb. 57	
10	0	Arthur Edmund Mansel	ᴾ 15 Oct. 50	ᴾ 9 Mar. 55	ᴾ 19 Feb. 58	
9	0	Robert Dymond........	ᴾ 17 Jan. 51	14 Sept. 55	ᴾ 21 May 58	
6	0	Jacob Camac Murphy ..	ᴾ 17 Feb. 54	14 Sept. 55	ᴾ 22 June 58	
6	0	William Morrison Bell ..	ᴾ 1 Sept. 54	ᴾ 3 Mar. 57	ᴾ 24 Aug. 58	
5	0	Charles Talbot Goff	ᴾ 18 May 55	9 Oct. 57	ᴾ 15 Oct. 58	
4	0	Richard Blundell	ᴾ 7 Mar. 56	ᴾ 19 Feb. 58	ᴾ 4 Mar. 59	
		LIEUTENANTS.			2 Col. Unett served with the 3rd Lt. Drs. throughout the campaign of 1842 in Affghanistan (Medal) and was present at the forcing of the Khyber Pass, storming the heights of Jugdulluck, action of Tezeen and Huftkotul, occupation of Caboul, storm and capture of Istaliff. He served also the Punjaub campaign of 1848-9, and was present at the affair of Ramnuggur, the passage of the Chenab at Wuzeerabad on the 1st Dec. 1848 with the force under Sir Joseph Thackwell, action of Sadoolapore, and battles of Chillianwallah (severely wounded) and Goojerat (Medal and two Clasps, and promoted to the brevet rank of Major).	
8	0	Joseph P. North,[7] *Adj.* ..	31 Dec. 52	ᴾ 2 Feb. 55		
6	0	Wm. Drury N. Lowe, s...	1 Dec. 54	ᴾ 10 Apr. 55		
5	0	Arthur Lautour	23 Oct. 55	9 Oct. 57		
3	0	John Unett............	ᴾ 31 July 57	ᴾ 28 May 58		
2	0	Henry Henzell Unett....	9 Jan. 58	ᴾ 24 Aug. 58		
2	0	Reginald Piffard	ᴾ 2 Feb. 58	ᴾ 24 Sept. 58		
2	0	John Ormsby Phibbs ..	3 Feb. 58	ᴾ 15 Oct. 58		
2	0	Fred. G. Forsyth Grant..	ᴾ 5 Mar. 58	ᴾ 4 Mar. 59		
5	0	Richard Jas. M. St.George	31 May 55	30 Mar. 58		
		CORNETS.				
3	0	Samuel Barrett	ᴾ 20 Mar. 57			
2	0	George Shippen Willes ..	ᴾ 14 May 58			
2	0	Henry Higgins	24 Aug. 58			
2	0	Edward Arthur Gore....	ᴾ 25 Aug. 58			
2	0	Daniel Henry Doherty ..	26 Oct. 58			
1	0	Anthony Strother	ᴾ 25 Mar. 59			
1	0	John Webb............	ᴾ 13 May 59			
1	0	Thomas Donaldson.....	ᴾ 22 July 59			
12	0	*Paymaster.*—Fred. Thomas Ongley Hopson,[6] 15 Feb. 56; *Cornet*, ᴾ 15 Aug. 48;				
8	0	*Adjutant.*—*Lieut.* Joseph P. North, 15 Nov. 55. [*Lt.* 15 March 53.				
2	0	*Quarter Master.*—Charles E. Nettles, 16 July 58; *Cor.* 30 Mar. 58.				
5	0	*Riding Master.*—James Alexander Dixon,[12] 21 Sept. 55.				
21	0	*Surgeon.*—Wm. Ord Mackenzie, M.D., *Assist.Surg.* 4 Jan. 39; *Surg.* 8 Jan.				
6	0	*Assist. Surg.*—John Crown Agnis, 11 Aug. 54. [47; *Surg.Maj.* 4 Jan. 59.				
14	0	*Vet. Surg.*—Benj. Chaning Rouse Gardiner,[13] 19 May 46; *1st Class*,1 July 59.				

Blue—*Facings* Scarlet.—*Agent*, Edward S. Codd, Esq.
[*Returned from the East Indies*, 12 May 1858.]

1 Lieut.General Lautour served in the Peninsula with the 11th Dragoons in 1811 and 12; he attacked with a squadron of that Regt., on the 26th Sept. 1811, near El Bodon, a French Cavalry Regt., which had captured the baggage of the Light Division, taking several prisoners, and covered the retreat of the 74th Regt., and five companies of the 60th Rifles from Ciudad Rodrigo. Present at the siege of Badajoz, battle of Salamanca, affair of Cavalry near the Tormes on the following day, when three French Battalions were taken, affairs of Callada, Camins, and Fenta da Poso. On 7th Sept. 1812, whilst in command of a squadron of the 11th Dragoons, he attacked and took prisoners a company of French Artillery near Valladolid, supporting the enemy's cavalry, during the time the British Army was crossing the Douro; he also repulsed, on 2nd Oct. 1812, at Monasteros in front of Burgos, an attack of the enemy's pickets and advanced guard, making one officer and many men prisoners. He was continually on outpost duty, and almost daily engaged with the enemy's skirmishers, and was slightly wounded in the retreat from Burgos by the bursting of a shell. Served the campaign of 1815 with the 23rd Light Dragoons, and was present in the actions of the 16th and 17th June, and at the battle of Waterloo, where he succeeded to the command of the Regiment and of the Brigade; was present also at the capture of Paris. He has received the War Medal with one Clasp for Salamanca.

3 Hon. Major Monckton served with the 29th Regt. throughout the Punjaub campaign of 1848-9, and was present at the passage of the Chenab, and battles of Chillianwallah (wounded) and Goojerat, and pursuit of the Sikhs with the force under Sir Walter Gilbert (Medal and two Clasps). Served with the army of the East, attached to the 4th Light Dragoons, and afterwards with the rank of Major in command of the Sultan's "Royal Regt. of Constantinople," with the cavalry under Major General Shirley.

7 Lieut. North served with the 6th Dragoons at the battle of the Tchernaya, siege and fall of Sebastopol (Medal and Clasp).

8 Paymaster Hopson served as Lieut. 10th Hussars in the Crimean campaign of 1855 (Medal with Clasp for Sebastopol).

12 Riding Master Dixon served the campaign in Affghanistan in 1842 (Medal), including the forcing of the Khyber Pass; served the Sutlej campaign of 1845-46, including the battles of Moodkee, Ferozeshah (severely wounded), and Sobraon (wounded) (Medal and two Clasps). Served also the Punjaub campaign of 1848-49, including the affair at Ramnuggur, passage of the Chenab, action of Sadoolapore (wounded), and battles of Chillianwallah and Goojerat (Medal and two Clasps).

13 Vet. Surgeon Gardiner served with the 7th Dragoon Guards throughout the Kaffir war of 1846-7 (Medal).

Head Quarters, Manchester.] **4th (*The Queen's Own*) *Regt. of Light Dragoons.*** 139

"TALAVERA" "ALBUHERA" "SALAMANCA" "VITTORIA" "TOULOUSE" "PENINSULA"
"AFFGHANISTAN" "GHUZNEE" "ALMA" "BALAKLAVA" "INKERMAN"
"SEVASTOPOL."

Years' Serv.		
62		Colonel.—💂 ⛨ Sir George Scovell,[1] KCB. *Adjutant,* 5 April 98; *Cornet,* 20 June 98; *Lieut.* 4 May 00; *Capt.* 10 March 04; *Major,* 30 May 11; *Lieut.Col.* 17 Aug. 12; *Col.* 27 May 25; *Major Gen.* 10 Jan. 37; *Lt. Gen.* 9 Nov. 46; *Gen.* 20 June 54; *Col.* 4th Light Dragoons, 18 Dec. 47.
Full Pay.	Half Pay.	
25	0	Lieut.Colonel.—Alexander Low,[2] *Cornet,* p 2 Oct. 35; *Lieut.* p 6 July 38; *Capt.* p 14 July 43; *Brev.Maj.* 20 June 54; *Maj.* 26 Oct. 54; *Brev.Lt. Col.* 12 Dec. 54; *Lieut.Col.* 1 May 57; *Col.* 12 Dec. 57.
20	0	Major.—George John Brown,[3] *Cornet,* p 17 April 40; *Lieut.* p 14 July 43; *Capt.* p 30 Jan. 46; *Brev.Major,* 12 Dec. 54; *Major,* 12 May 57.

		CAPTAINS.	CORNET.	LIEUT.	CAPTAIN.	BREV.-MAJ.
10	0	Hon.C.J. Keith-Falconer[4]	15 Feb. 50	p 31 Oct. 51	p 25 May 55	
10	0	Fiennes Cornwallis[5]	p 12 Apr. 50	26 Oct. 54	p 31 Aug. 55	
10	0	Chas. A. Gunter Browne[6]	p 13 Dec. 50	26 Oct. 54	p 21 Sept. 55	
12	0	Fred. J. Sandys Lindesay[7]	p 10 Mar. 48	p 2 Feb. 49	p 6 June 54	
10	0	Alex. Geo. Montgo. Moore	p 13 Dec. 50	p 6 July 52	p 9 May 56	
5	0	Hon. Fred. George Ellis	p 2 Aug. 55	p 3 Mar. 57	p 10 Oct. 57	
10	0	Archibald Philip Douglas	p 12 Apr. 50	p 14 Sept. 52	26 Feb. 58	
5	0	Edward William Blackett	1 June 55	21 Sept. 55	p 24 May 59	

4 Hon. Capt. Keith-Falconer served three years as a Midshipman, and was wounded in the boat action of H. M. S. *President* and *Eurydice* against the Arab pirates in the river Augozha, east coast of Africa, 23 Nov. 1847. Served the Eastern campaign of 1854-55 as Aide de Camp to Sir Richard England, including the battles of Inkerman and Tchernaya, and siege of Sebastopol; was also with the Light Cavalry Brigade at Eupatoria (Medal and Clasps, Sardinian Medal, and 5th Class of the Medjidie).

		LIEUTENANTS.				
6	0	Henry Jennings,[8] *Adj.*	5 Nov. 54	26 Feb. 55		
4	0	William Chaine	p 19 Dec. 56	p 30 June 57		
3	0	Warden Sergison	p 10 Mar. 57	p 4 Sept. 57		
4	0	William Hone Davis	29 Feb. 56	p 2 Feb. 58		
4	0	Frank Hodgkinson	26 Feb. 56	13 April 58		
3	0	Arth.W. De Capell Brooke	p 30 June 57	24 Aug. 58		
3	0	Alexander Fair Jones	p 18 Sept. 57	25 Jan. 59		
3	0	Russell England	24 Nov. 57	p 18 Feb. 59		
2	0	John Kennedy	p 14 May 58	p 24 May 59		
		CORNETS.				
2	0	Edward James Bradshaw	13 Aug. 58			
2	0	Conwy Grenv. H. Rowley	24 Aug. 58			
2	0	Theophilus Gist	p 7 Sept. 58			
1	0	Charles MatthewCalderon	13 May 59			
1	0	Harry Youl	1 July 59			
1	0	Nassau Clark	p 18 Mar. 59			

27	0	*Paymaster.*—George Thorne George,[5] 4 May 49; *Ens.* p 6 Sept. 33; *Lt.* p 9 Dec.	
6	0	*Adjutant.*—*Lieut.* Henry Jennings,[8] 23 March 55. [*Capt.* p 17 Jan. 45.	
2	0	*Quarter Master.*—James William Kelly, 15 Nov. 50; *Cornet,* 31 Aug. 58.	
3	0	*Riding Master.*—John Clark, 4 Sept. 57. [*Surgeon Major,* 1 Oct. 58.	
25	0	*Surgeon.*—Archibald Alexander, *Assist.Surg.* 20 Feb. 35; *Surg.* 3 Oct. 45;	
6	0	*Assist.Surg.*—John Charles Campbell, M.B., 23 June 54.	
4	0	*Veterinary Surgeon.*—Herbert Sewell, 14 Nov. 56.	

Blue—*Facings* Scarlet.—*Agents,* Messrs. C. Hopkinson & Co.
[*Returned from the Crimea,* 28 *May* 1856.]

1 Sir George Scovell served the campaign under Sir John Moore, terminating with the battle of Corunna, at which he was present as Deputy Assistant Quarter Master General. Afterwards in the Peninsula in the same department at the head-quarters under the Duke of Wellington, from Feb. 1809 to the end of that war in 1814, and was present at the passage of the Douro and pursuit of Marshal Soult; battles of Talavera, Busaco, and Fuentes d'Onor; sieges of Ciudad Rodrigo and Badajoz, battle of Salamanca, siege of Burgos, battles of Vittoria, the Pyrenees, Nivelle, and Nive; passage of the Adour, and battle of Toulouse. Served also the campaign of 1815, including the battle of Waterloo. Sir George has received the Gold Cross and one Clasp; and the Silver War Medal with eight Clasps; and has the 4th Class of St. Wladimir of Russia.
2 Colonel Low served the Eastern campaign of 1854-55, including the battles of Alma, Balaklava, Inkerman, and Tchernaya, and siege of Sebastopol, also present with the Light Cavalry Brigade at Eupatoria; at Inkerman he commanded the Regiment (Medal and Clasps, Brevet Lt.Col., Knight of the Legion of Honor, Sardinian Medal, and 4th Class of the Medjidie).
3 Major Brown served the Eastern campaign of 1854-55, including the battles of Alma, Balaklava, Inkerman (wounded), and Tchernaya, and siege of Sebastopol, also present with the Light Cavalry Brigade at Eupatoria (Medal and Clasps, Knight of the Legion of Honor, and 5th Class of the Medjidie).
5 Captain Cornwallis and Paymaster George served the Eastern campaign of 1854-55, including the battles of Alma, Balaklava, Inkerman, and Tchernaya, and siege of Sebastopol, also with the Light Cavalry Brigade at Eupatoria (Medal and Clasps, and 5th Class of the Medjidie).
6 Captain Browne served in the Crimea from 28th April to 20th July 1855, and has the Medal with Clasp for Sebastopol.
7 Captain Lindesay served with the 17th Regt. at the siege and fall of Sebastopol and assault of the Redan on the 8th Sept. 1855; also at the bombardment and surrender of Kinbourn (Medal and Clasp).
8 Lieut. Jennings served the Eastern campaign of 1854-55, including the battles of Alma, Balaklava (wounded), Inkerman, and Tchernaya, and siege of Sebastopol, also present with the Light Cavalry Brigade at Eupatoria (Medal and Clasps).

† C

140 5th (Royal Irish) Regt. of Light Dragoons (Lancers). [Head Quarters, Newbridge.

The Harp and Crown. "*Quis Separabit?*"

Years' Serv.			CAPTAINS.	CORNET.	LIEUT.	CAPTAIN.	BREV.-MAJ.
51		Colonel.—**♉ 🐉** Sir James C. Chatterton, *Bt.*¹KH. *Cor.* P23 Nov. 00; *Lt.* 6 June 11; *Capt.* P26 Mar. 18; *Major*, P22 July 24; *Lt.Col.* P18 Dec. 27; *Col.* 23 Nov. 41; *Maj.Gen.* 20 June 54; *Lt.Gen.* 13 Dec. 59; *Col.* 5 Drs. 23 Feb. 58.					
Full Pay 24	Half Pay 0						
20	0	*Lt.Colonel.*—Geo. Aug. Filmer Sulivan,² *Cor.* P29 July 36; *Lt.* P26 Feb. 41; *Capt.* P5 Apr. 44; *Maj.* 17 Feb. 54; *Bt.Lt.Col.* 12 Dec. 54; *Lt.Col.* 19 Feb. 58.					
		Major.—Robert Portal,³ *Ens.* P17 Jan. 40; *Lt.* P8 May 45; *Capt.* P9 June 46; *Bt.Major*, 6 June 56; *Major*, 10 Feb. 58.					
22	0		George E. Hillier⁴	14 Dec. 38	P10 Apr. 41	19 Mar. 47	30 June 54
13	0		William Hicks Slade⁵ ..	19 Mar. 47	P23 May 48	P 9 Mar. 55	20 July 58
6	0		Wm. G. Dunham Massy⁶	27 Oct. 54	9 Feb. 55	20 Feb. 57	
10	0		John Dynon⁸	2 Apr. 50	14 Sept. 55	26 Feb. 58	
9	0		Francis R. Charles Grant	P16 Sept. 51	P23 June 54	16 Mar. 58	
5	0		Thomas Wm. Vallance⁹ ..	9 Mar. 55	P25 May 55	P29 Apr. 59	
13	0		Amyatt Ernlé Brown¹⁰ ..	20 Mar. 47	P 2 Oct. 49	P12 Dec. 51	
10	0		John King Rendall......	P17 Sept. 50	P21 Apr. 54	P26 Mar. 58	
		LIEUTENANTS.					
7	0		Arthur Murray¹¹.........	17 June 53	23 Oct. 55		
5	0		Adolphus Murphy	....	7 Sept. 55		
5	0		Henry Norman Salis¹² ..	27 July 55	P11 Sept. 57		
3	0		Edwd. Fra. Weaver,¹³ *Adj.*	23 Oct. 57	17 Mar. 58		
5	0		Joseph Henry Cowan ..	P 7 Dec. 55	17 Mar. 58		
4	0		Fred. Walter Cardon....	P15 Feb. 56	26 Mar. 58		
3	0		William Edgeworth¹⁴....	P22 May 57	23 Oct. 57		
2	0		Robert Mather	16 Apr. 58	P22 April 59		
2	0		Richard J. Wyrley Birch	17 Apr. 58	P 6 May 59		
		CORNETS.					
2	0		Alexander Malcolmson ..	14 May 58			
2	0		John Chaffey	21 May 58			
2	0		Boyle Vandeleur	10 Sept. 58			
2	0		John O. Gowan Smith ..	5 Oct. 58			
2	0		Alexander Ewing	31 Dec. 58			
2	0	*Paymaster.*—John Akin Dyer, 15 March 58.					
3	0	*Adjutant.*—Lieut. Edward Francis Weaver,¹³ 5 March 58.					
1	0	*Quarter Master.*—George Griffith, 3 June 59.					
2	0	*Riding Master.*—William Rant, 6 Aug. 58.					
15	0	*Surgeon.*—Henry Huish, M.D., *A.S.* 31 Jan. 45; *Surg.* 15 Aug. 54.					
2	0	*Assistant Surgeon.*—John Atkinson, 10 March 58.					
15	0	*Veterinary Surgeon.*—William C. Lord, 20 Jan. 45; *1st Class*, 1 July 59.					

Facings Scarlet.—*Agent*, Henry Tucker Clack, Esq.

Note in right margin (captain column): *2 Lt.Colonel Sulivan served the Eastern campaign of 1854-55, including the affair of M'Kenzie's Farm, battles of Balaklava, Inkerman, and Tchernaya, siege and fall of Sebastopol (Medal and three Clasps, Knight of the Legion of Honor, and 5th Class of the Medjidie).*

3 Major Portal served the Eastern campaign of 1854-55, and was present at the battles of Alma, Balaklava, Inkerman, and Tchernaya, siege of Sebastopol, and with the Light Cavalry Brigade at Eupatoria; and was Aide de Camp to Lord George Paget during the period he commanded the Light Cavalry Brigade in the Crimea (Medal and Clasps, Sardinian Medal, and 5th Class of the Medjidie).

9 Captain Vallance served with the 95th Regt. at the siege and fall of Sebastopol from 22nd Aug. 1855 (Medal and Clasp).

Right vertical margin notes: *14 Lieut. Edgeworth served in the 8th Regt. at the siege of Delhi in 1857, and as a volunteer with the Artillery during the breaching of the city walls and the assault; was afterwards severely wounded in the action of Bolundshur.*

13 Lieut. Weaver served with the Royal Dragoons during the Eastern campaign of 1854-55, including the battles of Balaklava, Inkerman, and Tchernaya, and siege of Sebastopol (Medal and three Clasps).

1 Sir James Charles Chatterton served in the 12th Light Dragoons, now the Royal Lancers, in Portugal, Spain, Flanders, and France, from 1811 to 1818, including the affairs of Fuente Guinaldo and Aldea de Ponte; the sieges of Ciudad Rodrigo and Badajoz; frequently employed upon detached posts of observation and thanked for his exertions; the actions of Usagre, Llerena, Passage of the Tormes, near Salamanca (town), and attack of the enemy's rear-guard, Heights of San Christoval, Rueda, Castrajon, and battle of Salamanca; affairs at Tudela, Valladolid, Celadadel Caminho, to the investment and siege of Burgos, actions at Monasterio, Bridge of Baniel, Quintana Palla Venta del Pozo, and Cabezon, actions on the retreat from Burgos to Salamanca, thence to the combat and passage of the Huebra, Torrequemada and outposts to Ciudad Rodrigo, upon the advance of the army in 1813; the passage of the Ebro and Esin, action at Osma, and battle of Vittoria, actions at Villa Franca, Tolosa, to the siege and capture of San Sebastian. The actions on crossing the Bidassoa, and carrying the enemy's fortified entrenchments. The battle of the Nivelle, the actions at St. Jean de Luz, at Anglet, the Mayor's House, Bidart, the battles on the Nive from the 9th to the 13th Dec. 1813; the passage of the Adour, and investment of Bayonne; occupation of Bordeaux, the passage of the Garonne, and affairs at Etaliers or the passage of the Dordogne, besides various skirmishes and minor affairs. In 1815, the battles of Quatre Bras and Waterloo, to the advance on and capture of Paris. He has received the Cross of Knight of the Royal Hanoverian Guelphic Order, that of San Fernando of Spain, the War Medal and four Clasps for the battle of Salamanca, Vittoria, Nivelle, and Nive, and the Waterloo Medal. Received the commands of her Majesty to attend and bear the Great Banner on the occasion of the Funeral of the late illustrious Duke of Wellington, "in consideration of his long, faithful, and distinguished services."

4 Major Hillier acted as Aide du Camp to Brigadier Cureton in the action of Maharajpore, 29th Dec. 1843 (Medal); and served as Aide de Camp to the Governor General, with the army of the Sutlej, and was severely wounded in the action at Moodkee (Medal).

5 Major Slade served in the Crimea with the 6th Dragoons, and was present at the battle of the Tchernaya and fall of Sebastopol (Medal and Clasp).

6 Capt. Dunham Massy served at the latter part of the siege of Sebastopol, and commanded the Grenadiers of the 19th Regt. at the assault on the Redan on the 8th Sept., where he was dangerously wounded by a ball which passed through his left thigh, shattering the bone (Medal and Clasp, and Knight of the Legion of Honor).

8 Captain Dynon served with the 10th Lancers during the campaign in Affghanistan under Lord Keane, including the siege and capture of Ghuznee (Medal).

10 Captain Brown served with the 31st Regt. at the siege of Sebastopol from its landing on 22nd May, to 11th July 1855, including the attack of the 18th June (Medal and Clasp).

11 Lieut. Murray served with the 12th Lancers in the Crimea from 17th May 1855, including the siege and fall of Sebastopol, and various operations near Eupatoria under General D'Allonville (Medal and Clasp). Also served with a Squadron of the 12th Lancers with General Whitlock's Division of the Saugor and Nerbudda field force, from July to Dec. 1857.

12 Lieut. Salis served as a volunteer with the Cape Mounted Riflemen and on the Ordnance Staff during the Kaffir war of 1851-53 (Medal).

Mhow, Depot, Maidstone.] 6th (Inniskilling) Regiment of Dragoons. 141

The Castle of Inniskilling.—"WATERLOO," "BALAKLAVA," "SEVASTOPOL."

Colonel.—リ(?) Sir James Jackson,[1] KCB. KH. *Ens.* 9 Oct. 06; *Lt.* 25 Jan. 08; *Capt.* ᴾ 25 June 13; *Brevet-Major,* 18 June 15; *Brevet Lt.Col.* 25 May 26; *Major,* ᴾ 26 Apr. 27; *Lt.Col.* ᴾ 2 March 39; *Col.* 23 Nov. 41; *Major-Gen.* 11 Nov. 51; *Lt.Gen.* 26 Oct. 58; *Col.* 6 Drs. 11 June 56.

Lt.Colonels.—Charles Cameron Shute,[2] *Cornet,* ᴾ 19 July 34; *Lt.* ᴾ 13 May 39; *Capt.* ᴾ 5 Mar. 47; *Major,* 1 June 54; *Brevet Lt.Col.* 12 Dec. 54; *Lt.Col.* ᴾ 19 Feb. 58; *Col.* 21 Sept. 58.

Fred. Wellington John Fitz Wygram,[3] *Cornet,* ᴾ 28 July 43; *Lieut.* ᴾ 17 May 44; *Capt.* ᴾ 22 Dec. 48; *Major,* ᴾ 19 Feb. 58; *Lt.Col.* 26 July 58.

Majors.—Edmund D'Arcy Hunt,[3†] *Cornet,* ᴾ 29 Oct. 47; *Lt.* ᴾ 19 Oct. 49; *Capt.* ᴾ 15 Sept. 54; *Major,* 26 July 58.

James D. Cowell,[4] *Cornet,* ᴾ 18 July 34; *Lt.* ᴾ 17 May 37; *Capt.* ᴾ 9 June 48; *Major,* 26 July 58.

Years' Serv.			CORNET.	LIEUT.	CAPTAIN.	BREV-MAJ.
Full Pay	Half Pay					
54						
26	0					
17	0					
13	0					
26	0					
		CAPTAINS.				
8	0	Archibald Weir[5]	21 May 52	14 April 54	9 Oct. 57	
7	0	Wm. Sawrey Rawlinson[5]	ᴾ 10 June 53	6 Oct. 54	ᴾ 23 Oct. 57	
7	0	Nicholas De Jersey Lovell	ᴾ 20 Sept. 53	ᴾ 24 Nov. 54	ᴾ 19 Feb. 58	
6	0	Edward Finch Dawson[3]	ᴾ 15 Sept. 54	8 Dec. 54	ᴾ 21 May 58	
6	0	Arthur Finch Dawson[3]	ᴾ 17 Aug. 54	ᴾ 19 Jan. 55	ᴾ 2 July 58	
7	0	Hon. Ch.Wemyss Thesiger	ᴾ 5 Aug. 53	ᴾ 30 Dec. 53	ᴾ 2 July 58	
13	0	T. E. Anderson,[9] Q.M.2Apr.47	10 Nov. 54	9 Oct. 57	26 July 58	
6	0	Joseph Thomas Wetherall	ᴾ 24 Nov. 54	9 Oct. 57	ᴾ 26 July 58	
13	0	John Edward Swindley[7]	15 Jan. 47	22 Dec. 50	5 Mar. 58	
10	0	Henry Topham Clements[8]	ᴾ 17 May 50	21 July 57	ᴾ 31 May 59	
		LIEUTENANTS.				
5	0	William Moule,[3] Adj	22 June 55	23 Oct. 57		
3	0	Fred. Barclay Chapman	ᴾ 23 Oct. 57	26 Mar. 58		
3	0	Hon. Wm. Oct. B. Annesley	ᴾ 30 Oct. 57	ᴾ 28 May 58		
3	0	Hon. Edw. Rodon Bourke	18 Nov. 57	ᴾ 25 June 58		
3	0	John O'Neill	17 Nov. 57	ᴾ 13 July 58		
3	0	Edward Napier	31 Dec. 57	26 July 58		
5	0	George M. Billington[10]	ᴾ 30 Apr. 55	ᴾ 26 Dec. 56		
5	0	Burton John Daveney	30 Mar. 55	27 July 58		
5	0	Robert John Garnett	15 Jan. 58	ᴾ 24 Aug. 58		
5	0	Denison Montagu M. Inge	20 July 55	26 Mar. 58		
2	0	John Hardy	ᴾ 26 Feb. 58	ᴾ 13 May 59		
		CORNETS.				
2	0	John Baskerville	ᴾ 13 July 58			
2	0	Robert Davies[12]	23 Apr. 58			
2	0	Thomas Joseph FitzSimon	25 June 58			
2	0	Alex. Fred. Stewart	24 July 58			
2	0	Theodore Wm. Rathbone	ᴾ 30 July 58			
2	0	Henry A. Reade Revell	13 Aug. 58			
2	0	William Valentine King	14 Aug. 58			

Paym.—Thomas Smales,[13] 24 Sept. 58.
Adj.—Lt. Wm. Moule,[3] 15 Jan. 56.
Instructor of Musketry.—Lieut. Hon. E. R. Bourke, 14 Jan. 59.
Quarter Master.—John Kirkby Mountain,[5] 5 June 55.
Riding Master.—Joseph Malone, 7 Sept. 58.
Surgeon.—Francis Hastings Baxter,[3] M.D. 15 Aug. 54; *Assist.Surg.* 11 July 45.
Assist. Surgeons.—Oliver Barnett, 24 Nov. 54.
Robert Graves Burton,[11] M.D. 24 Feb. 54.
Veterinary Surgeon.—James Collins,[14] 23 June 54.

Scarlet—*Facings* Yellow.—*Agents,* Messrs. Cox & Co.

[*Returned from the Crimea,* 7 July 1856. *Embarked for India,* 6 Aug. 1858.]

1 Sir James Jackson served in the Peninsula, from April 1809 to the end of the war in 1814, including the battles of Oporto, Talavera, and Busaco; action at Pombal Redinha, and Foz d'Arouce (wounded), battle of Fuentes d'Onor (3rd and 5th May), first siege of Badajoz, action at El Bodon, siege and capture of Ciudad Rodrigo, siege and capture of Badajoz, battles of Salamanca, Vittoria (horse shot), Maya Pass, Pampeluna, 15th July, Pyrenees, 30th July, Nivelle, Nive, and Bayonne. Present at Waterloo, and with the army of occupation in France. Served in India and Arabia from 1819 to 1826, including the capture of Beni-Boo-Ali, as Military Secretary to Sir Lionel Smith, and for which service he was recommended by the Marquis of Hastings for the rank of Lieut.-Colonel. He has received the War Medal with nine Clasps for Busaco, Fuentes d'Onor, Ciudad Rodrigo, Badajoz, Salamanca, Vittoria, Pyrenees, Nivelle, and Nive.

2 Colonel Shute served in the 13th Lt. Dragoons with the Field Force employed in the reduction of Kurnool, East Indies; served with the 6th Dragoons the Eastern campaign of 1854-55 (as Assist. Adjutant General of the Cavalry Division since 23rd Nov. 1854), including the battles of Balaklava, Inkerman, and Tchernaya, and siege and fall of Sebastopol (Medal and Clasps, Brevet Lt.-Col., Knight of the Legion of Honor, and 5th Class of the Medjidie).

3† Major Hunt served with the 9th Lancers in the last Punjaub campaign, and was present at the battles of Chillianwallah and Goojerat (Medal and Clasps). Served the Eastern campaign with the 6th Dragoons, including the battles of Balaklava, Inkerman, and Tchernaya, and siege and fall of Sebastopol (Medal and Clasps, Sardinian Medal, and 5th Class of the Medjidie).

[Marginalia: 3 Lt.Col. Fitz Wygram, Captains E. F. Dawson and A. F. Dawson, Lt. Moule, and Qr.Master Mountain, served the Eastern campaign of 1854-55, including the battles of Balaklava, Inkerman, and Tchernaya, and siege and fall of Sebastopol (Medal and Clasp). Captain Weir has the 5th Class of the Medjidie.
4 Major Cowell served with the 3rd Light Dragoons throughout the campaign of 1842 in Affghanistan (Medal), and was present at the forcing of the Khyber Pass, capture of Mamoo Khail, storming the heights of Jugdulluck, actions of Tezeen and Huftkotul, and occupation of Caboul. He was present as Aide-de-Camp to Sir Joseph Thackwell in the action of Maharajpore on the 29th Dec. 1843 (Medal). He also served the Sutlej campaign of 1845-6, including the battles of Moodkee, Ferozeshah (charger killed), and Sobraon (Medals and two Clasps). Towards the close of the Sutlej campaign he officiated as Deputy Assistant Qr.Master General of the Cavalry Division. Served with the 10th Hussars in the Crimea from April 1855, including the capture of Tchorgoun, battle of the Tchernaya, siege and fall of Sebastopol (Medal and Clasp).
6 Captain Anderson served the Eastern campaign of 1854 with the 13th Light Dragoons; was under fire the day previous to the Alma, and present at the battles of Alma, Balaklava, and Inkerman (Medal and Clasps).
7 Captain Swindley served with the 12th Lancers in the Kaffir war of 1852-3 (Medal), and was at the action of the Berea. Also the Eastern campaign from 9th May 1855, including siege and fall of Sebastopol (Medal and Clasp), and commanded General Simpson's escort in the Crimea.
10 Lieut. Billington served with the 4th Regt. at the assault of the Fort on Boyt Island on 2nd April 1858 and was severely wounded.
11 Doctor Burton served with the 72nd Regt. the Eastern campaign of 1854-55 with the 11th Hussars including the battles of Alma, Inkerman, and siege of Sebastopol (wounded), and Tchernaya, during the Kaffir war of 1846-47 (Medal).
12 Cornet Davies served the Eastern campaign of 1854 with the 7th Dr. Gds. during the Eastern campaign of 1854-55, including the battles of Alma, Balaklava, and Sardinian Medal).
13 Paymaster Smales served in the Crimea as Chief Paymaster of the Turkish Contingent.
14 Veterinary Surgeon Collins served the Eastern campaign of 1854-55, including the battles of Balaklava and Inkerman, and siege and fall of Sebastopol (Medal and Clasps).]

142   7th (*The Queen's Own*) Regt. of Lt. Dragoons (*Hussars*.)   [Umballah. Dep. Canterbury.

"PENINSULA" "WATERLOO."

Years' Serv.		
Full Pay	Half Pay	
61		*Colonel.*—𝔚 Sir William Tuyll,[1] *KCH. Cor.* 22 Oct. 99; *Lieut.* 18 July 10; *Capt.* 7 April 04; *Major*, 20 Nov. 06; *Lieut.Col.* 13 June 11; *Col.* 27 May 25; *Major Gen.* 10 Jan. 37; *Lt.Gen.* 9 Nov. 46; *Gen.* 20 June 54; *Col.* 7th Hussars, 10 Mar. 46.
		Lieut. Colonels.—Sir William Russell,[2] *Bart.,CB.Cornet*, p 2 July 41; *Lt.* p 27 Feb. 46;
19	0	*Capt.* p 16 Apr. 47; *Major*, 13 Aug. 57; *Bt.Lt.Col.* 20 July 58; *Lt.Col.* p 12 Nov. 58.
15	0	William Babington, *Cornet*, p 11 Nov. 45; *Lieut.* p 9 Oct. 46; *Capt.* p 14 June 50; *Major*, p 12 Nov. 58; *Lt.Col.* p 13 May 59.
14	0	*Majors.*—William Dascon Bushe,[3] *Cornet*, p 27 Feb. 46; *Lt.* p 17 Apr. 47; *Capt.* p 8 June 52; *Bt.Maj.* 20 July 58; *Major*, 1 Jan. 59; *Bt.Lt.Col.* 26 Apr. 59.
9	0	Harrington Astley Trevelyan,[4] *Cornet*, p 17 Oct. 51; *Lt.* p 15 Feb. 53; *Capt.* 8 Dec. 54; *Major*, p 8 March 59.

		CAPTAINS.	CORNET.	LIEUT.	CAPTAIN.	BREV.MAJ.	BT.LT.COL.
10	0	Hon.I.DeV.T.W.Fiennes[5]	P 22 Nov. 50	P 8 June 52	P 3 Mar. 57	20 July 58	
11	8/12	David Philip Brown[6]	P 9 Feb. 49	P 16 Sept. 51	P 9 May 56		
12	7/12	James Aytoun[7]	P 22 Oct. 47	P 31 Oct. 51	P 24 June 56		
14	0	Thomas Heathcote Stisted[8]	3 April 46	P 10 Dec. 47	9 Oct. 57	26 Apr. 59	
10	0	Frank Garforth[9]	P 16 Aug. 50	P 30 Dec. 53	5 Mar. 58		
9	0	Charles William Paulet[7]	P 21 Nov. 51	14 Sept. 55	P 12 Nov. 58		
7	0	𝔚ℭ Hon. A. H. A. Anson[11]	P 27 May 53	8 Dec. 54	P 6 July 55	⟩ ⋅)	
8	0	Robert Hale	P 11 June 52	14 Sept. 55	1 Jan. 59		
3	0	John Gore	P 17 Feb. 57	5 Mar. 58	P 30 Sept. 59		
12	0	A. Eastfield Wilkinson[12]	P 11 Feb. 48	P 18 Jan. 50	5 Mar. 58		
		LIEUTENANTS.					
5	0	Richard Topham[13]	27 July 55	P 14 Mar. 56	6 Captain Brown has the Order of the Medjidie, 4th Class, for service in the Turkish Contingent. 7 Captains Aytoun and Paulet served in the Indian campaign from Feb. 1858 to March 1859 and was present at the repulse of the enemy's attack at the Alumbagh, siege and capture of Lucknow, affairs of Barree and Sirsee, action of Nawabgunge, occupation of Fyzabad, passage of the Goomtee at Sultanpore, throughout the Byswarra campaign, including the affairs of Daodpore (Captain Paulet only), Kandoo Nuddee and Hydergbur and pursuit of Benhi Madho's force to the Goomtee; also the Trans-Gogra campaign, including the affair near Churda and pursuit, taking of the fort of Meejeedia, attack on Bankee with pursuit to the Raptee, advance into Nepaul and affair at Sitkaghat (Medal and Clasp). 8 Captain Garforth served in the Indian campaign from Feb. 1858 to March 1859 and was present at the affair of Meengunge, siege and capture of Lucknow, affairs of Barree and Sirsee, action of Nawabgunge, occupation of Fyzabad, passage of the Goomtee at Sultanpore, throughout the Byswarra campaign, including the affairs of Kandoo Nuddee, Paleeghat, and Hyderghur, and pursuit of Benhi Madho's force to the Goomtee; also the Trans-Gogra campaign, including the affair near Churda and pursuit, taking the fort of Meejeedia, attack on Bankee with pursuit to the Raptee, advance into Nepaul and affair at Sitkaghat (Medal and Clasp).		
8	0	Henry John Wilkin,[14] (*Assist.Surg.* 13 Jan. 52)	2 Feb. 55	p 6 Feb. 57			
4	0	Hon.C.CravenMolyneux[16]	P 6 June 56	11 May 58			
5	0	John B. Phillipson[17]	21 Dec. 55	P 16 July 58			
3	0	Robt. DalrympleSteuart[18]	P 26 Aug. 57	P 19 Nov. 58			
3	0	Hon. Walter Harbord[19]	18 Dec. 57	P 19 Nov. 58			
4	0	J. Mould,[20] *Adj.*(*RM.*7Nov50)	16 Mar. 58	11 Mar. 59			
2	0	Charles H. Baillie	P 23 Mar. 58	P 11 Mar. 59			
2	0	Hon.A.Wm.E.M.Herbert	P 7 May 58	P 3 June 59			
2	0	Arthur Hamilton Scrope	P 13 July 58	P 28 Oct. 59			
7	0	James Giles[21]	P 30 Dec. 58	20 June 57			
		CORNETS.					
4	0	Herbert Owen Johnes	26 Feb. 56				
2	0	Edward Metcalfe	P 9 Nov. 58				
2	0	Edmund Hegan Kennard	P 26 Nov. 58				
1	0	Richard Simmons[22]	1 Jan. 59				
1	0	Henry Herbert Wombwell	P 11 Jan. 59				
1	0	Robert Masters	31 May 59				
2	0	Hen. Augustus Bushman	9 Nov. 58				

4	8/12	*Paymaster.*—George Elliott,[23] 18 Sept. 57; *Q. M.* 1 June 55.
4	0	*Adjutant.*—*Lieut.* John Mould,[20] 16 March 58.
2	0	*Instructor of Musketry.*—*Cornet* Edward Metcalfe, 13 Sept. 59.
3	0	*Quarter Master.*—Walter Borthwick,[23] 25 Aug. 57.
2	0	*Riding Master.*—William Bray,[27] 5 Oct. 58.
15	0	*Surgeon.*—Henry Kendall,[24] M.D. 6 Oct. 54; *Assist.Surg.* 16 Dec. 45.
6	0	*Assistant Surgeons.*—George Moulas Slaughter,[25] 13 Dec. 54.
3	0	Thomas Allen Thornhill,[26] M.B. 28 May 57.
5	0	*Veterinary Surgeon.*—John Barker,[23] 27 July 55.

Blue.—*Agents*, Messrs. Cox & Co.

[*Returned from Canada*, 19 Dec. 1842. *Embarked for India*, 27 Aug. 1857.]

1 Sir Wm. Tuyll served during part of the campaigns of 1793, 94, and 95 in the Netherlands; at the Helder in 1799; and in Portugal, Spain, and Walcheren in 1808 and 9, as Aide-de-Camp to the Marquis of Anglesey. Sir William has received the War Medal with one Clasp for Sahagun and Benevente.

2 Sir William Russell served in the Indian campaign from Feb. 1858 to March 1859 and was present at the repulse of the enemy's attack on the Alumbagh, siege and capture of Lucknow (brevet of Lt.Colonel). Commanded the 7th Hussars at the affairs of Barree and Sirsee, action of Nawabgunge, occupation of Fyzabad, passage of the Goomtee at Sultanpore, throughout the Byswarra campaign, including the affairs of Kandoo Nuddee, Paleeghat, Hyderghur, and pursuit of Benhi Madho's force to the Goomtee; also the Trans-Gogra campaign, including the affair near Churda and pursuit, taking the fort of Meejeedia, attack on Bankee with pursuit to the Raptee, advance into Nepaul and affair at Sitkaghat (several times mentioned in despatches, C.B., Medal and Clasp).

3 Lt.Col. Bushe served in the Indian campaign from Feb. 1858 to March 1859 and was present at the repulse of the enemy's attack on the Alumbagh, siege and capture of Lucknow, affair of Barree, action of Nawabgunge (mentioned in despatches), occupation of Fyzabad, passage of the Goomtee at Sultanpore, affair of Shahpore, throughout the Byswarra campaign, including the affairs of Kandoo Nuddee, Paleeghat, and taking the forts of Rehova and Reowlee; also the Trans-Gogra campaign, including the affair near Churda and pursuit, taking the fort of Mujeedia, attack on Bankee with pursuit to the Raptee, advance into Nepaul and affair at Sitkaghat (Brevets of Major and Lt.Colonel, Medal and Clasp).

4 Major Trevelyan served the Eastern campaign of 1854 with the 11th Hussars, including the affair of Bulganak, battles of Alma and Balaklava (wounded), and siege of Sebastopol (Medal and three Clasps, and 5th Class of the Medjidie).

5 Major Hon. I. Fiennes served in the Indian campaign from Feb. 1858 to March 1859 and was present at the affair of Meengunge, siege and capture of Lucknow, affairs of Barree and Sirsee, action of Nawabgunge, occupation of Fyzabad, passage of the Goomtee at Sultanpore, affairs of the Kandoo Nuddee, and Paleeghat, throughout the Trans-Gogra campaign as Cavalry Brigade Major, including passage of the Gogra at Fyzabad, affairs of Muchagawn and Kumdakotee, advance into Nepaul and affair at Sitkaghat (several times mentioned in despatches, Brevet of Major, Medal and Clasp).

7th (The Queen's Own) Regt. of Light Dragoons (Hussars). 143

8 Major Stisted served the Punjaub campaign of 1848-9 with the 3rd Light Dragoons, and was present at the affair of Ramnuggur, the passage of the Chenab at Wuzeerabad on the 1st Dec. 1848, with the force under Sir Joseph Thackwell, action of Sadoolapore, battles of Chillianwallah (wounded, and charger wounded) and Goojerat (Medal and two Clasps). Served with the 12th Lancers in the Crimea from 9th May 1855, including the siege and fall of Sebastopol (Medal and Clasp). Served with the 7th Hussars in the Indian campaign from Feb. 1858 to March 1859 and was present at the affair of Meengunge, siege and capture of Lucknow, affair of Barree, action of Nawabgunge, occupation of Fyzabad, passage of the Goomtee at Sultanpore, throughout the Byswarra campaign including the affairs of Doudpore, Kandoo Nuddee, Paleeghat, Hyderghur, and pursuit of Benhi Madho's force to the Goomtee; also the Trans-Gogra campaign, including the affair near Churda and pursuit, taking the fort of Meejeedia, attack on Bankee and pursuit to the Raptee, advance into Nepaul and affair at Sitkaghat (twice mentioned in despatches, Brevet of Major, Medal and Clasp).

11 Major Hon. A. Anson served with the Rifle Brigade at the siege of Sebastopol from Jan. 1855 (Medal and Clasp, and 5th Class of the Medjidie). Served in the Indian campaign of 1857-58 as Aide de Camp to General Grant, and was present at the siege and capture of Delhi (wounded), action at Bolundshuhur, the second relief of Lucknow and assault of the Secundra Bagh (wounded, and horse killed), assault and capture of Lucknow, and affairs at Koorsee and Barree; was thanked by the Governor General in Council and repeatedly mentioned in despatches (Medal and Clasps and Victoria Cross and Brevet of Major).

12 Captain Wilkinson served with the 9th Lancers in the Punjaub campaign of 1848-49, including the battles of Chillianwallah and Goojerat (Medal and Clasp).

13 Lieut. Topham served in the Indian campaign from Feb. 1858 to March 1859 and was present at the repulse of the enemy's attack on the Alumbagh, siege and capture of Lucknow, affairs of Barree (wounded) and Sirsee, action of Nawabgunge (contused), occupation of Fyzabad, passage of the Goomtee at Sultanpore, throughout the Byswarra campaign, including the affairs of Kandoo Nuddee, Paleeghat, and Hyderghur, and pursuit of Benhi Madho's force to the Goomtee; also the Trans-Gogra campaign, including the affair near Churda and pursuit, taking the fort of Meejeedia, attack on Bankee with pursuit to the Raptee, advance into Nepaul and affair at Sitkaghat (twice mentioned in despatches, Medal and Clasp).

14 Lieut. Wilkin served in the 11th Hussars throughout the Eastern campaign of 1854-55, including the affairs of Bulganac and M'Kenzie's Farm, battles of Alma, Balaklava, Inkerman, siege and fall of Sebastopol (Medal and four Clasps, and 5th Class of the Medjidie). Served in the 7th Hussars in the Indian campaign in Feb. and March 1858 (severely wounded in the operations before Lucknow) and from Dec. 1858 to March 1859 and was present at the affair of Meengungesiege and capture of Lucknow, throughout the Byswarra campaign, including the affair near Churda and pursuit, taking the fort of Meejeedia, attack on Bankee with pursuit to the Raptee, advance into Nepaul and affair of Sitkaghat (mentioned in despatches, Medal and Clasp).

16 Lt. Hon. C. Molyneux served in the Indian campaign from Feb. 1858 to March 1859 and was present at the repulse of the enemy's attack on the Alumbagh, siege and capture of Lucknow, affairs of Barree and Sirsee, action of Nawabgunge, occupation of Fyzabad, throughout the Byswarra campaign, including the affairs of Kandoo Nuddee, Paleeghat, and Hyderguuge, pursuit of Benhi Madho's force to the Goomtee; also the Trans-Gogra campaign, including the affair near Churda and pursuit, taking the fort of Meejeedia, attack on Bankee with pursuit to the Raptee, advance into Nepaul and affair at Sitkaghat (Medal and Clasp).

17 Lieut. Phillipson served in the Indian campaign from Sept. to Dec. 1858, including the affair of Daodpore (Medal).

18 Lieut. Steuart served in the Indian campaign from Feb. 1858 to March 1859 and was present at the repulse of the enemy's attack on the Alumbagh, siege and capture of Lucknow, affair of Barree, action of Nawabgunge, occupation of Fyzabad, passage of the Goomtee at Sultanpore, affair of Shahpore, throughout the Byswarra campaign, including the affairs of Kandoo Nuddee and Paleeghat, taking the forts of Rehora and Keowlie, and pursuit of Benhi Madho's force to the Goomtee; also the Trans-Gogra campaign, including the affair near Churda and pursuit, taking the fort of Meejeedia, attack on Bankee with pursuit to the Raptee, advance into Nepaul and affair at Sitkaghat (Medal and Clasp).

19 Lt. Hon. W. Harbord served in the Indian campaign from April 1858 to March 1859 and was present at the affair of Sirsee, action of Nawabgunge, occupation of Fyzabad, passage of the Goomtee at Sultanpore, throughout the Byswarra campaign, including the affairs of Kandoo Nuddee, Paleeghat, and Hyderghur, and pursuit of Benhi Madho's force to the Goomtee; also the Trans-Gogra campaign, including the affair near Churda and pursuit, taking the fort of Meejeedia, attack on Bankee and pursuit to the Raptee, advance into Nepaul and affair at Sitkaghat (mentioned in despatches, Medal and Clasp).

20 Lieut. Mould served as Adjutant of the 7th Hussars in the Indian campaign from Feb. 1858 to March 1859 and was present at the repulse of the enemy's attack on the Alumbagh, siege and capture of Lucknow, affairs of Barree and Sirsee, action of Nawabgunge (wounded), occupation of Fyzabad, passage of the Goomtee at Sultanpore, throughout the Byswarra campaign, including the affairs of Kandoo Nuddee, Paleeghat, and Hyderguuge, and pursuit of Benhi Madho's force to the Goomtee; also the Trans-Gogra campaign, including the affair near Churda and pursuit, taking the fort of Meejeedia, attack on Bankee with pursuit to the Raptee, advance into Nepaul and affair at Sitkaghat (Medal and Clasp).

21 Lieut. Giles served with the Persian expedition of 1857 (Medal). Was present at the suppression of the Mutiny at Aurungabad in 1857, and subsequently served as Adjutant of the left wing at the siege and capture of Dhar, action of Mundesore (wounded), battle of Goraria and relief of Neemuch; served with the Central India field force under Sir Hugh Rose in 1858 and was present at the siege and capture of Chandeyrie, siege and capture of Jhansi, battles of Betwa and Koonch, affairs during the advance on Calpee and action of Golowlee, capture of Calpee and pursuit, action of Morar, pursuit of rebels under Ferozeshah and action of Ranode (twice mentioned in despatches, Medal and Clasp).

22 Cornet Simmons served in the Indian campaign from Feb. 1858 to March 1859 and was present at the repulse of the enemy's attack on the Alumbagh, siege and capture of Lucknow, affairs of Barree and Sirsee, action of Nawabgunge, occupation of Fyzabad, passage of the Goomtee at Sultanpore, affair of Shahabad, throughout the Byswarra campaign, including the affairs of Kandoo Nuddee, Paleeghat, and Hyderghur, pursuit of Benhi Madho's force to the Goomtee; also the Trans-Gogra campaign, including the affair near Churda and pursuit, taking the fort of Meejeedia, attack on Bankee with pursuit to the Raptee, advance into Nepaul and affair at Sitkaghat (Medal and Clasp).

23 Paymaster Elliott, Qr.Master Borthwick, and Veterinary Surgeon Barker served in the Indian campaign from Feb. 1858 to March 1859 and was present at the repulse of the enemy's attack on the Alumbagh, siege and capture of Lucknow, affair of Barree, occupation of Fyzabad, passage of the Goomtee at Sultanpore, throughout the Byswarra campaign, including the affairs of Kandoo Nuddee and Hyderghur, also the Trans-Gogra campaign, including the affair near Churda and pursuit, taking the fort of Meejeedia, attack on Bankee and pursuit to the Raptee, advance into Nepaul and affair at Sitkaghat (Medal and Clasp).

24 Surgeon Kendall served with the 4th Lt. Drs. the Eastern campaign of 1854-55, including the affairs of Bulganac and M'Kenzie's Farms, battles of Alma, Balaklava, Inkerman, and Tchernaya, siege and fall of Sebastopol, and operations with the Light Cavalry Brigade at Eupatoria under General D'Allonville (Medal and four Clasps). Served with the 7th Hussars in the Indian campaign from Feb. 1858 to March 1859 and was present at the repulse of the enemy's attack on the Alumbagh, siege and capture of Lucknow, affairs of Barree and Sirsee, action of Nawabgunge, occupation of Fyzabad, passage of the Goomtee at Sultanpore, throughout the Byswarra campaign, including the affairs of Daodpore, Kandoo Nuddee, and Hyderghur, pursuit of Benhi Madho's force to the Goomtee; also the Trans-Gogra campaign, including the affair near Churda and pursuit, taking the fort of Meejeedia, attack on Bankee with pursuit to the Raptee, advance into Nepaul and affair at Sitkaghat (Medal and Clasp).

25 Assist.Surgeon Slaughter served in the Indian campaign from Feb. 1858 to March 1859 and was present at the affair of Meengunge, siege and capture of Lucknow, affairs of Barree and Sirsee, action of Nawabgunge, occupation of Fyzabad, passage of the Goomtee at Sultanpore, throughout the Byswarra campaign, including the affairs of Kandoo Nuddee, Paleeghat, and Hyderghur, pursuit of Benhi Madho's force to the Goomtee; also the Trans-Gogra campaign, including the affair near Churda and pursuit, taking the fort of Meejeedia, attack on Bankee with pursuit to the Raptee, advance into Nepaul and affair at Sitkaghat (Medal and Clasp).

26 Assist.Surgeon Thornhill served the campaign of 1857-58 against the Mutineers in India, including the action at Kudygunge, siege and fall of Lucknow, attack on the fort of Rooyah, action at Allygunge, and capture of Bareilly—wounded (Medal and Clasp).

27 Riding Master Bray served in the Indian campaign from March 1858 to March 1859 and was present at the affair of Barree, occupation of Fyzabad, passage of the Goomtee at Sultanpore, throughout the Byswarra campaign, including the affairs of Kandoo Nuddee, Paleeghat, and Hyderghur; also the Trans-Gogra campaign, including the affair near Churda and pursuit, taking the fort of Meejeedia, attack on Bankee with pursuit to the Raptee, advance into Nepaul and affair at Sitkaghat (Medal).

144 8th (*The King's R. Irish*) *Regt. of Lt. Drs.* (*Hussars.*) [Bombay. Depot,Canterbury.

Harp and Crown. "*Pristinæ virtutis memores.*"—"LESWARREE" "HINDOOSTAN" "ALMA" "BALAKLAVA" "INKERMAN" "SEVASTOPOL."

Years' Serv.		
44		**Colonel.**—George Charles, *Earl of* Lucan,[1] KCB. *Ens.* 29 Aug. 16; *Lt.* 24 Dec. 18; *Capt.* 16 May 22; *Maj.* 23 June 25; *Lt.Col.* 9 Nov. 26; *Col.* 23 Nov. 41; *Maj.Gen.* 11 Nov. 51; *Lt.Gen.* 24 Dec. 58; *Col.* 8th Hussars, 17 Nov. 55.
Full Pay	Half Pay	
30	0	**Lieut.Colonels.**—Rodolph de Salis,[2] *Cornet*, p 17 Dec. 30; *Lieut.* p 28 June 33; *Capt.* p 13 July 38; *Major*, p 19 Feb. 47; *Brevet Lt.Col.* 28 Nov. 54; *Lt.Col.* 2 Oct. 56; *Col.* 20 March 58.
19	0	Edward Seager,[3] *Cornet*, p 17 Sept. 41; *Lieut.* 29 June 43; *Capt.* 26 Oct. 54; *Major*, 31 Jan. 58; *Lt.Col.* p 5 Aug. 59.
20	0	**Majors.**—George Chetwode,[4] *Ens.* p 8 May 40; *Lieut.* p 10 Mar. 43; *Capt.* p 24 Feb. 54; *Brev.Maj.* 6 June 56; *Major*, 17 Sept. 57.
14	0	Fra. Edmund Macnaghten,[4] *Cornet* p 27 Oct. 46; *Lieut.* p 23 May 48; *Capt.* 8 Dec. 54; *Major*, p 5 Aug. 59.

		CAPTAINS.	CORNET.	LIEUT.	CAPTAIN.	BREV.-MAJ.
9	4	Edward Phillips[5]	p 11 July 51	p 24 Feb. 54	1 Aug. 56	
9	0	V.C. Clement W. Heneage[6]	p 19 Aug. 51	3 Sept. 54	p 12 May 57	20 July 58
12	0	John Puget[7]	p 12 Sept. 48	p 14 Oct. 51	p 5 June 57	
9	0	Robert Poore	5 Dec. 51	19 Jan. 55	17 Sept. 57	20 July 58
7	0	George Gooch Clowes[8]	p 11 Mar. 53	19 Jan. 55	p 17 Sept. 57	7 Oct. 59
19	0	Thomas Penton[9]	p 19 Nov. 41	p 26 Jan. 44	20 Feb. 57	
7	0	William Mussenden[11]	p 10 June 53	19 Jan. 55	31 Jan. 58	
16	0	Theodore Wirgman[12]	p 29 Nov. 44	3 Apr. 46	9 Oct. 57	
5	0	Peter Charles G. Webster	p 2 Feb. 55	p 12 May 57	p 13 May 59	
4	0	Robert Dunmore Napier	p 16 May 56	p 27 Mar. 57	p 22 June 58	
		LIEUTENANTS.				
5	0	Gurney Hanbury	p 17 Aug. 55	17 Sept. 57		
4	0	Hon. Everard Stourton	29 Feb. 56	17 Sept. 57		
3	0	Robert William Jenkins		20 Feb. 57		
7	0	John Mathew Biddle[13] (*Assist.Surg.* 3 June 53)	25 Sept. 57	5 Feb. 58		
3	0	Thomas Richards	26 Sept. 57	18 June 58		
3	0	Parry de Winton	p 9 Oct. 57	p 7 Dec. 58		
3	0	George Campbell Ross	p 19 June 57	p 30 July 58		
2	0	Richard William Palliser	8 Jan. 58	p 13 May 59		
2	0	Herbert Cromwell Collier[16]	15 Jan. 58	p 5 Aug. 59		
3	0	Walter T. Goldsworthy[15]	10 Oct. 57	30 Oct. 59		
		CORNETS.				
3	0	Dan.Dudley Valen.Maher	11 Oct. 57			
3	0	Michael Clarke, *Adj.*	16 Oct. 57			
2	0	Augustus Tonnochy[17]	28 April 58			
2	0	Edward Pulleyne	7 May 58			
2	0	Sebastian White Rawlins	5 Feb. 58			
1	0	John George Stopford	23 Aug. 59			
1	0	Lachlan Foster Jamieson	2 Dec. 59			

4 Majors Chetwode and Macnaghten served the Eastern campaign of 1854-55, including the battles of Alma, Balaklava, and Inkerman, affairs of Bulganak and M'Kenzie's Farm, and siege of Sebastopol (Medal and four Clasps). Major Chetwode commanded Lord Raglan's escort in the Crimea up to the time of his Lordship's death; he has the 5th Class of the Medjidie.

17 Assist.Surgeon Sherlock served the Eastern campaign of 1855, including the siege and fall of Sebastopol and assault on the Redan on the 18th June (Medal and Clasp).

21	0	**Paymaster.**—Henry Duberly,[16] 12 Nov. 47; *Ens.* p 28 Sept. 39; *Lt.* 15 April 42.
3	0	**Adjutant.**—*Cornet* Michael Clarke, 24 Nov. 59.
		Quarter Master.—
2	0	**Riding Master.**—John Pickworth, 31 Aug. 58.
12	0	**Surgeon.**—Jenkin Homfray Llewelyn,[14] 9 Feb. 55; *Assist.Surg.* 17 March 48.
6	0	**Assistant Surgeons.**—Henry Sherlock,[17] 15 Dec. 54.
0	0	Ralph Robert Scott, 28 July 54.
17	0	**Veterinary Surgeon.**—Edward Simpson Grey,[16] 24 April 43; *1st Class*, 1 July

Blue.—*Agents*, Messrs. Cox & Co. [59.

[*Returned from the Crimea*, 12 *May* 1856. *Embarked for India*, 5 *Oct.* 1857.]

1 Lord Lucan served the campaign of 1828 on the Staff of the Russian Army in Bulgaria (Russian War Medal and Commander of St. Anne of Russia). Commanded the Cavalry Division throughout the Eastern campaign of 1854, including the battles of Alma, Balaklava (wounded) and Inkerman, and siege of Sebastopol, (Medal and four Clasps, KCB., Commander of the Legion of Honor, and 1st Class of the Medjidie).

2 Colonel de Salis served the Eastern campaign of 1854-55, including the battles of Alma, Balaklava, Inkerman, and Tchernaya, affairs of Bulganak and M'Kenzie's Farm, and siege of Sebastopol, and commanded the Cavalry on the expedition to Kertch (Medal and four Clasps, Knight of the Legion of Honor, Sardinian Medal, and 5th Class of the Medjidie).

3 Lt.Col. Seager served the Eastern campaign of 1854, including the battles of Alma, Balaklava (wounded) and Inkerman, affairs of Bulganak and M'Kenzie's Farm, and siege of Sebastopol (Medal and four Clasps and 5th Class of the Medjidie).

5 Captain Phillips served the Eastern campaign of 1854-55, including the battles of Balaklava (horse shot) and Inkerman, and siege of Sebastopol (Medal and three Clasps).

6 Major Heneage served the Eastern campaign of 1854-55, including the battles of Alma, Balaklava, and Inkerman, siege of Sebastopol, and expedition to Kertch (Medal and four Clasps).

7 Captain Puget served on the expedition to Kertch, and at the siege of Sebastopol (Medal and Clasp).

8 Major Clowes served the Eastern campaign of 1854, including the battles of Alma and Balaklava, affairs of Bulganak and M'Kenzie's Farm, and siege of Sebastopol: was wounded and taken prisoner, and horse shot, at the battle of Balaklava (Medal and three Clasps).

[For remainder of Notes, see end of 10th Lt. Drs.

Exeter.] **9th (*The Queen's Royal*) *Regt. of Lt. Drs.* (*Lancers.*)** 145

The Royal Cyphor within the Garter. "PENINSULA" "PUNNIAR" "SOBRAON" "PUNJAUB"
"CHILLIANWALLAH" "GOOJERAT."

Years' Serv.							
Full Pay.	Half Pay.						
65		**Colonel.**—୴ ୱୋ Sir James Wallace Sleigh,[1] KCB. *Cornet*, Feb. 95; *Lieut.* 29 April 95; *Capt.* 25 Oct. 98; *Maj.* 14 June 05; *Lt.Col.* 14 Dec. 09; *Col.* 12 Aug. 19; *Maj.Gen.* 22 July 30; *Lt.Gen.* 23 Nov. 41; *Gen.* 20 June 54; *Col.* 9th Lancers, 24 Aug. 39.					
29	0						
25	0	**Lieut.Colonel.**—Archibald Little,[3] CB. *Cornet*, ᴾ 4 Oct. 31; *Lt.* ᴾ 31 Aug. 32; *Capt.* ᴾ 24 Feb. 37; *Major*, 5 Apr. 50; *Lt.Col.* 20 June 54; *Col.* 20 June 57.					
19	0	**Majors.**—William Drysdale,[3] CB. *Cornet*, ᴾ 29 Dec. 35; *Lt.* ᴾ 31 Aug. 38; *Capt.* ᴾ 29 Oct. 47; *Bt.Maj.* 19 Jan. 58; *Major*, 5 Mar. 58; *Bt.Lt.Col.* 20 July 58.					
		Aug. Fred. Steele,[4] *Ens.* ᴾ 18 Nov. 41; *Lt.* 17 Mar. 43; *Capt.* ᴾ 24 May 50; *Major*, ᴾ 22 June 58; *Bt.Lt.Col.* 26 Apr. 59.					

		CAPTAINS.	CORNET.	LIEUT.	CAPTAIN.	BREV.MAJ.	BT. LT.COL.
24	0	Josiah Rogers John Coles[5]	ᴾ 2 Sept. 36	ᴾ 22 Mar. 39	ᴾ 19 Mar. 47	20 July 58	9 Sept. 59
15	0	Chardin Philip Johnson[6]	ᴾ 14 Mar. 45	ᴾ 14 Apr. 46	ᴾ 19 Apr. 50	20 July 58	
8	0	Anthony Molloy Fawcett[7]	ᴾ 16 Apr. 52	ᴾ 28 Jan. 53	12 Jan. 55		
20	0	John Head[8]	ᴾ 15 Dec. 40	19 Nov. 42	18 Sept. 57		
13	0	Frederick Ellis[9]	ᴾ 13 Aug. 47	ᴾ 2 Oct. 49	11 Oct. 57		
14	0	Richard Shaw[10]	3 Apr. 46	5 Apr. 50	22 Mar. 58		
9	0	Charles David Rich[11]	ᴾ 17 June 51	ᴾ 23 Dec. 53	ᴾ 22 June 58		
10	0	Robert Mills[12]	8 Oct. 50	20 June 54	6 Nov. 58		
4	0	Robt. S.Wms. Bulkeley[12]†	ᴾ 12 May 54	14 Aug. 57	ᴾ 13 May 59		
		LIEUTENANTS.					
8	0	Roger Dawson Upton[13]..	ᴾ 23 Jan. 52	ᴾ 12 Oct. 52	3 Lt.Col. Drysdale served with the 4th Light Dragoons during the campaign in Affghanistan under Lord Keane, and was present at the siege and capture of Ghuznee (Medal). Served with the 9th Lancers in the action at Punniar, 29th Dec. 43 (Medal). The Sutlej campaign in 1845-46, including the battle of Sobraon (Medal). The Punjaub campaign of 1848-49, including the passage of the Chenab at Ramnuggur, and battles of Chillianwallah & Goojerat (Medal and Clasps). The Indian campaign of 1857-59 and present at Delhi during the siege operations, commanding the Regt. from 18th Aug. to the fall of the city—horse shot at the assault; commanded the Regt. with Greathed's column, in action at Bolundshuhur, horse shot (wounded), and present in the actions at Allyghur and Agra (mentioned in despatch); also present at the relief of Lucknow (Brevet of Lt.Colonel, CB., Medal and Clasps).		
6	0	James Goldie[14]	ᴾ 14 July 54	ᴾ 15 Jan. 56			
8	0	Arth. Gonne Bell-Martin[15]	ᴾ 27 Aug. 52	5 June 55			
4	0	Alexander Morrogh[16]....	ᴾ 9 June 56	9 Apr. 57			
4	0	John Evans[17]	ᴾ 22 July 56	20 June 57			
4	0	Piers Thursby[18]	ᴾ 19 Sept. 56	5 Mar. 58			
4	0	Samuel Ashton Pretor[19]	ᴾ 26 Dec. 56	22 Mar. 58			
3	0	Rd. Freer Thonger,[20] *Adj.*	17 June 57	13 July 58			
2	0	Thomas Stanton Starkey[19]	ᴾ 15 Jan. 58	ᴾ 23 July 58			
2	0	William Naper Carleton[19]	ᴾ 2 Feb. 58	6 Nov. 58			
		CORNETS.					
2	0	Fred. Robert C. Crofton[19]	26 Feb. 58				
2	0	Robert Bury	5 Mar. 58				
2	0	Charles Brome Bashford	30 Mar. 58				
2	0	Charles Agnew	4 June 58				
2	0	Henry John Hall	2 July 58				
2	0	Oliver Ormerod	17 Sept. 58				
1	0	Chas. Ashburnham Floyd	ᴾ 1 July 59				
2	0	**Paymaster.**—Maurice Hartland Mahon, 8 March 58.					
3	0	**Adjutant.**—*Lieut.* Richard Freer Thonger,[20] 16 Mar. 58.					
8	0	**Quarter Master.**—Peter House,[21] 12 Nov. 52.					
2	0	**Riding Master.**—Charles Clements Brooke, 15 June 58.					
14	0	**Surgeon.**—John James Clifford, M.D. 28 Aug. 57; *Assist.Surg.* 7 Aug. 46.					
5	0	**Assistant Surgeon.**—Samuel Fuller,[22] 23 July 55.					
2	0	**Veterinary Surgeon.**—Frederick Bailey,[23] [16 March 58.]	Blue—*Facings* Scarlet.—*Agents*, Messrs. Cox & Co.				

[*Returned from India, Oct.* 1859.]

1 Sir James Sleigh served in Flanders in 1795; in the actions in North Holland and the Helder, 10th and 19th Sept., and 2nd and 6th Oct. 1799. In the Peninsula in 1811 and 12. Commanded the 11th Dragoons at Waterloo, towards the close of which the command of the 4th Brigade devolved on him. In 1819 he accompanied his Regiment to India, and commanded the Cavalry division at the siege of Bhurtpore in 1825 & 6 (Medal). He has received the War Medal with one Clasp for Salamanca, and is a Knight of Maximilian Joseph of Bavaria.

2 Colonel Little served with the 9th Lancers in the Sutlej campaign in 1846, including the battle of Sobraon (Medal). Served as Brigadier in command of the Cavalry at the relief of Lucknow, and commanded the Post at Dilkoosha from 16th to 21th Nov. 1857, for which he received the thanks of the Commander in Chief and Governor General in Council, and CB. Commanded the Cavalry and three troops Horse Artillery at the battle of Cawnpore and pursuit of the Gwalior Mutineers on the 6th Dec., actions at Seraight and Khudargunge. Commanded the 1st Brigade of Cavalry at the siege of Lucknow, until severely wounded by a musket ball through the left elbow (twice mentioned in despatches, Medal and Clasps).

4 Lt.Colonel Steele served in the 98th Regt. with the expedition to the North of China in 1842 (Medal), and was present at the attack and capture of Chin Kiang Foo, and at the landing before Nankin. Commanded a Squadron of the 9th Lancers at the relief of Lucknow by Lord Clyde, battle of Cawnpore on 6th Dec. 1857, and action at Seraight; commanded two Squadrons in action at Shumshurbad (severely wounded); present during the siege of Lucknow from 2nd to 19th March, and in the Transgogra affair at Kumbakoti (mentioned in despatches, Brevet Lt.Colonel, Medal and Clasps).

5 Lt.Colonel Coles served with the 4th Light Dragoons in the campaign under Lord Keane in Scinde and Affghanistan in 1838-9, and was present at the taking of Ghuznee (Medal). Commanded a Squadron of the 9th Lancers at the relief of Lucknow by Lord Clyde in Nov. 1857, also at the battle of Cawnpore on 6th Dec., and action at Seraight, capture of Meangunge where his horse was killed in personal encounter with the enemy; commanded a detached force of Horse Artillery and Cavalry to cooperate with Brigadier Franks, also two Squadrons of the 9th Lancers in the attack on the Moosabagh, and commanded the Regiment during the summer campaign in Oude and Rohilcund including the actions at Rhodamow and Allygunge, capture of Bareilly, action at Shahjehanpore and pursuit to Mahoondee; present with Grant's force in the affair at Kundakote (thrice mentioned in despatches, Brevets of Major and Lt.Colonel, Medal and Clasp).

6 Major Johnson served in suppression of the Indian Mutiny in 1857-58, and commanded a Squadron of the 9th Lancers at the relief of Lucknow by Lord Clyde, battle of Cawnpore on 6th Dec., and action at Seraight; commanded the Cavalry, two Squadrons of the 9th Lancers and Hodson's Horse, at the action of Shumshabad; served on Sir Hope Grant's Staff at the siege and capture of Lucknow and action at Koorsee; commanded a Squadron throughout the summer campaign in Oude and Rohilcund, including actions at Rhodamow and Allygunge, capture of Bareilly, action at Shahjehanpore and pursuit to Mahoondee (twice mentioned in despatches, Brevet of Major, Medal and Clasp).

7 Captain Fawcett served the Eastern campaign of 1854-55 with the 50th Regt., including the battles of Alma and Inkerman, and siege of Sebastopol (Medal and Clasps). Served with the 9th Lancers the Indian campaign of 1857-59, commanded a

145a   9*th (The Queen's Royal) Regt. of Light Dragoons (Lancers).*

Squadron at the battle of Budlekeserai and throughout the siege and capture of Delhi (horse shot in repelling a sortie on 19th June); also with Greathed's column in the action at Bolundshur (horse shot) and Allyghur, and was senior officer of the Regt. in camp at Agra when the enemy attacked and commanded during the early part of the engagement, and in the action at Meraigunge; present at the relief of Lucknow by Lord Clyde, battle of Cawnpore on 6th Dec., and actions at Seraighat and Khudagunge, and capture of Mecangunge; commanded a Squadron at the siege of Lucknow from 2nd to 19th March, and throughout the summer campaign in Oude and Rohilcund, including actions at Rhodamow and Allygunge, capture of Bareilly, action at Shahjchanpore and pursuit to Mahomdee, and affair at Kumdakoti (Medal and Clasps).

8 Captain Head served in the Sutlej campaign in 1846, and was present at the battle of Sobraon (Medal). The Punjaub campaign of 1848-9, including the passage of the Chenab at Ramnuggur, and battles of Chillianwallah and Goojerat (Medal and Clasps). The Indian campaign in 1857-58, present at the battle of Budlekeserai and siege of Delhi, and commanded a detachment of the 9th Lancers at the actions of Gungaree and Pullealloe—severely wounded (twice mentioned in despatches, Medal and Clasp).

9 Captain Ellis served with the 9th Lancers in the last Punjaub campaign, and was present in the battles of Chillianwallah and Goojerat (Medal and Clasps).

10 Captain Shaw served in the suppression of the Indian Mutiny in 1858-59, commanded a Squadron of the 9th Lancers at the passage of the Gogra at Fyzabad, and at the affair of Kumdakoti (Medal).

11 Captain Rich served with the 9th Lancers at the relief of Lucknow by Lord Clyde in Nov. 1857, and with the Military Train in the force that remained in position at Alumbagh from the relief until the siege and capture of the City in March 1858, and was mentioned in despatch for services in action at Alumbagh (horse shot); served with the 9th Lancers throughout the campaign in Oude and Rohilcund including actions at Rhodamow and Allygunge, capture of Bareilly, action of Shahjchanpore and pursuit to Mahomdee; commanded a Squadron at the passage of the Gogra and affairs at Mutchleegaon and Kumdakoti (Medal and Clasps).

12 Captain Mills served with the 9th Lancers in the Sutlej campaign of 1845-6, and was present in the battle of Sobraon (Medal). Also the Punjaub campaign of 1848-9, including the passage of the Chenab, and battles of Chillianwallah and Goojerat (Medal and Clasps).

12† Captain Bulkeley served in the Indian campaign from Feb. 1858 to Juny. 1859 and was present at the affair of Mecangunge, siege and capture of Lucknow, affairs of Barree and Sirsee, action of Nawabgunge, occupation of Fyzabad, passage of the Goomtee at Sultanpore, throughout the Biswarra campaign, including the affairs of Kandoo Nuddee and Palecghat, taking the fort of Rehora, attack on and pursuit from Hyderghur; also the Trans-Gogra campaign, including the affair near Churda and pursuit. taking the fort of Meejeedin, and attack on Bankee with pursuit to the Raptee (Medal and Clasp).

13 Lieut. Upton served with a detachment of the 1st West India Regiment in the storm and capture of the strongly-stockaded town of Sabajee on the Gambia, in June 1853. Served with the 9th Lancers in suppression of the Indian Mutiny in 1857-59, and present at the battle of Budlekeserai (horse shot), siege of Delhi, siege and capture of Lucknow, the summer campaign in Oude and Rohilcund and actions at Rhodamow and Allygunge, capture of Bareilly, action at Shahjchanpore and pursuit to Mahomdee, passage of the Gogra at Fyzabad (Medal and Clasps).

14 Lieut. Goldie served with the 9th Lancers throughout the suppression of the Indian Mutiny in 1857-59, including the battle of Budlekeserai, siege operations assault and capture of Delhi, actions of Bolundshuhur and Allyghur, battle of Agra, affair of Kanouge, relief of Lucknow by Lord Clyde, battle of Cawnpore on 6th Dec., action at Seraighat, action at Shumshabad (in command of a Squadron), siege and capture of Lucknow, the summer campaign in Oude and Rohilcund and actions of Rhodamow and Allyghur, capture of Bareilly, action at Shahjchanpore and pursuit to Mahomdee, passage of the Gogra at Fyzabad, and affair at Kumdakoti (Medal and Clasps).

15 Lieut. Bell Martin served with the 9th Lancers throughout the suppression of the Indian Mutiny in 1857-59, including the battle of Budlekeserai, siege assault and capture of Delhi, actions of Bolundshuhur and Allyghur, battle of Agra, affair at Kanouge, relief of Lucknow by Lord Clyde, battle of Cawnpore on 6th Dec., actions at Seraighat and Khudagunge, capture of Mecangunge (officiated as Brigade Major of Cavalry), siege and capture of Lucknow, the summer campaign in Oude and Rohilcund and actions at Rhodamow and Allyghur, capture of Bareilly, action at Shahjchanpore and pursuit to Mahomdee (four times mentioned in despatches, Medal and Clasps).

16 Lieut. Morrogh served in the suppression of the Indian Mutiny in 1858-59, including the action at Shumshabad, siege and capture of Lucknow, the summer campaign in Oude and Rohilcund and actions at Rhodamow and Allygunge, capture of Bareilly, action at Shahjchanpore and pursuit to Mahomdee (Medal and Clasp).

17 Lieut. Evans served as a Volunteer on the personal staff of Major General Sir W. Williams in Asia Minor during the campaign of 1855-56 (Turkish Medal). Served with the 9th Lancers throughout the suppression of the Indian Mutiny in 1857-59, including the battle of Budlekeserai, action at Hujjufghur, and served as a volunteer with the Artillery in the advanced batteries during the siege operations assault and capture of Delhi; present with 9th Lancers at the actions of Bolundshur, Allyghur, and Agra, relief of Lucknow by Lord Clyde (horse killed), battle of Cawnpore on 6th Dec. and action at Seraighat, siege and capture of Lucknow, the Summer campaign in Oude and Rohilcund and actions of Rhodamow and Allygunge, capture of Bareilly, action at Shahjchanpore and pursuit to Mahomdee, and affair at Kumdakoti (Medal and Clasps).

18 Lieut. Thursby served in the suppression of the Indian Mutiny in 1857-59, including the action at Shumshabad, capture of Mecangunge, siege and capture of Lucknow with action at Moosabagh, the Summer campaign in Oude and Rohilcund and actions at Rhodamow and Allygunge, capture of Bareilly, action at Shahjchanpore and pursuit to Mahomdee, and affair at Kumdakoti (Medal and Clasp).

19 Lieuts. Pretor, Starkey, Carleton, and Cornet Crofton served in the suppression of the Indian Mutiny in 1858-59 including the affair at Kumdakoti (Medal).

20 Lieut. Thongor served with the 9th Lancers in the Sutlej campaign of 1845-46 and was present at the battle of Sobraon (Medal). The Punjaub campaign of 1848-49, including the passage of the Chenab, and battles of Chillianwallah and Goojerat (Medal and Clasps). Throughout the suppression of the Indian Mutiny in 1857-59, including the battle of Budlekeserai, the siege assault and capture of Delhi, and commanded a Troop of the 9th Lancers with Greathed's column in the actions of Bolundshuhur (wounded in personal encounter), Allyghur, Agra, and Kanoge; present at the relief of Lucknow by Lord Clyde, battle of Cawnpore on 6th Dec., actions at Seraighat and Khudargunge, siege and capture of Lucknow, the Summer campaign in Oude and Rohilcund and actions at Rhodamow and Allygunge, Bareilly, and Shahjchanpore, with pursuit to Mohumdee, and passage of the Gogra at Fyzabad (Medal and Clasps).

21 Quarter Master House served with the 9th Lancers in the battle of Punniar on 29th Dec. 1843 (Medal). The Sutlej campaign in 1846, including the battle of Sobraon (Medal). The Punjaub campaign of 1848-9, including the passage of the Chenab at Ramnuggur, and battles of Chillianwallah and Goojerat (Medal and Clasps). Throughout the suppression of the Indian Mutiny in 1857-59, including the battle of Budlekeserai, siege assault and capture of Delhi, actions at Bolundshuhur and Allyghur, battle of Agra, affair at Kanoge, relief of Lucknow by Lord Clyde, battle of Cawnpore on 6th Dec., action at Seraighat, occupation of Futtyghur, siege and capture of Lucknow, campaign in Oude and Rohilcund and affairs at Rhodamow and Allygunge, capture of Bareilly, action near Shahjchanpore and pursuit to Mohumdee, and passage of the Gogra at Fyzabad (Medal and Clasps).

22 Assist.Surgeon Fuller served with the 9th Lancers in the suppression of the Indian Mutiny in 1858-59, and was present at the capture of Mecangunge, siege and capture of Lucknow, the summer campaign in Oude and Rohilcund with actions at Rhodamow and Allygunge, capture of Bareilly, action near Shahjchanpore and pursuit to Mahomdee, passage of the Gogra at Fyzabad (Medal and Clasp).

23 Veterinary Surgeon Bailey served with the 9th Lancers in the suppression of the Indian Mutiny in 1858-59, and was present of the passage of the Gogra at Fyzabad, and affair at Kumdakoti (Medal).

Head Quarters at Hounslow.] **10th (*The Prince of Wales's Own*) Royal Regt. of Lt. Drs. (Hussars.)** 146

"PENINSULA" "WATERLOO" "SEVASTOPOL."

Years' Serv.		
Full Pay	Half Pay	
57		Col.—👤 H. Beauchamp, *Earl Beauchamp*,[1] *Cor.* 0 July 03; *Lt.* 24 May 04; *Capt.* 15 Jan. 07; *Maj.* 14 May 12; *Lt.Col.* 18 June 15; *Col.* 24 Mar. 22; *Maj.Gen.* 10 Jan. 37; *Lt.Gen.* 9 Nov. 46; *Gen.* 20 June 54; *Col.* 10th Huss. 23 June 43.
22	0	*Lieut.Colonel.*—John Wilkie,[2] *Cornet*, p 11 May 38; *Lieut.* p 29 May 40; *Capt.* p 17 May 44; *Major*, p 27 Feb. 52; *Lt.Col.* p 10 Feb. 54; *Col.* 28 Nov. 54.
12	0	*Major.*—Valentine Baker,[3] *Cornet*, p 1 Aug. 48; *Lieut.* 29 July 53; *Capt.* p 1 Aug. 56; *Major*, p 14 June 59.

		CAPTAINS.	CORNET.	LIEUT.	CAPTAIN.	BREV.MAJ.	BT. LT. COL.
19	0	Richard Playne Smith[4]..	p 26 Oct. 41	p 3 Apr. 46	p 27 Feb. 52		4 Capt.Smith served in the Crimean campaign in 1855, including the capture of Tchorgaun and siege of Sebastopol (Medal and Clasps).
8	0	Edward Levett[5]	p 17 Aug. 52	6 June 54	p 24 Nov. 57		
10	0	Arthur Herbert Cass[6]....	p 13 Dec. 50	p 5 Nov. 52	23 Apr. 58		
4	0	John Fife	14 Mar. 56	22 May 57	p 7 Sept. 58		
6	0	Robert Cooper Sawbridge	p 28 July 54	p 10 Aug. 55	p 6 Aug. 58		
9	0	Frederick Coates[7]	p 17 Jan. 51	p 26 July 53	14 Aug. 57		
4	0	Henry Atkins Bowyer ..	p 21 Nov. 56	p 24 Nov. 57	p 14 June 50		
5	0	Richard Newsham Pedder[8]	p 14 Dec. 55	5 Mar. 58	p 28 Oct. 59		
		LIEUTENANTS.					5 Captain Levett served the Eastern campaign of 1854-55 with the 19th Regiment, including the battle of Inkerman, siege and fall of Sebastopol, and assault on the Redan on the 8th September (Medal and Clasps). 6 Captain Cass served in the Crimean campaign in 1855, including the capture of Tchorgaun, battle of the Tchernaya, and siege of Sebastopol (Medal and Clasps). 7 Captain Coates served with the 7th Hussars in the Indian campaign of 1858, and was present at the repulse of the attack on the Alumbagh, siege and capture of Lucknow, affair of Burree, action of Nawabgunge, occupation of Fyzabad, passage of the Goomtee at Sultanpore, affairs of Khundoonuddee and Paleeghat (Medal and Clasp). 13 Paymaster Elrington, Qr.Master Fenn, and Surgeon Fraser served in the Crimean campaign in 1855, including the capture of Tchorgaun, battle of the Tchernaya, siege and fall of Sebastopol (Medal and Clasp).
5	0	Richard Lomax	23 Nov. 55	p 8 Jan. 58			
5	0	Edw. Picton Baumgarten	p 19 Jan. 55	p 11 Dec. 57			
3	0	Esdaile Lovell Lovell....	17 Nov. 57	p 15 June 58			
3	0	Ld. Ralph Drury Kerr, *adj.*	p 24 Nov. 57	p 15 June 58			
2	0	Crofton Toler Vandeleur .	p 15 Jan. 58	p 7 Dec. 58			
2	0	Thomas Shirley Ball	30 Apr. 58	p 18 Feb. 59			
2	0	Owen R. Slacke........	14 May 58	p 14 June 59			
2	0	Arthur Barthorp	13 July 58	p 17 June 59			
2	0	Edward Alexander Wood	16 July 58	p 30 Sept. 59			
		CORNETS.					
2	0	Wm. Morgan Maunder..	p 23 July 58				
2	0	Thomas Jas. W. Bulkeley	p 14 July 58				
1	0	Wilfrid Brougham	p 18 Feb. 59				
1	0	Smith Hill Child	p 5 Aug. 59				
1	0	Henry Price Holford[9] ..	p 26 Aug. 59				

22	0	*Paymaster.*—Richard John Elrington,[13] 2 Feb. 44; *Ens.* p 24 March 38; *Lieut.* p 29 May 39.
3	0	*Adjutant.*—*Lieut.* Lord Ralph Drury Kerr, 6 May 59.
14	0	*Quarter Master.*—John Fenn,[13] 19 May 46.
3	0	*Riding Master.*—Emanuel Simpson, 29 Dec. 57.
15	0	*Surgeon.*—Thomas Fraser,[13] M.D. 9 March 55; *Assist.Surg.* 16 Dec. 45.
6	0	*Assist.Surg.*—Lucas Geo. Hooper, 28 April 54. Blue.—*Agents*, Messrs. Cox & Co.
		Veterinary Surgeon.— [*Returned from the Crimea*, 2 June 1856.]

1 Lord Beauchamp served in the Peninsula with the 16th Dragoons from March 1809 to Sept. 1810, and again from Feb. 1814 to the end of that war, including the capture of Oporto, battle of Talavera, and passage of the Coa. Severely wounded in the neck, 26th Aug. 1810, in Massena's advance to the battle of Busaco. He has received the War Medal with one Clasp for Talavera.
2 Colonel Wilkie commanded the 10th Hussars in the Crimean campaign from the 17th April 1855, including the capture of Tchorgaun, battle of the Tchernaya, siege and fall of Sebastopol (Medal and Clasp, and 5th Class of the Medjidie).
3 Major Baker served with the 12th Lancers in the Kaffir war of 1852-53, and was present at the action of Borea (Medal). Served the Crimean campaign of 1855, and siege of Sebastopol, and was on the escort to the Commander-in-Chief at the final assault and capture of the town, and at the battle of Tchernaya (Medal and Clasp).
8 Captain Pedder served with the 7th Hussars in the Indian campaign from Feb. 1858 to March 1859 and was present at the repulse of the enemy's attack on the Alumbagh, siege and capture of Lucknow, affairs of Barree and Sirsee, action of Nawabgunge, occupation of Fyzabad, passage of the Goomtee at Sultanpore, throughout the Byswarra campaign, including the affairs of Kundoo Nuddee and Paleeghat, taking the fort of Rehora and pursuit of Benhi Madho's force to the Goomtee; also the Trans-Gogra campaign, including the affair near Churda and pursuit, taking the fort of Mecjeedia, attack on Bankee with pursuit to the Raptee, advance into Nepaul and affair at Sitkaghat (Medal and Clasp).
9 Cornet Holford served as Ensign 79th Highlanders in the Indian campaign of 1858, including the siege and capture of Lucknow (Medal and Clasp).

[*Continuation of Notes to 8th Dragoons.*]

9 Captain Penton served with the 3rd Light Dragoons throughout the Sutlej campaign of 1845-6, and was present at the battles of Moodkee (charger killed), Ferozeshah (charger killed), and Sobraon (Medal and two Clasps). Also throughout the Punjaub campaign of 1848-49, including the cavalry affair at Ramnuggur, passage of the Chenab at Wuzeerabad on the 1st December 1848, with the force under Sir Joseph Thackwell, action of Sadoolapore, and battles of Chillianwallah and Goojerat (Medal and two Clasps).
11 Captain Mussenden served the Eastern campaign of 1854-55, including the battles of Alma, Balaklava (horse shot), Inkerman, and Tchernaya, affairs of Bulganak and M'Kenzie's Farm, and siege of Sebastopol (Medal and four Clasps, and 5th Class of the Medjidie).
12 Captain Wirgman served in the Austrian Cavalry and Staff Corps, and was extra Aide-de-Camp to Field Marshal Prince Windisch-grætz in 1840, 41, and 42. Served in the Crimean campaign of 1855 with the 10th Hussars, in command of a Troop, and was present at the capture of Tchorgaun, battle of Tchernaya, siege and fall of Sebastopol (Medal and Clasp).
13 Lieut. Biddle served with the 60th Rifles at the siege and capture of Delhi (Medal and Clasp).
14 Surgeon Llewelyn served the Eastern campaign of 1854-55, including the battles of Alma, Balaklava, and Inkerman, siege and fall of Sebastopol (Medal and four Clasps).
15 Lieut. Goldsworthy served with the Volunteer Cavalry with Havelock's Column in 1857 and was present at the actions of Oonao and Busseerutgunge, and recapture of Busseerutgunge.
16 Lieut. Collier served on the Staff in the Persian campaign of 1857 (Medal).
17 Cornet Tonnochy served during the Indian Mutiny in the Meerut Volunteer Cavalry and was present in the actions of Barote, Golothee, Morepore, and Thanna Bhawim,—at Barote he was severely wounded, having personally encountered and killed the rebel leader Shahmul, for whose capture Government had offered a large reward; for his services he received a commission in the 8th Hussars, and subsequently in 1858 when in command of a party of Bombay Lancers and some Irregular Cavalry he attacked the rebels in the fort of Akajree in the Gwalior territory, and afterwards on their evacuating it he overtook and dispersed them at Gurodie in the Jhansi district (Medal).

147   11th (*or Prince Albert's Own*) *Regt. of Hussars.*   [Head Quarters at Birmingham.

The *Sphinx* with the words, "EGYPT" "SALAMANCA," "PENINSULA " "WATERLOO" "BHURT-PORE" "ALMA" "BALAKLAVA" "INKERMAN" "SEVASTOPOL."

Years' Serv.	Full Pay.	Half Pay.					
54			*Colonel.*—ജ ബഉ *Sir* Henry Wyndham,¹ KCB. *Ens.* 27 March 06; *Capt.* 8 June 09; *Major*, 9 Aug. 13; *Lieut.Col.* 20 Jan. 14; *Col.* 27 May 25; *Major Gen.* 10 Jan. 37; *Lt.Gen.* 9 Nov. 46; *Gen.* 20 June 54; *Col.* 11th Hus. 19 Nov. 47.					
21		0	*Lieut.Colonel.*—Broadley Harrison,² *Cornet*, ᴾ 11 Oct. 39; *Lieut.* ᴾ 7 Sept. 41; *Capt.* ᴾ 7 June 44; *Major*, ᴾ 5 Nov. 52; *Bt.Lt.Col.* 26 Oct. 58; *Lt.Col.* ᴾ 14 June 59.					
13		0	*Major.*—Charles Craufurd Fraser,³ *Cornet*, ᴾ 3 Dec. 47; *Lt.* ᴾ 14 June 50; *Capt.* ᴾ 21 April 54; *Bt.Major*, 20 July 58; *Major*, ᴾ 13 May 59.					

			CAPTAINS.	CORNET.	LIEUT.	CAPTAIN.	BREV.-MAJ.
6		0	Arthr. Lyttleton Annesley⁵	ᴾ 21 July 54	8 Dec. 54	ᴾ 24 Feb. 57	
12		0	Edward Harnett⁶	ᴾ 2 June 48	14 Oct. 51	5 Mar. 58	
5		0	William Cuninghame	28 Dec. 55	ᴾ 24 Feb. 57	ᴾ 23 Mar. 58	
5		0	Alex. Baring Bingham	3 Aug. 55	ᴾ 13 Mar. 57	ᴾ 21 May 58	
4		0	Daniel Shaw Stewart	ᴾ 13 June 56	ᴾ 10 April 57	ᴾ 23 July 58	
3		0	Albert Pool Garnett	ᴾ 6 Feb. 57	5 Mar. 58	ᴾ 14 June 59	
3		0	Arthur Cecil Tempest	ᴾ 3 Mar. 57	ᴾ 16 Mar. 58	ᴾ 30 Aug. 59	
5		0	Horace Montagu	ᴾ 13 Feb. 55	ᴾ 19 June 57	ᴾ 5 Aug. 59	

		LIEUTENANTS.			
3	0	John M'Loughlin,⁷ *Adj*		20 Feb. 57	
3	0	James Affleck Stewart	ᴾ 13 Mar. 57	ᴾ 26 Mar. 58	
3	0	Richard John Somers	ᴾ 2 April 57	ᴾ 21 May 58	
3	0	George Coke Robinson	ᴾ 3 April 57	ᴾ 22 June 58	
3	0	Paget Peploe Mosley	ᴾ 10 April 57	ᴾ 23 July 58	
2	0	Hon. Jas. D. Drummond	8 Jan. 58	ᴾ 8 Mar. 59	
2	0	John George Annesley	15 Jan. 58	ᴾ 14 June 59	
2	0	Francis de Burgh	17 Mar. 58	ᴾ 30 Aug. 59	
3	0	C. P. *Visc.* Royston⁸	ᴾ 20 Dec. 57	1 Jan. 59	

2 Lt.Col. Harrison served in the Crimean campaign in 1855, including the capture of Tchorgoun, siege and fall of Sebastopol (Medal and Clasp, and 5th Class of the Medjidie).

5 Captain Annesley served in the Crimea from 29th July 1855, including the siege and fall of Sebastopol (Medal and Clasp).

		CORNETS.	
2	0	Somerset Saunderson	ᴾ 28 May 58
2	0	Reginald Calvert	ᴾ 24 Dec. 58
1	0	James Gideon Pott	ᴾ 11 Jan. 59
1	0	Wastel Brisco	ᴾ 23 Aug. 59

6 Captain Harnett served in the Crimea from 14th July 1855, including the battle of Tchernaya, siege and fall of Sebastopol (Medal and Clasp).

10 Surgeon Crosse served the Eastern campaign of 1854-55, including the affair of Bulganak, battles of Alma, Balaklava, Inkerman, and Tchernaya, siege and fall of Sebastopol (Medal and Clasps, and Knight of the Legion of Honor).

26	0	*Paymaster.*—George Pott Erskine, 3 Nov. 43; *Ens.* ᴾ 11 July 34; *Lt.* ᴾ 1 Mar. 39.
3	0	*Adjutant.*—Lieut. John M'Loughlin,⁸ 10 Dec. 58.
7	0	*Quarter Master.*—Henry Kauntze,⁹ 1 April 53.
2	0	*Riding Master.*—Edmund Corbett, 5 Feb. 58.
20	0	*Surgeon.*—John Burton St. Croix Crosse,¹⁰ 16 June 48; *Assist.Surg.* 9 Oct. 40.
0	0	*Assist.Surgeon.*—Ormsby Bowen Miller,¹¹ 28 March 54.
3	0	*Veterinary Surgeon.*—Paul Anthony, 31 Aug. 57.

Blue.—*Agents*, Messrs. Cox & Co.

[*Returned from the Crimea, 26 July* 1856.]

1 Sir Henry Wyndham served the Peninsular campaigns of 1808, 9, 11, and 13, including the actions of Roleia, Vimiera, Benevente, Albuhera, Usagre, Morales de Toro, Vittoria, and the Pyrenees. Served also the campaign of 1815, and was severely wounded at Waterloo. He has received the War Medal with four Clasps for Roleia, Vimiera, Albuhera, and Vittoria.

3 Major Fraser served as Orderly Officer to Brigadier Campbell at the affair of Munseata near Allahabad, on the 5th Jan. 1858, and subsequently with the 7th Hussars in the Indian campaign from Feb. to July 1858 and from Dec. 1858 to March 1859 and was present at the affair of Moorngunge, siege and capture of Lucknow, affairs of Barree and Sirsee, action of Nawabgunge (severely wounded), throughout the Trans-Gogra campaign, including the affair near Churda and pursuit, taking the fort of Meejeedia, attack on Bankee with pursuit to the Raptee, advance into Nepaul and affair at Sitkaghat (twice mentioned in despatches, Brevet of Major, Medal and Clasp).

7 Lieut. M'Loughlin served throughout the Eastern campaign of 1854-55, including the affairs of Bulganak and M'Kenzie's Farm, battles of Alma, Balaklava, Inkerman, and Tchernaya, capture of Balaklava, siege and fall of Sebastopol, and operations near Eupatoria under General D'Allonville (Medal and four Clasps).

8 Lord Royston served with the 7th Hussars in the Indian campaign in 1858, including the advance into Nepaul and affair at Silkaghat (Medal).

9 Qr.Master Kauntze served with the 11th Hussars at the siege and capture of Bhurtpore in 1825-6 (Medal and one Clasp). Also the Eastern campaign of 1854 and up to 22nd Aug. 1855, including the affair of Bulganak, battles of Alma, Balaklava, and Inkerman, and siege of Sebastopol (Medal and Clasps).

11 Assist.Surgeon Miller served with the 77th Regt. throughout the Eastern campaign of 1854-55, including the battles of Alma and Inkerman, and siege of Sebastopol (Medal and Clasps, and 5th Class of the Medjidie).

Secunderabad. Depot, Maidstone.] **12th (*Prince of Wales's*) Royal Regt. of Lancers.** 148

The *Sphinx*, with the words, "EGYPT" "PENINSULA" "WATERLOO" "SEVASTOPOL."

Years' Serv.		
55	Full Pay	Half Pay

55 — *Colonel.*—₤ Sir Lovell Benjamin Lovell,[1] KCB. KH. *Cornet*, ᴾ 18 Dec. 05; *Lt.* ᴾ 19 May 08; *Capt.* ᴾ 12 Dec. 11; *Brev.Major*, 21 Jan. 19; *Maj.* ᴾ 28 Oct. 24; *Lt.Col.* ᴾ 21 Nov. 28; *Col.* 23 Nov. 41; *Major Gen.* 20 June 54; *Col.* 12th Lancers, 29 Nov. 56.

35 0 *Lt.Cols.*—Edward Pole,[2] *Cornet*, ᴾ 7 July 25; *Lt.* ᴾ 19 Sept. 26; *Capt.* ᴾ 18 Nov. 31; *Major* ᴾ 30 July 44; *Lieut.Col.* ᴾ 30 March 47; *Col.* 28 Nov. 54.

34 0 Lawrence Fyler,[3] *Ens.* ᴾ 7 Sept. 26; *Lieut.* ᴾ 10 July 28; *Capt.* ᴾ 7 Feb. 34; *Brev.Major*, 10 June 46; *Major*, ᴾ 7 April 48; *Brev.Lt.Col.* 20 June 54; *Lt.Col.* 7 July 57; *Col.* 26 Oct. 58.

35 0 Chas.Wm. Morley Balders,[3]† CB., *Cornet*, ᴾ 10 Nov. 25; *Lt.* ᴾ 25 Nov. 28; *Capt.* ᴾ 15 July 36; *Maj.* ᴾ 16 May 45; *Bt.Lt.Col.* 3 Apr. 46; *Col.* 20 June 54; *Lt.Col.* 8 Jan. 58.

14 0 *Majors.*—Thomas G. Alex. Oakes,[4] *Cornet*, ᴾ 16 Jan. 46; *Lt.* ᴾ 3 Sept. 47; *Capt.* ᴾ 22 Feb. 50; *Major*, ᴾ 1 Aug. 56; *Bt.Lt.Col.* 20 July 58.

21 0 Edw. Burgoyne Cureton,[5] *Cornet*, 21 June 30; *Lieut.* 10 Dec. 43; *Capt.* ᴾ 31 Jan. 51; *Brev.Maj.* 26 Dec. 56; *Major*, 7 July 57.

		CAPTAINS.	CORNET.	LIEUT.	CAPTAIN.	BREV.-MAJ.
19	0	J.DeM.M.Prior[6] l.c.26 Apr.59	31 Dec. 41	30 Apr. 46	8 July 51	20 July 58
25	0	George Horne[7]	ᴾ 19 June 35	ᴾ 28 Aug. 38	25 June 52	
16	0	Chandos Fred. Clifton[8]	ᴾ 31 May 44	ᴾ 29 Oct. 47	29 July 53	
11	0	Robt. HerbertHeath Jary[9]	ᴾ 23 Nov. 49	ᴾ 25 Apr. 51	ᴾ 1 May 55	
8	0	Adolph.UlickWombwell[10]	ᴾ 19 Aug. 52	ᴾ 23 Dec. 53	ᴾ 1 May 55	
17	0	Henry Elmhirst Reader[11]	24 Nov. 43	9 Aug. 45	ᴾ 1 Dec. 54	
12	0	Robert Campbell[12]	ᴾ 12 May 48	ᴾ 8 Feb. 50	29 Dec. 54	
14	0	Charles Joseph Harford	ᴾ 16 Jan. 46	ᴾ 27 Oct. 48	ᴾ 29 May 56	
10	0	William Wallis King	ᴾ 12 July 50	ᴾ 12 Nov. 52	ᴾ 19 Nov. 58	
10	0	Charles J. Watson Allen	ᴾ 14 June 50	ᴾ 3 June 53	ᴾ 27 May 56	
		LIEUTENANTS.				
8	0	Edward Brown,[9] *Adj.*	24 Aug. 52	3 Aug. 54		
8	0	Alexander Fletcher[15]	ᴾ 21 Sept. 52	ᴾ 4 Aug. 54		
7	0	Robert Edward Roe[16]	ᴾ 13 May 53	ᴾ 15 Sept. 54		
6	0	FrancisTheophilusBlunt[17]	ᴾ 4 Aug. 54	ᴾ 1 May 55		
6	0	Fitzhardinge Jones[17]†	ᴾ 15 Sept. 54	9 Nov. 55		
4	0	George Francis Morant	ᴾ 18 Apr. 56	ᴾ 1 Aug. 56		
4	0	John Charles Le Quesne	ᴾ 20 Apr. 56	7 July 57		
4	0	Erasmus Gower	ᴾ 20 July 56	9 Oct. 57		
4	0	Samuel Adams	ᴾ 19 Sept. 56	ᴾ 11 Dec. 57		
3	0	William Edward Shaw	24 Feb. 57	5 Mar. 58		
3	0	Frederick Swindley	17 Nov. 57	9 May 58		
3	0	James Hen. B. Vaughan	ᴾ 11 Dec. 57	7 Mar. 59		
5	0	William Lloyd Browne	ᴾ 15 Nov. 55	1 May 58		
		CORNETS.				
3	0	Arth. L'E. Ham. Holmes	15 Dec. 57			
3	0	David Roche Vandeleur	16 Dec. 57			
2	0	Adolph.J.S.C.Chichester	16 Mar. 58			
2	0	William Blacker	ᴾ 21 May 58			
2	0	Henry J. Russell Cruise[18]	22 May 58			
2	0	Jos. Devonsher Jackson	30 July 58			
1	0	Joseph Sefton	13 May 59			
1	0	James Elmsley Macaulay	1 July 59			
30	0	*Paymaster.*—Jas. Gustavus Hamilton Holmes,[15] 24 Feb. 37; *Ens.* ᴾ 11 June 30;				
8	0	*Adjutant.—Lieut.* Edward Brown,[9] 18 Oct. 53. [*Lt.* ᴾ 2 Aug. 33.]				
12	0	*Quarter Master.*—Michael Blake,[9] 18 July 48.				
3	0	*Riding Master.*—William St. Leger Stephens, 31 July 57.				
10	0	*Surgeon.*—Gavin Ainslie Turnbull,[15] 28 Dec. 55; *Assist.Surg.* 16 Aug. 50.				
6	0	*Assistant Surgeons.*—Edward Mason Wrench,[20] 3 Nov. 54.				
8	0	Samuel Gibson,[19] M.B. 23 Nov. 52.				
3	0	*Veterinary Surgeon.*—Charles Steel, 10 Aug. 57.				

Side notes for Captain column:
9 Capt.Jary, Lt.Brown and Qr.-Mr. Blake, served with the 12th Lancers in the Kaffir war of 1851-3 (Medal). Also in the Crimea from 9th May 1855, including the siege of Sebastopol (Medal and Clasp).

3 Colonel Fyler served with the 16th Lancers during the campaign in Affghanistan under Lord Keane, including the siege and capture of Ghuznee (Medal). Also at the battle of Maharajpore (Medal), 29 Dec. 1843; and in the campaign on the Sutlej in 1846 (Medal), including the battles of Buddiwal and Aliwal, at which last he was severely wounded by a musket shot whilst charging with the Squadron he commanded a large body of infantry with three guns in their front, and which he broke through and dispersed, being the last of the enemy's infantry which stood their ground; for this service he received the Brevet rank of Major. Served in the Punjaub campaign of 1848-9 with the 3rd Light Dragoons (Medal). Served in the Crimea with the 12th Lancers from 17th May 1855, and was present at the battle of the Tchernaya, siege and fall of Sebastopol (Medal and Clasp, and 5th Class of the Medjidie).

Blue.—*Facings* Scarlet.—*Agent*, Messrs. Cox and Co.

[*Returned from the Crimea*, 1 June 1856. *Embarked for India*, 16 Aug. 1856.]

1 Sir Lovell Benjamin Lovell served at the taking of Monte Video under Sir Sam. Auchmuty in 1807, and subsequently in the Peninsula, including the battles of Talavera, the Coa, Busaco, Fuentes d'Onor (wounded), Salamanca, Vittoria, the Pyrenees, Nive, Orthes, and Toulouse; actions or skirmishes near Talavera, Sexmiro, Val de la Mula, La Meares, Freixeda, Guarda, Coimbra, Valle, Venda de Sierra, Pombal, Redinha, Miranda, do Corvo, Coa, Galligos, Nave d'Aver, Espiga, near Fuentes d'Onor, Llerena, near Salamanca, St. Christoval, Rueda, Castrillos, Foncastin, Matylla, nt Burgos, Osma, Huarte, Pampeluna, Vale de Bustan, Pass of Maya, Lines of Ainho, Cambo, Hasparren, Helito, Garris, Sauveterre, St. Gladie, Buelho, Garlin, San Roman—total, ten general actions, forty minor actions or skirmishes, besides attending seven sieges; and was at the siege of Oporto, being one of the Military Reporters under Lord William Russell. He has received the War Medal with eleven Clasps for Busaco, Fuentes d'Onor, Badajoz, Salamanca, Vittoria, the Pyrenees, Nive, Orthes, and Toulouse.

2 Colonel Pole commanded the 12th Lancers in the Kaffir war of 1851-3 (Medal); in General Somerset's expedition over the Kei in 1851 he commanded the Cavalry and Artillery; and in 1852 he commanded several patrols and columns. Served in the Crimea from 9th May 1855, and was present at the capture of Tchorgoun, battle of Tchernaya, siege and all of Sebastopol, and at Eupatoria with the Light Cavalry Brigade (Medal and Clasp, and 5th Class of the Medjidie).

149   12th (Prince of Wales's) Royal Regt. of Lancers.

3† Colonel Balders served the Sutlej campaign of 1845-46, and commanded the 3rd Light Dragoons in the battles of Moodkee and Ferozeshah, and was wounded in the groin whilst charging the enemy's batteries at Ferozeshah on the evening of the 21st Dec. 1845 (Medal and Clasp, Brevet Lt.-Colonel, and *CB.*).

4 Lt.Colonel Onkes served with the 12th Lancers in the Kaffir war of 1851-3 (Medal). Served in the Crimea from 9 May 1855 (Medal and Clasp for Sebastopol, Sardinian Medal, and 5th Class of the Medjidie).

5 Major Cureton served with the 16th Lancers in the action at Maharajpore 20th Dec. 1843 (Medal); and with the 3rd Light Dragoons during the campaign of 1845-6 on the Sutlej; including the battles of Moodkee (severely wounded) and Sobraon, for which he has received a Medal and one Clasp ; and served with the 12th Lancers in the Kaffir war of 1851-53 (Medal). Served with the 12th Lancers in the Crimea from 31 July 1855, at the siege and fall of Sebastopol and at Eupatoria (Medal and Clasp).

6 Lt.Colonel Prior served with the 12th Lancers throughout the Kaffir war of 1851-53 (Medal), including the passage of, and operations across, the Kei. The Eastern campaign from 17th May 1855, including the battle of Tchernaya, siege and fall of Sebastopol, and operations near Eupatoria under General D'Allonville (Medal and Clasp). The Indian campaign of 1858-59 with the Saugor and Nerbudda field force, including the action of Banda where he commanded the left wing of the 12th Lancers, action of Jegungo and Kobrai, relief of Kirwee, and action at the storming of the heights of Punwarrie (mentioned in despatches, Brevets of Major and Lt. Colonel, Medal and Clasp).

7 Captain Horne served in the Crimea from 17th May 1855 (Medal and Clasp for Sebastopol).

8 Capt. Clifton served with the 9th Lancers in the campaign on the Sutlej in 1846, and was present at the battle of Sobraon (Medal). Served with the 12th Lancers in the Kaffir war in 1851-53 (Medal and mentioned in Dispatches) ; also in the Crimean campaign from 17th May 1855, including the battle of Tchernaya and siege of Sebastopol (Medal and Clasp).

10 Captain Wombwell served in the Crimea from 20th Aug. 1855 (Medal and Clasp for Sebastopol).

11 Captain Reader served in the pursuit of the enemy across the Indus in 1849 (Medal).

12 Captain Campbell served with the 34th Regt. at the siege of Sebastopol, in 1855 (Medal and Clasp).

15 Lieut. Fletcher, Paymaster Holmes, and Surgeon Turnbull served in the Crimea from 9th May 1855 (Medal and Clasp for Sebastopol).

16 Lieut. Roe served at the siege and fall of Sebastopol from 17th May 1855 (Medal and Clasp). Served as Brigade Major of Cavalry to the Saugor and Nerbudda Field Division and was present at the affairs cf Jejungo and Kubrai, general action of Banda, and surrender of the Rajah of Kirwee on 5th June 1858.

17 Lieut. Blunt served the Eastern campaign from 17th May 1855, including the battle of the Tchernaya, siege and fall of Sebastopol (Medal and Clasp).

17¼ Lieut. Jones served with the Saugor and Nerbudda field force during the Indian campaign in 1858-59, was present at the battle of Banda where he was severely wounded having received six sabre wounds; also present at the actions of Jegungo, Cobrai, and Lowherie, and several minor affairs (Medal).

18 Cornet Russell Cruise served in the French Army before Sebastopol as Lieut. and Adjutant in the 81st Regt., and was present at the battle of the Tchernaya and operations before Sebastopol, for which he has received the British War Medal and Clasp.

19 Assist.Surgeon Gibson served with the Saugor and Nerbudda field force in the Indian campaign in 1858-59, and was present at the storming of the heights of Punwarree and several minor affairs (Medal).

20 Assist.Surgeon Wrench served with the 34th Regt. at the siege of Sebastopol in 1854-55, and assault of the Redan on the 18th June (Medal and Clasp).

Head Quarters, ⎱ **13th *Regiment of Light Dragoons.*** 150
Edinburgh. ⎰
On the chances and appointments, the Motto, "*Viret in Æternum.*"—"PENINSULA" "WATERLOO" "ALMA"
"BALAKLAVA" "INKERMAN" "SEVASTOPOL."

Years' Serv.						
Full Pay.	Half Pay.					
57		*Colonel.*—🅱 🅼🅰 Hon. Edward Pyndar Lygon,[1] CB. *Sub-Lieut.* 1 June 03; *Lieut.* 7 Nov. 05; *Captain,* 15 Feb. 08; *Lieut.Colonel,* 27 April 15; *Colonel,* 27 April 22; *Major General,* 10 Jan. 37; *Lt.Gen.* 9 Nov. 46; *Gen.* 20 June 54; *Colonel,* 13th Light Dragoons, 29 Jan. 45.				
18	0	*Lieut.Colonel.*—Henry Holden, *Cornet,* p 22 Apr. 42; *Lieut.* p 30 Dec. 45; *Capt.* p 19 Mar. 47; *Major,* p 25 Sept. 55; *Lt.Col.* p 31 May 59.				
14	0	*Major.*—Arthur Tremayne,[2] *Cornet,* p 11 Sept. 46; *Lieut.* p 29 Oct. 47; *Capt.* p 4 Apr. 51; *Brev.Maj.* 12 Dec. 54; *Major,* p 31 May 59.				

		CAPTAINS.	CORNET.	LIEUT.	CAPTAIN.	BREV.MAJ.	BT.LT.COL.
9	0	Edward Lennox Jervis[3]. .	p 11 July 51	p 18 June 52	8 Dec. 54		
8	0	FitzRoy Donald Maclean[4]	p 19 Aug. 52	26 Oct. 54	p 18 Jan. 56		
12	0	Robert Macneill[5]	p 16 June 48	p 19 Apr. 50	9 Oct. 57		
5	1	John Dearden.	p 17 Mar. 54	8 Dec. 54	p 19 Jan. 57		
6	0	Henry Oldman Munn . .	p 4 Aug. 54	3 July 55	p 16 Apr. 58		
6	0	Thomas Price Gratrex[6] . .	24 Nov. 54	p 9 Oct. 55	p 24 Aug. 58		
10	0	Henry White	p 12 Apr. 50	p 21 Oct. 53	29 Dec. 54		
5		Stanley de Astel C. Clarke	3 Aug. 55	p 25 Jan. 56	p 14 June 59		
		LIEUTENANTS.					
6	0	George Gardner,[7] *Adj*. . . .	27 Sept. 54	9 Oct. 55			
3	0	Albert A. Erin Lethbridge	23 Oct. 57	p 14 May 58			
6	0	William Atkinson	p 6 Jan. 54	9 Nov. 55			
3	0	RichardWilliam Renshaw	p 16 Aug. 57	p 10 Sept. 58			
2	0	Robert Burdon	23 Mar. 58	p 24 Aug. 58			
3	0	Walter Sydney Tucker . .	p 10 Mar. 57	p 18 Jan. 59			
3	0	Francis James King	p 2 Oct. 57	12 July 58			
2	0	William Gore	17 Sept. 58	p 8 July 59			
2	0	Walter P. Bagenal.	31 Aug. 58	p 16 July 59			
		CORNETS.					
3	0	Thomas George Johnson[10]	27 Nov. 57				
2	0	Henry S. Lee Wilson. . . .	27 Feb. 58				
2	0	Geo. Croft Huddleston . .	p 26 Oct. 58				
1	0	John Saunders	p 22 July 59				

5 Captain Macneill served the Eastern campaign of 1854, including the affair of Bulganak, battles of Alma and Balaklava, also present with the Light Brigade at Eupatoria (Medal and three Clasps).

6 Captain Gratrex served the Eastern campaign of 1854, including the battles of Balaklava and Inkerman, and siege of Sebastopol (Medal and Clasps).

7 Lieut. Gardner served the Eastern campaign of 1854-5, including the affairs of Bulganak and M'Kenzie's Farm, battles of Alma, Balaklava (horse shot), and Inkerman, and siege of Sebastopol (Medal and four Clasps, and 5th Class of the Medjidie).

10 Cornet Johnson served the Eastern campaign of 1854-55, including the reconnaissance on the Danube, battles of Balaklava (horse wounded), Inkerman, and Tchernaya, siege of Sebastopol, and expedition to Eupatoria (Medal and three Clasps, French War Medal, and Knight of the Legion of Honor).

11 Paymaster Frith, Assist.Surg. Armstrong, and Vet. Surg. Towers served the Eastern campaign of 1854-55, including the affair of Bulganak, battles of Alma, Balaklava, Inkerman, and Tchernaya, and siege of Sebastopol; also present with the Light Brigade at Eupatoria (Medal and four Clasps;) Mr. Armstrong was with the reconnaissance on the Danube under Lord Cardigan.

26	0	*Paymaster.*—Edm. Bentley Frith,[11] 7 Sept. 41; *Ens.* p 31 Oct. 34; *Lt.* p 3 Nov. 37.
6	0	*Adjutant.*—*Lieut.* George Gardner,[7] 27 Sept. 54.
5	0	*Quarter Master.*—William Cresdee,[13] 2 March 55.
4	0	*Riding Master.*—Francis Levison Michael,[12] 11 July 56.
20	0	*Surgeon.*—Robert Carew Anderson, M.D. 18 May 49; *Assist.Surg.* 22 May 40.
6	0	*Assist.Surg.*—Lancelot Armstrong,[11] 7 April 54.
6	0	*Veterinary Surg.*—Thos. John Towers,[11] 12 May 54.

Blue—Facings Buff. Agents, Messrs. Cox & Co. [*Ret. from the Crimea,* 28 *May* 1856.]

1 General the Honourable Edward P. Lygon served in the Peninsula with the 2nd Life Guards, from Nov. 1812 to the end of that war in 1814, including the battle of Vittoria, for which he has received the War Medal with one Clasp. Served also the campaign of 1815, and was present at the battle of Waterloo. Fourth Class of St. Wladimir of Russia.

2 Major Tremayne served the Eastern campaign of 1854-55, including the reconnaissance on the Danube under Lord Cardigan, affairs of Bulganak and M'Kenzie's Farm, battles of Alma, Balaklava (horse shot), and Tchernaya, and siege of Sebastopol; also present with the Light Brigade at Eupatoria (Medal and three Clasps, Brevet Major, Knight of the Legion of Honor, and 5th Class of the Medjidie).

3 Capt. Jervis served the Eastern campaign of 1854-55, including the reconnaissance to Silistria with Lord Cardigan, affairs of Bulganak and M'Kenzie's Farm, battles of Alma, Balaklava (horse shot), Inkerman, and Tchernaya, and siege of Sebastopol; also present with the Light Brigade at Eupatoria (Medal and four Clasps).

4 Capt. Maclean served the Eastern campaign of 1854, including the battle of Alma (Medal and two Clasps).

12 Riding Master Michael served the Eastern campaign of 1854, including the affair of Bulganak and battle of Alma; also present with the Light Brigade at Eupatoria (Medal and two Clasps).

13 Qr.Master Cresdee served with the Light Brigade at Eupatoria, and has received the Crimean Medal.

[*Continuation of Notes to* 14*th Light Dragoons.*]

23 Lieut. Ridley served with the Persian expedition of 1857 and was present at the bombardment of Mohumra (Medal). Served with the Central India field force under Sir Hugh Rose in 1858 and was present at the capture of Loharic, action of Morar, and recapture of Gwalior (Medal and Clasp).

24 Paymaster Fetherstonhaugh served with the Central India field force under Sir Hugh Rose in 1858 and was present at the battle of Koonch, all the affairs during the advance on Calpee and action of Golowlee, capture of Calpee and pursuit, action of Morar, and recapture of Gwalior (Medal and Clasp).

25 Qr.Master Bennett served the Punjaub campaign of 1848-49 with the 14th Light Dragoons, including the action of Ramnuggur (severely wounded), battles of Chillianwallah and Goojerat, pursuit of the enemy across the Jhelum, and of the Affghans over the Indus through the Khyber Pass (Medal and Clasps).

26 Doctor Lofthouse served with the 10th Hussars in the Crimean campaign of 1855, including the siege and fall of Sebastopol, battle of the Tchernaya, and affair of 21st Sept. near Kertch (Medal and Clasp). Served with the 14th Lt. Drs. during the Indian campaigns of 1857 and 1858 under Sir Hugh Rose and Sir R. Napier, including the siege of Rahutghur, action of Barodia, relief of Saugor, siege and capture of Gurrakota, forcing the pass of Muddenpore, battle of Betwa, siege and fall of Jhansi, actions of Koonch and Golowlie, capture of the town and fort of Calpee, action of Morar, recapture of Gwalior, operations in Bundlecund and affairs of Garotha and Jachlone, and pursuit of Tantia Topee (Medal and Clasp).

27 Veterinary Surgeon Dawson served with the Persian expedition of 1857 (Medal). Served with the Central India field force under Sir Hugh Rose in 1858 and was present at the siege and capture of Rahutghur, relief of Saugor, capture of Gurrakota, at Malthone, siege and capture of Jhansi (Medal and Clasp).

151 [Kirkee, Bombay. Depot, Maidstone.] **14th (The King's) Regt. of Light Drs.** [Emb. for India, 24 May 1841.

The "PRUSSIAN EAGLE" "DOURO" "TALAVERA" "FUENTES D'ONOR" "SALAMANCA" "VITTORIA"
"ORTHES" "PENINSULA" "PUNJAUB" "CHILLIANWALLAH" "GOOJERAT."

Years' Serv.			
Full Pay	Half Pay		
60		Colonel.—Hon. Henry Murray,[1] CB. *Cornet*, 16 May 00; *Lt*. 11 June 01; *Capt*. 24 Aug. 02; *Major*, 26 March 07; *Lt.Col.* 2 Jan. 12; *Col*. 22 July 30; *Maj.Gen.* 28 June 38; *Lt.Gen.* 11 Nov. 51; *Gen*. 6 Feb. 55; *Col*. 14th Lt. Dragoons, 18 March 53.	
35	0	*Lt.Colonels.*—Charles Steuart,[2] CB. *Cornet*, 10 Dec. 25; *Lieut*. p 5 Feb. 29; *Capt*. p 9 Nov. 38; *Maj*. p 25 April 48; *Lt.Col*. 7 July 50; *Col*. 28 Nov. 54.	
31	4 2/13	Charles Philip Ainslie, 2*nd Lt*. 10 April 25; *Lt*. p 28 Jan. 26; *Capt*. p 16 Mar. 30; *Maj*. p 14 Oct. 42; *Lt.Col*. p 22 Oct. 47; *Col*. 28 Nov. 54.	
25	0	*Majors.*—Arthur Scudamore,[3] CB. *Cor.* p 29 May 35; *Lt*. 18 Feb. 38; *Capt*. p 22 Oct. 47; *Major*, 1 June 54; *Bt.Lt.Col*. 20 July 58.	
25	0	Richard Herbert Gall,[4] CB. *Cor.* p 3 July 35; *Lt*. 7 Dec. 38; *Capt*. p 31 Mar. 48; *Major*, 18 Sept. 57; *Bt.Lt.Col*. 24 Mar. 58.	

		CAPTAINS.	CORNET.	LIEUT.	CAPTAIN.	BREV.MAJ.	BT.LT.COL.
23	0	John Augustus Todd[5] ..	p 28 Apr. 37	p 14 June 39	27 Nov. 48	20 July 58	20 Dec. 59
17	1 7/13	Pearson Scott Thompson[6]	p 5 Aug. 42	p 7 June 44	p 3 Sept. 47	20 July 58	
22	0	Rich. Buckley Prettejohn[7]	p 23 Feb. 38	p 18 Oct. 39	17 Sept. 50	20 July 58	
19	0	Robert Johnston Brown[8]	p 31 Dec. 41	p 16 May 45	15 Mar. 53		
18	0	William M'Mahon[9]	p 26 Nov. 42	p 6 Nov. 46	p 27 May 53	20 July 58	
21	0	Arthur Need[11]	p 13 Oct. 39	p 17 June 42	1 June 54	20 July 58	
13	0	William D'Urban Blyth[12]	p 22 Oct. 47	22 Feb. 40	20 June 57		
12	0	Thomas Edward Gordon[13]	p 27 Oct. 48	17 Sept. 50	18 Sept. 57		
12	0	Charles Edwyn Wyatt[14]	p 18 July 48	p 8 Mar. 50	2 Feb. 58		

		LIEUTENANTS.			
9	0	Claudius Buchan. Whish[15]	19 Aug. 51	p 30 Sept. 53	
9	0	W.H.T. Clarke Travers[16]	p 20 Aug. 51	p 30 Sept. 53	
9	0	Standish Radley Jackson	p 12 Dec. 51	p 4 Nov. 53	
8	0	Robert Chadwick	p 17 Dec. 52	p 18 Nov. 53	
7	0	LawrenceSt.Patr.Gowan[17]	p 20 Sept. 53	1 June 54	
7	0	Edw.OrlandoV.Haldane[18]	p 30 Sept. 53	p 1 Dec. 54	
7	0	Lawrence Mackenzie[19] ..	p 18 Oct. 53	9 Oct. 55	
7	0	George Meyrick Dew[20] ..	p 18 Oct. 53	29 Feb. 56	
6	0	Wm. Henry S. Beamish[22]	p 1 Dec. 54	18 Sept. 57	
4	0	Richard Parnham Ridley[23]	18 Apr. 56	24 Nov. 57	

4 Lt.Colonel Gall served with the 14th Lt. Drs. throughout the Punjaub campaign of 1848-49, including the action of Ramnuggur with the charging squadrons and received a severe sabre wound in an effort to seize a Standard, battles of Chillianwallah and Goojerat. Served with the Persian expedition of 1857(Medal). Commanded the left wing of the Regt. in the Deccan field force at the suppression of the Mutiny at Aurungabad; also during the Mulwn campaign of 1857 and with the Central India Field force under Sir Hugh Rose in 1858, including the siege and capture of Dhar, action of Mundesore, battle of Gooraria and relief of Neemuch, siege and capture of Chandeyrie, siege and capture of Jhansi; commanded the force detached against the fort of Loharri and headed the stormers in the attack; present at the battle of Koonch and affairs during the advance on Calpee, including the action of Golowlie, also at the capture of Calpee and pursuit, and recapture of Gwalior (five times mentioned in despatches Brevet of Lt.Colonel, CB., Medal and Clasp).

		CORNETS.			
2	0	Francis Blake Eagle	8 Jan. 58		
2	0	Henry Bradley	5 Feb. 58		
2	0	Percy Dodgson	5 Feb. 58		
2	0	Wm. Atcherley Atcherley	5 Mar. 58		
2	0	William Sandys Browne	13 April 58		
2	0	Hon. Fred. Amherst	14 May 58		
2	0	Edw. Williams Pritchard	24 Aug. 58		

19	0	*Paymaster.*—William Fetherstonhaugh,[24] 15 June 49; *Ens.* p 8 Jan. 41; *Lt.* p 29 March 44.
		Adjutant.—
10	0	*Quarter Master.*—Thomas Bennett,[25] 9 Aug. 50.
4	0	*Riding Master.*—Joseph Raiker, 7 Nov. 56.
19	0	*Surgeon.*—William Arden, 25 July 51; *Assist.Surg.* 9 Apr. 41.
6	0	*Assist. Sury.*—Richard Chapman Lofthouse,[26] M.D. 14 July 54.
3	0	Robert Brown Forsyth Brown, 8 Dec. 57. [Blue—*Facings* Scarlet.
2	0	*Veterinary Surgeon.*—Henry Dawson,[27] 16 Mar. 58. [*Agents*, Messrs. Cox & Co.

1 General the Hon. Henry Murray served in Naples, Sicily, and Calabria, in 1806-7. Accompanied the expedition to Egypt in March 1807, and was present, as an Aide-de-Camp, at the attack on Alexandria, siege and storming of Rosetta, and on every other occasion when our troops were engaged. Served at Walcheren in 1809, including the siege and surrender of Flushing. Went with the 18th Hussars to the Peninsula in Jan. 1813; present at the crossing of the Eslar, and commanded the Regiment in support of the 10th Hussars at the action of Morales de Toro. Served also in the campaign of 1815, including the battle of Quatre Bras; commanded the rear regiment of the Column on the retreat during the following day; and, at the battle of Waterloo, he led the 18th Hussars in the brilliant charge of Sir Hussey Vivian's Brigade, at the conclusion of the action.

2 Colonel Steuart served with the 14th Lt. Drs. in the Punjaub campaign of 1848-9, including the battles of Chillianwallah (sabre wound) and Goojerat, pursuit of the enemy across the Jhelum, and of the Affghans over the Indus through the Khyber Pass (Medal and Clasps). Commanded a Cavalry Brigade in the Persian expedition of 1857 (Medal and CB.). Commanded the 2nd Brigade of the Central India Field Force under Sir Hugh Rose in 1858, and was present at the siege and capture of Rahutghur, relief of Saugor and capture of Gurrakota, forcing the Muddenpore Pass, siege and capture of Jhansi, battles of Betwa and Koonch (Medal and Clasp).

3 Lt.Colonel Scudamore served with the 4th Lt. Drs. throughout the campaign of 1838-39 in Affghanistan, including the siege and capture of Ghuznee (Medal). Served with the 14th Lt. Drs. throughout the Punjaub campaign of 1848-49, including the action of Ramnuggur (wounded), passage of the Chenab, battles of Chillianwallah and Goojerat—dangerously wounded (Medal and Clasps). Commanded the Regt. during the campaign of 1858 in Central India under Sir Hugh Rose and was present at the siege and capture of Rahutghur, action of Barodia, Relief of Saugor, capture of Gurrakota; commanded the detached force sent against Malthone; present at the siege and capture of Jhansi and commanded the outposts during the investment; present at the battle of Koonch and all the affairs during the advance on Calpee including the action of Golowlie; also at the action of Morar and recapture of Gwalior; also commanded a flying column for six months in the Gwalior and Jhansi districts (three times mentioned in despatches, Brevet of Lt.Colonel, CB., Medal and Clasp).

5 Lt.Col. Todd served with the 4th Lt. Drs. throughout the campaign of 1838-39 in Affghanistan, including the siege and capture of Ghuznee (Medal). Served with the 14th Lt. Drs. throughout the Punjaub campaign of 1848-49, including the action of Ramnuggur, passage of the Chenab, battles of Chillianwallah and Goojerat (Medal and Clasps). Served as Brigade Major of Cavalry with the Persian expedition of 1857 (Medal). Also as Brigade Major to the 2d Brigade of the Central India field

14th (The King's) Regt. of Light Dragoons. 151a

force under Sir Hugh Rose in 1858 and was present at the siege and capture of Rahutghur, relief of Saugor, capture of Gurrakota, forcing the Muddenpore pass, siege and capture of Jhansi, battles of Betwa with Koonch and affairs during the advance on Calpee and action of Golowlie; also the action of Morar, recapture of Gwalior and pursuit with action of Jowra Alipore; served as Assist. Adj. Gen. ; the Gwalior Division in pursuit of the Rebels and at the action of Ranode (mentioned in despatches, Brevet of Major, Medn. and Clasp).

6 Major Thompson served with the 7th Dragoon Guards against the Insurgent Boers in South Africa in 1846 ; and likewise in the Kaffir war of 1846-7 (Medal). Served with the 14th Lt. Drs. with the Central India field force under Sir Hugh Rose in 1858 and was present at the siege and capture of Jhansi; commanded the Cavalry at the capture of the fort of Loharri; present at the battle of Koonch, the various skirmishes before Calpee, action of Golowlie, and capture of the town and fort of Calpee; commanded the left wing of the Regt. at the action of Morar, the several engagements on the heights before Kotakaserai and Gwalior, and capture of the fort and city of Gwalior; commanded a field detachment for three months in Bundlecund, and in a successful attack against a very superior body of rebels at Garotha—thanked by the Governor of Bombay in Council (twice mentioned in despatches, Brevet of Major, Medal and Clasp).

7 Major Prettejohn served throughout the Punjaub campaign of 1848-49, including the action of Ramnuggur with the charging Squadrons, passage of the Chenab, battles of Chillianwallah and Goojerat, pursuit of the enemy across the Jhelum and of the Affghans over the Indus through the Khyber Pass (Medal and Clasps). Served with the Persian expedition of 1857 and was present at the bombardment of Mohumra (Medal). Also with the Central India field force under Sir Hugh Rose in 1858 and was present at the siege and capture of Rahutghur, action of Barodia, relief of Saugor, capture of Gurrakota, forcing the Muddenpore pass (wounded), siege and capture of Jhansi, Battles of Betwa and Koonch, affairs during the advance on Calpee, capture of Calpee, action of Morar and recapture of Gwalior and pursuit ending in the action of Jowra Alipore, action of Ranode—severely wounded (three times mentioned in despatches, Brevet of Major, Medal and Clasp).

8 Captain Brown served at the suppression of the Mutiny at Aurungabad in 1857, and with the Central India field force under Sir Hugh Rose in 1858 and was present at the siege and capture of Rahutghur, relief of Saugor, capture of Gurrakota and pursuit across the Beas, at Malthone, siege and capture of Jhansi (Medal and Clasp).

9 Major M'Mahon served in the Punjaub campaign of 1848-9; at the first siege of Mooltan, including the attack on the enemy's position in front of the advanced trenches, 12th Sept. 1848; with the charging squadrons of the 14th Lt. Dragoons at Ramnuggar (very severely wounded), and at the battles of Chillianwallah and Goojerat; was also present at the surrender of the Seikh army at Rawul Pindee, and pursuit of the Affghans to Peshawur (Medal and Clasps). Served with the Central India field force under Sir Hugh Rose in 1858 and was present at the siege and capture of Rahutghur, relief of Saugor, action of Barodia, at Malthone, siege and capture of Jhansi, battles of Betwa and Koonch (severely wounded), action of Morar, recapture of Gwalior, and commanded a flying column in operations against Bunjor Sing (twice mentioned in despatches, Brevet of Major, Medal and Clasp).

11 Major Need served the Punjaub campaign of 1848-49 as Aide-de-Camp to General Whish, and was present during the whole of the siege operations against and capture of Mooltan ; after which he was at the battle of Goojerat (Medal and Clasps). Served with the Persian expedition of 1857 (Medal). Also with the Central India field force under Sir Hugh Rose in 1858 and was present at the siege and capture of Rahutghur, relief of Saugor, capture of Gurrakota and pursuit across the Beas, forcing the Muddenpore Pass, siege and capture of Jhansi, battles of Betwa and Koonch, affairs during the advance on Calpee and action of Golowlie, capture of Calpee and pursuit, action of Morar, action resulting in the recapture of the town and fort of Gwalior, pursuit in 1858-9 and action of Ranode and pursuit of Tantia Topee (four times mentioned in despatches, Brevet of Major, Medal and Clasp).

12 Captain Blyth served throughout the Punjaub campaign of 1848-9, including the action of Ramnuggur (with the charging squadrons), passage of the Chenab, battles of Chillianwallah and Goojerat, pursuit of the enemy across the Jhelum, and of the Affghans over the Indus through the Khyber Pass (Medal and Clasps). Served with the Central India field force under Sir Hugh Rose in 1858 and was present at the capture of Loharri, battle of Koonch, various skirmishes before Calpee, action of Golowlee, capture of the town and fort of Calpee, action of Morar and severe engagements on the heights before Kolakaserai and Gwalior, capture of the fort and city of Gwalior (mentioned in despatches, Medal and Clasp).

13 Captain Gordon served in the Punjaub campaign of 1848-9, including the battles of Chillianwallah and Goojerat, pursuit of the enemy across the Jhelum, and of the Affghans over the Indus, through the Khyber Pass (Medal and Clasps). Served with the Central India field force under Sir Hugh Rose in 1858 and was present at the siege and capture of Chandeyrie, siege and capture of Jhansi, battle of Koonch, affairs during the advance on Calpee and action of Golowlie, capture of Calpee and pursuit, action of Morar, several engagements on the heights before Kotakaserai and Gwalior, recapture of the fort and city of Gwalior and pursuit of the rebels in 1858-59 (Medal and Clasp).

14 Captain Wyatt served in the Persian expedition of 1857 (Medal). Also in the Central India field force under Sir Hugh Rose in 1858 and was present at the siege and capture of Rahutghur, action of Barodia, relief of Saugor, capture of Gurrakota, forcing the Muddenpore pass, siege and capture of Jhansi (Medal and Clasp).

15 Lieut. Whish served as A. Q. M. Gen. of the Cavalry Division in the Persian Expedition of 1857 (mentioned in despatches and Medal).

16 Lieut. Travers served in the Persian expedition of 1857 (Medal). Also with the Central India field force under Sir Hugh Rose in 1858 and was present at the siege and capture of Rahutghur, capture of Gurrakota, forcing the Malthone Pass, siege and capture of Jhansi, battle of Koonch, all the affairs during the advance on Calpee and action of Golowlee, capture of Calpee and pursuit (Medal and Clasp).

17 Lieut. Gowan served with the Persian expedition of 1857 (Medal). Was present at the suppression of the Mutiny at Aurungabad; also with the Malwa field force in 1857 at the siege and capture of Dhar, action of Mundesore, battle of Goraria, and relief of Neemuch. Served with the Central India field force under Sir Hugh Rose in 1858 and was present at the siege and capture of Chandeyrie, siege and capture of Jhansi, battle of Koonch, affairs during the advance on Calpee and action of Golowlee, capture of Calpee, action of Morar, and action resulting in the recapture of the town and fortress of Gwalior; served in 1859 in pursuit of the Rebels and was in the successful attack on the 5th April (mentioned in despatches, Medal and Clasp).

18 Lieut. Haldane served with the Persian expedition of 1857 (Medal).

19 Lieut. Mackenzie served with the Persian expedition in 1857 and was present at the capture of Mohumrah (Medal). Was present in 1857 at the capture of the fort of Dhar and defeat of the rebels at Mundesore; served with the Central India field force under Sir Hugh Rose in 1858 and was present at the taking of the fort of Chandeyrie, siege and capture of Jhansi, battles of Betwa and Koonch, operations before Calpee with action of Golowlie and capture of the town and fort of Calpee, action of Morar and operations resulting in the capture of the fort and city of Gwalior, operations against the rebels in Bundlecund, acted as Brigade Major to the 2d Brigade Gwalior Division part of 1859.

20 Lieut. Dew served with the Persian expedition of 1857 (Medal). Was present at the suppression of the mutiny at Aurungabad in 1857, subsequently at the siege and capture of Dhar, action of Mundesore, battle of Goraria, and relief of Neemuch; served with the Central India field force under Sir Hugh Rose in 1858 and was present at the siege and capture of Rahutghur, relief of Saugor, capture of Gurrakota and pursuit across the Beas, at Malthone, siege and capture of Jhansi, battles of Betwa and Koonch, all the affairs during the advance on Calpee and action of Golowlee, capture of Calpee, action of Morar and recapture of Gwalior; served as Staff Officer to Colonel Scudamore's flying column in the autumn of 1858 and with Sir R. Napier in pursuit of Tantia Topee and Ferozeshah in 1849, and was present in the successful attack on the 5th April (mentioned in despatches, Medal and Clasp).

22 Lieut. Beamish served with the Persian expedition of 1857 (Medal). Was present at the suppression of the Mutiny at Aurungabad in 1857. Served with the Central India field force under Sir Hugh Rose in 1858 and was present at the siege and capture of Rahutghur, action of Barodia, relief of Saugor, capture of Gurrakota, at Malthone, siege and capture of Jhansi, battles of Betwa and Koonch (wounded), all the affairs during the advance on Calpee and action of Golowlee, capture of Calpee and pursuit, action of Morar, recapture of Gwalior, and operations against Brujor Sing (Medal and Clasp).

[For continuation of Notes, see end of 13th Lt. Drags.

15th (*The King's*) Regt. of Lt. Drs. (Hussars). [Head Quarters, Dublin.

"EMSDORF" "EGMONT-OP-ZEE" "VILLIERS EN COUCHE"
"SAHAGUN" "VITTORIA" "PENINSULA" "WATERLOO."

Years' Serv.			
Full Pay	Half Pay		
48		Colonel.—🎖️ 🎖️ Everard Wm. Bouverie,[1] Cor. P 2 Apr. 12; Lt. 15 Oct. 12; Capt P 9 Sept. 19; Bt.Major, 6 May 31; Lt.Col. P 4 Dec. 32; Col. 16 Sept. 45; Major Gen. 11 Nov. 51; Col. 15th Hussars 17 July 59.	
26	0	Lieut.Colonel.—Thomas R. Crawley,[2] Ensign, 19 Dec. 34; Lieut. 9 Mar. 42; Capt. P 13 Oct. 54; Maj. 26 Feb. 58; Lt.Col. P 23 Sept. 59.	
21	0	Major.—Henry Lee,[3] Cornet, P 12 Oct. 39; Lieut. P 29 July 44; Capt. P 8 Dec. 54; Major, P 23 Sept. 59.	

		CAPTAINS.	CORNET.	LIEUT.	CAPTAIN.	BREV.MAJ.
18	0	George Stoney Swinny, s.	P 14 June 42	12 Apr. 46	14 Sept. 55	
18	0	Horace Trower	P 30 Aug. 42	3 Apr. 46	2 Oct. 55	
16	0	William Veall Greetham	P 31 May 44	P 30 July 47	18 Sept. 57	
9	0	William Edington Stuart[4]	P 21 Nov. 51	14 Sept. 55	26 Feb. 58	
7	0	Pat.Alex.WatsonCarnegy[5]	P 16 Dec. 53	P 11 July 56	13 May 58	
6	0	Edwyn Walker	P 24 Nov. 54	P 14 Dec. 55	P 23 Sept. 59	
5	0	Robert Lesley Parker	P 13 Feb. 55	P 8 Jan. 56	P 4 Nov. 59	
4	0	Robert Penfold	P 14 Mar. 56	17 Nov. 57	P 16 Dec. 59	

		LIEUTENANTS.			
8	0	James Alston Clark	P 23 Nov. 52	P 10 Feb. 54	
5	0	Charles William Bell	P 1 June 55	P 9 May 56	
5	0	Henry Banks Wright	14 Sept. 55	P 17 July 57	
3	0	James Mann, *Adj*	17 Apr. 57	25 Jan. 59	
3	0	Arthur Randolph Mullings	P 17 July 57	P 25 Jan. 59	
2	0	Stewart Davies Cartwright	P 26 Mar. 58	23 Mar. 59	
3	0	Bryan Burrell	4 Dec. 57	P 23 Sept. 59	
2	0	Phineas Bury	8 Jan. 58	P 4 Nov. 59	
2	0	Montague Cecil Broun	P 15 Jan. 58	P 16 Dec. 59	

		CORNETS.		
2	0	Walter T. Edw. Bentinck	P 5 Feb. 58	
2	0	Fred. Geo. Lister Inglis	29 Oct. 58	
2	0	Geo. John Hooke Pearson	31 Dec. 58	
1	0	David Ricardo	P 13 May 59	
1	0	John Rob. Heron Maxwell	P 1 Apr. 59	
1	0	Benjamin Winthorp	P 28 Oct. 59	

2 Major Crawley was present at the closing operations before Mooltan and at the surrender of the citadel 22nd Jan. 1849. He served as extra Aide-de-Camp to Sir Henry Dundas commanding the Bombay Division of the army of the Punjaub during the march from Mooltan and the subsequent operations, and was present at the battle of Goojerat (Medal) and in the pursuit of the Sikh army to the river Jhelum.

3 Major Lee was present with the 16th Lancers in the action at Maharajpore, 29th Dec. 1843, and has received the Bronze Star.

8 Surgeon Watt served with the 23rd Fusiliers the Eastern campaign of 1854 and up to 24th March, 1855, including the battles of Alma and Inkerman, and siege of Sebastopol (Medal and three Clasps, and 5th Class of the Medjidie).

22	0	Paymaster.—Blayney T. Walshe,[7] 3 Oct. 48; Ens. P 28 Aug. 38; Lt. 31 Dec. 39.
3	0	Adjutant.—Lieut. James Mann, 1 May 57.
2	0	Quarter Master.—Benjamin Holloway, 5 Oct. 58.
3	0	Riding Master.—Maillard Noake, 20 Feb. 57.
16	0	Surgeon.—Wm. Godfrey Watt,[8] 28 March 54; Assist. Surg. 1 March 44.
3	0	Assistant Surgeon.—Charles Henry Browne,[10] 1 Aug. 57.
13	0	Veterinary Surgeon.—William Thacker,[9] 14 July 47; 1st Class, 1 July 59.

Blue—*Agents*, Messrs. Cox & Co.   *Irish Agents*, Sir E. R. Borough, Bt., Armit & Co.

[*Returned from Madras*, 20 June 1854.]

1 Major General Bouverie served in the Peninsular from October 1812, to the end of that war in 1814 and has received the War Medal with two Clasps for the battles of Vittoria and Toulouse. He served also the campaign of 1815, and was wounded at the battle of Waterloo.

4 Captain Stuart has received the Order of the Medjidie, 4th Class, for service in the Osmanli Cavalry.

5 Captain Carnegy served with the 2d Dragoon Guards in the Indian campaign in 1858-59, including the siege and capture of Lucknow (wounded), subsequent operations, action of Koorsee, the Oude campaign, action of Jamo, siege and capture of Birwah, and commanded a detached Squadron in the affair of Gooree (Medal and Clasp).

7 Paymaster Walshe served with the 9th Regt. throughout the campaign of 1842 in Affghanistan (Medal) under Sir George Pollock, including the storming the Khyber Pass, taking the Fort of Mamoo Khail, storming the heights of Jugdulluck, action in the Tezeen Valley, clearing the heights of Huftkotul, and storming the town of Istaliff. Served in the Kaffir war of 1851-53 (Medal).

9 Veterinary Surgeon Thacker served in the 12th Lancers in the Kaffir war of 1851-53 (Medal).

10 Assist.Surgeon Browne served in the Indian campaign from Nov. 1857 to April 1859, and was present at the siege and capture of the fort of Awah, also at the siege storm and capture of the town and fort of Kotah (Medal and Clasp).

Head Quarters, York. 16th *(The Queen's) Regt. of Lt. Drag. (Lancers).* 153

"TALAVERA" "FUENTES D'ONOR" "SALAMANCA" "VITTORIA" "NIVE"
"PENINSULA" "WATERLOO" "BHURTPORE" "AFFGHANISTAN"
"GHUZNEE" "MAHARAJPORE" "ALIWAL" "SOBRAON."

Years' Serv.						
Full Pay	Half Pay					
50		Colonel.—*¶ Hon. Sir* Edward Cust,[1] KCH. *Cor.* 15 Mar. 10; *Lt.* ᴾ 27 Dec. 10; *Capt.* ᴾ 9 Dec. 13; *Maj.* ᴾ 24 Oct. 21; *Lt.Col.* ᴾ 26 Dec. 26; *Col.* 23 Nov. 41; *Maj.Gen.* 11 Nov. 51; *Lt.Gen.* 14 May 59; *Col.* 16th Lancers, 9 Apr. 59.				
24	6½	Lieut.Colonel.—Charles John Foster,[2] *Cornet,* ᴾ 8 April 36; *Lt.* 21 Dec. 38; *Capt.* ᴾ 1 Dec. 47; *Major,* ᴾ 21 Sept. 52; *Lt.Col.* ᴾ 17 Feb. 57.				
13	0	Majors.—William Thomas Dickson, *Cornet,* ᴾ 23 Apr. 47; *Lieut.* ᴾ 25 Feb. 48; *Capt.* ᴾ 25 Apr. 51; *Major,* ᴾ 19 May 54; *Bt.Lt.Col.* 26 Oct. 58.				
13	0	Thomas Woollaston White, *Cornet,* ᴾ 7 May 47; *Lieut.* ᴾ 7 Apr. 48; *Capt.* ᴾ 23 Sept. 51; *Major,* ᴾ 2 Nov. 55.				

		CAPTAINS.	CORNET.	LIEUT.	CAPTAIN.	BREV.-MAJ.
12	0	Lancelot Halton	ᴾ 25 Feb. 48	ᴾ 13 April 49	ᴾ 12 Oct. 52	
11	0	David Barclay	ᴾ 13 April 49	ᴾ 2 Apr. 50	ᴾ 11 Oct. 53	
21	0	Patrick Dynon[3]	29 May 39	16 June 42	14 Sept. 55	
7	0	James Stewart	ᴾ 12 Aug. 53	ᴾ 13 Oct. 54	ᴾ 16 Mar. 58	
6	0	Hugh D'Arcy P. Burnell	ᴾ 14 July 54	14 Sept. 55	ᴾ 30 July 58	
6	0	Go. Wm. Hutton Riddell	ᴾ 21 July 54	ᴾ 2 Nov. 55	ᴾ 24 Dec. 58	
5	0	Francis Paynton Pigott	ᴾ 16 Mar. 55	ᴾ 18 Jan. 56	ᴾ 17 June 59	
4	0	Thomas Boyce	26 Feb. 56	ᴾ 15 May 57	ᴾ 17 June 59	
		LIEUTENANTS.				
5	0	Edwin Cowtan,[6] *Adj.*	26 Oct. 55	15 May 57		
4	0	Frederick Stoodley	14 Mar. 56	27 Nov. 57		
4	0	Arthur John Armstrong	ᴾ 3 June 56	ᴾ 11 Dec. 57		
4	0	Leonard Wilson Atkinson	ᴾ 7 Nov. 56	5 Mar. 58		
3	0	William Richd. Corballis	ᴾ 24 Feb. 57	ᴾ 23 Mar. 58		
3	0	Arthur Gooch	ᴾ 10 April 57	ᴾ 30 July 58		
2	0	Rich. Fielding Morrison[9]	ᴾ 30 Mar. 58	ᴾ 24 Dec. 58		
2	0	Morton Eagle Harmar	ᴾ 26 Oct. 58	ᴾ 17 June 59		
2	0	Thomas Francis Agg	27 Oct. 58	ᴾ 17 June 59		
		CORNETS.				
2	0	Francis Joseph Barron	ᴾ 19 Nov. 58			
1	0	Edward Philip Salter	ᴾ 11 Jan. 59			
1	0	Charles Anthony	ᴾ 12 Jan. 59			
1	0	George James Gilbard	18 Jan. 59			
3	0	Edwin Andrew Corbet	27 Nov. 57			
1	0	William John Wauchope	ᴾ 7 Oct. 59			

Captain column note: 9 Lieut. Morrison (late a Captain in the 51st F.) served with the 19th Regt. in the Eastern Campaign up to 28th Oct. 1854, including the battle of Alma and siege of Sebastopol (Medal and two Clasps). 10 Riding Master Brown served with the 16th Lancers during the campaign in Affghanistan, under Lord Keane, in 1839, including the siege and capture of Ghuznee (Medal).

24	0	*Paymaster.*—George Frederick Rosser,[7] 28 May 47; *Ens.* 20 Aug. 36.
5	0	*Adjutant.*—Lieut. Edwin Cowtan,[6] 26 Oct. 55.
13	0	*Quarter-Master.*—George Lamb,[8] 4 June 47.
3	0	*Riding Master.*—Thomas Brown,[10] 7 Sept. 58; *Cornet,* 29 Dec. 57.
15	0	*Surgeon.*—William Ker Park, 6 Oct. 54; *Assist.-Surg.* 31 Oct. 45.
5	0	*Assist.-Surgeon.*—Andrew Knox Rickards, 24 April 55.
12	0	*Veterinary Surgeon.*—Francis Frederick Collins, 8 Dec. 48.

Scarlet.—*Facings* Blue.—*Agents,* Messrs. Cox & Co.
[*Returned from Bengal,* 26 *Dec.* 1846.]

1 Sir Edward Cust joined the Duke of Wellington's army prior to the advance from Portugal in 1811, and continued with it up to the cantonments on the Adour in 1813, having been present with the 16th Light Dragoons at the battle of Fuentes d'Onor, and with the 14th Dragoons at the battles of Salamanca, Vittoria, the Pyrenees, Nivelle, and Nive, investment of Ciudad Rodrigo, siege of Badajoz, and generally in all the affairs of that period, until he quitted the Duke's army on promotion. He has received the War Medal with seven Clasps.

2 Lt. Colonel Foster served with the 16th Lancers during the campaign in Affghanistan under Lord Keane, including the siege and capture of Ghuznee (Medal). He served also at the battle of Maharajpore, 9th Dec. 1843 (Medal); and in the campaign on the Sutlej in 1846, including the battles of Buddiwal, Aliwal (as Aide de Camp to Brigadier Cureton), and Sobraon (Medal and Clasps).

3 Capt. Dynon served with the 16th Lancers during the campaign in Affghanistan nder Lord Keane, including the siege and capture of Ghuznee (Medal). He served also at the battle of Maharajpore (Medal), 9th Dec. 1843; and in the campaign on the Sutlej in 1846, including the battles of Buddiwal, Aliwal, and Sobraon (Medal and Clasps).

6 Lieut. Cowtan served with the 16th Lancers at the battle of Maharajpore, 29th Dec. 1843 (Medal); also in the Sutlej campaign in 1846, including the affair of Buddiwal, and battles of Aliwal and Sobraon (Medal and Clasps).

7 Paymaster Rosser was present at the siege and capture of Bhurtpore in 1825-6 (Medal). He served with the army of the Indus, under Lord Keane, in 1838 and 39, and was present at the capture of Ghuznee (Medal). He was also present in the action at Maharajpore, 29th. Dec. 1843 (Medal); and also at Buddiwal, Aliwal, and Sobraon (Medal and Clasps).

8 Qr.-Mast. Lamb served with the 16th Lancers during the campaign in Affghanistan under Lord Keane, including the siege and capture of Ghuznee (Medal). Also at the battle of Maharajpore (Medal) 29th Dec. 1843; and in the campaign on the Sutlej in 1846, including the battle of Buddiwal, Aliwal, and Sobraon (Medal and Clasps). Has also received a Medal for Meritorious Services.

17th Regt. of Light Dragoons (Lancers). [Gwalior, Bengal. Depot, Canterbury.]

"*Death's Head*," with the Motto, "*Or Glory.*"—"ALMA" "BALAKLAVA" "INKERMAN" "SEVASTOPOL."

Years' Serv. Full Pay	Half Pay					
55		*Colonel.*—김 Sir James Maxwell Wallace,[1] KH. *Cornet*, 14 Aug. 05; *Lieut.* 5 June 06; *Capt.* 22 Oct. 07; *Major*, 1 Jan. 17; *Lt.-Col.* 25 Sept. 23; *Colonel*, 28 June 38; *Major-Gen.* 11 Nov. 51; *Lt.-Gen.* 6 Feb. 55; *Colonel* 17th Lancers, 28 Jan. 54.				
20	0	*Lt.Colonels.*—Henry Roxby Benson,[2] *Cornet*, p 31 Jan. 40; *Lt.* p 15 April 42; *Capt.* p 27 June 45; *Maj.* 23 Oct. 54; *Lt.Col.* p 20 Sept. 56; *Col.* 23 Sept. 59.				
11	0	Alexander Learmonth,[3] *Cornet*, p 21 Aug. 49; *Lieut.* p 23 Aug. 50; *Capt.* 23 Oct. 54; *Major*, p 30 Sept. 56; *Lt.Col.* p 1 July 59.				
13	0	*Majors.*—Robert White,[4] *Cornet*, p 15 Oct. 47; *Lieut.* p 22 Dec. 48; *Capt.* p 26 Mar. 52; *Brev.Maj.* 12 Dec. 54; *Major*, 12 July 58.				
10	0	Sir William Gordon,[5] *Bt. Cornet*, p 14 June 50; *Lieut.* p 18 July 51; *Capt.* 26 Oct. 54; *Brev.Maj.* 7 Dec. 58; *Major*, p 1 July 59.				
		CAPTAINS.	CORNET.	LIEUT.	CAPTAIN.	BREV.-MAJ.
10	0	Lewis Edward Knight	p 17 Sept. 50	p 19 Aug. 51	7 Nov. 54	
27	0	John Macartney[6]	p 27 Sept. 33	p 19 Dec. 34	15 Mar. 53	
7	10/12	Sir Geo. Hector Leith, *Bt.*	p 10 July 52	26 Oct. 54	p 30 Mar. 55	
5	10/12	Drury Curzon Lowe[7]	p 28 July 54	7 Nov. 54	p 9 Nov. 56	
13	0	Henry Andrew Sarel[8]	p 13 July 47	p 15 Dec. 48	18 Sept. 57	24 Mar. 58
10	3/12	Charles Steel[9]	p 14 June 50	p 13 Oct. 54	p 30 June 57	
5	0	Walter Raymond Nolan	p 19 Jan. 55	p 10 April 57	p 22 Apr. 59	
6	0	John Gibsone[7]	8 Dec. 54	p 26 Feb. 56	27 May 59	
5	0	Henry Marshall	1 May 55	17 Sept. 57	p 1 July 59	
		LIEUTENANTS.				
6	0	James Duncan,[11] *Adj*	5 Nov. 54	10 April 57		
5	0	Hon. Wm. Henry Curzon[7]	13 July 55	17 Sept. 57		
5	0	Charles Waymouth	p 27 July 55	17 Sept. 57		
4	0	Robert Bainbridge	p 29 Feb. 56	p 2 Oct. 57		
5	0	Henry Evelyn Wood[12]	7 Sept. 55	p 1 Feb. 56		
5	0	Thomas Gonne	p 2 Nov. 55	p 11 Sept. 57		
3	0	James Harding	p 3 Oct. 57	p 24 Dec. 58		
2	0	Arthur James Billing	26 Feb. 58	p 7 Sept. 58		
3	0	Rob. Dennist. Macgregor	4 Oct. 57	27 May 59		
3	0	James George Scott	5 Oct. 57	p 16 Aug. 59		
3	0	Roger T. Goldsworthy[13]	9 Oct. 57	p 16 Aug. 59		
		CORNETS.				
4	0	John Illidge Fraser	p 25 Mar. 56			
4	0	H. W. Fortescue-Harrison	18 Jan. 56			
2	0	Henry Richard Abadie	6 Aug. 58			
3	0	Geo. John Brudenell Bruce	p 7 Aug. 57			
1	0	Henry William Young	23 Aug. 59			
1	0	George Rosser	26 Aug. 59			
1	0	Fred. William Blumberg.	p 15 Nov. 59			
2	0	*Paymaster.*—George Berkeley Belcher, 26 Nov. 58.				
6	0	*Adjutant.*—*Lieut.* James Duncan, 21 Nov. 56.				
4	0	*Quarter-Master.*—William Garland, 18 Apr. 56.				
2	0	*Riding-Master.*—George Pumfrett, 15 June 58.				
12	0	*Surgeon.*—James Kellie, M.D. 2 Oct. 57; *Assist.Surg.* 5 May 48.				
5	0	*Assist. Surgeons.*—Yorke Hobart Johnson, 24 Nov. 55.				
6	0	George Carleton Clery,[14] 13 Sept. 54.				
2	0	*Veterinary Surgeon.*—John Ferris, 17 Feb. 58.				

Blue—*Facings* White.—*Agents*, Messrs. Cox & Co.

[*Returned from the Crimea,* 14 *May* 1856. *Embarked for India,* 5 *Oct.* 1857.]

2 Colonel Benson served in the Crimea, and took command of the 17th Lancers on 14th Jan. 1855 (Medal and Clasp for Sebastopol), and 5th Class of the Medjidie.

3 Lt.Col. Learmonth served in the Eastern campaign of 1854-55 (Medal and Clasp).

4 Major White served in the Eastern campaign of 1854, including the affair of Bulganak, battles of Alma and Balaklava (severely wounded), and siege of Sebastopol (Medal and Clasps, Brevet Major, and 5th Class of the Medjidie).

5 Sir William Gordon served in the Eastern campaign of 1854-55, including the battle of Balaklava (wounded and horse shot) and siege of Sebastopol (Medal and Clasps, Knight of the Legion of Honor, and 5th Class of the Medjidie).

6 Captain Macartney was present with a squadron of the 19th Light Dragoons at Kurnool and in the action of Zorapore, on the 18th October 1839. Served with the 17th Lancers at the siege of Sebastopol and battle of the Tchernaya (Medal and Clasp).

1 Sir Maxwell Wallace, while serving at the Cape of Good Hope as Captain 21st Light Dragoons, was sent in 1812 in command of a squadron of that Regt. into Caffraria with Brigadier-General Graham's expedition, which in seven months of hard and severe work drove the Caffres across the Great Fish River. He served also the campaign of 1815, and was present in the action at Quatre Bras, the retreat on the 17th June, and battle of Waterloo. On the 16th June 1815 he was appointed, by Major General Baron Dornberg, Orderly Officer, to assist his Brigade-Major, Capt. Robais; the General's Aide-de-Camp, Captain Krachenburg, being taken prisoner the following day, he took Robais as Aide-de-Camp, and named Captain Wallace, Acting-Brigade-Major; and Robais being killed on the 18th, the Duke of Wellington confirmed Captain Wallace on the Major-General's recommendation.

7 Captains Lowe and Gibsone, and Lieut. Curzon, served in the Crimea (Medal and Clasp).

8 Major Sarel served with the 9th Lancers in the Punjaub campaign of 1848-49, including the battles of Chillianwallah and Goojerat (Medal and Clasps).

9 Captain Steel served in the Crimea from 29th July 1855.

11 Lieut. Duncan served the Eastern campaign of 1854-55, including the affair of Bulganak, battles of Alma, Balaklava (horse killed), and Inkerman (horse killed), and siege of Sebastopol (Medal and Clasps, Sardinian Medal, and 5th Class of the Medjidie).

[For continuation of Notes, see foot of next page.

Head Quarters, Aldershot.] **18th Regt. of Light Dragoons (Hussars).** 155

Years' Serv.			CORNET.	LIEUT.	CAPTAIN.	BREV. MAJ.
Full Pay	Half Pay					
49		*Colonel.*—ᴅ ᴅᴅ1 Edward Byam,[1] *Ens.* 11 Nov. 11; *Lt.* 29 Apr. 13; *Capt.* ᵖ2⁶ Aug. 19; *Major,* ᵖ 16 June 25; *Lt.-Col.* ᵖ 26 Sept. 26; *Col.* 23 Nov. 41; *Major Gen.* 11 Nov. 51; *Lt.Gen.* 16 Nov. 58; *Col.* 18th Drs. 23 Feb. 58.				
29	0	*Lieut. Colonel.*—Richard Knox, *Cor.* ᵖ28 June 31; *Lieut.* 20 April 34; *Capt.* 9 March 42; *Br.Maj.* 20 June 54; *Maj.* ᵖ 8 Dec. 54; *Lt.Col.* 19 Feb. 58.				
15	0	*Major.*—Soame Gambier Jenyns,[2] CB., *Cor.* ᵖ 30 Dec. 45; *Lieut.* ᵖ 24 Sept. 47; *Capt.* ᵖ20 Dec. 50; *Brev.Maj.* 12 Dec. 54; *Maj.* 19 Feb. 58.				
		CAPTAINS.				
21	0	Henry Brett	ᵖ 21 June 39	ᵖ 11 Feb. 42	ᵖ 25 July 51	
19	7½	Arthur John Loftus[3]	ᵖ 15 Dec. 40	3 May 44	ᵖ 13 Dec. 53	
12	0	W. Wedderburn Arbuthnot	ᵖ 5 Dec. 48	ᵖ 17 June 51	ᵖ 7 Sept. 55	
12	0	Henry Scott[4]	ᵖ 12 May 48	ᵖ 22 Feb. 50	26 Feb. 58	
4	0	George Eden Jarvis	ᵖ 1 Apr. 56	16 June 57	ᵖ31 Aug. 58	
10	0	John Wynter Jas. Gifford[5]	ᵖ12 July 50	ᵖ 1 Sept. 54	25 Jan. 59	
5	0	William Palliser	22 Apr. 55	ᵖ 31 Aug. 55	ᵖ 5 Aug. 59	
12	0	John Peyton	ᵖ 21 July 48	ᵖ 18 May 49	31 Aug. 58	
		LIEUTENANTS.				
5	0	John Dane		23 Mar. 55	ᵖ 19 June 55	2 Major Jenyns served in the Eastern campaign of 1854-55, including the reconnaissance on the Danube under Lord Cardigan (in command of the squadron 18th Lt. Drags.), battles of Balaklava (horse shot), Inkerman, and Tchernaya, and siege of Sebastopol; also present with the Light Brigade at Eupatoria (Medal and three Clasps): he was senior officer of the 18th Lt. Drags. out of the charge at Balaklava, and re-formed the Regiment, for which he received the brevet of Major and CB. Has also received the 5th Class of the Medjidie.
5	0	Wm. Pem. Hesketh,[6] *Adj.*		9 Mar. 55	6 Sept. 55	
5	0	Harmer Hardy		1 June 55	ᵖ 24 July 57	
5	0	William Coxon		20 July 55	ᵖ 9 Oct. 57	
3	0	William Henry Weldon	ᵖ 15 May 57	ᵖ 26 Feb. 58		
4	0	Thomas Phillips	ᵖ 26 Sept. 56	26 Mar. 58		
2	0	Richard Saunders	16 Mar. 58	5 Aug. 59		
2	0	William Henry O'Shea	17 Mar. 58	ᵖ 5 Aug. 59		
2	0	Hamlyn Huntingd. Harris	23 Mar. 58	ᵖ16 Sept. 59		
		CORNETS.				
2	0	James Clarke Hicks	26 Mar. 58			
2	0	Townley P. H. M. Filgate	27 Mar. 58			
2	0	Edmund Bernhard Leibert	13 Apr. 58			
1	0	Charles Arthur Tisdall	18 Jan. 59			
1	0	Harold Esdale Malet	18 Oct. 59			

23	1⁶/₁₂	*Paymaster.*—Wm. Betson,[8] 10 March 58; *Q.M.* 1 Nov. 35; *Hon.Capt.* 1 Sept. 56.	
5	0	*Adjutant.*—*Lieut.* Wm. Pemberton Hesketh,[6] 13 Dec. 59.	
2	0	*Quarter Master.*—Joseph Henry Pickles,[9] 23 March 58.	
2	0	*Riding Master.*—Edward Malcolm Greatrex, 14 May 58.	
20	0	*Surgeon.*—Edward Scott Docker, 14 May 51; *Assist.Surg.* 29 Dec. 40.	
3	0	*Assistant Surgeon.*—Maximilian Grant, M.D. 10 March 57.	
12	0	*Veterinary Surgeon.*—Austin Cooper Shaw, 21 Aug. 48.	

Facings Blue.—*Agents*, Messrs. Cox and Co.

1 Lieut.General Byam served the campaigns of 1812, 13, 14, and 15, including the battles of Salamanca Vittoria, Orthes, and Waterloo, besides minor affairs. Severely wounded by a grape-shot while carrying the regimental colour of the 38th at Salamanca, and slightly wounded at Waterloo. He has received the War Medal with three Clasps. Major-General Byam's first commission was an ensigncy in the 38th, with which Regt. he served two campaigns: all his other commissions and the rest of his service was in the 15th Hussars.

3 Captain Loftus served with the 10th Hussars in the Eastern campaign of 1855, and was present at the capture of Tchorgoum, battle of the Tchernaya and at the siege and fall of Sebastopol (Medal and Clasp and Turkish Medal). Served with the 2nd Dr. Guards in the Indian campaign in 1857-58, was present at the siege and capture of Lucknow, actions of Barree and Koorse in which he commanded a detached squadron and two Bengal Horse Artillery guns (mentioned in despatch, Medal and Clasp).

4 Captain Scott served in the 9th Lancers at the close of the Punjaub campaign in 1849 (Medal). Served as D. A. Q. M. General to Lugard's division from 28th Feb. 1858, and was present at the taking of the Dilkoosha, Martinière, Begum's Palace and capture of Lucknow; also at subsequent operations with detached column without Walpole; commanded a Squadron at the attack on Rodaghur, also at the action of Aligunge (Medal and Clasp).

5 Captain Gifford served with the 11th Lancers in the Crimea from 17 May 1855, including the capture of Tcherzoum, battle of the Tchernaya, siege and fall of Sebastopol (Medal and Clasp).

6 Lieut. Hesketh served with the 42nd Highlanders at the siege and fall of Sebastopol from July 1855, and received a contusion from a round shot in the trenches (Medal and Clasp).

8 Captain Betson served at the siege and capture of Bhurtpore in 1825-26 (Medal).

9 Qr.Master Pickles served with the 11th Hussars in the Eastern campaign of 1854-55, including the affair of Bulganne, battles of Alma, Balaklava, and Inkerman, and siege of Sebastopol (Medal and four Clasps).

[Continuation of Notes to 17th Lancers.]

12 Lieut. Wood served at the bombardment of Odessa as a Midshipman of H.M.S. *Queen*; and in the Naval Brigade as Aide-de-Camp to Captain Peel from 1st Oct. 1854 to 18th June, 1855, when he was severely wounded carrying up scaling ladders to the Redan; mentioned in Lord Raglan's dispatches (Medal with two Clasps, Knight of the Legion of Honor, 5th Class of the Medjidie, and Turkish Medal). Served in the Indian campaign of 1858 as Brigade Major in Somerset's Brigade, and was mentioned in General Michel's despatch.

13 Lieut. Goldsworthy served in the Indian campaign with the Volunteer Cavalry with Havelock's column in the actions of Oonao, Buscerutgunge, Boorbeacchowkee, Bithoor, Mungarwar, and Alumbagh, relief of Lucknow and its subsequent defence. Whilst in Lucknow served as an Assistant Engineer (Medal and Clasp).

14 Assist.Surgeon Clery served in the Crimea during parts of 1854-55 (Medal with Clasp for Sebastopol).

†D 2

Military Train.

Years' Serv.			
Full Pay	Half Pay		
23		**Colonel Commandant.**—William Montagu Scott M'Murdo,[1] CB. 1 April 57; *Ens.* 1 July 37; *Lt.* 5 Jan. 41; *Capt.* 7 July 43; *Brev.Maj.* 18 Feb. 48; *Bt. Lt.Col.* 21 Oct. 53; *Col.* 28 Nov. 54; *Maj.* 12 Oct. 55.	
28	3/12	**Brigade Major.**—Major Charles Robert Shervinton, Unattached.	
		Lieut.Colonels.—6 George Erskine,[3] *Ens.* 17 Aug. 32; *Lt.* ᴾ3 July 36; *Capt.* ᴾ1 May 40; *Bt.Maj.* 20 June 54; *Bt.Lt.Col.* 12 Dec. 54; *Maj.* 24 Aug. 55; *Lt.Col.* 26 Oct. 55.	
19	0	2 James Peter Robertson,[3] CB. *Ens.* 29 Oct. 41; *Lt.* ᴾ 30 Sept. 42; *Capt.* ᴾ21 Jan. 48; *Maj.* 20 Feb. 57; *Bt.Lt.Col.* 24 Mar. 58; *Lt.Col.* 4 Nov. 59.	
24	0	4 Bartholomew O'Brien,[4] *Ens.* ᴾ15 April 30; *Lt.* ᴾ13 July 38; *Capt.* 2 Aug. 50; *Bt.Maj.* 12 Dec. 54; *Major*, 20 Apr. 55; *Lt.Col.* 26 Oct. 58.	
16	0	**Majors.**—5 Joseph Salis,[5] *Ens.* 10 May 44; *Lt.* 8 Jan. 47; *Capt.* 7 Aug. 51; *Maj.* 20 Feb. 57.	
17	8/12	3 John M'Court,[6] *Ens.* 1 Jan. 43; *Lt.* 1 July 45; *Capt.* 9 Sept. 51; *Maj.* ᴾ 30 Mar. 58.	
15	0	1 Godfrey Cooper, *Ens.* ᴾ27 June 45; *Lt.* ᴾ2 Apr. 47; *Capt.* ᴾ4 Aug. 54; *Maj.* ᴾ15 June 58.	
15	3 2/12	7 Jas. M. Hill,[7] *Ens.* 1 Jan. 42; *Lt.* 10 Aug. 42; *Capt.* 1 Nov. 48; *Maj.* 4 Nov. 59.	

		CAPTAINS.	ENS., ETC.	LIEUT.	CAPTAIN.	BREV.-MAJ.
12	1 1/12	2 Arth. Wellesley Williams[8]	ᴾ 5 Nov. 47	ᴾ 2 Oct. 40	29 July 53	
8	7/12	4 James Hornby Buller[9]	ᴾ23 Jan. 52	11 Aug. 54	1 July 55	
10	7/12	2 James Henry Wyatt[10]	ᴾ20 Sept. 44	ᴾ26 June 46	ᴾ 3 Aug. 55	26 Apr. 59
16	1	1 William Robert Gray		7 Apr. 43	8 Jan. 47	15 Feb. 56
10	3/12	6 Henry R. Hoghton Gale[11]	ᴾ15 Feb. 50	ᴾ18 Feb. 53	ᴾ 2 May 56	
16	0	3 George P. Edw. Morrison	28 June 44	ᴾ 8 Sept. 46	20 Feb. 57	
10	0	1 William Robert Goodall	ᴾ12 Apr. 50	ᴾ15 Feb. 53	ᴾ10 Apr. 57	
7	0	3 James Powell[12]	27 May 53	15 Dec. 54	25 Sept. 57	
6	8/12	4 Chas.Josh.Tuffnell Oakes[13]	ᴾ10 June 53	8 Dec. 54	ᴾ 9 Jan. 57	
12	1 7/12	3 John Warden M'Farlan	8 Jan. 47	ᴾ22 Apr. 48	ᴾ24 June 56	
6	0	4 David Gibson[14]	5 Nov. 54	20 Feb. 57	26 Feb. 58	
13	0	3 Henry Ridge Wolrige	31 Mar. 47	ᴾ27 Dec. 50	27 Jan. 58	
3	0	6 Christian Wm. M'Niell		20 Feb. 57	ᴾ23 Apr. 58	
3	0	5 Arthur Hunt[15]		20 Feb. 57	ᴾ22 June 58	
7	0	1 Rob. Montague Hornby	ᴾ11 Mar. 53	ᴾ15 Dec. 54	ᴾ31 Aug. 58	
5	0	2 John Blake[16]	1 May 55	20 Feb. 57	8 Oct. 58	
8	0	2 George Pilkington Blake[17]	ᴾ 5 Nov. 52	30 July 54	17 Sept. 58	
12	0	6 Arthur Cassidy[18]	ᴾ17 Nov. 48	ᴾ14 June 50	15 June 58	
5	0	6 William Banks		11 May 55	7 Sept. 55	
5	0	5 Charles Fred. Hutton		2 Mar. 55	25 Jan. 56	
10	0	4 Thomas Edward Green	ᴾ17 May 50	ᴾ13 May 53	7 Sept. 55	
13	0	5 Edward Ring Berry[19]	29 Jan. 47	26 Apr. 49	1 Sept. 57	
3	0	5 William Corbett[20]		20 Feb. 57	15 Aug. 59	
5	0	1 St. John Willans[21]		30 April 55	25 Jan. 56	
9	0	7 J. Balcombe,[22] Q.M. 7 Nov. 51			1 April 57	
5	0	7 Henry Miller[23]†		2 Feb. 55	1 Feb. 56	
5	0	7 Joseph Harris		7 Sept. 55	1 Apr. 57	

		LIEUTENANTS.			
5	0	7 Thos. Hanmer Fletcher[23]		27 Aug. 55	
5	0	3 Thomas Witchell, Adj.		31 Aug. 55	
5	0	2 Lynch John Keogh		21 Sept. 55	
5	0	6 James Milne[42]	23 Nov. 55	1 Feb. 56	
4	0	5 J. Hesketh, Adj.	21 Feb. 56	20 Feb. 57	
3	0	5 ᵖᶜ George Symons[24]		20 Feb. 57	
3	0	1 Robert Bruce		20 Feb. 57	
3	0	2 John Devine[25]		20 Feb. 57	
3	0	6 C. W. Farwell		20 Feb. 57	
5	0	2 Wentworth Dawes	10 Mar. 55	9 Sept. 55	
5	0	1 Jn.Aug. Geo. Fred.Sewell		12 Feb. 55	
5	0	3 Frederic Bond	20 Feb. 57	25 Sept. 57	
5	0	6 John Walsh		7 Sept. 55	
5	0	1 Edward Jervis	23 Nov. 55	ᴾ15 Jan. 58	
5	0	1 Vincent Applin	23 Nov. 55	2 Feb. 58	
5	0	4 James Bodkin[26]	23 Nov. 55	2 Feb. 58	
5	0	5 Bernard H. Burke	23 Nov. 55	26 Feb. 58	
4	0	4 William Shackleton,[28] Adj.	12 Jan. 56	17 Mar. 58	
4	0	2 William Thompson,[29] Adj.	21 Jan. 56	17 Mar. 58	
4	0	1 John Briggs,[30] Adj.	28 Jan. 56	17 Mar. 58	
5	0	5 Robert Cope Hardy	20 July 55	ᴾ14 May 58	
3	0	3 Henry Keogh	9 Oct. 57	21 May 58	
2	0	6 Henry James Lane	ᴾ15 Jan. 58	ᴾ22 June 58	
3	0	3 Ruben Hill Powell	9 Oct. 57	30 June 58	
4	0	5 Emanuel Benjamin Bass	27 May 56	5 Mar. 58	
3	0	7 Isaac Cummin,[43] Adj.	17 Nov. 57	8 Oct. 58	
2	0	2 William Townley	30 Apr. 58	ᴾ17 Dec. 58	
2	0	1 Charles Williams	26 Feb. 58	ᴾ18 Feb. 59	

17 Captain George P. Blake served in the 84th Regt. with Havelock's Column in the actions of Onaoo, Busseerut Gunge (1st and 2nd),Boorbeake Chowkee, Bithoor, Mungawar, and Alum Bagh, relief of Lucknow, Sortie of 29th Sept. 1857, and storming of the Hirn Khana; with Outram's force at the Alum Bagh, also at the assault and capture of Lucknow, and relief of Azimghur.

18 Captain Cassidy served with the 78th Highlanders in the Persian war in 1857, including the night attack and battle of Kooshab, bombardment of Mohumrah, and expedition to Ahwaz. Served in Bengal with Havelock's Column from its first taking the field in July 1857, including the actions of Futtehpore, Aoung, Pandoo Nuddee,Cawnpore,Onao, Busseerutgunge (1st and 2nd), Boorbeakechowkee, Bithoor, and the several actions leading to and ending in the relief of Lucknow and subsequent defence; with Outram's force at Alumbagh including the repulse of the numerous attacks, and operations ending in the final capture of Lucknow; also throughout the campaign in Rohilcund under Lord Clyde, as Brigade Major to the 2d Brigade including the capture of Bareilly.

Military Train. 157

Years' Serv.		LIEUTENANTS.	ENSIGN.	LIEUT.	
Full Pay.	Half Pay.				
3	0	4 Jno. Huntingford Bridger	P 30 Jan. 57	P 25 Feb. 59	20 Captain Corbett served at the siege and fall of Sebastopol (Medal and Clasp). Also in the Indian Campaign of 1857-58, including the relief of Lucknow by Lord Clyde, occupation of the Alumbagh under Outram with the several engagements there, fall of Lucknow, relief of Azimghur, captures of Jugdispore—horse shot.
3	2	5 George Hall	22 Oct. 55	1 Feb. 56	
3	2	3 George Edwards	23 Nov. 55	1 Feb. 56	
3	2	2 H. Clarke	26 Dec. 55	1 Apr. 57	
2	0	6 Charles Turville Wilson	16 Mar. 58	P 11 Jan. 59	
4	0	6 John Taylor, Adj.	21 Feb. 56	15 Aug. 59	
4	0	4 Alexander M'Donald	2 Feb. 56	29 Nov. 59	21 Captain Willans served at the siege and fall of Sebastopol in 1854-55 (Medal and Clasp).
2	2 7/12	7 J. Watson		10 Sept. 55	
2	2 7/12	7 George James	23 Nov. 55	1 Feb. 56	22 Captain Balcombe served at the siege of Sebastopol from 22 Sept. 1854; also at the bombardment and capture of Kinbourn (Medal and Clasp).
2	2 7/12	7 James Pettigrew	1 Nov. 55	1 Feb. 56	
2	2 7/12	7 James Malley	1 Dec. 55	1 Apr. 57	
		ENSIGNS.			
2	0	5 Frank F. Perceval	P 23 Apr. 58		22† Captain Miller served at the siege of Sebastopol from March to July, 1855 (Medal and Clasp).
5	0	5 Henry Adams	31 Dec. 55		
2	0	2 Robert Warner Stone	P 23 July 58		23 Lieut. Fletcher served at the siege of Sebastopol in 1855 (Medal and Clasp).
4	0	3 Andrew Munro	20 Jan. 56		
4	0	4 William Laughton	21 Feb. 56		24 Lieut. Symons served with the Royal Artillery at the battle of Inkerman and siege of Sebastopol, and was severely wounded on the 6th June 1855 while unmasking the embrasures of a five-gun battery in the advanced right attack, under a terrific fire, for which he has received the Victoria Cross (Medal and Clasp, and Sardinian Medal).
4	0	1 Fergus M'Kenzie	21 Feb. 56		
2	2 3/12	3 George Ramsey	12 Jan. 56		
2	2 3/12	2 Robert Davies	21 Jan. 56		
2	2 7/12	1 Donat M'Mahon	9 Feb. 56		
1	0	7 John Matthew Benthall	20 Dec. 59		25 Lieut. Devine served the Eastern campaign of 1854-55, in the Royal Artillery and Turkish Contingent, including the battles of Alma, Balaklava, and Inkerman, sortie of 26th Oct., attacks of the Redan on 18th June and 8th Sept., siege and fall of Sebastopol, and capture of Kinbourn (Medal and four Clasps, and Knight of the Legion of Honor). Served in the Indian campaign of 1857-58 and was attached to the 9th Lancers at the advance on the Dilkoosha and Le Martiniere and throughout the operations resulting in the relief of Lucknow by Lord Clyde; present during the occupation of the Alumbagh under Outram with the several engagements there, fall of Lucknow, relief of Azimghur, capture of Jugdispore, and affair near Reotee.
		Paymasters.			
5	0	1 Maxwell Reeve, 5 Oct. 55.			
4	0	3 Obé Willans, 5 April 56.			
4	0	7 Thomas Bryson, 5 April 56.			
4	0	2 Benjamin Robert James,[31] 5 April 56.			
3	0	5 Grahame Craig, 1 April 57.			
4	0	6 George W. Macquarie,[32] 9 Sept. 56.			
2	0	4 Harry Lee Carter, 25 Aug. 58.			
		Adjutants.			
4	0	5 Lieut. J. Hesketh, 20 Feb. 57.			26 Lieut. Bodkin served in the Indian campaign of 1857-58, including the relief of Lucknow by Lord Clyde, occupation of the Alumbagh under Outram with the several engagements there, relief of Azimghur, and affair near Kusca.
4	0	4 Lieut. William Shackleton,[28] 20 Feb. 57.			
2	0	2 Lieut. William Thompson,[29] 20 Feb. 57.			
5	0	3 Lieut. Thomas Witchell, 12 Feb. 58.			
4	0	1 Lieut. John Briggs, 6 May 59.			27 Doctor D'Arcy served the siege of Sebastopol in 1854-55 (Medal and Clasp).
4	0	6 Lieut. John Taylor, 4 Nov. 59.			
3	0	7 Lieut. Isaac Cummin, 20 Dec. 59.			28 Lieut. Shackleton served the Eastern campaign of 1854-55, including the affair of M'Kenzie's farm, battles of Alma and Inkerman, sortie of 26th Oct., siege and fall of Sebastopol (Medal and three Clasps).
		Instructor of Musketry.			
4	0	Lieut. James Milne, 14 April 58.			
		Quarter Masters.			
11	0	7 Adam M'Bride, 2 Oct. 49.			33 Dr. Barry served with the 1st Battalion 60th Royal Rifles throughout the Punjaub campaign of 1848-9, was present at the siege of Mooltan, also at the battle of Goojerat, Feb. 21st 1849 (Medal and Clasps). Landed in the Crimea with the 13th Light Infantry, on the 30th June 1855, and was at the battle of the Tchernaya, siege and fall of Sebastopol (Medal and Clasp).
4	0	2 Theophilus Greenway,[34] 4 Feb. 56.			
4	0	1 William Lambert, 4 Feb. 56.			
4	0	4 John Gannon, 12 Feb. 56.			
4	0	3 J. Stalford, 16 Feb. 56.			
5	0	5 William M'Call, 14 Aug. 57; Cornet, 23 Nov. 55.			
1	0	6 Malcolm Keir, 2 Dec. 59.			

4	0	*Riding-Masters.*—3 William Matthews,[35] 10 March 57; *Cornet*, 12 Jan. 56.
4	0	2 Malachi Powell, 10 March 57; *Cornet*, 2 Feb. 56.
4	0	6 Thomas Ritchie,[37] 28 Aug. 57; *Cornet*, 12 Jan. 56.
17	0	*Surgeons.*—4 William Braybrooke, 2 Sept. 53; *Assist.Surg.* 13 June 43.
11	0	2 Alexander M'Arthur,[36] 11 May 55; *Assist.Surg.* 13 April 49.
14	0	3 Francis Reynolds, 8 Dec. 54; *Assist.-Surg.* 7 Aug. 46.
14	0	5 Alexander Mackay Macbeth,[38] 29 June 55; *Assist.Surg.* 11 July 46.
13	0	6 John Andrew Woolfreyes, 20 July 55; *Assist.Surg.* 13 July 47.
14	0	1 O'Connor D'Arcy,[27] *MD.* 2 Jan. 55; *Assist.Surg.* 2 Oct. 46.
14	0	4 Daniel Paterson Barry,[33] *MD.* 8 Dec. 54; *Assist.Surg.* 7 Aug. 46.
5	0	*Veterinary Surgeons.*—2 William Death, 11 May 55.
5	0	6 John James Channon, 15 Aug. 55.
5	0	4 Thomas Paton, 15 Aug. 55.
5	0	3 John Burr, 15 Aug. 55.
5	0	1 George Fleming, 28 Dec. 55.

Blue.—*Facings* White.—*Agent,* Sir John Kirkland.

1 Colonel M'Murdo served as Assistant Quartermaster-General of the Army under Sir Charles Napier during the campaign in Scinde in 1843 (Medal), and was present in the battle of Meeanee, in which his horse was shot under him—skirmish with the enemy while conducting Major Stack's Brigade from Muttaree to form a junction with Sir Charles Napier's force at Hydrabad; and battle of Hydrabad, where he received a sabre wound in the right breast. He again served as Assist.Quartermaster General to Sir Charles Napier's Army during the campaign against the Mountain and Desert tribes situated on the right bank of the Indus, early in 1845. Served in the Eastern campaign as Director General Land Transport Corps (Medal and Clasp for Sebastopol, Officer of the Legion of Honor, and 4th Class of the Medjidie).

2 Lt.Colonel Erskine served with the 33rd Regt. in the Eastern campaign of 1854-55, including the battle of Inkerman and siege of Sebastopol: he commanded the picquets of the Light Division on the 14th Oct. 1854, when they repulsed the attack made on them by the enemy (Medal and two Clasps, Brevet Lt.Colonel, and 5th Class of the Medjidie).

3 Lt.Colonel Robertson served with the 31st Regt. the Sutlej campaign of 1845-46, including the battles of Moodkee, Ferozeshah, Buddiwal, Aliwal, and Sobraon (Medal and three Clasps). Served in the Crimea from 22nd May 1855, including the siege of Sebastopol, and attacks on 18th June and 8th Sept. (Medal and Clasp). Commanded the Military Train, acting as Cavalry, in the Indian campaign of 1857-58, including the relief of Lucknow by Lord Clyde, occupation of the Alumbagh under Outram with the several engagements there and commanded the small force which repulsed the Enemy's Cavalry 3000 strong on the 16th March 1858, and fall of Lucknow; commanded the Cavalry of Lugard's Field Force from 29th March to 10th June, and was present at the relief of Azimghur capture of Jugdispore, and subsequent operations (Brevet of Lt.Colonel, and CB.).

4 Lt.Colonel O'Brien served with the 77th Regt. the Eastern campaign of 1854 and up to 26 March 1855, including the battles of Alma and Inkerman, and siege of Sebastopol (Brevet, Major, Medal and Clasps, and 5th Class of the Medjidie).

5 Major Salis served with the Cape Mounted Riflemen throughout the Kaffir war of 1846-47, against the insurgent Boers at Boem Plaats, in 1848, where he was dangerously wounded, and had his horse killed under him; also in the Kaffir war of 1850-53 (Medal), and when in command of a detachment at Graham's Town, he quelled a serious mutiny of the Native soldiers; served in the Crimea from Feb. 1855 (Medal and Clasp for Sebastopol). During a period of 13 years' service abroad he was in nineteen actions and skirmishes, and was frequently mentioned in public orders, for gallant and skilful conduct.

6 Major M'Court served as Brigade Major with the expedition against the King of Keenung, river Gambia, in the Actions of 6th, 7th, and 8th May 1849. Was present with the combined British and French Naval and Land Force at the attack and defeat of pirates in Basis Island, Jeba River, Dec. 1849. Commanded the British and Native Force during the Ashantee invasion of the Assin country, Gold Coast, in March and April 1852.

7 Major Hill served in the Kaffir war of 1846-47 (Medal). Served in the Crimea at the battle of Inkerman and siege of Sebastopol (Medal and two Clasps), after which as Major in the Turkish Contingent and commanded the Garrison Artillery at Kertch and Yenikali (4th Class of the Medjidie).

8 Captain Williams served with the 12th Lancers in the Kaffir war of 1851-53 (Medal); also at the siege of Sebastopol (Medal and Clasp).

9 Captain Butler served with the 57th Regt. in the Eastern campaign of 1854, and was very severely wounded in the trenches before Sebastopol, and again whilst being carried back to the camp (Medal and Clasp).

10 Major Wyatt served in the Indian campaign of 1857-58, including the relief of Lucknow by Lord Clyde, occupation of the Alumbagh under Outram with the several engagements there, fall of Lucknow, relief of Azimghur, capture of Jugdispore; commanded the Military Train acting as Cavalry throughout the Shahabad campaign (twice mentioned in despatches, Brevet of Major, Medal and Clasp).

11 Captain Gale landed with the 48th Regt. in the Crimea on the 21st April 1855, and served at the siege and fall of Sebastopol (Medal and Clasp).

12 Captain Powell served with the 30th Regt. in the operations against Kurnool in 1839. Landed in the Crimea with the Regt., did duty with it in the trenches at the siege of Sebastopol, and was selected to take charge of a party of the 39th, and to superintend the erection of a work under fire, for the efficient performance of which he was selected by Lord Raglan for Staff employ, and attached to the Land Transport Corps on 27th March 1855, the 8th Battalion of which he organized and commanded (Medal and Clasp).

13 Captain Oakes served with the Royals at the siege and fall of Sebastopol, from 11th July 1855 (Medal and Clasp).

14 Captain Gibson served the Eastern campaign of 1854-55, including the affair of M'Kenzie's Farm, battle of Balaklava (severely wounded in the head by several sabre cuts), and siege and fall of Sebastopol (Medal and two Clasps).

15 Captain Hunt served with the Field Train, Royal Artillery, in the Eastern campaign of 1855, and was present during the siege and fall of Sebastopol in the trenches with the siege train, at the bombardments of the 6th and 17th June (Medal and Clasp, and Knight of the Legion of Honor).

16 Captain John Blake served with the 47th Regt. at the siege and fall of Sebastopol (Medal and Clasp). Served in the Indian campaign of 1857-58, including the relief of Lucknow by Lord Clyde, and occupation of the Alumbagh.

19 Captain Berry served with the 61st Regt. in the Punjaub campaign of 1848-49, including the passage of the Chenab, battles of Sadoolapore, Chillianwallah, and Goojerat, and pursuit of the enemy to the Khyber Pass (Medal and two Clasps). Served in the Indian campaign in 1857, and was present at the siege, assault, and capture of Delhi, and action of Nujjufghur (Medal and Clasp).

29 Lieut. Thompson served in the Eastern campaign from May 1855, including the expedition to Kertch (Medal and Clasp). Served as Adjutant of the Military Train, acting as Cavalry, in the Indian campaign of 1857-58, including the relief of Lucknow by Lord Clyde, occupation of the Alumbagh under Outram with several engagements there, fall of Lucknow, relief of Azimghur, capture of Jugdispore, and subsequent operations.

30 Lieut. Briggs served with the 9th Regt. in the Crimea from Nov. 1854, including the siege of Sebastopol, and capture of the Cemetery and Suburbs under General Eyre (Medal and Clasp). Served in the Indian campaign of 1857-58, including the relief of Lucknow by Lord Clyde, occupation of the Alumbagh under Outram with the several engagements there, fall of Lucknow, relief of Azimghur, capture of Jugdispore, and subsequent operations.

31 Paymaster James served in the Indian campaign of 1857-58, including the relief of Lucknow by Lord Clyde, occupation of the Alumbagh under Outram, fall of Lucknow, and relief of Azimghur.

32 Paymaster Macquarie, previous to his having been appointed Paymaster, served in the army for 20 years, and as Captain in the 63rd Regt. in the Crimea from 6th Nov. 1854 to the end of Aug. 1855, including the siege of Sebastopol, expedition to Kertch, attack of the Redan on 18th June, and repulse of various night sorties (Medal and one Clasp).

34 Qr.Master Greenway served the Eastern campaign of 1854-55, including the battles of Alma and Inkerman, siege and fall of Sebastopol, bombardment and surrender of Kinbourn (Medal and three Clasps). Served in the Indian campaign of 1857-58, including the relief of Lucknow by Lord Clyde, occupation of the Alumbagh under Outram with the several engagements there, fall of Lucknow, relief of Azimghur, capture of Jugdispore, and subsequent operations.

35 Riding Master Matthews served with the Royal Dragoons during the Crimean war, and was present at the battles of Balaklava and Inkerman, the siege and fall of Sebastopol (Medal and Clasps).

36 Surgeon M'Arthur served the Eastern campaign of 1854-55, including the battles of Alma and Inkerman, and siege of Sebastopol (Medal and three Clasps). Was attached to the 9th Lancers at the advance on the Dilkoosha and Le Martiniere and throughout the operations resulting in the relief of Lucknow by Lord Clyde, and was wounded on the 14th Nov. 1857.

37 Riding Master Ritchie served with the Royal Artillery in the Eastern campaign of 1854-55, including the battle of Inkerman, siege and fall of Sebastopol in the trenches with the siege train, and at the bombardments of October, April, and 6th and 17th June; was wounded by the explosion of the French magazines of the 15th Nov. 1855 (Medal and Clasps).

38 Surgeon Macbeth served with the 29th Regt. in the Punjaub campaign of 1848-49, including the passage of the Chenab and battle of Chillianwallah (Medal).

42 Lieut. Milne served at the siege and fall of Sebastopol in 1855 (Medal and Clasp).

43 Lieut. Cummin served with the 90th Lt. Infantry in the Crimea from 5th Dec. 1854, including the siege and fall of Sebastopol, and assault of the Redan on the 8th Sept.—mentioned in despatches (Medal and Clasp).

1st (or Grenadier) Regiment of Foot Guards.
"LINCELLES" "CORUNNA" "BARROSA" "PENINSULA" "WATERLOO" "ALMA" "INKERMAN" "SEVASTOPOL."

Years' Serv. Full Pay.	Half Pay.	Colonel.—His Royal Highness Francis Albert Augustus Emanuel, The Prince Consort, Duke of Saxony, Prince of Saxe-Coburg and Gotha, KG, KT. K.P. GCB. GCMG. Field Marshal, 8 Feb. 1840; Col. Grenadier Gds., 23 Sept. 52.
34	1	Lt. Col.—Charles Algernon Lewis,¹ Cornet, P 13 Oct. 25; Lt. P 15 Aug. 26; Capt. P 12 Apr. 33; Capt.& Lt.Col. P 30 Dec. 45; Col. 20 June 54; Maj. 11 Jan. 58; Lt.Col. 13 Feb. 59.
29	0	Majors.—1 Fred. Wm. Hamilton,² CB. Ens. & Lt. 12 July 31; Lt. & Capt. 1 Dec. 36; Capt. & Lt.Col. P 3 April 46; Col. 20 June 54; Maj. 7 Dec. 58.
28	0	3 Hon. James Lindsay, Ens.& Lieut. P 16 Mar. 32; Lieut.& Capt. P 2 Dec.36; Capt. & Lieut.Col. P 14 Aug. 46; Col. 20 June 54; Major, 7 Dec. 58.
25	0	2 John Arthur Lambert, Ens. & Lieut. P 10 July 35; Lt. & Capt. P 11 Sept. 40; Capt. & Lt.Col. P 15 Nov. 50; Col. 28 Nov. 54; Maj. 13 Feb. 59.
24	0	Capts. & Lt.Cols.—2 VC. Hon. Hy. Hugh Manvers Percy,⁵ Ens.& Lt. P 1 July 36; Lt.& Capt. P 29 Dec. 40; Capt.& Lt.Col. P 7 Mar. 51; Col. 28 Nov.54.
23	0	1 Edward G. Wynyard,⁶ Ens. 12 May 37; Ens. & Lieut. P 9 Jan. 38; Lieut. & Capt. P 25 Oct. 42; Capt. & Lt.Col. 20 June 54.
22	0	3 Hon. Rd.Wm. Penn Curzon,⁷ CB.Ens. & Lt. P 14 July 38; Lt. & Capt. P 5 April 44; Brev.Maj. 28 May 53; Capt.& Lt.Col. 20 June 54; Col. 17 Nov. 57.
20	0	2 Ralph Bradford,⁸ Ens. & Lieut. P 30 Oct. 40; Lieut. & Capt. P 19 Dec. 45; Capt. & Lt.Col. 14 July 54.
20	0	1 Michael Bruce,⁹ Ens. & Lieut. P 15 Dec. 40; Lieut. & Capt. P 30 Dec. 45; Capt. & Lt.Col. 14 July 54.
32	0	3 Tho.Sydenham Conway,¹⁰CB., Ens. 14 Feb.28; Lt. P26April31; Capt.P9 Dec. 36; Brev.Maj. 4 July 43; Maj. 4 Feb. 53; Bt.Lt.Col. 20 June 54; Capt. & Lt.Col. 15 July 54; Col. 26 Oct. 58.
19	0	2 Charles Lennox Brownlow Maitland,¹¹ Ens.& Lt. P 9 April 41; Lt. & Capt. P 27 Mar. 46; Brev.Maj. 15 Sept. 48; Capt. & Lt.Col. 28 Sept. 54.
19	0	2 Lord Arthur Hay,¹² s. Ens. & Lieut. P 30 April 41; Lieut. & Capt. P 3 Apr. 46; Capt. & Lieut.Col. 19 Oct. 54.
20	0	3 Henry Edward Montresor,¹³ Ens. 15 Dec. 40; Ens. & Lieut. P 18 May 41; Lt. & Capt. P 18 May 46; Capt.& Lt.Col. 6 Nov. 54.
19	0	1 His Serene Highness Prince Wm. Aug. Edw. of Saxe Weimar,¹⁴ CB. Ens. 1 June 41; Ens.&Lt. P 8 June 41; Lt.&Capt. P 19 May 46; Brev.Maj. 20 June 54; Brev.Lt.Col. 12 Dec. 54; Capt. & Lt.Col. P 18 May 55; Col. 5 Oct. 55.
18	0	3 Jas. Fred. Dudley Crichton Stuart, Ens. & Lieut. P 25 Oct. 42; Lieut. & Capt. P 12 Feb. 47; Capt. & Lieut.Col. P 19 June 55.
20	0	3 Lord Frederick John FitzRoy,¹⁵ Ens. P 18 Sept. 40; Ens. & Lieut. P 14 July 43; Lieut. & Capt. P 31 Mar. 48; Capt. & Lt.Col. P 22 June 55.
18	0	3 Hy. Fred. Ponsonby,¹⁶ Ens. 27 Dec. 42; Ens. & Lt. P 16 Feb. 44; Lt. & Capt. P 18 July 48; Brev.Maj. 19 Oct. 49; Capt. & Lt.Col. P 31 Aug. 55.
17	0	1 C.Geo.Ellison,¹⁷ Ens. 23 Nov.43; Ens.& Lt. P 5 Apr.44; Lt.&Cap. P 10 Apr.49; Br. Maj. 12 Dec. 54; Br. Lt.Col. 2 Nov. 55; Capt. & Lt.Col. 8 July 56.
16	0	3 John Francis Cust, Ens. 26 July 44; Ens. & Lieut. P 2 Aug. 44; Lieut. & Capt. P 1 June 49; Capt. & Lieut.Col. P 16 Sept. 56.
15	9/12	1 Alfred Capel Cure,¹⁷† Ens. 30 July 44; Lieut. P 9 April 47; Capt. P 17 Aug. 52; Major, P 25 May 55; Brev. Lt.Col. 2 Nov. 55; Lt.Col. 18 Jan. 56.
16	0	1 John Hinde King,¹⁸† Ens.25 June 44; Lt. P 7 July 46; Capt.P 14 Oct.51; Br. Maj. 12 Dec. 54; Maj. 2 Oct.55; Br.Lt.Col. 2 Nov. 55; Lt.Col. 19 Dec. 56.
16	0	1 Wm. Henry Beaumont de Horsey,¹⁹ Ens. § Lieut. P 22 Nov. 44; Lieut. & Capt. P 22 Mar. 50; Brev. Maj. 12 Dec. 54; Capt. & Lieut.Col. P 13 Mar. 57.
15	0	1 Geo. W. A. Higginson,²⁰ Ens. & Lt. P 14 Feb. 45; Lt. & Capt. P 12 July 50; Bt.Maj. 12 Dec. 54; Bt. Lt.Col. 2 Nov. 55; Capt. & Lt.Col. P 10 Apr. 57.
15	0	2 Aug. Hen. Lane Fox,²¹ Ens. & Lt. P 16 May 45; Lt. & Capt. P 2 Aug. 50; Brev.Maj. 12 Dec. 54; Capt. & Lieut.Col. P 15 May 57.
17	0	2 Charles Wilson Randolph, Ens. P 10 Feb. 43; Lieut. 23 Mar. 45; Capt. P 15 Feb. 50; Capt. & Lieut.Col. P 17 July 57.
15	0	1 Edward Henry Cooper, Cor. P 16 May 45; Lt. P 11 Sept. 46; Capt. P 15 Aug. 48; Capt. & Lt.Col. P 17 Nov. 57.
14	0	2 Edwyn Sherard Burnaby,²³ Ens. & Lieut. P 3 Nov. 46; Lieut. & Capt. P 27 May 53; Brevet Major, 2 Nov. 55; Capt. & Lieut.Col. P 18 Dec. 57.
22	0	3 Alfred Tipping,¹⁸ Ens. P 22 June 38; Lieut. P 30 May 43; Capt. P 7 May 47; Brev.Maj. 12 Dec. 54; Capt. & Lt.Col. 11 Jan. 58.
17	0	2 VC. Sir Charles Russell, Bt.,²⁶ Ens. P 25 Aug. 43; Lt. P 9 June 46; Lt. & Capt. P 13 Sept. 53; Bt.Maj. 2 Nov. 55; Capt.& Lt.Col. P 23 April 58.
25	0	1 Henry Hume,²² CB. Ens. P 9 May 35; Lt. P 1 Dec. 37; Capt. P 19 Jan. 44; Maj. P 24 Dec. 52; Bt.Lt.Col. 12 Dec. 54; Lt.Col. 9 March 55.
14	0	2 Cameron Neville Hogge,²⁴ Ens. 1 Dec. 46; Ens.& Lt. P 6 Aug. 47; Lt. & Capt. P 24 Feb. 54; Capt. & Lt.Col. P 7 Dec. 58.
14	0	2 Sidney Burrard, Ens. & Lt. P 3 April 46; Lt. & Capt. P 2 May 51; Capt. & Lt.Col. 13 Feb. 59.
13	0	2 Sir Wm. Thomas Fra. Agnew Wallace, Bt., Ens. 20 July 47; Ens. & Lt. P 3 Mar. 48; Lt. & Capt. 20 June 54; Capt. & Lt.Col. P 20 July 59.
12	0	3 Frederick Charles Keppel. Ens. § Lt. P 31 Mar. 48; Lt. § Capt. 20 June 54; Capt. & Lt. Col. P 5 Aug. 59.

1st (or Grenadier) Regiment of Foot Guards.

Years' Serv. Full Pay	Half Pay	LIEUTS. AND CAPTAINS.	COR. 2D LT. OR ENSIGN.	ENSIGN AND LIEUT.	LIEUT. AND CAPTAIN.
11	0	2 W. A. M. Barnard,²⁵ *Maj.* 23 Oct. 57, *s.*	....	p 23 Feb. 49	14 July 54
11	0	3 Claud Alexander²⁸	....	p 11 May 49	14 July 54
10	0	3 John Murray²⁸	....	p 15 Mar. 50	14 July 54
14	0	1 Arthur Edw. Valette Ponsonby,²⁹ *s.*	26 June 46	p 9 Aug. 50	20 July 53
10	0	1 Sir John Montagu Burgoyne,³⁰ *Bart.*	....	p 16 Aug. 50	17 Oct. 54
9	0	2 Charles Napier Sturt,³¹ *s.*	....	p 14 Feb. 51	6 Nov. 54
9	0	2 Henry William Verschoyle³³	....	p 10 April 51	22 Dec. 54
9	0	1 Fred. Tho. Arthur Hervey Bathurst³³	....	p 16 May 51	22 Dec. 54
7	0	1 Robert Anstruther, *Adj.*	....	p 21 Jan. 53	p 8 June 55
7	0	2 Robert William Hamilton³⁵	....	p 27 May 53	p 18 June 55
7	0	1 Fitz Roy Aug. Talbot Clayton³⁴	....	p 8 July 53	p 13 July 55
11	0	2 Thomas Harvey Bramston³⁶	p 16 Feb. 49	6 June 54	20 Dec. 54
13	0	1 Rh. Lyons O. Pearson,³⁷ *s. Maj.* 2 Nov. 55	3 Dec. 47	p 4 April 51	20 Dec. 54
8	0	2 William Salisbury Ewart⁴²	p 9 July 52	p 11 Aug. 54	p 30 Mar. 55
11	0	2 Francis George Stapleton,³⁸ *s.*	30 Nov. 49	12 Mar. 52	p 10 Aug. 55
7	0	2 George Arthur Ferguson²⁴	....	p 15 Dec. 53	p 30 Nov. 55
7	0	1 S. A. B. *Earl of* Carrick²⁴	....	p 16 Dec. 53	p 7 Mar. 56
6	0	1 Henry Charles Eden Malet,²¹ *s.*	....	p 24 Feb. 54	p 26 Sept. 56
6	0	1 *Hon.* John Constantine Stanley,²⁴ *s.*	....	p 17 Mar. 54	p 7 Nov. 56
6	0	1 Edward Wm. Lloyd Wynne²⁴	....	p 27 June 54	p 13 Mar. 57
9	0	2 William Earle,⁴¹ *s.*	p 17 Oct. 51	6 June 54	p 16 Feb. 55
6	0	3 Clifton Gascoigne,²⁴ *s.*	6 June 54	27 Oct. 54	p 10 April 57
6	0	1 Fra. W. *Visc.* Hood.............	....	18 Nov. 54	p 15 May 57
6	0	3 William Lewis Stucley	....	1 Dec. 54	p 17 July 57
6	0	3 Henry Edward Clive	p 18 Aug. 54	8 Dec. 54	p 17 July 57
6	0	3 Henry Fanshawe Davies⁴⁹	....	19 Dec. 54	p 28 Aug. 57
6	0	1 Patrick Keith Murray	....	20 Dec. 54	p 11 Sept. 57
6	0	3 *Hon.* Sudeley Chas. G. Hanbury Tracy	....	21 Dec. 54	p 17 Nov. 57
6	0	3 William Henry Parnell	....	22 Dec. 54	p 18 Dec. 57
10	0	1 Rob. Hen. C. D. Lowe,⁴⁶ *Maj.* 19 Jan. 58	p 17 Sept. 50	27 Feb. 52	8 Jan. 58
6	0	1 Alfred Walter Thynne	p 25 Aug. 54	5 Jan. 55	p 23 April 58
5	0	2 Philip Smith, *Adj.*	....	19 Jan. 55	p 25 June 58
5	0	3 Reginald John Buller, *s*	....	p 9 Feb. 55	p 7 Dec. 58
5	0	3 Arch. Chas. Henry Douglas Pennant	....	p 16 Mar. 55	p 7 Dec. 58
6	0	2 George Henry Grey⁴⁷	7 Dec. 54	29 Dec. 54	10 May 58
5	0	1 Lewis Guy Phillips	....	p 15 June 55	p 24 June 59
5	0	2 John Julius Johnstone..........	....	p 20 July 55	p 20 July 59
7	0	2 *Hon.* Arthur Annesley	p 4 Nov. 53	p 10 Aug. 55	p 16 Aug. 59

Ensigns and Lieuts.

4	0	3 *Hon.* Wm. Edw. Sackville West, *Adj.*	....	p 7 Jan. 56	
4	0	3 Henry Osborne Gould	....	p 8 Jan. 56	
4	0	1 Edward Smith Bridges	....	p 4 Apr. 56	
4	0	3 *Hon.* Charles Ernest Edgcumbe ..	....	p 26 Sept. 56	
4	0	3 Norman Leslie Melville	....	p 27 Sept. 56	
4	0	2 Arthur Divett Hayter	....	p 14 Nov. 56	
3	0	3 Charles Berners Jarrett	....	p 10 April 57	
3	0	3 Alfred Molyneux Byng	....	p 15 May 57	
3	0	1 William Robert Gamul Farmer ...	....	p 30 June 57	
3	0	3 Thomas Ferdinand Fairfax	....	p 17 July 57	
3	0	3 Edmund Charles Nugent	....	p 7 Aug. 57	
3	0	2 Robert Thomas Lowndes Norton ...	....	p 28 Aug. 57	
3	0	3 Hugh Henry Cholmeley	....	p 11 Sept. 57	
3	0	2 Charles Fludyer	....	p 17 Nov. 57	
3	0	2 C. G. H. *Visc.* Hinchinbrook	....	p 18 Dec. 57	
2	0	1 Charles Wellesley Pakenham	....	12 Feb. 58	
2	0	1 *Hon.* Fred. Arthur Stanley	....	p 23 April 58	
2	0	1 Arthur P. *Visc.* Mahon	....	p 25 June 58	
2	0	2 Wm. Aug. Fred., *Viscount* Uffington	....	p 9 Nov. 58	
2	0	2 Henry Walter Hope.............	23 Apr. 58	p 7 Dec. 58	
2	0	3 *Hon.* Charles Geo. Cornwallis Eliot.	....	p 31 Dec. 58	
2	0	1 James T. Richard Lane Fox	p 5 Oct. 58	p 11 Mar. 59	
2	0	1 Leopold Richard Seymour	27 Oct. 58	p 24 June 59	
1	0	2 Henry Renebald Clinton	p 10 Jan. 59	p 29 July 59	
1	0	1 Robert Charles de Grey Vyner......	p 17 June 59	p 16 Aug. 59	

7	0	*Adjutants.*—1 Capt. Robert Anstruther, 3 Aug. 55.
4	0	3 Lt. *Hon.* Wm. Edw. Sackville West, 19 Nov. 58.
5	0	2 *Captain* Philip Smith, 25 Feb. 59.

1st (or Grenadier) Regiment of Foot Guards. 161

Years' Serv.		
Full Pay.	Half Pay.	
		Instructors of Musketry.—1 Captain Fitz Roy Aug. Talbot Clayton, 30 April 57.
		3 *Captain* Edward Henry Clive, 30 April 57.
		2 *Captain* John Julius Johnstone, 12 May 59.
30	0	*Quarter Masters.*—1 John Lilley,[30] 8 June 30.
9	0	2 John Atkinson, 28 Feb. 51.
5	0	3 Esau Collins, 2 March 55. [*A.S.* 13 April 38.
22	0	*Surgeon Major.*—3 George Eleazar Blenkins,[45] 24 Jan. 58 ; *Surgeon,* 1,Oct. 54 ;
20	0	*Battalion Surgeons.*—1 Charles R. Nicoll,[40] 29 Dec. 54; *A.S.* 26 June 40.
19	0	2 James John Marjoribanks Wardrop,[41] 2 Mar. 55; *Assist.Surg.* 21 May 41.
6	0	*Assistant Surgeons.*—3 Henry John Hughes Lawrence,[40] 24 Feb. 54.
7	0	3 Constantine Caridi Read,[40] 13 May 53.
6	0	1 Gilbert Prout Girdwood, 24 Nov. 54.
6	0	2 William Ralph Lane, 29 Dec. 54.
6	0	1 Frederick Gustavus Hamilton,[40] 28 April 54.
2	0	2 William Henry Pickford, M.B., 19 Feb. 58.
		Solicitor.—Edward White, 20 Feb. 55.

1st *Battalion returned from Portugal,* 1828.
2nd *Battalion returned from Canada,* 22 Oct. 1842.
3rd *Battalion returned from the Crimea,* June 1856.
Facings Blue.—*Agent, Sir* John Kirkland.

1 Colonel Lewis served during the latter part of the siege, and at the fall of Sebastopol (Medal and Clasp, and 5th Class of the Medjidie).
3 Colonel Hamilton served the Eastern campaign of 1854, including the battles of Alma, Balaklava, and Inkerman (severely wounded), and siege of Sebastopol (Medal and Clasps, Officer of the Legion of Honor, and 3rd Class of the Medjidie).
5 Colonel Hon. Henry Percy served the Eastern campaign of 1854-55, including the battles of Alma (wounded), Balaklava, and Inkerman (wounded), and siege of Sebastopol (Medal and Clasps, Aide de Camp to the Queen, Victoria Cross, Knight of the Legion of Honor, and 4th Class of the Medjidie).
6 Lt.Colonel Wynyard served in the Crimea in 1855 (Medal with Clasp for Sebastopol, and 5th Class of the Medjidie).
7 Colonel the Hon. R. W. P. Curzon served as Aide de Camp to Sir George Cathcart in the Kaffir war in 1852-3 (Medal), for which service he was promoted to the Brevet rank of Major. Served at the siege of Delhi in 1857, as Acting Quarter Master General of the Queen's troops (Colonel and *CB.*).
8 Lieut.Colonel Bradford served the Eastern campaign of 1854, including the battles of Alma, Balaklava, and Inkerman (severely wounded), and siege of Sebastopol (Medal and Clasps, and 5th Class of the Medjidie).
9 Lt.Colonel Bruce served in the Crimea (Medal).
1 (Colonel Conway served throughout the operations in Scinde (Medal), including the battles of Meeanee and Hyderabad ; and he commanded the Light Company (detached) at the previous defence of the Residency at Hyderabad. He served also the campaign in the Southern Mahratta country, and was present at the investment and capture of Panulla and Powughur.
11 Lieut.Colonel Maitland served the campaign of 1846-47 against the Kaffirs (Medal), as Military Secretary to Sir Peregrine Maitland, and received the rank of Brevet Major for his services. Served the Eastern campaign of 1854 as D. A. Adj.Gen. to the 4th Division, including the battles of Alma, Balaklava, and Inkerman (dangerously wounded), and siege of Sebastopol (Medal and Clasps, Knight of the Legion of Honor, and 5th Class of the Medjidie).
12 Lord Arthur Hay served the Sutlej campaign of 1845-6 as Aide de Camp to Lord Hardinge, and was present at the battle of Sobraon (Medal). Served also in the Crimea from 29th Dec. 1854 (Medal and Clasp, Sardinian Medal, and 5th Class of the Medjidie).
13 Lieut.Colonel Montresor served in the Crimea from 29th Dec. 1854 (Medal and Clasp, and 5th Class of the Medjidie).
14 Colonel Prince Edward of Saxe Weimar served the Eastern campaign of 1854, including the battles of Alma, Balaklava, and Inkerman, and siege of Sebastopol (wounded in the trenches, 19th Oct.) : Medal and Clasps, Knight of the Legion of Honor, and 4th Class of the Medjidie.
15 Lord Frederick FitzRoy served under Sir Robert Stopford during the operations on the coast of Syria in 1840 (Medal).
16 Lieut.Colonel Ponsonby served at the siege of Sebastopol from 13th Aug. 1855 (Medal and Clasp, and 5th Class of the Medjidie).
17 Lieut.Colonel Ellison landed in the Crimea on the 16th Oct. 1854, from which period he served as Brigade Major with the Brigade of Guards, and was present at the battles of Balaklava and Inkerman (promoted Brevet Major), and siege of Sebastopol (Medal and Clasps, Brevet of Major and Lieut.Col., Knight of the Legion of Honor, and 5th Class of the Medjidie).
17† Lieut.Colonel Cure served with the 55th Regt. at the siege of Sebastopol in 1855 ; commanded the party of the 55th at the attack on the Quarries, and commanded the Regiment from the middle of June to the 8th Sept., including the attacks of the Redan on the 18th June and 8th Sept.—severely wounded (Medal and Clasp, Brevet Lt.Colonel, Sardinian Medal, and 5th Class of the Medjidie).
18 Lt.Colonel Tipping served the Eastern campaign of 1854, including the battles of Alma, Balaklava, and Inkerman (severely wounded), and siege of Sebastopol (Medal and Clasps, Knight of the Legion of Honor, and 5th Class of the Medjidie).
18† Lt.Colonel King served with the 49th Regt. the Eastern campaign of 1854-55, including the battles of Alma and Inkerman, siege of Sebastopol, sortie on the 26th Oct., capture of the Quarries, and assaults of the Redan on the 18th June and 8th Sept.—severely wounded, left hand amputated (Medal and three Clasps, Brevet of Major and Lieut.Col., Knight of the Legion of Honor, Sardinian Medal, and 5th Class of the Medjidie).
19 Lt.Col. de Horsey served in the Eastern campaign of 1854, including the battle of Alma and siege of Sebastopol (Medal and Clasps, Brevet of Major, and 5th Class of the Medjidie).
20 Lieut.Colonel Higginson served throughout the Eastern campaign of 1854-55, as Adjutant 3rd Battalion Grenadier Guards, including the battles of Alma, Balaklava, and Inkerman (horse killed), siege and fall of Sebastopol; after which he served as Brigade Major of the Guards until the conclusion of the war (Medal and Clasps, Brevets of Major and Lieut.Col., Knight of the Legion of Honor, and 5th Class of the Medjidie).
21 Lt.Col. Lane Fox served in the Eastern campaign of 1854 as D. A. Adj.Gen., including the battle of Alma (Medal and Clasp, and 5th Class of the Medjidie).
22 Lt.Colonel Hume served the Eastern campaign of 1854-55 with the 95th, including the battles of the Alma (wounded, and horse killed under him) and Inkerman (severely wounded—shot through the thigh), siege and fall of Sebastopol, and sortie of 26th Oct. in command of the Regt.; he succeeded to the command of the Regt. at Inkerman, and received the brevet rank of Lieut.Colonel (Medal and Clasps, *CB.*, Knight of the Legion of Honor, and 4th Class of the Medjidie).

23 Lt.-Colonel Burnaby served in the Eastern campaign of 1854, including the battle of Inkerman and siege of Sebastopol (Medal and Clasps, Brevet Major, and 5th Class of the Medjidie).
24 Lt.Col. Hogge, Captains Ferguson, the Earl of Carrick, Malet, Stanley, Wynne, and Gascoigne served during the siege of Sebastopol (Medal and Clasp).
25 Major Barnard served at the siege of Sebastopol (Medal and Clasp, and 5th Class of the Medjidie). Served as Aide-de-Camp to Sir Henry Barnard commanding the force before Delhi (Brevet Major).
26 Sir Charles Russell served the Eastern campaign of 1854-55 (latterly as D. A. Q. M. Gen, 1st Division), including the battles of Alma, Balaklava, and Inkerman, and siege of Sebastopol (Medal and Clasps, Brevet Major, Victoria Cross, Knight of the Legion of Honor, and 5th Class of the Medjidie).
28 Captains Alexander and John Murray served in the Crimea from Dec. 1854, including the siege of Sebastopol (Medal and Clasp). Captain Alexander has the 5th Class of the Medjidie.
29 Captain Ponsonby served with the 43rd Light Infantry in the Kaffir war of 1851-53 (Medal), including the battle of the Berea. He served in the Crimea as Aide-de-Camp to Sir George Brown during the expedition to Kertch, attack of 18th June, and as Aide-de-Camp to Sir William Codrington on the 8th Sept. and fall of Sebastopol (Medal and Clasp, Sardinian Medal, and 5th Class of the Medjidie).
30 Sir John Burgoyne served in the Eastern campaign of 1854, including the battle of Alma (severely wounded): Medal and Clasp.
32 Captain Sturt served the Eastern campaign of 1854, including the battles of Alma, Balaklava, and Inkerman (severely wounded), and siege of Sebastopol (Medal and Clasps, Sardinian Medal, and 5th Class of the Medjidie).
33 Captains Verschoyle and Bathurst served the Eastern campaign of 1854-55, including the battles of Alma, Balaklava, and Inkerman, and siege of Sebastopol (Medal and Clasps, and 5th Class of the Medjidie). Captain Verschoyle was wounded in the trenches before Sebastopol on the 5th September 1855, and has also the Sardinian Medal.
34 Captain Clayton served in the Crimea (Medal and Clasp).
35 Capt. Hamilton served the Eastern campaign of 1854, including the battles of Alma (wounded), Balaklava, and Inkerman, and siege of Sebastopol (Medal and Clasps, Sardinian Medal, and 5th Class of the Medjidie).
36 Captain Bramston served with the Rifle Brigade in the Kaffir war of 1852-53 (Medal). Also the Eastern campaign of 1854-55, including the battles of Alma, Balaklava, and Inkerman, and siege of Sebastopol (Medal and Clasps, and 5th Class of the Medjidie).
37 Major Pearson served the Eastern campaign from April 1854 to July 1855, as Aide-de-Camp to Sir George Brown, including the battles of Alma and Inkerman, siege of Sebastopol, attack of the 18th June, and expedition to Kertch (Medal and Clasps, Brevet Major, Sardinian Medal, and 5th Class of the Medjidie).
38 Captain Stapleton served with the 43rd Regt. in the Kaffir war of 1851-53 (Medal).
39 Qr.-Master Lilley served in the Eastern campaign of 1854, including the battles of Alma and Balaklava (Medal and Clasps).
40 Surgeon Nicoll, and Assist.-Surgeons Lawrence, Read, and Hamilton served in the Crimea (Medal and Clasp).
41 Surgeon Wardrop served the Eastern campaign of 1854, including the battles of Alma, Balaklava, and Inkerman, and siege of Sebastopol (Medal and Clasps).
42 Captain Ewart served with the 93rd Highlanders in the Eastern campaign of 1854-55, including the battles of Alma and Inkerman, and siege of Sebastopol (Medal and Clasps).
43 Captain Davies served in the Royal Navy in the Burmese war (Medal).
44 Captain Earle served with the 49th Regt. the Eastern campaign of 1854-55, including the battles of Alma and Inkerman, siege of Sebastopol, sortie of 26th Oct., and assault of the Redan on 18th June (Medal and three Clasps, Sardinian Medal, and 5th Class of the Medjidie).
45 Surgeon Major Blenkins served in the Crimea from the 20th Dec. 1854 (Medal and Clasp, and 5th Class of the Medjidie).
46 Major Lowe served with the 74th Highlanders throughout the Kaffir war of 1851-53 (Medal). Served as Orderly officer to Major-Gen. Reed and as Aide-de-Camp to Sir A. Wilson at the siege and assault of Delhi (Brevet Major).
47 Captain Grey served at the siege and fall of Sebastopol, and attacks on the Redan on the 18th June and 8th Sept. (Medal and Clasp).

Coldstream Regiment of Foot Guards. 163
"LINCELLES."—The *Sphinx*, with the words "EGYPT" "TALAVERA" "BARROSA"
"PENINSULA" "WATERLOO" "ALMA" "INKERMAN" "SEVASTOPOL."

Years' Serv.			
67		**Colonel.**—其 其其 John *Earl of* Strafford,[1] GCB. & GCH. *Ens.* 30 Sept. 1793; *Lt.* 1 Dec. 93; *Capt.* 24 May 94; *Lt.Col.* 14 March 1800; *Col.* 25 July 10; *Major Gen.* 4 June 13; *Lt.Gen.* 27 May 25; *Gen.* 23 Nov. 41; *Field Marshal*, 2 Oct. 55; *Col.* Coldstream Guards, 15 Aug. 50.	
Full Pay.	Half Pay.		
34	0	**Lieut.Colonel.**—*Lord* Fred. Paulet,[3] CB., *Ens.* & *Lieut.* 11 June 26; *Lieut.* & *Capt.* p 21 Sept. 30; *Capt.* & *Lieut.Col.* p 8 May 46; *Col.* 20 June 54; *Maj.* 20 Feb. 55; *Lt.Col.* 26 Oct. 58.	
25	8/12	**Majors.**—1 Wm. Samuel Newton,[4] *Ens.* & *Lieut.* p 5 Dec. 34; *Lt.* & *Capt.* p 31 Dec. 39; *Capt.* & *Lt.Col.* p 25 Feb. 48; *Col.* 28 Nov. 54; *Maj.* 18 Nov. 56.	
23	0	2 Spencer Perceval,[5] *Ens.* & *Lieut.* p 13 Jan. 37; *Lieut.* & *Capt.* p 15 Oct. 41; *Capt.* & *Lt.-Col.* p 23 June 48; *Col.* 28 Nov. 54; *Major*, 26 Oct. 58.	
22	0	**Captains** & *Lieut.Colonels.*—1 Thomas Montagu Steele,[6] CB. *Cornet*, 12 Jan. 38; *Ens.* & *Lt.* p 20 July 38; *Lt.* & *Capt.* p 29 Mar. 44; *Capt.* & *Lt.Col.* p 31 Oct. 51; *Col.* 28 Nov. 54.	
24	0	2 William Mark Wood,[7] *Ensign*, p 22 July 36; *Lieut.* 24 May 41; *Capt.* p 20 Aug. 44; *Capt. & Lieut.-Col.* p 13 Dec. 53; *Col.* 28 Nov. 54.	
22	0	1 Charles Lygon Cocks,[5] *Ens.* p 28 July 38; *Ens. & Lieut.* p 24 Jan. 40; *Lieut.* & *Capt.* p 7 Aug. 46; *Capt.* & *Lt.-Col.* 20 June 54.	
21	0	2 James Halkett,[8] *Ens.* p 7 June 39; *Ens. & Lieut.* p 23 April 41; *Lieut.* & *Capt.* 1 July 47; *Capt.* & *Lt.-Col.* 20 June 54.	
20	0	1 Dudley Wilmot Carleton,[9] *2nd Lieut.* p 10 April 40; *Ens. & Lieut.* p 11 June 41; *Lieut.* & *Capt.* p 13 July 47; *Capt.* & *Lt.-Col.* 14 July 54.	
26	0	1 Arthur St. George H. Stepney,[10] CB. *Ens.* p 16 May 34; *Lieut.* p 10 Nov. 37; *Capt.* p 15 April 42; *Brevet Major*, 3 April 46; *Major*, p 9 July 50; *Brevet Lt.-Col.* 20 June 54; *Capt.* & *Lt.-Col.* 15 July 54; *Col.* 26 Oct. 58.	
30	0	1 JamesTalbot Airey,[11] CB. *s. Ens.* 11 Feb. 30; *Lieut.* p 3 May 33; *Capt.* p 22 July 42; *Major*, 11 Nov. 51; *Capt.* & *Lt.-Col.* 15 July 54.	
14	0	1 Ullick Canning, *Lord* Dunkellin,[13] *Ens.* & *Lieut.* p 27 Mar. 46; *Lieut.* & *Capt.* p 27 April 49; *Capt.* & *Lieut.-Col.* p 3 Nov. 54.	
16	0	1 William Gregory Dawkins,[14] *Ens.* p 2 Aug. 44; *Ens.* & *Lieut.* p 6 Sept. 44; *Lieut.* & *Capt.* p 25 April 48; *Capt.* & *Lieut.-Col.* 6 Nov. 54.	
21	0	2 Clement William Strong,[15] *Ens.* 18 Jan. 39; *Lieut.* 6 May 42; *Capt.* p 1 Sept. 48; *Capt.* & *Lt.-Col.* 6 Nov. 54.	
17	0	2 Francis Wm. Henry, *Earl of* Westmorland,[17] CB. *Ens.* 24 Feb. 43; *Lt.* 26 July 44; *Capt.* p 1 Aug. 48; *Brev. Maj.* 7 June 49; *Major*, p 22 April 53; *Brev. Lt.-Col.* 20 Sept. 54; *Lt.-Col.* 12 Dec. 54.	
16	0	2 *Hon.* Arthur Edward Hardinge,[18] CB. *Ens.* p 7 June 44; *Lt.* 22 Dec. 45; *Capt.* p 1 June 49; *Brevet Major*, 12 Dec. 54; *Capt.* & *Lt.-Col.* 20 Feb. 55; *Col.* 25 May 58.	
15	0	2 *Hon.* Percy Robert Basil Feilding,[19] *s. Ens.* p 8 Aug. 45; *Ens. & Lieut.* p 7 Aug. 46; *Lieut.* & *Capt.* 21 Aug. 51; *Brev.-Maj.* 12 Dec. 54; *Capt. & Lt.-Col.* p 23 Nov. 55.	
14	0	2 William Henry Reeve, *Ens.* & *Lieut.* p 29 Dec. 46; *Lieut.* & *Capt.* p 22 Aug. 51; *Capt.* & *Lt.-Col.* p 30 Nov. 55.	
13	0	2 Charles Baring,[20] *Ens.* & *Lieut.* p 2 July 47; *Lieut.* & *Capt.* p 29 April 53; *Brev.-Major*, 12 Dec. 54; *Capt.* & *Lieut.-Col.* p 21 Dec. 55.	
13	0	2 *Hon.* Henry Wm. John Byng, *Ens.* & *Lieut.* 27 Aug. 47; *Lieut.* & *Capt.* p 3 Mar. 54; *Capt.* & *Lt.-Col.* p 2 May 56.	
16	0	1 John Halkett Le Couteur,[20]† *2nd Lieut.* p 3 May 44; *Lieut.* 27 Mar. 46; *Capt.* 15 Mar. 53; *Brevet Major*, 2 Nov. 55; *Capt.* & *Lt.-Col.* 18 Nov. 56.	
13	0	2 Henry Armytage,[21] *Ens.* & *Lieut.* p 30 July 47; *Lieut.* & *Capt.* p 13 Dec. 53; *Bt.Major*, 12 Dec. 54; *Capt.* & *Lt.Col.* 26 Oct. 58.	
10	0	1 *VC* Gerald Littlehales Goodlake,[22] *2nd Lieut.* p 14 June 50; *Ens. & Lieut.* p 27 June 51; *Lieut.* & *Capt.* 14 July 54; *Bt.Major*, 14 June 56; *Capt.* & *Lt.Col.* p 29 Nov. 59.	
12	0	1 George, *Lord* Bingham,[23] *2nd Lieut.* p 29 Dec. 48; *Ens.* & *Lieut.* p 14 Oct. 51; *Lieut.* & *Capt.* 22 Aug. 54; *Bt.Major*, 17 July 55; *Capt.* & *Lt.-Col.* p 20 Dec. 59.	

		LIEUTENANTS AND CAPTAINS.	CORNET, OR ENSIGN.	ENSIGN AND LIEUT.	LIEUT. AND CAPTAIN.
13	0	1 P. Sambrook Crawley,[21] *Maj.*12Dec.54.	p 2 Mar. 47	p 23 June 48	14 July 54
9	0	1 Harvey Tower[21]	p 17 Jan. 51	p 21 Nov. 51	4 Sept. 54
8	0	1 Wm. H. *Visc.* Dangan[27] *Maj.* 26 Apr. 59	....	p 23 July 52	21 Sept. 54
8	0	2 Arthur James Fremantle, *Adj.*	10 Dec. 52	p 20 April 53	6 Nov. 54
8	0	1 *Hon.* Wm. Henry A. Feilding	13 Feb. 52	p 26 July 53	15 Dec. 54
7	0	1 Michael Walker Henenge[21]	....	p 13 Dec. 53	23 Dec. 54
9	0	1 *Lord* Eustace H. B. G. Cecil	p 21 Nov. 51	p 13 Jun. 54	20 Dec. 54
16	0	1 Christopher Edward Blackett[25]	21 Dec. 44	p 1 Oct. 47	4 Feb. 54
11	0	1 George Robert FitzRoy[26]	p 23 Nov. 49	p 8 Apr. 53	29 Dec. 54
11	0	2 *Hon.* Wm. Geo. Boyle,[28] *Maj.*12Dec.54.	p 9 Feb. 49	p 16 Sept. 51	p 13 Jan. 54
12	0	2 *VC* John Aug. Conolly[29] *Maj.* 17 July 55	p 25 Feb. 48	p 26 Aug. 50	22 Dec. 54
6	0	2 William Archer, *Visc.* Holmesdale.[32]	....	p 3 Mar. 54	4 Mar. 55

Coldstream Regiment of Foot Guards.

Years' Serv. Full Pay.	Years' Serv. Half Pay.	LIEUTENANTS AND CAPTAINS.	CORNET, 2D LIEUT. OR ENSIGN.	ENSIGN AND LIEUT.	LIEUT. AND CAPTAIN.
11	0	1 Hon. Richard Monck,³¹ Adj.	P 2 Mar. 49	P 17 Oct. 51	23 Mar. 55
10	0	2 Charles Greenhill	P 13 Dec. 50	P 22 Apr. 53	P 6 July 55
10	0	2 Henry Clarke Jervoise³³	P 13 Dec. 50	P 8 Apr. 53	P 6 Apr. 55
7	0	2 Hon. Henry Walter Campbell³⁵	P 13 May 53	21 Nov. 54	19 June 55
6	0	2 Julian Hamilton Hall		P 2 Aug. 54	P 13 Feb. 56
6	0	2 Godfrey James Wigram⁴¹		P 3 Aug. 54	P 14 Feb. 56
6	0	2 Arthur Lambton³⁴		P 4 Aug. 54	P 15 Feb. 56
8	0	2 Philip le Belward Egerton³⁷	P 23 Jan. 52	11 Aug. 54	23 Mar. 55
6	0	2 Hon. William Edwardes		P 24 Nov. 54	P 5 Feb. 58
5	0	1 Henry John Bagot Lane⁵		16 Jan. 55	26 Oct. 58
5	0	2 Alexander William Adair⁵		17 Jan. 55	P 6 May 59
5	0	1 William Fred. Ernest Seymour³⁶ ..		18 Jan. 55	P 13 May 59
5	0	1 Hon. Edward Henry Legge		P 12 Feb. 55	P 29 Nov. 59
5	0	2 Edward Strelley Pegge Burnell		P 13 Feb. 55	P 20 Dec. 59
		ENSIGNS AND LIEUTS.			
5	0	2 Fred. Horace Arthur Seymour		24 Apr. 55	
5	0	2 Richard Hasel Thursby		4 May 55	
5	0	2 Norman Burnand................	P 27 July 55	P 26 Oct. 55	
5	0	2 Fred. Charles Buller		P 30 Nov. 55	
4	0	2 William Wynne.................		P 13 Feb. 56	
4	0	2 Ellis Philip Fox Reeve		P 14 Feb. 56	
4	0	2 Hugh Bonham Carter		P 15 Feb. 56	
4	0	1 Hugh Granville Fortescue		1 Apr. 56	
4	0	1 John Fletcher Hathorn		P 19 Dec. 56	
3	0	1 Henry Arthur Herbert		P 30 Jan. 57	
2	0	1 Henry Robert Brand		10 Dec. 58	
1	0	1 Denzil Hugh Baring		P 6 May 59	
1	0	1 Hon. Frederick Charles Howard ...		P 13 May 59	
3	0	1 Reginald Arch. Edward Cathcart .	P 17 Nov. 57	P 21 Oct. 59	
3	0	1 Charles Walter Lee-Mainwaring....	18 Dec. 57	P 20 Nov. 59	
1	0	Hon. Vesey Dawson		P 20 Dec. 59	
8	0	*Adjutants.*—2 Capt. Arthur James Fremantle, 2 Oct. 55.			
11	0	1 Capt. Hon. Richard Monck, 8 Aug. 56.			
16	0	*Instructors of Musketry.*—1 Captain C. E. Blackett, 30 April 57.			
12	0	2 VC Brevet Major J. A. Conolly, 30 April 57.			
8	0	*Quarter Masters.*—2 Arthur Hurle, 13 Feb. 52.			
7	0	1 Alexander Falconer,³⁸ 1 July 53.			
28	0	*Surg. Maj.*—1 Jas. Monro, M.D. 20 Feb. 53; *Surg.* 4 April 51; *A.S.* 2 Nov. 32.			
9	0	*Batt. Surg.*—2 John Wyatt,³⁹ 9 April 57; *Assist. Surg.* 17 June 51.			
14	0	*Assistant Surgeons.*—1 Charles Vidler Cay, 12 June 46.			
6	0	2 John William Trotter,⁴⁰ 26 May 54.			
1	0	1 Robert Farquharson, M.D. 12 Jan. 59.			
1	0	2 Arthur Bowen Richards Myers, 26 Sept. 59.			
		Solicitor.—William George Carter, 29 Jan. 24.			

Facings Blue—*Agents,* Messrs. Cox & Co.
[1st *Battalion returned from the Crimea,* June 1856.]
[2nd *Battalion returned from Canada,* 29th Oct. 1842.]

1 Lord Strafford served with the 33rd in Flanders and in Holland in 1794 and 95, and was wounded at Geldermalsen. He served with the 3rd Guards in the expeditions to Hanover in 1805; to Copenhagen in 1807; and to Walcheren in 1809,—in the latter he was with the Reserve under Sir J. Hope, and commanded his advance, composed of the Grenadier Battalion of the Guards and a detachment of the 95th Rifles; in this command he charged a detachment of Dutch troops, taking some officers and upwards of a hundred men prisoners. In 1811 he joined the Brigade of Guards in Portugal; and in September of that year he was nominated to the command of a Brigade, in the 2nd Division under Lord Hill. He was present with it in all the movements and affairs with the enemy in the south of Spain—and during the period of the siege of Ciudad Rodrigo he was detached in command to Idanha Nova with his own Brigade and some cavalry to observe the movements of a corps of the enemy commanded by Gen. Foy, at Coria. Upon Lord Hill joining the main body of the Army at the commencement of the campaign of 1813, he was engaged in the several actions of Vittoria, of the Pyrenees, of Pampeluna, in which action he was wounded; in the crossing of the Nivelle and attack of the fortified camp,—wounded and had two horses shot under him; at Cambo, in driving the enemy's outposts and reconnoitring the Tête-de-Pont; in the passage of the Nive and the affair before Bayonne on the 13th Dec. 1813, when the 2nd Division was attacked by six Divisions of the French Army commanded by Marshal Soult; in this action he had a horse shot under him. On the 14th Feb. at the commencement of the campaign of 1814, he was engaged with the Rear Guard of the enemy at Espellette; and on the following day was employed in the attack of the heights above Garris. He was in the subsequent actions of Orthes and Aire; and he repulsed the enemy at Garlin. He was also engaged with his brigade at the battle of Toulouse. He commanded a Brigade of Guards at the battle of Waterloo; and commanded the first corps of the British Army from Waterloo to Paris,—took the fortified city of Peronne on the march, and subsequently possession of Paris by occupying the heights of Belle Ville and Montmartre. His Lordship has received the Gold Cross and one Clasp for Vittoria, Pyrenees, Nivelle, Nive, and Orthes; and the Silver War Medal with one Clasp for Toulouse; he is a Knight of Maria Theresa of Austria, and 2nd Class St. Wladimir of Russia.

3 Lord Frederick Paulet served the Eastern campaign of 1854, including the battles of Alma (horse killed), Balaklava, and Inkerman, and siege of Sebastopol (Medal and Clasps, Officer of the Legion of Honor, and 3rd Class of the Medjidie).

4 Colonel Newton served in the Eastern campaign of 1854, including the battles of Balaklava and Inkerman, and siege of Sebastopol (Medal and Clasps, and 5th Class of the Medjidie).

5 Colonel Perceval, Lieut. Col. Cocks, Captains Lane and Adair, served at the siege of Sebastopol (Medal and Clasp). Lieut. Col. Cocks has the 5th Class of the Medjidie.

6 Colonel Steele served the Eastern campaign of 1854-55 as Military Secretary to Lord Raglan, including the battles of the Alma, Balaklava, and Inkerman, and siege of Sebastopol (Medal and Clasps, CB., Aide-de-Camp to the Queen and Colonel, Officer of the Legion of Honor, Commander 2nd Class St. Maurice and St. Lazarus, and 3rd Class of the Medjidie).

Coldstream Regiment of Foot Guards. 165

7 Colonel Wood served the Eastern campaign of 1854, including the battles of Balaklava and Inkerman, and siege of Sebastopol (Medal and Clasps, and 5th Class of the Medjidie).

8 Lieut.-Col. Halkett served in the Eastern campaign of 1854, including the battles of Balaklava and Inkerman (severely wounded), and siege of Sebastopol (Medal and Clasps, Knight of the Legion of Honor, and 5th Class of the Medjidie).

9 Lieut.-Col. Carleton served in the Eastern campaign of 1854, including the battles of Balaklava and Inkerman, and siege of Sebastopol (Medal and Clasps, and 5th Class of the Medjidie).

10 Colonel Stepney served with the 29th Regt. in the Sutlej campaign of 1845-6; the command of the Regiment devolved upon him on the evening of the 21st Dec. at the battle of Ferozeshah, which he retained during the night of the 21st, and the action of the 22nd Dec. 1845 (wounded), and during the remainder of the active part of the campaign, until severely wounded by a grape-shot at the conclusion of the battle of Sobraon, 10 Feb. 1846 (Medal and Clasp, and CB.). Served at the siege of Sebastopol from January 1855 (Medal and Clasp, and 5th Class of the Medjidie).

11 Lieut.-Colonel Airey acted as Aide-de-Camp to Sir Robert Sale at the storming of the Khoord Cabool Pass in Oct. 1841, and had his horse shot under him. He served as Aide-de-Camp to Major-Gen. Elphinstone, in Affghanistan, from January 1841, and was present in every skirmish or sortie made by the garrison from the cantonments during the insurrection at Cabool, and was afterwards given up as a hostage. He acted as Aide-de-Camp to Sir John M'Caskill at the storming of Istaliff, and was present with the Buffs at the battle of Punniar (Medal). Served the Eastern campaign of 1854-55 as Assist.-Qr.-Mr. Gen. of the Light Division, including the battles of the Alma, Balaklava, and Inkerman, and siege of Sebastopol (Medal and Clasps, CB., Knight of the Legion of Honor, and 4th Class of the Medjidie).

13 Lord Dunkellin served in the Eastern campaign of 1854, including the battle of Alma and siege of Sebastopol, until taken prisoner in front of the trenches before daylight on the 22nd Oct. (Medal and Clasps, and 5th Class of the Medjidie).

14 Lieut.-Col. Dawkins served the Eastern campaign of 1854, including the battles of Alma and Balaklava, and siege of Sebastopol (Medal and Clasps, Knight of the Legion of Honor, and 5th Class of the Medjidie).

15 Lieut.-Col. Strong served the Eastern campaign of 1854, including the battles of Alma, Balaklava, and Inkerman, and siege of Sebastopol (Medal and Clasps, Knight of the Legion of Honor, Sardinian Medal, and 5th Class of the Medjidie).

17 Lord Westmorland served in the Punjaub campaign in 1846, and was present at the battle of Goojerat (Medal), for which he received the rank of Brevet-Major. Served also in the Eastern campaign of 1854, as Aide-de-Camp to Lord Raglan, including the battle of Alma, the Dispatches of which he conveyed to England, and received the rank of Brevet Lieut.-Colonel (Medal and Clasp, CB., Knight of the Legion of Honor, and 5th Class of the Medjidie).

18 Colonel Hon. A. E. Hardinge served as Aide-de-Camp to Lord Hardinge throughout the campaign on the Sutlej in 1845-6, and was present in the battles of Moodkee, Ferozeshah, and Sobraon, for which he has received a Medal and two Clasps; served the Eastern campaign of 1854-55 as D. A. Q. M. Gen. of the 3rd Division, including the battles of Alma, Balaklava, and Inkerman, and siege of Sebastopol (Medal and Clasps, Knight of the Legion of Honor, and 5th Class of the Medjidie).

19 Lieut.-Colonel Hon. Percy Feilding served the Eastern campaign of 1854 as Brigade Major to the Brigade of Guards at the battle of Alma, and on the staff of the 1st Division at the battles of Balaklava and Inkerman (severely wounded), and siege of Sebastopol (Medal and Clasp, Knight of the Legion of Honor, and 5th Class of the Medjidie).

20 Lieut.-Col. Baring served in the Eastern campaign of 1854, including the battle of Alma (severely wounded—arm amputated) (Medal and Clasp, Knight of the Legion of Honor, and 5th Class of the Medjidie).

20† Lieut.-Colonel Le Couteur served in the Eastern campaign from 11th Dec. 1854 until the fall of Sebastopol (Medal and Clasp, and Brevet Major). Employed as Assistant Engineer under the Q.M. General; also as Instructor of Musketry to the Turkish Contingent under Sir R. Vivian (5th Class of the Medjidie).

21 Lt.Col. Armytage, Major Crawley, and Capt. Tower, served the Eastern campaign of 1854, including the battles of Alma, Balaklava, and Inkerman, and siege of Sebastopol (Medal and Clasps, and 5th Class of the Medjidie). Lt.Col. Armytage and Captain Tower are Knights of the Legion of Honor. Major Crawley has also the Sardinian Medal.

22 Lt.Col. Goodlake served the Eastern campaign of 1854-55, including the battles of Alma, Inkerman, Balaklava, and Tchernaya, and siege and fall of Sebastopol. He volunteered for the Sharpshooters of the Brigade of Guards, commanded them for 42 days, and was engaged at the repulse of the sortie of 26th Oct. 1854; and he served on the Quarter-Master-General's staff from Feb. 1855 (Medal and Clasps, Brevet Major, Victoria Cross, Knight of the Legion of Honor, and 5th Class of the Medjidie).

23 Lord Bingham served the Eastern campaign of 1854 as Aide-de-Camp to Lord Lucan, including the battles of Alma, Balaklava, and Inkerman (Medal and Clasps, Knight of the Legion of Honor, and 5th Class of the Medjidie).

24 Captain Heneage served in the Eastern campaign of 1854-55, including the battles of Balaklava and Inkerman, and siege of Sebastopol (Medal and Clasps, and 5th Class of the Medjidie).

25 Captain Blackett served the Eastern campaign of 1854 with the 93rd Highlanders, including the battles of Alma and Balaklava, and siege of Sebastopol (Medal and Clasps, and 5th Class of the Medjidie).

26 Captain Fitzlloy served the Eastern campaign of 1854, in the 41st Regt., including the battles of Alma and Inkerman (severely wounded), and siege of Sebastopol (Medal and Clasps).

27 Lord Dangan served in the Crimea from the 17th July 1855, as Aide-de-Camp to Lord Rokeby (Medal and Clasp, and 5th Class of the Medjidie). Served as Aide de Camp to Lord Clyde in the Oude campaign (Medal and Brevet of Major).

28 Major Hon. W. G. Boyle served the Eastern campaign of 1854 as Aide-de-Camp to Sir De Lacy Evans, including the battles in the Crimea, and siege of Sebastopol (Medal and Clasps, and 5th Class of the Medjidie).

29 Major Conolly served the Eastern campaign of 1854 in the 49th Regt., including the battle of Alma and siege of Sebastopol; was dangerously wounded (shot through the body) at the repulse of the powerful sortie on the 26th October (Medal and Clasp, Victoria Cross, Sardinian Medal, and 5th Class of the Medjidie).

31 Captain Hon. R. Monck served with the 43rd Regt. in the Kaffir war in 1853 (Medal).

32 Lord Holmesdale served in the Eastern campaign of 1854, including the battles of Balaklava and Inkerman (severely wounded), and siege of Sebastopol (Medal and Clasps).

33 Captain Jervoise served the Eastern campaign of 1854-55, as Aide-de-Camp to General Airey, including the battles of Alma and Inkerman, and siege of Sebastopol (Medal and three Clasps, Sardinian Medal, and 5th Class of the Medjidie).

34 Captain Lambton served at the siege of Sebastopol (Medal and Clasp).

35 Captain Hon. H. W. Campbell served the Eastern campaign of 1854-55 as Aide-de-Camp to Sir William Codrington (Medal and Clasps, Knight of the Legion of Honor, and 5th Class of the Medjidie).

36 Captain Wm. F. E. Seymour served as a Midshipman with the Baltic Fleet in 1854 (Medal).

37 Captain Egerton served with the 2nd Battalion Rifle Brigade the Eastern campaign up to 13th April 1855, including the battle of Alma and siege of Sebastopol (Medal and Clasps).

38 Quartermaster Falconer served the Eastern campaign of 1854, including the battles of Alma, Balaklava, and Inkerman, and siege of Sebastopol (Medal and Clasps).

39 Surgeon Wyatt embarked with the 1st Battalion on the Eastern expedition, and served with it in Turkey and the Crimea until the end of the war; was present at the battles of Alma, Balaklava, and Inkerman (horse shot), and siege of Sebastopol (Medal and four Clasps, Knight of the Legion of Honor, and Turkish Medal).

40 Assist.Surgeon Trotter served the Eastern campaign of 1854-55, including the siege and fall of Sebastopol (Medal and Clasp).

41 Captain Wigram served at the siege of Sebastopol from 11th Dec. 1854 (Medal and Clasp, and 5th Class of the Mejidie).

Scots Fusilier Guards.

"LINCELLES"—The "*Sphynx*," with the words, "EGYPT" "TALAVERA" "BARROSA"
"PENINSULA" "WATERLOO" "ALMA" "INKERMAN" "SEVASTOPOL."

Years' Serv.		
Full Pay	Half Pay	
33	0	**Colonel.**—His Royal Highness George W. F. C. *Duke of* Cambridge,[1] KG. KP. GCB. GCMG. *Col.* 3 Nov. 37; *Major Gen.* 7 May 45; *Lieut.Gen.* 19 June 54; *Gen.* 15 July 56; *Colonel* of the Scots Fusilier Guards, 23 Sept. 52. *Lieut.Colonel.*—Edward Walter Forestier Walker,[2] CB. *Ens. & Lt.* ᵖ 8 Mar. 27; *Lt. & Capt.* ᵖ 18 Oct. 31; *Capt. & Lieut.Col.* ᵖ 6 Dec. 44; *Maj. & Col.* 20 June 54; *Lt.Col.* 14 June 58.
23	0	
25	0	*Majors.*—1 William John Ridley,[3] *Ens. & Lt.* ᵖ 19 June 35; *Lt. & Capt.* ᵖ 24 May 39; *Capt. & Lt.Col.* ᵖ 24 Nov. 48; *Col.* 28 Nov. 54; *Major*, 15 Dec. 54.
26	0	2 Francis Seymour,[4] CB. *Ens.* ᵖ 2 May 34; *Lt.* ᵖ 16 June 37; *Capt.* ᵖ 4 Sept. 40; *Capt. & Lt.Col.* ᵖ 28 June 50; *Col.* 28 Nov. 54; *Major*, 14 June 58.
23	0	*Captains and Lieut.Colonels.*—1 John Hamilton Dalrymple,[7] *Ens. & Lieut.* ᵖ 10 Nov. 37; *Lieut. & Capt.* ᵖ 31 Dec. 44; *Capt. & Lt.Col.* ᵖ 25 Mar. 53; *Col.* 28 Nov. 54.
21	0	2 Henry Percival de Bathe,[8] *Ens. & Lieut.* ᵖ 1 Nov. 39; *Lieut. & Capt.* ᵖ 14 Feb. 45; *Capt. & Lieut.Col.* ᵖ 17 Feb. 54; *Col.* 28 Nov. 54.
23	0	2 Fred. Charles Arthur Stephenson,[11] CB., *Ens. & Lieut.* 25 July 37; *Lieut. & Capt.* ᵖ 13 Jan. 43; *Capt. & Lieut.-Col.* 20 June 54.
19	0	1 Henry Poole Hepburn,[12] *Ens. & Lieut.* ᵖ 19 Feb. 41; *Lieut. & Capt.* ᵖ 2 Oct. 46; *Capt. & Lieut.-Col.* 20 June 54.
20	0	2 Francis Haygarth,[13] *Ens.* ᵖ 14 Feb. 40; *Ens. & Lieut.* ᵖ 21 May 41; *Lt. & Capt.* 30 Sept. 47; *Capt. & Lieut.-Col.* 14 July 54.
20	0	1 Hon. Richard Charteris, 2nd *Lieut.* ᵖ 2 Oct. 40; *Lieut.* ᵖ 7 Oct. 42; *Capt.* ᵖ 14 May 47; *Capt. & Lieut.-Col.* 14 July 54.
17	0	2 Henry Green Wilkinson, *Ens. & Lieut.* ᵖ 13 Jan. 43; *Lieut. & Capt.* ᵖ 10 Dec. 47; *Capt. & Lieut.-Col.* ᵖ 3 Nov. 54.
18	0	2 Hon. John Strange Jocelyn,[16] 2nd *Lieut.* ᵖ 7 Oct. 42; *Ens. & Lieut.* ᵖ 14 April 43; *Lieut. & Capt.* ᵖ 31 Mar. 48; *Capt. & Lieut.Col.* 6 Nov. 54.
14	0	1 Hon. Wm. Fred. Scarlett,[17] *Cornet,* ᵖ 14 April 46; *Ens. & Lieut.* ᵖ 12 June 46; *Lieut. & Capt.* ᵖ 23 Nov. 49; *Brev.Maj.* 12 Dec. 54; *Capt. & Lieut.Col.* ᵖ 24 April 55.
14	0	1 Augustus Wm. Henry Meyrick,[19] *Ens. & Lt.* ᵖ 8 Sept. 46; *Lt. & Capt.* ᵖ 22 Feb. 50; *Capt. & Lt.-Col.* ᵖ 22 June 55.
15	0	2 William Aitchison,[18] *Ensign,* ᵖ 21 Mar. 45; *Ens. & Lt.* ᵖ 2 Oct. 46; *Lt. & Capt.* ᵖ 24 May 50; *Capt. & Lt.-Col.* ᵖ 25 Mar. 56.
19	0	2 Edward Neville,[19] *Ens.* 1 June 41; *Lt.* ᵖ 29 Sept. 43; *Capt.* 30 Sept. 50; *Brev.Maj.* 12 Dec. 54; *Capt. & Lt.Col.* ᵖ 28 Nov. 56.
11	0	1 Reginald Gipps,[2b] *Ens. & Lieut.* ᵖ 10 April 49; *Lieut. & Capt.* 20 June 54; *Brev.-Maj.* 6 June 56; *Capt. & Lt.-Col.* ᵖ 2 Feb. 58.
14	0	2 Hon. Wenman Clarence Walpole Coke,[23] *Ens.* ᵖ 31 July 46; *Ens. & Lieut.* ᵖ 7 April 48; *Lieut. & Capt.* ᵖ 25 Mar. 53; *Bt. Major*, 2 Nov. 55; *Capt. & Lt.Col.* 14 June 58.
11	0	2 Francis Baring,[26] *Ens. & Lieut.* ᵖ 6 July 49; *Lieut. & Capt.* 14 July 54; *Bt. Major*, 2 Nov. 55; *Capt. & Lt.Col.* ᵖ 13 Aug. 58.
10	0	1 Henry Charles Fletcher, *Ens. & Lieut.* ᵖ 8 Nov. 50; *Lieut. & Capt.* ᵖ 3 Nov. 54; *Capt. & Lt.Col.* ᵖ 24 June 59.
7	0	1 James Ross Farquharson,[37] *Ens. & Lieut.* ᵖ 25 Mar. 53; *Lieut. & Capt.* ᵖ 26 Dec. 54; *Capt. & Lt.Col.* ᵖ 16 Aug. 59.
11	0	1 Raymond Herbert White, *Ens.* 10 Apr. 49; *Ens. & Lieut.* ᵖ 13 Apr. 52; *Lt. & Capt.* 20 Dec. 54; *Capt. & Lt.Col.* ᵖ 16 Sept. 59.
7	0	2 Francis Lambton,[21] *Ens.* ᵖ 22 Apr. 53; *Ens. & Lieut.* ᵖ 28 Oct. 53; *Lieut. & Capt.* ᵖ 22 June 55; *Capt. & Lt.Col.* ᵖ 4 Nov. 59.
13	0	1 William Mure,[32] 2nd *Lieut.* ᵖ 22 Oct. 47; *Ens. & Lieut.* ᵖ 11 July 51; *Lieut. & Capt.* 29 Dec. 54; *Capt. & Lt.Col.* ᵖ 16 Dec. 59.

		LIEUTENANTS AND CAPTAINS.	CORNET, 2D LIEUT. OR ENSIGN.	ENSIGN AND LIEUT.	LIEUT. AND CAPTAIN.
11	0	1 Hon. Roger Mostyn	....	ᵖ 23 Mar. 40	ᵖ 17 Feb. 54
8	0	1 George Grant Gordon,[41] *Adj.*	....	13 Feb. 52	20 Dec. 54
9	0	2 Hon. Hugh Annesley[31]	ᵖ 18 Apr. 51	29 July 53	7 Aug. 55
7	0	2 Archibald Campbell Campbell[37]† ..	ᵖ 24 June 53	ᵖ 17 Mar. 54	ᵖ 14 Aug. 55
6	0	1 Charles George Tottenham[19]	....	ᵖ 13 Jan. 54	8 Sept. 55
6	0	1 Hon. Charles Rowley Hay[39]	....	ᵖ 14 Apr. 54	15 Jan. 56
6	0	2 George Hay Moncrieff,[39] *Adj.*	6 June 54	ᵖ 4 Aug. 54	ᵖ 15 Jan. 56
14	1	2 David Hunter Blair	ᵖ 4 April 45	ᵖ 12 Nov. 47	ᵖ 5 Jan. 55
8	0	2 William John Rous[36]	ᵖ 11 June 52	ᵖ 25 Aug. 54	23 Oct. 55
6	0	2 Edward Marcus Beresford[40]	ᵖ 23 Aug. 54	3 Nov. 54	ᵖ 29 Apr. 56
12	0	1 Cecil Lennox Peel	ᵖ 1 Aug. 48	ᵖ 23 July 52	22 Aug. 55
6	0	1 Henry Jelf Sharp	....	22 Dec. 54	ᵖ 16 June 57
6	0	2 John Paynter	....	26 Dec. 54	ᵖ 25 Sept. 57
5	0	1 George Williams Knox	....	10 Jan. 55	ᵖ 25 Sept. 57

Scots Fusilier Guards.

Years' Serv. Full Pay	Years' Serv. Half Pay	LIEUTENANTS AND CAPTAINS.	CORNET, 2D LIEUT. OR ENSIGN.	ENSIGN AND LIEUT.	LIEUT. AND CAPTAIN.
5	0	1 Hon. Rodolph Trefusis		p 9 Feb. 55	p 2 Feb. 58
6	0	1 Godfrey Wentworth Beaumont[33] ..	p 17 Mar. 54	8 Dec. 54	p 5 Mar. 58
7	0	2 Richard Augustus Cooper[36]	p 8 July 53	21 Sept. 54	17 Nov. 57
6	0	1 Henry David Erskine	p 20 Oct. 54	p 26 Jan. 55	11 Feb. 59
5	0	2 Willoughby Sandilands Rooke		1 May 55	p 18 Mar. 59
5	0	2 Charles Shelley...............		p 6 July 55	p 24 June 59
5	0	2 John Fred. Buller Elphinstone		p 17 Aug. 55	p 16 Aug. 59
5	0	1 Frederick Palmer...............		21 Sept. 55	p 16 Aug. 59
5	0	1 Hon. Lionel Edward Massey	2 Sept. 55	26 Oct. 55	p 16 Aug. 59
5	0	1 Christopher Peach Pemberton		p 21 Dec. 55	p 16 Sept. 59
5	0	2 Henry George Bowden	7 Sept. 55	15 Jan. 56	p 4 Nov. 59
4	0	2 James Edward Ford		p 15 Jan. 56	p 10 Dec. 59
		ENSIGNS AND LIEUTENANTS.			
5	0	1 Sussex Vane Stephenson		2 Mar. 55	
4	0	2 Charles William White		p 15 Apr. 56	
4	0	1 Windsor Charles Cary Elwes		p 2 May 56	
4	0	1 Henry Hardinge Denne Stracey ..		p 28 Nov. 56	
3	0	1 Robert Augustus Dalzell		p 20 Mar. 57	
3	0	1 Robert Alfred Cunliffe		p 25 Sept. 57	
3	0	1 Gerard Smith		p 26 Sept. 57	
2	0	1 Archibald Alexander Speirs		p 2 Feb. 58	
2	0	1 Francis W. Garden Campbell		p 5 Mar. 58	
1	0	2 Stephen James Ram		p 18 Mar. 59	
2	0	2 Hon. Henry Thomas Fraser........	p 10 Sept. 58	p 24 June 59	
1	0	2 Henry Farquharson............		19 July 59	
1	0	2 Hon. Charles John Shore		p 16 Aug. 59	
1	0	2 Joseph Henry Watkins Thomas....		p 17 Aug. 59	
1	0	2 John J. H. H. Marq. of Tullibardine		p 16 Sept. 59	
1	0	2 Fred. St. John Newdigate Barne ..		p 4 Nov. 59	
8	0	Adjutants.—1 Captain George Grant Gordon,[41] 30 April 58.			
6	0	2 Captain G. H. Moncrieff,[39] 16 Sept. 59.			
5	0	Instructors of Musketry.—2 Captain H. G. Bowden, 1 April 57.			
5	0	1 Lieut. Sussex Vane Stephenson, 26 Oct. 57.			
7	0	Quarter-Masters.—1 George Allen,[41] 8 July 53.			
4	0	2 William Smith, 5 Sept. 56. [A.S. 8 Feb. 42.			
18	0	Surgeon-Major.—2 John Ashton Bostock,[34] M.D. 20 Mar. 57; Surg. 17 Feb. 54;			
13	0	Battalion-Surgeon.—1 Fred. Robinson,[41] M.D. 20 March 57; A.-S. 19 Nov. 47.			
7	0	Assistant-Surgeons.—2 Arthur Guy Elkington,[35] 11 Mar. 53.			
6	0	1 Francis Bramley Baker, 3 Mar. 54.			
6	0	2 Henry Turner,[42] 19 May 54.			
5	0	1 George Perry,[43] 29 Jan. 55.			

*Solicitor.—*Frederick Ouvry, 9 Nov. 58. *Facings* Blue.—*Agents,* Messrs. Cox & Co.
[1st Battalion returned from the Crimea, June 1856.]
[2nd Battalion embarked for the Netherlands, Nov. 1813, and returned from France, Jan. 1816. Served in Portugal from Dec. 1826 to March 1828.]

1 The Duke of Cambridge commanded the 1st Division of the Eastern Army throughout the campaign of 1854, including the battles of the Alma, Balaklava, and Inkerman (horse shot), and siege of Sebastopol (Medal and four Clasps).

2 Colonel Walker landed in the Crimea on the 22nd Sept. 1854, and commanded the Scots Fusilier Guards in the subsequent campaign, including the battles of Balaklava and Inkerman (received three wounds, one severe, and had his horse shot under him), siege of Sebastopol (wounded), and repulse of the sortie 26th Oct. (Medal and Clasps, CB., Officer of the Legion of Honor, Sardinian Medal, and 3rd Class of the Medjidie.

3 Colonel Ridley served the Eastern campaign of 1854, including the battles of Alma (horse shot), Balaklava, and Inkerman, siege of Sebastopol, and sortie on the 26th Oct. (Medal and Clasps, and 5th Class of the Medjidie.)

4 Colonel Seymour served the Eastern campaign of 1854-55, including the battles of Alma, Balaklava and Inkerman (wounded), siege of Sebastopol (severely wounded), and sortie on the 26th Oct. (Medal and Clasps, Officer of the Legion of Honor, and 4th Class of the Medjidie).

7 Colonel Dalrymple served in the Eastern campaign of 1854, including the battles of Alma (wounded) and Inkerman, and siege of Sebastopol (Medal and Clasps, and 5th Class of the Medjidie).

8 Colonels de Bathe and Lord Adolphus Tempest served in the Crimea from Nov. 1854, and were present at the siege and fall of Sebastopol (Medal and Clasp, and 5th Class of the Medjidie).

10 Lieut.-Colonel Meyrick and Captain Tottenham, served in the Crimea from Nov. 1854, and were present at the siege and fall of Sebastopol (Medal and Clasp, and 5th Class of the Medjidie).

11 Lieut.-Colonel Stephenson served in the Eastern campaign of 1854-55, including the battles of Alma, Balaklava, and Inkerman, siege of Sebastopol and sortie on the 26th Oct. (Medal and Clasps, Knight of the Legion of Honor, and 4th Class of the Medjidie).

12 Lieut.-Colonel Hepburn served in the Eastern campaign of 1854-55, including the battle of Alma (severely wounded), siege and fall of Sebastopol (Medal and Clasps, and 5th Class of the Medjidie).

15 Lieut.Colonel Haygarth served in the Eastern campaign of 1854, including the battle of Alma (severely wounded, shot through shoulder and thigh): Medal and Clasp, and 5th Class of the Medjidie.
16 Lieut.Colonel Hon. J. S. Jocelyn served in the Eastern campaign of 1854-55, including the battles of Alma, Balaklava, and Inkerman, siege of Sebastopol and sortie on 26th Oct.(Medal and Clasps, Knight of the Legion of Honor, and 5th Class of the Medjidie).
17. Lt.Colonel Hon. W. F. Scarlett served in the Eastern campaign of 1854-55, including the battles of Alma, Inkerman, and Balaklava, siege of Sebastopol and sortie on the 26th Oct.; was appointed extra Aide de Camp to Major General Sir James Yorke Scarlett on 3rd Nov. 1854, and rejoined his Regt. 1st April 1855 (Medal and Clasps, and 5th Class of the Medjidie).
18 Lieut.Colonel Aitchison served with the 1st Batt. 91st Regt. at the Cape of Good Hope from Dec. 1845 to March 1847; engaged in a severe affair with the Caffres 22nd May 1846, when his horse was shot under him (Medal).
19 Lieut.Colonel Neville served in the Eastern campaign of 1854-55 as Aide-de-Camp to Sir Richard England, including the battles of Alma, Balaklava, and Inkerman, and siege of Sebastopol (Medal and Clasps, Knight of the Legion of Honor, and 5th Class of the Medjidie).
21 Lt.Colonel Lambton served from Nov. 1854 at the siege and fall of Sebastopol (Medal and Clasp).
23 Lt.Colonel Hon. W. Coke served the Eastern campaign of 1854-55, including the siege of Sebastopol (wounded): Medal and Clasp, Brevet Major, Sardinian Medal, and 5th Class of the Medjidie.
25 Lt.Colonel Gipps served the Eastern campaign of 1854, including the battles of Alma (wounded, bayonet wound of hand), Balaklava, and Inkerman (severely wounded, shot through neck), siege of Sebastopol and sortie on the 26th Oct. (Medal and Clasps, Brevet Major, Knight of the Legion of Honor, and 5th Class of the Medjidie).
26 Lt.Col. Baring served the Eastern campaign of 1854-55, including the battles of Alma, Balaklava, and Inkerman (wounded), siege of Sebastopol and sortie on the 26th Oct., wounded by grape-shot at the siege (Medal and Clasps, Brevet Major, Knight of the Legion of Honor, and 5th Class of the Medjidie).
31 Capt. Hon. H. Annesley served with the 43rd Light Infantry in the Kaffir war of 1851-2-3 (Medal), and was severely wounded. Served with the Scots Fusilier Guards in the Eastern campaign of 1854, including the battle of Alma (severely wounded): Medal and Clasps.
32 Lt.Colonel Mure served with the 60th Rifles in the Kaffir war of 1851-53 (Medal); and the Eastern campaign with the 79th Regt., including the battles of Alma and Balaklava (Medal and Clasps).
33 Captain Beaumont served the Eastern campaign of 1854 with the 21st Fusiliers, including the battles of Alma, Balaklava, and Inkerman, and siege of Sebastopol (Medal and Clasps).
34 Doctor Bostock served in the Buffs at the battle of Punniar (Medal). Served in the Eastern campaign of 1854-55 with the Scots Fusilier Guards, including the battles of Alma, Balaklava, and Inkerman, siege of Sebastopol and sortie on the 26th Oct. (Medal and Clasps, and Knight of the Legion of Honor).
35 Assistant Surgeon Elkington served the Eastern campaign of 1854-55, including the battles of Balaklava and Inkerman (wounded), siege of Sebastopol, and sortie on the 26th Oct.(Medal and Clasps, and 5th Class of the Medjidie).
36 Captain Cooper served with the 93rd Highlanders throughout the Eastern campaign of 1854-55, including the battles of Alma and Balaklava, siege and fall of Sebastopol (Medal and three Clasps, Sardinian Medal, and 5th Class of the Medjidie).
37 Captain Farquharson joined the Battalion in the Crimea in the winter of 1854-55, and was at the siege of Sebastopol (severely wounded): Medal and Clasp, and 5th Class of the Medjidie.
37† Captain Campbell joined the Battalion in the Crimea in the winter of 1854-55 and was at the siege of Sebastopol—wounded (Medal and Clasp).
38 Captain Rous served with the 90th Light Infantry at the siege and fall of Sebastopol and was wounded at the assault of the Redan on the 8th Sept. (Medal and Clasp).
39 Captains Hay and Moncrieff served in the Crimea from May 1855, and were at the siege of Sebastopol (Medal and Clasp).
40 Captain Beresford joined the Battalion in the Crimea early in Sept. 1855, and was at the siege and fall of Sebastopol (Medal and Clasp).
41 Capt. Gordon, Doctor Robinson, and Quartermaster Allen served throughout the Eastern campaign of 1854-55, including the battles of Alma, Balaklava, and Inkerman, siege and fall of Sebastopol, and sortie of 26th Oct. (Medal and Clasps, and 5th Class of the Medjidie).
42 Assist.Surgeon Turner served in the Crimea from Dec. 1854, including the siege of Sebastopol (Medal and Clasp).
43 Assist.Surgeon Perry served in the Crimea from June 1855, including the siege of Sebastopol (Medal and Clasp).

1st Batt. Secunderabad.⎤
2nd Batt. China.   ⎦ **1st (*The Royal*) Regiment of Foot.**   169

The *King's Cypher* within the Collar of *St. Andrew*, and the *Crown* over it. In the second colour the *Thistle & Crown*.—"ST. LUCIA" "EGMONT-OP-ZEE." *The Sphinx*, "EGYPT" "CORUNNA" "BUSACO" "SALAMANCA" "VITTORIA" "ST. SEBASTIAN" "NIVE" "PENINSULA" "NIAGARA" "WATERLOO" "NAGPORE" "MAHEIDPOOR" "AVA" "ALMA" "INKERMAN" "SEVASTOPOL."

Years' Serv.		
66		*Colonel.*—10 *Right Hon.* Sir Edward Blakeney,[1] GCB. GCH. *Cornet*, 28 Feb. 1794; *Lt.* 24 Sept. 94; *Capt.* 24 Dec. 94; *Maj.* 17 Sept. 1801; *Lt.Col.* 25 April 08; *Col.* 4 June 14; *Maj.Gen.* 27 May 25; *Lt.Gen.* 28 June 38; *Gen.* 20 June 54; *Col.* 1st Foot, 21 Dec. 54.
Full Pay.	Half Pay.	
36	0	*Lt.Cols.*—1 Alexander Barry Montgomery,[2] CB. *Ens.* 25 Nov. 24; *Lt.* 30 Oct. 26; *Capt.* p 16 Aug. 33; *Maj.* p 5 Dec. 43; *Brev. Lt.Col.* 20 June 54; *Lt. Col.* 9 March 55; *Col.* 13 Jan. 58.
23	0	2 Edmund Haythorne,[3] *Ens.* 12 May 37; *Lt.* p 4 Oct. 39; *Capt.* 11 Sept. 44; *Brev. Major,* 7 June 49; *Major,* p 1 April 53; *Lt.Col.* p 12 May 54; *Col.* 28 Nov. 54.
29	8/12	1 Alex. Essex F. Holcombe,[3]† *Ens.* p 3 Dec. 30; *Lieut.* 12 Sept. 34; *Capt.* 22 July 42; *Major,* p 9 Aug. 50; *Lt.-Col.* 26 June 55.
40	0	*Majors.*—1 Burton Daveney,[4] *Ens.* 27 April 20; *Lieut.* p 7 July 25; *Capt.* p 8 Nov. 27; *Brev. Maj.* 23 Nov. 41; *Brev. Lt.Col.* 11 Nov. 51; *Major,* 10 Mar. 53; *Col.* 28 Nov. 54.
27	0	1 *Hon.* Cha. Dawson Plunkett,[5] *Ens.* p 11 Oct. 33; *Lieut.* p 10 Mar. 37; *Capt.* p 29 Dec. 43; *Brev.-Maj.* 20 June 54; *Major,* p 2 March 55; *Brev. Lieut. Col.* 2 Nov. 55.
29	0	2 Francis Gregor Urquhart,[6] *Ens.* p 18 Nov. 31; *Lieut.* p 16 Aug. 33; *Capt.* p 14 April 37; *Brev. Major,* 11 Nov. 51; *Major,* 26 June 55; *Brev. Lt. Col.* 2 Nov. 55.
27	0	2 Frederick R. Mein,[7] *Ens.* 22 Oct. 33; *Lt.* p 14 April 37; *Capt.* p 3 May 44; *Brev. Major,* 7 Sept. 55; *Major,* p 30 March 58.

		CAPTAINS.	ENSIGN.	LIEUT.	CAPTAIN.	BREV.-MAJ.
24	0	2 James Pollock Gore[8]	p 6 Feb. 36	p 20 Dec. 39	p 29 Oct. 47	6 June 56
14	2 3/12	2 Spencer Peel............	p 5 July 44	14 April 46	p 11 July 51	
16	0	1 Richard George Coles[9] ..	p 3 May 44	p 14 May 47	p 8 Sept. 54	
19	0	1 Frederick Wells[10]........	12 Oct. 41	2 Aug. 44	6 Nov. 54	2 Nov. 55
15	0	2 George Taaffe[11].........	p 19 Dec. 45	p 3 Sept. 47	29 Dec. 54	
15	0	2 Henry Francis Bythesea..	p 26 Sept. 45	p 2 Feb. 49	29 Dec. 54	
14	0	2 George Rowland........	p 30 Nov. 46	p 15 Nov. 50	29 Dec. 54	
13	0	1 John Alexander Chrystie[12]	p 2 July 47	20 July 51	p 12 Jan. 55	
11	0	2 E.T.St.LawrenceMccGwire	p 19 Oct. 49	p 21 May 52	p 19 Jan. 55	
11	0	1 Frederick Augustus Smith[13]	p 1 June 49	p 30 Aug. 52	p 30 Mar. 55	
10	0	2 MontaguAdamHen.Loggo[14]	p 15 Mar. 50	p 19 Mar. 53	17 June 55	
10	0	1 Wm. Fred. John Rudd[15]..	p 22 Nov. 50	p 27 May 53	25 June 55	
8	0	2 Richard L. Williams[16]....	p 14 May 52	6 June 54	p 15 May 57	
9	0	1 Fred. Harry Hope[15]......	p 16 Sept. 51	6 June 54	30 July 57	
6	1 1/12	2 Morgan James O'Connell[17]	p 27 May 53	8 Dec. 54	p 6 Sept. 55	
9	0	1 Fred. Pritzler Muller[18] ..	17 June 51	6 June 54	16 Mar. 58	
8	0	2 Edward Andrew Stuart[19] .	p 21 May 52	11 Aug. 54	30 Mar. 58	
7	0	1 Henry George White[20] ..	30 Dec. 53	29 Dec. 54	p 30 Mar. 58	
6	0	2 Rowland L.SidneyCurtois[11]	p 10 Mar. 54	29 Dec. 54	p 30 Mar. 58	
15	0	1 William Newcomen Watts	p 9 Dec. 45	21 Mar. 48	21 Sept. 55	
6	0	1 Sherlock Vignolles Willis[21]	p 9 June 54	12 Jan. 55	p 29 Oct. 58	
7	0	2 Richd. Abraham Manners[22]	12 May 53	p 18 Aug. 54	26 June 59	
6	0	1 Adolph. Halk. Versturme[23]	p 10 Feb. 54	12 Jan. 55	p 29 July 59	
7	0	1 Fred. J. Ponsonby Hill ..	13 May 53	12 Jan. 55	p 13 Dec. 59	
		LIEUTENANTS.				
8	0	2 Alexander W. Low[23]†	p 14 Sept. 52	6 Nov. 54		
7	0	1 James William Hassell[24]..	p 13 Sept. 53	8 Dec. 54		
8	0	1 Albert Seagrim[21]	p 12 Mar. 52	12 Jan. 55		
6	0	1 Duncan Cameron Brock[25].	14 July 54	12 Jan. 55		
6	0	1 James Creagh[26]	21 June 54	12 Jan. 55		
6	0	1 Joseph Hodgson Fawcett ..	p 4 Aug. 54	12 Jan. 55		
6	0	1 William Freeborn[11]	10 Aug. 54	1 May 55		
6	0	1 John James Heywood[27]*Adj.*	p 17 Aug. 54	14 May 55		
6	0	1 John Archibald Cumming..	p 25 Aug. 54	15 May 55		
5	0	2 *Hon.*T.O.WestenraPlunkett[16]	5 Jan. 55	15 May 55		
5	0	1 George Deane	25 Jan. 55	15 May 55		
5	0	1 John Heron Maxwell-Heron	26 Jan. 55	15 May 55		
5	0	2 William George Brown	9 Feb. 55	8 June 55		
5	0	2 George William Thompson	16 Feb. 55	17 June 55		
5	0	2 George Gilbert Stewart	20 Feb. 55	25 June 55		
5	0	2 Charles Boyes Steer	p 30 Mar. 55	26 June 55		
5	0	2 John Parker Gillmore.....	30 Mar. 55	17 Aug. 55		
5	0	2 Thomas Henry Townshend	10 Apr. 55	11 Sept. 55		

† E

170 1st (The Royal) Regiment of Foot.

Years' Serv. Full Pay.	Half Pay.		ENSIGN.	LIEUT.	
5	0	LIEUTENANTS. 2 St. George Gray	25 May 55	p 26 Oct. 55	3† Lt.-Col. Holcombe served with the 13th Lt. Inf. throughout the campaigns in Affghanistan from 1838 to 1842 inclusive, and commanded the rearguard of the 13th at the passage of the Kojak Pass on the 14th April 1839, when he repulsed the attacks of the enemy on the baggage of the army, and recaptured considerable public property; accompanied the Expedition to Girishk, and was present at the storm and capture of Ghuznee (Medal), assault and capture of the town and forts of Tootumdurrah, and took with two companies of the 13th the forts on the left of the enemy's position; storm of Jhoolghur, night-attack at Baboo Koosh Ghur, destruction of Khardurrah, assault of Perwandurrah, storming of the Khoord Cabool Pass, affair of Tezeen, forcing the Jugdulluck Pass (severely wounded), reduction of the fort of Mamoo Khail, heroic defence of Jellalabad, and sorties on the 14th Nov. and 1st Dec. 1841, 11th Mar., 24th Mar., and 1st April 1842; general action and defeat of Akbar Khan before Jellalabad (Medal), storming the heights of Jugdulluck, general action of Tezeen, and recapture of Cabool (Medal); commanded four companies of the 13th, which formed part of the force which proceeded under Sir Robert Sale towards Bameean for the purpose of bringing in the Cabool captives. Served in the Crimea from 30th June 1855, and at the siege of Sebastopol (Medal and Clasp). Present at the suppression of the Sepoy mutiny at Sukkur in Scinde in 1844. Has the 5th Class of the Medjidie. [12 Sept. 46.
5	0	2 Richard Llewelyn Roberts	11 May 55	20 Jan. 56	
5	0	2 Alexander Bruce Tulloch ..	23 May 55	30 July 57	
5	0	1 Charles Atkinson Logan ..	4 July 55	p 30 July 58	
5	0	1 William John Shanly	13 July 55	p 30 July 58	
4	0	2 Lloyd Evans	p 25 Jan. 56	p 18 Mar. 59	
5	0	2 Henry George Thomson ..	20 July 55	1 May 59	
5	0	1 John Richard Wheeler....	2 Oct. 55	26 June 59	
4	0	2 John Richard Palliser	1 Mar. 56	p 23 Aug. 59	
4	0	1 Alfred Bloomfield	p 7 Mar. 56	p 23 Aug. 59	
5	0	2 Arthur Trefusis Jones	21 June 55	26 Feb. 56	
5	0	ENSIGNS. 1 Wm. Mauger Davey	p 23 Nov. 55		
5	0	1 Thomas Arthur Mills	29 Feb. 56		
4	0	1 John Stansfeld	4 Apr. 56		
4	0	2 Emanuel Teale, Adj	18 Apr. 56		
3	0	2 Cresswell Keane Cha. Rooke	p 20 Mar. 57		
3	0	2 Fergus Farrell	p 22 May 57		
3	0	1 Alfred Moberly	11 Dec. 57		
2	0	2 Robert Cosens	p 12 Feb. 58		
2	0	1 Percy Bingham Schreiber	6 Aug. 58		
2	0	1 William Stewart Thorburn	p 24 Aug. 58		
2	0	1 Nathaniel Stevenson......	p 25 Aug. 58		
2	0	2 Artemas Thomas Aglen....	p 29 Oct. 58		
2	0	1 Thomas Atkinson	30 Oct. 58		
1	0	2 Edward Croker Frings	11 Mar. 59		
1	0	2 Hercules Akerman	13 May 59		
1	0	2 Henry Sedley Bainbridge ..	p 31 May 59		
1	0	2 Luke Frederic Scott	p 9 Sept. 59		
1	0	1 John Hammond	10 Sept. 59		
18	0	*Paymasters.* 2 Wm. John Bampfield,¹¹ 30 June 48; *Ens.* 18 Mar. 42; *Lieut.* 1 James Deacon,³⁰ 9 Oct. 55; *Ens.* 9 Aug. 54; *Lt.* 6 April 55.			
6	0				
4	0	*Adjutants.* 2 *Ensign* Emanuel Teale, 18 April 56.			
6	0	1 *Lieut.* John James Heywood, 20 Apr. 58.			
3	0	*Instructors of Musketry.*—1 *Ensign* Alfred Moberly, 15 June 59.			
2	0	2 *Ensign* A. T. Aglen, 25 Aug. 59.			
14	0	*Quarter-Masters.*—1 Joseph M'Gee,³¹ 8 Sept. 46.			
1	0	2 James Moore, 1 July 59.			
18	0	*Surgeons.*—1 Charles Bush Hearn,³² 16 Nov. 49; *Assist.-Surg.* 15 April 42.			
9	0	2 Charles Wm. Woodroffe, M.D. 26 June 58; *Assist.Surg.* 21 [March 51.			
7	0	*Assistant-Surgeons.* 2 Thomas Knox Birnie,³³ 7 Jan. 53.			
6	0	1 Robert Atkinson,³³ 5 May 54.			
6	0	2 Angus John Mackay,³⁹ M.D. 27 Oct. 54.			
6	0	1 John Wild Hulseberg,³⁴ 14 Dec. 54.			
2	0	1 Mathew Lawrence White, 22 Sept. 58.			
2	0	2 William White, 22 June 58.			

Facings Blue—Agents, Messrs. Cox & Co.

[1st Battalion returned from the Crimea, 3 July 1856. Embarked for India, 28 July 1857. Depot at Colchester.]
[2nd Batt. Foreign Service, 31 Jan. 1853. Depot at Birr.]

1 Sir Edward Blakeney accompanied the expedition under Major-Gen. White to the West Indies, and was present at the capture of Demerara, Berbice, and Essequibo, in 1796: In the course of this service he was three times taken prisoner by Privateers and suffered severe hardships. In 1799 he accompanied the expedition to Holland, and was present in the actions of the 10th and 19th Sept., and also in those of the 2nd and 6th October. In 1807 he sailed with the Royal Fusiliers to the Baltic; joined Lord Cathcart's expedition, and was present at the capture of the Danish Fleet and surrender of Copenhagen. In 1809 he was present at the capture of Martinique. In 1811 he sailed for Lisbon in command of the Fusiliers, and during that and the following campaigns of 1812, 13, and 14, he was present at the battles of Busaco and Albuhera— severely wounded through the thigh; action at Aldea de Ponte, sieges of Ciudad Rodrigo and Badajoz— severely wounded through the arm at the assault; battles of Vittoria, Pampeluna, Pyrenees, and Nivelle, besides various minor actions. In 1814 he joined the force against New Orleans, and was present at the assault of the lines before that place. In 1815 he joined the army in Belgium, and was present at the capture of Paris. Sir Edward has received the Gold Cross and one Clasp for Martinique, Albuhera, Badajoz, Vittoria, and Pyrenees; and the Silver War Medal with four Clasps for Busaco, Ciudad Rodrigo, Nivelle, and Nive; and is a Knight of the Tower and Sword of Portugal.

2 Colonel Montgomery served in Ava (Medal); also the Eastern campaign of 1854, and up to the 29rd August 1855, including the battles of Alma and Inkerman, and siege of Sebastopol (Medal and three Clasps, Sardinian Medal, and 4th Class of the Medjidie).

3 Colonel Haythorne served with the 98th Regt. on the China expedition in 1842 (Medal), and was present at the attack and capture of Chin Kiang Foo, and at the investment of Nankin. He served as Aide-de-Camp to Sir Colin Campbell in the Punjaub campaign of 1848-9, and was present at the battles of Sadoolapore, Chillianwallah, and Goojerat, and at the subsequent occupation of Peshawur (Medal). He commanded the Flank

1st (*The Royal*) Regiment of Foot. 171

Companies of the 98th on the expedition to the Kohat Pass with Sir Charles Napier, the Commander-in-Chief. Served with the 1st Batt. Royal Regt. from 29th August 1855, and at the siege and fall of Sebastopol (Medal and Clasp, and 5th Class of the Medjidie).

4 Colonel Daveney served in the Eastern campaign of 1854, including the battles of Alma and Balaklava, and siege of Sebastopol (Medal and three Clasps, and 5th Class of the Medjidie).

5 Lt.-Col. Hon. C. D. Plunkett served in Canada during the Rebellion of 1837-38. Also the Eastern campaign of 1854-55, including the battles of Alma and Inkerman, siege and fall of Sebastopol (Medal and Clasps, Brevet Lt.-Colonel, Knight of the Legion of Honor, Sardinian Medal, and 5th Class of the Medjidie).

6 Lt.-Colonel Urquhart landed in the Crimea with the 2nd Batt. on the 22nd April 1855, and was at the siege and fall of Sebastopol (Medal and Clasp, Brevet Lt.-Colonel, Sardinian Medal, and 5th Class of the Medjidie).

7 Major Mein served the Eastern campaign of 1854, and up to the 3rd May 1855, including the battles of Alma and Balaklava, and siege of Sebastopol (Medal and three Clasps, and 5th Class of the Medjidie).

8 Major Gore served with the 2nd Batt. in Canada during the rebellion in 1837-38, including the storm and capture of St. Charles and St. Eustache, and ulterior operations on the Richelieu and adjacent country. Was with the right wing on board the *Premier* when that transport was wrecked, in Nov. 1843, in the Gulf of St. Lawrence. Landed with the Battalion in the Crimea on the 22nd April 1855, and was at the siege and fall of Sebastopol, and wounded in the trenches on 6th July (Medal and Clasp).

9 Captain Coles served the Eastern campaign of 1854, and up to 5th Feb. 1855, including the battles of Alma and Inkerman, and siege of Sebastopol (Medal and three Clasps).

10 Major Wells served the Eastern campaign of 1854-55, including the battles of Alma and Inkerman, siege and fall of Sebastopol (Medal and three Clasps, Brevet Major, Knight of the Legion of Honor, and 5th Class of the Medjidie).

11 Captains Taaffe and Curtois, and Lt. Freeborn, and Paymaster Bampfield, landed in the Crimea with the 2nd Batt. on the 22nd April 1855, and were at the siege and fall of Sebastopol (Medal and Clasp). Lieut. Freeborn has the 5th Class of the Medjidie.

12 Captain Chrystie served the Eastern campaign of 1854-55, including the battles of Alma and Inkerman, siege and fall of Sebastopol (Medal and three Clasps, and 5th Class of the Medjidie).

13 Captain Smith served the Eastern campaign of 1854, and up to 2nd July 1855, including the battles of Alma and Inkerman, and siege of Sebastopol (Medal and three Clasps).

14 Captain Legge served at the siege of Sebastopol from 22nd April until wounded at the attack on the Quarries 8th June 1855 (Medal and Clasp).

15 Captains Rudd and Hope served the Eastern campaign of 1854-55, including the battles of Alma and Inkerman, and siege and fall of Sebastopol (Medal and Clasps, Sardinian Medal, and 5th Class of the Medjidie).

16 Captain Williams and Lieut. Hon. T. O. Plunkett served at the siege of Sebastopol from 29th Aug. 1855, and were wounded on 8th Sept. (Medal and Clasp).

17 Captain O'Connell served at the siege and fall of Sebastopol from 21st Nov. 1854 (Medal and Clasp, and 5th Class of the Medjidie).

18 Captain Muller served in the Eastern campaign of 1854-55, including the siege and fall of Sebastopol, from 15th April 1855 (Medal and Clasp).

19 Captain Stuart served at the siege of Sebastopol from 22nd April until severely wounded on 7th June 1855 (Medal and Clasp, and 5th Class of the Medjidie).

20 Captain White served at the siege of Sebastopol from 21st Nov. 1854 to 10th Aug. 1855 (Medal and Clasp).

21 Captain Willis served at the siege and fall of Sebastopol from 9th Dec. 1854 (Medal and Clasp, and 5th Class of the Medjidie).

22 Captain Manners served in the Eastern campaign of 1854-55, including the siege and fall of Sebastopol from 6th Jan. 1855 (Medal and Clasp, and 5th Class of the Medjidie).

23 Captain Versturme served with the 17th Regt at the siege and fall of Sebastopol from 19th May 1855 including assaults of the Redan on the 18th June and 8th Sept.; also present at the bombardment and surrender of Kinbourne (Medal and Clasp).

23† Lieut. Low served at the siege of Sebastopol from 16th June to 5th July 1855 (Medal and Clasp).

24 Lieuts. Hassell and Seagrim served at the siege and fall of Sebastopol from 20th Aug. 1855 (Medal and Clasp).

25 Lieut. Brock served at the siege and fall of Sebastopol from 23rd April 1855 (Medal and Clasp).

26 Lieut. Creagh served at the siege and fall of Sebastopol, from 27th Jan. 1855 (Medal and Clasp).

27 Lieut. Heywood served at the siege and fall of Sebastopol from 1st June 1855 (Medal and Clasp).

30 Paymaster Deacon served the Eastern campaign of 1854-55, including the battles of Balaklava and Inkerman, and siege and fall of Sebastopol (Medal and Clasps).

31 Qr.Master M'Gee served the Eastern campaign of 1854-55, including the battles of Alma and Inkerman, siege and fall of Sebastopol (Medal and Clasps).

32 Surgeon Hearn served in the Eastern campaign of 1854, and up to 20th March 1855, including the battles of Alma and Inkerman, and siege of Sebastopol (Medal and Clasps, and 5th Class of the Medjidie).

33 Assist.-Surgeons Birnie, Atkinson and Mackay served at the siege of Sebastopol in 1855 (Medal and Clasp).

34 Assist.-Surgeon Hulseberg served with the 8th Hussars the Eastern campaign of 1855, including the battle of the Tchernaya and fall of Sebastopol (Medal and Clasp).

2nd (The Queen's Royal) Regt. of Foot.

[1st Batt. Cape of Good Hope. 2nd Batt. Cephalonia.]

"The Paschal Lamb," with the mottos *"Pristinæ virtutis memor,"* and *"Vel exuviæ triumphant."* he Queen's Cypher within the Garter, having the Crown over it. On the Grenadiers' Caps, the King's Crest and the Queen's Cypher and Crown ; and on the Drums the Queen's Cypher. The Sphinx, with the words "EGYPT" "VIMIERA" "CORUNNA" "SALAMANCA" "VITTORIA" "PYRENEES" "NIVELLE" "TOULOUSE" "PENINSULA" "AFFGHANISTAN" "GHUZNEE" "KHELAT."

Years' Serv.			
54		Colonel.—John Spink,[1] KH. Ens. 2 Sept. 06; Lt. 9 March 07; Capt. 13 Oct. 12; Major, p 13 May 24; Lt.Col. p 20 May 26; Col. 23 Nov. 41; Major Gen. 11 Nov. 51; Lt.Gen. 26 Oct. 58; Col. 2nd Foot, 28 May 57.	
Full Pay	Half Pay		
30	0	Lieut.Colonels.—1 Stanhope William Jephson,[2] Ens. p 26 Nov. 30; Lt. p 10 Feb. 36; Capt. p 28 Dec. 41; Maj. p 4 Aug. 48; Lt.Col. 1 July 53; Col. 28 Nov. 54.	
22	3/12	2 Robert Bruce,[3] Ens. p 9 June 38; Lt. p 22 May 40; Capt. p 21 July 48; Bt. Maj. 28 May 53; Major, p 5 Sept. 56; Lt.Col. p 12 May 57.	
23	0	Majors.—1 Thomas Addison,[4] Ens. 15 Sept. 37; Lieut. 31 Jan. 39; Capt. p 16 Dec. 45; Bt.Maj. 28 May 53; Maj. 12 May 54; Bt.Lt.Col. 24 July 57.	
20	0	1 Demetrius Wyndham Grevis James,[5] Ens. p 31 Jan. 40; Lieut. p 15 Dec. 40; Capt. p 9 June 46; Maj. 1 Dec. 54.	
18	1	2 James Rose,[6] Ens. p 16 Nov. 41; Lt. 28 Dec. 46; Capt. p 5 Oct. 49; Bt.Maj. 12 Dec. 54; Major, 7 Sept. 55.	
20	8/12	2 Henry Reynolds Werge,[7] Ens. p 31 Dec. 39; Lt. 8 April 42; Capt. 19 Aug. 54; Bt.Major, 2 Nov. 55; Major, 19 Dec. 56.	

		CAPTAINS.	ENSIGN.	LIEUT.	CAPTAIN.	BREV.-MAJ.
19	0	1 E. S. Smyth[8] c. 23 Mar. 58	p 26 Jan. 41	29 May 43	p 4 Aug. 48	28 May 53
18	0	1 Richard Hill Rocke	7 Jan. 42	p 30 May 43	p 2 Nov. 49	
22	0	1 Frederick Connor[9]	p 29 Sept. 38	27 Jan. 40	10 Sept. 51	
13	0	1 Francis Lionel Oct. Attye[9]	1 Jan. 47	p 4 May 49	p 20 July 53	
16	0	1 George Wolfe	27 Sept. 44	3 Apr. 49	p 30 Dec. 53	
12	0	1 John Charles Weir[10]	p 9 June 48	p 2 Nov. 49	12 May 54	
11	0	1 John Thompson	p 19 Oct. 49	p 17 June 51	p 15 Jan. 56	
11	0	1 John Chalmers[11]	p 2 Mar. 49	p 17 June 51	24 Sept. 56	
8	0	1 Stanh. L. Douglas Willm[12]	p 15 Oct. 52	6 June 54	p 7 May. 56	
10	0	2 William Campbell[13]	p 12 Apr. 50	13 May 53	p 25 Jan. 56	
11	0	1 Charles Gibbs.........	p 23 Nov. 49	p 17 June 51	p 24 Oct. 56	
13	5/12	2 Robt Chas. Wm. Stuart[14]	p 22 May 46	18 July 50	12 Jan. 55	
10	5/12	2 William Charles Coghlan[17]	p 15 June 49	29 Apr. 53	13 July 55	
7	7/12	2 Nicholas Dunscombe[15] ..	p 23 Nov. 52	p 3 Feb. 54	2 Oct. 55	
9	2/12	2 Rupert George Brady[16] ..	p 17 Jan. 51	p 3 June 53	3 Nov. 55	
6	2/12	2 Francis John Hercy	p 28 Oct. 53	27 Oct. 54	p 9 Nov. 55	
5	1	2 Joseph Logan[18]	p 3 Feb. 54	8 Dec. 54	p 9 Nov. 56	
13	0	2 Robt. Henry Crampton[19]	p 5 Nov. 47	15 Aug. 50	17 Nov. 57	
12	0	2 Henry Brackenbury[21] ..	p 18 Aug. 48	25 June 50	13 Feb. 58	
9	0	2 Robert C. Thomson[9]	p 16 May 51	p 26 Mar. 52	20 Mar. 58	
9	0	2 William Henry Spencer[10]	p 18 June 51	p 8 Apr. 53	30 Mar. 58	
10	0	2 Wm. Wiltshire Lynch[22] ..	p 17 Sept. 50	p 13 Dec. 53	14 May 58	
9	0	1 William Webber Martin	p 12 July 51	p 29 July 53	p 26 Oct. 58	
8	0	1 John Cha. Tyrwhitt Drake	p 16 Apr. 52	6 June 54	p 26 Oct. 58	

		LIEUTENANTS.				
9	0	1 John Croome[23]	p 11 July 51	1 July 53		
8	0	1 George Pomeroy Colley	28 May 52	11 Aug. 54		
7	0	1 Thomas John	p 10 June 53	1 Dec. 54		
6	0	1 Henry Pye Phillipps, Adj.	12 May 54	p 15 Jan. 56		
7	0	1 Charles Squirl	p 29 July 53	24 Sept. 56		
5	0	1 Henry Hurd Mulock....	24 Apr. 55	p 24 Oct. 56		
5	0	1 Henry Grattan	15 June 55	p 6 Feb. 57		
5	0	2 James Wharton Hurrel..	15 June 55	p 5 June 57		
7	0	1 Daniel Litton Hewson ..	p 11 Oct. 53	16 June 57		
5	0	2 George Turnor	23 Feb. 55	14 Jan. 56		
5	0	2 Jas. McGellicuddy Magill	p 9 May 55	p 18 Jan. 56		
5	0	2 Charles de St. Croix	11 May 55	26 Feb. 56		
5	0	2 George Philips	6 Apr. 55	p 29 May 57		
5	0	2 DeLancy R. Anderson ..	15 June 55	p 14 July 57		
6	0	1 Henry Flood	21 July 54	17 Nov. 57		
5	0	1 Alexander Henry Haldane	20 July 55	12 Feb. 58		
5	0	1 Heber Reeve Tucker	30 Nov. 55	12 Feb. 58		
4	0	1 George F. Fra. Horwood	1 Feb. 56	12 Feb. 58		
4	0	2 John Melville Hatchell ..	26 Feb. 56	5 Mar. 58		
4	0	1 Henry Echalaz	p 24 June 56	26 Mar. 58		
4	0	1 Francis Roche Gubbins..	8 July 56	26 Mar. 58		
4	0	1 Arthur Wellesley Gosset.	p 24 Oct. 56	26 Mar. 58		
3	0	1 Henry Waring	p 5 June 57	13 Apr. 58		
4	0	2 Richard William Stokes .	27 Feb. 56	5 Oct. 58		
2	0	2 Sidney H.L.T. Widdrington	8 Jan. 58	p 11 Feb. 59		
2	0	2 Eustace Lovelace Hercy	p 5 Feb. 58	p 11 Feb. 59		
3	0	2 Frederick Squirl........	20 Nov. 57	p 31 May 59		

5 Major James served in the campaign in the Southern Mahratta country in 1844 (including the storm and capture of the fortress of Punella), and part of that in the Concan and Sawant Warree country in 1844 and 45. Also in the Kaffir war of 1851-52 (Medal), and with the expedition north of the Orange River in 1852-3.

8 Colonel Smyth served as Brigade Major to the Forces in the Southern Concan and Sawant Warree country during the campaign of 1844 and 45, including the storming of several stockades, and the investment and capture of the Forts of Monohur and Munsintosh. Served also in the Kaffir war of 1851-52 (Medal); with the expedition North of the Orange River in 1852-53, and afterwards as Deputy Assistant Quartermaster General of the 2nd Division.

17 Captain Coghlan served in the Crimea with the 50th Regt. from the 25th Aug. 1855 (Medal and Clasp for Sebastopol).

18 Captain Logan served with the 44th Regt. at the siege of Sebastopol, from 7th January to 1st July 1855, and was severely wounded at the attack on the 18th June (Medal and Clasp).

2nd (The Queen's Royal) Regiment of Foot. 173

Years' Serv.				
Full Pay.	Half Pay.	LIEUTENANTS.	ENSIGN.	LIEUT.
2	0	2 John Mackie Laurent ..	19 Feb. 58	P 18 Nov. 59
6	0	2 GilbertAlfred Nicholetts[25]	15 Dec. 54	9 Mar. 55
		ENSIGNS.		
3	0	2 Claude Scott S. Pinkerton	10 June 57	
3	0	2 Alexander Baird, *Adj.* ..	2 Oct. 57	
3	0	1 Alex.Plunk.VanHomrigh	19 Nov. 57	
2	0	1 Robert Alex. Crawford ..	20 Feb. 58	
2	0	1 Thomas Dudley Fosbroke	21 Feb. 58	
2	0	1 Thomas Kelly	22 Feb. 58	
2	0	2 Frederick Blake.........	23 Feb. 58	
2	0	2 James Campbell Stratford	5 Mar. 58	
2	0	1 Mello William Jackson..	26 Mar. 58	
2	0	1 John Fenton Boughey ..	27 Mar. 58	
2	0	2 Richard Arthur Corbet ..	28 Mar. 58	
2	0	1 Fra. Cha. Murhall Griffith	30 Mar. 58	
2	0	1 Albert Fred. Twyford ..	13 Apr. 58	
2	0	2 Edward George St. John	4 June 58	
2	0	2 Reginald Thoresby Gwyn	P 12 Nov. 58	
2	0	2 George Herbert Woodard	26 Oct. 58	
1	0	1 John Charles Grant	P 18 Mar. 59	
1	0	2 William Ward Bennitt ..	P 5 Aug. 59	
1	0	John Victor Bates........	P 15 Nov. 59	

19 Captain Crampton served with the 91st Regt. in the action with the Rebel Boers at Boem Plants, and was dangerously wounded.
21 Captain Brackenbury served in the Punjaub campaign of 1848-9 (Medal and Clasp), and was present at the battle of Goojerat, and with the field force in pursuit of the enemy to the Khyber Pass in March 1849; expedition to the Euzofzie country: in action with the enemy 11th and 14th Dec. 1849; present at the capture and destruction of the insurgent villages of Saggow, Pullee, Zoormundie, and Sheerkanee.
25 Lieut. Nicholetts served with the 68th Lt. Inf. at the siege and fall of Sebastopol from 6th Sept. 1855 (Medal and Clasp).

22	0	*Paymasters.*—1 Oliver Nicolls,[9] 25 Nov. 45; *Ens.* P 13 Jan. 38; *Lieut.* 16 [July 41.	
3	0	2 Robert Hamilton Simpson, 25 Sept. 57.	
3	0	*Adjutants.*—2 Ensign Alexander Baird, 2 Oct. 57.	
6	0	1 Lieut. Henry Pye Phillipps, 11 Jan. 59.	
5	0	*Instructors of Musketry.*—1 *Lieut.* A. H. Haldane, 6 Feb. 58.	
3	0	*Quarter Masters.*—1 William Mackie, 10 April 57.	
5	0	2 John Curran, 10 Oct. 55.	
19	0	*Surgeons.*—1 Henry Clinton Foss,[24] 17 June 51; *Assist.Surg.* 26 Feb. 41.	
10	1½	2 Daniel John Doherty, 20 July 55; *Assist.Surg.* 25 Sept. 49.	
5	0	*Assistant Surgeons.*—1 Henry Joseph Rose, 6 March 55.	
7	0	2 James Sinclair, M.D. 5 Aug. 53.	
2	0	1 Stephen Henry Marshall, 7 May 58.	
3	0	2 Henry Cole Peppin, 9 Nov. 57.	
2	0	1 Richard Beresford Carson, MB. 22 June 58.	

Facings Blue.—*Agents*, Messrs. Cox & Co.

[1st Battalion embarked for the *Cape of Good Hope,* 24 *June* 1851. *Depot, Walmer.*]
[2nd Battalion embarked for *Malta,* 12 *Feb.* 1858. *Depot, Walmer.*]

1 Lieut.General Spink served with the Light Company of the 12th Regt. in several actions in the Travancore war, East Indies. Severely wounded through the leg when leading a night attack against the enemy's position at St. Mary, in the island of Bourbon. Present also at the capture of the Isle of France, where his company armed with rifles formed the advance immediately on the disembarkation of the troops, and with which he was constantly engaged with the enemy during the three days' march on Port Louis.
2 Colonel Jephson served the campaign in Affghanistan and Beloochistan, including the storm and capture of Ghuznee (Medal) and of Khelat. He served also the campaign in the Southern Mahratta country in 1844 (including the storm of the Fortress of Punella), and that in the Concan in 1845: he commanded the storming party at the Western Heights of Punella (wounded).
3 Lt.Col. Bruce served with the 74th Highlanders throughout the Kaffir war of 1851-53 (Medal, and Brevet Major).
4 Lt.Colonel Addison served the campaign in Affghanistan and Beloochistan, including the storm and capture of Ghuznee (Medal) and of Khelat. Was employed as Major of brigade during the campaign in the Southern Mahratta country in 1844 (including the storm of Punella,—wounded), and that in the Concan in 1845. Also served in the last Kaffir war (Medal), and was severely wounded, 14 Oct. 1851, in action with the Caffres on the Waterkloof Heights: received the Brevet rank of Major at the close of the war.
6 Major Rose served with the 30th Regt. the Eastern campaign of 1854-55, including the battles of Alma and Inkerman (severely wounded), siege of Sebastopol, and sortie of 26th Oct. (Medal and Clasps, Brevet Major, and 5th Class of the Medjidie).
7 Major Werge served the Eastern campaign of 1854-55, including the battles of Alma and Inkerman, siege and fall of Sebastopol, sortie of 26th Oct., and as Brigade Major 1st Brigade, 2 nd Division, at the assault of the Redan on 8th Sept. (Medal and three Clasps, Brevet Major, and 5th Class of the Medjidie).
9 Captains Connor, Attye, and Thomson, and Paymaster Nicolls served in the Kaffir war of 1851-53 (Medal).
10 Captains Weir and Spencer served in the Kaffir war in 1852 (Medal); and with the expedition north of the Orange River in 1852-53.
11 Captain Chalmers served in the Kaffir war of 1851-52 (Medal); and with the expedition north of the Orange River in 1852-53.
12 Captain Willan landed in the Crimea with the 13th Lt. Infantry, and was present at the battle of the Tchernaya, siege and fall of Sebastopol (Medal and Clasp).
13 Captain Campbell served with the 71st Lt. Infantry in the Crimea—in the trenches at the siege and fall of Sebastopol, and on the expedition to Kertch (Medal and Clasp).
14 Captain Stuart landed in the Crimea with the 71st Regt. in 1855, and served in the trenches at the siege of Sebastopol and on the expedition to Kertch. In August he was appointed Brigade Major to the 2nd Brigade, Highland Division, and was present at the fall of Sebastopol (Medal and Clasp, and 5th Class of the Medjidie).
15 Captain Dunscombe served with the 46th Regt. at the siege of Sebastopol in 1854-55 (Medal and Clasp, and Sardinian Medal).
16 Captain Brady served with the 1st Royals at the siege and fall of Sebastopol from 1st June 1855 (Medal and Clasp).

22 Captain Lynch served in Persia with the Cavalry Division in 1857. Joined Havelock's force on its first taking the field, and was present in every action fought by that column (horse killed at Cawnpore). Served subsequently as second in command of the Volunteer Cavalry with the Oude field force, and was present in all the actions fought by that force until the relief of Lucknow on 25 Sept. 1857 (severely wounded, mentioned in Dispatches).
23 Lieut. Croome served in the Kaffir war in 1853 (Medal).
24 Surgeon Foss served with the 10th Regt. in the campaign on the Sutlej in 1846, and was present at the battle of Sobraon (Medal). Served with the Queen's Royals in the Kaffir war of 1851-52 (Medal); and with the expedition north of the Orange River in 1852-53.

[Continuation of Notes to 3rd Foot.]

16 Captain Pearson served in the Crimea from 3rd Sept. 1855, including the siege of Sebastopol and attack on the 8th Sept. (Medal and Clasp).
17 Captains Stewart and Reade served at the siege of Sebastopol in 1855, and belonged to the covering and ladder party at the assault of the Redan on the 8th Sept. 1855 (Medal and Clasp).
18 Captain Roe served at the siege of Sebastopol in 1855, and was Acting Adjutant of the Buffs at the assault of the Redan on the 8th Sept.—mentioned in Dispatches (Medal and Clasp, and Knight of the Legion of Honor).
19 Captain T. A. Cox served at the siege of Sebastopol in 1855, and was wounded at the assault of the Redan on the 8th Sept. (Medal and Clasp, and 5th Class of the Medjidie).
20 Lieut. Letts served at the siege of Sebastopol in 1855, and was dangerously wounded at the assault of the Redan on the 8th Sept. (Medal and Clasp, and 5th Class of the Medjidie).
21 Captain Newton served as Aide de Camp to Brigadier General Straubenzee at the siege of Sebastopol in 1855, and at the assault on the Redan on the 8th Sept. (Medal and Clasp).
22 Lieut. Peachey served the Eastern campaign of 1854-55 on the Army Medical Staff (Medal and Clasp).
23 Qr.Master Blisset served with the Buffs at the battle of Punniar, 29th Dec. 1843 (Medal). Also at the siege of Sebastopol in 1855, and assault of the Redan on the 8th Sept. (Medal and Clasp).
24 Surg. Burke served with the 50th Regt. throughout the campaign on the Sutlej in 1845-6, and was present at the battles of Moodkee, Ferozeshah, Aliwal, and Sobraon (Medal and three Clasps): in the two latter engagements, and to the end of the war, he was in medical charge of the Regiment. Served with the Buffs at the siege and assault of Sebastopol (Medal and Clasp).
25 Captain Eteson served with the 18th Royal Irish throughout the second Burmese war (Medal), including the capture of Martaban, Rangoon, Prome, and the Donabew stockades.
26 Captain Somerset served with the Cape Mounted Riflemen in the Kaffir war of 1847, and in that of 1850, 51, 52 (Medal).

3rd (E. Kent) Regt. of Foot (or The Buffs). 175

1st Batt. China.] 2nd Batt. Malta.

The *Dragon* "Douro" "Talavera" "Albuhera" "Pyrenees" "Nivelle" "Nive" "Peninsula" "Punniar" "Sevastopol."

Years' Serv.		
Full Pay	Half Pay	
48		Colonel.—🎖 Berkeley Drummond,¹ Ens. 5 March 12; Lt. & Capt. 4 July 15; Capt. & Lt.Col. ᵖ21 Dec. 26; Maj. & Col. 23 Nov. 41; Lt.Col. ᵖ31 Dec. 44; Maj.Gen. 11 Nov. 51; Lt.Gen. 9 Apr. 59; Col. 3rd Foot, 12 Dec. 57.
20	0	Lieut.-Colonels.—2 𝒱𝒞 Fred. Francis Maude,² CB. Ens. ᵖ13 Mar. 40; Lt. ᵖ27 Aug. 41; Capt. ᵖ10 Dec. 47; Major, 15 May 55; Brevet Lt.Col. 2 Nov. 55; Lt.Col. 14 Aug. 57.
15	0	1 George James Ambrose,³ Ens.ᵖ4 July 45; Lt. 5 Nov. 46; Capt. ᵖ12 Oct. 52; Brevet Major, 17 July 55; Major, ᵖ22 May 57; Lt.Col. ᵖ31 Dec. 57.
15	1⁰⁄₁₂	1 John Neptune Sargent,⁴ Ens. ᵖ19 Jan. 44; Lieut. ᵖ11 Sept. 46; Capt. 18 Nov. 53; Brev.Major, 2 Nov. 55; Major, 29 Feb. 56; Lt.Col. ᵖ29 July 59.
19	2	Majors.—2 John Hardman Burke,⁵ Ens. ᵖ1 Nov. 39; Lieut. ᵖ3 March 43; Capt. 6 June 54; Brev.Major, 12 Dec. 54; Major, 17 Aug. 55.
15	0	1 Henry John King, Ens. ᵖ8 Aug. 45; Lt. ᵖ23 April 47; Capt. ᵖ12 Nov. 52; Major, ᵖ31 Dec. 57.
16	0	1 Walter Pownall,⁸ Ens. ᵖ6 Dec. 44; Lieut. ᵖ18 Oct. 45; Capt. ᵖ6 Dec. 50; Major, 17 Sept. 58.
14	0	2 Fred. William Gore,⁹ Ens. ᵖ9 June 46; Lieut. ᵖ7 Apr. 48; Capt, ᵖ7 June 54; Major, ᵖ29 July 59.

		CAPTAINS.	ENSIGN.	LIEUT.	CAPTAIN.	BREV.-MAJ.
13	0	1 Rt. Sandfd. Warburton¹⁰	ᵖ 8 Oct. 47	ᵖ18 June 52	ᵖ 8 Dec. 54	
21	0	1 Thomas Kains¹¹	ᵖ29 Nov. 39	20 May 42	15 May 55	
14	0	1 Phil.H.Prender.Aplin¹⁰	21 Apr. 46	23 Sept. 51	15 May 55	
12	0	1 Penrose John Dunbar¹²	ᵖ 8 Dec. 48	ᵖ30 Jan. 52	15 May 55	
14	0	1 𝒱𝒞 Mark Walker¹³	25 Sept. 46	3 Feb. 54	15 May 55	6 June 56
13	0	1 E. K. Vaughan Arbuckle	ᵖ10 Dec. 47	ᵖ21 May 52	29 June 55	
8	0	1 William Ross Turner¹⁰	ᵖ23 Nov. 52	6 June 54	ᵖ22 May 57	
18	⁷⁄₁₂	2 Arthur Wellesley Joyce	17 Apr. 42	28 Mar. 44	3 Aug. 55	
15	⁹⁄₁₂	2 John Salmon Gordon	30 July 44	ᵖ20 Mar. 46	31 Aug. 55	
11	⁷⁄₁₂	2 Clifford Parsons	ᵖ16 Feb. 49	ᵖ10 Dec. 52	25 Sept. 55	
13	⁵⁄₁₂	2 John Otway Wemyss¹⁴	ᵖ 8 Dec. 46	ᵖ 8 June 52	31 Oct. 55	
7	⁹⁄₁₂	2 Chas. Moore B. Siree¹⁵	ᵖ18 Aug. 52	15 Sept. 54	18 Jan. 56	
7	⁷⁄₁₂	2 Chas. Knight Pearson¹⁶	ᵖ23 Nov. 52	15 June 55	ᵖ15 Feb. 56	
18	0	2 Henry Robert Cowell	15 Apr. 42	1 Mar. 44	7 Aug. 57	
8	0	2 William Jas. Newton²¹	ᵖ17 Dec. 52	ᵖ29 Sept. 54	ᵖ11 Sept. 57	
7	0	1 William Stewart¹⁷	ᵖ21 Jan. 53	ᵖ 8 Dec. 54	ᵖ16 Oct. 57	
7	0	1 George Noble Roe¹⁸	ᵖ18 Feb. 53	22 Dec. 54	ᵖ31 Dec. 57	
11	0	2 Jones Harper Reade¹⁷	10 Apr. 49	28 May 52	26 Feb. 58	
13	0	2 Francis Eteson²⁵	ᵖ 6 Aug. 47	15 Apr. 52	5 Mar. 58	
11	0	2 Hon. Geo. E. Somerset²⁶	13 Oct. 48	27 May 53	5 Mar. 58	
5	0	2 William Edmund Cater		31 Aug. 55	ᵖ25 June 58	
7	0	1 Talbot Ashley Cox¹⁹	ᵖ29 July 53	15 May 55	17 Sept. 58	
6	0	1 Henry Thomas Anley¹⁰	6 June 54	15 May 55	ᵖ10 Dec. 58	
6	0	1 Chas.JohnRoperTyler¹⁰	ᵖ25 Aug. 54	15 May 55	ᵖ16 Sept. 59	
		LIEUTENANTS.				
6	0	1 Harry A.Arth.Breedon⁸	21 July 54	*15 May 55		
6	0	1 Barnes John Caldecott⁸	ᵖ24 Aug. 54	15 May 55		
6	0	1 William Henry¹⁰	ᵖ29 Sept. 54	15 May 55		
6	0	1 George Grant Suttie¹⁰	ᵖ 8 Dec. 54	15 May 55		
6	0	2 Easton John Cox,¹⁰ s...	ᵖ 5 May 54	ᵖ 9 Feb. 55		
5	0	1 Arthur Worthington¹⁰	19 Jan. 55	1 June 55		
5	0	1 Francis Morley	13 May 55	1 Sept. 55		
5	0	2 Rd.Blackburn Leatham	14 May 55	8 Oct. 55		
5	0	2 Henry Parnell	23 May 55	9 Nov. 55		
5	0	2 Leyson Edwin Lewis	25 May 55	9 Nov. 55		
5	0	1 Alfred B. Letts,²⁰ Adj.	25 May 55	9 Nov. 55		
5	0	2 John Awdry	31 May 55	16 Nov. 55		
5	0	2 Lionel St. Aubyn	8 June 55	1 Feb. 56		
5	0	2 Charles Vercy	ᵖ25 Sept. 55	ᵖ14 Aug. 57		
5	0	1 Alfred George Huyshe	27 July 55	ᵖ11 Sept. 57		
5	0	1 Walter Aug. Daubeny	16 Nov. 55	ᵖ16 Oct. 57		
5	0	1 George Thomas Gape	ᵖ23 Nov. 55	ᵖ16 Oct. 57		
5	0	2 William Ker	29 Nov. 55	17 Nov. 57		
5	0	2 James H. Le Cocq	7 Dec. 55	ᵖ 2 Feb. 58		
5	0	2 Charles Deyman Baillie	6 Dec. 55	5 Mar. 58		
5	0	2 Albert Peachey²²	14 Dec. 55	23 Mar. 58		
4	0	2 John Cotter, Adj.	1 Feb. 56	23 Mar. 58		
4	0	2 George Edward Rundle	ᵖ26 Feb. 56	23 Mar. 58		
4	0	2 Hon.Jas.WilfridHewitt	1 Feb. 56	23 Mar. 58		
3	0	2 Robt. Burdett Morony	ᵖ30 Jan. 57	30 Mar. 58		
3	0	1 Felix Thomas Jones	ᵖ11 Sept. 57	ᵖ10 Dec. 58		

1 Lieut.General Drummond served in the 3rd Guards the campaign of 1814 in Holland, including the storming of Bergen-op-Zoom. Also the campaign of 1815, including the battles of Quatre Bras and Waterloo.

176 3rd (E. Kent) Regt. of Foot (or The Buffs).

Years' Serv.		LIEUTENANTS.	ENSIGN.	LIEUT.
Full Pay.	Half Pay.			
4	0	2 Shapland Graves	28 Feb. 56	6 July 59
3	0	1 Theophilus Jones	p 16 Oct. 57	p 16 Sept. 59
3	0	2 Fred. Taylor Hobson..	p 30 Oct. 57	p 30 Sept. 59
5	0	2 William Pitt Butts ..	19 July 55	19 Feb. 58

		ENSIGNS.		
3	0	2 John Law	p 12 May 57	
3	0	2 Robert Charles Hearn	17 Nov. 57	
3	0	1 Henry Thos. Halahan..	24 Nov. 57	
2	0	1 Dudley Geo. Cary Elwes	p 2 Feb. 58	
2	0	2 William Henry Irvine	6 Mar. 58	
2	0	1 Henry Kinahan	16 Mar. 58	
2	0	2 Charles Jas. Hamilton	17 Mar. 58	
2	0	2 James Edward Forster	18 Mar. 58	
2	0	1 William Fred. Kerr	23 Mar. 58	
2	0	1 Ernest Fred. Barnes ..	24 Mar. 58	
2	0	2 John Augustus Vivian	13 April 58	
2	0	1 Henry Harrison....	14 April 58	
2	0	2 Andrew Jackson	16 April 58	
2	0	1 Joseph Jas. B. Haydock	17 April 58	
2	0	2 Horace William Scriven	23 April 58	
2	0	1 Henry Manning[29]	15 Oct. 58	
2	0	2 John Raimond Trevilian	31 Dec. 58	

27 Doctor Barker joined the reserve Battalion 45th Regt., at Gibraltar, in March 1845, and proceeded to Monte Video, where he served in medical charge of that battalion during the siege of the city by the Argentine army, under General Oribe. He served the Kaffir campaign of 1846-7. Was present at Fort Cox with Sir Harry Smith at the outbreak of the Kaffir war in 1850, and served in medical charge of the 45th Regt. in the field during the whole of the campaign of 1851-53.
28 Paymaster Magill served with the 7th Dragoon Guards on the expedition against the insurgent Boers beyond the Orange River, Cape of Good Hope, in 1845. Also throughout the Kaffir war of 1846-47.
29 Ensign Manning was present at the battle of Punniar on 29th Dec. 1843 (Medal). Also at the siege of Sebastopol in 1855 and assault of the Redan on 8th Sept. (Medal and Clasp).

16	0	*Paymasters.*—1 Fred. Geo. Syms,[10] 25 June 47; *Ens.* 22 Mar. 44; *Lt.* 7 May 47.	
14	3⁰⁄₁₂	2 Henry Magill,[28] 18 Sept. 57; *Q. M.* 10 March 43.	
4	0	*Adjutants.*—2 *Lieut.* John Cotter, 1 Feb. 56.	
5	0	1 *Lieut.* Alfred Benwell Letts,[20] 15 Oct. 58.	
4	0	*Instructors of Musketry.*—2 *Lieut.* Shapland Graves, 14 Jan. 58.	
6	0	1 *Lieut.* H. A. A. Breedon, 6 Nov. 58.	
5	0	*Quarter-Masters.*—1 Thomas Blisset,[23] 19 June 55.	
4	0	2 George Pittendrigh, 1 Oct. 56.	
20	0	*Surgeons.*—1 Joseph Burke,[24] 22 Dec. 48; *Assist.-Surg.* 10 Jan. 40.	
15	0	2 Francis Oliver Barker,[27] M.D. 5 May 54; *Assist.-Surg.* 14 Feb. 45.	
6	0	*Assistant-Surgeons.*—1 Thomas Teevan,[10] 30 June 54.	
6	0	1 Theophilus Dolan, 1 Sept. 54.	
5	0	2 Henry McNeice, 6 Nov. 55.	
3	0	1 John Henry Beath, M.D, 15 Sept. 57.	
2	0	2 James Wilson, M.B., 5 Aug. 58.	

Facings Buff.—Agents, Messrs. Cox and Co.
[1st Batt. embarked for Malta, 2 April 1851. Depot, Limerick.]
[2nd Batt. embarked for Malta, 16 April 1858. Depot, Limerick.]

2 Lt.-Colonel Maude was present in the battle of Punniar (Medal) as Adjutant of the Buffs, and had his horse killed under him. Served at the siege of Sebastopol from 1855, and commanded the Buffs from 1st August till the final assault of the Redan on the 8th Sept., on which occasion he commanded the covering and ladder party of the 2nd Division furnished by his regt.; held a position inside the Redan for a considerable time—dangerously wounded—mentioned in dispatches (Medal and Clasp, Brevet Lt.-Col., Victoria Cross, Knight of the Legion of Honor, and 5th Class of the Medjidie).
3 Lt.-Colonel Ambrose served at the siege of Sebastopol from April 1855, commanded 200 men of the Buffs, and assisted in holding the Quarries with them on the night of the 7th June—dangerously wounded, mentioned in Dispatches. (Medal and Clasp, Brevet Major, Sardinian Medal, and 5th Class of the Medjidie).
4 Lt.-Col. Sargent served the Eastern campaign of 1854-55 with the 95th Regt., including the battles of Alma (wounded) and Inkerman, siege of Sebastopol, sortie of 26th Oct., and attack of the Redan on 8th Sept.—wounded (Medal and Clasps, Brevet Major, Knight of the Legion of Honor, and 5th Class of the Medjidie).
6 Major Burke served in the Eastern campaign of 1854-55 with the 88th Regt., including the battles of Alma and Inkerman, and siege of Sebastopol (Medal and Clasps, and 5th Class of the Medjidie).
8 Major Pownall, and Lieuts. Breedon and Caldecott, served at the siege of Sebastopol in 1855, and were wounded (Medal and Clasp).
9 Major Gore served with the 6th Regt. in the Kaffir wars of 1846-7, and of 1851-3 (Medal). Served with the Buffs at the siege of Sebastopol (Medal and Clasps). Nominated to the 4th Class of the Medjidie for service with the late Turkish Contingent.
10 Captains Warburton, Aplin, Turner, Anley, Tyler, and Lieuts. Henry, Suttie, E. J. Cox, and Worthington, Paymaster Syms, and Assist.-Surgeon Teevan, served at the siege of Sebastopol in 1855 (Medal and Clasp).
11 Captain Kains was present with the Buffs at the battle of Punniar (Medal). Also at the siege of Sebastopol in 1855, and assault of the Redan on the 8th Sept. (Medal and Clasp).
12 Captain Dunbar served at the siege of Sebastopol in 1855, and was wounded at the assault of the Redan on the 8th Sept. (Medal and Clasp).
13 Major Walker served the Eastern campaign of 1854-55 as Adjutant of the 30th Regiment, including the battles of the Alma (wounded) and Inkerman, siege of Sebastopol, and sortie on 26th October. On the night of the 21st April he volunteered and led a party which took and destroyed a Russian Rifle pit, for which he was mentioned in the Dispatches, and promoted into the Buffs. On the night of 9th June he was dangerously wounded in the trenches—right arm amputated (Medal and Clasps, Victoria Cross, and 5th Class of the Medjidie).
14 Captain Wemyss landed in the Crimea in 1855, and served in the trenches at the siege of Sebastopol, and on the expedition to Kertch; also served at the destruction of and affairs at Taman in Sept. 1855 (Medal and Clasp, and Sardinian Medal).
15 Captain Siree served with the 33rd Regt. in the Eastern campaign in 1854, and was severely wounded while carrying the colours at the battle of Alma (Medal and Clasp).

[For continuation of notes, see end of 2nd Foot.

1st Batt. East Indies.] 2nd Batt. Corfu. **4th (The King's Own) Regt. of Foot.** 177

"The Lion of England." "CORUNNA" "BADAJOZ" "SALAMANCA" "VITTORIA" "ST. SEBASTIAN" "NIVE" "PENINSULA" "BLADENSBURG" "WATERLOO" "ALMA" "INKERMAN" "SEVASTOPOL."

Years' Serv.		
Full Pay	Half Pay	
55		Colonel.—**19** Sir John Bell,[1] KCB. *Ens.* 1 Aug. 05; *Lieut.* 1 Oct. 07; *Capt.* 12 March 12; *Maj.* 21 June 13; *Lieut.-Col.* 12 April 14; *Col.* 6 May 31; *Major-Gen.* 23 Nov. 41; *Lt.-Gen.* 11 Nov. 51; *Col.* 4th Foot, 26 Dec. 53.
38	0	*Lt.-Colonels.*—1 Thomas Williams,[2] CB. *Ens.* p 12 Sept. 22; *Lt.* p 7 July 25; *Capt.* p 17 June 28; *Brev.-Maj.* 23 Nov. 41; *Major*, 1 June 45; *Brev. Lt.-Col.* 11 Nov. 51; *Col.* 28 Nov. 54; *Lt.-Col.* 7 Aug. 55.
27	1½	2 Ferdinand Whittingham,[3] CB. *Ens.* 2 Nov. 32; *Lt.* p 19 Feb. 36; *Capt.* p 30 April 41; *Brevet-Major*, 23 Dec. 42; *Major*, p 1 Oct. 47; *Brevet Lt.-Col.* 20 June 54; *Lt.-Col.* p 29 Aug. 56; *Col.* 26 Oct. 58.
24	0	1 William Wilby,[4] *Ens.* p 27 May 36; *Lt.* p 7 Oct. 37; *Capt.* p 10 Dec. 47; *Maj.* 7 Aug. 55; *Lt.Col.* 15 Feb. 59.
24	0	*Majors.*—1 Thomas Martin,[5] *Ens.* 27 May 36; *Lt.* 27 Oct. 39; *Capt.* 5 Dec. 51; *Major*, p 12 May 57.
21	8/12	2 George Latham Thomson,[6] *Ens.* p 27 July 38; *Lt.* 9 April 41; *Capt.* p 9 July 52; *Bt.Major*, 2 Nov. 55; *Bt.Lt.Col.* 26 Dec. 56; *Major*, 30 Jan. 57.
16	0	2 Wm. Gordon Cameron,[7] *Ens.* 24 May 44; *Ens. & Lt.* p 12 May 47; *Lt. & Capt.* p 15 July 53; *Brevet Major*, 24 April 55; *Major*, 23 Oct. 57.
16	0	1 Dominic Jacotin Gamble,[8] *Ens.* p 19 April 44; *Lt.* p 25 Feb. 45; *Capt.* p 16 July 52; *Brev.Maj.* 6 June 56; *Major*, 15 Feb. 59.

		CAPTAINS.	ENSIGN.	LIEUT.	CAPTAIN.	BREV.-MAJ.
13	0	2 Octavius Yorke Cocks[9] ..	p 30 Mar. 47	p 17 May 50	p 4 Aug. 54	
12	0	1 Aug. Edw. Henry Ansell[11]	22 Dec. 48	22 Aug. 50	29 Dec. 54	
12	0	2 Fred. Anthony Trevor[9] ..	p 15 Aug. 48	p 10 Feb. 52	p 19 Jan. 55	
10	0	2 Francis Fisher Hamilton[10]	p 18 Jan. 50	p 29 Apr. 53	p 2 Mar. 55	
8	0	1 J. Philip Bohun Forster[11]	p 10 July 52	15 Aug. 54	p 1 May 55	
10	0	1 James Paton[11]†	p 15 Feb. 50	6 June 54	6 May 55	
9	0	1 Thomas Sheppard[12]	p 14 Feb. 51	6 June 54	7 Aug. 55	
8	0	2 Cuthbert Eccles[13]	p 9 July 52	11 Aug. 54	18 Jan. 56	
8	1½	1 Augustus Joseph Sykes[12]	p 17 Aug. 52	p 15 Sept. 54	1 Feb. 56	
7	0	1 John Wimburn Laurie[15]..	2 Sept. 53	8 Dec. 54	p 12 May 57	
6	1	2 Henry John Bowyer[16] ..	p 13 May 53	8 Dec. 54	1 Feb. 56	
12	1	2 Donald Farrington	p 17 Dec. 47	p 28 Aug. 49	p 26 Oct. 55	
6	1	1 John Ralph Carr[19]	p 22 April 53	24 Sept. 54	p 2 Nov. 55	
6	1	2 Rawdon C. P. de Robeck[20]	p 18 Feb. 53	p 8 Sept. 54	p 16 Nov. 55	
12	0	2 Frederick Boehmer	1 Aug. 48	5 Dec. 50	6 Nov. 57	
6	0	1 Charles Patrick Stokes[22]	14 July 54	29 Dec. 54	p 8 Jan. 58	
7	0	1 John Howley[22]	p 2 Dec. 53	8 Dec. 54	15 Jan. 58	
9	0	2 Thos. Blakiston Houston	p 3 Jan. 51	p 18 Aug. 54	30 Mar. 58	
15	0	2 Alfred J. Douglas Smith	p 16 Dec. 45	p 28 Sept. 47	23 July 58	
11	0	2 William Congreve	30 Mar. 49	p 9 July 50	23 July 58	
13	0	1 John William Madden ..	p 29 Jan. 47	8 Sept. 54	23 July 58	
7	0	1 John M'Dowell Elliot[23]..	21 Oct. 53	29 Dec. 54	23 July 58	
6	0	1 Henry Budgen Maule[24]..	7 June 54	29 Dec. 54	15 Feb. 59	
8	0	1 James Constable[23]	p 21 Sept. 52	19 Jan. 55	2 Aug. 59	

		LIEUTENANTS.			
11	0	1 Rich. Alex. Law,[23] *Adj*...	p 2 Feb. 49	9 Feb. 55	1 Sir John Bell served in Sicily in 1806 and 7; in the Peninsula and France from July 1808 to Feb. 1809, and again from May 1809 to July 1814, including the battle of Vimiera, action at the bridge of Almeida, battle of Busaco, all the actions during the retreat of the French from Portugal, siege and storming of Ciudad Rodrigo, siege and storming of Badajoz, action at the heights of Castrillos, battle of Salamanca, action of Sabijana de Morillos, battles of Vittoria, the Pyrenees, Nivelle, Orthes, and Toulouse. Served afterwards with the army employed against Louisiana, from Dec. 1814 to June 1815. He has received the Gold Cross for the battles of the Pyrenees, Nivelle, Orthes, and Toulouse and the Silver War Medal with six Clasps for the other battles and sieges.
6	0	1 Chas. E. Bayard Breton[23]	15 Sept. 54	9 Feb. 55	
6	0	1 Thomas Burridge[9]......	5 Nov. 54	9 Mar. 55	
5	0	1 Edw. Crossweller George[23]	5 Jan. 55	9 Mar. 55	
5	0	1 John Clarence Boyce[23] ..	p 12 Jan. 55	6 May 55	
5	0	1 Charles Thomas Wilson..	10 Jan. 55	p 20 July 55	
5	0	2 William Fagan	10 April 55	p 3 Aug. 55	
5	0	2 Henry Arthur Blake	26 Jan. 55	7 Aug. 55	
5	0	2 Thomas Tanner	p 11 May 55	p 31 Aug. 55	
5	0	2 William Adams Nash....	2 Feb. 55	14 Dec. 55	
5	0	2 Edward Bromhead......	15 Feb. 55	21 Dec. 55	
5	0	1 John James Martin	16 Feb. 55	1 Feb. 56	
5	0	2 Joseph Daniel Dickinson	16 Mar. 55	1 Feb. 56	
5	0	1 Henry Arthur Grey Todd	1 May 55	23 Oct. 57	
5	0	2 Daniel Geran Clery	p 14 Sept. 55	p 23 Oct. 57	
5	0	2 George H. Kittoe	7 Sept. 55	p 8 Jan. 58	
5	0	1 Martin Samuel Sharpe..	p 23 Oct. 55	15 Jan. 58	
5	0	2 Richard Boyce	14 Dec. 55	5 Mar. 58	
5	0	2 Aug. Charles Twentyman	21 Dec. 55	15 June 58	
4	0	2 Francis Rynd	26 Feb. 56	15 June 58	
4	0	1 David Smith	p 26 Dec. 56	23 July 58	
3	0	1 Charles Edward Billing	p 15 May 57	p 30 July 58	
4	0	2 Edward Chinn	15 Feb. 56	p 6 Aug. 58	

178   4th (The King's Own) Regt. of Foot.

Years' Serv. Full Pay	Half Pay	LIEUTENANTS.	ENSIGN.	LIEUT.	
5	0	2 Stephen Weston Bent ..	p 19 Jan. 55	7 Aug. 58	6 Lt.-Colonel Thomson joined the Cape Mounted Rifles as a Provisional Ensign on the 3rd Feb. 1835, in which capacity he served until March 1858. Served in the Kaffir war of 1835 under Sir Benjamin d'Urban (Medal). Served in the Eastern campaign of 1854 and 55. Was at the battle of Alma (wounded), and throughout the siege and fall of Sebastopol. Appointed Deputy Assist.-Adj.-Gen. at Head Quarters 1st May 1855, and Assist.-Adjutant-General 10th April 56 (Medal and three Clasps, Knight of the Legion of Honor, 5th Class of the Medjidie, the Turkish Medal and Brevets of Major and Lt. Colonel).
3	0	2 Walter Francis Blake ..	p 2 Oct. 57	1 Oct. 58	
3	0	1 Charles Robin Hammond	24 Feb. 57	1 Oct. 58	
3	0	2 Oswald Robert Middleton	19 June 57	p 15 Oct. 58	
3	0	1 William John Holt	p 24 July 57	15 Feb. 59	
3	0	1 Christop. Rawes Durrant	p 6 Nov. 57	2 Aug. 59	
		ENSIGNS.			
3	0	2 Chas. Fred. Brockman, *Adj.*	17 Nov. 57		
3	0	2 James Henry M'Ewen ..	18 Nov. 57		
2	0	2 George Studdert	p 8 Jan. 58		
2	0	1 Walter Stewart Brown .	16 Mar. 58		
2	0	1 Francis Robert Sandys ..	26 Mar. 58		
2	0	2 William Paul Bridson ..	30 Mar. 58		7 Major Cameron served the Eastern campaign of 1854, including the battle of Alma and siege of Sebastopol,—severely wounded in the trenches, 20th Oct., while in command of the volunteer sharpshooters of the brigade of Guards (Medal and Clasps, Knight of the Legion of Honor, and 5th Class of the Medjidie). 8 Major Gamble served in the Eastern campaign and at the siege and fall of Sebastopol from May 1855 (Medal and Clasp).
2	0	1 William Thomas Freeman	p 21 May 58		
2	0	2 George William Hughes	28 May 58		
2	0	1 Herb. Munro Long Innes	2 July 58		
2	0	1 Richard Uniacke Bayly . .	p 24 Aug. 58		
2	0	1 George Augustus Sweny .	7 Sept. 58		
2	0	1 William Harry Stone....	8 Sept. 58		
2	0	2 Chas. Cartwright Sayce .	9 Sept. 58		
2	0	2 Jno. Wm. Goddard Telfer	17 Sept. 58		
2	0	1 Herbert Charles Borrett .	29 Oct. 58		
2	0	2 Lachlan MacLaine	p 9 Nov. 58		
2	0	2 Richard Annesley Knox..	7 Dec. 58		
1	0	2 George Hall Hall	p 18 Mar. 59		
1	0	2 Herbert John M. Williams	1 April 59		
1	0	1 Fred. Augustus Wright..	5 Aug. 59		

14	0	*Paymasters.*—1 Francis Edwin Maunsell,[12] 13 Sept. 53; *Ens.* p 12 June 46;
1	0	2 John Henry Gordon, 16 Sept. 59. [*Lt.* 29 Dec. 49.
11	0	*Adjutants.*—1 Lieut. Richard Alex. Law,[23] 21 Dec. 55.
3	0	2 Ensign Charles Fred. Brockman, 17 Nov. 57.
7	0	*Instructors of Musketry.*—1 Captain J. W. Laurie, 14 Nov. 56.
4	0	2 *Lieut.* Edward Chinn, 19 July 58.
6	0	*Quarter-Masters.*—1 William Connell,[12] 19 Sept. 54.
4	0	2 John Newey, 1 Oct. 50.
10	½	*Surgeons.*—1 John Gorringe,[26] M.D. 20 June 55; *Assist.-Surg.* 8 June 49
13	0	2 Henry Fisher, 2 Oct. 57; *Assist. Surg.* 7 June 47.
6	0	*Assistant-Surgeons.*—1 James Ekin,[27] M.B. 7 April 54.
6	0	1 John Lowe Erskine,[27] M.D. 1 Sept. 54.
2	0	2 Ebenezer Miller, M.D. 22 Jan. 58.
2	0	2 Joseph Vavasour Lane, 13 Oct. 58.
2	0	1 Edward Barrett Kearney, 22 Jan. 58.

Facings Blue.—*Agents*, Messrs. Cox & Co.

[1st Batt. returned from the Crimea, 19 July 56.   Embarked for Mauritius, 23 May 57. *Depot, Chichester.*]

[2nd Batt. embarked for Corfu, May 1859.   *Depot, Walmer.*]

2 Colonel Williams served in the Eastern campaign, landed in the Crimea from Gallipoli in March 1855, and commanded the 4th Regt. at the siege and fall of Sebastopol from 18th June 1855 (Medal and Clasp, CB., Knight of the Legion of Honor, and 4th Class of the Medjidie).

3 Colonel Whittingham served as Aide-de-Camp to Sir Hugh Gough throughout the operations of 1842 in China (Medal), and was present at Segoan, Chapoo, Woosung, Shanghae, and Chin Kiang Foo.

4 Lt.Colonel Wilby served at the siege and fall of Sebastopol (Medal and Clasp).

5 Major Martin served with the 18th Royal Irish throughout the China Expedition (Medal), and was present at the storming of Amoy, attack and capture of Chapoo, Woosung, Shanghai, and Chin Kiang Foo (where he commanded the Light Company), and investment of Nankin.

9 Captains Cocks and Trevor and Lieut. Burridge served the Eastern campaign of 1854-55, including the battles in the Crimea and siege of Sebastopol (Medal and three Clasps).

10 Captain Hamilton served the Eastern campaign of 1854-55, including the battles of Alma (wounded) and Inkerman, and the whole of the siege operations before Sebastopol until its fall (Medal and three Clasps, Sardinian Medal, and 5th Class of the Medjidie).

11 Captains Ansell and Forster served in the Eastern campaign and at the siege and fall of Sebastopol from March 1855 (Medal and Clasp).

11† Captain Paton served in the Eastern campaign of 1854-55, including the battle of Inkerman, siege and fall of Sebastopol; wounded (Medal and two Clasps, and Knight of the Legion of Honor).

12 Captains Sheppard and Sykes, Paymaster Maunsell, and Quarter-Master Connell, served the Eastern campaign of 1854-55, including the battles in the Crimea, siege and fall of Sebastopol (Medal and three Clasps). Captain Sykes has also the Sardinian Medal. Captain Sheppard has the 5th Class of the Medjidie.

13 Captain Eccles served throughout the Eastern campaign of 1854-55, including the battles of Alma and Inkerman, siege and fall of Sebastopol, and assaults of the 18th June and 8th Sept. (Medal and three Clasps, and 5th Class of the Medjidie).

15 Captain Laurie served at the siege and fall of Sebastopol from Nov. 1854, and was engaged in the repulse of the two sorties on the night of the 22nd Nov. 1854, and the following morning (Medal and Clasp, and 5th Class of the Medjidie).

16 Captain Bowyer served in the Eastern campaign from Nov. 1854, including the battle of Inkerman, siege and fall of Sebastopol (Medal and two Clasps).

4th (The King's Own) Regt. of Foot.

19 Captain Carr served with the 33rd Regt. the Eastern campaign of 1854-55, including the battles of Alma and Inkerman, siege and fall of Sebastopol, and assaults of the 18th June and 8th Sept. (Medal and Clasps, and 5th Class of the Medjidie).
20 Captain de Robeck served with the 80th Regt. in the Crimea from 31 Dec. 1854, including the siege and fall of Sebastopol and assaults of the 18th June and 8th Sept (Medal and Clasp).
22 Captains Stokes and Howley served at the siege and fall of Sebastopol from Nov. 1854 (Medal and Clasp). Captain Howley has also the Sardinian Medal.
23 Captains Elliot and Constable, Lieuts. Law, Breton, George, and Boyce, served at the siege and fall of Sebastopol (Medal and Clasp).
24 Captain Maule served at the siege of Sebastopol from Jan. 1855 (Medal and Clasp, and 5th Class of the Medjidie).
25 Doctor Gorringe, in the 1st Dragoons, served the Eastern campaign of 1854-55, including the battles of Balaklava and Inkerman, siege of Sebastopol, night attack on Russian outposts 19th Feb., and expedition to Kertch (Medal and three Clasps).
27 Assist.-Surgeons Ekin and Erskine served at the siege and fall of Sebastopol (Medal and Clasp).

[*Continuation of Notes to 5th Foot.*]

11 Major Meara served with the 5th Fusiliers in India during the Mutiny of 1857-58, and was present with Havelock's force in the actions of Mungarwar, capture of the Alumbagh, relief of Lucknow, and subsequent actions on the 26th and 27th, and Sortie of the 29th September. Succeeded to the command of the Regt. on the 6th October and commanded it until the end of the siege, and at the storming of the Engine House and King's Stables—mentioned in despatches and thanked by the Governor General in Council (Brevet Major). Served under Outram throughout the operations at the Alumbagh from Nov. 1857 to March 1858, and at the siege and capture of Lucknow under Lord Clyde; also in the Oude campaign of 1857-58, including the action of Buxar Ghat and defeat of the rebels under Bani Madhoo, capture of the fort of Omerah and destruction of several other forts (Medal and Clasps).
12 Captain Adair served during the Sepoy Mutiny in 1857-8, including Havelock's advance on Lucknow, actions at Mungarwar and Alumbagh, assault of Lucknow and relief of the Residency (horse shot) and sortie of the 26th Sept.; was severely wounded on 27th Sept., and specially noticed by General Havelock for gallantry on the 25th September.
15 Captain Macfarlane served with the 50th Regt. the Eastern campaign from Oct. 1854, including the battle of Inkerman, siege and fall of Sebastopol (Medal and Clasps).
16 Captain Macdonald served with the 39th Regt. in the Crimea from 31 Dec. 1854, including the siege and fall of Sebastopol and attacks of the 18th June and 8th Sept. (Medal and Clasps, and 5th Class of the Medjidie).
17 Captain Pocklington served with the 38th Regt. throughout the Eastern campaign of 1854-55, including the battle of Alma, and siege of Sebastopol (Medal and Clasps, and 5th Class of the Medjidie).
18 Captain Harkness served with the 55th Regt. throughout the Eastern campaign of 1854-55, including the battles of Alma and Inkerman, siege and fall of Sebastopol, sortie of 26th Oct. 54, and assault of the Redan on 8th Sept. (Medal and three Clasps, and 5th Class of the Medjidie).
19† Captain FitzRoy served during the Sepoy Mutiny in 1857-58 and was present at the relief of Lucknow by Lord Clyde including the attacks on the Dilkoosha, Martiniere, and Secunderbagh; with Outram's Division in the Alumbagh and engaged in the various operations there; also at the siege and capture of Lucknow.
21 Lieut. Massy joined Havelock's Column at Cawnpore on 15th Sept. 1857 and was present in the actions of Mungarwar and Alumbagh, assault on Lucknow and relief of the Residency, engaged thence at the taking of the Cawnpore battery, and storming of the Engine House and King's Stables; was subsequently with Outram's force in the Alumbagh and engaged in repelling the numerous attacks and in routing the enemy on 22nd Dec.; also at the siege and fall of Lucknow.
22 Lieut. Lewis was at the relief of Arrah and defeat of the Dinapore Mutineers at Jugdespore.
23 Captain Oldfield served in the Indian campaign of 1857-58, and was present at the relief of Arrah (wounded) and defeat of the Dinapore Mutineers at Jugdespore; with Havelock's force in the actions of Mungarwara and Alumbagh, and defence of the latter until arrival of Lord Clyde; actions of La Martiniere and relief of Lucknow; with Outram's force at the Alumbagh with repulse of numerous attacks, and operations ending in the capture of Lucknow; subsequently in the final campaign in Oude (Medal and Clasp).
24 Captain Mason was at the relief of Arrah (honorably mentioned) and defent of the Dinapore Mutineers at Jugdespore. Accompanied Havelock's Column from Cawnpore in Sept. 1857 and present in the actions of Mungarwar and Alumbagh, assault of Lucknow and relief of the Residency and various sorties thence. Served also with Outram's division before Lucknow including the action at Guilee.
25 Paymaster Forster was present at the capture of Lucknow and subsequent operations (Medal and Clasp).
26 Captain Cubitt served in India during the Mutiny of 1857-58, and was present at the action of Kudjwa under Sir Wm. Peel, at the relief of Lucknow by Lord Clyde, with the force in the Alumbagh under Outram from Nov. to March including the action of Gujuliee and the whole of the operations till the capture of Lucknow—wounded on 19th March 1858, was subsequently present in the Oude campaign of 1858-59, including the action of Buxar Ghat, capture of Umereen and other forts (Medal and Clasps).
27 Doctor Swettenham served with Havelock's Column in the action of Mungarwar, attack and capture of the Alumbagh, assault and relief of the Residency of Lucknow and its subsequent defence (wounded); present with Outram's division throughout the occupation of the Alumbagh and the Sorties thence, also at the capture of Lucknow by Lord Clyde, the subsequent campaign in Oude, including the action of Buxar Ghat, Doondiakera, and other minor affairs (Medal and two Clasps).
28 Doctor Reid served with the 91st Regt. in the Kaffir War in 1851-52 (Medal).

5th Regt. of Foot (Northumberland Fusiliers). [1st Batt. East Indies, 2nd Batt. Mauritius.]

"Quo Fata vocant," surmounting St. George and the Dragon. On the corners of the 2nd colour the Rose and Crown; on the caps the King's Crest; also St. George killing the Dragon. "WILHELMSTAHL" "ROLEIA" "VIMIERA" "CORUNNA" "BUSACO" "CIUDAD RODRIGO" "BADAJOZ" "SALAMANCA" "VITTORIA" "NIVELLE" "ORTHES" "TOULOUSE" "PENINSULA."

Years' Serv		
Full Pay	Half Pay	
54		Colonel.—彼此 William Lovelace Walton,¹ Ens. ᴾ 8 May 06; Lt. and Capt. 7 March 11; Capt. and Lt.-Col. ᴾ 20 Feb. 23; Col. 10 Jan. 37; Major-Gen. 9 Nov. 46; Lt.-Gen. 20 June 54; Col. 5th Foot, 20 Feb. 56.
36	0	Lt.-Colonels.—1 Philip Melmoth Nelson Guy,² CB. Ens. ᴾ 23 Sept. 24; Lt. ᴾ 12 June 28; Capt. ᴾ 29 Dec. 37; Maj. 20 July 47; Lt.-Col. ᴾ 21 May 50; Col. 28 Nov. 54.
21	2¾/₁₂	2 John A. Vesey Kirkland,³ 2nd Lt. ᴾ 22 Aug. 37; Lt. ᴾ 27 July 38; Capt. ᴾ G Sept. 44; Bt.-Major, 12 Dec. 54; Major, 17 July 55; Bt.-Lt.-Col. 26 Dec. 56; Lt.-Col. 26 Dec. 56.
21	0	1 William Chester Master,⁴ CB., 2nd Lt. ᴾ 23 April 39; Lieut. ᴾ 26 Oct. 41; Capt. ᴾ 29 Dec. 46; Major, 4 Sept. 57; Bt.Lt.Col. 24 Mar. 58; Lt.Col. 17 Dec. 58.
21	0	Majors.—1 George Bryan Milman,⁵ 2nd Lt. ᴾ 24 May 39; Lieut. 20 Sept. 42; Capt. ᴾ 29 Jan. 47; Major, 30 Sept. 57; Bt.Lt.Col. 24 March 58.
19	1⁴⁄₉	2 John Cowell Bartley,⁶ Ens. ᴾ 26 April 39; Lt. ᴾ 20 Oct. 40; Capt. 22 Aug. 50; Bt.-Major, 12 Dec. 54; Major, 21 Dec. 55.
19	0	2 William Lyons, Ens. 15 Jan. 41; Lieut. 12 Sept. 43; Capt. 8 Mar. 52; Major, 26 Dec. 57.
17	0	1 John Swaine Hogge,⁷ 2nd Lt. ᴾ 9 June 43; Lieut. 9 Nov. 46; Capt. 3 June 53; Major, 17 Dec. 58.

		CAPTAINS.	ENSIGN.	LIEUT.	CAPTAIN.	BREV.-MAJ.
7	0	2 Arthur Scott⁸	ᴾ 15 July 53	15 Dec. 54	ᴾ 31 Aug. 55	16 Aug. 59
6	0	1 George Carden⁹	11 Aug. 54	6 Nov. 54	9 Nov. 55	
6	0	1 Thomas Scovill Bigge¹⁰	ᴾ 7 June 54	21 Sept. 54	8 June 56	
14	0	1 Francis Henry Ponder	ᴾ 27 Mar. 46	ᴾ 30 July 47	24 Oct. 56	
14	0	1 Wm. Henry Petty Meara¹¹	24 Dec. 46	ᴾ 5 Dec. 51	4 Sept. 57	24 Mar. 58
14	0	2 Jas. Wallace Dunlop Adair¹²	21 April 46	3 Jan. 52	29 Sept. 57	
13	0	1 William Leach	ᴾ 21 July 47	ᴾ 20 May 53	6 Oct. 57	
13	⁹⁄₁₂	2 Albert Ernest Ross	22 Dec. 46	ᴾ 28 Dec. 49	ᴾ 6 Jan. 57	
7	1	2 Robt. Henry Macfarlane¹⁵	ᴾ 13 June 52	ᴾ 18 Oct. 53	ᴾ 24 April 55	
7	1	2 Norman Macdonald¹⁶	ᴾ 14 May 52	ᴾ 24 June 53	ᴾ 27 July 55	
6	1	2 Frederic Pocklington¹⁷	ᴾ 19 Oct. 53	8 Dec. 54	ᴾ 18 Jan. 56	
6	1	2 John Granville Harkness¹⁸	13 May 53	19 Aug. 54	18 Jan. 56	
11	0	1 Edw. Reginald Simmons¹⁹	29 June 49	29 Jan. 54	31 Oct. 57	
9	0	1 Geo. Hon. J. M. Chapman	ᴾ 21 Nov. 51	6 June 54	26 Dec. 57	
7	0	2 Fred. James Mylius	3 June 53	11 Aug. 54	25 Jan. 58	
14	0	2 S. Blomfield Kekewich	ᴾ 8 Dec. 46	29 Apr. 51	2 Feb. 58	
6	0	1 Horatio Walpole	1 Sept. 54	ᴾ 10 Mar. 57	ᴾ 16 Mar. 58	
6	0	2 Philip FitzRoy¹⁹†	ᴾ 6 Oct. 54	4 Sept. 57	ᴾ 13 April 58	
5	0	1 John Barnett Barker²⁰	ᴾ 22 June 55	29 Sept. 57	ᴾ 16 April 58	
7	0	1 Robert Moore	ᴾ 28 Oct. 53	ᴾ 15 May 55	ᴾ 7 Sept. 58	
7	0	1 John Robson Carlisle	ᴾ 10 June 53	ᴾ 6 Oct. 54	17 Dec. 58	
5	0	2 Edwin John Oldfield²³	ᴾ 31 Aug. 55	6 Oct. 57	ᴾ 4 Feb. 59	
4	0	2 Ed. Montgomery Mason²⁴	ᴾ 15 Feb. 56	19 Oct. 57	ᴾ 31 May 59	
4	0	2 Frank Astley Cubitt²⁶	29 Feb. 56	20 Oct. 57	ᴾ 20 Nov. 59	

		LIEUTENANTS.				
6	0	1 John Creagh, Adj.	28 April 54	15 Jan. 56		
6	0	1 George Eyre Massy²¹	24 Apr. 54	24 Oct. 56		
5	0	1 Edward Studley Lewis²²	1 May 55	24 Sept. 57		
4	0	1 Edward James Tyler	24 June 56	22 Oct. 57		
9	0	2 Edwin Biron	ᴾ 17 June 51	ᴾ 30 Mar. 55		
5	0	2 Edw. Wildman B. Villiers	24 April 55	4 Sept. 55		
5	0	2 William Thwaytes	23 April 55	5 Sept. 55		
5	0	2 Frederick Maycock	9 Mar. 55	ᴾ 7 Dec. 55		
5	0	2 John James Robinson	19 June 55	24 Dec. 55		
5	0	2 Nettervill John Barron	22 Mar. 55	22 Dec. 55		
5	0	2 John Rice Nowbolt	3 Aug. 55	ᴾ 15 Jan. 56		
5	0	1 James Morris Toppin	ᴾ 30 May 55	26 Feb. 56		
5	0	2 Henry Hartley Taylor	15 May 55	ᴾ 17 Feb. 57		
4	0	1 Edward Hoare	8 July 56	31 Oct. 57		
3	0	1 George Alex. Shegog	ᴾ 6 Jan. 57	26 Dec. 57		
3	0	1 Henry Bathe	ᴾ 13 Mar. 57	3 Jan. 58		
5	0	1 Charles Lewes Dashwood	ᴾ 9 Oct. 55	ᴾ 16 Mar. 58		
5	0	1 Charles John Miles	ᴾ 22 Oct. 55	ᴾ 13 Apr. 58		
4	0	1 William Enderby	ᴾ 7 Mar. 56	ᴾ 23 Apr. 58		
3	0	1 Fra. Stirling Brown Holt	26 Dec. 57	ᴾ 24 Aug. 58		
4	0	1 Gersham Herrick	28 Dec. 57	ᴾ 7 Sept. 58		
4	0	2 Samuel Richards	ᴾ 6 Sept. 56	1 Oct. 58		
3	0	2 James Vaughan Cooch	11 Sept. 57	2 Oct. 58		
3	0	2 Charles Sutton, Adj.	23 Oct. 57	2 Oct. 58		

7 Major Hogge served in the Indian campaign of 1857-58, and was present with the force in the Alumbagh, under Outram from Nov. to March, including the action of Gahilo and the whole of the operations until the capture of Lucknow (Medal and Clasp).

19 Captain Simmons served in the Indian campaign of 1858 including Lugard's operations in the Jugdespore Jungle, the command of the Southern Province of Shahabad in June and July, and operations in Oude in Nov. and Dec. (Medal).

20 Captain Barker was present at the action of Marigunge and relief of Lucknow; at the Alumbagh under Outram and engaged in repelling the numerous attacks and in routing the enemy on 22nd Dec. 57 and 25th Feb. 58 capturing guns; also present at the capture of Lucknow.

5th Regt. of Foot (Northumberland Fusiliers).

Years' Serv.		LIEUTENANTS.	ENSIGN.	LIEUT.	
Full Pay.	Half Pay.				
3	0	1 James Hartley	20 Dec. 57	12 Oct. 58	
3	0	2 Francis R. Bradford	30 Dec. 57	P 11 Jan. 59	
3	0	2 Wm. Charles Shoolbred..	31 Dec. 57	P 4 Feb. 59	
2	0	2 Jno. Cottingham Wadling	1 Jan. 58	P 7 Oct. 59	
3	0	2 Arthur Edward Flood ..	P 28 Aug. 57	28 May 59	
		ENSIGNS.			
2	0	1 Tho. D'Almaine Mackinlay	4 Jan. 58		1 Lieut.-General Walton served with the Coldstream Guards at the siege and capture of Copenhagen in 1807. He embarked for the Peninsula in 1808, and served the campaigns of 1809, 1810, and the first part of 1811; and was present at the passage of the Douro and capture of Oporto, the battles of Talavera and Busaco, the retreat to the Lines of Torres Vedras, and the subsequent advance to the Spanish frontier. He served also in Holland, Belgium, and France, from Nov. 1813 to Nov. 1818; and was present at the bombardment of Antwerp, the attack on Bergen-op-Zoom, the battles of Quatre Bras and Waterloo, and the capture of Paris: he was Acting Adjutant of the 2nd Battalion of his Regiment at Waterloo, and was appointed Brigade-Major to the 2nd Brigade of Guards on the march from that place to Paris. He served 40 years in the Coldstream Guards, and commanded the regiment upwards of six years. He has received the War Medal with two Clasps for Talavera and Busaco.
2	0	2 John Leslie	6 Jan. 58		
2	0	2 William Douglas Legge..	19 Feb. 58		
2	0	1 Adolphus Nicols	16 Mar. 58		
2	0	1 Robert Hull	23 Mar. 58		
2	0	1 John Johnson Bradshaw .	30 Mar. 58		
2	0	1 Fra. H. Denny Brome ..	31 Mar. 58		
2	0	1 Fred. Arthur Forsyth ..	1 Apr. 58		
2	0	1 Herbert S. Williams	23 Apr. 58		
2	0	1 Lucius John Blake......	4 June 58		
2	0	2 William Ford Longbourne	15 June 58		
2	0	1 William Church Ormond	13 July 58		
2	0	2 William Bevington Knox	13 Aug. 58		
2	0	2 John Igglesden Troup ..	P 26 Oct. 58		
2	0	1 William Henry Overton	P 29 Oct. 58		
2	0	2 Geo. Todderick Beasley..	26 Oct. 58		
1	0	2 Thomas Tarleton	P 18 Jan. 59		
1	0	2 David Gregory Beamish	23 Aug. 59		

14	0	*Paymasters.*—1 Fred. Blanco Forster,[25] 5 Dec.51; *Ens.* 12 Nov.46; *Lt.* 13 Oct.48.
3	0	2 James Wray, 7 Nov. 57.
6	0	*Adjutants.*—1 *Lieut.* John Creagh, 24 Sept. 57.
3	0	2 *Lieut.* Charles Sutton, 23 Oct. 57.
4	0	*Instructors of Musketry.*—1 *Lieut.* Edward James Tyler, 15 Sept. 57.
5	0	2 *Lieut.* E. W. B. Villiers, 17 Apr. 58.
3	0	*Quarter-Masters.*—1 Francis Drake, 17 Nov. 57.
2	0	2 Edward Henry Drake, 18 Jan. 58.
19	0	*Surgeons.*—1 William Kilner Swettenham,[27] M.D., 14 Oct. 51; *A. S.* 9 April 41.
18	0	2 Francis Reid,[28] MD. 25 Sept.49; *A. S.* 2 Aug. 42.
7	0	*Assist.-Surgeons.*—1 Thomas Ravenscroft Whitty, 25 Nov. 53.
2	0	2 John Williams Gillespie, M.D. 22 Jan. 58.
2	0	2 Peter Fred. Newland, 25 May 58.
2	0	1 Charles Henry Lect, 22 Jan. 58.
2	0	1 George Simpson Cameron, 7 May 58.

Facings Bright Green.—*Agents,* Messrs. Cox & Co.
[1st Batt. embarked for Mauritius, 25 July 47.   Depot, Colchester.]
[2nd Batt. embarked for Mauritius, Aug. 1858.   Depot, Pembroke.]

2 Colonel Guy commanded the Infantry Brigade of Hope Grant's Column at the defeat of the Rebels on 4th Nov. 1857 at Marigunge; commanded at the Alum Bagh from 13th to 30th Nov. during Sir Colin Campbell's advance to the relief of the Lucknow Garrison; from 1st Dec. 57 to 5th March 1858 commanded the 5th Fusiliers with Outram's Division at Alum Bagh and engaged in repelling the numerous attacks as also in attacking and routing the enemy on 22nd Dec. and 25th Feb. capturing guns; commanded the 3rd Infantry Brigade at the siege and capture of Lucknow, from 5th to 28th March (*CB.*).

3 Lt.-Col. Kirkland served the Eastern campaign of 1854, and up to 4th Aug. 1855, as D.A. Adj.-Gen. at head quarters, including the battles of Alma, Balaklava, and Inkerman, and siege of Sebastopol (Medal and Clasps, Brevets of Major and Lt.-Col., Sardinian Medal, and 5th Class of the Medjidie).

4 Lt.Col. Master commanded the 5th Fusiliers at the relief of Lucknow in Nov. 1857, and served with it in Outram's force at the Alum Bagh in all the operations of the succeeding months, and commanded the Regt. at the capture of Lucknow—several times mentioned in Dispatches (*CB.*).

5 Lt.Colonel Milman was present in the action at Marigunge and at the relief of Lucknow in Nov. 1857. Commanded a detachment during the advance on the Dilkhoosha and Martiniere (mentioned in Dispatches, and Brevet Lt.Col.); served with the 5th Fusiliers in Outram's force at the Alum Bagh in all the operations of the succeeding months including the capture of Lucknow. In 1848 when stationed at the Mauritius he was upset in a boat off Mahebourg together with five others whose lives were saved by his skill and courage in swimming, for which the Royal Humane Society conferred on him its Gold Medal.

6 Major Bartley served with the 4th Regt. the Eastern campaign of 1854-55, including the battles in the Crimea and siege of Sebastopol (Medal and three Clasps, Brevet Major, and 5th Class of the Medjidie).

8 Major Scott served with the 34th Regt. at the siege of Sebastopol in 1854-55 (Medal and Clasp, and 5th Class of the Medjidie). Served with the 5th Fusiliers during the Sepoy Mutiny of 1857-58, present at the relief of Arrah and defeat of the Dinapore Mutineers at Jugdespore (mentioned in dispatch); accompanied Havelock's Column in September to the relief of Lucknow, including the actions at Mungarwar and Alumbagh, assault on Lucknow and relief of the Residency with various Sorties thence—wounded on 6th October.

9 Captain Carden served with the 77th Regt. at the siege of Sebastopol from Dec. 1854 (Medal and Clasp).

10 Captain Bigge served with the 23rd Fusiliers at the siege of Sebastopol from the 18th Nov. 1854, including the assault of the Quarries on 7th June, and assaults of the Redan on the 18th June and 8th Sept., and was wounded in the trenches on the night of the 24th August (Medal and Clasp, and 5th Class of the Medjidie). Served with the 5th Fusiliers in the Indian campaign in 1857-58, including the defence of the Alumbagh in Oct. and Nov., relief of Lucknow by Lord Clyde, defence of the Alumbagh by Outram, capture of Lucknow, and campaign in Oude (Medal and Clasp).

[For continuation of Notes, see end of 4th Foot.

182 6th (*The Royal 1st Warwickshire*) *Regt. of Foot.* [1st Batt. East Indies. 2nd Batt. Gibraltar.

The Antelope."—On the three corners of the second colour," *The Rose and Crown.*"—And on the Grenadiers' caps, "*The King's Crest.*"—"ROLEIA" "VIMIERA" "CORUNNA" "VITTORIA" "PYRENEES" "NIVELLE" "ORTHES" "PENINSULA" "NIAGARA."

Years' Serv.						
Full Pay	Half Pay					
62		**Colonel.**—⑂ Henry James Riddell,[1] KH. *Ens.* Mar. 98; *Lieut.* 19 April 98; *Capt.* 24 Dec. 02; *Maj.* 10 Dec. 07; *Lt.-Col.* 4 June 13; *Col.* 22 July 30; *Major-Gen.* 23 Nov. 41; *Lt.-Gen.* 11 Nov. 51; *Gen.* 26 Sept. 57; *Col.* 6th Foot, 25 June 51.					
23	0	**Lieutenant Colonels.**—2 Robert W. Macleod Fraser,[2] *Lt.-Col.* 25 Nov. 57.				
18	0	1 James Elphinston Robertson,[3] *Ens.* ᴾ 8 Apr. 37; *Lt.* ᴾ 21 June 39; *Capt.* ᴾ 27 Oct. 43; *Brev.-Maj.* 20 June 54; *Major,* 10 May 55; *Lt.-Col.* 5 March 58.				
25	0	1 William Albert Stratton, *Ens.* 27 May 42; *Lt.* ᴾ 19 Nov. 44; *Capt.* ᴾ 30 Mar. 49; *Major,* ᴾ 15 April 56; *Lt.Col.* 6 May 58.				
17	0	**Majors.**—1 Edward James Blanckley,[4] *Ens.* 22 May 35; *Lieut.* 17 Jan. 38; *Capt.* 7 Aug. 46; *Brev.-Maj.* 6 June 56; *Maj.* 5 March 58.				
24	0	2 Henry Pratt Gore,[5] *Ens.* ᴾ 21 July 43; *Lieut.* ᴾ 10 June 46; *Capt.* ᴾ 26 Nov. 52; *Major,* 6 May 58.				
15	0	2 Hon. Francis Colborne,[6] CB., *Ens.* ᴾ 1 Oct. 36; *Lt.* ᴾ 18 Jan. 39; *Capt.* ᴾ 24 May 44; *Bt.-Major,* 21 Oct. 53; *Bt.-Lt.-Col.* 12 Dec. 54; *Major,* 16 Oct. 55; *Col.* 2 Apr. 58.				
		1 Charles Parker Catty,[7] *Ens.* ᴾ 2 May 45; *Lieut.* 29 Jan. 47; *Capt.* ᴾ 26 Aug. 53; *Major,* ᴾ 30 July 58.				

Years' Serv. F	H		CAPTAINS.	ENSIGN.	LIEUT.	CAPTAIN.	BREV.-MAJ.
15	0	1	Richard Thompson[8]	8 Aug. 45	ᴾ 12 Nov. 47	ᴾ 1 July 53	
18	0	1	Philip Aug. Mosse	16 Apr. 42	31 July 46	6 June 54	
14	0	1	John H. Ford Elkington,[9] l.c. 7 Dec. 58	28 Aug. 46	ᴾ 30 Mar. 49	2 Oct. 54	6 June 56
17	0	1	Henry Exley Jones	ᴾ 27 Oct. 43	9 June 46	4 July 54	
9	0	1	Robert Unwin	11 Apr. 51	ᴾ 9 July 52	ᴾ 15 Apr. 56	
13	0	2	Edward Lloyd[5]	ᴾ 12 Nov. 47	ᴾ 26 Dec. 51	20 Oct. 57	
7	1	2	Henry Broome Feilden[10]	ᴾ 21 Sept. 52	6 June 54	ᴾ 31 Aug. 55	
7	1	2	Charles Burch Phillipps[11]	23 Nov. 52	6 June 54	ᴾ 31 Aug. 55	
15	½	2	Wilsone Black[12]	11 Aug. 54	9 Feb. 55	ᴾ 9 Jan. 57	
5	0	2	Thomas John Grant	9 May 45	8 June 49	15 Dec. 57	
9	0	1	Walter Tyler Bartley	26 Dec. 51	ᴾ 26 Nov. 52	30 Dec. 57	
8	0	2	William Grove Annesley	ᴾ 23 Jan. 52	ᴾ 15 Feb. 53	15 Feb. 58	
8	0	2	Richard Henry Goodwin	ᴾ 24 Jan. 52	ᴾ 1 July 53	26 Feb. 58	
8	0	1	John Dawson[13]	28 May 52	6 June 54	5 Mar. 58	
8	0	1	John L. Otway Mansergh	ᴾ 9 July 52	6 June 54	6 May 58	
8	0	1	W. C. F. Burlton Bennett	ᴾ 17 Dec. 52	2 Oct. 54	ᴾ 28 May 58	
7	0	1	Thomas Folliott Powell	ᴾ 18 Feb. 53	ᴾ 8 Dec. 54	ᴾ 13 July 58	
7	0	1	Henry Parkinson	ᴾ 22 April 53	22 Dec. 55	ᴾ 13 July 58	
9	0	2	James Stillman[14]	2 Sept. 51	15 June 55	15 Nov. 57	
7	0	2	John Edward Tewart	ᴾ 8 July 53	ᴾ 15 Apr. 56	ᴾ 11 Mar. 59	
6	0	1	Richard Bolton	14 July 54	ᴾ 20 July 56	ᴾ 11 Mar. 59	
18	0	2	John Arthur Brockman	20 May 42	ᴾ 7 June 44	8 Nov. 55	
8	0	2	Lewis Blyth Hole	3 Dec. 52	ᴾ 7 June 54	29 Sept. 59	
6	0	2	Henry John Lawrell	8 Dec. 54	ᴾ 23 Nov. 55	ᴾ 18 Nov. 59	
			LIEUTENANTS.				
6	0	1	Richard Sheil	ᴾ 7 Dec. 54	ᴾ 25 Aug. 57		
8	0	2	John Grahame	10 Feb. 52	ᴾ 27 May 53		
5	0	2	John Augustus Staines	ᴾ 13 Feb. 55	25 Oct. 55		
5	0	1	Thos. Mortimer Kelson[16]	15 Mar. 55	16 Jan. 56		
5	0	2	David Garrick Protheroe	10 April 55	25 Jan. 56		
5	0	2	Rowland O'Connor	15 Mar. 55	26 Feb. 56		
5	0	2	Wm. Charles Wolseley	ᴾ 10 April 55	ᴾ 29 April 56		
5	0	2	Herbert Burrows Adcock	2 Mar. 55	ᴾ 17 Feb. 57		
5	0	1	Aubrey Wm. O. Saunders	22 Apr. 55	29 Dec. 57		
5	0	1	Thomas Bowen	23 Apr. 55	29 Dec. 57		
5	0	1	John Thomson Bowers	18 May 55	15 Jan. 58		
5	0	1	William Wastle[17]	30 Nov. 55	26 Jan. 58		
4	0	1	Dawson Kelly Evans	15 Jan. 56	15 Feb. 58		
4	0	1	James George Cockburn	ᴾ 15 Apr. 56	26 Feb. 58		
4	0	1	Charles Whyte	8 July 56	5 Mar. 58		
4	0	2	James Thomas Nugent	28 Feb. 56	16 April 58		
3	0	1	Patrick Browne Simpson	ᴾ 25 Aug. 57	ᴾ 23 April 58		
5	0	2	Henry Kitchener, *Adj.*	3 Aug. 55	6 May 58		
5	0	2	Edmund Hall	6 July 55	ᴾ 28 May 58		
4	0	1	George Gandy	ᴾ 22 Aug. 56	ᴾ 23 July 58		
3	0	2	Albert Henry Harrison	13 Dec. 57	ᴾ 29 Oct. 58		
3	0	2	George William Morland	15 Dec. 57	ᴾ 11 Jan. 59		
4	0	2	Thomas Hill Lucas	8 July 56	18 Jan. 59		
3	0	2	Chas. Edw. W. Roworth	17 Dec. 57	ᴾ 18 Mar. 59		
3	0	1	John Giffard	18 Dec. 57	ᴾ 25 Mar. 59		
3	0	2	David Barry Moriarty	19 Dec. 57	30 July 59		

1 General Riddell served as Deputy-Assist.-Quarter-Master-General at the capture of Copenhagen in 1807; and as Assistant-Quarter-Master-General on the eastern coast of Spain and at Genoa, with the army under Lord William Bentinck.

6th (The Royal 1st Warwickshire) Regt. of Foot. 183

Years' Serv. Full Pay	Half Pay	LIEUTENANTS.	ENSIGN.	LIEUT.
3	0	2 Wm. S. Selby Lowndes ..	20 Dec. 57	29 Sept. 59
3	0	1 Chas. Wm. Henry Wilson	20 Dec. 57	15 Nov. 59
3	0	1 Patrick Albert Howley ..	27 Feb. 58	p 29 Nov. 59
3	0	1 Bentinck L. Cumberland.	25 Sept. 57	p 7 Sept. 58
		ENSIGNS.		
2	0	1 William Smith	5 Mar. 58	
2	0	1 Thomas Greer Saunders..	6 Mar. 58	
2	0	1 Duncan D. Darroch Cotter	16 Mar. 58	
2	0	1 Jacob Biggs Hopkins ..	23 Mar. 58	
2	0	1 James FitzGerald	23 April 58	
2	0	1 Gust. W. Berry Collis ..	24 April 58	
2	0	1 Alex. Courtenay Hall ..	p 21 May 58	
2	0	2 Thomas Kent Neild	p 30 July 58	
2	0	2 William Grant	p 31 July 58	
2	0	2 Arthur Morton	p 29 Oct. 58	
2	0	2 James Bannatyne Blair..	11 Mar. 59	
2	0	2 Henry Mahony	1 Apr. 59	
2	0	2 Alfred Teevan..........	p 3 June 59	
1	0	2 William Harrison Falcon	p 4 June 59	
1	0	2 Henry Tringham Braidley	p 23 Aug. 59	
1	0	2 Theodosius Wm. Poulden	30 Sept. 59	
4	0	1 Frederick Helyar[19]	p 8 Jan. 58	
1	0	2 Henry Marvin	21 Oct. 59	

6 Colonel Hon. Francis Colborne served the Eastern campaign of 1854-55, as an Assist.-Qr.-Master General, including the battles in the Crimea, siege and fall of Sebastopol (Medal and Clasps, Brevet Lt.-Col., CB., Knight of the Legion of Honor, and 5th Class of the Medjidie).

14 Captain Stillman served with the Carabineers in the Crimea from 14 Aug. 1855, including the battle of Tchernaya, siege and fall of Sebastopol, and operations near Eupatoria (Medal and Clasp, and Turkish Medal). Was at Meerut at the outbreak of the Sepoy Mutiny on 10 May 1857 and served the campaign of that year, including the battles of the Hindun, siege and fall of Delhi, and subsequent operations under Brigadier Showers.

29 Doctor Cahill served with the 32nd Regt. at the first and second siege operations before Mooltan, including the capture of the city and surrender of the fortress. Also at the surrender of the fort and garrison of Cheniote and battle of Goojerat (Medal and Clasps).

7	0	*Paymasters.*—2 John O'Connor,[21] 3 Nov. 57 ; *Q. M.* 11 Mar. 53.	
2	0	1 Allan M'Donald, 26 Oct. 58.	
5	0	*Adjutants.*—2 *Lieut.* Henry Kitchener, 30 Oct. 57.	
	0	1 *Lieut.*	
5	0	*Instructors of Musketry.*—1 *Lieut.* A. W. O. Saunders, 23 Sept. 57.	
4	10/13	*Quarter-Masters.*—2 Samuel Haden, 25 Jan. 56.	
5	0	1 Patrick Sheeran, 27 July 55.	
12	0	*Surgeons.*—2 George Hyde,[22] M.D., 1 May 55 ; *Assist.-Surg.* 8 Dec. 48.	
14	0	1 Alex. Peile Cahill,[29] MD. 28 Aug. 57 ; *A. S.* 3 April 46.	
6	0	*Assistant-Surgeons.*—1 Alexander Robert Hudson, M.B. 26 May 54.	
5	0	1 Benjamin Cowan Kerr, 17 Nov. 55.	
2	0	1 William Hillman, 22 Jan. 58.	
2	0	2 Hampden Healy Maclean, 22 April 58.	
2	0	2 Thomas Ryan, 1 Sept. 58.	

Facings Blue.—*Agents*, Messrs. Cox and Co.

[1st Batt. embarked for the Cape of Good Hope, 28 Aug. 1846. Depot, Colchester.]
[2d Batt. embarked for Gibraltar, 18 May 58. Depot, Cork.]

2 Lt.-Col. Fraser acted as Staff Officer to a detachment sent from Bombay in 1837, against the Rebels in Canara. He served also with the 6th Regt. in the Kaffir war of 1846-47 (Medal).

3 Lt.-Col. Robertson served with the 6th Regt. in the Kaffir war of 1851-3 : commanded the Infantry, consisting of three companies of the 6th, and one company of the 73rd Regts. at the engagement of the Boomah Pass in the Amatola Mountains 24th Dec. 1850 (horse shot), and also in the skirmish on the following day between the Keiskamma Hoek and Fort White, when a large body of Kaffirs were defeated with great loss (mentioned in General Orders). Commanded the 6th Regt. on the 6th Feb. when attacked by a large force of Kaffirs between Fort Cox and Fort White, at which time a hundred of the enemy were killed (mentioned in General Orders). Appointed Commandant of Port Elizabeth and the district of Uitenhage in March 1851, and was placed in command of 300 levies and 100 mounted burghers for the purpose of keeping the Zuurberg Mountains clear of the enemy, and also the keeping open the communication between Port Elizabeth and Graham's Town. Was engaged in several minor affairs with the enemy from the above time to the close of the war in March 1853 (Medal).

4 Major Blanckley served with a detachment of the 6th Regt. sent from Bombay in 1837 against the rebels in Canara. Also in the Kaffir war of 1846-7 ; and throughout the whole of the Kaffir war and Hottentot rebellion of 1851-2-3, was present with the Regt. on nearly every patrol, and several times engaged with the enemy ; commanded the Regt. in a skirmish at the Caboula Hill, 29th June 1851, when it formed the rear-guard to the division then protecting a capture of 1,500 head of Gaika cattle (Medal).

5 Major Gore and Captain Lloyd served in the Kaffir war of 1851-3 (Medal).

7 Major Catty served throughout the Kaffir war of 1850-53 (Medal) : acted as Field Adjutant to the Infantry at the commencement of hostilities in the Boomah Pass, and on the following day, when incapacitated by wounds, was several times nearly taken prisoner. Present at Fort White when that post was stormed by a large force of the enemy, who were repulsed by the small garrison under Major Mansergh. In May 1851 he was appointed Commandant of an irregular corps of Europeans, designated "Catty's Rifles," and during thirteen months of the most active period of operations this corps did good and gallant service, being engaged in nearly every patrol of the 2nd Division, the same being frequently acknowledged in General Orders, and the various reports of Commanders of Divisions. On the disbandment of "Catty's Rifles," he rejoined his Regt. (the 6th), and proceeded with the expedition against the paramount chief Krell, and on his return to head-quarters was appointed to the command of Fort Grey, which he held till the cessation of hostilities, during which period, besides rendering the post perfectly defensible, waggons and cattle, which were on three occasions taken by the enemy and driven off, were recaptured by the garrison under Capt. Catty. Was twice severely wounded by musket balls in the Boomah Pass.

8 Captain Thompson served with the 6th Regt. in the Kaffir war of 1846-7. Also in that of 1851-2-3 ; was present at the operations in the Waterkloof in Sept. 1851 and in March 1852 ; and received a complimentary letter from Sir Harry Smith while in command of Fort Grey, for recapturing with a very small party a number of cattle taken by the enemy from the Government train (Medal).

6th (*The Royal 1st Warwickshire*) Regt. of Foot.

9 Lt.Col. Elkington served with the 6th Regt. in the Kaffir wars of 1847 and 1851-52 (Medal),—during which he was present at the operations in the Fish River, Waterkloof, Amatolas, and Trans-Kei Expeditions in command of the Light Company. He served as Assistant Quarter-Master-General to the Ottoman Contingent from its formation in May 1855, to the close of the war, for which he received the Brevet rank of Major and the 4th Class of the Medjidie.

10 Captain Feilden served with the 38th Regt. the Eastern campaign of 1854 and up to July 1855, including the battle of Alma and siege of Sebastopol, wounded (Medal and Clasps).

11 Captain Phillipps served with the 30th Regt. in the Crimea from 31 Dec. 1854, including the siege and fall of Sebastopol, and attacks of the 18th June and 8th Sept. (Medal and Clasp).

12 Captain Black served with the 42nd Highlanders in the Crimea from 14th July 1855, including the siege and fall of Sebastopol (Medal and Clasp).

13 Captain Dawson served with the 6th Regt. in the Kaffir war of 1846-47; also throughout that of 1850-53 (Medal), including the operations in the Fish River, Amatolas, and both the Trans-Kei Expeditions, on the latter of which as acting Adjutant.

16 Lieut. Kelson served with the 46th Regt. in the Crimea from the 13th Aug. 1855, including the siege and fall of Sebastopol (Medal and Clasp).

17 Lieut. Wastie served with the 6th Regt. in the Kaffir war of 1846-47; also throughout that of 1850-53 (Medal), including the operations in the Fish River, Amatolas, and both the Trans-Kei Expeditions.

19 Ensign Helyar served with the 42nd Highlanders in the Indian campaign in 1858, including the action of Khankur, defence of Jail (wounded), and subsequent operations at Shahjehanpore (Medal).

21 Paymaster O'Connor served with the 11th Regt. in the Crimea from 19th January 1855, including the siege and fall of Sebastopol, and assault of the 18th June (Medal and Clasp).

22 Doctor Hyde served in the Eastern campaign of 1854-55, and was specially mentioned and recommended for promotion in Sir Harry Jones' dispatch of 16th Sept. 1855 (Medal with Clasp for Sebastopol, and 5th Class of the Medjidie).

[Continuation of Notes to 7th Foot.]

15 Captain Clayhills served with the 93rd Highlanders in the Eastern campaign of 1854-55, including the battle of Balaklava, siege and fall of Sebastopol, and assault of the Redan on the 8th Sept. (Medal and two Clasps).

16 Captain Herbert served with the 31st Regt. in the Crimea from 22nd May 1855, including the siege and fall of Sebastopol, and attacks of the 18th June and 8th Sept. (Medal and Clasp).

17 Captain Daubeny served with the 90th Light Infantry in the Crimea from 5th Dec. 1854, including the capture of the Quarries, siege and fall of Sebastopol, attack of the Redan on the 18th June, and formed one of the storming party on the 8th Sept. (Medal and Clasp).

18 Captain Coope served with the 57th Regt. in the Crimea in 1855, including the siege and fall of Sebastopol, capture of the Quarries, and assault of the Redan on the 18th June; also at the bombardment and capture of Kinbourn (Medal and Clasp).

19 Captain Campbell served with the 72nd Highlanders in the Crimea from 13th June 1855, including the expedition to Kertch, siege and fall of Sebastopol (wounded in the Trenches on the 19th Aug.), and attacks of the 18th June and 8th Sept. (Medal and Clasp).

20 Captain Dowson served with the 29th Regt. throughout the Punjaub campaign of 1848-9, including the affair of Ramnuggur, passage of the Chenab, and battles of Chillianwallah and Goojerat (Medal and Clasps).

22 Captain Bennett served the Eastern campaign of 1854-55, including the battles of Alma and Inkerman siege of Sebastopol, and sortie on 26th Oct. (Medal and Clasps, and 5th Class of the Medjidie).

23 Captain Blackall served with the 40th Regt. in China (Medal), and was present at the first taking of Chusan.

24 Captain Plummer served at the siege of Sebastopol from 12th July 1855 (Medal and Clasp).

25 Lieuts. C. E. Hope, Browne, and Gardner, served at the siege of Sebastopol from 7th July 1855 (Medal and Clasp).

26 Paymaster Scott served the Eastern campaign of 1854-55, including the battles of Alma and Inkerman, and siege of Sebastopol (Medal and Clasps).

28 Quarter Master Metcalf served with the 40th Regt. throughout the Eastern campaign of 1854-55, including the battles of Alma and Inkerman, siege and fall of Sebastopol, sortie of 26th Oct., and assaults of the Redan on the 8th June and 8th Sept. (Medal and three Clasps).

29 Assist.-Surgeon Hale served in the Crimea from Jan. 1855, and was in the trenches during the bombardments of April and 7th June, and in the assault of 8th Sept. (Medal and Clasp, and Victoria Cross).

30 Assist.-Surgeon Ricketts served the Eastern campaign of 1854-55, including the battles of Balaklava and Inkerman, siege of Sebastopol, sortie of 20th October, and capture of Kertch and Yenikale (Medal and Clasps).

31 Captain Whigham served with the 42nd Highlanders in the Crimea from 2nd Dec. 1854, including the expedition to Kertch, siege and fall of Sebastopol, and assault of the outworks on the 18th June (Medal and Clasp).

33 Captain Wedderburne served with the 24th Regt. during the Punjaub campaign of 1848-49, and was present at the battle of Goojerat (Medal and one Clasp).

34 Captain Russell was at Meerut with the Carabineers at the outbreak of the Sepoy mutiny, and at Kurnaul when Colonel Gerrard was killed, was afterwards present with Seaton's Moveable Column at the battle of Gungaree where—his three senior officers being killed—he commanded the squadron of his Regt. and a detachment of the 9th Lancers, again on the 17th Dec. 1857 he commanded the Cavalry in the action of Puttcali where over 700 Sepoys were killed,—" to Lieut. Russell," writes Sir Thomas Seaton in his dispatch, " who commanded the Cavalry as well as to his brave companions in arms my thanks are specially due, for their gallantry in action and vigour in pursuit." He commanded the Cavalry also at Mynpooree where 250 of the rebels were killed, and was with his Regt. when General Penny was killed and Bareilly taken.

1st Batt. Peshawur.
2nd Batt. Gibraltar.

7th Regt. of Foot (Royal Fusiliers). 185

In the centre of the colours, The "*Rose*" within the "*Garter*" and the "*Crown*" over it. And in the corners of the second Colour, The "*White Horse*." "MARTINIQUE" "TALAVERA" "ALBUHERA" "BADAJOZ" "SALAMANCA" "VITTORIA" "PYRENEES" "ORTHES" "TOULOUSE" "PENINSULA" "ALMA" "INKERMAN" "SEVASTOPOL."

Years' Serv.		
Full Pay	Half Pay	
63		**Colonel.**—1) Sir Samuel Benj. Auchmuty,[1] KCB. *Ens.* 15 Oct. 97 ; *Lt.* 13 Mar. 00 ; *Capt.* 14 Nov. 05 ; *Maj.* 21 June 13 ; *Lt.-Col.* 12 Apr. 14 ; *Col.* 6 May 31 ; *Major-Gen.* 23 Nov. 41 ; *Lt.-Gen.* 11 Nov. 51 ; *Col.* 7th F. 18 Jan. 55.
16	0	**Lt.-Colonels.**—1 Richard William Aldworth,[2] *2nd Lt.* p 19 Aug. 44 ; *Lieut.* p 22 Oct. 47 ; *Capt.* 7 June 54 ; *Maj.* 27 May 56 ; *Lt.-Col.* p 20 March 57.
16	6/12	1 Reginald Yonge Shipley,[2]† *2nd Lt.* p 5 Dec. 43 ; *Lieut.* p 11 Dec. 46 ; *Capt.* p 30 April 52 ; *Brev. Maj.* 12 Dec. 54 ; *Major*, 19 June 55 ; *Lt.-Col.* 27 May 56.
		2 Poulett George Henry Somerset,[3]† CB. *Lt.-Col.* 2 Feb. 58.
17	0	**Majors.**—1 Charles Edward Watson,[3] *Ens.* p 13 Oct. 43 ; *Lt.* p 8 Aug. 45 ; *Capt.* p 24 Feb. 54 ; *Brev.-Major*, 2 Nov. 55 ; *Major*, 8 Jan. 56.
12	0	1 Thomas Tryon,[4] *Ens.* p 12 May 48 ; *Lieut.* p 1 Feb. 50 ; *Capt.* 21 Sept. 54 ; *Brev.-Maj.* 6 June 56 ; *Major*, p 20 March 57.
13	0	2 Hugh Robert Hibbert,[5] *Ens.* p 28 Sept. 47 ; *Lieut.* p 16 Aug. 50 ; *Capt.* 22 Dec. 54 ; *Brev.-Maj.* 2 Nov. 55 ; *Major*, 23 Oct. 57.
0	0	2 George William Wallace Carpenter,[7] *Ens.* p 17 June 51 ; *Lieut.* p 27 Jan. 54 ; *Capt.* p 12 Jan. 55 ; *Major*, p 13 May 59.

		CAPTAINS.	ENSIGN.	LIEUT.	CAPTAIN.	BREV.-MAJ.
9	0	1 Joshua Harry Cooper[6]	p 16 Sept. 51	p 24 Feb. 54	23 Mar. 55	
11	0	1 Thomas Wright Marten[9]	p 6 July 49	p 13 Dec. 53	19 June 55	
8	0	1 Lord Rich. Howe Browne[10]	p 23 Nov. 52	8 Dec. 54	p 13 July 55	
7	0	2 James Francis Hickie[11]	p 21 May 53	12 Jan. 55	p 3 Aug. 55	
6	0	1 George Henry Waller[13]	10 Aug. 54	22 Dec. 54	p 20 Mar. 57	
8	6/14	2 Robert Carr Glyn	p 13 Dec. 51	p 18 Feb. 53	p 30 Nov. 55	
6	0	1 Napier Douglas Robinson[14]	11 Aug. 54	12 Jan. 55	p 28 Aug. 57	
7	1	2 Jas. Menzies Clayhills[15]	p 23 Nov. 52	13 Aug. 54	p 31 Aug. 55	
9	1	2 George Flower Herbert[16]	p 15 Oct. 50	p 10 Dec. 52	9 Sept. 55	
7	1	2 Alfred Goodlad Daubeny[17]	p 23 Nov. 52	p 8 Sept. 54	30 Nov. 55	
5	1	1 William Jesser Coope[18]	p 17 Feb. 54	p 15 Sept. 54	26 Feb. 56	
8	1	2 John Thomas Campbell[19]	p 19 Aug. 51	6 June 54	p 29 July 56	
18	0	2 Cha. Sutherland Dowson[20]	3 June 42	p 27 Mar. 46	23 Oct. 57	
5	1	2 Robert Whigham[31]	6 June 54	8 Dec. 54	12 Sept. 56	
13	0	1 George Wedderburne[32]	p 3 Dec. 47	p 21 Dec. 49	2 Feb. 58	
14	0	2 Richard Harbord	p 22 Dec. 46	p 11 April 51	2 Feb. 58	
6	0	1 Adrian Bennett[22]	5 Nov. 54	9 Mar. 55	1 May 58	
14	0	1 Richard Barter[12]	28 Apr. 46	3 Apr. 49	17 Apr. 58	
22	0	1 Robert Blackall[23]	p 19 Jan. 38	6 Mar. 40	15 Mar. 53	
5	0	2 Baker Creed Russell[34]	2 Nov. 55	1 Aug. 56	p 18 Feb. 59	
11	0	1 Thos. Geo. Dupré Payn[35]	p 16 Feb. 49	25 Oct. 50	1 Oct. 58	
11	0	1 VC Hugh S. Cochrane	13 Apr. 49	p 15 Oct. 52	24 Aug. 58	
5	0	2 James Kennedy M'Adam	p 11 Jan. 55	19 June 55	p 24 May 59	
6	0	2 Heathcote Plummer[24]	15 Dec. 54	13 April 55	18 Sept. 59	

		LIEUTENANTS.				
5	0	2 John Emilius Elwes	p 12 Jan. 55	19 June 55		
6	0	1 Charles Errol Hope[23]	p 25 Aug. 54	26 July 55		
5	0	1 Henry Kerr	26 Jan. 55	27 July 55		
5	0	1 Robert Watson Sparks	16 Mar. 55	p 3 Aug. 55		
5	0	1 William Pryce Browne[25]	9 Mar. 55	19 Aug. 55		
5	0	1 James Anthony Gardner[25]	29 Mar. 55	9 Sept. 55		
5	0	1 Henry John Barnard	p 30 Mar. 55	9 Sept. 55		
5	0	1 Charles S. Courtenay	24 April 55	3 Oct. 55		
5	0	1 Francis Burton Cole	24 April 55	16 Oct. 55		
5	0	1 Alex. Nixon Montgomery	p 1 June 55	16 Nov. 55		
5	0	2 Cornelius Geo. O'Brien	19 July 55	p 16 Nov. 55		
5	0	2 Musgrave Watson	27 July 55	p 17 Nov. 55		
5	0	2 Francis John Foster	p 3 Aug. 55	28 Nov. 55		
7	0	1 Gwynne Orton Lewis, *Adj.*	p 27 May 53	23 Oct. 55		
5	0	2 Charles Gurney	21 Sept. 55	p 28 Aug. 57		
5	0	1 Henry Alexander Little	16 Mar. 55	p 29 May 57		
5	0	2 Thomas Burton Vandeleur	p 21 Sept. 55	23 Oct. 57		
5	0	1 Fitzmaurice Beauchamp	16 Oct. 55	p 26 Jan. 58		
5	0	1 Archibald James Arnott	6 July 55	p 19 Dec. 56		
5	0	2 Horace Sibbald Harrison	27 July 55	p 22 May 57		
5	0	2 William Hartrick	16 Nov. 55	14 July 57		
5	0	1 Anselm Tibeaudo	8 Oct. 55	13 April 58		
5	0	2 Edmund Waller	16 Nov. 55	p 30 July 58		
4	0	2 Hardinge Giffard Follett	p 20 Feb. 56	p 13 Aug. 58		
4	0	1 Edw. W. Cadwall. Lloyd	1 Apr. 56	p 24 Dec. 58		
4	0	1 Cart. Houstoun Kempson	p 4 Apr. 56	p 1 Apr. 59		
4	0	2 Douglas Flood	4 Apr. 56	p 24 May 59		
5	0	1 J. H. Randall Stoddart	16 Nov. 55	10 Oct. 57		
4	0	1 William John Frampton	12 Dec. 56	18 Sept. 59		

3† Lieut.-Colonel Somerset served the Eastern campaign of 1854, as Aide-de-Camp to Lord Raglan, including the battles of Alma, Balaklava, and Inkerman (horse killed by the explosion of a shell in him), and siege of Sebastopol (Medal and Clasps, and 4th Class of the Medjidie).

8 Captain Cooper served the Eastern campaign of 1854-55, including the sortie of 26th Oct., battle of Inkerman, and siege of Sebastopol; appointed Aide de Camp to Colonel Yea, and also present at the attack on the Quarries 7th June (wounded 8th June), and assault of the Redan on 18th June (Medal and Clasp, and 5th Class of the Medjidie).

12 Captain Barter served as Adjutant 75th Regt. throughout the East Indian campaign of 1857-58, including the battle of Badli ke Serai (severely wounded), siege, storm, and capture of Delhi, action of Bolundshur, affairs of Allighur and Akernbad, battle of Agra, skirmishes at Canoge and other places en route to Cawnpore, affairs of Maragunj and Alumbagh on the advance into Oude, occupation (after the relief) of the fortified outposts and camp before Lucknow, under Sir James Outram, and repulse of the enemy's attacks (Medal and Clasps).

7th Regt. of Foot (Royal Fusiliers).

Years' Serv. Full Pay.	Half Pay.	ENSIGNS.		ENSIGN.	
3	0	1	Arthur John Harrison ..	p 10 Mar. 57	7 Major Carpenter served in the Eastern campaign of 1854, and was wounded at the battle of Alma (Medal and Clasp).
3	0	2	Joseph Smith, Adj.	6 Nov. 57	27 Surgeon Mandeville served during the whole of the campaign under Sir George Berkeley against the Kaffirs in 1817, in medical charge of all the native levies. Accompanied the expedition in 1848 against the rebel Boers. Served also in the Kaffir war of 1850-51, and was present when a strong force of combined Kaffirs and Hottentots were defeated at Fort Brown on the 1st Oct. 1851, in their attempt to capture the cattle belonging to the Fort.
2	0	2	John Graydon Smith....	p 26 Jan. 58	
2	0	2	Edward Wynne Griffith	2 Feb. 58	
2	0	2	Vinc. Upton Langworthy	3 Feb. 58	
2	0	2	Henry Wm. Loveridge ..	4 Feb. 58	
2	0	2	Geo.Wm.Hy.Holyoake..	5 Feb. 58	
2	0	2	William Loraine Geddes	6 Feb. 58	
2	0	2	Edward Lloyd Gutacre..	7 Feb. 58	
2	0	2	Arthur Ashton	8 Feb. 58	
2	0	2	Charles Godfrey Bolam	9 Feb. 58	35 Captain Payn served with the 61st Regt. in the Indian campaign of 1857-58, including the siege, assault, and capture of Delhi, and action of Nujjufghur (Medal and Clasp).
2	0	2	Robert Fowler Butler ..	10 Feb. 58	
2	0	1	Fred. Charles Keyser ..	28 May 58	
2	0	1	Edward Bridges	p 4 June 58	
2	0	1	Henry W. Locke Paddon	6 Aug. 58	
2	0	1	Morris James Fawcett ..	p 31 Aug. 58	
1	0	1	Hon. Wollaston Rochfort	p 25 Jan. 59	
1	0	1	Charles James Hayter..	p 11 Mar. 59	
1	0	1	George Brooke Meares..	p 3 June 59	
1	0	1	Herbert Henry Rice....	p 24 June 59	

6	0	*Paymasters.*—1 John Mortimer Scott,[26] 15 Feb. 56; Qr.-Mr. 18 Aug. 54.
2	0	2 William Handasyde Buchanan, 19 Nov. 58.
3	0	*Adjutants.*—2 Ensign Joseph Smith, 6 Nov. 57.
7	0	1 *Lieut.* Gwynne Orton Lewis, 11 Aug. 58.
6	0	*Instructors of Musketry.*—1 *Captain* Adrian Bennett,[92] 1 May 57.
5	0	2 *Lieut.* H. S. Harrison, 1 Apr. 59.
4	0	*Quarter-Masters.*—1 Thomas Murphy, 4 April 56.
5	0	2 Timothy Metcalf,[26] 23 Oct. 57 ; *Ens.* 7 Dec. 55.
15	0	*Surgeons.*—1 Thomas Moorhead, M.D. 3 Nov. 54 ; *Assist.-Surg.* 24 Oct. 45.
14	0	2 Edward Wm. Thos. Mandeville,[27] 16 Feb. 55 ; *A.S.* 25 Sept. 46.
6	0	*Assistant-Surgeons.*—1 ỤC Thomas Egerton Hale,[29] M.D. 14 Dec. 54.
6	0	1 Charles Ricketts,[30] 28 April 54.
6	0	1 Thomas Sheehy, M.D. 26 May 54.
3	0	2 Michael Quinlan, 8 Dec. 57.
2	0	2 Edward Acton Gibbon, 1 Sept. 58.

Facings Blue.—*Agents,* Messrs. Cox & Co.

[1st Batt. ret. from Crimea, 27 June 56. Emb. for India, 21 July 57. Depot, Chatham.]
[2nd Batt. embarked for Gibraltar, 27 May 1858. Depot, Walmer.]

1 Sir Samuel Benj. Auchmuty served several years in the West Indies, and was present at the storming of Morne Fortunée, St. Lucia. In 1809 he accompanied the second Battalion Royal Fusiliers to Portugal, and was present at Oporto and Talavera as Major of Brigade to Sir Alex. Campbell; and at the battle of Busaco, the retreat of the army to and subsequent advance from the lines of Torres Vedras, and battle of Fuentes d'Onor, as Deputy Assistant Adjutant-General to the Sixth Division. On return to the Peninsula from sick leave he was appointed extra Aide-de-Camp to Sir Lowry Cole, and was in action with the Fourth Division at Vittoria and the Pyrenees,—at the latter was promoted to the Brevet rank of Major. Succeeding soon afterwards to the Regimental Majority, he commanded the light companies of Major-General Ross's Brigade, and served with them at Orthes and Toulouse,—at the latter was promoted Brevet Lieut.-Colonel. He has received the Gold Medal and one Clasp for the battles of Orthes and Toulouse; and the Silver War Medal with five Clasps for the other battles.
2 Lt.-Col. Aldworth served the Eastern campaign of 1854 up to 8th November, including the battles of Alma and Inkerman, siege of Sebastopol, and sortie of 26th October (Medal and Clasps).
2† Lt.-Col. Shipley served the Eastern campaign of 1854, including the battles of Alma and Inkerman (severely wounded), siege of Sebastopol, and sortie on 26th Oct., on which last occasion he commanded an outlying picket, and was warmly engaged (Medal and Clasps, Brevet Major, Sardinian Medal, and 5th Class of the Medjidie).
3 Major Watson served in the Eastern campaign of 1854, and was severely wounded at the battle of Alma (Medal and Clasp, and 5th Class of the Medjidie).
4 Major Tryon served in the Eastern campaign of 1854, including the battle of Inkerman, siege of Sebastopol, and sortie on 26th Oct. (Medal and Clasps).
5 Major Hibbert served the Eastern campaign of 1854-55, and was present at the battles of Alma (wounded) and Inkerman, and siege of Sebastopol, including sortie on 26th Oct. 1854, assault on the Redan 18th June 1855, and assault on the Redan on 8th Sept.—severely wounded (Medal and Clasps, Brevet Major, Knight of the Legion of Honor, Sardinian Medal, and 5th Class of the Medjidie).
9 Captain Marten served with the Royal Fusiliers at the siege of Sebastopol, from 17th June 1855, including the assaults of the Redan on the 18th June and 8th Sept., on which last occasion he succeeded to the command of the Regiment, led it across the ditch of that work, and subsequently brought it out of action—mentioned in Dispatches (Medal and Clasp).
10 Lord Richard Browne served at the siege of Sebastopol from 20th March 1855, including sorties on 22nd March and 9th May, defence of the Quarries 7th June, and assault on the Redan on the 18th June (severely wounded); also slightly wounded by the bursting of a shell in Sebastopol, 1st Dec. 1855 (Medal and Clasp, and 5th Class of the Medjidie).
11 Captain Hickie served at the siege of Sebastopol from 17th June 1855, including assaults on the Redan on 18th June and 8th Sept. (severely wounded): Medal and Clasp.
13 Captain Waller served at the siege of Sebastopol from 21st Nov. 1854, including sortie on 9th May, attack and capture of the Quarries 7th June (wounded), assault on the Redan 18th June (wounded), and was in the trenches on the 8th Sept. (Medal and Clasp, and Knight of the Legion of Honor).
14 Captain Robinson served at the siege of Sebastopol from 17th Feb. 1855, including the assault on the Redan on the 18th June (wounded): Medal and Clasp.

[For remainder of Notes, see end of 6th Foot.

1st Batt. Allahabad.
2nd Batt. Gibraltar.

8th (*The King's*) *Regiment of Foot.* 187

The "*White Horse*," on a red ground within the "*Garter*," and the "*Crown*" over it. In the three corners of the second colour, the "*Royal Cypher and Crown.*" "*Nec aspera terrent.*" The "*Sphinx*," with the words "EGYPT" "MARTINIQUE" "NIAGARA."

Years' Serv. Full Pay.	Half Pay.		
52		Colonel.—**P CB** Roderick Macneil,[1] *Ens.* 17 March 08; *Lt.* 9 May 09; *Capt* 1 Dec. 14; *Major,* 9 Aug. 21; *Lt.-Col.* 25 Jan. 22; *Col.* 10 Jan. 37; *Maj Gen.* 9 Nov. 46; *Lieut.-Gen.* 20 June 54; *Col.* 8th Foot, 18 Mar. 55.		
35	0	*Lt.-Colonels.*—1 John Longfield,[2] CB. *Ens.* P 23 June 25; *Lt.* P 26 Sept. 26; *Capt.* P 30 Jan. 35; *Major,* P 19 Nov. 44; *Lieut.Col.* 3 Apr. 46; *Col.* 20 June 54.		
35	1 6/12	2 Thomas Maitland Wilson, *Ens.* P 15 April 24; *Lt.* P 13 May 26; *Capt.* P 23 Dec. 31; *Br.-Maj.* 9 Nov. 46; *Major,* 18 Aug. 48; *Lt.-Col.* P 15 June 49; *Col.* 28 Nov. 54.		
21	0	1 Fred. Paul Haines,[3] *Ens.* P 21 June 39; *Lt.* P 15 Dec. 40; *Capt.* 10 May 46; *Bt.Maj.* 7 June 49; *Bt.Lt.Col.* 2 Aug. 50; *Major,* 15 Nov. 54; *Col.* 28 Nov. 54; *Lt.Col.* 24 April 55.		
29	0	*Majors.*—1 James Croft Brooke,[4] *Ens.* P 31 Oct. 31; *Lieut.* 2 Sept. 33; *Capt.* 31 March 46; *Major,* P 2 Oct. 48; *Brevet Lt.-Col.* 14 April 57.		
25	0	2 John Hindo,[5] CB. *Ens.* P 28 Feb. 35; *Lieut.* P 30 June 37; *Capt.* P 4 July 45; *Major,* 21 Oct. 57; *Brev.Lt.Col.* 19 Jan. 58.		
21	0	2 James Johnston, *Ens.* P 7 June 39; *Lieut.* P 13 May 42; *Capt.* P 21 Apr. 46; *Major,* 26 June 58.		
23	0	1 Alex. Cunningham Robertson,[6] *Ens.* P 15 Sept. 37; *Lieut.* P 20 Aug. 41; *Capt.* P 11 Nov. 45; *Bt.Maj.* 19 Jan. 58; *Bt.Lt.Col.* 20 July 58; *Maj.* 23 July 58.		

		CAPTAINS.	ENSIGN.	LIEUT.	CAPTAIN.	BREV.-MAJ.
25	0	1 Edwin Gream Daniell[7]..	P 2 Oct. 35	P 7 Sept. 38	P 25 Nov. 45	19 Jan. 58
21	0	1 William Bayly[8]	26 Jan. 39	23 June 42	29 May 48	13 Dec. 59
19	0	1 George Edward Baynes[9]	P 2 July 41	P 12 Dec. 43	17 Oct. 48	19 Jan. 58
13	0	2 John Millar Bannatyne[11]	P 17 Dec. 47	P 10 Jan. 51	P 22 April 53	19 Jan. 58
19	0	1 Astell Thomas Welsh[12] ..	P 21 May 41	26 July 44	17 Oct. 52	
8	0	2 De Vic Tupper[13]	P 15 Oct. 52	11 Aug. 54	15 Jan. 56	
12	0	1 Richard Raphael Mende[14]	P 6 Oct. 48	6 Oct. 51	P 31 Aug. 55	
15	0	1 John Whiteside[15]	19 Dec. 45	P 12 Nov. 47	14 Mar. 56	
18	0	1 Thomas George Souter[16].	21 May 42	28 Jan. 44	21 Oct. 57	
18	0	2 Daniel Beere[17]..........	4 May 42	3 Apr. 46	21 Oct. 57	
18	0	1 Ersk.NimmoSandilands[18]	21 May 42	3 Apr. 46	21 Oct. 57	
8	1	2 Swinnerton Halliday Dyer[19]	P 12 Dec. 51	P 24 Feb. 54	7 Sept. 55	
16	1	2 Rob. C. Dalrymple Bruce	10 Nov. 43	14 Apr. 46	21 Sept. 55	
19	2 2/12	2 Owen Wynne Gray[21]	9 Nov. 38	18 May 40	23 Oct. 57	
16	0	2 George Corry[22]	26 July 44	3 Apr. 46	15 Nov. 57	
13	0	2 John Vere W. Hen. Webb[23]	29 Jan. 47	P 21 Feb. 51	14 May 58	
13	0	1 Alexander Ross Bayly[24]..	2 Apr. 47	6 May 51	14 May 58	
12	0	2 Wm. Raymond Ximenes[25]	P 29 Dec. 48	25 May 53	14 May 58	
12	0	2 George Henry Cochrane .	2 Aug. 48	13 Dec. 51	21 May 58	
6	0	1 Fred. Bradford M'Crea[25]..	6 June 54	P 20 July 55	26 June 58	
4	0	1 Forster Longfield[26]......	15 Jan. 56	P 1 Aug. 56	P 24 Sept. 58	
8	0	1 William Fred. Metge[27] ..	P 13 Feb. 52	7 Sept. 55	P 22 Apr. 59	
7	0	2 William Edward Newall	P 12 May 53	26 July 55	26 Dec. 57	
6	0	2 John M'Queen[27]†	5 Nov. 54	8 Mar. 55	23 Sept. 59	
		LIEUTENANTS.				
5	0	1 Fred. Anderson Stebbing[28]	18 May 55	12 Apr. 56		
3	0	1 Alfred Downie Corfield..	P 1 Aug. 56	P 15 May 57		
4	0	1 Æneas Gordon Blair	7 Mar. 56	5 Sept. 57		
4	0	1 **VC** Andrew Moynihan[30]	2 May 56	16 Sept. 57		
4	0	1 Wm. Edw. Whelan,[30]†*Adj.*	P 16 May 56	18 Sept. 57		
5	0	2 James Q. Palmer	2 Mar. 55	26 Feb. 56		
5	0	2 Chas. Bradf. Brown,[32]*Adj.*	15 Mar. 55	26 Feb. 56		
5	0	2 Fred. Geo. Furlong Moore	15 May 55	26 Feb. 56		
5	0	2 James F. Macpherson ..	1 June 55	26 Feb. 56		
5	0	2 James O'Hara	8 Oct. 55	P 26 Dec. 56		
5	0	1 Charles Norris Fry[33]	16 Mar. 55	P 24 Feb. 57		
5	0	1 Richard Thos. B. Browne	26 Oct. 55	15 Nov. 57		
5	0	2 Edward Tanner	P 30 Nov. 55	7 Dec. 57		
4	0	1 Robert Yallop Stokes ..	P 12 Dec. 56	23 Mar. 58		
4	0	1 Reginald Whitting[39]	P 26 Dec. 56	23 Mar. 58		
5	0	1 Walter John Tarte	5 July 55	P 13 July 58		
5	.0	2 Henry Leeson	6 July 55	P 23 July 58		
3	0	1 Ashley George Westby ..	P 14 July 57	30 July 58		
3	0	2 James Seager Wheeley..	P 31 July 57	20 Sept. 58		
5	0	1 John William Hughes ..	1 May 55	1 Oct. 58		
5	0	2 James Magenis Lovekin	7 June 55	1 Oct. 58		
5	0	2 Wm. Theobald Butler ..	5 July 55	1 Oct. 58		
5	0	2 John Evans Freke Aylmer	27 July 55	1 Oct. 58		
5	0	1 Charles Dyneley Baynes	21 Sept. 55	1 Oct. 58		
3	0	2 Robert D. Forbes Shirreff	P 4 Sept. 57	1 Oct. 58		

1 Lieut. General Macneil served in Sir John Moore's retreat, and subsequently at Walcheren in 1809; in Swedish Pomerania in 1813; in Holland in 1814, including the attack on Bergen-op-Zoom; and the campaign of 1815, including the battle of Waterloo.

2 Colonel Longfield commanded the 2d Brigade at the siege of Delhi in 1857, the Reserve during the assault, and served in the City during the six days' fighting that ensued (CB.)

7 Major Daniell served with the 55th in China (Medal), and was present at Amoy, Chusan, and Chinhae, including the repulse of the night-attack; also the expedition to You-You, up the Ningpo River. Served in the 8th Regt. at the siege of Delhi, and was severely wounded when engaged with the mutineers on the 9th July 1857 (Brevet Major).

8th (The King's) Regiment of Foot.

Years' Serv. Full Pay.	Half Pay.	LIEUTENANTS.	ENSIGN.	LIEUT.	
3	0	2 John Coleberd Cooper ..	p 30 Oct. 57	p 26 Nov. 58	
3	0	2 Geo. N. James Bradford	20 Nov. 57	p 4 Feb. 59	
3	0	1 Philip Homer Page	12 Dec. 57	p 22 Apr. 59	
2	0	2 Chas. D. Ryder Madden	30 Mar. 58	p 26 Aug. 59	
2	0	2 William Bannatyne	27 Apr. 58	p 13 Dec. 59	
		ENSIGNS.			
3	0	2 Edward Emerson	6 Nov. 57		6 Lt.Col. Robertson served in the Anglo-Spanish Legion from July 1835 to June 1837. Received a Medal for the action of 5th May 1837; the cross of the 1st Class of San Fernando, for the actions of the 15th and 16th March 1837; and another medal for the storming of Irun, 17th May following: wounded in the face by a splinter in the general action on the heights of Ametzu, 1st Oct. 1836. Served with the 8th Regt. at the siege of Delhi in 1857, including repulse of Sorties on 9th, 14th, and 18th July (commanded the Regt.), and commanded detachments of 8th and 61st Regts. at the capture of four guns in front of the advanced picket on 12th Aug. Acted as D.A.Q.M.Gen. to Seaton's Column in Dec., including affairs of Gungaree, Puttiala, and Mynpoorie. Present during operations from 2nd to 22nd March 1858 resulting in the occupation of Lucknow in the capacity of Deputy Judge Advocate General to the Army in the field (Brevet Major).
3	0	1 Richard Chute	17 Nov. 57		
3	0	2 Thomas Palmer Senior..	18 Nov. 57		
3	0	2 Thos. Picton Fleetwood..	19 Nov. 57		
3	0	1 William James Watson..	21 Nov. 57		
3	0	1 Arundel Hill Cotter	11 Dec. 57		
3	0	1 John George Brown	13 Dec. 57		
2	0	1 Arthur Cook	16 Mar. 58		
2	0	2 William John Cooper ..	23 Mar. 58		
2	0	1 Cha. Blandford Crease ..	23 Mar. 58		
2	0	2 William W. Madden	2 July 58		
2	0	1 Jeremy Peyton Jones ..	3 July 58		
2	0	1 Robert Handcock	8 Oct. 58		
1	0	1 Walter Mowbray Johnston	28 Jan. 59		
1	0	2 Chas. Thos. Fred. Blair ..	29 Jan. 59		
1	0	2 Theodore Henry Skinner	p 1 Apr. 59		
1	0	1 William Albert Bridge..	p 3 June 59		
1	0	2 John R. Minshull Ford..	p 21 Oct. 59		

12	0	*Paymasters.*—1 G. Egerton Huddleston,[31] 23 Mar. 55; *Ens.* 30 Dec. 48; *Lt.* 2 John Falls, 4 Dec. 57. [p 27 June 54.	
3	0		
4	0	*Adjutants.*—1 Lieut. Wm. Edward Whelan, 30 April 58.	
5	0	2 *Lieut.* C. B. Brown,[32] 16 July 58.	
3	0	*Instructors of Musketry.*—1 Ensign William James Watson, 17 Feb. 59.	
5	0	2 *Lieut.* J. E. F. Aylmer, 30 May 59.	
4	10/12	*Quarter Masters.*—2 Thomas Massey Chadwick, 20 Sept. 55.	
1	0	1 John Keating, 23 Sept. 59.	
21	0	*Surgeons.*—1 Francis Charles Annesley;[35] *Assist.Surg.* 17 Sept. 30; *Surgeon*, 15 Aug. 48; *Surgeon Major*, 17 Sept. 59.	
14	0	2 John Madden,[36] 2 Oct. 57; *Assist.-Surg.* 8 Oct. 46.	
6	0	*Assistant Surgeons.*—1 William Henry Yates,[37] 24 Nov. 54.	
6	0	1 Thomas James Biddle,[38] 15 Aug. 54.	
2	0	2 William Jay, 22 Jan. 58.	
2	0	2 Joseph Edward O'Loughlin, 5 Aug. 58.	
2	0	1 Richard Westrop Saunders, M.D. 22 Jan. 58.	

Facings Blue.—*Agents*, Sir Chas. R. M'Grigor, Bt., and Walter M'Grigor, Esq.
[1st Batt. embarked for Bombay, 30 Apr. 46. Depot, Chatham.]
[2nd Batt. embarked for Gibraltar, 7 Sept. 58. Depot, Templemore.]

3 Colonel Haines' services:—On the formation of the Army of the Sutlej in 1845 he was appointed to officiate as Military Secretary to the Commander in Chief in India, Sir Hugh Gough, and in that capacity he was present at the battles of Moodkee and Ferozeshah (Medal and one Clasp); in the latter engagement he was severely wounded by grape shot at the attack on the enemy's works, his horse being killed under him at the same moment. At the recommendation of Lord Gough, he was promoted to a Company in the 10th Foot, without purchase. As Military Secretary to his Lordship, he served the Punjaub campaign of 1848-9, and was present at the affair of outposts at Ramnuggur, 22nd Nov. 1848, and subsequent operations resulting in the passage of the Chenab, and the battles of Chillianwallah and Goojerat (Medal and two Clasps); served with the 21st Fusiliers the Eastern campaign of 1854-55, including the battles of Alma, Balaclava, and Inkerman, and siege of Sebastopol (Medal and four Clasps, and 5th Class of the Medjidie).

4 Lt.-Colonel Brooke served with the 31st Regt. throughout the campaign of 1842 in Affghanistan (Medal) under General Pollock, and was present in the actions of Mazeena, Tezeen, and Jugdulluck (wounded), the occupation of Cabool, and the different engagements leading to it. He commanded a Company during the campaign, and received his wound whilst protecting some guns attached to the rear-guard. Served with the 8th Regt. at the siege of Delhi in 1857 including repulse of sorties on the 9th and 14th July, commanded the Regt. during the repulse of the enemy's attack on 23d July, present at the assault of the City and was one of the four Field Officers who commanded in the trenches—severely wounded.

5 Lt.Colonel Hinde served with the 8th Regt. in Delhi from 20th Sept. 1857; commanded the Regt. in the action of Bolundshur, affair of Allyghur, battle of Agra, action of Dilkoosha and relief of Lucknow under Lord Clyde; affair of the 2d and action of the 6th Dec. at Cawnpore, and action of Khudagunj (Brevet Lt. Col. and CB., and mentioned in despatches).

8 Major Wm. Bayly was present at the battle of Plattsburg in America in 1814. Served at the siege of Delhi from 28th June to 3d Sept. 1857, including repulse of Sorties on the 9th, 14th, 18th, and 23d July—commanded the two flank Companies on the last occasion.

9 Major G. E. Baynes served at the siege of Delhi in 1857, including repulse of Sorties on the 9th, 14th, 18th, and 23d July, and commanded the storming party of the 2d Column of attack at the assault of the City (Brevet Major).

11 Major Bannatyne served with the 8th Regt. at the siege and assault of Delhi in 1857, including repulse of Sorties on the 9th, 14th, and 18th July, and six days' fighting in the City (twice wounded); commanded the Regt. at the capture of the Burn Bastion on the night of the 19th Sept., and the Infantry of the Column which occupied the Jumna Musjid on the 20th September. Served as Brigade Major to Greathed's Moveable Column, including the action of Bolundshur, affair of Allyghur, and battle of Agra. Present as Brigade Major 3d Brigade of the army under Lord Clyde in the action of Dilkoosha and relief of Lucknow, affair of 2d and action of the 6th Dec. at Cawnpore, and action of Khudagunj (Brevet Major).

12 Captain Welsh served with the 80th Regt. in the Burmese war of 1852-53 (Medal); including the bombardment of Rangoon and subsequent operations of the 12th, 13th, and 14th April, and capture of the great Dagon Pagoda (with the storming party); bombardment and capture of Prome (specially thanked by the Governor General of India in Council), night-attack of the enemy on the camp on the heights of Prome, and expedition into the Poungdey district in Feb. and March 1853.

13 Captain Tupper served with the 38th Regt. throughout the Eastern campaign of 1854-55, including the battles of Alma, Inkerman, attack and capture of the Cemetery 18th June, siege and fall of Sebastopol (Medal and three Clasps).

14 Captain Meade was present as a Volunteer with the Artillery in the action at Agra on 5th July 1857. Served with the 8th Regt. at the relief of Lucknow under Lord Clyde; also at the affair of 2d and action of the 6th Dec. at Cawnpore, and the action at Khudagunj.

15 Captain Whiteside served throughout the campaign under General Pollock in Affghanistan in 1842 (Medal) and that on the Sutlej in 1845-46 (Medal and Clasps), including the battles of Moodkee, Ferozeshah, and Sobraon. Commanded the 8th Regt. whilst engaged on field service in Oude in Oct. 1858 and at the attack and capture of the fort and town of Sandee, and served in Oude during the campaign of 1858-59.

16 Captain Souter served in the Buffs in the action of Punniar 29th Dec. 1843 (Medal). Served with the 8th Regt. at the siege of Delhi in 1857, including repulse of Sorties on the 14th, 18th, and 23d July.

17 Captain Beere served at the siege of Delhi and was wounded at the assault of the City on the 14th Sept. 1857.

18 Captain Sandilands served with the 8th Regt. at the siege of Delhi in 1857 including repulse of Sorties on 14th, 18th, and 23d July (wounded by a splinter of a shell on the 10th August), and commanded the Light Company at the assault of the City (wounded); also present in the action of Dilkoosha and relief of Lucknow under Lord Clyde, the affair of the 2d and action of the 6th Dec. at Cawnpore, and action of Khudagunj.

19 Captain Dyer served with the 17th Regt. at the siege of Sebastopol from 2nd Jun. 1855, including assaults of the Redan on 18th June and 8th Sept.; was also at the bombardment and surrender of Kinbourn (Medal and Clasp, and 5th Class of the Medjidie).

21 Captain Gray served with the 39th at the affair of Gorapore, near Kurnool, on the 18th Oct. 1839; and also at the battle of Maharajpore, 29th Dec. 1843 (Medal).

22 Captain Corry was employed in various desultory operations against the Mutineers in India in 1857-58.

23 Captain Webb served at the siege and assault of Delhi in 1857, including repulse of Sorties on 9th and 14th July, capture of four guns on 12th Aug., and six days' fighting in the City; afterwards present in the action of Bolundshur, affair of Allyghur, and battle of Agra, the action of Dilkoosha and relief of Lucknow under Lord Clyde, affair of the 2d and action of 6th Dec. at Cawnpore, and action of Khudagunj.

24 Captain A. R. Bayly served at the siege and assault of Delhi including repulse of Sorties on 9th, 14th, and 18th July, and the six days' fighting in the City; afterwards present in the action of Bolundshur, affair of Allyghur, battle of Agra, action of Dilkoosha, and relief of Lucknow under Lord Clyde, affair of the 2d and action of 6th Dec. at Cawnpore, and action of Khudagunj.

25 Captains Ximenes and M'Crea served in Delhi from the 18th Sept. 1857, and was afterwards present in the action of Bolundshur, affair of Allyghur, battle of Agra, action of Dilkoosha and relief of Lucknow under Lord Clyde, the affair of the 2d and action of 6th Dec. at Cawnpore, and action of Khudagunj. Captain McCrea was also at the action of Kanonge, and served during the Oude campaign of 1858-59.

26 Captain Longfield served at the siege of Delhi in 1857 and repulse of Sorties on 9th, 14th, 18th, and 23d July, and capture of four guns on 12th Aug.; afterwards present in the action of Dilkoosha and relief of Lucknow under Lord Clyde, the affair of the 2d and action of 6th Dec. at Cawnpore, and action of Khudagunj also served in the Oude campaign of 1858-59 as Brigade Quartermaster to Brigadier Hale's force, and was present at the attack and capture of the fort and town of Sandee.

27 Captain Metge served at the siege and assault of Delhi in 1857, including repulse of Sorties on the 9th and 14th July, and was with the storming party of the Left Attack at the assault of the City (wounded); also served in command of the Police Cavalry with General Whitlock's Column in Bundlecund (Medal and Clasp).

27† Captain M'Queen served the Eastern campaign of 1854-55, including the battles of Alma, Balaklava, and Inkerman, siege and fall of Sebastopol, and assault on the batteries on the 18th June—wounded in the left arm (Medal and Clasps, and 5th Class of the Medjidie).

28 Lieut. Stebbing served at the siege and assault of Delhi in 1857 and during the six days' fighting in the City; afterwards present in the affairs of Gungaree, Puttiwalla, and Mynpoorie.

30 Lieut. Moynihan served with the 90th Light Infantry in the Crimea, from Dec. 1854, including the siege and fall of Sebastopol, and assault of the Redan on 8th Sept. with the storming party, being the first man to enter, and was made prisoner when rescuing the body of Lt. Swift from a party of Russians inside the Redan, but released by an advance of the British, after having been twice bayonetted; he held a position inside the Redan for a considerable time, and was again wounded in several places—mentioned in Dispatches (Medal and Clasp, and Victoria Cross). Served in the Indian campaign from Nov. 1857 and was present at the defeat of the rebels in the ravines of the Chumbul, attack and capture of Bhujah and Scorale; also served in the Oude campaign of 1858-59, including the attack and capture of the fort and town of Sandee.

30† Lieut. Whelan served in the Indian campaign from Nov. 1857 and was present at the defeat of the rebels in the ravines of the Chumbul, attack and capture of Bhujah and Scorale; served as Adjutant of the 8th Regt. in Oude during the campaign of 1858-59, including the attack and capture of the fort and town of Sandee.

32 Lieut. Brown served with the 63rd Regt. at the assault of the Redan and fall of Sebastopol, also at the bombardment and surrender of Kinbourn (Medal and Clasp).

33 Lieut. Fry served with the 18th Royal Irish in the Crimea (Medal).

34 Paymaster Huddleston served at the siege and capture of Delhi in 1857, also at the action of Bolundshur affair of Allyghur, battle of Agra, affair of the 2d and action of 6th Dec. at Cawnpore, and action of Khudagunj.

35 Surgeon Major Annesley served at the siege and capture of Delhi in 1857.

36 Surgeon Madden served with the 43rd Light Infantry in the Kaffir war of 1851-53 (Medal).

37 Assist.Surgeon Yates served with the 8th Regt. at the siege and capture of Delhi in 1857. Accompanied Greathed's Moveable Column in medical charge of the Regt. and present in the action of Bolundshur, affair of Allyghur, battle of Agra, action of Dilkoosha and relief of Lucknow under Lord Clyde, the affair of the 2d and action of 6th Dec. at Cawnpore, and action of Khudagunj.

38 Assist.Surgeon Biddle served with the 49th Regt. in the Crimea from 13th Sept. to 23d Dec. 1854 (Medal and Clasp for Sebastopol). Served with the 8th Regt. at the siege and assault of Delhi including repulse of Sorties on 14th, 18th, and 23d July, the capture of four guns on 12th Aug., the six days' fighting in the City, and capture of the Burn Bastion.

39 Lieut. Whitting served in the Indian campaign from March 1858, and acted as Staff Adjutant to a detachment at Sasseram and was engaged in the operations against the rebels in the jungles of Jugdeespore under Sir E. Lugard; also served the campaign of 1858-59 in Oude, including attack and capture of the fort and town of Sandee.

9th (The East Norfolk) Regiment of Foot. [2nd Batt. Corfu.

The figure of "*Britannia*," "ROLEIA" "VIMIERA" "CORUNNA" "BUSACO" "SALAMANCA" "VITTORIA" "ST. SEBASTIAN" "NIVE" "PENINSULA" "CABOOL 1842" "MOODKEE" "FEROZESHAH" "SOBRAON" "SEVASTOPOL."

Years' Serv.						
Full Pay	Half Pay					
60		Colonel.—1 Sir James Archibald Hope,[1] KCB. Ens. 12 Jan. 00; Lt. 3 June 01; Capt. 18 Feb. 06; Major, 6 March 11; Lt.Col. 21 June 13; Col. 22 July 30; Maj.Gen.23 Nov. 41; Lt.Gen. 11 Nov. 51; Gen. 12 June 59; Col. 9 F. 18 Feb.48.				
25	0	Lt.Colonels.—2 Charles Elmhirst,[2] Ens. p 14 Aug. 35; Lieut. p 17 Oct. 37; Capt. 22 Dec. 45; Major, p 8 June 52; Lt.Col. 9 March 55; Col. 20 May 58.				
25	0	1 Duncan Munro Bethune,[3] Ens. 17 Apr. 35; Lieut. 21 Mar. 38; Capt. 22 Dec.45; Major, 29 Dec. 54; Lt.Col. 24 Dec. 58.				
22	0	Majors.—1 Charles Henry Leslie,[4] Ens. p 20 July 38; Lt. 16 July 41; Capt. p 14 Apr. 46; Major, 20 Feb. 56.				
21	0	2 Alexander Tayler,[5] Ens. 21 June 39; Lt. 30 July 41; Capt. p 23 May 48; Major, 21 Oct. 57.				
16	8/12	2 William Sankey,[5]† Ens. p 19 April 44; Lt. p 8 Aug. 45; Capt. p 27 April 49; Bt.-Major, 12 Dec. 54; Bt. Lt.-Col. 2 Nov. 55; Major, 24 Feb. 57.				
17	0	1 George Harrington Hawes,[6] Ens. 24 Nov. 43; Lt. 4 Jan. 46; Capt. p 19 Sept. 48; Brev.Maj. 2 Nov. 55; Major, 24 Dec. 58.				

		CAPTAINS.	ENSIGN.	LIEUT.	CAPTAIN.	BREV.-MAJ.
17	0	1 Sydney Darling	30 May 43	4 July 45	p 29 Dec. 48	
14	0	1 John William Percy,[7] s.	21 Apr. 46	p 30 Mar. 47	p 8 June 52	
13	0	1 Hopton Bassett Scott,[9] s.	24 Dec. 47	p 28 Mar. 51	p 4 Aug. 54	26 Dec. 56
19	0	1 William Burden[11]	26 Oct. 41	13 Oct. 43	29 Dec. 54	
12	0	1 Henry John Wilkinson[12]	p 23 May 48	p 31 Oct. 51	6 Jan. 55	
14	0	1 Wm. Parker Terry[13]	2 Apr. 46	2 Apr. 52	21 June 55	
14	0	2 Bowen Van Straubenzee[14]	4 Apr. 46	p 25 Feb. 48	31 Aug. 55	
11	½	1 Arth. Oswald Richards[15]	p 1 Sept. 48	p 2 April 52	1 Feb. 56	
12	8/12	1 Jno. H. Houston Gaminell	p 15 Oct. 47	p 17 Dec. 52	p 9 Nov. 55	
12	0	2 William Daunt[12]	13 Sept. 48	p 15 Feb. 53	29 Feb. 56	
7	1	2 William Nugent[12]	p 2 April 52	6 June 54	p 13 June 56	
20	1	2 Henry Fletcher Marston[16]	8 Mar. 39	8 Aug. 41	23 June 52	
6	1	2 Donald Hay M'Barnet[17]..	p 21 Jan. 53	11 Aug. 54	7 Sept. 55	
6	1	2 Ambr. Marshall Cardew[18]	1 July 53	23 Sept. 54	27 June 56	
16	0	2 James Graham	3 May 44	29 Dec. 46	23 Oct. 57	
8	2⅕	2 George Spaight[19]	p 16 Mar. 50	p 18 June 52	5 Sept. 55	
15	0	2 Chas. Caldwell Grantham	16 Sept. 45	23 Oct. 47	23 July 58	
7	0	2 Henry Marcus Beresford	p 13 May 53	15 Dec. 54	p 30 July 58	
8	0	1 William Crosbie Harvey[12]	p 11 June 52	11 Aug. 54	p 7 Sept. 58	
8	0	1 Allen George Douglas[20]..	p 9 July 52	p 18 Aug. 54	24 Dec. 58	
6	0	1 Hon. Collingwood Vibart[19]	p 18 Aug. 54	12 Jan. 55	p 15 Apr. 59	
6	0	2 Thomas Grace[30]	5 Nov. 54	2 Mar. 55	1 Apr. 59	
6	0	2 Rolland V. S. Grimston[20]†	11 Aug. 54	8 Dec. 54	10 Dec. 58	
10	0	1 William Henry Peel[31]	p 14 June 50	p 24 Nov. 54	4 Mar. 59	
7	1/12	1 Hon. Fred. LePoer Trench	p 22 Jan. 53	p 25 May 55	13 May 59	
		LIEUTENANTS.				
6	0	1 H. Masterman Thompson[19]	6 June 54	29 Dec. 54		
6	0	1 Cha. James Borton,[12] Adj.	14 July 54	6 Jan. 55		
10	0	1 Thomas Tayler	p 18 Jan. 50	12 Jan. 55		
6	0	1 William Harris Burland[13]	p 25 Aug. 54	7 Mar. 55		
5	0	2 John Hunt Cumming	5 Jan. 55	9 Mar. 55		
5	0	1 William Aug. Elmhirst	p 12 Jan. 55	1 June 55		
5	0	1 Rich. Chas. Hen. Germon	p 16 Jan. 55	1 June 55		
5	0	1 Henry Geo. Hunt Grubbe	26 Jan. 55	5 June 55		
5	0	2 Henry Gipps	20 Feb. 55	9 Oct. 55		
5	0	2 Ar. F. Bing. Wright, Adj.	22 Mar. 55	1 Feb. 56		
5	0	2 John Haycroft Bolton	1 June 55	p 27 Jan. 57		
5	0	2 Edward D'Oyly Astley	9 Feb. 55	p 9 Oct. 55		
5	0	2 Spencer Field	2 Feb. 55	4 Feb. 56		
6	0	2 Thos. A. Massy Dickin	p 8 Dec. 54	p 15 Feb. 56		
5	0	2 Arthur V. B. Blanchard	6 April 55	p 3 Mar. 57		
5	0	1 William James Massy	20 July 55	p 11 Dec. 57		
5	0	2 W. H. Errington Ridsdale	1 May 55	15 Jan. 58		
4	0	1 Patrick William Hackett	p 25 Jan. 55	p 16 April 58		
4	0	2 Chas. Masterman Smyth	12 Dec. 56	p 14 May 58		
5	0	1 George Minchin Chadwick	11 May 55	23 July 58		
5	0	1 John Aplin[22]	5 June 55	23 July 58		
5	0	2 John Samuel Jeffares	9 Oct. 55	23 July 58		
3	0	2 James Lewis Bradshaw	p 27 Jan. 57	p 30 July 58		
4	0	2 Spencer Lynne	4 April 56	p 24 Aug. 58		
3	0	1 Charles Thomas Coote	p 17 Feb. 57	p 7 Sept. 58		
5	0	2 Archibald Shaw[32]	3 Aug. 55	1 Oct. 58		
3	0	2 Charles Smith Perry	p 29 May 57	2 Oct. 58		
3	0	1 Richard Roberts	p 11 Dec. 57	p 4 Mar. 59		
2	0	1 Brownlow Villiers Layard	19 Feb. 58	p 22 Apr. 59		
2	0	1 Francis Edward Eccles	16 Mar. 58	p 30 Sept. 59		

1 Sir James Hope served with the expedition to Hanover in 1805-6; to Zealand in 1807, including the siege of Copenhagen; to Sweden in 1808; in Portugal and Spain in 1808-9, including the action at Lugo and battle of Corunna. With the expedition to Walcheren in 1809; the Peninsular campaigns from 1810 to the end of that war in 1814, including the battle of Barrosa, siege of Ciudad Rodrigo, covering the siege of Badajoz, affairs in front of Salamanca and 2d Osma, battle of Vittoria, siege of San Sebastian, passages of the Bidassoa, Gave d'Oleron, and Gave de Pau, battles of the Nivelle, Nive, Orthes, & Toulouse. Sir James a has received the Gold Cross & Clasp for the battles of Vittoria, Nivelle, Nive, Orthes, and Toulouse; and the Silver War Medal with five Clasps for Corunna, Busaco, Ciudad Rodrigo, Badajoz, and Salamanca.

2 Colonel Elmhirst served with the 9th Regt. the campaign of 1842 in Affghanistan (Medal). Also in the Crimea from 5th June 1855, including the siege and fall of Sebastopol and assault of the battorie on 18th June (Medal and Clasp Knight of the Legion of Honour, an 5th Class of the Medjidie).

9th (*The East Norfolk*) Regiment of Foot. 191

Years' Serv			ENSIGNS.	ENSIGN.	
Full P. y.	Half Pay.				
3	0	1	Richard Fenton	17 Nov. 57	3 Lt.-Col. Bethune served the campaign in Affghanistan in 1842 (Medal),—as Adjutant of the 9th Regt. at the forcing of the Khyber Pass, and as Aide-de-Camp to Sir John M'Caskill at the action of Mamookail, forcing the Tezeen Pass, re-capture of Cabool, storm, capture, and destruction of Istaliff. He served also the campaign on the Sutlej in 1845-6 (Medal) as Aide-de-Camp to Sir John M'Caskill at the battle of Moodkee, where the Major General was killed,—as Aide de Camp to Brigadier Wallace (who was killed) at Ferozeshah (charger shot),—and in command of the Light Company of the 9th at Sobraon. Served at the siege of Sebastopol from Nov. 1854 to Feb. 1855 (Medal and Clasp, and 5th Class of the Medjidie).
3	0	2	Hillier Givins	19 Nov. 57	
2	0	1	Thomas Elmes	5 Mar. 58	
2	0	2	Edward Collins	23 Mar. 58	
2	0	2	Harry Elmhirst	14 May 58	
2	0	1	Arthur Henry Josselyn	p 21 May 58	
3	0	2	Nathaniel Forte	p 24 Aug. 58	
3	0	2	Edw. Wm. F. Leighton	p 7 Sept. 58	
3	0	1	Zachary Stanley Bayly	8 Sept. 58	
3	0	1	Arthur F. Piercy Cosens	9 Sept. 58	28 Paymaster Morrison served the Eastern campaign from Nov. 1854, including the siege and fall of Sebastopol (Medal and Clasp).
3	0	2	Ellsworth Pursdon	17 Sept. 58	
3	0	2	Richard Gadesden Dunn	p 20 Oct. 58	29 Captain Spaight served with the 31st Regt. in the Crimea from 22nd May to the end of June 1855, including the siege of Sebastopol and attack of the 18th June (Medal and Clasps).
3	0	2	George Waugh	p 19 Nov. 58	
3	0	1	Charles George Kane	7 Dec. 58	
1	0	2	James Edward Henning	18 Mar. 59	30 Captain Grace served with the 57th Regt. in the Crimea from 23 Sept. 1854, and was present at the battles of Balaklava and Inkerman, siege and fall of Sebastopol, storm and capture of the Quarries, storm of the Redan on the 18th June; also at the bombardment and capture of Kinbourne (Medal and three Clasps).
1	0	1	William Queale	p 15 Apr. 59	
1	0	1	John C. Ferguson Grier	6 May 59	
1	0	2	Wm. Hawkins Hathway	p 31 May 59	
1	0	1	Robert Dillon Hare	5 Aug. 59	
1	0	1	Herbert W. M. Baskerville	p 18 Oct. 59	31 Captain Peel served with the Cape Mounted Riflemen throughout the Kaffir war of 1850-53 (Medal and Clasp). 32 Lieut. Shaw served with the 59th Regt. at the siege and capture of Canton in Dec. 1858.

14	0	*Paymasters.*—1 Andrew Sievwright,[12] 2 Apr. 52; *Ens.* 1 Apr. 46; *Lt.* p 1 Sept. 48.
3	0	2 Walter Morrison,[28] 29 Dec. 57; *Ens.* 13 March 57.
5	0	*Adjutants.*—2 *Lieut.* Arthur F. B. Wright, 6 Nov. 57.
6	0	1 *Lieut.* Charles James Borton, 7 Oct. 59.
5	0	*Instructors of Musketry.*—2 *Lieut.* Henry Gipps, 26 April 58.
5	0	1 *Lieut.* George Minchin Chadwick, 15 May 59.
9	0	*Quarter Masters.*—1 William Banbury,[24] 8 July 51.
4	0	2 James Parrott Arrowsmith, 17 Jan. 56.
9	0	*Surgeons.*—1 James Carroll, M.B. 26 Jan. 58; *Assist. Surg.* 3 Jan. 51.
9	0	2 William Armstrong, 26 Jan. 58; *Assist. Surg.* 10 Jan. 51.
7	0	*Assist. Surgeons.*—1 John Coote Ovens,[25] 16 Dec. 53.
6	0	1 James Crosso Johnston,[27] 3 Nov. 54.
5	0	2 Charles Christopher Piper, 12 Sept. 55.
2	0	2 James Henry Jeffcoat, 5 Aug. 58.

F acings Yellow.—*Agents*, Messrs. Cox & Co.—*Irish Agents*, Sir E. R. Borough, Bt., Armit & Co.

[1st Batt. *returned from Canada*, 4 Nov. 57. *Depot, Limerick.*]
[2nd Batt. *embarked for Corfu* 30 Oct. 58. *Depot, Limerick.*]

4 Major Leslie served with the 80th Regt. the campaign on the Sutlej in 1845-6, including the battles of Moodkee, Ferozeshah, and Sobraon, for which he has received a Medal and two Clasps. In Nov. 1844 he was wrecked on one of the Andaman Islands in the transport *Briton*, with three Companies of the 80th Foot, and carried the Dispatches from the Island to Moulmein, during which time he was 22 days at sea in an open boat. Served at the siege of Sebastopol from 27th Nov. 1854 to 16th March 1855 (Medal and Clasp, and 5th Class of the Medjidie).
5 Major Tayler served the campaign of 1842 in Affghanistan (Medal); and that on the Sutlej (Medal), including the battles of Moodkee and Ferozeshah (severely wounded).
5† Lt.-Col. Sankey served the Eastern campaign up to 16th Dec. 1854, and from 13th July 1855, as D.A.Q.M.G., and from 31st Aug. as A.Q.M.G. to 1st Division, including the battles of Alma and Balaklava (charger killed), capture of Balaklava, siege and fall of Sebastopol (Medal and Clasps, Brevets of Major and Lieut.-Colonel, and 5th Class of the Medjidie).
6 Major Hawes served the Sutlej campaign of 1845-46, including the battles of Moodkee, Ferozeshah, and Sobraon Medal and Clasps). Also in the Crimea from the 27th Nov. 1854, including the siege and fall of Sebastopol, and assault on the batteries on the 18th June (Medal and Clasp, Brevet Major, and 5th Class of the Medjidie).
7 Captain Percy served in the Crimea from August 1855, including the siege and fall of Sebastopol (Medal and Clasp).
9 Major Scott served in the Crimea from Dec. 1854, including the siege and fall of Sebastopol, and assault of the batteries on the 18th June (Medal and Clasp, and Knight of the Legion of Honor).
11 Captain Burden served the campaign of 1842 in Affghanistan (Medal). Also at the siege of Sebastopol from Nov. 1854 to Feb. 1855 (Medal and Clasp).
12 Captains Wilkinson, W. Daunt, Nugent, and Harvey, Lieut. Borton, and Paymaster Sievwright, served in the Crimea from 27th Nov. 1854, including the siege and fall of Sebastopol, and assault on the batteries on the 18th June (Medal and Clasp). Captains Wilkinson and Daunt have the 5th Class of the Medjidie.
13 Captain Terry and Lieut. Burland served in the Crimea from 16th June 1855, including the siege and fall of Sebastopol, and assault on the batteries on the 18th June (Medal and Clasp).
14 Captain Straubenzee served with the 22nd Regt. at the first and second siege operations before Mooltan, including the action of Soorjkoond; he was severely wounded on the 27th Dec. 1848 (Medal and Clasp).
15 Captain Richards served at the siege of Sebastopol from 18th January to 17th May 1855 (Medal and Clasp).
16 Captain Marston served with the 41st Regt. the campaign of 1842 in (Affghanistan Medal) and was present in the engagements with the enemy on the 28th April in the Pisheen Valley; in that of the 29th May near Candahar, 30th Aug., at Goaine, 5th Sept. before Ghuznee, occupation and destruction of that fortress and of Cabool, expedition into Kohistan, storm, capture, and destruction of Istaliff, and in the various minor affairs in and between the Bolan and the Khyber Passes. Served with the 81st throughout the Burmese war of 1852-53; was on board the E. I. C. steam frigate *Feroze* during the naval action and destruction of the enemy's stockades on the Rangoon River; served during the succeeding three days' operations in the vicinity, and at the storm and capture of Rangoon (Medal and Clasp).
17 Captain M'Barnet served with the 79th Highlanders in the Crimea from 3rd June 1855, including the siege and fall of Sebastopol (wounded in the trenches on 24th August), assaults of the 18th June and 8th Sept., and expedition to Kertch and Yenikale (Medal and Clasp).
18 Captain Cardew served with the 19th Regt. in the Eastern campaign of 1854, and was severely wounded at the battle of Alma (Medal and Clasp).

[For remainder of notes see end of 10th Foot.

192   10th (*The North Lincolnshire*) *Regt. of Foot.*   [1st Batt. Plymouth.
                                                           [2nd Batt. C. of G. Hope

The "*Sphinx*," with the words, "EGYPT" "PENINSULA" "SOBRAON"
"PUNJAUB" "MOOLTAN" "GOOJERAT."

Years' Serv.		
63		Col.—ᗷ *Sir* Thomas M'Mahon,¹ *Bt.* GCB, *Ens.* 2 Feb. 97; *Lt.* 24 Oct. 99; *Capt.* 8 Oct. 03; *Maj.* 6 Nov. 06; *Lt.Col.* 4 May 09; *Col.* 4 June 14; *Maj.Gen.* 27 May 25; *Lt.Gen.* 28 June 38; *Gen.* 20 June 54; *Col.* 10th Foot, 28 Sept. 47.
Full Pay	Half Pay	
26	0	*Lt. Cols.*—2 William Fenwick,² CB., *Ens.* 26 Dec. 34; *Lt.* ᴾ 8 June 39; *Capt.* ᴾ 15 April 42; *Maj.* 13 Sept. 48; *Bt.Lt.Col.* 18 May 55; *Lt.Col.* 8 Jan. 58; *Col.* 26 July 58.
24	0	1 Henry Errington Longden,³ CB., *Ens.* 10 Sept. 36; *Lieut.* ᴾ 7 Aug. 40; *Capt.* ᴾ 26 Mar. 43; *Brev.Maj.* 7 June 49; *Maj.* 21 Feb. 50; *Bt.Lt.Col.* 8 Dec. 50; *Lt.Col.* 20 July 58; *Col.* 26 April 59.
40	⁸⁄₁₂	1 Mitchell George Sparks,³ᵗ *Ens.* 4 Nov. 19; *Lt.* 26 Dec. 23; *Capt.* 28 June 36; *Bt.Major,* 9 Nov. 46; *Bt.Lt.Col.* 20 June 54; *Major,* 8 Jan. 58; *Lt.Col.* 26 Oct. 58; *Col.* 25 Sept. 59.
28	0	*Majors.*—2 Richard Mordesley Best,⁴ *Ens.* ᴾ 20 April 32; *Lt.* ᴾ 16 Jan. 35; *Capt.* ᴾ 7 June 39; *Bt.Major,* 11 Nov. 51; *Major,* 8 Jan. 58; *Bt.Lt.Col.* 26 Oct. 58.
41	0	2 Thomas Byrne, *Ens.* 4 Nov. 19; *Lt.* 5 March 23; *Capt.* 22 Jan. 39; *Bt. Major,* 11 Nov. 51; *Major,* 8 Jan. 58; *Bt.Lt.Col.* 26 Oct. 58.
22	0	1 Henry Radford Norman,⁵ *Ens.* ᴾ 23 Feb. 38; *Lt.* 8 April 42; *Capt.* 4 Oct. 48; *Major,* 20 July 58; *Bt.Lt.Col.* 26 April 59.
22	0	1 Stephen Francis Charles Annesley,⁶ *Ens.* ᴾ 6 July 38; *Lt.* ᴾ 17 Aug. 41; *Capt.* ᴾ 22 Oct. 47; *Bt.Major,* 20 July 58; *Major,* 26 Oct. 58; *Bt.Lt.Col.* 24 June 50.

		CAPTAINS.	ENSIGN.	LIEUT.	CAPTAIN.	BREV. MAJ.
20	0	1 J.V. Harthals Montagu⁷	ᴾ 17 April 40	ᴾ 22 April 42	ᴾ 16 May 51	
27	⁶⁄₁₂	1 Samuel Burges Lamb ⁸	ᴾ 14 Dec. 32	ᴾ 5 Feb. 36	7 July 48	
21	0	1 Chas. Doyle Patterson⁹	21 June 39	4 Oct. 41	15 Mar. 53	19 Jan. 58
20	0	1 W.K. Orme¹⁰ ᵗ. ᶜ. 24 June 50	ᴾ 13 Mar. 40	ᴾ 31 Dec. 44	ᴾ 11 June 47	26 Oct. 58
15	0	2 Rich. Cormick Clifford¹²	17 Oct. 45	1 Jan. 47	30 July 57	
15	0	1 Cuthbert Barlow¹³	18 April 45	ᴾ 10 Dec. 47	8 Jan. 58	
15	0	1 John Montresor Smyth¹⁴	23 Sept. 45	ᴾ 7 July 48	8 Jan. 58	
15	0	1 Patrick Browne Lucas¹⁵	ᴾ 10 Oct. 45	4 Oct. 48	8 Jan. 58	
14	0	1 ᐯ℄ Joseph P.H. Crowe¹⁶	27 Oct. 46	17 Sept. 50	8 Jan. 58	20 Dec. 59
8	1⅔	2 Charles Hurt¹⁷....	ᴾ 17 June 51	30 Dec. 53	ᴾ 16 Nov. 55	
16	0	2 George Fred. Coryton..	2 Aug. 44	ᴾ 14 April 46	9 Jan. 58	
12	0	1 W.H.P. Gordon Bluett¹⁸	ᴾ 23 May 48	22 Feb. 49	30 Mar. 58	
13	0	2 John Edmund Whaite¹⁹	18 Dec. 47	21 Feb. 50	15 June 58	
15	0	2 Douglas Ernest Manners	18 Apr. 45	18 May 49	14 May 58	
10	0	2 Geo. C. Bartholomew²⁰†	ᴾ 17 May 50	ᴾ 13 Feb. 52	ᴾ 31 Aug. 58	
8	0	1 John Byron²¹	ᴾ 13 Feb. 52	14 June 54	ᴾ 22 June 58	
15	0	2 Robert Willock Davies	27 Feb. 45	7 Aug. 47	15 Jan. 58	
11	1⅔	2 George Ernest Bulger..	6 Nov. 47	ᴾ 5 Nov. 50	1 Oct. 58	
9	0	1 William James Hales²¹‡	ᴾ 19 Aug. 51	25 May 53	18 Jan. 56	
10	0	2 Henry Henderson ²² ..	ᴾ 13 Dec. 50	ᴾ 24 Dec. 52	24 Feb. 59	
12	0	2 Fred. Browne Sandwith²³	ᴾ 1 Dec. 48	9 Feb. 55	13 Mar. 59	
11	0	1 ᐯ℄ A. Cathcart Bogle²³‡	ᴾ 28 Dec. 49	ᴾ 18 Mar. 53	31 Aug. 58	
7	0	2 George Wm. Graham ²⁵	ᴾ 10 June 53	ᴾ 7 Sept. 55	ᴾ 18 Oct. 59	
5	0	1 Henry Rudkin Vigors..	2 Mar. 55	25 Jan. 57	ᴾ 20 Nov. 59	

		LIEUTENANTS.			
8	0	1 St. Andrew B. St. John²⁴	ᴾ 12 Mar. 52	23 April 55	1 Sir Thomas M'Mahon served with the Expedition under Sir Ralph Abercromby in 1800, destined for operations on the coast of Spain, at Cadiz, Ferrol, &c., and subsequently at the occupation of Malta. He served in the Peninsular war in 1809, 10, 11, and part of 1812, including the operations on the frontiers of Portugal and Spain, contiguous to the rivers Coa and Agueda; at the Lines of Torres Vedras, and at the subsequent advance therefrom on the retreat of the French Army. He commanded a corps of Portuguese Infantry, which was posted on the left of the Allied Army, during the battle of Fuentes d'Onor, protecting the fords on the Duas Casas, and covering Almeida. In 1813 he proceeded to the East Indies as Adjutant-General to the King's Forces, where he served for twelve years. In 1834 he was nominated Lieut.-Governor of Portsmouth, and commanded the troops in the South West District; and in 1839 he was appointed Commander-in-Chief of the Bombay Army, which command he held until 1847.
7	0	1 Percy Beale,²⁵ *Adj.*....	ᴾ 21 Jan. 53	23 Nov. 55	
5	0	1 Carteret A. Armstrong	20 July 55	4 Apr. 56	
5	0	1 M. M'Pherson Batye²⁷	23 Nov. 55	30 July 56	
4	0	1 John Ball²⁸	8 July 56	ᴾ 11 Dec. 57	
5	0	2 Chas. Proby Fitzgibbon	30 Mar. 55	25 Jan. 56	
5	0	2 Robert T. F. Stammers	25 May 55	ᴾ 14 May 56	
5	0	2 Spencer Edward Orr ..	6 April 55	10 Dec. 56	
5	0	2 Robert Annesley......	1 May 55	ᴾ 3 April 56	
5	0	2 Walter Hedger	16 July 55	ᴾ 29 May 57	
5	0	2 Wm. John Byde Martin	22 Oct. 55	ᴾ 14 Aug. 57	
4	0	1 Fred. Augustine Lynam³⁰	18 Jan. 56	15 Jan. 58	
4	0	2 ᐯ℄ James Craig,³¹ *Adj.*	25 Jan. 56	26 Jan. 58	
3	0	1 John Carr²⁹....	16 Oct. 57	26 Mar. 58	
6	0	1 Rich. Salisbury Bagge..	ᴾ 3 Nov. 54	25 June 58	
5	0	1 Philip Wride Matthews	ᴾ 14 Sept. 55	ᴾ 31 Aug. 58	
5	0	1 Herman Wayne	ᴾ 2 Oct. 55	ᴾ 21 May 58	
3	0	1 William Betson³²	17 Oct. 57	2 Oct. 58	
3	0	1 Theophilus Scott......	ᴾ 11 Dec. 57	2 Oct. 58	
5	0	2 Charles H. Newbatt ..	26 Oct. 55	2 Oct. 58	
5	0	2 Owen H. Strong......	22 Oct. 55	8 Oct. 58	
5	0	2 William Nassau Whitty	7 Nov. 55	8 Oct. 58	
3	0	1 John Rudge..........	ᴾ 11 Sept. 57	26 Oct. 58	
3	0	1 Henry Long W. Phillips	9 Oct. 57	24 Feb. 59	
2	0	2 John Dickson Power ..	26 Mar. 58	13 Mar. 59	
2	0	2 Hargood Thos. Snooke	30 Mar. 58	ᴾ 24 June 59	

10th (The North Lincolnshire) Regt. of Foot.

Years' Serv. Full Pay	Half Pay		LIEUTENANTS.	ENSIGN.	LIEUT.	2 Colonel Fenwick served with the 10th Regt. in the Sutlej campaign in 1846, including the battle of Sobraon (Medal). Served in the Indian Mutiny of 1857-58; commanded the Regt. at the actions of Chanda, Sultanpore, and Dhowraha, also at the siege and capture of Lucknow including the storming of the Emaumbara and Kaisabagh; commanded the advanced guard of Sir Edward Lugard's Column at the passage of the Tonse and relief of Azimghur; commanded the Regt. at the defeat of the rebels at Jugdispore (CB., Medal, and several times mentioned in despatches). 3† Colonel Sparks has received the Medal for services in China, having been present with the 49th Regt. before Nankin. He served with the 10th Regt. in the Punjaub campaign of 1848-9, and was present during the whole of the siege operations before Mooltan, including the action of Soorjkoond, carrying the heights before Mooltan, and surrender of the fortress; was afterwards present at the battle of Goojerat (Medal and Clasps). Did duty with the Murree volunteers during the Sepoy Mutiny in 1857 (Medal). 4 Lt.Col. Best served with the 10th in the Punjaub campaign of 1848-9, including the whole of the siege operations before Mooltan and surrender of the fortress; was afterwards present and slightly wounded in the leg at the battle of Goojerat (Medal and Clasps). 7 Captain Montagu served with the 10th Regt. in the Sutlej campaign in 1846 and was present in the battle of Sobraon (Medal).
2	0	1	Charles James Barnett	1 Apr. 58	P 18 Oct. 50	
2	0	2	Ernest Arch. Berger ..	2 Apr. 58	P 18 Nov. 59	
2	0	2	Richard Johnson	30 Apr. 58	P 29 Nov. 59	
2	0	1	Samuel Hercules Hayes	13 Mar. 58	P 30 Aug. 59	
			ENSIGNS.			
2	0	2	Geo.H.W.Tremenheere	23 Apr. 58		
2	0	2	John Lovel Kelly	1 May 58		
2	0	2	Abr. Richard Montfort	28 May 58		
2	0	2	William Malcolm	4 June 58		
2	0	2	Clift.deN.OrrStockwell	26 Apr. 58		
2	0	1	Thomas H. Powell....	10 Sept. 58		
2	0	1	Frederic Robertson....	8 Oct. 58		
2	0	1	John Bates Marston ..	9 Nov. 58		
2	0	1	Nicholas Whitton	12 Nov. 58		
2	0	2	William Whitla	13 Nov. 58		
1	0	1	Edward A. H. Roe....	28 Jan. 59		
1	0	2	Alexander Fraser	18 Mar. 59		
1	0	1	Robert Munro Dickinson	1 Apr. 59		
1	0	1	Samuel Fred. Peole ..	2 Apr. 59		
1	0	1	Henry E. Poole	24 June 59		
1	0	1	Henry P. Bluett	25 June 59		
1	0	2	Henry Masters Sproule	P 20 July 50		
1	0		George Wm. Carter ..	P 15 Nov. 59		

12	0	*Paymasters.*—1 James Murphy,[33] 1 June 55; *Qr.Mr.* 3 March 48.
2	0	2 Henry Barrett Bromley, 22 Feb. 58.
4	0	*Adjutants.*—VC 2 Lieut. James Craig,[31] 26 Jan. 58.
7	0	1 Lieut. Percy Beale,[50] 25 March 58.
5	0	*Instructors of Musketry.*—2 Lieut. S. E. Orr, 17 July 58.
3	0	1 Lieut. Theophilus Scott.
2	0	*Quarter Masters.*—2 William Sykes, 5 Feb. 58.
5	0	1 James Darker,[34] 3 Dec. 55.
19	0	*Surgeons.*—1 Chas. Alex. Gordon,[35] MD. CB. 10 July 46; *Assist.Surg.* 8 June 41.
11	0	2 Frederick Douglas, M.D. 2 Oct. 57; *Assist.Surg.* 30 March 49.
6	0	*Assist.Surgs.*—1 John Tulloch,[29] 7 June 54.
5	0	1 Thomas John Tucker, 18 July 55.
2	0	2 Theobald Fetherstone Langstaff, 22 Jan. 58.
2	0	2 William Langworthy Baker, 22 June 58.

Facings Yellow.—*Agents*, Messrs. Cox & Co.

[*1st Batt.* returned *from India, July* 1859. *Depot, Devonport.*]
[*2d Batt.* embarked *for Cape of Good Hope, Dec.* 1859. *Depot*, .]

3 Colonel Longden served with the 10th in the Sutlej campaign of 1845-6, and was present in the battle of Sobraon (Medal). He served also the Punjaub campaign of 1848-49, and was present during the whole of the siege operations before Mooltan, including the affair of the 9th Sept., storming the enemy's strongly-entrenched position before Mooltan 12th Sept., action of Soorjkoond, carrying the heights on 27th Dec. in command of the Regt., and surrender of the fortress as Field Engineer; afterwards present at the surrender of the fort and garrison of Cholilote, and battle of Goojerat (Medal and Clasps, and Brevet Major). Served in the Indian campaign of 1857-58,—commanded a field force in the Azimghur and Jounpore districts in 1857, including the capture of the fort of Atrowleea; commanded an advanced guard of picked marksmen and guns of Frank's force in its advance to Lucknow including the actions of Chanda, Umeerpore, and Sultanpore, and attack on the fort of Douraha; was attached to the Goorka Troops at the siege and capture of Lucknow; present at the storming of the Begum's House and Serai, storming of the Emaumbara and Kaisabagh, attack on the Moolvie in Abbasoodowlah's Kumbullah—mentioned in despatches; present with a wing of the 13th Lt. Inf. at the 1st relief of Azimghur; appointed chief of the staff to Lugard's force and present at the passage of the Touse, 2nd relief of Azimghur, capture of Jugdespore, and several skirmishes in its vicinity (Medal).

5 Lt.Col. Norman served with the 10th in the Sutlej campaign of 1845-6, and was present in the battle of Sobraon (Medal). He served also in the Punjaub campaign of 1848-9, and was present during the whole of the siege operations against Mooltan and surrender of the fortress, including the affair of the 9th Sept., storming the enemy's strongly-entrenched position before Mooltan, and commanded the troops in the advanced batteries of the camp during the action of Soorjkoond; afterwards present a the battle of Goojerat (Medal and Clasps). Commanded two companies when the Sepoys mutinied at Benares on 4th June 1857; commanded the selected marksmen of the Regt. with the Jounpore Field force including the actions of Chanda, Sultanpore, and Dhowraha; present with the Regt. at the repulse of the enemy near Ameerpore, siege and capture of Lucknow including the storming of the Emaumbara and the Kaisabagh; commanded the Regt. at the passage of the Tonse and forcing the enemy's position near Azimghur; present in the skirmish near Birheea, and at the defeat of the enemy at Jugdespore and subsequently repulsed them from that post; commanded the Regt. in the operations on the 26th May, 2nd and 4th June; was several times mentioned in Dispatches and promoted Brevet Major and Brevet Lt.Colonel (Medal).

6 Major Annesley served with the 37th Regt. in Ceylon during the rebellion in 1848. Served with the 10th Regt. in the Indian campaign of 1857-58, was present at the suppression of the Mutiny at Benares, capture of the fort of Atrowleea, advance on Lucknow including the actions of Chanda, Umeerpore, Sultanpore, and Douraha, siege and capture of Lucknow, commanded the advanced party into the Kaisabagh, commanded a party of volunteers occupying the large Mosque commanding the Kaisabagh—mentioned in despatches as having "highly distinguished himself;" afterwards present at the relief of Azimghur and subsequent operations at Jugdespore, Brevet of Major and Medal).

194   10th (*The North Lincolnshire*) Regt. of Foot.

8 Captain Lamb served during the Indian campaign of 1857-58 and was present at the action of Shahgunge 5th July and battle of Agra on 10th Oct. 1857 (Medal).
9 Major Patterson served with the 10th Regt. in the Sutlej campaign of 1845-6, including the battle of Sobraon (Medal). Also the Punjaub campaign of 1848-9, including the whole of the siege operations before Mooltan,—action of Soorjkoond, carrying the heights before Mooltan, capture of the Dowlat Gate (commanded the storming party), and surrender of the fortress: afterwards present at the battle of Goojerat (Medal and Clasps). Commanded three companies in Shahabad with Eyre's field force, action at Dilawur and capture of Jugdeespore 12 Aug. 1857—mentioned in Dispatches (Brevet Major, and Medal).
10 Lt.Col. Orme served with the 16th Lancers in the action of Maharajpore on 29 Dec. 1843 (Medal). Also in the Sutlej campaign in 1846 and was present in the actions at Buddiwal and Aliwal, in which last he received a severe bayonet wound when charging the Seikh infantry (Medal). Served with the 10th Regt. in the Indian campaign of 1857-58, including the advance on Lucknow and actions at Chanda, Umeerpore, and Sultanpore, siege and capture of Lucknow, relief of Azimghur, and operations against the rebels in the Jugdespore Jungle (Brevet of Major and Medal).
12 Capt. Clifford was present with the 10th at the battle of Goojerat (Medal).
13 Captain Barlow served the Punjaub campaign of 1848-9 with the 10th, including the whole of the siege operations before Mooltan, action of Soorjkoond, carrying the heights before Mooltan, capture of the Dowlat Gate (grape-shot wound), and surrender of the fortress: afterwards present at the battle of Goojerat (Medal and Clasps). Served in the Indian campaign of 1857-58, including the capture of Jugdespore with Eyre's force, capture of Atrowleea, actions of Chanda, Umeerpore, Sultanpore, and Douraha, siege and capture of Lucknow, relief of Azimghur, and operations in the Jugdespore jungle (Medal).
14 Captain Smyth served the Punjaub campaign of 1848-9 with the 10th, including the whole of the siege operations against Mooltan, storming the enemy's strongly-entrenched position, action of Soorjkoond, carrying the heights before Mooltan, capture of the Dowlat Gate, and surrender of the fortress: afterwards present at the battle of Goojerat (Medal and Clasps). Was engaged with the Dacca Mutineers at Jelpigoree in Dec. 1857 (Medal).
15 Captain Lucas served the Punjaub campaign of 1848-9 with the 10th, including the whole of the siege operations before Mooltan, affair of the 9th Sept., storming the enemy's strongly-entrenched position, and surrender of the fortress: afterwards present at the battle of Goojerat (Medal and Clasps). Served in the Indian campaign of 1857-58, including the advance on Lucknow and actions at Chanda, Umeerpore, and Sultanpore, siege and capture of Lucknow, relief of Azimghur, capture of Jugdespore and operations in its vicinity (Medal).
16 Major Crowe served with the 78th Highlanders in the Persian campaign in 1856 and was present in the action of Kooshab and bombardment of Mohumrah. Served in India with Havelock's Column from its first taking the field in 1857, including the actions of Futtehpore, Pandoo Nuddee, Cawnpore, Oonao, Buscerutgunge, Boorbeakechowkee (Victoria Cross for distinguished and gallant conduct), Mungurwar, and Alumbagh, relief of Lucknow (wounded), defence of Alumbágh under Outram, siege and capture of Lucknow, relief of Azimghur, and operations near Jugdespore (Medal).
17 Captain Hurt served with the Royals throughout the Eastern campaign of 1854-55, including the battles of Alma and Inkerman, siege and fall of Sebastopol, and with volunteer sharpshooters from 17th Oct. to 31st Dec. 1854 (Medal and Clasps, and Knight of the Legion of Honor).
18 Captain Bluett served with the 10th Regt. in the Punjaub campaign, including the latter part of the siege operations before Mooltan, and surrender of the fortress, and battle of Goojerat (Medal and Clasps). Served at the relief of Azimghur in April 1858, capture of Jugdespore and operations in its vicinity (Medal).
19 Captain Whaite served in the Punjaub campaign in 1846, including the latter part of the siege operations before Mooltan, surrender of that fortress, and battle of Goojerat (Medal and Clasps).
20† Captain Bartholomew commanded a wounded detachment of the 10th Foot during the operations against the rebels in the Shahabad district, from 9th Oct. 1858 to 4th Jan. 1859, and was several times engaged (Medal).
21 Captain Byron served in the 34th Regt. at the Siege of Sebastopol in 1854, and was wounded and taken prisoner in a Sortie by the Russians on the night of the 20th December (Medal and Clasp). Served in the Indian campaign in 1857-58, including actions at Cawnpore under Windham, siege and capture of Lucknow, and relief of Azimghur (Medal and Clasp).
21† Captain Hales served with the 18th Royal Irish in the Burmese campaign of 1852-53 (Medal). Also at the siege of Sebastopol from 30 Dec. 1854 (Medal and Clasp).
22 Captain Henderson served in the Indian campaign of 1857-58, and in June 1857 was attached to an Irregular Levy of 1400 men engaged in the district for the protection of Agra being also vested with the powers of Joint Magistrate in the district of Agra, Allyghur, and Muttra; present at the action of Agra on 5th July and was afterwards Assistant Field Engineer in the Fort; in October was appointed Orderly Officer to Col. Greathed, present at the action of Bulkhoosha and relief of Lucknow by Lord Clyde, the affair at Kanouge, affair of the 2nd Dec. and action of the 6th Dec. at Cawnpore; served afterwards as Aide de Camp to General Franks and present at the actions of Nusrutpore, Chanda, Umeerpore, Sultanpore, and Dhowraha, siege and capture of Lucknow (wounded by an explosion) including the storming of the Emaumbara and Kaisabagh (Medal).
23 Captain Sandwith served in the Indian campaign of 1857-58 and was present with the party of the 10th Regt. under Captain Dunbar (who was killed) at the attempt to relieve Arrah (wounded); advance to Lucknow and actions at Chanda, Umeerpore, and Sultanpore, siege and capture of Lucknow, storming of the Emaumbara and Kaisabagh, passage of the Touse, relief of Azimghur, capture of Jugdespore and operations in its vicinity (Medal).
23† Captain Bogle served with the 78th Highlanders during the Persian war in 1857, including the bombardment of Mohumrah (Medal). Served in Bengal with Havelock's Column from its first taking the field in 1857, including the actions of Futtehpore, Aoung, Pandoo Nuddee, Cawnpore, and Oonao, where he was severely wounded, and mentioned in Dispatches for " conspicuous gallantry "(Victoria Cross). Present at Cawnpore under Windham when attacked by the Gwalior Mutineers. Served as Adjutant to the Regt. in the force under Outram at Alumbagh, including the repulse of the numerous attacks, and also in the operations ending in the final capture of Lucknow. In Rohilcund in 1858 under Lord Clyde and at the action of Bareilly (Medal and Clasp).
24 Lieut. St. John served in the Indian campaign of 1857-58, including the advance to Lucknow and actions at Chanda, Umeerpore, Sultanpore, and Douraha, siege and capture of Lucknow, storming of the Emaumbara and Kaisabagh, relief of Azimghur, skirmish at Birheen, and action of Jugdespore, and was severely wounded at the action of Chutomah (Medal).
25 Captain Graham served in the Indian campaign of 1857-58, including the capture of the fort of Atrowleea, advance to Lucknow and actions at Chanda, Umeerpore, Sultanpore, and Douraha, siege and capture of Lucknow and storming of the Emaumbara and Kaisabagh (Medal).
26 Lieut. Beale served with the 10th Regt. in the Indian campaign of 1857-58, and was present at the Mutiny at Dinapore, defeat of the rebels by Eyre's force and capture of Jugdespore, advance to Lucknow and actions at Chanda, Umeerpore, and Sultanpore, siege and capture of Lucknow and led the storming party of the 10th Regt. at the storming of the Emaumbara and Kaisabagh (twice mentioned in despatch); as Adjutant of the Regt. he was present at the passage of the Touse, relief of Azimghur, capture of Jugdespore and operations in its vicinity; and was Staff Officer to Colonel Longden commanding in North Behar, during Sir J. Douglas' final operations in the winter of 1858-59 (Medal and Clasp).
27 Lieut. Battye served in the Indian campaign of 1857-58 and was present at the Mutiny at Dinapore and attempt to relieve Arrah; capture of Atrowleea, advance to Lucknow and actions at Chanda, Umeerpore, Sultanpore, and Douraha, siege and capture of Lucknow and storming of the Emaumbara and Kaisabagh (Medal

28 Lieut. Ball served in the Indian campaign of 1857-58, including the advance to Lucknow and actions at Chanda, Umeerpore, Sultanpore, and Douraha, siege and capture of Lucknow, relief of Azimghur, and operations near Jugdespore (Medal).

29 Lieut. Carr and Assist. Surgeon Tulloch served in the Indian campaign of 1857-58, including the suppression of the Mutiny at Benares, capture of Atrowleea, advance to Lucknow and actions at Chanda, Umeerpore, Sultanpore, and Douraha, siege and capture of Lucknow, relief of Azimghur, and operations near Jugdespore (Medal).

30 Lieut. Lynam served in the Indian campaign of 1857-58, and was at the Mutiny at Dinapore, capture of Atrowleea, advance to Lucknow and actions at Chanda, Umeerpore, Sultanpore, and Douraha, siege and capture of Lucknow, relief of Azimghur, and operations near Jugdespore (Medal).

31 Lieut. Craig served the Eastern campaign of 1854-55, including the battles of Balaklava and Inkerman (severely wounded), siege and fall of Sebastopol, and sortie of 26th Oct. (Medal and three Clasps, and Victoria Cross).

32 Lieut. Betson served with Brigadier Corfield's column at the affair at Peeroo on 11 May 1858, and with Lugard's force in the operations near Jugdespore (Medal).

33 Paymaster Murphy served with the 10th Regt. in the Sutlej campaign of 1845-46, including the battle of Sobraon (Medal). Also the Punjaub campaign of 1848-49, and was present during the whole of the siege operations before Mooltan, including the repulse of the enemy's night attack on 17th Aug. 1848, and surrender of the fortress; afterwards present at the battle of Goojerat (Medal and two Clasps).

34 Qr. Master Darker served with the 23rd Fusiliers in the Indian Campaign of 1857-58, including the relief of Lucknow by Lord Clyde, defeat of the Gwalior Contingent at Cawnpore, siege and fall of Lucknow (Medal and Clasps).

35 Doctor Gordon was present with the 16th Lancers at the battle of Maharajpore 29 Dec. 1843 (Medal). Had medical charge of a force in an expedition in 1848 on the West Coast of Africa, and was thanked in Despatch. Served in the Indian campaign of 1857-58,—in medical charge of Franks' force in its advance to Lucknow including the actions of Chanda, Umeerpore, and Badshagunge; was present with the 10th Regt. at the siege and capture of Lucknow; had medical charge of Lugard's force including the relief of Azimghur, capture of Jugdespore, and action of Chitowrah (twice mentioned in despatches, CB., Medal and Clasp).

[Continuation of Notes to 9th Foot.]

19 Captain Vibart and Lieut. Thompson served in the Crimea from 16th Feb. 1855, including the siege and fall of Sebastopol, and assault on the batteries on the 8th June (Medal and Clasp).

20 Captain Douglas served at the siege of Sebastopol from Nov. 1854 until the 18th June 1855, when he received a wound at the assault on the batteries (Medal and Clasp).

20† Captain Grimston served with the 93rd Highlanders in the Crimea from Jan. 1855, including the siege of Sebastopol, assault of the 18th June, and expeditions to Kertch (Medal and Clasp). Served in India at the battle of Cawnpore, the relief of and capture of Lucknow (wounded at the assault of the Begum's Palace), and engagements in Bareilly.

22 Lieut. Aplin served in the Crimea from the 27th June 1855, including siege and fall of Sebastopol (Medal and Clasp).

24 Qr. Master Banbury served in the campaign of 1842 in Affghanistan (Medal), including the forcing of the Khyber, Jugdulluck, and Tezeen Passes; actions of Mamookhail, Tezeen, and Huft Kotul; attack and capture of Istaliff. The Sutlej campaign of 1845-46, including the battles of Moodkee, Ferozeshah, and Sobraon (Medal and two Clasps). The campaign from Nov. 1854 to April 1855, including siege of Sebastopol (Medal and Clasp).

25 Assist. Surgeon Ovens served in the Crimea from 13th Nov. 1854, including the siege and fall of Sebastopol, and assault on the batteries on the 18th June (Medal and Clasp).

27 Assist. Surgeon J.C. Johnston served with the 9th Regt. in the Crimea from Jan. 1855, including the siege and fall of Sebastopol, and assault of the batteries on 18th June (Medal and Clasp).

11th (North Devonshire) Regt. of Foot. [1st Batt. Aldershot / 2nd Batt. Aldershot]

"SALAMANCA" "PYRENEES" "NIVELLE" "NIVE" "ORTHES" "TOULOUSE" "PENINSULA."

Years' Serv.		
57		**Colonel.**—Sir Richard Doherty,[1] *Ens.* P 10 Sept. 03; *Lieut.* 22 Nov. 04; *Capt.* 21 May 12; *Major,* P 16 Sept. 24; *Lieut.-Col.* P 26 Sept. 26; *Col.* 23 Nov. 41; *Maj.Gen.* 11 Nov. 51; *Lt.Gen.* 26 Oct. 58; *Col.* 11th Foot, 5 Sept. 57.
Full Pay	Half Pay	
34	1/2	**Lieut.Colonels.**—2 John Singleton, *Ens.* P 17 June 26; *Lieut.* P 31 Dec. 27; *Capt.* P 15 Feb. 30; *Major,* P 27 June 45; *Brev.Lieut.Col.* 20 June 54; *Lt.Col.* 1 July 58; *Col.* 26 Oct. 58.
42	0	1 Edward Moore, *Ens.* 21 May 18; *Lieut.* 7 Apr. 25; *Capt.* 7 Feb. 39; *Brev. Maj.* 11 Nov. 51; *Major,* 8 Jan. 58; *Bt.Lt.Col.* 26 Oct. 58; *Lt.Col.* 1 Apr. 59.
25	0	**Majors.**—1 Augustus Fred. Jenner, *Ens.* P 9 Oct. 35; *Lieut.* P 21 June 39; *Capt.* P 5 April 44; *Brev.Maj.* 5 June 55; *Major,* 26 Feb. 58.
19	0	1 John Walpole D'Oyly, *Ens.* P 17 Sept. 41; *Lieut.* P 5 Sept. 43; *Capt.* 15 June 40; *Major,* P 13 July 58.
21	14 3/4	2 Alex. Henry Louis Wyatt, *Ens.* P 17 Sept. 25; *Lieut.* P 24 Feb. 29; *Capt.* P 29 June 32; *Brev.Maj.* 9 Nov. 46; *Bt.Lt.Col.* 20 June 54; *Major,* P 7 Sept. 58; *Col.* 26 Oct. 58.
22	1 3/4	2 Thos. Peebles, *Ens.* P 17 Mar. 37; *Lt.* P 6 Feb. 41; *Capt.* 6 June 51; *Maj.* 1 Apr. 59.

			CAPTAINS.	ENSIGN.	LIEUT.	CAPTAIN.	BREV.MAJ.
16	0	1	John Roe	P 26 May 44	P 9 Oct. 46	P 30 Sept. 53	
17	0	1	Robert Neville	P 24 June 43	4 July 45	25 April 53	
17	2	1	Fred. Torrens Lyster[4]	20 June 41	P 1 Nov. 42	P 30 July 52	
12	0	1	Philip Philpot[5]	24 Nov. 48	P 7 Mar. 51	30 July 54	
13	0	1	Chu. Peregrine Teesdale	P 7 Jan. 47	P 18 Dec. 47	P 10 Aug. 55	
16	1/2	2	Richard Maunsell	P 29 Sept. 43	P 4 July 45	8 Jan. 58	
16	0	1	R. Wingfield Cardiff	6 Dec. 44	P 1 Dec. 48	8 Jan. 58	
16	1 3/4	2	Thomas Basil Tuite	P 31 Dec. 42	P 23 Aug. 44	21 Sept. 55	
5	1 3/4	2	Wm. Hen. Crompton[7]	P 17 Aug. 54	9 Feb. 55	P 7 Nov. 56	
17	0	2	Paget John Bourke[9]	P 30 June 43	9 Sept. 45	9 Jan. 58	
14	0	1	Harry Clayton Hague	P 28 Aug. 46	P 7 June 50	26 Feb. 58	
12	0	1	Geo.ToddingtonOsborn	P 1 Dec. 48	P 16 Sept. 51	P 21 May 58	
11	0	1	William Dutton Naper	29 June 49	P 30 Sept. 53	P 28 May 58	
14	0	2	Rt. Vaughan Dickens[10]	1 May 46	5 June 50	15 June 58	
11	0	1	Wm. Henry Clarkson	29 June 49	6 June 54	P 15 June 58	
10	0	1	Owen Davies	P 16 Aug. 50	6 June 54	P 13 July 58	
10	0	2	Richard Hotham	8 Oct. 50	11 Aug. 54	P 4 Aug. 58	
7	0	1	Thomas Hill	P 30 Sept. 53	23 Mar. 55	P 7 Sept. 58	
16	0	2	Chr. Rowl. Richardson[11]	P 16 Feb. 44	23 Dec. 45	24 Sept. 55	
12	0	2	John Henry Nott[12]	P 12 Sept. 48	P 14 Feb. 51	1 Oct. 58	
8	0	2	Marcus L. M'Causland	23 July 52	P 24 Mar. 54	P 2 Oct. 58	
5	0	2	Thomas Lindsay Stack	20 Feb. 55	20 July 55	P 11 Jan. 59	
5	0	2	Aug. Fred. De B. Dixon	10 Feb. 55	18 Jan. 56	P 22 Apr. 59	
9	0	2	Fra. Wm. Henry Petrie	P 15 May 51	P 18 Aug. 54	14 May 59	

LIEUTENANTS.

6	0	1	Edward Birch	P 24 Feb. 54	P 1 May 55
6	0	1	Stuart James Shortt	P 25 Aug. 54	7 Jan. 58
10	2 3/4	1	John William Poole	6 Nov. 47	4 Feb. 53
5	0	2	Hopton Scott Stewart	6 April 55	2 Aug. 55
5	0	2	Francis W. Osborne	10 April 55	P 3 Aug. 55
5	0	2	Morres Guard	20 Feb. 55	9 Oct. 55
5	0	2	John R. Kelsall[15]	11 May 55	P 7 Mar. 56
5	0	2	Edm. Joseph B. Donelan	16 Mar. 55	25 Mar. 56
5	0	1	Abraham Martin	11 May 55	15 Jan. 58
5	0	2	Henry Joseph Webb	15 May 55	15 Jan. 58
5	0	1	Francis Armstrong	1 June 55	15 Jan. 58
5	0	1	William Norman	8 June 55	26 Feb. 58
5	0	1	David Baker Gabb	P 9 June 55	23 Mar. 58
5	0	2	James Leslie Day	27 July 55	14 May 58
4	0	1	Thomas Davies	2 May 56	P 21 May 58
4	0	1	John Anthony Miers	8 July 56	P 28 May 58
4	0	1	William Taylor Corrie	P 7 Nov. 56	P 15 June 58
2	0	1	William Adam Smyth	5 Feb. 58	P 13 July 58
2	0	1	Alex. Miller Arthur, *Adj.*	19 Feb. 58	P 24 Aug. 58
5	0	2	Wm. Gerard Byron[19]	P 25 Sept. 55	P 7 Sept. 58
4	0	2	John Fred. Trotter	21 Nov. 56	19 Feb. 58
5	0	2	Benj. Oliver Johnson	P 5 June 55	1 Oct. 58
5	0	1	John Hichens Bamfield	6 July 55	1 Oct. 58
5	0	2	George Edge	25 Sept. 55	1 Oct. 58
2	0	2	Fred. James S. Whiteside	17 Mar. 58	P 2 Oct. 58
5	0	1	William Clegg	P 9 Oct. 55	5 Oct. 58
2	0	1	Stewart Charles Dixon	17 Jan. 58	P 28 Jan. 59
2	0	2	Percival Walsh Jordan	18 Mar. 58	P 22 Apr. 59
2	0	2	Thomas George Miles	18 Jan. 58	14 May 59
2	0	2	Jas. Farquharson Oliver	30 Mar. 58	P 17 June 59

1 Sir Richard Doherty served with the 90th Regt. at the capture of Martinique in 1809 (wounded), and at the capture of Guadaloupe in 1810, for which he has received the War Medal with two Clasps. Was knighted in 1841, on his return from Sierra Leone in consideration of his services on the coast, and of the satisfactory manner in which he had administered the government there.

12 Captain Nott served with the field force against the rebel Karens in Burmah in Jan. 1857, and on two occasions commanded a detachment of the 35th Regt. engaged with the enemy, and received a letter of approbation from the Governor General in Council.

13 Lieut. Byron served with the 38th Regt. in the Indian campaign in 1857-58, and was present at the assault and capture of Meangunge, siege and capture of Lucknow, and action at Barkee (Medal and Clasp).

11th (North Devonshire) Regt. of Foot.

Years' Serv.		ENSIGNS.	ENSIGN.
Full Pay.	Half Pay.		
2	0	2 William Joseph Tibbs	16 Mar. 58
2	0	1 George Price[16]	26 Mar. 58
2	0	2 William Arthur Irwin	31 Mar. 58
2	0	2 Joseph Mathers Gilbert	16 April 58
2	0	2 George Augustus Eliot	23 April 58
2	0	2 O. Campobello Robinson	1 May 58
2	0	2 William Miles Maskell	21 May 58
2	0	1 Henry Ralph Lewis	22 May 58
2	0	2 Edward Henry Hare	23 May 58
2	0	1 George Coote	p 28 May 58
2	0	2 Vyvyan Williams	4 June 58
2	0	1 Roper Dacre Tyler	p 13 July 58
2	0	1 David Halliday	p 30 July 58
2	0	1 Hugh Montil Toller	p 31 July 58
2	0	2 John Boyce	p 9 Nov. 58
1	0	1 Frederic Watson	p 29 July 59
1	0	2 Thomas Auchinleck	p 30 July 59
1	0	1 George Thobald	5 Aug. 59

4 Captain Lyster served with the 50th Regt. in the battle of Punniar (Medal). Previous to entering the British service he served in Portugal, in the Pedroite army, from 1833 to 1835, and was at the defence of Oporto, and in all the affairs from the raising of the siege to the termination of the war. He afterwards served in Spain under Sir De Lacy Evans, as Captain of Infantry, and under Espartero as Captain of Cavalry, and subsequently on the staff of General Don Diego Leon, whose escort he commanded from 1836 to 1841. Was twice decorated with the Order of St. Ferdinand for charges of cavalry at Allo and Berga, and with the Medals for the siege and capture of Irun and Morella; once severely wounded. Was present in the following actions and affairs in that country:—Fuenterabia (reconnaissance on), Ametzagana, San Marcos, Loyola, Aguirre, Oriamendi, Hernani, Urnietta, Irun (siege of), Lazarte, Usurbil, Andoin, Vera, Perdon, Otiera (reconnaissance on), Sesma, Belascoain, Aroniz, Santa Barbara (reconnaissance on), Valle de Berruera, Allo, Allo y dicastillo, Collander, Maniella y pena Cortada, Genebrosa, Canadette, Agua Viva, Segura (siege of), Castleotte (reconnaissance on), Castleotte (siege of), Valle de Lladres, Morella (siege of), Berga and its twenty-two redoubts; charged, with seven Lancers, Bosque's squadron, completely routing it, killing seven and capturing five horses.

5 Captain Philpot served with the 74th Regt. throughout the Kaffir war of 1851-53 (Medal).

2	0	Paymasters.—2 Richard Rodd Robinson, 26 Mar. 58.	
12	0	1 David Simpson, 15 June 58; Ens. 2 June 48.	
2	0	Adjutants.—1 Lieut. Alex. Miller Arthur, 26 Mar. 58.	
17	2	Instructors of Musketry.—1 Captain F. T. Lyster,[4] 20 Sept. 56.	
2	0	2 Lieut. F. J. S. Whiteside, 8 June 58.	
2	0	Quarter Masters.—2 William Charles Napier, 5 Feb. 58.	
1	0	1 Daniel Deacon, 18 Jan. 59.	
19	0	Surgeons.—1 Nesbitt Heffernan, M.B. 7 Nov. 51; Assist.-Surg. 11 June 41.	
15	0	2 William Thomas Black,[14] 20 July 55; Assist.-Surg. 25 Sept. 45.	
6	0	Assistant Surgeons.—1 Francis Henry Macfadin, 1 Dec. 54.	
7	0	1 Peter Divorty, M.B. 18 Nov. 53.	
2	0	2 Alexander Macintyre, M.D. 22 Jan. 58.	
2	0	2 Wilton Everet, 16 Nov. 58.	

Facings Green.

Agent, E. S. Codd, Esq.—Irish Agents, Sir E. R. Borough, Bt., Armit & Co.

[1st Battalion returned from New South Wales, 10 Feb. 58. Depot, Fermoy.]

7 Captain Crompton served with the 42nd Highlanders at the siege and fall of Sebastopol from July 1855 (Medal and Clasp).

9 Captain Bourke served in the Kaffir war of 1850-51 (Medal), and in 1852-53 in the Orange River Territory, where he commanded several successful patrols.

10 Captain Dickens served with the 64th Regt. in the Persian campaign of 1856-57, including the storm and capture of Reshire, surrender of Bushire, and bombardment of Mohumrah. Served in Bengal and N.W. Provinces in suppressing the mutiny in 1857-58; present with Havelock's column in the actions of Futtehpore, Aoung, Pandoo Nuddee, Cawnpore (wounded), and Bithoor; in an affair at Shirazpore under Brigadier Wilson; and was Assistant Engineer during the defence of Cawnpore.

11 Captain Richardson served the campaign on the Sutlej with the 9th Regt., and was present at the battles of Moodkee, Ferozeshah and Sobraon (Medal and two Clasps). Served in the Punjaub campaign of 1848-9 with the 61st Regt., and was present at Ramnuggur and the passage of the Chenab, the battles of Sadoolapore and Chillianwallah, and with the field force in pursuit of the enemy to the Khyber Pass in March 1849 (Medal and two Clasps). Served at the siege, assault, and capture of Delhi in 1857.

14 Surgeon Black served in the Kaffir war of 1847, and in that of 1851-53, and was present at the capture of Fort Armstrong from the Rebels on 22nd Feb. 1851 (Medal). Served also in the Crimea from 6th Sept. 1855 (Medal with Clasp for Sebastopol).

15 Lieut. Kelsall served with the 82nd Regt. at the siege and fall of Sebastopol from 25th Aug. 1855 (Medal and Clasp).

16 Ensign Price served with the 41st Regt. at the siege of Sebastopol in 1854-55 and was severely contused by a grape shot on the left shoulder in the advanced Rifle Pit on 8th June (Medal and Clasp).

12th (E. Suffolk) Regt. of Foot.

{1st Batt. Tasmania.
2nd Batt. Aldershot.

"MINDEN" "GIBRALTAR"—with the *Castle* and *Key*—"*Montis Insignia Calpe*"—"SERINGAPATAM" "INDIA."

Colonel.—👑 Charles Anthony Ferdinand Bentinck,[1] *Ens.* 16 Nov. 08; *Lt. and Capt.* 24 Sept. 12; *Brev.-Major*, 18 June 15; *Capt. and Lt.-Col.* 27 May 25; *Col.* 28 June 38; *Maj.* ᴾ 30 May 43; *Lt.-Col.* 9 Nov. 46; *Maj.-Gen.* 11 Nov. 51; *Lt.Gen.* 15 Jan. 58; *Col.* 12th Foot, 14 April 57.

Years' Serv.						
Full Pay.	Half Pay.					
52						
27	0	*Lt.-Cols.*—1 John Maxwell Perceval,[2] *CB. Ens.*ᴾ 21 June 33; *Lt.* ᴾ 18 Mar. 36; *Capt.* ᴾ 18 May 38; *Maj.*ᴾ 14 April 46; *Lt.Col.* ᴾ 2 April 50; *Col.* 28 Nov. 54.				
26	0	2 Thomas Brooke, *Ens.* ᴾ 31 Oct. 34; *Lieut.* ᴾ 29 July 36; *Capt.* ᴾ 15 May 40; *Major,* ᴾ 2 April 50; *Lt.Col.* ᴾ 19 May 54; *Col.* 28 Nov. 54.				
30	0	*Majors.*—1 John Francis Kempt, *Ens.* ᴾ 16 June 30; *Lt.* 19 May 37; *Capt.* 29 Apr. 42; *Major,* ᴾ 19 May 54; *Bt.Lt.Col.* 26 Oct. 58.				
20	1	2 Henry Meade Hamilton,[3] *Ens.* ᴾ 9 Aug. 39; *Lt.* ᴾ 26 Oct. 41; *Capt.* ᴾ 11 May 49; *Brev.Maj.* 12 Dec. 54; *Maj. Lt.Col.* 6 June 56.				
24	0	1 William James Hutchins, *Ens.* 2 Dec. 36; *Lt.* 2 Dec. 40; *Capt.* 20 Dec. 46; *Major,* 8 Jan. 58.				
14	0	2 Edward George Hibbert,[4] *Ens.* ᴾ 29 April 46; *Lt.* Oct. 48; *Capt.* ᴾ 28 May 52; *Bt.Maj.* 12 Dec. 54.				

		CAPTAINS.	ENSIGN.	LIEUT.	CAPTAIN.	BREV.MAJ.
18	0	1 Richard Atkinson	ᴾ18 Mar. 42	ᴾ18 Feb. 43	ᴾ30 Mar. 49	
18	0	2 James Wm. Espinasse[6]	ᴾ30 Apr. 42	ᴾ18 Aug. 43	23 June 50	
17	0	1 Wm. Henry Queade[5] ..	9 June 43	ᴾ27 June 45	ᴾ11 Apr. 51	
18	0	2 Thomas Dundas[7]	27 Dec. 42	ᴾ14 Apr. 46	ᴾ20 Feb. 52	
15	0	1 Thomas George Vereker	ᴾ23 May 45	ᴾ11 Dec. 46	ᴾ19 May 54	
14	0	2 Henry Robson	ᴾ27 Oct. 46	ᴾ2 Apr. 50	ᴾ27 June 54	
18	0	1 John Reynolds Palmer[6]	1 May 42	6 Jan. 46	26 Aug. 54	
18	0	2 Edward H. Foster,[6] *s.*	2 May 42	14 Apr. 46	14 Feb. 55	
13	2/12	1 Samuel Fairtlough[7] ..	25 Aug. 46	ᴾ22 Oct. 47	ᴾ27 July 55	
15	0	1 Edward Herrick [6]	ᴾ16 Dec. 45	ᴾ23 June 48	ᴾ29 May 57	
14	0	1 Henry Cole	9 Sept. 46	22 July 49	8 Jan. 58	
14	0	2 Frederick Bagnell[6] ..	20 Oct. 46	8 Aug. 49	8 Jan. 58	
6	1 2/12	1 Charles J. Cecil Sillery	21 Jan. 53	21 Sept. 54	9 Sept. 55	
15	0	2 Horatio Nelson Kippen	ᴾ18 Apr. 45	20 Apr. 49	9 Jan. 58	
11	0	1 Thos. Edmund Miller	ᴾ30 Mar. 49	13 Oct. 52	ᴾ19 Feb. 58	
10	0	2 Alexander M'Leod	17 Sept. 50	9 Feb. 55	26 Jan. 58	
11	0	1 John David Downing ..	ᴾ23 Nov. 49	ᴾ2 May 51	9 Oct. 56	
10	0	1 Aug. Johnnes Leeson ..	ᴾ14 June 50	ᴾ21 May 52	ᴾ13 April 58	
12	0	2 Geo. Glascott Newton	3 Nov. 48	14 May 52	30 Sept. 58	
12	0	2 Edward Marcon	13 Sept. 48	3 Dec. 52	30 Sept. 58	
11	0	1 John Lunan Wilkie ..	23 Nov. 49	ᴾ27 July 55	ᴾ26 Oct. 58	
13	0	2 Legh Richmond Parry	ᴾ30 July 47	3 June 53	20 Oct. 57	
10	0	2 Compton A. S. Dickins[8]	ᴾ13 Dec. 50	ᴾ20 May 53	17 June 55	
9	0	2 Samuel Henry Harford[9]	ᴾ18 Apr. 51	2 Dec. 53	ᴾ11 Mar. 59	

LIEUTENANTS.

11	0	1 Jas. Fielding Sweeney[6]	21 Aug. 49	ᴾ21 Oct. 53	
10	0	1 M. Caulfield Saunders	ᴾ17 May 50	ᴾ19 May 54	
11	0	2 Julius Henry Stirke[6] ..	18 Sept. 40	26 Aug. 54	
8	0	1 Fra. A. FitzGerald,*Adj.*	ᴾ21 Sept. 52	ᴾ16 May 56	
8	0	2 George Gibson,[6] *Adj.* ..	24 Dec. 52	3 April 57	2 Colonel Perceval commanded the reserve Battalion 12th Regt. in the Kaffir war of 1851-52, and for his services was nominated a CB. (Medal.)
7	0	2 John Warren	ᴾ12 Aug. 53	3 April 57	
6	0	1 Christopher Hodgson ..	1 Sept. 54	8 Nov. 55	
6	0	1 Coningsby M. Harward	ᴾ19 May 54	8 Jan. 58	3 Lieut.-Colonel Hamilton served the Eastern campaign of 1854-55 as D. A. Q. M. G., and as A. Q. M. G. from Oct. 1855, including the battle of Alma, capture of Balaklava, siege and fall of Sebastopol (Medal and Clasps, brevet of Major and Lieut.-Colonel, and 5th Class of the Medjidie).
6	0	2 Henry Nesbitt	22 Dec. 54	8 Jun. 58	
5	0	1 Wm. Dummer Jarvis .	8 June 55	8 Jan. 58	
5	0	2 Samuel Hall	13 Feb. 55	ᴾ10 Aug. 55	
5	0	2 George Morland......	23 Feb. 55	ᴾ26 Oct. 55	
6	0	1 Jno. Soame Richardson[11]	ᴾ30 Nov. 54	ᴾ23 Nov. 55	
5	0	2 Gilbert de Lacy Lacy [12]	14 Mar. 55	9 Dec. 55	
5	0	2 Frederick Alban......	8 June 55	ᴾ8 Jan. 56	
5	0	1 Matthew Coke	27 July 55	ᴾ2 Feb. 58	6 Capts. Espinasse, Palmer, Foster, Herrick, and Bagnell, Lieuts. Sweeney, Stirke, and Gibson, served in the Kaffir war of 1851-53 (Medal).
4	0	2 Reuben Fred. Magor ..	8 July 56	ᴾ23 Mar. 58	
5	0	1 Wm. Henry Crawhall .	ᴾ10 Aug. 55	ᴾ16 Apr. 58	
4	0	1 David Seymour	ᴾ1 Feb. 56	ᴾ23 Apr. 58	
5	0	1 Thophilus Henry Oliver	9 Oct. 55	1 Oct. 58	7 Capts. Dundas and Fairtlough served in the Kaffir war of 1852-53 (Medal).
5	0	1 William Keough	6 June 55	2 Oct. 58	
5	0	2 Joseph Oliver Johnson	7 Dec. 55	3 Oct. 58	
4	0	2 Robt. Brads. Moorhead	8 July 56	3 Oct. 58	9 Captain Harford served with the 56th Regt. in he Crimea from 25th Aug. 1855, and has the Medal with Clasp for Sebastopol.
3	0	1 Edward Jas. Dudgeon	ᴾ29 May 57	3 Oct. 58	
2	0	1 W.A. Featherstonehaugh	26 Mar. 58	ᴾ7 Dec. 58	
5	0	1 Henry Macgregor Lowry	31 Aug. 55	23 Mar. 58	
2	0	1 W. Crosbie Siddons Mair	28 May 58	ᴾ16 Apr. 59	
2	0	2 Robert Edward Dawson	30 Mar. 58	ᴾ26 Aug. 59	
2	0	2 Wm. S. Henry Dunlevie	31 Mar. 58	ᴾ28 Oct. 59	
2	0	2 John William Lloyd ..	ᴾ25 June 58	ᴾ4 Mar. 59	

12th (E. Suffolk) Regt. of Foot.

Years' Serv.		ENSIGNS.	ENSIGN.	
Full Pay	Half Pay			
2	0	1 Thos. Geo. D. Latouche	26 Jan. 58	11 Lieut. Richardson served with the 72nd Highlanders at the siege and fall of Sebastopol from 10th July 1855 (Medal and Clasp).
2	0	2 Thomas John Gray ..	27 Mar. 58	
2	0	2 Henry Magee	1 Apr. 58	12 Lieut. Lacy served with the 63rd Regt. at the siege and fall of Sebastopol from 3rd Sept. 1855; also at the bombardment and capture of Kinbourn (Medal and Clasp).
2	0	2 Edward Fiddes	2 Apr. 58	
2	0	2 Townsend George Gun	3 Apr. 58	
2	0	2 Henry J. Mac Donnell	4 Apr. 58	13 Doctor Dick served in the Kaffir War during portions of 1851-52 (Medal).
2	0	1 Charles Edward Hurst	25 Mar. 58	
2	0	2 Walter John Boyes ..	21 May 58	14 Surgeon Wodsworth served in the Kaffir war of 1851-53 (Medal). Served with the 12th Lancers in the Crimean campaign from 17th May 1855, including the battle of the Tchernaya, siege and fall of Sebastopol, and operations near Euputoria under General D'Allonville (Medal and Clasp). Also with the 12th Lancers during the suppression of the Indian mutiny, with the Nerbudda field force, and was present at the affairs of Jegunge and Kuhni, battle of Banda, and surrender of Rajah Kirwee (Medal).
2	0	2 Arthur Leroux Whipple	29 Oct. 58	
2	0	1 William Lewis Murphy	12 Nov. 58	
1	0	1 Edw. Cha. Colley Foster	11 Jan. 59	
1	0	1 Wm. Lawson Saunder	11 Mar. 59	
1	0	2 Robert Baynes Reed..	13 May 59	
1	0	1 Campbell Thos. Morris	p 23 Aug. 59	
1	0	1 William Mansell	24 Aug. 59	
1	0	1 Henry Smith Andrews	p 26 Aug. 59	
1	0	Hamilton John Wallace	p 13 Dec. 59	

9	0	*Paymasters.*—1 Walter Rice Olivey, 6 Apr. 55; *Ens.* p 14 Feb. 51; *Lt.* p 29 Oct. 52.
2	0	2 Robert William Burdett Desanges, 9 March 58.
8	0	*Adjutants.*—2 Lieut. George Gibson, 27 July 55.
8	0	1 Lieut. Francis Augustus FitzGerald, 1 Oct. 58.
11	0	*Instructors of Musketry.*—1 Lieut. J. F. Sweeney, 13 Feb. 58.
5	0	2 Lieut. Gilbert de Lacy Lacy, 28 Mar. 59.
6	0	*Quarter Masters.*—1 Robert Laver, 21 April 54.
2	0	2 William Ross, 14 May 58.
24	0	*Surgeons.*—1 W. Dick,[13] M.D. *A.S.* 13 May 36; *Surg.* 7 Aug. 46; *Surg. Maj.* 1 Oct. 58.
9	0	2 Dudley Clifton Wodsworth,[14] 26 Jan. 58; *Assist. Surg.* 10 Jan. 51.
6	0	*Assistant Surgeons.*—1 George Banks Floyer Arden, 9 June 54.
6	0	2 George Allan Hutton, 23 June 54.
2	0	1 Arthur Henry Francis Lynch, 7 May 58.
1	0	2 Joseph Wm. Carter Neynoe Murphy, 1 March 59.

Facings Yellow—*Agents*, Messrs. Cox & Co.
[1st Batt. embarked for Australia, 1 July 1854. Depot, Walmer.]
[2nd Batt. returned from Cape of Good Hope, Sept. 1858. Depot, .]

1 Lieut. General Bentinck served with two companies of the 2nd Battalion Coldstream Guards at the defence of Cadiz and the Isle of Leon from March 1810 to June 1811; was wounded at the battle of Barossa, which prevented him joining the first Battalion in Portugal. He was appointed Adjutant to the 2nd Battalion, and accompanied the six companies that were sent to Holland in 1813 under Lord Lynedoch, and was engaged in the successful attack of Merxem, bombardment of Antwerp, and operations against Bergen-op-Zoom. He was attached to the 2nd Division as D. A. Adjutant-General under Sir Henry Clinton at the battle of Waterloo and capture of Paris, for which he received the brevet rank of Major, and being appointed Assist. Adj.-General to the 2nd Division, he continued to serve in the army of occupation until its dissolution at the end of 1818. He has the Waterloo Medal, and also the War Medal with one Clasp.

4 Major Hibbert served in the 50th Regt. the Eastern campaign of 1854-55, including the battles of Alma and Inkerman, and siege of Sebastopol (Medal and Clasps, Brevet Major, Sardinian Medal, and 5th Class of the Medjidie).

5 Captain Queade served with a detachment of the 12th and 40th Regts. under Captain Thomas at the capture of a stockade occupied by Insurgents at the Ballarat Gold Fields in Australia on 3rd Dec. 1854.

8 Captain Dickins served with the 38th Regt. the Eastern campaign of 1854 and up to 19th July 1855, including the battles of Alma and Inkerman, and siege of Sebastopol; with Volunteer Sharpshooters from 17th Oct. to 20th Nov.; repulse of a sortie on 21st Dec.; commanded the Light Company in the attack of the Cemetery on the 18th June; was severely wounded in the advanced trenches on the 2nd July (Medal and three Clasps, and Knight of the Legion of Honor).

13th, or Prince Albert's Regt. of Lt. Inf. [1st Batt. Gorruckpore. 2nd Batt. Cape of G. Hope

The "**Sphinx**," with the words, " EGYPT" " MARTINIQUE" "AVA" "AFFGHANISTAN" "GHUZNEE"
A *Mural Crown*, superscribed " JELLALABAD" "CABOOL, 1842" " SEVASTOPOL."

Years' Serv.			
Full Pay	Half Pay		
66		*Colonel.*—**P QQ** Sir William Maynard Gomm,[1] GCB. *Ens.* 24 May 94; *Lt.* 16 Nov. 94; *Capt.* 25 June 03; *Major*, 10 Oct. 11; *Lieut.-Col.* 17 Aug. 12; *Col.* 16 May 29; *Maj-Gen.* 10 Jan. 37; *Lt.-Gen.* 9 Nov. 46; *Gen.* 20 June 54; *Col.* 13th Lt. Inf. 10 Mar. 46.	
24	1	*Lt. Colonels.*—1 Lord Mark Kerr,[2] CB. *Ens.* p 19 June 35; *Lt.* p 14 Sept. 38; *Capt.* p 26 June 40; *Maj.* p 25 July 51; *Lt.Col.* p 30 Dec. 53; *Col.* 28 Nov. 54.	
29	0	1 George King,[3] *Ens.* 13 April 31; *Lt.* p 16 Jan. 35; *Capt.* 2 Aug. 42; *Bt.Maj.* 20 June 54; *Maj.* 31 Aug. 55; *Bt.Lt.Col.* 26 Dec. 56; *Lt.Col.* 17 Nov. 57.	
35	0	2 Arthur Horne,[3]† *Ens.* p 19 Nov. 25; *Lt.* p 27 Nov. 28; *Capt.* p 21 Feb. 34; *Br.-Maj.* 9 Nov. 46; *Maj.* p 30 Mar. 49; *Brev. Lt.-Col.* 28 May 53; *Col.* 28 Nov. 54; *Lt.Col.* 8 Jan. 58.	
22	0	*Majors.*—1 John William Cox,[4] CB. *Ens.* 26 June 38; *Lt.* 22 Apr. 40; *Capt.* p 0 Apr. 47; *Bt.Maj.* 15 Dec. 54; *Major*, 25 Jan. 56; *Bt.Lt.Col.* 20 July 58.	
18	0	1 George Henry Tyler,[4] *Ens.* 23 July 42; *Lt.* 14 Apr. 46; *Capt.* p 8 Nov. 50; *Maj.* 17 Nov. 57; *Bt.Lt.Col.* 26 Apr. 59.	
16	0	2 William Lawes Peto,[5]† *Ens.* p 10 May 44; *Lt.* p 26 June 46; *Capt.* p 8 Feb. 50; *Major*, 21 May 58.	
20	0	2 Herbert Vaughan Mundell,[5] *Ens.* 2 Nov. 40; *Lt.* p 30 Dec. 45; *Capt.* 15 Mar. 53; *Major*, p 21 May 58.	

		CAPTAINS.	ENSIGN.	LIEUT.	CAPTAIN.	BREV.-MAJ.
14	0	1 Robert Peel[7]	p 21 July 46	p 8 Nov. 50	p 25 Nov. 53	
14	0	2 William Henry Kerr	p 31 July 46	p 24 Jan. 51	p 13 Jan. 54	20 July 58
22	0	1 Fred. Van Straubenzee[6]	p 17 Aug. 38	30 Apr. 41	6 June 54	26 Apr. 59
13	0	1 Robert B. Montgomery[6]	p 24 Sept. 47	p 12 Oct. 52	p 4 Aug. 54	
20	0	1 Gerald FitzGerald King[6]	p 3 Nov. 40	14 Oct. 42	26 June 55	
17	0	1 Melville Browne	24 Feb. 43	p 9 Apr. 47	26 June 55	
12	0	1 Edward Boyd[7]	p 29 Dec. 48	p 1 Apr. 51	26 June 55	
10	0	1 Arthur Bainbrigge[6]	p 14 June 50	p 6 May 53	26 June 55	
9	0	1 Charles Poore Long[6]	p 21 Nov. 51	p 25 Nov. 53	p 17 Aug. 55	
18	1	2 Charles Power Cobbe	13 July 41	3 Apr. 46	30 Aug. 55	
8	7½	2 Noel H. Bryan Vardon	p 12 Dec. 51	p 13 Jan. 54	25 Jan. 56	
10	1	2 Wm. Henry Grimston[13]	29 June 49	p 17 June 51	p 9 Nov. 55	
11	1½	2 Richard Morgan Hall[14]	p 31 Dec. 47	p 11 Dec. 49	15 May 55	
15	0	1 Geddes Sansom Twynam[16]	p 18 Oct. 45	p 23 July 47	11 Jan. 58	
15	0	2 John Cumming Clarke	11 Nov. 45	3 Sept. 47	11 Jan. 58	
12	0	2 J. Robertson Turnbull[15]	14 Jan. 48	p 4 May 49	11 Jan. 58	19 Jan. 58
8	0	1 Jno. Angerstein Rowley[6]	p 23 Nov. 52	6 June 54	14 Mar. 58	
7	0	1 Cornw. Hy. Chichester[6]	p 18 Feb. 53	11 Aug. 54	7 Apr. 58	
13	0	2 Samuel Head	1 Jan. 47	20 Nov. 48	31 Aug. 58	
7	0	1 George Henry Cobham[6]	p 22 Apr. 53	11 Aug. 54	p 7 Sept. 58	
10	0	1 O'Neil Stewart Segrave[6]	p 17 Sept. 50	p 19 Aug. 53	11 Feb. 59	
7	0	2 *Hon.* James C. Dormer[7]	p 12 May 53	p 18 Aug. 54	p 11 Mar. 59	14 June 59
11	0	2 Tho. Chevalier Robertson	10 Apr. 49	p 9 May 51	26 Oct. 58	
8	0	2 V C Alf. Stowell Jones[7]†	p 9 July 52	21 Sept. 55	16 Mar. 58	
		LIEUTENANTS.				
7	0	1 Hy. Lewis FitzGerald[9]	p 13 May 53	p 2 Feb. 55		
7	0	1 John Frederic Everett[6]	p 14 May 53	p 13 Feb. 55		
7	0	2 Richd. Nugent Clayton[6]	p 15 July 53	26 June 55		
7	0	2 Henry Edward Hall[6]	p 25 Nov. 53	26 June 55		
6	0	1 Phil. Edw. Victor Gilbert[9]	p 13 Jan. 54	26 June 55		
6	0	2 William Haslett[9]	p 18 Aug. 54	26 June 55		
6	0	1 Henry Gillett[10]	p 24 Aug. 54	26 June 55		
6	0	1 William Williams[11]	p 25 Aug. 54	26 June 55		
7	0	2 Thomas Tyler Gould	p 13 Dec. 53	26 June 55		
8	0	2 John Codd Conington	p 18 Dec. 52	6 July 55		
6	0	1 H. Alex. C. Wroughton	p 16 June 54	3 Aug. 55		
7	0	2 John J. Paterson Fox	19 Aug. 53	30 Aug. 55		
5	0	1 Allan Shafto Adair	p 2 Feb. 55	31 Aug. 55		
5	0	2 John Bond, *Adj.*	p 13 Feb. 55	25 Jan. 56		
5	0	1 Wm. Knox Leet, *Adj.*	4 July 55	p 1 Feb. 56		
5	0	1 John Fencott James	p 17 Aug. 55	p 7 Mar. 56		
5	0	1 Thomas McNeille Gill	1 June 55	10 Feb. 57		
5	0	2 Fredk. William Ruck	p 8 June 55	8 Jan. 58		
5	0	1 William Cox[23]	2 July 55	8 Jan. 58		
5	0	2 Charles Edwards Palmer	5 July 55	14 Mar. 58		
5	0	2 Edw. Lutwyche England	6 July 55	7 Apr. 58		
5	0	2 Aubrey Henzell	20 July 55	30 Apr. 58		
5	0	2 W. Strok. Cunninghame	2 Aug. 55	31 Aug. 58		
5	0	2 Alfred Gabriel Wynen	p 2 Oct. 55	31 Aug. 58		
4	0	1 Edward Bolger	25 Jan. 56	31 Aug. 58		
6	0	1 Fra. Drewó Edwards	p 28 Mar. 54	16 July 55		

4 Lt.-Col. Cox served in the 13th Light Infantry the campaigns of 1840, 41, and 42 in Affghanistan, and was present at the assault and capture of the town and fort of Tootumdurrah, storm of Jhoolghur, night-attack of Baboo Koosh Ghur, attack on Khardurrah, storming the Khoord Cabool Pass, affair of Tezeou, forcing the Jugdulluck Pass, reduction of the Fort of Mamoo Khail, heroic defence of Jellalabad and sorties on the 14th Nov. and 1st Dec. 1841, and 11th March, 24th March, and 1st April 1842; the general action with and defeat of the besieging force under Akbar Khan before Jellalabad on the 7th April; the storming of the Jugdulluck heights, general action at Tezeen, and recapture of Cabool, for which he has a Medal, as also another for Jellalabad. Served in the Crimea from 30th June 1855, and was at the battle of the Tchernaya, siege and fall of Sebastopol (Medal and Clasp, and 5th Class of the Medjidie).

13th, or Prince Albert's Regiment of Light Infantry.

Years' Serv. Full Pay.	Years' Serv. Half Pay.	LIEUTENANTS.	ENSIGN.	LIEUT.	
3	0	2 William Moffett	18 Dec. 57	30 Jan. 59	2 Lord Mark Kerr commanded the 13th Light Infantry in the Crimea from the 30th June 1855, and was at the battle of the Tchernaya, siege and fall of Sebastopol (Medal and Clasp, and 5th Class of the Medjidie).
2	0	2 Alured F. Cuninghame	29 Mar. 58	P 11 Mar. 59	
8	0	1 Charles Fraser	14 Sept. 52	10 Dec. 54	
2	0	1 Alex.MacmanusRowan	31 Mar. 58	P 7 Oct. 59	3 Lt.-Colonel King served throughout the campaigns in Affghanistan from 1838 to 1842 inclusive, including the storm and capture of Ghuznee (Medal), storming the Khoord Cabool Pass, affair of Tezeen, forcing the Jugdulluck Pass, reduction of the fort of Mamoo Khail, defence of Jellalabad, and surties on the 14th, Nov. and 1st Dec. 1841, 11th March, 24th March, and 1st April 1842, general action and defeat of Akbar Khan before Jellalabad (Medal), storming the heights of Jugdulluck, general action of Tezeen, and recapture of Cabool (Medal). Served in the Crimea from 30th June 1855, and was at the siege and fall of Sebastopol (Medal and Clasp, Knight of the Legion of Honor, and 5th Class of the Medjidie).
		ENSIGNS.			
2	0	2 Lloyd Picton Jenkins	27 Mar. 58		
2	0	1 Rich. Fitzgerald King	30 Mar. 58		
2	0	2 Arthur M'G. Denny	1 April 58		
2	0	2 Arthur Brooks	23 April 58		
2	0	2 Henry King Fenwick	24 April 58		
2	0	1 Pierce William Hughes	28 May 58		3† Colonel Horne served with the 12th Regt. in the Kaffir war of 1851-53 (Medal and Clasp).
2	0	1 Dudley Thomas Persse	29 May 58		
2	0	2 Robert Stuart Clarke	25 June 58		
2	0	1 Matthew John Bell	P 24 Aug. 58		Brevet Lt.-Colonel).
2	0	1 And. Cha. Cunningham	24 Sept. 58		4† Lt.-Col. Tyler landed with the Regt. in the Crimea on the 30th June 1855, and was present at the battle of the Tchernaya, siege and fall of Sebastopol (Medal and Clasp, and Knight of the Legion of Honor).
2	0	2 William James Hall	25 Sept. 58		
2	0	1 William Lea Smith	5 Oct. 58		
2	0	2 George Kemmis	P 9 Nov. 58		
2	0	1 Richard Hare Horne	12 Nov. 58		
2	0	1 Robert Warren	31 Dec. 58		
1	0	2 GerardSeptimusBurton	28 Jan. 59		
1	0	1 Charles Fred. Powell	29 Jan. 59		
1	0	2 JohnDroughtE.Mooney	P 18 Mar. 59		
1	0	2 Alex. Duke Simpson	P 3 June 59		
1	0	2 John A. P. K.Harwood	7 Oct. 59		
12	0	*Paymasters.*—1 Duncan Cameron M'Naughten,[12] 25 May 55; *Q.M.* 15 Aug.48.			
6	0	2 Thomas Calderhead Brown, 27 July 55; *Ens.* 5 Nov. 54; *Lt.* [15 May 55.			
5	0	*Adjutants.*—2 *Lieut.* John Bond, 13 April 58.			
5	0	1 *Lieut.* William Knox Leet, 2 Aug. 58.			
5	0	*Instructors of Musketry.*—2 *Lieut.* A. G. Wynen, 2 Nov. 58.			
2	0	1 *Ensign* Richard F. King, 16 May 59.			
5	0	*Quarter-Masters.*—1 Thomas Hoban,[21] 25 May 55; *Ens.* 12 Jan. 55.			
5	0	2 Thomas Argent, 9 Nov. 55.			
19	0	*Surgeons.*—1 James Jackson, *A.S.* 11 June 41 ; *Surg.* 21 May 52.			
18	0	2 Wm. Green Trousdell,[17] M. D. 13 Dec. 53; *Assist.Surg.* 8 Apr. 42.			
6	0	*Assistant-Surgeons.*—1 Peter Nevil Jackson,[22] 28 April 54.			
6	0	1 Arthur Edwin Temple Longhurst, 27 Oct. 54.			
5	0	1 Charles John Kirwan,[20] 20 Mar. 55.			
2	0	2 Nicholas Loftus Gray, 22 Jan. 58.			
2	0	2 John Stuart, 13 Oct. 58.			

Facings Blue.—*Agents*, Messrs. Cox & Co.

[1st Batt. embarked for Gibraltar 25 May 51. Depot, Fermoy.]
[2nd Batt. embarked for Cape of Good Hope 23 Feb. 1859. Depot, Fermoy.]

1 Sir William Gomm served in the expedition to the Helder, in 1799, including the action of the 19th Sept. at Bergen. Expedition on the coast of France and Spain, under Sir James Pulteney, in 1800. Expedition to Hanover in 1805; and that to Stralsund and Copenhagen in 1807. Campaign of 1808-9, including the battles of Roleia, Vimiera, and Corunna. Expedition to Walcheren, and siege of Flushing in 1809. Proceeded again to the Peninsula in 1810, where he served during the remainder of the war, the principal part of the time as an Assistant-Quarter-Master-General, including the battles of Busaco and Fuentes d'Onor, assault and capture of Badajoz, battle of Salamanca; action at Villa Muriel, battle of Vittoria, siege of San Sebastian, and battle of the Nive. Served also the campaign of 1815, including the battle of Waterloo. Sir William has received the Gold Cross and one Clasp for Badajoz, Salamanca, Vittoria, St. Sebastian, and Nive; and the Silver War Medal with six Clasps for Roleia, Vimiera, Corunna, Busaco, Fuentes d'Onor, and Nivelle; and is a Knight 2nd Class of St. Anne of Russia.

5 Major Mundoll served in New Zealand with a detachment of the 96th Regt. throughout the operations against the hostile natives, in 1845-46. He served on the Staff of the army in the Crimea in 1855 as D.A. Q.M. General, and was present at the fall of Sebastopol (Medal and Clasp).

5† Major Poto served with the 73rd Regt. in the Kaffir war of 1846-47 (Medal).

6 Captains Montgomery, King, Bainbridge, Long, Rowley, Chichester, Cobham, and Segrave, Lieuts. Everett, Clayton, Hall, and Gilbert, landed with the Regt. in the Crimea on the 30th June 1855, and were at the battle of the Tchernaya, siege and fall of Sebastopol (Medal and Clasp). Captains Montgomery, Long, and Cobham have the 5th Class of the Medjidie.

7 Major Hon. J. C. Dormer, Captains Peel and Boyd, landed with the Regt. in the Crimea on the 30th June 1855, and were at the battle of the Tchernaya, and siege of Sebastopol (Medal and Clasp).

7† Captain Jones was present at the battle of Budlekeserai and at Delhi throughout the siege operations including the assault and capture of the city, having been D.A.Q.M.G. to the Cavalry Brigade from 8th Aug. to 23d Sept. 1857. Served with the 9th Lancers in Greathed's pursuing column and was present in the actions of Bolundshuhur and Allyghur, and battle of Agra, where he was dangerously wounded, having received a musket shot wound and twenty-two sabre cuts. He was mentioned in the despatches, Sir Hope Grant's, on three different occasions, and has received the Victoria Cross for taking a 9-pounder gun with the assistance of some men from his squadron in the action at Budlekeserai (Medal and Clasp).

8 Major Straubenzee served the campaigns of 1840, 41, and 42, in Afghanistan with the 13th Light Infantry, including the assault and capture of the town and forts of Tootumdurrah, storm of Jhoolghur, night-attack at Baboo Koosh Ghur, destruction of Khardurrah, assault of Perwandurrah, storming the Khoord Cabool Pass, affair of Tezeen, forcing the Jugdulluck Pass, reduction of the fort of Mamoo Khail, heroic defence of Jellalabad, and surties on the 14th Nov. and 1st Dec. 1841, 11th March, 24th March, and 1st April 1842, general action and defeat of Akbar Khan before Jellalabad (Medal), storming the heights of Jugdulluck, general action of Tezeen, and recapture of Cabool (Medal). Landed with the Regt. in the Crimea on the 30th June 1855, and was at the battle of the Tchernaya, siege and fall of Sebastopol (Medal and Clasp, and 5th Class of the Medjidie).

9 Lieuts. Fitz Gerald and Haslett served at the siege and fall of Sebastopol from 3rd Sept. 1855 (Medal and Clasp). Lieut. Haslett served also in the Indian campaign in 1858, and was present with the Sarun field force at the actions of Amorah and the taking of Nuggur (Medal).
10 Lieut. Gillett served at the siege and fall of Sebastopol from 2nd Sept. 1855 (Medal and Clasp).
11 Lieut. Williams served at the siege and fall of Sebastopol from 7th Sept. 1855 (Medal and Clasp).
12 Paymaster M'Naughten landed with the Regt. in the Crimea on the 30th June 1855, and was at the siege and fall of Sebastopol (Medal and Clasp).
13 Captain Grimston served with the 2nd Regt. in the Kaffir war of 1851-52 (Medal), and with the expedition north of the Orange River in 1852-53.
14 Captain Hall landed with the 48th Regt. in the Crimea on the 21st April 1855, and served at the siege and fall of Sebastopol (Medal and Clasp).
15 Major Turnbull served as Aide-de-Camp to Sir H. Barnard, to Maj.-Gen. Reed, and to Sir A. Wilson, during the siege, assault, and capture of Delhi, in the action of Badli ke Serai and all the minor engagements (thanked by Governor General in Council, Brevet-Major).
17 Dr. Trousdell served with the 29th Regt. in the Punjaub campaign of 1848-9, and was present at the battles of Chillianwallah and Goojerat (Medal and two Clasps). Served the Eastern campaign of 1854-55, including the battles of Alma and Inkerman, and siege of Sebastopol (Medal and Clasps).
18 Captain Twynam served with the 61st Regt. at the siege and capture of Delhi in 1857 including the action of Nujifghur (Medal and Clasp).
20 Assist.-Surgeon Kirwan served at the siege of Sebastopol from the 14th to the 30th June 1855, including the assault of the 18th June (Medal and Clasp). Had medical charge of the left wing 13th Lt. Inf. in India in 1858 at the action of Amorah, assault and capture of Nuggur, and various actions of the Sarun field force (twice mentioned in despatches, and Medal).
21 Qr.-Master Hoban served with the 13th Lt. Infantry throughout the campaigns in Affghanistan from 1838 to 1842 inclusive, and was present at the storm and capture of Ghuznee (Medal), assault and capture of the town and fort of Tootumdurrah, storm of Jhoolghur, night-attack of Baboo Koosh Ghur, destruction of Khandurrah, assault of Perwandurrah, storming of the Khoord Cabool Pass, affair of Tezeen, forcing the Jugdulluck Pass, recapture of the fort of Mamoo Khail, heroic defence of Jellalabad and sorties of 14th Nov. and 1st Dec. 1841, 24th March and 1st April 1842, general action and defeat of Akbar Khan before Jellalabad 7th April (Medal), storming the heights of Jugdulluck, general action of Tezeen, and recapture of Cabool (Medal). Served in the Crimea from 30th June 1855, including the battle of the Tchernaya, siege and fall of Sebastopol (Medal and Clasp).
22 Assist.Surgeon Jackson served in the Eastern campaign of 1854-55, including the battles of Balaklava and Inkerman, and siege of Sebastopol (Medal and three Clasps).
23 Lieut. Cox was present in April 1858 in the actions at Amorah and the taking of Nuggur.

14th (The Buckinghamshire) Regt. of Foot. 202

1st Batt. Corfu.
2nd Batt. Mullingar.

On the Bear-skin Caps of the Grenadiers and Drummers, the *White Horse,* " *Nec aspera terrent.*"— "TOURNAY" "CORUNNA" "JAVA" "WATERLOO" "BHURTPORE." The *Royal Tiger,* superscribed "INDIA" "SEVASTOPOL."

Years' Serv.						
Full Pay	Half Pay					
77		Colonel.—Sir James Watson,[1] KCB. *Ens.* 24 June 83; *Lt.* 18 April 92; *Capt.* 11 Mar. 95; *Maj.* 3 Dec. 02; *Lt.-Col.* 15 May 06; *Col.* 4 June 14; *Maj.-Gen.* 19 July 21; *Lt.-Gen.* 10 Jan. 37; *Gen.* 11 Nov. 51; *Col.* 14th Regt. 24 May 37.				
35	0	*Lt.-Colonels.*—1 Ralph Budd,[2] *Ens.* 10 Mar. 25; *Lieut.* p 16 Mar. 26; *Capt.* 1 June 41; *Brev.-Maj.* 20 June 54; *Maj.* 15 May 55; *Lt.-Col.* p 27 Jan. 57.				
29	6	2 Sir James Edward Alexander,[3] *Cornet,* p 20 Jan. 25; *Lt.* p 26 Nov. 25; *Capt.* p 18 June 30; *Brevet-Major,* 9 Nov. 46; *Bt. Lt.-Col.* 20 June 54; *Major,* 29 Dec. 54; *Lt.-Col.* 26 March 58.; *Col.* 26 Oct. 58.				
18	0	*Majors.*—1 William Cosmo Trevor,[3]† *Ens.* 11 Mar. 42; *Lieut.* 22 Jan. 46; *Capt.* p 29 Nov. 50; *Brevet-Major,* 6 June 56; *Major,* p 27 Jan. 57.				
24	0	1 Edward John Holworthy, 2nd *Lieut.* p 12 Feb. 36; *Lieut.* p 25 Jan. 39; *Capt.* p 17 Oct. 45; *Major,* p 7 Mar. 56.				
19	3/12	2 John Dwyer,[4] *Ens.* p 19 July 31; *Lt.* 21 Nov. 34; *Capt.* 22 Jan. 46; *Bt.-Maj.* 2 Nov. 55; *Major,* 25 Sept. 57.				
26	0	2 William Douglas,[5] *Ens.* p 23 May 34; *Lt.* 1 Aug. 38; *Capt.* 18 Sept. 46; *Bt.-Maj.* 2 Nov. 55; *Major,* 8 Jan. 58.				

		CAPTAINS.	ENSIGN.	LIEUT.	CAPTAIN.	BREV.-MAJ.
18	0	1 Frederick Hammersley[6]	p 1 July 42	p 21 Apr. 46	p 25 Apr. 51	6 June 56
21	1 3/12	1 Plomer John Young[9]..	p 11 May 38	p 1 Nov. 39	25 Mar. 53	
14	0	1 Wm. Hanbury Hawley[7]	p 10 July 46	15 Feb. 50	29 Dec. 54	
13	0	1 Charles Edward Grogan	p 16 Apr. 47	p 28 Apr. 48	29 Dec. 54	
17	0	1 John Gittens Maycock[12]	p 2 June 43	p 4 Apr. 45	29 Dec. 54	
14	0	1 Martin Petrie, s.	14 Apr. 46	p 7 Jan. 48	p 5 May 54	
9	0	1 Daw. Stockley Warren[7]	p 19 Dec. 51	p 16 Dec. 53	p 10 Apr. 57	
8	0	1 Thomas Prittie Cosby[7]	p 23 Nov. 52	11 Aug. 54	p 24 July 57	
9	10/12	2 William Heywood[7] ..	p 15 Mar. 50	p 16 Jan. 52	15 May 55	
8	0	1 Walter Fred. Blunt[7] ..	p 24 Nov. 52	p 18 Aug. 54	p 2 Oct. 55	
7	5/12	2 Richard Hussey Vivian[7]	p 17 Aug. 52	6 June 54	p 9 Jan. 57	
12	0	1 Edw. D'H. Fairtlough[13]	p 20 Oct. 48	19 Oct. 50	8 Jan. 58	
14	0	2 Hugh Massy Lloyd ..	p 10 July 46	28 Sept. 47	5 Mar. 58	
12	0	2 Drury Richard Barnes[6]	p 7 Apr. 48	p 22 Aug. 51	16 Mar. 58	
6	0	2 Edward Wm. Saunders[7]	28 Mar. 54	p 29 Dec. 54	p 26 Mar. 58	
5	0	2 Hy. Theodore Vernede[9]	p 16 Jan. 55	15 May 55	p 30 July 58	
12	1	2 Edward Dyne Fenton[14]	p 13 Aug. 47	p 13 July 49	p 16 Oct. 57	
12	0	2 Alexander Strange	16 June 48[?]	p 4 Apr. 51	1 Oct. 58	
11	0	2 Henry Cowell[15] ,.....	12 Jan. 49	p 13 Apr. 52	1 Oct. 58	
9	0	2 Gage Hall Dwyer[10] ..	p 19 Aug. 51	28 Mar. 54	2 Oct. 58	
5	0	1 And. Alf. Le Mesurier[11]	19 Jan. 55	17 Aug. 55	p 5 Oct. 58	
20	0	1 Wm. Temple Parratt	p 5 Sept. 40	p 9 June 43	p 24 Oct. 45	15 Jan. 58
6	0	2 Ramsay Harman[13]	p 1 Sept. 54	9 Mar. 55	p 1 July 59	
6	0	2 John Owens[16]	9 Aug. 54	8 Dec. 54	25 June 58	
		LIEUTENANTS.				
6	0	1 Alexander Gordon[17] ..	11 Aug. 54	29 Dec. 54		
6	0	2 Fre.Gerard Armstrong[11]	p 18 Aug. 54	17 Feb. 55		
6	0	1 Jno. Donaldson Bradley[7]	p 25 Aug. 54	9 Mar. 55		
6	0	1 Hy. William Heaton[11]	22 Dec. 54	9 Mar. 55		
5	0	1 Charles Costin,[9] *Adj.*..	12 Feb. 55	1 Feb. 56		
5	0	2 Rich. A. Lynd Furneaux	13 Feb. 55	p 8 Feb. 56		
5	0	1 G. J. Newman Beamish	23 Mar. 55	p 17 Feb. 57		
5	0	2 Iver M'Iver ...,.....	1 May 55	p 24 Feb. 57		
5	0	1 John Taylor Casson ..	27 July 55	p 23 Oct. 57		
5	0	1 Peter Barlow	17 Aug. 55	p 30 Oct. 57		
5	0	2 John Glancy,[7] *Adj*	9 Mar. 55	8 Jan. 58		
5	0	2 Jas. Octavius Machell	15 May 55	8 Jan. 58		
5	0	2 Kenrick Hill	3 July 55	8 Apr. 57		
5	0	2 George Harwood Cope	p 25 May 55	7 May 57		
5	0	2 James Alex. Anderson	17 Aug. 55	p 2 Oct. 57		
5	0	1 George Robert Morgan	26 July 55	p 27 Nov. 57		
5	0	2 John Shaw Phelps[22] ..	15 June 55	9 Jan. 58		
5	0	1 Henry Augustus Burton	26 Oct. 55	26 Mar. 58		
4	0	1 Stephen Watson......	15 Jan. 56	15 June 58		
4	0	1 George Leslie Bryce ..	1 Feb. 56	15 June 58		
4	0	1 John Wilson	p 29 Feb. 56	15 June 58		
5	0	2 John Joseph Hill Carbery	p 23 Nov. 55	p 22 June 58		
5	0	2 Anthony Robert Keogh	5 July 55	1 Oct. 58		
3	0	1 Edward John Briscoe	p 24 Feb. 57	2 Oct. 58		
3	0	1 Francis Forbes Atkinson	23 Oct. 57	5 Oct. 58		
3	0	2 Henry John Harington	p 30 Oct. 57	p 10 Dec. 58		
3	0	2 Jas. Townsend Edwards	p 27 Nov. 57	p 10 Dec. 58		
3	0	2 John Bruckfield Frizell	p 26 Mar. 58	p 10 Dec. 58		
3	0	1 Rich. Seymour Lemon	p 29 Dec. 57	p 8 Oct. 58		
2	0	1 Joseph Laing	27 Mar. 58	p 1 July 59		

1 Sir James Watson served with the 14th Regt. on the Continent under the Duke of York in 1793 and 94 ; at the reduction of the islands of St. Lucie and Trinidad in 1796 and 97. Commanded the 14th Regiment at the capture of the Isles of France and Java, including the assault and capture of Djocjocarta ; commanded the expedition that captured the piratical state of Sambas in Borneo in 1813 ; at the capture of the fort of Hattras, and in the Pindarree and Mahratta wars ; actively assisted at the reduction of the fortress of Dhoomone Mundela (where he led the storming party), Gurra Kotah, and Asseerghur. Medal for Java.

2 Lt.-Colonel Budd served in the trenches at the siege of Sebastopol (Medal and Clasp, and 5th Class of the Medjidie).

† *a* 2

203—204 14th (The Buckinghamshire) Regt. of Foot.

Years' Serv.				
Full Pay	Half Pay	ENSIGNS.		ENSIGN.
2	0	2	James Stephen Johnson	13 April 58
2	0	2	Robert Langtry	14 April 58
2	0	2	Fra. Le Breton Butler	16 April 58
2	0	2	Wm. Bayford Lindsay	17 April 58
2	0	2	John Lawrence	18 April 58
2	0	2	William Jarvis Willis	23 April 58
2	0	2	Fred. Wm. Harington	p 28 May 58
2	0	1	Denis Creagh	6 Aug. 58
2	0	1	Henry Aug. Williams	6 Oct. 58
2	0	1	Henry Metcalfe	7 Oct. 58
2	0	1	Hon. M'Leod Hutchison	12 Nov. 58
1	0	1	William John Close	p 18 Jan. 59
1	0	1	Roger Hall	28 Jan. 59
1	0	1	John Daly	29 Jan. 59
1	0	1	Philip Alfred Riley	p 18 Mar. 59
1	0	2	Charles Curtis	24 May 59
1	0	2	Cecil Thomas M'Mahon	p 31 May 59
2	0	2	Cyrus Day	30 Mar. 58
1	0	1	Wm. Thornhill Blois	18 Oct. 59
1	0	1	Thomas Charles Watson	19 Oct. 59

3 Sir James Alexander served in the Madras Light Cavalry previous to being transferred to H.M. Dragoons. Was present with armies in the field during the first Burman, the Persian, Turkish, Portuguese, and Kaffir wars; and was on the personal staff of Generals Sir Benjamin d'Urban and Sir William Rowan, and employed on Government expeditions, exploring, and surveying in Africa and America. Served in the trenches at the siege of Sebastopol, including the assault on the 18th June, and commanded the 14th Regt. at the fall of the city (Medal and Clasp, Sardinian Medal, and 5th Class of the Medjidie). Was knighted by the Queen for services in Africa, and has received several decorations and War Medals, and 2d Class Lion and Sun of Persia.

3‡ Major Trevor served in the trenches at the siege and fall of Sebastopol, and assault of the 18th June (Medal and Clasp, Brevet Major and Sardinian Medal).

4 Major Dwyer served in the trenches at the siege and fall of Sebastopol, and assault of the 18th June (Medal and Clasp, Brevet Major, Knight of the Legion of Honor, and 5th Class of the Medjidie).

12	0	Paymasters.—1 Wm. Macdonnell, 22 Apr. 53; *Ens.* 18 Aug. 48; *Lt.* 25 June 52.
2	0	2 John Christopher Villiers Minnett, 19 March 58.
5	0	Adjutants.—1 Lieut. Charles Costin,⁹ 11 Sept. 57.
5	0	2 Lieut. John Glancy, 9 Feb. 58.
6	0	Instructors of Musketry.—1 Lieut. Henry Wm. Heaton, 20 May 58.
5	0	2 Lieut. J. A. Anderson, 19 July 58.
3	0	Quarter Masters.—1 William Andrew Armstrong,²¹ 4 Dec. 57.
4	2/12	2 James Spry, 31 Dec. 57; *Cornet*, 16 Dec. 55; *Lt.* 1 Apr. 57.
10	1/12	Surgeons.—1 George Smyth King,¹⁸ M.D. 29 June 55; *Assist.Surg.* 18 May 49.
18	0	2 John Elliot Carte, M.B. 18 Feb. 53; *Assist.Surg.* 31 Dec. 41.
6	0	Assist.Surgeons.—1 Thomas Macdougall Bleckley,¹⁹ M.B. 6 Jan. 54.
6	0	1 John Martin Hyde,²⁰ 3 Nov. 54.
2	0	2 Thomas Bennett, 22 Jan. 58.
2	0	2 Andrew Thomas Carbery, 16 Nov. 58.

Facings Buff—*Agents*, Messrs. Downes & Son.—*Irish Agents*, Sir E. R. Borough, *Bart.*, Armit & Co.

[1st *Batt. Foreign Service*, 25 *Apr.* 54. *Depot, Fermoy.*]

5 Major Douglas served in the trenches at the siege and fall of Sebastopol, and assault of the 18th June (Medal and Clasp, Brevet Major, and 5th Class of the Medjidie).

6 Major Hammersley served in the trenches at the siege and fall of Sebastopol, and assault of the 18th June (Medal and Clasp, Brevet Major, Sardinian Medal, and 5th Class of the Medjidie).

7 Captains Hawley, Warren, Cosby, Heywood, Blunt, Vivian, Saunders, Lieuts. Bradley and Glancy, served in the trenches at the siege and fall of Sebastopol, and assault of the 18th June (Medal and Clasp).

8 Captain Barnes served in a Local Battalion in the Kaffir war of 1846-47 (Medal), was present in several engagements, and accompanied the expedition into the Tambookie country.

9 Captains Young and Vernede, and Lieut. Costin, were present at the fall of Sebastopol (Medal and Clasp).

10 Captain Dwyer served in the trenches at the siege of Sebastopol and assault of the 18th June (Medal and Clasp).

11 Captain Le Mesurier, Lieuts. Armstrong and Heaton, served in the trenches at the siege and fall of Sebastopol (Medal and Clasp).

12 Captain Maycock served the Eastern campaign of 1854 in the 47th Regt., including the battles of the Alma (wounded) and Inkerman, siege of Sebastopol, and sortie of the 26th October (Medal and Clasps, Sardinian Medal, and 5th Class of the Medjidie).

13 Captains Fairtlough and Harman served in the trenches at the siege of Sebastopol (Medal and Clasp).

14 Captain Fenton served with the 53rd Regt. in the Punjaub campaign in 1849, including the battle of Goojerat (Medal and Clasp).

15 Captain Cowell served with the 75th Regt. at the Battle of Budlee ke Serai on the 8th June 1857 and at the siege of Delhi.

16 Captain Owens served with the 33rd Regt. in the Eastern campaign of 1854, including the battles of Alma and Inkerman (dangerously wounded), and siege of Sebastopol, twice wounded in the trenches (Medal and three Clasps, and 5th Class of the Medjidie).

17 Lieut. Gordon served the Eastern campaign of 1854-55, including the battles of Alma and Inkerman, and in the trenches at the siege and fall of Sebastopol, and assault of the 18th June (Medal and Clasps, and 5th Class of the Medjidie).

18 Doctor King served the Eastern campaign of 1854 and up to 2nd March 1855, including the battles of Alma and Inkerman, and siege of Sebastopol (Medal and three Clasps).

19 Assist.Surgeon Bleckley served in the trenches at the siege and fall of Sebastopol (Medal and Clasp).

20 Assist.Surgeon Hyde served in the trenches at the siege of Sebastopol, and at the assault of the 18th June (Medal and Clasp).

21 Quarter Master Armstrong served with the 49th Regt. throughout the operations in China (Medal), including the taking of Chusan (both operations), storm and capture of the heights above Canton, attack and capture of Amoy and the heights of Chinhae, occupation of Ningpo and repulse of the night attack, attack and capture of Chapoo, Woosung, and Chinkiangfoo. Also the Eastern campaign of 1854-55, including the battle of Alma, repulse of the sortie on 26th Oct. (severely wounded), siege and fall of Sebastopol (Medal and two Clasps).

22 Lieut. Phelps served at the siege of Sebastopol (as Assist.Surgeon from 14th Nov. 1854), and at the attack on the Redan on the 18th June (mentioned in despatches); also at the bombardment and capture of Kinbourn (Medal and Clasp, and 5th Class of the Medjidie).

[1st Batt. Jersey.
2nd Batt. Malta.] **15th (*The Yorkshire East Riding*) Regt. of Foot.** 205

"MARTINIQUE" "GUADALOUPE."

Years' Serv.		
Full Pay	Half Pay	
66		Colonel.—🟉 Sir Howard Douglas,¹ Bt. GCB, GCMG. 2nd Lieut. 1 Jan 94; Lieut. 30 May 94; Capt. 2 Oct. 99; Maj. 12 Oct. 04; Lt.Col. 31 Dec. 06; Col. 4 June 14; Major Gen. 19 July 21; Lt.Gen. 10 Jan. 37; Gen. 11 Nov. 51; Col. 15th Foot, 6 Oct. 51.
30	0	Lt. Colonels.—1 John A. Cole, Ens. 14 Jan. 30; Lt. 26 May 33; Capt. p 14 Dec. 38; Brev.Major, 11 Nov. 51; Maj. 2 Feb. 55; Lt.Col. 25 Aug. 56.
29	0	2 John Hope Wingfield, Ens. p 17 May 31; Lt. p 4 Oct. 33; Capt. p 18 Jan. 39; Brev.Major, 11 Nov. 51; Major, 25 Mar. 56; Lt.Col. 19 Feb. 58.
27	0	Majors.—1 Henry Grierson,³ Ens. p 9 Aug. 33; Lt. p 24 Feb. 37; Capt. p 6 May 42; Bt.Maj. 20 June 54; Major, 25 Aug. 56; Bt.Lt.Col. 17 Oct. 59.
25	0	2 William Fulton, Ens. p 10 April 35; Lt. p 11 Oct. 39; Capt. p 12 April 44; Bt.Major, 31 Aug. 55; Major, 19 Feb. 58.
27	0	2 George Ponsonby Hume, Ens. p 28 June 33; Lt. p 16 Dec. 36; Capt. p 20 Sept. 39; Bt.Major, 11 Nov. 51; Major, 20 Feb. 58; Bt.Lt.Col. 26 Oct. 58.
22	0	1 Algernon Robinson Sewell, Ens. p 16 Feb. 38; Lt. p 18 Sept. 40; Capt. p 28 June 50; Major, 12 Nov. 58.

		CAPTAINS.	ENSIGN.	LIEUT.	CAPTAIN.	BREV.MAJ.
21	0	1 Wm. Cairnes Armstrong	p 6 Sept. 39	p 1 July 42	p 23 Feb. 49	
20	0	1 Johnson Wilkinson³	p 4 Aug. 40	p 24 May 44	6 June 54	
15	0	1 Aug. Fred. Warburton, s.	p 13 June 45	p 29 Dec. 48	2 Oct. 54	
12	0	1 Andrew John Cowper	p 18 Aug. 48	p 12 Apr. 50	2 Feb. 55	
12	0	2 Francis Powell Hopkins	p 3 Oct. 48	p 24 May 50	16 Oct. 55	
10	0	1 Robert Wynne Price	p 16 Feb. 50	p 17 Oct. 51	25 Mar. 56	
9	0	1 Frederick Edward Lock	p 14 Feb. 51	6 June 54	p 11 Sept. 57	
9	0	1 Philip A. A. Twynam	p 12 Dec. 51	6 July 54	p 27 Nov. 57	
16	0	2 William Henry Eliot⁵	25 June 44	14 Apr. 46	9 Mar. 58	
14	0	1 James Wm. S. Moffatt	3 Nov. 46	11 May 49	9 Mar. 58	
13	0	2 Hugh Mackenzie⁶	30 Apr. 47	20 June 51	9 Mar. 58	
7	0	2 Aldred Oldfield	18 Feb. 53	2 Oct. 54	p 26 Mar. 58	
13	0	2 Richard Clancy	p 22 June 47	p 1 Dec. 48	30 Apr. 58	
15	0	1 Henry Nangle	17 Jan. 45	10 Apr. 49	21 May 58	
13	0	2 Charles Crawley	30 Apr. 47	22 Dec. 48	23 July 58	
6	0	2 Robert Tho. P. Cuthbert	14 July 54	13 Feb. 55	p 24 Aug. 58	
6	0	1 Archibald Butter⁷	p 11 Aug. 54	8 Dec. 54	17 Nov. 58	
6	0	1 Walter Goodwin Hawkins	p 23 Aug. 54	p 23 Mar. 55	23 Nov. 58	
6	0	2 William Robertson Tyler	p 24 Aug. 54	p 25 May 55	p 15 Apr. 59	
6	0	2 Fred. S. L'Est FitzRoy	p 13 Oct. 54	25 Mar. 55	p 22 July 59	
5	0	1 Alfred Grey⁹	11 Jan. 55	9 Mar. 55	1 Apr. 57	
12	0	1 Augustus Barton White¹⁰	22 Dec. 48	p 10 Jan. 51	p 4 Dec. 57	
9	0	2 Wm. Geo. H. T. Fairfax¹¹	p 21 Nov. 51	p 22 Dec. 54	p 18 Nov. 59	
6	0	2 Thomas Eccles Dickson	p 25 Aug. 54	16 Oct. 55	p 20 Dec. 59	
		LIEUTENANTS.				
6	0	1 Robert Coupe	15 Sept. 54	25 Mar. 56		
6	0	1 John Olpherts Kemmis	p 15 Dec. 54	p 20 Apr. 56		
5	0	1 William Starke	p 23 Mar. 55	p 27 May 56		
5	0	1 Richard Lewes Dashwood	18 May 55	p 9 Oct. 55		
5	0	2 Henry P. Shafto Orde	10 May 55	p 17 July 57		
5	0	1 Henry J. Hallowes, Adj.	11 May 55	p 11 Sept. 57		
5	0	1 George Joseph Maunsell	15 May 55	p 27 Nov. 57		
5	0	1 Fra. Robert Fishbourne	16 Mar. 55	26 Feb. 56		
5	0	2 F. H. Ehrenberg Allhusen	30 Mar. 55	p 12 Feb. 58		
5	0	1 John W. Coventry	24 May 55	12 Feb. 58		
5	0	1 John Low	p 6 July 55	23 Mar. 58		
4	0	2 Wm. Campbell Colquhoun	p 14 May 56	26 Mar. 58		
4	0	1 Francis Ironside Rawlins	p 25 Mar. 56	26 Mar. 58		
4	0	2 Magens James C. Browne	p 27 May 56	23 April 58		
5	0	2 Wm. Sugden Jemmett	17 Aug. 55	21 May 58		
5	0	2 Wm. St. Clair Tisdall	14 Sept. 55	21 May 58		
5	0	1 Cuthbert Willis	25 May 55	28 May 58		
4	0	2 Charles Edmund Layard	8 July 56	28 May 58		
3	0	1 Alfred Wintle	p 24 July 57	p 15 June 58		
3	0	1 Arthur Heaton	p 18 Sept. 57	p 16 July 58		
3	0	2 John Macdonald, Adj.	4 Dec. 57	24 Aug. 58		
5	0	2 Gerald Butler Beere	5 July 55	1 Oct. 58		
5	0	2 Russell Harris Vieth	21 Sept. 55	5 Oct. 58		
4	0	2 John Lewis Riall	p 8 Mar. 56	18 Jan. 59		
2	0	1 Henry W. R. de Coëtlogon	27 Mar. 58	p 3 June 59		
4	0	1 Thomas Marsh Horsfall	p 13 June 56	p 7 Sept. 58		
2	0	2 Robert Spencer Liddell	28 Mar. 58	p 22 July 59		
2	0	2 Robert Algeo Mostyn	20 Mar. 58	p 18 Nov. 59		
2	0	2 Henry Wm. K. Hawks	13 April 58	p 15 Nov. 59		

7 Captain Butter served with the 93rd Highlanders at the Siege and fall of Sebastopol from 3rd June 1855 (Medal and Clasp).

9 Captain Grey served with the 93rd Regt. in the Crimea from 9th Sept. 1855, and has the Medal with Clasp for Sebastopol.

10 Captain White served with the 12th Lancers in the Crimea from 16th Aug. 1855 and has the Medal with Clasp for Sebastopol.

11 Captain Fairfax served with the 31st Regt. in the Crimea from 22nd May 1855 and was present at the siege and fall of Sebastopol, and attacks of the 18th June and 8th Sept. (Medal and Clasp).

206 15th (*The Yorkshire East Riding*) Regt. of Foot.

Years' Serv		ENSIGNS.	ENSIGN.	
Full Pay.	Half Pay.			
2	0	1 George Luck	p 16 April 58	5 Captain Eliot, prior to entering the army, served for two years and a half in the Royal Navy, and was present in H. M. S. *Melville* in China,—at the taking of the Bogue Forts, and the operations before Canton (Medal).
2	0	1 George Wm. Hayne	17 April 58	
2	0	1 Geo. Onslow Churchill ..	23 April 58	
2	0	2 Francis Henry Garnett ..	24 April 58	
2	0	2 John J. Forsyth Grant ..	25 April 58	6 Capt. Mackenzie served with the 73rd Regt. throughout the Kaffir war of 1850-53 (Medal); also on the expedition to the Basuto country and battle of Berea.
2	0	1 Edward J. Boultbee	30 April 58	
2	0	2 Wilkinson Shaw........	21 May 58	
2	0	2 John Joseph Grier.	22 May 58	
2	0	1 De Burgho Edw. Hodge	p 13 July 53	
2	0	2 Walter Lawrence Martin	14 July 58	
2	0	1 Charles Clifton Tabor ..	p 31 Aug. 58	
2	0	1 Edward Cuthbert Ward..	7 Sept. 58	
2	0	2 Alex. Her. Arthur Smith	17 Sept. 58	
2	0	2 Geo. Ainsworth Fielding	8 Oct. 58	
1	0	1 Joseph M'Murray	1 Apr. 59	
1	0	2 Reginald Cartwright	p 16 Aug. 59	
1	0	1 Thos. Howard K. Fletcher	p 23 Aug. 59	
1	0	2 Henry Joseph Hadfield..	24 Aug. 59	
1	0	1 William Henry Hudson..	p 21 Oct. 59	

12	0	*Paymasters.*—1 Rd. Milbank Tilghman, 28 Oct. 53 ; *Ens.* p 29 Dec. 48 ; *Lieut.* 2 Robert Savery Rouse, 16 April 58. [p 28 June 50.
2	0	
5	0	*Adjutants.*—1 Lieut. Henry Jardine Hallowes, 4 Dec. 57.
3	0	2 Lieut. John Macdonald, 23 March 58.
6	0	*Instructors of Musketry.*—2 Captain R. T. P. Cuthbert, 15 March 58.
5	0	1 Lieut. G. J. Maunsell, 10 Feb. 59.
7	0	*Quarter Masters.*—1 Bryan Stratford, 5 Aug. 53.
2	0	2 Alexander R. Mitchell, 26 March 58.
21	0	*Surgeons.*—1 Thomas Rose Dyce, *Assist.Surg.* 7 June 39 ; *Surgeon*, 3 Aug. 49 ; [*Surgeon Major*, 7 June 59.
14	0	2 Usher Williamson Evans," M.D. 8 Dec. 54 ; *A.S.* 3 Apr. 46.
5	0	*Assist.Surgeons* —1 John Denis Healy, 5 May 55.
2	0	1 Edward Coffey, 22 Jan. 58.
2	0	2 James Hinton, 10 March 58.
2	0	2 Frederic Murray Chalk, 15 Aug. 58.

Facings Yellow.—*Agents*, Messrs. Cox & Co.
[*1st Battalion returned from Gibraltar*, 6 *June* 1857. *Depot, Pembroke*.]
[*2d Battalion embarked for Malta*, 25 *Nov.* 58. *Depot, Pembroke*.]

1 Sir Howard Douglas served in Portugal and Spain in 1808 and 9, and was present at the battle of Corunna. Served afterwards at Walcheren, including the siege and bombardment of Flushing. Returned to the Peninsula in 1811, and continued there during that year and to the end of the campaign of 1812, having in that time been employed on a special mission extending throughout the north of Spain, and was present at the operations on the Orbigo and Essler, and in the combined naval and military operations on the north coast of Spain in the early part of 1812, the attack and reduction of Lequetio, and afterwards at the siege of Astorga; the operations on the Douro, including the blockade of Zamora, the attack and reduction of the enemy's Forts on the Douro, and the siege of Burgos. Sir Howard has received the War Medal and one Clasp for Corunna, and is a Knight of Charles the 3rd of Spain.

3 Lt.Colonel Grierson and Capt. Wilkinson served with a detachment consisting of 200 of the 15th Regt. and Ceylon Rifles, under Capt. Lillie, in defeating the insurgents at Matole on the 29th July 1848, during the rebellion in the Kandian Provinces in Ceylon.

11 Doctor Evans served as a volunteer (his Regiment the 16th Lancers being at home) from the commencement of the war with Russia until promoted in December 1854, including the battles of Alma, Balaklava, and Inkerman, and in the trenches before Sebastopol (Medal and Clasps).

16th (The Bedfordshire) Regt. of Foot. 207

1st Batt. Aldershot.
2nd Batt. Clonmel.

Years' Serv.		
Full Pay.	Half Pay.	

Colonel.—Sackville Hamilton Berkeley,[1] *Ens.* 1 May 1800; *Lt.* 5 Nov. 00; *Capt.* 25 Dec. 04; *Maj.* 18 Feb. 08; *Lt.Col.* 20 June 11; *Col.* 27 May 25; *Major Gen.* 10 Jan. 37; *Lt.Gen.* 9 Nov. 46; *Gen.* 20 June 54; *Col.* 75 F. 16 Sept. 45; *Col.* 16 F. 22 Mar. 58.

Full	Half	
20	0	*Lieut.Colonels.*—2 Oliver Langley, *Ens.* p 19 Mar. 40; *Lt.* p 22 Mar. 44; *Capt.* p 22 Dec. 48; *Major,* 12 Oct. 57; *Lt.Col.* p 11 Jan. 59.
18	0	1 George John Peacocke, *Ens.* 8 July 42; *Lieut.* p 24 Oct. 45; *Capt.* p 21 June 50; *Major,* p 7 May 58; *Lt.Col.* p 18 Oct. 59.
34	0	*Majors.*—1 John Willett Payne Audain, *Ens.* 14 Dec. 26; *Lieut.* 2 Oct. 28; *Capt.* 27 May 42; *Bt.Major,* 20 June 54; *Major,* 18 April 56; *Bt.Lt.Col.* 7 Dec. 59.
28	0	2 John Henderson, *Ens.* p 20 Jan. 32; *Lieut.* 28 Nov. 34; *Capt.* p 10 Nov. 43; *Brevet Major,* 20 June 54; *Major,* 19 Feb. 58.
21	0	2 Cha. Lorenzo deWinton, *Ens.* p 15 Feb. 39; *Lieut.* 2 July 41; *Capt.* p 10 Mar 48; *Major,* 24 May 59.
19	0	1 Algernon Robert Garrett,[2] *Ens.* 1 June 41; *Lt.* p 27 Sept. 42; *Capt.* p 28 Apr. 48; *Bt.Maj.* 2 Nov. 55; *Major,* 31 Aug. 58.

		CAPTAINS.	ENSIGN.	LIEUT.	CAPTAIN.	BREV.-MAJ.
20	0	1 Charles Armstrong	p 25 Apr. 40	19 Aug. 42	p 2 Nov. 49	
21	0	1 Jno. Octavius Chichester	p 26 Oct. 39	27 May 42	21 Apr. 54	
20	0	1 Geo. Fred. Macdonald, *s.*	p 8 May 40	p 25 Aug. 43	6 June 54	
14	0	1 Jas. William Bostock[5]	p 1 May 46	p 20 Oct. 48	p 4 Aug. 54	
15	0	2 Charles Coote Grant	p 9 May 45	20 Aug. 49	18 Apr. 56	
10	0	1 Christr. Jas. Magnay[6]	p 12 Apr. 50	p 26 Mar. 52	16 Mar. 55	
16	0	2 Wm. Charles Bancroft, *s.*	25 June 44	21 April 46	26 Feb. 58	
14	0	1 George Burchard	p 2 Oct. 46	p 23 Mar. 49	9 Mar. 58	
14	0	2 Horace Ximenes[7]	p 27 Mar. 46	29 May 48	10 Mar. 58	
15	0	2 Edwd. O'Callaghan,[8] *s.*	10 Oct. 45	p 28 Dec. 49	10 Mar. 58	
12	0	2 John Welman Holyar	p 25 Nov. 48	p 23 July 52	10 Mar. 58	
9	0	1 John Watkins Freeman	p 21 Nov. 51	6 June 54	p 7 May 58	
8	0	2 G. C. S. Lombard	p 17 Aug. 52	p 10 Aug. 55	p 22 June 58	
6	0	1 Somerville G. C. Hogge	p 22 Sept. 54	11 Oct. 55	p 6 Sept. 58	
12	0	2 Walter Lawrence Ingles[9]	21 Jan. 48	8 Oct. 50	7 Sept. 58	
8	0	2 Edward Woolhouse[10]	p 15 Oct. 52	24 Apr. 55	7 Sept. 58	
9	0	2 John Hill Crosse	p 18 Apr. 51	11 Aug. 54	26 Oct. 58	
16	0	1 Geo. Hamilton Twemlow	p 11 Oct. 44	16 May 46	p 16 Nov. 55	
5	0	2 John George Dartnell	22 July 55	p 7 Nov. 56	13 May 59	
5	0	1 Richard Calvert Healy	9 April 55	19 Nov. 56	p 24 May 59	
5	0	2 A. Dingwall Thomson	11 May 55	p 26 Feb. 56	p 17 June 59	
17	0	2 James John Gordon	27 Sept. 43	11 Nov. 45	10 Aug. 55	
14	0	1 Andrew Gammell[11]	16 April 46	p 4 April 51	26 Feb. 58	
6	0	1 Lewis Stevens Rooke	p 18 Aug. 54	p 17 Aug. 55	p 30 Sept. 59	
5	0	2 Arthur Platt	1 May 55	p 22 May 57	p 18 Oct. 59	

LIEUTENANTS.

8	0	1 James Davis	p 16 Apr. 52	p 18 Aug. 54	
6	0	1 Wm. Henry Carter, *Adj.*	21 Apr. 54	27 July 55	
6	0	2 Henry Kelsall, *Adj.*	6 June 54	p 25 Sept. 55	
5	0	1 Geo. Palmer Lockwood	p 30 Mar. 55	29 Apr. 56	
5	0	2 Alexander Gibson	24 April 55	26 Feb. 58	
5	0	1 Wm. Robert Welch Lea	p 23 Oct. 55	26 Feb. 58	
5	0	2 Charles Wynn Isdell	23 Feb. 55	p 19 Dec. 56	
5	0	2 George Street	9 Nov. 55	23 Mar. 58	
5	0	2 Thomas Russell	p 23 Nov. 55	23 Mar. 58	
5	0	1 Bernard Heyer Westby	p 7 Dec. 55	23 Mar. 58	
4	0	1 Lancelot Le Feuvre	p 29 Apr. 56	23 Mar. 58	
4	0	2 Albert Andrew Pinson	30 Apr. 56	23 Mar. 58	
4	0	2 Albert Neame	p 2 May 56	p 23 Apr. 58	
4	0	1 James Henry Brabazon	8 July 56	p 7 May 58	
5	0	2 J. Armitage Chippindall	p 15 May 55	19 Sept. 55	
5	0	2 Charlton M. Rod. Reyne	11 May 55	4 June 58	
3	0	2 James Dunlop Knox	p 22 May 57	p 22 June 58	
5	0	1 Aubrey Palgrave Powis	1 May 55	7 Sept. 58	
5	0	2 Frederick Grant	14 Dec. 55	7 Sept. 58	
5	0	1 Fred. James Rogers	p 29 June 55	1 Oct. 58	
5	0	2 John Pyne	5 July 55	1 Oct. 58	
5	0	1 Abraham Anderson	7 Sept. 55	1 Oct. 58	
5	0	2 Robert Jones Birch	p 28 Dec. 55	5 Oct. 58	
5	0	2 John Pennefather	20 June 55	6 Mar. 58	
2	0	1 George Whitlam	26 Feb. 58	p 26 Nov. 58	
2	0	1 Charles James Horne	27 Feb. 58	p 31 May 59	
2	0	1 Frank Jefferson	23 Mar. 58	p 31 May 59	
2	0	2 Rich. Henry Freeman	p 2 Oct. 57	p 17 June 59	
2	0	1 Cecil Godwin	26 Mar. 58	p 30 Sept. 59	
2	0	2 C. Tempest Sheringham	27 Mar. 58	p 18 Oct. 59	

1 General Berkeley served at the capture of Surinam in 1804; of the Danish Islands of St. Thomas, St. John, and St. Croix, in 1807; and of Martinique in 1809, including the siege of Fort Bourbon. He has received the War Medal with two Clasps for Martinique and Guadaloupe.

2 Major Garrett served with the 46th Regt. and on the staff at the siege and fall of Sebastopol from 8th Nov. 1854 (Medal and Clasp, Brevet of Major, Sardinian Medal and 5th Class of the Medjidie).

11 Captain Gammell served in the 12th Lancers in the Crimea from 17th May 1855, including the capture of Tchorgoun, battle of the Tchernaya, siege and fall of Sebastopol, and various operations near Eupatoria (Medal and Clasp).

16th (The Bedfordshire) Regt. of Foot.

Years' Serv. Full Pay.	Half Pay.	ENSIGNS.	ENSIGN.	
2	0	1 Dan. J. Wood deMedewe	13 Apr. 58	5 Capt. Bostock served as acting Aide-de-Camp to Brigadier Campbell commanding the 2nd Cavalry Brigade of the Army of the Sutlej, and was present at the battle of Sobraon (Medal).
2	0	2 Geo. Lee Le M. Taylor	14 Apr. 58	
2	0	2 Rt. Wm. May Wetherell	15 Apr. 58	6 Captain Magnay served the Eastern campaign of 1854-55 with the 63rd Regt., including the battles of Alma, Balaklava, and Inkerman, siege, assaults, and fall of Sebastopol, expedition to Kertch, bombardment and capture of Kinbourn (Medal and Clasps, and 5th Class of the Medjidie).
2	0	2 Arthur Edward Cooch	16 Apr. 58	
2	0	1 Pierce M'Cunn	17 Apr. 58	
2	0	2 James Bell	18 Apr. 58	
2	0	2 Sydney Herbert Davies¹¹	19 Apr. 58	
2	0	2 Currer F. Busfield	24 Apr. 58	7 Captain Ximenes served in the 8th Regt. in Delhi from 20th Sept. 1857; afterwards as Orderly Officer to Colonel Greathed in the action of Bolundshur, affair of Allyghur, and battle of Agra, the action of Dilkoosha and relief of Lucknow under Lord Clyde, affair at Kanouge, affair of the 2nd and action of the 6th Dec. at Cawnpore, and action at Khudagunj.
2	0	1 Chas. Henry Woodmass	25 Apr. 58	
2	0	2 Henry Bowyer Smith	14 July 58	
2	0	1 Basil Clifton Westby	16 July 58	
2	0	2 Charles Platt	p 17 Sept. 58	
1	0	1 Edward Daly	28 Jan. 59	
1	0	1 Arthur Ewen Stabb	p 31 May 59	
1	0	2 Christr. Samuel Bailey	p 3 June 59	
1	0	1 Wm. Alex. Woodward	p 20 July 59	
1	0	1 Leonard B. A. Poynter	p 9 Sept. 59	
1	0	Richard Wood Robinson	p 28 Oct. 59	

18	0	*Paymasters.*—1 Thos. C. Higginson, 4 Apr. 56; *Ens.* Apr. 42; 10 *Lieut.* 8 July 46.
2	0	2 Mark Teversham, 23 April 58.
6	0	*Adjutants.*—2 *Lieut.* Henry Kelsall, 21 May 58.
6	0	1 *Lieut.* William Henry Carter, 13 May 59.
14	0	*Instructors of Musketry.*—1 *Captain* J. W. Bostock,⁸ 8 Oct. 56.
5	0	2 *Lieut.* A. Gibson, 23 July 58.
2	0	*Quarter Masters.*—2 James Winter, 26 March 58.
2	0	1 Richard Dent, 13 April 58.
15	0	*Surgeons.*—1 Wm. George Swan, M.D. 21 July 54; *Assist.-Surg.* 28 Feb. 45.
19	0	2 James Richard Ffennell, 10 Feb. 52; *Assist.-Surg.* 20 Nov. 41.
5	0	*Assistant Surgeons.*—1 Hector Ferguson, 30 July 55.
3	0	1 Joseph Richard Kehoe, 15 Sept. 57.
3	0	2 William Sly, 8 Dec. 57.
2	0	2 William Alexander Gardiner, 22 Sept. 58. [Armit & Co

Facings Yellow—*Agents*, Messrs. Barron & Smith. *Irish Agents*, Sir E. R. Borough, Bt

[1st Batt. returned from Canada, June 57. Depot, Templemore.]

8 Captain O'Callaghan served with the 51st throughout the Burmese war of 1852-53; on board the E.I.C. steam frigate *Feroze* during the naval action and destruction of the enemy's stockades on the Rangoon River; served during the succeeding three days' operations in the vicinity (including the storming of the White House Redoubt), and at the storm and capture of Rangoon (Medal and Clasp).

9 Captain Ingles served with the 32nd Regt. at the second siege of Mooltan in 1848-9, including the storm and capture of the city, and surrender of the fortress; also present at the subsequent surrender of the fort and garrison of Cheniote, and at the battle of Goojerat (Medal and Clasps).

10 Captain Woolhouse joined General Havelock's field force in Oude on 4th Aug. 1857, and was present in the actions of Busseerutgunge, Boorbeeake Chowkee, Bithoor, Mungarwar, and Alumbagh, assault and relief of Lucknow (severely wounded, right arm amputated).

11 Ensign Davies served as a midshipman in the Royal Navy at the bombardment of Odessa, the Naval bombardment of Sebastopol, and then in the Naval Brigade to the fall of Sebastopol (Medal and Clasp).

[*Continuation of Notes to 17th Foot.*]

21 Capt. James D. Travers served with the 12th Regt. in the Kaffir war of 1851-53 (Medal).

22 Major Johns served with the 38th Regt. at the siege and fall of Sebastopol from 3rd Sept. 1855 (Medal and Clasp).

23 Captain Joseph Oates Travers served with the 17th Regt. at the siege of Sebastopol from 29 Jan. 1855, including the assaults on the Redan on 18th June and 8th Sept.; also at the bombardment and surrender of Kinbourn (Medal and Clasp, and Knight of the Legion of Honor).

24 Captain Macreight served at the siege of Sebastopol from June 1855, and at the assault on the Redan on the 8th Sept.; also at the bombardment and surrender of Kinbourn (Medal and Clasp).

25 Lieuts. F. C. S. Dyer and Utterson served at the siege of Sebastopol from July 1855, and at the assault on the Redan on the 8th Sept. (Medal and Clasp); Lieut. Utterson was also at the bombardment and surrender of Kinbourn.

32 Lieuts. Hartwell and Webber served in the Crimea from Sept. 1855, and were at the bombardment and surrender of Kinbourn (Medal).

33 Lieut. Wilkinson served with the 95th Regt. in the Indian Campaign in 1858, and was present at the siege and capture of Awah and Kolakaseria, general action resulting in the capture of Gwalior, and siege and capture of Pouree (Medal).

1st Batt. Quebec.
2d Batt. Aldershot.] **17th (The Leicestershire) Regt. of Foot.** 210

Years' Serv.		
Full Pay	Half Pay	

The *Royal Tiger*, "HINDOOSTAN" "AFFGHANISTAN" "GHUZNEE" "KHELAT" "SEVASTOPOL."

Colonel.—🟊 Thomas James Wemyss,¹ CB. *Ens.* 14 Oct. 1800; *Lt.* 1 March 04; *Capt.* 30 Nov. 06; *Maj.* 21 June 13; *Lt.-Col.* 21 Jan. 19; *Col.* 10 Jan. 37; *Maj.-Gen.* 9 Nov. 46; *Lt.-Gen.* 20 June 54; *Col.* 17th Foot, 31 May 54.

Lieut. Colonels.—1 Arthur Lowry Cole,² CB. *Ens.* p 22 Aug. 34; *Lt.* p 20 Nov. 38; *Capt.* p 7 Sept. 41; *Major*, p 14 June 50; *Lt. Col.* 9 Mar. 55; *Col.* 9 Mar. 58.

2 G. Wm. Francklyn, *Ens.* p 30 Apr. 27; *Lt.* 23 Nov. 30; *Capt.* p 9 Dec. 36; *Maj.* p 27 Aug. 41; *Bt.Lt.Col.* 11 Nov. 51; *Col.* 28 Nov. 54; *Lt.Col.* 23 Oct. 55.

Majors.—1 William Gordon,⁵ *Ens.* p 20 July 38; *Lt.* p 3 Apr. 40; *Capt.* p 2 Feb. 49; *Bt.Maj.* 17 July 55; *Major*, 7 Sept. 55; *Bt.Lt.Col.* 6 June 56.

2 Alexander M'Kinstry,⁶ *Ens.* p 22 Feb. 39; *Lieut.* p 25 Sept. 40; *Capt.* 21 Aug. 49; *Brev.-Major*, 6 June 56; *Major*, 9 March 58.

🟊 2 John George Rawstorne,⁷ *Ens.* 22 July 13; *Lt.* 18 Aug. 14; *Capt.* 10 Oct. 38; *Bt.Maj.* 11 Nov. 51; *Bt.Lt.Col.* 26 Dec. 56; *Major*, 10 Mar. 58.

1 Richard John Ross O'Conor,⁸ *Ens.* p 12 Apr. 39; *Lt.* 1 Feb. 42; *Capt.* p 30 Nov. 49; *Brev.Maj.* 26 Dec. 56; *Major*, p 29 July 59.

Years			CAPTAINS.	ENSIGN.	LIEUT.	CAPTAIN.	BREV.-MAJ.
26	0						
31	1 10/12						
22	0						
21	0						
20	17 6/12						
21	0						
13	0	1 Dav. LatoucheColthurst⁹	p 20 July 47	p 10 Nov. 48	p 7 Sept. 52	
14	0	1 Philip M'Pherson¹⁰	27 Oct. 46	p 10 Mar. 48	p 24 Feb. 54	
12	0	1 George Tito Brice¹¹	22 Dec. 48	p 30 Nov. 49	p 7 April 54	2 Nov. 55
12	0	1 Clem. H. J. Heigham¹³	p 10 Nov. 48	p 16 Nov. 49	20 Dec. 54	
11	0	1 William Henry Earle¹⁴	p 13 Apr. 49	p 25 Oct. 50	20 Dec. 54	
10	0	1 Rich. Edmd. Williams¹⁵	p 16 Feb. 50	p 17 Oct. 51	19 June 55	
8	6/12	1 William Affleck King¹⁶	p 11 July 51	8 Dec. 54	p 14 Mar. 56	
9	1	2 JamesB. Horner Boyd¹⁷	p 22 Nov. 50	p 28 Oct. 53	p 22 June 55	
7	0	1 Anty. Powell Traherne¹⁸	p 29 July 53	6 June 54	p 4 Dec. 57	
7	9/12	2 W. Dalrym. Tompson¹⁹	p 15 Oct. 52	p 3 Mar. 54	14 Dec. 55	
9	0	1 Cecil M'Pherson²⁰	p 16 Sept. 51	6 June 54	9 Mar. 58	
18	0	2 Fred. Aug. Davidson	24 July 42	3 May 44	7 Aug. 57	
13	0	2 John Hunter	21 May 47	6 Dec. 50	10 Mar. 58	
12	0	2 William Tyler Stuart	20 Oct. 48	3 Mar. 53	10 Mar. 58	
10	0	1 Jas. Dalgairns Travers²¹	8 Oct. 50	8 Dec. 54	16 Mar. 58	
14	0	2 Charles Edward Johns²²	p 26 June 46	p 27 July 49	6 June 54	20 July 58
6	0	2 Edward John Lees¹¹	p 3 Mar. 54	29 Dec. 54	p 7 Sept. 58	
9	0	2 Norris Goddard	p 17 Jan. 51	p 1 Apr. 53	p 31 Aug. 58	
11	0	2 Francis Horatio Gee	4 Apr. 49	16 July 52	10 Sept. 58	
12	0	2 JohnCrawfordLangford	p 8 Dec. 48	p 6 Oct. 54	5 Oct. 58	
7	0	2 Charles Græme Grant	p 28 Oct. 53	8 Dec. 54	30 Jan. 59	
6	0	2 Joseph OatesTravers²³	6 June 54	29 Dec. 54	p 6 May 59	
6	0	1 Fred.Arch.Macreight²⁴	p 7 Apr. 54	12 Jan. 55	p 23 Sept. 59	
11	0	1 Hen. Hawley Smart²⁴†	20 Oct. 49	p 6 July 52	15 May 55	
		LIEUTENANTS.				
6	0	1 Fredk. Carr S. Dyer²⁵	p 24 Aug. 54	9 Feb. 55		
6	0	1 A. HammondUtterson²⁵	p 25 Aug. 54	9 Mar. 55		
6	0	1 William Robinson¹⁰	p 17 Nov. 54	9 Mar. 55		
5	0	1 Wm. Henry Parker²⁷	p 12 Jan. 55	19 June 55		
5	0	1 J. Moore ClarkeTravers	23 Mar. 55	p 31 Aug. 55		
5	0	2 Fra. Houlton Hartwell³²	25 Jan. 55	7 Sept. 55		
5	0	1 Fras.Jas. Berkeley, *Adj.*	8 June 55	p 14 Sept. 55		
5	0	2 Geo. Daniel Webber³²	26 Jan. 55	9 Nov. 55		
5	0	1 W.F. Aug. E. Presgrave	20 Feb. 55	12 Mar. 56		
5	0	1 Samuel Bradburne	p 29 Mar. 55	23 Mar. 58		
5	0	1 John T. Bolton Mayne	p 30 Mar. 55	23 Mar. 58		
5	0	2 John James Perceval	6 Apr. 55	23 Mar. 58		
5	0	2 Isaac Colquhoun	14 Dec. 55	14 May 58		
5	0	1 Thomas Rochfort Hunt	21 Dec. 55	13 June 58		
4	0	1 David Frederick Allen	p 18 Jan. 56	15 June 58		
4	0	2 James Urquhart Mosse	18 Apr. 56	15 June 58		
4	0	2 George Aug. Crickitt	9 Oct. 55	10 Sept. 58		
5	0	2 Alexander Fluder	p 30 Nov. 55	12 Nov. 58		
5	0	2 Edward Mason	29 Sept. 55	p 2 Oct. 57		
2	0	1 Duncan Malcolm Irvine	29 Mar. 58	p 18 Jan. 59		
2	0	1 Rob. G. Wynne Wrench	27 Mar. 58	30 Jan. 59		
2	0	2 Henry S. Wedderburn	30 Mar. 58	p 4 Feb. 59		
5	0	2 Francis Wood	19 July 55	p 25 June 58		
2	0	2 Thomas Braddell	31 Mar. 58	p 6 May 59		
2	0	2 Alex. Aitken Ross, *Adj.*	13 Apr. 58	29 July 59		
2	0	2 Hamilton Burnett	14 Apr. 58	p 29 July 59		
4	0	2 Hen. Clem. Wilkinson⁵³	15 Feb. 56	p 5 Aug. 59		
2	0	2 Richard Follett Bros	p 23 Apr. 58	p 28 Sept. 59		
2	0	1 Alex. M'Neil Caird	25 Apr. 58	p 28 Oct. 59		
2	0	1 Henry Charles Deane	27 Apr. 58	p 28 Oct. 59		

1 Lieut.-General Wemyss served with the Walcheren expedition in 1809, and subsequently in the Peninsula as Major of Brigade to the 50th, 71st, and 92nd, from the formation of that Brigade under Lord Howard in 1810, to its final embarkation at Bourdeaux in 1814; and was present in the different affairs during the retreat to the Lines near Lisbon, actions of Pombal, Redinha, Foz d'Arouce, battle of Fuentes d'Onor, surprise of Gerard at Arroyo de Molinos, storm of Fort Napoleon, and the siege of Almaraz, action of Alba de Tormes, defence of Bejar, battle of Vittoria (received the Brevet rank of Major), and the battles of the Nivelle, Cambo, Nive, Donna Maria (severely wounded), St. Pierre (wounded), Hellette, Garris, St. Palais, Tarbes, Arriveriette, Orthes, Aire, and Toulouse, besides numerous minor affairs. Served also against the Kandians in Ceylon. He has received the War Medal with seven Clasps.

24† Captain Smart served with the 1st Royals at the siege and fall of Sebastopol from 27th Jan. 1855 (Medal and Clasp).

211 17th (The Leicestershire) Regt. of Foot.

Years' Serv. Full Pay	Half Pay	ENSIGNS.	ENSIGN.	
2	0	2 Edward Arthur Elgin..	28 Apr. 58	27 Lieut. Parker served at the siege of Sebastopol, and was wounded at the assault on the Redan on the 8th Sept. 1855; also present at the bombardment and surrender of Kinbourn (Medal and Clasp).
2	0	1 Edward Jackson Harris	28 May 58	
2	0	1 Henry Grey MacGregor	29 May 58	
2	0	2 Herbert Kerr	4 June 58	28 Paymaster Howett served at the siege of Sebastopol from 6 Aug. 1855, and at the assault on the Redan on the 8th Sept.; also present at the bombardment and surrender of Kinbourn (Medal and Clasp).
2	0	1 Henry B. Jackson	25 June 58	
2	0	1 Edm. Sandilands Savage	2 July 58	
2	0	2 Lambart F. Wilson Dwyer	17 Sept. 58	
1	0	1 Jonathan Wm. Elmes ..	11 Jan. 59	29 Qr.-Master Campbell served at the siege of Sebastopol from Dec. 1854 to June 1855; also present at the bombardment and surrender of Kinbourn (Medal and Clasp).
1	0	1 William Fred. Woods..	28 Jan. 59	
1	0	1 Alfred John J. Ravenhill	11 Feb. 59	
1	0	2 Wm. Villett Rolleston..	P 17 June 59	30 Surgeon Ward served the Eastern campaign of 1854-55, including the affair of Mackenzie's Farm, battles of Alma, Balaklava, and Inkerman, siege of Sebastopol, repulse of the sortie on 26th Oct. 1854, and assault on the Redan on the 8th Sept.; also present at the bombardment and surrender of Kinbourn (Medal and Clasps, and Knight of the Legion of Honor).
1	0	1 Godfrey Wills Burleigh	P 18 June 59	
1	0	1 Charles W. B. Aylmer	24 June 59	
1	0	2 Fra. N. B. Groves Benson	19 July 59	
1	0	2 John Mush.........	P 29 July 59	
1	0	1 John Henry Thorold..	P 20 Aug. 59	
1	0	2 Charles Forbes Leith..	P 30 Sept. 59	
1	0	John Gathorne Wood	P 28 Oct. 59	31 Assist.-Surg. Gibaut served at the siege of Sebastopol from Feb. to Aug. 1855 (Medal and Clasp).
1	0	Henry Francis Dent ..	P 29 Oct. 59	

5	0	Paymasters.—1 Henry Hollis Howett,[28] 1 May 55.		
2	0	2 Noborne Gilpin Smith, 14 May 59.		
2	0	Adjutants.—2 Lieut. Alexander Aitken Ross, 13 Apr. 58.		
5	0	1 Lieut. Francis James Berkeley, 13 June 58.		
4	0	Instructors of Musketry.—2 Lieut. J. U. Mosse, 20 July 58.		
4	0	1 Lieut. D. F. Allen, 23 June 59.		
7	0	Quarter Masters.—1 John Campbell,[29] 29 April 53. [Apr. 57.		
4	1	2 James Falkner, 26 March 58; Cornet, 1 Dec. 55; Lt. 1		
13	0	Surgeons.—1 William Pearson Ward,[30] 26 June 55; Assist.Surg. 14 June 47.		
12	0	2 James Edward Clutterbuck, M.D. 2 Oct. 57; A.S. 22 Dec. 48.		
6	0	Assist.Surgeons.—1 Walter Moses Gibaut,[31] 3 Feb. 54.		
2	0	2 James Greer Cuppage, 10 March 58.		
2	0	William Chalmers, 14 Dec. 58.		
1	0	Alexander Allan, M.D. 12 Jan. 59.		

Facings White.—Agents, Cox & Co.—Irish Agents, Sir E. R. Borough, Bt. Armit & Co.
[1st Batt. embarked for Gibraltar, 24 April 1854. Depot, Limerick.]

2 Colonel Cole commanded the 17th Regt. at the siege of Sebastopol, and at the assault of the Redan on the 18th June—mentioned in Dispatches (Medal and Clasp, CB., and 5th Class of the Medjidie).

5 Lieut.-Col. Gordon served at the siege of Sebastopol from Dec. 1854; was present at the assault of the Redan on 18th June (mentioned in Dispatches), and commanded the 17th Regt. at the assault of the Redan on the 8th Sept. (mentioned in Dispatches), and at the bombardment and surrender of the Fortress of Kinbourn (Medal and Clasp, Brevet Lieut.-Colonel, Knight of the Legion of Honor, and 5th Class of the Medjidie).

6 Major M'Kinstry served at the siege of Sebastopol from Dec. 1854 to July 1855, including the assault on the Redan 18th June,—mentioned in Dispatches (Medal and Clasp, Brevet Major, Sardinian Medal, and 5th Class of the Medjidie).

7 Lt.-Col. Rawstorne served in the Peninsula, in the Chasseurs Britanniques, from Aug. 1813 to the end of the war, and was present at the battle of Orthes; he has received the War Medal with two Clasps. Present with the 91st in the Kaffir war of 1846-47 (Medal), and covered with his company the movement of a division of the force from the Doble Flats to the vicinity of Block Drift in April 1846 (wounded). On the renewal of operations in July 1846 he was entrusted for several months with the charge and defence of the Seminary at Block Drift, an isolated post, containing the magazines of the army, and maintaining the communications between the Colony and the divisions in the field. He commanded the detachment of the 91st on the expedition under Sir Harry Smith against the insurgent Boers in 1848, and had charge of the position at Botha's Drift, Orange River, to keep open the communication with the advanced column. For the manner in which he marched these troops to the camp of Sir Harry Smith, a distance of 250 miles, Sir Harry conferred on him the appointment of Brigade Major at Graham's Town.

8 Major O'Conor served at the siege of Sebastopol from Dec. 1854, and assault of the Redan on 18th June,—mentioned in Dispatches (Medal and Clasp, and 5th Class of the Medjidie).

9 Captain Colthurst served at the siege of Sebastopol from Dec. 1854 to Aug. 1855, and assault of the Redan on 18th June (Medal and Clasp).

10 Captain P. M'Pherson and Lt. Robinson served at the siege of Sebastopol, and assault on the Redan on the 8th Sept. 1855; also at the bombardment and surrender of Kinbourn (Medal and Clasp).

11 Major Brice and Captain Lees served at the siege of Sebastopol from 2 Jan. 1855, and at the assaults on the Redan on the 18th June and 8th Sept., also at the bombardment and surrender of Kinbourn (Medal and Clasp). Major Brice has the 5th Class of the Medjidie.

13 Captain Hoigham served at the siege of Sebastopol from Dec. 1854 to 1st June 1855 (Medal and Clasp).

14 Captain Earle served at the siege of Sebastopol from Dec. 1854 to Feb. 1855 (Medal and Clasp).

15 Capt. Williams served at the siege of Sebastopol from Dec. 1854 to June 1855 (Medal and Clasp), and received severe wounds causing loss of right eye, and a severe contusion of right leg, in the trenches on 21st May.

16 Captain King served the Eastern campaign of 1854-55 with the 4th Light Dragoons, including the battles of Alma, Balaklava, and Inkerman, and siege of Sebastopol (Medal and Clasps).

17 Captain Boyd served with the 17th Regt. at the siege of Sebastopol from Dec. 1854, including assaults of the Redan on 18th June and 8th Sept. (wounded in the trenches); was also at the bombardment and surrender of Kinbourn (Medal and Clasp).

18 Capt. Traherne served at the siege of Sebastopol from Dec. 1854, and assault of the Redan on 18th June; also at the bombardment and surrender of Kinbourn (Medal and Clasp).

19 Captain Tompson served at the siege of Sebastopol from Jan. 1855, including the assaults on the Redan on 18th June and 8th Sept. (dangerously wounded) (Medal and Clasp, and Knight of the Legion of Honor).

20 Captain C. M'Pherson served at the siege of Sebastopol from Dec. 1854, and at the assault on the Redan on the 18th June and 8th Sept.; also at the bombardment and surrender of Kinbourn (Medal and Clasp).

[For continuation of notes, see end of 10th Foot.

1st Batt. Secundrabad.
2nd Batt. Aldershot.

18th (*Royal Irish*) Regiment of Foot.

In the three corners of the second Colour, the *Lion of Nassau*, "*Virtutis Namurcensis Præmium.*" The *Sphinx*, "EGYPT." "*The Dragon,*" "CHINA" "PEGU" "SEVASTOPOL."

Years' Serv.		
Full Pay	Half Pay	
67		**Colonel.**—♚ Sir John Forster Fitzgerald,[1] KCB. *Ens.* 20 Oct. 93; *Lieut.* 31 Jan. 94; *Capt.* 9 May 94; *Major*, 25 Sept. 03; *Lieut.-Col.* 25 July 10; *Col.* 12 Aug. 19; *Major-Gen.* 22 July 30; *Lieut.-Gen.* 23 Nov. 41; *Gen.* 20 June 54; *Col.* 18th Regt. 9 March 50.
31	0	**Lt.-Colonels.**—1 Clement Alex. Edwards,[2] CB. *Ens.* 11 June 29; *Lt.* ᵖ 28 Nov. 34; *Capt.* ᵖ 13 Mar. 40; *Brev.-Maj.* 11 Nov. 51; *Maj.* 25 May 53; *Bt. Lt.Col.* 9 Dec. 53; *Col.* 28 Nov. 54; *Lt.Col.* 9 March 55.
23	0	1 George Fred. Stevenson Call,[3] *Ens.* ᵖ 7 Apr. 37; *Lieut.* ᵖ 20 Sept. 39; *Capt.* ᵖ 30 Dec. 42; *Brev.-Major*, 20 June 54; *Major*, 29 Dec. 54; *Brevet-Lieut.-Col.* 6 June 56; *Lt.-Col.* 18 Sept. 57.
18	0	2 Alfred Augustus Chapman, *Ens.* 20 May 42; *Lt.* ᵖ 17 Jan. 45; *Capt.* ᵖ 13 Apr. 49; *Major*, 15 May 55; *Lt.Col.* 17 Sept. 58.
19	0	**Majors.**—1 John Borrow,[6] *Ens.* ᵖ 16 Feb. 41; *Lieut.* ᵖ 23 Feb. 44; *Capt.* 1 Apr. 47; *Major*, 18 Sept. 57.
21	₁₂⁶	2 Anthony Wm. Samuel Freeman Armstrong,[7] *Ens.* ᵖ 21 June 39; *Lt.* 26 Jan. 41; *Capt.* 12 Dec. 52; *Bt.-Major*, 2 Nov. 55; *Major*, 18 Sept. 57.
19	0	1 Edmond Wm. Sargent,[8] *Ens.* 18 May 41; *Lieut.* 26 July 42; *Capt.* 25 May 53; *Major*, 9 March 58.
30	4 ₁₂⁸	2 Oliver Barker D'Arcey, *Ens.* ᵖ 8 April 26; *Lt.* ᵖ 9 Dec. 31; *Capt.* 19 Dec. 45; *Major*, 30 Sept. 56.

		CAPTAINS.	ENSIGN.	LIEUT.	CAPTAIN.	BREV.-MAJ.
17	0	1 Chas. Frederick Kelly[9]	2 Apr. 43	ᵖ 5 Dec. 47	ᵖ 4 Aug. 54	
18	0	1 Wm. Henry Graves...	25 Nov. 42	2 Feb. 44	29 Dec. 54	
14	0	1 John Swinburne[10]	5 Apr. 46	13 Sept. 48	29 Dec. 54	
13	0	1 Geo. Augustus Elliot[11]	ᵖ 10 Dec. 47	ᵖ 7 Mar. 51	26 Jan. 55	
9	0	2 Geo. Wm. Stacpoole[12]	ᵖ 18 Apr. 51	21 Mar. 53	22 June 55	
18	0	1 C. Jasper D. Annesley[13]	1 Nov. 42	11 Oct. 45	17 Aug. 55	
7	₁₂¹⁰	1 Wm. O'Bryen Taylor[12]	14 Sept. 52	6 June 54	ᵖ 2 May 56	
9	0	1 Geo. Hen. Pocklington[12]	5 Dec. 51	6 June 54	25 Sept. 57	
13	₁₂³	1 John Canavan[14]	16 Jan. 47	5 Aug. 51	9 Nov. 55	
14	0	1 ♚ ☩ Sir Henry M. Havelock,[15] *Bt. c.* 26 Apr. 59 }	31 Mar. 46	ᵖ 23 June 48	9 Oct. 57	19 Jan. 58
8	0	1 R. Hooy Jex-Blake[23] ..	23 Nov. 52	11 Aug. 54	9 Mar. 58	
10	0	1 Thos. Henry Stoddard	26 Oct. 41	5 June 44	10 Mar. 58	
13	0	2 John Inman	11 Jan. 47	1 Mar. 49	10 Mar. 58	
13	0	2 Wm. Dennis Chapman[17]	10 Dec. 47	1 Mar. 50	10 Mar. 58	
12	0	1 Alfred Macdonald	ᵖ 24 Nov. 48	ᵖ 30 Jan. 52	10 Mar. 58	
7	0	2 Rd. Pretyman Bishopp	ᵖ 8 July 53	ᵖ 10 Nov. 54	ᵖ 26 Mar. 58	
6	0	1 Charles James Coote[23]	14 July 54	20 Dec. 54	14 May 58	
7	0	2 Henry James Haydock[21]	ᵖ 16 Dec. 53	20 Feb. 55	13 Nov. 57	
9	₁₂⁶	2 Edw. Abbot Anderson ..	15 Nov. 50	6 June 54	ᵖ 14 May 58	
14	0	1 William Crozier[20]	20 Dec. 46	27 Feb. 50	10 Sept. 58	
7	0	2 James Tarrant Ring[23]..	ᵖ 11 Mar. 53	29 Dec. 54	10 Sept. 58	
6	0	2 Thos. Durand Baker[23]	ᵖ 18 Aug. 54	12 Jan. 55	ᵖ 26 Oct. 58	
6	0	1 William Kemp[22]	ᵖ 24 Aug. 54	12 Jan. 55	ᵖ 16 Aug. 59	
9	0	2 Hen. G. Austin Vicars[16]	ᵖ 17 Oct. 51	ᵖ 27 Oct. 54	13 Dec. 59	

		LIEUTENANTS.		
6	0	1 Jacob Francis Bryant..	ᵖ 6 Jan. 54	12 Jan. 55
6	0	1 Walter Blake Burke ..	6 June 54	12 Jan. 55
6	0	1 Fairfax Fearnley[24]	ᵖ 25 Aug. 54	20 Feb. 55
6	0	1 Edw. Langford Dillon[23]	1 Sept. 54	9 Mar. 55
6	0	1 Charles Hotham[22]	20 Oct. 54	9 Mar. 55
6	0	1 J. Shadwell Theobald[23]	ᵖ 10 Nov. 54	13 Apr. 55
5	0	1 Robert Isaac Adamson[23]	26 Jan. 55	10 June 55
5	0	1 Sydney Darvell	15 Mar. 55	ᵖ 23 Oct. 55
5	0	2 Rd. W.E. Dawson, *Adj*.	ᵖ 20 Feb. 55	18 Jan. 56
5	0	1 Hugh Shaw, *Adj*.	10 May 55	25 Sept. 57
5	0	2 Edward Abbott Noblett	31 May 55	9 Mar. 58
5	0	2 Thomas Charge Wray	11 May 55	27 Nov. 57
5	0	1 John Wily	1 June 55	23 Mar. 58
5	0	2 Henry Adams	6 July 55	23 Mar. 58
5	0	1 Richard Hillman Daniel	13 July 55	23 Mar. 58
5	0	2 Edward Hall	ᵖ 28 Dec. 55	23 Mar. 58
3	0	2 Malcolm J.R. Macgregor	ᵖ 20 June 57	ᵖ 23 Apr. 58
3	0	1 James Francis Daubeny	9 Jan. 57	14 May 58
5	0	2 Wm. Albert Le Mottée	19 June 57	ᵖ 23 July 58
5	0	2 Isaac William Home[25]	27 July 55	10 Sept. 58
5	0	2 John A. Julian Briggs	ᵖ 30 Aug. 55	10 Sept. 58
5	0	2 Wm. Hugh Thomas ..	14 Sept. 55	10 Sept. 58
5	0	1 Wm. Orme Bourke ..	9 Oct. 55	10 Sept. 58
5	0	2 John Bland Sawyer ..	29 June 55	2 Feb. 58

1 Sir John F. Fitzgerald joined the 46th Regt. at the age of sixteen in 1801. He commanded a Light Battalion and a Brigade in the Peninsula, and has received the Gold Cross for Badajoz, Salamanca, Vittoria, and the Pyrenees.

6 Major Borrow served with the Cape Mounted Rifles during the Kaffir war of 1846-47 (Medal); also against the insurgent Boers. Served with the 18th Royal Irish in Burmah from the advance against Prome in Sept. 1852 to the close of the war (Medal).

16 Captain Vicars served as Adjutant 61st Regt. at the siege, assault and capture of Delhi, and repulse of sorties on 4th, 9th, 18th (horse shot) and 23d July 1857 (Medal and Clasp).

213 18th (Royal Irish) Regiment of Foot.

Years' Serv.			ENSIGN.	LIEUT.	18 Dr. Peake served through-
Full Pay.	Half Pay.	LIEUTENANTS.			out the Kaffir war of 1851-53 (Medal).
3	0	2 Samuel Thomas Corrie	P 16 Oct. 57	27 Aug. 58	22 Captain Kemp and Lieut.
2	0	2 Wm. Fryer Thacker ..	13 Apr. 58	P 7 Dec. 58	Hotham served in the Crimea
2	0	1 Fra. Wallis Lipscomb..	23 Mar. 58	31 Jan. 59	from Dec. 1854, and were wounded at the assault on the outworks of Sebastopol 18th June 1855 (Medal and Clasp, and 5th Class of the Medjidie).
		ENSIGNS.			24 Lieut. Fearnley served in the Crimea from
2	0	1 Hervey Talbot........	16 Mar. 58		Dec. 1854 to July 1855, and was present in a
2	0	1 Cha. Henry Stevenson	26 Mar. 58		sortie on the 12th May, and at the assault on the
2	0	1 Geo. Lawson Hall Poole	14 Apr. 58		outworks of Sebastopol, 18th June: severely
2	0	1 Wm. Edward Twyning	15 Apr. 58		wounded (Medal and Clasp).
2	0	2 Edw. Ashhurst Marsland	24 Apr. 58		26 Qr.-Master Carney served throughout the war in China (Medal), including the attack on
2	0	2 George Aug. Nicolls ..	25 Apr. 58		Canton, taking of Amoy, Chapoo, Woosung,
2	0	2 Chas. Goring Minnitt..	30 Apr. 58		Shanghai, and Chinkiangfoo, and landing before
2	0	2 St. George Alex. Smith	1 May 58		Nankin. Accompanied the subsequent expedition under General D'Aguilar which assaulted
2	0	2 Thos. Boyle Meredith	2 May 58		and took the forts of the Bocca Tigris, those of
2	0	1 John Forbes Mosse....	21 May 58		the Stake Barrier, and of the city of Canton. Served throughout the Burmese war of 1852-53
2	0	1 Ferd. Ogilvy FitzGerald	22 May 58		(Medal), including the storming of the citadel of
2	0	1 Edmund Chas. Prichard	P 28 May 58		Rangoon, and capture of Prome. Served also
2	0	2 Chas. C. Yates Butler	16 July 58		in the Crimea, and was at the attack of the Cemetery on the 18th June and at the fall of Sebas-
2	0	1 Wright Sherlock......	23 July 58		topol (Medal and Clasp).
2	0	1 Walter Carroll	5 Oct. 58		27 Qr. Master Godfrey served with the Royal
2	0	2 Chas. Orchard Cornish	26 Nov. 58		Engineers in the expedition in the Baltic in 1854,
1	0	2 Jno. Boddington Jackson	P 4 Feb. 59		and was present at the siege and capture of Bomarsund (Medal). Served with the R. Engineers
1	0	1 Charles Dawson	P 25 Mar. 59		in the trenches before Sebastopol from 18th Dec.
1	0	2 William Henry Herbert	29 July 59		1854 to the close of the siege, and was present at
1	0	2 Henry Gordon Heath..	5 Aug. 59		the taking of the Rifle Pit on 21st April, and the sortie on the right sap right attack on 30th August (Medal and Clasp).
16	0	Paymasters.—1 Chas. Edw. Preston, 6 Jan. 54; Ens. 26 July 44; Lt. P 19 Mar. 47.			
17	1 2/12	2 John Cornes,24 15 Nov. 47; {Q.M. 25 June 41; Cor. 2 Oct. 46; Lt. P 23 Mar. 47.			
5	0	Adjutants.—2 Lieut. Richard Wm. Erskine Dawson, 1 May 58.			
5	0	1 Lieut. Hugh Shaw, 29 Nov. 59.			
5	0	Instructors of Musketry.—1 Lieut. John Wily, 12 May 59.			
5	0	2 Lieut. Edward A. Noblett, 26 July 59.			
9	0	Quarter-Masters.—1 Thomas Carney,26 14 Oct. 51.			
2	0	2 Cornelius Godfrey,27 26 March 58.			
12	0	Surgeons.—1 Thomas Crawford,19 M.D. 9 Feb. 55; Assist. Surg. 18 Feb. 48.			
11	0	2 George William Peake,18 M.D. 2 Oct. 57; Assist. Surg. 25 Sept. 49.			
3	0	Assist.-Surgeons.—1 Frederick Ffolliott, 1 Aug. 57.			
3	0	1 Richard Armstrong Hyde, 17 Aug. 57.			
2	0	2 William Isaac Spencer, 22 Apr. 58.			
1	0	2 Hunter Alexander Coghlan, 1 March 59.			
2	0	1 John Henry Halked Tothill, 22 June 58.			

Facings Blue.—Agents, Messrs. Cox & Co.

[1st Batt. returned from Crimea, 18 July 56. Emb. for India, 11 Nov. 57. Depot, Buttevant.]
[2nd Batt. Depot, Templemore.]

2 Colonel Edwards served with the 18th Royal Irish throughout the war in China (Medal), and was present at the attack upon Canton, at the taking of Amoy, Chapoo, Woosung, Shanghai and Chinkiangfoo, and at the concluding operations before Nankin; was employed on the staff during the war, and afterwards appointed by Lord Gough Assistant Quarter-Master-General to the force in China. He served also with the 18th in the Burmah war from July 1852 to the conclusion (Medal); was at the taking of Prome, and employed on a detached command for six months, when the provinces of Padoung and Kanghein were cleared of the enemy, after several skirmishes and severe marches, by the detachments under his command. In January 1853 he led a party on special service from Prome to Arracan, for which service the Government of India and General Godwin recorded their approbation. Served at the siege and fall of Sebastopol from Dec. 1854 (Medal and Clasp, CB., Knight of the Legion of Honor, and 3rd Class of the Medjidie). Received the Brevet of Lt.-Col. for his services in Burmah, and that of Colonel for services in the Crimea. Commanded the Brigade at Mhow, at the termination of the Mutiny in 1858-59, and received the thanks of the Governor General in Council, for the promptness of measures, whereby the rebels under Tantia Topee were prevented entering Kandeish.

3 Lt.-Colonel Call served with the 18th Royal Irish throughout the whole of the China expedition (Medal). Was present at the first capture of Chusan, attack of the Forts of the Bocca Tigris, storming of the height and Forts at Canton, and destruction of the Forts and capture of Amoy. Was employed on the Staff in China in 1841-2 as Sub. Assist. Comm.-Gen. Served throughout the Burmese war of 1852-3 (Medal) as Brigade Major to the 1st Bengal-Brigade, and for a part of the period as Assist. Adj.-Gen. of the Pegu Division. Was present at the destruction of the Stockades at the entrance of the Rangoon River, at the operations before, and subsequent storming of, the Citadel of Rangoon, at the capture of Prome, and repulses of the enemy from that position. Served at the siege of Sebastopol from Dec. 1854 (Medal and Clasp, Brevet Lt.-Colonel, Sardinian Medal, and 5th Class of the Medjidie).

7 Major Armstrong served with the 18th Royal Irish throughout the war in China (Medal), including the storming and capture of the heights and forts above Canton (carried the colors), capture of Amoy, second capture of Chusan, attack on Chinhae, Ningpo, Segoan, and Chinkiangfoo. Commanded the guard at the west gate of Ningpo on the morning of the 10th March 1842, when at the head of 28 men he repulsed a column of 3000 Chinese, and captured a stand of the enemy's colors, for which service he was thanked in Orders by Lord Gough, and mentioned in the Dispatches. Served in Burmah from January 1853 until the end of the war (Medal), and commanded a detachment consisting of four Companies of the 18th Royal Irish during the whole of the successful operations in the Donabew district, including the 17th March 1853, when the 18th Royal Irish stormed and carried the first stockade, and also the 19th March, when the stronghold of the Burmese chief, Meah Toon, was stormed, and after considerable loss captured. Served in the Crimea from 30th Dec. 1854 to 11th Aug. 1855, and led the attack against the batteries at the Dock Yard Creek, and was wounded (Medal and Clasp, Brevet Major, Knight of the Legion of Honor, and 5th Class of the Medjidie).

8 Major Sargent served with the 18th Royal Irish on the China expedition (Medal), and was present at Woosung, Shanghai, Chinkiangfoo, and Nankin. Was subsequently Aide-de-Camp to Sir John Davis in China for three years, and acting Aide-de-Camp to General D'Aguilar during the expedition which assaulted and took the Forts of the Bocca Tigris in the Canton River; received a severe contusion on the head, and was favourably recommended by Sir John Davis to Lord Palmerston for his services on this occasion. Was appointed Adjutant of the 18th at the storming of Rangoon on Lieut. and Adj. Doran being killed, and served throughout the Burmese war of 1852-53 (Medal).

9 Capt. Kelly served in the 18th Royal Irish with the expedition under General D'Aguilar in April 1847. Also the latter part of the Burmese war, and was present at the night-attack on the height at Prome in January 1853 (Medal). Served at the siege of Sebastopol from Dec. 1854 (Medal and Clasp).

10 Captain Swinburne served with the 32nd at the first and second siege operations before Mooltan, including the attack on the enemy's position in front of the advanced trenches 12th Sept. 1848 (wounded in the right hand); also the storm and capture of the city, and surrender of the fortress; was also present at the surrender of the fort and garrison of Cheniote 9th Feb. 1849, and subsequently at the battle of Goojerat (Medal and two Clasps). Served with the 18th Royal Irish throughout the Burmese war of 1852-53 (Medal); was at the capture of Martaban; on board H. M. S. *Rattler* during that ship's engagement with and destruction of the stockades in front of Rangoon; present at the operations in front of Rangoon on the 11th, 13th, and 14th April; at the subsequent capture of Prome, and minor skirmishes. Served at the siege of Sebastopol from Dec. 1854 (Medal and Clasp).

11 Captain Elliot served with the 18th Royal Irish throughout the Burmese war of 1852-53 (Medal); was with the storming party at the capture of Martaban; on board H. M. S. *Rattler*, at the destruction of the river stockades; and on land at that of those on the Dallah side; in the operations in front of Rangoon on the 12th and 13th April 1852, including the capture of the White House stockade; also at the storm and capture of Rangoon (wounded). Served at the siege of Sebastopol from 20 Aug. 1855 (Medal and Clasp).

12 Captains Stacpoole, Taylor, and Pocklington, served in the Burmese campaign of 1852-53 (Medal). Served also at the siege of Sebastopol (Medal and Clasp). Capt. Taylor has the 5th Class of the Medjidie.

13 Captain Annesley served with a detachment of 30 of the Ceylon Rifles, which defeated the insurgents in the first and second attack on Kornegalle on the 30th and 31st July, during the suppression of the rebellion in the Kandian Provinces in 1848.

14 Captain Canavan served with the 18th Royal Irish throughout the Burmese war of 1852-53 (Medal), including Martaban, Rangoon, Prome, and minor skirmishes on the right bank of the Irrawaddy.

15 Sir Henry Havelock served as a D.A.Q.M.Gen. in the Persian expedition from 15 Feb. 1857, including the bombardment and capture of Mohumrah (Medal). Served throughout the Indian campaigns of 1857-59 as Aide de Camp to General Havelock from 7th July, in the actions of Futtehpore, Aoung, Pandoo Nuddee, and Cawnpore, and as D.A.Adj.Gen. to the force 20 July, 1857, in the actions of Oonao, Busscerut Gunge (horse shot), Nawabgunge, Boorbeenke Chowkee, Bithoor, Mungarwar, and Alumbagh, and relief of Lucknow on 25th Sept—dangerously wounded by musket ball through left elbow, and horse shot; defence of the Residency until relieved by Lord Clyde on 17th Nov., on which day again severely wounded by a rifle ball through left shoulder. Within a month joined the Jounpore field force under Gen. Franks as D.A.Adj.Gen., and was present at the actions of Nusrutpore, Chanda, Umeerpore, and Sultanpore. Present with the 4th Division before Lucknow from 4th March till its fall, including the storming of the Lesser Emaumbarra and the Kaiserbagh. Served as D. A. Adj.Gen. from 29th March with Lugard's column, and present at the relief of Azimghur; operations to 4th June (sabre cut on right hand) against the Jugdespore rebels, including the attack on that stronghold and eight minor skirmishes. As D. A. G. in the disturbed districts of Ghazeepore and Behar under Brigadier Douglas from 16th June to Nov. 1858, including the operations in the former district in July and August, and the campaign in Shahabad in Oct. and November. Commanded a detached body of 250 Mounted Riflemen and Cavalry in pursuit of the rebels after they evacuated Jugdespore on 18th Oct., intercepted and turned them from the Soane river, and three times engaged and defeated them, once at Nonadee on 20th Oct., inflicting considerable slaughter. Commanded a detachment of Hodson's Horse with the Army in Oude under Lord Clyde, and present at the skirmish at Burgudeea, capture of Musjeedia, and final action on the Raptee on 31st Dec. 1858. Served till the conclusion of the campaign in command of the 1st Regt. Hodson's Horse. Was repeatedly mentioned in Dispatches, has received the Victoria Cross, and the Brevets of Major and Lt.Colonel.

17 Captain Chapman served with the 29th Regt. throughout the Punjaub campaign of 1848-49, including the passage of the Chenab, and battles of Chillianwallah and Goojerat (Medal and Clasps).

19 Dr. Crawford served with the 51st Regt. throughout the Burmese war of 1852-35; was on board the E.I.C. steam-frigate *Ferooz* during the naval action and destruction of the enemy's stockades in the Rangoon River; served during the succeeding three days' operations in the vicinity, and at the storm and capture of Rangoon (including the storming of the White House Redoubt); also at the storm and capture of Bassein, 10th May (Medal).

20 Captain Crozier served with the 27th Regt. during the Kaffir war of 1846-47 (Medal).

21 Captain Haydock served with the 90th Lt. Inf. at the siege and fall of Sebastopol from 10th Aug. 1855, and was with the storming party at the assault of the Redan on the 8th Sept.—wounded (Medal and Clasp). Also during the Indian campaign of 1857-58 and was present with Havelock's Column at the actions of Mungawar and Alumbagh, relief and subsequent defence of Lucknow, defence of the Alumbagh under Outram, siege and fall of Lucknow (Medal and Clasps).

23 Captains Jex-Blake, Coote, Ring, and Baker, Lieuts. Dillon, Theobald, and Adamson, served in the Crimea from December 1854, and were at the siege of Sebastopol (Medal and Clasp). Captain Baker has the Sardinian Medal. Captain Coote has the 5th Class of the Medjidie.

24 Paymaster Cornes served with the 53rd Regt. in the campaign on the Sutlej in 1846 (Medal and Clasps), and commanded the rear guard at Buddiwal when cut off by the enemy's cavalry, and effected his retreat in an orderly manner in the face of the entire Seik cavalry,—his conduct on this occasion afterwards elicited the Duke of Wellington's "cordial approbation and thanks for the gallantry and judgment he displayed in protecting the baggage and sick in the movement towards Loodiana, when attacked by a large force of the enemy on the 21st January." He was also present at the battles of Aliwal and Sobraon. At Buddiwal he was wounded in the leg, and his horse was shot under him. Served with the 79th Regt. the Eastern campaign of 1854, including the battle of Alma and siege of Sebastopol (Medal and Clasp).

25 Lieut. Home served with the 34th Regt. at Cawnpore under General Windham in the actions with the Gwalior Contingent on the 26th, 27th and 28th Nov. 1857; also present at the capture of Lucknow, and at the relief of Azimghur with Lugard's Column (Medal and Clasp).

[*Continuation of Notes to 19th Foot.*]

13 Captain Goren served in 1854-55, at the battle of Inkerman, siege of Sebastopol (wounded), and storming of the Redan on the 8th Sept.: dangerously wounded (Medal and Clasps, and 5th Class of the Medjidie).

14 Captain Anderson served with the 51st throughout the Burmese war of 1852-53; on board the E. I. C. steam frigate *Sesostris* during the naval action and destruction of the enemy's stockades on the Rangoon River; and served during the succeeding three days' operations in the vicinity, and at the storm and capture of Rangoon, and at the assault and capture of Bassein, 19th May 1852 (Medal and Clasp).

15 Captain Kirke served in 1855 at the siege of Sebastopol (Medal and Clasp).

16 Lieut. Evans served in 1855 at the siege of Sebastopol (severely wounded), and at the storming of the Redan on the 8th Sept. (Medal and Clasp).

17 Lieut. Thompson served the Eastern campaign of 1854-55, including the battles of Alma (carried the colours) and Inkerman and siege of Sebastopol (Medal and Clasps, and Sardinian Medal).

18 Captain Forbes and Lieut. Browne served at the latter part of the siege of Sebastopol, and at the assault on the Redan on the 8th Sept. (Medal and Clasp).

19 Lieut. Molesworth served in the Crimea from May 1855, and was engaged in the attack on the Quarries 7th June, and in the attacks of the Redan on 18th June and 8th Sept. (severely wounded); Medal and Clasp.

20 Captain Martin was dangerously wounded at the assault on the Redan on the 8th Sept. 1855 (Medal and Clasp).

21 Paymaster Palmer served the Eastern campaign of 1854-55, including the battles of Alma and Inkerman, siege and fall of Sebastopol (Medal and Clasps).

215   19th (*The* 1*st Yorkshire North Riding*) *Regt. of Foot.* [1st Batt. Bengal. 2nd Batt. Aldershot.

"ALMA"   "INKERMAN"   "SEVASTOPOL."

Years' Serv.		
Full Pay.	Half Pay.	
57		Colonel.—**PGA** Sir William Rowan,[1] KCB. *Ens.* 4 Nov. 03; *Lieut.* 15 June 04; *Capt.* 19 Oct. 08; *Major,* 3 March 14; *Lt.-Col.* 21 Jan. 19; *Col.* 10 Jan. 37; *Maj.-Gen.* 9 Nov. 46; *Lt.-Gen.* 20 June 54; *Col.* 19th Foot, 15 June 54.
		Lt.-Colonels.—1 George Valentine Edw. Mundy,[2] *CB. Ens. & Lt.* 27 Feb. 35;
25	1/12	*Lt. & Capt.* p 1 May 40; *Bt.-Major,* 11 Nov. 51; *Bt. Lt.-Col.* 12 Dec. 54; *Major,* 29 Dec. 54; *Lt.-Col.* 19 Sept. 55.
17	0	1 Robert Onesiphorus Bright,[3] *Ens.* p 9 June 43; *Lt.* p 2 April 47; *Capt.* p 23 Jan. 52; *Major,* 15 Sept. 55; *Brev. Lt.-Col.* 26 Dec. 56; *Lt.-Col.* 28 Nov. 57.
17	1/12	2 Robert Warden,[3]† *Ens.* p 12 Oct. 41; *Lt.* p 4 April 45; *Capt.* p 6 Aug. 47; *Bt.-Major,* 12 Dec. 54; *Major,* 31 Aug. 55; *Bt. Lt.-Col,* 2 Nov. 55; *Lt.-Col.* 26 Sept. 56.
17	0	*Majors.*—1 George Bingham Jenings,[4] *Ens.* p 21 July 43; *Lt.* p 4 April 45; *Capt.* 1 July 53; *Major,* 30 Sept. 56.
13	0	1 Edward Chippindall,[5] *Ens.* p 10 Dec. 47; *Lt.* p 9 Jan. 49; *Capt.* p 23 Dec. 53; *Brev.-Maj.* 2 Nov. 55; *Major,* 28 Nov. 57.
11	2	2 Lumley Graham,[6] *Ens.* p 13 Aug. 47; *Lt.* p 28 Feb. 51; *Capt.* p 7 June 54; *Bt.-Major,* 12 Dec. 54; *Major,* 7 March 56; *Bt. Lt.-Col.* 6 June 56.
26	0	2 Robert Bates,[7] *Ens.* 6 June 34; *Lieut.* p 25 Dec. 38; *Capt.* 15 Oct. 45; *Bt.-Major,* 6 June 56; *Major,* 9 March 58.

		CAPTAINS.	ENSIGN.	LIEUT.	CAPTAIN.	BREV.-MAJ.
13	0	1 Hugh Francis Massy[7]†	p 7 Aug. 47	9 July 50	p 3 Feb. 54	
11	0	2 L. Douglas Hay Currie[8]	p 2 Feb. 49	p 23 Jan. 52	29 Dec. 54	
14	0	1 Richard Doyle Barrett[9]	14 April 46	9 April 48	29 Dec. 54	
11	0	2 George Clay[9]	p 18 Sept. 49	p 31 Dec. 52	29 Dec. 54	
11	0	2 Hen. Turner Unlacke[11]	p 21 Dec. 49	1 July 53	31 Aug. 55	
12	0	1 Charles Henry Lambert	p 13 Oct. 48	p 28 Jan. 53	p 14 Sept. 55	
8	0	1 Edw.Rob.WardBayley[12]	p 13 Feb. 52	p 17 Feb. 54	14 Sept. 55	
6	0	1 Edw. St. John Griffiths	27 Oct. 54	9 Mar. 55	p 24 July 57	
6	0	2 Edw. Nassau Kindersley	15 Dec. 54	9 Mar. 55	p 7 Aug. 57	
7	0	1 Ames Goren[13]	p 11 Mar. 53	6 Nov. 54	28 Nov. 57	
16	0	1 John RichardsonStuart	23 Mar. 44	13 Dec. 47	9 Mar. 58	
14	0	2 Philip Doyne Vigors	p 9 Oct. 46	p 19 July 50	9 Mar. 58	
13	0	2 John Anderson[14]	p 25 June 47	18 Apr. 51	9 Mar. 58	
13	0	1 Edwin Fletcher Foster	p 23 Apr. 47	7 Jan. 53	9 Mar. 58	
15	0	2 Henry S. G. S. Knight	2 Sept. 4	3 June 47	p 30 Oct. 57	
9	0	1 Fred. Mont. Alison,[10] *s.*	p 17 Oct. 51	1 Sept. 54	13 Apr. 58	26 Apr. 59
6	0	2 John Henry Kirke[15]	p 17 Feb. 54	p 10 Nov. 54	p 30 Apr. 58	
14	0	2 Wm.Fred.Tho.Marshall	13 Mar. 46	7 Feb. 51	2 July 58	
9	0	1 Thomas Conway Lloyd	p 18 Apr. 51	24 Apr. 55	p 13 July 58	
12	0	2 **VC** Hen.Edw.Jerome[27]	21 Jan. 48	30 Apr. 52	23 July 58	1 July 59
5	0	1 Francis Davis[10]	5 Jan. 55	11 May 55	p 24 Dec. 58	
5	0	1 George Forbes[16]	p 12 Jan. 55	10 July 55	p 24 May 59	
5	0	1 RobertConollyMartin[20]	26 Jan. 55	31 Aug. 55	p 31 May 59	
5	0	2 William John Foster[26]	21 Feb. 55	2 Oct. 55	p 8 July 59	

		LIEUTENANTS.				
6	0	1 Godfrey Baldwin	6 June 54	8 Dec. 54		
6	0	1 Edward Wm. Evans[16]	7 June 54	8 Dec. 54		6 Lt.-Colonel Graham served with the 43rd Regt. in the Kaffir war of 1851-53 (Medal). Served the Eastern campaign of 1854-55, part of the time as Aide-de-Camp to Major-General Eyre, including the battle of Alma and siege of Sebastopol; was severely wounded 29th Aug. 1855, occasioning amputation of right arm (Medal and Clasps, Brevets of Major and Lt.-Colonel, Knight of the Legion of Honor, and 5th Class of the Medjidie).
6	0	1 Thos. Thompson,[17] *Adj.*	11 Aug. 54	12 Jan. 55		
6	0	1 Henry John Browne[18]	22 Nov. 54	17 Feb. 55		
6	0	1 Richard Molesworth[19]	23 Nov. 54	9 Mar. 55		
6	0	2 James Robert Dalton	24 Nov. 54	9 Mar. 55		
5	0	1 Chas.Vincent Hiffernan	13 Feb. 55	15 Sept. 55		
5	0	1 William Henry Moffatt	16 Mar. 55	p 12 Dec. 56		
5	0	1 Alex. Brooke Morgan	6 April 55	28 Nov. 57		
5	0	2 Charles Hereford	17 Aug. 55	p 17 July 57		
5	0	2 John Binnie Mackenzie	17 Aug. 55	p 4 Dec. 57		7 Major Bates served with the 45th Regt. in the Kaffir war of 1846-47 (Medal).
5	0	1 Henry Thompson	11 May 55	26 Mar. 58		
5	0	1 James Knox	30 April 55	26 Mar. 58		
5	0	2 Francis Edw. Biddulph	15 May 55	26 Mar. 58		7† Capt. Massy served in the Eastern campaign (Medal and Clasp for Sebastopol).
5	0	1 Conyng. Cours Backas	3 Aug. 55	26 Mar. 58		
5	0	2 George Douglas Harris	17 Aug. 55	15 June 58		
5	0	2 Thomas Dennis Rew	26 Oct. 55	15 June 58		8 Captain Currie served in the Eastern campaign of 1854, and was severely wounded at the battle of Alma (Medal and Clasp).
5	0	2 William Robert Iles	16 Nov. 55	15 June 58		
4	0	2 Robert Henry Hackett	4 Apr. 56	15 June 58		
4	0	2 George Rogers	p 15 Jan. 56	p 22 June 58		9 Captains Barrett and Clay served the Eastern campaign of 1854, and part of 1855, including the battles of Alma and Inkerman, and siege of Sebastopol (Medal and Clasps, and 5th Class of the Medjidie).
5	0	2 Beauchamp Colclough	4 July 55	13 July 58		
5	0	2 Cha. Jas. Forbes Smith	27 July 55	13 July 58		
4	0	2 Arth. WestbrookeBurton	p 2 Dec. 56	16 July 58		
3	0	1 Fred. George Frith	p 3 Mar. 57	4 Nov. 58		10 Captain Davis served at the siege and fall of Sebastopol from 3rd Sept. 1855 (Medal and Clasp).
2	0	2 George Francis Vesey[30]	14 Apr. 58	p 11 Feb. 59		
2	0	2 Thomas H. Kirby	15 Apr. 58	p 11 Feb. 59		
2	0	1 Robert Biscoe	16 Apr. 58	p 24 May 59		
2	0	1 Horace Arthur Wells	24 Apr. 58	p 2 Dec. 59		
2	0	2 Philip Downes Williams	26 Apr. 58	p 2 Dec. 59		

19th (The 1st Yorkshire North Riding) Regt. of Foot. 216

Years' Serv. Full Pay.	Half Pay.	ENSIGNS.	ENSIGN.
2	0	1 William Bennett	26 Mar. 58
2	0	1 John C. Taylor Humfrey	27 Mar. 58
2	0	2 Brumhead Rogers	30 Apr. 58
2	0	2 William Read, *Adj*	7 May 58
2	0	2 Duncan Campbell Affleck	14 May 58
2	0	2 Edgar Angelo Dickenson	28 May 58
2	0	1 Aug. Mourant Handley	2 July 58
2	0	1 James Francis Fraser	3 July 58
2	0	1 Francis Herbert Evans	4 July 58
2	0	1 Robert Guyer Traill	16 July 58
2	0	1 Cortlandt Skinner	6 Aug. 58
2	0	2 Geo. Hewetson Reynolds	15 Oct. 58
2	0	1 Const. Chas. B. Tribe	19 Nov. 58
2	0	2 Martin Tucker	24 Dec. 58
1	0	2 Alexander Bredin	11 Mar. 59
1	0	2 William Joseph Lynch	p 18 Mar. 59
1	0	1 Henry Stokes	p 31 May 59
1	0	2 Geo. Archibald Warden	p 3 June 59
1	0	2 Daniel James Mansergh	p 14 June 59

22 Surgeon Hassard served in the Kaffir war of 1851-53—horse shot in the Waterkloof (Medal).
23 Assist. Surgeon Hiffernan served the Eastern campaign of 1854-55, including the battles of Alma and Inkerman, and siege of Sebastopol (Medal and Clasps).
24 Assist. Surgeon J. C. Smith served with the 21st Regt. during 1855 at the siege and fall of Sebastopol, and expedition to Kinbourn (Medal and Clasp).
26 Major Alison served with the 72nd Highlanders in the Crimea from 13th June 1855, including the expedition to Kertch, siege and fall of Sebastopol, and attack of the 18th June (Medal and Clasp).
28 Captain Foster served with the 46th Regt. at the siege and fall of Sebastopol from 18th Aug. 1855 (Medal and Clasp).
33 Lieut. Vesey served as a Midshipman in the Baltic Fleet in 1854 (Medal).
31 Doctor Chalmers served with the 18th Royal Irish during the last Burmese war (Medal). Also in the trenches at the siege and fall of Sebastopol (Medal and Clasp).

6	0	*Paymasters.*—1 Thomas Palmer,[21] 7 Dec. 55; *Qr. Master*, 21 April 54.	
2	0	2 Frank William Dundee, 23 March 58.	
6	0	*Adjutants.*—1 Lieut. Thomas Thompson,[17] 21 Sept. 55.	
2	0	2 Ensign William Read, 17 May 58.	
2	0	*Instructors of Musketry.*—1 *Ensign* R. G. Traill, 15 June 59.	
5	0	2 *Lieut.* C. J. F. Smith, 16 Nov. 59.	
2	0	*Quarter Masters.*—2 John James Macdonald, 30 March 58.	
2	0	1 Charles Usherwood,[33] 7 Sept. 58.	
14	0	*Surgeons.*—Wm. Kelman Chalmers,[31] M.D. 12 Jan. 55; *Assist. Surg.* 13 Nov. 46.	
9	0	Henry Bolton Hassard,[22] 26 Jan. 58; *Assist. Surg.* 14 Mar. 51.	
6	0	*Assistant Surgeons.*—1 Exham Long Hiffernan,[23] 16 June 54.	
6	0	1 James Castor Smith,[24] 1 Sept. 54.	
2	0	2 Donald Macpherson, 10 March 58.	
1	0	2 Thomas Hewlett, 1 Feb. 59.	
1	0	1 Charles Edward Wikeley, 12 Jan. 59.	

Facings Green.—*Agents*, Messrs. Cox & Co.

[1st Batt. returned from Crimea, 28 June 56. Emb. for India, 22 July 57. Depot, Chatham.]

1 Sir William Rowan served with the 52nd Regt. in Sicily in 1806-7; on the expedition to Sweden in 1808; in Portugal and Spain under Sir John Moore, from August 1808 to the embarkation of the Army at Corunna, at the bombardment and capture of Flushing in 1809; in Portugal in 1811, including the action at Sabugal; in the Peninsula and south of France, from January 1813 to the end of the war, including the battles of Vittoria and the Pyrenees; attack of the entrenched camp at Vera during the passage of the Bidassoa River; attack of the fortified positions of La Rhune and Sarre during the passage of the river Nivelle, battle on passing the river Nive, and attack by the French of the heights of Arcanguez; battles of Orthes and Toulouse, and intermediate affairs. Served also the campaign of 1815, and was present at the battle of Waterloo and capture of Paris, when he was appointed Commandant of the first arrondissement of that city. Promoted to Brevet-Major for the battle of Orthes, and Brev. Lt. Colonel for services in the field. He has received the War Medal with six Clasps.

2 Lieut. Colonel Mundy served in the Coldstream Guards during the Canadian Rebellion in 1838-39. Served in the 33rd Regt. throughout the Eastern campaign of 1854-55, including the battles of Alma (horse shot) and Inkerman (commanded the Regt.), siege and fall of Sebastopol (severely wounded in the trenches), attack on the Rifle Pits 19th April, and that of the Redan on the 18th June—wounded (Medal with three Clasps, C.B., Brevet Lt. Colonel, Knight of the Legion of Honor, Sardinian Medal, and 5th Class of the Medjidie).

3 Lt. Col. Bright served the Eastern campaign of 1854-55, including the battles of Alma and Inkerman, siege of Sebastopol, and storming of the Redan on the 8th September (Medal and Clasps, Knight of the Legion of Honor, and 5th Class of the Medjidie).

3* Lt. Colonel Warden served with the 19th Regt. the Eastern campaign of 1854-55, including the battles of Alma (severely wounded) and Inkerman, siege of Sebastopol (wounded); was of the party that first held the Quarries; commanded 400 of the 97th Regt. in the trenches at the assault of the 18th June; succeeded to the command of the 19th Regt. at the storming of the Redan on the 8th Sept. (severely wounded), and took the Brigade out of action (Medal and three Clasps, Brevets of Major and Lt. Col., Knight of the Legion of Honor, Sardinian Medal, and 5th Class of the Medjidie).

4 Major Jenings served the Eastern campaign of 1854 (Medal and Clasp).

5 Major Chippindall served with the 32nd Regt. during the latter part of the siege operations before Mooltan, and was present at the surrender of that Fortress; also at the surrender of the Fort and Garrison of Cheniote, and at the battle of Goojerat (Medal and Clasps). Served the Eastern campaign of 1854-55, with the 19th Regt., including the affair of Bulganak, battles of Alma and Inkerman, in the trenches during the whole of the siege operations before Sebastopol, assaults of the Redan on the 18th June and 8th Sept.; wounded (Medal and Clasps, Brevet Major, Knight of the Legion of Honor, and 5th Class of the Medjidie).

11 Captain Uniacke served the Eastern campaign of 1854-55, including the battle of Alma, siege of Sebastopol, and storming of the Redan on the 8th Sept. (Medal and Clasps, Sardinian Medal, and 5th Class of the Medjidie).

12 Captain Bayley served the Eastern campaign of 1854-55, including the battle of Alma, siege of Sebastopol (wounded), and storming of the Redan; wounded (Medal and Clasps, Sardinian Medal, and 5th Class of the Medjidie).

27 Major Jerome served in the Indian campaign of 1857-59, including operations against the rebel tribes in Goojerat, storm and capture of Chundairee—led the storming party, siege and capture of Jhansi where under a murderous fire he assisted in rescuing Ensign Secoal who was severely wounded—mentioned in dispatches; also present at the action of Koonch and at the various engagements before Calpee—severely and dangerously wounded, mentioned in dispatches, Brevet of Major (Medal and Clasp, and Victoria Cross).

33 Qr. Master Usherwood served the Eastern campaign of 1854-55, including the battles of Alma and Inkerman, and siege of Sebastopol (Medal and three Clasps).

[For continuation of Notes, see end of 18th Foot.

20th (The East Devonshire) Regt. of Foot. [1st Batt. Lucknow. 2nd Batt. Dublin.

"MINDEN" "EGMONT-OP-ZEE" The *Sphinx*, with the words "EGYPT" "MAIDA" "VIMIERA" "CORUNNA" "VITTORIA" "PYRENEES" "ORTHES" "TOULOUSE" "PENINSULA" "ALMA" "INKERMAN" "SEVASTOPOL."

Years' Serv.			
Full Pay	Half Pay		
43		**Colonel.**—Marcus Beresford, 2nd *Lt.* P 4 Sept. 17; *Lt.* 1 Feb. 21; *Capt.* P 16 Sept. 24; *Major,* P 26 Sept. 26; *Lt.Col.* P 6 Nov. 27; *Col.* 23 Nov. 41; *Maj. Gen.* 20 June 54; *Lt.Gen.* 7 Dec. 59; *Col.* 20th Foot, 22 Sept. 58.		
19	0	**Lieut. Colonels.**—2 Wm. Pollexfen Radcliffe,¹ *Ens.* P 12 Mar. 41; *Lieut.* P 2 Aug. 42; *Capt.* P 25 July 51; *Bt.Maj.* 12 Dec. 54; *Major,* 29 Aug. 56; *Lt.-Col.* 26 Mar. 58.		
19	5/12	1 John Cormick,² *Ens.* P 27 Aug. 41; *Lt.* P 25 Oct. 42; *Capt.* P 12 April 50; *Bt.Major,* 17 July 55; *Major,* 18 Sept. 57; *Lt.Col.* P 24 Dec. 58.		
14	0	1 George Bennett,³ *Ens.* P 20 Dec. 46; *Lt.* 8 Mar. 52; *Capt.* 29 Dec. 54; *Brev. Major,* 20 July 58; *Major,* P 24 Dec. 58; *Lt.Col.* P 28 Oct. 59.		
19	0	**Majors.**—1 Edward Alan Holditch,⁴ *CB. Ens.* P 2 July 41; *Lt.* 26 July 44; *Capt.* P 22 Feb. 50; *Bt.Major,* 2 Aug. 50; *Bt.Lt.Col.* 28 May 53; *Col.* 28 Nov. 54; *Major,* 26 Mar. 58.		
37	12 3/12	2 ⚑ Archibald Campbell,⁵ *Ens.* 7 March 11; *Lt.* 5 March 12; *Capt.* P 27 Oct. 37; *Bt.Major,* 11 Nov. 51; *Bt.Lt.Col.* 16 March 58; *Major,* 23 April 58.		
9	0	2 Wm. Drummond Scrase Dickins,⁶ *Ens.* P 19 Aug. 51; *Lt.* P 7 June 54; *Capt.* P 20 Feb. 55; *Bt.Maj.* 20 July 58; *Maj.* P 28 Oct. 59.		
8	0	1 Augustus Riversdale Warren,⁷ *Ens.* P 12 Mar. 52; *Lieut.* P 16 June 54; *Capt.* P 1 May 55; *Major,* P 13 Dec. 59.		

		CAPTAINS.	**ENSIGN.**	**LIEUT.**	**CAPTAIN.**	**BREV.-MAJ.**
15	0	1 Thomas Casey Lyons⁸	P 31 Aug. 45	P 2 Nov. 49	P 27 July 55	26 Apr. 59
8	0	2 Baringtn. G. Dashwood	P 13 Feb. 52	P 20 Oct. 54	P 10 Aug. 55	
9	5/12	2 Wm. Lewis D. Meares¹¹	29 Nov. 50	P 11 Oct. 53	16 Oct. 55	
7	0	1 Geo. Edmond Francis¹²	P 22 April 53	9 Feb. 55	P 31 July 57	
5	0	1 Fre. Lockwood Edridge¹³	P 19 Feb. 55	10 Aug. 55	P 7 Aug. 57	
13	0	1 John T. Nicolls O'Brien	11 Sept. 47	5 May 50	2 Feb. 58	26 Apr. 59
18	0	2 Thomas Aldridge	21 May 42	3 Apr. 46	4 Sept. 57	
14	1 5/12	2 Augustus William Ord	P 2 Sept. 44	P 6 Aug. 47	P 17 Oct. 51	
18	0	2 Samuel Sharpe	8 Nov. 42	8 Jan. 47	26 Mar. 58	
14	0	2 Richard Hull Lewis¹⁴	29 Dec. 46	P 3 Mar. 48	26 Mar. 58	
13	0	2 Edw. Monckton Jones	8 Jan. 47	27 Apr. 49	26 Mar. 58	
14	0	2 Geo. G. Gower Munro	16 Apr. 46	P 21 Aug. 49	26 Mar. 58	
7	0	1 Hect. Barlow Vaughan¹⁶	P 30 Dec. 53	8 Dec. 54	26 Mar. 58	
5	0	2 Cha. Gustavus Rochfort	9 Mar. 55	P 10 Aug. 55	P 30 Mar. 58	
6	0	1 John Jas. S. O'Neill¹⁷	6 June 54	29 Dec. 54	3 June 58	
12	3	2 Allen Noble Adams¹⁹	P 27 June 45	P 3 Sept. 47	10 Mar. 58	
14	0	1 Henry Evans Quin	24 Aug. 46	12 Oct. 52	10 Sept. 58	
6	0	1 Patrick Geraghty²¹	5 Nov. 54	17 Feb. 55	10 Sept. 58	
5	0	2 W. F. Forbes Gordon²²	1 May 55	P 27 Sept. 55	P 24 Dec. 58	
5	0	1 Edw. Aug. Patrickson²³	26 Jan. 55	11 May 55	5 May 59	
5	0	1 William David Nunn²⁵	20 Feb. 55	21 Sept. 55	P 29 July 59	
18	1 5/12	2 Rodney Payne O'Shea	16 July 41	20 Apr. 44	16 May 56	
5	0	2 George Blair Duffin²⁷	4 May 55	P 16 Oct. 55	P 28 Oct. 59	
5	0	1 George Gethin²⁸	15 June 55	P 16 Oct. 55	P 13 Dec. 59	
		LIEUTENANTS.				
5	0	1 Francis Geo. Holmes²⁴	16 Feb. 55	15 June 58		
5	0	1 *Hon.* Adol. E. P. Vereker²⁶	2 Mar. 55	16 Oct. 55	3|† Lieut. Blount served in the Indian campaign of 1857-58, including the actions of Chanda, Umeerpore, and Sultanpore, siege and capture of Lucknow, subsequent operations in Oude and affair of Mohan (Medal and Clasp).	
5	0	2 J. Hen. Herbert St. John	30 Mar. 55	P 29 Feb. 56		
5	0	1 Joseph Cooke Cox	31 Aug. 55	P 19 June 57		
5	0	1 Conroy Fahle²⁹	P 29 Apr. 55	30 Mar. 58		
5	0	2 Chas. Fred. Houghton	1 May 55	26 Feb. 56		
5	0	1 O. Tudor Burne,³⁰ *Adj.*	15 May 55	10 Apr. 58		
6	0	2 John Armstrong,³¹ *Adj.*	8 Sept. 54	23 Mar. 55		
5	0	2 Stephen Egan	9 Oct. 55	28 May 58		
5	0	2 Robert Blount³¹†	P 15 Oct. 55	3 June 58		
5	0	2 Charles Kyrle Chatfield	2 Nov. 55	15 June 58		
4	0	2 Samuel Johnstone	8 Feb. 56	15 June 58		
4	0	1 Fred. Gowland Horn³²	29 Feb. 56	15 June 58		
3	0	2 John Aldridge	P 19 June 57	P 29 June 58		
5	0	2 Hen. Parker Chapman	14 June 55	10 Sept. 58		
5	0	2 Frederick Fox	15 June 55	10 Sept. 58		
5	0	2 Henry Archdall	6 July 55	10 Sept. 58		
5	0	1 Frederick Wright³³	13 July 55	10 Sept. 58		
5	0	1 Hy. Fra. Geo. Webster	10 Aug. 55	10 Sept. 58		
5	0	1 Nadolig Xim. Gwynne	9 Oct. 55	10 Sept. 58		
4	0	1 Frederick Mansel³⁴	4 Apr. 56	10 Sept. 58		
2	0	2 Hub. C. Z. de Stackpoole	13 April 58	P 24 Dec. 58		
2	0	1 Harry Russell Bowlby	23 April 58	P 11 Jan. 59		
2	0	1 William Unwin³⁵	10 Apr. 58	11 Apr. 59		
2	0	1 Renouard Henry James	14 April 58	16 Apr. 59		
2	0	2 William Glencross	16 April 58	5 May 59		

20th (*The East Devonshire*) Regt. of Foot.

Years' Serv. Full Pay.	Years' Serv. Half Pay.	LIEUTENANTS.	ENSIGN.	LIEUT.	
2	0	1 Robert Fraser........	30 April 58	p 29 July 59	
2	0	2 Charles Henry Webster	2 May 58	p 16 Sept. 59	
2	0	1 Charles Enys	3 May 58	p 28 Oct. 59	
2	0	1 James Smyth........	2 July 58	p 13 Dec. 59	33 Lieut. Wright served with the 56th Regt. at the siege and fall of Sebastopol from 25th Aug. 1855 (Medal and Clasp).
		ENSIGNS.			
2	0	1 George Edward Bolger	1 May 58		
2	0	1 George R. Gibbs......	25 June 58		34 Lieut. Mansel served in the operations in Oude in 1858, and was present at the affairs of Mohan, Meangunge, also at Churda and fort of Musjeedia (Medal).
2	0	1 Charles A. Vernon....	26 June 58		
2	0	1 Cliff. Gabourel Gibaut	3 July 58		
2	0	1 Ed. Alex. Hawtrey Parks	6 Aug. 58		35 Lieut. Unwin served in the Indian campaign of 1857-58, including the actions of Chanda, Umeerpore, and Sultanpore, siege and capture of Lucknow, subsequent operations in Oude and affairs of Churda and fort of Musjeedia (Medal and Clasp).
2	0	2 Geo. Frederic Harris..	31 Dec. 58		
1	0	1 George Duncan Wahab	28 Jan. 59		
1	0	1 Charles Simeon Elliott	18 Mar. 59		
1	0	1 Thomas Alfred Davies	p 19 Mar. 59		
1	0	1 Charles Edward Hussey	p 20 Mar. 59		36 Paymaster Gibbs served in the Indian campaign in 1858, including the capture of Lucknow, and affairs of Churda and fort of Musjeedia (Medal and Clasp).
1	0	1 Baldwin K. Whiteford	24 June 59		
1	0	2 Champion Jones......	25 June 59		
1	0	1 Zachary Macaulay....	23 Aug. 59		37 Qr.Master Cole served the Eastern campaign of 1854-55, including the battles of Alma (wounded), Balaklava, and Inkerman, siege and fall of Sebastopol (Medal and four Clasps).
1	0	2 Robert Nicholas Bird..	30 Aug. 59		

11	0	*Paymasters.*—1 John Matthews Gibbs,[36] 19 Oct. 49.	
2	0	2 Augustus Bolle de Lasalle, 18 May 58.	
6	0	*Adjutants.*—2 *Lieut.* John Armstrong,[31] 21 May 58.	
5	0	1 *Lieut.* Owen Tudor Burne,[30] 10 Sept. 58.	
6	0	*Instructors of Musketry.*—1 *Captain* John James S. O'Neill, 4 Dec. 57.	
5	0	2 *Lieut.* C. K. Chatfield, 2 Aug. 58.	
2	0	*Quarter-Masters.*—2 John Cole,[37] 26 March 58.	
4	0	1 William Smith,[38] 18 Jan. 56.	
18	0	*Surgeons.*—1 Edward Howard,[39] 24 Feb. 54; *Assist.-Surg.* 29 April 42.	
18	0	2 Thomas Guy, M.D. 1 July 53; *Assist.Surg.* 28 Jan. 42.	
5	0	*Assistant-Surgeons.*—1 Henry Kelsall,[40] 8 Sept. 55.	
6	0	1 Francis John Shortt, 6 Aug. 55.	
4	0	1 John Munday,[41] 4 Feb. 56.	
5	0	2 John Henry Gouldsbury Meares, 16 May 55.	
1	0	2 Hammerton Crump, M.D. 1 March 59.	

Facings Yellow.—*Agents*, Messrs. Cox and Co.

[*Returned from the Crimea*, 19 *July* 56. *Embarked for India*, 6 *Aug.* 57. *Depot, Chatham.*]

1 Lt.Col. Radcliffe served the Eastern campaign of 1854-55 with the 20th Regt., including the battles of Alma (as Aide-de-Camp to acting Brigadier-General Horn), Balaklava, and Inkerman, siege of Sebastopol, and affair of the 18th June (Medal and Clasps, Brevet Major, Sardinian Medal, and 5th Class of the Medjidie). Served in the Indian campaign of 1857-58 and was present at the actions of Chanda, Ameerapore, and Sultanpore, and at the siege and capture of Lucknow—wounded, and twice mentioned in despatches.

2 Lt.Col. Cormick was present with the 40th Regt. in the action of Maharajpore, 29th Dec. 1843 (Medal). Served with the 18th Royal Irish the Burmah campaign of 1852-53, including the capture of Martaban, Rangoon, and Prome (Medal). Served also at the siege of Sebastopol from Dec. 1854, and was wounded 18th June 1855 (Medal and Clasp, Brevet Major, and 5th Class of the Medjidie).

3 Lt.Col. Bennett served the Eastern campaign of 1854 with the 20th Regt., including the battles of Alma, Balaklava, and Inkerman (severely wounded), and siege of Sebastopol (Medal and Clasps, and 5th Class of the Medjidie). Served in the Indian campaign of 1857-58 and was present at the actions of Chanda, Umeerpore, and Sultanpore (as Orderly Officer to Brigadier Evelegh), siege and capture of Lucknow, subsequent operations in Oude and affairs of Churda and fort of Musjeedia (mentioned in despatches, Brevet of Major, Medal and Clasp).

4 Colonel Holditch served as Aide-de-Camp to Sir Harry Smith throughout the campaign on the Sutlej (Medal and Clasps), and was present in the battles of Moodkee, Ferozeshah (wounded), Buddiwal, Aliwal, and Sobraon (severely wounded). He served also as Aide-de-Camp to Sir Harry in the action with and defeat of the Rebel Boers at Boem Plaats (South Africa) 29 Aug. 1848; and in the Kaffir campaigns from 1850 to 1852 (Medal). He served with the 80th Regiment in the Burmese war of 1853 (Medal), and was with the expedition under Sir John Cheape against the robber chief Myattoon, and succeeded to the command of the right wing at the assault and capture of his stronghold on the 19th March (appointed a *CB.*).

5 Lt.Colonel Campbell served with the 77th Regt. in the Peninsula from Aug. 1812 to the end of that war in 1814, and was present at the blockade of Bayonne and repulse of the sortie. Served with the 30th Regt. at the siege of Sebastopol in 1855, and was wounded at the assault on the Redan on the 8th Sept. (Medal and Clasp, and 5th Class of the Medjidie).

6 Major Dickins served at the siege and fall of Sebastopol from 26th Jan. 1855; also present at the capture of Kinbourn (Medal and Clasp, and 5th Class of the Medjidie). Served in the Indian campaign of 1857-58 and was present at the actions of Chanda, Umeerpore, and Sultanpore, siege and capture of Lucknow, subsequent operations in Oude, and affair of Meangunge (Brevet of Major, Medal and Clasp).

7 Major Warren served at the siege and fall of Sebastopol from 26th Jan. 1855; also present at the capture of Kinbourn (Medal and Clasp). Served in the Indian campaign of 1857-58, including the actions of Chanda, Umeerpore, and Sultanpore, siege and capture of Lucknow (wounded), subsequent operations in Oude and affairs of Mohan and Meangunge, also at Churda, and fort of Musjeedia (Medal and Clasp).

8 Major Lyons served with the 20th Regt. in the Indian campaign of 1857-58, and commanded the selected marksmen of the Regt. in the actions of Chanda, Umeerpore, Sultanpore, and fort of Dhowraha whence he assisted in bringing away two guns under a heavy fire; was present at the siege and capture of Lucknow, the subsequent operations in Oude and affair of Mohan, and commanded four Companies at Morar Mow and Beerah, fort of Simree and action of Buxar Ghat; served as Brigade Major to the 2nd Brigade Oude force and was present at the capture of fort Oomreah (three times mentioned in despatches, Medal and Clasp, and Brevet Major).

† H

20th (The East Devonshire) Regt. of Foot.

9 Captain Dashwood served in the Indian campaign of 1857-58, including the actions of Chanda, Umeerpore, and Sultanpore, siege and capture of Lucknow, subsequent operations in Oude, affairs of Buxarghat, Churda, and fort of Musjeedia (Medal and Clasp).

11 Captain Meares served at the siege and fall of Sebastopol from 15 July 1855 (Medal and Clasp); also present at the capture of Kinbourn.

12 Captain Francis served in the Indian campaign of 1857-58, including the actions of Chanda, Umeerpore, and Sultanpore, siege and capture of Lucknow (Medal and Clasp).

13 Captain Edridge served at the siege of Sebastopol and capture of Kinbourn (Medal and Clasp). Also in the Indian campaign from August 1858, including the trans-Gogra operations under Lord Clyde (Medal).

14 Captain Lewis served with the Grenadier Company of the 94th in the action with and destruction of a desperate band of insurgent fanatics at Teermanam Coonettos in Malabar.

16 Captain Vaughan served throughout the Eastern campaign of 1854-55, including the battles of Alma and Inkerman, siege and fall of Sebastopol and affair of the 18th June; also present at the capture of Kinbourn (Medal and Clasps, Sardinian Medal, and 5th Class of the Medjidie). Served in the Indian campaign of 1857-58, including the actions of Chanda, Umeerpore, and Sultanpore, siege and capture of Lucknow, subsequent operations in Oude and affairs of Churda, fort of Musjeedia, and Bankee—commanded a detachment (Medal and Clasp).

17 Captain O'Neill served at the siege and fall of Sebastopol from 30th May 1855, and was wounded at the affair of the 18th June; also present at the capture of Kinbourn (Medal and Clasp). Served in the Indian campaign of 1857-58, including the actions of Chanda, Umeerpore, and Sultanpore, siege and capture of Lucknow, subsequent operations in Oude and affairs of Meangunge, Beerah (thanked in despatch), Buxar Ghat (as Brigade Major), Churda, and fort of Musjeedia (Medal and Clasp).

19 Captain Adams served with the 7th Dr. Gds. in the Kaffir war in 1847 (Medal).

21 Captain Geraghty served in the Eastern campaign of 1854-55, including the battles of Alma, Balaklava, and Inkerman, and siege of Sebastopol (Medal and four Clasps). Served in the Indian campaign of 1857-58 as Adjutant of the 20th Regt. and was present at the actions of Chanda, Umeerpore, and Sultanpore, and at the siege and capture of Lucknow (Medal and Clasp).

22 Captain Gordon served in the Indian campaign of 1857-58, and was present with the selected marksmen of the Regt. at the actions of Chanda, Umeerpore, and Sultanpore, fort of Dhowraha, siege and capture of Lucknow, subsequent operations in Oude and affair of Meangunge, also at Churda and fort of Musjeedia (Medal and Clasp).

23 Captain Patrickson served at the siege of Sebastopol and capture of Kinbourn (Medal and Clasp). Served in the Indian campaign of 1857-58, including the actions of Chanda, Umeerpore, and Sultanpore, siege and capture of Lucknow, subsequent operations in Oude and affairs of Meangunge, Simree, Beerah, Buxar Ghat, Churda, fort of Musjeedia, and Bankee (Medal and Clasp).

24 Lieut. Holmes served at the siege and fall of Sebastopol from 1st June 1855, and was wounded at the affair of the 18th June; also present at the capture of Kinbourn. Served in the Indian campaign of 1857-58, including the actions of Chanda, Umeerpore, and Sultanpore, siege and capture of Lucknow, subsequent operations in Oude and affairs of Mohan, Meangunge, and Morar Mow (as Orderly Officer to Brigadier Evelegh), fort of Simree, Beerah, Buxar Ghat, Churda, fort of Musjeedia, and Bankee (Medal and Clasp).

25 Captain Nunn served at the siege and fall of Sebastopol from 15th July 1855; also at the capture of Kinbourn (Medal and Clasp). Served in the Indian campaign of 1857-58, including the actions of Chanda, Umeerpore, and Sultanpore, siege and capture of Lucknow, subsequent operations in Oude and affairs of Mohan, Hussengunge, Meangunge (as Orderly Officer to Brigadier Evelegh), Churda, fort of Musjeedia, and Bankee (Medal and Clasp).

26 Lieut. Hon. A. Vereker served at the siege and fall of Sebastopol from 3rd Sept. 1855, and also at the capture of Kinbourn (Medal and Clasp). Served in the Indian campaign of 1857-58 with the selected marksmen of the Regt. in the actions of Chanda, Umeerpore, Sultanpore, fort of Dhowraha, siege and capture of Lucknow, subsequent operations in Oude and affairs of Churda, fort of Musjeedia, and Bankee—as Adjutant to a detachment (Medal and Clasp).

27 Captain Duffin served in the Indian campaign of 1857-58, including the actions of Chanda, Umeerpore, and Sultanpore, siege and capture of Lucknow, subsequent operations in Oude and affairs of Morar Mow, fort of Simree, Beerah, and Buxar Ghat (Medal and Clasp).

28 Captain Gethin served in the Indian campaign of 1857-58, including the actions of Chanda, Umeerpore, and Sultanpore, siege and capture of Lucknow, subsequent operations in Oude and affairs of Meangunge, Churda, and fort of Musjeedia (Medal and Clasp).

29 Lieut. Fahie served in the Indian campaign of 1857-58, including the actions of Chanda, Umeerpore, and Sultanpore, siege and capture of Lucknow, subsequent operations in Oude, and affairs of Churda and fort of Musjeedia (Medal and Clasp).

30 Lieut. Burne served in the Indian campaign of 1857-58 on the Staff of Brigadier Evelegh, and was present at the actions of Chanda, Umeerpore, and Sultanpore, siege and capture of Lucknow, subsequent operations and affairs of Mohan, Hussengunge, Meangunge, Morar Mow, and fort of Simree; was also present as Adjutant of the Regt. at the affairs of Churda and fort of Musjeedia (several times mentioned in despatches, Medal and Clasp).

31 Lieut. Armstrong served with the 40th Regt. throughout the operations in Candahar, Affghanistan, in 1841-42 (Medal). Also in the battle of Maharajpore (Medal).

32 Lieut. Horn served in the operations in Oude during Dec. 1858, and was present at the affairs of Churda and fort of Musjeedia (Medal).

38 Qr.Master Smith served the Sutlej campaign in 1845, and was severely wounded at the battle of Ferozeshah (Medal); served also the Punjaub campaign of 1848-49, including the passage of the Chenab nd battles of Chillianwallah and Goojerat (Medal and two Clasps).

39 Surgeon Howard served the Eastern campaign of 1854-55, including the battles of Alma and Inkerman, siege of Sebastopol, and assault of the 8th Sept. (Medal and Clasps, and 5th Class of the Medjidie). Served in the Indian campaign of 1857-58, including the actions of Chanda, Umeerpore, and Sultanpore, siege and capture of Lucknow (Medal and Clasp).

40 Assist.Surgeon Kelsall served in the Indian campaign of 1857-58, including the actions of Chanda, Umeerpore, and Sultanpore, siege and capture of Lucknow, subsequent operations in Oude and affairs of Meangunge, Morar Mow, fort of Simree, Beerah, and Buxar Ghat, also Churda and fort of Musjeedia, and Bankee (Medal and Clasp).

41 Assist.Surgeon Munday served in the Indian campaign of 1857-58, including the actions of Chanda, Umeerpore, and Sultanpore, siege and capture of Lucknow, subsequent operations in Oude and affairs of Hussengunge and Meangunge (Medal and Clasp).

1st Batt. Malta.
2nd Batt. Aldershot. **21st Regt. of Foot (Royal North British Fusiliers).** 220

The Thistle within the Circle of St. Andrew, "*Nemo me impune lacessit*," The King's Cypher and Crown "BLADENSBURG" "ALMA" "INKERMAN" "SEVASTOPOL."

Years' Serv.						
53		Colonel.—**田 田田** Sir De Lacy Evans,[1] GCB. *Ens.* 1 Feb. 07; *Lt.* 1 Dec. 08; *Capt.* 12 Jan. 15; *Maj.* 11 May 15; *Lt.-Col.* 18 June 15; *Col.* 10 Jan. 37; *Maj.-Gen.* 9 Nov. 46; *Lt.-Gen.* 20 June 54; *Col.* 21st Fusiliers, 29 Aug. 53.				
Full Pay.	Half Pay.	*Lt.Colonels.*—1 John Ramsay Stuart,[2] CB, *2nd Lt.* P 20 Jan. 32; *Lt.* 9 Aug.				
28	0	35; *Capt.* P10 Jan. 40; *Maj.* P 9 Feb. 49; *Lt.-Col.* 15 Nov. 54; *Col.* 15 Feb. 58.				
23	0	2 Edward W. D. Lowe,[3] CB., *Ens.* 20 May 37; *Lt.* P 12 Mar. 41; *Capt.* P 23 May 45; *Major*, 1 July 57; *Bt.Lt.Col.* 24 Mar. 58; *Lt.Col.* 26 Sept. 58.				
		Majors.—1 John Thos. Dalyell,[4] *2nd Lieut.* 14 May 47; *Lieut.* P 21 June 50;				
13	0	*Capt.* P 23 Apr. 52; *Brev.-Major*, 12 Dec. 54; *Major*, 3 Aug. 55.				
12	6/12	2 Geo. Neeld Boldero,[5] *2nd Lieut.* 8 Oct. 47; *Lieut.* 3 April 49; *Capt.* P 7 May 52; *Brev.-Major*, 12 Dec. 54; *Major*, 18 Sept. 58.				
20	4 5/12	1 Humphrey Gray,[6] *Ens.* 25 Mar. 36; *Lieut.* 1 July 38; *Capt.* 15 Feb. 50; *Brev.-Major*, 6 June 56; *Major*, 26 March 58.				
10	0	2 Edwin A. Tucker Steward,[7] *Ens.* P 15 Mar. 50; *Lt.* P 2 April 52; *Capt.* 15 Nov. 54; *Brev.-Major*, 6 June 56; *Major*, P 14 May 58.				

		CAPTAINS.	ENSIGN.	LIEUT.	CAPTAIN.	BREV.-MAJ.
13	0	1 Wm. Pole Collingwood[8]	P 23 Mar. 47	P 15 Nov. 50	P 28 July 54	26 Dec. 56
12	4	1 Saml. Wm. Hy. Hawker[9]	19 Jan. 44	21 Apr. 46	P 14 Apr. 48	25 Sept. 59
10	0	2 John Aldridge[10]	P 12 April 50	P 23 Apr. 52	29 Dec. 54	6 June 56
9	0	1 Crofton Peddie	P 17 Oct. 51	23 Nov. 52	29 Dec. 54	
15	0	1 Fre. R. Eyre Burnside[11]	P 27 June 45	19 Nov. 47	12 Jan. 55	
8	0	2 Alfred Templeman[12]	P 26 Mar. 52	P 4 Mar. 53	2 Feb. 55	
8	0	1 John Charles Sheffield[13]	P 14 May 52	P 18 Mar. 53	P 2 Feb. 55	
8	0	2 Wm. Hy. Carleton,[14] *s*.	P 11 June 52	P 22 April 53	11 May 55	
8	1/12	1 Roger Killeen[15]	20 Feb. 52	6 June 54	3 Aug. 55	
7	1/12	1 John George Image[16]	23 Nov. 52	P 28 July 54	P 31 Aug. 55	
8	0	1 Shadwell Hy. Clerke[17]	3 Dec. 52	6 Nov. 54	26 Mar. 58	
17	0	1 Charles Hill Fresson	9 June 43	7 Jan. 48	5 Mar. 58	
14	0	2 Francis George King	14 Apr. 46	30 Nov. 49	26 Mar. 58	
6	0	1 Thomas Bruce[18]	P 14 July 54	12 Jan. 55	P 14 May 58	
12	0	2 Geo. Fred. Gildea	P 14 Apr. 48	P 6 Aug. 52	10 Sept. 58	
12	0	2 Alexander Walker[19]	1 Aug. 48	6 June 54	10 Sept. 58	
8	0	2 Geo. Harmer Pering[20]	P 12 Mar. 52	11 Aug. 54	27 Apr. 58	
6	0	2 S. G. Bower St. Clair[21]	P 28 July 54	12 Jan. 55	P 28 Jan. 59	
6	0	1 William Cairnes	6 June 54	8 Dec. 54	29 Jan. 59	
6	0	1 Tho. Burchell Hollway[22]	10 Aug. 54	12 Jan. 55	P 29 Apr. 59	
7	0	2 Augustus Breedon[23]	P 19 Mar. 53	29 Dec. 54	13 Oct. 58	
8	0	1 Alfred Holt[25]	P 12 Oct. 52	9 Feb. 55	P 30 Aug. 59	
15	0	2 John Henderson[25]	P 18 April 45	2 Dec. 46	P 18 Mar. 53	
6	0	2 Rob. Beatty Henderson	P 20 Feb. 54	13 Feb. 55	P 13 Dec. 59	
		LIEUTENANTS.				
9	2	2 J.G. M'Donald Tulloch[24]	26 Dec. 51	12 Jan. 55		
7	0	1 Rich. W. Cha. Winsloe[26]	P 11 June 53	P 6 Oct. 54		
6	0	1 Isaac Tristram Coffin[26]	22 Dec. 54	23 Mar. 55		
5	0	2 Thomas Hennis Green[26]	P 11 Jan. 55	1 May 55		
5	0	1 Arth. Grey Hazlerigg[29]	P 16 Jan. 55	11 May 55		
5	0	1 Sept. Sherson Connell	24 May 55	P 31 Aug. 55		
5	0	1 Tho. H. Sherwood	15 June 55	P 9 Oct. 55		
5	0	1 Pet. Herbert Delamere[30]	2 Mar. 55	5 Dec. 55		
5	0	1 Robert Cook, *Adj*.	P 4 Apr. 55	P 6 Feb. 57		
5	0	1 Francis Novil Reade	P 29 Mar. 55	31 Oct. 57		
6	0	2 Hy. Wellingt. Hartford	24 Mar. 55	16 Mar. 55		
5	0	1 William Henry Ker	P 30 Mar. 55	30 Mar. 58		
5	0	1 George Will. Furlong[31]	5 Apr. 55	15 June 58		
5	0	2 Edw. Thos. Bainbridge	6 Apr. 55	15 June 58		
5	0	1 Francis Wm. Hamilton	20 July 55	15 June 58		
5	0	2 Jas. Hy. Patrickson,[32] *Assist.-Surg.* 14 July 54	3 Aug. 55	15 June 58		
5	0	2 Edw. Wood Pearman	P 10 Aug. 55	15 June 58		
5	0	2 Robert Bruce Gaskell	16 Nov. 55	15 June 58		
2	0	1 George Albert Grant	P 26 Jan. 58	P 16 July 58		
2	0	1 Edw. E. Digby Boycott	P 2 Feb. 58	P 16 July 58		
3	0	2 Ernest Lewis	P 2 July 57	23 July 58		
5	0	2 Jas. A. Ogilvy Carnegy	3 Aug. 55	10 Sept. 58		
5	0	1 George O'Connell	14 Dec. 55	10 Sept. 58		
5	0	2 George Gilmour	3 July 55	1 Oct. 58		
2	0	2 Alfred William Channer	16 Mar. 58	P 28 Jan. 59		
2	0	1 Fred. George Jackson	30 Mar. 58	P 6 May 59		
2	0	1 Edward Bussell	1 Apr. 58	P 30 Aug. 59		
2	0	2 James Browne	31 Mar. 58	P 13 Dec. 59		
5	0	2 Henry Alex. Donald[37]	P 23 Nov. 55	15 Jan. 57		

13 Captain Sheffield served the Eastern campaign of 1854-55, including the battles of Alma and Inkerman, siege and fall of Sebastopol (Medal and three Clasps, and 5th Class of the Medjidie). 14 Captain Carleton served the Eastern campaign of 1854-55, including the battles of Alma, Balaklava, and Inkerman, siege and fall of Sebastopol, attack of the Redan on 18th June, and expedition to Kinbourn (Medal and four Clasps, and Knight of the Legion of Honor). 15 Captain Killeen served the Eastern campaign of 1854-55, including the battles of Alma, Balaklava, and Inkerman, siege and fall of Sebastopol, attack on the Redan on the 18th June, and capture of Kinbourn; at Inkerman he commanded a Company and under a heavy fire rescued the Regimental Colour and was severely wounded on the occasion, but did not quit the field (Medal and four Clasps, and Knight of the Legion of Honor). 25 Captain John Henderson was present at the defeat of the insurgents at Matale on the 29th July, during the suppression of the rebellion in the Kandian provinces in Ceylon in 1848, and afterwards commanded a detachment in those provinces during the whole time martial law was in force.

† H 2

221 21st Regt. of Foot (*Royal North British Fusiliers*).

Years' Serv. Full Pay.	Years' Serv. Half Pay.	ENSIGNS.	ENSIGN.	
2	0	2 William Thorburn	16 Apr. 58	
2	0	2 Edward Fred. Pole ..	23 Apr. 58	
2	0	2 John Blaksley	7 May 58	19 Captain Walker served as Adjutant with a wing of the 45th Regt. in the Kaffir war of 1850-53 (Medal), and was mentioned by the Commander in Chief there for gallant conduct in repulsing and pursuing a large body of the enemy at Fort Cox on the 26th Sept. 1851 ; he was also three times noticed in despatches.
2	0	2 William C. Ralston ..	25 June 58	
2	0	1 William R. MacPherson	26 June 58	
2	0	1 Howard Plestow Cox..	27 June 58	
1	0	1 Frederick Packman ..	2 July 58	
2	0	1 John Dudley E. Crosse	p 30 July 58	
2	0	1 Walter Nowell Carey ..	p 6 Aug. 58	
2	0	2 James Ferguson, *Adj*..	5 Oct. 58	
1	0	1 Jno. Popham Mainwaring	11 Jan. 59	
2	0	2 Francis Meik Salmond.	31 Dec. 58	
1	0	1 Michael Thunder	28 Jan. 59	
2	0	2 Clement John Sneyd ..	26 Oct. 58	
1	0	1 John Hornby Conor ..	11 Mar. 59	
1	0	2 Edward Walker	p 31 May 59	
1	0	2 Francis Farquharson ..	p 1 June 59	
1	0	1 John Talbot Coke	24 June 59	

29	0	*Paymasters.*—2 George Thompson, 1 Oct. 58 ; *Q.M.* 13 Sept. 31.
1	0	1 Thomas Joseph Atkinson, 25 Jan. 59.
2	0	*Adjutants.*—2 *Ensign* James Ferguson, 4 Feb. 59.
5	0	1 *Lieut*. Robert Cooke, 23 Sept. 59.
2	0	*Instructors of Musketry.*—2 *Ensign* John Blaksley, 9 Feb. 59.
2	0	1 *Lieut.* Edw. Essex Digby Boycott, 6 May 59.
5	0	*Quarter-Masters.*—1 J. Grahame,[33] 17 Aug. 55.
3	1	2 Francis Foley,[36] 12 Feb. 56.
17	0	*Surgeons.*—1 David Reid Mackinnon,[33] 28 Mar. 54 ; *Assist.Surg*. 12 Dec. 43.
8	0	2 Thomas Llewellyn Nash, M.D. 18 Jan. 59 ; *Assist.Surg*. 5 Mar. 52.
8	0	*Assistant-Surgeons.*—1 Arthur Jackson Greer,[34] 23 July 52.
6	0	1 John Henry West,[35] M.D. 24 March 54.
2	0	2 Thomas Walsh, 25 May 58.
1	0	2 Edwin Granville Ley, M.D. 1 March 59.

Facings Blue.—*Agents*, Messrs. Cox & Co.
[1st Batt. *Foreign Service*, 16 *Aug*. 54. *Depot, Birr*.]

1 Sir De Lacy Evans served in India in 1807, 8, 9, and 10. Portugal, Spain, and France in 1812, 13, and 14. America, part of 1814-15. Belgium and France in 1815, 16, 17, and 18. In Spain in 1835, 36, and 37. Present during the operations against Ameer Khan and the Pindarries, capture of the Mauritius, part of the retreat from Burgos, action on the Hormaza (wounded), battle of Vittoria, investment of Pampeluna, battle of the Pyrenees, investment of Bayonne (horse shot), actions of Vic Bigorre and Tarbes battle of Toulouse (horse shot) battle of Bladensburg (horse shot), capture of Washington, attack on Baltimore, operations before New Orleans (boarding and capture of American Flotilla,)—action 25th Dec. wounded severely—unsuccessful assault, Jan. (wounded severely), battle of Quatre Bras, retreat of 17th of June, Waterloo (horse shot and one sabred), investment and capitulation of Paris. Continued on Staff of Allied Army of Occupation in France. Accepted under an allied Power (1835) command of an auxiliary British and Spanish corps of army by sanction and desire of the English Government, by order of the King in Council. Acted, while so employed, in conjunction with the British forces (under Lord J. Hay), and through mediation of British authorities:—raising investments of San Sebastian and Bilboa, action of Arinbau, capture of port and castle of Passages. Defeated the enemy in general actions on the 5th of May, 6th of June, 1st of October (wounded) 1836; also 10th and 15th of March 1837. Attacked near Hernani, 10th March, by the *élite* of the Carlist army, 16,000 strong (about double the allied force), and obliged to retreat about one mile, but with a less loss in killed and wounded (600) than that of the enemy. Resumed the offensive the following month—capture of Hernani by escalade, 14th May—of Oyarzun, 16th May—of Yrun, by storm 17th May—of Fontarabia by capitulation, 18th May. Those, and other minor affairs, were for the most part, severely contested, and cost (including those of the enemy) above ten thousand killed and wounded. Excepting occasionally two or three stragglers, generally without arms, the Legion never lost (under his command) prisoners, artillery, or equipage, though utterly contrary statements repeatedly appeared at the time—while he took from the enemy 100 officers, 1000 men, thirty pieces of cannon, several entrenched positions, fortified towns and posts, with an extensive and most important strategical tract of the insurgent territory, including their main line of retreat, communication and supply. Thenceforth "The frontier was effectually closed against the entrance of resources to the Carlists, except by the small mountain passes, which are only accessible to foot passengers, or mules lightly laden"—(British Commissioners' Dispatch, Parliamentary Paper)—and thus did this auxiliary corps decisively contribute to the successful termination of the war. He holds the rank of Lieut.-General in the national army of Spain, by licence of a British royal warrant ; also, honoured by Her Majesty for these services with the Cross of Commander of the Bath, and by the government of Spain with the Grand Crosses of St. Ferdinand and Charles III. Received his Company, Majority, and Lieut.-Colonelcy in the British service for conduct against the enemy. Sir De Lacy has received the War Medal with three Clasps for Vittoria, Pyrenees, and Toulouse. Commanded the 2nd Division in the Eastern campaign of 1854, including the battles of the Alma (wounded), Balaklava, and Inkerman, and siege of Sebastopol, comprising the repulse of the powerful sortie on the 26th Oct. 1854 (Medal and Clasps, *G CB*., Grand Officer of the Legion of Honor, and 1st Class of the Medjidie).

2 Colonel Stuart served the Eastern campaign of 1854 and latter part of 1855, including the battles of Alma, Balaklava, and Inkerman, siege and fall of Sebastopol (Medal and Clasps, and 5th Class of the Medjidie).

21st Regt. of Foot (Royal North British Fusiliers).

3 Lt.Colonel Lowe served with the 32nd Regt. at the first and second siege operations before Mooltan, including the attack on the enemy's position in front of the advanced trenches on 12th Sept. 1848, on which occasion he succeeded to the command of the companies of the 32nd Regt. that were engaged; he was also present at the action of Soorjkoond, storm and capture of the city and surrender of the fortress of Mooltan, surrender of the fort and garrison of Cheniote, and battle of Goojerat (Medal and Clasps). Served throughout the suppression of the Indian Mutiny of 1857-59; commanded the 32d during the defence of the Residency of Lucknow till wounded on 26th September; commanded a sortie of 150 men of the Regt. when 7 guns were captured and the enemy's position carried; commanded a party of the Regt. sent out to assist the rear guard of Havelock's force in protecting their heavy guns and ammunition on their coming into Lucknow (thanked in despatch); was slightly wounded on 20th Aug., and severely wounded on 26th Sept. 1857 (mentioned in the despatches of Sir J. Inglis and the Governor General, Brevet of Lt.Colonel, and CB.). Commanded the 32d at the defeat of the Gwalior Rebels at Cawnpore on 6th Dec.; was with it in the field Oude from July 1858 to Jan. 1859 (in command from 1 Dec. 1858), including the reduction of fort Tyrhool. Commanded an advanced post of all arms nearest to the fort of Amethee until Lord Clyde advanced upon it (Medal and Clasp).

4 Major Dalyell served the Eastern campaign of 1854 and the early part of 1855, including the battles of Alma, Balaklava, and Inkerman, and siege of Sebastopol (Medal and four Clasps, Brevet Major, and 5th Class of the Medjidie).

5 Major Boldero served with the 21st Fusiliers in the Eastern campaign of 1854 and up to 27th April 1855, including the battles of Alma and Inkerman (severely wounded in left arm), and siege of Sebastopol (Medal and three Clasps, Brevet Major, Sardinian Medal, and 5th Class of the Medjidie).

6 Major Gray was present with the 39th Regt. in the battle of Maharajpore (Medal), and was severely wounded. Served with the 21st Fusiliers the latter part of the Crimean campaign of 1855, including the siege and fall of Sebastopol; commanded the Regiment during the expedition to Kinbourn (Medal and Clasp, and Brevet Major).

7 Major Steward served the Eastern campaign of 1854-55, including the battles of Alma, Balaklava, and Inkerman, siege and fall of Sebastopol, attack on the Redan on the 18th June, and the expedition to Kinbourn (Medal and four Clasps, and Brevet Major).

8 Major Collingwood served with the 37th Regt. in the Rebellion of 1848 in Ceylon. Served with the 21st Fusiliers during 1855 at the siege and fall of Sebastopol, and on the expedition to Kinbourn (Medal and Clasp); from Nov. 1855 to Nov. 1856 he commanded a Battalion of the Land Transport Corps. Commanded the troops on board the *Spartan* steamer when wrecked on the Dog Rocks, Coast of Africa, on 5th July 1856, on returning from the Crimea, and for his services throughout this trying occasion, he received the Brevet rank of Major.

9 Major Hawker served during 1855 at the siege and fall of Sebastopol (wounded in the trenches) and attack on the Redan on the 18th June; also the expedition to Kinbourn (Medal and Clasp, and 5th Class of the Medjidie).

10 Major Aldridge served the Eastern campaign of 1854-55, including the battle of Alma, siege and fall of Sebastopol, and attack on the Redan on the 18th June; also the expedition to Kinbourn (Medal and Clasps, and Brevet Major).

11 Captain Burnside served in the Punjaub campaign of 1848-9, and was present at the battle of Goojerat, and with the field force in pursuit of the enemy to the Khyber Pass in March 1849 (Medal and Clasp); expedition into the Euzofzle country; in action with the enemy 11th and 14th Dec. 1849; present at the capture and destruction of the insurgent villages of Saggow, Pullee, Zoormundie, and Sheerkanee. Expedition to Kohat against the Affredie Tribe, 10th, 11th, and 13th Feb. 1850.

12 Captain Templeman served the Eastern campaign of 1854-55, including the battles of Alma, Balaklava, and Inkerman (wounded in the hand), siege and fall of Sebastopol, and attack on the Redan on the 18th June; also the expedition to Kinbourn (Medal and four Clasps, and Knight of the Legion of Honor).

16 Captain Inuge served the Eastern campaign of 1854 and early part of 1855, including the battles of Alma and Inkerman, siege of Sebastopol, and attack on the Redan on the 18th June (severely wounded), where he commanded the party carrying the wool-bags to fill the ditch (Medal and three Clasps, and Knight of the Legion of Honor).

17 Captain Clerke served the Eastern campaign of 1854-55, including the battles of Alma and Inkerman, siege and fall of Sebastopol, attack on the Redan on the 18th June, where he commanded the scaling-ladder party, and was mentioned in Dispatches; served as Adjutant at the fall of Sebastopol and expedition to Kinbourn (Medal and Clasps, and Sardinian Medal).

18 Captain Bruce served during the latter part of 1855 at the siege and fall of Sebastopol, and attack on the Redan on the 18th June; also the expedition to Kinbourn (Medal and Clasp).

20 Captain Pering served in the 89th Regt. at the Siege and Fall of Sebastopol from 15th Dec. 1854, and attacks of the 18th June and 8th Sept. (Medal and Clasp, and 5th Class of the Medjidie).

21 Captain St. Clair served the Eastern campaign of 1854-55, including the battle of Alma (shot through the arm) and siege of Sebastopol (Medal and Clasps): at Alma he acted as Interpreter to the army, after which he served as Aide-de-Camp to General Eyre. Has received the 5th Class of the Medjidie.

22 Captain Hollway served the early part of 1855 at the siege and fall of Sebastopol, and attack on the Redan on the 18th June (Medal and Clasp).

23 Captain Breedon served with the 89th Regt. at the siege of Sebastopol from 29th June to 10th July 1855 (Medal and Clasp).

24 Lt. Tulloch served during the latter part of 1855 at the siege and fall of Sebastopol (Medal and Clasp).

26 Captain Holt, Lieuts. Winsloe, Coffin, and Green, served the latter part of 1855 at the siege and fall of Sebastopol, and expedition to Kinbourn (Medal and Clasp).

29 Lieut. Hazlerigg served during the latter part of 1855 at the siege and fall of Sebastopol (Medal and Clasp).

30 Lieut. Delamere served the latter part of the campaign of 1855, including the siege and fall of Sebastopol, and the expedition to Kinbourn (Medal and Clasp).

31 Lt. Furlong served in the Eastern campaign of 1854-55 at the siege of Sebastopol (Medal and Clasp).

32 Lieut. Patrickson served the Eastern campaign of 1854-55, including the battles of Alma and Balaklava, siege and fall of Sebastopol, and expedition to Kinbourn (Medal and three Clasps).

33 Quarter-Master Grahame and Surgeon Mackinnon served the Eastern campaign of 1854-55, including the battles of Alma, Balaklava, and Inkerman, siege and fall of Sebastopol, and expedition to Kinbourn (Medal and four Clasps). Surgeon Mackinnon is a Knight of the Legion of Honor, and has the 5th Class of the Medjidie.

34 Assist.-Surgeon Greer served the Eastern campaign of 1854 and early part of 1855, including the Battles of Alma, Balaklava, and Inkerman, siege of Sebastopol, and attack on the Redan on the 18th June—mentioned in Dispatches (Medal and four Clasps, and 5th Class of the Medjidie).

35 Assist.-Surgeon West served the Eastern campaign of 1854-55, including the battles of Alma and Inkerman, siege and fall of Sebastopol, and expedition to Kinbourn (Medal and three Clasps).

36 Qr.Master Foley served with the 31st Regt. in the Sutlej campaign of 1845-46, including the battles of Moodkee, Ferozeshah, Buddiwal, Aliwal, and Sobraon—severely wounded (Medal and three Clasps). Served in the Crimea from 22 May 1855, including the siege and fall of Sebastopol and attacks of the 18th June and 8th September (Medal and Clasp).

37 Lieut. Donald served with the 10th Regt. in the Indian campaign of 1857-58, including the suppression of the Mutiny at Benares, capture of Atrowleea, advance to Lucknow and actions at Chanda, Unceerpore, Sultanpore, and Douraha, siege and capture of Lucknow, relief of Azimghur, and operations near Jugdespore (Medal).

22nd (The Cheshire) Regt. of Foot.

[1st Batt. Dublin.
2nd Batt. Malta.

"SCINDE" "MEEANEE" "HYDERABAD."

Years' Serv.		
60	Full Pay	Half Pay

Colonel.—1 Sir William F. P. Napier,[1] KCB. *Ens.* 14 June 00; *Lt.* 18 Apr. 01; *Capt.* 2 June 04; *Maj.* 30 May 11; *Lt.-Col.* 22 Nov. 13; *Col.* 22 July 30; *Major-Gen.* 23 Nov. 41; *Lt.-Gen.* 11 Nov. 51; *Gen.* 17 Oct. 59; *Col.* 22nd Regt. 19 Sept. 53.

22	0	**Lieut.-Colonels.**—1 Francis Pym Harding,[2] CB. *Ens.* p 16 Mar. 38; *Lieut.* p 18 Dec. 40; *Capt.* 29 Jan. 47; *Major*, p 27 Oct. 54; *Brev. Lieut.-Col.* 12 Dec. 54; *Lt.-Col.* 25 Sept. 57; *Col.* 9 Sept. 58.
22	0	2 David Anderson, *Ens.* 28 Dec. 38; *Lt.* 15 May 41; *Capt.* p 2 Feb. 49; *Maj.* p 8 July 56; *Lt.-Col.* 5 March 58.
16	0	**Majors.**—1 Sir George Abercrombie Robinson, *Bart. Ens.* 26 July 44; *Lt.* p 14 Aug. 46; *Capt.* p 11 Dec. 49; *Major*, p 25 Sept. 57.
18	0	1 John Higgin Graham, *Ens.* 6 May 42; *Lt.* p 7 Mar. 45; *Capt.* p 7 May 52; *Major*, 5 March 58.
19	0	2 Herbert Geo. Bowden,[3] *Ens.* 30 Apr. 41; *Lt.* p 30 May 43; *Capt.* 22 Feb. 53; *Major*, 5 March 58.
27	0	2 Henry Draper Nevill,[4] *Ens.* p 16 Aug. 33; *Lt.* p 20 Jan. 37; *Capt.* p 5 Dec. 43; *Bt.-Major*, 20 June 54; *Major*, 6 March 58.

		CAPTAINS.	ENSIGN.	LIEUT.	CAPTAIN.	BREV.-MAJ.
14	0	1 E. Simeon Webber Smith	21 Apr. 46	p 30 July 47	p 4 Aug. 54	
14	0	1 Thomas Young, s.	p 22 May 46	p 26 May 48	p 27 Oct. 54	
15	0	2 William Mills Molony	p 8 Aug. 45	p 1 Dec. 48	10 Jan. 55	
11	0	1 William McBean	30 Nov. 40	p 8 June 52	p 2 Nov. 55	
12	0	1 James Legh Thursby[5]	p 10 Sept. 48	p 8 June 52	p 14 Sept. 55	
15	0	1 Trevor Goff[6]	p 25 July 45	p 7 April 48	p 15 Sept. 54	
7	0	2 E. Napoleon L'Estrange	p 18 Feb. 53	23 June 55	p 22 May 57	
7	0	1 Bonar Millett Deane ..	p 12 Mar. 53	p 2 Nov. 55	p 25 Sept. 57	
7	0	1 Thomas Tyacke	p 1 July 53	p 2 Nov. 55	p 23 Oct. 57	
14	0	2 William Couch	20 Oct. 46	p 10 Nov. 47	16 Mar. 58	
12	0	1 Arthur Lloyd Monk ..	18 Aug. 48	p 11 Nov. 51	16 Mar. 58	
14	0	1 Austin Peter O'Malley	15 Aug. 46	3 April 49	17 Mar. 58	
14	0	2 George Fuller Walker[7].	14 April 46	13 Sept. 49	17 Mar. 58	
6	0	1 Hy. G. Lyon Campbell	p 27 Oct. 54	p 23 Nov. 55	p 17 Mar. 58	
14	0	2 Peter Edward Quin ..	22 May 46	21 Sept. 50	26 Mar. 58	
13	0	2 Avary Jordan Davern[9]	20 Jan. 47	3 Jan. 53	26 Mar. 58	
6	0	2 Oliv. Gaspard De Lancey[8]	24 Nov. 54	9 Mar. 55	p 26 Mar. 58	
14	0	1 Henry Albert Norris ..	p 21 July 46	p 30 Mar. 49	15 June 58	
14	0	2 Wm. Ivers Lutman ..	p 25 Sept. 46	27 Apr. 49	23 July 58	
13	0	1 John Fred. Trydell ..	23 Mar. 47	23 June 52	23 July 58	
8	0	1 Wm. Theod. Hickman[10]	p 9 July 52	6 June 54	p 5 Feb. 58	
5	0	2 Thomas Clowes Hinds	p 10 Aug. 55	p 7 Dec. 55	p 5 Aug. 59	
5	0	2 Thomas Smith Robin	7 Sept. 55	p 8 July 56	p 23 Aug. 59	
6	0	2 John William Trevor[11]	7 June 54	9 Oct. 54	20 April 58	

LIEUTENANTS.

			ENSIGN.	LIEUT.
6	0	1 Rt. C. Dobbs Ellis, *Adj.*	p 4 Aug. 54	p 2 Nov. 55
5	0	2 Henry Proctor	21 Mar. 55	9 Sept. 55
5	0	1 Stephen Winthrop....	p 9 Nov. 55	p 2 Oct. 57
5	0	1 Charles Tucker	p 23 Nov. 55	p 23 Oct. 57
5	0	2 George Turner	1 May 55	3 Nov. 55
5	0	1 Edw. Standish Baker..	5 July 55	p 27 Jan. 57
4	0	2 Charles Watkins	p 16 May 56	23 Mar. 58
4	0	2 Jas. St. Geo. Armstrong	p 8 July 56	23 Mar. 58
4	0	2 Herbert Cha. Patton, *Adj.*	9 July 56	26 Mar. 58
3	0	1 Henry Leigh	p 22 May 57	p 26 Mar. 58
5	0	2 Anthony Gardner	p 18 May 55	p 12 May 57
3	0	1 Francis Edw. Holyoake	p 11 Sept. 57	p 4 June 58
5	0	1 Thomas Gilling Gilling	p 23 Oct. 55	p 15 June 58
5	0	2 Wm. Sheffield Harding	24 Apr. 55	13 July 58
5	0	1 Alex. Daniel Gilson ..	23 Mar. 55	16 July 58
5	0	2 Henry Edw. Harrison.	31 Aug. 55	16 July 58
5	0	1 Edw. Murray Cookesley[15]	31 Aug. 55	15 Mar. 58
5	0	2 William Busfeild	19 June 55	24 Sept. 58
3	0	2 Wm. Conyngham Plunket	p 9 Oct. 57	1 Oct. 58
3	0	1 Fra. Shorard Chichester	p 31 July 57	1 Oct. 58
5	0	2 Jonas Dolmage	p 30 Mar. 55	5 Oct. 58
3	0	1 Edg. Wainwright Bishop	p 22 May 57	p 5 Mar. 58
2	0	1 Harry H. Palmer Vivian	5 Feb. 58	p 25 Jan. 59
2	0	2 Robert Henry Dillon ..	24 Mar. 58	p 3 June 59
2	0	2 George Henry Burt ..	23 Mar. 58	p 5 Aug. 59
2	0	1 Geo. Hamilton French	25 Mar. 58	p 23 Aug. 59
2	0	1 Robert Arthur Denny	p 26 Mar. 58	p 23 Aug. 59
2	0	1 Alf. Geo. Drake Pocock	30 Mar. 58	p 30 Sept. 59
2	0	2 Ernest Adolphus Carey	13 Apr. 58	p 7 Oct. 59
2	0	2 William S. Ward	16 Apr. 58	p 18 Nov. 59

3 Major Bowden served throughout the operations in Scinde (Medal), including the battles of Meeanee and Hyderabad, in the former of which he was wounded in the breast. He served also the campaign in the Southern Mahratta country in 1844-5, including the investment and capture of the Forts of Punella and Pownghur.

6 Captain Goff served with the 45th Regt. in the Kaffir war of 1846-47 (Medal).

10 Captain Hickman served with the 50th Regt. in the Crimea from 2nd Sept. 1855— (Medal with Clasp for Sebastopol).

11 Captain Trevor served with the 55th Regt. in the Crimea from 22nd Nov. 1854 to 11 June 1855, and was present at the siege of Sebastopol and attack and capture of the Rifle Pits on the night of the 18th April 1855, dangerously wounded (Medal and Clasp).

22nd (The Cheshire) Regt. of Foot.   224—225

Years' Serv.				
Full Pay.	Half Pay.	ENSIGNS.	ENSIGN.	
2	0	2 Rich. N. Cartwright Foll	23 Apr. 58	12 Surgeon Carey served with the 64th Regt. in the Persian campaign of 1856-57, including the storm and capture of Reshire, surrender of Bushire, night attack and battle of Kooshab. Served in Bengal and N.W. Provinces in suppressing the mutiny in 1857-58 in medical charge of 500 men; present in the actions of Futtehpore, Aoung, Pandoo Nuddee, Cawnpore, Onao, Buseerut Gunge (1st and 2nd), Boorheakchowkee, Bithoor, Mungurwar, Alumbagh, and first relief of Lucknow with Havelock's Column; present in three sorties from the Residency, also at the defence of Cawnpore—severely wounded.
2	0	1 Wm. Cunliffe Powys..	24 Apr. 58	
2	0	1 Michael Fenton	30 Apr. 58	
2	0	2 Percy Sandford Nevile	1 May 58	
2	0	2 Henry James Oliver ..	14 May 58	
2	0	2 William Pilsworth	6 Aug. 58	
2	0	1 Fred. Wm. Best Parry .	7 Aug. 58	
2	0	1 Geo. Rob. Hy. Daubeney	P 7 Sept. 58	
2	0	1 John Godfrey Hughes .	29 Oct. 58	
2	0	2 John David Cove Thomas	P 9 Nov. 58	
1	0	2 Henry Allen Gosset ...	28 Jan. 59	13 Assist.-Surgeon Pollard served the Eastern campaign of 1854-55 with the 93rd Highlanders, including the affair of Bulganac, battles of Alma and Balaklava, capture of Balaklava, capture of Kertch and Yenikale, siege and fall of Sebastopol, and attacks of the 18th June and 8th September (Medal and three Clasps, and 5th Class of the Medjidie).
1	0	1 Louis Rich. G. Vaughan	1 Apr. 59	
1	0	1 James Allan Parke.....	P 3 June 59	
1	0	2 Alex. George Fraser ..	P 29 July 59	
1	0	2 Harry Bromley Pitman	P 5 Aug. 59	
1	0	2 Albert Garner Richards	P 9 Sept. 59	
1	0	1 A. Eugene Tollemache	P 28 Oct. 59	14 Qr.-Master Clinton served with the 82nd Regt. in the Crimea from 2nd Sept. 1855 (Medal with Clasp for Sebastopol).
1	0	1 Henry Peregrine Leader	P 4 Nov. 59	
1	0	2 Walter Benson Hutton	P 5 Nov. 59	

2	0	*Paymasters.*—2 George Montgomerie Davidson, 1 April 58.
2	0	1 George Waller Vesey, 8 Dec. 58.
6	0	*Adjutants.*—1 Lieut. Robert Conway Doblis Ellis, 2 Oct. 57.
4	0	2 Lieut. Herbert Charles Patton, 4 March 59.
5	0	*Instructors of Musketry.*—2 Lieut. George Turner, 20 April 58.
3	0	1 Lieut. Henry Leigh, 10 Feb. 59.
11	0	*Quarter-Masters.*—1 Michael Clinton,[14] 27 July 49.
2	0	2 George Wohlman, 5 March 58.
12	0	*Surgeons.*—1 Andrew Leith Adams, M.D. 25 Sept. 55 ; *Assist. Surg.* 1 Dec. 48.
9	0	2 Thomas Carey,[12] 26 Jan. 58 ; *Assist. Surg.* 24 Jan. 51.
6	0	*Assist.-Surgs.*—1 John Joseph Adrien, 10 Feb. 54.
6	0	1 William Henry Pollard,[13] 7 April 54.
2	0	2 Francis Henry Preston, 10 March 58.
1	0	2 James Edward Clark, 1 Feb. 59.

Facings Buff.—*Agent*, A. Lawrie, Esq.
[1st Batt. returned from India, 28 July 1855.   *Depot, Parkhurst.*]
[2nd Batt. embarked for Malta, 11 May 1859.   *Depot, Parkhurst.*]

---

1 Sir William Napier served at the siege of Copenhagen and battle of Kioge in 1807; Sir John Moore's campaign of 1808-9; the subsequent Peninsular campaigns from 1809 to the end of that war in 1814, and was present in many of the soul-stirring scenes which he has described with so much ability in his admirable "History of the Peninsular War," including the action of the Coa (wounded), battle of Busaco, actions of Pombal, Redinha, and Casal Nova—severely wounded at the head of six Companies supporting the 52nd: action of Foz d'Arouce, battle of Salamanca, passage of the Huebra, action of Vera when Soult attempted to relieve San Sebastian, and again when the Allies passed the Bidassoa; battles of the Nivelle and Nive—wounded in defending the churchyard of Arcangues ; battle of Orthes. Served also in the campaign of 1815. Sir William has received the Gold Medal and two Clasps for Salamanca, Nivelle, and Nive, at which battles he commanded the 43rd Light Infantry, and also in many minor actions, and the Silver War Medal with three Clasps for Busaco, Fuentes d'Onor, and Orthes.

2 Colonel Harding served with the Lt. Company at defence of the Residency at Hyderabad, and was afterwards severely wounded at the battle of Meeanee (Medal). Served the Eastern campaign of 1854 as Aide-de-Camp to General Pennefather, including the battles of the Alma, Balaklava, and Inkerman (severely wounded), and siege of Sebastopol (Medal and Clasps, Brevet Lt.-Col., CB., Knight of the Legion of Honor, and 5th Class of the Medjidie).

4 Major Nevill served in Canada during the rebellion of 1837 and 1838, and was engaged with the rebels at St. Charles and at St. Eustache. Served also in the Eastern campaign of 1854, and up to the 16th June 1855, when he was appointed to the command of Russian prisoners on the Bosphorus ; he was present at the battles of Alma and Inkerman, and siege of Sebastopol (Medal and three Clasps, and 5th Class of the Medjidie).

5 Capt. Thursby served with the 9th Regt. in the Crimea from 27th Nov. 1854, including the siege and fall of Sebastopol, and assault on the batteries on the 18th June (Medal and Clasp).

7 Captain Walker served as Adjutant of the 8th Regt. at the siege and assault of Delhi (severely wounded), including repulse of sorties on 9th (horse shot), 14th, 18th, and 23rd July 1857; afterwards present in the actions of Bolundshur and Allighur, battle of Agra, action of Dil Kooshn and relief of Lucknow under Lord Clyde, affair of the 2nd and action of the 6th Dec. at Cawnpore, and action of Khudagunj.

8 Captain De Lancey served with the 47th Regt. at the siege and fall of Sebastopol from Sept. 1855 (Medal and Clasp). Was awarded the Silver Medal of the Royal Humane Society on 10th April 1858, in consideration of " noble, gallant, and humane conduct displayed on the night of 27th May 1857, in having jumped from the deck of the steam troop ship *Adelaide* to endeavour to save Private Patrick Dempsey, 47th Regt., who had fallen overboard at sea, on passage from Malta to Gibraltar."

9 Captain Davern served with the 53rd Regt. in the Punjaub campaign in 1849, including the battle of Goojerat (Medal and Clasp). Expedition against the Hill Tribes on the Peshawur frontier in 1851-52. Campaigns in India in 1857-58, including the actions of Kallee Nuddee and Shumshabad, storm and capture of Meeangunge, siege and capture of Lucknow, and minor affairs.

15 Lieut. Cookesley served with the 97th Regt. in Bengal in suppressing the mutiny in 1857-58,—with the Jounpore field force in the actions of Chanda, Ummeerpore, and Sultanpore, afterwards at the siege and capture of Lucknow.

23rd (Royal Welsh Fusiliers) Regt. of Foot. [1st Batt. Lucknow. 2nd Batt. Malta.

The *Prince of Wales's Feathers,* "*Ich Dien;*" the *Rising Sun,* the *Red Dragon,* the *White Horse,* "*Nec aspera torrent;*" "MINDEN," the *Sphinx,* "EGYPT" "CORUNNA" "MARTINIQUE" "ALBUHERA" "BADAJOZ" "SALAMANCA" "VITTORIA" "PYRENEES" "NIVELLE" "ORTHES" "TOULOUSE" "PENINSULA" "WATERLOO" "ALMA" "INKERMAN" "SEVASTOPOL."

Years' Serv.	Full Pay	Half Pay					
56			Colonel.—🌣 Henry Rainey,¹ CB. KH., *Ens.* 24 Aug. 04; *Lieut.* 1 Nov. 04; *Capt.* 13 Apr. 09; *Maj.* 21 June 17; *Lt.-Col.* 15 Aug. 22; *Col.* 10 Jan. 37; *Maj.-Gen.* 9 Nov. 46; *Lt.-Gen.* 20 June 54; *Col.* 23rd F. 22 May 55.				
			Lt.-Colonels.—1 Samuel Wells, CB. *Ens.* 9 Apr. 25; *Lt.* ᵖ 8 Oct. 29; *Capt.*				
35	0		ᵖ 15 Sept. 37; *Major,* 16 Sept. 51; *Lt.-Col.* 9 May 56.				
23	0		1 Robert Pratt,³ CB., *Ens.* ᵖ 16 June 37; *Lt.* ᵖ 27 June 39; *Capt.* ᵖ 23 Sept. 45; *Major,* 29 Dec. 54; *Lt.Col.* 9 Sept. 55.				
18	0		2 𝓥ℂ Edward William Deddington Bell,⁴ *2nd Lt.* 15 April 42; *Lt.* ᵖ 17 Nov. 43; *Capt.* 18 Dec. 48; *Bt.-Major,* 12 Dec. 54; *Major,* 23 March 55; *Bt. Lt.-Col.* 26 Dec. 56; *Lt.-Col.* 8 Jan. 58.				
11	0		*Majors.*—1 Edward Gascoigne Bulwer,⁶ CB., *2nd Lt.* ᵖ 21 Aug. 49; *Lt.* ᵖ 13 Dec. 50; *Capt.* 21 Sept. 54; *Major,* 29 Jan. 58; *Bt.Lt.Col.* 26 Apr. 59.				
15	0		2 James Gubbins,⁷ *Ens.* 19 Dec. 45; *Lt.* ᵖ 13 Apr. 49; *Capt.* ᵖ 18 Feb. 53; *Bt.-Major,* 12 Dec. 54; *Major,* 29 Aug. 56.				
11	0		1 Henry D'Oyley Torrens,⁸ *2nd Lt.* 18 Sept. 49; *Lt.* 8 May 51; *Capt.* 21 Sept. 54; *Bt.Major,* 6 June 56; *Major,* 18 Oct. 58; *Bt.Lt.Col.* 26 Apr. 59.				
10	0		2 Jervoise Clarke Jervoise, *Ens.* ᵖ 13 June 50; *Lieut.* ᵖ 9 May 51; *Capt.* 21 Sept. 54; *Bt. Major,* 20 July 58; *Major,* ᵖ 2 Dec. 59.				

			CAPTAINS.	ENSIGN.	LIEUT.	CAPTAIN.	BREV.MAJ.
9	0		2 Bevil Granville⁶	ᵖ 16 May 51	ᵖ 6 June 54	16 Mar. 55	2 pr. 59
9	0		2 Fred. Fletcher Vane¹⁰	ᵖ 17 Oct. 51	ᵖ 23 June 54	23 Mar. 55	4 June 58
7	0		1 *Hon.* Savage Mostyn¹¹	ᵖ 13 May 53	21 Sept. 54	8 June 55	
13	0		1 Geo. Hy. John Heigham	ᵖ 22 June 47	ᵖ 10 Feb. 54	ᵖ 6 July 55	26 Apr. 59
7	0		1 Cha. G. Campb. Norton¹²	ᵖ 21 Jan. 53	12 Jan. 55	ᵖ 7 Sept. 55	
7	0		2 Geo. Phipps Prevost¹⁴	ᵖ 26 Aug. 53	12 Jan. 55	ᵖ 22 May 57	
5	1¾		2 Sydney Crohan Millett¹⁴	16 June 54	21 Sept. 54	30 Nov. 55	
6	0		1 𝓥ℂ Thos. B. Hackett¹⁵	ᵖ 7 June 54	9 Feb. 55	ᵖ 26 Jan. 58	
18	1¾		2 Robert Douglas²⁶	2 Apr. 41	28 Dec. 42	6 July 55	
14	¾		2 David Reid²⁷	31 Mar. 46	ᵖ 25 Feb. 48	14 July 57	
14	0		1 Wm. Munnings Lees..	ᵖ 14 Apr. 46	18 Aug. 48	26 Mar. 58	
14	0		1 Donald Maclean Fraser²⁸	8 May 46	10 June 49	26 Mar. 58	
14	0		2 Jos. FitzTho. Shadwell	ᵖ 26 June 46	8 Jan. 51	26 Mar. 58	
12	0		1 Rob. Philip Armstrong²⁹	ᵖ 25 Feb. 48	6 June 54	26 Mar. 58	
6	0		1 Charles Monsell¹³†	22 Sept. 54	8 Dec. 54	26 Mar. 58	
6	0		1 𝓥ℂ Luke O'Connor¹⁶	5 Nov. 54	9 Feb. 55	24 Aug. 58	
6	0		1 Charles G. Blane¹⁷ ..	6 Nov. 54	9 Feb. 55	ᵖ 6 Sept. 58	
8	0		2 Edward Armstrong³⁰ .	16 Apr. 52	5 Oct. 54	7 Sept. 58	
28	0		2 Chas.S.S.EvansGordon	12 Oct. 32	ᵖ 3 June 36	ᵖ 20 Dec. 42	20 June 54
6	0		1 *Hon.* Nathl. Fiennes¹⁸..	16 Nov. 54	25 Feb. 55	18 Oct. 58	
6	0		2 James De Vic Tupper²⁰	15 Dec. 54	9 Mar. 55	1 Apr. 59	
6	0		1 John Lawrence¹⁹	28 Nov. 54	9 Mar. 55	ᵖ 28 Oct. 59	
5	0		2 Charles Fred. Gregorie	12 Feb. 55	30 June 55	ᵖ 4 Nov. 59	
5	0		1 Philip Henry Knight..	16 Mar. 55	9 Sept. 55	ᵖ 2 Dec. 59	
			LIEUTENANTS.				
6	0		1 James Williamson²⁰ .	29 Dec. 54	23 Mar. 55		
5	0		2 Alfred Markland Law³¹	15 Mar. 55	27 July 55		
5	0		1 John Tilly	6 Apr. 55	9 Sept. 55		
5	0		1 Edwin Utterton¹⁹	30 Apr. 55	10 Sept. 55		
5	0		1 Wm. Dowdesw. Bloxsome	1 May 55	30 Sept. 55		
5	0		2 Gust. Wm. H. Bussell	10 May 55	16 Oct. 55		
5	0		2 Arthur Hill.........	11 May 55	16 Oct. 55		
7	0		2 Jno. Keate S. Henderson	ᵖ 13 Sept. 53	9 Feb. 55		
5	0		2 Fred. Wollaston Hutton	ᵖ 18 May 55	ᵖ 27 Mar. 57		
5	0		2 William Romilly	ᵖ 19 July 55	ᵖ 22 May 57		
5	0		2 Wriothe. Aug. FitzRoy	20 July 55	ᵖ 5 Mar. 58		
5	0		2 Jas. Harford Walwyn .	ᵖ 25 July 55	30 Mar. 58		
5	0		1 Wm. Jolliffe Twyford .	26 July 55	23 Apr. 58		
5	0		2 Charles James Wrench	8 Oct. 55	29 May 58		
5	0		2 Annesley Cary	9 Oct. 55	4 June 58		
5	0		1 John W. W. Costley²²	15 Oct. 55	4 June 58		
5	0		2 George Packe........	16 Oct. 55	4 June 58		
5	0		2 Allan Graham	30 Nov. 55	4 June 58		
4	0		2 Harry Charles Willes .	ᵖ 14 Mar. 56	4 June 58		
6	0		2 Cha. Cameron Lees, *Adj.*	7 June 54	15 Jan. 58		
3	0		1 Geo. Fred. Russell Colt³²	ᵖ 27 Mar. 57	7 Sept. 58		
2	0		1 Arch. Rob. Winstanley	ᵖ 5 Mar. 58	13 Oct. 58		
2	0		1 Frederick Gerard	30 Mar. 58	18 Oct. 58		
2	0		1 Lorenzo George Lysons	16 Apr. 58	ᵖ 26 Oct. 58		
2	0		1 Henry Edmund Stanley	ᵖ 23 Apr. 58	ᵖ 18 Jan. 59		

13† Captain *Hon.* S. Mostyn served at the siege of Sebastopol in 1855, including the attack of the Redan on the 18th June (Medal and Clasp).

13† Captain Monsell served the Eastern campaign of 1854-55, including the battles of Alma and Balaklava, siege and fall of Sebastopol, and both attacks on the Redan (Medal and Clasps).

23rd (Royal Welsh Fusiliers) Regt. of Foot. 227

Years' Serv. Full Pay.	Years' Serv. Half Pay.	LIEUTENANTS.	ENSIGN.	LIEUT.	
2	0	2 George William Lewis	p 24 Apr. 58	p 18 Jan. 59	
2	0	1 A. Mitchell Molyneux.	7 May 58	p 14 June 59	4 Lt.-Colonel Bell served
.2	0	1 John Henry Tulloch ..	30 Apr. 58	p 13 Dec. 59	the Eastern campaign of 1854-
2	0	1 Gerald Geo. Liddell ..	14 May 58	p 13 Dec. 59	55, including the battle of
2	0	1 Sam. Wm. Ralph Sadler	5 June 58	p 13 Dec. 59	Alma, where he personally captured and secured the first gun
		ENSIGNS.			taken from the Russians, and
4	0	1 Nicholas Gosselin	8 Jan. 56		afterwards succeeded to the
2	0	1 Francis Palmer Jones .	4 June 58		command of the 23rd Fusiliers, and brought it
2	0	1 Thos. James Bowyer..	6 June 58		out of action; he was also at the battle of Inkerman and siege of Sebastopol, and was com-
2	0	1 Henry Fred. Seagram .	7 June 58		plimented in General Orders for distinguished
2	0	1 Rob. Albert Evans Hay	8 June 58		conduct while in command of a working party,
2	0	1 Robert Cæsar Bacon ..	13 July 58		2 April 1855, under a heavy fire from the enemy (Medal and Clasp, Brevet Major, Victoria
2	0	1 James Clayton, Adj...	30 July 58		Cross, Knight of the Legion of Honor, and 5th
2	0	1 Wm. Robert Murray ..	6 Aug. 58		Class of the Medjidie).
2	0	1 Eugene Mervin Roe ..	10 Sept. 58		7 Major Gubbins served the Eastern campaign of 1854 as Aide-de-Camp to Sir De Lacy
2	0	2 Henry Olivier Lloyd ..	5 Oct. 58		Evans, including the battles of the Alma and
2	0	2 George Wildes	26 Oct. 58		Inkerman (severely wounded) and siege of Sebastopol (Medal and Clasps, and 5th Class of
2	0	2 Charles Morgan......	p 30 Oct. 58		the Medjidie).
2	0	2 John Francis Sparrow	p 9 Nov. 58		8 Lt.Col. Torrens served in the Eastern campaign as Aide-de-Camp to Brig.-General Torrens, including the battle of Inkerman (wounded) and siege of Sebastopol; was appointed
1	0	2 Joseph Napier	p 18 Mar. 59		
1	0	2 Henry Francis Hutton	1 Apr. 59		
1	0	2 Edm. B. Knowles Lacon	p 29 July 59		D. A. Q. M. Gen. at Head Quarters in Feb. 1855, and served in that capacity until the end of the war, having been present at both attacks on the Redan (Medal and Clasps, Brevet Major, Knight of the Legion of Honor, and 5th Class of the Medjidie).

1	0	*Paymasters.*—2 George Knox Leet, 2 July 58.	
12	0	1 Tho. Newton Young, 1 Jan. 57 ; Q.M. 9 Apr. 47 ; Ens. 21 July 48 ; Lt. 3 Jan.	
6	0	*Adjutants.*—2 Lieut. Charles Cameron Lees, 2 July 58.	[54.
2	.0	1 Ensign James Clayton, 3 June 59.	
6	0	*Instructors of Musketry.*—1 Lieut. James Williamson, 1 Nov. 56.	
5	0	2 Lieut. George Packe, 29 Aug. 59.	
2	0	*Quarter-Masters.*—2 George Burden, 13 April 58.	
10	0	1 Michael O'Donnell,[33] 1 June 55 ; Ens. 29 Nov. 50.	
19	0	*Surgeons.*—1 Patrick Sinclair Laing,[23] 6 Jan. 54 ; Assist.-Surg. 8 Apr. 41.	
9	0	2 Alex. Scott Fogo,[31]† M. D. 31 Dec. 58 ; Assist.Surg. 7 Oct. 51.	
6	0	*Assist.-Surgs.*—1 VC Henry Thos. Sylvester,[24] M.D. 3 Mar. 54.	
5	0	1 Charles Fred. Morris,[25] 2 Feb. 55.	
5	0	1 John Noble Shipton, 23 Mar. 55.	
2	0	2 Richard William Berkeley, 22 April 58.	
2	0	2 John Greig, M.B. 14 Dec. 58.	

Facings Blue.—*Agents,* Messrs. Cox & Co.

[*Returned from the Crimea,* 19 *July* 56. *Emb. for China,* 16 *June* 57. *Depot, Chatham.*]
[2nd *Battalion embarked for Malta* 8 Feb. 59. *Depot, Deal.*]

1 Lieut.General Rainey served with the 82nd at the siege and capture of Copenhagen in 1807; with Sir Brent Spencer's expedition off the coast of Spain, and at Cadiz on surrender of the French fleet; from thence joined Sir Arthur Wellesley's army at Mondego Bay, and was afterwards present at the battles of Roleia, Vimiera, and Corunna, also the retreat under Sir John Moore. Accompanied the Regiment to Walcheren in 1809, and was present at the surrender of Middleburgh, siege and capture of Flushing. Joined the army in the Peninsula in May 1812, and served as Aide-de-Camp to Sir Thomas Bradford during the siege of the Forts of Salamanca, battle of Salamanca, capture of Madrid, siege of Burgos, and retreat therefrom. Served afterwards in the Portuguese service in advance through the Tras-os-Montes in 1813, at the battle of Vittoria, actions of Villa Franca and Toloso, storm of the fortified convent in front of San Sebastian, at both the sieges and storm of San Sebastian, passage of the Bidassoa, battle of the Nivelle, battles of the Nive on the 9th and 10th Dec.—severely wounded; wounded also at the siege of San Sebastian. Served in France with the Army of Occupation from the capitulation of Paris in 1815 to the end of 1818. He has received the War Medal with eight Clasps.
3 Lt.Colonel Pratt served with the 41st throughout the campaign of 1842 in Affghanistan (Medal), and was present in the engagements with the enemy on the 28th April in the Pisheen Valley; in those of the 29th May near Candahar, 30th Aug. at Gonine, 5th Sept. before Ghuznee; at the occupation and destruction of that Fortress and of Cabool, the Expedition into Kohistan, storm, capture, and destruction of Istaliff, and the various minor affairs in and between the Bolan and the Khyber Passes. Served at the siege of Sebastopol, was present at the attacks of the Redan on the 18th June and 8th Sept.—wounded (Medal and Clasp, and Brevet of Lieut.-Col. dated 2 Nov. 1855, Sardinian Medal, and 5th Class of the Medjidie). Joined Sir Colin Campbell's army before Lucknow on 14th Nov. 1857 and was at the relief of the Garrison, also at the defeat of the Gwalior Contingent at Cawnpore on 6th Dec., and at the fall of Lucknow in March 1858 when he commanded the Left Column of attack on and occupation of the Iron Bridge from 11th to 15th March and was mentioned in the Dispatches; commanded a Column in the chain of operations by Lord Clyde against the rebels in Dec. 1858 and Jan. 1859 when they were driven from Oude into the Nepaul territory (Medal and Clasps, and CB.).
6 Lt.Col. Bulwer and Major Granville served in the Eastern campaign of 1854-55, including the battles of Alma and Inkerman, and siege of Sebastopol (Medal and three Clasps).
10 Major Vane served the Eastern campaign of 1854-55, including the battle of Inkerman (wounded), siege and fall of Sebastopol, attack of the Quarries, and attacks of the Redan on the 18th June and 18th Sept.—severely wounded (Medal and Clasps, and 5th Class of the Medjidie).
12 Captain Norton served in the Indian campaign of 1857-58, including the relief of Lucknow by Lord Clyde, defeat of the Gwalior Contingent at Cawnpore, siege and capture of Lucknow and operations across the Goomtee under Outram—mentioned in despatches (Medal and two Clasps).
14 Capt. Prevost served at the siege and fall of Sebastopol from 17th June 1855, including assaults of the Redan on the 18th June and 8th Sept.—wounded (Medal and Clasp).

227a 23rd (Royal Welsh Fusiliers) Regt. of Foot.

14† Captain Millett served in the Eastern campaign of 1854-55, including the battles of Alma and Inkerman, siege and fall of Sebastopol: he was severely wounded at the attack on the Redan on the 8th Sept. (Medal and three Clasps, Sardinian Medal, and 5th Class of the Medjidie).

15 Lieut. Hackett served at the siege of Sebastopol from June 1855, including the assault of the Redan on the 18th June (Medal and Clasp). Served in the Indian campaign of 1857-58, including the relief of Lucknow by Lord Clyde, battle of Cawnpore on 6th Dec., siege and capture of Lucknow (Medal and Clasp and Victoria Cross.)

16 Captain O'Connor served the Eastern campaign of 1854-55, including the battles of Alma (severely wounded) and Inkerman, siege and fall of Sebastopol, attack on the Quarries, and assaults of the 18th June and 8th Sept.—dangerously wounded (Medal and Clasps, Victoria Cross, Sardinian Medal, and 5th Class of the Medjidie). Served in the Indian campaign of 1857-58, including the relief of Lucknow by Lord Clyde, defeat of the Gwalior Contingent at Cawnpore, siege and capture of Lucknow and operations across the Goomtee under Outram (Medal and two Clasps).

17 Captain Blane served at the siege of Sebastopol in 1855, including the attack of the Redan on the 18th June, and was wounded in the trenches on 30th June (Medal and Clasp). Served in the Indian campaign of 1857-58, including the siege and capture of Lucknow and operations across the Goomtee under Outram (Medal and Clasp).

18 Captain Hon. N. Fiennes served at the siege and fall of Sebastopol from 17th June 1855, including assaults of the Redan on the 18th June and 8th Sept. (Medal and Clasp).

19 Capt. Lawrence and Lt. Utterton served at the siege and fall of Sebastopol in 1855, including the assault of the Redan on 8th Sept. (Medal and Clasp). Lieut. Utterton served in the Indian campaign of 1857-58, including the relief of Lucknow by Lord Clyde, defeat of the Gwalior Contingent at Cawnpore, siege and capture of Lucknow—mentioned in despatches (Medal and Clasp).

20 Captain Tupper and Lieut. Williamson served at the siege and fall of Sebastopol in 1855, including the assault of the Redan on 8th Sept.—severely wounded (Medal and Clasp). Lieut. Williamson served in the Indian campaign of 1857-58, including the relief of Lucknow by Lord Clyde, defeat of the Gwalior Contingent at Cawnpore, siege and capture of Lucknow and operations across the Goomtee under Outram (Medal and two Clasps).

22 Lieut. Costley served the Indian campaign of 1857-58 as Interpreter to the 23rd Fusiliers and was present at the capture of Furruckabad, siege and capture of Lucknow including operations across the Goomtee; was afterwards Adjutant to a Sikh Corps in the disturbed districts of Buxar and Behar from May to Sept. under Brigadier Douglas—mentioned in despatches (Medal and Clasp).

23 Surgeon Laing served the campaign under Sir Charles Napier against the Mountain and Robber Tribes situated on the right bank of the Indus early in 1845. Served in the Eastern campaign of 1854-55 (Medal and Clasp). Joined the 23rd Fusiliers in Bundlecund in Jan. 1858 and served at the siege and capture of Lucknow (Medal and Clasp).

24 Doctor Sylvester served at the siege and fall of Sebastopol, and at the assault of the Redan on the 8th Sept. 1855, on which occasion he was mentioned in Sir James Simpson's Dispatch "for his courage in going to the front under heavy fire to assist the wounded." (Medal and Clasp, Victoria Cross, and Knight of the Legion of Honor). Served in the Indian campaign of 1857-58, including the relief of Lucknow by Lord Clyde, defeat of the Gwalior Contingent at Cawnpore, siege and capture of Lucknow (Medal and Clasps).

25 Assist.-Surgeon Morris served at the siege of Sebastopol in 1855 (Medal and Clasp).

26 Captain Douglas served with the Buffs at the battle of Punniar (Medal).

27 Captain Reid served with the 61st Regt. in the Punjaub campaign of 1848-49, including the capture of the Sikh Forts of Rungur, Nungul, and Muraree, affair at Ramnuggur, passage of the Chenab, battles of Chillianwallah and Goojerat, pursuit of the Affghan army to the Khyber Pass, and occupation of Peshawur (Medal and two Clasps). Served under Sir Colin Campbell on the expedition into the hill country around Mitchnee, and was present at the destruction of the forts and strongholds of the Momunds and other Hill Tribes.

28 Captain Fraser served with the 80th Regt. in the Burmese war of 1852, and was present at the capture of Martaban, in the operations before Rangoon on the 12th, 13th, and 14th April, and storming of the Great Dagon Pagoda; also at the capture of Prome (Medal).

29 Captain R. P. Armstrong served with the 77th Regt. during the siege of Sebastopol in 1855, including the attacks on the 18th June and 8th Sept.— wounded (Medal and Clasp).

30 Captain Edward Armstrong served in the 3rd West India Regt. in the affray with the natives of Sabajee, West Coast of Africa, on the 10th July, 1855, in which he lost his right arm and received six other wounds. Served with the 75th Regt. in India during the Mutiny, including the whole of the siege operations against Delhi and was severely wounded at the assault.

31 Lieut. Law served in the Indian campaign of 1857-58, including the siege and capture of Lucknow and operations across the Goomtee (Medal and Clasp).

31† Doctor Fogo served the Eastern campaign of 1854-55, including the battles of Alma and Balaklava, and siege of Sebastopol (Medal and Clasps, and 5th Class of the Medjidie).

32 Lieut. Colt served in the Indian campaign of 1857-58, including the siege and fall of Lucknow (Medal and Clasp).

33 Qr. Master O'Donnell served the Sutlej campaign of 1845-46, including the battle of Sobraon (Medal). Also the Punjaub campaign of 1848-49, and was present during the whole of the siege operations against Mooltan: including the storming of the enemy's strongly-entrenched position 12th Sept. 1848, action of Soorjkoond, carrying the heights before Mooltan and surrender of the fortress. Also present at the battle of Goojerat (Medal and Clasps). Served in the Indian campaign of 1857-58, and was present at the Mutiny at Dinapore, advance to Lucknow and actions at Chanda, Umeerpore, Sultanpore, and Douraha, siege and capture of Lucknow and storming of the Emaumbara and Kaizabagh, relief of Azimghur, and operations near Jugdespore (Medal).

1st Batt. India.
2nd Batt. Aldershot.]**24th (*The 2nd Warwickshire*) *Regt. of Foot.*** 228

The *Sphinx*, with the words, "EGYPT" "CAPE OF GOOD HOPE" "TALAVERA" "FUENTES D'ONOR"
"SALAMANCA" "VITTORIA" "PYRENEES" "NIVELLE" "ORTHES" "PENINSULA"
"PUNJAUB" "CHILLIANWALLAH" "GOOJERAT."

Years'Serv.		
Full Pay.	Half Pay.	
51		Colonel.—泠Hon. John Finch,¹ CB. Cornet 5 Oct. 09; Lt. P 20 Dec. 10; Capt. P 17 Feb. 14; Major, P 5 Mar. 18; Brevet Lt.-Col. 25 Oct. 23; Lieut.-Col. P 12 Dec. 26; Col. 28 June 38; Major-Gen. 11 Nov. 51; Lt.-Gen. 20 Feb. 55; Col. 24th Foot, 19 June 56.
35	0	Lieut.-Colonels.—1 William Gustavus Brown,² Ens. 7 July 25; Lt. 11 May 30; Capt. 10 May 44; Maj. 15 Jan. 49; Lt.-Col. P 21 Dec. 49; Col. 28 Nov. 54.
21	0	2 Chas. Henry Ellice,³ CB. Ens. & Lt. 10 May 39; Lt. & Capt. P 8 Aug. 45; Major, P 21 Dec. 49; Lieut.-Col. P 8 Aug. 51; Col. 28 Nov. 54.
35	0	1 Augustus George Blachford,³† Ens. P 12 Nov. 25; Lieut. P 12 Dec. 26; Capt. 17 Aug. 41; Maj. 14 Jan. 49; Bt. Lt.Col. 7 June 49; Col. 28 Nov. 54; Lt. Col. 30 March 58.
23	0	Majors.—1 Edmund Wodehouse, Ens. P 24 Mar. 37; Lieut. P 15 Jan. 41; Capt. P 28 Apr. 46; Major, P 8 Aug. 51; Bt. Lt.-Col. 12 Dec. 57.
22	0	2 Louis Howe Bazalgette,⁴ Ens. 26 June 38; Lieut. P 24 Sept. 41; Capt. 7 Apr. 48; Major, 30 March 58.
19	0	1 John Henry Lutman,⁵ Ens. 8 Jan. 41; Lieut. P 16 June 43; Capt. 14 Jan. 49; Major, 17 Apr. 58.
14	10/12	2 Hon. Daniel Greville Finch,⁶ Ens. P 2 May 45; Lt. P 22 Dec. 46; Capt. P 30 Dec. 53; Bt.Major, 2 Nov. 55; Major, 6 Nov. 57.

		CAPTAINS.	ENSIGN.	LIEUT.	CAPTAIN.	BREV.-MAJ.
22	9/12	2 Francis Chas. Skurray	P 7 Oct. 37	8 April 42	14 Jan. 49	
18	0	1 Andrew J. Macpherson⁷	19 Apr. 42	26 July 44	14 Jan. 49	19 Jan. 58
18	0	1 George Fred. Berry⁸ ..	7 Jan. 42	P 25 Apr. 45	20 Oct. 49	
17	0	1 John Bulk.Thelwall,⁹ CB.	P 4 Aug. 43	3 April 46	P 21 Dec. 49	26 Apr. 59
18	0	1 Hy. Macdonald Burns	20 May 42	23 June 48	20 July 56	
10	0	2 Richard Thomas Glyn⁹†	P 16 Aug. 50	P 24 June 53	7 Sept. 55	
10	0	1 William Winniett¹⁰ ..	18 Jan. 50	28 July 54	21 Dec. 55	
14	0	1 Robert G.A. de Montmorency¹¹	P 25 Aug. 46	14 Jan. 49	8 July 57	
16	0	1 Robert Halahan	17 May 44	1 Jan. 49	21 July 57	
15	0	1 Rich. Henry Travers¹³	P 9 Dec. 45	5 Jan. 49	P 7 Aug. 57	
15	0	1 James Stewart¹⁴	27 Feb. 45	5 Jan. 49	16 April 58	
12	0	1 Richard Henry Holland	P 20 Oct. 48	P 1 Dec. 49	16 April 58	
16	0	2 Thomas Clark........	26 April 44	23 July 46	27 Mar. 55	
11	0	2 Fred. Cha.D'E.Barclay¹⁶	P 27 April 49	P 15 July 53	P 5 Mar. 58	
12	0	1 Wm. Vesey Munnings¹⁷	P 10 Mar. 48	P 1 Feb. 50	17 April 58	
13	0	1 Montague Browne¹⁸ ..	19 Nov. 47	6 June 51	17 April 58	
12	0	2 Charles Hunter	P 14 Apr. 48	P 1 Aug. 51	10 Sept. 58	
11	0	1 James Tennent Tovey	23 Nov. 49	P 8 Aug. 51	10 Sept. 58	
9	0	2 Hen.H.Godwin-Austen¹⁹	26 Dec. 51	12 Oct. 54	P 29 Oct. 58	
10	0	2 Edmund Watkin Kent	P 17 May 50	P 1 May 55	P 31 Dec. 58	
5	0	2 Edmund Fred. Tarte ..	P 23 Mar. 55	15 Mar. 56	P 7 May 58	
8	0	2 William Plumer Gaskell	21 Sept. 52	29 Dec. 54	P 1 Apr. 59	
4	0	2 John Johnstone	8 July 56	21 July 57	P 5 Aug. 59	
5	0	2 Henry Jas. Hitchcock..	22 Feb. 55	P 21 Sept. 55	P 21 Oct. 59	

LIEUTENANTS.

11	0	1 R.Josh.LoganCrutchley	23 Nov. 49	26 June 52	
11	0	1 Sam.JohnJames Burns²¹	P 11 May 49	P 26 Nov. 52	1 Lieut.-Gen. Hon. John Finch served in the 15th Light Dragoons the Peninsular campaigns of 1813 and 1814, and was present at the battle of Vittoria (sabre wound), blockade of Pampeluna, affair of Tarbes, and battles of Orthes and Toulouse, besides outpost affairs. Served as Aide-de-Camp to Viscount Combermere with the army of occupation in France; accompanied his lordship, as Military Secretary, to the West Indies in 1817; to Ireland in 1822 (receiving for his services the brevet rank of Lieut.-Col. in 1823), and to India in 1825; present at the siege and capture of Bhurtpore, for which he was nominated a CB., and has received Medals for Vittoria, Orthes, Toulouse, and Bhurtpore.
8	0	1 Alfred William Adcock	P 17 Dec. 52	4 May 55	
6	0	1 Wal. Bernardino Logan	P 5 May 54	20 July 56	
5	0	1 John Cordeiro Warne	23 Mar. 55	26 Feb. 56	
5	0	1 Alex.John Colvin Birch	2 Mar. 55	3 Nov. 56	
4	0	1 George Scott	2 Oct. 55	8 July 57	
5	0	1 Robt.Paterson Fox,²⁰ Adj.	20 July 55	P 27 Nov. 57	
5	0	2 Edward Trevor Dunn	7 Sept. 55	31 Oct. 56	
5	0	2 William Franklin ..	14 Sept. 55	16 April 58	
3	0	1 John Moore G. Tongue	24 Feb. 57	16 April 58	
4	0	1 Jona. Christian Thomas	27 Feb. 56	16 April 58	
5	0	2 Hy. Burmester Pulleine	16 Nov. 55	4 June 58	6 Major Hon. D. G. Finch served with the 68th Light Infantry throughout the Eastern campaign of 1854–55, including the battles of Alma and Inkerman, siege and fall of Sebastopol (Medal and Clasps, Brevet Major, and 5th Class of the Medjidie).
5	0	1 Henry Chas. Marsack²⁶	1 May 55	13 July 58	
3	0	1 ArthurWm.FitzMaurice	P 7 Aug. 57	7 Sept. 58	
5	0	2 John Foot	5 July 55	10 Sept. 58	
5	0	2 Arth. Coleman Hallowes	18 July 55	10 Sept. 58	
5	0	2 Rob. Napol.Surplice,Adj.	25 July 55	10 Sept. 58	
5	0	2 Dav. W. Balfour Ogilvy	21 Sept. 55	10 Sept. 58	
3	0	1 George Clarkson Ross .	9 Oct. 57	10 Sept. 58	
2	0	1 HughBackhouseChurch	15 Jan. 58	24 Sept. 58	
5	0	2 Rob. S. Brydges Leech	P 8 Oct. 55	29 Oct. 58	
2	0	1 Thomas Pierce Butler²⁷	P 23 April 58	P 7 Dec. 58	
4	0	2 Charles Fred. Lloyd ..	P 1 Aug. 56	23 July 58	

229—230   24th (The 2nd Warwickshire) Regt. of Foot.

Years' Serv.						
Full Pay	Half Pay	LIEUTENANTS.	ENSIGN.	LIEUT.		
2	0	1 Redmond O'Mahony..	23 Mar. 58	3 Jan. 59	20 Lieut. Fox was engaged with the enemy at Cawnpore on 26th, 27th, and 28th Nov. 1857; at the capture of the town of Meergunj; and at the siege of Lucknow under Lord Clyde. 26 Lieut. Marsack served with the 40th Regt. at the siege and fall of Sebastopol from 18 Aug. 1855 (Medal and Clasp) 23 Qr.-Master Airey served with the 13th Regt. throughout the campaigns in Affghanistan from 1838 to 1842 inclusive, and was present at the storm and capture of Ghuznee (Medal), assault and capture of the town and forts of Tootumdurrah, storm of Jhoolghur, night-attack at Baboo Koosh Ghur, destruction of Khardurrah, assault of Perwandurrah, storming of the Khoord Caboul Pass, affair of Tezeen, forcing the Jugdulluck Pass, reduction of the fort of Mamoo Khail, defence of Jellalabad (Medal) and sorties on the 14th Nov. and 1st Dec. 1841, 11th Mar., 24th Mar. and 1st April 1842; general action and defeat of Akbur Khan before Jellalabad, storming the heights of Jugdullnck, general action of Tezeen, and recapture of Caboul (Medal). 27 Lieut. Butler as a Lieut. 56th Regt. served at the siege and fall of Sebastopol from 25th Aug. 1855 (Medal and Clasp).	
2	0	2 Rich. Arch. Farquharson	24 April 58	18 Mar. 50		
2	0	2 E. Henry B. Sawbridge,	P 30 April 58	P 5 Aug. 59		
2	0	2 W. R. Bigsby Chamberlin	1 May 58	P 21 Oct. 50		
5	0	2 Wm. Alex. Henry Plasket	6 July 55	P 18 Jan. 50		
5	0	2 Oliver Goldsmith	23 Mar. 55	18 Jan. 50		
		ENSIGNS.				
2	0	1 Fra. Massey Pearson..	25 April 58			
2	0	1 Chas. Henry Fellowes	26 April 58			
2	0	2 Charles A. Hewitt....	7 May 58			
2	0	1 William Mugill	30 April 58			
2	0	2 Geo. Vaughan Wardell	14 May 58			
2	0	1 Edw. F. Aug. MacCarthy	21 May 58			
2	0	2 Henry Dewé	22 May 58			
2	0	1 John Fletcher Caldwell	28 May 58			
2	0	2 Rob. Henry Burrell Airey	30 April 58			
2	0	1 Alex. Carden Hennessy	4 June 58			
2	0	2 Fra. Arth. Holmes Yonge	5 June 58			
2	0	2 Wm. Wynne Goodrich	P 15 June 58			
2	0	1 Charles Wm. Story ..	12 Nov. 58			
2	0	1 Wm. Maxwell Brander	31 Dec. 58			
1	0	1 Henry Fra. Brouncker..	P 28 Jan. 59			
1	0	1 Henry Albert Harrisson	1 Apr. 50			
1	0	2 William Hitchcock ...	P 31 May 59			
1	0	2 George Paton	P 23 Aug. 59			
1	0	2 Charles James Bromhead	30 Aug. 59			

10	0	*Paymasters.*—1 Fra. Freeman White, 11 July 56; *Ens.* P 15 Feb. 50; *Lt.* P 5 May [54.			
7	0	2 Robert Champion Streatfeild,²² 8 June 58; *Ens.* P 12 Aug. 53;			
5	0	*Adjutants.*—1 Lieut. Robert Paterson Fox,²⁰ 16 July 58. [*Lt.* P 26 Oct. 55.			
5	0	2 Lieut. Robert Napoleon Surplice, 22 Oct. 59.			
2	0	*Instructors of Musketry.*—1 Lieut. T. P. Butler, 24 May 59.			
5	0	2 Lieut. Wm. Franklin, 31 Oct. 59.			
14	0	*Quarter-Masters.*—1 Thos. Airey,²³ 28 May 52; *Ens.* 21 April 46; *Lt.* 5 Jan. 49.			
2	0	2 John Cusack,²⁶ 13 April 58.			
10	0	*Surgeons.*—1 Richard Gamble, M.D. 12 March 52; *Assist.-Surg.* 8 June 41.			
12	0	2 James Lewis Holloway, 2 Oct. 57; *Assist. Surg.* 17 Mar. 48.			
6	0	*Assist.-Surgeons.*—1 Charles Carroll Dempster,²⁵ 5 May 54.			
3	0	1 Robert Sutherland, 19 Oct. 57.			
2	0	2 John Colahan, M.D. 25 May 58.			
6	0	2 Thomas Smith Hollingsworth, 3 Nov. 54.			
2	0	2 Joseph Salkeld Johnston, M.D. 7 May 58.			

Facings Green.—*Agents,* Messrs. Cox & Co.
[1st Batt. embarked for India, 8 May 46.   Depot, Chatham.]

2 Colonel Brown served throughout the Punjaub campaign, and was present with the 24th at the passage of the Chenab and battles of Sadoolapore, and Chillianwallah (wounded), and as Major of the 29th Regt. at the battle of Goojerat (Medal and Clasps).

3 Colonel Ellice commanded the detachment of Troops at the defeat of the Jhelum mutineers on the 7th July 1857, and was severely wounded in two places (one dangerous) and horse shot—nominated CB.

3† Colonel Pinchford served with the 24th in the Punjaub campaign of 1848-9 (Medal), including the passage of the Chenab and battles of Sadoolapore, Chillianwallah (succeeded to the command of the Regt.), and Goojerat (Medal and Clasps).

4 Major Bazalgette served in the Punjaub campaign of 1848-9, and was present at the passage of the Chenab and battles of Sadoolapore, Chillianwallah (severely wounded), and Goojerat (Medal and Clasps).

5 Major Lutman served in the Punjaub campaign of 1848-9, including the passage of the Chenab and battles of Sadoolapore, Chillianwallah, and Goojerat (Medal and Clasps).

7 Major Macpherson served in the Punjaub campaign of 1848-9, and was present at the passage of the Chenab and battles of Sadoolapore and Chillianwallah—severely wounded (Medal and Clasps). Served in the Indian campaign of 1857-58, and was present with a detachment of the 24th Regt. at the defeat of the Jhelum mutineers on the 7th July 1857, and succeeded to the command (Brevet Major); served subsequently in command of the 22nd Regt. Punjaub Infantry.

8 Capt. Berry served in the Punjaub campaign of 1848-9, including the passage of the Chenab, and battles of Sadoolapore, Chillianwallah (slightly wounded), and Goojerat (Medal and Clasps). Served in India during the Mutiny of 1857-58,—commanded the Station of Murree (Punjaub) when attacked by Hillmen on the night of 1st Sept. 57 and during proceedings of the three following days. In Nov. 57 raised, under orders of Sir John Lawrence at Lahore, a Battalion of Seikhs 1200 strong and proceeded down to North Western Provinces with it in Jan. 1858; was attached to Maxwell's Column and present at the taking of Calpee (Medal).

9 Major John B. Thelwall served in the Punjaub campaign of 1848-9, and was present at the passage of the Chenab, and battles of Sadoolapore, Chillianwallah (severely wounded), and Goojerat (Medal and Clasps).

9† Captain Glyn served with the 82nd Regt. in the Crimea from 2nd Sept. 1855 (Medal with Clasp for Sebastopol).

10 Capt. Winniett served with the 4th Regt. at the siege of Sebastopol from April 1855 (Medal and Clasp).

11 Captain De Montmorency served with a detachment of the 24th Regt. at the defeat of the Jhelum mutineers on the 7th July 1857.

13 Capt. Travers served the Punjaub campaign of 1848-9, and was present with the 10th Regt. during the whole of the siege operations before Mooltan, action of Soorjkoond, and surrender of the fortress of Mooltan; afterwards present at the battle of Goojerat (Medal and Clasps).

14 Captain Stewart served in the Punjaub campaign of 1848-9, and was present from the battle of Goojerat (Medal).

16 Captain Barclay served with the 10th Regt. in the Kaffir war of 1851-53 (Medal).

17 Captain Munnings served as Adjutant of the 24th Regt. in the Punjaub during the Indian Mutiny of 1857. Was on board the ship *Eastern Monarch* when burnt at Spithead on 3rd June 1859; was mentioned in Lt. Col. Allen's dispatch, and received a letter from Captain Morris, bearing testimony to his coolness and judgment on this trying occasion.

19 Captain Godwin-Austen served in the Burmese war in 1853, as Aide de Camp to General Godwin (Medal).

1st Batt. Gibraltar. ⎤
Depot, Athlone. ⎦   **25th (*The King's own Borderers*) Regt. of Foot.**   281

The *King's Crest* in two corners of the Colour, "*In Veritate Religionis confido.*" The *Arms of Edinburgh*, "*Nisi Dominus frustra;*" with the *White Horse* in the third corner of the Colour. "*Nec aspera terrent,*" "MIN-DEN" "EGMONT-OP-ZEE." The *Sphinx.* "EGYPT."—Flank Companies, "MARTINIQUE."

Years' Serv.			
40		𝔓 𝔎ℬ Sir Henry Somerset,¹ KCB., KH., Cornet, 5 Dec. 11; *Lieut.* 30 Dec. 12; *Capt.* 6 Oct. 15; *Major,* ᴾ 25 March 23; *Lt.-Col.* ᴾ 17 July 24; *Col.* 28 June 38; *Maj.Gen.* 11 Nov. 51; *Lt.Gen.* 29 Jan. 57; *Col.* 25 F. 3 Sept. 56.	
Full Pay.	Half Pay.		
27	0	*Lt.-Colonels.*—1 Samuel B. Hamilton, *Ens.* 20 Sept. 33; *Lt.* ᴾ 14 July 37; *Capt.* ᴾ 12 Jan. 30; *Brev.Major,* 11 Nov. 51; *Major,* 4 July 54; *Lt.Col.* ᴾ 24 Nov. 57.	
30	0	2 Andrew Timbrell Allan,² *Ens.* 20 Sept. 30; *Lt.* 28 Dec. 32; *Capt.* ᴾ 31 Dec. 41; *Major,* ᴾ 26 Dec. 51; *Bt.Lt.Col.* 26 Oct. 58; *Lt.Col.* 12 Dec. 59.	
20	0	*Majors.*—Andrew Pitcairn,³ *Ens.* ᴾ 15 May 40; *Lieut.* ᴾ 15 April 42; *Capt.* ᴾ 8 June 52; *Brev.Major,* 2 Nov. 55; *Major,* 2 Sept. 56.	
18	7/12	Francis Fane,³† *Ens.* ᴾ 27 Aug. 41; *Lt.* ᴾ 12 Dec. 43; *Capt.* ᴾ 10 Jan. 51; *Maj.* 18 Feb. 59.	
24	0	Henry Torrens Walker, *Ens.* 28 Oct. 36; *Lt.* ᴾ 4 July 39; *Capt.* 16 Sept. 51; *Major,* 12 Dec. 59.	
16	1/12	Mawdistly Gaussen Best,⁴ *Ens.* ᴾ 12 Dec. 43; *Lt.* ᴾ 21 July 46; *Capt.* ᴾ 7 Mar. 51; *Bt.Maj.* 20 July 58; *Major,* ᴾ 13 May 59.	

		CAPTAINS.	ENSIGN.	LIEUT.	CAPTAIN.	BREV.-MAJ.	BT.LT.COL.
18	0	George Bent	10 April 42	ᴾ 13 Oct. 43	15 Mar. 53		
18	0	Charles D. Pogson.....	9 April 42	ᴾ 10 May 44	15 Mar. 53		
19	0	Cha. Jas. Stewart Wallace	5 Nov. 41	ᴾ 20 Dec. 44	4 July 53		
16	0	Thomas Edwin Blomfield	24 May 44	ᴾ 8 Oct. 47	23 Oct. 55		
12	0	Nicholas Appleby Spoor⁵	ᴾ 7 April 48	ᴾ 16 Jan. 52	ᴾ 8 Dec. 54		
15	0	Astley Campbell Smith..	ᴾ 11 Nov. 45	11 June 48	9 May 56		
12	0	Thomas Rowland⁶......	ᴾ 27 Oct. 48	4 Mar. 53	2 Mar. 56		
11	0	F. Charlesworth Kennedy⁷	18 Sept. 49	ᴾ 17 Oct. 51	ᴾ 24 Nov. 57		
5	0	Henry Pears	1 June 55	8 Jan. 56	ᴾ 11 Jan. 59		
5	0	Tho. Winter Sheppard ..	6 Apr. 55	9 Sept. 55	ᴾ 30 Sept. 59		
13	0	𝒱𝒞 S. Hill Lawrence⁸..	12 Dec. 47	ᴾ 22 Feb. 50	1 July 57	24 Mar. 58	
11	0	George Skene Hallowes..	16 Feb. 49	21 Oct. 51	10 Sept. 58		
11	0	John Richard Harvey ..	9 Mar. 49	24 July 52	12 Dec. 59		
10	0	John O'Hea	ᴾ 17 Feb. 50	ᴾ 7 Sept. 52	12 Dec. 59		
10	0	Arthur Cotton Young ..	ᴾ 15 Feb. 50	ᴾ 21 May 52	13 Dec. 59		
11	0	John Wilkinson⁹	9 Mar. 40	13 July 52	13 Dec. 59		
9	0	Henry Helsham¹⁰	ᴾ 14 Mar. 51	ᴾ 12 Oct. 52	13 Dec. 59		
10	0	Arthur Sisson Cooper ..	ᴾ 22 Nov. 50	11 Mar. 53	13 Dec. 59		
11	0	Thomas Edward Gordon .	21 Aug. 49	2 Dec. 53	13 Dec. 59		
9	0	Edmund Garland Horne¹¹	ᴾ 12 Dec. 51	6 June 54	13 Dec. 59		
8	0	𝒱𝒞 A. Spicer Cameron¹²	ᴾ 9 July 52	ᴾ 1 Sept. 54	13 Dec. 59		
5	0	Fred. Aug. Magrath¹³ ..	ᴾ 7 Dec. 55	16 June 57	13 Dec. 59		
		LIEUTENANTS.					
5	0	Fred. Stephen Terry	15 May 55	3 Apr. 57			
5	0	Charles H. Layard......	23 Oct. 55	ᴾ 10 Apr. 57			
5	0	George Kirwan	10 Aug. 55	ᴾ 3 Mar. 57			
5	0	Gerald Fitzgerald	30 Nov. 55	ᴾ 30 June 57			
5	0	Horatio Bland	ᴾ 7 Dec. 55	ᴾ 14 July 57			
4	0	Charles Pell Heigham ..	ᴾ 29 Feb. 56	ᴾ 17 Nov. 57			
4	0	Charles Edward Hill....	ᴾ 4 Apr. 56	ᴾ 24 Nov. 57			
4	0	Raymond South Paley .	9 May 56	ᴾ 7 May 58			
4	0	John Stubbs	8 July 56	15 Oct. 58			
3	0	Henry George Ramadge	ᴾ 17 Apr. 57	29 Oct. 58			
3	0	Arthur W.A. Nelson Hood	19 June 57	ᴾ 11 Feb. 59			
2	0	Nath. Cricklow Ramsay	ᴾ 14 July 58	ᴾ 11 Mar. 59			
3	0	Henry M. Cornwall Legh	ᴾ 17 Nov. 57	ᴾ 30 Sept. 59			
5	0	Geo. Augustus Eliott...	15 Mar. 55	16 Oct. 55			
4	0	Francis Geo. Coleridge¹⁴	ᴾ 11 Jan. 56	ᴾ 12 Dec. 59			

1 Sir Henry Somerset served the campaigns of 1813, 14, and 15, including the battles of Vittoria, Orthes, Toulouse, and Waterloo. During a protracted service on the frontiers of the Cape of Good Hope, he held a command in the various arduous operations against the Kaffir tribes. He has received the War Medal with three Clasps, and the Kaffir Medal.

2 Colonel Allan served with a detachment 57th Regt. against the Rebels in Canara in 1837. Commanded the 2nd Infantry Brigade in the Eusofzie campaign of 1858. Commanded the troops on board the ship *Eastern Monarch* when she blew up and caught fire at Spithead on the 3rd June 1859, on which occasion a General Order was issued expressing the Commander in Chief's gratification at the conduct of Lt.Col. Allan, and officers and men, and another conveying the Queen's approbation of the discipline and good order displayed under such trying circumstances.

3 Major Pitcairn served the Eastern campaign of 1854-55, including the battles of Alma and Balaklava, expedition to Kertch, siege and fall of Sebastopol, and assault on the outworks 18th June (Medal and Clasps, Brevet Major, Sardinian Medal, and 5th Class of the Medjidie).

3† Major Fane raised and commanded the Peshawur Light Horse during the Indian Mutiny of 1857-59.

4 Major Best served with the 34th Regt. at the siege and fall of Sebastopol from 10 Aug. 1855, and assault of the Redan on the 8th Sept. (Medal and Clasp).

5 Capt. Spoor served with the 6th Regt. in the Kaffir war of 1851-53 (Medal).

231a 25th (*The King's own Borderers*) Regt. of Foot.

Years' Ser Full Pay.	Half Pay.	ENSIGNS.	ENSIGN.	
3	0	Louis James Lambert ..	P 30 June 57	6 Captain Rowland served with the 1st Royals at the siege of Sebastopol from 20 Aug. 1855 (Medal and Clasp).*
3	0	Geo.T.Lyder Carwithen..	P 27 Nov. 57	7 Capt. Kennedy served with the 51st Regt. throughout the Burmese war of 1852; was on board the E.I.C. steam sloop *Sesostris* during the naval action and destruction of the enemy's stockades on the Rangoon River; served during the succeeding three days' operations in the vicinity (including the storming of the White House Redoubt), and at the storm and capture of Rangoon; also at the assault and capture of Bassein, 19th May (Medal).
2	0	Fowell Buxton Johnston	P 21 May 58	
2	0	Henry James Harvey ..	5 June 58	
2	0	Ernest Hen. Paul Vivian	P 9 Nov. 58	
2	0	Charles Robert Leslie ..	12 Nov. 58	
2	0	James Long Watson	31 Dec. 58	
1	0	Robert Crossman	P 11 Feb. 59	8 Major Lawrence served with the 32d Regt. in the Punjaub campaign of 1848-49 including the second siege operations before Mooltan, including the storm and capture of the city, and surrender of the fortress; also at the surrender of the fort and garrison of Cheniote, and battle of Goojerat (Medal and Clasps). Served during the Indian Mutiny in 1857-58; commanded the Head Quarters 32d Regt. at the evacuation of Fort Muchee Bhawan on 1st July 1857, and from that date was engaged in the defence of the Residency of Lucknow until its final relief on 24th Nov. by Lord Clyde, during the greater part of which he commanded the Redan Battery; led a sortie on 7th July and a division of another on 26th Sept. where his Company captured a 9-pounder gun at the point of the bayonet—mentioned in despatches by Sir John Inglis and the Governor General, and received the Victoria Cross (Brevet of Major, Medal and Clasp).
1	0	Reginald Blewitt Dowling	P 31 May 59	
1	0	Alex. Bain Chisholm	P 7 Oct. 59	
				8† Captain Young served with the 61st Regt. at the siege and assault of Delhi including the action of Nujjufghur, and was severely wounded at the assault, causing the loss of the use of the right arm (Medal and Clasp).
30	0	*Paymasters.*—1 Wm. Brumell, 30 Sept. 42; *Ens.* 11 June 30; *Lieut.* 10 Oct. 24.		
		Adjutants.—		
5	0	*Instructors of Musketry.*—1 *Lieut.* F. S. Terry, 6 Feb. 59.		
11	0	*Quarter-Masters.*—1 Robert Malcolm, 27 April 49.		
14	0	*Surgeons.*—1 Jonas King Carr, M.D. 11 May 55; *Assist.Surg.* 24 July 46.		
13	0	2 Charles Robert Robinson, 1 May 55; *Assist.Surg.* 12 Nov. 47.		
6	0	*Assist.Surgeons.*—1 Charles Beaufoy, 23 Dec. 54.		
2	0	1 James Clerk Rattray, M.D. 1 Dec. 58.		
6	0	2 James Gideon Creasy, 14 Dec. 54.		
1	0	2 Edward Corrigan Markey, 1 Mar. 59.		

Facings Blue.—*Agent*, Sir John Kirkland.
[*Returned from Madras* 7 *Aug.* 1855. *Embarked for Gibraltar* 13 *Jan.* 1858.]

9 Captain Wilkinson served with the 80th in the Burmese war of 1852-53, and was present at the capture of Martaban, operations before Rangoon on the 12th, 13th, and 14th April, and capture of the Great Dagon Pagoda with the storming party; and he was severely wounded when in command of the detachment 80th Regt., at the assault and capture of Myattoon's stronghold, on the 19th March 1853 (Medal).

10 Captain Helsham served with the 53rd Regt. in the Indian campaign of 1857-58, including the actions of Chutra, Gopalgunge, Khodagunge and entry into Futtehghur, affair of Shumshabad, storm and capture of Menangunge, siege and capture of Lucknow—wounded (mentioned in despatches, Medal and Clasp).

11 Captain Horne served as Adjutant of the 48th Regt. in the Crimea from 27th April 1855, and at the siege and fall of Sebastopol—wounded 18th Aug. (Medal and Clasp, and 5th Class of the Medjidie).

12 Captain Cameron served with the 72nd Highlanders in the Crimea from 13th June 1855, including the expedition to Kertch, siege and fall of Sebastopol, and attack of the 18th June (Medal and Clasp). From the 9th Oct. 1855 to the 8th March 1856 he served as Assistant Engineer to the Highland Division. Served in the Indian campaign and received the Victoria Cross for conspicuous bravery on the 30th March 1858 at Kotah, in having headed a small party of men and attacked a body of armed fanatic rebels strongly posted in a loop-holed house with one narrow entrance; stormed the house and killed three rebels in single combat, having lost half of one hand by a stroke from a tulwar (Medal).

13 Captain Magrath served with a Company of the 84th Regt. forming part of the garrison of Lucknow from its first investment; afterwards with Outram's force at the Alum Bagh, also at the assault and capture of Lucknow, relief of Azimghur, and pursuit of Koer Singh (Medal and Clasp).

14 Lieut. Coleridge served with the 42d Highlanders the campaign of 1857-58 against the Mutineers in India, including the actions at Cawnpore (6th Dec. 57), Seriaghat, Kudygunge, and Shumsabad, siege and fall of Lucknow, attack on the fort of Rooyah, action at Allyghur, attack and capture of Bareilly (Medal and Clasp).

Dublin. Depot at Belfast.] **26th (The Cameronian) Regt. of Foot.** 232

The Sphinx "EGYPT" "CORUNNA" "CHINA."—The Dragon.

Colonel.—[?] Philip Bainbrigge, CB.[1] Ens. 30 June 00; Lieut. 13 Nov. 00; Capt. 17 Oct. 05; Major, 15 Oct. 12; Lt.-Col. 21 June 17; Col. 10 Jan. 37; Maj.-Gen. 9 Nov. 46; Lt.-Gen. 20 June 54; Col. 26th Foot, 31 Mar. 54.

Lieut.-Colonel.—Andrew T. Hemphill, Ens. 7 Apr. 25; Lt. 16 Apr. 29; Capt. 3 July 39; Major, 11 Feb. 46; Lt.-Col. P 8 Dec. 46; Col. 20 June 54.

Majors.—Francis Carey, Ens. P 22 May 35; Lt. P 2 Sept. 37; Capt. P 7 July 43; Brev.-Maj. 20 June 54; Major, 26 July 54.

Richard Wollaston Clerke, Ens. P 12 April 44; Lieut. P 22 Dec. 46; Capt. P 7 April 54; Major, P 8 Jan. 58.

Full Pay	Half Pay	CAPTAINS.	ENSIGN.	LIEUT.	CAPTAIN.	BREV.-MAJ.
25	0	William Thomas Betts[5]	24 Nov. 35	15 Nov. 39	6 June 54	
11	0	Walter Fitzgerald Kerrich	P 19 Oct. 49	P 30 July 52	P 7 June 54	
11	0	Robt. Creighton Granville	P 2 Mar. 49	P 5 Nov. 50	26 July 54	
11	0	William Mosse	21 Aug. 49	P 5 Dec. 51	P 25 Aug. 54	
15	0	C. R. Berkeley Calcott[6]..	11 Oct. 45	22 Dec. 48	P 30 Mar. 55	
10	0	Edw. H. Pierce Elderton	P 13 Dec. 50	P 1 April 53	P 30 Mar. 55	
9	0	Henry Charles Hardinge	P 14 Mar. 51	P 27 Sept. 53	P 5 Sept. 56	
25	8 2/12	W. M'Donald, *l.c.* 14 Aug. 59	P 5 April 27	P 31 Aug. 30	8 April 42	20 June 54
9	0	John Colling	P 13 Dec. 51	P 28 April 54	P 8 Jan. 58	
8	0	Edward Arch. Collins	P 23 Jan. 52	6 June 54	28 Jan. 59	
8	0	William Eliott Lockhart	P 17 Aug. 52	6 June 54	P 3 June 59	
7	0	Matthew Holford Hale ..	P 13 May 53	9 July 54	P 3 June 59	

LIEUTENANTS.

7	0	Estcourt Day	P 22 April 53	P 7 June 54	
7	0	Geo. Wilbraham Northey	P 27 Sept. 53	26 July 54	1 Lieut.-General Bainbrigge served in the Peninsula in the Quarter-Master-General's department from 1810 to the end of that war in 1814, and was present at the Lines of Torres Vedras, part of the siege of Olivença, siege of Ciudad Rodrigo, last siege of Badajoz, affair of the Guarena, battle of Salamanca, part of the siege of Burgos, affair of Villa Muriel, retreat from Burgos to Ciudad Rodrigo, battles of Vittoria and the Pyrenees, part of the last siege of San Sebastian, battle of the Nive, and actions near Bidart, Bussussary, and Villa Franque; actions of Garris, Tarbes, and Vic Bigorre, and battle of Toulouse. He has received the War Medal with seven Clasps. 5 Captain Betts served throughout the China expedition (Medal), and were present at Chusan, Canton, defence of Ningpo, at Chapoo, Woosung, Shanghae, Chin Kiang Foo, and Nankin. 8 Captain Meldrum served throughout the China expedition (Medal), including the operations before Canton, attack of the sea batteries of Amoy, capture of Golongso, defence of Ningpo, capture of Chapoo, Woosung, Shanghae, and Chinkiangfoo, and landing at Nankin.
6	0	Geo. Edm. Phipps Trent	P 17 Mar. 54	P 8 Sept. 54	
6	0	James Armstrong	P 7 June 54	P 10 Nov. 54	
6	0	George Walton Appleby	P 18 Aug. 54	P 30 Mar. 55	
6	0	Joseph Lowndes	P 24 Aug. 54	P 30 Mar. 55	
6	0	George Meldrum,[8] *Adj*.	11 Aug. 54	P 11 May 55	
6	0	William Beers	P 25 Aug. 54	P 23 Oct. 55	
6	0	Edward Kempson	P 27 Oct. 54	29 Oct. 56	
6	0	Henry Aug. Barton	P 10 Nov. 54	30 Oct. 57	
6	0	Morris Robinson	1 Dec. 54	P 8 Jan. 58	
5	0	William Henry Salwey..	10 Aug. 55	P 23 Apr. 58	
5	0	Thomas Turner	P 28 Dec. 55	28 Jan. 59	
4	0	George Philip Fawkes ..	8 July 56	P 3 June 59	
4	0	Philip Conway Story	P 5 Sept. 56	P 3 June 59	

ENSIGNS.

4	0	William Manjin	19 Apr. 56	
3	0	Lancelot Allgood Gregson	18 Dec. 57	
2	0	Hon. W. H. Bruce Ogilvy	P 15 Jan. 58	
2	0	Charles Henry Wills	P 16 Mar. 58	
2	0	Oswald Cresswell	P 23 Apr. 58	
2	0	Henry P. Wolferstan	25 June 58	
2	0	Henry C. Sharp	2 July 58	
1	0	William Barton Wade ..	11 Mar. 59	
1	0	George Douthwaite	P 3 June 59	
1	0	Jas. Ross Gray Buchanan	P 14 June 59	

5	0	*Paymaster.*—James Bridge, 24 Oct. 56; Cor. 23 Nov. 55; Lt. 1 Feb. 56.
6	0	*Adjutant.*—*Lieut.* George Meldrum, 11 Aug. 54.
7	0	*Instructor of Musketry.*—*Lieut.* G. W. Northey, 1 Aug. 58.
3	0	*Quarter-Master.*—Archibald Hall, 2 Oct. 57.
10	0	*Surgeon.*—John Coates, M.D. 25 Jan. 56; *Assist.Surg.* 2 April 50.
3	0	*Assist.-Surgeons.*—John M'Letchie, 28 Sept. 57.
2	0	John Davidge, 5 Aug. 58. [Borough, Armit & Co.

Facings Yellow.—*Agents*, Messrs. Cox & Co.—*Irish Agents*, Sir E. R.

[*Returned from Bermuda*, 31 Oct. 1859.]

6 Capt. Calcott served with the 10th Regt. during the Punjaub campaign of 1848-9, including the whole of the siege operations before Mooltan, the action at Soorjkoond, capture of the Suburbs, and surrender of the fortress on the 22nd January 1849; also present with the Regt. at the battle of Goojerat (Medal and two Clasps). Served also as a staff officer under Maj.-Gen. Storks, commanding on the Bosphorus during the Russian war in 1855-56.

[*Continuation of Notes to 27th Foot.*]

8 Major Freer served as a Volunteer with the 75th Regt. at the action of Budle-ke-Serai on 8th June 1857, and in all the subsequent affairs in which the 75th Regt. was engaged during the siege of Delhi; commanded the "Stables" Piquet at the capture of four field pieces at "Ludlow Castle" on the 12th August; was severely wounded near the Burn Bastion on the afternoon of the assault of Delhi (Medal).

10 Captain Gresson served as a Volunteer in the Peshawur Light Horse at Peshawur during the Indian Mutiny of 1857-58. Was on board the ship "Eastern Monarch" when she blew up and caught fire at Spithead on 3d June 1859.

10† Lieut. Simeon served as a Volunteer with the 61st Regt. at the siege, assault, and capture of Delhi in 1857, including repulse of sorties on the 4th, 9th, and 18th July, and the action of Nujufghur.

11 Qr. Master Trenor served throughout the Kaffir war of 1846-7 (Medal).

12 Captain Urquhart served with the Reserve of the Army of the Indus at the reduction of Fort Munaro in Scinde in Feb. 1839. Debarked in command of a detachment under a brisk fire at Bushire for the protection of the Political Resident there. Was present with the expeditionary force in China, from the first capture of Chusan up to the attack on the heights above Canton (Medal), and in the course of these operations he commanded a company specially selected for desultory services, and was frequently mentioned in the Dispatches, in one " as having rendered important service while in charge of the enemy's Naval Arsenal Canton."

233   [Emb. for India. 5 July 54.]   **27th (or Inniskilling) Regt. of Foot.**   [Serving in India. Depot, Buttevant.

A Castle with Three Turrets; St. George's colours flying in a blue Field. The White Horse. "*Nec aspera terrent.*" "ST. LUCIA." The *Sphinx*, with the words "EGYPT" "MAIDA" "BADAJOZ" "SALAMANCA" "VITTORIA" "PYRENEES" "NIVELLE" "ORTHES" "TOULOUSE" "PENINSULA" "WATERLOO."

Years' Serv		
Full Pay	Half Pay	
58		**Colonel.**—Ɖ Edward Fleming,[1] CB. *Ens.* 24 June 02; *Lieut.* 6 July 04; *Capt.* 30 May 07; *Major*, 1 April 13; *Lieut.-Col.* 18 July 16; *Col.* 10 Jan. 37; *Major Gen.* 9 Nov. 46; *Lt.Gen.* 20 June 54; *Col.* 27th Regt. 19 Sept. 53.
		Lt.-Cols.—Robert Julian Baumgartner,[2] CB. *Ens.* p 27 Sept. 33; *Lt.* p 30 June
26	1¾	37; *Capt.* p 23 April 41; *Major*, 23 Sept. 51; *Lt. Col.* 12 Dec. 54.
23	0	Herman Stapylton, *Ens.* p 4 Aug. 37; *Lieut.* p 19 Mar. 41; *Capt.* p 1 Dec. 46; *Major*, 9 Oct. 56; *Lt.Col.* 5 Aug. 59.
16	0	**Majors.**—Barclay Thomas, *Ens.* 31 Dec. 44; *Lt.* 19 Nov. 47; *Capt.* p 8 Nov. 50; *Major*, p 25 Jan. 59.
14	0	Richard Freer,[3] *Ens.* 22 May 46; *Lt.* 13 Dec. 49; *Capt.* 23 Mar. 55; *Brev. Maj.* 19 Jan. 58; *Major*, p 18 Oct. 59.

		CAPTAINS.	ENSIGN.	LIEUT.	CAPTAIN.	BREV.-MAJ.
15	0	John Vize O'Donnell	p 25 Nov. 45	p 11 Feb. 48	p 15 June 49	
23	0	Edw. Nassau Molesworth[4]	p 1 Dec. 37	p 2 Apr. 41	2 Dec. 51	3 June 59
13	0	James Henry Creagh	19 Nov. 47	p 21 June 50	p 6 May 53	
21	0	John Samuel Manly[7]	15 Feb. 39	p 20 Oct. 43	26 May 54	
13	0	Charles Warren[5]	23 April 47	p 18 Sept. 49	26 May 54	
19	0	John Ball Campbell[6]	2 July 41	20 Sept. 43	27 Jan. 55	
15	0	William Croker	p 25 Jan. 46	p 22 June 47	p 12 May 54	
7	0	Henry Mitford[8]	p 23 Dec. 53	23 Sept. 54	8 Aug. 56	
9	0	Henry Bethune Patton	26 Dec. 51	p 14 April 54	p 26 Oct. 58	
14	0	Richard John Evans[9]	4 Apr. 46	p 28 Sept. 47	13 Aug. 57	
8	0	Francis Eastwood Murphy	p 12 Mar. 52	26 May 54	p 25 Jan. 59	
8	0	William Henry Gresson[10]	p 13 Mar. 52	26 May 54	p 18 Oct. 59	
		LIEUTENANTS.				
10	0	W. Hamil. Twemlow, *Adj.*	p 15 Mar. 50	p 9 July 52		
8	0	William Henry Davis	p 9 July 52	26 May 54		
8	0	Walter Macpherson	p 16 Apr. 52	p 15 July 53		
8	0	Wm. S. Church Pinwill	p 23 Nov. 52	28 May 54		
7	0	George Stewart White	4 Nov. 53	29 Jan. 55		
6	0	Charles Edward Stewart	p 14 April 54	1 May 55		
6	0	Andrew David Geddes	6 June 54	p 7 Sept. 55		
5	0	Robert Lloyd	1 May 55	9 Oct. 56		
5	0	Henry Scott Simeon[10]†	1 June 55	p 19 Dec. 56		
5	0	William Magenis Stafford	8 June 55	p 3 April 57		
4	0	Fred. Richard Attwood	p 7 Mar. 56	p 1 May 57		
8	0	William James Surman[9]†	11 June 52	4 Aug. 54		
4	0	Henry Monteath Caine	p 10 Dec. 56	p 19 June 57		
3	0	Laurence Wm Desborough	6 Jan. 57	12 Oct. 57		
3	0	Aiskew Clay	p 1 May 57	p 26 Oct. 58		
3	0	Francis Coffey	p 9 Nov. 58	p 21 Oct. 59		
		ENSIGNS.				
4	0	Albert Dixon	26 Feb. 56			
3	0	Richard Hamilton	p 18 Sept. 57			
2	0	George Power Cobbe	15 Jan. 58			
2	0	Frederick Tottenham	29 Oct. 58			
2	0	Ormsby Cox	9 Nov. 58			
1	0	James M. Vernon Cotton	p 18 Mar. 59			
1	0	William Herring	p 18 Nov. 59			

[37; *Capt.* 9 Nov. 46.]

20	2½	**Paymaster.**—John Urquhart,[12] 1 Feb. 50; *2nd Lt.* 14 July 28; *1st Lt.* 26 May
10	0	**Adjutant.**—*Lieut.* Walter Hamilton Twemlow, 23 Nov. 54.
8	0	**Instructor of Musketry.**—*Lieut.* W. S. C. Pinwill, 16 Dec. 58.
6	0	**Quarter-Master.**—John Trenor,[11] 28 April 54.
16	0	**Surgeon.**—Mark Stanley Todd, 28 March 54; *Assist.-Surg.* 22 Nov. 44.
6	0	**Assist.-Surgeons.**—John M'Leod Cameron, M.B. 26 May 54.
6	0	Leonard Kidd, M.B. 26 May 54.
3	0	Alexander Stevenson Russell, 1 Aug. 57.

Facings Buff.—*Agents*, Messrs. Cox & Co.

1 Lieut.-General Fleming served with the 31st Regt. in Sicily, and part of the Grenadier Battalion in Calabria in 1806 under Sir John Stuart. In Egypt in 1807 under General Mackenzie Fraser, at the taking of Alexandria, and storming of Rosetta, when he obtained his Company in action. Joined the expedition under Sir David Baird to Corunna, and served the Peninsular campaigns of 1808, 9, 10, and 11, including the passage of the Albuera with the advanced Brigade, the pursuit of Massena from Santarem, battles of Talavera, Busaco, and Albuhera (very severely wounded in the head); and commanded the Light Company of his Regiment, forming part of the advance, at the spirited affair with and retreat of the enemy from Campo Mayor to Badajoz on the 25th March 1811. Served in the West Indies from 1813 to 1819, including the expedition up the river St. Mary's, in Georgia, United States of America; in the East Indies from 1820 to 1823 inclusive, and in Canada from 1829 to 1833. He has received the Silver War Medal with three Clasps.

2 Lt. Colonel Baumgartner served the Eastern campaign of 1854-55 with the 28th Regt., including the battles of Alma and Inkerman, siege of Sebastopol, and affair on the 18th June in the Cemetery (succeeded to the command of the Regt.); was wounded in the trenches 17th Aug. 1855 (Medal and Clasps, CB., Sardinian Medal, and 4th Class of the Medjidie).

Ahmednuggur. Depot, Fermoy.] **28th (*The North Gloucestershire*) Regt. of Foot.** 234

The *Sphinx*, with the words "EGYPT" "CORUNNA" "BARROSA" "ALBUHERA" "VITTORIA" "PYRENEES" "NIVELLE" "NIVE" "ORTHES" "PENINSULA" "WATERLOO" "ALMA" "INKERMAN" "SEVASTOPOL."

Years' Serv.		
Full Pay	Half Pay	
47		

34	0	Colonel.—Sir Henry John Wm. Bentinck,[1] KCB. *Ens.* 25 Mar. 13; *Lt. & Capt.* 18 Jan. 20; *Capt. & Lt.-Col.* 16 May 20; *Col.* 23 Nov. 41; *Maj.-Gen.* 20 June 54; *Col.* 28th Foot, 11 Oct. 54.
34	0	Lieut.-Colonels.—Frank Adams,[2] CB. *Ens.* P 30 Dec. 26; *Lt.* 23 Mar. 32; *Capt.* P 31 Dec. 33; *Maj.* 29 Oct. 43; *Lieut.-Col.* P 16 July 52; *Col.* 28 Nov. 54.
21	0	Percy Archer Butler,[3] *Ens.* P 1 Mar. 39; *Lt.* 2 May 42; *Capt.* P 4 Apr. 45; *Brev. Maj.* 12 Dec. 54; *Major*, 9 Oct. 55; *Brev.Lt.Col.* 6 June 56; *Lt.Col.* 17 Sept. 58.
18	0	Majors.—Thomas Maunsell,[4] *Ensign*, P 27 May 42; *Lieut.* P 23 May 45; *Capt.* 8 Oct. 50; *Brev.-Maj.* 2 Nov. 55; *Major*, P 9 Jan. 57.
21	0	William Roberts,[5] *Ens.* P 1 Nov. 39; *Lieut.* 19 July 43; *Capt.* P 17 Aug. 52; *Bt.-Maj.* 2 Nov. 55; *Major*, 17 Sept. 58.

		CAPTAINS.	ENSIGN.	LIEUT.	CAPTAIN.	BREV.-MAJ
14	0	Henry R. Crewe Godley[7]	P 25 Sept. 46	P 21 July 48	P 17 Feb. 54	6 June 56
18	0	Sussex L. A. B. Messiter[8]	5 Nov. 42	P 24 May 44	29 Dec. 54	
13	0	William Gordon Shute[9]	P 26 Nov. 47	P 30 Mar. 49	26 Jan. 55	
13	0	Simpson Hackett[10]	31 Dec. 47	P 16 July 52	P 16 Mar. 55	
8	0	James Williams[14]	P 21 Sept. 52	20 Nov. 54	P 25 Sept. 55	
11	0	James Graham Turner[11]	P 30 Mar. 49	P 18 Oct. 53	9 Oct. 55	
8	13	Hill Faulconer Morgan[12]	P 23 Sept. 51	5 Oct. 55	15 Jan. 56	
15	0	Daniel Antoine Baby[13]	28 Feb. 45	P 1 Aug. 48	P 17 July 57	
6	0	Charles David Ingham[18]	P 17 Feb. 54	8 Dec. 54	P 26 Mar. 58	
6	0	John Godfrey Day[16]	P 3 Mar. 54	12 Jan. 55	P 7 May 58	
7	0	Tho. Sutton Kirkpatrick[21]	P 18 Oct. 53	8 Dec. 54	17 Sept. 58	
16	0	John William Preston	26 Jan. 44	P 13 Nov. 46	P 17 July 57	

		LIEUTENANTS.			
6	0	Francis Brodigan[19]		6 June 54	8 Jan. 55
6	0	William Alfred Steward[17]		7 June 54	12 Jan. 55
7	0	Edw. Percival Vaughan[21]	P 29 July 53	P 16 June 54	
9	0	Charles Geo. Mackenzie	P 21 Feb. 51	13 Feb. 55	
6	0	Frederick C. Irwin[18]	3 Nov. 54	9 Mar. 55	
6	0	Edward Fox Angelo[11]	15 Dec. 54	13 April 55	
6	0	Thomas Edmund Adams[11]	29 Dec. 54	13 April 55	
5	0	Alexander Lyon Emerson	P 12 Jan. 55	13 July 55	
5	0	Gordon Charles S. Ducat	24 April 55	26 Nov. 58	
5	0	Charles Thackeray	14 May 55	P 5 May 58	
5	0	Francis Edward Webb	15 May 55	P 7 May 58	
5	0	Mark Farley Wade	6 July 55	17 Sept. 58	
5	0	Alexander Humfrey	19 July 55	13 June 59	
5	0	Thomas Horniblow	20 July 55	7 Oct. 59	

1 Sir Henry Bentinck left England with the Guards the 22nd Feb. 1854, and commanded that Brigade during the Eastern campaign until the 8th November, including the battles of Alma, Balaklava, and Inkerman (wounded in the arm), siege of Sebastopol, and in support of the 2nd Division at the repulse of the sortie of 26th October. Was appointed to the 4th Division after the fall of Sir George Cathcart, but prevented by wound and ill-health from joining it till the 1st June 1855; continued in command until the 10th October (Medal and Clasps, KCB., Commander of the Legion of Honor, Sardinian Medal, and 2nd Class of the Medjidie).

3 Lt.-Col. Butler served the Eastern campaign of 1854-55, including the battles of Alma and Inkerman, siege and fall of Sebastopol (Medal and three Clasps, Brevet of Major and Lt.-Col., Knight of the Legion of Honor, and 5th Class of the Medjidie).

		ENSIGNS.			
5	0	Edward Brett		30 Nov. 55	
5	0	Fred. Rance,[25] *Adj.*		9 Oct. 55	
2	0	Jerome O'Brien		P 5 Feb. 58	
2	0	Arthur St. George Cuff		6 Feb. 58	
2	0	Arthur Holden Turner		P 5 Mar. 58	
2	0	Ellis Houlton Ward		P 23 April 58	
2	0	Arthur Howard Southey		P 21 May 58	
2	0	Sam. F. Fred. Auchmuty		P 13 July 58	
2	0	Robert Burn Singer		24 Sept. 58	
1	0	Nathaniel Robert Slator		29 July 59	

6	0	Paymaster.—Henry A. Berry,[22] 14 Dec. 55; *Ens.* 11 Aug. 54.	
5	0	Adjutant.—Ensign Frederick Rance,[25] 8 Aug. 56.	
5	0	Instructor of Musketry.—Ensign Edward Brett, 20 June 57.	
5	0	Quarter-Master.—Thomas Lumsden, 14 Dec. 55.	
18	0	Surgeon.—Benjamin William Marlow,[23] M.D. 24 Feb. 54; *A.-S.* 25 Feb. 42.	
6	0	Assist.-Surgeons.—William Henry Brice,[6] 6 Jan. 54.	
6	0	Charnney Graves Irwin,[24] 24 Feb. 54.	
2	0	William Gerard Don, M.D., 22 Jan. 58.	

Facings Yellow.— *Agts.*,Messrs. Cox & Co.—*Irish Agts.*,Sir E.R. Borough, *Bt.*, Armit & Co.
[*Embarked for Turkey*, 22 Feb. 1854.]

2 Colonel Adams commanded the 28th Regt. throughout the Eastern campaign of 1854-55, including the battles of Alma and Inkerman, siege and fall of Sebastopol, and affair on 18th June in the Cemetery. Succeeded to the command of the Brigade on Sir Wm. Eyre being wounded, and brought it out of action (Medal and three Clasps, CB., Officer of the Legion of Honor, Sardinian Medal, and 3rd Class of the Medjidie).

28th (*The North Gloucestershire*) Regt. of Foot.

4 Major Maunsell served in the 32nd Regt. the Punjaub campaign of 1848-9, and was present at the first and second siege operations before Mooltan, including the attack on the enemy's position in front of the advanced trenches on the 12th Sept. 1848 (slightly grazed by a bullet), the action of Soorjkoond, storm and capture of the city, and surrender of the fortress; afterwards present at the surrender of the fort and garrison of Cheniote, and at the battle of Goojerat (Medal and two Clasps); was severely wounded at Mooltan on the 21st January 1849. Served the Eastern campaign of 1854-55 in the 28th Regt., including the battles of Alma and Inkerman, and siege of Sebastopol, during which he commanded the volunteer sharpshooters of the 3rd Division until severely wounded on the 30th Dec., for which service he was made honourable mention of in Division Orders of 3 Jan., 1855, and promoted Brevet-Major (Medal and three Clasps, Sardinian Medal, and 5th Class of the Medjidie).

6 Major Roberts and Assist.-Surg. Brice served the Eastern campaign of 1854-55, including the battles of Alma and Inkerman, siege and fall of Sebastopol, and affair in the Cemetery (Medal and three Clasps). Major Roberts is a Knight of the Legion of Honor, and has the 5th Class of the Medjidie.

7 Major Godley served the Eastern campaign of 1854-55, including the battles of Alma and Inkerman, siege of Sebastopol, and affair in the Cemetery (severely wounded): Medal and three Clasps, Brevet Major, and 5th Class of the Medjidie.

8 Captain Messiter served the Eastern campaign of 1854-55, including the battles of Alma and Inkerman, siege and fall of Sebastopol (Medal and Clasps, Sardinian Medal, and 5th Class of the Medjidie).

9 Captain Shute served the Eastern campaign until Jan. 1855, including the battles of Alma and Inkerman, and siege of Sebastopol (Medal and three Clasps).

10 Captain Hackett served the Eastern campaign of 1854-55 as Adjutant of the 28th Regt., including the battles of Alma and Inkerman, siege and fall of Sebastopol, and affair in the Cemetery (Medal and three Clasps, and 5th Class of the Medjidie).

11 Captain Turner, Lieuts. Angelo and Adams, served the Eastern campaign of 1855, including the siege of Sebastopol (Medal and Clasp).

12 Captain Morgan served the Eastern campaign of 1854-55, including the battles of Alma and Inkerman, and siege of Sebastopol, severely wounded in the trenches, 3rd June, by two musket-balls in the right leg (Medal and three Clasps, and 5th Class of the Medjidie).

13 Captain Baby served with the 98th Regt. in the Punjaub campaign of 1848-49 (Medal).

14 Captain Williams served the Eastern campaign of 1854-55, including the battles of Alma and Inkerman, siege and fall of Sebastopol, and affair in the Cemetery. Served in Turkey from Feb. 1856 as Aide-de-Camp to Major-General Smith, Commanding Osmanli Irregular Cavalry, until the disbandment of that force (Medal with three Clasps, 4th Class of the Medjidie, and Lt.-Col. Turkish Army).

17 Lieut. Steward served in the Crimea from the 20th Jan. 1855, including the siege and fall of Sebastopol and the affair in the Cemetery on the 18th June (Medal and Clasp).

18 Captains Ingham and Day, and Lieut. Irwin, served the Eastern campaign of 1855, including the siege and fall of Sebastopol, and affair in the Cemetery (Medal and Clasp).

19 Lieut. Brodigan served the Eastern campaign of 1855, including the siege of Sebastopol and affair in the Cemetery—severely wounded (Medal and Clasp).

21 Captain Kirkpatrick and Lieut. Vaughan served the Eastern campaign of 1855, including the siege of Sebastopol (Medal and Clasp).

22 Paymaster Derry served the Eastern campaign of 1854-55, including the battles of Alma and Inkerman, siege of Sebastopol, and affair in the Cemetery (Medal and three Clasps).

23 Surgeon Marlow served the Eastern campaign of 1854-55, including the battles of Alma and Inkerman, and siege of Sebastopol (Medal and three Clasps, and Knight of the Legion of Honor).

24 Assist.-Surg. Irwin served in the Eastern campaign of 1854-55, including the battle of Alma and siege of Sebastopol (Medal and Clasps).

25 Ensign Rance served the Eastern campaign of 1854-55, including the battles of Alma and Inkerman, in the trenches at the siege and fall of Sebastopol, and assault of the 18th June (Medal and three Clasps).

[*Continuation of Notes to 29th Foot.*]

Camp to Gen. Luard at the relief of Azimghur and action of Jugdeespore (mentioned in dispatch); as Brigade Major at the reduction of Dehayon, Tirhol (mentioned in dispatch), and other of the Oude forts, also at the surrender of Amethic (Medal and Clasp).

7 Captain Kneebone served with the 29th throughout the Punjaub campaign in 1848-9, including the passage of the Chenab, and battles of Chillianwallah and Goojerat (Medal and Clasps).

9 Captain Clarke served with the 93rd Highlanders the Eastern campaign of 1854-55, including the battles of Alma and Balaklava, siege and fall of Sebastopol, capture of Kertch and Yenikali (Medal and three Clasps, and Turkish Medal). Also the Indian campaign in 1857-59, including relief of Lucknow by Lord Clyde, battle of Cawnpore on 6th Dec., pursuit of the enemy and capture of their guns at Sernighat, action at Kallee Nuddie; taking of Futtehghur, expedition to Mowh under Brigadier Hope, siege and capture of Lucknow (mentioned in Sir E. Lugard's despatches), and subsequent affairs ending in the capture of Bareilly (Medal and Clasps).

10 Captain Wilkie served with the 97th Regt. at the siege of Sebastopol from 16 June 1855 (Medal and Clasp). Also in the Indian campaign of 1857-58, and was present with the Jounpore field force in the actions of Chanda, Ummeerpore, and Sultanpore, and afterwards at the siege and capture of Lucknow (Medal and Clasp).

11 Lieut. Bailey served the campaigns in Affghanistan of 1838-42, and was present at the storming of Ghuznee (Medal), and the forts of Totumdurrah and Joolghur, the engagements in forcing the passes from Cabool to Jellalabad, and in defence of the latter, including the general action of the 7th April 1842 (Medal); also present at the affairs of Jugdulluck and Tezeen, and the recapture of Cabool (Medal).

12 Qr.Master Aylett served with the 20th Regt. throughout the Eastern campaign of 1854-55, including the battles of Alma and Inkerman, siege and fall of Sebastopol, and affair of the 18th June (Medal and Clasps). Also in the Indian campaign of 1857-58, including the actions of Chanda, Umeerpore, and Sultanpore, siege and capture of Lucknow, subsequent operations in Oude, and affairs of Churda, and fort of Musjeedia (Medal and Clasp).

13 Doctor Moorhead served with the 32nd Regt. at the first and second siege operations before Mooltan, including the capture of the city and surrender of the fortress (Medal and Clasp).

Preston, Depot, Weedon.] **29th (The Worcestershire) Regt. of Foot.** 236

"ROLEIA" "VIMIERA" "TALAVERA" "ALBUHERA" "PENINSULA" "FEROZESHAH" "SOBRAON" "PUNJAUB" "CHILLIANWALLAH" "GOOJERAT."

Years' Serv.		
56	Full Pay	Half Pay

Col.—39 Ulysses, *Lord* Downes,[1] KCB. *Ens.* 31 Mar. 04; *Lt.* 12 Nov. 04; *Capt.* 4 Sept. 06; *Maj.* 31 Mar. 11; *Lt.Col.* 5 Sept. 12; *Col.* 27 May 25; *Maj.Gen.* 10 Jan. 37; *Lt.Gen.* 9 Nov. 46; *Gen.* 20 June 54; *Col.* 29th Regt. 15 Aug. 50.

23	0	*Lieut.Colonel.*—John Ross Wheeler, *Ens.* 30 July 28; *Lieut.* p 25 Dec. 29; *Capt.* p 15 Dec. 40; *Major*, 11 Nov. 51; *Bt.Lt.Col.* 26 Oct. 59; *Lt.Col.* 13 Dec. 59.
22	0	*Majors.*—Edward Henry Westropp,[3] *Ens.* p 2 Nov. 38; *Lt.* 8 Apr. 42; *Capt.* 5 Aug. 47; *Maj.* 20 July 58.
17	0	Lindsay Farrington,[3] *Ens.* 23 June 43; *Lieut.* 27 Sept. 44; *Capt.* p 9 July 50; *Major*, 13 Dec. 59.

		CAPTAINS.	ENSIGN.	LIEUT.	CAPTAIN.	BREV.MAJ.
20	0	Hugh George Colvill[4]	10 Jan. 40	3 Aug. 41	10 Dec. 52	
18	0	Henry George Walker[5]	p 29 Apr. 42	31 Dec. 43	15 Mar. 53	
17	0	John Mackenzie Lyle[3]	p 19 May 43	p 2 Sept. 45	6 Aug. 53	
16	0	Augustus Alexander Dick[6]	p 31 Dec. 44	20 Mar. 46	9 Jan. 54	
15	0	Frederick Kneebone[7]	19 Dec. 45	20 Mar. 46	13 June 55	
18	0	Fred. Dobson Middleton[8]	30 Dec. 42	18 Aug. 48	p 6 July 52	20 July 58
10	0	Heneage Charles Chester	p 16 Aug. 50	p 28 May 52	12 Oct. 57	
11	0	Somerset Molynx. Clarke[9]	p 23 Nov. 49	p 5 Mar. 52	20 Dec. 54	
6	0	Hales Wilkie[10]	p 18 Aug. 54	3 Jan. 55	p 24 July 57	
6	0	Richard Edwyn Barry	p 3 Feb. 54	14 Sept. 55	p 24 Sept. 58	
5	0	Nathaniel Polhill Ledgard	p 1 May 55	27 July 55	p 29 Apr. 59	
11	0	John James Hood Gordon	p 21 Aug. 49	9 Jan. 54	13 Dec. 59	

		LIEUTENANTS.			
11	0	H. W. Somerville Carew	21 Aug. 49	20 June 54	1 Lord Downes was appointed Aide-de-Camp to Sir John Cradock, whom he accompanied to Portugal in Nov. 1808, where Sir John held the chief command until May 1809, when he was succeeded by the Duke of Wellington, with whom Lord Downes continued as Aide-de-Camp and Assistant Military Secretary during the whole war, and was present at the battles of Talavera (slightly wounded), Busaco, Fuentes d'Onor, and El Bodon; sieges of Ciudad Rodrigo and Badajoz, battles of Salamanca, Vittoria, and the Pyrenees; siege of San Sebastian, battles of the Nivelle (horse shot), Nive, and Toulouse (slightly wounded). His Lordship has received the Gold Cross & one Clasp for Vittoria, Pyrenees, Nivelle, Nive, & Toulouse; and the Silver War Medal and six Clasps for Talavera, Busaco, Fuentes d'Onor-Ciudad Rodrigo, Badajoz, and Salamanca.
7	0	Geo. Wm. Fred. D. Smith	13 May 53	13 June 55	
8	0	Thomas Pattison Wood	p 23 Nov. 54	p 10 Nov. 54	
5	0	Edward Gorton	p 26 July 55	p 9 Nov. 55	
5	0	Fred. Stirling Eckersall	27 July 55	4 Dec. 55	
5	0	John James Bailey,[11] *Adj.*	3 Aug. 55	10 June 57	
5	0	George F. Hart	15 June 55	10 June 57	
5	0	William Winn	30 Nov. 55	13 Aug. 57	
4	0	John North Bomford	29 Feb. 56	20 July 58	
4	0	Alfred Godfrey Black	8 July 56	23 July 58	
4	0	Kenrick Verulam Bacon	p 12 Dec. 56	17 Sept. 58	
3	0	George Edward Fursdon	3 Mar. 57	26 Oct. 58	
3	0	Lancelot Amelius Shadwell	p 12 May 57	p 20 Apr. 59	
4	0	Wm. Montague Cochrane	p 26 Feb. 56	p 13 May 59	
3	0	William Boycott	18 Dec. 57	13 Dec. 59	

		ENSIGNS.		
3	0	Howell Davis	19 Dec. 57	
2	0	Francis William Prittie	26 Mar. 58	
2	0	Alfred Fawcett	30 Mar. 58	
2	0	Elsden P. Henry Everard	p 24 Aug. 58	
2	0	Robert Berkeley	24 Sept. 58	
2	0	Henry Wasey Kindersley	29 Oct. 58	
2	0	Jas. Henry Herbert Croft	12 Nov. 58	
1	0	Fred. Charles Ruxton	p 3 June 59	
1	0	William Graham Arnold	p 4 June 59	
1	0	Ernest Aug. Prid. Bruce	p 20 Dec. 59	

4	0	*Paymaster.*—John Edward Longden, 26 Dec. 56.
5	0	*Adjutant.*—Lieut. John James Bailey,[11] 29 Feb. 56.
3	0	*Instructor of Musketry.*—Ensign William Boycott, 31 Jan. 59.
5	0	*Quarter-Master.*—James Aylett,[12] 9 Feb. 55.
18	0	*Surgeon.*—Edward Moorhead,[13] M.D. 25 May 55; *Assist.-Surg.* 2 Aug. 42.
5	0	*Assist.-Surgeons.*—William Langford Farmer, 24 April 55.
3	0	Walter John,[ ] 9 Nov. 57.

Facings Yellow—*Agents*, Messrs. Cox & Co.

[*Returned from Bengal* 18 *Sept.* 1859.]

3 Majors Westropp and Farrington, and Captain Lyle, served with the 29th in the Sutlej campaign of 1845-46, and were present at the battles of Ferozeshah and Sobraon (Medal and Clasp). Major Farrington served also in the Punjaub campaign of 1848-49, including the passage of the Chenab and battles of Chillianwallah and Goojerat (Medal and Clasps).

4 Captain Colvill served with the 39th Regt. in the action of Maharajpore (Medal), 29 Dec. 1843 (severely wounded).

5 Captain Walker served with the 29th Regt. in the campaign on the Sutlej, including the battles of Ferozeshah and Sobraon—wounded (Medal and Clasp); at Ferozeshah he was acting Aide-de-Camp to the Governor-General, and had a horse shot under him.

6 Capt. Dick served with the 29th Regt. in the Sutlej campaign of 1845-46 and was present at the battle of Ferozeshah (Medal and Clasp). Also throughout the Punjaub campaign in 1848-49, including the passage of the Chenab, and battles of Chillianwallah and Goojerat (Medal and two Clasps). Served with the 8th Regt. during the Indian Mutiny, and was present in the action of Dilkoosha and relief of Lucknow and Cawnpore by Lord Clyde (Medal and Clasp).

8 Major Middleton served with the 58th Regt. at the assault and capture of Kawiti's Pah, also during 1846-47 in the southern part of New Zealand, including the repulse of the attack on Wanganui (mentioned in dispatch) and subsequent affairs there. Served as a Volunteer during the Santhal rebellion in India. Served in the Indian campaign of 1857-58;—as Orderly Officer to General Franks in the action of Sultanpore and subsequent affairs on the advance to Lucknow (three times mentioned in dispatches); as Aide de Camp to Gen. Lugard at the siege and capture of Lucknow, and storming of the Martinière, Banks' House, Begum's Kotee, and Moulvy's Mosque (mentioned in dispatch, and Brevet Major); as Deputy Judge Advocate, and Aide de

[For remainder of Notes, see preceding page.]

237   30th (*The Cambridgeshire*) *Regt. of Foot.*   [Head Qrs. Curragh.
                                                       Depot, Parkhurst.

The *Sphinx*, with the words "EGYPT" "BADAJOZ" "SALAMANCA" "PENINSULA"
"WATERLOO" "ALMA" "INKERMAN" "SEVASTOPOL."

Years' Serv.		
Full Pay	Half Pay	
56		Col.—George, *Marquis of* Tweeddale,¹ KT. CB. *Ens.* June 04 ; *Lt.* 12 Oct. 04 ; *Capt.* 14 May 07 ; *Maj.* 14 May 12 ; *Lt.Col.* 21 June 13 ; *Col.* 27 May 25 ; *Maj.-Gen.* 10 Jan. 37 ; *Lt.Gen.* 9 Nov. 46 ; *Gen.* 20 June 54 ; *Col.* 30th F. 7 Feb. 46.
26	0	Lieut.-Colonel.—James Thomas Mauleverer,² CB. *Ens.* P 18 Apr. 34 ; *Lieut.* P 19 Aug. 36 ; *Capt.* P 28 July 43 ; *Major,* P 21 May 52 ; *Lt.Col.* 30 Sept. 54 ; *Col.* 30 Sept. 57.
16	0	Majors.—Thomas Henry Pakenham,³ *Ens.* P 12 July 44 ; *Lt.* P 10 Mar. 47 ; *Capt.* P 24 Sept. 50 ; *Brev.Maj.* 12 Dec. 54 ; *Maj.* 9 Sept. 55 ; *Brev.Lt.Col.* 6 June 56.
22	0	Robert Dillon,⁴ *Ens.* P 8 June 38 ; *Lieut.* P 29 Nov. 39 ; *Capt.* P 30 Nov. 49 ; *Maj.* 15 Feb. 56.

Years Full	Half	CAPTAINS.	ENSIGN.	LIEUT.	CAPTAIN.	BREV.-MAJ.
13	0	Fra. Topping Atcherley⁵	P 4 June 47	P 4 Aug. 48	P 16 Dec. 53	17 July 55
11	0	Charles Mingaye Green⁶	P 20 April 49	P 17 May 50	30 Sept. 54	2 Nov. 55
11	0	William John Brook⁷	P 19 Oct. 49	P 21 May 52	29 Dec. 54	
10	0	Edwd. Newstead Falkner⁸	P 22 Nov. 50	P 7 Jan. 53	29 Dec. 54	
8	0	Lachlan Macpherson⁹	P 17 Dec. 52	P 6 Jan. 54	17 Aug. 55	
8	0	Jas. Cavendish Hobbs¹⁰	23 Nov. 52	11 Aug. 54	7 Sept. 55	
6	0	Edward Nicholas Hill¹¹	10 Mar. 54	P 18 Aug. 54	9 Sept. 55	
6	0	Stamer Gubbins¹²	6 June 54	P 3 Nov. 54	27 Nov. 57	
6	0	Charles John Moorsom¹³	21 July 54	8 Nov. 54	P 4 Dec. 57	
7	0	John Pennock Campbell¹⁴	13 May 53	6 Nov. 54	30 April 58	
6	0	Henry Corbet Singleton¹¹	11 Aug. 54	8 Dec. 54	P 24 Sept. 58	
8	0	William, Deedes¹⁷	P 13 Feb. 52	11 Aug. 54	23 Mar. 55	

LIEUTENANTS.

6	0	Alfred John Austin¹⁵	7 June 54	6 Nov. 54	1 Lord Tweeddale served in the Peninsula as an Assistant-Quarter-Master-General, and has received the Gold Medal for the battle of Vittoria, in which action he was wounded, as also at Busaco. Served also in the American war, and was again wounded.
6	0	Joseph Fleming¹¹	P 18 Aug. 54	8 Dec. 54	
8	0	H. L'Estnge.Herring,*Adj.*	P 17 Aug. 52	26 Jan. 55	
6	0	Edward St. George Smyth	24 Nov. 54	9 Mar. 55	
6	0	Nathaniel Wm. Massey	8 Dec. 54	9 Mar. 55	
8	0	Francis John Connell¹⁶	13 Feb. 52	P 13 Nov. 52	
5	0	Chas.Jas.Palmer Clarkson	P 18 Jan. 55	18 May 55	17 Captain Deedes served with the Rifle Brigade the Eastern campaign of 1854, including the battles of Alma and Inkerman, and siege of Sebastopol (Medal and three Clasps).
5	0	Hyde Sergison-Smith	P 25 Jan. 55	9 Sept. 55	
5	0	Robert Olphert Campbell	9 Feb. 55	25 Sept. 55	
5	0	Charles Tyner	15 May 55	30 April 58	
5	0	Henry F. Morewood	18 May 55	31 Aug. 58	
5	0	Montagu D. Stevenson	9 Oct. 55	P 24 Sept. 58	
4	0	Decimus Montagu	P 10 Dec. 56	P 29 Oct. 58	
3	0	John William Green	P 17 Nov. 57	P 11 Mar. 59	
2	0	Frd. Harcourt Williamson	P 5 Mar. 58	P 5 Aug. 59	

ENSIGNS.

4	0	Octavius Boyce	25 Jan. 56	
4	0	Alex. Webster M'Kenzie	1 Feb. 56	
2	0	William Glascott	16 Mar. 58	
2	0	*Hon.* Leo.Wm. H. Powys	P 21 May 58	
2	0	Pelham T. Pelham	25 June 58	
2	0	Richard Nagle	7 Sept. 58	
2	0	Henry Horace Eden	P 13 July 58	
2	0	Joshua E. C. C. Lindesay	8 Sept. 58	
1	0	William Vesey Brownlow	P 29 Apr. 59	
2	0	David Matthew La Touche	17 Dec. 58	

3	0	Paymaster.—George Fead Lamert, 6 Oct. 57.
8	0	Adjutant.—*Lieut.* Henry L'Estrange Herring, 24 Feb. 57.
6	0	Instructor of Musketry.—*Captain* Charles John Moorsom, 18 Dec. 56.
6	0	Quarter Master.—John Moon,¹⁰ 1 June 55 ; *Ens.* 5 Nov. 54 ; *Lt.* 9 March 55.
16	0	Surgeon.—Raphael Woolman Read, 28 Dec. 55 ; *Assist.-Surg.* 31 May 44.
6	0	Assist.Surgs.—David Milroy,¹⁰ M.D. 7 April 54.
2	0	Wallace Lindsay, 5 Aug. 58.

Facings Yellow.—*Agents*, Messrs. Cox & Co.
[*Returned from Gibraltar,* 11 *September* 1857.]

2 Colonel Mauleverer served with the 17th Regt. throughout the Affghanistan and Beloochistan under Lord Keane, and was present at the storm and capture of Ghuznee (Medal) and of Khelat. Served the Eastern campaign of 1854-55, with the 30th, including the battle of the Alma (horse shot), shortly after which he succeeded to the command of the Regiment, and was present at the battle of Inkerman (severely wounded), siege of Sebastopol, sortie of 26th Oct. 1854, and assault on the Redan 8th Sept. 1855—wounded (Medal and Clasps, mentioned in Dispatches, CB., Officer of the Legion of Honor, Sardinian Medal, and 4th Class of the Medjidie).
3 Lieut.-Col. Pakenham served in the Eastern campaign of 1854, and was slightly and also severely wounded at the battle of Alma (Medal and Clasp, Brevets of Major and Lt.Colonel, Sardinian Medal, and 5th Class of the Medjidie).
4 Major Dillon served at the siege of Sebastopol (Medal and Clasp, and Sardinian Medal).
5 Major Atcherley served in the Eastern campaign of 1854-55, including the battle of Alma, siege of Sebastopol, repulse of the sortie on 26th Oct. 1854 (severely wounded in the arm, and mentioned in Dispatches), and assault on the Redan on the 8th Sept. 1855—mentioned in despatches (Medal and Clasps, Brevet-Major, Knight of the Legion of Honor, and 5th Class of the Medjidie).

30th (The Cambridgeshire) Regt. of Foot. 238

6 Major Green served the Eastern campaign of 1854-55, including the battles of Alma and Inkerman, siege of Sebastopol, sortie of 26th Oct. 1854, and assault on the Redan on the 8th Sept. (Medal and Clasps, and mentioned in Dispatches, Brevet Major, Knight of the Legion of Honor, and 5th Class of the Medjidie).

7 Captain Brook served in the Crimea from 8th Sept. 1855, as D. A. Q. M. G. 4th Division (Medal and Clasp).

8 Captain Falkner served the Eastern campaign of 1854-55, attached to the Commissariat, including the battles of Alma and Inkerman, the siege of Sebastopol, and repulse of the sortie on the 26th Oct. (Medal and Clasps).

9 Captain Macpherson served the Eastern campaign of 1854-55, including the battles of Alma and Inkerman, siege of Sebastopol, and sortie of 26th Oct. (Medal and Clasps, and 5th Class of the Medjidie).

10 Captain Hobbs, Qr.Master Moon, and Assistant Surgeon Milroy, served the Eastern campaign of 1854, including the battles of the Alma and Inkerman, and siege of Sebastopol (Medal and Clasps). Assist. Surgeon Milroy has the 5th Class of the Medjidie.

11 Captains Hill and Singleton, and Lieut. Fleming, served at the siege of Sebastopol in 1855 (Medal and Clasp).

12 Captain Gubbins served at the siege of Sebastopol in 1855, and sortie of 5th June—mentioned in Dispatch (Medal and Clasp, and Knight of the Legion of Honor).

13 Captain Moorsom served at the siege of Sebastopol, and at the assault on the Redan on the 8th Sept. 1855, where he was severely wounded in the left arm (Medal and Clasp).

14 Captain Campbell served the Eastern campaign of 1854-55, including the battles of Alma and Inkerman, siege of Sebastopol, and sortie of 26th Oct. 1854 (Medal and Clasps, and 5th Class of the Medjidie).

15 Lieut. Austin served at the siege of Sebastopol in 1855, and at the assault on the Redan on the 8th Sept. (Medal and Clasp, and 5th Class of the Medjidie).

16 Lieut. Connell served at the siege of Sebastopol, and at the attack on the Redan on the 18th June 1855 (Medal and Clasp).

[Continuation of Notes to 31st Foot.]

4 Major Eagar served the campaign of 1842 in Affghanistan, including the actions of Mazeena, Tezeen, and Jugdulluck, the occupation of Cabool, and the different engagements leading to it (Medal). Served in the Crimea from 11th June 1855, as Brigade Major of 2nd Brigade 1st Division from 10th Aug. 1855, to 17th Jan. 1856, and was present at the siege of Sebastopol and attacks on the 18th June and 8th Sept. (Medal and Clasp, Brevet Major, Knight of the Legion of Honor, and 5th Class of the Medjidie).

5 Major Swaffield, Captains Baldwin, Schreiber, Swettenham, and Mitchell, Lieuts. Cassidy, Pyler, Pepper, and Bayley, served in the Crimea from 22nd May 1855, including the siege of Sebastopol and attacks on the 18th June and 8th Sept. (Medal and Clasp). Major Swaffield and Captain Schreiber have the 5th Class of the Medjidie.

6 Capt. Law served with the 31st throughout the campaign of 1842 in Affghanistan (Medal), including the actions of Mazeena, Tezeen, and Jugdulluck, the occupation of Cabool, and the different engagements leading to it. He served also the Sutlej campaign of 1845-46, including the battles of Moodkee, Ferozeshah, Buddiwal, Aliwal, and Sobraon (severely wounded): Medal and three Clasps.

8 Captains Macbean and Leeson and Lieut. Rycroft, served in the Crimea from 6th Aug. 1855, including the siege of Sebastopol and attack on the 8th Sept. (Medal and Clasp). Captain Leeson has the 5th Class of the Medjidie.

10 Captain Prevost served in the Crimea from 22nd May 1855, including the siege and fall of Sebastopol and attack of the 8th Sept.; he was wounded on the 17th June (Medal and Clasp).

11 Captain Harcourt was at the battle of the Alma (Medal and Clasps).

12 Captain M'Gregor served with the 14th Lt. Dragoons in the campaign with the Central India Field Force under Sir Hugh Rose.

15 Captain Cary served in the Crimea from 22nd May to 23rd Aug. 1855, including the siege of Sebastopol and attack on the 18th June (Medal and Clasp).

16 Surgeon Atkinson served with the 31st Regt. in the Crimea from 7th July 1855, including the siege and fall of Sebastopol, and attack of the Redan on the 8th Sept. 58 (Medal and Clasp).

17 Assist.Surgeon Grant served in the Crimea from 12th Nov. to 28th Dec. 1854, and from 31st July 1855, including the siege of Sebastopol, and attack on the 8th Sept. (Medal and Clasp).

18 Lieut. Hamilton served in the Crimea from 22nd May to 15th June 1855 (Medal and Clasp for Sebastopol).

31st (*The Huntingdonshire*) Regt. of Foot.

India, Depot, Chatham.

"TALAVERA" "ALBUHERA" "VITTORIA" "PYRENEES" "NIVELLE"
"NIVE" "ORTHES" "PENINSULA" "CABOOL, 1842" "MOODKEE"
"FEROZESHAH" "ALIWAL" "SOBRAON" "SEVASTOPOL."

Years' Serv.		
Full Pay.	Half Pay.	
47		**Colonel.**—Peter Edmonstone Craigie,[1] CB. *Ens.* p 3 June 13; *Lt.* p 29 Sept 14; *Capt.* p 24 Oct. 21; *Major*, p 10 Aug. 26; *Lt.Col.* 21 Nov. 34; *Col.* 23 Dec. 42; *Maj.Gen.* 20 June 54; *Col.* 31 F. 20 Feb. 59.
		Lieut.-Colonels.—Frederick Spence,[2] *Ens.* 24 Dec. 29; *Lt.* p 1 Nov. 31; *Capt.*
31	0	28 June 44; *Maj.* 15 June 55; *Brev.Lt.Col.* 26 Dec. 56; *Lt.Col.* 7 Dec. 58.
32	1 9/12	William Sutton,[3] *Ens.* p 5 June 27; *Lieut.* p 16 Mar. 30; *Capt.* p 30 July 36; *Brev.Maj.* 9 Nov. 46; *Major,* p 6 Oct. 48; *Brev.Lt.Col.* 15 Sept. 48; *Lt.Col.* 11 Nov. 51; *Col.* 28 Nov. 54.
		Majors.—Robert John Eagar,[4] *Ens.* 11 June 30; *Lt.* p 25 Jan. 33; *Capt.* p 8
30	0	Oct. 44; *Brev.Maj.* 2 Nov. 55; *Major,* 21 Dec. 55.
14	0	Charles James Orton Swafield,[5] *Ens.* 27 Feb. 46; *Lt.* p 21 Jan. 48; *Capt.* p 19 Apr. 50; *Major,* 7 Dec. 58.

		CAPTAINS.	ENSIGN.	LIEUT.	CAPTAIN.	BREV.MAJ.
14	0	George Walter Baldwin[5]	4 Apr. 46	p 20 July 49	p 31 Oct. 51	
20	0	Robert Law[6]	8 Feb. 40	27 July 42	5 May 54	
18	1 10/12	William Fred. Macbean[8]	p 31 Oct. 40	30 Sept. 42	p 27 Aug. 52	
14	0	Samuel Christian	5 Apr. 46	p 11 Sept. 49	15 June 55	
11	0	Arthur John Schreiber[5]	30 Nov. 49	p 31 Oct. 51	15 June 55	
10	0	Charles Prevost[10]	p 16 Aug. 50	p 17 Aug. 52	27 July 55	
9	0	Thos. Eaton Swettenham[5]	9 Sept. 51	p 18 Feb. 53	p 12 Feb. 58	
5	1	Jno.S.Chandos Harcourt[11]	p 6 Jan. 54	30 Sept. 54	26 Feb. 56	
9	0	Alexander Mitchell[5]	p 12 Dec. 51	5 May 54	7 Dec. 58	
13	0	Alex. Edgar M'Gregor[12]	2 Apr. 47	p 29 May 49	26 Feb. 58	
8	0	Annesley Cary[15]	p 12 Mar. 52	6 June 54	p 1 July 59	
8	0	Ralph Leeson[8]	p 21 Sept. 52	11 Aug. 54	p 29 Nov. 59	

		LIEUTENANTS.			
8	0	Fred. Young Cassidy[5]	p 11 June 52	6 June 54	
7	0	John W. Townsend Fyler[5]	p 21 Jan. 53	15 June 55	
6	0	George Nicholson Pepper[5]	6 June 54	15 June 55	
6	0	George Bayley[5]	p 24 Aug. 54	15 June 55	
6	0	George John Hamilton[16]	p 22 Sept. 54	15 June 55	
6	0	Thos. Christian Rycroft[8]	p 22 Dec. 54	15 June 55	
5	0	Robert Froke Gould	13 Apr. 55	15 June 55	
8	0	H. K. Johnstone Waldron	9 July 52	p 23 Dec. 53	
5	0	Hugh Pollexfen Doane	24 Apr. 55	9 Sept. 55	
5	0	Arthur Jebb	22 June 55	p 15 Feb. 56	
5	0	Colin Campbell M'Intyre	4 July 55	p 21 May 58	
5	0	John T. Austin Gardiner	23 Oct. 55	7 Dec. 58	
5	0	William Hill James	19 July 55	1 Oct. 58	

2 Lt.Col. Spence served in the Crimea from 22nd May 1855, including the siege of Sebastopol, and attacks on the 18th June and 8th Sept.; commanded the Regt. from 13th Nov. (Medal and Clasp, Knight of the Legion of Honor, and 5th Class of the Medjidie).

3 Colonel Sutton served throughout the Kaffir wars of 1834-35, 1846-47, and 1851-52. At the commencement of the latter war he defeated a large force which made an attack on Fort Beaufort, a very important success at that period (Medal).

		ENSIGNS.		
4	0	William Edward Tibbetts	26 Feb. 56	
4	0	Reginald Edward Huxam	27 Feb. 56	
3	0	Fra.Wm.H.Davies Butler	11 Sept. 57	
3	0	Andrew Hamilton	p 16 Oct. 57	
2	0	Arthur Johnson Danyell	16 Mar. 58	
2	0	Alex. G. Selwyn Maynard	p 28 May 58	
2	0	John Mich. Bradley Wood	p 23 July 58	
2	0	Isaac Parsons	p 30 July 58	
2	0	Alex. Cumming Gow	p 9 Nov. 58	
1	0	George Moore Lambert	p 26 Aug. 59	
3	0	**Paymaster.**—William Edmund Adams, 10 March 57.		
		Adjutant.—*Lieut.*		
6	0	**Instructor of Musketry.**—*Lieut.* G. N. Pepper, 11 Dec. 58.		
2	0	**Qr. Master.**—Chrystopher Kettyles, 2 July 58.		
9	0	**Surgeon.**—Thomas Johnston Atkinson,[16] 20 Jan. 58; *Assist.-Surg.* 28 Feb. 51.		
6	0	**Assistant Surgeons.**—William Grant,[17] 9 June 54.		
3	0	Byng Thomas Giraud, M.D. 9 Nov. 57.		
2	0	Charles Hervé Giraud, 10 March 58.		

Facings Buff.—*Agents,* Messrs. Cox and Co.
[*Embarked for Corfu, 24 January* 1853.]

1 Major General Craigie served with the 2nd Battalion 52nd Light Infantry the campaign of 1813-14 in Holland under Lord Lynedoch, including both attacks on the fortified village of Merxem—in the latter of which he led the advance party of Major Gen. Sir Herbert Taylor's Brigade. In May 1841 he embarked at Calcutta in command of the 55th Regiment for China (Medal), and served with the Expeditionary Force under Lord Gough till the end of the War, and was senior Field Officer serving with the force in the field and consequently second in command from the period of its sailing from Hong Kong in August and during the whole of the active operations which took place during the following five months. He commanded a Brigade or Column of attack at the assault and capture of the fortified cities of Amoy, Chusan (2nd capture)—on which occasion it happened that the whole of the engagement devolved upon his Brigade—and Chinhae. Subsequently, when the Head Quarters of the force proceeded to the Yeang-tze Keang, he was appointed by Lord Gough to the responsible command of the Island of Chusan, which he held for eight months until the return of the Force after the treaty of peace had been signed at Nankin. For his conduct on the above occasions (as stated in Lord Gough's despatches) he was promoted to the rank of Colonel and appointed an Aide de Camp to the Queen and a Companion of the Bath. [For remainder of notes see preceding page.

Dover. Depot, Devonport.] **32nd (The Cornwall) Regt. of Foot (Light Infantry).**

"ROLEIA" "VIMIERA" "CORUNNA" "SALAMANCA" "PYRENEES" "NIVELLE" "NIVE" "ORTHES". "PENINSULA" "WATERLOO" "PUNJAUB" "MOOLTAN" "GOOJERAT" "LUCKNOW."

Years' Serv.						
Full 62		Col.—Ᵽ Sir Willoughby Cotton,[1] GCB. & KCH. Ens. 31 Oct. 98; Lt. & Capt. 25 Nov. 99;				
Full Pay.	Half Pay.	Capt. & Lt.Col. 12 June 11; Col. 25 July 21; Maj.Gen. 22 July 30; Lt.Gen. 23 Nov. 41; Gen. 20 June 54; Col. 32nd Regt. 17 Apr. 54.				
21	0	Lt.Colonel.—James Dodington Carmichael,[2] CB. Ens. ᴾ 12 July 39; Lieut. 11 May 41; Capt. ᴾ 18 April 45; Major, 20 Feb. 55; Bt.Lt.Col. 1 Feb. 56; Lt.Col. 26 Nov. 57.				
36	8 5/12	Majors.—William Bell,[3] Ens. 30 Nov. 15; Lt. 26 Apr. 28; Capt. 2 July 41; Bt.Maj. 20 June 54; Major, 23 March 58; Bt.Lt.Col. 16 Jan. 59.				
15	0	Charles Clapcott,[4] Ens. ᴾ 18 Apr.45; Lt. ᴾ 12 June 46; Capt. ᴾ 23 July 52; Maj. 26 Sept. 58.				

		CAPTAINS.	ENSIGN.	LIEUT.	CAPTAIN.	BREV.MAJ.	BT.LT.COL.
20	0	Robert Stacy Colls[5]	14 Feb. 40	24 Apr. 43	20 Feb. 55	26 Apr. 59	
14	0	Alfred Bassano[6]	3 Apr. 46	24 May 48	15 Oct. 56	24 Mar. 58	
15	0	William Rudman[7]	22 Dec. 45	ᴾ 11 Feb. 48	15 May 57	24 Mar. 58	
14	0	Horatio Priestley[8]	28 Aug. 46	19 June 48	3 Apr. 57		
13	0	John Birtwhistle[9]	ᴾ 11 Dec. 47	3 Sept. 49	28 June 57		
12	0	William James Anderson	15 Aug. 48	ᴾ 16 Sept. 51	11 Aug. 57		
10	0	Charles Rodick Ricketts[11]	8 Oct. 50	ᴾ 31 Dec. 52	14 Sept. 57		
10	0	John Edmondstoune[12]	ᴾ 15 Oct. 50	ᴾ 5 Jan. 55	2 Oct. 57	24 Mar. 58	
9	0	Charles Marshall Foster[13]	ᴾ 18 April 51	14 Apr. 55	26 Nov. 57	24 Mar. 58	
5	0	Edwin Harmar[14]	ᴾ 23 Mar. 55	ᴾ 15 June 55	23 Mar. 58		
11	0	Richard Henry Magenis[15]	10 Apr. 49	ᴾ 5 May 54	25 Feb. 55	20 July 58	
5	0	Edw. Aug.T.Cunynghame	9 Oct. 55	ᴾ 26 Feb. 56	ᴾ 11 Mar. 59		
		LIEUTENANTS.					
5	0	Henry Elkins Bennett[8]	ᴾ 14 Sept. 55	ᴾ 29 Apr. 56			
4	0	Henry Sparke Stabb,[8] Adj.	ᴾ 29 Apr. 56	1 Aug. 56			
5	0	James Strachan[16]	30 Aug. 55	1 July 57			
4	0	Charles Edw. Lane Bluett	15 Jan. 56	5 Feb. 58			
4	0	Edmund Lakin	26 Feb. 56	5 Feb. 58			
5	0	Alex. James Badgley[11]	1 June 55	ᴾ 8 Jan. 58			
3	0	John Garforth[17]	19 June 57	6 Feb. 58			
5	0	Henry Mant Gilby[18]	17 Aug. 55	ᴾ 9 Nov. 58			
3	0	James Thomas Gray[17]	17 Nov. 57	30 Apr. 58			
5	0	A. R. Wm. Thistlethwayte	18 Mar. 55	26 Oct. 55			
5	0	George Walker[19]	11 May 55	27 Nov. 57			
5	0	Samuel Black Noble[11]	18 May 55	ᴾ 23 Mar. 58			
3	0	Timothy Morris	18 Nov. 57	9 Aug. 58			
2	0	Cha. Geoffrey Stanley	ᴾ 5 Feb. 58	26 Sept. 58			
2	0	Cornelius Francis Clery	5 Mar. 58	ᴾ 3 June 59			
		ENSIGNS.					
2	0	Arthur Bishop	ᴾ 12 Feb. 58				
2	0	William Trickett Goad[20]	13 Feb. 58				
2	0	Chas. E. Le M. Cherry	23 Mar. 58				
2	0	Walter Philip Walshe	31 Mar. 58				
2	0	Herbert Rich. Hardinge	14 May 58				
2	0	Frank A. Horridge	2 July 58				
2	0	David Bond	ᴾ 7 Sept. 58				
2	0	Fred. Nassau Golding	29 Oct. 58				
2	0	Chas. Hamilton Trueman	29 Oct. 58				
1	0	Hugh Wm.Mort.Cathcart	ᴾ 3 June 59				
12	0	Paymaster.—John Giddings,[21] 28 Nov. 56; Qr.Master, 13 Sept. 48.					
4	0	Adjutant.—Lieut. Henry Sparke Stabb,[8] 9 Aug. 58.					
4	0	Instructor of Musketry.—Lieut. Edmund Lakin, 27 Aug. 59.					
4	0	Quarter Master.—Francis Stribling,[22] 28 Nov. 56.					
8	0	Surgeon.—William Boyd,[23] 7 Sept. 58; Assist.Surg. 12 March 52.					
5	0	Assist.Surgeons.—William Henry Harris,[24] 10 March 55.					
6	0	ᵥⅭ William Bradshaw,[25] 15 Aug. 54.					

1 Sir Willoughby Cotton served with the 3rd Guards on the expedition to Hanover in 1805; and on that to Copenhagen in 1807, where he was appointed Deputy Assistant Adjutant General to the reserve under the Duke of Wellington, and was present at the battle of Kioge. In 1809 he accompanied the Duke to Spain, and served as Deputy Assistant Adjutant General to the Light Division during the whole of the campaign of the retreat to Torres Vedras and the subsequent advance, the former containing a series of skirmishes and the battle of the Coa. Returned to England on promotion in June 1811, and rejoined the Peninsular army in 1813; he was present at the battle of Vittoria, commanded the Light Companies at the passage of the Adour, and the pickets of the 2nd Brigade of Guards at the repulse of the sortie from Bayonne. He commanded a Division of Sir Archibald Campbell's army in the Burmese war; and also of the army under Lord Keane in Affghanistan, and was present at the assault and capture of Ghuznee (Medal). Sir Willoughby has received the War Medal and three Clasps; also First Class of Dooranee Empire.

5 Major Colls served with the 39th Regt. in the battle of Maharajpore (Medal). Served with the 32nd in the Punjaub campaign of 1848-49, and was present at the second siege operations before Mooltan, including the storm and capture of the city, and surrender of the fortress; also present at the surrender of the garrison of Cheniote, and at the battle of Goojerat (Medal and Clasps). Served during the Indian Mutiny in 1857-59, and present as Field Engineer to the force under Brigadier Berkeley at the capture of the forts of Dehaign and Tyrhool (mentioned in despatches); also as D.A.Q.M. General to Brigadier Pinckney's force during the campaign in Oude (Brevet of Major, Medal).

Facings White.—Agents, Messrs. Cox & Co.
[Embarked for India, 31 May 1846; returned home, 25 Aug. 1859.]

2 Lt.Colonel Carmichael served with the 32nd Regt. at the first and second siege operations before Mooltan, and was at the action of Soorjkoond; led the right column of attack at the storm and capture of the city of Mooltan (wounded), and was present at the surrender of the fortress, as also at the surrender of the fort and garrison of Cheniote, and at the battle of Goojerat (Medal and Clasps). Commanded the Regt. in the Indian campaign at the attack and capture of the forts of Dehaign and Tyrhool under Brigadier Berkeley; again at the action of Daodpore and defent of the Nusseerabad Mutineers under Brigadier Horsford, and was thanked in that officer's despatch "for the able manner in which he commanded the Infantry." Served the campaign for the Reduction of Oude,—commanded a moveable column, which, acting under the orders of and in conjunction with Lord Clyde's force, was sent in pursuit of the rebel chief Beni Maddoo, to drive him and his troops across the river Gogra, which object the column successfully accomplished—mentioned in Lord Clyde's despatch as "distinguished for the decision and celerity of his movements" (CB., Medal).
3 Lt.Colonel Bell was present at the battle of Goojerat (Medal and Clasps).
4 Major Clapcott served with the 32nd Regt. at the first and second siege operations before Mooltan, including the attack on the enemy's position in front of the advanced trenches on 12th Sept. 1848, the action of Soorjkoond, storm and capture of the city, and surrender of the fortress; also present at the surrender of the fort and garrison of Cheniote, and at the battle of Goojerat (Medal and Clasps).

32nd (The Cornwall) Regt. of Foot (Light Infantry).

6 Major Bassano served with the 32d Regt. at the first and second siege operations before Mooltan, including the attack on the enemy's position in front of the advanced trenches on 12th Sept. 1848, the action of Soorjkoond, storm and capture of the city, and surrender of the fortress; also present at the surrender of the fort and garrison of Cheniote, and at the battle of Goojerat (Medal and Clasps). Served during the Indian Mutiny in 1857-59; was in action at Chinhut on 30th June 1857 (severely wounded), and from that date engaged in the defence of the Residency of Lucknow until its final relief by Lord Clyde on 24th Nov. 1857; engaged in a sortie on 26th Sept. when seven guns were captured, and was in command of the Regt. from 27th Sept. to 24th Nov. (mentioned in despatches by Sir John Inglis and the Governor General, Brevet of Major); also engaged in the defeat of the Gwalior rebels at Cawnpore on 6th Dec. 1857, and in part of the subsequent campaign in Oude (Medal and Clasp).

7 Major Rudman served with the 62nd Regt. in the campaign on the Sutlej (Medal and Clasp), including the battles of Ferozeshah and Sobraon.

8 Captain Priestley, Lieuts. Bennett and Stabb served during the Indian Mutiny in 1857-59, and were present at the capture of the forts Dehaign and Tyrool, action of Doadpore, and throughout the Oude campaign (Medal).

9 Captain J. Birtwhistle served with the 32nd Regt. in the Punjaub campaign of 1848-49 including the second siege operations before Mooltan, including the storm and capture of the city, and surrender of the fortress; also at the surrender of the fort and garrison of Cheniote, and battle of Goojerat (Medal and Clasps).

11 Captain Ricketts, Lieuts. Badgley and Noble served during the Indian Mutiny in 1858-59, and were present at the action of Doadpore, and throughout the Oude campaign (Medal).

12 Major Edmondstoune served during the Indian Mutiny in 1857-59; defended the Iron Bridge over the river Goomtee with fifty men to cover the retreat from Chinhut on 30th June 1857, and from that date engaged in the defence of the Residency of Lucknow until its final relief on 24th November by Lord Clyde; led a sortie on 29th Nov., and was twice severely wounded, on 28th July and 29th Nov.—mentioned in despatches by Sir John Inglis and the Governor General (Brevet of Major); subsequently engaged in the defeat of the Gwalior rebels at Cawnpore on 6th Dec., at the capture of the forts of Dehaign and Tyrool, and throughout the Oude campaign (Medal and Clasp).

13 Major Foster served in the Indian Mutiny in 1857-58 and was in action with the rebel force at Chinhut on the 30th June 1857, and from that date engaged in the defence of the Residency of Lucknow until its final relief by Lord Clyde on 24th Nov.,—was severely wounded during the siege and mentioned in despatches by Sir John Inglis and the Governor General; was subsequently engaged in the defeat of the Gwalior rebels at Cawnpore on 6th Dec. 1857 (Medal and Clasp and Brevet of Major).

14 Captain Harman served during the Indian Mutiny in 1857-58 and was in action with the rebel force at Chinhut on 30th June 1857, and from that date engaged in the defence of the Residency of Lucknow until its final relief on 24th Nov. by Lord Clyde (severely wounded, leg fractured by a round shot, mentioned in despatches by Sir John Inglis and the Governor General, Medal and Clasp).

15 Major Magenis served with the 90th Light Infantry at the siege and fall of Sebastopol; commanded a party of the Regt. at the taking of the Rifle Pits on the 19th April 1855, and was of the storming party at the assault of the Redan on the 8th Sept.—mentioned in Dispatches (Medal and Clasp, and 5th Class of the Medjidie). Also during the Indian campaign of 1857-58,—present with Havelock's Column at the actions of the 21st and 23rd Sept., relief and subsequent defence of Lucknow, defence of the Alumbagh under Outram, and fall of Lucknow (Brevet of Major, Medal and Clasp).

16 Lieut. Strachan served during the Indian Mutiny in 1857-59 and was present at the capture of the forts of Dehaign and Tyrhool, and the Oude campaign (Medal).

17 Lieuts. Garforth and Gray served during the Indian Mutiny in 1858-59, including the Oude campaign (Medal).

18 Lieut. Gilby served with a detachment of the 88th Regt. in the operations at Cawnpore under General Windham, and was severely wounded at the attack against the Gwalior Contingent on 26 Nov. 1857 (Medal).

19 Lieut. Walker served with the 88th Regt. at the siege and fall of Sebastopol in 1855, was wounded in the trenches on the 8th Aug., and twice severely wounded at the final attack on the Redan (Medal and Clasp and Turkish Medal). Served in the Indian campaign in 1857-58 and was present at the repulse of the Gwalior Contingent at Bogneepore and fall of Calpee under Sir Hugh Rose (Medal).

20 Ensign Goad served during the Indian Mutiny in 1858-59; as a Volunteer with the 79th Highlanders at the siege and capture of Lucknow by Lord Clyde; subsequently with the 32d Regt. at the capture of the forts of Dehaign and Tyrhool, action of Doadpore, and throughout the Oude campaign (Medal and Clasp).

21 Paymaster Giddings served at the first and second siege operations before Mooltan, including the action of Soorjkoond, storm and capture of the city, and surrender of the fortress; also at the surrender of the fort and garrison of Cheniote and battle of Goojerat (Medal and Clasps). Served during the Indian Mutiny in 1857-59 and was engaged in the defence of the Residency of Lucknow from 30th June until its final relief on 24th Nov. by Lord Clyde, during part of which time he acted as Adjutant of the Regiment and was also in temporary charge of posts in addition to other duties; was subsequently engaged in the defeat of the Gwalior rebels at Cawnpore on 6th Dec. 1857 (Medal and Clasp).

22 Qr. Master Stribling served during the Indian Mutiny in 1857-59 and was engaged in the defence of the Residency of Lucknow from the 30th June until its final relief on 24th Nov. by Lord Clyde (mentioned in despatches by Sir John Inglis); was subsequently engaged in the defeat of the Gwalior rebels at Cawnpore on 6th Dec., capture of the forts of Dehaign and Tyrhool, action of Doadpore, and throughout the Oude campaign (Medal and Clasp).

23 Surgeon Boyd served during the Indian Mutiny in 1857-59 and was engaged in the defence of the Residency of Lucknow from 30th June until its final relief on 24th Nov. by Lord Clyde, during which time he officiated as Medical Officer in charge of the European Garrison Hospital besides having charge of the 32d Regt.,—was promoted Surgeon "for eminent services" rendered throughout the whole siege of Lucknow and mentioned in despatches by Sir John Inglis and the Governor General; present also at the defeat of the Gwalior rebels at Cawnpore on 6th Dec., and accompanied the 32d Regt. in several minor excursions after the mutineers both before and subsequent to the siege of Lucknow (Medal and Clasp).

24 Assist. Surgeon Harris served in the Crimea from 22nd May 1855, including the siege and fall of Sebastopol, the attack of the 18th June, and battle of the Tchernaya (Medal and Clasp). Also served during the Indian Mutiny in 1857-59, including the Oude campaign (Medal).

25 Assist. Surgeon Bradshaw served with the 50th Regt. at the siege and fall of Sebastopol from 8th Nov. 1854 (Medal and Clasp and Turkish Medal). Served with the 90th Lt. Inf. during the Indian campaign of 1857-58 and was present with Havelock's column at the actions of the 21st and 23rd Sept. (wounded), relief and subsequent defence of Lucknow, defence of the Alumbagh under Outram, and fall of Lucknow (Medal and Clasps, and Victoria Cross).

33rd (or *The Duke of Wellington's*) Regt. of Foot. 242

Serving in India. Depot, Fermoy.

"SERINGAPATAM" "WATERLOO." The Crest and Motto of the Duke of Wellington.
"ALMA" "INKERMAN" "SEVASTOPOL."

Years' Serv.			
Full Pay	Half Pay		
53		Colonel.—🂱 🂿🂱 Sir Charles Yorke,[1] KCB., *Ens.* 22 Jan. 07; *Lt.* 18 Feb. 08; *Capt.* 24 Dec. 13; *Major*, 9 June 25; *Lt.Col.* 30 Nov. 26; *Col.* 23 Nov. 51; *Maj.Gen.* 11 Nov. 51; *Lt.Gen.* 13 Feb. 59; *Col.* 33rd Foot, 27 Sept. 55.	
33	0	*Lt.-Colonels.*—John Douglas Johnstone,[2] CB. *Ens.* p 15 Aug. 27; *Lt.* 16 Mar. 30; *Capt.* p 19 Oct. 38 ; *Major*, p 3 Oct. 48 ; *Lt.Col.* 9 Mar. 55 ; *Col.* 9 Mar. 58.	
21	0	John E. Collings,[4] *Ens.* 21 June 39; *Lieut.* 22 Jan. 42 ; *Capt.* p 3 Oct. 48 ; *Major*, 19 Sept. 55 ; *Brev.-Lieut.-Col.* 6 June 56 ; *Lt.-Col.* 17 Nov. 57.	
20	0	*Majors.*—Edw. Westby Donovan,[5] *Ens.* 10 Jan. 40 ; *Lieut.* 14 June 42 ; *Capt.* 22 Dec. 48; *Bt.-Maj.* 17 July 55 ; *Major*, 26 Oct. 55 ; *Bt. Lt.-Col.* 26 Dec. 56.	
20	0	Henry Chas. Fitzgerald,[7] *Ens.* p 25 Sept. 40; *Lieut.* 9 Oct. 42 ; *Capt.* p 2 Jan. 52 ; *Brev.-Major*, 26 Dec. 56 ; *Major*, 17 Nov. 57.	

Years	Serv.	CAPTAINS.	ENSIGN.	LIEUT.	CAPTAIN.	BREV. MAJ.
18	0	Thomas Wickham [9]	p 25 Oct. 42	p 22 Dec. 46	p 25 Mar. 53	6 June 56
18	0	Richard Lacy, s.		11 Mar. 42	p 27 Sept. 44	6 June 54
14	0	Basil Fanshawe [10]		p 14 Apr. 46	p 3 Oct. 48	29 Dec. 54
14	0	Frederic Smith Vacher [11]		8 Dec. 46	p 20 Oct. 48	29 Dec. 54	6 June 56
13	0	Chas. Carter Barrett [13]	p 22 Jan. 47	10 Sept. 49	29 Dec. 54	
12	0	William Henry Parry [15]	p 20 Oct. 48	p 2 Jan. 52	19 Jan. 55	
12	0	Alex. Bruce Wallis [16]		22 Dec. 48	p 6 July 52	24 Aug. 55	
10	0	Buxton Martin Kenrick [15]	p 18 Jan. 50	p 21 Sept. 52	19 Sept. 55	
10	6/12	Edward Barker Prescott [17]	p 15 Mar. 50	p 8 April 53	26 Oct. 55	
7	1	John James Greenwood [12]		15 Oct. 52	21 Sept. 54	19 Sept. 56	
7	0	John Thornton Rogers [20]	p 13 May 53	6 Nov. 54	p 27 Nov. 57	
9	0	John Trent [21]		p 19 Aug. 51	p 3 June 53	28 May 59	
16	0	John M'Kay M'Kenzie		29 July 44	11 Feb. 46	30 July 56	
		LIEUTENANTS.				
6	0	Charles Whateley Willis [23]	10 Aug. 54	12 Jan. 55		
6	0	Arthur Edw. Aug. Ellis [21]	11 Aug. 54	12 Jan. 55		
6	0	Hn. R.H. deMontmorency [18]	p 18 Aug. 54	12 Jan. 55		
6	0	John Douglas Johnstone [25]	27 Oct. 54	9 Feb. 55		
6	0	Francis A. Ball [24]	3 Nov. 54	9 Feb. 55		
7	0	John Henry Campbell	2 Dec. 53	16 Feb. 55		
6	0	Geo. Talbot Worthington	15 Dec. 54	9 Mar. 55		
5	0	Rich. Radcliffe Twining	p 25 Jan. 55	5 June 55		
5	0	Birchall G. Graham, *Adj.*	18 Feb. 55	19 June 55		
5	0	George Aug. Vaughan	20 Feb. 55	24 Aug. 55		
6	0	William Bally	p 15 Sept. 54	9 Sept. 55		
5	0	Richard Statham	p 10 Mar. 55	19 Sept. 55		
5	0	Randal Howland Roberts	14 Mar. 55	16 Oct. 55		
5	0	Arthur M. Peter Browne	8 June 55	18 Jan. 56		
5	0	Henry Gillespie Boyd	25 July 55	28 May 59		
		ENSIGNS.				
5	0	Murray D. V. T. Grant	21 Sept. 55			
5	0	William Henry Gore	9 Oct. 55			
5	0	James Maurice Shipton	14 Oct. 55			
5	0	Marcus Lynch	15 Oct. 55			
5	0	Frederick Easton	16 Oct. 55			
4	0	Charles Francis Mundy	18 Jan. 56			
3	0	James Philips	p 27 Nov. 57			
2	0	Rowland Hill Fawcett	p 15 May 58			
1	0	Edwin Jervis	p 23 Aug. 59			

1 Sir Charles Yorke served in the Peninsula with the 52nd Regt., and was present at the battles of Vimiera, Fuentes d'Onor, Salamanca, Vittoria, Pyrenees, Nivelle (wounded), Nive, and Orthes (severely wounded), and at the sieges of Ciudad Rodrigo and Badajoz (wounded), for which he has received the War Medal with ten Clasps. He served also the Waterloo campaign.

2 Colonel Johnstone served the Eastern campaign of 1854-55, including the siege of Sebastopol: he was Field Officer in command of the trenches at the taking of the Quarries on the 7th June; commanded the 33rd Regt. in the assault on the 18th June, and was severely wounded by grape-shot; left arm amputated (Medal and Clasp, CB., and 5th Class of the Medjidie).

4 Lieut.Col. Collings served the Eastern campaign of 1854-55, including the battles of Alma and Inkerman, siege and fall of Sebastopol, and assault on the 18th June (Medal and Clasps, Brevet Lt.-Col., Knight of the Legion of Honor, Sardinian Medal, and 5th Class of the Medjidie).

7 Major Fitzgerald served in the Eastern campaign of 1854, and was severely wounded at the battle of Alma (Medal and Clasp, and 5th Class of the Medjidie).

6	0	*Paymaster.*—John Thompson,[26] 25 May 55; *Ens.* 5 Nov. 54; *Lieut.* 9 March 55.
6	0	*Adjutant.*—*Lieut.* Birchull George Graham, 17 Feb. 57.
5	0	*Instructor of Musketry.*—Ensign Marcus Lynch, 2 Sept. 59.
6	0	*QuarterMaster.*—Edward Vyse,[26] 14 July 54.
14	0	*Surgeon.*—William Hanbury,[27] 3 Nov. 54; *Assist. Surg.* 3 Apr. 46.
7	0	*Assist.Surgeons.*—John Ogilvy,[28] M.B. 15 July 53.
6	0	Thomas Clark,[29] 7 April 54.
5	0	Alexander Robert Kilroy, 12 April 55.

Facings Red.—*Agents*, Messrs. Cox & Co.

[*Returned from the Crimea*, 19 *July* 1856. *Embarked for the Mauritius*, 4 Feb. 1857.]

5 Lt.Col. Donovan served in the Eastern campaign of 1854-55, including the battles of Alma and Inkerman, and siege of Sebastopol—severely wounded in the trenches on the 16th of April (Medal and three Clasps, Brevet of Major, Knight of the Legion of Honor, and 5th Class of the Medjidie).

9 Major Wickham served at the siege of Sebastopol, and was severely wounded at the attack on the Redan on the 18th June (Medal and Clasp, and Brevet Major).

10 Captain Fanshawe served at the siege of Sebastopol in 1855, and at the assault on the Redan on the 18th June (Medal and Clasp).

[For remainder of Notes, see second page of 34th Foot.

34th (The Cumberland) Regt. of Foot. [Serving in India. Depot, Colchester.]

"ALBUHERA" "ARROYO DOS MOLINOS" "VITTORIA" "PYRENEES"
"NIVELLE" "NIVE" "ORTHES" "PENINSULA" "SEVASTOPOL."

Years' Serv.		
78		Colonel.—🅱 Sir Thomas Makdougall Brisbane,[1] *Bart.* GCB. GCH. *Ens.* 10 Jan. 1782; *Lieut.* 30 July 91; *Capt.* 12 April 93; *Major*, 5 Aug. 95; *Lieut.-Col.* 4 April 1800; *Col.* 25 July 10; *Major-Gen.* 4 June 13; *Lieut.-Gen.* 27 May 25; *Gen.* 23 Nov. 41; *Col. 34th Regt.* 16 Dec. 26.
Full Pay.	Half Pay.	
26	0	*Lieut.-Colonels.*—Richard Denis Kelly,[2] CB. *Ens.* 7 March 34; *Lt.* ᴾ 30 July 36; *Capt.* ᴾ 24 Sept. 41; *Major*, ᴾ 17 March 48; *Brev. Lt.-Col.* 12 Dec. 54; *Lt.-Col.* 9 March 55; *Col.* 30 Jan. 58.
25	0	John Simpson,[3] CB. *Ens.* ᴾ 13 Mar. 35; *Lieut.* ᴾ 3 Nov. 37; *Capt.* ᴾ 26 Jan. 44; *Major*, 29 Dec. 54; *Brev. Lt.-Col.* 17 July 55; *Lt.-Col.* 28 July 57.
24	0	*Majors.*—John Gwilt,[4] *Ens.* ᴾ 25 Nov. 36; *Lt.* ᴾ 10 Aug. 38; *Capt.* ᴾ 14 Feb. 45; *Brev.-Maj.* 17 July 55; *Major*, 26 Oct. 55; *Brevet Lieut.-Col.* 6 June 56.
19	0	James Maxwell,[5] *Ens.* ᴾ 24 Sept. 41; *Lieut.* ᴾ 13 Oct. 43; *Capt.* ᴾ 22 June 47; *Brev.-Major*, 2 Nov. 55; *Major*, 28 July 57.

		CAPTAINS.	ENSIGN.	LIEUT.	CAPTAIN.	BREV.MAJ.
15	0	Joseph Jordan[7]	ᴾ 14 Feb. 45	27 Mar. 48	ᴾ 29 Oct. 52	2 Nov. 55
26	5⅚	Francis P. Cassidy	ᴾ 25 Nov. 28	13 Dec. 31	10 Nov. 48	20 July 58
12	0	David Steuart	ᴾ 17 Mar. 48	ᴾ 26 Oct. 49	29 Dec. 54	
12	0	Granville William Puget[13]	ᴾ 14 Apr. 48	ᴾ 1 Feb. 50	29 Dec. 54	
24	0	Arthur George Shawe	1 April 36	23 Aug. 39	7 Feb. 51	
11	0	Edward Herman Marsh[13]	ᴾ 23 Nov. 49	ᴾ 17 Sept. 50	19 June 55	
11	0	Arth.Trevor L.Chapman[13]	ᴾ 24 Nov. 49	ᴾ 7 Mar. 51	26 Oct. 55	
10	0	Abel Woodroffe Boyce[16]..	ᴾ 17 May 50	ᴾ 29 Oct. 52	25 Aug. 57	
10	0	John Leslie Moore[17]	ᴾ 17 Sept.50	ᴾ 13 Sept. 53	4 June 58	
8	0	Thomas Harry Saunders[19]	ᴾ 9 July 52	15 Dec. 54	26 Aug. 58	
15	0	Charles Nedham[8]	28 Feb. 45	1 Aug. 48	8 Jan. 58	
7	0	Francis Peel[20]	ᴾ 25 Nov. 53	20 Dec. 54	ᴾ 13 May 59	
		LIEUTENANTS.				
9	0	Edmund P. L. Mathew..	ᴾ 9 Sept.51	6 June 54		
6	0	John Francis Wyse[21]	6 June 54	29 Dec. 54		
6	0	Rupert Inglis Cochrane[13]	14 July 54	9 Feb. 55		
5	0	Wm. Matthew Dunbar[17]..	5 Jan. 55	23 Mar. 55		
5	0	Tyssen Sowley Holroyd[17]	ᴾ 12 Jan. 55	8 June 55		
5	0	Henry Lampen[17]	26 Jan. 55	19 June 55		
6	0	Alexander Watson[17]	14 July 54	19 June 55		
5	0	Spencer Ley Greaves[17]	15 Feb. 55	19 June 55		
5	0	Julius Dyson Laurie[22]	16 Feb. 55	13 July 55		
5	0	Rich. Jn. P. Leeson,[17] *Adj.*	16 Mar. 55	27 July 55		
5	0	George Malcolm	6 July 55	29 Nov. 57		
3	0	John Bruen Rutledge	20 Feb. 57	25 Sept. 57		
5	0	Richard Newton	ᴾ 28 Dec. 55	ᴾ 5 Oct. 58		
5	0	Henry Theoph. Sheppard	14 Oct. 55	10 Sept. 58		
		ENSIGNS.				
3	0	T. H. M'Dougall Murray	ᴾ 4 Dec. 57			
3	0	Lutley Jordan	24 Nov. 57			
2	0	Charles Edward Leeson..	16 Mar. 58			
2	0	Andrew George Walker..	17 Mar. 58			
2	0	Charles Michael Fox..	ᴾ 13 Apr. 58			
2	0	Charles Hamilton Webb	13 July 58			
2	0	John MacCarthy O'Leary	ᴾ 17 Sept. 58			
2	0	James L. N. Willis	13 Nov. 58			
1	0	Gerald Brenan	28 Jan. 59			
1	0	Henry E. Sharpe	24 June 59			
6	0	*Paymaster.*—Terence Rowan,[24] 16 Sept. 59; *Q.M.* 28 April 54.				
5	0	*Adjutant.*—Lieut. Richard John Philip Leeson,[17] 19 Sept. 56.				
5	0	*Instructor of Musketry.*—Lieut. J. D. Laurie,[22] 21 April 57.				
		Quarter Master.—				
14	0	*Surgeon.*—Michael Fenton Manifold, 8 Dec. 54; *Assist.Surg.* 22 May 46.				
6	0	*Assist.Surgeons.*—Wallace Haward,[24] 7 June 54.				
2	0	Frederick Pennington, 22 April 58.				
2	0	Edward Masterson, 22 April 58.				

1 Sir Thomas Brisbane joined the Duke of York's army in the beginning of the war, and was present in every action except that of the 22nd May 93, when he was confined from a wound received in the action of the 18th of the same month. He was subsequently present at the taking of various islands, forts, &c. in the West Indies, under Sir Ralph Abercromby. Sir Thomas has received the Gold Cross and one Clasp for Vittoria, Pyrenees, Nivelle, Orthes, and Toulouse (where he was wounded); and the Silver War Medal with one Clasp for the Nive.

8 Captain Nedham served in the 10th Regt. the Punjaub campaign of 1848-9, including the whole of the siege operations before Mooltan, affair of 9th Sept., storming the enemy's strongly-entrenched position, capture of the Dowlut Gate, action of Soorjkoond, and surrender of the fortress; afterwards present at the battle of Goojerat (Medal and Clasps).

Facings Yellow.—*Agents*, Messrs. Cox & Co.
[*Returned from the Crimea, June* 1856. *Embarked for India,* 7 *Aug.* 1857.]

2 Colonel Kelly served at the siege of Sebastopol in 1855; commanded the Guard in the trenches on the 22nd March, when he was wounded and taken prisoner in a sortie of the Russians (Medal and Clasp, Brev. Lt.Col., Knight of the Legion of Honor, and 5th Class of the Medjidie).

3 Lt.Colonel Simpson served at the siege of Sebastopol in 1854-55; commanded a party in the assault (wounded) and capture of the Quarries; also present at the assault of the Redan on the 8th Sept. (Medal and Clasp, Brevet Lt.Col., Knight of the Legion of Honor, Sardinian Medal, and 5th Class of the Medjidie).

34th (The Cumberland) Regt. of Foot. 244

4 Lieut.Col. Gwilt served at the siege of Sebastopol in 1854-55; was present at the capture of the Rifle Pits on the 19th April, and commanded the 34th Regt. at the assault of the Redan on the 18th June—severely wounded (Medal and Clasp, Brevet of Major and Lt.-Col., Knight of the Legion of Honor, and 5th Class of the Medjidie).

5 Major Maxwell served at the siege of Sebastopol in 1854-55, and was severely wounded by the bursting of a shell in the trenches, 25th May (Medal and Clasp, Brevet Major, and 5th Class of the Medjidie).

7 Major Jordan served at the siege of Sebastopol in 1855, sortie of the 22nd March, capture of the Rifle Pits 19th April, sortie of 9th May, and assault of the Redan on the 18th June—severely wounded (Medal and Clasps, Brevet Major, Sardinian Medal, and 5th Class of the Medjidie).

13 Captains Puget, Marsh, and Chapman, and Lt. Cochrane, served at the siege of Sebastopol in 1854 5 (Medal and Clasp). Lt. Cochrane has the 5th Class of the Medjidie.

16 Captain Boyce served at the siege of Sebastopol in 1855, and assaults on the Redan on the 18th June and 8th Sept. (Medal and Clasp, Sardinian Medal, and 5th Class of the Medjidie).

17 Captain Moore, Lieuts. Dunbar, Holroyd, Lampen, Watson, Greaves, and Leeson, served at the siege of Sebastopol in 1855 (Medal and Clasp).

19 Captain Saunders served at the siege of Sebastopol in 1855, and was severely wounded at the capture of the Quarries on the 7th June (Medal and Clasp).

20 Captain Peel served at the siege of Sebastopol in 1855, and was wounded at the assault of the Redan on the 18th June (Medal and Clasp, and Sardinian Medal).

21 Lieut. Wyse served at the siege and fall of Sebastopol in 1854-55, including sortie of 21st Dec. 54, assaults of the Redan on the 18th June and 18th Sept., and was contused when in charge of Rifle Pits on 25th July 55 (Medal and Clasp, and 5th Class of the Medjidie).

22 Lieut. Laurie served at the siege of Sebastopol in 1855, and was severely wounded at the assault of the Redan on the 8th Sept., was also wounded on a former occasion (Medal and Clasp).

24 Paymaster Rowan and Assist.Surgeon Haward served at the siege of Sebastopol in 1854-55 (Medal and Clasp).

[*Continuation of Notes to 33rd Foot.*]

11 Major Vacher served with the 33rd Regt. in the campaign of 1854 until November, when he was appointed Assistant Engineer, right attack, and served in the trenches until Feb. 1855, when he was transferred to the General Staff, and held the appointment of D. A. Q. M. Gen. at Head Quarters during the remainder of the war (Medal and three Clasps, Brevet Major, Knight of the Legion of Honor, and 5th Class of the Medjidie).

12 Captain Greenwood served with the 33rd Regt. in the Eastern campaign of 1854, and was severely wounded while carrying the colours at the battle of Alma (Medal and Clasp).

13 Captain Barrett served the Eastern campaign of 1854-55 as Adjutant of the 33rd Regt., including the battles of the Alma and Inkerman, and siege of Sebastopol (Medal and three Clasps, and 5th Class of the Medjidie).

15 Captains Parry and Kenrick served in the Eastern campaign of 1854, including the battle of Inkerman, and siege of Sebastopol (Medal and Clasps).

16 Captain Wallis carried a colour at the Alma, and although severely wounded through the thigh remained with the Regt. until after the close of the action (Medal and Clasp, and Sardinian Medal).

17 Captain Prescott served at the siege of Sebastopol in 1855, and was severely wounded on the 15th August (Medal and Clasp).

18 Lieut. *Hon.* R. H. de Montmorency served at the siege of Sebastopol and at the attack of the Redan on the 8th Sept. (Medal and Clasp, and Sardinian Medal).

20 Captain Rogers served at the siege of Sebastopol from 13th Nov. 1854 until the fall of the place, and was present at the assaults on the Redan on the 18th June and 8th Sept. (Medal and Clasp).

21 Captain Trent served at the siege of Sebastopol, and was wounded at the assault on the Redan on the 8th Sept. 1855 (Medal).

22 Captain M'Kenzie served with the 53rd Regt. in the Sutlej campaign in 1846, including the affair of Buddiwal, and actions of Aliwal and Sobraon (Medal and Clasps).

23 Lieut. Willis served at the siege of Sebastopol in 1855, and assaults on the Redan on the 18th June and 8th Sept.—wounded (Medal and Clasp).

24 Lieuts. Ellis and Ball served at the siege of Sebastopol (Medal and Clasp).

25 Lieut. Johnstone served at the siege of Sebastopol in 1855, and at the assault on the Redan on the 18th June (Medal and Clasp).

26 Paymaster Thompson and Qr.Master Vyse served the Eastern campaign of 1854-55, including the battles of Alma and Inkerman, and siege of Sebastopol (Medal and three Clasps).

27 Surgeon Hanbury served with the 24th in the Punjaub campaign of 1848-9, including the passage of the Chenab, and battles of Sadoolapore, Chillianwallah, and Goojerat (Medal and Clasps). Served in the Crimea during the winter and spring of 1854-55 (Medal and Clasp for Sebastopol).

28 Assist.Surgeons Ogilvy and Clark served the Eastern campaign of 1854-55, including the battles of Alma and Inkerman, siege of Sebastopol, and assaults on the Redan on the 18th June and 8th Sept. (Medal and Clasps). Assist.Surgeon Clark has also the Sardinian Medal.

35th (Royal Sussex) Regiment of Foot. [Meerut. Depot, Chatham.]

"MAIDA."

Years' Serv.						
Full Pay	Half Pay					
54		*Colonel.*—John Leslie,[1] KH., *Ens.* 7 Aug. 06; *Lt.* 2 June 08; *Capt.* 30 Nov. 09; *Major,* p 1 Jan. 19; *Lieut.Col.* p 29 Aug. 26; *Col.* 23 Nov. 41; *Major-Gen.* 11 Nov. 51; *Lt.Gen.* 26 Oct. 58; *Col.* 35 Foot, 26 Sept. 57.				
		Lieut.Colonels.—John M'Neill Walter,[2] CB., *Ens.* p 31 July 35; *Lt.* 3 July 39;				
25	0	*Capt.* 29 Sept. 47; *Major,* p 2 Dec. 53; *Lt.Col.* p 17 Oct. 56.				
20	0	Charles Beamish, *Ens.* p 26 Apr. 31; *Lieut.* p 20 Mar. 35; *Capt.* p 31 Dec. 39; *Brev.Major,* 11 Nov. 51; *Major,* 20 June 54; *Bt.Lt.Col.* 26 Oct. 58. *Lt.Col.* 16 Sept. 59.				
22	0	*Majors.*—Patrick Wm. Sydenham Ross, *Ens.* p 9 Nov. 38; *Lieut.* p 2 Sept. 42; *Capt.* 16 Jan. 49; *Major,* p 17 Oct. 59.				
23	0	Thomas Teulon, *Ens.* p 29 Dec. 37; *Lieut.* p 15 Dec. 40; *Capt.* p 31 Dec. 47; *Brev.Major,* 9 Apr. 59; *Major,* 16 Sept. 59.				

		CAPTAINS.	ENSIGN.	LIEUT.	CAPTAIN.	BREV.MAJ
21	0	Robert Henry Price	p 31 Dec. 39	p 3 May 44	p 23 June 48	
20	0	Archibald Tisdall	26 June 40	p 20 Sept. 44	p 11 May 49	
18	0	William Ranby Goate ..	15 April 42	29 May 45	p 14 Dec. 49	
16	0	M. Villiers Sankey Morton	p 3 May 44	p 2 Apr. 47	20 June 54	
17	0	Chas. Fred Browne	19 May 43	9 June 46	p 22 April 53	
14	0	Samuel Fritche Blyth ..	28 Apr. 46	p 23 June 48	16 May 56	
18	0	Robert Crosse Stewart[6]..	25 Oct. 42	10 Sept. 45	7 Feb. 55	20 July 58
13	0	Charles John Patterson..	p 2 Oct. 47	16 Sept. 51	p 10 Feb. 54	
16	0	Wm. Henry Ballingull ..	p 5 Apr. 44	11 Oct. 46	30 May 57	
11	0	Ranulph Charles Lee ..	p 21 Aug. 49	p 28 Mar. 54	30 Aug. 58	
9	0	John Ormsby Vandeleur	p 21 Nov. 51	20 June 54	p 3 June 59	
8	0	John Davis............	p 13 Feb. 52	20 June 54	16 Sept. 59	
		LIEUTENANTS.				
12	0	Alfred John Ford[8]......	18 Aug. 48	p 18 July 51		5 Lieutenant Pohle served with the Field Force against the rebel Karens in Burmah in Jan. 1857, and was severely wounded. Served with Lt.Col. Walter's Column against the rebels in the Shahabad district from June to Oct. 1858.
8	0	Edward Tedlie	p 23 Nov. 52	23 June 54		
8	0	Robert J. Gordon Grant[3]	24 Jan. 52	p 10 Dec. 52		
7	0	C. G. MacGregor Skinner	p 13 May 53	p 7 June 54		
6	0	Thomas Lloyd	p 3 Mar. 54	p 24 Nov. 54		
6	0	Albert John Revell	p 28 Mar. 54	26 Jan. 55		
6	0	Mars Mourier Pohle[5]....	p 24 Nov. 54	p 3 Aug. 55		6 Major Stewart served as D.A.A. Gen. to the 2nd Division at the capture of Lucknow in March 1858 and was severely wounded (Brevet Major).
5	0	Woodford Wright Sherlock	p 13 July 55	p 9 May 56		
5	0	Richard Trimen	p 21 Sept. 55	16 May 56		
5	0	Richard Ross	2 Oct. 55	9 May 56		
5	0	Robert Henry W. Troup .	p 15 May 55	p 30 Jan. 57		8 Lieut. Ford served in Shahabad from July to Nov. 1858 and was present at the affairs of Rampore, Pawara, and Pemaon
4	0	Richard Parsons........	9 May 56	p 15 May 57		
5	0	Wm. Henry Bayly Payn	7 Dec. 55	24 Apr. 58		
4	0	Robert Hill Ross, *Adj.* ..	16 May 56	30 Aug. 58		
3	0	Henry Edmund Fryer ..	p 30 Jan. 57	p 17 Dec. 58		
3	0	Timothy John Dillon ..	p 15 May 57	p 15 Nov. 59		
		ENSIGNS.				
4	0	Thomas Broun	8 July 56			
2	0	Edward Laws..........	p 13 July 58			
2	0	Fred. Bowdler Gipps....	6 Aug. 58			
2	0	William Poste	24 Aug. 58			
2	0	William Trocke	p 7 Sept. 58			
2	0	Charles John Stone	20 Oct. 58			
1	0	Arthur C. Crookshank ..	11 Jan. 59			

18	0	*Paymaster.*—John Mills Hewson, 28 Sept. 47; *Ens.* 28 March 42; *Lt.* 29 Dec. 43.	
4	0	*Adjutant.*—*Lieut.* Robert Hill Ross, 5 April 57.	
6	0	*Instructor of Musketry.*—*Lieut.* Thomas Lloyd, 11 Dec. 58.	
6	0	*Quarter Master.*—Michael McLoughlin, 13 Jan. 54.	
21	0	*Surgeon.*—James Walker Chambers, M.D., *A.S.* 4 Oct. 39.; *Surg.* 6 Aug. 47;	
6	0	*Assistant Surgeons.*—Edward Thiselton, 20 June 54. [*Surg.Maj.* 4 Oct. 59.	
2	0	Richard Thomas Golty Catton, 7 May 58.	
2	0	John Mahon, 22 June 58.	

Facings Blue.—*Agent,* Sir John Kirkland.

[*Embarked for India,* 31 *July* 1854.]

1 Lieut.General John Leslie was at the taking of Travancore in 1808 and at the capture of Bourbon and the Isle of France in 1810; after which he served in Java and was present in the engagements of the 10th, 22nd, and 26th August 1811. He served also in the Pindaree war in 1817, and with the Army of Occupation in France. He has received the War Medal with one Clasp for Java.

2 Lt.Colonel Walter served throughout the Kaffir campaign of 1846-7 as Adjutant of the 90th Light Infantry, and Field Adjutant of the 1st Division (Medal). Served with the 53rd Regt. in the Punjaub campaign in 1849, and was present at the battle of Goojerat (Medal and Clasp). Also with a Brigade on the Peshawur frontier in 1851-52. Served with the 35th Regt. in the Indian campaign of 1858-59; commanded the Arrah field force in the actions of Sirthoon, Brumineegunge, Rampoorperoiora Jemaon, and Kareesath; subsequently a light column in the operations in Shahabad, including the action before Noncodhee (CB. and Medal).

3 Lieut. Grant was present at the storm and destruction of the fortified native Mandingo town of Sabajee, on the Gambia on the 1st June 1853.

Head Qrs. Plymouth.
Depot, Athlone.] **36th (*The Herefordshire*) Regt. of Foot.**

"Firm." "HINDOOSTAN" "ROLEIA" "VIMIERA" "CORUNNA" "SALAMANCA"
"PYRENEES" "NIVELLE" "NIVE" "ORTHES" "TOULOUSE" "PENINSULA."

Years' Serv.						
Full Pay	Half Pay					
55		Colonel.—🅑 William Henry Scott,[1] *Ens.* 27 Oct. 05; *Lt. & Capt.* 28 March 11; *Capt. & Lt.-Col.* 5 July 15; *Col.* 10 Jan. 37; *Major-Gen.* 9 Nov. 46; *Lt.-Gen.* 20 June 54; *Col.* 36th Foot, 31 Oct. 54.				
19	6/12	*Lt.-Col.*—John Josiah Hort,[2] *Ens.* 20 Nov. 40; *Lieut.* ᴾ 30 Sept. 42; *Capt.* ᴾ 29 Dec. 46; *Maj.* 12 Dec. 54; *Brev.-Lt.-Col.* 2 Nov. 55; *Lt.-Col.* 1 Feb. 56.				
30	0	*Majors.*—Wm. R. Haliday, *Ens.* ᴾ 12 Feb. 30; *Lt.* 3 Mar. 33; *Capt.* ᴾ 11 Nov. 36; *Bt. Maj.* 9 Nov. 46; *Maj.* ᴾ 3 Aug. 49; *Bt. Lt.-Col.* 20 June 54; *Col.* 13 Dec. 59.				
24	0	James Nugent, *Ens.* ᴾ 15 April 36; *Lieut.* 11 Jan. 39; *Capt.* ᴾ 22 Sept. 43; *Brev.-Major*, 20 June 54; *Major*, 16 Oct. 57.				

		CAPTAINS.	ENSIGN.	LIEUT.	CAPTAIN.	BREV. MAJ.
23	0	Edward Charles Butler, s.	ᴾ 13 Jan. 37	ᴾ 5 Mar. 41	ᴾ 23 Aug. 44	23 Sept. 56
19	0	Rickard Lloyd	ᴾ 2 April 41	ᴾ 22 Sept. 43	6 June 54	
8	0	Ralph Edward Carr[3]	ᴾ 13 Feb. 52	ᴾ 10 June 53	25 Jan. 56	
11	0	Edwin William Philips[7]	ᴾ 18 Sept. 49	21 Oct. 53	ᴾ 3 June 56	
8	0	Joshua Cunliffe Ingham[8]	ᴾ 23 Nov. 52	ᴾ 18 Aug. 54	ᴾ 27 July 55	
12	0	Waring Alex. Biddle[6]	ᴾ 18 Feb. 48	5 Oct. 49	13 July 55	
10	0	Henry Robert Twyford	ᴾ 22 Nov. 50	ᴾ 28 May 52	ᴾ 15 May 57	
8	0	Robert B. Lloyd	ᴾ 17 Aug. 52	9 Mar. 55	ᴾ 4 June 58	
6	0	F. X. De Coucy Orange.	6 June 54	ᴾ 30 Mar. 55	ᴾ 1 Oct. 58	
6	0	Fred. Willoughby Harris	ᴾ 20 Oct. 54	ᴾ 8 June 55	ᴾ 18 Feb. 59	
9	0	Alexander Fred. Stewart	ᴾ 19 Aug. 51	11 Aug. 54	ᴾ 9 Sept. 59	
5	0	William C. Hill	10 April 55	ᴾ 21 Sept. 55	2 Dec. 59	
		LIEUTENANTS.				
5	0	Horace Edward Willett	15 June 55	ᴾ 8 Jan. 56		
5	0	Augustus Henry Hartford	1 June 55	30 June 56		
5	0	Richard Lloyd Hawkes	30 Nov. 55	21 Sept. 56		
4	0	Charles George Mahon	15 Jan. 56	16 Oct. 57		
8	0	William Henry Paul	ᴾ 14 May 52	ᴾ 27 June 54		
4	0	Clement Sheriff T. Sale	31 Jan. 56	ᴾ 18 Dec. 57		
4	0	Joseph O. Walter Scott	ᴾ 8 Feb. 56	23 Mar. 58		
4	0	Tho. Maunsell Le Mesurier	ᴾ 29 Feb. 56	23 Mar. 58		
4	0	Charles Dere James	1 Mar. 56	26 Mar. 58		
4	0	Arthur Francis Kelsey, *Adj.*	12 Dec. 56	ᴾ 4 June 58		
2	0	Edward Dorrien Newbolt	ᴾ 2 Feb. 58	ᴾ 1 Oct. 58		
2	0	*Hon.* Chas. J. Fox Powys	23 Mar. 58	ᴾ 18 Feb. 59		
3	0	William Neal	12 Dec. 57	ᴾ 23 July 58		
3	0	Clifford Wilson	16 Oct. 57	ᴾ 9 Sept. 59		
2	0	Amelius Taylor	26 Mar. 58	2 Dec. 59		
		ENSIGNS.				
2	0	Hardinge Rich. Stracey	27 Mar. 58			
2	0	Christopher Spurgeon	ᴾ 4 June 58			
2	0	William Rushton	ᴾ 29 Oct. 58			
2	0	George Cotton Dumergue	ᴾ 30 Oct. 58			
2	0	Clements Moffatt Bond	30 Mar. 58			
1	0	Henry Edward Stopford	18 Jan. 59			
1	0	John Dickinson Atkinson	ᴾ 18 Mar. 59			
2	0	Stainsby Henry Pigott	26 Nov. 58			
1	0	Edward Staples Bond	ᴾ 9 Sept. 59			

1 Lt.-Gen. Scott proceeded to the Peninsula in 1808, and was present with the Scots Fusilier Guards at the passage of the Douro, capture of Oporto, subsequent retreat of Soult's army, and battle of Talavera, where he was wounded through the body, and being left there in hospital, he was made prisoner. He commanded the Scots Fusilier Guards for upwards of three years. Has received the War Medal with one Clasp for Talavera.

2 Lt.-Col. Hort served the Eastern campaign of 1854-55 with the 4th Regt., including the battles of Alma and Inkerman, siege and fall of Sebastopol (Medal and three Clasps, Br.-Lt.-Col., Sardinian Medal, and 5th Class of the Medjidie).

3 Captain Carr served with the 39th Regt. at the siege and fall of Sebastopol in 1855, and at the attacks on 18th June and 8th Sept. (Medal and Clasps, and Knight of the Legion of Honor).

4 Doctor Jopp served with the Queen's Royals during the campaign of 1844-45 in the Southern Concan and Sawant Warree country including the storming of several stockades, and the investment and capture of the Forts of Monohur and Munsuntosh.

2	0	*Paymaster.*—William Causabon Frend, 30 March 58.	
4	0	*Adjutant.*—Lieut. Arthur Francis Kelsey, 15 Apr. 59.	
4	0	*Instructor of Musketry.*—Lieut. T. M. Le Mesurier, 20 Dec. 59.	
5	0	*Quarter Master.*—Joseph Brookes, 30 Mar. 55.	[*Surg. Maj.* 22 Feb. 59.
21	0	*Surgeon.*—James Jopp,[4] M.D. *Assist. Surg.* 22 Feb. 39; *Surgeon*, 1 Jan. 47;	
7	0	*Assist. Surgeons.*—John Richard Tobin, 21 Oct. 53.	
6	0	Stephen Massett Webb,[5] M.D. 19 May 54.	

Facings Grass Green.
Agents, Messrs. Cox & Co.—*Irish Agents*, Sir E. R. Borough, *Bt.*, Armit & Co.
[*Returned from Jamaica*, 7 July 1857.]

5 Assist. Surgeon Webb served at the siege of Sebastopol during the winter of 1854-55 (Medal and Clasp).
6 Captain Biddle served wi h the 28 h Regt. the Eastern campaign until Jan. 1855, including the battles of Alma and Inkerman, and siege of Sebastopol (Medal and three Clasps).
7 Captain Philips served with the 56th Regt. at the siege and fall of Sebastopol, and was wounded on 4th Sept. 1855 (Medal and Clasp).
8 Captain Ingham served in the 57th Regt. in the Crimea from Jan. 1855, including the siege and fall of Sebastopol, storming of the Redan on the 18th June and attack of the 8th Sept., also the bombardment and surrender of Kinbourn (Medal and Clasp, and 5th Class of the Medjidie).

37th (The North Hampshire) Regt. of Foot.

[Serving in India. Depot, Colchester.

"MINDEN" "TOURNAY" "PENINSULA."

Years' Serv.			
Full Pay	Half Pay		
51		**Colonel.**—John Fraser,[1] *Ens.* 10 April 09; *Lieut.* 12 Sept. 11; *Capt.* 28 Jan. 13; *Brev.-Maj.* 31 Oct. 18; *Maj.* p 21 June 21; *Brev.-Lt.-Col.* 24 May 27; *Col.* 23 Nov. 41; *Maj.-Gen.* 20 June 54; *Lt.Gen.* 17 Oct. 59; *Col.* 37th Foot, 11 Jan. 58.	
25	0		
23	0	**Lieut. Colonels.**—Egerton Charles Wm. Miles Milman,[2] *Ens. & Lt.* p 24 April 35; *Lt. & Capt.* p 5 Feb. 41; *Capt. & Lt.Col.* p 7 April 48; *Col.* 28 Nov. 54.	
23	0	Edward D. Atkinson, *Ens.* p 6 Oct. 37; *Lieut.* p 28 July 40; *Capt.* p 20 Feb. 46; *Brev.-Maj.* 3 April 58; *Major*, 15 June 58; *Lt.Col.* p 26 Nov. 58.	
20	0	**Majors.**—Henry Macmanus Sall,[3] *Ens.* 8 Dec. 37; *Lieut.* 1 Sept. 40; *Capt.* 12 Sept. 48; *Major*, 26 Oct. 58.	
		Robert Prescott Harrison, *Ens.* p 28 July 40; *Lt.* p 17 June 42; *Capt.* p 8 Feb. 50; *Major*, p 26 Nov. 58.	

		CAPTAINS.	ENSIGN.	LIEUT.	CAPTAIN.	BREV.MAJ.
19	0	Raymond Richard Pelly[6]	p 26 Jan. 41	20 May 44	p 7 June 50	
18	0	Joseph Jones	7 Jan. 42	29 Dec. 45	16 June 53	
16	0	John William Boissier[4]	p 31 Dec. 44	p 3 April 46	p 30 Jan. 52	
18	0	Wm. Joseph Bazalgette	p 17 June 42	p 30 Dec. 45	6 June 54	
19	0½	John Richard Heaton	19 Dec. 34	22 Aug. 37	p 24 Feb. 43	20 June 54
17	0	Charles Luxmoore[7]	p 17 Nov. 43	p 1 May 46	p 26 Oct. 55	
15	0	Edward Joseph N. Burton	p 13 June 45	p 20 Nov. 46	20 Mar. 56	
13	0	John Brown	5 Feb. 47	p 1 Aug. 48	15 June 57	
8	0	John Derring Collum	p 9 July 52	p 8 July 53	15 June 58	
11	0	George William Savage	23 Nov. 49	p 13 Sept. 53	26 Oct. 58	
8	0	Fred. John Nash Ind	p 23 Nov. 52	p 25 Aug. 54	p 7 Dec. 58	
7	0	Edw. Robt. Bigsby Barnes[3]	p 24 June 53	p 10 Aug. 55	p 6 May 59	
		LIEUTENANTS.				
10	0	William Henry Henzell	p 12 April 50	6 June 54		
8	0	Cha. Edw. Ascough Evered	p 23 Jan. 52	11 Aug. 54		
7	0	S. Lavalliere Curgenven	p 9 July 53	31 Aug. 55		
13	0	R. Bunn, *Adj.* Q.M. 3 Dec. 47.	p 18 Sept. 53	26 Oct. 55		
7	0	Bezsin Reece	p 13 Sept. 53	p 26 Oct. 55		
6	0	James Frederick Reyne	6 June 54	20 Mar. 56		
6	0	Henry Edward Glass	p 17 Mar. 54	p 7 Sept. 56		
5	0	James Drummond Græme	14 June 55	31 July 57		
5	0	Geo. Goodridge Fraser	3 Aug. 55	31 July 57		
5	0	Tho. Sheridan Gore Jones	7 Sept. 55	28 Mar. 58		
4	0	Samuel Hawkes	3 June 56	p 21 May 58		
5	0	George John Usil Mason	p 28 Dec. 55	15 June 58		
4	0	Francis Charteris Forbes	8 July 56	26 Oct. 58		
4	0	Michl. Andrews Borthwick	p 19 Dec. 56	p 7 Dec. 58		
3	0	Albert Jones	30 Oct. 57	p 6 May 59		
		ENSIGNS.				
3	0	William Hodgkinson	6 Nov. 57			
3	0	William Belcher	17 Nov. 57			
2	0	John Ennis	15 Jan. 58			
2	0	Fra. Openshaw Sargeant	p 28 May 58			
2	0	John Reilly	4 June 58			
2	0	Henry Bullen	p 30 July 58			
2	0	Charles Edward King	24 Sept. 58			
2	0	John Everard Whitting	19 Nov. 58			
1	0	Thomas Noble Holton	p 18 Jan. 59			
1	0	Norcliffe Gilpin	p 31 May 59			
12	0	**Paymaster.**—Raynsford Taylor, 15 Feb. 56; *Ens.* p 8 Dec. 48; *Lt.* 5 May 53.				
13	0	**Adjutant.**—*Lieut.* Richard Bunn, 15 Sept. 53.				
4	0	**Instructor of Musketry.**—*Lieut.* Samuel Hawkes, 4 June 57.				
7	0	**Quarter Master.**—William Crutchley, 13 Sept. 53.				
14	0	**Surgeon.**—James William Fleming,[5] 2 Oct. 57; *Assist. Surg.* 27 Oct. 46.				
6	0	**Assistant Surgeons.**—William Ramsay,[6] M.D. 15 Dec. 54.				
3	0	William Samuel Chapman, 15 Sept. 57.				
2	0	Isaac Hoysted, 16 May 58.				

Facings Yellow.—Agents, Messrs. Price & Boustead.
[Embarked for Ceylon, 18 Nov. 1840.]

3 Captain Barnes volunteered on the outbreak of the Kaffir war in 1850, and was appointed a Lieut. in a native corps, and served under Sir Harry Smith and Sir George Cathcart from January 1851 until March 1853. He accompanied the first patrol that left King William's Town on the 30th Jan. 1851, and was present at the engagements of the 17th February, 6th March, 10th April, of 1851, and at the passage of the Kei on the 4th December of the same year; besides many other minor encounters with the enemy during the war (Medal)

5 Major Sall served with the 10th Foot in the Punjaub campaign of 1848-9, including the whole of the siege operations before Mooltan, repulse of the enemy and night-attack upon the British camp at Muttee Thol 17th Aug. 1848; action of Soorjkoond and capture of the enemy's guns Nov. 7th; carrying the heights and suburbs before Mooltan Dec. 27th; and surrender of the fortress 22nd Jan. 1849; after which joined with the Mooltan force the army under Lord Gough, and was present at the battle of Goojerat (Medal and two Clasps).

8 Surgeon Fleming served in Ceylon during the rebellion of 1848.

1 Lt. General Fraser served in the Peninsula with the 24th, from June 1809 to June 1813, including the action at Foz d'Arouce, battle of Busaco, battle of Fuentes d'Onor, on 3rd and 5th May, siege of Ciudad Rodrigo, covering the siege of Badajoz, battle of Salamanca, capture of Madrid, and siege of Burgos, where he was at the taking of the Horn Work, 19th Sept.; and he led the storming party to the breach formed by the mine on the 4th Oct. Employed in the field throughout the whole of the Kandian rebellion in Ceylon in 1817 and 18, as Aide-de-camp to the Commander of the Forces. He has received the War Medal with four Clasps.

2 Colonel Milman served with the Coldstream Guards in the Canadian rebellion in 1838. Served in India during the mutiny, and commanded a field force in the Ghazeepore district in Dec. 1857 preventing the rebels crossing the Goggra and Ganges at their junction, and at Azimghur on 16 March 1858; was engaged with the Enemy at Atrowlea and Koelsa on 1st March. Commanded the left wing 37th Regt. at Azimghur until relieved by Lugard's force on 15 April; held a ridge on the Benares road with a small picquet against a large force of mutineers on 9 April and secured the passage of a large convoy of stores and ammunition into the Azimghur entrenchment (Medal).

8 Captain Pelly served in the Indian campaign of 1857-58, and was engaged with the Enemy at Atrowlea and Koelsa (mentioned in despatches); besieged in Azimghur and sortie thence; proceeded with Brigadier Douglas' column in pursuit of Koer Sing, and present in the actions of 17th and 20th April (Medal).

4 Captain Boissier served with the 32nd Regt. at the second siege operations before Mooltan, including the surrender of the fort and garrison of Cheniote, and at the battle of Goojerat (Medal and Clasp).
Doctor Ramsay served in the Crimea from 28 May 1855 to the end of a Wing 37th Regt. in the Indian campaign of 1858, in medical charge of a Wing 37th Regt. in the action at Atrowlea, besieged in Azimghur and subsequent operations (Medal).

Serving in India.
Depot, Colchester.

38th (The 1st Staffordshire) Regt. of Foot. 248

"MONTE VIDEO" "ROLEIA" "VIMIERA" "CORUNNA" "BUSACO" "BADAJOZ" "SALAMANCA"
"VITTORIA" "ST. SEBASTIAN" "NIVE" "PENINSULA" "AVA" "ALMA"
"INKERMAN" "SEVASTOPOL."

Years' Serv.		
Full Pay	Half Pay	
64		Col.—**Hon.** Hugh Arbuthnott,[1] CB. Ens. 18 May 06; Lt. 15 Sept. 96; Capt. 20 Mar. 99; Maj. 23 Nov. 04; Lt.-Col. 9 May 11; Col. 19 July 21; Maj.-Gen. 22 July 30; Lt.-Gen. 23 Nov. 41; Gen. 20 June 54; Col. 38th Regt. 4 Apr. 43.
45	0	Lieut.-Colonels.—James Pattoun Sparks,[2] CB. Ens. 27 July 15; Lt. 30 July 18; Capt. 5 Sept. 26; Br.-Maj. 23 Nov. 41; Brev. Lt.-Col. 11 Nov. 51; Maj. 6 July 52; Col. 28 Nov. 54; Lt.-Col. 9 March 55.
32	0	Wm. O'Grady Haly,[3] CB. Ens. p 17 June 28; Lt. p 19 July 31; Capt. p 25 Apr. 34; Maj. p 19 May 46; Lt.Col. p 27 Dec. 50; Col. 28 Nov. 54.
19	0	Majors.—James S. Hawker Farrer,[4] Ens. 2 April 41; Lieut. p 2 June 43; Capt. p 28 April 48; Brev.-Maj. 12 Dec. 54; Major, 29 June 55.
22	0	William James Loftus,[5] Ens. p 9 Nov. 38; Lt. p 8 Nov. 42; Capt. p 19 July 50; Major, 29 July 55; Brev Lt.-Col. 2 Nov. 55.

		CAPTAINS.	ENSIGN.	LIEUT.	CAPTAIN.	BREV. MAJ.
18	0	Edw. T. Gloster[6],[c. 20 July 58]	p 13 May 42	3 Jan. 45	p 30 July 52	6 June 56
13	0	Horatio Page Vance[8]	p 3 Dec. 47	p 20 Dec. 50	p 4 Aug. 54	20 July 58
12	0	James Thomas Craster[9]	19 Sept. 48	p 17 Oct. 51	22 Dec. 54	
10	0	Hon. Cha. J. Addington[10]	p 16 Aug. 50	p 30 July 52	29 Dec. 54	20 July 58
7	0	Const.Wm.Sept.Gaynor[11]	p 18 Oct. 53	p 18 Aug. 54	p 14 Aug. 57	
7	0	Henry Charles Evans	p 22 April 53	2 Feb. 55	p 25 June 58	
6	0	William Kidston Elles[12]	6 June 54	2 Feb. 55	p 13 July 58	
14	0	George Aug. M'Nair	13 Nov. 45	p 30 June 48	10 Mar. 58	
12	0	David William Martin	p 16 June 48	p 1 June 49	30 Sept. 58	
7	0	W.deW.RocheThackwell[13]	p 10 June 53	15 Dec. 54	p 20 Feb. 58	
12	0	Bendyshe Walton[14]	p 16 June 48	p 8 Feb. 50	p 8 Jan. 56	24 Mar. 58

		LIEUTENANTS.			
7	0	Jno. Fred. Clinton Boyle[17]	21 Jan. 53	8 Dec. 54	
6	0	George Wm. Fred. Snell[21]	7 June 54	2 Feb. 55	
6	0	Philip Homan Eyre,[22] Adj.	10 Aug. 54	2 Feb. 55	
6	0	Arth. Johnson Allix Ewen[23]	11 Aug. 54	2 Feb. 55	
6	0	Walter Hume[26]	p 23 June 54	9 Mar. 55	
5	0	Rob. Johnston Stansfeld[21]	26 Jan. 55	17 June 55	
6	0	Arthur Alexander Wilkie[27]	6 June 54	29 June 55	
5	0	Alexander Walker	19 Feb. 55	29 July 55	
5	0	John Alex. Caldecott[28]	2 Mar. 55	16 Aug. 55	
5	0	John Thomas Carroll	16 Mar. 55	29 Feb. 56	
4	0	Arthur William Barron	6 Sept. 55	25 Oct. 56	
5	0	John Mayo[25]	30 Mar. 55	7 July 57	
5	0	James Hughes Pope	29 June 55	p 14 Aug. 57	
5	0	Wm. Henry Russell Skey	19 July 55	24 Aug. 58	
4	0	Andrew Macdonald Grote[35]	p 26 Feb. 56	p 31 Dec. 58	
4	0	Edward Conduit Bicknell	26 Feb. 56	p 31 Dec. 58	
5	0	Alfred Stokes	27 July 55	12 Nov. 58	

		ENSIGNS.		
5	0	Arthur Bailey	31 Aug. 55	
2	0	Dyas Ringrose Lofthouse	p 13 July 58	
2	0	Norman Drumm. Pringle	10 Sept. 58	
2	0	John Barrett Brady	p 9 Nov. 58	
2	0	William Uvedale Miller	12 Nov. 58	
1	0	Benj. Parnell Bromhead	18 Jan. 59	
1	0	John Smyth Nelson	28 Jan. 59	
1	0	John Barnes Sparkes	5 Aug. 59	

1 General the Hon. Hugh Arbuthnott served with the 49th Regt. at the Helder in 1799; also on the expedition to the Baltic, and battle of Copenhagen in 1801. In July 1807 embarked with the expedition to Zealand, and was present at the siege and capture of Copenhagen. Accompanied the expedition to Sweden, and afterwards to Portugal and Spain under Sir John Moore, and was present at the battle of Corunna. Served also in the Peninsula under the Duke of Wellington, & commanded the 52nd Regt. at the battle of Busaco, for which he has received the Gold Medal: he has also received the Silver War Medal with two Clasps for Corunna and Fuentes d'Onor; and the Naval War Medal for Copenhagen.

4 Major Farrer served in the Eastern campaign of 1854-55, including the battles of Alma and Inkerman, and siege of Sebastopol (Medal and Clasps, Brevet Major, and 5th Class of the Medjidie).

5 Lt.-Colonel Loftus served throughout the Eastern campaign of 1854-55, including the battles of Alma and Inkerman, and siege and fall of Sebastopol, attack and occupation of the Cemetery on the 18th June (Medal with three Clasps, Brevet Lieut.-Colonel, Sardinian Medal, and 5th Class of the Medjidie).

20	0	Paymaster.—James Twibill,[34] 23 June 54; Ens. 7 May 40.	
6	0	Adjutant.—Lieut. Philip Homan Eyre, 22 Apr. 59.	
6	0	Instructor of Musketry.—Captain W. T. Elles, 4 May 57.	
5	0	Quarter Master.—Robert Smith,[29] 7 Dec. 55.	
14	0	Surgeon.—Thomas Fred. Wall,[30] 12 Jan. 55; Assist. Surg. 20 Nov. 46.	
7	0	Assist. Surgeons.—Digby William Lawlor,[31] 10 June 53.	
6	0	James Henry Lewis,[32] 24 March 54.	
6	0	Thomas Wright,[33] 21 April 54.	

Facings Yellow.—Agents, Cox & Co.

[Returned from the Crimea, 19 July 1856. Embarked for India, 4 Aug. 1857.]

2 Colonel Sparks served on the N. E. frontier of the Cape of Good Hope against the Kaffirs in 1817; on the expedition into Kaffraria under Col. Brereton in 1818; in the action at Graham's Town 22nd April 1819, and the campaign of the same year in Kaffraria under Col. Wiltshire; on the N. E. frontier when the Kaffirs invaded it in Dec. 1834, and during the war which ensued he commanded a local corps—the Graham's Town Volunteers—with the Colonial Commission of Lt.-Colonel. In 1848 he was sent from Jamaica to the Mosquito Coast, in consequence of the death of H. M.'s Agent and Consul-General, to attend to British interests there, and received the thanks of H. M.'s Government. Served throughout the Eastern campaign of 1854-55, except from the middle of Feb. to the end of May 1855 (sent to England on duty); succeeded to the command of the 38th Regt. on the morning of the 18th June when Lt.-Col. Louth was wounded,

38th (The 1st Staffordshire) Regt. of Foot.

was the senior unwounded officer of the 2nd Brigade 3rd Division at the close of the action, and commanded it for ten days. Has the Kaffir Medal, the Crimean Medal with three Clasps for Alma, Inkerman, and Sebastopol, and the Sardinian Medal, is a CB., an Officer of the Legion of Honor, and has the 4th Class of the Medjidie).
3 Colonel Haly served the Eastern campaign of 1854-55, including the battles of Alma (charger killed) and Inkerman (received four bayonet wounds), capture of Balaklava, siege and fall of Sebastopol, and sortie on 26th Oct. (Medal and Clasps, CB., Officer of the Legion of Honor, and 3rd Class of the Medjidie).
6 Lt.Colonel Gloster served in the Eastern campaign of 1854-55, including the battles of Alma and Inkerman, siege and fall of Sebastopol (Medal with three Clasps, and Brevet Major). Served the Indian campaign of 1857-58, and was dangerously wounded at the capture of Lucknow (Brevet of Lt.Colonel, Medal and Clasp).
8 Major Vance served at the siege of Sebastopol from Jan. to the end of April 1855 (Medal and Clasp, and Turkish Medal). Also in the Indian campaign, and was present at the storm and capture of Mecangunge, siege and capture of Lucknow, affairs of Barree and Nuggur (Brevet of Major, Medal and Clasp).
9 Captain Craster served in the Eastern campaign of 1854, including the battles of Alma and Inkerman, and siege of Sebastopol (Medal and three Clasps).
10 Major Hon. C. J. Addington served the Eastern campaign of 1854 and up to 20th June 1855, including the battles of Alma and Inkerman, siege of Sebastopol, attack and occupation of the Cemetery on the 18th June—severely wounded (Medal and three Clasps, and 5th Class of the Medjidie).
11 Captain Gaynor served the Eastern campaign of 1854 and until 25th Feb. 1855, including the battles of Alma and Inkerman, and siege of Sebastopol, and was shot through the leg in the trenches on 21st Feb. (Medal and three Clasps, and Sardinian Medal).
12 Captain Elles served at the siege and fall of Sebastopol in 1854-55, including the attack and occupation of the Cemetery on the 18th June (Medal and Clasp, and Knight of the Legion of Honor).
13 Captain Thackwell served with the 39th Regt. in the Crimea from 31st Dec. 1854, including the siege and fall of Sebastopol, and attacks of the 18th June and 8th September (Medal and Clasp, and 5th Class of the Medjidie).
14 Major Walton served with the 53rd Regt. in the Punjaub campaign in 1849 and was present at the battle of Goojerat (Medal and Clasp). With the expedition against the Hill Tribes on the Peshawur frontier in 1851-52. Campaign in India in 1857, including the relief of Lucknow by Lord Clyde, and was severely wounded at the storming of the Secunderbagh (mentioned in despatches, Medal and Clasp, and Brevet Major).
17 Lieut. Boyle served with the 38th Regt. throughout the Eastern campaign of 1854-55, including the battles of Alma (carried the colours) and Balaklava, siege and fall of Sebastopol, attack and occupation of the Cemetery on the 18th June (Medal and three Clasps).
21 Lieuts. Snell and Stansfeld served at the siege and fall of Sebastopol from 1st June 1855, including the attack and occupation of the Cemetery on the 18th June (Medal and Clasp).
22 Lieut. Eyre served in the Eastern campaign from 10th Nov. 1854 to 10th May 1855, including the siege of Sebastopol (Medal and Clasp).
23 Lieut. Ewen served at the siege and fall of Sebastopol from 13th Jan. 1855, including the attack and occupation of the Cemetery on the 18th June (Medal and Clasp, and Sardinian Medal).
25 Lieut. Mayo served at the siege and fall of Sebastopol from 29th Aug. 1855 (Medal and Clasp).
26 Lieut. Hume served at the siege and fall of Sebastopol from 1st July 1855 (Medal and Clasp).
27 Lieut. Wilkie served at the siege and fall of Sebastopol from 23rd July 1855 (Medal and Clasp).
28 Lieut. Caldecott served in the Crimea from 7th Sept. 1855, and was at the fall of Sebastopol (Medal and Clasp).
29 Qr.Master Smith served at the siege and fall of Sebastopol, including the attack and occupation of the Cemetery (Medal and Clasp).
30 Surgeon Wall served at the siege and fall of Sebastopol from 19th Dec. 1854, and at the attack of the 18th June 1855 (Medal and Clasp).
31 Assist.Surgeon Lawlor served throughout the Eastern campaign of 1854-55, including the battles of Alma and Inkerman, siege and fall of Sebastopol, and attack of the 18th June (Medal and three Clasps, and 5th Class of the Medjidie).
32 Assist.Surgeon Lewis served throughout the Eastern campaign of 1854-55, including the battles of Alma and Inkerman, siege and fall of Sebastopol, attack and occupation of the Cemetery (Medal and three Clasps).
33 Assist.Surgeon Wright served with the 26th Regt. the Eastern campaign of 1854-55, including the battles of Alma and Inkerman, and siege of Sebastopol (Medal and Clasps).
34 Paymaster Twibill served throughout the Eastern campaign of 1854-55, including the battles of Alma and Inkerman, siege and fall of Sebastopol, and attack of the 18th June (Medal and three Clasps).
35 Lieut. Grote served with the 95th Regt. in the Indian campaign of 1858, including the siege and capture of Awah and Kotah, battle of Kotah ka Seria, general action resulting in the capture of Gwalior, siege and capture of Pourie (Medal).

[*Continuation of Notes to* 39th *Regiment.*]

8 Captain Agnew served in the Crimea from Dec. 1854 to Feb. 1855 (Medal and Clasp).
9 Captain Milligan and Lieut. Smyth served at the siege and fall of Sebastopol in 1855, and at the attacks on the 18th June and 8th Sept. (Medal and Clasps, and 5th Class of the Medjidie).
10 Captain Turner served with the 79th Highlanders throughout the Eastern campaign of 1854-55, including the battles of Alma and Balaklava, siege and fall of Sebastopol, and assault of the 8th September (Medal and three Clasps). Also in the Indian campaign and present at the siege and capture of Lucknow in March 1858 (Medal and Clasp).
11 Major Snodgrass landed with the army at Old Fort, 14th Sept. 1854, as Aide de Camp to Major General Sir John Campbell, and was present at the battles of Alma and Inkerman, siege of Sebastopol, expedition to Kertch, and assault on the Redan 18th June (severely wounded); present with the 38th Regt. at the close of the campaign (Medal and three Clasps, Brevet Major, Sardinian Medal, and 5th Class of the Medjidie). Served also with the 38th Regt. in the Indian campaign of 1857-58, and was present in several engagements and at the siege and capture of Lucknow (Medal and Clasp).
12 Lieut. Bennett served at the siege and fall of Sebastopol in 1855, including the attacks of the 18th June and 8th Sept. (Medal and Clasp, and Sardinian Medal).
13 Lieuts. Stokes and Murray served at the siege and fall of Sebastopol in 1855 (Medal and Clasp).
14 Lieut. Newport served at the siege of Sebastopol (Medal and Clasp).
15 Paymaster Benison was present at that lamentable catastrophe the burning of the *Kent* East Indiaman in the Bay of Biscay, on the 1st March 1825. He served with the 31st Regt. throughout the campaign of 1842 in Affghanistan (Medal) under Major-General Pollock, including the actions of Mazeena, Tezeen, and Jugdulluck, the occupation of Cabool, and the different engagements leading to it. He served also the campaign on the Sutlej, and was present in the battles of Moodkee, Ferozeshah, Buddiwal, Aliwal, and Sobraon, and was one of only five officers who escaped being wounded (Medal and three Clasps). Served with the 39th Regt. in the Crimea from 9th Dec. 1854 to 30th April 1856, including the siege and fall of Sebastopol (Medal and Clasp).
16 Surgeon Woodman and Assist.Surgeon Ross served at the siege and fall of Sebastopol in 1855, and at the attack on the 18th June (Medal and Clasp).
17 Lieuts. Raper, Palmer, and Gosselin served in 1855 at the siege and fall of Sebastopol, and final assault on the 8th Sept. (Medal and Clasp).
19 Quarter Master Blurton served the Eastern campaign of 1854-55 including the battles of Alma, Balaklava, and Inkerman, siege and fall of Sebastopol (Medal and Clasp).
20 Lieut. Sharples was present at the battle of Maharajpore 20th Dec. 1843 (Medal): he served also at the siege and fall of Sebastopol in 1855, including attacks on the 18th June and 8th Sept. (Medal and Clasp).

Foreign Service, 19 April 54.
Bermuda, Dep. Templemore. **39th (*The Dorsetshire*) Regt. of Foot.** 250—251

"*Primus in Indis.*" "PLASSEY" "GIBRALTAR" with the *Castle and Key*, "*Montis Insignia Calpe*" "ALBUHERA" "VITTORIA" "PYRENEES" "NIVELLE" "NIVE" "ORTHES" "PENINSULA" "MAHARAJPORE" "SEVASTOPOL."

Years' Serv.						
Full Pay	Half Pay					
58		Colonel.—🎖️ 🎖️ Richard Lluellyn,¹ CB. *Ens.* 24 July 02; *Lieut.* 7 April 04; *Capt.* 28 Feb. 05; *Maj.* 23 April 12; *Lt.-Col.* 18 June 15; *Col.* 10 Jun. 37; *Maj.-Gen.* 9 Nov. 46; *Lt.-Gen.* 20 June 54; *Col.* 39th Foot, 17 Jan. 53.					
26	0	Lieut.-Colonel.—William Munro,² CB. *Ens.* p 20 June 34; *Lieut.* p 1 April 36; *Capt.* 2 July 44; *Maj.* p 7 May 52; *Lt.-Col.* p 11 Nov. 53; *Col.* 28 Nov. 54.					
23	0	*Majors.*—Thomas Wright Hudson,³ *Ens.* p 16 June 37; *Lieut.* 30 Oct. 40; *Capt.* 7 Dec. 45; *Brev.-Maj.* 2 Nov. 55; *Major,* p 16 Nov. 55.					
22	0	Robert Hamilton Currie,⁴ *Ens.* p 28 Dec. 38; *Lieut.* p 14 Feb. 40; *Capt.* p 10 Feb. 52; *Brev.-Major,* 6 June 56; *Major,* p 30 Oct. 57.					

		CAPTAINS.	ENSIGN.	LIEUT.	CAPTAIN.	BREV. MAJ.
17	0	William Leckie⁵	10 Nov. 43	16 April 45	p 2 Apr. 52	6 June 56
14	0	Charles Denison Pedder⁶	p 7 July 46	p 27 Dec. 50	p 7 May 52	
21	0	Wm. Newport Tinley⁷	p 15 Nov. 39	p 11 June 41	27 May 53	
11	0	Robert Broome Baker	p 4 May 49	p 2 Apr. 52	p 24 June 53	
10	0	W. Hucks Harding Warner	p 1 Feb. 50	p 7 May 52	p 11 Nov. 53	
16	0	James Agnew⁸	22 Oct. 44	p 23 June 48	29 Dec. 54	
11	0	Thomas Fraser Dixon	10 April 49	p 10 Feb. 52	29 Dec. 54	
8	0	Charles Milligan,⁹ *s.*	p 11 June 52	p 11 Nov. 53	26 June 55	
9	0	W. H. Wilson Hawtayne	p 17 Jan. 51	p 10 July 52	p 4 Aug. 54	
8	0	William Gammell⁶	p 12 Mar. 52	p 11 June 53	p 17 July 57	
8	0	Francis Charles Turner¹⁰	p 9 July 52	6 June 54	p 15 June 55	
12	0	Arch. Camp. Snodgrass¹¹	p 6 Oct. 48	p 7 Nov. 51	29 Dec. 54	17 July 55
		LIEUTENANTS.				
8	0	T. Westropp Bennett¹²	p 17 Dec. 52	6 June 54		
9	0	Aug. Frederic Raper,¹⁷ *Adj*	p 16 May 51	p 12 May 54		
7	0	Edward John Stokes¹³	p 11 June 53	15 Dec. 54		
6	0	James Gibbons Smyth⁹	p 25 Aug. 54	9 Feb. 55		
6	0	Henry Bolton Newport¹⁴	1 Sept. 54	9 Feb. 55		
6	0	John Henry Murray¹³	p 8 Sept. 54	9 Feb. 55		
5	0	William Henry Palmer¹⁷	p 12 Jan. 55	18 Feb. 55		
6	0	John Tryon	p 17 Feb. 54	23 Mar. 55		
6	0	Edward Gatty	p 24 Mar. 54	6 Apr. 55		
5	0	Thos. Reginald Gosselin¹⁷	25 Jan. 55	27 July 55		
5	0	Fred. Standish Hore	9 Mar. 55	p 31 Aug. 55		
5	0	Francis Henry Chambers	26 Jan. 55	10 Nov. 55		
5	0	John Sharples²⁰	3 Aug. 55	p 14 Dec. 55		
5	0	Copner Francis Oldfield	p 23 Sept. 55	p 31 Aug. 58		
5	0	John Barthol. Corballis	p 25 Sept. 55	p 3 June 59		
		ENSIGNS.				
5	0	Abel Henry Woodroofe	p 16 Nov. 55			
5	0	Rich. Albert Vercoe Pope	p 21 Dec. 55			
2	0	Chauncy Arthur Taylor	13 April 58			
2	0	Frederick Trotter	p 15 June 58			
2	0	Oliver John Bradford	p 17 Sept. 58			
2	0	Fred. William Clarkson	p 12 Nov. 58			
2	0	Edward John Armytage	20 Feb. 58			
1	0	John DuB. Blennerhassett	22 Apr. 59			
1	0	Hugh Stewart	p 14 June 59			
1	0	Richard L. Leir	24 June 59			
19	0	*Paymaster.*—Samuel Benison,¹⁵ 5 Nov. 52; *QuarterMaster,* 13 July 41.				
9	0	*Adjutant.*—Lieut. Augustus Frederic Raper, 21 Aug. 58.				
6	0	*Instructor of Musketry.*—Lieut. Edward Gatty, 24 Aug. 58.				
5	0	*Quarter Master.*—George Blurton,¹⁹ 27 July 55.				
16	0	*Surgeon.*—George Thomas Woodman,¹⁶ M.D. 7 Apr. 54; *Assist. Surg.* 29 Nov. 44.				
7	0	*Assist. Surgs.*—John Halyburton Ross,¹⁶ M.B., 16 Dec. 53.				
2	0	Robert Lindsay, M.B. 14 Dec. 58.				

1 Lieut. General Lluellyn entered the army as a Captain with temporary rank in the 52nd Regt., and was present with it at Ferrol, Cadiz, and in the Mediterranean, in 1800 and 1801, and on the conclusion of peace was placed on half-pay; but on war soon after breaking out, he relinquished his temporary commission, and re-entered the service; and having in Feb. 1805 obtained a Company by purchase in the 28th Regt., he accompanied it to the Peninsula in 1809, and was present at the battle of Busaco, defence of the Lines of Lisbon, advance on Campo Mayor, investment of Olivença, siege of Badajoz, battle of Albuhera, surprise and capture of a French corps at Arroyo de Molino, attack and capture of the Forts and Bridge of Almaraz, advance on Aranjuez and Madrid, occupation of Bordeaux, and other services of minor importance. In 1815 he embarked with his Regiment for the Netherlands, where he was personally engaged with it in the battles of Quatre Bras and Waterloo, in the latter of which he was severely wounded, and received for his conduct in the field the brevet rank of Lt.-Colonel and the Companionship of the Bath. He has received the War Medal with two Clasps for Busaco and Albuhera.

Facings Green.—Agents, Messrs. Cox & Co.
Irish Agents, Sir E. R. Borough, Bt., Armit & Co.

2 Colonel Munro served as Adjutant of the 39th in the action of Maharajpore, and was severely wounded (Medal). Commanded the Regt. at the siege and fall of Sebastopol, and commanded the supports of the 1st Brigade 3rd Division at the attack on the 18th June 1855 (Medal and Clasp, Knight of the Legion of Honor, and 4th Class of the Medjidie).

3 Major Hudson served at the siege and fall of Sebastopol in 1855, and at the attacks on the 18th June and 8th Sept. (Medal and Clasp, Brevet Major, Sardinian Medal, and 5th Class of the Medjidie).

4 Major Currie served with the 39th Regt. in the action of Maharajpore, 29th Dec. 1843, and was wounded (Medal). Also at the siege and fall of Sebastopol in 1855, and at the attacks on the 18th June and 8th Sept. (Medal and Clasp, Brevet Major, and 5th Class of the Medjidie).

5 Major Leckie served at the siege and fall of Sebastopol in 1855, and at the attacks on the 18th June and 8th Sept. (Medal and Clasp, Brevet Major, and Knight of the Legion of Honor).

6 Captains Pedder and Gammell served at the siege of Sebastopol in 1855, and at the assault on the Redan on the 18th June (Medal and Clasp).

7 Captain Tinley served with the 39th Regt. in the action of Maharajpore, 29th Dec. 1843 (Medal). Also at the siege and fall of Sebastopol in 1855, and at the attacks on the 18th June and 8th Sept. (Medal and Clasp).

252 40th (*The 2nd Somersetshire*) *Regt. of Foot.* [Emb. for N.S. Wales, 14 July 52; Serving at Melbourne. Depot at Birr.

The *Sphinx*, with the word "EGYPT" on the caps of the Flank Companies. "MONTE VIDEO" "ROLEIA" "VIMIERA" "TALAVERA" "BADAJOZ" "SALAMANCA" "VITTORIA" "PYRENEES" "NIVELLE" "ORTHES" "TOULOUSE" "PENINSULA" "WATERLOO" "CANDAHAR" "GHUZNEE and CABOOL, 1842," "MAHARAJPORE."

Years' Serv.		
Full Pay	Half Pay	
66		**Colonel.**—Sir Alexander Woodford,[1] GCB. GCMG. *Ens.* 6 Dec. 94; *Lt.* 15 July 95; *Capt.* 11 Dec. 99; *Capt. & Lt.-Col.* 8 Mar. 10; *Col.* 4 June 14; *Major-Gen.* 27 May 25; *Lieut.-Gen.* 28 June 38; *Gen.* 20 June 54; *Col.* 40th Foot, 25 April 42.
22	0	**Lieut.-Colonel.**—Arthur Leslie, *Ens.* p 20 Nov. 38; *Lieut.* p 6 May 42; *Capt.* p 3 April 46; *Major,* p 25 June 52; *Lt.Col.* 6 Aug. 58.
29	0	**Majors.**—Thomas L. K. Nelson,[2] *Ens.* 25 Nov. 31; *Lt.* 29 Jan. 36; *Capt.* p 10 July 46; *Major,* 15 Feb. 56.
17	0	Hans Thomas Fell White, *Ens.* p 12 May 43; *Lt.* p 14 May 47; *Capt.* p 13 Dec. 50; *Major,* 28 Oct. 59.

		CAPTAINS.	ENSIGN.	LIEUT.	CAPTAIN.	BREV.MAJ.
13	0	Robert Hare, s.	p 7 May 47	p 18 Aug. 48	p 25 June 52	
11	0	Fred. Samuel Blyth	p 4 May 49	p 19 July 50	p 23 Dec. 53	
21	0	Edw. Hungerford Eagar[4]	p 13 April 39	16 July 41	6 June 54	
12	0	George Owen Bowdler[5]	26 May 48	p 18 Sept. 49	23 Mar. 55	
20	0	Justin E. D. MacCarthy	16 Dec. 40	29 Mar. 44	29 Dec. 54	
22	0	Dudley Clarges Hill, s.	9 Jan. 38	p 10 Sept. 41	p 4 May 49	
10	0	W. H. Horndon Messenger	p 19 July 50	p 5 Nov. 52	p 4 Dec. 57	
8	0	Charles Fleetwood Shawe[6]	p 13 Mar. 52	p 11 Oct. 53	p 20 Mar. 57	
9	0	Thomas Bailey Richards[5]	p 15 May 51	p 28 May 52	6 Aug. 58	
10	⅞	William Lawrence Murphy	11 Jan. 50	p 30 May 51	14 May 58	
9	0	Geo. Aug. Bentley Buckle	p 14 Feb. 51	24 Feb. 54	p 29 Oct. 58	
9	0	Theophilus Bolton	p 21 Nov. 51	6 June 54	p 22 Apr. 59	
11	0	Fred. C. H. S. Baddeley	p 20 Oct. 49	p 23 Dec. 53	28 Oct. 59	
		LIEUTENANTS.				
8	0	Arthur Fred. Fitz Simons	p 9 July 52	6 June 54		
8	0	Ar. M. Champion-Möller	p 9 July 52	17 Nov. 54		
7	0	Edw. Henry Melville Tod	p 23 Dec. 53	p 15 Dec. 54		
7	0	Charles Francis Brooke	p 23 Dec. 53	22 Dec. 54		
6	0	L. Nesbitt Lloyd	1 Sept. 54	12 Jan. 55		
6	0	Alfred Cook	p 15 Dec. 54	25 April 55		
5	0	Richard Armstrong	8 April 55	15 Feb. 56		
5	0	William Gibson	5 June 55	p 7 Dec. 55		
5	0	Hy. Ross-Lewin Morgan	1 May 55	p 27 Mar. 57		
5	0	George Hobbs	9 April 55	p 5 Mar. 58		
5	0	William Dowman	11 May 55	21 May 58		
4	0	Denis Jackson	8 Jan. 56	p 18 Feb. 59		
5	0	John Vander Horst Rees	p 6 Oct. 55	p 29 Apr. 59		
5	0	De Neufville Lucas	17 Aug. 55	28 Oct. 59		
		ENSIGNS.				
5	0	Tho. Ormsby Johnston, *adj*	28 Dec. 55			
4	0	John Thomas Whelan	15 Feb. 56			
4	0	Frederick Dudgeon	22 July 56			
3	0	Oliver Geo. W. D'Arcey	12 May 57			
2	0	Robert Brooks Clarke	p 5 Mar. 58			
2	0	Martin Morphy	2 July 58			
2	0	Edward Stack	17 Sept. 58			
1	0	Stepney P. E. Mansergh	11 Jan. 59			
1	0	Richard Crundel Brook	p 31 May 59			
1	0	Edward Toseland	19 July 59			

[5] Captains Bowdler and Richards served with a detachment of the 12th and 40th Regts. under Captain J. W. Thomas, 40th Regt., at the capture of a Stockade occupied by insurgents at the Ballarat Gold Fields in Australia, on 3rd Dec. 1854.

[6] Captain Shawe served with the 4th Dr.Gds. in the Crimea from 5 Aug. 1855, including the battle of the Tchernaya, siege and fall of Sebastopol (Medal and Clasp).

[7] Assist.Surgeon Stiles served in the Crimea attached to the Buffs from June 1855 (Medal and Clasp).

[4] Captain Eagar served with the 40th Regt. throughout the operations in Candahar and Affghanistan in 1841:42, and was severely wounded at Beni Badam (Medal); served also in the battle of Maharajpore—wounded (Medal). Served in the Crimea from Feb. to Aug. 1855 as acting field officer of the Land Transport Corps (Medal and Clasp).

23	⅞	*Paymaster.*—Henry Butler Stoney, 12 Oct. 52; *Ens.* p 5 May 37; *Lt.* p 11 Sept. [40]; *Capt.* 28 May 52.
5	0	*Adjutant.*—Ensign Thomas Ormsby Johnson, 24 Aug. 58.
5	0	*Instructor of Musketry.*—Lieut. William Gibson, 16 Oct. 57.
4	0	*Quarter Master.*—Francis Barnes, 19 Sept. 56.
15	0	*Surgeon.*—Henry Frederic Robertson, 2 Oct. 57; *Assist.Surg.* 19 Dec. 45.
6	0	*Assist. Surgeons.*—Thomas Mines, 1 Dec. 54.
5	0	Bradford Stiles,[7] 14 April 55.

Facings Buff.—*Agents,* Messrs. Cox & Co.

[1] Sir Alexander Woodford served in the 9th Regt. in North Holland, and was severely wounded on the 19th Sept. 1799. Served in the Coldstream Guards at the capture of Copenhagen in 1807. Served on the Staff in Sicily in 1808, 9, and 10. Commanded the Light Battalion of the Brigade of Guards, at the siege of Ciudad Rodrigo, battle of Salamanca, capture of Madrid, and at the siege of Burgos. Commanded first Battalion Coldstream Guards at the battle of Vittoria, capture of San Sebastian, at the Nivelle, the Nive, and investment of Bayonne. Commanded the second Battalion at the battle of Waterloo, surrender of Paris, and during the occupation in France. Sir Alexander has received the Gold Medal and two Clasps for the battle of Salamanca, Vittoria, and the Nive; and the Silver War Medal with one Clasp for Ciudad Rodrigo and Nivelle; and he is a Knight of Maria Theresa of Austria, and Fourth Class of St. George of Russia.

[2] Major Nelson served with the 40th Regt. throughout the operations in Candahar and Affghanistan in 1841-42 (Medal), also in the battle of Maharajpore, 29th Dec. 1843. Severely wounded and horse shot (Medal); he was Adjutant of the Regt. in the second Affghan campaign in 1842, as well as at Maharajpore.

Head Quarters, Jamaica.\
Depot, Devonport. **41st (The Welsh) Regiment of Foot.** 253

The Prince of Wales's Plume,"Gwell Angeu na Chywilydd." "DETROIT" "QUEENSTOWN" "MIAMI" "NIAGARA" "AVA" "CANDAHAR, GHUZNEE, and CABOOL, 1842" "ALMA" "INKERMAN" "SEVASTOPOL."

Years' Serv.			
Full Pay	Half Pay		
59		Colonel.—Charles Ashe a'Court-Repington,[1] CB. KH. Ens. 17 Dec. 01; Lt. 2 Sept. 02; Capt. 25 July 04; Major, 26 Feb. 11; Lt.Col. 19 May 13; Col. 22 July 30; Major Gen. 23 Nov. 41; Lt.Gen. 11 Nov. 51; Gen. 20 Feb. 56; Col. 41st Foot, 5 Feb. 48.	
16	0	Lieut.Colonel.—Julius Edmund Goodwyn,[2] CB. Ens. P 5 Jan. 44; Lt. P 6 June 45; Capt. P 3 May 50; Maj. P 15 Sept. 54; Lt.Col. 12 Dec. 54; Col. 19 Mar, 58.	
10	0	Majors.—Henry Stratton Bush,[3] Ens. P 16 Mar. 50; Lieut. P 26 Nov. 52; Capt. P 24 Nov. 54; Major, P 7 Nov. 56.	
14	1	Henry Warter Meredith,[4] Ens. P 6 June 45; Lieut. P 3 Nov. 46; Capt. P 25 June 52; Brevet Major, 12 Dec. 54; Major, 8 Jan. 56.	

		CAPTAINS.	ENSIGN.	LIEUT.	CAPTAIN.	BREV.MAJ.
10	0	Fred. Cherburgh Bligh[6]..	P 15 Mar. 50	P 25 June 52	P 15 Sept. 54	26 Dec. 56
13	0	Chas. Pelgue Bertram[6]	P 6 Feb. 47	P 22 Feb. 50	29 Dec. 54	6 June 56
10	0	William Allan[7]	P 12 July 50	P 11 Nov. 53	29 Dec. 54	
19	0	George Hyde Page[8]	P 23 April 41	P 12 May 43	26 Jan. 55	20 July 55
14	0	John Edmund Harvey ..	P 14 Aug. 46	P 9 Aug. 50	P 23 Mar. 55	
15	0	Hy. Vauslt. Pennefather	28 Feb. 45	18 Aug. 48	P 3 Aug. 55	
6	0	Wal. McClellan Lambert[10]	P 13 Jan. 54	P 22 Sept. 54	18 Jan. 56	
6	0	George Peddie[12]	P 10 Feb. 54	6 Nov. 54	26 Feb. 56	
10	0	Arthur Robert Fowler[13]..	P 12 July 50	P 2 Mar. 55	P 22 May 57	
6	0	Henry Seymour Hill[14] ..	7 June 54	8 Dec. 54	15 Feb. 59	
6	0	Edw. L. Barnwell Lowry[15]	10 Aug. 54	8 Dec. 54	P 14 June 59	
6	0	Robert Eustace Maude[17]	P 22 Sept. 54	11 Jan. 55	P 13 Dec. 59	
		LIEUTENANTS.				
6	0	Henry James Nowlan[16]..	11 Aug. 54	8 Dec. 54		
11	0	Irving Francis Kennedy	P 18 May 40	9 Feb. 55		
6	0	James Baird[18]	5 Nov. 54	9 Mar. 55		
6	0	Arthur Henry Wavell[20]..	14 Dec. 54	9 Mar. 55		
6	0	Isaac King, Adj.....	22 Dec. 54	9 Mar. 55		
5	0	W. H. Gardner Cornwall	10 Jan. 55	27 July 55		
5	0	Richard Pack..........	2 Feb. 55	18 Jan. 56		
5	0	Francis Michell	27 July 55	P 31 Dec. 57		
4	0	Milrea Tellet Quayle....	15 Jan. 56	7 Oct. 58		
4	0	Ashton Henry Warner ..	1 Feb. 56	20 Jan. 59		
3	0	Ralph Sadler	P 31 Dec. 57	15 Feb. 59		
2	0	Edw. Fra. Brown Brooke	23 April 58	P 14 June 59		
2	0	John Caulfield	16 June 58	P 26 Aug. 59		
2	0	Nathaniel Montgomery..	20 Nov. 58	P 26 Aug. 59		
2	0	Montagu Tho. Ball Michell	26 Nov. 58	P 13 Dec. 59		
		ENSIGNS.				
3	0	Henry E. G. Crean Lynch	P 24 Nov. 57			
2	0	Thomas P. A. Bracken..	15 June 58			
2	0	Jno. Tremenheer Johnston	19 Nov. 58			
1	0	Charles Miller	18 Mar. 59			
1	0	Seymour FitzJohn Clarke	19 Mar. 59			
1	0	George West Barnes ..	29 Apr. 59			
1	0	Edgar Younghusband....	P 23 Aug. 59			
1	0	John Wright Westby....	P 28 Oct. 59			
1	0	Arthur Gray	P 4 Nov. 59			
1	0	Henry Webb Byng	P 16 Dec. 59			
5	0	Paymaster.—James Simpson, 26 Aug. 59; Q.M. 12 June 55.				
6	0	Adjutant.—Lieut. Isaac King, 29 Aug. 56.				
11	0	Instructor of Musketry.—Lieut. I. F. Kennedy, 8 Nov. 58.				
2	0	Quarter Master.—Charles Ward, 29 Oct. 58.				
14	0	Surgeon.—James Leitch, M.D. 1 May 55; Assist.Surg. 23 Jan. 46.				
6	0	Assist. Surgeons.—Frederick Tydd Abbott,[23] 7 April 54.				
5	0	George Langford Hinde,[24] 15 May 55.				

1 General a'Court-Repington was detached on a separate command in 1806 to the Adriatic, to attack the islands of Tremitis, and in the same year he assisted at the siege of Scylla. In 1807 he served in Egypt, and was present at the capture of Alexandria, and in the action near Rosetta. At the siege and capture of Santa Maura he was in charge of the Quarter Master General's department: he was also at the siege of Capri in the same year. He was Aide de Camp to the Adjutant General when the enemy landed in Sicily in 1809, and commanded the advance-guard to which nearly 1000 prisoners surrendered, and he personally captured the enemy's standard. Served afterwards on the staff in Sicily, Spain, and Italy, and was present at the siege of Tarragona, action at Villa Franca, and retreat from thence; subsequently at the occupation of Leghorn, capture of Genoa, siege of Savona, and lastly at the surrender of Naples in 1815. He is a Commander of St. Ferdinand and Merit of Naples, and Knight of St. Maurice and Lazare of Sardinia.

2 Colonel Goodwyn served the Eastern campaign of 1854-55, including the battles of Alma and Inkerman, siege of Sebastopol, repulse of the sortie on 26th Oct., affair on 18th June (wounded), and assault on the Redan 8th Sept. (Medal and Clasps, Knight of the Legion of Honor, and 5th Class of the Medjidie).

Facings White.—*Agents*, Messrs. Cox & Co.

[*Returned from the Crimea*, 15 July 1856. *Embarked for Jamaica*, 3 April 1857.]

3 Major Bush served the Eastern campaign of 1854-55, including the battles of Alma and Inkerman (severely wounded), siege of Sebastopol, and repulse of the sortie on 26th Oct. (Medal and Clasps, and Sardinian Medal).

4 Major Meredith served the Eastern campaign of 1854-55, including the battles of Alma and Inkerman (severely wounded), siege of Sebastopol, and repulse of the sortie of 26th Oct. (Medal and three Clasps Brevet Major, and 5th Class of the Medjidie).

5 Major Bligh served in the Eastern campaign of 1854-55, including the battle of Inkerman (severely wounded), siege of Sebastopol, repulse of the sortie on 26th Oct. and assault of the Redan on 8th Sept. (Medal and Clasps).

6 Major Bertram served at the siege of Sebastopol from Feb. 1855 (Medal and Clasp, and Brevet Major).

7 Captain Allan served the Eastern campaign of 1854-55, including the battles of Alma and Inkerman, siege and fall of Sebastopol, repulse of the sortie on 26th Oct., and assault of the Redan on the 8th Sept. (Medal and Clasps, and Knight of the Legion of Honor).

41st (The Welsh) Regiment of Foot.

8 Major Page served in the 58th Regt. in New Zealand, and was present at the storming of Kawiti's Pah, 11th Jan. 1846, and he defeated the Natives in a night-attack on his post on the river Hutt, 16th May following. Present at the skirmish at Taitai, 16th June, commanded a detachment at the capture of the Chief Te Rauperaha and at the skirmish in Horokiwi Valley; present at the attack and repulse of the enemy on the settlements and stockades of Wanganui 19th May; and in the action of the 19th July 1847 he directed a charge which repulsed the enemy.

10 Captain Lambert served at the siege of Sebastopol from Feb. to March 1855 (Medal and Clasp).

12 Captain Peddie served at the siege of Sebastopol from Nov. 1854 (Medal and Clasp, and Sardinian Medal).

13 Captain Fowler served throughout the Kaffir war of 1851-53 (Medal), and was present at the taking of Fort Armstrong, the operations in the Waterkloof, the Amatolas, and other actions of the First Division. Whilst on duty with his Regiment in the Amatolas he received serious injuries which obliged him to return to England.

14 Captain Hill served at the siege of Sebastopol from Nov. 1854 (Medal and Clasp, and 5th Class of the Medjidie).

15 Captain Lowry served at the siege of Sebastopol from Nov. 1854, and was wounded at the assault of the Redan on the 8th Sept. (Medal and Clasp, and 5th Class of the Medjidie).

16 Lieut. Nowlan served at the siege of Sebastopol from Feb. 1855 (Medal and Clasp).

17 Captain Maude served at the siege of Sebastopol, and was wounded at the attack on the Redan 8th Sept. 1855 (Medal and Clasp).

18 Lieut. Baird served the Eastern campaign of 1854-55, including the battles of Alma and Inkerman, siege of Sebastopol, sortie of the 26th Oct., and assault of the Redan on the 8th Sept. (wounded 9th June 1855): Medal and Clasps.

20 Lieut. Wavell served at the siege of Sebastopol from June 1855 (Medal and Clasp).

23 Assist.Surgeon Abbott served the Eastern campaign of 1854-55, including the battles of Alma and Inkerman (Medal and Clasps).

24 Assist.Surg. Hinde served at the siege and fall of Sebastopol from 30th July 1855 (Medal and Clasp).

[Continuation of Notes to 43rd Foot.]

5 Captain Glover and Lieut. Sargent served with the 51st Regt. throughout the Burmese war of 1852 (Medal); on board the E. I. C. steam frigate *Ferooz* during the naval action and destruction of the enemy's stockades on the Rangoon River; during the succeeding three days' operations in the vicinity, and at the storm and capture of Rangoon.

6† Captain Horan served with the 41st Regt. during the whole of the campaign of 1842 in Affghanistan (Medal), and was present in the engagements with the enemy on 28th March and 28th April in the Pisheen Valley; in that of the 29th May near Candahar, 30th Aug. at Gonine, 5th Sept. before Ghuznee, occupation and destruction of that fortress and of Cabool, expedition into Kohistan, storm, capture, and destruction of Istaliff, and in the various minor affairs in and between the Bolan and the Khyber Passes.

8 Captain Mure served with the 43rd Light Infantry in the Kaffir war of 1851-53 (Medal). Served also in the Crimea from 29th July to 29th Sept. 1855, as Aide-de-Camp to Major-Gen. Markham (Medal and Clasp for Sebastopol, and 5th Class of the Medjidie).

8† Captain Hudson served as Adjutant 64th Regt. throughout the Persian campaign of 1856-57, including the storm and capture of Reshire, surrender of Bushire, night attack and battle of Kooshab, and bombardment of Mohumrah. Served in Bengal and N. W. Provinces in suppressing the mutiny in 1857-59; present with Havelock's column in the actions of Futtehpore, Aoung, Pandoo Nuddee, Cawnpore, Onao, Buscerut Gunge (1st and 2nd), Boorbeakeechowkee, Bithoor, Alumbagh, and first relief of Lucknow; present in all subsequent operations, including three sorties, until the second relief of Lucknow (thanked by Governor General in Council); served in defence of Cawnpore and defeat of the Gwalior mutineers, and actions of Kala Nuddee and Kerkeroulie, and capture of Bareilly: acted as D. A. Adj. Gen. with Sir H. Havelock at Mohumrah and at Alumbagh.

9 Lieut. Medhurst served with the 51st Regt. throughout the Burmese war of 1852 (Medal); on board the E. I. C. steam sloop *Sesostris* during the naval action and destruction of the enemy's stockades on the Rangoon River; served during the succeeding three days' operations in the vicinity (including the storming of the White House Redoubt) and at the storm and capture of Rangoon; also at the assault and capture of Bassein 19th May.

11 Lt. Morley served with the 51st Regt. throughout the Burmese war of 1852 (Medal); on board the E.I.C. steam frigate *Ferooz* during the naval action and destruction of the enemy's stockades on the Rangoon River; served during the succeeding three days' operations in the vicinity (including the storming of the White House Redoubt), and at the storm and capture of Rangoon.

12 Doctor Barclay served in the Kaffir war of 1846-7, and in that of 1851-2-3 (Medal).

Serving in India, Depot, Stirling.] *42nd (The Royal Highland) Regt. of Foot.* 255

Years' Serv.		
61		St. Andrew, "Nemo me impune lacessit."—The *Sphinx*, "EGYPT" "CORUNNA" "FUENTES D'ONOR" "PYRENEES" "NIVELLE" "NIVE" "ORTHES" "TOULOUSE" "PENINSULA" "WATERLOO" "ALMA" "SEVASTOPOL."
Full Pay.	Half Pay.	Colonel.—13 Sir James Douglas,¹ KCB. *Ens.* 10 July 1799; *Lieut.* 19 June 1800; *Capt.* 16 Sept. 02; *Major*, 16 Feb. 09; *Lieut.-Col.* 30 May 11; *Col.* 10 July 21; *Maj-Gen.* 22 July 30; *Lt.-Gen.* 23 Nov. 41; *Gen.* 20 June 54; *Col.* 42nd Foot, 10 April 50.
18	0	Lt.-Colonels.—Frederick Green Wilkinson,² *Ens.* P27 Dec. 42; *Lieut.* P13 Aug. 47; *Capt.* P17 Oct. 51; *Major*, 9 Oct. 55; *Lt.Col.* 16 March 58.
25	0	Edward Ramsden Priestley,³ *Ens.* 27 Nov. 35; *Lt.* P13 Jan. 38; *Capt.* P20 Oct. 43; *Brev.-Maj.* 20 June 54; *Major*, 3 April 57; *Lt.Col.* 10 Aug. 58.
14	0	Majors.—John Chetham M'Leod,⁴ *Ens.* 21 Apr. 46; *Lieut.* P17 Nov. 48; *Capt.* 29 Dec. 54; *Major*, 16 March 58.
13	0	John Drysdale,⁵ *Ens.* 22 June 47; *Lieut.* 12 Oct. 52; *Capt.* 12 Jan. 55; *Brev. Maj.* 20 July 58; *Major*, 10 Aug. 58.

		CAPTAINS.	ENSIGN.	LIEUT.	CAPTAIN.	BREV.-MAJ.
11	0	George Fraser⁶	P 6 July 49	P 13 Jan. 54	P 6 Apr. 55	
12	0	William Crofton Ward⁷	18 Aug. 48	20 May 53	24 Apr. 55	
8	0	Duncan Macpherson⁸ ..	P25 June 52	6 June 54	P24 Apr. 55	
9	0	Joseph Cha. Ross Grove⁹	9 Sept. 51	6 June 54	17 July 55	
8	0	Wm. G. Everard Webber¹⁰	P 23 Nov. 52	11 Aug. 54	10 Aug. 55	
10	0	Rowland Hill Gordon¹¹ ..	P 12 Dec. 50	31 Dec. 52	23 Feb. 55	
8	0	Fra. Cunningham Scott⁹	P 24 Nov. 52	P18 Aug. 54	6 Sept. 55	
7	0	Herbert Henry Moseley¹²	3 June 53	8 Dec. 54	9 Oct. 55	
6	0	Adam Ferguson¹³	P18 Aug. 54	9 Feb. 55	P 1 May 57	
6	0	William Baird¹⁴.........	P17 Nov. 54	9 Mar. 55	P22 May 57	
6	0	John Wilson¹⁵	10 Aug. 54	9 Feb. 55	16 Mar. 58	
5	0	William Green¹⁷.........	P16 Jan. 55	13 April 55	19 Aug. 59	
		LIEUTENANTS.				
5	0	V̇C̈F.E.H.Farquharson¹⁸	19 Jan. 55	24 April 55		
6	0	W. Wood,⁹*adj.*(*q.m.*5May54)	16 Feb. 55	25 May 55		
5	0	Murdoch Macleod¹⁹	20 Feb. 55	1 June 55		
5	0	George Wm. Cockburn²⁰	23 Feb. 55	17 July 55		
5	0	Hon. Rand. Hy. Stewart²¹	2 Mar. 55	10 Aug. 55		
5	0	Richard Korr Bayly²² ..	16 Mar. 55	2 Oct. 55		
5	0	George Armand Furse¹⁹..	P 29 Mar. 55	9 Oct. 55		
5	0	Charles Shuttleworth .	P23 April 55	P23 Oct. 55		
5	0	Thomas Mansfield James	P11 May 55	P 23 Nov. 55		
5	0	Jonathan Wynyard Haynes	P25 May 55	P23 Nov. 55		
5	0	William Underwood	P 5 June 55	P23 Nov. 55		
5	0	William Thomas Fraser	1 May 55	P 14 Dec. 55		
4	0	James William Mitchell..	15 Feb. 56	28 Aug. 57		
5	0	William James²²	P 30 Mar. 55	16 Apr. 58		
5	0	Arthur James Ceely²² ..	10 Aug. 55	20 June 58		
5	0	James Edmund Christie²²	17 Aug. 55	19 Aug. 59		
		ENSIGNS.				
5	0	William Henry Spooner¹⁹	P 9 Oct. 55			
5	0	Samuel Gordon McDakin²²	23 Oct. 55			
4	0	William Sanders Walter¹⁹	25 Jan. 56			
4	0	Henry Wemyss Feilden²¹	P 1 Feb. 56			
4	0	Geo. Thos. Carus Moore	12 Dec. 56			
3	0	Edmund Whitehead	P22 May 57			
2	0	Alex. Ferrier Kidston ..	P 9 Nov. 58			
1	0	Henry Brooke	P 5 Aug. 59			

1 Sir James Douglas accompanied the Expedition to South America under Gen. Craufurd on the Quarter-Master-General's Staff, and was engaged in the attack on Buenos Ayres. Subsequently in the same capacity he proceeded to Portugal with the Expedition under Sir Arthur Wellesley : was senior officer of the Quarter-Master-General's Department on the landing of the army ; and was present at the battles of Roleia, Vimiera, and Corunna. Joined the Portuguese army with the command of a Regiment in 1809 ; was present at the passage of the Douro, and battles of Busaco, Fuentes d'Onor, Salamanca, and the Pyrenees (wounded); after which he obtained command of the 7th Portuguese Brigade, & commanded it in the battles of the Nivelle, Nive, Orthes, and Toulouse (twice wounded, occasioning the loss of a leg). Sir James has received the Gold Cross and three Clasps for Busaco, Salamanca, Pyrenees, Nivelle, Nive, Orthes, and Toulouse.

5	0	Paymaster.—James Arnold Bazalgette,²⁵ 24 April 55.
6	0	Adjutant.—Lieut. William Wood,⁹ 16 Feb. 55.
5	0	Instructor of Musketry.—Lieut. William Thomas Fraser, 27 May 59.
1	0	Quarter-Master.—John Simpson, 7 Oct. 59.
13	0	Surgeon.—John Sheldon Furlong,²⁷ M.D. 9 Feb. 55; *Assist.Surg.* 19 Nov. 47.
6	0	Assistant-Surgeons.—Alexander Maclean,²⁸ 7 April 54.
6	0	Alfred Hooper,²⁹ 16 June 54.
3	0	William Alexander Mackinnon,³⁰ 23 Oct. 57.

Facings Blue.—Agents, Messrs. Cox & Co.
[*Returned from the Crimea, July 1856. Embarked for India, 14 Aug. 1857.*]

2 Lt.Colonel Wilkinson served the Eastern campaign until Oct. 1854, including the battle of Alma and siege of Sebastopol (Medal and Clasps, and 5th Class of the Medjidie). Served the campaign of 1857-58 against the Mutineers in India, including the action of Kudygunge, siege and fall of Lucknow, attack on the fort of Rooyah, action at Allygunge, and capture of Bareilly.
3 Lt.Colonel Priestley served the campaign of 1857-58 against the Mutineers in India, including the actions at Kudygunge and Shumsabad, siege and fall of Lucknow and assault of the Martiniere and Banks' Bungalow (mentioned in despatch), attack on the fort of Rooyah, action at Allygunge, and capture of Bareilly.

256   42nd (*The Royal Highland*) *Regt. of Foot.*

6 Captain Fraser served the campaign of 1857-58 against the Mutineers in India, including the actions at Kudygunge and Shumsabad, siege and fall of Lucknow and assault of the Martiniere and Banks' Bungalow, attack on the fort of Rooyah, action at Allygunge, and capture of Bareilly.

7 Captain Ward served throughout the Eastern campaign of 1854-55, including the battles of Alma and Balaklava, expedition to Kertch and Yenikale, siege and fall of Sebastopol (received a slight contusion from the fragment of a shell in the trenches (Medal and Clasps, and 5th Class of the Medjidie). Served the campaign of 1857-58 against the Mutineers in India, including the actions at Kudygunge and Shumsabad, siege and fall of Lucknow and assault of the Martiniere and Banks' Bungalow, attack on the fort of Rooyah, action at Allygunge, attack and capture of Bareilly.

8 Captain Macpherson served the campaign of 1857-58 against the Mutineers in India, including the action at Kudygunge, siege and fall of Lucknow and assault of the Martiniere and Banks' Bungalow, attack on the fort of Rooyah, action at Allygunge, attack and capture of Bareilly.

9 Captains Grove and Scott and Lieut. Wood served throughout the Eastern campaign of 1854-55, including the battles of Alma and Balaklava, expedition to Kertch and Yenikale, siege and fall of Sebastopol (Medal and Clasps. Captains Grove and Scott have the 5th Class of the Medjidie, and Lieut. Wood is a Knight of the Legion of Honor). Served the campaign of 1857-58 against the Mutineers in India, including the actions at Cawnpore (6 Dec. 57), Seringhat, Kudygunge, and Shumsabad, siege and fall of Lucknow and assault of the Martiniere and Banks' Bungalow, attack on the fort of Rooyah, action at Allygunge, attack and capture of Bareilly.

10 Captain Webber served throughout the Eastern campaign of 1854-55, including the battles of Alma and Balaklava, expedition to Kertch and Yenikale, siege and fall of Sebastopol (Medal and Clasps).

11 Captain Gordon served with the 38th Regt. throughout the Eastern campaign, including the battles of Alma and Inkerman, siege of Sebastopol, and commanded the party of the 38th which was engaged in repulsing the sortie on the 20th Dec., for which he was honorably mentioned by Lord Raglan and promoted into the Coldstream Guards (Medal and Clasps).

12 Captain Moseley served the campaign of 1857-58 against the Mutineers in India, including the actions at Kudygunge and Shumsabad, siege and fall of Lucknow and assault of the Martiniere and Banks' Bungalow.

13 Captain Ferguson served at the siege and fall of Sebastopol from 14th July 1855 (Medal and Clasp).

14 Captain Baird served at the siege of Sebastopol from July 1855 (Medal and Clasp). Served the campaign of 1857-58 against the Mutineers in India, including the actions at Kudygunge and Shumsabad, siege and fall of Lucknow, attack on the fort of Rooyah, action at Allygunge, attack and capture of Bareilly.

15 Captain Wilson served the Eastern campaign of 1854-55, including the battle of Balaklava, expedition to Kertch and Yenikale, siege and fall of Sebastopol (Medal and Clasps, and 5th Class of the Medjidie). Served the campaign of 1857-58 against the Mutineers in India, including the actions at Cawnpore (6th Dec.), Seriaghat, and Kudygunge, siege and fall of Lucknow and assault of the Martiniere and Banks' Bungalow, attack on the fort of Rooyah, action at Allygunge, attack and capture of Bareilly.

17 Captain Green served at the siege of Sebastopol from 14th July 1855 (Medal and Clasp). Served the campaign of 1857-58 against the Mutineers in India, including the actions of Kudygunge and Shumsabad, siege and fall of Lucknow, and assault of the Martiniere and Banks' Bungalow, attack on the fort of Rooyah, action at Allygunge, attack and capture of Bareilly.

18 Lieut. Farquharson served at the siege of Sebastopol from 14th July 1855 (Medal and Clasp). Served the campaign against the Mutineers in India, including the actions at Cawnpore (6th Dec. 57), Seriaghat, Kudygunge, and Shumsabad, siege and fall of Lucknow and assault of the Martiniere and Banks' Bungalow (severely wounded).

19 Lieuts. Macleod and Furse, Ensigns Spooner and Walter served the campaign of 1857-58 against the Mutineers in India, including the actions at Kudygunge and Shumsabad, siege and fall of Lucknow and assault of the Martiniere and Banks' Bungalow, attack on the fort of Rooyah, action at Allygunge, attack and capture of Bareilly.

20 Lieut. Cockburn served the campaign of 1857-58 against the Mutineers in India, including the actions at Cawnpore (6th Dec. 57), Seriaghat, Kudygunge, and Shumsabad, siege and fall of Lucknow and assault of the Martiniere and Banks' Bungalow, attack on the fort of Rooyah (wounded), and action at Allygunge.

21 Lieut. the Hon. R. Stewart served at the siege of Sebastopol from 14th July 1855 (Medal and Clasp). Served the campaign of 1857-58 against the Mutineers in India, including the actions at Kudygunge and Shumsabad, siege and fall of Lucknow, attack on the fort of Rooyah, action at Allygunge, attack and capture of Bareilly.

22 Lieuts. Bayly, James, Ceely, and Christie and Ensign McDakin served the campaign of 1857-58 against the Mutineers in India, including the actions at Cawnpore (6th Dec. 57), Seriaghat, Kudygunge, and Shumsabad, siege and fall of Lucknow and assault of the Martiniere and Banks' Bungalow, attack on the fort of Rooyah, action of Allygunge, attack and capture of Bareilly.

24 Ensign Feilden served the campaign of 1857-58 against the Mutineers in India, including the actions at Cawnpore (6th Dec. 57), Seriaghat, Kudygunge, and Shumsabad, siege and fall of Lucknow, and assault of the Martiniere and Banks' Bungalow.

25 Paymaster Bazalgette served at the siege of Sebastopol from 22d June 1855 (Medal and Clasp). Served the campaign of 1857-58 against the Mutineers in India, including the action at Kudygunge, siege and fall of Lucknow, attack on the fort of Rooyah, action at Allygunge, and capture of Bareilly.

27 Surgeon Furlong served throughout the Eastern campaign of 1854-55, including the affair of Bulganak, battles of Alma, Balaklava, and Inkerman, expedition to Kertch and Yenikale, siege and fall of Sebastopol (Medal and Clasps, and 5th Class of the Medjidie). Served the campaign of 1857-58 against the Mutineers in India, including the actions at Cawnpore (6th Dec. 57), Seriaghat, Kudygunge, and Shumsabad, siege and fall of Lucknow, attack on the fort of Rooyah, action at Allygunge, and capture of Bareilly.

28 Assist. Surgeon Maclean served the Eastern campaign up to the 30th Oct. 1854, and from 17th Feb. 1855, including the battle of Balaklava, expedition to Kertch and Yenikale, siege and fall of Sebastopol (Medal and Clasps). Served the campaign of 1857-58 against the Mutineers in India, including the actions at Kudygunge and Shumsabad, siege and fall of Lucknow, attack on the fort of Rooyah, action at Allygunge, and capture of Bareilly.

29 Assist. Surgeon Hooper served in the Eastern campaign from 8th Nov. 1854—Medal and Clasp for Sebastopol. Served the campaign of 1857-58 against the Mutineers in India, including the actions at Cawnpore (6th Dec. 57), Seringhat, Kudygunge, and Shumsabad, siege and fall of Lucknow, attack on the fort of Rooyah, action at Allygunge, and capture of Bareilly.

30 Assist. Surgeon Mackinnon served the Eastern campaign of 1854-55 with the 42nd Highlanders, including the battles of Alma and Balaklava, expedition to Kertch, siege and fall of Sebastopol, and assault of the outworks on the 18th June (Medal and Clasp).

Emb. for C. of G. Hope, 10 Oct. 51.
Serving in India. Dep. Chatham.] **43rd (*Monmouthshire*) *Regt. of F.(Lt. Inf.*)**

"VIMIERA" "CORUNNA" "BUSACO" "FUENTES D'ONOR" "CIUDAD RODRIGO" "BADAJOZ" "SALAMANCA" "VITTORIA" "NIVELLE" "NIVE" "TOULOUSE" "PENINSULA."

Years' Serv.		
Full Pay.	Half Pay.	
59		Colonel.—🝆 Sir James Fergusson,¹ KCB. *Ens.* 20 Aug. 01; *Lt.* 9 Feb. 04; *Capt.* 1 Dec. 06; *Major,* 3 Dec. 12; *Lt.-Col.* 16 May 14; *Col.* 22 July 30; *Major-Gen.* 23 Nov. 41; *Lieut.-Gen.* 11 Nov. 51; *Col.* 43rd Foot, 26 Mar. 50.
34	0	*Lieut.-Colonels.*—Geo. Talbot, *s., Ens.* 2 Feb. 26; *Lieut.* ᴾ 9 Sept. 28; *Capt.* ᴾ 3 Apr. 35; *Br. Maj.* 9 Nov. 46; *Maj.* 29 July 53; *Brev. Lt.-Col.* 20 June 54; *Lt.-Col.* 7 Nov. 56; *Col.* 18 Feb. 58.
23	0	James Maurice Primrose,² *Ens.* 6 Jan. 37; *Lieut.* 7 May 41; *Capt.* 11 Apr. 48; *Maj.* 9 Feb. 55; *Lt.-Col.* ᴾ 20 March 57.
13	0	*Majors.*—Henry Jackson Parkin Booth,⁴ *Ensign,* 11 June 47; *Lieut.* ᴾ 9 Aug. 50; *Capt.* 29 July 53; *Major,* ᴾ 3 April 57.
19	0	Francis Hutchinson Synge, *Ens.* ᴾ 7 Sept. 41; *Lieut.* ᴾ 9 June 46; *Capt.* ᴾ 17 Oct. 51; *Major,* ᴾ 24 July 57.

		CAPTAINS.	ENSIGN.	LIEUT.	CAPTAIN.	BREV.-MAJ.
20	0	Thomas Hugh Cockburn	ᴾ 6 Mar. 40	15 April 42	9 Sept. 51	20 July 58
22	3¹⁄₁₂	William John Dorehill⁶..	ᴾ 16 Jan. 25	10 Mar. 38	11 Jan. 50	
16	0	John Geo. C. Disbrowe..		2 Feb. 44	ᴾ 31 Mar. 48	20 June 59
22	0	Thomas Edmonds Holmes	ᴾ 28 Dec. 38	8 April 42	15 Aug. 52	
13	0	Henry B. Harrison Rocke	ᴾ 10 Dec. 47	ᴾ 26 Apr. 50	ᴾ 17 Aug. 52	
10	0	Fiennes Middleton Colvile	ᴾ 14 Aug. 50	ᴾ 23 Nov. 52	ᴾ 9 Oct. 55	
10	0	Robert Coke Glover⁵ ..	ᴾ 18 Jan. 50	ᴾ 5 Dec. 51	30 Jan. 57	
18	0	Thomas Horan⁶†		27 May 42	ᴾ 23 Sept. 45	24 April 55
11	0	Henry Trafford Trafford⁷	31 Mar. 49	6 June 54	ᴾ 3 Apr. 57	
9	¹⁄₁₂	Charles Reginald Mure⁸	ᴾ 16 Aug. 50	29 July 53	ᴾ 8 Jan. 56	
8	0	Wm. Stewart Richardson	23 Nov. 52	9 Feb. 55	ᴾ 24 Aug. 58	
7	0	John Hudson⁸†	ᴾ 22 April 53	ᴾ 9 Mar. 55	23 July 58	
		LIEUTENANTS.				
11	0	Samuel Tomyns Sargent⁵	18 May 49	9 July 52		
10	0	Fred. Edward Medhurst⁹.	ᴾ 14 June 50	24 Jan. 53		
10	0	Arthur G. Evelyn Morley¹¹	ᴾ 17 Sept. 50	25 April 53		
6	0	Hon. Arthur Ern. Harris	14 April 54	23 Mar. 55		
6	0	Herbert Johnes Berners	ᴾ 7 June 54	ᴾ 13 Apr. 55		
6	0	Harry Armstrong Brett..	ᴾ 8 Sept. 54	ᴾ 1 May 55		
6	0	Thomas Collings Maguire	ᴾ 25 Aug. 54	ᴾ 10 Aug. 55		
6	0	Fred. Guy Eaton Glover.	ᴾ 9 Sept. 54	29 Aug. 55		
5	0	Arthur R. Close	ᴾ 13 Apr. 55	ᴾ 9 Oct. 55		
5	0	Harry Gorton..........	ᴾ 1 May 55	ᴾ 14 Dec. 55		
5	0	Stanley Crozier	8 June 55	ᴾ 8 Jan. 56		
5	0	Chris. Hore Hatchell....	6 July 55	ᴾ 5 Sept. 56		
5	0	William Livesay	26 Oct. 55	ᴾ 3 Apr. 57		
4	0	Hugh Osborne Bateman	ᴾ 6 Mar. 56	ᴾ 24 July 57		
4	0	D'Urban W. Farrer Blyth	ᴾ 7 Mar. 56	24 May 58		
4	0	Henry Charles Talbot ..	ᴾ 5 Sept. 56	ᴾ 24 Aug. 58		
4	0	Thomas McGoun	8 July 56	ᴾ 22 April 59		
		ENSIGNS.				
3	0	George Garland,⁴ *Adj.* ...	6 Feb. 57			
3	0	John E. Kingston Morley	14 Mar. 56			
3	0	Gerald Henry Baird Young	ᴾ 3 April 57			
3	0	Ernest Villiers	ᴾ 24 July 57			
2	0	Joseph Hogarth.........	ᴾ 31 Aug. 58			
2	0	Robert Mercer Tod	ᴾ 7 Sept. 58			
1	0	John M'Neill	ᴾ 17 Sept. 58			
2	0	Charles Salmon	29 Oct. 58			
2	0	*Paymaster.*—Horatio Morgan, 17 Sept. 58.				
3	0	*Adjutant.*—Ensign George Garland,⁴ 6 Feb. 57.				
12	0	*Instructor of Musketry.*—Lieut. S. T. Sargent, 13 Oct. 58.				
2	0	*Quarter Master.*—Arthur Williams, 29 Oct. 58.				
17	0	*Surgeon.*—Alexander Barclay,¹² M.D. 13 April 52; *Assist.-Surg.* 22 Dec. 43.				
6	0	*Assistant-Surgeons.*—Charles Dodgson Madden, M.D. 14 Dec. 54.				
4	0	John James Henry, 18 Jan. 56.				
3	0	James Good, 3 Oct. 57.				

Notes column (right side):
2 Lt. Colonel Primrose served with the 43rd in the Kaffir war of 1851-53 (Medal).
4 Major Booth and Ensign Garland served with the 43rd in the Kaffir war of 1851-53 (Medal).
6 Captain Dorchill served with the Buffs in the battle of Punniar (Medal), and was severely wounded on the right side of his breast.

Facings White.—*Agents,* Messrs. Cox & Co.

1 Sir James Fergusson served the campaign of 1808-9, including the battles of Vimiera and Corunna, Expedition to Walcheren in 1809. Peninsular campaigns from March 1810 to the end of that war in 1814, including the passage of the Coa, near Almeida, battle of Busaco, actions at Pombal, Redinha, Miranda de Corvo, Foz d'Arouce, and Sabugal; battle of Fuentes d'Onor, sieges and assaults of Ciudad Rodrigo and Badajoz, battle of Salamanca, action of San Munos, passage of the Bidassoa, battle of the Nivelle, battles of the Nive on the 9th, 10th, 11th, 12th and 13th Dec. 1813; and investment of Bayonne. Major-General Fergusson has received five wounds, viz. at Vimiera, slightly; at the storming of Ciudad Rodrigo, severely in the body and slightly in the foot; at Badajoz, slightly in the side by a splinter of a shell in the trenches, and in the head at the assault. He has received the Gold Medal for Badajoz, as senior surviving Officer of the Light Division Storming Party; and he also served in the Storming Party at Ciudad Rodrigo and at the taking of the outworks of that place Fort Reynard. He has also received the Silver War Medal) with eight Clasps.

7 Capt. Trafford served with the 51st Regt. in Burmah from Sept. 1852 to the end of the war, and was present with Capt. Irby's detachment of four Companies with Brigadier-General Cheape's force during the whole of the successful operations in the Donabew district, ending in the assault and capture, on the 19th March 1853, of the stronghold of the Burmese chief Myattoon (Medal). [For remainder of Notes see end of 41st Foot.

44th (The East Essex) Regt. of Foot. [Serving in India. Depot, Colchester.

The Sphinx, "EGYPT" "BADAJOZ" "SALAMANCA" "PENINSULA" "BLADENSBURG" "WATERLOO" "AVA" "ALMA" "INKERMAN" "SEVASTOPOL."

Years' Serv. 47

Colonel.—◆ Thomas Reed,[1] CB. *Cornet*, 26 Aug. 13; *Lt*. p 2 May 15; *Capt*. p 19 Feb. 24; *Major*, p 15 June 26; *Lt.Col*. p 11 Aug. 29; *Col*. 23 Nov. 41; *Major Gen*. 20 June 54; *Col*. 44 F. 2 Aug. 58.

Full Pay.	Half Pay.	
25	0	*Lt.Colonels.*—Charles William Dunbar Staveley,[2] CB. *2nd Lt.* p 6 Mar. 35; *Lieut*. p 4 Oct. 30; *Capt*. p 6 Sept. 44; *Major*, 7 Dec. 50; *Lt.Col*. 12 Dec. 54; *Col*. 9 Mar. 58.
25	0	William MacMahon,[3] *Ens*. p 6 Nov. 35; *Lieut*. 28 Feb. 40; *Capt*. 17 May 45; *Maj*. 12 Dec. 54; *Brev. Lt.Col*. 2 Nov. 55; *Lt.Col*. 28 Aug. 57.
19	0	*Majors*.—Andrew Browne,[4] *Ens*. p 30 Apr. 41; *Lt*. 14 Oct. 42; *Capt*. p 8 Sept. 46; *Brev.Maj*. 12 Dec. 54; *Maj*. 31 Aug. 55; *Brev.Lt.Col*. 6 June 56.
21	2	John Hackett,[5] *Ens*. 17 Nov. 37; *Lt*. 28 Aug. 39; *Capt*. 25 July 51; *Brev. Major*, 12 Dec. 54; *Major*, 7 Sept. 55.

		CAPTAINS.	ENSIGN.	LIEUT.	CAPTAIN.	BREV.-MAJ.
17	0	William Faussett[7]	7 July 43	p 23 Aug. 44	p 23 Mar. 49	17 July 55
18	0	John Robinson[8]	26 Oct. 42	p 22 Dec. 43	30 Jan. 51	2 Nov. 55
14	0	Richard Preston[9]	p 27 Feb. 46	p 24 Nov. 48	20 Dec. 54	2 Nov. 55
14	0	William Fletcher[10]	p 6 Nov. 46	p 21 Mar. 51	12 Jan. 55	6 June 56
12	0	Fred. Wm. Gregory[11]	29 Dec. 48	24 Mar. 53	19 June 55	
13	0	Hon.R.Baillie-Hamilton[13]	p 7 May 47	p 26 Dec. 51	29 June 55	
7	0	Alex. W. Cobham[11]	p 2 Dec. 53	8 Dec. 54	p 10 April 57	
6	0	Fra. Dalrymple Walters[18]	6 June 54	9 Feb. 55	p 12 May 57	
6	0	Arthur William Staveley[22]	16 June 54	9 Feb. 55	p 11 Sept. 57	
6	0	A. de Montmorcy. Fleming	11 Aug. 54	9 Feb. 55	p 7 Dec. 58	
9	0	George Ingham[12]	p 21 Mar. 51	6 June 54	17 Dec. 58	
6	0	John Jennings Kendall[16]	p 18 Aug. 54	9 Mar. 55	p 31 Dec. 58	
		LIEUTENANTS.				
7	0	Wm. Arthur Wood[14]	13 May 53	11 Aug. 54		
6	0	George Evatt Acklom[16]	p 13 Jan. 54	8 Dec. 54		
6	0	Matthew Skinner Smith[18]	7 June 54	9 Feb. 55		
6	0	Peter McInnis[20]	10 Aug. 54	9 Feb. 55		
6	0	Thomas Orton Howorth[21]	29 Dec. 54	9 Mar. 55		
5	0	Edw.Cha.P.Pigott,[19] *Adj*.	p 16 Jan. 55	19 June 55		
5	0	Elliott Arthur Raymond	18 Feb. 55	19 June 55		
5	0	James Kay	10 Feb. 55	19 June 55		
5	0	Azim Salvator Birch	20 Feb. 55	29 June 55		
5	0	Robt. Montresor Rogers[15]	21 Feb. 55	3 Aug. 55		
5	0	Geo. Cuthbertson Bower[15]	22 Feb. 55	17 Aug. 55		
5	0	George Egerton Hodgson	16 Mar. 55	7 Dec. 55		
5	0	Philip Morton Pitt	6 Apr. 55	7 Dec. 55		
5	0	Samuel Handy Halahan	1 May 55	30 Mar. 58		
5	0	Aug. Richard Trimmer	23 Nov. 55	17 Dec. 58		
4	0	Richard Yarde Foley	p 1 Feb. 56	p 31 Dec. 58		
3	0	Henry William Heane	p 10 April 57	p 3 June 59		
		ENSIGNS.				
5	0	Francis O'Neill[23]	6 Dec. 55			
5	0	Charles Bassett Lewis	p 7 Dec. 55			
2	0	Arthur J. Roberts	8 Oct. 58			
2	0	Cha. Elphinstone Rennie	19 Nov. 58			
1	0	Constantine Maguire	p 25 Jan. 59			
1	0	Wm. John E.G. Sutherland	11 Mar. 59			
1	0	Charles Hussey Walsh	13 May 59			
1	0	Henry de Parny Rennick	p 5 Aug. 59			

1 Major General Thomas Reed served the campaign of 1815, and was present at the battle of Waterloo. In 1846 he commanded a Brigade of the Army of the Sutlej, and was wounded and had a horse killed under him at the battle of Ferozeshah (Medal). Commanded the force besieging Delhi in June and July 1857 (Medal and Clasp).

2 Colonel Staveley served the Eastern campaign of 1854-55, including the battles of Alma and Balaklava (volunteered his services as Aide-de-Camp to the Duke of Cambridge), siege of Sebastopol, and attack and occupation of the Cemetery and Suburbs on the 18th June—succeeded to the command of the 44th Regt., and commanded the Regt. at the fall of Sebastopol (Medal and Clasps, CB., Sardinian Medal, and 5th Class of the Medjidie).

5	0	*Paymaster*.—Richard Gillham Thomsett,[24] 25 Jan. 56; *Qr.Mr.* 27 July 55.
5	0	*Adjutant*.—*Lieut*. Edward Charles Pemberton Pigott,[19] 8 March 59.
		Instructor of Musketry.—
4	0	*Quarter Master*.—William Hart,[26] 25 Jan. 56.
15	0	*Surgeon*.—James Mee,[34] 5 May 54; *Assist.Surg.* 28 March 45.
3	0	*Assistant Surgeons*.—James Bowyer Baker, 28 May 57.
3	0	Charles James Kinahan, 27 May 57.
5	0	Edmund Greswold M'Dowell, 6 Nov. 55.

Facings Yellow.—*Agents*, Messrs. Cox & Co.
[*Returned from the Crimea, June* 1856. *Embarked for India*, 26 *Aug.* 1857.]

3 Lieut.Colonel MacMahon served the Eastern campaign of 1854-55, including the battles of Alma and Inkerman, siege and fall of Sebastopol, and attack and occupation of the Cemetery and Suburbs on the 18th June (Medal and Clasps, Knight of the Legion of Honor, Sardinian Medal, and 5th Class of the Medjidie).

4 Lieut.Colonel Browne served the Eastern campaign of 1854, including the battle of Alma and siege of Sebastopol, and was severely wounded in the trenches on the 20th October by a shell, occasioning amputation of right arm and part of left hand (Medal and Clasps, Brevets of Major and Lt.Col., Knight of the Legion of Honor, and 5th Class of the Medjidie).

44th (The East Essex) Regt. of Foot.

5 Major Hackett served in the Eastern campaign of 1854-55 as D. A. Q. M.Gen., including the battles in the Crimea and siege of Sebastopol (Medal and Clasps, Brevet Major, Sardinian Medal, and 5th Class of the Medjidie).
7 Major Faussett served the Eastern campaign of 1854-55, including the battles of Alma and Inkerman, siege and fall of Sebastopol, and attack and occupation of the Cemetery on the 18th June; he was Brigade Major in the 3rd Division from 23rd April 1855 (Medal and Clasps, Brevet Major, Sardinian Medal, and 5th Class of the Medjidie).
8 Major Robinson served the Eastern campaign of 1854-55, including the battles of Alma and Inkerman, siege and fall of Sebastopol, attack and occupation of the Cemetery on the 18th June, and was Aide-de-Camp to Brigadier-General Spencer in the trenches at the fall of Sebastopol 8th Sept., and in the expedition to and capture of the Forts of Kinbourn (Medal and Clasps, Brevet Major, Knight of the Legion of Honor, and 5th Class of the Medjidie).
9 Major Preston served the Eastern campaign of 1854-55, including the battles of Alma and Inkerman, siege and fall of Sebastopol, attack and occupation of the Cemetery on the 18th June (Medal and Clasps, Brevet of Major, Knight of the Legion of Honor, and 5th Class of the Medjidie).
10 Major Fletcher served the Eastern campaign of 1854-55, including the battles of Alma and Inkerman, siege and fall of Sebastopol, attack and occupation of the Cemetery on the 18th June (Medal and Clasps, Brevet of Major, Sardinian Medal, and 5th Class of the Medjidie).
11 Captains Gregory and Cobham served the Eastern campaign of 1845-55, including the battles of Alma and Inkerman, siege and fall of Sebastopol, attack and occupation of the Cemetery on the 18th June (Medal and Clasps, and 5th Class of the Medjidie).
12 Captain Ingham served the Eastern campaign of 1854-55, including the battles of Alma and Inkerman, siege and fall of Sebastopol, and attack and occupation of the Cemetery on the 18th June (Medal and Clasps).
13 Captain Hon. R. Baillie-Hamilton served the Eastern campaign of 1854-55, including the battles of Alma and Inkerman, siege and fall of Sebastopol, and capture of Kinbourn—as Aide de Camp to General Spencer (Medal and Clasps, and Sardinian Medal).
14 Lieut. Wood served the Eastern campaign of 1854-55, including the battles of Alma and Inkerman, siege and fall of Sebastopol (contusion from a round shot in the trenches 17th Oct. 54), and attack and occupation of the Cemetery on the 18th June (Medal and Clasps, and Sardinian Medal).
15 Lieuts. Rogers and Bower were at the fall of Sebastopol (Medal and Clasp).
16 Lieut. Acklom served at the siege of Sebaspotol, including the attack on the 16th June (Medal and Clasp).
18 Captains Walters and Kendall, and Lieut. Smith, served at the siege and fall of Sebastopol in 1855, including the attack on the 18th June (Medal and Clasp).
19 Lieut. Pigott served in the trenches before Sebastopol and at its fall (Medal and Clasp).
20 Lieut. McInnis served in the Crimea (Medal and Clasp).
21 Lieut. Howorth served at the siege of Sebastopol, including the attack on the 18th June—severely wounded (Medal and Clasp).
22 Capt. Staveley served in the trenches before Sebastopol (Medal and Clasp).
23 Ensign O'Neill served in the Eastern campaign of 1854-55, including the battle of Alma and siege of Sebastopol (Medal and Clasps).
24 Paymaster Thomsett and Surgeon Mee served the Eastern campaign of 1854-55, including the battles of Alma and Inkerman, siege and fall of Sebastopol (Medal and Clasps).
26 Qr.Master Hart served the Eastern campaign of 1854-55, including the battles of Alma and Inkerman, siege and fall of Sebastopol, attack and occupation of the Cemetery on the 18th June (Medal and Clasps).

[Continuation of Notes to 45th Foot.]

7 Captain Hobbs served the Kaffir campaign of 1850-53 (Medal); commanded the rear-guard of the 91st Regt. as a volunteer on 29th Dec. 1850, when two officers and twenty-two men were killed, and one officer and eighteen men wounded; was appointed Captain Commandant of a native force of 330 men, which he commanded for several months on patrol through the Amatolas and Waterkloof; in Dec. 1851 he was again attached to the 91st Regt. as a volunteer; rejoined the 45th Regt. early in 1852, and accompanied it on every patrol through the Waterkloof and Amatolas until the termination of the war; was several times named in General Orders.
11 Ensign Guernsey served in the Kaffir war of 1846-47, and in the field against the Enemy in the Orange River Sovereignty between 24th Dec. 1850 and 6 Feb. 1853 (Medal).
13 Quarter Master Power served with the 60th Rifles in the Kaffir war of 1851, 52, 53 (Medal).
14 Lieut. Pearson served with the 95th Regt. in the Indian campaign in 1858, including the siege and capture of Kotah, battle of Kota ka Serai, general action resulting in the capture of Gwalior, siege and capture of Gwalior (Medal).

260   **45th (*The Nottinghamshire*) Regt. of Foot.** [Preston.
Depot, Parkhurst.

"ROLEIA" "VIMIERA" "TALAVERA" "BUSACO" "FUENTES D'ONOR" "CIUDAD RODRIGO"
"BADAJOZ" "SALAMANCA" "VITTORIA" "PYRENEES" "NIVELLE" "ORTHES"
"TOULOUSE" "PENINSULA" "AVA."

Years' Serv.						
Full Pay.	Half Pay.					
40		*Colonel.*—Sir Hugh Henry Rose,[1] GCB. *Ens.* p 8 June 20; *Lt.* p 24 Oct. 21; *Capt.* p 22 July 24; *Major,* p 30 Dec. 26; *Lt.Col.* p 17 Sept. 39; *Col.* 11 Nov. 51; *Major Gen.* 12 Dec. 54; *Col.* 45 F. 20 July 58.				
31	0	*Lieut.-Colonel.*—Henry Cooper,[2] *Ens.* p 26 Feb. 29; *Lieut.* p 5 Apr. 31; *Capt.* p 13 Nov. 35; *Major,* 10 Sept. 45; *Lt.Col.* 19 July 48; *Col.* 28 Nov. 54.				
31	0	*Majors.*—William R. Preston, *Ens.* p 24 Sept. 29; *Lieut.* p 22 Feb. 33; *Capt.* p 18 Oct. 39; *Major,* 19 July 48; *Bt. Lt.-Col.* 20 Feb. 55.				
22	0	Henry John Shaw, *Ens.* p 23 Mar. 38; *Lieut.* p 7 June 39; *Capt.* p 1 July 42; *Major,* p 4 Nov. 53; *Bt.Lt.Col.* 26 Oct. 58.				

		CAPTAINS.	ENSIGN.	LIEUT.	CAPTAIN.	BREV.-MAJ.
25	0	Geo. A. L. Blenkinsopp[3] *Lieut.-Col.* 19 June 56.	p 4 Sept.35	p 31 May 39	p 29 Mar. 44	22 Dec. 48
21	0	Henry Woodbine Parish,[4] *s*	p 9 Mar. 39	15 Apr. 42	p 6 Feb. 46	6 June 56
21	0	Stephen Bilton Gordon[5]	7 June 39	15 Apr. 42	19 July 48	
30	0	Henry Downe Griffith	13 June 30	6 Apr. 36	p 20 Oct. 43	20 June 54
18	0	Rob. Beckford Johnstone[6]	27 May 42	10 Sept. 45	p 4 Nov. 53	
18	0	James M'Crea,[5] *s*......	23 May 42	p 30 Aug. 44	6 June 54	
18	0	Henry Leach[6]	p 22 July 42	15 Oct. 45	p 4 Aug. 54	
14	0	Fred. Robert Grantham[5]	p 6 Fe'y. 46	p 22 June 49	p 13 Oct. 54	
13	0	George Lamont Hobbs[7] .	29 Jan. 47	p 22 June 49	p 4 Dec. 57	
9	0	Thomas Aug. Burrowes	25 April 51	11 Aug. 54	p 26 Feb. 58	
13	0	Charles Lewis Griffin[8] ..	19 Mar. 47	p 3 Aug. 49	19 Feb. 58	
11	0	Henry Lucas[9]..........	p 22 June 49	6 June 54	p 24 Aug. 58	
9	0	James John Wood......	p 14 Feb. 51	11 Aug. 54	31 Dec. 58	
		LIEUTENANTS.				
9	0	Henry Safe Willoughby	p 17 June 51	p 15 Sept. 54		
8	0	E. Gambier Eliot Atherley	p 23 Nov. 52	p 13 Oct. 54		
7	0	Richard Blair, *Adj.*	p 18 Mar. 53	17 Nov. 54		
7	0	Richard Grey........	22 Apr. 53	p 17 Nov. 54		
7	0	George Champagne Close	p 4 Nov. 53	p 21 Sept. 55		
6	0	John Ingle Preston	16 June 54	p 15 Feb. 56		
6	0	Fred. Wm. Swann Webber	p 18 Aug. 54	28 Nov. 57		
6	0	Caulfield Fra. Beamish ..	14 July 54	10 Feb. 58		
6	0	Adam Perry	p 17 Nov. 54	p 26 Feb. 58		
5	0	Edward O'Neill	11 May 55	16 Mar. 58		
4	0	Henry Blakeney Hayward	8 July 55	p 24 Aug. 58		
5	0	Wyrley Birch[10]	2 Mar. 55	17 Aug. 55		
5	0	George Weir Cosens	p 2 Oct. 55	p 11 Mar. 59		
4	0	James Franklin	25 Oct. 54	17 Nov. 57		
5	0	William Pearson[14]	p 13 July 55	p 26 Nov. 58		
		ENSIGNS.				
3	0	William Kershaw	p 20 Mar. 57			
3	0	James Hett Tennant	p 4 Dec. 57			
3	0	Robert J. Callwell	p 18 Dec. 57			
2	0	Charles Harrison Hignett	p 12 Feb. 58			
2	0	Forbes William Guernsey[11]	6 Aug. 58			
2	0	Henry Hodson Hooke ..	13 Aug. 58			
2	0	Edward Browne	p 17 Sept. 58			
2	0	Francis Dixon Johnson..	p 29 Oct. 58			
2	0	Richard Albert Nolan ..	p 19 Nov. 58			
1	0	Henry James B. Hancock	11 Mar. 59			
7	0	*Paymaster.*—John David Blythe, 3 June 53.				
7	0	*Adjutant.*—*Lieut.* Richard Blair, 16 March 58.				
3	0	*Instructor of Musketry.*—Ensign R. J. Callwell, 26 July 59.				
13	0	*Quarter-Master.*—Richard Power,[13] 28 May 47.				
13	0	*Surgeon.*—Thomas Connor O'Leary,[12] M.B. 9 Feb. 55; *Assist.Surg.* 6 Aug. 47.				
7	0	*Assist.-Surgeons.*—Alexander Fisher Bartley, 14 Jan. 53.				
7	0	James Arthur Hanbury, M.B. 30 Sept. 53.				

Notes column:
2 Colonel Cooper commanded the Reserve Battalion 45th Regt. in the Kaffir war of 1846-47, and a Wing of the Regt. throughout the Kaffir war of 1850-53 (Medal), and was appointed Commandant of the Natal Colony at the close of the war.

3 Lt.-Col. Blenkinsopp served the Kaffir campaign of 1847 (Medal); and he commanded the detachment of the 45th Regt. in the action with and defeat of the Rebel Boers at Boem Plaats (South Africa) 29th Aug. 1848.

5 Captains Gordon, Johnstone, M'Crea, and Grantham, served in the Kaffir war of 1846-47 (Medal).

6 Captain Leach served in the Kaffir war of 1846-47, and in that of 1852-53 (Medal).

8 Captain Griffin served in the Kaffir war of 1850-53 as Fort Adjutant at Fort Hare (Medal).

9 Captain Lucas served throughout the Kaffir war of 1850-53 (Medal).

10 Lieut. Birch served with the 88th Regt. at the siege and fall of Sebastopol, from 11 Aug. 1855, and at the attack of the Redan on 8th Sept. (Medal and Clasp).

Facings Green.—*Agents,* Messrs. Cox and Co.

[*Returned from the Cape of Good Hope, 2nd June 1859.*]

1 Sir Hugh Rose served the Syrian campaign of 1840-41 (Medal, *CB.*, Cross of St. John of Jerusalem of Prussia, and sword of honor from the Sultan). Served the Eastern campaign of 1854-55 as the Queen's Commissioner at the Head Quarters of the French Army, and was wounded before Sebastopol (Medal and Clasps, Major General, *KCB.*, Commander of the Legion of Honor, and third Class of the Medjidie). Commanded the Central India Field Force throughout the Mutiny of 1857-58, including the relief of Saugor, capture of Ratghur, Shahghur, and Chundehree, siege and capture of Jhansi and Calpee, and various other engagements terminating in the storm and capture of Gwalior and restoration of the Maharajah Scindia to his capital (*GCB.*).

4 Major Parish served the Kaffir campaign of 1846-47 (Medal). Was in command of two Companies of the 45th Regt., a Detachment of Cape M. Rifles, and 900 Zulus, sent from Natal to aid Major Warden in the Sovereignty, from Aug. 1851 to July 1852.

12 Surgeon O'Leary served with the 68th Lt. Inf. at the siege and fall of Sebastopol from 18th March 1855 (Medal and Clasp, and 5th Class of the Medjidie).

[*For remainder of Notes see preceding page.*]

Eastern Army, 14 Oct. 54.
East Indies.
Depot, Buttevant.

46th (The South Devonshire) Regt. of Foot. 261

"DOMINICA" "SEVASTOPOL."

Years' Serv. Full Pay	Half Pay					
42		Colonel.—Sir John Lysaght Pennefather,[1] KCB. Cor. 14 Jan. 18; Lt. 20 Feb. 23; Capt. 5 Nov. 25; Maj. 22 March 31; Lt.-Col. 18 Oct. 39; Col. 19 June 46; Maj.-Gen. 20 June 54; Col. 46th Foot, 19 Nov. 54.				
25	0	Lieut.-Colonels.—Alexander Maxwell,[3] CB. Ens. p 19 June 35; Lt. p 28 Dec. 38; Capt. p 27 Sept. 42; Major, p 19 Sept. 48; Lt. Col. 12 Dec. 54; Col. 12 Dec. 57.				
25	0	Arthur George Vesey,[4] Ens. p 29 May 35; Lt. p 25 Aug. 37; Capt. p 22 July 42; Brev. Maj. 20 June 54; Major, 29 Dec. 54; Lt. Col. 31 Aug. 58.				
20	0	Majors.—Colin Fred. Campbell,[5] Ens. 1 May 40; Lieut. 10 Mar. 42; Capt. p 13 Aug. 47; Major, p 11 May 55; Brev.-Lt.-Col. 2 Nov. 55.				
18	0	Charles Rowley Platt, Ens. p 30 Sept. 42; Lt. 26 July 44; Capt. p 17 Oct. 51; Maj. p 18 Oct. 59.				

		CAPTAINS.	ENSIGN.	LIEUT.	CAPTAIN.	BREV.-MAJ.
16	0	James George Clarke[8]	26 Apr. 44	22 Feb. 47	p 20 Jan. 54	
16	0	Albert Nicholas[7]	p 6 Dec. 44	p 13 Aug. 47	p 28 Apr. 54	
19	0	Henry Fuller Sandwith	p 30 Oct. 41	26 Apr. 44	6 June 54	
15	0	George Fred. Dallas,[10] s.	p 16 May 45	p 28 Apr. 48	p 22 Sept. 54	6 June 56
14	0	Charles S. M'Alester[7]	p 6 Nov. 46	p 10 Nov. 48	29 Dec. 54	
11	0	Alfred Henry Waldy[8]	p 14 Dec. 49	p 1 Apr. 53	29 Dec. 54	
8	0	Thomas Douglas Forde[8†]	p 15 Oct. 52	p 20 Jan. 54	p 5 June 55	
7	0	George Henry Knapp[9]	p 11 Mar. 53	9 June 54	p 29 May 57	
7	0	William Thomas Waldy[12]	p 22 Apr. 53	6 June 54	p 17 July 57	
7	0	Richard Coote[12]	p 11 Nov. 53	22 Sept. 54	p 24 Aug. 58	
6	0	Hon. Carr Wm. Hamond[12]	p 20 Jan. 54	8 Dec. 54	p 23 Aug. 59	

		LIEUTENANTS.			
6	0	Edw. Hawker Helyar[9]	p 4 Feb. 54	8 Dec. 54	1 Sir John Pennefather served in Sir Charles Napier's campaign in Scinde, and commanded the Infantry Brigade at the battle of Meeanee (Medal), and was shot through the body: he was also at the destruction of the Fort of Imaumghur. Served throughout the Eastern campaign of 1854, in command of a brigade in the 2nd division at the battle of the Alma (horse twice wounded) and siege of Sebastopol (including the repulse of the powerful sortie on the 26th October), and in command of the division at and after the battle of Inkerman (horse killed under him). (Medal and Clasps, KCB. Grand Officer of the Legion of Honor, Commander 1st Class of St. Maurice and St. Lazarus, and 2nd Class of the Medjidie.)
6	0	Edward Townshend[9]	p 28 Apr. 54	9 Feb. 55	
6	0	Percy Malcolm Jones[11]	14 July 54	9 Feb. 55	
6	0	Richard Edw. Brookes[12]	15 Sept. 54	9 Mar. 55	
6	0	Andrew Whitten[12]	5 Nov. 54	9 Mar. 55	
6	0	John Spencer Churchill[12]	15 Dec. 54	9 Mar. 55	
5	0	Charles John Burgess[12]	p 16 Jan. 55	p 4 May 55	
5	0	Frank Grieve	20 Feb. 55	6 July 55	
5	0	Peter And. John Ducrow	6 July 55	p 2 July 58	
5	0	Vesey Daly	1 June 55	31 Aug. 58	
5	0	Allan Joshua Kentish	p 17 Aug. 55	p 31 Aug. 58	
4	0	Charles Benj. Cole Speke	p 12 Jan. 56	p 23 Aug. 59	
1	3½	Thomas Murphy		8 Jan. 56	

		ENSIGNS.			
5	0	Stewart James Carlow	2 Oct. 55		
4	0	Geo. T. Delme Radcliffe	15 Feb. 56		3 Colonel Maxwell served at the siege of Sebastopol in 1854-55 (Medal and Clasp, Knight of the Legion of Honor, and 5th Class of the Medjidie). 5 Lieut.-Col. Campbell served at the siege of Sebastopol in 1854-55, and was wounded in the trenches (Medal and Clasp, Brevet Lt.-Colonel, Knight of the Legion of Honor, Sardinian Medal, and 5th Class of the Medjidie).
4	0	Robert Bole Morrow	26 Feb. 56		
4	0	John Dwyer, Adj.	25 Mar. 56		
3	0	Rd. F. Armytage Howorth	p 14 July 57		
2	0	William Gordon M'Crae	p 13 July 58		
2	0	Fra. Lloyd Priestley	16 July 58		
2	0	Henry Boscawen Scott	p 7 Sept. 58		
2	0	Lawrence W. Herchmer	p 12 Nov. 58		
2	0	William Francis Spencer	31 Dec. 58		
1	0	Henry Whatley Estridge	p 30 Sept. 59		
15	0	Paymaster.—Henry Wm. Sibley,[14] 27 Oct. 54; Ens. 17 Oct. 45; Lt. 9 Feb. 48.			
4	0	Adjutant.—Ensign John Dwyer, 25 Mar. 56.			
6	0	Instructor of Musketry.—Lieut. Andrew Whitten, 15 Jan. 57.			
6	0	Quarter-Master.—George Sanderson,[14] 28 April 54.			
11	0	Surgeon.—Edward Touch,[15] MD. 2 Oct. 57; Assist. Surg. 16 Nov. 49.			
8	0	Assistant-Surgeons.—John Meane,[16] 24 Dec. 52.			
5	0	John George Faught, 5 Jan. 55.			
2	0	William Venour, 22 Sept. 58.			

Facings Yellow.—*Agents*, Messrs. Cox & Co.
Irish Agents, Sir E. R. Borough, Bt., Armit & Co.

4 Lt.-Col. Vesey served at the siege of Sebastopol in 1854-55 (Medal and Clasp, and 5th Class of the Medjidie).
7 Captains Nicholas and M'Alester served at the siege of Sebastopol in 1854-55 (Medal and Clasp, and 5th Class of the Medjidie).
8 Captains Clarke and Waldy served at the siege of Sebastopol in 1854-55 (Medal and Clasp).
8† Captain Forde served at the siege and fall of Sebastopol from 8th Nov. 1854, as Aide-de-Camp to Maj.-Gen. Garrett from 1st Dec. 1854 (Medal and Clasp, and 5th Class of the Medjidie).
9 Captain Knapp, Lieuts. Helyar (wounded at Inkerman) and Townshend, served the Eastern campaign of 1854-55, including the battles of the Alma, Balaklava, and Inkerman, and siege of Sebastopol (Medal and Clasps). Captain Knapp has also the Sardinian Medal. Lieut. Townshend has the 5th Class of the Medjidie).

46th (The South Devonshire) Regt. of Foot.

10 Major Dallas served in the Eastern campaign of 1854, including the siege of Sebastopol and battle of Inkerman, where he succeeded to the command of the two Companies 46th Regt. (Medal and Clasps, Brevet Major, Knight of the Legion of Honor, and 5th Class of the Medjidie).

11 Lieutenant Jones served in the Eastern campaign of 1855, during a considerable portion of which he acted as an Assistant Engineer (Medal and Clasp, and 5th Class of the Medjidie).

12 Captains Waldy, Coote, and Hamond, Lieuts. Brookes, Whitten, Churchill, and Burgess, served at the siege of Sebastopol in 1854-55 (Medal and Clasp).

14 Paymaster Sibley and Quarter-Master Sanderson served at the siege of Sebastopol in 1854-55 (Medal and Clasp).

15 Doctor Touch served at Aboo in Rajpootana in 1857 as Assist. Surgeon 83rd Regt. when a large detachment of the Joudpore Legion mutinied and attacked the barracks and station, and was officially thanked by the Officer commanding the Deesa field brigade in a letter which was read to the Regt. for having in the absence of the Officer commanding the detachment of the 83rd Regt. who was sick, "at the commencement of the attack so ably directed the convalescents upon the points most exposed to the attack of the mutineers." By the conduct of the detachment 83rd Regt. the lives of 136 European women and children were saved. Served in medical charge of the 83rd at the siege, assault and capture of Kotah, action of Sanganeer, battle of Bunass, and night attack on the enemy's camp at Seekur (Medal).

16 Assist.Surgeon Meane served with the 31st Regt. in the Crimea from 22nd May 1855, including the siege and fall of Sebastopol, and attacks of the 18th June and 8th Sept., and received a contused wound on the knee from a shell in the trenches on 17th June (Medal and Clasp).

[Continuation of Notes to 47th Foot.]

1 Lieut.General Shaw Kennedy served with the 43rd Light Infantry at the siege of Copenhagen and battle of Kioge in 1807. In 1808 with the Corps of Sir David Baird from Corunna to Sahagun, and in the retreat under Sir John Moore. In 1809 with the Light Division in the march from Lisbon to Talavera, where he became Adjutant of the 43rd. Served as Aide-de-Camp to General Robert Craufurd during 1809 and 1810, and was present in the numerous affairs that took place between the Coa and Agueda, and severely wounded at the action of Almeida. Served at the siege of Ciudad Rodrigo, and at the assault of the Fort and of the place. Stood with General Craufurd when, in the assault, he placed himself on the crest of the glacis, where he fell mortally wounded. Was the bearer of the Duke of Wellington's summons to the Governor demanding the surrender of the place. Served with the 43rd at the siege and storming of Badajoz, during the investment of the forts of Salamanca, the advance and retreat from that place to the Douro, the action of Salamanca, and the investment of the Retiro and occupation of Madrid. Served as Aide-de-Camp to General Baron Alton on the retreat from Madrid to Salamanca, and in the affairs that took place between Salamanca and Rodrigo. Served as the only officer of the Quarter-Master General's Department to the 3rd Division of the Army, in the actions of Quatre Bras and Waterloo. Reconnoitred for the line of march of the Division on the 17th of June from Piermont and the Ligny Road, crossing the Dyle at Ways, a line of march separate from the rest of the Army, and a movement of great delicacy, being performed in open day in presence of Napoleon's advance. On the 18th of June was allowed, in presence of the Duke of Wellington, to form the Division in an order of battle new and unusual, that of oblongs in exchequer, to meet the formidable masses of Cavalry seen forming in its front, and in this formation the Division resisted repeatedly, with perfect success, attacks of Cavalry and Artillery probably as formidable as any known in military history. On the 18th was struck on the side and disabled for some time; and had one horse killed and one wounded. Commanded at Calais, during the three years of the Army of Occupation, the establishment formed there to keep up the communication between the Army and England. Served nine years as Assistant Adjutant-General at Manchester, during periods of disturbance, and generally in command. Organized the Constabulary Force of Ireland. After attaining the rank of Major General, was named by the Duke of Wellington to several very important commands. Has received the War Medal with three Clasps.

10 Captain Waddilove served the Eastern campaign of 1854-55, including the battles of Alma and Inkerman (wounded), capture of Balaklava, siege of Sebastopol, sortie on 26th Oct., and storming the Quarries on 7th June (Medal and Clasps).

11 Captains Croker and Bloomfield, and Lieut. Hawkes, served at the siege and fall of Sebastopol in 1855 (Medal and Clasp).

12 Captain Straton served at the siege and fall of Sebastopol in 1855 (Medal and Clasp).

13 Captain Garnier served at the siege of Sebastopol in 1855 (Medal and Clasp).

14 Qr.Master M'Intosh and Assist.Surgeon White served the Eastern campaign of 1854-55, including the battles of Alma and Inkerman, capture of Balaklava, siege and fall of Sebastopol, and sortie on 26th Oct. (Medal and Clasps).

15 Doctor Singleton served in the Kaffir war of 1851-53 (Medal).

16 Assist.Surgeon Grange served on the Staff and subsequently in the 47th Regt. in the Eastern campaign from 13th Nov. 1854, including the siege and fall of Sebastopol and assault of the 8th Sept. (Medal and Clasp). Was detached from his Regt. for special service in India during the Mutiny of 1857-58 and was in medical charge of a Squadron of the 2nd Dragoon Guards at the action of Azimghur on 7th April 1858—horse shot (Medal).

17 Lieut. Powell served with the 90th Lt. Infantry with General Havelock in his advance on Lucknow up to the taking of the Alumbagh; present in the defence of the Alumbagh, and relief of Lucknow by Lord Clyde and was severely wounded (Medal and Clasp).

Head Quarters, Shorncliffe. Depot, Cork.] **47th (The Lancashire) Regt. of Foot.** 263

"TARIFA" "VITTORIA" "ST. SEBASTIAN" "PENINSULA" "AVA" "ALMA"
"INKERMAN" "SEVASTOPOL."

Years' Serv						
Full Pay	Half Pay					
55		Colonel.—反 ԱՄ James Shaw Kennedy,[1] CB. *Ens.* 18 Apr. 05; *Lt.* 23 Jan. 06; *Capt.* 16 July 12; *Major,* 18 June 15; *Lt.-Col.* 21 Jan. 19; *Col.* 10 Jan. 37; *Maj.Gen.* 9 Nov. 46; *Lt.Gen.* 20 June 54; *Col.* 47th Foot, 27 Aug. 54.				
32	8/12	*Lt.Colonel.*—Thomas Conyngham Kelly,[2] CB., *Ens.* 3 April 28; *Lt.* p 31 Aug. 30; *Capt.* 6 May 43; *Major,* p 20 July 49; *Lt.Col.* 15 June 55.				
20	0	*Majors.*—Robert William Lowry,[3] *Ens.* p 29 Dec. 40; *Lieut.* 12 May 43; *Capt.* p 18 Feb. 48; *Major,* 15 June 55; *Brev.Lt.Col.* 26 Dec. 56.				
19	0	Henry Call Lodder,[4] *Ens.* p 51 Jan. 41; *Lieut.* p 19 Apr. 44; *Capt.* p 19 Sept. 48; *Major,* 25 June 58.				

		CAPTAINS.	ENSIGN.	LIEUT.	CAPTAIN.	BREV.-MAJ.
17	0	Chas. Courtenay Villiers[5]	p 12 May 43	p 30 Jan. 46	p 27 Dec. 50	2 Nov. 55
14	0	Thomas Roper[6]	p 30 Jan. 46	p 24 Dec. 47	6 June 54	
12	0	Richd. George Ellison,[7] s.	p 18 Feb. 48	p 14 June 50	29 Dec. 54	
12	0	Jasper Lucas[8]	p 23 June 48	5 Sept. 49	2 Oct. 55	
17	0	John Thos. Chandler[9]	24 Mar. 43	p 10 Oct. 45	16 Nov. 55	
9	0	Thomas Palmer[8]	p 14 Feb. 51	8 Dec. 54	p 2 Oct. 57	
8	0	Hen. Bowles Geo. Stokes[8]	p 23 Jan. 52	8 Dec. 54	p 6 Nov. 57	
8	0	Grainville Waddilove[10]	p 23 Nov. 52	8 Dec. 54	19 Feb. 58	
6	0	Edward Croker[11]	p 10 Feb. 54	12 Jan. 55	p 30 Mar. 58	
6	0	James A. Bloomfield[11]	6 June 54	9 Feb. 55	p 15 June 58	
6	0	James Murray Straton[12]	p 3 Nov. 54	9 Mar. 55	p 25 June 58	
6	0	Brownlow North Garnier[13]	p 21 July 54	9 Feb. 55	p 6 May 59	
		LIEUTENANTS.				
6	0	Richard Parker Hawkes[11]	p 24 Aug. 54	9 Feb. 55		
6	0	W. Carnegy de Balinhard	p 25 Aug. 54	9 Feb. 55		
6	0	Thomas Young[7]	5 Nov. 54	9 Mar. 55		
6	0	Wm. C. Rodney Mylius	15 Dec. 54	9 Mar. 55		
5	0	C. Van R. Conway Gordon	12 Jan. 55	4 May 55		
5	0	Henry Gem, *Adj.*	19 Jan. 55	17 Aug. 55		
5	0	Ernest Peake Newman	22 Feb. 55	27 Aug. 55		
5	0	George William Davern	13 Mar. 55	2 Oct. 55		
5	0	Gerald Fitzgerald King	14 Mar. 55	1 Feb. 56		
5	0	George Dudley Dawson	16 Mar. 55	26 Feb. 56		
5	0	George Ourry Clarke	p 5 June 55	p 26 Dec. 56		
4	0	George Henry Powell[17]	p 1 Feb. 56	p 23 Apr. 58		
4	0	John Stanley	1 Feb. 56	p 15 June 58		
5	0	Henry Adolphus Meyer	p 20 July 55	8 Oct. 58		
2	0	George Vachell Boyd	p 13 Apr. 58	p 24 May 59		
		ENSIGNS.				
5	0	Roderick John Hanley	2 Oct. 55			
4	0	Andrew John Hicks	p 8 Jan. 56			
2	0	Fred. George Berkeley	p 13 July 58			
2	0	John Frederic Bell	p 14 July 58			
2	0	Dudley North	p 10 Sept. 58			
2	0	Charles Fred. Surplice	8 Oct. 58			
2	0	George Strickland	11 Jan. 59			
1	0	Charles Atty	29 Apr. 59			
1	0	William Seton Dent	p 29 July 59			
1	0	Jerome Richard Murphy	18 Jan. 59			

Note column (right side): 2 Lt.Colonel Kelly served with the 31st Regt. in the Crimea from 22nd May to the end of June 1855, including the attack of the outworks of Sebastopol on the 18th June (Medal and Clasp, and 5th Class of the Medjidie).

3 Lt.Col. Lowry served the Eastern campaign of 1854-55, including the battles of Alma and Balaklava, capture of Balaklava, siege and fall of Sebastopol. Served on the Staff of the Adjutant-General's Department in the Crimea and at Scutari (Medal and Clasps, Brevet of Lt.Colonel, and 5th Class of the Medjidie).

4 Major Lodder served the Eastern campaign of 1854, including the battle of Alma, capture of Balaklava, and siege of Sebastopol (Medal and Clasps).

5 Major C. C. Villiers served the Eastern campaign of 1854-55, including the battles of Alma and Inkerman, capture of Balaklava, siege and fall of Sebastopol, and sortie of 26th Oct. (Medal and Clasps, Brevet Major, Knight of the Legion of Honor, and 5th Class of the Medjidie).

18	1 4/12	*Paymaster.*—Henry Charles Watson, 6 Apr. 55; *Ens.* p 18 June 41; *Lt.* 29 Dec. [42; *Capt.* 1 Dec. 54.
5	0	*Adjutant.*—Lieut. Henry Gem, 22 June 58.
5	0	*Instructor of Musketry.*—Lieut. Ernest Peake Newman, 17 June 57.
14	0	*Quarter-Master.*—William M'Intosh,[14] 25 Sept. 46.
14	0	*Surgeon.*—William Singleton,[15] MD. 2 Oct. 57; *Assist.Surg.* 10 July 46.
7	0	*Assistant-Surgeons.*—William Alexander White,[14] MD. 18 Oct. 53.
6	0	Henry Grange,[16] 1 Sept. 54.

Facings White.—*Agents,* Messrs. Cox & Co.—*Irish Agents,* Messrs. Cane & Sons.

[*Returned from Gibraltar,* 25 August 1857.]

6 Captain Roper served in the Eastern campaign of 1854-55, and was wounded at the siege of Sebastopol and present at its fall (Medal and Clasp).

7 Captain Ellison and Lieut. Young served the Eastern campaign of 1854-55, including the battles of Alma and Inkerman, capture of Balaklava, siege of Sebastopol, and sortie on 26th Oct. (Medal and Clasps). Lieut. Young was wounded at the Alma. Capt. Ellison has also the Sardinian Medal, and 5th Class of the Medjidie.

8 Captains Lucas, Palmer, and Stokes served the Eastern campaign of 1854-55, including the battles of Alma and Inkerman, capture of Balaklava, siege and fall of Sebastopol, sortie on 26th Oct., and storming the Quarries on 7th June (Medal and Clasps, and 5th Class of the Medjidie).

9 Captain Chandler served with the 10th Regt. in the Sutlej campaign of 1845-6, including the battle of Sobraon (Medal). Also the Punjaub campaign of 1848-9, including the whole of the siege operations before Mooltan, affair of the 9th Sept. (wounded), storming the enemy's strongly-entrenched position, carrying of the heights before Mooltan, and surrender of the fortress: afterwards present at the battle of Goojerat (Medal and Clasps).

[For remainder of Notes, see preceding page.]

264   48th (*The Northamptonshire*) Regt. of Foot.   [East Indies. Depot at Cork.

"DOURO" "TALAVERA" "ALBUHERA" "BADAJOZ" "SALAMANCA" "VITTORIA" "PYRENEES" "NIVELLE" "ORTHES" "TOULOUSE" "PENINSULA" "SEVASTOPOL."

Years' Serv.						
Full Pay	Half Pay					
61		Colonel.—⑬ Sir James Henry Reynett,[1] KCH. Ens. 25 Nov. 99; Lt. 14 March 00; Capt. ᵖ24 March 04; Maj. 8 April 13; Lt.Col. 1 June 14; Col. 22 July 30; Maj.Gen. 23 Nov. 41; Lt.Gen. 11 Nov. 51; Col. 48th Foot, 25 Nov. 50.				
30	0	Lieut.-Colonels.—Benjamin Riky,[2] Ens. ᵖ9 Nov. 30; Lt. 30 May 34; Capt. ᵖ8 Sept. 38; Br.Maj. 11 Nov. 51; Maj. ᵖ20 Feb. 52; Lt.Col. ᵖ13 Dec. 53; Col. 28 Nov. 54.				
32	0	Archibald Neil Campbell,[3] Ens. 14 Aug. 28; Lt. 8 April 31; Capt. 1 Nov. 42; Bt.Major, 9 Dec. 53; Major, 22 June 55; Lt.Col. 9 Mar. 58.				
23	0	Majors.—John Guise Rogers Aplin,[4] Ens. ᵖ7 Oct. 37; Lt. ᵖ23 Apr. 41; Capt. 20 Nov. 45; Bt.Maj. 17 July 55; Major, 20 Apr. 58.				
14	0	Robert Blakeney,[6] Ens. ᵖ3 Nov. 46; Lieut. ᵖ10 Sept. 47; Capt. ᵖ2 Apr. 52; Brev.Maj. 6 June 56; Maj. ᵖ24 Sept. 58.				

		CAPTAINS.	ENSIGN.	LIEUT.	CAPTAIN.	BREV.-MAJ.
13	0	Oliver Matthew Latham[5]	ᵖ29 Jan. 47	ᵖ13 Apr. 49	ᵖ20 Feb. 52	
16	0	James Mancor	5 July 44	ᵖ20 July 47	27 Dec. 52	
13	0	William Henry Cairnes,[7,8]	ᵖ2 Apr. 47	ᵖ3 Aug. 49	ᵖ13 Dec. 53	
17	0	Wm. Robert Williamson[8]	ᵖ5 Dec. 43	17 Nov. 48	6 June 54	
15	0	John Richard Loyett[10]	ᵖ28 Nov. 45	ᵖ2 Mar. 47	15 May 55	
12	0	William Henry Knight[7]	13 Oct. 48	ᵖ2 Aug. 50	15 May 55	
10	8/12	Fra. Constantine Trent[11]	ᵖ18 Sept. 40	ᵖ2 Apr. 52	ᵖ21 Dec. 55	
11	0	John Bedingfeld[5]	ᵖ14 Dec. 49	27 Dec. 52	ᵖ31 Dec. 57	
19	0	Geo. Perceval Drought[12]	ᵖ2 July 41	ᵖ10 Mar. 44	16 Oct. 55	
11	0	Frederick John Castle[7]	30 Mar. 49	ᵖ7 Mar. 51	16 Mar. 58	
6	0	Henry Francis Brooke[9]	6 June 54	15 May 55	ᵖ24 Sept. 58	
6	0	William Cumming[15]	ᵖ8 Dec. 54	15 May 55	ᵖ30 Aug. 59	
		LIEUTENANTS.				
9	0	Edward Feneran[7]	ᵖ14 Mar. 51	6 June 54		
8	0	Arthur George Wyse[14]	ᵖ14.May 52	11 Aug. 54		
8	0	Richard Eyre[10]	ᵖ17 Dec. 52	15 May 55		
6	0	James Farquhar[10]	ᵖ24 Aug. 54	15 May 55		
8	0	George Thomas Miller	25 Jan. 52	ᵖ15 Feb. 53		
5	0	Edward Benbow	23 Mar. 55	ᵖ27 July 55		
5	0	John Rawlins[5]	9 Apr. 55	16 Oct. 55		
5	0	Henry J. Wm. Wilkinson[3]	13 Apr. 55	16 Oct. 55		
5	0	Colin Campbell	14 June 55	ᵖ10 Oct. 55		
5	0	Corwallis Wade Browne	ᵖ24 May 55	ᵖ12 Dec. 56		
5	0	Geo. Nugent R. Goddard	1 June 55	ᵖ5 Oct. 58		
5	0	Pembr. O'M. H. Marshall	15 June 55	15 Mar. 59		
5	0	Charles Henry Chauncy	15 Oct. 55	ᵖ30 Aug. 59		
5	0	Thomas Hall	ᵖ28 Dec. 55	ᵖ21 Oct. 59		
		ENSIGNS.				
2	0	Edward Cecil Brown	16 Mar. 58			
2	0	Pulteney Edwd. Bowlby	30 Mar. 58			
2	0	John Walter Keyworth	13 Apr. 58			
2	0	William Rapp Tudor	ᵖ28 May 58			
2	0	Reginald Pennell	ᵖ13 July 58			
2	0	William Farley	ᵖ12 Nov. 58			
2	0	Charles Wheler Hume	19 Nov. 58			
1	0	Edwin Augustus Windsor	ᵖ3 June 59			
1	0	St. John Bally	ᵖ4 Nov. 59			
1	0	Wm. Richard Vandeleur	ᵖ16 Dec. 59			
3	0	Paym. Alex.Wm. McKenzie, 6 Feb. 57.				
9	0	Adjut.—Lt. E. G. Horne,[13] 14 July 54.				
9	0	Instructor of Musketry.—Lieut. Edward Feneran, 14 Aug. 58.				
5	0	Quarter Master.—John Maitland,[17] 3 Aug. 55.				
15	0	Surgeon.—Geo. Aug. Fred. Shelton,[7] M.B. 5 May 54; Assist.-Surg. 3 Jan. 45.				
5	0	Assist. Surgeons.—Jean Valleton de Boissiere, M.D, 12 June 55.				
3	0	John Gordon Grant, 19 Oct. 57.				
5	0	William Henry Leslie, M.B. 7 May 55.				

Facings Buff.—Agent, Sir John Kirkland.—Irish Agents, Messrs. Cane and Sons.

[*Embarked for Corfu*, 22 Feb. 1853.]

2 Colonel Riky commanded the 48th Regt. in the Crimea from 21st April 1855, at the siege and fall of Sebastopol (Medal and Clasp, Knight of the Legion of Honor, and 5th Class of the Medjidie).
4 Major Aplin served the Eastern campaign of 1854-55, including the battles of Alma and Inkerman, siege and fall of Sebastopol, and affair in the Cemetery. Wounded while in command of the sharpshooters of the 28th Regt. (Medal and three Clasps, Brevet Major, Knight of the Legion of Honor, and 5th Class of the Medjidie).
5 Captains Latham and Bedingfeld, Lieuts. Rawlins and Wilkinson, served at the siege and fall of Sebastopol from 3rd Sept. 1855 (Medal and Clasp). Lieut. Wilkinson served also on detached duty in the Dockyard from 14th January to 14th March 1856.
6 Major Blakeney served in the Crimea from 2nd June 1855, at the siege and fall of Sebastopol, and on detached duty in the Dockyard from 14th January to 14th March 1856 (Medal and Clasp and Brevet Major).

48th (The Northamptonshire) Regt. of Foot.

7 Captains Cairnes, Knight, Castle, and Brooke, Lieut. Feneran, and Surgeon Shelton, landed with the Regt. in the Crimea on the 21st April 1855, and served at the siege and fall of Sebastopol (Medal and Clasp). Captain Cairnes has also the Sardinian Medal. Capt. Knight has the 5th Class of the Medjidie.

8 Captain Williamson served in the Crimea at the siege of Sebastopol from 21st April to 28th July 1855 (Medal and Clasp).

10 Captain Lovett, and Lieuts. Eyre and Farquhar, landed with the 48th Regt. in the Crimea, served at the siege and fall of Sebastopol, and on detached duty in the Dockyard from 14th January to 14th March 1856 (Medal and Clasp). Capt. Lovett has the 5th Class of the Medjidie.

11 Captain Trent served in the Crimea from 21st April 1855, including the siege and fall of Sebastopol—wounded on 4th June (Medal and Clasp, and 5th Class of the Medjidie).

12 Captain Drought served with the 62nd Regt. the Sutlej campaign in 1846, including the affair of Buddiwal, and actions of Aliwal and Sobraon (Medal and Clasps). Also the Eastern campaign of 1854-55, including the battles of Sebastopol from 13th Nov. 1854 (Medal and Clasp).

14 Lieut. Wyse served in the Crimea from 14th May to 7th Sept. 1855, and at the siege of Sebastopol (Medal and Clasp).

15 Captain Cumming served in the Crimea at the siege of Sebastopol from 21st April to 7th August 1855 (Medal and Clasp).

17 Qr.Master Maitland was present at the attack and capture of Coorg, in the East Indies, in April 1834; served also in the Crimea from 21st April 1855, at the siege and fall of Sebastopol (Medal and Clasp).

[Continuation of Notes to 49th Foot.]

5 Captain Beresford served in the Eastern campaign of 1854-55, including the siege of Sebastopol and assault of the Redan on the 18th June (Medal and Clasp).

6 Captain Gostling served the Eastern campaign of 1854, including the battle of Alma, siege of Sebastopol, and sortie of 26th Oct. (Medal and three Clasps).

7 Captains Astley and Corban and Lieut. Mackay served in the Eastern campaign of 1854-55, including the battles of Alma and Inkerman, siege of Sebastopol, and sortie of 26th Oct. (Medal and three Clasps).

9 Captain Armstrong served the Eastern campaign of 1854-55, including the battles of Alma and Inkerman, siege and fall of Sebastopol, sortie of 26th Oct., and assaults of the Redan on 18th June and 8th Sept. (Medal and three Clasps, and Knight of the Legion of Honor).

10 Captain Hopkins served the Eastern campaign of 1854-55, including the battle of Inkerman, siege and fall of Sebastopol, sortie on 26th Oct., capture of the Quarries, and assaults of the Redan on 18th June and 8th Sept. (Medal and two Clasps, and 5th Class of the Medjidie).

11 Captains FitzGerald and Young served the Eastern campaign of 1854-55, including the siege and fall of Sebastopol, capture of the Quarries with the storming party, and assaults of the Redan on 18th June and 8th Sept. (Medal and Clasp). Captain Young was severely wounded at the Quarries, and has also the Sardinian Medal. Capt. FitzGerald has the 5th Class of the Medjidie.

12 Captain Chatfield served the Eastern campaign of 1854-55, including the siege of Sebastopol, capture of the Quarries with the storming party, and assault of the Redan on 18th June: was wounded in the trenches on 3rd Sept. 1855 (Medal and Clasp, and Sardinian Medal).

13 Captain Gibson served as Adjutant of the 49th Regt. at the siege and fall of Sebastopol from 19th June 1855, and assault of the Redan on 8th Sept. (Medal and Clasp).

14 Captains Scoones and Roberts, Lts. Savary and Davies, served in the Crimea, and were present at the siege and fall of Sebastopol, and assaults of the Redan on 18th June and 8th Sept. (Medal and Clasp).

16 Lieut. Eustace served in the Crimea, and was present at the siege of Sebastopol and capture of the Quarries with the storming party, and was severely wounded (Medal and Clasp).

17 Lieuts. Rogers, Madan, and Powell, and Assist.Surgeon Calder, served in the Crimea, and were present at the siege and fall of Sebastopol, and assault of the Redan on 8th Sept. (Medal and Clasp).

18 Paymaster Michell served with the 49th Regiment throughout the whole of the operations in China (Medal), commencing with the first taking of Chusan, and terminating with the demonstration before Nankin, including the storm and capture of the heights above Canton, attack and capture of Amoy, second capture of Chusan, attack and capture of the heights of Chinhae, occupation of Ningpo, and repulse of the night-attack; attack and capture of the enemy's entrenched camp on the heights of Segoan, attack and capture of Chapoo, Woosung, and Chin Kiang Foo. Served the Eastern campaign of 1854-55, including the battles of Alma and Inkerman, sortie of 26th Oct., and siege of Sebastopol (Medal and three Clasps).

19 Surgeon Bews served in the Crimea from May 1855 (Medal and Clasp).

20 Assist.Surgeon Hannan served the Eastern campaign of 1854-55, including the battles of Alma and Inkerman, siege and fall of Sebastopol, sortie of 26th Oct., capture of Rifle Pits on 19th April, capture of the Quarries, and assaults of the Redan on 18th June and 8th Sept. (Medal and three Clasps, and 5th Class of the Medjidie).

49th (*The Princess Charlotte of Wales's, or the Hertfordshire*) *Regt. of Foot.*

[Head Qrs. Barbadoes.
Depot, Belfast.]

"EGMONT-OP-ZEE" "COPENHAGEN" "QUEENSTOWN" "CHINA" "The Dragon."
"ALMA" "INKERMAN" "SEVASTOPOL."

Years' Serv.		
Full Pay	Half Pay	
56		Colonel.—💂 ⚔ Sir Edward Bowater,[1] KCH. *Ens.* 31 Mar. 04; *Lt. & Capt.* 23 Aug. 09; *Capt. & Lt.-Col.* 25 July 14; *Col.* 12 Oct. 26; *Maj. Gen.* 10 Jan. 37; *Lt.-Gen.* 9 Nov. 46; *Gen.* 20 June 54; *Col.* 49th Foot, 24 Apr. 46.
32	0	
38	0 4/12	Lt.-Colonel.—John Thornton Grant,[2] CB. *Ens.* 28 Apr. 28; *Lt.* 12 Nov. 30; *Capt.* 30 July 42; *Brevet-Maj.* 20 June 54; *Maj.* 29 Oct. 54; *Brev. Lt.-Col.* 12 Dec. 54; *Lt.Col.* 22 Dec. 54; *Col.* 12 Dec. 57.
15	0	Majors.—Thomas White,[3] *Ens.* 7 Dec. 15; *Lt.* P 25 Aug. 24; *Capt.* 5 Oct. 38; *Brev.Maj.* 11 Nov. 51; *Major,* 1 June 55; *Bt. Lt. Col.* 12 Aug. 58. Cadwallader Adams,[4] *2nd Lt.* P 2 Sept. 45; *Lt.* P 23 Mar. 47; *Capt.* P 5 Dec. 51; *Brev.Maj.* 12 Dec. 54; *Brev. Lt.Col.* 6 June 56; *Major,* 19 Dec. 56.

		CAPTAINS.	ENSIGN.	LIEUT.	CAPTAIN.	BREV.-MAJ.
17	0	M.W. De la PoerBeresford[5]	24 Feb. 43	19 Dec. 44	6 June 54	
12	0	Fanshawe W. Gostling[6]	P 23 May 48	P 8 Nov. 50	19 Dec. 54	
11	0	Richard D. Astley[7]	P 20 Apr. 49	P 21 Feb. 51	29 Dec. 54	
10	0	William Watts Corban[7]	P 12 July 50	P 3 Feb. 54	29 Dec. 54	
9	0	T. P. St. Geo. Armstrong[9]	31 Jan. 51	6 June 54	20 Mar. 55	
7	0	John Hopkins[10]	P 22 Apr. 53	P 18 Aug. 54	9 Sept. 55	
6	0	Charles FitzGerald[11]	P 27 Jan. 54	29 Oct. 54	2 Oct. 55	
6	0	George Kemp Chatfield[12]	P 3 Feb. 54	6 Nov. 54	P 19 Aug. 56	
5	1	William Young[11]	P 3 Mar. 54	6 Nov. 54	P 19 Aug. 56	
5	½	Charles Edgar Gibson[13]	P 12 May 54	8 Dec. 54	P 9 Jan. 57	
6	0	Henry Dalton Scoones[14]	7 July 54	8 Dec. 54	P 4 June 58	
7	0	Chas. John C. Roberts[14]	P 21 Jan. 53	9 Mar. 55	P 6 May 59	

		LIEUTENANTS.		
6	0	Thomas Fox Eustace[16]	11 Aug. 54	29 Dec. 54
6	0	Harry Denham T. Savary[14]	P 25 Aug. 54	29 Dec. 54
6	0	Edward Mackay[7]	5 Nov. 54	2 Mar. 55
6	0	Henry James Davies[14]	10 Nov. 54	9 Mar. 55
6	0	Henry Gordon Rogers[17]	1 Dec. 54	9 Mar. 55
6	0	William Madan[17]	14 Dec. 54	9 Mar. 55
6	0	Frederick Powell[17]	15 Dec. 54	P 9 Mar. 55
5	0	Edward John Cresswell	15 Mar. 55	P 31 Aug. 55
5	0	Robert Hall Spratt	26 Jan. 55	2 Oct. 55
5	0	John Thos. Lyon Cobham	24 Apr. 55	P 21 May 58
5	0	John Isaac Nason	14 Sept. 55	P 4 June 58
5	0	George Donovan	2 Oct. 55	P 6 May 59
2	0	George Shirley	28 May 58	11 July 59
2	0	Alex. Dingwall Fordyce	P 4 June 58	P 30 Aug. 59

		ENSIGNS.	
2	0	Robert Oliver Aldworth	29 May 58
2	0	Robert Emslie Henry	P 25 June 58
2	0	Thomas Cooper Hincks	P 24 Aug. 58
2	0	William John Gillespie	P 31 Aug. 58
2	0	John Jamison R. Russell	24 Sept. 58
2	0	William Stevenson	26 Nov. 58
2	0	John Holmes	27 Nov. 58
1	0	Henry Topp	P 14 June 59
1	0	Edwin Glass Fern	16 Sept. 59
1	0	Edgar Lonsdale	P 29 Nov. 59

1 Sir Edward Bowater served with the 3rd Guards at the siege and taking of Copenhagen in 1807; and subsequently in the Peninsula from Dec. 1808 to Nov. 1809, and again from Dec. 1811 to the end of that war in 1814, including the passage of the Douro and taking of Oporto, battles of Talavera and Salamanca, capture of Madrid, siege of Burgos, battle of Vittoria, siege of San Sebastian, passage of the Bidassoa, and battle of the Nive (Mayor's house). Served also the campaign of 1815, including the battles of Quatre Bras and Waterloo, Wounded at Talavera, and again at Waterloo. Sir Edward has received the War Medal and five Clasps for Talavera, Salamanca, Vittoria, Nivelle, and Nive.

3 Lt. Col. White served with the 32nd Regt. in Canada during the rebellion in 1837-38, and was present in the action of St. Eustache.

4 Lt.Col. Adams served the Eastern campaign of 1854-55 as Aide-de-Camp to General Adams during 1854, including the battles of the Alma and Inkerman (wounded), siege of Sebastopol, sortie on 26th Oct., and assaults of the Redan on 18th June and 8th Sept. (Medal and three Clasps, Brevet of Major and Lt.-Col., Knight of the Legion of Honor, and 5th Class of the Medjidie).

25	0	*Paymaster.*—Henry Seymour Michell,[18] 9 April 47; *Ens.* P 22 May 35; *Lieut. Adjutant.—Lieut.* [22 Mar. 39.
5	0	*Instructor of Musketry.—Lieut.* R. H. Spratt, 17 Aug. 58.
4	0	*Quarter-Master.*—Charles James Kerridge, 21 Nov. 50.
12	0	*Surgeon.*—John Hamilton Bews,[19] 1 May 55; *Assist.-Surg.* 22 Dec. 48.
6	0	*Assistant Surgeons.*—James Hannan,[20] 7 April 54.
6	0	William Menzies Calder,[17] 26 May 54.

Facings Green.—*Agents,* Messrs. Cox & Co.

[Returned from the Crimea, 15 July 1856. Embarked for Barbadoes, 27 Feb. 1857.]

2 Colonel Grant served with the 49th Regiment throughout the whole of the operations in China (Medal), commencing with the first taking of Chusan, and terminating with the demonstration before Nankin, including the storm and capture of the heights above Canton, attack and capture of Amoy, second capture of Chusan, attack and capture of the heights of Chinhae, occupation of Ningpo, and repulse of the nightattack, attack and capture of the enemy's entrenched camp on the heights of Segoan, attack and capture of Chapoo, Woosung, and Chin Kiang Foo (wounded). Served the Eastern campaign of 1854-55 in command of the 49th from the battle of Inkerman, including the battles of Alma and Inkerman, siege and fall of Sebastopol, sortie on 26th Oct., and assaults of the Redan on the 18th June and 8th Sept.; commanded the working party, 600 strong, from the Light and 2nd Divisions that had to turn the enemy's work after the Quarries were carried, and he was engaged during the night in working and repelling the three attempts made by the Russians to retake the position (Medal and three Clasps, CB., Officer of the Legion of Honor, Sardinian Medal, and 4th Class of the Medjidie).

[For continuation of Notes, see preceding page

Serving in Ceylon. Depot, Parkhurst.] **50th (The Queen's Own) Regt. of Foot.**

The *Sphinx* with the words "EGYPT" "VIMIERA" "CORUNNA" "ALMARAZ" "VITTORIA" "PYRENEES" "NIVE" "ORTHES" "PENINSULA" "PUNNIAR" "MOODKEE" "FEROZESHAH" "ALIWAL" "SOBRAON" "ALMA" "INKERMAN" "SEVASTOPOL."

Years' Serv.		
Full Pay	Half Pay	
52		Colonel.—Sir Richard England,[1] GCB. KH., *Ens.* 25 Feb. 08; *Lieut.* 1 June 09; *Capt.* 11 June 11; *Major*, 4 Sept. 23; *Lt.-Col.* 29 Oct. 25; *Col.* 28 June 38; *Major-Gen.* 11 Nov. 51; *Lt.-Gen.* 4 June 56; *Col. 50th Foot*, 20 Sept. 54.
28	0	Lieut.-Colonel.—Richard Waddy,[2] CB. *Ens.* 17 Aug. 32; *Lt.* 4 May 36; *Capt.* 18 Nov. 41; *Major*, 14 Feb. 52; *Lt.-Col.* 3 March 54; *Col.* 28 Nov. 54.
19	0	Majors.—Henry Edwin Weare,[3] *Ens.* 22 Oct. 41; *Lieut.* p 22 Dec. 43; *Capt.* p 26 May 48; *Brev.-Maj.* 12 Dec. 54; *Major*, 22 Dec. 54; *Brevet-Lt.-Col.* 6 June 56.
25	0	Francis Gilbert Hamley,[4] *Ens.* p 7 Aug. 35; *Lt.* p 25 July 37; *Capt.* 2 Nov. 43; *Bt.Major*, 20 June 54; *Major*, 8 Jan. 58.

		CAPTAINS.	ENSIGN.	LIEUT.	CAPTAIN.	BREV.-MAJ.
16	0	John Purcell[6]	29 Mar. 44	7 Feb. 46	p 13 April 52	
13	0	Andrew C. Knox Lock[6†]	p 28 Sept. 47	p 8 June 49	p 12 Aug. 53	2 Nov. 55
11	0	Philip Limborch Tillbrook[7]	11 Apr. 49	p 24 Sept. 50	p 18 Oct. 53	
18	0	Richard Moore Barnes[8]	p 1 Nov. 42	5 July 45	3 Mar. 54	
21	2 3/12	William Hardinge[9]	p 10 Mar. 37	24 Apr. 39	12 Mar. 52	
11	0	Daniel William Tupper[10]	2 Feb. 49	p 19 Mar. 52	22 Dec. 54	2 Nov. 55
10	1 3/12	Alfred John Lane	p 9 Feb. 49	p 11 July 51	29 June 55	
8	0	George William Bunbury	p 12 June 52	p 2 Sept. 53	27 July 55	
8	0	Edw. Crawfurd Antrobus[11]	p 23 Nov. 52	11 Aug. 54	p 3 Aug. 55	
8	0	John Thompson[12]	27 Feb. 52	3 Mar. 54	25 Sept. 55	
7	0	Arthur Evelyn Fyler[14]	18 Oct. 53	6 Nov. 54	p 11 Feb. 59	
8	0	Robert Richardson Ellis	p 23 Nov. 52	p 27 Oct. 54	23 July 58	
		LIEUTENANTS.				
7	0	M.deS. M'K.G.A. Clarke[13]	p 18 Feb. 53	p 25 Aug. 54		
6	0	Fred. Leycester Barwell[15]	3 Mar. 54	8 Dec. 54		
6	0	Robert H. Patrick Doran[18]	6 June 54	8 Dec. 54		
6	0	Thomas Denote Leo[19]	7 June 54	9 Dec. 54		
6	0	Clement Richd. Johnson[20]	11 Aug. 54	12 Jan. 55		
6	0	Hon. Chas. C. Chetwynd[21]	p 25 Aug. 54	9 Feb. 55		
6	0	C. Aug. Fitzgerald Creagh	8 Sept. 54	9 Feb. 55		
6	0	Edmund Leach	3 Nov. 54	9 Feb. 55		
6	0	Frederic Falkner	15 Dec. 54	9 Mar. 55		
5	0	Robert Charles Goff[7]	p 16 Jan. 55	9 Mar. 55		
5	0	Charles Fred. Young	19 Jan. 55	20 July 55		
5	0	Thos. Millard Benton Eden	22 Feb. 55	26 Feb. 56		
5	0	William Henry Wilson	p 31 May 55	23 Aug. 58		
5	0	Henry Evelyn W. Preston	p 9 Nov. 55	p 11 Feb. 59		
5	0	Charles Richard King, *Adj.*	1 June 55	11 Mar. 59		
4	0	George Henry Turner	p 8 Feb. 56	p 11 Mar. 59		
		ENSIGNS.				
4	0	William Henry Barker	26 Feb. 56			
4	0	William Richard White	p 5 Dec. 56			
2	0	Rob. Stuart MacGregor	p 12 Feb. 58			
2	0	Robert C. T. Atthill	p 29 Oct. 58			
2	0	John Walter Walkem	12 Nov. 58			
2	0	William L. Fleury	11 Jan. 59			
1	0	John H. VanderMeulen	p 18 Mar. 59			
2	0	Richard Oliffe Richmond	2 July 58			
1	0	James ffranck Rolleston	p 17 June 59			

[1] Sir Richard England served at the attack on Flushing in 1809; and in the operations in Sicily in 1810-11. Joined the army in Paris in 1815. Commanded the 75th Regt. several years. Commandant of Kaffraria, and employed throughout the Kaffir war of 1836-37 (Medal). Commanded the Bombay Division in the Affghan war of 1842 (Medal), including actions of 28th March and 28th April in the Pisheen Valley in their advance to Candahar, and of the 17th and 18th Aug. on the Kojuck Heights, and 10th Oct. in the Bolan Pass in their retreat to the Indus. Commanded the third Division of the Crimean army in 1854-55, including the battles of Alma and Inkerman, affair of 18th June, and the siege duties against the Russian forts which covered the south side of Sebastopol from their first investment till 2nd Aug. 1855 (Medal and Clasps, *GCB.*, 1st Class of the Medjidie, Grand Officer of the Legion of Honor, and Sardinian Medal).

[2] Colonel Waddy was present with the 50th Regt. at the battle of Punniar (Medal). Served the Eastern campaign of 1854-55 in command of the 50th, including the battles of Alma and Inkerman, and siege of Sebastopol. Mentioned in Lord Raglan's Dispatches for distinguished conduct in command of the trenches when the enemy made a sortie in force—wounded in the trenches, 13th Oct. 54 (Medal and Clasps, *CB.*, Knight of the Legion of Honor, Sardinian Medal, and 4th Class of the Medjidie).

12	0	Paymaster.—John Nowlan,[14] 14 April 54; *Ens.* 29 Dec. 48; *Lt.* p 18 April 51.
5	0	Adjutant.—Lieut. Charles Richard King, 4 March 59.
5	0	Instructor of Musketry.—Lieut. H. E. W. Preston, 15 Dec. 58.
6	0	Quarter Master.—John Turner,[25] 13 Dec. 54; *Ens.* 10 Aug. 54.
11	5/6	Surgeon.—James Fraser, M.D. 25 Sept. 55; *Assist.Surg.* 20 Oct. 48.
6	0	Assist. Surgeons.—George Frederick Davis,[23] 7 April 54.
6	0	Joseph Johnston, M.D. 27 Oct. 54.

Facings Blue.—*Agents*, Messrs. Cox & Co.

[*Returned from the Crimea, August 1856. Embarked for Ceylon, 30 June 1857.*]

3 Lieut.Col. Weare served with the 32nd Regt. the Punjaub campaign of 1848, including the first siege operations before Mooltan (Medal and Clasp). Served the Eastern campaign of 1854 as D. A. Adj. General at Head Quarters, including the affair of Bulganak and battle of Alma (severely wounded). In 1855 he served at the siege of Sebastopol, and was appointed A. Q. M. General (Medal and two Clasps, Brevets of Major and Lt.-Col., Sardinian Medal, and 5th Class of the Medjidie).

4 Major Hamley served in the 19th Regt. in the Kaffir war of 1851-53 (Medal).

6 Capt. Purcell, with a detachment of the 50th, was wrecked on the Andaman Islands in Nov. 1844, where he remained for 55 days, suffering great privation. He served on the Sutlej (Medal), and was at Buddiwal, and severely wounded at Aliwal while carrying the colours.

6† Major Lock served throughout the Eastern campaign of 1854-55, including the battles of Alma and Inkerman, siege and fall of Sebastopol (Medal and Clasps, Brevet Major, Knight of the Legion of Honor, and 5th Class of the Medjidie).

268   50th (The Queen's Own) Regt. of Foot.

7 Captain Tillbrook and Lieut. Goff served during the latter part of the siege of Sebastopol (Medal and Clasp).
8 Capt. Barnes served the Sutlej campaign of 1845-6 (Medal and one Clasp), including the battles of Moodkee and Ferozeshah (severely wounded). Served also during the latter part of the siege of Sebastopol (Medal and Clasp).
9 Captain Hardinge served with the 39th Regt. in the battle of Maharajpore (Medal).
10 Major Tupper served the Eastern campaign of 1854-55, including the battles of Alma and Inkerman, siege and fall of Sebastopol (Medal and Clasps, Brevet of Major, and 5th Class of the Medjidie).
11 Captain Antrobus served the Eastern campaign of 1854-55, including the battles of Alma and Inkerman, and siege of Sebastopol (Medal and Clasps, and 5th Class of the Medjidie).
12 Captain Thompson served the Sutlej campaign of 1845-6, and was present at the battles of Moodkee, Ferozeshah, Aliwal, and Sobraon: was wounded by the explosion of a gun limber at Ferozeshah, and very severely wounded by grape-shot in right breast at Sobraon (Medal and three Clasps). Served the Eastern campaign of 1854-55, including the battles of Alma and Inkerman, and siege of Sebastopol (Medal and Clasps, and 5th Class of the Medjidie).
13 Lieut. Clarke served the Eastern campaign until severely wounded and taken prisoner in a sortie on the trenches before Sebastopol, 21st Dec. 1854, having been present at the battles of Alma and Inkerman (Medal and Clasps, Sardinian Medal, and 5th Class of the Medjidie).
14 Captain Fyler and Paymaster Nowlan served the Eastern campaign of 1854-55, including the battles of Alma and Inkerman, siege and fall of Sebastopol (Medal and Clasps).
15 Lieut. Barwell served at the siege of Sebastopol from Nov. 1854 to March 1855 (Medal and Clasp).
18 Lieut. Doran served at the siege of Sebastopol from 22nd Nov. 1854 (Medal and Clasp).
19 Lieut. Lee served at the siege of Sebastopol from 2nd Dec. 1854 (Medal and Clasp, and 5th Class of the Medjidie).
20 Lieut. Johnson served at the siege of Sebastopol from 16th June 1855 (Medal and Clasp).
21 Lieut. Hon. C. C. Chetwynd served at the siege of Sebastopol from 2nd July 1855 (Medal and Clasp).
23 Assist. Surgeon Davis served at the siege of Sebastopol from Jan. 1855 (Medal and Clasp).
25 Quartermaster Turner served with the 50th Regt. at the battle of Punniar, 29th Dec. 1843 (Medal). Also the Sutlej campaign of 1845-46, including the battles of Moodkee, Ferozeshah, Aliwal, and Sobraon (Medal and three Clasps). Served the Eastern campaign of 1854-55, and was present at the battles of Alma and Inkerman, and during the whole siege and fall of Sebastopol (Medal and Clasps).

[*Continuation of Notes to* 51st *Foot.*]

capture of Kittoor in the Dooab, in Dec. 1824. Served also throughout the whole of the campaign in Affghanistan under Lord Keane; present at the capture of the fortress of Ghuznee, 23rd July 1839, upon which occasion he was appointed KCB.; and while in command of the Bombay column of the army of the Indus he captured the fortress of Khelat on the 13th Nov. following, for which service he was created a Baronet. Has received the Silver War Medal with seven Clasps; also First Class Dooranée Empire.
2 Colonel Errington served with the 51st during the war in Burmah from April to Dec. 1852; was on board the E. I. C. steam sloop *Sesostris* during the naval action and destruction of the enemy's stockades on the Rangoon River; served during the succeeding three days' operations in the vicinity, and commanded the Regiment at the storm and capture of Rangoon: he also commanded the troops engaged at the assault and capture of Bassein, 19th May (wounded), and received the especial approbation of the Governor-General in Council for his services upon this occasion (Medal and Clasp, and Brevet Lt.-Colonel).
3 Lt.Col. Irby served with the 51st throughout the Burmese war of 1852-53: on board the E. I. C. frigate *Sesostris* during the naval action and destruction of the enemy's stockades on the Rangoon River; served during the succeeding three days' operations in the vicinity, and at the storm and capture of Rangoon; also at the assault and capture of Bassein 19th May. Commanded a Detachment consisting of four Companies of the 51st with Brigadier-General Cheape's force during the whole of the successful operations in the Donabew district, ending in the assault and capture, on the 19th March 1853, of the stronghold of the Burmese chief Myat-toon (Medal and Clasp).
4 Major Dickson served with the 51st in Burmah from Feb. 1853 to the end of the war, and was present with Captain Irby's Detachment of four Companies with Brigadier-General Cheape's force until shortly before the capture of Myattoon's stronghold, when he was left in command of a Detachment to protect the sick and wounded of the force (Medal and Clasp).
5 Major Agg served with the 51st throughout the Burmese war of 1852-53; on board the E. I. C. steam frigate *Feroze* during the naval action and destruction of the enemy's stockades on the Rangoon River; served during the succeeding three days' operations in the vicinity (including the storming of the White House Redoubt), and at the storm and capture of Rangoon; also at the assault and capture of Bassein, 19th May (Medal and Clasp).
6 Capt. Madden served with the 51st throughout the Burmese war of 1852-53: on board the E. I. C. steam sloop *Sesostris* during the naval action and destruction of the enemy's stockades on the Rangoon River; served during the succeeding three days' operations in the vicinity (including the storming of the White House Redoubt), and at the storm and capture of Rangoon; also at the assault and capture of Bassein 19th May (Medal and Clasp).
11 Captain Reed served as Aide de Camp to General Reed when he commanded at the siege of Delhi, and was present in all the actions that took place there from the 8th June to 17th July 1857, and volunteered afterwards to serve with the 61st Regt. before Delhi (Medal and Clasp).

[Serving in India. Depot, Chichester.] **51st (*The 2nd Yorkshire West Riding*) or**
The King's Own Light Infantry Regt.
"MINDEN"   "CORUNNA"   "SALAMANCA"   "VITTORIA"   "PYRENEES"   "NIVELLE"   "ORTHES"
"PENINSULA"   "WATERLOO"   "PEGU."

Years' Serv.		
Full Pay	Half Pay	
65		Col.—**D** Sir Thomas Willshire,[1] *Bart.*, KCB. *Ensign*, 25 June 95; *Lieut.* 5 Sept. 05; *Capt.* 28 Aug. 04; *Maj.* 21 Sept. 13; *Lt.Col.* 4 Dec. 15; *Col.* 10 Jan. 37; *Maj.Gen.* 9 Nov. 46; *Lt.Gen.* 20 June 54; *Col.* 51st Foot, 26 June 49.
		Lieut.Colonels.—Arnold Chas. Errington,[2] *Ens.* p 4 Feb. 26; *Lt.* 13 Sept. 31;
34	0	*Capt.* p 14 July 37; *Maj.* p 25 July 45; *Br.Lt.Col.* 9 Dec. 53; *Col.* 28 Nov. 54; *Lt.Col.* p 13 Feb. 55.
23	0	Augustus Henry Irby,[3] *Ens.* p 15 July 37; *Lieut.* p 5 Oct. 41; *Capt.* 9 Aug. 50; *Brev.Major*, 6 June 56; *Major*, p 19 Sept. 56; *Lt.Col.* 18 Sept. 57.
21	0	*Majors.*—John Henry Dickson,[4] *Ens.* 15 Nov. 39; *Lt.* 20 May 42; *Capt.* 15 Mar. 53; *Major*, 18 Sept. 57.
10	0	William Agg,[5] *Ens.* p 15 Oct. 50; *Lt.* 19 May 53; *Capt.* p 13 Feb. 55; *Major*, p 17 Sept. 58.

		CAPTAINS.	ENSIGN.	LIEUT.	CAPTAIN.	BREV.-MAJ.
17	0	Saml. Alexander Madden[6]	p 7 July 43	4 July 45	6 June 54	
11	0	Stewart Alex. Cleeve[7]	20 Jan. 49	p 4 Apr. 51	p 1 June 55	
16	0	George Warde[8]	p 22 Nov. 44	p 10 Nov. 48	p 17 Dec. 52	
9	0	Charles Acton[9]	p 12 Dec. 51	6 June 54	p 8 Jan. 56	
8	0	Hon. R. De Anyers Willis	9 July 52	11 Aug. 54	p 4 Apr. 56	
6	0	Geo. Hen. Hibbert Ware[10]	6 June 54	p 3 Nov. 54	22 Dec. 55	
15	0	R. G. Sanders Mason	4 July 45	18 May 49	18 Sept. 57	
6	0	Fra. Jas. Buch. Reed[11] *s.*	11 Aug. 54	13 Feb. 55	p 17 Nov. 57	
7	0	Malcolm Chas. Farrington	10 June 53	p 3 Nov. 54	23 June 58	
6	0	Augustus Brigstocke	p 24 Aug. 54	p 13 Feb. 55	p 17 Sept. 58	
8	0	Charles James Hughes	15 May 52	25 Jan. 54	p 1 Apr. 59	
5	0	Percy Chaplin	p 13 Feb. 55	p 1 June 55	p 15 Nov. 59	
		LIEUTENANTS.				
6	0	Martin Budd Lewin	p 3 Nov. 54	p 4 Apr. 56	7 Captain Cleeve served as Adjutant of the 51st Light Infantry throughout the Burmese war of 1852-53; on board the E.I.C. steam frigate *Feyooz* during the naval action and destruction of the enemy's stockades on the Rangoon River; served during the succeeding three days' operations in the vicinity (including the storming of the White House Redoubt), and the storm and capture of Rangoon (Medal and Clasp).	
6	0	Eust. Beaumont Burnaby	14 July 54	p 5 Sept. 56		
5	0	Wm. Charles Edw. Scott	10 Apr. 55	p 19 Sept. 56		
5	0	Riland W. Oldham	1 May 55	p 16 Jan. 57		
5	0	Chas. L. Baillie Hamilton	9 Apr. 55	18 Sept. 57		
5	0	Arthur W. Crowe Read	15 May 55	p 17 Nov. 57		
5	0	Edmund Moresby Crowe	11 May 55	23 Mar. 58		
5	0	William Clements, *Adj.*	18 May 55	23 Mar. 58		
5	0	Smeeton Walker	p 27 July 55	23 Mar. 58		
4	0	William Henry Saunders	p 8 Jan. 56	9 May 58		
4	0	Henry Chambers	p 4 Apr. 56	20 May 58	8 Captain Warde has received the 4th Class of the Medjidie for service, as Major, with the Turkish Contingent.	
4	0	Edward Dudley Oliver	p 22 Aug. 56	23 June 58		
4	0	Henry Steuart Tompson	p 5 Sept. 56	p 24 Sept. 58		
3	0	Robert Norton Cobb	p 16 Jan. 57	p 1 Apr. 59		
3	0	W. Price Llewellyn Lewes	p 17 Nov. 57	p 15 Nov. 59	9 Captain Acton served with the 51st in Burmah from Feb. 1853 to the end of the war, and was present with Capt. Irby's Detachment of four Companies with Brigadier-General Cheape's force during the whole of the successful operations in the Donabew district, ending in the assault and capture, on the 19th March 1853, of the stronghold of the Burmese chief Myattoon (Medal and Clasp).	
		ENSIGNS.				
4	0	Fred. Thomas Humfrey	p 26 Sept. 56			
2	0	Empson Edw. Middleton	30 Mar. 58			
2	0	Dudley Villiers Stuart	31 Mar. 58			
2	0	Robert Stratford	25 June 58			
2	0	George S. Robertson	26 June 58			
2	0	Arthur Shaen Carter	24 Sept. 58		10 Captain Hibbert Ware served with the 97th Regt. at the siege and fall of Sebastopol from 20th Nov. 1854, and was severely wounded in the night of the 30th Aug. in a sortie made by the Russians on our trenches (Medal and Clasp, and Sardinian Medal).	
2	0	John Vesey Nugent	p 9 Nov. 58			
1	0	Hen. Montague Trenchard	p 3 June 59			
1	0	George Beverley Bird	p 4 June 59			
2	0	*Paymaster.*—George Henry Shuttleworth, 8 June 58.				
5	0	*Adjutant.*—Lieut. William Clements, 18 May 55.				
5	0	*Instructor of Musketry.*—Lieut. Wm. C. E. Scott, 16 Dec. 58.				
5	0	*Quarter-Master.*—Thomas Lawrence, 29 June 55.				
14	0	*Surgeon.*—Alexander Smith, M.D. 12 Jan. 55; *Assist.Surg.* 7 Aug. 46.				
5	0	*Assist.-Surgeons.*—George Thomas Bourke, 8 April 55.				
5	0	John Folliott, 7 May 55.				
3	0	George Samuel Burnside, 1 Aug. 57.				

Facings Blue.—*Agent*, A. Laurie, Esq.

[*Returned from Malta, June* 1856. *Embarked for India,* 8 *Oct.* 1857.]

1 Sir Thomas Willshire served with the 38th Regt. in the West Indies from August 1797 to June 1800; the campaign of 1808-9, including the battles of Roleia and Vimiera, retreat to, and battle of, Corunna. Accompanied the expedition to Walcheren in 1809. Served afterwards in the Peninsula from June 1812 to the end of that war in 1814; commanded the Light Company at the battle of Salamanca (twice wounded), on the retreat from Burgos and action at Villa Muriel, the action of Osma, battle of Vittoria, first assault of San Sebastian, also second assault and capture, when he received the brevet rank of Major. Commanded a Brigade of Light Companies at the passage of Bidassoa, battle of Nivelle, and battles of the Nive on the 9th, 10th, and 11th Dec. 1813, for which services he was in 1815 appointed Brevet Lieut.-Colonel. Repulsed with three hundred men the attack of ten thousand Kaffirs upon the open village of Graham's Town, on the frontier of the Cape of Good Hope, on the 22nd April 1819, and commanded during the subsequent operations against the Kaffirs in the same year. Served afterwards in the East Indies from May 1822 to 1840. Commanded a wing of the 46th Regt. at the

[For continuation of Notes, see preceding page.

† L 2

52d (Oxfordshire) Rt. of Foot (Lt. Infantry).

[Emb. for India, 30 June 53. Depot, Chatham.

"HINDOOSTAN" "VIMIERA" "CORUNNA" "BUSACO" "FUENTES D'ONOR"
"CIUDAD RODRIGO" "BADAJOZ" "SALAMANCA" "VITTORIA" "NIVELLE"
"NIVE" "ORTHES" "TOULOUSE" "PENINSULA" "WATERLOO."

Years' Serv.						
Full Pay	Half Pay					
66		Colonel.—₱ Sir Archibald Maclaine,¹ KCB. *Ens.* 16 Apr. 94; *Lt.* 29 Apr. 95; *Capt.* 22 Dec. 04; *Major*, 4 Oct. 10; *Lt.Col.* 25 Jan. 13; *Col.* 22 July 30; *Major Gen.* 23 Nov. 41; *Lieut.Gen.* 11 Nov. 51; *Gen.* 5 June 55; *Col. 52nd F.* 8 Feb. 47.				
25	0	*Lieut.-Colonels.*—George Campbell,² CB. *Ens.* ᴾ 13 Mar. 35; *Lieut.* 21 Dec. 38; *Capt.* ᴾ 26 Jan. 41; *Major*, ᴾ 21 May 50; *Lt.Col.* 27 May 53; *Col.* 28 Nov. 54.				
32	0	John Leslie Dennis,³ *Ens.* 25 April 28; *Lieut.* 22 Sept. 30; *Capt.* 17 May 41; *Major*, ᴾ 29 Nov. 44; *Brevet Lt.Col.* 2 Aug. 50; *Col.* 28 Nov. 54; *Lt.Col.* 29 Dec. 54.				
23	0	*Majors.*—C. A. Denison, s. *Ens.* ᴾ 22 Sept. 37; *Lieut.* ᴾ 11 May 39; *Capt.* ᴾ 26 Oct. 41; *Bt. Major*, 20 June 54; *Bt.Lt.Col.* 23 Oct. 55; *Major*, 11 July 56.				
22	0	William Corbett, *Ens.* ᴾ 23 Nov. 38; *Lt.* ᴾ 31 Jan. 40; *Capt.* ᴾ 19 June 46; *Major*, 15 Oct. 58.				

		CAPTAINS.	ENSIGN.	LIEUT.	CAPTAIN.	BREV.-MAJ.
18	0	Arthur Lennox Peel	ᴾ 2 Sept. 42	ᴾ 1 May 46	ᴾ 22 Aug. 51	
16	0	James Johnes Bourchier	ᴾ 28 June 44	ᴾ 13 July 47	ᴾ 15 Oct. 52	
16	0	Hon. Ernest Geo. Curzon	ᴾ 13 Dec. 44	ᴾ 18 Feb. 48	ᴾ 12 Nov. 52	
14	0	George Charles Synge⁵ ..	ᴾ 16 Jan. 46	ᴾ 14 Apr. 48	27 May 53	19 Jan. 58
12	0	Hon. D. John Monson ..	ᴾ 16 June 48	ᴾ 22 Aug. 51	ᴾ 20 July 55	
10	0	Charles Kenrick Crosse⁷	ᴾ 12 July 50	ᴾ 15 Oct. 52	ᴾ 15 Apr. 56	19 Jan. 58
9	0	Fred. Albert Champion, s.	31 Jan. 51	ᴾ 12 Nov. 52	11 July 56	
10	0	Seymour John Blane⁸ ..		ᴾ 28 June 50	ᴾ 9 Oct. 54	19 Jan. 58
9	0	Walter James Stopford⁹	ᴾ 16 Sept. 51	ᴾ 11 Mar. 53	15 Oct. 58	
8	0	Arthur Henley	ᴾ 14 May 52	26 Aug. 53	ᴾ 15 Apr. 59	
8	0	Hon.Geo.H.WindsorClive	ᴾ 21 Sept. 52	ᴾ 20 Jan. 54	ᴾ 17 June 59	
10	0	Alexander Hope Graves¹⁰.	13 Dec. 50	12 Dec. 52	23 Sept. 59	
		LIEUTENANTS.				
7	0	Thos. Archer Julian, *Adj.*	ᴾ 13 May 53	ᴾ 6 July 55		
8	0	Robert Westropp Ellis ..	ᴾ 14 May 52	ᴾ 29 Dec. 54		
5	0	George Cruden Fraser ..	ᴾ 6 July 55	18 Apr. 56		
5	0	Stephen Murphy	2 Nov. 55	ᴾ 16 May 56		
5	0	Rich. Davies Burroughs	3 Aug. 55	11 July 56		
4	0	Henry Richard Beattie..	ᴾ 14 Mar. 56	7 Sept. 57		
4	0	Thomas Simpson	ᴾ 16 May 56	15 Sept. 57		
4	0	William Owen	24 June 56	29 Nov. 57		
4	0	Charles Keyworth.....	ᴾ 27 May 56	13 Apr. 58		
4	0	Richard Wingfield.....	8 July 56	ᴾ 31 Dec. 58		
4	0	Reginald G. Wilberforce	15 Feb. 56	ᴾ 15 Apr. 59		
3	0	Chas. Middle. Prendergast	18 Dec. 57	ᴾ 24 May 59		
3	0	Thomas Brett Cowburn..	19 Dec. 57	ᴾ 17 June 59		
4	0	Sydenham Lott Pidsley .	ᴾ 7 Nov. 56	23 Sept. 59		
5	0	Chas. O'L. L. Prendergast	23 Oct. 55	11 Sept. 57		
		ENSIGNS.				
2	0	Henry Atkinson Adair ..	16 Mar. 58			
2	0	Edmund Pakenham¹⁰ ..	23 Mar. 58			
2	0	Willoughby B. P. Burrell	ᴾ 7 May 58			
2	0	John Philip Mickleburgh	8 Oct. 58			
2	0	John Charles Wm. Lever	9 Nov. 58			
1	0	Henry Crawley Norris ..	ᴾ 18 Jan. 59			
1	0	Vesey Edmund Knox ..	ᴾ 3 June 59			
1	0	Edward Stewart Ker ..	ᴾ 17 June 59			
1	0	Henry Fred. Barker	ᴾ 19 July 59			
2	0	Francis Edward Dowler..	ᴾ 29 Oct. 58			

2 Colonel Campbell commanded the 52nd Light Infantry at the defeat of the Sealkote mutineers on the banks of the Ravee on the 12th and 16th July 1857, and commanded the third column at the assault of Delhi (Medal and Clasp).

3 Colonel Dennis served with the 49th Regt. in China (Medal), and was present at Chusan (both operations), Canton and Amoy; after which he was employed as a military magistrate at Chusan. In August 1840, a determined and desperate band of insurgent fanatics having defeated a native force which had been marched against them, killing a European officer and several Sepoys, Major Dennis, with a force consisting of the Grenadier Company of the 40th and 100 Sepoys of the Madras Native Infantry, encountered them at a Pagoda near Teermanam Coonettos, in Malabar. On the approach of our troops these madmen, armed with matchlocks, spears, swords, and war knives, rushed out upon the detachment, and a sanguinary conflict ensued, terminating in the destruction of the entire Mopla band, 64 in number, three of whom were killed by Major Dennis, who received a contusion on the chest and a few slight wounds.

15	0	*Paymaster.*—Francis Wm. Fellows, 3 June 53; *Ens.* ᴾ 16 Dec. 45; *Lieut.* 29 [Oct. 47.
7	0	*Adjutant.*—Lieut. Thomas Archer Julian, 8 April 58.
4	0	*Instructor of Musketry.*—Lieut. C. Keyworth, 15 June 59.
15	0	*Quarter Master.*—William Knott, 25 Feb. 45.
10	½	*Surgeon.*—John Coghlan Haverty, 29 June 55; *Assist.Surg.* 27 Apr. 49.
5	0	*Assistant Surgeons.*—Charles Alex. Innes,¹² M.D. 14 March 55.
5	0	Henry Alex. Gogarty, 29 Aug. 55.
3	0	Alexander Thorburn McGowan, M.D. 15 Sept. 57.

Facings Buff.—*Agents,* Sir Charles R. M'Grigor, *Bt.*, and Walter M'Grigor, Esq.

1 Sir Archibald Maclaine's services:—Mysore campaign of 1799 against Tippoo Sultan, including the battle of Mallavelly, siege and storming of Seringapatam, where he received three wounds, from the effects of which he was confined in hospital for upwards of a year. Capture of the Danish settlement of Tranquebar, and the Polygar war in 1801, including the battle of Ardingy, and affair of Serungapore, where he was wounded. Mahratta war of 1802, 3, and 4, against Scindia, Holkar, and the Bera Rajah, including the storming of Julnaghur, siege and storming of Gawilghur, siege of Asseerghur (wounded), and battle of Argaum. Ordered home in 1804, in consequence of severe wounds received in the different actions from 1799 to 1804. Peninsular campaigns of 1810, 11, and 12, including the defence of Cadiz, the defence of Matagorda (an outwork of Cadiz, and a ruined redoubt when taken possession of from the enemy), from 22nd February to 22nd April 1810, during which long period Sir Archibald, then a Captain in the old 94th Regiment, with a very small force under his command, most gallantly kept at bay 8,000 of the enemy under Marshal Soult, who conducted the siege, and did not evacuate until ordered to do so by Lieut.-General Sir Thomas Graham, his men being nearly all either killed or wounded. Served also at the battle of Barrosa (dangerously wounded, and his horse killed) and capture of Seville. Sir Archibald has received the War Medal and one Clasp for Barrosa. Is a Knight of Charles the Third of Spain,

52nd (The Oxfordshire) Regt. of Foot (Lt. Infantry).

5 Major Synge served as a Brigade Major at the siege and assault of Delhi (Brevet of Major, Medal and Clasp).

7 Major Crosse served with the 52nd at the defeat of the Sealkote mutineers on the banks of the Ravee on the 12th and 16th July 1857; also at the siege, assault (led in the storming party of the 3rd Column) and occupation of Delhi from 14th Aug. 1857 (Brevet of Major, Medal and Clasp).

8 Major Blane served with the Scots Fusilier Guards throughout the Eastern campaign of 1854-55, including the battles of Balaklava and Inkerman (wounded), siege and fall of Sebastopol, and sortie of the 26th Oct. (Medal and Clasps, Sardinian Medal, and 5th Class of the Medjidie). Served as Brigade Major to General Nicholson at the defeat of the Sealkote mutineers at Goodaspore on the 12th and 16th July 1857, action at Nujjufghur, siege and assault of Delhi,—three times mentioned in Dispatches and thanked by the Governor General (Brevet of Major, Medal and Clasp).

9 Captain Stopford served as Adjutant of the 52nd Lt. Infantry during the Indian Mutiny and was present at the defeat of the Sealkote Mutineers on the banks of the Ravee on the 12th and 16th July 1857, also at the siege assault, and occupation of Delhi from 14th Aug. 1857 (Medal and Clasp).

10 Captain Graves served with the 18th Royal Irish in the Burmese war of 1852-53 (Medal).

12 Doctor Innes served in the Crimea from the 26th May 1855, including the siege and fall of Sebastopol and bombardment of the 18th June; was also with the expedition to Kertch (Medal and Clasp).

13 Ensign Pakenham served in the Indian campaign of 1857-58, including the siege and fall of Lucknow and assault of the Martinière and Banks' Bungalow (Medal and Clasp).

[*Continuation of Notes to 53rd Foot.*]

22 Lieut. Macneill served as Adjutant of the 53rd Regt. in the Indian campaign of 1857-58, including the action of Khujwah, relief of Lucknow by Lord Clyde, battle of Cawnpore on 6th Dec. (severely wounded), action of Khodagunge and entry into Futtehghur, affair of Shumshabad, storm and capture of Meangunge, siege and capture of Lucknow and affair of Koorsie (Medal and Clasps).

23 Lieut. Stoney served in the Indian campaign of 1857-59, including the action of Khodagunge and entry into Futtehghur, affair of Shumshabad, storm and capture of Meangunge, siege and capture of Lucknow, affair of Koorsie, passage of the Gogra at Fyzabad on 25th Nov. (as Orderly Officer to Lt.Col. Payn), action of Toolsepore, and minor affairs (Medal and Clasps).

24 Lieut. Bagnall served in the Indian campaign of 1857-59, including the action of Khodagunge and entry into Futtehghur, storm and capture of Meangunge, siege and capture of Lucknow, affair of Koorsie, and passage of the Gogra at Fyzabad on 25th Nov. (Medal and Clasp).

25 Lieut. Smythe served in the Indian campaign of 1857-59, including the action of Chutra, storm and capture of Meangunge, siege and capture of Lucknow, affair of Koorsie, passage of the Goomtee and occupation of Sultanpore, passage of the Gogra at Fyzabad on 25th Nov., action of Toolsepore, and minor affairs (mentioned in despatches, Medal and Clasp).

26 Lieut. Truell served in the Indian campaign of 1857-59, including the action of Khujwah, relief of Lucknow by Lord Clyde, battle of Cawnpore on 6th Dec. and pursuit of the Gwalior Contingent to Serai Ghat, action of Khodagunge and entry into Futtehghur, affair of Shumshabad, storm and capture of Meangunge, siege and capture of Lucknow, affair of Koorsie, passage of the Goomtee and occupation of Sultanpore, passage of the Gogra at Fyzabad on 25th Nov., action of Toolsepore, and minor affairs (mentioned in despatches, Medal and Clasps).

27 Lieut. Prince served in the Indian campaign of 1857-59, including the action of Khujwah, relief of Lucknow by Lord Clyde, battle of Cawnpore on 6th Dec. and pursuit of the Gwalior Contingent to Serai Ghat, action of Khodagunge and entry into Futtehghur, affair of Shumshabad, storm and capture of Meangunge, siege and capture of Lucknow, affair of Koorsie, passage of the Gogra at Fyzabad on 25th Nov., action of Toolsepore, and minor affairs (Medal and Clasps).

28 Lieut. Barr served in the Indian campaign of 1858-59, including the passage of the Goomtee and occupation of Sultanpore, passage of the Gogra at Fyzabad on 25th Nov., action of Toolsepore, and minor affairs (Medal).

29 Lieut. Bell, Ensigns Auchinleck and Rolls served with the Oude field force in 1858-59, and were present at the action of Toolsepore and minor affairs (Medal).

30 Ensign Pye served with the 40th Regt. at the battle of Maharajpore on 29th Dec. 1843 (Bronze Star). With the 31st Regt. during the Sutlej campaign of 1845-46, including the battles of Moodkee, Ferozeshah, Aliwal, and Sobraon (Medal and Clasps). Served with the 53rd Regt. in the Punjaub campaign of 1848-49 (Medal). Campaign in 1852 against the Hill Tribes on the Peshawur frontier in 1852. Indian campaign of 1857-59, including the action of Khujwah, relief of Lucknow by Lord Clyde (severely wounded), battle of Cawnpore on 6th Dec. and pursuit of the Gwalior Contingent to Serai Ghat, action of Khodagunge and entry into Futtehghur, affair of Shumshabad, storm and capture of Meangunge, siege and capture of Lucknow, affair of Koorsie, passage of the Goomtee and occupation of Sultanpore (Medal and Clasps, and Victoria Cross).

31 Paymaster Thompson served in the Indian campaign of 1857-59, including the battle of Cawnpore on 6th Dec. and pursuit of the Gwalior Contingent to Serai Ghat, action of Khodagunge and entry into Futtehghur, siege and capture of Lucknow, and passage of the Gogra at Fyzabad on 25th Nov. (Medal and Clasp).

32 Qr.Master Marshall served in the Sutlej campaign of 1845-46, including the affair of Buddewal, and actions of Aliwal and Sobraon (Medal and Clasp). Punjaub campaign of 1848-49, including the battle of Goojerat (Medal and Clasp). Campaign of 1851-52 against the Hill Tribes on the Peshawur frontier. Indian campaign of 1857-59, including the action of Khujwah, relief of Lucknow by Lord Clyde, battle of Cawnpore on 6th Dec. and pursuit of the Gwalior Contingent to Serai Ghat, action of Khodagunge and entry into Futtehghur, affair of Shumshabad, storm and capture of Meangunge, siege and capture of Lucknow, affair of Koorsie, passage of the Gogra at Fyzabad on 25th Nov., action of Toolsepore and minor affairs (Medal and Clasps).

33 Doctor Grant served in the Kaffir war of 1847 (Medal). Served with the 53rd Regt. in the campaign of 1851-52 against the Hill Tribes on the Peshawur frontier. Indian campaign of 1857-59, including the action of Khujwah, relief of Lucknow by Lord Clyde, battle of Cawnpore on 6th Dec. and pursuit of the Gwalior Contingent to Serai Ghat, action of Khodagunge and entry into Futtehghur, affair of Shumshabad, storm and capture of Meangunge, siege and capture of Lucknow, affair of Koorsie, passage of the Goomtee and occupation of Sultanpore, passage of the Gogra at Fyzabad on 25th Nov., action of Toolsepore (horse killed), and minor affairs (mentioned in despatches, Medal and Clasps).

34 Assist.Surgeon Hungerford served in the Crimea from 11th March 1855 and has the Medal with Clasps for Sebastopol. Served with the 53rd Regt. during the Indian campaign of 1857-58, including the action of Khodagunge and entry into Futtehghur, storm and capture of Meangunge, siege and capture of Lucknow, and affair of Koorsie (Medal and Clasp).

36 Assist.Surgeon Ashton served in the Indian campaign of 1858-59, and was present with the 79th Highlanders at the storm and capture of Rampore Cassie, and passage of the Gogra at Fyzabad, present with the 53rd Regt. at the action of Toolsepore, and minor affairs (Medal).

272 [Embarked for India, 28th Aug. 44.] **53rd (*The Shropshire*) Regt. of Foot.** [Calcutta. Depot, Chatham.

"NIEUPORT" "TOURNAY" "ST. LUCIA" "TALAVERA" "SALAMANCA" "VITTORIA"
"PYRENEES" "NIVELLE" "TOULOUSE" "PENINSULA" "ALIWAL" "SO-
BRAON" "PUNJAUB" "GOOJERAT."

Years' Serv.			
Full Pay.	Half Pay.		
56		*Colonel.*—William Sutherland,[1] CB., *Ens.* 15 Dec. 04; *Lt.* 1 July 06; *Capt.* 18 Aug. 14; *Major*, 25 Sept. 17; *Lt.Col.* 16 May 22; *Col.* 10 Jan. 37; *Major Gen.* 9 Nov. 46; *Lt.Gen.* 20 June 54; *Col. 53rd F.* 25 May 55.	
27	0	*Lieut.Colonels.*—Frederick English,[2] CB., *Ens.* P 22 March 33; *Lt.* P 17 June 36; *Capt.* P 15 Dec. 40; *Brevet Major*, 11 Nov. 51; *Major*, 16 May 56; *Lt.Col.* 2 Nov. 57.	
18	0	William Payn,[3] CB., *Ens.* P 27 May 42; *Lt.* P 12 Jan. 44; *Capt.* P 14 Mar. 51; *Bt. Maj.* 6 June 56; *Maj.* 2 Nov. 57; *Bt.Lt.Col.* 24 Mar. 58; *Lt.Col.* 13 July 58.	
17	0	*Majors.*—Annesley Paul Gore,[4] *Cornet*, P 7 Apr. 43; *Lt.* P 8 Jan. 47; *Capt.* P 11 Sept. 49; *Major*, 19 Nov. 57.	
20	0	Thomas Moubray,[5] *Ens.* 5 June 40; *Lieut.* 25 Feb. 42; *Capt.* 15 Mar. 53; *Major*, 6 Aug. 58.	

Years		CAPTAINS.	ENSIGN.	LIEUT.	CAPTAIN.	BREV.-MAJ.
16	0	John H. Lothian	P 31 Dec. 44	28 May 48	P 15 Feb. 53	
17	0	Wm. F. Adams Colman[6]	15 June 43	10 Mar. 45	15 Mar. 53	
21	0	George Robert Hopkins[7]	28 Aug. 39	26 July 44	7 Nov. 53	24 Mar. 58
20	0	Joseph Maycock[7]†	P 20 Oct. 40	29 Apr. 42	4 Feb. 53	24 Mar. 58
16	0	Frederick Arthur Walter[8]	26 Jan. 44	23 Jan. 46	P 26 Nov. 52	
14	0	George Newton Fendall[9]	11 Dec. 46	P 4 May 49	P 7 Nov. 56	24 Mar. 58
16	0	Henry Buck[10]	28 July 44	22 Feb. 46	29 Sept. 57	20 July 58
18	0	George Herbert Cox[11]	17 Apr. 42	7 July 43	23 Oct. 57	
14	0	Jas. Winsmore Corfield[12]	28 Aug. 46	P 16 June 48	18 Nov. 57	
13	0	John Alexander Dalzell[13]	30 Jan. 47	P 14 Mar. 51	10 Nov. 57	26 Apr. 59
11	0	Graham Taylor[14]	10 April 49	P 9 May 51	6 Aug. 58	
8	0	Sidney Godolphin Quicke[15]	9 July 52	6 June 54	8 Aug. 55	

		LIEUTENANTS.				
11	0	Fred. Richard Solly Flood[16]	P 21 Aug. 49	P 8 Aug. 51		
9	0	Thomas Acton[18]	25 July 51	P 6 May 53		
11	0	Wale Rymer Byrne[19]	9 April 49	20 Oct. 53		
9	0	Wm. Henry Jas. Clarke[19]†	19 Aug. 51	P 2 Dec. 53		
8	0	Thomas Charles Ffrench[20]	21 May 52	9 Oct. 55		
6	0	*VC* Alfred Kirke Ffrench[21]	P 10 Feb. 54	21 Oct. 55		
8	0	John M. Macneill[22]	P 17 Dec. 52	27 Feb. 56		
5	0	Richard Annesley Eyre	1 June 55	3 Sept. 56		
5	0	Robert Fannin Stoney[23]	P 26 July 55	P 7 Nov. 56		
4	0	Charles Bagnall[24]	8 July 56	P 9 Jan. 57		
4	0	Joseph C. Smythe[25]	9 May 56	26 Mar. 57		
4	0	Robert Holt Truell[26]	P 13 June 56	29 Sept. 57		
4	0	Robert Prince[27]	P 11 Aug. 56	10 Nov. 57		
3	0	William Lamb Barr[28]	P 17 Nov. 57	11 May 58		
3	0	John Charles Bell[29]	11 Dec. 57	3 Dec. 58		

		ENSIGNS.		
3	0	Wm. Lowry Auchinleck[29]	29 Dec. 57	
2	0	Samuel James Nicholls	P 8 Jan. 58	
2	0	Francis Tuach Rolls[29]	15 Jan. 58	
2	0	Robert Brown	30 Mar. 58	
2	0	*VC* Charles Pye,[30] *Adj.*	2 July 58	
2	0	Henry John Beckwith	30 Dec. 58	
2	0	George Beresford Deare	31 Dec. 58	
1	0	Charles Henry Bonney	11 Mar. 59	
1	0	Herbert Boyles Osborne	P 31 May 59	

5	0	*Paymaster.*—Robert Thompson,[31] 1 Nov. 55.
2	0	*Adjutant.*—*VC* Ensign C. Pye,[30] 30 May 59.
5	0	*Instructor of Musketry.*—*Lieut.* R. A. Eyre, 6 Feb. 59.
8	0	*Quarter Master.*—Thomas Marshall,[32] 30 July 52.
14	0	*Surgeon.*—James Simpson Grant,[33] M.D. 28 Aug. 57; *Assist.Surg.* 25 Sept. 46.
6	0	*Assistant Surgeons.*—Richard Hungerford,[34] 26 May 54.
5	0	Robert Henry Beale,[35] 22 Feb. 55.
3	0	William Ashton,[30] M.B. 15 Sept. 57.

Facings Red.—*Agents*, Messrs. Cox & Co.

Captain Colman, while on passage to India in the Transport *Briton*, was wrecked on the Lesser Andaman in Nov. 1844, and remained on that island fifty-one days, suffering very severe privations. He served with the 80th Regt. throughout the Sutlej campaign of 1845-6, and was present in the battles of Moodkee, Ferozeshah, and Sobraon (Medal and two Clasps).

35 Assist. Surgeon Beale served with the 31st Regt. in the Crimea from 4th June 1855, including siege and fall of Sebastopol, and attacks of the Redan on the 18th June and 8th Sept.(Medal and Clasp). Served with the 53rd Regt. in the Indian campaign of 1858-59, including the storm and capture of Menngunge, siege and capture of Lucknow, affair of Koorsie, passage of the Goomtee and occupation of Sultanpore, passage of the Gogra at Fyzabad on 25th Nov., and minor affairs (Medal and Clasp).

1 Lt.General Sutherland commanded the few troops on the Gold Coast in the successful operations and actions against the Ashantees, whom he defeated and dispersed (about 20,000 strong) in June and July 1824.

2 Lt.Colonel English served during the Indian campaign of 1857-59, and while in command of the Left Wing 53d Regt. 180 strong, with 100 Seikhs, attacked and routed at Chutra a force of 1000 Mutineers, chiefly of the Ramghur Battalion, taking all their guns, treasure, and camp equipage—thanked by the Commander in Chief and nominated a CB. Was thanked by the Governor General for having cleared the Behar District of the mutinous Sepoys of the 32d N.I. whom he encountered and defeated at Gopalgunge; commanded the 53d Regt. at the action of Khodagunge and entry into Futtehghur, and the affair of Shumshabad; commanded the right column of attack at the storm and capture of Meuingunge; commanded the 53d throughout the siege and capture of Lucknow, and the affair of Koorsie, also at the passage of the Gogra at Fyzabad on 23d Nov., the action of Toulsepore (horse wounded), and minor affairs (Medal and Clasp).

3 Lt.Colonel Payn served with the 53rd Regt. in the Sutlej campaign of 1845-6, including the affair of Buddiwal and actions of Aliwal and Sobraon (Medal and Clasp), Punjaub campaign of 1849, including the battle of Goojerat (Medal and Clasp), campaign of 1851-52 against the Hill Tribes on the Peshawur frontier. Served in the Crimea in command of a Regiment of the Turkish Contingent, and was present with that force from June 1855, until its disbandment in May 1856 (received the Brevet of Major, and the 4th Class of the Medjidie). Served in the Indian campaign of 1857-58, including the actions of the 26th, 27th and 28th Nov. at Cawnpore under General Windham, battle of Cawnpore on 6th Dec. and pursuit of the Gwalior Contingent to Serai Ghat, action of Khodagunge and entry into Futtehghur, affair of Shumshabad, storm and capture of Meangunge in command of the left attack, siege and capture of Lucknow, and affair of Koorsie; commanded the 53d throughout the hot weather campaign and passage of the Goomtee and occupation of Sultanpore, present with the Regt. at the passage of the Gogra at Fyzabad on 25th Nov., action of Toolsepore, and minor affairs (mentioned five times in despatches, Brevet of Lt.Colonel, C.B., Medal and Clasp).

4 Major Gore served with the 7th Drag. Guards against the Insurgent Boers in South Africa in 1845, also throughout the Kaffir war of 1846-7 (Medal). Served with the 53d Regt. during the Indian campaign of 1857-58, including the action of Khujwah, relief of Lucknow by Lord Clyde, battle of Cawnpore on 6th Dec. and pursuit of the Gwalior Contingent to Serai Ghat, action of Khodagunge and entry into Futtehghur, affair of Shumshabad, storm and capture of Meangunge, siege and capture of Lucknow, and affair of Koorsie (Medal and Clasps).

5 Major Moubray served in the Punjaub campaign (Medal). Also in the Indian campaign of 1857-58, including the action of Khujwah (wounded), relief of Lucknow by Lord Clyde, battle of Cawnpore on 6th Dec. and pursuit of the Gwalior Contingent to Serai Ghat, action of Khodagunge and entry into Futtehghur, and affair of Shumshabad (Medal and Clasp).

7 Major Hopkins served in the Sutlej campaign in 1846, including the affair of Buddiwal, and actions of Aliwal and Sobraon (Medal and Clasp). Campaign of 1851-52 against the Hill Tribes on the Peshawur frontier. Indian campaign of 1857-58, including the action of Khujwah, relief of Lucknow by Lord Clyde, battle of Cawnpore on 6th Dec. and pursuit of the Gwalior Contingent to Serai Ghat, action of Khodagunge and entry into Futtehghur, affair of Shumshabad, storm and capture of Meangunge, siege and capture of Lucknow—wounded (mentioned in despatch, Brevet of Major, Medal and Clasp).

7† Major Maycock served in the Indian campaign of 1857-8 and was present as a D.A.Q.M.General with Havelock's force in all the actions in Oude during the 1st and 2nd advance for the relief of Lucknow; also at the battle of Bithoor, and at the defence of the Alumbagh from 25th Sept. to 14th Nov.; served on the Staff of the Q.M.Gen. at the relief of Lucknow by Lord Clyde (twice contused and horse wounded), and present at the battle of Cawnpore (three times mentioned in despatches, Brevet of Major, Medal and Clasp).

8 Captain Walter served during the Indian campaign in 1858-59, including the passage of the Gogra at Fyzabad on 25th Nov., action of Toolsepore, and minor affairs (Medal).

9 Major Fendall served against the Hill Tribes on the Peshawur Frontier in 1851-52. The Indian campaign of 1857-59, including the actions of Chutra, Gopalgunge, Khodagunge and entry into Futtehpore, and affair of Shumshabad; served as Brigade Major at the assault and capture of Meangunge and also at the siege and capture of Lucknow, after which he officiated as D.A. Quarter Master General at Lucknow until the close of the rebellion in Oude (mentioned in despatches, Brevet Major, Medal and Clasp).

10 Major Buck served in the Sutlej campaign in 1846, including the affair of Buddiwal, and actions of Aliwal and Sobraon (Medal and Clasp). Punjaub campaign in 1849, including the battle of Goojerat (Medal and Clasp). Indian campaign of 1857-59, including the action of Khodagunge and entry into Futtehghur, storm and capture of Meangunge, siege and capture of Lucknow, affair of Koorsie, passage of the Goomtee and occupation of Sultanpore, passage of the Gogra at Fyzabad on 25th Nov., action of Toolsepore, and minor affairs (Medal and Clasp, and Brevet of Major).

11 Captain Cox served in the Punjaub campaign (Medal). Campaign of 1851-52 against the Hill Tribes on the Peshawur frontier. Indian campaign of 1857-58, and was second in command of the 4th Seikhs in the pursuit of the Mutineers from the Jullundur force; also served in the trans Gogra campaign of 1859 (Medal).

12 Captain Corfield served in the Punjaub campaign of 1848-49 (Medal). Campaign of 1851-52 against the Hill Tribes on the Peshawur frontier. Indian campaign of 1857-58, and was severely wounded at the action of Khujwah (Medal).

13 Major Dalzell served in the Punjaub campaign in 1849, including the battle of Goojerat (Medal and Clasp). Campaign of 1851-52 against the Hill Tribes on the Peshawur frontier. Indian campaign of 1857-58, including the action of Khodagunge and entry into Futtehghur, passage of the Gogra at Fyzabad on 25th Nov., action of Toolsepore, and minor affairs (Medal and Brevet of Major).

14 Captain Taylor served the campaign of 1851-52 against the Hill Tribes on the Peshawur frontier. Indian campaign of 1857-58, including the actions of Chutra, Gopalgunge, Khodagunge and entry into Futtehghur, affair of Shumshabad, storm and capture of Meangunge, siege and capture of Lucknow (Medal and Clasp, and mentioned in despatches).

15 Captain Quicke served with the 38th Regt. in the Eastern campaign of 1854-55, including the battle of Inkerman, siege and fall of Sebastopol; with Volunteer Sharpshooters from 20th Nov. to 31st Dec., attack and occupation of the Cemetery on the 18th June (Medal and three Clasps, and 5th Class of the Medjidie).

16 Lieut. Flood served the campaign of 1851-52 against the Hill Tribes on the Peshawur frontier. Indian campaign of 1857-59, including the relief of Cawnpore on 29th Nov., action there on the 6th Dec. and pursuit of the Gwalior Contingent to Serai Ghat, action of Khodagunge and entry into Futtehghur, affair of Shumshabad, storm and capture of Meangunge, siege of Lucknow (as Aide de Camp to General Mansfield, and severely wounded), hot weather campaign in Oude and passage of the Goomtee and occupation of Sultanpore; served as Aide de Camp to General Mansfield during the Baiswara and trans Gogra campaign (mentioned in despatches, Medal and Clasp).

18 Lieut. Acton served in the Indian campaign of 1857-59, including the action of Khujwah (severely wounded), storm and capture of Meangunge, siege and capture of Lucknow and affair of Koorsie, passage of the Goomtee and occupation of Sultanpore; served as Brigade Major at the storm and capture of Rampore Cassie, at the passage of the Gogra at Fyzabad on 25th Nov., and minor affairs (mentioned in despatches, Medal and Clasp).

19 Lieut. Byrne served in the campaign of 1851-52, against the Hill Tribes on the Peshawur frontier. Indian campaign of 1857-59, including the relief of Lucknow by Lord Clyde, battle of Cawnpore on 6th Dec. and pursuit of the Gwalior Contingent to Serai Ghat, action of Khodagunge and entry into Futtehghur, storm and capture of Meangunge, siege and capture of Lucknow, affair of Koorsie, passage of the Goomtee and occupation of Sultanpore, passage of the Gogra at Fyzabad on 25th Nov., action of Toolsepore, and minor affairs (Medal and Clasp).

19† Lieut. Clarke served in the Indian campaign of 1857-59, including the actions of Chutra, Gopalgunge, Khodagunge and entry into Futtehghur, storm and capture of Meangunge, siege and capture of Lucknow, affair of Koorsie, passage of the Gogra at Fyzabad on 25th Nov., action of Toolsepore, and minor affairs (mentioned in despatches, Medal and Clasp).

20 Lieut. T. C. Ffrench served in the Indian campaign of 1857-58, including the relief of Lucknow by Lord Clyde (wounded) battle of Cawnpore on 6th Dec. and pursuit of the Gwalior Contingent to Serai Ghat, action of Khodagunge and entry into Futtehghur, storm and capture of Meangunge, siege and fall of Lucknow and affair of Koorsie; served subsequently with the Oude Military Police, and when in command of 500 of that force, defeated a body of rebels 1000 strong with two guns posted in the village of Rahcemabad, was also present at the attack on the fort of Birwah (Medal and Clasp).

21 Lieut. A. K. Ffrench served in the Indian campaign of 1857-59, including the relief of Lucknow by Lord Clyde, battle of Cawnpore on 6th Dec. and pursuit of the Gwalior Contingent to Serai Ghat, action of Khodagunge and entry into Futtehghur, storm and capture of Meangunge, siege and capture of Lucknow, affair of Koorsie, passage of the Goomtee and occupation of Sultanpore, passage of the Gogra at Fyzabad on 25th Nov., action of Toolsepore, and minor affairs (Medal and Clasps, and Victoria Cross).

[For remainder of Notes, see end of 52nd Foot.

54th (The West Norfolk) Regt. of Foot.

[Serving in India. Depot, Colchester.]

The *Sphinx*, with the words "MARABOUT" "EGYPT" "AVA."

Years' Serv.		
Full Pay	Half Pay	
30		**Colonel.**—Sir William John Codrington,[1] KCB. *Ens.* P 22 Feb. 21; *Ens. & Lt.* P 24 Apr. 23; *Lieut. & Capt.* P 20 July '26; *Capt. & Lt.Col.* P 8 July 36; *Col.* 9 Nov. 46; *Maj.Gen.* 20 June 54; *Lieut.Gen.* 6 June 54; *Col. 54th Foot*, 11 Aug. 56.
30	1 5/12	**Lt.Colonels.**—Charles Edward Michel, *Ens.* P 25 Nov. 28; *Lt.* 23 Nov. 33; *Capt.* P 2 Feb. 38; *Major,* P 25 June 47; *Bt.Lt.Col.* 28 Nov. 54; *Lt.Col.* 26 Feb. 56.
35	0	Charles Herbert,[2] CB. *Ens.* P 19 Nov. 25; *Lt.* P 10 Oct. 26; *Capt.* P 27 Sept. 33; *Maj.* P 25 Apr. 45; *Bt.Lt.Col.* 20 June 54; *Lt.Col.* 2 June 57; *Col.* 19 Aug. 58.
20	0	**Majors.**—John Charles Hill Jones, *Ens.* P 16 Dec. 40; *Lieut.* P 30 Dec. 42; *Capt.* P 9 Nov. 49; *Major,* 5 Sept. 56.
18	0	William Freeland Brett, *Ens.* P 1 Apr. 42; *Lieut.* 6 Dec. 44; *Capt.* 25 June 51; *Maj.* P 14 Aug. 57; *Brevet Lt.Col.* 11 Nov. 57.

Years' Serv.		CAPTAINS.	ENSIGN.	LIEUT.	CAPTAIN.	BREV.-MAJ.
18	0	James Sinclair Thomson	P 25 Nov. 42	13 June 46	P 9 July 52	
18	0	John S. Ferguson Fowke	P 30 Dec. 42	14 June 46	4 Mar. 53	
17	0	Prideaux William Gillum[4]	P 28 Oct. 43	P 31 Dec. 47	P 4 Aug. 54	11 Nov. 57
16	0	W. Ed. Freeman O'Brien	6 Dec. 44	P 2 Mar. 49	1 Dec. 54	
11	0	Wm. Hill Dawe Clarke	29 June 49	P 17 Jan. 51	P 2 Feb. 55	
13	0	Edward Thomas Shiffner[4]	P 31 Dec. 47	P 13 Dec. 50	P 15 Feb. 56	
7	0	Francis Geo. C. Probart[3]	18 Nov. 53	21 Sept. 54	29 Feb. 56	
11	0	J. Sackville Swann	1 June 49	25 June 51	5 Sept. 56	
11	0	Charles Alex. Thomson	P 19 Dec. 49	11 Nov. 51	26 Sept. 56	
13	0	Charles FitzRoy Barnett	P 12 Nov. 47	3 Apr. 49	P 5 June 57	
10	0	Robert Baret Stokes	22 Oct. 50	6 June 54	P 14 Aug. 57	
10	0	And. Robert Guy Evered	P 15 Mar. 50	11 Aug. 54	P 19 Nov. 58	

		LIEUTENANTS.				
11	0	Edward Cliffe	P 28 Dec. 49	6 June 54		
6	0	Wm. Arthur Galbraith[4]	P 10 Feb. 54	P 2 Feb. 55		[4] Major Gillum, Captain Shiffner, Lts. Galbraith, Bayly, and Cronyn, were at the taking of the forts of Lechean and Tirhol in Oude in June 1858 (Medal).
6	0	Francis Geo. S. Parker	P 18 Aug. 54	P 2 Feb. 55		
6	0	John Stevenson	P 25 Aug. 54	P 1 Feb. 56		
6	0	Vere Temple Bayly[4]	3 Nov. 54	P 29 Feb. 56		
7	0	Henry Ridout Floyd	P 10 June 53	1 Dec. 54		[5] Surgeon Dowding served with the Eastern Army in 1854-55.
6	0	Joseph Wm. Hughes, *Adj.*	P 1 Dec. 54	26 Sept. 56		
5	0	George Cronyn[4]	P 2 Feb. 55	P 5 June 57		[6] Assist.Surgeon Reid served with the Royals at the siege and fall of Sebastopol from 15th July 1855 (Medal and Clasp).
5	0	John Ayton Wood	11 May 55	P 14 Aug. 57		
4	0	Joshua Gladwyn Jebb	P 1 Feb. 56	13 Feb. 58		
4	0	Lancelot Kerby Edwards	P 7 Mar. 56	30 Mar. 58		
4	0	Matthew Wm. Edw. Gosset	8 July 56	P 31 Aug. 58		
4	0	George Fowler[7]	8 July 56	3 June 59		
4	0	Sir Chas. W. Burdett, Bt.	18 Jan. 56	15 Aug. 59		
3	0	James Chute	P 5 June 57	P 26 Aug. 59		

		ENSIGNS.				
3	0	Dudley B. Coppinger	24 Feb. 57			
3	0	Warren Edward Evans	P 24 July 57			
3	0	Charles Gooden Loveridge	P 14 Aug. 57			
2	0	Robert Magill	16 Mar. 58			
2	0	James Hearn Tarleton	P 14 May 58			
2	0	Henry Lambard	P 13 July 58			
2	0	Charles Samuel Chapman	P 31 Aug. 58			
2	0	William Patrick Hodnett	26 Oct. 58			
1	0	Wm. Edmund Wilkinson	P 28 Oct. 59			

14	0	*Paymaster.*—William Marriott, 22 Aug. 51; *Ens.* 12 June 46.
6	0	*Adjutant.*—Lieut. Joseph Wm. Hughes, 21 June 58.
6	0	*Instructor of Musketry.*—Lieut. Fra. Geo. S. Parker, 8 May 57.
9	0	*Quarter Master.*—Thomas Hipkin, 6 July 52; *Ens.* 1 Aug. 51.
15	0	*Surgeon.*—William Mills Dowding,[5] 19 May 54; *Assist.Surg.* 9 May 45.
6	0	*Assistant Surgeons.*—George Youell, 20 May 54.
6	0	Alexander Reid,[6] 26 May 54.
3	0	Charles Bartholomew Mathew, 9 Nov. 57.

Facings Green.—*Agents*, Messrs. Cox & Co.

[*Returned from Gibraltar, June* 1856. *Embarked for India*, 15 *August* 1857.]

1 Sir William Codrington commanded a Brigade of the Light Division, and afterwards a Division throughout the Eastern campaign of 1854-55, including the battles of Alma and Inkerman, siege and fall of Sebastopol (Medal and Clasps, KCB., Commander of the Legion of Honor, Grand Cross of the Military Order of Savoy, and 1st Class of the Medjidie). From October 1855, and until the evacuation of the Crimea, he was Commander in Chief of the Eastern Army.

2 Colonel Herbert commanded the 75th Regt. during the operations against Delhi and was wounded in the action of the 8th June and again at the assault of Delhi (*CB.*).

3 Captain Probart served with the 95th Regt. at the siege and fall of Sebastopol from 24th Nov. 1854 (Medal and Clasp, and 5th Class of the Medjidie).

7 Lieut. Fowler served the Indian campaign of 1857-58,—with the Malwa Field Force in the actions before Dhar, siege and capture of that fort, actions before Mundesore, battle of Ghouraria and the three days' subsequent operations there; present with the Central India Field Force in the actions before Chundarie and during the siege and assault of that fort; also in the actions before and siege and storming of the Fort and Town of Jhansi, and was severely wounded when leading a storming party on a Palace outside the town (Medal).

Head Qrs. Curragh.]
Depot, Plymouth.] **55th (The Westmoreland) Regt. of Foot.** 274

"CHINA."—"The Dragon."—"ALMA." "INKERMAN." "SEVASTOPOL."

Years' Serv.						
Full Pay	Half Pay					
60		*Colonel.*—🅱 Sir James Holmes Schoedde,¹ KCB. *Ens.* May 1800; *Lt.* 8 Oct. 01; *Capt.* ᴾ 19 Sept. 05; *Bt.-Maj.* 21 June 13; *Maj.* ᴾ 20 Jan. 25; *Lt.-Col.* 20 Mar. 29; *Col.* 23 Nov. 41; *Maj.-Gen.* 20 June 54; *Col.* 55th Foot, 28 May 57.				
13	0	*Lt.Colonel.*—Robert Hume,² *Ens.* ᴾ 9 April 47; *Lieut.* ᴾ 30 Nov. 49; *Capt.* 21 Sept. 54; *Brev.Maj.* 2 Nov. 55; *Maj.* 20 April 58; *Lt.Col.* ᴾ 8 Oct. 58.				
15	0	*Majors.*—Thomas Southwell Brown,³ *Ens.* 14 Nov. 45; *Lieut.* ᴾ 26 May 48; *Capt.* ᴾ 4 Aug. 54; *Major*, 10 Sept. 56.				
11	0	Richard England,⁴ *Ens.* ᴾ 18 Sept. 49; *Lt.* ᴾ 17 Aug. 52; *Capt.* 29 Dec. 54; *Major*, ᴾ 22 July 59.				

		CAPTAINS.	ENSIGN.	LIEUT.	CAPTAIN.	BREV.-MAJ.
11	0	John Richard Hume⁷ ..	ᴾ 19 Oct. 49	ᴾ 26 Nov. 52	29 Dec. 54	
11	0	Edw. Marcus Armstrong⁸	ᴾ 18 Sept. 49	ᴾ 24 June 53	2 Feb. 55	
7	0	Wm. Hamilton Richards¹⁰	ᴾ 14 May 53	ᴾ 15 Sept. 54	ᴾ 1 June 55	
7	0	Edm. Fortescue Twysden¹¹	ᴾ 24 June 53	21 Sept. 54	ᴾ 20 July 55	
13	0	Sylvester W.F.M.Wilson,s	ᴾ 12 Nov. 47	ᴾ 11 May 49	ᴾ 31 Aug. 55	
8	7/12	Geo. Anthony Morgan,¹² s.	ᴾ 16 Sept. 51	6 June 54	9 Sept. 55	
6	0	John George Echalaz¹³ ..	ᴾ 12 May 54	21 Sept. 54	ᴾ 5 Mar. 58	
6	0	Edwyn Fred. Temple¹⁵ ..	ᴾ 19 May 54	15 Dec. 54	ᴾ 22 June 58	
6	0	John H. Sharpe¹⁷	3 Nov. 54	2 Mar. 55	ᴾ 8 Oct. 58	
5	0	George Fortescue Park..	23 Feb. 55	ᴾ 3 Aug. 55	ᴾ 17 June 59	
6	0	Fred. Fitz Wm. T. Hobbs	15 Dec. 54	8 June 55	ᴾ 29 July 59	
12	0	Wm. Hodnett Rowland..	ᴾ 2 Aug. 48	ᴾ 29 Oct. 52	23 July 58	
		LIEUTENANTS.				
6	0	Francis Williams¹⁶	21 Sept. 54	29 Dec. 54		1 Sir James Schoedde served the Egyptian campaign of 1801. Served also in the Peninsula from 1808 to the end of the war, including the battles of Roleia, Vimiera, Talavera, Busaco, Fuentes d'Onor, sieges of Ciudad Rodrigo and Badajoz, battles of Salamanca, Vittoria, Pyrenees, Nivelle, Nive, Orthes, and Toulouse, besides numerous minor actions and skirmishes. He has received a gold Medal from the Grand Seignior for the Egyptian campaign; the gold Medal for Nivelle; and the silver War Medal with fourteen Clasps for the other battles and sieges, and for Egypt. Commanded a brigade in China (Medal) at the attack and capture of Chapoo, Woosung, Shanghai, and Chin Kiang Foo.
5	0	Percy Lytton Bellamy ..	ᴾ 16 Jan. 55	7 Aug. 55		
5	0	Palms Spread Morgan ..	9 Mar. 55	2 Oct. 55		
5	0	Cotton Edwin Theobald .	14 Mar. 55	2 Oct. 55		
5	0	Wm.FitzJohn LeP.Trench	15 Mar. 55	2 Oct. 55		
5	0	Robt. Fitz Gerald Dalton	23 Mar. 55	23 Oct. 55		
5	0	Edwin Charles Hilton ..	ᴾ 27 July 55	ᴾ 21 Dec. 55		
5	0	James Francis Morton ..	ᴾ 26 Oct. 55	ᴾ 5 Mar. 58		
5	0	Mark M. Gillies	15 June 55	20 Apr. 58		
5	0	Osborne S. Delano-Osborne	2 Nov. 55	ᴾ 22 June 58		
4	0	George Hyde Harrison ..	ᴾ 14 Mar. 56	ᴾ 8 Oct. 58		
5	0	Thomas Dunn,¹⁸ *Adj.*....	31 Aug. 55	28 Mar. 59		
4	0	Wm. Martin Frobisher ..	ᴾ 19 Dec. 56	28 Mar. 59		
3	0	Philip William Justice ..	29 Dec. 57	ᴾ 17 June 59		
2	0	Hen. Whewell Dan. Riley	ᴾ 5 Mar. 58	ᴾ 29 July 59		
		ENSIGNS.				
2	0	Charles F. Faber	ᴾ 30 Apr. 58			
2	0	Geo. W. Yates FitzGerald	ᴾ 24 Apr. 58			
2	0	David Anderson Ogden..	14 May 58			
2	0	Alfred Hervey Kay	ᴾ 13 July 58			
2	0	Francis Holt Tate	ᴾ 9 Nov. 58			
2	0	Herbert Richard Hudson	12 Nov. 58			
1	0	Francis Barnston	11 Mar. 59			
1	0	William King	ᴾ 17 June 59			
1	0	Frederick Baird	ᴾ 23 Aug. 59			
2	0	Loftus Nunn	7 Dec. 58			
6	0	*Paymaster.*—Henry Burke,¹⁹ 14 July 57; *Ens.* 10 Aug. 54; *Lt.* 6 Nov. 54.				
5	0	*Adjutant.*—Lieut. Thomas Dunn,¹⁸ 13 Aug. 58.				
4	0	*Instructor of Musketry.*—Lieut. G. H. Harrison, 5 Nov. 58.				
2	2 10/14	*Quarter Master.*—Samuel Millward, 20 Dec. 55.				
10	0	*Surgeon.*—Ethelbert Henry Blake,²¹ M.D. 7 Jan. 53; *Assist.-Surg.* 16 Nov. 41.				
6	0	*Assist.Surgeons.*—William Jasper Rendell,²² 26 May 54.				
6	0	George Henry Finlay, 6 Oct. 54.				

Facings Green.—*Agents*, Messrs. Cox and Co.
[*Returned from Gibraltar*, 12 *September* 1857.]

2 Lt.Colonel Hume served the Eastern campaign of 1854-55, including the battles of Alma and Inkerman (severely wounded), siege and fall of Sebastopol, repulse of the sortie of 26th Oct., and assaults of the Redan on the 18th June and 8th Sept.—severely wounded, and mentioned in Dispatches (Medal and three Clasps, Brevet Major, Knight of the Legion of Honor, and 5th Class of the Medjidie).

3 Major Brown served the Eastern campaign of 1854-55, including the battles of Alma and Inkerman, and siege of Sebastopol (Medal and Clasps, and 5th Class of the Medjidie).

4 Major England served the Eastern campaign of 1854 as Aide-de-Camp to Sir Richard England, including the battle of Inkerman and siege of Sebastopol (Medal and Clasps, and 5th Class of the Medjidie).

7 Captain John Hume served the Eastern campaign of 1854-55, including the battles of Alma and Inkerman, siege and fall of Sebastopol, repulse of the sortie of 26th Oct., assaults of the Redan on the 18th June and 8th Sept.—severely wounded and mentioned in Dispatches (Medal and three Clasps, and Knight of the Legion of Honor).

8 Captain Armstrong served in the Eastern campaign of 1854-55, including the battle of Alma—severely wounded (Medal and Clasp).

55th (The Westmoreland) Regt. of Foot.

10 Captain Richards served the Eastern campaign of 1854-55, including the battles of Alma (carried the Colors) and Balaklava, siege and fall of Sebastopol, and assaults of the Redan on the 18th June and 8th Sept. —wounded and mentioned in Dispatches (Medal and Clasps, and 5th Class of the Medjidie).

11 Captain Twysden served in the Eastern campaign of 1854-55, including the battles of Alma and Inkerman, and siege of Sebastopol—wounded (Medal and Clasps).

12 Captain Morgan served with the 55th Regt. in the Eastern campaign of 1854-55, including the battles of Alma and Inkerman, siege and fall of Sebastopol, and sortie of 26th October. During the latter months of the siege was Aide-de-Camp to Brigadier-General Warren, and as such was severely wounded at the assault of the Redan on the 8th Sept. Mentioned in Dispatches (Medal and three Clasps, and 5th Class of the Medjidie).

13 Captain Echalaz served at the siege of Sebastopol from Dec. 1854 to April 1855 (Medal and Clasp).

15 Captain Temple served at the siege and fall of Sebastopol (Medal and Clasp).

16 Lieut. Williams served with the 55th Regt. in China (Medal), and was present at the taking f Amoy, second capture of Chusan, attack and capture of the heights of Chinhae and repulse of the night-attack, expedition to You-You up the Ningpo River, attack and capture of Chapoo (wounded), Woosung, Shanghai, and Chinkiangfoo. Served the Eastern campaign of 1854-55, including the battles of Alma (mentioned in Division Orders) and Inkerman, siege of Sebastopol, sortie on 26th Oct., attack on the Quarries 7th June (mentioned in Dispatches), and acted as Adjutant 55th Regt. at the assault of the Redan on the 18th June (Medal and three Clasps, and 5th Class of the Medjidie).

17 Captain Sharpe served at the siege of Sebastopol from Sept. 1855 (Medal and Clasp).

18 Lieut. Dunn served the Eastern campaign of 1854-55, including the battles of Alma and Inkerman, and siege and fall of Sebastopol, sortie of 26th Oct., and assaults of the Redan on the 18th June and 8th Sept. (Medal and three Clasps).

19 Paymaster Burke served with the 55th Regt. in China (Medal), and was present at the taking of Amoy, the second capture of Chusan, occupation of Ningpo, repulse of the night-attack on Chinhae, expedition to You-You up the Ningpo River, taking of Chapoo, and operations in the Woosung and Yang-tse Kiang Rivers. Served the Eastern campaign of 1854-55, including the battles of Alma and Inkerman, siege and fall of Sebastopol, repulse of the sortie on 26th Oct., and assault of the Redan on 8th Sept. (Medal and three Clasps, and 5th Class of the Medjidie).

21 Doctor Blake served with the 98th Regt. in China (Medal), and was present at the storm and capture of Chinkiangfoo. Served the Eastern campaign of 1854-55 (Medal and Clasps), including the battles of Alma and Inkerman, the siege of Sebastopol, and repulse of the sortie on 26th Oct. 1854.

22 Assist.Surgeon Rendell served with 41st and 45th Regts. at the siege and fall of Sebastopol from 20th March 1855 (Medal and Clasp).

Serving in India, Depot, Colchester.

56th (The West Essex) Regt. of Foot. 276

"MORO" "GIBRALTAR." With the Castle and Key, "Montis Insignia Calpe."
"SEVASTOPOL."

Years' Serv.		
47		Colonel.—John Home Home, Ens. P 19 Jan. 13; Lt. & Capt. P 30 June 15; Capt. & Lt.Col. P 10 May 57; Maj. & Col. P 11 Sept. 40; Lt.Col. 15 Apr. 45; Maj.Gen. 11 Nov. 51; Lt.Gen. 22 Sept. 58; Col. 56th F. 17 Oct. 59.
Full Pay	Half Pay	
28	0	Lieut. Colonels.—Richard Walter Lacy,[2] Ens. 23 Mar. 32; Lieut. 15 Sept. 37; Capt. 1 May 46; Major, 13 July 55; Lieut.-Col. P 16 May 56.
27	0	Alfred Thomas Heyland,[3] CB. Ens. P 4 April 33; Lieut. P 8 July 36; Capt. P 13 Dec. 42; Brev.-Maj. 20 June 54; Major, 1 Dec. 54; Brev. Lt.-Col. 12 Dec. 54; Lt.-Col. 5 June 55; Col. 20 Mar. 58.
21	0	Majors.—George William Paty, Ens. P 6 Sept. 39; Lieut. P 18 Feb. 42; Capt. P 6 Feb. 46; Maj. 23 April 55.
21	0	John James Bull,[2] Ens. P 8 June 39; Lieut. P 16 Nov. 41; Capt. P 20 Dec. 43; Brev.-Maj. 20 June 54; Maj. P 16 May 56.

		CAPTAINS.	ENSIGN.	LIEUT.	CAPTAIN.	BREV.-MAJ.
19	0	Richard Anderson[4]	8 Jan. 41	P 7 Apr. 43	P 20 Dec. 46	26 Dec. 56
19	0	Wm. George Margesson[4]	P 16 July 41	P 12 Sept. 43	P 8 Nov. 50	
18	0	Fox Maule Ramsay[2]	P 18 Feb. 42	P 7 June 44	P 7 Feb. 51	
15	0	Henry John Tolcher	P 28 Nov. 45	P 29 Dec. 46	P 3 Feb. 54	
14	0	William Watkin Bassett	P 6 Feb. 46	P 28 Jan. 48	6 June 54	
14	0	William Clutterbuck	P 3 Apr. 46	3 Oct. 48	P 4 Aug. 54	
14	0	Morton Robert Eden[2]	19 May 46	P 21 Aug. 49	P 22 Sept. 54	
14	0	Hugh Eccles	1 May 46	P 15 June 49	23 Apr. 55	
12	0	Marcell Conran[2]	P 28 Jan. 48	P 12 Oct. 49	13 July 55	
18	0	Robt. Gordon Cumming[5]	22 July 42	22 Dec. 45	13 July 55	
10	0	William Alex. Godley[2]	8 Oct. 50	21 Oct. 53	P 6 Feb. 57	
13	2 7/12	Charles Russell Colt[7]	P 16 May 45	9 Nov. 46	P 3 Feb. 54	
		LIEUTENANTS.				
7	0	James Fleming Baxter[2]	P 10 June 53	6 June 54		
7	0	Francis Charles Hill[2]	21 Oct. 53	P 18 Aug. 54		
6	0	Henry Williams,[2] Adj.	11 Aug. 54	25 May 55		
6	0	Augustine William Massy	P 8 Sept. 54	P 29 June 55		
6	0	Henry George Monk	P 7 April 54	13 July 55		
6	0	Arthur William Turner[2]	P 22 Sept. 54	13 July 55		
7	0	George Stamer Gubbins	8 July 53	20 July 55		
10	0	John William Huskisson	8 Nov. 50	19 Jan. 55		
7	0	Robert Thomas Thompson[2]	11 Mar. 53	27 July 55		
6	0	Livius Sherwood King	P 7 Apr. 54	3 Aug. 55		
5	0	Arthur Nassau Bolton[2]	29 June 55	9 Mar. 57		
6	0	Meyrick Beaufoy Field[6]	3 Nov. 54	9 Mar. 55		
5	0	Augustus Spiller	3 Aug. 55	P 11 Jan. 59		
5	0	William Bell	31 Aug. 55	P 25 Jan. 59		
5	0	Reginald Bythell	P 2 Oct. 55	P 8 Apr. 59		
5	0	Charles Swinhoe	27 July 55	8 Sept. 59		
		ENSIGNS.				
4	0	John Charley	P 7 Mar. 56			
2	0	Caleb Coote Lloyd	P 12 Feb. 58			
2	0	Henry John Nuthall	19 Nov. 58			
2	0	Thomas Durell Sullivan	7 Dec. 58			
2	0	Arthur Rowley Heyland	31 Dec. 58			
2	0	James Landon Watt	P 25 Jan. 58			
1	0	George Dixwell Grimes	P 8 Apr. 59			
1	0	John Philip Burnett	P 30 Aug. 59			

3 Colonel Heyland served with the 95th Regt. in the Eastern campaign of 1854-55, including the battle of Alma (severely wounded—arm amputated), siege and fall of Sebastopol (Medal and Clasps, Brevet Lt.Colonel, Sardinian Medal, and 4th Class of the Medjidie).

4 Major Anderson and Capt. Margesson served at the siege and fall of Sebastopol from 25th Aug. 1855 (Medal and Clasp, and Knight of the Legion of Honor).

5 Capt. Cumming served the campaign of 1845-6 on the Sutlej with the 9th Regt, and has received the Medal and two Clasps for Moodkee, Ferozeshah, and Sobraon.

6 Lieut. Field served with the 30th Regt. at the siege and fall of Sebastopol from 30th May 1855 and was severely wounded at the assault on the Redan on the 8th Sept (Medal and Clasp).

5	0	Paymaster.—Hamilton Finlay, 14 Dec. 55.
6	0	Adjutant.—Lieut. Henry Williams,[2] 11 Aug. 54.
7	0	Instructor of Musketry.—Lieut. Robert Thomas Thompson, 5 May 57.
5	0	Quarter Master.—James M'Grath,[2] 1 May 55.
14	0	Surgeon.—William Deeble,[2] 12 Jan. 55; Assist.-Surg. 27 Oct. 46.
6	0	Assistant Surgeons.—Duncan Campbell Taylor, M.D., 26 May 54.
3	0	James Parr, 28 May 57.
2	0	William Cathcart Boyd, 22 Jan. 58.

Facings Purple.—Agents, Messrs. Cox & Co.

[Returned from the Crimea, August 1856. Embarked for India, 24 August 1857.]

2 Lt.Colonel Lacy, Major Bull, Captains Ramsay, Eden, Conran and Godley, Lts. Baxter, Hill, Williams, Turner, Thompson, and Bolton, Qr.Master M'Grath, and Surgeon Deeble, landed with the 56th Regiment at the Crimea on the 25th Aug. 1855, and have received the Medal with Clasp for Sebastopol.

7 Captain Colt served with the 3rd Light Dragoons in the Sutlej campaign in 1846, and was present at the battles of Aliwal and Sobraon (Medal and one Clasp); served also in the Punjaub campaign of 1848-9, as Aide-de-Camp to Major-General Gilbert and was present at the affair of Ramnugger, and battles of Chillianwallah and Goojerat (Medal and two Clasps).

57th (The West Middlesex) Regt. of Foot.

[Poonah. Depot, Cork. Emb. for Corfu, 28 Feb. 53.

"ALBUHERA" "VITTORIA" "PYRENEES" "NIVELLE" "NIVE" "PENINSULA" "INKERMAN" "SEVASTOPOL."

Years' Serv. Full Pay.	Years' Serv. Half Pay.	
56		**Colonel.**—**乃 犯** Sir James Frederick Love,[1] KCB., KH., *Ens.* 26 Oct. 04; Lt. 5 June 05; *Capt.* 11 July 11; *Brev. Maj.* 16 March 15; *Brev. Lt. Col.* 5 May 25; *Major,* 9 July 30; *Lieut. Col.* 6 Sept. 34; *Col.* 28 June 38; *Major Gen.* 11 Nov. 51; *Lt. Gen.* 26 Sept. 57; *Col.* 57 F. 24 Sept. 56.
23	0	**Lt. Colonels.**—Henry James Warre,[2] CB. *Ens.* 3 Feb. 37; *Lt.* 1 June 41; *Capt.* p 8 Jan. 47; *Major,* 7 Nov. 54; *Lt. Col.* 9 March 55; *Col.* 9 Mar. 58.
20	0	Wm. Inglis,[3] *Ens.* 7 Feb. 40; *Lt.* p 31 Dec. 41; *Capt.* p 26 Oct. 49; *Brev.-Maj.* 12 Dec. 54; *Major,* 9 Feb. 55; *Brev. Lt. Col.* 2 Nov. 55; *Lt. Col.* 21 May 58.
19	0	**Majors.**—Robert Abraham Logan, *Ens.* 26 Oct. 41; *Lieut.* p 3 Mar. 43; *Capt.* p 7 Mar. 51; *Major,* 19 June 55.
13	0	Henry Butler,[4] *Ens.* p 2 Mar. 47; *Lt.* p 23 Mar. 49; *Capt.* 6 Nov. 54; *Brev. Maj.* 6 June 56; *Major,* p 21 May 58.

		CAPTAINS.	ENSIGN.	LIEUT.	CAPTAIN.	BREV.-MAJ.
14	0	James Stewart[5]	29 Jan. 46	10 Nov. 48	p 12 Oct. 52	
16	0	Jason Hassard[6]	3 Oct. 44	18 May 48	6 June 54	2 Nov. 55
12	0	Chas. Wm. St. Clair[7]	18 July 48	p 24 Jan. 51	7 Nov. 54	6 June 56
11	0	William Edward Brown[8]	10 April 49	p 26 Dec. 51	29 Dec. 54	
10	0	Arthur Maxwell Earle[9]	p 18 Jan. 50	p 15 Feb. 53	20 Dec. 54	6 June 56
9	0	Thomas Nind Woodall	p 18 Apr. 51	6 June 54	29 Dec. 54	
16	0	Thomas Wm. John Lloyd	21 Dec. 44	20 Dec. 46	26 Jan. 55	
6	0	Henry Bird[10]	10 Aug. 54	9 Nov. 54	p 29 May 57	
6	0	John Robert Wilmot[11]	p 16 Aug. 54	29 Dec. 54	p 10 Mar. 58	
6	0	Fred. Spencer Schomberg[12]	p 17 Aug. 54	9 Feb. 55	p 21 May 58	
6	0	Sir Robert Douglas, *Bart.*	p 18 Aug. 54	9 Feb. 55	p 21 May 58	
6	0	Alfred Fred. Adolp. Slade[13]	15 Sept. 54	9 Feb. 55	p 23 Aug. 59	

		LIEUTENANTS.			
6	0	Wm. Aldersey Jas. Shortt[14]	6 June 54	7 Nov. 54	
6	0	Hon. Douglas M. Shute	15 Dec. 54	9 Mar. 55	1 Sir James Fred. Love served with the 52nd Regt. in the expedition to Sweden under Sir John Moore, and afterwards in Portugal and Spain, including the advance into Spain, retreat to, and battle of Corunna, besides the different affairs on the retreat. Served afterwards in the Peninsula with the Light Division, including the storming of Ciudad Rodrigo, and all the affairs and battles in which the Light Division took a part up to 1812. During the campaign in Holland under Lord Lynedoch, he was present at the attack on the fortified village of Merxem, and the bombardment of Antwerp. Present in the several affairs before New Orleans, and in the attack on that place, on which occasion he had two horses shot under him, and was slightly wounded in the arm by a rifle-ball. Served also the campaign of 1815, and received four severe wounds at the battle of Waterloo, when the 52nd Regiment charged the French Imperial Guards. He has received the War Medal with four Clasps for Corunna, Busaco, Fuentes d'Onor, and Ciudad Rodrigo.
6	0	Charles George Clarke[11]	29 Dec. 54	9 Mar. 55	
5	0	Hickman Rose Russell[15]	p 16 Jan. 55	29 Mar. 55	
5	0	G. Rowland Waugh[16] *Adj.*	12 Feb. 55	19 June 55	
5	0	Bathurst Chas. Bayntun[11]	13 Feb. 55	1 July 55	
5	0	Samuel Hopper Powell[15]	14 Mar. 55	p 31 Aug. 55	
5	0	Edward Mills	23 Feb. 55	8 Oct. 55	
5	0	Edward Gould Hasted[15]	2 Mar. 55	26 Feb. 56	
5	0	Edward Bratton	15 Mar. 55	26 Feb. 56	
5	0	Wyndham A. R. Thompson	16 Mar. 55	26 Feb. 56	
5	0	Thomas H. Tragett	13 Apr. 55	26 Feb. 56	
5	0	John Parkinson	27 July 55	p 21 May 58	
5	0	Reginald Alb. Hoby Cox	2 Nov. 55	p 3 June 59	
4	0	Charles Mansfield Clarke	1 Mar. 56	p 18 Nov. 59	

		ENSIGNS.			
5	0	Henry Francis Emly	19 July 55		
5	0	Walt. DeWarrenne Waller	20 July 55		
4	0	Acheson M'Clintock	27 Feb. 56		
4	0	Paul Francis Clarke	29 Feb. 56		
2	0	Richard Edward Brown	p 15 Jan. 58		
2	0	Robert Murray	p 16 Mar. 58		
2	0	Francis Henry Clayton	p 28 May 58		
1	0	Arthur Cecil Manners	p 4 Feb. 59		
1	0	Henry D. Chevers Barton	p 24 June 59		
21	0	**Paymaster.**—Mark Matthews,[17] 28 July 43; *Ens.* 29 May 39; *Lt.* 23 Nov. 40.			
5	0	**Adjutant.**—Lieut. George Rowland Waugh,[16] 12 Feb. 55.			
6	0	**Instructor of Musketry.**—Lieut. Wm. Aldersey James Shortt, 11 Sept. 57.			
2	2¾	**Quarter Master.**—Thomas Martindale, 25 Oct. 55.			
16	0	**Surgeon.**—William MacAndrew,[18] M.D., 23 Mar. 55; *Assist.-Surg.* 6 Dec. 44.			
6	0	**Assistant Surgeons.**—Michael James Griffin, 22 Sept. 54.			
6	0	William Ferguson, 22 Sept. 54.			
2	0	James Davis, 10 March 58.			

Facings Yellow.—*Agents,* Messrs. Cox & Co.
Irish Agents, Messrs. Cane & Sons.

2 Colonel Warre served at the siege of Sebastopol from March 1855, and commanded the 57th Regt. at the assaults on the Redan on the 18th June (after Colonel Shadforth was killed) and 8th Sept.; also at the bombardment and surrender of Kinbourn (Medal and Clasp, CB., and 5th Class of the Medjidie).

3 Lieut. Colonel Inglis served in the Crimea from 23rd Sept. 1854, including the battles of Balaklava and Inkerman (commanded the 57th Regt. after Captain Stanley was killed, and was honorably mentioned in Lord Raglan's Dispatch), siege and fall of Sebastopol, assault of the Redan on 18th June, and expedition to Kinbourn (Medal and three Clasps, Brevets of Major and Lieut.-Colonel, Knight of the Legion of Honor, and 5th Class of the Medjidie).

4 Major Butler served in the Crimea from 23rd Sept. 1854, including the battles of Balaklava and Inkerman (carried the Colors after Lieut. Hague was killed) siege and fall of Sebastopol, assault of the Redan on 18th June, and expedition to Kinbourn (Medal and three Clasps, Brevet Major, and Knight of the Legion of Honor).

5 Captain Stewart served from 6 Sept. 1855, at the siege and fall of Sebastopol, also in the expedition to Kinbourn (Medal and Clasp).

Major Hassard served at the siege of Sebastopol from 14th Nov. 1854, and was with the storming column at the assault of the Redan on the 18th June and 8th Sept.; was also with the expedition to Kinbourn (Medal and Clasp, Brevet Major, and 5th Class of the Medjidie).

7 Major St. Clair served in the Eastern campaign from 23rd Sept. 1854, including the battles of Balaklava and Inkerman (horse shot under him), siege of Sebastopol, and attack on the Redan, 18th June —severely wounded; acted as Assist.Adj.Gen. to the forces on the Bosphorus, Dardanelles, &c., from July 1855 to Aug. 1856 (Medal and Clasps, Brevet Major, and Sardinian Medal).

6 Captain Brown served at the siege of Sebastopol from 5th Feb. 1855, including the attacks of the Redan on the 18th June (with the Storming Column) and 8th Sept.; also at the bombardment and surrender of Kinbourn (Medal and Clasp, and 5th Class of the Medjidie). Commanded a party of the 57th Regt. with the Column under Brigadier Coghlan at the attack and capture of the Arab village of Sheik Othman on the 18th March 1858 (mentioned in despatch, and thanked in General Orders).

9 Major Earle served in the Eastern campaign from 23rd Sept. 1854 as Aide-de-Camp to Brigadier-Gen. Goldie, who was killed at Inkerman; was wounded in the trenches 3rd Nov. 1854. Appointed Brigade-Major in 4th Division 17th Nov.; and present with Sir Colin Campbell commanding the assaulting column on the 18th June; with Major-Gen. Spencer in the assault of the 8th Sept.; and with Lord West at the capture of Kinbourn (three times mentioned in despatches, Medal and three Clasps, Brevet Major, Knight of the Legion of Honor, and 5th Class of the Medjidie).

10 Captain Bird served at the siege and fall of Sebastopol from 1st June 1855, and at the capture of the Quarries, and assault of the Redan on the 18th June; also at the bombardment and capture of Kinbourn (Medal and Clasp).

11 Captain Wilmot, Lieuts. Clarke and Bayntun, served at the fall of Sebastopol, and at the bombardment and capture of Kinbourn (Medal and Clasp).

12 Captain Schomberg served at the siege and fall of Sebastopol in 1855, attack of the Redan on the 8th Sept. bombardment and capture of Kinbourn (Medal and Clasp).

13 Captain Slade served the Eastern campaign from 15th Nov. 1854, including the siege of Sebastopol and repulse of two night sorties, attack and capture of the Quarries, and storming of the Redan on the 18th June; severely wounded in two places (Medal and Clasp, Sardinian Medal, and 5th Class of the Medjidie).

14 Lieut. Shortt served at the siege and fall of Sebastopol from 15th Nov. 1854, and at the storming of the Quarries, and of the Redan on the 18th June; also at the bombardment and capture of Kinbourn (Medal and Clasp, and 5th Class of the Medjidie).

15 Lieuts. Russell, Powell, and Hasted, served in the Crimea from Sept. 1855, and were present at the bombardment and capture of Kinbourn (Medal).

16 Lieut. Waugh served at the siege and fall of Sebastopol from 19th May 1855, and at the attack on the Redan on the 18th June; also at the bombardment and capture of Kinbourn (Medal and Clasp).

17 Paymaster Matthews served in the Crimea from the 22nd Sept. 1854, including the siege and fall of Sebastopol, attack and surrender of Kinbourn (Medal and Clasp).

18 Dr. MacAndrew served in the Eastern campaign from 2nd May 1855, including the expedition to Kertch, siege and fall of Sebastopol, bombardment and capture of Kinbourn (Medal and Clasp).

[*Continuation of Notes to* 58*th Foot.*]

3 Major Hood was employed in the year 1846 as Secretary on a Special Public Mission to the Argentine Republic to settle the difference on the part of the combined Powers of England and France, and General Rosa, the Governor of Buenos Ayres. Served at the siege of Sebastopol in 1855 (wounded), and commanded the ladder party of the Buffs at the assault of the Redan on 8th Sept.—wounded; commanded the Regt. from 13 Sept. to 27 Dec. 1855, and marched it into the Karabelnaia on 17th Sept. with Colors, &c., these being the first English Colors that entered Sebastopol (Medal and Clasp, Brevet Major, and 5th Class of the Medjidie).

5 Major Thompson was present at every action, assault, and skirmish which took place during the operations carried on in 1845 and 46 under Lieut.-Col. Hulme, and subsequently under Colonel Despard, against the insurgent chiefs in the north of New Zealand. He was thanked in General Orders by Sir Robert Nickle, commanding the Forces in Australia, for "the promptitude with which he checked the insubordination among the detachments proceeding under his command to New Zealand on board the *Egmont* in April 1854."

8 Captain Battiscombe served with the 68th Light Infantry the Eastern campaign of 1854-55, including the battle of Alma, siege and fall of Sebastopol, and was wounded on 12th January 1855 (Medal and Clasps, and 5th Class of the Medjidie).

9 Captain Hall served with the 14th Regt. in the Crimea in 1855, including the siege and fall of Sebastopol and assault of the 18th June (Medal and Clasp).

11 Lieut. Hill served as a midshipman in the Indian Navy in the Burmese war in 1853 (Medal and Clasp).

12 Lieut. Perryn served with the 90th Light Infantry in the Indian Campaign of 1857-58, including the relief of Lucknow by Lord Clyde, defence of the Alumbagh under Outram, siege and capture of Lucknow (Medal and Clasp).

13 Qr.Master Slattery was present in New Zealand at the taking and destruction of Pomare's Pah on 30th Apr. 1845, attack on Heki's Pah, destruction of the Waikiri Pah, storming of Kawitti's Pah, capture and destruction of Rhuapekapeka 11th Jan. 1856.

15 Assist.Surgeon Worthington served with the 34th Regt. in the Crimea from Jan. 1855 and was present at the siege and fall of Sebastopol, and with the storming party at the capture of the Quarries on 7th June (Medal and Clasp). Served also with the 34th in the Indian campaign in 1857-58, including Windham's action at Cawnpore, capture of Lucknow, and relief of Azimghur (Medal and Clasp).

279   58th (*The Rutlandshire*) Regt. of Foot.   [Aldershott, Depot, Birr.

"GIBRALTAR"—with the *Castle and Key*, "*Montis Insignia Calpe.*"—The *Sphinx*, with the words "EGYPT" "MAIDA" "SALAMANCA" "VITTORIA" "PYRENEES" "NIVELLE" "ORTHES" "PENINSULA."

Years' Serv. 57

Full Pay.	Half Pay.					
		Colonel.—Edward Buckley Wynyard,[1] CB., *Ens.* 17 Dec. 03; *Lt.&Capt.* 7 Jan. 08; *Brev. Maj.* 25 March 13; *Capt. & Lt.Col.* 28 April 14; *Col.* 22 July 30; *Major Gen.* 23 Nov. 41; *Lt.Gen.* 11 Nov. 51; *Col.* 58th Regt. 31 Jan. 51.					
35	0	**Lt.Colonel.**—Cyprian Bridge,[2] *Ens.* 8 April 25; *Lt.* ᴾ 31 Jan. 28; *Capt.* ᴾ 16 Dec. 36; *Major,* ᴾ 30 Dec. 42; *Bt.Lt.Col.* 20 June 54; *Lt.Col.* 26 Oct. 58; *Col.* 26 Oct. 58.					
15	9/12	**Majors.**—Charles Hood,[3] *Ens.* ᴾ 26 June 44; *Lt.* ᴾ 20 Nov. 46; *Capt.* ᴾ 7 Nov. 51; *Brevet Major,* 2 Nov. 55; *Major,* 8 Jan. 56.					
16	0	George Henry Wynyard,[4] *Ens.* 3 May 44; *Lt.* 19 Sept. 48; *Capt.* ᴾ 9 Oct. 55; *Major,* ᴾ 14 June 59.					

		CAPTAINS.	ENSIGN.	LIEUT.	CAPTAIN.	BREV.-MAJ.
24	0	Charles Wm. Thompson[5]	ᴾ 23 Dec. 36	ᴾ 3 May 39	12 May 43	20 June 54
19	0	Leslie Jenkins Thompson	17 Sept. 41	18 Aug. 47	31 Aug. 55	
9	0	Rob. Children Whitehead[6]	7 Oct. 51	ᴾ 18 Aug. 54	30 Nov. 55	
9	0	Henry G. C. Burningham[7]	ᴾ 14 Mar. 51	ᴾ 29 July 53	31 Aug. 55	
12	0	William Davies Shipley	ᴾ 3 Mar. 48	20 Aug. 49	13 Apr. 58	
6	1	H. Lumsden Battiscombe[8]	ᴾ 8 July 53	11 Aug. 54	14 Jan. 56	
7	0	Angus William Hall[9]	ᴾ 16 Dec. 53	15 Dec. 54	ᴾ 23 Oct. 57	
7	0	Dawson Townley	24 June 53	26 Jan. 55	ᴾ 14 June 59	
6	0	John Horner	ᴾ 30 Aug. 54	6 April 55	15 June 59	
5	0	William Dunn Bond	ᴾ 9 Mar. 55	ᴾ 17 Aug. 55	20 July 59	
6	0	Andrew H. Russell	3 Nov. 54	31 Aug. 55	ᴾ 5 Aug. 59	
5	0	Henry Hingeston	11 May 55	ᴾ 26 Oct. 55	ᴾ 16 Dec. 59	
		LIEUTENANTS.				
5	0	William Russell Russell	16 Mar. 55	ᴾ 12 Dec. 56		
5	0	George Marriner	15 May 55	ᴾ 25 Aug. 57		
5	0	Octavius William Hill[11]	1 June 55	ᴾ 8 Jan. 58		
5	0	John Augustus Tighe	10 April 55	26 Feb. 58		
5	0	Bartie Maclaren	26 Oct. 55	13 Apr. 58		
5	0	Charles Henry S. Jones	21 Dec. 55	1 Oct. 58		
4	0	Robert Wm. Archibald	15 Feb. 56	26 Oct. 58		
4	0	Bertie Shiffner	18 July 55	23 Apr. 58		
4	0	James Pringle	8 July 56	ᴾ 31 May 59		
4	0	Henry John Wynyard	ᴾ 12 Dec. 56	ᴾ 14 June 59		
3	0	William Bolton, *Adj.*	15 Dec. 57	15 June 5		
2	0	John Valentine Hesse	ᴾ 8 Jan. 58	15 June 5		
2	0	George Onslow	26 Feb. 58	20 July 5		
5	0	George Edward Perryn[12]	8 Oct. 55	ᴾ 24 Feb.		
2	0	Thomas Egerton Jones	ᴾ 24 Aug. 58	ᴾ 20 Dec. 59		

		ENSIGNS.		
3	0	Alex. William M'Crae	ᴾ 25 Aug. 57	
2	0	Fred. Florence Murray	5 Oct. 58	
2	0	William Henry Webb	ᴾ 29 Oct. 58	
2	0	Charles Edward Foster	31 Dec. 58	
1	0	William Henry Key	ᴾ 17 June 59	
1	0	Conway Ric. Dobbs Reeves	ᴾ 18 June 59	
1	0	William Nunnington	8 July 59	
1	0	Richard Dane	ᴾ 5 Aug. 59	
1	0	Henry N. Reeve Storks	6 Aug. 59	
		Paym.—Aldborough Rundle, 3 June 50.		
3	0	*Adjutant.*—*Lt.*Wm. Bolton, 6 Apr. 58.		
5	0	*Instructor of Musketry.*—*Captain* Henry Hingeston, 9 Nov. 58.		
2	0	*Quarter Master.*—Mathew Slattery,[13] 23 July 58.		
19	1 7/12	*Surgeon*—Henry Downes, MD. *A.S.* 1 Nov. 39; *Surg.* 19 Jan. 49; *Surg.Maj.*		
6	0	*Assist.Surgeons.*—Richard Jukes Worthington,[15] 26 May 54. [7 Sept. 55.		
4	0	William Barry, 25 Jan. 56.		

4 Major G. H. Wynyard commanded and led a storming party from the left stockade into the breach at Kawiti's Pah on the 11th Jan. 1846; and also served as Aide-de-Camp to Governor Grey in the valley of the Hutt, and the Horakiwi Valley during the operations in the South in the same year.
6 Captain Whitehead served with the 97th Regt. at the siege and fall of Sebastopol from 20 Nov. 1854, and was on the storming party at the assault of the Redan on the 8th Sept. (Medal and Clasp, and 5th Class of the Medjidie).
7 Capt. Burningham served with the Buffs in the Crimea in 1855, and was wounded at the siege of Sebastopol (Medal and Clasp, and 5th Class of the Medjidie).

[Armit & Co.
Facings Black.—*Agents,* Messrs. Cox & Co.—*Irish Agents,* Sir E. R. Borough, *Bt.,*
[*Returned from New Zealand,* 5 *March* 59.]

1 Lieut. General Wynyard served with the army in Sicily from 1808 to March 1810, when he was severely wounded at the attack on Santa Maura, for which he subsequently obtained the Brevet rank of Major; he was also present and on the staff with the force that occupied Ischia and Procida.
2 Colonel Bridge served with the 58th throughout the whole of the operations in the North of New Zealand from April 1845 to Jan. 1847. He commanded the Regiment in the action at Mawie; planned and conducted a night-attack in boats up the Waikari River against a rebel tribe, which he routed, and destroyed their Pah (thanked by the Governor and Council). Again commanded the Regt. on the second expedition against the rebel chiefs Heki and Kawiti; re-captured a hill at the head of the Regiment on the morning of the 1st July 1845 at Ohiawhi, and led one of the storming parties at the assault on the Pah on that afternoon, and was at the capture of the Pah at Ohinawai on the 11th July, and also at the assault and capture of Kawiti's Pah at Ruapekapeka on the 11th Jan. 1846. (Several times named in Dispatches, &c.)

[For remainder of Notes see preceding page.

Emb. for Hong Kong, 12 June 1849, Cape of Good Hope. Depot, Athlone.

59th (*The 2nd Nottinghamshire*) Regt. of Foot. 280

"CAPE OF GOOD HOPE" "CORUNNA" "JAVA" "VITTORIA" "ST. SEBASTIAN" "NIVE" "PENINSULA" "BHURTPORE."

Years' Serv.			
55			
Full Pay.	Half Pay.		
31	0		
30	0		
26	0		

Colonel.—Jeremiah Taylor,¹ Ens. 28 Feb. 05; Lt. 1 Oct. 07; Capt. 2 Oct. 17; Major, p 1 April 24; Lt.Col. p 22 March 27; Col. 23 Nov. 41; Major Gen. 20 June 54; Lt.Gen. 17 July 59; Col. 59 Foot, 8 Sept. 57.

Lt.Colonel.—Henry Hope Graham,² CB., Ens. p 15 Oct. 29; Lt. p 7 Sept. 32; Capt. p 7 Nov. 34; Major, p 14 Apr. 46; Lt.Col. p 20 Apr. 53; Col. 28 Nov. 54.

Majors.—Arnold E. Burmester,³ Ens. 31 Aug. 30; Lt. p 7 Mar. 34; Capt. p 16 Mar. 38; Brev.Major, 11 Nov. 51; Major, p 29 Apr. 53; Bt.Lt.Col. 13 Apr. 58.

William Wynne Lodder,⁴ Ens. p 7 Mar. 34; Lt. p 5 June 35; Capt. p 6 Feb. 41; Brev.Major, 20 June 54; Major, 21 July 55; Bt.Lt.Col. 1 Nov. 58.

		CAPTAINS.	ENSIGN.	LIEUT.	CAPTAIN.	BREV.-MAJ.
24	0	Robert William Romer⁵	p 30 Sept. 36	15 Jan. 40	p 2 Feb. 49	13 Apr. 58
17	0	Charles Kendal Bushe⁶..	p 14 Apr. 43	p 14 Apr. 46	p 11 May 49	13 Apr. 58
18	0	Mathew Pennefather Lloyd	p 30 Dec. 42	p 11 July 45	p 6 July 49	
16	7/2	Charles Stuart Baker ..	29 Mar. 44	p 8 Jan. 47	p 11 April 51	
20	0	Joseph de Montmorency⁴	p 14 Aug. 40	p 14 Apr. 45	p 14 Sept. 52	
20	0	John King	p 10 July 40	p 29 Apr. 42	p 29 April 53	
15	0	Edward Fred. Chadwick	10 Oct. 45	p 16 Feb. 49	p 4 Aug. 54	
15	0	Jas. Stanhope Pat. Clarke⁴	p 26 Sept. 45	p 23 Nov. 48	p 31 Aug. 55	
18	0	James Leyne⁴	20 May 42	1 Oct. 45	21 July 55	
13	0	Henry Kean⁶†	29 Oct. 47	p 11 April 51	14 Sept. 55	
11	0	Wm. Hamilton Thompson	18 Sept. 49	p 22 Oct. 52	24 June 57	
8	0	Isaac Bomford Bomford	p 9 July 52	6 June 54	p 5 Aug. 59	
		LIEUTENANTS.				
10	0	James Lawson⁷	p 13 Dec. 50	3 Dec. 52		
10	0	Monteford Spread Morgan	p 15 Oct. 50	p 8 April 53		
7	0	Frederick Drage	p 21 Jan. 53	p 21 Oct. 53		
8	0	Rob. Jefferson Spofforth⁴	p 12 Mar. 52	6 June 54		
8	0	Robt. Staveley Shinkwin⁸	p 17 Dec. 52	p 18 Aug. 54		
6	0	S. Lee H. Hamilton Ffinney⁴	6 June 54	9 Feb. 55		
6	0	Benj. Henry Burge,⁹ Adj.	p 18 Aug. 54	21 July 55		
6	0	George Joy⁴	p 25 Aug. 54	14 Sept. 55		
6	0	John Shephard⁴	20 Oct. 54	18 Jan. 56		
5	0	Herbert Edw. Geo. Crosse	11 May 55	p 9 Nov. 55		
5	0	Robert Cuming⁴........	15 June 55	p 17 April 57		
5	0	Arthur Hesilrige	1 June 55	30 Dec. 57		
5	0	Henry Edward Harrow..	20 July 55	11 Aug. 58		
5	0	Launcelot Charles Brown	29 Feb. 56	p 5 Aug. 59		
4	0	Jas. Dillon Macnamara¹²	2 May 56	p 20 Dec. 58		
		ENSIGNS.				
5	0	John M'Mullin⁴........	16 Nov. 55			
4	0	Gerald FitzGibbon	8 July 56			
2	0	Cha. Stuart Wms. Furlong	26 Feb. 58			
2	0	Charles Wollaston Hutton	23 Mar. 58			
2	0	John Trohear Rudd	p 30 Apr. 58			
2	0	Edward Gunter	31 Dec. 58			
1	0	Louis Philip Gould	11 Jan. 59			
1	0	Henry Turner Herchmer	p 25 Mar. 59			
1	0	Patrick Chalmers	p 23 Aug. 59			

21	1¾	Paymaster.—Francis Levett Bennett,¹¹ 29 Oct. 47; Ens. p 25 July 37; Lt. [p 5 July 39.
6	0	Adjutant.—Lieut. Benjamin Henry Burge,⁹ 31 Dec. 58.
4	0	Instructor of Musketry.—Lieut. Launcelot Charles Brown, 28 Sept. 57.
2	0	QuarterMaster.—Samuel Cordue,⁴ 15 Jan. 58.
18	0	Surgeon.—Robert McWharrie, M.D. 4 Nov. 53; Assist.-Surg. 11 March 42.
2	0	Assist.Surgeons.—Walter Crisp, 5 Aug. 58.
2	0	Walter Barnett Ramsbottom, M.B. 10 March 58.

Facings White.—*Agents,* Messrs. Downes & Son.—*Irish Agents,* Sir E. R. Borough, Bt., Armit & Co.

[Right margin notes:] 2 Colonel Graham commanded the 2nd Brigade of the expeditionary force employed against Canton during the operations before that city and at its capture in Dec. 1857 (C.B.). 3 Lt.Colonel Burmester commanded the 59th Regt. at the operations before Canton and capture of the city (Brevet of Lt.-Colonel). 4 Lt.-Col. Lodder, Captains de Montmorency, Clarke, and Leyne, Lts. Spofforth, Ffinney, Joy, Shephard, Cuming, and Brown, and Ensign M'Mullin and Qr.Master Cordue were present at the operations before and capture of Canton in 1857. 11 Paymaster Bennett served the Sutlej campaign of 1845-46 as Lieut. 9th Foot, including the battles of Moodkee, Ferozeshah, and Sobraon (Medal and Clasps). Served the Eastern campaign with the 44th Regt. including the battle of Alma and the siege of Sebastopol (Medal and Clasp).

[Far right margin:] 9 Lieut. Burge served as AidedeCamp to Colonel Graham at the assault and capture of Canton on 29th Dec. 1857; accompanied the force to the Peiho in June, and was present at the assault of Namtaw on 11th Aug. 1858.

8 Lieut. Shinkwin was present at the attack and capture of Fort Lin and the heights behind Canton on 28th Dec., and at the storming and capture of the city (wounded) on 29th Dec. 1857; also at the affair at the White Cloud Mountains, and afterwards with the expedition to the Gulf of Pehchell.

1 Lieut.General Taylor served in the Peninsula with the 9th Regt. from Aug. 1808 to Feb. 1813, and again from Oct. 1813 to the end of the war in 1814, including the battles of Vimiera (wounded), Busaco, Salamanca, retreat from Burgos, action of Villa Muriel (wounded), and repulse of the Sortie from Bayonne. He has the War Medal with four Clasps for Vimiera, Busaco, Fuentes d'Onor and Salamanca.

5 Major Romer was employed as Aide de Camp to the French Admiral during the operations before and capture of Canton in 1857 (Brevet of Major). Commanded the detachment of the 59th Regt. at the storming and capture of Namtow on 11th Aug. 1858.

6 Major Bushe was present at the operations before and capture of Canton in 1857 (Brevet Major), and at the storming and capture of Namtow on 11th Aug. 1858.

6† Captain Kean was present at the attack and capture of Canton on the 28th and 29th Dec. 1857, and subsequent operations; commanded a detachment of the 59th Regt. with the Expedition to the White Cloud Mountains in June 1858, and accompanied the Regt. to the Gulf of Pecheli.

7 Lieut. Lawson was present at the operations before and capture of Canton in 1857; was engaged on the expedition from Canton to the White Cloud Mountains in June, and at the storming and capture of Namtow on 11th Aug. 1858.

12 Lieut. Macnamara was engaged in the expedition from Canton to the White Cloud Mountains in June, and at the storming and capture of Namtow on 11th Aug. 1858.

60th (*The King's Royal Rifle Corps*).

"*Celer et audax*," "ROLEIA" "VIMIERA" "MARTINIQUE" "TALAVERA" "FUENTES D'ONOR" "ALBUHERA" "CIUDAD RODRIGO" "BADAJOZ" "SALAMANCA" "VITTORIA" "PYRENEES" "NIVELLE" "NIVE" "ORTHES" "TOULOUSE" "PENINSULA" "PUNJAUB" "MOOLTAN" "GOOJERAT."

Years' Serv.		
Full Pay.	Half Pay.	
40		*Colonel-in-Chief.*—℗ General Hugh, *Viscount* Gough, KP., GCB., 21 Jan. 54. *Colonels Commandant.*—2 ℗ ᴳᶜᴮ *Sir* William George Moore,¹ KCB., *Ens.* 18 April 11; *Lt.* 10 Sept. 12; *Capt.* 14 April 14; *Maj.* 21 Jan. 19; *Lt.-Col.* 12 Jan. 24; *Col.* 28 June 38; *Maj.-Gen.* 11 Nov. 51; *Lt.-Gen.* 5 June 55; *Col.* 60th Rifles, 26 Jan. 56.
61		1 ℗ Joseph Paterson,² *Ens.* ᴾ 17 May 99; *Lt.* 7 Feb. 01; *Capt.* 23 Oct. 06; *Maj.* 29 Sept. 14; *Lt.-Col.* ᴾ 31 Dec. 25; *Col.* 28 June 38; *Maj.-Gen.* 11 Nov. 51; *Lt.Gen.* 26 Aug. 58; *Col.Comm.* 60th Rifles, 14 April 57.
34	0	*Lieut.Colonels.*—1 Maurice Griffin Dennis,³ CB., *Ens.* 9 May 26; *Lt.* 5 July 27; *Capt.* ᴾ 15 Dec. 37; *Major*, ᴾ 2 May 45; *Brevet Lt.-Col.* 7 June 49; *Lt.-Col.* 19 Oct. 51; *Col.* 28 Nov. 54.
32	0	1 *Sir* John Jones, KCB.,⁴ *Ensign,* ᴾ 12 June 28; *Lieut.* ᴾ 2 Dec. 31; *Capt.* ᴾ 16 July 41; *Major*, ᴾ 20 July 49; *Lt.-Col.* 20 June 54; *Col.* 19 Jan. 58.
32	0	3 Wm. Fanshawe Bedford,⁵ *2nd Lt.* ᴾ 18 Dec. 28; *Lt.* ᴾ 28 June 33; *Capt.* ᴾ 23 July 41; *Maj.* ᴾ 12 Oct. 49; *Br.-Lt.-Col.* 28 May 53; *Col.* 28 Nov. 54; *Lt.Col.* 23 Mar. 55.
33	0	3 Henry Bingham,⁶ *2nd Lieut.* ᴾ 30 April 27; *Lieut.* ᴾ 28 Sept. 32; *Capt.* 25 June 41; *Major*, 19 Oct. 51; *Lt.-Col.* 19 June 57.
27	0	2 Francis Roger Palmer,⁸ CB. *Ens.* ᴾ 15 Mar. 33; *Lieut.* ᴾ 24 April 35; *Capt.* ᴾ 11 Mar. 42; *Maj.* 20 June 54; *Lt.-Col.* 22 June 58.
26	0	2 Webbe Butler, *2nd Lieut.* ᴾ 19 Sept. 34; *Lieut.* ᴾ 15 Dec. 40; *Capt.* 26 July 44; *Major*, 23 Mar. 55; *Lt.Col.* 9 Sept. 58.
20	0	4 William Pretyman,¹⁰ *Ens.* ᴾ 8 May 40; *Lt.* ᴾ 5 Aug. 42; *Capt.* ᴾ 11 Sept. 49; *Bt.Maj.* 2 Nov. 55; *Major*, 9 Sept. 56; *Bt.Lt.Col.* 26 Dec. 56; *Lt.Col.* ᴾ 29 Apr. 59.
20	0	*Majors.*—3 Henry Friend Kennedy,⁹ *2nd Lieut.* ᴾ 11 Sept. 40; *Lieut.* 7 Apr. 42; *Capt.* ᴾ 20 Oct. 48; *Major*, ᴾ 17 Aug. 55.
24	0	1 Charles Napier North,¹¹ *Ensign,* 20 May 36; *Lieut.* 28 Dec. 38; *Capt.* 28 Dec. 48; *Major*, 19 June 57; *Bt.Lt.Col.* 20 July 58.
22	0	4 Robert B. Hawley,¹³ *Ens.* 28 Aug. 38; *Lt.* ᴾ 31 Dec. 39; *Capt.* 10 Jan. 57; *Bt.-Maj.* 2 Nov. 55; *Major*, 5 Sept. 56.
19	0	2 George Waldegrave Bligh,¹⁴ *2nd Lieut.* 12 Mar. 41; *Lieut.* 26 July 44; *Capt.* ᴾ 12 Oct. 49; *Major*, 24 Apr. 58.
19	0	2 Gibbes Rigaud,¹⁴ *2nd Lieut.* ᴾ 11 June 41; *Lieut.* 26 July 44; *Capt.* ᴾ 16 Aug. 50; *Major*, 22 June 58.
19	0	1 *Sir* Edward FitzGerald Campbell, *Bt.*¹⁵ *s.* *2nd Lt.* 2 July 41; *Lt.* 26 July 44; *Capt.* ᴾ 27 Dec. 50; *Bt.Major*, 19 Jan. 58; *Major*, 9 Sept. 58.
19	0	4 Peter Burton Roe, *2nd Lieut.* ᴾ 23 July 41; *Lieut.* 26 July 44; *Capt.* ᴾ 17 June 51; *Major*, ᴾ 29 Apr. 59.
19	0	3 James Fraser, *2nd Lieut.* ᴾ 10 Sept. 41; *Lieut.* 26 July 44; *Capt.* ᴾ 7 Jan. 53; *Major*, 18 Oct. 59.

		CAPTAINS.	ENSIGN.	LIEUT.	CAPTAIN.	BREV.-MAJ.
20	0	1 Thomas Biggs	ᴾ 2 Oct. 40	15 Nov. 43	8 Apr. 53	
17	0	4 Randle J. Feilden	ᴾ 31 Mar. 43	ᴾ 25 Feb. 45	23 Dec. 53	
17	0	1 Hen. Francis Williams¹⁶	19 May 43	ᴾ 20 Dec. 44	ᴾ 3 Mar. 54	19 Jan. 58
17	0	2 D.D.Muter,¹⁷ *t.c.* 20 July 58	14 April 43	ᴾ 17 Jan. 45	31 May 54	19 Jan. 58
17	0	3 C. A. Boswell Gordon¹⁸	ᴾ 21 April 43	ᴾ 13 June 45	6 June 54	6 June 56
20	0	1 John Maguire¹⁹	ᴾ 7 Feb. 40	4 July 43	20 June 54	20 July 58
16	0	2 Hen. Edward Warren¹⁴	ᴾ 5 Jan. 44	ᴾ 30 Dec. 45	ᴾ 4 Aug. 54	
21	⁴⁄₁₂	1 John Robert Wilton²⁰	20 Dec. 38	3 Dec. 41	14 July 54	19 Jan. 58
19	0	3 Alfred J. FitzGerald¹⁶	ᴾ 30 Apr. 41	ᴾ 13 Feb. 46	23 Mar. 55	
16	0	3 Francis Dawson	29 July 44	ᴾ 22 June 47	23 Mar. 55	
16	0	3 John Prevost Battersby	30 July 44	ᴾ 28 Jan. 48	23 Mar. 55	
16	0	3 J. Lambert Edw. Baynes	31 July 44	ᴾ 24 Feb. 48	23 Mar. 55	
16	0	3 Bernard Edw. Ward²¹	1 Aug. 44	ᴾ 5 May 48	23 Mar. 55	20 July 55
15	0	3 Vincent Tongue⁹	ᴾ 14 Feb. 45	28 Dec. 48	23 Mar. 55	
15	0	4 R. Harcourt Robinson	ᴾ 25 Feb. 45	ᴾ 20 July 49	23 Mar. 55	
15	0	2 Robt. Wilmot Brooke²²	ᴾ 30 Dec. 45	ᴾ 12 Oct. 49	23 Mar. 55	
14	0	2 Fran. Charteris Fletcher	ᴾ 31 July 46	ᴾ 16 Aug. 50	23 Mar. 55	
14	0	2 Edward Bowles,²³ *s.*	ᴾ 14 Aug. 46	ᴾ 16 Aug. 50	23 Mar. 55	
13	0	1 R. J. Eust. Robertson¹⁶	ᴾ 5 Mar. 47	ᴾ 27 Dec. 50	23 Mar. 55	
11	0	2 Hugh P. Montgomery¹⁴	ᴾ 21 Aug. 49	ᴾ 28 Oct. 53	ᴾ 17 Aug. 55	
9	0	1 C. D. C. Ellis¹⁴	17 Jan. 51	20 June 54	ᴾ 14 Dec. 55	
9	0	2 *Hon.* Atholl C. J. Liddell	ᴾ 16 May 51	20 June 54	ᴾ 21 Dec. 55	
12	0	1 William Tedlie²³	ᴾ 5 May 48	ᴾ 13 Apr. 52	25 Jan. 56	20 July 58
12	0	1 Conyngham Jones²⁴	ᴾ 25 Feb. 48	21 Oct. 52	6 May 56	26 Apr. 59
12	0	3 Geo. C. Henry Waters²⁵	ᴾ 21 Jan. 48	ᴾ 18 Mar. 53	ᴾ 1 May 57	
15	0	3 C. H. Spen. Churchill²⁶	ᴾ 10 Oct. 45	ᴾ 24 Sept. 47	ᴾ 4 Aug. 54	2 Nov. 55
11	0	1 Geo. Bliss MacQueen²⁷	9 Mar. 40	2 Oct. 53	19 June 57	

60th (The King's Royal Rifle Corps). 282

Years' Serv. Full Pay.	Half Pay.		CAPTAINS.	ENSIGN.	LIEUT.	CAPTAIN.	BREV.-MAJ.
11	⅞	3	Hon. John Colborne 28	5 Aug. 48	P 14 Mar. 51	1 Feb. 56	
11	0	3	Henry Semple	11 Sept. 49	P 16 Dec. 53	P 25 May 57	
9	1/12	4	Edward Aug. Stotherd 29 ..	7 Feb. 51	4 Feb. 54	8 Jan. 56	
8	⅔	4	Robert Crowe 31	P 17 May 51	20 May 54	P 15 Apr. 56	
8	2/12	4	Wm. Spicer Cookworthy 32	P 14 Mar. 51	P 18 Oct. 53	22 Aug. 56	
9	0	4	Charles Williamson	P 11 July 51	11 Aug. 54	P 16 Oct. 57	
11	0	4	Rowley Willes Hinxman 33	23 Nov. 49	P 3 Mar. 54	15 Jan. 58	
9	0	4	Francis Stewart Travers ..	P 20 Aug. 51	18 Aug. 54	15 Jan. 58	
8	0	4	Wykeham Leigh Pemberton 31	P 23 Apr. 52	P 25 Aug. 54	23 Mar. 58	
8	0	4	Henry Pardoe Eaton 35 ...	P 11 June 52	23 Mar. 55	23 Apr. 58	
7	0	2	Fra. Dundas Farquharson..	P 18 Feb. 53	23 Mar. 55	24 Apr. 58	
7	0	4	John James Phillipps ...	P 27 May 53	23 Mar. 55	P 14 May 58	
6	0	1	James Durham Dundas 36..	P 3 Mar. 54	23 Mar. 55	22 June 58	
6	0	1	Herbert George Deedes 37..	11 Aug. 54	23 Mar. 55	P 2 July 58	
6	0	3	John D'Olier George.....	P 23 Aug. 54	23 Mar. 55	P 2 July 58	
6	0	1	James Hare 33	P 17 Mar. 54	23 Mar. 55	9 Sept. 58	
17	0	2	John William Medhurst 37†	P 20 Jan. 43	15 Sept. 45	4 Apr. 56	
6	0	4	James Joseph Collins	P 25 Aug. 54	23 Mar. 55	P 19 July 59	
18	1 5/12	2	Jas. Hy. Lawrence-Archer 38†	P 15 Dec. 40	P 22 Dec. 54	23 Aug. 59	
6	0	2	D. G. Neville Watts-Russell	P 29 Sept. 54	23 Mar. 55	P 29 Nov. 59	
6	0	2	Arthur William Knox Gore	P 8 Dec. 54	11 May 55	P 16 Dec. 59	

LIEUTENANTS.

6	0*	2	Llewellyn Edmund Traherne	P 24 Aug. 54	23 Mar. 55		21 Major Ward served as Aide-de-Camp to Colonel Viscount Melville during the campaign in the Punjaub of 1848-49, including the second siege operations before Mooltan and battle of Goojerat (Medal and two Clasps). Served with a detachment of the 60th during operations in the Euzofzie country in Dec. 1849, and acted as Staff Officer to the European portion of the force sent against the Affreedies in the Kohat Pass in Feb. 1850.
7	0	1	Anthony Carlisle 38	P 20 Sept. 53	P 22 Sept. 54		
6	0	2	James Arthur Morrah	P 8 Sept. 54	11 May 55		
6	0	2	Hon.R. Prendergast Vereker	29 Dec. 54	11 May 55		
5	0	1	Francis Vernon Northey ..	22 Mar. 55	27 July 55		
5	0	1	Philip Julian Curtis 39	23 Mar. 55	3 Aug. 55		
5	0	1	William F. Carleton	30 Mar. 55	P 17 Aug. 55		
5	0	3	James Forbes, Adj.......	5 Apr. 55	23 Oct. 55		
5	0	3	Robert Morris Hazen	6 Apr. 55	23 Oct. 55		
5	0	3	George Ffrench Stehelin ...	7 Apr. 55	26 Oct. 55		
5	0	3	Burnet Bell Forsyth	10 Apr. 55	26 Oct. 55		26 Major Churchill served in the Kaffir war of 1846-47 (Medal). Also the Eastern campaign of 1854-55, including the battles of Alma and Inkerman, and siege of Sebastopol—wounded in the trenches (Medal and Clasps, Brevet Major, and 5th Class of the Medjidie). Served the campaign in Rohilcund in 1858, including the actions of Bugawalla and Nugena, relief of Moradabad, action on the Dojura, assault and capture of Bareilly, attack and bombardment of Shahjehanpore defeat of the rebels and relief of the garrison, capture of the fort of Bunnai, pursuit of the enemy to the left bank of the Goomtee, and destruction of the fort of Mahundee.
5	0	1	Cromer Ashburnham 40	20 Apr. 55	26 Oct. 55		
5	0	2	George Kennedy Shaw	22 Apr. 55	P 26 Oct. 55		
5	0	1	Augustus Morgan 41	21 Apr. 55	25 Jan. 56		
5	0	2	Kennett Gregg Henderson..	23 Apr. 55	6 May 56		
5	0	1	Fred. Austin 42	8 May 55	P 9 May 56		
5	0	3	Edward Campbell Ainslie ..	9 May 55	P 9 May 56		
5	0	2	Jas. Sturgeon Hamilton Algar	10 May 55	P 9 May 56		
5	0	3	Joseph John Bradshaw	1 June 55	P 9 May 56		
5	0	4	Norman FitzGerald Uniacke	23 Oct. 55	P 7 Mar. 56		
6	0	1	G.C.Kelly,40 Adj.(Q.M.2Apr.54)	1 May 55	16 Nov. 56		
5	0	2	Matthew Tilford, Adj.....	31 May 55	17 Mar. 57		28 Captain Hon. J. Colborne served at the siege of Sebastopol in 1855 (Medal and Clasp). 31 Captain Crowe served the Eastern campaign of 1854-55 with the 93rd Highlanders, expedition to the Sea of Azoff, capture of Kertch and Yenikale, and siege and fall of Sebastopol (Medal and three Clasps, and Knight of the Legion of Honor). 32 Captain Cookworthy served throughout the Eastern campaign of 1854-55, including the battles of Alma and Balaklava, siege and fall of Sebastopol (Medal and three Clasps, and Sardinian Medal). 33† Mr. Sparrow served in the Kaffir war of 1847, and in that of 1852-53 (Medal). Was in medical charge of a strong force sent from Natal to aid Major Warden in the Sovereignty, from Sept. 1851 to July 1852. Served at the siege of Sebastopol in 1855 (Medal and Clasp).
5	0	4	Fred. Simon A. Orchard 41..	8 June 55	17 Mar. 57		
5	0	3	James Kiero Watson	20 July 55	P 1 May 57		
5	0	3	Chas. Christoph. Willoughby	P 20 July 55	31 May 57		
5	0	3	Jenico Preston 43	P 14 Sept. 55	19 June 57		
5	0	3	Robert John Hickman	20 Oct. 55	P 25 Aug. 57		
5	0	1	John Owen Young 45	23 Oct. 55	P 25 Aug. 57		
5	0	3	William Norcott Manners	16 Mar. 55	23 Oct. 55		
5	0	4	Fred. H. Anson Hamilton..	P 25 Jan. 55	16 Nov. 55		
5	0	4	Harry Robert Milligan ..	16 Feb. 55	23 Nov. 55		
5	0	4	Wm. M. Miller Fortescue..	26 Jan. 55	P 25 Jan. 56		
5	0	3	George Hatchell..........	22 Oct. 55	27 Sept. 57		
5	0	3	Arthur Tufnell	9 Nov. 55	15 Jan. 58		
5	0	1	Richard Fra. Jennings 46 ..	23 Nov. 55	15 Jan. 58		
5	0	2	Frank Sadlier Brereton ...	14 Dec. 55	13 Feb. 58		
4	0	1	William Greer Turle 46	1 Feb. 56	23 Mar. 55		
4	0	1	Cary Hampton Borrer	8 Feb. 56	23 Apr. 58		
4	0	3	Henry Stephen Hodges....	29 Feb. 56	24 Apr. 58		
4	0	4	Alfred Lewis	14 Mar. 56	21 May 58		
4	0	4	George Henry Mackenzie..	P 9 May 56	21 May 58		
4	0	1	Stanley Mortimer 47	14 May 56	21 May 58		
4	0	4	William John Evered Poole	15 May 56	21 May 58		
4	0	2	Newton Jones Pauli	27 May 56	P 4 June 58		
4	0	1	Ashley Henry Woodgate ..	P 19 Sept. 56	P 15 June 58		
3	0	2	William Henry Moseley ..	P 1 May 57	P 15 June 58		
3	0	4	Wm. Lewis Kinloch Ogilvy	18 June 57	P 15 June 58		
4	0	2	Alfred Spencer Heathcote 19	16 May 56	22 June 58		
4	0	1	James Walker King	8 July 56	P 6 Aug. 58		
4	0	2	Fred. Augustus Campbell ..	5 Dec. 56	9 Sept. 58		

† M

283 60th (The King's Royal Rifle Corps).

Years' Serv. Full Pay.	Years' Serv. Half Pay.	LIEUTENANTS.	ENSIGN.	LIEUT.
3	0	3 Hugh Saint George Barton	19 June 57	P 9 Nov. 58
3	0	3 George Hewitt Trotman ..	P 12 May 57	13 Aug. 59
3	0	4 Richard Albert Massy	28 Aug. 57	P 16 Aug. 59
3	0	4 Julius Lovell	P 24 Feb. 57	P 30 Sept. 59
3	0	4 Richard Russell Gubbins ..	19 June 57	P 7 Oct. 59
4	0	4 Charles Henry Cox	26 Dec. 56	P 4 Nov. 59
3	0	4 Walter Langford Sainsbury	P 25 Aug. 57	P 16 Dec. 59
3	0	2 John Barrott L. Nevinson	P 24 July 57	P 16 Dec. 50
		ENSIGNS.		84 Assistant Surgeon Young served with the 2nd Batt. Rifle Brigade in the Crimea, and was present throughout the siege of Sebastopol (Medal and Clasp).
3	0	1 Eaton Stannard Steward ..	P 26 Aug. 57
3	0	1 Henry Richard Treeve	27 Aug. 57
4	0	4 Latham C. Brownrigg, Adj.	28 Feb. 56
3	0	1 Henry John Barker	P 14 Aug. 57	48 Qr.Master FitzGibbon served with the 45th Regt. in the Kaffir war of 1846-7 (Medal).
3	0	2 Rt. FitzWilliam de B. Barry	P 30 Oct. 57
3	0	1 Henry Brodrick	P 27 Nov. 57	50 Qr.Master Walker served with the 71st Highlanders at the siege of Sebastopol and expedition to Kertch and Yenikale from 13th Feb. 1855 (Medal and Clasp).
3	0	3 John East Hunter Peyton..	18 Dec. 57
2	0	2 Pierce O'Brien Butler	2 Feb. 58
2	0	1 Julius Tottenham	P 5 Feb. 58
2	0	4 Reginald H. Beadon......	P 6 Feb. 58	51 Doctor Young served throughout the Eastern campaign of 1854-55, including the battles of Alma, Balaklava, and Inkerman, siege and fall of Sebastopol, and expedition to Kertch (Medal and four Clasps).
2	0	3 George D. Anderson......	26 Mar. 58
2	0	1 John William Marshall....	27 Mar. 58
2	0	2 Richard Meade	28 Mar. 58
2	0	2 Charles Bateman Prust ..	29 Mar. 58
2	0	3 Harcourt James Lees	30 Mar. 58
2	0	4 Pennyman White Worsley	31 Mar. 58
2	0	4 Astley Fellowes Terry	1 April 58
2	0	4 John Gustavus Crosbie....	23 Apr. 58
2	0	1 Nesbit Willoughby Wallace	26 Mar. 58
2	0	1 Charles Gosling..........	14 May 58
2	0	1 Marcus William O'Rorke..	25 Apr. 58
2	0	2 Arthur Morris	P 21 May 58
2	0	4 Alexander Borthwick	P 22 May 58
2	0	2 Redvers Henry Buller	P 23 May 58
2	0	2 Henry M. Pryor	25 June 58
2	0	3 G.Ed.Graham Foster Pigott	14 July 58
2	0	2 Charles Pierson Cramer ..	P 24 Aug. 58
2	0	3 Edward Digby O'Rorke ..	P 31 Aug. 58
2	0	4 John Charles Mariette ..	15 Oct. 58
2	0	4 John Miller	P 9 Nov. 58
1	0	4 Courtenay Forbes Terry..	8 Apr. 59
1	0	2 Hon.Walt.CourtenayPepys	P 14 June 59
1	0	3 Francis William Robins ..	P 22 July 59
1	0	3 Francis Wallace Grenfell .	P 5 Aug. 59
1	0	3 Barnard Henry Davidson	P 16 Aug. 59
1	0	3 John William Rhodes....	P 7 Oct. 59
1	0	2 Aubrey Vero O'Brien	P 18 Oct. 59
1	0	1 RichardF.St.And.St.John	P 15 Nov. 59
1	0	4 John Edward Pratt Barlow	P 16 Dec. 59
1	0	Charles Louis C. de Robeck	P 22 Oct. 59
11	0	Paymasters.—2 Francis FitzPatrick, 2 March 55; Ens. P 19 Oct. 49; Lt. 31 May 54.
5	0	3 Frederick Thomas Patterson, 19 June 55.
19	⁶⁄₁₂	1 John Henry Chads,²³ 29 May 57; Ens. 9 Jan. 41; Lt. 12 May 44; Capt. 15 Jun. 56.
5	0	4 Edward Charles Grant, 28 Dec. 55.
5	0	Adjutants.—3 Lieut. James Forbes, 5 Apr. 55.
6	0	1 Lieut. George Charles Kelly, 1 May 55.
5	0	2 Lieut. Matthew Tilford, 9 Oct. 55.
4	0	4 Ensign Latham Coddington Brownrigg, 18 Jan. 59.
6	0	Instructors of Musketry.—3 Lieut. James Kiero Watson, 1 Aug. 57.
5	0	2 Lieut. Frank Sadlier Brereton, 28 Aug. 57.
5	0	4 Lieut. Wm. N. Manners, 22 March 58.
13	0	Quarter Masters.—2 Luke FitzGibbon,⁴⁸ 15 Oct. 47.
5	0	1 William Hunter,⁴⁹ 13 July 55.
12	0	4 Thomas Walker,⁵⁰ 10 March 48.
2	0	3 Robert Duncan, 13 Aug. 58.
21	0	Surgeons.—2 Henry James Schooles, M.D. Assist.Surg. 28 June 39; Surgeon, [1 Oct. 47; Surgeon Major, 22 July 59.
15	0	3 Geo.Waterloo Pennington Sparrow,⁸³† 6 July 55; A.S. 25 Sept. 45.
14	0	1 Edward William Young,⁵¹ M.D. 8 Dec. 54; A.S. 7 Aug. 46.
12	⁶⁄₁₂	4 James Crerar, 6 Apr. 55; A.S. 3 Sept. 47.

60th (The King's Royal Rifle Corps).

Years' Serv. Full Pay.	Half Pay.		
6	0	Assistant Surgeons.—2	Grahame Young,[34] 5 May 54.
6	0	3	Thomas John Murphy, 28 April 54.
6	0	3	James Macartney, 6 Oct. 54.
4	0	1	Ebenezer John Hatchell, 15 Jan. 56.
3	0	2	Robert Owen Hayden, 15 Sept. 57.
3	0	1	Frederick William Wade, 15 Sept. 57.
3	0	1	William Silver Oliver,[44] M.D. 15 Sept. 57.
3	0	3	Seth Sam, 9 Nov. 57.
3	0	2	James Doran, M.D. 9 Nov. 57.
. 2	0	4	John Alexander Lamb, 22 June 58.
1	0	4	Alexander Campbell M'Tavish, 12 Jan. 59.

[1st Battalion embarked for India, July 1845. Depot, Winchester.]
[2nd Batt. emb. for the Cape of Good Hope, June 1851. In India. Depot, Winchester.]
[3rd Battalion embarked for India, 7 July 1857. Depot, Winchester.]
[4th Battalion, Waterford. Depot, Winchester.]

Regimentals Green—Facings Scarlet.—Agents, Sir C. R. M'Grigor, Bt., and Walter M'Grigor, Esq.

1 Sir William George Moore served in the Peninsula with the 52nd, and was present at the sieges of Ciudad Rodrigo, Badajoz, and St. Sebastian, and at the battles of Salamanca, Vittoria, Nivelle, and Nive, for which he has received the War Medal with seven Clasps. He was also at the repulse of the sortie from Bayonne as Aide-de-Camp to Sir John Hope, and was severely wounded and taken prisoner with that General. He served also the Waterloo campaign on the staff of the Quarter-Master-General.

2 Lieut.General Paterson served with a corps of Cavalry as a volunteer in the Rebellion in Ireland in 1798. He served the Egyptian campaign of 1801 in the 28th Regt., and was present in the actions of the 8th, 13th, and 21st March, as also at the capture of Grand Cairo and Alexandria. In 1805 he accompanied Lord Cathcart's expedition to the Continent. He served in the 77th in the Peninsula and South of France during the campaigns of 1811, 12, 13, and 14, including the affair at El Bodon, siege and capture of Ciudad Rodrigo and of Badajoz, investment of Bayonne and repulse of the sortie, besides various skirmishes. When the rebellion broke out in Canada in 1837 he volunteered his services, which were accepted. Served five years in the West Indies. He has received the Gold Medal from the Grand Seignior for the Egyptian campaign, and the Silver War Medal with three Clasps for Egypt, Ciudad Rodrigo, and Badajoz.

3 Colonel Dennis served with the 1st Battalion 60th Rifles during the second siege operations at Mooltan, and commanded the Battalion 27th Dec. 1848, when the enemy's outposts and suburbs of Mooltan were captured (wounded); was afterwards present at the battle of Goojerat, pursuit of the fugitive Sikh army until its final surrender at Rawul Pindee, and expulsion of the Affghan force beyond the Khyber Pass (Medal and two Clasps).

4 Sir John Jones served the campaign of 1857-58 against the Mutineers in India; commanded the 1st Batt. 60th Rifles at the actions on the Hindun of 30th and 31st May, battle of Budlee ke Serai and forcing the heights before Delhi on 8th June, throughout the siege operations before Delhi, action of the 19th June, attack on the Subzee Mundi on 18th July (commanded column of attack), and covering the assaulting columns at the storming of the City on the 14th September. Commanded the left attacking column within the City from 15th to 20th Sept., forced through the City blew open the gates and took possession of the Palace on 20th September 1857. Commanded as Brigadier General the Roorkee Field Force throughout the operations in Rohilcund from 17th April to 21st May 1858, including the actions of Bugawalla and Nugena, relief of Moradabad, action on the Dojura, assault and capture of Bareilly, attack and bombardment of Shahjehanpore defeat of the rebels and relief of the garrison, capture of the fort of Bunnai, pursuit of the enemy to the left bank of the Goomtee, and destruction of the fort of Mahundee (CB. and Colonel for distinguished service in the field. Good Service pension, and KCB.).

5 Colonel Bedford served in the Kaffir war of 1851-53 (Medal, and Brevet Lt.Colonel).

6 Lt.Colonel Bingham served with the 1st Battalion 60th Rifles during the second siege operations at Mooltan, including the siege and storm of the town, and capture of the citadel. Afterwards at the battle of Goojerat, pursuit of the Sikh army, and expulsion of the Affghan force beyond the Kyber Pass. Commanded the Companies of the 60th engaged against the Hill Tribes in the Euzofzye country 11th Dec. 1849, and was severely wounded in the head (Medal and two Clasps).

8 Lt.Colonel Palmer served in the campaign of 1857-58 against the Mutineers in India, including the siege operations before Delhi from 22nd Aug., assault and capture of the City with the final attack on and occupation of the Palace. Commanded the 1st Batt. 60th Rifles throughout the campaign in Rohilcund, including the actions of Bugawalla and Nugena, relief of Moradabad, action on the Dojura, assault and capture of Bareilly, attack and bombardment of Shahjehanpore defeat of the rebels and relief of the garrison, capture of the fort of Bunnai, pursuit of the enemy to the left bank of the Goomtee, and destruction of the fort of Mahundee (CB.).

9 Major Kennedy, and Captain Tongue, served the Punjaub campaign of 1849 (Medal and two Clasps), and were present during the second siege operations at Mooltan (including the siege and storm of the town and capture of the citadel), battle of Goojerat, pursuit of the Sikh army until its final surrender at Rawul Pindee, the occupation of Attock and Peshawur, and expulsion of the Affghan force beyond the Khyber Pass. Served also in the expedition against the Affredies in the Kohat Pass in Feb. 1850.

11 Lt. Col. North served the Punjaub campaign of 1849 (Medal and two Clasps), and was present during the second siege operations at Mooltan (including the siege and storm of the town and capture of the citadel), battle of Goojerat, pursuit of the Sikh army until its final surrender at Rawul Pindee, occupation of Attock and Peshawur, and expulsion of the Affghan force beyond the Khyber Pass. Served with Havelock's Column in 1857 attached to 78th Highlanders and on the Staff in the actions of Futtehpore, Aoung, Pandoo Nuddee, Cawnpore, Oonao, Buseerutgunge (29th July), Bithoor, Alum Bagh, and Relief of Lucknow—slightly wounded (thanked by Governor General in Council and in Gen. Outram's despatches for "valuable services").

12 Lt.Colonel Pretyman served the Eastern campaign of 1854-55 with the 33rd Regt., up to 20th Feb. 1855, when he was appointed Brigade Major to 1st Brigade, Light Division; was present at the battles of Alma and Inkerman, siege of Sebastopol, and assaults on the 18th June and 8th Sept. (Medal and Clasps, Brevet Major, Knight of the Legion of Honor, and 5th Class of the Medjidie).

13 Major Hawley served with the 89th Regt. at the siege and fall of Sebastopol from 9th Jan. 1855, and attacks on the 18th June and 8th Sept. (Medal and Clasp, Brevet Major, Sardinian Medal, and 5th Class of the Medjidie).

14 Majors Bligh and Rigaud, Captains Warren, Montgomery, and Ellis, served in the Kaffir war of 1851-53 (Medal).

15 Sir Edward Campbell served the Punjaub campaign of 1849 (Medal and two Clasps), and was present during the second siege operations at Mooltan (including the siege and storm of the town and capture of the citadel), battle of Goojerat, pursuit of the Sikh army until its surrender at Rawul Pindee, occupation

60th (*The King's Royal Rifle Corps*).

of Attock and Peshawur, and expulsion of the Affghan force beyond the Khyber Pass. Served with the expedition against the Affreedies in the Kohat Pass in 1850 as Aide-de-Camp to Sir Charles Napier. Served from 3rd July during the siege operations before Delhi, assault and capture of the City with the final attack on and occupation of the Palace on 20th Sept. 1858 (Brevet Major).

16 Major Williams, Capts. FitzGerald and Eustace Robertson, served with the 1st Battalion 60th Rifles during the second siege operations at Mooltan, including the siege and storm of the town, and capture of the citadel. Afterwards at the battle of Goojerat, the pursuit of the Sikh army, and the expulsion of the Affghans beyond the Khyber Pass. Also present during the operations in the Euzofzye country, and capture of the insurgent villages on the 11th and 14th Dec. 1849. Capt. Eustace Robertson served in the expedition against the Affreedies in the Kohat Pass in Feb. 1850 (Medal and two Clasps). Major Williams served also in the campaign of 1857 against the Mutineers in India, including the actions on the Hindun of the 30th and 31st May, battle of Budlee ke Serai and taking of the heights before Delhi on 8th June, subsequent siege operations to 16th August—severely wounded on 19th June (Brevet Major).

17 Lt.Colonel Muter served in the Punjaub campaign in 1848-49, including the siege and capture of Mooltan, battle of Goojerat, pursuit and surrender of Shere Sing, occupation of Attock and Peshawur (Medal and two Clasps). Served the campaign of 1857-58 against the Mutineers in India; commanded a Wing of 60th Rifles at Meerut in suppressing insurgent villagers from 10th May to 26th Aug.; present with the 1st Battalion from 6th Sept. at the siege of Delhi, assault and capture of the City on 14th Sept. with the final attack on and occupation of the Palace on 20th Sept.—succeeded to the command of the attacking Column on Kishingunge on 14th Sept. on the fall of Major Reid (Brevet Major). Served as D.A.Adj.General to the Roorkee Field Force during the campaign in Rohilcund, including the actions of Bugawalla and Nugena, relief of Moradabad, action on the Dojura, assault and capture of Bareilly, attack and bombardment of Shahjehanpore defeat of the rebels and relief of the garrison, capture of the fort of Bunnai, pursuit of the enemy to the left bank of the Goomtee, and destruction of the fort of Mahundee (Brevet Lt.Colonel).

18 Major Gordon served as a volunteer at the first attack upon Mooltan, and with the 1st Battalion 60th Rifles through the Punjaub campaign in 1848-9, including the siege of Mooltan and battle of Goojerat (Medal and two Clasps, Fourth Class of the Medjidie for service with the Turkish Contingent).

19 Major Maguire served with the 55th Regt. in China (Medal), at Amoy, Chusan, and Chinhae; and with the 60th throughout the Punjaub campaign of 1848-9, including the siege and storm of the town and capture of the citadel of Mooltan, battle of Goojerat, and subsequent operations (Medal and two Clasps). Served throughout the campaign in Rohilcund in 1858, including the actions of Bugawalla and Nugena, relief of Moradabad, action on the Dojura, assault and capture of Bareilly, attack and bombardment of Shahjehanpore defeat of the rebels and relief of the garrison, capture of the fort of Bunnai, pursuit of the enemy to the left bank of the Goomtee, and destruction of the fort of Mahundee; commanded a wing of the 1st Batt. 60th Rifles at the attack and destruction of Shahabad; commanded the Battalion in the action of Bunkagong (Brevet of Major, Medal).

20 Major Wilton served in the 55th Regiment during the Chinese expedition (Medal), and was present at the operations before Nankin. Served in the 1st Batt. 60th Rifles in the campaign of 1857 against the Mutineers in India, including the actions on the Hindun, battle of Budlee ke Serai and taking the heights before Delhi on 8th June, and subsequent siege operations to 1st Sept. 1857 (Brevet Major).

22 Capt. Brooke served with the 1st Battalion 60th Rifles during the second siege operations at Mooltan, including the siege and storm of the town and capture of the citadel of Mooltan; afterwards at the battle of Goojerat, pursuit of the Sikh army under Rajah Shere Sing until its final surrender at Rawul Pindee, occupation of Attock and Peshawur, and expulsion of the Affghan force under the Ameer Dost Mahomed beyond the Khyber Pass; was wounded at Mooltan 27th Dec. 1848 (Medal and two Clasps). Served also in the Kaffir war of 1851-53 (Medal).

23 Captains Bowles, Tedlie and Chads served in the campaign in Rohilcund in 1858, including the actions of Bugawalla and Nugena, relief of Moradabad, action on the Dojura, assault and capture of Bareilly, attack and bombardment of Shahjehanpore defeat of the rebels and relief of the garrison, capture of the fort of Bunnai, pursuit of the enemy to the left bank of the Goomtee, and destruction of the fort of Mahundee. Captain Tedlie served as D.A.Q.M.Gen. to the Roorkee Field Force.

24 Major Jones served the campaign against the Mutineers in India from 3rd June 1857, including the battle of Budlee ke Serai and taking the heights before Delhi, the subsequent siege operations until severely wounded on 23rd June. Served the campaign in Rohilcund in 1858, including the actions of Bugawalla and Nugena, relief of Moradabad, action on the Dojura, assault and capture of Bareilly, attack and bombardment of Shahjehanpore defeat of the rebels and relief of the garrison, capture of the fort of Bunnai, pursuit of the enemy to the left bank of the Goomtee, and destruction of the fort of Mahundee, attack on and destruction of Shahabad.

25 Captain Waters served from 18th July 1857 at the siege of Delhi, assault and capture of the City, and final attack on and occupation of the Palace; was wounded on 6th August and again at the assault on 14th Sept.

27 Captain MacQueen was engaged with the Mutineers near Cawnpore on the 26th and 27th Nov., and commanded a company of the 34th Regt. at the defence of Cawnpore from 28th Nov. to 24th Dec. 1857. Served with the 1st Battalion 60th Rifles the campaign in Rohilcund in 1858, including the actions of Bugawalla and Nugena, relief of Moradabad, action on the Dojura, assault and capture of Bareilly, attack and bombardment of Shahjehanpore defeat of the rebels and relief of the garrison, capture of the fort of Bunnai, pursuit of the enemy to the left bank of the Goomtee, and destruction of the fort of Mahundee, attack on and capture of Shahabad.

29 Captain Stotherd served with the 93rd Highlanders the Eastern campaign of 1854 and up to the 14th July 1855, including the battles of Alma and Balaklava, siege of Sebastopol, and expedition to Kertch (Medal and three Clasps).

33 Captains Hinxman and Hare served in the campaign of 1857 against the Mutineers in India from 7th June, including the battle of Budlee ke Serai and taking the heights before Delhi, the subsequent siege operations, assault and capture of the City with the final attack on and occupation of the Palace.

34 Captain Pemberton served in India during the Mutiny and was severely wounded at Cawnpore on the 27th Nov. 1857 (Medal).

35 Captain Eaton served in the campaign of 1857 against the Mutineers in India from 3rd June, including the battle of Budlee ke Serai and taking the heights before Delhi, the subsequent siege operations (dangerously wounded on 10th Sept.), assault and capture of the City with the final attack on and occupation of the Palace.

36 Captain Dundas served in the campaign of 1857 against the Mutineers in India from 7th June, including the battle of Budlee ke Serai and taking the heights before Delhi, the subsequent siege operations to 6th Aug. (wounded on 19th June). Served the campaign of 1858 in Rohilcund, including the actions of Bugawalla and Nugena, relief of Moradabad, action on the Dojura, assault and capture of Bareilly, attack and bombardment of Shahjehanpore defeat of the rebels and relief of the garrison, capture of the fort of Bunnai, pursuit of the enemy to the left bank of the Goomtee, and destruction of the fort of Mahundee.

37 Captain Deedes served with the 1st Battalion 60th Rifles the campaign of 1857-58 against the Mutineers in India, including the actions on the Hindun, battle of Budlee ke Serai and taking the heights before Delhi, the subsequent siege operations (wounded on 12th June), assault and capture of the City with the final attack in and occupation of the Palace. Served as Aide de Camp to Brigadier Jones during the campaign in Rohilcund, including the actions of Bugawalla and Nugena, relief of Moradabad, action on the Dojura, assault and capture of Bareilly, attack and bombardment of Shahjehanpore defeat of the rebels and relief of the garrison, capture of the fort of Bunnai, pursuit of the enemy to the left bank of the Goomtee, and destruction of the fort of Mahundee. Served as extra Aide de Camp to Sir A. Wilson at the siege and capture of Lucknow.

60th (The King's Royal Rifle Corps).

37† Captain Medhurst served with the 10th Regt. in the Sutlej campaign in 1846, and was present at the battle of Sobraon (Medal). Served in the Indian campaign of 1857-58 and present at the Mutiny at Dinapore and attempt to relieve Arrah in July 1857, advance on Lucknow and actions at Chanda, Umeerpore, Sultanpore, and Douraha, siege and capture of Lucknow, relief of Azimghur, operations in the Jugdespore Jungle and capture of that place; subsequently commanded a detachment in garrison at Arrah and was engaged in several skirmishes in its vicinity (Medal).

38 Lieut. Carlisle served from 12th Nov. 1857 against the Mutineers in India, including the operations at Cawnpore on 26th, 27th, and 28th Nov. and its defence till the defeat of the Gwalior Mutineers on 6th Dec. and action of Kalleo Nuddee; campaign in Rohilcund, including the actions of Bugawalla and Nugena, relief of Moradabad, action on the Dojura, assault and capture of Bareilly, attack and bombardment of Shahjehanpore defeat of the rebels and relief of the garrison, capture of the fort of Bunnai, pursuit of the enemy to the left bank of the Goomtee, and destruction of the fort of Mahundee, attack on and destruction of Shahabad.

38† Captain Lawrence-Archer served with the 24th Regt. throughout the Punjaub campaign of 1848-49, including the battles of Sadoolapoore, Chillianwallah (wounded), and Goojerat (Medal and Clasps).

39 Lieut. Curtis served in the campaign of 1857 against the Mutineers in India, including the actions on the Hindun, battle of Budlee ke Serai and taking the heights before Delhi, subsequent siege operations, assault and capture of the City with the final attack on and occupation of the Palace; was wounded on the 13th June and again at the assault on 14th September.

40 Lieuts. Ashburnham, Jennings, Kelly, and Heathcote served the campaign of 1857-58 against the Mutineers in India, including the actions on the Hindun, battle of Budlee ke Serai and taking the heights before Delhi, subsequent siege operations, assault and capture of the City with the final attack on and occupation of the Palace; campaign in Rohilcund, including the actions of Bugawalla and Nugena, relief of Moradabad, action on the Dojura, assault and capture of Bareilly, attack and bombardment of Shahjehanpore defeat of the rebels and relief of the garrison, capture of the fort of Bunnai, pursuit of the enemy to the left bank of the Goomtee, and destruction of the fort of Mahundee, attack and destruction of Shahabad. Lieut. Heathcote was wounded before Delhi on 17th June.

41 Lieut. Morgan served in the campaign of 1857-58 against the Mutineers in India, including the battle of Budlee ke Serai and taking the heights before Delhi, subsequent siege operations, assault and capture of the City with the final attack on and occupation of the Palace; campaign in Rohilcund, including the actions of Bugawalla and Nugena, relief of Moradabad, action on the Dojura, assault and capture of Bareilly, attack and bombardment of Shahjehanpore defeat of the rebels and relief of the garrison, capture of the fort of Bunnai, pursuit of the enemy to the left bank of the Goomtee, and destruction of the fort of Mahundee, attack and destruction of Shahabad.

42 Lieut. Austin was engaged in active service in India in 1857 in dispersing Insurgent Villagers. Served the campaign in Rohilcund in 1858, including the actions of Bugawalla and Nugena, relief of Moradabad, action on the Dojura, assault and capture of Bareilly, attack and bombardment of Shahjehanpore defeat of the rebels and relief of the garrison, capture of the fort of Bunnai, pursuit of the enemy to the left bank of the Goomtee, and destruction of the fort of Mahundee, attack and destruction of Shahabad.

43 Lieut. Preston served the campaign in Rohilcund in 1858, including the actions of Bugawalla and Nugena, relief of Moradabad, action on the Dojura, assault and capture of Bareilly, attack and bombardment of Shahjehanpore defeat of the rebels and relief of the garrison.

44 Lieut. Orchard, and Doctor Oliver served the campaign 'in Rohilcund in 1858, including the actions of Bugawalla and Nugena, relief of Moradabad, action on the Dojura, assault and capture of Bareilly, attack and bombardment of Shahjehanpore defeat of the rebels and relief of the garrison, capture of the fort of Bunnai, pursuit of the enemy to the left bank of the Goomtee, and destruction of the fort of Mahundee, attack on and destruction of Shahabad.

45 Lieut. Young was engaged in active service in India in 1857 in dispersing Insurgent Villagers.

46 Lieut. Turle served in the campaign of 1857 against the Mutineers in India, including the actions on the Hindun, battle of Budlee ke Serai and taking the heights before Delhi, the subsequent siege operations until dangerously wounded on 10th August.

47 Lieut. Mortimer served in the campaign of 1857-58 against the Mutineers in India, including dispersion of Insurgent Villagers, siege of Delhi from 7th Sept., assault and capture of the City, with the final attack on and occupation of the Palace; campaign in Rohilcund, including the actions of Bugawalla and Nugena, relief of Moradabad, action on the Dojura, assault and capture of Bareilly, attack and bombardment of Shahjehanpore defeat of the rebels and relief of the garrison, capture of the fort of Bunnai, pursuit of the enemy to the left bank of the Goomtee, and destruction of the fort of Mahundee, attack on and destruction of Shahabad.

49 Qr. Master Hunter served in the Punjaub campaign of 1848-49, including the siege and capture of Mooltan from 28th Dec. 48 to 22nd Jan. 49, battle of Goojerat, pursuit and surrender of Shere Sing, occupation of Attock and Peshawur (Medal and two Clasps). Served the campaign of 1857-58 against the Mutineers in India, including the actions on the Hindun, battle of Budlee ke Serai and attack of the heights before Delhi, subsequent siege operations, assault and capture of the City with the final attack on and occupation of the Palace; campaign in Rohilcund, including actions of Bugawalla and Nugena, relief of Moradabad, action on the Dojura, assault and capture of Bareilly, attack and bombardment of Shahjehanpore defeat of the rebels and relief of the garrison, capture of the fort of Bunnai, pursuit of the enemy to the left bank of the Goomtee, and destruction of the fort of Mahundee, attack and destruction of Shahabad.

61st (*The South Gloucestershire*) Regt. of Foot. [Mauritius. Depot, Pembroke.

The Sphinx, with the words, "EGYPT" "TALAVERA" "SALAMANCA" "PYRENEES" "NIVELLE" "NIVE" "ORTHES" "TOULOUSE" "PENINSULA"—Flank Companies, "MAIDA" "PUNJAUB" "CHILLIANWALLAH" "GOOJERAT."

Years' Serv.		
Full Pay	Half Pay	
60		**Colonel.**—⦿ ⦿⦿⦿ John Reeve,¹ *Ens.* 23 Oct. 00; *Lieut. and Capt.* 11 April 05; *Capt. and Lieut.-Col.* 25 Dec. 13; *Col.* 22 July 30; *Major.-Gen.* 23 Nov. 41; *Lt.-Gen.* 11 Nov. 51; *Gen.* 7 Dec. 59; *Col.* 61st Foot, 11 Oct. 52.
35	0	**Lieut.-Colonels.**—William Jones,² CB. *Ens.* 10 April 25; *Lieut.* P 12 Dec. 26; *Capt.* P 24 Nov. 35; *Maj.* 26 July 44; *Lt.-Col.* P 29 Dec. 48; *Col.* 28 Nov. 54.
25	0	Charles Clement Deacon,³ CB. *Ens.* P 28 Aug. 35; *Lieut.* P 2 Dec. 37; *Capt.* 26 July 44; *Maj.* 19 Aug. 49; *Lt.-Col.* P 11 May 55.
29	0	**Majors.**—Henry Garner Rainey,⁴ *Ens.* 12 April 31; *Lieut.* 8 June 33; *Capt*; P 27 Dec. 42; *Major,* P 20 April 49; *Brevet-Lt.-Col.* 22 Aug. 56.
18	0	John Patrick Redmond,⁵ *Ens.* 7 Jan. 42; *Lt.* P 29 Sept. 43; *Capt.* 20 May 48; *Major,* P 11 May 55.

		CAPTAINS.	ENSIGN.	LIEUT.	CAPTAIN.	BREV.-MAJ.
18	0	Alexander Wm. Gordon⁶	P 11 Mar. 42	P 3 May 44	P 20 Dec. 48	19 Jan. 58
18	0	Wm. Ed. Durand Deacon⁷	3 June 42	P 26 Jan. 44	28 July 49	19 Jan. 58
20	0	Robert Cecil Dudgeon⁸ ..	P 28 Aug. 40	26 July 44	20 July 50	
18	0	Hon. E. Hillm. Burnside⁹	27 Dec. 42	26 July 44	P 2 Sept. 51	19 Jan. 58
18	0	Edw. Thomas Wickham¹⁰	P 19 Aug. 42	26 July 44	13 Feb. 52	
16	0	Drought Rich. Croasdaile	3 May 44	23 April 46	15 Mar. 53	
15	0	Robert Greig¹¹	P 22 July 45	20 Nov. 47	P 11 May 55	
13	0	Thomas Maitland Moore¹⁴	20 July 47	5 June 49	2 Oct. 57	
11	0	Stephen M'Donough¹⁵ ..	10 Apr. 49	P 7 June 50	27 July 58	
6	0	Henry N. Cotton Thurston	22 Dec. 54	13 Apr. 55	P 24 Dec. 58	
11	0	Thomas John Sadleir¹⁶ ..	27 April 49	13 Feb. 52	28 May 59	
13	0	Thomas Rice Hamilton ..	P 12 Nov. 47	P 4 Apr. 51	27 Feb. 58	
		LIEUTENANTS.				
10	0	Arthur Cotton Young¹⁸ ..	P 15 Feb. 50	P 21 May 52	3 Lt.-Col. Deacon served in the Punjaub campaign of 1848-9, present at the passage of the Chenab, and in the battles of Sadoolapore, Chillianwallah, and Goojerat, and with the field force in pursuit of the enemy to the Khyber Pass in March 1849 (Medal and two Clasps). Expedition into the Euzofzie country; in action with the enemy 11 and 14 Dec. 1849; present at the capture and destruction of the insurgent villages of Saggow, Pullee, Zoormundie, and Sheerkanee on those days, in which he commanded the portion (300 men) of his Regt. employed. Commanded the 61st Regt. at the siege, assault, and capture of Delhi in 1857 and at the repulse of the Sortie of 23rd Aug., and commanded the Column which assaulted and took the Magazine in the city of Delhi on 16th September (CB.).	
9	0	H. G. Austin Vicars,¹⁹ *Adj.*	P 17 Oct. 51	P 27 Oct. 54		
11	0	Robert Hutton	P 29 May 49	19 Jan. 55		
8	0	John Sloman²⁰	P 17 Aug. 52	P 11 May 55		
8	0	Charles John Griffiths²¹ ..	P 17 Dec. 52	P 7 Sept. 55		
8	0	Henry John Yonge²²	24 July 52	15 Dec. 55		
5	0	Thomas Bruce Hutton²³	P 19 Jan. 55	27 July 55		
5	0	Charles Henry Boileau²⁴	31 Aug. 55	P 7 May 57		
4	0	Thomas Casement²⁵	P 8 Feb. 56	1 Sept. 57		
4	0	Edwyn Brenton Andros²⁶	P 7 Mar. 56	8 Sept. 57		
3	0	Miah Murphy..........	P 31 July 57	27 July 58		
3	0	Arthur Jolliffe Tuffnell²⁷	P 15 May 57	1 Oct. 58		
3	0	Edward Waugh Rumsey	P 27 Nov. 57	P 30 Aug. 59		
5	0	Samuel F. Sewell	14 June 55	8 Dec. 56		
3	0	Frederick John Fane....	18 Dec. 57	13 Dec. 59		
		ENSIGNS.				
3	0	James Graham Hamilton	18 Dec. 57			
2	0	William Sydney Nugent..	12 Feb. 58			
2	0	William Edward Ness ..	5 Mar. 58			
2	0	Chas. Hercules Atkinson	P 15 June 58			
2	0	John Robert Cockle	P 24 Aug. 58			
2	0	Edward Ellis Borton	12 Nov. 58			
1	0	John David Wedgwood..	P 31 May 59			
1	0	William Fraser	5 Aug. 59			
1	0	Geo. Ernest P. Madden..	P 28 Oct. 59			

10	0	*Paymaster.*—William Dowler,¹⁰ 26 Mar. 58; *Ens.* 22 Oct. 50; *Lt.* 24 Sept. 55.	
9	0	*Adjutant.*—Lieut. Henry George Austin Vicars,¹⁹ 20 Feb. 55.	
2	0	*Instructor of Musketry.*—Ensign W. S. Nugent, 1 Dec. 58.	
4	0	*Quarter-Master.*—John Dowler,²⁹ 22 July 56.	
10	0	*Surgeon.*—Herbert Taylor Reade, 3 Nov. 57; *Assist. Surg.* 8 Nov. 50.	
5	0	*Assistant Surgeons.*—Alfred Hoyte,³⁰ 27 March 55.	Facings Buff.
3	0	Charles Mackinnon, 28 Sept. 57.	Agents, Messrs. Cox & Co.

[*Embarked for India,* 1 July 1845.]

1 General Reeve served with the Grenadier Guards in Sicily in 1806-7; Sir John Moore's campaign in 1808-9, and was present at the battle of Corunna. With the expedition to Walcheren in 1809. Went to Cadiz in 1811, and remained in the Peninsula until the beginning of 1814; present at the passage of the Bidassoa, battles of the Nivelle and Nive. Served also the campaign of 1815, including the battles of Quatre Bras and Waterloo, storming of Peronne and capture of Paris. Remained with the Army of Occupation until its return to England in 1818. He has received the War Medal with three Clasps.

2 Colonel Jones served with the 61st in the Punjaub campaign of 1848-9, was present at the passage of the Chenab, and in the battles of Sadoolapore and Chillianwallah; after which he commanded the Regt. at the battle of Goojerat; and he commanded a portion of Sir Walter Gilbert's field force, consisting of a troop of Bengal Horse Artillery and the 61st Regt. in pursuit of the enemy to the Khyber Pass in March 1849 (Medal and two Clasps, and CB.). Commanded as Brigadier the 2nd Infantry Brigade at the siege of Delhi in 1857 and repulse of the Sortie of the 9th July; commanded the 2nd Column at the assault on the 14th Sept., during which the command of the 1st Column devolved on him on the fall of General Nicholson, he continued in command of both Columns during the six days' fighting within the City until its final capture on the 20th September.

4 Lt. Col. Rainey served throughout the whole of the operations in China (Medal), commencing with the first taking of Chusan, and terminating with the demonstration before Nankin, including the storm and capture of the heights above Canton, attack and capture of Amoy, second capture of Chusan, attack and

61st (The South Gloucestershire) Regt. of Foot.

capture of the heights of Chinhae, occupation of Ningpo, repulse of the night-attack on Ningpo, attack and capture of the enemy's entrenched camp on the heights of Segoan, attack and capture of Chapoo, Woosung, and Chinkiangfoo. Served with the 61st Regt. at the siege, assault, and capture of Delhi, and commanded the Wing engaged at the action of Nujjufghur.

5 Major Redmond served throughout the Punjaub campaign of 1848-49, and was present at the passage of the Chenab, and in the battles of Sadoolapore, Chillianwallah, and Goojerat, and with the field force in pursuit of the enemy to the Khyber Pass (Medal and two Clasps). Expedition into the Eusufzie country. Skirmishes near Saggow and Zoormundio on 11th and 14th Dec. 1849. Commanded the flank companies 61st Regt. with the force under Sir Colin Campbell at the forcing of the Kohat Pass in Feb. 1850. Commanded detachment 61st Regt. which repulsed the attack of the mutinous Sepoys on the magazine at Ferozepore on 13th May 1857, and was severely wounded. Served at the siege (from 14th Aug.), assault, and capture of Delhi.

6 Major Gordon served at the siege, assault, and capture of Delhi, and commanded the Reserve at the action of Nujjufghur (Bt. Major).

7 Major Deacon served in the Punjaub campaign of 1848-9; present at the passage of the Chenab, and in the battles of Sadoolapore, Chillianwallah, and Goojerat, and with the field force in pursuit of the enemy to the Khyber Pass in March 1849 (Medal and two Clasps). Served the siege and assault (severely wounded) of Delhi, and at the action of Nujjufghur (Bt. Major).

8 Captain Dudgeon served on the Staff from 7th March 1858 in the Dooab and Rohilcund and was present at the action of 30th April and 5th May and throughout the operations leading to the fall of Bareilly.

9 Major Burnside served in the Punjaub campaign of 1848-9; present at the passage of the Chenab, and in the battles of Sadoolapore, Chillianwallah, and Goojerat, and with the field force in pursuit of the enemy to the Khyber Pass in March 1849 (Medal and two Clasps). Served as Brigade Major to the 3rd Infantry Brigade at the siege, assault, and capture of Delhi (severely wounded), and repulse of the sortie of the 9th July 1857—wounded (Bt. Major).

10 Captain Wickham and Paymaster Dowler served in the Punjaub campaign of 1848-9; present at the passage of the Chenab, and in the battles of Sadoolapore, Chillianwallah, and Goojerat, and with the field force in pursuit of the enemy to the Khyber Pass (Medal and two Clasps). Paymaster Dowler served at the siege, assault, and capture of Delhi in 1857, and of Nujjufghur.

11 Captain Greig served in the Punjaub campaign of 1848-9 (Medal and Clasp), was present at the passage of the Chenab, and in the battles of Sadoolapore and Goojerat, and with the field force in pursuit of the enemy to the Khyber Pass in March 1849; expedition into the Euzofzie country; in action with the enemy 11th and 14th Dec. 1849; present at the capture and destruction of the insurgent villages of Saggow, Pullee, Zoormundie, and Sheerkanee.

14 Captain Moore served in the Punjaub campaign of 1848-9, and was present at the battle of Goojerat, and with the field force in pursuit of the enemy to the Khyber Pass in March 1849 (Medal and Clasp); expedition to Kohat against the Affreedie Tribe 10th, 11th, 12th, and 13th Feb. 1850. Served at the siege, assault, and capture of Delhi in 1857 (wounded), and action of Nujjufghur.

15 Captain M'Donough served in the Punjaub campaign of 1848-9, was present at the passage of the Chenab, and battles of Chillianwallah (wounded) and Goojerat, and with the field force in pursuit of the enemy to the Khyber Pass in March 1849 (Medal and two Clasps). Served at the siege, assault, and capture of Delhi and action of Nujjufghur.

16 Captain Sadleir served against the Hill Tribes on the Peshawur frontier in 1851. Also in the Indian campaign of 1857-59; commanded a dogra contingent under General Van Courtlandt in Hurriana and led the attack on the rebel position at Khyrakee on 19th June 1857, relieved Hansic 12th July, action at Hissar, and commanded the Infantry employed in the attack on and destruction of the rebel village of Mungalee; acted also as staff officer of the force during the time it was actively engaged. Commanded the 4th Oude Cavalry (Military Police) during the campaign in Oude in 1858-59, and was present at the destruction of Selimpore, actions of Kintore, Dacoodpore, Bursingpore, and Burtapore (received the thanks of Government on three occasions, Medal).

18 Lieut. A. C. Young served at the siege and assault of Delhi including the action of Nujjufghur, and was severely wounded at the assault causing the loss of the use of the right arm.

19 Lieut. Vicars served as Adjutant 61st Regt. at the siege, assault, and capture of Delhi, and repulse of Sorties on 4th, 9th, 18th (horse shot), and 23rd July 1857.

20 Lieut. Sloman served from 1st July 1857 as Orderly Officer to Brigadier Wm. Jones at the siege, assault, and capture of Delhi, and repulse of Sorties on 9th July and 23rd August.

21 Lieut. Griffiths served at the siege and capture of Delhi and repulse of Sorties on 4th and 9th July 1857 (wounded).

22 Lieut. H. J. Yonge served at the siege of Delhi including repulse of Sorties on 18th July and 12th August.

23 Lieut. T. B. Hutton served with the 21st Fusiliers during the latter part of 1855, and at the siege and fall of Sebastopol, and the expedition to Kinbourn (Medal and Clasp). Served with the 61st Regt. at the siege, assault and capture of Delhi in 1857, including repulse of Sorties on 4th, 18th, and 23rd July, and 1st August (wounded).

24 Lieut. Boileau served with the 61st Regt. at the siege, assault, and capture of Delhi (and as a Volunteer with the Artillery from 26th Aug. till its fall), including repulse of sorties on 4th 18th and 23rd July, and 1st Aug. 1857.

25 Lieut. Casement served at the siege of Delhi and was present at the repulse of Sorties on 4th and 18th July and 1st Aug. 1857.

26 Lieut. Andros served at the siege, assault, and capture of Delhi, including repulse of Sorties on 4th, 9th (wounded) and 18th July and action of Nujjufghur.

27 Lieut. Tuffnell served with the 93rd Highlanders at the relief of the Garrison of Lucknow in Nov. 1857, at the defence of Cawnpore and defeat of the Gwalior Mutineers there and at Serai Ghat, also present at the action of Kalee Nuddee.

28 Qr. Master Dowler served at the siege and capture of Delhi.

30 Assist. Surgeon Hoyte served at the siege, assault, and capture of Delhi, including the action of Nujjufghur.

62nd (The Wiltshire) Regt. of Foot. [For Service, 11 Feb. 54. Nova Scotia. Dep. Belfast.

"NIVE" "PENINSULA" "FEROZESHAH" "SOBRAON" "SEVASTOPOL."

Years' Serv.	Full Pay.	Half Pay.					
47			*Colonel.*—13 William Thomas Knollys,¹ *Ens.* 9 Dec. 13; *Lieut. & Capt.* 25 Sept. 17; *Capt. & Lt.-Col.* P 31 Dec. 27; *Col.* 23 Nov. 41; *Major-Gen.* 20 June 54; *Colonel,* 62nd Foot, 16 Nov. 58.					
18	0		*Lieut.-Colonel.*—William Lenox Ingall,² CB. *Ens.* 27 Dec. 42; *Lieut.* 23 July 45; *Capt.* P 7 Feb. 51; *Maj.* 8 June 55; *Lt.Col.* 25 Oct. 55.					
15	0		*Majors.*—James Daubeny,³ CB. *Ens.* 4 July 45; *Lieut.* P 28 April 46; *Capt.* P 6 July 52; *Maj.* 8 June 55; *Brevet Lt.-Col.* 2 Nov. 55.					
15	0		M'Kay Rynd,⁴ *Ens.* P 16 Dec. 45; *Lieut.* P 5 Mar. 47; *Capt.* P 2 Sept. 53; *Maj.* 25 Oct. 55.					

			CAPTAINS.	ENSIGN.	LIEUT.	CAPTAIN.	BREV.-MAJ.
12	0		Geo. Hampden Wilkieson⁵	P 8 Dec. 48	P 7 Feb. 51	6 June 54	
13	0		G. Stoddart Whitmore⁶ ..	23 Jan. 47	P 21 May 50	7 July 54	6 June 56
15	0		Samuel George Carter⁷..	13 June 45	18 July 48	21 July 54	
11	0		Charles M. S. L. Gwynne⁸	P 13 Apr. 49	P 23 Sept. 51	P 17 Nov. 54	
11	0		Joseph Sanderson¹⁰	25 Sept. 49	16 Aug. 52	29 Dec. 54	
8	0		Graham Hay¹¹	P 18 Aug. 52	P 28 Oct. 53	P 16 Feb. 55	
8	0		Edward Hunter¹²	P 17 Aug. 52	P 2 Sept. 53	8 June 55	
8	0		Bradney Todd Gilpin⁸ ..	P 17 Dec. 52	28 Mar. 54	8 June 55	
11	0		Holt Waring Clerke¹³....	23 Nov. 49	P 26 Mar. 52	8 June 55	
7	0		Chas. Campbell Cubitt¹⁴	P 26 July 53	P 3 Nov. 54	9 Sept. 55	
7	0		Geo. Wm. B. Hughes¹⁵ ..	P 2 Sept. 53	P 17 Nov. 54	25 Oct. 55	
6	0		Herrick Augustus Palmer¹⁶	P 27 Jan. 54	8 Dec. 54	P 20 May 57	

LIEUTENANTS.

6	0		Wm. Bromley Davenport¹⁷	7 Apr. 54	15 Dec. 54
6	0		Thomas Milsom,¹⁸ *Adj.*..	31 Aug. 54	9 Feb. 55
6	0		Robert Scott Machell ..	1 Sept. 54	9 Feb. 55
6	0		John Joshua Rowan	24 Nov. 54	9 Mar. 55
5	0		William Montagu Tharp..	5 Jan. 55	9 Mar. 55
5	0		John Manners Kerr	25 Jan. 55	4 May 55
5	0		Lorenzo G. Dundas¹⁹....	P 26 Jan. 55	8 June 55
5	0		Conrad Sawyer	9 Mar. 55	8 June 55
5	0		Wm. Lane Robinson Scott	14 Mar. 55	9 Sept. 55
5	0		Adolphus Fred. Walsh ..	16 Mar. 55	9 Sept. 55
5	0		George Fox Grant	23 Mar. 55	23 Oct. 55
5	0		Archibald George Keen..	7 Oct. 55	P 14 Dec. 55
5	0		Matt. Beachcroft Harrison	11 May 55	26 Feb. 56
5	0		Macdonald Hall	23 Oct. 55	P 24 June 56
4	0		Arthur Lloyd Reade	26 Feb. 56	P 10 Sept. 58

ENSIGNS.

5	0		John Paine Sargent	23 Oct. 55
3	0		Jules Victor Le Blond ..	18 Dec. 57
2	0		John Medows Theobald..	P 5 Feb. 58
2	0		Charles W. Brown......	P 30 Apr. 58
2	0		Arthur Lake	P 13 July 58
2	0		Fred. Howes Horneman..	8 Oct. 58
2	0		Samuel Waring	29 Oct. 58
2	0		John Henry Pagan	P 9 Nov. 58
1	0		Edward Hoare Reeves ..	P 18 Jan. 59
1	0		John L. Bland	24 June 59

11	0	*Instructor of Musketry.*—Capt. J. Sanderson, 28 July 56.
6	0	*Paymaster.*—William Dring,²⁰ 7 Sept. 55; *Ens.* 5 Nov. 54; *Lieut.* 26 Feb. 55.
6	0	*Adjutant.*—Lieut. Thomas Milsom, 2 March 55.
5	0	*Quarter Master.*—James Gamble,²¹ 2 Feb. 55.
19	0	*Surgeon.*—Frederick Wm. Tupper, 26 Dec. 51; *Assist. Surg.* 8 June 41.
6	0	*Assistant Surgeons.*—Sydney Alder, 3 Nov. 54.
6	0	James Petrie Street,²² M.D. 9 June 54.

Facings Buff.—*Agent,* Edward S. Codd, Esq.
Irish Agents, Sir E. R. Borough, *Bt.,* Armit & Co.

4 Major Rynd served in the trenches before Sebastopol from 19th May 1855 to the end of the siege (Medal and Clasp, and 5th Class of the Medjidie).

5 Captain Wilkieson served at the siege of Sebastopol in 1854-55, including the sortie of 6th April, and attack on the Quarries 8th June, and on the Redan 18th June (Medal and Clasp, Sardinian Medal, and 5th Class of the Medjidie).

6 Major Whitmore served in the latter part of the Kaffir war in 1847. Was in the action of Boem Plants and defeat of the Insurgent Boers in 1848. Served throughout the Kaffir war of 1851-52, and was present with the 2nd Division in nearly every affair, including the storming of the Iron Mountain. Commanded Sir Harry Smith's escort from March to Nov. 1851, during which time he was repeatedly employed as a staff officer with the various columns on patrol. Acted as Major of Brigade to the 2nd Division from Nov. 1851 to Oct. 1852; and as Brigade Major to the Cavalry Brigade in the Expedition under Sir George Cathcart, ending in the battle of Berea. He has had two horses shot under him in action, and has been repeatedly thanked in Brigade and Division Orders, as well as in the General Orders and Dispatches of Sir H. Smith and of Sir G. Cathcart (Medal). Brevet Major, and 4th Class of the Medjidie, for Service with the Turkish Contingent.

1 Major-General Knollys served with the Scots Fusilier Guards from the 6th March to the end of the Peninsular War in 1814, and was present at the blockade of Bayonne, repulse of the sortie—on which occasion Sir Henry Sullivan and ten officers of the Guards were killed or died of their wounds.

2 Lt.-Colonel Ingall served the Sutlej campaign of 1845-46, including the battles of Ferozeshah (wounded) and Sobraon (Medal and Clasps). Served also at the siege of Sebastopol in 1854-55, including the sortie of 6th April, and attack on the Quarries on the 8th June—wounded (Medal and Clasp, CB., Knight of the Legion of Honor, Sardinian Medal, and 5th Class of the Medjidie).

3 Lt.-Colonel Daubeny served with the 62nd at the siege of Sebastopol in 1854-55, including the sortie of 6th April, and attack on the Quarries 8th June (succeeded to the command), on the Redan 18th June (commanded the Regt.), and again on the 8th Sept. (Medal and Clasp, Bt.Lt.-Col., Knight of the Legion of Honor, and 5th Class of the Medjidie).

7 Captain Carter served with the 51st Regt. during the war in Burmah from April to August 1852; was on board the E. I. C. steam sloop *Sesostris* during the naval action and destruction of the enemy's stockades on the Rangoon River, served during the succeeding three days' operations in the vicinity, and at the storm and capture of Rangoon; also at the assault and capture of Bassein 19th May (severely wounded). Was mentioned in General Godwin's Dispatches as "deserving the best consideration of Government" for his services at the capturing by storm the enemy's stronghold and entrenched position south of Bassein, armed with sixteen guns and twenty gingalls; and honoured with the best thanks of the Governor-General in Council (Medal).

8 Captains Gwynne and Gilpin served at the siege of Sebastopol in 1854-55 (Medal and Clasp).

10 Captain Sanderson served the Sutlej campaign of 1845-46, including the battles of Ferozeshah and Sobraon (Medal and Clasps).

11 Captain Hay served at the siege of Sebastopol in 1854-55, including the attack on the Quarries (Medal and Clasp, and 5th Class of the Medjidie).

12 Captain Hunter served at the siege of Sebastopol in 1854-55, including the sortie of 5th May, attack on the Quarries 8th June, and on the Redan 8th Sept.—wounded (Medal and Clasp, Knight of the Legion of Honor, and 5th Class of the Medjidie).

13 Captain Clerke served at the siege of Sebastopol from May 1855, including the attack on the Quarries (Medal and Clasp).

14 Captain Cubitt served at the siege of Sebastopol in 1854-55, including the sorties of 6th April and 10th May, and attack on the Quarries, and of the Redan on 18th June, and was wounded in the trenches on 28th May (Medal and Clasp, and 5th Class of the Medjidie).

15 Captain Hughes served at the siege of Sebastopol and taking of the Quarries (Medal and Clasp).

16 Captain Palmer served at the siege of Sebastopol in 1855, and was taken prisoner at the attack on the Redan on the 8th Sept. (Medal and Clasp, and 5th Class of the Medjidie).

17 Lieut. Davenport served at the siege of Sebastopol in 1855, and was severely wounded at the attack on the Redan on the 8th Sept. (Medal and Clasp, and 5th Class of the Medjidie).

18 Lieut. Milsom served at the siege of Sebastopol in 1855, including the attack on the Quarries on 8th June, and on the Redan 18th June and 8th Sept. (Medal and Clasp).

19 Lieut. Dundas served at the siege of Sebastopol in 1855, and at the attack on the Redan on the 8th Sept. (Medal and Clasp).

20 Paymaster Dring served the Sutlej campaign of 1845-46, and was wounded at the battle of Ferozeshah (Medal). Served also at the siege of Sebastopol in 1855, including sorties of 5th and 10th May, and attack on the Redan on the 8th Sept. (wounded: Medal and Clasp).

21 Quarter Master Gamble served the Sutlej campaign of 1845-46, including the battles of Ferozeshah (severely wounded) and Sobraon (Medal and Clasp).

22 Doctor Street served in the Crimea from 10th May 1855, including the siege and fall of Sebastopol, and attacks of the Redan on the 18th June and 8th Sept. (Medal and Clasp).

[*Continuation of Notes to 63rd Foot.*]

10 Captains Paterson and Bowles, Paymaster Ingram, Ass't.Surgeons Mills and O'Dell, and Qr.Master Linford, served throughout the Eastern campaign of 1854-55, including the battles of Alma, Balaklava, and Inkerman, siege, assaults, and fall of Sebastopol, expedition to Kertch, bombardment and capture of Kinbourn (Medal and Clasps). Captain Paterson has also the Sardinian Medal. Captains Paterson and Bowles have the 5th Class of the Medjidie.

11 Captain Marson served the Eastern campaign of 1854-55, including the siege, assaults, and fall of Sebastopol (Medal and Clasp), expedition to Kertch, bombardment and capture of Kinbourn.

13 Capt. Hunt served at the siege, assaults, and fall of Sebastopol from 31st January 1855 (Medal and Clasp).

14 Captains Hand and Dumaresq served the Eastern campaign of 1855, including the expedition to Kertch, siege, assaults, and fall of Sebastopol, bombardment and capture of Kinbourn (Medal and Clasp).

15 Captain Beamish served in the Crimea from 12th November 1854, including the siege and fall of Sebastopol, repulse of various sorties, attacks of the 18th June and 8th September, expedition to Kertch, bombardment and capture of Kinbourn (Medal and Clasp).

17 Lieut. Pye served at the siege and fall of Sebastopol from 5th Aug. 1855 (Medal and Clasp).

18 Lieuts. Moore, Archer, Ramsbottom, and Griffiths, and Surgeon Crisp, served at the siege and fall of Sebastopol in 1855; also at the bombardment and capture of Kinbourn (Medal and Clasp).

19 Lieuts. Bruce and Vieth served at the siege and fall of Sebastopol; also at the bombardment and capture of Kinbourn (Medal and Clasp).

290   63rd (*The West Suffolk*) *Regt. of Foot.*   [For. Service, 22 July 54. Nova Scotia. Depôt, Belfast.

"EGMONT-OP-ZEE" "MARTINIQUE" "GUADALOUPE" "ALMA"
"INKERMAN" " SEVASTOPOL."

Years' Serv.		
Full Pay	Half Pay	
61		Colonel.—**19** Thomas Kenah,[1] CB. *Ens.* 14 Aug. 99; *Lt.* 9 May 00; *Capt.* 3 Mar. 04; *Major*, 5 Nov. 12; *Lieut.-Col.* 27 Dec. 13; *Col.* 22 July 30; *Maj.-Gen.* 23 Nov. 41; *Lt.-Gen.* 11 Nov. 51; *Col.* 63rd Foot, 25 Nov. 50.
27	0	*Lieut.-Colonel.*—Thomas Harries,[3] *Ens.* P 19 July 33; *Lieut.* P 2 May 34; *Capt.* P 26 Jan. 44; *Major*, 6 Nov. 54; *Brevet-Lt.-Col.* 6 June 56; *Lt.Col.* 17 Sept. 58.
23	0	*Majors.*—William Fred. Carter,[4] *Ens.* P 1 Dec. 37; *Lieut.* 2 April 41; *Capt.* 4 June 47; *Brev.-Maj.* 2 Nov. 55; *Maj.* P 7 March 56.
14	0	Francis Douglas Grey,[5] *Ens.* 9 May 46; *Lieut.* P 13 Aug. 47; *Capt.* P 4 Nov. 53; *Major*, 17 Sept. 58.

		CAPTAINS.	ENSIGN.	LIEUT.	CAPTAIN.	BREV.-MAJ.
13	0	Chas. Le Mesurier Carey[6]	P 13 Aug. 47	P 18 Jan. 50	6 Nov. 54	6 June 56
12	0	F. T. Logan Paterson[10] ..	26 May 48	P 26 Dec. 51	29 Dec. 54	
9	0	Robert Bennett[7]	P 17 Oct. 51	6 June 54	P 24 Apr. 55	
11	0	Vere Hunt Bowles[10]	P 10 April 49	P 12 Aug. 53	8 July 55	
7	0	Archibald Wybergh[12]	P 13 May 53	6 Nov. 54	P 21 Sept. 55	
11	0	William Fitz Roy	P 29 May 49	P 10 Feb. 54	2 Nov. 55	
10	0	Edward Joseph Hunt[13]..	P 17 Sept. 50	P 23 Dec. 53	24 Feb. 56	
8	0	Charles Augustus Hand[14]	P 11 June 52	6 June 54	P 14 July 57	
11	0	Francis Retallack, *s*	P 2 Nov. 49	P 18 June 52	P 22 May 57	
6	0	Alex. Macleay Dumaresq[14]	1 Sept. 54	9 Feb. 55	P 4 Dec. 57	
6	0	Geo. Perceval Beamish[15]	23 June 54	10 Nov. 54	26 Mar. 58	
6	0	Walter Sam. Marson[11] ..	5 Nov. 54	2 Mar. 55	17 Sept. 58	
		LIEUTENANTS.				
6	0	Stewart Hervey Bruce[16]..	P 17 Nov. 54	2 Mar. 55		
6	0	Charles Colquhoun Pye[17]	14 Dec. 54	8 Mar. 55		
6	0	Stephen Moore[18]........	15 Dec. 54	9 Mar. 55		
6	0	Richard Hallilay Archer[18]	20 Dec. 54	9 Mar. 55		
5	0	Geo. W. Clutterbuck, *Adj.*	12 Jan. 55	1 May 55		
5	0	John Rd. Ramsbottom[10]	19 Jan. 55	8 July 55		
5	0	Arthur Geo. F. Griffiths[18]	13 Feb. 55	27 July 55		
5	0	Fred. Harris Dawes Vieth[19]	16 Feb. 55	27 July 55		
8	0	Thomas Coote Grant	P 23 Jan. 52	6 June 54		
5	0	George Rochfort Byron ..	30 Mar. 55	P 26 Oct. 55		
5	0	William Grogan Graves..	16 Mar. 55	P 23 Nov. 55		
5	0	Richard Wm.B. Crowther	26 July 55	P 15 Jan. 56		
5	0	James Power Boyd	10 Aug. 55	P 9 Nov. 58		
5	0	Charles Henry Kinahan	P 2 Nov. 55	P 24 June 59		
5	0	Wm. Lancelot Knowles..	P 7 Dec. 55	25 Aug. 59		
		ENSIGNS.				
4	0	Geo. W. Wynford Knapp	P 25 Jan. 56			
2	0	Francis Thomas Hulton	P 19 Nov. 58			
2	0	James Stewart Smyth ..	P 20 Nov. 58			
2	0	Thomas Atkinson	P 10 Nov. 58			
2	0	Thornton Scovell	30 Dec. 58			
1	0	John P. Mayers Burton .	P 11 Jan. 59			
1	0	Charles Ellison Terrot ..	18 Jan. 59			
1	0	Major Dawson Hill	P 3 June 59			
1	0	Daniel Fox Tarratt	P 1 July 59			
1	0	John Thacker..........	30 Sept. 59			
8	0	*Paymaster.*—Henry Ingram,[10] 7 Dec. 55; *Qr.M.* 16 July 52.				
5	0	*Adjutant.—Lieut.* George Watlin Clutterbuck, 12 Nov. 58.				
5	0	*Instructor of Musketry.—Lieut.* R. W. Barnardiston Crowther, 23 Oct. 59.				
5	0	*Quarter Master.*—James Linford,[10] 28 Dec. 55.				
12	0	*Surgeon.*—Henry Crisp,[18] M.B. 22 June 55 ; *Assist.-Surg.* 3 Nov. 48.				
6	0	*Assist. Surgeons.*—William Wilson Mills,[10] 28 March 54.				
6	0	Francis O'Dell,[10] 28 July 54.				

Facings Green.—*Agent*, Edward S. Codd, Esq.
Irish Agents, Sir E. R. Borough, *Bt.* Armit & Co.

1 Lt. General Kenah served in Holland in 1799, and was present in the action of the 19th of Sept., as well as in several other minor affairs. In Egypt, under Sir Ralph Abercromby in 1801; in Sicily from 1808 to 1812; subsequently on the eastern coast of Spain, as Assistant, and afterwards as Deputy-Adjutant-General at the Head of the Department, and was present at the battle of Castalla, as also several other affairs. Served also at the siege and capture of Genoa in April 1814. He has received the Gold Medal from the Grand Seignior for the Egyptian campaign, and also the Silver War Medal with one Clasp.

7 Captain Bennett served the Eastern campaign of 1854, including the battles of Alma, Balaklava, and Inkerman (severely wounded and horse shot) and siege of Sebastopol (Medal and Clasps).

12 Captain Wybergh served throughout the Eastern campaign of 1854-55, including the battles of Alma and Balaklava, expedition to Kertch, siege, assaults, and fall of Sebastopol, bombardment and capture of Kinbourn (Medal and Clasps, and 5th Class of the Medjidie).

3 Lt. Colonel Harries served the Eastern campaign of 1854, including the battles of Alma, Balaklava, and Inkerman (severely wounded), and siege of Sebastopol (Medal and Clasps, Brevet Lt.-Colonel, Knight of the Legion of Honor, and 5th Class of the Medjidie).
4 Major Carter served throughout the Eastern campaign of 1854-55 with the 63rd Regt., including the battles of Alma, Balaklava, and Inkerman, expedition to Kertch, siege, assaults, and fall of Sebastopol (succeeded to the command of the Regt. at the last attack), bombardment and capture of Kinbourn (Medal and Clasps, Brevet Major, Knight of the Legion of Honor, and 5th Class of the Medjidie).
5 Major Grey served as an Ensign in the 24th Bengal N. I. during the campaign on the Sutlej, and was present at the battle of Ferozeshah (Medal); served with the 63rd Regt. at the siege and fall of Sebastopol from 6 Sept. 1855 (Medal and Clasp), as also at the bombardment and capture of Kinbourn.
6 Major Carey served the Eastern campaign of 1854, and up to July 1855, including the battles of Alma, Balaklava, and Inkerman, and siege of Sebastopol (Medal and Clasps, and Brevet Major).

[For remainder of notes see preceding page.

Emb. for Bombay, Jan. 1849.
Serv. in India. Dep. Canterbury.] **64th (*The 2nd Staffordshire*) Regt. of Foot.** 291
"ST. LUCIA" "SURINAM."

Years' Serv.		
Full Pay	Half Pay	
54		Colonel.—19 James Freeth,[1] KH., *Ens.* 25 Dec. 06; *Lt.* 30 May 09; *Capt.* 21 April 14; *Major*, 21 Jan. 19; *Lt.-Col.* 11 July 26; *Col.* 23 Nov. 41; *Maj.-Gen.* 11 Nov. 51; *Lt. Gen.* 26 Oct. 58; *Col.* 64th Foot, 13 Aug. 55.
22	0	Lieut.-Colonels.—George Wm. Powlett Bingham,[2] CB. *Ens.* p 16 Feb. 38; *Lt.* 8 April 42; *Capt.* p 12 Sept. 48; *Major*, 10 Dec. 56; *Lt.Col.* 29 Nov. 57.
16	0	Neville Hill Shute,[4] *Ens.* p 22 Mar. 44; *Lt.* p 25 Sept. 46; *Capt.* p 9 Aug. 50; *Major*, 29 Nov. 57; *Br.Lt.Col.* 24 March 58; *Lt.Col.* 2 Sept. 59.
26	0	*Majors.*—Thomas Anderson,[5] *Ens.* 16 May 34; *Lieut.* p 29 Dec. 37; *Capt.* 22 Aug. 48; *Major*, 16 March 58.
17	0	Robert Mockler,[6] *Ens.* 12 Sept. 43; *Lt.* 12 Jan. 48; *Capt.* 9 May 51; *Brev.Maj.* 24 Mar. 58; *Major*, 2 Sept. 59.

		CAPTAINS.	ENSIGN.	LIEUT.	CAPTAIN.	BREV.-MAJ.
17	0	Henry Francis[7]	p 23 June 43	14 Sept. 45	15 Mar. 53	24 Mar. 58
15	0	Alfred Picton Bowlby[8]	31 Oct. 45	12 Mar. 48	15 Mar. 53	24 Mar. 58
14	0	Charles Thompson[9]	p 19 June 46	p 2 June 48	28 Oct. 53	
16	0	Winter Goode[10]	p 26 Apr. 44	p 28 Aug. 46	p 25 June 52	24 Mar. 58
13	0	William John Chads[11]	p 12 Nov. 47	p 12 Sept. 48	30 June 54	15 Dec. 54
13	0	Chamb. Henry Hinchliff	p 9 Apr. 47	p 3 Aug. 49	p 8 Feb. 56	
16	0	Matthew Fanning[12]	1 Feb. 44	14 Apr. 46	29 Nov. 57	
15	0	Godfrey Lyon Knight[13]	28 Feb. 45	17 Mar. 48	29 Nov. 57	
12	0	Frederick J. Hutchison[14]	22 Dec. 48	9 May 51	29 Nov. 57	
11	0	Stand. de Crey. O'Grady[15]	p 16 Feb. 49	5 Dec. 51	29 Nov. 57	
11	0	Valentine Ryan[15]	30 Nov. 49	2 Jan. 52	16 Mar. 58	
11	0	David Mortimer Murray	14 Dec. 49	p 26 Nov. 52	2 Sept. 59	

LIEUTENANTS.

10	0	Alfred John Tuke	p 15 Feb. 50	8 Jan. 53	
9	0	Alexander Benison[16]	p 18 Apr. 51	30 June 54	
7	0	Louis D'Acosta[18]	14 Mar. 53	23 Nov. 55	
5	0	Francis Du Bois Lukis[19]	p 30 Mar. 55	p 14 Dec. 55	
5	0	Robert Richard Fennessy	19 June 55	p 8 Feb. 56	
5	0	Geo. Hy. John Haldane[20]	p 23 Mar. 55	p 1 Apr. 56	
5	0	Chas. Hy. Laprimandaye	p 10 Aug. 55	p 29 Apr. 56	
5	0	John Thomas Pack,[22] *Adj.*	31 Aug. 55	p 24 July 57	
5	0	John William Taylor[23]	23 Nov. 55	29 Nov. 57	
4	0	Arthur W. L. Mirehouse[24]	p 1 Apr. 56	20 Nov. 57	
4	0	David Gardiner[25]	4 Dec. 56	30 Mar. 58	
5	0	Henry Edward Couper	5 Sept. 55	p 1 Mar. 57	
3	0	Henry Davies	p 24 July 57	22 Apr. 59	
3	0	William Henry Ashe	6 Nov. 57	2 Sept. 59	
5	0	George Robert Daniel	16 Nov. 55	p 16 Dec. 59	

4 Lt.Colonel Shute served with the 64th Regt. in Bengal and N. W. Provinces in suppressing the mutiny in 1857-58; present with Havelock's column in the actions of Futtehpore, Aoung, Pandoo Nuddee, Cawnpore, Onao, and Busseerut Gunge (1st and 2nd), Boorbeakeehowkee, Bithoor, Mungurwarra, Alumbagh, and first relief of Lucknow; present in three sorties, two of which he commanded (thanked by the Governor General in Council). Served in defence of Cawnpore and defeat of the Gwalior mutineers; also in the actions of Kala Nuddee and Kerkerouile, and capture of Bareilly (Brevet Lt.Colonel).

7 Major Francis served in Bengal and N. W. Provinces in suppressing the mutiny in 1857-58; served in defence of the Alumbagh, in the actions at the Dilkoosha, second relief of Lucknow, defence of Cawnpore, defeat of the Gwalior mutineers, and actions of Kala Nuddee and Kerkerouile, and capture of Bareilly.

ENSIGNS.

4	0	William James Voules	24 Jan. 56	
4	0	James George Anderson	26 Feb. 56	
2	0	Fred. Edward Wilson	5 Jan. 58	
2	0	Charles Hamilton Sams	p 12 Feb. 58	
2	0	Herbert Small Janvrin	19 Feb. 58	
2	0	Herbert Grant	2 July 58	
2	0	Henry Fred. Scobell	p 31 Aug. 58	
1	0	Arthur Richard Alston	24 June 59	
1	0	Tho. Albert Bray Wright	16 Sept. 59	

21	0	*Paymaster.*—James Howes,[31] 1 Oct. 47; *Quarter-Master*, 6 Sept. 39.
5	0	*Adjutant.*—*Lieut.* John Thomas Pack, 23 July 58.
4	0	*Instructor of Musketry.*—*Lieut.* David Gardiner, 8 March 59.
1	0	*Quarter-Master.*—Alexander Ross, 20 Dec. 59.
21	0	*Surgeon.*—Jas. Gordon Inglis,[27] M.D., CB. *Asst.Surg.* 29 Mar. 39; *Surg.* 29 Mar.
6	0	*Assist.Surgeons.*—Ed. Louis Lundy,[30] 7 April 54. [52; *Surg.Maj.* 29 Mar. 59.
3	0	George Parsons Wall, 19 Oct. 57.
5	0	Claudius Edward Le Febure, 30 July 55.

Facings Black.—*Agents*, Messrs. Cox & Co.

1 Lieut. General Freeth served in the Peninsula and France from May 1809 to Jan. 1814, and was present at the following actions and sieges; viz. :—Fuentes d'Onor, capture of Ciudad Rodrigo and Badajoz, battles of Salamanca, Burgos, Vittoria, and Pyrenees, near Pampeluna, Nivelle, and Nive, for which he has received the War Medal with eight Clasps.

2 Colonel Bingham served with the 64th Regt. in the Persian campaign of 1856-57, including the storm and capture of Reshire, surrender of Bushire, night attack and battle of Kooshab. Served in Bengal and N. W. Provinces in suppressing the mutiny in 1857-58; present with Havelock's column in the actions of Futtehpore, Aoung, Pandoo Nuddee, Cawnpore, Busseerut Gunge (1st and 2nd), Boorbeakeehowkee, and Bithoor; commanded a convoy with provisions from Cawnpore to Alumbagh; served in defence of the Alumbagh and afterwards in the actions at La Martiniere and the second relief of Lucknow; commanded the Regt. during the defence of Cawnpore and defeat of the Gwalior mutineers; also present in the actions of Kala Nuddee and Kerkerouile, and capture of Bareilly (CB).

5 Major Anderson served with the 64th Regt. in the Persian campaign of 1856-57, including the storm and capture of Reshire, surrender of Bushire, night attack and battle of Kooshab, and bombardment of Mohumrah. Served in Bengal and N. W. Provinces in suppressing the mutiny in 1857-58; present with Havelock's column in the actions of Futtehpore, Aoung, Pandoo Nuddee, Cawnpore, Onao, and Busseerut Gunge.

6 Major Mockler served in the Persian campaign of 1856-57, including the storm and capture of Reshire, surrender of Bushire, and night attack and battle of Kooshab (severely wounded by round shot). Served in the Indian campaign of 1857-58, including the actions of Kala Nuddee and Kerkeroulie, Bareilly, Shajehanpore, Bunnow, and Mahombdie.

8 Major Bowlby served with the 64th Regt. in the Persian campaign of 1856-57, including the storm and capture of Reshire, surrender of Bushire, night attack and battle of Kooshab, and bombardment of Mohumrah. Served in the N. W. Provinces in suppressing the mutiny in 1857-58 ; succeeded to the command of the regiment, on the death of Colonel Wilson and Major Stirling, in the operations at Cawnpore under Gen. Windham (mentioned in despatches as having distinguished himself, Brevet of Major), defence of Cawnpore and defeat of the Gwalior mutineers, and actions of Kala Nuddee and Kerkeroulie, and capture of Bareilly.

9 Captain Thompson served in Bengal and N. W. Provinces in suppressing the mutiny in 1857-58 ; commanded the escort which safely conveyed the treasure from Gya to Calcutta (thanked by the Governor General in Council) ; present in the operations at Cawnpore under Gen. Windham, defence of Cawnpore and defeat of the Gwalior mutineers, and action of Kala Nuddee.

10 Major Goode served in the Persian campaign of 1856-57 (Medal and Clasp), including the storm and capture of Reshire, surrender of Bushire, night attack and battle of Kooshab, and bombardment of Mohumrah ; commanded the flank companies in the expedition to Ahwaz, for which he was thanked by the Governor General in Council. Served in Bengal and N. W. Provinces in suppressing the mutiny in 1857-58 ; present with Havelock's column in the actions of Futtehpore, Aoung, Pandoo Nuddee, Cawnpore, Onao, Buscerut Gunge (1st and 2nd), Boorbeakechowkee, and Bithoor; subsequent defence of the Alumbagh, actions at La Martiniere and second relief of Lucknow, defence of Cawnpore, defeat of the Gwalior mutineers, and actions of Kala Nuddee and Kerkeroulie, capture of Bareilly, and several minor affairs (Medal and Clasps, and Brevet of Major).

11 Major Chads served as Aide-de-Camp to General Godwin throughout the Burmese war of 1852-53, and was present at the assault and capture of Martaban, the destruction of the river stockades at Rangoon, attack on the White House Stockade, 12th April (wounded, but did not quit the field), and operations of the two following days, concluding with the storm of the Great Shoe Dagon Pagoda Stockade ; also present at the captures of Bassein and Pegu, the relief of the beleaguered garrison at Pegu, and the operations of the four following days, during which the enemy in force were driven out of three entrenched positions (Medal and Brev. Major) : received the thanks of the Governor-General in Council on six separate occasions during the war. Served as a volunteer at the bombardment and capture of Bomarsund in the Baltic expedition of 1854 (Medal). Served as Staff Captain at Smyrna from April to Sept. 1855, and as Commandant with rank of Assist. Adj. Gen. at Smyrna and Abydos (Dardanelles from 1st Sept. to 27th Oct. 1856).

12 Captain Fanning served with the 64th Regt. in the Persian campaign of 1856-57, including the storm and capture of Reshire, surrender of Bushire, night attack and battle of Kooshab, and bombardment of Mohumrah. Served in the N. W. Provinces in suppressing the mutiny in 1857-58 ; commanded a detachment in the action of Khugwa, present in the defence of Cawnpore and defeat of the Gwalior mutineers, and actions of Kala Nuddee and Kerkeroulie, and capture of Bareilly.

13 Captain Knight served in the Persian campaign in 1857, including the bombardment of Mohumrah. Served in Bengal and N. W. Provinces in suppressing the mutiny in 1857-58 ; present in the operations at Cawnpore under Gen. Windham, defence of Cawnpore and defeat of the Gwalior mutineers, and action of Kala Nuddee.

14 Captain Hutchison served in the Persian campaign of 1856, including the storm and capture of Reshire and surrender of Bushire. Present in the action of Kerkeroulie, capture of Bareilly, and attack of Mohundee (Medal and Clasp).

15 Captains O'Grady and Ryan served in the N. W. Provinces in suppressing the mutiny in 1857-58 ; present in the operations at Cawnpore under Gen. Windham (Capt. Ryan acting as his Aide de Camp), defence of Cawnpore and defeat of the Gwalior mutineers, and actions of Kala Nuddee and Kerkeroulie, and capture of Bareilly.

16 Lieut. Benison served in the Persian campaign of 1856-57, including the storm and capture of Reshire, surrender of Bushire, night attack and battle of Kooshab, and bombardment of Mohumrah. Served in Bengal and N. W. Provinces in suppressing the mutiny in 1857-58 ; present with Havelock's column in the actions of Futtehpore, Aoung, Pandoo Nuddee, Cawnpore, Onao, Buscerut Gunge (1st and 2nd), Boorbeakechowkee, and Bithoor; operations at Cawnpore under Gen. Windham, defence of Cawnpore and defeat of the Gwalior mutineers, action of Kerkeroulie, and capture of Bareilly.

18 Lieut. D'Acosta served in the Persian campaign of 1856-57, including the bombardment of Mohumrah. Served in Bengal and N. W. Provinces in suppressing the mutiny in 1857-58, including the defence of Cawnpore ; also present in the action of Kerkeroulie and capture of Bareilly.

19 Lieut. Lukis served in the Persian campaign of 1856-57, including the night attack and battle of Kooshab and bombardment of Mohumrah. Served in Bengal and N. W. Provinces in suppressing the mutiny in 1857-58 ; present with Havelock's column in the actions of Futtehpore, Aoung, Pandoo Nuddee, Cawnpore, Onao, Buscerut Gunge (1st and 2nd), Boorbeakechowkee, and defence of Cawnpore ; also present in the action of Kerkeroulie and capture of Bareilly.

20 Lieut. Haldane served the Persian campaign of 1856-57, including the storm and capture of Reshire, surrender of Bushire, night attack and battle of Kooshab, bombardment of Mohumrah, and expedition to Ahwaz. Served in Bengal and N. W. Provinces in suppressing the mutiny in 1857-58 ; present with Havelock's column in the actions of Futtehpore, Aoung, Pandoo Nuddee, Cawnpore (wounded), Onao, Buscerut Gunge (1st and 2nd) ; was an Assistant Field Engineer in the defence of the Alumbagh (mentioned in Dispatches) ; present at the actions of Dilkoosha and second relief of Lucknow, defence of Cawnpore and defeat of the Gwalior mutineers, and actions of Kala Nuddee and Kerkeroulie, and capture of Bareilly.

22 Lieut. Pack served with the 64th Regt. throughout the Persian campaign of 1856-57, including the storm and capture of Reshire, surrender of Bushire, night attack and battle of Kooshab, bombardment of Mohumrah, and expedition to Ahwaz. Served in Bengal and N. W. Provinces in suppressing the mutiny in 1857-58, including the operations at Cawnpore under General Windham (as Acting Adjutant), defence of Cawnpore and defeat of the Gwalior mutineers, and actions of Kala Nuddee and Kerkeroulie, and capture of Bareilly.

23 Lieut. Taylor served in the Persian campaign of 1856-57, including the night attack and battle of Kooshab, and bombardment of Mohumrah. Served in Bengal and N. W. Provinces in suppressing the mutiny in 1857-58 ; present with the escort conveying treasure from Gya to Calcutta, operations at Cawnpore under General Windham, defence of Cawnpore and defeat of the Gwalior mutineers, and action of Kala Nuddee.

24 Lieut. Mirehouse served in Bengal and N. W. Provinces in suppressing the mutiny in 1857-58, including the actions of Futtehpore, Aoung, Pandoo Nuddee, Cawnpore, Onao, Buscerut Gunge (1st and 2nd), and Bithoor with Havelock's column, defence of the Alumbagh, actions of La Martiniere and second relief of Lucknow, defence of Cawnpore and defeat of the Gwalior mutineers, and actions of Kala Nuddee and Kerkeroulie, and capture of Bareilly.

25 Lieut. Gardiner served the campaign of 1844-45 in the Southern Mahratta country, including the capture of the forts of Panulla, Powughur, Monahur, and Munsuntoosh.

27 Doctor Inglis served the Punjaub campaign of 1848-9 with the 10th Regt., including the whole of the siege operations before Mooltan (the greater part of which in medical charge of the Regt.), and battle of Goojerat (Medal and Clasps). Served with the 64th Regt. in the Persian campaign of 1856-57, including the capture of Reshire, surrender of Bushire, night attack and battle of Kooshab, and bombardment of Mohumrah. Served in Bengal and N. W. Provinces in suppressing the mutiny in 1857-58, including operations at Cawnpore under General Windham, defence of Cawnpore and defeat of the Gwalior mutineers, and actions of Kala Nuddee and Kerkeroulie, and capture of Bareilly.

31 Paymaster Howes was present at the action of Kerkeroulie and capture of Bareilly.

30 Assist. Surgeon Lundy served the Eastern campaign of 1854-55 with the 79th, including the battles of Alma and Balaklava, siege of Sebastopol, and assaults of the 18th June and 8th Sept., expedition to Kertch and Yenikale, was wounded in the trenches before Sebastopol on 29th July 1855 (Medal and Clasps). Served with the 64th Regt. in the Persian campaign in 1857, including the night attack and battle of Kooshab, and surrender of Mohumrah. Served in Bengal and N. W. Provinces in suppressing the mutiny in 1857-58, including the actions of Futtehpore, Aoung, Pandoo Nuddee, and Cawnpore with Havelock's Column, operations at Cawnpore under General Windham, defence of Cawnpore and defeat of the Gwalior mutineers, and action of Kala Nuddee.

Serving in N.Zealand.] 65th (*The 2d Yorkshire N. Riding*) *Regt. of Ft.*   293
Depot, Birr.

The *Royal Tiger*, superscribed "INDIA" "ARABIA."

Years' Serv.							
Full Pay.	Half Pay.						
57		Colonel.—P Robert Bartlett Coles,[1] *Cornet*, P 20 Aug. 03; *Lieut.* 1 May 05; *Capt.* P 8 Sept. 08; *Maj.* P 24 Oct. 21; *Lt.-Col.* P 19 Sept. 26; *Col.* 23 Nov. 41; *Major-Gen.* 11 Nov. 51; *Lt.Gen.* 26 Oct. 58; *Col.* 65th Foot, 25 July 57.					
32	0	*Lieut.Colonel.*—Charles Emilius Gold, *Ens.* P 20 Mar. 28; *Lt.* P 28 Oct. 31; *Capt.* P 5 Feb. 36; *Major,*P 4 Oct. 44; *Lieut.-Col.* 30 Dec. 45; *Col.* 20 June 54.					
34	0	*Majors.*—Alfred Francis W. Wyatt, *Ens.* P 12 Dec. 26; *Lt.* P 23 Apr. 29; *Capt.* P 19 Sept. 34; *Maj.* P 23 Sept. 45; *Bt. Lt.Col.* 20 June 54; *Col.* 26 Oct. 58.					
43	7	James Patience,[2] *Ens.* 5 April 10; *Lieut.* 24 Oct. 11; *Capt.* 13 Nov. 27; *Bt.Maj.* 23 Nov. 41; *Major*, 30 Dec. 45; *Brev.Lt.Col.* 11 Nov. 51; *Col.* 28 Nov. 54.					

		CAPTAINS.	ENSIGN.	LIEUT.	CAPTAIN.	BREV.-MAJ.
32	0	Geo. F. Murray *l.c.* 26 Oct. 58	26 Apr. 48	P 29 June 32	P 5 Jan. 39	11 Nov. 51
30	0	William Pym Young ..	P 26 Oct. 30	P 27 Nov. 35	12 Sept. 43	20 June 54
19	0	Robert Henry MacGregor	P 31 Dec. 41	P 13 June 45	P 28 May 52	
17	0	James Paul[4]	8 Nov. 43	19 Dec. 45	P 2 Sept. 53	
13	0	Fra. Beaumaris Bulkeley	P 22 June 47	18 Sept. 51	P 8 Dec. 54	
14	0	Charles Blewitt	P 8 May 46	22 Dec. 48	P 1 May 55	
21	0	Frederick Rice Stack[3] ...	1 June 39	7 Jan. 42	5 Aug. 53	
18	0	Henry Ferdinand Turner	8 Feb. 42	8 Oct. 45	18 Nov. 56	
12	0	Thomas Geo. Strange ..	P 22 Dec. 48	P 27 June 51	12 Aug. 57	
14	7/12	James Barton	P 13 June 45	19 Aug. 50	29 Dec. 54	
9	0	John Owen Jones Priestley	7 Feb. 51	P 26 July 53	P 24 Sept. 58	
9	0	Fred. Stansfield Herries	4 Apr. 51	P 25 Nov. 53	P 7 Dec. 58	
		LIEUTENANTS.				
9	0	George Buck	P 14 Feb. 51	P 2 Sept. 53		
8	0	A. Nicholson Magrath ..	14 May 52	6 June 54		
8	0	Frederick Bailie.........	P 11 June 52	6 June 54		
8	0	Lionel Smith Warren ..	P 23 Nov. 52	P 18 Aug. 54		
7	0	Charles James Urquhart	P 2 Sept. 53	P 1 May 55		
7	0	Edmund Jacob Whitbread	P 25 Nov. 53	P 7 Sept. 55		
6	0	Walter Higgin..........	P 28 Mar. 54	P 2 Oct. 55		
6	0	Joseph William Lewis ..	28 Apr. 54	P 28 Dec. 55		
6	0	Henry Stratton Bates ..	P 18 Aug. 54	P 30 June 57		
6	0	Arthur Branthwayt Toker	P 25 Aug. 54	12 Aug. 57		
6	0	William Popham Wrixon	20 Oct. 54	17 Nov. 57		
5	0	Arthur Henry Lewis, *Adj.*	15 June 55	P 19 Feb. 58		
5	0	Falcon Peter Leonard ..	10 Aug. 55	6 July 58		
4	0	George Pennefather	13 Jan. 56	P 7 Dec. 58		
4	0	George Robert Chevalier	14 Jan. 56	P 7 Dec. 58		
		ENSIGNS.				
4	0	Edward Vernon White ..	15 Feb. 56			
4	0	John Shrews Talbot	16 Feb. 56			
4	0	Andrew Pagan	8 July 56			
3	0	Henry Moseley Muttit ..	9 Oct. 57			
2	0	Windle Hill St. Hill	12 Feb. 58			
2	0	Villars Butler	16 Mar. 58			
2	0	Augustus Tabuteau	P 9 Nov. 58			
2	0	William Alexander......	7 Dec. 58			
1	0	William Byam	P 25 Jan. 59			
2	0	Thomas Henry Fernley..	P 9 Nov. 58			
24	0	*Paymaster.*—J. Williams Marshall, 3 Apr. 46; *Ens.* P 2 Sept. 36; *Lt.* P 19 Mar. 41.				
5	0	*Adjutant.*—*Lieut.* Arthur Henry Lewis, 19 Feb. 58.				
6	0	*Instructor of Musketry.*—*Lieut.* Arthur Branthwayt Toker, 11 Sept. 58.				
9	0	*Quarter-Master.*—Edward Withers, 21 Nov. 51.				
15	0	*Surgeon.*—Thomas Esmonde White, M.D. 2 Oct. 57; *Assist.Surg.* 26 Sept. 45.				
3	0	*Assistant-Surgeons.*—Alexander Neill, 15 Sept. 57.				
3	0	Eugene M'Shane, 15 Sept. 57.				

3 Captain Stack served as an Ensign in the 45th Regt. at Newport in Monmouthshire during the Chartist Riots of Nov. 1839, when his father's Company of that Regt. defeated a body of nearly 5000 armed men led on by the ex-Mayor of Newport, Mr. John Frost, who attacked the town with the treasonable intention of commencing a revolution in the Government of the country. The defeat of this insurrectionary host after eleven were killed on the spot and about thirty or forty wounded, was characterized at the time in the Imperial Parliament as having been the means of saving the whole of England from anarchy and rebellion. For this service each of the three officers of the Company received the thanks of the Queen and of the Commander in Chief, and also the thanks from the counties of Monmouthshire, Glamorganshire, and Brecknshire. In April 1855 he was promoted to a Majority in the Turkish service, and served at Constantinople, Bayukdere, and the entrenched camp at Kertch during the winter of 1855 until the disbandment of the Anglo-Ottoman Force, and has received the 4th Class of the Medjidie and a Lt. Colonel's commission from the Sultan.

Facings White.—*Agent*, E. S. Codd, Esq.
Irish Agents, Sir E. R. Borough, Bt., Armit & Co.
[*Embarked for New South Wales*, 18 May 1846.]

1 Lieut.General Coles served in India under Lord Lake the latter part of 1804 and the campaigns of 1805 and 6. On the termination of the war in India he returned to England; was promoted to a company, and embarked for Spain; served the campaign of 1808-9 under Sir John Moore, including the action at Lugo and retreat to Corunna. Accompanied his regiment on the expedition to the Scheldt in 1809; landed at Walcheren; was present at the siege and surrender of Flushing, and remained with the force on the island until it was evacuated. Joined the army under the Duke of Wellington in the Peninsula in 1813, was present at the passage of the Bidassoa, the battles of the Nivelle and Nive, the passage of the Adour, the investment of Bayonne and repulse of the sortie. Marched to Bourdeaux and embarked for North America in 1814, was present at the passage of the Saranac and the action of Plattsburg. Served in Canada till the latter part of 1826, when he was promoted to a Lieut.-Coloneley unattached. Has received the Silver War Medal with three Clasps for Corunna, Nivelle, and Nive.

2 Colonel Patience was present at the surrender of Martinique, and at the capture of Les Saintes and Guadaloupe, in 1815.
4 Capt. Paul served with the 31st throughout the campaign of 1845-6 on the Sutlej, and was present in the battles of Moodkee, Ferozeshah (wounded), Buddiwal, Aliwal and Sobraon; Medal and three Clasps. He carried the Queen's color of the 31st at Moodkee and Ferozeshah.

66th (*The Berkshire*) Regt. of Foot. [Serving in India. Depot, Colchester.

"DOURO" "TALAVERA" "ALBUHERA" "VITTORIA" "PYRENEES"
"NIVELLE" "NIVE" "ORTHES" "PENINSULA."

Years' Serv.		
73	Full Pay.	Half Pay.

Colonel.—⑨ Richard Blunt,[1] *Ens.* 31 Jan. 1787; *Lieut.* 23 Feb. 91; *Capt.* 12 July 93; *Major*, 17 May 96; *Lieut.Col.* 23 Aug. 99; *Col.* 25 Oct. 1809; *Major Gen.* 1 Jan. 12; *Lt.Gen.* 27 May 25; *Gen.* 23 Nov. 41; *Col.* 66th Regt. 25 Mar. 35.

16	0	Lieut.Colonels.—Charles Edmund Law,[2] *Cornet*, P 2 Feb. 44; *Lt.* P 8 May 46; *Capt.* P 26 Dec. 51; *Major*, P 7 July 54; *Lt.Col.* P 5 Jan. 55; *Col.* 12 July 58.
34	0	George Maxwell, *Ens.* P 23 Feb. 26; *Lieut.* 29 May 28; *Capt.* 21 Oct. 43; *Brev.Maj.* 20 June 54; *Major*, 9 Jan. 55; *Lt.Col.* 14 Aug. 57.
18	0	Majors.—Tom Benson, *Ens.* P 8 Nov. 42; *Lt.* P 8 Aug. 45; *Capt.* P 30 Mar. 49; *Major*, P 25 Aug. 57.
14	0	Webster Thomas Gordon, *Ens.* P 1 Dec. 46; *Lieut.* P 12 Sept. 48; *Capt.* P 14 May 52; *Major*, 1 Jan. 59.

		CAPTAINS.	ENSIGN.	LIEUT.	CAPTAIN.	BREV.-MAJ.
13	0	George Watson	P 9 Apr. 47	14 Nov. 48	P 28 April 54	
16	0	Charles Wm. Aylmer ..	21 Dec. 44	P 28 Aug. 46	P 1 Sept. 54	
13	0	Arch. Hamilton Dunbar	P 28 Sept. 47	P 30 Mar. 49	P 3 Nov. 54	
13	0	Charles Perrin	P 24 Dec. 47	P 4 May 49	1 Dec. 54	
15	0	John Walker	P 25 Nov. 45	P 13 July 49	9 Jan. 55	
12	0	Richard Horner Paget ..	1 Dec. 48	P 6 June 51	P 19 Jan. 55	
11	0	Alfred Torrens	9 Mar. 49	P 17 Oct. 51	P 13 Feb. 55	
9	0	Charles James Knox Gore	P 16 May 51	P 6 May 53	P 8 June 55	
9	0	James Galbraith	P 12 Dec. 51	6 June 54	P 29 Feb. 56	
9	0	Sir C.F.WheelerCuffe, Bt.	P 16 May 51	P 21 April 54	P 20 Mar. 57	26 Apr. 59
9	0	James Lorenzo Verschoyle	P 13 Dec. 51	11 Aug. 54	P 28 Aug. 57	
11	0	Edward Jas. Storey	9 Jan. 49	25 June 52	1 Jan. 59	
		LIEUTENANTS.				
9	0	Leslie Eames	P 17 June 51	P 28 April 54		
9	0	Wm. Henry Jones Westby	P 17 Oct. 51	6 June 54		
8	0	Alfred Austin.........	P 11 June 52	P 8 Sept. 54		
8	0	Fred. Hugh Irwin Day ..	P 9 July 52	P 3 Nov. 54		
6	0	C. J. Thornton Duesbury	P 21 April 54	1 Dec. 54		
6	0	Richard Thomas Hughes	P 28 April 54	9 Jan. 55		
6	0	Alfred Trigge	21 July 54	P 26 Jan. 55		
6	0	Henry Charles Spearman	P 24 Aug. 54	P 13 Feb. 55		
6	0	John Baring Short	P 25 Aug. 54	P 20 July 55		
6	0	Charles Valentine Oliver	P 8 Sept. 54	P 29 Feb. 56		
6	0	Charles Augustus Shortt	6 June 54	P 20 Mar. 57		
6	0	John Tobin Ready.....	P 9 Sept. 54	P 28 Aug. 57		
5	0	Wm.Trevelyan HodyCox	P 13 Feb. 55	P 2 July 58		
4	0	James Howe Mardon ..	P 7 Mar. 56	1 Jan. 59		
		ENSIGNS.				
4	0	Edward Richardson	8 July 56			
3	0	Thomas Gambell	P 27 Mar. 57			
3	0	John Mahony, *Adj.*	25 Aug. 57			
3	0	Walter Cecil Strickland..	P 28 Aug. 57			
3	0	Rob. Gibbings Westropp	28 Aug. 57			
2	0	Francis Edward Browne	P 13 July 58			
2	0	John Tulloch Nash[5]	14 July 58			
2	0	Charles Tennant Wallace	13 Aug. 58			
2	0	Charles Langley Whitty	19 Nov. 58			
1	0	George Dalton Michell ..	11 Mar. 59			
1	0	Alfred Chamberl. Addison	18 Mar. 59			
14	0	*Paymaster*.—George Pollard, 17 Aug. 55; *Qr.Master*, 28 July 46.				
3	0	*Adjutant*.—*Ensign* John Mahony, 25 Aug. 57.				
6	0	*Instructor of Musketry*.—*Lieut.* Richard Thomas Hughes, 5 Feb. 57.				
6	0	*Quarter Master*.—Henry Hammond, 17 Mar. 54.				
9	0	*Surgeon*.—William Sim Murray, M.B. 26 Jan. 58; *Assist.Surg.* 10 Jan. 51.				
6	0	*Assistant Surgeons*.—William Hemphill,[4] M.D. 14 July 54.				
2	0	James M'Crevey, M.D. 22 Jan. 58.				
2	0	George Alexander Moorhead, 22 July 58.				

Right column notes:
4 Assist.Surgeon Hemphill served with the 48th Regt. in the Crimea from 21st April 1855, including the siege and fall of Sebastopol, and detached duty in the Dockyard from 14th Jan. to 14th March 1856 (Medal and Clasp).

5 Ensign Nash served as a Volunteer with the Bengal Yeomanry Cavalry during the Indian Mutiny of 1857-58, and was present in the actions at Belwa in Oude (wounded by musket shot in thigh), Amorah on 5th March 58, Thilga (wounded by sabre cut on head), Amorah on 25th April (horse shot) and 9th June, and Hurriah (Medal).

Facings Green.—*Agents*, Messrs. Cox & Co.
[*Returned from Gibraltar, June* 1856. *Embarked for India*, 29 *Aug.* 1857.]

1 General Blunt served in Lord Moira's expedition, and in Flanders in 1794 and 95, and was actively employed in the West Indies from 1795 until 1802. He has since served in Hanover, Madeira, and in the Peninsula. Is a Commander of the Tower and Sword of Portugal.
2 Colonel Law served with the 9th Lancers in the Sutlej campaign in 1846, including the battle of Sobraon (Medal).

China, Depôt, Athlone.] **67th (*The South Hampshire*) Regt. of Foot.** 295

"BARROSA"—"PENINSULA"—The *Royal Tiger*, superscribed, "INDIA."

Years' Serv.		
Full Pay.	Half Pay.	
52		**Colonel.**—ｐ Francis John Davies,¹ *Ens.* ᴾ 3 Feb. 08; *Lieut.* ᴾ 26 Jan. 09; *Capt.* ᴾ 12 Aug. 13; *Capt. & Lieut.-Col.* ᴾ 30 Apr. 27; *Col.* 23 Nov. 41; *Maj.-Gen.* 20 June 54; *Lt.Gen.* 14 Aug. 59; *Col.* 67th F. 15 Jan. 58.
22	0	**Lt. Colonels.**—Thomas Edmond Knox, *Ens.* 26 Jan. 38; *Lieut.* ᴾ 24 June 42; *Capt.* 31 July 46; *Major*, ᴾ 17 Aug. 52; *Lt.Col.* 17 Sept. 58.
21	0	John Wellesley Thomas,² *Ens.* 7 June 39; *Lt.* 7 Sept. 41; *Capt.* ᴾ 14 May 47; *Brev. Maj.* 3 Dec. 54; *Maj.* 25 April 55; *Lt.Col.* 31 Dec. 58.
26	0	**Majors.**—John Porter, *Ens.* ᴾ 28 Mar. 34; *Lieut.* ᴾ 29 Dec. 37; *Capt.* ᴾ 6 Oct. 43; *Brev.Maj.* 20 June 54; *Major*, 17 Sept. 58.
25	0	Charles Barnard Hague, *Ens.* ᴾ 5 Sept. 35; *Lt.* ᴾ 30 Dec. 37; *Capt.* ᴾ 5 Dec. 43; *Brev.Maj.* 20 June 54; *Major*, 31 Dec. 58.

		CAPTAINS.	ENSIGN.	LIEUT.	CAPTAIN.	BREV.-MAJ.
24	0	Henry Collette.........	ᴾ 26 Aug. 36	22 Jan. 39	ᴾ 23 Feb. 44	6 Jan. 55
18	0	Robert Hudson Wood ..	ᴾ 11 Mar. 42	ᴾ 5 Dec. 43	ᴾ 28 Aug. 49	
17	0	Dugald Stewart Miller, s.	ᴾ 24 Feb. 43	ᴾ 11 July 45	ᴾ 31 Jan. 51	
14	0	Henry Crofton	ᴾ 8 Sept. 46	ᴾ 19 Nov. 47	ᴾ 17 Jan. 51	
15	0	Daniel Thompson, s.	ᴾ 11 July 45	ᴾ 16 Apr. 47	ᴾ 30 Nov. 55	
7	0	Henry C. Worthington³	ᴾ 21 Jan. 53	11 Aug. 54	ᴾ 9 May 56	
6	0	Frederick William Jebb⁴.	ᴾ 23 June 54	16 Nov. 54	8 July 56	
14	0	Edward Daubeny	29 Dec. 46	ᴾ 28 Aug. 49	15 Jan. 58	
11	0	Arthur Henry Coney	10 Apr. 49	ᴾ 8 June 52	ᴾ 15 June 58	
10	0	George T. Horton Atchison	25 Oct. 50	6 June 54	17 Sept. 58	
19	0	William Francis Stehelin⁷	30 Apr. 41	20 Dec. 42	3 Mar. 50	
17	0	Thomas Stack⁶	18 Feb. 43	18 Nov. 45	29 Apr. 56	
6	0	Malachy Nugent	ᴾ 5 May 54	21 Sept. 55	11 Aug. 59	
		LIEUTENANTS.				
6	0	Arthur Forbes Robertson	ᴾ 20 Oct. 54	ᴾ 30 Nov. 55		
5	0	John Richard Crane	31 May 55	ᴾ 15 Jan. 56		
6	0	Edward Coxen	19 Oct. 54	1 June 56		
5	0	Edmund Henry Lenon ..	15 June 55	ᴾ 14 Nov. 56		
4	0	Thomas Dawson.......	1 Feb. 56	ᴾ 17 July 57		
5	0	Wm. Henry Bell Kingsley	1 June 56	30 Oct. 57		
4	0	Charles Edward Morgan	25 Mar. 56	ᴾ 30 Oct. 57		
4	0	George Thomson	8 July 56	23 Mar. 58		
4	0	William Digby Lloyd ..	ᴾ 8 Aug. 56	23 Mar. 58		
3	0	George Masters Cardew	19 June 57	ᴾ 15 June 58		
3	0	Nathaniel Burslem	20 Feb. 57	12 Feb. 58		
3	0	Charles William Creyke	17 July 57	ᴾ 24 Sept. 58		
4	0	John Trevor Hall Gardiner	ᴾ 14 Nov. 56	31 Dec. 58		
3	0	Charles Henry B. Turner	25 Sept. 57	11 Aug. 59		
		ENSIGNS.				
3	0	James Hardie Fraser....	ᴾ 30 Oct. 57			
3	0	George Baker	18 Dec. 57			
2	0	Alfred Adams Price	5 Mar. 58			
2	0	Lorenzo Nickson Mosse	26 Mar. 58			
2	0	Miles Charles Seton	30 Mar. 58			
2	0	John Worthy Chaplin ..	13 Apr. 58			
2	0	Wm. Southby Middleton.	ᴾ 13 July 58			
2	0	Cha. Preice Killeen, *Adj.*	17 Sept. 58			
1	0	Arthur James Poole ..	11 Jan. 59			
1	0	Geo. Chas. Henry Holmes	ᴾ 18 Feb. 59			
1	0	Henry William Pollard ..	30 Sept. 59			
6	0	**Paymaster.**—John Andrew Pope,⁵ 24 March 54.				
2	0	**Adjutant.**—Ensign Charles Preice Killeen, 17 Sept. 58.				
6	0	**Instructor of Musketry.**—Lieut. Edward Coxen, 26 Jan. 58.				
3	0	**Quarter Master.**—John Staniforth, 24 Feb. 57.				
10	0	**Surgeon.**—Jones Lamprey, MB., 3 Nov. 57; *Assist.Surg.* 8 Oct. 50.				
7	0	**Assistant Surgeons.**—Alex. Clark Ross, M.D. 1 July 53.				
3	0	Robert Heard, M.D. 15 Sept. 57.				
2	0	James George Stewart Mathison, 5 Aug. 58. [Armit & Co.				

Notes on right column:

2 Lt.Col. Thomas served with the 40th Regt. throughout the operations in Candahar and Affghanistan in 1841-42 (Medal); also in the action of Maharajpore 29th Dec. 1843—wounded (Medal); commanded detachments of the 12th and 40th Regiments at the capture of a stockade occupied by Insurgents at the Ballarat Gold Fields in Australia, on 3rd Dec. 1854, for which he received the rank of Major.

3 Capt. Worthington served with the 28th Regt. as Adjutant the Eastern campaign of 1855, including the siege and fall of Sebastopol (Medal and Clasp, and Turkish Medal).

4 Captain Jebb served with the 23rd Fusiliers at the siege and fall of Sebastopol from 14th Nov. 1854 (Medal and Clasp).

5 Paymaster Pope served with the 47th Regt. the Eastern campaign of 1854-55, including the battles of Alma and Inkerman, siege and fall of Sebastopol, and sortie of 26th Oct. (Medal and Clasps).

6 Captain Stack served throughout the operations in Scinde (Medal), including the destruction of Imaumghur and the battles of Meeanee and Hyderabad (severely wounded). Was afterwards present at Panulla, Pownghur, Munnahur, and Munsuntosh.

Facings Yellow.—*Agents*, Messrs. Cox & Co.—*Irish Agents*, Sir E. R. Borough, Bt.,

[*Returned from the West Indies*, 28 March 1857. *Emb. for India*, 18 Sept. 1858.]

1 Lieut.General Davies served in the Peninsula with the 52nd, and was present at the battles of Fuentes d'Onor, Salamanca, Vittoria and the Pyrenees, and at the siege of Badajoz (wounded), for which he has received the War Medal with five Clasps.

7 Captain Stehelin served with the 29th Regt. in the Sutlej campaign of 1845-46, including the battles of Ferozeshah and Sobraon (Medal and Clasp).

68th (The Durham) Regt. of Foot. (Lt. Inf.) [Serving in India. Depot at Fermoy.]

"SALAMANCA" "VITTORIA" "PYRENEES" "NIVELLE" "ORTHES" "PENINSULA"
"ALMA" "INKERMAN" "SEVASTOPOL."

Years' Serv.						
53		Colonel.—ᵖ Robert Christopher Mansel,¹ KH. Ens. 29 Jan. 07; Lt. 27 Jan. 08; Capt. ᵖ 4 Feb. 13; Brev.Maj. 5 July 21; Maj. ᵖ 9 June 25; Lt.Col. ᵖ 10 June 26; Col. 23 Nov. 41; Maj.Gen. 11 Nov. 51; Lt.Gen. 26 Oct. 58; Col. 68th F. 4 June 57.				
Full Pay	Half Pay					
10	0	Lieut.Colonels.—Henry Harpur Greer, Ens. ᵖ 10 Sept. 41; Lt. ᵖ 20 Aug. 44; Capt. ᵖ 31 Dec. 47; Major, 29 Dec. 54; Lt.Col. ᵖ 18 Feb. 59.				
34	0	Robert Clifford Lloyd, Ens. ᵖ 30 Dec. 26; Lieut. ᵖ 8 June 30; Capt. ᵖ 3 June 36; Brev.Major, 9 Nov. 46; Major, 3 Sept. 47; Brev.Lt.Col. 20 June 54; Lt.-Col. ᵖ 17 July 57; Col. 9 Sept. 59.				
16	0	Majors.—Horatio Harbord Morant,⁵ Ens. ᵖ 20 Aug. 44; Lieut. ᵖ 3 Nov. 46; Capt. ᵖ 21 Oct. 53; Brev.Major, 26 Dec. 56; Major, ᵖ 17 Nov. 57.				
14	0	Fred. Stuckley Savage,⁶ Ens. ᵖ 30 Jan. 46; Lieut. ᵖ 31 Dec. 47; Capt. 10 Mar. 54; Brev.Maj. 6 June 56; Major, ᵖ 18 Feb. 59.				

		CAPTAINS.	ENSIGN.	LIEUT.	CAPTAIN.	BREV.-MAJ.
21	1⁹⁄₁₂	W. Hervey FitzGerald⁷..	ᵖ 5 May 37	5 Jan. 41	9 Dec. 51	
17	0	John Cassidy⁸.........	19 May 43	ᵖ 14 Apr. 46	6 Nov. 54	
14	0	C. U. Shuttleworth⁸ ..	ᵖ 18 Sept. 46	ᵖ 12 May 48	1 Dec. 54	
12	0	Harrison W. J. Trent ...	ᵖ 14 Apr. 48	ᵖ 1 July 53	29 Dec. 54	
10	0	Cavendish C. FitzRoy⁹..	ᵖ 22 Nov. 50	ᵖ 20 Jan. 54	29 Dec. 54	
14	0	James Spratt	8 May 46	ᵖ 11 May 49	12 Jan. 55	
7	0	Hugo Shelley Light¹¹ ..	ᵖ 21 Oct. 53	ᵖ 25 Aug. 54	ᵖ 17 Nov. 57	
6	0	Edward Rich. Fox Vicars¹³	ᵖ 5 May 54	24 Nov. 54	ᵖ 7 May 58	
9	0	Sheffield Grace¹⁵.......	ᵖ 17 Oct. 51	8 Dec. 54	ᵖ 15 June 58	
6	0	F.DeLuttrell Saunderson¹⁷	28 July 54	8 Dec. 54	ᵖ 11 Feb. 59	
5	0	Reynold Alleyne Clement	6 July 55	ᵖ 7 Dec. 55	ᵖ 7 Dec. 58	
7	0	Geo. John Arata Oakley¹⁰	14 May 53	ᵖ 16 Mar. 55	4 Apr. 59	
		LIEUTENANTS.				
7	0	Aubrey Harvey Tucker¹²	ᵖ 13 Sept. 53	6 Nov. 54		10 Captain Oakley served with Havelock's field force in the action at Alum Bagh and at the relief of Lucknow (severely wounded in the head); with Outram's force at the Alum Bagh, also at the capture of Lucknow, and relief of Azimghur (Medal and two Clasps).
6	0	Edward Deshon¹⁴	6 June 54	1 Dec. 54		
6	0	Edmund Peel Ethelston¹⁵	ᵖ 24 Aug. 54	9 Feb. 55		
6	0	J.HobartCulmeSeymour¹⁵	ᵖ 25 Aug. 54	9 Feb. 55		
6	0	John Blood¹⁵	8 Sept. 54	9 Feb. 55		
9	0	John Ponsonby Cox¹⁶ ..	21 Nov. 51	2 Mar. 55		
6	0	Thomas Reeder Clarkson¹⁵	14 Dec. 54	9 Mar. 55		
5	0	Geo. Stanislaus Thornton¹⁵	5 Jan. 55	9 Mar. 55		19 Surgeon Best served in the field against the enemy in the Orange River Sovereignty in 1850-51, and in the Kaffir war of 1852-53 (Medal)
5	0	Henry J. R. Villiers-Stuart	ᵖ 16 Jan. 55	15 Mar. 55		
5	0	Wm. Henry T. Duesbery	2 Feb. 55	8 June 55		
5	0	Cha. Ern. Beaty-Pownall	24 Apr. 55	ᵖ 8 Jan. 56		
5	0	Geo. Faulkner Wilkinson	28 Mar. 55	26 Feb. 56		20 Ensign Craig served the Eastern campaign of 1854-55, including the battles of Alma and Inkerman, siege and fall of Sebastopol, sortie of 26th Oct., and as a volunteer with the storming party on the 8th Sept. (Medal and three Clasps).
5	0	James O. D. Annesley ..	30 Mar. 55	ᵖ 17 Nov. 57		
5	0	William Algernon Kay ..	5 June 55	ᵖ 7 May 58		
5	0	Charles Covey, Adj.	8 June 55	22 June 58		
5	0	Arthur Francis Marshall	15 May 55	ᵖ 22 June 58		
5	0	Cyril Blackburne Tew ..	ᵖ 27 July 55	ᵖ 11 Feb. 59		
4	0	Henry George Cavendish	ᵖ 26 Feb. 56	ᵖ 23 Aug. 59		
5	0	Henry John Evans	19 July 55	17 Nov. 57		
		ENSIGNS.				
4	0	William Weston Turnor .	1 Feb. 56			
4	0	Leonard Bolden	ᵖ 27 Feb. 56			
4	0	John Pitts Briggs	28 Feb. 56			
3	0	Rob.G.Craig,²⁰ q.m.20Feb.57	14 Aug. 57			
2	0	Horatio Gordon Robley..	ᵖ 14 May 58			
2	0	Richard Clayton	ᵖ 21 May 58			
2	0	Charles Clifton Hood ..	ᵖ 13 July 58			
1	0	George Fowler Caldecott	ᵖ 25 Feb. 59			
1	0	Alfred Gordon Howard..	ᵖ 21 Oct. 59			
5	0	Paymaster.—Frederick Francis Fereday, 9 Nov. 55.				
5	0	Adjutant.—Lieut. Charles Covey, 28 Sept. 56.				
12	0	Quarter-Master.—Thomas Tunks,¹⁸ 14 Apr. 48.				
18	0	Surgeon.—Thomas Best,¹⁹ 13 Apr. 52; Assist.Surg. 22 Apr. 42.				
6	0	Assistant-Surgeons.—Augustus Patrick Meyers Corbett,¹⁹† M.D. 27 Oct. 54.				
5	0	Clement Williams, 5 Jan. 55.				
3	0	Augustus Oliver Applin, 3 Oct. 57.				[Arnit & Co.

Facings Green.—Agents, Messrs. Cox & Co. Irish Agents, Sir E. R. Borough, Bt.,
[Returned from Corfu, 14 August 1857. Embarked for India, Dec. 1857.]

1 Lieut.General Mansel served with the 10th Regt.in the Mediterranean; subsequently with the 53rd in the Peninsula, and was severely wounded at Toulouse, for which battle he has the War Medal with one Clasp.

5 Major Morant served the Eastern campaign to the 8th Nov. 1854, including the battles of Alma and Inkerman and siege of Sebastopol (fracture of right arm in the trenches). Served as Aide-de-Camp to Br.Gen. Shirley from 10th Sept. 1855 (Medal and three Clasps).

6 Major Savage served throughout the Eastern campaign of 1854-55, including the battles of Alma, Balaklava, and Inkerman, siege and fall of Sebastopol (Medal and Clasps, Brevet Major, and 5th Class of the Medjidie).

7 Captain FitzGerald served in the Anglo-Spanish Legion during 1835-37; was severely wounded in the action of the 5th May near St. Sebastian, and has two Crosses and a Medal for his conduct and services.

8 Captains Cassidy and Shuttleworth served the Eastern campaign of 1854-55, including the battles of Alma and Inkerman, siege and fall of Sebastopol (Medal and Clasps). Captain Shuttleworth has the 5th Class of the Medjidie.

9 Capt. FitzRoy served the Eastern campaign until sent home on promotion early in 1855, including the battles of Alma and Inkerman, siege and fall of Sebastopol (Medal and Clasps, and 5th Class of the Medjidie).

11 Captain Light served in the Eastern campaign of 1854, including the battle of Alma and siege of Sebastopol (Medal and Clasps).

12 Lieut. Tucker served the Eastern campaign of 1854-55, including the battles of Alma and Inkerman, siege and fall of Sebastopol (Medal and Clasps, and Knight of the Legion of Honor).

13 Captain Vicars served in the Crimea during the siege and fall of Sebastopol (Medal and Clasp).

14 Lieut. Deshon served in the Crimea during the siege and fall of Sebastopol from 13th Nov. 1854 (Medal and Clasp).

15 Captain Grace, Lieuts. Ethelston, Seymour, Blood, Clarkson, and Thornton, served in the Crimea during the siege and fall of Sebastopol (Medal and Clasp). Captain Grace has also the Sardinian Medal.

16 Lieut. Cox served with the Cape Mounted Riflemen throughout the Kaffir war of 1852-53, and was present at the battle of Berea (Medal).

17 Captain Saunderson served at the siege and fall of Sebastopol from 2nd Dec. 1854 (Medal and Clasp, and Sardinian Medal).

18 Quarter Master Tunks served the Eastern campaign of 1854-55, including the battles of Alma and Inkerman, siege and fall of Sebastopol (Medal and Clasps).

19† Assist.Surg. Corbett served in the Crimea during the siege and fall of Sebastopol (Medal and Clasp, and 5th Class of the Medjidie).

298 69th (The South Lincolnshire) Regt. of Foot. [Serving in India. Depot, Fermoy.]
"JAVA" "BOURBON" "WATERLOO" "INDIA."

Years' Serv.			
Full Pay	Half Pay		
49		**Colonel.**—[P] Ernest Frederic Gascoigne,[1] *Ens.* 2 May 11; *Lt.* 13 May 13; *Capt.* 6 July 15; *Major,* P 19 May 25; *Lt.-Col.* P 3 June 28; *Col.* 23 Nov. 41; *Maj. Gen.* 20 June 54; *Col.* 69th Foot, 3 Apr. 58.	
27	0	**Lieut.-Colonels.**—David Elliot Mackirdy, *Ens.* P 5 April 33; *Lieut.* P 30 Dec. 36; *Capt.* P 26 June 41; *Maj.* P 22 Feb. 50; *Lt.Col.* 25 Aug. 53; *Col.* 28 Nov. 54.	
22	0	Percival Fenwick, *Ens.* P 28 Sept. 38; *Lieut.* P 1 Nov. 40; *Capt.* P 14 May 47; *Major,* P 19 June 57; *Lt.Col.* P 22 Apr. 59.	
25	0	**Majors.**—James Handasyde Edgar, *Ens.* P 9 Oct. 35; *Lieut.* P 28 June 39; *Capt.* 20 Jan. 47; *Major,* 17 Nov. 57.	
20	0	Augustus Barnard Hankey, *Ens.* P 30 Oct. 40; *Lieut.* P 20 June 45; *Capt.* P 20 May 49; *Major,* P 22 Apr. 59.	

		CAPTAINS.	ENSIGN.	LIEUT.	CAPTAIN.	BREV.-MAJ.
28	1½	George Hughes Messiter	15 June 30	29 Sept. 34	3 Sept. 47	26 Oct. 58
19	0	Edward Bowen	1 June 41	P 2 Sept. 45	P 29 June 49	
15	0	George Bagot	P 20 June 45	P 25 Sept. 46	P 8 June 52	
14	0	Francis Gamble Blood	12 June 46	P 14 Apr. 48	25 Aug. 53	
14	0	James Smyth	P 25 Sept. 46	P 12 Sept. 48	6 June 54	
13	0	H. Beauchamp Brady, *s.*	P 24 Dec. 47	P 8 June 52	P 3 Aug. 55	
11	0	Thomas Henry Charleton	11 May 49	21 Jan. 53	P 25 Jan. 56	
8	0	Robert Aufrère Leggett	P 11 June 52	P 28 Oct. 53	P 30 June 57	
14	0	Richard FitzGerald	18 Sept. 46	P 10 Nov. 48	17 Nov. 57	
8	0	Roberts Torrens Pratt[4]	11 June 52	P 9 June 54	24 Aug. 58	
7	0	Rich. Cooper Hutchison	11 Mar. 53	11 Aug. 54	P 14 June 59	
7	0	James W. H. Anderson	30 Sept. 53	P 6 July 55	P 13 Dec. 59	
		LIEUTENANTS.				
7	0	Charles West Hill	18 Feb. 53	6 June 54	4 Captain Pratt served as Orderly Officer to Brigadier Hon. Adrian Hope in the storming of the Secunder Bagh, Shah Nujeef, 32nd Mess House, and Moti Mahal, at the relief of the Lucknow garrison, afterwards present with Outram's force at the Alum Bagh, also at the storm and capture of Lucknow (commanded a company at the storming of the Kaisar Bagh), and relief of Azimghur.	
6	0	Henry Scott Turner	P 25 Aug. 54	P 3 Aug. 55		
6	0	Romain Flem.Stirke, *Adj.*	6 June 54	16 Aug. 55		
5	0	Edward Boyle	6 July 55	P 25 Jan. 56		
6	0	Charles Richard Williams	5 May 54	25 Sept. 55		
5	0	James John Osmer	1 June 55	P 24 June 56		
5	0	Edward Marwood Vincent	14 Sept. 55	P 22 July 56		
5	0	Robert Boucher Clarke	8 June 55	P 14 July 57		
5	0	John Whiteford	13 Sept. 55	17 Nov. 57		
5	0	Richard Alexander Skues	6 July 55	14 May 57		
4	0	Henry Harrison Bartlett	15 Feb. 56	17 Sept. 58		
4	0	Redmond B. C. Daubeny	27 Feb. 56	1 Oct. 58		
4	0	Henry Charles St. George	29 Feb. 56	3 June 59		
3	0	Frederick Hotham Dyke	P 30 June 57	P 14 June 59		
4	0	Pearson Thomas Beames	8 July 56	P 13 Dec. 59		
		ENSIGNS.				
4	0	Peter Shuttleworth	9 May 56			
4	0	Edward Williams	P 24 June 56			
3	0	George Edward Brace	P 14 July 57			
3	0	T. Hyde Crawley Boevey	P 22 May 57			
3	0	Robert Lestock Thorpe	17 Nov. 57			
2	0	William F. Butler	17 Sept. 58			
2	0	Lambert John Rob. Disney	26 Oct. 58			
1	0	Frederic Knight	P 29 July 59			
1	0	Alexander Irvine	30 Aug. 59			

13	0	**Paymaster.**—Robert Smyth, 10 Nov. 54; *Qr.Mr.* 3 Sept. 47.	
6	0	**Adjutant.**—*Lieut.* Romain Fleming Stirke, 3 June 59.	
3	0	**Instructor of Musketry.**—*Ensign* George Edward Brace, 4 March 59.	
6	0	**Quarter Master.**—William Bustard, 15 Dec. 54.	
19	0	**Surgeon.**—Huntley Geo. Gordon, M.D. 22 April 53; *Assist. Surg.* 31 Dec. 41.	
5	0	**Assist.-Surgeons.**—James Robert Crawford, 2 April 55.	
3	0		John Henderson Whittaker, 3 Oct. 57.
3	0		Francis Madden, 19 Oct. 57.

Facings Green.—*Agents*, Messrs. Cox & Co.

[*Returned from Barbadoes*, 14 May 1857. *Embarked for India*, 17 Nov. 1857.]

1 Major General Gascoigne served in the Peninsula from July 1813 to May 1814, including the passage of the Bidassoa, battles of the Nivelle and Nive, and the investment of Bayonne. Served afterwards in the American war, and was present at the battle of Bladensburg and capture of Washington, where he was severely wounded. He has received the War Medal with three Clasps for San Sebastian, Nivelle, and Nive.

70th (The Surrey) Regt. of Foot. 299

Emb. for Bengal, 18 Jan. 1849. Depot, Canterbury.

Years' Serv.		
Full Pay.	Half Pay.	
56		**Colonel.**—[1] George William Paty,[1] CB. KH. *Ens.* 28 April 04; *Lt.* 7 May 05; *Capt.* 28 April 08; *Maj.* 2 June 14; *Lt.-Col.* 4 Sept. 17; *Col.* 10 Jan. 37; *Maj.-Gen.* 9 Nov. 46; *Lt.-Gen.* 20 June 54; *Col.* 70th F. 8 May 54.
38	1½	**Lieut. Colonels.**—Thomas James Galloway, *Ens.* p 13 Sept. 21; *Lieut.* 2 June 25; *Capt.* p 27 Dec. 27; *Brev.-Maj.* 23 Nov. 41; *Maj.* 14 June 42; *Lt.-Col.* 22 Dec. 48; *Col.* 28 Nov. 54.
28	0	Trevor Chute, 2nd *Lieut.* p 10 Aug. 32; *Lieut.* p 28 Oct. 36; *Capt.* p 2 Aug. 39; *Major,* p 23 April 47; *Lieut.-Col.* p 14 Dec. 49; *Col.* 28 Nov. 54.
24	0	**Majors.**—Thomas Edmonds Mulock, *Ens.* p 18 Mar. 36; *Lieut.* p 29 Nov. 39; *Capt.* p 8 May 46; *Bt.Maj.* 26 Oct. 58; *Major,* 6 Feb. 59.
16	0	George A. Ryan, *Ens.* p 31 May 44; *Lieut.* p 31 Dec. 45; *Capt.* p 15 Nov. 50; *Major,* p 16 Dec. 59.

		CAPTAINS.	ENSIGN.	LIEUT.	CAPTAIN.	BREV.-MAJ.
19	0	Sydney Cosby Jackson..	p 10 Sept. 41	p 25 June 44	p 8 Nov. 50	
22	0	Oswald Pilling	30 Nov. 38	23 June 43	9 Apr. 52	
19	0	Arch. John O. Rutherfurd	p 18 May 41	7 July 46	15 Mar. 53	
17	0	William Cooper[4]	5 June 43	31 Oct. 45	26 Jan. 55	
16	0	Chas. A. Poyntz James[6]	22 Dec. 44	10 Apr. 46	15 Sept. 57	
15	0	Paul Fred. de Quincey[7]..	p 2 May 45	31 July 46	9 Jan. 58	
13	0	Oates Joseph Travers ..	20 Jan. 47	22 Dec. 48	18 July 58	
12	0	Arthur Saltmarshe	22 Dec. 48	p 17 Jan. 51	6 Feb. 59	
7	0	James Green	p 21 Jan. 53	p 5 June 55	p 16 Aug. 59	
11	0	George Richards Greaves.	30 Nov. 49	p 16 Jan. 52	11 Oct. 59	
4	0	Robert Eckford	p 8 Aug. 56	p 14 July 57	p 25 Mar. 59	
7	0	Henry Turner[8]	p 16 Dec. 53	10 Dec. 56	p 16 Dec. 59	
		LIEUTENANTS.				
8	0	Alex. Cha. Hughes Tovey	p 23 Jan. 52	26 Jan. 55		
6	0	Charles William Quin ..	6 June 54	13 May 55		
10	0	Henry Berkeley Good ..	p 22 Nov. 50	30 July 56		
7	0	Thos. Deering Backhouse	13 May 53	15 Sept. 57		
6	0	C.G.StuartMenteath, *Adj*	p 13 Jan. 54	18 May 58		
3	0	William Henry Ralston..	18 Dec. 57	23 July 58		
5	0	Henry Leake	19 July 55	30 July 58		
2	0	John Beldham	15 Jan. 58	24 Sept. 58		
5	0	Eustace Cey	6 July 55	p 30 June 57		
3	0	Arthur William Crozier	11 Sept. 57	12 Jan. 59		
2	0	Alex. Boydell Wright ..	5 Mar. 58	6 Feb. 59		
4	0	Arthur Strong Gilbert ..	22 Aug. 56	24 May 59		
2	0	Herbert John Hill......	p 13 July 58	p 3 June 59		
2	0	Charles Roger	p 12 Nov. 58	p 23 Sept. 59		
2	0	Christopher Garsia.....	23 Mar. 58	11 Oct. 59		
		ENSIGNS.				
2	0	Cha. Clarke Richardson .	26 Mar. 58			
2	0	Charles Hamilton Prior .	30 July 58			
2	0	Norman Huskisson	24 Sept. 58			
2	0	John Fred. Aug. Grierson	31 Dec. 58			
1	0	Robert Stuart Riddell ..	11 Mar. 59			
1	0	James M'Pherson	24 May 59			
1	0	John Robert Collins	p 31 May 59			
1	0	W. Saunders Ford Feneran	24 June 59			
1	0	Henry Bally	p 4 Nov. 59			

8 Captain Turner served in the Persian campaign of 1856-57, including the storm and capture of Reshire, surrender of Bushire, night attack and battle of Kooshab. Served in Bengal and N. W. Provinces in suppressing the mutiny in 1857-58; present in an affair near Futtehpore under Major Eyre, also in the actions of Mungarwar, Alumbagh, and first relief of Lucknow with Havelock's column, present in two sorties from the Residency, the defence of Cawnpore and defeat of the Gwalior mutineers, and actions of Kala Nuddee and Kerkeroulie, and capture of Bareilly.

9 Paymaster Thompson served with the 2nd Batt. Royal Regt. throughout the Mahratta war, with the army in the Deccan, under Sir John Doveton, in the years 1817, 18, and 19. Also, during the Burmese war from Jan. 1825 until its conclusion in 1826 (Medal).

15	0	*Paymaster.*—Michael Thompson,[9] 10 Nov. 54; *Qr.Mr.* 31 Oct. 45.
6	0	*Adjutant.*—*Lieut.* Charles Granville Stuart Menteath, 16 Dec. 59.
5	0	*Instructor of Musketry.*—*Lieut.* H. Leake, 16 Apr. 59.
5	0	*Quarter Master.*—William Nevell, 1 June 55. [June 43.
17	0	*Surgeon.*—George Cunninghame Meikleham,[10] M.D. 28 Mar. 54; *Assist.Surg.* 16
6	0	*Assist. Surgeons.*—Henry James Rogers, 16 June 54.
5	0	James Francis Deakin, M.D. 28 July 55.
5	0	Joseph Watts, 5 April 55.

Facings Black.—*Agents,* Messrs. Cox & Co.

1 Lieut. General Paty served on the expedition to Copenhagen in 1807. Served afterwards in the Peninsula from June 1811 to the end of that war in 1814, including the siege and capture of Badajoz, battle of Salamanca, retreat from Madrid to Burgos, battles of Vittoria, the Pyrenees and Nivelle, battles of the Nive on the 9th, 10th, 11th, 12th, and 13th Dec. 1813, besides various minor affairs. He has received the War Medal with six Clasps; and is a Commander of St. Bento d'Avis and Knight of the Tower and Sword of Portugal.

4 Captain Cooper served with the 18th Royal Irish throughout the campaign of 1852-53 in Burmah (Medal).

6 Captain James served with the 50th Regt. in the campaign on the Sutlej, and was present in the battles of Aliwal and Sobraon (Medal and one Clasp).

7 Captain de Quincey was present with the 8th Regt. at the battle of Sobraon (Medal).

10 Doctor Meikleham served with the 51st during the war in Burmah, from April to June 1852; was on board the E. I. C. steam sloop *Sesostris* during the naval action and destruction of the enemy's stockades in the Rangoon River; served during the succeeding three days' operations in the vicinity (including the storming of the White House Redoubt), and at the storm and capture of Rangoon (Medal and Clasp). Joined the Eastern expedition in March 1854, and served in Turkey till after the end of the war, and was present at the siege of Sebastopol and assault of the Redan on 18th June (Medal and Clasp).

[Emb. for Corfu, March 1853.] **71st (Highland) Regt. of Ft. (L. I.)** [Serving in India. Depot, Perth.

"HINDOOSTAN" "CAPE OF GOOD HOPE" "ROLEIA" "VIMIERA" "CORUNNA"
"FUENTES D'ONOR" "ALMARAZ" "VITTORIA" "PYRENEES" "NIVE" "ORTHES"
"PENINSULA" "WATERLOO" "SEVASTOPOL."

Years' Serv.			Rank and Name	ENSIGN.	LIEUT.	CAPTAIN.	BREV.-MAJ.
Full Pay.	Half Pay.						
55			*Colonel.*—1) Thomas Erskine Napier,¹ CB. *Ens.* 3 July 05; *Lt.* 1 May 06; *Capt.* 27 Oct. 08; *Brev.-Maj.* 26 Dec. 13; *Brev.-Lt.-Col.* 21 June 17; *Col.* 10 Jan. 37; *Major,* 19 May 43; *Maj.-Gen.* 9 Nov. 46; *Lt.-Gen.* 02 June 54; *Col.* 71st F. 16 May 57.				
25	0		*Lieut. Colonels.*—William Hope,⁴ CB. *Ens.* p 4 Sept. 35; *Lieut.* p 24 Mar. 38; *Capt.* p 30 May 45; *Major,* 31 Oct. 55; *Lt.Col.* 26 Dec. 57.				
20	0		George Whitworth Talbot Rich,⁵ *Ens.* p 12 June 40; *Lt.* p 15 Apr. 42; *Capt.* p 12 Nov. 47; *Brevet Major,* 6 June 56; *Major,* p 2 Oct. 57; *Bt.Lt.Col.* 29 July 58; *Lt.Col.* 4 Dec. 59.				
18	0		*Majors.*—James Arthur Gore, *Ens.* 17 Apr. 42; *Lieut.* p 16 Dec. 45; *Capt.* p 8 June 52; *Major,* p 4 Mar. 59.				
19	0		Henry Loftus,⁶ *Ens.* 26 Oct. 41; *Lt.* p 4 Aug. 43; *Capt.* p 22 Dec. 48; *Brev. Maj.* 26 Dec. 56; *Major,* 4 Dec. 59.				
			CAPTAINS.	ENSIGN.	LIEUT.	CAPTAIN.	BREV.-MAJ.
18	0		Arthur Charles Parker¹⁰	4 Mar. 42	p 16 Feb. 44	p 26 Dec. 51	7 Dec. 58
16	0		John Ignatius Macdonell⁸	p 26 Apr. 44	p 8 Dec. 46	29 Dec. 54	
15	0		Charles Francis Smith¹¹ ..	p 30 May 45	p 19 Mar. 47	29 Dec. 54	
15	0		Wm. Francis Segrave	p 8 Aug. 45	p 12 Nov. 47	29 Dec. 54	
10	0		Francis Bonham⁹	p 14 June 50	p 20 Sept. 53	p 17 Apr. 57	
9	0		Fred. William Lambton⁷	p 16 Sept. 51	p 22 Sept. 54	p 23 Oct. 57	19 July 59
9	0		James Dalgleish¹³	6 June 51	7 July 54	26 Dec. 57	
7	0		Edward P. Wade Browne⁶	p 12 Aug. 53	29 Dec. 54	p 12 Nov. 58	
7	0		Charles James Mounsey⁹	p 20 Sept. 53	29 Dec. 54	p 4 Mar. 59	
7	0		John C. H. Poyer Callen⁸	p 28 Oct. 53	9 Feb. 55	p 1 Apr. 59	
8	0		Courtenay H. Salt. Scott⁸	p 17 Aug. 52	8 Dec. 54	p 5 Aug. 59	
6	0		William O'Malley¹³	6 June 54	9 Feb. 55	4 Dec. 59	
			LIEUTENANTS.				
6	0		Robt. Barttelot Aldridge⁷	p 6 June 54	9 Feb. 55		
6	0		C. J. H. Howard	31 Dec. 54	9 Mar. 55		
5	0		Arthur Kindersley Blair .	p 12 Jan. 55	1 June 55		
5	0		Robert Lewis	p 16 Jan. 55	31 Oct. 55		
5	0		Stratton Boulnois	22 Feb. 55	p 30 Jan. 57		
5	0		Robert Heron	30 Mar. 55	p 17 Nov. 57		
5	0		Le Marchant James Carey	10 April 55	26 Dec. 57		
5	0		Wm. Fred. Vernon Harris	1 June 55	15 April 58		
5	0		Robert James Isacke	7 Sept. 55	17 June 58		
5	0		James Hay Campbell, *Adj.*	16 Nov. 55	p 26 Nov. 58		
5	0		Francis Fawkes	14 Dec. 55	p 11 Jan. 59		
4	0		John Boulderson	p 1 Feb. 56	p 11 Mar. 59		
3	0		John Henry Leslie	p 30 Mar. 57	p 1 Apr. 59		
3	0		Richard Kane..........	p 11 Sept. 57	p 5 Aug. 59		
			ENSIGNS.				
3	0		Rich. Courtenay Musgrave	p 17 Nov. 57			
3	0		John Younger Allan	p 18 Nov. 57			
2	0		Arthur Edward Morgan	8 Jan. 58			
2	0		Henry Brooke Wilson ..	p 24 Aug. 58			
1	0		Henry Craster	p 18 Jan. 59			
1	0		Edward Francis Brownlow	p 11 Feb. 59			
1	0		Charles Balfour Murray .	p 18 Mar. 59			
1	0		Hugh Fraser	p 31 May 59			
1	0		Henry Gleed Dods......	p 5 Aug. 59			
1	0		Edw. Gordon Lillingston	p 30 Aug. 59			
1	0		Francis Brodie	p 21 Oct. 59			
19	3		*Paymaster.*—Joseph Cartmail,¹⁴ 25 Aug. 54; *Ens.* 7 Dec. 38.				
5	0		*Adjutant.*—Lieut. James Hay Campbell, 26 Nov. 58.				
			Instructor of Musketry.—				
4	0		*Quarter-Master.*—Robert Anderson,¹³ 29 April 56.				
14	0		*Surgeon.*—William Simpson,¹⁵ M.D. 8 Dec. 54; *Assist.-Surg.* 1 May 46.				
6	0		*Assistant-Surgeons.*—Walter Leach, 24 Nov. 54.				
5	0		Edwin Wilson, 19 May 55.				
3	0		John Warren, 9 Nov. 57.				

1 Lt.-General Napier served with the 52nd Regt. at the siege of Copenhagen and battle of Kioge in 1807. Aide-de-Camp to Sir John Hope on the expedition to Sweden in 1808; and subsequently in Sir John Moore's campaign in Spain, including the retreat to, and battle of, Corunna. In Sicily with the Regiment until the autumn of 1810. Served afterwards in the Peninsula on the staff, including the defence of Cadiz, battle of Fuentes d'Onor, second siege of Badajoz, battles of Salamanca, Vittoria, Nivelle, and the Nive—including the various engagements near the Mayor's house—slightly wounded on the 10th Dec., and severely on the 11th—lost left arm. He has received the War Medal with seven Clasps.

Facings Buff.—*Agents,* Messrs. Cox & Co.

4 Lt.-Colonel Hope landed in the Crimea in 1854, and served in the trenches and at the siege of Sebastopol, and on the expedition to Kertch (Medal and Clasp, Knight of the Legion of Honor, and 5th Class of the Medjidie).

5 Lt.Col. Rich landed in the Crimea in 1855, served in the trenches at the siege of Sebastopol, and was present at its fall (Medal and Clasp, and Brevet Major).

6 Major Loftus served in the Crimea in 1855, including the siege and fall of Sebastopol, expedition to Kertch, affairs at and destruction of Taman (Medal and Clasp, and 5th Class of the Medjidie).

7 Major Lambton and Lieut. Aldridge landed in the Crimea in 1855, served in the trenches at the siege of Sebastopol, and were present at its fall (Medal and Clasp).

71st (Highland) Regt. of Foot (L.I.)

8 Captains Macdonell, Browne, Callen, and Scott, landed in the Crimea in 1855, and served in the trenches at the siege of Sebastopol, and on the expedition to Kertch (Medal and Clasp). Captain Scott served at the destruction of and affairs at Taman in Sept. 1855.

9 Captains Bonham and Mounsey landed in the Crimea in 1854, and served in the trenches at the siege of Sebastopol and expedition to Kertch (Medal and Clasp). Captain Mounsey served at the destruction of and affairs at Taman in Sept. 1855. Captain Bonham has the 5th Class of the Medjidie.

10 Major Parker served in the Crimea from Dec. 1854-57, including the siege and fall of Sebastopol, expedition to Kertch, affairs at and destruction of Taman (Medal and Clasp, and 5th Class of the Medjidie).

11 Captain Smith landed and served in the Crimea in 1855 (Medal and Clasp).

13 Captains Dalgleish and O'Malley, and Qr.Master Anderson landed in the Crimea in 1855, and served at the siege of Sebastopol and expedition to Kertch (Medal and Clasp). Captain O'Malley served at the destruction of and affairs at Taman in Sept. 1855.

14 Paymaster Cartmail landed in the Crimea in 1855 (Medal and Clasp).

15 Doctor Simpson landed in the Crimea in 1854, and served at the siege of Sebastopol (Medal and Clasp).

[Continuation of Notes to 72nd Highlanders.]

only cavalry with the 1st Division throughout the war, and was present in all its operations; commanded the Regt. in the action of Berea; repeatedly mentioned in Dispatches and General Orders. Commanded a Cavalry Brigade in Central India in 1858-59, and defeated the rebels under Tantia Topee at Burod (Medal).

4 Lt.Colonel Thellusson served in the Eastern campaign of 1855, including the expedition to Kertch, siege and fall of Sebastopol, and attack of the 18th June (Medal and Clasp, Knight of the Legion of Honor, and 5th Class of the Medjidie).

5 Major Norman, Captains Robinson, Crombie, Hunter, Couthupe, Lieuts. Basset, Beresford, Campion, Brownlow, St. John, Ensign M'Kay, and Surgeon Seaman, served in the Eastern campaign in 1855, including the expedition to Kertch, siege and fall of Sebastopol, and attack of the 18th June (Medal and Clasp).

6 Captain Rice served at the siege and fall of Sebastopol in 1855 (Medal and Clasp).

7 Major Rocke, Captains Stewart and Vesey served in the Crimea from 13th June 1855, including the expedition to Kertch, siege and fall of Sebastopol, and attack of the 18th June (Medal and Clasp, and 5th Class of the Medjidie).

8 Captain Hastings served in the Persian war in 1857, including the night attack and battle of Kooshab and bombardment of Mohumrah. Served in Bengal in the several actions leading to and ending in the relief of the Residency at Lucknow (severely wounded).

9 Lieuts. Hon. A. T. FitzMaurice and Burges served in the Eastern campaign in 1855, including the expedition to Kertch, siege of Sebastopol, and attack of the 18th June (Medal and Clasp).

10 Lieut. Stockwell served at the siege of Sebastopol in 1855 (Medal and Clasp).

11 Paymaster Webster served in the Eastern campaign in 1855, including the expedition to Kertch and siege of Sebastopol (Medal and Clasp).

12 Qr.Master Munro served in the Eastern campaign in 1855, including the expedition to Kertch, siege and fall of Sebastopol (Medal and Clasp).

13 Assist.Surgeon Rutter served in the Crimea in 1854-55 during the siege and at the fall of Sebastopol (Medal and Clasp).

72d (Duke of Albany's own Highlanders) Reg. of Ft. [Serving in India. Depot, Aberdeen.]

The Duke's Cypher and Coronet.

"HINDOOSTAN" "CAPE OF GOOD HOPE" "SEVASTOPOL."

Years' Serv.						
Full Pay	Half Pay					
55		Colonel.—¹³ Sir John Aitchison,[1] KCB. Ens. 25 Oct. 05; Lt. and Capt. 22 Nov. 10; Capt. and Lt.-Col. 15 Dec. 14; Col. 20 May 36; Major-Gen. 23 Nov. 41; Lt.Gen. 11 Nov. 51; Col. 72nd Highlanders, 29 Dec. 51.				
20	0	Lieut.Colonels.—William Parke,[2] CB. Ens. ᴾ15 Dec. 40; Lt. ᴾ27 Sept. 42; Capt. 9 Jan. 49; Major, ᴾ1 Dec. 54; Lt.Col. ᴾ23 Nov. 55; Col. 26 Apr. 59.				
24	0	Charles Henry Somerset,[3] CB., s. Ens. ᴾ30 July 36; Lieut. 20 Sept. 39; Capt. 8 Jan. 47; Maj. ᴾ17 May 50; Lt.Col. ᴾ28 Jan. 53; Col. 28 Nov. 54.				
19	0	Majors.—Alexander Dalton Thellusson,[4] Ens. ᴾ12 Oct. 41; Lieut. ᴾ8 Oct. 44; Capt. ᴾ28 Dec. 49; Major, ᴾ23 Nov. 55; Bt.Lt.Col. 20 July 58.				
18	0	Richard Rocke,[7] Ens. ᴾ20 May 42; Lieut. ᴾ 8 Nov. 44; Capt. ᴾ8 Mar. 50; Brev. Major, 26 Dec. 56; Major, 6 Mar. 58.				

		CAPTAINS.	ENSIGN.	LIEUT.	CAPTAIN.	BREV.MAJ.
17	0	Douglas Robinson[5]	ᴾ17 Mar. 43	ᴾ19 Mar. 47	2 Dec. 50	
16	0	Charles J. Wm. Norman[5]	ᴾ 8 Nov. 44	ᴾ 8 Oct. 47	ᴾ 7 Oct. 51	20 July 58
14	0	Alexander Crombie[5]	ᴾ 8 May 46	25 Jan. 49	6 June 54	
13	0	Hon. H. W. FitzMaurice	ᴾ19 Mar. 47	ᴾ28 Dec. 49	ᴾ 4 Aug. 54	
13	0	Tho. Cha. Hardinge Best	ᴾ12 Nov. 47	25 April 50	1 Dec. 54	
12	0	Cecil Rice[6]	1 Dec. 48	ᴾ 2 Aug. 50	ᴾ 1 Dec. 54	7 Oct. 59
11	0	C. Fleming Hunter[5]	ᴾ 9 Mar. 49	2 Dec. 50	22 June 55	
10	0	Wm. Drum. Ogilvy Hay	ᴾ17 May 50	ᴾ14 Oct. 51	22 June 55	
10	0	Hon. Bentinck Coathupe[5]	ᴾ12 July 50	ᴾ14 Oct. 51	22 June 55	
10	0	John Campbell Stewart[7]	ᴾ16 Aug. 50	ᴾ25 June 52	6 Mar. 58	
20	0	Douglas Hastings[8]	20 Mar. 40	8 Apr. 42	15 Mar. 53	
10	0	Chas. C. Wellesley Vesey[7]	8 Nov. 50	6 June 54	ᴾ15 Apr. 59	

		LIEUTENANTS.		
8	0	Edward James Upton	ᴾ 21 Sept. 52	1 Dec. 54
7	0	Hon.Alex.T.FitzMaurice[9]	ᴾ13 May 53	ᴾ 1 Dec. 54
7	0	Gustavus Lambert Basset[5]	ᴾ10 June 53	ᴾ 1 Dec. 54
7	0	M. de la Poer Beresford[5]	ᴾ 2 Dec. 53	22 June 55
6	0	Stapleton Dresing Burges[9]	6 June 54	22 June 55
6	0	William Henry Campion[5]	ᴾ18 Aug. 54	22 June 55
6	0	Francis Brownlow[5]	ᴾ 8 Sept. 54	22 June 55
6	0	Robert St. John[5]	3 Nov. 54	22 June 55
6	0	Charles M. Stockwell[10]	17 Nov. 54	22 June 55
6	0	Hercules Edwin Brown	ᴾ 1 Dec. 54	26 Feb. 56
5	0	Charles Stewart Murray	19 June 55	26 Feb. 56
5	0	James Robert Kildahl	21 June 55	23 Mar. 58
5	0	Henry Arthur Crane	6 July 55	7 Sept. 58
5	0	James Drummond Stewart	4 July 55	ᴾ15 May 59

1 Sir John Aitchison served in 1807 at the siege and capture of Copenhagen. Embarked in 1808 for the Peninsula, and in 1809 was present at the passage of the Douro, capture of Oporto, and subsequent pursuit of Soult's army to Salamonde. He was wounded in the arm at the battle of Talavera, while carrying the King's colour, which was also shot through. He served the campaigns of 1810, 12, 13, and 14, and was present at the battle of Busaco and retreat to the lines of Torres Vedras; battle of Salamanca, capture of Madrid, siege of Burgos, and retreat from thence into Portugal; affair at Osma, battle of Vittoria, affair at Tolosa, siege of San Sebastian, battles of the Nivelle and the Nive, passage of the Adour, investment of Bayonne, siege of the citadel, and repulse of the sortie. He has received the War Medal with six Clasps. He was Lieut.-Colonel of the Scots Fusilier Guards when promoted to Major-General, and had commanded that Regiment upwards of four years. Served in India as Major-General on the Staff of the Madras Presidency from June 1845 to Nov. 1851, in command of the Mysore division (including Coorg), and of the Provinces of Malabar and Canara.

		ENSIGNS.	
5	0	John Price Mackinnon	22 June 55
5	0	George M'Kay[5]	2 Aug. 55
5	0	Francis George Sherlock	17 Aug. 55
5	0	Matthew John Baillie	14 Dec. 55
4	0	Albert Tanner	27 Feb. 56
3	0	Herbert Barron	ᴾ27 Mar. 57
3	0	Henry Francis Campbell	ᴾ 3 Mar. 57
2	0	James Thomson, Adj.	15 Oct. 58
2	0	Arthur Rice	31 Dec. 58
1	0	Thomas Francis Pardoe	ᴾ31 May 59
16	0	Paymaster.—Rowland Webster,[11] 29 May 49; Ens. 12 Jan. 44; Lt. ᴾ25 July 45.	
2	0	Adjutant.—Ensign James Thomson, 31 Dec. 58.	
5	0	Instructor of Musketry.—Ensign George M'Kay,[5] 30 July 57.	
5	0	Quarter Master.—Donald Munro,[12] 30 Nov. 55.	
19	0	Surgeon.—Wm. Campbell Seaman,[5] M.D. 16 May 51; Assist.-Surg.16 Feb. 41.	
6	0	Assistant Surgeons.—Theodore William Rutter,[13] M.D. 9 June 54.	
6	0		George M'Gusty Carolan, 23 Dec. 54.
5	0		Morgan Jones Jones, 15 Feb. 55.

Facings Yellow.—*Agents*, Messrs. Cox and Co.

[*Returned from the Crimea*, 30 *July* 1856. *Embarked for India*, 26 *August* 1857.]

2 Colonel Parke served in the Crimean campaign in 1855, in command of the 72nd Highlanders from July, including the expedition to Kertch, siege and fall of Sebastopol, and assaults of 18th June and 8th Sept. (Medal and Clasp, Knight of the Legion of Honor, and 5th Class of the Medjidie). Served in India in 1857-59, was appointed 1st Class Brigadier and commanded 2nd Brigade of the Rajpootanah field force from March 1858 to July 1859, including the siege and fall of Kotah on which occasion he commanded the leading column of assault; subsequently throughout the operations in Central India in 1858-59, and pursuit of the rebel forces under Tantia Topee and Rao Sahib, who were attacked and defeated at Oodeypore in Dec. 1858 by the 2nd Brigade R. F. Force). Received the thanks of the Governor General of India and of the Governor in Council of Bombay; Aide de Camp to the Queen, CB. and Colonel, Medal and Clasp).

3 Colonel Somerset served as Aide-de-Camp to Sir Benjamin D'Urban during the Kaffir war in 1835. In 1841 he accompanied Major Smith's expedition towards Natal, served in the Kaffir war of 1846-47 as Aide-de-Camp to Col. Somerset, and afterwards to Sir George Berkeley. Served throughout the Kaffir war of 1850-53 (Medal). In Dec. 1850 took the Head Quarters of the Cape Mounted Riflemen into the field, on the 29th commanded that portion of the Regt. with the 1st Division in action (horse wounded); commanded the storming party at the capture of Fort Armstrong; commanded the wing of the C. M. Riflemen, the [For remainder of Notes, see preceding page.

73rd Regiment of Foot. 303

"MANGALORE" "SERINGAPATAM" "WATERLOO."

Em. for C. of G. Hope, 20 Sept. 45.] Dinapore. Depot, Chatham.

Colonel.—Chesborough Grant Falconar,[1] KH. *Ens.* p 1 Sept. 95; *Lt.* 1 Nov. 99; *Capt.* 26 Dec. 05; *Brev.-Maj.* 12 Aug. 19; *Maj.* p 26 June 23; *Lt.-Col.* p 22 Oct. 25; *Col.* 28 June 38; *Maj.Gen.* 11 Nov. 51; *Lt.Gen.* 20 July 58; *Col.* 73rd Foot, 11 Feb. 57.

Lieut. Colonels.—George Hankey Smith,[3] *Ens.* p 7 May 18; *Lt.* p 7 Feb. 22; *Capt.* p 8 Apr. 26; *Bt.-Maj.* 23 Nov. 41; *Maj.* 20 July 49; *Bt.Lt.Col.* 11 Nov. 51; *Col.* 28 Nov. 54; *Lt.Col.* 21 May 58.

Majors.—Thomas Ross, *Ens.* p 23 March 38; *Lieut.* p 18 May 41; *Capt.* p 4 June 47; *Major*, p 22 Oct. 52; *Bt.Lt.Col.* 26 Oct. 58.
Hugh Maurice Jones,[4] *Ens.* p 22 Apr. 46; *Lt.* p 9 Aug. 50; *Capt.* p 1 July 53; *Bt.Major*, 20 July 58; *Major*, 11 Feb. 59.

Years' Serv.						
Full Pay	Half Pay	CAPTAINS.	ENSIGN.	LIEUT.	CAPTAIN.	BREV.MAJ.
65						
42	0					
22	0					
14	0					
20	0	W. E. Bowes,[5] *s. l.c.* 26 Oct. 58	19 June 40	p 22 July 42	p 3 Aug. 49	28 May 53
18	0	George Renny[6]	1 Nov. 42	1 May 44	p 28 Dec. 49	
15	0	Godfrey James Burne[6]	p 23 May 45	p 26 May 48	p 18 Apr. 51	
19	0	Wm. Creagh O'Brien[8]	p 19 Nov. 41	26 June 44	21 Dec. 52	
11	0	William Henry Barry	p 18 Sept. 49	p 17 Sept. 50	p 18 Feb. 53	
11	0	J. C. Gawler,[10] *l.c.* 18 Feb. 59	9 Feb. 49	p 12 July 50	p 14 Apr. 54	20 July 55
15	0	Frederick Reeve	p 24 Oct. 45	p 8 Oct. 47	6 June 54	
13	0	James Whittaker Barnes[11]	5 Nov. 47	p 6 July 49	22 Sept. 54	
10	0	Alex. Allan Aitchison	p 17 May 50	p 18 Apr. 51	p 17 Feb. 57	
9	0	Spencer V. Fra. Henslowe	p 18 Apr. 51	21 Dec. 52	p 27 Nov. 57	
10	0	Albert H. Godfrey	p 8 Feb. 50	p 4 Apr. 51	21 May 58	
9	0	Richard James Hereford	20 June 51	p 22 April 53	2 July 58	
8	0	Philip Gibaut	12 Oct. 52	6 June 54	p 4 Nov. 59	
		LIEUTENANTS.				
9	0	Fred. Tichfield Greatrex		5 Dec. 51	11 Aug. 54	
7	0	Mathew Smith Blyth		p 13 May 53	31 Aug. 55	
6	0	Wm. John Lane Milligan		6 June 54	p 17 Apr. 57	
6	0	William Mitford		22 Sept. 54	p 28 Aug. 57	
5	0	Hugh Fraser		p 12 Jan. 55	p 27 Nov. 57	
6	0	William Gordon, *Adj.*		15 Sept. 54	23 Mar. 58	
5	0	William Bayley		9 Feb. 55	14 May 58	
5	0	Thomas Wm. Shore Miles		1 May 55	21 May 58	
5	0	Archibald Henry Sharp		7 Sept. 55	2 July 58	
5	0	Wm. Henry Samuel Pigott		7 Dec. 55	9 July 58	
4	0	Hast. D'Oyly Farrington		8 July 56	10 July 58	
3	0	William Clarke		p 17 Feb. 57	p 1 Oct. 58	
3	0	Thomas Monsell Warren		p 17 Apr. 57	2 Nov. 58	
2	0	Arch. C. Fall Armstrong		22 June 58	p 13 Dec. 59	
2	0	James Fraser		28 May 58	p 16 Dec. 59	
		ENSIGNS.				
3	0	Arthur Hare Palmer		p 29 Dec. 57		
2	0	James Trench Turner		13 April 58		
2	0	James Kirk		15 June 58		
2	0	Hugh F. Hacket Gibsone		p 13 July 58		
2	0	St. John Dupond Galwey		p 30 July 58		
2	0	Bolton Jas. Alf. Monsell		7 Sept. 58		
2	0	Thos. Nepean Edw. Kenny		31 Dec. 58		
1	0	Henry Synge		23 Aug. 59		
1	0	Sydenham Clith. M'Gill		p 13 Dec. 59		

22	0	**Paymaster.**—Loftus Cassidy, 30 June 54; *Ens.* p 9 Nov. 38; *Lieut.* 11 June 41;	
6	0	**Adjutant.**—*Lieut.* William Gordon, 4 Nov. 59.	[*Capt.* 6 June 54.
2	0	**Instructor of Musketry.**—*Ensign* James Trench Turner, 26 Feb. 59.	
2	0	**Quarter Master.**—Jonathan Gortly Scott, 24 Feb. 59.	
19	0	**Surgeon.**—Edward Booth, 13 Feb. 52; *Assist.-Surg.* 11 June 41.	
3	0	**Assistant Surgeons.**—Robert Thomas Scott, 8 Dec. 57.	Facings Green.
2	0	John Anderson, M.B. 10 March 58.	Agents, Messrs.
2	0	John M'Kinnel, M.D. 22 April 58.	Cox & Co.

1 Lieut.General Falconar joined the 61st Regt. at the Cape in February 1801, and accompanied it to Egypt, joining General Baird's army at Cosier—crossed the Desert with it, and remained in the Army of Egypt until 1803. In 1804 and 1805 he served in the campaign in Italy under Sir James Craig. Served with the 78th Highlanders the campaign of 1806 in Italy under Sir John Stuart—at the battle of Maida, siege of Scylla, capture of Catrone, &c. In 1807, the campaign in Egypt, including the attack on the fortified heights and forts of Alexandria, 1st affair at Lake Elcho and Elhamet, investment and siege of Rosetta, actions at Rosetta and Elhamet 21st April. Served the campaign of 1814 and 1815 in Holland and Flanders—commanded Light Infantry 78th at both attacks on Merxem, attack of French at Brescat, and bombardment of Antwerp. Has received the Egyptian Gold Medal; also the Silver War Medal with two Clasps for Egypt and Maida, at which last battle he had a horse shot under him when acting as Aide de Camp to General Acland.

[Marginal notes: 2 Captains Renny and Burne served in the Kaffir war of 1851-53 (Medal), including the operations in the Amatolas, Fish River, Waterkloof, and Trans-Kei expeditions. 6 Captain O'Brien served in the action of Manarjpore (wounded), in the 40th Regt. in the Bronze Star. 8 Captain Barnes served as Lieut. and Adj. in Major Hogg's Battalion of Native Infantry in the Kaffir war of 1846-47; was present in several engagements, accompanied the expedition into the Tamboökie country in August, and that over the Kei in Dec. 1846. Served with the 73rd Regt. in the Kaffir war in 1851 (Medal). 10 Lt.-Col. Gawler served with the 73rd Regt. throughout the Kaffir war of 1850-53 (Medal and Bt. Major); commanded the Light Company in nearly all the principal actions in Kaffirland and in the Colony, as also at the battle of Berea; served at different periods during the operations as Field Adjutant and as D.A. Qr. Master General to the Divisions under Colonel Eyre, and was honourably mentioned eight times in official Reports; was appointed District Adjutant of Natal at the close of the war. In Sept. 1855 was appointed Special Magistrate to Umhala's tribe in British Kaffraria, just as that Chief was attempting the cattle killing and corn destroying insurrection; succeeded in bringing about a reaction among a large number of Kaffirs who placed themselves under his authority in opposition to their Chiefs, and who were thus formed into one friendly tribe under him as their Chief, he procured evidence by their instrumentality to convict almost all the Kaffir leaders of treasonable practices, having thus broken up their power he was permitted to invade with his tribe the territory of the paramount Chief Kreli and succeeded in driving him beyond the Bashee,—Kreli's territory was thus added to British Kaffraria and occupied in villages by Lt.-Col. Gawler's Kaffirs. For the foregoing services he received the public thanks of the Cape Government and was gazetted Lt.-Colonel in the Army on 18th Feb. 1859. 3 Colonel Smith served in the Kaffir war of 1846-7, and was severely wounded. In Sir George Berkeley's General Order of 17th Dec. 1847 he was mentioned in the following handsome terms:—"The Lieut. General begs to thank Major Smith, 73rd Regt., who has commanded the Head Quarter Camp during the whole of the active operations, for the zeal and ability which he has shown" (Medal). 4 Major Jones served with the 13th Lt. Inf. in the Crimea from 30th June 1855, including the battle of the Tchernaya, siege and fall of Sebastopol (Medal and Clasps), and 5th Class of the Medjidie. 5 Lt.-Col. Bewes served the Kaffir campaign of 1846-7 (Medal) with the 45th Regt.]

304 [Foreign Service, 11 Mar. 51.] **74th (Highland) Reg. of Foot.** [Serving in India. Depot, Aberdeen.

The *Elephant*, superscribed "SERINGAPATAM" "ASSAYE" "BUSACO" "FUENTES D'ONOR" "CIUDAD RODRIGO" "BADAJOZ" "SALAMANCA" "VITTORIA" "PYRENEES" "NIVELLE" "ORTHES" "TOULOUSE" "PENINSULA."

Years' Serv.							
52		Colonel.—19 Charles Augustus Shawe,[1] *Ens.* p 26 May 08; *Lt. & Capt.* p 23 April 12; *Capt. & Lt.-Col.* p 28 April 25; *Major & Col.* p 8 Aug. 37; *Major-Gen.* 9 Nov. 46; *Lt.Gen.* 20 June 54; *Col.* 74th Foot, 24 Nov. 56.					
Full Pay.	Half Pay.						
37	0 6/12	Lieut. Colonels.—John MacDuff,[2] *Ens.* 10 Feb. 14; *Lieut.* 26 June 27; *Capt.* p 13 April 30; *Major*, 13 Nov. 47; *Lieut.Col.* p 8 June 49; *Col.* 28 Nov. 54.					
19	1 4/12	James Villiers,[3] *Ens.* p 31 Dec. 39; *Lt.* p 24 Sept. 41; *Capt.* p 24 Dec. 47; *Bt. Maj.* 12 Dec.54; *Maj.* 4 May 55; *Bt. Lt.Col.* 17 July 55; *Lt.Col.* 15 June 58.					
22	0	Majors.—Walter Douglas Phillipps Patton,[4] *Ens.* p 28 Sept. 38; *Lt.* p 3 Nov. 40; *Capt.* p 19 May 46; *Maj.* 27 Feb. 52; *Bt. Lt. Col.* 28 May 53; *Col.* 28 Nov. 54.					
15	0	William Kelty M'Leod, *Ens.* 6 June 45; *Lieut.* p 31 July 46; *Capt.* p 24 Sept. 50; *Maj.* 27 Jan. 58.					
		CAPTAINS.	ENSIGN.	LIEUT.	CAPTAIN.	BREV.MAJ.	
14	0	John Jago	p 16 Jan. 46	p 19 Feb. 47	p 7 Mar. 51		
14	0	Lewis Augustus Brydon[6]	1 May 46	p 21 July 48	27 Feb. 52		
14	0	Henry Wellington Palmer[6]	p 7 Aug. 46	10 Nov. 48	17 Aug. 52		
13	0	James Falconer[8]	4 Nov. 47	2 Aug. 49	29 July 53		
22	0	James Stewart Menzies .	p 10 Feb. 38	24 Oct. 39	15 Mar. 53		
13	0	Augustus Davies	p 4 June 47	p 3 Aug. 49	16 Dec. 53		
21	1 6/12	Fred. J. B. Priestley	2 Mar. 38	8 Apr. 42	21 Jan. 53		
43	3 7/12	9 W. J. Impett,[9] c. 25 Mar. 59	14 Apr. 14	p 5 Oct. 20	30 Jan. 35	9 Nov. 46	
11	0	Fred. B. Thackeray[6] ...	p 14 Dec. 49	7 Nov. 51	p 5 Sept. 56		
9	0	Cavendish Venables [10] ..	p 19 Aug. 51	7 Aug. 54	19 June 55		
10	0	Hon. John B. J. Dormer	p 15 Mar. 50	p 21 Apr. 54	p 22 June 55		
9	0	Charles Wylde Sherlock	p 21 Nov. 51	p 5 Nov. 52	p 6 May 59		
		LIEUTENANTS.					
9	0	Thomas William Lawson[6]	p 22 Aug. 51	17 Aug. 52			
11	0	Henry Jameson	23 Mar. 49	p 21 Sept. 52			
8	0	William Shapter Hunt ..	p 6 July 52	30 June 54			
8	0	Norman S. M'Crummen	23 Nov. 52	8 Sept. 54			
8	0	Robert Frederick Martin	p 17 Dec. 52	p 10 Nov. 54			
6	0	Frederick Nind Woodall	p 24 Mar. 54	15 Dec. 54			
7	0	John Thomas Evans	p 11 Mar. 53	6 June 54			
6	0	Abel Straghan	p 30 July 54	p 8 July 56			
9	0	Henry Currie, *Adj.*	p 16 Sept. 51	p 7 June 54			
6	0	A. Wm. Chalmers Magrath	p 24 Mar. 54	p 5 Sept. 56			
6	0	Colin Hugh Thomson ..	p 6 Oct. 54	p 5 Sept. 56			
4	0	Robert Elphinstone Deare	p 8 July 56	p 9 Jan. 57			
6	0	Arthur Angelo	13 Oct. 54	15 Jan. 58			
4	0	Augustus Daniel Keane..	0 July 56	27 Jan. 58			
4	0	Edwin Tarver Sainsbury.	p 5 Sept. 56	p 18 Mar. 59			
3	0	Francis Pavy	p 9 Jan. 57	p 13 May 59			
		ENSIGNS.					
2	0	Charles John Rolleston..	30 Mar. 58				
2	0	Norman Magnus MacLeod	31 Mar. 58				
2	0	Robert Langley Clowes..	13 Apr. 58				
2	0	Edward Bradby	p 24 Aug. 58				
2	0	Arthur Meredith Duff ..	p 1 Oct. 58				
2	0	Peter M'Laren	29 Oct. 58				
2	0	William Henry Beere....	19 Nov. 58				
1	0	George Wm. Monk Hall .	p 31 May 59				
1	0	Charles H. Dougherty ..	24 June 59				
0	0	*Paymaster.*—Roger Sheehy, 13 May 59.					
0	0	*Adjutant.*—Lieut. Henry Currie, 30 July 58.					
11	0	*Instructor of Musketry.*—Lieut. H. Jameson, 12 Apr. 58.					
4	0	*Quarter Master.*—George Watson,[17] 27 May 56.					
10	0	*Surgeon.*—James Macbeth,[15] M.D. 12 Aug. 53; *Assist.-Surg.* 3 Dec. 41.					
5	0	*Assistant Surgeons.*—Wm. Robt. Burkitt,[16] 17 Apr. 55.					
3	0	Arthur Chester, 1 Aug. 57.					
2	0	Robert Gillespie, M.D. 1 Sept. 58.					

Facings White.—*Agents*, Messrs. Cox & Co.

2 Colonel MacDuff served in India upwards of 14 years with the 40th Regt., including the operations in 1840 in Lower and Upper Scinde; also the campaigns in Beloochistan, Candahar, and Cabool during 1841-42, and has received the Medal inscribed "Candahar, Ghuznee, Cabool." Was with the 40th Regt. in the operations against the Gwalior state in 1843-4, and commanded the Grenadier Company at the battle of Maharajpore (Medal). In 1852 he commanded the 1st Infantry Brigade with the force under Sir George Cathcart in the advance across the Orange and Caledon rivers, Southern Africa, into the Basuto Chief Moshesh's country; afterwards he commanded the force encamped at the Dhoonie Station in Kaffraria, until the end of the Kaffir war in 1853 (Medal).

6 Captains Brydon, Palmer, and Thackeray, and Lieut. Lawson, served throughout the Kaffir war in 1851—53 (Medal).

9 Colonel Impett served the campaign of 1815 with the 71st Regt., and was present at the battle of Waterloo.

1 Lieut.-General Shawe served the campaigns of 1810, 1811, and part of 1812, in the Peninsula, including the battle of Busaco. Served also in Holland and Belgium from Nov. 1813 to 1814, and was severely wounded at Bergen-op-Zoom. He has received the War Medal with three Clasps for Busaco, Fuentes d'Onor, and Ciudad Rodrigo.

4 Colonel Patton served with the 74th throughout the Kaffir war of 1851-53 (Medal), and was present in all the operations; commanded the Regt. from Nov. 1851 until Oct. 1852; for his services he was promoted to the rank of Lieut. Colonel. Served in the Eastern campaign of 1854, and was present at the battles of Balaklava and Inkerman, and siege of Sebastopol; was also present throughout the battle of the Alma with Lord Raglan's Staff as an amateur (Medal and four Clasps, and 5th Class of the Medjidie).

8 Capt. Falconer served as Adjutant of the 74th in the Kaffir war and Hottentot Rebellion of 1851-53 (Medal), and was present in all the operations in which the Regt. was engaged; served as Field Adjutant to the Brigade under Lieut.-Colonel Fordyce, until that officer was killed in Nov. 1851; accompanied the force under Sir George Cathcart, which crossed the Orange River against the Basuto Chief Moshesh in 1852; served as Brigade-Major in the first Brigade of that force, and received the thanks of Colonel Eyre commanding the Infantry, and of Lieut.Col. MacDuff commanding the Brigade. Commanded three Companies of the 74th on field service in the Southern Mahratta Country in 1858-59, during the Indian Mutiny.

74th (Highland) Regiment of Foot. 305

10 Captain Venables served with the 57th Regt. in the Crimea from Sept. 1854, and was present at the battles of Balaklava and Inkerman (wounded), siege and fall of Sebastopol, storming of the Quarries, and attack of the Redan on the 8th of June ; also present at the bombardment and capture of Kinbourn (Medal and Clasps, and 5th Class of the Medjidie).
15 Dr. Macbeth served with the 10th Foot in the Sutlej campaign of 1845-6, including the battle of Sobraon (Medal). Served also in the Punjaub campaign of 1848-9, and was present during the siege operations before Mooltan (till ordered away on duty with sick and wounded), including the affair of the 9th Sept., and storming the enemy's entrenched position on the 12th September (Medal and Clasp).
16 Assist. Surgeon Burkitt served in the Crimea in 1855, and was at the assaults on Sebastopol on the 18th June and 8th Sept. (Medal and Clasp).
17 Quarter Master Watson served in the Kaffir War of 1851-53 (Medal).

[Continuation of Notes to 75th Foot.]

4 Lt.Colonel Mollan served in the Indian campaign of 1857-59,—commanded the 75th Regt. with Outram's force at Alumbagh, from Dec. 1857 to Feb. 1858, including repulse of attacks on 12th and 16th Jan. and minor affairs. Served as Brigade Major with the Rifle Brigade at the siege and capture of Lucknow, and actions of Koorsee, Barce, Simree, Nawabgunge (horse killed by round shot), and Sultanpore, operations terminating in the passage of the Goomtee on 28th Aug., action at Daodpore and capture of the enemy's guns, surrender of the forts of Ameethie and Shunkerpore (frequently mentioned in despatches, Medal and Clasp, Brevet Lt. Colonel, and CB.).
5 Lt.Colonel Gordon served in the campaigns against the Kaffir Tribes of South Africa in 1834-35 (Medal). Also as Assistant Engineer during 1837 and 1838, on the eastern frontier of the Cape Colony; and employed under Colonel Lewis, commanding Royal Engineers, to execute a confidential survey (trigonometrical and statistical) on that frontier. Served in the Indian campaign of 1857-58, commanding the 75th Regt. during the capture of Delhi from the 15th Sept., and was wounded on the 18th leading the assault on the Hubshee-ka-Phatcck ; planned and carried out the forward movement of the right attack within the city, surprising and capturing the Burra Bastion at its gorge on the evening of the 19th, retaining it under a constant fire until the next morning when the enemy evacuated Delhi. Proceeded with Greathed's Column and commanded the Regt. in the actions of Bolundshuhur, Allyghur, Akrabad, Agra, and Kanoj, advance into Oude and minor affairs ending in the relief of Lucknow; subsequently with the Oude field force in front of the city until 14th Feb.—specially mentioned in Outram's despatch for "judgment and coolness" in defending the left advanced outpost of the Camp during a night attack made by a very large force of the enemy on the 16th Jan., which he repulsed with severe loss (Medal and Clasps, and Brevet Lt.Colonel).
6 Major Brookes served as Field Adjutant to the Troops on the first line of defence during the Kaffir war of 1834-35 (Medal). Was Brigade Major to the force of Occupation in the conquered province of Queen Adelaide from April to Dec. 1836; and District Adjutant at Fort Beaufort from Jan. 1837 to Dec. 1842; received the special thanks of Sir George Napier the Governor and Commander in Chief at the Cape of Good Hope in a letter dated 5th July 1839 for service in the field. Served during the Indian campaign of 1857-58 from the outbreak on the 12th May, including the siege and capture of Delhi (part of the time in command of the 75th Regt.), pursuit of the enemy and actions of Bolundshuhur, Allyghur, Aerabad, Agra, and Kanoj, advance into Oude and affairs of Maragunge and Alumbagh, occupation after the relief of Lucknow of the fortified outposts and camp with Outram's force, and repulse of the enemy's attacks (Medal and Clasps and Brevet of Major).
10 Major Drew served with the 75th Regt. throughout the campaign before Delhi in 1857, including the battle of Badulee ke Serai ; commanded the Grenadier Company at the assault of Delhi and ultimately the Regt.; accompanied Colonel Greathed's pursuing column and was present at the affairs of Allyghur and Akbarabad, and battles of Bolundshuhur and Agra; served in the advance into Oude under Sir Colin Campbell, and on the relief of the Garrison of Lucknow remained with General Outram's force at Alumbagh, and took part in the several repulses of the enemy (Medal and Clasps, and Brevet of Major).
11 Captain Smith served the campaign in Oude and relief of the Garrison of Lucknow, afterwards at the Alum Bagh, and took part in the several repulses of the enemy (Medal and Clasp).
12 Captain Malan served in the 7th Fusiliers at the siege and fall of Sebastopol from 12th June 1855 (Medal and Clasp).
13 Captain Justice served during the Indian campaign of 1857, and was present at the siege of Delhi from 23d June to 13th Sept. (in command of the Light Company), storm and capture of the city (Medal and Clasp).
14 Lieut. Pelley served during the Indian campaign of 1857-58, from the outbreak on 12th May, including the battle of Budleckaserai, siege, storm and capture of Delhi, pursuit of the enemy and actions of Bolundshuhur, Allyghur, Acrabad, Agra, Kanoj, advance into Oude and affairs of Maragunge and Alumbagh, occupations after the relief of Lucknow of the fortified outposts and camp with Outram's force, and repulse of the enemy's attacks (Medal and Clasps).
15 Captain Pym served in the Indian campaign of 1857-58, including the battle of Budleckaserai, and siege operations against Delhi from 23d June to 8th Aug. (Medal and Clasp).
16 Lieut. Hurford served in Burmah (Medal).
17 Lieut. Brocas served in the Indian campaign of 1857-58, including the occupation, after the relief of Lucknow, of the fortified outposts and camp with Outram's force, and repulse of the enemy's attacks (Medal).
18 Lieut. Row served in the Indian campaign of 1857 from the outbreak on 12th May, including the battle of Budleckaserai, siege, storm and capture of Delhi (Medal and Clasp).
19 Lieut. Morris served in the Indian campaign of 1857-58, including the occupation, after the relief of Lucknow, of the fortified outposts and camp with Outram's force, and repulse of the enemy's attacks; also present at the battle of Cawnpore on 6th Dec. (Medal).
20 Lieut. Wadeson served in the Indian campaign of 1857 from the outbreak on 12th May, including the battle of Budleckaserai, siege operations before Delhi and repulse of sorties on 12th and 15th June, and of night attacks on the camp on 19th and 23d June, and 14th and 18th July, storming (severely wounded) and capture of Delhi (Medal and Clasp, and Victoria Cross).
21 Lieut. Streets served in the Indian campaign of 1857, and was present at the affairs with the Sealkote Mutineers on the banks of the Ravee on the 12th and 16th July, also at the assault (severely wounded) and capture of Delhi (Medal and Clasp).
22 Paymaster Chambers served in the Indian campaign of 1857 from the outbreak on 12th May, including the battle of Budleckaserai, siege (wounded on 8th June), storm and capture of Delhi (Medal and Clasp).
23 Qr.Master Dunlop served in the Indian campaign of 1857 from the outbreak on 12th May, including the battle of Budleckaserai, storm and capture of Delhi (Medal and Clasp).
24 Doctor Domenichetti served on the Staff of General Havelock on his first taking the field in 1857, and was present in the actions of Futtehpore, Aoung, Pandoo Nuddee, Cawnpore, Buseerutgunge, Bithoor, and Alumbagh, also the defence of the Alumbagh (thanked by the President of the Council of India). Served with the 75th Regt. before Lucknow under Gen. Outram in two attacks upon his position.

[Embarked for Bengal, 7 May 49.] **75th Regiment of Foot.** [Serving in India. Depot, Chatham.

Years' Serv.		
52		The *Royal Tiger*, superscribed "INDIA" "SERINGAPATAM."

Colonel.—St. John Augustus Clerke,[1] KH. *Ens.* 13 Oct. 08; *Lt.* 6 June 11; *Capt.* p 11 Mar. 19; *Major*, p 26 May 25; *Lt.Col.* p 30 Dec. 28; *Col.* 23 Nov. 41; *Major Gen.* 20 June 54; *Col.* 75th Foot, 22 Mar. 58.

Full Pay	Half Pay	
29	0	**Lieut.Colonels.**—William Radcliffe, *Ens.* p 27 Sept. 31; *Lt.* p 24 April 35; *Capt.* p 7 June 44; *Bt.Major*, 18 Dec. 55; *Major*, 13 Apr. 58; *Lt.Col.* 26 Oct. 58.
27	0	Legendre Charles Bourchier,[3] *Ens.* p 5 April 33; *Lt.* p 12 May 36; *Capt.* p 20 July 38; *Bt.Maj.* 11 Nov. 51; *Maj.* 12 Dec. 51; *Bt.Lt.Col.* 9 Aug. 58; *Lt.Col.* 7 Oct. 59.
33	0	**Majors.**—Edward Knollys, *Ens.* p 18 Oct. 27; *Lt.* p 2 Nov. 30; *Capt.* p 17 Feb. 37; *Brev.Maj.* 11 Nov. 51; *Maj.* 2 June 57; *Brevet Lt.Col.* 11 Jan. 58.
20	0	Wm. Campbell Mollan,[4] CB. *Ens.* p 10 Jan. 40; *Lieut.* p 2 April 41; *Capt.* p 13 Oct. 43; *Brev.Maj.* 20 June 54; *Major*, 7 Oct. 59.

		CAPTAINS.	ENSIGN.	LIEUT.	CAPTAIN.	BREV.MAJ.
27	0	C. E. P. Gordon,[5] l.c.10 Jan.58	13 Dec. 33	p 17 Feb. 37	p 25 Apr. 45	29 Aug. 57
27	0	William Brookes[6]	11 Jan. 33	16 Sept. 36	28 Jan. 48	19 Jan. 58
25	1	John H. Cox,[7] l.c. 26 Apr. 59	p 10 Oct. 34	p 11 July 37	31 Mar. 48	19 Jan. 58
18	0	Thomas Clement Dunbar[8]	1 Apr. 42	p 31 Mar. 43	p 25 Apr. 51	19 Jan. 58
15	0	Thomas Milles	p 25 Apr. 45	3 April 49	p 15 May 57	
18	0	George William Muriel	24 June 42	29 July 45	2 June 57	
15	0	Browning Drew[10]	p 7 Mar. 45	p 8 Jan. 47	13 June 57	24 Mar. 58
18	0	Wm. John Jas. Smith[11]	20 May 42	7 Sept.43	5 Oct. 57	
6	0	Charles H. Malan[12]	6 Nov. 54	9 Mar. 55	p 4 June 58	
8	0	William Clive Justice[13]	10 Dec. 52	p 20 July 55	p 22 Apr. 59	
7	0	Charles Melville Pym[15]	p 10 June 53	9 June 57	p 18 Oct. 59	

		LIEUTENANTS.			
11	0	Ernest Le Pelley[14]	20 Oct. 49	27 Aug. 52	7 Lt.Colonel Cox served in the Indian campaign of 1857-59, and acted as Staff Officer in the affair of Kudjwah on 1st Nov. 1857; served as a Brigade Major with Lord Clyde's force at the relief of the Residency of Lucknow (horse shot); present at the battle of Cawnpore and fight at Subadah Tank the same day, affair of Seraighat, action of Kala Nuddee, affair of Shumshabad, siege and capture of Lucknow, affair of Rayeah, and capture of Bareilly, capture of the fort of Muttoulic (six times mentioned in despatches, Brevets of Major and Lt.Colonel, Medal and Clasp). 8 Major Dunbar has the Medal for the Punjaub campaign. Served with the flank companies 98th Regt. in the force under Sir Colin Campbell at the forcing of the Kohat Pass in Feb. 1850. Served during the Indian campaign of 1857 from the outbreak on 12th May, including the battle of Budleekaserai, siege, storm, and capture of Delhi—wounded in the hand in the trenches on 12th Sept. (Medal and Clasp, and Brevet of Major).
11	0	William Henry Urquhart	p 9 Feb. 49	p 10 June 53	
9	0	Thomas Carlisle	p 17 Jan. 51	p 23 June 54	
8	0	Henry Payne Hurford[16]	16 Jan. 52	13 June 57	
5	0	Reginald Brocas[17]	9 Feb. 55	p 9 Oct. 55	
4	0	George Home Row[18]	p 18 Jan. 56	19 June 57	
3	0	Mont.Cholmeley Morris[19]	p 22 May 57	15 Sept. 57	
3	0	VC Rich. Wadeson,[20] *Adj.*	2 June 57	19 Sept. 57	
3	0	James Streets[21]	19 Sept. 57	1 Nov. 57	
4	0	Frederick Cornwall	27 Feb. 56	p 21 Feb. 58	
3	0	John Thomas H. Butt	30 Oct. 57	1 Oct. 58	
4	0	Hugh Barton Gladstones	p 26 Feb. 56	p 22 Apr. 59	
4	0	Irving Stening Allfrey	p 29 July 56	16 Apr. 58	
2	0	Denzil Hammill	16 Jan. 58	p 18 Oct. 59	
2	0	Fred. Francis Daniell	13 Aug. 58	p 16 Dec. 59	

		ENSIGNS.		
5	0	Henry O'Brien	16 Oct. 55	
4	0	Wilmsdorf G. Mansergh	8 Feb. 56	
2	0	George Benjamin Singer	15 Jan. 58	
2	0	Charles Finnerty	17 Jan. 58	
2	0	F. Bullen Morris	p 13 July 58	
2	0	J. Tarby	8 Oct. 58	
2	0	Harry Philip Dawson	p 9 Nov. 58	
2	0	Anthony Rowband	31 Dec. 58	
1	0	Alfred John Buckle	p 15 Nov. 59	
2	0	Alfred Sinclair Leatham	p 9 Nov. 58	
20	0	**Paymaster.**—David Francis Chambers,[22] 26 Jan. 49; *Ens.* p 31 Jan. 40; *Lt.*		
3	0	**Adjutant.**—VC *Lieut.* Richard Wadeson,[20] 11 March 59. [6 May 42.		
9	0	**Instructor of Musketry.**—*Lieut.* T. Carlisle, 1 Nov. 58.		
13	1	**Quarter Master.**—John Dunlop,[23] 9 Feb. 49; *Ens.* 1 May 46.		
14	0	**Surgeon.**—Richard Domenichetti,[24] M.D. 10 June 57; *Assist.Surg.* 3 April 46.		
3	0	**Assistant Surgeons.**—Harry Reid, M.D. 8 Dec. 57.		
2	0	Charles William Semple, 22 Apr. 58.		
2	0	Robert Woods, 13 Oct. 58.		

Facings Yellow.—*Agent*, E. S. Codd, Esq.

1 Major General Clerke served with the old 94th at Cadiz during the siege, in the Lines of Torres Vedras, during the retreat from Santarem; having been present in the actions of Pombal, Redinha, Condeixa, Foz d'Arouce, Sabugal, and Fuentes d'Onor. He joined the 77th Regt. (also in the Peninsula) on promotion, and served with it in the actions of El Bodon and Aldea de Ponte, at the siege and assault of Cuidad Rodrigo, siege of Badajoz, assault and capture of Port Picurina, and storming of the castle of Badajoz (severely wounded in the right knee); he has received the War Medal with three Clasps. For the affair at Redinha he was promoted, and his services at Picurina and the storming of Badajoz were voluntary and were duly recognised by his superiors.

3 Lt.Col. Bourchier served with the 17th throughout the campaign in Affghanistan and Beloochistan under Lord Keane, and was present at the storm and capture of Ghuznee (Medal) and of Khelat, at which last he was twice wounded.

[For remainder of Notes, see preceding page.

Head Quarters, Dublin.]
Depot, Belfast.   **76th Regiment of Foot.**   307

The *Elephant*, circumscribed "HINDOOSTAN" "NIVE" "PENINSULA."
Colonel.—💰 William Jervois,[1] KH. *Ens.* 7 April 04; *Lieut.* 8 Aug. 04; *Capt.* 14 July 08; *Major,* 19 Dec. 13; *Lieut.Col.* 22 Sept. 14; *Col.* 10 Jan. 37; *Major Gen.* 9 Nov. 46; *Lt.Gen.* 20 June 54; *Col.* 76th Foot, 10 May 53.

Lieut.Colonels.—Henry Smyth,[2] CB. *Ens.* ᴘ 28 June 33; *Lieut.* ᴘ 28 Oct. 36; *Capt.* ᴘ 2 Dec. 42; *Major,* ᴘ 12 May 48; *Lt.Col.* ᴘ 30 Dec. 53; *Col.* 28 Nov. 54.
Majors.—Richard Gardiner, *Ens.* 12 May 14; *Lieut.* 29 Sept. 25; *Capt.* ᴘ 5 April 33; *Maj.* 11 Nov. 45; *Brev.Lt.Col.* 20 June 54; *Col.* 26 Oct. 58.
Henry Craigie Brewster, *Ens.* ᴘ 18 Oct. 33; *Lieut.* ᴘ 19 Aug. 36; *Capt.* ᴘ 9 Nov. 39; *Brev.Maj.* 11 Nov. 51; *Maj.* 15 Jan. 58; *Bt.Lt.Col.* 26 Oct. 58.

Years' Serv. Full Pay	Half Pay	CAPTAINS.	ENSIGN.	LIEUT.	CAPTAIN.	BREV.MAJ.
56						
27	0					
46	0					
27	0					
25	0	C. Fenwick, *l. c.* 26 Oct. 58	ᴘ 4 Sept. 35	ᴘ 7 April 37	ᴘ 3 April 40	11 Nov. 51
25	0	Morley S. Tynte Dennis	ᴘ 18 Sept. 35	ᴘ 28 Nov. 37	ᴘ 10 Nov. 43	20 June 54
24	0	Thomas Tydd	ᴘ 3 June 36	ᴘ 19 Oct. 38	3 Sept. 47	26 Oct. 58
14	0	Thomas William Cator	29 Dec. 46	ᴘ 30 July 47	ᴘ 12 Nov. 52	
21	0	Henry Hearne Lacy	ᴘ 1 Feb. 39	ᴘ 16 Apr. 41	6 June 54	
21	0	Charles O'Donoghue	29 Aug. 39	ᴘ 20 Dec. 42	21 July 54	
20	0	Wilford Brett, *s.*	ᴘ 29 May 40	ᴘ 13 Jan. 43	29 June 55	
14	0	James Fox Bland	ᴘ 8 Dec. 46	14 Oct. 51	ᴘ 15 Feb. 56	
24	4	T.B. Mortimer, *l.c.* 25 Mar. 59	ᴘ 16 Nov. 32	2 July 37	ᴘ 24 Sept. 41	20 June 54
15	0	James Cumming Clarke	ᴘ 28 Mar. 45	ᴘ 4 June 47	15 Jan. 58	
6	4⁰⁄₁₂	Edward G. Waldy[3]	ᴘ 8 July 53	8 Dec. 54	ᴘ 9 Jan. 57	
12	0	John Geddes	25 Aug. 48	6 June 54	7 Sept. 58	
		LIEUTENANTS.				
9	0	Charles Thos. Caldecott	ᴘ 4 Apr. 51	11 Aug. 54		
10	0	John Henry Tripp	ᴘ 12 July 50	ᴘ 22 April 53		
9	0	John Vincent	ᴘ 2 May 51	20 June 55		
9	0	Edward Wm. Fred. Acton	5 Dec. 51	ᴘ 13 July 55		
6	0	John Augustine Palliser	ᴘ 1 Sept. 54	ᴘ 14 Mar. 56		
6	0	Luke E. O'Connor, *adj.*	3 Nov. 54	ᴘ 15 Apr. 56		
5	0	John M'Dermid Allardice	20 Feb. 55	25 Jan. 56		
5	0	James Henry Linton	10 May 55	2 Oct. 55		
5	0	Henry Filkes Hooper	6 July 55	12 Feb. 58		
4	0	Richard Wm. Beachey	ᴘ 15 Apr. 56	10 Sept. 58		
5	0	Thos. Trophimus Hodges	6 Sept. 55	22 July 50		
5	0	Edward Harrison	23 Nov. 55	5 Aug. 59		
4	0	Edward Harding	8 July 56	ᴘ 16 Aug. 59		
5	0	Seaton Ralph Forster[4]	23 Nov. 55	17 Sept. 58		
2	0	Edward Le Breton Butler	26 Jan. 58	ᴘ 13 Dec. 59		
		ENSIGNS.				
2	0	Godfrey Treve Faussett	ᴘ 5 Feb. 58			
2	0	Edmund Austin	12 Feb. 58			
2	0	Henry Bouverie Pusey	ᴘ 21 May 58			
2	0	Ernest Rogby Bartleet	ᴘ 28 May 58			
2	0	Albert E. Pearse	2 July 58			
2	0	Augustus George West	ᴘ 9 Nov. 58			
1	0	Joseph Alex. Greene	ᴘ 18 Jan. 59			
1	0	William Monro	8 Apr. 59			
1	0	John Talbot	ᴘ 28 Oct. 59			

3 Captain Waldy served with the 28th Regt. the Eastern campaign of 1854-55, including the battles of Alma and Inkerman, siege and fall of Sebastopol, and affair in the Cemetery (Medal and three Clasps, and 5th Class of the Medjidie).

4 Lt. Forster served with the 84th Regt. in the Indian campaign of 1858, and was present with Brigadier Douglas' column in the action of Burrahpore, assault and capture of Jugdespore, and subsequent operations (Medal).

16	0	*Paymaster.*—Robert Thos. Hearn, 30 Sept. 51; *Ens.* 19 Aug. 44; *Lt.* 29 May 47.	
6	0	*Adjutant.*—Lieut. Luke E. O'Connor, 2 Feb. 58.	
10	0	*Instructor of Musketry.*—Lieut. J. H. Tripp, 1 May 58.	
2	2₁₃	*Quarter Master.*—John Packwood, 20 Dec. 59; *Cornet,* 21 Jan. 56.	
24	0	*Surgeon.*—Robert Thomas Scott, *Assist.Surg.* 15 July 36; *Surgeon,* 7 Aug. 46; [*Surg. Major,* 1 Oct. 58.	
7	0	*Assistant Surgeons.*—Duncan Alex. Campbell Fraser, M.D. 28 Oct. 53.	
6	0	John Macartney, 9 June 54.	

Facings Red.—*Agents,* Messrs. Cox and Co.—*Irish Agents,* Sir E. R. Borough, *Bt.,* Armit, & Co.
[*Returned from Nova Scotia,* 13 *Oct.* 1857.]

1 Lieut.General Jervois accompanied the 89th Regt. on the expedition to Hanover in 1805. In 1810 he was appointed to the staff of Lord Blayney; accompanied him on the expedition to Malaga, and was slightly wounded in the attack on the Fortress of Frangerola. In 1813 he was appointed to the staff of Sir Gordon Drummond, and embarked with him for Canada, where, during the operations of that and the following year, he was present in almost every action fought with the American Army either in that Province or on the Frontier, including the storming of Port Niagara, Lewistown, the attacks on Black Rock and Buffalo, operations against the forts and batteries of Oswego, and action of Lundy's Lane. He received the brevet rank of Major for Buffalo, and that of Lieut.Colonel for Lundy's Lane.

2 Colonel Smyth commanded the 68th Light Infantry throughout the Eastern campaign of 1854-55, including the battles of Alma and Inkerman (horse killed), siege and fall of Sebastopol (Medal and Clasps, CB., Officer of the Legion of Honor, Sardinian Medal, and 4th Class of the Medjidie).

308 77th (*The East Middlesex*) Regt. of Foot. [East Indies. Depot, Chatham.

The Plume of the Prince of Wales.—"SERINGAPATAM" "CIUDAD RODRIGO" "BADAJOZ" "PENINSULA" "ALMA" "INKERMAN" "SEVASTOPOL."

Years' Serv.			
Full Pay.	Half Pay.		
57		*Colonel.*—₽ George Leigh Goldie,¹ CB. *Cornet*, 3 Sept. 03; *Lieut.* 14 Mar. 05; *Capt.* 4 Dec. 06; *Major*, 20 June 11; *Lieut.Col.* 12 Aug. 19; *Col.* 10 Jan. 37; *Maj.Gen.* 9 Nov. 46; *Lt.Gen.* 20 June 54; *Col.* 77th Foot, 22 Dec. 54.	
19	0	*Lieut.Colonels.*—Hon. Aug. Geo. Charles Chichester, *Ens.* ᵖ 19 Feb. 41; *Lt.* ᵖ 22 Nov. 42; *Capt.* ᵖ 3 Aug. 49; *Maj.* ᵖ 6 July 55; *Lt.Col.* 16 June 58.	
38	0	Thomas Josephus Deverell, *Ens.* 7 Nov. 22; *Lieut.* 25 June 29; *Capt.* ᵖ 30 Aug. 31; *Bt.Maj.* 9 Nov. 46; *Maj.* 3 Sept. 47; *Bt.Lt.Col.* 20 June 54; *Lt.Col.* 24 Aug. 58; *Col.* 26 Oct. 58.	
15	0	*Majors.*—Henry Kent,³ *Ens.* ᵖ 8 Aug. 45; *Lieut.* ᵖ 23 Aug. 50; *Capt.* 27 Sept. 54; *Major*, 24 Aug. 58.	
20	0	Henry Alfred Macdonald, *Ens.* 30 Dec. 40; *Lieut.* ᵖ 10 Nov. 43; *Capt.* 26 Jan. 55; *Major*, ᵖ 4 Nov. 59.	

Full	Half	CAPTAINS.	ENSIGN.	LIEUT.	CAPTAIN.	BREV.MAJ.
9	0	Wm. Joseph Carden⁴ ..	5 Dec. 51	6 June 54	ᵖ 2 Mar. 55	
8	0	Rd. Butler Willington⁵	ᵖ 16 Apr. 52	ᵖ 13 May 53	20 Apr. 55	
7	0	Frederick John Butts⁶ ..	ᵖ 18 Mar. 53	ᵖ 18 Aug. 54	20 Apr. 55	
7	0	Wm. N. Morris Orpen⁷	ᵖ 14 May 53	27 Sept. 54	ᵖ 5 June 55	
7	0	Matthew Wm. Dickson⁸	22 Apr. 53	ᵖ 18 Aug. 54	24 July 55	
6	0	H. M. Lamont Colquhoun	ᵖ 18 Aug. 54	29 Dec. 54	ᵖ 17 July 57	
6	0	George Edward Leggett⁹	ᵖ 25 Aug. 54	29 Dec. 54	ᵖ 30 Apr. 58	
6	0	James M. Daly¹⁰.......	4 Nov. 54	9 Feb. 55	ᵖ 4 June 58	
7	0	Wm.Tho.ExhamFosbery¹¹	ᵖ 11 Mar. 53	2 Feb. 55	16 June 58	
6	0	Thomas Peter Harvey¹² ..	27 Oct. 54	9 Feb. 55	24 Aug. 58	
13	0	Edward Lister Green¹² †	22 Jan. 47	ᵖ 6 Oct. 48	2 Feb. 58	
6	0	John George Skene	29 Dec. 54	9 Mar. 55	ᵖ 4 Nov. 59	

		LIEUTENANTS.			
5	0	Marcus A. Waters¹³ ..	26 Jan. 55	ᵖ 23 Feb. 55	
6	0	William Minister¹⁴......	5 Nov. 54	9 Mar. 55	
6	0	Herbert Fred. L. Browne	1 Dec. 54	9 Mar. 55	
5	0	Wm. M. Dixwell Alderson	ᵖ 16 Jan. 55	20 Apr. 55	
5	0	Charles B. Knowles¹⁵....	20 Feb. 55	20 Apr. 55	
5	0	Aubrey Thomas Butts ..	9 Mar. 55	ᵖ 25 May 55	
5	0	Phil. Secklemore Dauncey	15 Mar. 55	ᵖ 5 June 55	
5	0	Charles Bertram Saunders	22 Feb. 55	4 Sept. 55	
5	0	Harcourt Mort. Bengough	ᵖ 22 Mar. 55	3 Oct. 55	
5	0	John Jordan	9 Oct. 55	ᵖ 3 Apr. 58	
5	0	Hen. StewartWeigall,*Adj.*	6 July 55	24 Aug. 58	
5	0	John Wordsworth	8 Nov. 55	ᵖ 4 Mar. 59	
5	0	Reginald Hoskins	ᵖ 7 Dec. 55	ᵖ 3 June 59	
4	0	Percy Kirk	1 Feb. 56	ᵖ 4 Nov. 59	
4	0	Randle Jackson	12 Dec. 56	ᵖ 18 Nov. 59	

		ENSIGNS.			
5	0	Cecil Percival Stone	6 Nov. 55		
5	0	Henry Reginald Bate ..	9 Nov. 55		
5	0	John Lenthal Davids....	31 Aug. 55		
2	0	Oscar Henry Blount	ᵖ 28 May 58		
2	0	George Augustus White..	19 Nov. 58		
1	0	Edward Nicholas Mosley	ᵖ 18 Mar. 59		
1	0	Wm. Samuel Henderson	ᵖ 31 May 59		

1 Lieut.General Goldie served in the Peninsula from March 1809 to Nov. 1813, including the passage of the Douro, battles of Talavera, Busaco, and Albuhera, covering sieges of Badajoz, affairs of Arroyo, de Molino, and Campo Mayor, battles of Vittoria and the Pyrenees, besides minor actions and skirmishes. Severely wounded in the Pyrenees on the 30th July 1813 by a musket-ball, which is still lodged in the lungs—this wound was long considered mortal. He has received the Gold Medal for Albuhera, and the Silver War Medal with four Clasps for Talavera, Busaco, Vittoria, and Pyrenees. He held an important command in the disputed territory in Canada in 1838-39.
4 Capt. William Carden served in the Eastern campaign of 1854-55, including the siege of Sebastopol (Medal and Clasp).
17 Assist.Surgeon Hoysted served with the 59th Regt. at the operations before and capture of Canton on 29th Dec. 1857.

6	0	*Instructor of Musketry.*—Capt. H. M. L. Colquhoun, 30 Dec. 56.
17	0	*Paymaster.*—Wm. Fortescue Scott,¹⁶ 13 Jan. 54; *Ens.* 15 July 43; *Lt.* 18 Feb 48.
5	0	*Adjutant.*—Lieut. Henry Stewart Weigall, 4 Nov. 59.
6	0	*Quarter Master.*—Henry Blissett,¹⁶ 3 Nov. 54.
12	9/12	*Surgeon.*—Thomas Rhys, 20 July 55; *Assist.Surg.* 3 June 48.
6	0	*Assistant Surgeons.*—Alexander Humfrey,¹⁶ 28 April 54.
5	0	George Clarence Hyde, 17 Jan. 55.
5	0	Thomas Norton Hoysted,¹⁷ 28 Sept. 55.

Facings Yellow.—*Agents*, Messrs. Alx. F. Ridgway & Sons.

[*Returned from the Crimea*, 23 July 1856. *Embarked for Australia*, 4 June 1857.] †

3 Major Kent served the Eastern campaign of 1854-55, including the battles of Alma and Inkerman, and siege of Sebastopol (Medal and Clasps, and 5th Class of the Medjidie).
5 Capt. Willington served the Eastern campaign of 1854-55, including the battles of Alma and Inkerman, and siege of Sebastopol (Medal and Clasps, Sardinian Medal, and 5th Class of the Medjidie).
6 Capt. Butts served the Eastern campaign of 1854-55, including the battles of Alma and Inkerman, siege of Sebastopol, and attack on the Redan on the 8th Sept.—severely wounded (Medal and Clasps, and 5th Class of the Medjidie).
7 Captain Orpen served at the siege of Sebastopol in 1855 (Medal and Clasp).
8 Captain Dickson served in the Eastern campaign of 1854-55, including the battles of Alma and Inkerman, and siege of Sebastopol, until severely wounded 8th June (Medal and Clasps).
9 Captain Leggett served at the siege of Sebastopol from December 1854, and was wounded at the attack on the Redan on the 8th Sept. (Medal and Clasp).

77th (*The East Middlesex*) Regt. of Foot.

10 Captain Daly served at the siege of Sebastopol in 1855 (Medal and Clasp).

11 Captain Fosbery served at the siege of Sebastopol from July 1855, and was dangerously wounded—left leg amputated (Medal and Clasp).

12 Captain Harvey served at the siege and fall of Sebastopol from the 7th June 1855, and at the assault of the Redan on the 8th Sept.; he was selected to cross the open space, under a heavy fire, to stop the fire of our own eight-gun battery (Medal and Clasp).

12† Captain Green served in the Kaffir wars of 1847 and 1850-53 (Medal), was severely wounded in the former war when commanding the rear-guard, and in the latter war served as Aide de Camp to Major General Somerset, and D.A.Qr.Mas.Gen. with the head-quarters of Sir George Cathcart.

13 Lieut. Waters served with the 53rd Regt. during the campaign against the Hill Tribes on the Peshawur frontier in 1851-52. Served with the 77th Regt. in the Crimea from 11th June 1855, including the siege and fall of Sebastopol, and was present at the assault on the 18th June, and engaged at the storming of the Redan on the 8th Sept.—severely contused (Medal and Clasp).

14 Lieut. Minister served in the Eastern campaign of 1854-55, including the battles of Alma and Inkerman, and siege of Sebastopol (Medal and Clasps).

15 Lieut. Knowles served at the siege of Sebastopol in 1855, and was severely contused at the assault on the Redan on the 8th Sept. (Medal and Clasp).

16 Paymaster Scott, Qr.Master Blissett, and Assist.Surgeon Humfrey, served the Eastern campaign of 1854-55, including the battles of Alma and Inkerman, and siege of Sebastopol (Medal and Clasps). Assist.-Surgeon Humfrey has also the Sardinian Medal. Paymaster Scott has the 5th Class of the Medjidie.

[*Continuation of Notes to 78th Foot.*]

28 Assist.Surgeon M'Master served in the Persian war in 1857, including the night attack and battle of Kooshab, and bombardment of Mohumrah. Left Allahabad with Havelock's column in July 1857, and was present in all the operations resulting in the recapture of Cawnpore and in the first advance into Oude and subsequent engagements up to 12th August; present on the second advance into Oude and in all the actions ending in the relief of the Residency of Lucknow and subsequent defence including several sorties (wounded); with Outram's force at Alumbagh until the capture of Lucknow.

29 Doctor Skipton served with the 49th Regt. at the siege and fall of Sebastopol from 22 May 1855 (Medal and Clasp). Was attached to the 14th Lt. Dragoons in the Central India field force under Sir Hugh Rose in 1858, and was present at the siege and capture of Rahatghur, relief of Saugor, capture of Gurrakotah and pursuit across the Beas; at Malthone, siege and capture of Jhansi, capture of the fort of Loharree (mentioned in despatches), and various affairs during the advance on Calpee, action of Golowlee, capture of the fort and arsenal of Calpee, action of Morar, and recapture of Gwalior (Medal and Clasps).

Record of the Services of the 78th Highlanders.

Raised by letter of Service dated 7th March 1793; inspected and passed July 1793; proceeded to Holland September 1794; returned to England May 1795; proceeded to Quiberon August 1795; returned January 1796; proceeded to the Cape of Good Hope 1796; to Calcutta February 1797; to Bombay February 1803; to Goa February 1807; to Java August 1811; returned to England July 1817; proceeded to Ireland November 1817; embarked for Ceylon April 1826; returned to England February 1838; embarked for India April 1842. Proceeded on active service to Persia in Jan. 1857, returned to Bombay in May 1857, thence immediately to Bengal. Returned to England, Sept. 1859.

78th (Highland) Regt. of F. (or Ross-shire Buffs.) [Fort George. Depot, Fort George.

"*Cuidich'n Rhi.*"—The *Elephant*, superscribed "ASSAYE" "MAIDA" "JAVA."

Years' Serv. Full Pay.	Half Pay.					
57		**Colonel.**—Sir William Chalmers,[1] CB. KCH. Ens. 9 July 03; Lieut. 25 Oct. 03; Capt. 27 Aug. 07; Major, 26 Aug. 13; Lieut. Col. 18 June 15; Col. 10 Jan. 37; Major Gen. 9 Nov. 46; Lt. Gen. 20 June 54; Col. 78th Foot, 30 Sept. 53.				
22	0	**Lt. Col.**—John Alexander Ewart,[2] CB. Ens. 27 July 38; Lieut. 15 April 42; Capt. p 12 May 48; Brev. Maj. 12 Dec. 54; Major 29 Dec. 54; Brev. Lt. Col. 2 Nov. 55; Lt. Col. 16 April 58; Col. 26 April. 59.				
31	0	**Majors.**—Henry Hamilton,[4] CB. Ens. p 13 Aug. 29; Lieut. p 20 Nov. 33; Capt. p 29 April 42; Major, p 19 April 50; Bt. Lt. Col. 9 July 57.				
35	0	Colin Campbell M'Intyre,[5] CB. Ens. 9 Apr. 25; Lieut. p 17 July 28; Capt. p 28 Apr. 37; Major, 19 June 50; Bt. Lt. Col. 5 Sept. 57.				

		CAPTAINS.	ENSIGN.	LIEUT.	CAPTAIN.	BREV. MAJ.	BT. LT. COL.
21	0	Jas. Duncan MacAndrew[6]	p 15 Mar. 39	p 21 May 41	p 6 Oct. 48		
23	0	Græme Alex. Lockhart[7]	p 8 Dec. 37	8 April 42	p 19 Apr. 50	24 Mar. 58	13 Dec. 59
21	0	Thos. R. Drummond Hay[8]	p 2 Aug. 39	p 5 Nov. 41	p 17 Nov. 48	19 Jan. 58	
20	0	Alexander Mackenzie[9] ..	p 7 Feb. 40	8 April 42	15 Mar. 53	20 July 58	
19	0	Lawrence P. Bouverie[11]	p 7 Sept. 41	28 Dec. 42	p 22 Dec. 54	19 Jan. 58	20 July 58
18	0	Wm. M'Gregor Archer[12],	p 1 April 42	24 Oct. 44	13 Dec. 56		
15	0	Thomas Anderson	23 May 45	p 10 Dec. 47	17 Aug. 57		
14	0	T. C. Belmore St. George[13]	p 29 Dec. 46	p 10 Nov. 48	2 Feb. 58		
12	0	Alfred W. Pym Weekes[10]	p 6 Oct. 48	p 14 Sept. 52	10 Sept. 58		
9	⅙	Oswald Barton Feilden[14]	p 17 Sept. 50	p 15 July 53	p 23 Nov. 55		
11	0	Augustus Edm. Warren[15]	p 2 Feb. 49	p 5 Nov. 52	p 20 July 55		
	0	John Finlay[16]	p 14 Feb. 51	p 22 Dec. 54	10 Sept. 58		
		LIEUTENANTS.					
7	0	Geo. Digby Barker,[20] *Adj.*	p 21 Jan. 53	p 16 Mar. 55			
8	0	Melville Aug. Walker[21]..	p 18 Aug. 52	6 July 55			
7	0	Frederick Henry Walsh[22]	p 18 Mar. 53	p 21 Sept. 55			
4	0	Edw. Jackson Fitzsimons	20 Feb. 56	p 5 June 57			
4	0	William Thomson	8 July 56	19 July 57			
4	0	Richard Pierce Butler ..	p 17 Oct. 56	29 July 57			
3	0	John Nathaniel Gower..	p 1 May 57	20 Nov. 57			
3	0	Wm. Hen. S. M. Browne[23]	19 June 57	23 Mar. 58			
5	0	Richard Clay...........	2 Nov. 55	30 Mar. 58			
4	0	Thomas Mackenzie....	p 8 Feb. 56	30 Apr. 58			
3	0	Thomas Hinde Thompson	27 Nov. 57	10 Sept. 58			
3	0	Malcolm M'Neill	18 Dec. 57	p 24 Dec. 58			
4	0	R. Cuninghame C. Graham	p 1 Apr. 56	p 11 Mar. 59			
3	0	Henry Anthony Ingles ..	18 Dec. 57	p 9 Sept. 59			
5	0	Henry B. Savory[24].....	9 Oct. 55	24 Sept. 57			
		ENSIGNS.					
2	0	Sir Alex. M. Mackenzie, *Bt*	p 12 Feb. 58				
2	0	Andrew Murray........	p 7 Feb. 58				
2	0	Thomas Owen S. Davies	16 Mar. 58				
2	0	Alex. B. Ker Williamson	23 Mar. 58				
2	0	James Baron Baillie	30 Mar. 58				
2	0	Jas. Tho. S. Richardson	30 Apr. 58				
2	0	James Hart	10 Sept. 58				
2	0	Henry Swanson	26 Nov. 58				
2	0	John Ingle	13 April 58				
1	0	William Charles Smith ..	p 16 Sept. 59				
22	0	**Paymaster.**—Joseph Webster,[25] 22 April 53; Ens. 23 Nov. 38.					
7	0	**Adjutant.**—Lieut. George Digby Barker, 5 Nov. 58.					
3	0	**Instructor of Musketry.**—Lieut. T. H. Thompson, 18 Aug. 59.					
4	0	**Quarter Master.**—Charles Skrine,[26] 12 Sept. 56.					
18	0	**Surgeon.**—Joseph Jee,[27] CB. 23 June 54; Assist. Surg. 15 Apr. 42.					
5	0	**Assist. Surgeons.**—Valentine Mumbee M'Master,[28] 27 Mar. 55.					
6	0	Samuel Stacy Skipton,[29] M.D. 9 June 54.					

Side notes:
10 Captain Weekes served in the Persian war in 1857, including the night attack and battle of Kooshab, bombardment of Mohumrah.
14 Captain Feilden served in the 72nd Highlanders at the siege and fall of Sebastopol from 16th July 1855 (Medal and Clasp).
15 Captain Warren served with the 82nd Regt. at the siege of Sebastopol from 2nd Sept. 1855 (Medal and Clasp). Also in the Indian campaign of 1857-59, and was present at the relief of Lucknow by Lord Clyde, defeat of the Gwalior Contingent at Cawnpore, action of Khodagunge, and occupation of Futteghur,—acting successively as Orderly Officer to Brigadier Russell, Col. Hale, and Sir John Inglis; served the Rohilcund campaign, including the defence of the Jail and subsequent operations at Shahjehanpore, and actions of Khankur and Bunkagaon (Medal and Clasp).
16 Captain Finlay served in the Persian war in 1857, including the night attack and battle of Kooshab, bombardment of Mohumrah, and expedition to Ahwaz. Served in Bengal with Havelock's column from its first taking the field in 1857, including the actions of Futtehpore, Aoung, Pandoo Nuddee, Cawnpore, Oonao, Busserutgunge (1st and 2nd), and in the several actions leading to and ending in the relief of the Residency of Lucknow and subsequent defence; with Outram's force at Alumbagh, including the repulse of the numerous attacks and operations, ending in the final capture of Lucknow. Indian campaign of 1857-59, and was present with Havelock's Column at the actions of the 21st and 23rd Sept., the relief of Lucknow, subsequent defence of Lucknow (wounded), defence of the Alumbagh under Outram, final capture of Lucknow, and subsequent operations in Oude (Medal and Clasps).
24 Lieut. Savory served with the 90th Lt. Inf. during the Indian campaign of 1857-59, and was present with Havelock's Column at the actions of the 21st and 23rd Sept., the relief of Lucknow (wounded), defence of the Alumbagh under Outram, final capture of Lucknow, and subsequent operations in Oude (Medal and Clasps).

Facings Buff.—*Agents*, Messrs. Cox & Co.
[*Returned from India, Sept. 1859.*]

1 Sir William Chalmers served in Sicily in 1806 and 7; campaigns of 1808-9 in Portugal and Spain; expedition to Walcheren, including bombardment of Flushing; at Cadiz in 1810 and 11; and all the succeeding Peninsular campaigns, including the battle of Barrosa, attack of the enemy on the heights near Moresco, affair of Senhora de la Pena, battle of Salamanca, action of San Munos, battle of Vittoria, attack at Maya, battles of the Pyrenees on the 30th and 31st July, repulse of the enemy in his attack of the heights of St. Antonio, 31st August, attack of the enemy's forts near Sarre, 9th Oct. 1813, battle of Nivelle, besides a great many minor affairs and skirmishes on the advance to Madrid and capture of the Retiro. He was present with the army in the Peninsula during almost all the sieges, and was engaged in the following affairs during the retreat from Burgos, viz. Olmos, Monasterio, bridge of Valladolid, and passage of the Huebra. Served also in the Netherlands in 1814 and 15, including the battle of Waterloo, capture of Paris, and posterior operations in France, to Aug. 1817. He was severely wounded in assault of the entrenchments at Sarre, and has had nine horses killed or wounded under him in action, three of them at Waterloo. During the above campaigns he was on the staff, except at Waterloo. Subsequently to his services in Sir John Moore's campaign and Lord Chatham's expedition, he was, in the course of about four years (from 5th March 1811 to 18th June 1815), in seventeen engagements, six of them general actions—exclusive of sieges; and for his conduct in the field he was twice promoted, viz. to the brevet rank of Major at the battles of the Pyrenees, and of Lieut.-Colonel at the battle of Waterloo, on which occasion he commanded the left wing of the 52nd Regt. He has received the War Medal with eight Clasps.

78th (Highland) Regt. of Foot. 311

2 Colonel Ewart served throughout the Eastern campaign of 1854-55; present with the 93rd at the battle of Alma, and until after the occupation of Balaklava; appointed a D.A.Q.M.G. 26th Sept. 1854, and as such was present at the battles of Balaklava and Inkerman, and throughout the siege operations before Sebastopol up to 13th Feb. 1855, when he rejoined the 93rd on promotion; accompanied the expedition to the Sea of Azoff, and was at the capture of Kertch and Yenikali; afterwards present at the siege and fall of Sebastopol, and assaults on the 18th June and 8th Sept. (Medal and four Clasps, Brevet of Major and Lt.Col., Knight of the Legion of Honor, Sardinian Medal, and 5th Class of the Medjidie). Served in Bengal during the Indian Mutiny; was at an engagement near Bunnoe, and afterwards at the final relief of Lucknow; held for a short time a command consisting of three squadrons of Cavalry 5 guns and 500 Infantry (specially named in despatches and appointed a CB.); and on the 16th Nov. commanded the leading party of stormers at the assault of the Secunderbagh, on which occasion he personally captured a colour, receiving two sabre wounds in an encounter with the two Native Officers who were defending it; was again (very severely) wounded by a cannon shot (left arm carried away) when in action with the Gwalior rebels at Cawnpore on the 1st Dec. 1857 (Medal and Clasp, Aide de Camp to the Queen and Colonel).

4 Lt.-Colonel H. Hamilton joined Sir Hope Grant's column advancing to the relief of Lucknow in Nov. 1857; commanded a Battalion of Detachments in the skirmish before and in the attack and capture of Bunterah, as also during the operations resulting in the relief of the Garrison of Lucknow; commanded 78th Highlanders during the occupation and defence for three months of Alumbagh, and in the closing operations against Lucknow; was present at the affair of Gailee. Served in the Rohilcund campaign in Apr. 1858, and commanded the 78th at the capture of Bareilly (CB.).

5 Lt.Colonel M'Intyre served in the Persian campaign of 1857; commanded the 78th Highlanders on the expedition to Borazjoon, in the night attack and battle of Kooshab, and present at the bombardment of Mohumrah (received thanks of Government). Accompanied Havelock's force from Cawnpore in September for the relief of Lucknow, and was in the actions during that advance on the morning that Havelock entered the City, he was thrown into the Alumbagh with 250 men and four guns to protect the sick and wounded, the reserve ordnance park, ammunition, treasure chest, &c., and the camp followers of the whole force; from 25th Sept. to 7th Oct. was surrounded by the enemy and all communication cut off, was then reinforced from Cawnpore by 250 men and two guns, and further by 500 men and four guns on 25th Oct.; held the position, still surrounded by the enemy, for 52 days until the approach of Lord Clyde's force; was wounded on 23d Sept., and horse shot by the splinter of a shell when about to mount him on 25th Sept.; received thanks of Government. Proceeded with Commander in Chief's force and commanded advance in attacks on Dilkoosha and La Martiniere, and was present in the after operations ending in the relief of the garrison of Lucknow (mentioned in despatches). Was with Outram's force during the reoccupation for upwards of three months of the Alumbagh and at the repulse of all the attacks on that position. Was with Brigadier Campbell's force in the third advance on Lucknow, and in the operations of that force until the final capture of the city (CB.).

6 Captain MacAndrew served with the 40th Regt. throughout the operations in Candahar in Affghanistan in 1841 and 42, and has received the Medal inscribed "Candahar, Ghuznee, Cabool, 1842." Served with the 78th Highlanders in the Persian war in 1857, including the night attack and battle of Kooshab, bombardment of Mohumrah, and expedition to Ahwaz.

7 Lt.Col. Lockhart served with the 78th Highlanders in the Persian war in 1857, including the night attack and battle of Kooshab, and bombardment of Mohumrah. Served in Bengal in the several actions leading to and ending in the relief of the Residency at Lucknow (wounded) and commanded the Regt. during the subsequent defence, also commanded two sorties (wounded), and was mentioned in Dispatches; served with Outram's force at Alumbagh, including the repulse of numerous attacks, also in the operations ending in the final capture of Lucknow (Brevet Major).

8 Major Hay served in the Persian war in 1857, including the night attack and battle of Kooshab, as Brigade Major (Brevet Major), and bombardment of Mohumrah. Served in Bengal in the several actions leading to and ending in the relief of the Residency at Lucknow and its subsequent defence; served with Outram's force at Alumbagh, including the repulse of the numerous attacks and operations ending in the final capture of Lucknow.

9 Major Mackenzie served in the Persian war in 1857, including the night attack and battle of Kooshab and bombardment of Mohumrah. Served in Bengal with Havelock's column from its first taking the field in 1857, including the actions of Futtehpore, Aoung, Pandoo Nuddee, Cawnpore, Onao, Buseerut Gunge (1st and 2nd), Boorbeakechowkee, and Bithoor (severely wounded); with Grant's column in the attack on Bunterah (severely wounded and horse killed); with Outram's force at Alumbagh, including the repulse of the numerous attacks, and in the operations ending in the final capture of Lucknow.

11 Lt.Col. Bouverie served in the Persian war in 1857 as a Brigade Major, including the bombardment of Mohumrah (Brevet Major). Served with the 78th Highlanders in Bengal with Havelock's column from its first taking the field in 1857, including the actions of Futtehpore, Aoung, Pandoo Nuddee, Cawnpore, Onao, Buscerutgunge (1st and 2nd), Boorbeakechowkee, and Bithoor; as Brigade Major in the several actions leading to and ending in the relief of Lucknow and subsequent defence; with Outram's force at Alumbagh, including the repulse of the numerous attacks, and in the operations ending in the final capture of Lucknow (Brevet of Lt.Colonel, Medal and Clasp).

12 Captain Archer served in the Persian war in 1857, including the bombardment of Mohumrah. Served in Bengal in 1857, at Bithoor with Havelock's column, skirmish before Bunterah, operations resulting in the second relief of Lucknow, with Outram's force at Alumbagh including the repulse of the numerous attacks, and operations ending in the final capture of Lucknow.

13 Captain Belmore St. George served with the 3rd Light Dragoons throughout the Punjaub campaign of 1848-49 (Medal).

20 Lieut. Barker served in the Persian war in 1857, including the night attack and battle of Kooshab, bombardment of Mohumrah, and expedition to Ahwaz. Served in Bengal with Havelock's column from its first taking the field in 1857, including the actions of Futtehpore, Aoung, Pandoo Nuddee, Cawnpore, Onao, Buscerutgunge (1st and 2nd), Boorbeakechowkee, and the several actions leading to and ending in the relief of the Residency of Lucknow and subsequent defence, including several sorties (wounded); with Outram's force at Alumbagh including the repulse of the numerous attacks, and in the operations ending in the final capture of Lucknow, where he officiated as D.A.Q.M. Gen. 1st Division, and was mentioned in Dispatches.

21 Lieut. Walker served in the Persian war in 1857, including the night attack and battle of Kooshab, and bombardment of Mohumrah. Served in Bengal with Havelock's column from July 1857, including the actions of Cawnpore, Onao, Buscerutgunge (1st and, 2nd) and Bithoor, the several actions leading to and ending in the relief of the Residency at Lucknow and subsequent defence; with Outram's force at Alumbagh including the repulse of the numerous attacks and operations ending in the final capture of Lucknow.

22 Lieut. Walsh served in the Persian war in 1857, including the night attack and battle of Kooshab, and bombardment of Mohumrah. Served in Bengal with Havelock's column in the several actions leading to the relief of Lucknow; present in the defence of Alumbagh for six weeks; operations resulting in the second relief of Lucknow; with Outram's force at Alumbagh including repulse of numerous attacks, and operations ending in the final capture of Lucknow.

23 Lieut. Browne served under Gen. Windham when Cawnpore was attacked by the Gwalior Mutineers in Nov. 1857; subsequently with Outram's force at Alumbagh, including the repulse of the numerous attacks, and operations ending in the final capture of Lucknow; also the campaign in Rohilcund and capture of Bareilly.

25 Paymaster Webster was present at the battle of Platsburg, and various skirmishes in 1814. Served in the Persian war in 1857, including the bombardment of Mohumrah.

26 Qr.-Master Skrine served in the Persian war in 1857, including the night attack and battle of Kooshab, and bombardment of Mohumrah. Served in Bengal with Havelock's column from its first taking the field in 1857, including the actions of Futtehpore, Aoung, Pandoo Nuddee, Cawnpore, Onao, Busecrutgunge (1st and 2nd), Bithoor, and the several actions leading to and ending in the relief of the Residency of Lucknow and subsequent defence; with Outram's force at Alumbagh, including the repulse of the numerous attacks, and operations ending in the final capture of Lucknow.

27 Surgeon Jee served in the Persian war in 1857, including the night attack and battle of Kooshab, and bombardment of Mohumrah. Served with Havelock's column in the several actions leading to and ending in the relief of the Residency of Lucknow and subsequent defence; with Outram's force at Alumbagh, including the repulse of the numerous attacks, and operations ending in the final capture of Lucknow; present with Brigadier Campbell's column in the affairs of 20th and 21st May; also at the capture of Bareilly.

[For remainder of Notes, see end of 77th Foot.

312

79th Regt. of Foot (Cameron Highlanders). [Serving in India, Depot, Stirling.

"EGMONT-OP-ZEE,"—The Sphinx, "EGYPT" "FUENTES D'ONOR", "SALAMANCA" "PYRENEES" "NIVELLE" "NIVE" "TOULOUSE" "PENINSULA" "WATERLOO" "ALMA" "SEVASTOPOL."

Years' Serv		
54		Colonel.—**D** William Henry Sewell,[1] CB., Ens. 27 March 06; Lt. 26 Feb. 07; Capt. 12 March 12; Maj. 3 March 14; Lt.Col. 21 June 17; Col. 10 Jan. 37; Maj.Gen. 9 Nov. 46; Lt.Gen. 20 June 54; Col. 79th Foot, 24 March 54.
Full Pay.	Half Pay.	
27	0	Lieut.Colonels — Sir John Douglas,[2] KCB., Ens. P 6 Sept. 33; Lt. P 8 July 36; Capt. P 8 June 41; Brev.Maj. 1 Nov. 42; Maj. P 24 Dec. 52; Brev.Lt.Col. 20 June 54; Lt.Col. 13 Aug. 54; Col. 1 Aug. 57.
25	0	Richard Chambre Hays Taylor,[3] CB. Ens. 11 Dec. 35; Lieut. P 29 Mar. 39; Capt. P 23 Aug. 44; Maj. 8 Aug. 54; Lt.Col. 12 Dec. 54; Col. 21 May 58.
20	0	Majors.—Thomas Bromhead Butt,[4]† Ens. P 3 April 40; Lieut. P 2 Aug. 42; Capt. P 2 Apr. 47; Maj. P 17 July 57; Bt.Lt.Col. 26 Apr. 59.
20	0	Wm. Chauval Hodgson,[4] Ens. P 18 Sept. 40; Lieut. P 10 Feb. 43; Capt. P 11 June 47; Brev.Maj. 2 Nov. 55; Major, 7 Aug. 57.

		CAPTAINS.	ENSIGN.	LIEUT.	CAPTAIN.	BREV.MAJ.	BT.LT.COL.
15	0	Keith Ramsay Maitland[5]	P 4 July 45	P 25 Aug. 46	P 24 Dec. 52	20 July 58	
18	0	Alex.Cockburn M'Barnet[6]	19 Aug. 42	28 Nov. 45	P 10 Mar. 54	20 July 58	
14	0	George Murray Miller[5]	P 30 Jan. 46	P 2 Apr. 47	P 4 Aug. 54	26 Apr. 59	
14	0	Edward William Cuming[10]	P 24 July 46	P 31 Mar. 48	8 Oct. 54		
11	0	Hy. Holford Stevenson[7]	29 June 49	P 24 Dec. 52	29 Dec. 54	20 July 58	
10	0	Philip Perceval[8]	P 16 Aug. 50	6 June 54	P 27 Mar. 55		
6	0	Francis Gore Currie[10]	P 3 Mar. 54	22 Aug. 54	P 17 Feb. 57		
6	0	John Macdonald Leith[11]	P 17 Mar. 54	P 6 Oct. 54	P 15 May 57		
6	0	George Thomas Scovell[12]	6 June 54	8 Oct. 54	P 16 June 57		
6	0	Donald M'Donald[14]	6 June 54	1 Dec. 54	P 17 July 57		
7	9/12	George Alex. Harrisson	P 23 Nov. 52	8 Aug. 54	P 13 July 55		
10		Simon George Newport[12]†	3 Aug. 41	2 July 44	6 June 54		
		LIEUTENANTS.					
6	0	William Henry Mackesy[14]	11 Aug. 54	8 Dec. 54			
7	0	John Edward Allen[14]	P 13 May 53	10 Jan. 55			
6	0	John Miller M'Nair[14]	P 18 Aug. 54	9 Feb. 55			
6	0	Wm. John M. Crawfurd[16]	P 25 Aug. 54	9 Feb. 55			
7	0	Havilland J. De Carteret[17]	P 25 Nov. 53	9 Feb. 55			
6	0	James Young[15]†	2 Oct. 54	9 Feb. 55			
6	0	Wm.Barclay G. Cleather[14]	13 Oct. 54	9 Feb. 55			
6	0	Fra. Pembrtn. Campbell[14]	3 Nov. 54	9 Mar. 55			
6	0	Chas. Edward McMurdo[14]	17 Nov. 54	9 Mar. 55			
5	0	Rich. B. Roland Bedford	19 Jan. 55	7 Sept. 55			
5	0	Edward Everett[6]	1 Mar. 55	P 14 Sept. 55			
5	0	Neil Campbell[16]	22 Feb. 55	21 Sept. 55			
5	0	Douglas Alleyne[11]	23 Feb. 55	P 2 Nov. 55			
5	0	Arthur Walker[12]	9 Mar. 55	P 16 June 57			
5	0	Douglas Wimberley[12]	24 May 55	P 15 Jan. 56			
5	0	Wm. Buxton Robertson	16 Mar. 55	P 28 Aug. 57			
5	0	Robert Stewart,[18] Adj.	P 13 July 55	17 June 59			
5	0	R. P. O. P., Lord Louth	P 3 Aug. 55	P 17 June 59			
5	0	Albert Newby Clay[18]	7 Sept. 55	P 1 July 59			
5	0	Thomas Ballard Dougal[12]	P 14 Sept. 55	9 Sept. 59			
5	0	Gardon Duff[18]	P 28 Dec. 55	P 28 Oct. 59			
		ENSIGNS.					
3	0	Wm. Henry M'Causland[18]	P 24 Feb. 57				
3	0	Alex. Peter B. Baillie	P 14 Aug. 57				
4	0	Gilbert Walter Coventry	1 Feb. 56				
1	0	Rt. MacGowan Borthwick	P 18 Jan. 59				
1	0	Alexander Bruce Murray	P 18 Mar. 59				
1	0	Albert Charles Wood	P 19 Mar. 59				
1	0	Alfred Hutton	P 31 May 59				
1	0	William Seaman Thomson	P 31 May 59				
1	0	Arthur Hume	P 29 July 59				
1	0	John Brebner	P 18 Jan. 59				

1 Lt. Gen. Sewell was appointed Aide de Camp to General Beresford, and proceeded with the expedition that left England in 1807. Joined the Duke of Wellington's army in Portugal in 1808. Was present with Sir John Moore's army in its advance and in its retreat to Corunna. Was with the Duke's Head Quarters through the Peninsular war as Aide de Camp to Lord Beresford, and was present at the battles of Corunna, Talavera (actions on the Coa and Agueda, with the Light Division), Busaco, the sieges of Ciudad Rodrigo, Badajoz, St. Sebastian, battles of the Nivelle, Nive, before Bayonne (10th, 11th, and 13th Dec.), Orthes, and Toulouse, besides Cavalry affairs and skirmishes. Had six horses killed and wounded under him in general actions. Has received the War Medal with ten Clasps. Served twenty-eight years in India,

4 Major Hodgson served the Eastern campaign of 1854-55, including the battles of Alma and Balaklava, expedition to Kertch and Yenikale, siege and fall of Sebastopol, and assaults of the 18th June and 8th Sept. (Medal and three Clasps, Brevet of Major, Knight of the Legion of Honor, and 5th Class of the Medjidie). Served in the Indian Campaign of 1858-59, including the siege and capture of Lucknow (Medal and Clasp).

‡‡ Lt.Colonel Butt served in the Indian campaign of 1858-59, including the siege and capture of Lucknow, in command of the 79th Highlanders from Nov. 1858 to Jan. 1859 (Brevet of Lt.Colonel, Medal and Clasp).

5 Majors Maitland and Miller served the Eastern campaign of 1854, and early part of 1855, including the battles of Alma and Balaklava, and siege of Sebastopol (Medal and three Clasps). Served in the Indian campaign of 1858-59, including the siege and capture of Lucknow. Major Miller was severely wounded through the body (Brevet of Major, Medal and Clasp).

6 Major M'Barnet served throughout the Eastern campaign of 1854-55, including the battles of Alma and Balaklava, siege and fall of Sebastopol, assaults of the 18th June and 8th Sept., expedition to Kertch and Yenikale (Medal and three Clasps, and 5th Class of the Medjidie). Served in the Indian campaign of 1858-59, including the siege and capture of Lucknow (Brevet of Major, Medal and Clasp).

0	0	Paymaster.—David Cant,[13] 24 June 56; Ens. 10 Aug. 54; Lieut. 8 Dec. 54.
5	0	Adjutant.—Lieut. Robert Stewart,[18] 18 Feb. 59.
5	0	Instructor of Musketry.—Lieut. Albert Newby Clay, 8 July 59.
6	0	Qr.Master.—William McGill,[10] 14 Nov. 56; Ens. 5 Nov. 54; Lt. 9 Mar. 55.
10	0	Surgeon.—Thomas Goldie Scot,[20] M.D. 18 Feb. 53; Assist.Surg. 14 Dec. 41.
6	0	Assist.Surgeons.—Andrew Knox Drysdale,[22] 24 March 54.
5	0	Patrick Kilgour,[12] 17 Jan. 55.
2	0	George Scott Davie, M.D. 1 Nov. 58.

Facings Green.—Agents, Messrs. Cox & Co.

[Returned from the Crimea, 3 July 1856. Embarked for India, 31 July 1857.]

2 Sir John Douglas served the Eastern campaign of 1854-55 in command of the 79th Highlanders, including the battles of Alma and Balaklava, siege of Sebastopol, assault of the 18th June and expedition to Kertch and Yenikale (Medal, and three Clasps, CB., Sardinian Medal, and 4th Class of the Medjidie). Served in the Indian campaign of 1857-59; commanded the Infantry in the action of Secundra; commanded a Brigade during the siege of Lucknow, taking the Residency, Iron Bridge, Great Emaumbarra, and several other important positions; afterwards commanded the Infantry of the

79th Regt. of Foot (Cameron Highlanders).

Azimghur field force and present in the action at Tigra, taking of Azimghur, detached in pursuit of Koer Singh, actions at Azimghur, Munnear, Sheoporeghat, and various operations in and around Jugdespore and the jungles, and pursuit to Buxar. On 15th June 1858 appointed to command the troops in the Azimghur and Jounpore districts, and on 25th June to the command of the disturbed districts of Behar, Dinahpore, Ghazepore, Shahabad, and constantly engaged in pursuing the rebels during the hot and wet seasons; took the field after the rains, defeated the rebels at Kurisath and drove them into the jungle, took Jugdespore, pursued and drove the rebels into the Kymore Hills, killing 1200; campaign in the Kymore Hills and successful night attack at Sulya Duhar. On 15th Jan. 1859 appointed to command the troops in Palamow and Chota Nagpore, engaged in pursuing the rebels in Palamow (frequently mentioned in despatches and thanked by the Governor General of India, Brevet of Colonel, KCB., Medal and Clasp).

3 Colonel Taylor served the Eastern campaign of 1854-55, including the battles of Alma and Balaklava, and siege of Sebastopol (Medal and Clasps, and 5th Class of the Medjidie). Commanded the 79th Highlanders from Feb. to 16th Nov. 1858 in the Indian campaign including the siege and capture of Lucknow, and commanded a Brigade in Oude from Nov. 1858 to Jan. 1859 (mentioned in despatches, CB., Brevet of Colonel, Medal and Clasp).

7 Major Stevenson served throughout the Eastern campaign of 1854-55, including the battles of Alma and Balaklava, siege and fall of Sebastopol, assaults of the 18th June and 8th September, expedition to Kertch and Yenikale (Medal and three Clasps, Sardinian Medal, and 5th Class of the Medjidie). Served in the Indian campaign of 1858-59, including the siege and capture of Lucknow; served as a Brigade Major from Feb. 1858 to the close of the campaign (frequently mentioned in despatches, Brevet of Major, Medal and Clasp).

8 Captain Percival served the Eastern campaign of 1854-55, including the battles of Alma and Balaklava, siege of Sebastopol, assault of the 18th June, expedition to Kertch and Yenikale (Medal and three Clasps). Served in the Indian campaign of 1858-59, including the siege and capture of Lucknow (Medal and Clasp).

10 Captains Cuming and Currie and Quarter Master McGill served throughout the Eastern campaign of 1854-55, including the battles of Alma and Balaklava, siege and fall of Sebastopol, assaults of the 18th June and 8th September, expedition to Kertch and Yenikale (Medal and three Clasps, and 5th Class of the Medjidie). Captain Currie and Qr. Master McGill served in the Indian campaign of 1858-59, including the siege and capture of Lucknow (Medal and Clasp).

11 Capt. Leith served the Eastern campaign of 1854-55, including the battle of Balaklava; siege and fall of Sebastopol, assaults of 18th June and 8th Sept., and expedition to Kertch and Yenikale (Medal and two Clasps, and 5th Class of the Medjidie). Served in the Indian campaign of 1858-59, including the siege and capture of Lucknow (Medal and Clasp).

12 Captain Scovell, Lieuts. Wimberley, Walker, and Dougal, and Assist.-Surgeon Kilgour, served in the suppression of the Indian Mutiny in 1858, including the siege and capture of Lucknow (Medal and Clasp). Lieut. Walker served throughout the Indian campaign as Aide de Camp to Brigadier Douglas and was thrice mentioned in despatches (Medal).

12† Captain Newport served with the 30th Regt. in the action of Maharajpore on 29 Dec. 1843 (Medal). Also at the siege and fall of Sebastopol in 1855 (Medal and Clasp).

14 Captain M'Donald, Lieuts. Mackesy, Allen, M'Nair, Cleather, F. P. Campbell, McMurdo, and Alleyne served at the siege and fall of Sebastopol from July 1855, and assault of 8th Sept. (Medal and Clasp). Served in the Indian campaign of 1858-59, including the siege and capture of Lucknow (Medal and Clasp).

15 Paymaster Cant served the Eastern campaign of 1854-55, including the battles of Alma and Balaklava, siege of Sebastopol, and assault of 18th June (Medal and three Clasps). Served in the Indian campaign of 1858-59, including the siege and capture of Lucknow (Medal and Clasp).

15† Lieut. Young served throughout the Eastern campaign of 1854-55, including the battles of Alma and Balaklava, siege and fall of Sebastopol, assaults of the 18th June and 8th September, expedition to Kertch and Yenikale (Medal and three Clasps, and Knight of the Legion of Honor), served in the suppression of the Indian Mutiny in 1858, including the siege and capture of Lucknow (Medal and Clasp).

16 Lieuts. Crawfurd and Neil Campbell, served at the siege of Sebastopol from July 1855 (Medal and Clasp). Served in the Indian campaign of 1858-59, including the siege and capture of Lucknow (Medal and Clasp).

17 Lieut. De Carteret served at the siege and fall of Sebastopol from June 1855, including the assaults of 18th June and 8th Sept. (Medal and Clasp). Served in the Indian campaign of 1858-59, including the siege and capture of Lucknow (Medal and Clasp).

18 Lieuts. Everett, Stewart, Clay, and Duff, and Ensign M'Causland served in the Indian campaign of 1858-59, including the siege and capture of Lucknow (Medal and Clasp).

20 Surgeon Scot served the Eastern campaign of 1854-55, including the battle of Alma and siege of Sebastopol (Medal and two Clasps, and 5th Class of the Medjidie). Served in the Indian campaign of 1858-59, including the siege and capture of Lucknow (Medal and Clasp).

22 Assist.Surgeon Drysdale served the Eastern campaign of 1854-55, including the battles of Alma and Balaklava, and siege of Sebastopol (Medal and three Clasps). Served in the Indian campaign of 1858-59, including the siege and capture of Lucknow (Medal and Clasp).

[Continuation of Notes to 80th Foot.]

6 Major Young served the campaign on the Sutlej with the 80th, including the battles of Moodkee, Ferozeshah, and Sobraon (wounded); Medal and two Clasps. Served in the Indian campaign in 1858-59; commanded the Head Quarter wing of the 80th Regt. with a column in Oude; at the capture of the fort of Simree, at Bera and Doondeakeira (Brevet of Major, Medal).

7 Major Smith served with the 80th Regt. in the Burmese war of 1852, and was present at the capture of Martaban, operations before Rangoon on the 12th, 13th, and 14th April, and capture of the Great Dagon Pagoda (with the storming party), and capture of Prome (Medal). Served in the Indian campaign of 1858-59 including the capture of Calpee and campaign in Oude (Medal).

8 Captain Hon. J. H. M. Browne, Lts. Mortimer and St. Leger served in the Indian campaign in 1858-59 and were present at the capture of Calpee (Medal).

9 Captain Hume served in the Burmese war of 1852-53, including the bombardment and capture of Prome and subsequent operations (Medal). Served in the Indian campaign in 1858-59 (Medal).

10 Major Miller served in the last Burmese war, and was engaged in the principal actions (Medal). Has the 4th Class of the Medjidie for service with the late Turkish Contingent. Served in the Indian campaign in 1858-59, including the engagement on the banks of the Jumna, and campaign in Oude, and commanded the Infantry at the capture of the fort of Simree, at Bera and Doondeakeira (Medal).

11 Captain Woods served with the Buffs in the action of Punniar, 29th Dec. 1843 (Medal).

12 Captain Nunn served with the 80th Regt. in the Burmese war of 1852, and was present at the capture of Martaban, operations before Rangoon on the 12th, 13th, and 14th April, and capture of the Great Dagon Pagoda (with the storming party), and capture of Prome (Medal). Served in the campaign in Oude in 1858-59, and present at the capture of Simree fort, Bera, and Doondeakeira (Medal).

13 Captain Amiel and Lieut. Whitehead served with the 80th Regt. in the Burmese war of 1852, and were present at the capture of Martaban, operations before Rangoon on the 12th, 13th, and 14th April, and capture of the Great Dagon Pagoda (with the storming party), and capture of Prome (Medal). Served in the Indian campaign in 1858-59,—Lt. Whitehead was at the capture of Calpee (Medal).

14 Captain Dudgeon served in the campaign in Oude in 1858-59 (Medal).

15 Captain Borrowes served in the Burmese war of 1853 as Adjutant of the 80th Regt. (Medal). Also in the campaign in Oude from 18th Jan. 1858, including the affair at Hurra, action at Morar Mow with the 1st Sikh Cavalry, capture of Simree fort (wounded) as Orderly Officer to Major Miller, and affair at Bussingpore as Staff Officer to Colonel Christie (Medal).

16 Captain Sullivan served with the 80th Regt. in the Burmese war of 1852-53, including the bombardment and capture of Prome and subsequent operations (Medal). Has the 4th Class of the Medjidie for service in the late Turkish Contingent. Served in the suppression of the Indian Mutiny, and was present with the Camel Corps at the battle of Golowlie and taking of Calpee on 22nd and 23rd May 1858 (Medal).

17 Lieut. Crawfurd served in Burmah in 1853 (Medal). Also in the campaign in Oude in 1858-59, including the capture of Simree fort and defence of Poorwah (Medal).

18 Captain Maxwell and Lieut. Huskisson served in the campaign in Oude in 1858-59, including the capture of Simree fort, Bera, and Doondeakeira.

19 Lieuts. Trevor, Gower, Goddard, Beaumont, O'Connor, and Howard, and Doctor Frank served in the Indian campaign of 1858-59 (Medal).

314   80th Regt. of Foot (Staffordshire Volunteers).   [East Indies, Depot, Buttevant.

The *Sphinx*, with the words "EGYPT" "MOODKEE" "FEROZESHAH" "SOBRAON" "PEGU."

Years' Serv.		
Full Pay	Half Pay	
55		**Colonel.**—[P][TM] Thomas Wm. Robbins,¹ *Ens.* 26 Sept. 05; *Lt.* 5 May 08; *Capt.* 25 May 09; *Major*, 24 Dec. 18; *Lt.Col.* 24 Oct. 21; *Col.* 10 Jan. 37; *MajorGen.* 9 Nov. 46; *Lt.Gen.* 20 June 54; *Col.* 80th F. 12 Mar. 55.
24	0	**Lieut.Colonels.**—Sam. Tolfrey Christie,² CB. *Ens.* P 22 Jan. 36; *Lt.* P 13 July 38; *Capt.* 28 Aug. 45; *Maj.* 31 Oct. 52; *Bt.Lt.Col.* 9 Dec. 53; *Col.* 28 Nov. 54; *Lt.Col.* 5 Mar. 58.
29	0	Robert Hawkes,³ *Ens.* P 2 Dec. 31; *Lieut.* 8 July 37; *Capt.* P 11 Oct. 44; *Brev.Maj.* 16 Dec. 56; *Major*, 5 Mar. 58; *Lt.Col.* 4 May 59.
20	0	**Majors.**—Edward Hardinge,⁴ *Ens.* P 11 Jan. 40; *Lt.* P 31 Dec. 41; *Capt.* P 22 Dec. 48; *Major*, 4 May 59.
16	0	Hamilton Charles Smith,⁷ *Ens.* P 8 Oct. 44; *Lt.* 24 Dec. 45; *Capt.* 1 May 53; *Major*, P 18 Oct. 59.

		CAPTAINS.	ENSIGN.	LIEUT.	CAPTAIN.	BREV.MAJ.	BT.LT.COL.
21	0	George Dean Pitt, s.....	11 Oct. 39	19 Jan. 44	P 4 May 49		
19	0	George Samuel Young⁶	16 July 41	26 July 44	31 Oct. 52	26 Apr. 59	
14	0	Hon.Jno.HoweM.Browne⁸	27 Feb. 46	11 Dec. 46	6 June 54		
15	0	Bliss John Hume⁹	11 Nov. 45	P 17 Mar. 48	P 4 Aug. 54		
15	0	Frederick Miller¹⁰	16 May 45	P 4 April 46	1 Dec. 54	6 June 56	
19	0	Richard William Woods¹¹.	P 27 Aug. 47	30 Dec. 48	12 Apr. 56		
13	0	Jas. L. Winniett Nunn¹²	29 Oct. 47	P 22 Feb. 50	P 27 Nov. 57		
15	0	Charles Frederick Amiel¹³	P 16 May 45	P 25 Sept. 46	5 Mar. 58		
14	0	James John Dudgeon¹⁴...	20 Mar. 46	P 22 Dec. 48	30 Mar. 58		
8	0	Erasmus Borrowes ¹⁵ ...	P 13 Feb. 52	1 May 53	P 24 May 59		
11	0	George Sullivan¹⁶	9 Jan. 49	P 31 Oct. 51	4 May 59		
8	0	Horatio Pettus Batcheler	23 Nov. 52	6 June 54	P 26 Aug. 59		
6	0	Robert James Maxwell¹⁸	P 25 Aug. 54	P 1 Apr. 56	P 18 Oct. 59		

LIEUTENANTS.

11	0	William Whitehead¹³....	22 Aug. 49	17 Aug. 52	
8	0	F. B N. Craufurd,¹⁷ *Adj.*	P 21 Sept. 52	6 June 54	
8	0	William Picton Mortimer⁸	24 Nov. 52	11 Aug. 54	
6	0	Hen. HungerfordSt.Loger⁶	P 18 Aug. 54	1 Dec. 54	
6	0	William Gordon Trevor¹⁹	P 31 Aug. 54	P 27 Nov. 57	
6	0	H. B. B. Leveson Gower¹⁹	P 1 Sept. 54	12 Feb. 58	
6	0	F. FitzClarence Goddard¹⁹	2 Sept. 54	5 Mar. 58	
6	0	Wm. Beaver B. Christie²⁰	13 Oct. 54	30 Mar. 58	
5	0	Samuel Geo. Huskisson¹⁶	15 May 55	1 Jan. 59	
3	0	Alexander Ewing	30 Oct. 57	20 July 58	
5	0	Christian B. Steward....	P 7 Dec. 55	23 July 58	
4	0	Dudley Beaumont¹⁹ ...	8 July 56	4 May 59	
3	0	Valentine O'Connor¹⁹ ...	P 17 Feb. 57	P 26 Aug. 59	
2	0	Walter Howard¹⁹	16 Mar. 58	P 26 Aug. 59	
2	0	Joseph Bramley Ridout..	13 Apr. 58	P 18 Oct. 59	

ENSIGNS.

2	0	Henry James Brown	12 Feb. 58	
2	0	Samuel Pollock Muirhead	26 Nov. 58	
2	0	Thomas Bernard Michell	19 Feb. 58	
1	0	Samuel Harrison	6 May 59	
1	0	Charles George Norris ..	P 31 May 59	
1	0	John Hugh Green	1 July 59	
1	0	Patrick Joseph Cowan ..	P 29 July 59	
1	0	Paul Swinburne	P 28 Oct. 59	
1	0	Alfred R. Bayly Dowling	P 29 Oct. 59	

13	0	*Instructor of Musketry.*—Capt. James Loftus W. Nunn, 23 Sept. 57.
7	0	*Paymaster.*—Wellington Browne,²¹ 1 July 55; *Q.M.* 22 April 53.
8	0	*Adjutant.*—Lieut. Fred. B. Numa Craufurd,¹⁷ 24 May 59.
5	0	*Quarter Master.*—William Maloney,²³ 23 Oct. 55.
16	0	*Surgeon.*—John Alex. Wm. Thompson, M.D. 26 Feb. 56; *Asst.Surg.* 19 Nov. 44.
6	0	*Assist.Surgeons.*—Philip Frank,¹⁹ M.D. 14 Dec. 54.
3	0	William Jackson, 9 Nov. 57.
3	0	James Inkson, M.D. 19 Oct. 57.

Facings Yellow.—*Agents*, Messrs. Cox & Co.

[*Returned from Bengal*, 16 *June* 54. *Emb. for Cape of Good Hope*, 25 *July* 56.]

Notes (right column, Captains section):
1 Lt.General Robbins served in Sicily in 1806-7 with the 1st Brigade of Guards under Sir John Moore. Subsequently with the 7th Hussars in the Peninsula and France in the campaigns of 1813 and 14, including the investment and surrender of Pampeluna, the battles of Orthes and Toulouse, with several intermediate affairs of outposts. Served also in Flanders in 1815 with the 7th Hussars; was present at Quatre Bras, and commanded a squadron of the Rear Guard in the affair at Genappe, also at the battle of Waterloo, where he was severely wounded. He has received the War Medal with two Clasps for Orthes and Toulouse.

3 Lt.Colonel Hawkes served in the Burmese war of 1852-53 as Brigade Major to the second Bengal Brigade, and was present at the relief of the garrison of Pegu, and in the subsequent operations against the enemy in that vicinity (Medal). Served in the Indian campaign of 1858-59 (Medal).

23 Qr.Master Maloney served the Sutlej campaign of 1845-46, including the battles of Moodkee, Ferozeshah, and Sobraon (Medal and two Clasps). Served also in the Burmese war of 1852-53, including the capture of Martaban, operations before Rangoon, and capture of Prome (Medal and Clasp). Served in the Indian campaign of 1858-59, including the affair of Hurra, Simree, Bera, Doondeakeira, and Bussingpore (Medal).

20 Lieut. Christie served in the Indian campaign of 1858-59, including the capture of Calpee, campaign in Oude and capture of Simree fort, Bera, Doondeakeira, and affair of Bussingpore (Medal).

21 Paymaster Browne served in the campaign in Oude in 1858-59 (Medal).

2 Colonel Christie served with the 80th Regt. throughout the Burmese war of 1852-53; present at the capture of Martaban (where he commanded the storming party), at the operations before Rangoon on the 12th, 13th, and 14th April—on the 14th commanded the skirmishers in front of the light guns during the advance on Rangoon, and was with the storming party at the capture of the great Dagon Pagoda; also present at the capture of Prome, and received the especial thanks of the Governor General of India in Council for his services on that occasion; and commanded the flank companies of his Regt. at the affair of the stockades on the heights opposite Prome, 12 Nov. 1852, and also at the repulse of the night-attack (Medal and Brevet of Lieut.Colonel). Served in the Indian campaign of 1858-59, commanded a moveable column in the Futtehpore district during the siege of Lucknow; engaged with the enemy on the banks of the Jumna on 5th March 1858; also commanded a field force detached from the Commander in Chief's camp during the latter part of the campaign in Oude; was wounded on 23rd Dec. 1858 and had a horse shot under him (CB., Medal).

4 Major Hardinge was present with the 39th Regt. in the action of Maharajpore on the 29th Dec. 1843 (Medal). Served with the 80th Regt. the Sutlej campaign of 1845-6, including the battles of Moodkee and Sobraon (Medal and one Clasp). Also in the Burmese war of 1852-53, and was present at the capture of Prome and subsequent night-attack of the enemy on the heights. Commanded a detachment at the defence of the post of Toomboo, 22nd Dec. 1852, and at several operations in its vicinity in Jan. and Feb. 1853. Present at the capture of the intrenched position of Tomah and at the destruction of the force of Moung-Shoe-Moung (Medal).

[For remainder of Notes, see preceding page.

[Emb. for India, 1 July 58. Depot, Chatham.] **81st Regt. of Foot (Loyal Lincoln Volunteers). 315**

"MAIDA" "CORUNNA" "PENINSULA."

Years' Serv.			
Full Pay	Half Pay		
66		*Colonel.*—Thomas Evans,¹ CB. *Ens.* 3 Dec. 94; *Lt.* 1 Oct. 95; *Capt.* 19 Nov. 03; *Major*, 6 Feb. 12; *Lt.-Col.* 13 Oct. 12; *Col.* 22 July 30; *Major-Gen.* 28 June 38; *Lt.Gen.* 11 Nov. 51; *Gen.* 18 May 55; *Col.* 81st F. 12 July 47.	
27	0	*Lieut.-Colonels.*—Henry Renny,² *Ens.* ᴾ 27 Dec. 33; *Lieut.* ᴾ 7 Aug. 35; *Capt.* 29 May 44; *Major*, ᴾ 17 Nov. 48; *Lieut.Col.* 27 May 53; *Col.* 28 Nov. 54.	
43	8/12	Matthew Smith,³ *Ens.* 16 Sept. 16; *Lieut.* 31 Dec. 23; *Capt.* 8 Feb. 34; *Brev.-Major*, 23 Dec. 42; *Major*, 22 Dec. 45; *Brev. Lt.-Col.* 7 June 49; *Lt.Col.* 20 June 54; *Col.* 28 Nov. 54.	
21	0	*Majors.*—John Arthur Gildea, *Ens.* ᴾ 23 Aug. 39; *Lieut.* ᴾ 30 Apr. 41; *Capt.* ᴾ 14 April 48; *Major*, 9 Apr. 56.	
29	0	John B. Flanagan, *Ens.* 8 Feb. 31; *Lieut.* 28 Aug. 35; *Capt.* 11 Nov. 45; *Brev.Major*, 13 Mar. 58; *Major*, 12 Dec. 59.	

Years Full	Half	CAPTAINS.	ENSIGN.	LIEUT.	CAPTAIN.	BREV.MAJ.
17	0	Robert Bruce Chichester⁵	ᴾ 20 Oct. 43	5 Apr. 47	ᴾ 7 Oct. 51	
21	0	John Bourchier	24 Aug. 39	2 July 41	27 May 53	
21	0	James Woods⁶	31 Dec. 39	ᴾ 6 May 42	27 May 53	
19	0	Charles James Skerry	10 Sept. 41	29 May 44	27 May 53	
18	0	Wm. Benjamin Browne⁷	ᴾ 16 Aug. 42	ᴾ 18 April 45	25 Jan. 54	
13	0	George Betts	ᴾ 10 Dec. 47	ᴾ 20 June 51	ᴾ 15 June 55	
17	0	Alfred Wright	10 Nov. 43	21 Apr. 46	16 June 55	
15	0	Valens Tonnochy⁸	ᴾ 2 Sept. 45	20 Mar. 46	20 June 54	
13	0	William Egerton Todd	21 May 47	ᴾ 7 Mar. 51	9 Apr. 56	
9	0	Hugh Arthur Chichester	ᴾ 17 Jan. 51	ᴾ 13 Apr. 52	ᴾ 18 Apr. 56	
9	0	Rich. Granville Charlton	18 Jan. 51	27 May 53	ᴾ 16 Aug. 59	
9	0	Stanley John Lowe	ᴾ 18 Apr. 51	27 May 53	12 Dec. 59	
		LIEUTENANTS.				
9	0	Geo. Wm. Moyse Harmer	ᴾ 19 Apr. 51	27 May 53		
9	0	Richard Swift	ᴾ 21 Nov. 51	31 Oct. 52		
10	0	William Minchin Harnett	ᴾ 12 July 50	ᴾ 25 Mar. 53		
8	0	James Alexander Deans⁶	ᴾ 15 Oct. 52	ᴾ 13 Oct. 54		
8	0	Walter Musgrave⁵	11 June 52	19 Jan. 55		
7	0	William Dare Sladen	ᴾ 13 Dec. 53	9 Feb. 55		
6	0	Henry John Faircloth⁵	15 Dec. 54	13 Apr. 55		
6	0	Tristram Chas. S. Speedy⁵	6 June 54	23 Oct. 55		
6	0	Daniel Weir	ᴾ 10 Nov. 54	8 Apr. 56		
5	0	Henry Harrison Briscoe⁵	ᴾ 16 Nov. 55	ᴾ 22 July 56		
8	0	Henry John Fane	ᴾ 9 July 52	1 Dec. 54		
5	0	George Fred. Jellicoe	23 Oct. 55	9 Sept. 57		
4	0	Fred. Keppel FitzRoy	ᴾ 22 July 56	25 Oct. 57		
4	0	Wm. Hy. MuntonJackson⁵	5 Dec. 56	ᴾ 5 Aug. 59		
2	0	William Henry Warren	23 Mar. 58	ᴾ 20 Dec. 59		
		ENSIGNS.				
3	0	Sydney William Bell	ᴾ 6 Jan. 57			
2	0	Michael Curry, *Adj.*	2 Feb. 58			
2	0	Thomas George Kerans	16 Mar. 58			
2	0	Cowper Rochfort	30 Mar. 58			
2	0	Henry Maturin	16 Apr. 58			
2	0	Thomas Rogers	26 Oct. 58			
1	0	Robert John MacDonnell	ᴾ 26 Aug. 59			

30	0	*Paymaster.*—Wm. Fred. Nixon, 8 Jan. 41; *Ens.* 3 Aug. 30; *Lieut.* ᴾ 22 Jan. 36.	
2	0	*Adjutant.*—Ensign Michael Curry, 24 Sept. 58.	
9	0	*Instructor of Musketry.*—Lieut. Richard Swift, 27 Sept. 58.	
16	0	*Quarter Master.*—Charles Correll,⁵ 28 June 44.	
12	0	*Surgeon.*—Grahame Auchinleck,⁷ M.D. 2 Oct. 57; *Assist.Surg.* 22 Dec. 48.	
6	0	*Assist. Surgeons.*—William Henry Corbett,¹⁰ M.D. 15 Dec. 54.	Facings Buff.—
5	0	Herman Bicknell,⁶ 16 May 65.	Agents, Messrs.
3	0	William James Mullan, 15 Sept. 57.	Cox & Co.

Side notes:

Emb. for India, 1 July 58, under Sir G. Cotton.

² Colonel Renny commanded the 1st Brigade in the Eusoofzie expedition of 1858 under Sir G. Cotton.

⁶ Captain Woods, Lt. Deans and Assist.Surgeon Bicknell served against the rebels in the Goojira district in 1857.

⁷ Captain Browne commanded the Head Quarter wing of the 81st Regt. in the Eusoozie expedition in 1858.

[For remainder of Notes, see second page of 84th Foot

³ Colonel Smith served as Major of Brigade with the army under General Pollock during the campaign of 1842 in Affghanistan (Medal), and was present (as D. A. Adj.Gen. of the Inf. Div.) at the forcing of the Khyber Pass, action at Mamoo Khail, forcing the Tezeen and Huft Kotul Passes, attack and capture of Istaliff (received the Brevet rank of Major). He served with the 29th in the Punjaub campaign in 1848-9, including the passage of the Chenab, and battle of Chillianwallah (wounded) and he commanded the 24th Regt. at the battle of Goojerat (Medal and Clasps).

⁵ Captain Chichester, Lieuts. Musgrave, Faircloth, Speedy, Briscoe and Jackson, and Qr. Master Correll, served in the Eusoofzie expedition in 1858.

sorties, with severe loss, on the 5th and 12th Aug. 1814, before Fort Erie, by the pickets under his command; assault of Fort Erie, and the series of affairs on the Niagara frontier. For these services, and conducting the 2nd Battalion of the King's Regiment from New Brunswick to Canada, through the Wilderness, General Evans has had honourable mention made of his name in the London Gazettes, and in General Orders on ten several occasions; and so unremitted have been this officer's services in all quarters, that this officer, two only were in the West Indies (as Captain in the 8th and Aide de Camp to Sir Gordon Drummond) in England. Wounded in three places at Sackett's Harbour; contused and had his horse shot at Fort Erie, from his gaiery and shivered at Lundy's Lane;

¹ General Evans's services:—Entered the army in 1793 as a volunteer, and enlisted 150 men for the service. Operations in the West Indies and Ireland in 1794 and 95 ; capture of Demerara and Berbice in 1796. Captured returning from South America, and kept a close prisoner in France in 1797. Operations at Minorca and Guernsey in 1798 and 99 ; ditto on the coast of Spain, Malta, and Marmorice, in 1800. Egyptian campaign of 1801 (Medal), including the actions of the 8th, 13th, and 21st of March : battle of Rahmanie on the Nile, and reduction of that fortress, sieges and surrender of Cairo and Alexandria (as Lieut. and Adjutant of the 8th). Operations at Gibraltar in 1802 and 3 ; ditto in the West Indies (as Captain in the 8th and Aide-de-Camp to Sir Gordon Drummond) in 1804, 5, and 6. Operations in Nova Scotia in 1807 and 8 ; ditto in the Canadas (as Aide-de-Camp and Military Secretary to Sir G. Drummond) in 1809, 10, and 11. Campaigns of 1812, 13, and 14, in Upper Canada (as Brigade-Major, discharging duties of Deputy-Adjutant-General, and in command of the 8th), including the preparation of the force against Detroit and Michilimackinac, the defence of Fort George, and destruction of the enemy's attacking batteries, and directing the reinforcements on Queenston, which enabled Major General Sheaffe to defeat and capture the American army, after General Brock's fall in a gallant attempt on the enemy with inadequate means. Assault on Sackett's Harbour, expulsion of the enemy's army from Forty Mile Creek, and capture of his army *materiel*, with many prisoners ; battle of Chippewa, covering the army's retirement on Fort George, and retrograde on Twenty Mile Creek, until resuming the offensive. Night-attack on the enemy's investing forces of Fort George, on which the American commander, General Swift, was slain. Battle of Lundy's Lane, two repulses of the enemy's [Continued on the margin.

† O 2

82nd Regt. of F. (The Prince of Wales's Volunteers).

[Serving in India. Depot, Canterbury.]

The Prince of Wales's Plume.—"ROLEIA" "VIMIERA" "VITTORIA" "PYRENEES" "NIVELLE" "ORTHES" "PENINSULA" "NIAGARA" "SEVASTOPOL."

Colonel.—

Years' Serv. Full Pay.	Half Pay.					
27	0	Lieut.Colonels.—Edward Blagden Hale,² CB. Ens. ᴾ2 Aug. 33; Lt. ᴾ20 Jan. 36; Capt. ᴾ5 Feb. 41; Major, ᴾ21 Nov. 51; Lt.Col. 7 Sept. 55; Col. 26 Apr. 59.				
10	1½	Hon. Percy Egerton Herbert,³ CB. Ens. 17 Jan. 40; Lt. ᴾ7 Sept. 41; Capt. ᴾ19 June 46; Maj. ᴾ27 May 53; Bt.Lt.Col. 28 May 53; Col. 28 Nov. 54; Lt.Col. 9 Feb. 55.				
27	0	Majors.—David Watson,⁴ Ens. ᴾ12 July 33; Lt. ᴾ24 Oct. 35; Capt. 3 June 41; Brev.-Maj. 20 June 54; Major, ᴾ1 Sept. 54; Brev. Lt.-Col. 26 Dec. 56.				
22	0	Charles Thomas Vesey Bunbury,⁵ Ens. 30 Oct. 38; Lt. 26 Dec. 40; Capt. ᴾ16 Feb. 49; Major, ᴾ13 Mar. 57.				

		CAPTAINS.	ENSIGN.	LIEUT.	CAPTAIN.	BREV.-MAJ.	BT.LT.COL.
17	0	Henry Chris. Marriott⁶..	ᴾ 5 Sept. 43	ᴾ19 June 46	ᴾ 2 Feb. 49	26 Apr. 59	
21	0	George Edmund Halliday⁷	ᴾ23 Aug. 39	ᴾ15 Apr. 42	10 Aug. 49	26 Apr. 59	
15	0	Samuel Peters Jarvis....	ᴾ14 June 45	15 Jan. 47	ᴾ21 Sept. 52	26 Apr. 59	
15	0	Wm. Roberts Farmar⁸..	ᴾ25 Feb. 45	11 April 46	ᴾ13 May 53	26 Apr. 59	
14	0	William Alex. Bailie⁹....	28 Aug. 46	10 Aug. 49	ᴾ 4 Aug. 54		
18	0	Stanley Slater ¹⁰	16 Apr. 42	4 Apr. 47	31 Jan. 55		
11	0	Robert Maule¹¹	18 Sept. 49	ᴾ16 Dec. 53	7 Sept. 55		
7	0	Hon. Chandler Wilkinson¹²	ᴾ11 Mar. 53	11 Aug. 54	ᴾ 1 May 57		
8	0	Jno. Frederick Pilkington¹³	ᴾ17 Dec. 52	6 June 54	9 Jan. 58		
11	0	Patrick Hunter	ᴾ15 June 49	ᴾ 6 July 52	ᴾ29 Dec. 57		
15	0	VCHerb. T. Macpherson¹⁴	28 Feb. 45	13 July 48	6 Oct. 57	20 July 58	
3	0	Edward M. Palliser		20 Feb. 57	ᴾ14 May 58		
		LIEUTENANTS.					
7	0	John Sidney Hand⁹		ᴾ13 May 53	ᴾ18 Aug. 54		
8	0	RFH. Macgregor Skinner¹⁵		ᴾ17 Dec. 52	ᴾ18 Aug. 54		
7	0	Chas. Edw. Gore Browne¹⁶		ᴾ16 Dec. 53	ᴾ 1 Sept. 54		
6	0	Cecil James East⁹		ᴾ18 Aug. 54	5 June 55		
6	0	Henry Dyke Marsh¹⁷....		ᴾ 1 Sept. 54	ᴾ20 July 55		
6	0	Edward Hugo Budgen¹⁸ .		12 Sept. 54	6 Sept. 55		
6	0	Charles Spencer,¹⁹ Adj. .		6 Oct. 54	7 Sept. 55		
5	0	Daniel Sullivan²⁰		21 Apr. 55	7 Sept. 55		
5	0	James Athol Brock²¹....		22 Apr. 55	7 Sept. 55		
5	0	William Carden Seton²²		23 Apr. 55	7 Sept. 55		
9	0	Louis Walter Fisher²⁴†..		ᴾ17 June 51	9 Feb. 55		
7	0	Chas. Studdert Maunsell²³		ᴾ18 Feb. 53	21 Sept. 55		
7	0	Graham Mylne²¹		ᴾ20 Sept. 53	22 Sept. 55		
5	0	Wm. Henry Craven Allen		11 May 55	27 Oct. 55		
5	0	George Porter²⁵		22 June 55	26 Feb. 56		
7	0	William Boyd O'Malley..		ᴾ21 Jan. 53	ᴾ23 Oct. 55		
5	0	Bertram C. Henderson ..		4 Sept. 55	ᴾ10 Mar. 57		
5	0	Thomas Ryan		24 Apr. 55	30 Nov. 57		
5	0	Edward Seppings Lock²⁶		2 Oct. 55	20 Jan. 58		
		ENSIGNS.					
5	0	Edward Snow Mason²⁷ ..		ᴾ 9 Oct. 55			
5	0	Henry Mount Parkerson²⁸		23 Nov. 55			
4	0	James Johnston²⁹		ᴾ25 Jan. 56			
4	0	Charles Paget Miller³⁰..		26 Feb. 56			
5	0	Nicholas Mourant Brock³⁰		ᴾ21 Dec. 55			
3	0	Charles Neville³¹........		ᴾ20 Mar. 57			
2	0	John Butler MacKenna..		30 Mar. 58			
2	0	William Reeves Bunbury		31 Mar. 58			
2	0	Charles Worthy		7 Dec. 58			
2	0	Charles Henry Marchant		25 Apr. 58			

14	0	Paymaster.—Wm. Hughes,³² 1 Apr. 56; Ens. 9 Sept. 46; Lt. 2 June 49.	
6	0	Adjutant.—Lieut. Charles Spencer,¹⁹ 26 Jan. 59.	
2	0	Instructor of Musketry.—Ensign W. R. Bunbury, 3 Sept. 59.	
4	0	Quarter Master.—John Connor,³³ 1 April 56.	
15	0	Surgeon.—Henry Day Fowler,³¹ 20 July 55; Assist.Surg. 19 Dec. 45.	
6	0	Assistant Surgeons.—Rowland Winburn Carter,³⁵ 28 July 54.	
5	0	William Henry Muschamp,³⁶ 23 Jan. 55.	
2	0	Robert Spence, 31 Dec. 58.	

Facings Yellow.—Agents, Messrs. Cox & Co.

[Returned from the Crimea, 11 August 1856. Embarked for China, 20 May 1857.]

3 Colonel Hon. Percy Herbert served with the 43rd Light Infantry in the Kaffir War of 1851-53 (Medal); also in the Expedition into the Orange River Sovereignty, including the battle of Boven. Served as Assist.Qr.Master General to the 2nd Division of the Eastern Army from its formation to Nov. 1855, and subsequently as Quarter Master General to the Army of the East until June 1856; was present at the battle of Alma (wounded), affair of 26th October, battle of Inkerman, siege and fall of Sebastopol (wounded), (Medal and Clasps), Aide de Camp to the Queen, CB., Officer of the Legion of Honor, Commander of 2nd Class of St. Maurice and St. Lazarus, and 3rd Class of the Medjidie.

82nd Regt. of Foot (The Prince of Wales's Volunteers). 317

2 Colonel Hale served in the N.W. Provinces and Oude in suppressing the Mutiny in 1857-59; commanded three companies of the 82d Regt. at the relief of Lucknow by Lord Clyde, and succeeded to the command of the 5th Brigade on Brigadier Russell being severely wounded and Colonel Biddulph killed (wounded and horse killed by a round shot); commanded the 82nd during the latter part of the defence and at the battle of Cawnpore, and the 5th Brigade at the action of Khodagunge, subsequent occupation of Futtehghur; served throughout the Rohilcund campaign and was left in command of the post of Shahjehanpore on the advance of the army under Lord Clyde to Bareilly (wounded); commanded the Regt. at the actions of Kankur and Bunkagaon; was appointed to the command of a Brigade for field service in Oude in Oct. 1858 and held it to the end of the campaign (frequently mentioned in despatches, CB., Colonel, Medal and Clasp).

4 Lt.Colonel Watson served at the siege of Sebastopol from 2d Sept. 1855 (Medal and Clasp). Served in the N.W. Provinces in suppressing the Indian Mutiny in 1857-58 and was present in the operations at Cawnpore under Windham, defeat there of the Gwalior Contingent, actions of Kala Nuddee and Khankur, siege of the Jail and subsequent operations at Shahjehanpore, affairs of Mahomdee, Shahabad, and Bunkagaon (Medal).

5 Major Bunbury served at the siege of Sebastopol from 2nd Sept. 1855 (Medal and Clasp).

6 Major Marriott served at the siege and fall of Sebastopol from 2nd Sept. 1855 (Medal and Clasp). Served in the N.W. Provinces in suppressing the Indian Mutiny in 1857-58 and was present in the operations at Cawnpore under Windham, defeat there of the Gwalior Contingent, actions of Kala Nuddee and Khankur, siege of the Jail and subsequent operations at Shahjehanpore (Brevet of Major and Medal).

7 Major Halliday served at the siege and fall of Sebastopol from 2d Sept. 1855 (Medal and Clasp). Served in the N.W. Provinces in suppressing the Indian Mutiny in 1858 and was present at the actions of Khankur, siege of the Jail and subsequent operations at Shahjehanpore (Brevet of Major and Medal).

8 Major Farmar served with the 50th Regt. in the Sutlej campaign in 1846, and was present at the affair of Buddiwal and action of Aliwal (Medal), at which last action he was severely wounded in the right thigh by a grape-shot while carrying the Queen's colour. Served with the 82nd Regt. in the Indian campaign in 1857-58, including the actions at Cawnpore on the 26th, 27th and 28th Nov., and 6th Dec, capture of Futtehghur, action at Kankur, capture of Bareilly, relief of Shahjehanpore, and actions around (Medal, and Brevet of Major).

9 Captain Baillie and Lieuts. Hand and East served at the siege and fall of Sebastopol from 2d Sept. 1855 (Medal and Clasp). Lieut. East served in the Indian campaign in 1857, and was severely wounded at Cawnpore on 26th Nov. (Medal).

10 Captain Slater served in the N.W. Provinces in suppressing the Indian Mutiny in 1857-59 and was present in the operations at Cawnpore under Windham, defeat there of the Gwalior Contingent, advance on and occupation of Furruckabad including destruction of Tuttcha and action of Khodagunge, also present at the action of Khankur, advance on and capture of Bareilly, bombardment and relief of Shahjehanpore and subsequent affairs of the 15th and 18th May 1858, capture of the fort of Bunnai, destruction of Mahomdee, attack and destruction of the fort of Shahabad, and action of Bunkagaon (Medal).

11 Captain Maule served at the siege and fall of Sebastopol from 2d Sept. 1855 (Medal and Clasp). Served during the suppression of the Indian Mutiny in 1857-59, in Oude and Rohilcund comprising the action of Khankur, defence of the Jail of Shahjehanpore and affairs subsequent to its relief, capture of the fort of Bunnai, attack and destruction of the forts of Mahomdee and Shahabad, and action of Bunkagaon (Medal).

12 Captain Wilkinson served at the siege and fall of Sebastopol from 2d Sept. 1855 (Medal and Clasp). Served in the N.W. Provinces in suppressing the Indian Mutiny in 1857-58 and was present at the second relief of Lucknow, defeat of the Gwalior Contingent at Cawnpore, actions of Kala Nuddee and Bunkagaon, siege of the Jail and subsequent operations at Shahjehanpore and affairs at Mahomdee and Shahabad (Medal and Clasp).

13 Captain Pilkington served at the siege and fall of Sebastopol from 2nd Sept. 1855 (Medal and Clasp). Served in India during the suppression of the Mutiny in 1857-59 and was present at the action of Khankur, the Rohilcund campaign and defence of the Jail at Shahjehanpore, attack and occupation of Shahabad, and affair at Bunkagaon (Medal).

14 Major Macpherson served in the Persian war in 1857 as Adjutant 78th Highlanders, including the night attack and battle of Kooshab, and bombardment of Mohumrah. Served in Bengal with Havelock's Column, present in the actions of Onao (wounded), Buseerutgunge (1st and 2nd), Boorbeakechowkee, and Bithoor, and in the several actions leading to and ending in the relief of the Residency at Lucknow and subsequent defence (Victoria Cross); with Outram's force at Alumbagh including the repulse of the numerous attacks, and served as a Brigade Major in the operations ending in the final capture of Lucknow (wounded).

15 Lieut. Skinner served in the N.W. Provinces in suppressing the Indian Mutiny in 1857-58 and was present at the second relief of Lucknow, defeat of the Gwalior Contingent at Cawnpore, actions of Kala Nuddee and Khankur, siege of the Jail and subsequent operations at Shahjehanpore, affairs of Mahomdee and Bunkagaon (Medal and Clasp).

16 Lieut. Browne served as Adjutant of the 82d Foot in the N.W. Provinces in suppressing the Indian Mutiny in 1857-59 and was present in the operations at Cawnpore under Windham, defeat there of the Gwalior Contingent, action of Khankur, defence of the Jail of Shahjehanpore and affairs subsequent to its relief (Medal).

17 Lieut. Marsh served at the siege and fall of Sebastopol from 2d Sept. 1855 (Medal and Clasp). Served in the N.W. Provinces in suppressing the Indian Mutiny in 1857-58 and was present in the operations at Cawnpore under Windham, defeat there of the Gwalior Contingent, actions of Kala Nuddee, Khankur, and Bunkagaon, capture of Bareilly, relief of Shahjehanpore, and affairs of Mahomdee and Shahabad (Medal).

18 Lieut. Budgen served in the Crimea from 23rd Nov. 1854 (Medal and Clasp for Sebastopol, and 5th Class of the Medjidie).

19 Lieut. Spencer served in the N.W. Provinces in suppressing the Indian Mutiny in 1858 and was present at the defence of the Jail at Shahjehanpore and subsequent operations (Medal).

20 Lieut. Sullivan served in the Eastern campaign of 1854-55, and was present with the 30th Regt. at the battles of Alma and Inkerman, siege of Sebastopol to May 1855, and sortie of 26th Oct. 1854 (wounded), for which last he was mentioned in the Dispatches. Served afterwards with the 82nd Regt. at the siege and fall of Sebastopol from 2nd Sept. 1855 (Medal and Clasps). Also in the N.W. Provinces in suppressing the Indian Mutiny in 1857-59 and was present in the operations at Cawnpore under Windham, defeat there of the Gwalior Contingent, destruction of the fort of Tettcha, actions of Khodagunge and Khankur, defence of the Jail of Shahjehanpore and subsequent affairs, capture of the fort of Bunnai and destruction of the forts of Mahomdee and Shahabad (Medal).

21 Lieut. Brock served in the suppression of the Indian Mutiny in 1857-58, including the expedition against the rebel villages near Allahabad, capture of Bareilly, relief of Shahjehanpore, destruction of Bunnai, attack and destruction of Mahomdee and Shahabad and subsequent operations, and action of Bunkagaon (Medal).

22 Lieut. Seton served in the suppression of the Indian Mutiny in 1857-58, including the defeat of the Gwalior Contingent at Cawnpore, the Rohilcund campaign and capture of Bareilly, attack and bombardment of Shahjehanpore and subsequent operations, affairs of Khankur and Bunkagaon, attack and capture of Shahabad (Medal).

23‡ Lieut. Fisher served during the suppression of the Indian mutiny in 1857-58 in Oude and Rohilcund, and was present at the defence of the Jail at Shahjehanpore and affairs subsequent to its relief (Medal).

23 Lieut. Maunsell served in the N.W. Provinces in suppressing the Indian Mutiny in 1857-58 and was present in the operations at Cawnpore under Windham, defeat there of the Gwalior Contingent, and actions of Kala Nuddee and Khankur, capture of Bareilly and relief of Shahjehanpore (Medal).

24 Lieut. Mylne served in the N.W. Provinces in suppressing the Indian Mutiny in 1857-59, acted as Adjutant to part of the Regt. at the second relief of Lucknow, present at the battle of Cawnpore, action of Khodagunge, occupation of Futtehghur, the Rohilcund campaign (as Orderly Officer to Brigadier Stisted) and capture of Bareilly, relief of Shahjehanpore and subsequent affairs, attack and destruction of the fort of Shahabad, actions of Khankur and Bunkagaon, and was Orderly Officer to Brigadier Hale in Oude from Oct. 1858 to the end of the campaign (Medal and Clasp).

25 Lieut. Porter served in the N.W. Provinces in the suppression of the Indian Mutiny in 1857-58, including the operations at Cawnpore under Windham, and defeat there of the Gwalior Contingent, destruction of Tettcha, actions of Goorsaginge and Khankur, defence of the Jail of Shahjehanpore, attack and capture of the fort of Bunnai, destruction of Mahomdee and subsequent operations, capture and destruction of Shahabad, and action of Bunkagaon (Medal).

26 Lieut. Lock served in the N.W. Provinces in suppressing the Indian Mutiny in 1858 and was present at the action of Khankur, defence of the Jail and subsequent operations at Shahjehanpore, affairs of Shahabad, Mahomdee, and Bunkagaon (Medal).

27 Ensign Mason served in suppressing the Indian Mutiny in 1857-58, including the operations at Cawnpore under Windham, defeat there of the Gwalior Contingent, action of Khankur, taking of Bareilly, subsequent operations in Rohilcund, and defence of Powayne (Medal).

28 Ensign Parkerson served in the N.W. Provinces in suppressing the Indian Mutiny in 1857-58 including the second relief of Lucknow, defeat of the Gwalior Contingent at Cawnpore, action of Kala Nuddee; defence of the Jail and subsequent operations at Shahjehanpore (Medal).

317a   82nd Regt. of Foot (The Prince of Wales's Volunteers).

29 Ensign Johnston served in the N.W. Provinces in suppressing the Indian Mutiny in 1857-58 and was present at the operations at Cawnpore under Windham, defeat there of the Gwalior Contingent, actions of Kala Nuddee and Khankur, defence of the Jail and subsequent operations at Shahjehanpore (Medal).
30 Ensigns Miller and Brock served in the Indian Mutiny in 1857, including the actions around Cawnpore on 26th, 27th, and 28th Nov., under Gen. Windham, battle of Cawnpore on 6th Dec., and capture of Futtehghur (Medal).
31 Ensign Neville served in suppressing the Indian Mutiny 1857-59, including the advance on and occupation of Furruckabad, capture of Bareilly, relief of Shahjehanpore and pursuit, actions of Shahabad, Khankur, and Bunkagaon (Medal).
32 Paymaster Hughes served with the 22nd Regt. the campaign of 1842-3 in Scinde, including the destruction of Imaumghur, and battles of Meeanee and Hyderabad (Medal). Also the campaign in the Southern Mahratta Country in 1844-5, and was present at the investment and capture of the forts of Panulla and Pownghur. Served with the 82nd Regt. in the N.W. Provinces in suppressing the Indian Mutiny in 1857-58, including the operations at Cawnpore under Windham, defeat there of the Gwalior Contingent, action of Kala Nuddee, occupation of Furruckabad, defence of the Jail and subsequent operations at Shahjehanpore (Medal).
33 Quartermaster Connor served the campaign of 1842-43 in Scinde under Sir Charles Napier, including the battles of Meeanee and Hyderabad (Medal). Served also the campaign of 1844-45 in the Southern Mahratta country including the taking of the forts of Punella and Pownghur.
34 Surgeon Fowler served in suppressing the Indian Mutiny in 1858-59, including the operations at Cawnpore under Windham, advance on Futtehghur, campaign in Rohilcund, affair at Sungancer, and defence of Shahjehanpore.
35 Assist.Surgeon Carter served with the 29th Regt. at the siege and fall of Sebastopol and at the capture of Kinbourn (Medal and Clasp). Served with the 82nd Regt. in the suppression of the Indian Mutiny in 1858, including the actions of Khankur and Bunkagaon (Medal).
36 Assist.Surgeon Muschamp served at the siege and fall of Sebastopol in 1855 and attack of the 18th June (Medal and Clasp), served in the N.W. Provinces in suppressing the Mutiny of 1857-58, including the operations at Cawnpore under Windham, defeat there of the Gwalior Contingent, actions of Kala Nuddee and Khankur, capture of Bareilly, relief of Shahjehanpore, and affairs of Mahomdee, Shahabad, and Bunkagaon (Medal).

[*Continuation of Notes to* 83*rd Foot.*]

3 Lt.Colonel Austen served during the suppression of the Indian Mutiny, including the affair of Sangancer on 8th Aug 1858, defeat of the Gwalior rebels at Kotaria, and commanded the Head Quarters of the 83rd Regt. at the surprise and attack on the rebels at Seekur on 21st Jan. 1859 (Medal).
6 Captains Molony and Wright, and Lieut. Coote served in suppressing the Indian Mutiny and was present at the affair of Sangancer, and defeat of the Gwalior rebels at Kotaria on the 14th Aug. 1858 (Medal).
8 Captain Pigott served in suppressing the Indian Mutiny and was present at the reduction of the fort of Arrah in Jan. 1858, siege of Kotah and its capture by assault, affair at Sangancer, and defeat of the Gwalior rebels at Kotaria (Medal).
9 Captain Baumgartner served as Assist.Adj.General of the Rajpootana field force and was present at the attack on the fort of Arrah in Sept. 1857, and at the siege of Kotah and its capture by assault on the 30th March 1858 (Medal).
10 Captain Sprot served with the force under General Woodburn in the affair at Aurungabad in 1857 (Medal).
11 Captain Meurant was present at the surprise of and attack on the rebels in Seekur on 21st Jan. 1859 (Medal).
12 Lieut. Colthurst served as Adjutant of the 83rd Regt. during the suppression of the Indian Mutiny and was present at the siege of Kotah and its capture by assault on 30th March 1858, affair of Sangancer, defeat of the Gwalior rebels at Kotaria, surprise of and attack on the rebels at Seekur (Medal).
13 Lieut. Wakefield served at the attack on the fort of Arrah in Sept. 1857 (Medal).
14 Lieut. Gandy was present at the siege of Kotah in March 1858 (Medal).
15 Lieut. Gore was present at the siege and capture of Kotah on 30th March 1858, affair at Sangancer, defeat of the Gwalior rebels at Kotaria, surprise of and attack on the rebels at Seekur (Medal).
16 Lieut. Browne was present at the attack on the fort of Arrah in Sept. 1857 and at its reduction in Jan. 1858 (Medal).
17 Lieuts. Minheer and Pennefather were present at the siege of Kotah and its capture by assault on the 30th March 1858 (Medal).
18 Lieut. Beazley served with the force which attacked and destroyed the town of Malageah W. coast of Africa in May 1855, served with the 82nd Regt. at the affair of Sangancer 8th Aug. 1858, defeat of the Gwalior rebels at Kotaria, surprise and attack of the rebels at Seekur (Medal).
19 Lieut. Wardell was present at the reduction of the fort of Arrah in Jan. 1858, at the siege of Kotah and its capture by assault, affair at Sangancer, defeat of the Gwalior rebels at Kotaria, surprise of and attack on the rebels at Seekur (Medal).
20 Lieut. Huyshe was present at an affair with the rebels at Kussanah on the 10th Feb. 1859 (Medal).
21 Lieut. Onslow was present at the siege of Kotah and its capture by assault on 30th March 1858, affair of Sangancer, defeat of the Gwalior rebels at Kotaria, and affair at Kossanah (Medal).
22 Lieut. Chamley was present at an affair with the rebels at Nhumbaira in Sept. 1857 and commanded a detachment of the 83rd Regt. in the fort of Neemuch during its defence in Nov. 1857, present at the siege of Kotah and its capture by assault, affair at Sangancer, and defeat of the Gwalior rebels at Kotaria (Medal).
23 Lieut. Karslake was present at the siege of Kotah and its capture by assault, affair at Sangancer, and defeat of the Gwalior rebels at Kotaria (Medal).
24 Ensign Haaley was present at the reduction of the fort of Arrah in Jan. 1858, at the siege of Kotah and its capture by assault, defeat of the Gwalior rebels at Kotaria, surprise on and attack of the rebels at Seekur (Medal).
25 Qr.Master Hayes was present at the surprise of and attack on the rebels at Seekur (Medal).

Embarked from Bombay, 11 Jan. 1849. **83rd *Regiment of Foot.*** Serving in India. Depot, Chichester. **318**

"CAPE OF GOOD HOPE" "TALAVERA" "BUSACO" "FUENTES D'ONOR" "CIUDAD RODRIGO" "BADAJOZ" "SALAMANCA" "VITTORIA" "NIVELLE" "ORTHES" "TOULOUSE" "PENINSULA."

Years' Serv.						
Full Pay	Half Pay					
60	0	Colonel.—1) Sir Frederick Stovin,[1] KCB. KCMG. *Ens.* 22 Mar. 1800; *Lt.* 7 Jan. 01; *Capt.* 24 June 02; *Major,* 27 April 12; *Lt.Col.* 26 Aug. 13; *Col.* 22 July 30; *Maj.Gen.* 23 Nov. 41 ? *Lt.Gen.* 11 Nov. 51; *Gen.* 14 Aug. 59; *Col.* 83rd Regt. 1 Sept. 48.					
26	0	*Lieut.Colonels.*—Edward Steele,[2] CB. *Ens.* P 18 April 34; *Lieut.* P 15 Mar. 39; *Capt.* P 19 Mar. 47; *Maj.* 19 Jan. 55; *Lt.Col.* 13 Apr. 58.					
22	0	Charles Wilson Austen,[3] *Ens.* P 14 Dec. 38; *Lieut.* P 15 Dec. 40; *Capt.* P 1 Dec. 48; *Maj.* 16 May 56; *Lt.Col.* 26 Oct. 58.					
29	0	*Majors.*—John Heatly,[4] *Ens.* 20 Sept. 31; *Lieut.* 28 Mar. 34; *Capt.* P 17 Nov. 43; *Brev. Maj.* 20 June 54; *Bt.Lt.Col.* 19 Jan. 58; *Maj.* 13 Apr. 58.					
23	0	James Florence Murray, *Ens.* P 28 Nov. 37; *Lieut.* P 7 Jan. 42; *Capt.* 14 Nov. 47; *Major,* 26 Oct. 58.					

		CAPTAINS.	ENSIGN.	LIEUT.	CAPTAIN.	BREV. MAJ.
21	0	Edward William Bray[5]..	21 June 39	21 Jan. 41	P 14 June 50	
18	0	Edward Bowen Cooke ..	P 16 Aug. 42	8 May 46	P 17 May 50	
15	0	John Sharman Molony[6]	P 23 May 45	29 June 48	15 Mar. 53	
17	0	Richard Rodes Wyvill[7]..	P 14 Apr. 43	P 4 June 47	P 22 Oct. 52	
15	0	Henry De Renzy Pigott[8]	P 22 July 45	P 19 Sept. 48	7 May 54	
15	0	T. Mowbray Baumgartner[9]	P 4 April 45	P 26 Nov. 47	P 19 Aug. 56	
16	0	Thomas Parker Wright[6]	2 Feb. 44	7 Aug. 46	5 Oct. 57	
16	0	James Verling Ellis	29 Mar. 44	P 8 Sept. 46	24 Oct. 57	
12	0	Frederick Dickinson	18 Aug. 48	P 2 Feb. 49	13 Apr. 58	
12	0	John Sprot[10]	P 19 Sept. 48	P 29 May 49	14 July 58	
12	0	Richard Thomas Sweeny	P 1 Dec. 48	3 June 51	2 Sept. 58	
12	0	Edward Meurant[11]......	P 10 Nov. 48	7 May 54	26 Oct. 58	
		LIEUTENANTS.				
9	0	Jas. Nich. Colthurst,[12] *Adj.*	14 Oct. 51	P 11 May 55		
7	0	Julian Wakefield[13].....	22 Apr. 53	P 20 July 55		
7	0	Thomas Gethin Coote[6] ..	P 13 May 53	10 Jan. 56		
5	0	Henry Gandy[14]	P 23 Oct. 55	P 18 Apr. 56		
5	0	Charles Clitherow Gore[15]	30 Nov. 55	P 2 May 56		
5	0	Peter Clifford Browne[16]..	27 July 55	16 May 56		
5	0	William Minheer[17]....	31 Aug. 55	P 27 June 56		
8	0	George Gant Beazley[18] ..	P 17 Aug. 52	1 Dec. 54		
5	0	Geo. Wm. Henry Wardell[19]	3 Aug. 55	2 Aug. 56		
4	0	Geo. Lightfoot Huyshe[20]	P 18 Apr. 56	P 19 Aug. 56		
5	0	Guildford Macleay Onslow[21]	20 Feb. 55	26 Feb. 56		
4	0	William Henry Iviny ..	P 14 Mar. 56	5 Oct. 57		
4	0	Braithwaite Chamley[22] ..	P 9 May 56	24 Oct. 57		
5	0	Nicholas Pennefather[17] ..	P 19 Aug. 56	P 26 Jan. 58		
4	0	James Rob. A. Colebrooke	P 18 April 56	P 5 Mar. 58		
3	0	Frederick Karslake[23]	19 June 57	2 Sept. 58		
5	0	Wm. Forbes Anderson ..	2 Oct. 58	26 Oct. 58		
		ENSIGNS.				
3	0	John Healey[24]	4 Dec. 57			
2	0	Hubert Cornish Whitlock	P 5 Feb. 58			
2	0	Michael Murphy	P 6 Feb. 58			
2	0	James Edmund Brymer	30 Mar. 58			
2	0	Littleton Albert Powys..	P 20 Oct. 58			
2	0	Reginald Kennett Gibb..	12 Nov. 58			
1	0	Frederick Ford	28 Jan. 59			
2	0	Henry Albert Fuller	26 Nov. 58			
17	0	*Paymaster.*—John Dennis Swinburne, 2 Mar. 49; *Ens.* 25 Mar. 43; *Lt.* 3 Oct. 46.				
9	0	*Adjutant.*—*Lieut.* James Nicholas Colthurst,[12] 2 Aug. 56.				
5	0	*Instructor of Musketry.*—*Lieut.* W. F. Anderson, 20 Dec. 57.				
8	0	*Quarter Master.*—Patrick Hayes,[25] 5 Nov. 52.				
16	0	*Surgeon.*—Robert Browne, 14 July 56; *Assist.Surg.* 1 March 44.				
5	0	*Assist.Surgeons.*—William Sharp, 3 Feb. 55.				
3	0	Thomas Rawlings Mould, 31 May 57.				
2	0	Edward O'Connell, 22 Sept. 58.				

Notes for Heatly's service column: 4 Lt.Col. Heatly served with the 49th Regt. and as Deputy Assistant Adjutant General, throughout the operations in China, and was present at Chusan, Canton, Amoy, Chusnan, Chinhae, Ningpo, Chapoo, Woosung, Chinkiangfoo, and Nankin (Medal). Served on the staff of General Havelock in the Persian war in 1856 (Brevet of Lt. Colonel). Commanded a detachment of the 83rd Regt. at the attack on the fort of Arrah in Sept. 1857 and at its reduction in Jan. 1858; commanded three companies of the Regt. during the siege of Kotah and at its capture by assault; present at an affair with the rebels at Koosanah on the 10th Jan. 1859.

5 Capt. Bray served with the 31st Regt. throughout the campaign of 1842 in Affghanistan under Maj. Gen. Pollock, and was present in the actions of Mazeena, Tezeen, & Jugdulluck, the occupation of Caboul, and the different engagements leading to it (Medal).

7 Capt. Wyvill served with the 90th Regt. in Kaffirland during the whole of the war of 1846-7 (Medal). Served with the 83rd Regt. in suppressing the Indian Mutiny and was present at the attack on the fort of Arrah in Sept. 1857, and at the siege of Kotah and its capture by assault on the 30th March 1858 (Medal).

Facings Yellow.—*Agents,* Messrs. Cox & Co.

1 Sir Frederick Stovin served at the Ferrol in 1800; in Germany in 1805; at the siege and capture of Copenhagen in 1807; with the expedition to Sweden in 1808; in Spain and Portugal in 1808-9, including the retreat to and battle of Corunna. With the expedition to Walcheren and at the capture of Flushing in 1809; subsequently in the Peninsula, and was second in command at the first defence of Tarifa; Aide-de-Camp to Sir Thomas Picton at the siege and capture of Ciudad Rodrigo and Badajoz. Assistant Adjutant General to the 3rd Division at the battle of Salamanca, capture of Madrid and the Retiro, retreat therefrom and subsequent advance, passage of the Ebro, battles of Vittoria, Pyrenees, Nivelle, and Orthes, action at Vic Bigorre, and battle of Toulouse. Served also at New Orleans, where he was wounded. Sir Frederick has received the Gold Cross and two Clasps for Salamanca, Vittoria, Nivelle, Nive, and Orthes; and the Silver War Medal with three Clasps for Corunna, Ciudad Rodrigo, and Badajoz.

2 Lt.Colonel Steele served with the 83rd Regt. during the insurrection in Canada in 1838 and was present at the affair at Prescott. Served during the suppression of the Indian Mutiny and commanded the Regt. at the siege of Kotah and its capture by assault on 30th March 1858, affair of Sanganeer, and defeat of the Gwalior rebels at Kotaria on 14th Aug. 1858 (CB. and Medal).

[For remainder of Notes, *see* preceding page.]

319   84th *(York and Lancaster) Regt. of Foot.*   [Sheffield. Depot, Pembroke.

The Union Rose, "NIVE" "PENINSULA" "INDIA."

Years' Serv.						
Full Pay	Half Pay					
65		Colonel.—Sir George Augustus Wetherall,[1] KCB. KH. *Lieut.* 29 July 95 ; *Capt.* 13 May 05 ; *Major,* 12 Aug. 19 ; *Lieut.-Col.* 11 Dec. 24 ; *Col.* 28 June 38 ; *Major-Gen.* 11 Nov. 51 ; *Lt.-Gen.* 8 Sept. 57 ; *Col.* 84th F. 15 June 54.				
22	0	*Lieut.-Colonel.*—Thomas Lightfoot,[2] CB. *Ens.* 1 June 38 ; *Lt.* p 30 Oct. 40 ; *Capt.* 26 June 51 ; *Bt.Major,* 24 Mar. 58 ; *Major,* 2 July 58 ; *Lt.Col.* 4 Apr. 59.				
21	0	*Majors.*—Spier Hughes, *Ens.* p 31 Dec. 39 ; *Lt.* 8 Apr. 42 ; *Capt.* 15 Mar. 53 ; *Major,* 10 Sept. 58.				
10	0	Frederic Arthur Willis,[3] CB. *Ens.* 27 Sept. 44 ; *Lt.* p 8 May 46 ; *Capt.* p 16 Jan. 52 ; *Bt. Major,* 24 Mar. 58 ; *Major,* 4 Apr. 59 ; *Bt.Lt.Col.* 26 Apr. 59.				

		CAPTAINS.	ENSIGN.	LIEUT.	CAPTAIN.	BREV.MAJ.
18	0	Walter C. E. Snow......	11 April 42	22 Nov. 44	9 Jan. 55	
18	0	Cornelius Cha. Rolleston[4]	20 May 42	7 July 45	2 Feb. 55	24 Mar. 58
16	0	David O'Brien[5]	22 Nov. 44	20 May 46	21 July 57	24 Mar. 58
18	0	Wm. M'Geachy Keats[6]..	p 14 Oct. 42	21 April 46	26 Sept. 57	
11	0	Frederick Hardy[7]	p 23 Nov. 49	p 6 June 51	27 Nov. 57	
14	0	Geo. Fred. Tod Whitlock[8]	p 11 Dec. 46	26 June 51	13 Apr. 58	
9	0	John Penton[9]	p 6 June 51	p 13 Sept. 53	22 Aug. 58	
10	0	Robert Barry[10]	p 17 May 50	2 Feb. 55	10 Sept. 58	
8	0	Hon.Wm.Henry Herbert[11]	p 11 June 52	p 25 Aug. 54	p 16 Nov. 55	
5	0	Harry B. Crohan[12].....	1 June 55	7 Dec. 55	p 19 Nov. 58	
6	0	James Hudson[13]........	p 3 Nov. 54	9 Feb. 55	25 June 58	
6	0	John Francis Sparke[14] ..	p 23 Aug. 54	9 Dec. 54	p 25 Feb. 59	

		LIEUTENANTS.				
4	0	Rob. Fraser Humphrey[15]	29 Feb. 56	28 June 57		
4	0	Hugh Pearce Pearson[16]..	28 Feb. 56	25 Aug. 57		
4	0	Egbert Charles S. Hely..	8 July 56	26 Sept. 57		
4	0	Montgomery Williams ..	p 22 July 56	29 Nov. 57		
5	0	Hon. Latham Brownrigg.	25 May 55	17 Nov. 57		
5	0	Thomas White	16 Aug. 55	p 17 Nov. 57		
3	0	Henry Shawe Jones	p 25 Aug. 57	22 Aug. 58		
3	0	Charles Thomas Horan..	17 Nov. 57	7 Sept. 58		
3	0	William Charles Driberg	11 Dec. 57	10 Sept. 58		
3	0	V C Geo. Lambert,[17] *Adj.*	12 Dec. 57	17 Sept. 58		
3	0	Fra.Edw.Edwards Wilson	p 17 Nov. 57	p 1 Oct. 58		
4	0	Andrew Stewart........	26 Feb. 56	7 May 58		
2	0	Thomas Griffin[18].......	2 Feb. 58	4 Apr. 59		
3	0	Alexander Jason Hassard	p 17 July 57	p 9 Nov. 58		

		ENSIGNS.				
2	0	Henry Arkwright	2 July 58			
2	0	William Frank Wheatley	16 July 58			
4	0	James M. Thos. Simpson	p 4 Apr. 56			
2	0	John Hunter Knox	30 Mar. 58			
2	0	Arthur Henry Messiter[19]	12 Nov. 58			
2	0	John Henry B. Isherwood	p 10 Dec. 58			
2	0	Richd. H. O'Grady Haly	6 Nov. 58			
2	0	William Kemmis	30 Dec. 58			
2	0	John Gerald Wilson	31 Dec. 58			
1	0	William Clayton Clayton	p 31 May 59			

1	0	*Paymaster.*—William Vanderkiste, 23 Aug. 59.
3	0	*Adjutant.*—V C *Lieut.* George Lambert,[17] 2 July 58.
3	0	*Instructor of Musketry.*—*Lieut.* W. C. Driberg, 21 Oct. 59.
2	0	*Quarter Master.*—John Nally, 5 Oct. 58.
19	0	*Surgeon.*—James M'Grigor Grant, 29 Nov. 50 ; *Assist.Surg.* 6 Nov. 40.
3	0	*Assistant Surgeons.*—Henry Patrickson Gregory, 19 Oct. 57.
5	0	William Henry Jenkins, 24 Sept. 55.

Facings Yellow.—*Agents,* Messrs. Cox & Co.

[*Returned from India,* 1 Sept. 1859.]

1 Sir George Aug. Wetherall was in action with a squadron of French frigates in the Mozambique Channel in June 1810 ; in the attack of a squadron of French frigates in port S.E. of the Isle of France in July 1810. At the attack and conquest of Java in 1811, as Aide-de-Camp to Major-Gen. Wetherall, for which he has received the War Medal with one Clasp. He was appointed a CB, for his distinguished services in the suppression of the insurrection in Canada.

2 Lt.Colonel Lightfoot served as Brigade Major to the 5th Brigade at the second relief of Lucknow and at the defeat of the Gwalior rebels at Cawnpore, present at the passage of the Kala Nuddee, commanded the 84th Regt. from the 23rd Jan. 1858 at the Alum Bagh, capture of Lucknow, relief of Azimghur, and pursuit of Koer Sing (several times mentioned in despatches, Brevet Major, Medal and Clasp).

3 Lt.Col. Willis was present with General Havelock's field force in the actions of Oonao and Buscerut Gunge on 29th July 1857; commanded the 84th Regt. in the actions of Buscerut Gunge on the 5th Aug., Boorbeake Chowkee on 12th Aug., at Bithoor on the 16th Aug., at Mungawar on 21st Sept., at Alumbagh on 23rd Sept., and relief of Lucknow on 25th Sept. (wounded in left knee and right thigh); commanded the right column at the storming of the Hirn Khannah on 16th Nov., and was thanked in Division Orders by General Havelock. Was with General Outram's force at the Alumbagh from 26 Nov. 1857 to 9 March 58—commanded the 84th up to 6th Jan.; present at the fall of Lucknow; accompanied Gen. Lugard's force and present at the relief of Azimghur; proceeded with Brigadier Douglas's column in pursuit of the rebel chief Koer Sing, and present in the actions of 17th and 20th April (mentioned in Dispatches, *CB.*, and Brevets of Major and Lt.Colonel, Medal and Clasps).

4 Major Rolleston served at the second relief of Lucknow and commanded a picquet post until the evacuation (mentioned in despatches, Brevet Major); present with Outram's force at the Alum Bagh, also at the assault and capture of Lucknow (Medal and Clasps).

5 Major O'Brien commanded a Company of the 84th Regt. forming part of the garrison of Lucknow from its first investment and was severely wounded in the right arm; afterwards present with Outram's force at the Alum Bagh, also at the assault and capture of Lucknow (several times mentioned in Dispatches, Brevet Major, Medal and Clasps).

6 Captain Keats served with Havelock's field force in the actions of Oonao, Buscerut Gunge, Boorbeenke Chowkee, Mungawar, and Alumbagh. Accompanied the Commander in Chief's force at the second relief of Lucknow, afterwards with Outram's force at the Alum Bagh, also at the assault and capture of Lucknow, relief of Azimghur, and with Brigadier Douglas' Column in pursuit of Koer Sing (Medal and Clasp).

7 Captain Hardy served as Orderly Officer to Brigadier Russell at the second relief of Lucknow, at the Alum Bagh, and at the capture of Lucknow; also present at the relief of Azimghur and pursuit of Koer Sing (Medal and Clasp).

8 Captain Whitlock commanded a detachment 84th Regt. at Gya in a skirmish with the mutinous 5th Irregular Cavalry on 8th Sept. 1857; present with Outram's force at the Alum Bagh, also at the assault and capture of Lucknow, and relief of Azimghur (Medal and Clasp).

9 Captain Penton served in the Indian campaign of 1857-58,—joined Havelock's force at Cawnpore, present in the actions of Mungawar and Alumbagh, headed a party which stormed and took possession of a gate through which the relieving force had to pass on its way to the Residency of Lucknow, commanded a Company in the sortie of 29th Sept. when a number of guns was taken, and at the storming of the Hirn Khannah he extricated his Commanding Officer Major Willis from a mine pit while exposed to a heavy fire from three points and was the first in through the breach; present with Outram's force at the Alumbagh; at the fall of Lucknow commanded three companies of the 84th Regt. at the storming of the Kaisabagh; served with Lugard's Column and present in the actions of the 17th and 26th April, relief of Azimghur, and pursuit of Koer Sing (Medal and Clasps).

10 Captain Barry joined Havelock's force on its first taking the field, and was present in the actions of Futtehpore, Aoung, Pandoo Nuddee, Cawnpore, Oonao, Buscerut Gunge (1st and 2nd), Bithoor, Mungawar, and Alumbagh, relief of Lucknow (severe contusion of right side), and commanded a Company at the storming the Hirn Khannah; with Outram's force at the Alum Bagh, also at the capture of Lucknow, and relief of Azimghur (Medal and Clasps).

11 Captain Hon. W. H. Herbert served with the 46th Regt. at the siege of Sebastopol in 1854-55 (Medal and Clasp).

12 Captain Crohan served with Havelock's Column in the action at Bithoor, and was Aide de Camp to Brigadier Franklyn with Outram's force at the Alum Bagh, and at the siege and capture of Lucknow, also present at the relief of Azimghur (Medal and Clasp).

13 Captain Hudson served with the 97th Regt. in the Indian campaign of 1857-58, and was present in the actions of Chanda, Umeerpore, and Sultanpore, and at the siege and capture of Lucknow (Medal and Clasp).

14 Captain Sparke served with the 68th Lt. Inf. at the siege and fall of Sebastopol, from 19th May 1855 (Medal and Clasps).

15 Lieut. Humphrey served with Havelock's Column in the actions of Buscerut Guhge, Boorbeake Chowkee, Bithoor, Mungawar, and Alum Bagh, relief of Lucknow; with Outram's force at the Alum Bagh, assault and capture of Lucknow (Medal and Clasps)

16 Lieut. Pearson srrved throughout the operations of the Column under Havelock, including the actions of Futtehpore, Aoung, Pandoo Nuddee, Cawnpore (wounded), Oonao, Buscerut Gunge (1st and 2nd), Boorbeake Chowkee, Bithoor, Mungawar, and Alum Bagh, relief of Lucknow, commanded a Company of the 84th Regt. in the Sortie of 26th Sept. 1857, and at the storming of the Hirn Kanah; with Outram's force at the Alum Bagh, also at the assault and capture of Lucknow, relief of Azimghur, and pursuit of Koer Singh (Medal and Clasp).

17 Lieut. Lambert served with Havelock's Column in the actions of Oonao, Buscerut Gunge (1st and 2nd), Boorbeake Chowkee, Bithoor, Mungawar, and Bithoor, relief of Lucknow (severely wounded), and storming of the Hirn Khana (Victoria Cross); with Outram's force at the Alum Bagh, also at the assault and capture of Lucknow, and relief of Azimghur (Medal and Clasps).

18 Lieut. Griffin served with Havelock's Column in the actions of Oonao, Buscerut Gunge (1st and 2nd), Boorbeake Chowkee, Bithoor, Mungawar, and Alum Bagh, and relief of Lucknow; with Outram's force at the Alum Bagh, also at the assault and capture of Lucknow, and relief of Azimghur (Medal and Clasps).

19 Ensign Messiter served in the Indian campaign in 1857-58, and was present during the operations at Cawnpore under General Windham, battle of Cawnpore on 6th Dec., siege and capture of Lucknow, and relief of Azimghur (Medal and Clasp).

[*Continuation of Notes to 81st Foot.*]

8 Captain Tonnochy served with the 29th Regt. in the Sutlej campaign in 1846, including the battle of Sobraon (Medal). Served also in the Punjaub campaign of 1848-49, including the passage of the Chenab, and battles of Chillianwallah and Goojerat (Medal and Clasps). Served as a Brigade Major in the Eusoozie expedition in 1858.

9 Doctor Auchinleck served in the Burmese war of 1852-53. Also in the Eusoozie expedition in 1858 (Medal).

10 Assist.Surgeon Corbett served in the Crimean campaign of 1854-55, including the siege of Sebastopol (Medal and Clasp).

85th (Buck. Volunteers) The King's Lt. Inf. Regt. [Emb. for Mauritius, 8 Jan. 58. C.G.Hope. Depot at Pembroke.

"Aucto splendore resurgo."

"FUENTES D'ONOR," "NIVE," "PENINSULA," "BLADENSBURG."

Years' Serv.						
Full Pay	Half Pay					
66		Colonel.—1) Sir John Wright Guise,¹ Bart. KCB. Ens. 4 Nov. 94; Lt. and Capt. 25 Oct. 98; Capt. and Lt.-Col. 25 July 05; Col. 4 June 13; Maj.-Gen. 12 Aug. 10; Lt.-Gen. 10 Jan. 37; Gen. 11 Nov. 51; Col. 85th Lt. Inf. 1 June 47.				
26	0	Lieut.Colonel.—John William Grey, Ens. P 16 May 34; Lieut. P 1 June 38; Capt. P 31 Mar. 43; Major, P 17 Dec. 52; Lt.-Col. 28 April 57.				
19	0	Majors.—William Williamson, Ens. P 16 Nov. 41; Lieut. P 22 Nov. 44; Capt. P 1 Aug. 51; Major, P 16 Oct. 55.				
18	0	Robert Maunsell, Ens. P 24 June 42; Lt. P 28 Mar. 45; Capt. P 7 Nov. 51; Major, 28 April 57.				

Years' Serv.		CAPTAINS.	ENSIGN.	LIEUT.	CAPTAIN.	BREV.-MAJ.
16	0	George Thompson......	P 23 Feb. 44	31 Mar. 47	P 29 Oct. 52	
12	0	Hon.Edmund John Boyle	P 12 Sept. 48	P 12 Dec. 51	P 16 Dec. 53	
15	0	William Henry Orme,⁵ s.	P 24 Jan. 45	3 Apr. 46	P 13 Jan. 54	1 July 59
12	0	John Armitage	P 10 Nov. 48	P 19 Mar. 52	P 28 Apr. 54	
11	0	Lord John Hy. Taylour	P 14 Dec. 49	P 3 Dec. 52	P 31 Aug. 55	
9	0	John Athorpe	P 16 Sept. 51	P 17 Dec. 52	P 2 Oct. 55	
0	0	Charles Wells Hogge....	P 12 Dec. 51	P 28 Jan. 53	P 16 Oct. 55	
8	0	Montagu Barton	P 16 Apr. 52	P 15 July 53	P 8 Jan. 56	
12	0	William Thomas Baker...	7 Jan. 48	P 9 July 52	29 Aug. 56	
8	0	John Bayley	P 21 Sept. 52	P 26 Aug. 53	28 April 57	
8	0	Devereux Herbert Mytton	P 22 Sept. 52	P 16 Dec. 53	P 30 Apr. 58	
7	0	Waller Ashe	P 21 Jan. 53	P 28 Apr. 54	P 7 Dec. 58	
		LIEUTENANTS.				
7	0	William Hallowes	P 22 Jan. 53	6 June 54	3 Major Orme served with the 3rd Light Dragoons during the Sutlej campaign of 1848-9, and was present at the battles of Moodkee and Ferozeshah, at which last he was severely wounded in the arm (Medal and one Clasp).	
7	0	Augustine FitzGerald ..	P 18 Feb. 53	11 Aug. 54		
7	0	Henry Manners Chichester	P 19 Feb. 53	11 Aug. 54		
7	0	William Henry Mathew..	P 11 Mar. 53	11 Aug. 54		
7	0	Edward Musgrave Beadon	P 12 Mar. 53	P 2 Mar. 55		
7	0	Rob. Kirkpatrick Taylor	P 15 July 53	P 31 Aug. 55		
5	0	Lambert Houlton Ward	P 9 Mar. 55	P 14 Sept. 55		
5	0	Boles Reeves	1 May 55	P 9 Oct. 55		
5	0	Finch White	30 April 55	P 16 Nov. 55		
5	0	William Galbraith	1 June 55	P 30 Nov. 55		
5	0	K. Wm. Herbert Noyes..	8 June 55	P 15 Jan. 56		
6	0	James Murray Grant....	1 Sept. 54	29 Aug. 56		
5	0	Stephen Henry K. Wilson	3 Aug. 55	28 April 57		
5	0	Francis Arthur Thomas..	P 29 Nov. 55	P 30 Apr. 58		
5	0	Chester Doughty	P 30 Nov. 55	P 7 Dec. 58		
		ENSIGNS.				
5	0	Wm. Henry Urquhart ..	P 7 Dec. 55			
4	0	Wm. Chipchase Henderson	P 15 Jan. 56			
4	0	Wm. Henry Drage, Adj.	9 May 56			
4	0	George Henry Stace	8 July 56			
3	0	William Fred. Hancocks	P 1 May 57			
3	0	C. Colvill Parkinson....	15 May 57			
3	0	Frederick Holmes A'Court	19 June 57			
2	0	Loftus L. Astley Cooper..	P 30 Apr. 58			
2	0	Arthur A. Capel........	19 Nov. 58			
1	0	Geo. Rob. S. Ramsbottom	P 1 Apr. 59			
1	0	Fred. Willock Garnett ..	P 29 Nov. 59			
9	0	Paymaster.—John R. Rouse, 3 June 59; Q.M. 12 Dec. 51.				
4	0	Adjutant.—Ensign Wm. Henry Drage, 2 March 58.				
4	0	Instructor of Musketry.—Ensign G. H. Stace, 15 Jan. 58.				
2	2⅚	Quarter Master.—William Hill Watts, 15 Feb. 56.				
16	0	Surgeon.—John William Johnston, M.D., 29 June 55; Assist.-Surg. 8 June 44.				
3	0	Assistant Surgeons.—Henry Carden Herbert, 15 Sept. 57.				
5	0	Nathaniel Norris, 2 Apr. 55.				

Facings Blue.—Agents, Messrs. Cox & Co.

1 Sir John Guise served with the 3rd Guards at Ferrol, Vigo, and Cadiz, in 1800; the Egyptian campaign of 1801 (Medal), including the actions of the 8th and 21st March, and 17th August, attack of the fortress of Marabout on the following day, action of the 22nd August, investment and capture of Alexandria. Expedition to Hanover in 1805-6. Proceeded to the Peninsula in 1809, and commanded the Light Battalion of the Guards with a Rifle Company of the 60th attached, on the retreat to the lines in 1810, battle of Busaco, and subsequent retreat, lines of Torres Vedras, several actions on the advance from thence in 1811, and battle of Fuentes d'Onor. Present also at the siege and captures of Ciudad Rodrigo and Badajoz. Commanded the 1st Battalion of the 3rd Guards at the battle of Salamanca, capture of Madrid, siege of Burgos and retreat from thence, advance in 1813, battle of Vittoria, siege and capture of San Sebastian, passage of the Bidassoa, battles of the Nive, passage of the Adour, investment of Bayonne and repulse of the sortie—during the latter part of the action he commanded the 2nd Brigade of Guards in consequence of Sir E. Stopford being wounded. Sir John has received the Gold Cross for Fuentes d'Onor, Salamanca, Vittoria, and Nive; and the Silver War Medal and one Clasp for Busaco.

Gosport.
Depot, Templemore.] **86th (The Royal County Down) Regt. of Ft.** 322

On the Colours & Appointments, the *Harp* and *Crown*, with the Motto "*Quis separabit?*"
"INDIA"—The *Sphinx*, with the words "EGYPT" "BOURBON"—On the Buttons, the *Irish Harp* and *Crown*.

Colonel.—🄿 ꓩ🄰 Lord James Hay,[1] *Ens.* 23 Jan. 06; *Lieut.* 6 Aug. 07; *Capt.* 8 Feb. 10; *Lieut.-Col.* 26 Mar. 18; *Col.* 10 Jan. 37; *Major-Gen.* 9 Nov. 46; *Lt.-Gen.* 20 June 54; *Col.* 86th Foot, 8 May 54.

Years' Serv.						
54						
Full Pay	Half Pay					
38	3¾	Lieut. Colonel.—Robert Henry Lowth,[2] CB. *Ens.* ᴾ4 Feb. 19; *Lieut.* ᴾ1 April 24; *Capt.* ᴾ15 May 27; *Brev. Maj.* 23 Nov. 41; *Brev.Lt.Col.* 11 Nov. 51; *Maj.* 30 Apr. 52; *Col.* 28 Nov. 54; *Lt.Col.* 10 Aug. 55.					
32	0	*Majors.*—Wm. Kier Stuart,[3] *Ens.* 6 Mar. 28; *Lt.* ᴾ28 Sept. 30; *Capt.* 8 Apr. 42; *Brev.Major*, 20 June 54; *Major*, 29 Sept. 54; *Bt.Lt.Col.* 20 July 58.					
33	0	Giles Keane, *Ens.* 21 June 27; *Lieut.* 22 Feb. 31; *Capt.* 23 Oct. 42; *Brev.-Major*, 20 June 54; *Major*, 10 Aug. 55; *Bt.-Lt.-Col.* 24 March 58.					

		CAPTAINS.	ENSIGN.	LIEUT.	CAPTAIN.	BREV.-MAJ.
24	0	John Perkins Mayers ..	ᴾ29 July 36	ᴾ23 Apr. 39	ᴾ27 Jan. 43	20 June 54
24	0	Harvey Wel. Pole Welman[4]	2 April 36	28 Dec. 38	9 Jan. 46	22 Mar. 58
22	0	Joshua Henry Kirby	ᴾ10 Aug. 38	8 Apr. 42	30 Apr. 52	
19	0	Charles Osborne Creagh[5]	18 June 41	ᴾ 5 Aug. 42	1 Mar. 54	
18	0	John Jerome	9 Apr. 42	14 Nov. 43	ᴾ28 Mar. 54	
21	0	Charles Darby[6]	6 Sept. 39	ᴾ30 July 42	10 Dec. 54	20 July 58
13	0	Maxwell Lepper	ᴾ13 Aug. 47	ᴾ23 Feb. 49	ᴾ25 Sept. 55	20 July 58
14	0	George Hewish Adams ..	14 April 46	ᴾ25 July 51	ᴾ25 Jan. 56	
10	0	Robert Edward Henry[7]..	ᴾ14 June 50	ᴾ10 Feb. 54	ᴾ25 June 58	
14	0	Ralph FitzGibbon Lewis	27 Oct. 46	30 July 49	2 July 58	
11	0	William Knipe	ᴾ19 Oct. 49	5 June 53	26 Aug. 59	
14	0	Benjamin Aylett Branfill	5 Apr. 46	ᴾ10 Dec. 47	9 Oct. 57	
		LIEUTENANTS.				
9	0	J. K. Douglas Mackenzie[7]†	24 Jan. 51	1 Mar. 54		
8	0	Augustus Nicholas Wilson	ᴾ15 May 52	29 Sept. 54		
9	0	Alfred Robert Ord......	5 Dec. 51	23 Jan. 55		
6	0	John F. Whitmore Mullen	7 June 54	27 July 55		
6	0	James Creagh	7 June 54	10 Aug. 55		
5	0	John William Fry[10]	25 May 55	28 Dec. 55		
5	0	Julius Drake Brockman[8]	10 Aug. 55	14 Sept. 57		
4	0	Gilbert Sidney Jackson	ᴾ19 Sept. 56	ᴾ25 June 58		
5	0	Duncan Stewart,[12] *Adj.*..	3 July 55	ᴾ 2 Oct. 55		
4	0	Charles Keane	1 Apr. 56	8 Oct. 58		
2	0	Matthew Edw. Leadbitter	30 Mar. 58	ᴾ14 June 59		
5	0	William Ker Gray	1 May 55	ᴾ17 July 57		
4	0	Thomas Yardley[13]	ᴾ 7 Mar. 55	ᴾ 7 Sept. 58		
5	0	Joshua James Bowness ..	2 Mar. 55	23 Oct. 55		
2	0	John Wells............	23 Mar. 58	18 Oct. 59		
		ENSIGNS.				
2	0	William Saunders	26 Mar. 58			
2	0	George Edw. A. Hilliard ..	13 Apr. 58			
2	0	Richard Jebb Posnett ..	ᴾ13 July 58			
2	0	Charles Henry Jackson..	2 July 58			
2	0	Francis Glasse Marshall..	ᴾ 7 Sept. 58			
2	0	Henry Valentine Cullinan	9 Nov. 58			
1	0	John William Boulcott ..	ᴾ14 June 59			
1	0	Edw. Berkeley Philipps..	ᴾ17 June 59			
2	0	John Edm. Monro Sperrin	19 Nov. 58			
27	0	*Paymaster.*—Charles Fade Heatly, 17 Dec. 47; *Ens.* 19 Apr. 33; *Lt.* 7 July 37.				
5	0	*Adjutant.*—*Lieut.* Duncan Stewart,[12] 3 June 59.				
5	0	*Quarter Master.*—William Lane, 31 Aug. 55.				
2	0	*Instructor of Musketry.*—*Ensign* C. H. Jackson, 12 Sept. 59.				
10	0	*Surgeon.*—Joseph Sawyers, M.D., 26 Jan. 58 ; *Assist.-Surg.* 29 Nov. 50.				
5	0	*Assistant Surgeons.*—Thomas Stawell Barry,[9] 22 Feb. 55.				
6	0	Edward Canny Ryall,[15] 22 Sept. 54.				

Facings Blue.—*Agents*, Messrs. Cox & Co.
[*Returned from India, 15 Aug. 1859.*]

Notes in margin: 1 Lord James Hay served in the Peninsula, and was present at the battles of Vimiera, Talavera, Busaco, Fuentes d'Onor, Vittoria, Pyrenees, Nivelle, and Nive, for which he has received the War Medal with eight Clasps. He served also the Waterloo campaign. 4 Major Welman served with the 17th Regt. during the campaign of 1838 and 39 in Affghanistan and Beloochistan under Lord Keane, & was present at the storm & capture of Ghuznee (Medal), and of Khelat, at which last he was with the advance-guard under Col. Pennycuick. 5 Captain Creagh served with a party of Volunteers attached to the Scinde Camel Corps during Sir Charles Napier's Campaign of 1845 against the mountain and desert tribes on the right bank of the Indus. Also on the Head Quarter Staff of the Azimghur field force during the Campaign of 1858 in the N. W. Provinces of India, and was present at the action of 6th April before Azimghur and in the intrenchment of that place from 6th to 14th April when besieged by Koer Sing's force. Also at the assault of Jugdespore, actions at Jelowra 11th and 29th May, Melahi, and skirmishes in the Jugdespore Jungle (Medal). 6 Major Darby served during Sir Chas. Napier's campaign against the Mountain and Desert Tribes situated on the right bank of the Indus, early in 1845, with a detachment of 200 men—volunteers from the 13th to the 39th Regt.

Right margin: acted as Orderly Officer to Brigadier General Jones in the action at Shahjehanpore on 14th May; was present at the action of Mohunpore on 26th May; wounded, and mentioned in despatches (Medal) and at the siege and capture of the fort of Pownie in August, and at the battle of Azimghur on 6th April, and specially thanked; commanded two squadrons of Irregular Cavalry at the siege and capture of the fort of Pownie in August, and at the action of Beejapore on 6th Sept.—wounded, and mentioned in despatches (Medal) [For remainder of Notes see second page of 86th Foot.

10 Lieut. Fry served with the Central India Field Force under Sir Hugh Rose, and was present at the actions of Kooneh and Golowlie, siege and capture of Calpee and of Gwalior, and taking of Pourie (Medal). 12 Lieut. Stewart served in the Indian campaign in 1858, and was present with the 13th Light Infantry

2 Colonel Lowth when Brigadier commanding at Kurrachee disarmed the 21st Regt. Bombay N.I. on the night of the 13th Sept. 1857. Served with the Central India field force in 1858 in command of the 8th Regt. and was present at the siege storm and capture of the strong hill fort of Chundairee, battle of the Betwa, siege storm and capture of the town and fortress of Jhansi, action of Kooneh, operations before Calpee from 16th to 21st May, battle of Gowlowlie, capture of the town and fort of Calpee, battle of Morar, battle of and capture of the town and fortress of Gwalior (several times mentioned in despatches, Brevet of Colonel, distinguished service pension, CB., Medal and Clasp).

3 Lt. Colonel Stuart commanded the 86th Regt. at the disarming of 4 companies of the 27th Bombay N I. at Rutnagherry on 11th Aug. 1857. Present at the siege storm and capture of Chandaree 17th March 1858 ; commanded left attack before Jhansi 30th March to 2d April; led the only successful escalade attack at the storm of Jhansi and commanded the party of the 86th Regt. in the fight of the stable of Ji ansi (Brevet of Lt.Colonel); led the storming party (wing of the 86th Regt.) at Kooneh; present in all the actions before Calpee 13th to 21st May and commanded the pickets on 20th May; battle of Gowlowlee, capture of Calpee, battle of Morar, and capture of Gwalior (several times mentioned in despatches, Medal and Clasps).

Embarked for Bengal, 21 April 1840.] **87th *Regt. of Foot (Royal Irish Fusiliers).*** [Serving in India. Depot, Buttevant.

"MONTE VIDEO" "TALAVERA."—*An Eagle, with a Wreath of Laurel above the Harp, in addition to the Arms of the Prince of Wales, in commemoration of their distinguished Services on various occasions, and particularly at the Battle of* "BARROSA" "TARIFA" "VITTORIA" "NIVELLE" "ORTHES" "TOULOUSE" "PENINSULA" "AVA."

Years' Serv. Full Pay	Half Pay					
49		Colonel.—🏵 ⚜ Sir James Simpson,[1] GCB. *Ens.* 3 April 11; *Lt. and Capt.* 25 Dec. 13; *Capt. and Lt.-Col.* 28 April 25; *Col.* 28 June 38; *Maj.-Gen.* 11 Nov. 51; *Lt.-Gen.* 29 June 55; *Gen.* 8 Sept. 55; *Col.* 87th Foot, 29 June 55.				
25	0	Lieut.Colonels.—Alexander Murray,[2] 2nd *Lieut.* ᴾ 24 Apr. 35; *Lieut.* 23 Oct. 39; *Capt.* ᴾ 20 Aug. 44; *Major,* ᴾ 30 Dec. 53; *Lieut.Col.* ᴾ 2 Nov. 55.				
13	1	Henry Ralph Browne,[3] *Ens.* 3 April 46; *Lt.* ᴾ 19 Sept. 48; *Capt.* ᴾ 28 Dec. 49; *Brev.Maj.* 2 Nov. 55; *Maj.* 1 Feb. 56; *Lt.Col.* ᴾ 15 June 58.				
17	0	Majors.—Alexander Hugh Cobbe, 2nd *Lieut.* 16 June 43; *Lieut.* ᴾ 10 Jan. 45; *Capt.* ᴾ 21 July 48; *Major,* ᴾ 2 Nov. 55.				
23	0	Charles Fred. Campbell, *Ens.* 15 Sept. 37; *Lieut.* ᴾ 28 Aug. 40; *Capt.* 2 Oct. 46; *Bt. Major,* 26 Oct. 58; *Major,* ᴾ 14 June 59.				

		CAPTAINS.	ENSIGN.	LIEUT.	CAPTAIN.	BREV.-MAJ.
22	0	Louis Herries Hamilton[5]	6 Apr. 38	ᴾ 17 Jan. 40	22 Dec. 46	20 July 55
18	0	James Bailie	ᴾ 20 Dec. 42	ᴾ 14 Feb. 45	ᴾ 22 Feb. 50	
29	0	William Francis Ring[6]	28 Oct. 31	8 May 35	15 Mar. 50	26 Dec. 56
17	0	William Hanmer	ᴾ 22 Dec. 43	ᴾ 3 Oct. 45	ᴾ 12 Oct. 49	
17	0	John Theophilus Ussher[7]	ᴾ 30 May 44	14 April 46	1 Jan. 54	
13	0	William Wiltshire	ᴾ 13 July 47	3 April 49	ᴾ 6 July 55	
8	0	Hon. D'Arcy G. Osborne	ᴾ 17 Aug. 52	ᴾ 9 Oct. 55	ᴾ 30 Nov. 55	
8	0	Jas. Arch. Ruddell Todd[8]	ᴾ 17 April 52	6 June 54	ᴾ 13 July 55	
17	0	John Hallowes	ᴾ 10 Mar. 43	ᴾ 27 June 45	ᴾ 17 July 57	
17	0	Ormond FitzGerald	6 Jan. 43	1 April 47	26 Oct. 58	
11	0	Rob. Gibson (*Q.M.* Apr. 47)	3 April 40	ᴾ 22 Feb. 50	18 Feb. 59	
9	0	Colmer Lynch	17 June 51	ᴾ 6 July 55	ᴾ 8 July 59	
		LIEUTENANTS.				
11	0	Edw. Hen. John Meredyth	ᴾ 18 May 49	ᴾ 8 Apr. 53		
10	0	Anthony Butler	ᴾ 13 Dec. 50	ᴾ 30 Sept. 53		
8	0	Joseph Noble Beasley	ᴾ 17 Aug. 52	ᴾ 24 June 53		
12	0	Thomas Law Roberts	ᴾ 19 Sept. 48	ᴾ 27 Dec. 50		
11	0	Charles Edmund Goddard	5 April 49	ᴾ 30 Dec. 53		
8	0	Edward Dampier Cockell	ᴾ 10 Dec. 52	ᴾ 11 Nov. 53		
7	0	Robert Lampen	ᴾ 30 Sept. 53	ᴾ 30 Nov. 55		
7	0	John Rawson Simpson	ᴾ 30 Dec. 53	ᴾ 30 Nov. 55		
8	0	Walter Carr Mackinnon	ᴾ 24 Aug. 52	ᴾ 17 July 57		
4	0	Benj. D'Urban Musgrave	25 Jan. 56	15 Mar. 58		
4	0	George William Marsden	ᴾ 8 Feb. 56	7 Sept. 58		
4	0	John Graham Leadbitter	15 Feb. 56	ᴾ 18 Mar. 59		
4	0	Fred. Flood Devereux	8 July 56	ᴾ 18 Mar. 59		
3	0	Richard Throckmorton	ᴾ 24 July 57	ᴾ 24 June 59		
		ENSIGNS.				
2	0	Rentone Geo. F. Poynter	26 Mar. 58			
2	0	George Robert Storey	30 Mar. 58			
2	0	Adrian A. Von Beverhoudt	31 Mar. 58			
2	0	John Hooker Vowell	7 Sept. 58			
2	0	John Leigh Hollest	17 Sept. 58			
2	0	Robert Atkin Hickson	6 Nov. 58			
2	0	Edw. Willoughby Pardoe	31 Dec. 58			
1	0	Alf. Herbert Hugh Smith	ᴾ 25 Mar. 59			
1	0	Charles Shortt Dicken	ᴾ 29 July 59			
2	0	Paymaster.—Arthur Anderson, 16 Aug. 50; *Ens.* 5 Mar. 58.				
		Adjutant.—				
18	0	Quarter Master.—Hy. Thomas,[10] 20 Apr. 49; *Ens.* 11 Apr. 42; *Lt.* 22 Dec. 45.				
20	0	Surgeon.—Richard George Davys Banon,[11] 1 July 53; *Assist.-Surg.* 30 Oct. 40.				
3	0	Assist.Surgeons.—David Chambers M'Fall, 15 Sept. 57.				
3	0	Philip Broke Smith, M.D. 15 Sept. 57.				
2	0	John Collins, M.D. 24 Mar. 58.				

2 Lt.-Col. Murray served in the 18th on the China expedition (Medal), and was present at Canton, Amoy, Chusan, Chinhae, Ningpo, Segoan, Chapoo (wounded), Shanghai, Woosung and Chin Kiang Foo.

3 Lt.-Colonel Browne served with the 9th Regt. in the Crimea from 27th Nov. 1854, including the siege and fall of Sebastopol and assault of the batteries on the 18th June (Medal and Clasp, and Brevet Major, Knight of the Legion of Honor, and 5th Class of the Medjidie).

5 Major Hamilton served as Assist.-Adjutant-General in the Burmah war (Medal); name twice honorably mentioned in General Godwin's Dispatches, and in Orders of the Governor-General.

7 Capt. Ussher served the campaign of 1844-5 in the Southern Mahratta country, with the 22nd, and was present at the investment and capture of the Forts of Panulla and Pownghur. Was on board the troop ship "Eastern Monarch" when she blew up and was destroyed by fire at Spithead on 3 June 1859.

8 Captain Todd served with the 1st Batt. Royals the Eastern campaign of 1854-55, including the battles of Alma and Inkerman, siege and fall of Sebastopol (Medal and Clasps, and Knight of the Legion of Honor).

Facings Blue.—*Agents*, Messrs. Cox & Co.

1 Sir James Simpson served in the Peninsula from May 1812 to May 1813, including the latter part of the defence of Cadiz, and the attack on Seville. Served also the campaign of 1815, and was severely wounded at Quatre Bras. He served as second in command to Sir Charles Napier during the campaign against the Mountain and Desert Tribes situated on the right bank of the Indus, early in 1845. Served in the Eastern campaign in 1855, first as Chief of the Staff and afterwards as Commander-in-Chief, including the siege and fall of Sebastopol (Medal and Clasp), *GCB*., Grand Cross of the Legion of Honor, Grand Cross of the Military Order of Savoy, and 1st Class of the Medjidie).

6 Major Ring served in 1855-56 with the Anglo-Turkish Army as Deputy Quarter-Master General (Brevet Major, 4th Class of the Medjidie, and Colonel Imperial Turkish Army).

10 Qr. Mr. Thomas served the campaign on the Sutlej in 1845-6 with the 9th Regt., including the battles of Moodkee, Ferozeshah, and Sobraon (Medal and Clasps).

11 Surgeon Banon served with the army on the Sutlej, and was taken prisoner by the Sikhs at the affair of Buddiwal; after a captivity of twenty-five days, twelve of which in irons, he was released, on the advance of the British forces on Lahore.

Serving in India. Depôt, Colchester.]   **88th Regt. of Foot (Connaught Rangers).**   324

The *Harp and Crown,* "*Quis separabit?*" The *Sphinx*, "EGYPT" "TALAVERA" "BUSACO" "FUENTES D'ONOR" "CIUDAD RODRIGO" "BADAJOZ" "SALAMANCA" "VITTORIA" "NIVELLE" "ORTHES" "TOULOUSE" "PENINSULA" "ALMA" "INKERMAN" "SEVASTOPOL."

Years' Serv.		
Full Pay	Half Pay	
54		**Colonel.**—p Horatio George Broke,[1] *Ens.* 29 May 06; *Lt.* 15 Feb. 08; *Capt.* p 18 Mar. 13; *Bt.Major,* 28 July 14; *Major,* p 12 June 23; *Bt.Lt.Col.* 20 July 30; *Col.* 23 Nov. 41; *Maj.Gen.* 20 June 54; *Col.* 88th Regt. 24 Dec. 58.
22	0	**Lieut. Colonels.**—George Vaughan Maxwell,[2] CB., *Ens.* p 2 Feb. 38; *Lt.* p 26 Apr. 39; *Capt.* p 6 Dec. 44; *Maj.* p 28 July 54; *Bt.-Lt.-Col.* 12 Dec. 54; *Lt.-Col.* 23 Mar. 55; *Col.* 23 Mar. 58.
21	0	Edward Herbert Maxwell,[3] *Ens.* p 26 Apr. 39; *Lieut.* p 16 Nov. 41; *Capt.* p 8 Oct. 47; *Major,* 8 June 55; *Bt.-Lt.-Col.* 2 Nov. 55; *Lt.-Col.* 16 June 57.
19	0	**Majors.**—Hon. John Jocelyn Bourke,[4] *Ens.* p 21 May 41; *Lt.* p 22 July 42; *Capt.* p 1 June 49; *Maj.* 27 May 56; *Bt.Lt.Col.* 26 Apr. 59.
19	0	Edmund Gilling Maynard,[5] *Ens.* p 31 Dec. 41; *Lt.* p 23 Jan. 46; *Capt.* p 14 July 54; *Bt. Major,* 2 Nov. 55; *Major,* 16 June 57; *Bt.Lt.Col.* 26 Apr. 59.

		CAPTAINS.	ENSIGN.	LIEUT.	CAPTAIN.	BREV.-MAJ.
16	0	Ben. Banbury Mauleverer[6]	p 30 Aug. 44	p 8 Oct. 47	p 28 July 54	6 June 56
20	0	Joshua Grant Crosse[7] ..	p 25 Sept. 40	p 30 Aug. 44	30 Aug. 54	26 Dec. 56
17	0	Thomas Gore[8]	p 3 Mar. 43	p 19 Feb. 47	29 Dec. 54	6 June 56
14	0	H.J.Le Marchant Baynes[7]	14 Apr. 46	p 12 Sept. 48	29 Dec. 54	
13	0	John Edward Riley[8]†...	p 8 Oct. 47	p 18 June 52	26 Jan. 55	
11	0	Shurlock Henning[9] ...	p 20 April 49	6 June 54	23 Mar. 55	
9	0	George Richard Browne[10]	p 17 June 51	11 Aug. 54	p 24 Apr. 55	4 June 58
8	0	Emil. C. Delmé Radcliffe[12]	p 9 July 52	p 18 Aug. 54	8 June 55	26 Apr. 59
6	0	William Charles Pearson[13]	p 5 May 54	p 6 Oct. 54	8 June 55	
5	6/13	Lewis John Fillis Jones[14]‡	14 July 54	8 Dec. 54	27 May 56	
6	0	William Lambert[16]	p 16 Aug. 54	8 Dec. 54	27 Nov. 57	
6	0	Frederick Hall[15]	p 17 Aug. 54	9 Feb. 55	p 23 Mar. 58	
		LIEUTENANTS.				1 Major General Broke accompanied the 52nd on the expedition to Copenhagen in 1807; and the following year on that to Portugal, and was present at the battle of Vimiera, the advance into Spain and retreat under Sir John Moore. In 1809 he served on the Walcheren expedition. In 1811 he joined the Light Division on the retreat of Massena from the lines of Lisbon, and served in Spain till the end of the war. In 1812 he joined Sir Henry Clinton as Aide de Camp, at the siege of Burgos, and was shot through the lungs while serving with him at the battle of Orthes. He served with the Army of Occupation in France from 1815 to 1818 as Aide de Camp to Sir Henry Clinton. Has the War Medal with four Clasps for Vimiera, Salamanca, Nive, and Orthes.
11	0	George Priestley[14]	30 Mar. 49	29 Dec. 54		
6	0	Robert Vernor[17]	p 18 Aug. 54	9 Feb. 55		
6	0	Ernest Aug. Perceval[16] .	p 15 Sept. 54	9 Feb. 55		
6	0	John Evans[15]†	13 Oct. 54	9 Feb. 55		
6	0	Edward Hopton[18]	p 27 Oct. 54	9 Feb. 55		
5	0	Caleb Robertson	p 12 Jan. 55	15 Apr. 55		
5	0	Lucas Clements Scott[20]..	p 16 Jan. 55	21 May 55		
6	0	Holt Waring[15]	p 27 June 54	8 June 55		
5	0	George Stretton Watson[20]	28 Feb. 55	8 June 55		
5	0	Edgar Edw. Austin, *Adj.*	1 Mar. 55	8 June 55		
5	0	Theobald Burke[15]	15 Mar. 55	17 Aug. 55		
5	0	Fred. Napleton Dew ...	16 Mar. 55	21 Sept. 55		
5	0	John D. Garner Dodgin .	23 Mar. 55	16 Oct. 55		
5	0	Edw. C. Mallet de Carteret	p 6 Apr. 55	16 Oct. 55		
5	0	Mortimer Neville Woodard	24 Apr. 55	16 Oct. 55		
5	0	John Irwin	1 May 55	26 Oct. 55		
5	0	H. Garrett Moore	7 June 55	p 26 Oct. 55		
5	0	Rowley Miller	21 Sept. 55	p 14 Dec. 55		
6	0	William John Saul.....	p 13 Oct. 54	p 26 Feb. 58		
5	0	James Buchanan Whitla	26 Oct. 55	p 29 Apr. 59		
		ENSIGNS.				
5	0	Patrick Dwyer[21]	16 Aug. 55			
5	0	William Hatfield	p 28 Dec. 55			
4	0	Lewis Mans. Buchanan ..	29 Feb. 56			
2	0	Thomas H. Cuthbertson .	16 Mar. 58			
1	0	Arthur Allen Owen	p 31 May 59			
1	0	Henry Griffith Bowen ..	p 28 Oct. 59			
16	5	**Paymaster.**—Michael Joseph Cunningham,[21] 24 Oct. 56; *Ens.* 14 Dec. 54; *Lt.* [13 April 55.
5	0	**Adjutant.**—Lieut. Edgar Edward Austin, 20 June 58.
5	0	**Instructor of Musketry.**—Ensign Patrick Dwyer, 17 March 59.
5	0	**Quarter Master.**—Matthew Evans,[20] 28 Dec. 55.
9	0	**Surgeon.**—Archibald Henry Fraser, 26 Jan 58; *Assist.Surg.* 21 Feb. 51.
6	0	**Assist.Surgeons.**—Thomas Robert Williams,[27] M.B. 24 March 54.
6	0	Richard William Meade,[28] 1 Sept. 54.
5	0	John Copeland Knipe, 14 March 55.

Facings Yellow.—*Agents,* Sir C. R. M'Grigor, *Bt.,* and Walter M'Grigor, Esq.
[*Returned from the Crimea,* 19 *July* 1856. *Embarked for India,* 15 *July* 1857.]

2 Colonel G. V. Maxwell served the Eastern campaign of 1854-55, including the battles of Alma and Inkerman, siege of Sebastopol, attack on the Quarries 7th June; commanded the 88th Regt. at the attacks on the Redan on the 18th June and 8th Sept.—severely wounded (Medal and Clasps, and *CB.*, Brevet Lt.-Col., Knight of the Legion of Honor, Sardinian Medal, and 4th Class of the Medjidie).

3 Lt.-Colonel E. H. Maxwell served the Eastern campaign of 1854-55, including the battles of Alma and Balaklava, siege of Sebastopol, attack on the Quarries 7th June, and on the Redan 18th June and 8th Sept. Medal and Clasps, Brevet Lt.-Col., Knight of the Legion of Honor, and 5th Class of the Medjidie).

88th Regt. of Foot (Connaught Rangers).

4 Lt.Colonel Hon. J. J. Bourke served the Eastern campaign of 1854-55, including the battles of Alma and Inkerman, and siege of Sebastopol (Medal and Clasps, and 5th Class of the Medjidie).

5 Lt.Colonel Maynard served at the siege of Sebastopol, the attack on the Quarries 7th June (severely wounded), and attacks on the Redan on the 18th June and 8th Sept. (Medal and Clasp, Brevet Major, Sardinian Medal, and 5th Class of the Medjidie).

6 Major Maulverer served at the siege of Sebastopol, and was severely wounded at the attack on the Redan on the 8th Sept. (Medal and Clasp, and Brevet Major).

7 Major Crosse and Captain Baynes served the Eastern campaign of 1854, including the battles of Alma and Inkerman (severely wounded), and siege of Sebastopol (Medal and Clasps, and Brevet Major).

8 Major Gore served the Eastern campaign in 1854-55, including the battles of Alma and Inkerman, siege of Sebastopol, attack on the Quarries 7th June, and on the Redan 18th June and 8th Sept. (Medal and Clasps, Brevet Major, and Sardinian Medal).

8† Captain Riley served the Eastern campaign of 1854-55, including the battles of Alma and Inkerman and siege of Sebastopol (Medal and Clasps, and Sardinian Medal).

9 Captain Honning served in the Eastern campaign of 1854-55, including the battle of the Alma, siege of Sebastopol, and attack on the Redan 8th Sept. (Medal and Clasps).

10 Major Browne served the Eastern campaign of 1854-55, including the battles of Alma and Inkerman, siege of Sebastopol, and attack on the Redan on the 18th June—dangerously wounded, right arm amputated (Medal and Clasps, and Knight of the Legion of Honor). Served in the Indian campaign in 1857-58, and was present at the relief of Lucknow by Lord Clyde, and at the fall of Calpee under Sir Hugh Rose (Medal).

12 Major Radcliffe served in the Eastern campaign of 1854-55, including the battle of Alma and siege of Sebastopol (Medal and Clasps).

13 Captain Pearson served at the battle of Inkerman, siege of Sebastopol, attack on the Quarries, and attacks on the Redan on the 18th June and 8th Sept. (Medal and Clasps, and 5th Class of the Medjidie).

13† Captain Jones served in the 7th Fusiliers the Eastern campaign from 20th Oct. 1854, and was present at the battle of Inkerman (wounded) and siege of Sebastopol, including sorties on the 26th Oct., 5th April (wounded), and 9th May, attack and capture of the Quarries on 7th June (wounded), and assault of the Redan on 18th June (severely wounded in three places); he was also wounded in the trenches on 27th March (Medal and Clasps, and 5th Class of the Medjidie).

14 Lieut. Priestley served at the siege of Sebastopol, and assaults on the Redan on the 18th June and 8th Sept., in which last he commanded the Grenadier Company (Medal and Clasp, and Sardinian Medal).

15 Captain Hall, Lieuts. Waring and Burke, served at the siege of Sebastopol, and attack on the Redan on the 8th Sept. (Medal and Clasp).

15† Lieut. Evans served at the siege of Sebastopol, attack on the Quarries 7th June, on the Redan 18th June, and was wounded in the trenches 8th Aug. (Medal and Clasp). Served in the Indian campaign, and when Adjutant of the Regt. was very severely wounded (compound fracture of the right leg by a musket ball) in action with the Gwalior rebels at Cawnpore on 27th Nov. 1857 (Medal).

16 Captain Lambert and Lieut. Perceval served at the siege of Sebastopol, including the attack on the Quarries, and attack on the Redan on the 18th June and 8th Sept.—severely wounded (Medal and Clasp). Lieut. Perceval has the 5th Class of the Medjidie.

17 Lieut. Vernor served at the siege of Sebastopol, attack on the Quarries, and attack on the Redan on the 18th June and 8th Sept. (Medal and Clasp, and 5th Class of the Medjidie).

18 Lieut. Hopton served at the siege of Sebastopol, attack on the Redan 18th June and 8th Sept. (severely wounded): Medal and Clasp.

20 Lieuts. Scott and Watson served at the siege of Sebastopol, and were severely wounded at the attack on the Redan on the 8th Sept. (Medal and Clasp).

21 Ensign Dwyer served the Eastern campaign of 1854-55, including the battles of Alma and Inkerman, siege of Sebastopol, and attack on the Quarries severely wounded by musket shot in left thigh and right leg (Medal and three Clasps).

24 Paymaster Cunningham served with the 18th Royal Irish in the Crimea from Dec. 1854, and was present at the siege of Sebastopol (Medal and Clasp).

27 Assist.Surgeon Williams served the Eastern campaign of 1854-55, including the battle of Alma and Inkerman, and siege of Sebastopol (Medal and Clasps).

28 Assist.Surgeon Meade served with the 88th Regt. at the siege of Sebastopol (Medal and Clasp).

29 Qr.Master Evans served throughout the Eastern campaign of 1854-55 (Medal and three Clasps).

[*Continuation of Notes to 88th Foot.*]

7 Captain Henry served with the Central India Field Force under Sir Hugh Rose in 1857-58, and was present at the siege and capture of Dhar, engaged in the actions of Mundesoor and Goodaren, siege and assault of Chundaree, siege and capture of Jhansi, battles of Baitwa and Kooneh, actions at and in front of Calpee, and the actions of 16th and 19th June 1858; was appointed SubAssist.Commissary General to the 1st Brigade and acted as Aide de Camp to Brigadier Stuart in most of the engagements (Medal).

7† Lieut. Mackenzie served with the Malwa, Nerbudda, and Central India field forces in 1857-58; present at the siege and capture of Dhar, operations at Mundesore and battle of Goodaria, siege storm and capture of Chundaree and also of the fortress of Jhansi, action of Kooneh and operations before Calpee (Medal and Clasp).

8 Lieut. Brockman entered the Royal Navy in 1847; was actively employed during the Kaffir war of 1851-52 (Medal). Served in H.M.S. *Hermes* at the first attack on the stockades in the Rangoon River, was present at the attack and taking of Martaban and afterwards at the storm and capture of Rangoon 11 Apr. 1852 (Medal and Clasp). Afterwards was in several actions with Pirates on the coast of China. Served in the Central India field force under Sir Hugh Rose from Feb. 1858 to Jan. 1859, including the capture of the strong hill fort of Chundaree, siege storm and capture of Jhansi, action of Kooneh, operations before Calpee, battle of Gowlowlee capture of Calpee, battle of Morar, and capture of Gwalior; captured a battery of 3 guns on the heights before Gwalior and turned them on the enemy (mentioned in despatches, Medal and Clasp).

9 Assist.Surgeon Barry served with the 71st at the capture of Kertch and Yenikale, and with the 90th at the siege and fall of Sebastopol, and was of the storming party at the assault of the Redan on the 8th Sept. 1855 (Medal and Clasp).

13 Lieut. Yardley served with the 13th Lt. Infantry in the Indian Campaign of 1857-58, and was present at the 1st relief of Azimghur as Orderly Officer to Lord Mark Kerr, and at the subsequent operations in that district; also at the defeat of the rebels at Banpore Thannah, actions at Demuriagunge, trans-Gogra campaign and action of Soolsepore (Medal).

15 Assist.Surg. Ryall served the Eastern Campaign of 1854-55, including the siege and fall of Sebastopol and assault on the outworks on 18th June (Medal and Clasp).

Serving in India, Depot, Fermoy.

89th Regiment of Foot. 326—327

The *Sphinx*, "EGYPT" "JAVA" "NIAGARA" "AVA" "SEVASTOPOL."

Colonel.—Charles George James Arbuthnot, *Ens. & Lt.* 26 Dec. 16; *Capt.* ᵖ 16 March 20; *Major*, ᵖ 3 July 23; *Lieut.Col.* ᵖ 1 Oct. 25; *Col.* 28 June 38; *Major Gen.* 11 Nov. 51; *Lt. Gen.* 13 Mar. 58; *Col.* 89th Foot, 9 July 57.

Lieut. Colonels.—Augustus Hallifax Ferryman,[1] CB. *Ens.* ᵖ 27 June 34; *Lieut.* 30 June 37; *Capt.* ᵖ 16 April 41; *Major*, ᵖ 22 Dec. 43; *Lt.Col.* ᵖ 24 Nov. 48; *Col.* 28 Nov. 54.

William Boyle,[5] *Ens.* 6 Dec. 38; *Lieut.* ᵖ 21 May 41; *Capt.* ᵖ 4 Jan. 50; *Brev.Major*, 2 Nov. 55; *Major*, 17 Nov. 57; *Lt.Col.* 13 Oct. 58.

Majors.—Edward Buller Thorp, *Ens.* 12 June 46; *Lieut.* ᵖ 2 Feb. 49; *Capt.* ᵖ 11 Mar. 53; *Major*, 9 May 58.

John Atkinson, *Ens.* ᵖ 22 Oct. 47; *Lieut.* 17 Jan. 51; *Capt.* ᵖ 4 Aug. 54; *Major*, 13 Oct. 58.

Years' Serv.		CAPTAINS.	ENSIGN.	LIEUT.	CAPTAIN.	BREV.MAJ.	BT. LT. COL.
Full Pay	Half Pay						
44							
26	0						
22	0						
14	0						
13	0						
17	0	John M. Cuppage[7]	10 Nov. 43	ᵖ 8 Aug. 45	20 Dec. 54	6 June 56	
12	0	Charles Heycock[10]	ᵖ 31 Mar. 48	ᵖ 5 Dec. 51	30 Dec. 54		
12	0	Robert Selby[11]	ᵖ 3 Oct. 48	ᵖ 20 Feb. 52	16 Jan. 55		
11	0	Wm. Cecil George Pery[12]	ᵖ 2 Feb. 49	ᵖ 6 Aug. 52	26 Jan. 55		
14	0	Rich. Fra. Holmes[13]	26 Sept. 46	8 Apr. 53	28 Aug. 57		
9	0	Francis Knatchbull[16]	ᵖ 5 Dec. 51	6 June 54	17 Nov. 57		
8	0	Barnes Slyfield Robinson[17]	17 Dec. 52	8 Dec. 54	9 May 58		
7	0	Richard Edward Beck[18]	ᵖ 18 Mar. 53	8 Dec. 54	10 Aug. 58		
14	0	Fra. Hen. Digby Marsh	31 Mar. 46	11 Sept. 51	26 Mar. 58		
6	0	John Arthur Barstow[6]	ᵖ 18 Aug. 54	26 Jan. 55	ᵖ 10 Dec. 58		
5	0	Montague C. Browning[20]	ᵖ 14 Jan. 55	27 Mar. 55	ᵖ 10 Dec. 58		
12	0	De Vic Valpy	ᵖ 20 Oct. 48	ᵖ 5 Oct. 49	26 Mar. 58		

LIEUTENANTS.

6	0	Montfort H. Trant Lloyd[20]	6 June 54	16 Jan. 55
6	0	Henry Lewis Harvest[20]	13 Oct. 54	9 Feb. 55
8	0	Simpson Hackett Hobbs	ᵖ 19 Dec. 52	6 Apr. 55
5	0	William Drage	ᵖ 15 Jan. 55	31 Mar. 55
5	0	Robert Johnston	ᵖ 16 Jan. 55	7 Sept. 55
5	0	Josias Dunn	9 Feb. 55	21 Oct. 55
5	0	Burchall Helme	ᵖ 9 Mar. 55	23 Oct. 55
5	0	Geo. Francis Dowdeswell	24 May 55	26 Feb. 56
5	0	Robert Bulkeley Baldwin	1 June 55	ᵖ 17 July 57
5	0	Henry Bishop	15 June 55	27 Apr. 58
5	0	Alexander Dixon Grier	6 July 55	10 Aug. 58
5	0	Rob. G. Newbigging, *Adj.*	20 July 55	13 Oct. 58
4	0	William Pott	8 Jan. 56	ᵖ 10 Dec. 58
5	0	William Sealy	23 Oct. 55	25 Mar. 59
5	0	Stephen William Sewell	9 Nov. 55	28 Sept. 58

ENSIGNS.

3	0	William Atthill	20 Dec. 57
2	0	James Shaw Hay	17 Sept. 58
2	0	Rich. Nathan Hubbersty	24 Sept. 58
2	0	William Herbert Rudall	ᵖ 8 Oct. 58
2	0	Augustus William Price	26 Nov. 58
1	0	William Grinfield Ostler	ᵖ 11 Jan. 59
1	0	Geo. J. Whitaker Hayward	12 Jan. 59
1	0	Charles William Burton	29 July 59
1	0	Charles Vernon Hassall	ᵖ 28 Oct. 59

15 Capt. Holmes served at the siege and fall of Sebastopol from 26th Jan. 1855, and attacks on the 18th June and 8th Sept. (Medal and Clasp).
16 Captain Knatchbull served at the siege of Sebastopol from 15th Dec. 1854, and attack on the 18th June (Medal and Clasp).
17 Captain Robinson served at the siege and fall of Sebastopol from 5th Jan. 1855, and attacks of the 18th June and 8th Sept (Medal and Clasp, and 5th Class of the Medjidie).
18 Captain Beck served at the siege and fall of Sebastopol from 12th March 1855, and attacks on the 18th June and 8th Sept. (Medal and Clasp).
20 Captain Browning, and Lieuts. Lloyd and Harvest, served at the siege and fall of Sebastopol from 20th Aug. 1855, and attack on the 8th Sept. (Medal and Clasp).
21 Paymaster Scott and Quartermaster Sibbald served at the siege and fall of Sebastopol from 15th Dec. 1854, and attacks on the 18th June and 8th Sept. (Medal and Clasp).
22 Surgeon Gilborne served with the 8th Hussars in Bulgaria from 5th June 1854. Served with the 89th Regt. at the siege and fall of Sebastopol, and attacks on the 18th June and 8th Sept. (Medal and Clasp).
25 Assist. Surgeon Price served with the 14th Regt. at the siege and fall of Sebastopol from 21st July 1855 (Medal and Clasp).

21	0	*Paymaster.*—Robert Scott,[21] 20 Feb. 52; *Ens.* 31 May 39; *Lieut.* ᵖ 14 May 43.	
5	0	*Adjutant.*—Lieut. Robert G. Newbigging, 10 Dec. 58.	
5	0	*Instructor of Musketry.*—Lieut. B. Helme, 20 Apr. 59.	
5	0	*Quarter Master.*—William Sibbald,[21] 14 Sept. 55.	
14	0	*Surgeon.*—Richard Gilborne,[22] 8 Dec. 54; *Assist.-Surg.* 2 Oct. 46.	
5	0	*Assistant Surgeons.*—James Bonnyman, M.D. 13 Dec. 55.	
6	0	William Henry Price,[25] 26 May 54.	
2	0	Thomas Walsh, 13 Oct. 58.	

Facings Black.—*Agent*, Sir John Kirkland.

[*Embarked for Turkey*, 20 April 1854.]

1 Colonel Ferryman commanded the 89th Regt. at the siege and fall of Sebastopol from 15th Dec. 1854, and attacks on the 18th June and 8th Sept. (Medal and Clasp), Knight of the Legion of Honor, and 4th Class of the Medjidie).
5 Lt. Colonel Boyle served at the siege and fall of Sebastopol, and was present at the attack of the 8th Sept. as Aide-de-Camp to Sir James Simpson. Served also as Assistant Military Secretary to Sir William Codrington until the evacuation of the Crimea (Medal and Clasp, Brevet Major, Knight of the Legion of Honor, and 5th Class of the Medjidie).
6 Captain Barstow served at the siege and fall of Sebastopol from 29th June 1855, and attack on the 8th Sept. (Medal and Clasp).
7 Major Cuppage served at the siege and fall of Sebastopol from 15th Dec. 1854, and attacks of the 18th June and 8th Sept. (Medal and Clasp, Brevet Major, Knight of the Legion of Honor, and 5th Class of the Medjidie).
10 Captain Heycock served at the siege and fall of Sebastopol from 5th Jan. 1855, and attacks on the 18th June and 8th Sept. (Medal and Clasp, and 5th Class of the Medjidie).
11 Captain Selby served at the siege of Sebastopol from 15th Dec. 1854 to 10th Feb. 1855 (Medal and Clasp).
12 Captain Pery served at the siege and fall of Sebastopol from 15th Dec. 1854, and attacks on the 18th June and 8th Sept. (Medal and Clasp, and 5th Class of the Medjidie).

90th Regt. of Foot (Perthshire Volunteers). (Light Infantry.)

[Seetapore, Oude. Depot, Canterbury.]

Years' Serv.					
Full Pay	Half Pay				
40		**"ANDORA." The Sphinx. "EGYPT" "MARTINIQUE" "GUADALOUPE" "SEVASTOPOL."**			

Colonel.—<s>p</s> Alexander Fisher Macintosh,[1] KH. *Cor.* 31 Oct. 11; *Lt.* p 11 June 12; *Capt.* p 9 June 16; *Major,* p 18 Sept. 23; *Lt.Col.* p 15 Dec. 25; *Col.* 28 June 38; *Maj.Gen.* 11 Nov. 51; *Lt.Gen.* 2 Aug. 58; *Col.* 90th F. 4 March 57.

22	0	**Lieut.Colonels.**—Wm. Paston Purnell,[2] CB. *Ens.* 24 March 38; *Lieut.* p 25 June 41; *Capt.* p 16 June 48; *Major,* 19 Jan. 55; *Lt.Col.* 9 Oct. 55; *Col.* 24 Mar. 58.
19	0	Thomas Smith,[3] CB. *Ens.* p 16 July 41; *Lt.* p 16 Sept. 45; *Capt.* p 20 Apr. 49; *Brev.Maj.* 2 Nov. 55; *Maj.* 30 Nov. 55; *Brev.Lt.Col.* 6 June 56; *Lt.Col.* 13 Nov. 57.
15	0	**VC Majors.**—John Christopher Guise,[4] *Ens.* p 6 June 45; *Lieut.* p 13 Oct. 48; *Capt.* 6 June 54; *Major,* 13 Nov. 57; *Bt.Lt.Col.* 24 Mar. 58.
13	0	William Pattison Tinling,[5] *Ens.* p 4 June 47; *Lt.* p 20 Apr. 49; *Capt.* p 8 Sept. 54; *Bt.Maj.* 6 June 56; *Major,* 24 Dec. 57; *Bt.Lt.Col.* 26 Apr. 59.

		CAPTAINS.	ENSIGN.	LIEUT.	CAPTAIN.	BREV.-MAJ.
12	0	H.H. Crealock[6] l.c. 20 July 58	p 13 Oct. 48	p 24 Dec. 52	29 Dec. 54	26 Dec. 56
8	0	Garnet Joseph Wolseley[7] l.c. 26 Apr. 59	12 Mar. 52	16 May 53	26 Jan. 55	24 Mar. 58
11	0	James Horne Wade[8]	p 2 Feb. 49	p 24 Feb. 54	2 Feb. 55	20 July 58
9	0	James Clerk Rattray[10]	p 17 Jan. 51	11 Aug. 54	9 Sept. 55	
8	0	Lawrence N.D. Hammond	23 Nov. 52	p 4 Aug. 54	p 8 July 56	
6	0	Leonard H. Lloyd Irby[11]	p 5 May 54	8 Dec. 54	p 24 Feb. 57	
6	0	Percy Julius Deverill[12]	11 Aug. 54	26 Jan. 55	1 Oct. 57	
7	0	Oswald William Every[13]	p 26 Aug. 53	2 Feb. 55	30 Oct. 57	
6	0	H. Holyoake Goodricke[14]	p 28 Apr. 54	20 Feb. 55	24 Dec. 57	
23	0	Fred. Edward Sorell	p 11 Aug. 37	1 Jan. 41	17 Sept. 50	
14	0	Wm. Thomas M'Grigor	28 Apr. 46	p 1 Dec. 48	10 Mar. 58	
5	0	Robert Trotter Knox[15]	15 May 55	13 July 55	26 Sept. 58	

		LIEUTENANTS.			
6	0	Charles B. Wynne[16]	p 24 Nov. 54	25 Feb. 55	
5	0	Ivan S. Andrew Herford[17]	10 Feb. 55	29 Apr. 55	
5	0	Henry Bingham	16 Feb. 55	9 Sept. 55	
5	0	William Knight	p 16 Mar. 55	23 Oct. 55	
5	0	Charles Dawson Barwell	5 Apr. 55	30 Nov. 55	
6	0	**VC** William Rennie, *Adj.*	11 Aug. 54	30 Nov. 55	
5	0	George Robert Miller	6 Apr. 55	p 7 Dec. 55	
5	0	Henry Carver Treacher	p 13 Apr. 55	p 7 Dec. 55	
5	0	Apsley Cherry	p 11 May 55	18 Jan. 56	
5	0	Edward Cooper Wynne	15 May 55	p 18 Jan. 56	
5	0	Edward Carter	25 May 55	p 8 Feb. 56	
5	0	Louis Worthington Wilmer	23 Oct. 55	25 Sept. 57	
5	0	Gerald Andrew Agnew	p 8 Nov. 55	28 Sept. 57	
5	0	Annesley Eyre	30 Nov. 55	13 Nov. 57	
4	0	George Gregg	p 18 Jan. 56	20 Apr. 58	
6	0	Charles Hunt Bindon	15 Dec. 54	25 June 58	
	0	Joseph Outram	13 Apr. 58	p 5 Aug. 59	

1 Lieut.General Macintosh served in the Peninsula with the 3rd Dragoon Guards from Aug. 1812 to the end of that war in 1814, including the retreat from Madrid to Salamanca, and action at Alba de Tormes, retreat of Ciudad Rodrigo and action at San Munos, passage of the Tormes above Salamanca, and attack on the French rear-guard under General Villate, action at Hormasa before Burgos, battle of Vittoria, investment of Pampeluna, action at Tarbes, attack on the French cavalry rear-guard at St. Gaudens, and battle of Toulouse. He has received the War Medal with two Clasps for Vittoria and Toulouse.

3 Lt.Colonel Smith served at the siege and fall of Sebastopol from 5th Dec. 1854 (Medal and Clasp, Brevets of Major and Lt.Col., Knight of the Legion of Honor, Sardinian Medal, and 5th Class of the Medjidie).

		ENSIGNS.			
4	0	Henry James Edgell[21]	p 15 Feb. 56		
4	0	James Felix Haig	p 1 Apr. 56		
5	0	Samuel Roden Handy	16 Oct. 55		
3	0	John Williamson	p 24 Feb. 57		
2	0	David Patterson Murray	25 June 58		
2	0	Francis Russell	2 July 58		
2	0	Oscar Wm. de Thoren	13 Aug. 58		
2	0	Fred. Hone Charleton	12 Nov. 58		

11	0	**Paymaster.**—Thomas Cassidy,[22] 11 April 55; *Q.M.* 4 May 49.
6	0	**Adjutant.**—**VC** *Lieut.* William Rennie, 30 Nov. 55.
5	0	**Instructor of Musketry.**—*Lieut.* C. D. Barwell, 2 March 59.
6	0	**Quarter Master.**—David Jackson,[24] 15 Dec. 54; *Ens.* 10 Aug. 54.
12	0	**Surgeon.**—Patrick Joseph Clarke, 11 May 55; *Assist.Surg.* 17 March 48.
3	0	**Assistant Surgeons.**—Edward Joseph Crane, 18 Aug. 57.
6	0	George Bell Poppelwell,[27] 9 June 54.
3	0	Charles George Lumsden, 28 May 57.

Facings Buff.—*Agent*, Andrew Lawrie, Esq.

[*Returned from the Crimea,* 23 *July* 1856. *Embarked for China,* 15 *April* 1857.]

2 Colonel Purnell served at the siege of Sebastopol (Medal and Clasp, and 5th Class of the Medjidie).
4 Lt.Colonel Guise served in the Crimea from 5th to 24th Dec. 1854 (Medal with Clasp for Sebastopol).
5 Lt.Colonel Tinling served with the 90th Lt. Infantry in the Crimea at the siege and fall of Sebastopol from 10th Aug. 1855, and was severely wounded at the assault of the Redan on the 8th Sept. (mentioned in despatches, Medal and Clasp, and Brevet Major). Served with Havelock's force in the advance to and relief of Lucknow in its subsequent defence; with Outram's force at the Alumbagh; at the final assault and capture of Lucknow, and subsequent operations in Oude (Medal and two Clasps, and Brevet of Lt.Colonel).
6 Lt.Colonel Crealock served in the Crimea from 5th Dec. 1854 to 10th Feb. 1855, and again from 28th March 1855, including the siege and fall of Sebastopol (Medal and Clasp, Brevet Major, and 5th Class of the Medjidie).

7 Lt.Col. Wolseley served with the 80th Regt. in the Burmese war of 1852-53 (Medal); was with the expedition under Sir John Cheape against the robber chief Myattoon, and severely wounded when leading the storming party against that chief's stronghold on the 10th March (mentioned in Di-patches). Landed in the Crimea with the 90th Light Infantry on 5th Dec. 1854, and employed in the trenches as Acting Engineer until Seba-topol was taken; was engaged in the assault and defence of the Quarries on 7th June, and on duty in the trenches at the attack of the 18th June: severely wounded in a sortie 30th Aug. when in charge of the advanced sap—several times mentioned in Dispatches (Medal and Clasp, Knight of the Legion of Honor, and 5th Class of the Medjidie).

8 Major Wade served with the 90th Light Infantry at the siege and fall of Sebastopol from 4th Dec. 1854 and was of the storming party at the assault of the Redan on the 8th Sept.—severely wounded and mentioned in despatches (Medal and Clasp, Sardinian Medal, and 5th Class of the Medjidie). Also during the Indian campaign of 1857-58,—present with Havelock's Column at the actions of the 21st and 23d Sept., relief and subsequent defence of Lucknow (mentioned in despatches), defence of the Alumbagh under Outram, and fall of Lucknow (Brevet of Major, Medal and Clasps).

10 Captain Rattray served at the siege and fall of Sebastopol from 4th Dec. 1854, and was severely wounded at the assault of the Redan on the 8th Sept. (Medal and Clasp).

11 Captain Irby served at the siege of Sebastopol from 5th Dec. 1854 to 20th March 1855 (Medal and Clasp). Served in Oude from 28th Oct. 1857 until the end of the Rebellion, including the defence of the Alumbagh, relief of Lucknow by Lord Clyde, defence of the Alumbagh under Outram, siege and fall of Lucknow (Medal and Clasps).

12 Captain Deverill served at the siege and fall of Sebastopol from 5th Dec. 1854, and was severely wounded at the assault of the Redan on the 8th Sept. (mentioned in despatches, Medal and Clasp). Also during the Indian campaign of 1857-58, and present at the defence of Alumbagh under Outram, the capture of Lucknow and subsequent operations in Oude (Medal and Clasp).

13 Captain Every served at the siege and fall of Sebastopol from 10th Aug. 1855 (Medal and Clasp).

14 Captain Goodricke served at the siege and fall of Sebastopol from 31st Aug. 1855, and was severely wounded at the assault of the Redan on the 8th Sept. (Medal and Clasp).

15 Captain Knox served during the Indian Mutiny in 1857-59; was present, attached to 64th Regt. at the action of Soorajpore, and did duty with a detachment 84th Regt. during the defence of the Alumbagh in Oct. and Nov. 1857, and final relief of the garrison of Lucknow on 24th Nov. by Lord Clyde; subsequently engaged in the defeat of the Gwalior rebels at Cawnpore on 6th Dec., the capture of the forts of Dehaign and Tyrool, action of Doudpore, and throughout the Oude campaign (Medal and Clasp).

16 Lieut. Wynne served at the siege and fall of Sebastopol from 12th July 1855, and was of the storming party at the assault of the Redan on the 8th Sept. (Medal and Clasp). Served in the Indian campaign from July 1857, including the relief of Lucknow by Lord Clyde, with Outram at the Alumbagh, and subsequent capture of Lucknow (mentioned in Sir J. Outram's despatches). Served with Grant's field force through the hot weather campaign (Medal and Clasp).

17 Lieut. Herford served at the siege and fall of Sebastopol from 7th Sept. 1855, and assault of the Redan on the 8th Sept. (Medal and Clasp).

21 Ensign Edgell served in the Indian campaign from 12th Aug. 1857, and was present at the defence of the Alumbagh during Lord Clyde's relief of Lucknow and afterwards under Outram, the capture of Lucknow, and subsequent operations in Oude (Medal and Clasp).

23 Paymaster Cassidy served in the expedition to the Umzimkulu against the revolted Kaffir chief Todo in 1844; also as a volunteer with the rank of Captain in the Cape Town Levies during the Kaffir war of 1851-52 (Medal). Served with the 21st Fusiliers in the Crimea, and was present at the battles of Alma, Balaklava, and Inkerman, and siege of Sebastopol (Medal and four Clasps).

24 Quarter-Master Jackson served throughout the Kaffir war of 1846-47 (Medal). Served also in the Crimea during the siege and fall of Sebastopol from 5th Dec. 1854 (Medal and Clasp).

27 Assist.-Surgeon Poppelwell served on the Staff in the Eastern campaign of 1854-55, and was present with the 31st Regt. at the siege of Sebastopol, and attack of the Redan on the 18th June (Medal and Clasp). Served with General Havelock's field force in the actions of 21st and 23rd Sept. 1857, the relief of Lucknow, and storming the Hirn Khannah.

91st (*The Argyllshire*) Regt. of Foot. [Foreign Service, Dec. 1854. Indi̇a. Depot, Chatham.

"ROLEIA" "VIMIERA" "CORUNNA" "PYRENEES" "NIVELLE" "NIVE" "ORTHES" "TOULOUSE" "PENINSULA."

Years' Serv.						
Full Pay	Half Pay					
52		Colonel.—**1** Hon. Charles Gore,[1] CB. KII., *Ens.* 21 Oct. 08; *Lieut.* 4 Jan. 10; *Capt.* 13 March 15; *Maj.* 21 Jan. 19; *Lt.-Col.* 19 Sept. 22; *Col.* 10 Jan. 37; *Maj.-Gen.* 9 Nov. 46; *Lt.-Gen.* 20 June 54; *Col.* 91st F. 8 Aug. 55.					
33	0					
28	0	Lt.-Cols.—John Francis Glencairn Campbell,[2] CB. *Ens.* 25 Oct. 27; *Lt.* p 27 Aug. 29; *Capt.* p 23 Nov. 32; *Maj.* 8 July 43; *Lt.-Col.* 14 Apr. 46; *Col.* 20 June 54.					
		Bertie Edward Murray Gordon, *Ens.* p 26 Oct. 32; *Lt.* p 24 July 35; *Capt.* p 23 Apr. 41; *Maj.* p 13 Oct. 48; *Bt.Lt.Col.* 30 Sept. 55; *Lt.Col.* 31 Aug. 58.					
21	0	*Majors.*—Wm. Tho. Laird Patterson, *Ens.* p 22 Feb. 39; *Lt.* p 12 Oct. 41; *Capt.* p 20 April 49; *Major,* p 14 Dec. 55.					
25	0	Henry J. Savage,[3] *Ens.* 5 June 35; *Lt.* p 11 May 38; *Capt.* 8 July 43; *Brev. Major,* 20 June 54; *Major,* 31 Aug. 58.					

		CAPTAINS.	ENSIGN.	LIEUT.	CAPTAIN.	BREV.MAJ.
10	0	Wm. Benj. Battiscombe..	p 15 Mar. 50	21 May 52	p 10 Nov. 54	
10	0	John Charles Sweny	p 12 Dec. 50	p 24 Aug. 52	p 9 Feb. 55	
9	0	Mal. Potter Macqueen, s.	p 18 Apr. 51	p 23 Apr. 53	p 7 Sept. 55	
9	0	Thomas Thornhill Lane..	p 19 Aug. 51	1 Jan. 54	p 14 Dec. 55	
8	0	Charles Goddard Dewell	8 June 52	p 10 Mar. 54	p 17 Nov. 57	
11	0	William Squirl[11]........	p 11 May 40	p 8 July 51	5 Mar. 58	
9	0	Henry Aubrey Bond ..	4 Apr. 51	24 Aug. 53	23 Mar. 58	
8	0	Henry Wood	p 17 Aug. 52	p 19 May 54	p 23 July 58	
9	0	Lloyd Henry Thomas[12]..	p 17 Oct. 51	p 17 Feb. 54	13 Aug. 58	
8	0	Alex. Cuningh. Bruce ..	p 18 June 52	p 17 Mar. 54	31 Aug. 58	
7	0	Henry William Gregg ..	p 21 Jan. 53	p 10 Nov. 54	28 Sept. 58	
7	0	William Rust D'Eye....	p 13 May 53	p 9 Feb. 55	p 4 Nov. 59	
		LIEUTENANTS.				
7	0	Tho. Erskine Arthur Hall	2 Sept. 53	5 June 55		
6	0	Wm. Prescod Gurney ..	p 17 Feb. 54	p 6 July 55		
6	0	John Edward Burton....	p 19 May 54	p 14 Dec. 55		
7	0	Francis Pike	p 22 Apr. 53	7 Oct. 55		
6	0	W. Overbeck Wade, *Adj.*	10 Mar. 54	27 Nov. 57		
5	0	Aug. Frederic Perkins ..	p 9 Feb. 55	p 27 Nov. 57		
5	0	Elliot Armstrong	8 June 55	p 11 Dec. 57		
5	0	Hubert Plunkett Burke..	p 10 July 55	5 Mar. 58		
5	0	John Macleod Tingcombe	p 7 Dec. 55	p 23 July 58		
4	0	Edward Kelly Obbard ..	8 July 56	13 Aug. 58		
3	0	Robert Powell Jones	p 19 June 57	31 Aug. 58		
3	0	Charles Hollway	p 7 July 57	28 Sept. 58		
3	0	John Edward Buller....	p 4 Dec. 57	15 Dec. 58		
3	0	William Hunter Baillie..	p 11 Dec. 57	2 July 59		
3	0	Henry Hamilton	p 15 Dec. 57	p 4 Nov. 59		
		ENSIGNS.				
3	0	Horace Ralph Spearman .	18 Dec. 57			
2	0	Charles Lacon Harvey ..	5 Mar. 58			
2	0	George Francis Robertson	p 23 Apr. 58			
2	0	William Grant	13 Aug. 58			
2	0	Henry Cæsar Kemm	7 Sept. 58			
2	0	Robert Butt Wesley	12 Nov. 58			
1	0	Arthur Elkington	28 Jan. 59			
1	0	Thomas Gerard Elrington	29 July 59			

2 Colonel Campbell commanded the infantry force which formed part of the expedition against the Insurgent Boers, beyond the Orange River, South Africa, in April 1845; and he commanded the Reserve Battalion, 91st Regt., throughout the whole of the Kaffir war of 1846-7, and was specially mentioned in Colonel Somerset's Dispatches of the 17th and 18th Apr. 1846, as also in Lieut.-Gen. Sir George Berkeley's General Order of the 17th Dec. 1847, as having conducted and commanded one of the columns of attack against the chief Sandilli, which concluded the war (Medal).

8 Major Savage served with the detachment of the 91st in the expedition against the Insurgent Boers beyond the Orange River, South Africa, in 1845; also in the Kaffir war of 1846-7; and in that in 1852-53 (Medal).

11 Captain Squirl served as a Lieutenant in the Austrian Army under Marshal Radetzki in 1848-49, and was present at the battles of Mortara and Novara. Served in the Kaffir War of 1850-53 (Medal).

12 Captain Thomas served throughout the Kaffir war of 1852-53, and was in every action in the Waterkloof in which the 91st Regt. were engaged (Medal).

8	0	*Paymaster.*—John Anthony Kysh, 7 Nov. 50; *Ens.* 6 July 52; *Lt.* 28 April 54	
6	0	*Adjutant.—Lieut.* Walter Overbeck Wade, 27 Nov. 57.	
7	0	*Instructor of Musketry.—Lieut.* Thomas Erskine Arthur Hall, 20 March 57.	
13	0	*Quarter Master.*—James Paterson, 1 Oct. 47.	
18	0	*Surgeon.*—Miah William Murphy,[16] 3 March 54; *Assist. Surg.* 22 July 42.	
6	0	*Assist. Surgs.*—Robert Watson, 24 May 54.	
2	0	Hugh Mackay Macbeth, 22 June 58.	
2	0	John M'Lean Marshall, 1 Sept. 58.	

Facings Yellow.—*Agent,* Andrew Lawrie, Esq.

1 Lieut.-General Hon. Charles Gore joined the 43rd in the Peninsula in July 1811, and was present and one of the storming party of Fort San Francisco at the investment of Ciudad Rodrigo; also at the siege and storming of that fortress and of Badajoz, battle of Salamanca, as Aide-de-Camp to Sir Andrew Barnard; and in a similar capacity to Sir James Kempt in the battles of Vittoria, the Nivelle, the Nive (9th, 10th, and 11th Dec.), Orthes, and Toulouse. He was also in the action of San Milan, capture of Madrid, storming of the heights of Vera, bridge of Yauzi, and all the skirmishes of the Light Division from 1812 to the close of the war in 1814; after which he accompanied Sir James Kempt with the troops sent to Canada under his command; returned to Europe in time for the campaign of 1815, and was first and principal Aide-de-Camp to Sir James Kempt, and present at the battles of Quatre Bras (horse shot), and Waterloo (three horses shot), and capture of Paris. He has received the War Medal with nine Clasps.

16 Surgeon Murphy served with the 80th Regt. during the Burmese war of 1852-53, and was present at the taking of Prome; also present as Staff Surgeon to the Bengal division with Sir J. Cheape's force at Donabew, and wounded in the attack on the enemy's stockade on the 19th March 1853 (Medal).

Emb. for Corfu, 3 Mar. 51.
In India. Depot, Stirling.

92nd (Gordon Highlanders) Regt. of Foot. 331

"EGMONT-OP-ZEE" "MANDORA"—The Sphinx, "EGYPT" "CORUNNA" "FUENTES D'ONOR" "ALMARA" "VITTORIA" "PYRENEES" "NIVE" "ORTHES" "PENINSULA" "WATERLOO."

Years' Serv.		
Full Pay.	Half Pay.	
57		Colonel.—꘏ Sir John M'Donald,[1] KCB. Ens. 17 Dec. 03; Lt. 21 March 05; Capt. 7 Sept. 09; Major, 26 Aug. 13; Lt.Col. 4 Sept. 17; Col. 10 Jan. 37; Major Gen. 9 Nov. 46; Lt.Gen. 20 June 54; Col. 92nd Foot, 25 May 55.
36	12⁶	Lieut.Colonels.—Mark Kerr Atherley, Ens. p28 Aug. 23; Lt. p 13 Aug. 25; Capt. p 25 Nov. 28; Brev.Major, 23 Nov. 41; Maj. 9 Nov. 46; Lt.Col. p 23 Nov. 49; Col. 28 Nov. 54.
32	0	Archibald Inglis Lockhart, CB. Ens. p 31 Dec. 28; Lieut. p 11 June 30; Capt. p 19 Aug. 36; Bt.Maj. 9 Nov. 46; Maj. p 23 Nov. 49; Bt.Lt.Col. 20 June 54; Lt.Col. 26 Dec. 57; Col. 7 Dec. 58.
37	0	Majors.—Robert Macleod Sutherland, Ens. 25 Dec. 23; Lt. 7 Aug. 24; Capt. 5 Oct. 41; Bt.Maj. 20 June 54; Maj. 25 Sept. 55; Bt.Lt.Col. 2 Apr. 59.
29	0	Kenneth Douglas Mackenzie,[2] Ens. p 25 Nov. 31; Lt. p 19 Aug. 36; Capt. p 27 Sept. 44; Brev.Maj. 12 Dec. 54; Bt.Lt.Col. 2 Nov. 55; Maj. 26 Dec. 57.

		CAPTAINS.	ENSIGN.	LIEUT.	CAPTAIN.	BREV.MAJ.
25	0	Edward Eldridge Haines	p 26 June 35	p 1 Feb. 39	p 3 Apr. 46	26 Dec. 56
17	0	Chris. Monteith Hamilton	p 3 Feb. 43	p 27 Sept. 44	p 12 Nov. 47	16 Jan. 59
16	0	Forbes Macbean	p 27 Sept. 44	p 8 Aug. 45	p 3 Aug. 49	
16	0	Arthur Welling. Cameron	6 Dec. 44	p 27 Mar. 46	p 28 Jan. 53	
14	0	John Henry St. John	20 Nov. 46	p 23 Nov. 49	26 July 55	7 Dec. 58
11	0	Gibson Stott	p 9 Mar. 49	p 23 Apr. 52	25 Sept. 55	
7	0	George Hubert Parker	p 21 Jan. 53	p 14 April 54	p 18 Sept. 57	
9	0	Lionel Holmes	p 18 Apr. 51	p 24 Mar. 54	p 9 Oct. 57	
7	0	Henry Ritchie Wallace	p 14 May 53	p 6 July 55	p 6 Nov. 57	
6	0	Percy Feilding Gooch	p 14 April 54	25 Sept. 55	p 24 May 59	
6	0	Robert L.Grant M'Grigor[7]	p 27 Oct. 54	p 27 May 56	p 4 Feb. 59	
6	0	Theodore Gordon	p 29 Sept. 54	25 Sept. 55	p 16 Sept. 59	
		LIEUTENANTS.				
6	0	Gordon Stonhouse Hughes	p 14 July 54	p 29 June 55		
8	0	James Moorhead	23 Nov. 52	3 Oct. 55		
6	0	George Hollings Best	10 Feb. 55	4 Oct. 55		
5	0	L. W. Maxwell Lockhart	9 Feb. 55	4 Oct. 55		
5	0	Robert Bruce M'Ewen	24 Apr. 55	4 Oct. 55		
5	0	William Kilvert	30 Apr. 55	4 Oct. 55		
7	0	Chas. Alex. Humfrey, Adj.	11 Mar. 53	p 26 May 54		
6	0	R. W. S. Raper Hunton[6]	14 Sept. 54	16 Nov. 55		
7	0	Edmund Spry Tritton	22 April 53	30 Nov. 55		
5	0	John Crosland Hay	15 May 55	p 14 Dec. 55		
5	0	Alex. Forbes Mackay	p 25 July 55	p 8 Jan. 56		
5	0	Cockburn M'Barnet	p 27 July 55	p 18 Jan. 56		
5	0	Francis Roberts	17 Sept. 55	p 17 April 57		
5	0	Adam Clerk Rattray	2 Nov. 55	p 9 Oct. 57		
2	0	George Foyle Fawcett	28 Mar. 58	p 7 Sept. 58		
5	0	Gilbert Edward Campbell	1 Oct. 55	p 23 Aug. 59		
5	0	Rich. Jas. S. Carruthers	2 Oct. 55	p 30 Sept. 59		
		ENSIGNS.				
5	0	Henry Abigail Ellis	7 Sept. 55			
5	0	Adam Eddington	28 Sept. 55			
5	0	Robert Alexander Emmet	p 21 Sept. 55			
4	0	William Grisdale Hicks	p 8 Jan. 56			
4	0	D. Baird Hope Johnstone	1 Feb. 56			
3	0	Alex. Robert A. Boyd	p 17 April 57			
3	0	Thomas Rendall Morris	p 25 Aug. 57			
1	0	David M. Makgill Crichton	p 31 May 59			
1	0	Maurice Thom.Carmichael	p 28 Oct. 59			
1	0	Grant Tomlinson	p 4 Nov. 59			

1 Sir John M'Donald's services:—Expedition to South America, and assault of Buenos Ayres; Peninsula, from Nov. 1808 to 1813, and in the south of France from March 1814, including the battle of Busaco, Lines of Torres Vedras, affairs at Redinha, Pombal, and Campo Mayor, first siege of Badajoz, battle of Albuhera, third siege and assault of Badajoz, affairs at Alva de Tormes, battles of Vittoria, the Pyrenees, 25th (had two horses shot under him), 30th and 31st July, and Toulouse. Wounded in the head and right thigh at the assault of Buenos Ayres, 5th July 1807; in the left leg and right groin in the Pyrenees 30th July; and in the right shoulder and lungs at the assault of the fortified rock on the mountain Aroila, and surprising the enemy's post in the valley of Banen Pyrenees, 2nd Oct. 1813. He has received the Gold Medal and one Clasp for Vittoria and the Pyrenees; and the Silver War Medal with four Clasps for Busaco, Albuhera, Badajoz, and Toulouse.

6 Lieut. Hunton served with the Eastern Army from Nov. 1854 as Ensign in the Mounted Staff Corps (Medal and Clasp for Sebastopol).

5	0	Paymaster.—James George, 21 May 55; Q. M. 12 Jan. 55; Ens. 3 June 56.
7	0	Adjutant.—Lieut. Charles Alex. Humfrey, 21 May 58.
5	0	Instructor of Musketry.—Lieut. A. F. Mackay, 31 May 59.
4	0	Quarter Master.—John Dewar, 3 June 56.
9	0	Surgeon.—Thomas Bussett Reid, 5 Oct. 58; Assist.Surg. 16 May 51.
5	0	Assistant Surgeons.—Samuel Black Roe, 4 Aug. 55.
3	0	David Shorter Skinner, 28 Sept. 57.
3	0	James Langdale, M.D. 15 Sept. 57.

Facings Yellow.—Agent, Andrew Lawrie, Esq.

2 Lt.-Colonel Mackenzie served the Eastern campaign of 1854-55 as a Brigade-Major in the Light Division, including the battles of the Alma and Inkerman, and siege of Sebastopol (Medal and Clasps, Brevets of Major and Lt.-Col., Knight of the Legion of Honor, Sardinian Medal, and 5th Class of the Medjidie).

7 Captain M'Grigor served at the siege (wounded) and assault of Delhi in 1857 and during the six days' fighting in the City; afterwards present in the action of Bolundshur, affair of Allyghur, battle of Agra, action of Dilkoosha and relief of Lucknow under Lord Clyde, affair of the 2d and action of 6th Dec. at Cawnpore, and action of Khudagunj; also served the campaign of 1858-59 in Oude (Medal and Clasp).

93rd (Sutherland Highlanders) Regt. of Foot.

[Serving in India — Depôt, Aberdeen]

"CAPE OF GOOD HOPE" "ALMA" "BALAKLAVA" "SEVASTOPOL."

Years' Serv		
Full Pay	Half Pay	
52		Colonel.—☉ Colin, *Lord Clyde*,[1] GCB. *Ens.* 26 May 08; *Lt.* 28 June 09; *Capt.* 9 Nov. 13; *Major*, 26 Nov. 25; *Lt. Col.* 26 Oct. 32; *Col.* 23 Dec. 42; *Maj. Gen.* 20 June 54; *Lt. Gen.* 4 June 56; *Gen.* 14 May 58; *Col.* 93rd Highlanders, 15 Jan. 58.
25	0	*Lieut. Colonels.*—Alex. Sebastian Leith Hay,[2] CB. *Ens.* p 25 Dec. 35; *Lieut.* p 26 Apr. 39; *Capt.* p 31 Mar. 48; *Major*, p 21 Oct. 53; *Lt. Col.* 12 Dec. 54; *Col.* 16 April 58.
25	0	Henry William Stisted,[3] CB. *Ens.* p 4 Dec. 35; *Lt.* p 29 Sept. 38; *Capt.* p 29 April 42; *Major*, p 26 May 48; *Lt. Col.* p 19 April 50; *Col.* 28 Nov. 54.
19	8/12	*Majors.*—Robert Lockhart Ross,[5] *Ens.* p 15 Dec. 40; *Lt.* 27 June 45; *Capt.* 11 June 52; *Bt.-Major*, 12 Dec. 54; *Major*, 8 Jan. 56; *Bt. Lt.-Col.* 26 Dec. 56.
24	0	George Cornwall,[6] *Ens.* p 8 July 36; *Lt.* p 9 Mar. 38; *Capt.* 9 June 48; *Bt. Major*, 24 Mar. 58; *Major*, 16 April 58.

		CAPTAINS.	ENSIGN.	LIEUT.	CAPTAIN.	BREV. MAJ.
14	0	Wm. G. Alex. Middleton.	24 July 46	p 3 Aug. 49	6 June 54	20 July 58
13	0	Wm. Donald Macdonald[7]	p 4 June 47	p 1 Oct. 50	10 Oct. 54	26 Dec. 56
12	0	Fred. William Burroughs[8]	p 31 Mar. 48	p 23 Sept. 51	p 10 Nov. 54	20 July 58
15	0	E. S. Fra. Geo. Dawson[9]	25 Nov. 45	11 June 52	29 Dec. 54	24 Mar. 58
24	8	James Montagu Brown	17 April 28	14 Oct. 36	1 Jan. 47	26 Oct. 58
9	0	Reginald Stewart Williams	17 Jan. 51	p 21 Oct. 53	15 Aug. 55	
6	0	Edward Welch[11]†	10 Mar. 54	10 Oct. 54	12 Mar. 58	
6	0	VC William M'Bean[13]	10 Aug. 54	8 Dec. 54	16 April 58	
10	0	Wm. Wallingfrd. Knollys[14]	22 Oct. 50	p 5 Nov. 50	6 Nov. 54	
14	0	Charles Hugh Levinge[15]	2 Apr. 46	p 19 Feb. 57	10 June 57	
6	0	Ewen H. D. Macpherson[12]	p 3 Nov. 54	9 Feb. 55	p 13 May 59	
14	0	Whiteford John Bell[13]†	13 Nov. 46	23 Mar. 49	23 July 58	
		LIEUTENANTS.				
6	0	Arthur C. Nightingale[12]	p 10 Nov. 54	9 Mar. 55		
6	0	Maxwell Wither Hyslop[12]	p 8 Dec. 54	9 Mar. 55		
8	0	George Roe Fenwick[17]	23 Nov. 52	28 Nov. 54		
5	0	Wm. Gordon Alexander[12]	p 16 Jan. 55	1 May 55		
6	0	Anthony Olivier Tabuteau	p 6 Oct. 54	1 May 55		
5	0	Edward Septinus Wood	9 Feb. 55	10 June 55		
5	0	Samuel Edward Wood	16 Feb. 55	14 June 55		
5	0	Charles Warner Losack	1 Mar. 55	27 July 55		
5	0	Roderick dhu G. H. Burgoyne	2 Mar. 55	15 Aug. 55		
5	0	George Cecil Gooch	29 Mar. 55	p 23 Oct. 55		
5	0	FitzRoy M'Pherson,[15] *Adj.*	8 Mar. 55	2 Nov. 55		
5	0	Edward Court Haynes	p 25 May 55	p 2 Nov. 55		
5	0	George Greig	9 Mar. 55	8 Jan. 56		
5	0	Waller Scott Mackenzie	11 May 55	17 Nov. 57		
5	0	George Forbes Robertson	19 July 55	13 Dec. 57		
5	0	Geo. John Malcolm Taylor	3 Aug. 55	12 Mar. 58		
5	0	Rt. K. A. Dick Cunyngham	10 Aug. 55	16 Apr. 58		
5	0	John E. Deans Campbell	2 Oct. 55	p 10 Dec. 58		
5	0	Fra. Rawdon Macnamara	28 Dec. 55	p 13 May 59		
		ENSIGNS.				
5	0	Charles Hastie	2 Nov. 55			
4	0	Wm. Fullarton Fullarton	8 Jan. 56			
4	0	Charles Dennis Potts	p 18 Jan. 56			
4	0	Dunlop Hay	14 Mar. 56			
2	0	Robert Wm. Thew Gordon	26 Feb. 58			
2	0	Henry Thomas Butter	25 June 58			
2	0	William Forbes	10 Dec. 58			
1	0	Charles Edward Condell	p 18 Jan. 59			
1	0	Edward Augustus Raikes	p 14 June 59			

5 Lt. Colonel Ross served the Eastern campaign of 1854-55 with the 93rd Highlanders, including the battles of Alma, Balaklava, and siege of Sebastopol (Medal and Clasps, Brevet Major and Sardinian Medal, and 5th Class of the Medjidie).

6 Major Cornwall served the Eastern campaign of 1854-55 with the 93rd Highlanders, including the battles of Alma and Balaklava, capture of Balaklava, expedition to the Sea of Azoff and capture of Kertch and Yenikale; afterwards present at the siege and fall of Sebastopol, and assaults of the 18th June and 8th Sept.—wounded in the trenches on the 3rd Aug. 1855 (Medal and three Clasps, and Knight of the Legion of Honor).

10	0	*Paymaster.*—Stephen Blake,[18] 26 Jan. 49; *Ens.* p 4 Oct. 44; *Lieut.* p 21 July 46.
5	0	*Adjutant.*—*Lieut.* FitzRoy M'Pherson,[16] 16 April 58.
6	0	*Instructor of Musketry.*—*Lieut.* A. O. Tabuteau, 11 Dec. 58.
5	0	*Quarter Master.*—John Joiner,[19] 6 July 55.
16	0	*Surgeon.*—Wm. Munro,[20] M.D. 5 May 54; *Assist. Surg.* 6 Dec. 44.
7	0	*Assist. Surgeons.*—William Sinclair,[21] 2 Sept. 53.
6	0	Robert Menzies, 24 Feb. 54.
7	0	James Nicholas Bell,[21] M.D. 1 April 53.

Facings Yellow.—*Agents*, Messrs. Cox and Co.

[*Returned from the Crimea*, 15 July 1856. *Embarked for China*, 10 June 1857.]

1 Lord Clyde served with the 9th Regt. in the Peninsula and at Walcheren, and was present at the battle of Vimiera, in the advance and retreat of the army under Sir John Moore, and battle of Corunna; at the battle of Barrosa and the defence of Tarifa. He was attached to the army of Ballesteros at the latter end of 1812, and was present at several affairs; also in an expedition to relieve Tarragona; was at the affair of Osma, battle of Vittoria, siege of St. Sebastian, where he received two severe wounds, and passage of the Bidassoa, where he was again severely wounded. Served in

93rd (Sutherland Highlanders) Regt. of Foot. 333

America in 1814-15 in the 60th Rifles. Was Brigade Major of the troops engaged in quelling the insurrection in Demerara in 1823. Commanded the 98th Regt. in the expedition to China in 1842, including the capture of Chinkiangfoo and subsequent operations near to Nankin. Commanded the 3rd Division of the army of the Punjaub throughout the Punjaub campaign of 1848-9, including the affair of Ramnuggur, passage of the Chenab, affair of Sadoolapore, battles of Chillianwallah (wounded) and Goojerat, and the final operations. He was constantly employed in 1851 and 1852, when Brigadier General commanding the Peshawur districts, in operations against the Hill Tribes surrounding the valley, including the forcing of the Kohat Pass under Sir Charles Napier, and repeated affairs with the Momunds, who finally made terms after their defeat at Punj Pao by a small detachment of cavalry and horse artillery under his immediate command, the combined tribes numbering upwards of 8,000 men. In 1852 he commanded an expedition against the Ootmankhail and Ranazai Tribes, whom he attacked in their valleys, and destroyed the strongly-defended village of Nowadund, the fortified village of Pranghur, and he finally routed them with great slaughter at Iskakote, where they mustered 8,000 men, while his force was under 3,000 men. Commanded the Highland Brigade and Highland Division throughout the Eastern campaign of 1854-55, including the battles of the Alma and Balaklava, and the siege of Sebastopol (Medal and Clasps, *GCB*., Grand Officer of the Legion of Honor, Grand Cross of St. Maurice and St. Lazarus, and 1st Class of the Medjidie); has also received the War Medal with five Clasps, the Chinese Medal, the Punjaub Medal with two Clasps, and was nominated KCB. after the Punjaub campaign. Wounded at the second relief of Lucknow 16th Nov. 1857.

2 Colonel Leith Hay served in Canada during the Rebellion, and was in the affair at Prescot. Served the Eastern campaign of 1854 up to 8th Feb. 1855, and again from 13th Aug. 1855, including the battles of Alma and Balaklava, siege and fall of Sebastopol, and commanded the 93rd Highlanders at the assault on the 8th Sept. (Medal and Clasps, Knight of the Legion of Honor, and 5th Class of the Medjidie, and Turkish Medal). Commanded the 93rd Highlanders at the relief of Lucknow 14th to 25th Nov. 1857, defeat of the Gwalior Contingent at Cawnpore on 6th Dec. and pursuit to Seraighat, siege and capture of Lucknow; commanded the Highland Brigade at the battle of Bareilly, and served in the Oude campaign in 1858-59, including the actions Purgaon and Russoulpore, and evacuation of the fort of Mittoula (Brevet of Colonel, Medal and Clasp).

3 Colonel Stisted served with the Queen's Royals during the campaign in Affghanistan and Belooch is ta under Lord Keane, including the storm and capture of Ghuznee (wounded) and of Khelat (Medal for Ghuznee). Served with the 72nd Highlanders in the Persian war in 1857; commanded a Brigade in the night attack and battle of Kooshab (*CB*.), and the 78th at the bombardment of Mohumrah. Served with Havelock's column in 1857, present in the action at Bithoor, commanded the Regt. in the several actions leading to and ending in the relief of the Residency at Lucknow. Succeeded to the command of the 1st Brigade on the death of General Neil on 25th Sept. and held that command during the whole of the operations throughout the defence of the Residency, also for two months with Outram's force at Alumbagh including the repulse of several attacks, and the operations ending in the final capture of Lucknow (frequently mentioned in Dispatches). Served the Rohilcund campaign in Apr. 1858, and commanded the 2d Brigade at the capture of Bareilly.

7 Major Macdonald served the Eastern campaign of 1854, as Provost Marshal (Medal and Clasps for Alma, Balaklava, Inkerman, and Sebastopol, and 5th Class of the Medjidie). Appointed D.A.A.G. and D.A.Q.M.G. 8 Jan. 1855 – at Scutari to the 13th Aug. 1856. Appointed D.A.A.G. to the force in China from 23rd March to 10th Nov. 1857. Served with the 93rd Highlanders the campaign of 1857-58 in the Doab, Oude, and Rohilcund, including the capture of Lucknow, Bareilly, and Furruckabad.

8 Major Burroughs served throughout the Eastern campaign of 1854-55, including the battles of Alma and Balaklava, expedition to Kertch and Yenikale, siege and fall of Sebastopol (Medal and three Clasps, Turkish Medal, and 5th Class of the Medjidie). Also in the Indian campaign in 1857-58, including the relief of Lucknow by Lord Clyde with assaults on the Secundrabagh and the Shahnujeev (was the first through the breach at the storming of the Secundrabagh and received a sabre cut on the head), battle of Cawnpore on 6th Dec. and pursuit to Seraighat, action of Khodagunge, storming of the Beegum Khotee and capture of Lucknow—severely wounded, blown up (Brevet of Major, Medal and Clasp).

9 Major Dawson served in the 45th the Kaffir campaign of 1846-7, and that of 1851-2 (Medal). Served the Eastern campaign of 1854, and up to 8th Feb. 1855, with the 93rd Regt., including the battles of Alma and Balaklava, and siege of Sebastopol (Medal and Clasps).

11† Captain Welch served at the siege and fall of Sebastopol from 14th July 1855 (Medal and Clasp). Served in the Indian campaign from Sept. 1857 to Apr. 1858, including the relief of Lucknow (severely wounded, the ball still lodged), assault of the Secunderbagh, action of Cawnpore, and final capture of Lucknow (Medal and Clasp).

12 Captain Macpherson, Lieuts. Nightingale, Hyslop, and Alexander, served at the siege and fall of Sebastopol from 14th July 1855 (Medal and Clasp).

13 Captain M'Bean served at the siege and fall of Sebastopol from 10th Dec. 1854 (Medal and Clasp, and 5th Class of the Medjidie).

14 Captain Knollys served with the Scots Fusilier Guards in the Eastern campaign up to Sept. 1854, including the siege of Sebastopol (Medal and Clasp).

15 Captain Levinge served with the 29th Regt. throughout the Punjaub campaign of 1848-49, including the passage of the Chenab, and battles of Chillianwallah and Goojerat (Medal and Clasps).

15† Captain Bell served in the Southern Mahratta Country in 1858, and commanded a Company of the 74th Highlanders at the assault and capture of the town and hill fort of Nurgoond on 1st and 2nd June.

16 Lieut. FitzRoy M'Pherson served in the Indian campaign of 1857-58 (Medal).

17 Lieut. Fenwick served with the 1st Battalion of the Royals the Eastern campaign of 1854, and up to 19th May 1855, including the battles of Alma and Inkerman, and siege of Sebastopol (Medal and three Clasps).

18 Paymaster Blake served throughout the Eastern campaign of 1854-55, including the battles of Alma and Balaklava, siege of Sebastopol, expedition to Kertch and Yenikali (Medal and Clasps). Served the Indian campaign of 1857-59, including the relief and capture of Lucknow, and subsequent operations in Rohilcund and Oude (Medal and Clasp).

19 Qr.Master Joiner served at the siege and fall of Sebastopol from 6th July 1855 (Medal and Clasp).

20 Doctor Munro served as Assistant Surgeon of the 91st Regt. throughout the Kaffir war of 1846-7 (Medal); Surgeon of the 93rd Highlanders during the campaign in the Crimea, including the battles of Alma and Balaklava, and siege of Sebastopol (Medal and three Clasps, and 5th Class of the Medjidie). Also served in India during the suppression of the mutiny and was present in the operations for the relief of Lucknow by Lord Clyde, battle of Cawnpore on 6th Dec. 1857 and pursuit, action near Futtehghur, siege and fall of Lucknow, campaign in Rohilcund and attack on Fort Rugia, actions at Allygunge and Bareilly, campaign in Oude and actions of Posgaon and Russulpore, and attack on fort Metlioulie (Medal and Clasp).

21 Doctor Bell served with the 79th Highlanders the Eastern campaign of 1854-55, including the battle of Balaklava, siege and fall of Sebastopol, and assaults of the 18th June and 8th Sept. (Medal and two Clasps).

22 Asst.Surgeon Sinclair served at the siege of Sebastopol from 13th Oct. 1854 to 21st March 1855 (Medal and Clasp).

94th Regiment of Foot. [Depot, Chatham. India.

Years' Serv. Full Pay	Half Pay					
55		Colonel.—10 George Powell Higginson,¹ Ens. 6 Nov. 05; Lt. and Capt. 3 April 11; Capt. and Lt.Col. 26 Oct. 20; Col. 10 Jan. 37; Major Gen. 9 Nov. 46; Lt.Gen. 20 June 54; Col. 94th Foot, 29 Jan. 55.				
25	3¹⁹/₁₂	Lieut.Colonels.—Charles James Conway Mills, Ens. p 26 Dec. 34; Lt. p 28 Aug. 38; Capt. p 25 June 41; Maj. p 22 Aug. 51; Lt.Col. 11 July 56.				
25	0	Henry George Buller, Ens. p 26 June 35; Lt. p 8 June 38; Capt. 5 June 44; Major, 1 July 54; Lt.Col. 18 Sept. 57.				
24	0	Majors.—Wm. Henry Kirby, Ens. 14 Oct. 36; Lieut. p 28 Dec. 38; Capt. 7 Dec. 45; Maj. 29 Dec. 54; Bt.Lt.Col. 26 Apr. 59.				
22	0	Septimus Lyster,³ Ens. p 28 Dec. 38; Lieut. 18 Aug. 41; Capt. p 6 Oct. 48; Major, 18 Sept. 57.				

		CAPTAINS.	ENSIGN.	LIEUT.	CAPTAIN.	BREV.MAJ.
25	0	Edward Smyth Mercer⁴	p 6 Mar. 35	p 11 June 36	23 Mar. 49	
16	0	Haydon Lloyd Cafe	p 27 Sept. 44	p 9 Dec. 45	p 28 Dec. 49	
12	0	Wm. West James Bruce⁶	25 Apr. 48	p 3 Aug. 49	29 July 53	
16	0	Henry Hamilton Pratt	p 25 June 44	9 Nov. 46	p 29 Dec. 54	
13	0	Thomas George Gardiner	p 15 May 47	12 Aug. 49	p 5 Nov. 52	
12	0	Charles William St.John	11 Feb. 48	f 6 Oct. 48	p 17 Aug. 55	
11	0	Osmond DeLancey Priaulx	4 Apr. 49	4 Oct. 52	p 31 July 57	
11	0	Robert A. Boothby Tod	30 Nov. 49	1 July 54	p 14 Aug. 57	
9	0	John Murray	p 17 Jan. 51	21 July 54	p 19 Nov. 58	
8	0	George Lake Hedley	p 12 Oct. 52	p 29 Dec. 54	p 18 Jan. 59	
12	0	Thos. Goodricke Peacocke	p 15 Aug. 48	9 Jan. 55	17 Apr. 58	
3	3¹/₁₂	Courtney W. A. T. Kenny⁷	23 June 54	16 Nov. 54	26 Oct. 55	

		LIEUTENANTS.			
8	0	Sydenham Malthus, Adj.	p 24 Feb. 52	11 Aug. 54	
8	0	Arthur Charles Elliot	p 23 Nov. 52	29 Dec. 54	
6	0	Josiah Robert Rolls	p 29 Dec. 54	p 17 Aug. 55	
5	0	Francis Hamilton Elliot	24 Jan. 55	p 14 Sept. 55	
6	0	Poltimore Ridgway	31 Aug. 54	p 19 Aug. 56	
5	0	William Collum	15 Mar. 55	30 Nov. 55	
5	0	John Murriot Aytoun	p 12 Jan. 55	p 31 July 57	
5	0	Arthur Chute	4 May 55	p 14 Aug. 57	
5	0	Arthur Brinckman	11 May 55	15 Jan. 58	
5	0	Robert Wingfield Cox	15 May 55	23 Mar. 58	
4	0	Charles Butler	p 19 Aug. 56	p 14 Mar. 59	
4	0	William Ferrier Godfrey	8 July 56	p 13 April 59	
3	0	George James Teevan	24 Nov. 57	p 22 June 58	
3	0	Henry Samuel Hall	p 31 July 57	p 17 June 59	
3	0	Caulfield French	p 6 Nov. 57	12 July 59	

		ENSIGNS.			
2	0	Ramsay Stewart	p 5 Feb. 58		
2	0	Edward Logan Stohelin	6 Aug. 58		
2	0	Henry Farrer	p 12 Nov. 58		
2	0	Percival Richards	12 Nov. 58		
2	0	Philip Rob. Anstruther	31 Dec. 58		
1	0	Jas. Brabazon Pilkington	p 18 Jan. 59		
1	0	John Mackinlay	p 22 July 59		
1	0	John Joseph Blake	p 29 July 59		
1	0	James Browne	p 30 July 59		
1	0	Walter Gregory Buller	30 Sept. 59		

1 Lt.General Higginson served with the Grenadier Guards in Sicily in 1807, in the campaign in the north of Spain with Sir John Moore in 1808-9, and was present at the battle of Corunna. Went with the expedition to Walcheren in 1809. Joined his Regiment in Portugal in 1812, and advanced with the army into Spain in 1813; commanded a detachment of the Grenadier Guards at the storming and capture of San Sebastian, 31st August in the same year, entered France by the Pyrenees, was present at the passages of the Nive, the Nivelle, and the Adour, also during the investment of Bayonne. Embarked with his Regiment at Bordeaux when the army left France in 1814. Went with reinforcements to the Netherlands in June 1815, arrived at Paris shortly after its capture, and remained in France during the three years of its occupation by the Allied Army. In 1830 he was appointed Aide de Camp to Lord Hill, then Commander in chief, and continued on his staff upwards of twelve years, until his Lordship's resignation of office from ill health. He has received the War Medal with four Clasps.

4 Captain Mercer served in the Turkish Contingent at Varna, and in the entrenched camp at Kertch, commanding successively the 3rd (Albanians), 6th, and 8th Regiments (4th Class of the Medjidie).

20	0	Paymaster.—Henry John Wahab, 8 Dec. 54; Ens. p 22 May 40; Lt. p 16 Aug. 42; [Capt. 21 July 54.
8	0	Adjutant.—Lieut. S. Malthus, 21 May 59.
		Instructor of Musketry.—
4	0	Quarter Master.—Thomas Harper, 21 Nov. 56.
12	0	Surgeon.—Andrew Acres Stoney, 11 May 55; Assist.Surg. 22 Dec. 48.
3	0	Assist. Surgeons.—Edward M'Grath, 1 Aug. 57.
5	0	James Greig Leask, M. B. 28 Aug. 55.
3	0	John Wallace, 2 June 57.

Facings Green.—Agents, Messrs. Cox & Co.

[Returned from Gibraltar, June 1856. Embarked for India, 8 Dec. 1857.]

3 Major Lyster served in the War of Succession in Spain as Lieut. of Infantry, and was present in the operations before San Sebastian, and was severely wounded through the body in the attack upon the fortified heights of Arambura near Hernani.

6 Capt. Bruce served with the 74th Highlanders throughout the Kaffir war of 1851-53 (Medal), and was wounded on the 26th June 1851.

7 Captain Kenny served with the 88th Regt. at the siege of Sebastopol from 22d Jan. to June 1855, and was severely wounded at the attack of the Quarries (Medal and Clasp).

Serving in India. Depot, Fermoy.]   **95th (The Derbyshire) Regt. of Foot.**   335
"ALMA" "INKERMAN" "SEVASTOPOL."

Years' Serv.			
	Full Pay.	Half Pay.	
60			**Colonel.**—1) Sir Francis Cockburn,¹ *Ens.* 16 Oct. 00; *Lieut.* 6 April 03; *Capt.* 3 March 04; *Maj.* 27 June 11; *Lieut.Col.* 27 Oct. 14; *Col.* 10 Jan. 37; *Major Gen.* 9 Nov. 46; *Lt.Gen.* 20 June 54; *Col.* 95th Foot, 26 Dec. 53.
18	0		**Lieut. Colonels.**—Julius Aug. Robert Raines,² CB. *Ens.* 28 Jan. 42; *Lt.* 5 April 44; *Capt.* p 13 Apr. 52; *Brev.Maj.* 24 April 55; *Major*, 1 May 57; *Lt.Col.* 17 Nov. 57; *Col.* 20 July 58.
16	0		Hon. Fred. Aug. Thesiger,³ *2nd Lt.* p 31 Dec. 44; *Ens. & Lt.* p 28 Nov. 45; *Lt. & Capt.* p 27 Dec. 50; *Bt.Maj.* 2 Nov. 55; *Capt. & Lt.Col.* p 28 Aug. 57.
17	0		**Majors.**—George Courtenay Vialls,⁴ *Ens.* p 20 Jan. 43; *Lieut.* p 22 May 46; *Capt.* p 25 Mar. 53; *Brev.Maj.* 6 June 56; *Major*, p 29 May 57; *Bt.Lt.Col.* 20 July 58.
13	0		Hon. Eyre C. Henry Massey,⁵ *Ens.* p 8 Oct. 47; *Lt.* p 21 Nov. 51; *Capt.* p 14 Jan. 53; *Bt.Major*, 2 Nov. 55; *Major*, 17 Nov. 57; *Bt.Lt.Col.* 20 July 58.

		CAPTAINS.	ENSIGN.	LIEUT.	CAPTAIN.	BREV.MAJ.
21	3 4/12	Hon. Edward S. Plunkett⁶	p 17 June 36	p 11 May 41	7 Mar. 51	26 Dec. 56
16	0	Edward Spicer Charlton⁷	23 Mar. 44	p 3 Mar. 48	21 Sept. 54	
15	0	Henry Foster⁸	p 25 Nov. 45	9 June 48	21 Sept. 54	20 July 58
12	0	G. Lynedoch Carmichael⁹	p 15 Dec. 48	p 22 Oct. 52	29 Dec. 54	15 Nov. 59
7	0	Edmund Davidson Smith¹⁰	p 22 Apr. 53	6 June 54	5 June 55	
13	0	Henry Edward Moore¹²	p 3 Sept. 47	p 17 May 50	p 24 Nov. 54	
6	0	John W. Inglis Stockwell¹³	11 Aug. 54	8 Dec. 54	p 29 May 57	
6	0	Jonathan Benison¹¹	6 June 54	8 Dec. 54	17 Nov. 57	
6	0	Robert Wield¹⁵	10 Aug. 54	8 Dec. 54	2 Apr. 58	
6	0	Charles Fred. Parkinson¹⁶	21 Sept. 54	9 Feb. 55	p 26 Nov. 58	
6	0	John North Crealock¹⁷	p 13 Oct. 54	9 Feb. 55	p 6 May 59	
9	0	George Robertson¹⁸	p 17 June 51	9 Feb. 55	p 16 Dec. 59	
		LIEUTENANTS.				
6	0	John Budgen¹⁹	3 Nov. 54	9 Mar. 55	3 Lt.Col. Hon. F. A. Thesiger served with the Grenadier Guards at the siege and fall of Sebastopol from 31st May 1855 (Medal and Clasp, Brevet Major, Sardinian Medal, and 5th Class of the Medjidie).	
6	0	Robert M. B. Maurice¹⁹†	4 Nov. 54	9 Mar. 55		
6	0	John Sexton,²¹† *Adj.*	5 Nov. 54	9 Mar. 55		
6	0	Norton Knatchbull²⁰	29 Dec. 54	9 Mar. 55		
5	0	John Joseph Bacon²¹	p 12 Jan. 55	6 April 55		
5	0	John Henry Waterfall	p 19 Jan. 55	5 June 55	24 Lieut. Paske served at the siege and fall of Sebastopol from 25th Aug. 1855 (Medal and Clasp). Served in 1858 at the siege and capture of Kotah. 28 Paymaster Morris served in 1858 at the siege and capture of Kotah, battle of Kota ka Seria, general action resulting in the capture of Gwalior (Medal).	
5	0	Arch. Macdonell Rawlins²²	15 Mar. 55	p 10 Aug. 55		
5	0	Henry Gresham Paske²¹	23 Mar. 55	7 Nov. 55		
5	0	Charles Edward Fisher²⁵	p 28 Mar. 55	p 30 Nov. 55		
5	0	Joseph Gabbett	30 Mar. 55	p 14 Dec. 55		
5	0	William Fleming	28 April 55	1 Feb. 56		
5	0	William R. Willans²²	29 April 55	29 Feb. 56		
5	0	John Nicholas	30 April 55	p 6 Feb. 57		
5	0	Charles James Holbrook²²	15 May 55	17 Nov. 57		
5	0	Robert Macnee²⁶	1 June 55	2 Apr. 58	29 Assist. Surgeon Clarke and Qr. Master Campbell served the Eastern campaign of 1854-55, including the battles of Alma and Inkerman, siege of Sebastopol, and sortie on 26th Oct. (Medal and Clasps). Served in 1858 at the siege and capture of Kotah, battle of Kota ka Seria, general action resulting in the capture of Gwalior, siege and capture of Pouree (Medal).	
5	0	Edward Chapple²⁶	31 Aug. 55	p 24 May 59		
6	0	James Alexander Stubbs	6 June 54	24 Nov. 57		
5	0	Lewis Cubitt	p 30 Nov. 55	16 Dec. 59		
		ENSIGNS.				
5	0	Leonard Knipe²⁷	p 7 Dec. 55			
4	0	Robert Anderson²⁶	29 Feb. 56			
2	0	John Henry Prior	8 Jan. 58			
2	0	Henry V. Brooke	25 June 58			
2	0	Wm. Geo. Remfry Herd	p 26 Nov. 58			
1	0	Edward Warren Golding	p 18 Jan. 59			
1	0	Bolton Waller Faulkner	p 14 June 59			
1	0	Arthur Thomas Helme	p 26 Aug. 59			

3	0	*Paymaster.*—Maxwell Kirwan Morris,²⁸ 10 March 57.	
6	0	*Adjutant.*—Lieut. John Sexton,²⁰† 9 Oct. 55.	
6	0	*Instructor of Musketry.*—Capt. John North Crealock,¹⁷ 28 Aug. 56.	
6	0	*Quarter Master.*—John Campbell,²⁹ 7 April 54.	
15	0	*Surgeon.*—Henry March Webb, M.B. 8 Dec. 54; *Assist.Surg.* 23 Sept. 45.	
7	0	*Assistant Surgeons.*—John Clarke,²⁹ 13 Dec. 53.	
3	0	Robert Arthur Elliott, 30 May 57.	
5	0	William Sharpe, 6 July 55.	

Facings Yellow.—*Agents,* Messrs. Price & Boustead.

[Returned from the Crimea, July 1856. Embarked for the Cape of Good Hope, June 1857.]

1 Sir Francis Cockburn served in South America in 1807; in the Peninsula in 1809 and 1810; and in Canada from 1811 to 1814.

2 Colonel Raines served the Eastern campaign of 1854-55, including the battles of Alma, Inkerman, and Tchernaya; served as an Assistant Engineer throughout the siege and fall of Sebastopol (wounded in the trenches 17th Oct.) and present at the attack of the Redan on the 18th June (Medal and Clasps, Brevet Major, Sardinian Medal, and 5th Class of the Medjidie). Commanded the troops at the assault and capture of Rowa on 6th Jan. 1858; commanded the left wing 95th Regt. at the siege and capture of Awah, on 24th Jan.; commanded the 95th at the siege and capture of Kotah, and commanded the 3rd assaulting column on 30th March; commanded the Infantry of Brigadier Smith's Column at the battle of Kota ka Seria before Gwalior on 17th June and in the general action on the 19th June (wounded by a musket-ball in the left arm) which resulted in the capture of the city and fortress of Gwalior, and present at the siege and capture of Pouree on 24th Aug. 1858 (frequently mentioned in despatches Medal and Clasps, Colonel, and CB.).

95th (The Derbyshire) Regt. of Foot.

4 Lt.Colonel Vialls served the Eastern campaign of 1854-55, including the battle of Inkerman (severely wounded), siege of Sebastopol, and sortie on 26th Oct. (Medal and Clasps, and Brevet Major). Served in 1858 at the siege and capture of Kotah, battle of Kota ka Seria, general action resulting in the capture of Gwalior, siege and capture of Pouree (mentioned in despatches, Medal).

5 Lt.Col. Hon. E. C. H. Massey served at the siege and fall of Sebastopol from 22nd Nov. 1854 (Medal and Clasp, Bt. Major, Knight of the Legion of Honor, and 5th Class of the Medjidie). Served in 1858 at the siege and capture of Kotah, battle of Kota ka Seria, general action resulting in the capture of Gwalior, siege and capture of Pouree (mentioned in despatches, Medal).

6 Major Hon. E. S. Plunkett served at the siege of Sebastopol from 10th Dec. 1854 to July 1855, including the capture of the Quarries on 7th June, and present in the trenches during the attack of the Redan on the 18th June (Medal and Clasp, and Brevet Major); has also the 4th Class of the Medjidie for service in the late Osmanli Horse Artillery. Served in 1858 at the siege and capture of Awah and Kotah, battle of Kota ka Seria, and general action resulting in the capture of Gwalior (Medal).

7 Capt. Charlton served in the Eastern campaign of 1854-55, including the battles of Alma and Inkerman, siege of Sebastopol, and sortie on 26th Oct. (Medal and Clasp).

8 Major Foster served in 1858 at the siege and capture of Awah and Kotah, battle of Kota ka Serai, general action resulting in the capture of Gwalior, siege and capture of Pouree, and action of Bejapore (mentioned in despatches, Brevet of Major, and Medal).

9 Major Carmichael served the Eastern campaign of 1854-55, including the battles of Alma and Inkerman, siege and fall of Sebastopol, and sortie on 26th Oct. (Medal and Clasps, Knight of the Legion of Honor, and 5th Class of the Medjidie). Served in 1858 at the siege and capture of Kotah (Medal).

10 Capt. Smith served the Eastern campaign of 1854, including the battles of Alma and Inkerman, siege of Sebastopol, and sortie on 26th Oct.—wounded in the head in the trenches 17th Oct. (Medal and Clasps). Served in 1858 at the siege and capture of Awah and Kotah, and general action resulting in the capture of Gwalior (Medal).

12 Captain Moore served in 1858 at the siege and capture of Kotah, battle of Kota ka Serai, general action resulting in the capture of Gwalior, siege and capture of Pouree (Medal).

13 Capt. Stockwell served at the siege and fall of Sebastopol from 18th Jan. 1855 (Medal and Clasp, and 5th Class of the Medjidie). Served in 1858 at the siege and capture of Awah and Kotah, battle of Kota ka Seria, general action resulting in the capture of Gwalior, siege and capture of Pourie (Medal).

14 Capt. Benison served at the siege and fall of Sebastopol from 23rd Dec. 1854, including the capture of the Rifle Pits on 19th April, capture of the Quarries on 7th June, and was present in the trenches during the attacks of the Redan on 18th June and 8th Sept. (Medal and Clasp, and 5th Class of the Medjidie). Served in 1858 at the siege and capture of Awah (Medal).

15 Captain Wield served in the Eastern campaign in 1854-55, including the siege and fall of Sebastopol, and was dangerously wounded in the trenches 22 Aug. 55 (Medal and Clasp, and 5th Class of the Medjidie).

16 Captain Parkinson served at the siege and fall of Sebastopol from 30th May 1855, and was wounded at the attack on the Redan on 8th Sept. (Medal and Clasp). Served in 1858 at the siege and capture of Kotah (Medal).

17 Captain Crealock, in 1858 served at the siege and capture of Kotah, battle of Kota ka Serai (wounded), and general action resulting in the capture of Gwalior (Medal).

18 Captain Robertson served with the 12th Regt. in the Kaffir war of 1851-53 (Medal). Served with the 95th Regt. at the siege and fall of Sebastopol from 26th Jan. 1855 (Medal and Clasp, and 5th Class of the Medjidie). Served in 1858 at the siege and capture of Kotah (Medal).

19 Lieut. Budgen served at the siege and fall of Sebastopol from 16th Aug. 1855 (Medal and Clasp). Served in 1858 at the siege and capture of Kotah, battle of Kota ka Seria, general action resulting in the capture of Gwalior, siege and capture of Pourie, and action of Bejapore (mentioned in despatches, Medal).

19† Lieut. Maurice served at the siege and fall of Sebastopol from 16th Aug. 1855 (Medal and Clasp). Served in 1858 at the siege and capture of Kotah, battle of Kota ka Seria, and general action resulting in the capture of Gwalior (mentioned in despatches, Medal).

20 Lieut. Knatchbull served at the siege of Sebastopol from 10th June 1855 (Medal and Clasp). Served in 1858 at the siege and capture of Kotah, battle of Kota ka Seria, general action resulting in the capture of Gwalior, siege and capture of Pourie (mentioned in despatches, Medal).

20† Lieut. Sexton served the Eastern campaign of 1854-55, including the battles of Alma and Inkerman, siege and fall of Sebastopol, and sortie of 26th Oct. (Medal and Clasps, and Knight of the Legion of Honor). Served in 1858 at the siege and capture of Kotah, battle of Kota ka Seria, general action resulting in the capture of Gwalior, siege and capture of Pourie (mentioned in despatches, Medal); was severely burnt by an explosion of powder while serving a gun captured from the enemy and turned on them.

21 Lt. Bacon served at the siege of Sebastopol from 11 July 55 (Medal and Clasp). Served in 1858 at the siege and capture of Kotah, battle of Kota ka Seria, general action resulting in the capture of Gwalior, siege and capture of Pouree (Medal).

22 Lts. Rawlins, Willans, and Holbrook, served in 1858 at the siege and capture of Awah and Kotah, battle of Kota ka Seria, general action resulting in the capture of Gwalior, siege and capture of Pouree (Medal).

25 Lieut. Fisher served in 1858 at the siege and capture of Kotah, battle of Kota ka Serai, general action resulting in the capture of Gwalior, siege and capture of Pouree, dangerously wounded (Medal).

26 Lieuts. Macnee and Chapple, and Ensign Anderson, served in 1858 at the siege and capture of Awah and Kotah, battle of Kota ka Serai, and general action resulting in the capture of Gwalior (Medal).

27 Ensign Knipe served in 1858 at the siege and capture of Awah (Medal).

Head Quarters, Manchester. ⎱
Depot, Parkhurst.   ⎰ **96th Regiment of Foot.**   337

Years' Serv.						
Full Pay	Half Pay					
48		Colonel.—여 대대 Mildmay Fane,[1] Ens. 11 June 12; Lt. 25 Sept. 13; Capt. 28 July 14; Major, 2 March 20; Lt.Col. 12 June 23; Col. 28 June 38; Maj. Gen. 11 Nov. 51; Lt.Gen. 30 Jan. 55; Col. 96th Foot, 11 Aug. 55.				
25	0	Lt.Col.—Edward W. Scovell, Ens. 29 Dec. 35; Lieut. p 2 Nov. 38; Capt. p 13 Dec. 42; Brev.Maj. 20 June 54; Major, 28 Jan. 56; Lt.Col. 8 July 56.				
24	0	Majors.—Richard Roundell Currer, Ens. 16 Sept. 36; Lieut. p 27 Sept. 39; Capt. p 20 Oct. 46; Major, p 15 April 56.				
14	0	Hon. Aug. Murray Cathcart,[2] Ens. 25 Sept. 46; Lt. p 21 July 48; Capt. p 21 Oct. 53; Bt.Major, 12 Dec. 54; Major, 15 April 56; Bt.Lt.Col. 6 June 56.				

		CAPTAINS.	ENSIGN.	LIEUT.	CAPTAIN.	BREV.MAJ.
15	0	Arthur Henry C. Snow, s.	30 Dec. 45	p 10 Mar. 48	13 Dec. 53	
16	0	Geo. Fred. Campbell Bray	22 Mar. 44	27 Jan. 46	1 Feb. 55	
18	0	John Smith Cannon.....	28 Jan. 42	14 Apr. 46	28 Jan. 56	
14	0	Patrick James John Grant	14 Apr. 46	p 28 Apr. 48	p 15 Apr. 56	
15	0	E. D. Justin Mac Carthy	p 2 Sept. 45	18 Aug. 48	8 July 56	
13	0	George B. Cumberland..	p 13 Aug. 47	p 15 June 49	p 27 Nov. 57	
9	0	Jas. Buchanan Kirk	p 17 Oct. 51	1 Feb. 55	p 31 Dec. 57	
6	0	Rouse Douglas Douglas	p 15 Sept. 54	p 2 Nov. 55	p 30 Apr. 58	
8	0	James Briggs..........	13 Feb. 52	31 Aug. 55	p 21 May 58	
5	0	George Kerr Hallett	30 Aug. 55	p 27 Nov. 57	p 1 Apr. 59	
5	0	Alfred Edward Cookson	p 16 Oct. 55	p 15 Jan. 58	p 14 June 59	
4	0	Edmund John Scovell ..	25 Mar. 56	p 30 Apr. 58	p 7 Oct. 59	
4	0	William Osborne Barnard	p 15 Apr. 56	21 May 58	p 18 Nov. 59	
		LIEUTENANTS.				
7	0	George Irwin Thompson	19 Aug. 53	p 9 Oct. 55		
8	0	John Whitty	p 15 Oct. 52	16 Oct. 55		
5	0	Elias Wm. Dixon Gray ..	11 May 55	28 Jan. 56		
5	0	William Cameron Geddes	15 Oct. 55	p 15 Apr. 56		
5	0	John Thomas French....	26 July 55	8 July 56		
5	0	Walter Barnes Pugh, Adj.	16 Nov. 55	p 13 June 56		
5	0	Edward Johnston	9 Oct. 55	30 Mar. 58		
4	0	A. Gowrie Mancra	29 Feb. 56	p 21 May 58		
3	0	James Morrison Kirkwood	p 24 July 57	p 1 Apr. 59		
3	0	Charles Edward-Wright	p 27 Nov. 57	p 15 Apr. 59		
2	0	Marriott Aytoun	p 15 Jan. 58	p 14 June 59		
2	0	Henry Houghton	13 Apr. 58	p 8 July 59		
2	0	Edward Hogg	15 Apr. 58	p 7 Oct. 59		
2	0	Francis Reid	p 14 May 58	p 7 Oct. 59		
2	0	John Leslie Toke	p 21 May 58	p 18 Nov. 59		
		ENSIGNS.				
4	0	Albert Jackson Harcourt	8 July 56			
2	0	Wm. R. Estridge Durrant	p 22 June 58			
2	0	Edw. Barrett H. Curteis	p 1 June 59			
1	0	Frederick Henniker	24 June 59			
1	0	Fred. John Josselyn	p 29 July 59			
1	0	Justinian Henry Strong .	p 30 July 59			
1	0	Francis Lennox Geo. Grey	26 Aug. 59			
1	0	William Yates Foot	p 18 Oct. 59			
1	0	James Moubray........	p 28 Oct. 59			
1	0	Aug. Fred. Arthur Hill..	p 18 Nov. 59			
12	0	Paymaster.—William Thompson, 27 July 55; Q.M. 25 Feb. 48.				
5	0	Adjutant.—Lieut. Walter Barnes Pugh, 6 May 59.				
5	0	Instructor of Musketry.—Lieut. E. W. D. Gray, 21 May 58.				
3	0	Quarter Master.—James Jamieson, 28 Aug. 57.				
18	0	Surgeon.—Benjamin Swift, M.D. 13 Jan. 54; Assist.Surg. 8 Apr. 42.				
6	0	Assistant Surgeons.—Hamilton Mitchell, 21 July 54.				
6	0	John Joseph Mulock, 5 May 54.				

Facings Yellow.—Agents, Messrs. Cox & Co.

[Returned from Gibraltar, 10 June 1857.]

1 Lieut.General Fane served in the Peninsula from Dec. 1812 to March 1814, including the battle of Vittoria, assault and capture of San Sebastian, and battles of the Nive on 9th and 13th Dec. 1813. Served also the campaign of 1815, including the battles of Quatre Bras and Waterloo, at the former of which he was severely wounded. He has received the War Medal and three Clasps for Vittoria, San Sebastian, and Nive.

2 Lt.Colonel Hon. A. M. Cathcart accompanied the 93rd Highlanders to Turkey, and on the embarkation for the Crimea he was appointed Extra Aide-de-Camp to his uncle Sir George Cathcart, with whom he was present at the battles of Alma, Balaklava, and Inkerman (promoted Brevet Major), where Sir George was killed; rejoined the 93rd, but having been appointed a Deputy Assist. Adjutant General, he was attached to the Light Division, and was present in all the operations in which it was engaged, including both attacks on the Redan and fall of Sebastopol—mentioned in Despatches (Medal and Clasps, Brevet Lt.Colonel, Sardinian Medal, and 5th Class of the Medjidie).

97th (*The Earl of Ulster's*) Regt. of Foot.

Serving in India. Depot, Colchester.

"*Quò fas et gloria ducunt.*"—"SEVASTOPOL."

Years' Serv.			
Full Pay	Half Pay		
50		**Colonel.**—Edmund Finucane Morris,[1] CB. *Ens.* 21 June 10; *Lt.* 21 Apr. 13; *Capt.* 1 Dec. 25; *Major,* p 13 Sept. 33; *Lt.Col.* p 22 Nov. 36; *Col.* 23 Dec. 42; *Maj.Gen.* 20 June 54; *Col.* 97th Foot, 14 May 59.	
21	0	**Lt. Cols.**—Fowler Burton,[2] *Ens.* p 30 Aug. 39; *Lieut.* 15 Apr. 42; *Capt.* p 14 June 50; *Major,* 2 Nov. 55; *Br. Lt.Col.* 26 Dec. 56; *Lt.Col.* 15 Mar. 58.	
19	4/12	Wm. West Turner,[3] CB. *Ens.* 19 Feb. 41; *Lt.* 27 Dec. 42; *Capt.* p 27 May 53; *Bt.Maj.* 17 July 55; *Bt.Lt.Col.* 2 Nov.55; *Major,* 9 Nov. 55; *Lt.Col.* 4 June 59.	
17	0	**Majors.**—Septimus Moore Hawkins,[4] *Ens.* p 2 June 43; *Lt.* p 30 Aug. 44; *Capt.* p 23 Dec. 53; *Brev.Maj.* 20 July 58; *Major,* 4 June 59.	
13	1 5/12	James William Dewar,[5] *Ens.* p 1 July 46; *Lt.* p 12 May 50; *Capt.* 6 Nov. 54; *Bt.Maj.* 2 Nov. 55; *Major,* 23 Mar. 58.	

		CAPTAINS.	ENSIGN.	LIEUT.	CAPTAIN.	BREV.MAJ.
18	0	Archibald Richd. Harenc[8]	p 15 Apr. 42	p 25 Apr. 45	6 June 54	20 July 58
16	0	Thomas Venables[6]	p 28 June 44	p 8 Dec. 46	p 18 Aug. 54	
18	0	Edward D. Harvest	17 Apr. 42	p 6 Feb. 46	29 Dec. 54	
14	0	Edward Kent Jones[10]	21 Apr. 46	p 30 Nov. 49	29 Dec. 54	
13	0	Wm. Richard Annesley[9]	p 10 Dec. 47	p 6 Dec. 50	29 Dec. 54	
14	0	Osborne Barwell Cannon[11]	p 6 Nov. 46	p 23 Dec. 53	23 Mar. 55	
6	0	Charles Henry Browne[12]	11 Aug. 54	8 Dec. 54	p 15 May 57	
8	10/12	Roger Swire[13]	p 18 Feb. 52	p 7 Apr. 54	p 23 Nov. 55	
14	0	Lynch Stapleton Cotton	p 8 Sept. 46	p 27 May 48	16 Mar. 58	
11	0	Henry Browne[14]	9 Nov. 49	15 Aug. 52	4 June 58	
14	0	George Augustus Ferris [14]	8 Dec. 46	30 Apr. 49	20 July 58	
6	0	Isaac Harmond[15]	5 Nov. 54	9 Mar. 55	4 June 59	

		LIEUTENANTS.			
6	0	Jonathan Morgan[15]*	p 10 Mar. 54	6 Apr. 55	
8	0	Rob. Tho. Fra. Hamilton[16]	23 Jan. 52	13 Apr. 55	14 Capt. Ferris served with the 29th Foot throughout the Punjaub campaign of 1848-49, including the passage of the Chenab, and battles of Chillianwallah and Goojerat (Medal and Clasps).
6	0	Andrew George Onslow[18]	p 17 Mar. 54	p 8 Sept. 54	
5	0	Maurice G. B. FitzGerald[19]	p 16 Jan. 55	25 May 55	
5	0	John Edwin Dickson Hill[19]	13 Feb. 55	19 Aug. 55	
5	0	Arthur Robert N. Gould[21]	20 Feb. 55	31 Aug. 55	
5	0	John Wright Shaw[8]	22 Mar. 55	9 Sept. 55	16 Lieut. Hamilton served in Bengal in suppressing the Mutiny in 1857-58, and was with the Jounpore field force in the actions of Nusrutpore (as Orderly Officer to Colonel Ingram, and mentioned in despatches), Chanda, Ummeerpore, and Sultanpore, and afterwards at the siege and capture of Lucknow and storming of the Kaisa Bagh (Medal and Clasp).
5	0	David J. Dickson Safford[17]	23 Mar. 55	9 Sept. 55	
7	0	James Clephane Minto[26]	19 Aug. 53	9 Sept. 55	
7	0	Robert Geo. Macdonald[8]	26 July 53	21 Sept. 55	
5	0	Frederick Wyer Parker[27]	19 June 55	p 11 Dec. 57	
5	0	Robert Wheatley Barbor	20 July 55	5 Mar. 58	
5	0	Robert Smith,[20] Adj.	9 Sept. 55	6 Aug. 58	
5	0	Rich. B. Hamilton Lowe[8]	16 Oct. 55	14 Feb. 59	
5	0	John Cooper	1 Nov. 55	4 June 59	26 Lieut. Minto served with the irregular forces under Sir George Cathcart during the Kaffir war of 1851-53 (Medal).

		ENSIGNS.		
5	0	Robert Thompson	8 Nov. 55	
5	0	Robert Lefroy	7 Dec. 55	27 Lieut. Parker served in the suppression of the Mutiny in India from Nov. 1857.
5	0	Henry Grantham Fulford[8]	21 Dec. 55	
4	0	Thomas Evans Stuart	1 Apr. 56	
3	0	Robert Gray[8]	p 10 Apr. 57	
3	0	Hy. Champanto Crespin	p 11 Dec. 57	
2	0	Peter Lawless[28]	10 Sept. 58	
2	0	Thomas Candler Wharton	11 Sept. 58	
1	0	A. P. Martin	17 June 59	
1	0	Thomas Thompson Irvine	23 Aug. 59	
13	0	*Instructor of Musketry.*—Captain W. R. Annesley, 16 Oct. 56.		
13	0	*Paymaster.*—Thomas Smith,[72] 28 July 54; *Ens.* 28 May 47; *Lieut.* 2 Aug. 50.		
5	0	*Adjutant.*—Lieut. Robert Smith,[20] 30 Nov. 55.		
5	0	*Quarter Master.*—William John Woodruffe,[23] 2 Nov. 55.		
10	0	*Surgeon.*—Alexander Macrae, M.D. 26 Jan. 58; *Assist.-Surg.* 5 Nov. 50.		
7	0	*Assistant Surgeons.*—Joshua Henry Porter,[21] 17 June 53.		
6	0	Edward Malcolm Sinclair,[25] M.D. 28 Mar. 54.		
3	0	Thomas Sharkey, 1 Aug. 57.		

Facings Sky Blue.—*Agents,* Messrs. Cox & Co.

[*Returned from the Crimea, 24 July 1856. Embarked for India, 6 Aug. 1857.*]

1 Major General Morris served in the American war with the 49th, and was present at the various operations at Fort George, and at the actions of Stoney Creek and Plattsburg. Accompanied the regiment on the China expedition (Medal), and commanded a brigade at the storming and capture of the heights above Canton, for which service he was made a CB. Commanded a brigade at the attack and capture of the city of Amoy, and at the second capture of Chusan. Commanded the centre column of attack at the capture of the heights of Chinhae. Commanded the force at Ningpo, and repulsed the enemy with great slaughter in their attack on that city. Commanded a brigade at the attack and capture of the enemy's entrenched camp on the heights of Segoan, at the attack and capture of the city of Chapoo, and at the attack and capture of the enemy's position at Woosung.

2 Lt.Col. Burton served at the siege of Sebastopol from 20th Nov. 1854 to 5th July 1855; commanded the Light Company, 97th Regt., in the sortie on the night of the 20th Dec. 1854, and succeeded in driving the Russians out of the most forward parallel, from which the Guard had been compelled to withdraw, and retained its possession (Medal and Clasp, Brevet Lt.Colonel, Sardinian Medal, 5th Class of the Medjidie, and Turkish Medal). Served in Bengal in suppressing the Mutiny in 1857-59, with the Jounpore field force in the action and capture of Fort Nusrutpore (commanded the Sharpshooters of the Brigade), actions of Chanda, Ummeerpore, and Sultanpore (mentioned twice and thanked in despatch), siege and capture of Lucknow and storming of the Kaiserbagh; afterwards served in Central India (Medal and Clasp).

97th (*The Earl of Ulster's*) Regt. of Foot.

3 Colonel Turner served with the 26th Cameronians in China, and was present at the defence of Ningpo, action of Tseko, storm and capture of Chapoo, Woosung, Shanghai, and Chinkiangfoo, and demonstration before Nankin (Medal). Served with the 15th Regt. in Ceylon, and during the Kandian rebellion of 1848. Served with the 7th Fusiliers in the Eastern campaign during the siege of Sebastopol in 1855, including the sorties of 5th April and 9th May, assault and capture of the Quarries on 7th June (in command of the storming party of his Regt. and slightly wounded), assault of the Redan on 18th June (brought the Regt. out of action), assault of the Redan on 8th Sept. (in command of the Regt. and wounded), and was commandant of the Karabelnaia at Sebastopol from 3rd Dec. 1855 to the end of June 1856 (Medal and Clasp, Brevets of Major and Lt.Colonel, CB., Knight of the Legion of Honor, and 5th Class of the Medjidie). Served in Bengal in suppressing the Mutiny in 1857-58, with the Jounpore field force in the actions of Chanda, Ummeerpore, and Sultanpore, afterwards at the siege and capture of Lucknow.

4 Major Hawkins served at the siege and fall of Sebastopol from 12th July 1855 (Medal and Clasp). Served in Bengal in suppressing the Mutiny in 1857-58, with the Jounpore field force in the actions of Nusrutpore, Chanda, Ummeerpore, and Sultanpore, afterwards at the siege and capture of Lucknow.

5 Major Dewar served in the 49th Regt. the Eastern campaign of 1854-55, including the battles of Alma and Inkerman (contused wound), siege and fall of Sebastopol, sortie of 26th Oct., capture of the Quarries, and assaults of the Redan on 18th June and 8th Sept., and was Town Major of Sebastopol from 9th Sept. 1858 till the Embarkation of the Army for England (Medal and three Clasps, Brevet Major, and Knight of the Legion of Honor).

6 Major Harenc, Captain Venables, Lieuts. Shaw, Macdonald, and Lowe, Ensigns Fulford and Gray served in Bengal in suppressing the Mutiny in 1857-58,—with the Jounpore field force in the actions of Nusrutpore, Chanda, Ummeerpore, and Sultanpore, afterwards at the siege and capture of Lucknow.

9 Captain Annesley served in the Crimea from 20th Nov. to Dec. 1854 (Medal with Clasp for Sebastopol). Served in the suppression of the Mutiny in India from Nov. 1857.

10 Captain Jones served at the siege and fall of Sebastopol from 4th Sept. 1855 (Medal and Clasp). Served in Bengal in suppressing the Mutiny in 1857-58, with the Jounpore field force in the actions of Nusrutpore, Chunda, Ummeerpore, and Sultanpore, afterwards at the siege and capture of Lucknow.

11 Captain Cannon served at the siege of Sebastopol from 20th Nov. 1854 to 14th June 1855 (Medal and Clasp).

12 Captain Charles H. Browne served at the siege of Sebastopol from 4th May 1855, and was on the storming party at the assault of the Redan on the 8th Sept.—wounded (Medal and Clasp, Sardinian Medal, and 5th Class of the Medjidie). Served in Bengal in suppressing the Mutiny in 1857-58, with the Jounpore field force in the actions of Nusrutpore, Chanda, Ummeerpore, and Sultanpore, afterwards at the siege and capture of Lucknow.

13 Captain Swire served at the siege of Sebastopol from Dec. 1854, latterly as Aide-de-Camp to Brigadier-General Wyndham, and led the assaulting party at the attack on the Redan on the 8th Sept., and was dangerously wounded, was also at the assault of the Redan on 18th June (Medal and Clasp, Sardinian Medal, and 5th Class of the Medjidie).

14 Captain Henry Browne was present with General Havelock's field force, and was severely wounded in the left arm, leg, and hip at the storming of Oomao on 29th July 1857; afterwards at the Alum Bagh, assault and capture of Lucknow, relief of Azimghur, and pursuit of Koer Singh.

15 Captain Harmond served at the siege of Sebastopol from 20th Nov. 1854 to 25th May 1855, and was engaged in a Sortie on 22nd March—received a bayonet wound in the left hand (Medal and Clasp). Served in Bengal in suppressing the Mutiny in 1857-58, and present with the Jounpore field force in the actions of Nusrutpore, Chanda, Ummeerpore, and Sultanpore, afterwards at the siege and capture of Lucknow (Medal and Clasp).

16 Lieut. Morgan served at the siege and fall of Sebastopol from 31st July 1855 (Medal and Clasp). Served in Bengal in suppressing the Mutiny in 1857-58, with the Jounpore field force in front with the Skirmishers in the actions of Nusrutpore, Chanda, Ummeerpore, and Sultanpore; was one of the stormers at Fort Dhowrara and assisted in bringing out two guns under a close fire; was afterwards at the attack and capture of Lucknow and storming of the Kaiser Bagh (thanked in despatches).

17 Lieut. Safford served in Bengal in suppressing the Mutiny in 1857-58,—with the Jounpore field force in the actions of Chanda, Ummeerpore, and Sultanpore, afterwards at the siege and capture of Lucknow.

18 Lieut. Onslow served in Bengal in suppressing the Mutiny in 1857-58, with the Jounpore field force in front with Skirmishers in the actions of Nusrutpore, Chanda, Ummeerpore, and Sultanpore; was afterwards at the siege and capture of Lucknow and storming of the Kaiser Bagh.

19 Lieuts. FitzGerald and Hill served at the siege of Sebastopol from 31st July 1855, and were on the ladder party at the assault on the Redan on the 8th Sept. (Medal and Clasp). Lieut. FitzGerald served in Bengal in suppressing the Mutiny in 1857-58, with the Jounpore field force in the actions of Nusrutpore, Chanda, Ummeerpore, and Sultanpore; was one of the stormers at Fort Dhowrara and assisted in bringing out two guns under a close fire; was afterwards at the siege and capture of Lucknow.

20 Lieut. Smith served at the siege and fall of Sebastopol from 20th Nov. 1854, and sortie of the 20th Dec. (Medal and Clasp). Served in Bengal in suppressing the Mutiny in 1857-58, with the Jounpore field force in the actions of Nusrutpore, Chanda, Ummeerpore, and Sultanpore, afterwards at the siege and capture of Lucknow.

21 Lieut. Gould served in Bengal in suppressing the Mutiny in 1857-58, with the Jounpore field force in front with the Skirmishers in the actions of Nusrutpore, Chanda, Ummeerpore, and Sultanpore; was one of the stormers at Fort Dhowrara and assisted in bringing out two guns; was afterwards at the attack and capture of Lucknow and storming of the Kaiser Bagh (thanked in despatches).

22 Paymaster Smith served at the siege of Sebastopol from 20th Nov. 1854 (Medal and Clasp). Served in Bengal in suppressing the Mutiny in 1857-58,—with the Jounpore field force in the actions of Nusrutpore, Chanda, Ummeerpore, and Sultanpore, afterwards at the siege and capture of Lucknow.

23 Qr.-Master Woodruffe served at the siege of Sebastopol from 20th Nov. 1854 (Medal and Clasp).

24 Assist.-Surgeon Porter served at the siege of Sebastopol from 20th Nov. 1854 (Medal and Clasp, and 5th Class of the Medjidie). Served in Bengal in suppressing the mutiny in 1857-58,—with the Jounpore field force in the actions of Nusrutpore, Chanda, Ummeerpore, and Sultanpore, afterwards at the siege and capture of Lucknow.

25 Doctor Sinclair served at the siege of Sebastopol from 20th Nov. 1854 (Medal and Clasp). Served in Bengal in suppressing the Mutiny in 1857-58,—with the Jounpore field force in the actions of Chanda, Ummeerpore, and Sultanpore, afterwards at the siege and capture of Lucknow.

26 Ensign Lawless served at the siege and fall of Sebastopol from 20 Nov. 1854, including the assault of the Redan on the 8th Sept.—severely wounded, ball through left thigh and right arm (Medal and Clasp, and Knight of the Legion of Honor). Served in Bengal in suppressing the Mutiny in 1857-58 with the Jounpore field force (Medal).

[*Continuation of Notes to 98th Foot.*]

2 Colonel Rainier and Captain Grantham served in the 98th with the expedition to the north of China in 1842 (Medal), and were present at the attack and capture of Chinkiangfoo, and at the landing before Nankin.

7 Captains Ellerman and Blackett, Lieuts. Gardiner, Heywood, Gregory, and Smith, and Assist.-Surgeon Collis served in the Peshawur Expeditionary force on the Euzofzie frontier under Sir Sydney Cotton in April and May, 1858, and at the affair with the Hindostanee fanatics on the heights of Satana on the 4th May.

9 Captains Edwards and Reid served in the Punjaub campaign of 1848-49 (Medal); served also with the Flank Companies 98th Regt. in the force under Sir Colin Campbell, at the forcing of the Kohat Pass in Feb. 1850. Served in the Peshawur Expeditionary force on the Euzofzie frontier under Sir Sydney Cotton in April and May 1858, and at the affair with the Hindostanee fanatics on the heights of Satana on the 4th May.

10 Captain Cleveland served in the Punjaub campaign of 1848-49 (Medal). Served in the Peshawur Expeditionary force on the Euzofzie frontier under Sir Sydney Cotton in April and May 1858, and at the affair with the Hindostanee fanatics on the heights of Satana on the 4th May.

12 Paymaster Leigh was present at the storm and destruction of the fortified native Mandingo town of Sabajee on the Gambia, on the 1st June 1853.

13 Qr.-Master Walsh served with the 9th Regt. throughout the campaign of 1842 in Affghanistan under Sir George Pollock, including the storming of the Khyber Pass, action of Mamoo Khail, storming the heights of Jugdulluck, forcing the Tezeen Pass, clearing the heights of Huft Kotul, recapture of Cabul, assault of the Istaliff (Medal). Served in the Sutlej campaign of 1845-46, including the battles of Moodkee and Ferozeshah—severely wounded (Medal and Clasp), also in the Punjaub campaign of 1848-49 (Medal).

98th Regiment of Foot.

[Serving in India. Depot, Canterbury.]

"*The Dragon*" "CHINA" "PUNJAUB."

Years' Serv.							
Full Pay	Half Pay						
50		**Colonel.**—William Lindsay Darling,[1] Ens. 13 Dec. 01; Lieut. 23 June 02; Capt. 13 June 08; Major, 14 April 14; Lt.Col. 21 June 17; Col. 10 Jan. 37; Maj.Gen. 9 Nov. 46; Lt.Gen. 20 June 54; Col. 98th F. 17 April 54.					
24	0	**Lieut.Colonels.**—Daniel Rainier,[2] Ens. p 4 March 36; Lieut. p 11 May 38; Capt. p 27 May 42; Maj. p 3 Sept. 50; Lt.Col. p 1 April 53; Col. 28 Nov. 54.					
31	0	Henry Bates,[4] Ens. 0 July 29; Lt. 28 Nov. 33; Capt. p 8 Aug. 45; Bt.Maj. 19 June 46; Bt.Lt.Col. 7 June 49; Maj. p 11 Oct. 53; Col. 28 Nov. 54; Lt.Col. 18 Sept. 57.					
19	0	**Majors.**—Francis Peyton,[5] Ens. p 20 Jan. 41; Lieut. p 27 May 42; Capt. p 3 Sept. 50; Major, p 12 May 54; Bt.Lt.Col. 26 Oct. 58.					
21	0	Granville George Chetwynd Stapylton,[6] Ens. 15 June 39; Lieut. 13 Jan. 42; Capt. p 28 April 48; Major, 18 Sept. 57.					

		CAPTAINS.	ENSIGN.	LIEUT.	CAPTAIN.	BREV.MAJ.	BT.LT.COL.
24	0	Francis Haden Crawford	14 Oct. 36	p 15 Dec. 40	p 1 Oct. 50		
23	0	Edward John Ellerman[7]	p 10 Feb. 37	p 4 Sept. 40	9 July 50		
19	0	Edward Grantham[2]	p 5 Oct. 41	17 Mar. 43	28 May 52		
19	0	S. Hen. Hutchins Edwards[6]	26 Nov. 41	18 Dec. 43	p 28 May 52		
16	0	G. D. Dickson Cleveland[10]	p 10 May 44	p 2 Sept. 45	p 11 Oct. 53		
18	0	Molyneux Batt	28 Dec. 42	11 Sept. 44	22 Nov. 54		
11	0	Frederick Rhodes	p 18 Sept. 49	p 8 Oct. 50	p 14 Apr. 54		
17	0	Robert Reid[9]	p 23 June 43	p 25 Jan. 45	10 Apr. 57		
17	0	Henry Wallace Stroud[11]	19 Mar. 45	18 Aug. 47	18 Sept. 57		
14	0	Attilio Schoberras	21 Apr. 46	p 21 Jan. 48	9 Mar. 58		
6	0	William Blackett[7]	p 20 Dec. 54	p 9 Nov. 55	p 17 Dec. 58		
5	0	William Langmead Lewes	23 Mar. 55	p 2 Oct. 55	p 8 July 59		
		LIEUTENANTS.					
11	0	Wm. Henry Joseph Lance	p 18 Sept. 49	p 7 Feb. 51			
8	0	Samuel Cooper Walker	p 11 June 52	7 Sept. 55			
11	0	Thomas Gardiner[7]	p 20 April 49	p 3 Sept. 50			
5	0	David J. Copeland Jones	8 June 55	p 19 Aug. 56			
5	0	Sidney Henry Heywood[7]	24 May 55	9 Nov. 55			
5	0	Thomas Francis Lloyd	22 June 55	p 15 May 57			
5	0	Kingston Brett	7 Sept. 55	18 Sept. 57			
5	0	Edw. Frank Gregory,[7] Adj.	p 9 Nov. 55	p 30 Oct. 57			
5	0	Charles Henry Griffin	2 Nov. 55	5 Mar. 58			
4	0	Geo. Washington Smith[7]	p 1 Feb. 56	23 Apr. 58			
4	0	George Thomas West	8 July 56	15 Oct. 58			
7	0	Tho. R. Devereux Bingham	p 13 Dec. 53	9 Jan. 58			
3	0	George Benjamin Wolseley	18 Sept. 57	24 Aug. 58			
3	0	Thos. Thomson Simpson	p 30 June 57	p 26 Aug. 59			
3	0	Thomas Francis Swinford	p 23 Oct. 57	p 18 Nov. 59			
		ENSIGNS.					
4	0	Charles Graham Heathcote	p 19 Aug. 56				
3	0	Percival Herbert Dobbs	25 Sept. 57				
2	0	Robert Thorp	p 2 Feb. 58				
2	0	William O'Toole	5 Mar. 58				
2	0	Richard Townley	p 21 May 58				
2	0	James George Ballantyne	p 28 May 58				
2	0	W. Henry Simmonds	31 Dec. 58				
1	0	Stafford Willard Vardow	p 31 May 59				
1	0	Edward Haughton	p 28 Oct. 59				
11	0	**Paymaster.**—Henry Leigh,[12] 8 Sept. 54; Lieut. 24 Nov. 49; Lieut. p 23 Jan. 52.					
5	0	**Adjutant.**—Lieut. Edward Frank Gregory, 8 May 58.					
11	0	**Instructor of Musketry.**—Lieut. W. H. J. Lance, 6 July 58.					
5	0	**Quarter Master.**—William Walsh,[13] 29 June 55.					
12	0	**Surgeon.**—Neil Henry Stewart, M.D. 22 June 55; Assist.Surg. 1 Dec. 48.					
6	0	**Assist.Surgeons.**—James McNeill Beatty, 14 Dec. 54.					
5	0	William Collis,[7] 14 Sept. 55.					
2	0	Samuel Archer, 5 Aug. 58.					

Facings White.—**Agents**, Downes & Son.

[*Returned from Bengal, May* 1855. *Embarked for India,* 3 *Oct.* 1857.]

4 Colonel Bates served as Aide-de-Camp to Sir Robert Dick (who was killed) in the battle of Sobraon (Medal); and was appointed after that action Aide-de-Camp to the Commander in Chief in India, in which capacity he served the Punjaub campaign of 1848-9, and was present at the affair of Ramnuggur and battles of Chillianwallah and Goojerat (Medal and two Clasps).

5 Lt.Colonel Peyton served in the 98th with the Expedition to the north of China in 1842 (Medal), and was present at the attack and capture of Chinkiangfoo, and at the landing before Nankin. He also served with the Flank Companies at the forcing of the Kohat Pass, in the force under Sir Colin Campbell in Feb. 1850. Served also in the Punjaub campaign of 1848-49 (Medal). Commanded four Companies of the 98th Regt. in the Peshawur expeditionary force on the Euzofzic frontier under Sir Sidney Cotton in April and May 1858, and at the affair with the Hindostanee fanatics on the heights of Sarana on 4th May.

6 Major Stapylton served in the 13th Light Infantry the campaigns of 1841 and 1842 in Affghanistan, and was present at the storming of the Khoord Cabool Pass, affair of Tezeen, forcing the Jugdulluck Pass, reduction of the Fort of Mamoo Khail, heroic defence of Jellalabad, and sorties on the 14th Nov. and 1st Dec. 1841, 11th March, 24th March, and 1st April 1842; the general action, with defeat of the besieging force under Akbar Khan before Jellalabad on the 7th April; the storming of the Jugdulluck Heights, general action at Tezeen, and recapture of Cabul, for which he has a Medal, as also for Jellalabad.

11 Captain Stroud served in the Punjaub campaign of 1848-49 (Medal).

1 Lieut.General Darling served at the reduction of Guadaloupe in 1810, and was severely wounded in the left knee by a musket-shot in storming the heights of Matauba. Proceeded to the Peninsula, and joined the 51st Light Infantry at Castello Branco in May 1812; engaged on the heights of San Christoval; the battle of Salamanca, and surrender of the Retiro at Madrid; employed with his regiment before Burgos; and after the retreat from thence he was attacked by typhus fever, and sent to England for recovery in May 1813. Rejoined the army on the heights of Echallar in September following, and was present at the battle of Nivelle, and the subsequent attack of the heights of St. Pé. Appointed Major of Brigade in Dec. 1813, and attached to Major General Hay's brigade in the 5th Division, and was employed throughout the blockade and operations before Bayonne. Appointed Assistant Adjutant General to the 5th Division in April 1814, and remained in charge of that department until the embarkation of the division in Aug. 1814. On the renewal of the war in 1815 he was re-appointed to the staff as Assistant Adjutant General, and attached to the 4th Division, under Sir Charles Colville; employed with his division in the operations connected with the battle of Waterloo, the storming of Cambray, and capitulation of Paris. He received the War Medal with three Clasps for Guadaloupe, Salamanca, and Nivelle.

[For continuation of Notes, see preceding page.]

East Indies, Depot, Cork.] **99th (*Lanarkshire*) Regiment of Foot.** 341

Years' Serv.			ENSIGN.	LIEUT.	CAPTAIN.	BREV.MAJ.
61		Colonel.—*P* Sir John Hanbury,[1] KCH. *Ens.* 20 July 99; *Lieut.* 26 Sept. 99; *Capt.* 3 June 02; *Lt.Col.* 20 Dec. 12; *Col.* 25 July 21; *Major Gen.* 22 July 30; *Lt.Gen.* 23 Nov. 41; *Gen.* 20 June 54; *Col.* 99th F. 6 Oct. 51.				
Full Pay.	Half Pay.					
34	2½	Lieut.Colonels.—George Marmaduke Reeves, *Ens.* 1 July 24; *Lt.* P 8 April 26; *Capt.* P 27 April 27; *Bt.Maj.* 23 Nov. 41; *Bt.Lt.Col.* 11 Nov. 51; *Maj.* 20 June 54; *Col.* 28 Nov. 54; *Lt.Col.* 17 Sept. 58.				
32	0	Philip Smyly, *Ens.* P 27 Mar. 28; *Lieut.* P 18 June 30; *Capt.* P 18 July 34; *Brev. Maj.* 9 Nov. 46; *Bt.Lt.Col.* 20 June 54; *Maj.* 24 Nov. 57; *Lt.Col.* 26 Oct. 58; *Col.* 16 Jan. 59.				
35	0	Majors.—Henry James Day, *Ens.* 10 Feb. 25; *Lieut.* 11 June 29; *Capt.* 16 July 41; *Bt.Maj.* 20 June 54; *Maj.* 17 Sept. 58; *Bt.Lt.Col.* 13 Feb. 59.				
11	8/12	Montagu Hamilton Dowbiggin,[2] *Ens.* P 30 June 48; *Lt.* P 16 Sept. 51; *Capt.* 29 Dec. 54; *Bt.Major*, 17 July 55; *Major*, 1 Feb. 56.				
		CAPTAINS.				
23	0	Charles Blamire............	P 25 July 37	16 July 41	P 22 Feb. 50	
22	0	Patrick Johnston,[4] s.....	P 20 Nov. 38	P 18 July 41	17 Feb. 51	
21	0	Lempster R. Elliot[5]	9 Aug. 39	P 28 Dec. 41	6 June 54	
14	0	Fred. Wm. Despard	29 Jan. 46	P 23 Mar. 49	13 May 55	
11	0	Loftus John Nunn.........	P 23 Mar. 49	P 12 Oct. 52	P 25 Sept. 55	
8	0	John Hart Dunne[6]........	P 21 Sept. 52	P 27 Jan. 54	27 July 55	
13	0	Wm. H.D. Reeves Welman	P 10 Dec. 47	6 June 54	P 30 Oct. 57	
11	0	Henry Fred. W. Ely	P 22 June 49	6 June 54	P 17 Nov. 57	
12	0	Francis Seymour Gaynor	P 1 Aug. 48	P 6 Dec. 54	17 Sept. 58	
8	0	Thomas Holling. Clarkson	P 21 Sept. 52	14 Aug. 54	P 8 Apr. 59	
11	0	Wm. Speke Dickinson ...	P 4 May 49	6 Aug. 53	26 Oct. 58	
6	0	Charles Burton...........	P 19 June 54	P 1 June 55	16 May 59	
6	0	Malcolm Brown Purcell..	20 June 54	P 21 Sept. 55	P 22 July 59	
		LIEUTENANTS.				
6	0	G. Rob. Stewart Black, *Adj.*	P 18 Aug. 54	P 29 Aug. 56		
5	0	William John Kempson ..	8 June 55	P 16 Jan. 57		
5	0	Thomas Lowrie Grenville	5 July 55	P 30 June 57		
6	0	Henry James Day........	15 Dec. 54	30 Oct. 57		
5	0	Eustace Wilberforce Jacob	6 July 55	24 Nov. 57		
5	0	George Richards Harvey	25 Sept. 55	P 24 Nov. 57		
5	0	George Clayton	P 23 Oct. 55	P 11 Dec. 57		
4	0	Edward Colpoys Johnson[10]	P 26 Feb. 56	P 7 Sept. 58		
5	0	Aug. Wm. Hy. Atkinson	2 Nov. 55	17 Sept. 58		
4	0	Edward Beevor Batcheler	P 29 Aug. 56	P 15 Oct. 58		
4	0	Martin Joseph Browne ..	8 July 56	26 Oct. 58		
3	0	Alexander Gray..........	P 1 May 57	P 22 Apr. 59		
3	0	Henry Richmond Sayce	P 7 July 57	6 May 59		
3	0	Horace Townsend	P 24 Nov. 57	16 May 59		
3	0	Charles Coates	P 11 Dec. 57	P 22 July 59		
		ENSIGNS.				
3	0	Albert Lancelot Walker..	18 Dec. 57			
2	0	Philip Homan ffolliott ..	P 7 Sept. 58			
2	0	Chas. BruceHen. Somerset	17 Sept. 58			
2	0	Edward Egan............	P 19 Nov. 58			
1	0	Joseph Ward	25 Jan. 59			
1	0	Kearns Deane Tanner ..	P 28 Jan. 59			
1	0	Walter Skipper	P 31 May 59			
1	0	Joseph Arthur Stanford .	22 July 59			
2	0	Geo. Wm. Vernon Cotton	22 May 58			
1	0	Forbes Lugard Story	P 5 Aug. 59			

Notes alongside (right column):

[4] Capt. Johnston commanded the Light Company of the 90th at the storming of Kawiti's Pah at Ohaeawai on the 1st July 1845 (where he was slightly wounded on the forehead), and destruction of the same on the 10th July; again at the destruction of Arratua's Pah on 16th July; also at the destruction and capture of Kawiti's Pah at Ruapekapeka in Jan. 1846.

[5] Captain Elliot volunteered with the 58th on that Regt. proceeding to New Zealand, and served throughout the northern and southern campaigns of 1845 and 1846; was present at Okaihau, Ohaeawai, Ruapekapeka, and Horokiwi, and in several skirmishes in the north.

[6] Captain Dunne served the Eastern campaign of 1854 and early part of 1855, including the battles of Alma, Balaklava, and Inkerman, siege of Sebastopol, and attack on the Redan on the 18th June (Medal and four Clasps, and 5th Class of the Medjidie).

[10] Lieut. Johnson served in the Eastern campaign of 1854 in the Commissariat department, and was present at the battle of Alma (Medal and one Clasp).

[9] Surgeon Todd served with the 71st Regt. in the Crimea in 1855, the greater part of the time in medical charge of the Regt.—including the siege of Sebastopol and expedition to Kertch (Medal and Clasp).

12	22 3/12	Paymaster.—Charles Schomberg Thomas, 1 Aug. 55; *Ens.* 24 Aug. 24; *Lt.* 4
6	0	Adjutant.—Lieut. George Robert Stewart Black, 6 May 59. [Apr. 27.
5	0	Instructor of Musketry.—Lieut. W. J. Kompson, 7 Aug. 59.
2	0	Quarter Master.—John Johnston, 24 Sept. 58.
10	0	Surgeon.—Richard Cooper Todd,[9] 3 Nov. 57; *Assist.Surg.* 24 Sept. 50.
3	0	Assistant Surgeons.—George Whitla, 15 Sept. 57.
3	0	James Whinyates George Allen, 12 Nov. 57.
2	0	Samuel Halliday Macartney, 5 Aug. 58.

Facings Yellow.—*Agents*, Messrs. Cox & Co.—*Irish Agents*, Sir E. R. Borough, Bt., Armit & Co.

[*Returned from Australia*, 29 May 1856. *Emb. for India*, Sept. 1858.]

1 Sir John Hanbury served the Egyptian campaign of 1801 as a Lieutenant in the 58th, including the actions of the 8th, 13th, and 21st March; and has received the Gold Medal from the Grand Seignior. He was Aide-de-Camp to Major General Warde in the campaign of 1808-9, and was present on Sir John Moore's retreat, and at the battle of Corunna. He served with the 1st Guards at Walcheren in 1809, and subsequently in the Peninsular campaign, including the retreat from Burgos, passage of the Bidassoa and Adour, battles of Nivelle and Nive, investment of Bayonne and repulse of the sortie. He has received the War Medal with four Clasps for Egypt, Corunna, Nivelle, and Nive.

2 Major Dowbiggin served the Eastern campaign of 1854-55, including the battle of Alma, siege of Sebastopol and capture of Kinbourn (Medal and Clasps, Brevet Major, Knight of the Legion of Honor, and 5th Class of the Medjidie).

342 100th (*The Prince of Wales' Royal Canadian*) Regt. of Foot. [Gibraltar.

Colonel.—Henry Viscount Melville,[1] KCB. *Ens. & Lt.* 18 Nov. 10; *Capt.* P 1 Apr. 24; *Major*, P 11 July 26; *Lt. Col.* P 3 Dec. 29; *Col.* 28 Nov. 41; *Major Gen.* 20 June 54; *Col.* 100 F.

Lieut. Colonel.—George de Rottenburg,[2] CB. *Ens.* 7 Apr. 25; *Lt.* P 27 Apr. 27; *Capt.* P 19 July 32; *Bt. Major*, 31 Dec. 41; *Bt. Lt. Col.* 11 Nov. 51; *Col.* 28 Nov. 54; *Major*, 7 May 58; *Lt. Col.* 14 May 58.

Majors.—James Henry Craig Robertson, *Ens.* 2 July 20; *Lt.* 30 Dec. 35; *Capt.* 27 Feb. 42; *Bt. Maj.* 20 June 54; *Bt. Lt. Col.* 6 June 56; *Major*, 7 May 58.

VC Alexander Roberts Dunn,[3] 29 June 58.

Years' Serv. Full Pay	Years' Serv. Half Pay	CAPTAINS.	ENSIGN.	LIEUT.	CAPTAIN.	BREV. MAJ.
41	—					
31	4					
30	1					
2	0					
22	1 8/12	Tho. Maths. Luz Weguelin	P 23 Dec. 36	P 28 June 39	P 20 Dec. 43	20 June 54
9	7/12	Robert Bethune Ingram..	P 14 July 50	11 Aug. 54	9 Sept. 55	
5	0	Henry Cook[4]	15 June 55	31 Aug. 55	1 June 58	
4	0	James Clery[5]	P 18 Jan. 56	P 11 July 56	1 June 58	
5	0	Henry George Browne[6]..	31 Aug. 55	15 Oct. 56	1 June 58	
2	0	John Clarke	....	....	29 June 58	
2	0	Ter. W. Waverley Smythe[7]	....	....	29 June 58	
2	0	George Macartney[8]	....	....	29 June 58	
2	0	Charles John Clark	....	....	29 June 58	
2	0	Richard Charles Price	....	....	29 June 58	
12	6/12	William Alfred Swift....	P 11 Feb. 48	16 July 50	P 13 Mar. 57	
6	0	George Bell Coulson[9] ..	13 Oct. 54	9 Feb. 55	P 20 Dec. 50	
		LIEUTENANTS.				
6	0	John Lee,[10] *Adj.*	5 Nov. 54	9 Mar. 55		
6	0	James Lamb[11]	5 Nov. 54	9 Mar. 55		
5	0	Fred. William Benwell ..	19 Feb. 55	9 Mar. 55		
5	0	Henry Lionel Nicholls ..	24 Jan. 55	9 Mar. 55		
5	0	Joseph Dooley	21 Feb. 55	25 June 55		
5	0	Richard Lane Bayliff....	19 Mar. 55	16 Oct. 55		
2	0	John Fletcher[12]	....	29 June 58		
2	0	Louis Adolphe Casault ..	....	29 June 58		
2	0	L. C. A. L. de Bellefeuille	....	29 June 58		
2	0	Philip Derbishire	....	29 June 58		
2	0	Alfred Edwin Rykert ..	....	29 June 58		
2	0	Charles Henry Carriere..	....	29 June 58		
2	0	Henry Theod. Duchesney	....	29 June 58		
2	0	Brown Wallis	....	23 July 58		
3	0	Const. M'D. Moorsom[13]	6 Nov. 57	P 20 Dec. 59		
		ENSIGNS.				
2	0	Frederick Morris	28 June 58			
2	0	John Gibbs Ridout	29 June 58			
2	0	Henry Edward Davidson.	29 June 58			
2	0	Charles Arkoll Boulton..	23 July 58			
2	0	Thomas Henry Baldwin .	24 July 58			
2	0	William Palmer Clarke .	13 Aug. 58			
2	0	Horatio William Lawrell	8 Oct. 58			
1	0	Robert Edw. C. Jarvis ..	19 July 59			
1	0	George John Skinner ..	16 Sept. 50			

2	0	*Paymaster.*—Joseph Hutchison, 14 May 58.	
6	0	*Adjutant.*—Lieut. John Lee,[10] 1 June 58.	
2	0	*Instructor of Musketry.*—Ensign Frederick Morris, 10 Sept. 58.	
2	0	*Quarter Master.*—George Grant, 30 Apr. 58.	
17	0	*Surgeon.*—William Barrett, M.B. 28 Mar. 54; *Assist. Surg.* 20 Oct. 43.	
3	0	*Assist. Surgeons.*—Thomas Liddard, 3 Oct. 57.	
3	0	Daniel Murray, M.D. 19 Oct. 57.	

Facings Blue.—Agents, Messrs. Cox & Co.

[*Embarked for Gibraltar*, 7 May 1859. *Depot, Isle of Wight.*]

1 Lord Melville commanded the 83rd during the suppression of the insurrection in Lower Canada in 1837; and also in repelling the attacks of the American Brigands who landed near Prescott, Upper Canada, in 1838. Commanded the Bombay column of the army throughout the Punjaub campaign of 1848-9, including the siege and storm of the town and capture of the citadel of Mooltan, battle of Goojerat, and subsequent operations (Medal and Clasps, and KCB.).

2 Colonel de Rottenburg served in Canada during the rebellion and received the Brevet rank of Major for services there whilst employed on a Particular Service.

3 Major Dunn as a Lieut. in the 11th Hussars served the Eastern campaign of 1854, including the battles of Alma and Balaklava and siege of Sebastopol (Medal and Clasps, and Victoria Cross).

4 Captain Cook was present with the 32nd Regt. in the action of Chinhut 30 June 1857 and throughout the defence of the Lucknow Residency; commanded the outpost at Innes' House during the first part of the siege, and at Sago's House during the latter part; commanded two Sorties, in one of which he took a gun in battery at the head of twenty men, for which he was mentioned in General Inglis' despatch as having "highly distinguished himself" (Medal and Clasp).

12 Lieut. Fletcher was actively employed during the suppression of the Rebellion in Canada in 1847-49 in the Montreal Volunteers.

13 Lieut. Moorsom served as a Naval Cadet in the Baltic from March to August 1854 (Medal).

5 Captain Clery served with the 32nd Regt. in the action of Chinhut 30 June 1857 and throughout the defence of the Lucknow Residency, where he commanded one of the most exposed outposts and led a Sortie—was mentioned in General Inglis' despatches and received the thanks of the Governor General in Council (Medal and Clasp).

7 Captain Smythe served in the Incorporated Militia in Canada during the suppression of the insurrection in 1837-38 and was present at the action of Windmill Point. Subsequently he was placed in command of the 1st Rifle Corps of Upper Canada in which he served until joining the 100th Regt.

8 Captain Macartney served as an officer of the Militia in Canada during the suppression of the insurrection, and was present at the siege of Navy Island.

9 Captain Coulson served with the 49th Regt. from the 15th June to 20th July at the siege of Sebastopol and assault of the Redan on 18th June (Medal and Clasp).

10 Lieut. Lee served with the 17th Regt. at the siege of Sebastopol from Dec. 1854 to May 1855 (Medal and Clasp).

6 Captain Browne commanded the Grenadiers of the 32nd Regt. at Chinhut on 30th June 1857, and was present in the Lucknow Residency throughout the Siege, he led a Sortie and spiked two guns, and was twice wounded—once severely, and was thanked by the Governor General (Medal and Clasp).

11 Lieut. Lamb served with the 50th Regt. including the Eastern campaign of 1854-55, battles of Alma and Inkerman, siege and fall of Sebastopol (Medal and Clasps, Sardinian Medal and 5th Class of the Medjidie).

Rifle Brigade. 343

"COPENHAGEN" "MONTE VIDEO" "ROLEIA" "VIMIERA" "CORUNNA" "BUSACO" "BARROSSA"
"FUENTES D'ONOR" "CIUDAD RODRIGO" "BADAJOZ" "SALAMANCA" "VITTORIA" "NIVELLE" "NIVE"
"ORTHES" "TOULOUSE" "PENINSULA" "WATERLOO" "ALMA" "INKERMAN" "SEVASTOPOL."

Years' Serv.		
		Colonel-in-Chief.—Field Marshal His Royal Highness Francis Albert Augustus Charles Emanuel *Duke of* Saxony, *Prince of* Saxe Coburg & Gotha, KG, KT, KP, GCB, GCMG, 23 Sept. 52.
55		*Colonels Commandant.*—1 $\mathbb{P}$ $\mathbb{C}\mathbb{R}$ *Sir* Harry George Wakelyn Smith,[1] *Bart.* GCB., 2nd *Lieut.* 8 May 05; *Lieut.* 15 Aug. 05; *Capt.* 28 Feb. 12; *Major*, 29 Sept. 14; *Lieut.-Col.* 18 June 15; *Col.* 10 Jan. 37; *Major-Gen.* 9 Nov. 46; *Lieut.Gen.* 20 June 54; *Col. Comm.* Rifle Brigade, 16 April 47.
54		2 $\mathbb{P}$ *Sir* George Brown,[2] GCB. KH. *Ens.*23 Jan. 06; *Lt.* 8 Sept. 06; *Capt.* 20 June 11; *Major*, 26 May 14; *Lt.-Col.* 29 Sept. 14; *Col.* 6 May 31; *Maj.-Gen.* 23 Nov. 41; *Lt.-Gen.* 11 Nov. 51; *Gen.* 7 Sept. 55; *Col. Comm.* Rifle Brigade, 18 Jan. 55.
Full Pay.	Half Pay.	
27	0	*Lt.Colonels.*—3 Alfred H. Horsford,[3] CB. 2*nd Lt.* ᴾ 12 July 33; *Lt.* ᴾ 23 April 39; *Capt.* ᴾ 5 Aug. 42; *Maj.* ᴾ 26 Dec. 51; *Brev. Lt.Col.* 28 May 53; *Col.* 28 Nov. 54; *Lt.Col.* 2 Feb. 55.
24	1 7/12	2 Percy Hill, CB. *Ens.* ᴾ 24 April 35; *Lieut.* ᴾ 5 Oct. 38; *Capt.* ᴾ 23 Jan. 46; *Major*, ᴾ 22 Oct. 50; *Lt.Col.* ᴾ 29 Dec. 54; *Col.* 29 Dec. 57.
23	0	3 Alexander Macdonell,[b] CB. 2*nd Lieut.* ᴾ 23 June 37; *Lieut.* ᴾ 11 May 41; *Capt.* ᴾ 24 Oct. 45; *Brev. Maj.* 12 Dec. 54; *Maj.* 22 Dec. 54; *Brevet Lieut.Col.* 17 July 55; *Lt.Col.* 16 June 57; *Col.* 20 July 58.
34	10/12	2 *Sir* Robert Walpole,[6] KCB. 2*nd Lt.* ᴾ 11 May 25; *Lt.* ᴾ 26 Sept. 26; *Capt.*ᴾ 24 Jan. 34; *Maj.* ᴾ 31 May 44; *Bt.Lt.Col.* 2 July 47; *Col.* 28 Nov. 54; *Lt.Col.* 17 Oct. 56.
21	0	4 Fred. Robert Elrington,[7] 2*nd Lieut.* ᴾ 7 June 39; *Lieut.* 23 Nov. 41; *Capt.* ᴾ 22 May 46; *Brevet Major*, 12 Dec. 54; *Major*, 29 Dec. 54; *Brev.Lt.Col.* 26 Dec. 56; *Lt.Col.* ᴾ 1 Sept. 57.
21	0	1 Lord Alex. G. Russell,[8] 2*nd Lt.* ᴾ 11 July 39; *Lt.* 15 Apr. 42; *Capt.* ᴾ 7 Aug. 46; *Bt. Maj.* 28 May 53; *Maj.* 29 Dec. 54; *Bt. Lt.Col.* 6 June 56; *Lt.Col.* ᴾ 17 Dec. 58.
20	0	*Majors.*—1 Henry Hardinge,[9] 2*nd Lt.* ᴾ 19 June 40; *Lt.* ᴾ 5 Aug. 42; *Capt.* ᴾ 7 May 47; *Brevet Major*, 12 Dec. 54; *Major*, 23 March 55.
19	0	3 Julius Richard Glyn,[10] CB. *Ens.* 16 July 41; *Lt.* ᴾ 13 Oct. 43; *Capt.* ᴾ 9 June 48; *Bt. Major*, 12 Dec. 54; *Bt.Lt.Col.* 6 June 56; *Maj.* 5 June 57.
26	0	2 William Aug. Fyers,[11] CB. *Ens.* ᴾ 17 Oct. 34; *Lt.* ᴾ 29 May 36; *Capt.* ᴾ 7 May 47; *Bt. Major*, 2 Nov. 55; *Bt.Lt.Col.* 26 Dec. 56; *Major*, 16 June 57.
18	0	4 Edward Newdigate,[13] 2*nd Lieut.* 29 May 42; *Lieut.* 14 Apr. 46; *Capt.* ᴾ 30 Apr. 52; *Bt. Major*, 2 Nov. 55; *Major*, 31 Aug. 57.
17	0	4 *Hon.* Gilbert Elliot,[14] 2*nd Lieut.* ᴾ 7 July 43; *Lieut.* ᴾ 11 Sept. 46; *Capt.* ᴾ 12 Oct. 52; *Bt. Major*, 12 Dec. 54; *Major*, 31 Aug. 57.
16	0	3 Chas. Vernon Oxenden,[16] 2*nd Lieut.* ᴾ 23 Aug. 44; *Lieut.* ᴾ 13 July 47; *Capt.* 6 June 54; *Bt.Maj.* 6 June 56; *Maj.* ᴾ 1 Sept. 57; *Bt.Lt.Col.* 26 Apr. 59.
18	0	2 Hercules Walker,[12] 2*nd Lt.* 22 May 42; *Lt.* ᴾ 30 Dec. 45; *Capt.* ᴾ 8 Aug. 51; *Brev. Major*, 6 June 56; *Major*, 29 Nov. 57.
15	0	1 Edmund Manningham Buller,[18] 2*nd Lt.* 11 Oct. 45; *Lieut.* ᴾ 24 Sept. 47; *Capt.* 26 Sept. 54; *Major*, ᴾ 17 Dec. 58.

		CAPTAINS.	ENSIGN.	LIEUT.	CAPTAIN.
17	0	4 *Hon.* W. J. Colville,[15] *Maj.* 8 Sept. 55	22 Nov. 43	ᴾ 14 May 47	ᴾ 11 Oct. 53
15	0	1 *Hon.* James Stuart,[19] *Maj.* 17 July 55.	ᴾ 24 Oct. 45	ᴾ 15 Oct. 47	6 Nov. 54
15	0	1 *Hon.*LeicesterCurzon,[20] *s. l.c.*8 Sep. 55	ᴾ 29 Nov. 45	ᴾ 12 Nov. 47	22 Dec. 54
14	0	3 John Ross,[21] *Major*, 6 June 56; *l.c.* 20 July 58, *s.*	14 Apr. 46	ᴾ 29 Dec. 48	29 Dec. 54
13	0	2 Arthur James Nixon,[28] *Maj.* 20 July 58	30 Apr. 47	ᴾ 31 Oct. 51	do
13	0	2 Arthur Fred.Warren,[25] *Maj.* 2 Nov. 55	ᴾ 23 July 47	ᴾ 11 Oct. 53	do
11	0	3 𝔙ℭClaud T. Bourchier,[24]†*Maj.*17 July55	10 Apr. 49	6 June 54	do
9	0	4 Edward William Blackett[29]	ᴾ 14 Feb. 51	6 June 54	9 Feb. 55
15	0	3 Horace Fred. Hill	20 June 45	ᴾ 2 Mar. 49	23 Mar. 55
15	0	1 Henry John Maclean	30 May 45	ᴾ 15 June 49	do
9	0	3 Hen. R. L. Newdigate,[28]*Maj.* 20 July 58	ᴾ 16 Sept. 51	6 June 54	do
9	0	3 Adolphus Haggerston Stephens[30] ..	ᴾ 17 June 51	ᴾ 24 Feb. 54	do
9	0	3 George Smyth Windham[31]	ᴾ 21 Nov. 51	11 Aug. 54	do
8	0	3 Boyd Francis Alexander	ᴾ 11 June 52	ᴾ 25 Aug. 54	do
7	0	1𝔙ℭWm.Js.MontgomeryCuninghame[34]	ᴾ 11 Mar. 53	ᴾ 12 Nov. 54	ᴾ 8 June 55
11	0	2 Henry Wilmot, *Maj.* 20 July 58......	ᴾ 29 May 49	ᴾ 17 Oct. 51	ᴾ 1 May 55
8	0	2 RiversdaleRich.Glyn,[35] *Maj.* 20 July 58	ᴾ 16 Apr. 52	26 Oct. 54	ᴾ 10 Aug. 55
12	0	2 *Hon.* Lewis W. Milles,[36]*Maj.* 20 July 58	ᴾ 28 Apr. 48	ᴾ 20 June 51	ᴾ 10 Apr. 55
17	6/12	2 Martin Dillon,[37] *Maj.* 20 July 58	18 Mar. 43	14 Nov. 44	ᴾ 2 Nov. 55
13	7/12	2 Charles William Earle[37]†	24 Dec. 46	ᴾ 28 Feb. 51	23 Mar. 55
6	0	3 George Ernest Rose[64]	....	ᴾ 24 Aug. 54	ᴾ 2 May 56
6	9/12	1 William Norris[65]	ᴾ 17 Mar. 54	6 June 54	ᴾ 8 Jan. 56
7	9/12	4 Reginald Henry Graham[66]	3 Dec. 52	15 Dec. 54	ᴾ 8 Feb. 56
6	0	1 *Lord* Edw. Wm. Pelham Clinton ..	ᴾ 9 June 54	8 Dec. 54	ᴾ 1 Sept. 57

344 Rifle Brigade.

Years' Serv. Full Pay.	Half Pay.		CAPTAINS.	ENSIGN.	LIEUT.	CAPTAIN.
7	½	4	Hon. Jossylin Francis Pennington..	p 21 Jan. 53	p 13 Oct. 54	p 8 Feb. 56
5	½	4	Fitzhardinge Kingscote[67]	p 7 April 54	6 Nov. 54	26 Feb. 56
5	¼	4	Charles Vaue FitzRoy[68]	6 June 54	6 Nov. 54	25 Mar. 56
6	½	4	Robert Henry Evans[69]............	p 3 Mar. 54	8 Dec. 54	p 1 April 56
8	½	4	Godfrey Clerk, Major, 20 July 53	5 Dec. 51	p 25 Mar. 53	p 29 June 56
6	0	2	John Brett[38]	13 July 54	22 Dec. 54	24 Nov. 57
6	0	2	FitzRoy William Fremantle[52]......	14 July 54	22 Dec. 54	p 24 Nov. 57
6	0	2	George Robert Saunders[39]†	15 July 54	29 Dec. 54	29 Nov. 57
6	0	4	Christopher Edward Musgrave[39] ..	16 July 54	29 Dec. 54	p 12 Feb. 58
6	0	4	Charles Browne Dashwood........	17 July 54	29 Dec. 54	p 19 Feb. 58
6	0	1	John Plumptre Carr Glyn[39]	p 25 Aug. 54	29 Dec. 54	12 Mar. 58
6	0	2	James Singer[53]	5 Nov. 54	29 Dec. 54	30 April 58
6	0	4	VC John Simpson Knox[51]	5 Nov. 54	29 Dec. 54	30 April 58
6	0	4	John Croft Moore[41]	17 Nov. 54	29 Dec. 54	p 7 May 58
6	0	1	Richard Tryon	21 Nov. 54	20 Feb. 55	p 13 July 58
6	0	3	Stewart Smyth Windham	p 25 Aug. 54	9 Feb. 55	7 Sept. 58
6	0	1	William Trevor Rooper[39]	14 Dec. 54	23 Mar. 55	p 10 Sept. 58
6	0	3	James Frederick Henley	24 Dec. 54	23 Mar. 55	p 5 Oct. 58
6	0	2	Arthur Loftus Tottenham[39]......	8 Dec. 54	23 Mar. 55	7 Dec. 58
6	0	1	John Clerk[37]	6 June 54	23 Mar. 55	p 17 Dec. 58
7	0	2	John Byron Blenkinsopp Coulson[55]	....	p 28 Oct. 53	p 9 Oct. 55
6	0	1	Palmer Whalley	15 Sept. 54	23 Mar. 55	p 3 June 59
5	0	1	Robert Edw. Stuart Harington[70]....	4 Jan. 55	11 May 55	p 3 June 59
5	0	3	Grenville Charles Lane[40].........	5 Jan. 55	11 May 55	p 3 June 59
7	0	3	Henry Wood[58]	p 12 May 53	p 22 Sept. 54	p 5 Aug. 59
5	0	3	Frederic Carl Payne[41]	p 16 Jan. 55	11 May 55	p 18 Nov. 59

LIEUTENANTS.

6	0	1	Walter J. H. Ruthven[39]	15 Dec. 54	23 Mar. 55
6	0	1	John Constantine Pester	15 Dec. 54	23 Mar. 55
5	0	2	Christopher Rice Havard Nicholl[39]	17 Jan. 55	11 May 55
5	0	2	Frederick Edward Sotheby[59]	18 Jan. 55	11 May 55
5	0	1	Hector Stewart Vandeleur	p 26 Jan. 55	11 May 55
5	0	1	Charles Thomas Bunbury	p 2 Feb. 55	8 June 55
5	0	2	William Hall Eccles[41]	12 Feb. 55	19 June 55
5	0	3	Edmund Fortescue	13 Feb. 55	22 June 55
5	0	1	Charles George Slade	18 Feb. 55	6 July 55
5	0	3	Walter Richard Lascelles	p 20 Feb. 55	6 July 55
5	0	4	Frederic Arthur Riley[41]	1 Mar. 55	27 July 55
5	0	3	Cecil Webb Cragg[40]	p 2 Mar. 55	2 Aug. 55
5	0	2	David Alexander Gordon, Adj.	21 Mar. 55	p 31 Aug. 55
5	0	1	Henry B. Hollinshead Blundell, Adj.	30 Mar. 55	p 31 Aug. 55
5	0	3	Geoffrey Lewis Austin	6 Apr. 55	p 31 Aug. 55
5	0	4	Sydney Carr Glyn[56]..............	21 Apr. 55	p 31 Aug. 55
5	0	3	Charles Edward Buckley	9 Mar. 55	9 Sept. 55
5	0	3	Andrew Green	20 May. 55	10 Sept. 55
5	0	3	Lewis Percival	21 May. 55	23 Oct. 55
5	0	3	FitzRoy Stephen, Adj.	22 Mar. 55	23 Oct. 55
5	0	4	Edmund George Johnson	23 Mar. 55	23 Oct. 55
5	0	2	Henry Martin Moorsom	24 Apr. 55	11 Nov. 55
6	0	4	Daniel Bishop Davy	p 10 Feb. 54	p 20 Feb. 55
5	0	2	George Mark L. Egerton..........	p 30 Apr. 55	23 Dec. 55
5	0	4	William Henry Deedes	1 May. 55	p 15 Jan. 56
5	0	4	Herbert Alex. St. John Mildmay[60]..	4 May. 55	14 Mar. 56
5	0	4	Clinton Frazer Henshaw..........	10 May. 55	14 Mar. 56
5	0	4	Henry Lamplugh Wickham	11 May. 55	p 3 Mar. 57
5	0	1	Hon. Alan Joseph Pennington[61]....	17 May. 55	p 22 May 57
5	0	2	Henry Charles Geast Dugdale	5 June 55	p 1 Sept. 57
5	0	2	Hugh Lawton	18 May. 55	27 Nov. 57
5	0	3	Emanuel Jeames	25 May. 55	27 Nov. 57
5	0	2	William Causabon Purdon	8 June 55	p 27 Nov. 57
5	0	1	John Hillary Allaire	14 June 55	29 Nov. 57
5	0	2	Edward John Fryer..............	15 June 55	12 Feb. 58
5	0	4	George Augustus Curzon	23 June 55	12 Feb. 58
5	0	1	John William Russell	8 June 55	p 12 Feb. 58
5	0	1	Lewis Vaughan Williams	6 July 55	p 19 Feb. 58
5	0	2	Frederick Ames	19 July 55	12 Mar. 58
5	0	1	Edward Palmer	20 July 55	26 Mar. 58
5	0	1	Ernest Henry Buller	p 25 July 55	30 Apr. 58
5	0	2	Fred. William Ramsbottom	27 July 55	10 May 58
5	0	4	William Steward Travers[74]......	3 Aug. 55	11 May 58
5	0	1	William George Swinhoe.........	p 18 Oct. 55	23 Aug. 58
5	0	3	James Edward Vaughan	20 Oct. 55	7 Sept. 58
5	0	4	Fred. Wm. Marsh Chalmers[71]	22 Oct. 55	7 Sept. 58

Rifle Brigade.

Years' Serv. Full Pay	Half Pay	LIEUTENANTS.	ENSIGN.	LIEUT.
5	0	3 Arthur Blundell Geo. Sandys Hill ..	23 Oct. 55	7 Sept. 58
5	0	3 Arthur Ruck Keene	p 9 Nov. 55	p 7 Sept. 58
5	0	1 Aylmer H. T. H. Somerset	21 Nov. 55	p 10 Sept. 58
5	0	2 Alex. Angus Airlie Kinloch	22 Nov. 55	p 24 Sept. 58
5	0	3 Albert Divett Rickman	p 29 Nov. 55	21 Oct. 58
5	0	2 Cornelius Davenport Broadbent....	30 Nov. 55	p 19 Nov. 58
5	0	1 Thomas Roworth Parr............	p 30 Nov. 55	28 Nov. 58
5	0	2 James Hook	28 Dec. 55	9 Dec. 58
4	0	3 Edward Henry Chamberlin	p 8 Jan. 56	p 31 May 59
4	0	4 *Hon.* Cuthbert Ellison Edwardes ..	15 Feb. 56	p 31 May 59
4	0	4 Francis Markham	16 Mar. 56	p 3 June 59
4	0	2 William Arbuthnot..............	25 Mar. 56	p 3 June 59
3	0	4 John Francis Mair Winterscale	p 3 Mar. 57	p 3 June 59
3	0	4 Cecil George Assheton Drummond..	p 23 Oct. 57	p 18 Nov. 59
3	0	4 Rowland Egerton	24 Oct. 57	p 18 Nov. 59
		ENSIGNS.		
4	0	2 William James Kempt Myers	25 Jan. 56	
3	0	2 Charles Walker Robinson.........	27 Nov. 57	64 Captain Rose served with the Coldstream Guards at the siege and fall of Sebastopol from 11th Dec. 1854 (Medal and Clasp).
3	0	1 Archdale Robert Palmer	p 28 Nov. 57	
2	0	1 Wilmot Grant	2 Feb. 58	
2	0	1 *Lord* Edward Cavendish	p 19 Feb. 58	65 Captain Norris served at the siege of Sebastopol from Dec. 1854, and was severely wounded in the trenches (Medal and Clasp).
2	0	2 FitzRoy Wilson.................	21 Feb. 58	
2	0	2 Lucius F. B. Cary[72]	22 Feb. 58	
2	0	1 *Hon.* Fred. Noel Somerville.......	p 26 Feb. 58	
2	0	2 George Stanley Byng	27 Feb. 58	66 Captain Graham served with the 14th Regt. at the siege of Sebastopol from 10th Jan. 1855 (Medal and Clasp).
2	0	2 Charles Francis Blackett.........	30 Mar. 58	
2	0	4 *Hon.* John Abercromby	p 7 May 58	
2	0	4 Gerald Edmund Boyle...........	2 June 58	67 Captain Kingscote served with the 41st Regt. at the siege and fall of Sebastopol from 15th Nov. 1854, including the storming of the Quarries, and the assault of the Redan on 8th Sept. (Medal and Clasp, and 5th Class of the Medjidie).
2	0	4 Christopher Hatton Turnor.......	3 June 58	
2	0	1 John Ormsby Vandeleur	4 June 58	
2	0	1 Arthur Wilson Patten	5 June 58	
2	0	2 Robert Hamilton Lloyd Anstruther	25 June 58	
2	0	2 Hugh William Reid	30 July 58	
2	0	1 John Charles Stephen Fremantle ..	2 Jan. 58	
2	0	3 James Dunlop	26 Oct. 58	
2	0	1 *Lord* Adelbert Percy Cecil	p 29 Oct. 58	68 Captain FitzRoy served with the 41st Regt. at the siege and fall of Sebastopol from 15th Nov. 1854, including the storming of the Quarries, and the assault of the Redan on 8th Sept. (Medal and Clasp, and 5th Class of the Medjidie).
2	0	4 W. H. J. C. *Visc.* Glentworth......	p 30 Oct. 58	
2	0	4 George Roberts Noseley, *Adj.*......	31 Oct. 58	
2	0	1 John Stewart Hardy.............	30 Dec. 58	
2	0	2 *Hon.* Albert Hood	31 Dec. 58	
1	0	3 *Hon.* Edward Lawless	p 11 Jan. 59	
1	0	1 Walter Caradoc Smith............	p 28 Jan. 59	69 Captain Evans served with the 90th Light Infantry at the siege of Sebastopol from 5th Dec. 1854 to 16th Feb. 1855 (Medal and Clasp).
1	0	3 *Hon.* Thomas Charles Scott	p 11 Mar. 59	
1	0	4 Charles Fairfield	12 Mar. 59	
1	0	2 Christopher Johnston	1 Apr. 59	
2	0	4 Francis Ernest Kerr	31 Aug. 58	73 Surgeon La Presle in Medical Charge of the 84th Regt. joined General Havelock's force on its first taking the field in 1857, and was present in the actions of Futtehpore, Aoung, Pandoo Nuddee, Cawnpore, Oonao, Buscerut Gunge (1st and 2nd), Boorbeake Chowkee, Bithoor, Mungawar, Alum Bagh, and relief of Lucknow; with Outram's force in the Alum Bagh and repulse of the several attacks, also at the assault and capture of Lucknow.
1	0	3 George John FitzRoy Smith	p 3 June 59	
1	0	4 *Hon.* Edward Courtenay Vaughan ..	p 14 June 59	
1	0	2 Alexander Stuart Harington	p 15 June 59	
1	0	3 George Anson Hillyard...........	16 June 59	
1	0	3 George Larcom	17 June 59	
1	0	3 George Caulfield	p 22 July 59	
1	0	3 Alfred Ames	p 23 July 59	
1	0	4 Leopold Victor Swaine...........	p 24 July 59	
1	0	3 Thomas Lander Mitchell-Innes	24 June 59	
1	0	*Hon.* Thomas John Wynn	p 28 Oct. 59	
1	0	Richard Winstanley Ormerod......	18 Nov. 59	
1	0	*Hon.* Charles North	p 19 Nov. 59	
1	0	Frederick William Duncombe......	p 20 Nov. 59	
17	0	*Paymasters.*—1 John Edw. Large,[45] 8 Aug. 51; *Ens.* p 10 Nov. 43; *Lt.* 1 May 46.		
9	0	2 Mich. W. Lade Coast, 1 Dec. 54; *Ens.* p 3 Jan. 51; *Lt.* 21 July 54.		
14	0	3 Thomas Gough, 14 Sept. 55; *Qr. Master*, 14 Aug. 46.		
11	0	4 Henry Peacocke,[47] 27 Oct. 57; *Q.M.* 21 Aug. 49.		
5	0	*Adjutants.*—1 *Lieut.* Henry Blundell H. Blundell, 27 Nov. 57.		
5	0	3 *Lieut.* FitzRoy Stephen, 10 Feb. 58.		
5	0	2 *Lieut.* D. A. Gordon, 25 June 58.		
2	0	4 *Ensign* George Roberts Noseley, 31 Oct. 58.		
5	0	*Instructors of Musketry.*—2 *Lieut.* Henry Martin Moorsom, 27 Aug. 56.		
6	0	3 *Captain* Stewart Smyth Windham, 5 April 57.		
6	0	4 *VC Captain* J. S. Knox, 7 Jan. 58.		
5	0	1 *Lieut.* Charles George Slade, 19 April 58.		

† Q

846 *Rifle Brigade.*

Years' Serv.		
Full Pay.	Half Pay.	
5	0	*Quarter Masters.*—3 Henry Harvey,⁴⁶ 24 April 55.
5	0	2 George Rogers, 14 Sept. 55.
3	0	4 Duncan M'Intyre, 16 Oct. 57.
3	0	1 William Higgins,⁴⁷ 4 Dec. 57.
10	0	*Surgeons.*—1 Robert Bowen,⁴⁹ 26 Dec. 51 ; *Assist.Surg.* 18 May 41.
13	0	4 Jas. Edward Scott,⁵⁰ M.D. 9 Feb. 55 ; *Assist.Surg.* 11 June 47.
14	0	3 Joseph Thomas La Presle,⁷³ 2 Oct. 57 ; *Assist.Surg.* 22 Dec. 46.
11	0	2 Henry Martyn Fraser, M.D. 2 Oct. 57 ; *Assist.Surg.* 11 Sept. 49.
6	0	*Assist.Surgs.*—1 John Ignatius Purcell Williams,⁴⁴ 14 July 54.
6	0	2 John By Cole Reade,⁵¹ 24 March 54.
6	0	3 Alexander Guthrie, M.D. 28 April 54.
6	0	1 Fra. S. Bennet Francois de Chaumont,⁶² M.D. 28 Apr. 54.
5	0	3 John Storey, 7 Dec. 55.
6	0	3 David Cullen,⁶³ M.D. 1 Sept. 54.
3	0	2 Alexander Frederick Bradshaw, 27 May 57.
5	0	4 George Buly, 4 Apr. 55.
2	0	4 Charles Seward, 22 Apr. 58.
1	0	2 David Ritchie Pearson, M.D. 12 Jan. 59.

Regimentals Green.—*Facings* Black.—*Agent,* Sir John Kirkland.
1st *Batt. returned from the Crimea,* 7 *July* 1856. *Hd.Qrs., Portsmouth. Depot, Winchester.*
2nd *Batt. returned from Crimea, June* 56. *Emb. for India,* 9 *Aug.* 57. *Depot, Winchester.*
3rd *Battalion embarked for India,* 26 *July* 1857. *Depot, Winchester.*
4th *Battalion embarked for Malta, Aug.* 1858. *Depot, Winchester.*

1 Sir Harry Smith served with the Rifle Brigade at the siege, storm, and taking of Monte Video under Sir S. Auchmuty, and at the assault upon Buenos Ayres under Brigadier-General Craufurd. Employed with the troops in Spain under Sir John Moore, from the battle of Vimiera to the embarkation of the troops at Corunna. Embarked for the Peninsula under Major-General Robert Craufurd in 1809 ; was seriously wounded in the action upon the bridge of the Coa near Almeida. Commanded a Company in the pursuit of Massena from the Lines of Lisbon ; at the actions of Redinha, Condeixa, and Foz d'Arouce. Appointed Brigade-Major to the 2nd Light Brigade in the Light Division, and was present in the action of Sabugal, battle of Fuentes d'Onor, siege and storm of Ciudad Rodrigo, siege and storm of Badajoz, battles of Salamanca and Vittoria, attack of the heights of Vera and passage of the Bidassoa, battle of Sarre, attack upon the position of St. Jean de Luz and heights of Arcangues, battle of Orthes, affair at Tarbes, and battle of Toulouse. Appointed Assistant Adjutant-General to the troops under Major-General Ross destined against Washington, and was present at the battle of Bladensburg and destruction of Washington. Brought home Dispatches, and went out again immediately under Sir Edward Pakenham, and was present at the attack upon the enemy's lines near New Orleans. After the death of Sir Edward he was appointed Military Secretary to Sir John Lambert, commanding the Army, and was present at the siege and taking of Fort Bowyer. Appointed Assist.-Quarter-Master-General to the 6th Division of the Army under the Duke of Wellington, and was present at the battle of Waterloo. In 1828 he was appointed D. Q. M. Gen. at the Cape of Good Hope, and commanded a division under Sir Benjamin D'Urban throughout the operations against the Kaffir tribes in 1834 and 1835. In 1840 he proceeded to the East Indies as Adjutant-General, and was nominated a *KCB*, for the action of Maharajpore, in which battle he was present as Adjutant-General ; and for his distinguished services in the campaign on the Sutlej and brilliant victory over the Seikhs at Aliwal, he was nominated a *GCB*, and afterwards created a Baronet. Finally, as Governor and Commander-in-chief at the Cape of Good Hope, he attacked and defeated the rebel Boers at Boem Plaats 29th Aug. 1848. Sir Harry has received the War Medal and twelve Clasps.

2 Sir George Brown served at the siege and capture of Copenhagen in 1807, in the Peninsula from Aug. 1808 to July 1811 ; and again from July 1813 to May 1814, including the battle of Vimiera, passage of the Douro and capture of Oporto, with the previous and subsequent actions ; battle of Talavera (severely wounded through both thighs), action of the Light Division at the bridge of Almeida, battle of Busaco, the different actions during the retreat of the French army from Portugal, action at Sabugal, battle of Fuentes d'Onor, siege of San Sebastian, battles of the Nivelle and Nive, and the Investment of Bayonne. Served afterwards in the American war, and was present at the battle of Bladensburg and capture of Washington. Slightly wounded in the head and very severely in the groin at Bladensburg. He has received the War Medal with seven Clasps. Commanded the Light Division throughout the Eastern campaign of 1854-55, including the battles of the Alma (horse shot under him), Balaklava, and Inkerman (severely wounded—shot through the arm), and siege of Sebastopol (Medal and four Clasps, *GCB*., Grand Cross of the Legion of Honor, 1st Class of the Medjidie, and Sardinian Medal).

3 Colonel Horsford served with the Rifle Brigade in the Kaffir war of 1846-47, and commanded the 1st Battalion in that of 1852-53 (Medal and Brevet Lt.-Colonel). Also commanded the 1st Battalion in the Eastern campaign of 1854, including the battles of the Alma, Balaklava, and Inkerman, and siege of Sebastopol (Medal and Clasps, *CB*., Sardinian Medal, and 5th Class of the Medjidie).

5 Colonel Macdonell served in the Kaffir war of 1846-47 (Medal). Also in the Eastern campaign of 1854 as Aide-de-Camp to Sir George Brown, and present at the affair of Bulganac, capture of Balaklava and battles of Alma and Inkerman ; commanded the 2d Battalion from May 1855 to the fall of Sebastopol, including the defence of the Quarries on 7th June, and assaults of the Redan on the 18th June and 8th Sept. (Medal and Clasps, Brevets of Major and Lt.Col., *CB*., Knight of the Legion of Honor, Sardinian Medal, and 5th Class of the Medjidie).

6 Sir Robert Walpole commanded a Brigade in the actions at Cawnpore in Nov. 1857, and afterwards a Division at the relief of Lucknow and subsequent operations under Lord Clyde (Medal and Clasp, and *CB*.).

7 Lt.-Col. Elrington served the Eastern campaign of 1854, including the battles of Alma and Inkerman, and siege of Sebastopol (Medal and Clasps, Brevet Major, Knight of the Legion of Honor, and 5th Class of the Medjidie).

8 Lord Alexander Russell served in the Kaffir war of 1852-53 (Medal) as D. A. Q. M. G. to the 1st Division, and was present at the battle of Berea: received the brevet rank of Major. Served also at the siege of Sebastopol from June 1855 (Medal and Clasp, Brevet Lt.-Colonel, Sardinian Medal, and 5th Class of the Medjidie).

9 Major Hardinge served in the Kaffir war from Nov. 1846 until its termination in 1847 ; and in that of 1852-53 (Medal). Also in the expedition against the insurgent Boers N. E. of the Great Orange River in Aug. 1848, when he was present and slightly wounded in the action at Boem Plaats. Served the Eastern campaign of 1854, including the battles of Alma and Inkerman, and siege of Sebastopol (Medal and Clasps, Brevet Major, and 5th Class of the Medjidie).

10 Lt.Col. Glyn served as Field Adjutant to the force under Sir Harry Smith in the action with and defeat of the rebel Boers at Boem Plaats (horse killed). Served in the Kaffir war of 1852-53 (Medal). Also the Eastern campaign as a Brigade Major and Assist.Adj.Gen. in the Light Division, including the battles of Alma and Inkerman, and siege of Sebastopol (Medal and Clasps, Brevets of Major and Lt.Col., Knight of the Legion of Honor, and 5th Class of the Medjidie). Served the Indian campaigns of 1857-59, including the defeat of the Gwalior Contingent at Cawnpore on 6th Dec., final capture of Lucknow, action at Nawabgunge (commanded Battalion) and subsequent operations (Medal and Clasp, and *CB*.). Commanded the 3d Battalion during the Indian Mutiny, including the Skirmish at Secundra, siege and capture of Lucknow and subsequent operations (Brevet of Colonel, Medal and Clasp).

Rifle Brigade. 347

11 Lt.Col. Fyers served in the 40th throughout the operations in Candahar and Affghanistan in 1841 and 1842 (Medal), and was present in the actions at Kale Shukh, Kunje Kuk, Pangwaie, Tiloo Khan, and Baba Wallie; also at the relief of Khelat-I-Ghilzee; subsequently at Killa Azlem, Goaine, Ghuznee, and occupation of Cabool; and in all the affairs in which the Candahar Division of the Army of Affghanistan, under General Nott, was engaged in its progress through the Khoord Cabool, Tezeen, Jugdulluck, and Khyber Passes. Served the Eastern campaign of 1854-55 with the 2nd Batt. Rifle Brigade, including the battle of Alma, siege and fall of Sebastopol, and attack on the Redan on 8th Sept. In October 1854 he commanded a party of Rifles and 23rd Fusiliers from Pickets of the Light Division, and repulsed an attack made by the enemy's riflemen on our pickets, and he commanded the covering party of 200 men on the attack of the Redan (Medal and Clasps, Brevets of Major and Lieut.Col., Knight of the Legion of Honor, and 5th Class of the Medjidie).

12 Major Walker served at the siege of Sebastopol from Jan. 1855 (Medal and Clasp, Brevet Major, and 5th Class of the Medjidie).

13 Major Edward Newdigate served the Eastern campaign of 1854, including the battles of Alma and Inkerman (wounded), and siege of Sebastopol (Medal and Clasps, Brevet Major, Knight of the Legion of Honor, and 5th Class of the Medjidie).

14 Major Hon. G. Elliot was Aide de Camp to Sir Geo. Cathcart in the Kaffir war of 1852-53 (Medal); and he was also present at the battle of Berea. Served the Eastern campaign of 1854-55 as D. A. Q. M. G. to the 4th Division, including the battle of Alma and siege of Sebastopol (Medal and Clasps, Brevet Major, Sardinian Medal, and 5th Class of the Medjidie).

15 Major Hon. W. J. Colville served in the Eastern campaign of 1854-55, including the battle of Alma, siege and fall of Sebastopol (Medal and two Clasps, Brevet Major, Knight of the Legion of Honor, Sardinian Medal, and 5th Class of the Medjidie).

16 Lt.Colonel Oxenden served on the Eastern Frontier of the Cape of Good Hope against the Kaffir Tribes in 1846-7-8 (Medal), and was engaged in the successful operations in the Amatola Mountains against Sandilli. Served at the siege and fall of Sebastopol from June 1855 (Medal and Clasp, and Brevet Major).

18 Major E. M. Buller served in the Kaffir war of 1846-47, and in that of 1852-53 (Medal).

19 Major Hon. James Stuart served in the Eastern campaign of 1854 (Medal and Clasp), including the battle of Alma and siege of Sebastopol, and commanded the covering party leading the attack on the Redan on the 18th June (Medal and Clasps, Brevet Major, Sardinian Medal, and 5th Class of the Medjidie).

20 Lt.Col. Hon. L. Curzon served in the Kaffir war of 1852-53 (Medal); also at the battle of Berea. Served the Eastern campaign of 1854-55 as Assistant Military Secretary to Lord Raglan, and afterwards to General Simpson (Medal and Clasps, Brevets of Major and Lt.-Col., Knight of the Legion of Honor, Sardinian Medal, and 5th Class of the Medjidie).

21 Major Ross served in the Eastern campaign, including the battles of Alma and Inkerman, and siege of Sebastopol until Feb. 1855 (Medal and Clasps, Brevet Major, and 5th Class of the Medjidie).

25 Major Warren served in the Eastern campaign of 1854-55, including the battle of Alma and siege of Sebastopol (Medal and Clasps, Brevet Major, and 5th Class of the M djidie).

28 Majors Nixon and H. R. L. Newdigate served in the Eastern campaign of 1854, including the battle of Alma (Medal and Clasps). Major Nixon has the 5th Class of the Medjidie.

28† Major Bourchier served in the Kaffir war of 1852-53 (Medal). Also in the Eastern campaign of 1854, including the battles of Alma, Balaklava, and Inkerman (as Aide de Camp to General Torrens), siege of Sebastopol, night attack and capture of the Ovens, where he succeeded to the command of the detachment of Riflemen on the death of Lieut. Tryon, for which he was mentioned in the Dispatches, and promoted Brevet Major (Medal and Clasps, Victoria Cross, Knight of the Legion of Honor, and 5th Class of the Medjidie). Served in the Indian campaign of 1857-58, including the siege and capture of Lucknow and battle of Nawabgunge (M dal and C.a-p).

29 Capt. Blackett served the Eastern campaign of 1854-55, including the battles of Alma, Balaklava, and Inkerman, and siege of Sebastopol; commanded a ladder party at the assault of the Redan on the 18th June (mentioned in Dispatches) and was dangerously wounded—left leg amputated (Medal and Clasps, and Knight of the Legion of Honor).

30 Captain Stephens served at the siege of Sebastopol from Jan. to April 1855 (Medal and Clasp).

31 Captain Windham served in the Eastern campaign, including the battles of Alma and Balaklava, and siege of Sebastopol until April 1855 (Medal and three Clasps).

34 Captain Cuninghame served the Eastern campaign of 1854-55, including the battles of Alma, Balaklava, and Inkerman, siege and fall of Sebastopol, attack and capture of the Rifle Pits on the night of 20th Nov. 54 (mentioned in Dispatches), and attack on the Ovens (Medal and four Clasps, Victoria Cross, and 5th Class of the M djidie).

35 Major Riverdale Glyn served the Eastern campaign of 1854-55 with the 8th Hussars, including Lord Cardigan's reconnaissance on the Danube, affairs of Bulganac, and M'Kenzie's Farm, battles of Alma, Balaklava, Inkerman, and Tchernaya, and siege of Sebastopol; promoted to a Company in the 1st Batt. Rifle Brigade in Aug. 1855, and served with the reserve at the storming of the Redan on the 8th Sept. (Medal and Clasps). Served the campaign of 1857-59 in India with the 2nd Battalion, including the siege and capture of Lucknow, and subsequent operations in Oude, and action of Nawabgunge, also the operations in the Nepaulese frontier (Medal and Clasp, and Brevet of Major).

36 Major Hon. L. W. Milles served with the 43rd Light Infantry in the Kaffir war in 1851-52 (Medal). Served in India during the rebellion of 1857-58, and was severely wounded at Cawnpore on the 28th Nov. 1857.

37 Major Dillon served with the 98th Regt. in the Punjaub campaign of 1848-49 (Medal), also with the Flank Companies in the force under Sir Colin Campbell at the forcing of the Kohat Pass in Feb. 1850.

37† Captain Earle served on the staff of Sir George Cathcart in the Kaffir war of 1851-53 (Medal).

38 Captain Brett served in the Kaffir war of 1846-47, and that of 1852-53 (Medal); and he was severely wounded at the battle of Boem Plaats in 1848. Served the Eastern campaign of 1854-55, including the battles of Alma and Inkerman and siege of Sebastopol (Medal and Clasps, and Knight of the Legion of Honor).

39 Captains Musgrave, J. P. C. Glyn, Rooper, and Tottenham, Lieuts. Ruthven and Nicholl, served at the siege of Sebastopol in 1855 (Medal and Clasp).

39† Captain Saunders served at the siege of Sebastopol from Jan. 1855, and was with the covering party leading the attack on the Redan on the 18th June (Medal and Clasp, Sardinian Medal, and 5th Class of the Medjidie).

40 Captain Lane and Lieut. Cragg served in the Eastern campaign of 1855, including the siege and fall of Sebastopol (Medal and Clasp).

41 Captains Moore and Playne, Lieuts. Eccles and Riley, served at the siege of Sebastopol in 1855, and were wounded at the attack on the Redan on the 8th Sept. (Medal and Clasp). Captain Moore has also the Sardinian Medal.

42 Paymaster Peacocke served in Kaffraria in the campaign of 1846; and with one of the columns which penetrated the Amatola Mountains in the Spring of 1847 (Medal). He served also with the troops under Sir Harry Smith which crossed the Orange River in 1848 to suppress the insurrection of the Dutch Boers, and was present in the action of Boem Plants. Served the Eastern campaign of 1854-55, including the battle of Alma, siege and fall of Sebastopol (Medal and Clasps).

43 Surgeon Bowen served in the Kaffir war of 1852-53 (Medal), and acted as Principal Medical Officer to the expedition against the Kaffir Chief Kreli, in Aug. 1852. Was shipwrecked in H. M. S. *Birkenhead* off Danger Point, Cape of Good Hope, 26th Feb. 1852. Served the Eastern campaign of 1854-55, including the battles of Alma and Inkerman and siege of Sebastopol (Medal and Clasps).

44 Assist.Surgeon Williams served the Eastern campaign of 1854-55, including the battles of Alma, Balaklava, and Inkerman, and siege of Sebastopol (Medal and Clasps).

348   *Rifle Brigade.*

45 Paymaster Large served in the Kaffir war of 1852-53 (Medal); also the Eastern campaign of 1854-55, including the battles of Alma and Inkerman, siege and fall of Sebastopol (Medal and Clasps).
46 Quarter Master Harvey served in the Eastern campaign, including the battles of Alma and Inkerman, and siege of Sebastopol until June 1855 (Medal and three Clasps, also the Medal for distinguished conduct in the Field).
47 Qr.Master Higgins served in the Kaffir war of 1846-47, and in that of 1852-53 (Medal). Also the Eastern campaign of 1854-55, including the battles of Alma, Balaklava, and Inkerman, and siege of Sebastopol (Medal and Clasps).
50 Doctor Scott served with the Rifle Brigade in the Kaffir war of 1852-53, including the expedition beyond the Kei in Aug. 1852, and the final clearing of the Waterkloof. Embarked with the Rifle Brigade and served throughout the Eastern campaign of 1854-55,—from March 1855 as Surgeon of the 41st Regt. (Medal and four Clasps, and 5th Class of the Medjidie).
51 Assist.Surgeon Reade served the Eastern campaign of 1854-55, including the battles of Alma and Inkerman, siege of Sebastopol, and sortie of 26th Oct. (Medal and Clasps).
52 Captain Fremantle served in the Eastern campaign from Nov. 1854 to June 1855, and was severely wounded in the attack of the Redan on the 18th June (Medal and Clasp, and Sardinian Medal).
53 Captain Singer served the Eastern campaign of 1854-55, including the battles of Alma and Inkerman, and siege of Sebastopol (Medal and Clasps, and 5th Class of the Medjidic).
54 Captain Knox served the Eastern campaign of 1854-55, including the battles of Alma, Balaklava, and Inkerman, siege of Sebastopol, repulse of the sortie on 26th Oct., and with the ladder party in the attack of the Redan on the 18th June (mentioned in Dispatches), when he was severely wounded by grape-shot—left arm amputated at the shoulder (Medal and Clasps, Victoria Cross, and Knight of the Legion of Honor).
55 Captain Coulson served with the Grenadier Guards at the siege of Sebastopol (Medal and Clasp).
56 Lieut. Sydney Carr Glyn served at the siege and fall of Sebastopol from 6th Sept. 1855, including the assault on the Redan on the 8th Sept. (Medal and Clasp).   It 57
57 Captain Clerk served at the siege of Sebastopol (Medal and Clasp).
58 Captain Wood served with the 30th Regt. at the siege and fall of Sebastopol from 20th May (Medal and Clasp).
59 Lieut. Sotheby served at the siege and fall of Sebastopol in 1855 and storming of the Redan of 8th Sept. (Medal and Clasp).
60 Lieut. Mildmay served the Eastern campaign of 1855, including the siege and fall of Sebastopol (Medal and Clasp).
61 Lieut. Hon. A. J. Pennington served on board H.M.S. *Bellerophon* as Midshipman at the bombardment of Sebastopol on 17th Oct. 1854 (Medal and Clasp).
62 Doctor de Chaumont served the Eastern campaign of 1854-55, including the siege and fall of Sebastopol (Medal and Clasp).
63 Doctor Cullen was attached to the 68th and 48th Regts. for nine months during the siege of Sebastopol; and was with the 4th Light Dragoons on the cavalry expedition to Eupatoria (Medal and Clasp).
70 Captain Harington served at the siege and fall of Sebastopol from the 8th Sept. 1855 (Medal and Clasp).
71 Lieut. Chalmers served in the Indian campaign of 1857-58, including the recapture of Cawnpore, siege and capture of Lucknow; also affairs of Koorsee and Nawabgunge under Sir Hope Grant; and latterly on the personal staff of that General (Medal and Clasp).
72 Ensign Cary served five years in the Royal Navy, and was on board H.M.S. *Albion* with the Black Sea fleet in 1854-55, including the bombardment of Sebastopol on 17 Oct. 1854 (Medal and Clasp).
74 Lieut. Travers served in the Indian campaign and was severely wounded at Cawnpore on the 27th Nov. 1857.

[*Continuation of Notes to 1st West India Regt.*]

2 Colonel O'Connor commanded a brigade of detachments,—1st, 2nd, and 3rd West India Regts.—Enrolled Pensioners, Royal Gambia Militia; Commander Bradshaw, officers, sailors, and marines of H.M.'s ship *Resistance*, against the Mahometan Rebels of Combo; stormed, captured, and totally destroyed the strongly stockaded town of Sabajee on the 1st June 1853, and acquired, by treaty, a valuable tract of territory; the sense entertained by H.M. Government of the very effective manner in which this service was performed by Colonel O'Connor and the officers and men under him was conveyed by the Duke of Newcastle in a despatch to Col. O'Connor. On the 17th July 1855, he attacked and repulsed a numerous force of Mahometans commanded by Omar Hadajee, the Black Prophet, on which occasion 29 men were killed, and 53 wounded, of 240 British, and Colonel O'Connor was severely wounded in the right arm and left shoulder. On 4th Aug. 1855, he commanded the combined British and French forces against the Mahometan rebels of Upper and Lower Combos, and after four hours' fighting in the Pass of Baccow Kouko, stormed their stockade, and totally routed the rebel forces, with a loss of 500 killed and wounded. For these services Colonel O'Connor was created a *CB.*, and placed on the list of officers receiving rewards for distinguished services.
4 Major Murray commanded the centre division of the brigade, and was engaged at the storming and capture of the stockades of Sabajee on 1st June 1853.
6 Major Fetcher commanded the detachments of the 1st and 3rd West India Regiments which destroyed the town of Malageah, Western Africa, in May 1855, but with severe loss, owing to the overwhelming force of the enemy.
9 Lieut. Strachan commanded a detachment of the 1st W. I. Regt. at Danish Accra, Gold Coast, during the Rebellion of 1854. He also commanded a division at the destruction of the large Mandingo town of Malcaghea, near Sierra Leone, 22nd May 1855, where, out of a force of 150 men, upwards of 70 men and 4 officers were killed or wounded.

1st West India Regiment of Foot. 349

"DOMINICA" "MARTINIQUE" "GUADALOUPE."

Years' Serv. Full Pay	Years' Serv. Half Pay					
56		Colonel.—🏵 ⚜ Sir George Bowles,¹ KCB. Ens. 20 Dec. 04; Lt. and Capt. 1 Feb. 10; Maj. 18 June 15; Lt.Col. 14 June 21; Col. 10 Jan. 37; Maj Gen. 9 Nov. 46; Lt.Gen. 20 June 54; Col. 1st W. I. Regt. 9 Sept. 55.				
33	0	Lt.Cols.—Luke Smyth O'Connor,² CB. Ens. ᴾ 27 Apr. 27; Lt. 22 Mar. 31; Capt. ᴾ 17 Jan. 34; Brev.Maj. 9 Nov. 46; Maj. 1 Jan. 47; Brev.Lt.Col. 3 Feb. 53; Col. 28 Nov. 54; Lt.Col. 21 Sept. 55.				
41	6/12	Henry Dunn O'Halloran, Ens. 1 Nov. 18; Lieut. ᴾ 28 June 27; Capt. ᴾ 1 Sept. 38; Brevet Major, 11 Nov. 51; Brevet Lieut.Col. 4 Feb. 53; Major, 23 Aug. 54; Col. 28 Nov. 54; Lt.Col. 26 Mar. 58.				
28	0	Majors.—Augustus Wm. Murray,⁴ Ens. ᴾ 28 Dec. 32; Lieut. ᴾ 28 Nov. 37; Capt. ᴾ 25 Nov. 42; Brev.-Major, 20 June 54; Major, 4 Dec. 57.				
18	1 6/12	Robert Follett Synge,⁵ Ens. ᴾ 20 Oct. 40; Lt. 26 Sept. 42; Capt. 6 June 54; Maj. ᴾ 15 June 58.				

		CAPTAINS.	ENSIGN.	LIEUT.	CAPTAIN.	BREV.-MAJ.
17	0	Richard D'Oyly Fletcher⁶	ᴾ 21 Apr. 43	ᴾ 19 Apr. 44	ᴾ 9 Apr. 47	26 Oct. 58
21	0	Robert Hughes	2 June 39	18 June 41	6 Apr. 48	17 July 59
18	0	Henry Anton	14 Jan. 42	3 Mar. 43	21 May 54	
11	0	Alexandre Bravo	ᴾ 6 July 49	ᴾ 15 Feb. 50	ᴾ 29 Sept. 54	
17	0	James Alexander Fraser	27 Oct. 43	ᴾ 8 Aug. 45	16 Mar. 55	
17	0	James Shortall Macauley	18 Aug. 43	18 Nov. 44	ᴾ 30 Nov. 55	
15	0	John Fanning	30 Dec. 45	6 Apr. 48	11 July 57	
7	0	Henry Francis Luke	ᴾ 13 May 53	ᴾ 17 Feb. 54	ᴾ 6 Nov. 57	
14	0	George Thorne	29 April 46	10 April 49	4 Dec. 57	
12	0	William James Ross	12 May 48	31 May 50	30 July 59	
5	0	James Dixon Mackenzie	10 Apr. 55	ᴾ 7 Nov. 56	ᴾ 7 Oct. 59	
5	0	William Alexander Dobie	6 April 55	ᴾ 24 Feb. 57	ᴾ 29 Nov. 59	

		LIEUTENANTS.			
12	0	Angus William Mackay	23 May 48	13 Jan. 51	
8	0	W. H. P. Fitz M. Strachan⁹	14 Feb. 52	ᴾ 25 Feb. 53	1 Sir George Bowles served in the north of Germany in 1805 and 6 under Lord Cathcart. Present at the siege and capture of Copenhagen in 1807. In the Peninsula from 1809 to 1814 (excepting the winters of 1810 and 11), and was present at the passage of the Douro; battles of Talavera, Salamanca, and Vittoria; sieges of Ciudad Rodrigo, Badajoz, Burgos, and San Sebastian; capture of Madrid; passages of the Bidassoa, Nivelle, Nive, and Adour; and the investment of Bayonne. Present at the battles of Quatre Bras and Waterloo, and at the capture of Paris. He has received the War Medal with six Clasps. 5 Major Synge served with the Cameronians on the China expedition (Medal), and carried the colors of the regiment at the repulse of the night attack on Ningpo, the attack and capture of Chapoo, the taking of Shanghae and Woosung, the storming of Chin Kiang Foo, and the operations before Nankin. [Notes continued on preceding page.]
6	0	Wm. Walker W. Johnston	4 Aug. 54	30 Mar. 55	
6	0	J. Richd. O'Meara Lawler	29 Dec. 54	6 July 55	
5	0	Thomas Edmunds	24 April 55	26 Oct. 55	
5	0	James Moffitt	17 Aug. 55	14 Sept. 56	
6	0	Christopher Fred. Holt	6 Jan. 54	22 June 55	
5	0	Alex. M. W. Samson	25 Sept. 55	31 Oct. 56	
5	0	C. Lionel John FitzGerald	15 Mar. 55	15 Jan. 56	
5	0	John M'Auley	1 Oct. 55	9 April 57	
5	0	Arthur Wm. C. Nowlan	2 Nov. 55	11 July 57	
5	0	Joseph Alexander Smith	7 Dec. 55	20 Aug. 57	
5	0	Augustus Sullivan	14 Dec. 55	30 Oct. 57	
4	0	Charles Pressly Pender	31 Oct. 56	15 Jan. 58	
4	0	Richard Brew	5 Dec. 56	30 Apr. 58	
4	0	Thomas George Mawe	12 Dec. 56	7 Sept. 58	
3	0	Cornelius O'Callaghan	30 Jan. 57	7 Dec. 58	
2	0	Arthur James Plunkett	26 Jan. 58	ᴾ 4 Feb. 59	
3	0	Herbert G. Panter, Adj.	1 May 57	18 Feb. 59	
3	0	William Ormsby	17 July 57	30 July 59	
3	0	Augustus Temple	23 Oct. 57	28 Aug. 59	
3	0	Thomas Bunbury Eames	30 Oct. 57	27 Sept. 59	
2	0	Joseph Bourke	26 Oct. 58	ᴾ 13 Dec. 59	

		ENSIGNS.		
2	0	George Fred. Gavin	19 Feb. 58	
2	0	Michael Clare Garsia	26 Mar. 58	
2	0	Francis Nolan	14 May 58	
1	0	Thomas Alphonso Cary	13 May 59	
1	0	Anthony Thos. Wilkinson	14 May 59	
1	0	Henry Hopewell Smith	22 July 59	
1	0	John Atkinson	30 Sept. 59	
1	0	Charles Francis Barry	30 Sept. 59	
1	0	James Sealy	28 Oct. 59	
1	0	Henry Charles Mansergh	15 Nov. 59	

7	0	Paymaster.—William Thomson, 28 Oct. 59; Q.M. 17 June 53.	
3	0	Adjutant.—Lieut. Herbert Gauntlett Panter, 23 Sept. 59.	
2	0	Instructor of Musketry.—Lieut. A. J. Plunkett, 26 Nov. 59.	
1	0	Quarter-Master.—Patrick Maloney, 18 Nov. 59.	
0	0	Surgeon.—James Davys, 4 Sept. 57; Assist.Surg. 9 Sept. 51.	
5	0	Assist.-Surgs.—Frederick Mackenzie Skues, 28 Feb. 55.	
5	0	James Kelly, 17 July 55.	
2	0	Patrick Barrett Kearney, 1 Nov. 58.	

Facings White.—*Agents*, Messrs. Cox & Co.

2nd West India Regiment of Foot.

Colonel.—₽ *Sir* Robert John Harvey,[1] CB., *Ens.* 8 Oct. 03; *Lt.* 24 Mar. 04; *Capt.* 2 Jan. 06; *Maj.* 25 July 11; *Lt.Col.* 21 June 13; *Col.* 22 July 30; *Maj.Gen.* 23 Nov. 41; *Lt.Gen.* 11 Nov. 51; *Gen.* 17 July 59; *Col.* 2d W. I. Regt. 15 June 48.

Lieut.Colonels.—Henry Wase Whitfeild, *Ens.* 13 Feb. 28; *Lt.* 28 Oct. 31; *Capt.* 15 April 42; *Maj.* 14 Feb. 53; *Lt.Col.* 3 Feb. 54; *Col.* 28 Nov. 54.

Thomas Gibbings, *Ens.* 15 Jan. 47; *Lieut.* 27 April 49; *Capt.* ᴾ 22 Oct. 52; *Major*, ᴾ 9 June 54; *Lieut.Col.* ᴾ 29 Apr. 56.

Majors.—James Owen Bovill,[3] *2nd Lieut.* ᴾ 23 Mar. 47; *Lieut.* ᴾ 20 Oct. 48; *Capt.* ᴾ 16 Dec. 53; *Major*, ᴾ 29 April 56.

Thomas Hardwick Smith,[9] *Ens.* 9 Feb. 49; *Lieut.* ᴾ 10 Dec. 52; *Capt.* ᴾ 19 Aug. 56; *Major*, ᴾ 7 May 58.

Years' Serv. Full Pay	Half Pay	CAPTAINS.	ENSIGN.	LIEUT.	CAPTAIN.	BREV.-MAJ.
57		*Colonel* (see above)				
32	0					
13	0					
13	0					
11	0					
23	0	Jas. Delamain Mends ..	ᴾ 3 Nov. 37	26 Oct. 39	29 July 47	26 Oct. 58
21	0	Wm. M'Carthy Murray..	22 Feb. 39	4 Aug. 41	1 July 51	
12	0	John Deane Reece......	ᴾ 29 Dec. 48	ᴾ 28 Aug. 49	ᴾ 28 Jan. 53	
20	0	Wm. Elliot Mockler[6]....	8 May 40	15 April 42	14 Feb. 53	
7	0	William Hill[8]...........	20 May 53	21 Sept. 54	ᴾ 30 Nov. 55	
16	0	George James Ivey	1 Nov. 44	15 Jan. 47	15 Mar. 56	
12	0	Richard Henry Willcocks	ᴾ 3 Nov. 48	13 May 53	ᴾ 17 July 57	
13	0	Rokeby S.Wilkinson Jones	13 Aug. 47	11 July 51	15 June 58	
12	0	James Lambert Byrne ..	14 Oct. 48	26 Dec. 51	15 Jan. 59	
15	0	Francis Delmahoy Wyatt	11 April 45	22 Aug. 49	10 Sept. 58	
6	0	Wm. C. O'Shaughnessy..	ᴾ 16 June 54	3 Aug. 55	ᴾ 30 Sept. 59	
4	0	John Bellamy	ᴾ 31 Oct. 56	ᴾ 30 June 57	ᴾ 20 Dec. 59	
		LIEUTENANTS.				
11	0	Lloyd R. Creak Drouet[5]..	9 Feb. 49	27 Apr. 52		
11	0	Horatio James Wise	28 April 49	14 Feb. 53		
8	0	William Davis[10].......	24 Aug. 52	ᴾ 18 Oct. 53		
7	0	James Kingsley Maunsell	20 Sept. 53	2 Feb. 55		
7	0	John Harger	12 Nov. 53	1 June 55		
5	0	S. Sewell Davenport ..	31 Jan. 55	11 May 55		
5	0	James Gerrard King	7 Sept. 55	ᴾ 14 Mar. 56		
5	0	M. Wm. Bidwell Edwardes	23 Oct. 55	17 Oct. 56		
5	0	Mchl. John Macnamara..	26 Oct. 55	15 May 57		
5	0	Charles T. Edwards	2 Nov. 55	30 June 57		
5	0	Martin Lynch........	14 Dec. 55	14 Aug. 57		
4	0	Charles Bury Cradock ..	9 May 56	16 Sept. 57		
4	0	William Henry McCoy..	24 Oct. 56	16 Oct. 57		
3	0	Henry Albert Platt	ᴾ 6 Jan. 57	26 Feb. 58		
5	0	Holwell Hely H. Walshe	3 July 55	ᴾ 7 July 57		
3	0	Francis Adam Knapp ..	ᴾ 1 July 57	ᴾ 7 May 58		
3	0	Charles Edward Russell .	24 Feb. 57	15 June 58		
5	0	Tho. Macmillan Fogo, *Adj.*	1 June 55	26 Feb. 56		
5	0	Ernest Theodore Evans..	15 Nov. 55	10 Sept. 58		
7	0	Robert Eyre	17 Oct. 57	22 Nov. 58		
7	0	Edward M'Mahon Forbes	7 Nov. 57	15 Jan. 59		
5	0	Arthur G. Smith	ᴾ 21 Dec. 55	17 Sept. 58		
5	0	George William Reade ..	31 Aug. 55	21 May 58		
		ENSIGNS.				
3	0	George Massy Studdert..	29 Dec. 57			
2	0	Lionel Lowdham Brett..	15 Jan. 58			
2	0	Robert Straker Turton ..	26 Feb. 58			
2	0	Sidney Watkin Williams	ᴾ 5 Mar. 58			
2	0	Fred. Ludwig Mathews..	ᴾ 28 May 58			
2	0	Henry Lowry.........	13 Aug. 58			
2	0	Charles D'Obree Bowers	26 Oct. 58			
2	0	Ambrose Madden	24 Dec. 58			
1	0	William Berry Drinan ..	13 May 59			
1	0	William George Gow	22 July 59			
1	0	George Fletcher Coward..	26 Aug. 59			

Paymaster.—William Neilson, 4 Dec. 57.
Adjutant.—*Lieut.* Thomas Macmillan Fogo, 28 Oct. 59.
Instructor of Musketry.—*Ensign* F. L. Mathews, 27 July 59.
Quarter Master.—Thomas Kelly, 2 Oct. 55.
Surgeon.—Richard Edward FitzGibbon, 22 July 56; *Assist.Surg.* 10 Jan. 51.
Assist.Surgs.—Charles Bagot, M.B. 15 Sept. 57.
Charles FitzRoy Somerset Macauley, 20 Apr. 59.
George Harman Harris, 22 June 58.

Facings Yellow.—**Agents,** *Sir* C. R. M'Grigor, *Bt.*, and W. M'Grigor, Esq.

---

1 Sir Robert Harvey served as Assistant-Quarter-Master-General of the British and of the Portuguese armies in Portugal, Spain, and France, from 1809 to the close of the war in 1814, and was present at the battles of the passage of the Douro and Busaco, second siege of Badajoz, siege and storm of Ciudad Rodrigo and Badajoz, battle of Salamanca, siege of Burgos, battles of Vittoria, Pyrenees (slightly wounded), Nivelle, Nive, Orthes, and Toulouse, besides numerous minor affairs. From 1809 to 1811 he was employed in procuring intelligence of the enemy in advance of the army, in organising nine Portuguese Guerilla Corps, the officers of which presented him with an elegant sword in testimony of his services with them; and in resisting the attempt of the enemy's passage of the Tagus at Chamusca. From 1811 to 1814 he was the organ of communication between the Duke of Wellington and the Portuguese troops. Sir Robert has received the Gold Medal for the battle of Orthes; the Silver War Medal with nine Clasps; and is a Commander of St. Bento d'Avis and Knight of the Tower and Sword of Portugal.

3 Major Bovill served with a detachment of 30 of the Ceylon Rifles, which defeated the insurgents in the first and second attack on Kornegalle on the 16th, 17th, and 18th Jan. 1836, in the general actions on the 10th and 31st July, during the suppression of the rebellion in the Kandian Provinces in 1848.

5 Lt. Drouet was present at the storm and destruction of the fortified Native Mandingo town of Sabajee on the Gambia, on the 1st June 1853.

6 Captain Mockler served as Captain in the Anglo-Spanish Legion, and was present in the operations on the heights of Ariaban in Alava on the 16th, 17th, and 18th Jan. 1836, 16th, 17th, 18th March in front of San Sebastian on the 5th May (Medal), 1st Oct. 1836, 10th, 15th, and 16th March (wounded), storm and capture of Irun 16th and 17th May 1837 (Medal), besides several skirmishes.

8 Captain Hill served with the 95th Regt. the Eastern campaign of 1854-55, including the battles of Alma and Inkerman, siege of Sebastopol, and sortie on the 26th Oct. (Medal and Clasps).

9 Major Smith served with the 18th Royal Irish in the Burmese war of 1852-53 (Medal); was present at the capture of Martaban, at the operations before Rangoon on the 12th, 13th, and 14th April, at the capture of Great Dagon Pagoda (with the storming party), and capture of Prome. Also served with a force detached for the purpose of clearing the right bank of the Irrawaddy of the enemy, from November 1852 to March 1853, against the town of Sabajee on the Gambia was employed as staff officer a considerable portion of the period.

10 Lieut. Davis commanded a party of the 2nd West India Regt. which was wounded on 16th July 1855, and was wounded.

3rd West India Regiment of Foot. 352

Years' Serv.			
Full Pay	Half Pay		
63		*Colonel.*—Ⓟ Wm. Wood,[1] CB. KH. *Ens.* 27 Jan. 97; *Lieut.* 27 Dec. 97; *Capt.* 3 Dec. 02; *Maj.* 14 May 07; *Lt.-Col.* 8 April 13; *Col.* 22 July 30; *Maj.-Gen.* 23 Nov. 41; *Lt.-Gen.* 11 Nov. 51; *Gen.* 31 Aug. 55; *Col.* 3rd West India Regt. 8 Feb. 49.	
18	0	*Lieut.-Colonels.*—Wm. John Chamberlayne, *Ens.* ᴾ 25 Nov. 42; *Lt.* 6 Dec. 44; *Capt.* 31 Aug. 54; *Major,* ᴾ 27 Jan. 57; *Lt.-Col.* ᴾ 19 Feb. 58.	
16	3 6/12	Henry Edward M'Gee,[2] *Ens.* ᴾ 4 Sept. 40; *Lieut.* ᴾ 3 Feb. 43; *Capt.* ᴾ 8 Aug. 45; *Major,* ᴾ 14 Apr. 54; *Bt.Lt.Col.* 12 Dec. 54; *Lt.Col.* 31 Aug. 55.	
18	0	*Majors.*—Edward Conran, *Qr.-M.* 2 Dec. 42; *Ens.* 17 Oct. 45; *Lt.* ᴾ 5 Nov. 47; *Capt.* ᴾ 4 Feb. 53; *Major,* ᴾ 15 May 55.	
11	0	Wm. Beverley Robinson, *Ens.* 27 Apr. 49; *Lieut.* 26 Aug. 51; *Capt.* ᴾ 24 Mar. 54; *Major,* ᴾ 26 Mar. 58.	

		CAPTAINS.	ENSIGN.	LIEUT.	CAPTAIN.	BREV.-MAJ.
26	0	Jas. Travers *l.c.* 25 Sept. 59	28 Nov. 34	29 July 36	15 Apr. 42	20 June 54
24	0	Rich. Plunket Ireland[5]..	23 Dec. 36	28 Dec. 38	17 July 49	
18	0	James Francis Birch, *s.* .	7 Jan. 42	30 Dec. 42	6 Apr. 55	
10	0	Fred. Geo. Nuttall Clarke	ᴾ 17 May 50	ᴾ 17 Oct. 51	ᴾ 15 May 55	
6	0	Alexander Dunlop......	ᴾ 9 June 54	24 April 55	ᴾ 29 Dec. 57	
6	0	Henry Rowland........	ᴾ 31 Aug. 54	24 Apr. 55	ᴾ 26 Mar. 58	
6	0	Wm. Rice Mulliner	ᴾ 1 Sept. 54	21 Sept. 55	ᴾ 26 Mar. 58	
13	0	William John Russwurm[7]	5 Feb. 47	28 April 49	13 Aug. 58	
13	0	Robert William Harley..	8 Oct. 47	29 April 49	1 Oct. 58	
5	0	Francis John Green	22 Nov. 55	ᴾ 15 Apr. 56	ᴾ 10 Dec. 58	
3	0	Fred. Wm. John Dugmore	ᴾ 16 June 57	ᴾ 20 Dec. 57	ᴾ 23 Sept. 59	
22	2	Henry Fred. Saunders[8]..	30 July 36	27 Dec. 37	18 Apr. 51	24 Mar. 58

		LIEUTENANTS.			
14	0	Parr W. Kingsmill, *Adj.*	7 Aug. 46	16 April 50	
12	0	Claudius Kerr	12 Sept. 48	5 June 51	
11	0	Henry James Rainsford[7] .	15 June 49	10 Sept. 51	
9	0	Thomas Maurice Quill[7]..	19 Aug. 51	14 Aug. 53	
7	0	Alfred Aug. Richardson..	18 Nov. 53	16 Mar. 55	
6	0	William Cody[10]	10 Nov. 54	19 Aug. 56	
5	0	Francis Shearman......	19 Jan. 55	5 Sept. 56	
5	0	James Bower Jackson ..	2 Nov. 55	ᴾ 17 Oct. 56	
5	0	Thomas Dunn	16 Oct. 55	16 June 57	
4	0	Francis Graham Dunn ..	15 Apr. 56	15 Jan. 58	
6	0	H.C. De la Poer Beresford	ᴾ 22 Sept. 54	ᴾ 30 June 57	
5	0	James John Plumridge[9]	24 Apr. 55	17 Nov. 57	
4	0	Ebenezer Rogers	24 Oct. 56	13 Aug. 58	
4	0	Thomas Davies Mahon ..	14 Nov. 56	1 Oct. 58	
2	0	Stephen George Allman..	5 Mar. 58	ᴾ 11 Feb. 59	
4	0	Wm. Aug. Trydell Helden	7 Mar. 56	23 Mar. 58	
2	0	John Moore	6 Aug. 58	ᴾ 1 Apr. 59	

		ENSIGNS.		
3	0	Duncan Forbes Murray..	1 May 57	
3	0	Thomas Francis Beamish	25 Aug. 57	
3	0	Robert John Stewart....	11 Sept. 57	
3	0	Richard Wilson	ᴾ 23 Oct. 57	
2	0	William Gavin..........	26 Jan. 58	
2	0	John Croly	15 Oct. 58	
1	0	Fred. Chandos Clifton ..	18 Jan. 59	
1	0	Richard Webster	11 Mar. 59	
1	0	T. Calclough M'Cormick	13 May 59	
1	0	Thomas Croft..........	ᴾ 22 July 59	
1	0	George Francis O'Grady .	23 July 59	
1	0	*Paymaster.*—William Henry Browning, 14 June 59.		
14	0	*Adjutant.*—Lieut. Parr Wm. Kingsmill, 28 May 54.		
5	0	*Instructor of Musketry.*—Lieut. James Bower Jackson, 19 Feb. 57.		
5	0	*Quarter-Master.*—Martin Doorly, 16 Oct. 55.		
14	7/12	*Surgeon.*—Deodatus William Eaton, 11 May 55; *Assist.Sury.* 24 Oct. 45.		
2	0	*Assist.-Surgs.*—John Gillespie Richardson, 10 Mar. 58.		
2	0	Hugh Deane Massy, 10 Mar. 58.		
2	0	William Declan Carbery, 5 Aug. 58.		

Facings Blue—*Agents,* Messrs. Downes & Son.

2 Lt. Colonel M'Gee served the Eastern campaign of 1854-55 with the 19th Regt., including the battles of Alma (wounded) and Inkerman, and siege of Sebastopol (Medal and three Clasps, Brevet Lt.Col., and 5th Class of the Medjidie).

1 General Wood served six years in the West Indies. Accompanied the expedition to Hanover in 1805. He next served the campaign of 1808-9, including the battle of Corunna. Subsequently at the siege of Flushing, he volunteered to storm the enemy's entrenchments, which he carried; and in November he was again sent to Walcheren to cover the embarkation of the troops when the island was evacuated. In 1810 he proceeded to the Mediterranean, where he served three years, and on being promoted, in 1813, to the Lieut.-Colonelcy of the 85th, he joined the army in Spain. In 1814 he accompanied the 85th to America, and commanded it at the battle of Bladensburg, where he received four severe wounds, had a horse shot under him, and was obliged to surrender himself as a prisoner of war. He has received the War Medal with one Clasp for Corunna. On 14th March 1841 he was appointed Commander of the Forces in the Windward and Leeward Islands, where he served the usual period of five years.

10 Lieut. Cody served with the Royals during the Canadian rebellion of 1837-38, including the affairs of St. Charles and St. Eustache.

5 Capt. Ireland accompanied an expedition 80 miles up the Gambia in 1849, on which service he commanded a field battery of artillery, consisting of three light six-pounders, two three-pounders, and a howitzer, having personally trained the men and horses for the occasion, and was most favourably mentioned in the public Dispatches, and recommended for promotion. He was also at the storm and destruction of the town of Bumbacoo, and in the subsequent engagements with the enemy.

7 Captain Russwurm, Lieuts. Rainsford and Quill, were present at the storm and destruction of the fortified native Mandingo town of Sabajee on the Gambia, on the 1st June 1853.

8 Major Saunders served on the west coast of Africa from 1836 to 1841,—present with the expeditionary force in the Interior in 1837; employed on a mission to convey Dispatches to the French at Senegal in 1838; commanded the troops at a riot up the Gambia in 1838, and whilst at night patrolling captured a gun. Was attached to the 64th Regt. at Cawnpore in Nov. 1857, and 9 Lieut. Plumridge served with the 9th Regt. at the siege and fall of Sebastopol (Medal and Clasp).

8 Major Saunders ... mentioned in the Dispatches as having distinguished himself (Brevet Major and Medal).

353 Ceylon Rifle Regiment.

Years' Serv. Full Pay	Years' Serv. Half Pay					
27	0	*Lieut.Colonel.*—William Twisleton Layard,[1] *2nd Lt.* ᴾ 22 Feb. 33; *Lt.* ᴾ 22 Nov. 36; *Capt.* ᴾ 16 Aug. 39; *Maj.* ᴾ 28 Sept. 47; *Bt.Lt.Col.* 28 Nov. 54; *Lt.Col.* 12 June 50.				
30	0	*Majors.*—James Mitchell Macdonald,[2] *2nd Lt.* 26 Oct. 30; *Lt.* ᴾ 29 July 36; *Capt.* ᴾ 9 May 45; *Brev.Maj.* 6 June 56; *Maj.* ᴾ 4 Mar. 59; *Bt.Lt.Col.* 26 Apr. 59.				
21	0	William Charles Vanderspar, *2nd Lt.* ᴾ 16 Aug. 39; *Lt.* 9 Oct. 42; *Capt.* ᴾ 28 Sept. 47; *Brev.Maj.* 23 Nov. 58; *Major*, ᴾ 20 Dec. 59.				
		CAPTAINS.	ENSIGN.	LIEUT.	CAPTAIN.	BREV.-MAJ.
23	3	Lionel Hook[4]	5 Sept. 34	4 Dec. 38	27 April 49	
17	0	Edw. Frederick Tranchell	30 May 43	20 June 45	28 Jan. 53	
13	0	Richard Henry Brook[6]..	15 Jan. 47	13 Sept. 51	ᴾ 10 Aug. 55	
13	0	Alex.Maxwell Rutherford[6]	16 Jan. 47	30 July 52	ᴾ 15 Apr. 56	
11	0	Rupert Campbell Watson	9 Mar. 49	21 Sept. 54	ᴾ 27 June 56	
18	0	David Stewart[7]	7 Nov. 42	ᴾ 11 Nov. 45	29 Aug. 56	
8	0	James Meaden	27 Feb. 52	ᴾ 10 Aug. 55	ᴾ 15 May 57	
15	0	Geo. Adolphus Tranchell	20 June 45	9 Jan. 47	23 Apr. 58	
5	0	Chas. Hamilton Roddy ..	8 June 55	ᴾ 7 Mar. 56	ᴾ 24 Sept. 58	
8	0	Henry Edward Watson..	ᴾ 17 Dec. 52	9 Nov. 55	ᴾ 25 Jan. 59	
13	0	Wm. Joseph Gorman	13 Jan. 47	12 Sept. 51	12 June 59	
11	0	James Campbell Fielding	10 Apr. 49	16 Mar. 55	15 Aug. 59	
9	0	B. Cha.Wm. C. Bloxsome[8]	ᴾ 18 Apr. 51	6 June 54	23 July 58	
6	0	Thos. Geo. O'D. Hervey	13 Oct. 54	29 Aug. 56	ᴾ 20 Dec. 59	
		LIEUTENANTS.				
9	0	Gother Mann Parsons ..	17 Oct. 51	17 Aug. 55	8 Captain Bloxsome served with the 9th Regt. in the Crimea from 27th Nov. 1854 and was present at the siege and fall of Sebastopol and assault of the batteries on the 18th June (Medal and Clasps).	
5	0	Frederick Blair Staples..	24 Apr. 55	ᴾ 1 Aug. 56		
5	0	Charles Lynott	6 July 55	ᴾ 12 Sept. 56		
5	0	John James Cahill Miller	27 July 55	ᴾ 15 May 57		
5	0	William Guy, *Adj*......	28 Aug. 55	ᴾ 26 Jan. 58		
5	0	Benj. Stephen Du Jardin	5 July 55	23 Apr. 58		
5	0	Orby Montgomery Hunter	ᴾ 17 Aug. 55	23 July 58		
5	0	Andrew Murray Walker	30 Aug. 55	23 July 58		
5	0	Francis Archibald Stewart	31 Aug. 55	ᴾ 24 Sept. 58		
5	0	Wm. Biddulph Pinchard	31 Aug. 55	15 Oct. 58		
5	0	Thomas Gash..........	18 July 55	ᴾ 10 Apr. 57		
3	0	Fenton Josiah Hort	ᴾ 15 May 57	ᴾ 4 Feb. 59		
4	0	Arthur Hansard........	25 Mar. 56	12 June 59		
3	0	Joseph Albert Denton ..	6 Jan. 57	15 Aug. 59		
3	0	Charles Mesham	ᴾ 16 Oct. 57	ᴾ 20 Dec. 59		
		ENSIGNS.		4 Captain Hook served with the 9th Regt. throughout the campaign of 1842 in Affghanistan (Medal), under Sir George Pollock, and was present at the forcing of the Khyber Pass, storming of Mamookail, storming the heights of Jugdulluck, affair in the Tezeen Valley, storming of the Tezeen and Huft Kotul Mountains, occupation of Cabool, expedition into Kohistan, storm, capture, and destruction of Istaliff. He served as Adjutant of the 9th Regt. the campaign of 1845-6 on the Sutlej, and was present in the battles of Moodkee, Ferozeshah (horse shot under him), and Sobraon, for which he has received a Medal and two Clasps. 12 Ensign Arrowsmith served with the 31st Regt. at the siege of Sebastopol from 22d May to 15th Aug. 1855 (Medal and Clasp).		
3	0	Guy Wm. Fred. L'Estrange	ᴾ 23 Oct. 57			
2	0	Fred. Thomas Tegart....	ᴾ 26 Jan. 58			
2	0	John James	30 Mar. 58			
2	0	Henry Dickson Demain	23 Apr. 58			
2	0	Francis Pearson Murray..	ᴾ 6 Aug. 58			
2	0	Michael Joseph Tighe ..	7 Sept. 58			
2	0	Fred. Chenevix Baldwin	24 Sept. 58			
2	0	Thomas Fletcher Roddy	ᴾ 5 Oct. 58			
2	0	Henry Whalley Mellis ..	6 Oct. 58			
2	0	J. Williams Arrowsmith[12]	9 Nov. 58			
1	0	Alfred Randall	19 July 59			
1	0	Edward Negus Wood....	ᴾ 22 July 59			
1	0	John Glover	26 Aug. 59			
8	0	*Paymaster.*—Henry Dudley, 5 Mar. 52.				
5	0	*Adjutant.*—Lieut. William Guy, 1 Oct. 58.				
12	0	*Quarter-Master.*—Thomas Miller,[13] 8 July 53; *2nd Lieut.* 11 Feb. 48.				
19	0	*Surgeon.*—Henry Lionel Cowen, 5 May 54; *Assist.-Surg.* 17 June 41.				
6	0	*Assist.-Surgs.*—Joseph John Thompson, 14 July 54.				
6	0	Edward Gregg Noott,[14] 10 Feb. 54.				

Regimentals *Green*—Facings Black.—*Agent*, Sir John Kirkland.

1 Lt.-Colonel Layard was in the Royal Navy for nearly four years before he entered the Army, and served in the Burmese war, having been present at the taking of Rangoon, the capture of Syriam, and various other engagements; after which he accompanied the combined Naval and Military Expedition up the Bassein River, and was present at the capture of Negrass and Bassein; has received the Medal for Ava. Commanded the troops in the district of Korneagalle, Ceylon, during the Rebellion of 1848.
2 Lt Col. Macdonald commanded a detachment consisting of a Company of the 37th Regt. and half a Company of the Ceylon Rifles in Korneagalle, during the Rebellion in the Kandian Provinces, Ceylon, in 1848.
6 Captains Brook and Rutherford served with Capt. Lillie's detachment in defeating the insurgents at Matalé, on 29th July, during the suppression of the Rebellion in the Kandian Provinces in 1848.
7 Captain Stewart was present with the " Buffs" in the battle of Punniar, and has received the Bronze Star.
13 Quartermaster Miller served with the 98th with the Expeditionary Force in the river Yang-tze-Kiang in China (Medal), and was present at the capture of Chinklangfoo, and at the investment of Nankin.
14 Assist.Surgeon Noott served with the 50th Regt. in the Crimea from the landing up to 16th Nov. 1854, and again from 7 July 1855, including the battles of Alma and Inkerman, siege and fall of Sebastopol (Medal and Clasps).

Cape Mounted Riflemen. 354

"CAPE OF GOOD HOPE."

Years' Serv. Full Pay.	Half Pay.	
		Lieut.Colonels.—Robert Newport Tinley,[1] *Ens.* 4 April 32; *Lieut.* p 19 July 33;
28	0	*Capt.* p 15 Dec. 40; *Brev.Major*, 11 Nov. 51; *Major*, p 10 Feb. 52; *Lt.Col.* 9 Mar. 55; *Col.* 28 May 58.
34	0	George Staunton,[2] *Ens.* p 5 Oct. 26; *Lt.* p 15 Feb. 31; *Capt.* p 8 June 39; *Maj.* p 28 Mar. 45; *Lt.Col.* p 20 July 49; *Col.* 28 Nov. 54.
33	0	**Majors.**—Thomas Donovan,[3] *Ens.* 15 Mar. 27; *Lieut.* 16 May 33; *Capt.* 19 Nov. 41; *Br.Maj.* 15 Sept. 48; *Maj.* 11 Nov. 51; *Br.Lt.Col.* 31 Aug. 55.
15	0	George Jackson Carey,[4] *Ens.* p 22 July 45; *Lieut.* 1 Apr. 47; *Capt.* p 6 Oct. 48; *Maj.* p 28 Jan. 53; *Brev.Lt.Col.* 28 May 53; *Col.* 28 Nov. 54.

		CAPTAINS.	ENSIGN.	LIEUT.	CAPTAIN.	BREV.MAJ.
23	0	J. Armstrong,[6] c. 28 Nov. 54	p 28 Oct. 37	7 Feb. 40	8 Jan. 47	22 Dec. 48
25	0	Thomas Hare[7]	27 Mar. 35	6 Nov. 38	1 Apr. 47	26 Oct. 58
21	0	Frederick Campbell[8]	2 Mar. 39	16 Feb. 41	1 Apr. 47	26 Oct. 58
20	0	J. J. Bisset,[9] c. 28 Nov. 54, s.	7 Feb. 40	16 Feb. 44	1 Apr. 47	15 Sept. 48
15	0	Arnold More Knight[10]	p 14 Feb. 45	29 Jan. 46	p 16 Nov. 49	
16	0	John M'Donnell[11]	p 28 June 44	8 Jan. 47	11 Nov. 51	
14	0	Charles Van Notten Pole	never	p 14 Aug. 46	p 24 Aug. 52	
17	0	Chas. Harland Bell[12]	24 Mar. 43	2 Sept. 44	p 2 Mar. 55	6 June 56
12	0	Ralph Lovel Thursby[13]	p 1 Aug. 48	p 14 May 52	p 14 Dec. 55	
15	0	James Fischal Boyes[14]	3 Jan. 45	22 Jan. 47	10 Apr. 57	
14	0	John Harvey[15]	25 Aug. 46	1 Apr. 47	23 Mar. 58	
12	0	Thomas John Lucas	p 6 Oct. 48	p 28 Jan. 53	p 1 July 59	
		LIEUTENANTS.				
5	0	Jno. Theodore Cartwright	p 2 Feb. 55	p 5 Sept. 56		
5	0	Christopher Jno. Barnard	p 6 Apr. 55	p 5 Sept. 56		6 Colonel Armstrong was appointed Provisional Ens. C. M. Rifles 19th Mar. 1835, and served throughout the Kaffir war of that period. He was present in the attack on the Amatola April 1846, and served on the Staff of Major General Somerset during the war of that period, as Field Adjutant, and subsequently as Aide de Camp, and was present at the action of the Gwanga. Commanded three squadrons of the C. M. Rifles under Sir Harry Smith against the rebel Boers over the Orange River, and was in the action at Boom Plaats 29th August 1848, where he was severely wounded, and had his horse shot under him, for which he received the rank of Brevet Major. Was selected by Sir Harry Smith to form and command a corps of Irregular Horse ("Armstrong's Horse") during the war of 1852-3, and was on several occasions mentioned in general orders, having commanded detachments in various successful affairs against the enemy, for which he received the rank of Brevet Lieut.Colonel (Medal).
8	0	Richard Rorke	18 June 52	24 Feb. 57		
6	0	Edward Alexander Lynar	10 Mar. 54	15 May 57		
6	0	Charles B. Marshall, *Adj.*	p 7 June 54	15 Jan. 58		
5	0	Wm. Erskine Woodrooffe	9 Mar. 55	15 Jan. 58		
5	0	William Nicolson	20 July 55	12 Feb. 58		
5	0	Duncan C. L. Fitzwilliams	2 Nov. 55	p 12 Feb. 58		
5	0	Talbot de Bashall Hughes	30 Nov. 55	23 Mar. 58		
5	0	H. R. Morin Humphreys	21 Dec. 55	30 Mar. 58		
4	0	Edward Yewd Brabant	p 13 June 56	p 11 Mar. 59		
4	0	Charles Currie	p 27 Sept. 56	p 1 July 59		
4	0	James Henry Randell	p 30 Sept. 56	p 23 Sept. 59		7 Major Hare served in the Kaffir war during 1847 (Medal).
		ENSIGNS.				
4	0	Chas. Harrington Harris	p 26 Sept. 56			
4	0	DeLacy R. F. Wooldridge	21 Nov. 56			
3	0	Walter J. Wyatt	24 Feb. 57			
3	0	Thomas Herrick	p 22 May 57			
2	0	Tho. H. V. Dalrymple Hay	p 26 Jan. 58			
2	0	Charles Henry Marillier	12 Feb. 58			
2	0	Cha. Jas. M. Hallewell	13 Feb. 58			
2	0	George Lidwill Harnette	p 16 July 58			
1	0	William Henry Salis	13 May 59			
1	0	Arthur Hales	p 18 Oct. 59			
1	0	Hamilton Sabine Pasley	p 16 Dec. 59			
1	0	Edward Vanrenen	p 20 Dec. 59			
7	0	*Paymaster.*—John Gregory Gurney, 6 May 53.				
6	0	*Adjutant.*—*Lieut.* Charles B. Marshall, 18 April 56.				
2	0	*Instructor of Musketry.*—*Ens.* C. H. Marillier, 7 Sept. 58.				
4	10/12	*Quarter Master.*—John Landrey, 5 Feb. 58; *Cor.* 1 Dec. 55; *Lt.* 1 Apr. 57.				
5	0	*Riding Master.*—Clark Morris, 5 June 55.				
15	0	*Surgeon.*—Alex. George Montgomery, *A.S.* 9 Dec. 45; *Surgeon*, 2 Oct. 57.				
3	0	*Assist. Surgeons.*—Edward L'Estrange, M.D. 15 Sept. 57.				
2	0	Henry Knaggs, 22 Apr. 58.				
21	0	*Veterinary Surgeon.*—John Kingsley, 29 March 39; *1st Class*, 1 July 59.				

Regimentals Green.—*Facings* Black.—*Agent*, Sir John Kirkland.

1 Colonel Tinley served the campaign against the Rajah of Coorg in 1834. He was also present in the battle of Maharajpore, 29th Dec. 1843 (Medal), and was severely wounded. Served at the siege and fall of Sebastopol in 1855; commanded the 30th Regt. in the attack on the 18th June; and commanded the trench guard, left attack, where a strong sortie of 2,000 Russians was made against the chevaux de frise, Woronzoff Road, on the night of the 2nd Aug., and which was successfully repulsed; also present at the attack on the 8th Sept. (Medal and Clasp, Knight of the Legion of Honor, and 5th Class of the Medjidie).

2 Colonel Staunton served with the 10th Regt. in the Sutlej campaign in 1846, including the battle of Sobraon (Medal). Commanded the 31st Regt. in the Crimea from 22nd May 1855, and was present at the siege of Sebastopol and attacks on the Redan on the 18th June and 8th Sept.; commanded 2nd Brigade 4th Division as a Brigadier General from 13th Nov. (Medal and Clasp, Knight of the Legion of Honor, Sardinian Medal, and 4th Class of the Medjidie).

3 Lt.Col. Donovan served against the Fiteani tribe in 1828 under Colonel Somerset. Commanded an advanced post in the Neutral territory, Cape of Good Hope, in 1832 and 33. Served against the insurgent Boers in 1845. Was actively employed throughout the whole of the Kaffir war of 1846 and 47 (Medal), and commanded the advanced guard in forcing the passage of the Fish River Jungle from Fort Peddie to Trompeter's Dritt in May 1846, when the troops were engaged with the whole of Pato's tribe for upwards of three hours: previous to the action on the Gwanga he led as a volunteer a small party into the jungle, where

he had a personal rencontre with four armed Kaffirs (the Chief Zeto and one of his Captains being of the party), two of whom he slew single-handed. For the above services he received the brevet rank of Major. Commanded the troops in the Sovereignty during the Kaffir war of 1851-53; crossed the Orange River in Feb. 1851 (effecting the passage with guns, wagons, &c., in a temporary boat constructed on the occasion) to assist in the protection of the Albert District, and on the 28th March following, with one troop Cape M. Rifles, one six-pounder, and a small Burgher force, defeated a large body of Tambookies and Basutos, under the chiefs Moocrose, Umhali, and Spepere, leaving upwards of 300 of the enemy dead on the field.

4 Colonel Carey served throughout the Kaffir war of 1846 and 47, during which he had a horse wounded under him. Also throughout the war of 1850-52 (Medal), in which he was slightly wounded, and had a horse killed under him. For the above services he was promoted to the Brevet rank of Lt.Col.

8 Major Campbell served as a volunteer, and afterwards as a provisional ensign in the Cape M. R. throughout the Kaffir campaign of 1835 (Medal). In 1844 he proceeded in command of a troop to Port Natal, and was engaged against the revolted Zoolu chief Todo. In Sept. 1848 he commanded three squadrons at Bloom Fountain, and advanced to Wimburgh for the suppression of the Dutch Boor rebellion. Served throughout the Kaffir war of 1851-52-53, including the operations in the Amatolas, passage of and operations across the Kei in Dec. 1852, and other desultory operations. Commanded a squadron with the force under Sir George Cathcart against the Baralong Chief Mosesh, in Dec. 1852 and Jan. 1853, which service concluded the war. He received a serious injury while actively engaged against the enemy at Buffalo Post, 27 Feb. 1852, by the dislocation of the right ankle and fracture of the bone of the leg.

9 Colonel Bisset served through the Kaffir war of 1835-6, as a volunteer, and as Ensign and Lieut. in a battalion of Native Infantry. He was Field Adjutant to a division of troops proceeding to Colesberg in Dec. 1842 to suppress a rebellion of the Boers. He served through the Kaffir war of 1845-6-7, at the commencement of which he was appointed Deputy Assist. Qr.Master General. Was present at the battle of the Gwanga, and all the minor affairs with the Kaffirs, and was twice slightly wounded. He was repeatedly thanked in General Orders by successive General Officers, and finally received the brevet of Major for his services during the campaign. At the close of the war, he was appointed Brigade Major of British Kaffraria; and on the breaking out of the war in 1850 he was severely wounded in the first engagement with the enemy in the Amatola Mountains (Medal).

10 Capt. Knight served the Sutlej campaign of 1845-46 with the 16th Lancers, and was present at the affair of Buddiwal, and in the battles of Aliwal and Sobraon (Medal and Clasp). Served in the Kaffir was of 1847, with the 7th Dragoon Guards, when he commanded the Cavalry Escort of Sir Harry Smith. Also during the Kaffir war of 1851-3 (Medal) with the Cape M. Riflemen, including the action of Berea. Served again on the Staff of Sir Harry Smith, and subsequently on that of his successor, Sir George Cathcart.

11 Capt. M'Donnell served throughout the Kaffir war of 1846-47 (Medal), during which he commanded several successful skirmishing parties. Led the successful attack under Sir George Berkeley against a large body of Kaffirs posted in one of their strongest positions at the Sohoto Mountain, where they treacherously murdered Major Baker and four other officers two days previously. Was present in the action with and defeat of the insurgent Boers at Boom Plaats 29th Aug. 1848, and on Major Armstrong being severely wounded he commanded the Cape M. Riflemen during the latter part of the engagement.

12 Major Bell served throughout the Kaffir war of 1850-52 (Medal) on the staff of Major General Somerset, commanding the 1st Division, and was present in every engagement with the division; commanded a detachment of Cape Mounted Rifles at the Kaffir attack on Fort Hare and Alice, 21 Jan. 1851, when the enemy were repulsed with great loss.

13 Captain Thursby served in the Kaffir war of 1850-53 (Medal), and was severely wounded in action on the Fish River Bush 9th Sept. 1851.

14 Captain Boyes served throughout the Kaffir war of 1846-47, including the action of the Gwanga (Medal).

15 Captain Harvey served with the Cape Mounted Riflemen on several commandos against the Kaffir tribes, between 1827 and 1831. Throughout the Kaffir war of 1834-35 including the engagement in Bushman River Ports 15th Jan. 1835, several others in the Trompeter's Port, pursuit and capture of the Chief Boko. Served with Colonel Somerset's division during the Kaffir war of 1846, and present at every engagement in which the division was in, including the battle of the Gwanga. Acted as Adjutant to a detachment C. M. R. under Colonel Napier, in the Kaffir war of 1850-53 (Medal).

Royal Canadian Rifle Regiment. 356

Years' Serv. Full Pay	Years' Serv. Half Pay					
27	0	*Colonel.*—The Lieut.General Commanding the Forces in Canada, for the time being.				
25	4½	*Lt.Col.*—Wilmot Henry Bradford,[1] *Ensign*, P 24 May 33; *Lieut.* P 26 Aug. 36; *Capt.* P 27 Aug. 41; *Major*, P 8 Aug. 51; *Lt.Col.* 29 Dec. 54.				
		Majors.—FitzWilliam Walker, *Ens.* P 31 Dec. 30; *Lieut.* P 17 June 36; *Capt.* P 21 June 39; *Brev.Maj.* 11 Nov. 51; *Major*, 19 Feb. 58; *Bt.Lt.Col.* 26 Oct. 58.				
13	0	Kenneth Mackenzie Moffatt, *Ens.* P 5 Nov. 47; *Lieut.* P 2 Apr. 50; *Capt.* P 29 Dec. 54; *Major*, P 24 Sept. 58.				

		CAPTAINS.	ENSIGN.	LIEUT.	CAPTAIN.	BREV.-MAJ.
19	0	William Henry Sharpe	22 July 41	14 Apr. 46	17 Aug. 55	
17	0	Charles Walter Grange[2]	P 3 Nov. 43	P 2 May 45	P 31 Dec. 47	1 May 59
14	0	Windsor Henry Humphreys	P 24 July 46	P 29 Oct. 47	P 21 Sept. 55	
9	0	Francis Gordon Hibbert[3]	5 April 51	P 23 Nov. 52	P 8 June 58	
19	0	John Weyland	23 July 41	14 Apr. 46	19 Feb. 58	
18	0	Edward Benjamin Wilson	14 Jan. 42	14 Apr. 46	19 Feb. 58	
11	0	George Mignan Innes	P 20 Aug. 49	9 Aug. 54	19 Feb. 58	
10	0	John Barton Taylor[4]	P 12 June 50	P 13 Dec. 53	P 11 Dec. 57	
9	0	Henry Basil Houson	P 22 Nov. 51	P 7 June 45	P 19 Sept. 56	
6	0	William Fleming Marson	P 29 Dec. 54	P 14 Dec. 55	P 9 Nov. 58	
13	1¾	Henry Elliott Bayly	14 Apr. 46	11 Oct. 49	P 1 Dec. 54	
7	0	John Shuter Davenport M'Gill[5]	P 16 Dec. 53	23 Mar. 55	P 14 May 58	
		LIEUTENANTS.				
8	0	Winnicett Lockhart Melville	20 Oct. 52	6 June 54		
5	0	John Fellows Armstrong	12 Feb. 55	25 May 55		
5	0	Robert Persse	6 July 55	19 Feb. 58		
5	0	Philip Chas. Coffin Savago	20 July 55	19 Feb. 58		
4	0	Alexander Moore Armstrong	8 Jan. 56	26 Feb. 58		
4	0	Richard William Barrow	P 2 May 56	26 Feb. 58		
5	0	George Traill Munro	5 June 55	15 Jan. 58		
4	0	William Henry Surman	P 25 Jan. 56	15 Jan. 58		
2	0	Edward Whyte	30 Mar. 58	P 8 Apr. 59		
3	0	George John Chas. Whittington	P 14 July 57	P 23 Apr. 58		
5	0	Mortimer James Macdonald	P 9 Nov. 55	2 July 58		
5	0	Fred. Herbert Suckling[6]	29 Mar. 55	29 June 55		
4	0	Thomas Merrett	15 Jan. 56	23 Mar. 58		
4	0	Arthur Bambrick Mitchell	2 May 56	20 Dec. 59		
		ENSIGNS.				
2	0	Fred. John Atkinson Dunn	1 April 58			
2	0	David Miller, *Adj.*	16 Apr. 58			
2	0	Ernest C. Wilford	17 Apr. 58			
2	0	Thomas Harman Bond	30 April 58			
3	0	Thomas Bradley Thornett[7]	23 May 57			
2	0	Edw. Rodney Cecil Pechell	28 May 58			
2	0	Wm. Tho. Philippe Bernard	25 June 58			
1	0	Thomas Henry Selwyn Donovan	3 June 59			

2 Major Grange served as an officer of Militia in Canada during the suppression of the insurrection, and was present at the siege of Navy Island. He commanded the Enrolled Pensioners in the expedition against the king of Kenung up the Gambia in May 1849. He also commanded the detachments of the 1st and 3rd W. I. Regts. in the Expedition sent up the river Sherebro with H. M. S. *Alert* and *Pluto* in June and July 1849.

8 Paymaster Bernard served in the Crimea with the 82nd Regiment from 2nd September 1855 (Medal with Clasp for Sebastopol.

9 Doctor Rambaut was present at the defeat of the insurgents at Matolo on the 29th July, during the suppression of the rebellion in the Kandian Provinces in Ceylon in 1848.

10 Assist.Surgeon Meadows served with the 9th Regt. in the Crimea from Dec. 1854, including the siege and fall of Sebastopol, and assault of the batteries on the 18th June (Medal and Clasp).

19	0	*Paymaster.*—Luke FitzGerald Bernard,[8] 8 Dec. 48; *Ens.* P 6 Aug. 41; *Lieut.* P 3 May 44.
2	0	*Adjutant.*—Ensign David Miller, 16 April 58.
2	0	*Instructor of Musketry.*—Ensign Ernest C. Wilford, 23 Feb. 59.
3	0	*Quarter Master.*—Abraham Cook, 12 May 57.
13	0	*Surgeon.*—John Rambaut,[9] M.D. 20 July 55; *Assist.Surg.* 29 Jan. 47.
6	0	*Assistant Surgeons.*—Robert Wyatt Meadows,[10] 26 May 54.

Regimentals Green.—*Facings* Scarlet.—*Agent*, Sir John Kirkland.

1 Lt.Colonel Bradford served the Eastern campaign of 1854, including the battle of Alma (Medal and Clasp, and 5th Class of the Medjidie).
3 Captain Hibbert served in the Kaffir War of 1851-53, and was wounded in action at Waterkloof on 4 March 1852 (Medal).
4 Captain Taylor served with the 9th Regt. in the Crimea from 16th Feb. 1855, including the siege and fall of Sebastopol, and assault of the batteries on the 18th June (Medal and Clasp).
5 Captain M'Gill served with the 60th Rifles in the campaign of 1857 against the Mutineers in India, including the actions on the Hindun, battle of Budlee ke Serai and forcing the heights before Delhi, the subsequent siege operations, assault and capture of the City with the final attack on and occupation of the Palace (contusion on 19th June).
6 Lieut. Suckling served with the 45th Regt. during the Kaffir war of 1846-47 (Medal); and with the 18th Royal Irish during the Burmese war of 1852-53 (Medal), including Martaban, the White House Stockade, and the storming of the Dagon Pagoda at Rangoon.
7 Ensign Thornett served the Punjaub campaign of 1848-49 in the 3rd Light Dragoons, including the affair at Ramnuggur, passage of the Chenab, actions of Sadoolapore, Chillianwallah, and Goojerat (Medal and two Clasps).

St. Helena Regiment.

Years' Serv. Full Pay	Years' Serv. Half Pay					
23	0	Lieutenant Colonel.—William Forbes Macbean, Ens. 7 July 37; Lieut. 7 Jan. 42; Capt. 8 June 49; Major, 15 Jan. 58; Lt.Col. 1 May 59.				
28	2	Major.—Henry Gahan, Ens. p 13 June 30; Lieut. p 15 June 32; Capt. p 6 Mar. 40; Bt.Maj. 11 Nov. 51; Bt.Lt.Col. 26 Oct. 58; Major, 1 May 59.				

		CAPTAINS.	ENSIGN.	LIEUT.	CAPTAIN.	BREV.-MAJ.
15	0	Robert Alexander Loudon....	p 16 Sept. 45	8 June 49	p 25 June 52	
17	0	John H. Prenderville	10 Nov. 43	18 Aug. 48	26 July 57	
10	0	Edmund Charles Barnes	p 14 June 50	p 1 May 55	15 Jan. 58	
8	0	Henry Tayler	p 25 June 52	15 Aug. 55	p 12 Feb. 58	
7	0	Jno. Baldwin Hainault Rainier	p 16 Dec. 53	p 24 Oct. 56	1 May 59	
		LIEUTENANTS.				
11	0	John M'Namee, Adj.........	2 Feb. 40	3 Aug. 55		
7	0	Adolphus William Campbell	18 Feb. 53	26 July 57		
5	0	John Glass Gordon Stuart....	1 June 55	p 1 May 57		
4	0	George Stackpole Furnell	2 May 56	4 June 58		
4	0	John Lysaght Hewson	6 June 56	1 May 59		
4	0	William Russell Nash	p 12 Dec. 56	p 5 Aug. 59		
		ENSIGNS.				
3	0	Anthony Edmond Donelan ..	28 Aug. 57			
2	0	Edward Drummond Hay	13 Aug. 58			
2	0	George Vantier Lambe	p 12 Nov. 58			
1	0	Thomas England	3 June 59			

11	0	Adjutant.—Lieut. John M'Namee, 4 June 58.
7	0	Instructor of Musketry.—Captain J. B. H. Rainier, 6 Dec. 58.
7	0	Quarter Master.—John Hobson Wright, 26 July 53.
17	0	Surg.—John Mullins, 6 Oct. 54; Assist.Surg. 13 Oct. 43.
6	0	Assistant Surgeon.—James Jardine, 15 Dec. 54.

Facings Buff.—Agent, Sir John Kirkland.

Royal Newfoundland Companies.

Years' Serv. Full Pay	Years' Serv. Half Pay					
30	3 6/12	Major. John James Grant,[1] Ens. 9 Mar. 26; Lt. p 12 Feb. 28; Capt. 22 Mar. 44; Bt.Major, 12 Dec. 54; Major, 17 July 55.				

		CAPTAINS.	ENSIGN.	LIEUT.	CAPTAIN.	BREVET MAJOR.
19	0	Walter Saxton Bold	6 Aug. 41	25 Nov. 42	7 Sept. 55	
9	0	Thomas Hanrahan[2]	1 Nov. 51	28 May 54	18 Jan. 59	
		LIEUTENANTS.				
9	0	A. Saunders Quill, Adj.	21 Nov. 51	31 Aug. 55		1 Major Grant served the Eastern campaign of 1854-55, including the battles of Balaklava and Inkerman, siege and fall of Sebastopol (Brevet of Major, Medal and three Clasps).
5	0	Daniel Edward Daly....	p 9 Feb. 55	7 Sept. 55		
16	0	William John Coen	23 Feb. 44	30 Mar. 49		
		ENSIGNS.				
3	0	William Gillmor........	4 Sept. 57			
1	0	William Cavanagh	20 Dec. 59			

| 9 | 0 | Adjutant.—Lieut. Arthur Saunders Quill, 31 Aug. 55. |
| 7 | 0 | Assistant Surgeon.—William Mackenzie Skues, M.B., 29 July 53. |

Facings Blue.—Agent, Sir John Kirkland.

2 Captain Hanrahan was present at the storm and destruction of the fortified native Mandingo town of Sabajee on the Gambia on the 1st June 1853.

Gold Coast Artillery Corps. 358

Years' Serv. F.P.	H.P.		ENSIGN.	LIEUT.	CAPTAIN.	BREV.-MAJ.
18	0	Major.—Henry Bird,[1] Ens. p 27 Sept. 42; Lieut. p 18 Apr. 45; Capt. 9 Sept. 51; Brev.Major, 6 June 56; Major, 21 Nov. 56; Bt.Lt.Col. 28 Jan. 59.				
		CAPTAINS.				
15	0	Thomas Cochrane[2]	25 Apr. 45	9 Jan. 47	25 Jan. 55	28 Jan. 59
9	0	Joseph Brownell[3]	10 Sept. 51	10 Feb. 53	23 Nov. 55	
20	1	Charles Augustus Daniell[4]	p 18 Jan. 39	p 10 Apr. 40	2 May 56	
14	0	Cha.Hy.T.B. de Ruvignes[5]	30 July 46	p 2 Nov. 49	11 Sept. 57	
6	0	Jas. Trevor W. Andrews	1 Dec. 54	23 Nov. 55	26 Nov. 58	
4	0	Edw. N. Robt. Gatehouse[3]	26 Feb. 56	21 Nov. 56	19 July 59	
		LIEUTENANTS.				
4	0	Charles Hewett[6]	1 April 56	16 Jan. 57		
3	0	Henry Augustus Williams	3 Apr. 57	16 June 57		
3	0	Francis John Bolton[3]	4 Sept. 57	9 Nov. 58		
2	0	Thomas G. Danger, Adj.	28 May 58	9 Nov. 58		
2	0	Edwin Hewett	15 June 58	26 Nov. 58		
2	0	John James Mathew	30 July 58	25 Mar. 59		
2	0	Edmund Westropp Smyth	17 Dec. 58	19 July 59		
		ENSIGNS.				
1	0	Edward Moore	25 Jan. 59			
1	0	Gisborne Horner	25 Mar. 59			
1	0	James Thomson	19 July 59			
2	0	Adjutant.—Lieut. Thomas G. Danger, 22 Apr. 59.				
4	0	Instructor of Musketry.—Captain Edward Nath. Robert Gatehouse, 24 July 58.				

5 Captain de Ruvignes served with the 80th Regt. in the Burmese war of 1852-3 (Medal); was present at the capture of Prome, and repulse of the enemy's night-attack. Served with the force which escorted elephants from India across the Gonin Tonug Mountains, and in pursuit of the Woozeer Monung Shera Monung's force, resulting in the destruction and capture of the entrenched position of Tonesh.

Facings Blue.—Agent, Sir John Kirkland.

1 Lt.Colonel Bird commanded a detachment of 131 men of the Gold Coast Artillery in defence of Christiansborg Castle against a Rebel force of 4000 men, in Sept. and Oct. 1854, during the bombardment of that and the adjacent towns of Labody and Tacin by H. M. S. *Scourge*—wounded (Brevet of Major). Administered the Government of the Gold Coast during the successful expedition against the Crobboes, 50 miles in the Interior, in Sept. Oct. and Nov. 1858 (Brevet of Lieut.Colonel).
2 Major Cochrane commanded the Expedition against the Crobboes in Sept. Oct. and Nov. 1858, including the action of the Crobboe Heights on the 18th Sept. (Brevet of Major).
3 Captains Brownell and Gatehouse and Lieut. Bolton served with the Expedition against the Crobboes in Sept. Oct. and Nov. 1858, including the action of the Crobboe Heights on the 18th September.
4 Captain Daniell served in the 55th Regt. on the China expedition (Medal), and was present at the attack and capture of Amoy, Chusan, and Chin-kiang-foo. Served with the Gold Coast Artillery with the Expedition against the Crobboes during Oct. and Nov. 1858.
6 Lieut. Charles Hewett served with the Expedition against the Crobboes during Oct. and Nov. 1858.

School of Gunnery.

Commandant & Superintendent	Colonel J. W. Mitchell.
Chief Instructor	Colonel W. B. Gardner.
Brigade Major	Lieut.Colonel S. E. Gordon.
Instructors in Gunnery	Major F. B. Ward.
	Captain R. J. Hay.
	Major E. Taddy.
Carbine Instructor	Captain T. Brown.
Adjutant & QuarterMaster	Captain H. H. Alderson.

School of Musketry and Inspectors of Musketry.

Commandant & Inspector General of Instruction	Major General C. C. Hay.
Assistant Commandant, Major, and Chief Instructor	Colonel Wilford, 17 June 56. [6 May 59.
Dep. Assist. Adj. Gen.	John M'Kay, Ens. 25 Aug. 54; Lt. 9 Mar. 55; Capt.
Captain Instructors	Captain Edward O'Callaghan, 16 F.
	Captain Samuel Fairtlough, 12 F.
Lieutenant Instructors	Lieut. John M'Dermid Alladice, 76 F. } Provisional.
	Lieut. Arthur Walker, 79 F.
Paymaster	G. B. C. Crespigny, 1 April 55; Major, 20 June 54.
Quarter Master, with rank of Lieut.	James Slack,[1] 22 Apr. 59; Ens. 15 Jan. 56.
Surgeon	John Foster, M.D. h.p. 73 F.

Inspectors of Musketry.

1. HEAD QUARTERS DISTRICT.—Kent, Sussex (except Chichester), Surrey, Berks, Oxford, Buckingham, Middlesex, Essex, Hertford, Bedford, Huntingdon, Cambridge, Suffolk, Norfolk, Monmouth, Worcester, Hereford, North and South Wales, except Flint and Denbigh . . . . The Inspector General.
2. ALDERSHOT . . . . Capt. M'Crea, 45 F.
3. SOUTH WESTERN.—Hants (except Aldershot), Dorset, Wilts, Isle of Wight, Chichester, Gloucester, Somerset, Devon, Cornwall, Jersey, Guernsey, and Alderney . Capt. P. Johnstone, 99 F.
4. NORTHERN.—Scotland, Northumberland, Cumberland, Durham, Westmoreland, Yorkshire, Lancashire, Cheshire, Derbyshire, Lincoln, Flint, Denbigh, Salop, Staffordshire, Warwickshire, Leicestershire, Rutland, Northamptonshire, and Notts . Capt. Hill, 40 F.
5. DUBLIN.—Dublin, Wicklow, Donegal, Londonderry, Antrim, Tyrone, Fermanagh, Monaghan, Armagh, Down, Mayo, Sligo, Leitrim, Cavan, Meath, Louth, Galway, Roscommon, Longford, Westmeath, and Kildare . . . . Brev.Lt.Col. Bewes, 73 F.
6. CORK.—Cork, King's County, Queen's County, Clare, Limerick, Tipperary, Kilkenny, Carlow, Wexford, Kerry, and Waterford . . . . Capt. D. Thompson, 67 F.
7. NORTH AMERICA . . . . Capt. Lacy, 33 F.
8. CAPE OF GOOD HOPE AND MAURITIUS . . . . Bt.Major Scott, 9 F.
9. AUSTRALIAN COLONIES . . . . Capt. G. D. Pitt, 80 F.
10. MALTA, GOZO, THE IONIAN ISLANDS, AND GIBRALTAR . . . . . Capt. Snow, 66 F.

1 Lieut. Slack served throughout the Eastern campaign of 1854-55, including the battles of Alma, Balaklava, and Inkerman, siege, assaults and fall of Sebastopol, expedition to Kertch, bombardment and capture of Kinbourn (Medal and four Clasps, and 5th Class of the Medjidie; also Medal for distinguished conduct at the battle of Inkerman).

CHATHAM GARRISON.

COMMANDANT.—*Major General* Henry Eyre.
MAJOR OF BRIGADE.—*Brevet-Major* Gordon, 23 F.

Invalid Depot.

Years' Serv. Full Pay.	Half Pay.	
46	1 3/12	*Superintendent.*—**CB** Henry Anderson,[1] *Ens.* 22 July 13; *Lieut.* 15 June 15; *Capt.* 12 Feb. 36; *Brevet-Major,* 9 Nov. 46; *Brevet Lt.-Col.* 20 June 54; *Major,* 25 May 55; *Col.* 20 June 59.
10	0	*Staff Captains.*—Thomas Andrews Rawlins, *Ens.* p 17 Nov. 41; *Lieut.* p 29 Dec. 43; *Capt.* p 5 Feb. 47; *Bt.Major,* 26 Oct. 58.
17	0 10/12	James FitzHerbert de Tessier,[5] *Ens.* p 13 Sept. 33; *Lt.* 1 Apr. 36; *Capt.* p 6 May 42; *Bt.Major,* 20 June 54; *Bt.Lt.Col.* 17 Oct. 59.
5	0	*Adjutant.*—Henry Saville,[2] *Lt. & Adj.* 22 Oct. 55.
47	0	*Paymasters.*—John Henry Matthews,[3] 21 Oct. 13. [Feb. 23.
40	0	John MacKenzie Kennedy,[4] 30 Oct. 28; *Ens.* 24 Feb. 14; *Lt.* p 6

1 Colonel Anderson served the campaigns of 1814 and 15 in Holland and the Netherlands, including the action at Merxem, bombardment of Antwerp, storming of Bergen-op-Zoom, and actions at Quatre Bras and Waterloo. Severely wounded at Waterloo by a musket-ball, which broke the left shoulder, passed through the lungs, and made its exit at the back, breaking the scapula.
2 Lieut. Saville served the Eastern campaign of 1854-55, including the battle of Inkerman, siege and fall of Sebastopol (Medal and Clasps).
3 Paymaster Matthews served in the Nepaul war in 1814 and 15; at the capture of Hattrass; in the Mahratta war in 1817 and 18; at the capture of Bhurtpore; and the campaign of 1842 in Affghanistan under General Pollock.
4 Paymaster Kennedy served as Paymaster of the 22nd Regiment in Scinde during the campaign under Sir Charles Napier in 1843 (Medal).
5 Lt.Colonel de Tessier served in Scinde, in command of a detachment, protecting the stores and ammunition of the army tracked up the Indus. Served also in the Light Company of the 17th during the campaign in Affghanistan and Beloochistan, and was present at the storm and capture of the fortresses of Ghuznee and Khelat, for which he has received the Medal.

CAVALRY DEPOT AT MAIDSTONE.

COMMANDANT.—*Col.* Charles Wm. Morley Balders, CB. 12th Drs.
ASSIST.COMM.—*Lt.-Col.* C. H. Teush-Hecker, Unatt.
RIDING MASTER.—*Brev.Major* Wm. Griffin Sutton,[3] Unatt. 31 Oct. 56.
ADJUTANT.—*Capt.* William Miller,[1] h.p. 2 Drs. 14 Nov. 56.
PAYMASTER.—Edward George Cubitt, 16 Feb. 44; *Ens.* p 9 Dec. 31; *Lt.* p 28 Apr. 37.
QUARTER MASTER.—John Swindley, 1 Nov. 39.
VETERINARY SURGEON.—Charles Curtis Brett, 8 March 33; *1st Class,* 1 July 59.

CAVALRY DEPOT AT CANTERBURY.

COMMANDANT.—*Colonel* John C. Hope Gibsone, Unatt. 17 Nov. 57.
MAJORS.—*Major* Edward Tomkinson, Unatt. 17 Nov. 57.
Major John Wycliffe Thompson, Unatt. 11 Aug. 48.
RIDING MASTER.—*Captain* John Kemp, h. p. 4 F. 19 Feb. 58.
ADJUTANT.—*Captain* John Yates,[4] Unatt. 24 Oct. 59.
INSTRUCTOR OF MUSKETRY.—*Cornet* Edward Pulleyne, 8 Hussars, 1 Apr. 59.
PAYMASTER.—John Stephenson,[2] 30 April 47; *Cor.* 16 Feb. 44; *Lt.* 25 Sept. 45.
QUARTERMASTER.—John Thompson, 3 Oct. 48.

1 Captain Miller served the Eastern campaign of 1854-55 with the Scots Greys, including the affair of M'Kenzie's Farm, battles of Balaklava and Inkerman, and siege of Sebastopol (Medal and Clasps).
2 Paymaster Stephenson served with the 17th Lancers in India from Feb. 1814 to 1823, including the campaign of 1817-18 against the Pindarees. Also the Eastern campaign of 1854-55, including the affair of Bulganac, battles of Alma, Balaklava, and Inkerman (acting as Adjutant), and siege of Sebastopol (Medal and Clasps).
3 Major Sutton has the 4th Class of the Medjidie for Service with the Turkish Contingent.
4 Captain Yates served with the 11th Hussars the Eastern campaign of 1854-55, including the affair of Bulganac, battles of Alma, Balaklava, and Inkerman, and siege of Sebastopol (Medal and four Clasps, and Sardinian Medal).

DEPOT BATTALIONS.

1st Depot Battalion (India Depots). Chatham.

Years' Serv. Full Pay.	Half Pay.	
48	1/12	*Lieut.Colonel.*—Henry Jervis,[1] *Ens.* 19 Dec. 11; *Lt.* 29 Dec. 14; *Capt.* p 19 Sept. 26; *Bt.Maj.* 23 Nov. 41; *Maj.* p 27 Sept. 42; *Lt.Col.* p 8 Mar. 50; *Col.* 28 Nov. 54.
17	1 1/12	*Majors.*—Henry Disney Ellis,[4] *Ens.* 14 June 42; *Lieut.* p 31 Jan. 45; *Capt.* p 21 Sept. 52; *Brev.Major,* 2 Nov. 55; *Major,* 18 Jan. 56.
10	0	Fred. Ernest Appleyard,[47] *Ens.* p 14 June 50; *Lt.* p 12 Oct. 52; *Capt.* 29 Dec. 54; *Bt.Major,* 26 Dec. 56; *Major,* p 31 Aug. 58.
29	0	*Staff Captain.*—Henry Jackson, *Ens.* p 5 April 31; *Lt.* p 20 Sept. 33; *Capt.* 27 Dec. 42; *Brevet Major,* 20 June 54.
10	0	*Adjutant.*—Leonard Sidebottom,[11] 31 Oct. 56; *Ens.* p 13 Dec. 50; *Lieut.* p 23 Nov. 52; *Capt.* 8 Jan. 56.
5	0	*Paymaster.*—William Summerfield, 1 July 55.
11	0	*Quarter Master.*—James Menzies, 4 May 49; *Ens.* 27 April 49. [1 Oct. 58.
27	0	*Surgeon.*—Andrew Maclean, M.D., *A.S.* 4 Oct. 33; *Surg.* 1 Mar. 44; *Sury.Maj.*

Instructor of Musketry.—*Captain* R. H. Travers, 24 F. 1 Mar. 58.
Depots.—7 F. 24 F. 35 F. 43 F. 53 F. 77 F.

Years' Serv.		
Full Pay.	Half Pay.	*Depot Battalions.* 360

2nd Depot Battalion (India Depots). Chatham.

Full Pay	Half Pay	
		Lieut.Colonel.—Robert Newton Phillips,² *Ens.* p 27 May 36; *Lieut.* p 2 Oct.
24	0	40; *Capt.* p 12 Jan. 44; *Maj.* p 17 Oct. 41; *Brev. Lt.Col.* 28 May 53; *Lieut.Col.* 29 July 53; *Col.* 28 Nov. 54.
27	0	*Majors.*—William Little Stewart,²⁴ *Ens.* p 12 April 33; *Lieut.* 13 Jan. 37; *Capt.* p 28 July 43; *Brev.Major*, 20 June 54; *Major*, p 15 May 57.
22	4/1½	Fred. Geo. Thomas Deshon,¹¹ *Ens.* 29 Dec. 37; *Lt.* 5 Jan. 41; *Capt.* 30 Nov. 49; *Bt.Major*, 2 Nov. 55; *Major*, 16 Mar. 58.
22	0	*Adjutant.*—Richard Roney,⁶ 3 March 57; *Ens.* p 14 Sept. 38; *Lieut.* 30 April 41; *Capt.* 16 July 50.
34	13 6/1½	*Paymaster.*—Edwin Griffiths,¹⁶ 11 Jan. 33; *2nd Lt.* 6 Jan. 13; *Lt.* 12 Nov. 13.
5	0	*Quarter Master.*—William M'Kay, 27 July 55.
		Instructor of Musketry.—*Captain* P. Geraghty, 20 F. 7 Nov. 59.
		Depots.— 20 F. 23 F. 31 F. 52 F. 73 F.

3rd Depot Battalion (India Depots). Chatham.

23	6/1½	*Lieut.Colonel.*—Charles Edward Fairtlough,²³ *Ens.* p 12 May 37; *Lieut.* p 31 Dec. 39; *Capt.* 25 Aug. 46; *Brev.Major*, 17 July 55; *Major*, 26 Feb. 56; *Lieut.Col.* p 7 March 56.
13	2/1½	*Majors.*—Charles Elgee,³⁹ *Ens.* 14 Apr. 46; *Lieut.* p 18 Feb. 48; *Capt.* 29 Dec. 54; *Bt.Major*, 2 Nov. 55; *Major*, 26 Mar. 58.
23	0	Rupert Barber Deering,⁴⁶ *Ens.* p 3 Mar. 37; *Lt.* 17 Oct. 39; *Capt.* 8 June 49; *Major*, 26 Oct. 58.
15	0	*Adjutant.*—Francis Barry Drew, 23 Aug. 59; *Ens.* p 23 May 45; *Lt.* 17 Aug. 48; *Capt.* p 21 Nov. 51.
40	7	*Paymaster.*—Monkhouse Graham Taylor, 26 Aug. 36; *Ens.* p 10 June 13; *Lt.* p 5 Sept. 22.
4	9/1½	*Quarter Master.*—William Goldby, 12 July 55.
		Instructor of Musketry.—*Captain* Alfred Wright, 81 F. 7 Nov. 58.
		Depots.—8 F. 19 F. 75 F. 81 F. 91 F. 94 F.

4th Depot Battalion (India Depots). Canterbury.

17	0	*Lieut.Colonel.*—James Wells Armstrong,⁵ CB. *Ens.* p 18 Aug. 43; *Lieut.* p 29 Nov. 44; *Capt.* 20 Jan. 51; *Brev.Maj.* 12 Dec. 54; *Maj.* 29 Dec. 54; *Brev.Lt.Col.* 17 July 55; *Lt.Col.* 2 Oct. 55; *Col.* 1 Oct. 58.
18	1 2/1½	*Majors.*—Dawson Cornelius Greene,²⁴ *Ens.* p 3 July 40; *Lt.* p 14 Jan. 42; *Capt.* 11 Dec. 49; *Bt.Major*, 2 Nov. 55; *Major*, 7 Nov. 56.
26	0	Joseph Henry Laye,⁵ *Ens.* p 2 May 34; *Lt.* 1 Dec. 37; *Capt.* p 26 Mar. 41; *Bt.Major*, 20 June 54; *Bt.Lt.Col.* 28 Nov. 54; *Major*, 31 Mar. 58.
10	0	*Adjutant.*—Hon. Bernard Mathew Ward,³ 1 Oct. 56; *Ens.* p 12 July 50; *Lt.* p 10 Feb. 54; *Capt.* p 14 March 56.
15	0	*Paymaster.*—Samuel Williams,¹⁶ 23 May 53; *Q.M.* 18 Apr. 45.
6	0	*Quarter Master.*—Thomas Vousden,²¹ Oct. 56; *Ens.* 5 Nov. 54; *Lt.* 20 Feb. 58.
		Instructor of Musketry.—*Capt.* A. J. O. Rutherfurd, 70 F. 12 Nov. 58.
		Depots attached to the Battalion.—64 F. 70 F. 82 F. 90 F. 98 F.

5th Depot Battalion. Parkhurst.

35	0	*Lieut.Colonel.*—Edmund Richard Jeffreys,¹⁰ CB. *Ens.* 16 June 25; *Lt.* 11 Oct. 27; *Capt.* p 2 Feb. 38; *Maj.* p 12 May 43; *Br.Lt.Col.* 20 June 54; *Lt.Col.* 16 March 55; *Col.* 1 Apr. 58.
16	0	*Major.*—Fred. Biscoe Tritton, *2nd Lt.* p 22 Mar. 44; *Lt.* p 8 May 46; *Capt.* p 23 Sept. 51; *Major*, p 24 Aug. 58.
20	0	*Adjutant.*—Hercules Atkin Welman,¹⁴ 4 May 55; *Ens.* p 17 Jan. 40; *Lieut.* 16 Mar. 43; *Capt.* p 3 Feb. 47; *Bt.Major*, 26 Oct. 58.
37	0	*Paymaster.*—Francis Feneran,⁸ 15 Dec. 37; *Qr.Master*, 1 Dec. 23.
8	0	*Quarter Master.*—Thomas Moore,¹¹ 21 May 52.
22	0	*Surgeon.*—Jas. T. Oswald Johnston, M.D., *Assist.Surg.* 3 Aug. 38; *Surgeon*, 29 Dec. 46; *Surgeon Major*, 1 Oct. 58.
		Instructor of Musketry.—*Captain* S. B. Gordon, 45 F. 10 Mar. 58.
		Depots attached to the Battalion.—1st and 2d Batts. 22 F. 30 F. 45 F. 50 F. 96 F. 100 F.

6th Depot Battalion. Walmer.

19	0	*Lieut.Colonel.*—Edmund Aug. Whitmore,³† *Ens.* p 6 Aug. 41; *Lt.* 10 July 46; *Capt.* p 1 June 49; *Bt.Maj.* 12 Dec. 54; *Maj.* 29 Dec. 54; *Lt.Col.* 15 Feb. 56.
12	0	*Major.*—William Rickman,¹⁴ *Ens.* p 12 Sept. 48; *Lieut.* p 31 Oct. 51; *Capt.* p 24 March 54; *Brevet Major*, 24 April 55; *Major*, 1 Feb. 56.
13	0	*Adjutant.*—William Edward Wallace, 15 Apr. 59; *Cornet*, p 3 Sept. 47; *Lt.* p 9 Nov. 49; *Capt.* 9 July 54.
25	0	*Paymaster.*—Hugh S. S. Burney,² 31 July 46; *Ens.* p 29 Dec. 35; *Lt.* p 14 June 39
13	0	*Quarter Master.*—Timothy Morris,¹ 28 May 47; *Ens.* 15 Jan. 47.
		Instructor of Musketry.—*Capt.*
		Depots attached to the Battalion.—1st & 2d Batts. 2 F. 2d Batt. 4 F. 2d Batt. 7 F. 12 F.

Depot Battalions.

Years' Serv. Full Pay	Half Pay	
		7th Depot Battalion. Winchester.
38	0	*Lieut.Colonel.*—Wm. Sherbrook Ramsay Norcott,[10] CB., 2nd *Lieut.* 13 June 22; *Lieut.* 16 June 25; *Capt.* 21 Feb. 40; *Major*, 1 Aug. 47; *Brev. Lieut. Col.* 12 Dec. 54; *Lieut. Col.* 22 Dec. 54; *Col.* 29 June 55.
13	1 2/12	*Majors.*—Alastair M'Ian M'Donald,[20] *Ens.* p 27 March 46; *Lieut.* p 12 Nov. 47; *Capt.* 6 June 54; *Brev.Major*, 12 Dec. 54; *Major*, 17 July 55.
21	0	Arthur Wombwell,[3] *Ens.* p 5 April 39; *Lt.* p 29 Oct. 41; *Capt.* p 8 May 46; *Bt.Maj.* 2 Nov. 55; *Major*, 24 Feb. 57.
11	2 8/12	*Adjutant.*—Peter MacDonald, 1 Oct. 56; *Qr.Mr.* 19 May 46; 2*nd Lieut.* 8 Sept. 46; *Lieut.* 10 Jan. 50; *Capt.* 3 Feb. 54.
28	0	*Paymaster.*—John Wheatley,[4] 12 Oct. 48; *Ens. & Adj.* 20 July 32; *Lt.* 3 Apr. 35.
12	0	*Quarter Master.*—William Watson,[7] 25 April 48.
		Instructor of Musketry.—*Captain* Thomas Biggs, 60 F. 15 July 58.
		Depots attached to the Battalion.—1st, 2nd, and 3rd Batts. 60 F. 1st, 2nd, 3rd, and 4th Batts. Rifle Brigade.
		8th Depot Battalion. Pembroke.
32	3 2/12	*Lieut.Colonel.*—Henry Phipps Raymond, *Ens.* 9 April 25; *Lieut.* p 17 March 27; *Capt.* p 21 March 34; *Brevet Major*, 9 Nov. 46; *Major*, p 17 Dec. 47; *Lieut.Col.* p 17 Jan. 51; *Col.* 28 Nov. 54.
25	0	*Major.*—Charles Lavallin Nugent,[30] *Ens.* p 21 Aug. 35; *Lt.* 4 Feb. 38; *Capt.* p 16 Nov. 41; *Major*, p 18 July 51; *Bt.Lt.Col.* 26 Nov. 57.
12	0	*Adjutant.*—George Ley Woolferston Dodsley Flamstead,[13] 23 Aug. 50; *Ens.* p 28 Apr. 48; *Lt.* p 30 May 51; *Capt.* 10 Sept. 58.
23	0	*Paymaster.*—Julius Brockman Travers,[14] 9 May 45; 2*nd Lieut.* 8 July 37; *Lieut.* 8 Apr. 42.
14	0	*Quarter Mas.*—Patrick Hopkins,[13] 5 Nov. 52; *Ens.* 14 Apr. 46; *Lt.* 26 June 50.
		Instructor of Musketry.—*Capt.* T. Rowland, 25 F. 16 Jan. 58.
		Depots attached to the Battalion.—2 Batt. 5 F. 15 F. 61 F. 85 F.
		9th Depot Battalion (India Depots). Colchester.
22	0	*Lieut.Colonel.*—George Dixon,[17] CB., *Ens.* p 30 Dec. 28; *Lieut.* p 26 Dec. 34; *Capt.* p 29 Nov. 39; *Major*, p 27 Dec. 50; *Brev. Lieut.Col.* 12 Dec. 54; *Lieut.Col.* 20 April 55; *Col.* 20 May 58.
14	1	*Majors.*—Charles Carew de Morel,[18] *Ens.* p 24 Oct. 45; *Lieut.* p 29 May 49; *Capt.* p 23 Nov. 52; *Brev.Major*, 12 Dec. 54; *Major*, 21 Sept. 55.
11	1 4/12	Geo. Edw. Brown Westhead,[31] *Ens.* p 7 Apr. 48; *Lt.* p 25 Jan. 50; *Capt.* 29 Dec. 54; *Bt.Major*, 2 Nov. 55; *Major*, 17 Feb. 57.
16	0	*Adjutant.*—Samuel Dunning, 18 Aug. 54; *Ens.* 16 Feb. 44; *Lieut.* 7 Oct. 47; *Capt.* 14 July 54.
32	0	*Paymaster.*—Charles Boyse Roche,[3] 30 Nov. 38; *Ens.* 18 Jan. 28; *Lt.* 21 June 32.
15	0	*Quarter Master.*—QM Alexander Hendry,[9] 2 Sept. 45.
		Instructor of Musketry.—*Captain* R. G. Coles, 1 F. 16 June 56.
		Depots.—1 Batt. 1 F. 54 F. 56 F. 66 F. 88 F.
		10th Depot Battalion (India Depots). Colchester.
21	0	*Lieut.Colonel.*—John Alfred Street,[7] CB. *Ens.* p 29 Nov. 39; *Lt.* p 5 Oct. 41; *Capt.* 7 Jan. 48; *Brev.Maj.* 12 Dec. 54; *Maj.* 20 Dec. 54; *Lt.Col.* 19 June 55; *Col.* 11 Aug. 58.
17	0	*Majors.*—Frederick West,[32] *Ens.* p 11 Aug. 43; *Lt.* p 29 Jan. 47; *Capt.* p 3 Aug. 49; *Major*, p 27 July 55.
16	2/12	William Warry,[35] *Ens.* p 26 Jan. 44; *Lt.* p 12 Feb. 47; *Capt.* p 14 May 52; *Bt.Major*, 2 Nov. 55; *Major*, 15 June 58.
11	0	*Adjutant.*—Innis Colin Munro, 4 Mar. 59; *Ens.* 10 Apr. 49; *Lt.* 14 July 53; *Capt.* 1 Oct. 58.
3	0	*Paymaster.*—Samuel Daniel, 30 Jan. 57.
6	0	*Quarter Master.*—John Henry Anderson,[9] 30 June 54.
		Instructor of Musketry.—*Capt.* A. T. L. Chapman, 34 F. 8 Nov. 58.
		Depots.—5 F. 34 F. 37 F. 38 F. 44 F. 97 F.
		11th Depot Battalion. Plymouth.
22	2 10/12	*Lieut.Colonel.*—Hugh Dennis Crofton,[48] *Ens.* p 13 Mar. 35; *Lt.* 29 Dec. 37; *Capt.* p 9 Aug. 39; *Major*, p 30 Dec. 45; *Bt.Lt.Col.* 20 June 54; *Lt.Col.* 9 Mar. 55; *Col.* 26 Oct. 58.
12	1 7/12	*Major.*—George Skipwith,[40] *Ens.* p 3 Nov. 46; *Lt.* p 15 Oct. 47; *Capt.* p 11 Nov. 53; *Brev.Maj.* 2 Nov. 55; *Major*, 1 Feb. 56.
17	0	*Adjutant.*—John Hanham,[5] 1 Oct. 56; *Ens.* p 22 Dec. 43; *Lt.* p 23 Dec. 45; *Capt.* p 12 July 50.
35	2/12	*Paymaster.*—Thomas Miller Creagh,[17] 21 June 39; *Ens.* 23 Feb. 25; *Lt.* 6 Mar. 26.
5	0	*Quarter Mas.*—John Fred. Grier,[4] 14 Nov. 56; *Ens.* 5 Nov. 54; *Lt.* 9 March 55.
		Instructor of Musketry.—*Capt.* Lyle, 20 F. 1 Mar. 58.
		Depots.—10 F. 32 F. 41 F. 55 F.

Years' Serv.	
Full Pay.	Half Pay.

12th Depot Battalion. *Athlone.*

26 | 0 | *Lieut.Colonel.*—Arthur Cyril Goodenough,²³ CB. *Ens.* ᴾ 8 April 34; *Lieut.* ᴾ 25 Nov. 36; *Capt.* ᴾ 26 Oct. 41; *Major*, 27 March 48; *Brevet Lieut.-Col.* 6 Jan. 55; *Lt.Col.* 26 Oct. 55; *Col.* 24 June 58.

13 | 8/12 | *Major.*—John Nason,²⁷ *Ens.* 9 May 46; *Lieut.* ᴾ 4 Sept. 49; *Capt.* 29 Oct. 54; *Brevet Major*, 17 July 55; *Major*, 1 Feb. 56.

6 | 0 | *Adjutant.*—William Little,¹⁰ 1 Oct. 56; *Ens.* 10 Aug. 54; *Lieut.* 8 Dec. 54; *Capt.* 27 May 56.

40 | 8 | *Paymaster.*—ᵁ Geo. Thos. Benson,⁶ 20 May 36; *Ens.* 13 Feb. 12; *Lt.* 25 Aug. 13.

14 | 0 | *Quarter Master.*—John Desmond,⁹ 12 June 46.

Instructor of Musketry.—Captain W. H. Thompson, 59 F. 22 Jan. 58.
Depots attached to the Battalion.—25 F. 36 F. 50 F. 67 F.

13th Depot Battalion. *Birr.*

28 | 0 | *Lt.Colonel.*—John Wm. Sidney Smith,¹⁵ *Ens.* 3 Feb. 32; *Lieut.* 4 Aug. 37; *Capt.* ᴾ 7 Aug. 40; *Brevet-Major*, 11 Nov. 51; *Major*, 29 Dec. 54; *Lieut.Col.* 29 July 55; *Col.* 2 Sept. 58.

17 | 1 | *Major.*—William Hardy,¹⁶ *Ens.* ᴾ 27 Sept. 42; *Lieut.* ᴾ 8 May 46; *Capt.* ᴾ 12 Oct. 52; *Brev.Maj.* 12 Dec. 54; *Major*, 1 Oct. 56.

10 | 0 | *Adjutant.*—Hon. Somerset Richard Hamilton Ward,⁹ 18 Mar. 59; *Ens.* 8 Nov. 50; *Lt.* ᴾ 11 Nov. 53; *Capt.* 10 Sept. 58.

17 | 1 | *Paymaster.*—William Young,⁹ 1 Sept. 54; *Ens.* 19 Nov. 41; *Honorary rank of Captain*, 1 July 59.

4 | 0 | *Quarter Master.*—Jeremiah Moloney,¹⁰ 29 April 56.

Instructor of Musketry.—Captain E. H. Eagar, 40 F. 20 Sept. 56.
Depots attached to the Battalion.—2nd Batt. 1 F. 21 F. 40 F. 58 F. 65 F.

14th Depot Battalion. *Belfast.*

13 | 0 | *Lieut.Colonel.*—Thomas Francis Hobbs,²⁸ 2nd *Lt.* 15 Jan. 47; *Lt.* ᴾ 21 May 50; *Capt.* ᴾ 2 April 52; *Major*, 11 May 55; *Lt.Col.* ᴾ 8 Mar. 59.

26 | 0 | *Major.*—Hew Dalrymple Fanshawe, *Ens.* 4 July 34; *Lt.* ᴾ 25 May 38; *Capt.* ᴾ 13 May 42; *Br.Maj.* 20 June 54; *Maj.* ᴾ 27 July 55; *Bt.Lt.Col.* 25 Oct. 59.

10 | 8/12 | *Adjutant.*—John Martley,¹⁷ 14 July 57; *Ens.* 6 July 49; *Lieut.* ᴾ 3 June 53; *Capt.* 13 July 55.

18 | 0 | *Paymaster.*—Edwin Robert Wethered,⁷ 30 June 54; *Ens.* ᴾ 5 Aug. 42; *Lieut.* ᴾ 24 May 44; *Capt.* 6 June 54.

2 | 0 | *Quarter Master.*—Edward Coghlan, 2 Feb. 58.

Instructor of Musketry.—Captain C. O'Donoghue, 76 F. 18 Jan. 58.
Depots attached to the Battalion.—26 F. 49 F. 62 F. 63 F. 76 F.

15th Depot Battalion (India Depots). *Buttevant.*

38 | 7 8/12 | *Lieut.Colonel.*—William Devonish Deverell,³⁴ *Ens.* 4 May 15; *Lt.* 16 Nov. 20; *Capt.* 7 Apr. 37; *Maj.* 5 Mar. 47; *Bt.Lt.Col.* 28 Nov. 54; *Lt.Col.* 7 Apr. 58.

17 | 2 1/12 | *Majors.*—William A. Armstrong,¹³ *Ens.* ᴾ 1 Nov. 40; *Lt.* 28 July 43; *Capt.* 3 Dec. 52; *Bt.-Major*, 2 Nov. 55; *Major*, 14 Dec. 55.

10 | 2 8/12 | Herbert Russell Manners,³⁸ *Ens.* 28 Aug. 38; *Lt.* 7 Jan. 42; *Capt.* 13 Nov. 46; *Major*, ᴾ 8 Jan. 56.

12 | 0 | *Adjutant.*—James Harwood Rocke,¹⁸ 28 Aug. 57; *Ens.* ᴾ 4 Aug. 48; *Lieut.* ᴾ 1 March 50; *Capt.* 1 Dec. 54.

1 | 0 | *Paymaster.*—John Holland, 14 Aug. 55; 2nd *Lt.* 26 March 28; *Lt.* 15 Nov. 36.

Quarter Master.—Thomas Lee, 1 July 59; *Ens.* 18 Jan. 59.
Instructor of Musketry.—Capt. R. W. Woods, 80 F. 1 Nov. 57.
Depots attached to the Battalion.—18 F. 27 F. 46 F. 80 F. 87 F.

16th Depot Battalion. *Templemore.*

32 | 1 | *Lieut.Colonel.*—William Irwin, *Ens.* ᴾ 15 Nov. 27; *Lt.* 19 Nov. 30; *Capt.* ᴾ 26 April 39; *Maj.* 18 Jan. 48; *Lt.Col.* ᴾ 26 Dec. 51; *Col.* 28 Nov. 54.

18 | 0 | *Major.*—Ellis James Charter, *Ens.* ᴾ 25 Oct. 42; *Lt.* ᴾ 16 Dec. 45; *Capt.* 15 Mar. 53; *Major*, ᴾ 8 Mar. 59.

16 | 0 | *Adjutant.*—George Stacpole Coxon,⁴ 24 Aug. 58; *Ens.* ᴾ 29 Mar. 44; *Lt.* 29 Jan. 47; *Capt.* 24 Nov. 57.

15 | 0 | *Paymaster.*—George Bodlo,¹¹ 8 April 53; *Ens.* 23 May 45; *Lt.* 21 Feb. 46.

3 | 1 4/12 | *Quarter Master.*—R. P. Brooks,¹³ 30 July 58; *Cornet*, 14 Dec. 55; *Lt.* 1 Apr. 57.

Instructor of Musketry.—Captain G. F. Macdonald, 16 F. 14 May 59.
Depots attached to the Battalion.—2 B. 8 F. 2 B. 18 F. 16 F. 86 F. 39 F.

17th Depot Battalion. *Limerick.*

28 | 0 | *Lieut.Colonel.*—Arthur Borton,⁹ CB. *Ens.* ᴾ 13 July 32; *Lt.* ᴾ 3 Apr. 35; *Capt.* 30 July 41; *Bt.Major*, 3 Apr. 46; *Maj.* ᴾ 19 Sept. 48; *Lt.Col.* ᴾ 10 June 53; *Col.* 28 Nov. 54.

19 | 0 4/12 | *Major.*—Gustavus Nigle Kingscote Anker Yonge,³⁷ *Ens.* ᴾ 22 Aug. 34; *Lt.* 29 June 37; *Capt.* 1 Jan. 47; *Major*, ᴾ 15 Jan. 56.

23 | 1 | *Adjutant.*—John Henry Grant,¹⁹ 23 Oct. 57; *Ens.* 2 Apr. 36; *Lt.* 15 Dec. 40; *Capt.* 17 Jan. 51.

12 | 0 | *Paymaster.*—Alex. Fair,¹⁰ 28 Jan. 53; *Quarter Master*, 7 July 48.

11 | 0 | *Quarter Master.*—John Burke,¹² 29 Dec. 54; *Ens.* 4 Sept. 40; *Lt.* 22 Feb. 53.

Instructor of Musketry.—Brevet Major George T. Brice, 17 F. 1 Jan. 57.
Depots attached.—1st and 2nd Batts. 3 F. 1st and 2d Batts. 9 F. 17 F.

Full Pay.	Half Pay.	
		18th Depot Battalion. Fermoy.
28	0	*Lieut.Colonel.*—Caledon Richard Egerton,²⁰ *Ens.* 15 June 32; *Lieut.* ᵖ 28 March 34; *Capt.* ᵖ 15 March 39; *Brev. Major*, 11 Nov. 51; *Major*, ᵖ 5 Dec. 51; *Lieut. Col.* 9 March 55; *Col.* 18 Apr. 58.
22	0	*Major.*—George King,⁴¹ *Ens.* ᵖ 19 Oct. 38; *Lieut.* ᵖ 7 Feb. 40; *Capt.* ᵖ 5 Nov. 47; *Major*, 30 Apr. 58.
10	0	*Adjutant.*—Thomas Lynden Bell,¹² 1 Oct. 56; *Ens.* ᵖ 17 May 50; *Lieut.* ᵖ 17 Feb. 54; *Capt.* 30 Nov. 55.
26	0	*Paymaster.*—Stephen Lawson, 6 Jan. 43; *Ens.* 26 Dec. 34; *Lieut.* 22 Jan. 39.
5	0	*Quarter Master.*—Patrick Higgins, 1 July 55.
		Instructor of Musketry.—*Captain* R. Nevill, 11 F.
		Depots attached to the Battalion.—11 F. 2d Batt. 13 F. 14 F. 28 F.
		19th Depot Battalion (India Depots). Fermoy.
25	9/12	*Lieut.Colonel.*—Isaac Moore, *Ens.* 20 Feb. 35; *Lieut.* 29 June 38; *Capt.* 20 Feb. 44; *Brev.Major*, 12 Dec. 54; *Major*, 9 Sept. 55; *Lieut.Col.* 30 Nov. 55.
16	1	*Majors.*—John Lawrie,³³ *Ens.* ᵖ 22 Dec. 43; *Lieut.* ᵖ 7 Nov. 47; *Capt.* ᵖ 3 Dec. 52; *Brev.Major*, 2 Nov. 55; *Major*, 18 Jan. 56.
14	0	Charles Raleigh Chichester,²¹ *Ens.* 31 Mar. 46; *Lt.* ᵖ 1 Sept. 48; *Capt.* ᵖ 6 Dec. 50; *Bt.Major*, 6 June 56; *Major*, 15 Mar. 58.
18	0	*Adjutant.*—Richard Young,¹ 30 Apr. 58; *Ens.* 22 July 42; *Lt.* 28 July 44; *Capt.* 15 Mar. 53.
30	0	*Paymaster.*—Ernest Aug. Hawker,¹³ 19 Oct. 38; *Ens.* 30 Sept. 30; *Lieut.* ᵖ 8 July 36.
5	0	*Quarter Master.*—William Drage,¹⁴ 21 Feb. 55.
		Instructor of Musketry.—*Captain* A. B. Wallis, 33 F. 13 Dec. 56.
		Depots attached to the Battalion.—1st Batt. 13 F. 33 F. 68 F. 69 F. 89 F. 95 F.
		20th Depot Battalion. Cork.
26	0	*Lieut.Colonel.*—Richard T. Farren,³⁰ CB. *Ens.* 30 May 34; *Lieut.* 31 Jan. 40; *Capt.* 3 Jan. 45; *Major*, ᵖ 27 Dec. 50; *Brev.Lieut.Col.* 12 Dec. 54; *Lieut. Col.* 9 March 55; *Col.* 12 Dec. 57.
25	0	*Major.*—George Mein,¹² *Ens.* 19 June 35; *Lieut.* 21 Apr. 39; *Capt.* ᵖ 3 Nov. 46; *Brevet Major*, 30 June 54; *Major*, 8 July 56.
19	0	*Adjutant.*—Robert John Hughes,⁸ 1 Oct. 56; *Ens.* 7 Jan. 41; *Lieut.* 30 Aug. 43; *Capt.* 7 Sept. 55.
30	9/12	*Paymaster.*—MorrisRobinsonCampbell,20Aug.41;*Ens.* 2July29; *Lt.*19 Dec. 35.
5	0	*Quarter Master.*—Thomas Knight, 20 May 55.
		Instructor of Musketry.—*Captain* W. H. Cairnes, 48 F. 9 Aug. 59.
		Depots attached to the Battalion.—2nd Batt. 6 F. 47 F. 48 F. 57 F. 99 F.
		21st Depot Battalion. Chichester.
28	0	*Majors.*—Edward W. C. Wright,⁸ *Ens.* 21 Dec. 32; *Lt.* ᵖ 13 Nov. 35; *Capt.* ᵖ 2 July 41; *Bt.Major*, 26 Feb. 52; *Bt.Lt.Col.* 6 June 56; *Major*, 6 Aug. 58.
8	2 1/12	Francis Edward Drewe,⁴² *Ens.* ᵖ 17 May 50; *Lt.* ᵖ 23 Sept. 51; *Capt.* 21 Sept. 54; *Bt.Major*, 6 June 56; *Major*, 8 July 56.
11	0	*Adjutant.*—Frederick Beswick,¹⁶ 9 Feb. 55; *Ens.* 23 March 49; *Lt.* 19 March 52; *Capt.* 29 Dec. 54.
23	2 6/12	*Paymaster.*—Robert Thomas Browne Boyd, 26 March 41; *Ens.* ᵖ 20 Feb. 35; *Lieut.* ᵖ 15 Feb. 39.
6	0	*Quarter Master.*—William Browne, 10 March 54.
20	0	*Surgeon.*—Alexander Gibb,¹ M.D. 18 Sept. 40; *Assist. Surg.* 10 Jan. 40.
		Instructor of Musketry.—*Capt.* Edw. Wm. Bray, 83 F. 22 July 58.
		Depots attached to the Battalion.—4 F. 51 F. 83 F.
		22nd Depot Battalion (India Depots). Stirling.
40		*Majors.*—Edward A. G. Muller,²⁵ *Ens.* 3 Feb. 20; *Lieut.* 11 Aug. 25; *Capt.* ᵖ 11 Jan. 33; *Brev.Major*, 9 Nov. 46; *Brev. Lieut.-Col.* 20 June 54; *Major*, 29 Dec. 54; *Col.* 26 Oct. 58.
11	0	ᵛᶜ Fred. Cockayne Elton,⁴⁴ *Ens.* ᵖ 19 Jan. 49; *Lt.* ᵖ 30 Apr. 52; *Capt.* 29 Dec. 54; *Bt.Major*, 2 Nov. 55; *Major*, 22 June 58.
11	0	*Adjutant.*—Bache Harpur Heathcote, 8 Jan. 58; *Ens.* ᵖ 21 Aug. 49; *Lt.* ᵖ 20 Feb. 52; *Capt.* ᵖ 14 Sept. 55.
21	0	*Paymaster.*—John Peter Hall,¹² 11 Apr. 51; *Ens.* ᵖ 26 April 39; *Lieut.* 23 April 41; *Capt.* 15 Feb. 50.
5	0	*Quarter Master.*—Alexander M'Gregor,⁵ 25 May 55.
		Instructor of Musketry.—*Captain* W. G. E. Webber, 42 F. 12 May 59.
		Depots attached to the Battalion.—42 F. 71 F. 79 F. 92 F.

Depot Battalions. 364

Years' Serv.		
Full Pay.	Half Pay.	
25	0	**23rd Depot Battalion. Aberdeen.**
		Majors.—Charles Henry Gordon,⁴³ CB. *Ens.* ᴾ 24 Nov. 35; *Lt.* ᴾ 28 July 38; *Capt.* ᴾ 13 May 42; *Bt.Maj.* 20 June 54; *Major*, 10 Oct. 54; *Bt.Lt.Col.* 6 June 56.
11	1 3/12	Patrick Robertson,⁴⁵ *Ens.* 7 Apr. 48; *Lt.* 5 Dec. 51; *Capt.* 29 Dec. 54; *Bt. Major*, 17 July 55; *Major*, 3 Apr. 57.
12	0	*Adjutant.*—Francis Padfield,⁷ 1 Oct. 56; *Ens.* ᴾ 7 April 48; *Lieut.* 6 June 54; *Capt.* 21 Sept. 55.
15	0	*Paymaster.*—Robert Wm. Duff, 19 Jan. 49; *Ens.* ᴾ 20 June 45; *Lt.* ᴾ 9 June 46.
11	0	*Quarter Master.*—Robert Jameson,⁸ 11 May 49.
		Instructor of Musketry.—Captain T. Anderson, 78 F. 1 Feb. 58.
		Depots.—72 F. 74 F. 93 F.
		AGENT, Sir John Kirkland.

Paymaster of Detachments, Portsmouth.
Alexis Corcoran,⁵ 8 July 42; *Ens.* 30 Nov. 38; *Lt.* 8 April 42.

Convalescent Establishment, Yarmouth.
Commandant.—Captain Edwyn Stanhope Jervois, h.p. 7 F.
Paymaster.—Charles Scarlin Naylor,¹ 8 May 35; *Ens.* 1 Sept. 12; *Lt.* 25 Dec. 15; *Capt.* 9 May 34.

Isle of Man.
Staff Captain to command Detachments and Pensioners.—Edward John Dickson, 1 Sept. 54; *Ens.* ᴾ 27 Sept. 39; *Lt.* ᴾ 14 Oct 42; *Capt.* ᴾ 13 Apr. 49.

Depot Medical Staff Corps.
Staff Captain.—Stonehouse George Bunbury, 2nd *Lt.* ᴾ 28 June 33; *Lt.* ᴾ 25 Dec. 38; *Capt.* 30 Dec. 46; *Brevet-Major*, 6 June 56.
Assist. Staff Captain.—Richard Sweet Cole, *Ens.* ᴾ 12 Aug. 36; *Lt.* ᴾ 25 Dec. 38; *Capt.* 28 Feb. 51.

War Services of the Battalion Field Officers.

1 Colonel Jervis served in the 72nd Highlanders the Kaffir campaigns of 1834-35 (Medal).

2 Colonel Phillips served with the 43rd Light Infantry in the Kaffir war of 1851-3 (Medal), and was promoted Brevet Lt.-Col. for his services.

3 Major Wombwell served with the 46th Regt. at the siege of Sebastopol in 1854-55 (Medal and Clasp, Brevet-Major, and 5th Class of the Medjidie).

3† Lt.-Colonel Whitmore served the Eastern campaign of 1854 as Aide-de-Camp to Sir George Brown including the battles of the Alma (horse shot) and Inkerman, and siege of Sebastopol (Medal and Clasps, Knight of the Legion of Honor, and 5th Class of the Medjidie).

4 Major Ellis served with the 33rd Regt. at the siege of Sebastopol in 1855 (wounded 15th Aug.), and at the assaults of the Redan on the 18th June and 8th Sept. (wounded) (Medal and Clasp, Brevet Major, and 5th Class of the Medjidie).

5 Colonel Armstrong served the Eastern campaign of 1854-55 (during 1854 as a Major of Brigade in the 2nd Division), and was present at the battles of Alma, Balaklava, and Inkerman (horse killed), and siege of Sebastopol, sortie on 26th Oct. (horse shot); commanded the left column of the storming party at the capture of the Quarries—twice severely wounded, first by a grape-shot in the thigh, and afterwards by the explosion of a Fougass (Medal and four Clasps, Brevets of Major and Lt.-Colonel, Knight of the Legion of Honor, and 4th Class of the Medjidie).

6 Lt.Colonel Laye was engaged in the assault and capture of Kawiti's Pah, in New Zealand, 11 Jan. 1846; also served throughout the campaign of 1846 and 47, and commanded the troops at Wanganui on the 19th May 1847, when the Natives attacked the Settlement and were repulsed, for which service he was promoted Brevet Lt.Colonel. In 1855 he joined the staff in Turkey, and was appointed Assistant Military Secretary to Lord Wm. Paulet, commanding the troops on the Bosphorus.

7 Colonel Street served in the 98th Regt. with the expedition to the North of China in 1842 (Medal) and was present at the attack and capture of Chinkiangfoo, and at the landing before Nankin. Embarked for the Crimea 18th Sept. 1854, as Brigade Major, 1st Brigade, 4th Division; was present at the battles of Balaklava and Inkerman, siege and fall of Sebastopol, and expedition to Kinbourn (Medal and three Clasps, Brevet Major, CB., Sardinian Medal, and 4th Class of the Medjidie).

8 Lt.-Colonel Wright served during the Kaffir war of 1846-47; also that of 1852-53, on the staff (Medal). Was senior surviving officer of the troops embarked in H.M.S. *Birkenhead*, which vessel was wrecked off Danger Point, Cape of Good Hope, on the night of the 26th Feb. 1852. Promoted to the rank of Major and awarded a pension of 100l. per annum for "distinguished services;" and subsequently promoted to the rank of Lieut.-Colonel for " service in the field,"

9 Colonel Borton served with the 9th Regt. the campaign of 1842 in Affghanistan (Medal), and that of 1845-46 on the Sutlej, including the battles of Moodkee and Ferozeshah (Medal and Clasp)—in the latter he succeeded to the command of the Regt. and was severely wounded. Served also the campaign in the Crimea, in command of the Regiment, from 27th Nov. 1854, including the siege and fall of Sebastopol, and assault on the batteries on the 18th June (Medal and Clasp, Knight of the Legion of Honor, and 3rd Class of the Medjidie).

10 Colonel Jeffreys served with the 88th Regt. the Eastern campaign of 1854, and was present at the battles of Alma and Inkerman (wounded—at the latter he commanded the Regt.) and the siege of Sebastopol (Medal and Clasps, and 5th Class of the Medjidie).

11 Major Deshon served with the 22nd Regt. in Scinde, and was present at the battle of Hyderabad (Medal). He served also the campaign in the Southern Mahratta country in 1844-5, and was present at the investment and capture of the Forts of Panulla and Pownghur, as also in the operations against the Forts of Munnahur and Munsuntosh in the Southern Concan. Landed in the Crimea with the 48th Regt., served at the siege and fall of Sebastopol, and commanded a portion of the Regiment detached on duty in the Dockyard from 14th January to 14th March 1856 (Medal and Clasp, Brevet Major, and 5th Class of the Medjidie).

12 Major Mein served with the 13th Regt. in Affghanistan in 1838, 39, 40, and 41, and was present at the storm and capture of Ghuznee (Medal), assault and capture of the town and forts of Tootamdurrah, storm of Joolghur, night attack at Baboo Koosh Ghur, destruction of Kardurrah, assault of Perwandurrah, and storming the Khoord Cabool Pass, where he was dangerously wounded and sent into Cabool, and was consequently present with the force under Major-General Elphinstone, during the insurrection at Cabool, and on the disastrous retreat, until taken prisoner at Tezeen on the 8th Jan. 1842;

he was released with the other Cabool captives in September following. Was specially mentioned for gallant conduct during the disastrous retreat from Cabool in 1842, by Sir Robert Peel when moving a vote of thanks in the House of Commons to the Army of the Indus in 1843 at the conclusion of the Affghan War.

13 Major Armstrong served with the 17th Regt. at the siege and fall of Sebastopol from 10th May 1855, and attacks of the Redan on the 18th June and 8th Sept., also at the bombardment and surrender of Kinbourn (Brevet Major, Medal and Clasp, and 5th Class of the Medjidie).

14 Major Rickman served with the 77th Regt. in the Crimea from Nov. 1854, including the siege of Sebastopol and sortie of 22nd March (Medal and Clasp, Brevet Major, Knight of the Legion of Honor, and 5th Class of the Medjidie).

15 Colonel Smith commanded a detachment of the 38th Regiment in co-operation with a Naval expedition under Captain Loch in the ascent, in boats, of the river St. Juan de Nicaragua, Central America, in 1848, including the assault and capture of the port of Serapiqui, and surrender of the Forts of Castillo Viejo and St. Carlos. He also accompanied Captain Loch to the town of Grenada, and was present at the deliberations and conclusion of a treaty with the Nicaragua Commissioners. Served the Eastern campaign of 1854-55, including the battles of Alma and Inkerman, siege of Sebastopol, capture and occupation of the Cemetery and suburbs on the 18th June, and was senior officer of the 38th at the close of the war (Medal and three Clasps, Knight of the Legion of Honor, and 4th Class of the Medjidie).

16 Major Hardy served the Eastern campaign of 1854, and commanded the detachment of two companies 40th Foot at the battles of the Alma, Balaklava, and Inkerman (severely wounded in right shoulder), and siege of Sebastopol (Medal and Clasps, Brevet Major, and 5th Class of the Medjidie).

17 Colonel Dixon served with the 77th Regt. the Eastern campaign of 1854-55, including the battles of Alma and Inkerman, and siege of Sebastopol (Medal and Clasps, Brevet Lt.-Colonel, CB., Knight of the Legion of Honor, and 4th Class of the Medjidie).

18 Major de Morel served in the Eastern campaign of 1854-55 as Aide-de-Camp to General Estcourt, including the battles of Alma, Balaklava, and Inkerman, and siege of Sebastopol (Medal and Clasps, Brevet Major, Knight of the Legion of Honor, and 5th Class of the Medjidie).

19 Colonel Norcott served the Eastern campaign of 1854-55; held the independent command of a wing of the 2nd Batt. Rifle Brigade at the battle of the Alma—horse killed—(markedly named in the first Dispatch), as also before Sebastopol on its first bombardment. From 1st February 1855 he commanded the 1st Battalion engaged in the siege operations (Medal and Clasps, Brevets of Lt.-Col. and Colonel, Aide-de-Camp to the Queen, CB., Officer of the Legion of Honor, Sardinian Medal, and 3rd Class of the Medjidie).

20 Major M'Donald served the Eastern campaign of 1854 as Aide-de-Camp to General Pennefather, including the battles of the Alma (severely wounded) and Inkerman (severely wounded), and siege of Sebastopol (Medal and Clasps, Brevet Major, and 5th Class of the Medjidie).

21 Major Chichester served at the siege of Sebastopol from 20th Nov. 1854 (Medal and Clasp, and Brevet Major). Served in Bengal in suppressing the Mutiny in 1857-58, with the Joumpore field force in the action of Nusrutpore, during part of which he commanded the reserve consisting of a Regt. of Goorkas and a wing of the 97th Regt.; commanded the Selected Marksmen of the 97th with the Joumpore field force, including the actions of Chanda, Ummeerpore, and Sultanpore; advanced with 2 Subalterns and 90 men in support at the attack of Fort   and passing through the village stormed two faces of the entrenchments from the opposite side, and assisted in bringing out two guns under a close fire; was afterwards at the siege and capture of Lucknow and storming of the Kaisor Bagh (thrice thanked in despatches).

22 Major Stewart served with the 1st Royals the Eastern campaign up to 23rd April 1855, including the battles of Alma and Inkerman and siege of Sebastopol (Medal and three Clasps, and 5th Class of the Medjidie).

23 Lt.-Col. Fairtlough served the Eastern campaign of 1854 with the 63rd Regt., including the battles of Alma, Balaklava, and Inkerman (severely wounded), and siege of Sebastopol (Medal and Clasps, Brevet Major, Sardinian Medal, and 5th Class of the Medjidie).

24 Major Greene served with the 43rd Light Infantry in the Kaffir war of 1851-53 (Medal). Nominated to the 4th Class of the Medjidie for service with the Turkish Contingent.

25 Colonel Muller served with the 1st Royals in the Burmese war, under Sir Archibald Campbell (Medal).

26 Colonel Goodenough served at the siege of Sebastopol in 1854-55, and commanded the 34th Regt. at the assault of the Redan on the 8th September (Medal and Clasp, Brevet Lt.-Col., Knight of the Legion of Honor, and 5th Class of the Medjidie).

27 Major Nason served at the siege of Sebastopol from May 1855, including the assault on the Quarries (lt Major), and on the Redan on 18th June and 8th Sept. (Medal and Clasp, and 5th Class of the Medjidie).

28 Lt.Colonel Hobbs served at the siege of Sebastopol in 1855, and commanded the 21st Fusiliers at the attack on the Redan on the 18th June (Medal and Clasp, and 5th Class of the Medjidie).

29 Colonel Egerton served at the siege and fall of Sebastopol from 15th Dec. 1854, and attacks on the 18th June and 8th Sept. (Medal and Clasp, Sardinian Medal, and 5th Class of the Medjidie).

30 Colonel Farren served with the 47th Regt. the Eastern campaign of 1854-55,—present uninterruptedly with the expeditionary force from the commencement of the war with Russia to the breaking up of the army in the Crimea at the conclusion of peace,—including the battles of Alma and Inkerman, capture of Balaklava, sortie on 26th Oct., siege and fall of Sebastopol. Commanded the 47th Regt. at the battle of Inkerman and uninterruptedly during the siege of Sebastopol (the trenches) from 5th Nov. 1854 to 8th Nov. 1855, including the attacks of the 18th June and 8th Sept.; at Inkerman he was the senior officer of the 2nd Brigade 2nd Division coming out of action—mentioned in Dispatches (Medal and Clasps, Brevet of Lt.-Col., CB., Officer of the Legion of Honor, Sardinian Medal, and 4th Class of the Medjidie).

31 Major Brown Westhead served with the 34th Regt. in the Crimea from 9th Dec. 1854 to 24th July 1855, including the siege of Sebastopol, sortie of 9th May, capture of the Rifle Pits on 19th April, and capture of the Quarries—severely wounded (Medal and Clasp, Brevet Major, and 5th Class of the Medjidie).

32 Major West landed in the Crimea with the 48th Regt. on the 21st April 1855, and served at the siege of Sebastopol (Medal and Clasp, Knight of the Legion of Honor, and 5th Class of the Medjidie).

33 Major Lawrie served in the Crimea in 1854-55, including the siege of Sebastopol, assault and capture of the Cemetery on the 18th June (Medal and Clasp, and 5th Class of the Medjidie).

34 Lt.-Col. Deverell served the Deccan campaigns of 1816, 17, and 18; in the Persian Gulf in 1819 and 20, including the capture of the Arab fortresses of Ras-el-Khyma and Zyah; and in the Burmese war from Nov. 1825 until the peace in 1826, including the capture of Donabew, attacks on the height near Prome, of Maloon, and of several stockades.

35 Major Warry served with the 34th Regt. at the siege of Sebastopol from Feb. to 30th July 1855, and was severely contused in the trenches on the 18th June (Medal and Clasp, and Brevet Major).

36 Lt.Colonel Nugent served in the field in New Zealand during 1845-46; commanded the advanced guard which penetrated the forest surrounding Ruapekapeka, and was present at the capture of that Pah on 11th Jan. 1846.

37 Major Yonge served with the Queen's Royals throughout Lord Keane's campaign in Affghanistan and Beloochistan, and was severely wounded at the storming of Ghuznee (Medal). He served also the campaign in the Southern Mahratta country in 1844 (including the storm of the fortress of Punella), and that of the Concan in 1845.

38 Major Manners served throughout the Burmese War of 1853-53, and was present with the 51st Light Infantry on board the E. I. C. steam frigate *Feroze* at the attack and destruction of the enemy's batteries and stockades on the Rangoon River on the 11th April 1852; on the following day commanded the skirmishers which covered the disembarkation and advance of the storming party at the capture of the White House Redoubt; at the final assault and taking of Rangoon he commanded the Escort of the Major General Commanding, and at the storm and capture of Rangoon (Medal). Was appointed Brigade Major to the 1st Madras Brigade in Sept. 1852, and was present at the engagement on the heights of Prome (Medal and Clasp).

Depot Battalions.—War Services.

39 Major Elgee served with the 47th Regt. at the siege of Sebastopol in 1855 (Medal and Clasp, and Brevet Major).
40 Major Skipwith served throughout the Eastern campaign of 1854-55 with the 41st Regt., including the battles of Alma and Inkerman, siege and fall of Sebastopol, and repulse of the powerful sortie of 26th Oct. (Medal and three Clasps, Brevet Major, Knight of the Legion of Honor, Sardinian Medal, and 5th Class of the Medjidie).
41 Major King served with the 55th Regt. on the China expedition (Medal), at Amoy, Chusan, Chinhae (including repulse of night-attack), Chapoo, Woosung, Shanghae, and Chin Kiang Foo. Also the Eastern campaign of 1854, including the battle of Alma and siege of Sebastopol (Medal and Clasps).
42 Major Drewe served with the 23rd Fusiliers the Eastern campaign of 1854-55, including the battles of Alma and Inkerman, siege and fall of Sebastopol, attack of the Quarries, also attacks of the 18th June and 8th Sept.—wounded and mentioned in Dispatches (Medal and three Clasps, Brevet Major, Knight of the Legion of Honor, and Sardinian Medal).
43 Lt.Colonel Gordon served with the 93rd Highlanders the Eastern campaign of 1854 and up to 11th July 1855, including the battles of Alma and Balaklava, expedition to the Sea of Azoff, capture of Kertch and Yenikali, and siege of Sebastopol (Medal and Clasps, Brevet Lt.Colonel, and 5th Class of the Medjidie). Served in the Indian campaign under Sir Colin Campbell from Sept. 1857 to April 1858, including the relief of Lucknow, action at Cawnpore, and final capture of Lucknow ; at the relief of Lucknow from 13th to 24th Nov. commanded the 53rd Regt., for which he was made a CB. ; commanded left wing 93rd Highlanders at the storming of the Begum's Palace, and specially mentioned in despatches as commanding a part of the 93rd in dislodging the enemy from their last position in Lucknow.
44 Major Elton served with the 55th Regt. the Eastern campaign of 1854-55, including the battle of Inkerman, siege and fall of Sebastopol, Sortie of 26th Oct., attack on the Quarries (mentioned in despatches), and assault of the Redan on the 8th Sept. (mentioned in despatches); was wounded in the trenches on 10th Aug. (Medal and Clasps, Brevet Major, Victoria Cross, Knight of the Legion of Honor, and 5th Class of the Medjidie).
45 Major Patrick Robertson served in the Cape Mounted Rifles during the Kaffir war of 1850-51 (Medal), was appointed Field Captain in command of the local force of "Armstrong's Horse;" in which capacity he was engaged in many most successful operations against the enemy, including the affair against Seyola's tribe, April 16, 1851, where he captured 200 head of cattle, and had his horse killed under him; and more particularly at the combined attack on the Amatolas June 28, 1851, where he captured nearly 2000 head of cattle; repeatedly had the honor of receiving the highest commendation in General Orders, and special mention in the despatches of Sir Harry Smith, then Governor and Commander-in-Chief. Served throughout the Eastern campaign of 1854-55 with the 4th Regt., including the battles in the Crimea, siege and fall of Sebastopol ; was mentioned in the despatches in high terms by Lord Raglan and by General Eyre, for the "spirited manner" in which, on the night of the 22nd Nov. 1854, and following morning, he twice repulsed the Russian attack upon an advanced position before Sebastopol; served as Aide-de-Camp to Sir William Eyre since 17th April 1855, including the attack and occupation of the Cemetery on 18th June (Medal and Clasps, Brevet Major, Knight of the Legion of Honor, and 5th Class of the Medjidie).
46 Major Deering served as Brigade Major to Colonel Despard's force in the operations against and assault on the rebel chief's Pah at Ohuiawai in New Zealand on 1st July 1845 (mentioned in despatch), also at the destruction of Anatuale's Pah on 16th July.
47 Major Appleyard served with the 80th in the Burmese war of 1852 (Medal), and was present at the capture of Martaban, operations before Rangoon on the 12th, 13th, and 14th April, and capture of the Great Dagon Pagoda, with the storming party ; also at the capture of Prome. Served the Eastern campaign of 1854-55 with the Royal Fusiliers, and was present at the battles of Alma (wounded) and Inkerman, and siege of Sebastopol, including sorties on 5th April and 9th May, defence of the Quarries 7th June, and assault on the Redan 18th June—wounded (Medal and Clasps, Knight of the Legion of Honor, and 5th Class of the Medjidie).
48 Colonel Crofton served in the Eastern campaign of 1854 with the 20th Regt., including the battle of Alma, siege of Sebastopol, and battle of Inkerman (severely wounded and horse shot). He commanded the Regt. at Alma and a wing at Inkerman (Medal and three Clasps, Knight of the Legion of Honor, and 5th Class of the Medjidie).

Adjutants.

1 Captain Young served with the 98th Regt. in the Punjaub campaign of 1848-49 (Medal).
2 Captain Hon. B. M. Ward served with the 47th Regt. the Eastern campaign of 1854-55, including the battle of Inkerman, siege of Sebastopol, and sortie of 26th Oct. (Medal and Clasps, and Sardinian Medal).
4 Captain Coxon served in the Orange River Sovereignty, Cape of Good Hope, in 1851, where he was dangerously wounded (shot through both thighs) in an encounter with Boers and Hottentots.
5 Captain Hanham served the Sutlej campaign of 1845-46, including the battles of Moodkee (wounded), Ferozeshah, and Sobraon (Medal and Clasps).
6 Captain Roney served as Major in the 1st Jager Corps, British German Legion, from its formation, accompanied it to the East, and was eventually appointed to the command of the corps.
7 Captain Padfield served the Eastern campaign of 1854-55 as Adjutant of the 20th Regt., including the battles of Alma, Balaklava, and Inkerman (wounded, and horse shot under him), and siege operations against Sebastopol—severely wounded (Medal and Clasps).
8 Captain Hughes has the 4th Class of the Medjidie for Service with the late Turkish Contingent.
9 Captain Hon. S. R. H. Ward served with the 72nd Highlanders in the Crimea in 1855, including the expedition to Kertch, siege and fall of Sebastopol, and attack of the 18th June (Medal and Clasp).
10 Captain Little served in the Eastern campaign of 1854-55, including the siege of Sebastopol (wounded 28th March), attack on the Quarries 7th June, and on the Redan 18th June (Medal and Clasp).
11 Captain Sidebottom served with the Buffs at the siege of Sebastopol in 1855 (Medal and Clasp).
12 Captain Bell served the Eastern campaign of 1854-55, including the battles of Alma and Inkerman, siege and fall of Sebastopol, and affair in the Cemetery (Medal and three Clasps, and Sardinian Medal).
13 Captain Flamstead served with the 18th Royal Irish throughout the Burmese war of 1852-53 (Medal), including the destruction of the stockades in the Rangoon River, capture of Rangoon and Prome, and the greater part of the operations against Myattoon in the Donabew district.
14 Major Welman commanded a detachment of the 80th, embarked in the private schooner *Ariel*, at the capture by surprise of the piratical schooner *Hannah* in a harbour of the Mercury Islands on the 26th Oct. 1843, for which he received the thanks of the Governor of New Zealand, and the approbation of the Duke of Wellington. He served the campaign on the Sutlej in 1845-6 as Adjutant of the 80th, including the battles of Moodkee, Ferozeshah, and Sobraon (Medal and two Clasps).
16 Capt. Beswick served in the Eastern campaign up to 8th Nov. 1854, as Adjutant of the 38th Regt., including the battles of Alma and Inkerman, and siege of Sebastopol (Medal and three Clasps).
17 Captain Marlley served in the Crimea with the 56th Regt. from 25th Aug. 1855 (Medal with Clasp for Sebastopol).
18 Captain Rocke served with the 2nd Regt. in the Kaffir war of 1851-53 (Medal).
19 Captain Grant served with the 2nd Foot during the campaign of 1844-45, in the Southern Concan and Sawant Warree country, including the storming of several stockades and the investment and capture of the Forts of Monohur and Munsyntosh.

Paymasters.

1 Captain Naylor served at the siege and capture of Loghur, Konreo, Ryghur, and several small Hill Forts in the Southern Mahratta country in 1818. Served in the Serwent Warree State, and was severely wounded in both legs (compound fracture of the right) at the assault of Roree, 13th Feb. 1819. Served also in the Burmese war in 1825 and 1826; and at the capture of Kurrachee in Lower Scinde in 1839. Has received the India Medal with a Clasp for Ava.

2 Paymaster Burney served with the 51st throughout the Burmese war of 1852-53; on board the E.I.C. steam frigate *Feroze* during the naval action and destruction of the enemy's stockades on the Rangoon River; during the succeeding three days' operations in the vicinity, and at the storm and capture of Rangoon.

3 Paymaster Roche served in the 34th Regt. in the Crimea from 9th Dec. 1854 (Medal and Clasp for Sebastopol).

4 Paymaster Wheatley served with the 42nd the Eastern campaign of 1854, including the battles of Alma and Balaklava, and siege of Sebastopol (Medal and three Clasps).

5 Paymaster Corcoran served with the 48th Regt. the Coorg campaign in April 1834.

6 Paymaster Benson served in the Peninsula from July 1812 to the end of the war, including the battles of Vittoria, the Pyrenees (wounded in the arm), Pampeluna, Nivelle, Nive, Orthes, and Toulouse, and has received the War Medal with five Clasps. Served also in the American war, and was severely wounded in the right breast by a rifle-ball at Plattsburgh. Served the Eastern campaign of 1854-55, including the battles of Alma and Inkerman, and siege of Sebastopol (Medal and Clasps, and Turkish Medal).

7 Captain Wethered served in the Eastern campaign of 1854, including the battle of Alma (Medal and Clasp).

8 Paymaster Fenoran served the campaign of 1814 in Holland; also that of 1815, including the battle of Waterloo.

9 Captain Young served with the 22nd Regt. the campaign of 1844-45 in the Southern Mahratta country, and was present at the investment and capture of the Forts of Panulla and Pownghur.

10 Paymaster Fair served with the 44th in the retreat from Cabool, and was taken prisoner at Gundamuck after receiving four wounds. He served with the 50th at the battle of Punniar (Medal), and the campaign on the Sutlej (Medal and three Clasps), including the battles of Moodkee, Ferozeshah, Aliwal, and Sobraon.

11 Paymaster Bodle served in the 80th Regt. throughout the Sutlej campaign of 1845-6, including the battles of Moodkee, Ferozeshah, and Sobraon (Medal and two Clasps). Also in the Burmese war of 1852, including the capture of Martaban, operations before Rangoon on the 12th, 13th, and 14th of April, and capture of the Great Dagon Pagoda (with the storming party), and capture of Prome (Medal).

12 Captain Hall served with the 14th Regt. at the siege and fall of Sebastopol (Medal and Clasp).

13 Paymaster Hawker served with the 21st Fusiliers the Eastern campaign of 1854-55, including the battles of Alma, Balaklava, and Inkerman, siege and fall of Sebastopol, and expedition to Kinbourn (Medal and four Clasps).

14 Paymaster Travers served with the 31st Regt. in the Crimea from 22nd May 1855, including the siege and fall of Sebastopol, and attacks of the 18th June and 8th Sept. (Medal and Clasp).

15 Paymaster Griffiths served the campaigns of 1813 and 14 in the Peninsula. Served also in the American War, including the capture of Washington, battle before Baltimore, the several operations on the coast, the several attacks upon the enemy's lines before New Orleans, and taking of Fort Bowyer. In the Batteries upon the banks of the Mississippi at the blowing-up of a man-of-war schooner.

16 Paymaster Williams served with the 90th Light Infantry throughout the Kaffir war of 1846-47 (Medal), in the Crimea during the siege and fall of Sebastopol from 5th Dec. 1854 (Medal and Clasp, and Turkish Medal). In the Indian campaign in 1857-58 including the actions at Cawnpore in Dec., and subsequently at the fall of Lucknow (Medal and Clasp).

17 Paymaster Creagh served the Eastern campaign of 1854-55, including the battle of Alma and siege of Sebastopol (Medal and Clasps).

Quarter Masters.

1 Quarter Master Morris served with the 30th Regt. the Eastern campaign of 1854-55, including the battle of Inkerman, siege of Sebastopol, and sortie of 26th Oct. (Medal and Clasps).

2 Qr. Master Vousden served with the 21st Fusiliers the Eastern campaign of 1854, including the battles of Alma, Balaklava, and Inkerman (severely wounded in left leg), and siege of Sebastopol (Medal and four Clasps).

3 Quarter Master Anderson served with the 40th Regt. throughout the operations in China, including the first taking of Chusan, storm and capture of Canton, capture of Amoy, second capture of Chusan, capture of the heights of Chinhae, occupation of Ningpo and repulse of the night-attack, capture of Chapoo, Woosung, and Chinkiangfoo. Served the Eastern campaign of 1854-55, including the battles of Alma and Inkerman, siege and fall of Sebastopol, and sortie of 26th Oct. (Medal for China, Crimean Medal with three Clasps, and Medal for Meritorious Conduct).

4 Qr. Master Grier served with the 88th Regt. the Eastern campaign of 1854-55, including the battles of Alma and Inkerman, siege of Sebastopol, attack of the Quarries (wounded), and attack of the Redan on 18th June (Medal and Clasps).

5 Qr. Master M'Gregor served throughout the Eastern campaign of 1854-55, including the battles of Alma and Balaklava, expedition to Kertch and Yenikale, siege and fall of Sebastopol (Medal and Clasps). Served the campaign of 1857-58 against the Mutineers in India, including the action at Kudygunge, siege and fall of Lucknow, attack on the fort of Rooyah, action at Allygunge, and capture of Bareilly.

6 Qr. Master Hendry served the campaign of 1815, and was present at the battles of Quatre Bras and Waterloo, and capture of Paris.

7 Qr. Master Watson served with the 80th Regt. at the siege of Sebastopol, from 15th Dec. 1854, to 4th July 1855, and at the attack on the Redan on the 18th June (Medal and Clasp).

8 Qr. Master Jameson served with the 79th Highlanders the Eastern campaign of 1854-55, including the battles of Alma and Balaklava, siege and fall of Sebastopol, assaults of the 18th June and 8th Sept., and expedition to Kertch (Medal and three Clasps, and Sardinian Medal).

9 Qr. Master Desmond served in the Crimea with the 97th Regt. from Nov. 1854, to 27th June 1855, and has received the Medal and Clasp for Sebastopol.

10 Qr. Master Moloney served with the 55th Regt. on the China expedition, and was present at the capture of Amoy and Chusan and storming of Chinkiangfoo (Medal).

11 Quar. Master Moore served with the 31st Regt. the Affghanistan campaign of 1842, including the actions of Mazeena, Tezeen, and Jugdulluck, re-occupation of Cabool, and the different engagements leading to it (Medal). Also the Sutlej campaign of 1845-46, including the actions of Moodkee, Ferozeshah, Buddiwal, Aliwal, and Sobraon (Medal and three Clasps). Served with the 88th Regt. the Eastern campaign of 1854-55, including the battles of Alma (wounded) and Inkerman, siege and fall of Sebastopol (Medal and three Clasps, and 5th Class of the Medjidie).

12 Qr. Master Burke served in the 22nd Regt. in the campaign in the Southern Mahratta country in 1844 and 1845, and was present at the storm of the Pettahs on 27th Nov., and of the forts of Panulla and Pownghur.

13 Qr. Master Hopkins served with the 31st Regt. in the Crimea from 22nd May 1855, including the siege and fall of Sebastopol, and attacks of 18th June and 8th Sept. (Medal and Clasp).

Royal Malta Fencible Regiment. 368

14 Qr.Master Drage served in the Crimea with the Grenadier Guards from April to October 1855, and with the 31st Regt. to the end of the siege (Medal with Clasp for Sebastopol).
15 Qr.Master Brooks served with the Grenadier Guards the Eastern campaign of 1854-55, including the battles of Alma, Balaklava, and Inkerman, siege and fall of Sebastopol, and Sortie of 26th Oct. (Medal and four Clasps).

Surgeon.

1 Doctor Gibb served in the expedition against the insurgent Boers beyond the Orange River in 1845; also throughout the Kaffir war of 1846-47, and that of 1850-53 (Medal), and was present at several engagements.

Royal Malta Fencible Regiment.

Lieut. Colonel.—*Antonio Maltei, 12 Nov. 58.
Major.—*Salverio Gatt, 12 Nov. 58; *Brevet Major*, 26 Oct. 58.
Captains.
- *Felice Rizzo, 20 July 47 ; *Brevet Major*, 26 Oct. 58.
- *Giuseppe Gouder, 12 March 52.
- *Georgio Virtu, 26 June 52.
- *William Gatt, 23 Oct. 57.
- *Giuseppe Cavarra, 22 June 58.
- *Giuseppe Sesino, 12 Oct. 58.

Lieutenants.
- *Filippo Eynaud, 12 March 52.
- *Loreto Bonavita (*Adj.*), 7 May 52.
- *Giuseppe de Piro, 26 June 52.
- *James Lazzarini, 13 Feb. 56.
- *Saverio de Piro, 23 Oct. 57.
- *Henry Montanaro, 22 June 58.
- *Marquis* Filippo Giacomo Cassar Desain, 12 Nov. 58.

Ensigns.
- *Michael Portelli, 12 March 52.
- *Thomas Emmanuel Bonavia, 12 Oct. 52.
- *Frederick Gatt, 25 June 58.
- *Joseph Speranza, 26 June 58.
- *Paolo Bernard, 17 Sept. 58.
- *John Rutter, 4 Feb. 59.

Paymaster.—Vincenzo Rizzo, 25 Feb. 17.
Adjutant.—*Lieut. Loreto Bonavita, 12 Feb. 47.
Instructor of Musketry.—*Ensign* Thomas Emmanuel Bonavia, 20 May 58.
Quarter Master.—*Giovanni Enriquez, 17 March 56.
Surgeon.—Ludovico Bernard, M.D. 9 May 49 ; *Assist.-Surg.* 27 Jan. 43.
Assistant Surgeon.—Carmelo Ellul, M.D., 9 Aug. 49.

Facings Blue.—*Agent, Sir* John Kirkland.

[*Continuation of Notes to Recruiting Staff.*]

12 Paymaster Furlong was in the action before Genoa, and the taking of that city, 7th April, 1814. Served afterwards in the American war, including the operations in the Chesapeake, battle of Bladensburg and capture of Washington, action before Baltimore, and the subsequent service in the Chesapeake ; operations of the army before New Orleans, the actions of the 2nd Dec. 1814, and 1st Jan. 1815, and storm of the American lines before New Orleans ; taking of Port Bowyer. On board the *Golden Fleece* transport when attacked by an American privateer, off the island of St. Domingo, 28th Nov. 1814.
13 Paymaster Marshall served with the 6th Dragoons the Eastern campaign of 1854-55, including the battles of Balaklava and Inkerman, and siege of Sebastopol (Medal and Clasps).
14 Paymaster Robinson served at the siege of Asseerghur in March and April 1819.
15 Lieut. J. B. Hamilton has received the War Medal with one Clasp for Salamanca.
16 Lieut. B. H. Edwards served in the Peninsula from 1811 to the end of that war in 1814, including the siege and storming of Badajoz (wounded) with the 9th Portuguese Regiment of the Line ; and in the 43rd Light Infantry at the battles of Salamanca, Vera, Nivelle (wounded), Nive, Tarbes, and Toulouse. He has received the War Medal with six Clasps.
17 Lieut. Spence served the campaigns of 1813 and 14, in Spain and France, with the 84th, and was present at the passage of the Bidassoa, battles of Nivelle and Nive, and actions near Bayonne. He has received the War Medal with two Clasps.
18 Paymaster FitzGerald served with the 60th Rifles in the Caffir war in 1851-52 (Medal) ; and with the 30th Regt. in the Eastern campaign of 1854, including the battle of Inkerman and siege of Sebastopol (Medal and Clasps).

Recruiting Staff.

Inspecting Field Officers.

Years' Serv. Full Pay.	Years' Serv. Half Pay.	
46	3/12	Thomas Armstrong Drought,[1] *Ens.* 11 Nov. 13; *Lieut.* p 16 Oct. 17; *Capt.* p 10 Oct. 22; *Major*, p 31 Dec. 30; *Lt.-Col.* p 21 Mar. 45; *Col.* 20 June 54.
32	4	William Sullivan,[2] CB. *Ens.* p 14 Oct. 24; *Lt.* p 8 Apr. 26; *Capt.* p 21 June 31; *Maj.* p 27 Aug. 41; *Lt.-Col.* p 11 Sept. 46; *Col.* 20 June 54.
32	0	David Russell,[3] CB. *Cornet,* p 10 Jan. 28; *Lt.* p 1 Oct. 29; *Capt.* p 5 Apr. 33; *Major*, 7 July 45; *Lt.Col.* p 10 Dec. 47; *Col.* 28 Nov. 54.
42	4/12	Edward Basil Brooke, 2nd *Lt. R. Art.* 15 Dec. 17; *Lt.* p 9 Apr. 25; *Capt.* p 11 July 26; *Maj.* p 5 July 31; *Lt.Col.* 9 Nov. 46; *Col.* 20 June 54.
37	0	Charles Franklyn,[4] CB. *Ens.* p 17 July 23; *Lt.* p 8 April 26; *Capt.* p 10 July 28; *Major*, p 28 Dec. 33; *Lieut.Col.* 16 Sept. 45; *Col.* 20 June 54.
41	0	Walter Hamilton,[5] CB. *Ens.* p 28 Jan. 19; *Lt.* p 15 Apr. 24; *Capt.* p 15 Mar. 33; *Brev.Maj.* 9 Nov. 46; *Major*, p 10 Dec. 47; *Lt.Col.* 2 Oct. 49; *Col.* 28 Nov. 54.
32	7	John Rowland Smyth,[6] CB. *Cor.* p 5 July 21; *Lt.* p 26 May 25; *Capt.* p 22 Apr. 26; *Major*, p 17 Aug. 41; *Bt.Lt.Col.* 19 June 46; *Lt.Col.* p 10 Dec. 47; *Col.* 20 June 54.

Paymasters.

40	5 8/12	Henry Balthasor Adams,[9] 30 Oct. 1828; *Ens.* 23 Feb. 15; *Lieut.* 12 June 17; *Capt.* p 17 Sept. 25.
32	6/13	Charles Henry Peirse, 23 Aug. 39; *Ens.* p 6 Dec. 27; *Lieut.* 18 July 30.
30	21 9/12	Charles John Furlong,[12] 22 April 24; 2nd *Lieut.* 29 Sept. 08; *Lieut.* 3 Jan. 10.
43	0	James Robinson,[14] 26 Dec. 37; *Ens.* 20 Nov. 17; *Lieut.* 24 April 20.
32	0	William Henry FitzGerald,[18] 20 Sept. 39; *Ens.* 17 Jan. 28; *Lt.* p 31 May 33.
6	0	Daniel Bartlett, 1 Aug. 54.
22	0	Robert Collins Craigie, 3 Nov. 43; *Ens.* p 2 Feb. 38; *Lt.* p 16 Nov. 41.
12	0	Edward M'Mullin,[10] 15 Oct. 50; *Q.M.* 17 Nov. 48.
17	7/12	James Marshall,[13] 4 May 55; *Q.M.* 14 Apr. 43.

		ADJUTANTS.	ENSIGN.	LIEUT.	ADJUTANT.
28	1 8/12	Charles Pratt Hamilton..........	29 June 30	p 13 Mar. 35	24 Feb. 43
34	16 9/12	p James Banbury Hamilton[15]	25 Sept. 09	p 23 July 12	6 Dec. 44
31	17 1/12	p Benjamin Hutchins Edwards[16]	14 May 12	21 Oct. 13	7 Mar. 47
17	0	Robert Alexander Dagg..........	2 Jan. 43	15 Mar. 46	17 Sept. 47
24	0	p John Spence[17].....	22 April 36	11 Jan. 40	10 Mar. 48
18	0	William Freeme Wyndowe........	p 20 Apr. 42	5 July 44	12 April 50
19	0	William Frederick Lowrie	2 April 41	20 April 43	24 June 53
24	0	George Griffin	16 Dec. 36	22 Feb. 39	26 May 54
11	0	Edward Barnes Goodman	4 May 49	21 May 54	25 July 59

1 Colonel Drought commanded the entire of the troops during the successful suppression of the Rebellion in the Kandian Provinces in Ceylon in 1848;—was thanked in General Orders, and most honourably mentioned throughout in the Dispatches of the Governor and of the Commander of the Forces.

2 Colonel Sullivan served the Eastern campaign of 1854, as Assistant Adjutant-General to the Light Division, including the battles of the Alma, Balaklava, and Inkerman (horse shot), and siege of Sebastopol (Medal and Clasps, CB., Knight of the Legion of Honor, and 4th Class of the Medjidie).

3 Colonel Russell commanded the 5th Brigade at the second relief of Lucknow—severely wounded and particularly mentioned in despatches as having much distinguished himself (C.B.); commanded 1st Brigade under Outram at the repulse of several attacks on the Alumbagh; at the fall of Lucknow he commanded 2nd Brigade which stormed the Imaumbarra and captured the Kaiserbagh.

4 Colonel Franklyn commanded the 2nd Brigade at the Alum Bagh in Feb. and March 1858, and subsequently the 1st Division, and was present at the defeat of the enemy's attack on the 25th-26th Feb.; commanded the 1st Division of the army at the Alumbagh when the position was attacked on the 16th March 1858, by the enemy in great force under the command of the Moulvie, which attack was successfully repulsed (C.B.).

5 Colonel Hamilton commanded a Brigade during the Persian war in 1857, and was present at the bombardment of Mohumrah. Commanded the 78th Highlanders in Havelock's Column from its first taking the field in 1857, including the actions at Futtehpore, Aoung, Pandoo Nuddee, Cawnpore (horse shot), Onao, Buseerut Gunge on 29th July and 5th Aug. (horse killed by a round shot), Boorbeakechowkee, and Bithoor; commanded the left Infantry Brigade in the several actions leading to and ending in the relief of the Residency at Lucknow and its subsequent defence; served with the force under Outram at Alumbagh, including the repulse of the numerous attacks (frequently mentioned in Dispatches, CB., and a pension for distinguished service in the field).

6 Colonel Smyth served with the 16th Lancers at the siege of Bhurtpore, under Lord Combermere (Medal). He was also present with the Regiment in the action of Maharajpore 29th December 1843 (Medal); and in the campaign on the Sutlej in 1846, including the battles of Buddiwal and Aliwal, in the last of which he commanded the Regiment until severely wounded in the thigh by a musket-ball whilst charging the enemy's infantry and guns (Medal and Clasps).

9 Captain Adams served four years in Western Africa, and was present at the various affairs and skirmishes which took place at the different parts of the coast at which he was stationed, including the attack upon, and destruction of, Fort Albredn, and capture of the town of Barra, in the river Gambia, in 1817. Served subsequently in Caffraria, Cape of Good Hope; and with the 71st Highlanders in Upper and Lower Canada.

10 Paymaster M'Mullin served with the 48th Regt. the campaign against the Rajah of Coorgh in April 1834. Served also in the Crimea from 21st April 1855, including the siege and fall of Sebastopol (Medal and Clasp).

[For remainder of Notes, see preceding page.

370

Royal Regiment of Artillery.

The Royal Arms and supporters, with a Cannon, and the Motto "*Ubique*" over the Gun, and "*Quo fas et gloria ducunt*" below it.

The figures prefixed to the Names denote the Brigades to which the Officers belong.—H.B. Horse Brigade.—G.C. Gentleman Cadet Company.—R.H.E. Riding House Establishment.—*d*. Depot Brigade.

Years' Serv. Full Pay / Half Pay		COLONELS-COMMANDANT.	SECOND LIEUT.	FIRST LIEUT.	CAPTAIN.	BREVET-MAJOR.	MAJOR.	BREVET-LT.-COL.	LT.-COL.	BREVET-COLONEL.	COLONEL.	COLONEL COMM.	MAJOR-GENERAL.	LIEUT.-GENERAL.	GENERAL.
66	0	3 Joseph Webbe Tobin	1 Jan. 91	4 Aug. 94	4 Feb. 00	1 Jan. 12	20 Dec. 14	19 July 21	6 Aug. 25	...	31 Dec. 27	16 Aug. 46	10 Jan. 37	9 Nov. 46	20 June 54
65	0	8 Thomas John Forbes	6 Mar. 95	13 April 95	9 Sept. 02	4 June 13	17 Oct. 23	...	29 July 25	...	8 Dec. 47	8 Dec. 47	10 Jan. 37	9 Nov. 46	20 June 54	16 Jan. 59
65	0	H.B. Sir Hew Dalrymple Ross,¹ GCB.	do	10 May 96	1 Sept. 03	31 Dec. 11	29 July 25	21 June 13	do	22 July	1 Nov. 48	25 Nov. 41	11 Nov. 51	28 Nov. 54
63	0	6 Frederick Campbell³	12 Jan. 97	16 July 99	29 July 04	4 June 14	...	...	28 Nov. 28	30	11 June 38	10 Mar. 52	11 Aug. 52	11 Nov. 51	28 Sept. 59
63	0	6 George Turner,⁴ CB.	14 Jan.	do	do	do	...	...	35 Nov.	...	28 June	11 Aug. 52	do	do	
63	0	4 Sir Rob. Wm. Gardiner,⁵ GCB. KCH.	7 April 97	do	12 Oct. 04	27 April 12	...	3 Mar. 14	30 Dec. 28	22 July	30 24 Nov. 39	22 Mar. 53	23 Nov. 41	11 Nov. 51	28 Nov. 54
63	0	11 Peter Margetson Wallace⁶	10 May 97	do	15 Nov.	4 June 14	The Regimental		31 Dec.		23 Nov. 41	21 June 53	20 June 54	28 Nov. 54	
63	0	3 Richard Jones⁷	12 May 97	do	5 Dec. 04	do	rank of Major was	31 Dec. 28		do	1 Jan. 54	do		
63	0	14 E. C. Whinyates,⁸ CB. KH.	11 Mar. 98	2 Oct. 99	8 July 05	18 July	15 rank of	31 July 30		do	1 April 55	20 June 54	1 June 56	
62	0	5 John Michell,⁹ CB.	do	do	20 Sept.	29 Sept. 14	Major was abolished	do		14 June	14 June 56	28 Nov. 54	do	
60	0	4 Wm. Green-fields Power,¹⁰ CB. KH.	31 May 00	11 Feb. 02	13 June 07	21 Sept. 13	abolished	21 June 17	12 June 35	10 Jan. 37	4 May 46	16 Dec. 56	9 Nov. 46	20 June 54	4 Feb. 57
59	0	7 Thomas Dynely,¹¹ CB.	1 Dec. 01	1 July 03	23 May 08	18 June 15	6th Nov.		10 Jan. 37 23 Nov. 41		9 Nov. 46	4 Feb.	20 June 54	16 Dec. 56	
58	0	13 George Cobbe¹²	9 Oct. 29	7 Sept. 01	2 June 06	12 Aug. 10	1827.				1 Apr. 46	29 Aug. 57	do	4 Feb. 57	
56	4/₁₂	9 Alex. Carslile Mercer¹³	20 Dec.	1 Dec.	8 Dec.	do			5 June 35			16 Jan. 59	do	29 Aug. 57	
57	0	1 Sir Wm. M. Geo. Colebrooke,¹⁸ CB. KH.	17 Aug. 02	12 Sept. 04	27 Sept. 10	1 June 13		22 July 30	10 Jan. 37	9 Nov. 46	1 Nov. 46	25 Sept. 59	20 June 54	16 Jan. 50	
		Rem. from Corps, having Rank of *General Officers* (Regimentally placed).													
59	0	Henry Alex. Scott¹⁴	28 Apr. 01	20 Apr. 03	1 Feb. 05	27 May 25			10 Aug. 36		9 Nov. 46	20 June 54		25 Sept. 50	
58	0	Henry Charles Russel¹⁵	1 Apr. 02	12 Sept.	15 July	09 12 April 14			10 Jan. 37		do	do			
57	0	3 William Cator,¹⁶ CB.	7 May 03	do	1 May	3 Aug. 14		22 July 30	do		do	do	28 Nov. 54		
57	0	Henry Wm. Gordon¹⁷	17 Aug.	do	3 Aug. 09	12 April 30			do		1 Nov. 48	20 Nov. 54			
57	0	William Wylde,¹⁹ CB.	8 Sept. 03	6 Dec.	16 Mar. 12	22 July 30		19 Aug. 36	20 Nov. 39	9 Nov. 46	8 Jan. 49	20 June 54			
57	0	9 Alexander Maclachlan²⁰	do	do	17 June	do		1 June 32	11 April 40		11 Nov. 51	14 June 56			
53	2½	9 Edward Sabine²¹	22 Dec.	3 20 July	04 24 Jan. 13	10 Jan. 37			25 Jan. 41		do	6 Jan. 55			
57	0	Francis Rawdon Chesney²²	9 Nov. 04	20 Sept. 05	20 June 15	2 Dec. 35			18 April 42		18 Mar. 52	29 Aug. 57			
32	3¹⁰/₁₂	13 William Bell¹³	28 Nov. 04	2 Dec. 05	3 July 15	10 Jan. 37			do		do	16 Dec. 54			
49	6⁴/₁₂	5 William Brereton,²⁴ CR. KH.	10 May 04	1 June 05	06 30 Sept. 16	21 Jan. 19		10 Jan. 37	17 Aug. 43	11 Nov. 51	24 June 54	9 Aug. 58			
49	6¼	3 Poole Vallancey Encland²⁵	do	do	11 Mar. 17	19 Jan. 35			do		17 Feb. 54	26 Oct. 58			
52	2	5 Richard Hardinge,²⁶ KH.	23 May 06	19 Dec.	06 17 July 23	28 June 28		5 April 45	20 June 54						
53	1	Browne Willis	4 Oct. 06	1 Feb. 08	29 July 25				1 April 46						
52	0	Thomas Gordon Higgins²⁷	do	do	do	do		2 April 41	9 Nov. 51	24 Jan. 57	26 Oct. 58				
52	0	4 Wm. Cochrane Anderson¹³	3 Nov. 07	1 Aug. 08	6 Nov. 27	23 Nov. 41			9 Nov. 54			26 Oct. 58			
52	1	3 Richard Say Armstrong²⁹	17 Dec. 07	22 Mar. 09	do	16 Jan. 59									
51	0	3 Jn. Bloomfield,³⁰ *Insp. Gen. of Artillery*	28 Apr. 10	17 Dec. 13	7 Feb. 32	9 Nov. 46		do	1 Nov. 48	25 Sept. 59					
43	0	Sir Richard James Dacres,³⁶ KCB. s.	15 Dec.	17 29 Aug. 25	25 18 Dec. 37	11 Nov. 51		23 Feb. 52	23 Feb. 55	29 June 55					
35	0	John Edward Dupuis,³⁸ CB.	13 Feb. 25	8 Nov. 27	15 June 40	8 Jan. 47		22 April 53	17 Aug.	2 Nov. 55					
35	0	Sir Wm. Fenwick Williams,³⁹ *Bart.* KCB.	14 July 25	16 Nov. 27	13 Aug. 40	22 Mar. 48		31 Mar. 48	18 Sept. 55	29 Nov. 54					do

Years' Service. Full Pay	Years' Service. Half Pay		Colonels.	Second Lieut.	First Lieut.	Captain.	Brevet Major.	Brevet Lt.-Col.	Lt.-Col.	Brevet Colonel.	Colonel.
51	0	1	P W Francis Warde [30]	4 Mar. 09	8 Mar. 12	3 July 30	9 Nov. 46	....	7 May 47	....	13 Sept. 54
51	0	2	P W William Bates Ingilby [31]	1 Apr. 09	9 April	22 July 30	do	....	do	....	6 Nov. 54
51	0	3	P Henry Pester [32]	1 May 09	16 June	do	do	....	20 July 47	....	28 Nov. 54
50	0	8	P Henry Palliser [34]	4 June	18 Feb. 14	27 Sept.	do	....	1 Nov. 48	28 Nov. 54	13 Dec. 54
46	1 4/12	2	P W Burke Cuppage [35]	17 Dec. 12	20 June 15	20 July 34	do	....	8 Jan. 49	do	6 Jan. 55
41	6 7/12	5	Robert Burn	do	do	14 Aug.	do	....	29 Mar.	do	do
42	3 4/12	6	Daniel Thorndike	1 May 15	8 May 19	28 Dec. 35	do	....	27 May 50	do	do
43	2 8/12	8	Charles Gostling	do	22 April 20	19 April 36	do	....	20 June	do	7 Feb.
42	2 6/12	9	Charles Bertie Symons	10 July 15	2 Dec. 21	1 July	do	....	22 Dec.	do	25 Feb.
44	0	*d*	*Edmund Neal Wilford*	16 Dec. 16	3 Jan. 25	10 Jan. 37	....	....	6 June 51	do	1 April 55
44	0	14	Wm. Henry Pickering	do	9 April 25	do	....	....	11 Nov.	do	do
43	0	4	Thomas Peters Flude	7 July 17	29 July 25	29 Jan. 37	11 Nov. 51	....	30 Dec.	do	15 May 55
42	3/12	11	Charles William Wingfield	8 July 18	1 April 26	30 Dec. 37	do	....	18 Mar. 52	do	24 Sept.
42	3/12	*d*	*Alexander Tulloh*	8 July 18	10 July 26	20 April 38	do	....	1 April 52	do	18 Oct.
40	1 3/12	11	Henry Poole	5 Oct. 18	1 Feb. 27	13 Nov.	do	....	do	do	2 Nov. 55
40	1	H.B.	Henry George Teesdale	8 Dec. 19	26 May 27	23 May 39	do	....	do	do	23 Feb. 56
39	6/12	H.B.	Noel Thomas Lake, [37] CB.	5 July 20	5 July	10 Aug.	do	....	do	do	do
39	9/12	12	Piercy Benn	3 Feb. 21	13 Oct.	14 Aug.	do	....	31 Aug. 52	do	7 June 56
36	0	5	Ashton Ashton Shuttleworth, *s.*	10 Dec. 24	8 Nov.	21 Apr. 40	do	....	7 Dec.	do	14 June
35	0	13	John Hill	10 Apr. 25	12 Nov. 27	22 July	do	....	21 June 53	do	7 July 56
35	0	13	Henry Joseph Morris [40]	29 July 25	1 Jan. 28	27 Sept.	do	....	12 Jan. 54	do	24 Jan. 57
35	0	12	John M'Coy	do	3 Jan.	25 Jan. 41		....	24 Jan.	do	23 Feb. 57
34	0	14	John Wray Mitchell, *s.*	18 Oct. 26	9 Dec.	1 Apr. 41	....	....	17 Feb. 54	do	26 May 57
32	0	7	Rob. Fitzgerald Crawford	19 May 28	12 May 29	do	....	....	do	do	21 July 57
32	0	*d*	*John St. George*, [41] CB., *s.*	do	11 July	do	....	....	do	do	29 Aug. 57
32	0	10	William Robert Nedham [42]	do	12 July	do	....	....	do	do	22 Dec. 57
32	0	6	Edward Charles Warde, [43] CB., *s.*	do	30 June 30	5 June 41	....	....	do	do	5 June 58
32	0	9	John William Ormsby	6 Aug. 28	22 July	16 Sept.	....	....	17 Mar. 54	do	9 Aug. 58
32	0	7	Arthur Joseph Taylor, [44] *s.*	do	22 July	25 Sept. 41	....	....	30 May 54	do	2 Oct. 58
32	0	3	George Maclean [45]	do	5 Aug.	1 Oct.	....	....	do	do	26 Oct. 58
31	0	*d*	*William Harrison Askwith* [46]	18 Dec. 29	6 Nov.	23 Nov. 41	28 Jan. 42	20 June 54	20 June 54	20 June 57	do
31	0	10	Franklin Dunlop, [47] CB. *s.*	do	25 Nov.	do	20 June 54	....	do	do	do
31	0	4	Francis Dick	do	26 Nov.	do	do	....	do	do	16 Jan. 59
31	0	1	Charles James Dalton	do	29 Apr. 31	do	do	....	do	do	25 Sept. 59
			Lieutenant-Colonels.								
31	0	H. B.	*Sir* David Edward Wood, [48] KCB.	18 Dec. 29	30 June 31	23 Nov. 41	20 June 54	....	20 June 54	2 Nov. 55	
30	0	4	Fred. Marow Eardley-Wilmot	6 Nov. 30	27 Sept.	7 April 42	do	....	do	20 June 57	
30	0	8	James William Fitzmayer, [49] CB.	do	26 Oct.	12 April	do	....	do	2 Nov. 55	
30	0	6	Geo. Robert Harry Kennedy	do	27 Oct.	13 April	do	....	do	20 Aug. 57	

Royal Artillery.

Years' Service.		LIEUTENANT-COLONELS.	SECOND LIEUT.	FIRST LIEUT.	CAPTAIN.	BREVET-MAJOR.	BREVET-LIEUT. COL.	LIEUT. COL.	BREVET COLONEL.
Full Pay	Half Pay								
30	0	12	Chas. Vansittart Cockburn	6 Nov. 30	2 Feb.	32 13 April 42	20 April 54	....	20 June 54	20 Sept. 57
29	0	4	John Henry Francklyn,[50] CB.	26 July 31	23 June	do	do	....	6 June	28 June 57
29	0	H. B.	Gloucester Gambier,[51] CB.	do	31 July	do	do	....	6 July	6 July 57
29	0	4	Edward Walter Crofton[52]	do	29 Aug.	2 Aug.	do	....	6 Nov.	6 Nov. 57
29	0	13	Gilbert John Lane Buchanan	16 Dec. 31	1 Aug.	33 4 April 43	do	....	28 Nov.	28 Nov. 57
29	0	2	Henry Aylmer	do	21 Nov.	do	do	....	13 Dec.	13 Dec. 57
29	0	6	Alexander Irving,[53] CB.	do	10 Mar. 34	4 May	do	....	do	do
29	0	13	St. John Thomas Browne	20 June 32	11 July	18 May	15 Sept. 48	....	do	do
28	0	5	Charles Bingham, *Deputy Adjt. Gen.*	do	20 July	17 Aug.	20 June 54	....	16 Dec. 54	16 Dec. 57
28	0	13	Henry Sebastian Rowan,[54] CB.	do	14 Aug.	18 Aug.	22 May 46	20 June 54	do	14 Oct. 57
28	0	12	John Noble Arbuthnot Freese,[55] CB.	do	9 Sept.	22 Aug.	20 June 54	....	6 Jan. 55	6 Jan. 58
28	0	10	Fred. Darby Cleaveland[56]	do	25 Sept.	1 Sept.	do	....	do	do
28	0	7	Henry Austin Turner	do	20 Nov.	14 Jan. 44	28 Nov. 54	....	do	do
28	0	9	Thomas Beckett Feilding Marriott	20 Dec.	21 Nov.	30 Mar.	do	....	13 Jan. 55	13 Jan. 58
28	0	5	Thomas Elwyn, s.	do	29 Dec.	1 April	29 Sept. 54	....	7 Feb. 55	7 Feb. 58
28	0	3	Charles James Wright	do	30 Dec.	do	do	....	do	do
28	0	1	George Augustus Fred. De Rinzy	do	28 Jan. 35	do	do	....	25 Feb. 55	25 Feb. 58
28	0	10	William Hamilton Elliot	do	4 April	14 May 44	do	....	8 Mar. 55	8 Mar. 58
28	0	1	Peter Maclean	do	5 May	15 April	do	....	do	do
28	0	7	Anthony Benn	do	2 Sept. 36	5 April 45	do	....	1 April 55	1 Apr. 58
27	0	12	Wm. Thomas Crawford,[57] CB.	21 June 33	1 July	5 April	do	....	do	do
27	0	10	Pierrepont Henry Mundy	20 Dec. 33	2 July	10 April	do	....	do	do
27	0	3	William Henderson	do	13 July	6 May 37	do	....	do	do
27	0	13	William James Smythe	do	10 Jan.	9 May	12 Dec. 54	....	15 May 55	15 May 58
27	0	7	David William Paynter,[58] CB.	do	do	21 May	do	....	1 June	2 Nov. 55
26	0	14	Sir George Robert Barker,[59] KCB. s.	21 June 34	do	14 June	28 May 53	....	29 June	29 June 58
26	0	14	Peter Pickmore Faddy[60]	do	do	3 Sept.	do	....	13 Aug.	13 Aug. 58
26	0	H. B.	Arthur Thomas Phillpotts[61]	do	do	29 Oct.	do	....	1 Sept.	1 Sept. 58
26	0	2	William Bethel Gardner	19 Dec. 34	do	30 Nov.	do	....	24 Sept. 55	24 Sept. 58
26	0	d	John Henry Lefroy	do	do	12 Dec.	do	....	do	do
26	0	11	Charles James Buchanan Riddell,[62] CB.	do	do	26 Feb. 46	do	....	18 Oct. 55	
26	0	10	Arthur George Burrows	do	do	1 April 46	do	....	2 Nov. 55	
26	0	H. B.	Edward Price,[63] CB.	do	28 Jan.	do	do	....	do	
26	0	7	James William Domville	do	6 Feb.	do	do	....	do	
26	0	6	Edwin Wodehouse,[64] CB. *Aide de Camp to the Queen, Assist. Adj. Gen.*	do	22 Feb.	do	do	....	do	14 June 59
26	0	d	Geo. Ashley Maude,[65] CB. *Crown Equerry*	18 June	27 Mar.	do	12 Dec. 54	....	23 Feb. 56	
25	0	5	Evan Maberly,[66] CB.	do	24 June	do	do	....	do	
25	0	9	Wm. Manley Hall Dixon	do	30 Oct.	do	do	....	do	
25	0	d	Collingwood Dickson,[67] CB. *Aide de Camp to the Queen, Assist. Adj. Gen. in Ireland*	18 Dec.	29 Nov. 37	do	22 May 46	20 June 54	do	29 June 55
25	0	6	George Graydon[68]	do	23 Mar. 38	do	do	....	7 June 56	

Years' Service			LIEUTENANT-COLONELS.	2ND LIEUT.	1ST LIEUT.	CAPTAIN.	BREVET MAJOR.	BREVET LIEUT.-COL.	LIEUT.-COL.	BREVET COLONEL
Full Pay	Half Pay									
25	0	11	Henry Paget Christie	18 Dec. 38	11 June 38	1 April 46	......	......	14 June 56	......
24	0	14	James Benjamin Dennis	18 Jan.	28 June	do	......	......	1 Jan. 57	......
24	0	14	John Travers[69]	do	6 Oct.	6 April 46	......	......	24 Jan.	......
24	0	4	*Hon.* George Talbot Devereux[70]	do	13 Nov.	13 April	28 May 53	......	28 Feb.	......
24	0	1	Spencer Delves Broughton[71]	do	23 May 39	23 June	2 Nov. 55	26 Dec. 56	21 July 57	......
24	0	12	Allan Hamilton Graham	do	3 July	8 July	......	......	29 Aug. 57	......
24	0	11	John Miller Adye,[72] CB	13 Dec.	7 July 36	29 July	22 Sept. 54	12 Dec. 54	15 Sept. 57	......
24	0	*d*	*Frederick Alex. Campbell*	30 Dec.	10 Aug. 36	14 Oct.	......	......	do	......
24	0	8	Henry Philip Goodenough	do	13 Aug.	9 Nov. 46	......	......	22 Dec. 57	......
24	0	9	George Bucknall Shakespear	do	11 Sept.	do	......	......	26 May 58	......
23	0	5	Richard Henry Crofton	5 May	20 Nov. 37	do	......	......	5 June 58	......
23	0	8	Murray Octavius Nixon	14 Dec.	25 Feb. 37	do 40	......	......	9 Aug. 58	......
23	0	8	Henry Lynedoch Gardiner[73]	do	16 Mar.	do	20 July 55	......	26 Oct. 58	......
23	0	9	Robert Parker Radcliffe	do	13 May	do	......	......	do	......
23	0	13	Thomas Knox[74]	do	15 June	do	13 Apr. 58	......	do	......
23	0	3	Charles Wright Younghusband[75]	do	19 June	28 Nov.	26 Oct. 58	......	16 Jan. 59	......
22	0	3	Robert Corcyra Romer	6 June	20 July 38	15 Mar. 47	26 Dec. 54	26 Dec. 56	2 Mar. 59	20 July 58
22	0	11	Charles Lawrence D'Aguilar,[76] CB	do	22 July	22 April	2 Nov. 55	26 Dec. 56	15 May 59	......
22	0	2	Hugh Archibald Beauch. Campbell,[71] CB	do	31 July	7 May	28 May	......	23 May 59	......
22	0	1	Robert Talbot	do	13 Aug.	28 May	26 Oct. 58	......	25 Sept. 59	......
21	0		Arnold Thompson[77]	19 Mar.	18 Aug. 39	20 July 47	26 Oct.	......	......	......
			CAPTAINS.							
21	0	*d*	*Henry Clerk*	19 Mar.	13 Aug. 39	27 Sept. 47	16 Nov. 58	......		
21	0	7	Francis Beckford Ward[78]	do	31 Dec.	21 Dec.	2 Nov. 55	......		
21	0	H.B.	John Jas. Brandling,[79] CB	do	25 Jan.	1 May	12 Dec. 54	......		
21	0	3	Alfred Romaine Wragge[80]	do	18 Mar.	30 May 48	......	......		
21	0	4	Frederick Wm. Haultain	do	1 Apr. 41	30 June	......	......		
21	0	3	Frederick John Travers,[81] *s.*	do	do	do	24 Mar. 58	2 Nov. 55		
21	0	*VC*	Matthew Charles Dixon[82]	do	11 Apr.	do	17 July	26 Dec. 56		
21	0	H.B.	John Turner,[83] CB	do	7 May	do	12 Dec. 54	......		
21	0	1	Edward Henry Fisher[84]	do	5 June	do	......	......		
21	0	6	Robert Frederick Mountain	do	17 Aug.	do	......	......		
21	0	13	Samuel Cleaveland	do	16 Sept.	do	......	......		
21	0	*d*	*Edward Mourrier Boxer*	20 Dec.	17 Nov.	do	......	......		
21	0	5	Chas. Scudamore Longden[85]	do	23 Nov. 39	do 48	24 Mar. 58	26 Apr. 59		
21	0	H.B.	Wm. Alex. Middleton,[86] CB	18 Dec.	do	do	24 Mar.	......		
20	0	14	James Robert Gibbon,[84] CB	do	do	40	30 July 58	20 July 58		
20	0	9	John R. Anderson,[57] CB	do	do	41	12 Dec. 54	......		
19	0	H.B.	Henry Fra. Strange,[86] CB	19 June	7 April 41	do 42	12 Dec. 54	2 Nov. 55		
19	0	10	William Hamilton Cox	do	13 April	do 42	......	......		
19	0	7	Richard O'Connell	do	do	do	2 Nov. 55	......		
19	0	2	Miller Clifford[84]	do	do	do	......	......		

Royal Artillery. 374

Years' Serv. Full Pay.	Years' Serv. Half Pay.		CAPTAINS.	2d LIEUT.	1st LIEUT.	CAPTAIN.
19	0	8	Charles Taylor Du Plat, *Equerry to H. R. H. The Prince Consort*	19 June 41	27 April 42	30 June 48
19	0	3	Mortimer Adye,[19] *Major* 2 Nov. 55	do	28 April	9 Oct.
18	0	4	Chas. Trigance Franklin,[90] CB. *Maj.* 12 Dec. 54	1 Jan. 42	14 July	14 Oct.
18	0	8	Alexander Cæsar Hawkins,[91] *Maj.* 2 Nov. 55.....	do	2 Aug.	1 Nov. 48
18	0	14	Barclay Lawson	do	4 Oct.	do
18	0	8	Andrew Pellett Scrimshire Green	do	1 Nov.	do
18	0	a.c.	Edward Arthur Williams	do	3 Nov.	do
18	0	9	Neil M'Innes Mackay[92]......................	do	7 Dec.	do
18	0	13	Wm. James Eston Grant,[93] *Maj.* 2 Nov. 55......	do	31 Dec. 42	do
18	0	10	Joseph Clark Childs........................	do	4 Apr. 43	do
18	0	H.B.	George Vanderheyden Johnson[94]	do	do	do
18	0	13	Adolphus Frederick Connell[92]	do	do	16 Nov. 48
18	0	10	Robert Barlow M'Crea,[95] *Maj.* 8 Apr. 50	18 June 42	do	28 Nov.
18	0	8	John Lindredge Elgee	do	do	8 Jan. 49
18	0	14	John Desborough	do	6 April 43	15 Feb.
18	0	7	George Shaw,[91] *Major* 2 Nov. 55, *Brigade Major, Woolwich*	do	3 May	9 April
18	0	10	Aug. Fred. Fra. Lennox,[92] *Major* 2 Nov. 55......	do	4 May	7 May
18	0	H.H.E.	Charles Stuart Henry,[96] *l. c.* 2 Nov. 55	do	15 May	19 May
18	0	12	Philip Gosset Pipon,[97] *Maj.* 12 Dec. 54.........	do	18 Aug.	5 Sept.
18	0	6	J. Davenport Shakespear,[98] *Maj.* 12 Dec. 54....	do	9 Sept.	6 Mar. 50
17	0	d	*Edward Bruce Hamley*,[99] *l. c.* 2 Nov. 55	11 Jan. 43	15 Sept.	14 May
17	0	2	George Thomas Field,[100] *Major* 2 Nov. 55	do	30 Oct.	23 May 50
17	0	8	Arthur Comyn Pigou[92]	do	8 Nov.	do
17	0	H.B.	Hon. David M'Dowall Fraser,[101] *Maj.* 2 Nov. 55; *l. c.* 26 Apr. 50	do	14 Jan. 44	27 May 50
17	0	6	Charles John Strange,[102] *Major* 2 Nov. 55	do	30 Mar.	11 June
17	0	H.B.	Horace Parker Newton,[92] *Maj.* 2 Nov. 55......	do	1 Apr. 44	8 July
17	0	d	*Alexander Cameron Gleig*[94]	do	do	9 July
17	0	9	*Hon.* Wm. C. Yelverton,[103] *Maj.* 12 Dec. 54	do	14 Apr. 44	16 July
17	0	4	George Henry Vesey[92]	do	15 Apr.	6 Aug.
17	0	10	Stapylton Robinson	17 June 43	do	2 Oct.
17	0	6	M. A. Shrapnel Biddulph,[104] *l.c.* 6 June 56	do	26 Apr. 44	4 Oct.
17	0	3	Henry Arthur Vernon[91]	do	28 Apr.	15 Oct.
17	0	9	Gus. Hamil. L. Milman,[105] *s. Maj.* 2 Nov. 55...	do	15 May	11 Nov.
17	0	d	J. F. Lodington Baddeley,[106] *Maj.* 12 Dec. 54....	do	17 Jan. 45	22 Feb. 51
17	0	7	George Lee Chandler	do	do	1 April
17	0	H.B.	Chas. G. Arbuthnot,[105] *Major* 2 Nov. 55.......	do	1 Feb. 45	4 April
17	0	11	Charles Richard Ogden Evans..............	do	4 Feb.	6 June
17	0	2	Guy Rotton,[107] *Major* 13 Apr. 58	do	5 April 45	2 July
17	0	11	Francis W. Hastings,[105] *Major* 2 Nov. 55	do	do	24 July
17	0	4	Henry Augustus Smyth[91]....................	20 Dec. 43	do	11 Aug.
17	0	12	Paul Winsloe Phillipps	do	10 April 45	2 Sept.
17	0	7	Frederick Hugh Chancellor	do	17 April	11 Nov. 51
17	0	7	Charles Waller, *s.*	do	9 May	do
17	0	1	Rd. King Freeth, D.A.Q.M.Gen. *Woolwich*	do	1 May	30 Nov. 51
17	0	13	Fra. M. Maxwell Ommanney,[108] *Maj.* 20 July 58	do	3 Sept.	2 Jan. 52
17	0	1	Edmund Palmer,[109] *Major* 20 July 58	do	4 Sept.	14 Jan.
17	0	H.B.	Leopold Grimston Paget[110]..................	do	29 Oct.	3 Feb.
17	0	4	Henry Mercer[111]	do	12 Dec.	23 Feb.
16	0	9	George Colclough[112]	19 June 44	20 Feb. 46	18 Mar.
16	0	4	Thomas Walter Milward[111]	do	1 April 46	1 April 52
16	0	12	Henry L. Chermside,[113] *Maj.* 12 Dec. 54.....	do	do	do
16	0	5	Frederick William Craven Ord..............	do	do	do
16	0	5	William Conyngham Lynch Blosse[114].........	do	do	1 May 52
16	0	7	Matthew Bligh Forde	do	do	5 June
16	0	1	William Townsend Barnett	do	do	6 July
16	0	d	*Archibald Edw. Harbord Anson*,[115] *Superintend. of Police at the Mauritius*	do	do	9 July
16	0	11	S. Enderby Gordon,[116] *l. c.* 2 Nov. 55	do	do	28 July
15	2	11	Edward Moubray,[117] *Major* 2 Nov. 55	20 Dec. 43	10 April 44	25 Sept. 51
16	0	6	John Geo. Boothby,[118] *Maj.* 12 Dec. 54.........	19 June 44	1 April 46	5 Aug. 52
16	0	12	Charles Neville Lovell	19 Dec. 44	do	18 Aug.
16	0	1	James Francis Eaton Travers	do	do	31 Aug.
16	0	6	*Hon.* Edw. T. Gage,[119] *l. c.* 2 Nov. 55.........	do	do	1 Sept.
16	0	13	Neville Saltren Keats Bayly[120]...............	do	do	27 Sept.
16	0	3	George Barstow,[121] *Major* 12 Dec. 54.........	do	do	11 Nov.
16	0	4	George Leslie	do	do	7 Dec.
16	0	13	Rob. Emilius F. Craufurd,[122] *Maj.* 6 June 56.....	19 June 44	do	22 Mar. 53
16	0	14	Charles Wright	19 Dec.	do	22 April

Royal Artillery.

Years' Serv. Full Pay.	Years' Serv. Half Pay.	CAPTAINS.	2D LIEUT.	1ST LIEUT.	CAPTAIN.
16	0	14 John Everett Thring,[123] *Major* 20 July 58..........	19 Dec. 44	1 April 46	19 May 53
16	0	6 William Magrath King[124].....................	do	do	20 May
16	0	5 Henry Lambert Fulke Greville	do	do	21 June
16	0	3 Hugh Bent[125]..............................	do	do	22 July
16	0	5 Francis Robert Glanville	do	do	6 Sept.
16	0	d Henry Jervis White Jervis	do	do	18 Sept.
15	0	5 William Lovelace Dumaresq	18 June 45	do	22 Sept.
15	0	H.B.Gaspard Le Marchant Tupper,[126] *Major* 12 Dec. 54.	do	do	26 Sept.
15	0	10 Henry Heyman[127]	do	do	29 Nov. 53
15	0	4 Dixon Edw. Hoste,[128] CB. *Maj.* 12 Dec. 54	do	do	24 Jan. 54
15	0	2 Edward Taswell[129]............................	do	do	17 Feb. 54
15	0	14 John Singleton,[130] *Major* 12 Dec. 54	do	do	do
15	0	6 Wm. Edm. M. Reilly,[131] CB., *s. Major* 2 Nov. 55..	18 Dec. 45	3 April 46	do
15	0	8 William Boyd Saunders[132]	do	6 April	do
15	0	11 Cha. H. Smith[133] *Maj.* 6 June 56 ; *l.c.* 26 Apr. 59......	do	13 April	do
15	0	G.C. Hen. Terrick Fitz Hugh[105] *Maj.* 6 June 56	do	13 April	do
15	0	2 John Lawrance Bolton[134]	do	26 May	do
15	0	d George Henry John Alex. Fraser	do	23 June	do
14	0	11 France James Soady,[131] *Maj.* 6 June 56	1 May 46	29 July	do
14	0	14 Joseph Godby,[105] *Maj.* 6 June 56	do	20 Oct.	do
14	0	1 Domi. Sarsfield Greene,[133] *Maj.* 24 Mar. 58	do	9 Nov. 46	do
14	0	4 Wm. W. Barry,[136] *Maj.* 2 Nov. 55 ; *l.c.* 24 Mar. 58....	do	do	do
14	0	9 George Hatton Colomb	do	do	do
14	0	14 Archibald Motteux Calvert, *s.*................	do	do	do
14	0	2 O'Brien Bellingham Woolsey, *s.*..............	6 Aug. 46	26 Nov. 46	do
14	0	d Alfred Wilkes Drayson	do	28 Nov. 46	do
14	0	8 Cadwallader William Elgee[74]	do	1 Jan. 47	do
14	0	5 Edm. J. Carthew,[131] *Major* 2 Nov. 55.........	do	1 Feb.	24 Feb. 54
14	0	1 George Harrison Ann Forbes	do	15 March	7 Mar.
14	0	2 Robert John Hay	do	7 May 47	17 Mar.
14	0	9 Alexander John MacDougall	do	do	30 May 54
14	0	6 John Spurway,[157] *Maj.* 6 June 56	do	28 May 47	do
14	0	6 George Ramsay Craik Young[74]................	do	1 July	17 June
14	0	2 J. E. Michell,[138] *Major* 2 Nov. 55 ; *l.c.* 26 Apr. 59	16 Dec. 46	27 Sept. 47	20 June 54
14	0	5 Geo. Cecil Henry,[137]† *Maj.* 2 Nov. 55......	do	23 Oct.	do
14	0	d Thomas Picton Warlow	do	23 Nov.	do
14	0	12 Philip Bedingfeld	do	24 Nov.	do
14	0	11 Richard Paget Campbell Jones	do	14 Mar. 48	do
14	0	d Reginald Onslow Farmer	do	30 May	do
14	0	13 Charles Maitland Govan	do	30 June 48	do
14	0	10 Chas. Henry Ingilby,[139] *Major* 12 Dec. 54	do	do	do
14	0	10 Robert Poole Gabbett, *r.*	do	do	28 June 54
13	0	3 H. Peel Yates,[110] *Maj.* 12 Dec. 54 ; *l.c.* 26 Apr. 59......	2 May 47	do	6 July
13	0	d Charles Edward Mainwaring.................	do	do	3 Aug.
13	0	1 W. J. Williams,[141] *s.Major* 2 Nov. 55	do	do	24 Aug.
13	0	1 Charles Fred. Young,[142] *Maj.* 26 Apr. 59........	do	do	13 Sept.
13	0	d Sanford Freeling, *s.*..........................	do	do	21 Sept. 54
13	0	9 Oliver Robert Stokes........................	do	do	do
13	0	14 J. Farrell Pennycuick,[143] *Maj.* 12 Dec. 54	do	do	do
13	0	12 Walter John Grimston	do	do	28 Sept. 54
13	0	8 C. E. Oldershaw,[144] *Major* 2 Nov. 55...........	do	do	29 Oct. 54
13	0	4 Nath. Octavius Simpson Turner,[145] *Maj.* 6 June 56 ; *l. c.* 26 Apr. 59........	do	do	6 Nov. 54
		SECOND CAPTAINS.			
13	0	11 Hon. Leonard A. Addington	1 Oct. 47	30 June 48	24 Nov. 54
13	0	5 Arthur Vandeleur,[146] *Maj.* 6 June 56	do	do	28 Nov. 54
13	0	d Andrew Orr	do	do	do
13	0	H.B.Charles Rowland Hill	do	do	do
13	0	H.B.Patrick John Campbell[147]	do	do	8 Dec. 54
13	0	11 VC Fra. C. Maude,[148] CB. *Maj.* 19 Jan. 58 ; *l.c.* 20 July 58	do	do	13 Dec. 54
13	0	2 Arthur William Twiss[149]	do	do	do
13	0	9 Reginald Curtis,[150] *Major* 6 June 56	do	do	do
13	0	13 Allan Sievwright[151]	do	do	do
13	0	4 Frederic Southcote Scale[151]	do	do	do
13	0	10 John De Luttrell Saunderson	do	do	16 Dec.
13	0	3 Philip Dickson,[152] *Major* 2 Nov. 55............	do	do	20 Dec. 54

Royal Artillery. 376

Years' Serv. Full Pay.	Half Pay.		SECOND CAPTAINS.	2ND LIEUT.	1ST LIEUT.	CAPTAIN.	
13	0	d	Edward Jackson Bruce...............	1 Oct. 47	30 June 48	3 Jan.	55
13	0	5	W. Powell Richards,[153] *Maj.* 6 June 56	do	do	6 Jan.	
13	0	6	J. Edward Hope,[154] *Major* 2 Nov. 55	do	do	do	
13	0	7	Algernon Brendon,[155] *Maj.*6 June 56	do	do	do	
13	0	9	James de Havilland,[156]*Maj.* 6 June 56	do	do	13 Jan.	55
13	0	H.B.	George Allix Wilkinson	do	do	26 Jan.	
13	0	d	W. Wind. Aug. Lukin,[157] *Maj.*2 Nov. 55..........	do	do	7 Feb.	55
13	0	11	C. Edm. Walcott,[158] *Major* 2 Nov. 55...........	18 Dec. 47	do	do	
13	0	8	♥︎𝕮 Gronow Davis,[159] *Maj.* 28 Aug. 57...........	do	do	25 Feb.	55
13	0	14	Edgar G. Bredin,[160] *Major* 6 June 56	do	do	do	
13	0	d	W. John Bolton,[161] *Major* 2 Nov. 55	do	do	8 Mar.	
13	0	7	Frederick Close, *Adj.*......................	do	do	1 Apr.	55
13	0	7	James Sinclair,[162] *Major* 2 Nov. 55	do	do	do	
13	0	8	HenryLynchTalbot,[163]*Maj.* 20 July 58..........	do	do	do	
13	0	14	Willoughby James Wilson[164]................	do	do	do	
13	0	2	W. H. R. Simpson,[165] *Maj.* 6 June 56, *Adj.*......	do	do	do	
13	0	3	Lewis W. Penn,[166] *Major* 2 Nov. 55, *Adj.*........	do	do	do	
13	0	8	William Morris,[167] *Adj.*...................	do	do	do	
13	0	11	Henry Renny	do	do	do	
13	0	1	Charles Paulett Rotton,[168] *Adj.*.............	do	17 Aug. 48	do	
13	0	d	Thomas Edmund Byrne,[169] *Adj.*.............	do	14 Oct.	do	
12	0	1	Edward Taddy,[170] *Maj.* 2 Nov. 55	27 June 48	1 Nov. 48	do	
12	0	2	Charles Johnston[171]......................	do	do	do	
12	0	13	Tho. Sam. Poer Field,[172]*Maj.* 4 Nov. 50	do	do	do	
12	0	14	Lawrence Augustus Bradshaw	do	do	do	
12	0	11	J. M'C. Campbell,[173] *Maj.* 26 Apr. 59, *Adj.*	do	do	do	
12	0	13	William French	do	do	do	
12	0	10	♥︎𝕮 Frederick Miller,[174] *Maj.* 2 Nov. 55	19 Dec. 48	19 Dec. 48	13 Apr.	55
12	0	5	Robert Wolseley Haig.....................	do	do	9 May	
12	0	d	Chas. Henry Owen,[175] *Maj.*,2 Nov. 55	do	do	15 May	
12	0	10	Geo. Ald. Milman,[176] *s. Maj.* 6 June 56........	do	8 Jan. 49	29 May	
12	0	6	Robert Boyle,[177] *s.*.....................	do	15 Feb.	1 June	
12	0	H.B.	Lambert Henry Denne,[177] *Adj.*	do	2 May	23 June	
12	0	14	George Malcolm Pasley[178]	do	7 May	29 June	55
12	0	6	P. W. L'Estrange,[179] *Maj.*2 Nov. 55	do	19 May	do	
12	0	3	Charles Edwd. Burt,[180] *Maj.* 6 June 56	do	28 June	do	
12	0	9	Constantine Lemon H. McTernan	do	31 Aug.	do	
12	0	2	Hazlitt Irvine,[160] *Maj.*6 June 56.............	do	4 Sept.	6 July	55
12	0	1	Claud George William Lascelles, *s.*..........	do	5 Sept.	12 Aug.	
12	0	H.B.	Shadwell M. Grylls,[181] *Maj.* 6 June 56.........	do	3 Nov. 49	13 Aug.	55
12	0	3	Regd. H. Champion[182] *Maj.* 2 Nov. 55, *r.*......	do	6 Mar. 50	17 Aug.	
11	0	4	Luke Brabazon Brabazon...................	20 June 49	14 May	23 Aug.	
11	0	d	*Thomas Longworth Dames*[163]	do	23 May 50	1 Sept.	
11	0	10	Charles Carpenter	do	do	7 Sept.	
11	0	H.B.	Wm. Gilly Andrews[184] *Maj.*2 Nov.55..........	do	27 May 50	10 Sept.	55
11	0	14	Alexander Henry Murray,[185] *Adj.*...........	do	20 June	do	
11	0	4	John Alexander Phillips Adams	do	8 July	do	
11	0	6	Roderick Mackenzie[186]*Maj.*2 Nov. 55.........	do	9 July	24 Sept.	55
11	0	4	Robert Horseley R. Rowley................	do	16 July	do	
11	0	11	Wm. George Le Mesurier,[157] CB. *Maj.* 2 Nov. 55; *l.c.* 20 July 58	do	6 Aug.	28 Sept.	55
11	0	7	Falkland Carey	do	10 Aug.	10 Oct.	
11	0	12	Henry Heberden[188].......................	do	2 Oct.	18 Oct.	
11	0	6	Trevor Charles Molony	do	4 Oct.	27 Oct.	
11	0	2	Andrew Noble	do	17 Nov.	2 Nov.	55
11	0	4	Henry Lowther Balfour	do	1 Nov.	do	
11	0	d	George Kepple Taylor	do	5 Dec.	do	
11	0	6	Richard Oldfield, *Adj.*...................	19 Dec. 49	22 Dec.	do	
11	0	9	Herbert Mark Gar. Purvis.................	do	22 Feb. 51	1 Jan.	56
11	0	H.B.	W. H. Goodenough,[189] *Maj.* 20 July 58.........	do	1 April	23 Feb.	56
11	0	H.B.	Albert Henry Wilmot Williams[190]...........	do	do	do	
11	0	3	Wm. Smyth Maynard Wolfe[191]	do	4 April	do	
11	0	1	Charles Fred. Cockburn[168]	do	6 June	do	
11	0	2	Henry Hamilton Conolly[192]	do	2 July	do	
11	0	7	Walter Chidiock Nangle[168]................	do	24 July	do	
11	0	12	Henry Strover[168]	do	26 July	do	
11	0	7	Campbell Hardy	do	11 Aug.	do	
11	0	6	Lewis Frederick Hall	do	25 Sept.	do	
11	0	11	Fred. Cockburn Griffin[193]	do	3 Oct.	do	

Royal Artillery.

Years' Serv. Full Pay.	Half Pay.		SECOND CAPTAINS.	2ND LIEUT.	1ST LIEUT.	CAPTAIN.
11	0	12	John Henry Peile	19 Dec. 49	11 Nov. 51	23 Feb. 56
11	0	7	John Kelly	do	do	do
10	0	13	John Stirling Stirling	19 June 50	30 Nov. 51	4 Mar.
10	0	H.B.	Fredk. Thos. Whinyates[194]	do	30 Dec.	25 June
10	0	14	William Nool Waller[195]	do	2 Jan. 52	19 July
10	0	3	E. T. Willoughby Purcell[95]	do	14 Jan. 52	21 July
10	0	14	Alured C. Johnson[196] Maj. 26 Apr. 59...	do	17 Jan.	1 Jan. 57
10	0	12	Cecil Brooke LeMesurier, Adj.	do	3 Feb.	13 Jan.
10	0	10	Henry Sheridan Elliot	do	16 Feb.	24 Jan.
10	0	2	Hy. Plantagenet Prescott Phelips[197]	do	18 Mar.	21 Feb.
10	0	13	Augustus Wm. Johnson[197]†	do	1 Apr. 52	23 Feb.
10	0	5	John Andrew Price[198]	do	do	26 March
10	0	H.B.	Augustus Henry King[199]	do	do	20 April
10	0	10	Robert James Cairnes, Adj.	do	do	26 May
10	0	d	Richard Roynon Jones[200]	do	5 June 52	6 July
10	0	5	John Wheler Collington, Adj.	do	4 July	14 July
10	0	8	John Henry Brown[201]	19 Dec. 50	6 July	21 July
10	0	H.B.	Walter Aston Fox Strangways[202]	do	9 July	20 Aug.
10	0	4	Thomas Arthur John Harrison	do	28 July	21 Aug.
10	0	13	John Donald George Higgon	do	5 Aug.	29 Aug.
10	0	6	Geo. Sisson Harward[203]	do	18 Aug.	25 Sept.
10	0	13	James Meredith Collingwood Vibart, Adj. ..	do	31 Aug.	10 Oct.
10	0	R.H.E.	William Booth[204]	do	1 Sept.	12 Nov.
10	0	11	William Lambert Yonge, Dep. Assist. Adj. General	do	2 Sept.	17 Nov. 57
10	0	6	Charles Booth Brackenbury[204]	do	27 Sept.	do
10	0	H.B.	Edwin Markham[205]†	do	22 Oct.	do
10	0	12	Henry Richard Porter	do	11 Nov.	do
10	0	4	Edmund Penrose Bingham Turner	do	7 Dec.	do
10	0	9	Frederick Nurse Cromartie	do	31 Dec.	22 Dec. 57
10	0	6	Leonard Sumner Joyce	do	18 Feb. 53	14 Jan. 58
10	0	8	Ralph Gore[204]	do	22 Mar.	do
9	0	3	VC C. C. Teesdale,[205] CB. s. Maj. 15 Jan. 58	18 June 51	22 April	do
9	0	2	James Lyons[161]	do	19 May	21 Feb. 58
9	0	10	Charles Edward Torriano[206]	do	20 May	22 Feb. 58
9	0	2	John Tatton Butler Brown[207]	do	21 June	do
9	0	11	Charles James Tyler[204]	do	28 June	28 April 58
9	0	12	George Joseph Smart[207]	do	12 July	5 May
9	0	5	Alex. Walter Armstrong Ogilvie[208]	do	18 Sept.	26 May 58
9	0	14	Robert Henry Newbolt[209]†	do	22 Sept.	do
9	0	1	Thomas Mahon	do	26 Sept.	5 June 58
9	0	9	Charles Edward Stirling[209]	do	3 Oct.	do
9	0	9	William Carey, Adj.	do	20 Nov.	22 June 58
9	0	14	Thomas Bland Strange[210]	17 Dec. 51	21 Nov.	16 Sept.
9	0	7	Francis Lyon[211]	do	29 Nov.	26 Oct. 58
9	0	4	Markham Le Fer Taylor,[212] Adj.	do	2 Dec.	do
9	0	3	Edward Keate[209]	do	12 Jan. 54	3 Nov.
9	0	12	Thomas Wright Blakiston[213]	do	24 Jan.	7 Dec.
9	0	8	Arthur Lister Kaye[213]	do	28 Jan.	3 Jan. 59
9	0	4	Jones Julian Smith[213]	do	17 Feb. 54	16 Jan.
9	0	14	Eardley Maitland[214]	do	do	15 Feb.
9	0	3	Maurice Edward Covey Stocker	do	do	2 March
9	0	d	John Lardner Clarke[215]	do	do	1 April 59
9	0	9	Henry Thornhill[213]	do	do	do
9	0	d	Arthur Thornton Gratwicke Pearse[216] ...	do	do	do
9	0	6	Thomas Priaulx Carey	do	do	do
9	0	1	William Francis Walker	do	do	do
8	0	8	Geoffrey Joseph Shakerley[213]	23 June 52	do	do
8	0	13	Henry James Alderson[217]	do	do	do
8	0	d	Alexander Hadden Hutchinson	do	do	do
8	0	1	Fred. George Ravenhill[216]	do	do	do
8	0	d	Thomas Henry Pitt[213]	do	do	do
8	0	8	Frederic Lee Hopkinson Lyon[219]	do	do	do
8	0	3	Charles Lennox Tredcroft[80]	do	do	15 May 59
8	0	1	George William Holmes	do	do	17 May
8	0	5	John Edward Ruck-Keene[220]	do	do	23 May
8	0	10	Henry Archdall Doyne[221]	do	do	24 May
8	0	9	John Theophilus Daubuz[222]	do	do	28 June
8	0	10	Robert Hodson	do	do	10 July
8	0	12	Ernest Courtenay Vaughan[221]	do	do	21 July

Royal Artillery.

Years' Serv.					
Full Pay.	Half Pay.	SECOND CAPTAINS.	2ND LIEUT.	1ST LIEUT.	CAPTAIN.
8	0	5 Frederick Sidney Maude	23 June 52	17 Feb. 54	5 Sept. 59
8	0	5 Francis Towry Adeane Law [223]	22 Dec. 52	do	25 Sept. 59
8	0	d Major Francis Downes [223]	do	do	14 Nov.
8	0	1 Francis Henry William Nisbett [224]	do	do	do
8	0	4 Falkland George Edgeworth Warren [225]	do	do	do
8	0	4 Henry Clement Swinnerton Dyer [226]	do	do	do
		LIEUTENANTS.			
8	0	2 Thomas Lloyd Still [222]	22 Dec. 52	17 Feb. 54	
8	0	G.C. Joseph Hanwell [222]	do	do	
8	0	6 Joshua Frederick Betty.................	do	do	
8	0	7 John Kelly Holdsworth	do	do	
8	0	11 Maurice Henry Fitzmaurice [227]	do	do	
8	0	H.B. Wilbraham Digby Milman [228]	do	do	
8	0	14 Henry Richmond Martin	do	do	
8	0	14 William Alexander Patrick Wyllie	do	do	
7	0	0 Charles Gray Johnson [222]	8 April 53	24 Feb. 54	
7	0	9 Henry Cardew [222]	do	7 March	
7	0	3 Horace Percival [229]	22 June 53	12 March	
7	0	H.B. Henry Thomas Arbuthnot [230]	do	16 May	
7	0	11 Robert Biddulph [231]	do	30 May 54	
7	0	11 William Stirling [232]	do	do	
7	0	H.B. Peter Edward Hill [233]	do	17 June	
7	0	H.B. S. John Mildmay Maxwell [234]	do	20 June 54	
7	0	7 Champagne L'Estrange [223]	do	do	
7	0	H.B. Arthur Kennedy Rideout [235]	21 Dec. 53	do	
7	0	H.B. William Henry Watson [160]	do	do	
7	0	10 Edw. Chichester Bolton................	do	do	
7	0	9 Oliver H. Atkins Nicolls [229]	do	do	
7	0	12 James Barton	do	do	
7	0	1 Ch. Jas. Hope Johnstone	do	do	
7	0	3 Benjamin Geale Humfrey [91]	do	28 June 54	
7	0	9 Charles Watson Wilson.................	do	1 July	
7	0	14 Legh Delves Broughton [236]	do	6 July	
7	0	H.B. Geo. Alb. Aug. Walker [223].............	do	14 July	
6	0	H.B. Fran. Walter de Winton [237]............	11 April 54	17 July	
6	0	H.B. Aug. H. Carr Hamilton [74]..............	do	19 July	
6	0	14 Edm. Charles Cuthbert [238]..............	do	3 Aug.	
6	0	5 Pilkington Jackson	do	4 Aug.	
6	0	4 Jervis Tucker [239]	do	24 Aug.	
6	0	13 Brymer Francis Schreiber [222]............	do	13 Sept.	
6	0	14 Michael Tweedie [218]..................	do	21 Sept. 54	
6	0	12 Robert Loftus Tottenham [93].............	do	do	
6	0	5 Richard O'Hara	do	do	
6	0	H.B. Hugh Chetham Lyle [222]...............	do	do	
6	0	G.C. Leonard Griffiths [240]	do	do	
6	0	11 Wm. R. Lluellyn	do	28 Sept. 54	
6	0	12 Henry J. F. Ellis Hickes [237].............	do	4 Oct.	
6	0	12 Fred. George Baylay	14 Aug. 54	23 Oct.	
6	0	6 Noel Hamlyn Harris [201]................	do	24 Oct.	
6	0	12 Oswald Carr [74]......................	do	29 Oct.	
6	0	4 Henry Whitby Briscoe [201]...............	do	6 Nov. 54	
6	0	1 Wm. George Martin [223]................	do	do	
6	0	H.B. Philip Hen. Sandilands...............	do	24 Nov.	
6	0	H.B. William James Hall [237]..............	do	28 Nov. 54	
6	0	H.B. Morton Parker Eden	do	do	
6	0	G.C. Chas. Dalrymple Gilmour [222]...........	do	do	
6	0	H.B. Edward John Ward [241]	do	30 Nov. 54	
6	0	H.B. Alex. Dickson Burnaby [212].............	do	8 Dec.	
6	0	14 Wilmot B. Edw. Ellis	do	13 Dec. 54	
6	0	5 Charles George Luard	do	do	
6	0	5 Henry A. D. de Vismes [222]...............	do	do	
6	0	d Vivian Dering Majendie [243]	23 Oct. 54	do	
6	0	G.C. Jas. Edward Blackwell	do	do	
6	0	14 Sir John Wm. Campbell, Bt. [91]...........	do	16 Dec. 54	
6	0	H.B. Æmelius De Vic Tupper [222]............	do	do	
6	0	H.B. John Cha. Fra. Ramsden [244]............	do	20 Dec. 54	
6	0	H.B. Francis Arthur Whinyates [245]..........	do	27 Dec. 54	
6	0	H.B. Frederick Coulthurst Elton [108]..........	do	1 Jan. 55	
6	0	H.B. Charles Richard Franklen [222]..........	do	3 Jan.	
6	0	5 Clennell Collingwood................	do	6 Jan. 55	
6	0	14 Frederick Augustus Anley [91]	do	do	

† s

Royal Artillery.

Years' Serv. Full Pay.	Half Pay.	LIEUTENANTS.	2ND LIEUT.	1ST LIEUT.
6	0	4 Lewis Paxton Walsh[223]	23 Oct. 54	6 Jan. 55
6	0	14 Power D. Le Poer Tronch[246]	do	13 Jan.
6	0	2 William Rooke[224]	do	26 Jan.
6	0	1 Sidney Augustus Bazalgette[247]	do	7 Feb. 55
6	0	10 Charles D. Bevan[224]	20 Dec. 54	do
6	0	5 William Henry Newcome	do	13 Feb. 55
6	0	6 John Robert King	do	25 Feb. 55
6	0	H.B. Charles Orde Browne[212]	do	do
6	0	3 Thomas Cuming	do	6 Mar. 55
6	0	H.B. Charles E. Southouse Scott[212]	do	8 Mar. 55
5	0	12 Henry Dowdeswell Pitt	28 Feb. 55	do
5	0	13 Hale Young Wortham[248]	do	1 Apr. 55
5	0	H.B. Henry Barlow Maule[212]	do	do
5	0	4 Charles Wills Walrond	do	do
5	0	2 Wm. James Smith-Neill[249]	do	do
5	0	14 Henry Le Guay Geary[212]	do	do
5	0	d Walter Brook Rice[250]	do	do
5	0	6 George Uchter Knox	do	do
5	0	4 William Norton Perssé	do	do
5	0	3 Osborne Hall Goodenough	do	do
5	0	2 James Hamilton Pringle Anderson[251]	do	do
5	0	11 Joseph N. Portlock Dadson	do	do
5	0	9 Hy. Chamberlayne Farrell[224]	do	do
5	0	3 Edward M'Laughlin	do	do
5	0	13 Charles Fyshe Roberts[212]	do	do
5	0	4 Arthur Stewart Hunter[224]	do	do
5	0	8 G. R. Thackery Stevenson	do	do
5	0	6 George Adam Crawford	do	do
5	0	2 Townsend Aremberg de Moleyns[223]	......	20 Apr. 55
5	0	3 John Booth Richardson[95]	......	do
5	0	2 William Henry Wardell[95]	......	do
5	0	H.B. Frederick John George Hill[224]	......	do
5	0	8 William Henry Izod	......	do
5	0	12 Robert Charles Walter Campbell	......	do
5	0	13 James Douglas Strange	......	do
5	0	7 Arthur John Henry Wynne	......	do
5	0	H.B. Turner Van Straubenzee	......	do
5	0	H.B. Henry Webster Shakeley	......	do
5	0	2 John Robert Dyce[74]	......	31 July 55
5	0	7 Kenneth Monro	......	do
5	0	H.B. Edmund Staveley[252]	......	do
5	0	11 Wallace Gilmour[253]	......	do
5	0	14 Robert Preston Lewis Welch	......	do
5	0	11 Henry Edmeades[251]	......	do
5	0	13 John Macvicar Burn[259]	......	do
5	0	5 Stuart James Nicholson	......	do
5	0	11 William Smith[228]	......	do
5	0	13 Walter Newman	......	do
5	0	14 Edmund John Tremlett	......	do
5	0	5 Thomas Auriol Robinson	......	do
5	0	13 George Murray Lyon Campbell	......	do
5	0	12 George Edwin Maule	......	do
5	0	6 William Dobree Carey	......	do
5	0	6 Alexander Grant Miller	......	do
5	0	12 Edmund Charles Macnaghten	......	1 Aug. 55
5	0	R.H.E. Lawe. Hector Hardress Parsons	......	do
5	0	3 Ramsay Weston Phipps	......	do
5	0	9 James Charles Cavendish	......	do
5	0	H.B. Robert Sandham	......	do
5	0	5 George Erskine Callander	......	do
5	0	4 Algernon Augustus Stewart	......	do
5	0	R.H.E. Hon. Robert Villiers Dillon[74]	......	do
5	0	11 Edmund Sidney Burnett[255]	......	do
5	0	11 FitzRoy Somerset Talbot	......	do
5	0	7 Francis Duncan	......	24 Sept. 55
5	0	11 John Ryder Oliver[256]	......	do
5	0	11 Edward Egan	......	do
5	0	13 James Corry Jones Lowry[260]	......	do
5	0	14 James Peattie Morgan[261]	......	do
5	0	2 George Grote Hannen[107]	......	do
5	0	13 Philip M'Lourin Guille	......	do
5	0	14 Arthur Ford[257]	......	do

Royal Artillery. 380

LIEUTENANTS.	LIEUT.	LIEUTENANTS.	LIEUT.
4 Francis Montague Smith	24 Sept. 55	d Henry Pountney Darwall	10 Aug. 56
9 Francis Arthur Mant	do	11 Edward Roden Cottingham[266]	do
d Frederick Howlett	do	10 George Russell Salmon	do
3 Richard Handcock	do	9 Joseph Thomas Barrington	do
d Charles Mills Molony	do	11 John Claudius Auchinleck[267]	do
H.B. George Arbuthnot[269]	do	4 George Sheppard Harvey	do
6 Richard Sadleir	do	9 Samuel Cotter Kyle[268]	do
2 William Ruxton Barlow	do	8 William Stopford Maunsell	do
14 Robert Callwell Smith	do	14 Herbert Leonard Mitchell	do
H.B. Chas. Stewart Vardon Wilson	1 Oct. 55	6 Edward Vicars Boyle	18 Oct. 56
H.B. John de Burgh Rochfort[74]	do	7 Henry Martin Borton	do
7 Rowland Burdon Webster	do	10 Edwin William Sandys	20 Dec. 56
11 Charles David Chalmers[232]	do	3 John Minton Maunsell	do
7 Samuel Parr Lynes	do	14 George Lloyd Engström	do
11 Charles Hart Pickering[228]	do	8 Conway Richard Reeves	do
12 Bowes Lennox Forsters	do	6 Michael John Sexton	do
14 James Robertson[263]	do	10 William Scott	do
7 Edward Augustus Slessor	19 Dec. 55	12 Hugh Latimer Ellaby	8 April 57
13 Louis C. Aug. Adrian de Cetto[261]	do	8 Vincent Frederick Tufnell	15 May 57
4 Henry Anderson	do	9 Richard Butler Stoney	do
1 Charles Trench	do	8 John Henry Blackley	do
7 Henry Colebrooke Lewes	do	8 Robert Carstairs Drysdale	do
14 Hon. Ralph Hare	do	6 Henry Williams Dicken	do
7 Arthur Sutherland Macartney	do	11 William Sampson Brown[269]	do
3 Alexander Doull	6 March 56	9 Henry John Palliser	do
12 Robert Emmett Cane	do	7 Benjamin John Bonnor	do
2 Archibald Hamilton Bell	do	8 Charles Thornhill	do
13 George Budd	do	14 Charles Eversfield Bethune[211]	do
12 John Haughton	do	11 Joseph Egerton Cockburn	do
13 Francis Sadleir Stoney[258]	do	8 Sidney Parry	do
12 Henry Rogers Ievers	do	9 William Rice Bowen	do
1 Thomas Clarke	do	6 Arthur Harness	23 June 57
4 William Godeffroy Brancker	do	3 Eugene Hay Cameron	do
10 Donald Roderick Cameron[96]	do	8 Henry de Stuteville Isaacson	do
10 William Henry Noble	do	4 Henry Cole Magenis	do
4 Richard Newton Young	do	4 Edward James Walker	1 Oct. 57
9 George O'Connor	do	6 Edward Ommanney Hollist	do
10 William Kemmis	7 April 56	6 Frederick Swaine LeGrice	do
4 Richard Philip Perry	do	4 Henry Montague Hozier	do
5 Edward Taylor Warry	do	5 Thomas Bramston Hamilton	do
5 Henry Bond	do	12 Arthur Hamilton Gorges	do
2 Henry Geary Hill	do	2 Thomas Charles Price	do
5 Wm. Morritt Barneby Walton	do	3 Wm. Fras. Moore Hutchinson	do
6 Richard Pendrill Waddington	do	8 Albert Thornton Wodehouse	do
d Henry Brackenbury[265]	do	5 Clinton Heywood Sabine Pasley	do
5 Charles Alfred Gorham	do	5 John Philip Nolan	do
1 William Henry Graham	do	10 Osmond Francis Le Mottée	do
5 Alexander William Duncan	do	9 Henry Wedderburn Isacke	do
9 George Fred. Stanley Chambers	do	9 Patrick Fitzgerald Gallwey	do
6 William Southwell Curzon	do	6 Buddle Atkinson	do
5 Samuel Dunlop	do	7 Charles Henry Fairfax Ellis	do
12 Edward Lyons	do	7 John Fletcher Owen	do
9 William Michael Tollner	do	1 John Egerton Gubbins	do
13 George Bertie Benjamin Hobart	do	6 Alexander Ramsay Cruikshank	do
14 Harry Adair Tracey[211]	do	8 John Heathfield Stratton	do
12 William Strahan	do	8 Walter George Stirling	do
8 Alexander Macdonell Bonar	do	10 James Robert Davies Cooke	do
9 Henry John Francis Shea	do	10 Edward Smith Gordon	do
8 Horace Hervey Webber	21 June 56	12 Francis Thomas Lloyd	do
10 Wentworth Hy. King-Harman	do	10 George James Gillios	do
6 Thomas Strong Seccombe	do	6 George Cumine Strahan	do
9 Robert David Dewar Hay	do	d Henry St. John Vaughan Le Marchant Thomas	do
6 Joseph Chas. Smyth-Windham	do		
1 William Bruce Raikes Hall	do	9 Granville Deedes	do
8 William Thomas Budgen	do	d George Conrad Sartorius	do
5 Edward Broadrick	do	4 Henry Francis Phillpotts	do
6 Edward Hovell Thurlow	do	3 Henry Miles Burgess	do
11 Hon. Alexander Stewart	do	8 Darell Robert Jago	do
6 William Walpole Murdoch	do	2 Archibald Wm. Montgomerie	do
8 Francis Hume Dodgson	10 Aug. 56	5 Thomas Challoner Martelli	do
14 Edward Delaval Tarleton[211]	do	8 John Chas. D'Urban Murray	do

Royal Artillery.

LIEUTENANTS.	LIEUT.	LIEUTENANTS.	LIEUT.
13 Arthur John Rait	1 Oct. 57	7 Anthony Oliver Molesworth	22 June 59
12 Henry Manvers Moorson	do	11 Harry Dacres Evans	do
1 George John Burgmann	do	1 James Murray Murray	do
7 Charles Edw. Hood Symons	23 Dec. 57	10 Norman Spencer Perceval	do
4 Henry Gratwicke Hasler	do	3 Walter John Tatham	do
13 Herbert Lionel Gwyn	do	3 Henry Fra. Peterkin Lewis	do
8 Charles Edward Elwyns	do	11 James Mainwaring Douglas	do
12 Henry Maxwell Robertson	do	7 Fra. Laurence Gore Little	do
14 John Murray Traill	do	10 John Randal Wilmer	do
7 Ernest St. George Cobbold	do	6 Dudley Maryon Wilson	do
7 Wm. Adw. M'Pherson Gordon	do	4 Robert Henry Grant	do
8 William Arthur Roberts	do	2 Hugh Allen Mackey	do
10 Duncan Norton Taylor	do	1 Percy Charles Whalley	do
14 Francis Beresford	do	4 Trevor Bruce Tyler	do
13 Thomas Maynard Hazlerigg	do	10 Dudley North Allan	do
5 Julian Frederick Sandeman	do	4 Henry Metcalfe	3 Sept. 59
7 Vincent Wells	do	2 Edwin Marshall	Dec. 59
3 Robert Power Saunders[05]	do	1 Chas. Edmund Baker Leacock	do
2 William Trelawny Scott	1 Mar. 58	1 Henry Gordon Palmer	do
9 Robt. Smythe Muir Mackenzie	22 June 58	10 Marcus F. H. M'Causland	do
1 Flemyng George Gyll	do	9 Thomas Jesson	do
4 Seymour Hood Toogood	do	10 Simon Simpson	do
6 Evelyn Baring	do	11 Christopher Wm. Townsend	do
2 Henry Norris Jones	do	13 Francis Forster Barham	do
1 Henry Bond	do	1 George Augustus Noyes	do
4 Arthur Fred. Pickard	do	3 Henry St. John Cole Bowen	do
3 Thomas Burnett	do	10 Edmund Hill Wickham	do
12 Samuel Holworthy Desborough	do	3 Robert Joseph Pratt Saunders	do
4 Lionel Gye	do	1 Vincent Wing	do
8 Charles Henry Hamilton	do	4 Seymour de Lacy Lacy	do
5 Ashton John Shuttleworth	1 Oct. 58	3 Norton Lawrence Porter	do
2 Albert Lake Collins Smithett	do	1 Frederick Schack	do
1 John Robert Jennings Bramly	do	10 Henry Llewelyn Williams	do
14 Arch. Wm. Fred. Campbell	do	11 William Reynolds Stirke	do
3 Lionel Herbert Noyes	do	13 Pringle David Barclay	do
4 Geo. Walter Chas. Rothe	do	13 Henry Graves	do
4 Basil de Beauvoir Tupper	do	2 Thomas John Jones	do
4 Henry Hills Goodeve	do	2 Richard Tracey Mullett	do
9 George Best	21 Dec. 58	1 James Lancaster Bell	do
4 Clement Walford Bellairs	do	10 Henry Edward Baines	do
5 Adrian de Montmorency Prior	do	1 Henry Tho. Thompson Sandes	do
6 Joseph Sladen	1 Apr. 59	1 James Robert Yule	do
3 Samuel Pasfield Oliver	do	4 Robert Townsend Farquhar	do
8 Charles Smith Harvey	do	8 John Younger	do
10 Robert Henderson Robertson	do	2 Thomas Mulrenan	do
1 Arthur John Cullen	do	3 Charles John Deshon	do
2 Joseph Thos. Maher Loughnan	do	1 Francis Cha. Hughes Hallett	do
10 Orlebar Frederic Layton	do	6 William Francis Nelson	do
9 Charles Frederick Dixon	do	2 Hugh Fife Ashley Brodie	do
2 Robert Berkeley Butt	do	6 Edward Ireland	do
3 William Macaulay Glasgow	do	6 Richard William Chute	do
5 Charles Crosthwaite	22 June 59	11 Geo. Mackenzie Bent Hornsby	

Royal Artillery. 383

Inspector General.
꜀꜀꜀ *Major General* John Bloomfield.
Aide de Camp, VC Major Teesdale, CB.
Deputy Adjutant General.
Colonel Charles Bingham, 1 April 58.
Assistant Adjutant General.
Colonel E. Wodehouse, CB. 1 Oct. 57.
Deputy Assistant Adjutant General.
2nd Capt. W. L. Yonge, 17 July 58.
Adjutants.
8 2nd *Capt.* W. Morris, 3 April 55.
7 2nd *Capt.* F. Close, 16 June 55.
6 2nd *Capt.* Rich. Oldfield, 18 Dec. 55.
H.B. 2nd *Capt.* L. H. Denne, 28 July 56.
12* 2nd *Capt.* C. B. Le Mesurier, 6 July 57.
14 2nd *Capt.* A. H. Murray, 21 July 57.
3 2nd *Capt.* L. W. Penn, m. 23 July 57.
2* 2nd *Capt.* W. H. R. Simpson, m. 20 Aug. 57.
5* 2nd *Capt.* J. W. Collington, 10 Oct. 57.
1* 2nd *Capt.* C. P. Rotton, 22 Dec. 1857.
10* 2nd *Capt.* R. J. Cairnes, 14 Jan. 1858.
4* 2nd *Capt.* Markham le Fer Taylor, 5 March 59.
d 2nd *Capt.* Ths. Edm. Byrne, 24 March 59.
9 2nd *Capt.* W. Carey, 17 May 59.
11* 2nd *Capt.* J. M'C. Campbell, m. 17 June 59.
13* 2nd *Capt.* J. M. C. Vibart, 17 June 59.
Chief Paymaster.
William Marvin, 24 Feb. 58; *Q.M.* 10 Sept. 44; *Honorary rank of Major*, 1 April 58.
Paymasters.
d John Sargent, 1 Sept. 58; *Lt.* 12 July 55.
H.B. Edward Gibbs, 1 Sept. 58.
2 Henry William Vyner, 24 May 59.
8 Henry George Augustus Powell, 23 Feb. 55; *Ens.* 23 Jan. 46; *Lt.* 27 July 49.
3 Augustus Staveley Murray, 17 June 59.
5 William Archibald Kidd, 10 June 53; *Ens.* P 20 Nov. 46; *Lt.* P 22 Dec. 48.
6 James Scott,[278] 24 June 59; *Ens.* 5 Nov. 54; *Lt.* 2 Mar. 55.
10 John Baylis Thompson, 21 June 59.
1 Wm. Piers Brisley, 8 July 59.
4 Thomas Richardson Griffiths, 8 July 59.
9 Nathaniel Eyre Robbins, 8 July 59.
14 David Aikman Patterson, 28 July 59; *Ens.* P 4 Apr. 45; *Lt.* 29 July 47; *Capt.* 16 Oct. 57.
11 Henry Lewis de la Chaumette, 8 Aug. 59.
Quarter Masters.
8 Thomas Hassall, 12 April 50.
1 John Cass, 1 April 52.
13 Wm. Reuben Kirkman, 17 Feb. 54.
d Thomas Hendley (*Commissary of Stores*), 1 July 54.
3 James Black, 27 Oct. 54.
6 William Stewart, 27 Mar. 55.
14 William Hoge, 1 Apr. 55.
10 John McDonald Hains, 21 April 56.
   Charles Wharry (*Superintendent of Schools*), 6 May 56.
   George Grant (*Com. of Clothing*), 8 May 56; *Hon. rank of Capt.* 6 May 59.
12 Richard Keating, 1 Sept. 56.

Henry Penson, 11 Oct. 56.
9 William Armstrong, 1 April 57.
5 William Cairns, 1 April 57.
7 John Morris, 1 April 57.
4 John Williams, 1 April 57.
   John Cochran (*Commissary of Stores*), 15 April 57. *
   George William Taylor (*Inspector of Clothing*), 15 Jan. 58.
H.B. George Marvin (*Commissary of Stores*), 1 Oct. 58.
11 William Lloyd, 1 Nov. 58.
2 James Murphy, 13 May 59.
G.C. George Alex. Shepherd, 4 Nov. 59.
Veterinary Surgeons.
John S. Stockley,[270] 18 Aug. 49.
Hicks Withers,[271] 6 March 54.
Matthew John Harpley,[272] 24 April 54
John Thomas Cochrane,[273] 9 June 54.
Francis Cotterell,[274] 24 June 54.
Wm. Barry Lord, 1 Oct. 54.
Gabriel Isles Rollings,[275] 1 Feb. 55.
Thomas John Williamson, 5 Mar. 55.
Christopher Sanderson,[276] 22 May 55.
Edwin Harrison, 28 June 55.
James Cleaveland, 28 June 55.
Daniel Hinge, 1 July 55.
Frederick Horne Rush Spratt, 10 Sept. 55.
John Bunn Wm. Skoulding,[277] 9 Nov. 55.
Edward Kelly, 26 Feb. 56.
John Bolton Hall, 26 Feb. 56.
George Longman, 10 Aug. 57.
Charles Steel, 25 Aug. 57.
John Tatam, 10 Aug. 57.
John Baldock, 10 Aug. 57.
Joseph Ball, 23 Sept. 57.
William Dorrofield, 14 Sept. 57.
James Lambert, 12 Oct. 57.
William Partridge,[279] 16 July 55.
*Henry Hussey, 14 Sept. 57.
*James Woodyer Callow, 14 Dec. 57.
Chaplains.
Rev. Matthew R. Scott, 10 April 37.
Rev. Walter Melvill Wright, 1 Sept. 50.
Company of Gentlemen Cadets.
Governor.—Col. E. N. Wilford.
Capt. Com.—E. A. Williams, 1 Nov. 48.
2nd Capt.—Bt. *Major* Fitzhugh, 6 June 56.
Lieuts.—J. Hanwell, 17 Feb. 54.
   L. Griffiths, 21 Sept. 54.
   C. D. Gilmour, 28 Nov. 54.
   J. E. Blackwell, 13 Dec. 54.
Qr. Mast.—Geo. Alex. Shepherd, 4 Nov. 59.
Riding Establishment.
Superintending: Captain Charles Stuart Henry (*Lt. Col.*), 2 Nov. 55.
Riding Masters.
Lieut. William Boylin, 2 June 54.
Lieut. Thomas Bishop, 9 May 55.
Lieut. James Everett, 1 Aug. 55.
William Norton, 23 March 58.
William Donald, 1 Apr. 59.
John Barnett, 27 Aug. 59.
George Dann, 27 Aug. 59.

* *Temporary Rank only.*

Royal Artillery

Years' Serv. Full Pay	Half Pay	SURGEONS MAJOR.	ASSIST. SURGEON.	SURGEON.	SURGEON MAJOR.
31	0	d John Atkins Davis	10 Aug. 29	24 Jan. 44	13 Oct. 53
21	0	11 Rich. Coffin Elliot,[1] CB.......	7 June 39	1 Jan. 53	21 May 55
24	0	13 Wm. Alston Dassauville, MD..	14 June 36	25 July 49	1 Oct. 58
24	0	d James Somerville Litle[2]	2 Nov. 36	23 Oct. 49	do
23	0	d George Thomas Ferris[3]	26 Sept. 37	1 Apr. 50	do
22	0	d Melborne Broke Gallwey	18 June 38	3 Jan. 51	do
21	1¾	d John Bent[5]†.............	11 Sept. 38	8 Nov. 52	21 Dec. 55
		SURGEONS.			
19	0	10 Wm. Hen. Mackintosh, MD. .	10 April 41	1 April 54	
18	0	d Henry Briscoe, MD..........	27 May 42	13 April 55	
16	0	H.B. James Macmillan Scott Fogo[4]	5 Mar. 44	13 April 55	
14	0	12 Edward Schaw Protheroe[5]	18 April 46	16 Mar. 55	
15	0	7 Edward Gilborne[6]	1 May 45	5 Nov. 55	
11	0	6 William Perry[7]	23 Oct. 49	20 July 55	
17	0	14 Hugh Crawford Walshe,[8] MD..	6 May 43	8 Dec. 54	
14	0	5 Stanhope Hunter Fasson,[9] MD..	1 July 46	23 Mar. 55	
14	0	1 Matthew Combe,[10] MD.......	20 July 46	24 April 55	
10	1¾	4 John Duff, MD..............	3 Aug. 49	8 Jan. 56	
9	1	3 Thomas Park[11].............	1 April 50	21 Dec. 55	
9	0	2 Howell Walters Voss	3 Jan. 51	26 Jan. 58	
10	0	9 Arthur Rudge	1 Apr. 50	2 Oct. 57	
19	1/12	8 Rich. Francis Valpy De Lisle[12]	27 Aug. 41	5 Nov. 52	
12	0	d John Riggs Miller Lewis[12]†MD.	11 Feb. 48	7 Dec. 55	
		ASSISTANT SURGEONS.			
7	0	H.B. Jos. C. Hornsby Wright,[13] MD..	1 Jan. 53		
7	0	H.B. John Alex. M'Munn,[17] MD..	13 Oct. 53		
6	0	13 Joseph Barker[16]	15 July 54		
6	0	H.B. Henry Clifford	do		
6	0	11 William Haughton,[18] MB......	28 April 54		
5	0	d Wm. George Nicholas Manley	20 Feb. 55		
6	0	d Sampson Roch	14 Dec. 54		
6	0	H.B. Randolph Webb[26]	15 Dec. 54		
6	0	13 John Henry Hearn..........	13 Oct. 54		
6	0	H.B. Thomas Tarrant[27]	16 June 54		
5	0	6 Edwin James Hopwood	29 Jan. 55		
6	0	11 George Sharp	13 April 55		
6	0	14 Robert Augustus Chapple[19] ..	28 April 54		
5	0	14 Thomas Jerram Orton[28]	17 Jan. 55		
6	0	H.B. Jas. Balfour Cockburn,[15] MD..	3 March 54		
6	0	12 Albert Hawkins[20]	15 April 54		
7	0	H.B. William Beale Wallis	27 May 53		
6	0	13 William Younge Jeeves[21]	7 April 54		
6	0	12 Joseph Fletcher Lougheed[22] ..	15 Aug. 54		
5	0	11 Andrew Robertson Smith[29]....	21 Feb. 55		
5	0	11 John Whittle Rimmer	2 April 55		
5	0	13 Richard Uniacke Cashman, MD.	18 May 55		
5	0	d Henry Richard Lobb Veale[30]..	14 May 55		
6	0	11 James Horridge Finnemore ..	23 June 54		
6	0	6 Jeffery Allen Marston, MD. ··	10 Nov. 54		
6	0	5 Stephen Henry Dickerson ...	23 Dec. 54		
5	0	13 Alf. Joseph Lumby Hepworth .	26 Jan. 55		
5	0	5 William Fletcher[24]	4 May 55		
5	0	11 Francis Hyde Forshall	3 Oct. 55		
3	0	H.B. Robert Lower[25]	1 Aug. 57		
3	0	14 Henry Foljambe Paterson	19 Oct. 57		
3	0	14 Robert David Burn, MD.	19 Oct. 57		
3	0	7 Melville George Jones........	10 Oct. 57		
5	0	H.B. John Wood	10 Jan. 57		
3	0	14 Joseph Marmaduke Taylor....	15 Sept. 57		
3	0	14 Decim. Filius de Hodgson, MD.	28 Sept. 57		
3	0	13 George Davidson Milne,[31] MD.	15 Sept. 57		
3	0	14 Robert Walter Clifton.......	28 Sept. 57		
3	0	11 William Tanner	9 Nov. 57		
3	0	12 William James Cumming, MD.	9 Nov. 57		
2	0	10 John Sarsfield Comyn.......	22 Jan. 58		
6	0	14 Alexander Dudgeon Gulland[23]	23 June 54		
4	0	3 Eugene Francis O'Leary	9 Feb. 56		
4	0	2 Samuel Pratt Woodfull	9 Feb. 56		
2	0	9 Edward Hardinge...........	10 March 58		
2	0	10 James Johnson d'Altera	22 April 58		

3† Surgeon Major Bent served in the Crimea from 30th Apr. 1855 (Medal and Clasp for Sebastopol and 5th Class of the Medjidie).

1 Surgeon Major Elliot served the Eastern campaign of 1854-55, including the affairs of Bulganac and M'Kenzie's Farm, the battles of Alma, Balaklava, and Inkerman, capture of Balaklava, and siege of Sebastopol (Medal and Clasps, CB., Knight of the Legion of Honor, and 5th Class of the Medjidie). Served in India in 1857-58, and was present at the action of Pandoo Nuddee, operations of the 27th, 28th, and 29th Nov. before Cawnpore and battle there on the 6th Dec. (twice mentioned in despatches, Medal).

6 Surgeon Gilborne served the Eastern campaign of 1854, including the affairs of Bulganac and M'Kenzie's Farm, battles of Alma and Balaklava, capture of Balaklava, siege of Sebastopol, and repulse of the sortie on the 26th Oct. 1854 (Medal and Clasp).

9 Doctor Fasson served in the Kaffir war of 1847; and throughout that of 1851-52 (Medal), and was present at the engagement with the Basuto tribes at the Berea 20th Dec. 1852. Served the Eastern campaign of 1854-55, including the affairs of Bulganak and M'Kenzie's Farm, the battles of Alma, Balaklava, and Inkerman, capture of Balaklava, siege and fall of Sebastopol, and repulse of the sortie on the 26th Oct. 1854 (Medal and Clasps, and Knight of the Legion of Honor).

10 Doctor Combe served the Eastern campaign of 1854-55, including the battles of Alma, Balaklava, and Inkerman, the siege of Sebastopol, and repulse of the sortie on 26th Oct. 1854 (Medal and Clasps, and 5th Class of the Medjidie).

12 Surgeon De Lisle served with the 4th Regt. throughout the Eastern campaign of 1851-55, including the battles of Alma and Inkerman, siege and fall of Sebastopol (Medal and three Clasps, and Knight of the Legion of Honor).

13 Doctor Wright served the Eastern campaign of 1854-55, including the battles of Alma, Balaklava, and Inkerman (Medal and four Clasps).

15 Doctor Cockburn served in the Eastern campaign of 1854-55, including the expedition to Kertch and Yenikali, and siege of Sebastopol (Medal and Clasps).

Royal Artillery. 385

Years' Serv. Full Pay.	Half Pay.	ASSISTANT SURGEONS.	ASSIST. SURGEON.	
2	0	8 George Ralph Tate, MD.	10 March 58	25 Assist.Surgeon Robert Lewer served in the Royal Navy during the operations in the Baltic and was present at the bombardment of Sweaborg (Medal).
2	0	4 Albert Stanley Knight Prescott	6 May 58	
2	0	8 John Robinson............	22 Sept. 58	33 Assist.Surgeon Steuart served in the Crimea during the winter of 1854-55, and has the Medal with Clasp for Sebastopol.
3	0	H.B.Jn.Trehane May Symons, MD.	8 Dec. 57	
2	0	1 John Montgomery Fiddes, MB..	1 Nov. 58	
2	0	9 Joseph Bourke	25 May 58	
2	0	8 Francis Roberts Hogg, MD....	5 Aug. 58	
2	0	1 William Graves	22 Sept. 58	
2	0	4 William Temple, MB.........	1 Nov. 58	
2	0	4 Henry Harrison	16 Nov. 58	
2	0	8 Benjamin Burland, MB.	1 Dec. 58	
2	0	9 Alfred Lewer................	1 Dec. 58	
1	0	8 Edmund Thomas Palmer	12 Jan. 59	
2	0	3 A.Wm.PultneyPinkerton,MD..	22 June 58	
1	0	4 William Taylor Morgan, MD..	1 Feb. 59	
2	0	9 Langer Carey, MD.	13 Oct. 58	
6	0	7 Herbert Chalmers Miles [32]....	23 Dec. 54	
1	0	7 Charles William Griffith	12 Jan. 59	
1	0	9 George Arthur Grant........	12 Jan. 59	
2	0	11 Robert Cardiff Crean	1 Sept. 58	
6	0	4 William Ramsay Steuart[33]....	11 Aug. 54	
2	0	4 Alexander Richmond........	13 Oct. 58	

2 Surgeon Major Litle served in the field during the rebellion in Canada of 1839-80.
3 Surgeon Major Ferris served in India in 1857-58, and was present at the relief of Lucknow by Lord Clyde, battle of Cawnpore on 6th Dec., siege and capture of Lucknow (Medal and Clasp).
4 Surgeon Fogo served in the Crimea from the April bombardment of 1855 until the final evacuation, and was in medical charge of the left siege train at the fall of Sebastopol (Medal and Clasp).
5 Surgeon Protheroe served in the Eastern campaign of 1854-55, including the battle of Inkerman and siege of Sebastopol (Medal and Clasps).
7 Surgeon Perry served in the Eastern campaign of 1854-55, including the battles of Alma and Inkerman, siege of Sebastopol, and sortie on 26th Oct. (Medal and Clasps, Sardinian Medal, and 5th Class of the Medjidie).
8 Doctor Walshe served in the expedition against the Insurgent Boers beyond the Orange River, South Africa, in 1845. He also accompanied Colonel Somerset's Division throughout the Kaffir war of 1846-47, and was present in all the engagements that took place. Served in the Crimea from Jan. 1855, and was at the fall of Sebastopol (Medal and Clasp, and 5th Class of the Medjidie).
11 Surgeon Park served in the Eastern campaign of 1854-55, including the battle of Inkerman, siege of Sebastopol, and repulse of the sortie on the 20th October 1854 (Medal and Clasps, and Knight of the Legion of Honor).
12† Doctor Lewis served with the Rifle Brigade in the expedition against the insurgent Boers, north of the Orange River, and was present at the action of Boem Plaats on 29th August 1818.
16 Assist.Surgeon Barker served in India in 1858, and was present at the siege and capture of Lucknow, and actions of Sirsoe and Nawabgunge (Medal and Clasp).
17 Doctor M'Munn served in the Eastern campaign of 1854-55, including the siege of Sebastopol (Medal and Clasp).
18 Assist.Surgeon Haughton served in the Eastern campaign of 1854-55, including the battle of Inkerman and siege of Sebastopol (Medal and Clasps, and 5th Class of the Medjidie). Served in the Indian campaign in 1857-58, including the action of Kalee Nuddee, affair of Ramgunga, siege and capture of Lucknow, actions of Bareilly, Shahjehanpore, and Mohumdee (Medal and Clasp).
19 Assist.Surgeon Chapple served the Eastern campaign of 1854-55 (Medal and Clasps, and 5th Class of the Medjidie).
20 Assist.Surgeon Hawkins served with the 4th Regt. at the siege and fall of Sebastopol (Medal and Clasp).
21 Assist.Surgeon Jeeves landed with the army at Old Fort, and was present at the battles of Alma and Inkerman, served in the trenches during the siege and bombardment of Sebastopol, and was present at the assault and capture of the Cemetery, for which he was mentioned in Dispatches (Medal and three Clasps, and Knight of the Legion of Honor).
22 Assist.Surgeon Lougheed served in the Eastern campaign in medical charge of the Royal Engineers right attack, during the winter of 1854-55; was present in the trenches with the Royal Artillery during the two final bombardments of Sebastopol, and was specially mentioned and recommended for promotion in Sir Harry Jones' Dispatch of 16th Sept. 1855 (Medal and Clasp, and 5th Class of the Medjidie. Was present at the capture of Canton in Dec. 1857.
23 Assist.Surgeon Gulland served at the siege of Sebastopol and expedition to Kertch (Medal and Clasp).
24 Assist.Surgeon Fletcher served at the siege and fall of Sebastopol from 26th Aug. 1855 (Medal and Clasp).
26 Assist.Surgeon Webb served in India in 1857-58, and was present at the actions of Banda and Chitrakote (mentioned in despatch, Medal).
27 Assist.Surgeon Tarrant served in India in 1857-58, and was present at the battle of Cawnpore on 6th Dec., action of Kalee Nuddee, and affair of Kankur (Medal).
28 Assist.Surgeon Orton served with the Royal Artillery in the trenches before Sebastopol in 1855 and at the assault of the Redan on the 8th Sept. (Medal and Clasp). Served with the Central India field force under Sir Hugh Rose in 1858, and was present at the siege and capture of the fort of Chandairee, siege and capture of Jhansi, battle of the Betwa, action at Koonch, actions of 17th and 18th May, and of 21st May at Golowlie and capture of Calpee; was afterwards present in various actions in the Bundlekund district (Medal).
29 Assist.Surgeon Smith served in India in 1857-58, and was present at the actions of Secundra, Chanda, and Sultanpore, siege and capture of Lucknow, and relief of Azimghur (Medal and Clasp).
30 Assist.Surgeon Veale served in India and was severely wounded at the relief of Lucknow by Lord Clyde (Medal and Clasp).
31 Assist.Surgeon Milne served in India in 1857-58 and was present at the actions of Sornon and Tiroul (wounded), capture of the village and fort of Dchaign, attack and capture of Tiroul (Medal).
32 Assist.Surgeon Miles served in the Medical Staff during the Crimean War in 1855 (Medal and Clasp). Served with the 83rd Regt. In the Indian campaign of 1857-58, and was present at the affair of Nimbkeira (severely wounded), siege of Neemuch, field operations against Awah, and subsequent destruction of the adjacent towns, also at the capture of Kotah (Medal).

Coast Brigade of Artillery.

Years' Serv.		
Full Pay	Half Pay	

MAJOR.

13 | 0 | James Campbell, *2nd Lieut.* 1 July 47; *Capt.* 10 May 55; *Major,* 4 Nov. 59.

CAPTAINS.

3 | 2 7/12 | Henry M'Gorrery, *Lieut.* 31 Jan. 55; *Capt.* 7 Sept. 55.
3 | 2 7/12 | William Handyside, *Lieut.* 3 May 55; *Capt.* 7 Sept. 55.
3 | 2 7/12 | William Henry, *Lieut.* June 54; *Capt.* 16 Nov. 55.
5 | 0 | VC Andrew Henry,[1] *Lt.* 15 May 55; *Capt.* 28 Nov. 55.
2 | 2 7/12 | John Mackenzie, *Lieut.* 22 Sept. 55; *Capt.* 1 Feb. 56.
13 | 0 | William Elliott, *Qr.Master,* 8 Feb. 47; *Capt.* 4 Nov. 59.
3 | 2 7/12 | James Rogan,[2] *Deputy Assist.Commissary,* 1 April 54; *Capt.* 4 Nov. 59.

SECOND CAPTAIN.

3 | 0 | John Sweeny,[3] *Cornet,* 20 Feb. 57; *Lieut.* 17 Mar. 58; *Capt.* 4 Nov. 59.

LIEUTENANTS.

3 | 2 7/12 | James MacGillivray,[2] *Deputy Assist.Commissary,* 25 July 54; *Lieut.* 4 Nov. 59.
1 | 0 | James Scott, 4 Nov. 59.
1 | 0 | Robert Kettle, 4 Nov. 59.
1 | 0 | David Anderson, (*Qr.Master*) 4 Nov. 59.
1 | 0 | Charles Phillips, 4 Nov. 59.
1 | 0 | James Thomas Cole, (*Adj.*) 4 Nov. 59.
1 | 0 | James Thomson, 4 Nov. 59.
1 | 0 | George M'Murray, 4 Nov. 59.
1 | 0 | *Adjutant.—Lt.* J. T. Cole, 4 Nov. 59.
1 | 0 | *Qr.Master.—Lt.* D. Anderson, 4 Nov. 59.

Agents, Messrs. Cox and Co.

1 Captain Andrew Henry served in the Eastern campaign of 1854-55, including the battles of Alma, Balaklava, and Inkerman, and siege of Sebastopol (Medal and Clasps), and has received the Victoria Cross "for defending the guns of his battery against overwhelming numbers of the enemy at the battle of Inkerman, and continuing to do so until he had received twelve bayonet wounds."

2 Captain Rogan and Lieut. M'Gillivray served at the siege of Sebastopol in 1854-55 (Medal and Clasp).

3 Captain Sweeny served in the Royal Artillery throughout the China Expedition of 1840-43 (Medal), including the capture of Chusan, attack on Chuenpee, destruction of the Bocca Tigris Forts, storm and capture of the heights above Canton, of Amoy, Chusan, Chinhae, Ningpo,—and repulse of the night attack, attack and capture of the enemy's entrenched camp on the heights of Segoan, of Chapoo, Woosung, Shanghae, and Chinkiangfoo, and the landing before Nankin; served in the Crimea from April 1855 at the siege and fall of Sebastopol (Medal and Clasp). He has also the Medal for Meritorious Service.

1 Sir Hew Ross served in the Peninsula and France from 9th June 1809 to Feb. 1814, including the action of the Coa, battle of Busaco, actions of Pombal, Redinha (wounded in the shoulder), Casal Nova, Foz d'Arouce (wounded in the leg), and Sabugal; battle of Fuentes d'Onor, action of Aldea de Ponte, sieges of Ciudad Rodrigo and Badajoz (dangerously wounded in the head); action at Castrajon, capture of forts at and battle of Salamanca, capture of Madrid and the Retiro, affairs of San Munoz and San Milan, battles of Vittoria, and the Pyrenees from 26th to 30th July, passage of the Bidassoa, Nivelle, and Nive; battle near Bayonne, 13 Dec. 1813. Served also the campaign of 1815, and was present at the battle of Waterloo. Sir Hew has received the Gold Cross and two Clasps for Busaco, Badajoz, Salamanca, Vittoria, Nivelle, and Nive; the Silver War Medal with three Clasps for Fuentes d'Onor, Ciudad Rodrigo, and Pyrenees; and is a Knight of the Tower and Sword of Portugal, and 2nd Class St. Anne of Russia.

3 General Campbell served the Egyptian campaign of 1801, including the actions of the 8th, 13th, and 21st March, capture of Rosetta, several affairs on the march to, and capture of Cairo, and afterwards at the capture of Alexandria. Medal for services in Egypt.

4 Lieut. General Turner was at the capture of the Cape of Good Hope in 1806. Served also in the Peninsula from Dec. 1813 to the end of the war, including the battles of Orthes and Toulouse, and the affairs of Vic Bigorre and Tarbes. He has received the Gold Medal and one Clasp for Orthes and Toulouse.

5 Sir Robert Gardiner's services:—capture of Minorca in 1798; campaign in Portugal and Spain, including the battles of Rolcia, Vimiera, and Corunna; expedition to Walcheren; Peninsular campaigns from early in 1810 to the end of the war in 1814, including the battle of Barrosa, capture of Badajoz, battle of Salamanca, siege of Burgos, affair of Morales, battles of Vittoria, Orthes, and Toulouse; campaign of 1815, including the battle of Waterloo. Sir Robert has received the Gold Cross and two Clasps for Barrosa, Badajoz, Salamanca, Vittoria, Orthes, and Toulouse; and the Silver War Medal with three Clasps for Rolcia, Vimiera, and Corunna; and is a Knight 2nd Class of St. Anne of Russia. In 1848 he was appointed Governor and Commander-in-Chief of Gibraltar, and continued in that command until the 26th August 1855.

6 Lieut. General Wallace was on board the *Phœnix* Letter of Marque when she beat off a French Privateer near Barbadoes in Dec. 1800. Present at the siege of Flushing in 1809; and he commanded the Artillery at the attack of Sackets Harbour, United States, in 1813.

7 Lieut. General Richard Jones served in Holland in 1799, including the battles of Zuyp, Hoorn, Egmont, and Limmen. Present at the capture of Paris, and with the Army of Occupation until 2nd Dec. 1818.

8 Lieut. General Whinyates served in the expedition to the Helder and campaign in North Holland in 1799; expedition to Madeira in 1801, and to Copenhagen 1807; Peninsular campaigns from Feb. 1810 to July 1813, including the battles of Busaco and Albuhera; affairs at Usagre, Aldea de Ponte, and San Munos, attack and defeat of General Lalleman's cavalry at Ribera, and many other affairs. Served also the campaign of 1815, and was severely wounded in the left arm at Waterloo. He has received the Silver War Medal with two Clasps for Busaco and Albuhera.

9 Lieut. General Michell served the campaign in Holland in 1799; in the Peninsula and south of France from Aug. 1813 to May 1814, including siege of San Sebastian, passage of the Bidassoa, Nivelle, and Nive, battles of Orthes and Toulouse; in America from May 1814 to May 1815, including the attack of Washington, Baltimore, and New Orleans, and other operations on the coast. Attached to the Prussian army in reducing the fortresses in the Netherlands. He has received the Gold Medal and one Clasp for Orthes and Toulouse; and the Silver War Medal with three Clasps for St. Sebastian, Nivelle, and Nive.

10 General W. G. Power served in Spain, Portugal, and France, from 14th Oct. 1808 to 4th June 1814, including the battle of Talavera, sieges of Ciudad Rodrigo (wounded), and Badajoz, capture of French works at Almaraz, reduction of forts at, and battle of Salamanca, siege of Burgos (wounded), siege of San Sebastian from 11th July to 8th Sept. 1813, passage of the Bidassoa, the Nive, and the Adour, battle of Orthes, investment of Bayonne, and various minor actions. Led the reserve to the support of the assaulting party of Fort La Picurina during the last siege of Badajoz, and the Commandant surrendered to him personally. He has the Silver War Medal with nine Clasps.

11 Lieut. General Dyncley's services:—Campaign of 1805 in Italy under Sir Jas. Craig; and that in Calabria in 1806 under Sir John Stuart, including the battle of Maida and siege of Scylla. Peninsular campaigns from July 1811, to November 1813, including the siege of Ciudad Rodrigo (wounded in the head), siege of forts at Salamanca (wounded in the face), heights of St. Christovel, battle of Salamanca, defence of the Bridge of Simancas, affairs at Morales de Toro and San Munos, battles of Vittoria, and the Pyrenees. Campaign of 1815, including the battle of Waterloo. Taken prisoner at Malanahenda near Madrid, 11th Aug. 1812, when engaged with the rear-guard of Joseph Bonaparte's army; escaped from the enemy, and rejoined the army the 23rd of the same month. He has received the Silver War Medal with five Clasps.

12 Lieut. General Cobbe served the campaign in the West Indies in 1801, under Lieut. Gen. Sir Thos. Trigge.

13 Lieut. General Mercer served in South America in 1807, and commanded the rear-guard left in occupation of the citadel of Monte Video to cover the embarkation of the garrison. Served the campaign of 1815 in command of a battery of Horse Artillery, including the action of Quatre Bras, the Cavalry affairs of the following day, and battle of Waterloo (wounded), where he saved two squares of Brunswick Infantry, previously dis-

388   War Services of the Officers of the Royal Artillery.

located by a heavy cannonade, from being broken by a charge of Cuirassiers—and this by disobeying the Duke of Wellington's positive order, "To withdraw the men from their guns, if charged home, into the adjacent squares of Infantry:" the charge was defeated, though persevered in to within ten yards of the guns' muzzles. Three several attacks were in a similar manner defeated; was afterwards at the action of St. Denis and capture of Paris.

14 Maj.Gen. Scott served in the expedition to Walcheren, and was at the siege of Flushing.

15 Major General Russel was actively employed as acting Brigade-Major during the insurrection of the slaves in Jamaica in 1832.

16 Lieut.General Cator served the campaign of Walcheren and siege of Flushing. In the Peninsula and south of France from the end of 1809 to the termination of the war in 1814, including the defence of Cadiz, lines at Torres Vedras and at Santarem, battle of Barrosa (wounded), affair at Osma, battle of Vittoria, affair at Tolosa, passage of the Bidassou, and at the attack of Bidassoa by the French, battles of Nivelle and Nive, and four days' engagements in front of Bayonne. He has received the Silver War Medal with four Clasps.

17 Major General H. W. Gordon's services :—Expedition to Naples, Dec. 1805, and subsequent occupation of Sicily; battle of Maida, and attack and surrender of the Rock of Scylla, 1806. He has received the Silver War Medal with one Clasp for Maida.

18 Sir Wm. Colebrooke's services :—Campaigns of 1809 and 10 in India; expedition to Java in 1811, including the action of Weltyvreden, in batteries before Cornelis (until wounded in the groin 22nd August), and the siege and capture of Jokjakarta. Expedition to Palembang, in Sumatra, 1813; campaign of 1817 and 18, in India, against the Pindarrees and Mahrattas; campaign of 1818 and 19 in Southern India. Present also at the sieges of Ras-el-Kyhma and Zaya, Arab fortresses. Sir William has received the Silver War Medal with one Clasp for Java.

19 Major General Wylde served in Holland in 1813 and 14, and commanded a battery before Antwerp and at the attack on Bergen-op-Zoom. Was attached to the Horse Artillery with the Army of Occupation in France. In April 1834 succeeded Lord William Russell as Military Commissioner at the head-quarters of Don Pedro's army in Portugal, and continued with them until the Convention of Evora Monte; and subsequently from Nov. 1834 to 1840 at the head-quarters of the Spanish Army, and in all the general actions during that period, including the raising of the siege of Bilboa, for which he received the thanks of the Spanish Cortes. In Portugal, again, in 1846, during the Civil War, and signed the Convention of Oporto. He is a Knight of Charles the Third, 2nd Class St. Fernando, and Commander of Isabella the Catholic.

20 Major General Maclachlan served in Spain in 1813 and 14. He is a Knight of St. Maurice and Lazare.

21 Major General Sabine served the campaign on the Niagara Frontier in 1814, and commanded the batteries at the siege of Fort Erie in August and September.

22 Major Gen. Chesney was employed, from 1829 to 1832, in examining the principal parts of Western Asia; during which time, assisted only by a few Arabs, he descended the river Euphrates upon a Raft; and his reports to Government led to a Parliamentary vote to extend our commercial relations in that quarter, and open a communication with India through Arabia. His Majesty, through the Duke of Wellington, having conferred on him the rank of Colonel on a particular service, he sailed early in 1835 with a detachment of artillery, another of sappers, a proportion of seamen, and thirteen military and naval officers; with whose assistance Colonel Chesney accomplished the extraordinary achievement of transporting two iron steam vessels across Syria, and floating them in a perfect state on the Upper Euphrates, not very far from Aleppo. In the early part of the navigation thus commenced, a fearful hurricane carried the smaller vessel and twenty of her men to the bottom, Colonel Chesney and eight others being saved by swimming. The Commander, however, persevered; and in the remaining vessel he not only completed the surveys of the river Euphrates, Tigris, and Kareen, but continued the undertaking until it was turned over in the following year to the East India Company. His late Majesty warmly approved of the intrepidity manifested in continuing the service after the calamitous loss of one-half of his force, and the brevet rank of Major was bestowed on him by the King, which was followed by that of Lieut.-Colonel by command of the Queen.

23 Maj.Gen. Bell's services:—Capture of the islands of St. Thomas and St. Croix in 1807; siege of fort Desaix, Martinique; capture of Les Saintes, near Guadaloupe, and bombardment and driving from the anchorage the French fleet in 1809; capture of Guadaloupe and adjacent islands in 1810. Served in the Peninsula and France from July 1813 to July 1814, including the passage of the Bidassoa, Nivelle, Nive, and four days' engagements near Bayonne; passage of the Adour, investment of Bayonne, affairs at Vic Bigorre, and Tarbes, passage of the Garonne, and subsequent operations to the battle of Toulouse where he was slightly wounded. Served also the campaign of 1815, including the battles of Quatre Bras and Waterloo, and capture of Paris. He has the Silver War Medal with five Clasps.

24 Major Gen. Brereton served in Spain, France, and the Netherlands, from December 1809 to June 1815, and was present at the defence of Cadiz and of Fort Matagorda (wounded), the Artillery of which last place he commanded. He served in the batteries at the siege of San Sebastian; was present in the battles of Barrosa (wounded), Vittoria, the Pyrenees, Orthes, Toulouse, Quatre Bras, and Waterloo (severely wounded), actions on the retreat from Burgos, at San Munos, near Salamanca, Helette, St. Palais, Sauveterre, Aire, and Tarbes. He commanded a Division, as second in command, of the expedition under Major-General D'Aguilar, which assaulted and took the Forts of the Bocca Tigris in the Canton River, those of the Staked Barrier, and of the city of Canton, spiking 879

War Services of the Officers of the Royal Artillery. 389

pieces of heavy ordnance. He has received the Silver War Medal with six Clasps. Was on board the flag-ship *Britannia* during the naval action of the allied fleets with the defences of Sebastopol on the 17th Oct. 1854, and directed the rockets fired from that ship against the forts and city: has received the Crimean War Medal with Clasp for Sebastopol.

25 Major Gen. England served the expedition to the Weser in 1805 and 6; to the Cape of Good Hope and South America in 1806 and 7; campaign of 1813 in the Peninsula, including the battle of Vittoria and siege of San Sebastian, for which he has received the Silver War Medal with two Clasps.

26 Major Gen. Hardinge served in the Peninsula from Aug. 1812, to the end of the war in 1814, including the battle of Vittoria, siege of San Sebastian, battles of Orthes and Toulouse, affairs at Osma, Tolosa, Bidassoa, and Tarbes. Served also the campaign of 1815, and was present at Ligny and Quatre Bras. He has received the Silver War Medal with four Clasps.

27 Major General Gordon Higgins commanded the Royal Artillery in the Syrian campaign from August 1840 to the evacuation of that country in Dec. 1841 (Medal), and was present at the bombardment and capture of Beyrout and of St. Jean d'Acre.

28 Major General Anderson's services:—Siege and capture of Flushing, and the subsequent operations in 1809; Bombardment of Antwerp, also previous and subsequent operations in 1813 and 1814; campaign of 1815, including the battle of Waterloo, and captures of Cambray and Paris.

29 Major General Armstrong served at Walcheren in 1809; and in Canada from May 1810 to July 1815, including the capture of a detachment on river Raisin, the cutting out of an enemy's vessel when in command of a gun-boat at Prescott, at Fort Erie during a cannonade of 17 hours; at the loss of Fort George, actions at Stoney Creek, and Black Rock, investment of Fort George, capture of Fort Niagara, Black Rock, and town of Buffalo, action at Streets Creek, and Chippawa, and at the siege of Fort Erie under an almost constant fire for about five weeks. Slightly wounded at Fort George, 27th May 1813.

30 Colonel Fras. Warde was present at the defence of Cadiz and at the battle of Waterloo.

31 Colonel Ingilby served in the Peninsula from July 1810 to Jan. 1813, including the sieges of Ciudad Rodrigo, Forts of Salamanca (wounded), and Burgos; and the battles of Busaco, Fuentes d'Onor, and Salamanca. Served also the campaign of 1815, and was present at the battle of Waterloo. He has received the Silver War Medal with four Clasps.

32 Colonel Pester was present at the defence of Cadiz, and at the battle of Barrosa, where he was severely wounded. He has received the Silver War Medal with one Clasp for Barrosa.

33 Major Gen. Bloomfield served in the Peninsula and France, from March 1813 to June 1814, including the battle of Vittoria, siege of San Sebastian, crossing the Bidassoa, and battles of the Nivelle, Nive, Orthes, and Toulouse. Served also the campaign of 1815, including the battle of Waterloo. He has received the Silver War Medal with six Clasps.

34 Colonel Palliser served in the Peninsula and France, from November 1812 to May 1814, including the siege of San Sebastian, and battles of Vittoria, Orthes, and Toulouse, for which he has received the Silver War Medal with four Clasps. Served subsequently in the American war, including the battles of Bladensburg and Baltimore, capture of Washington, and operations before New Orleans. With the army of occupation in France from June 1815 to November 1818, and present at the capture of Paris.

35 Colonel Cuppage served in the Peninsula and France, from February to August 1814, and was present at the repulse of the sortie from Bayonne. Served also the campaign of 1815, including the battle of Waterloo.

36 Sir Richard Dacres served the Eastern campaign of 1854-55, including the affairs of Bulganac and M'Kenzie's Farm, and battles of Alma, Balaklava, and Inkerman (horse killed): commanded the Royal Artillery at the repulse of the Russians in the sortie from Sebastopol on the 26th October; succeeded to the command of the Royal Artillery at the siege and fall of Sebastopol after Br.-General Strangways was killed at Inkerman on the 5th Nov. 1854 (Medal and Clasps, *KCB.*, Commander of the Legion of Honor, Commander 1st Class Military Order of Savoy, and 2nd Class of the Medjidie).

37 Colonel Lake commanded the Artillery of the Light Division in the Eastern campaign of 1854-55, including the affairs of Bulganac and M'Kenzie's Farm, and the battles of Alma (horse shot), Balaklava, and Inkerman (horse shot), and siege of Sebastopol (Medal and four Clasps, Officer of the Legion of Honor, and 4th Class of the Medjidie).

38 Major Gen. Dupuis served on the north coast of Spain in 1836, 7, and 8, in co-operation with the Spanish army, including the field actions of the 10th, 12th, 14th, and 16th March, and the action of Hernani, on the 14th May 1837, besides various other minor affairs. Served the Eastern campaign of 1854-55, including the battles of Alma, Balaklava, and Inkerman, siege and fall of Sebastopol (Medal and Clasps, *CB.*, Commander of the Legion of Honor, Sardinian Medal, and 3rd Class of the Medjidie). Commanded the Royal Artillery in India from Oct. 1857 to Feb. 1859, and was present at the action of Pandoo Nuddee 26th Nov., operations of the 27th, 28th and 29th Nov. before Cawnpore, and battle there on the 6th Dec. 1857—twice mentioned in despatches (Medal).

39 Sir William Fenwick Williams commanded the Turkish army at the defence of Kars, and for his distinguished services was promoted Major-General, nominated a *KCB.*, and created a Baronet; has also received the First Class of the Turkish Order of the Medjidie, and is a Grand Officer of the French Legion of Honor.

40 Colonel Morris served in the Eastern campaign of 1854-55, and was present at the siege and fall of Sebastopol (Medal and Clasp, and 5th Class of the Medjidie).

41 Colonel St. George served the Eastern campaign of 1855, and commanded the siege train at the fall of Sebastopol (Medal and Clasp, *CB.*, Officer of the Legion of Honor, and 4th Class of the Medjidie).

42 Colonel Nedham served at the siege of Sebastopol in 1855 in command of the Artillery of the Third Division (Medal and Clasp, and 5th Class of the Medjidie).

43 Colonel E. C. Warde served in the Eastern campaign of 1855, in command of the siege train before Sebastopol, and was present at the bombardments of April and (June 6th and 17th), (Medal and Clasp, *CB.*, Officer of the Legion of Honor, and 4th Class of the Medjidie).

44 Colonel Taylor served at the siege and fall of Sebastopol in 1855 in command of the Artillery of the Highland Division (Medal and Clasp, and 5th Class of the Medjidie).

45 Colonel Maclean served at the siege and fall of Sebastopol in 1855 in command of the Artillery of the Light Division (Medal and Clasp, and 5th Class of the Medjidie).

46 Colonel Askwith has the decorations of 1st Class St. Fernando, Commander Isabella the Catholic, and Knight of Charles the Third.

47 Colonel Dunlop commanded the Troops in China from the breaking out of hostilities in 1856 to the end of April 1857. In Jan. 1857, suffered severely from an attempt made by the Chinese to poison the inhabitants of Hong Kong by mixing arsenic with the bread sold on the 16th of January. Commanded the Artillery at the capture of Canton in Dec. 1857 (*CB.*).

48 Sir David Edward Wood commanded the Royal Artillery on the Eastern frontier of the Cape of Good Hope during the insurrection of the Boers and Caffres in 1842-43. Served in the Eastern campaign of 1854-55, and was present at the battles of Balaklava and Inkerman, the siege and fall of Sebastopol, and repulse of the sortie on the 26th Oct. 1854 (Medal and Clasps, *CB.*, Officer of the Legion of Honor, and 4th Class of the Medjidie). Commanded the Royal Horse Artillery in India from Oct. 1857 to Feb. 1859, and was present at the action of Pandora, and as Brigadier commanded the Field Artillery at the siege and capture of Lucknow—four times mentioned in despatches (Medal and Clasp).

49 Colonel Fitzmayer served the Eastern campaign of 1854-55, including the affairs of Bulganac and M'Kenzie's Farm, battles of Alma and Inkerman, siege and fall of Sebastopol, and repulse of the sortie on the 26th October 1854; was complimented on parade by Sir De Lacy Evans for his manner of bringing the Artillery at the Alma under "the hottest fire," and was again thanked by Sir De Lacy, and twice mentioned in his Dispatch on the repulse of the sortie on 26th October 1854 (Medal and Clasps, *CB.*, Officer of the Legion of Honor, and 4th Class of the Medjidie).

50 Colonel Francklyn served in the Eastern campaign of 1855, and commanded the siege train of the left attack before Sebastopol, and was present at the bombardments of the 6th and 17th June (Medal and Clasp, *CB.*, and 5th Class of the Medjidie).

51 Colonel Gambier served in the Eastern campaign of 1854 in command of the siege train before Sebastopol, and was present at the bombardment of October, and at the battle of Inkerman (severely wounded, Medal and Clasps, *CB.*, and 5th Class of the Medjidie).

52 Colonel E. W. Crofton served in Spain during the Christino and Carlist war in 1837 and 1838, and was taken prisoner by the Carlists (1st Class St. Fernando). Nominated to the 3rd Class of the Medjidie for Services, as a Brigadier, with the late Osmanli Cavalry.

53 Colonel Irving served the Eastern campaign of 1854-55, including the battle of Inkerman and siege of Sebastopol; commanded the Artillery of the left attack at the bombardment in October and during the three last months of 1854 (Medal and Clasps, *CB.*, and 5th Class of the Medjidie).

54 Colonel Rowan served the Syrian campaign (Medal). Also the Eastern campaign of 1854-55, including the battle of Inkerman and siege of Sebastopol, in the trenches with the siege train and bombardment of October (Medal and Clasps, *CB.*, and 5th Class of the Medjidie).

55 Colonel Freese served on the China expedition, and was slightly wounded at Chinkiangfoo. Served in the Eastern campaign of 1854-55, including the battle of Inkerman and siege of Sebastopol, in the trenches with the siege train and bombardment of October (Medal and Clasps, *CB.*, and 5th Class of the Medjidie).

56 Colonel Cleaveland served on the north coast of Spain in 1837-39, in co-operation with the Spanish army towards the conclusion of the war in St. Sebastian and its vicinity.

57 Colonel Crawford served in India from Sept. 1857 to Jan. 1858, and as Brigadier commanded the Artillery at the relief of Lucknow by Lord Clyde and also the Artillery attached to the Commander in Chief's force at the battle of Cawnpore, 6th Dec. (mentioned in despatches, *CB.*, Medal and Clasp).

58 Colonel Poynter served the Eastern campaign of 1854, including the affairs of Bulganac and M'Kenzie's Farm, the battles of Alma, Balaklava, and Inkerman, and siege of Sebastopol (Medal and Clasps, *CB.*, and 5th Class of the Medjidie).

59 Sir George Robert Barker served the Eastern campaign of 1854-55, including the battles of Alma and Balaklava, expedition to Kertch (in command of Royal Artillery), siege of Sebastopol, including the command of the batteries of the left attack at the fall of the fortress (Medal and Clasps, *CB.*, Knight of the Legion of Honor, and 4th Class of the Medjidie). Served the Indian campaign of 1857-58, was present at the affair of Kaloe Nuddee, as Brigadier commanded the Siege Artillery at the siege and capture of Lucknow, commanded the Column which defeated the rebels 5000 strong at Jamo, subsequently assaulted and took the fort of Birwa after eight hours firing (twice mentioned in despatches, *KCB.*, Medal and Clasp).

60 Colonel Paddy commanded the R. Artillery in the engagement at Port Natal against the revolted Zoolu chief Foro in 1840. He served in the Kaffir war of 1852 in command of the Royal Artillery, and was named in the official Dispatches, especially in

that relating to the capture of the Kaffir chief Macomo's stronghold, called "Macomo's Den," on the 10th March. Also commanded the R. Artillery at the battle of Berea against the Basuta tribes under the Chief Moshesh (horse shot) 20th Dec. 1852, and was again mentioned in Dispatches, and received the Brevet rank of Major for his services (Medal). Commanded as Brigadier the column detached from the Saugor field force, which defeated the rebel force at Kentee in Bundlecund on 4th March 1859 (mentioned in despatches, Medal).

61 Colonel Phillpotts served at the siege and fall of Sebastopol in 1855 (Medal and Clasp, and 5th Class of the Medjidie); has also received the Syrian Medal of 1841.

62 Colonel Riddell commanded the Siege Artillery of Outram's force on the left bank of the Goomtee at the siege and capture of Lucknow in March 1858, also commanded the Artillery of Lugard's Column at the affair of Tigree, relief of Azimghur, operations in the Jungle and capture of Jugdespore (three times mentioned in despatches, *CB*., Medal and Clasp).

63 Colonel Price commanded the Artillery of the Rajpootana field force under General Roberts at the capture of Kotah on 30 March 1858, and at the action of Saugor, and defeat of the rebels on the right bank of the Bunnas (mentioned in despatches, *CB*., and Medal).

64 Colonel Wodehouse served the Eastern campaign of 1854-55, including the affairs of Bulganac and M'Kenzie's Farm, the battles of Alma, Balaklava, and Inkerman (horse killed), siege of Sebastopol, and repulse of the sortie on the 26th October 1854 (Medal and Clasps, *CB*., Knight of the Legion of Honor, and 5th Class of the Medjidie).

65 Lt.Colonel Maude served the Eastern campaign of 1854 in command of a troop of Royal Horse Artillery, including the affairs of Bulganac and M'Kenzie's Farm, the battles of the Alma and Balaklava (dangerously wounded and horse shot), and siege of Sebastopol (Medal and Clasps, *CB*., and 5th Class of the Medjidie).

66 Colonel Maberly commanded the Artillery of the Jounpore field force under General Franks in the actions of Chanda and Sultanpore; also present at the siege and capture of Lucknow in March 1858, and with Grant's Column in the actions at Koorsee and Barree (four times mentioned in despatches, *CB*., and Medal and Clasp).

67 Colonel Dickson served on the staff of Lord Raglan during the campaign of 1854-55, and was present at the affairs of Bulganac and M'Kenzie's Farm, the battles of Alma and Inkerman, capture of Balaklava, expedition to Kertch, and siege of Sebastopol (wounded 4th Feb. 1855): commanded the right siege train, and was present at the bombardment of October, April, and June 17th (Medal and Clasps, *CB*., Aide-de-Camp to the Queen and Colonel, Victoria Cross, Officer of the Legion of Honor, and 2nd Class of the Medjidie). He is also a Knight of Charles the Third, 1st Class St. Fernando, and Knight of Isabella the Catholic.

68 Lt.Col. Graydon served in the Eastern campaign of 1854-55, including the siege of Sebastopol, and expedition to Kertch (Medal and Clasp).

69 Lt.Colonel John Travers served in the Eastern campaign of 1854-55, including the siege and fall of Sebastopol (Medal and Clasp).

70 Lt.Colonel the Hon. G. T. Devereux served in the Kaffir war of 1852 (Medal); and was present at the engagement with the Basuta tribes at Berea 20th Dec.: named in the official Dispatch, and received the Brevet rank of Major for his services.

71 Lt.Cols. Broughton and Hugh Campbell, *CB*., served in the Eastern campaign of 1854-55, in the trenches with the siege train before Sebastopol, and at the bombardment of April and of June (6th and 17th): Medal and Clasp, Knight of the Legion of Honor, and 5th Class of the Medjidie.

72 Lt.Colonel Adye served the Eastern campaign of 1854-55 as Assist. Adj. General of Royal Artillery, and was present at the affairs of Bulganac and M'Kenzie's Farm, the battles of the Alma, Balaklava, and Inkerman, capture of Balaklava Castle, siege and fall of Sebastopol) Medal and Clasps, *CB*., Officer of the Legion of Honor, and 4th Class of the Medjidie). Served in India in 1857-58 as Assist.Adj.General of Royal Artillery, and was present at the action of Pandoo Nuddy 26 Nov., operations before Cawnpore under Gen. Windham 27th, 28th, and 29th Nov., battle of Cawnpore and defeat of the Gwalior Contingent 6th Dec. 1857 (three times mentioned in despatches, Medal).

73 Lt.Colonel H. L. Gardiner served in the operations at Prescott in Upper Canada in 1838. Also in the pursuit of Tantia Topee in Central India in 1858.

74 Lt.Colonel Knox, Captains C. W. Elgee, and G. R. C. Young, Lieuts. A. H. C. Hamilton, Carr, Dyce, Hon. R. V. Dillon, Rochfort, and Cane were at the capture of Canton in Dec. 1857.

75 Lt.Colonel Younghusband served in the Eastern campaign of 1854, including the battle of Inkerman and siege of Sebastopol (Medal and Clasps).

76 Colonel D'Aguilar served the Eastern campaign of 1854-55 (Medal and Clasps, *CB*., and 5th Class of the Medjidie), including the battle of Inkerman (horse shot) and siege of Sebastopol, in the trenches with the siege train, and at the bombardment of October. Served the Indian campaign of 1857-58, and commanded the Artillery of General Franks' force at the action of Secundra, also commanded the Royal Horse Artillery at the siege and capture of Lucknow (three times mentioned in despatches, and Brevet of Colonel).

77 Lt.Colonel Thompson served at the siege and fall of Sebastopol in 1855 (Medal and Clasp, and 5th Class of the Medjidie).

78 Major Ward served at the siege and fall of Sebastopol in 1855, and at the battle of Tchernaya (Medal and Clasp, Sardinian Medal, and 5th Class of the Medjidie).

79 Major Brandling served the Eastern campaign of 1854-55 in command of a troop of Royal Horse Artillery, including the affairs of Bulganac and M'Kenzie's Farm, the battles of

Alma, Balaklava, and Inkerman, capture of Balaklava, siege and fall of Sebastopol (Medal and Clasps, *CB.*, Knight of the Legion of Honor, and 5th Class of the Medjidie).

80 Captains Wragge and Tredcroft, served in the Eastern campaign of 1855, including the siege of Sebastopol, in the trenches with the siege train, and at the bombardment of April (Medal and Clasp). Captain Tredcroft has the 5th Class of the Medjidie.

81 Major F. J. Travers commanded the Artillery with Grant's force from 30th Oct. to 10th Dec. 1857 throughout the operations resulting in the relief of Lucknow and defeat of the Gwalior Contingent at Cawnpore; was senior officer R. A. In the action of 2nd Nov.; commanded the Artillery sent against Jellalhabad Nov. 13th; was wounded in the advance of 16th-17th Nov.; mentioned in despatches and thanked by Governor General in Council (Brevet of Major, Medal and Clasp).

82 Lt.Colonel Dixon served in the Eastern campaign in 1855, in the trenches with the siege train before Sebastopol, and at the bombardments of April, and 6th and 17th June (Medal and Clasp, Brevets of Major and Lt.-Colonel, Victoria Cross, Knight of the Legion of Honor, and 5th Class of the Medjidie).

83 Lt.Col. John Turner was present at the capture of Port Natal on the 26th June 1842. Served also the Eastern campaign of 1854-55, including the affair at M'Kenzie's Farm, the battles of Alma and Inkerman, siege of Sebastopol, and repulse of the sortie on the 26th October 1854 (Medal and Clasps, *CB.*, Knight of the Legion of Honor, and 5th Class of the Medjidie). Received the Brevet of Lieut.-Col. for distinguished service at the battle of Alma in crossing the river with two guns, ascending the heights and enfilading the Russian columns.

84 Captain Fisher and Major Clifford served at the siege and fall of Sebastopol in 1855 (Medal and Clasp). Major Clifford has the 5th Class of the Medjidie.

84† Major Gibbon served at the siege and fall of Sebastopol in 1855 (Medal and Clasp). Served with Outram's force throughout the operations on the left bank of the Goomtee at the siege and capture of Lucknow in March 1858, and commanded the Artillery with Grant's Column in the action of Sirsee—severely wounded (5 times mentioned in despatches, Brevet of Major, *CB.*, Medal and Clasp).

85 Major Longden commanded the Mortar battery in the operations resulting in the relief of Lucknow by Lord Clyde in Nov. 1857 (wounded), and at the battle of Cawnpore on 6th Dec. (twice mentioned in despatches, Brevet of Major, Medal and Clasp).

86 Lt.Colonel Middleton served in the Indian campaign of 1857-58, including the relief of Lucknow by Lord Clyde (wounded, and horse shot), battle of Cawnpore, actions of Serai Ghat (commanded the Artillery), Chanda, and Sultanpore, siege and capture of Lucknow, action of Barree, capture of Rampore Kussie (commanded the Artillery), and affair of Muchagawn (nine times mentioned in despatches, Brevets of Major and Lt.Colonel, *C.B.*, Medal and Clasps).

87 Lt.Col. Anderson served during the operations on the Yiang-tse-Kiang in China in 1842, including the storm and capture of Chin Kiang Foo; also at the demonstration before Nankin (Medal). Served the Eastern campaign of 1854-55, including the affairs of Bulganac and M'Kenzie's Farm, battle of Alma, capture of Balaklava, and siege of Sebastopol (Medal and Clasps, *CB.*, and 5th Class of the Medjidie). Served in India in 1857-58, and was at the action of Pandora where a portion of his troop acted as Cavalry; commanded the Artillery of Grant's division at the capture of Meangunge, also at the siege and capture of Lucknow (four times mentioned in despatches, Brev. of Lt.Col., Medal and Clasp).

88 Lt.Colonel H. F. Strange served the Eastern campaign of 1854-55, including the affairs of Bulganac and M'Kenzie's Farm, the battles of Alma and Inkerman, siege and fall of Sebastopol, in the trenches with the siege train, and at the bombardments of Oct., April, and June (6th and 17th): Medal and Clasps, *CB.*, Knight of the Legion of Honor, and 5th Class of the Medjidie.

89 Major M. Adye served in the Eastern campaign of 1854-55, in the trenches at the siege and fall of Sebastopol, and at the bombardment of June 6th (severely wounded): Medal and Clasp, and 5th Class of the Medjidie.

90 Major Franklin served the Eastern campaign of 1854-55, including the battle of Alma and siege of Sebastopol (Medal and Clasps, *CB.*, and 5th Class of the Medjidie).

91 Majors Hawkins and Shaw, Lieuts. Humfrey, Sir John Campbell and Anley, served in the Eastern campaign in 1855, in the trenches with the siege train before Sebastopol, and at the bombardments of April and June (6th and 17th): Medal and Clasp, and Sardinian Medal. Majors Hawkins and Shaw have the 5th Class of the Medjidie.

92 Captains Mackay and Connell, Major Lennox, Captain Pigou, Major Newton, Captains Vosey and H. Smyth, served at the siege and fall of Sebastopol in 1855 (Medal and Clasp). Majors Lennox and Newton and Capt. Pigou have the 5th Class of the Medjidie.

93 Major Grant served in the Eastern campaign from 18th Jan. 1855, in the trenches with the siege train, including the siege and fall of Sebastopol, and bombardments of April and June (6th and 17th): Medal and Clasp, Brevet Major, Knight of the Legion of Honor, and 5th Class of the Medjidie.

94 Captains Johnson, Gloig, and Vernon, served in the Eastern campaign of 1854-55, including the siege and fall of Sebastopol (Medal and Clasp). Captain Johnson has the 5th Class of the Medjidie.

95 Major M'Crea in command of 3 batteries R. Artillery and a detachment of the 41st Regt. (with Capt. Purcell, Lts. Tottenham, Richardson, Wardell, Saunders, and Cameron) was present in the revolution which upset the Emperor Faustin in Hayti in Jan. 1859; landed and protected the Europeans at Port au Prince, and carried off the Emperor his

War Services of the Officers of the Royal Artillery. 393

family and ministers: received the thanks of the English and the French Governments, and the Brevet of Major.

96 Lt.Col. Henry served in the Eastern campaign of 1855, in the trenches with the siege train before Sebastopol (severely wounded), and at the bombardments of April and June (6th and 17th): Medal and Clasp, Brevets of Major and Lt.Col., Sardinian Medal, and 5th Class of the Medjidie.

97 Major Pipon served the Eastern campaign of 1854-55, including the affairs of Bulganac and M'Kenzie's Farm, the battles of Alma and Balaklava, siege and fall of Sebastopol (Medal and Clasps, Brevet Major, Sardinian Medal, and 5th Class of the Medjidie).

98 Major Shakespear served the Eastern campaign of 1854-55, including the affairs of Bulganac and M'Kenzie's Farm, the battles of Alma, Balaklava (horse shot), and Inkerman, and siege of Sebastopol (Medal and Clasps, Brevet Major, and 5th Class of the Medjidie).

99 Lt.Colonel Hamley served the Eastern campaign of 1854-55, including the affairs of Bulganac and M'Kenzie's Farm, the battles of Alma (horse shot), Balaklava, and Inkerman (horse killed), the siege and fall of Sebastopol, and repulse of the sortie on the 26th October 1854 (Medal and Clasps, Brevets of Major and Lt.Col., Knight of the Legion of Honor, Sardinian Medal, and 5th Class of the Medjidie).

100 Major Field served the campaign of 1854-55 as D. A. Q. M. G. to the Royal Artillery, and was present at the siege and fall of Sebastopol, and with the Expedition to Kertch (Medal and Clasp, Knight of the Legion of Honor, and 5th Class of the Medjidie).

101 Lt.Colonel Hon. D. M'D. Fraser served in the Eastern campaign of 1854-55, including the battle of Inkerman and siege of Sebastopol (Medal and Clasps, and 5th Class of the Medjidie). Commanded a Troop of Royal Horse Artillery in the action at Hyderghur 29th Nov. 1858, defeat of a rebel force at Bujeedia, capture of Fort Mujeedia, and action at Bankee (Brevet of Lt.Colonel, Medal).

102 Major C. J. Strange served at the siege of Sebastopol in 1855, in the trenches with the siege train, and at the bombardments of April and 6th June (Medal and Clasp, and 5th Class of the Medjidie).

103 Major Hon. W. C. Yelverton served in the Eastern campaign of 1854-55, including the battle of Inkerman (horse killed), siege and fall of Sebastopol, and repulse of the sortie on the 26th October 1854 (Medal and Clasps, and 5th Class of the Medjidie).

104 Lieut.Col. Biddulph served the Eastern campaign of 1854-55, including the battles of Alma, Balaklava, and Inkerman, and siege and fall of Sebastopol (Medal and Clasps, Knight of the Legion of Honor, and 5th Class of the Medjidie).

105 Majors Milman, Arbuthnot (twice wounded), Hastings, Fitz Hugh, and Godby served at the siege and fall of Sebastopol, in the trenches with the siege train, and at the bombardments of 6th and 17th June (Medal and Clasp). Majors Milman, Arbuthnot, Hastings, and Fitz Hugh have the 5th Class of the Medjidie.

106 Major Baddeley served the Eastern campaign of 1854 as Adjutant to the Artillery of the Light Division, including the affairs of Bulganac and M'Kenzie's Farm, the battles of Alma, Balaklava, and Inkerman (severely wounded), capture of Balaklava, siege of Sebastopol, and repulse of the sortie 26th Oct. (Medal and four Clasps, Knight of the Legion of Honor, and 5th Class of the Medjidie).

107 Major Guy Rotton and Lt. Hannen served at Canton with the force under Rear Admiral Seymour in 1856-57; were also present at the capture of Canton in Dec. 1857.

108 Major Ommanney was present at the affair of Futtyabad 6 March 1858; commanded the Artillery of the 1st Brigade Central India Field Force under Sir Hugh Rose at the capture of Chandairee Fort, siege and capture of Jhansi and action on the Betwa; also commanded the Artillery of that force in the attack on Koonch and capture of Calpee; and served with Duff's Column at the affair of Sahao (mentioned in despatches, Brevet of Major, Medal).

109 Major Palmer served in the Indian campaign of 1857-59, and commanded a field battery of Royal Artillery with Whitlock's field division in the action at Bandah, action at Chitrakote with Carpenter's force, and defeat of a body of the Gwalior Contingent at Koleri (twice mentioned in despatches, Brevet of Major, and Medal).

110 Captain Paget served in India in 1857-59, and was present with Malcolm's field force at the defeat of a body of rebels near Nurgoond, storm and occupation of the Petah and capture of the fort of Nurgoond, and defeat of Tantia Topee at Chupra Burode (twice mentioned in despatches, Medal).

111 Capts. Mercer and Milward served the siege of Sebastopol in 1855 (Medal & Clasp).

112 Captain Colclough was nominated to the 4th Class of the Medjidie for services with the late Osmanli Horse Artillery.

113 Major Chermside served in the Eastern campaign of 1854-55, including the battle of Inkerman and siege of Sebastopol as Adjutant to the siege train (Medal and Clasp, and 5th Class of the Medjidie).

114 Captain Blosse served at the siege and fall of Sebastopol in 1855 (Medal and Clasp).

115 Captain Anson served at the siege of Sebastopol in 1855 in the trenches with the siege train, and at the bombardments of 6th and 17th June (Medal and Clasp, and 5th Class of the Medjidie).

116 Lt.Colonel Gordon served in the Eastern campaign of 1854-55, including the battles of Alma, Balaklava, and Inkerman, siege and capture of Sebastopol (Medal and Clasps, Sardinian Medal, Brevets of Major and Lt.Col., and 5th Class of the Medjidie). Served in India in 1857-58, and was present at the action of Pandora (mentioned in despatches, Medal).

394   *War Services of the Officers of the Royal Artillery.*

117 Major Moubray served in the Eastern campaign of 1854-55, including the battle of Inkerman, siege and fall of Sebastopol (wounded in the trenches) with the Siege train, bombardments of October and April, and battle of Tchernaya (Medal and Clasps, Brevet Major, Knight of the Legion of Honor, Sardinian Medal, and 5th Class of the Medjidie).

118 Major Boothby served the Eastern campaign of 1854-55, including the affair of M'Kenzie's Farm, the battles of Alma and Inkerman, the siege of Sebastopol, and repulse of the sortie on the 26th Oct. 1854 (Medal and Clasps, Knight of the Legion of Honor, and 5th Class of the Medjidie).

119 Lt.Col. Hon. E. T. Gage served the Eastern campaign of 1854-55 as Brigade-Major to the Royal Artillery, and was present at the affairs of Bulganac and M'Kenzie's Farm, the battles of Alma, Balaklava, and Inkerman, capture of Balaklava, siege and fall of Sebastopol (Medal and Clasps, Brevets of Major and Lt.Col., Sardinian Medal, and 5th Class of the Medjidie); was also present with the Turkish army under Omar Pasha during the operations at Rudchuck and Giurgevo, in the summer of 1854, and has received the Gold Medal for the campaign on the Danube, awarded to him by the Turkish Government.

120 Captain Bayly served in India in 1858, and commanded a small force sent from Kurrachee to reduce a fort on Beyt Island, and was dangerously wounded on 2nd April.

121 Major Barstow served the Eastern campaign of 1854-55, including the affairs of Bulganac and M'Kenzie's Farm, the battles of Alma, Balaklava, and Inkerman, and siege of Sebastopol (Medal and Clasps, and 5th Class of the Medjidie). Was present at the capture of Canton in Dec. 1857.

122 Major Craufurd served in 1855 with the siege train at the siege and fall of Sebastopol, and bombardment of 17th June; was also with the Kertch expedition (Medal and Clasp, and 5th Class of the Medjidie).

123 Major Thring served at the siege and fall of Sebastopol in 1855 (Medal and Clasp). Served in India in 1857-58 including the actions of Secundra, Chanda, and Sultanpore, siege and capture of Lucknow, and relief of Azimghur (five times mentioned in despatches, Brevet of Major, Medal and Clasp).

124 Captain King served during the Kaffir war of 1846 (Medal), from April to Nov. of that year, and commanded the Artillery at the attack of Fort Peddie.

125 Captain Bent was nominated to the 4th Class of the Medjidie for services, as Brigade Major, with the late Osmanli Horse Artillery.

126 Major Tupper served the Eastern campaign of 1854-55, including the battles of Balaklava and Inkerman (wounded), the siege and fall of Sebastopol, and repulse of the sortie on the 26th October 1854 (Medal and Clasps, Brevet Major, Sardinian Medal, and 5th Class of the Medjidie).

127 Captain Heyman served at the siege and fall of Sebastopol in 1855 (Medal and Clasp, and 5th Class of the Medjidie).

128 Major Hoste served the Eastern campaign of 1854-55, including the battles of Alma, Balaklava, and Inkerman, the siege of Sebastopol, and repulse of the sortie on the 26th October 1854 (Medal and Clasps, *CB.*, and 5th Class of the Medjidie).

129 Captain Taswell served in the Eastern campaign of 1854, including the siege of Sebastopol (Medal and Clasp).

130 Major Singleton served the Eastern campaign of 1854-55, including the affairs of Bulganac and M'Kenzie's Farm, the battles of Alma, Balaklava, and Inkerman, the siege and fall of Sebastopol, and repulse of the sortie on the 26th October 1854 (Medal and Clasps, Knight of the Legion of Honor, and 5th Class of the Medjidie). Served in India in 1858, and commanded the Artillery in the repulse of the mutinous Sepoys at Mooltan on 31st March.

131 Majors Reilly (Brigade Major), Soady, and Carthew, served in the Eastern campaign of 1854-55, in the trenches with the siege train before Sebastopol, and at the bombardments of April and June (6th and 17th): Medal and Clasp, and 5th Class of the Medjidie. Majors Carthew and Reilly are Knights of the Legion of Honor. Major Reilly is a *CB*. Major Soady served in the Indian campaign in 1858-59, and commanded a field battery attached to the force under Lt.Col. Walker in the attack and defeat of the rebels occupying the fort and jungle of Bungaon, in April 1859 (Medal).

132 Major Saunders served at the siege and fall of Sebastopol in 1855 (Medal and Clasp).

133 Lt.Colonel C. H. Smith served at the siege and fall of Sebastopol, in the trenches with the siege train, and at the bombardments of 6th and 17th June (Medal and Clasp, and Brevet of Major). Served the Indian campaign of 1857-58, including the battle of Cawnpore on 6th Dec., and affair of Kalee Nuddy, and commanded the Artillery at the affair of Kankur, and operations before Sandee (twice mentioned in despatches, Brevet of Lt.Colonel, Medal).

134 Captain J. L. Bolton served in the Eastern campaign of 1854-55, including the siege of Sebastopol (Medal and Clasp). Served in India in 1857-58, and commanded the Artillery in the action at Pertabghur—wounded (Medal).

135 Major D. S. Greene served in India in 1857-58, including the action of Pandoo Nuddee, operations of the 27th, 28th and 29th Nov. before Cawnpore and battle there on the 6th Dec. (four times mentioned in despatches, Brevet of Major, and Medal).

136 Lt.Colonel Barry served the Eastern campaign of 1854-55, including the battles of Alma, Balaklava, and Inkerman, and siege and fall of Sebastopol (Medal and Clasps, Brevet Major, Sardinian Medal, and 5th Class of the Medjidie). Served in India in 1857-58, including the relief of the garrison of Lucknow, battle of Cawnpore, siege and capture of Lucknow—severely wounded (twice mentioned in despatches, Brevet of Lt.Colonel, Medal and Clasps).

War Services of the Officers of the Royal Artillery. 395

137 Major Spurway served the Eastern campaign of 1854-55, including the battle of Inkerman, siege and fall of Sebastopol (Medal and Clasp, Brevet Major, and Knight of the Legion of Honor).

137† Major Henry served the Eastern campaign of 1854-55, including the battle of Inkerman, siege and fall of Sebastopol (Medal and Clasps, Brevet Major, Knight of the Legion of Honor, Sardinian Medal, and 5th Class of the Medjidie). Served in the Indian campaign in 1858-59 and commanded a field battery attached to Colonel Kelly's force in the attack and defeat of the rebel forces posted on the first range of the Nepaul Hills, on 25th and 28th March 1859 (mentioned in despatch, Medal).

138 Lt.Colonel Michell served the Eastern campaign of 1854-55, including the battles of Alma and Balaklava, and siege of Sebastopol (Medal and Clasps, Brevet Major, Sardinian Medal, and 5th Class of the Medjidie). Served the Indian campaign of 1857-58, including the storm and capture of Meangunge, siege and capture of Lucknow, and commanded the Royal Horse Artillery at the affair of Tigree, relief of Azimghur, action near Azimutghur, operations in the Jungle and capture of Jugdespore, attack and capture of Tiroul (four times mentioned in despatches, Brevet of Lt.Colonel, Medal and Clasp).

139 Major Ingilby served the Eastern campaign of 1854-55, including the affairs of Bulganac and M'Kenzie's Farm, the battles of Alma, Balaklava, and Inkerman (severely wounded), the siege of Sebastopol, and repulse of the sortie on the 26th October 1854 (Medal and Clasps, Brevet Major, Sardinian Medal, and 5th Class of the Medjidie).

140 Lt.Colonel Yates served the Eastern campaign of 1854, including the affair at M'Kenzie's Farm, battles of Alma and Inkerman, siege of Sebastopol, and repulse of the sortie on the 26th October 1854 (Medal and Clasps, Brevet Major, Sardinian Medal, and 5th Class of the Medjidie). Served the Indian campaign of 1857-58, present at the action of Secundra, siege and capture of Lucknow, commanded Royal Horse Artillery at the affairs of Saragunge on 23rd and 29th July, also commanded the Artillery in the actions at Sultanpore on 13th and 28th Aug. 1858 (three times mentioned in despatches, Brevet of Lt.Colonel, Medal and Clasp).

141 Major W. J. Williams served at the siege and fall of Sebastopol in 1855 (wounded), in trenches with siege train, and at bombardments of 6th and 17th June (Medal and Clasp, and 5th Class of the Medjidie).

142 Major C. P. Young served in India in 1858, and was present at the siege and capture of Lucknow, relief of Azimghur, operations in the Jungle and capture of Jugdespore (twice mentioned in despatches, Brevet of Major, and Medal).

143 Major Pennycuick served in the Eastern campaign of 1854-55, including the battle of Inkerman, and siege of Sebastopol (Medal and Clasps, Sardinian Medal, and 5th Class of the Medjidie). Served in the Indian campaign of 1857-58, including the relief of Lucknow by Lord Clyde, battle of Cawnpore on 6th Dec., actions of Serin Ghat, Chanda, and Sultanpore, siege and capture of Lucknow, and action of Barree (Medal and Clasps).

144 Major Oldershaw served in the Eastern campaign of 1855, including the siege of Sebastopol in the trenches with the siege train and bombardment of April; was employed on special service in 1855-56 (Medal and Clasp, Brevet of Major, and 5th Class of the Medjidie).

145 Lt.Col. N. O. S. Turner served at the siege and fall of Sebastopol in 1855 (Medal and Clasp, Brevet of Major, and 5th Class of the Medjidie). Served in India in 1858, and was present at the siege and capture of Lucknow, affair of Tigree, relief of Azimghur, action near Azimutghur, operations in the Jungle and capture of Jugdespore (three times mentioned in despatches, Medal and Clasp).

146 Major Vandeleur served the Eastern campaign of 1854-55, including the affairs of Bulganac and M'Kenzie's Farm, battle of Alma, and siege of Sebastopol (Medal and Clasp).

147 Captain P. J. Campbell served in the Kaffir war of 1851-53 (Medal). Also at the siege and fall of Sebastopol in 1855 (Medal and Clasp).

148 Lt.Colonel F. C. Maude commanded the Royal Artillery throughout the operations with General Havelock's Column in 1857 including the defeat of the Rebels at Futtehpore, actions of Aoung, Pandoo Nuddee, Cawnpore, Oonao, Busseerut Gunge, Mungarwar, relief and defence of the Residency of Lucknow; with Outram's force at the Alumbagh from Jan. to March 1858; also at the siege and capture of Lucknow (repeatedly mentioned in despatches, Brevets of Major and Lt.Col., *CB.*, Victoria Cross, Medal and Clasps).

149 Captain Twiss served at the siege of Sebastopol in 1855 (Medal and Clasp). Served at Canton with the force under Rear Admiral Seymour in 1856-57.

150 Major R. Curtis served at the siege and fall of Sebastopol in 1855, in the trenches with the siege train (Medal and Clasp).

151 Captains Sievwright and Seale served at the siege and fall of Sebastopol in 1855 (Medal and Clasp).

152 Major Dickson served the Eastern campaign of 1854-55, including the battles of Alma and Balaklava, siege and fall of Sebastopol, in the trenches with the siege train, and at the bombardments of April, and 6th and 17th June (Medal and Clasps, Knight of the Legion of Honor, and 5th Class of the Medjidie).

153 Major Richards served the Eastern campaign of 1854-55, including the affairs of Bulganac and M'Kenzie's Farm, the battles of Alma (horse shot), Balaklava, and Inkerman (horse killed), siege of Sebastopol and repulse of the sortie on the 26th Oct. 1854 (Medal and Clasps, and Knight of the Legion of Honor).

154 Major Hope served in the Eastern campaign of 1854-55, including the battle of Inkerman, siege and fall of Sebastopol (wounded), in the trenches with the siege train, and

† T

at the bombardments of October, April, and 6th and 17th June (Medal and Clasps, Brevet Major, Knight of the Legion of Honor, and 5th Class of the Medjidie).

155 Major Brendon served the Eastern campaign of 1854-55, including the affairs of M'Kenzie's Farm, the battles of Alma and Inkerman, the siege of Sebastopol, and repulse of the sortie on the 26th Oct. 1854 (Medal and Clasps, and 5th Class of the Medjidie).

156 Major de Havilland served the Eastern campaign of 1854-55, including the battles of Alma and Balaklava, and siege of Sebastopol (Medal and Clasps and Brevet Major).

157 Major Lukin served the Eastern campaign of 1854-55, including the battles of Alma, Balaklava, and Inkerman, and siege of Sebastopol, in the trenches with the siege train, and at the bombardments of April and June (6th and 17th) (Medal and Clasps, Knight of the Legion of Honor, and 5th Class of the Medjidie).

158 Major Walcott served at the siege of Sebastopol in 1855 (Medal and Clasp, Brevet of Major, and 5th Class of the Medjidie). Served in the Indian campaign of 1857-58, including the action of Futtehghur, battle of Cawnpore on 6th Dec., and action of Sherghur Ghat (mentioned in despatch, Medal).

159 Major Davis served at the siege and fall of Sebastopol, and at the battle of Tchernaya, in 1855 (Medal and Clasp, Victoria Cross, and 5th Class of the Medjidie).

160 Major Bredin and Lieut. Watson served in the Eastern campaign of 1854-55, including the battle of Inkerman and siege of Sebastopol (Medal and Clasps, and Brevet Major). Major Bredin was nominated to the 4th Class of the Medjidie for services with the late Osmanli Horse Artillery.

161 Major W. J. Bolton served in the Eastern campaign of 1854-55, in the trenches with the siege train before Sebastopol, and at the bombardments of October, April, and 6th and 17th June (Medal and Clasp, Knight of the Legion of Honor, and 5th Class of the Medjidie).

162 Major Sinclair served the Eastern campaign of 1854-55, in the trenches during the bombardment of the 17th Oct. 1854, with the 18-pounder guns at the battle of Inkerman, and bombardment of 10th April 1855. Severely wounded, left thigh fractured, left arm broken, and left hand smashed (Medal and Clasps, Brevet Major, Sardinian Medal, and 5th Class of the Medjidie).

163 Major H. L. Talbot served in the Indian campaign of 1857-58, including the relief of Lucknow by Lord Clyde, battle of Cawnpore on 6th Dec., siege and capture of Lucknow, actions of Barree and Sirsee (Medal and Clasps).

164 Captain W. J. Wilson served in 1855 in the trenches, as Adjutant of the Left Siege Train at the siege of Sebastopol and bombardments of 6th and 17th June; also present at the fall of Sebastopol and battle of the Tchernaya (Medal and Clasp, and 5th Class of the Medjidie).

165 Major Simpson and Captain Lyons served in the Eastern campaign of 1854-55, including the battle of Inkerman, siege of Sebastopol, in the trenches with the siege train, and bombardments of Oct. and Apr. (Medal and Clasps, and Knights of the Legion of Honor).

166 Major Penn served in the Eastern campaign of 1854-55, as an Assistant Engineer, with the siege train in the trenches before Sebastopol, and at the bombardments of October, April, and June (6th and 17th); he was also at the battle of Inkerman (Medal and Clasps, Brevet Major, Sardinian Medal, and 5th Class of the Medjidie).

167 Captain Morris served the Eastern campaign of 1854, including the battles of Balaklava and Inkerman, and siege of Sebastopol (Medal and Clasps, and 5th Class of the Medjidie).

168 Captain Rotton served at the siege and fall of Sebastopol in 1855 (Medal and Clasp).

169 Captain Byrne served at the siege and fall of Sebastopol in 1855, and with the Expedition to Kertch (Medal and Clasp).

170 Major Taddy served the Eastern campaign of 1854-55, including the affairs of Bulganac and M'Kenzie's Farm, the battles of Alma, Balaklava, and Inkerman, and siege of Sebastopol (Medal and Clasps, Bt.Major, Sardinian Medal, and 5th Class of the Medjidie).

171 Captain C. Johnston served in India in 1857-58 and was present at the battle of Cawnpore on 6th Dec. (Medal).

172 Major Field served in the Kaffir war of 1851-2 (Medal). Served in India in 1858, and was present with the Central Indian Field force at the attack and capture of Fort Lahorle, attack on Koonch, and capture of Calpee (mentioned in despatch, Medal).

173 Major J. M'C. Campbell served in the Indian campaign of 1857-58, including the action of Kalee Nuddee, siege and capture of Lucknow, assault and capture of Fort Birwah (twice mentioned in despatches, Medal and Clasp, and Brevet Major).

174 Major Miller served the Eastern campaign of 1854-55, including the battles of Alma, Balaklava, and Inkerman, the siege of Sebastopol and repulse of the sortie on the 26th Oct. 1854 (Medal and Clasps, Brevet Major, Victoria Cross, Knight of the Legion of Honor, and 5th Class of the Medjidie).

175 Major Owen served the Eastern campaign of 1854-55, including the battle of Inkerman, siege and fall of Sebastopol, in the trenches with the siege train, and bombardments of October, April, and 6th and 17th June (Medal and Clasps, Knight of the Legion of Honor, and 5th Class of the Medjidie).

176 Major G. A. Milman served in the Eastern campaign of 1854, in the trenches with the siege train before Sebastopol, and at the bombardments of April and 6th and 17th June (Medal and Clasp, Brevet Major, and 5th Class of the Medjidie).

177 Captains R. Boyle and Donne served at the siege and fall of Sebastopol in 1855 (Medal and Clasp).

178 Captain Pasley was nominated to the 4th Class of the Medjidie for services with the late Turkish Contingent.

179 Major P. W. L'Estrange served in the Eastern campaign of 1854-55, in the trenches with the siege train before Sebastopol, and at the bombardments of April and 6th and 17th June—wounded (Medal and Clasp, Brevet Major, Sardinian Medal, and 5th Class of the Medjidie).

180 Majors Burt and Irvine served in the Eastern campaign in 1855, in the trenches with the siege train before Sebastopol, and at the bombardments of April and 6th and 17th June (Medal and Clasp, Brevet Major, and 5th Class of the Medjidie).

181 Major Grylls served the Eastern campaign of 1854-55, including the affairs of Bulganac and M'Kenzie's Farm, the battles of Alma, Balaklava, and Inkerman, capture of Balaklava, and siege of Sebastopol (Medal and Clasps).

182 Major Champion served in the Eastern campaign of 1854-55, including the battle of Inkerman, siege and fall of Sebastopol, in the trenches with the siege train, and at the bombardments of April and 6th and 17th June —wounded (Medal and Clasps, Brevet Major, Sardinian Medal, and 5th Class of the Medjidie).

183 Captain Dames served in the Eastern campaign of 1854-55, including the siege and fall of Sebastopol (Medal and Clasp).

184 Major Andrews served in the Eastern campaign of 1854-55, including the battle of Inkerman, siege and fall of Sebastopol (Medal and Clasps, Brevet Major, Sardinian Medal, and 5th Class of the Medjidie).

185 Captain Murray was nominated to the 4th Class of the Medjidie for services with the late Osmanli Horse Artillery.

186 Major Mackenzie served in the Eastern campaign of 1854-55, including the battle of Inkerman, siege and fall of Sebastopol, in the trenches with the siege train, and bombardments of October, April, and 6th and 17th June, also at the bombardment and capture of Kinbourn (Medal and Clasps, Knight of the Legion of Honor, and 5th Class of the Medjidie).

187 Lt.Colonel W. G. Le Mesurier served the Eastern campaign of 1854-55, including the affairs of Bulganac and M'Kenzie's Farm, the battles of Alma and Balaklava, siege and fall of Sebastopol (Medal and Clasps, Brevet Major, Sardinian Medal, and 5th Class of the Medjidie). Served in the Indian campaign of 1857-58 in command of a battery of Artillery, including the action of Kalee Nuddee, affair of Ramgunga, siege and capture of Lucknow, action of Bareilly, attack and capture of Fort Burmi, and capture of Rampore Kussiah (four times mentioned in despatches, Brevet of Lt.Colonel, CB., Medal and Clasp).

188 Captains Heberden, Cockburn, Nangle, and Strover, served at the siege and fall of Sebastopol in 1855 (Medal and Clasp).

189 Major Goodenough served in the Indian campaign of 1857-58, including the action of Pandoo Nuddee, siege and capture of Lucknow, attack and capture of Fort Birwah—severely wounded (three times mentioned in despatches, Brevet of Major, Medal and Clasp).

190 Captain A. H. W. Williams served at the siege and fall of Sebastopol in 1855 (Medal and Clasp). Served in India in 1858, and was engaged in the repulse of the mutinous Sepoys at Mooltan on 31st March.

191 Capt. W. Wolfe served at the siege and fall of Sebastopol, and on the expedition to Kertch in 1855 (Medal and Clasp).

192 Captain Conolly served in the Crimea in 1855, in the trenches with the siege train before Sebastopol (wounded), and at the bombardments of April and 6th and 17th June (Medal and Clasp, and Knight of the Legion of Honor).

193 Captain Griffin served in the Crimea, and was present at the final bombardment and fall of Sebastopol (Medal and Clasp).

194 Capt. F. T. Whinyates served in the Eastern campaign of 1854-55, including the battle of Balaklava, siege and fall of Sebastopol (Medal and Clasps, and 5th Class of the Medjidie).

195 Captain Waller served in India in 1857-58, and was present in the actions of Secundra, Chanda, and Sultanpore, siege and capture of Lucknow, relief of Azimghur, and capture of Jugdespore (three times mentioned in despatches, Medal and Clasp).

196 Major A. C. Johnson served at the siege and fall of Sebastopol in 1855 (Medal and Clasp). Served in India in 1858, and was present at the siege and capture of Lucknow, and actions of Sirsee and Nawabgunge (Brevet of Major, Medal and Clasp).

197 Captain Phelips served in the Eastern campaign of 1854, including the battle of Alma and siege of Sebastopol (Medal and Clasps).

197† Captain A. W. Johnson served in India in 1858, and commanded the Artillery in the attack on a fort in Beyt Island on the 2nd April.

198 Captain Price and Lieut. Elton served in 1855 at the siege and fall of Sebastopol (Captain Price was wounded), in the trenches with the siege train, and at the bombardments of April, and 6th and 17th June (Medal and Clasp, and Knights of the Legion of Honor).

199 Captain King served the Eastern campaign of 1854-55, including the affairs of Bulganac and M'Kenzie's Farm, battles of Alma, Balaklava, and Inkerman, siege and fall of Sebastopol, repulse of the sortie on the 26th Oct. 1854, and was Aide de Camp to General Markham on the final assault on the Redan 8th Sept. Mentioned in Dispatches (Medal and Clasps, Knight of the Legion of Honor, and 5th Class of the Medjidie).

200 Captain R. R. Jones served in the Eastern campaign of 1854-55, including the siege of Sebastopol (Medal and Clasp).

201 Captain J. H. Brown, Lieuts. Harris and Briscoe served in 1855 at the siege of Sebastopol in the trenches with the siege train, and at the bombardments of April, and 6th and 17th June (Medal and Clasp). Captain Brown and Lt. Harris are Knights of the Legion of Honor. Lt. Briscoe has the 5th Class of the Medjidie.

398   *War Services of the Officers of the Royal Artillery.*

202 Captain Strangways served the Eastern campaign of 1854-55, including the affairs of Bulganac and M'Kenzie's Farm, battles of Alma, Balaklava, and Inkerman, capture of Balaklava, siege and fall of Sebastopol (Medal and Clasps, and Knight of the Legion of Honor).

203 Captain Harward served in the Eastern campaign of 1854-55, including the battle of Inkerman and siege of Sebastopol, in the trenches with the siege train, and bombardments of October, April, and 6th and 17th June (Medal and Clasps, and 5th Class of the Medjidie).

204 Captains Booth, Brackenbury, Gore, J. T. B. Brown, and Tyler (wounded), served at the siege and fall of Sebastopol in 1855 (Medal and Clasp). Captain Brown has the 5th Class of the Medjidie. Captain Tyler served in the Indian campaign in 1858-59, and acted as Staff Officer to Lt.Col. Walker in the attack and defeat of the rebel force which occupied the fort and jungle of Bungnon (mentioned in despatch, Medal).

205 Major Teesdale served as Aide de Camp to Major Gen. Sir W. F. Williams during the whole of the blockade of Kars, and at the battle on the heights above that town on the 29th Sept. 1855. Successfully held the Redoubt called "Yuksek Tabia" for the space of seven and a half hours under a very heavy fire on the 29th Sept. 1855, and was mentioned in the Dispatch. Received a severe contusion from a grape-shot in the leg. The rank of Lieut.-Col. and the third class of the Turkish Imperial Order of the Medjidie were conferred upon him by the Sultan. In a letter from the Foreign Office, dated 7th March 1855, Her Majesty's Government conveyed their sense of approval of his efforts in averting from the garrison of Kars the horrors that they suffered from famine in the preceding winter. In virtue of his rank of Lt.-Col. in the Turkish Service he received the Order of Companion of the Bath and that of 4th Class of the Legion of Honor. Has also received the Victoria Cross.

205† Captain Markham served the Eastern campaign of 1854-55, including the affair at M'Kenzie's Farm, battles of Alma and Inkerman, siege of Sebastopol, and repulse of the sortie on the 26th Oct. 1854 (Medal and Clasps, and Knight of the Legion of Honor). Served in India in 1858, and was present at the action of Secundra on 23rd Jan. (Medal).

206 Captain Torriano served in the Eastern campaign of 1854-55, including the battle of Inkerman, siege of Sebastopol in the trenches with the siege train, and bombardments of October, April, and 6th and 17th June (Medal and Clasps, and Knight of the Legion of Honor). Served in India in 1857-58, and was present at the action of Pandora, storm and capture of Meangunge, siege and capture of Lucknow, and captures of the forts of Dehnia and Tirol in Oude (Medal and Clasp).

207 Captain Smart served in India in 1857-58, and was present at the actions of Chanda and Sultanpore, siege and capture of Lucknow, actions of Barree, Sirsee, and Nawabgunge (twice mentioned in despatches, Medal and Clasp).

208 Captain Ogilvie served the Eastern campaign of 1854-55, including the battles of Alma, Balaklava, and Inkerman, siege and fall of Sebastopol (Medal and Clasps, and 5th Class of the Medjidie).

208† Captain Newbolt served in India in 1857-59, and was present at the attack and defeat of the rebel force posted in the first range of the Nepaul Hills, in March 1859 (Medal).

209 Captains C. E. Stirling and Keate served at the siege of Sebastopol in 1855 (Medal and Clasp).

210 Capt. T. B. Strange served in India in 1857-58, and was present at the actions of Chanda, Sultanpore, and Dhowrara, siege and capture of Lucknow, actions of Koorsee, Nawabgunge, Seragunge, affairs of 23rd and 29th July, passage of the Goomtee at Sultanpore including affairs of 25th 26th 27th and 28th August, and Doadpore 20th Oct. (four times mentioned in despatches, Medal and Clasp).

211 Captain Francis Lyon, Lieuts. Tracey (wounded), Tarleton, and Bethune served the Indian campaign of 1858, were present at the siege and capture of Lucknow and several minor affairs (Medal and Clasp).

212 Captain M. Taylor, Lieuts. Charles O. Browne, C. E. S. Scott (wounded), Maule, Geary, and Roberts (wounded), served in 1855 in the trenches, with the siege train at the siege and fall of Sebastopol, and bombardments of 6th and 17th June and August. Lieut. Roberts was subsequently very severely wounded by the explosion of the French powder magazine in camp on the 15th Nov. 1855 (Medal and Clasp). Lieuts. Browne, Maule, and Roberts have also the Sardinian Medal. Captain Taylor, Lieuts. Scott and Geary have the 5th Class of the Medjidie.

213 Captains Blakiston, A. L. Kaye, J. J. Smith, Thornhill, Shakerley, and Pitt, served at the siege and fall of Sebastopol (Medal and Clasp).

214 Captain Eardley Maitland served throughout the operations with Havelock's Column in 1857, including the actions of Futtehpore, Aoung, Pandoo Nuddee, Cawnpore, Oonao, Buscerutgunge, Mungawara, and Alumbagh, relief and defence of the Residency at Lucknow, with Outram's force in the Alumbagh from Jan. to March 1858, siege and capture of Lucknow, and actions at Selimpore and Sundeela in the ensuing Oude campaign (Medal and Clasps).

215 Captain J. Lardner Clarke served in the Eastern campaign of 1854-55, including the siege of Sebastopol (Medal and Clasp).

216 Captain Pearse served at the siege and fall of Sebastopol in 1855 (Medal and Clasp, and 5th Class of the Medjidie). Served in India in 1858, and was present at the capture of Kotah on 30th March (Medal).

217 Captain Alderson served the Eastern campaign of 1854-55, including the battles of

Alma and Inkerman, and siege of Sebastopol, in the trenches with the siege train, and bombardments of October, April, and 6th and 17th June (Medal and Clasps, and Knight of the Legion of Honor).

218 Captain Ravenhill and Lieut. Tweedie served at the siege and fall of Sebastopol, and battle of Tchernaya (Medal and Clasp).

219 Capt. Fred. L. H. Lyon served in the Eastern campaign of 1854-55, including the siege of Sebastopol, and in the trenches with the siege train at the bombardments of April, and 6th and 17th June (Medal and Clasp). Served in the Indian campaign in 1857-58, including the action of Pandora, storm and capture of Meaungunge, siege and capture of Lucknow, action of Barree, capture of Rampore Kussie, affairs of Muchagawn Tigree, relief of Azimghur, operations in the Jungle and capture of Jugdespore (Medal and Clasp).

220 Captain Ruck-Keene served in the Eastern campaign of 1854-55, including the battle of Inkerman, siege and fall of Sebastopol (wounded), in the trenches with the siege train, and bombardments of October, April, and 6th and 17th June (Medal and Clasps, and Knight of the Legion of Honor).

221 Captains Doyne and Vaughan served in 1855 at the siege and fall of Sebastopol, in the trenches with the siege train, and bombardments of 6th and 17th June (Medal and Clasp). Captain Vaughan is a Knight of the Legion of Honor. Captain Doyne has the 5th Class of the Medjidie.

222 Captain Daubuz, Lieuts. Still, Hanwell, C. G. Johnson, Cardew, Schreiber, Lyle, Gilmour, de Vismes, Tupper, and Franklen, served at the siege and fall of Sebastopol (Medal and Clasp).

223 Captains Law and Downes, Lieuts. C. L'Estrange, Walker, W. G. Martin, Walsh, and de Moleyns, served at the siege of Sebastopol in 1855 (Medal and Clasp).

224 Captain Nisbett, Lieuts. Rooke, Bevan, Farrell, Hunter, and F. J. Hill, served at the siege and fall of Sebastopol in 1855 (Medal and Clasp).

225 Captain Warren served in the Indian campaign of 1857-58, including the relief of Lucknow by Lord Clyde, battle of Cawnpore on 6th Dec., storm and capture of Meaungunge, siege and capture of Lucknow, actions of Barree and Sirsee, capture of Forts Rehora and Koorlee (mentioned in despatch, Medal and Clasp).

226 Captain Dyer served at the siege and fall of Sebastopol in 1855 (Medal and Clasp). Served the Indian campaign of 1857-58, including the relief of Lucknow by Lord Clyde, battle of Cawnpore on 6th Dec., action of Kalee Nuddee, affair of Ramgunga, siege and capture of Lucknow, actions of Bareilly, Shahjehanpore, and Mohumdee (mentioned in despatch, Medal and Clasps).

227 Lieut. Fitzmaurice served in the Indian campaign of 1857-58, including the relief of Lucknow by Lord Clyde, battle of Cawnpore on 6th Dec., siege and capture of Lucknow, and relief of Azimghur (twice mentioned in despatches, Medal and Clasps).

228 Lieuts. Milman (wounded 16th Nov., and horse shot), Wm. Smith, and Pickering served in the Indian campaign of 1857-58, including the relief of Lucknow by Lord Clyde, battle of Cawnpore on 6th Dec., actions of Serai Ghat (Lt. Milman commanded the Battery and was mentioned in despatches), Chanda, and Sultanpore, siege and capture of Lucknow, and action of Barree (Medal and Clasps). Lieut. Pickering was present in the attack and defeat of the rebel force which occupied the fort and jungle of Bungaon, in April 1859 (mentioned in despatch, Medal).

229 Lieuts. Percival and Nicolls served in the Eastern campaign of 1854; and Lieut. Nicolls served also at the siege and fall of Sebastopol (Medal and Clasp).

230 Lieut. H. T. Arbuthnot served the Eastern campaign of 1854-55, including the affair at M'Kenzie's Farm, battles of Alma and Inkerman, siege and fall of Sebastopol, and repulse of the sortie on the 26th Oct. 1854 (Medal and Clasps, and Knight of the Legion of Honor). Served in the Indian campaign of 1857-58, including the action of Secundra, attack on a fort near Moonsheegunge, siege and capture of Lucknow, capture of forts Rehora and Koorlee (mentioned in despatch, Medal and Clasp).

231 Lieut. Biddulph served the Eastern campaign of 1854-55, including the battles of Alma and Balaklava, siege and fall of Sebastopol, and expedition to Kertch (Medal and Clasps, and 5th Class of the Medjidie). Served in the Indian campaign of 1857-58, including the action of Kalee Nuddee, siege and capture of Lucknow (as D.A.Q.M.Gen. of Art.), action of Jamo, and affair of Daoodpoore. Served as D.A.Adj.Gen. of the Oude force under Sir Hope Grant from Oct. 1858, and present in the operations in the Byswarra district, passage of the Gogra and various actions on the Nepaul frontier, also operations there in 1859 terminating in the forcing of the Jerwah Pass (several times mentioned in despatches, Medal and Clasp).

232 Lieut. Wm. Stirling served the Eastern campaign of 1854-55, including the affairs of Bulganac and M'Kenzie's Farm, the battles of Alma, Balaklava, and Inkerman, the siege and fall of Sebastopol, and repulse of the sortie on the 26th October 1854 (Medal and Clasps, and Knight of the Legion of Honor). Served as Brigade Major of Artillery with Rajpootana field force at the capture of Kotah on 30th March 1858 (Medal).

233 Lieut. P. E. Hill served in the Eastern campaign of 1854-55, including the battles of Balaklava and Inkerman, siege and fall of Sebastopol (Medal and Clasps, and 5th Class of the Medjidie).

234 Lieut. Maxwell served the Eastern campaign of 1854-55, including the affairs of Bulganac and M'Kenzie's Farm, battles of Alma, Balaklava, and Inkerman, siege and fall of Sebastopol and repulse of the Sortie on 26th Oct. 1854 (Medal and four Clasps, and Knight of the Legion of Honor). Served in the Indian campaign of 1857-58, in-

cluding the action of Pandora, storm and capture of Meangunge, siege and capture of Lucknow, affair of Tigree, relief of Azimghur, operations in the Jungle and capture of Jugdespore (Medal and Clasp).

235 Lieut. Rideout served in the Eastern campaign of 1854-55, including the battle of Inkerman, siege and fall of Sebastopol, in the trenches with the siege train, and bombardments of October, April, 6th and 17th June, and August (Medal and Clasps, and Knight of the Legion of Honor).

236 Lieut. Broughton served the Eastern campaign of 1854-55, including the affair at M'Kenzie's Farm, the battles of Alma and Inkerman, siege and fall of Sebastopol and repulse of the sortie on the 26th Oct. 1854·(Medal and Clasps, and Knight of the Legion of Honor).

237 Lieuts. De Winton (wounded), Hickes, and Hall, served in the Eastern campaign of 1854-55, including the siege and fall of Sebastopol, in the trenches with the siege train, and bombardments of April and 6th and 17th June (Medal and Clasp, and Knights of the Legion of Honor). Lieut. Hall was present at the siege and capture of Lucknow in March 1858 (Medal and Clasp).

238 Lieut. Cuthbert served in 1855 at the siege and fall of Sebastopol in the trenches with the siege train, and bombardments of 6th and 17th June (Medal and Clasp, and 5th Class of the Medjidie). Served in the Indian campaign of 1857-59, including the action of Pandora, defence of the Alumbagh in Feb. and March, siege and capture of Lucknow, subsequent operations in Oude and action of Barree (four times mentioned in despatches, Medal and Clasp).

239 Lieut. Tucker served in the Eastern campaign of 1854-55, including the siege and fall of Sebastopol (Medal and Clasp).

240 Lieut. Leonard Griffiths served in the Eastern campaign of 1854-55, including the siege of Sebastopol, and in the trenches with the siege train at the bombardments of April, and 6th and 17th June (Medal and Clasp, and 5th Class of the Medjidie).

241 Lieut. Ward served at the siege and fall of Sebastopol (Medal and Clasp, Sardinian Medal, and 5th Class of the Medjidie).

242 Lieut. Burnaby served at the siege and fall of Sebastopol (Medal and Clasp). Served in India in 1858, and was present at the siege and capture of Lucknow, and actions of Sirsee and Nawabgunge (Medal and Clasp).

243 Lieut. Majendie served at the siege and fall of Sebastopol (Medal and Clasp). Served in India in 1858, and was present at the siege and capture of Lucknow, and action of Sirsee (Medal and Clasp).

244 Lieut. Ramsden served at the siege and fall of Sebastopol and expedition to Kertch in 1855 (Medal and Clasp). Served in the Indian campaign of 1857-58, including the action of Pandora, siege and capture of Lucknow (mentioned in despatch, Medal and Clasp).

245 Lieut. F. A. Whinyates served at the siege and fall of Sebastopol (Medal and Clasp). Served in the Indian campaign of 1857-58, including the battle of Cawnpore on 6th Dec., action of Futtehghur, and affair of Kankur (Medal).

246 Lieut. Trench served in 1855 at the siege and fall of Sebastopol and expedition to Kertch (Medal and Clasp).

247 Lieut. Bazalgette served in the Eastern campaign of 1855, including the siege of Sebastopol and expedition to Kinbourn (Medal and Clasp).

248 Lieut. Wortham served at the siege and fall of Sebastopol in 1855 (Medal and Clasp). Served in India in 1858, and was present at the attack on a fort occupied by rebels on Beyt Island.

249 Lieut. Smith-Neill served in India in 1857-58 and was present at the Alumbagh in Feb. and March, siege and capture of Lucknow, and action of Nawabgunge (Medal and Clasp).

250 Lieut. Rice served in 1855 with the siege train at the siege of Sebastopol, and bombardments of 6th and 17th June (Medal and Clasp).

251 Lieut. Anderson served at the siege and fall of Sebastopol in 1855 (Medal and Clasp). Also at the capture of Canton in Dec. 1857.

252 Lieuts. Staveley and Chalmers served in the Indian campaign of 1857-58, including the action of Kalee Nuddee, affair of Ramgunga, siege and capture of Lucknow, actions of Bareilly, Shahjehanpore, and Mohumdee (Medal and Clasp).

253 Lieut. Gilmour served in India in 1857-58, and was present at the action of Pandora, and battle of Cawnpore on 6th Dec. (Medal).

254 Lieut. Edmeades served in India in 1857-58, and was present at the action of Kalee Nuddee, battle of Cawnpore on 6th Dec., and action of Sherghur Ghat (Medal).

255 Lieut. Burnett served in the Indian campaign in 1857-58, including the relief of Lucknow by Lord Clyde, battle of Cawnpore on 6th Dec., siege and capture of Lucknow, actions of Barree and Sirsee (Medal and Clasp).

256 Lieut. Oliver served in the Indian campaign in 1857-58, including the action of Pandoo Nuddee, operations of the 27th, 28th and 29th Nov. before Cawnpore, and battle there on 6th Dec., actions of Kalee Nuddee and Ramgunga, siege and capture of Lucknow, actions of Bareilly, Shahjehanpore, and Mohumdee (mentioned in despatch, Medal and Clasp).

257 Lieut. Ford served in India in 1857-58, including the relief of Lucknow (wounded) by Lord Clyde, affair of Bundah, at the Alumbagh from Jan. to March, siege and capture of Lucknow (mentioned in despatch, Medal and Clasps).

War Services of the Officers of the Royal Artillery.

258 Lieut. F. S. Stoney served in India in 1858, and was present at the attack on a fort occupied by rebels on Beyt Island.

259 Lieut. Burn served in India in 1857-58, and was present at the capture of Nurgoond on 1 June 1858 (Medal).

260 Lieut. Lowry served in India in 1857-58, and was present at the affair of Futtyabad, capture of Chandairee fort, action of Sahno, siege and capture of Jhansi, capture of Fort Lahorie, attack on Koonch, and capture of Calpee (twice mentioned in despatches, Medal).

261 Lieut. Morgan served in India in 1857-58, and was present at the action of Bandah (Medal).

262 Lieut. George Arbuthnot served in India in 1857-58 and was present at the capture of Rathghur, relief of Saugor, forcing the pass at Nudinpore, siege and capture of Jhansi, and attack on Koonch (Medal).

263 Lieut. Robertson served in India in 1857-58 and was present at the relief of Azimghur and capture of Jugdespore (mentioned in despatch, Medal).

264 Lieut. de Cetto served in India in 1857-58, and was present at the affair of Futtyabad, capture of Chandairee Fort, siege and capture of Jhansi, and action of Betwa (Medal).

265 Lieut. Brackenbury served in India in 1857-58, and was present at the action of Bandah (Medal).

266 Lieut. Cottingham served in India in 1857-58, and was present at the action of Pandora, and action and capture of Tiroul (Medal).

267 Lieut. Auchinleck served in India in 1857-58, and was present at the action of Kalee Nuddee, battle of Cawnpore on 6th Dec., and affair of Kankur (Medal).

268 Lieut. Kyle served in India in 1857-58, and was present at the actions of Secundra, Chanda, and Sultanpore, siege and capture of Lucknow, relief of Azimghur, action near Azimutghur, operations in the Jungle and capture of Jugdespore (mentioned in despatch, Medal and Clasp).

269 Lieut. W. S. Brown served in India in 1857-58, and was present at the attack on Bunterah, relief of Lucknow by Lord Clyde, affair of Gaillee, in the Alumbagh from Jan. to March, siege and capture of Lucknow (mentioned in despatches, Medal and Clasps).

270 Veterinary Surgeon Stockley served the Eastern campaign of 1854-55, including the affairs of Bulganac and M'Kenzie's Farm, taking of Balaklava, battles of Alma, Balaklava, and Inkerman, siege and fall of Sebastopol (Medal and Clasps, and Knight of the Legion of Honor).

271 Veterinary Surgeon Withers served the Eastern campaign of 1854-55, including the affairs of Bulganac and M'Kenzie's Farm, battles of Alma, Balaklava, and Inkerman, siege of Sebastopol and repulse of the sortie on the 26th Oct. 1854 (Medal and Clasps). Served also in the Indian campaign of 1857-58, including the relief of Lucknow by Lord Clyde, battle of Cawnpore on 6th Dec., actions of Seria Ghat, Chanda, and Sultanpore, siege and capture of Lucknow, and action of Barree (Medal and Clasps).

272 Veterinary Surgeon Harpley served the Eastern campaign of 1854-55, including the affairs of Bulganac and M'Kenzie's Farm, battles of Alma, Balaklava, and Inkerman, siege of Sebastopol and repulse of the Sortie on the 26th Oct. 1854 (Medal and Clasps). Served in India in 1857-58, and was present at the action of Pandora, storm and capture of Meangunge, siege and capture of Lucknow (Medal and Clasps).

273 Veterinary Surgeon Cochrane served at the siege and fall of Sebastopol in 1855 (Medal and Clasp).

274 Veterinary Surgeon Cotterell served in the Eastern campaign of 1854-55, including the siege and fall of Sebastopol (Medal and Clasp).

275 Veterinary Surgeon Rollings was present at the siege and capture of Lucknow in March 1858 (Medal and Clasp).

276 Veterinary Surgeon Sanderson served at the siege and fall of Sebastopol in 1855 (Medal and Clasp). Served in India in 1857-58 and was present at the action of Kankur (Medal).

277 Veterinary Surgeon Skoulding served in India in 1857-58, and was present at the capture of Nurgoond (Medal).

278 Paymaster Scott served with the 55th Regt. in China (Medal), and was present at the capture of Amoy, second capture of Chusan, and repulse of the night-attack on Chinhae. Served the Eastern campaign of 1854-55, including the battles of Alma and Inkerman, the siege of Sebastopol, repulse of the Sortie on 26th Oct. 1854, and attack on the Quarries on 7th June—wounded and mentioned in despatches (Medal and Clasps, and Sardinian Medal).

279 Veterinary Surgeon Partridge served with the 17th Lancers in the Crimea from 17 Feb. 1855 and has the Medal with Clasp for Sebastopol.

FIELD TRAIN DEPARTMENT.

1 Commissary W. L. M. Young served the Eastern campaign of 1854-55, including the battles of Alma, Balaklava, and Inkerman, and siege of Sebastopol (Medal and Clasps, Knight of the Legion of Honor, and 5th Class of the Medjidie).

2 Deputy Assistant Commissary Clark served in the right attack at the siege and fall of Sebastopol from May 1855 (Medal and Clasp). Served with the expedition in China in 1857-58.

Corps of Royal Engineers.

The Royal Arms and Supporters, with a Cannon, and the Motto, "*Ubique*" over the gun, and "*Quo Fas et Gloria ducunt*" below it.

Years'Serv. Full Pay	Half Pay	COLONELS COMMANDANT.	SECOND LIEUT.	FIRST LIEUT.	CAPTAIN.	BREVET-MAJOR.	BREVET-LT.-COL.	LT.-COL.	BREVET-COL.	COLONEL.	COLONEL COMN.	MAJOR-GENERAL.	LIEUT.-GENERAL.
67	0	*Sir* G. Whitmore, KCH *Gen.*20June54	18 Sept. 93	5 Feb. 96	28 Feb. 01	4 June 13		21 July 13		23 Mar. 25	1 Apr. 46	10 Jan. 37	9 Nov. 46
67	0	F. Rennell Thackeray, CB.[1] *do.*	do	18 June 96	18 Apr. 01	9 May 10		do		2 June 25	29 Apr. 46	do	do
66	0	Gustavus Nicolls,[2] *do.*	6 Nov. 94	3 Mar. 97	30 Mar. 02	4 May 13		1 Sept. 13		29 July 25	28 Jan. 51	do	do
63	0	*Sir* Charles Wm. Pasley, KCB.[3]	1 Dec. 97	28 Aug. 99	1 Mar. 05	5 Feb. 12	27 May 15	20 Dec. 14	22 July 30	12 Nov. 31	28 Nov. 53	23 Nov. 41	11 Nov. 51
62	0	*Sir* J. Fox Burgoyne, *Bt.*GCB.[4] *Gen.*5 Sept. 55; *Inspect.–Gen. of Fortifications*	29 Aug. 98	1 July 00	1 Mar. 05	6 Feb. 12	27 Apr. 12	do	do	10 Jan. 37	22 Nov. 54	28 June 38	11 Nov. 51
50	0	Charles Greae Ellicombe, CB.[6]		1 July 01	1 July 06	27 Apr. 12	21 Sept.13	23 Mar. 25	do	do	20 May 56	23 Nov. 41	20 June 54
58	0⁷⁄₁₂	George Judd Harding, CB.[8]	1 Oct. 02	1 Dec. 02	18 Nov. 07	19 July 21		30 July 25	28 June 38	22 Nov. 41	10 May 59	11 Nov. 51	23 Nov. 58
49	5⁸⁄₁₂	John Oldfield, KH.[11] Removed from the Corps, having the Rank of Major-General	2 April 06	1 July 06	1 May 11	22 July 30		12 Nov. 31	23 Nov. 41	9 Nov. 46	25 Oct.	20 June 54	10 May 59
54	7⁄₁₂	*Sir* John Mark Fred. Smith, KH.[10]	1 Dec. 05	1 Mar. 06	1 May 11			16 Mar. 30		9 Nov. 46		20 June 54	25 Oct. 59
52	0	*Sir* Harry David Jones, KCB.[14]	17 Sept. 08	24 June 09	12 Nov. 15	10 Jan. 37	11 Nov. 51	7 Sept. 40	11 Nov. 51	7 July 58		12 Dec. 54	
52	0	William Cuthbert Ward[13]	10 May 08	24 June 09	21 July 13	15 Jan. 37		9 Dec. 37		11 Nov. 51		18 Aug. 58	
45	6⁷⁄₁₂	William Redman Ord[16]	25 Apr. 09	29 May 10	21 July 13	do		18 Mar. 45		17 Feb. 54		1 Nov. 58	
43	0	Henry John Savage[17]	30 Sept.	1 May 11	1 Dec. 15	do		22 May 45		21 Mar. 54		23 Nov. 58	
50	7⁄₁₂	Lewis Alexander Hall	21 July 10	1 May 11	12 Jan. 25	28 June 38		1 Apr. 46	20 June 54	23 Sept. 54		10 May 59	
42	5⁄₁₂	Daniel Bolton[19]	14 Dec. 11	1 July 12	7 June 25	do		9 Nov.	do	13 Dec. 54		20 June 59	
40	5	Thomas Foster[24]	1 Sept. 15	7 Sept. 19	10 Jan. 37	29 Mar. 39		11 Nov. 51	20 June 54	4 June 56		25 Oct. 59	
		COLONELS.											
48	0	Charles Wright[20]	1 July 12	1 Mar. 13	29 July 25	28 June 38	28 Nov. 54	4 Feb. 47	28 Nov. 54	3 Jan. 55			
47	0	Henry Sandham	20 July 13	15 Dec.	1 May 34	9 Nov. 46	do	9 Aug. 48	do	21 May 55			
40	5⁄₁₂	Henry Powell Wulff	1 Aug. 14	1 July	15	23 Sept. 36	do	5 July 51	do	27 Oct. 55			
38	7⁵⁄₁₂	Montgomery Williams[23]	24 Mar. 15	1 May	16	10 Jan. 37	do	14 July 51	do	10 June 56			
41	0	John Isaac Hope	1 Sept. 15	1 July	21	do		11 Nov. 51	28 Nov. 54	11 Aug. 56			
45	7⁄₁₂	Richard John Stotherd	do	13 Mar. 24	do	11 Nov. 51		24 Nov.	do	10 Sept. 56			
45	0	Alexander Gordon[25]	do	2 Dec. 24	do	do		6 Dec. 51	do	2 Sept. 57			
45	0	Cowper Rose	do	12 Jan. 25	do	do		28 Jan. 52	do	25 Nov. 57			
44	0	Wm. Biddlecomb Marlow[26]		23 Mar. 25	28 Mar. 37	7 July 46		1 April	do	12 Aug. 58			
44	0	Benjamin Spicer Stehelin	1 Aug. 16	2 June 25	31 Mar. 38	11 Nov. 51		19 Sept. 53	do	1 Nov. 58			
44	0	Henry Servante	do	29 July 25	27 May 39	do		17 Feb. 54	do	23 Nov. 58			
44	0	Henry Owen Crawley	do	17 Aug. 26	do	do		do	do	10 May 59			
42	2	John Twiss	do	do	20 Sept. 39	11 Nov. 51		do	do	20 June 59			
35	0	Edward Frome[27]	11 May 25	24 Sept.	28 Nov. 39	15 Sept. 48		do	do	25 Oct. 59			
		LIEUTENANT-COLONELS.		6 Dec. 25	7 Sept. 39	11 Nov. 51							
35	0	Charles Edmund Wilkinson	6 Aug. 25	26 Feb. 28	19 July 41			17 Feb. 54	28 Nov. 54				
35	0	William Turnbull Renwick	do	7 Nov. 28	9 Mar.			21 Mar. 54	do				
35	0	William E. Delves Broughton	do	24 Feb. 29	1 April			20 June 54	20 June 57				
34	0	Richard J. Nelson	7 Jan. 26	22 May 29	1 Sept. 41			20 June 54	20 June 57				

399

Years' Serv. F.P. H.P.	LIEUTENANT-COLONELS.	SECOND LIEUT.	FIRST LIEUT.	CAPTAIN.	BREVET-MAJOR.	BREVET-LIEUT.-COL.	LIEUT.-COL.	BREVET-COLONEL.
34 0	George Burgmann	15 March 26	27 Feb. 29	30 Sept. 41	......	......	20 June 54	20 June 57
34 0	John Chaytor	do	16 Feb. 30	23 Nov. 41	......	......	26 Oct. 54	20 Oct. 57
34 0	Sir William Thomas Denison, KCB. Governor General of New South Wales	do	22 June 30	do	20 June 54	......	13 Dec. 54	13 Dec. 57
34 0	Edw. Wm. Durnford,[29] A. Adj. Gen. Dublin	22 Sept. 26	5 Feb. 31	23 Feb. 42	do	......	do	13 Dec. 57
34 0	Edward Thomas Lloyd[30]	do	24 June 31	28 June 42	do	......	do	do
34 0	Henry James	do	6 Oct. 31	24 Oct. 42	19 Feb. 47	......	16 Dec. 54	16 Dec. 58
34 0	William Robinson	do	7 Oct. 31	16 Mar. 43	20 June 54	......	22 Dec. 54	22 Dec. 58
34 0	Thomas Rawlings Mould	do	12 Nov. 31	4 Apr. 43	do	......	3 Jan. 55	3 Jan. 58
34 0	George Wynne	4 May 27	18 Mar. 32	27 May	do	......	13 Jan.	13 Jan.
33 0	Henry Drury Harness, CB.	24 May 27	20 Sept. 32	30 June	do	......	do	do
33 0	Edmund Twiss Ford	30 Aug. 27	5 Feb. 33	15 Nov.	do	......	do	13 Jan. 58
32 0	William Yolland	12 April 28	4 Sept. 33	19 Dec.	do	......	do	do
31 0	Charles Erskine Ford	29 April 29	1 May	10 Jan. 44	28 Nov. 54	......	do	13 Jan. 58
30 0	Richd. Clement Moody, Chief Commissioner of Lands and Woods of British Colombia	5 Nov.	25 June	6 Mar. 44	......	......	do	28 Apr. 58
29 0	F. A. Yorke, Insp. R. M. Academy, Woolwich	5 Oct. 31	2 Aug. 35	20 June 45	......	24 April 55	1 April 55	1 Apr. 58
29 0	Charles Francis Skyring[31]	do	19 Aug. 35	16 Aug.	......	......	do	do
29 0	Robert Gorges Hamilton	29 May 32	5 Dec. 35	18 Dec.	......	......	do	do
28 0	William Charles Hadden[33]	do	6 Feb. 36	26 Dec. 45	......	......	21 May	21 May 58
28 0	Roger Stuart Beatson	do	13 May 36	18 Mar. 45	......	......	27 Oct. 55	......
28 0	Sampson Freeth	26 Sept.	13 May 36	18 Mar.	......	......	23 Feb. 56	......
27 0	John Graham M'Kerlie	27 Feb. 33	23 Sept. 36	1 April	......	......	10 June	......
27 0	William George Hamley	5 Aug. 33	25 Sept. 36	1 May	......	......	14 June	......
27 0	Andrew Beatty	1 Dec. 33	6 Nov. 36	22 May	......	......	1 Aug. 56	29 June 55
27 0	John W. Gordon,[34] CB., Dep. Adj.-General	do	10 Jan. 37	12 July 45	12 Dec. 54	......	11 Aug.	......
27 0	Marcus Dill	do	do	1 April 46	......	......	10 Sept.	......
27 0	Philip John Bainbrigge	do	do	do	......	......	29 Oct.	......
27 0	Archibald P. G. Ross	do	do	do	......	......	2 Sept. 57	......
26 0	Edmund Ogle	9 June 34	do	do	......	......	25 Nov.	......
26 0	Conolly M'Causland	9 June 34	do	do	......	......	2 Dec.	......
26 0	John Cameron	12 Dec. 34	do	do	14 June 58	......	12 Aug. 58	......
26 0	John Summerfield Hawkins	do	do	do	20 July 58	......	23 Nov. 58	......
26 0	James Holt Freeth	19 Dec. 34	31 Jan. 37	do	28 May 53	26 Oct. 58	1 Apr. 59	......
26 0	Charles Duesbery Robertson[37]	do	23 Feb. 37	do	2 Aug. 58	......	do	......
25 0	Charles Fanshawe	18 June 35	28 Mar. 37	do	12 Dec. 54	24 Apr. 55	20 June 59	2 Nov. 55
24 0	Fred. Edward Chapman,[38] CB	18 June 36	31 Mar. 38	do	13 Apr. 58	......	13 Oct. 59	......
24 0	Gother Frederick Mann	18 June 36	5 May 38	do	12 Aug. 58	......	25 Oct. 59	......
23 0	Spencer Westmacott	5 May 37	1 Aug. 38	do	26 Aug. 58	......	......	......
23 0	William Collier Menzies							

Corps of Royal Engineers.

Years' Serv. Full Pay.	Half Pay.	CAPTAINS.	SECOND LIEUT.	FIRST LIEUT.	CAPTAIN.
23	0	Robert Michael Laffan, *Major*, 26 Oct. 58	5 May 37	1 Apr. 39	1 May 46
23	0	Arthur Henry Freeling, *Major*, 26 Oct. 58	14 Dec. 37	27 May 39	27 July 46
23	0	Harry St. Geo. Ord,[41] *Maj.* 8 Sept. 54; *Lt. Gov. of Dominica*	do	do	29 Oct. 46
23	0	Hampden Clement Blamire Moody, *Maj.* 26 Oct. 58	do	22 Sept. 39	9 Nov. 46
23	0	John Lintorn Arabin Simmons,[42] CB. *Maj.* 14 July 54; *l.c.* 12 Dec. 54; *Col.* 12 Dec. 57; *Consul General at Warsaw*	do	15 Oct. 39	do
23	0	George Archibald Leach, *Major*, 26 Oct. 58	do	28 Nov. 39	do
23	0	Philip John Stapleton Barry, *Major*, 26 Oct. 58	do	3 Apr. 40	17 Nov. 46
23	0	Henry Arthur White, *Major*, 26 Oct. 58	do	28 July	26 Jan. 47
23	0	Paul Bernard Whittingham, *Major*, 26 Oct. 58	do	28 July	4 Feb.
22	0	James William Gosset, *Major*, 26 Oct. 58	16 June 38	7 Sept.	1 March
22	0	George Clement Baillie, *Major*, 26 Oct. 58	do	10 Feb. 41	22 Mar.
22	0	Thomas Bernard Collinson, *Major*, 26 Oct. 58	do	9 Mar.	16 Apr.
22	0	George Bent,[45] CB. *Maj.* 1 Sept. 54; *l.c.* 2 Nov. 55; *Col.* 25 Oct. 59; *Aide de Camp to the Queen*	do	1 Apr. 41	16 Apr.
22	0	Edm. Yeamans Walcott Henderson, *Maj.* 26 Oct. 58	do	do	22 Apr.
21	0	John Bayly, *Major*, 1 Nov. 58	10 Mar. 39	16 Sept. 41	3 Sept.
21	0	Henry C. C. Owen,[46] CB. *Maj.* 17 July 55; *l.c.* 6 June 56	do	30 Sept.	28 Oct.
21	0	Wm. Fran. Drummond Jervois,[47] *Maj.* 29 Sept. 54	do	8 Oct.	13 Dec.
21	0	Thomas Lionel John Gallwey, *Major* 14 May 59	do	23 Nov.	2 Feb. 48
21	0	Richard Burnaby, *Major*, 9 Sept. 59	do	7 Dec.	14 April 48
21	0	Albert O'Donnel Grattan	do	23 Feb. 42	26 Feb. 49
21	0	Hon. Hussey Fane Keane,[49] *Maj.* 2 Nov. 55	do	28 June 42	14 Aug. 49
21	0	Charles John Gibb,[50] *May*, 2 Nov. 55	20 Dec. 39	16 Mar. 43	16 April 50
21	0	Charles Gordon Gray	do	1 May	21 Sept. 50
20	0	Wm. Driscoll Gossett, *Treasurer of British Columbia*	20 June 40	27 May	11 Nov. 50
20	0	Charles Sim, *Surveyor Gen. of Ceylon*	do	11 Sept.	5 July 51
20	0	Fairfax Charles Hassard,[52] *Maj.* 14 Nov. 55	do	23 Sept.	14 July
20	0	Douglas Galton	18 Dec. 40	1 Oct.	31 Aug.
20	0	Henry Young Darracott Scott	do	19 Dec.	11 Nov.
20	0	George Ross	do	10 Jan. 44	11 Nov.
20	0	James Robert Mann, *Surveyor General of the Mauritius*	do	20 June	24 Nov.
19	0	John Williamson Lovell,[55] CB. *Maj.* 12 Dec. 54	19 June 41	16 Aug.	6 Dec.
19	0	Millington Henry Synge	do	30 Oct.	20 Dec.
19	0	Edward Wolstenholme Ward	do	18 Dec.	28 Jan. 52
18	0	E. F. Bourchier,[56] CB. *Maj.* 24 April 55; *l.c.* 2 Nov. 55	1 Jan. 42	26 Dec.	9 Aug. 52
18	0	Henry Grain	do	22 Feb. 45	22 April 53
18	0	John Marshall Grant	do	18 Mar.	17 Dec. 53
18	0	Jas. Frankfort Manners Browne,[57] CB. *Maj.* 17 July 55; *l.c.* 26 Dec. 56	do	1 April	7 Feb. 54
18	0	FitzRoy Molyneux Henry Somerset	do	22 April	17 Feb.
18	0	Horace Wm. Montagu[59] *Maj.* 24 April 55; *l.c.* 2 Nov. 55	do	1 May	do
18	0	Valentine Thomas Mairis	do	22 May	do
18	0	*Francis Fowke*	18 June 42	1 April 46	do
18	0	*Charles Richard Binney*	do	do	do
17	0	Frederick Henry Rich	11 Jan. 43	do	do
17	0	Francis Rawdon Chesney	do	do	do
17	0	Thos. Andrew Lumsden Murray	do	do	do
17	0	Wm. Lawtie Morrison	17 June 43	do	do
17	0	Anth. Chas. Cooke,[61] *Maj.* 2 Nov. 55	do	do	do
17	0	Thomas Inglis	do	do	do
17	0	Ben Hay Martindale	do	do	do
17	0	Charles Scrope Hutchinson	20 Dec. 43	do	do
17	0	Henry Wray	do	do	do
17	0	*Charles Pasley*	do	do	do
17	0	John Stokes,[63] *Maj.* 6 June 56	do	do	do
16	0	Andrew Clarke	19 June 44	do	do
16	0	Francis Du Cane,[64] *Maj.* 6 June 56	do	do	do
16	0	John Yerbury Moggridge	do	do	do
16	0	*John Gordon Jervois*	19 Dec. 44	do	21 Mar. 54
16	0	Henry Whatley Tyler	do	do	31 Mar. 54
16	0	John Cromie Blackwood De Butts	do	do	20 June 54
16	0	Walter Samuel Stace	do	do	do
16	0	Gwavas Speedwell Tilly	do	do	do

Corps of Royal Engineers. 402

Years' Serv. Full Pay	Years' Serv. Half Pay	CAPTAINS.	2ND LIEUT.	1ST LIEUT.	CAPTAIN.
16	0	Edw. Stanton,[65] CB. *M.* 12 Dec, 54, *l.c.* 2 Nov. 5 *Assist. Adj. General*	19 Dec. 44	1 April 46	20 June 54
15	0	Charles Cornwallis Chesney	18 June 45	do	22 July
15	0	Louis John Amadée Arnlit,[67] *Maj.* 2 Nov. 55	do	do	15 Nov.
15	0	Charles Brisbane Ewart,[68] *Maj.* 2 Nov. 55	do	do	13 Dec. 54
15	0	Chas. B. P. N. H. Nugent, *Maj.* 2 Nov. 55	18 Dec. 45	do	do
15	0	Edward Belfield	do	do	do
15	0	Hon. George Wrottesley	do	do	16 Dec. 54
15	0	Edward C. A. Gordon, *Maj.* 2 Nov. 55	do	do	do
15	0	Whitworth Porter,[71] *Maj.* 2 Nov. 55	do	do	3 Jan. 55
15	0	John Joshua Wilson	do	do	13 Jan. 55
14	0	Joshua Henry Smith	1 May 46	1 May 46	do
14	0	Anthony Reynolds Vyvyan Crease	do	27 July 46	do
14	0	Edward Metcalfe Grain[73]	do	29 Oct.	14 Mar. 55
14	0	Augustus Meyer Lockner	do	9 Nov. 46	1 April 55
14	0	Philip Ravenhill,[75] *Maj.* 2 Nov. 55	do	do	do
14	0	Herbert Taylor Siborne	6 Aug. 46	do	do
14	0	Charles Style Akers	do	do	do
14	0	Berdoe Amherst Wilkinson	do	17 Nov. 46	do
14	0	L. Nicholson,[76] CB. *M.* 2 Nov. 55, *l.c.* 20 July 58	do	26 Jan. 47	do
14	0	George Edmond Lushington Walker	do	4 Feb. 47	do
		SECOND CAPTAINS.			
14	0	Francis Edward Cox, *Major*, 26 Apr. 59	6 Aug. 46	20 Feb. 47	1 April 55
14	0	Sidney Bayton Farrell	do	1 March	do
14	0	Charles William Barry	17 Dec. 46	16 Apr. 47	do
14	0	Charles Herbert Sedley,[77] *Maj.* 2 Nov. 55	do	do	16 April 55
14	0	Richard Warren	do	14 July	14 May
14	0	Hon. John James Bury	do	1 Sept.	21 May
13	0	Richard Hugh Stotherd	2 May 47	28 Oct.	21 May
13	0	William Hatt Noble	do	13 Dec.	1 June
13	0	Henry Schaw	do	2 Feb. 48	1 June
13	0	Edward Nicholas Heygate	do	12 Feb.	7 June
13	0	George Hamilton Gordon	do	9 April	19 June
13	0	Charles John Fowler[79]	do	19 June 49	15 Aug.
13	0	Alexander Ross Clarke	1 Oct. 47	1 July	8 Sept.
13	0	Francis Horatio De Vere,[80] *Major*, 2 Nov. 55	do	16 April 50	27 Oct. 55
13	0	Henry Raymond Pelly	do	21 Sept. 50	23 Feb. 56
13	0	Robert Mann Parsons	do	do	do
13	0	Frederic Brine[62]	do	11 Nov. 50	do
13	0	Arthur A'Court Fisher,[83] *Major*, 22 Sept. 58	do	5 July 51	do
13	0	Geo. M. Stopford,[81] *Major*, 22 Sept. 58, *Adj.*	do	14 July	do
13	0	Edward Bridge	do	31 Aug.	do
13	0	Montagu Stopford Whitmore[86]	do	11 Nov.	29 Feb. 56
13	0	VC How. C. Elphinstone,[57] *Major*, 22 Sept. 58	18 Dec. 47	11 Nov.	20 April
13	0	Charles Edward Cumberland	do	13 Nov.	10 June
13	0	Henry Reynolds Luard	1 Oct. 47	24 Nov.	14 June
13	0	*William Coles Phillpotts*	18 Dec. 47	6 Dec.	11 Aug.
13	0	Amelius Beauclerck Fyers	do	20 Dec.	18 Aug.
13	0	Alexander Stephen Creyke[90]	do	28 Jan. 52	10 Sept.
13	0	James Grantham	do	1 April 52	4 Dec.
13	0	Lionel Charles Barber	do	3 Oct. 52	20 May 57
13	0	George Reid Lempriere,[91] *Instructor of Musketry*	do	22 April 53	26 May
13	0	James Ponsonby Cox	do	14 May 53	2 Sept.
13	0	Henry George Savage	do	17 Dec. 53	1 Oct.
12	0	VC W. O. Lennox,[93] *M.* 24 Mar. 58, *l.c.* 26 Apr. 59	27 June 48	7 Feb. 54	25 Nov.
12	0	Arthur Leahy,[94] *Major* 23 Sept. 58	do	17 Feb.	2 Dec. 57
12	0	Edward Loftus Bland	do	do	1 Feb. 58
12	0	Anthony William Durnford	do	do	18 March
12	0	Donald Alexander Frazer	do	do	1 April
12	0	Edmond Frederick DuCane	19 Dec. 48	do	16 April
12	0	William Crossman	do	do	12 Aug.
11	0	Willoughby Digby Marsh	19 Dec. 49	do	13 Aug.
11	0	William James Stuart[95]	do	do	20 Aug.
10	0	*John Clayton Cowell*,[98] *Major*, 23 Sept. 58	19 June 50	do	22 Sept. 58
10	0	Robert Hawthorn	do	do	do
10	0	VC Gerald Graham[99]	do	do	28 Oct. 58
10	0	Charles Elwin Harvey	19 Dec. 50	do	23 Nov.
10	0	Robert William Duff	do	do	1 Dec.
10	0	*George Philips*[96]	do	do	15 Dec.
9	0	Charles Nassau Martin[97]	18 June 51	do	4 Jan. 59
9	0	Francis Edward Pratt[101]	do	do	1 April

Corps of Royal Engineers.

Years' Serv. Full Pay.	Half Pay.	SECOND CAPTAINS.	2ND LIEUT.	1ST LIEUT.	CAPTAIN.
9	0	John Mervin Cutcliffe Drake[100]	17 Dec. 51	17 Feb. 54	1 April 59
9	0	Edward Renouard James[102]	do	do	do
8	0	*William Bailey*	23 June 52	do	do
8	0	Frederick Edward Blackett Beaumont	do	do	do
8	0	Charles George Gordon,[103] *Adjutant*	do	do	do
8	0	Oliver Haldam Stokes[104]	do	do	do
8	0	James Bevan Edwards[112]	22 Dec. 52	do	do
7	0	John Fretcheville Dykes Donnelly[105]	22 June 53	do	do
7	0	John Edwin Cornes	do	do	do
7	0	Alexander De Courcy Scott[106]	do	do	do
7	0	Carew Louis Augustus O'Grady	do	do	26 April 59
7	0	Lonsdale Augustus Hale	21 Dec. 53	21 Mar. 54	10 May
7	0	Wm. Henry Hart Davis Dumaresq[107]	do	31 Mar.	24 May
7	0	Arthur Reid Lempriere	do	20 June	20 June
7	0	George Longley[113]	do	20 June 54	19 Sept. 59
6	0	Peter Henry Scratchley[109]	11 April 54	do	1 Oct. 59
6	0	Gustavus Nicolls Kelsall[109]	do	do	13 Oct. 59
		LIEUTENANTS.			
6	0	Charles John Darrah[110]	14 Aug. 54	14 Aug. 54	
6	0	John Popham Maquay	do	do	
6	0	Robert Nicholl Dawson	do	16 Aug. 54	
6	0	Edward Osborne Hewett	do	20 Oct.	
6	0	Frederick Mould	do	23 Oct.	
6	0	Constantine Phipps Carey	do	15 Nov.	
6	0	William Butler Gossett	do	13 Dec. 54	
6	0	Robert Grant	23 Oct. 54	do	
6	0	Edward Harding Stewart	do	do	
6	0	Edward Donald Malcolm	do	16 Dec. 54	
6	0	Arthur Robert Mac Donnell	do	22 Dec.	
6	0	James Hamilton Wilson	do	3 Jan. 55	
6	0	Charles Anne Law de Montmorency	do	13 Jan. 55	
6	0	Hon. William Le Poer Trench	do	do	
6	0	Francis Arthur Marindin	20 Dec. 54	do	
6	0	Moreton John Wheatley	do	do	
6	0	Edward Coysgarne Sim	do	do	
5	0	William Adolphus Frankland	28 Feb. 55	1 Mar. 55	
5	0	William Simeon Boileau	do	14 Mar. 55	
5	0	Alexander Dirom	do	1 April 55	
5	0	Walter Moncrieff Thriepland Campbell	do	do	
5	0	Douglas Gosset Waldegrave Moncrieff	do	do	
5	0	Morgan Crofton Molesworth	do	do	
5	0	Richard Betton Rimington	do	do	
5	0	Percy Guillemard Llewellyn Smith	do	do	
5	0	James Makgill Heriot Maitland	....	20 April 55	
5	0	Charles Edmund Webber	....	do	
5	0	Edward Robert Festing	....	do	
5	0	Allan Eliott Lockhart	....	do	
5	0	Richard Decie	....	do	
5	0	George Watts Stockley	....	do	
5	0	John Ashton Papillon	....	do	
5	0	Gordon Douglas Pritchard	....	31 July 55	
5	0	Edward Saumerez Tyler	....	do	
5	0	Edward Thomas Brooke	....	do	
5	0	Richard Harrison	....	do	
5	0	Edward Henry Courtney	....	do	
5	0	Richard Mainwaring Forman Sandford	....	do	
5	0	Richard Bullen	....	do	
5	0	Henry Helsham Jones	....	1 Aug. 55	
5	0	Arthur Tillard Storer	....	do	
5	0	John Thomas Twigge	....	do	
5	0	Reginald Gother Thorold	....	do	
5	0	George Sackville Berkeley	....	do	
5	0	Gustavus Holmes Brooke	....	do	
5	0	Edward Mitchell	....	do	
5	0	John Garnier	....	do	
5	0	Robert Murdoch Smith	....	24 Sept. 55	
5	0	Charles William Wilson	....	do	
5	0	William Newsome[111]	....	15 Oct. 55	
5	0	John Knox Tisdall	....	19 Dec. 55	
5	0	William Gustavus Temple Stace	....	do	
5	0	John Barrett Lennard	....	do	
4	0	George Swetenham	....	7 April 56	

Corps of Royal Engineers.

LIEUTENANTS.	LIEUT.	LIEUTENANTS.	LIEUT.
Daniel Corrie Walker	7 April 56	Honorius Sisson Sitwell	23 Dec. 57
Robert Home	do	Charles Albert Lyon Campbell	do
John Brand Paterson	do	William John Engledue	do
Herbert Locock	do	William Sherer Maud	do
Frederick Hinne	do	George Vivian Sivewright	do
William Keith	do	Henry Somerset Clive	do
Ferdinal Beckwith Maingay	21 June 56	Dallas Gordon Jones	do
Henry Frederick Chapman Lewin	do	Arthur Blayney Coddington	do
Arthur George Durnford	do	Henry Fyers Turner	do
Montague Lambert	do	William Innes	22 June 58
G. Ed. Langham Somerset Sanford	18 Oct. 50	Robert Mitchell Campbell	do
Shearman Godfrey Bird	do	Hamilton Tovey	do
Edward Fraser Spearman Lloyd	do	Richard Nicholas Buckle	do
Henry Darley Crozier	20 Dec. 56	Robert Athorpe	do
Henry Spencer Palmer	do	James Fellowes	do
Robert Barton	do	Rd. Henry Beaumont Beaumont	do
Robert Owen Jones	do	George Le Breton Simmons	do
Valentine Gardner Clayton	do	*Richard Harry Williams	1 Oct. 58
Henry Cooper Seddon	do	*Jasper Gustavus Silvester Davies	do
Allan May	21 Feb. 57	*Edmund DonoughCollinsO'Brien	do
Frederick Wm. Richard Clements	15 May 57	*William Joseph Carroll	21 Dec. 58
Edward Micklem	do	*Samuel Anderson	do
Frederick Tynte Warburton	do	*Charles Woodward	do
George Goodall	do	*Robert Young Armstrong	do
Arthur Parnell	do	*Robert John Bond	do
Grant Blunt	do	*Arthur Kyle Haslett	do
Charles Edward Luard	do	*George Edward Grover	do
Bruce Brine	do	*Charles Harland Craigie Halkett	do
Alexander Charles Hamilton	23 June 57	*George Henry Law Pole	do
Harry Parnell Cole	do	*Charles Bowen	do
Bayard Clark Cochrane	do	*George William Johnson	do
Charles Crawford	1 Oct. 57	*William Hutchinson Mulloy	do
Frederick Augustus Le Mesurier	do	*William Randall Slacke	do
Charles Richard Tierney Davidson	do	*Edward Toler Wynne	do
Bruce Hull Melville	do	*Francis George Oldham	do
Charles John Moysey	do	*George Allen Gun	do
Richard Charles Price	do	*Geo. Gordon Chamberlin Bigsby	do
Thomas Lyster	do	*James Octavius Playfair	do
Joseph Allan Millar	do	*John Charles Ardagh	1 Apr. 59
Edward Pelham Hardinge	do	*James Jameson Robertson	do
John Roberts Hogg	do	*William Emmerson Peck	do
Napier George Sturt	do	*Edmund Stephens	do
Thomas Pilkington White	do	*Christopher Josiah Russell	do
Charles John O'Neill Ferguson	do	*John Mabbott Morgan	do
George Herbert Bolland	do	*Arthur Balfour Haig	22 June 59
Richard Warren Stewart	do	*Henry Cautley	do
William Salmond	do	*Albany Featherstonhaugh	do
George Mansell Collings	23 Dec. 57	*Joseph Henry Satterthwaite	do
Robert Hamilton Vetch	do	*Ernest Marsh Lloyd	do
George Warren	do	*John Cosmo Macpherson	do
Edward Nicolls Peters	do	*Thomas Howard	do
John Henry Crowdy	do	*Frederick Bailey	do

Deputy Adjutant General.—Colonel John Wm. Gordon, CB. 18 Oct. 56.
Assistant Adj. Gen.—Lt.Col. Edward Stanton, CB.
Instructor of Musketry.—Captain George Reid Lempriere, 4 Oct. 56.
Adjutants.—Major George Montagu Stopford, 1 Oct. 57.
    Captain Charles George Gordon, 2 May 59.
Chief Paym.—William Marvin, 24 Feb. 58; Q. M. 10 Setp. 44; *Hon. rank of Maj.* 1 Apr. 58.
Paymasters.—Charles Wilkinson, 1 Sept. 58.
    George Pringle, 5 Aug. 59.
Quarter Masters.—William Young, 1 April 53.
    Thomas William John Connolly, 26 June 55.
    Michael Bradford, 17 Dec. 55.
    David Youle, 14 Jan. 58.
Quarter Master and Commissary of Clothing.—James Mutch, 22 Dec. 56.
    Establishment at Chatham for instructing the Corps in Military Field Works.
Director.—Colonel Henry Sandham.

Royal Engineer Train.

Lieut. and Adjutant.—Mathias Moore, 24 Feb. 59.   Scarlet.—
Veterinary Surgeon.—Thomas Walton Mayer, 10 Oct. 56.   Facings, Blue Velvet.

N. B. The officers in Italics are holding civil employment.

War Services of the Officers of the Royal Engineers.

1 General Thackeray was at the capture of Surinam in 1799; St. Martin's and St. Bartholomew's in 1801; directed the siege of Scylla Castle in 1806; and that of the Fortress of Santa Maura in 1809. Served with the army in Spain in 1812; at the battle of Castalla and siege of Tarragona in 1813, and remained with the army until 1814.

2 General Nicolls went out with a reinforcement of several Regts. to Gibraltar on the war breaking out with Spain in 1796, and remained blockaded in that fortress two and a half years; proceeded from thence to the West Indies in 1799. Went as Commanding Engineer with Lt.-Gen. Sir George Prevost to Nova Scotia in 1808, under expectations of hostilities with America. Remained there until the war broke out in 1812, and was actively employed in the protection of the frontiers of Nova Scotia and New Brunswick, and was present at the capture of Moose Island, Castine and Belfast. Commanding Engineer in Canada part of 1814 and 15.

3 Sir Charles Pasley's services:—defence of Gaeta, in 1806; battle of Maida; siege of Copenhagen in 1807; campaign of 1808-9, including several skirmishes, and battle of Corunna. Reconnoitered the enemy's coast under the fire of batteries, and was afterwards at the siege of Flushing. Received a bayonet-wound through the thigh, and a musket-wound, which injured the spine, in leading a storming party to attack an advanced work occupied by the French on the Dike in front of Flushing, 14th Aug. 1809. Sir Charles has received the Silver War Medal with two Clasps for Maida and Corunna.

4 Sir John Burgoyne embarked in 1800 on the expedition to Egypt under Sir Ralph Abercromby, but was detached at Malta to be employed in blockade of La Valetta, and was present at its capture. Joined the army in Sicily in 1806, and embarked as Commanding Engineer with the expedition to Egypt under Major-General Mackenzie Fraser, and served at the assault of the lines of Alexandria and siege of Rosetta. Was next employed as Commanding Engineer with Sir John Moore's expedition from Messina, and afterwards under the same General in Sweden in 1808. Sailed in the same year with the expedition to Portugal under Sir John Moore, and was present in the retreat to Corunna, in which he blew up the bridge at Benevente in presence of the enemy. Joined the army in Portugal under Sir Arthur Wellesley in April 1809, and was attached to the 3rd (Sir Thomas Picton's) Division; was engaged at the passage of the Douro, affair of Salamonde, retreat to the lines of Torres Vedras, (blew up Fort Conception in presence of the enemy,) battle of Busaco, first siege of Badajoz, action of Elbodon, action of Aldea de Ponte, siege and capture of Ciudad Rodrigo,—accompanied the 3rd Division in the assault and obtained his Brevet of Major for services at the siege; siege and capture of Badajoz,—accompanied the 3rd Division in the assault and escalade of the Castle, and obtained his Brevet of Lt.-Colonel for services at this siege; served as Commanding Engineer at the siege and capture of the Forts of Salamanca, and battle of Salamanca; served as Commanding Engineer at the capture of Madrid and the Retiro, and siege of Burgos (wounded); advance in 1813, battle of Vittoria (horse shot under him), siege of San Sebastian (wounded in the assault), conducted the siege of the Castle of San Sebastian as Commanding Engineer, Sir R. Fletcher having been killed in the preceding assault; action of the Bidassoa, battles of the Nivelle and Nive, passage of the Adour, blockade of Bayonne and repulse of the sortie. Accompanied the expedition to New Orleans as Commanding Engineer, and served in the attack on the enemy's entrenched position, and capture of Fort Bowyer. Joined the Army of Occupation at Paris on his return from New Orleans. In 1827, accompanied the army to Portugal as Commanding Engineer under Lt.-General Sir W. Clinton. Sir John has received the Gold Cross and one Clasp for Badajoz, Salamanca, Vittoria, St. Sebastian, and Nive; and the Silver War Medal with three Clasps for Busaco, Ciudad Rodrigo, and Nivelle; and, at the recommendation of the Duke of Wellington, the Portuguese order of the Tower and Sword was conferred upon him. In Jan. 1854 he proceeded to Turkey on a special mission, and prior to the sailing of the expedition to the Crimea, was appointed Lieut.-General on the Staff of the Eastern Army; was engaged at the battles of Alma, Balaklava, and Inkerman, and conducted the British portion of the siege of Sebastopol until ordered home in February 1855 (Medal and four Clasps). For his services at the siege of Sebastopol Sir John was created a Baronet and promoted to the rank of General; he has also received the 1st Class of the Turkish Order of Nishid Medjidie, and the decoration of Grand Officer of the Legion of Honor. Sir John is also a Knight Grand Cross of the Bath.

6 Lieut.-General Ellicombe served in the Peninsula from Nov. 1811 to the end of the war, including the siege and storm of Ciudad Rodrigo, siege and storm of Badajoz, retreat from Burgos, advance of the army and crossing the Ebro, battle of Vittoria, as Brigade-Major; siege and storm of San Sebastian, 15th July to 9th Sept. 1813; passage of Bidassoa, battles of Nivelle and Nive (10th, 11th and 12th Dec. 1813); passage of the Adour, blockade of Bayonne and repulse of the sortie. He has received the Gold Medal for San Sebastian, and the Silver War Medal with five Clasps for Ciudad Rodrigo, Badajoz, Vittoria, Nivelle, and Nive.

8 Lieut. General Harding served with the army in Sicily in 1812; on the eastern coast of Spain in 1813, including the battle of Castalla, attack of Denia, and siege of Tarragona. In 1815 he served as Commanding Engineer with the Prussian army under Prince Augustus of Prussia at the sieges of Maubeuge, Landrecy, Marienburg, Philippeville, and Rocroy; and continued with the Army of Occupation until 1818.

10 Sir Frederick Smith served in 1809 at the siege of the castle of Ischia and the cap-

ture of that Island and Procida in the Bay of Naples, also at the capture of Zante and Cephalonia. In 1810, in the action before the investment of the fortress of Santa Maura as Deputy Assistant Quarter Master General, and at the siege and capture of the Fortress as an Officer of Royal Engineers.

11 Lieut. General Oldfield served in North America in 1807-8 and 9. In Holland and the Netherlands in 1814. From March to June 1815, he served as second in command of the Engineer Department in the Netherlands—as Brigade Major to the corps of Royal Engineers in the Netherlands and France, from March, 1815, to the withdrawal of the Army of Occupation in December 1818 : present at the battle of Waterloo, and capitulation of Paris. Was Commanding Royal Engineer in the Canadas from 1839 to 1843.

13 Major General Ward served with the army in Sicily in 1811 and 12 ; was present at the action of Castalla, attack of Denia, and siege of Tarragona in 1813 ; served with the army in the Netherlands in 1814.

14 Sir Harry Jones served in the expedition to Walcheren in 1809. Also the campaigns of 1810, 11, 12, 13, and 14, including the actions and sieges of Cadiz, Tarragona (1811), Badajoz (1812), Vittoria, St. Sebastian, passage of the Bidassoa, Nivelle, Nive, Bayonne. Wounded leading the Forlorn Hope at the first assault of St. Sebastian. He has received the Silver War Medal with five Clasps. In Feb. 1815 joined the army under General Lambert in Dauphin Island; by the return of an American Flag of Truce, was sent to New Orleans on a special duty: landed at Ostend 18th June 1815. Appointed Commanding Engineer in charge of the fortifications on Montmâtre, after the entrance of the British troops into Paris, in 1815; appointed a Commissioner to the Prussian Army of Occupation in 1816. Appointed a Brigadier General for particular service in the Baltic in 1854, and commanded the British forces at the siege operations against Bomarsund, in the Aland Isles (Baltic Medal), and for his services in the Baltic was promoted Major General. Appointed, 10th February, to command the Royal Engineers in the Eastern campaign of 1855, which he retained until the fall of Sebastopol; was wounded in the forehead by spent grape-shot on the 18th June (Medal and Clasp, *KCB.*, Commander 1st Class of the Military Order of Savoy, and 2nd Class of the Medjidie). Formed one of the Council of War held in Paris in January 1856, when he received the Cross of Commander of the Legion of Honor.

16 Major General Ord served in Spain during 1810, 11, 12, 13, and one-half of 1814, including the sieges of Cadiz and Tarragona.

17 Major General Savage served in the Peninsula from Nov. 1813 to the end of the war, including the investment of Bayonne and repulse of the sortie.

19 Major General Bolton served in the Peninsula from Oct. 1813 to the end of the war.

20 Colonel Wright was wounded by a musket-ball through the thigh, 12th Oct. 1821, at Zante, in an attack made by the Greeks upon a Turkish man-of-war.

23 Colonel Montgomery Williams served in the Kaffir campaigns of 1834-5 under Sir Benjamin D'Urban (Medal).

24 Major General Foster was actively employed in Canada during the rebellion in 1837, 8, and 9; and was favourably noticed in the Dispatches of the Commander of the Forces, and upon the special recommendation of Sir John Colborne received for his services the Brevet rank of Major.

25 Colonel Alex. Gordon served, as senior officer, in Demerara, during the insurrection of the Negroes, in 1823 and 1824. He was mentioned in General Orders, and received the thanks of the Court of Policy of the United Colony of Demerara and Essequibo.

26 Colonel Marlow was commanding Royal Engineer at the storming of Kawiti's Pah at Owrawui in New Zealand on the 1st July 1845, and the subsequent destruction of the same. Also at the burning of Aretua's Pah, and at the storming of Kawiti's Pah on the 11th Jan. 1846; for these services he received the Brevet rank of Major.

27 Colonel Walpole commanded the Royal Engineers on the eastern frontier of the Cape of Good Hope during the Kaffir war of 1846-7, was twice wounded on the 8th June 1846 (Medal and Brevet Major).

29 Colonel Durnford served as Executive Engineer in the combined Naval and Military expedition up the Canton River in April 1847, and was present at the capture of eight Forts, viz.:—North and South Wangtong, at the Bocca Tigris ; Pachow and Wookongtap, at the Barrier; Zig-zag, Segment, Shameen, and Dutch Folly, at Canton.

30 Colonel Lloyd served with the Army of the East from May to Oct. 1855 as Commanding Royal Engineer at Constantinople, and from 14th Oct. to the termination of hostilities as Commanding Royal Engineer with the Army in the Crimea, during which period the total destruction of the Docks at Sebastopol was effected under his directions. He has the Crimean Medal, and is a Knight of the Legion of Honor.

31 Colonel Skyring served the Syrian campaign of 1840-41 (Medal).

33 Colonel Hadden was actively employed in Canada during the Rebellion in 1837-39, and was engaged with the rebels at St. Eustache and St. Benoit.

35 Colonel John W. Gordon served the Eastern campaign of 1854 and up to July 1855, including the battle of Alma, and siege of Sebastopol (Medal and Clasps, Brevets of Major, Lt.Col., and Colonel, *C.B.*, Officer of the Legion of Honor, Sardinian Medal, and 3rd Class of the Medjidie).

37 Lt.Colonel Robertson served in command of the Royal Sappers and Miners in B. Kaffraria during the Kaffir war of 1850-3, and was several times mentioned in General Orders (Medal, and Brevet Major).

38 Colonel Chapman proceeded on a special mission to Constantinople in Jan. 1854,

Was employed surveying the positions at Bulair, Adrianople, and Buguk Tchekmadgie, previous to the arrival of the British forces in Turkey; was attached to the 1st Division, and accompanied it to Bulgaria, and Bulganak, and M'Kenzie's Farm; also present at the battles of Alma and Inkerman. Served throughout the siege of Sebastopol, during the early part of which he was Director of the left attack, and in the latter part he was executive Engineer to the Forces. Was several times mentioned in official Dispatches, and received the Brevet ranks of Major, Lt.Colonel, and Colonel, *CB.*, Medal and three Clasps, Officer of the Legion of Honor, Sardinian Medal, and 3rd Class of the Medjidie.

41 Major St. George Ord served as Brigade Major in the combined French and English expedition to the Baltic in 1854, and was at the siege and capture of Bomarsund, for which he received Brevet rank.

42 Colonel Simmons was employed for three years in the disputed territory on the N.E. frontier of the United States in constructing works for its defence and in making military explorations. Happening to be in Turkey in 1853 he was specially employed by Lord Stratford de Redcliffe on several important services: joined Omer Pasha in March 1854; escorted the new Governor into Silistria after the former one had been killed, and was present during part of the siege of that fortress; laid out and threw up the lines of Slobodzie and Georgevo on the Danube, having entire charge of the operation with 20,000 men of all arms under his command, a Russian army of 70,000 men being within seven miles: was present during the occupation of Wallachia and had frequent charge of reconnaissances upon the enemy's rear. Went to the Crimea in Dec. 1854 to concert with the allied Commanders in Chief as to the movements of the Turkish army: was present at the battle of Eupatoria, laid out and threw up the entrenched camp round that place; afterwards was before Sebastopol from April 1855 until after its fall, and then went to Mingrelia and was present at the forced passage of the Ingur, where he commanded the division which crossed the river and turned the enemy's position capturing his works and guns: Omer Pasha in his dispatch attributed the success of the day chiefly to Lieut.Col. Simmons. He served as Her Majesty's Commissioner to the Ottoman army throughout the war and was employed in all the negotiations having reference to the movements of Omar Pasha's army. Has received the Crimean Medal and Clasp, the Turkish Gold Medal for the Danubian campaign, the Order of Medjidie 3rd Class, and a Sword of Honor from the Turkish Government; also the 4th Class of the Legion of Honor.

45 Colonel Bent went to Turkey with the Eastern expedition in April 1854; served with the Turkish army on the Danube from June to Dec. 1854, and was present at the battle of Giurgevo. Served at the siege and fall of Sebastopol from Jun. 1855,—for the last six months as Director of the left attack (Medal and Clasps, Brevets of Major and Lt.Col., and *CB.*; also the Order of Medjidie, and Turkish Gold Medal, and a Knight of the French Legion of Honor).

46 Lt.Colonel Owen served at the Cape of Good Hope in the campaign against the insurgent Boers in 1845, and in the Kaffir war of 1846-7 (Medal). Served in the Crimea from Feb. to May 1855, and lost left leg at the siege of Sebastopol (Medal and Clasps, *CB.*, Officer of the Legion of Honor, and 5th Class of the Medjidie).

47 Major Jervois served at the Cape of Good Hope during the Kaffir war of 1846-7, and made a military sketch of 2000 square miles of Kaffirland,—1,100 of which he surveyed during the war.

49 Major Hon. H. F. Keane served in the Crimea from 31 Dec. 1854, including the siege and fall of Sebastopol, and battle of the Tchernaya (Medal and Clasp, and 5th Class of the Medjidie).

50 Major Gibb served at the Cape of Good Hope from August 1841 to April 1848 accompanied the overland expedition to Port Natal, and commanded the Royal Engineers during all the operations connected with the capture of that settlement in May and June 1842. Served the Eastern campaign from Nov. 1854, including the siege and fall of Sebastopol (Medal, and 5th Class of the Medjidie).

52 Major Hassard served the Eastern campaign from Nov. 1854, including the siege and fall of Sebastopol, sortie 11th May, and expedition to Kertch and Yenikale (Medal, Brevet Major, Sardinian Medal, and 5th Class of the Medjidie).

55 Major Lovell served the Eastern campaign up to Nov. 1854, and was present at the battle of the Alma and siege of Sebastopol (Medal and Clasps, Brevet of Major, 5th Class of the Medjidie, and Turkish Medal).

56 Lt.Col. Bourchier served in the Kaffir campaign of 1846, during a portion of which he commanded a Native levy (Medal). Served throughout all the operations of the Eastern campaign of 1854-55, including the battles of Alma and Inkerman, and as Brigade Major to the Royal Engineers at the siege and fall of Sebastopol — wounded (Medal and three Clasps, Brevets of Major and Lt.Colonel, *CB.*, Knight of the Legion of Honor, and 5th Class of the Medjidie).

57 Lt.Col. Browne served for nearly six months in the trenches before Sebastopol; was present at the repulse of sorties on 22nd March and 5th April; was engaged at the capture and defence of the Quarries, and senior Engineer Officer employed forming lodgments in and communications to that outwork, for which service he was honourably mentioned in Dispatches, and received the Brevet of Major. Succeeded Colonel Tylden as Directing Engineer of the right attack, and in the execution of the duties of that appointment was severely wounded by a rifle ball on 24th August,—left arm broken, shot through the shoulder, and jaw injured (Medal and Clasp, Brevets of Major and Lt.Col., *CB.*, Knight of the Legion of Honor, Sardinian Medal, and 5th Class of the Medjidie).

War Services of the Officers of the Royal Engineers.

59 Lt.Col. Montagu served the Eastern campaign of 1854-55, including the battles of Alma and Inkerman; also at the siege of Sebastopol until 2nd March, when he was taken prisoner during a sortie, but discharged, and afterwards present at the fall of Sebastopol (Medal and Clasps, Brevets of Major and Lt.Col., Knight of the Legion of Honor, Sardinian Medal, and 5th Class of the Medjidie).

61 Major Cooke served in the Crimea from July 1855, including the siege and fall of Sebastopol (Medal and Clasps, Brevet Major, and 5th Class of the Medjidie).

63 Major Stokes served in the Kaffir Wars of 1846-47 and 1850-51 (Medal); was thanked by the Commander in Chief for gallant conduct in the action of the Gwanga on 8 June 1846, and again on 25th July for opening communication through the heart of the enemy's country. In 1851 was appointed D.A.Q.M. General of the Field Force and assisted to organize some 3000 Hottentot Levies, and was engaged in all the operations of the Division from Feb. to July 1851, and repeatedly mentioned in General Orders. In 1855 was appointed Chief Engineer to the Turkish Contingent and raised and organized the Engineer Corps and Train of that force. Was employed in fortifying Kertch during the winter of 1855-56 (Brevet Major, and 4th Class of the Medjidie). In July 1856 was appointed Her Majesty's Commissioner for the Danube, under the Treaty of Paris.

64 Major Du Cane served in the Crimea from 13th April to 2d Sept. 1855, including the siege of Sebastopol (Medal and Clasp, and Brevet of Major).

65 Lt.Col. Stanton was attached to the Q. M. G.'s Staff with the expedition across the Orange River under Sir George Cathcart in 1852, and was present at the action of Berea. Served the Eastern campaign of 1854-55, including the attack on the Port of Odessa, the battles of Alma and Inkerman, and siege of Sebastopol (Medal and Clasps, Brevets of Major and Lt.Col., *CB.*, Knight of the Legion of Honor, Sardinian Medal, and 5th Class of the Medjidie).

67 Major Armit served at the siege of Sebastopol from Feb. to July 1855, and was severely wounded in the batteries on the 4th April (Medal and Clasp, and 5th Class of the Medjidie).

68 Major Ewart proceeded to Turkey on special service in Jan. 1854; joined the army in the East on its arrival, and served with it uninterruptedly until its return in June 1856, including one year as Major of Brigade, R.E. (Medal with four Clasps, Brevet Major, Knight of the Legion of Honor, Sardinian Medal, and 5th Class of the Medjidie).

71 Major Porter served the Crimean campaign from Feb. to May 1855, including the siege of Sebastopol (Medal and Clasp, Brevet Major, and 5th Class of the Medjidie).

73 Captain E. M. Grain served in the trenches before Sebastopol during the winter of 1854-55 (Medal and Clasp).

75 Major Ravenhill served the Eastern campaign of 1854-55, including the battles of Alma and Inkerman, and siege of Sebastopol (Medal and Clasps, and 5th Class of the Medjidie).

76 Lt.Colonel Nicholson served at the siege and fall of Sebastopol from August 1855, commanded 4th Company R.E. at Kinbourn, and was in immediate directions of the works for the destruction of Sebastopol Dockyard (Medal and Clasp, Brevet Major, and 5th Class of the Medjidie). Served in the Indian campaign from 12th Dec. 1857 to 23rd Dec. 1858 and was present at the capture of Lucknow (Brevet of Lt.Colonel, *CB.*, Medal and Clasp), has been frequently mentioned in despatches.

77 Major Sedley served at the siege of Sebastopol from June to September 1855 (Medal and Clasp, Brevet Major, and 5th Class of the Medjidie).

79 Captain Fowler served throughout the Kaffir war of 1851-53 (Medal).

80 Major de Vere proceeded to Turkey on special service in Feb. 1854; joined the Eastern army in May, and served with it throughout the campaign of 1854-55, and was present at the battles of Alma and Inkerman, siege and fall of Sebastopol (Medal and Clasps, Brevet Major, Knight of the Legion of Honor, Sardinian Medal, and 5th Class of the Medjidie).

82 Capt. Brine served as a volunteer the campaign of 1855, including the siege and fall of Sebastopol; did duty in the trenches of the right attack (Medal and Clasp).

83 Major Fisher served at the siege of Sebastopol in 1855, and led a storming party in the assault of the 18th June (Medal and Clasp, Knight of the Legion of Honor, and 5th Class of the Medjidie).

84 Major Stopford served in the Eastern campaign of 1854-55, including the battles of Alma, Balaklava, and Inkerman, and siege of Sebastopol, as Aide de Camp to Sir John Burgoyne (Medal and Clasps, Sardinian Medal, and 4th Class of the Medjidie, and Turkish Medal). Was charged with organising and laying down the Field Electric Telegraph in the Crimea.

86 Captain Whitmore was selected for service as Senior Captain of the Engineer Corps attached to the Turkish Contingent in May 1855, and served with it in the Crimea from October until June following, commanding Engineers at Yenikale during the winter of 1855-56, and selected to organise the Turkish Corps of Engineers, which he commanded with the rank of Kaimakam (Lieut.Colonel) until the force was handed over to the Sultan. Has received the 4th Class of the Medjidie.

87 Major Elphinstone served the Eastern campaign of 1854-55, including the battles in the Crimea, siege and fall of Sebastopol (Medal and Clasp, Knight of the Legion of Honor, and 5th Class of the Medjidie).

90 Captain Creyke served in the Crimea from Sept. to Nov. 1854, including the siege of Sebastopol (Medal and Clasp, and Turkish Medal).

91 Captain Lempriere served with the Army in Turkey, Bulgaria, and the Crimea, in 1854-55, including the battle of Inkerman and siege of Sebastopol: served also under Selim Pacha in 1854 at Radut Kall, Charakou, Soukam-Kall, &c. (Medal and Clasps, and Turkish Medal).

93 Lt. Colonel Lennox landed in the Crimea in Oct. 1854, and was present at the four bombardments of Sebastopol and battle of Inkerman (Medal and two Clasps, Victoria Cross, Sardinian Medal, and 5th Class of the Medjidie).

94 Major Leahy joined the Army of the East at Varna, and served throughout the campaign of 1854-55, latterly as D.A.Q.M.G. to the Royal Engineers (Medal and three Clasps, Sardinian Medal, and 5th Class of the Medjidie).

95 Captain Stuart served during the operations of 1856-58 at Canton; was present at the capture and demolition of French Folly Fort and at the formation of defensive position at the Factories; led the French Storming Party at the assault of Canton, and was thanked by the French Naval Commander in Chief.

96 Captain Philips served in the Crimea from Sept. 1854 to Feb. 1855 (Medal and Clasps, and 5th Class of the Medjidie).

97 Captain Martin served at the siege of Sebastopol from Sept. 1854 to Feb. 1855 (Medal and Clasp, Knight of the Legion of Honor, and 5th Class of the Medjidie).

98 Major Cowell embarked on board the Baltic Fleet with a detachment of Royal Sappers and Miners in Feb. 1854; in July was appointed Aide de Camp to Brigadier General Harry Jones, and served as such at the operations against Bomarsund (Baltic Medal); accompanied General Jones as Aide de Camp to the Crimea in Jan. 1855, and continued with him until his return to England (Medal with Clasp for Sebastopol, Knight of the Legion of Honor, and 5th Class of the Medjidie).

99 Captain Graham served at the siege of Sebastopol and assault of the Redan on the 18th June 1855 (Medal and Clasp, Victoria Cross, Knight of the Legion of Honor, and 5th Class of the Medjidie).

100 Captain Drake served at the siege of Sebastopol from Nov. 1854 to May 1855 (Medal and Clasp, Knight of the Legion of Honor, and 5th Class of the Medjidie).

101 Captain Pratt served during the operations crossing the Danube in July 1854, and received the Turkish Gold Medal for that campaign. Served during the Crimean campaign until the end of May 1855 (Medal and Clasp, Sardinian Medal, and 5th Class of the Medjidie).

102 Captain James served at the siege of Sebastopol from Feb. 1855 until taken prisoner of war on 2nd July (Medal and Clasp, and 5th Class of the Medjidie). Was attached to the Turco-Russian Boundary Commissions in Bessarabia and Asia in 1856-57.

103 Captain Gordon served in the trenches before Sebastopol from Dec. 1854 to the close of the siege (wounded on 6th June 1855). Accompanied the column under Sir John Campbell at the attack of the Redan on the 18th June; accompanied the Company of Sappers attached to the expedition to Kinbourn, and present at the surrender of that fort. Was employed in the demolition of the docks of Sebastopol; and subsequently employed on the Turco-Russian Boundary Commissions in Bessarabia and Asia in 1856-57 (Medal and Clasp, Knight of the Legion of Honor, and Turkish Medal).

104 Captain Stokes served at the siege of Sebastopol from Sept. 1854 to March 1855 (Medal and Clasp).

105 Captain Donnelly served throughout the Eastern campaign of 1854-55, including the battles in the Crimea, siege and fall of Sebastopol (Medal and Clasps, and Knight of the Legion of Honor).

106 Captain Scott served at the siege of Sebastopol in June 1855 (Medal and Clasp).

107 Captain Dumaresq served during 1855 at the siege and fall of Sebastopol; did duty in the trenches of the right attack (Medal and Clasp).

108 Captain Scratchley served at the siege and fall of Sebastopol from Aug. 1855 (Medal and Clasp).

109 Captain Kelsall served at the siege of Sebastopol, right attack, from Aug. 1855 (Medal and Clasp).

110 Lieut. Darrah served at the siege of Sebastopol from June to Aug. 1855 (Medal and Clasp).

111 Lieut. Newsome has received the 5th Class of the Medjidie.

112 Captain Edwards served in the Crimea from 14th Sept. 1855, and was employed in the demolition of the Docks of Sebastopol, and has received the Crimean and Turkish Medals. Served in India in 1857-59, and commanded a Company of the Royal Engineers throughout the campaign in Central India under Sir Hugh Rose, was present at the siege and storming of Chandairee, siege and storming of Jhansi, actions of the Betwah, Koonch, and Goolowlee, capture of Calpee, action before and capture of Gwalior, and present at the capture of Tantia Topee and commanded the only Europeans there (several times mentioned in despatches, Medal).

113 Captain Longley was dangerously wounded at the attack on the forts at the mouth of the Peiho on the 25th June 1859.

411

Corps of Royal Marines. (Light Infantry.)

"GIBRALTAR"—The *Globe*, with the motto "*Per Mare, per Terram.*" The Crown—The Anchor & Laurel—The Cypher of George the Fourth.

(Post in the Line, between the 49th and 50th Regiments.)

Division	Year's Full Pay	Serv. Half Pay		2ND LIEUT.	1ST LIEUT.	CAPTAIN.	MAJOR.	LIEUT.-COLONEL.	COLONEL.	COL. COM-MANDANT.	MAJOR-GENERAL.	LIEUT.-GENERAL.	GENERAL.
			GENERALS.										
..	58	4 6/12	ȹ Charles Menzies,¹ KH.	17 Feb. 98	21 Dec. 03	13 Apr. 13	10 Jan. 37	10 July 37	10 July 44	17 Aug. 48	20 June 54	20 June 55	1 July 57
..	57	0	Ł John Rawlins Coryton²	6 July 03	15 Aug. 05	31 July 26	23 Nov. 41	6 May 44	25 May 49	23 Dec. 51	20 June 55	6 Feb. 57	8 Sept. 58
			LIEUTENANT-GENERALS.										
..	56	0	Ṯ Samuel Burdon Ellis,³ CB. ..	1 Jan. 04	29 Apr. 06	15 Nov. 26	6 May 41	26 May 41	3 Nov. 51	18 Oct. 52	20 June 55	20 Feb. 57	
..	53	2 10/12	Ṯ Thomas Wearing⁴	5 May 04	24 Apr. 07	20 Dec. 27	23 Nov. 41	18 Dec. 46	20 Nov. 51	9 June 54	do	1 July 57	
..	49	7	James Irwin Willes⁵	12 Nov. 04	27 July 08	15 Oct. 29	6 May 42	4 Jan. 48	18 Oct. 52	1 Aug. 54	do	8 Sept. 58	
			MAJOR-GENERALS.										
..	44	10 3/4	ȹ Henry Ivatt Delacombe⁶	21 Oct. 05	30 June 09	12 Oct. 32	9 Nov. 46	25 May 49	9 June 54	22 June 55	14 July 55		
..	50	4 4/12	ȹ John Alexander Philips⁷ ..	26 Aug. 06	17 July 13	27 May 34	do	4 Sept. 51	1 Aug. 54	do	6 Feb. 57		
..	51	1	ȹ Fortescue Graham,⁸ CB.	17 Nov. 08	6 May 25	10 July 37	11 Nov. 51	26 Nov. 51	20 June 54	do	20 Feb. 57		
..	51	0	ȹ S. Robt. Wesley,⁹ *Dep.Adj.G.*	26 June 09	24 Nov. 27	16 Nov. 37	do	23 Nov. 52	13 Dec. 54	30 Oct. 55	1 July 57		
..	44	4 11/12	John Tatton Brown¹⁰	21 May 11	14 Nov. 29	28 Feb. 39	do	13 Dec. 52	22 June 55	22 June 55	8 Sept. 58		
			COLONELS COMMANDANT.										
Wo.	37	0	Anthony B. Stransham¹⁴	1 Jan. 23	12 Oct. 32	12 Feb. 42	15 Apr. 42	9 June 54	28 Nov. 54	8 Sept. 58			
Cha.	37	0	Edward Rea¹⁵	3 Feb. 23	do	19 Mar. 42	20 June 54	21 June 54	6 Feb. 57	11 Aug. 59			
Por.	37	0	Alexander Anderson¹⁶	13 May 23	12 Oct. 32	5 May 42	20 June 54	7 July 54	20 Feb. 57	21 Nov. 59			
Art.	36	0	John Fraser¹⁷	8 May 24	23 Apr. 33	29 Sept. 42	do	21 Oct. 54	1 April 57	21 Nov. 59			
Ply.	35	0	Thomas Holloway,¹⁸ CB.	17 Mar. 25	9 Dec. 33	23 Nov. 42	do	20 Nov. 54	13 Mar. 57	21 Nov. 59			
			COLONELS 2ND COMMANDANT.										
Wo.	34	0	Fielding Alex. Campbell¹⁹	23 Sept. 26	27 May 34	21 Sept. 42	20 June 54	21 Feb. 55	21 Feb. 58				
Cha.	34	0	George Evans Hunt²⁰	16 Dec. 26	do	3 May 44	..	do	do				
Por.	33	0	John Mitchell²¹	5 Oct. 27	29 Nov. 34	6 May 44	..	22 June 55	22 June 58				
Ply.	33	0	Thomas Lemon,²² CB.	8 Oct. 27	5 Feb. 35	10 July 44	..	do	13 Apr. 58				
			LIEUTENANT COLONELS.										
Cha.	33	0	Thomas Charles Cotton Moore²³	4 Dec. 27	26 Oct. 35	31 Oct. 44	..	22 June 55	22 June 58				
Wo.	32	0	Art.SandysStawellWalsh,²⁴†CB.	12 Apr. 28	6 Dec. 36	26 Aug. 46	..	28 June 56					
Ply.	32	0	John George Augustus Ayles²⁴	13 May 28	10 Jan. 37	10 Oct. 46	..	5 July 56					
Cha.	32	0	John Hawkins Gascoigne²⁴	4 June 28	23 May 37	9 Nov. 46	..	6 Feb. 57					
Cha.	31	0	Robert John M'Killop²⁵	4 Mar. 29	10 July 37	9 Dec. 46	..	do					
Wo.	31	0	Wm. Friend Hopkins,²⁶ CB. ⎫ (c. 20 Dec. 59) ⎭	27 Apr. 29	do	20 Apr. 47	12 Dec. 54	6 Feb. 57	20 Dec. 59				

Royal Marines.

Division	Years' Serv. Full Pay.	Half Pay.	LIEUTENANT-COLONELS.	2ND LIEUT.	FIRST LIEUT.	CAPTAIN.	BREV.-MAJ.	LIEUT.-COL.	COLONEL.
Art.	31	0	Henry Carr Tate	30 June 29	10 July	4 May 47		6 Feb. 57	14 Dec. 57
Art.	31	0	George Colt Langley [27] (c. 14 Dec. 57)	30 June	do	do 47	13 Dec. 54	20 Feb. 57	
Ply.	30	0	Edward Hocker,[29] CB.	30 Jan. 30	do	27 July		1 April 57	
Por.	30	0	Simon Fraser[30]	23 Feb.	do	do	12 Dec. 54	25 Feb. 58	
Cha.	30	0	William Henry March[33]	20 Nov.	do	11 Aug. 47	do	14 July 59	
Por.	29	0	Gallway Byng Payne[34]	17 May 31	· do	4 Dec.	do	11 Aug. 59	
Por.	29	0	Joseph Oates Travers,[35] Assist. Adjt. Gen.	10 Sept.	do	27 Dec.	13 Apr. 58	8 Sept. 59	
Ply.	28	0	Robert Murray Curry[36]	22 Feb. 32	do	4 Jan. 48		7 July 59	
Wo.	28	0	Edward Stanley Browne	19 Mar.	28 Sept. 37	4 May		12 July	
Por.	28	0	William Robert Maxwell[38]	11 July	15 Dec. 37	17 May		11 Aug.	
Ply.	28	0	Thomas Dudley Fosbroke[39]	30 Nov. 32	1 Jan. 38	17 May 48	17 Oct. 59	21 Nov. 59	
Wo.	27	0	Charles Joseph Hadfield[40]	15 Feb. 33	26 Apr. 38	do	25 Oct. 59	10 Dec. 59	
Por.	27	0	Richard Carr Spalding[41]	7 May 33	4 May 38	do	7 Dec. 59	20 Dec. 59	
			CAPTAINS.						
Cha.	27	0	Hayes Marriott,[42] r.	11 Oct. 33	16 June 38	17 May 48	12 Dec. 54		
Por.	27	0	Samuel Netterville Lowder,[43] Inst. of Musketry	1 Nov. 33	7 Nov. 38	do	2 Nov. 55		
Por.	26	0	Edw.T.ParkerShewen[47] Inst. of Gunnery	28 Feb. 34	7 Feb. 40	31 Aug. 48			
Wo.	26	0	George Lambrick,[48] r.	14 Mar. 34	2 Mar. 40	1 Oct. 48			
Cha.	25	0	Richard Geo. Connolly, Inst. of Gunnery	26 Dec.	13 Nov. 40	25 Apr. 49			
Por.	25	0	Augustus Dover Lyddon Farrant,[50] r.	31 July 35	do.	1 May 49			
Ply.	23	0	Chas. Ogilvy Hamley,[52] Inst. of Musketry	27 Feb. 37	20 Jan. 41	21 Aug. 49	12 Dec. 54		
Por.	23	0	Wm. Stratton Aslett,[53] r.	26 July 37	5 Mar. 41	3 Oct. 49	13 Apr. 58		
Ply.	23	0	William Francis Foote,[54] r.	1 Aug. 37	29 Mar. 41	16 Nov. 49			
Por.	23	0	Wm. Grigor Suther,[55] Inst. of Musketry	do	11 May 41	28 Feb. 50			
Por.	23	0	William Ramsay Searle[57]	17 Oct. 37	do	28 Feb. 51			
Wo.	23	0	Charles Louis[59]	21 Nov. 37	13 May 41	23 May 51	15 Sept. 58		
Wo.	23	0	Richard King Clavell,[60] Inst. of Gunnery	do	3 July 41	23 May 51			
Wo.	23	0	Penrose Charles Penrose[62]	19 Dec. 37		22 Sept. 51			
Cha.	23	0	Geo. Brydges Rodney,[63] Inst. of Musketry						
Art.	23	0	John Maurice Wemyss,[64] CB.	19 Dec. 37	14 Aug. 41	6 Oct. 51	2 Nov. 55	31 May 59	
Cha.	22	0	Peregrine Henry Fellowes, r.	31 Mar. 38	30 Oct. 41	12 Nov. 51	do.		
Wo.	22	0	Wm. Christ. Parkin Elliott[66] r.	8 May 38	12 Feb. 42	19 Nov. 51	8 Sept. 54		

Royal Marines. 413

Div.	Years' Serv. F.p.	H.p.	CAPTAINS.	2ND LIEUT.	1ST LIEUT.	CAPTAIN.	
Ply.	22	0	Charles William Adair,[67] r	8 May 38	12 Feb. 42	26 Nov.	51
Ply.	22	0	William Jolliffe [68]	12 June 38	19 Mar.	10 Jan.	52
Por.	22	0	Robert Seppings Harrison,[69] r.	do	5 May	14 Jan.	
Art.	22	0	G. G. Alexander,[71] CB. l. c. 2 Nov. 55	14 Aug. 38	17 June	19 Jan.	52
Por.	22	0	Charles Frederick Menzies[72]	21 Aug.	27 June	14 June	52
Cha.	22	0	John Huskisson [74]	4 Dec.	18 July	17 Aug.	
Cha.	22	0	John Henry Stewart,[75] r.	18 Dec. 38	17 Aug.	18 Oct.	
Cha.	22	0	David Blyth[76]	do	29 Sept.	13 Nov.	52
Cha.	21	0	James Ainslie Stewart,[78] r............	11 May 39	21 Nov.	23 Nov.	52
Por.	21	0	James Pickard [79]	do	23 Nov.	do	
Cha.	21	0	Henry Charles Penrose Dyer[80]	11 May 39	23 Nov.	13 Dec.	52
Ply.	21	0	Wm. Alfred G. Wright[82] *Inst. of Gunnery*	24 Sept.	12 April 43	18 Jan.	53
Ply.	20	0	George Wentworth Forbes............	17 Nov. 40	12 Aug. 43	8 April	
Por.	23	0	Jermyn Charles Symonds [83]	19 Dec. 37	17 Aug. 41	26 April	
Art.	19	0	G. Aug. Schomberg,[84] *Maj.* 2 Nov. 55; *l.c.* 15 Sept. 58, *Instructor of Laboratory.*	16 Mar. 41	21 Sept. 43	1 July	
Ply.	19	0	Fleetwood John Richards, r	do	3 May 44	15 Aug.	53
Cha.	19	0	Hugh Hamilton Goold	do	6 May	do	
Cha.	19	0	Arthur Butcher	do	10 July	do	
Ply.	19	0	George Drury[64]†	do	12 July	18 Oct.	53
Cha.	19	0	Edward Andrée Wylde [85]	18 May 41	21 Dec.	17 Feb.	54
Wo.	19	0	Ebenezer Tristram Thomas Jones......	15 June 41	21 Jan. 45	24 Feb.	54
Por.	19	0	Joseph Henry Jolliffe[85]†	do	do	do	
Wo.	19	0	John William Alexander Kennedy[86] ...	do	do	do	
Por.	19	0	Rob. Boyle,[87] *Maj.* 28 Aug. 57; *l.c.* 16 Aug. 59	do	do	do	
Ply.	19	0	Simon Ridley Little[87]†	do	17 April 45	do	
Por.	19	0	John Elliott[88]	do	5 May	do	
Por.	19	0	Charles M'Arthur,[70] r	6 July 41	9 Aug.	do	
Por.	19	0	Hamond Weston Gwyn[69]	do	16 Aug.	do	
Art.	19	0	Chas. Loudon Barnard [90]	17 Aug. 41	18 Aug.	do	
Wo.	19	0	Henry George Johnstone Davies	do	7 April 46	do	
Wo.	19	0	Rodney Vansittart Allen [91]	do	do	do	
Ply.	19	0	Nevinson Willoughby de Courcy	do	11 Apr. 46	do	
Wo.	19	0	George Webb	31 Aug. 41	25 June	19 April	54
Ply.	19	0	William Mansell Mansell [86]	do	26 Aug.	28 April	
Cha.	18	0	Wm. Godfrey Rayson Masters [92]	15 Feb. 42	9 Nov.	21 June	
Wo.	18	0	Richard Parke,[93] *Major*, 13 Apr. 58	do	26 Nov.	7 July	
Por.	18	0	Thomas Magin [94]	19 April 42	24 Dec.	31 July	
Por.	18	0	Charles Slaughter[95]	do	20 April 47	1 Aug.	
Cha.	18	0	Fermor Bonnycastle Gritton [96]	17 May 42	10 May 47	21 Oct.	
Wo.	18	0	Henry John Tribe[97]	14 June	27 July 47	20 Nov.	
Art.	18	0	J. Wm. Collman Williams [98]	7 July 42	do	20 Nov.	
Art.	18	0	Hugh Stukely Buck	do	do	7 Dec.	
Ply.	18	0	Thomas Valentine Cooke,[99] *Major*, 15 Sept. 58	do	do	19 Dec.	
Art.	18	0	Geo. Stephen Digby,[100] CB., *Maj.* 2 Nov. 55	16 Aug. 42	do	27 Dec.	
Por.	18	0	William Edward Farmar	18 Oct. 42	do	13 Feb.	55
Cha.	18	0	J. Cha. Downie Morrison,[101] *Maj.* 15 Sept. 58	do	do	21 Feb.	
Cha.	18	0	Alfred De Hochepied Nepean	15 Dec. 42	do	1 March	55
Por.	18	0	George Edw. Owen Jackson,[102] *Maj.* 13 Apr. 58	27 Dec. 42	do	do	
Wo.	18	0	Edward Price Usher[103]............	do	do	29 March	55
Ply.	18	0	Michael Spratt [104]	do	do	22 June	55
Wo.	17	0	Julius Bunce	4 Jan. 43	do	do	
Ply.	17	0	Henry Treffry Fox [105]	15 Aug.	11 Aug. 47	do	
Wo.	17	0	Edward Lawes Pym [106].............	21 Aug.	25 Aug.	do	
Cha	16	0	Charles John Ellis,[107] *Major*, 15 Sept. 58 ..	16 Mar. 44	21 Dec.	14 July	55
Art.	16	0	William Sandom Davis [108]	3 May	21 Dec.	2 Aug.	
Ply.	16	0	Edmund Charles Domville [109]	6 May	27 Dec.	5 Sept.	
Ply.	16	0	Frederick Edward Budd [110]..........	17 July	4 Jan. 48	27 Sept.	
Por.	16	0	Benjamin Bousfield Herrick [110]†	27 Dec.	21 March 48	18 Dec.	55
Cha	16	0	Francis Harry Noott[111]	27 Dec. 44	27 May 48	28 June	56
Art.	15	0	William Pitt Draffen [112]	2 July 45	do	5 July	
Por.	15	0	William James Kinsman [110]	do	do	10 July	
Wo.	15	0	John Tunstall Haverfield, r..........	14 Oct. 45	do	16 Sept.	
Cha.	15	0	Ponsonby May Carew Croker[112]†......	16 Dec.	do	18 Oct.	
Cha.	15	0	George Bayles Heastey	29 Dec. 45	do	12 Dec.	
Por.	15	0	Henry Adair, *Artillery*, r.	do	do	19 Dec.	
Art.	15	0	Henry Way Mawbey [113]	do	do	3 Jan.	57

Royal Marines.

Div.	Years' Serv. F.p.	H.p.	CAPTAINS.	2ND LIEUT.	1ST LIEUT.	CAPTAIN.
Art.	14	0	Fred. Llewellyn Alexander[114]	16 Feb. 46	27 May 48	16 March 57
Ply.	14	0	John Basset Prynne[105]	5 May 46	do	1 April
Cha.	14	0	Charles Osborn Baker[115]	do	do	22 June
Wo.	14	0	Philip Harris[116]	18 Aug. 46	do	27 July
Ply.	14	0	William James Dunn, r.	do	do	1 Sept.
Cha.	14	0	John Horndon Parry	do	do	8 Sept.
Por.	14	0	Richard Kennett Willson..........	do	do	17 Oct.
Art.	14	0	Edmund Henry Cox[117]	do	do	2 Dec.
Wo.	14	0	Edmund Brighouse Snow[110]†	do	do	2 Dec.
Cha.	14	0	James Taylor	do	do	1 Feb. 58
Ply.	14	0	John Barlow Butcher[118]	28 Dec. 46	do	do
Art.	14	0	Edward Henderson Starr [119]	do	do	2 Feb. 58
Wo.	13	0	Edward Joseph Ridgway Connolly[120] ...	16 Feb. 47	do	25 Feb.
Art.	13	0	Edward Ralph Horsey[121]	do	do	3 July
Wo.	13	0	Arthur Ellis [122]	20 Apr. 47	do	14 July
Ply.	13	0	George Bazalgette[97]	10 May 47	do	11 Aug.
Cha.	13	0	Edward Gough M'Callum[123]	do	do	11 Aug.
Art.	13	0	Richard Turberville Ansell [121]	do	do	8 Sept.
Art.	13	0	George Henry Wriford [121]	do	do	10 Dec.
Art.	13	0	John Poore [125]	do	12 June 48	19 Jan. 59
Por.	13	0	George Gregory [126]............	3 Aug. 47	8 Aug.	19 Feb.
Wo.	13	0	Henry George Elliot [127]	do	17 Aug.	7 March 59
Art.	13	0	Henry Hewett [128]	20 Sept. 47	28 Aug.	14 April 59
Por.	13	0	Edward M'Arthur [129]........	do	31 Aug.	do
Por.	13	0	Henry Bradley Roberts [130]	18 Oct. 47	1 Oct.	do
Ply.	13	0	James Shute[131]	do	11 Oct.	do
Wo.	13	0	John Busteed Seymour[132]	9 Dec. 47	26 Oct.	do
Wo.	13	0	Arthur John Stuart	14 Dec. 47	1 March 49	do
Cha.	13	0	Charles Barker Parke[133]	30 Dec. 47	9 March	do
Ply.	13	0	John Yate Holland[134]	do	5 April	do
Por.	13	0	Nugent Macnamara [135]........	do	25 April	4 May 59
Cha.	12	0	Archibald Alex. Douglas,[136] *Maj*. 17 June 59	12 Feb. 48	25 May	7 May 59
Cha.	12	0	Charles Loftus Tottenham Usher [137]	do	do	do
Por.	12	0	George Lascelles Blake [138]	do	12 July 49	do
Wo.	12	0	Osborne Frederick Charles Fraser[139]	14 Mar. 48	11 Aug.	do
Ply.	12	0	William Henry Worthy Bennett[140]	do	21 Aug.	do
Ply.	12	0	George Leslie	do	19 Sept.	do
Wo.	12	0	William Penn Burton[141]	16 May 48	16 Nov.	do
Wo.	12	0	Nicholas Bennett Dalby[142]	do	20 Jan. 50	do
Por.	12	0	Enbule Daysh Thelwall [143]	29 June 48	28 Feb. 51	do
Ply.	12	0	Richard Pentland Henry[145]........	do	23 May	do
Cha.	12	0	Charles Louis Atterbury Farmar,[146]	do	24 July	25 May 59
Por.	12	0	Charles Jolliffe [147]	do	4 Sept. 51	do
Ply.	12	0	Henry Lindsay Searle [148]	do	do	7 July 59
Cha.	12	0	Harry Lewis Evans[149]	do	17 Sept. 51	12 July
Ply.	12	0	William Richard Jeffreys[150]	25 July	6 Oct.	11 Aug.
Wo.	12	0	V⚔ George Dare Dowell,[151]	25 July 48	6 Oct. 51	22 Sept.
Wo.	12	0	Theophilus Vaughton	15 Aug. 48	7 Nov.	7 Oct. 59
Ply.	12	0	William Taylor[153]	do	19 Nov.	8 Nov. 59
Por.	12	0	Horatio Nelson Charles Blanckley[140]	do	14 Jan. 52	do
Ply.	12	0	Edward Fitzgerald Pritchard[154]	19 Sept. 48	19 Jan.	15 Nov. 59
Ply.	12	0	Charles William Carrington[155]..........	do	23 Feb.	21 Nov.
Ply.	12	0	Robert William Bland Hunt[156]	do	13 March	22 Nov.
Cha.	12	0	John Frederick Hawkey[157]	do	10 May	8 Dec.
Por.	12	0	Edward Spry[158]......	do	14 June	10 Dec. 59
Wo.	12	0	Frederick George Pym[159]...........	do	14 June	20 Dec.
			FIRST LIEUTENANTS.			
Cha.	12	0	Henry Fallowfield Cooper,[160] *Quarterm*.	14 Nov. 48	17 Aug. 52	
Cha.	12	0	Joseph Hamilton Maskery,[161] *Adjutant*..	do	18 Sept.	
Cha.	12	0	William Henry Hore West[162]	do	18 Oct.	
Ply.	12	0	Henry Colton Mudge[163]	do	26 Oct.	
Wo.	12	0	Ambrose Wolrige,[164] *Quartermaster*	10 Dec. 48	13 Nov.	
Cha.	12	0	Thomas George Sholton Meheux[161].......	30 Dec. 48	23 Nov. 52	
Por.	12	0	William Tauzia Savary [165]..............	do	do	
Art.	12	0	George Brydges [167]	do	13 Dec. 52	
Por.	11	0	John Michael De Courcy Meade[168]......	20 Feb. 49	27 Dec.	
Wo.	11	0	George Oliver Evans[169].............	do	18 Jan. 53	
Por.	11	0	Francis Walton[170]........	do	19 Jan.	
Wo.	11	0	Richard John Hardy Douglas[171]	do	8 April	
Cha.	11	0	Jacob Richards Lloyd [172]	do	8 April	
Cha.	11	0	Frederick Herbert Ruel[173]	do	5 May	

Royal Marines.

Div.	Years' Serv F.p.	Years' Serv H.p.	First Lieutenants.	2nd Lieut.	1st Lieut.
Ply.	11	0	George Naylor,[171] *Adjutant*	20 Feb. 49	19 July 53
Cha.	11	0	Francis William Thomas,[175] *Adjutant*	28 June 49	15 Aug. 53
Cha.	11	0	Henry Dickonson Nightingale[176]	do	do
Cha.	11	0	John Cobb[177]	do	1 Sept. 53
Wo.	11	0	William Henry Clements[178]	do	18 Oct.
Cha.	11	0	Frederick William Arthur Boyd	do	21 Oct.
Cha.	11	0	Cuthbert Ward Burton,[179] *Quartermaster*	do	8 Dec.
Wo.	11	0	James Conway Travers,[180] *Adjutant*	14 Aug. 49	14 Feb. 54
Ply.	11	0	Frederick Lewis David	do	16 Feb.
Cha.	10	0	James Stirling Mould[182]	3 Jan. 50	17 Feb.
Art.	10	0	Fred. Augustus Foster,[183] *Qr.Master*	do	24 Feb. 54
Por.	10	0	Philip Harington,[165] *Adjutant*	do	do
Art.	10	0	Francis Worgan Festing,[184] *Adjutant*	3 July 50	do
Wo.	10	0	William Addis Delacombe[165]	do	do
Wo.	10	0	Henry Eyre Wyatt Lane[185]	30 Dec. 50	do
Por.	10	0	Wm. F. Portlock Scott Dadson,[186] *Qr.Master*	do	do
Wo.	10	0	Charles Frederick Short[187]	do	do
Ply.	10	0	Francis Lean,[188] *Adjutant*	do	do
Por.	9	0	John Blackwood Colwell[165]	4 Mar. 51	do
Ply.	9	0	Henry Swale[169]	20 April 51	do
Cha.	9	0	Cuthbert Fetherstone Daly[190]	26 June 51	do
Por.	9	0	William Sanders[191]	do	do
Art.	9	0	Edw. Congreve Langley Durnford,[192] *Adjutant*	30 Dec. 51	do
Art.	9	0	Edward Gladstone[193]	do	do
Ply.	9	0	Ussher Lee Morris,[180] *Adjutant*	do	do
Cha.	9	0	Arthur Charles Joshua M'Meekan[194]	do	do
Por.	9	0	George Frederick Walker[197]	do	do
Art.	8	0	William Pitman[195]	1 July 52	do
Ply.	8	0	Henry Laws Harrison[194]	do	do
Por.	8	0	Thomas Herbert Alexander Brenan[166]	20 July 52	do
Art.	8	0	Geoffrey Mairis[196]	27 Dec. 52	do
Art.	8	0	Charles Sidney Williams[132]†	do	do
Wo.	8	0	Charles Bullen Hugh Mitchell[197]	do	do
Por.	8	0	John Maitland Lennox,[198] *Adjutant*	do	do
Cha.	8	0	Thomas Bent[199]	do	do
Art.	8	0	John Wm. Henry Chafyn Grove Morris[132]	do	do
Art.	8	0	Francis Edward Halliday[121]	do	14 March 54
Wo.	8	0	Frederick Ley	do	21 March
Wo.	8	0	John Frederick Sanders[200]	do	19 April
Por.	8	0	James Pulteney Murray[201]	do	28 April
Ply.	7	0	Charles Hope Clendon[194]	18 April 53	8 May
Cha.	7	0	George Weatherall Thomas Hemmans[100]	do	9 June
Cha.	7	0	Fitzmaurice Creighton[137]	do	21 June
Ply.	7	0	Charles James Dundas Napier[202]	30 June 53	7 July
Ply.	7	0	Wingrove Laugharne Tinmouth[203]	do	19 July
Por.	7	0	Charles Bulkeley Nurse[204]	2 Aug. 53	31 July
Art.	7	0	Robert Woollcombe[121]	do	1 Aug.
Ply.	7	0	Jelinger Henry Symons[194]	3 Aug. 53	21 Oct.
Ply.	7	0	Howard Sutton Jones[194]	do	10 Nov.
Art.	7	0	Richard Augustus Fitzgerald Studdert[205]	30 Dec. 53	20 Nov. 54
Art.	7	0	Harry Boscawen Savage[206]	do	do
Cha.	7	0	Charles Francis Coppin[207]	do	4 Dec. 54
Por.	7	0	Robert Abernethie Brutton[208]	do	7 Dec.
Wo.	7	0	Albert Higman[132]		10 Dec.
Art.	6	0	Hollis Henry Nott[209]	7 Jan. 54	27 Dec.
Cha.	6	0	John Richard Mascall[132]	do	13 Feb. 55
Ply.	6	0	Anthony Malone	21 Jan. 54	21 Feb.
Wo.	6	0	Melville Suther[210]	do	21 Feb.
Ply.	6	0	Thomas Prothero Newall[185]	do	1 March 55
Por.	6	0	Frederick Gasper le Grand[211]	20 March 54	do
Wo.	6	0	Samuel James Graham[212]	do	do
Por.	6	0	Robert Frederick Tayler[213]	do	do
Ply.	6	0	James William Vaughan Arbuckle	do	do
Por.	6	0	Albert Henry Ozzard[214]	do	do
Por.	6	0	Edward Brace Pritchard[215]	do	do
Wo.	6	0	George Frederick Blake[194]	do	do
Wo.	6	0	Alexander Donellan[216]	do	29 March 55
Art.	6	0	Otway Wheeler Cuffe	do	10 April
Wo.	6	0	Henry Villiers Forbes[185]	do	2 June
Cha.	6	0	Ardley Henry Falwasser Barnes[217]	do	22 June 55
Art.	6	0	Henry Brasnell Tuson	19 April 54	do
Wo.	6	0	Gustavus Francis Munro	do	do

Royal Marines.

Division.	Years' Serv. F.p.	H.p.	FIRST LIEUTENANTS.	2ND LIEUT.	1ST LIEUT.
Ply.	6	0	Arthur Huntly Hill Walsh[132]	19 April 54	2 June 55
Ply.	6	0	Alex. Bassett Stephen Shairp[218]	do	do
Cha.	6	0	John Cairncross[219]	do	5 July 55
Por.	6	0	Henry Dixon[219]	do	10 July
Art.	6	0	Wm. Henry Townsend Morris Dodgin	do	14 July
Cha.	6	0	Charles Stark[220]	do	2 Aug.
Art.	6	0	John Chesterton Crawford[221]	24 June 54	2 Aug.
Art.	6	0	John Charles Ready Colomb	do	2 Aug.
Cha.	6	0	Morgan Henry Price[220]	do	5 Sept.
Ply.	6	0	James Smail[222]	do	27 Sept.
Ply.	6	0	John Delves Broughton[223]	do	24 Nov.
Por.	6	0	Ponsonby Ross Holmes[224]	do	18 Dec.
Ply.	6	0	Alfred Henry Pascoe[225]	do	1 March 56
Art.	6	0	Robert Ballard Gardner	25 Sept. 54	22 March
Cha.	6	0	Lennox George Rodney[226]	do	4 June
Por.	6	0	Daniel Conner[227]	do	28 June
Por.	6	0	William Henry Wroot[228]	do	5 July
Por.	6	0	Charles Durham Hocart Robilliard[229]	do	10 July
Art.	11	0	Joshua Rowland Brookes[229]†	28 June 49	11 July
Por.	6	0	William Godfrey Hale[227]	25 Sept. 54	24 July
Ply.	9	0	Joseph George Shanks[230]	30 Dec. 51	24 Feb. 54
Cha.	6	0	Edward Willis[231]	25 Sept. 54	5 Aug. 56
Ply.	6	0	Francis Joseph Parry[232]	do	16 Sept.
Wo.	6	0	Charles Edward Macdonald[233]	do	18 Oct.
Ply.	6	0	William Henry Speer[231]	do	7 Nov.
Art.	6	0	John Frederick Crease[221]	20 Dec. 54	12 Dec.
Art.	6	0	Colpoys Parkyns Heaslop	do	19 Dec.
Cha.	6	0	John Martley Sadleir[219]	24 June 54	18 Sept. 55
Wo.	6	0	Charles Hugh Standbridge[226]	20 Dec. 54	6 Oct. 57
Por.	6	0	Vernon William Sims	do	17 Oct.
Wo.	6	0	Rose Lambert Price[238]†	do	28 Nov.
Por.	6	0	Horatio Guy Campbell[233]	do	2 Dec.
Wo.	6	0	Thomas Meyrick Hewett	do	2 Dec.
Wo.	6	0	George Johnston	do	1 Feb. 58
Art.	5	0	Thomas Brewer[235]	23 April 55	do
Art.	5	0	Robert Lennox Bourchier	do	2 Feb. 58
Por.	5	0	Archibald Macintosh	do	25 Feb.
Por.	5	0	Henry Thomas Stanes Davis	do	13 March
Por.	5	0	Clement Winstanley Carlyon	do	3 July
Wo.	5	0	William Stirling[236]	do	14 July
Wo.	5	0	William Winkworth Allnutt[237]	do	29 July
Ply.	5	0	Henry Towry Miles Cooper[238]	do	11 Aug. 58
Ply.	5	0	Fred. Edward Molyneux St. John[234]	do	do
Ply.	5	0	Andrew Wm. Douglas Smith[238]†	do	8 Sept. 58
Art.	5	0	William Crosbie Hesketh	8 May 55	14 Sept.
Por.	5	0	John Christopher Hore	do	2 Nov.
Por.	5	0	Arthur Hill	do	15 Nov.
Por.	5	0	William Nicholas Gibson Johnson	do	10 Dec.
Por.	5	0	John Macdonald Moody	do	19 Jan. 59
Por.	5	0	Sechwell Ray Buckle	do	19 Feb.
Por.	5	0	Edward Charles Sparshott[231]	do	7 March 59
Ply.	5	0	Charles Lanyon Owen[239]	do	11 March 59
Por.	5	0	George Francis Gamble	do	14 Apr. 59
Por.	5	0	Samuel Edward Weatherall Hemmans	do	do
Por.	5	0	Edward Hillman White	do	do
Wo.	5	0	Alfred Fonblanque[240]	17 Aug. 55	do
Por.	5	0	Mackey Andrew Herbert James Heriot[210]	do	do
Art.	5	0	Joseph Robert Leeds	do	do
Wo.	5	0	Benjamin Dutton Kennicott	do	do
Ply.	5	0	George Clement Boase	do	do
Wo.	5	0	William Morris Pritchett[234]	do	do
Ply.	5	0	William Vincent Bowen Hewett	do	do
Por.	5	0	George Maunsell Shewell	do	do
Cha.	5	0	John Miller Hamilton	do	do
Por.	5	0	John Sims Bontein[242]	do	do
Wo.	5	0	James Woodward Scott[243]	do	do
Wo.	5	0	Samuel Travers Collins[210]	do	do
Art.	5	0	George Lyon Tupman	26 Oct. 55	do
Ply.	5	0	George Henry Elliot	do	do
Por.	5	0	William Wynch George Back Willis	do	do
Por.	5	0	George William Oliver	do	do
Cha.	5	0	John Gore Fitzgerald	do	do

Royal Marines. 417

Division.	Years' Serv. P v.	Years' Serv. H. p.	FIRST LIEUTENANTS.	2ND LIEUT.	1ST LIEUT.
Wo.	5	0	William Edward Despard	26 Oct. 55	14 Apr. 59
Cha.	5	0	Walter Julius Barker[210]	do	do
Art.	5	0	Cuthbert Collingwood Suther		4 May 59
Cha.	5	0	Edwin Forbes Thompson[210]	do	5 May 59
Por.	5	0	Henry Sturt Lewis	do	7 May 59
Ply.	5	0	William Henry Smith[213]	do	do
Por.	5	0	John Straghan[211]	do	do
Wo.	5	0	William Henry Poyntz[213]	do	do
Ply.	5	0	Thomas Linley Grant	do	do
Ply.	5	0	Augustine Evans	do	do
Por.	5	0	Robert Reginald Augustus Woodforde[210]	do	do
Ply.	5	0	James Alfred Godfrey[213]	do	do
Por.	5	0	Langham Rokeby[244]	do	do
Por.	5	0	William Armstrong[213]	31 Oct. 55	do
Art.	5	0	Charles William Fothergill	13 Nov. 55	do
Cha.	5	0	Robert James Pascoe	do	do
Cha.	5	0	Henry Cowley Bowker	23 Nov. 55	do
Art.	5	0	Henry Ives de Kantzow	do	do
Art.	5	0	Sidney Thomas Bridgford	do	do
Cha.	5	0	John William Waller O'Grady[213]	do	do
Cha.	5	0	Graham Hewett	do	do
Por.	5	0	Henry Monckton Kay	do	do
Por.	5	0	Nowell Fitz Upton Way	do	do
Por.	5	0	Ernest Augustus Macy	do	do
Ply.	4	0	George Majendie Vivian	23 June 56	do
Ply.	4	0	Charles Edward Servante[211]	do	do
Ply.	4	0	Edward O'Donovan Powell	do	do
Wo.	4	0	James Anderson Morice	do	do
Wo.	4	0	Daniel Thomas Woodriff	do	do
Ply.	4	0	William Younghusband	do	do
Cha.	4	0	William Henry Nantes	24 Dec. 56	25 May 59
Por.	4	0	Matthew Henry Farquharson	do	do
Ply.	4	0	Martin Hogge	do	7 July 59
Cha.	4	0	Joseph Philips	do	12 July
Ply.	4	0	Charles Robert Ricketts	do	26 July
Art.	4	0	Charles James Kinsman	do	11 Aug. 59
Art.	3	0	William Davis Welch	24 June 57	20 Sept.
Art.	3	0	William Stewart	do	do
Por.	3	0	George Bentham Morris	do	22 Sept. 59
Wo.	3	0	Robert Patrick	24 June 57	7 Oct. 59
Cha.	3	0	Jacob Mortimer Wier Silver	do	8 Nov. 59
Ply.	3	0	James Weir Inglis	6 Oct. 57	do
Art.	3	0	Corry Beverley Smith	17 Oct.	do
Wo.	3	0	Henry Harford Strong	3 Dec.	15 Nov. 59
Cha.	3	0	Duncan Gordon Campbell	14 Dec.	21 Nov. 59
Cha.	3	0	Thomas Palmer Norton	14 Dec.	22 Nov. 59
Art.	2	0	Arthur French	4 Feb. 58	8 Dec. 59
Art.	2	0	Richard Archibald Gorges	do	10 Dec. 59
Wo.	2	0	Henry Eyre Russell	do	20 Dec. 59

SECOND LIEUTENANTS.

Division.	Years' Serv. P v.	Years' Serv. H. p.		2ND LIEUT.	1ST LIEUT.
Por.	2	0	Robert Good Sharpe	25 Feb. 58	
Ply.	2	0	Thomas Martin Whale	13 March	
Ply.	2	0	Edward Owen Browne Gray	29 April	
Wo.	2	0	William Repton Friend Hopkins	3 July	
Por.	2	0	Alfred Emanuel Otter	14 July	
Art.	2	0	Frederic Amelius Ogle	29 July	
Art.	2	0	Francis Edmund Begbie	11 Aug. 58	
Por.	2	0	George Harrie Thorn Colwell	do	
Art.	2	0	James Samuel Derriman	8 Sept. 58	
Art.	2	0	Edward Ellice Hill	14 Sept.	
Por.	2	0	Hugh William Bamber	2 Nov.	
Art.	2	0	Herbert Everitt	15 Nov.	
Ply.	2	0	Henry Evelyn Sturt	10 Dec.	
Wo.	1	0	William Henry Vallack Tom	19 Jan. 59	
Cha.	1	0	Robert Charles Harvey	19 Feb.	
Wo.	1	0	Charles Frederick La Coste	7 March	
Ply.	1	0	John Dudley Fosbroke	11 March	
Por.	1	0	Owen Thomas Jones	14 Apr. 59	
Por.	1	0	Francis Harwood Poore	do	
Ply.	1	0	Edward Kinsman	do	
Wo.	1	0	Henry William Frampton	do	

Royal Marines.

Division	Years' Serv. F.p.	Years' Serv. H.p.	SECOND LIEUTENANTS.	2ND LIEUT.
Cha.	1	0	Sydney Vere Alston	14 Apr. 59
Ply.	1	0	Edward Lee Rose	do
Ply.	1	0	Laurence Paulet Shawe	do
Cha.	1	0	George Stevens Nash	do
Por.	1	0	Frederick Warwick Gray	2 May 59
Cha.	1	0	Edward Henry Moore	do
Por.	1	0	Francis Hastings Edmund Owen	do
Por.	1	0	Henry Holdsworth Kelly	do
Por.	1	0	Andrew Donald	do
Cha.	1	0	James Wm. Adams Elliott Lillicrap	do
Por.	1	0	Francis Bacon	do
Ply.	1	0	William Rolt Triscott	do
Wo.	1	0	Edward James Westby	do
Ply.	1	0	John William Clapperton	do
Wo.	1	0	Roland Lewis Agassiz	do
Ply.	1	0	Frederick Robert Beechey	do
Ply.	1	0	St. Andrew St. John	12 May 59
Wo.	1	0	Charles Rowley Brand	do
Por.	1	0	Edward Willoughby Grenville Byam	do
Por.	1	0	John Ignatius Morris	do
Por.	1	0	Gerald Altham Heseltine	do
Wo.	1	0	Henry Seton Bourchier	do
Cha.	1	0	John Holland	do
Cha.	1	0	Henry Luxmoore Stirling	do
Ply.	1	0	Edward Benjamin Steele Perkins	do
Wo.	1	0	William Murray Swinton	do
Cha.	1	0	George John Airey	do
Cha.	1	0	Francis Fosbery Evans	do
Ply.	1	0	Robert William Francis Holt	do
Por.	1	0	Robert Hoare Dwyer	17 May 59
Por.	1	0	Alexander George Anson	17 June 59
Por.	1	0	Robert Calder Allen	do
Por.	1	0	Alfred Wilmot Johnston	do
Cha.	1	0	Edward Moulton Messiter	do
Por.	1	0	John Layland Needham	18 June 59
Por.	1	0	James Inman	do
Por.	1	0	William George Tomlin Bickford	do
Por.	1	0	George Anne Greenwell Martin	do
Wo.	1	0	Henry Bevan Isaacson	do
Por.	1	0	John Midlane Dyer	do
Por.	1	0	Henry Fuller	22 June 59
Ply.	1	0	James Lecky	30 June 59
Cha.	1	0	William Taylor Miller	28 July 59
Ply.	1	0	James Maurice O'Connor	do
Cha.	1	0	Ringrose Drew Tully	do
Wo.	1	0	Robert Bedford Hitchcock	26 Aug. 59
Wo.	1	0	Joe Drury Bottomley	11 Sept. 59
Wo.	1	0	John Serjeant	20 Sept. 59
Ply.	1	0	Henry Ainslie Alfred Turner	do
Wo.	1	0	Reginald Phillips Baker	do
Cha.	1	0	Henry Arthur Thomas	do
Wo.	1	0	John Alfred Sweny	17 Nov. 59

ROYAL MARINE ARTILLERY. 419
Head Quarters, Portsmouth.

Colonel Commandant—John Fraser, 21 Nov. 1850.
Lieut.Colonel—Henry Carr Tate, 1 April 57.
    George Colt Langley, 20 Dec. 59. (*Col.*) 14 Dec. 59.
    John Maurice Wemyss, CB. (*Lt.Col.*), (*Acting Lt.Col.*) 6 Oct. 51.
    Geo. Gardiner Alexander, CB. (*Lt.Col.*) (*Acting Lt.Col.*) 19 Jan. 52
    G. Aug. Schomberg (*Lt.Col.*) (*Acting Lt.Col.*) 24 Feb. 54.

Captains.

Chas. L. Barnard, 28 April 54.	Fred. L. Alexander, 8 Sept. 57.
John W. C. Williams, 20 Nov. 54.	Edmund Henry Cox, 2 Feb. 58.
Hugh Stukely Buck, 7 Dec. 54.	Edward Henderson Starr, 7 May 59.
Geo. Stephen Digby, CB. (*Major*), 27 Dec. 54.	Edward Ralph Horsey, 7 May 59.
William Sandom Davis, 2 Aug. 55.	Richard Tuberville Ansell, 25 May 59
William Pitt Draffen, 5 July 56.	George Henry Wriford, 25 May 59
Henry Adair, 19 Dec. 56.	John Poore, 21 Nov. 59.
Henry W. Mawbey, 6 Feb. 57.	Henry Hewett, 21 Nov. 59.

First Lieutenants.

George Brydges, 13 Dec. 52.	Joshua Rowland Brookes, 11 July 56.
Fred. Aus. Foster (*Qr.Master*), 24 Feb. 54.	John Frederick Crease, 12 Dec. 56.
Francis Worgan Festing, *Adj.* 24 Feb. 54.	Colpoys Parkyns Heaslop, 19 Dec. 56.
Edw. C. Langley Durnford, *Adj.* 24 Feb. 54	Thomas Brewer, 1 Feb. 58.
Edward Gladstone, 24 Feb. 54.	Robert Lennox Bourchier, 2 Feb. 58.
William Pitman, 24 Feb. 54.	William Crosbie Hesketh, 14 Sept. 58.
Charles Sidney Williams, 24 Feb. 54.	Joseph Robert Leeds, 14 Apr. 59.
John Wm. Henry C. Grove Morris, 24 Feb. 54.	George Lyon Tupman, 14 Apr. 59.
Francis Edward Halliday, 14 March 54.	Cuthbert Collingwood Suther, 4 May 59.
Robert Woolcombe, 1 Aug. 54.	Charles William Fothergill, 7 May 59.
Rich. Augustus Fitzgerald Studdert, 3 Jan. 55.	Henry Ives De Kantzow, 7 May 59.
Harry Boscawen Savage, 3 Jan. 55.	Sidney Thomas Bridgford, 7 May 59.
Hollis Henry Nott, 3 Jan. 55.	Charles James Kinsman, 11 Aug. 59.
Otway Wheeler Cuffe, 10 April 55.	William Davis Welch, 20 Sept. 59.
Henry B. Tuson, 22 June 55.	William Stewart, 20 Sept. 59.
W. H. T. M. Dodgin, 14 July 55.	Corry Beverley Smith, 8 Nov. 59.
John Chesterton Crawford, 30 Aug. 55.	Arthur French, 8 Dec. 59.
J. C. R. Colomb, 2 Aug. 55.	Richard Archibald Gorges, 10 Dec. 59.
R. B. Gardner, 22 March 56.	

Second Lieutenants.

Fred. Amelius Ogle, 29 June 59	Edward Ellice Hill, 29 July 59
Francis Edmund Begbie, 29 June 59.	Herbert Everitt, 29 July 59.
James Samuel Derriman, 29 July 59.	

    Adjutants.—1*st Lieut.* Francis Worgan Festing, 25 Jan. 59.
        1*st Lieut.* E. C. L. Durnford, 1 Nov. 59.
    Quartermaster.—Fred. Aug. Foster, 24 Sept. 59.

STAFF OFFICERS OF THE ROYAL MARINES.

Deputy Adjutant-General.—𝔇 *Major-General* Samuel Robert Wesley, 13 Dec. 54.
Assistants Adjutant-General.—
        Lieut. Colonel.—Joseph Oates Travers, 20 Dec. 50.
        Office, 7, *New Street, Spring Gardens, S. W.*

Adjutants.

Cha.	1*st Lieut.* Fras. Wm. Thomas, 15 Sept. 57.	Ply.	1*st Lieut.* Ussher Lee Morris, 11 July
Por.	—— John M. Lennox, 25 Feb. 58.	Art.	—— E. C. L. Durnford, 1 Nov. 59.
Wo.	—— James C. Travers, 21 July 58.	Por.	—— Francis Lean, 22 Nov. 59.
Cha.	—— J. Hn. Maskery,[129] 10 Mar. 59.	Ply.	—— Philip Harington, 14 Dec. 59.
Wo.	—— George Naylor, 16 May 59.		

Quarter Masters.

Wo.	1*st Lieut.* Ambrose Wolrige, 6 Nov. 55.	Por.	John Lewis, 1 Sept. 57.
Cha.	—— Henry F. Cooper, 29 July 57.	Wo.	Matthew Brickdale, 1 Sept. 57.
Ply.	—— Cuthbert Ward Burton, 18 Apr. 59	Cha.	William Scott, 1 Sept. 57.
Art.	—— F. A. Foster, 24 Sept. 59.	Art.	William Healey, 1 Nov. 59.
Por.	—— Wm. F. Portlock S. Dadson, 23 Dec. 59.		

Paymasters.

Cha.	George Hookey,[245] 23 March 36; 2*nd Lt.* 27 Jan. 06; 1*st Lt.* 8 Aug. 11; *Capt.* 12 Oct. 32.
Wo.	George Watson,[246] 1 July 53; 2*nd Lt.* 20 Dec. 12; 1*st Lt.* 27 June 32; *Capt.* 30 June 41.
Ply.	Thomas Brown Gray,[247] 16 Feb. 54; 2*nd Lt.* 31 Jan. 25; 1*st Lt.* 1 Oct. 33; *Capt.* 5 Nov. 42.
Por.	Walter Cossar,[248] 13 March 57; 2*nd Lt.* 10 Aug. 30; *Lt.* 10 July 37; *Capt.* 27 July 47.
Art.	Joseph Edward Wilson Lawrence,[71] 17 Nov. 59; 2*d Lt.* 27 Dec. 38; 1*st Lt.* 5 Nov. 42; *Capt.* 13 Nov. 52; *Bt.Major*, 2 Nov. 55.

Barrack Masters.

Cha.	𝔇 Ambrose A. R. Wolrige,[249] 5 June 32; 2*d Lt.* 4 July 03; 1*st Lt.* 15 Aug. 05; *Capt.* 31 July 26.
Ply.	Isaac Toby,[250] 21 March 42; 2*nd Lt.* 3 Apr. 10; 1*st Lt.* 9 Sept. 28; *Capt.* 22 May 38.
Por.	Hy. Atkins M'Callum,[251] 30 Nov. 57; 2*nd Lt.* 24 Oct. 37; 1*st Lt.* 11 May 41; *Capt.* 1 May 51.
Wo.	Hen. Hotham M'Carthy,[252] 30 Nov. 57; 2*nd Lt.* 30 Jan. 38; 1*st Lt.* 24 Nov. 41; *Capt.* 7 Nov. 51.
Art.	Thomas Quin Meade, 1 Nov. 59; 2*d Lt.* 24 July 44; 1*st Lt.* 4 Jan. 48; *Capt.* 30 Oct. 55.

Deputy Inspectors of Hospitals.

Wo.	Oliver Evans, M.D., 17 Jan. 49.	Cha.	Jas. Wingate Johnston, M.D. 21 Dec. 57.

Staff Surgeons.

Ply.	Andrew Millar,[253] M.D. 12 Aug. 48.	Por.	Charles Dean Steel,[254] 1 Oct. 57.

Assistant-Surgeons.

Cha.	James Nicholas Dick, 30 Aug. 58.		Ply.	Wm. Henry Woods,[256] M.D. 9 Sept. 54.
Por.	Wm. Gordon Jas. Ayre,[255] 17 Jan. 57.		Wo.	Charles Hall Chambers,[260] 17 May 56.
Por.	James Sproule,[256] 30 June 58.		Wo.	Geo. B. Newton [259]
Ply.	N. C. Hatherly,[257] 23 Dec. 53.			

Scarlet—Facings Blue. Artillery—*Blue*—Facings Red. *Agent*, Laming W. Tear, Esq.

War Services of the Officers of the Royal Marines.

1 General Menzies was attached to Lord Nelson's squadron off Boulogne, where he participated in all the desperate cutting-out affairs on the French coast against Buonaparte's flotilla. Commanded a detachment of Royal Marines landed at Port Jackson during an insurrection of convicts, in March 1804 ; by his promptitude and exertions the town of Sydney, and indeed the colony, was in a great measure preserved, and tranquillity restored. On the 22nd June 1806, he was in one of the boats of His Majesty's Ship *Minerva*, cutting out five vessels from under Fort Finisterre ; and on the 11th July following he was in the barge which, when 50 miles from where the frigate lay at anchor, captured by boarding the *Buena Dicha* Spanish privateer, of three times the force of the boat, after a sharp conflict: this attack was planned by General Menzies. Commanded and headed the Marines at the storming of Fort Finisterre, being the first who entered the Fort. In boats cutting out the Spanish vessel of war, *St. Joseph*, from the Bay of Arosa, where he landed and made prisoner the Spanish Commodore, who delivered to him his sword. Commanded the Marines at the capture of Fort Guardia. Slightly wounded cutting out the French corvette, *La Moselle*, from under a battery in Basque Roads. Taking of Fort Camarinus and gun-boats from under its protection. Repeatedly engaged in severe boat-actions, and against batteries. Right arm amputated. Received a sword of honour from the Patriotic Fund. Commanded the Royal Marine Artillery from 1837 to 1844. Is a Knight of Charles the 3rd of Spain, and a Knight of the Tower and Sword of Portugal.

2 General Coryton served as a Midshipman in the Royal Navy, on board the *Severn* and *Hunter*, from February 1800 until December 1802, and was engaged with the batteries at the Isle of Bas. In 1803 he entered the Royal Marines, and served in the *Spartiate*, off Brest, in the West Indies, and at Trafalgar, in which battle Captain Sir Francis Laforey states that "Lieut. Coryton rendered himself conspicuous by his gallant conduct." Embarked in 1806 in the *Argo*, and served until 1809 on the coast of Africa, Canary Isles, West Indies, and Spanish Main; was landed in command of a detachment at Winebah, on the coast of Africa, against a native army; at the storming and capture of a battery at Teneriffe, and attempt at cutting out an enemy's vessel (severely wounded). Engaged with the enemy on thirty occasions —several times hand to hand—and repeatedly wounded. General Burn stated that "Lieut. Coryton distinguished himself by a series of brilliant and successful achievements not surpassed by a subaltern of any Service." Mentioned for "conspicuous zeal and gallantry" at the siege and blockade of St. Domingo, and at the battering of Fort St. Jerome in 1809. At the cutting out of the French National Felucca *Joseph*, of seven guns and sixty-two men. At the City of St. Domingo, on the 9th March 1809, he commanded the gig, which, owing to her superior pulling, boarded the vessel fifteen minutes before the other boats; he maintained himself until their arrival, when they found him engaged single-handed with eight or ten of the enemy, refusing to surrender, although wounded in nine different places with sabres. After his return to England he was voted a sword from the Patriotic Fund. Has received the War Medal with one Clasp.

3 Lieut.General S. B. Ellis's services:— The general action with the combined fleets of France and Spain, off Cape Finisterre, 22nd July 1805; battle of Trafalgar, 21st October following; the Walcheren expedition in 1809, and in the *Lavinia*, the leading frigate of ten, forcing the passage of the Scheldt under a heavy fire from the batteries of Flushing and Cadsand. Capture of the island of Guadaloupe, in January 1810. Employed, in 1812 and 13, off the coasts of France, Spain, and Portugal. Taking of the American frigate *President*, January 1814; various successful affairs of boats in North America. Bombardment and reduction of Fort Munora in Scindo in February 1839; and, landing, the 25th of the following month, with the detachment of his corps at Bushire, under a smart fire from the Persians, for the protection of the East India Company's Political Resident, and in possession of the Residency until the 30th, when that agent was embarked in safety. China expedition, and as senior officer in command of the Royal Marines at the capture of Chusan on the 5th July 1840, battle of Chuenpee, 7th January 1841, wherein he commanded the advance (promoted Brevet Major) ; bombardment of the Bogue Forts, assault and capture of the Island of North Wantung, 26th February; the advance on Canton, March 8th ; storming and taking the heights and forts before the walls of Canton, 26th May (promoted Lieut.Colonel); capture of the strongly-fortified Island of Colongso, near Amoy, 26th August ; 2nd capture of Chusan, 1st October ; assault and capture of citadel and city of Chinhae, 10th October ; advance on and entry into Ningpo, 13th October ; in garrison and command of Tay-woong-kaou fortress in the river and near

to Canton, from 6th April to 24th May 1841; and on similar duties at Ningpo and Chusan, with Battalion of Royal Marines, from 10th October to 27th January 1842, following (Medal for China and *CB*., also the War Medal with two Clasps).

4 Lieut.General Wearing was wounded at Trafalgar (War Medal with one Clasp).

5 Lieut.General Willes's services:— Sir Richard Strachan's action, 4th November 1805; West Indies 1808 to 1812, including the capture of the city of St. Domingo in 1809; South Beveland, winter of 1813; operations in the *Chesapeake* under Sir George Cockburn; capture of Washington; advance to Baltimore, in 1814; capture of Cumberland Island on the coast of Georgia, and of the town of Saint Mary's, 1814; coast of Africa, 1817; East Indies, 1832 to 1835. Various boat and other services. Has received the War Medal with one Clasp.

6 Major General Delacombe served on board the *Tonnant* covering the embarkation of Sir John Moore's army at Corunna, and afterwards in various boat affairs in Basque Roads, in 1809, and at the defence of Cadiz the following year. In 1812 he was at the destruction of the batteries of Languelio, after charging with the bayonet and defeating a battalion of the French 52nd Regiment of the Line of a very superior force. In 1813 he was on board the *Imperieuse* at the attack on the batteries and tower of post D'Anzo, after which he was landed and the enemy driven from their posts, which were destroyed, and a convoy of 29 vessels laden with ship timber for Toulon brought out; he was afterwards at the attack on Leghorn under Sir Josias Rowley. Independent of the above, he has been employed on various and repeated boat service; partially engaged with the French fleet off Toulon; and several times with the Neapolitan squadron, gun-boats, and batteries in the Bay of Naples.

7 Major General Philips served as a Midshipman on board H.M.S. *Belleisle* at the battle of Trafalgar. As an officer of Royal Marines, he was present at the storming of three of the enemy's entrenched batteries and siege of Santa Maura, and frequently employed in boat affairs on the coasts of Italy and Dalmatia. In April 1812 he joined the first Battalion; served with it in Spain and in America, including the storming of the enemy's entrenched camp at Hampton in Virginia, and frequent affairs with the enemy there. Detached to Canada and served under Commodore Sir James Yeo, on the Lakes Ontario, Erie, and Champlain. Has received the War Medal with one Clasp.

8 Major General Graham served with the army in the Battalion formed of the Marines of the squadron at the taking of Walcheren in 1809. Also served in the 1st Battalion in Portugal and in operations on the north coast of Spain, at the taking and defence of Castro. Proceeded with the battalion to America, where it was brigaded under Sir Sidney Beckwith at the attack upon Norfolk, and the taking of Hampton, and several small places. The brigade being broken up, he went with the battalion to Canada; whilst there, he was sent with a detachment in command of a division of gun boats to attack a battery at the head of Lake Champlain, with which they were engaged some hours. Returned with the battalion to the coast of America, and was at the attack and taking of Fort Point Petre and the town of St. Mary's, in Georgia; shortly after his promotion in 1837, he exchanged to join the battalion in Spain. He was afterwards at the demonstration before Nankin in China (Medal). Commanded the R. M. Battalion in the Brigade under General Jones, acting in conjunction with the French army at the bombardment and surrender of the forts at Bomarsund, Aland Isles, in Aug. 1854 (Medal and *CB*.).

9 Major General Wesley served in a Battalion of Marines formed from the squadron under Sir Alex. Cochrane at the attack and capture of Guadaloupe, St. Martin's and St. Eustatia in 1810. In blockading squadrons off Brest, L'Orient, and Basque Roads, including several successful boat affairs under the Batteries of Rochelle and Isle d'Aix in 1811. In coast operations, north of Spain; and, with the 1st Battalion of Marines, in Portugal, in 1812. At the attack on Norfolk, and the entrenched camp of Hampton, &c. in the *Chesapeake*. Served the campaigns of 1813 and 14 at the advanced posts in Lower Canada, and in command of a division of seven gun-boats employed blockading the enemy's flotilla at Platsburg. At the defence of La Cole Mill. Adjutant to a Light Corps formed of the flank companies of the 2nd West India Regiment and Marine Battalions at the attack and capture of Fort Peter, the fortified positions of St. Mary's and Cumberland Island (coast of Georgia). In command of a detachment of Artillery in H. M. S. *Phæton* assisted in repelling an attack of Algerine gun-boats in 1821. Adjutant to a battalion under Colonel Owen serving in co-operation with the Spanish army in 1836-7, including the affair before Fuenterabia, 11 July 1836, the field actions of the 10th, 12th, and 14th March, and of Hernani, 16 March 1837. Served as Captain in the same battalion until the Force under Lord John Hay was withdrawn in 1840. He has received the Military War Medal with one Clasp for Guadaloupe, and is a Knight 1st Class of St. Fernando.

10 Major General Brown's services:—attack on French forts at Ciota June 1812; attack and capture of the town of L'Escalia, in the Bay of Rosas, 1812; partial engagement with the French fleet, near Toulon, 1813; attack of Algiers; destruction of Greek pirates at Porto Bono, Isle of Candia, June 1826. Has received the War Medal with one Clasp, as also the Turkish Medal for services on the Coast of Syria in 1840-41.

14 Colonel Stransham served at the battle of Navarino, 21st Oct. 1827 (War Medal and Clasp). Served on the China expedition in 1840-41 (Medal); was Adjutant and Brigade-Major at the attack on Chuenpee; commanded the Royal Marines at the storming of the Whampoo batteries, at the reduction of Macao Fort which he garrisoned and commanded: at the capture of several small forts on 17th March 1841, he was severely wounded by an explosion, and mentioned for his gallantry; was Adjutant at the capture of Canton, and until the end of the war: for these services he received the Brevet rank

of Major on obtaining his Company. Served with the combined expedition to the Baltic from March to July 1854 (Medal).

15 Colonel Rea served with the R. M. Battalion on the north coast of Spain against the Carlists in 1837-38; and with the combined expedition to the Baltic in 1854 (Medal).

16 Colonel Anderson was at the battle of Navarino in 1827; at the commencement of the action he boarded, with his men, one of the Turkish ships, and captured the flag: the following day he was a volunteer in the boats for the purpose of cutting out the in-shore squadron. Served with the Army of Occupation in Portugal, and was for some time quartered at Fort St. Julian in Oct. 1827. Served throughout the campaign on the coast of Syria in 1840; at the storming of Sidon he planted the British colours on the walls; was encamped at D'Jouni; at the attack and capture of Beyrout; the bombardment and surrender of St. Jean d'Acre; the surrender of Jaffa, and a volunteer in the expedition against Gaza; during the latter part of the time he was Adjutant to the R. M. Battalion. Has received the War Medal with two Clasps, and the Turkish Silver Medal.

17 Colonel Fraser commanded a battalion of Royal Marines in the Crimea at the siege of Sebastopol in 1854 (Medal and Clasp, and Turkish Medal).

18 Colonel Holloway commanded a battalion of Royal Marines in the Crimea during the siege of Sebastopol in 1854-55, until its fall, and was employed at the occupation of Kertch, and advance on Yeni Kalé, also at the surrender of Kinbourn (Medal and Clasp, Officer of the Legion of Honor, Sardinian Medal, 4th Class of the Medjidie, and Turkish Medal). In Aug. 1857 was appointed to command a Brigade ordered for special service in China; was present during the blockade of the Canton river, landing before and storming of Canton—wounded (CB.), and was appointed one of the three Allied Commissioners for the government of that Province in 1858.

19 Colonel F. A. Campbell served with the R. M. Battalion on the north coast of Spain. Served with the combined force before the town of Sebastopol during the siege in 1854-55; was on the expedition to and occupation of Kertch, and advance on Yeni Kalé; commanded the First Battalion of the R. M. Brigade serving in the Crimea, until the fall of Sebastopol, also with expedition to and surrender of Kinbourn (Medal and Clasp, 4th Class of the Medjidie, and Turkish Medal).

20 Colonel Hunt served on the coast of Syria in 1840-41 (Medals).

21 Colonel Mitchell served with the R. M. Brigade in the Crimea in 1855; also at the surrender of Kinbourn (Medal, and Turkish Medal).

22 Colonel Lemon served with the Royal Marine Battalion on the north coast of Spain; also on the China expedition in 1842. Commanded the Provisional Battalion at the operations before and storming of Canton 29 Dec. 1857 (Brevet rank of Colonel and *CB*). Commanded the Brigade on the expedition to the North of China and at the attack on the forts at the Peiho on 25th June 1859 (severely wounded in the head, and mentioned in despatches).

23 Colonel Moore was at the destruction of 58 piratical vessels at Cho-Keum in October 1849. Accompanied the expedition to the Baltic in 1855 (Medal).

23† Lt.Colonel Walsh commanded a Battalion on the China expedition of 1857-58, including the blockade of the Canton river, the landing before and storming of Canton (*CB*).

24 Lt.Col. Ayles served at the battle of Navarino in 1827 (Medal). Commanded the Royal Marines at the capture of Aden, 19th January 1839; and was also at the destruction of 29 war junks in China in 1840.

24† Lt.Colonel Gascoigne served in the Baltic in July and Aug. 1854 (Medal).

25 Lt.Colonel M'Killop served with the R. M. Battalion in conjunction with the French army at the bombardment and surrender of the Forts of Bomarsund in Aug. 1854 (Medal)

26 Colonel Hopkins served with the R. M. Brigade in the Crimea in 1854-55: in command of the 1st Battalion on the heights of Balaklava at the attack of the Russians upon that place, and from the time of its landing until detached in command of four companies to join the Light Division of the Army before Sebastopol, with which he remained doing duty in camp and in the advanced trenches during the siege from Nov. 1854 to March 1855, and commanded the Royal Marines engaged at the battle of Inkerman (mentioned in Dispatches, and promoted Brevet Major): afterwards commanded the 1st Battalion at Balaklava from March to June 1855 (Medal and three Clasps, Brevet Lt.Col., *CB*., Knight of the Legion of Honor, Sardinian Medal, 4th Class of the Medjidie, and Turkish Medal).

27 Colonel Langley served in the operations on the north coast of Spain in command of the detachment of Royal Marines of H.M.S. *Castor*, during 1834 and two following years, and was severely wounded on the 9th June 1836, defending the heights of Passages against a very superior force of Carlists,—for his conduct on this occasion he was awarded the 1st Class of the Order of San Fernando. He served subsequently on the North Coast of Spain from 1838 to 1840, and had the same Order conferred on him a second time for his general services in Spain.

29 Lt.Colonel Hocker served in Syria in 1840 and was at the storming of Sidon and bombardment of Acre (Medal and Clasp, and Turkish Medal). Commanded a Battalion on the China expedition of 1857-58, including the blockade of the Canton river, the landing before and storming of Canton.

30 Lt.Col. Simon Fraser served throughout the campaign in Syria (Medal and Clasp, and Turkish Medal), including the storming and capture of Sidon (in command of three companies which forced the Citadel Gate), surrender of Beyrout, bombardment and capture of St. Jean d'Acre. Served with the R. M. Brigade in the Crimea in 1854-55, including

the battle of Balaklava, and siege of Sebastopol, acted as Major in the Marine Batteries, and in command of No. 3 Battery was actively engaged at the battle of Balaklava (Medal and two Clasps, Brevet Major, 5th Class of the Medjidie, and Turkish Medal).

33 Lt.Col. March served with the R. Marine Battalion on the north coast of Spain from 1836 to 1840, and was present in all the affairs in which the battalion took part, including the battle of Hernani. Served with the R. M. Brigade during the campaign in the Crimea, and siege of Sebastopol; was attached to the Light Division of the Army at the battles of Balaklava and Inkerman—severely wounded (Medal and three Clasps, Brevet Major, Knight of the Legion of Honor, Sardinian Medal, 5th Class of the Medjidie, and Turkish Medal).

34 Lt.Col. Payne served in R. Marine Battalion on the north coast of Spain during the Carlist war in 1838-39. Served in the Crimea from 18th Sept. 1854 to the termination of the siege of Sebastopol. Commanded Battalion of R. Marines in occupation and defence of Eupatoria in Oct. 1854; also the 2nd Battalion in camp near Baidar from June 1855, attached to Sir Colin Campbell's Brigade (Medal and Clasp, Brevet of Major, Sardinian Medal, 5th Class of the Medjidie, and Turkish Medal).

35 Lt.Col. Travers served with the R. M. Battalion on the north coast of Spain during the Carlist war. On the coast of Syria in 1841 (Medal and Clasp, and Turkish Medal). Served with the Baltic expeditions in 1854-55, and was on board a gun-boat during the bombardment of Sweaborg in August (Medal). Served as Brigade Major to the Royal Marines on the China expedition of 1857-58, including the blockade of the Canton river, operations before and storming of Canton (Brevet Major), and was wounded in action with the Braves and destruction of villages near the White Cloud Mountains; was appointed Assistant Quarter Master General to the Expedition in Aug. 1858.

36 Lt.Colonel Curry served the Syrian campaign of 1840,—at D'Jouni, the storming of Sidon, and bombardment of Acre (Medal and Clasp, and Turkish Medal). Served in the Baltic in the latter part of 1855 (Medal).

38 Lt.Colonel Maxwell served on the China expedition, and was present at the battle of Chuenpee, attack of batteries of Anunghoy and North Wantung, advance on Canton, storming the heights and entrenched camp of Canton, bombardment of Colongso (Medal).

39 Lt.Colonel Fosbroke was employed on shore against the Natives in New Zealand in 1846. Served with the R. M. Battalion at the bombardment and surrender of the forts of Bomarsund in Aug. 1854. Served with the expedition to the Baltic in 1855, and was landed to destroy a telegraph station (Medal).

40 Lt.Colonel Hadfield served with the R. M. Brigade in the Crimea during the siege and fall of Sebastopol, and also at the surrender of Kinbourn (Medal and Clasp, and Turkish Medal).

41 Lt.Colonel Spalding served in command of a Company throughout the operations in Syria, in 1840, and was slightly wounded at the attack on Gebail (War Medal with one Clasp, and Turkish Medal). Served as Provost-Marshal on the Staff of the Army in the Crimea in 1856 until its evacuation.

42 Major Marriott served two years with the expeditionary force in China, and was present at the first capture of Chusan; assisted at the demolition of the Bogue Forts in the Canton River; participated in the actions of the first and second Bars; was engaged in the destruction of all the enemy's sea and river defences, including the fortresses of French Folly and Hoqua's Fort; bombardment and taking of Macao Passage Fort; storming of the Bird's Nest Battery, and finally at the combined attack on the enemy's position and entrenched camp on the heights above Canton (Medal). Was in the action with the batteries and expulsion of the Russian Garrison from Redout Kaleh, 19th May 1854. Served with the R. M. Brigade in the Crimea until Feb. 1855, after which with the combined force at the battle of Balaklava and before Sebastopol until its fall; acted as Field Officer to the battalion, landed at Kertch, and occupation of Yeni Kalé; and was also at the surrender of Kinbourn (Medal and two Clasps, Brevet Major, 5th Class of the Medjidie, and Turkish Medal).

45 Major Lowder served on the coast of Syria in 1840 (Medals). Was in the action at Esknaes in the Gulf of Finland, 20 May 1854; also at the operations before Bomarsund and in action with the forts 15th August; and commanded the detachment of Royal Marines at the surrender of Fort Prasto, 16th Aug. 1854. Served with the Baltic expedition in 1855, including the destruction of a Fort and shelling an Encampment, blowing up of Fort Svartholm and barracks, destruction of the barracks at Lovisa, shelling a Cossack encampment and landing at Kounda Bay, destruction of a Cossack barrack, action with a Russian steamer, gunboats, and a battery near Wiborg, and with the batteries of Fredericksham, capture of the Island of Kotka and destruction of military stores, and bombardment of Sweaborg (Medal, and Brevet Major).

47 Capt. Shewen was employed during the whole of the campaign on the coast of Syria, including the storming and capture of Sidon, surrender of Beyrout, and bombardment and fall of St. Jean d'Acre; served also with the battalion at the camp at D'Jouni (War Medal and Clasp, and Turkish Medal).

48 Captain Lambrick served in Spain with the R. M. Battalion, and was wounded 12th July 1836; he is a Knight 1st Class of St. Fernando.

50 Captain Farrant served with the Royal Marine Battalion in Syria (Medal), at D'Jouni, the storming and capture of Sidon, and bombardment of Acre. Served also in China in 1842 (Medal). He has received the War Medal and one Clasp.

52 Captain Hamley served in Syria in 1840 (Medal and Clasp, and Turkish Medal),

War Services of the Officers of the Royal Marines.

at Caiffa and Tsour, the bombardment of Acre, and at D'Jouni. Also with the R. M Battalion at the bombardment and surrender of the forts of Bomarsund in Aug. 1854. Served with the Baltic expedition in 1855, including the destruction of a Telegraph Station, and shelling a large body of Russian troops (Medal).

53 Major Aslett served as Brigade Major to the Royal Marines in the Crimea in 1854 and part of 1855, including the battle of Balaklava; was present during the whole of the siege and fall of Sebastopol; also at the surrender of Kinbourn (Medal and Clasps, Brevet Major, 5th Class of the Medjidie, and Turkish Medal).

54 Major Foote served on the China expedition of 1857-58, including the blockade of the Canton river, and was Major of the Provisional Battalion at the landing before and storming of Canton; commanded the Royal Marines at the assault and capture of the walled town of Namtow—mentioned in despatches (Brevet of Major).

55 Captain Suther served with the R. M. Battalion on the north coast of Spain during the Carlist War. Has received the War Medal with Clasp, as also the Turkish Medal for services on the coast of Syria in 1840-41.

57 Captain Searle served the Syrian campaign (Medal and Clasp, and Turkish Medal); was at D'Jouni, the attack on the fortified position of Gebail, at the surrender of Beyrout, and the storming of Sidon. Served with the Baltic expedition in 1855, including the action with a battery at the mouth of the Narva 18th June—wounded (Medal).

59 Captain Louis served in Syria at the storming of Sidon, and at D'Jouni (Medal and Clasp, and Turkish Medal). Served with the Baltic expeditions in 1854 and 1855, including the action with a battery at the mouth of the Narva on 18th June; was severely wounded by the explosion of an infernal machine on 21st June (Medal).

60 Captain Clavell served with the R. M. Battalion at D'Jouni in Syria in 1840 (Medal and Clasp, and Turkish Medal) as Acting Engineer. Was severely wounded by an explosion of gunpowder while firing a salute on board H. M. S. *Camperdown*. Served in the R. M. Battalion at the bombardment and surrender of Bomarsund in Aug. 1854, and operations there (Baltic Medal). In 1855 he was before Sebastopol until its fall; was employed on the staff of the army as Provost-Marshal on the expedition to Kertch and Yeni Kalé, as also at the surrender of Kinbourn, and operations there (mentioned in despatches, Medal and Clasp, 5th Class of the Medjidie, and Turkish Medal).

62 Major Penrose served with the Royal Marine Battalion on the north coast of Spain in 1838. Also in China in 1841-2 (Medal), during the operations in the Yangtse-Kiang. Landed on 24th Oct. 1856 for the protection of the British Factory at Canton; commanded the Royal Marines at the storming of the breach in the wall of Canton on 29th October, and throughout the subsequent operations—mentioned in Dispatches (Brevet Major).

63 Major Rodney served in Spain during the Carlist war. Served with the R. M. Battalion at Eupatoria in 1854, and with the Brigade in the Crimea as Aide-de-Camp and Brigade-Major at the battle of Balaklava and during the siege and fall of Sebastopol; was also at the surrender of Kinbourn (Medal and two Clasps, Brevet Major, Knight of the Legion of Honor, 5th Class of the Medjidie, and Turkish Medal).

64 Major Wemyss served with the R. M. Battalion at D'Jouni in Syria in 1840 (Medal and Clasp, and Turkish Medal). Served with the Baltic expeditions in 1854 and 1855, and commanded the mortars of the flotilla during the bombardment of Sweaborg (mentioned in Dispatches, Medal, Brevet Major, and *CB*.).

66 Major Wm. Elliott served in Syria in 1840 (Medal and Clasp, and Turkish Medal). Served as Brigade Major to the Royal Marines at the bombardment and capture of the forts of Bomarsund in Aug. 1854, for which he received the brevet rank of Major. Was with the Baltic expedition in 1855, including an action with six Russian gun-boats off Cronstadt on 15th August; and served again in the Baltic in 1856 (Medal).

67 Captain Adair served in Syria in 1840 (Medal and Clasp, and Turkish Medal), and was slightly wounded in the assault upon Gebail. Served before Sebastopol during its siege and fall, and with the R. M. Battalion at the occupation of Kertch and Yeni Kalé as also at the surrender of Kinbourn (Medal and Clasp, 5th Class of the Medjidie, and Turkish Medal).

68 Captain William Jolliffe served the Syrian campaign of 1840—at D'Jouni, the storming of Sidon, and bombardment of Acre (Medal and Clasp, and Turkish Medal). Served also with the Baltic expedition in 1854 (Medal).

69 Captain Harrison served in the operations on the coast of Syria, including the attacks on the fortress of D'Jebail, and bombardment and capture of Acre (Medal and Clasp, and Turkish Medal). He served also in New Zealand, and was present at the taking of the fortified Pah at Ruapekapeka on the 11th January 1846. Was with the Baltic expeditions in 1854 and 1855 (Medal).

70 Captain M'Arthur served with the expedition to the Baltic in 1855 (Medal).

71 Lt. Colonel Alexander served with the Baltic expedition in 1854 (Medal). Commanded the R. M. Artillery serving with the Brigade in the Crimea in 1854-55, and was employed in the siege train in the batteries before Sebastopol during its siege and fall, and was also at the bombardment and surrender of Kinbourn (Medal and Clasp, Brevets of Major and Lt. Colonel, *CB*., Knight of the Legion of Honor, Sardinian Medal, 4th Class of the Medjidie, and Turkish Medal).

72 Captain Menzies served with the Baltic expeditions in 1854, 1855, and 1856 (Medal).

74 Captain Huskisson served on the coast of Syria in 1840 (Medal and Clasp and Turkish Medal). Served in China and at Canton during the war in 1856.

War Services of the Officers of the Royal Marines.   425

75 Captain J. H. Stewart served the Syrian campaign of 1840,—at D'Jouni, the storming of Sidon, and bombardment of Acre (War Medal and Clasp, and Turkish Medal).

76 Captain Blyth served on the coast of Syria in 1840 (Medal and Clasp, and Turkish Medal). Served the Eastern campaign of 1854-55 with the Royal Marines, including the battle of Balaklava and siege of Sebastopol, and was attached to the Light Division of the army in the trenches, and at the battle of Inkerman (Medal and three Clasps, Knight of the Legion of Honor, 5th Class of the Medjidie, and Turkish Medal).

77 Major Lawrence acted as Aide de Camp to Capt. Hotham, R.N. while taking and destroying the batteries, &c. at Punta Obligada, in the river Parana, on the 20th Nov. 1845. Served with the Baltic expedition in 1855, and commanded the Marine Artillery of a Division of gun-boats at the bombardment of Sweaborg (mentioned in Dispatches, Medal, and Brevet Major).

78 Captain J. A. Stewart served throughout the campaign in Syria in 1840,—at the camp at D'Jouni as Acting Engineer, the storm and capture of Sydon, surrender of Beyrout, bombardment and capture of St. Jean d'Acre (War Medal and Clasp and Turkish Medal). Served also on the coast of Africa for two years, commanded a detachment of Marines at the destruction of several Barracoons, and liberated 1200 slaves in 1845; was attacked by large numbers of Africans at Kabenda, three miles inland, and effected a safe retreat to the beach with three men mortally wounded.

79 Captain Pickard served on the China expedition, and was present at the battle of Chuenpee, attack of batteries of Anunghoy and North Wantung, advance on Canton, storming the heights of Canton, bombardment of Colongso (Medal).

80 Captain Dyer served at Monte Video during the Civil War in 1844. At Borneo Proper in an engagement with pirates, and at the defeat of their forces, and destruction of their stockades in Malloodoo Bay in 1845. Served with the Baltic expedition in 1855, and again in 1856 (Medal).

82 Captain Wright served on the coast of Syria in 1840 (Medals).

83 Captain Symonds served with the R. Marine Battalion against the Carlists on the North Coast of Spain. Served with the Baltic expedition in 1855 (Medal), and engaged with the batteries at the bombardment of Sweaborg on 9th August. Served in China with the expeditionary force in 1858-59.

84 Lt.Colonel Schomberg served with the Baltic expedition in 1855 (Medal), and commanded Marine Artillery of a Division of gun-boats at the bombardment of Sweaborg (mentioned in Dispatches, and promoted to Brevet Major). Commanded the R.M. Artillery with the Brigade in China in 1857-58, including the blockade of the Canton river, was in command of the Mortar battery at the bombardment of Canton, and present at the assault and capture (Brevet Lt.Colonel).

84† Captain Drury served in Burmah during the war in 1852 (Medal and Clasp). Served with the Baltic expedition in 1855, including the bombardment of Sweaborg (Medal).

85 Captain Wylde served with the R. M. Battalion at the occupation of Kertch and Yeni Kalé; was before Sebastopol until its fall; also at the surrender of Kinbourn (Medal and Clasp, and Turkish Medal.

85† Captain J. H. Jolliffe served on the China expedition in 1842, and with the blockading force in the Baltic until the declaration of peace in 1856.

86 Captains Kennedy and Mansell were present in an engagement with Pirates at Borneo, and defeat of their forces and destruction of their stockades in Malloodoo Bay in 1845. Captain Mansell served on the China expedition of 1857-58, including the operations at Canton, with the storming and capture of the city.

87 Lt.Colonel Boyle commanded the detachment of Royal Marines in the expedition up the St. Juan de Nicaragua, and was present at the storming of Fort Serapagui, and surrender of others in 1848, and was mentioned in the Dispatches. Served in China during the last war, was present at the capture of the forts and blockade of the Canton river, landed for the protection of the Factories, and was at the storming on 29th Oct. 56 (mentioned in despatches); engaged in all the subsequent operations, at the destruction of Mandarin Junks in Fatsham Creek (mentioned in despatches, and Brevet Major), landing before and storming of Canton. Commanded the Royal Marines of the fleet on the expedition to the North of China, and at the capture of the forts at the mouth of the Peiho river (mentioned in despatches, and Brevet of Lt.Colonel).

87† Captain Little served on the China expedition of 1857-58, including the operations at Canton, with the storming and capture of the city.

88 Captain John Elliott served with the China expedition in 1842 (Medal). Was in H. M. S. Fox during the action with the stockade batteries, and destruction of the Burmese war-boats in the Rangoon River, on the 10th Jan. 1852; commanded the Royal Marines at the destruction of the same stockades on the 4th April; landed in command of the Marines during the whole of the operations against Rangoon, from the 11th to the 17th April; commanded the Marines on the expedition to Mobee against the army of the Governor of Rangoon (officially thanked); and afterwards at the storm and capture of the city of Bassein (wounded, and honourably mentioned in both Naval and Military Dispatches), as also the Royal Marines embarked in the steam flotilla on the Irrawaddy, and severely wounded on the advance to Prome (honourably mentioned in Governor-General's Dispatch): Medal and Clasp. Served in the R. M. Battalion in co-operation with the French army at the bombardment and surrender of the forts of Bomarsund, in Aug. 1854 (Baltic Medal). With the combined force during the siege of Sebastopol in 1855, the ex-

pedition to Kertch and Yeni Kalé, and action with the outer forts of Sebastopol on the 17th June (Medal and Clasp, 5th Class of the Medjidie, and Turkish Medal). Has also the Medal for the Kaffir War.

89 Captain Gwyn served with the R. M. Brigade in the Crimea in 1855, and was also at the surrender of Kinbourn (Medal and Clasp, and Turkish Medal).

90 Captain Barnard served in the Royal Navy in Syria in 1840 (Turkish Medal and Naval War Medal with one Clasp). In the Parana, and commanded the first division of the rocket party at St. Lorenzo, in action with the batteries on 4th June 1846.

91 Captain Allen served on the China expedition. Also with the R. M. Brigade in the Crimea in 1855, and at the surrender of Kinbourn (Medal and Clasp, and Turkish Medal).

92 Captain Masters served in India during the Mutiny in 1857-58. Served with the Expedition to the North of China, and commanded the 2nd Battalion at the attack on the forts at the Peiho on 25 June 1859—severely wounded, and mentioned in despatches.

93 Major Parke served on the China expedition of 1857-58, and was at the blockade of the Canton river, and Major of the 1st Battalion at the landing before and storming of the city (Brevet of Major). Accompanied the Expedition to the North of China, and in command of the 1st Battalion at the attack on the forts at the Peiho on 25th June 1859, and brought the Brigade out of action (mentioned in despatches).

94 Captain Magin served with the Baltic expedition of 1854 (Medal). Served on the China expedition of 1857-58; was shipwrecked in H.M.S. *Raleigh*, afterwards present at the capture of Mandarin war junks in Escape and Fatshan Creeks, commanded the garrison of Macao fort during the blockade of the Canton river, and present at the landing before and storming of Canton.

95 Captain Slaughter served with the Baltic expedition in 1854 (Medal). Also in China with the expeditionary force in 1858-59, accompanied the Expedition to the North, and present at the attack on the forts at the Peiho (wounded).

96 Captain Gritton served on the China expedition of 1857-58, including the blockade of the Canton river, the storm and capture of the city.

97 Captains Tribe and Bazalgette served on the China expedition of 1857-58, including the blockade of the Canton river, the landing before, storm and capture of the city. Capt. Tribe was in action with the Braves near the White Cloud Mountains.

98 Captain Williams was severely wounded at Lagos, Western Africa, 26th Dec. 1851, in spiking the guns to protect H. M. steamer *Teazer*, then aground.

99 Major Cooke served on the China expedition of 1857-59, including the blockade of the Canton river, the landing before and capture of Canton in command of one of the storming Companies; served afterwards as D.A.Q.M.General to the army in garrison at Canton (Brevet of Major).

100 Major Digby served in 1855 in command of the R. M. Artillery in the flotilla of mortar-boats employed against Sebastopol during its siege and fall; also at the bombardment and surrender of Kinbourn; was several times mentioned in Dispatches (Medal and Clasp, Brevet Major, CB., Knight of the Legion of Honor, 5th Class of the Medjidie, and Turkish Medal).

101 Major Morrison was present when the Batteries of Obligado in the river Parana were attacked and carried, 20th Nov. 1845. Served on the China expedition of 1857-58, including the blockade of the Canton river, the landing before, storm and capture of the city. Served as Provost Marshal to the expedition and afterwards as D.A.A.General to the army in garrison at Canton (Brevet of Major).

102 Major Jackson was at the bombardment of Odessa 22nd April 1854. Served with the R. M. Brigade in the Crimea at the battle of Balaklava and during the siege of Sebastopol in 1854-55 (Medal and two Clasps, 5th Class of the Medjidie, and Turkish Medal). Served on the China expedition of 1857-58, including the blockade of the Canton river, and as Major of the Battalion at the landing before and storming of Canton (Brevet Major).

103 Captain Usher served at the bombardment of Odessa 22d April; commanded the detachment landed at the capture of Eupatoria; was the senior officer of his corps engaged in the attack on the outer forts and works of Sebastopol on 17th Oct., and employed in the blockading force before that town until Dec. 1854 (Medal and Clasp, and Turkish Medal). Served on the China expedition of 1857-58, including the blockade of the Canton river, the landing before, storm and capture of the city. In 1858 he served with the Allied Garrison in Canton as Provost Marshal to the Army.

104 Captain M. Spratt served with the R.M. Battalion at Eupatoria, and with the Brigade in the Crimea; was present at the battle of Balaklava, and during the siege and fall of Sebastopol, part of the time as Adjutant of a battalion; he was also at the surrender of Kinbourn (Medal and two Clasps, 5th Class of the Medjidie, and Turkish Medal). Served on the China expedition of 1857-58, including the blockade of the Canton river, the landing before and capture of the city.

105 Captains Fox and Prynne served in the Baltic in July and Aug. 1854 (Medal). Served on the China expedition of 1857-58, including the blockade of the Canton river, the landing before and capture of the city.

106 Captain Pym served on the China expedition of 1857-58, including the blockade of the Canton river, the landing before, storm and capture of the city. In 1858 he served on the Staff of the Army as Captain Superintendent of the Canton Police force.

107 Major Ellis served in the Kaffir war of 1846-47 (Medal). Served with the Baltic expedition in 1854 (Medal); was Adjutant to the 2nd Battalion during the siege of Sebas-

War Services of the Officers of the Royal Marines.

topol and at the battle of Balaklava in the same year, and Aide-de-Camp to Colonel Hurdle at its fall, as also at the surrender of Kinbourn (Medal and two Clasps, Sardinian Medal, 5th Class of the Medjidie, and Turkish Medal). Served with the China expedition of 1857-58 as Aide de Camp to Colonel Holloway, including the blockade of the Canton river, the landing before, storm and capture of the city (Brevet of Major). Appointed Major of Brigade to the Royal Marines in August 1858.

108 Captain Davis was at the destruction of 23 vessels, with storehouses, timber, and stores, at Uleaborg on the 1st and 2nd June 1854; at the destruction of a vessel and 80 stacks of timber, at Tornea on the 8th June; at the partial bombardment of Bomarsund 1st June; in action with its forts on the 10th and 15th August, and at the operations before, and its surrender (Baltic Medal). Served with the combined force during the siege of Sebastopol, until its fall, and was engaged with the outer forts on several occasions; was employed co-operating with the Turkish army at the attack on Eupatoria, 17th Feb.; accompanied the Kertch expedition; was at the blockade of Odessa, and at the bombardment and surrender of Kinbourn (Medal and Clasp, 5th Class of the Medjidie, and Turkish Medal).

109 Captain Domville was landed in 1845 with a detachment of Royal Marines for the protection of British property at Monte Video. He was there detached for service in the Parana, and was present at the attack and capture of the ports of Obligado, and forcing the passage of the river. Commanded a detachment at Rat Island, off Monte Video, and was at the defence of Colonia in the river Plate in March and April 1847.

110 Captains Budd and Kinsman served with the Baltic expedition in 1854 (Medal). Served on the China expedition of 1857-58, including the blockade of the Canton river, the landing before and capture of Canton.

110† Captains Herrick and Snow served with the Baltic expeditions in 1854 and 1855 (Medal).

111 Captain Noott served in the White Sea, blockading the Russian ports during the summer of 1854.

112 Captain Draffen served in the Baltic the latter part of 1854 (Medal); was at the blockade of Odessa, and before Sebastopol during the siege in 1855 (Medal and Clasp, and Turkish Medal).

112† Captain Croker served on the China Expedition of 1857-59, including the blockade of the Canton River, the landing before, storm and capture of Canton; Expedition to the North, as Brigade Major, and attack on the forts at the Peiho (wounded, and mentioned in despatches).

113 Capt. Mawbey was in action with the forts of Bomarsund, 10th Aug. 1854; and he commanded the Royal Marine Artillery in the battalion, during the operations against and surrender of the forts (Medal).

114 Capt. Alexander was present during the siege of Sebastopol until its fall, and in action with the outer batteries on 20th April; at Eupatoria during the defence of the lines against the Russian army 17th Feb.; also at the bombardment and surrender of Kinbourn (Medal and Clasp, and Turkish Medal).

115 Captain Baker was in action with the Russian batteries on Hangoe-head, 22nd May 1854. Served with the Baltic expedition in 1855, including the bombardment of Sweaborg (Medal).

116 Captain Harris served in the Kaffir war of 1851-2 (Medal).

117 Captain Cox was at the action with the batteries, and expulsion of the Russian garrison from Redout Kaleh, 19th May 1854, and variously employed on that coast; was the senior officer of R. M. Artillery at the attack by the combined fleets on the outer forts and works of Sebastopol on the 17th October, and employed in the blockading force during the siege, until March 1855 (Medal and Clasp, 5th Class of the Medjidie, and Turkish Medal).

118 Captain Butcher served in Burmah during the war in 1853 (Medal and Clasp). Present before Sebastopol in 1854-55 until its fall; served in co-operation with the Turks at the defence of Eupatoria 17th Feb., and was at the bombardment of Kinbourn (Medal and Clasp, and Turkish Medal).

119 Captain Starr served with the Baltic expedition in 1854 (Medal); also in the flotilla of mortar-boats employed before Sebastopol until its fall, and at the bombardment and surrender of Kinbourn (Medal and Clasp, Knight of the Legion of Honor, and Turkish Medal).

120 Captain Connolly served with the Baltic expedition in 1854 (Medal).

121 Captains Horsey and Wriford, Lieuts. Halliday and Woollcombe, served with the Baltic expedition in 1855, and in the flotilla of mortar-boats during the bombardment of Sweaborg (Medal).

122 Captain Arthur Ellis served in the Black Sea during the siege of Sebastopol in 1855 (Medal and Clasp, and Turkish Medal).

123 Captain M'Callum was present at the attack on the outer batteries of the harbour of Petropaulovski, 31st August; landed 4th Sept. at an attack on the same batteries, and succeeded to the command of the Royal Marines on the death of Capt. Parker, and was wounded in the head; was at the capture of two Russian vessels on the 7th Sept. 1854. Served with the China expedition of 1857-58, and commanded a division of the Royal Marines of the fleet at the attack and capture of the forts at the mouth of the Peiho river on 20th May—mentioned in despatches.

124 Captain Ansell was at the bombardment of Odessa, 22nd April, and was made

prisoner by the Russians when H. M. S. *Tiger* was stranded and burnt, 12th May 1854. Served with the Baltic expedition in 1855, and in the flotilla of gunboats during the bombardment of Sweaborg (Medal).

125 Captain Poore served with the R. M. Battalion in the operations against and surrender of the forts of Bomarsund in Aug. 1854. Also with the Baltic expedition in 1855, and in the flotilla of mortar boats during the bombardment of Sweaborg (Medal).

126 Captain Gregory was present at the bombardment of Odessa 22nd April 1854; served with the R. M. Battalion at the occupation of Eupatoria in 1854, and with the Brigade in the Crimea during the siege of Sebastopol in 1854-55 (Medal and Clasp, 5th Class of the Medjidie, and Turkish Medal).

127 Captain H. G. Elliot served as Adjutant to the 1st Battalion in the Crimea during the siege and fall of Sebastopol in 1854-55, and at the battle of Balaklava, also at the surrender of Kinbourn. Was present at the bombardment of Odessa, 22nd April; commanded a detachment employed in covering the ships' companies of H.M.S. *Albion* and *Vesuvius* on the 25th and 26th of September 1854, when employed removing wounded Russians from the battle field of the Alma on those days, and covered the embarkation of the unarmed parties on the latter day when obliged to retreat in consequence of the advance of a strong force of the enemy's cavalry; for his conduct on this occasion he received the thanks of Sir S. Lushington (Medal and Clasps, 5th Class of the Medjidie, and Turkish Medal).

128 Captain Hewett served with the R. M. Battalion in the operations against and surrender of the forts of Bomarsund in Aug. 1854 (Medal). In 1855 he served in charge of a mortar in the flotilla employed against Sebastopol during the siege, and also at the bombardment and surrender of Kinbourn (Medal and Clasp, Knight of the Legion of Honor, and Turkish Medal).

129 Captain M'Arthur was at the attack and destruction of the piratical stockades, &c. at Lagos, Western Africa, in Dec. 1851. Also at the bombardment of Odessa, 22nd April 1854; employed in making observations on the coast of Georgia, &c.; in action with the batteries, and expulsion of the Russian garrison from Redout Kaleh on 19th May; at the shelling of a Russian camp in the bay of Katcha during the landing of the allied armies on the 14th September; present at the combined attack on the outer forts and works of Sebastopol on 17th October, and with the blockading force before that town during the siege, until Dec. 1854 (Medal and Clasp, 5th Class of the Medjidie, and Turkish Medal).

130 Captain Roberts was in the action with the batteries and expulsion of the Russian garrison from Redout Kaleh on the 19th May 1854. Served with the R. M. Brigade during the siege of Sebastopol; was employed as Assistant-Engineer at Balaklava, and with the Royal M. Artillery in the siege train before Sebastopol in 1854-55 (Medal and Clasp, Knight of the Legion of Honor, 5th Class of the Medjidie, and Turkish Medal).

131 Captain Shute served in the Royal Navy during the operations on the coast of Syria (Turkish Medal and Naval War Medal with one Clasp). In 1854-55 he served with the R. M. Brigade in the Crimea, part of the time as Quartermaster of Brigade, during the siege and fall of Sebastopol, and at the battle of Balaklava, and commanded a Company at the capture of Kinbourn (Medal and Clasps, 5th Class of the Medjidie, and Turkish Medal); he was also at the bombardment of Odessa 22nd April 1854.

132 Captain Seymour, Lieuts. Grove Morris, Higman, Mascall, and Walsh, served with the Baltic expedition in 1855 (Medal). Lt. Walsh served also with the expedition to the Baltic until the declaration of peace in 1856.

132† Lieut. C. S. Williams served with the Baltic expedition in 1855 (Medal). Served with the China expedition of 1857-59, including the blockade of the Canton river, bombardment, storm and capture of the city; expedition to the North and attack on the forts at the Peiho (wounded).

133 Captain Parke served in the Black Sea in the latter part of 1855.

134 Captain Holland commanded a detachment employed on board H.M.S. *Fury*, and on shore at the capture and destruction of 23 piratical vessels and 250 guns in Bias Bay (China), on the 1st Oct. 1849; and in H.M.S. *Medea* at the destruction of 13 piratical vessels and 120 guns at Kuto (China), on the 4th and 5th March 1850. Served in boats of H.M.S. *Hastings* on the Irawaddy in the autumn of 1852, in action with Burmese troops at Meet-tha on 30th September, and on shore at the capture and occupation of Prome (Medal and Clasp).

135 Captain Macnamara served with the combined force before Sebastopol during the siege and at its fall; was the senior officer of R. M. Artillery employed in the Sea of Asof in June 1855, and was landed at Taganrog, Marioupol, and Ghirsk, to destroy Government stores, &c. (mentioned in Dispatches); present at the bombardment and surrender of Kinbourn (Medal and two Clasps, 5th Class of the Medjidie, and Turkish Medal).

136 Major A. A. Douglas was at the bombardment of Odessa, 22nd April 1854. Served in the breaching batteries before Sebastopol in 1854, and at the bombardments from 1854, until its fall, and was wounded 21st April (Medal and Clasps, Knight of the Legion of Honor, Sardinian Medal, 5th Class of the Medjidie, and Turkish Medal).

137 Captain Usher and Lieut. Creighton served in the Baltic in the latter part of 1855 (Medal).

138 Captain G. L. Blake was landed with detachments for the protection of British subjects and property at Singapore, in May 1854. Landed in Oct. 1856 for the protection of the British factories at Canton; was at the destruction of Chinese war junks in Escape

and Fatshan Creeks on 27th May and 1st June 1857, twice landed and attacked and defeated parties of Chinese soldiers (mentioned in despatches); blockade of the Canton river and storming of Canton.

139 Captain Fraser served as Adjutant to the R. M. Battalion at the bombardment and surrender of the forts of Bomarsund in Aug. 1854 (Medal).

140 Captains Bennett and Blanckley served during the summer of 1855, blockading the Russian ports in the White Sea.

141 Captain W. P. Burton was in the boats at the attack on Gamla Carleby, in the Gulf of Bothnia, on the 7th June 1854. Served with the Baltic expedition in 1855, and was at the bombardment of Sweaborg, and employed in the Rocket boats on the nights of 9th and 10th August (Medal).

142 Captain Dalby served as Acting Quartermaster of the R. M. Brigade in the Crimea during the siege of Sebastopol in 1854 (Medal and Clasp, 5th Class of the Medjidie, and Turkish Medal).

143 Captain Thelwall was at the destruction of 14 vessels and a vast quantity of stores at Brahested on the 30th May 1854; at the destruction of 23 vessels, storehouses, &c. at Uleaborg on the 1st and 2nd June; at the destruction of a vessel and 80 stacks of timber at Tornea on 8th June; at the operations against Bomarsund, and in action with the forts on the 15th August (Medal). In 1855 he was present during the siege of Sebastopol until its fall, and was in action with the outer forts on the 19th June; engaged shelling the batteries in Soujak Bay, and expelling the Russian garrison 12th March, and in action with the batteries at Soujak Kulé 13th March; assisted at the landing of the troops at Kinbourn, and at the bombardment of that fort (Medal and Clasp, 5th Class of the Medjidie, and Turkish Medal).

145 Captain Henry served with the Baltic expedition in 1854 (Medal). Served throughout the war of 1856-58 in China, including the storming of the breach in the walls of Canton (mentioned in despatches) and operations there; occupation of Macao forts, destruction of Mandarin junks in Fatsham Creek, blockade of the Canton river, storm and capture of Canton.

146 Captain Farmar was present at the occupation of Petropolovski in 1855.

147 Captain Jolliffe served with the R. M. Brigade in the Crimea in 1854, and in command of a battery at Balaklava; was attached to the Royal Artillery in the siege train before Sebastopol during the bombardments in 1855, and at its fall; was also at the bombardment and surrender of Kinbourn (Medal and Clasps, Knight of the Legion of Honor, 5th Class of the Medjidie, and Turkish Medal).

148 Captain Searle was at the action of Ecknaes in the Gulf of Finland, 20th May 1854; in action with the forts of Bomarsund, 15th August; and at the surrender of Fort Prasto on the 16th August. Served with the Baltic expedition in 1855, and in the mortar-boat flotilla during the bombardment of Sweaborg (Medal).

149 Captain H. L. Evans served with the R. M. Battalion in co-operation with the French army at the attack and surrender of the forts of Bomarsund in Aug. 1854. Served with the Baltic expedition in 1855, including the destruction of telegraph stations on 29th June, and the shelling of a large body of Russian troops on 1st July (Medal). Commanded a Company throughout the China expedition of 1857-59, including the blockade of the Canton river, storm and capture of the city, and action with the Braves near the White Cloud Mountains; accompanied the Expedition to the North as Adjutant of the 2nd Battalion, and was at the attack on the forts at the Peiho (mentioned in despatches).

150 Captain Jeffreys served with the R. M. Battalion in co-operation with the French army at the attack and surrender of the forts of Bomarsund in Aug. 1854 (Medal). In 1855 he was present with the combined force before Sebastopol during its siege and fall, and in action with the outer forts on 17th June; acted as Quartermaster to the R. M. Battalion at the occupation of Kertch and Yeni Kalé, and commanded a company at the surrender of Kinbourn (Medal and Clasp, and Turkish Medal).

151 Captain Dowell was in action with the Russian batteries on Hangoe-head, 22nd May 1854. Served with the Baltic expedition in 1855, and was engaged with the enemy on the 8th June; present at the destruction of a fort and barracks, and the shelling an encampment on the 23rd June; destruction of thirty vessels in the Bay of Werolax on 30th June; landing at Lovisa, and burning the Government houses, &c., on 5th July; shelling a Cossack encampment on 10th July; destruction of a Cossack barrack, &c., 12th July; action with a steamer, gun boats, and a battery near Wiborg on 13th July, and was mentioned in the Dispatches for his gallantry in assisting to save the crew of a boat under fire, for which he has received the Victoria Cross; engaged with the batteries at Frederiksham on 21st July; occupation of the Island of Kotka, and destruction of the stores, &c., on 26th July, and bombardment of Sweaborg (Medal).

153 Captain Wm. Taylor served the Eastern campaign of 1854-55 with the R. M. Brigade in the Crimea, including the battle of Balaklava, siege and fall of Sebastopol, and commanded a company at the surrender of Kinbourn (Medal and two Clasps, 5th Class of the Medjidie, and Turkish Medal).

154 Captain E. F. Pritchard was at the bombardment of Odessa 22nd April 1854; served the Eastern campaign of 1854-55 with the R. M. Brigade, and was attached to the Light Division of the army in the trenches before Sebastopol during the winter; was Adjutant to the 2nd Battalion at the fall of Sebastopol, and at the surrender of Kinbourn (Medal and Clasps, 5th Class of the Medjidie, and Turkish Medal).

155 Captain Carrington was at the bombardment of Odessa 22nd April 1854; served the

Eastern campaign with the R. M. Brigade, including the battle of Balaklava, siege and fall of Sebastopol, also at the surrender of Kinbourn (Medal and Clasps, and 5th Class of the Medjidie). Served the campaign of 1857-59 in China as Quartermaster of the 1st Battalion and was at the operations before and storming of Canton; expedition to the North, and wounded at the attack on the forts at the Peiho.

156 Captain R. W. B. Hunt served with the R. M. Battalion in the operations against and surrender of the forts of Bomarsund in Aug. 1854 (Medal).

157 Captain Hawkey was at the storming and destruction of the inner batteries and stockades at the Sulina mouth of the Danube, 8th July 1854. Served the Eastern campaign with the R. M. Brigade, including the battle of Balaklava, siege and fall of Sebastopol; was also at the surrender of Kinbourn (Medal and two Clasps, 5th Class of the Medjidie, and Turkish Medal). Served on the China expedition of 1857-59, including the blockade of the Canton river, storm and capture of the city, the latter part of the time as Adjutant of the 1st Battalion; expedition to the North, and attack on the forts at the Peiho (mentioned in despatches).

158 Captain Spry was at the bombardment of Odessa 22nd April 1854; served the Eastern campaign with the R. M. Brigade, including the battle of Balaklava, siege and fall of Sebastopol, also at the surrender of Kinbourn (Medal and two Clasps, 5th Class of the Medjidie, and Turkish Medal).

159 Captain F. G. Pym served the Eastern campaign with the Royal Marines attached to the Light Division, including the battles of Balaklava and Inkerman and siege of Sebastopol (Medal and three Clasps, Knight of the Legion of Honor, 5th Class of the Medjidie, and Turkish Medal). Commanded a detachment throughout the Indian campaign of 1857-58 (Medal). Has received the Silver Medal from the Royal Humane Society.

160 Lieut. H. F. Cooper served with the R. M. Battalion at the defence of Eupatoria and with the Brigade in the Crimea during the siege and fall of Sebastopol; latterly as Acting Quartermaster; was Quartermaster of the 1st Battalion at the surrender of Kinbourn (Medal and Clasp, 5th Class of the Medjidie, and Turkish Medal).

161 Lieut. Muskery served in the Black Sea the latter part of 1855. Served as Adjutant of the 2nd Battalion on the China expedition of 1857-58, including the blockade of the Canton river, operations before and capture of the city.

162 Lieut. West served at the blockade in the Baltic in 1854; was present during the operations against the Aland Islands, including the capture of an Earthen battery on the 8th August, and in the action with the forts of Bomarsund on the 15th August. In 1855 he accompanied the Baltic expedition; was in action with steamers and a battery on 21st June, and at the bombardment of Sweaborg (Medal). Served also with the expedition to the Baltic until the declaration of peace in 1856.

163 Lieut. Mudge served with the Baltic expedition in 1855, was engaged with the batteries of Fredericksham on 21st July, occupation of the fortified island of Kotka and destruction of barracks, &c., there on 26th July, also at bombardment of Sweaborg (Medal).

164 Lieut. Ambrose Wolrige served in the Baltic in August and September 1854 (Medal); served the Eastern campaign of 1854 with the R. M. Brigade, including the battle of Balaklava, and was with the Light Division of the army at the battle of Inkerman, and in the trenches during the whole winter; present with the combined force before Sebastopol during the siege, and at its fall in 1855; served as Adjutant to the R. M. Battalion on the Kertch expedition and occupation of Yeni Kalé, was also at the surrender of Kinbourn (Medal and three Clasps, Sardinian Medal, 5th Class of the Medjidie, and Turkish Medal).

165 Lieuts. Meheux, Harington, Delacombe, and Colwell, served with the Baltic expedition in 1854 (Medal).

166 Lieuts. Savary and Brenan served in the Baltic in July and Aug. 1854 (Medal). Lt. Brenan accompanied the Expedition to the North of China and was wounded at the attack on the forts at the Peiho on 25 June 1859.

167 Lieut. Brydges served with the Baltic expeditions in 1854 and 1855, and commanded a mortar in the flotilla during the bombardment of Sweaborg (Medal).

168 Lieut. Meade served the Eastern campaign of 1854-55 with the R. M. Brigade, including the battle of Balaklava and siege of Sebastopol (Medal and two Clasps, 5th Class of the Medjidie, and Turkish Medal). Served on the China expedition of 1857-58, including the blockade of the Canton river, operations before and capture of the city; afterwards as Quarter Master of the 2nd Battalion.

169 Lieut. G. O. Evans served the Eastern campaign with the R. M. Brigade, including the battle of Balaklava, siege and fall of Sebastopol, also at the surrender of Kinbourn—as Quarter Master of the 2nd Battalion; was appointed Aide de Camp to Colonel Holloway in Sept. (Medal and two Clasps, 5th Class of the Medjidie, and Turkish Medal). Served on the China expedition of 1857-58, including the blockade of the Canton river, storm and capture of the city. In January 1858 he was appointed D.A.Q.M. General to the force in garrison at Canton, and afterwards Assistant Superintendent of the Police Force in that city.

170 Lieut. Walton served with the R. M. Brigade at the siege of Sebastopol in 1854-55 (Medal and Clasp, 5th Class of the Medjidie, and Turkish Medal). Served with the expedition to the Baltic until the declaration of peace in 1856.

171 Lieut. R. J. H. Douglas served with the R. M. Battalion at the defence of Eupatoria in 1854, and with the R. M. Brigade at the siege of Sebastopol in 1854-55 (Medal and Clasp, 5th Class of the Medjidie, and Turkish Medal). Served on the China expe-

dition of 1857-59, including the blockade of the Canton river, storm and capture of the city; expedition to the North, and wounded at the attack on the forts at the Peiho.

172 Lieut. Lloyd served the Eastern campaign with the R. M. Brigade, including the battle of Balaklava, siege and fall of Sebastopol; and was also at the bombardment and surrender of Kinbourn (Medal and two Clasps, 5th Class of the Medjidie, and Turkish Medal).

173 Lieut. Ruel was at the action with the batteries and expulsion of the Russian garrison from Redout Kaleh, 19th May 1854. Served with the R. M. Brigade in the Crimea from 1854 to Feb. 1855, and with the combined force before Sebastopol during its siege and fall; commanded a Company at the occupation of Kertch and Yeni Kalé, and was also at the surrender of Kinbourn (Medal and Clasp, 5th Class of the Medjidie, and Turkish Medal).

174 Lieut. Naylor served with the R. M. Battalion at the attack and surrender of the forts of Bomarsund in Aug. 1854. Served with the Baltic expedition in 1855, and was at the bombardment of Sweaborg (Medal).

175 Lieut. Thomas served with the R. M. Battalion at Eupatoria in 1854, and with the Brigade in the Crimea during the siege and fall of Sebastopol, and was also at the surrender of Kinbourn (Medal and Clasp, 5th Class of the Medjidie, and Turkish Medal).

176 Lieut. Nightingale served throughout the Burmese war of 1852 in H.M.S. *Fox* (Medal and Clasp).

177 Lieut. Cobb served on the China expedition of 1857, including the blockade of the Canton river, storm and capture of the city.

178 Lieut. Clements was present at the attack on the batteries at Petropaulovski on 31st August, landed on 4th Sept. at an attack on the same batteries (severely wounded), and was at the capture of two Russian vessels on 7th Sept. 1854. Served in the China war of 1857-58, including the blockade of the Canton river, storm and capture of Canton, expedition to the North, and landed at the bombardment and capture of the forts at the mouth of the Peiho river on 20th May.

179 Lieut. Cuthbert W. Burton has received the Burmese Medal. On the landing of the Royal Marines for the protection of the British factories at Canton on 24 Oct. 1856 he was appointed Adjutant of that force, and was present at the storming of the breach in the wall on the 29th Oct. (mentioned in despatches) and subsequent operations; destruction of Chinese war junks in Fatshan Creeks on 1st June 1857; blockade of the Canton river, and as Adjutant of the Provisional Battalion at the storming of Canton and its subsequent military occupation.

180 Lieuts. J. C. Travers and Ussher Morris served with the Baltic expeditions in 1854 and 1855, including the action with a battery at the mouth of the Narva on 18th June, and at the bombardment of Sweaborg (Medal). Lieut. Travers served as Adjutant of the 1st Battalion on the China expedition of 1857-58, including the blockade of the Canton river, the landing before, storm and capture of the city; was appointed Aide de Camp to Colonel Holloway in Aug. 1858.

182 Lieut. Mould was present at the attacks on the Russian batteries at Petropaulovski on 31st August and 4th Sept., and at the capture of two Russian vessels on 7th Sept. 1854.

183 Lieut. Foster served with the Baltic expedition in 1854 (Medal). In 1855 he was present with the combined force before Sebastopol during the siege, and was employed in the occupation of the Sea of Azof in June, and destruction of the enemy's ships and magazines at Taganrog, Marioupol, Ghirsk, &c.; served in command of a mortar in the flotilla, and was several times engaged in firing on the town of Sebastopol until its fall; also in action with the outer batteries on the 18th June; was in command of a mortar at the bombardment and surrender of Kinbourn; was several times mentioned in Dispatches (Medal and two Clasps, 5th Class of the Medjidie, and Turkish Medal).

184 Lieut. Festing served with the Baltic expedition in 1854 (Medal). Commanded a mortar in the flotilla employed against Sebastopol until its fall, and was also at the bombardment and surrender of Kinbourn (Medal and Clasp, Knight of the Legion of Honor, and Turkish Medal). Served with the China expedition of 1857-58 as Adjutant of the Artillery, including the blockade of the Canton river, bombardment and storm of the city.

185 Lieuts. Lane, Newall, and Forbes served with the expeditions to the Baltic in 1854 and 1855 (Medal).

186 Lieut. Dadson served with the R. M. Battalion, in co-operation with the French army, at the bombardment and surrender of the forts of Bomarsund, in Aug. 1854, and was on picquet in the breaching battery during the battering of Fort Nottick on 15th Aug., and served with the Allied expedition to the Baltic, from March to Dec. of that year (Medal). Joined the combined force before Sebastopol in Jan. 1855, and was present at the siege until May; accompanied the Kertch expedition, and the advance on and occupation of Yeni Kalé, and commanded a Company in camp there until June; afterwards present at the siege and fall of Sebastopol, and at the surrender of Kinbourn (Medal and Clasp, and Turkish Medal). Served on the China expedition of 1857-58, including the blockade of the Canton river, the landing before Canton, and dangerously wounded by a gingal ball (right arm shattered) while with the scaling ladders at the storm and capture of the city.

187 Lieut. Short served with the Baltic expedition in 1854 and again in the latter part of 1855 (Medal). Served on the China expedition of 1857-58, including the blockade of the Canton river, the landing before, storm and capture of the city.

188 Lieut. Lean was at the surrender of Fort Nottick, Aland Isles, 15th Aug. 1854. Served with the expedition to the Baltic in 1855, including the bombardment of Sweaborg, during which he was serving with a detachment in a gunboat of the flotilla (Medal).

189 Lieut. Swale was landed with detachments for the protection of British subjects and property at Singapore, in May 1854. Was landed in Oct. 1856 for the protection of the British factories at Canton, engaged in the storming of the breach in the wall of that city on 29th October and wounded in the neck by a musket ball (mentioned in despatches); was in the boats at the capture of French folly fort on 5th Dec.; at the destruction of Chinese war junks in Escape and Fatshan Creeks on 27th May and 1st June 1857; blockade of the Canton river, storm and capture of the city.

190 Lieuts. Daly and Hemmans served with the Baltic expeditions of 1854, 1855, and 1856 (Medal).

191 Lieut. Wm. Sanders served with the R. M. Battalion at the bombardment and surrender of the forts of Bomarsund in Aug. 1854. Also with the Baltic expedition in 1855, including the action with a battery at the Mouth of the Narva on the 18th June (Medal).

192 Lieut. Durnford served with the R. M. Battalion at the operations against and surrender of the forts of Bomarsund in Aug. 1854,—the latter part of the time doing duty as Assistant Engineer. Served with the Baltic expedition in 1855, and was in command of a mortar in the flotilla during the bombardment of Sweaborg (Medal).

193 Lieut. Gladstone served with the Baltic expedition in 1854 (Medal). Also in the Black Sea in the latter part of 1855 and until the declaration of peace in 1856.

194 Lieuts. M'Meekan, Walker, Harrison, Clendon, Symons, H. S. Jones, and G. F. Blake, served with the Baltic expedition in 1854 (Medal).

195 Lieut. Pitman served in the Baltic in July and Aug. 1854 (Medal), and subsequently in 1854 before Sebastopol until its fall, and was in command of a mortar in the flotilla employed during the siege; occupation of the Sea of Azof, bombardment of Taganrog, and destruction of ships, stores, &c., there; also at Marioupol and other towns on the coast, where he was landed; was in the mortar flotilla at the bombardment and surrender of Kinbourn (Medal and two Clasps, Knight of the Legion of Honor, 5th Class of the Medjidie, and Turkish Medal).

196 Lieut. Mairis served the Eastern campaign of 1854-55 with the R. M. Brigade, including the battle of Balaklava and siege of Sebastopol (Medal and two Clasps, 5th Class of the Medjidie, and Turkish Medal). Served with the expedition to the Baltic until the declaration of peace in 1856.

197 Lieut. Mitchell served with the Baltic expeditions in 1854 and 1855, and was employed in the Rocket Boats on the 9th Aug. at the bombardment of Sweaborg (Medal). Served with the expedition to the Baltic until the declaration of peace in 1856.

198 Lieut. Lennox served as orderly officer to Colonel Graham, R. M., during the operations against and surrender of the forts of Bomarsund in Aug. 1854 (Medal). Joined the combined force before Sebastopol in Jan. 1855; served with the R. M. Battalion at the occupation of Kertch and Yeni Kalé in May, and with the Brigade in the Crimea from Aug. until the fall of Sebastopol (Medal and Clasp, and Turkish Medal).

199 Lieut. Bent served with the R. M. Battalion at the bombardment and surrender of the forts of Bomarsund in Aug. 1854 (Medal). Landed at Tana and Woodlark Islands in July 1858 to destroy the villages and operate against the natives.

200 Lieut. J. F. Sanders served with the R. M. Battalion at the bombardment and surrender of the forts of Bomarsund in Aug. 1854. Served also with the Baltic expedition in 1855 (Medal). Served with the expedition to the Baltic until the declaration of peace in 1856.

201 Lieut. Murray served with the R. M. Battalion at the bombardment and surrender of the forts of Bomarsund in Aug. 1854 (Medal). Served with the combined force before Sebastopol in 1855, and with the R. M. Brigade until the termination of the siege; was also at the surrender of Kinbourn (Medal and Clasp, and Turkish Medal).

202 Lieut. Napier served the Eastern campaign of 1854 with the R. M. Brigade, including the battle of Balaklava; attached to the Light Division in the trenches and at the battle of Inkerman; with the combined force before Sebastopol during the siege in 1855, and with the expedition to Kertch and occupation of Yeni Kalé (Medal and three Clasps, Sardinian Medal, 5th Class of the Medjidie, and Turkish Medal). Served on the China expedition of 1857-58, including the blockade of the Canton river, the landing before and capture of the city.

203 Lieut. Tinmouth served in the Baltic in July and Aug. 1854 (Medal); also with the R. M. Brigade in the Crimea at the siege of Sebastopol from Feb. to Aug. 1855 (Medal and Clasp, and Turkish Medal).

204 Lieut. Nurse served in the Baltic in July and Aug. 1854 (Medal); also with the combined force before Sebastopol in 1854-55 until its fall; with the battalion at the occupation of Kertch and advance on Yeni Kalé, also at the bombardment of Kinbourn (Medal and Clasp, and Turkish Medal).

205 Lieut. Studdert served in the Crimea in 1855, and on the expedition to Kinbourn (Medal, and Turkish Medal). Served on the China expedition of 1857-58, including the blockade of the Canton river, bombardment, storm and capture of the city.

206 Lieut. Savage served throughout the China war of 1856-58, including the bombardment of Canton, capture of the Forts in the river, and landed for the protection of the factories; blockade of the river, landing before, bombardment and capture of Canton, expedition to the North and capture of the forts at the mouth of the Peiho river and operations there.

207 Lieut. Coppin served with the Baltic expeditions of 1854 and 1855 (Medal). Served with the China expedition of 1857-59, including the blockade of the Canton river, opera-

War Services of the Officers of the Royal Marines. 433

tions before and capture of the city; expedition to the North and wounded at the attack on the forts at the Peiho.

208 Lieut. Brutton served with the combined force before Sebastopol during the siege in 1854-55, and with the expedition to Kertch and Yeni Kalé (Medal and Clasp, and Turkish Medal).

209 Lieut. Nott served on the China expedition of 1857-58, including the blockade of the Canton river, bombardment and storming of the city, expedition to the North and capture of the forts at the mouth of the Peiho river and operations there.

210 Lieut. Melville Suther served before Sebastopol from 1854 until its fall; also at Kertch and Yeni Kalé, and at the bombardment of Kinbourn (Medal and Clasp, and Turkish Medal).

211 Lieut. le Grand served at the siege of Sebastopol from 1854 until its fall; was also at the capture of Kertch, and occupation of Yeni Kalé, and at the surrender of Kinbourn (Medal and Clasp, and Turkish Medal).

212 Lieut. Graham served with the Baltic expeditions in 1854 and 1855, including the destruction of Telegraph Stations on 29th June, and the shelling a large body of troops on 1st July (Medal).

213 Lieut. R. F. Taylor served with the R. M. Brigade in the Crimea from Feb. 1855, until the fall of Sebastopol (Medal and Clasp, and Turkish Medal).

214 Lieut. Ozzard served with the R. M. Brigade in the Crimea in 1855, and with the combined force before Sebastopol during the siege; also with the expedition to Kertch, advance on and occupation of Yeni Kalé; was in action with outer defences of Sebastopol on 17th June (Medal and Clasp, and Turkish Medal). Served on the China expedition of 1857-58, and was at the destruction of war junks in Escape and Fatshan Creeks, capture of Chuenpee fort, and blockade of the Canton river.

215 Lieut. E. B. Pritchard joined the R. M. Brigade in the Crimea in Feb. 1855, and served with it until the fall of Sebastopol; was also at the surrender of Kinbourn (Medal and Clasp, and Turkish Medal).

216 Lieut. Donellan served with the Baltic expedition in 1855, including the bombardment of Sweaborg (Medal).

217 Lieut. Barnes served in the operations in the Canton river in 1856-58; was in Macao fort when attacked by junks on 4th January, at the destruction of war junks in Fatsham Creek, landed to destroy a village, storm and capture of Canton.

218 Lieut. Shairp served with the Baltic expedition in 1855, including the destruction of Telegraph Stations on 29th June, and the shelling a large body of troops on 1st July (Medal).

219 Lieuts. Cairncross, Dixon, and Sadleir served with the Baltic expedition in 1855 (Medal). Lieut. Dixon served also with the expedition to the Baltic until the declaration of peace in 1856.

220 Lieuts. Stark and M. H. Price served with the Baltic expedition in 1855, including the bombardment of Sweaborg (Medal). Lt. Price served in China in 1857-58, including the blockade of and operations in the Canton river, the landing before and storming of the city.

221 Lieuts. Crawford and Crease served on the China expedition of 1857-58, including the blockade of the Canton river, bombardment and storming of the city. Lt. Crawford accompanied the expedition to the North and was present at the attack on the forts at the Peiho on 25 June 1859 (severely wounded, and mentioned in despatches).

222 Lieut. Smail served with the Baltic expedition in 1855 (Medal). He commanded the Launch of H.M.S. *Esk* in action at the capture of a Mandarin junk and a Snake-boat, the former of which was set on fire and destroyed, the latter brought off under a heavy fire from an armed village, in a branch of the Canton River on the 6th July 1857, was employed in the blockade of the river and subsequent operations.

223 Lieut. Broughton served in the Crimea during the latter part of 1855 (Medal). Served on the China expedition of 1857-58, including the blockade of the Canton river, the landing before and capture of the city.

224 Lieut. Holmes served with the Baltic expedition in 1855, including the destruction of a fort, and shelling an encampment on 23rd June, blowing up of Fort Svartholm and barracks on 4th July, destruction of the barracks at Lovisa on 5th July, shelling a Cossack encampment and landing at Kounda Bay on 11th July, destruction of a Cossack barracks, &c. on 12th July, action with a Russian steamer, gun-boats, and a battery near Wiborg on 13th July; also with the batteries of Fredericksham on 21st July, capture of the Island of Kolka, and destruction of military stores on 26th July, and bombardment of Sweaborg (Medal). Served also with the expedition to the Baltic, until the declaration of peace in 1856.

225 Lieut. Pascoe served with the Baltic expedition in 1855 (Medal). Served in China during the war and was present at the destruction of war junks in Fatsham Creek on 1st June 1857, and blockade of the Canton river.

226 Lieuts. Rodney and Standbridge served with the Baltic expedition in 1855 (Medal).

227 Lieuts. Conner and Hale served with the Baltic expedition in 1855 (Medal). Also with the China expedition of 1857-58, including the blockade of the Canton river, the landing before and capture of the city.

228 Lieut. Wroot served with the Baltic expeditions of 1855 and 1856 (Medal). Also with the China expedition, including the blockade of the Canton river, the landing before and capture of the city.

229 Lieut. Robilliard served with the Baltic expedition in 1855, including the action with a battery at the mouth of the Narva on 18th June, and bombardment of Sweaborg (Medal).

229† Lieut. Brookes served with the Baltic expedition in 1854, and with the R. M. battalion at the attack and surrender of the forts of Bomarsund (Medal). In 1855 he was present with the combined force before Sebastopol during the siege, until May, when he accompanied the expedition to Kertch, and served with the R. M. Artillery in the gun-boats during the occupation of the Sea of Azof, including the attack on, and destruction of, Government stores, &c., at Taganrog on 3rd June; at Marioupol on 5th June, and at Ghiesk on 6th June (officially mentioned). Commanded a mortar in a flotilla employed against Sebastopol on several occasions, from 15th of August until the capture of that place (honorably mentioned). Also in command of a mortar at the bombardment and surrender of Kinbourn on 17th October (officially mentioned). Served as a captain of Artillery with the Turkish Contingent from March 1856, until disbanded, and was Garrison Adjutant to the Artillery at Kertch. Has received the Crimean Medal with two Clasps, is a Knight of the Legion of Honor, has the 5th Class of the Medjidie, and Turkish Medal.

230 Lieut. Shanks served with the R. M. Battalion at Eupatoria in 1854, and with the Brigade in the Crimea during the siege of Sebastopol in 1855 (Medal and Clasp, 5th Class of the Medjidie, and Turkish Medal).

231 Lieut. E. Willis served with the Baltic expedition in 1855 (Medal). Also with the China expedition of 1857-59, including the blockade of the Canton river, the landing before, storm and capture of the city; expedition to the North and wounded at the attack on the forts at the Peiho on 25 June 1859.

232 Lieut. F. J. Parry served with the R. M. Brigade in the Crimea at the siege and fall of Sebastopol, also at the surrender of Kinbourn (Medal and Clasp, and Turkish Medal). Also with the China expedition of 1857-58, including the blockade of the Canton river, the landing before and capture of the city.

233 Lieuts. Macdonald and H. G. Campbell served in the Black Sea in the latter part of 1855. Lieut. Macdonald served also in the Crimea during the latter part of 1855 (Medal).

234 Lieuts. Speer, St. John, Sparshott, and Pritchett, served on the China expedition of 1857-58, including the blockade of the Canton river, the landing before, storm and capture of the city.

235 Lieut. Brewer was present at the bombardment of Jeddah on 25 July 1858.

236 Lieut. Stirling served in India during the mutiny and was severely wounded in the action at Kudjwa on 1st Nov. 1857, and present with the field force during the operations of 1857-58 (Medal).

237 Lieut. Allnutt served in China during the war of 1856-58, and was present at the capture of the forts and blockade of the Canton river, landed for the protection of the factories, at the storming on 20th Oct. 1856 (mentioned in despatches), all the subsequent operations, destruction of war junks in Fatsham Creek, the landing before and storming of Canton, expedition to the North and capture of the forts at the mouth of the Peiho river.

238 Lieut. H. T. M. Cooper served in China during the war of 1856-58, and was present at the capture of the forts and blockade of the Canton river, landed for the protection of the factories, destruction of war junks in Fatsham Creek on 1st June 1857, the landing before, assault and capture of Canton, expedition to the North and bombardment and capture of the forts at the mouth of the Peiho river.

238† Lieuts. R. L. Price and A. W. D. Smith served on the China Expedition of 1857-59, including the blockade of the Canton river, the landing before, storm and capture of the city; expedition to the North and attack on the forts at the Peiho (wounded, Lt. Smith severely).

239 Lieut. Owen was wrecked in H.M.S. *Raleigh* and served in China in 1857-58, was at the destruction of Mandarin junks in Escape and Fatsham Creeks, blockade of the Canton river, storm and capture of the city.

240 Lieuts. Fonblanque, Heriot, Collins, Barker, Thompson, and Woodforde served on the China expedition of 1857-58, including the blockade of the Canton river, the landing before, storm and capture of the city. Lts. Heriot and Collins accompanied the expedition to the North and were wounded (Lt. Collins severely) at the attack on the forts at the Peiho on 25th June 1859.

241 Lieuts. Straghan and Servante served on the China expedition of 1857-58, including the blockade of the Canton river. Lt. Straghan accompanied the expedition to the North and was wounded at the attack on the forts at the Peiho on 25th June 1859 (mentioned in despatches).

242 Lieut. Bontein served with the expeditionary force during the operations at Canton in 1858.

243 Lieuts. Scott, W. H. Smith, Poyntz, Godfrey, Armstrong, and O'Grady served on the China expedition of 1857-58, including the blockade of the Canton river, the landing before and capture of the city.

244 Lieut. Rokeby served on the China expedition of 1857-59, including the blockade of the Canton river, the landing before, storm and capture of the city, action with the Braves and destruction of villages near the White Cloud Mountains—severely wounded; expedition to the North as Aide de Camp to Colonel Lemon, and attack on the forts at the Peiho on 25th June 1859 (mentioned in despatches).

245 Capt. Hookey served as Volunteer 1st class, in His Majesty's ship *Prince of Wales*, from Jan. to Dec. 1805, and was in the general action of the 22nd Dec. 1805. Served in the West Indies, from 1806 until 1809, including the capture of Les Saints, and Martinique, and several actions in boats cutting out French vessels, and destroying batteries, &c. From 1809 to 1811 served on board H. M. S. *Theban*, blockading the French flotilla at Boulogne;

several times in action with them. Assisted in the boats cutting out a large French lugger at Dieppe. From 1812 to 1814 served on board His Majesty's ship *Daphne*, in the Baltic, and was several times in action with Danish gun-boats in the Belt. Has received the War Medal with one Clasp.

246 Captain Geo.Watson served as Quartermaster of the Royal Marine Battalion employed in co-operation with the troops of the Queen of Spain in 1837, and was wounded 16th March.

247 Captain T. B. Gray served at the battle of Navarino in 1827. Also in a battalion under Colonel Owen, on the north coast of Spain in 1836-7-8, in co-operation with the Spanish army, including the field actions of the 10th, 12th, and 14th March, and the action of Hernani, 16th March 1837: he was subsequently appointed Adjutant to the force under Colonel Parke. He served as Captain on the coast of Portugal and in the Tagus during the civil war in 1846-7, and was landed with his detachment from H. M. S. *Superb*, to guard the captured divisions of the rebel army under Count das Antas, prisoners in Fort St. Julian. Has received the War Medal with one Clasp.

248 Captain Cossar served on the coast of Syria in 1840 (Medals).

249 Capt. Ambrose A. R. Wolrige served in the year 1809 with Lord Cochrane in the Basque Roads; and in the same year was engaged in action with gun-boats in the Baltic. From 1810 to 1812 defence of Cadiz and Tarifa. Severely wounded at South Beveland in 1814, and received a reward from the Patriotic Fund. Present at the battle of Algiers in 1816. Has received the War Medal with four Clasps.

250 Captain Toby served from 1810 to 12 inclusive, on the coast of France. From 1813 to 16, with the 1st Battalion (Royal Marines) in America, and on the Lakes of Canada. Since the Peace, he has served in the Mediterranean, on the coasts of Africa, and South America. He has been frequently engaged in boat actions with batteries, &c. &c.

251 Captain M'Callum served the Syrian campaign of 1840 (Medal and Clasp, and Turkish Medal),—at D'Jouni, and bombardment of Acre. Served the Eastern campaign of 1854-55 with the R. M. Brigade, including the battle of Balaklava, and was with the battalion attached to the Light Division in the trenches during the winter; in 1855 he was with the combined force before Sebastopol until its fall; with the battalion in the expedition to Kertch and occupation of Yeni Kalé; and with the Brigade at the surrender of Kinbourn (Medal and Clasps, 5th Class of the Medjidie, and Turkish Medal).

252 Captain M'Carthy served on the coast of Syria in 1840 (Medals and Clasp).

253 Doctor Millar has received the War Medal and Clasp and the Turkish Medal for service in Syria in 1840.

254 Staff Surgeon Steel was employed in the *Cyclops* as Assist.Surgeon during the whole of the operations on the coast of Syria. As Surgeon of the *Arethusa* in the attack on Odessa, also on Sebastopol on the 17th October; and as Surgeon of the *Russell* in the Baltic. He has four Medals and two Clasps, the 5th Class of the Medjidie, and Turkish Medal.

255 Assist.Surgeon Ayre served in the Crimea (Medal and Clasp, and Turkish Medal).

256 Assist.Surgeon Sproule served with the Baltic expedition in 1854 (Medal), and in the Crimea from Jan. 1855, including the expedition to Kertch, siege and fall of Sebastopol, and expedition to Kinbourn (Medal and Clasp, and Turkish Medal).

257 Assist.Surg. Hatherly served as medical officer of the expedition up the San Juan Nicaragua, in 1848, and was present at the storming of Fort Scrapaqui (mentioned in Dispatches).

258 Doctor Woods served in the Burmese war in 1852, including the capture of Prome (Medal).

259 Assist.Surgeon Newton has the Burmah Medal. Was Assist.Surgeon of H.M.S. "Bittern" during her successful cruises on the coast of China and under fire in boat attacks upon Pirates on eleven occasions. Attached to the forces operating against Canton and present at the assault of the city; served in the boats at the attack on the French Folly and destruction of the fleet of War Junks, and again at the capture of French Folly fort.

260 Assist.Surgeon Chambers was present at the attack upon Lagos in 1851. Served in both the Baltic expeditions (Medal).

COMMISSARIAT DEPARTMENT.

	Commissary General in Chief.	Deputy Asst. Commis. Gen.	Assistant Commis. Gen.	Deputy Commis. Gen.	Commissary General.	Station.
	John William Smith,[1] CB.	1 Dec. 33	24 Dec. 44	30 Dec. 54	27 Nov. 58	*London.*
	Commissaries General.					
19	William Bishop	13 July 24	24 July 34	29 Dec. 49	1 Apr. 59	*Malta.*
	Thomas Christie Bartrum Weir	15 July 26	11 Apr. 36	do	do	*Canada.*
	William Henry Drake,[5] CB.	16 Apr. 35	16 Dec. 45	1 Jan. 55	21 June 59	*C.of G.H*
	Deputy Commissaries General.					
20	Henry Bowers[2]	25 Dec. 14	13 Dec. 33	24 Dec. 44		
	Charles Williams	25 Dec. 14	1 July 40	6 Jan. 54		*Western Australia.*
	William Fisher Mends	1 July 37	15 June 43	do		*West Indies.*
	Fred. Thomas Mylrea	10 Sept. 30	6 Dec. 39	1 Jan. 55		*Melbourne.*
	Ferguson Thos. Coxworthy	7 June 25	24 Dec. 41	do		
	Thomas Graham[4]	11 Dec. 34	15 June 44	do		*Nova Scotia.*
	Francis Bisset Archer	2 Jan. 34	16 Dec. 45	2 Jan. 56		*Ionian Islands.*
	Philip Turner	28 June 38	26 Dec. 46	do		*China.*
	Henry Browne Morse[6]	1 July 40	8 Dec. 46	do		*Jamaica.*
	Leonce Routh[7]	do	20 Dec. 49	do		*Bermuda.*
	Frederick Stanley Carpenter[8]	24 Dec. 41	20 Dec. 49	do		*Gibraltar.*
	Montague Wm. Darling[9]	26 Dec. 40	6 Jan. 54	1 Aug. 56		
	Wm. James Tyrone Power,[10] CB. ..	24 Dec. 44	1 Jan. 55	do		*London.*
	William Henry Maturin	20 Jan. 37	26 Dec. 40	11 Nov. 59		*War Office.*
	Randolph Routh[4]	do	do	do		*Mauritius.*
	Assistant Commissaries General.					
	Wm. Robert Alex. Lamont	5 Oct. 32	16 Dec. 45			*Pembroke.*
	Stephen Owen	do	do			
	George Shepheard	20 Jan. 37	26 Dec. 46			*Ionian Islands.*
	John William Bovell[1]	do	do			*Tasmania.*
	Maximilian Malassez	28 June 38	do			*Jamaica.*
	Charles Thos. Malassez	20 May 28	20 Dec. 49			*Malta.*
	Alexander Edwards	20 Jan. 37	do			*Dublin.*
	George Darley Lardner	1 July 40	do			*Honduras.*
	William Le Mesurier[2]	23 Dec. 42	17 Sept. 50			
	William Spearman Archer[4]	28 June 38	28 Dec.			*Malta.*
	John Salusbury Davenport[13]	do	do			*Cape of Good Hope.*
	James Aug. Erskine[3]...........	do	do			
	Humphrey Stanley Jones[16]	1 July 40	5 Jan. 53			*New Zealand.*
	George Horne.................	do	do			*Malta.*
	Henry Ashton	do	do			*Western Australia.*
	Thomas Wroot Midwood[4]........	do	do			*China.*
	William Palmer[1]	do	do			*Nova Scotia.*
	Edm. John M'Mahon[4]	1 July	6 Jan. 54			*Nova Scotia.*
	Edward Strickland[5]	20 Dec.	do			
	Kean Osborn[6]..................	24 Dec. 41	do			*Aldershot.*
	Alfred Salwey[7]	24 Dec. 44	15 Jan.			*London.*
	Henry Wm. Woodforde Plant......	26 Dec. 40	1 Jan. 55			*Canada.*
	Thomas Wm. Goldie......	26 Dec. 40	do			*Bahamas.*
	George Atkinson	23 Dec. 42	do			*Portsmouth.*
	Fred. Henry Ibbetson	do	do			*West Indies.*
	Edward Barrington de Fonblanque[8]	do	do			*China.*
	James Douglas Willan[11]	do	do			*St. Helena.*
	Robert Clement Major...........	19 Dec. 43	do			*West Indies.*
	Redmond Uniacke[4]	do	do			*London.*
	James Knight Goold	do	do			*Bermuda.*
	Douglas Bennet Clarke	do	do			*Cork.*
	Robert May Gardiner[16]	do	do			*Curragh.*
	Fitzjames Edward Watt	do	do			*War Office.*
	James Bell Lundy[4]	24 Dec. 44	do			*Belfast.*
	Robert Cumming[16]	16 Dec. 45	do			*Canada.*
	Villiers W. Cæsar Hawkins[4]	19 Dec. 45	do			*West Indies.*
	Conrad Potgièter[17],............	26 Dec. 46	do			*Cape of Good Hope.*
	Thomas Williams[14]	16 Dec. 45	1 Jan. 56			*Curragh.*
	Henry Curll[9]	17 Oct. 44	2 Jan. 56			*West Indies.*
	John Banner Price	17 Oct. 44	2 Jan. 56			*Canada.*
	Charles H. Sheil[9]	24 Dec. 44	do			
	Hector John Macaulay...........	do	do			*Melbourne.*
	Henry Connell	do	do			*New Zealand.*
	Frederick Wm. Waldron	26 Dec. 46	do			*Bermuda.*
	Henry Moore.................	do	do			*Mauritius.*
	Henry Bartlott[10]	do	do			*New Zealand.*
	Alexander Crowder Crookshank[12] ..	do	do			*Chatham.*
	Henry Robinson[9]	do	do			*China.*
	Philip Rolleston[15].............	20 Dec. 48	do			*Edinburgh.*
	George Joseph Webb[4]	16 Dec. 45	1 Aug. 46			*Cape of Good Hope.*

Commissariat Department. 436

	Deputy Asst. Commis. Gen.	Assistant Commis. Gen.	Station.
John Francis Rogers [4]	28 Dec. 47	1 Aug. 50	*China.*
Charles Garrow Blanc [4]	8 Dec. 48	do	
Charles Palmer [16]	29 Dec.	do	*Devonport.*
Charles Bagot Smith [19]	29 Dec. 48	1 Aug. 56	*Cape of Good Hope.*
James Magloire Montague Gaudet	5 Jan. 53	7 July 58	*Gambia*
Arthur Wm. Downes	29 Dec. 51	27 Oct. 58	*Gibraltar.*
Robert Baker [1]	24 Dec. 44	11 Nov. 59	*The Curragh.*
Charles Wm. Eichbauen	16 Dec. 45	do	*Cape of Good Hope.*
Geo. Alexander Skinner [1]	do	do	*London.*
Arthur F. Adams	do	do	*New Zealand.*
James Hardy Tubby [1]	26 Dec. 46	do	*Newfoundland.*

Deputy Assistant Commissaries General.

	Deputy Asst. Commis. Gen.	Station.		Deputy Asst. Commis. Gen.	Station.
John M. M. Sutherland	16 Dec. 45	*W. Australia*	Croker Lovell Pennell	2 Jan. 50	*Jamaica*
B. J. Montanaro	do	*Malta*	Arthur Lewis Chaplin [3]	do	*Tasmania*
Widdrington Tinling	26 Dec. 46	*Barbadoes*	Owen Edward Hayter [3]	do	*C. of G. Hope*
Henry Maule	28 Dec. 47	*Tasmania*	Hy. Clutterbuck Lewis [3]	do	*China*
Robert Henry Smith [1]	do	*C. of G. Hope*	Wm. F. G. Servantes [8]	do	*China*
Charles Swain [2]	29 Dec. 48	*Gibraltar*	Alf. Robt. Thompson [14]	do	*West Indies*
Edward Ibbetson	do	*Ionian Islands*	Charles Wm. Charlier [1]	do	*St. Helena*
Robert Booth [3]	do	*C. of G. Hope*	Francis Charles Blunt	do	*Jamaica*
Justus Hy. Thompson [4]	29 Dec. 49	*Manchester*	Edwin Litchfield	1 Aug. 50	*C. of G. Hope*
Theodre. E. M'Clintock [5]	do	*China*	Alfred Ernest Petrie	do	*Tasmania*
John Henry Sale [6]	do	*Tasmania*	Chas. Davis O'Connor [13]	7 Sept. 56	*C. of G. Hope*
Wm. John Fagan	do	*Aldershot*	Geo. Hutchison Phillips	16 Oct. 57	*C. of G. Hope*
Arch. Donald M'Lean	do		Wm. Henry Newland	9 June 58	*London*
Alex. Wm. Turner [3]	19 Jan. 50	*Canada*	Robert Dalrymple Ross	17 Sept. 58	
Thomas Forsyth Moore	28 Dec. 50	*Ionian Islands*	Thos. Sutton Marshall	11 Nov. 59	*China*
Lathan Wm. Blacker [1]	do	*C. of G. Hope*	Aug. Morton Festing	do	*Honduras*
Geo. B. Bennett [1]	do	*C. of G. Hope*	Edward Charles Saunder	do	*China*
Fred. Geo. Swan	do	*Shorncliffe*	Frederick Casolani	do	*Ionian Islnds.*
Edward L. Ward	8 Feb. 51	*Woolwich*	John Fitzm. Manning	do	*Newfoundl.*
John Blood Gallwey	29 Dec. 51		Edward Cattell	do	
James Long	do	*Dublin.*	Sidney Reynett Brown	do	*Canada*
D. Campbell Napier	do	*Colchester*	Tho. Buttorw. Prissick	do	*Nova Scotia*
Jas. A. F. Mitchell	do	*Sierra Leone*	John Manley Rattle	do	*West Indies*
William C. Ball	14 Feb. 52	*W. Australia*	Welles. G. W. Robinson	do	*C. of G. Hope*
Henry J. Brownrigg [7]	2 July 52	*Bermuda*	Henry John Wyld	do	*Canada*
John Murray	21 Dec. 52	*London*	Charles D'Oyly Forbes	do	*China*
E. Mills	5 Jan. 53	*Malta*	Francis Innes	do	*Aldershot*
Wm. M. Rogers	do	*Canada*	Wm. Worthing. Moore	do	*C. of G. Hope*
Arthur Kay [1]	do	*C. of G. Hope*	Robert Stanes	do	*C. of G. Hope*
David Standen [1]	do	*C. of G. Hope*	Edw. F. G. Greenwood	do	*Melbourne*
Donald Maclean [1]	do		John Philip Wilkinson	do	*Gibraltar*
Joseph Marsh [6]	do	*Malta*	Robert Edward Hunter	do	*Gold Coast*
George Rennie [6]	do	*W. Australia*	Edward Courtney	do	*C. of G. Hope*
James Wm. Murray [8]	3 Mar. 53	*C. of G. Hope*	Ashley Cowper Ryland	do	*Tasmania*
Arthur Thesiger West	6 Jan. 54	*Curragh*	Henry Wm. Hackman	do	*Bahamas*
Walter T. M'Kinstey	do	*West Indies*	William Ogilvy	do	*Canada*
Robert Grey D. Selby	do	*Ionian Islands*	William Oakley Chislett	do	*New Zealand*
Jas. S. C. Sutherland [12]	do	*Nova Scotia*	Geo. Rawstorne Gibson	do	*Honduras*
Charles Foster [6]	do	*China*	Fred. Basset Wingfield	do	*C. of G. Hope*
James Bailey [9]	do	*Bermuda*	John Draper	do	*New Zealand*
Matthew Bell Irvine	do	*Canada*	Alexander Ewing	do	*China*
Geo. Joseph Wrentmore	do	*N. S. Wales*	John Leslie Robertson	do	*Tasmania*
Horace Travers	do	*W. Australia*	John Henry Randall	do	*C. of G. Hope*
J. Mainwaring Lindsey	7 Nov. 54	*Gold Coast*	Robert Lee Matthews	do	*Jamaica*
George Twining	1 Jan. 55	*Bermuda*	Tho. Aug. Le Mesurier	do	*Nova Scotia*
Luke R. Castray [1]	do	*C. of G. Hope*	Geo. Wm. White Ingram	do	*Gibraltar*
A. Foulkes Cookesley [10]	do	*C. of G. Hope*	Horace Neville Thurp	do	*London*
Fra. C. Colquhoun [4]	do	*C. of G. Hope*	Hy. B. Arth. Middleton	do	*West Indies*
Geo. Ramsay Primrose [6]	do	*West Indies*	Arthur Lawr. Haliburton	do	*Nova Scotia*
Matthew Winter	17 Feb. 55	*China*	William Roger Snow	do	*Aldershot*
John Buckle Barlee [2]†	28 Feb. 55	*C. of G. Hope*	Wm. Hy. Sut. Marshall	do	*China*
Alexander Clerk [11]	30 Mar. 55	*New Zealand*	Edward Estridge	do	*West Indies*
Arthur S. Baynes [11]	9 June 55	*China*	Ivan Ran. C. C. Graham	do	*Jamaica*
Edward Turnbull	2 Jan. 56	*Gambia*	Edwin Dunn	do	*Melbourne*
Fred. Souter Monk [6]	do	*S. Australia*	Charles Walter Penrice	do	*Nova Scotia*
Robert Handley Dundee	do	*C. of G. Hope*	Nathaniel Taylor	do	*China*
Edwd. Daniel Lawrence	do		Edmund John Johnstone	do	
Wm. Elmfreville Green [6]	do	*C. of G. Hope*	Paul Geo. Fred. Furse	do	

1 Mr. J. W. Smith is a CB., and a Knight of the Legion of Honor.
2 Mr. Bowers served in the Peninsula, and has received the War Medal with one Clasp for St. Sebastian.
4 Messrs. Graham and R. Routh have the Kaffir Medal.
5 Mr. Drake served throughout the Eastern campaign of 1854-55, including the Commissariat charge of the Expedition to Kertch (Medal and three Clasps for Balaklava, Inkerman, and Sebastopol, CB., Knight of the Legion of Honor, Officer of St. Maurice and St. Lazarus, and 4th Class of the Medjidie).
6 Mr. Morse served at the siege of Sebastopol (Medal and Clasp, and 5th Class of the Medjidie).
7 Mr. Leonce Routh served the Eastern campaign of 1854-55, including the battle of Alma and siege of Sebastopol (Medal and Clasps, and 5th Class of the Medjidie).
8 Mr. Carpenter served in the Eastern campaign of 1854-55, including the battle of Alma and siege of Sebastopol (Medal and Clasps, Knight of the Legion of Honor, and 4th Class of the Medjidie).
9 Mr. Darling served in the Eastern campaign of 1854-55, with the Light Division, including the battles of Alma and Inkerman, and siege of Sebastopol (Medal and Clasps, Knight of the Legion of Honor, and 5th Class of the Medjidie).
10 Mr. Power served in the Kaffir war (Medal). Served the Eastern campaign of 1854-55 with the 2nd Division at the battles of Alma and Inkerman, and siege of Sebastopol (Medal and Clasps, and 5th Class of the Medjidie).

Assistant Commissaries General.

1 Messrs. Bovell, W. Palmer, Baker, Skinner and Tubby have received the Medal for the Kaffir war.
2 Mr. Le Mesurier was present at the storm and destruction of the Mandingo town of "Bambacoo," up the Gambia, 6th May 1849; also at the storm and partial destruction of the chief's town, "Keenung," on the following day, and during the action and defeat of the enemy on the 8th May, on the Plain of Quenella.
3 Mr. Erskine served as a Captain of the 8th Regiment Anglo-Spanish Legion in 1835-6, and has received a Medal for St. Sebastian, 5th May, and the Cross of First Class of the Order of San Fernando for Altza, 6th June 1836.
4 Messrs. W. S. Archer, Midwood, M'Mahon, Unjacke, Lundy, Hawkins, Webb, Rogers and Blanc, served at the siege of Sebastopol (Medal and Clasp). Mr. M'Mahon has the 5th Class of the Medjidie.
5 Mr. Strickland served with the 1st Division at the battle of Alma (Medal and Clasp).
6 Mr. Osborn served in the Kaffir war (Medal); also at the siege of Sebastopol (Medal and Clasp, Knight of the Legion of Honor, and 5th Class of the Medjidie).
7 Mr. Salwey was present at the storm and destruction of the Native Mandingo town of Sabajee on the Gambia 1st June 1853.
8 Mr. de Fonblanque served with the 3rd Division at the battles of the Alma and Inkerman, and siege of Sebastopol (Medal and Clasps, and 5th Class of the Medjidie).
9 Messrs. Curll, Sheil and Robinson have received the Medal for the Kaffir war.
10 Mr. Bartlett served with the 4th Division at the battles of Alma and Inkerman and siego of Sebastopol (Medal and Clasps; has also received the Medal for the Kaffir war).
11 Mr. Willan was present at the battle of Alma and siege of Sebastopol (Medal and Clasps).
12 Mr. A. C. Crookshank served throughout the Eastern campaign of 1854-55,—in Commissariat charge of the Cavalry Division from the landing in the Crimea, present at the affairs of Bulganac and M'Kenzio's Farm, battles of Alma, Balaklava, Inkerman, and Tchernaya and siege of Sebastopol (Medal and Clasps, and 5th Class of the Medjidie). Served on the China expedition of 1857-58 in Commissariat charge of the Expeditionary Field Force, and was present at the capture of Canton.
13 Mr. Davenport served the Syrian campaign of 1840 (Medal).
14 Mr. Williams served in the Kaffir war (Medal). Also the Eastern campaign of 1854-55, including the battle of Alma and siege of Sebastopol (Medal and Clasps).
15 Mr. Rolleston served with the 1st Division throughout the Eastern campaign of 1854-55, including the battles of Alma, Balaklava, and Inkerman, and siege of Sebastopol (Medal and Clasps, and 5th Class of the Medjidie).
16 Messrs. Gardiner, Cumming and Palmer served in the Kaffir war (Medal); also at the siege of Sebastopol (Medal and Clasp).
17 Mr. Potgieter has received the Kaffir Medal.
18 Mr. H. S. Jones has the 4th Class of the Medjidie for service with the late Osmanli Cavalry.
19 Mr. Smith served in the Kaffir war (Medal). Also the Eastern campaign of 1854-55, including the battle of Alma and siege of Sebastopol (Medal and Clasp).

Deputy Assistant Commissaries General.

1 Messrs. R. H. Smith, Blacker, Bennett, Kay, Standen, Maclean, Castray, and Charlier, have received the Medal for the Kaffir war.
2 Mr. Swain served with the 2nd Division in Bulgaria in 1854, and with the 4th Division from the landing at Old Fort, and was present at the battles of Alma and Inkerman, and siege of Sebastopol (Medal and Clasps). He was subsequently appointed Assistant Commissary General (1st Jan. 1856), and had the charge of the Military Chest and Staff Paymaster's duties at Scutari, until the breaking up of that establishment in August 1856.
2* Mr. Barlee served with the 4th Division throughout the Eastern campaign of 1854-55, including the battles of Alma and Inkerman and siege of Sebastopol (Medal and three Clasps).
3 Messrs. Booth, A. W. Turner, Chaplin, Hayter, and Lewis, served at the siege of Sebastopol (Medal and Clasp).
4 Messrs. J. H. Thompson and F. C. Colquhoun served the Eastern campaign of 1854-55 with the 2nd Division at the battles of Alma and Inkerman and siege of Sebastopol (Medal and three Clasps).
5 Mr. M'Clintock has received the Medal for the Kaffir war of 1851-52. He was in Commissariat charge of a strong force which marched from Natal to the Orange River Sovereignty to the assistance of the troops at Bloemfontein against the Basuto chief Moshesh, from Aug. 1851 to July 1852.
6 Messrs. Sale, Marsh, Rennie, Foster, Primrose, Monk, and Green, served in the Kaffir war (Medal), also at the siege of Sebastopol (Medal and Clasp).
7 Mr. Brownrigg served throughout the Eastern campaign of 1854-55 with the 3rd Division, including the battles of Alma and Inkerman, and siege of Sebastopol (Medal and three Clasps, and Turkish Medal).
8 Messrs. J. W. Murray and Servantes served with the Heavy Cavalry at the battles of Balaklava and Inkerman and siege of Sebastopol (Medal and Clasps).
9 Mr. Bailey served in the Kaffir war (Medal); also throughout the Eastern campaign of 1854-55, including the battle of Alma and siege of Sebastopol (Medal and two Clasps).
10 Mr. Cookesley served with the Head Quarters of the army throughout the Eastern campaign of 1854-55, including the battles of Alma, Balaklava, and Inkerman, and siege of Sebastopol (Medal and four Clasps).
11 Messrs. A. Clark and A. S. Baynes served the Eastern campaign of 1854-55 with the Light Division, including the battles of Alma and Inkerman, and siege of Sebastopol (Medal and three Clasps).
12 Mr. Sutherland served with the Light Cavalry at the battles of Alma, Balaklava, and Inkerman, and siege of Sebastopol (Medal and Clasps).
13 Mr. O'Connor served with detachments of 1st, 2nd, and 3rd West India Regts. that proceeded from Gambia in Oct. 1854 to the assistance of the troops besieged in Christianborg Castle, Gold Coast, and with the expedition against the Kings and Chiefs of the Moriah country, Western Africa, in Nov. 1854.
14 Mr. A. R. Thompson was present at the battle of Alma and siege of Sebastopol (Medal and Clasps).

MEDICAL DEPARTMENT.

Years service.	Full Pay Half pay		Hospital Assist.	Assist.-Surgeon	Surgeon	Surgeon Major	Deputy Insp-Gen.	Inspec.-General	Where Stationed
26	0	*Director General.* Thos. Alexander,[1] CB. (*Director Gen.* 22 June 58)	...	10 Oct. 33	30 May 45	3 Mar. 54	12 Jan. 55	22 June 58	
		Inspectors General of Hospitals.							
33	10	William Linton,[2] MD. CB.	9 Dec.	26 18 Jan. 27	2 July 41	17 Mar. 48	28 Mar. 54	7 Dec. 58	East Indies.
34	2½	John Forrest,[3] MD. CB.	10 Nov.	25 9 Feb. 26	2 July 41	21 May 50	28 May 54	31 Dec. 58	Malta.
34	0	William Charles Humfrey[4]	10 Jan.	26 18 Jan. 27	2 July 41	14 Mar. 51	15 Aug. 54	do	Dublin.
27	0	John Robert Taylor,[5] CB.	...	31 May 33	14 June 42	3 Mar. 54	1 Feb. 55	do	Chatham.
34	0	James Brown Gibson, MD. CB.	14 Dec.	26 12 Jan. 29	2 July 41	19 May 51	1 May 55	do	Aldershott.
32	0	Thomas Galbraith Logan,[13] MD.	8 May	28 29 July 30	30 Aug. 42	5 Nov. 52	21 Dec. 55	8 Apr. 59	London.
33	1 4/12	David Dumbreck,[6] MD. CB.	3 Nov.	25 12 Jan. 26	2 July 41	10 Sept. 47	28 Mar. 54	19 July 59	Cape of Good Hope.
		Deputy Inspectors General of Hospitals.							
33	0	Daniel Maclachlan, MD. (*Chelsea Hospital only*).	14 Aug.	27 21 Feb. 28	...	...	23 Feb.	49 Chelsea Hospital.	
44	11	Charles Whyte	19 Sept.	15 14 May 16	24 Aug.	26 30 Dec. 36	6 Jan. 54	Bombay.	
34	0	Thomas Atkinson,[7] MD.	22 Dec.	25 11 May 26	6 Nov.	40 25 Sept. 46	28 Mar. 54	Ceylon.	
25	0	Robert Lawson,[9] MD.	...	15 May	35 16 Dec.	45 27 Oct. 46	8 Dec. 54	Jamaica.	
33	1	Thomas David Hume,[11] MD.	26 Oct.	27 11 Oct. 27	2 July	41 26 Nov. 52	29 June 55	Cork.	
33	0	James Edmund Williams[12]	...	11 May	27 23 July	41 23 Oct.	49 20 July 55	Madras.	
34	0	Samuel Maitland Hadaway	29 Nov.	26 29 July	30 2 Aug.	42 21 Sept. 52	25 Jan. 56	Umballah, Bengal.	
24	0	Archibald Gordon,[14] MD. CB.		28 June	36 12 Sept.	48 27 Oct.	54 25 Jan. 56	Dublin.	
20	1 3/12	V.C Jas. Mouat,[15] CB.		14 Dec.	38 3 Nov.	48 9 Feb.	55 7 Dec. 58	New South Wales.	
26	0	Thomas Ross Jameson,[16] MD.		10 Jan.	34 5 Dec.	43 28 Mar.	54 51 Mar. 58	West Indies.	
25	0	Arthur Anderson,[17] MD.		16 Oct.	35 16 Dec.	45 do	do	Calcutta.	
24	0	John Charles Graham Tice,[18] MD. CB.		15 Jan.	36 23 Jan.	46 do	do	Lucknow, Bengal.	
30	0	James Edward Thomas Parratt[19]		11 Mar.	30 22 Feb.	44 1 April 54	do	Woolwich.	
25	0	John Drope M'Illree		20 Feb.	35 8 Dec.	45 20 Oct. 54	do	Nora Scotia.	
20	1 6/12	George Stewart Beatson,[20] MD.		13 July	38 28 Aug.	46 8 Dec. 54	do	Corfu.	
26	0	George Taylor[21]		16 May	34 30 May	45 12 Jan. 55	do	Montreal.	
21	8	Joshua Paynter[22]		11 Jan.	39 11 Feb.	48 9 Feb. 55	do	Gibraltar.	
23	12/12	Patrick Gammie[23]		17 June	36 2 Mar.	47 1 May 55	do		
24	12/12	Richard Dane,[24] MD.		17 July	35 21 July	46 25 May 55	do	Curragh.	
26	0	Charles Scott,[25] MD. CB.		7 Nov.	34 9 May	45 7 Sept. 58	do		
24	0	Archibald Stewart[26]		19 Feb.	36 12 Feb.	47 1 Oct. 58	do		
23	0	Francis William Innes,[27] MD. CB.		10 Feb.	37 2 Feb.	49 do	do	Shorncliffe.	
19	0	John Fraser,[28] MD. CB.		20 Aug.	41 24 Aug.	52 ...	do		
18	0	John Harrie Ker Innes,[29] CB.		8 April	42 11 Mar.	53 ...	do		
18	0	William Mure Muir,[30] MD.		22 Nov.	42 24 Feb.	54 ...	do	China.	
17	0	Thomas Longmore[31]		3 Feb.	43 3 Mar.	54 ...	do	Colchester.	
24	0	Samuel Currie,[32] MD.		14 Oct.	36 12 Feb.	47 1 Oct. 58	18 Jan. 59	China.	
28	0	George Cherilew, MD.		2 Nov.	32 5 Dec.	43 15 May 55	26 April 59	Mauritius.	
25	0	Richard James O'Flaherty[33]		9 Jan.	35 23 May	45 28 Mar. 54	19 July 59	Portsmouth.	
24	0	T. Graham Balfour, MD.		29 April	36 1 Aug.	48 29 April 56	22 July 59	London.	
21	0	Henry Mapleton,[34] MD.		12 July	39 13 July	47 12 July 59	26 Aug. 59	London.	

440   *Medical Department.*

Years' Service. Full Pay	Half Pay	Surgeons Major.	HOSPITAL-ASSISTANT.	ASSISTANT-SURGEON.	SURGEON.	SURGEON MAJOR.		WHERE STATIONED.
38	0	John Clark, MD.	4 Oct. 27	29 July 30	17 June 42	5 Nov.	52	Canada.
30	2½	William Odell, MD.	14 Feb. 28	9 Nov. 30	21 Apr. 43	3 Mar.	54	Canada.
25	1½⁄₁₂	George Gordon Robertson, MD.	....	12 Aug. 34	25 June 44	28 Mar.	54	York.
26	0	Robert Smith.	....	26 Sept. 34	8 Dec. 45	do		Dublin.
24	0	Joseph Samuel Prendergast,[1] MD.	....	10 Feb. 36	22 May 46	do		Chatham.
25	0	John Thomson Telfer	....	17 July 35	9 June 46	do		China.
25	0	George Carr	....	24 July 35	7 Aug. 46	do		Bermuda.
24	0	Henry Pilleau	....	22 Jan. 36	14 April 46	7 June		Belfast.
25	10⁄₁₂	Collis C. John Delmege,[4] MD.	....	15 May 35	13 March 46	10 Nov.		Plymouth.
24	10⁄₁₂	George Anderson[5]	....	12 June 35	16 Dec. 45	8 Dec.		Edinburgh.
23	9⁄₁₂	James Guy Piers Moore[6]	....	3 Mar. 37	12 June 46	do		Cape of Good Hope.
23	9⁄₁₂	William Denny	....	13 Jan. 37	7 Aug. 46	12 Jan.	55	China.
21	3⁄₁₂	John Gillespie Wood,[7] MD.	....	11 Jan. 39	10 Dec. 47	9 Feb.		West Indies.
20	1⁴⁄₁₂	William Leslie Langley,[8] MD.	....	do	30 Mar. 47	16 Feb.		Liverpool.
23	1¹⁵⁄₁₂	Edward John Burton, MD.	....	11 May 38	27 June 45	do		Canterbury.
26	0	Henry Hadley,[9] MD.	....	28 Nov. 34	23 Mar. 47	23 Mar.	55	Channel Islands.
20	1⁷⁄₁₂	Frederick Foaker[10]	....	19 Oct. 38	24 Apr. 47	1 May	55	Malta.
19	2⁴⁄₁₂	Henry Cooper Reade	....	31 May 39	3 Sept. 47	22 June	55	West Indies.
25	0	Charles Cowan[11]	....	27 March 35	16 Feb. 44	29 June	55	Dublin.
23	6⁄₁₂	William Carson, MD.	....	7 Oct. 36	28 Aug. 46	do		London.
22	5⁄₁₂	William Home,[12] MD.	....	12 Jan. 38	13 Nov. 46	do		Depot Batt. Birr.
20	7⁄₁₂	Edw. Wm. Stone,[13] MD.	....	5 Oct. 38	17 March 48	6 July		Glasgow.
19	1¼⁄₁₂	John Mure, MD.	....	24 Dec. 39	24 Dec. 47	20 July	55	D. Batt. Winchester.
20	1½⁄₁₂	William Sall,[14] MD.	....	10 May 39	13 July 46	3 Nov.	55	West Australia.
27	0	James Macgregor	....	24 July 34	13 Dec. 44	7 Dec.	55	Ceylon.
20	1⁷⁄₁₂	Robert Templeton, MD.	....	6 May 33	5 April 47	8 Jan.	55	Bristol.
19	0	John Davies[16]	....	22 Nov. 39	27 Oct. 48	31 Aug.	56	Yarmouth.
17	0	Thomas Patrick Matthew[17]	....	12 Dec. 43	11 Sept. 49	1 Oct.	58	Chatham.
34	0	John Maitland, MD.	16 Dec. 26	12 June 28	3 Dec. 41	do	58	Stirling.
20	0	Adam Thomas Jackson, MD.	29 Nov. 27	27 July 39	24 Feb. 42	do		Athlone.
33	0	Thomas Coke Gaulter, MD.	22 Mar. 27	20 July 30	25 Feb. 42	do		Chelsea Hospital.
25	1½⁄₁₂	Gideon Dolmage	....	10 Dec. 33	5 April 44	do		Aldershot.
25	0	John Charles Cameron, MD.	....	27 Mar. 35	15 Apr. 44	do		Walmer.
25	0	Francis Robert Waring[18]	....	8 May 35	15 Dec. 45	do		Ceylon.
24	0	Robert Keating Prendergast	....	7 Oct. 36	14 April 46	do		Belfast.
23	0	John Grant	....	9 June 37	10 July 46	do		Nova Scotia.
22	0	James Stewart[19]	....	17 April 38	5 Aug. 46	do		Malta.
25	0	Edward Mockler.[20]	....	25 Sept. 35	7 Aug. 46	do		Fermoy.
23	0	Alex. Douglas Taylor, MD.	....	15 Sept. 37	7 Aug. 46	do		Fermoy.

Medical Department.

Years' Service.			HOSPITAL-ASSISTANT.	ASSISTANT-SURGEON.	SURGEON.	SURGEON MAJOR.	WHERE STATIONED.
Full Pay	Half Pay						
		Surgeons Major.					
24	0	Joseph Ambrose Lawson, M.D.		11 June 36	19 April 47	1 Oct. 58	Corfu.
23	0	Henry Franklin[21]		29 Dec. 37	10 Feb. 52	do	Chatham.
25	0	Melville Neale, M.D.		18 Sept. 35	19 Mar. 52	do	Royal Mil. College.
22	0	Arthur Saunders Thomson, M.D.		19 Oct. 38	6 Aug. 47	19 Aug. 58	Mauritius.
21	0	John Donald		23 Aug. 39	18 July 48	23 Aug. 59	
21	0	Duncan Donald M'Cay M'Donald[22]		4 Oct. 39	6 Oct. 48	4 Oct. 59	Cork.
		Staff Surgeons.					
19	0	George Williamson, M.D.		26 March 41	13 July 47		Chatham.
21	0	John Stuart Smith, M.D.		22 Nov. 39	27 Oct. 48		New Zealand.
21	0	George Murray Webster, M.D.		6 Dec. 39	1 Dec. 48		New South Wales.
21	0	James Alex. Fraser,[2] M.D.		22 Dec. 39	22 Dec. 48		East Indies.
19	0	Sandford M'Vittie Lloyd, M.D.		5 Mar. 41	22 Dec. 48		Aberdeen.
16	0	John William Mostyn, M.D.		8 Mar. 44	16 Mar. 49		Maidstone.
20	0	John Summers, M.D.		29 May 40	28 Aug. 49		Chatham.
17	2¹¹/₁₂	Luke Barron, M.D.		10 July 40	25 Sept. 49		Chatham.
20	0	James Carroll Dempster, M.D.		29 Dec. 40	5 Nov. 50		
19	1	George Thomas Galbraith,[3] M.D.		17 Sept. 41	3 Jan. 51		China.
19	0	Eneas Macintosh Macpherson[4]		21 Aug. 40	14 Oct. 51		Cape of Good Hope.
19	0	Thomas Waller Barrow[5]		8 June 41	26 Dec. 51		Jamaica.
19	0	John Ewing[9]		21 May 41	12 Mar. 51		Dublin.
19	0	William Home Fairbairn,[16] M.D.		11 June 41	16 April 52		London.
19	0	Ludovic Charles Stewart[6]		8 June 41	11 June 52		East Indies.
19	0	William Rutherford,[7] M.D.		2 July 41	11 June 52		China.
19	0	Edward Frederic Kelaart		16 July 41	16 July 52		Ceylon.
16	0	John Thomas Watson Bacot		10 May 44	3 Dec. 52		Pembroke.
16	0	Robert Villiers George,[1] M.D.		10 Nov. 43	4 Feb. 53		
13	0	Wm. Freeman Daniell, M.D.		26 Nov. 47	11 Mar. 53		China.
17	0	Edward Menzies		29 Oct. 41	26 July 53		China.
15	0	George Frederick Bone, M.D.		9 Dec. 45	21 Oct. 53		East Indies.
14	0	Thomas Parr		21 July 46	21 Oct. 53		
18	0	William Nelson Irwin[12]		2 Dec. 42	3 Mar. 54		Yarmouth.
14	3⁷/₁₂	Robert Lewins,[8] M.D.		13 Dec. 42	3 Mar. 54		China.
17	0¹/₁₂	William Walterweld[31]		20 Jan. 43	3 Mar. 54		Malta.
16	0	Thomas Moore Sunter,[10] M.B.		6 Oct. 43	28 Mar. 54		Honduras.
17	1¹/₁₂	Vere Webb[13]		13 Oct. 43	28 Mar. 54		
16	0	Alfred Crocker[11]		26 Jan. 44	do 54		Chatham.
18	1¹/₁₂	George William Powell		20 Aug. 44	do 54		Chatham.
18	0	James Pritchard Moline[46]		7 Oct. 42	15 Aug. 54		Gibraltar.
15	0	Wm. Fred. Torcato Ivey[13]		30 May 45	15 Aug. 54		Chatham.
15	0	Henry Somers, M.D.		17 Oct. 45	do 54		
15	0	George Saunders[14], M.D.		16 Dec. 45	20 Oct. 54		C. of G. Hope.
14	0	David Stuart Erskine Bain,[15] M.D.		23 Jan. 46	3 Nov. 54		West Indies.

† x

Medical Department.

Years' Serv. Full Pay.	Half Pay.	Staff Surgeons.	ASSISTANT SURGEON.	SURGEON.	WHERE STATIONED.
18	0	Orlando Sawle Donnall..........	1 Nov. 42	3 Nov. 54	West Indies.
16	0	Edward Bailey Tuson	20 Aug. 44	10 Nov.	Canada.
14	0	John Dunlop,[27] M.D.	3 Apr. 46	8 Dec. 54	
13	0	Henry Fowle Smith,[43] M.D......	23 Mar. 47	12 Jan. 55	London.
16	1	Edward William Bawtree, M.D...	24 Nov. 43	19 Jan.	Corfu.
14	8/12	Wellington Wellesley W. Poole[19]..	1 Aug. 45	9 Feb.	East Indies.
12	0	Anthony Dickson Home[20]	17 Mar. 48	9 Feb.	China.
13	0	Dudley Hanley, M.D............	20 July 47	16 Feb.	Templemore.
14	0	Robert Thornton[21].............	6 July 46	24 April	Jamaica.
13	0	Henry Shearley Sanders	5 Mar. 47	do	Gravesend.
11	0	Philip Henry Eustace Cross[22]	3 April 49	15 May	Colchester.
15	0	John Small[23]..................	30 Dec. 45	10 July	Mauritius.
9	1 6/12	Charles Walter Poulton	18 Sept. 49	20 July	Mil. Prison, Gosport.
12	0	Waldegrave Rock Thompson, M.D.	30 Nov. 48	14 Sept. 55	
11	7/12	Wm. Walton Somerville, M.D. ..	22 Dec. 48	8 Jan. 56	Cork.
14	0	Henry Vereker Bindon[17]	12 June 46	25 May 56	
9	0	Thomas Ligertwood,[24] M.B.	14 Nov. 51	20 Oct.	East Indies.
9	0	John Hendley[25]	14 Mar. 51	5 Dec. 56	
16	0	Charles Hamilton Fasson[26]	12 July 44	19 Feb. 57	Plymouth.
14	0	William Lapsley................	7 Aug. 46	28 Aug. 57	East Indies.
14	0	Henry Clinton Martin	20 Mar. 46	11 Sept.	
14	0	Brinsley Nicholson,[50] M.D.	25 Sept. 46	2 Oct. 57	
13	0	Gordon Kenmure Hardie,[28] M.D...	12 Feb. 47	2 Oct.	East Indies.
13	0	Edward Dawson Allinson	31 May 47	do	East Indies.
13	0	Henry Higgins Jones, M.D......	10 Dec. 47	do	East Indies.
12	0	David Field Rennie, M.D.......	19 Sept. 48	do	
10	0	John Irvine,[33] M.D.	15 Mar. 50	do	London.
10	0	Robert McGregor	19 April 50	do	East Indies.
10	0	John Gibbons[19]	7 June 50	3 Nov.	East Indies.
10	0	Robert M'Nab,[47] M.D.	8 Nov. 50	26 Jan. 58	Glasgow.
10	0	Robert Beresford Smyth,[34] M.D. ..	15 Nov. 50	26 Jan. 58	Yarmouth.
10	0	Daniel Macqueen, M.D..........	15 Nov. 50	do	Colchester.
9	0	George Peacocke, M.D.	10 Jan. 51	do	East Indies.
9	0	George Edwin Gains	21 Feb. 51	do	East Indies.
9	0	John Edward Moffatt[32]...........	14 Mar. 51	do	East Indies.
9	0	John Hoffman, M.D.............	4 April 51	25 June	Chatham.
9	0	Benjamin Tydd[34]†.............	25 April 51	16 July	Buttevant.
9	0	George Pain	8 May 51	30 July	China.
9	0	William James Ingham[35]........	9 May 51	24 Aug.	Curragh.
9	0	Francis Holton, M.B.	23 May 51	24 Aug.	East Indies.
9	0	Francis Walters Knox[36].........	17 June 51	24 Sept.	East Indies.
13	0	Thomas Blatherwick	4 June 47	31 Dec.	Canada.
9	0	John Knox Leet...............	27 June 51	do	Cape of Good Hope.
9	0	James M'Grigor Laing	25 July 51	do	East Indies.
9	0	Geo. Paul Minchin Woodward, M.D.	12 Sept. 51	do	East Indies.
9	0	William Arthur Thomson, M.B. ..	14 Oct. 51	do	Bahamas.
9	0	Robert Thomas Buckle,[37] M.D. ..	14 Oct. 51	do	East Indies.
9	0	Colin Matheson Milne Miller, M.D.	7 Nov. 51	do	Chatham.
9	0	Francis Cogan	26 Dec. 51	do	Ceylon.
8	0	Patrick M'Dermott[38]..........	2 Jan. 52	do	East Indies.
8	0	John Lyster Jameson...........	2 Jan. 52	do	East Indies.
8	0	Arthur Bell	23 Jan. 52	do	East Indies.
8	0	Edward Arthur Brien	11 Mar. 52	do	Gold Coast.
7	0	Charles Thompson Abbott........	18 Mar. 52	do	Sierra Leone.
8	0	Theodore Gordon Bone,[39] M.D. ..	12 Mar. 52	18 Jan. 59	Canada.
8	0	John Campbell,[41] M.D...........	27 Feb. 52	25 Feb.	Corfu.
8	0	Henry Bowles Franklyn,[40] M.D. ..	26 Mar. 52	11 Mar.	Chatham.
8	0	John Phillips Cunningham, M.D. .	13 Apr. 52	11 Mar.	Limerick.
8	0	Thomas George FitzGerald[42]	do	8 Apr.	London.
8	0	John O'Neal	do	5 May	East Indies.
8	0	Duncan Robertson Rennie[44]	7 May 52	18 Nov. 59	
8	0	Cornelius Clark Rutherford[45]	7 May 52	2 Dec. 59	
5	0	William Skeen, M.D.	8 Mar. 55	13 Dec. 59	Gambia.
5	0	Patrick Andrew M'Dermott......	27 Sept. 55	16 Dec. 59	

Medical Department.

Full Pay	Half Pay	Apothecaries.	ASSISTANT SURGEON.	APOTHECARY &c.	WHERE STATIONED.
35	18 7/12	⒆ Joseph Schembri	17 Jan. 07	14 Oct. 13	Corfu.
45	0	Francis Matthias Bassano	{ Dispenser } { 4 April 15 }	18 Apr. 25	London.
6	0	John M'Intosh		1 Sept. 54	C. of G. Hope.
5	0	F. Fernandez		20 Feb. 55	China.
4	0	John Andrews		5 Dec. 56	Malta.
		Assistant Surgeons.		ASSIST.SURG.	
19	0	Thomas Joliffe Tufnell		11 June 41	Dublin.
7	1 4/12	David Ogilvy Hoile, M.D.		14 Oct. 51	Stirling.
8	0	Thomas Clark Brady[1]		21 May 52	Ceylon.
8	0	Edward Walker Skues, M.D.		11 June	Honduras.
8	0	John Smith Chartres		do	Parkhurst.
8	0	Benjamin Lane[2]		23 July	London.
8	0	Thomas William Fox, M.B.		do	Canada.
8	0	Watkin Sandom Whylock,[52] M.D. ...		25 Dec. 52	
7	0	John James Scott[3]		21 Jan. 53	C. of G. Hope.
7	0	Robert Speedy		11 Mar.	C. of G. Hope.
7	0	Johnston Ferguson		22 April	Mauritius.
7	0	William Snell		6 May 53	
7	0	William Tydd Harding		13 May	Corfu.
7	0	Augustus Frederick Turner		26 July	C. of G. Hope.
7	0	William Stewart, M.D.		29 July	Parkhurst.
6	1 4/12	Peter Davidson, M.D.		5 Aug. 53	Aberdeen.
7	0	Francis Lewis Fitzgerald		12 Aug.	China.
7	0	Wynne Peyton Frazer.............		21 Oct.	Jamaica.
7	0	Humphrey John Gillett Atkinson ...		28 Oct.	Dublin.
7	0	Frederick William Moore		do	Eastbourne.
7	0	John Eldon Young,[12] M.D.		do	Nova Scotia.
6	0	George Evans		24 March 54	
6	0	William Marshall Webb[21]		28 March 54	East Indies.
6	0	David Woods		7 April 54	Canada.
6	0	Alfred Malpas Tippetts[4]		do	West Indies.
6	0	Edward Young Kellett[5]...........		28 April	Corfu.
6	0	Samuel Joseph Bayfield[6]		5 May	Gibraltar.
6	0	Thomas Stephenson Teevan		19 May	Gold Coast.
6	0	Allen Bryson,[7] M.D.		19 May	Jamaica.
6	0	Robert William Jackson		26 May 54	Dublin.
6	0	Henry Titterton[8]..................		26 May	Tasmania.
6	0	Leslie Ogilby Patterson		20 June	East Indies.
6	0	Edmund Humphrey Roberts[10].....		23 June	Canterbury.
6	0	John Sparrow[23]		30 June 54	
6	0	Arthur Salter		14 July 54	
6	0	Daniel O'Donovan, M.D.		14 July	Plymouth.
6	0	Richard Wolseley[9]		28 July	Pembroke.
6	0	Francis Collins,[14] M.D.		1 Sept.	Winchester.
6	0	William Thomas Paliologus		1 Sept.	Walmer.
6	0	John Vernon Seddall,[17] M.D.		13 Oct.	New Colombia.
6	0	Tertius Ball		3 Nov.	West Indies.
6	0	Andrew Semple		10 Nov.	Nova Scotia.
6	0	William Fleming Cullen[6]†........		1 Dec.	Bermuda.
6	0	William Carden Roe[16]............		1 Dec.	Birr.
6	0	Robert Graham Dickson, M.D. ...		14 Dec.	Corfu.
5	0	Henry Lloyd Randell[11]		5 Jan. 55	Jamaica.
5	0	John Michael		10 Jan.	Templemore.
5	0	William Stockwell		31 Jan.	Malta.
5	0	Thomas Kennedy...............		30 March	West Indies.
5	0	David Stranaghan,[18] M.D.........		8 April	Canada.
5	0	Robert Turner		17 April	Malta.
5	0	Charles Moore Jessop[19]		do	Hong Kong.
5	0	William Henry Leslie, M.B.		7 May	East Indies.
5	0	Alexander Crawford Robertson ...		1 June	Limerick.
5	0	James Alfred Turner		7 July	China.
5	0	Thomas Butler Power O'Brien ...		29 Sept.	Belfast.
5	0	Nicholas Ffolliott		13 Oct.	Portsmouth.
5	0	John Goodwin		5 Dec.	Hong Kong.
5	0	Curtiss Martin		15 Dec.	Gold Coast.
4	0	Augustus Morphew		18 Jan. 56	Gambia.
4	0	William O'Halloran		18 Feb.	
4	0	William Page		23 Feb.	China.
4	0	Frederick Oakes		5 Dec.	Gambia.
3	0	Thomas Chaytor Beale		27 Mar. 57	Gambia.
3	0	Alexander Watt Beveridge,[15] M.D.....		15 Sept. 57	
3	0	William Alexander		28 Sept.	East Indies.

Medical Department.

Assist.Surg.		Stationed at		Assist.Surg.	Stationed at
Charles O'Callaghan	6 Nov. 57		Hunt Johnson Bailey	12 Jan. 59	Chichester.
James Jameson, M.D.	9 Nov. 57	Canada.	Henry Walker	do	East Indies.
George Bouchier	do		William Hensman	do	C. of G. Hope.
Edward Brock	8 Dec. 57	C. of G. Hope.	Arthur Sanderson	do	do
James Gorman	22 Jan. 58	Ceylon.	John M'Gilp	do	
James Mackay, M.D.	18 Feb.		William Armstrong	do	East Indies.
James Lander	5 Mar.	Gold Coast.	John Jas. Colin Rogers	do	Corfu.
William Curran	10 Mar. 58	Pembroke.	J. Smeeton Allanby, M.D.	1 Feb. 59	East Indies.
John Henry Hunt[20]	do	Canada.	George Calvert	do	Gambia.
Wm. Michael Trestrail	16 April		Thomas Seward, M.D.	do	C. of G. Hope.
Charles Gray	22 April 58	China.	James Watson	do	Colchester.
John Carlaw	do	China.	James Dow Sainter	1 March 59	China.
James Thompson	do	Fermoy.	John Clarke, M.D.	do	East Indies.
James Paxton, M.D.	do	Canada.	William Millar	do	East Indies.
Edward Hopkins	do	East Indies.	King John Parr	do	Cork.
John Niven	do	New Zealand.	William Orr	do	East Indies.
Fra. L. Gower Gunn	23 April 58	Gold Coast.	Edwin Parsonage, M.D.	do	East Indies.
Fitzgerald Edw. Scanlan	30 April 58	C. of G. Hope.	Colin Alex. Fraser	do	China.
Geo. Richd. Woolhouse	7 May 58	East Indies.	Henry S. Edw. Schroeder	do	Sierra Leone.
Arthur Croker	7 May 58	East Indies.	Geo. Carson Gribbon	20 Apr 59	Templemore.
Wm. Astle Hope, M.B.	do	East Indies.	Wm. Ligertwod, M.D.	do	Shorncliffe.
John Bradshaw	do	Gold Coast.	George Cardell	do	Portsmouth.
Thos. Turville Gardner	do	East Indies.	James Land	do	Templemore
Andrew Moffitt	25 May 58	Fermoy.	Morgan S. Grace	do	Winchester.
Richard John W. Orton	do	China.	Cha. Edw. Smith, M.D.	do	Yarmouth
Charles Rattray, M.D.	do	China.	Joseph Hy. Thos. King	do	East Indies.
Julius Wiles	4 June 58	East Indies.	Alex. Jennings, M.D.	do	Shorncliffe.
Henry William Devlin.	do		Charles Wyat Watling	do	Canterbury.
Thos. Michael O'Brien	do	East Indies.	Maurice Tracey	do	Canterbury.
Horatio Scott	do	New Zealand.	George Simon	do	Dover
Wm. Percy P. Mackesy	1 July 58	East Indies.	Florence T. M'Carthy	do	Cork.
John Mackenzie, M.D.	5 Aug. 58	China.	Thomas Heazle	do	Colchester.
John Walsh	do	Gibraltar.	Robert Tate, M.D.	do	Yarmouth
John Kinahan	do	China.	Sidney K. Ray	do	Colchester.
Samuel Argent	do	China.	Greville Ewing Tait	do	Winchester.
George Palatiano, M.D.	18 Aug. 58	Corfu.	George A. Davidge	do	Buttevant.
Frederick O'Conor	26 Aug.	Chatham	Valentine Maher	do	China.
Cha. D. Campbell, M.D.	1 Sept. 58		William Langston	do	Chatham.
Austin Jonas Ferguson.	do	Ceylon.	Alex. Edw. Bartlet	do	Plymouth.
James Speedy	do	Ceylon.	Robert Storey	do	Chichester.
St. John Killery	22 Sept. 58		John Adsetts	13 June 59	Woolwich.
Lancelot Andr. White.	22 Sept. 58	Ceylon.	Edw. Harf. Lloyd, MB.	do	Woolwich.
William Holmes	do	Mauritius.	Jas. Y. Donaldson, M.D.	do	Yarmouth.
Edmond Hoile, M.D.	do	China.	Oliver Codrington	do	Portsmouth.
Thos. Alex. C. Macarthur	do	China.	Edwin Drew	do	Woolwich.
Charles Longmore	do	China.	John Adcock, M.D.	do	Colchester.
Richard White	do	Fermoy.	Howison Y. Howison MD	do	Chelsea
Tobias Barnwell	do		Geo. Fred. Spry	do	Woolwich.
Charles Benjamin Mosse	8 Oct.	Jamaica.	John Tho. Melburn	do	Chatham.
Francis Alfred Turton	13 Oct. 58	East Indies.	John Alfred Illingworth	do	do
George Forbes Adams	do	do	Rob. Alex. P. Grant	do	Aberdeen.
Charles Farran Squire	do	East Indies.	Arthur Herbert Orpen	do	Chatham.
Francis Ed. M'Farland	1 Nov. 58	do	Alex. Thomson, M D.	do	do
Thomas Ramsay	do	do	Geo. Henry Dyer	do	do
Wm. K. Stewart, M.D.	do	do	James A. B. Horton, MD.	5 Sept. 59	Gold Coast.
Jas. Jos. M'Carthy, M.D.	16 Nov. 58	Cork.	W. Brough. Davies, MD.	5 Sept. 59	Gold Coast.
James Martin	do		James T. Tulloch, MD.	11 Oct. 59	Colchester.
James W. Lougheed	do	East Indies	Arthur Charles Gay e	do	Plymouth.
George Smith	22 Nov. 58	do	W. Evelyn Alston, MD.	do	Athlone.
Rt. Austen Allen, M.D.	do	Ceylon.	Joseph Sumpner Joyner.	do	Athlone.
Thomas Hession	1 Dec. 58	East Indies.	Colin Henderson	do	Fermoy.
Edwin Wilkes	do	do	John Alex. Scott	do	Belfast.
Geo. Edward Gascoyen	do	do	Arnold Royle	do	Colchester.
Alexander Mackay	do	do	Wm. Dumville Smythe	do	Chatham.
William Rob. Kerans	14 Dec. 58	Belfast.	Thomas Wood, MD.	do	Chichester.
Edw. Litton Low, M.B.	do	Athlone.	James Bell Jardine	do	Fermoy.
Thomas Murtagh	do	Athlone.	John E. Stewart, MD.	do	Woolwich.
George Park, M.D.	do	East Indies	Henry Cramer Guinness	do	Chatham.
J. Shand Duncan, M.D.	do	do	Alx. Oswld. Cowan, MD.	do	Chatham.
Richard Henry	do	do	Jas. Sam. Currie Collier	do	Chatham.
R. Muir Gilchrist, MD.	do	do	William Creagh	15 Oct. 59	Fermoy.

Medical Department.

Acting Assistant Surgeons.

	Assist.Surg.	Stationed at		Assist.Surg.	Stationed at
Harvey Rowe, M.D.	10 Sept. 57	Isle of Wight.	Wm. Warman Coleman	30 Mar.	5 Woolwich.
Thomas Callaway	17 Nov.		John Benbow, M.D.	5 April	Curragh.
Theodore Gross, M.D.	12 Feb. 58	Jersey.	George Cowper Rose	do	Fermoy.
John Mills Willis	16 Mar.	Devonport.	John Craven	do	Limerick.
Percy Lee	23 Mar.	Portsmouth.	James William Crow	30 April	Buttevant.
Joseph Thomas Mitchell	30 Mar.	Deal.	Merrick Lloyd Burrows	30 April	Yarmouth.

Uniform, Scarlet.—*Agent,* Sir John Kirkland.

Veterinary Medical Department.

Principal Veterinary Surgeon.
John Wilkinson, 12 July 54; Veterinary Surgeon, 27 April 26.

Staff Veterinary Surgeons.
John Wm. Gloag,[1] *Vet.Surg.* 29 June 32; *1st Class V.S.* 1 July 59; *Staff V.S.* 4 Nov. 59.
Matthew Poett,[2] *Vet.Surg.* 21 April 37; *1st Class V.S.* 1 July 59; *Staff V.S.* 4 Nov. 59.
James Geo. Philips, *Vet.Surg.* 28 Aug.38; *1st Class V.S.* 1 July 59; *Staff V.S.* 4 Nov. 59.
Thomas Hurford,[3] *Vet.Surg.* 25 Jan. 39; *1st Class V.S.* 1 July 59; *Staff V.S.* 4 Nov. 59.

Acting Veterinary Surgeons.

Martin Mence	25 July 55	Henry Dunsford	8 July 59
Edwin Thomas Cheesman	16 July 58	Greatrex Naden	23 Aug.
John Mills	8 July 59		

[1] Mr. Gloag served with the 11th Hussars the Eastern campaign of 1854-55, including the affair of Bulganak, battles of Alma, Balaklava, Inkerman, and Tchernaya, siege and fall of Sebastopol (Medal and Clasps, Knight of the Legion of Honor, and 5th Class of the Medjidie).
[2] Mr. Poett served with the Royal Dragoons in the Eastern campaign of 1854-55, including the siege of Sebastopol and battle of Balaklava (Medal and two Clasps).
[3] Mr. Hurford served with the 12th Lancers in the Crimea, and has the Medal with Clasp for Sebastopol.

Purveyor's Department.

Purveyor in Chief.—James Scott Robertson, 7 April 55.—London.
Deputy do.—David Fitzgerald,[5] 31 Oct. 55; *Purveyor,* 15 Dec. 54.—Cape of Good Hope.

PURVEYORS.	PURVEYOR'S CLERK.	DEPUTY PURVEYOR.	PURVEYOR.	STATIONED AT
ⓓ Wm. Henry Clapp[1]	1 July 09	15 Oct. 12	27 Apr. 53	Cork.
ⓓ George Pratt[2]	25 Sept. 09	3 June 13	do.	Chatham.
ⓓ Matthew Wreford[3]	14 Oct. 12	3 Sept. 29	do.	Canterbury.
William Macdonnell	....	....	do.	Dublin.
Wm. J. A. Tucker	....	....	do.	Woolwich.
J. M'Innes Green	....	....	do.	Barbadoes.
Kentish Jenner	....	....	do.	Portsmouth.
William Anderson	....	....	do.	
Charles John Minney	....	....	7 Apr. 54	China.
Selkirk Stuart	....	....	15 Aug.	C. of G. Hope.
Thomas Arthur Corlett	....	....	1 Sept.	Melbourne.
William Stamford Rogers	....	....	19 Jan. 55	Jersey.
Joseph William Macdonnell, M.D.	....	....	3 Feb.	China.
Sydney C. Harrington	....	....	20 Feb.	Shorncliffe.
David Elvy Robb	....	....	21 Feb.	Halifax, N. S.
Augustus Pigott	....	....	22 Feb.	Curragh.
Charles Coward	....	....	31 Mar.	Canterbury.
T. O. Hagger	....	....	1 July	Cape Town.
Edward Morris	....	....	13 Oct.	Aldershot.
James Holmes	....	....	do.	Gibraltar.
John L'Estrange Lenny Buchanan	....	....	do.	Corfu.
George Whittaker Mellish	....	....	1 Nov. 56	Montreal.
Charles Barrett Knapp	....	....	10 Mar. 57	China.
Gregson Bridgett	....	....	1 April	London.
Richard Maitland Lonsdale	....	....	10 Feb. 58	Edinburgh.
Charles E. Wrench	....	....	19 Nov. 58	Ceylon.
William Amey	....	....	25 Mar. 59	
John Bush	....	....	28 Oct. 59	Malta.
George W. Rippon	....	....	20 Dec. 59.	

War Services of the Officers of the Medical Department.

Director General.

1 Mr. Alexander served with the 60th Rifles in the Kaffir war of 1851-53 (Medal), and was principal Medical Officer of the Expedition across the Kei in 1851, as also of Kaffraria for some months—was thanked in orders. Proceeded with the first troops of the Eastern Army to Gallipoli as principal Medical Officer; was in Medical Charge of the Light Division of the Eastern Army from its first taking the field throughout the campaign of 1854-55, until the Division left the Crimea for England, without being absent from duty for a single day, and was present at the affair of Bulganac, battles of Alma and Inkerman, capture of Balaklava, siege and fall of Sebastopol, sortie on 26th Oct., assaults of the Redan on 18th June and 8th Sept.; and was principal Medical Officer of the Kertch Expedition: was noticed in Lord Raglan's Dispatch after Inkerman, "for his able exertions as deserving to be most honourably mentioned"; also in General Codrington's Dispatches after the fall of Sebastopol (Medal and three Clasps, *CB*., and Knight of the Legion of Honor).

Inspectors General and Deputy Inspectors General.

2 Doctor Linton preceded the army to the East in 1854 on a special mission of inspection throughout Roumelia. Served with the army at Scutari and in Bulgaria; accompanied it to the Crimea, and was present at the affair of Bulganac, battles of Alma, Balaklava, and Inkerman, sortie on 26th Oct., opening of the siege of Sebastopol, and every succeeding bombardment until its fall; was noticed in Lord Raglan's Dispatches of 11th Nov. 1854, " for his able exertions as deserving of being most honourably mentioned" (Medal and Clasps, *CB*., and 4th Class of the Medjidie).

3 Doctor Forrest served in the expedition against the Rajah of Kolapore in 1827. Also in the expedition against the Insurgent Boers beyond the Orange River, South Africa, in 1845; and in the Kaffir war of 1846 (Medal). Was in medical charge of the 3rd Division of the Eastern Army at Gallipoli and Bulgaria, and accompanied the expedition to the Crimea in Sept. 1854; was present at the affair of Bulganac, capture of Balaklava, battles of Alma and Inkerman, and siege of Sebastopol; and was noticed in Lord Raglan's Dispatch after Inkerman, "for his able exertions as deserving to be most honourably mentioned" (Medal with three Clasps, *CB*., 4th Class of the Medjidie, Turkish Medal, and Honorary Physician to the Queen).

4 Mr. Humfrey served at the siege of Sebastopol in 1854-55 (Medal and Clasp, and 4th Class of the Medjidie).

5 Mr. Taylor served with the 29th the Sutlej campaign of 1845-46, including the battles of Ferozeshah and Sobraon (Medal and Clasp); and with the 80th Regt. the Burmese war of 1852-53, including the capture of Murtaban, the operations before Rangoon on the 12th, 13th, and 14th April, and capture of the Great Dagon Pagoda; also at the capture of Prome (Medal and Clasp). Was in medical charge of the 3rd Division before Sebastopol from 20th March 1855 to the end of the War, including the assaults of the 18th June and 8th Sept. (*CB*., Medal and Clasp).

7 Doctor Atkinson served the campaign of 1847 in Kaffraria, under Sir George Berkeley (Medal). The following year he accompanied Sir Harry Smith's expedition over the Orange River against the insurgent Boers, and was present at the battle of Boem Plaats—remaining on the field with the wounded, the troops having pursued the enemy onwards. Was left in sole charge of the General Hospital and Garrison of Graham's Town during the Kaffir and Hottentot rebellion, from Jan. 1851 to March 1852.

8 Dr. Dumbreck, prior to the breaking out of hostilities, was despatched on special service early in 1854 to the expected seat of war, and traversed on his mission Servia, Bulgaria, and part of Roumelia, crossing the Balkan on his route; he was subsequently for a short time principal medical officer with the army, and served with it in the field as Senior Deputy Inspector General, and was present in this capacity and was attached to Head Quarters at the affair of Bulganac, the Alma, capture of Balaklava, battles of Balaklava and Inkerman, and siege of Sebastopol (Medal and four Clasps, *CB*., and 4th Class of the Medjidie).

9 Doctor Lawson was present at the storm and destruction of the fortified native Mandingo town of Sabajee, on the Gambia, 1st June 1853. Served in the Crimea from 8th November 1854 to 15 Jan. 55 (Medal and Clasp for Sebastopol, and 4th Class of the Medjidie).

11 Doctor Hume served at the siege of Sebastopol (Medal and Clasp, and 5th Class of the Medjidie).

12 Mr. Williams has received the 5th Class of the Medjidie.

13 Doctor Logan served with the 53rd the Sutlej campaign of 1845-6, and was present at the affair of Buddiwal, and in the actions of Aliwal and Sobraon (Medal and one Clasp). Served also at the siege of Sebastopol during 1855, and was present at the taking of the Quarries on 7th June, at the assault of the 18th June, and as Principal Medical Officer of the Highland Division at the final assault on the 8th Sept. (Medal and Clasp, and 5th Class of the Medjidie).

14 Doctor Gordon served with the 53rd Regt. in the Sutlej campaign in 1846, including the affair of Buddiwal, and actions of Aliwal and Sobraon (Medal and Clasp). Served in medical charge of the 24th Regt. throughout the Punjaub campaign of 1848-49, and was present at the battles of Sadoolapore, Chillianwallah, and Goojerat (Medal and Clasps). Served in the Eastern campaign of 1854-55, present at the affair of Bulganac, battle of Alma, and capture of Balaklava, and P.M. Officer of the 2nd Division throughout the siege and fall of Sebastopol; also P.M.O. of the Kinbourn Expedition (Medal and Clasps, *CB*., and Knight of the Legion of Honor). Principal Medical Officer with the Expeditionary force to China in 1857, and present at the capture of Canton. P.M.O. throughout the campaign in Oude in 1858-59 (Medal).

15 Mr. Mouat served with the 6th Dragoons and on the Medical Staff the Eastern campaign of 1854-55, including the battle of Balaklava and siege of Sebastopol (Medal and Clasps, *CB*., and Knight of the Legion of Honor).

War Services of the Officers of the Medical Department.

16 Doctor Jameson served in the Kaffir war of 1846-7 (Medal). Served in Turkey and Russia from April 1854 to July 1856 (5th Class of the Medjidie).

17 Doctor Arthur Anderson served the Eastern campaign of 1854 and up to 13th June 1855, including the battles of Alma, Balaklava, and Inkerman, and siege of Sebastopol; was P.M.O. 4th Division at Balaklava and Inkerman (Medal and four Clasps, and Knight of the Legion of Honor).

18 Doctor Tice served throughout the Eastern campaign of 1854-55, in medical charge of the 2nd Brigade Light Division, and was present at the affair of Bulganac, battles of Alma and Balaklava, and siege of Sebastopol; was principal medical officer of the station when the battle of Balaklava was fought (Medal with Clasps, 5th Class of the Medjidie, and Turkish Medal). Served in the Indian war of 1857-58 as P.M.O. of H.M.'s troops east of Lucknow from Oct. 1857 to Jan. 1858; subsequently in medical charge of all the Infantry divisions at the siege and capture of Lucknow; as P.M.O. of the Rohilcund field force throughout that campaign, including the attack on fort Roowah, action of Allygunge, and capture of Bareilly (Medal and Clasp, C.B.).

19 Mr. Parratt served in the operations in the Yeang tse Kiang in China (Medal), including the storm and capture of Chin Kian-Foo. He was also present at the demonstration before Nankin.

20 Doctor Beatson served as Surgeon of the 51st Lt. Infantry throughout the Burmese war of 1852-53 (Medal and Clasp); was present on board the steam frigate *Feroze*, in the action with and destruction of the stockades in the Rangoon River, and during the three days' operations ending in the capture of the Great Dagon Pagoda; at the defence of Prome and repulse of the night attack.

21 Mr. George Taylor has the 5th Class of the Medjidie.

22 Mr. Paynter served with the Rifle Brigade in the Kaffir war of 1846-47 (Medal). Served also throughout the Eastern campaign of 1854-55; was present as Surgeon of the 13th Light Dragoons at the affair of Bulganac, and battles of Alma, Balaklava, and Inkerman; and as 1st Class Staff Surgeon in the 3rd and 4th Divisions during the siege and at the fall of Sebastopol; also accompanied the expedition to Kertch (Medal and four Clasps, and 5th Class of the Medjidie).

23 Mr. Gammie served the Sutlej campaign of 1845-6 (Medal and Clasps); was present with the 80th Regt. at the battles of Moodkee and Ferozeshah; and in medical charge of the 31st at Buddiwal, Aliwal, and Sobraon.

24 Doctor Dane served the Punjaub campaign of 1846, including the battle of Goojerat (Medal).

25 Doctor Scott served at the first and second siege operations before Mooltan, including the capture of the city, and surrender of the fortress. Also at the surrender of the fort and garrison of Cheniote, and battle of Goojerat (Medal and Clasps). Promoted Staff Surgeon of the First Class "for eminent services throughout the whole siege of Lucknow."

26 Mr. Stewart served with the 9th Lancers in the campaign on the Sutlej in 1846, and was present at the battle of Sobraon (Medal). He served with the 14th Lt. Drs. throughout the Punjaub campaign of 1848-9, including the battles of Ramnuggur, Chillianwallah, and Goojerat (Medal and Clasps).

27 Doctor F. W. Innes served as Superintending Surgeon to the force under Havelock and Outram from 21st July 1857 until the fall of Lucknow in March 1858 and was thanked by the Governor General for "his unwearied attention to the sick and wounded"—was present in the actions of Oonao, Busseerutgunge (both), Boorbeeakeechowkee, Bithoor, Mungarwar, Alumbagh, occupation of Alumbagh under Outram, siege and capture of Lucknow. Served with the Azimghur field force in all the minor actions until the expulsion of the Rebels from the Jugdespore Jungle; served also in Shahabad until the final suppression of the rebellion in that district (Medal and Clasps, and C.B.).

28 Doctor Fraser served throughout the Eastern campaign of 1854-55, including the battles of Alma and Inkerman, and siege of Sebastopol (Medal and Clasps, and Knight of the Legion of Honor).

29 Mr. J. H. K. Innes served as a volunteer in the Crimea (his regiment being in India) from the commencement of the year until Aug. 1856, and was engaged in the attack of the Redan on the 18th June (Medal and Clasp, Turkish Medal Medjidie). Served throughout the Indian campaign of 1857-58 with the 1st Battalion 60th Rifles, including the actions on the Hundun (wounded and horse shot), battle of Budlee ke Serai, storming the heights before Delhi, siege, assault, and capture of the City. Served as Principal Medical Officer of Sir John Jones' force throughout all the subsequent operations in Rohilcund, and with Brigadier Troup's force in Oude during the winter of 1858-59 (Medal and Clasp, C.B.).

30 Doctor Muir served with the 33d Regt. throughout the Eastern campaign of 1854-55, including the battles of Alma and Inkerman, siege and fall of Sebastopol (Medal and three Clasps, and Knight of the Legion of Honor).

31 Mr. Longmore served throughout the Eastern campaign of 1854-55, including the battles of Alma and Inkerman, and the whole siege of Sebastopol (Medal and Clasps, and Knight of the Legion of Honor).

32 Doctor Currie served with the 16th Lancers at the battle of Maharajpore, 29 Dec. 1843 (Medal). Also in the campaign on the Sutlej in 1846, including the affair at Buddiwal, and actions of Aliwal and Sobraon (Medal and Clasp).

33 Mr. O'Flaherty served in the Crimea from 17th Sept. 1854 (Medal and Clasp, and 5th Class of the Medjidie).

34 Doctor Mapleton served with the 40th Regt. in the action of Maharajpore (Medal).

Surgeons Major.

1 Doctor J. S. Prendergast accompanied the Eastern Expedition in 1854 as surgeon of the 77th Regt. While in Bulgaria he was appointed to the personal staff of Lord Raglan, and attended him in the field at the battle of Alma, and in all the other actions until his Lordship's death, when he accompanied his remains to England (Medal and Clasps, and 5th Class of the Medjidie).

4 Dr. Delmege served throughout the whole Kaffir war of 1846-7, at first in medical charge of the 27th Regiment, and subsequently on promotion, as a Staff Surgeon (Medal). Served also in Turkey during the campaign of 1854-55, from Nov. 1854 to the fall of Sebastopol (Medal and Clasp).

5 Mr. George Anderson served the Eastern campaign of 1854 and from 15th March 1855 (Medal and Clasps, and 5th Class of the Medjidie).

6 Mr. Moore served the Eastern campaign of 1854-55, including the affair of Bulganac, battle of Alma, capture of Balaklava, sortie of 26th Oct., battle of Inkerman, and siege of Sebastopol (Medal and Clasps, and 5th Class of the Medjidie).

7 Doctor Wood served the Eastern campaign of 1854-55 as Surgeon 42nd Highlanders, including the affair of Bulganac, battles of Alma and Balaklava, and as 1st Class Staff Surgeon in the 2nd Division at the assault of the Redan on the 18th June and during the siege of Sebastopol up to its fall (Medal and three Clasps, 5th Class of the Medjidie, and Turkish Medal).

8 Doctor Langley served the Eastern campaign of 1854-55 and has the Medal and Clasp for Sebastopol, and the Turkish Medal.

9 Doctor Hadley served with the 40th Regt. at the taking of the fort of Munora and Kurrachee, in Lower Scinde, in Feb. 1839; and served in the subsequent campaign against the Beloochees and action at Dadur, in Upper Scinde, in 1840. Served in the Crimea from 30th April 1855 (Medal and Clasp, and 5th Class of the Medjidie).

10 Mr. Foaker served throughout the Eastern campaign of 1854-55, as Surgeon 38th Regt., and as 1st Staff Surgeon, including the battles of Alma and Inkerman, siege and fall of Sebastopol, and expedition to Kinbourn (Medal and Clasps).

11 Mr. Cowan served with the 18th in China (Medal), and was present during the operations against Canton, and at the attack and capture of Chapoo, Shanghai, Woosung, and Chin Kiang Foo; also in the Punjaub campaign of 1848-49 (Medal).

12 Doctor Home served in the Crimea from 27th July 1855 (Medal and Clasp for Sebastopol, and 5th Class of the Medjidie).

13 Doctor Stone served with the 14th Lt. Dragoons against Kolapore in 1844-45. Served also in the Crimea (Medal and Clasp for Sebastopol).

14 Doctor Sall served in the Kaffir war of 1852-53 (Medal).

16 Mr. Davies served with the 49th Regt. the Eastern campaign of 1854-55, including the battles of Alma and Inkerman, siege of Sebastopol, and sortie on 26th Oct. (Medal and Clasps, Sardinian Medal, and 5th Class of the Medjidie).

17 Mr. Matthew served in the Crimea (Medal and Clasp, and Knight of the Legion of Honor).

18 Mr. Waring served in the Kaffir war of 1847 (Medal).

19 Mr. Stewart served with the 18th Royal Irish Regt. in the China war in 1841-42 (Medal); in 1852-53 in the second Burmese war (Medal); and landed in 1854 in the Crimea with the Regt. (Medal and Clasp).

20 Mr. Mockler served with the 10th Regt. in the Punjaub campaign of 1848-49, including the latter part of the siege operations before Mooltan, the surrender of that fortress, and battle of Goojerat (Medal and Clasps).

21 Mr. Franklin served with the 3rd Light Dragoons throughout the campaign of 1842 in Affghanistan (Medal), and was present at the forcing of the Khyber Pass, storming the heights of Jugdulluck, action at Tezeen and Huftkotul, occupation of Cabool, and capture of Istaliff. Also the Sutlej campaign of 1845-6, including the battles of Moodkee and Ferozeshah (Medal and one Clasp).

22 Mr. M'Donald served with the 25th Regt. on the expedition against the insurgent Boers and taking of Port Natal in June 1842. Also with the 73rd Regt. throughout the Kaffir War of 1851-3 (Medal), and accompanied the expedition into Kreli's country in Dec. 1851 as Senior Medical Officer.

Staff Surgeons.

1 Doctor George served with the 12th Lancers in the Kaffir war of 1851-52-53 (Medal); was present at the battle of the Beren on the 20th Dec. 1852.

2 Doctor Fraser served with the 74th Regt. throughout the Kaffir war of 1851-52-53.

3 Doctor Galbraith served with the 99th in New Zealand, and was present at Ohaeawai and Ruapekapeka. He was the senior medical officer present during the greater part of the operations in the southern district of New Zealand: at several skirmishes in the valley of the Hutt; also at the Horokiwi on the 6th Aug. 1846.

4 Surgeon Macpherson served with the 40th Regt. at Candahar, at the relief of Khelat-i-Ghilzie, and in various minor operations in Affghanistan in 1841-42 (Medal). With the 53rd Regt. during part of the Sutlej campaign of 1845-46. And with the 9th Lancers in the Punjaub campaign of 1848-49, including the passage of the Chenab at Ramnuggur, and battle of Chillianwallah (Medal and Clasps).

5 Mr. Barrow served in the Queen's Royal Regt. in the campaign of 1844 in the Southern Mahratta country (including the storming of the fortress of Punella), and that in the Concan in 1845. Served also during the Kaffir war in 1852-53 (Medal).

6 Mr. L. C. Stewart served with the 29th Regt. throughout the Punjaub campaign in 1848-9, including the passage of the Chenab, and the battles of Chillianwallah and Goojerat (Medal and Clasps).

7 Doctor Rutherford served with the 62nd the Sutlej campaign of 1845-46, and was in medical charge of the Regt. at the battle of Sobraon (Medal). Served in the Eastern campaign of 1854-55, including the siege of Sebastopol (Medal and Clasp).

8 Doctor Lewins served with the 63rd Regt. the Eastern campaign of 1854 and up to the 13th January 1855, including the battles of Alma, Balaklava, and Inkerman, and siege of Sebastopol (Medal and four Clasps).

War Services of the Officers of the Medical Department. 450

9 Mr. Ewing served with the 95th Regt. in the Indian campaign in 1858, including the siege and capture of Kotah, battle of Kota ka Seria, and general action resulting in the capture of Gwalior (Medal).

10 Mr. Sunter served in the Crimea during the siege of Sebastopol from 29th July 1855 (Medal and Clasp, and Turkish Medal).

11 Surgeon Crocker landed in the Crimea with the 2nd Batt. Royals on 22 Apr. 1855 and was at the siege and fall of Sebastopol (Medal and Clasp).

12 Mr. Irwin was in medical charge of the 27th Regt. from the 1st July 1846, and during the Kaffir war of 1846, 47, 48 (Medal); and in medical charge of the 1st Division in the field, in the operations under Major General Hare, from July until November 1846.

13 Surgeon Ivey served with the army in Turkey and Bulgaria in 1854, and in the Crimea in the 31st Regt. in 1855, including the siege of Sebastopol (Medal and Clasp).

14 Surgeon Saunders served in medical charge of the 47th Regt. the Eastern campaign of 1854-55, including the battles of Alma and Inkerman, capture of Balaklava, siege of Sebastopol, and sortie on 26th Oct. (Medal and Clasps).

15 Doctor Bain served at the siege and fall of Sebastopol from 13th May 1855 (Medal and Clasp).

16 Doctor Fairbairn served with the 41st throughout the campaign of 1842 in Affghanistan, and was present at the engagements on the 28th March and 28th April in the Pisheen Valley; in those near Candahar, at Goaine, and before Ghuznee; occupation and destruction of that fortress and of Cabool; expedition into Kohistan; storm, capture, and destruction of Istaliff, and the various minor affairs in and between the Bolan and the Khyber Passes (Medal).

17 Surgeon Bindon served in the Kaffir war of 1846-47, and in that of 1851-53 (Medal).

18 Surgeon Webb served with the 10th Regt. throughout the Punjaub campaign of 1848-9, including the whole of the siege operations before, and surrender of, Mooltan, and battle of Goojerat (Medal and two Clasps). Served with the 46th Regt. at the siege of Sebastopol in 1854-55 (Medal and Clasp).

19 Surgeon Poole served in the Kaffir war of 1851-53 (Medal).

20 Surgeon Home served in the Eastern campaign of 1854-55, including the battle of Alma and siege of Sebastopol (Medal and Clasps).

21 Mr. Thornton served the Eastern campaign of 1854-55, including the affairs of Bulganak and M'Kenzie's Farm, battles of Alma, Balaklava, and Inkerman, siege and fall of Sebastopol (Medal and Clasp, and 5th Class of the Medjidie).

22 Mr. Cross served in the Crimea from the 3rd Feb. 1855 and has the Medal and Clasp for Sebastopol.

23 Mr. Small served in the Kaffir war of 1851-53 (Medal).

24 Surgeon Ligertwood served in the Crimea (Medal and Clasp, and Knight of the Legion of Honor).

25 Surgeon Hendley was present in an engagement between the British troops and the Mahometans of Combo in the Gambia, on the 17th July 1855, and received contusions on the chest and forehead from musket-balls. He served also with the combined forces of the French and English on the 4th Aug. following, when the stockaded town of Sabajee was taken and destroyed.

26 Surgeon Fasson served with the 53rd in the campaign on the Sutlej, and was present at Buddiwal and Aliwal (Medal). He served with the 14th Lt. Drs. throughout the Punjaub campaign of 1848-49, including the battles of Ramnuggur, Chillianwallah, and Goojerat (Medal and Clasps).

27 Doctor Dunlop served with the 32nd Regt. during the Punjaub campaign of 1848-49, and was present at the first and second siege operations before Mooltan, including the capture of the city and surrender of the fortress; also present at the surrender of the fort and garrison of Cheniote, and battle of Goojerat (Medal and Clasps). Served the Eastern campaign of 1854-55, including the battles of Alma and Inkerman, siege of Sebastopol, and attack on the Redan on the 18th June and 8th Sept. (Medal and Clasps).

28 Surgeon Hardie served with the 53rd Regt. in the Punjaub campaign in 1849 and was present at the battle of Goojerat (Medal and Clasp).

29 Surgeon Gibbons served the Eastern campaign of 1854-55, including the battles of Alma and Inkerman, siege and fall of Sebastopol (wounded 20th Oct. 54, by a shell in the trenches), and attack and occupation of the Cemetery on the 18th June; was especially mentioned in Lord Raglan's Dispatches for his exertions (Medal and Clasps, and Knight of the Legion of Honor). Served the Indian campaign of 1857-58 in medical charge of the 32nd Lt. Inf. and was present at the successful attack on the entrenched position at Dehaygain, capture of the fort of Dirhool, action at Dondpore, affair at Jugdespore, surrender of the forts of Amethie and Lurkerpore, and accompanied the column under Colonel Carmichail which drove Beni Madhoo across the Gogra (Medal).

30 Doctor Nicholson served as Staff Assist. Surgeon in the Kaffir war of 1847-48, and with the 60th Rifles in the Kaffir war of 1851-53 (Medal).

31 Mr. Weld served with the 47th Regt. in the Eastern campaign of 1854-55, including the siege and fall of Sebastopol (Medal and Clasp).

32 Surgeon Moffatt served with the 2nd Regt. in the Kaffir war of 1851-53 (Medal).

33 Doctor Irvine served throughout the operations with Havelock's Column in 1857 in Medical charge of the Royal Artillery (Maude's), including the actions of Futtehpore, Aoung, Pandoo Nuddee, Cawnpore, Oonao, Busserut Gunge, Mungawarra, and Alumbagh, relief and defence of the Residency at Lucknow (mentioned in despatches); with Outram's force in the Alumbagh from Nov. 1857 to March 1858, and at the siege and capture of Lucknow by Lord Clyde (Medal and Clasps).

34 Doctor Smyth served the Eastern campaign of 1854-55, including the battle of Balaklava and siege of Sebastopol (Medal and two Clasps).

34† Surgeon Tydd served in the Eastern campaign of 1854-55 including the affair of Bulganac and battle of Alma (Medal and Clasp, and Turkish Medal).

451   *War Services of the Officers of the Medical Department.*

35 Surgeon Ingham was present and in Medical Charge of the 52nd Lt. Inf. at the action with the Sealkote mutineers at Trimmos Ghat Goorsdaspore on 12th and 16th July 1858, and at the siege and capture of Delhi.

36 Mr. Knox served with the 56th Regt. in the Crimea from 25 Aug. 1855 and has the Medal and Clasp for Sebastopol.

37 Doctor Buckle served in the Persian campaign of 1856, including the storm and capture of Reshire and surrender of Bushire.

38 Mr. M'Dermott served the Eastern campaign of 1854-55, including the battles of Alma and Balaklava, siege and fall of Sebastopol (Medal and Clasps).

39 Doctor Bone served the Eastern campaign of 1854-55, including the affair of Mackenzie's Farm, battles of Alma, Balaklava, and Inkerman, siege of Sebastopol, repulse of the sortie on 26th Oct. 1854, and assault on the Redan on the 8th Sept. 1855; also present at the bombardment and surrender of Kinbourn (Medal and Clasps).

40 Doctor Franklyn served the Indian campaign of 1857-58 with the Royal Horse Artillery, including the attack on Secundra, storm and capture of Mecangunge, capture of Lucknow, with Azimghur field force in the affairs of 9th and 10th June (was several times mentioned in despatches, twice for gallantry and once for general ability and zeal, Medal and Clasp).

41 Mr. Campbell served in charge of head-quarter staff and escort during the Kaffir war of 1852-3 (Medal); accompanied the expedition across the Kei in Aug. 1852; was present at the last and effectual clearing of the Waterkloof, and, accompanying the expedition beyond the Orange River against the Basuto chief Moshesh, was present at the Berea.

42 Surgeon FitzGerald served in the Crimea from 8th to 20th May 1855 (Medal and Clasp, and 5th Class of the Medjidie).

43 Doctor H. F. Smith served throughout the Eastern campaign of 1854-55; was attached to Head Quarters and not absent a single day from duty; had medical charge of Staff belonging to Adjutant and Quarter Master General's Departments, and subsequently on the personal Staff of Sir James Simpson and Sir William Codrington; present at Bulganac, Alma, Balaklava, Inkerman, siege and fall of Sebastopol (Medal and four Clasps, and 5th Class of the Medjidie).

44 Surgeon Rennie served with the 10th Regt. in the Indian campaign of 1857-58, and was present at the mutiny at Dinapore in medical charge of the Regt. capture of Atrowleea in medical charge of the field force, advance to Lucknow including actions of Chanda, Umeerpore, and Sultanpore; siege and capture of Lucknow, relief of Azimghur including passage of the Tonse and affair at Binheeah; capture of Jugdespore, and action at Chitowrah (Medal and Clasp).

45 Surgeon Rutherford served with the 2nd Dragoons in the Crimean campaign from 17th Nov. 1854, including the battle of the Tchernaya, siege and fall of Sebastopol (Medal and Clasp).

46 Surgeon Moline served with the 22nd Regt. during the campaign of 1844-45 in the Southern Mahratta country; and was present at the taking of the forts of Panulla and Pownghur.

47 Doctor Robert M'Nab served in suppressing the Indian Mutiny in 1857-58, and was present with the 64th Regt. in the operations at Cawnpore under General Windham, defeat of the Gwalior mutineers on 6th Dec., and action of Khulee Nuddee (Medal).

Assistant Surgeons.

1 Assist.Surgeon Brady served on the Medical Staff and in the 57th Regt. the Eastern campaign from May 1854 to Dec. 1855, including the battles of Balaklava and Inkerman, siege and fall of Sebastopol, attack of the Redan on the 18th June, and expedition to Kinbourn (Medal and three Clasps, and Knight of the Legion of Honor).

2 Mr. Lane served with the 80th Regt. in the Burmese war of 1852-53, including the attack on the outpost of Tomboo and several operations in its vicinity (Medal).

3 Assist.Surgeon Scott served with the 57th Regt. in the Eastern campaign of 1854-55, including the battles of Balaklava and Inkerman, and siege of Sebastopol, and was specially reported to Lord Raglan for gallantry and devotion to duty under the thickest fire of the enemy on the field of Inkerman (Medal and three Clasps).

4 Assist.Surgeon Tippetts served with the 7th Fusiliers the Eastern campaign of 1854-55, including the affair at Bulganac, battles of Alma and Inkerman, and siege of Sebastopol (Medal and Clasps).

5 Assist.Surgeon Kellett served in the Crimea at the siege and fall of Sebastopol (Medal and Clasp).

6 Assist.Surgeon Bayfield served with the 19th Regt. at the siege and fall of Sebastopol (Medal and Clasp).

6† Assist.Surgeon Cullen served in the Eastern campaign of 1854-55 (Medal and Clasp for Sebastopol).

7 Assist.Surgeon Bryson served with the 97th Regt. at the siege and fall of Sebastopol from 20th Nov. 1854, and was on the storming party at the assault of the Redan on the 8th Sept. (Medal and Clasp).

8 Assist.Surgeon Titterton served in the Eastern campaign in 1854-55, including the battle of Balaklava, siege and fall of Sebastopol, and attacks of the 18th June and 8th Sept. (Medal and Clasps).

9 Mr. Wolseley served the Eastern campaign of 1854-55 with the 20th Regt., including the battles of Alma, Balaklava, and Inkerman (wounded) siege and fall of Sebastopol, and assaults of the 18th June and 8th Sept. (Medal and Clasps).

10 Mr. Roberts served with the 72nd Highlanders in the Crimea from 13th June 1855, including the expedition to Kertch, siege and fall of Sebastopol, and attacks of the 18th June and 8th Sept. (Medal and Clasp, and Turkish Medal). Served with the 79th Highlanders in the Indian campaign of 1857-58, including the siege and capture of Lucknow, attack on the fort of Rooyah, action of Allygunge, and capture of Bareilly (Medal and Clasp).

War Services of the Officers of the Medical Department. 451a

11 Assist. Surgeon Randell served with the 62nd Regt. in the Crimea from 4th July 1855, including the siege and fall of Sebastopol, and assault of the Redan on the 8th Sept. (Medal and Clasp).

12 Doctor Young served at the siege and fall of Sebastopol in 1854-55 (Medal and Clasp).

13 Mr. Patterson served in medical charge of the field force employed against the rebel Kareens in Burmah in 1856 and was present in six engagements.

14 Doctor Collins served during the Sepoy Mutiny in 1857-58 and was present at the relief of Lucknow by Lord Clyde including the attacks on the Dilkoosha, Martiniere, and Secunderbagh; with Outram's Division in the Alumbagh and engaged in the various operations there; also at the siege and capture of Lucknow.

15 Doctor Beveridge served with the 78th Highlanders in the Indian campaign and was present with Outram's force in the Alumbagh, including the repulse of numerous attacks, and operations ending in the final capture of Lucknow (Medal and Clasp).

16 Mr. Roe served with the 89th Regt. at the siege of Sebastopol from 2nd March to 28 June 1855 and attack on the 18th June (Medal and Clasp).

17 Doctor Seddall served with the 33rd Regt. at the siege and fall of Sebastopol in 1855, and assault of the Redan on the 8th Sept. (Medal and Clasp).

18 Doctor Stranaghan served in the Crimea from 19th May 1855, including the siege and fall of Sebastopol and attack of the 7th and 18th June, and final assault of the 8th Sept. (Medal and Clasp).

19 Assist. Surgeon Jessop served with the Scots Fusilier Guards in the Crimea from June 1855 (Medal and Clasp). Was present doing duty with the Royal Artillery at the capture of Canton on 28 Dec. 1857.

20 Mr. Hunt has received the Silver Medal of the Royal Humane Society for intrepid conduct in saving life.

21 Mr. Webb served with the 19th Regt. in the Crimean campaign of 1854-55, including the battles of Alma and Inkerman, siege and fall of Sebastopol (Medal and Clasps).

22 Doctor Whylock served with the 75th Regt. at the siege of Delhi and at the battle of Budleekaserai, where he killed two of the enemy, one in close combat thereby saving the life of an European soldier.

23 Mr. Sparrow served with the 98th Regt. in the Peshawur Expeditionary force on the Euzofzic frontier under Sir Sydney Cotton in April and May 1858, and at the affair with the Hindostance fanatics on the heights of Satana on the 4th May.

Purveyors.

1 Mr. Clapp has received the War Medal with two Clasps for St. Sebastian and Nivelle.

2 Mr. Pratt joined the army in the Peninsula in Jan. 1810, and was present at the siege and capture of San Sebastian, and with the head-quarters during the operations in the Pyrenees. He has received the War Medal with two Clasps.

3 Mr. Wreford served in the Peninsula from 1812 to the end of that war in 1814, and was present with head quarters during the operations in the Pyrenees in July, August, and September 1813. He accompanied the expedition under the late Lord Keane to New Orleans, and was present with the troops in all the affairs before that city; after which he served in France, and recently in Turkey. He has received the War Medal with one Clasp.

5 Mr. Fitzgerald has received the 5th Class of the Medjidie.

STAFF OFFICERS OF PENSIONERS.

MILITARY SUPERINTENDENT.— *Sir* Alexander Murray Tulloch, KCB, 31 May 44; *Ens.* ᵽ0 April 26; *Lt.* 30 Nov. 27; *Capt* 12 March 38; *Brevet Major*, 29 March 39; *Major*, 6 Aug. 41; *Brevet Lieut.Col.* 31 May 44; *Lieut.Col.* 10 Feb. 52; *Col.* 20 June 54; *Maj.Gen.* 9 Sept. 59.

ASSISTANT MILITARY SUPERINTENDENT.—John ffolliott Crofton,(1) 22 July 52; *Ens.*, 18 Dec. 24; *Lt.* ᵽ29 Aug. 26; *Capt.* ᵽ17 July 35; *Major*, ᵽ15 April 42; *Lt.Col.* 7 Aug. 46; *Col.* 20 June 54.

STATION.	Years' Regtl. Serv.	Cornet, Ensign, &c.	LIEUT.	CAPTAIN.	BREVET-MAJOR.	Appointed Staff Officer.
GREAT BRITAIN.						
ABERDEEN.—GeorgeMunro,Unatt.*l.c.*26Oct.58	24	20 Jan. 14	29 Mar.21	10 July 40	11 Nov.51	29 June42
AYR.—Charles Edmund Thornton	16	ᵽ30 Dec. 42	ᵽ20 Aug.44	ᵽ19 Sept.48	..	1 Jan. 50
BATH.—John Forbes(8), Unatt. *c.* 25 Oct. 59..	28	21 Nov. 11	21 Oct. 13	13 Oct. 36	9 Nov. 16	18 Sept.43
BIRMINGHAM.—Henry M. Smyth, h.p. 44 F.	19	7 June 31	ᵽ20 Mar. 35	24 May 45	26 Nov. 57	11 Feb. 52
BOLTON.—William Pilsworth, Unatt.	23	ᵽ24 May 33	18 Mar.38	9 Nov. 46	26 Oct. 58	1 Oct. 55
BRIGHTON.—Arthur Hill Hull, Unatt.	6	24 Aug.25	6 Nov.27	24 Oct. 56	..	6 July 43
BRISTOL.— { M. R. S. Whitmore, h.p. 10 Drs. / *l c.* 22 Mar. 58	10	26 June27	ᵽ 5 Aug.28	ᵽ16 Feb. 38	11 Nov.51	11 Oct. 42
CAMBRIDGE.—Michael Edward Smith, Unatt.	20	ᵽ 3 Nov. 37	ᵽ20 Dec.39	10 Dec. 52	..	1 July 58
CANTERBURY.—John O. Burridge,Unatt.	14	ᵽ 9 Nov.30	1 Sept.36	29 Dec. 53	..	9 Dec. 44
CARDIFF.—Henry William Wily (27), Unatt.	14	27 June38	15 Nov.39	31 Oct. 51	..	21 Apr. 52
CARLISLE.—Thomas William Prevost, h.p. 42 F.	10	18 June41	ᵽ 5 April44	ᵽ 9 Feb. 49	..	11 Sept. 50
CARMARTHEN.—*Capt.* James Bailie, 9 F.	19	28 Nov. 34	31 Dec. 30	3 Oct. 48	..	16 Nov.58
CHATHAM.—Rich. Jenkins,Unatt.*l.c.* 15 Jan. 58	20	ᵽ 1 Feb. 27	ᵽ 4June 28	ᵽ16 June 37	11 Nov.51	1 July 46
CHESTER.—James Hunter, Unatt.	8	ᵽ17 Nov. 37	ᵽ27 Sept. 39	19 Dec. 56	..	18 Sept.44
COVENTRY.—Charles Pattison, h. p. 56 F.	14	ᵽ 7 Oct. 36	ᵽ30 Aug. 39	ᵽ10 Dec. 47	25 Mar. 59	1 July 50
DERBY.—Fred. Nassau Dore (31), h.p. 5 F.	16	26 Oct. 41	14 Jan.44	ᵽ13 Sept.53	..	1 Oct. 57
DUNBEE.—Wm John Kirk, Unatt.	14	27 Sept.31	ᵽ27 Oct. 37	24 Feb. 54	..	24 Feb. 44
EDINBURGH.— { Colonel Fred. Hope, Unatt.. / Jas. Waddell-Boyd, h.p. 14 F.	22	5 Feb. 36	2 May 38	1 May 46	10 Oct. 58	1 April 57
EXETER.—Arthur Pigott, h.p.20 F.	16	ᵽ24 Apr. 35	2 July 38	ᵽ25 Aug. 43	20 June 54	20 Aug.50
FALMOUTH.—T. W. J. McDougall, h.p. R. Mar.	10	10 Mar. 28	5 July 30	ᵽ30 Sept.55	..	20 May 43
GLASGOW.— { W. Campbell,Unatt. *c.* 26 Oct. 58 / George Sinclair (3), Unatt.	12	ᵽ23 June 25	ᵽ25 June 29	ᵽ20 Sept.33	9 Nov. 46	27 Nov.43
	9	17 Feb. 14	ᵽ14 June 21	28 Oct. 53	..	1 July 42
GLOUCESTER.—H. C. C. Somerset, h.p. 27 F.	11	ᵽ 4 Oct. 33	ᵽ14 July 37	ᵽ23 June 43	20 June 54	1 Jan. 44
HALIFAX.—J. E.Orange(4),h.p.34F.*c.*13 Dec. 58	20	10 Apr. 25	15 Oct. 27	ᵽ27 Dec. 33	9 Nov. 46	13 Feb. 44
HULL.—Charles Shipley Teale, Unatt.	19	7 Apr. 25	10 Dec. 27	22 May 43	20 June 54	12 Nov. 44
INVERNESS.—A. Houstoun, h.p. 4 F. *c.*28 Nov.54	18	ᵽ 4 Dec. 23	ᵽ19 Nov. 25	ᵽ12 Dec. 26	23 Nov. 41	22 July 42
IPSWICH.— { S. A. Capel, h.p. 51 F. Qr. M. / 11 Oct. 33	13	7 July 37	25 May 39	ᵽ30 July 44	22 Aug. 56	15 Mar. 47
JERSEY, { J. F. DuVernet (5), h.p. R. / GUERNSEY, &c. Afr. Corps, *c.* 9 Apr. 59	19	27 Mar.25	ᵽ 8April 26	ᵽ24April 35	9 Nov. 46	30 Oct. 44
LEEDS.— { J. Sampson (26), h.p. 8 Gar. Bn. / *l.c.* 27 May 58	24	29 Nov. 10	9 Dec. 13	23 May 38	11 Nov.51	28 Mar.43
LEICESTER.—J. Chester (10), h.p. York Chass.	15	ᵽ 2 Oct. 40	ᵽ 1 July 42	ᵽ30 Dec. 47	26 Feb. 50	1 May 58
LINCOLN.—George W. Raikes, h.p. 76 F.	18	ᵽ14 Dec. 32	ᵽ23 Oct. 35	ᵽ22 Dec. 46	26 Oct. 58	8 July 50
LIVERPOOL. { H.B.H. Rogers, Unatt. *c.* 7 Dec. 59 / Henry Cole Faulkner, Unatt.	15	ᵽ17 Jan. 28	ᵽ12 April 33	ᵽ14 Oct. 36	9 Nov. 46	27 July 47
	14	ᵽ13 Nov.35	ᵽ18 May 39	9 Nov. 49	..	1 Apr. 54
LONDON DISTRICT. { *Northern Div.* Jas.Jno.Graham (23), Unatt. *c.*26Oct.58	16	ᵽ28 Oct. 24	ᵽ 8 Apr. 26	ᵽ25 Feb. 30	9 Nov. 46	4 Apr. 51
Regent's Pk. Bks. { Fred.G. Christie, Unatt.	13	8 April 34	20 July 38	ᵽ30 May 45	12 Dec. 57	1 Oct. 45
Eastern Div. { John Pelling Pigott(7),Unatt.	15	ᵽ15 Feb. 39	ᵽ28 Jan. 42	ᵽ19 Dec. 45	31 Mar.56	1 Apr. 51
Tower Hill. { Robert M'Nair (28), Unatt..	25	22 Oct. 12	24 Mar. 14	12 April 50	..	8 Dec. 52
Southern Div. { Fra. Percy Nott, h.p. *Kennington Com.* 1Gar.Bn.*l c.*26Oct.58	19	23 June 25	10 May 26	1 Nov. 40	11 Nov. 51	28 Mar. 43
Western Div. { G. H. F. Campbell, h. p. / *Chelsea Hosp.* Staff C. *c.* 26 Oct. 58..	12	never.	ᵽ11 June 30	ᵽ27 July 32	9 Nov. 46	1 Oct. 40
{ Richard S. O'Brien, h. p. 36 F..	10	25 Nov. 31	19 Aug. 36	18 April 45	17 July 57	22 Nov.50
Woolwich Div. { D. H. Mackinnon (33), Unatt.	15	ᵽ 1 July 26	ᵽ23 Mar. 38	ᵽ15 Oct. 47	13 Dec. 58	11 Feb. 54
Deptford Div.—Walter Warde, Unatt.	11	ᵽ29 June 32	ᵽ 4 May 35	ᵽ25 Oct. 42	20 June 54	18 Sept.43
LYNN.—Edm. John Cruice (14), Unatt.	24	9 April 25	13 June 30	5 Apr. 44	18 May 55	1 Jan. 55
MANCHESTER.— { A. F. Bond, h.p. Staff Corps / *l.c.* 26 Aug. 58	16	3 April 28	ᵽ20 June 32	ᵽ12 Oct. 38	11 Nov.51	24 Sept.40
{ Wm. Ready (9), Unatt.	20	19 May 25	28 June 27	24 Jan. 45	6 July 57	8 Oct. 46
NEWCASTLE-ON-TYNE.— { H. C. Powell, Unatt. / *l.c.* 17 July 59...	18	9 April 25	ᵽ17 Jan. 29	8 April 42	20 June 54	5 May 42
NORWICH.—J. Cockburn, Unatt. *l c.* 20 July 58	13	12 April 27	ᵽ23 Aug. 33	ᵽ 8 June 38	11 Nov. 51	1 July 44
NORTHAMPTON.—Thos. Smith, Unatt.	17	ᵽ13 Sept.31	ᵽ 4 July 34	19 Nov. 47	13 Feb. 50	1 Sept. 52
NOTTINGHAM.—Valen. Fred. Story, Unatt.	13	ᵽ30 Oct. 25	ᵽ22 Jan. 27	ᵽ26 May 48	30 Sept.55	25 June40
OXFORD.—Fred. Smythe, Unatt.	10	ᵽ24 Feb. 37	ᵽ10 July 40	24 Oct. 56	..	24 Feb. 45
PAISLEY.—George Bayly, Unatt.	28	10 Feb. 25	17 April30	8 May 46	26 Oct. 58	5 Apr. 52
PERTH.— { ᵽ A. Campbell(11),h.p. 2 Ceylon / R. *c.* 26 Oct. 58...........	15	26 April10	29 July 13	11 June29	9 Nov. 46	30 June42
{ ᵽ E. Trevor(12),h.p. R. Art. *c.* 26 Oct. 58	35	4 June 10	17 Dec. 13	23 June32	9 Nov. 46	29 April45
PLYMOUTH.— { ᵽ W. T. Blewett Mounsteven (13), h. p. 79 F. *c.* 1 May 59)	32	25 Nov.13	25 Oct. 20	8 May 35	9 Nov.46	1 Jan. 47
{ H. Russell,h.p.60 F. *l.c.* 20Feb.59	11	ᵽ16 May 34	ᵽ24 Mar. 37	ᵽ10 Sept.41	20 June 54	7 Nov. 43
PORTSMOUTH. { E.S.Farmar,Unatt.*c.*13 Nov.58 / J. K. Willson (15), h.p. R.M. *l.c.* 20 June 59	27	2 Jan. 17	ᵽ10 Jan. 22	ᵽ18 Oct. 33	9 Nov. 46	1 Oct. 45
	27	10 Oct. 32	7 Feb. 42	20 June54	23 Jan. 47
PRESTON.—Geo. Robert Pole, Unatt.	20	11 Aug.25	24 April28	27 Sept.44	9 Nov. 46	7 July47
SALISBURY.—Charles Edward Astell, h.p. 45 F.	14	ᵽ24 Feb. 37	ᵽ22 June 39	ᵽ 3 Oct. 48	..	1 July 50
SHEFFIELD.—Matthew Cassan, Unatt.	18	ᵽ13 Dec. 31	19 May 38	13 Mar. 44	6 Feb. 55	1 Feb. 47
SHREWSBURY.—Henry Wm. Goodwyn, Unatt.	21	ᵽ 9 Dec. 36	ᵽ26 June40	3 Apr. 49	..	1 April 57
SOUTHAMPTON.—William Lacy, Unatt.	19	20April26	30 Aug. 27	6 Dec. 44	14 April 57	15April45

Staff Officers of Pensioners. 453

STATION.	Years' Regtl. Serv.	Cornet, Ensign, &c.	LIEUT.	CAPTAIN.	BREVET-MAJOR.	Appointed Staff Officer.
GREAT BRITAIN—*Continued.*						
STAFFORD NORTH, BURSLEM } M.F. Steele (17), Unatt.	10	9 April 25	16 Feb. 31	28 Oct. 53	..	6 Sept. 43
STIRLING.—William Peddie (18), Unatt.	8	2 Jan. 10	30 Jan. 12	7 Oct. 53	..	1 July 42
STOCKPORT.—Donald Wm. Tench (10), h.p. 15 Drs	23	31 July 28	p3 Dec. 31	1 Oct. 44	8 Dec. 56	1 Jan. 56
TAUNTON.—Geo. W. Meehan, Unatt. 9 Sept. 50	24	17 April 28	14 April 36	15 April 42	20 June 54	1 Dec. 52
THURSO.—J. P. Stuart, Unatt.	15	30 Dec. 38	3 Oct. 40	4 Mar. 53	..	1 Jan. 55
TROWBRIDGE.—John Lawson, Unatt.	13	p10 Oct. 22	p17 Aug. 26	8 Oct. 55	..	8 Oct. 45
WOLVERHAMPTON.—W. Follows (20) h.p. 18 Drs.	16	13 Sept. 32	28 May 36	26 July 44	19 June 56	7 Mar. 49
WORCESTER.—Rob. Frd. Middlemore (2), Unatt.	21	19 Dec. 34	p12 July 39	19 May 45	5 Sept. 56	1 Oct. 55
YORK.—William Francis Webster, Unatt.	10	p6 Feb. 23	p12 July 33	28 Oct. 53	..	8 Nov. 43
IRELAND.						
ARMAGH.— { p Wm. O'Neill (22), Unatt. l.c. 14 May 59 }	19	12 Aug. 12	22 May 18	28 Dec. 41	20 June 54	15 Apr. 52
ATHLONE.—James Wm. Graves (24), Unatt.	18	24 Oct. 34	31 May 30	26 Jan. 44	28 Nov. 54	15 Nov. 51
BALLYMENA.—Henry Wm. Baco, Unatt.	21	15 Feb. 33	27 July 38	7 July 48	..	1 Jan. 57
BELFAST.— { W. M'Pherson, Unatt. c. 17 Oct. 50	18	p22 Nov. 21	22 Sept. 25	p17 Sept. 36	9 Nov. 46	10 Oct. 42
{ Wm. Child, Unatt. l.c. 23 Nov. 58	30	13 Nov. 22	11 Aug. 26	2 April 41	20 June 54	15 Aug. 52
BIRR.—Geo. Butler Stoney, h.p. 20 F.	15	p13 May 36	p11 Jan. 39	10 Dec. 44	4 June 57	1 July 50
CARLOW.—William Frederick Harvey, Unatt.	25	p11 April 26	p13 Aug. 29	5 Aug. 42	20 June 54	1 Jan. 51
CAVAN.—Fra. Thos. Meik (34), Unatt.	20	p 1 Nov. 28	p 4 May 32	3 Apr. 46	22 Sept. 58	21 Jan. 55
CLONMEL.—John F. A. Hartle, Unatt.	22	21 Feb. 34	p11 Nov. 36	10 Jan. 51	..	1 Nov. 55
CORK.— { Ed. O. Broadley, Unatt. l.c. 26 Oct. 58	15	p15 Aug. 26	p29 Sept. 29	p28 Sept. 39	11 Nov. 51	8 Nov. 43
{ Geo. Thomson (25), CB., E. I. Co.'s Serv. l.c. 4 Aug. 54	...	...	...	...	...	26 June 49
DROGHEDA.— { Frederick G. Bull, h.p. 60 F. l.c. 22 Sept. 58 }	21	25 Oct. 27	p 8 Feb. 31	p23 Nov. 38	11 Nov. 51	28 Feb. 51
DUBLIN.— { Owen Lloyd Ormsby, Unatt. l.c. 26 Oct. 58 }	11	p21 Dec. 32	p 2 Feb. 38	p 1 Nov. 39	11 Nov. 51	9 May 43
{ Robert R. Harris, h.p. 60 F. l.c. 26 Oct. 58	25	19 Oct. 20	18 Aug. 24	31 Oct. 40	11 Nov. 51	1 Oct. 44
ENNIS.—Henry Thomas Richmond (36), Unatt.	18	21 Nov. 41	9 June 43	15 Mar. 53	..	1 July 59
ENNISKILLEN.—John Edw. Sharp (16), h.p. 17 F	22	p24 Apr. 35	p 9 Feb. 38	p17 Dec. 47	2 April 59	1 Jan. 57
GALWAY.—Benj. Bloomfield Keane, Unatt.	21	8 May 35	p11 Jan. 39	8 Jan. 47	26 Oct. 58	1 Apr. 55
KILKENNY.—Jacob Glynn Rogers, Unatt.	14	6 Oct. 14	p 8 Mar. 18	28 Oct. 53	..	3 Nov. 43
LIMERICK.—Wm. Garstin, h.p. 24 Drs.	25	28 Oct. 24	20 May 28	2 Aug. 42	20 June 54	11 Dec. 48
LONDONDERRY.— { Digby St. Vincent Hamilton, Unatt. }	23	p30 Aug. 33	30 Nov. 37	9 Nov. 46	26 Oct. 58	1 July 56
LONGFORD.—Wm. Mauleverer, h.p. 58 F.	14	p31 Aug. 30	p13 Jan. 37	p22 July 42	20 June 54	20 Nov. 43
MONAGHAN.— { Oliver Nicolls Chatterton, h.p. Rifle Br. }	20	p23 July 33	p 5 Aug. 36	15 Aug. 48	..	1 July 56
NEWRY.—J. Stuart, h.p. 84 F. c. 12 June 59.	15	20 April 15	p15 Dec. 25	13 Nov. 35	9 Nov. 46	14 Dec. 43
OMAGH.—Alexander Maclean, h.p.	21	15 Mar. 30	p28 Jan. 42	p23 July 52	..	23 May 59
ROSCOMMON.—Adam Campbell, Unatt.	21	19 Apr. 36	19 Feb. 38	22 Aug. 49	..	1 July 56
SLIGO.—Robert Law, 31 F.	20	8 Feb. 40	27 July 42	5 May 54	..	16 Nov. 59
TRALEE.—Pat. Day Stokes, h.p. 4 F.	12	p22 Oct. 33	p13 Jan. 38	p 8 Nov. 44	4 Feb. 57	20 Nov. 43
TULLAMORE.—Geo. Fred. Moore (21), Unatt.	16	25 Oct. 39	9 Nov. 41	p21 May 47	20 Oct. 58	1 Aug. 55
WATERFORD.—Cha. Reed Driver (30), h.p. R.M.	17	18 Oct. 42	27 July 47	21 Feb. 55	..	1 Feb. 59
CANADA.						
Military Superintendent.—J.G.D. Tulloch, h.p. 84 F. *Lt.-Col.* 9 Feb. 55 }	14	18 July 30	14 Feb. 34	22 Aug. 41	20 June 54	1 July 42
John P. Ferris (35), Unatt.	14	20 Nov. 40	14 Apr. 46	26 July 53	..	1 Jan. 55
Thomas Bourke, h.p. 37 F.	22	p 9 May 34	2 May 37	27 Mar. 48	12 June 59	1 Oct. 57
Thomas Hodgetts, Unatt.	0	4 Sept. 30	13 Mar. 35	28 Dec. 53	..	27 Dec. 43
NEW ZEALAND.						
1st Batt.—Head-Quarters, Onehunga. Wm. H. Kenny, h.p. 61 F. l.c. 9 Apr. 59 (*Commanding*). }	16	3 April 28	15 Mar. 32	p12 Oct. 41	20 June 54	11 July 43
2nd Batt.—Head-Quarters, Howick.						
TASMANIA.						
Fred. Brown Russell, h.p. 3 Dr. Gds.	24	2 Nov. 26	18 Feb. 30	13 Sept. 42	20 June 54	6 Nov. 49
WESTERN AUSTRALIA.						
John Bruce (29), h.p. 56 F. (*Local rank of Lt.-Col.* 26 Sept. 54) }	22	31 July 28	p12 April 13	19 Aug. 42	20 June 54	23 Jan. 50
Charles Finnerty, Unatt.	0	25 Oct. 50	6 June 54	5 Mar. 57	...	6 May 59

Scale of Allowance in addition to Half-Pay.

1st Class.—10s. 6d. per diem. 2nd Class.—8s. 6d. per diem.

In the event of the Staff Officer of Pensioners being subject to additional expense in consequence of his employment in aid of the Civil Power at a distance from head-quarters, he will also receive a further allowance of five shillings a day while necessarily detained from home, together with the amount of travelling charges thus incurred by him.

Contingent Allowances.

For 70 enrolled men, one shilling a day; 100 and upwards, one shilling and sixpence a day; 200 and upwards, two shillings a day; Officers with Brevet rank have two shillings a day in addition.

Any Captain applying to the Secretary of State for War to be appointed a Staff Officer of Pensioners should answer distinctly the following questions as to his qualifications:—

1st. What is his age? Whether on full or half-pay? Whether serving abroad or at home?
2nd. Has he completed fifteen years' service on full pay, and in what corps?
3rd. What is the date of his commission as Captain?
4th. Has he received the difference when placed on half-pay? Did he retire at his own request, from ill-health or from wounds?
5th. Has he served as Adjutant or Paymaster, or on the Staff in any capacity likely to qualify him for the duties of Staff Officer of Pensioners?
6th. Has he certificates of ability and fitness from officers under whom he served?

N.B. Officers under or above the rank of Captain, or whose appointment would involve immediate Brevet rank, or who, having received the difference, are not prepared to repay it, are ineligible for the appointment of Staff Officer of Pensioners.

War Services of Staff Officers of Pensioners.

1 Colonel Crofton was appointed Persian Interpreter to the force under Brigadier-General Litchfield, in August 1832, and served with it throughout the arduous operations in Parkur, and against the tribes in the N.W. Desert, which ended in the taking of Balmeer.
2 Major Middlemore served in the latter part of the Kaffir war of 1846-47; also throughout that of 1851-53 (Medal) as second senior officer of the Reserve Battalion 91st Regiment, and frequently commanded it in various engagements, and was present in every affair the Battalion was engaged in during the war; commanded 120 men with Eyre's Division in his first attack on the Amatolas and Noble Valley.
3 Captain Sinclair served the campaign of 1814 in Holland as a volunteer, and was severely wounded at the attack on the fortified village of Merxem on the 2nd Feb. 1814.
4 Colonel Orange served in the Burmese war in 1825, and has received the Indian War Medal for Ava.
5 Colonel Du Vernet served with the 45th Regiment in the Burmese war in 1825-26.
7 Major J. P. Pigott served with the 32nd Regiment at the 1st and 2nd siege operations before Mooltan, including the attack on the suburbs on the 27th Dec. 1848, storm and capture of the city, and surrender of the fortress; was also present at the surrender of the fort and garrison of Cheniote, and battle of Goojerat (Medal and Clasps). Served the Eastern campaign of 1854-55 with the Ambulance Corps (Medal and Clasps, and Brevet Major).
8 Colonel Forbes served in the Cape Mounted Riflemen in the Kaffir campaigns of 1834-5.
9 Major Ready served as Adjutant of the 11th Light Dragoons at the siege and capture of Bhurtpore in 1825-6 (Medal).
10 Major Tench served with the 45th Regiment during the Kaffir war of 1846-47 (Medal), and was afterwards present in the action with the insurgent Boers at Boem Plaats.
11 Colonel Campbell served in the Peninsula with the 4th Portuguese Regt. from 20 May 1810 to the end of that war in 1814, including the battle of Busaco, Lines of Torres Vedras, action of Campo Mayor, battle of Albuhera, first and second sieges of Badujoz, action at Arroyo de Molino, battles of Vittoria, Pyrenees, Pampeluna (severely wounded in the side); on the 27th July with the Company he commanded he defended the hill where the principal attack of that day was made, and drove the French thrice from it at the point of the bayonet, for which he was promoted to the Brevet Rank of Captain in the Portuguese Army, as stated in the *Gazette* of 11th Aug. 1813— "Em consequencia da sua boa conducta no Campo de Batalha." Also present at the battle of the Nive on 9th Dec., and in that before Bayonne on the 13th December. On the 20th Dec. 1813 he commanded four companies of his Regt., with which he took the Island of Holriague on the river Adour, and captured a number of prisoners and a quantity of provisions and forage, which were forwarded to Lord Hill's head-quarters. Afterwards present at the battle of Orthes, the action at Aire, and battle of Toulouse. Head severely injured 24th June 1813, when pursuing the enemy to Pampeluna. Has received the Silver War Medal with seven Clasps, and a Gold Cross from the King of Portugal for his services in five campaigns.
12 Colonel Trevor served the campaign of 1814 in Holland; and that of 1815 in Flanders and France, and was present at the battle of Waterloo and captures of Cambray and Paris.
13 Colonel Mounsteven served the campaign of 1815, and was severely wounded at the battle of Waterloo.
14 Major Cruice served with the 6th Regiment in the Kaffir war in 1851 (Medal).
15 Lt.Col. Willson served as Adjutant to the Royal Marines of the Mediterranean fleet; in that capacity with the 1st Battalion in the operations on the coast of Syria (Naval War Medal, and one from the Sultan); was at the attack and capture of Sidon; and on board the *Princess Charlotte* at the battle of St. Jean d'Acre. Served four years in the Royal Navy prior to his appointment as Second Lieutenant.
16 Major Sharp served in the 2nd Batt. of the Royals in Canada during the rebellion in 1838. Landed with the Battalion in the Crimea on the 22nd April 1855, and was at the siege and fall of Sebastopol (Medal and Clasp, and 6th Class of the Medjidie).
17 Captain Steele served at the capture of Java in 1811 as an officer of Royal Marines, and has received the War Medal with one Clasp.
18 Capt. Peddie served in Holland with the 21st Fusiliers in 1813 and 14, and was present at the attack on Merxem, the bombardment of the French fleet at Antwerp, and assault on Bergen-op-Zoom.
19 Major Chester served with the 53rd Regt. in the Sutlej campaign of 1845-46, including the affair at Buddiwal, and battles of Aliwal (wounded) and Sobraon (severely wounded by a musket ball through the body): Medal and Clasp.
20 Major Follows was present with the 43rd Light Infantry in the attack on New Orleans in Jan. 1815. He landed with his Regt. at Ostend on the 18th June following, and was present at the capture of Paris.
21 Captain George Fred. Moore served with the 10th Regt. in the early part of the siege operations before Mooltan in 1848 (Medal), including the affair of the 9th Sept., and the storming of the enemy's strongly-entrenched position; was severely wounded in the thigh on 4th November.
22 Lt.Col. William O'Neill served as a volunteer with the 83rd Regt. from 1st Feb. 1812 to the 12th of August following, when he was appointed to an ensigncy in that regiment, present with it at the battle of Salamanca capture of Madrid and the Retiro, retreat from Madrid and Salamanca, battle of Vittoria, blockade of Pampeluna, battles of the Pyrenees (from 27th to 30th July), Nivelle, Nive, and Orthes, actions of Sauveterre, Vic Bigorre, and Tarbes, and battle of Toulouse, besides several affairs and skirmishes; he has received the War Medal with eight Clasps. He served afterwards in Ceylon during the Kandian war in 1817, 18, and 19, and was the individual officer who made the two Kandian chiefs, together with many of their followers, prisoners, which at once put an end to that formidable rebellion, and for which he received the thanks, in General Orders, of the Governor and Commander-in-Chief Sir Robert Brownrigg, as also of the Duke of York.
23 Colonel Graham has the 3rd Class of the Medjidie for Service with the late Turkish Contingent.
24 Major Graves served with the 18th in China (Medal) from Sept. 1840 to June 1847, and was present at the storming and capture of the heights above Canton, attack and capture of Amoy, second capture of Chusan, attack and capture of the heights of Chinghae, occupation of Ningpo, and repulse of the night-attack, attack and capture of the enemy's entrenched camp on the heights of Segoan, attack and capture of Chapoo, Woosung, Shanghai, and Chin Kiang Foo, and demonstration before Nankin. He was also present at the operations in the Canton river, under Major-Gen. D'Aguilar in April 1847, and was selected as the officer to remain in command at the Factories when the force was withdrawn, for the purpose of organizing and drilling the Associated Gentlemen Volunteers at Canton.
25 Lieut.Colonel Thomson commanded the Engineers and corps of Pontoniers during the campaign in Arracan in 1824, and was present at the attacks on Paddown, Mahatee, and Arracan city (Medal). In 1838 was appointed Chief Engineer to the army of the Indus, and commanded the detachments of British troops which first crossed that river; afterwards constructed a bridge of boats over it, for which he received thanks in General Orders, as also for opening a passage for the army through the Bolan Pass and over the Amran Mountains. Reconnoitred the fortress of Ghuznee and proposed a plan of attack, which being successful, he received the thanks of the Commander in Chief, and afterwards of the Governor General of India (Medal and CB.).
26 Lt. Col. Simpson served the campaign in Tuscany, and was in the action before Genoa, and at the capture of that city in 1814. Served in the expedition to the Chesapeak, and was in the action at Bladensburg, and at the capture of Washington, 24th Aug. 1814. Present in the action before Baltimore, Sept. 1814. Served in Florida, and was in the action before New Orleans 8th Jan. 1815; also at the capture of Fort Bowyer.
27 Captain Wily served the campaign on the Sutlej (Medal and three Clasps), including the battles of Moodkee, Ferozeshah, Aliwal, and Sobraon, in which last engagement, and during the hottest part of the contest, he suc-

ceeded to the command of the 50th Regt., and brought it out of the action; his gallantry in the hand-to-hand conflict with the enemy attracted and called forth the marked and written approbation of Sir Harry Smith and Brigadier Penny, and for which he was noted by Lord Gough " as one worthy of reward for meritorious conduct in action with the enemy."

28 Captain M'Nair served during the American war in the campaigns of 1813 and 14 on the borders of Lake Ontario, and on the Niagara frontier, including the investment of Fort George, action at Black Rock and capture of the town of Buffalo; siege of Fort Erie, and the action at the sortie, 17th Sept. 1814, beside other affairs. Prisoner of war about six months.

29 Lt.Colonel Bruce served as Assistant Adjutant General to the Force under Sir George D'Aguilar in 1857, which captured the Bogue, Bocca Tigris, and Barrier Forts in the Canton River, mounting in all 879 pieces of heavy ordnance. He was also present at the operations before Canton.

30 Captain Driver was landed at Monte Video for the protection of British property in 1845, and served there until July 1847, the last five months as Major of Brigade. Served as Major of the 2nd Battalion Royal Marines in China from Aug. 1857 to Jan. 1858, including the blockade of the Canton river.

31 Captain Doro served with the Buffs in the battle of Punniar (Medal). Served with the 20th Regt. at the siege of Sebastopol (wounded) from the 11th July 1855, also at the capture of Kinbourn (Medal & Clasp).

33 Major Mackinnon served with the 16th Lancers in the campaign in Affghanistan of 1838-39 under Lord Keane, and was present at the siege and capture of Ghuznee (Medal). Several also throughout the Sutlej campaign of 1845-46, and was present at the affair of Buddiwal (charger killed under him by a round shot), and battles of Aliwal and Sobraon (Medal and Clasp).

34 Major Meik served with the 16th Lancers throughout the campaign in Affghanistan, under Lord Keane, including the siege and capture of Ghuznee (Medal). He was also present in the battle of Maharajpore (Medal), on the 29th Dec. 1843; and in 1846 he served in the campaign on the Sutlej (Medal), including the actions at Buddiwal, Aliwal, and Sobraon.

35 Captain Ferris served in the Burmese war in 1825-26 (Medal).

36 Captain Richmond served with the 98th Regt. in the Punjaub campaign of 1848-49 (Medal), and with the flank companies in Sir Colin Campbell's force, at the forcing of the Kohat Pass in Feb. 1850.

CHAPLAINS' DEPARTMENT.

Chaplain General to the Forces .... $\mathfrak{P}$ The Rev. George Robert Gleig,[1] A.M. 2 July 46 ...... *War Office.*

Chaplains to the Forces (2nd Class) under the Warrant of 5 Nov. 1858.

Rev. Henry Press Wright†	1 Jan. 59	Canterbury	Rev. W. Helps	11 July 56	St. Helena
— J. E. Sabin	1 Jan. 59	Aldershot			

Chaplains to the Forces under the Warrant of 1847.

Rev. Robert Wm. Browne, A.M.	1 Apr. 47	London	Rev. E. W. Milner, M.A.	1 Oct. 56	Portsmouth
— William Hare, A.M.	27 June 49	Woolwich	— Charles J. Hort	1 Oct. 56	Pembroke
— W.WalrondJackson,A.M.	21 Dec. 46	Barbadoes	— Hugh Hulcutt†	1 Oct. 56	
— Robert Hamilton†	24 Mar. 54	Templemore	— J. A. Crozier,† B.A.	1 Oct. 56	Gibraltar
— Henry W.M.Egan,†A.M.	13 Jan. 55	Parkhurst	— Wm. Sykes,† A.M.	1 Oct. 58	C. of G. Hope
— George Lawless,† A.M.	22 Dec. 55	Cephalonia	— L. J. Parsons	20 Oct. 57	Dublin
— Henry Hare	22 Feb. 56	Malta	— Robert L. M'Ghee	13 Apr. 58	Curragh

Chaplains to the Forces (3rd Class) under the Warrant of 1 Jan. 1859.

Rev. Charles Green, A.M.	1 Feb. 56	Chatham	Rev. D. Robertson	1 June 56	Quebec
— J. T. Twining, D.D.	1 Apr. 56	Halifax, N.S.	— T. H. M. Bartlett	2 May 57	Kingston, Canada
— Robert Halpin †	13 Nov. 49	Dublin	— E. J. Rogers	26 Mar. 59	Montreal
— Geo. WinneLangmead,A.M.	15 May 55	Plymouth	— Geo. Dacre,[3] A.M.	17 Apr. 59	Curragh

Chaplains to the Forces (4th Class) under the Warrant of 1 Jan. 1859.

Rev. L. Parsley (Rom. Cath.)	1 Apr. 47	Dublin	Rev. Edwin Smith	1 Oct. 56	Malta
— Henry M'Dougall	22 July 47	Jamaica	— C.A.AsshetonCraven,†A.M.	22 Oct. 57	Chatham
— Thomas Gardner	27 Mar. 51	Cork	— George Wylde	25 Feb. 58	Preston
— M. C. Odell	6 Dec. 53	Mauritius	— Henry Ovenden Wrench	18 Mar. 58	Zante
— James Leith Moody	7 Apr. 54	Winchester	— Wm. Watson Wood	1 July 58	Malta
— Henry E. Maskew	23 June 54	Aldershot	— Pat. Benton,A.M.(Presb.)	1 July 58	London
— J. H. Gilborne[2]	4 Sept. 54	Sheffield	— Wm. Anderson (Presb.)	1 July 58	Chatham
— W. F. Hobson	17 Nov. 54	Shorncliffe	— James Young (Presb.)	16 Oct. 58	Shorncliffe
— Francis Cannon (Presb.)	2 Mar. 55	Aldershot	— John Dick (Presb.)	16 Oct. 58	Dublin
— Dudley Somerville	6 Mar. 55	London	— George Ruggles Fisher	30 Oct. 58	London
— S. B. Windsor	10 Mar. 55	Portsmouth	— Fred. James Abbot	1 Apr. 59	China
— J. D'Arcy W. Preston	11 Apr. 55	Shorncliffe	— Michael Cuffe, R.C.	1 Apr. 59	Dublin
— Thomas Coney, M.A.	5 May 55	Aldershot	— Thomas Moloney, R.C.	1 Apr. 59	Chatham
— Milward Crooke	18 May 55	Birr	— John O'Flaherty, R.C.	1 Apr. 59	Gibraltar
— Henry Robinson	21 May 55	Walmer	— Joseph M'Sweeney, R.C.	1 Apr. 59	Aldershot
— HoraceN.Wheeler,†A.M.	28 May 55	Newbridge	— Joseph O'Dwyer, R.C.	1 Apr. 59	
— JohnVirtue(Rom.Cath.)	24 June 55	Aldershot	— Wm. George Morley, R.C.	1 Apr. 59	Chatham
— T.Unsworth(Rom.Cath.)	10 July 55	Aldershot	— Robert Shepherd, R.C.	1 Apr. 59	Colchester
— E. L. Walsh	5 Aug. 55	Colchester	— James Hamilton, R.C.	1 Apr. 59	Curragh
— LeonardH.St.George,B.D.	1 Sept. 55	Hong Kong	— John Fra. Browne, R.C.	1 Apr. 59	Gosport
— J.J. Mahe (Rom.Cath.)	19 Sept. 55	China	— Thomas Coghlan, R.C.	1 Apr. 59	Plymouth
— Fred. F. Thompson	1 Oct. 55	Malta	— Charles Morgan, R.C.	1 Apr. 59	Woolwich
— Alex. Henderson (Presb.)	16 Oct. 55	Curragh	— Edmond Butler, R.C.	1 Apr. 59	Halifax N.S.
— Jas.Hy.Beresford Harris	22 Oct. 55	Chichester	— Michael Hogan, R.C.	1 Apr. 59	Dover
— Thomas Molesworth	19 Nov. 55	Chatham	— James Carey, R.C.	1 Apr. 59	Portsmouth
— T.Richard Maynard, M.A.	5 Dec. 55	Dover	— Richard Blake, R.C.	1 Apr. 59	
— Wm.Sam.Sturges, M.A.	2 Jan. 56	Devonport	— Geo. Campbell Williams	14 May 59	Woolwich
— Charles Moore	1 Oct. 56	Gibraltar	— Alfred West	20 Sept. 59	Aldershot

⁂ The Chaplains with a † after their names served in the Crimea during the siege of Sebastopol, and have received the Medal.

1 Mr. Gleig served in the Peninsular campaigns of 1813 and 14 as a subaltern in the 85th, including the siege of San Sebastian, the passage of the Bidassoa, battle of the Nivelle, where he was wounded in the foot and arm, battle of the Nive (slightly wounded), and investment of Bayonne (War Medal with three Clasps). Served afterwards in the American war at Bladensburg (wounded), Baltimore (wounded), New Orleans (received a bayonet wound), and Fort Bowyer.

2 Mr. Gilborne served with the 3rd Division before Sebastopol from Oct. 1854, including the battle of Inkerman, and until Jan. 1856, when he was invalided home by reason of a broken leg (Medal and Clasp).

3 Mr. Dacre served in the Kaffir war of 1851-53 (Medal).

STAFF, &c. OF GREAT BRITAIN.

DISTRICTS.

Districts.	General and other Officers.	Aides de Camp.	Staff.
NORTHERN.—Head Quarters at Manchester. Lancashire, Cheshire, Shropshire, Flintshire, Denbighshire, Isle of Man, Northumberland, Cumberland, Durham, Westmoreland, York, Derby, Nottingham, Leicester, and Rutland, Warwick, Stafford, Northampton, and Worcester.	Lt.Gen. Sir John L. Pennefather, KCB. Col. Marriott, R. Art. Col. Hamilton, R. Eng.	Capt. Ellison, 47 F. Major Paget Bayly (Unatt.)	Assist.Adj.Gen. Col. R. Wilbraham, CB. Unatt. Assist.Qr.Mas.Gen. Lt.Col. L. Shadwell, Unatt.
SOUTH WEST.—Head Qrs. Portsmouth. Wilts, Dorset, and Hants.	Major Gen. Hon. Sir J. Y. Scarlett, KCB. Col. Lake, R. Art. Maj.Gen. Foster, R. Eng.	Lt.Col. Lugard, Unatt.	Assist.Qr.M.Gen. Colonel E. A. Somerset, CB. Unatt. Assist.Adj.Gen. Lt.Col. J.Conolly, Unatt. Town Major. Capt. J. Breton, Unatt.
WESTERN.—Head Quarters, Devonport. Devon, Cornwall, and Somerset, exclusive of Bristol and its vicinity.	Maj.Gen. W. N. Hutchinson Col. Pester, R. Art. Col. Wright, R. Eng.		Major of Brigade. Captain Kirk, 96 F. Town Major at Exeter. Lt.Col. J.B.Mann, Unatt.
SOUTH-EASTERN.—Kent, Surrey, Sussex, except the troops at Woolwich, Chatham, Sheerness, the batteries on the river Thames, Maidstone, Aldershot, Croydon, and Chichester, Hertford, Norfolk, Suffolk, Cambridge, and Huntingdon.	½ Lieut.Gen. R. C. Mansel, KH. Col. Cuppage, R. Art. Col. Stothord, R. Eng.	Capt. Mansel, 3 Drs. Major J. Forster, Unatt.	Assist.Adj.Gen. Col. H. W.Bunbury, CB. h. p. 23 F. Assist. Qr.-M. Gen. Lt.Col. H. A.Ouvry, CB. h. p. 6 Drs.
JERSEY.	Maj.Gen. G. C. Mundy. Col. Cleaveland, R. Art. Col. Renwick, R. Eng.		Fort Major & Adjt. ½ Col. John Fraser.
GUERNSEY AND ALDERNEY.	Maj.General M. J. Slade, Lieut.Gov. Col. Dunlop, CB. R. Art. Col. Burgmann, R. Eng.		Fort Major and Adjt. of Guernsey, Col. J.H. Bainbrigge. Town Major of Alderney ½ Col. W. A. Le Mesurier

RECRUITING DISTRICTS.

York. Consisting of the counties of Northumberland, Durham, York, Lincoln, Nottingham, Leicester, and Rutland.	Insp.Fd.Off. Col. C. Franklyn, CB. Adj. . . . Lt. Lowrie Paymaster . . C. H. Peirse *Superintending Officers.* Lt. Massey, 30 F...... Nottingham. Lt. Mackay, 40 F. ....Newcastle-on-Tyne. Lt. Gilby, 32 F........Lincoln.	Bristol. Consisting of the counties of Gloucester, Somerset, Devon, Cornwall, Dorset, Wilts, Hereford, Worcester, Warwick, Monmouth, and South Wales.	Insp. F. Off. Col. W. Hamilton, CB. Adj. ½ Lt. J. B. Hamilton, 6 Dec. 44. Paymaster . . . C. J. Furlong. *Superintending Officer.* Lt. M'Innis, 44 F....... Birmingham. Lt. Biron, 5 F....... Taunton. Lt. Russell, 23 F. .... Newport. Lt. Stammers, 10 F. .... Exeter.
Liverpool. Consisting of the counties of Lancashire, Chester, Cumberland, Westmoreland, Derby, Stafford, Salop, and North Wales.	Insp. F. Off. Col. J. R. Smyth, CB. Adj. ½ Lt. B. H. Edwards, 7 May 47 Paymaster . . E. M'Mullin. *Superintending Officer.* Lt. Emerson, 8 F....... Manchester. Lt. Davies, 10 F. ...... Preston.	London. Consisting of the counties of Middlesex, Surrey, Kent, Sussex, Essex, Suffolk, Norfolk, Cambridge, Huntingdon, Northampton, Bedford, Buckingham, Oxford, Berks, Hants, and Herts.	Insp. Fd. Off. Col. D. Russell, CB. Adj. Lt. W. F. Wyndowe. Paymaster D. Bartlett. *Superintending Officers.* Lt. Levett, 1 Dr. Gds... London. (Cavalry Subdivision.) Lt. FitzGerald, 97 F....... Ipswich. Lt. Davy, Rifle Br. .... Reading. Lt. Fagan, 4 F. .... Cambridge. Lt. Lockhart, 92 F. .... Reigate.

ALDERSHOT.
(Including Artillery at Christchurch and Cavalry at Hounslow.)

COMMANDING THE DIVISION	½ Lieut.Gen. W. T. Knollys.
Aides de Camp	{ Captain E. W. Blackett, Rifle Br. { Lieut. W. Palliser, 18 Drs.
Assistant Adjutant General................	Colonel J. Stewart Wood, CB. Unatt.
Deputy Assist.Adjutant General	Major Nugent, Unatt.
Assistant Quartermaster General	Colonel J. Clark Kennedy, CB. h.p. 18 F.
Deputy Assistant Quartermaster General....	Captain T. Young, 22 F.
Camp Quartermaster	Captain Richard Brennan, h.p. Land Transport Corps.
COMMANDING ROYAL ARTILLERY	Colonel Phillpotts.
Brigade Major	Brevet Major G. Milman.
COMMANDING ROYAL ENGINEERS	Colonel F. E. Chapman, CB.

Cavalry Brigade.

COMMANDING BRIGADE.....................	Major Gen. J. Lawrenson, h. p.
Aide de Camp	Captain Lyon, 2 Life Gds.
Brigade Major	Captain Godman, 5 Dr. Gds.

1st Infantry Brigade.

COMMANDING BRIGADE.....................	Major Gen. Lord Wm. Paulet, CB.
Aide de Camp	Captain C. Milligan, 30 F.
Brigade Major	Captain R. C. W. Stuart, 2 F.

2nd Infantry Brigade.

COMMANDING BRIGADE.....................	Major Gen. Hon. A. A. Spencer, CB. h. p. 44 F.
Aide de Camp	Captain A. Oldfield, 15 F.
Brigade Major	Captain Currie, 19 F.

3rd Infantry Brigade.

COMMANDING BRIGADE.....................	Major Gen. A. J. Lawrence, CB. h. p. Rifle Br.
Aide de Camp	Brevet Major C. E. Oldershaw, R. Art.
Brigade Major	Captain Wm. Deedes, 39 F.

Staff, &c. of Great Britain.

CAMP AT SHORNCLIFFE AND DOVER.
(Including the troops at Brighton and Canterbury, and a Battery of Artillery at Sheerness.)

COMMANDING DIVISION..........................	ꝓ *Lt.Gen.* R. C. Mansel, *KH.*
Aides de Camp	{ Captain A. E. Mansel, 3 Drs. Major J. Forster, Unatt.
Assistant Adjutant General................	Colonel H. W. Bunbury, *CB.* h. p. 23 F.
Assistant Quartermaster General.........	Lt.Col. H. A. Ouvry, *CB.* h. p. 9 Drs.

1st Infantry Brigade.

COMMANDING BRIGADE...........................	Major Gen. J. R. Craufurd.
Aide de Camp	Captain Malet, Gr. Gds.
Brigade Major	Brevet Major W. A. M. Barnard, Gr. Gds.

2nd Infantry Brigade.

COMMANDING BRIGADE...........................	ꝓ *Major Gen.* W. F. Williams, *KH.*
Aide de Camp	Captain Eteson, 3 F.
Brigade Major	Captain W. H. Charleton, 21 F.

COLCHESTER.

COLONEL ON THE STAFF	ꝓꝓ Colonel H. K. Bloomfield.
Brigade Major	Major Charles Cooch, Unatt.

STAFF, &c. OF SCOTLAND.

General Officer.	Station.	Aide de Camp.	Staff.
Major Gen. *Visc.* Melville, *KCB.*	Edinburgh	Major D. Jones, Unatt.	Assist. Adj. Gen. Col. W. A. M'Cleverty, Unatt. Staff Adjut......... Lieut. E. B. Goodman.
Col. FitzMayer, *CB.* R.Art.	Inverness, or Fort George		Fort Major .... Major A. C. Anderson, Unatt.
Col. Skyring, R. Eng.			Chaplain............. *Rev.* David Arthur.

RECRUITING DISTRICTS.

		Superintending Officers.
Glasgow.	Insp. F. Off. Major-Gen. A. C. Van N. Pole Adj........ ꝓ Lt. John Spence, 10 March 48. Paymaster..James Marshall	Lt. Carew, 29 F. ....Aberdeen
Edinburgh	Paymaster..Rob. Collings Cragie Adjutant ..John O'Neill, 8 Feb. 42.	Lt. Tulloch, 21 F..................Inverness

---

STAFF, &c. OF IRELAND.

General Commanding the Forces. | Captain Moore, 4 Drs., *Aide de Camp.*
ꝓꝓꝓ Gen. Lord Seaton, *GCB.*, *GCMG.*, & *GCH.* | Captain Prendergast, 2 Drs., *Aide de Camp.*
Commanding R. Artillery, Col. Ormsley | *Military Secretary,* Lt.Colonel *Hon.* James Colborne, Unatt.

ADJUTANT GENERAL'S DEPARTMENT. (*Head Quarters—Dublin.*)
Deputy Adjutant Gen. Col. S. Brownrigge, *CB.* Unatt. | *Dep. Assist. Adj. General,* Major Wm. Bellairs, Unatt.

QUARTER MASTER GENERAL'S DEPARTMENT. (*Head Quarters—Dublin.*)
Dep.Quart. Mast. Gen. Col. E.R. Wetherall,*CB.*,Unatt. | *Assist. Dep. Qr. Mast. Gen.* Captain Branfill, 16 F.
Commanding R. Artillery, Col. Ormsby | *Assist. Adj. General to R. Art.* ꝓꝓ Col. C. Dickson, *CB.*

ROYAL ARTILLERY AND ROYAL ENGINEERS.
Command. R. Engineers, Colonel Frome. | *Assist. Adjutant General,* Colonel Durnford.

AIDES DE CAMP TO HIS EXCELLENCY THE LORD LIEUTENANT.

Capt. *Hon.* L. A. Ellis	. Kilkenny Militia	Captain E. A. Shuldham .	. S. Cork Militia
Lieut. A. P. Cockerell	. N. Gloucester Militia	Captain W. W. Moore .	. Co. Dublin Militia
Capt. C. Lascelles	. R. Art.	Captain R. G. Buller .	. Gr. Gds.
Bt. Major F. R. Foster	. 4 Dr. Gds.	Commander Glyn .	. Royal Navy
Extra.		Lieut. R. Donaldson .	. Meath Militia
Ens. A. F. Gore .	. Longford Militia		

DISTRICTS.

Districts.	General Officers.	Aides de Camp.	Staff.
Dublin.—Head Quarters, Dublin.	ꝓ Major Gen. E. F. Gascoigne. Col. Gambier, *CB.* R. Art. Col. Lloyd, R. Eng.	Captain Gascoigne, Gr. Gds.	*Assist. Adj. Gen.* Lt.Col. R. Blane, *CB.* Unatt. *Town Major.* Lt.Col. H. B. J. Wynyard, Unatt.
Cork.—Head Quarters, Cork.	Major Gen. John Eden, *CB.* Lt. Col. Shakespear, R. Art. Lt. Col. J. H. Freeth, R. Eng.	Major Hammersley, 14 F.	*As. Adj. Gen.* Lt.Col. H. Smith, Unatt. *As. Qua. M. Gen.* Col. A. J. Reynell-Pack, *CB.* h. p. *Fort Major.* ꝓ Lt. J. Black, Charles Fort.

DUBLIN DIVISION.

COMMANDING THE DIVISION	Major-Gen. E. F. Gascoigne.
Aide-de-Camp	Captain Gascoigne, Gr. Gds.
Assistant-Quartermaster-General	Lieut.-Col. *Hon.* P. R. B. Feilding, Coldst. Gds.

Cavalry Brigade.

COMMANDING BRIGADE	Major-Gen. Wm. Parlby, h. p. 10 Hussars.
Aide-de-Camp	Captain Gratrex, 13 Drs.
Brigade Major	Major A. Elliot, Unatt.

1st Infantry Brigade.

COMMANDING BRIGADE	Major-Gen. J. B. Gough, *CB*.
Aide-de-Camp	Captain A. F. Warburton, 15 F.
Brigade Major	Major C. F. T. Daniell, Unatt.

2nd Infantry Brigade.

COMMANDING BRIGADE	Major-Gen. A. A. T. Cunynghame, *CB*. h. p. 51 F.
Aide-de-Camp	Captain C. Ellis, 60 F.
Brigade Major	Captain G. A. Morgan, 55 F.

CAMP AT THE CURRAGH OF KILDARE.

COMMANDING BRIGADE	Major-Gen. Horatio Shirley, *CB*. h. p. 88 F.
Aide-de-Camp	Captain G. R. Beresford, h. p. 7 F.
Brigade Major	Major Nathaniel Steevens.
Assistant-Quartermaster-General	Lt.-Col. George W. Mayow, Unatt.

RECRUITING DISTRICTS.

Northern. Head Quarters, Belfast. Consisting of the counties of Antrim, Armagh, Donegal, Down, Fermanagh, Londonderry, Louth, Monaghan, and Tyrone.	Insp. F.Off. *Colonel* W. Sullivan, *CB*. Adj. Lieut. Griffin 24 June 53 Paymaster . . . . Jas. Robinson *Superintending Officer*. Lieut. Coupe, 15 F. *Omagh*.	Leitrim, Longford, Mayo, Meath, Queen's, Roscommon, Sligo, Westmeath, Wicklow, Carlow and Kilkenny.	*Superintending Officers*. Lt. Knight, 90 F............ *Athlone*. Lt. Wilson, 86 F............ *Boyle*.
Centre. Head Quarters, Dublin. Consisting of the countiesof Cavan, Dublin, Galway, Kildare, King's.	Insp. Field. *Off*. . Col. E. B. Brooke Adj. Lt. C. P. Hamilton 24 Feb. 48 Paymaster . . Capt. H. B. Adams.	Southern. Head Quarters, Cork. Consisting of the counties of Clare, Cork, Kerry, Kilkenny, Limerick, Tipperary, Waterford, and Wexford.	Insp. Fd. *Off*. Col. T. A. Drought. Adj. . Lt. R. A. Dagg,17Sept.47. Paymaster . . Wm. H. Fitzgerald. *Superintending Officers*. Ens. Bell, 16 F. .... *Limerick*. Lt. Ker, 3 F. .... *Clonmel*.

STAFF, &c., ON FOREIGN STATIONS.

AUSTRALIA.

New South Wales.
Captain General and Governor in Chief.................Colonel Sir Wm.Thos. Denison, *KCB*.R.Eng. *Sydney*.
    Aide-de-Camp................................
Major of Brigade ....Major Charles Nasmyth, Unatt.

Victoria.
Captain-General & Governor-in-Chief ....Sir Henry Barkly, *KCB*.
    Military Secretary..............................Captain Bancroft, 16 F.
Major-Gen. on the Staff..................................Major Gen. T. S. Pratt, *CB*. *Melbourne*.
    Assistant Military Secretary ....
    Aide-de-Camp ....Lt.Col. Robert Carey.
Deputy Adjutant-General ....Lt. Forster, R. Art. *Melbourne*.
Major of Brigade ....Captain R. Hare, 40 F. *Melbourne*.

Western Australia.
Governor and Commander-in-Chief...........................Arthur Edward Kennedy, Esq.

South Australia.
Captain-General and Governor-in-Chief..........Sir Richard Graves Mac Donnell, *CB*., *Adelaide*.
    Private Secretary ....

Tasmania.
Captain-General and Governor-in-Chief..................Sir Henry Edward Fox Young, *CB*., *Hobart Town*.
    Aide-de-Camp................................
Commanding the Forces...................................Col. J. M. Perceval, *CB*. 12 F. do.
Assist. Adjutant-General ....Lieut.-Colonel Bradshaw, Unatt. do.
Commanding Royal Engineers..............................Colonel Broughton.

New Zealand.
Governor and Commander-in-Chief ....Col. T. G. Browne, *CB*. late of 41 F.
Commanding the Forces...................................Colonel Gold, 65 F.
Deputy Quarter-Master General ....Lieut.-Col. Charles Sillery, h. p.
Major of Brigade ....Capt. Stack, 65 F. ....*Auckland*.
Commanding Royal Engineers..............................Colonel Mould.

BAHAMAS.

Governor and Commander-in-Chief............. ....Charles John Bayley, Esq.
    Fort Adj. ....Lieut. Edwardes, 2 W. I. R.

Staff, &c., on Foreign Stations.

BERMUDA.
Governor and Comm.-in-Chief	Colonel Freeman Murray, h.p.
Fort Adj.	
Commanding Royal Artillery	Colonel H. A. Turner.
Commanding Royal Engineers	Lt.Col. S. Freeth.

BRITISH COLOMBIA.
Governor and Commander in Chief	James Douglas, CB.
Lieut. Governor	Colonel R. C. Moody, R. Eng.

CAPE OF GOOD HOPE.
Governor and Commander-in-Chief	Sir George Grey, KCB.
Military Secretary	
Commanding the Forces & Lt.-Governor	Major Gen. R. H. Wynyard, CB.
Military Secretary	Captain Shipley, 58 F.
Aides-de-Camp	
Commanding Brigade	Colonel W. J. D'Urban, Unatt.
Aide-de-Camp	
Assistant-Adjutant-General	Colonel Bisset, Cape M.R., *King William's Town*.
Deputy Quarter-Master General	Col. E. S. Smyth, 2 F.
Brigade Major	Ü Lt.Col. Wm. Carruthers, Unatt. *Cape Town*.
Commanding Royal Artillery	Colonel J. N. A. Freese, CB.
Commanding Royal Engineers	Colonel Cowper Rose.

CEYLON.
Governor and Commander-in-Chief	Sir Henry George Ward, GCMG.
Aide-de-Camp	Bt.Major D. W. Tupper, 50 F.
Major-General on the Staff	Ü Major-Gen. H. F. Lockyer, CB. KH.
Assistant Military Secretary	Major Henry George Woods, Unatt.
Aide-de-Camp	Captain Ingles, 16 F.
Dep. Adj. Gen....Lt.Col. H. L. Maydwell, h.p. Depot Batt.	Dep Q. M. Gen..Col. Garvock, Unatt.
Commanding Royal Artillery...Lt.Col. Graham.	Commanding Royal Engineers..Col. Wilkinson.

EAST INDIES.
Captain-General and Governor-in-Chief	Charles John, *Earl* Canning, GCB.
Military Secretary	Major Sir E. S. Campbell, 60 F.
Aide-de-Camp	Captain Hon. J. C. Stanley, Gr. Gds.
Commander-in-Chief	Ü General *Lord* Clyde, GCB.
Military Secretary	Colonel A. C. Sterling, CB., Unatt.
Aides-de-Camp	{ Major F. Alison, 10 F. Major Hon. J. C. Dormer, 13 F.
Chief of the Staff	
Aide-de-Camp	
Adjutant-General	Colonel Hon. Wm. Lygon Pakenham, CB. Unatt.
Deputy-Adjutant-General	Lt.Col.K. D. Mackenzie, 93 F.
Assistant-Adjutant-General	
Quarter-Master-General	Colonel George Congreve, CB. h.p. 29 F.
Major of Brigade at Calcutta	Major Blanc, 52 F.

Bengal.
Major-General on the Staff	Major-Gen. Charles Ash Windham, CB.
Aide-de-Camp	Captain Swire, 97 F.
Major-General on the Staff	Major-Gen. Sir Sydney John Cotton, KCB.
Aide-de-Camp	Captain L. S. Cotton, 97 F.
Major-General on the Staff	Ü Major-Gen. Sir Robert Garrett, KCB. KH.
Aide-de-Camp	Major G. F. Dallas, 46 F.
Major-General on the Staff	Major-Gen. Sir John E. W. Inglis, KCB.
Aide de Camp	Lieut. Fletcher, 48 N.I.
Commanding Royal Artillery	Colonel Sir G. R. Barker, KCB.
Commanding Royal Engineers	Colonel H. D. Harness, CB.

Madras.
Governor	Sir Charles Edward Trevelyan, KCB.
Military Secretary	
Aide-de-Camp	
Commander-in-Chief	Lt.-Gen. Sir Patrick Grant, KCB.
Military Secretary	Colonel F. P. Haines, 8 F.
Aides-de-Camp	{ Lt. H. J. Fane, 81 F.
Deputy-Adjutant-General	Lt.-Col. Charles A. Denison, 2 F.
Deputy Quarter-Master-General	Colonel George Talbot, 43 F.
Major of Brigade at Madras	Major Sir C. F. W. Cuffe, *Bart*. 66 F.
Lieut.Gen. on the Staff	Lieut.-Gen. Marcus Beresford
Aide-de-Camp	
Maj.-Gen. on the Staff	Major-Gen. P. E. Craigie, CB.
Aide-de-Camp	Captain Champion, 52 F.
Commanding Royal Artillery	Colonel J. M. Adye, CB.

Bombay.
Governor	John, *Lord* Elphinstone, GCB.
Military Secretary	Major Visc. Dangan, Coldst. Gds.
Aide-de-Camp	Lieut. E. A. Ellis, 33 F.
Commander-in-Chief	Ü ☙ Lieut.-Gen. Sir Henry Somerset, KCB. KH.
Military Secretary	
Aides-de-Camp	{ Capt. E. L. Greene, 77 F. Lt. Hon. A. Stewart, R. Art.
Deputy Adjutant-General	Colonel C.H. Somerset, CB. 72 F.
Assistant Adjutant General	Lt.Colonel Ross, 93 F.
Major of Brigade at Bombay	Captain Cleeve, 51 F.
Major-General Commanding Poonah Division	Major-Gen. Sir Hugh Henry Rose, GCB.
Aide-de-Camp	Captain George E. Rose, Rifle Br.
Major-General on the Staff	Major-Gen. Sir John Michel, KCB.
Aide-de-Camp	Lt.Colonel Elkington, 6 F.
Commanding Royal Artillery	Colonel G. J. L. Buchanan.
Commanding Royal Engineers	Lt.Colonel J. F. M. Browne, CB.

Staff, &c. on Foreign Stations.

FALKLAND ISLANDS.
Governor and Commander-in-Chief Captain Thomas Edward Laws Moore, R.N.
Commanding Detachments . . . Capt. Charles Compton Abbott, 7 Aug. 57; Ens. 22 July 42; Lt. 24 May 44;
Capt. 26 Mar. 58.

GIBRALTAR.
Governor and Commander-in-Chief . . . . Lt.Gen. *Sir* William J. Codrington, *KCB*.
   Assist. Mil. Sec. . . . . . Captain W. Earle, Gr. Gds.
   Aides-de-Camp . . . . . { Capt. *Hon.* H. W. Campbell, Colds. Gds.
                                       { Lt. A. W. Hood, 25 F.
Commanding Brigade . . . . . Major Gen. R. Rumley, Unatt.
   Aide-de-Camp
Assist. Adj.-Gen. . . . . . . Colonel Lacy, Unatt.
Brigade-Major . . . . Captain Osborne, 11 F.
Commanding Royal Artillery . . . . Colonel A. A. Shuttleworth.
Commanding Royal Engineers . . . . Colonel B. S. Stehelin.
Town Adjutant . . . . . . Captain Bernard Morgan,[1] 8 July 56; *Ens.* 11 July 54;
                                           Lt. 5 Nov. 54; *Capt.* 3 Oct. 55.
Garrison Quarter-Master . . . . . * Lt. Wm. Hume, h. p. Qr.-M. 72 F.
1 Captain Morgan served the Eastern campaign of 1854-55, including the battles of Alma and Inkerman, siege of Sebastopol, and capture of the Rifle Pits on the 18th April—contused (Medal and Clasps).

HELIGOLAND.
   Lieut.-Governor . . . . . Richard Pattinson, Esq.

HONG KONG.
Governor and Commander-in-Chief of Hong Kong . . . Sir Hercules George Robert Robinson*
Lieutenant-Governor . . . .
Town Major . . . .

Expeditionary Force in China.
Lieut.General Commanding . . . . Lt.Gen. *Sir* J. Hope Grant, *KCB*.
Lieut.General on the Staff . . . . Lt.Gen. *Sir* W. R. Mansfield, *KCB*.
Major-General on the Staff . . . . Major-Gen. *Sir* Charles T. Van Straubenzee, *KCB*.
   Aide-de-Camp . . . . . . Captain B. van Straubenzee, 9 F.
Military Secretary . . . . . . Colonel *Hon.* St. George G. Foley, *CB*. Unatt.
Assistant Adj.-Gen. . . . . . Lt.Col. F. C. A. Stephenson, *CB*. Scots Fus. Gds.
Assist. Qr.-Mas.-General . . . . Lt.Col. Joseph Oates Travers, R. Marines.
Dep. Assist. Qr.-Mas.-Gen. . . . . .
Commanding Royal Artillery . . . . Colonel W. T. Crawford, *CB*.
Commanding Royal Engineers . . . . Lt.Colonel G. F. Mann.

IONIAN ISLANDS.
Comprising *Corfu, Vido, Paxo, Santa Maura, Cefalonia, Zante, Ithaca* and *Calamos*, and *Cerigo*.
Lord High Commissioner . . . . . . Colonel *Sir* Henry Knight Storks, *KCB*. Unatt.
   Aides-de-Camp . . . . . . { Major John Peel, Unatt.
Major-General on the Staff . . . . Major-General *Sir* George Buller, *KCB*.
   Assist. Mil. Sec. . . . . . Lt.-Col. *Hon.* L. Curzon, Rifle Br.
   Aide-de-Camp . . . . . . Captain A. E. V. Ponsonby, Gr. Gds.
Dep.-Quarter-Mast. General . . . . Lieut.-Col. Arthur James Herbert, Unatt.
Major of Brigade . . . . . . VC Major Hamilton, Unatt.
Commanding Royal Artillery . . . . Colonel A. Irving, *CB*.
Commanding Royal Engineers . . . . Colonel G. Wynne.

JAMAICA, (including HONDURAS.)
Captain-General and Governor-in-Chief . . . . . Henry Charles Darling, Esq.
   Aide-de-Camp and Military Secretary . . . .
Major-General on the Staff & Lt. Governor . . . . Major Gen. Edw. Wells Bell
   Assistant Military Secretary . . . . Capt. Birch, 3 W. I. R.
   Aide-de-Camp . . . . Lieut. H. S. Stewart, 11 F.
Dep. Adj. Gen. . . . . Lt.Col. J. W. Reynolds, Unatt.
Commanding Royal Artillery . . . . Captain G. L. Chandler.
Commanding Royal Engineers . . . . Lt.Colonel C. M'Causland.
Garrison Quarter Master . . . . Ensign Williams, 2 W. I. R.
Superintendent at Honduras . . . . Fred. Seymour, Esq.
Fort Adjutant at Honduras . . . . Lieut. C. B. Cradock, 2 W. I. Regt.

MALTA.
Governor and Commander-in-Chief . . . . . Lieut.General *Sir* J. Gaspard Le Marchant.
   Aides-de-Camp . . . . . . { Lt. Romilly, 23 F.
   Assistant Military Secretary . . . . Capt. W. Brett, 76 F.
   Assistant Adjutant-General . . . . Lt.Col. G. H. S. Willis, Unatt.
   Deputy Qr. M. General . . . . . Bt. Lt.-Col. E. G. Hallewell, Unatt.
   Town Major . . . . Lt.Col. B. C. Mitford, Unatt.
Commanding 1st Brigade . . . . . Major-Gen. C. Warren, *CB*.
   Aide-de-Camp . . . . . . Captain J. W. Trevor, 22 F.
   Brigade-Major . . . . . . Major *Hon.* W. J. Colville, Rifle Br.
Commanding 2nd Brigade . . . . . Major-Gen. F. Horn, *CB*, h. p. 20 F.
   Aide-de-Camp . . . . . . Lieut. E. J. Cox, 3 F.
   Brigade Major . . . . . . Captain S. W. F. M. Wilson, 55 F.
Commanding Royal Artillery . . . . Colonel E. C. Warde, *CB*.
Commanding Royal Engineers . . . . Colonel H. O. Crawley.

MAURITIUS.
Governor and Commander-in-Chief . . . . William Stevenson, Esq. *CB*.
   Aide-de-Camp . . . .
Major-General on the Staff . . . . Major-Gen. Henry Wm. Breton.
Assist. Mil. Sec. Major A. A. Nelson, Unatt.
   Aides-de-Camp . . . . { Capt. C. W. Aylmer, 66 F.
Dep. Quarter-Master Gen. . . . . Lt.-Col. H. F. F. Johnson, h. p. 5 F.
Commanding Royal Artillery . . . . Colonel V. C. Cockburn.
Commanding Royal Engineers . . . .

Staff, &c. on Foreign Stations.

NEWFOUNDLAND.
Governor and Commander in Chief .... Sir Alexander Bannerman.
Aide de Camp ....

NORTH AMERICA.
Comprising all the Provinces within and adjacent thereto.

Captain General & Governor in Chief	Right Hon. Sir Edmund Walker Head, *Bart.*
Aide de Camp	Capt. Retallack, 63 F.
Lieut.General on the Staff	Lt.Gen. *Sir* William Fenwick Williams, *Bart.*
Military Secretary	Major W. J. Williams, R. Art.
Aides de Camp	Captain O. B. Woolsey, R. Art.
	Lieut. Grant, R. Eng.

Canada.

Colonel on the Staff (Comm. R. Art.)	Col. A. J. Taylor	Montreal.
Major of Brigade	Capt. Charles Waller, R. Art.	
Colonel on the Staff (Comm. R. Eng.)	Colonel H. Servante	Ditto.
Assist. Adj. Gen.	Colonel *Hon.* Robert Rollo, Unatt.	Montreal.
Dep. Quarter Master General	Colonel G. T. C. Napier, *CB.* Unatt.	Montreal.
Town Major	Lt. Ens. C. Macdonald, h. p. 50 F.	Ditto.
— —	Bt.Major Alfred Knight, Unatt.	Quebec.
— —	Colonel Bourchier, h.p.	Kingston.
Fort Adjutant	Michael Dowd	Isle-aux-Noix.

Nova Scotia.

Lieutenant Governor	The Earl of Mulgrave.
Aide de Camp	Captain Stapleton, Gr. Gds.
Commanding Brigade	Maj.Gen. C. Trollope, *CB.* h.p. 62 F.
Aide de Camp	Capt. Armstrong, 10 F.
Brigade Major	Capt. J. W. Percy, 9 F.
Assist. Quarter Master Gen.	Lt.Col. C. F. Fordyce, *CB.* Unatt.
Town Major	Colonel A. F. Ansell, Unatt.
Commanding Royal Artillery	Colonel A. Benn.
Commanding Royal Engineers	Colonel R. J. Nelson.

New Brunswick.

Lieut.Governor	Hon. John Henry Thomas Manners Sutton.	
Town Major	Lieut. T. E. Jones, h.p. 4 F.	*St. John's*.

Prince Edward's Island.

Lieut.Governor	George Dundas, Esq.

SAINT HELENA.

Governor	Sir Edward Drummond Hay.
Aide de Camp	
Fort Adjutant	Lieut. A. W. Campbell, St. Helena Regt.
Commanding Royal Artillery	Colonel G. Maclean.
Commanding Royal Engineers	Lt.Col. A. Beatty.

WESTERN COAST OF AFRICA.

Sierra Leone.
Captain General and Governor in Chief .... Colonel Hill, h.p. 2 West India Regt.

Gambia.
Governor and Commander in Chief .... Colonel George A. K. d'Arcy.

Gold Coast.

Governor and Commander in Chief	Sir Benjamin Chilley Pine.	
Garrison Adjutants	Lieut. Temple 1 West India Regt.	Sierra Leone.
	Lieut. Molony, do.	Gambia.
Paymasters of Detachments	John Ashwood, 31 Dec. 58	Sierra Leone.
	William Mansergh Alma, 18 Feb. 59	Gambia.

WINDWARD AND LEEWARD ISLANDS.

Major General commanding the Troops	Major Gen. Sir A. Josias Cloete, *CB. KH.*	Barbadoes.
Assistant Military Secretary	Major Parish, 45 F.	
Aide de Camp	Capt. Gostling, 49 F.	
Dep. Adj. Gen.	Colonel Edw. Rowley Hill, h.p. 63 F.	Barbadoes.
Dep. Assist. Qr. Mas. Gen.	Captain A. F. Stewart, 36 F.	Barbadoes.
Major of Brigade	Captain Beresford, 49 F.	
Governor and Commander in Chief of Barbadoes, Grenada, St. Vincent, Tobago, and St. Lucia, and their Dependencies,	Francis Hincks, Esq.	Barbadoes.
Aide de Camp	Lieut. Beresford, 3 W. I. R.	
Lieutenant Governors	Edward John Eyre, Esq.	St. Vincent.
	James Vickery Drysdale, Esq.	Tobago.
	Cornelius Kortright, Esq.	Grenada.
	H. H. Breen, Esq.	St. Lucia.
Governor & Com. in Chief of Leeward Islands	Ker Baillie Hamilton, Esq.	St.Christophers and Anguilla.
Lieutenant Governors	Major Harry St. George Ord, R. Eng.	Dominica.
	E. E. Rushworth, Esq.	Montserrat.
Officers administering the Government	Sir Carlo Arthur Henry Rumbold, *Bart.*	Nevis.
	Thomas Price, Esq.	Virgin Islands.
Governor and Commander in Chief of Trinidad	Robert William Keate, Esq.	
Governor and Com. in Chief of British Guiana	Philip E. Wodehouse, Esq.	Demerara.
Fort Adj. Lieut. Davies, 49 F. ... Trinidad	Fort Adj. ...Lieut. Eustace, 40 F.	St. Lucia.
——— Lieut. Kerr, 3 W. I. R. ...... Demerara		

MILITARY AND CIVIL DEPARTMENTS.

WAR OFFICE.
Prin. Sec. of State, Rt. Hon. Sidney Herbert, *MP.*
Under Secretaries { Sir Benjamin Hawes, KCB.
of State, { Earl de Grey and Ripon.
Assistant do. .... John R. Godley, Esq.
Sec. for Military
Correspondence, } Maj.Gen. Sir Edward Lugard, *KCB.*

Chief Examiner of Army Accounts, F. J. Prescott, *Esq.*

ORDNANCE BRANCH.
Inspector General { ꝑ General Sir John F. Burgoyne,
of Fortifications { Bart., *GCB.*
Deputy do., Lt. Colonel H. C. C. Owen, *CB.*
Assists. do. ...... { Major Jervoise.
  { Captain Bolfield.
  { Captain Galton.
Director General of } Capt. J. C. Caffin, *CB.* R.N.
Stores and Clothing, }
Assistant do., George D. Ramsay, *Esq.*
Director of Contracts, Thomas Howell, *Esq.*
Accountant General, R. C. Kirby, *Esq. CB.*

MANUFACTURING DEPARTMENTS.
Superintendent of Royal Gun { Sir Wm. G. Anderson,
Factories, Woolwich { *CB.*
Do. of R. Carriage Department, Woolwich, Colonel A. Tulloh, R. Art.
Do. of R. Laboratories, Woolwich, Capt. F. M. Boxer, R. Art.
Do. of R. Factories of Small Arms, Enfield, Lt. Col. W. M. H. Dixon, R. Art.
Superintendent of Royal Powder Factories, Waltham Abbey, Col. W. H. Askwith, R. Art.

ARMY PAY OFFICE.
Paymaster Gen., Rt. Hon. W. F. Cowper, *MP.*

JUDICIAL DEPARTMENT.
Judge Advocate General } Right Hon. Thomas Emerson
of the United Kingdom } Headlam, *MP.*
Deputy ditto Stephen Charles Denison, *Esq.*
Office, 35, Great George Street, Westminster.

COUNCIL OF EDUCATION.
President ...... H. R. H. The General Commanding in Chief (*ex officio*).
Vice President.. Major Gen. Duncan A. Cameron, *CB.*
  { Major Gen. Joseph E. Portlock, ret.
  { f. p. R. Eng.
Members ...... { Lt. Col. Joseph E. Addison, h. p. 97 F.
  { Col. T. Elwyn, R. Art.
  { Rev. Henry Moseley, *MA.*
Secretary ...... Captain Doveton D. Greentree, Unatt.

INSPECTOR OF REGIMENTAL COLOURS.
Albert Wm. Woods, Esq. Lancaster Herald.
Heralds' College, Doctors' Commons.

ROYAL MILITARY COLLEGE AT SANDHURST.
(*Comprising the Staff College and the Cadets' College.*)
COMMISSIONERS.
Ex Officio.
H. R. H. The General Commanding in Chief *President.*
The Secretary of State for War .... *Vice President.*
The Adjutant General.
The Quarter Master General.
The Governor of the Royal Military College.
Specially appointed.
ꝑ General Sir Howard Douglas, *Bt. GCB. GCMG.*
ꝑ ——— Hon. Henry Murray, *CB.*
ꝑ ——— Sir George Brown, *GCB.*
ꝑ ꝗꝗ General Sir Hew D. Ross, *GCB.* R. Art.
ꝑ ꝗꝗ ——— Sir James Simpson, *GCB.*

ꝑ ꝗꝗꝗ General Sir George Scovell, *KCB.*
Lieut. Gen. Sir Charles Yorke, *KCB. Military Sec.*
ꝑ Major General James Freeth, *KH.*
ꝑ ——— Forster, *KH. Dep. Adj. Gen.*
Colonel Hon. Alex. Gordon, *CB., Dep. Qv. Mr. Gen.*
Sir Benjamin Hawes, *KCB. Under Secretary for War.*

Governor, ꝑ Maj. Gen. Sir Harry D. Jones, *KCB.* R. E.
Lt. Gov. ꝑ Col. C. R. Scott, h. p.
Major and Superintendent of Studies, Col. William C. E. Napier, Unatt.
Adjutant, William Patterson,[2] 12 Feb. 58; Ens 17 Apr. 42; Lt. 14 Apr. 46; Capt. 13 July 55.
Captains of Companies of Gentlemen Cadets.
Br. Major Garnet Man.
Captain William Paterson,[3] Ens. 11 Dec. 46; Lt. 13 Oct. 51; Capt. p 25 Mar. 56.
Riding Master.—Capt. J. H. T. Warde, Unatt.
Chaplain, Rev. H. Le M. Chepmell, *DD.*
Paymaster, Lieut. Wm. Leigh Hilton.
Quarter Master.—John Davies, 26 Nov. 58.
Surgeon, Edward Bradford, *Deputy Insp. Gen. on h. p.*
Assistant Surg. Melville Neale, *M.D.*, *Surgeon Major.*

Professors and Masters.
  { Rev. F. W. Vinter, *M.A.*
  { Rev. A. Deck, *M.A.*
Mathematics and Arith- { Rev. Samuel Howlett, *B.A.*
metic .... { Rev. R. H. Walker.
  { G. Hester.
  { Henry R. Greer.
  { Colonel W. H. Adams, Un.
Fortification .... { Captain Geo. Philips, R. Eng.
  { Capt. Robert Petley, Unatt.
Military Surveying . . { Capt. R. W. Taylor, Unatt.
  { Lieut. C. E. Palmer, 13 F.
Military History . . . Captain C.C. Chesney, R. Eng.
Landscape Drawing . . Edward de la Motte
History, Geography, and } Rev. George E. Cole, *M.A.*
Classics ..... } Rev. E. M. Heale, *M.A.*
French .... { A. Aigré de Charente.
  { G. Bouily.
  { Paul Baume.
  { A. Talandier.
German ...... { Dr. J. Ehrenbaum.
  { Carl Dressner.

STAFF COLLEGE.
Commandant.—Colonel P. L. MacDougall,[1] h. p. *Adj.*

Professors.
Mathematics.................. { Rev. J. F. Twisden, *MA.*
  { B. T. Moore, *BA.*
Fortification and Artillery...Capt. Mainwaring, R. Art.
Military History ....Lt. Col. Hamley, R. Art.
Military Topography ....Capt. S. B. Farrell, R. Eng.
Military Administration... { Capt. W. Walker, late of
  { 60 F.
French ....G. Cambier.
German ....F. Demmler.
Hindostanee..................John Dowson.

STUDENTS.

Senior Division.	Junior Division.
Capt. W. C. Nanule, R. Art.	Lieut. R. Home, R. Eng.
Lieut. C. G. Goff, 50 F.	Captain P. G. B. Lake, 100 F.
Lieut. A. H. Wavell, 41 F.	Bt. Maj. J. R. Turnbull, 13 F.
Capt. H. J. Wilkinson, 9 F.	Captain W. T. Stuart, 17 F.
Captain H.F. Morgan, 28 F	Captain C. O. Creagh, 86 F.
ꝒЄ Capt. A. S. Jones, 18 Hussars.	Lieut. F. W. Hutton, 23 F.
Captain E. M. Palliser, 82 F.	Lieut. K. Monro, R. Art.
Captain R. B. Stokes, 54 F.	Lieut. F. S. Stoney, R. Art.
Lieut. Taylor, R. Marines.	Captain J. P. Battersby, 60 F.
Captain H. Bird, 57 F.	Captain G. Hay, 62 F.
	Captain J. S. Swan, 54 F.
	Capt. W. E. Lockhart, 26 F.
	Bt. Maj. R. C. Stewart, 85 F.
	Lieut. T. E. A. Hall, 91 F.
	Cnpt. M. Creagh, 4 Dr. Gds.

1 Colonel MacDougall was employed on particular service in the Crimea, acting on the Quarter Master General's Staff to the Kertch Expedition (Medal and Clasp for Sebastopol).
2 Captain Patterson served with the 32nd Regt. in the 1st and 2nd siege operations before Mooltan, including the storm and capture of the city; he was also present at the surrender of the fort and garrison of Cheniote, and at the battle of Goojerat (Medal and Clasps). Served with the force under Sir Colin Campbell against the Affghan Tribes of the Caboot frontier in 1852.
3 Captain Paterson served with the 80th Regiment in the Burmese war of 1852-53 (Medal), including the bombardment and capture of Prome, repulse of the subsequent night-attack, reconnaissance at Lthaymow, advance on Meeaday, and capture and destruction of two of the enemy's stockades beyond it.

GARRISONS.

BELFAST.
Town Maj. Lieut. Peter Stuart.

DARTMOUTH.
Gov.... Ar. Howe Holdsworth

DUNCANNON FORT.
Fort Maj. Lieut. Thos. Austin

EDINBURGH CASTLE.
Chaplain. Rev. James Millar

GRAVESEND & TILBURY FORT.
Fort Maj. Col. Thos. Kelly, KC.

LONDONDERRY & CULMORE.
Gov. ꝑ ꝕꝕ Field Marshal John Earl of Strafford, GCB. & GCH.

MILFORD HAVEN.
Gov.. Sir John Owen, Bt.

STIRLING CASTLE.
Chaplain.. Rev. Chas. Rogers, LL.D.

TOWER OF LONDON.
Constable.. ꝑ Field Marshal Visct. Combermere, GCB. GCH.

Lieut... ꝑ ꝕꝕ Lieut.Gen. Sir George Bowles, KCB.

Dep. Lieut. ..M.Gen. Lord De Ros
Major..Lt.Col.F.A.Whimper,Unatt.
Chaplain..Rev. Henry Melvill, BD.

MILITARY ESTABLISHMENTS.

ROYAL HOSPITAL, CHELSEA.
Governor, ꝑ Gen. Right. Hon. Sir Edw. Blakeney, GCB. GCH.
Lt.Governor, ꝑ ꝕꝕ Gen. Sir Alex. Woodford, GCB., GCMG.
Major.—ꝑ Colonel Sir John Morillyon Wilson, CB. KH.
Adjutant.—John James Charles Irby,[1] Ens. r 17 Jan. 51; Lt. 8 Oct. 54; Hon. Capt. 1 May 58.
Secretary, Alexander James Moorhead, Esq.
Chaplain, Rev. George Mathias, M.A.
Physician & Surgeon, Local Deputy Inspector General Daniel Maclachlan, M.D.
Deputy Surgeon, Thos. Coke Gaulter, M.D., Surg. Major.
Assistant-Surgeon.—
Quartermaster, James Farrier.
Chief Clerk, F. H. Talman, Esq.

Captains of Invalids.
ꝑ John Davern, h. p. 27 F.
ꝑ Charles Edwards, h. p. 71 F.
ꝑ John Ford, h. p. 3 W. I. Regt.
W. Chadwick, of late 5 R. Veteran Batt.
John Harrison, Unatt.
John Dowman, Unatt.

COMMISSIONERS ROYAL MILITARY ASYLUM.
Ex Officio.
H. R. H. The General Commanding in Chief President.
The Secretary of State for War .... Vice President.
The Bishop of London.
The Bishop of Winchester.
The Paymaster General.
The Adjutant General.
The Quarter Master General.
The Governor of Chelsea Hospital.
The Lieut.Governor of Chelsea Hospital.
The Governor of the Royal Military College.
The Colonel of the 1st Life Guards.
The Colonel of the 2nd Life Guards.
The Judge Advocate General.
The Under Secretary for War.

Specially appointed.
General Sir Howard Douglas, Bt. GCB. GCMG.
——— Sir Hew D. Ross, GCB. R. Art.
Rt. Hon. Sidney Herbert.
Rt. Hon. Laurence Sullivan.
General Hon. Henry Murray, CB.
——— Sir James Simpson, GCB.
——— Sir George Scovell, KCB.
Lieut.General James Freeth, KH.
Major General W. F. Forster, KH. Dep. Adj.Gen.

Commandant.—Colonel Charles Crutchley.
Secretary & Adjutant, Lt.Col. Edw. Adams, Unatt.
Quarter Master, William Cousins.
Surgeon.—
Chaplain.—Rev. W. S. O. Dusautoy.

ROYAL HOSPITAL, KILMAINHAM.
Master.—The Commander of the Forces in Ireland.
Joint Dep. Masters.—The Deputy Adjutant General in Ireland,
The Deputy Quarter Master General, do.

Captains on the Establishment.
ꝑ Thomas Gibbons, h. p. Unatt.

Adjutant.—Capt. John Chadwick, h. p. 15 Drs.
Physician and Surgeon.—William Carte,[2] 13 Aug. 58; Assist.Surg. 23 June 54.
Chaplain.—Rev. George Hare.
Secretary, Registrar and Treasurer.—Geo. F. Dunn.
Solicitor.—Robert Disney, Esq.

ROYAL HIBERNIAN MILITARY SCHOOL, DUBLIN.
Commandant.—Colonel Geo. F. Mylius, Unatt.
Secretary & Adjutant.—Major T. B. Speedy, Unatt.
Surgeon, Francis Bowen, M.D. 31 May 59; A.S.22 Dec. 54.
Chaplain.—Rev. W. A. Neville.

MILITARY PRISONS.
Inspector General.—Colonel Sir Joshua Jebb, KCB. ret. full pay, R. Engineers, Home Office.
Aldershot.—Gov. Capt. A. P. Miller, late of 29 F.
Med. Off., Dep. Insp. Gen. Tho. Fox, M.D. h. p.
Fort Clarence.—Gov., Capt. R. Manners, late of 79 F.
Med. Off., J. Connoll, h. p. Dep. Insp. Gen.
Gosport.—Gov., Capt. J. Curtin, late of 93 F.
Med. Off., Staff Surg. W. Poulton.
Weedon.—Gov., Capt. C. S. Boyle, late of 72 F.
Med. Off., Assist.Surg. H. Fraser, h. p. 66 F.
Devonport.—Med. Off., R. W. Woollcombe, h. p.
Greenlaw, near Pennycuick.—Gov., Major John C. Campbell, late of 9 Drs.
Med. Off., Dr. Campbell, h. p. 93 F.
Dublin.—Gov., Major J. H. Rutherford, ret. f. p. R. Eng
Med. Off., Staff Assist. Surg. T. J. Tuffnell.
Cork.—Gov., Capt. Barnham, late of 15 F.
Med. Off., Dr. Bain, h. p. 34 F.
Limerick.—Gov.,
Gibraltar.—Gov. Fred. Brome, late of 46 F.
Montreal.—Gov Major H. W. Campbell, late of 79 F.
Blue—Facings Red.——Agent, Sir John Kirkland

EAST INDIA DEPOT, RECRUITING OFFICERS, AND MILITARY SEMINARY.

DEPOT AT WARLEY, IN ESSEX.
Commandant .... Col. John Thomas Leslie, CB.
2nd in Command........ Lieut.Col. W. Falconer Hay,
Paymaster .... Lt.Col. S. J. Stevens, CB,
Adjutant & Qr.-Master... Capt. Francis Tower.
Lieutenants............... { Lt. H. Price, B. Inf.
                           { Lt. C. J. Nicholson, do.
Surgeon .... Duncan Stewart, M.D.
Assist.Surgeon .... A. T. J. Cooke.

RECRUITING OFFICERS.
Lt.Col. Henry Brown Smith.. Bristol.
Lt.Col. George Thomson, CB. Cork.
Colonel Henry Brown ......London,28, Soho Square.
Lt.Col. James Roxburgh...... Belfast.
Captain Daniel Bayley........ Dublin.
Captain Henry Vibart Glogg .. Edinburgh.
Lieut.Col. Wm. Turner ...... Liverpool.

---

1 Captain Irby served the Eastern campaign of 1854-55, including the battles of Alma and Inkerman, capture of Balaklava, siege of Sebastopol, repulse of sortie on 26th Oct. 1855, and storming the Quarries on 7th June 1855—severely wounded, left leg amputated (Medal and three Clasps).
2 Mr. Carte served in the Eastern campaign of 1854-55, including the battles of Balaklava and Inkerman, siege of Sebastopol, and Sortie of 26th Oct. (Medal and Clasps).

ROYAL INDIAN MILITARY COLLEGE AT ADDISCOMBE.

Public Examiner and Inspector	Lieut.Gen. Sir J. M. Frederick Smith, KH. R. Eng.	Surgeon	Edward Westall.
Lieut.Governor	Maj.Gen. Sir Fred. Abbott, CB. late of Bengal Engineers.	Orderly Officers	Lt. G. C. H. Armstrong, Bengal Inf. Lt. A. D. Toogood, do.
Staff Officer	Lt.Col. Thomas Donnolly, late of Bombay Infantry.	Public Examiner in the Oriental Department	Horace H. Wilson, MA.

Professors and Masters.

Mathematics and Classics	Rev. Jonathan Cape, AM. Rev. Alfred Wrigley, MA. Rev. W. H. Johnstone, MA. (Chaplain) Rev. R. Inchbald, MA. Rev. Geo. R. Roberts, MA.	Landscape Drawing	A. Penley. John Callow.
		Hindustani	Lt.Col. M. J. Rowlandson, late Madras Inf. Cotton Mather.
Fortifications and Artillery	John T. Hyde, MA. Major F. Ditmas, late Madras Engineers.	French	Leon Contanseau.
		Geology and Mineralogy	D. T. Ansted, AM.
		Chemistry	Edward Frankland.
		Sword Exercise	Joseph Stephenson.
Military Surveying & Drawing	Captain J. Ouchterlony, Madras Engineers. Captain P. Francis, do.	Clerk for passing Cadets and Assist.Surgeon	John Hollyer, Military Depart. India House.

MILITARY STORE DEPARTMENT.

PRINCIPAL MILITARY STOREKEEPERS
(With relative Military rank of Lieut.-Colonel).

Alexander Stewart .... PORTSMOUTH
Capt.HenryWm.Gordon,[1] CB. WOOLWICH
Jeremy Jones .... TOWER

MILITARY STOREKEEPERS
(With relative Military rank of Lieut.-Colonel).

Joseph Pellatt .... DEVONPORT
H. Tatum .... MALTA
T. C. Martelli .... GIBRALTAR
J. C. Saunder[2] .... DUBLIN
C. S. Elliott .... LONDON
W. Morris .... CHATHAM

DEPUTY MILITARY STOREKEEPERS
(With relative Military rank of Major).

E. C. King .... TOWER
F. M. Cromartie .... BARBADOES
Joseph Leacock .... JAMAICA
T. Pearce .... TOWER
J. Baker .... TOWER
R. Macfarlane .... MAURITIUS
George Pett .... CAPE TOWN
G. Wyatt .... CORFU
W. L. Penno .... BERMUDA
W. H. G. Johnstone .... COLOMBO
*J. C. Rowland .... HONG KONG
*E. Pongelley .... CORK HARBOUR
R. R. Pringle .... HALIFAX, N. S.
A. Gun .... MONTREAL
R. Douglas .... HOBART TOWN
*John Gange .... DOVER
Thomas Gibbs .... EDINBURGH
S. G. Bake .... GRAHAM'S TOWN
W. H. Parkyn .... WOOLWICH
*John Drew .... SIERRA LEONE
*James St. George .... HYDE PARK
C. K. Cleeve .... TOWER

ASSISTANT MILITARY STOREKEEPERS
(With relative Military rank of Captain).

*John Greensill .... STIRLING
B. Wright .... DUBLIN
James Windsor .... ATHLONE
R. A. T. Walker .... FORT GEORGE
*P. Drouet .... BAHAMAS

*W. A. Holwell .... DOVER
Augustus Wright .... PRIDDY'S HARD
G. Stokes .... GIBRALTAR
*T. A. G. Satchwell .... PURFLEET
F. A. Galletley .... CHESTER
*John B. Cole .... TOWER
W. C. Moore .... TOWER
S. B. Maclean .... KINGSTON, C. W.
W. O'Neill .... TOWER
W. M. King .... MALTA
*B Major T. R. Agnew .... TIPNER
*P. Wilkinson .... SYDNEY
*J. T. Knight .... TILBURY
*Henry Topping .... ST. HELENA
H. De R. Maxwell .... PEMBROKE DOCK
*John Tunbridge .... NEWFOUNDLAND
*William S. Forster .... TRINIDAD
*Richard Rogers .... HONDURAS
E. M. Moore .... PORTSMOUTH
D. J. Fretz .... POINT DE GALLE
*C. H. Cooper .... WEEDON
*W. H. Tapp .... QUEBEC
*G. W. Barry .... ST. LUCIA
*Wm. H. Horatio Scott[3] .... GRAHAM'S TOWN
F. H. Glinn .... TRINCOMALEE
G. G. Munro .... WOOLWICH
John Isaac Lilley[4] .... PIMLICO
W. Green .... PIMLICO
John Shepherd .... UPNOR
*Joseph Pearson .... SYMON'S TOWN
*Corn. Sharpe .... HARWICH
*George F. C. Peter .... CAPE TOWN
*Goodman Sandes .... ALDERNEY
*Henry W. Piers .... KING WILLIAM'S TOWN
*W. B. Stapley .... BULL POINT
*R. M. Ozanne .... GUERNSEY
*T. S. Ford .... ZANTE
J. O. Hamley .... AUCKLAND, N. Z.
*James Duncan .... MARCHWOOD
G. Kane .... TOWER
*George C. Holden .... PORT NATAL
G. Bayly .... JERSEY
John Durnford .... TOWER
S. Wright .... DEVONPORT
*William Foster .... SHEERNESS
T. Thomson .... ZANTE.
J. R. Dombrain .... DUBLIN
J. R. Hamilton .... GAMBIA
W. E. Webster .... HYDE PARK
A. H. Young .... WOOLWICH

The * denotes those acting as Barrackmasters.
Uniform Blue, Facings Red.

1 Captain Gordon joined the army in the Crimea in March 1855, having, when a captain on half-pay, been appointed by the Secretary of State for War to superintend the collection of surplus clothing and stores. In Aug. 1855 he was appointed Ordnance Storekeeper, and in that capacity, on peace being proclaimed, was ordered to superintend the embarkation of the material and stores of the several departments of the army, with the exception of that of the Commissariat, but including those of the Medical, Land Transport, and Army Works Corps, as well as the Railway,' so that every article with the army might be accounted for by him to the War Department.
2 Mr. Saunder has received the Medal for the Kaffir wars.
3 Mr. Scott has received the Medal for the Kaffir wars.
4 Mr. Lilley served in the Field Train of the Royal Artillery the Eastern campaign of 1854-55, and was present with the 1st Division in the affair of McKenzie's Farm, battles of Alma, Balaklava, and Inkerman, throughout the siege and at the fall of Sebastopol and capture of Kadikoi (Medal with four Clasps, Knight of the Legion of Honor, and Turkish Medal). In Dec. 1855 was appointed Deputy Storekeeper in the War Department, and assisted Captain Gordon in carrying out the duties until the evacuation of the Crimea.

BARRACK-MASTERS.

*** BARRACK-MASTERS of 1st Class Stations have the relative rank of MAJOR;—2nd Class, of CAPTAIN.

GREAT BRITAIN.

ABERDEEN—*Captain* J. Forbes
ALDERSHOT—၃ ၏ Thomas Smith [1]
1st Assist. Barrack-Master D.T.Grant, late Lt.44 F.
2nd Do.   Do.   ..Capt. W. Peel, late 1 Drs.
BIRMINGHAM, Coventry, and Nottingham—Lt.Col. J. R. Heyland
BRIGHTON—J. B. Hawkes,[2] late Capt. 3 Drs.
BRISTOL—C. Marr, late Capt. 12 Drs.
CANTERBURY—P. A. Barnard
CHATHAM, &c.—Capt. J. Buckley
COLCHESTER—Capt. Sir Wm. O'Malley
DEVONPORT—Captain J. Stawell
DOVER—Capt. R. D. Macdonald, late 42 F.
DUNDEE and Perth—၃ Major D. J. MacQueen, KH.
EDINBURGH, &c.—Capt. R. S. Wickham
EXETER ၃ Maj. G. W. DeRenzy[14]
GLASGOW, Hamilton, &c.—Major Rt. Douglas Barbor
GOSPORT—Captain F. P. Laye
HOUNSLOW & Hampton Ct.—၃ Lt.Col. H. Edmonds[10]
HYTHE, &c.—R. S. Kelly
JERSEY—Captain J. E. Acklom

LEEDS, &c.—Captain Brickenden
MAIDSTONE—Major H. W. Dennie,[16] r. f. p 28 F.
MANCHESTER—၃၏ Capt. G. Drummond[5]
NEWCASTLE—L. R. Shawe
NEWPORT, Cardiff, &c.—Lt.Col. Wm. Bell
NORWICH—J. T. Downman
PARKHURST—Lieut.G. H.Sanders,[9] h.p. 30 F.
PLYMOUTH—J. R. Nason
PORTSMOUTH—S. W. Hall [17]
PRESTON—Capt. G. H. Wilkins
REGENT'S PARK, &c.—၃၏ Col. F. Browne, CB.
ST. JAMES'S PARK, &c.—၃၏ Captain L. White [15]
SHEFFIELD—၃၏ Capt. P. Minchin [11]
SHORNCLIFFE—J. G. Wright
TOWER & CROYDON—Captain W. Fuller
WALMER—၏ T. Stephens, late 1 F.
WEYMOUTH, &c.—Captain E. J. Otway
WINCHESTER—Maj.Gen. R. F. Romer
WINDSOR—E. Harrison
WOOLWICH—Major E. Sutherland
  Assistant—J. Sanderson

IRELAND.

BELFAST, Carrickfergus &
  Downpatrick .... Wm. Biston Frizell
BIRR, Banagher, Shannon
  Bridge, and Portumna Captain J. Campbell
BUTTEVANT, Mallow, and
  Mill-street .... ၃ Captain B. Gaynor [6]
CAHIR, Clogheen, & New
  Inn........................Lieut. A. T. Munro
CASTLEBAR, Foxford, Bal-
  linrobe, and Westport..Lieut. J. Nagel [12]
CLONMEL, Ballinamult, &
  Carrick-on-Suir........Capt. W. A. Stewart
CORK and Ballincollig....၃ Major J. N. Gossett [7]
CURRAGH ....Capt. E. C. Munns
DERRY, Lifford, & Omagh Lieut. W. Barton, late of 76 F.
DUBLIN:—
PORTOBELLO, Beggar's Bush
  and Pigeon House Fort ..၃ Capt. R. Jeffreys [10]
RICHMOND, Island Bridge,
  and Magazine Fort ......၃ Capt. J. Kirkman [4]

ROYAL BARRACKS, Mount-
  joy, R. Infirmary, & Ship
  Street.................Lieut. John Orr
DUNDALK ....J. Shrapnel
FERMOY and MitchelstownR. A. Daniell
GALWAY, Dunmore, Lough-
  rea, and Oughterarde ..၃ Lieut. J. Hughes[8]
KILKENNY & Castlecomer. Lieut. J. S. N. Green
KINSALE—G. A. F. Cary, late Capt. 31 F.
LIMERICK ....၃ Capt. Robt. Mackintosh[3]
LONGFORD, Granard, Ros-
  common, &c ....Captain W. Adam
MULLINGAR ....Major H.W.B.Warburton
NEWBRIDGE, Naas, and
  Maryborough ....Captain R. Vivian
SLIGO, Ballyshannon, and Belleek..W. Potterfield
TEMPLEMORE and Thurles Lieut. Graves Ackland
TRALEE and Newcastle—Sir R. Colleton, Bt. late of 45 F.
WATERFORD and New Ross—H. Jephson, late Lt. 87 F.

FOREIGN STATIONS.

BARBADOES—Maj. F. Percy Lea, Unatt.
BERMUDA—Capt. P. P. Trotman
CAPE OF GOOD HOPE:—
KING WILLIAM'S TOWN—Capt. Geo. Allen
FORT BEAUFORT—Captain C. M. Creagh
KEISKAMMA—W. Knight
GIBRALTAR—Capt. T. Townsend, late of 60 Foot
CORFU—၏ Major J. Daniell
JAMAICA:—
NEWCASTLE, &c.—Capt. B. C. Boothby, h.p. 95 F.

SPANISH TOWN, &c. ......
MAURITIUS—၏ Lieut. J. S. Sedley
MALTA—Capt. W. Fisher
       M. G. L. Meason, late Capt. 8 Drs.
NOVA SCOTIA AND NEW
  BRUNSWICK:—
FREDERICTON............George Priestley
HALIFAX ....Capt. Fred. Wm. Smith
TASMANIA:—
Hobart Town ....J. D. Mackay

War Services of the Barrack-Masters.

1 Major Smith served with the Rifle Brigade during the Peninsular war from 1808 to its termination in 1814, and was present at the actions of Calcavellas, Royales, Constantino, Betanzos, El Burgo, Corunna, Gallegos, Barquillo, and the Coa—dangerously wounded ; siege and storm of Ciudad Rodrigo, siege and storm of Badajoz, battle of Salamanca, advance to and capture of Madrid, action of San Milan, battle of Vittoria, action at Echalar, both attacks of Vera, battle of the Nivelle, action of Arcangues, battle of Orthes, action of Tarbes, and battle of Toulouse. Served also the campaign of 1815, including the battle of Waterloo. He has the War Medal with ten Clasps.

2 Captain Hawkes served the Sutlej campaign of 1845-6, including the battles of Moodkee, Ferozeshah (horse shot), and Sobraon (wounded): Medal and two Clasps.

3 Captain Mackintosh has received the War Medal with six Clasps for Fuentes d'Onor, Badajoz, Salamanca, Vittoria, St. Sebastian, and Nive.

4 Capt. Kirkman served with the Rifle Brigade during the campaigns of 1810, 11, 12, 13, and 14, in the Peninsula, including the actions and defence of Cadiz, siege of Tarragona, battle of Barrosa, actions near Fuente Guinaldo and Aldea de Ponte, siege and capture of Ciudad Rodrigo (volunteered the storming party), siege and capture of Badajoz (volunteered, and accompanied the forlorn hope, and was wounded in the head), battle of Salamanca, advance to and capture of Madrid, subsequent retreat through Spain, affairs of San Munoz and San Milan, battle of Vittoria, and three days' severe skirmishing in following the enemy to Pampeluna, which ended in the capture of their last gun ; action at Echalar, passage of the Bidassoa, various actions in the Pyrenees, battle of Nivelle (gun-shot wound in the right arm), action of Arcangues, and passage of the Nive. Served also the campaign of 1815 in Belgium. He has received the War Medal with eight Clasps.

5 Captain Drummond served with the Rifle Brigade in the Peninsula, and was present at Ciudad Rodrigo, Badajoz, Castrijon, Salamanca, Alba de Tormes, Madrid, San Munos, Castalla, San Milan, Vittoria, Pyrenees, Bridge of Zansi, Port d'Achard, Bridge of Vera, Bidassoa, Nivelle, Arcangues, Nive, Orthes, St. Germain, Tarbes, St. Simon, and Toulouse (Medal and eight Clasps). Also the campaign of 1815, including Quatre Bras, Genappe, and Waterloo.

6 Captain Gaynor served in the Peninsula with the Portuguese army during 1808, 9, and 10, when he was wounded and taken prisoner at Arroyo del Puerco, when employed on the reconnoitring service.

7 Major Gossett served with the Rifle Brigade in the Peninsula from Oct. 1813 to July 1814, including the battle of the Nive on the 9th, 10th, 11th, 12th and 13th Dec., passage of the Gave d'Oleron, battle of Orthes, actions at Tarbes and Tournefeuille, and battle of Toulouse. Served afterwards in the American war, and was constantly engaged near New Orleans from 23rd Dec. 1814, to the 7th Jan. 1815, and was also present at the attack on New Orleans on the 8th Jan.—wounded in the head. He has the War Medal with three Clasps.

8 Lieut. Hughes served in the Peninsula with the 57th Regt. from 1810 to the end of that war in 1814, and was present at the Battle of Busaco, first siege of Badajoz, battle of Albuhera,—severely wounded through the left thigh; retreat from Madrid, battles of Vittoria, the Pyrenees on the 28th and 30th July, and the Nivelle,—severely wounded in the right thigh, where the ball remained for nine years. He has the War Medal with five Clasps.

9 Lieut. Sanders served in the Austrian army in 1849-51; was present at the battle of Novara, and served the campaign against Garibaldi in the Roman States, for which he has a Medal. Served as Adjutant of the 30th Regt. at the siege of Sebastopol in 1855; was in the trenches at the attacks of the 8th and 18th of June, and was twice severely and once slightly wounded at the assault of the Redan on the 8th Sept.—left leg amputated—mentioned in despatches (Medal and Clasp, and Sardinian Medal).

10 Lt. Colonel Edmonds served in the Peninsula with the 66th Regt. from March 1809 to the end of that war in 1814, and was slightly wounded at the battle of Talavera.

11 Captain Minchin served in the 51st Regt. the campaign and battle of Corunna. On the expedition to Walcheren, and at the siege of Flushing. Embarked with the Regt. for Lisbon in Jan. 1811, and was present at the battle of Fuentes d'Onor, covering the siege of Ciudad Rodrigo, two sieges of San Christoval, covering the second siege of Badajoz, affair near Val Moresco, battle of Salamanca, capture of Madrid and the Retiro, covering the siege of Burgos, actions of Monasterio and Quintana Pulla, and retreat into Portugal; battles of Vittoria and the Pyrenees, covering the siege of San Sebastian, action of Lesaca (severely wounded), and occupation of Bordeaux. Served also in the campaign of 1815, including the battle of Waterloo, capture of Cambray, and capitulation of Paris. He has received the War Medal with four Clasps.

12 Lieut. Nagel served the Punjaub campaign of 1848-49 with the 61st Regt., and was present at the affair of Ramnuggur, and battles of Sadoolapore and Chillianwallah, at which last he lost a leg (Medal and Clasp).

13 Lt. Colonel Heyland served with the 7th Fusiliers at the siege of Sebastopol from 7th July 1855, and was severely wounded in command of the Regiment at the assault of the Redan on the 8th Sept. (Medal and Clasp, Sardinian and Turkish Medals, and 5th Class of the Medjidie).

14 Major De Renzy served at Walcheren in 1809, and was present at the siege and capture of Flushing. Served afterwards in the Peninsula in the 82nd Regt., and at the battle of Vittoria he was most severely wounded by a cannon-shot,—right arm amputated. He has received the War Medal with one Clasp.

15 Captain White served on the expedition to the Elbe and Weser under Lord Cathcart; the principal campaigns in the Peninsula under the Duke of Wellington, including the operations on the Coa during the siege and battle of Almeida, the siege of Ciudad Rodrigo, the siege and storming of Badajoz, the battle of Salamanca, capture of Madrid and the Retiro, the siege of Burgos and affair on retreat at Muriel. The campaigns in Flanders and France under Lord Lynedoch and the Duke of Wellington, including the attack on Merxem, bombardment of Antwerp, the affair of Fort Frederick, Hendrick, and siege of Bergen-op-Zoom, the battle of Waterloo, storming of Cambray, and capitulation of Paris. He has received the War Medal with three Clasps.

16 Captain Jeffreys entered the corps of Royal Marines as 2nd Lieut. in 1803, and was appointed to the Marine Artillery in the following year. He served off Boulogne, and also in the action under Lord Cochrane at Basque Roads, as senior officer of Marine Artillery, on board the *Etna* bomb vessel. In 1811 he proceeded with the marine Battalion, commanded by the late Sir Richard Williams, to Portugal, and returned to England in 1812. In 1813 he obtained a company in the Glamorgan Militia, and having volunteered the same year into the 53rd Regt., he landed in Spain, and proceeded to join the army at Toulouse. He has received the Naval War Medal with one Clasp for Basque Roads.

17 Mr. Hall served with the 73rd Regt. during a portion of the Kaffir war of 1847, and was Barrack Master of British Kaffraria during the war of 1852-53.

18 Major Dennie served with the 28th Regt. in the Crimea in 1855, and was present at the siege of Sebastopol (Medal and Clasp); had half the right foot and a greater part of the left amputated, owing to frost bite, in consequence of which he was placed on the retired list (Pension).

REGIMENTAL PAY, &c.

ANNUAL PAY OF COLONELS.

CORPS.		If appointed on or before the 31st March, 1834.	If appointed after the 31st March, 1834.
Life Guards and Horse Guards, *without other emolument*......		1,800*l*.	1,800*l*.
1st Dragoon Guards (*in lieu of emoluments from Clothing* 800*l*.)		1,100	1,000
Other Regiments of Cavalry (do. do. 450*l*.)		1,000	900
Grenadier Guards (do. do. 1,000*l*.)		1,200	1,200
Coldstream and Scots Fusilier Gds. (do. do. 1,000*l*.)		1,000	1,000
Regular Infantry (do. do. 600*l*.)		600	500
West India Regiments (do. do. 600*l*.)		—	500

DAILY PAY OF OFFICERS.

RANKS.	Life Guards & Horse Guards.	Foot Guards.	Drg.Gds. and Dragns.	Foot.	Royal Artillery.		Royal Enginrs.	Royal Marines
					Horse Brigade.	Foot.		
	l. s. d.	*l. s. d.*	*l. s. d.*	*l. s. d.*	*l. s. d.*	*l. s. d.*	*l. s. d.*	*l. s. d.*
Colonel Commandant	—	—	—	—	3 0 0	2 14 9½	2 14 9½	1 18 6
Colonel 2nd Commandant	—	—	—	—	—	—	—	1 0 0
Colonel	—	—	—	—	1 12 4	1 6 3	1 6 3	—
Lieut.Colonel	1 9 2	1 6 9	1 3 0	0 17 0	1 7 1	0 18 1	{18 1 / 16 1}	}17 0
Major	1 4 5	1 3 0	0 19 3	0 16 0	—	—	—	0 16 0
Captain	0 15 1	0 15 6	0 14 7	0 11 7	0 16 1	0 11 1	0 11 1	0 11 7
Do. having higher Rank by Brevet	—	—	—	0 13 7	0 18 1	0 13 1	0 13 1	0 13 7
Lieutenant	0 10 4	0 7 4	0 9 0	0 6 6	0 9 10	0 6 10	0 6 10	0 6 6
Do. after 7 years' service	—	—	—	0 7 6	0 10 10	0 7 10	0 7 10	0 7 6
Cornet and Ensign	0 8 0	0 5 6	0 8 0	0 5 3	—	0 5 7	0 5 7	0 5 3
Paymast. { On Appointment	—	—	0 12 6	0 12 6	—	—	—	
After 5 years' service	—	—	0 15 0	0 15 0	—	—	—	
15 do.	—	—	0 17 6	0 17 6	—	—	—	}16 6
20 do.	—	—	1 0 0	1 0 0	—	—	—	
25 do.	—	—	1 2 6	1 2 6	—	—	—	
Adjutant	0 13 0	0 10 0	0 10 0	§0 3 6	†0 10 8	0 18 6	0 10 0	0 6 6
Quar. { On Appointment	0 0 6	0 6 0	0 8 0	0 6 6	—	—	—	—
Mast. { After 10 years' service ...	—	0 8 6	0 10 6	0 8 6	10 10 0	0 7 10	0 8 0	0 4 8
15 do.	—	0 10 0	0 12 0	0 10 0				

† If 2d Capt. 17s. 9d.   ‡ If 2d Capt. 12s. 9d.   § In addition to the pay as a Subaltern.

COMMISSARIAT DEPARTMENT.

	Full Pay.		Charge Pay.	Half Pay.	Retired Pay.	Length of Full Pay Service to give a claim to Retirement.	Age at which, in the absence of exceptional circumstances, Retirement shall be compulsory.
	On attaining the Rank.	After five years' service in last Rank.					
	£ s. d.	£ s. d.	£ s. d.	£ s. d.	£ s. d.		
Commissary General	3 0 0	3 0 0	..	1 10 0	2 0 0	30 years.	65 years.
Deputy Commissary General	1 10 0	1 10 0	0 10 0	0 15 0	1 5 0	do	60 years.
Assistant Commissary General	0 15 0	1 0 0	0 5 0	0 10 0	0 15 0	do	55 years.
Deputy Assistant Comm. General ..	0 10 0	0 12 6	0 2 6	0 6 3	0 9 4	do	55 years.

MEDICAL DEPARTMENT.

RANKS.	After 30 Years' Service on full pay.	After 25 Years' Service on full pay.	After 20 Years' Service on full pay.	After 15 Years' Service on full pay.	After 10 Years' Service on full pay.	After 5 Years' Service on full pay.	Under 5 Years' Service on full pay.
	£ s. d.	£ s. d.	£ s. d.	£ s. d.	£ s. d.	£ s. d.	£ s. d.
Inspector General	2 5 0	2 5 0	2 0 0*	..	..	..	0 12 6
Deputy Inspector General	1 14 0	1 10 0	1 8 0*	..	..	..	..
Surgeon Major	..	1 5 0	1 2 0	..	..	..	..
Surgeon	..	..	..	0 18 0	0 15 0*	..	..
Assistant Surgeon	..	..	..	..	0 13 0	0 11 6	0 10 0

* Or on promotion, should these periods of service not be already completed.

MEDICAL DEPARTMENT ON HALF PAY.

	Rates of Half Pay after a Service on Full Pay of						
	30 Years.	25 Years.	20 Years.	15 Years.	10 Years.	5 years.	Under 5 yrs.
	£ s. d.	£ s. d.	£ s. d.	£ s. d.	£ s. d.	£ s. d.	£ s. d.
Inspector General	1 17 0	1 13 6	1 10 0	..	..	..	..
Deputy Inspector General.........	1 5 6	1 2 6	1 1 0	..	..	..	..
Surgeon Major.......................	0 18 6	0 16 6	..	..	..	..	..
Surgeon................................	..	..	..	0 13 6	0 11 0	..	..
Assistant Surgeon ..	..	..	..	..	0 10 0	0 8 0	0 5 0

VETERINARY MEDICAL DEPARTMENT.

	Service on Full Pay.					
	After 25 Years.	After 20 Years.	After 15 Years.	After 10 Years.	After 5 Years.	On appointmt
	£ s. d.	£ s. d.	£ s. d.	£ s. d.	£ s. d.	£ s. d.
Staff Veterinary Surgeons......	1 3 0	1 2 0	1 1 0	..	..	..
Veterinary Surgeons, 1st Class	1 0 0	0 17 0	0 15 6	0 14 6	*0 12 6	..
Veterinary Surgeons	0 14 0	0 14 0	0 14 0	0 13 0	0 11 6	0 10 0
Veterinary Surgeons who entered the Service prior to the date of this Warrant..	0 17 6	0 15 0	0 14 0	0 13 0	0 11 6	0 10 0

HALF PAY.—(Not Brevet.)

VETERINARY MEDICAL DEPARTMENT ON HALF PAY.

	After 25 Yrs.	After 20 Yrs.	After 15 Yrs.	After 10 Yrs.	After 5 Yrs.	After 3 Yrs.	Under 3 Years.
	£ s. d.	£ s. d.	£ s. d.	£ s. d.	£ s. d.	£ s. d.	
Staff Veterinary Surgeon	0 15 0	0 14 0	The half pay of his former rank.				
Veterinary Surgeon, 1st Class	0 13 0	0 11 0	0 10 0	0 9 0	The half pay of his former rank.		
Veterinary Surgeon, Do.			0 9 0	0 8 0	0 7 0	0 4 0	Temporary half pay at 4s. a day for a period equal to that for which the Officer has served on full pay.
Veterinary Surgeons who entered the Service prior to the date of this Warrant	0 10 0	0 9 0	0 9 0	0 8 0	0 7 0	0 4 0	

REGIMENTAL RANK.	OLD RATE.		NEW RATE.	
	Cavalry	Infant.	Cavalry	Infant.
	£ s. d.	£ s. d.	£ s. d.	£ s. d.
Colonel	0 13 0	0 12 0	0 15 0	0 14 6
Lieutenant-Colonel	0 10 0	0 8 6	0 12 0	0 11 0
Major	0 8 0	0 7 6	0 10 0	0 9 6
Captain	0 5 6	0 5 0	0 7 6	0 7 0
Lieutenant	0 3 0	0 2 4	0 4 8	0 4 0
Do. above Seven Years standing	—	—	—	0 4 6
Do. of Five Years standing, and if at the Battle of Waterloo	—	—	0 5 2	—
Cornet, 2d Lieutenant, or Ensign	0 2 6	0 1 10	0 3 6	0 3 0
Paymaster* above 5 and under 10 years actual service as Paymaster	—	—	0 6 0	0 6 0
————10————15	—	—	0 8 0	0 8 0
————15————20	—	—	0 10 0	0 10 0
————20 years actual service as Paymaster	—	—	0 13 0	0 13 0
————30 Years do. do.	—	—	0 15 0	0 15 0
Adjutant, if not commissioned as Lieutenant	—	—	0 4 0	0 4 0
Quarter-Master† under 5 Years Service§	—	—	0 3 0	0 3 0
Above 5 and under 10	—	—	0 4 0	0 4 0
————10———15	—	—	0 5 0	0 5 0
————15 Years total Service, of which 10 as Quarter-Master	—	—	0 5 6	0 5 6
————20 Years, of which 10 as Quarter-Master	—	—	0 6 0	0 6 0
————25 do. of which 10 do.	—	—	0 7 0	0 7 0
————30 do. of which 10 do.	—	—	0 8 0	0 8 0

* If of less than 5 Years' actual service as Paymaster, the Half Pay of his former Commission.
† Or the Half Pay of his former Commission.
N.B.—Previous Service of 10 Years' duration or upwards, on Full Pay in other Ranks as a Commissioned Officer, after the Paymaster shall have completed 15 Years' actual Service as such, to reckon as equivalent to 5 Years' Service as Paymaster.
‡ If appointed from any other Commission in the Army, and retiring before having completed 7 Years' Service as Quarter-Master, the Half Pay of his former Commission. § If he shall have previously served 3 Years as a Non-commissioned Officer.

RATES OF HALF-PAY FOR THE ROYAL ARTILLERY AND ROYAL ENGINEERS.

	s. d.		s. d.		s. d.
Lieutenant-Colonel	11 8	First Lieut. above seven years	4 8	Resident Surgeon	10 0
Major	10 1	Second Lieut.	3 2¼	Surgeon	7 0
Captain	7 4	Quarter-Master	4 8	First Assistant Surgeon	4 0
First Lieutenant	4 2	Surgeon-General	20 0	Second do.	2 0

Prices of Commissions.

RANK.	Full Price of Commissions.	Difference in value between the several Commissions in succession.	Difference in value between Full and Half-pay.
	l. s.	l. s.	l. s. d.
Life Guards.			
Lieutenant-Colonel	7250 0	1000 0	
Major	5350 0	1850 0	
Captain	3500 0	1715 0	
Lieutenant	1785 0	525 0	
Cornet	1200 0		
Royal Regiment of Horse Guards.			
Lieutenant-Colonel	7250 0	1000 0	
Major	5350 0	1850 0	
Captain	3500 0	1900 0	
Lieutenant	1600 0	400 0	
Cornet	1200 0		
Dragoon Guards and Dragoons.			
Lieutenant-Colonel	6175 0	1600 0	1533 0 0
Major	4575 0	1350 0	1352 0 0
Captain	3225 0	2035 0	1034 3 4
Lieutenant	1190 0	350 0	692 13 4
Cornet	840 0		300 0 0
Foot Guards.			
Lieutenant-Colonel	9000 0	700 0	
Major, with rank of Colonel	8300 0	3500 0	
Captain, with rank of Lieut.-Colonel	4800 0	2750 0	
Lieutenant, with rank of Captain	2050 0	850 0	
Ensign, with rank of Lieutenant	1200 0		
Regiments of the Line.			
Lieutenant-Colonel	4500 0	1300 0	1314 0 0
Major	3200 0	1400 0	949 0 0
Captain	1800 0	1100 0	511 0 0
Lieutenant	700 0	250 0	365 0 0
Ensign	450 0		150 0 0
Fusilier Regiments and Rifle Corps.			
First Lieutenant	700 0	200 0	365 0 0
Second Lieutenant	500 0		200 0 0

OFFICERS

ON THE
RETIRED FULL PAY, AND HALF PAY,
INCLUDING THE ROYAL REGIMENT OF ARTILLERY, CORPS OF ROYAL ENGINEERS, ROYAL MARINES, STAFF, AND MILITARY DEPARTMENTS.

N.B. *Officers whose names are in Italics are on retired full pay.*

CAPTAINS.

	CORNET, 2d LIEUT., or ENSIGN.	LIEUT.	CAPTAIN.	WHEN PLACED ON HALF PAY.
Acton, Wm. Molesworth Cole,[1] 77 Foot..	17 Sept. 50	2 April 52	29 Dec. 54	5 Oct. 58
Adair, Richard Bratton, Royal Artillery..	16 June 38	12 Aug. 40	7 May 47	20 Dec. 54
Addy, John,[†] Land Transport Corps ..	....	6 Sept. 55	1 Feb. 56	
Allen, Charles Davers, Unattached	17 Sept. 12	20 May 13	2 April 41	27 Dec. 42
𝔓 *Allen, John Penn, 1 Prov. Bn. of Mil.	never	never	25 Dec. 13	1814
Allen, Ralph Shuttleworth, R. Art., *Maj.* R. Cornwall and Devon Miners	18 June 36	1 May 39	4 May 46	11 Aug. 51
*Allen, Robert, 5 Foot	never	never	25 Dec. 13	25 Sept. 14
𝔓 Alpe, Hamond,[2] 18 Dragoons	11 Feb. 08	12 April 09	13 Jan. 20	15 Nov. 21
Anketell, Moutray, Royal Artillery	1 Oct. 47	30 June 48	16 Dec. 54	10 Oct. 57
Anton, Alexander,[3] 8 West India Regt. ..	14 Sept. 04	25 Dec. 04	29 Feb. 16	25 Sept. 17
Arbuthnott, John, *Viscount*, Irish Brigade	27 Mar. 01	21 April 03	28 Aug. 04	8 Sept. 08
Arbuthnott, *Hon.* John, Unattached	23 June 25	8 April 26	25 June 30	25 June 30
Archdall, Audley Mervyn, Royal Artillery	19 Dec. 44	1 April 46	31 Dec. 52	12 Aug. 55
𝔓 Archdall, Henry, 84 Foot	25 Sept. 04	14 Nov. 05	26 Aug. 13	23 April 18
𝔓 Armstrong, John,[4] 88 Foot	7 Aug. 03	26 Sept. 04	5 Jan. 15	25 Mar. 16
Atchison, Henry Alexander, Unattached..	7 April 25	7 Aug. 28	27 Feb. 35	12 July 44
Atchison, Thomas, R. Artillery, *Lt.-Col. Comm. Lancashire Artillery Militia*	9 June 04	5 Dec. 04	17 Feb. 14	
Atkinson, Thomas Geo. B.,[4] Unatt.	6 June 54	9 Feb. 55	1 April 57	
Bailey, Charles, Royal Engineers	25 April 26	21 June 30	23 Nov. 41	15 Nov. 43
Bailie, James, Unattached	28 Nov. 34	31 Dec. 39	3 Oct. 48	22 April 49
Baker, George Granville, Unattached....	1 Aug. 34	23 July 38	18 Aug. 48	18 Aug. 48
Baker, James Swayne, Royal Engineers	19 Mar. 30	23 Feb. 42	6 Aug. 49	27 Jan. 55
Baker, Richard D., Unattached	13 Sept. 11	10 Dec. 30	5 Oct. 41	11 July 51
Baker, Robert,[5] 57 Foot	31 Jan. 07	22 May 06	22 July 10	4 May 20
𝔓 Baker, William, 60 Foot	3 Dec. 02	19 Nov. 03	11 Oct. 10	22 Dec. 55
Balck, George Philip, Unattached	20 Oct. 29	17 April 35	1 June 38	26 June 38
Bamford, Robert Carter,[6] 63 Foot	5 Sept. 34	12 July 39	6 June 54	10 Nov. 56
Barclay, Edward, Unattached	12 July 27	14 Feb. 34	3 Dec. 47	3 Dec. 47
Barnes, Richard Knowles, Royal Marines	6 Mar. 10	4 June 28	26 April 38	13 Nov. 40
𝔓 Barwell, Osborne,[7] Unattached	12 Sept. 11	2 April 12	1 Aug. 26	24 Jan. 28
Basset, Arthur,[8] Unattached	12 Dec. 51	20 April 53	15 Feb. 56	6 June 56
Batchellor, Samuel George, R. Artillery	18 Dec. 47	30 June 48	8 Mar. 55	28 Sept. 55
Bathurst, Benjamin, R. Artillery	14 Dec. 37	11 April 40	9 Nov. 46	16 Feb. 52
𝔓 𝔇𝔞 Baynes, Geo. Macleod,[9] R. Art. ...	4 April 07	1 Feb. 08	1 Aug. 27	25 Sept. 34
Bayntun, Charles, Queen's Rangers ...	Mar. 03	15 Oct. 93	1 Feb. 08	17 Nov. 08
Bell, William,[9] 89 Foot	3 Mar. 08	9 May 11	25 Nov. 24	26 Mar. 41
Bennett, James, Unattached	9 April 09	2 Dec. 13	20 Feb. 23	31 May 27
Bentley, Alex. C. Downing, 7 Foot.....	9 Apr. 25	17 Aug. 32	18 June 41	8 Jan. 47
Beresford, George Robert,[11] 7 Foot ...	17 Oct. 51	18 Aug. 54	21 May 55	17 July 57
Bernard, Peter, Unattached	29 Jan. 24	11 Feb. 26	5 Nov. 29	17 May 31
Bernard, Thomas, Unattached, *Lt.-Col. King's County Militia*	24 Apr. 35	26 Apr. 39	26 Apr. 44	3 Sept. 47
Bernard, William, Unattached........	17 Nov. 25	25 Jan. 26	25 Jan. 41	14 Feb. 45
Berry, James Parsons,[12] York Chasseurs	8 Jan. 07	26 Jan. 08	7 July 43	8 Sept. 46
*Bettesworth, Henry, 4 Foot	never	never	25 Dec. 13	25 Sept. 14
𝔇𝔞 Biddulph, Theophilus, 6 Dragoons ..	22 Dec. 04	22 May 06	14 Sept. 14	25 Mar. 16
𝔓 Birch, James,[13] R. Engineers	12 July 09	1 May 11	20 Dec. 14	24 Sept. 25
𝔓 Bishop, James,[14] 23 Foot	25 May 04	23 Dec. 04	27 June 11	2 May 22
Blackall, John, 98 Foot	6 July 09	8 July 13	14 Nov. 16	25 Nov. 18
Blacker, John Robert,[10] Unattached	22 April 53	20 Jan. 54	30 Mar. 58	6 Aug. 59
Blakely, Alex. Theophilus, R. Artillery ..	19 June 44	1 Apr. 46	1 Apr. 52	18 Aug. 52
Bland, James, Unattached, *Paymaster, Aberdeen Militia*	4 Sept. 04	25 Aug. 09	12 Feb. 20	23 Dec. 31
Bloomfield, Edwin, 10 Foot...........	13 Aug. 04	23 April 05	15 April 13	6 July 26
Bond, Wadham Wyndham, Unattached, *Adjutant, Armagh Militia*	4 Nov. 36	9 Mar. 39	24 Nov. 54	24 Nov. 54
Boothby, Basil Charles,[15] 95 Foot, *Barrackmaster at Jamaica*	2 Sept. 53	21 Sept. 54	1 Feb. 56	10 Nov. 56

Y

Captains.

	CORNET, ETC.	LIEUT.	CAPTAIN.	WHEN PLACED ON HALF PAY.
Boteler, Robert, R. Engineers	11 May 25	20 Oct. 26	15 Aug. 40	9 Mar. 41
Boulton, Richard, Coldstream Guards ..	11 April 94	never	13 July 97	25 Dec. 02
Bowen, John Watts, 56 Foot	19 Feb. 07	28 Jan. 08	12 May 14	25 Dec. 14
Bowman, Henry Samuel, Unattached, *Adjutant, Edinburgh County Militia*	13 Oct. 43	1 April 47	20 June 54	24 Nov. 54
⅏ Brander, Tho. Coventry,[16] 59 Foot ..	27 June 11	30 Mar. 14	1 June 39	28 Feb. 40
Brannan, James, Unattached	6 June 16	25 Dec. 23	25 July 45	25 July 45
Brenan, John,[17] 53 Foot, *Capt. Dublin City Militia*	17 Sept. 39	30 Apr. 41	28 Dec. 49	7 May 52
Breton, John,[18] Unatt., *Town Major at Portsmouth*	2 Dec. 42	26 July 44	2 Dec. 53	2 Nov. 55
Brettingham, Richard Wheatley, R. Art. *Major, Dublin City Artillery Militia*	19 June 41	13 April 42	30 June 48	1 Jan. 55
Bridge, George, 3 F., *Gentleman-at-Arms*	16 April 29	21 Sept. 32	28 Jan. 44	4 Nov. 53
Bridge, Robert Onslow,[19] Royal Marines .	2 April 22	12 Oct. 32	12 Feb. 42	16 Aug. 44
Brine, Andrew Gram,[20] 42 Foot	15 Apr. 42	18 Apr. 45	13 Sept. 48	23 July 52
⅏ Broughton, Robert Edwards,[21] 0 Foot		29 Oct. 07	9 July 12	19 Nov. 18
⅏ ⅏ Brown, Thomas,[22] 79 Foot	23 Oct. 06	15 Dec. 07	20 July 15	25 Feb. 16
⅏ Browne, Peter Rutledge Montague, Unatt., *Major, South Down Militia*	31 Oct. 11	24 Dec. 12	29 Aug. 20	28 June 31
Browne, Valentine,[23] Unattached	16 April 12	10 Aug. 15	19 Dec. 56	19 Dec. 56
Buchanan, John Grahame, Unattached .	15 Feb. 16	9 April 25	2 Aug. 39	2 Aug. 39
⅏⅏⅏ Burges, Som. Wald.,[21] 5 W. India R.	1 Oct. 12	never	20 Oct. 14	8 May 17
Burnaby, Edwin, Unattached	4 Nov. 19	12 June 23	8 April 26	12 Oct. 26
Burnett, Rich. Parry,[25] Vet. Company .	10 July 99	5 May 00	13 June 05	1 Nov. 16
⅏ Burton, John Curzon,[26] Royal Artillery	4 April 07	1 Feb. 08	6 Nov. 27	25 Nov. 33
Butler, Richard Alexander, Unattached..	29 July 19	25 Sept. 23	10 Sept. 25	5 Nov. 29
Butler, Walter, Unatt., *Captain, South Mayo Militia*	15 Dec. 25	10 Sept. 20	20 Sept. 44	2 May 51
Butt, John Wells, Unattached	16 Jan. 16	2 Mar. 26	20 Nov. 40	28 July 43
Bygrave, Joseph, Unattached	never	never	25 Dec. 13	8 May 28
Caffin, Wm. Geo. Chart, Royal Artillery	16 Dec. 25	30 June 28	18 Mar. 41	14 April 41
Cahill, Patrick,[26]† Unattached	10 Aug. 54	22 Dec. 54	2 Dec. 59	2 Dec. 59
Campbell, Henry J. Montgomery, R. Art.	16 Dec. 46	1 May 48	20 June 54	4 Aug. 54
Campbell, John,[27] 26 F. *Barrack Mr. at Birr*	2 April 12	1 April 13	26 Dec. 25	10 Sept. 30
⅏ Campbell, William,[28] Unattached ...	28 Feb. 11	25 June 12	12 April 27	28 June 31
Cannon, Rouquier John, Royal Artillery .	20 June 40	23 Nov. 41	30 June 48	27 Oct. 55
Capadose, Henry, Unattached..........	26 Feb. 28	17 May 34	29 Dec. 46	29 Dec. 46
Carloss, John Baxter, 96 Foot..........	11 Sept. 06	29 Sept. 09	7 April 25	15 Mar. 33
⅏ Carnegie, W. F. Lindsay,[29] Royal Art.	22 Dec. 03	20 July 04	1 July 13	1 Dec. 19
Carr, Ralph,[30] Royal Marines	9 April 12	17 Mar. 31	13 Nov. 40	5 Mar. 41
Carter, John Money, Unatt. *Adjutant Monmouth Militia*	18 May 32	7 Aug. 35	18 Sept. 39	21 April 46
Cary, William Lucius, Unattached	11 Jan. 15	{ *25 Dec 13 3 May 15	26 May 25	20 Jan. 32
Casey, Thomas Page,[31] Royal Marines ..	20 June 43	27 July 47	22 June 55	1 Feb. 58
Cator, John Farnaby, R. Art., *Lt.-Col. Comm. Kent Militia Artillery*	18 June 35	5 April 37	1 April 46	3 Feb. 52
Cathcart, *Hon.* Adolphus F., Unattached	7 Nov. 22	9 June 25	13 July 32	27 July 32
⅏ Caulfield, Daniel,[32] 7 Foot	4 April 05	18 June 07	26 May 23	14 Sept. 32
⅏ Chaloner, John, Independent Company	14 June 00	2 Nov. 03	11 Feb. 08	21 June 13
⅏ Chancellor, John,[33] 61 Foot	30 Jan. 00	19 May 07	14 Sept. 09	10 July 23
Chapman, John James,[34] Royal Artillery	13 Sept. 05	1 June 06	21 April 20	2 June 29
Charlton, Saint John, 14 Dragoons......	10 Feb. 14	10 Nov. 14	12 Oct. 20	25 Oct. 21
Chawner, Edward Hoare, Unattached .	9 June 25	10 June 26	7 Sept. 32	7 Sept. 36
Cheese, Joseph,[34]† Land Transport Corps	....	31 Aug. 55	1 Feb. 56	
Chepmell, Charles, Unattached	May 04	23 Nov. 04	1 Oct. 12	25 April 22
Chesshire, Edward, 49 Foot	20 Oct. 96	11 May 97	15 Dec. 04	24 Sept. 17
Chichester, Arthur, Liverpool Regt.	27 Sept. 01	14 Jan. 02	12 Dec. 05	
Chichester, Arthur Charles, Unattached ..	12 Dec. 26	10 Nov. 29	3 April 35	8 Aug. 45
Clark, John Stephens, 72 Foot	27 Sept. 42	30 Dec. 45	25 April 50	10 Nov. 56
Clayfield, Edward Ireland, Unattached ..	19 July 15	28 Mar. 22	17 Sept. 25	17 Sept. 25
Clive, Edward, Unattached	27 April 15	21 Jan. 19	23 June 25	22 May 28
Cockburn, Alexander, Unattached	4 Dec. 32	27 May 36	13 Dec. 42	7 Nov. 51
Cole, *Hon.* Henry Arthur, Unatt.	17 Jan. 28	12 Feb. 30	6 Mar. 35	3 July 41
Collis, Peter, Unattached	11 Mar. 12	14 June 15	3 Feb. 32	28 Aug. 38
Colliss, John, Royal Marines	26 Mar. 13	7 Mar. 32	11 May 41	4 Sept. 49
Colman, Wm. Thomas, Unattached.....	7 Sept. 15	13 June 30	3 Dec. 41	14 Oct. 51
⅏ Colvile, Frederick,[35] Scots Fusilier Gds.	22 Sept. 08	never	9 Dec. 13	25 Feb. 19
Cook, Wm. Surtees, Unatt., *Adjutant 1st Somerset Militia*	27 June 34	5 Jan. 39	30 Dec. 45	28 April 46

Captains. 472

Name	CORNET, ETC.	LIEUT.	CAPTAIN.	WHEN PLACED ON HALF PAY.
Cookes, George,[36] Unattached	14 July 37	29 April 42	2 April 50	2 April 50
⁋ Costley, Theoph. Byers,[37] 45 Foot	9 May 05	1 Jan. 07	7 Oct. 13	25 Dec. 14
Cotton, Edward Antonius,[38] R. Artillery	1 July 06	1 Feb. 08	29 July 25	29 July 25
⁋ Courtenay, William Allan,[39] Unatt.	14 June 09	23 Aug. 12	26 Dec. 51	26 Dec. 51
⁋ Cox, Charles,[40] 41 Foot	17 Sept. 03	16 May 05	14 April 08	9 Nov. 15
Cradock, Adam Williamson, 15 Foot	9 July 03	21 Mar. 05	7 Oct. 12	25 Nov. 14
Craig, Aylmer Strangford,[49]† Gold Coast Artillery Corps	18 Nov. 53	24 Feb. 54	16 Dec. 57	26 Nov. 58
Cranfield, George Darley, Unattached	16 June 06	12 May 07	7 April 25	14 Sept. 26
Cremer, James Smith, Royal Artillery	7 July 17	29 July 25	2 June 37	4 May 40
Cresswell, George,[41] Unattached	16 Aug. 50	11 Mar. 53	31 Mar. 55	28 Aug. 57
Crofton, Walter Fred., CB. Royal Artillery	21 June 33	25 May 36	17 Jan. 45	1 Feb. 45
Crookshank, Chichester Graham,[42] Sub-Inspector of Militia	25 Mar. 36	29 Dec. 38	18 July 48	8 Jan. 56
Crosbie, *Sir* William, *Bart.*, Unattached	4 Mar. 13	13 July 15	24 Feb. 17	1 June 26
Cross, William Jennings, Unattached	1 April 19	1 Dec. 25	29 Aug. 26	29 Aug. 26
Cuddy, Alexander Daniel, Unattached	10 Oct. 22	18 May 26	13 Dec. 39	9 April 41
Cuppage, Alexander, Unattached	25 Aug. 09	29 Dec. 12	28 Mar. 16	11 June 30
Curtis, Henry,[43] Royal Artillery	22 Dec. 03	20 July 04	25 Jan. 13	21 April 21
Custance, Neville, 1 R. Veteran Batt.	2 July 12	9 Sept. 13	15 June 26	12 Oct. 26
⁋ Davern, John,[44] 27 Foot, *Captain of Invalids, Royal Hospital, Chelsea*	27 Mar. 06	11 Nov. 07	31 Aug. 15	8 June 30
Davies, Arthur, Unattached	22 Nov. 21	17 Feb. 25	3 Oct. 26	3 Oct. 26
*Davies, John, 4 Foot	never	never	27 Nov. 09	25 Dec. 09
Davies, John, Royal Artillery	4 April 08	20 June 09	6 Nov. 27	9 Sept. 34
Davis, Alfred,[46] Unattached	21 Sept. 15	27 May 19	19 Jan. 26	13 Aug. 30
De la Condamine, Thomas, Unattached	16 June 14	18 Mar. 25	15 June 32	15 June 32
De Lisle, Hirzel Fred., Unattached	23 Sept. 13	12 Feb. 24	2 April 26	14 Feb. 28
D'Erp, Balthazar, *Baron*, 60 Foot	never	never	30 Dec. 97	5 Nov. 00
Despard, Philip Henry, Unattached	17 Mar. 25	22 Nov. 27	10 Feb. 43	10 Feb. 43
Des Vœux, *Sir* Henry Wm., *Bart.*, Unatt.	8 April 25	9 Feb. 26	26 Nov. 29	22 Aug. 34
Donnelly, George, Land Transport Corps	....	22 Sept. 55	1 Feb. 56	1 April 57
Dore, William Henry, Unattached	8 Dec. 37	27 Sept. 39	17 Dec. 46	5 June 57
Dorehill, George, Unattached	20 Nov. 38	25 Sept. 40	15 Mar. 53	20 May 53
Douglas, Henry Hamilton, 78 Foot	12 Mar. 14	14 April 18	30 June 24	16 July 25
⁋Douglas, Joseph,[47] Unatt. *Military Knight of Windsor*	14 July 08	20 Dec. 10	8 April 26	14 Aug. 28
Douglas, Robert, Unattached	12 Oct. 15	10 Aug. 26	9 Mar. 49	9 Mar. 49
Dowland, John, 67 Foot	1 Nov. 04	28 Mar. 05	1 June 15	16 Nov. 18
Dowman, John,[48] Unattached, *Capt. of Invalids, Royal Hospital, Chelsea*	28 Sept. 30	21 Dec. 32	3 Sept. 47	3 Sept. 47
Dresing, Charles,[49] 3 Foot	19 Feb. 36	2 June 38	2 July 45	10 Nov. 56
⁋ ⁋ Dromgoole, N. Fleming, 35 Foot	1 Nov. 04	4 July 05	29 July 13	25 June 17
Du Bourdieu, John, 87 Foot	28 Feb. 28	8 July 34	20 Sept. 42	10 Nov. 43
Du Cane, Robert, 9 Foot	3 April 46	28 April 48	15 Nov. 50	8 Feb. 56
Duncan, William,[50] Royal Artillery	10 May 05	1 June 06	11 Mar. 17	15 Mar. 25
Dunne, Richard, Unattached	8 April 25	2 Mar. 26	16 May 34	23 Nov. 38
Dutton, Charles, Unattached	10 May 10	15 Oct. 12	30 Oct. 40	24 June 42
⁋ ⁋⁋ Eaton, Charles,[51] 10 Foot	4 Dec. 06	7 June 08	21 April 14	14 Aug. 23
⁋ ⁋⁋ Edwardes, David John,[52] R. Artill.	1 Nov. 05	1 June 06	1 June 25	29 July 26
⁋ ⁋⁋ Elliott, Richard Chas., Unattached	5 June 09	23 June 11	28 Aug. 27	28 Aug. 27
⁋ ⁋⁋ Elliott, William,[53] 14 Foot	4 Jan. 10	27 Nov. 12	14 April 18	22 Jan. 24
⁋ Ellis, Hercules,[54] Unattached	5 Aug. 07	20 April 09	11 Aug. 25	4 Nov. 36
Emerson, John,[55] Unattached	30 July 07	12 April 09	13 Feb. 27	23 Sept. 36
ℂ Enderby, Samuel,[56] York Chasseurs	31 Oct. 11	16 April 12	27 May 19	17 Feb. 32
Evelegh, George Carter, Royal Artillery	20 Dec. 33	10 Jan. 37	17 April 45	9 May 45
Evelegh, John Henry, Unatt.	8 April 25	28 Jan. 26	20 Jan. 32	19 Dec. 40
Fairtlough, Wm. Haviland,[57] Unatt.	12 Aug. 36	29 Dec. 38	9 Sept. 51	9 Sept. 51
Farmar, Richard,[58] Royal Marines	8 May 38	12 Feb. 42	23 Dec. 51	1 Feb. 58
Finey, Alen George, Unattached	26 July 08	19 April 10	5 June 27	5 June 27
Fisher, Seth Nuttall, Unattached	12 Feb. 24	13 May 26	3 April 35	23 June 43
Fisk, William Hawley, Unattached, *Adjutant, South Devon Militia*	27 April 15	25 Oct. 15	8 April 26	17 Feb. 37
FitzGerald, Thos. B. Vandeleur,[60] R. Mar.	14 Oct. 45	27 May 48	11 July 56	27 July 57
*Fitzherbert, John, 80 Foot	never	never	25 Dec. 13	1814
Ford, Charles,[61] Royal Artillery	1 July 06	1 Feb. 08	29 July 25	7 May 33
Forde, William,[62] Unattached	4 July 05	12 June 07	27 July 20	7 July 25
Foskett, Joseph, Unatt., *Major, Hertford Militia*	24 April 23	22 Oct. 25	7 Nov. 26	31 Aug. 30

Y 2

473 Captains.

	ENSIGN, ETC.	LIEUT.	CAPTAIN.	WHEN PLACED ON HALF PAY.
Fraser, Evan Baillie, Unattached.......	9 Jan. 23	15 Dec. 25	12 Dec. 26	14 June 33
₽ Fraser, Thomas,⁶³ 83 Foot	16 Jan. 08	19 Feb. 08	2 July 12	25 June 17
Fraser, Thomas,⁶⁴ R. Marines	26 Nov. 28	10 July 37	26 Nov. 46	23 Jan. 51
*Frederick, Sir Richard, Bart., 9 Foot ..	never	never	27 Nov. 99	25 May 02
French, Acheson, Grenadier Guards	17 June 07	17 Dec. 07	7 April 25	9 Nov. 30
₽ Furnace, Norbury,⁶⁵ 60 Foot	25 Dec. 06	16 Mar. 08	30 Dec. 19	3 April 23
Fyers, Henry Thomas, Royal Artillery, Major, R. Lancashire Art. Militia	26 July 31	13 July 32	13 April 42	12 May 49
₽ Fyfe, William,⁶⁵ 92 Foot	2 June 04	29 Aug. 05	16 Sept. 13	25 Dec. 14
₽ Gapper, Edmund, 83 Foot	1 Aug. 04	5 May 05	3 June 12	25 June 17
Garth, Thomas, 15 Dragoons	23 Nov. 15	6 June 16	24 Aug. 20	25 Oct. 21
₽ Gascoyne, Thos. Bamber,⁶⁷ 9 Ceylon Reg.	5 Nov. 07	25 Mar. 09	7 Feb. 22	13 May 36
₽ Gee, Francis,⁶⁸ Unattached	18 Sept. 40	5 June 43	13 Sept. 53	13 Sept. 53
₽ Gibbons, Thomas,⁶⁹ Unatt., Capt. of Invalids, R. Hospital, Kilmainham	9 Sept. 12	7 April 25	7 Aug. 40	7 Aug. 40
Gichard, Wm. Robert, Royal Artillery ..	19 Mar. 30	27 Sept. 40	24 Nov. 47	15 Oct. 50
₽ Gilbert, Francis Yarde,⁷⁰ R. Engineers	1 May 11	10 June 11	23 Mar. 25	6 June 25
Gilbert, James Anthony, Royal Artillery	16 Dec. 16	28 Feb. 25	10 Jan. 37	28 Nov. 37
*Giles, Joseph, 9 Foot	never	never	25 Dec. 13	25 Sept. 14
Gilleland, John, Unatt. Q.M., 5 Mar. 47	18 Mar. 53	14 Sept. 55	9 Jan. 57	9 Jan. 57
Gillespie, John, Unattached	31 May 39	7 Jan. 42	8 June 55	8 June 55
Ginger, Joseph,⁷¹ 6 Foot	25 Sept. 03	6 Mar. 05	1 May 11	21 Dec. 26
₽ Glasse, Francis, 25 Foot	14 Aug. 01	9 Jan. 02	18 Sept. 06	8 Jan. 18
Glegg, Edward Holt, Unattached	3 Aug. 26	21 June 31	23 April 39	31 Jan. 45
Gleig, Charles Edward Stuart, 92 Foot ..	1 June 41	24 June 42	9 Nov. 46	10 Nov. 56
Godber, Robert, Land Transport Corps ..	....	7 Feb. 55	7 Sept. 55	1 April 57
Gold, Henry Yarburgh, Unattached	11 April 25	18 Sept. 28	5 April 31	25 Feb. 45
Goode, John,⁷³ Unattached	5 Sept. 11	12 Nov. 12	20 Feb. 35	20 Feb. 35
Goodwin, S. Osnaburgh, Unattached ..	25 Dec. 13	31 Oct. 22	22 Dec. 35	8 Feb. 39
Gordon, James, 3 West India Regt.	27 Nov. 23	26 May 26	12 Nov. 29	15 Mar. 31
Gould, John Stillman,⁷⁴ 63 Foot........	30 Sept. 42	28 June 44	20 July 49	10 Nov. 56
Granger, John, Land Transport Corps ..	....	1 Oct. 53	1 Feb. 56	1 April 57
Grant, James, Unattached	20 Dec. 21	30 June 26	6 Mar. 27	6 Mar. 27
Grant, John, 24 Foot................	15 Feb. 10	5 Mar. 13	13 Aug. 30	14 Dec. 32
Grantt, John, 72 Foot	16 Dec. 95	23 June 96	27 Dec. 14	25 Dec. 17
Graves, William H., Unattached........	6 Jan. 08	26 Oct. 08	8 April 25	23 Nov. 36
Gray, Basil, Unattached	30 July 28	31 Jan. 34	20 Nov. 39	20 June 45
Greentree, Doveton Downes,⁷⁵ Unatt., Secretary to Council of Education	9 May 45	9 Jan. 47	8 Jan. 58	8 Jan. 58
Greenwood, Joseph,⁷⁶ Unattached	6 May 36	27 Oct. 36	31 Mar. 46	23 April 58
₽ Gregor, Gordon Wm. Fra.,⁷⁷ 23 Foot ..	23 May 06	14 May 07	17 June 31	25 Dec. 14
₽ Grimes, John, 76 Foot	6 Oct. 08	1 Nov. 10	25 May 22	30 May 22
Guthrie, William, Unattached..........	22 April 26	20 Mar. 27	24 Feb. 37	13 Aug. 47
₽ Gwynne, Henry Lewis Edward,⁷⁹ 62 Foot	25 April 05	26 June 06	23 Aug. 10	25 Feb. 17
Handcock, Hon. Robt. French, R. Art., Lt.-Col. Comm. Dublin City Art.	26 July 31	23 Dec. 32	1 Nov. 42	9 Oct. 48
Hanley, Malachi, Land Transport Corps..	28 May 47	11 April 51	9 Sept. 57	16 Aug. 59
₽₽ Harris, William, Unattached	16 April 12	21 Jan. 13	2 June 25	8 June 30
₽ ₽₽ Harrison, Hugh,⁸¹ 5 Foot	21 Nov. 05	18 June 07	11 June 12	16 May 22
Harrison, John,⁸² Unatt. Captain of Invalids, Royal Hospital, Chelsea	20 July 15	28 Oct. 24	3 Dec. 29	15 Mar. 39
₽ Harrison, John,⁸³ 82 Foot, Adjutant, Royal Mid Lothian Yeomanry Cav.	25 June 24	13 Aug. 25	27 Oct. 35	25 Oct. 42
Hart, Richard,⁸⁵ 66 Foot	27 Mar. 05	25 April 06	25 Mar. 25	19 May 25
Hartman, Gustavus Adolphus,⁷² Unatt...	10 May 44	9 Feb. 47	10 Nov. 54	10 Nov. 54
Hartshorn, William, Unatt., Adjutant 6 Lancashire Militia	20 Dec. 43	3 April 46	8 Aug. 51	12 Jan. 55
Harvey, John, Royal Artillery, Major, Donegal Artillery Militia	18 June 35	23 June 37	1 April 46	26 May 46
*Haselfoot, Charles, 3 Foot	never	never	25 Dec. 13	25 Aug. 14
Haviland, Francis, Unattached	24 Nov. 35	20 Sept. 37	30 April 52	30 April 52
Hawke, Hon. Stanhope, Unattached	17 July 23	12 May 25	26 Sept. 26	2 Dec. 31
Hawker, Charles, Unatt..............	22 Feb. 31	20 July 32	25 Aug. 43	14 Sept. 52
Hawkey, Henry Cha. M.,⁸⁶ R. Marines	27 Sept. 08	18 Nov. 40	13 July 49	14 June 52
Hawkins, George Palmer, Unattached ..	30 Nov. 09	6 Jan. 11	15 May 27	15 May 27
Hawkins, John, Unattached..........	25 Aug. 06	3 Nov. 08	1 July 20	7 Sept. 26
₽ Hay, William,⁸⁷ 15 Foot, Colonel, Berwick Artillery Militia	9 Mar. 07	14 Jan. 08	2 May 11	25 April 12
₽ Healy, John,⁸⁸ 39 Foot............	4 June 08	8 Sept. 08	26 June 23	25 Jan. 42
Heard, William Hodder, 86 Foot	16 Sept. 27	10 Dec. 33	20 Sept. 44	1 June 49

Captains. 474

	2D LIEUT. ETC.	LIEUT.	CAPTAIN.	WHEN PLACED ON HALF PAY.
Heath, Macclesfield William, R. Engineers	1 Aug. 14	1 July 15	13 May 36	25 May 38
*Heathcote, Cockshutt, 53 Foot	never	never	25 Dec. 13	25 Dec. 14
Henderson, David, 10 Foot	28 Nov. 00	23 Jan. 08	5 Jan. 15	25 Feb. 16
Hertford, R. S. C., *Marquis of*, KG., 22 Drs.	24 Feb. 20	24 Oct. 21	25 Mar. 23	17 April 23
₰ ꝙ Hill, Henry,[89] Unatt., *Adjutant Cheshire Yeomanry Cavalry*	19 Jan. 15	5 May 15	28 June 36	28 June 36
Hilker, Henry,[69]† Land Transport Corps	....	26 Feb. 55	7 Sept. 55	1 April 57
Hinde, Henry Reynolds, 36 Foot	29 Jan. 00	13 Jan. 02	29 Nov. 03	25 Mar. 11
Hingston, Francis Bernard, Unattached..	13 Oct. 08	5 Dec. 11	1 Oct. 50	1 Oct. 50
₰ ꝙ Hodges, George Lloyd,[90] CB., Unatt. *Consul General at the Hague*	28 Aug. 00	7 Jan. 08	31 Dec. 30	31 Dec. 30
Hodges, Thomas Eardley,[91] Unattached..	29 Jan. 12	4 Feb. 14	17 Dec. 41	17 Dec. 41
₰ Hollinsworth, Henry.[92] Unattached, *Military Knight of Windsor*	3 Dec. 25	29 May 28	28 June 50	28 June 50
Hopkins, Henry, 11 Garrison Battalion ..	7 Oct. 02	24 June 03	21 Aug. 06	2 Nov. 09
Hornbrook, Thomas Beckford, R. Marines	25 Aug. 99	1 Sept. 04	8 May 24	5 Jan. 26
Horsford, George Fabic, Unattached	30 Jan. 23	20 April 36	14 June 42	2 Aug. 42
Horsley, Nicholas,[93] Unattached	18 Mar. 13	5 Oct. 15	16 Jan. 46	16 Jan. 46
Hotham, Augustus, Unattached	20 Dec. 21	19 May 25	19 Dec. 26	28 Dec. 32
Hotham, George,[94] R. Engineers........	24 Mar. 15	1 May 16	10 Jan. 37	17 Aug. 39
₰ Houlton, Sir George, 43 F., *Ensign of Yeomen of the Guard*	20 Nov. 06	6 Oct. 08	2 Nov. 16	25 Mar. 17
Howard deWalden, C. A., *Lord*, GCB., 8F. *Envoy Ex.& Min. Plenipo. at Brussels*	• never	14 April 17	3 Oct. 22	3 Oct. 22
Hudson, Charles, Land Transport Corps	....	25 Jan. 55	1 May 55	1 April 57
Humbley, Wm. Wellington Waterloo,[95] Un.	27 Mar. 35	15 Dec. 38	29 April 56	23 Oct. 57
Humphreys, John Goullin,[56] Coldst. Gds.	14 May 07	14 July 08	8 April 25	18 Nov. 31
Hunt, John, Unattached	11 Dec. 12	9 April 15	10 Oct. 45	10 Oct. 45
Hunter, George James,[97] Royal Artillery	1 Oct. 08	13 Mar. 11	6 Nov. 27	23 Oct. 33
Hunter, James, Unattached............	17 Nov. 37	27 Sept. 39	19 Dec. 56	19 Dec. 56
Hussey, Thomas,[98] Royal Marines	28 April 97	18 July 03	24 Sept. 10	1 Sept. 14
Hutchinson, Fred. Jas. Taggart, Unatt., *Major, Fife Artillery Militia*	18 Dec. 27	17 May 31	17 Mar. 38	27 May 42
Imlach, Alexander, Unattached	9 Nov. 15	7 Jan. 42	10 Sept. 47	10 Sept. 47
Inge, Chas., Unatt., *Maj.*, 1 *Stafford Mil.*	7 Jan. 30	26 Feb. 36	27 Mar. 40	28 Jan. 46
Irwin, Thomas, 6 Dragoons	26 Aug. 09	29 Oct. 12	3 Dec. 18	25 Oct. 21
Isaac, John Matcham,[99] Unattached	4 Nov. 26	3 Sept. 21	11 July 45	10 Sept. 50
James, Demetrius Grevis,[100] Royal Marines	19 April 96	8 June 99	29 June 08	25 Feb. 12
Jarvis, Sir Samuel Raymond,[101] 7 Drs. ..	7 April 06	19 June 06	7 Sept. 15	25 Jan. 23
₰ *Jeffreys, Richard, 53 Foot, *Barrack-master at Dublin*	....	....	25 Dec. 13	25 Sept. 14
Jervois, Edwyn Stanhope, 7 F., *Comm. of Convalescent Depot at Yarmouth*	13 July 49	28 Mar. 54	16 Nov. 55	31 July 57
Johnson, Yarrall, 63 Foot............	12 Aug. 03	22 Dec. 04	9 June 13	3 July 23
Joliffe, Sir W. G. H., *Bt.*, Bourbon Regt...	10 April 17	26 Aug. 19	22 April 24	24 June 24
Jones, James,[102] Royal Marines	....	....	8 June 10	1 Sept. 14
Jones, Vaughan, Unattached	12 Nov. 07	12 Jan. 09	19 Dec. 56	19 Dec. 56
₰ Jones, William,[103] 52 Foot	25 Feb. 08	5 Jan. 09	30 Sept. 19	5 June 23
₰ *Jones, Wm., 1 Provisional Batt. of Mil.	never	never	25 Dec. 13	25 Oct. 44
Kaye, Wilkinson Lister, Royal Artillery..	11 Dec. 15	1 May 22	12 July 36	4 May 43
Keane, George Michael, Unattached....	27 Mar. 23	27 Aug. 25	19 Dec. 26	17 Mar. 37
Keats, John Smith, Royal Waggon Train	16 Dec. 16	2 Mar. 25	5 July 29	31 May 33
Kemp, John, 4 F., *R. M. at Canterbury*	10 Mar. 48	29 May 49	14 Aug. 57	19 Feb. 58
₰ Kenmare, Thomas,[104] Earl of, 16 Drags.	6 Aug. 07	14 July 08	12 Aug. 12	25 Mar. 19
Kenny, Steph., [106] Unatt. *Adj. Stirling. Mil.*	8 June 41	26 July 44	15 Mar. 53	15 Dec. 54
₰ Ker, Richard Hall,[107] Unattached	31 May 10	10 June 13	6 Feb. 35	6 Feb. 35
Kerr, Robert Dundas, Royal Engineers ..	19 June 44	1 April 46	17 Feb. 54	28 Dec. 58
₰ *Kettilby, James,[105] 51 Foot	never	never	25 Dec. 13	25 Aug. 15
₰ King, James,[109] 73 Foot	25 Sept. 06	10 Dec. 06	28 Feb. 11	1 Jan. 18
₰ King, John Duncan,[110] Unattached, *Military Knight of Windsor*....	28 Aug. 06	18 Feb. 08	16 Mar. 30	28 Dec. 30
King, Sir R. Duckworth, *Bt.*, Unattached	28 Feb. 22	29 May 25	22 April 26	5 Feb. 36
Kingsley, James Bell, Unattached	10 Nov. 13	9 Nov. 14	21 May 41	21 May 41
*Kinneir, Joseph Hall, 2 Prov. Bn. of Mil.	never	never	25 Dec. 13	1814
₰ Kirby, Michael, 65 Foot	25 June 12	20 Feb. 16	31 May 21	19 April 23
Kirwan, Henry, 15 Foot	18 April 00	28 Nov. 00	22 May 04	25 July 12
Knight, Brook John, Royal Staff Corps..	26 Oct. 26	8 June 30	26 June 35	2 Aug. 44
Knipe, Geo. M. 36 F., *Adj. Carlow Militia*	22 Feb. 39	20 May 42	6 June 54	22 Dec. 54
Kyrle, J. Ernle Money, R. Staff Corps, *Adjutant, Hereford Militia*	10 April 33	5 Oct. 38	22 July 42	29 Jan. 47
Labalmondiere, Douglas W. P., 45 Foot, *Assist. Commissr. of Metrop. Police*	21 June 33	25 May 38	7 June 44	26 April 50

475 *Captains.*

	ENSIGN, ETC.	LIEUT.	CAPTAIN.	WHEN PLACED ON HALF PAY.
₽ Lambert, *Sir* Henry John,[111] *Bt.*, 86 Foot	6 April 09	never	27 May 13	12 Aug. 15
Lamotte, Chas. Wyndham, Unattached ..	6 Nov. 27	28 Oct. 31	22 July 36	10 Nov. 37
Langrishe, Hugh Henry, Unattached	never	5 July 15	27 April 25	27 Oct. 25
Langley, George Richard, Unattached ..	24 Nov. 12	7 Jan. 14	26 April 44	26 April 44
₽ ⓆⓂ Langton, Edward,[112] 52 Foot.	23 May 05	25 July 05	12 May 12	8 April 17
Lanphier, J. Philips Cosby, 25 Foot	27 Mar. 06	7 Sept. 09	19 April 18	6 Oct. 25
₽ Latham, Matthew,[113] Portuguese Service	15 Nov. 05	8 April 07	11 Feb. 13	20 April 13
Law, James Horton, Unattached.	22 July 13	7 May 18	9 Sept. 25	11 Jan. 28
Lawlor, Provo William,[114] R. Artillery ..	1 July 06	1 Feb. 08	8 April 25	20 April 30
₽ Lawrence, W. Hudson,[115] R. Artillery	28 April 10	17 Dec. 13	2 Feb. 32	8 Aug. 40
*Laxon, John, 7 Foot	never	never	25 Dec. 13	25 Sept. 14
Lazenby, James, Unattached	15 June 55	14 Jan. 56	18 Mar. 59	18 Mar. 59
Lea, Samuel Percy, Unattached, *Maj.,* } *South Mayo Militia*	6 July 38	8 April 42	18 Feb. 53	18 Feb. 53
Leatham, James Birley, Unatt., *Lieut,* } *Denbigh Yeomanry Cavalry*	5 Feb. 30	9 Jan. 30	23 Aug. 50	23 Aug. 50
Lee, William, Royal Marines	22 Aug. 21	12 Oct. 32	12 Feb. 42	10 Aug. 49
Le Marchant, Edward,[116] 57 Foot	12 April 50	3 Dec. 52	20 Dec. 54	6 May 59
Lempriere, Henry, Royal Artillery	16 June 38	13 Aug. 40	1 July 47	17 Feb. 54
Leonard, Henry Bates, Royal Marines ..	31 Aug. 41	21 May 46	14 Mar. 54	17 Oct. 57
Lewis, Alexander, Unattached	15 June 97	27 May 01	13 June 11	22 Mar. 27
Lindsay, Wm. Chacon, Royal Artillery ..	11 Sept. 12	1 April 15	23 Oct. 33	3 July 27
₽ Litchfield, Richard,[117] Royal Artillery	26 Nov. 08	5 Sept. 11	6 Nov. 27	6 Nov. 39
Little, Robert John,[118] Royal Marines ..	4 July 03	15 Aug. 05	31 July 26	30 Nov. 57
Loftus, Frederick, Unattached.	7 Oct. 19	9 June 25	8 April 26	8 April 26
Logan-Home, Geo. Home,[119] R. Marines, } *Major, Berwick Artillery Militia* ..	1 July 23	20 Feb. 33	17 June 42	26 Oct. 48
Lyon, George, Unattached	8 Nov. 21	31 May 25	30 Dec. 26	30 Dec. 26
₽ M'Donald, Donald,[121] R. Engineers ..	12 Sept. 08	24 June 09	20 Oct. 13	28 Sept. 24
M'Intyre, Angus,[122] Unattached	26 Aug. 07	2 April 10	27 Aug. 24	9 July 29
Macdonald, Ranald, Unattached.	18 July 15	3 Dec. 18	19 Nov. 30	22 Mar. 33
Macdonald, Ronald, 12 Foot	5 Feb. 01	26 July 04	2 Jan. 12	20 April 20
₽ Mac Donnell, Ewen,[123] Unattached ..	20 Jan. 14	27 Mar. 23	6 May 35	28 Nov. 37
₽ Macfarlane, Andrew,[124] 91 Foot	20 Oct. 04	26 Oct. 04	10 Sept. 12	25 Feb. 16
Mac Gregor, John,[125] Unattached	19 Oct. 09	28 Nov. 11	29 Sept. 27	28 Mar. 34
Mackay, Henry Fowler, Unattached ..	9 June 25	12 Jan. 26	12 Feb. 30	26 Mar. 41
Mackenzie, Alexander, Unattached.	30 Nov. 15	8 April 25	1 Aug. 26	7 Mar. 34
₽Muckenzie, Alex. Wedder,[126] 3 Garr. Batt.	14 Jan. 07	11 Jan. 08	23 Jan. 12	6 Nov. 17
Maclean, James,[127] 103 Foot	22 July 13	8 Nov. 14	22 Nov. 21	18 Sept. 23
Mac Queen, James,[131] Unattached	14 Apr. 46	10 May 50	30 Sept. 56	14 Jan. 59
Malcolm, John Dundas,[128] 28 Foot	1 Nov. 42	29 Mar. 44	29 Dec. 54	14 July 57
₽ Mancor, Andrew,[129] 59 Foot	26 Oct. 04	16 June 07	3 Sept. 12	1 Aug. 16
March, C. H. G. L., *Earl of*, Unatt...	24 May 39	27 Sept. 42	27 Sept. 44	27 Sept. 44
ⓆⓂ Marcon, Edward, 79 Foot.	11 May 11	20 May 13	3 Jan. 22	6 Feb. 23
Margesson, Philip Davos, Royal Artillery	1 May 40	9 Nov. 40	17 Feb. 54	15 Feb. 59
Mason, John Monck,[130] Unattached	27 Sept. 15	25 Oct. 35	3 April 46	3 April 46
ⓆⓂ Master, Richard Thomas,[132] Gr. Gds.	21 Jan. 13	never	1 July 15	25 Feb. 19
ⓆⓂ Maunsell, John Edm.,[133] R. Artillery	14 June 05	1 June 09	24 Mar. 17	14 Nov. 26
Maxwell, Henry, Unattached	4 Mar. 13	13 Jan. 14	10 April 23	18 May 26
₽ Meech, Thomas Crosby,[134] 62 Foot....	5 Sept. 05	26 Dec. 05	1 Oct. 12	3 May 21
₽ Mends, Hugh Bowen, R. Staff Corps..	13 Nov. 06	27 Nov. 06	12 Feb. 14	26 Feb. 29
Menzies, John, Unattached.	18 Oct. 31	16 Aug. 35	15 Dec. 48	15 Dec. 48
Meredith, Boyle,[135] Unattached	29 Mar. 10	1 July 13	1 Oct. 50	1 Oct. 50
Michell, Walter Taylor, Royal Marines ..	10 June 94	24 April 95	21 Dec. 03	5 Oct. 13
Midgley, Benjamin, Unatt., *Adjutant,* } *3rd Stafford Militia*.	11 Dec. 37	16 April 41	27 Aug. 52	27 Aug. 52
Miller, William, 2 Drs. *Adjutant of* } *Cavalry Depot at Maidstone*	7 July 46	20 June 50	30 Sept. 54	10 Nov. 56
Millerd, Thomas, Unattached	20 Mar. 22	27 Feb. 24	8 April 26	8 April 26
Mitchell, Thomas Peter,[136] 69 Foot.	1 June 00	5 April 01	11 April 11	3 June 13
Montgomerie, Alexander,[138] Unattached..	24 Sept. 41	23 Nov. 42	16 Nov. 55	19 Nov. 55
₽ Montgomery, Alex. Rich.,[139] 23 Foot..	16 May 05	28 May 06	17 Sept. 12	16 Dec. 19
ⓆⓂ Moore, James Stewart, 24 Dragoons	1 Aug. 11	7 April 13	15 April 19	25 Dec. 24
Moore, Thomas,[140] Royal Marines	14 Jan. 01	15 Aug. 05	21 Nov. 10	30 Nov. 57
₽ Morgan, Edward,[141] 75 Foot, *Lt.-Col.* } *Commandant R. Merioneth Militia*	never	4 Feb. 08	5 Mar. 12	22 Aug. 22
₽ Morle, John,[142] 3 West India Regt.....	18 Aug. 08	14 Sept. 09	2 Sept. 13	29 April 19
₽ Morris, Samuel,[143] 28 Foot	31 Jan. 05	2 April 06	25 Nov. 13	25 Dec. 14
Morrish, Henry George, Royal Marines	6 Dec. 13	11 June 32	13 May 41	3 Nov. 41

Captains. 476

	2D LIEUT. ETC.	LIEUT.	CAPTAIN.	WHEN PLACED ON HALF PAY.
₽ Morrison, Hans, 60 Foot............	7 May 07	15 Feb. 08	13 Feb. 27	6 Dec. 27
Morshead, Pentyre Anderson, Royal Art.	19 Mar. 39	1 Oct. 41	30 June 48	9 Oct. 48
Mottley, Thomas Martin, Royal Artillery	11 Dec. 15	15 Nov. 24	10 Jan. 37	30 Dec. 37
Mullen, John, Unatt.	9 Mar. 43	26 Mar. 46	18 Nov. 53	18 Nov. 53
Murray, Charles Robert, Unattached....	1 Aug. 22	19 May 25	8 April 26	25 Nov. 28
Murray, George, Unattached	25 June 30	12 Aug. 34	30 Aug. 39	25 Feb. 48
Murray, Henry, Royal Artillery	20 June 32	24 Oct. 34	9 Sept. 43	15 May 44
Nestor, James, 19 Foot................	16 Sept. 04	15 Nov. 05	24 Oct. 11	14 Mar. 22
Newburg, Ar. R. Camac, Unattached....	25 April 17	16 July 21	17 June 23	21 May 25
Newenham, Richard, Unattached	14 June 31	5 Feb. 36	4 Oct. 44	4 Aug. 54
Nicholas, James, Royal Marines	21 Sept. 05	6 April 09	4 June 31	30 Sept. 33
Nicholls, John, Unattached	12 Feb. 18	7 Dec. 38	14 Jan. 48	14 Jan. 48
Nicholson, Chris. Hampden, Unattached	3 Mar. 25	14 Jan. 26	5 July 31	9 April 41
₽ Nicholson, Huntley,[144] Grenadier Gds.	10 Oct. 11	5 Aug. 13	24 Mar. 33	17 Sept. 39
₽ Nicolls, Augustus,[145] Unattached	5 Oct. 09	1 Sept. 13	17 Mar. 37	17 Mar. 37
Nooth, Henry Stephen, 6 Dr. Guards....	never	14 May 12	29 Jan. 24	13 May 24
Norman, Ralph, Land Transport Corps..	....	26 Aug. 55	1 Feb. 56	1 April 57
Norman, Robert,[146] Unattached	7 Sept. 26	2 Sept. 29	25 Aug. 42	31 July 46
Norton, James Roy, Unatt., *Paymaster, Northampton Militia*	9 April 25	17 Dec. 30	29 Dec. 43	3 April 46
Oates, William Coape, Glengarry Fencibles	22 Aug. 11	7 Oct. 13	27 July 15	25 Aug. 16
O'Flanagan, John, 33 Foot	24 Jan. 45	1 Oct. 46	4 Dec. 57	23 Sept. 59
₽ ᴍᴍ Ormsby, Arthur,[118] Unattached ..	2 June 14	27 Jan. 23	15 Jan. 36	25 Aug. 37
Ormsby, Augustus Howard,[149] Unattached	29 June 24	22 Mar. 26	3 Feb. 43	9 April 47
Ouseley, William, Unattached..........	20 May 18	31 Jan. 22	9 June 25	9 Aug. 31
ᴍᴍ Packe, Geo. Hussey,[150] 21 Dragoons	24 June 13	6 Jan. 14	27 June 16	25 Mar. 17
*Page, Robert, 9 Foot	never	never	25 Dec. 13	25 Sept. 14
ᴍᴍ Pakenham, William, Royal Artillery	30 Aug. 04	10 April 05	20 Dec. 14	1 July 22
₽ Palmer, Edward Despard,[151] 67 Foot..	1 Feb. 00	22 May 00	7 Sept. 00	13 Nov. 17
₽ Pardey, John Quin,[152] 87 Foot	18 July 11	17 Dec. 12	31 Dec. 28	28 June 44
Parkin, John Bawden, Royal Artillery ..	27 June 48	1 Nov. 48	1 April 55	6 July 57
Paterson, Edward James, Royal Artillery	18 June 42	22 Aug. 43	3 Nov. 49	13 Sept. 54
₽ Pemberton, G. Keating,[153] Royal Artil.	5 Mar. 10	17 Dec. 13	3 Oct. 31	8 July 34
Pennyman, James White, Sub-Insp. of Mil.	1 July 12	21 July 13	8 April 20	1 Jan. 33
Penruddocke, Thomas, Scots Fus. Gds. ..	15 Nov. 97	never	25 Nov. 09	25 Dec. 02
Peploe, Daniel Peploe, Unattached	5 Oct. 15	11 July 22	12 Dec. 26	18 Dec. 28
Petley, Robert, Unatt., *Professor of Military Surveying, R. Military College*	24 Dec. 29	12 Aug. 34	18 Jan. 59	18 Jan. 59
Phelips, Richard, Royal Artillery	20 Dec. 43	30 Nov. 45	16 Feb. 52	17 June 54
Phillips, Fred. Hervey Bathurst, R. Art.	1 May 46	14 Oct. 46	17 Feb. 54	21 Sept. 54
Pieters, Charles,[154] Unattached	4 Aug. 14	9 Sept. 19	12 May 54	12 May 54
Pigott, Robert, 1 Garrison Battalion	16 June 04	13 Nov. 04	9 July 07	25 June 16
Pilgrim, John Bunce, Unattached	4 Dec. 32	16 Sept. 37	14 June 42	14 June 50
Pitts, Francis, Unattached	25 Nov. 21	17 Feb. 25	15 April 36	15 April 36
Pode, William,[155] 33 Foot	8 June 09	12 Jan. 11	17 May 21	25 Oct. 21
Pollock, William Paul, Royal Artillery ..	18 Dec. 40	20 Dec. 41	30 June 48	19 May 49
Pope, James, 6 Foot..................	31 Mar. 48	11 Nov. 52	11 Jan. 59	20 Dec. 59
₽ Porteous, Alexander,[157] 60 Foot	17 July 06	23 July 07	20 April 15	25 July 15
₽ Potter, Thomas,[158] Portuguese Service	13 Nov. 00	2 Mar. 09	25 Oct. 14	25 Dec. 16
Powell, Peter, 2 West India Regt.	26 Oct. 04	2 Mar. 06	4 Feb. 13	26 Feb. 30
₽ Price, David,[159] 36 Foot	25 Dec. 05	23 April 07	8 Oct. 12	25 Dec. 14
₽ Price, Rice,[160] 57 Foot	Mar. 08	21 July 08	27 April 20	25 Dec. 21
* Prickett, William, Royal Waggon Train	never	never	25 Dec. 13	25 June 16
₽ Quentin, Geo. Edward, Portuguese Ser.	28 July 08	17 May 09	25 Dec. 14	25 Dec. 16
Ralph, Joseph, Unattached............	1 Jan. 26	11 June 30	16 Dec. 45	16 Dec. 45
Ramsay, Francis, Royal Artillery	20 Dec. 32	12 June 35	15 April 44	1 May 48
₽ ᴍᴍ Randall, George,[161] Unattached ..	22 Feb. 11	15 April 11	18 June 15	13 Oct. 25
Randolph, Francis, Royal Engineers....	11 Sept. 15	13 April 21	10 Jan. 37	15 Oct. 39
Read, Constantine, Royal Staff Corps....	7 Nov. 16	7 April 25	24 Aug. 32	24 Aug. 32
Reeves, Thomas, 24 Foot	7 Sept. 04	9 Oct. 05	25 June 07	8 April 19
Rice, Charles Augustus, Royal Engineers	2 May 47	26 Feb. 49	1 Aug. 45	15 Dec. 58
Rich, John Sampson,[152] Royal Artillery..	1 Mar. 08	30 April 09	9 Dec. 28	6 Nov. 30
Rich, Robert James Evelyn, 66 Foot	12 Aug. 24	29 June 26	1 Feb. 31	14 Feb. 31
Richards, George, Royal Marines	25 Jan. 08	18 Oct. 09	19 April 12	18 Mar. 13
Richardson, Mervyn, Unattached	19 July 15	2 May 24	4 Feb. 26	4 Feb. 26
₽ Richardson, Thomas,[163] 7 Dragoons....	3 Sept. 07	10 Mar. 08	22 May 16	4 Sept. 17
*Rickards, William, 64 Foot	never	never	25 Dec. 13	25 Aug. 14
*Riddlesden, Richard, 4 Foot	never	never	25 Dec. 13	25 Sept. 14
*Ridgway, Samuel, 85 Foot............	never	never	25 Dec. 13	1814
Roberts, Julius, Royal Marines	16 Mar. 41	16 Mar. 44	15 Aug. 53	24 Sept. 55
Robertson, Alexander, Unattached	16 Nov. 09	28 Nov. 10	6 Mar. 27	6 Mar. 27

Captains.

	CORNET, ETC.	LIEUT.	CAPTAIN.	WHEN PLACED ON HALF PAY.
Robertson, Frederick,[164] Royal Artillery..	22 Dec. 03	20 July 04	23 July 13	10 Oct. 21
*Robertson, John, 14 Foot	never	never	25 Dec. 13	25 Sept. 14
Rollo, Robert A.,[165] Royal Artillery	17 Aug. 03	12 Sept. 03	29 Dec. 10	12 April 20
Rose, Hugh, Unattached	31 Dec. 12	25 May 19	28 June 50	28 June 50
Rose, William, 97 Foot................	8 Feb. 04	3 Sept. 94	15 Nov. 94	1 Mar. 98
Ross, Gillian Maclaine, Unattached	8 May 35	9 Aug. 39	4 Sept. 48	15 Feb. 56
Rous, *Hon.* Wm. Rufus, Portuguese Serv.	never	17 Dec. 12	18 Nov. 18	24 April 23
𝔓 Rudkin, Mark,[166] 47 Foot	12 July 05	29 Jan. 07	21 Jan. 15	15 May 28
Runnacles, Anthony, Royal Artillery	11 Dec. 15	22 Sept. 23	10 Jan. 37	27 Mar. 37
St. John, Fred. Arthur,[173] Unattached ..	28 July 44	5 Mar. 47	23 Mar. 55	28 Jan. 59
Savage, Henry, Royal Marines	2 Dec. 11	22 July 30	26 Aug. 40	3 May 44
Savile, Henry Bourchier Osborne, Rl. Art.	14 Dec. 37	21 April 40	9 Nov. 46	20 May 53
Sayer, Frederic,[167] 23 Foot, *Police Magistrate for Gibraltar* .... }	5 Nov. 50	14 Sept. 52	29 Dec. 54	27 Mar. 57
Scott, Charles,[168] Royal Marines........	13 Feb. 06	16 Jan. 12	19 Mar. 34	11 April 36
Sealy, Francis, 97 Foot................	19 Nov. 30	21 Dec. 32	5 Oct. 38	16 July 41
Senhouse, William Wood, 88 Foot	7 April 37	20 July 39	14 Oct. 51	28 Dec. 55
𝔓 Seward, Elliot,[169] Royal Artillery	29 Sept. 04	3 July 05	10 May 15	16 Jan. 18
Seymour, Edward Adolphus, R. Artillery	27 June 48	1 Nov. 48	1 April 55	27 Aug. 56
Sheppard, Walter Cope, Unattached	8 May 23	10 Nov. 25	9 April 29	25 June 31
Sherwen, Peter, Unattached............	21 June 39	22 July 44	10 Aug. 55	10 Aug. 55
Shoveller, William King, Royal Marines, *Chief Officer of Coast Guard* ...... }	2 Oct. 20	10 July 37	6 May 47	14 July 48
𝔓 Sisson, Joseph,[170] Unattached	18 Sept. 06	26 Aug. 08	7 April 25	14 Sept. 26
Slater, Henry Francis, Royal Artillery ..	1 May 15	6 Nov. 20	4 June 36	19 Aug. 39
Small, Robert, Unattached	4 Oct. 11	29 Sept. 14	29 Oct. 25	29 Oct. 25
Smith, William,[171] Unattached..........	26 July 38	13 June 40	14 April 46	1 Aug. 48
Smith, William, Land Transport Corps..	....	15 Sept. 55	1 Feb. 56	1 April 57
Spratt, Henry,[171]+ Royal Marines	27 Sept. 42	27 July 47	1 Mar. 52	22 Nov. 59
Spurin, John,[172] Royal Marines	7 Feb. 97	19 Nov. 01	22 July 09	15 Sept. 26
𝔓 𝔐 Stewart, Duncan,[174] Unattached ..	13 June 05	1 Jan. 07	3 Aug. 15	25 Dec. 26
Stewart, Mervyn, Royal Artillery	1 May 46	9 Nov. 46	17 Feb. 54	13 April 55
𝔓 *Still, Nathaniel Tyron,[175] 5 Foot	....	....	25 Dec. 13	25 Sept. 14
Stockenstrom, *Sir* And.*Bt*.R.Corsican Ran.	12 Sept. 11	7 June 14	25 May 20	20 July 20
Strange, Charles, Unattached	6 May 19	5 Dec. 23	21 Nov. 28	21 Nov. 28
Straubenzee, Charles, 6 West India Regt.	28 Oct. 95	5 Sept. 96	14 Dec. 04	15 Oct. 07
Stuart, *Hon.* Arch. Geo., 6 West I. Regt.	30 April 29	30 Aug. 31	25 May 39	11 July 45
Stuart, *Hon.* John, Unattached	12 July 15	14 Nov. 16	27 Aug. 25	27 Aug. 25
Studdert, George, Unattached	3 June 36	19 July 38	3 Aug. 49	30 Sept. 59
Sullivan, John,[176] Unattached	9 July 37	31 Dec. 39	28 Oct. 53	28 Oct. 53
Tallan, Lawrence,[177] Unattached	1 Nov. 21	27 Aug. 24	22 Aug. 37	8 Aug. 45
Taylor, Fra. Manby Shawe, Unatt......	never	6 May 13	5 Oct. 20	13 April 26
Taylor, Fra. Richard, 44 F., *Professor of Military Surveying, R. Mil. Coll.* }	28 May 42	16 May 45	21 May 50	25 May 59
Taylor, James, Gold Coast Artillery Corps	11 Aug. 54	11 May 55	23 Oct. 57	19 July 59
𝔓 Taylor, John,[178] Unattached	30 July 12	14 July 14	1 Oct. 50	1 Oct. 50
Taylor, Wm. Ryves Nash, Royal Artillery	18 June 42	1 Aug. 43	10 July 49	5 Dec. 50
Telfer, James Drummond, Royal Artillery	11 Jan. 43	7 Mar. 44	27 May 50	24 Aug. 54
𝔓 * Terry, John,[179] 74 Foot	never	never	25 Dec. 13	25 Sept. 14
* Terry, Stephen, 8 Foot	never	never	5 Dec. 99	3 Sept. 01
Thompson, Edward, Royal Staff Corps ..	9 Nov. 07	1 Mar. 10	13 June 16	10 Aug. 19
𝔓 Thompson, James,[160] 80 Foot	19 June 06	15 Oct. 07	23 May 16	25 Jan. 17
𝔓 Tittle, John Moore,[181] Unattached	7 July 08	1 Nov. 10	28 June 50	28 June 50
Tobin, John, Unatt. *Adj. N. Glouces. Mil.*	28 Dec. 25	16 Aug. 27	30 Oct. 40	28 Aug. 46
Torriano, C. Strangways,[182] Royal Artillery	25 April 06	22 Oct. 06	22 Dec. 23	15 April 29
Troyer, Anthony, 4 Ceylon Regt.	1 Mar. 03	2 Dec. 04	15 July 13	15 June 15
𝔓 Tweedie, Michael,[183] Royal Artillery ..	1 May 09	17 June 12	22 July 30	17 Dec. 33
Vansittart, Francis, Royal Artillery	20 Dec. 43	7 Oct. 45	17 Jan. 52	21 Feb. 57
Varlo, George, Royal Marines	18 June 03	24 April 05	15 July 03	23 Aug. 05
Varlo, Henry,[184] Royal Marines	7 April 37	28 Jan. 41	19 Sept. 49	13 Mar. 55
𝔓 Vaughan, Herbert Henry,[185] Unatt. ..	29 June 09	16 Jan. 12	4 Sept. 23	25 Jan. 31
Vavasour, Mervin, R. Engineers........	19 Mar. 39	23 Feb. 42	11 July 49	22 April 53
Veitch, Thomas George, Unattached	17 Aug. 26	10 July 28	26 June 35	1 July 42
𝔓 Ventry, T. T. Arcm. *Lord*, 43 Foot....	never	6 Feb. 07	8 Aug. 11	11 Dec. 17
Verner, John Donovan, Unatt.	24 Sept. 41	23 Aug. 44	6 July 52	10 Aug. 55
Vernon, Bowater Henry, Unattached	17 Oct. 16	8 July 24	28 Jan. 26	28 Jan. 26
Vernon, Leicester Viney Samwell, R. Eng	1 Aug. 16	29 July 25	15 Oct. 39	4 Mar. 40
𝔓 Vetch, James,[166] R. Eng., *Engineer to Hydrographic Dept. of Admiralty* }	1 July 07	1 Mar. 08	21 July 13	11 Mar. 24
Vokes, Thomas, Land Transport Corps ..	....	3 Feb. 55	7 Sept. 55	1 April 57
Wake, Richard William, R. African Corps	10 April 25	22 April 26	16 July 30	25 May 32

Captains. 478

	2D LIEUT. ETC.	LIEUT.	CAPTAIN.	WHEN PLACED ON HALF PAY.
₽ Walker, William, 24 Foot	6 July 09	13 June 11	22 Mar. 15	15 June 13
Walsh, John, Royal Artillery	23 Nov. 04	1 Dec. 05	20 June 15	24 Feb. 25
Ward, Henderson,[187] Royal Marines	21 Aug. 43	29 Oct. 47	10 July 55	10 Dec. 58
Ward, William, R. West India Rangers, Adj. Cornwall and Devon Miners..	18 July 26	4 Dec. 32	9 May 43	29 Dec. 46
Warde, John Henry Turner, Unatt., Riding Master, R. Military Coll...	21 June 33	22 May 35	16 Dec. 53	16 Dec. 53
*Warner, Richard, 5 Foot	never	never	25 Dec. 13	25 Sept. 14
₽ Watkins, William Nowell,[168] 48 Foot..	16 June 03	2 June 04	8 Mar. 10	25 Oct. 21
Watson, Andrew Vincent, Unatt. Capt. Limerick Artillery Militia	21 Dec. 32	18 May 33	20 Oct. 43	7 April 54
Webb, Theodosius, R. Eng.	18 June 35	18 Aug. 37	1 April 46	14 Mar. 51
Welch, Stephen J. W. F., Cape Regt.	27 Aug. 25	19 Sept. 26	6 Sept. 27	6 Sept. 27
₽ Wellings, George,[169] Unattached	14 Feb. 11	14 Nov. 11	23 Mar. 15	25 June 25
₤₤ Wells, Fortescue,[190] Royal Artillery..	4 Oct. 06	1 Feb. 08	29 July 25	29 July 25
Wemyss, James, Unattached, Major, Fife Artillery Militia	10 April 17	31 Jan. 21	22 Oct. 25	22 Oct. 25
Wetherall, Charles,[191] Unattached	15 Aug. 13	8 Aug. 16	29 June 24	27 June 34
Whalley, George Briscoe, Unattached	12 Dec. 26	12 Jan. 30	9 July 35	2 April 41
₽ Whitley, James,[194] 9 Foot	22 Aug. 05	17 Dec. 06	17 June 13	25 Feb. 16
Willan, Wm. Moffat Douglas, R. Art., Adj. Pembroke Artillery Militia	18 June 35	28 Nov. 37	1 April 46	9 July 50
Williams, Hugh, Royal Engineers	17 Dec. 46	19 Aug. 47	24 May 55	4 Jan. 59
₽ Williams, James,[194] 11 Foot	9 April 07	10 Aug. 08	14 Sept. 13	25 Feb. 16
Williamson, John, Unattached	30 Dec. 26	16 July 30	30 Oct. 40	15 Aug. 48
Wills, Thomas Lake,[195] Royal Marines	12 Feb. 07	3 Dec. 01	9 Aug. 09	27 Nov. 15
Wilson, Edward, 57 Foot	5 June 06	9 Feb. 08	28 June 10	25 Feb. 16
Wilson, James, Coldstream Gds.	19 May 14	20 Dec. 24	7 April 37	5 May 37
Wilson, Joseph Fraser, Unattached	5 April 10	10 June 11	13 Feb. 27	13 Feb. 27
*Winnington, Hen. Jeffreys, 39 Foot	never	never	25 Dec. 13	25 Sept. 14
Wise, William, 72 Foot	21 Feb. 27	17 May 31	23 Nov. 41	13 July 47
Wood, Fred. Aug. Percy, Royal Marines	27 Dec. 42	27 July 47	13 Mar. 55	22 Sept. 59
Wood, Henry,[196] 3 Dragoons	10 July 37	16 Nov. 41	10 Jan. 51	1 Dec. 54
₽ Wood, James,[197] Royal Marines	25 April 12	14 May 31	13 Nov. 40	4 Aug. 43
Woodward, John, Unattached	5 Nov. 29	10 May 33	12 June 40	6 June 51
Workman, Thomas, Unattached	3 Jan. 11	2 April 12	3 Aug. 30	8 Mar. 31
Wright, George, Royal Marines	11 July 03	25 Oct. 05	31 July 26	30 Sept. 33
Wulff, Kenelm Chandler, Royal Artillery	29 Oct. 08	12 July 11	6 Nov. 27	6 Nov. 27
Wyatt, Samuel, Royal Artillery	28 Feb. 07	1 Feb. 08	1 Mar. 27	19 April 36
Wyndham, Alex. Wadham, Unattached..	16 Mar. 20	25 Nov. 24	12 Dec. 26	26 July 27
Wynne, John, Royal Artillery	16 Dec. 20	1 Aug. 27	13 Aug. 39	13 Sept. 39
Wynter, Robert, Royal Artillery	26 July 31	22 Jan. 33	31 Dec. 42	1 May 43
Yates, John, Unatt. (Q.M. 6 July 52) Adjutant, Cavalry Depot, Canterbury	22 Sept. 54	20 Dec. 55	18 Oct. 59	18 Oct. 59
Young, Henry, Unattached	30 June 25	1 Aug. 26	3 Nov. 37	30 Dec. 45

War Services of the Captains.

1 Captain Acton served with the 77th Regt. the Eastern campaign of 1854, and up to 9th Feb. 1855, including the battles of Alma and Inkerman and siege of Sebastopol (Medal and three Clasps, and 5th Class of the Medjidie).

1† Captain Addy served with the 5th Dr. Gds. during the Eastern campaign of 1854-55, including the battles of Balaklava, Inkerman, and Tchernaya, and siege of Sebastopol (Medal and three Clasps).

2 Captain Alpe served in the Peninsula with the 4th Dragoons, and has received the War Medal with five Clasps for Talavera, Albuhera, Salamanca, Vittoria, and Toulouse.

3 Captain Anton has the War Medal with two Clasps for Martinique and Guadaloupe.

4 Captain John Armstrong (h.p. 88 F.) has received the War Medal with five Clasps for Busaco, Fuentes d'Onor, Ciudad Rodrigo, Badajoz, and Salamanca.

4† Captain Atkinson served at the siege of Sebastopol in 1854-55 (Medal and Clasp).

5 Captain Robert Baker has received the War Medal with one Clasp for Java.

6 Captain Bamford served with the 63rd Regt. the Eastern campaign up to Jany. 1855, including the battles of Alma, Balaklava, and Inkerman, and siege of Sebastopol (Medal and Clasps).

7 Captain Barwell has the War Medal with two Clasps for Vittoria and Toulouse.

8 Captain Basset served the Eastern campaign with the 1st Dragoons, including the battle of Balaklava and siege of Sebastopol (Medal and Clasp).

9 Captain Baynes served in the Peninsula, from Sept. 1812 to the end of the war in 1814, including the battles of the Pyrenees (30th July), Nivelle and Toulouse, for which he has received the War Medal with three Clasps. Served also the campaign of 1815, and was present at the battles of Quatre Bras and Waterloo.

War Services of the Captains.

9† Captain Bell served at the capture of the Isle of France in 1810. Also at the taking of the following Forts in the Concan, East Indies, viz., Seedghur, Bugwuntghur, Ryghur, in 1818; Newtee and Raree, in 1819; at the first and last places led the storming parties, as also at the taking of a stockade commanding a ford near Bugwuntghur.

10 Captain Blacker served with the 18th Royal Irish at the siege and fall of Sebastopol from 30th Dec. 1854 (Medal and Clasp).

11 Captain Beresford served with the 88th Regt. the Eastern campaign of 1854-55, including the battles of Alma and Inkerman, siege of Sebastopol, attack on the Quarries, and attack on the Redan on the 18th June and 8th Sept.—severely wounded (Medal and Clasps, and Knight of the Legion of Honor).

12 Captain Berry served nearly five years with the army in Sicily, and was present at the taking of the islands of Ischia and Procida. Served on board the *Weazle* brig, cutting out gunboats on the coast of Calabria in 1811.

13 Captain Birch served at the defence of Cadiz.

14 Captain Bishop has the War Medal with three Clasps for Vittoria, Pyrenees, and Nivelle.

15 Captain Boothby served with the 95th Regt. in the Eastern campaign of 1854, and was severely wounded at the battle of Alma—foot amputated (Medal and Clasp, and Sardinian Medal).

16 Captain Brander served the campaign of 1815 with the 1st Dragoon Guards, and was present at the battle of Waterloo.

17 Captain Brenan served throughout the operations in Scinde (Medal), including the destruction of Imaumgur and the battles of Mecanee and Hyderabad (severely wounded). Was afterwards present at Panulla, Pownghur, Munnahur, and Munsuntosh.

18 Captain Breton served with the 53rd Regiment in the Sutlej campaign of 1845-46, including the affair of Buddiwal, and actions of Aliwal and Sobraon—wounded (Medal and Clasps).

19 Captain Robert Onslow Bridge served with the expeditionary force in China (Medal), including the attack on Chuenpe and operations before Canton in 1841.

20 Captain Brine served with the 32d Regiment in the second siege operations before Mooltan (Medal), including the storm and capture of the city on the 2d Jan. 1849: he was severely wounded on the 16th Jan.

21 Captain Broughton served in the Peninsula with the 9th Regt., and was present at the battles of Vimiera, Fuentes d'Onor, and Salamanca, for which he has the War Medal with three Clasps.

22 Captain Thomas Brown served with the 79th at the siege of Copenhagen, in 1807; and subsequently in the Peninsula from Jan. 1810 to the end of that war in 1814, including the defence of Cadiz, battle of Busaco (slightly wounded), lines of Torres Vedras, pursuit of Massena, action of Foz d'Arouce, battles of Fuentes d'Onor and Salamanca, siege of Burgos, battles of the Pyrenees, Nivelle, Nive, and Toulouse. Served also the campaign of 1815, and was severely wounded at Quatre Bras. He has received the War Medal with seven Clasps.

23 Captain Valentine Browne served with the 13th Regt. in the West Indies, and was present at the action of L'Ecole; also at the siege of Plattsburg in America.

24 Captain Burges served in the Peninsula, France, and Flanders, and was severely wounded at Waterloo. He has received the War Medal with two Clasps for Nivelle and Nive.

25 Captain Burnett has received the War Medal with one Clasp for Guadaloupe.

26 Captain J. C. Burton served on the eastern coast of Spain from March 1813 to the end of that war in 1814.

26† Captain Cahill served throughout the whole of the operations in China (Medal), commencing with the first taking of Chusan, and terminating with the demonstration before Nankin, including the storm and capture of the heights above Canton (wounded), attack and capture of Amoy, second capture of Chusan, attack and capture of the heights of Chinhae, occupation of Ningpo, repulse of the night-attack on Ningpo, attack and capture of Chapoo, Woosung, Shanghae, and Chin Kiang Foo. Served the Eastern campaign of 1854, was present at the battle of the Alma (carried the regimental colour) and siege of Sebastopol; received the thanks of Sir De Lacy Evans in Orders for the able assistance rendered to Major Fordyce, 47th Regiment, in the trenches, on the 18th of Oct., when in charge of a working party; and was severely wounded at the repulse of the sortie on the 26th of October (Medal and Clasp).

27 Captain John Campbell (h. p. 26 F.) served at New Orleans with the 5th West India regt.

28 Captain William Campbell served in the Peninsula with the 30th from August 1811 to June 1813, including the siege of Ciudad Rodrigo, siege and storming of Badajoz, battle of Salamanca, capture of Madrid and the Retiro, siege of Burgos, and affair on retreat at Villa Muriel. He has received the War Medal with three Clasps.

29 Captain Carnegie served in Portugal from Nov. 1809 to 1811, and has received the War Medal with one Clasp for Fuentes d'Onor.

30 Captain Carr served in the North Sea, on the coast of France, and North and South America from 1812 to 1815.

31 Captain Casey served with the R. M. Battalion attached to the Light Division of the army in the trenches before Sebastopol in 1854-55, and with the R. M. Brigade until its fall; was also at the surrender of Kinbourn (Medal and Clasp).

32 Captain Caulfield served in the Mediterranean and the Peninsula with the 44th from April 1806 to the end of that war in 1814, including the captures of Santa Maura, and the Islands of Ischia and Procida; also the siege of Tarragona. Served also in the American war, including the actions of Bladensburg, Baltimore, and New Orleans, at which last he was slightly wounded.

33 Captain Chancellor has received the War Medal and one Clasp for Talavera.

34 Captain Chapman served with the expedition to Walcheren, and was present at the siege of Flushing.

34† Captain Cheese served with the 39th Regt. in the operations against Kurnool in 1839; and on 29th Dec. 1843, in the action of Maharajpore—wounded (Medal). Served in 1855 at the siege and fall of Sebastopol (Medal and Clasp).

35 Captain Colvile embarked in 1810 with the Guards for Cadiz, then besieged, and was present at the battle of Barrosa. He served afterwards with the Peninsular army as Aide-de-Camp to Lord Lynedoch, and was present at the siege of Ciudad Rodrigo, the action of El Bodon, battle of Vittoria, the two sieges of San Sebastian, and passage of the Bidassoa; he then proceeded to Holland, and was present at the affair of Merxem, and the attack on Bergen-op-Zoom. He has received the War Medal with four Clasps.

36 Captain Cookes served in the 3d Light Dragoons during the Sutlej campaign of 1845-6, and was present in the battles of Moodkee, Ferozeshah, and Sobraon (Medal and two Clasps).

37 Captain Costley served in the Peninsula with the 45th, and was present at the battles of Busaco, Fuentes d'Onor, Salamanca, Vittoria, and the Pyrenees, and at the sieges of Ciudad Rodrigo and Badajoz: he has received the War Medal with seven Clasps.

38 Captain Cotton served at the capture of the islands of Ischia and Procida, in 1809; also at the siege of Genoa, in 1814.

39 Captain Courtenay served in the Peninsula from 1811 until severely wounded in the Pyrenees in 1813. He has received the War Medal with one Clasp for the battle of Vittoria.

40 Captain Charles Cox has received the War Medal with one Clasp for Talavera.

40† Captain Craig served as a Lieutenant in the 62nd Regt. in the Sutlej campaign in 1845, and was present at the battle of Ferozeshah (Medal), where he was severely wounded by a cannon ball, causing amputation of the right arm.

41 Captain Cresswell served with the 89th Regt. at the siege of Sebastopol from 15th Dec. 1854 to 15th Feb. 1855 (Medal and Clasp).

42 Captain Crookshank, when proceeding to Van Diemen's Land in charge of a convict guard, received several severe wounds by the accidental discharge of a pistol, in an attempt made by the prisoners to surprise the guard.

43 Captain Curtis served at Walcheren in 1809, and was present at the attack of Ter Vere and siege of Flushing.

44 Captain Davern served with the 88th at the attack on Buenos Ayres, 5th July 1807. At the defence of Cadiz in 1800 and 10; subsequent campaigns in the Peninsula, including the pursuit of the French from the Lines of Torres Vedras, action at Sabugal, battle of Fuentes d'Onor, second siege of Badajoz, action at El Bodon, siege and capture of Ciudad Rodrigo, third siege and capture of Badajoz (wounded at the assault), battles of Salamanca, Vittoria, Pampeluna, and the Pyrenees; passage of the Bidassoa, battles of Nivelle, Nive, and Orthes (wounded); actions at Vic Bigorre, Tarbes, and Hasparen, battle of Toulouse, and various other minor affairs. Served afterwards in the American war and was present in the action in Plattsburg. He has received the War Medal with ten Clasps.

46 Captain Alfred Davis was present with a squadron of the 22nd Light Dragoons at the battle of Maheidpore, 21st Dec. 1817; and at the taking of Talneir in 1818.

47 Captain Joseph Douglas served as 2nd Lieut. R. Marines on board H. M. S. *Hindostan* in the North Sea, off Texel, in 1804, watching the movements of the Dutch Fleet. On 4th June 1805 was employed in the boats of the *Loire* cutting out the boats of the *Confiance*, 490 tons, off Muros Bay, coast of Spain, and storming two batteries under Sir James Yeo (Medal). On 24th Nov. 1805 on board the *Loire* during the engagement with and capture, off Rochfort, of the French 44 gun frigate *Libre*. In 1808 he was gazetted to an Ensigncy in the 32nd Foot, and the following year served on the Walcheren expedition, siege of Flushing, and ascent of the Scheldt. In Dec. 1810 promoted to Lieut. in the 45th, with which Regiment he served the Peninsular campaigns of 1813 and 14, and was present at the battles of Nivelle, Nive, Orthes, and Toulouse, at which last he was severely wounded in the right arm by a musket ball, when carrying the King's color: he has received the War Medal with four Clasps.

48 Captain John Dowman served with the 40th Regt. throughout the operations in Affghanistan, in 1841-42 (Medal). Served as Aide-de-camp to Major General Dennis in the battle of Maharajpore on the 29th Dec. 1843 (Medal, and mentioned in despatch).

49 Captain Dresing was present at the storming of Kawiti's Pah at Ruapekapeka, New Zealand, on 11th Jan. 1846, after which he proceeded to the valley of the Hutt, and served there during different operations.

50 Captain Duncan served with the expedition to Bremen in Germany in 1805. Also in the American war, including the capture of Moose Island.

51 Captain Eaton served in the Peninsula, France, and Flanders with the Rifle Brigade, and has received the War Medal with seven Clasps for Barrosa, Vittoria, Pyrenees, St. Sebastian, Nivelle, Orthes, and Toulouse.

52 Captain Edwardes served in the Peninsula from Jan. 1813 to June 1814, and was present at the battle of Vittoria, siege of San Sebastian, passage of the Bidassoa and of the Adour, and investment of Bayonne: has the War Medal with four Clasps for Vittoria, San Sebastian, Nivelle, and Nive. He served also the campaign of 1815, including the battle of Waterloo.

53 Captain William Elliott served with the 2nd Life Guards in the Peninsula, France, and Flanders, and was present at the battle of Vittoria, at Pampeluna, the Pyrenees, Toulouse, Waterloo, and capture of Paris: has the War Medal with two Clasps for Vittoria and Toulouse.

54 Captain Hercules Ellis served in the Peninsula with the 88th, from March 1809 to the end of that war in 1814, including the first siege of Badajoz, and battles of Busaco, Fuentes d'Onor, Vittoria, and the Pyrenees.

War Services of the Captains.

55 Captain Emerson served with the 35th at the taking of Santa Maura, storming of the enemy's outposts, and at the taking of the Ionian Islands.

56 Captain Enderby served with the 22nd Light Dragoons at Belgaum and Sholapore, in 1818; and with the 16th Lancers at Bhurtpore in 1825-6. In addition to the above he served three years in the royal navy as midshipman, and was on board H.M.S. *Defence* at the battle of Trafalgar.

57 Captain Fairtlough served with the 55th on the China expedition (Medal), and was present at Amoy, Chusan, Chinhae (including the night attack), Chapoo, Woosung, Shanghae, and Chin Kiang Foo.

58 Captain Farmar served on the China expedition, and was present at the battle of Chuenpee, attack of the Anunghoy batteries, advance on Canton, capture of the heights of Canton, capture of Colongso, second capture of Chusan, assault and capture of the citadel and city of Chinhae, entry into Ningpo (Medal). Served with the Baltic expeditions in 1854 and 1855 (Medal).

60 Captain T. B. V. FitzGerald was present at the bombardment of Odessa 22nd April 1854. Served during the siege of Sebastopol in 1854-55, and was several times in action with the outer defences (Medal and Clasp); commanded a Company in the R. battalion at the occupation of Kertch, and advance on Yeni Kalé, and was encamped there until the embarkation of the English army in June 1855.

61 Captain Charles Ford served at the siege of Flushing, in 1809; and at New Orleans, in 1814.

62 Captain William Forde (Unattached) served with the 15th at the capture of Guadaloupe in 1810, for which he has received the War Medal with one Clasp.

63 Captain Thomas Fraser (83rd Foot) was present at the operations before Ter Vere and Flushing in 1809. He served also in the Peninsula from Sept. 1813 until the end of that war, and afterwards at Genoa.

64 Captain Thomas Fraser (Royal Marines) was presented with a piece of plate by the Merchants on the occasion of his being landed for the protection of British property at Lima, during the revolution in Dec. 1835, when the place was in possession of the rebels.

65 Captain Furnace served in the Peninsula with the 61st, and was present at the battles of Talavera, Busaco, Salamanca, Pyrenees, Nivelle, Nive, Orthes, and Toulouse, for which he has received the War Medal with eight Clasps.

66 Captain Fyfe served with the 92d with the expedition under Sir John Moore to Sweden in 1808, and afterwards in Portugal and Spain, including the battle of Corunna. He next served on the Walcheren expedition, after which he joined the army under the Duke of Wellington in the lines of Torres Vedras, and was present at the battle of Fuentes d'Onor, at Arroyo de Molino, Almarez, Alba de Tormes, Vittoria, Maya Pass (twice wounded), and Pyrenees on 25th, 30th, and 31st July, at the Nivelle, the Nive, Garris, Ariverette, Orthes, and Aire (severely wounded), besides various minor affairs and skirmishes. He has received the War Medal with seven Clasps.

67 Captain Gascoyne served in the Peninsula with the 83rd from 1809 to 1813, and was severely wounded in the leg at the battle of Salamanca. Served also in Ceylon as Deputy-Assistant-Adjutant-General during the Kandian rebellion in 1818. He has received the War Medal with two Clasps for Busaco and Salamanca.

68 Captain Gee served with the 39th Regt. in the Peninsula from 1811 to 1814, and was present at Vittoria, Stewart's Rock, near Maya; Pyrenees, Pampeluna, Nivelle, Nive, Bayonne, Garris, Orthes, and Toulouse, and has received the War Medal with six Clasps. He was also present in the battle of Maharajpore, 29 Dec. 1843 (Medal).

69 Captain Gibbons served in the rebellion in Ireland, and was at the taking of the French near Ballinamuck, 8th Sept. 1798. Served also in the Peninsula from Sept. 1811 to the end of that war in 1814, including the covering of the sieges of Ciudad Rodrigo and Badajoz, forcing the enemy out of Llerena on the night of the 25th March 1812, actions near Usagre (wounded in the right hand) and Llerena, affair with the enemy's cavalry 21st June, battle of Salamanca, and capture of the French rear-guard on the following day; captures of Madrid and Valladolid, investment and siege of Burgos, retreat from thence, blockade of Pampeluna, battles of the Pyrenees, 28th, 29th, and 30th July; Pass of Maya, battles of the Nivelle and Nive, blockade of Bayonne, from 11th Dec. 1813 to 22nd Feb. 1814; battle of Orthes, actions of Vic Bigorre and Tarbes. He has received the War Medal with five Clasps. Since the Peace of 1815 he served eight years in the Mediterranean and was an eye-witness of the war on the Morea between the Greeks and Turks. He also served nine years in India.

70 Captain F. Y. Gilbert served in the Peninsula from Dec. 1812 to the end of that war in 1814, and has received the War Medal with four clasps for Vittoria, Pyrenees, Nivelle, and Nive.

71 Captain Ginger was present with the 81st at the battle of Maida, for which he has received the War Medal with one Clasp.

72 Captain Hartman was nominated to the 4th Class of the Medjidie for service with the Turkish Contingent.

73 Captain Goode served in the American war, including the operations in the Chesapeake, battles of Bladensburg and capture of Washington and Alexandria, action near Baltimore, and destruction of the American flotilla. Served also at the attack and capture of Guadaloupe, in 1815.

74 Captain Gould served with the 63rd Regt. in the Eastern campaign of 1854, including the battle of Alma (Medal and Clasp).

75 Captain Greentree served on the Persian expedition; left foot carried away by a round shot, causing loss of leg in the action at Khooshab, 8th Feb. 1857.

76 Captain Greenwood served with the 31st Regt. throughout the campaign of 1842 in Affghanistan under Major-General Pollock, and was present in the actions of Mazeena, Tezeen, and Jugdulluck, the occupation of Cabool, and the different engagements leading to it (Medal).

77 Captain Gregor served with the 23rd at the capture of Martinique in 1809, and subsequently in the Peninsula, including the battles of Albuhera (severely wounded), Vittoria, and the Pyrenees: he has received the War Medal with four Clasps.

79 Captain Gwynne served in the Peninsula with the 62nd, and has received the War Medal with two Clasps for Nivelle and Nive.

81 Captain Hugh Harrison served in the Peninsula with the 32nd, and has received the War Medal with one Clasp for Salamanca. He served also the campaign of 1815, and was severely wounded at Waterloo.

82 Captain John Harrison (Unatt.) served with the 45th in the Burmese war in 1825 (Medal).

83 Captain John Harrison (h. p. 82nd Foot) served in the Peninsula with the 18th Hussars from Jan. 1813 to the end of that war, and was present at the battles of Vittoria, in the Pyrenees, Nivelle, Nive, Orthes, and Toulouse, as also in the minor actions of the Esla, at Morales de Toro, near Hillette, and at the bridge of Croix d'Orade (wounded in the hand). He has received the War Medal with five Clasps.

85 Captain Hart served with the 78th at the capture of Java in 1811, for which he has received the War Medal with one Clasp.

86 Captain Hawkey served the Syrian campaign of 1840 (Medal and Clasp, and Turkish Medal).

87 Captain William Hay served in the Peninsula with the 16th Light Dragoons, and was present at the battles of Talavera, Busaco, and Fuentes d'Onor, for which he has received the War Medal with three Clasps.

88 Captain Healy served in the Peninsula with the 7th Fusiliers, and was present at the battles of Talavera, Busaco, Albuhera, Orthes, and Toulouse, for which he has received the War Medal with five Clasps.

89 Captain Henry Hill served in the Peninsula with the 11th Light Dragoons from May 1811 to June 1813, and was present at the action near El Bodon, battle of Salamanca, with the advance and rear-guard to and on the retreat from Burgos. Served also the campaign of 1815, and was present at the battle of Waterloo. He has the War Medal with one Clasp for Salamanca.

89† Captain Hilliker served with the 3rd Light Dragoons the campaign of 1842 in Affghanistan (Medal), including the forcing of the Khyber Pass, storming the heights of Jugdulluck, actions of Tezeen and Huft Kotul, occupation of Cabul, and capture of Istaliff. Served also the Punjaub campaign of 1848-49, including the affair at Ramnuggur, passage of the Chenab, action of Sadoolapore, and battles of Chillianwallah and Goojerat (Medal and two Clasps).

90 Captain G. Lloyd Hodges served in the Peninsula, from 1810 to 1814, including the battles of Vittoria and the Pyrenees, besides various minor actions and skirmishes. Served also the campaign of 1815, and was present at the battles of Quatre Bras and Waterloo. Commanded the Auxiliary land forces under the orders of his Imperial Majesty the Duke of Braganza, in Portugal, in 1832 and 1833. Was also present at the attack on the Egyptian Forces under Ibrahim Pasha, by the Turkish Army, commanded by Commodore Sir Charles Napier, on the heights above Beyrout in Syria, 10th Oct. 1840. He has been three times wounded in the course of his services. He has received the War Medal with one Clasp for Vittoria.

91 Captain T. E. Hodges served at the capture of Genoa in 1814, and subsequently in the American war, including the capture of Washington and engagements at Baltimore and New Orleans.

92 Captain Hollinsworth served the campaign of 1799, in Holland, including the actions of the 10th Sept., 2nd and 6th October. The Egyptian campaign of 1801, including the actions of the 17th and 25th August. At the battle of Maida, 1806. Campaign of 1808-9, including the battles of Vimiera and Corunna. Expedition to Walcheren, 1809. Peninsular campaigns from Oct. 1812 to the end of that war in 1814, including the battle of Vittoria, actions at Roncesvalles, in the Pyrenees (28th July, 1st and 2nd Aug.); affairs on entering France, and battle of Orthes, at which last he was severely wounded in the right thigh. He has received the War Medal with nine Clasps.

93 Captain Horsley served the campaign of 1813 and 14 in Germany and Holland, and was severely wounded (three wounds) at the storming of Bergen-op-Zoom.

94 Captain George Hotham served at the bombardment of Algiers, under Lord Exmouth.

95 Captain Humbley served with the 9th Lancers in the Sutlej campaign in 1846, including the battle of Sobraon (Medal).

96 Captain Humphreys served with the 15th at the capture of Martinique and the Saintes, in 1809; and of Guadaloupe, in 1815. He has received the War Medal with one Clasp for Martinique.

97 Captain George James Hunter served during the campaign of 1814 on the Niagara frontier, including the action at Chippewa and attack on Fort Erie.

98 Captain Hussey served in Egypt under Sir Ralph Abercromby, in 1801; for which he has received the Turkish Gold Medal, and the Silver War Medal with one Clasp. Was at the attack on the Citadel at Cassis, 18 Aug. 1813; when the battery was carried by escalade by the Royal Marines, and 27 vessels captured.

99 Captain Isaac served with the Cape Mounted Rifles in several affairs and skirmishes in the Kaffir war of 1835-36 (Medal).

100 Captain James has received the War Medal with one Clasp for Copenhagen.

101 Sir Samuel Raymond Jarvis served with the 25th at the capture of Martinique in 1809, and of Guadaloupe in 1810, for which he has received the silver War Medal with two Clasps.

102 Captain James Jones served in the Royal Marine battalion at the capture of St. Elmo, Capua, and Gaeta, in 1799. Also in Egypt under Sir Ralph Abercromby, in 1801; and has received the Turkish Gold Medal, and the Silver War Medal with one Clasp.

103 Captain William Jones (h. p. 52nd F.) served in the Peninsula with the 14th Dragoons, and was present at Busaco, Badajoz, Vittoria, and Nivelle, for which he has received the War Medal with four Clasps.

War Services of the Captains.

104 Lord Kenmare landed with the first expedition to Portugal on the 3rd Aug. 1808, as a lieutenant in the 40th, and served during the campaigns of 1808, 9, 10, 11, and 12, including the battles of Roleia and Vimiera, capture of Lisbon, battles of Talavera and Busaco, the retreat to the lines of Torres Vedras, action of Redinha, capture of Campo Mayor, siege of Olivenca, first and third sieges of Badajoz, siege of Ciudad Rodrigo ; and at the battle of Salamanca, capture of Madrid and subsequent retreat into Portugal, he commanded the light company of the 40th. He has received the War Medal with eight Clasps.

106 Captain Stephen Kenny served with the 60th Rifles in the Kaffir War of 1851-53 (Medal).

107 Captain Ker served with the 37th at the investment of Bayonne, in 1814.

108 Captain Kettilby served the campaign of 1808-9 with the 23rd Fusiliers, and has received the silver War Medal with one Clasp for Corunna.

109 Captain James King served in the West Indies, and was present at the capture of the city of St. Domingo, in 1809. Served afterwards in the Peninsula in the 87th, from Jan. 1812 to June 1813, and was severely wounded at the battle of Vittoria, for which he has received the War Medal with one Clasp.

110 Captain J. D. King served in Holland and the Peninsula, from July 1809 to the end of that war in 1814, including the capture of Walcheren and siege of Flushing; battle of Busaco, action at Fuente Guinaldo, affair at Aldea de Ponte, action of Osma, battle of Vittoria, and battles of the Pyrenees on the 25th, 26th, 27th, and 28th July, 1813,—severely wounded in the right shoulder on the 28th. Present also at the capture of Paris, in 1815. He has received the War Medal with three Clasps.

111 Sir Henry John Lambert served in the Peninsula with the Grenadier Guards, and was present at the battles of Barrosa and Salamanca, for which he has received the War Medal with two Clasps.

112 Captain Langton served in the Peninsula and also the Waterloo campaign with the 52nd, and has received the War Medal with four Clasps for Corunna, Fuentes d'Onor, Ciudad Rodrigo, and Salamanca.

113 Captain Latham served in the Peninsula with the Buffs, and was present at the battles of Busaco and Albuhera (wounded), for which he has received the War Medal with two Clasps.

114 Captain Lawlor served in the American war, under Sir Gordon Drummond.

115 Captain W. H. Lawrence served in the Peninsula from April 1813 to the end of that war in 1814, including the siege of Tarragona.

116 Captain Le Marchant served with the 49th Regt. in the Eastern Campaign of 1854-55, including the battles of Alma and Balaklava, siege of Sebastopol, and capture of the Quarries with the storming party—severely wounded, left arm fractured (Medal and three Clasps, and 5th Class of the Medjidie),

117 Captain Litchfield served at Walcheren in 1809; also the Peninsular campaigns of 1812, 13, and 14, including the action at Puerto del Almarez, and battles of Vittoria, Orthes, and Toulouse, —for which he has received the War Medal with three Clasps. He served afterwards in the American war, including the action at Plattsburg.

118 Captain Little served in the channel fleet and at the blockade of Ferrol and Corunna in 1803-4. Appointed to the Royal Marine Artillery on the formation of that corps in 1804, and was employed in various bomb vessels on the enemy's coast co-operating with the land forces, or on detached service. In command of the mortars in the *Vesuvius* bomb at the attack of Boulogne. Defence of Cadiz in 1809 ; and subsequently at the blockade of Rochfort, where he commanded a storming party in a successful night attack on the coast, on which occasion he received the particular thanks of the Admiralty, and was rewarded by the Patriotic Fund:—at the commencement of this attack he was severely wounded by a musket-ball shattering the wrist, which rendered amputation of the right hand necessary. He has the War Medal with one Clasp.

119 Captain Logan-Home's services :—co-operation with the French Army in the Morea. Siege of Patras. Co-operation with the Spanish Forces and Legion near San Sebastian.

121 Captain Donald M'Donald served at Walcheren, in 1809; and at the defence of Cadiz.

122 Captain Angus M'Intyre served with the 41st in the American war.

123 Captain Mac Donnell served the campaign of 1814 with the 61st, including the affair of Tarbes, and battle of Toulouse, for which he has received the War Medal with one Clasp.

124 Captain Macfarlane served in the Peninsula with the 91st, and was present at the battles of Roleia, Vimiera, and Corunna, for which he has received the War Medal with three Clasps.

125 Captain John Mac Gregor served in the East Indies, with the Royals, and was severely wounded at the battle of Mahidpore, 22nd Dec. 1817, and again at the assault on Fort Talneir, 27th Feb. 1818.

126 Captain A. Wedder Mackenzie has received the War Medal with three Clasps for Busaco, Fuentes d'Onor, and Salamanca.

127 Captain Maclean embarked in Nov. 1813, for the western coast of Africa, where he served on several expeditions, and was present in almost every affair and skirmish that took place on the various parts of the coast at which he was stationed with the Royal African Corps and 2nd West India Regiment, from Jan. 1814 to May 1822, including the attack and capture of the town of Barra, River Gambia, in July 1817.

128 Captain Malcolm served with the 28th Regt. in the Crimea from Jan. to 5th July 1855, including the siege of Sebastopol and affair in the Cemetery. Severely wounded (Medal and Clasp).

129 Captain Mancor served the campaign of 1808-9 with the 59th, and has received the Silver War Medal with one Clasp for Corunna.

War Services of the Captains. 484

130 Captain J. M. Mason served in Canada, Flanders, and France, in 1814 and 15; also in Canada in 1838, and commanded a company of volunteers at the taking of Grand Brule.

131 Captain James MacQueen served with 16th Lancers throughout the campaign of 1838-39 in Affghanistan, and was present at the siege and capture of Ghuznee (Medal). He was afterwards present at the battle of Maharajpore on the 29th Dec. 1843 (Medal); served also in the Sutlej campaign in 1846, and was present at the affair of Buddiwal, and battles of Aliwal (wounded), and Sobraon (Medal and Clasp). He was present with the 3rd Lt. Drs. throughout the Punjaub campaign of 1848-9, including the affair of Ramnuggur, the passage of the Chenab at Wuzzeerabad on the 1st Dec. 1848 with the force under Sir Joseph Thackwell, action of Sadoolapore, and battles of Chillianwallah and Goojerat (Medal and two Clasps)

132 Captain Master went with the expedition to the Hague in the 2d battalion of the Grenadier Guards, and served the campaign of 1813 and 14 in Holland, including the taking of Merxem, bombardment of Antwerp, and storming of Bergen-op-Zoom. Served also the campaign of 1815, and carried the King's Colour of the 3rd battalion Grenadier Guards at the battles of Quatre Bras and Waterloo ; he was also present with the storming party at Peronne, and subsequently at the capture of Paris.

133 Captain Maunsell served the campaign of 1815, and was present at the battle of Waterloo.

134 Captain Meech served two campaigns in the Peninsula with the 39th, in Lord Hill's Division.

135 Captain Meredith served with the 13th Regt. in the last American War, and was present at the capture of Plattsburg in 1813, and at the battle of La Cole Mill.

136 Captain T. P. Mitchell served with the 1st Royals throughout the Egyptian campaign of 1801 and has received the Turkish Gold Medal. Served with the 69th Regt. at the reduction of Bourbon and the Mauritius in 1810, and of Java in 1811, where he was severely wounded on the 22d August. He has received the War Medal with two Clasps.

138 Captain A. Montgomerie served with the 10th Regt. in the Sutlej campaign in 1846, including the battle of Sobraon (Medal).

139 Captain A. Rich. Montgomery served at the siege of Copenhagen in 1807; and subsequently in the Peninsula, including the storming of Badajoz, affairs previous to and battle of Salamanca, and retreat to Madrid. He has received the War Medal with two Clasps.

140 Captain Thomas Moore served in H.M.S. *Amphion* from May 1803 to July 1811 ; was in the action with and capture of four Spanish frigates off Cape St. Mary's; action with flotilla of gun-boats in Gibraltar Bay ; cutting out a schooner in Corsica ; a severe action with a French frigate, and driven on shore under the batteries in the Bay of Rosas in 1808. Served at the taking of Pessara, and capture of large convoys. Commanded the marines at the taking of Cortelazza in 1809, and taking six gun-boats. Commanded the marines of the squadron at the taking of Grao and large convoys laden with military stores, after a most sanguinary action with a garrison of French troops at the point of the bayonet, when the whole of the garrison were killed, wounded, or made prisoners,—for this action and previous services he was made Brevet Captain. Present also at the capture of several other towns on the coast of the Adriatic, and destruction of convoys. He was senior officer of marines in the action off Lissa, 13 March 1810. Was twice very severely wounded, and twice rewarded from the Patriotic Fund. He has been in upwards of 30 successful contests with the enemy, and frequently officially mentioned for gallantry. Has received the War Medal with three Clasps.

141 Captain Edward Morgan embarked with the 7th Fusiliers for Portugal, in March 1810, and was present at the battles of Talavera, Busaco, and Albuhera, where he was severely wounded in the knee, and disabled for nearly twelve months. In April 1813 he rejoined the regiment, in the Peninsula, and was present at the battles of Vittoria, the Pyrenees, Nivelle, Nive, Orthes, and Toulouse; after which he accompanied the Fusiliers to America, and was present at the attack on New Orleans, in January 1815. He has the War Medal with eight Clasps.

142 Captain Morle served in the Queen's in Sir John Moore's retreat; at the siege of Flushing; and subsequently in the Peninsula, including the battles of Vittoria, Pampeluna, Nivelle, Nive, and Toulouse, besides several affairs of outposts. He has received the War Medal with four Clasps.

143 Captain Samuel Morris served in the Peninsula with the 28th, and was present at the battles of Barrosa, Vittoria, Nivelle, Nive, Orthes, and Toulouse, for which he has received the War Medal with six Clasps.

144 Captain Huntley Nicholson served in the Peninsula with the 42nd from July 1813 to the end of that war in 1814, including the battles of the Nivelle, Nive, Orthes, and Toulouse, for which he has received the War Medal with four Clasps. Present at the quelling of the mutiny at Barrackpore, in Dec. 1824. Served also in the Burmese war, including the engagements near Prome on the 20th, 25th, and 26th Nov. 1825.

145 Captain Aug. Nicolls served in the Peninsula with the 66th from Feb. 1810 to the end of that war in 1814, including the battles of Busaco, Albuhera, Vittoria, Orthes, and Toulouse. for which he has received the War Medal with five Clasps: he was also present at the actions of Arroyo de Molino, Garris, and Aire.

146 Captain Norman served with the 31st throughout the campaign of 1842 in Affghanistan, and was present in the actions of Mazeena, Tezeen, and Jugdulluck, the occupation of Cabool, and in the different engagements leading to it, and has received the medal. He was present with the 40th at Maharajpore, and has received the Bronze star.

148 Captain Arthur Ormsby served in the Peninsula from March 1809 until 1811, and was present at the crossing of the Douro, and in the Lines of Torres Vedras. He served the campaign of 1815 with the 14th, and was present at the battle of Waterloo and storming of Cambray,

at which last he was slightly wounded. Served afterwards in the East Indies, and was present at the siege and capture of Hattras; also in the Deccan campaign of 1817 and 18; and the siege and capture of Bhurtpore under Lord Combermere.

149 Captain A. H. Ormsby served in the Burmese war from Sept. 1824 to Jan. 1826, and was present at the siege and capture of Aracan, and in the Tulack expedition. Mentioned in Col. Wetherall's dispatch for distinguished gallantry in action with the rebels at St. Eustache and St. Benoit, in Canada, 14th Dec. 1837.

150 Captain Packe served the campaign of 1815, with the 13th Dragoons, and was slightly wounded at Waterloo.

151 Captain E. D. Palmer served on the expedition to Ferrol in 1800; the Egyptian campaign of 1801, including the action at the landing (with the 1st Division) and those of the 13th and 21st March. Served also at the siege and capture of the Fort of Balaguer on the Eastern Coast of Spain. He has received the Silver War Medal with one Clasp for Egypt.

152 Captain Pardey served in the Peninsula from Feb. 1813 to the end of that war in 1814, and has received the War Medal with one Clasp for Toulouse.

153 Captain Pemberton served in the Peninsula from Feb. 1814 to the end of that war.

154 Captain Pieters served in the American War in Canada in 1814 and 15; also in the late Rebellion in Canada.

155 Captain Pode served with the 33rd the campaigns of 1813 and 14 in Germany and Holland, including the actions at Merxem, bombardment of Antwerp, and storming of Bergen-op-Zoom, where he was severely wounded and taken prisoner.

157 Captain Porteous served in the Peninsula with the 61st and was present at the battles of Busaco, Fuentes d'Onor, Orthes, and Toulouse, for which he has received the War Medal with four Clasps.

158 Captain Thomas Potter served in the Peninsula and has received the War Medal with eight Clasps for Corunna, Barrosa, Badajoz, Vittoria, Pyrenees, Nivelle, Nive, and Orthes.

159 Captain David Price served in the Peninsula with the 36th and was present at the battles of Roleia, Vimiera, Corunna, Salamanca, Orthes, and Toulouse, for which he has received the War Medal with six Clasps.

160 Captain Rice Price served in the Peninsula from Nov. 1811 to the end of that war in 1814, and was present at the battles of Vittoria, Pampeluna, 28th July (severely wounded in the left groin, where the ball still remains), and the Nive 9th and 13th Dec. 1813, for which he has received the War Medal with three Clasps. Served subsequently in the American war.

161 Captain Randall served in the Peninsula with the 1st Life Guards and has received the War Medal with one Clasp for Vittoria : he served also the Waterloo Campaign.

162 Captain J S Rich served at Walcheren in 1809; and in Holland from Dec. 1813 to May 1814.

163 Captain Thomas Richardson served in the Peninsula with the 20th Light Drags. and was present at the battles of Roleia and Vimiera, for which he has the War Medal with two Clasps.

164 Captain Frederick Robertson whilst serving with the land and naval forces on the coast of North America in 1813, was mentioned in terms of commendation in four different despatches. He has received the Naval Silver War Medal with one Clasp, inscribed "April and May Boat Service, 1813."

165 Captain Robert A. Rollo served in Egypt, in 1807.

166 Captain Rudkin served with the 50th during the campaigns in the Peninsula, from 1808 to 1813 inclusive, and also on the Walcheren expedition; he was present at the battles of Vimiera and Corunna, occupying the lines at Torres Vedras, battles of Fuentes d'Onor (wounded), action of Arroyo de Molino, covering the siege of Badajoz, surprise of Almarez, and battles of Vittoria and the Pyrenees, at which last he was wounded and taken prisoner. He has received the War Medal with five Clasps.

167 Captain Sayer served in the Eastern campaign of 1854 in the 23rd Fusiliers, and was present at the affair of Bulganak and battle of Alma; had charge of the Land Transport of the Light Division in Bulgaria and the Crimea; was very severely wounded at the Alma while serving as a Volunteer with the 23rd Fusiliers (Medal and Clasp, 5th Class of the Medjidie, and decorated personally by the Emperor Napoleon with the Legion of Honor).

168 Captain Charles Scott has received the War Medal with one Clasp for Navarino, 1827.

169 Captain Seward served in the Peninsula from Oct. 1810 to Feb. 1813, including the siege of the forts and battle of Salamanca; siege of Burgos, from 19th Sept. to 21st Oct. 1812.

170 Captain Sisson served in the Peninsula with the 81st and was present at the battle of Corunna, for which he has received the War Medal with one Clasp.

171 Captain William Smith served with the 45th in the Burmese war.

171† Captain Spratt served with the Baltic expedition in 1854 (Medal).

172 Captain Sparin assisted in cutting out a French privateer at Palamos, 8th November 1813.

173 Captain S . John served with the 1st Battalion 60th Rifles during the second siege operations at Mooltan, including the siege and storm of the town, and capture of the citadel. Afterwards at the battle of Goojerat, the pursuit of the Sikh army, and the expulsion of the Affghans beyond the Khyber Pass (Medal and Clasps). Also present during the operations in the Euzofyze country, and capture of the insurgent villages on the 11th and 14th Dec. 1849.

174 Captain Duncan Stewart served with the 42nd in the campaigns in the Peninsula, France, and Flanders, and was present at the battles of Salamanca, the Pyrenees (28th July to 2nd Aug.), Nivelle, Nive (9th to 13th Dec.), Orthes (shot through the left hand), and Quatre Bras (severely wounded in the left thigh, the ball remaining lodged). He has received the War Medal with five Clasps).

175 Captain Still served in the Peninsula and has received the War Medal with two Clasps for Busaco and Fuentes d'Onor.

176 Captain Sullivan served with the 3rd Light Dragoons the campaign in Affghanistan, in

War Services of the Captains. 485a

1842 (Medal), and was present at the forcing of the Khyber Pass, storming the heights of Jugdulluck, action of Tezeen and Huftkotul, and occupation of Cabool. Served the Sutlej campaign of 1845-6, including the battles of Moodkee, Ferozeshah, and Sobraon (Medal and two Clasps): he officiated as Major of Brigade to the 1st Cavalry Brigade at Ferozeshah; and had three horses shot under him in the actions of the 18th, 21st, and 22nd Dec. 1845. Served also the Punjaub campaign of 1848-9; and commanded a Troop at the battle of Goojerat (Medal and Clasp).

177 Captain Tallan served with the 41st throughout the Burmese war, and was present at the capture of Rangoon, attack on Kemundine and on Pagoda Point, capture of Syriam, the several engagements in front of Rangoon from the 1st to the 15th Dec. 1824, capture of Tantabain, siege of Denobiu from 25th of March until its capture on the 2nd April 1825, engagements near Prome on the 1st, 2nd, and 5th Dec. following, capture of Meloom and of Pagahm Mew. Served also in Upper and Lower Scinde and in Beloochistan, in 1840 and 1841. Has the Medal for Ava.

178 Capt. John Taylor served in the Peninsula with the 91st and was present at the battles of the Pyrenees, Nivelle, Nive, and Orthes, for which he has the War Medal with four Clasps.

179 Captain John Terry has received the War Medal with one Clasp for the battle of Toulouse.

180 Captain James Thompson went out with others on board the *Union* transport, to join the 1st Battalion 36th Regiment, then serving with General Whitelock's expedition in South America; but as the whole force had left, when they arrived at the River Plate, they ultimately returned to England. In 1808, he served with the 36th in Portugal, and was present at the battles of Roleia and Vimiera. In 1809, on the Walcheren expedition, including the capture of Ter Vere and Flushing. Served again in the Peninsula from 1811 to the end of that war in 1814, and was present with the 36th in every action in which it was engaged, including the battle of Salamanca, siege of Burgos, and battles of the Pyrenees, Nivelle, Nive, Orthes, and Toulouse; and commanded a Company throughout, after his Captain was killed at Salamanca. Has received the War Medal with eight Clasps.

181 Captain Tittle served in the 38th, on the Walcheren expedition in 1809; also the Peninsular campaigns, from April, 1811, to the end of that war in 1814, including the storming of Badajoz, battle of Salamanca, various skirmishes on the retreat from Burgos, action at Osma, battle of Vittoria, siege of San Sebastian, and investment of Bayonne. In 1819 he served on Commando through Cafferland. At the siege of San Sebastian he acted as an engineer, and was severely wounded on the 31st August, whilst showing a ford to Col. Fernes of the Portuguese service. He has received the War Medal with four Clasps.

182 Captain Torriano served at Walcheren, and was present at the siege of Flushing.

183 Captain Tweedie was present in the batteries of the Faro, under Sir James Stewart. Served also the campaign of 1814, in the south of France, including the battle of Toulouse, for which he has received the War Medal with one Clasp.

184 Captain Henry Varlo served the campaign in Syria in 1840 (Medal) at D'Jouni, and bombardment of Acre (War Medal with one Clasp and the Turkish Medal). Served with the Baltic expedition in July and Aug. 1854 (Medal).

185 Captain H. H. Vaughan served in the Peninsula with the 67th, from July 1810 to Jan. 1812, including the battle of Barrosa and defence of Cadiz. Served afterwards in the East Indies, including the Mahratta campaigns of 1817 and 18; and sieges of Rhygur, Amulneer, and Asseerghur. He has received the War Medal with one Clasp for Barrosa.

186 Captain Vetch has received the War Medal with two Clasps for Barrosa and Badajoz; and he served also at the defence of Cadiz.

187 Captain Henderson Ward served on the China expedition of 1857-58, including the blockade of the Canton River, the landing before and capture of Canton.

188 Captain Watkins served in the Peninsula and was present at the battles of Busaco, Albuhera, Vittoria, Pyrenees, Nivelle, Nive, Orthes, and Toulouse, for which he has received the War Medal with eight Clasps.

189 Captain Wellings served in the Peninsula and has received the War Medal with two Clasps for St. Sebastian and Nive.

190 Captain Wells served at Madeira, in 1807 and 8; at Walcheren in 1809; and the campaign of 1815, including the battles of Quatre Bras and Waterloo.

191 Captain Wetherall served in the Mahratta war in 1817, 18, and 19, with the 22nd Light Dragoons, and was engaged at Bodamy, Belgaum, Sholapore, and Capaul Droog.

192 Captain Whitley served in the Peninsula with the 9th and was present at the battles of Roleia, Vimiera, Corunna, Busaco, and Salamanca, for which he has received the War Medal with five Clasps.

194 Captain James Williams served in the Peninsula with the 11th and was present at the battles of Busaco and Salamanca, for which he has received the War Medal with two Clasps.

195 Captain Wills served in the 1st Battalion Royal Marines during the American War in 1813-15; distinguished himself at the attack upon Hampton; attacked Point Pitre, garrisoned it with 150 men, and retained possession of it until it was destroyed.

196 Captain Henry Wood served with the 3rd Light Dragoons throughout the campaign of 1842 in Affghanistan (Medal), and was present at the forcing of the Khyber Pass, capture of Mammoo Khail, storming the heights of Jugdullugk, action at Tezeen and Huft Kotul, and occupation of Cabool. Served also in the Punjaub campaign of 1849, and was present at the battles of Chillianwallah and Goojerat (Medal and two Clasps).

197 Captain James Wood served from 1812 to 1815 at the Texel, Flushing, Cherbourg, Basque Roads, north coast of Spain, and San Sebastian. During the war he served also in the West Indies, St. Helena, and Madeira.

LIEUTENANTS.

	CORNET, 2d LIEUT. or ENSIGN.	LIEUT.	WHEN PLACED ON HALF PAY.
Ackland, Graves, 61 Foot, *Barrackmaster at Templemore*	18 Nov. 13	23 April 18	7 June 19
ℙ Addison, John,¹ 2 Dragoon Guards	1 Sept. 14	17 Oct. 16	6 June 22
Alder, Walter K., Royal Marines..........	1 Nov. 03	1 Feb. 06	7 Oct. 14
*Allen, George, 88 Foot	never	25 Dec. 13	25 Mar. 16
Alley, Tottenham, Royal Corsican Rangers	23 Aug. 10	5 June 11	25 July 16
ℙ Altenstein, Henry,² *Baron*, 6 W. India Rt.	16 Jan. 09	10 Nov. 09	9 Dec. 24
Amyott, Richard Garret, Royal Marines....	2 Aug. 99	21 Aug. 04	5 Dec. 14
Andrew, Charles, Royal Artillery	28 April 10	17 Dec. 13	19 Dec. 20
*Arden, William, 4 Foot	never	25 Dec. 13	25 Sept. 14
ℙ Armstrong, Francis Wheeler,³ Coldst. Gds.	1 Sept. 08	21 June 10	24 Oct. 22
Armstrong, John, 40 Foot	19 Oct. 09	23 April 12	25 Feb. 16
ℙ Armstrong, John Cooper,⁴ R. Art. Drivers	1 Jan. 07	17 Dec. 08	1 July 16
Armstrong, Montgomery, R. York Rangers	10 June 13	25 May 15	25 Dec. 18
Armstrong, Richard, 70 Foot	16 May 07	7 Mar. 10	12 Mar. 18
Arnott, Alexander, 26 Foot	27 April 00	28 Feb. 12	25 Mar. 17
Atkin, John, 88 Foot....................	30 Jan. 12	19 Oct. 15	25 Feb. 16
Atkinson, John, 98 Foot	28 Feb. 05	12 Sept. 05	25 Nov. 18
ℙ Austin, Edward Frederick,⁵ 47 Foot	11 July 11	30 Sept. 13	9 Jan. 14
Austin, Thomas,⁶ 5 Royal Vet. Batt. Fort Major of Duncannon Fort	17 May 10	6 Dec. 19	
ℙ Ayshford, Aaron Moore,⁷ 12 Foot	17 Aug. 09	15 April 12	31 Mar. 14
Bailey, James Alderson,⁸ 60 Foot........	5 May 14	21 Dec. 15	3 Jan. 22
ℙ Baillie, Andrew,⁹ 30 Foot	29 June 09	27 June 11	3 July 17
Bain, John, 61 Foot	20 April 09	11 April 11	2 Dec. 14
ℂℳ Bain, William, 33 Foot	22 April 12	14 Aug. 15	25 Mar. 17
Bainbrigge, Thomas Parker, 48 Foot	1 Oct. 07	3 May 10	20 Nov. 23
Baker, George, Royal Marines............	16 Dec. 11	27 July 30	3 Feb. 31
Bale, William, 3 Foot	9 July 06	28 Oct. 07	23 Oct. 16
Balinhard, John Allen Carnegy de, 13 Drags.	11 June 30	29 Mar. 33	1 June 40
Ball, Howell, Garrison Company	20 May 13	18 Mar. 15	
ℙ Ball, Robert,¹⁰ 59 Foot................	27 Oct. 07	14 Nov. 09	22 Oct. 16
Ball, William, 22 Foot..................	25 Jan. 10	11 Mar. 13	9 Nov. 20
Baring, Frederick, 51 Foot	15 Nov. 11	8 Feb. 13	4 Aug. 37
Barlow, John Thomas, 93 Foot	8 Aug. 05	19 Mar. 07	20 Dec. 19
Barnetson, Alexander, 92 Foot............	1 Mar. 06	29 Sept. 07	28 Mar. 22
Barrett, Thomas, 3 Foot	15 April 13	8 June 15	25 Feb. 16
Barry, St. George Ryder, 13 Dragoons	23 June 14	25 Oct. 15	14 Nov. 16
Bartlet, Frederick George, 7 Foot	20 Aug. 13	18 May 20	7 Oct. 24
Bate, Frederick, Royal Artillery Drivers....	1 Dec. 12	15 July 13	1 Nov. 14
ℙ Bayly, Frederick,¹¹ Royal Artillery......	5 June 09	21 June 12	20 June 29
Bayly, Geo. Augustus, 57 Foot............	29 April 36	5 Jan. 41	22 Dec. 46
Bayly, Thomas, 1 Foot	25 Aug. 13	19 Oct. 14	25 Mar. 16
ℙ Beamish, Bernard,¹² 84 Foot	5 Feb. 08	11 Oct. 08	25 Oct. 21
Beauchamp, Charles Eustace, Royal Artillery	5 Oct. 18	15 Mar. 27	6 Feb. 37
Belford, William, 48 Foot................	18 Mar. 13	25 Jan. 25	25 Nov. 33
Bell, Samuel, 90 Foot	15 Sept. 08	3 Jan. 11	25 Dec. 18
Bennett, Bryan O'Donnell, 77 Foot	26 May 14	24 April 16	30 Mar. 26
ℙ Bennett, James, 14 Dragoons	19 Nov. 12	21 Oct. 13	25 Mar. 16
Benson, Wm. Welbore H., 30 Foot	7 July 25	11 Dec. 28	7 Feb. 40
ℙ Benwell, Thomas,¹³ 4 Foot	21 Sept. 13	17 Mar. 15	25 Feb. 16
Bezant, John,⁴¹ Royal Marine Artillery....	3 Feb. 06	5 Sept. 11	6 Mar. 15
ℙ Birch, George,¹⁵ 64 Foot	15 Aug. 11	20 Aug. 12	15 Mar. 17
ℙ *Black, John*,¹⁶ 3 R. Veteran Batt., *Fort-Major of Charles Fort and Kinsale* ..	15 June 09	30 Dec. 10	
Blair,, Thomas Newenham, 7 West India Regt.	23 Sept. 12	15 June 15	25 April 16
Blake James Bunbury, 43 Foot	25 Jan. 25	5 Sept. 26	12 Mar. 29
Blake, John, Royal Artillery	5 July 13	4 July 15	22 Jan. 25
Bland, Robert John, 70 Foot	29 Aug. 11	12 June 15	8 Nov. 17
Bleazby, Fra. Bernard, Land Trans. Corps	23 Nov. 55	1 Feb. 56	1 April 57
Bloomfield, J. A. D. *Lord, GCB.*, Coldst. Gds., *Envoy Extr. and Minister Plenipotentiary at Berlin*	never	9 April 18	25 Dec. 18
Blythe, Joseph Harry F.,¹⁷ 88 Foot	6 June 54	8 June 55	1 Aug. 57
Boghurst, Edward, Royal Artillery	4 June 10	17 Feb. 14	1 Aug. 21
Boileau, John Peter, 90 Foot	18 Mar. 13	11 July 16	14 Aug. 17
Bolton, Samuel, 23 Foot	4 May 09	29 Mar. 10	27 April 15
Bond, William Spittle, Royal Marines	16 Mar. 01	15 Aug. 05	2 Feb. 15
Bovill, Edward, 29 Foot	3 Sept. 12	16 Sept. 13	2 May 17
Bowdler, George Andrew, 99 Foot	18 May 08	22 Sept. 08	30 Oct. 17

Lieutenants. 487

	CORNET, ETC.	LIEUT.	WHEN PLACED ON HALF PAY.
Bowles, Humphrey, 22 Dragoons	May 02	20 July 02	20 July 02
Bradburne, Francis, 16 Dragoons	8 June 15	3 Sept. 16	3 Sept. 16
₽ Bradshaw, Francis Green,[19] 52 Foot	5 Jan. 05	5 Dec. 05	12 Mar. 18
Brainer, James Louttit, Royal Marines	13 Mar. 38	21 Dec. 41	21 Dec. 44
₡₡ Bramwell, John,[20] 92 Foot	29 July 13	18 July 15	25 Feb. 17
₡ Brattle, Thomas,[21] Royal Marines	8 July 03	15 Aug. 05	11 Aug. 14
₡₡ Brearey, Christ. Spencer,[22] 27 Foot...	21 July 08	2 Nov. 09	5 May 25
₽ ₡₡ Brice, Alexander Adair,[23] 66 Foot ..	8 Aug. 11	21 May 12	5 Oct. 20
₽ *Bridger, John, 1 Prov. Batt. of Militia..	never	30 Mar. 14	1814
₽ Brown, Charles,[25] 50 Foot.............	8 Mar. 10	7 Oct. 13	25 Dec. 14
₡₡ Brown, Eugene, 91 Foot	14 Sept. 09	9 July 12	25 April 17
Brown, Francis Carnac, 80 Foot	27 July 07	1 April 10	8 July 18
Brown, John, 82 Foot	16 April 07	26 Aug. 08	10 Dec. 12
₡₡ Browne, *Hon.* William, 52 Foot	19 Sept. 11	26 Nov. 12	3 Jan. 22
Brumby, Charles, Meuron's Regt.	29 Oct. 12	25 Feb. 14	25 Oct. 16
₽ Bubb, Anthony,[26] 61 Foot.............	20 Feb. 12	16 Dec. 13	25 Dec. 14
₽ Buchanan,Wm.Theophilus,[27] 13 Dragoons	10 Dec. 12	2 Sept. 13	25 July 16
Buckeridge, Francis Hotchkin, 30 Foot	6 April 20	7 April 25	13 April 26
Buckley, William Henry, Unattached......	4 Oct. 21	28 July 25	2 Nov. 32
Buller, John, 85 Foot	22 Aug. 05	19 Mar. 07	7 Oct. 19
Bunyon, Charles Spencer, Unattached	1 Aug. 26	16 July 29	16 Sept. 36
Burlton, George Le Hardy,[28] R. Marines ..	10 May 48	26 Feb. 51	26 Mar. 57
Burn, Henry Wilson, 1 Foot.............	25 Nov. 13	2 Mar. 16	21 Nov. 28
Burn, James, 72 Foot	13 Oct. 08	10 Feb. 11	25 June 14
₡₡ Burnet, John, 52 Foot...............	27 May 13	8 May 15	25 Feb. 16
Burroughes, Thomas D'Eye, 14 Dragoons ..	4 May 20	24 Oct. 21	24 Oct. 21
Burslem, James Godolphin,[29] R. Artillery	24 Sept. 96	1 June 98	1 Mar. 19
Busteed, John, 16 Foot.................	2 April 12	29 Sept. 14	25 Mar. 17
Busteed, Michael, 57 Foot	30 Nov. 09	8 Aug. 11	25 July 13
₡₡ Butler, Whitwell,[30] Scots Fusilier Guards	never	12 Jan. 14	25 Feb. 19
₽ Butterworth, Henry,[31] 35 Foot	25 Aug. 07	27 April 09	11 May 20
Byng, *Hon.*Gerald Fred. F., 53 Foot, *Gentleman Usher of the Privy Chamber*..	Nov. 99	26 Jan. 01	
₽ Cahill, Nicholas,[32] 36 Foot	10 Mar. 08	30 Aug. 10	11 May 15
Cameron, Donald, 42 Foot	13 Dec. 04	7 Aug. 05	5 June 06
₽ Cameron, Donald,[33] 60 Foot...........	never	7 May 11	23 Sept. 19
Cameron, Duncan, 1 Foot	22 April 13	21 April 14	27 June 16
Cameron, James, 77 Foot...............	25 Aug. 08	21 Mar. 11	10 July 17
Cameron, John, 49 Foot	25 Dec. 13	7 July 37	9 June 43
₽ Cameron, Lachlan Maclean,[34] Unattached	13 Oct. 12	20 May 14	26 Feb. 29
Campbell, Alexander,[35] Royal Marines	10 Sept. 05	10 Oct. 08	1 Sept. 14
Campbell, Charles, 99 Foot	24 June 13	29 Sept. 14	25 Sept. 18
₽ Campbell, Charles William,[36] 39 Foot ..	21 May 09	2 May 11	17 April 17
Campbell, James,[37] 41 Foot	24 Feb. 15	24 Oct. 34	5 Dec. 43
Campbell, Rupert,[38] 38 Foot............	26 Sept. 31	7 July 37	27 July 38
Cannon, James, 3 Garrison Battalion......	4 Jan. 15	22 June 15	25 Nov. 16
Carew, Robert, 41 Foot.................	20 July 15	8 April 25	11 Aug. 43
₽ Carey, Michael,[39] 40 Foot	27 Oct. 08	7 Mar. 11	7 Sept. 32
₽ Carnaby, Alexander,[40] 76 Foot	2 Nov. 09	24 Nov. 14	25 Mar. 17
Carr, Ralph,[41] 21 Foot.................	2 July 11	27 Jan. 14	16 April 17
Cassan, Edward Sheffield, West India Ran.	18 July 10	25 June 12	19 Dec. 22
Chads, William Catherwood, Royal Marines	15 Oct. 05	5 June 10	1 Sept. 14
Chadwick, Jno.[42] 15 Dr. *Adj. Kilmainham Hospital, with honorary rank of Capt.*	27 Feb. 52	25 Oct. 54	29 April 56
Chadwick, Wm.,[43] 5 R. Vet. Batt., *Capt. of Invalids, Royal Hospital, Chelsea*	18 Jan. 10	18 Jan. 12	
₽ Challis, John Henry,[44] 1 Royal Vet.Batt.	26 Feb. 08	1 Sept. 08	
Chamberlayne, J. Chamberlayne, Royal Art.	5 July 09	24 Oct. 12	1 April 26
Chambers, John, Royal Marines	17 Sept. 27	27 May 34	16 June 37
Chambres, Wm. Chambres, R. Marines	3 Oct. 05	18 Nov. 09	1 Sept. 14
Champion, Edward Kendall, Unattached ..	7 July 14	12 Feb. 24	29 Dec. 25
Chatfield, Frederick, 20 Foot	24 Nov. 18	19 Nov. 21	19 Nov. 21
Chevalier, Charles, Land Transport Corps ..	?	7 Sept. 55	1 April 57
₡ Cinnamond, Joseph,[45] Royal Marines ..	2 Nov. 03	22 Feb. 06	25 April 15
Clare, Benjamin, 60 Foot...............	21 Dec. 12	11 Dec. 14	25 Dec. 18
Clark, Edward Stevens, 44 Foot..........	30 Jan. 12	10 June 13	25 Mar. 17
Clarke, Walter, 24 Dragoons	18 July 16	9 Nov. 18	1 Sept. 20
Clarke, William,[46] Royal Marines	18 July 03	15 Aug. 05	1 Jan. 16
Clay, Wm. Waldegrave Pelham, 43 Foot ..	1 July 13	19 April 21	10 Oct. 22
₽ Cobbold, Frederick,[47] Unattached	23 Aug. 10	15 Aug. 11	2 Feb. 30
*Cochrane, William, 32 Foot	never	25 Dec. 13	25 Sept. 14

z 2

Lieutenants.

	2D LIEUT. ETC.	LIEUT.	WHEN PLACED ON HALF PAY.
Cockburn, Phineas Charles, 70 Foot	30 Dec. 13	23 Feb. 15	18 Sept. 23
Colclough, M'Carty, 62 Foot	25 April 11	23 Sept. 13	25 May 17
Cole, John William, 21 Foot	16 July 07	16 Nov. 09	13 Nov. 17
Collis, William, Royal Marines	22 April 06	1 July 12	1 Sept. 14
𝔓 Colls, William,⁴⁶ York Light Infantry	1 Feb. 16	25 Sept. 17	26 Feb. 18
Coningham, William, 63 Foot	24 Nov. 13	4 April 16	13 Mar. 17
𝔓 Cooke, Adolphus, 76 Foot	30 Mar. 09	16 July 12	9 Aug. 21
Coombe, Joseph,⁴⁹ Royal Marines	1 Jan. 00	7 Sept. 04	25 Oct. 05
*Cooper, Charles Kelly, 52 Foot	never	25 Dec. 13	25 Oct. 14
Cooper, Samuel, 2 Foot	12 July 21	10 Sept. 25	25 Dec. 28
Coote, Richard Gethin Creagh,⁵⁰ 35 Foot	25 Sept. 13	10 May 15	1 Feb. 31
Coppinger, John Murray, Royal Marines	14 April 26	19 May 34	30 Mar. 35
Corham, William, Royal Marines	4 Mar. 06	13 Nov. 98	5 Dec. 01
Cosby, William,⁵¹ 5 West India Regt.	18 Sept. 04	8 May 06	2 April 18
𝔓 𝔘𝔄 Cottingham, Thomas,⁵² 52 Foot	11 May 12	5 Aug. 13	25 Dec. 18
Courtenay, George Henry, 6 Foot	9 Mar. 32	8 April 36	4 Mar. 42
Covenay, James, 60 Foot	never	20 Feb. 16	23 Oct. 17
𝔓 Cowley, Charles,⁵³ 39 Foot	24 May 00	10 Sept. 12	18 July 16
𝔓 𝔘𝔄 Cox, Charles Thomas,⁵⁴ 71 Foot	29 June 09	29 May 11	25 Oct. 21
Crauford, William, 70 Foot	22 May 12	24 Aug. 15	25 Mar. 17
Crause, Charles, Royal Marines	3 Aug. 00	12 Dec. 04	31 Oct. 14
Crispo, Sidney Smith, Royal Marines	11 Mar. 28	18 July 36	7 Nov. 37
Crookshank, Richard, 4 Dragoon Guards	23 July 12	4 Feb. 13	25 Sept. 14
Crow, William, 9 Foot	Sept. 00	18 Nov. 99	25 Nov. 02
Crowe, Joseph, 60 Foot	26 Oct. 10	29 Mar. 12	28 June 19
Crowe, Robert, Land Transport Corps	23 Nov. 55	1 April 57	1 April 57
Crozier, Acheson,⁵⁶ Royal Marines	2 July 03	15 Aug. 05	1 May 17
𝔓 Cubitt, Edward George,⁵⁷ 4 Dragoons	31 Oct. 11	23 Jan. 12	8 Jan. 24
Cumming, Alexander, 26 Foot	27 Jan. 14	6 Oct. 14	25 Dec. 14
Curzon, Hon. John Henry Roper, 37 Foot	14 Oct. 24	15 Nov. 27	30 Dec. 31
𝔓 Cusine, John,⁵⁸ Unattached	22 Mar. 10	4 Mar. 13	13 Dec. 26
𝔓 Dalgairns, William,⁵⁹ 55 Foot	7 Sept. 09	5 July 10	24 July 17
Dalgleish, Robert, 73 Foot	1 April 12	1 July 13	25 June 17
𝔓 D'Alton, Edw.Richd.⁶⁰ Chass.Britanniques	3 June 12	7 Sept. 13	1814
Daly, Edward Nugent, 63 Foot	19 April 44	16 Sept. 45	29 Aug. 47
Dalzell, William John, Royal Artillery	1 May 15	29 July 20	17 Jan. 24
Dames, Mansell, 6 Dragoons	6 Feb. 12	25 May 15	25 Mar. 16
Daniel, Peter Fane Edge,⁶¹ Royal Marines	4 April 34	26 Aug. 40	11 Oct. 48
𝔓 Darcy, Isaac Roboteau,⁶² 8 R. Vet. Batt.	15 April 07	2 Oct. 09	
Daubuz, James Barill, Unattached	3 Aug. 20	24 Oct. 21	22 Mar. 27
Davidson, James Batchelor, 2 W. India Regt.	25 May 32	13 Aug. 35	25 Feb. 42
Davies, David,⁶¹Royal Marines, *Captain R.* *Carmarthen Militia*	21 Nov. 06	1 Oct. 13	8 May 27
Davis, William Henry, 8 West India Regt.	21 Jan. 13	25 May 15	18 April 17
Davys, Edmund Soden, 90 Foot	11 Nov. 08	16 May 11	25 Dec. 18
Dean, Robert, 16 Dragoons	1 Jan. 13	5 June 15	20 Oct. 16
Deane, Henry Allen Murray, 4 Foot	5 Dec. 43	1 Dec. 46	15 June 58
𝔓 Delamain, Edward Smith,⁶⁵ 60 Foot	20 Feb. 11	28 July 14	2 July 29
𝔓 Delmé, Henry Peter,⁶⁶ 88 Foot	7 Mar. 11	3 Sept. 12	25 Feb. 16
*Denford, Charles, 95 Foot	never	25 Dec. 13	1814
Denison, George, 19 Foot	18 June 12	29 Jan. 18	20 July 20
Desbarres, Henry Windham, Unattached	26 May 14	8 Dec. 14	2 Feb. 26
𝔘𝔄 Dickson, Charles Lennox, Unattached	11 June 12	21 April 14	7 Sept. 26
Dickson, David, 42 Foot	8 Dec. 15	23 Dec. 24	3 July 28
Diddep, John, 41 Foot	27 July 15	18 Oct. 36	13 Sept. 43
Digges, Charles, West India Rangers	4 Mar. 13	11 May 15	3 Oct. 18
𝔓 Dighton, Robert,⁶⁷ Unattached	27 April 09	7 Sept. 12	7 Nov. 34
Dillon, Edward Walter Percy,⁶⁸ 63 Foot	21 April 08	5 Oct. 09	23 Dec. 19
Dillon, Thomas, 8 R. Veteran Battalion	3 July 06	2 Feb. 09	
Dobyns, Robert William, 7 W. India Regt.	19 July 09	27 Mar. 11	2 Sept. 16
𝔓 𝔘𝔄 Dodwell, George, 23 Dragoons	6 July 04	25 April 05	30 May 16
Donnelly, John, 2 R. Veteran Battalion	21 Nov. 13	18 July 15	
Doswell, Henry,⁶⁹ Royal Marines	18 Sept. 05	1 Feb. 09	1 April 17
𝔓 Dowker, Thomas,⁷⁰ 38 Foot	20 April 09	15 Mar. 10	24 Nov. 14
Downer, Geo. P. Maxwell, York Lt. Inf. Vol.	3 Feb. 14	19 Jan. 15	25 Mar. 17
Doyne, Robert Stephen, 7 Dragoons	22 Sept. 25	28 Sept. 26	17 Sept. 29
Dreghorn, Allan Hamilton, 7 R. Vet. Batt.	26 Mar. 12	6 May 13	
𝔓𝔘𝔄 Drummond,Geo.Duncan,⁷¹3R.Vet.Bn.	30 May 17	23 Jan. 18	13 25 June 26
Drury, Henry,⁷² Royal Marines	19 Oct. 37	11 May 41	31 Jan. 51
𝔘𝔄 Dunnicliffe, Henry,⁷³ Royal Artillery	12 Dec. 11	20 Dec. 14	1 April 19
Dyer, Robert Turtliff,⁷⁴ Royal Marines	16 Feb. 05	27 July 08	14 Dec. 14

Lieutenants. 489

	ENSIGN, ETC.	LIEUT.	WHEN PLACED ON HALF PAY.
Eagles, Edward, Bampfield, Royal Marines	29 Sept. 04	28 Mar. 07	1 Sept. 14
ᵱ Eccles, Cuthbert,⁷⁵ 83 Foot	19 Nov. 12	20 May 14	25 Mar. 17
Ede, Denzil, Royal Marines	7 June 99	18 Aug. 04	1 Jan. 16
Ede, John, Royal Marines	14 Mar. 96	1 Jan. 99	
ᵱ Edwards, Charles,⁷⁶ 71 Foot, *Capt. of Invalids, Royal Hospital, Chelsea*....	27 Sept. 13	24 Dec. 18	3 Mar. 25
ᵱ Edwards, Thomas,⁷⁷ 66 Foot	11 April 09	8 Oct. 12	8 July 19
ᵱ Edwards, Wright,⁷⁸ 58 Foot	2 Sept. 12	10 Nov. 13	11 July 22
Elliot, Henry,⁷⁹ Royal Marines	11 July 03	5 Nov. 05	11 Dec. 16
Ellis, William, 89 Foot	1 Feb. 10	9 June 12	25 Jan. 17
Erskine, Robert, Royal African Corps	2 April 22	25 June 24	5 July 31
ᵱ Evans, John,⁸⁰ 28 Foot	1 Mar. 10	13 April 13	25 Dec. 14
ᵱ Evans, Ralph,⁸¹ 62 Foot	24 Sept. 12	16 Feb. 14	25 May 17
ᵱ Evans, Thomas,⁸² 38 Foot	26 Nov. 12	19 Jan. 14	25 Feb. 17
Fergusson, James, 57 Foot	23 June 13	21 April 14	25 Feb. 16
Ffennell, Richard, 98 Foot	25 April 06	26 Oct. 06	10 Dec. 18
Fitz Gerald, Richard Henry, Unattached ..	1 Oct. 12	23 Mar. 15	26 May 25
Fitz Gibbon, William, 83 Foot	29 May 11	10 Sept. 13	25 Sept. 17
Fonblanque, John Sam. Mar. de Grenier, 21 F.	3 Jan. 10	18 June 12	25 Mar. 17
Foot, Randall, 14 Foot	11 July 26	6 Aug. 29	3 Feb. 32
ᵱ Foote, John Hollis Rolle,⁸⁴ 9 Foot	18 April 11	29 April 13	25 Feb. 16
Ford, Arthur White, 2 R. Veteran Battalion	27 April 09	3 Oct. 11	
ᵱ Ford, John,⁸⁵ 3 West India Regt., *Captain of Invalids, Royal Hospital, Chelsea*	25 May 09	30 May 11	15 Nov. 21
*Forster, John Augustus, 2 Prov. Bn. of Militia	never	25 Dec. 13	1814
Fortescue, John Mill, 103 Foot	19 Aug. 13	7 Mar. 16	1 Oct. 17
Fowler, William, Royal Marines	11 May 96	1 Nov. 99	1 July 20
ᵱ ᵺ Fraser, Andrew Simon,⁸⁶ Unattached	16 Sept. 13	20 July 15	18 Jan. 27
ᵱ Fraser, David,⁸⁷ 82 Foot	9 May 11	2 Dec. 13	25 Mar. 17
Freeman, Alfred P. Isidore Walsh, 15 Foot	1 Oct. 96	14 May 12	22 Feb. 16
French, Hyacinth, 97 Foot	27 July 09	17 May 13	25 Dec. 18
French, William, 36 Foot	8 May 06	11 Nov. 07	3 Aug. 20
Fullarton, John, 71 Foot	22 July 13	7 Dec. 14	7 April 16
Fuller, W., Ceylon Regt., *Adj. Sussex Militia*	25 June 44	12 July 47	23 July 52
Gale, William, 1 Dragoons	12 April 15	26 June 17	22 Sept. 20
*Gamlen, Chas. Arthur, 3 Prov. Batt. of Mil.	never	16 Mar. 14	1814
Garden, John Campbell, Newfoundland Fenc.	16 Dec. 07	4 Oct. 10	25 June 16
Gardiner, Wm. Gregory, Rifle Brigade	21 Mar. 11	12 Aug. 12	24 May 21
ᵱ ᵺ Gardner, Andrew, 27 Foot	14 Nov. 11	30 Sept. 13	25 Mar. 17
Garstin, James, 15 Foot	26 Oct. 07	12 Nov. 09	10 Nov. 17
Gatty, Joseph, 60 Foot	10 Dec. 11	26 Oct. 12	13 Nov. 17
ᵱ Geddes, James,⁸⁸ 43 Foot	17 Mar. 13	9 June 14	25 Dec. 14
Gibb, Harry Wm. Scott, Royal Artillery ..	11 July 14	27 Sept. 18	1 Dec. 22
Gibbon, Stephen, 29 Foot	20 May 12	10 Nov. 14	1 May 17
Gibbons, Thomas, Royal Artillery	8 June 04	1 Dec. 05	1 Jan. 36
ᵱ *Gibson, Wm. Joseph,* 8 R. Veteran Batt.	27 Sept. 04	11 Mar. 06	
ᵱ Gilder, Matthew William,⁸⁹ 6 Foot	19 July 10	26 Aug. 13	16 April 17
*Gill, George,*⁹⁰ Royal Marines	29 Jan. 06	26 Aug. 11	1 Sept. 14
Gill, George,⁹¹ Royal Marines	30 Dec. 48	13 Dec. 52	29 July 58
Gillman, Wm. Howard, R. Artillery Drivers	18 Dec. 12	16 July 13	1 July 16
ᵱ Gillmore, Joseph Albert,⁹² 27 Foot	12 Nov. 12	1 Sept. 14	7 Aug. 17
ᵺ Glendinning, Thomas, 60 Foot	9 Dec. 12	13 Dec. 13	15 27 Sept. 17
ᵺ Glynn, Henry, 40 Foot	25 Nov. 13	20 Sept. 15	25 Feb. 16
ᵱ Goodall, William,⁹³ 52 Foot	30 Mar. 09	21 Dec. 09	6 June 16
Gordon, Alexander, 92 Foot	22 May 06	3 Mar. 08	25 Oct. 10
ᵱ Gordon, George,⁹⁴ 85 Foot	20 Feb. 12	6 Jan. 14	30 Dec. 19
Gordon, John Ponsonby, Unattached	17 Jan. 22	15 Aug. 26	15 Aug. 26
Grant, Charles, 81 Foot		5 Jan. 78	13 May 83
Grant, George Colquhoun, 2 Ceylon Regt...	15 June 09	2 Jan. 11	19 Dec. 22
*Grant, James, Royal Waggon Train	never	25 Dec. 13	25 June 16
*Grant, James, Royal Waggon Train	never	25 Dec. 13	25 Sept. 14
ᵱ Grant, John,⁹⁶ Royal Artillery	1 Oct. 08	8 May 11	21 Oct. 25
ᵱ Grant, John,⁹⁷ Unattached	5 Oct. 09	15 April 13	31 Aug. 38
Grape, Henry,⁹⁸ Royal Marines	3 Oct. 00	9 April 05	22 Oct. 14
Gray, John, 9 F., *Adj. King's Own Militia*	1 Jan. 47	19 May 49	5 Nov. 52
Greatrex, Charles Butler, Royal Marines ..	15 Oct. 05	1 June 10	1 Sept. 14
Greaves, Charles, Unattached	25 Oct. 27	8 June 30	9 May 34
Green, Samuel, 78 Foot	10 Sept. 12	23 Dec. 24	
Greene, Edward,⁹⁹ Royal Artillery	13 Dec. 13	1 Aug. 16	1 Feb. 19
Greer, William, 11 Foot	6 July 09	9 July 12	25 May 17
Greetham, John Henry, Unattached	2 April 22	25 June 24	23 Mar. 32

Lieutenants.

	CORNET, ETC.	LIEUT.	WHEN PLACED ON HALF PAY.
P ⚔ Grier, Robert,[100] 44 Foot	26 Feb. 10	13 May 12	27 Mar. 17
Griffin, John, 37 Foot	8 May 11	23 Sept. 13	25 May 17
Griffith, Charles,[101] Royal Marines	2 July 03	15 Aug. 05	
P *Grimes, Robert*,[102] Royal Artillery	4 Mar. 09	16 Mar. 12	
Grove, Charles Thomas, 14 Foot	4 June 12	13 Oct. 14	24 Feb. 16
P Grueber, Daniel,[103] 30 Foot	24 Dec. 12	21 April 14	25 Mar. 17
Guest, Edward, 2 Royal Veteran Battalion	25 Aug. 07	10 Sept. 12	
Hadwen, Thomas, 80 Foot	21 May 18	18 Mar. 24	13 Feb. 38
P ⚔ Haggup, William,[105] Unattached	30 Aug. 10	13 May 12	14 Feb. 52
Haire, John, 1 Garrison Battalion	12 Nov. 06	18 Feb. 08	14 Sept. 15
Hallilay, Richard Goddard,[106] Roy. Marines	20 June 47	14 July 48	13 Feb. 54
Hallowes, Brabazon Miller, Land Trans.Cor.	30 Nov. 55	1 April 57	1 April 57
P Hamer, Michael Greathead,[107] 5 Foot	6 April 09	23 April 12	2 April 18
P Hamilton, George, Unattached	29 April 13	4 Aug. 15	22 Sept. 37
P ⚔ Hamilton, John,[108] 2 Line Batt. German Legion	26 July 12	17 Aug. 13	25 Mar. 16
Harden, William, 2 Garrison Battalion	22 Feb. 10	22 Oct. 13	25 Feb. 16
Hardman, Henry Anthony, 7 West India Regt.	16 June 06	15 Jan. 07	25 April 16
Hargrove, John Langford, 10 R. Vet. Batt.	18 Oct. 10	28 Mar. 12	
P*Harland, John, 1 Prov. Batt. of Militia	never	25 Feb. 14	1814
Harris, Charles, 60 Foot	11 Aug. 13	12 June 16	25 Oct. 17
Hart, John, 2 Foot	13 June 11	12 Aug. 13	25 Dec. 18
P *Hasleham, William Gale*,[109] 6 R. Vet. Batt.	11 Feb. 08	25 Aug. 09	
Hassard, Richard, Royal Irish Artillery		20 Oct. 94	
Hatheway, Charles, New Brunswick Fencibles	25 Mar. 13	25 Aug. 14	25 April 16
Hay, Alexander Murray, Unattached	10 Nov. 14	22 July 24	12 April 33
Hearn, John Fleming,[110] 60 Foot	5 May 08	18 Feb. 10	25 Oct. 22
⚔ Hearne, George Henry, 4 Foot	16 Mar. 09	20 Oct. 10	20 Aug. 16
*Heath, Thomas, 38 Foot	never	25 Dec. 13	25 Sept. 14
Heddle, Alexander, Royal African Corps	4 May 09	20 Mar. 10	25 Dec. 21
Henderson, James Allen, 10 Foot	28 Mar. 10	26 Feb. 12	25 Sept. 18
P Henderson, William,[111] 5 Foot	4 July 11	17 Oct. 14	25 May 17
Herrick, Edward Henry, 15 Foot	8 Oct. 12	22 June 15	25 Mar. 16
P Herron, Samuel,[112] 24 Foot	7 Sept. 09	30 May 11	6 Nov. 23
Hewat, William, 62 Foot	19 Sept. 11	22 Oct. 13	25 May 17
Hewett, James Waller, 1 Foot	9 May 11	7 July 13	24 Jan. 18
Higginbotham, Henry, 22 Dragoons	13 May 13	2 April 18	25 Sept. 20
*Hilder, Jesse, 15 Foot	never	25 Dec. 13	25 Sept. 14
P Hilliard, Christopher,[113] 5 Foot	7 July 08	22 Feb. 10	25 Nov. 18
Hilton, Wm. Legh, 98 Foot, *Paymaster, Royal Military College*	21 May 12	1 Dec. 14	22 Feb. 22
*Hinde, Edward, Rifle Brigade	never	25 Dec. 13	1814
P Hine, John,[114] Unattached	1 Aug. 27	30 April 32	8 May 40
⚔ Hodder, Edward,[115] 69 Foot	20 July 13	10 Aug. 15	25 Nov. 16
P Hodgson, Alderson,[116] 2 Foot	25 Jan. 10	22 Aug. 11	22 June 20
P Holgate, Edward Milton,[117] 82 Foot	8 May 11	23 Sept. 13	25 Jan. 16
Holland, Rupert Charles,[118] Royal Marines	27 Sept. 05	11 Aug. 09	1 April 17
P Hollis, William Henry,[119] 57 Foot	26 Aug. 07	5 May 08	24 July 17
P ⚔ Holman, Charles, 52 Foot	10 Sept. 12	11 Nov. 13	25 Dec. 18
Holmes, Charles Wm. Scott D., 3 Dragoons	21 April 14	7 Sept. 15	13 April 17
P Home, John, 3 Foot	11 Oct. 10	26 Nov. 12	3 July 17
Home, William, York Light Infantry	24 Nov. 04	7 Jan. 06	15 Jan. 24
P Hopkins, William Randolph,[121] 5 Foot	14 Sept. 08	5 Oct. 13	25 July 16
Houghton, William, 15 Foot, *Paymaster, Antrim Artillery Militia*	6 Feb. 12	4 May 15	1 Oct. 48
Hubbard, James, Royal Marines	1 Nov. 05	20 Aug. 10	1 Sept. 14
Hughes, Edward, 19 Foot	12 Nov. 12	9 Sept. 13	25 Dec. 18
Hughes, Henry Francis, Glengarry Fencibles	8 June 09	6 Feb. 12	25 Aug. 16
P *Humfrey, Robert Blake*,[122] 9 R. Vet. Batt.	30 April 12	23 Sept. 13	
P Humphreys, Cha. Gardiner,[123] 14 Dragoons	9 May 11	11 Mar. 13	4 Sept. 17
P Hunt, Michael,[124] 61 Foot	13 April 09	8 Aug. 11	2 Mar. 15
Hunter, Thomas, 18 Dragoons	25 Feb. 16	27 Nov. 18	10 Nov. 21
Hunter, William Dodsworth, 64 Foot	23 April 05	17 April 06	25 Nov. 16
P Hutchinson, John,[125] 60 Foot	12 Nov. 12	6 Nov. 15	24 April 23
Hutton, William, Royal Marines, *Chief Officer of Coast Guard*	26 Nov. 24	14 May 33	28 Sept. 37
Huyghue, Samuel, 60 Foot	30 Aug. 10	26 Jan. 15	25 Oct. 17
P Inglis, Edward,[126] 3 Dragoon Guards	1 Oct. 12	17 June 13	25 Mar. 16
Inman, Thomas Withy, 45 Foot	4 Jan. 10	7 Oct. 13	16 Mar. 15
P ⚔ Innes, Alexander,[127] Unattached	19 July 10	15 Oct. 12	24 Nov. 28
Innes, Robert, 48 Foot	2 Dec. 13	4 April 15	25 Dec. 28

Lieutenants. 491

Name	2D LIEUT. ETC.	LIEUT.	WHEN PLACED ON HALF PAY.
Irvine, Robert, 7 West India Regiment	22 July 13	4 May 15	11 July 16
Irving, Robert, 32 Foot..................	16 May 11	7 July 14	26 Oct. 15
Irwin, Alexander,[128] 3 Foot	4 Mar. 13	24 Nov. 14	13 Jan. 37
Irwin, John Robert,[129] 54 Foot	25 Feb. 08	28 Dec. 09	18 Feb. 14
ℙ𝕎 Isaacson, Egert.Cha. H.,[130] Gar.Comp.	30 Dec. 12	14 July 14	25 Sept. 23
Jackson, Frederick, 27 Foot, *Adjutant,* Leicester Yeomanry Cavalry	24 Aug. 26	8 Sept. 32	29 Aug. 34
Jackson, William, 64 Foot	3 Oct. 11	29 June 15	15 Mar. 17
Jameson, William, 37 Foot	21 May 12	2 Feb. 14	7 Aug. 17
Jappie, William, 14 Foot	14 May 11	29 April 13	25 Mar. 17
Jeffreyson, George, 2 Royal Vet. Battalion	28 July 95	12 Jan. 96	
ℙ Jeffries, Joseph,[131] 1 Foot	8 May 11	5 July 13	14 May 18
Jones, Jeremy, 60 Foot...................	9 May 11	10 Feb. 13	9 April 19
Jones, Thomas Edward, 4 Foot, *Town Major at St. John's, New Brunswick*	6 Feb. 46	14 May 49	17 June 53
ℙ Jordan, Edward,[132] 26 Foot	25 Aug. 07	10 Aug. 08	16 Oct. 17
Kane, John Joseph, 4 Foot	21 Oct. 13	4 May 15	25 Mar. 17
Kayes, William, 73 Foot	14 May 12	10 Aug. 14	25 Mar. 15
Kean, John Henry, Land Transport Corps..	26 Dec. 55	1 April 57	1 April 57
ℙ Kearnes, John,[133] 08 Foot.................	5 Jan. 14	26 Feb. 18	25 July 19
ℙ Keep, William Thornton,[134] 28 Foot	29 Aug. 11	8 Sept. 13	25 Dec. 14
Kennedy, John Pitt, 42 Foot	23 Mar. 49	15 Mar. 53	11 Nov. 53
*Kennedy, P. Henry, 2 Prov. Batt. of Militia	never	25 Dec. 13	1814
Kerr, John Henry, 104 Foot	21 Jan. 13	23 Nov. 20	15 Mar. 21
Kersteman, Harry Gobins, Royal Artillery..	12 Dec. 11	20 Sept. 14	2 Sept. 22
King, William, Royal Artillery	19 June 41	13 April 42	3 Nov. 47
Knight, Frederick Charles,[135] Royal Marines	9 July 44	29 Dec. 47	24 July 56
Knight, William, 28 Foot................	14 Feb. 05	28 May 07	3 Dec. 18
ℙ Knox, Francis,[136] 31 Foot..................	23 Mar. 08	23 May 10	14 Aug. 17
ℙ Lacy, Samuel Walter,[137] 10 Foot........	4 Oct. 10	16 Sept. 13	24 June 24
La Grange, Jas. Warrington, 3 Dragoon Gds.	10 Mar. 14	5 Oct. 15	25 Mar. 16
*Lambert, John, 2 Prov. Battalion of Militia	never	25 Mar. 14	1814
Lander, Alfred, Land Transport Corps	....	22 Sept. 55	1 April 57
Lander, Wm. Henry, do.	....	7 Sept. 55	1 April 57
ℙ Lane, Ambrose,[138] 83 Foot................	28 May 11	28 July 13	25 June 17
Lane, Charles Henry John, Unattached	26 Mar. 18	27 May 24	1 Jan. 50
Lane, John, Unattached	22 June 15	30 Dec. 26	24 April 28
ℙ Langdon, Colwell,[139] 60 Foot	6 April 09	21 Dec. 09	30 Sept. 19
Latham, John, 92 Foot...................	1 July 13	14 July 14	25 Dec. 14
Laye, George, 24 Foot	14 July 14	29 April 19	24 Mar. 25
Leach, Henry, Scots Fusilier Guards	never	5 July 15	25 Dec. 18
Leathes, Edward, 8 Dragoons	14 Nov. 10	25 Sept. 23	6 May 24
Leavach, John, 3 West India Regiment....	17 Aug. 09	3 July 11	17 Feb. 20
ℙ Leggett, John,[140] 3 Dragoon Guards	28 Feb. 08	15 Sept. 08	16 Oct. 16
Leslie, Angus, 93 Foot	12 Mar. 12	10 Feb. 14	25 Mar. 17
ℙ L'Estrange, George,[141] Scots Fusilier Gds.	16 Jan. 12	17 June 13	11 July 22
L'Estrange, Torriano Francis,[142] Coldst. Gds.	20 Oct. 14	16 Oct. 17	16 Nov. 20
Lewis, Henry,[143] Royal Marines	1 Sept. 06	4 Aug. 13	1 Sept. 14
Lewis, Thomas, 3 Garrison Battalion	12 May 14	10 Oct. 15	25 Nov. 16
Lewis, William, 19 Foot	12 Mar. 10	10 May 14	20 July 20
ℙ Lindsey, Henry John,[144] Unattached	5 Dec. 11	11 Jan. 16	31 Jan. 28
Lisle, Benjamin de, Canadian Fencibles....	6 Dec. 10	2 Sept. 12	11 Oct. 16
ℂ Lister, John,[145] Royal Marines	23 Feb. 05	27 July 08	26 Nov. 25
Little, John William, Unattached	1 Jan. 19	12 Mar. 24	11 July 29
ℙ𝕎 Lloyd, Edward Bell, 16 Dragoons	30 May 11	11 Mar. 12	25 Aug. 19
Locke, William, 5 Dragoon Guards........	9 June 14	3 July 17	20 Mar. 23
ℙ Long, Edmund Slingsby,[147] 23 Foot	3 Aug. 04	8 Aug. 05	5 Aug. 13
Lonsdale, Alured, 84 Foot................	20 May 26	3 Aug. 30	8 April 36
ℙ 𝕎 Lonsdale, William,[146] 4 Foot	1 Feb. 10	15 May 12	25 Mar. 17
Lovelace, Henry Philip, Unattached	25 Aug. 00	24 May 11	23 Aug. 27
*Lovett, Joseph Venables, 3 Prov. Batt. Mil.	never	25 Feb. 14	1814
Lovett, Thomas, Royal Artillery	1 April 09	17 April 12	1 Mar. 22
ℙ Lowry, Armar,[149] 45 Foot................	31 Dec. 12	28 July 14	25 Dec. 14
Lowry, John,[150] 95 Foot	7 June 10	24 Dec. 12	13 July 20
ℙ 𝕎 Lucas, Jasper,[151] 32 Foot	6 Jan. 13	19 July 15	25 Mar. 17
Lynam, Charles, 15 Foot	25 June 12	16 Nov. 15	25 Mar. 16
Lynch, Edward Crean, 22 Foot	11 Dec. 23	21 Jan. 26	8 April 34
Lyster, Arthur O'Neil, 46 Foot	2 Sept. 24	13 June 30	7 Sept. 33
Lyster, Henry, 7 Dragoons	29 May 17	7 Sept. 20	25 Oct. 21
M'Annally, Charles, 84 Foot..............	26 Nov. 06	31 Dec. 07	5 Oct. 20

Lieutenants.

	ENSIGN, ETC.	LIEUT.	WHEN PLACED ON HALF PAY.
M'Carthy, Justin Thadeus Courtney, R. Mar.	17 Jan. 33	13 Jan. 38	10 May 30
𝔓 M'Crohan, Denis Eugene,[152] 3 R. Vet. Batt.	16 May 12	21 Oct. 13	
M'Dermott, James, 20 Dragoons	15 Oct. 12	31 Mar. 14	25 Mar. 16
𝔓 M'Dermott, Thomas,[153] 7 Royal Veteran Batt., *Military Knight of Windsor* ..	1 Nov. 94	25 Feb. 05	
M'Donald, Colin, 72 Foot	25 Nov. 08	21 Feb. 11	25 Feb. 16
Macduff, Alex., 100 Foot	23 Feb. 09	9 July 12	15 May 18
M'Gregor, John, 46 Foot	12 May 20	22 Dec. 24	25 Dec. 28
M'Intosh, W., Land Transport Corps	1 Dec. 55	1 April 57	1 April 57
M'Intyre, Peter,[156] Royal Marines	21 Sept. 05	16 May 09	1 Sept. 14
M'Kenzie, John, Canadian Fencibles	31 Dec. 12	8 Sept. 14	11 Oct. 16
M'Kinnon, John, 104 Foot	18 Dec. 06	15 Mar. 10	25 July 17
𝔓 M'Laren, Alexander Donald,[157] 91 Foot	3 June 12	31 Mar. 14	25 Feb. 16
M'Leroth, Thomas, Royal Marines	17 June 13	16 April 32	22 April 33
M'Loughlin, Patrick,[158] 50 Foot	17 Sept. 46	13 Oct. 48	13 Sept. 53
M'Namara, Michael, 60 Foot	2 Nov. 00	18 Oct. 10	28 June 19
𝔓 M'Nicol, Nicol,[159] 27 Foot	14 May 12	10 Feb. 14	16 April 17
M'Niel, Donald, Cape Regt.	23 Aug. 10	4 June 14	17 July 18
M'Pherson, Alex., R. Art. Riding Troop ..	...	1 Jan. 36	
𝔓 M'Pherson, Æneas,[160] 59 Foot	25 June 12	26 Sept. 13	25 April 16
M'Rae, Farquhar,[161] 66 Foot	24 June 05	21 Jan. 08	7 Feb. 22
M'Rae, Theodore, Royal African Corps ...	26 July 15	14 May 18	25 Dec. 18
Macalpine, James, 8 Dragoons	5 Mar. 12	15 Aug. 13	25 July 20
Macartney, Charles, 11 Dragoons	11 Dec. 28	13 Nov. 34	1 Nov. 38
𝕼 Macdonald, Stephen, 1 Light Infantry Battalion German Legion	22 Dec. 12	5 April 14	25 April 16
Mac Gregor, John,[162] 4 Royal Veteran Batt.	9 May 11	26 Jan. 14	
𝔓 Mac Kay, Lachlan,[163] 42 Foot	31 Oct. 11	23 Sept. 13	18 Jan. 31
Mackay, Hugh Donald, 5 West India Regt.	1 April 13	31 Mar. 14	1 Oct. 17
𝔓 Mackay, Neil,[164] 76 Foot	9 May 05	27 Feb. 06	25 Oct. 19
Mackenzie, William, 3 Dragoons	20 July 15	7 Sept. 20	25 Oct. 21
Maclauchlan, James Augustus, 104 Foot ..	5 Mar. 12	24 Feb. 14	25 July 17
Macpherson, Duncan, 52 Foot	26 Mar. 08	2 Jan. 12	13 Dec. 16
Magee, W., Land Transport Corps	23 Nov. 55	1 Feb. 56	1 April 57
ℒ Magin, William,[165] Royal Marines	2 July 03	15 Aug. 05	25 Sept. 09
Maher, Martin, R. Veteran Batt., Paymaster, Glamorgan Militia	6 April 09	17 Jan. 11	
Mahon, Edmond, 70 Foot	12 Mar. 12	15 June 15	4 Nov. 17
Mahon, James, 26 Foot	2 Jan. 12	2 Feb. 14	25 Dec. 14
March, Leopold George Fred., R. Marines, *Vice-Consul at San Sebastian*	5 Feb. 33	26 April 38	3 July 41
Marshall, Ralph, 89 Foot	3 Feb. 08	12 April 10	12 June 23
Marshall, Thomas, Royal Marines	2 Sept. 98	1 April 04	14 Aug. 07
Martin, William Neufville, 64 Foot	15 April 12	3 Mar. 14	15 Mar. 17
Mason, Francis, 8 Garrison Battalion	25 June 05	9 Oct. 06	22 Mar. 10
𝔓 Mathison, John Augustus,[166] 77 Foot ...	8 May 11	12 Aug. 13	25 Mar. 17
𝕼 Matthews, John Powell, 10 Foot	3 Nov. 14	7 April 25	31 Dec. 30
*Mawby, Joseph, 3 Prov. Bn. of Militia	never	9 Mar. 14	1814
Maxwell, John, 8 West India Regt.	18 July 11	24 Dec. 12	1816
Meares, John,[167] Royal Marines	20 Mar. 09	18 Sept. 27	2 Oct. 28
𝔓 Mellish, William,[168] Royal Waggon Train	20 Nov. 05	17 Nov. 08	16 Mar. 15
Mercer, Alexander, 42 Foot	15 April 13	1 June 15	25 Mar. 17
𝕼 Middleton, Thos. Falkner, 1 Drag. Gds.	28 Oct. 13	4 May 15	25 July 16
𝔓 Miles, George,[169] 7 Foot	25 May 09	16 May 11	14 Mar. 22
Miller, William, Royal Artillery	10 July 15	7 April 21	25 Jan. 25
Miller, Zaccheus,[170] Royal Marines	20 May 97	19 July 03	
𝔓 *Milne, James Miles,* 5 Royal Vet. Batt.	2 Mar. 08	31 Mar. 10	
Milnes, Alfred Shore, Royal Artillery	5 July 13	15 Jan. 16	5 Sept. 22
Milnes, Thomas Milnes Smith, 28 Foot ..	28 Nov. 11	9 Feb. 15	25 Mar. 17
Minchin, Charles Humphrey, R. Engineers	1 Jan. 14	1 Aug. 14	24 June 19
Minchin, George, New Brunswick Fencibles	25 Mar. 13	25 Dec. 14	25 May 16
𝔓 Mitchell, Robert,[171] 28 Foot	15 Feb. 10	11 Feb. 13	25 Mar. 17
𝔓 Mogridge, James Edward,[172] 34 Foot...	11 April 09	28 June 10	2 Oct. 17
Monck, Charles Stanley, 44 Foot	10 Oct. 11	31 Dec. 12	25 Mar. 17
Money, George, 12 Foot	1 Jan. 12	15 July 13	25 Mar. 17
Moore, James Adolphus,[173] Royal Marines..	14 Oct. 05	14 May 10	8 Sept. 20
*Moore, Joshua John, 14 Foot	never	25 Dec. 13	25 Sept. 14
*Moore, Samuel, 38 Foot	never	25 Dec. 13	25 Sept. 14
𝔓 𝕼 Moorhead, Charles,[174] 71 Foot	23 Aug. 10	3 Sept. 12	25 Dec. 18
𝔓 Moreton, Moses,[175] 54 Foot	26 Nov. 07	28 April 08	4 Sept. 17

Lieutenants. 493

	2D LIEUT. ETC.	LIEUT.	WHEN PLACED ON HALF PAY.
Morgan, Thomas, Royal Marines.........	2 Oct. 00	30 Mar. 05	17 Oct. 14
Morley, Edward Lacy, Royal York Rangers	16 Aug. 10	13 Jan. 13	25 Mar. 17
P Morphy, Richard,[176] 3 Foot............	2 April 12	26 Aug. 13	25 Mar. 17
Mosley, Godfrey Goodman,[175]† 7 Foot	1 May 46	11 May 49	19 Nov. 58
Mosse, Henry Alexander, 94 Foot	31 Dec. 07	4 Jan. 10	25 Mar. 19
P Mostyn, Robert,[177] 81 Foot	28 Aug. 08	26 Sept. 11	18 April 17
QM MountEdgcumbe,E.A.,*Earl of*,[178]Gr.Gds.	never	12 Jan. 14	25 Feb. 19
Mountford, Joseph,[179] Royal Marines......	12 April 06	2 June 12	1 Sept. 14
P Munro, Frederick,[160] Royal Artillery	20 Dec. 09	3 Sept. 13	23 June 24
QM Muro, George,[161] Grenadier Guards....	never	14 April 14	15 June 20
Murphy, John, Land Transport Corps	....	22 Sept. 55	1 April 57
P Murray, Francis,[182] 94 Foot	29 June 09	7 July 14	25 Dec. 18
*Myers, William, 2 Prov. Bn. of Militia....	never	25 Dec. 13	1814
Nagel, John, Ceylon Regiment, *Barrack Master at Castlebar*	20 Dec. 46	5 Jan. 49	17 June 51
Nangle, George, 76 Foot	29 Jan. 06	30 June 08	4 Sept. 17
P Nantes, Richard,[183] 55 Foot, *Military Knight of Windsor*	never	19 Oct. 09	25 Dec. 14
Napier, Duncan Campbell, Meuron's Regt.	24 Feb. 14	4 May 15	5 Aug. 16
Nason, Henry, 8 West India Regt........	10 Sept. 11	29 Feb. 16	25 Dec. 16
Neame, Charles Covell, 13 Foot	20 May 42	14 Feb. 45	27 May 56
Nesfield, William Andrews, 48 Foot	26 June 12	30 Mar. 14	25 Dec. 18
*Newbolt, Francis, Royal Waggon Train ..	never	25 Dec. 13	25 Sept. 14
P Newton, Hibbert,[181] 32 Foot............	27 July 09	13 April 13	25 Mar. 17
Newton, John, 15 Dragoons..............	16 Sept. 95	2 Dec. 95	23 Aug. 02
Newton, Thomas Charles, R. Waggon Train	23 April 13	7 Sept. 15	25 Aug. 16
Newton, Walter, 21 Dragoons	6 Aug. 09	2 Nov. 10	2 Aug. 20
QM Nicholson, John,[185] 14 Foot, *Quartermaster, East York Militia*	25 Dec. 13	5 April 15	25 Mar. 16
P Nicholson, Richard, 5 Foot	27 Dec. 10	7 Oct. 13	25 July 16
C Nicolas, Paule Harris,[186] Royal Marines..	6 July 05	27 July 08	1 Sept. 14
Nicoll, Samuel James,[146]† Royal Marines ..	24 June 54	10 Sept. 55	26 July 59
Nisbett, Henry, 24 Dragoons	20 Mar. 06	16 Feb. 09	25 Dec. 18
P QM Nixon, Wm. Richmond,[187] 52 Foot..	26 July 10	11 May 12	25 Nov. 19
P Norman, William,[188] 69 Foot	7 Mar. 10	14 May 12	25 April 26
Norris, Robert, 20 Dragoons	9 May 16	18 Mar. 18	31 Dec. 18
O'Connor, Bernard Richard, 44 Foot	18 May 09	22 Nov. 10	18 July 16
P O'Connor, Maurice,[189] 97 Foot	10 Aug. 08	25 Oct. 10	20 Jan. 20
O'Dell, Edm. Westropp, 98 Foot..........	12 Sept. 05	13 Aug. 07	25 Sept. 18
O'Kelly, James, 4 Foot..................	8 Mar. 10	16 Nov. 12	20 Mar. 23
*Oliver, John, 33 Foot	never	25 Dec. 13	25 Sept. 14
Ollerton, James, Land Transport Corps	....	6 Sept. 55	1 April 57
O'Neill, Henry, Unattached..............	30 June 25	29 Aug. 26	11 July 37
QM Onslow, Phipps Vansittart,[191] R. Artillery	17 Dec. 07	16 Dec. 08	9 Dec. 24
P O'Reilly, John, 11 Foot................	25 April 11	16 Sept. 13	25 May 16
Ormsby, Henry Michael, 36 Foot	2 Jan. 12	1 Oct. 12	25 Mar. 17
P Ormsby, James,[192] 25 Dragoons	10 Oct. 06	14 Mar. 08	10 Feb. 20
P Ormsby, Sewell, 6 Foot	7 Mar. 05	8 Jan. 07	11 Dec. 17
Orr, James,[193] Royal Marines	26 Nov. 04	27 July 08	1 April 17
P QM *Orr, John*,[194] 8 Royal Veteran Batt.	3 Oct. 11	29 April 13	
Oughton, James, 61 Foot................	20 Feb. 12	20 Oct. 16	25 Mar. 19
QM Pagan, Samuel Alex.,[195] 55 Foot	31 Oct. 11	7 April 14	14 Feb. 22
Pannell, Robert, 60 Foot	30 Mar. 12	2 Aug. 13	25 June 19
Parke, Samuel, 2 Garrison Battalion	9 Feb. 09	4 Mar. 11	7 Sept. 15
Parker, Kenyon Stevens,[196] Royal Marines, *A Queen's Counsel*................	26 Nov. 05	15 Jan. 11	1 Sept. 14
P Parratt, Hillebrant Mered.,[197] R. Art. *Lieut.-Col. 2nd Royal Surrey Militia*	29 Oct. 08	11 July 11	12 Sept. 22
P QM Parry, James,[198] 28 Foot	10 Sept. 12	27 Jan. 14	25 Mar. 17
*Parry, Thomas, 3 Prov. Bn. of Militia....	never	25 Feb. 14	1814
Paton, George, 22 Dragoons.............	12 July 10	1 July 12	25 Sept. 16
Patterson, John Williams, 60 Foot, *Inspecting Lieut. of Coast Guard*	18 April 11	3 Sept. 12	11 Oct. 19
P Paxton, Archd. Frederick,[200] 11 Dragoons	26 June 11	19 Dec. 11	23 July 17
Peach, John Carroll, Royal African Corps..	3 Sept. 12	25 Aug. 14	25 Feb. 19
Peacocke, Warren William Richard, 17 Foot	18 Jan. 39	1 April 42	13 Aug. 47
Pearse, Edward Octavius, Royal Marines, *Adjutant, R. Anglesey Militia*	16 May 48	24 Nov. 40	30 April 58
Peel, Edmund, 25 Foot..................	15 Mar. 15	13 Mar. 17	2 May 22
Peers, Henry de Linné, 53 Foot	20 Jan. 12	22 July 13	17 Aug. 20

Lieutenants.

	ENSIGN, ETC.	LIEUT.	WHEN PLACED ON HALF PAY.
P Penfold, Edward,[202] 12 Dragoons	29 Aug. 11	25 Mar. 12	25 Mar. 17
P Pennefather, Richard,[203] 87 Foot	14 June 10	26 Sept. 11	31 July 17
P Pennington, Rowland,[204] 5 R. Vet. Batt.	8 Sept. 08	23 May 11	
P Pepper, Theobald,[205] 3 Dragoon Guards	14 Sept. 08	27 June 11	25 Mar. 16
Percy, Francis, 51 Foot	22 July 13	16 Oct. 17	25 Dec. 18
Perham, John, Royal Marines	26 June 06	9 Feb. 13	9 Sept. 26
Perham, William, Royal Marines	20 Sept. 05	20 Feb. 00	1 Sept. 14
Perry, Henry, Royal Waggon Train	5 Jan. 05	18 Aug. 14	31 Jan. 15
Perry, Richard Lavite, 44 Foot	20 Dec. 10	3 Sept. 12	25 Mar. 17
Philips, Henry,[204] Riding Troop, Royal Art.	25 Mar. 28	31 July 35	9 May 55
Pickard, Henry William,[206] Royal Artillery	17 Dec. 12	21 May 15	29 April 31
Pictet, Armand Jacques,[207] Unatt., Consul at Geneva	9 Feb. 15	6 April 26	21 Feb. 28
Pictet, Frederick, 60 Foot	25 June 12	22 Jan. 14	24 Sept. 19
Pigou, Lawrence, 2 Dragoon Guards	17 Nov. 14	8 Aug. 10	25 Mar. 17
Pinniger, Broome, 6 West India Regiment	2 April 12	1 Dec. 13	28 Dec. 17
Playfair, Andrew William, 104 Foot	26 April 10	7 Nov. 11	25 July 17
*Plowman, Thomas, Royal Waggon Train	never	25 Dec. 13	25 Sept. 14
Plunkett, Thomas Richard, 18 Dragoons	6 Mar. 11	1 July 13	6 Oct. 25
P Poe, Purefoy,[208] 30 Foot	13 June 09	1 July 13	17 April 17
☿ Polhill, William,[209] 23 Dragoons	1 July 13	13 Dec. 15	10 Jan. 19
Porter, Henry, Royal Marines	7 July 03	15 Aug. 05	9 Sept. 14
Porter, Robert, 7 Foot	7 Dec. 09	3 Mar. 12	11 April 16
Powell, James Bruce, 12 Foot	22 June 00	26 Feb. 12	16 April 18
Pridham, William,[210] Royal Marines	13 July 99	18 Aug. 04	23 Oct. 16
P *Priest, John*,[211] R. Artillery Drivers	13 July 05	1 Jan. 06	
Pringle, James, 81 Foot	3 Aug. 09	5 Aug. 13	18 April 17
Probyn, John, 20 Foot	4 June 01	14 April 04	16 June 08
Puddicombe, Robert Bruce, Royal Marines	20 Feb. 34	10 May 39	22 Nov. 44
Rainsforth, Charles, 67 Foot	2 Sept. 12	5 Feb. 16	28 Feb. 20
Rainsforth, Charles, Unattached	2 Feb. 15	8 April 25	19 May 25
Ramsden, George, Royal Artillery	10 July 15	7 Nov. 21	30 Mar. 25
Rankine, David, Rifle Brigade	25 Feb. 13	17 Nov. 14	25 Dec. 18
P Ratcliff, William,[212] 1 Garrison Battalion	25 Aug. 07	13 April 09	6 Dec. 14
P Read, Robert,[213] Unattached	21 Mar. 11	23 April 13	26 May 25
Reeves, *Lewis Buckle*,[214] Royal Marines	23 April 04	12 Mar. 07	1 April 17
Renny, *Henry Laws*, Royal Engineers	20 July 13	15 Dec. 13	
Reveley, George Williamson, 30 Foot	15 May 11	6 July 14	20 June 19
P Reynett, William France,[215] 73 Foot	20 July 09	28 Feb. 11	24 Dec. 18
☿ Reynolds, Thos. Matthew,[216] 12 Foot	20 Feb. 12	10 Mar. 14	8 April 24
P Ribton, *Sir John, Bt.*,[217] 23 Foot	6 Feb. 11	25 June 12	5 Feb. 18
Rich, Henry, 4 West India Regiment	21 Jan. 12	4 Feb. 13	30 Nov. 20
Richardes, William Eardley,[218] R. Artillery	11 July 14	25 Jan. 19	12 May 24
Richmond, Sylvester,[219] 48 Foot	9 Aug. 11	24 April 13	3 Oct. 22
Ricketts, Alfred, 9 Foot	8 July 13	22 Dec. 14	25 Feb. 16
Rideout, Henry Wood, 19 Foot	21 Sept. 15	19 April 18	20 July 26
Riet, William Van der, Cape Regiment	6 June 14	13 April 15	25 Dec. 16
Rigby, Samuel, New Brunswick Fencibles	28 June 10	3 Nov. 11	27 June 16
Ritchie, James, 1 Foot	20 Feb. 17	21 Feb. 27	25 Sept. 27
Robb, David, 25 Dragoons	14 July 08	16 Oct. 09	6 Jan. 20
Robertson, George Duncan, 21 Foot	4 Aug. 40	9 Nov. 43	20 Oct. 48
P ☿ Robertson, James,[221] 79 Foot	6 Jan. 14	20 July 15	25 Feb. 16
Robinson, George, 60 Foot	15 Sept. 08	7 Nov. 09	25 April 19
P ☿ Robinson, James,[222] 50 Foot	10 Dec. 07	17 May 10	20 Mar. 23
Robinson, John, 85 Foot	14 Mar. 05	8 Jan. 07	30 Sept. 19
Robinson, Isaac Byrne, 92 Foot	17 Dec. 18	3 Nov. 25	8 Feb. 43
P Robinson, William Henry, 45 Foot	28 Nov. 11	27 Aug. 13	11 Feb. 15
*Rochfort, John, 100 Foot	never	25 Dec. 13	25 Sept. 14
P Rogers, Adam,[223] 6 Garrison Battalion	25 Oct. 07	15 Mar. 09	4 Feb. 15
Rogers, John, Royal Marines	10 April 11	30 June 29	14 May 31
Rollo, James, 59 Foot	27 Mar. 12	5 Aug. 13	25 May 16
ℭ Rooke, Lewis,[224] Royal Marines	6 Oct. 14	20 Jan. 08	1 Sept. 14
Rooney, Bernard, 2 Garrison Battalion	4 Nov. 13	24 May 15	24 Oct. 15
Rose, John, Irish Brigade	12 Feb. 04	13 Feb. 94	11 Oct. 98
Roscingrave, Matthew, 10 Foot	2 April 07	11 Feb. 08	25 Sept. 17
Ross, Emilius, Unattached	10 Aug. 15	26 June 27	28 June 30
P ☿ Ross, Ewen,[225] 92 Foot	13 April 09	26 Nov. 12	25 Mar. 17
ℭ *Rotely, Lewis*,[226] Royal Marines	27 July 07	27 July 08	
Rothwell, William, Unattached	10 July 11	25 Nov. 13	12 Oct. 26
Rouse, Richard,[227] Royal Marines	3 Nov. 98	18 Aug. 04	13 Dec. 05

Lieutenants. 495

	2D LIEUT. ETC.	LIEUT.	WHEN PLACED ON HALF PAY.
Rowan, John Hill, Unattached	15 Nov. 27	8 July 32	31 Aug. 30
Russell, Henry James, 60 Foot	4 Aug. 08	10 Aug. 13	25 Aug. 19
𝔓 Rutherford, James,228 23 Foot	15 Feb. 10	27 Oct. 14	15 June 15
Ryan, John Dennis, 22 Dragoons	29 Aug. 15	10 Oct. 16	25 Sept. 20
Rybot, Henry Day,229 Royal Marines	20 Aug. 52	24 Feb. 54	11 Mar. 59
St. John, John, 12 Foot	15 July 13	9 Aug. 15	25 Mar. 17
St. John, Richard Fleming, Royal Artillery	16 Dec. 16	8 April 25	1 Oct. 30
Sanders, David Morison, Unattached	12 May 13	9 Mar. 20	25 May 26
Sanders, Gilbert H., 30 Foot, *Barrack Master at Parkhurst*	15 Dec. 54	17 Aug. 55	31 Aug. 58
Sandwith, Geo. Aug. Elliott,230 R. Marines	14 Oct. 05	25 April 10	1 Sept. 14
Sargent, Samuel, 1 Royal Veteran Battalion	1 Nov. 09	17 Oct. 10	20 Feb. 23
Sarsfield, Bingham, Unattached	1 Aug. 11	30 Dec. 14	27 July 26
Saunders, Andrew Childers, 1 Dragoons	19 Aug. 13	31 Mar. 14	25 Mar. 16
𝔓 Saunders, Robert Francis,231 68 Foot	16 Mar. 09	7 Dec. 09	8 Jan. 20
𝕸 Saunders, Robert John,232 Royal Artillery	26 Nov. 08	11 Aug. 11	1 April 21
𝔓 Sawkins, William,233 3 Garrison Battalion	26 Dec. 11	6 Jan. 14	25 July 17
Sawyers, John, Royal Marines	24 Dec. 04	27 July 08	14 June 18
Schneider, Robert Wilmot, Unattached	10 April 25	8 April 26	29 Nov. 27
Scobell, John,234 Royal Marines	27 Jan. 96	20 Oct. 97	27 Nov. 02
𝔓 Scott, David,235 7 Royal Veteran Battalion	28 Nov. 11	25 Jan. 13	
𝔓 Scott, Percy, 98 Foot, *Captain, commanding Isle of Wight Militia*	22 June 12	28 Nov. 15	20 Aug. 17
𝕸 Sedley, John Somner,237 R. Staff Corps, *Barrack-Master at the Mauritius*	6 May 13	23 Oct. 17	25 Dec. 18
Segrave, O'Neil, Unattached	23 June 25	13 May 26	26 Mar. 30
Shadforth, Henry J. Tudor, Unattached	14 Oct. 19	4 Dec. 23	21 Mar. 29
Shafto, William Henry, 16 Foot	5 Aug. 13	28 Sept. 15	25 Mar. 17
Sharpe, John, 54 Foot	14 April 08	19 April 09	10 Sept. 12
Sharpin, Henry, 53 Foot	4 Feb. 13	7 Nov. 15	10 Feb. 32
Shaw, George, Unattached	17 May 14	4 Sept. 23	13 July 26
Shaw, Samuel, 4 Foot	17 Oct. 05	20 Sept. 08	30 Sept. 19
Simpson, James, 89 Foot	23 May 11	23 Sept. 13	28 Nov. 16
*Singleton, Jonathan Felix, 2 Prov. Bn. of Mil.	never	25 Dec. 13	1814
Slaney, Moreton, 25 Dragoons	21 Nov. 05	24 Aug. 07	1 Dec. 20
Smith, Alexander,236 Royal Marines	12 Sept. 99	1 Sept. 04	15 Dec. 06
Smith, Edward Atkins, 31 Foot	25 July 09	2 May 11	11 April 22
*Smith, Henry Pascoe, 12 Foot	never	25 Dec. 13	25 Sept. 14
Smith, Henry Porter, Rifle Brigade	16 June 14	24 June 10	24 May 21
Smith, James Berridge, 21 Dragoons	1 Oct. 12	26 Aug. 13	30 Oct. 23
𝕸 Smith, James Ramsay,239 38 Foot	13 Oct. 14	20 Mar. 24	6 July 26
Smith, Leonard Fleming, 26 Foot	5 June 12	19 May 14	14 May 15
Smith, Peter, Royal Artillery Drivers	never	30 April 04	
𝔓 Smith, Ralph,240 53 Foot	22 Sept. 08	22 Mar. 10	8 May 23
𝔓 Smith, Robert,241 1 Foot	4 April 05	20 Feb. 06	11 July 16
Smith, William,242 Royal Artillery Drivers	14 Jan. 07	3 Mar. 09	1 July 16
𝔓 𝕸 Smith, William,243 71 Foot	1 Sept. 13	19 July 15	25 Feb. 16
Smyth, Thomas, 34 Foot	29 June 09	28 Aug. 11	25 Jan. 17
𝔓 Smyth, William,244 Scots Fusilier Guards	16 May 11	3 June 19	30 Dec. 19
Souter, Richard, 40 Foot	25 Sept. 35	4 Oct. 44	12 June 46
𝔓 Spaight, Henry,245 2 Dragoon Guards	3 Mar. 14	11 Oct. 21	23 June 25
Spalding, Warner Reeve, 8 R. Vet. Batt.	26 Mar. 07	13 Nov. 10	
𝕸 Sperling, John,246 Royal Engineers	14 Dec. 11	1 July 12	24 Jan. 24
Spottiswood, Andrew, 21 Foot	4 July 11	3 Feb. 14	25 Mar. 17
Sproule, Edward,247 60 Foot	26 Jan. 08	1 Feb. 10	5 Nov. 18
𝔓 Stacey, Edwin,248 12 Dragoons	30 May 11	26 Mar. 12	25 Aug. 14
𝕸 Stainforth, George,249 23 Foot	29 July 13	19 July 15	25 Mar. 17
Stansfield, Robert, 20 Foot, *Major, 6 West York Militia*	19 Sept. 26	2 Nov. 32	4 Aug. 37
𝔓 Stapleton, Richard,250 Unatt., *Chief Officer of Coast Guard*	19 April 14	7 April 25	24 May 27
Stapleton, William Bull, Staff Corps of Cav.	26 Nov. 12	25 Feb. 13	9 Nov. 15
𝔓 Staveley-Shirt, John,251 4 Foot	25 Dec. 06	9 Mar. 09	12 Nov. 18
𝔓 Stawell, William,252 98 Foot	19 Sept. 11	9 Nov. 15	25 Dec. 17
Steade, Charles, 60 Foot	never	22 Feb. 16	23 Oct. 17
Steele, Arthur Charles,253 Royal Marines	28 Dec. 40	27 May 48	31 May 56
Stewart, Mervyn, 21 Dragoons	12 Jan. 15	25 Jan. 16	10 July 20
Stobart, Henry,254 Royal Artillery, *Honorary Colonel, Durham Artillery Militia*	12 Dec. 11	29 Aug. 14	10 July 26
Stronach, William, Royal Engineers	24 Mar. 15	11 Nov. 16	31 Dec. 24

Lieutenants.

	CORNET, ETC.	LIEUT.	WHEN PLACED ON HALF PAY.
Stuart, Charles George, 88 Foot	9 May 11	20 April 14	25 Mar. 16
ℙ Stuart, George Evans,[255] 61 Foot	28 Feb. 12	20 Jan. 14	25 Dec. 14
Stuart, Peter, 1 Royal Veteran Battalion	never	14 Oct. 06	
ℚℕ Stuart, Robert Thomson,[256] 28 Foot	5 Aug. 13	18 July 15	25 Mar. 17
Stuart, William,[257] Royal Marines	24 April 04	24 Mar. 07	25 June 16
Sutherland, Sutherland Hall, 65 Foot	22 June 15	15 Feb. 16	4 April 23
Suttie, Sir Geo. Grant, Bart. Scots. Fus. Gds.	never	17 April 17	25 Dec. 18
Swain, Henry Thomas, R. Marines	10 Nov. 42	27 July 47	14 June 52
Swanson, Thomas, 42 Foot	25 May 08	25 Oct. 10	17 Mar. 13
Sweeting, George, 7 Foot	never	4 Aug. 14	16 Dec. 19
Swiny, Shapland William, 39 Foot	16 May 11	29 April 13	11 July 16
Symonds, William, 60 Foot	27 Jan. 07	2 July 07	25 Mar. 17
ℙ Syret, James,[258] 9 Foot	23 Jan. 12	26 Aug. 13	25 Mar. 17
Talbot, William, Land Transport Corps	7 Dec. 55	1 April 57	1 April 57
Tane, Thos. James Waldegrave,[259] R. Marines	2 July 03	15 Aug. 05	17 Aug. 14
ℙ Tatlock, Thomas,[260] 62 Foot	8 Mar. 09	15 Aug. 11	2 Oct. 17
Taylor, John, 74 Foot	25 Dec. 13	1 June 20	25 Nov. 21
Taylor, Joseph Henry, Unattached	16 Dec. 19	26 July 26	2 Feb. 30
Taylor, Nathaniel, 90 Foot	21 May 12	13 July 15	25 Dec. 18
* Thackeray, Joseph, 51 Foot	never	25 Dec. 13	25 Sept. 14
Thiballier, Hubert, 35 Foot	3 July 06	26 Dec. 06	11 June 18
ℙ Thompson, Benjamin,[261] 1 R. Vet. Batt.	11 July 11	29 Aug. 16	
Thompson, John, Unattached	15 May 28	15 Aug. 34	26 May 38
ℙ Thompson, Ralph Keddey,[262] 26 Foot	26 Mar. 12	21 Oct. 13	2 April 18
ℙ Thompson, Tho. James,[263] Unattached	10 Nov. 08	24 May 10	28 Dec. 26
Thomson, Joseph, 15 Foot	20 April 13	7 Sept. 15	25 Mar. 16
ℙ Thornton, John,[264] 42 Foot	27 Aug. 07	2 Aug. 10	17 July 17
Thorold, Frederick, Unattached	3 Oct. 26	16 Jan. 29	18 May 32
ℚℕ Tighe, Daniel,[265] Grenadier Guards	never	20 Nov. 14	15 Feb. 21
Tisdall, James, 10 Foot	3 Jan. 11	14 April 13	25 Jan. 16
Tolcher, Christopher, 2 Foot	20 July 15	9 July 18	25 Dec. 18
Torkington, Henry Theodore, 16 Foot	14 Aug. 35	26 June 38	20 Mar. 42
Tour, Augustus de la, R. Foreign Artillery	26 July 10	1 Mar. 15	1 Feb. 17
ℙ Town, Edward,[266] Dillon's Regiment	26 Nov. 12	17 Mar. 14	9 Nov. 15
ℙℚℕ Townsend, John,[267] Royal Artillery	21 Dec. 08	1 Dec. 11	6 Feb. 26
Townsend, Joseph, Royal Engineers	1 Sept. 15	20 Dec. 22	21 April 23
Townsend, Robert Lawrence, 18 Dragoons	2 Dec. 13	13 Jan. 20	30 Aug. 21
Trant, William, 80 Foot	23 April 07	25 May 08	11 Dec. 17
Travers, Joseph O., 60 Foot		29 Aug. 22	7 Sept. 22
Travers, Lyon Conway,[268] 60 Foot	20 July 44	22 June 47	13 Dec. 53
Trebeck, Thomas, Royal Artillery	11 Dec. 15	18 June 24	18 June 24
Tristram, Barrington, Royal Artillery	11 Sept. 12	11 May 15	1 Feb. 10
Trollope, Right Hon. Sir John, Bt., 10 Drs.	10 July 17	24 Oct. 22	25 Sept. 23
Tucker, Richard Franklin, Royal Marines	17 Aug. 41	4 Feb. 46	8 April 53
ℙ ℚℕ Tudor, Charles, 23 Dragoons	6 April 04	20 Oct. 08	25 Jan. 18
Tudor, Henry, 37 Foot	1 June 14	5 May 16	5 April 21
Tunstall, Gabriel, Unattached	13 Jan. 14	25 July 16	8 Nov. 27
ℙ Tunstall, William,[269] 36 Foot	11 May 09	21 Jan. 12	22 April 19
ℙ Turner, Thomas,[270] 23 Foot	25 Aug. 07	16 Mar. 09	25 Dec. 14
Turner, Young, Sicilian Regiment	19 April 10	1 May 11	25 June 16
Twyford, John, Royal Marines	10 Oct. 05	15 Mar. 10	1 Sept. 14
Urquhart, Donald, 60 Foot	27 Oct. 10	30 Mar. 12	25 Dec. 17
ℙ Vallancey, Richard,[271] 1 Foot	1 Sept. 07	20 July 09	23 July 18
Vereker, Henry, 18 Foot	25 Sept. 11	11 Feb. 13	11 Feb. 17
ℙ Vereker, Henry Thomas,[272] 62 Foot	23 April 07	29 Sept. 08	7 May 22
Vernon, John Russell, 1 Foot	30 June 25	7 Aug. 27	28 Sept. 30
ℙ Vesey, John,[273] 76 Foot	21 Sept. 09	2 Aug. 10	21 Oct. 17
Vieth, Frederick William, Unattached	14 Mar. 11	3 Aug. 13	29 Dec. 25
Wade, George, 18 Foot	9 May 11	14 Jan. 13	25 Mar. 17
Walbridge, Henry William, York Chasseurs	3 Nov. 08	2 Jan. 12	30 Dec. 19
ℙ Walker, Alexander,[274] 96 Foot	27 Oct. 07	26 Feb. 11	25 Dec. 18
Walker, James, 96 Foot	14 Oct. 13	23 May 16	25 Dec. 18
Walker, James, Royal African Corps	12 Nov. 12	16 Feb. 14	25 Dec. 18
Wall, Richard, 7 Royal Veteran Battalion	7 Nov. 05	1 May 09	
ℙ Wallace, Hugh Ritchie,[275] 7 Foot	14 July 09	16 Nov. 09	9 July 18
ℙ Waller, Kilner, 57 Foot	20 Sept. 10	25 Feb. 13	3 April 16
ℙ Walsh, Lawrence De Courcy, 34 Foot	14 May 07	8 June 09	25 Aug. 23
Ward, Henry,[276] Royal Marines	30 Jan. 07	11 Dec. 13	23 Feb. 30
Wardell, John, 19 Foot	17 Mar. 11	1 Aug. 18	20 July 20
Waring, Edward, Royal African Corps	8 Dec. 25	15 Mar. 27	25 Feb. 29
ℚℕ Watson, Andrew,[277] 24 Foot	10 June 13	16 Aug. 15	25 Sept. 23

Lieutenants.

	ENSIGN, ETC.	LIEUT.	WHEN PLACED ON HALF PAY.
P Watson, George,[276] Unattached	28 Feb. 12	22 Oct. 12	14 Sept. 32
Watson, Thomas Brereton, 8 Foot	23 Nov. 09	21 Nov. 11	18 April 16
P Watson, Sir William Henry,[279] 6 Drs. ..	11 Nov. 11	7 May 12	25 Mar. 16
Wauch, David, 6 Dragoon Guards	8 Nov. 10	19 May 14	25 July 14
P Weir, William,[280] 27 Foot	31 Mar. 08	17 Oct. 11	25 July 17
P Whimster, James,[281] Sicilian Regt.......	27 Nov. 10	5 Aug. 13	25 June 16
P White, George,[282] 36 Foot.............	28 Feb. 12	13 May 13	25 Mar. 17
White, Henry, 63 Foot.................	20 Sept. 44	31 July 46	29 Aug. 47
White, William,[263] Royal Marines	13 Sept. 08	10 May 23	27 Jan. 36
Whiteford, John, 13 Foot...............	12 Sept. 11	8 Aug. 15	25 Mar. 17
Whiting, George Wm.,[264] R. Mar., Chief Officer of Coast Guard	2 Jan. 38	4 Nov. 41	25 June 46
Wightman, James Thomas, 67 Foot, Adjutant, South Notts Yeomanry Cavalry	24 Feb. 43	5 Apr. 44	30 May 51
Wigley, George James,[285] 63 Foot	13 July 08	25 Mar. 10	20 May 19
P Wigton, James,[286] 9 Foot	25 Mar. 08	2 Sept. 08	25 Mar. 15
QM Wilkinson, Henry,[267] 40 Foot	8 May 10	12 May 12	14 May 16
Wilkinson, John Alexander, 24 Foot	6 Oct. 08	3 Oct. 11	11 Sept. 23
Williams, C. P., Land Transport Corps	....	7 Sept. 55	1 April 57
P Willis, George Brander,[286] Royal Artillery	2 May 08	17 Nov. 09	3 April 23
Wilson, Henry, 89 Foot.................	21 July 25	29 Nov. 27	11 Oct. 31
Wilson, John Henry, 97 Foot	15 June 09	16 May 13	17 July 17
Wilson, W.Henry Bowen Jordan,Gar. Comp.	10 Sept. 25	12 Oct. 26	1 Feb. 31
Winckworth, John, 75 Foot..............	14 Nov. 10	22 Feb. 16	16 July 17
P Windle, John Shepard,[269] 53 Foot	11 Dec. 06	25 Jan. 08	16 May 22
Winne, John James,[290] Royal Marines	16 April 32	16 Nov. 37	15 Aug. 48
Wisdom, John, 17 Foot.................	25 Dec. 06	10 Dec. 07	20 July 09
P QM Wood, Frederick,[291] 11 Dragoons....	28 April 04	14 June 05	25 Mar. 17
Wood, George Horsley, 67 Foot	25 Nov. 13	12 April 21	29 Jan. 27
P Wood, Henry,[292] 23 Foot	25 Mar. 13	13 Aug. 18	11 Nov. 24
P Woods, Wm.,[293] 6 Dragoons, Adjutant, Northumberland Yeomanry Cavalry ..	7 April 08	28 Dec. 09	15 Feb. 16
Worsley, George, 39 Foot................	8 Dec. 03	21 Mar. 05	10 Sept. 12
P QM Wray, Hugh Boyd,[294] 40 Foot	23 Jan. 11	10 Sept. 12	19 April 17
Wright, Edward, 35 Foot...............	Dec. 01	13 Aug. 02	25 Oct. 02
Wright, John, 27 Foot	8 June 09	10 Sept. 12	25 July 17
QM Wright, William,[295] Rifle Brigade	11 Mar. 13	20 July 15	25 Dec. 18
Wrighte, William, 3 Foot	20 May 12	26 May 14	19 April 17
Yarnold, Benjamin, Royal Marines........	23 July 12	17 Sept. 31	29 Nov. 34
Young, Henry Harman, 31 Foot	3 April 06	25 Nov. 08	22 Jan. 18
Young, Henry, 6 Royal Veteran Battalion	31 May 09	1 Aug. 11	
Young, John George, 90 Foot	20 Jan. 14	12 Aug. 24	14 May 29
Young, Robert, 1 Royal Veteran Battalion	3 Oct. 11	6 Sept. 14	

War Services of the Lieutenants.

1 Lieut. Addison served in the Peninsula and was present at the battles of Vittoria and the Pyrenees, for which he has received the War Medal with two Clasps.

2 Baron Altenstein has received the War Medal with one Clasp for Talavera.

3 Lieut. F. W. Armstrong served in the Peninsula and was present at the battles of Talavera, Busaco, Albuhera, Salamanca, Vittoria, Pyrenees, Nivelle, Orthes, and Toulouse, and at the siege of Badajoz: he has received the War Medal with ten Clasps.

4 Lieut. J. Cooper Armstrong served at Copenhagen, in 1807; and in the Peninsula from 1812 to 1814.

5 Lieut. E. F. Austin served in the Peninsula with the 47th and was present at the battles of Vittoria, Nivelle, and Nive, and at the siege of St. Sebastian, for which he has received the War Medal with four Clasps.

6 Fort-Major Austin served in the 35th Regt. during the campaign of 1813-14 in Holland, including the first investment of Bergen-op-Zoom, both actions at Merxem: he was severely wounded in the left arm when engaged with the enemy's pickets on the night of the 1st Feb. 1814; and in following up the advantage (after the second capture of Merxem) to the gates of Antwerp, his left leg was struck off by a cannon-ball, and his left side lacerated by another round shot.

7 Lieut. Ayshford served in the Peninsula and was present at the battles of Busaco and Fuentes d'Onor, and at the siege of Ciudad Rodrigo. He has the War Medal with three Clasps.

8 Lieut. J. A. Bailey served with the 69th Regt. in Belgium, and with the Army of Occupation in France.

9 Lieut. Andrew Baillie served in the Peninsula with the 30th and was present at the battles of Fuentes d'Onor and Salamanca, and at the sieges of Ciudad Rodrigo and Badajoz. He has received the War Medal with four Clasps.

10 Lieut. Robert Ball has received the War Medal with one Clasp for the battle of Nivelle.

11 Lieut. Frederick Bayly served in the Peninsula from June 1810 to the end of that war in 1814, including the battles of Busaco and Castalla. In the American war in 1814 and 15, including the attacks on Baltimore and New Orleans, at which last he was slightly wounded. With the Prussian army in 1815, at the taking of the fortresses of Maubeuge, Landrecies, Philippeville, and Rocroy.

12 Lieut. Beamish was present with the 84th at the battle of the Nive, for which he has received the War Medal with one Clasp.

13 Lieut. Benwell joined the 4th in the Peninsula, as a volunteer, and was present at the action of Osma, battle of Vittoria, the several stormings and capture of San Sebastian, passage of the Bidassoa and attack on the Heights, battles of Nivelle and Nive, investment of Bayonne, and repulse of the sortie. Served afterwards in the American war, at Bladensburg, Washington, Baltimore, and New Orleans, at which last he was several times wounded, and severely by grape-shot. He has received the War Medal with four Clasps.

14 Lieut. Bezant was wounded at the attack on the French fleet in Aix Roads. Served at the bombardment and surrender of Flushing, 1809. Was in command of the Artillery in Fort Massarene at the defence of Anholt by the Royal Marines in 1811. War Medal with two Clasps.

15 Lieut. Birch served in the Peninsula with the 10th and was present at the sieges of Tarragona in 1812 and 13, at the battle of Castalla, retreat from Ordal and Villa Franca to Tarragona, and the siege of Barcelona in 1814.

16 Fort-Major Black served in the Peninsula with the 74th, and was present in the actions of Aldea de Ponte and Fuentes Guinaldo, capture of Madrid and the Retiro, retreat from Madrid into Portugal, passage of the Ebro, battle of Vittoria, action at the Maya Pass, battles of the Pyrenees on the 27th July and 2nd Aug., passage of the Bidassoa, blockade of Pampeluna, battles of Nivelle and Nive (9th to 13th Dec.), actions of Vic Bigorre, Tarbes, and Sauveterre, battle of Orthes, action at Aire, and battle of Toulouse, besides various minor affairs. He has received the War Medal with six Clasps.

17 Lieut. Blythe served with the 88th Regt. in the Crimea from 11th Aug. 1855, including the siege and fall of Sebastopol and attack of the Redan on the 8th Sept. (Medal and Clasp).

19 Lieut. Bradshaw served in the Peninsula and was present at the battles of Vittoria and Toulouse, for which he has received the War Medal with two Clasps.

20 Lieut. Bramwell served the campaign of 1815 with the 92nd, and was severely wounded at Quatre Bras,—right leg amputated.

21 Lieut. Brattle served in the battle of Trafalgar, on board H. M. S. *Africa*, 64. Joined the force under General Whitelock at Monte Video, in 1807. In action with Danish gun-boats near Copenhagen, 20th Oct. 1808 (severely wounded). Served afterwards with the Channel Fleet off Brest, Basque Roads, and Belleisle. Has received the War Medal with two Clasps.

22 Lieut. Brearey served on the Walcheren expedition in 1809, and was present at the siege and reduction of Flushing. He served also the campaigns of 1814 and 1815 in Holland and the Netherlands, including the action at Merxem, bombardment of Antwerp, storming of Bergen-op-Zoom, battle of Waterloo, storming of Cambray, and capture of Paris.

23 Lieut. Brice served in the Peninsula with the 23rd, from May 1812 to the end of that war in 1814, and was present at the battles of Salamanca, Vittoria, and the Pyrenees (wounded). Served also the campaign of 1815, including the battle of Waterloo, storming of Cambray, and capture of Paris. He has received the War Medal with two Clasps.

25 Lieut. Charles Brown served in the Peninsula with the 50th and was present at the surprise and capture of Fort Napoleon at Almaraz, retreat from Madrid, affair at Fuente Decana, defence of, and repulse of the enemy at Alba de Tormes ; repulse of the enemy on the rear-guard ; repulse of the enemy at Bejar ; battle of Vittoria, action at Pampeluna, daily skirmishing to the summit of the Pyrenees ; defence of the pass of Maya (thanked by Sir W. Stewart), battle of the Pyrenees, and action with the enemy's rear-guard ; various affairs on the road to Roncesvalles ; battle of the Nivelle, and attack on the rear-guard ; action at Cambo ; passage of the Nive, battle of St. Pierre, Bayonne (wounded), affairs at Hellette and Arriverette, (bayonet wound in the hand), attack of the heights of Garris, and action at St. Palais (severely wounded). He has received the War Medal with four Clasps.

26 Lieut. Bubb served in the Peninsula with the 61st and was present at the battles of the Pyrenees, Nivelle, Nive, and Orthes, for which he has received the War Medal with four Clasps.

27 Lieut. Wm. T. Buchanan landed at Passages in Spain, and was engaged almost daily during the march of Lord Hill's division across the Pyrenees, as also frequently on the banks of the Bidassoa. He was afterwards present at the battles of Bayonne, Orthes, and Toulouse. He has received the War Medal with four Clasps for Nivelle, Nive, Orthes, and Toulouse.

28 Lieut. Burlton was present in 1854-55, before Sebastopol during its siege and fall ; with the R. M. Battalion at the occupation of Kertch and Yeni Kale ; in action with the outer forts of Sebastopol on 17th June ; and at the bombardment and surrender of Kinbourn (Medal and Clasp).

29 Lieut. Burslem served at the siege of Houat, and commanded a detachment of Artillery in a night attack on the batteries of Morbihan. Landed at Ferrol with the army under the command of Sir James Pulteney, and was attached to the reserve on the heights. Served the campaign of 1801 in Egypt, including the siege of Aboukir and battle of Alexandria, at which latter he lost his right leg by a cannon-shot. Medal for services in Egypt.

War Services of the Lieutenants.

30 Lieut. W. Butler served the campaign of 1815 with the 3rd Guards, and was present at the battle of Waterloo.

31 Lieut. Butterworth served in the Peninsula with the 32nd and was present at the battles of Roleia, Vimiera, Talavera, Salamanca, Pyrenees, and Nivelle, for which he has received the War Medal with six clasps.

32 Lieut. Cahill served in the Peninsula with the 36th, and has received the Silver War Medal with four Clasps for the Pyrenees, Nive, Orthes, and Toulouse.

33 Lieut. Donald Cameron (h. p. 60 Foot) served in the Peninsula with the 7th Fusiliers from Aug. 1811 to the end of that war in 1814, including the actions at Fuentes Guinaldo and Adea de Ponte, battle of Salamanca, Vittoria, the Pyrenees, St. Marcial near St. Sebastian, 31st Aug., Nivelle, Nive, and Orthes (wounded). He was afterwards present at the assault on New Orleans, and at the capture of Paris. He has the War Medal with six Clasps.

34 Lieut. L. M. Cameron served the campaigns of 1813 and 14 in the Peninsula, and was present at the battle of the Pyrenees on the 28th, 29th, and 30th July, the blockade of Pampeluna, battle of the Nivelle, battle of the Nive from 9th to 13th Dec., investment of Bayonne, and battle of Toulouse. Served also during the late Canadian Rebellion, and commanded a party of Volunteers on the Niagara frontier. He has received the War Medal with four Clasps.

35 Lieut. Alex. Campbell, Royal Marines, served in the action off Ferrol, 1805; and in action with a Danish Flotilla off Maudal, 1810. War Medal with one Clasp.

36 Lieut. C. W. Campbell served in the Peninsula with the 39th and was present at the battles of the Pyrenees, Nivelle, Orthes, and Toulouse, for which he has received the War Medal with four Clasps.

37 Lieut. James Campbell (h. p. 41st), served the campaign in Affghanistan with the 41st and was present at the action of Hykulzie on the 28th March 1842.

38 Lieut. Rupert Campbell served the campaign of 1806, in Sicily and Italy, including the skirmish at Eufemia, battle of Maida, attack on and taking of the Castle of Scylla, also the capture of Catrone. Campaign of 1807, in Egypt, including the attack on the forts and heights of Alexandria, and capture of that city on the 19th, 20th, and 21st March; also the attacks in the Desert, and siege of Rosetta. Campaign in Holland and the Netherlands in 1814 and 15, including both the actions of Merxem, and bombardment of Antwerp, where he rendered important personal service to his late Majesty King William IV., then present with the army as Duke of Clarence. He has received the War Medal with one Clasp for Maida.

39 Lieut. Michael Carey served in the Peninsula with the 83rd, from March 1809 to the end of that war in 1814, including the passage of the Douro, battles of Talavera (severely wounded in the head) and Busaco, first siege of Badajoz, battle of Fuentes d'Onor, siege of Ciudad Rodrigo, siege and storming of Badajoz, battles of Salamanca, Orthes, and Toulouse, for which he has received the War Medal with eight Clasps.

40 Lieut. Carnaby served in the Peninsula with the 76th and has received the War Medal with two Clasps for the battles of the Nivelle and Nive.

41 Lieut. Carr served with the 21st in Sicily in 1813-14; and at the reduction of Genoa in 1814. Also in America at Bladensburg, Washington and New Orleans, at which last place on the 8th January 1815, he was severely wounded. Served with the regiment at Paris, and at Valenciennes in 1816 and 1817.

42 Captain John Chadwick served in the Eastern campaign of 1854 as Adjutant of the 17th Lancers, including the affair of Bulganac, battle of Alma, siege of Sebastopol, and battle of Balaklava, where he was severely wounded and taken prisoner, having also had his horse killed (Medal and three Clasps).

43 Captain Wm. Chadwick, prior to entering the army, served as a Midshipman on board H. M. sloop *Moselle* in 1806-7, in which he saw a great deal of active service, and accompanied Sir Richard Strachan's flying squadron sent in pursuit of Jerome Bonaparte's fleet. He served in Madras, Ceylon, and Bengal from 1808 to 1816.

44 Lieut. Challis served in the Peninsula and has received the War Medal with one Clasp for the battle of Vimiera.

45 Lieut. Cinnamond has received the War Medal with one Clasp for the battle of Trafalgar.

46 Lieut. William Clarke assisted in cutting out the French Corvette *Cesar*; capture of the French squadron, 1806; bombardment of Copenhagen, 1807; capture of Russian *Sewolod*, 1808. Lost his right leg in action with a division of the French fleet off Toulon, 5th Nov. 1813. War Medal with two Clasps.

47 Lieut. Cobbold served in the Peninsula with the 1st Dragoons, and has received the War Medal with one Clasp for the battle of Toulouse.

48 Lieut. Colls served in the Peninsula and was present at the battles of Roleia, Vimiera, Corunna, and Salamanca, for which he has received the War Medal with four Clasps.

49 Lieut. Coombe served in Egypt in 1801, and has received the Egyptian medal.

50 Lieut. R. G. C. Coote served in the Burmese war.

51 Lieut. Cosby served with the 63rd at the capture of Martinique in 1809 and of Guadaloupe in 1810, for which he has received the War Medal with two Clasps.

52 Lieut. Cottingham served in the Peninsula with the 52d in the campaigns of 1812, 13, and 14, and was present at the storming and capture of Badajoz (as a volunteer), battles of Salamanca, Vittoria, Pyrenees, Nivelle, Nive, Orthes, and Toulouse for which he has received the War Medal with eight Clasps. He served also the campaign of 1815, including the battle of Waterloo.

53 Lieut. Cowley served in the Peninsula, and has received the Silver War Medal with one Clasp for Toulouse.

54 Lieut. Charles Thomas Cox served with the 71st during the campaigns of 1810, 11, 12, 13 14, and 15, in the Peninsula, France, and Flanders, including the retreat to and occupation of the lines of Torres Vedras, the subsequent pursuit of Massena through Portugal, action of Sobral, battles of Fuentes d'Onor (wounded), actions of Arroyo de Molino, Almaraz, and Alba de Tormes, covering the sieges of Badajoz, the advance to and retreat from Madrid, battle of Vittoria,—severely wounded and taken prisoner, a musket ball having passed through the lungs and lodged in his body; being unable to keep up with the enemy, they left him on the field when they were hard pressed and under a cannonade from the British artillery. Present at the invasion of France from the Pyrenees, and subsequent actions of the Nivelle, Nive, Cambo, Garris, St. Palais, Arriverietc, Hellette, Orthes, Aire, Tarbes, Urt, Toulouse, and many affairs of piquets, &c. At the battle of Waterloo he received a contusion on the hip from the fragment of a shell, but was present at the capture of Paris, and served three years with the Army of Occupation. In 1821, the change of position of the ball received at Vittoria compelled him to relinquish the active duties of his profession and retire on half-pay. He has received the War Medal with six Clasps.

56 Lieut. Crozier served at the attack on the enemy's works on the right bank of the Mississippi, when he turned the enemy's flank and captured a field piece.

57 Lieut. Cubitt served in the Peninsula with the 4th Dragoons and was present at the battles of Vittoria and Toulouse, for which he has received the War Medal with two Clasps.

58 Lieut. Cusine served in the Peninsula and was present at the battles of Roleia and Vimiera, for which he has received the War Medal with two Clasps.

59 Lieut. Dalgairns served in the Peninsula with the 7th Fusiliers, and was present at the battle of Busaco, occupation of the lines of Torres Vedras, advance after Massena, taking of Olivença, 1st siege of Badajoz, battles of Albuhera and Vittoria, investment of Pampeluna and battles of the Pyrenees; after which he went to Holland with Sir James Graham's Army as Adjutant of the 55th Regt., and was wounded at the storming of Bergen-op-Zoom, and taken prisoner. He has received the War Medal with four Clasps.

60 Lieut. E. R. D'Alton served in the Peninsula and was present at the battles of the Pyrenees and Orthes, for which he has received the War Medal with two Clasps.

61 Lieut. Daniel served in China in 1841 (Medal).

62 Lieut. Darcy served in the Peninsula with the 60th and was present at the battles of Roleia and Vimiera, for which he has received the War Medal with two Clasps.

64 Captain David Davies, Royal Marines, was serving on board the *Java* when captured by the American frigate *Constitution* (wounded).

65 Lieut. Delamain served with the 2nd battalion of the 67th in Spain from the latter part of 1811 to the close of that war, including the sieges of Cadiz, Tarragona, and Barcelona, the affair of Villa Franca, and others connected with the army on the Eastern coast of Spain. He was also present at the siege and capture of Asseerghur in the East Indies, in 1819.

66 Lieut. Delmé served in the Peninsula with the 88th, and was present at the battle of Vittoria, sortie from Pampeluna, battles of the Pyrenees, the Nivelle, the Nive, and Orthes, actions of Vic Bigorre and Tarbes, and battle of Toulouse; served afterwards in the American war, and was present in the action of Plattsburg, and the passage of the Sarinac. He has received the War Medal with six Clasps.

67 Lieut. Dighton served in Spain and Portugal, from April 1810 to July 1812, including Massena's retreat. Served also in the South of France in 1814, and was present at the investment of Bayonne and repulse of the sortie,—slightly wounded.

68 Lieut. E. W. P. Dillon accompanied the expedition to Walcheren in 1809, and was present at the siege and capture of Flushing. Served also at the reduction of Guadaloupe in 1815.

69 Lieut. Doswell was present at the passage of the Dardanelles, 1807.

70 Lieut. Dowker served in the Peninsula with the 53rd and was present at the battles of Talavera, Buscaco, Vittoria, Pyrenees, Nivelle, and Nive, for which he has received the War Medal with six Clasps.

71 Lieut. Drummond served in the Peninsula with the Rifle Brigade and was present at the sieges of Ciudad Rodrigo and Badajoz, and at the battles of Salamanca, Pyrenees, Nivelle, Nive, Orthes, and Toulouse, for which he has received the War Medal with eight Clasps. He served also the Waterloo campaign.

72 Lieut. Drury commanded the Royal Marines at the attack by the English and French on the fortified position of Tamatave in Madagascar in 1845.

73 Lieut. Dunnicliffe served the campaign of 1815, and was present at the battles of Quatre Bras and Waterloo.

74 Lieut. Dyer served at the capture of a convoy of 27 vessels, and the storming of the citadel of Cassis, which was taken by escalade by the Royal Marines, 18 Aug. 1813.

75 Lieut. Eccles served in the Peninsula with the 61st, and was present at the battles of the Nivelle, Nive (9th to 13th Dec.), Orthes, and Toulouse, besides various minor affairs. He has received the War Medal with four Clasps.

76 Captain Charles Edwards served in the Peninsula with the 47th, from July 1813 to the end of that war in 1814, including the second assault and capture of San Sebastian, passage of the Bidassoa, battle of the Nivelle, battles of the Nive on the 9th, 10th, 11th, 12th, and 13th Dec. 1813, and blockade of Bayonne. Served also the campaigns of 1817 and 18 in Malwa against the Mahrattas. He has received the War Medal with three Clasps.

77 Lieut. Thomas Edwards served in the Peninsula with the 20th and was present at the battles of Nivelle, Nive, Orthes, and Toulouse, for which he has the War Medal with four Clasps.

78 Lieut. Wright Edwards served in the Peninsula with the 59th and was present at the

War Services of the Lieutenants.

battles of Vittoria, Nivelle, and Nive, and at the siege of St. Sebastian, for which he has received the War Medal with four Clasps.

79 Lieut. Henry Elliot served in the Royal Marine Battalion at the capture of Java (wounded, and War Medal with one Clasp). Was at the attack on the enemy's works on the right bank of the Mississippi.

80 Lieut. John Evans (h. p. 28th Foot) served in the Peninsula with the 28th and was present at the battles of Busaco, Albuhera, Vittoria, Pyrenees, Nivelle, Nive, Orthes, and Toulouse, for which he has received the War Medal with eight Clasps.

81 Lieut. Ralph Evans served in the Peninsula with the 62nd and was present at the battle of the Nivelle, for which he has received the War Medal with one Clasp.

82 Lieut. Thomas Evans served the campaigns of 1813 and 14 with the 38th Regt., including the battles of the Nivelle and the Nive, the investment of Bayonne, and repulse of the sortie. He has received the Silver War Medal with two Clasps.

84 Lieut. J. H. R. Foote served in the Peninsula with the 2nd Battalion. 5th Regt., and was present in the actions of El Bodon, Aldea de Ponte, and Fuentes Guinaldo, sieges of Ciudad Rodrigo and Badajoz, besides minor affairs and skirmishes, and has received the Silver War Medal with two Clasps. In 1813 he joined the army in Canada and was present in the action at Plattsburg, besides skirmishes.

85 Captain John Ford served the campaigns of 1809, 10, 11, 13, and 14, and was present at the siege of Flushing, defence of Cadiz, and battle of Fuentes d'Onor, Nivelle, Nive, and Toulouse, besides other actions of less importance. Served as an assistant engineer during four of the campaigns. He has received the War Medal with four Clasps.

86 Lieut. A. S. Fraser served in the Peninsula with the 42nd and was present at the battles of the Pyrenees, Nivelle, and Nive, for which he has received the War Medal with three Clasps. He served also the campaign of 1815, and was slightly wounded at Quatre Bras.

87 Lieut. David Fraser served in the Peninsula with the 82nd and was present at the battles of Nivelle and Orthes, for which he has received the War Medal with two Clasps.

88 Lieut. James Geddes was present with the 42nd at the battle of Toulouse (severely wounded), for which he has received the War Medal with one Clasp.

89 Lieut. Gilder served in the Peninsula with the 6th and was present at the battles of Vittoria, Pyrenees, Nivelle, and Orthes, for which he has received the War Med. with four Clasps.

90 Lieut. Gill (ret. f. p. R. Marines) served at the storming of Fort Cornelis and capture of Java in 1811, for which he has received the War Medal with one Clasp.

91 Lieut. Gill (h. p. R. Marines) served on board H.M.S. *Winchester* during the Burmese war of 1852-53 (Medal and Clasp) : commanded a detachment of Royal Marines, and took part in the attack on Meatoon's Stockade near Donabew. On the 12th Aug. 1853 he was in an engagement against pirates in the China Seas. Served with the Baltic expedition in 1855 (Medal). Served in China as Quarter Master of the 2d Battalion during the war from Aug. 1857 to March 1858, including the blockade of the Canton river, capture of Canton, and subsequent operations. He has also the Medal for the Kaffir war of 1852.

92 Lieut. Gillmore served in the Peninsula and was present at the battles of Nivelle, Nive, Orthes, and Toulouse, for which he has received the War Medal with four Clasps.

93 Lieut. Goodall served with the Queen's Royals on the Walcheren expedition in 1809; and subsequently in the Peninsula, from Feb. 1811 to June 1813, including the operations before Ciudad Rodrigo and Badajoz, storming the Forts and battle of Salamanca, siege of Burgos, and retreat from thence. He has received the War Medal with one Clasp for Salamanca.

94 Lieut. George Gordon served in the Peninsula with the 42nd and was present at the battles of Nivelle, Nive, Orthes, and Toulouse, for which he has received the War Medal with four Clasps.

96 Lieut. John Grant (R. Artillery) served with the expedition to Walcheren, and was present at the siege of Flushing. Served afterwards in the Peninsula from Oct. 1813 to Feb. 1814.

97 Lieut. John Grant (Unattached) served in the 92nd Highlanders in the Peninsula from Aug. 1811 to Dec. 1813, including the storming of Fort Napoleon at Almaraz, retreat from Madrid, defence of Alba de Tormes, and battles of Vittoria and the Pyrenees, and various minor affairs. Wounded in the side at the Maya Pass. He has received the War Medal with one Clasp for Vittoria.

98 Lt. Grape served in the actions in Algesiras Bay and Straits of Gibraltar in 1811 (Medal).

99 Lieut. Edward Greene served with the battering train attached to the Prussian besieging army, and was employed in taking several fortresses on the French frontier in July and Aug. 1815.

100 Lieut. Grier served in the Peninsula with the 44th and was present at the battles of Fuentes d'Onor and Salamanca and at the siege of Badajoz, for which he has received the War Medal with three Clasps. He served also the campaign of 1815, and was severely wounded at Quatre Bras.

101 Lieut. Charles Griffith served at the capture of the French frigate *Etoile* in 1814, and has received the War Medal with one Clasp.

102 Lieut. Grimes served in the Peninsula from March 1811 to Sept. 1812, and was present at the siege of Ciudad Rodrigo, and the successful siege of Badajoz, at which latter he was severely wounded in the right thigh by a cannon-shot. He has the War Medal with two Clasps.

103 Lieut. Grueber has received the War Medal with one Clasp for the battle of Toulouse.

105 Lieut. Haggup served in the Peninsula with the Rifle Brigade and was present a the battles of Busaco, Fuentes d'Onor, Salamanca, Pyrenees, Nivelle, and Toulouse, and at the sieges of Ciudad Rodrigo and Badajoz, for which he has received the War Medal with eight Clasps. He served also the Waterloo campaign.

106 Lieut. Hallilay was employed in the gun-boats at the destruction of the Chinese piratical fleet in the Tonquin River in 1849.

107 Lieut. Hamer served with the 5th on the Walcheren expedition in 1809, and was present at the siege and surrender of Flushing (slightly wounded, and horse shot under him). He served afterwards in the Peninsula, and has received the Silver War Medal with three Clasps for the battles of the Nivelle, the Nive, and Orthes. Served also in the last American war; and with his regiment rejoined the Duke of Wellington's army at Paris.

108 Lieut. John Hamilton served in the Peninsula with the 2nd Line Battalion German Legion, and has received the Silver War Medal with three Clasps for Vittoria, Nivelle, and Nive.

109 Lieut. Hasleham served in the Peninsula and was present at the battles of Talavera and Busaco, for which he has received the War Medal with two Clasps.

110 Lieut. J. F. Hearn served with the 60th at the capture of Martinique in 1809 and of Guadaloupe in 1810, for which he has received the War Medal with two Clasps.

111 Lieut. William Henderson served in the Peninsula with the 5th and was present at the battles of Salamanca, Vittoria, Pyrenees, Nivelle, Nive, Orthes, and Toulouse, for which he has received the War Medal with seven Clasps.

112 Lieut. Herron served in the Peninsula with the 74th, and has received the Silver War Medal with seven Clasps for Busaco, Fuentes d'Onor, Ciudad Rodrigo, Badajoz, Salamanca, Vittoria, and Pyrenees.

113 Lieut. Hilliard served in the Peninsula with the 5th and was present at the battles of Busaco, Fuentes d'Onor, Vittoria, Pyrenees, Nivelle, Nive, Orthes, and Toulouse, and at the sieges of Ciudad Rodrigo and Badajoz, for which he has received the War Medal with ten Clasps.

114 Lieut. Hine served in the Peninsula with the 48th from April 1809 to the end of that war in 1814, including the battles of Oporto, Talavera, and Albuhera (twice wounded); assault and capture of Ciudad Rodrigo and Badajoz, battles of Salamanca (wounded), Vittoria, Pyrenees, Nivelle, Nive, Orthes, and Toulouse. He has received the War Medal with ten Clasps.

115 Lieut. Hodder served with the 2nd battalion of the 69th during the campaigns of 1814 and 15, in Holland and Flanders, and was present at the attack on Merxem, the bombardment of Antwerp, assault on Bergen-op-Zoom, and battles of Quatre Bras and Waterloo, at which last he was severely wounded.

116 Lieut. Hodgson served in the Peninsula with the 4th Dragoon Guards during the campaigns of 1811, 12, and 13.

117 Lieut. Holgate served in the Peninsula in 1813 with the 82nd Regt.

118 Lieut. Rupert Charles Holland served in boats of *Thalia* at the capture of the French 6 gun privateer *Requin*, in 1808; and at the siege of Flushing and occupation of South Beveland in 1809. In *Euryalus* 36 gun frigate, at the defence of Cadiz and Matagorda, and Blackwood's action off Toulon in 1810; in her barge at the cutting out of the French privateer *Intrepide* in 1811; in command of her marines took a field-piece and stormed two batteries; at the capture of the 10 gun xebec *La Fortune* and twenty sail of Merchant Vessels in Calvacie Roads; in the same ship when she simultaneously drove on shore the French storeship *Balleine* of 28 guns, and compelled a gabarre of 30 guns and a large schooner to take refuge under the land batteries; and he participated in her numerous boat services from 1810 to 1814, including the ascent of the Potomac, capture of Washington and of Alexandria, and attack of Baltimore. In *Queen Charlotte* at Algiers, and personally commended by the Admiral for his services on that occasion. He has received the Silver War Medal with two Clasps.

119 Lieut. Hollis served in the Peninsula with the 57th and was present at the battle of Busaco, for which he has received the War Medal with one Clasp.

121 Lieut. Hopkins served in the Peninsula with the 5th Regt. and was present at the battle of Busaco, in pursuit of Massena from Santarem, actions of Pombal, Condeixa, Foz d'Arouce, and Sabugal, battle of Fuentes d'Onor, affair of El Bodon, siege and storming of Ciudad Rodrigo, where he carried the color taken in,—the other Ensign and the six Sergeants fell on the breach, and no other Regt. took colors—the siege and storm of Badajoz, and has received the War Medal with four Clasps. In 1816, was placed on half-pay in consequence of wounds.

122 Lieut. Blake Humfrey served in the Peninsula and was present at the battles of Nivelle and Nive, for which he has received the War Medal with two Clasps.

123 Lieut. C. G. Humphreys served in the Peninsula with the 14th Lt. Dragoons and was present at the battles of Salamanca, Vittoria, Pyrenees, Nivelle, Nive, Orthes, and Toulouse, for which he has received the War Medal with seven Clasps.

124 Lieut. Hunt served in the Peninsula with the 24th, and has received the Silver War Medal with seven Clasps for Busaco, Fuentes d'Onor, Ciudad Rodrigo, Salamanca, Vittoria, Pyrenees, and Nivelle.

125 Lieut. Hutchinson has received the War Medal with one Clasp for the battle of Corunna.

126 Lieut. Inglis served in the Peninsula with the 3rd Dragoon Guards and has received the War Medal with one Clasp for the battle of Toulouse.

127 Lieut. Alexander Innes served in the Peninsula with the 42nd and was present at the battle of Toulouse, for which he has received the War Medal with one Clasp. He served also the Waterloo campaign.

128 Lieut. Alexander Irwin served at the siege and capture of Hattras in 1816-17; the Mahratta campaign of 1817 and 18; in the Burmese war in 1825 and 26.

129 Lieut. J. R. Irwin served with the 63rd at the capture of Guadaloupe in 1810, for which he has received the War Medal with one Clasp.

130 Lieut. Isaacson served in the Peninsula with the 52nd, and was present at the battles of Nivelle and Orthes, for which he has received the War Medal with two Clasps. He served also the Waterloo campaign.

War Services of the Lieutenants.

131 Lieut. Jeffries served in the Peninsula with the Royals and was present at the battle of Salamanca, for which he has received the War Medal with one Clasp.

132 Lieut. Jordan served the campaign of 1808-9 with the 26th and was present at the battles of Roleia and Vimiera, for which he has received the War Medal with two Clasps.

133 Lieut. Kearnes served in Ireland during the Rebellion of 1798, and was present in the battles of New Ross and Vinegar Hill. Accompanied the 68th Regt. to the West Indies in 1800, and was wounded on the 12th April, 1802, at Prince Rupert's in Dominica, when quelling the mutiny of the 8th West India Regt. In June 1803 he sailed from Barbadoes with the expedition against the French, Dutch, and Danish West India Islands, and received high commendation for his conduct in the storming of an outwork in front of the redoubt of Morne Fortune in St Lucia. In 1809, sailed with the expedition for Walcheren, and present at the siege and capture of Flushing. In June 1811, joined the Duke of Wellington's army, and was present with the covering army at the sieges of Ciudad Rodrigo and Badajoz, at the actions of Moresco and on the heights of Salamanca, battle of Salamanca, taking of Madrid and the Retiro, siege of Burgos, actions of Osma and San Munos, battles of Vittoria (wounded), Pyrenees (at Lasaca), and Nivelle, action at Hastingues, and battle of Orthes. He has received the Silver War Medal with five Clasps.

134 Lieut. Keep served in the Peninsula with the 28th and was present at the battles of Vittoria, Pyrenees, and Nivelle, for which he has received the War Medal with three Clasps.

135 Lieut. F. C. Knight served with the Baltic expedition of 1854 (Medal).

136 Lieut. Knox served the Peninsular campaigns of 1808, 9, 10, 11, and 12 with the 2nd battalion of the 31st, including the battles of Talavera (severely contused on the head by a musket ball), Busaco, Albuhera, and Arroyo de Molino, retreat to Portugal, occupation of the Lines of Torres Vedras, and pursuit of Massena, besides several minor affairs. He has received the War Medal with three Clasps.

137 Lieut. Lacy served in the Peninsula with the 82nd and was present at the battles of Vittoria and the Pyrenees, for which he has received the War Medal with two Clasps.

138 Lieut. A. Lane (h. p. 83rd F.) served in the Peninsula with the 83rd and was present at the siege of Badajoz and battles of Salamanca, Vittoria, Nivelle, and Orthes, for which he has received the War Medal with five Clasps.

139 Lieut. Langdon served in the Peninsula and South of France with the 39th, and has received the Silver War Medal with three Clasps for Busaco, Albuhera, and Nive.

140 Lieut. Leggett served in the Peninsula with the 3rd Dragoon Guards and was present at the battles of Vittoria and Toulouse, for which he has the War Medal with two Clasps.

141 Lieut. George L'Estrange served in the Peninsula with the 31st and was present at the battles of Vittoria, Pyrenees, Nivelle, Nive, Orthes, and Toulouse, for which he has received the War Medal with six Clasps.

142 Lieut. T. F. L'Estrange served in the 7th Fusiliers with the Army of Occupation in France.

143 Lieut. Henry Lewis was severely wounded in the action with and capture of the *Renommée* and *Néréide* and surrender of the Isle de la Passe, 1811. War Medal with one Clasp.

144 Lieut. Lindsey served in the Peninsula with the 11th and was present at the battle of Salamanca, for which he has received the War Medal with one Clasp.

145 Lieut. Lister served at the battle of Trafalgar; also at the passage of the Dardanelles in 1807. Has received the War Medal with one Clasp.

147 Lieut. E. S. Long served in the Peninsula with the 7th Hussars, and has received the Silver War Medal with one Clasp for Sahagun and Benevento.

148 Lieut. Wm. Lonsdale served in the Peninsula with the 4th and was present at the battle of Salamanca, for which he has the War Medal with one Clasp. He served also the Waterloo campaign.

149 Lieut. Armar Lowry served in the Peninsula with the 45th and was present at the battle of Orthes, for which he has received the War Medal with one Clasp.

150 Lieut. John Lowry served with the 8th in the American war of 1812, 13, and 14, and was present in the actions of Prescot, Sackett's Harbour (severely wounded), Chippewa, Lundy's Lane (contused), assault on Fort Erie, and sortie (severely wounded) in Sept. 1814, and was severely wounded through the body in action at Sackett's Harbour.

151 Lieut. Lucas served in the Peninsula with the 32nd and was present at the battle of Toulouse, for which he has the War Medal with one Clasp. He served also the Waterloo campaign.

152 Lieut. M'Crohan served in the Peninsula with the 4th and was present at the siege of Badajoz and battle of Vittoria, for which he has the War Medal with two Clasps.

153 Lieut. Thomas M'Dermott served in the Irish Rebellion in 1798. Also the Staff Corps of Cavalry in the Peninsula, and was present at the battles of the Pyrenees, Orthes, and Toulouse, for which he has received the War Medal with three Clasps.

156 Lieut. M'Intyre has received the War Medal with one Clasp for the capture of the Dutch frigate *Guelderland*, 19 May 1808.

157 Lieut. M'Laren served in the Peninsula with the 91st and was present at the battles of the Pyrenees, Nivelle, Nive, Orthes, and Toulouse, for which he has received the War Medal with five Clasps.

158 Lieut. M'Loughlin served with an expedition, under Major Hill, eighty miles up the Gambia, in 1849, which stormed and destroyed the fortified town of Bambacoo, 6 May; attacked and partially destroyed the fortified town of Keenung, 7 May; action and defeat of the enemy on the plains of Quenella (wounded). Also present with a detachment of the 2nd and 3rd West India Regiments, in the combined attack of a British and French Naval and Land Force, under Commodore Fanshawe, in the attack and total defeat of Pirates at the Island of Basis, Jeba River, Western Africa, 12 Dec. 1849.

159 Lieut. Nicol M'Nicol served in the Peninsula with the 27th and was present at the battles of Vittoria, Pyrenees, Nivelle, Orthes, and Toulouse, for which he has received the War Medal with five Clasps.

160 Lieut. Æneas M'Pherson served in the Peninsula and South of France with the 59th, and has received the Silver War Medal with four Clasps for Vittoria, St. Sebastian, Nivelle, and Nive.

161 Lieut. F. M'Rae was present with the 78th at the battle of Maida, for which he has received the War Medal with one Clasp.

162 Lieut. MacGregor served with the 24th during the Nepaul campaigns of 1814, 15, and 16, and was present at the taking of Harriapore.

163 Lieut. Lachlan Mac Kay served in the Peninsula with the 42nd from 1812 to the end of that war in 1814, including the battles of the Pyrenees, Nivelle, Nive, Orthes, and Toulouse, for which he has received the War Medal with five Clasps.

164 Lieut. Neil Mackay has the War Medal with one Clasp for the battle of Corunna.

165 Lieut. Magin has received the War Medal with one Clasp for Trafalgar.

166 Lieut. Mathison served in the Peninsula with the 77th and was present at the sieges of Ciudad Rodrigo and Badajoz, and at the battles of Vittoria, Pyrenees, Nive, Orthes, and Toulouse, for which he has received the War Medal with seven Clasps.

167 Lieut. Meares was at the capture of the town of Groa, and a convoy of twenty-five vessels on 28 June, 1810. Landed at Ortona 12th Feb. 1811, captured eleven vessels and destroyed two large magazines after planting the British colours at the gate of the town. Wounded at the battle of Lissa 13th March. Landed with his detachment 27th July, near Ragoniza, captured and destroyed twenty-eight vessels after the defeat of 300 French soldiers. Present at the capture of *Pomone* and *Persanne* 29th Nov. 1811. Has received the War Medal with three Clasps.

168 Lieut. Mellish served in the Peninsula and has received the War Medal with one Clasp for Badajoz.

169 Lieut. George Miles served in the Peninsula with the 5th Dr. Guards from 1811 to the end of that war in 1814, including the action at Llerena, battle of Salamanca, capture of the French rear-guard on the following day, capture of Madrid, siege of Burgos, and retreat into Portugal, battle of Vittoria, investment of and action on the heights before Pampeluna, and battle of Toulouse. He has received the War Medal with three Clasps.

170 Lieut. Zaccheus Miller served in Egypt in 1801 (Medal). Was present in the action with the French fleet and capture of four of their ships on the coast of Ireland on 12th Oct. 1798. Served in the R. M. Battalion at the surrender of the Castles of Ovo, Novo, and St. Elmo, and of the fortified towns of Capua and Gaeta in June and July 1799. Was at the blockade of Malta in 1800, including the capture of Admiral Perree's squadron on 18th Feb., and of the *Guillaume Tell* on 31st March. Has the War Medal with two Clasps.

171 Lieut. Mitchell served in the Peninsula with the 28th from 1810 to 1813 inclusive, and was present at the battle of Barrosa, storming of Badajoz, and battle of Vittoria (severely wounded), besides various minor affairs. He has received the War Medal with three Clasps.

172 Lieut. Mogridge served in the Peninsula with the 34th and was present at the battles of Albuhera, Vittoria, Orthes, and Toulouse, for which he has the War Medal with four Clasps.

173 Lieut. J. A. Moore served in the American war.

174 Lieut. Moorhead served in the Peninsula with the 71st and was present at the battles of Nivelle, Nive, Orthes, and Toulouse, for which he has received the War Medal with four Clasps. He served also the Waterloo campaign.

175 Lieut. Moreton served in the Peninsula and South of France with the 58th, and has the War Medal with six Clasps for Vittoria, Pyrenees, Nivelle, Nive, Orthes, and Toulouse.

176 Lieut. Morphy served in the Peninsula with the Buffs and was present at the battles of the Pyrenees and Nive, for which he has received the War Medal with two Clasps.

176† Lieut. Mosley served with the 20th Regt. in the Eastern campaign of 1854-55, including the battles of Alma and Inkerman, and siege of Sebastopol (Medal and Clasps).

177 Lieut. Mostyn served the campaign of 1808-9 with the 81st, and has received the Silver War Medal with one Clasp for Corunna.

178 Lord Mount Edgcumbe served with the Grenadier Guards at the battle of Waterloo.

179 Lieut. Mountford served at the destruction of the French vessels *Arienne, Andromaque,* and *Mamelouck,* 22 May, 1812. War Medal with one Clasp.

180 Lieut. Frederick Munro served in the Peninsula from March 1812 to the end of that war in 1814, including the sieges of the forts at Salamanca, Burgos, and San Sebastian, and the battles of Salamanca, Vittoria, the Bidassoa, and St. Jean de Luz. He has received the War Medal with four Clasps.

181 Lieut. Mure served the Waterloo campaign with the Grenadier Guards.

182 Lieut. Francis Murray served in the Peninsula with the old 94th, from Jan. 1810 to the end of that war in 1814, including the defence of Cadiz from Jan. to Sept. 1810, lines of Torres Vedras, the pursuit of Massena, actions at Redinha, Condeixa, and Sabugal; battle of Fuentes d'Onor, second siege of Badajoz, action of El Bodon, siege and storm of Ciudad Rodrigo, siege and storm of Badajoz, battle of Salamanca, capture of Madrid, battles of Vittoria, the Pyrenees, Nivelle, and Orthes; action of Vic Bigorre, and battle of Toulouse. He has received the War Medal with ten Clasps.

183 Lieut. Nantes served with the 7th Fusiliers in the Peninsula and South of France in 1811, 12, 13, and 14, and was present at the siege of Ciudad Rodrigo, and commanded a company in the action of the Guarena, and at the battles of Salamanca and Toulouse. He was slightly wounded at the Guarena; most severely at Salamanca, his right arm having been broken in two places; and again slightly wounded at the battle of Orthes. He was also accidentally hurt by

one of his own men, and carried off the field in the operations at the Nive. He has received the War Medal with five Clasps.

184 Lieut. Hibbert Newton served in the Peninsula with the 32nd, and has received the Silver War Medal with one Clasp for Salamanca.

185 Lieut. John Nicholson served the Waterloo campaign with the 14th Foot, including the taking of Cambray.

186 Lieut. Nicolas served at the battle of Trafalgar. Was in the boats at an attack upon a convoy in Basque Roads, and at the destruction of a second in the harbour of Fosse de l'Oye in 1810. Has the War Medal with two Clasps.

186† Lieut. Nicoll served with the Baltic expedition in 1855, including the bombardment of Sweaborg (Medal).

187 Lieut. Nixon served in the Peninsula with the 52nd and was present at the battles of Fuentes d'Onor and Orthes, and siege of Badajoz, for which he has received the War Medal with three Clasps. He served also the Waterloo campaign.

188 Lieut. Norman served in the Peninsula and was present at the sieges of Ciudad Rodrigo and Badajoz, and at the battles of Albuhera, Salamanca, Vittoria, and Pyrenees, for which he has received the War Medal with six Clasps.

189 Lieut. Maurice O'Connor served in the Peninsula with the 88th, and was present at the battles of Fuentes d'Onor, Pyrenees, Nivelle, Nive, Orthes, and Toulouse, for which he has received the War Medal with six Clasps.

191 Lieut. Onslow served at the siege of Flushing in 1809; the campaign of 1814 in Holland, including the bombardment of the French fleet at Antwerp. Campaign of 1815, including the battle of Waterloo.

192 Lieut. James Ormsby served in the Peninsula with the 83rd and was present at the battles of Busaco, Fuentes d'Onor, and Salamanca, for which he has received the War Medal with three Clasps.

193 Lieut. James Orr was present at the capture of Linois' Squadron in 1806. Served with the Royal Marine Battalions in the Walcheren expedition, 1809; and at the capture of Java, 1811, for which he has the War Medal with one Clasp. Commanded the detachment sent to reduce the Island of Madura in 1811.

194 Lieut. John Orr (8 R. Vet. Bn.) accompanied the 1st battalion of the 42nd to the Peninsula in April 1812, and joined the army at Salamanca, during the siege of the forts in that city; present at the battle of Salamanca, siege of Burgos, and storming of San Michael; retreat to Portugal, advance in 1813, and all the actions in the Pyrenees. Served also the campaign of 1815, including the battles of Quatre Bras and Waterloo. Slightly wounded at Burgos, and severely at Waterloo. He has received the War Medal with two Clasps.

195 Lieut. Pagan served the campaign of 1815 with the 33rd, and was severely wounded at Waterloo.

196 Lieut. Kenyon S. Parker served in 1806 in the boats at the capture of the French corvette *Cesar*, and was present at the capture of the French frigate squadron off Rochefort. In 1809 he acted as Paymaster of the R. M. Battalion on the Walcheren expedition. In 1813 he was at the capture of Fiume and other places in the Adriatic, and commanded the Royal Marines at the destruction of guns and a battery at Ragoniza and Pola. Was afterwards employed with the Austrian army, and present at the capture of Trieste. Has received the War Medal with one Clasp.

197 Lieut. Parratt served at Walcheren in 1809; and in the Peninsula from 1811 to the end of that war in 1814, including the defence of Cadiz, siege of San Sebastian, battle of Nivelle, actions at Vic Bigorre and Tarbes, and battles of Orthes and Toulouse. He has received the War Medal with five Clasps.

198 Lieut. James Parry served in the Peninsula with the 28th and was present at the battles of Nivelle, Nive, Orthes, and Toulouse, for which he has received the War Medal with four Clasps. He served also the Waterloo campaign.

200 Lieut. Paxton served in the Peninsula with the 11th Lt. Dragoons and was present at the battle of Salamanca, for which he has received the War Medal with one Clasp.

201 Lieut. Philips was nominated to the 4th Class of the Medjidie for service with the Turkish Contingent.

202 Lieut. Penfold served in the Peninsula with the 12th Lt. Dragoons, and was present at the battles of Vittoria, Nivelle, and Nive, for which he has received the War Medal with three Clasps.

203 Lieut. Pennefather served in the Peninsula with the 77th, and was present at the sieges of Ciudad Rodrigo and Badajoz (wounded), for which he has received the War Medal with two Clasps.

204 Captain Pennington served in the Peninsula from June, 1809, and during the greater part of the subsequent campaigns, including the battle of Busaco, where he commanded one of the advance piquets of the 3d division on the morning of the action, and was sharply engaged with the enemy; retreat to the lines of Torres Vedras, advance from thence, actions and affairs at Leria, Redinha, Pombal, Roblida, Condeixa, Foz d'Arouce, Guarda, and Sabugal; battles of Fuentes d'Onor, siege of Badajoz (wounded in the right thigh), actions at Campo Mayon El Bodon, and Guinaldo; affairs and actions in the Pyrenees, St.Pé (contused wound), Hasparrere and Grassietta; battles of Nivelle, Nive, and Orthes (severely wounded), besides several other affairs of posts and piquets during the war. He has received the War Medal and seven Clasps.

205 Lieut. Pepper served in the Peninsula, and was present at the battles of Talavera, Barrosa, and Toulouse, for which he has received the War Medal with three Clasps.

206 Lieut. Pickard served the campaign of 1814 in Lower Canada, under Sir George Prevost and was present at the attack on Plattsburg. Served also the campaign of 1815 in Upper Canada under Sir Gordon Drummond.

207 Lieut. A. J. Pictet served in the Burmese war with the Royals, and was present at the taking of Donabew.

208 Lieut. Poe served in the Peninsula with the 39th and was present at the battles of Albuhera, Vittoria, and Pyrenees, for which he has received the War Medal with three Clasps.

209 Lieut. Polhill served the Waterloo campaign with the 16th Lt. Dragoons.

210 Lieut. Pridham served in Egypt in 1801 (War Medal with one Clasp, and the Turkish Medal). Was present at the siege and surrender of Genoa,—at the battle of Copenhagen in 1807, and disembarked at Figueras, co-operating with the British army at Lisbon, in 1808. Served on the coast of Spain in 1809, and in Portugal in 1811-12. Was in the 1st Battalion during the war in North America in 1813-15. Has received the War Medal with one Clasp.

211 Lieut. Priest served in Portugal and Spain in 1808 and 9, and was present at the battle of Corunna, for which he has received the War Medal with one Clasp.

212 Lieut. Ratcliff served in the Peninsula and was present at the battle of Corunna, for which he has received the War Medal with one Clasp.

213 Lieut. Robert Read served in the Peninsula with the 38th and was present at the siege of Badajoz (severely wounded at the assault), for which he has the War Medal with one Clasp.

214 Lieut. L. Buckle Reeves served in the *Victory* at Trafalgar (severely wounded). Was present at the defeat of the French forces at Babagué, near St. Louis, 9th July 1809 ; took possession of and garrisoned fort St. Louis, which he retained seven months. War Medal with one Clasp.

215 Lieut. Reynett served in the Peninsula with the 45th and was present at the battle of Vittoria, for which he has received the War Medal with one Clasp.

216 Lieut. Reynolds served the campaigns of 1813, 14, and 15, in Germany, Holland, and the Netherlands, including the action of Goerde, attack upon Merxem, defence of Fort Frederick Heny against the French Fleet, battle of Quatre Bras, retreat on the following day, and battle at Waterloo (severely wounded by a cannon shot in the left thigh). In 1818 he served the campaign in the interior of Ceylon, and commanded a small Division, a detachment of which captured Madugalla, one of the three Chiefs.

217 Sir John Ribton served in the Peninsula with the Rifle Brigade and was present at the battles of the Pyrenees, Nive, Orthes, and Toulouse, for which he has received the War Medal with four Clasps.

218 Lieut. Richardes served the campaign of 1815, and was present at the sieges of Maubeuge, Philippeville and Landrecies.

219 Lieut. S. Richmond served with the 49th in the American war and was present at the action of Chrystler's Farm, for which he has received the War Medal with one Clasp.

221 Lieut. James Robertson served in the Peninsula, and has received the Silver War Medal with four Clasps for Corunna, Busaco, Fuentes d'Onor, and Salamanca. He served also the campaign of 1815 with the 79th, and was severely wounded at Quatre Bras.

222 Lieut. James Robinson served in the Peninsula with the 32nd and was present at the battles of Salamanca, Vittoria, Nivelle, Nive, Orthes, and Toulouse, for which he has received the War Medal with six Clasps. He served also the campaign of 1815, and was severely wounded at Quatre Bras.

223 Lieut. Adam Rogers served in the Peninsula and was present at the battle of Talavera, for which he has received the War Medal with one Clasp.

224 Lieut. Rooke served at the battle of Trafalgar, for which he has the War Medal with one Clasp. Served with the 2nd Bat. Royal Marines, during the War in North America, in 1813-15.

225 Lieut. Ewen Ross served in the Peninsula with the 92nd, and was present at the battle of Fuentes d'Onor, siege of Badajoz, actions at Arroyo de Molino (severely wounded), Almaraz, and Alba de Tormes. Also the campaign of 1815, and was severely wounded at Quatre Bras. He has received the War Medal with one Clasp for Fuentes d'Onor.

226 Lieut. Rotely served in the *Victory* at Trafalgar (severely contused), and succeeded to the command of the small arm men, on the death of Captain Adair, R.M. Employed blockading the French squadron in the Chesapeake. Present at the capture of the *Topaze*, and the reduction of Martinique, 1809. Actively employed in boat actions in North America and the West Indies, and assisted at the capture of 100 armed and other vessels. War Medal with two Clasps.

227 Lieut. Rouse has the War Medal with one Clasp for the battle of Copenhagen, 1801.

228 Lieut. Rutherford served in the Peninsula with the old 94th, and was present at the defence of Cadiz in 1810, lines of Torres Vedras, pursuit of Massena, actions at Pombal, Redinha, Condeixa, and Sabugal; battle of Fuentes d'Onor, second siege of Badajoz, battles of Vittoria, Pyrenees, and Nivelle; passage of the Gave d'Oleron, battle of Orthes, action of Vic Bigorre, and battle of Toulouse. He has received the War Medal with seven Clasps.

229 Lieut. Rybot served with the Baltic expedition in 1854 (Medal).

230 Lieut. Sandwith assisted in cutting out a Turkish ship at Sigri in 1807 ; served in the 1st Battalion Royal Marines, during the whole of the American War in 1813-15.

231 Lieut. R. F. Saunders served in the Peninsula with the 67th and was present at the battle of Barrosa, for which he has received the War Medal with one Clasp.

232 Lieut. R. J. Saunders served the campaign of 1815 and was present at the battle of Waterloo.

233 Lieut. Sawkins served in the Peninsula with the 50th and was present at the battles of Vittoria, Pyrenees, Nivelle, Nive, Orthes, and Toulouse, for which he has received the War Medal with six Clasps.

234 Lieut. Scobell served at the battle of the Nile (Medal), and in the Marine Battalion at the capitulation of St. Elmo, Capua, and Gaeta, in 1799.

235 Lieut. David Scott has received the War Medal with three Clasps for Egypt, Martinique, and Albuhera.

War Services of the Lieutenants. 507

237 Lieut. Sedley served the Waterloo campaign with the Royal Staff Corps.
238 Lieut. Alexander Smith served in the actions in Algesiraz Bay and the Straits of Gibraltar in 1801; at the reduction of St. Domingo in 1802; pursuit of Villeneuve to the West Indies; capture of the Spanish frigate "Amfitrite," and assisting disabled ships and prizes after the battle of Trafalgar in 1805; commanded a detachment in the action off St. Domingo, headed the Royal Marines at the boarding of the "Jupiter" and hauled down the flag, 6th Feb. 1806. Has the Silver War Medal with two Clasps.
239 Lieut. J. R. Smith served the Waterloo campaign with the 14th Foot.
240 Lieut. Ralph Smith served in the Peninsula with the 23rd and was present at the battles of Vittoria, Pyrenees, Nivelle, Nive, Orthes, and Toulouse, for which he has received the War Medal with six Clasps.
241 Lieut. Robert Smith was present with the 26th at the battle of Corunna, for which he has received the War Medal with one Clasp.
242 Lieut. W. Smith (Royal Artillery Drivers) served at Walcheren, in 1809; and the campaigns of 1813, 14, 15, in Holland, Belgium, and France, and was wounded at Merxem.
243 Lieut. William Smith (h. p. 71st Foot) served the Waterloo campaign with the 71st Light Infantry.
244 Lieut. William Smyth (h. p. Scots Fus. Gds.) served in the Peninsula with the 31st and was present at the battles of Vittoria and the Pyrenees, for which he has received the War Medal with two Clasps.
245 Lieut. Spaight served in the Peninsula and was present at the battles of Nivelle and Orthes, for which he has received the Silver War Medal with two Clasps.
246 Lieut. Sperling served the campaigns of 1814 and 15 in Holland and Flanders, and led the right column in the assault of Bergen-op-Zoom.
247 Lieut. Sproule served with the 69th at the capture of Java in 1811, for which he has received the War Medal with one Clasp.
248 Lieut. Stacey served in the Peninsula with the 12th Lt. Dragoons and was present at the battles of Vittoria, Nivelle, and Nive, for which he has received the War Medal with three Clasps.
249 Lieut. Stainforth served the Waterloo campaign with the 23rd Fusiliers.
250 Lieut. Richard Stapleton served as a Volunteer at the defence of Cadiz.
251 Lieut. Staveley-Shirt served in the Peninsula with the 4th and was present at the battles of Corunna, Vittoria, Nivelle, and Nive, and at the siege of St. Sebastian, for which he has received the War Medal with five Clasps.
252 Lieut. Stawell served in the Peninsula with the 48th and was present at the battles of Vittoria, Pyrenees, Orthes, and Toulouse, for which he has the War Medal with four Clasps.
253 Lieut. Steele was wounded in the trenches before Sebastopol, 24th Oct. 1854, and served with the R. M. Artillery during the whole of the operations there during that year; he was also at the bombardment of the outer forts on 17th October. In 1855 he served in the siege batteries until the fall of Sebastopol, and was wounded 12th April during the bombardment mentioned in Dispatches); also present at the bombardment of Kinbourn (Medal and Clasp, (and Knight of the Legion of Honor).
254 Lieut. Stobart served in the American war under Sir Gordon Drummond.
255 Lieut. G. E. Stuart served in the Peninsula with the 61st and was present at the battles of Busaco, Salamanca, Pyrenees, Nivelle, Nive, Orthes, and Toulouse, for which he has received the War Medal with seven Clasps.
256 Lieut. R. T. Stuart served the Waterloo campaign with the 28th Foot.
257 Lieut. William Stuart served under Sir Samuel Hood in the West Indies. At Copenhagen. In the Mediterranean on board the *Cyane* 28 guns under Sir Thomas Staines, when that officer lost his arm in action with the *Cérès* 40 gun Neapolitan frigate. Gun-boats and batteries in the bay of Naples, on the 27th June 1809. Served also at the reduction of Trieste, in 1814. Has received the War Medal with one Clasp.
258 Lieut. Syret served in the Peninsula with the 9th and was present at the siege of St. Sebastian, and battles of Vittoria, Nivelle, and Nive, for which he has received the War Medal with four Clasps.
259 Lieut. Tane has received the War Medal with one Clasp for Trafalgar.
260 Lieut. Tatlock served in the Peninsula with the 3rd Dragoons, and was present at the battles of Vittoria and Toulouse, for which he has received the War Medal with two Clasps.
261 Lieut. Benjamin Thompson served in the Peninsula with the 48th and was present at the battles of Talavera, Albuhera, Nivelle, and Orthes, and at the sieges of Ciudad Rodrigo and Badajoz, for which he has received the War Medal with six Clasps.
262 Lieut. R. K. Thompson served in the Peninsula with the 47th and was present at the battl of Vittoria and siege of St. Sebastian, for which he has received the War Medal with two Clasps.
263 Lieut. T. J. Thompson served in the Peninsula with the 34th and was present at the battle of Albuhera, for which he has received the War Medal with one Clasp.
264 Lieut. Thornton served in the Peninsula with the old 94th from Feb. 1810 to Feb. 1814, including the defence of Cadiz from April to Sept. 1810, Lines of Torres Vedras, actions of Redinha, Condeixa, and Sabugal; battle of Fuentes d' Onor, second siege of Badajoz, action of El Bodon, siege of Ciudad Rodrigo, siege and assault of Badajoz, battle of Salamanca, capture of Madrid, battles of Vittoria, the Pyrenees, and Nivelle, at which last he was dangerously wounded through the neck by a musket-ball, which carried away the lower part of the ear. He has received the War Medal with seven Clasps.
265 Lieut. Tighe served the Waterloo campaign with the Grenadier Guards.
266 Lieut. Town served in the Peninsula and was present at the siege and storming of

Badajoz (with the Portuguese army), retreat from Burgos, battle of Vittoria, affair of Tolosa, both sieges of San Sebastian, passage of the Bidassoa and carrying of the lofty mountains of the left bank of the river; the whole of the operations against Bayonne, and sortie therefrom. He served afterwards in the American war,—at the battle of Bladensburg, capture of Washington, and action near Baltimore. He has received the War Medal with two Clasps for Vittoria and San Sebastian.

267 Lieut. John Townsend served in the Peninsula and was present at the battles of Nivelle and Nive, for which he has received the War Medal with two Clasps. He served also the Waterloo campaign.

268 Lieut. L. C. Travers served with the 1st Battalion, 60th Rifles, during the second siege operations at Mooltan, including the siege and storm of the town and capture of the Citadel. Was afterwards at the battle of Goojerat, pursuit of the Sikh army under Rajah Shore Sing, until its final surrender at Rawul Pindee, occupation of Attock and Peshawur, and expulsion of the Affghan force, under the Ameer Dost Mahomed, beyond the Khyber Pass (Medal and Clasps).

269 Lieut. W. Tunstall served in the Peninsula with the 36th and was present at the battle of Nivelle, for which he has received the War Medal with one Clasp.

270 Lieut. Thos. Turner served in the Peninsula with the 23rd and was present at the battles of Corunna, Vittoria, and Nivelle, for which he has received the War Medal with three Clasps.

271 Lieut. Vallancey served in the Peninsula with the Royals, and was present at the battles of Busaco, Fuentes d'Onor, Salamanca, Nivelle, and Nive, and at the siege of Badajoz, for which he has received the War Medal with six Clasps.

272 Lieut. H. Thomas Vereker served in the Peninsula with the 83rd, and has received the Silver War Medal with three Clasps for Busaco, Fuentes d'Onor, and Salamanca.

273 Lieut. Vesey served in the Peninsula with the 76th and was present at the battles of Nivelle and Nive, for which he has received the War Medal with two Clasps.

274 Lieut. Alexander Walker served in the Peninsula with the old 97th and was present at the battles of Vimiera, Talavera, Busaco, and Albuhera, for which he has received the War Medal with four Clasps.

275 Lieut. H. R. Wallace served in the Peninsula with the 7th Fusiliers and was present at the battles of Busaco, Albuhera, Salamanca, Orthes, and Toulouse, and at the sieges of Ciudad Rodrigo and Badajoz, for which he has received the War Medal with seven Clasps.

276 Lieut. Ward was at the capture of Java in 1811 (War Medal with one Clasp).

277 Lieut. Andrew Watson served the Waterloo campaign with the 33rd Foot.

278 Lieut. George Watson served in the Peninsula with the 3rd Dragoons from June 1813 to the end of that war in 1814, and was present at the battle of Toulouse.

279 Lieut. Sir Wm. H. Watson served the campaigns of 1813 and 14 in Spain and France with the Royal Dragoons, and has received the War Medal with one Clasp for the battle of Toulouse.

280 Lieut. William Weir served in the Peninsula with the 27th and was present the siege of Badajoz, and battles of Busaco, Vittoria, Pyrenees, and Nivelle, for which he has received the War Medal with five Clasps.

281 Lieut. Whimster served in the Peninsula, and has received the War Medal with three Clasps for Corunna, Busaco, and Fuentes d'Onor.

282 Lieut. George White served in the Peninsula with the 36th and was present at the battle of Salamanca, for which he has received the War Medal with one Clasp.

283 Lieut. William White has received the War Medal with one Clasp for the battle of Algiers, 27 Aug. 1816.

284 Lieut. Whiting served on the Chinese expedition, and was present at the battle of Chuenpee, attack of the Anunghoy batteries, advance on Canton, capture of the heights of Canton, capture of Colongso, second capture of Chusan, assault and capture of the citadel and city of Chinhae.

285 Lieut. Wigley served at the capture of Martinique in 1809 and of Guadaloupe in 1810, for which he has received the War Medal with two Clasps.

286 Lieut. Wigton served in the Peninsula with the 9th and was present at the battles of Vimiera and Salamanca, for which he has received the War Medal with two Clasps.

287 Lieut. Henry Wilkinson served the Waterloo campaign with the 40th Foot.

288 Lieut. Willis served at Walcheren, and was present at the siege of Flushing. Served also the Peninsular campaigns of 1811, 12, and 14, including the 2nd and 3rd sieges of Badajoz, investment of Bayonne, and repulse of the sortie. He has received the War Medal with one Clasp for Badajoz.

289 Lieut. Windle served with the 10th at the siege of Scylla Castle, in 1808. Present with the Anglo-Sicilian army during the whole of its operations on the coast of the Faro, against Murat. With the army on the eastern coast of Spain, in 1812 and 13.

290 Lieut. Winne served with the Royal Marines, on the North Coast of Spain in 1837-38. Was landed in 1845 with a detachment at Monte Video for the protection of British subjects and property during the siege of that city by the Argentine army under General Oribe, and was in garrison there until the end of the Civil war.

291 Lieut. Frederick Wood was severely wounded at Waterloo.

292 Lieut. Henry Wood served in the Peninsula with the 76th, from June 1813 to the end of that war in 1814, including the siege of San Sebastian, passage of the Bidassoa, battles of Nivelle and Nive, and investment of Bayonne. Served afterwards in the American war, and was present in the action of Plattsburg. He has received the War Medal with two Clasps.

293 Lieut. Woods served in the Peninsula with the 48th in 1810 and 1811, and with the 4th Dragoon Guards in 1812, including the Lines of Torres Vedras, pursuit of Massena, and the

operations in the Alemtejo; action of Campo Mayor, siege of Olivença, and first siege of Badajoz; with Colonel Colborne's Brigade, when, by a rapid advance, several convoys were intercepted, and the country cleared to Guadalcanal and the fortified post of Benelcazar; battle of Albuhera, where he received two wounds and some severe contusions, and was taken prisoner in the charge of the Polish Lancers, but subsequently escaped and rejoined the army on its advance. He has received the War Medal with one Clasp.

294 Lieut. Wray served with the 40th in the Peninsula and was present at the battles of Vittoria and the Pyrenees, for which he has received the War Medal with two Clasps. He next accompanied the regiment on the New Orleans expedition, and subsequently served the campaign of 1815 and was present at the battle of Waterloo, after which he was specially employed as acting engineer officer on Sir John Lambert's staff, on the line of march to Paris.

295 Lieut. Wm. Wright (h. p. Rifle Brigade) served in Holland in 1813 and 1814, and was present at the attack on Merxem and bombardment of the French fleet at Antwerp. Served also the campaign of 1815, and was severely wounded at Waterloo.

2ND LIEUTENANTS, CORNETS, AND ENSIGNS.

	CORNET, 2d LIEUT. or ENSIGN.	WHEN PLACED ON HALF PAY.
Agassiz, Lewis,[1] Royal Marines	21 Aug. 09	14 May 17
Ainslie, Robert, 77 Foot	14 Mar. 83	8 May 83
Alexander, George, Land Transport Corps	31 Dec. 55	1 April 57
Anderson, William, Royal Marines	12 July 09	1 Jan. 16
Armstrong, Wm., Land Transport Corps	21 Feb. 56	1 April 57
Astley, Ralph, Land Transport Corps	21 Feb. 56	1 April 57
Atkinson, Charles, Royal Marines	11 Nov. 11	11 Aug. 14
Backhouse, John Iggulden, Royal Marines	17 Mar. 31	26 Feb. 36
Baillie, Thomas, 14 Foot	20 July 15	15 April 19
Baird, John, Land Transport Corps	22 Jan. 56	1 April 57
Barrett, William Newman, 60 Foot	6 May 13	30 Sept. 19
Barrow, John Edward,[1]† 20 Foot	16 Mar. 55	10 Jan. 57
Barry, James, Royal Marines	30 July 11	
Baugh, James, Royal Marines	7 Dec. 12	1 Sept. 14
* Bell, John, 3 Provisional Battalion of Militia		1814
Berkeley, Hon. G.C.Grantley Fitzhardinge, 82 F.	7 Nov. 16	28 Aug. 23
Bignell, Charles Philips, Royal Artillery	18 Oct. 26	7 Sept. 29
Black, James, Royal Waggon Train	8 July 15	25 June 16
Black, Thomas, 19 Foot	24 Feb. 14	22 May 23
Blake, Edward John,[2] Royal Marines	26 Mar. 12	1 Jan. 16
Bolomey, Louis William James, 2 Light Infantry Battalion German Legion	26 Sept. 13	24 Feb. 16
Bowden, George, Royal Marines	30 July 10	1 Jan. 16
Branch, George Ferguson,[3] Royal Marines	16 April 32	14 July 37
⁋ * Brew, Charles,[4] 2 Prov. Battalion of Militia	Dec. 13	1814
Brisac, Douglas Pettiward,[5] Royal Marines	12 June 12	1 Jan. 16
Bruyeres, Henry Pringle, Royal Engineers, Captain of Sandown Castle	1 Sept. 15	21 Feb. 23
Burrowes, Peter, Land Transport Corps	18 Mar. 56	1 April 57
Burton, Emanuel, Unattached	17 Aug. 15	14 Sept. 26
Butcher, John Lewis, 8 West India Regiment	18 Oct. 09	1816
Cain, Michael, Land Transport Corps	21 Jan. 56	1 April 57
* Cameron, James, 3 Provisional Batt. of Militia		1814
Campbell, Colin,[6] Royal Marines	28 Oct. 09	26 Oct. 14
Campbell, James, Royal Marines	2 Sept. 08	17 June 13
Campbell, James, 92 Foot	11 Nov. 13	25 Dec. 14
Carden, Paul Kyffin,[7] Royal Marines	22 Jan. 11	3 Aug. 20
Carey, John Westropp,[8] 30 Foot	23 June 14	30 Dec. 19
Chambers, Montague, 71 F., *A Queen's Counsel*	9 Nov. 15	1 Oct. 18
Child, George Richard, Royal Marines	24 July 09	14 Nov. 17
Christie, John, Royal Marines	15 April 47	15 April 47
Clarke, Joseph, Land Transport Corps	21 Jan. 56	1 April 57
Coleman, Charles,[9] Royal Marines	13 Feb. 98	1 Jan. 03
Collier, James, Royal Marines	26 July 08	24 Oct. 11
Collins, Richard Geo., Land Transport Corps	21 Jan. 56	1 April 57
Collins, Stephen Edward, Royal Marines	14 Dec. 12	1 Sept. 14
Cooper, John, Land Transport Corps	21 Feb. 56	1 April 57
Couche, Richard, Royal Marines	28 April 08	15 Sept. 17
Crossgrove, James, 104 Foot	29 July 13	4 Feb. 19
D'Anfossy, *Le Chevalier*, R. Foreign Artillery	29 June 15	1 Aug. 15
Davis, John Henry, Royal Marines, *Chief Officer of Coast Guard*	21 May 08	
Davis, William, Royal Marines	12 Aug. 09	
⁋ Deanan, Thos.,[13] Bradshaw's Recruiting Corps	28 April 14	11 July 22
De Beauvoir, *Sir* John Edmund, *Bart.* 104 Foot	3 Mar. 14	14 May 18
De Fauche, Charles, 60 Foot	15 June 15	25 Mar. 17
Devereux, George Alfred, Royal Marines	2 Oct. 09	12 Aug. 14
Dillon, John, 3 Dragoon Guards	5 Mar. 18	1 April 24
Dillon, Theobald Augustus, 58 Foot	21 April 14	25 Feb. 16
Dixon, John Smart, 94 Foot	20 July 15	4 Jun. 21
Dodd, Chas. Wm. M., Newfoundland Fencibles	6 Aug. 13	25 June 16
⁋ Donovan, Henry Douglas,[14] 9 Foot	25 Aug. 13	13 Feb. 17
Downer, George, Royal Marines	15 April 47	15 April 47
Drinkwater, Thomas,[15] Royal Marines	4 April 09	1 Jan. 16
Dufresne, Louis Flavien,[16] Canadian Fencibles	13 Nov. 13	11 Oct. 16
Duncan, William, 2 Garrison Battalion	2 June 14	6 Feb. 15
Durnford, And. M. Isaacson, 2 R. Vet. Batt.	18 May 20	
Elliott, John Furzer,[17] Royal Marines	4 June 09	23 April 19

2nd Lieutenants, Cornets, and Ensigns. 512

	CORNET, ETC.	WHEN PLACED ON HALF PAY.
Ensor, James,[18] Royal Marines	19 Mar. 97	31 May 02
Evans, Daniel, Royal Marines	16 Dec. 12	1 Sept. 14
Eyre, Thomas Dowling, Royal Marines	11 Nov. 11	28 Dec. 14
Findlay, James, Land Transport Corps	21 Feb. 56	1 April 57
Fitz Gerald, John, 29 Foot	19 Aug. 13	25 Oct. 21
Flexman, James,[19] Royal Marines	27 Jan. 08	11 Jan. 16
Flint, William Richard,[20] Royal Marines	3 Sept. 10	1 Jan. 16
Forbes, John, 107 Foot	1 June 96	29 Nov. 98
Ford, William,[21] Royal Marines	29 April 09	6 Jan. 19
Fosbery, Henry William, 12 Foot	17 Feb. 14	25 Oct. 21
Frett, John, Royal Marines	21 Feb. 14	1 Sept. 14
Gage, John Ogle, 9 Dragoons	25 Dec. 13	8 May 23
Gardner, John, 7 Royal Veteran Battalion	28 Sept. 15	
Gatt, Arthur, Land Transport Corps	23 Nov. 55	1 April 57
Gillbee, James, Sicilian Regiment	13 April 13	25 Mar. 16
Gillies, Walter, Royal Marines	29 April 47	29 April 47
Glanville, Francis (*Lieut.*), 19 Dragoons	20 April 15	11 April 22
Glass, Archibald, Land Transport Corps	21 Feb. 56	1 April 57
Graham, Humphrey, Hanger's Recruiting Corps	19 July 98	
Grant, John, Bradshaw's Recruiting Corps	4 July 98	4 July 98
Gritton, Henry, Royal Marines	8 Sept. 08	20 Feb. 17
Gunn, William, Bourbon Regiment	23 Aug. 15	24 April 16
Gunthorpe, Joshua Rowley, Royal Marines	4 June 95	16 Oct. 95
Hallum, James, Royal Marines	31 Mar. 08	30 Mar. 20
Hammond, William,[22] Royal Marines	17 Oct. 14	1 Jan. 16
ꝕ Handcock, Tobias,[24] 27 Foot	4 May 15	26 Mar. 16
ꝕ Harwood, Edward,[25] 32 Foot	12 Oct. 13	25 Dec. 14
ꝕ Haydon, Robert Luckcombe,[26] 20 Foot	24 Feb. 14	1 April 19
Hayes, Henry Horace, 81 Foot	5 Jan. 16	25 June 18
Hayter, George, Royal Waggon Train	10 June 13	25 June 14
Hepburn, John, Land Transport Corps	21 Feb. 56	1 April 57
Howett, Frederick, Royal Marines	9 Sept. 12	1 Jan. 16
Hewson, George, 24 Foot	2 April 12	25 Dec. 14
Hoare, Charles Vyvyan, Royal Marines	12 Mar. 11	3 Aug. 15
ꝕ Holland, Thomas Edward,[28] 83 Foot	25 Dec. 13	14 Jan. 19
Hoyland, John, Royal Sappers and Miners	1 April 16	1 Mar. 17
ꝕ Jagger, Joseph,[30] Royal Artillery Drivers	16 July 13	1 Aug. 16
Jeffery, James, Royal Marines	16 April 49	16 April 49
Jenkins, John, Royal Marines	19 Jan. 10	1 Jan. 16
Johnstone, Hamilton Trail, Royal Marines	25 Aug. 10	1 Jan. 16
Jones, Stopford Thomas, 61 Foot	15 Nov. 10	25 Mar. 16
Jop, Robert, 25 Foot	11 May 15	25 April 16
Kennett, Charles Leighton, 4 West India Regt.	21 Sept. 15	20 April 20
Lamborn, John Sherrard, Royal Marines	24 Aug. 32	24 July 35
Lane, George Dawkins, Royal Marines	15 Feb. 12	1 Jan. 16
Langdale, Marmaduke Robert, 9 Foot	17 June 02	25 July 02
Leatham, Francis, 62 Foot	4 Nov. 13	25 April 17
Lee, Frederick Richard, 96 Foot	6 Dec. 13	21 Dec. 15
Lee, John, 78 Foot	8 Sept. 14	25 April 16
Lee, Robert Newton, 2 Ceylon Regiment	29 June 15	13 Nov. 23
Leech, James William, 34 Foot	17 July 55	1 April 57
Lewis, Stephen, 73 Foot	19 May 14	6 July 20
Lloyd, Henry Vereker, 86 Foot	31 Jan. 16	25 Oct. 21
Lloyd, Samuel,[32] Royal Marines, *Chief Officer of Coast Guard*	24 Feb. 09	10 April 16
Loft, John Henry, 15 Dragoons	30 Dec. 13	12 Mar. 18
Long, Fitzjames, R. Marines	1 Apr. 51	1 Apr. 51
Lyons, Anthony Munton, Royal Marines	3 Nov. 12	1 Sept. 14
M'Conechy, James, Royal Marines	10 Mar. 12	1 Jan. 16
M'Lachlan, Neil, 64 Foot	7 Sept. 04	7 Sept. 04
M'Leod, Norman, 6 Foot	11 Aug. 14	8 Mar. 21
ꝕ ꝕ Macdonald, Colin,[33] 50 Foot, *Town Major at Montreal*	*30 Jan. 35; 28 Jan. 48	28 Jan. 48
Maclean, Alexander, Newfoundland Fencibles	24 June 13	25 June 16
ꝕ Maclean, Saml.[34] Royal Sappers and Miners	22 April 15	1 Mar. 17
Manico, Edward,[35] Royal Marines	2 Feb. 11	1 Jan. 16
Mason, Richardson, 94 Foot	14 April 13	25 Dec. 18
ꝕ *Mead, Charles,*[36] Royal Artillery Drivers	1 May 13	
Molesworth, Robert Sackville, Royal Marines	5 May 46	5 June 48
Montgomery, Robert, 95 Foot	2 Dec. 13	25 Jan. 19
Moore, Charles William, Royal Marines	31 May 09	22 Sept. 17

2nd Lieutenants, Cornets, and Ensigns.

Name	2D LIEUT. ETC.	WHEN PLACED ON HALF PAY.
* Moore, John, 1 Provisional Batt. of Militia..		1814
Morehouse, George, New Brunswick Fencibles	25 Oct. 13	25 April 16
P Mortashed, John,[37] 35 Foot	27 Jan. 14	25 Oct. 21
P Morgan, John,[38] Royal Marines	25 July 12	
Murray, Adam, 84 Foot	18 Jan. 16	13 Feb. 18
Orme, Herbert Lewis, R. Marines	15 April 47	15 April 47
Palling, Henry, 95 Foot	8 July 13	25 Jan. 19
Philipps, George, Royal Marines, *Chief Officer of Coast Guard*	15 April 12	1 Jan. 16
Pitt, Henry, Royal Marines	2 Sept. 12	1 Jan. 16
Porter, John Hall, Royal Marines	4 Feb. 11	1 Jan. 16
Potts, Thomas, Royal Marines	15 April 47	15 April 47
Poussin, Balthazard, Corsican Rangers	23 Dec. 13	25 Mar. 16
Pulliblank, Edward Cooper, Royal Marines	18 July 09	16 Jan. 16
Raye, Henry Robert,[39] Royal Marines	14 Dec. 12	1 Sept. 14
Read, Thomas, Royal Marines	1 Feb. 06	7 May 10
Rickard, Martin, Royal Waggon Train	25 Dec. 13	25 Dec. 18
Ridge, James Stuart, 6 West India Regiment	22 Feb. 14	29 June 20
Robertson, William, Royal Sappers and Miners	1 July 12	
Ross, Henry Paget Bayly, Royal Marines	16 Dec. 12	1 Sept. 14
Ross, John, 6 Garrison Battalion	20 Oct. 10	4 Feb. 15
Savage, Rowland, 1 Foot	2 Dec. 14	12 Mar. 18
Shawe, Wm. Lowe, Land Transport Corps	2 Feb. 56	1 April 57
P Shore, John,[41] Royal Artillery Drivers	19 May 13	15 Nov. 14
Silver, T. R.,[40] 11 Drs., *Adj. W. Kent Yeomanry*	5 Nov. 54	10 Nov. 56
Simpson, John Bridgman, (*Cornet,*) 48 Foot..	17 Oct. 16	5 Aug. 24
Simpson, John W., Royal Marines	2 Aug. 10	1 Jan. 16
Skues, George, Royal Marines	25 Oct. 13	1 Sept. 14
Smith, John, Royal Sappers and Miners	1 June 11	
※ Smith, Wm. Slaytor,[42] (Lt. 17 Oct. 08,) 72 F. *Adjt. Yorkshire Hussars, Yeomanry Cav.*	25 Dec. 06	8 Nov. 19
Smithwick, Robert,[43] Royal Marines	3 Oct. 10	1 Jan. 16
Spark, John,[44] Royal Sappers and Miners	8 April 12	
Standish, Richard, Royal Marines	28 June 11	1 Jan. 16
Swaffield, Robert Hassall, Royal Marines	22 Feb. 11	1 Jan. 16
P Sweeney, Francis Bernard,[47] 62 Foot	20 Jan. 14	25 April 17
Tasker, George, Land Transport Corps	12 Jan. 56	1 April 57
Temple, Gustavus Hancock, Royal Marines	15 May 09	18 Mar. 13
Teynham, G. H. R., *Lord,* Royal Artillery	16 Dec. 16	2 Jan. 21
Thierry, Lewis de,[18] Royal Marines	8 Feb. 14	1 Sept. 14
Thomas, Mark, 98 Foot	9 Nov. 15	25 Nov. 18
Thomson, George, 12 Foot	5 May 14	25 Jan. 18
Todd, William, Royal Marines	2 Feb. 10	1 Jan. 16
Turnbull, William George, 73 Foot	12 Aug. 13	25 June 18
P Veitch, William,[49] 58 Foot	30 Jan. 12	30 May 16
Wade, Thomas, Royal Marines	5 Dec. 08	1 Jan. 16
Walsh, George, 45 Foot	14 April 14	25 June 20
Waters, Wm. Henry, Land Transport Corps	3 Jan. 56	1 April 57
Watson, Atherton, 91 Foot	31 May 91	12 April 93
Watts, David John, Royal Marines	20 May 08	1 Jan. 16
Wilson, John, Land Transport Corps	31 Dec. 55	1 April 57
Wolff, Alexander Joseph, 11 Foot	25 Dec. 21	11 Nov. 24
Wood, John, Land Transport Corps	29 Feb. 56	1 April 57
Woodcock, Frederick, Royal Marines	3 Aug. 12	20 Feb. 15
Woolhouse, Andrew Mackason, Unattached	13 Aug. 25	17 July 28
Wright, John, Glengarry Fencibles	17 Aug. 15	25 Aug. 16

War Services of Second Lieutenants, Cornets, and Ensigns.

1 Lieut. Agassiz served in the 3rd Battalion Royal Marines during the American War in 1815.
1† Ensign Barrow served with the 20th Regt. at the siege of Sebastopol from 15th July 1855, also at the capture of Kinbourn (Medal and Clasp).
2 Lieut. Blake served in the Adriatic, and in co-operation with the Austrian army at the reduction of Trieste and Venice in 1813. Was severely wounded in defending the town of Commacchio in Italy against the French. War Medal with one Clasp.
3 Lieut. Branch served with the Royal Marines in the North of Spain in 1836.
4 Ensign Brew accompanied the 2nd Prov. Batt. of Militia to the South of France, in 1814.
5 Lieut. Brisac served in North America, with the 3rd Battalion Royal Marines, during the war of 1814-15.
6 Lieut. Colin Campbell was at the attack and surrender of the Island of Augusta. Landed 1st February at Port Buffalo; carried an eminence that commanded the town. At the attack of the sea batteries, and surrender of the island of Curzola, 3rd February. At the capture of the Devil's Island, 14th April. Attacked a body of French troops at St. Cataldo, and by a resolute advance with the bayonet, dislodged them from a strong position, making twenty-six of them prisoners, and assisted in the capture of the vessel from which they had debarked on 24th April, 1813.
7 Lieut. Carden served at the capture of a battery and sixteen vessels near Languelia, 10th May 1812; also at the reduction of Leghorn in 1813.
8 Ensign J. W. Carey served the Egyptian campaign of 1801 (War Medal with one Clasp).
9 Lieut. Coleman was present in the action with the French fleet and capture of four of their ships on the coast of Ireland on 12th Oct. 1798 (Medal and one Clasp).
13 Ensign Deaman served in the Peninsula and was present at the battles of Vittoria, Pyrenees, Nivelle, Nive, Orthes, and Toulouse, for which he has received the War Medal with six Clasps.
14 Ensign Donovan served in the Peninsula and was present at the battles of the Pyrenees, Nivelle, and Orthes, and at the siege of St. Sebastian, for which he has received the War Medal with four Clasps.
15 Lieut. Drinkwater served in the attack on the enemy's works on the right bank of the Mississippi, and has received the War Medal with one Clasp.
16 Ensign Dufresne served in the American war, and was present at the action of Chateauguay, for which he has received the War Medal with one Clasp.
17 Lieut. Elliott served in the R. M. Battalion at the capture of Java in 1811 (War Medal with one Clasp).
18 Lieut. Ensor has received the War Medal with one Clasp for the defence of St. Marron.
19 Lieut. Flexman acted as Quartermaster to the R. M. Battalion on the Walcheren expedition in 1809.
20 Lieut. Flint was severely wounded at the capture of four American vessels in the Rappamock, in 1813. War Medal with one Clasp.
21 Lieut. Ford was frequently employed in cutting-out expeditions during the war, and was severely wounded in one, in June 1810.
23 Lieut. Hammond served with the Royal Marines during the war in North America in 1813, and received a commission as 2nd Lieutenant, for his zeal and able management in training the refugee blacks, previous to their being embodied in the battalion under Major Lewis, R.M.
24 Ensign Handcock served the Waterloo campaign with the 27th Foot.
25 Ensign Harwood served in the Peninsula and was present at the sieges of Ciudad Rodrigo and Badajoz, and at the battles of Nive and Orthes, for which he has received the War Medal with four Clasps.
26 Ensign R. Luckcombe Haydon served in the Peninsula and was present at the battle of Barrosa, for which he has received the War Medal with one Clasp.
28 Ensign Holland served the Waterloo campaign with the 4th Foot.
30 Lieut. Jagger served in the Peninsula, and was present at the battle of Talavera. Served also the campaign of 1815, including the battle of Waterloo.
32 Lieut. Samuel Lloyd landed with the Royal Marines, on the 8th June, 1813, and drove the French soldiers from the town of Omago; also destroyed a battery and captured four vessels. Headed the attack on the town of Fiume and capture of ninety vessels, two batteries, and a quantity of stores, on 3rd July (wounded). Landed at Bocca-Ré and spiked the guns, 5th July. Attacked and captured the fortress of Faressina, mounting five eighteen-pounders; disabled the guns and destroyed the works, 7th July. Present at the capture of a convoy of twenty-one vessels at Rovigno, 2nd August, 1813. Served in co-operation with the Austrian army, and was at the reduction of Trieste.
33 Ensign Macdonald served the campaigns of 1811, 12, 13, 14, and 15, with the 79th, including the siege of Ciudad Rodrigo, covering last siege of Badajoz, battle of Salamanca, capture of Madrid, sieges of Burgos, subsequent retreat through Spain, battles of the Pyrenees (28th and 30th July), Nivelle, Nive, Toulouse, and Waterloo, besides various minor affairs, and was four times severely wounded, viz. in the right thigh at the battle of the Pyrenees, in the right groin at the Nive, in the right leg and right cheek at Waterloo. He has received the War Medal with five Clasps. He served in Canada during the Rebellion of 1837-38.
34 Lieut. Samuel Maclean served the Campaign of 1808-9, and has received the Silver War Medal with one Clasp for Corunna.
35 Lieut. Manico participated in boat actions on the coast of Puglia, the capture or destruction of ninety-one vessels and nearly 100 guns in the batteries in 1813. Served in the Royal Marine Battalion in the Chesapeake, was at the attack on Baltimore, and in a boat at the re-capture of the armed schooner, *Franklin*, in 1814. At the capture of a convoy and attack on the batteries at Corigeon in 1815.

War Services of Second Lieutenants, Cornets, and Ensigns.

36 Lieut. Mead served in the campaigns of 1814 and 15 in the Peninsula, France, and Flanders, and was present at the capture of Paris.

37 Ensign Mortashed served in the Peninsula and was present at the battles of the Pyrenees, Nive, Orthes, and Toulouse, for which he has received the War Medal with four Clasps.

38 Lieut. Morgan served in 1812 with the 2nd Batt. Royal Marines in the North of Spain, and in 1813 with the Expeditionary Army under Sir Sydney Beckwith on the North Coast of America, and was present at the attack on Norfolk in the Chesapeake, at the capture of Hampden, Queenstown, and Portsmouth in North Carolina, when the U. S. brig *Anaconda* of 18 guns and *Otter* 16-gun schooner were taken; was also at other boat and landing affairs in the Chesapeake. In 1814 present at the assault and capture of the town and forts of Oswego, also at the second attack (wounded). Served on the Lakes under Sir James Yeo, and on shore with the right division of the Army on the Quarter Master General's Staff until the end of the war.

39 Lieut. Raye has received the War Medal with one Clasp for St. Sebastian.

40 Cornet Silver served with the 11th Hussars the Eastern campaign of 1854, including the affair of Bulganak and battle of Alma (Medal and Clasp).

41 Lieut. Shore served in the Peninsula from Sept. 1813 to the end of that war in 1814.

42 Lieut. W. S. Smith served the Waterloo campaign with the 10th Hussars.

43 Lieut. Smithwick was present at the destruction of the French ships *Arienne* and *Andromaque* of forty guns, and *Mamelouck* of sixteen guns, on 22nd May, 1812, and has received the War Medal with one Clasp.

44 Lieut. Spark was present at the battle of Maida, for which he has received the War Medal with one Clasp.

47 Ensign Sweeney has received the Silver War Medal with two Clasps for Nivelle and Nive.

48 Lieut. de Thierry served with the 3rd Battalion Royal Marines, during the American War in 1814.

49 Ensign Veitch served in the Peninsula with the 48th and was present at the battles of Orthes and Toulouse, for which he has received the War Medal with two Clasps.

PAYMASTERS.

Name	CORNET, 2d LIEUT. or ENSIGN.	LIEUT.	PAY-MASTER.	HONORARY MAJOR.	WHEN PLACED ON HALF PAY.
Aitken, Alexander, 42 Foot	.. ..	.. ..	26 Aug. 13	.. ..	17 Feb. 21
ᵖ Barlow, Cuthbert,¹ 22 Foot	7 Jan. 10	13 Jan. 14	3 Jan. 28	.. ..	1 Jan. 57
ᵖ Bartley, George,² 54 F. (*Capt.*0Dec.21)	25 Oct. 07	13 Apr. 09	23 June 25	18 Oct. 59	22 Aug. 51
Bedford, William Devaynes,³ 87 Foot	6 April 26	31 Jan. 27	28 April 37	.. ..	28 April 50
Belfield, William,⁴ 88 Foot	13 May 42	29 July 43	9 Feb. 49	.. ..	24 Oct. 56
Bell, William, 56 Foot	.. ..	.. ..	12 Dec. 11	.. ..	19 Aug. 19
Boggis, Jas. Edwd. 55 F. (*Capt.*26 July 44) *Adjutant, West Essex Militia*	12 July 33	17 Oct. 34	8 Sept. 46	.. ..	22 Apr. 53
Boustead, John, Ceylon Rifle Regiment	.. ..	.. ..	21 June 10	.. ..	1 May 36
ᵖ Bowden, Wm. Carey,⁵ 21 Dragoons	.. ..	.. ..	12 May 08	.. ..	4 Nov. 24
Boyd, Alex.⁶ 11 F.	14 Sept. 08	9 Aug. 09	8 Feb. 21	15 June 58	15 June 58
Boyd, Richard, Land Transport Corps	.. ..	23 Nov. 55	7 April 56	.. ..	1 April 57
ᵖ Boyle, James,⁷ 21 Foot	21 July 08	6 Feb. 12	3 Nov. 25	.. ..	1 May 32
Brough, Richard, 83 Foot	.. ..	*25 Dec. 13	7 Oct. 24	.. ..	2 Mar. 49
Burn, James,⁸ 4 Foot (*Capt.* 19 Dec. 34)	1 Oct. 11	16 June 13	6 Feb. 35	.. ..	26 Jan. 49
Castle, Wm., Cavalry Depot (*Capt.*10June26)	25 Jan. 16	7 Apr. 25	16 Feb. 29	1 Oct. 58	1 Oct. 58
Court, John, 73 Foot	2 Nov. 08	7 Feb. 11	22 July 36	.. ..	14 Dec. 49
ᵖ Cowper, Henry,⁹ 7 Line Bn. Ger. Leg.	.. ..	.. ..	1 Mar. 06	.. ..	25 Sept. 16
Cox, Charles, 75 Foot	.. ..	.. ..	29 Jan. 06	.. ..	7 May 29
Cox, Douglas Leith, 47 Foot	30 Nov. 09	29 Oct. 12	25 Sept. 40	.. ..	1 Sept. 48
ᵖ Crawford, William,¹⁰ 2 Dragoons	17 Aug. 15	25 June 19	24 Mar. 29	.. ..	1 Jan. 49
Crowe, George William, 27 Foot	.. ..	.. ..	7 Mar. 11	.. ..	25 Dec. 24
Dana, Wm. Pulteney, 6 Garrison Batt.	.. ..	.. ..	25 April 07	.. ..	25 Dec. 16
ᵖ Davies, Richard,¹¹ 74 Foot	6 June 11	31 Dec. 12	1 Dec. 25	.. ..	20 Aug. 41
ᵖ Dickson, Francis,¹³ 52 Foot	12 Mar. 12	27 Jan. 14	26 July 27	9 Sept. 59	3 June 53
Dive, Hugh, 10 Foot	.. ..	.. ..	31 Mar. 08	.. ..	21 Aug. 23
Durnford, Geo. Aug.¹⁵ 39 F. (*Capt.*13Feb.27)	28 June 06	10 Mar. 10	13 Feb. 27	9 Sept. 59	5 Nov. 52
Espinasse, James,¹⁷ 1 F. (*Capt.* 11 July 37)	8 Feb. 21	7 April 25	8 Feb. 39	.. ..	9 Oct. 55
Evans, Edward, 78 Foot	24 Mar. 25	5 Jan. 27	30 July 44	.. ..	22 Apr. 53
ᵖ Fugion, Edward,¹⁹ Depot Battalion	4 May 09	25 July 11	23 Dec. 19	9 Sept. 59	1 April 51
Gapper, Peter, 104 Foot	20 June 05	25 Dec. 06	14 Nov. 16	.. ..	11 Nov. 19
Geddes, Adam Gordon, 10 R. Vet. Batt.	.. ..	.. ..	31 Mar. 14	.. ..	25 June 21
ᵖ ᵐ Gordon, James,²¹ 92 Foot	.. ..	.. ..	4 April 05	.. ..	2 Mar. 20
Gregg, Charles Francis, Depot Batt.	16 Dec. 31	14 Feb. 34	26 Mar. 41	.. ..	18 Sept. 57
ᵖ Hall, Henry William, 39 Foot	.. ..	.. ..	4 April 05	.. ..	29 July 19
Hall, William Sanford, 53 Foot	19 Dec. 11	22 Apr. 13	10 July 40	.. ..	11 Nov. 53
ᵖ Halpin, William,²⁵ 1 Lt. Dr. Germ. Leg.	.. ..	.. ..	6 Jan. 07	.. ..	25 June 16
Head, Hy. Bond, 2 Dr.Gds. (*Capt.*21Mar.45)	.. ..	23 Dec. 36	21 June 39	.. ..	30 May 45
Heath, Edwin, 88 Foot	.. ..	*1814	28 June 27	.. ..	30 Aug. 39
Hely, Joseph,²⁶ Cavalry Depot	16 Feb. 39	11 Nov. 45	1 Dec. 48	.. ..	1 Sept. 56
ᵖ ᵐ Hilliard, Henry,²⁷ 68 Foot	25 Feb. 08	16 Nov. 09	22 Mar. 21	.. ..	10 May 39
Holdsworth, Samuel,²⁸ 82 Foot	31 Dec. 07	1 Nov. 09	22 Sept. 25	.. ..	27 Aug. 41
Hunter, Edward,²⁹ 98 Foot, (*Capt.*18 May 38)	13 July 09	11 Aug. 13	27 Mar. 40	.. ..	21 Aug. 49
Jefferson, Richard, Ceylon Regt.	23 Oct. 23	1 Sept. 26	6 May 36	.. ..	8 Sept. 46
ᵖ Jellicoe, Richard,³⁰ Recruiting Dist.	17 June 07	.. ..	24 Feb. 14	1 Sept. 56	1 Sept. 56
Johnson, Ralph Boetler, 45 Foot	.. ..	.. ..	27 Oct. 10	.. ..	25 June 15
ᵖ Jones, Michael,³¹ 80 Foot	.. ..	.. ..	21 April 98	.. ..	25 Aug. 19
King, Thomas, 98 Foot	.. ..	.. ..	5 Sept. 11	.. ..	25 Dec. 18
Kyffin, Rt.Willington,12 F. (*Capt.*11Sept.40)	14 May 12	23 Dec. 13	17 Sept. 41	.. ..	6 April 55
ᵖ M'Leod, Martin,³³ 25 Foot	8 Oct. 12	18 Jan. 15	15 Jan. 24	.. ..	15 Jan. 30
Mackay, James Duff, 50 Foot	.. ..	.. ..	26 Nov. 12	.. ..	25 Dec. 14
Mackenzie, Hugh Baillie, Depôt Batt.	1 Feb. 13	.. ..	24 May 29	.. ..	1 April 56
MacKinnon, Edmund Vernon, 5 Dr. Gds.	29 April 36	27 Mar. 40	30 June 48	.. ..	6 April 55
ᵖ Maclaurin, David Scott Kin.,³⁵ 1 Dr. Gds., *Dep.Assist.Com.Gen.*7 Mar. 14	.. ..	.. ..	18 Sept. 23	.. ..	30 July 44
Manders, Thomas, 6 Dr.Gds. Adjutant *Wilts Yeomanry Cavalry*	30 July 35	6 Oct. 38	25 Sept. 49	.. ..	5 Jan. 55
ᵖ Middleton, John,³⁶ Recruiting Dist., (*Captain*, 7 April 25)	10 Mar. 08	4 Oct. 09	25 Nov. 20	1 July 56	1 July 56
ᵖ ᵐ Moore, George,³⁷ 32 Foot	1 Oct. 12	6 Dec. 13	19 Oct. 26	9 Sept. 59	16 Apri 52
O'Keefe, James,³⁸ 48 Foot	.. ..	.. ..	16 Jan. 12	.. ..	1 April 37
ᵖ Pennington, James Masterson,³⁹ 48 Foot	5 Feb. 07	31 Jan. 08	26 Jan. 16	9 Sept. 59	1 July 50
Perry, Charles James, 87 F. (*Q.M.* 23July44)	22 Dec. 48	30 Nov. 49	3 May 55	.. ..	16 Aug. 59
Prior, Lodge Morres Murray,⁴¹ 12 Lancers	12 Sept. 11	9 Dec. 13	6 July 20	9 Sept. 59	3 Oct. 48
Ratcliff, Thomas Hanson, 9 Dragoons	3 Apr. 40	16 Aug. 42	3 Sept. 47	.. ..	24 Sept. 58
ᵖ ᵐ Robinson, P. Vyvyan,⁴² 88 Foot	.. ..	.. ..	28 Jan. 13	.. ..	28 June 27
ᵖ Rodgers, James,⁴³ 26 Foot	17 May 27	.. ..	7 Oct. 36	.. ..	1 June 37
ᵖ Rofe, Samuel,⁴⁴ 14 Light Dragoons	.. ..	.. ..	3 Sept. 12	9 Sept. 59	25 Jan. 50
South, Charles,⁴⁵ 20 F.	9 Dec. 13	17 Dec. 18	23 Aug. 27	4 April 55	4 April 55
Stevens, William,⁴⁶ Land Transport Corps (*Captain*, 25 Jan. 50)	.. ..	24 Apr. 55	5 Apr. 56	.. ..	1 April 57

Paymasters.

	ENSIGN, ETC.	LIEUT.	PAY-MASTER.	HONORARY MAJOR.	WHEN PLACED ON HALF PAY
Stuart, William, 36 Foot, *Q.M.* 10 July 35 (*Honorary Captain* 30 Mar. 58)	.. ..	.. ..	11 Jan. 50	.. ..	30 Mar. 58
ℬ Telford, Wm. 17 F. (*Capt* 2 *April* 41) Paymaster, *North Lincoln Militia* ..	5 Dec. 11	25 Aug. 13	20 Oct. 48	.. ..	1 May 55
Terry, Henry, 99 Foot	13 Sept. 10	19 May 14	27 Dec. 27	.. ..	1 June 35
Thompson, George Ash, 85 Foot	16 Mar. 15	22 May 17	27 Jan. 20	9 Sept. 59	6 June 51
ℬ ℬ Thomson, James Crooke,[49] 1 Foot..	.. ..	.. ..	31 Jan. 11	.. ..	22 Oct. 16
Thorp, John, 63rd Foot.................	27 Sept. 33	5 June 35	8 Oct. 44	.. ..	7 Dec. 55
Timbrell, Sydney James,[50] 6 Foot	27 May 42	10 Nov. 43	9 May 51	.. ..	26 Oct. 58
ℬ Timbrell, Thomas Richardson,[51] 58 Foot (*Q.M.* 19 *Nov.* 30)	.. ..	.. ..	25 Oct. 42	.. ..	3 June 59
ℬ Tovey, Alexander, 24 Foot	22 Oct. 13	11 June 18	4 Feb. 19	.. ..	29 Mar. 42
Trick, Thomas, 1 R. Veteran Battalion ..	.. ..	.. ..	14 Sept. 09	.. ..	12 July 14
Wardell, Charles, 42 Foot...............	1 Sept. 10	20 Dec. 13	7 Feb. 21	.. ..	25 Jan. 28
Wardell, Wm. Hen.,[55] R. Canadian Regt.	15 Aug. 15	21 Feb. 22	18 Dec. 28	18 Dec. 57	18 Dec. 57
Ware, Robert,[52] 49 Foot	25 Oct. 12	25 Sept. 13	28 June 31	.. ..	9 Apr. 47
ℬ White, John Lewis,[53] 81 Foot	.. ..	.. ..	25 Feb. 13	.. ..	8 Oct. 18
White, Lawr. L. Esmonde, 89 Foot.....	18 Jan. 31	26 June 35	29 Sept. 43	.. ..	17 Jan. 51
Wood, Peter Valentine, 14 F. (*Capt.* 13 Feb.28)	17 Sept. 07	3 Jan. 11	2 Aug. 31	.. ..	11 Apr. 51
ℬ Woodgate, John,[46] Recruiting Dist. (*Capt.* 20 Feb. 12)	17 Oct. 05	11 Feb. 08	25 June 29	1 Oct. 58	1 Oct. 58
ℬ Wright, James,[54] 94 Foot.............	.. ..	.. ..	25 Mar. 10	.. ..	25 Dec. 18

War Services of the Paymasters.

1 Paymaster Barlow, previous to entering the Army, served three years as a Midshipman in the Royal Navy. He served afterwards in the Peninsula from Aug. 1810 to April 1812; the campaign against Nepaul in 1815; and the Mahratta campaigns of 1817 and 1818, and was present at the battle of Jubblepore, 19th Dec. 1817. He was present with the 10th Regt. at the battle of Sobraon (Medal); and with the 9th Lancers at the passage of the Chenab at Ramnuggur, and the battles of Chillianwallah and Goojerat (Medal and Clasps).

2 Major Bartley served the Corunna campaign, and subsequently in the Peninsula from March 1811, to the end of the war, and was engaged at Almarez, Alba de Tormes, Baighar, Vittoria, Pyrenees 25th, 26th, and 27th July, Pampeluna 28th and 30th July. He has received the War Medal with two Clasps.

3 Paymaster Bedford served as Major and Deputy Assistant Adjutant-General to the Anglo-Spanish Legion, during 1835 and part of 1836; and was engaged in the village of Mendigur and heights of Arlaban, in Alava, on the 16th, 17th, and 18th Jan. 1836.

4 Paymaster Belfield served with a detachment of the 17th, with Lieut. Col. Outram's Light Brigade, in the Southern Mahratta campaign of 1844-5, and was present in all its operations, including the capture of Gotea, 21st, and storming of Monohur Stockades and Fort, 25th Jan. 1845, at which place this detachment formed the storming party, and suffered very seriously. Served with the 88th in the Eastern campaign of 1854-55, including the battles of Alma and Balaklava, siege of Sebastopol, and attack on the Redan on the 18th June and 8th Sept. (Medal and Clasps).

5 Paymaster Bowden served in the Peninsula with the Queen's Royals : in 1808 he went with Sir Arthur Wellesley's Expedition to Portugal and was present at the battle of Vimiera; afterwards with Sir John Moore during the campaign and retreat to Corunna in 1808-9. Subsequently he accompanied his Regt. to Walcheren and was present at the siege and capture of Flushing. Embarked again with his Regt. for Lisbon in Jan. 1811, and was present at the battle of Fuentes d'Onor, covering the siege of Badajoz, siege of the Forts and battle of Salamanca, and siege of Burgos. He has received the War Medal with three Clasps for Vimiera, Corunna, and Salamanca.

6 Major Boyd accompanied the Expedition to Walcheren and was present at the siege of Flushing.

7 Paymaster Boyle served in the Peninsula from May 1809 to the end of that war in 1814, including the battle of Busaco, retreat to Torres Vedras, pursuit of Massena, actions of Foz d'Arouce and Campo Mayor, siege and capture of Olivença, assault and capture of Badajoz, capture of Madrid and the Retiro, battles of Vittoria and the Pyrenees. Slightly wounded in the ear at Fort St. Christoval, 10th May 1813, and again in the face in the Pyrenees, 28th July 1813. He has received the War Medal with eight Clasps.

8 Captain Burn served the campaign in the Eastern Islands, and was at the taking of Macassar in 1814. Served the Mahratta campaign of 1817 and 18, and was severely wounded at Bhurtpore in 1826.

9 Paymaster Cowper served on the expedition to Stralsund and Copenhagen in 1807; to Sweden with Sir John Moore, in 1808; thence the same year to Portugal, where he served until July 1811; thence to Malta, Sicily, and Genoa, until the peace. He has received the War Medal with two Clasps for Talavera and Fuentes d'Onor; also the War Medal bestowed by the King of Hanover to every officer, non-commissioned officer, and soldier of the German Legion, in commemoration of the services of the corps.

War Services of the Paymasters.

10 Paymaster Crawford served the Waterloo campaign with the 2nd Dragoons.

11 Paymaster Davies served in the Peninsula from Sept. 1811 to the end of that war in 1814, including the capture of Fort Picurina and Badajoz, battles of Salamanca, Vittoria, Pyrenees, Nivelle, Torbes, Orthes, and Toulouse. He has received the War Medal with seven Clasps.

13 Major Dickson served with the 10th Regt. in Spain, from early in 1813 until the end of the war; was present at the attack of the pass Col de Balaguer, second siege of Tarragona, attack of the pass of Ordal, under Lord Wm. Bentinck, and the blockade of Barcelona. Proceeded to India in 1818, and served in the 41st throughout the Burmese war of 1824-26 (Medal), and was present in most of the actions in which the regt. was engaged. Was at the siege of Collapore in 1817. Also in Scinde and Affghanistan from Nov. 1840 to Feb. 1843 (Medal), and was with the force under General Nott during its march from Candahar, Ghuznee, Cabul, Jellalabad, and Khyber Pass, to Ferozepore, in 1842-43.

15 Major Durnford served at the capture of the Isle of France in 1810; in the expedition to Java in 1811; capture of Kandy in 1815; in the Kandyan rebellion in 1817 and 18; and in the action of Maharajpore, 29 Dec. 43.

17 Captain Espinasse served the Eastern campaign of 1854 to 8th Sept. 1855, including the siege of Sebastopol (Medal and Clasp).

19 Major Fugion served in the Peninsula from July 1809, to the end of the war in 1814, including the battle of Salamanca, siege of Burgos, and battle of Orthes. He has received the War Medal and two Clasps for Salamanca and Orthes.

21 Paymaster Gordon served in the Peninsula with the 92nd and has received the War Medal with seven Clasps for Corunna, Fuentes d'Onor, Vittoria, Pyrenees, Nive, Orthes, and Toulouse. He served also the Waterloo campaign.

25 Paymaster Halpin served in the Peninsula, and has received the War Medal with four Clasps for Salamanca, Vittoria, Orthes, and Toulouse.

26 Paymaster Hely served as a Captain in the 1st Lancers of the late Anglo-Spanish Legion, in 1835 and 36, and was engaged at the castle of Guevara, the stronghold of the Cavlists; and afterwards at Mendegur, Azua, and heights of Arlaban in Alava on the 16th, 17th, and 18th Jan. 1836; also at the passage of the Urumea on the 28th May, and commanded the squadron which took Passages on that day. Again on the right of the lines when Alza was attacked; together with the constant skirmishes in front of Vittoria. Served in the Eastern campaign as Paymaster 11th Hussars, including the battles of Balaklava and Inkerman (Medal and Clasps).

27 Paymaster Hilliard served in the Peninsula from June 1809 to the end of that war in 1814, including the battle of Busaco, action of Campo Mayor, first siege of Badajoz, battle of Albuhera, affairs at Arroyo de Molino and Almaraz. Served also the campaign of 1815, including the battles of Quatre Bras and Waterloo, at which latter he was severely wounded. He has received the War Medal with two Clasps.

28 Paymaster Holdsworth served on the expedition against Belle Isle, in June 1800; at the siege and capture of Flushing, in 1809; in the Peninsula from June 1812 to the end of that war in 1814, including the battles of Vittoria, Maya Pass, Heights of Pampeluna 30th (wounded in the wrist by a musket-ball and contused on the shoulder) and 31st July, Heights of Lesaca 31st Aug., battles of Nivelle and Orthes. He has received the War Medal with three Clasps.

29 Captain Hunter served in the 98th with the Expedition to the North of China in 1842 (Medal), including the attack and capture of Chin Kiang Foo, and landing before Nankin.

30 Major Jellicoe served at the capture of Heligoland in 1807. Frequently engaged in boats in the North Seas and Baltic, and in several affairs with Danish gunboats and the Russians during 1808, 9, and 11. Served two years on the island of Anholt, and commanded a Company at the defeat of the Danes in their attack of the island in 1811,—the garrison taking prisoners more than double their own numbers. Served afterwards in the Peninsula. He has received the Naval War Medal as a Lieut. of Royal Marines, for the battle of Anholt, 27 March 1811.

31 Paymaster Jones has received the War Medal with one Clasp for the Egyptian campaign of 1801.

33 Paymaster M'Leod served in the Peninsula with the 27th and was present at the battles of Nivelle, Nive, Orthes, and Toulouse, for which he has received the War Medal with four Clasps.

35 Paymaster Maclaurin served in the Peninsula during the campaign of 1813, and that in Holland in 1814: subsequently at Waterloo, and with the army of occupation, as Deputy Assistant Commissary General. He has received the War Medal with one Clasp for Nivelle.

36 Major Middleton served in the Peninsula and France with the 95th Rifles from 13th March 1810 to 18th July 1814, and was present in every action in which the 3rd Batt. of that corps was engaged, namely—the battle of Barrosa, siege and capture of Ciudad Rodrigo, where he served with the storming party, and was severely hurt by the explosion of a magazine on the rampart; siege and storming of Badajoz, actions on the heights of San Christoval and at Castrajan, battle of Salamanca, capture of Madrid, action at San Milan, battles of Vittoria and the Pyrenees, storming the heights of Echalar and of Vera, battles of the Nivelle and Nive, actions near Bayonne of the 9th, 10th, 11th, 12th, and 13th Dec. 1813 (horse shot under him on the 10th), action at Tarbes, and battles of Orthes and Toulouse, besides various affairs of outposts. He has received the War Medal with ten Clasps.

37 Major Moore served the campaign of 1814 in Holland, including the action at Merxem, and bombardment of Antwerp; present at Waterloo. He served also at the 1st and 2nd

siege operations before Mooltan, and was present at the surrender of the fortress. Also at the surrender of the fort and garrison of Cheniote, and battle of Goojerat.

38 Paymaster O'Keefe served with the 48th Regt. at the attack and capture of Coorg, in the East Indies, in April 1834.

39 Major Pennington served in the Peninsula with the 5th, from June 1809 to May 1814, including the battle of Busaco, actions at Torres Vedras, Leria, Redinha, Pombal, Robleda, Condeixa, Foz d'Arouce, Guarda, and Sabugal; battle of Fuentes d'Onor, 1st siege of Bajadoz in May and June 1811 (on the 9th June commanded a party of 1 sergeant and 30 men, which drove the enemy's piquet from the foot of the breach); actions at Campo Mayor, El Bodon, and Fuente Guinaldo; siege and storm of Ciudad Rodrigo (received two contusions in the trenches by the explosion of a 13-inch shell), siege and storm of Badajoz, battle of Salamanca, capture of Madrid, battles of Vittoria, Pyrenees, Nivelle, Nive, Orthes, and Toulouse. He has received the War Medal and eleven Clasps.

41 Major Prior served the campaign of 1817 in the East Indies against the Pindarrees.

42 Paymaster Robinson served the Waterloo campaign with the 69th Foot.

43 Paymaster Rodgers served in the Peninsula from May 1813 to the end of that war in 1814, including the siege of Tarragona. Served afterwards in the East Indies, and was present at Amulnier, Malligaum, and Asseerghur.

44 Major Rofe served in the Peninsula from Oct. 1812 to the end of that war in 1814, and has the Silver War Medal with four Clasps for Vittoria, Pyrenees, Nivelle, and Orthes.

45 Major South received the thanks of the Commander of the Forces in Ireland on 30 Apr. 1818 for capturing and conveying into Sligo a smuggler, while in command of a detachment on the Coast of Ireland. He accompanied a wing of the 20th Regt. as Adjutant in 1824-27 for the reduction of Hill Forts in the Southern Mahratta country. Sailed with the Brigade of Guards to the East as their Brigade Paymaster, and was present with the Brigade in its services in 1854-55, and has received the Medal with four Clasps for Alma, Balaklava, Inkerman, and Sebastopol.

46 Captain Stevens served with the 49th Regt. throughout the operations in China (Medal), commencing with the first taking of Chusan and terminating with the landing before Nankin, including the storm and capture of the heights above Canton, attack and capture of Amoy, second capture of Chusan, attack and capture of the height of Chinhae, occupation of Ningpo and repulse of the night-attack, capture of Chapoo, Woosung, Shanghae, and Chinkiangfoo.

49 Paymaster J. C. Thomson served in the Peninsula, and has received the War Medal with two Clasps for the battles of Orthes and Toulouse. Served also the Waterloo campaign.

50 Paymaster S. J. Timbrell served the Sutlej campaign of 1845-6, and was present in the battles of Moodkee, Ferozeshah, Buddiwal, Aliwal, and Sobraon, in which last he had both his thigh-bones broken by grape-shot (Medal and Clasps).

51 Paymaster T. R. Timbrell was present, as a volunteer, with the old 94th, at battles of the Nive on the 9th, 10th, 11th, and 13th Dec. 1813; and at the action at Sauveterre, battles of Orthes and Toulouse, and other minor affairs in the south of France, as an Ensign with the 87th Regt. He has received the War Medal and three Clasps.

52 Paymaster Ware served with the 38th in the Burmese war, and was present at the capture of Rangoon and subsequent operations before that place (Medal). Served with the 49th throughout the operations in China, except Segoan (Medal).

53 Paymaster John Lewis White served in the Peninsula with the 68th and has received the War Medal with two Clasps for Nivelle and Orthes.

54 Paymaster Wright served in the Peninsula with the late 94th, from April 1810 to the end of that war in 1814, including the defence of Cadiz, lines of Torres Vedras, pursuit of Massena, actions of Redinha, Condeixa, Foz d'Arouce, and Sabugal; battle of Fuentes d'Onor, siege and storm of Ciudad Rodrigo, siege and storm of Badajoz, battle of Salamanca, retreat from Madrid to Portugal, battles of Vittoria, Pyrenees, Nivelle, and Orthes; action at Vic Bigorre, and battle of Toulouse. He has received the War Medal with ten Clasps.

55 Major William H. Wardell, previous to entering the Army, served five years as a Midshipman in the Royal Navy, and was at the capture of Java in 1811 (Medal), and also upon the expedition to Palembang, Sumatra, in the year following. He has lost his right arm from a contusion received in the naval service.

56 Major Woodgate has the War Medal with four Clasps for Vimiera, Talavera, Fuentes d'Onor, and Ciudad Rodrigo.

ADJUTANTS.

	CORNET, 2d LIEUT. or ENSIGN.	LIEUT.	ADJUTANT	WHEN PLACED ON HALF PAY.
Crause, John,[1] Recruiting District	29 Dec. 08	25 April 11	6 April 15	25 May 17
Ellis, Richard, 97 Foot................	29 Jan. 07	17 July 12	2 Feb. 09	25 Dec. 18
Farnan, John, 8 Foot..................	7 April 13	10 Aug. 14	7 April 13	25 Feb. 16
Fraser, Alexander,[2] New Brunswick Fenc.	25 Mar. 13	24 June 15	25 Mar. 13	25 Feb. 16
Henry, John,[3] 91 Foot	9 June 14	never	9 June 14	25 Feb. 16
Kyle, J., Land Transport Corps..........	....	....	21 Feb. 56	1 April 57
Leith, John Kenneth, 12 Foot	12 June 17	never	12 June 17	17 Sept. 18
Mitchell, J. H., Land Transport Corps ..	....	....	21 Feb. 56	1 April 57
Mitchell, Thomas, Land Transport Corps	....	....	21 Feb. 56	1 April 57
Osborne, Francis,[4] 62 Foot	9 Dec. 10	never	9 Dec. 19	15 Mar. 21
Parlour, William, 6 West India Regiment	5 Aug. 13	5 Mar. 16	5 Aug. 13	28 Dec. 17
Peacocke, George, 88 Foot	never	never	31 Mar. 83	27 April 83
Thompson, Tho., Ross & Cromarty Fen. Inf.	never	never	6 June 99	1802

1 Lieut. Crause served in the Peninsula and was present at the battle of Salamanca, for which he has received the War Medal with one Clasp.
2 Colonel Fraser served in the American war with the 49th, and highly distinguished himself in the night attack upon the American army at Stoney Creek, where he bayoneted seven of the enemy and took the American General Winder prisoner. He is now a Colonel of Militia in Upper Canada.
3 Ensign Henry has received the War Medal with eleven Clasps for Martinique, Albuhera, Ciudad Rodrigo, Badajoz, Salamanca, Vittoria, Pyrenees, Nivelle, Nive, Orthes, and Toulouse.
4 Ensign Osborne served the campaign of 1808-9, and has received the Silver War Medal with one Clasp for Corunna.

QUARTER-MASTERS.

	QUARTER-MASTER.	HONORARY RANK OF CAPTAIN.	WHEN PLACED ON HALF PAY.
Allen, George, Royal Sappers and Miners	1 April 53	.. ..	25 June 55
p Andrews, John, 4 Dragoon Guards	20 June 34	1 July 59	3 Oct. 48
Armstrong, Charles, 12 Lancers	7 July 37	1 July 59	18 July 48
Armstrong, John, 58 Foot	25 April 05	.. ..	16 Dec. 19
Austin, Norton, Royal Marines	25 July 46	22 Aug. 57	22 Aug. 57
Banyard, John, 16 Foot	3 Mar. 48	13 April 58	13 April 58
Barnes, Samuel, Royal Artillery	1 Feb. 08	1 July 59	1 April 44
Baxter, Jas., Canadian Regt.	15 July 35	4 April 56	
Bilham, David,[1] 20 F. 2nd Lancashire Militia	17 Sept. 41	9 Feb. 55	9 Feb. 55
p ꟼ Bishop, William,[2] 1 Life Guards	19 June 15	.. ..	13 Nov. 27
Black, James,[3] Ceylon Regiment	10 Aug. 26	1 July 59	30 May 43
Blackburne, William, 91 Foot (Ens. 20 Oct. 46)	1 Aug. 48	.. ..	27 July 55
Blay, Samuel Sutton, 72 Foot	5 Mar. 12	.. ..	25 June 16
p Booth, Jonathan,[4] 60 Foot	4 May 26	1 July 59	27 July 38
p ꟼ Brannan, John,[5] 60 Foot (Ens. 5 Sept. 35)	18 Sept. 35	1 July 59	28 May 47
Breading, John Remington, Depot Battalion	23 June 48	2 Dec. 59	2 Dec. 59
Byrne, Francis Henry, R. Military Asylum	22 May 40	.. ..	1 July 47
Carroll, James, 18 Foot	4 June 29	.. ..	23 July 44
Carroll, Patrick, 78 Foot	7 Aug. 46	12 Sept. 56	12 Sept. 56
Carson, John,[6] 73 Foot	28 Nov. 45	24 Feb. 57	24 Feb. 57
p ꟼ Carter, John Henry,[7] 1 Life Guards	25 Oct. 26	.. ..	1 Jan. 31
Clark, Geo. Alex., Royal Artillery	1 Nov. 48	1 Nov. 58	1 Nov. 58
Clarke, William, Royal Staff Corps	24 April 28	.. ..	25 Aug. 29
Clarkson, Walter, 15 Hussars (Cornet 20 Aug. 44)	1 Sept. 48	5 Oct. 58	5 Oct. 58
Cockburn, James, 8 Dragoons	13 July 15	.. ..	24 June 24
Cole, George, 35 Foot	15 Dec. 40	1 July 59	13 Jan. 54
p Collins, Francis,[8] 11 Hussars	6 Feb. 34	1 July 59	5 Mar. 47
Conolly, Patrick, 20 Foot	19 Aug. 27	1 July 59	17 Sept. 41
Cooper, Thomas,[9] Royal Marines	15 July 46	23 Oct. 57	23 Oct. 57
p ꟼ ꟼ Copeland, Geo.[10] Scots Fus. Gds. Paym. Cambridge Mil...	7 April 37	1 July 59	2 Sept. 51
Copeland, Thomas, Land Transport Corps	16 Feb. 56	.. ..	1 April 57
Cowell, John, Depot Batt.	20 Oct. 43	15 April 66	15 April 66
Crabtree, Abra.[11] 3 Drs. (Cor. 17 Sept. 41)	25 Nov. 42	16 July 58	16 July 58
Crawford, George,[12] 80 Foot (Ens. 18 Sept. 46)	21 May 47	.. ..	22 April 53
Crispin, George, 67 Foot Ens. 22 March 39; 7 Lancashire Militia	25 Oct. 39	24 Feb. 57	24 Feb. 57
Croker, John Charles, 6 Foot; 5 West York Militia	28 July 46	26 Sept. 56	
p Crooks, William Smedley,[13] 2 Life Guards	7 Jan. 28	.. ..	1 Jan. 31
Daines, Charles,[14] 74 Foot	24 Sept. 41	27 May 56	27 May 56
Dandy, John, 90 Foot	7 Mar. 22	.. ..	7 Sept. 26
ꟼ Davidson, James,[15] 41 Foot	14 Feb. 28	.. ..	22 July 36
Dibbin, George, Royal Marines	7 July 46	22 Aug. 57	22 Aug. 47
Doherty, Daniel,[16] Depot Batt.	28 July 41	1 Oct. 56	1 Oct. 56
Dougherty, Wm., Depot Batt.	3 May 44	26 Mar. 58	26 Mar. 58
p Duke, Jones,[17] 39 Foot	10 Jan. 37	1 July 59	9 July 50
Dunbar, Charles, Royal Artillery	2 July 46	1 April 57	1 April 57
Edwards, George, 85 Foot	25 Oct. 27	1 July 59	30 April 41
Edwards, Thomas Willock,[18] 84 Foot	3 Dec. 12	1 July 59	17 Feb. 32
Elliott, Archibald,[19] 41 Foot (Ens. 31 Mar. 48)	21 July 48	29 Oct. 58	29 Oct. 58
p ꟼ Emmott, William,[20] Royal Horse Guards, Adjutant, Worcestershire Yeomanry Cavalry	25 Sept. 28	.. ..	1 Jan. 31
Farrants, James, 103 Foot	9 May 11	.. ..	29 Mar. 18
Farrell, James, 84 Foot	12 May 37	1 July 59	23 May 48
FitzGerald, Thomas, Depot Batt.	23 Jan. 47	14 May 58	14 May 58
Forbes, John, 91 Foot	6 Sept. 39	.. ..	1 Aug. 48
p Fox, Samuel,[22] 96 Foot	19 July 39	1 July 59	25 Feb. 48
France, Richard, Grenadier Guards	24 Dec. 29	1 July 59	28 Feb. 51
Fraser, Chas., 49 F. (Ens. 4 Sept. 43), 2nd Somerset Militia	28 Aug. 46	30 June 54	30 June 54
Freeburn, James, Royal Artillery	1 April 46	21 April 56	21 April 56
Gates, William, Royal Artillery	15 Nov. 09	1 July 59	24 Mar. 41
ꟼ ꟼ Goddard, Sam.,[23] 14 Foot, Mil. Knt. of Windsor	20 Mar. 23	1 July 59	11 Mar. 53
ꟼ ꟼ Grant, Charles,[24] 23 Foot	5 July 44	1 July 59	17 Mar. 54
Green, Owen,[24]† 55 Foot	7 June 54	.. ..	25 Oct. 59
Grigg, James Wm.[25] 55 Foot	22 June 39	7 June 54	7 June 54
Grimwood, Thomas, 56 Foot	25 Nov. 11	.. ..	25 July 14
p ꟼ Hall, John,[26] 6 West India Regiment	29 Sept. 14	.. ..	14 Jan. 19
Hall, William, 17 Dragoons	10 May 31	1 July 59	6 July 52
Hamilton, Richard, 37 Foot	2 Nov. 37	1 July 59	9 Nov. 49
ꟼ ꟼ Hardy, Luke, New Brunswick Fencibles	13 Jan. 25	.. ..	3 Aug. 26
Haviland, John, 2 Dr. Gds.	15 July 36	5 Jan. 55	5 Jan. 55

Quarter-Masters. 521

	QUARTER-MASTER.	HONORARY RANK OF CAPTAIN.	WHEN PLACED ON HALF PAY.
P QM Heartley, Andrew,[27] Royal Horse Guards, *Military Knight of Windsor*	12 Dec. 22	.. ..	1 Jan. 31
Hill, John,[27]† 4 Dragoons	22 June 49	15 Nov. 59	15 Nov. 59
Hilton, James, Royal Sappers and Miners	9 Nov. 35	1 July 59	14 Jan. 48
Hives, Thomas Walter,[28] 40 Foot, *Hampshire Militia*	25 Oct. 42	19 Sept. 56	19 Sept. 56
Hollis, James, 69 Foot, *Paymaster Stirling Militia*	3 Nov. 37	1 July 59	27 July 49
Holt, William, 95 Foot, *Dublin City Militia*	3 Dec. 41	7 April 54	7 April 54
Hornby, William, 66 Foot	1 Feb. 27	1 July 59	27 Sept. 42
Huddlestone, Thomas, Land Transport Corps	16 Feb. 56	.. ..	1 April 57
P Hudson, Edward,[29] 23 Foot	28 Sept. 09	.. ..	25 Dec. 14
Hume, Wm., 72 F., *Town Adjutant at Gibraltar*	24 April 38	.. ..	23 July 47
Jackson, Henry, Royal Horse Guards	28 April 27	.. ..	1 Jan. 31
Jerome, Joseph, 86 Foot	23 Mar. 26	1 July 59	17 Mar. 54
Jones, Joseph, 33 Foot, *Northumberland Militia*	25 Oct. 42	14 July 54	14 July 54
Joyce, Edward, 63 Foot (*Ens.* 4 Sept. 40)	9 Oct. 40	1 July 59	16 July 52
Kelly, Rich. Seymour, R. Staff Corps (*Barrack Master at Hythe*)	26 Jan. 26	.. ..	8 June 38
P QM Kerr, William,[30] 28 Foot (*Ens.* 7 July 37)	1 June 38	.. ..	23 July 44
P QM Kinkee, Frederick,[31] 19 Dragoons	8 June 24	.. ..	18 Aug. 25
Landers, James, 8 Dragoons	29 Nov. 39	1 July 59	17 Mar. 54
Langford, Alexander, 5 Dragoon Guards	18 June 41	1 July 59	8 July 53
M'Clellan, James Creighton,[32] 10 Dragoons	28 Jan. 19	1 July 59	19 May 46
M'Clenahan, Thomas, 2 Garrison Battalion	4 Nov. 13	.. ..	25 Dec. 16
M'Donald, Bernard, 59 Foot	20 July 47	15 Jan. 58	15 Jan. 58
McQueen, D., 92 Foot (*Ens.* 14 Nov. 41)	6 Dec. 44	12 Jan. 55	12 Jan. 55
P Mackay, Donald,[33] 42 Foot	12 Oct. 04	.. ..	18 Mar. 13
Mackenzie, John, 7 Foot	16 Mar. 20	.. ..	2 Jun. 23
Mackintosh, William,[34] 93 Foot (*Ens.* 27 Jan. 14)	22 June 20	1 July 59	13 Dec. 39
P Manley, John,[35] 36 Foot	22 Oct. 12	.. ..	25 Dec. 14
Mansfield, John,[36] 2 Foot	27 Oct. 46	10 April 57	10 April 57
Mansfield, William,[37] 22 Foot	21 April 11	.. ..	9 April 29
Mayne, Henry,[39] 49 Foot, *Paymaster, Worcester Militia*	23 June 37	1 July 59	5 Nov. 50
Midwinter, Thomas, 1 Life Guards	19 June 15	.. ..	1 June 28
P Miller, George,[40] 2 Life Guards	21 Sept. 21	.. ..	1 Jan. 31
Missett, Joseph, 1 Dragoon Guards	30 Mar. 38	1 July 59	23 Apr. 52
Moir, William,[41] 58 Foot	15 Oct. 47	.. ..	23 July 58
P Morgan, John,[42] 52 Foot	1 Jan. 24	1 July 59	29 Dec. 37
Morris, William, 19 Foot	15 Oct. 14	.. ..	26 April 27
Mulhall, John, 17 Foot, *Adjt. R. N. Lincoln Militia*	17 Aug. 41	.. ..	29 April 53
Murray, James,[43] 24 Foot	4 Dec. 17	1 July 59	16 Aug. 42
Neill, William, 85 Foot	25 April 41	1 July 59	12 Dec. 51
QM Nelson, Michael, 2 Dragoons (*Ens.* 4 Dec. 35)	25 Dec. 35	1 July 59	16 Aug. 50
Newland, William, 90 Foot	15 Sept. 37	.. ..	15 Dec. 54
Nicoll, James, Royal Artillery	1 Jan. 43	1 April 57	1 April 57
P Nowlan, John,[44] 62 Foot (*Ens.* 20 Nov. 40)	29 Oct. 41	2 Feb. 55	2 Feb. 55
Oliphant, George, Royal Artillery	1 July 47	1 Oct. 58	1 Oct. 58
QM Parry, John Evans,[45] 7 Dragoons	12 Oct. 41	25 Aug. 57	25 Aug. 57
QM Partridge, John, 1 Dragoons	18 July 34	1 July 59	26 Oct. 49
QM Paton, Edward,[46] 42 Foot	19 June 40	5 May 54	5 May 54
P Payne, John,[47] Gr. Gds.	31 Aug. 15	5 Dec. 55	5 Dec. 55
Pegley, Robert, 4 Royal Veteran Battalion	24 Feb. 20	.. ..	25 July 21
P Pratt, David,[48] (*Cor.* 5 Sept. 11; *Lt.* 26 Oct. 12), 16 Drs.	25 Jan. 16	1 July 59	23 Sept. 36
Preston, John Wm. 76 Foot (*Ens.* 11 June 12; *Lt.* 10 Dec. 16)	12 June 28	1 July 59	9 Feb. 49
Rafferty, George William, 6 Foot	4 Mar. 42	.. ..	28 June 44
Riordan, John, 98 Foot (*Ens.* 31 Dec. 44; *Lt.* 10 July 48)	21 Aug. 49	.. ..	1 April 53
P Roberts, John,[49] 81 Foot	28 April 08	.. ..	25 June 29
Rorke, Michael, Cape Mounted Rifles (*Ens.* 19 Nov. 41)	10 May 44	7 June 54	7 June 54
Russell, Richard, 25 Dragoons	.. ..	.. ..	25 Jan. 20
Ruston, William, Royal Marines	23 June 46	22 Aug. 57	22 Aug. 57
Salamono, Paolo, Malta Fencibles	25 Jan. 39	.. ..	13 July 55
P Sanderson, Joseph Prossor,[50] 47 Foot	28 May 07	.. ..	28 May 18
Scoltock, Samuel,[51] Depot Batt.	13 Mar. 46	29 April 56	29 April 56
P Scott, James,[52] 9 Foot, *Mil. Knight of Windsor*	17 Dec. 07	1 July 59	8 July 51
Sears, John,[57] 64 Foot (*Ens.* 8 May 40; *Lt.* †19 Mar. 47)	1 Oct. 47	20 Dec. 59	20 Dec. 59
Shean, Robert,[51] 51 Foot	20 Aug. 44	29 June 55	29 June 55
P Shirley, John,[54] Royal Horse Guards	14 Sept. 26	.. ..	1 Jan. 31
Sinclair, Donald, 93 Foot, *Paymaster, Antrim Militia*	22 Mar. 44	6 July 55	6 July 55
Smith, Thomas, Cavalry Depot	26 June 35	27 May 56	27 May 56
Smith, Wm. Honey, 6 Foot	8 Jan. 56	.. ..	5 June 57
P QM Steel, Joseph,[55] 1 Life Guards	10 Oct. 26	.. ..	1 Jan. 31
Steele, Alexander, Royal Artillery	1 July 44	1 April 57	1 April 57
Stephens, John,[56] Royal African Corps	14 Sept. 15	.. ..	9 Dec. 31

	QUARTER-MASTER.	HONORARY RANK OF CAPTAIN.	WHEN PLACED ON HALF PAY.
Swaine, Joseph,[58] 1 Foot	20 Nov. 46	1 July 59	1 July 59
Taylor, John, Depot Batt.	25 Aug. 46	1 Oct. 56	1 Oct. 56
Taylor, Richard, Rifle Brigade	29 Mar. 39	.. ..	21 Aug. 49
Thomson, William, 22 Foot	17 Mar. 14	.. ..	25 Dec. 14
p *QM* Troy, Thomas,[60] Royal Horse Guards	5 Aug. 13	.. ..	25 Dec. 28
Tyler, Henry, 76 Foot	3 Sept. 47	2 Feb. 58	2 Feb. 58
p *QM* Waddell, William,[61] 1 Dragoons	8 July 13	.. ..	1 Mar. 27
Wakefield, William, 3 W. Ind. Regt. (*Ens.* 1 Feb. 38.)	13 Dec. 39	.. ..	16 Apr. 47
Wall, Michael,[62] 61 Foot (*Ens.* 6 Nov. 40)	16 Feb. 41	22 July 56	22 July 56
Wallis, Samuel,[63] 69 Foot	1 Feb. 23	1 July 59	3 Nov. 37
Walsh, Thomas, 44 Foot	27 Oct. 43	27 July 55	27 July 55
Walsh, William, 21 Foot	16 June 08	.. ..	31 Jan. 28
p Ward, John,[64] 30 Foot	21 Oct. 24	1 July 59	28 May 47
Webster, Robert, 5 Foot	19 July 47	30 July 58	30 July 58
p Webster, William,[65] 2 Life Guards	11 Mar. 22	.. ..	1 Jan. 31
White, James, Royal Artillery	1 Feb. 56	1 April 57	1 April 57
Williamson, Thomas, Depot Battalion, 1st *Lanark Militia*	22 Nov. 44	6 April 55	6 April 55
QM Willox, James,[67] 54 Foot	27 Sept. 27	1 July 59	11 Sept. 46
Wright, Thomas,[66] 9 Dragoons	11 Aug. 25	1 July 59	17 Aug. 38
*p Wynne, Rich. Miles,[69] 3 Prov. Batt. of Militia, *late Major*, Denbigh Militia	25 Dec. 13	.. ..	1814

War Services of the Quarter Masters.

1 Captain Bilham served the Eastern campaign of 1854 with the 20th Regiment, including the battle of Alma, and siege of Sebastopol (Medal and Clasps).

2 Quarter Master Bishop served in the Peninsula and has received the War Medal with two Clasps for Vittoria and Toulouse. He served also the Waterloo Campaign.

3 Captain Black served the campaigns of 1813 and 14, in Germany and Holland, and was present at the attack upon Bergen-op-Zoom.

4 Captain Booth served the campaign in Spain from Oct. 1808 to Jan. 1809, and has received the War Medal with one Clasp for Corunna.

5 Captain Brannan served in the Peninsula, France, and Flanders, from July 1809, to the end of the war, including the battle of Busaco; 1st siege of Badajoz; battle of Albuhera (severely wounded); actions of Arroyo del Molinos and Castlo Murrenito; battles of Vittoria (slightly wounded), the Pyrenees, 7th, 10th, 25th, and 31st July, Nivelle, Nive, 9th Dec., and before Bayonne 13th Dec. (slightly wounded), St. Palais, Orthes, Lambeige, Toulouse, Quatre Bras, and Waterloo. He has received the War Medal with eight Clasps.

6 Captain Carson served with the 73rd Regt. in the Kaffir War of 1846-47 (Medal).

7 Quarter Master J. H. Carter served in the Peninsula with the 1st Life Guards, and has received the War Medal with two Clasps for Vittoria and Toulouse. He served also the Waterloo Campaign.

8 Captain Francis Collins served in the Peninsula from Oct. 1809 to the end of that war in 1814, including the Battle of Busaco, retreat to the lines of Torres Vedras and subsequent advance, battle of Fuentes d'Onor, siege of Ciudad Rodrigo, battle of Salamanca, capture of Madrid, siege of Burgos and retreat to the frontiers of Portugal, battle of Vittoria, siege of San Sebastian, crossing of the Bidassoa, battle of the Nive, passage of the Adour, investment of Bayonne and repulse of the sortie, on which occasion he was wounded through the left arm. He has received the War Medal with six Clasps.

9 Captain Cooper has received the Medal for service in Syria in 1840.

10 Captain Copeland served in the Peninsula, from March 1813, to the end of the war, including the battle of Vittoria, siege of San Sebastian, passage of the Bidassoa, the Nive, and the Adour, investment of Bayonne, and repulse of the sortie. Also the campaign of 1815, including the battles of Quatre Bras and Waterloo. He has received the War Medal with two Clasps for Vittoria and the Nive.

11 Captain Crabtree served with the 3rd Light Dragoons throughout the campaign of 1842 in Affghanistan, and was present at the forcing of the Khyber Pass, storming the heights of Jugdulluck, action of Tezeen and Huftkotul, and occupation of Cabool (Medal). Served the Sutlej campaign of 1845-6, and was present at the battles of Moodkee (charger killed), Ferozeshah, and Sobraon (severely wounded) (Medal and two Clasps). Served also in the Punjaub campaign of 1848-9, and was present at the affair of Ramnuggur, the passage of the Chenab at Wuzeerabad on 1st Dec. 1848, with the force under Sir Joseph Thackwell, and battles of Chillianwallah and Goojerat (Medal and two Clasps).

12 Quarter Master Crawford served with the 8th Regt. the Sutlej campaign of 1845-6, including the battles of Moodkee, Ferozeshah, and Sobraon (Medal and two Clasps).

13 Quarter Master Crooks served in the Peninsula with the 2nd Life Guards and has received the War Medal with two Clasps for Vittoria and Toulouse.

14 Captain Daines served with the 74th Regt. in the Kaffir war of 1851-52 (Medal).

War Services of the Quarter-Masters. 523-4

15 Quarter Master Davidson served the campaigns of 1814 and 15 in Holland, Flanders, and France, including the action at Merxem, bombardment of Antwerp (wounded), storming of Bergen-op-Zoom, battles of Quatre Bras and Waterloo (twice wounded), and capture of Paris.

16 Captain Doherty served with the 38th Regiment in the Eastern campaign of 1854-55, and has the Medal and two Clasps for Inkerman and Sebastopol.

17 Captain Duke served in the Peninsula, and has received the Silver War Medal with two Clasps for Orthes and Toulouse.

18 Captain T. W. Edwards served in the East Indies from Nov. 1796 to 1830, during which long period he was actively employed in nearly all the campaigns and engagements which took place, commencing with the battle of Malavelly, and terminating with the Burmese war. Medal for the capture of Seringapatam.

19 Captain Elliott served with the 41st Regt. the Eastern campaign of 1854-55, including the battles of Alma and Inkerman, and siege of Sebastopol (Medal and Clasps).

20 Quarter Master Emmott served in the Peninsula from Oct. 1812 to the end of that war in 1814, and was present at the battle of Vittoria. Served also the campaign of 1815, including the battle of Waterloo.

22 Captain Fox served in the Peninsula, and has received the Silver War Medal with two Clasps for Nivelle and Nive.

23 Captain Goddard served the Campaign of 1815, including the battle of Waterloo, and storming of Cambray. In 1817 he was present at the siege of Hattras, and served the Campaign of 1817-18 in the Deccan. Also present at the siege and storming of Bhurtpore in 1825-6 (Medal).

24 Captain Charles Grant served the Campaign of 1815, and was severely wounded at Quatre Bras. He served as acting Quarter Master in the Grenadier Guards during the insurrection in Canada in 1838-39.

24† Quarter Master Green served the campaign against the Rajah of Coorg in April 1834. Served the China war (Medal), including the taking of Amoy, Chusan, Chinhae (also night attack), Ningpo, Chapoo, Woosung, Shanghae, and operations in the Woosung and Yeng-tse Kiang Rivers. Served the Eastern campaign of 1854-55, including the battles of Alma and Inkerman, siege and fall of Sebastopol (Medal and Clasps).

25 Captain Grigg served with the 55th Regiment in China (Medal); at Amoy, Chusan, Chinhae (including repulse of night attack), Chapoo, Woosung, Shanghae, and Chinkiungfoo.

26 Quarter Master John Hall served the Egyptian campaign of 1801. Also in the Peninsula, and has received the War Medal with two Clasps for Egypt and Salamanca. He served also the Waterloo Campaign.

27 Quarter Master Heartley served in the Peninsula from Oct. 1812 to the end of that war in 1814, and was present at the battle of Vittoria. Served also the campaign of 1815, including the battle of Waterloo. He has received the War Medal with two Clasps for Vittoria and Toulouse.

27† Captain Hill served as Deputy Provost Marshal to the Bombay column of the Army of the Indus during the whole of the time it was in the field (from Dec. 1838 to Feb. 1840), and was present at the storm and capture of Ghuznee (Medal); served the Eastern campaign of 1854-55, including the battles of Alma, Balaklava, Inkerman, and Tchernaya, and siege of Sebastopol, also with the Light Cavalry Brigade at Eupatoria (Medal and Clasps).

28 Captain Hives served with the 40th Regt. throughout the operations at Candahar and in Affghanistan in 1841-42 (Medal); was also in the battle of Maharajpore (Medal).

29 Quarter Master Hudson joined the 23rd in 1796, and was on the expedition with the flank companies to Ostend in 1798, and taken prisoner. The following year he served the campaign in Holland, including the landing at the Helder, and the actions of the 10th and 19th Sept., 2nd and 6th October. In 1801 he served the Egyptian campaign, including the action on the landing, and those of the 12th, 13th, and 21st March (severely wounded). In 1805 he served in Hanover; and in 1807 on the expedition to Denmark, and was present in the actions of the 17th and 24th August in front of Copenhagen. From 1810 to 1814 he served in the Peninsula, and was present at the battle of Albuhera, the siege and storming of Badajoz, and other actions during the above period. He has the War Medal with three Clasps.

30 Quarter Master Kerr served in the Peninsula and was present at the battles of Busaco, Albuhera, Nivelle, Nive, Orthes, and Toulouse, for which he has received the War Medal with six Clasps. He served also the Waterloo campaign.

31 Quarter Master Kinkee served in the Peninsula, France, and Flanders, from Jan. 1813 to the end of the war in 1815, including the action at Morales de Toro, and battles of Vittoria, Pyrenees, Orthes, and Waterloo. He has received the War Medal with two Clasps.

32 Captain M'Clellan served throughout the campaigns of 1813 and 14 on the Niagara Frontiers, including the action before Fort George, Blackrock, Buffalo, Chippewa, Lundy's Lane, Niagara, before Fort Erie, Cook's mills, and pass of Grand River. Received a contusion in the head by a musket shot at the moment of passing through the enemy's line in the charge at Chippewa 4th July 1814.

33 Quarter Master Mackay served in the Peninsula, and has received the War Medal with two Clasps for Busaco and Fuentes d'Onor.

34 Captain Mackintosh has received the War Medal with two Clasps for Martinique and Guadaloupe.

35 Quarter Master Manley served in the Peninsula, and has received the War Medal with four Clasps for Roleia, Vimiera, Corunna, and Salamanca.

36 Captain Mansfield served with the 2nd Regt. in the Kaffir War of 1851-53 (Medal).

37 Quarter Master Mansfield served during twenty years in the East Indies, including the

storming of Fort Barabatty in 1803, where he was wounded; and the Mahratta campaigns of 1804, 5, and 6, under Lord Lake. Served also at the capture of the Isle of France, in 1810.

39 Captain Mayne served throughout the whole of the operations in China (Medal) with the 49th Regt., and as Brigade Quartermaster, including the storm and capture of the heights above Canton, attack and capture of Amoy, second capture of Chusan, attack and capture of the heights of Chinhae, occupation of Ningpo, repulse of the night attack on Ningpo, attack and capture of the enemy's entrenched camp on the heights of Segoan, attack and capture of Chapoo, Woosung, and Ching Kiang Foo.

40 Quarter Master Miller served in the Peninsula with the 2nd Life Guards, and has received the War Medal with one Clasp for Vittoria.

41 Quarter Master Moir was present at the destruction of Pomare's Pah on 30th April 1845, at the attack on Heki's Pah at Mawio 8th May, destruction of the Waikiri Pah 16th May, storming of Kawiti's Pah at Ohiawai 1st July (severely wounded on the right leg), and capture of Kawiti's Pah at Ruapekapeka 11th Jan. 1847.

42 Captain Morgan served throughout the whole of the Peninsular war, with the exception of a few months, including the following battles, sieges, &c., viz., Corunna, Almeida, Busaco, Pombal, Redinha, Miranda de Corvo, Condeixa, Foz d'Arouce, Sabugal, Fuentes d'Onor, Ciudad Rodrigo (a volunteer on the storming party, and wounded in the left leg), and Badajoz (again a volunteer on the storming party, and severely contused on the head). He has received the War Medal with seven Clasps.

43 Captain Murray's services:—Egyptian campaign of 1801 (War Medal and Clasp); capture of the Cape of Good Hope in 1806; Nepaul campaigns of 1814, 15, and 16; Mahratta war, in 1817 and 18.

44 Captain Nowlan served in the Peninsula with the 11th Regt. in 1813-14, and has received the War Medal with four Clasps for the battles of Nivelle, Nive, Orthes, and Toulouse.

45 Captain Parry served the campaign of 1815 with the 7th Hussars, and was wounded in the hand at the battle of Waterloo.

46 Captain Patton served the campaign of 1815 with the 42nd Highlanders and was present at the battles of Quatro Bras and Waterloo.

47 Captain Payne served in Sicily in 1806 and 7; in 1808 and 9 in Spain, and present in the actions of Sahagun, Benevente, Lugo, and Corunna; subsequently at Walcheren. He served also the campaigns of 1812, 13, 14, and 15, in the Peninsula, France, and Flanders, and was present in the actions of the Pyrenees, siege and capture of San Sebastian, passage of the Bidassoa and of the Nive, battle of Nivelle, action at the Mayor's House, sortie and investment of Bayonne, battles of Quatre Bras and Waterloo, capture of Peronne and of Paris, and subsequently with the Army of Occupation. He has received the War Medal with three Clasps for Corunna, Nivelle, and Nive.

48 Captain Pratt served in the Peninsula from April 1809 to the end of that war in 1814, including the passage of the Douro, and battles of Talavera, Busaco, Fuentes d'Onor, Salamanca, Vittoria, and investment of Bayonne. Served also at Bhurtpoer, under Lord Combermere. He has received the War Medal with five Clasps.

49 Quarter Master John Roberts served on Lord Moira's expedition and with the Duke of York, in 1794 and 1795, and was present at the siege of Nimeguen and other affairs of importance. From 1795 to 1801 he served in Hanover, Madeira, and the West Indies, and was present at the taking of the Danish and Swedish Islands, and he served also against the Brigands in Gadarne, and against the Caribs in St. Vincent. From 1808 to 1810 he served in the Peninsular Campaigns, including the passage of the Douro, battle of Talavera, and several affairs of outposts. He has received the War Medal with two Clasps.

50 Quarter Master Sanderson served in the Peninsula with the 40th and has received the War Medal with six Clasps for Badajoz, Vittoria, Pyrenees, St. Sebastian, Orthes, and Toulouse.

51 Captain Scoltock served with the 46th Regt. at the capture of Kittoor in Dec. 1824.

52 Captain Scott served in Holland in 1799, and was present in the action of the 19th Sept. Served also in the Peninsula from Aug. 1808 to Aug. 1809, and again from Jan. 1813 to June 1814, including the battle of Vimiera, capture of Oporto, battle of Vittoria, siege of San Sebastian, battles of the Nive on the 9th, 10th, and 11th Dec. 1813. He has received the War Medal with five Clasps.

53 Captain Shean served with the 51st Regt. throughout the Burmese war of 1852-53 (Medal); on board the E. I. C. steam frigate *Ferooz* during the naval action and destruction of the enemy's stockades on the Rangoon River; during the succeeding three days' operations in the vicinity, and at the storm and capture of Rangoon.

54 Quarter Master Shirley served in the Peninsula from Oct. 1812 to May 1813, and again from Jan. 1814 to the end of that war, and has received the War Medal with one Clasp for the battle of Toulouse.

55 Quarter Master Steel served in the Peninsula with the 1st Life Guards and has received the War Medal with two Clasps for Vittoria and Toulouse.

56 Quarter Master John Stephens served in the Nepaul war in the East Indies.

57 Captain Sears served with the 39th Regt. the campaign against the Rajah of Coorg in 1834; the operations against Kurnool in 1839, and at the battle of Maharajpore on the 29th Dec. 1843 (Medal). Was present with the 64th Regt. at the landing in Persia on 7th Dec. 1856, at the storm and capture of Reshire, and bombardment and surrender of Bushire.

58 Captain Swaine served with the 1st Royal at the siege and fall of Sebastopol from the landing of the 2nd battalion on the 22d April 1855 (Medal and Clasp).

60 Quarter Master Troy served in the campaigns in the Peninsula, France, and Flanders with

the Royal Horse Guards, and was present at every action in which that Regt. was engaged, including the battle of Waterloo. He has the War Medal with two Clasps for Vittoria and Toulouse.

61 Quarter Master Waddell served in the Peninsula and has received the War Medal with three Clasps for Fuentes d'Onor, Vittoria, and Toulouse. He served also the Waterloo Campaign.

62 Captain Wall served with the 61st Regt. in the Punjaub campaign of 1848-49, and was present at the passage of the Chenab, battles of Sadoolapore, Chillianwallah, and Gojeerat, and with the field force in pursuit of the enemy to the Khyber Pass (Medal and two Clasps).

63 Captain Wallis served in the Burmese war.

64 Captain Ward served in the Peninsula with the 30th from March 1809 to June 1813, including the defence of Cadiz from 4th June to 25th Sept. 1810; occupation of the Lines of Torres Vedras, pursuit of Massena, actions of Sabugal, Almeida, and Barba del Puerco, battle of Fuentes d'Onor, siege of Badajoz, and action of Villa Muriel. Served the campaign of 1814 in Holland, under Sir Thomas Graham; and that of 1815, under the Duke of Wellington. He has received the War Medal with three Clasps.

65 Quarter Master William Webster served in the Peninsula with the 2nd Life Guards and has received the War Medal with one Clasp for Vittoria.

67 Captain Willox served with the 54th in Stralsund under General Gibbs in 1813, and the subsequent campaign in Holland under Lord Lynedoch, including the attack on Merxem and bombardment of Antwerp. He served also the campaign of 1815, including the storming and capture of Paris; and finally in the Burmese war, including the attack and capture of Mahatee, and the assault and capture of Arracan.

68 Captain Wright served in South America in 1807, under General Whitelock; also at Walcheren in 1809, including the siege of Flushing.

69 Major Wynne served the campaign of 1808-9 in Spain as Deputy Assist. Commissary General with Sir John Moore's army; and served with the 3rd Provisional Battalion of Militia in the south of France in 1814.

COMMISSARIAT DEPARTMENT.

COMMISSARIES-GENERAL.

Adams, *George*,[1] CB. ....27 Mar. 56
p Adams, Joseph Hollingworth[2] 20 Jan. 37
p Carey, Tupper[3] ....24 Dec. 44
p Coffin, *Sir* Edward Pine[4] .... 1 July 40
p Dobree, John Saumarez[6] .... 1 June 52
p Drake, John[7] ....30 Aug. 33
p Dunmore, Thomas,[8] CB. ....25 Dec. 14
p Fildcr, William,[9] CB. ...... 1 July 40
Hewetson, William[10] ....23 Dec. 43
p Laidley, John[5] .... 2 Jan. 56
p Maclean, *Sir* George,[11] KCB. 29 Dec. 49
Ramsay, Thomas Warton ...... 1 Jan. 55
Robinson, Wm. Henry .... 1 Jan. 55
Wild, Henry James .... 6 Jan. 54

DEPUTY COMMISSARIES GENERAL
RETIRED WITH HONORARY RANK OF
COMMISSARIES GENERAL.

Bland, John.................15 May 59
Clarke, Charles Anthony ......15 May 59
p Dinwiddie, Gilbert Hamilton[12]15 May 59
Greig, William Isaac ....17 Sept. 59
p Watt, James Duff[13] ....15 May 59
p Wilson, James ....15 May 59

DEPUTY-COMMISSARIES-GENERAL.

p Barney, Richard[1] ....19 July 21
p Booth, William,[2] CB. ......18 Dec. 18
p Daniel, John Edgcumbe[5] ....26 Dec. 46
p Fletcher, William .... 6 Jan. 54
Forbes, Charles John..........25 July 15
Goldsmith, Oliver .... 5 Jan. 53
Green, William ....16 Dec. 45
Hopkins, Samuel..............25 Dec. 14
Lane, John...................29 Dec. 49
Lindsey, Robert.............. 5 Jan. 53
p Lukin, William .... 2 Sept. 14
p Major, Francis Wm. A.C.[6] ..16 Dec. 45
p Nugent, Geo, Stph, N. Hodges[10] 22 Oct. 16
Osborn, Thomas..............28 June 38
Rae, Thomas .... 5 Jan. 53
Singer, Paulus Æmilius ...... 1 April 00
p Spurrier, John ....10 Sept. 30
Stickney, Thomas ....11 Aug. 46
Swain, Charles .... 1 Jan. 55
p Telfer, Buchan Fraser[12].....25 Dec. 14
Thompson, James ....16 Dec. 45
Thomson-Sinclair, William ....26 Dec. 46
p Wemyss, William[13] ....25 Dec. 14
p White, George ....20 Nov. 6
Woodhouse, James, CMG. .... 7 June 25
p Wybault, Joseph William.... 2 Jan. 56

ASSISTANT COMMISSARIES GENERAL
RETIRED WITH HONORARY RANK OF
DEPUTY COMMISSARIES GENERAL.

p Bayley, Henry Addington....15 May 59
Pryce, Josiah ....15 May 59
Stanton, William ....15 May 59
Stevens, William ....15 May 59

ASSISTANT-COMMISSARIES-GENERAL.

Brathwaite, Frederick .... 5 Jan. 53
Beech, William ....24 Feb. 10
Carr, Samuel ....24 Dec. 41
p Chalmers, Andrew[1] ....20 Jan. 37

Charters, Robert............. 1 July 40
Child, George................ 4 May 15
Clarke, Henry[2] ....28 Dec. 50
Comper, John Thomas .... 2 Jan. 56
Courtenay, George Townsend ..26 Sept. 06
Cramer, Henry John .... 4 May 15
Crookshank, George .... 3 Aug. 14
Dalrymple, William Henry ...29 Dec. 49
p Darling, Henry Charles...... 1 July 40
Davidson, Peter Fraser........19 July 21
De Smidt, Johannes[2]..........24 Dec. 44
Feilde, Fulford Bastard ....23 Dec. 43
Gem, Thomas................. 1 Jan. 55
Grindlay, Robert ....30 July 25
Hewetson, William .... 2 Jan. 56
Hoffay, Ernest Albert .... 1 July 40
Julyan, Primrose G. .... 2 Jan. 56
Knowles, Francis Edward....:.14 Feb. 53
Lithgow, William ....22 Oct. 16
Looker, William..............23 Dec. 43
Low, William ....28 June 38
Priaulx, Henry .... 5 Jan. 53
Ragueneau, Charles ....10 Sept. 30
p Reed, James William[4] ...... 1 July 40
p Riddell, Archibald[5] ....10 Sept. 30
p Roberts, Peter[6] .... 1 July 40
Robinson, William............16 Dec. 45
Spearman, *Sir* Alex. Young, *Bt.* 10 Oct. 16
Trew, Thomas Eggar..........24 Dec. 41
p Wemyss, Charles[8] .... 1 July 40
p Wybault, Patrick Robert[11]...25 Dec. 14
Yeoland, George..............10 Sept. 30

DEPUTY-ASSISTANT-COMMISSARIES-
GENERAL.

p Anderson, John David[1] ....11 Oct. 14
p Bain, George[2] ....20 May 28
Beltz, Samuel ....31 Mar. 14
Billings, Francis Thomas ...... 9 Sept. 14
Cellem, Robert ....27 Feb. 51
De Smidt, John Pascal Larkins.. 1 July 40
p Dilke, William[3]............22 Oct. 16
Dougan, George Augustus......28 Dec. 50
p Eyl, John George[4] ....25 Dec. 14
Fuxardo, Aug. Maria Guaxardo 25 Dec. 14
Freeborn, John ....25 Dec. 14
Graham, Frederick ....22 Oct. 16
p Greig, William[5]............25 April 15
Harper, Charles ....22 Oct. 16
Harris, Anthony Charles ......25 Dec. 14
Kirkland, *Sir* John........... 4 May 15
Lee, David Ross .... 7 June 42
Le Mesurier, Henry .... 4 May 14
Macpherson, James ....10 Sept. 30
Montgomerie, Frederick ......22 Oct. 16
Paille, Peter Francis .... 1 July 40
Parish, *Sir* Woodbine, *KCH*...30 April 14
Parker, Frederick Saintbury ..26 Dec. 46
Petrie, Samuel, *CB*..........25 Dec. 14
Richardson, Fran. Mosely.....25 Dec. 14
Robinson, Augustus Facey ....25 April 15
p Sisson, Marcus Jacob[6] ......22 Oct. 16
Stanton, William ....19 July 21
Stayner, Thomas Allen ....11 May 13
Telfer, George Home .... 2 Jan. 56
Tomes, John ....24 Dec. 41
Williams, W. J............... 5 Nov. 16
Wilson, Thomas..............10 Sept. 30

War Services of the Commissariat Officers.

Commissaries General.

1 Mr. George Adams served the Eastern campaign of 1854-55, including the battle of Alma and siege of Sebastopol (Medal and Clasps, *CB.*, and 4th Class of the Medjidie).
2 Mr. J. H. Adams has received the War Medal with one Clasp for Talavera.
3 Mr. Carey has received the War Medal with seven Clasps for Talavera, Busaco, Fuentes d'Onor, Ciudad Rodrigo, Badajoz, Salamanca, Orthes, and Toulouse.
4 Sir Edward Pine Coffin has the War Medal with three Clasps for Corunna, Vittoria, and Toulouse.
5 Mr. Laidley has received the War Medal with three Clasps for Fuentes d'Onor, Ciudad Rodrigo, and St. Sebastian.
6 Mr. Dobree has received the War Medal with eight Clasps for Sahagun and Benevente, Barrosa, Vittoria, St. Sebastian, Nivelle, Nive, Orthes, and Toulouse.
7 Mr. Drake has received the War Medal with two Clasps for Corunna and Busaco.
8 Mr. Dunmore has received the War Medal with one Clasp for Corunna.
9 Mr. Pilder has received the War Medal with nine Clasps for Talavera, Albuhera, Salamanca, Vittoria, Pyrenees, Nivelle, Nive, Orthes, and Toulouse. Commanded the Commissariat of the Expeditionary Force untill the end of July 1855, including the battles of Alma, Balaklava, and Inkerman, and siege of Sebastopol (Medal and Clasps, and 3rd Class of the Medjidie).
10 Mr. Hewetson previous to entering the Commissariat in 1806 served as a midshipman in the East India Company's marine, and was present in 1804 on board the *Earl Campden*, Commodore Dance, in the memorable action and repulse by the China fleet of the French squadron, under Admiral Linois, off the Straits of Singapore (grant from the Patriotic Fund). In 1806 at the taking of the Cape of Good Hope, and received a severe contusion when in command of a boat landing troops in Lospardo Bay, and subsequently present with a party of seamen at the battle of Blueberg. In 1811-12 he served on the Frontier in Commissariat charge with the force under Colonel Graham employed in expelling the Kaffirs from the Zeurfeldt. In 1814-15 served in the American War with the army in North America, and on the termination of hostilities, on a special mission into the United Staics. In 1815, joined the army in France.
11 Sir George Maclean served in the Peninsula and South of France, and has received the War Medal with two Clasps for the battles of Orthes and Toulouse. Served in the Kaffir War of 1851-53 (Medal) and was knighted in recognition of his services on returning from the Cape in 1854. Served as Chief of the Commissariat with the Army in the East during the latter part of the siege of Sebastopol (Medal and Clasp, KCB., Commander 2nd Class of the Sardinian Order of St. Maurice and St. Lazarus, and 4th Class of the Turkish Order of the Medjidie).
12 Mr. Dinwiddie served in the Peninsula, and has received the War Medal with one Clasp for Vittoria; also the Syrian Medal.
13 Mr. Watt served in the Peninsula, and has received the War Medal with six Clasps for Salamanca, Pyrenees, Nivelle, Nive, Orthes, and Toulouse; also the Kaffir Medal.

Deputy Commissaries General.

1 Mr. Barney has received the War Medal with two Clasps for Corunna and Busaco.
2 Mr. Booth has received the War Medal with ten Clasps for Corunna, Talavera, Busaco, Salamanca, Vittoria, Pyrenees, Nivelle, Nive, Orthes, and Toulouse.
5 Mr. Daniel has received the War Medal with seven Clasps, for Salamanca, Vittoria, Pyrenees, Nivelle, Nive, Orthes, and Toulouse.
8 Mr. Major has received the War Medal with six Clasps for Salamanca, Vittoria, Pyrenees, Nivelle, Orthes, and Toulouse.
10 Mr. Nugent has received the War Medal with five Clasps for Roleia, Vimiera, Talavera, Busaco, and Fuentes d'Onor.
12 Mr. Telfer has received the War Medal with one Clasp for Corunna.
13 Mr. William Wemyss has received the War Medal with ten Clasps for Roleia, Vimiera, Corunna, Talavera, Busaco, Fuentes d'Onor, Salamanca, Vittoria, Nivelle, and Nive.

Assistant Commissaries General.

1 Mr. Chalmers has the War Medal with four Clasps for Salamanca, Vittoria, Nivelle, and Nive.
2 Messrs. Henry Clarke and Johannes de Smidt have received the Kaffir Medal.
4 Mr. Reed has received the War Medal with one Clasp for Vittoria.
5 Mr. Riddell has the War Medal with four Clasps for Salamanca, Vittoria, Orthes, and Toulouse.
6 Mr. Roberts has received the War Medal with one Clasp for Nive.
8 Mr. Wemyss has the War Medal with four Clasps for Salamanca, Vittoria, Nivelle, and Nive.
11 Mr. Wybault has the War Medal with three Clasps for Busaco, Fuentes d'Onor, and Salamanca.

Deputy Assistant Commissaries General.

1 Mr. Anderson has received the War Medal with one Clasp for Salamanca.
2 Mr. Bain has received the War Medal with three Clasps for Nive, Orthes, and Toulouse.
3 Mr. Dilke has received the War Medal with five Clasps for Vittoria, Pyrenees, Nivelle, Nive, and Orthes.
4 Mr. Eyl has the War Medal with three Clasps for Ciudad Rodrigo, Salamanca, and Vittoria.
5 Mr. Greig has received the War Medal with three Clasps for Vittoria, Orthes, and Toulouse.
6 Mr. Sisson has received the War Medal for Salamanca, Vittoria, and the Pyrenees.

529

MEDICAL DEPARTMENT.

	HOSPITAL ASSISTANT	ASSISTANT SURGEON.	SURGEON.	STAFF SURGEON.	ASSIST.-INSPEC. OR PHYSICIAN.	BREVET-DEP.-INSP.	DEPUTY INSP.-GEN.	INSPECTOR GENERAL.	WHEN PLACED ON HALF PAY.
DIRECTOR-GENERAL.									
Smith, *Sir* Andrew, *MD. KCB. (Director General,* 25 Feb. 53)	15 Aug. 25	27 Oct. 25	.. ..	7 July 37	.. ..	.. ..	19 Dec. 45	7 Feb. 51	22 June 58
PRINCIPAL INSPECTOR-GENERAL.									
Somerville, William, *MD. (Principal Insp.Gen.,* 28 Dec. 15	25 Mar. 95	.. ..	Mar. 05	.. ..	.. ..	.. ..	25 Mar. 05	never	25 Dec. 16
INSPECTORS-GENERAL.									
Barry,[1] James, *MD.*	5 July 13	7 Dec. 15	.. ..	22 Nov. 27	.. ..	.. ..	16 May 51	7 Dec. 58	19 July 59
Bell,[1] William, *MD.*	24 Aug. 12	4 Mar. 13	15 Mar. 31	7 June 44	.. ..	.. ..	12 Mar. 52	7 Dec. 58	7 Dec. 58
Borland, James,[2] *MD.*	20 Dec. 92	never	2 April 94	Sept. 25	.. ..	.. ..	5 Dec. 26	99 22 Jan. 07	25 May 16
Davy, John, *MD.*	18 May 13	9 Nov. 15	1 Feb. 21	29 Mar. 21	.. ..	.. ..	13 Oct. 40	22 Dec. 48	3 Feb. 49
Dawson, William, *MD.*	18 Oct. 13	9 June 14	3 April 21	29 Dec. 37	8 Nov. 27	.. ..	13 Oct. 40	21 Oct. 53	28 Nov. 56
Fergusson, Andrew,[3] *MD. Honorary Physician to the Queen*	21 June 13	20 July 15	28 Nov. 34	11 Jan. 39	.. ..	.. ..	19 July 50	7 Dec. 58	7 Dec. 58
Franklin, Henry,[4] *CB.*	13 Aug. 08	29 June 09	26 May 14	19 Nov. 30	.. ..	.. ..	14 Jan. 42	25 June 47	29 Nov. 50
French, James,[5] *MD. CB.*	.. ..	8 Feb. 10	9 Dec. 14	1 Aug. 42	.. ..	.. ..	10 Dec. 45	12 Mar. 52	12 Mar. 52
Grant, *Sir* Jas. Robt.[6] *MD. CB. KH.*	22 Jan. 92	24 Feb. 94	never	.. ..	.. ..	.. ..	16 April 07	14 July 14	25 Mar. 19
Gunning, John,[7] *CB.*	never	never	.. ..	30 July 94	.. ..	.. ..	17 Sept. 12	1 Feb. 16	1 Oct. 16
Hall, *Sir* John,[8] *MD. KCB.*	24 June 11	12 Sept. 22	.. ..	8 Nov. 27	.. ..	.. ..	25 Sept. 46	28 Mar. 54	1 Jan. 57
Henry, Walter[9]	11 April 11	19 Dec. 15	8 June 26	4 Jan. 39	.. ..	.. ..	16 Dec. 45	5 June 55	5 June 55
MacAndrew, *Sir* John,[10] *MD. KCB. Hon. Physician to the Queen*	27 June 09	15 Feb. 10	30 April 22	7 July 46	.. ..	.. ..	21 Oct. 23	28 Nov. 56	7 Dec. 58
Maclean, Charles,[11] *MD.*	8 July 09	27 Dec. 10	14 June 25	5 Aug. 42	.. ..	.. ..	19 Jan. 49	18 Sept. 57	18 Sept. 57
Mahony, Montagu Martine,[12] *MD.*	.. ..	29 Sept. 08	3 June 13	11 Aug. 35	30 Aug. 39	.. ..	20 Oct. 41	19 Sept. 49	19 Jan. 49
Melvin, Alex.[13] *Honorary Surgeon to the Queen*	26 July 10	26 Sept. 11	10 Dec. 23	3 Aug. 26	.. ..	.. ..	21 Feb. 51	7 Dec. 58	7 Dec. 58
Munro, William	6 Sept. 08	16 Feb. 09	22 June 15	5 Jan. 26	.. ..	.. ..	22 Dec. 48	5 June 55	5 June 55
Pym, *Sir* William, *MD. KCH.*	.. ..	.. ..	.. ..	.. ..	.. ..	.. ..	20 Dec. 16	25 Oct. 16	25 Sept. 16
Scott, Daniel,[14] *MD.*	8 Feb. 13	18 Mar. 24	17 Oct. 34	.. ..	.. ..	.. ..	2 Aug. 50	18 Sept. 57	25 Sept. 57
Skey, Joseph, *MD.*	.. ..	.. ..	.. ..	18 July 05	11 Dec. 23	.. ..	26 Dec. 15	Feb. 29	29 Mar. 49
Stewart, Alexander,[15] *MD.*	14 June 09	27 Dec. 10	13 May 24	24 Nov. 25	.. ..	.. ..	16 Dec. 45	32 Mar. 52	12 Mar. 52
Stewart, Arthur,[16] *MD.*	5 Nov. 05	10 April 06	3 Sept. 12	9 Nov. 26	27 Sept. 27	26 Nov. 18	9 Dec. 36	16 Dec. 45	16 Dec. 45
Thomas, Morgan[17]	.. ..	14 July 04	11 Nov. 11	.. ..	14 July 36	.. ..	16 Jan. 41	1 April 50	1 April 50

							DEPUTY INSP.-GEN.	HONORARY INSP.-GEN.	WHEN PLACED ON HALF PAY.
DEPUTY-INSPECTORS-GENERAL, WITH HONORARY RANK OF INSPECTORS GENERAL									
Armstrong, Daniel	6 Sept. 13	22 Dec. 14	30 Oct. 28	16 May 51	16 Feb. 55	13 July 57	13 July 57		
Austin, William, *MD.*	21 Nov. 11	4 Mar. 13	21 Nov. 28	19 Jan. 49	16 Feb. 55	5 May 57	5 May 57		
Carter, John Collis, *MD.*	10 Jan. 14	2 June 25	19 Nov. 38	6 Nov. 40	16 Feb. 55	5 Oct. 58	5 Oct. 58		
Dempster, John,[22] *MD.*	4 Oct. 13	1 Sept. 14	4 Mar. 36	27 Oct. 48	12 Mar. 52	8 Jan. 59	18 Jan. 59		
Dowse, Richard[18]	24 Jan. 14	25 Jan. 15	8 Jan. 36	27 April 49	16 Feb. 55	17 Jan. 57	7 Jan. 57		
Halahan, John Wallon, *MD., Royal Artillery*	.. ..	5 Dec. 08	5 June 43	1 April 54	7 Dec. 58	7 Dec. 58			
Hall, Thomas	19 May 15	30 June 25	29 May 40	29 1 April 43	16 Feb. 54	7 Dec. 58	12 May 57		
Henderson, James,[19] *MD.*	5 Aug. 09	13 Feb. 11	20 Apr. 26	27 July 55	18 Dec. 57	17 Dec. 58	1 Dec. 58		
Miller, John,[20] *MD.*	9 July 12	8 Feb. 16	4 Jan. 38	19 Nov. 47	16 Feb. 55	1 Jan. 57	1 Jan. 57		
Richardson, John[21]	9 July 05	18 Feb. 08	5 Jan. 26	20 Nov. 46	16 Feb. 55	1 Jan. 57	1 Jan. 57		

Medical Department.

	HOSPITAL ASSISTANT SURGEON.	ASSIST.-SURGEON.	SURGEON.	STAFF SURGEON.	ASSIST.-INSPEC.	BREVET-DEP.-INSP.-GEN.	DEPUTY INSP.-GEN.	WHEN PLACED ON HALF PAY.
DEPUTY INSPECTORS GENERAL.								
Barry, William,[1] *MD.*	15 April 08	4 Jan. 10	never	19 Nov. 21	..	..	10 Nov. 25	25 June 28
Chapman, John Strange[2]	15 Dec.	25 28 Sept. 26	5 Oct. 41	7 Nov. 51	..	..	5 May 54	6 Oct. 54
Collier, Charles,[3] *MD.*	Sept. 06	4 Oct. 25	Aug. 09	4 June 12	..	3 Feb. 25	22 July 30	9 Jun 38
Dartnell, George Russell	30 Nov.	20 20 Oct. 25	4 Jan. 39	14 Mar. 45	..	..	24 Nov. 54	16 Jan. 57
Daun, Robert,[4] *MD.*	22 Oct.	03 17 Dec. 03	4 Aug. 14	19 Jan. 32	..	..	20 Jan. 32	16 May 32
Hartle, Robert[5]	1 Dec.	96 22 Nov. 01	25 Feb.	04 28 Jan. 13	..	6 Mar. 23	22 July 30	16 Aug. 31
Macdonell, Alexander Sheriff[6]	15 Nov.	27 29 July	30 2 Dec.	42 28 Mar. 54	..	..	1 Feb. 55	26 April 59
Menzies, Duncan[7]	1 Nov.	27 29 July	30 24 June	42 24 Aug. 52	..	..	6 Oct. 54	30 Aug. 56
Ogilvie, Alexander, *MD.*, Royal Artillery	..	11 10 Aug.	29 1 Jan. 43	..	..	22 Sept. 55	1 Feb. 57
Shortt, John,[9] *MD.*	June 04	19 Dec.	04 25 Mar. 24	never	..	..	10 Nov. 43	17 June 47
West, Sir Augustus,[10] *MD.*	26 May 04	7 Nov. 05	never	25 Mar. 18	1 June 08	29 April 18	18 Nov. 24	18 Nov. 24

						WHEN PLACED ON HALF PAY.		
ASSISTANT INSPECTORS.								
Durie, William, *KH.* (Ordnance)	never	20 Nov. 97	18 Nov. 05	never	26 Sept.	14 14 Sept. 36		
Knight, Edward,[11] *MD.*	never	never	never	never	16 July	09 16 Sept. 14		
Maclagan, David,[12] *MD.*	never	10 Sept. 07	never	never	26 May	14 16 June 15		
Wright, James,[13] *MD.*	..	23 June 04	8 Sept. 08	never	26 May	14 25 Oct. 19		

	HOSPITAL ASSISTANT SURGEON.	ASSIST. SURGEON.	SURGEON.	SURGEON MAJOR.	HON. DEP. INSP. GEN.	WHEN PLACED ON HALF PAY.		
SURGEONS MAJOR, WITH HONORARY RANK OF DEPUTY INSPECTOR GENERAL.								
Battersby, Robert	22 Dec.	25 28 Sept. 26	2 July 41	3 Mar. 54	3 Nov. 56	3 Nov. 56		
Blakeney, Edward Hugh	..	17 Oct. 34	19 Dec. 45	1 Oct. 58	18 Nov. 59	18 Nov. 59		
Boyes, Charles Robert,[14] *MD.*	17 Aug.	26 22 Nov. 27	2 July 41	12 Jan. 55	3 Nov. 56	3 Nov. 56		
Bradford, Edward, *Surgeon R. Military College; Homo. Surgeon to the Queen*	5 Dec.	26 20 Mar. 28	24 Sept. 41	16 Apr. 52	7 Dec. 58	7 Dec. 58		
Chisholm, Stewart[15]	..	30 Nov.	13 11 Sept. 38	1 June 46	7 Dec. 58	7 Dec. 58		
Connell, James	16 June	25 10 Nov. 25	2 July 41	12 Mar. 52	7 Dec. 58	7 Dec. 58		
Dempsey, Charles, Royal Artillery	..	22 July	28 1 Jan. 43	1 Jan. 53	2 Aug. 59	2 Aug. 59		
Fox, Thomas, *MD.*	15 Mar.	27 29 July 30	2 July 41	12 Jan. 55	7 Dec. 58	7 Dec. 58		
Graves, John Stewart[16]	22 Feb.	26 28 Sept. 26	2 July 41	1 Oct. 58	7 Dec. 58	7 Dec. 58		
Hunter, Thomas,[17] *MD.*	..	18 April 34	23 July 44	6 Oct. 54	29 July 59	29 July 59		
Lucas, William, *Surgeon R. Military Asylum*	3 Nov.	25 25 May 26	17 June 42	1 July 53	7 Dec. 58	7 Dec. 58		
M'Gregor, James	5 Jan.	26 12 Apr. 29	26 Feb. 41	12 Jan. 52	7 Dec. 58	7 Dec. 58		
Mostyn, Thomas,[18] *Honorary Surgeon to the Queen*	9 Nov.	10 19 Dec. 11	6 Oct. 25	1 Oct. 58	7 Dec. 58	7 Dec. 58		
Parry, William	20 Dec.	13 7 Mar. 22	17 April 38	16 Mar. 55	3 Nov. 56	3 Nov. 56		
Savage, Johnson, *MD.*, Royal Artillery	..	15 Dec. 30	1 June 46	1 Oct. 58	16 Sept. 59	16 Sept. 59		

530

Medical Department.

SURGEONS OF THE FIRST CLASS, AND SURGEONS MAJOR.	HOSPITAL ASSIST., &c.	ASSISTANT SURGEON.	SURGEON.	FIRST CLASS SURGEON.	WHEN PLACED ON HALF PAY.
℞ Anderson, Andrew,[1] MD.	1 Mar. 05	4 Feb. 08	25 June 12	Regimental	23 Aug. 33
℞ Berry, Titus[2]	......	......	24 June 03	2 Jan. 06	25 Feb. 16
℞ Boggie, John,[3] MD.	17 Oct. 99	8 Jan. 01	15 Oct. 07	15 Oct. 12	25 Feb. 16
Brown, George, Gr. Gds. (*Surgeon Major,* 29 Dec. 54)	21 April 25	12 Jan. 26	26 June 40	......	24 Jan. 58
Brown, Robert	8 July 99	11 Jan. 00	11 Dec. 06	8 June 00	25 May 16
Burrell, William Henry, MD.	24 June 15	12 April 21	5 May 37	16 Dec. 45	24 June 54
Burton, Edward	9 May 11	21 Jan. 13	......	1 June 26	15 Sept. 37
Coates, William Henry	8 April 94	......	16 June 95	28 Feb. 12	
Colelough, Anthony Cæsar[5]	......	11 Nov. 02	14 April 13	19 Nov. 30	21 Aug. 40
Cotton, Thomas Forrest[6]	4 Oct. 13	17 Aug. 15	13 Mar. 35	30 Dec. 45	15 June 49
Dobson, William	6 May 15	22 Sept. 25	29 Mar. 30	19 July 50	5 Nov. 52
℞℞ Finnie, William[7]	25 June 12	12 Nov. 12	26 Oct. 26	25 Mar. 36	5 Mar. 41
℞ Fraser, Arch. Campbell[8]	......	Dec. 08	20 July 15	7 Nov. 34	11 Jan. 39
℞ ℞℞ Galliers, William[9]	2 May 03	25 Mar. 04	10 Sept. 07	7 Sept. 15	25 July 16
℞ Glasco, John[10]	......	21 April 08	8 Feb. 16	20 April 26	20 Sept. 39
Grant, John	......	11 April 00	15 Oct. 03	3 Aug. 15	25 April 16
Greatrex, Edw., Coldst. Gds. (*Surgeon-Major,* 2 Sept. 45)	24 Nov. 25	16 Nov. 26	14 April 43	......	4 April 51
℞ Griffith, John[11]	6 April 06	7 May 07	17 Sept. 12	9 Sept. 13	25 April 14
℞ Harrison, John,[12] Gren. Gds. (*Surgeon-Major,* 17 Mar. 37).	......	29 June 09	29 April 24	......	17 April 40
Hunter, Robert Hope Alston[13]	10 Jan. 27	15 June 30	2 July 41	30 July 47	10 Feb. 52
℞ ℞℞ Hunter, Wm.[14] MD., Coldst. Gds. (*Surg.-Maj.* 16 Mar. 38).	......	10 Feb. 14	4 Sept. 36	......	2 Sept. 45
℞ ℞℞ Jeyes, Samuel,[15] MD.	14 Nov. 11	28 Nov. 11	2 May 22	7 Dec. 38	17 Dec. 41
℞ ℞℞ Jones, Wm.,[16] MD.	12 Nov. 05	21 Nov. 05	3 Sept. 12	Regimental	10 May 31
Judd, Wm. Hen. Scots Fusil. Gds. (*Surg.-Maj.* 22 July 45) *Surg. in Ordinary to the Prince Consort*	......	1 Jan. 18	12 July 27	......	17 Feb. 54
℞ Lightbody, John[17]	20 Aug. 04	20 June 05	15 Oct. 12	3 Mar. 37	2 Aug. 42
M'Munn, Robert Andrew,[18] MD.	22 Nov. 13	1 Nov. 14	1 Nov. 33	13 July 47	27 Oct. 48
Mair, John, MD.	8 Nov. 21	10 Nov. 25	30 Oct. 40	2 Aug. 50	12 Nov. 52
℞ Murray, Dennis, MD.	9 Nov. 12	22 June 15	23 Nov. 32	18 Sept. 46	10 Sept. 47
Palmer, Charles Quartley	18 Oct. 13	17 April 17	30 Dec. 34	14 July 43	18 Sept. 46
Pickering, John, MD.	24 April 10	29 April 13	......	29 June 32	
Quigley, Thos. Haswell, Ordnance	......	3 Nov. 12	26 Aug. 30	24 Jan. 44	1 Jan. 53
Richardson, Thomas, Scots Fusil. Gds. (*Surgeon Major* 17 Feb. 54)	......	4 Dec. 23	22 July 45	......	20 Mar. 57
Richardson, William, MD. Ordnance	......	17 April 27	10 April 41	25 July 49	15 Oct. 53
Robertson, Peter, MD.	24 Nov. 25	12 Jan. 26	2 July 41	18 Sept. 49	15 May 55
Roe, Peter Henry, Staff	......	3 Sept. 47	27 May 53	4 Sept. 57	13 Dec. 59
℞ ℞℞ Scott, Robert, MD.	24 June 10	5 Nov. 12	......	8 Nov. 27	19 June 35
Sievwright, Francis[20]	7 June 13	13 Mar. 17	25 Sept. 35	2 Aug. 42	1 Nov. 56
Sinclair, Alexander, MD.	20 July 15	9 May 16	28 Aug. 35	20 Sept. 39	11 Mar. 51
℞ ℞℞ Smith, Thomas,[21] MD.	20 Mar. 12	2 July 12	13 July 26	4 Jan. 39	27 Dec. 46
℞ Stratton, Robert[22]	25 Sept. 99	21 Mar. 00	3 Sept. 13	30 Sept. 13	27 Dec. 14
Teevan, Stephenson, MD.	22 Dec. 25	23 Nov. 26	4 Sept. 40	25 Sept. 46	24 July 56
White, Moses, MD.	4 April 14	5 May 25	29 July 36	16 Dec. 45	19 Nov. 47
℞ Widmer, Christopher[23]	June 04	15 Aug. 05	24 Oct. 11	5 Nov. 12	25 Feb. 17
Williams, Thomas, MD.	3 Nov. 25	28 Sept. 26	26 Jan. 41	15 June 49	5 Nov. 52
Wright, James Dennis, Gren. Gds. (*Surgeon-Major,* 7 Feb. 45)	......	11 Nov. 24	11 May 32	......	29 Dec. 54

Medical Department.

SURGEONS.	HOSPITAL-ASSIST.,&c.	ASSISTANT SURGEON.	SURGEON.	WHEN PLACED ON HALF PAY.
࿓ Abell, Joseph,[1] 60 Foot	4 Nov. 05	10 April 06	15 July 13	25 Dec. 18
Abercrombie, John, 60 Foot	9 June 98	6 Mar. 99	19 June 00	30 Sept. 19
Allan, Robert, 17 Foot	22 Nov. 27	29 July 30	1 Nov. 42	18 Feb. 53
࿓ Allardyce, James,[2] 5 Garrison Batt.	never	4 Aug. 01	30 Mar. 09	29 May 23
࿓ Anderson, Thomas, 3 Foot	25 June 95	27 June 98	4 April 00	20 July 26
Ayton, Robinson,[5] 34 Foot	23 Sept. 05	1 May 06	10 Sept. 12	25 Nov. 28
࿓ Bacot, John,[6] 21 Dragoons	never	2 July 03	9 June 14	14 Dec. 20
Bain, William, MD. 34 F. Med. Officer Military Prison at Cork	24 June 15	30 June 25	20 Dec. 37	22 Dec. 48
Bannatine, Richard, Staff.		17 Sept. 39	10 Oct. 49	23 June 54
࿓ Bartley, John Metge,[7] MD. 39 Foot		27 Dec. 10	31 Aug. 26	26 July 53
࿓ Bolton, Robert Henry,[10] MD., 78 Foot	26 Nov. 07	9 Feb. 09	7 Oct. 13	23 Mar. 26
Breslin, Wm. Irwin, MD., Depot Batt.	9 Feb. 26	8 Mar. 27	2 July 41	15 Aug. 56
࿓ Brown, Frederick,[11] MD., 73 Foot	19 May 08	4 Jan. 10	8 Sept. 25	22 June 26
࿓ Brown, Josh.[12] Staff Corps of Cavalry	19 Jan. 08	25 Feb. 08	28 Oct. 13	25 Feb. 19
Browne, Alexander, MD. 37 Foot	16 June 25	3 Aug. 26	22 Nov. 39	2 Aug. 50
Brush, John Ramsay,[13] MD., Staff		8 June 41	2 April 52	11 Oct. 56
Cahill, Alexander, 25 Foot	20 Aug. 03	15 Oct. 07	25 Aug. 09	17 Mar. 14
Campbell, James, 28 Foot	24 Feb. 20	25 Oct. 25	10 June 35	30 July 44
࿓ Campbell, John,[14] MD., 93 F. Med. Officer Military Prison at Greenlaw	25 Mar. 13	27 July 15	27 Dec. 33	30 Mar. 49
Clark, Thomas, 19 Foot			16 Sept. 95	25 Dec. 00
Coghlan, John, 86 Foot	9 Nov. 12	19 Sept. 22	5 Sept. 34	20 Nov. 44
Colchester, Thomas, Ordnance	never	27 Jan. 27	16 Jan. 41	5 April 47
Cole, Robert John, MD., 1 West India Regt.		27 Aug. 41	24 Dec. 52	1 Oct. 56
Collings, Adolphus, MD., 40 Foot		26 Feb. 41	20 Nov. 46	24 Aug. 58
Connel, Abra. Jas. Nisbot, MD. 2 Life Gds.	10 Mar. 25	16 June 25	22 Nov. 39	23 May 51
࿓ Coombe, Charles,[15] Coldstream Gds.	never	April 01	14 Nov. 05	26 Nov. 12
Cowper, George Alex. MD. 56 F.		30 Mar. 38	22 Dec. 46	16 Nov. 49
࿓ Cross, James,[16] 83 Foot	7 Jan. 11	11 Mar. 13	19 Nov. 30	5 May 37
Cuddy, Stephen,[17] Ordnance	never	1 Aug. 06	1 Nov. 14	1 Jan. 19
Cunningham, Alexander,[18] 86 Foot	13 July 04	26 Oct. 04	6 Feb. 12	5 Sept. 34
Daunt, William,[19] MD., 6 Dragoons	12 Sept. 07	3 Mar. 08	12 May 14	16 Feb. 44
Davidson, James,[20] 50 Foot	24 June 15	30 Oct. 25	28 July 40	30 June 48
Davies, Henry, MD., 100 Foot	3 Aug. 03	20 Oct. 08	5 Sept. 11	15 May 18
࿓ Dealey, Charles,[22] 81 Foot	Feb. 11	4 Mar. 13	19 Oct. 32	30 May 45
Eddie, Wm. Cruickshank,[23] Cape Regt.	1 May 25	12 Jan. 26	26 Mar. 41	1 April 51
࿓ Este, Michael Lambton,[24] 1 Life Guards	never	4 Sept. 00	3 Oct. 12	6 Nov. 35
Ewing, Joseph, 95 Foot		7 Sept. 09	4 Dec. 35	12 Sept. 48
Farr, George, Ordnance		1 June 30	1 June 46	15 Aug. 55
Forster, John, MD.,[27] 73 Foot, Surgeon, School of Musketry at Hythe	22 Nov. 13	9 Nov. 15	1 April 36	30 May 45
Fraser, Hugh, 60 Foot, Medical Officer of Weedon Military Prison	10 May 13	26 Jan. 15	30 Dec. 34	30 June 43
Fraser, Peter,[28] 8 Foot	16 July 12	10 Dec. 12	6 Dec. 36	3 Dec. 41
Fraser, Robert Winchester, MD., Staff		15 April 42	23 May 48	22 July 56
࿓ Freer, John, MD., 97 Foot	21 Jan. 07	16 Nov. 09	24 Feb. 25	21 Nov. 28
Galcani, Michael,[29] MD., 46 Foot	12 Nov. 12	16 June 25	7 Nov. 34	17 Feb. 43
Garrett, George, MD., 70 Foot	1 May 97	4 Sept. 06	18 June 12	17 Jan. 28
࿓㺊 Gilder, Frederick,[30] Coldstream Gds.	never	9 June 14	16 Mar. 38	14 April 43
࿓ Griffin, George, 85 Foot	11 June 11	28 April 14	26 Sept. 34	5 Dec. 43
࿓ Griffith, Moses,[31] 20 Foot	4 Nov. 09	24 Oct. 11	8 Feb. 27	4 Sept. 40
Grogan, John, MB., Staff		16 April 41	14 Nov. 51	24 Sept. 58
Gulliver, George, Royal Horse Guards	17 May 27	12 June 28	2 June 43	1 April 53
࿓ Hair, Archibald,[32] MD., R. Horse Gds.	never	12 Nov. 12	12 Jan. 26	2 June 43
Harthill, Robert,[33] 69 Foot	never	29 Dec. 37	27 Oct. 46	19 Nov. 47
࿓ Henderson, Duncan,[34] MD., 5 Foot	24 Oct. 11	16 Apr. 12	23 Mar. 26	13 July 47
࿓ Heriot, John,[35] MD., 6 Dragoon Gds.	11 May 04	8 Nov. 04	16 April 12	11 June 52
࿓㺊 Hichens, Richard,[36] Ordnance	never	1 Sept. 06	22 July 15	1 April 16
Home, Alex. George, MD. 2 Dragoon Gds.	6 Oct. 26	18 Jan. 27	24 Mar. 43	2 April 52
Horniblow, George, MD., Staff		15 Mar. 44	23 June 54	11 Oct. 56
Ingham, Charles Thomas,[37] MD., 54 Foot	24 May 10	8 Aug. 10	25 June 26	5 April 44
Jameson, David, MD., 1 Dragoons	10 June 06	15 Oct. 07	6 Mar. 17	29 Mar. 39
࿓ Johnson, Sir Edward,[38] MD., 39 Foot	April 07	19 Nov. 07	15 July 13	25 Mar. 16
࿓ Kettle, William, 49 Foot		Aug. 05	10 April 06	26 Aug. 13	25 Dec. 14
Kingdom, Edw. Wm. Clemishaw, MD., Staff		25 Feb. 48	2 Oct. 57	25 Feb. 59
Knox, George, 6 Foot	19 June 15	23 June 25	11 July 40	13 Dec. 43
࿓ Lewis, Thos.,[40] MD., Staff	8 July 11	9 Sept. 13	19 Nov. 30	22 Dec. 48
Lloyd, Evans Garnons, Rifle Brigade	25 Jan. 27	18 Oct. 27	6 Aug. 41	13 Feb. 52

Medical Department.

SURGEONS.	HOSPITAL-ASSIST.,&c.	ASSISTANT SURGEON.	SURGEON.	WHEN PLACED ON HALF PAY.
Lloyd, William,[41] M.D., 36 Foot	12 May 15	9 Nov. 15	18 Sept. 35	1 June 41
℗ Lorimer, William,[42] 40 Foot	10 June 11	22 June 15	3 Nov. 37	27 Oct. 48
M'Diarmid, John Duncan, Staff	......	4 Dec. 35	7 Aug. 46	17 Sept. 50
℗ ⚕ M'Donald, Alexander,[45] M.D., Ord.	never	2 Sept. 07	30 Sept. 26	1 Sept. 38
Macarthur, Peter,[46] 1 Royal Veteran Bat.	24 May 95	8 Dec. 04	5 Sept. 05	29 July 14
Maclise, William,[47] Staff	......	22 Dec. 42	3 Mar. 54	27 Oct. 56
℗ Macnish, William,[48] M.D., 23 Foot	10 Aug. 03	4 Aug. 04	6 June 09	20 May 24
Marshall, Thornton, Staff	......	11 April 45	12 Jan. 55	18 Nov. 59
Millar, James, M.D., Staff	......	7 June 33	14 Feb. 45	18 July 48
Minto, James Clephane, Cape M. R.	29 Mar. 27	29 July 30	30 June 43	10 July 55
Moore, John Wardrop, St. Helena Regt.	8 May 28	20 July 30	10 Feb. 43	6 Oct. 54
Morgan, Alex. Braithwaite, 57 Foot	21 Dec. 15	27 Oct. 25	22 Nov. 39	20 Jan. 43
Morison, James, 67 Foot	......	14 Oct. 36	25 Sept. 46	16 June 50
Murtagh, John,[49] M.D., 6 Foot	5 Dec. 26	11 Feb. 30	2 July 41	7 May 52
℗ Neill, Matthew,[50] 56 Foot	10 Jan. 14	6 Nov. 23	29 Dec. 37	9 April 41
Nelson, Wm. Fred., Ordnance	......	12 Feb. 13	26 Oct. 30	5 Feb. 45
Nicolson, Patrick, M.D., 75 Foot	......	31 Dec. 33	28 Mar. 45	24 Dec. 47
Nivison, James Finlayson,[51] Staff	24 June 15	30 June 25	20 Sept. 39	8 Jan. 47
O'Brien, Francis, 60 Foot	12 July 15	27 Oct. 25	11 Jan. 39	23 Jan. 46
O'Callaghan, Patrick, M.D., 11 Hussars	18 July 26	21 Feb. 28	3 Feb. 43	14 Oct. 51
℗ Paterson, James,[52] M.D., 42 Foot	7 June 10	22 Aug. 11	25 May 26	26 Feb. 41
⚕ Pearson, Richard Arthur,[53] M.D., 87 F.	30 Apr. 11	13 May 13	19 Nov. 30	2 Mar. 47
℗ ⚕ Perston, David,[54] M.D., 13 Drag.	19 Oct. 08	1 Feb. 10	17 Feb. 25	30 May 43
Piper, Samuel Ayrault,[55] M.D., Prov. Batt.	never	27 Dec. 06	20 Feb. 23	22 Dec. 46
Pollok-Morris, William,[56] M.D., 53 Foot	8 Sept. 03	24 Oct. 03	8 Oct. 18	14 July 25
℗ Prichard, Octavius, New Bruns. Fenc.	21 Jan. 07	25 Feb. 08	13 May 13	26 Mar. 18
⚕ Riach, John,[61] M.D., 67 Foot	18 May 12	2 July 12	19 Nov. 30	19 Nov. 41
Robertson, John,[62] M.D., 13 Foot	29 Dec. 25	13 Mar. 26	14 Dec. 41	4 April 51
℗ Rogers, Wm. Reynolds,[64] 10 Dragoons	22 Aug. 11	7 Nov. 11	3 Aug. 26	14 Dec. 41
Seaton, Thomas, Ordnance	never	23 Oct. 12	25 Aug. 30	1 Nov. 42
℗ Shekleton, Robert,[66] 51 Foot	never	5 Nov. 07	9 Sept. 13	25 April 29
℗ Shorland, James,[67] 96 Foot	7 Oct. 07	29 June 09	14 July 14	20 Aug. 41
Sidey, James, M.D., 6 Dragoons	1 Dec. 25	12 Jan. 26	2 July 41	27 Feb. 52
Sinclair, John Hartley, M.D., Depot Batt.	14 April 26	21 Dec. 26	2 July 41	1 May 55
Smith, George Roche, 2 Foot	......	13 Sept. 35	12 Dec. 49	17 June 51
Smyth, Robert Dunkin, 2 Drag.	19 May 25	12 Oct. 25	6 Nov. 40	21 July 54
Spencer, Richard, York Rangers	7 April 00	5 June 00	9 July 03	25 Feb. 21
Staunton, Charles Fred. M.D. R. Art.	......	13 Nov. 30	1 June 46	10 Mar. 57
℗ Stephenson, George Alex.,[70] 55 Foot	......	14 May 07	28 Oct. 13	21 Feb. 51
℗ Stewart, John Edmonstone,[71] 1 W. I. Rgt.	10 Dec. 10	25 June 12	2 Nov. 30	24 Dec. 52
Stuart, Hugh Lindsay, 38 Foot	28 Dec. 20	15 Dec. 25	17 Sept. 30	28 Aug. 46
Tighe, James Lowry, 12 Lancers	24 June 15	20 Oct. 25	10 Jan. 40	1 Dec. 48
Turner, William, 7 Royal Veteran Batt.	9 June 98	15 May 02	9 Aug. 10	15 June 15
Tweddell, Fenwick Martin, Military Train	......	8 Jan. 47	15 May 55	11 Mar. 59
℗ Vallange, William, M.D., 60 Foot	8 July 06	7 Dec. 09	19 Jan. 15	9 Oct. 23
Wallace, William, M.D., 14 Foot	17 Aug. 26	8 Mar. 27	2 July 41	7 Jan. 53
℗ Ward, John Richard,[73] Scots Fus. Gds.	......	21 Aug. 06	4 Dec. 23	12 July 27
Warren, Jas. Low, M.D., 7 Dragoons	14 July 15	19 Feb. 24	17 April 38	27 Oct. 46
White, Peter, 72 Foot	21 Dec. 07	15 Nov. 10	7 Oct. 13	20 Oct. 25
Whitfield, Charles Tomlins, Ordnance	never	20 May 12	1 June 30	1 July 42
℗ Wilkins, William Mortimer,[75] 41 Foot	10 Jan. 14	22 June 25	23 Dec. 36	5 May 54
℗ Williams, William,[76] 99 Foot	9 July 09	19 Dec. 11	21 Sept. 30	3 June 42
Wilson, Robert,[77] M.D. Staff	......	25 Aug. 48	9 Feb. 55	1 Jan. 56
Wood, Arthur,[79] M.D. Staff	22 Dec. 25	19 Nov. 26	21 Aug. 40	1 Nov. 56
Wright, Robert, 2 Prov. Bn. of Militia	never	never		1814
Wybrow, William, 17 Dragoons	never	26 Dec. 96	3 July 99	11 Sept. 28
℗ Wyer, John,[80] 19 Foot	......	9 Sept. 13	13 April 32	18 Oct. 39
Young, Colin, M.D., 6 Royal Veteran Batt.	never	1 Mar. 98	15 Oct. 07	25 May 21
Young, James,[81] M.D., 48 Foot	18 Mar. 24	14 Aug. 24	18 Oct. 30	18 Feb. 53
℗ ⚕ Young, Wm. Henry,[82] M.D., 28 F.	19 Dec. 11	4 Feb. 13	4 Sept. 28	3 Nov. 54

ASSISTANT-SURGEONS.	HOSPITAL-ASSISTANT	ASSISTANT SURGEON.	WHEN PLACED ON HALF PAY.
Apreece, Thomas, Ordnance	never	21 June 10	25 Oct. 15
Bowen, Francis, *MD.*, *Staff Surgeon, Royal Hibernian Military School*	......	22 Dec. 54	2 Dec. 59
Bowling, John, Scots Fusilier Guards	......	12 July 27	31 Dec. 52
P Bremner, Alexander,[1] 3 Foot	6 July 10	3 Sept. 12	25 Dec. 18
Browne, Francis, 26 Foot	12 Oct. 26	24 July 28	20 July 32
Butler, George, Staff	......	7 Oct. 42	20 Oct. 48
P Campbell, Alexander, 3 Dragoon Guards	24 Feb. 14	13 July 15	11 July 34
P Cannon, Æneas,[2] *MD.*, Ordnance	11 June 11	23 July 11	1 Dec. 23
Chislette, Henry, 81 Foot	......	15 Dec. 04	7 May 12
Douglas, John, 8 Foot	Aug. 10	26 Sept. 11	25 Feb. 16
P Eddowes, James,[3] Ordnance	never	25 Aug. 10	1 Sept. 20
W Evers, George,[4] 14 Foot	3 June 15	23 Dec. 24	15 Dec. 25
Fitzmaurice, George Lionel, Ordnance	6 July 29	1 July 31	18 June 38
P Furnival, John James,[5] *MD.*, Ordnance	never	1 Dec. 09	1 Mar. 19
P Hewat, Richard, 65 Foot	4 Jan. 11	15 June 15	22 Nov. 27
Holden, Horatio Nelson, 21 Foot	1 Feb. 27	2 Aug. 31	21 Nov. 34
Hollier, Edward, 37 Foot	......	7 Oct. 13	23 Mar. 32
Huggins, John, 58 Foot	10 Jan. 14	28 Dec. 15	2 Aug. 33
P W Kenny, Matthias,[6] *MD.*, Ordnance	never	1 Dec. 10	4 Jan. 19
Knott, William, 6 Dragoons	16 June 15	5 May 25	4 Dec. 35
La Cloche, Thomas, 7 Royal Veteran Batt.	7 Nov. 97	24 Dec. 02	1 Feb. 33
M'Lean, George Gordon, 35 Foot	7 Feb. 14	1 Sept. 14	9 April 18
Mac Bain, Giles, 62 Foot	15 Feb. 10	19 Mar. 12	25 Aug. 14
Martin, George, 67 Foot	Feb. 09	28 Feb. 11	12 June 17
Martin, James, 9 Foot	29 Dec. 14	10 Oct. 16	6 Jan. 25
Morice, David, *MD.*, 60 Foot	never	29 May 35	6 June 45
Mullarky, Daniel, 27 Foot	22 Nov. 13	6 Oct. 25	25 May 27
Nugent, Morgan, Ordnance	8 Dec. 12	20 Nov. 13	1 Oct. 27
P O'Beirne, James,[7] *MD.*, Ordnance	never	11 Oct. 10	1 Aug. 17
O'Donnell, John, 77 Foot	7 Mar. 14	25 Jan. 25	25 April 26
Reilly, William, Staff	......	1 Nov. 13	25 Dec. 22
Rolland, James Henderson, Staff	29 May 28	29 July 30	28 Oct. 36
Ross, William Baillie, *MD.*, 5 Roy. Vet. Batt.	7 April 25	16 June 25	26 April 33
Sprague, John Hanmer, 8 Royal Vet. Batt.	5 May 10	14 June 10	25 July 16
Swift, Richard, 60 Foot	never	19 Aug. 13	15 Aug. 34
P Thompson, John,[8] Ordnance	never	1 Dec. 09	1 April 26
P Tobin, John,[9] 9 Dragoons	7 Dec. 09	19 Dec. 11	25 Dec. 18
P Venables, Robert,[10] *MD.*, Ordnance	28 Aug. 11	11 Nov. 11	9 Aug. 24
W Verner, Edw. Donovan,[11] Ordnance	9 June 13	29 Nov. 13	1 Dec. 18
Wilkinson, George Anderson, 76 Foot	......	17 Dec. 47	29 Feb. 56
Woodley, Richard, *MB.*, 41 Foot	......	14 April 46	2 Mar. 55
Woollcombe, Robert Wm., Staff, *Medical Officer of Devonport Military Prison*	......	28 Mar. 45	1 Feb. 57
Wyer, George Goforth, 3 Foot	......	21 Feb. 51	1 May 55

APOTHECARIES.		APOTHECARY.	
P Graham, John[1]	19 April 08	31 Aug. 09	25 Dec. 16
P Jones, Samuel	Aug. 09	31 Aug. 09	
Simpson, James Woolley	24 June 11	18 May 15	5 Dec. 56

PURVEYOR.		DEPUTY-PURVEYOR	PURVEYOR
P Usher, William	....	13 Nov. 00	2 June 14

DEPUTY PURVEYORS.

P Croft, Jonathan ......16 April 12	P O'Reilly, Henry Wm. 5 Jan. 09
P Findley, Thomas[1] ....10 Mar. 14	Pierce, Thomas Estwick..17 Jan. 22
P Harrington, Joseph.... 9 Sept. 13	P Soare, Charles ......15 Oct. 12
P Newcombe, Joseph,[4] ..26 May 15	P Winter, George[5] ....15 Oct. 12

HOSPITAL ASSISTANTS.

Blackwood, John........25 April 14	Bruce, Alexander ...... 4 July 15
Brereton, Charles........ 9 Nov. 13	

War Services of the Medical Officers.

Inspectors General.

1 Doctor Bell served the campaign of 1814 in Holland, including both the attacks on Merxem and bombardment of Antwerp. Served also throughout the war in China with the 26th (Medal), at Chusan, Canton, Ningpo, Tacke, Chapoo, Shanghai, Woosung, Chin Kiang Foo, and Nankin.

2 Dr. Borland entered the Army in 1792, as Surgeon's Mate of the 42nd Regt., from which he was promoted to the Staff the following year, and served two campaigns in Flanders, under the Duke of York. From 1795 to 1798 he served as Staff Surgeon in St. Domingo, remaining in the Island until evacuated by the British Troops. In 1799 he served the campaign in North Holland. From 1810 to 1816 he was employed at the head of the Medical Department in the Mediterranean, and he accompanied to Naples the troops which, under General M'Farlane, assisted the Austrians in expelling Murat; and he was also present with a division of the Army which proceeded from Genoa to Marseilles, and blockaded Toulon. During the expedition to the Scheldt Dr. Borland volunteered the duty of a mission to Walcheren at the head of a commission appointed to enquire into the nature of the alarming malady prevailing amongst the troops. Their report was approved by Government and ordered by a vote of the House of Commons to be printed and circulated. He is a Knight of St. Maurice and Lazare.

3 Doctor Fergusson served in the American War.

4 Mr. Franklin served in the Peninsula from Sept. 1808 to the end of the war, including the battles of Vittoria, Pampeluna, Pyrenees, Nivelle, Orthes, and Toulouse, and siege of Badajoz, for which he has received the War Medal with six Clasps. Served also in the American War, including the battle of Plattsburgh. He served in India from April 1812, to June 1850; was present at the battles of Chillianwallah and Goojerat, in the Punjaub campaign (Medal and two Clasps, and CB.).

5 Doctor French served with the 4th Regt. in the Peninsula from May 1812 to the end of that war in 1814, including the battles of Salamanca and Vittoria, siege of the castle of San Sebastian, passage of the Bidassoa and of the Nivelle, and actions of the Nive in Dec. 1813. He served in the American war at the battle of Bladensburg, and in all the operations before Baltimore and New Orleans. Served with the 49th (also as Superintending Surgeon from April 1841, until towards the close of active operations), throughout the war in China (Medal), including the capture of Chusan, storming of the heights and forts above Canton, taking of Amoy, sortie and repulse of the night attack on Ningpo, and capture of Chupoo, Woosung, Shanghae, and Chin Kiang Foo, and investment of Nankin. He has received the War Medal with five Clasps.

6 Sir James Grant served as Hospital-Assistant in the campaign of 1793 with the army under the Duke of York. In 1795 he was senior Staff Surgeon to the expedition for the capture of the Cape of Good Hope. In 1809 he served throughout the Walcheren campaign, in which he was appointed Inspector to the Forces in the Field, having the charge at the bombardment of Flushing, and in South Beveland. He served the campaigns of 1813 and 14 in Holland and Belgium as chief of the department. In 1815 he served the campaign of Waterloo as chief of the medical department of the Duke of Wellington's army; and he continued as medical chief of that army during the three years' occupation of France. He is a Knight 2nd Class of St. Anne of Russia.

7 Mr. Gunning served in Holland and Flanders in 1793, 94, and 95. Embarked with the Peninsular Army in 1808 as Surgeon to the Commander-in-Chief and Staff Surgeon, and was afterwards made Deputy Inspector and Surgeon-in-Chief, and served until the close of that war in 1814: he has received the War Medal with eleven Clasps for Roleia, Vimiera, Talavera, Busaco, Fuentes d'Onor, Ciudad Rodrigo, Badajoz, Salamanca, Vittoria, St. Sebastian, and Orthes. He was also at Waterloo as Surgeon-in-Chief of the Army, and was honored with the Order of the Netherlands Lion by the King of Holland, for his attendance upon the then Prince of Orange who was wounded on the Field of Battle.

8 Sir John Hall served the campaign of 1815 in F ders. Served the campaign of 1847 in Kaffraria, as head of the Medical Department under Sir George Berkeley, and was thanked in General Orders (Medal). In 1848 he accompanied Sir Harry Smith across the Orange River, as principal medical officer of the force employed against the emigrant Boers,—was present at the battle of Boem Plaatz, and specially mentioned in Sir Harry's Dispatch, for services on the field, and subsequently thanked in General Orders. Was principal medical officer of the army in Kaffraria under Sir Harry Smith during the campaign of 1851, and thanked in General Orders on his being ordered to India. Served as Principal Medical Officer of the Eastern Army from the 18th June 1854 to 5th July 1856 without being absent from duty for a single day; was present at the affairs of Bulganac, and M'Kenzie's Farm, battles of Alma (mentioned in Dispatches), Balaklava, Inkerman, and Tchernaya, capture of Balaklava, siege and fall of Sebastopol, taking of the Rifle Pits and Quarries, assault of the Redan on the 18th June (Medal and four Clasps, KCB., Officer of the Legion of Honor, and 3rd Class of the Medjidie).

9 Mr. Henry served with the 66th Regiment in the Peninsula from May 1811 to the close of the war at Toulouse, including the last siege of Badajoz, battle of Vittoria, and actions in the Pyrenees; battles of the Nivelle and Nive, engagement at Garris, battle of Orthes and action at Aire. He served also with the same corps in the Nepaulese War in India in 1816-17, and in the two Canadian Rebellions of 1837-38. Mr. Henry was present with his Regiment in St. Helena during the last four years of the life of Napoleon; and after his death was charged with the duty of preparing the bulletin of the post-mortem appearances of the body, which was published by the British Government. He has received the War Medal with six Clasps.

War Services of the Medical Officers.

10 Sir John MacAndrew served in the expedition to Walcheren in 1809, including the taking of Terveer and Fort Ramakins, and siege of Flushing, also with the army in South Beveland. Served in the Peninsula in Lord Hill's Division from 1811 to 1813, was present at the siege of Badajoz, retreat from Burgos. Was present at the capture of Fort Minora, and the surrender of Kurrachee, Lower Scinde. Senior medical officer of the army sent for the relief of the force employed against the Fort of Kujjuck, Upper Scinde. Present during the investment of Candahar, end of 1841 and beginning of 1842. Senior medical officer of the force sent for the relief of Kelat-i-Ghilzie; senior medical officer of Sir W. Nott's army from October 1841 to the 1st Jan. 1843, present at the actions of Kallee Shuk, Runja Ruk, Panjwaure, and Tilloo Khan, Baba Walla, battle of Gowine, storming the heights of Bellool (Ghuznee), capture of Ghuznee, affairs of Bene Bedam and Mydam, affair with the rear-guard from Soorkab to Gundamuck (Khoord Cabul Pass), affair with the rear-guard from Lundikhana to Ali Musjeed (Khyber Pass). Acted as principal medical officer, Queen's troops at the battle of Maharajpore, 29th Dec. 1843. Senior medical officer in the Kandian provinces during the rebellion in 1848. Served as Principal Medical Officer in N.W. Provinces of Bengal during the Mutiny in 1857-58, and was present at the siege and storm of Delhi, and capture of Lucknow.

11 Doctor Maclean served at Walcheren in 1809; and in the Peninsula from Feb. 1810 to the end of that war in 1814, including the battles of Busaco, Salamanca, Vittoria, and the Pyrenees, crossing the Bidassoa, and battles of Nivelle and Toulouse (War Medal with six Clasps).

12 Doctor Mahony served in the Peninsula from April 1809 to the end of the war, including the passage of the Douro, battle of Talavera,—taken prisoner and marched to Verdun; battle of Busaco, siege of Olivença, battle of Albuhera, affair of Aldea de Ponte, sieges of Ciudad Rodrigo and Badajoz, affair of Fuenta de la Prima, battle of Salamanca, capture of Madrid, battle of Vittoria, affair of Roncesvalles, battle near Pampeluna, affair of Echalar, assault of San Sebastian, battles of Nivelle, Orthes, and Toulouse. Present also in the attack on New Orleans, 8th Jan. 1815; and subsequently at the capture of Paris. He has the War Medal with thirteen Clasps.

13 Mr. Melvin served at the capture of Guadaloupe in 1815.

14 Doctor Scott served in the Peninsula from March 1813 to the end of the war.

15 Dr. Alex. Stewart served in the Peninsula from 1809 to the end of that war in 1814, including the siege of the forts and battle of Salamanca, siege of Burgos, battles of the Pyrenees, the Nivelle, the Nive, Orthes, and Toulouse. He has received the War Medal with six Clasps.

16 Doctor Arthur Stewart served on the expedition to South America in 1807; in the Peninsula from March 1809 to Sept. 1812; the campaign of 1815; including the battle of Waterloo. He has received the War Medal with four Clasps for Busaco, Fuentes d'Onor, Ciudad Rodrigo, and Badajoz.

17 Mr. Thomas's services:—Campaign in Italy in 1805, including the occupation of Sicily. Descent on the coast of Calabria, battle of Maida, and siege of Scylla Castle in 1806. Expedition to Sweden, under Sir John Moore; and subsequently in Portugal and Spain, up to the retreat to Corunna, in 1808-9. Capture of Guadaloupe in 1815. He has received the Silver War Medal with two Clasps.

18 Mr. Dowse served at the surrender of Martinique and Guadaloupe in 1815.

19 Doctor Henderson served at the capture of Guadaloupe in 1810 (Medal and Clasp). In the campaigns of 1813, 14, and 15, in Lower Canada, including Plattsburg (in medical charge of the 13th Regt.). Throughout the whole of the Burmese war, under Sir Archibald Campbell, with the 13th and 41st Regiments (in medical charge); was present at the storming and capture of the island of Cheduba, the attack and capture of Donabu, Melloon, Paghmmew (Medal and Clasp). In 1834 he was at the capture of Coorg, as Surgeon of the 48th Regt. In 1842 with the 3rd Light Dragoons in Affghanistan, and present at the forcing of the Khyber Pass, the storming of the heights of Jugdulluck, action of Tezeen and Huftkotul, and occupation of Cabool (Medal). Served in the Punjaub campaign of 1848-49, including the affair of Ramnuggur, action of Sadoolapore, and battles of Chillianwallah and Goojerat (Medal and two Clasps).

20 Dr. Miller served the campaigns of 1813 and 14 in Spain and the South of France; with the Expedition to New Orleans; and the campaign of 1815 under the Duke of Wellington. He has received the Silver War Medal with four Clasps for the Pyrenees, Nivelle, Nive, and Orthes.

21 Mr. Richardson served at the capture of the Cape of Good Hope in 1806; reduction of Monte Video, and campaign of 1806 and 7 in South America; campaigns of 1808 and 9 in the Peninsula, including the battles of Roleia and Vimiera, for which he has received the War Medal with two Clasps.

22 Doctor Dempster served with 38th Regt. throughout the Burmese war, including the capture of Rangoon, storm and capture of the stockades of Kincardine and Kamaroot, battles of Rangoon, Kokein, &c.

Deputy Inspectors General.

1 Doctor Barry served in the Peninsula from Aug. 1808 to Aug. 1811, and again from Aug. 1813 to the end of that war in 1814, and has received the War Medal with four Clasps for Busaco, Nivelle, Orthes, and Toulouse. He served also the campaign of 1815, including the battle of Waterloo.

2 Mr. Chapman served throughout the campaign in Affghanistan under Lord Keane, and was present at the storm and capture of Ghuznee (Medal).

3 Doctor Collier served at the capture of Martinique, in 1809; and in the Peninsula from the latter part of 1812 to the end of that war in 1814, including the battles of Vittoria, Orthes, and Toulouse. He has received the War Medal with four Clasps.

War Services of the Medical Officers.

4 Doctor Daun served at the capture of the Cape of Good Hope in 1806. Also the campaign of 1815, including the battle of Waterloo.

6 Mr. Hartle served on the expedition to St. Lucia in 1803, and accompanied the storming party of Morne Fortunée. Present at Dominica when the French attacked the island in 1805; served also at the capture of the islands of St. Thomas and St. Croix in 1807; and Martinique in 1809, including the actions of the 1st and 2nd Feb. Also at the capture of Guadaloupe in 1815. He has received the War Medal with one Clasp for Martinique.

7 Mr. Menzies served with the 45th on the expedition to the Umzincula, and engaged against the revolted Zoola chief Fodo, in 1847. Applied to join the expedition to Turkey and embarked early in April 1854; was employed from the period of his arrival in the East, at Scutari, where he was Principal Medical Officer from 26th June to the 1st Jan. 1855, during which period he had to make the necessary arrangements for the accommodation of the sick and wounded of our army, and received all the wounded sent from the seat of war after the three great battles of the Alma, Balaklava, and Inkerman, besides the numerous sick that were almost daily arriving from the field,—these duties being of so overwhelming a nature, and having many other difficulties to contend with, his health gave way under this pressure of duty, which compelled him to relinquish his position and return to England.

8 Mr. Macdonell served with the 80th Regt. the Sutlej campaign of 1845-46, including the battles of Moodkee, Ferozeshah, and Sobraon (Medal and two Clasps). Served in the Crimea from 17 Sept. 54 (Medal and Clasps, and 4th Class of the Medjidie).

9 Doctor Shortt served in the Peninsula from Sept. 1810 to the end of that war in 1814, and subsequently in the American war.

10 Sir Augustus West served in Hanover in 1805; at Copenhagen and Sweden in 1807; in Portugal and Spain in 1808; at Walcheren in 1809; and in the Peninsula from 1809 to the end of that war in 1814, and has received the War Medal with seven Clasps for Busaco, Ciudad Rodrigo, Salamanca, Vittoria, St. Sebastian, Nivelle, and Nive; and is a Commander of the Tower and Sword of Portugal.

11 Doctor Knight served at Walcheren in 1809.

12 Doctor Maclagan served at Walcheren in 1809. Also in the Peninsula from Dec. 1811 to the end of that war in 1814, and has received the War Medal with six Clasps for Badajoz, Salamanca, Vittoria, Pyrenees, Nivelle, Nive.

13 Doctor Wright served at the capture of Martinique in 1809, for which he has received the War Medal with one Clasp.

14 Doctor Boyes served the Punjaub campaign of 1848-49 (Medal).

15 Mr. Chisholm served in the campaign of 1815, including Waterloo, and the capture of Paris. Was engaged in both Rebellions in Upper Canada. Accompanied several naval expeditions against the brigands on Lake Ontario, and among "the Thousand Islands," and served in the gun-boats with the Marines and Indians during the attack and surrender at Mill Point. Was the only medical officer of the regular force on the field, and a volunteer during the sharp conflict with the rebels and Americans near Prescott, 13th Nov. 1838, where upwards of 80 of the small force were killed and wounded, including the two officers who landed with the expedition. Received high commendation in the official communications of the Commander of the Forces, "in admiration of his conduct," and for the "valuable services" he rendered on that occasion. The General commanding in chief directed "his congratulations" to be sent to Mr. Chisholm "with reference to his exertions in that affair;" and the Master General expressed by "minute" his gratification "at conduct so creditable and so honourable to him."

16 Mr. Graves served with the 4th Light Dragoons during the campaign in Affghanistan under Lord Keane, and was present at the siege and capture of Ghuznee (Medal). Served also in the Crimea with the 68th Regt. in 1854-55, and was present at the battle of Inkerman (Medal and Clasps).

17 Doctor Hunter served the Eastern campaign of 1854-55, including the battles of Alma and Balaklava, and siege of Sebastopol (Medal and Clasps, and 5th Class of the Medjidie).

18 Mr. Mostyn served in the Peninsula, from Jan. 1811 until the end of the war, including the siege of Badajoz, April 1812, battles of Salamanca, Vittoria, and the Pyrenees; storming of San Sebastian with the Volunteer party; battles of Orthes and Toulouse. Served in the American war, including the action at Plattsburg. Present on the 18th June at Waterloo. He has received the War Medal with eight Clasps for Badajoz, Salamanca, Vittoria, Pyrenees, St. Sebastian, Nivelle, Nive, and Toulouse. Served with the 27th Regt. in the Kaffir wars of 1834-35 and 1846-47 (Medal).

Surgeons of the First Class, &c.

1 Doctor Andrew Anderson served in Naples and Calabria, and was present at the battle of Maida and siege of Scylla Castle. Expedition to Walcheren and siege of Flushing in 1809. Peninsula, from Dec. 1809 to Nov. 1813, including the defence of Cadiz, battles of Busaco. Fuentes d'Onor, and Salamanca; siege of Burgos Castle, and actions in the Pyrenees. He has received the War Medal with five Clasps.

2 Mr. Berry served in the Peninsula, and has received the Silver War Medal with one Clasp for Vittoria.

3 Doctor Boggie served the Egyptian campaign of 1801. Also in the Peninsula, and has received the War Medal with five Clasps for Egypt, Roleia, Vimiera, Talavera, and Fuentes d'Onor.

5 Mr. Colclough served in the Mahratta war from Aug. 1812 to Dec. 1813; the Kandian

War Services of the Medical Officers.

campaign of 1815, including the capture of Kandy in the island of Ceylon. Deccan campaigns of 1818 and 19, including the storm and capture of Capaul Droog.

6 Mr. Cotton served with the 14th Foot at the siege and capture of Bhurtpore in 1825-6.

7 Mr. Finnie served the Waterloo campaign with the Royals.

8 Mr. Fraser served in the Peninsula and has received the War Medal with three Clasps for Corunna, Nivelle, and Nive.

9 Mr. Galliers served in the Peninsula with the Royals and has received the War Medal with two Clasps for Vittoria and St. Sebastian. He served also the Waterloo campaign.

10 Mr. Glasco served in the Peninsula with the 83rd and has received the War Medal with nine Clasps for Talavera, Fuentes d'Onor, Ciudad Rodrigo, Badajoz, Salamanca, Vittoria, Pyrenees, Nivelle, and Nive.

11 Mr. John Griffith served at the capture of Martinique in 1809, and subsequently in the Peninsula: he has received the War Medal with four Clasps for Martinique, Busaco, Fuentes d'Onor, and Vittoria.

12 Mr. Harrison served in the Walcheren expedition 1809; at Cadiz and in the Peninsula in 1811, 12, and 13; expedition to Holland, 1814; Netherlands and France from 1814 till 1818. Present at the assault of Seville, bombardment of Antwerp, storming of Bergen-op-Zoom, battles of Quatre Bras and Waterloo, and taking of Peronne.

13 Mr. Robert H. A. Hunter served in medical charge of the Belgaum field force in Canara, in 1837. Also in medical charge of the Queen's Royals during the campaign in Affghanistan and Beloochistan, including the capture of Ghuznee and Khelat. Medal for Ghuznee.

14 Doctor William Hunter served with the Coldstream Guards at the blockade of Bayonne in 1814; also the campaign of 1815, including the battle of Waterloo.

15 Doctor Joyes joined the 15th Hussars in 1811, and remained in that Regiment for twenty-eight years; he served in the Peninsula from Jan. 1813 to the end of that war in 1814, including the affair at Morales, battles of Vittoria, Pyrenees, Orthes, and Toulouse. Also the campaign of 1815, and was present at Waterloo. He has received the War Medal with three Clasps.

16 Doctor Jones served in the Peninsula as an Assistant Surgeon of the Rifle Brigade and from Sept. 1812 as Surgeon of the 40th, and has received the War Medal with twelve Clasps for Corunna, Busaco, Fuentes d'Onor, Ciudad Rodrigo, Badajoz, Salamanca, Vittoria, Pyrenees, Nivelle, Nive, Orthes, and Toulouse. He served also the Waterloo campaign.

17 Mr. Lightbody served at Gibraltar during the epidemic in 1804; with the army in Sicily in 1807 and 8; in the Peninsula from March 1812 to April 1813; and again from April 1814 to the end of the war, including the defence of Alba de Tormes and retreat from Salamanca.

18 Doctor M'Munn served the campaigns of 1813, 14, and 15 in Holland and Flanders, including the action at Merxem and bombardment of Antwerp.

20 Mr. Sievwright served with the 59th Regt. at the siege and capture of Bhurtpore in 1825-26 (Medal).

21 Doctor Smith served the campaigns of 1813, 14, and 15, including the battles of Vittoria, the Pyrenees, Nivelle, Orthes, Toulouse, and Waterloo. He has received the War Medal with five Clasps.

22 Mr. Stratton served at the capture of Martinique in 1809, and of Guadaloupe in 1810, for which he has received the War Medal with two Clasps.

23 Mr. Widmer served in the Peninsula and has received the War Medal with five Clasps for Talavera, Busaco, Fuentes d'Onor, Salamanca, and Vittoria.

Surgeons.

1 Mr. Abell served in Hanover in 1805 with the 95th (Rifle Brigade); at the siege of Copenhagen and battle of Kioge, in 1807; with the army under Sir John Moore on the retreat to Corunna; in the Peninsula in 1810; and with the 60th in America from 1814 to 1818.

2 Mr. Allardyce has received the War Medal with two Clasps for Vimiera and Corunna.

5 Mr. Ayton served at the capture of Martinique in 1809, for which he has received the War Medal with one Clasp.

6 Mr. Bacot served in the Peninsula and has received the War Medal with four Clasps for Corunna, St. Sebastian, Nivelle, and Nive.

7 Doctor Bartley served in the Peninsula, and was present at the battle of Salamanca, for which he has received the War Medal with one Clasp.

10 Doctor R. H. Bolton served in the Peninsula and has received the War Medal with two Clasps for Roleia and Vimiera.

11 Doctor Frederick Brown served in the Peninsula and has received the War Medal with one Clasp for Albuhera.

12 Mr. Josh. Brown served in the Peninsula and has received the War Medal with five Clasps for Busaco, Albuhera, Vittoria, Pyrenees, and Nivelle.

13 Dr. Brush served with the 26th on the China expedition (Medal), and was present at the repulse of the night-attack on Ningpo, at the attack and capture of Chapoo, Woosung, Shanghae, and Chin Kiang Foo, and at the landing before Nankin. Served throughout the Eastern campaign of 1854-55 with the 93rd Regt. and Scots Greys, including the affair of M'Kenzie's Farm, capture of Balaklava, battles of Balaklava, Inkerman, and Tchernaya, siege and fall of Sebastopol (Medal and three Clasps).

14 Doctor John Campbell served the campaigns of 1813 and 14 in the Peninsula and has re-

ceived the War Medal with two Clasps for Pyrenees and Orthes. He served afterwards at New Orleans.

15 Mr. Coombe served the Egyptian campaign of 1801. Also in the Peninsula, and has received the War Medal with three Clasps for Egypt, Talavera, Busaco, and Fuentes d'Onor.

16 Mr. Cross served in the Peninsula, and has received the Silver War Medal with four Clasps for Badajoz, Nivelle, Orthes, and Toulouse.

17 Mr. Cuddy served at the capture of Martinique in 1809 for which he has received the War Medal with one Clasp.

18 Mr. Cunningham served the campaigns of 1813 and 14 in Upper Canada, under Sir Gordon Drummond.

19 Doctor Daunt served at the capture of Madeira in 1807; of Martinique in 1809 (for which he has received the War Medal with one Clasp); and of Arracan in 1825.

20 Mr. Davidson served with the 50th in the battle of Punniar (Medal). Also the campaign on the Sutlej (Medal), including the battles of Moodkee and Ferozeshah.

22 Mr. Dealey served in the Peninsula in 1811 and 1812, and was present at the battle of Albuhera, and first siege of Badajoz.

23 Mr. Eddie served in the Kaffir War of 1846-7.

24 Mr. Este served the Egyptian campaign of 1801 (Medal), including the actions of the 8th (slightly wounded), 13th, and 21st March, and siege of Alexandria. Served also in the Peninsula from Oct. 1812 to the end of that war in 1814, including the battles of Vittoria, Pampeluna, Orthes, and Toulouse. He has received the War Medal with three Clasps.

27 Doctor John Forster served the campaign of 1814 in Holland.

28 Mr. Peter Fraser served in the American war, and was present at the capture of Oswego.

29 Doctor Galeani joined the army in Sicily, in 1812, and was employed in the field until landed at Leghorn, 14th March 1814. Present in the campaign of Italy with the advanced army, including the taking of the Castle of St. Maria, in Spezia, action at Seshi, siege and surrender of Genoa, and taking of the castle of Savona and Novi.

30 Mr. Gilder served the Waterloo campaign with the Grenadier Guards.

31 Mr. M. Griffith served in the Peninsula from Jan. 1810 to the end of that war in 1814, including the battles of Busaco and Fuentes d'Onor, siege and assault of Ciudad Rodrigo, siege and assault of Badajoz, battles of Salamanca, Vittoria, Pyrenees, Nivelle, Nive, and Orthes, action at Vic Bigorre (wounded), and battle of Toulouse. Served also in India, Arabia, and the Burmese Empire, from May 1818, including sieges of Asseerghur, Ras-el-Kyma, and Zaia, siege and assault of Dwarka, affair of Beni-Boo-Ali, assault of a fortress on the banks of the Pegu River, assault of Syrian Pagoda, siege of Donabew, and battle near Prome. He has received the War Medal with nine Clasps.

32 Doctor Hair's services :—Peninsular campaigns from Nov. 1812 to the end of that war in 1814, including the battle of Vittoria, siege of San Sebastian in August and Sept. 1813, battles of the Nivelle, Nive, and Orthes, and the affairs of Vera. Subsequently in the action in front of New Orleans, and, finally, at the capture of Paris. He has received the War Medal with five Clasps.

33 Mr. Harthill served with the 9th throughout the campaign of 1842 in Affghanistan (Medal) under General Pollock.

34 Doctor Henderson served in the Peninsula, and was present at the siege of Badajoz, and both the actions of Salamanca, 18th and 22nd July 1812. He has received the War Medal with two Clasps.

35 Doctor Heriot served in the Peninsula from June 1809, to the end of the war, including the battles of Talavera and Salamanca, siege of Burgos, and battles of Vittoria, the Pyrenees, Nivelle, and Orthes, and has received the War Medal with six Clasps.

36 Mr. Hichens served the Waterloo campaign.

37 Doctor Ingham served in the American war, and was present at the battles of Fort George, Chippewa, and at the Falls of Niagara.

38 Sir Edward Johnson served in the Peninsula and has received the War Medal with one Clasp for Corunna, and is a Knight of Charles the Third of Spain.

40 Doctor Thomas Lewis served in the Peninsula from July 1811 to June 1813.

41 Doctor William Lloyd served the campaign in Flanders in 1815; also in the interior of Ceylon during the Kandian rebellion in 1817.

42 Mr. Lorimer served in the Peninsula from June 1810 to end of that war in 1814.

45 Doctor M'Donald served in the Peninsula and has received the War Medal with six Clasps for Sahagun and Benevente, Corunna, Salamanca, Vittoria, Orthes, and Toulouse. He served also the Waterloo campaign.

46 Mr. Macarthur was severely wounded at the storming of Seringapatam.

47 Mr. Maclise served with the 90th Regt. in the Kaffir war of 1846-47 (Medal); and on the Staff in the Eastern campaign of 1854-55, and was present at the battle of Alma (Medal and Clasps).

48 Doctor Macnish served with the expedition to Hanover in 1805; expedition to South America under General Whitelock, in 1806 and 7; campaign of 1808 and 9, in the Peninsula, including the battles of Roleia and Vimiera for which he has received the War Medal with two Clasps. Expedition to Walcheren, including the siege of Flushing.

49 Doctor Murtagh, with the effective men of the wing of the 6th Regt. stationed at Aden, formed part of an expedition of 500 men under the command of Lieut.-Colonel Pennycuick, which destroyed the Arab posts of Sheik Medi and Sheik Othman, and skirmished between those places on the 6th Oct. 1841.

50 Mr. Neill served the Peninsular campaign of 1814.
51 Mr. Nivison served in Upper and Lower Canada during the Rebellion in 1837 and 38.
52 Doctor Paterson served in the Peninsula from Sept. 1810 to Dec. 1811. Served also in the Burmese war.
53 Doctor Pearson served the Waterloo campaign.
54 Doctor Perston served in the Peninsula from Jan. 1809 to April 1813, including the combat of Foz d'Arouce, battle of Salamanca (for which he has received the War Medal with one Clasp), capture of Madrid, siege of Burgos, and retreat therefrom. Served also the campaign of 1815, and was present at the battles of Quatre Bras and Waterloo, and capture of Paris.
55 Doctor Piper served twenty years in the East Indies, and was present at the destruction of the Dutch Squadron in Sourabaya in 1809. Accompanied the expedition under Admiral Drury to Macoa, in China, as auxiliaries to the Portuguese, in 1809. Served also with the Army of Reserve during the Pindarree war from 1816 to 1821.
56 Doctor Pollok-Morris served in the East Indies from 1805 to 1823. He was in the action at sea with the French squadron under Admiral Linois, in the *Marengo*, 84, on the voyage to Madras, in Aug. 1805; he was at the siege and capture of the fortress of Adjighur in Bundlekund, in 1809; and he served throughout the Nepaul war in 1814 and 1815, including the sieges of Kalunga, of Nahn, and of Jeytuck.
61 Doctor Riach served the campaigns of 1813 and 14, in Germany and Holland, including the action of Goerde in Hanover, 16th Sept. 1813; affair near Antwerp in Jan. 1814; attack on Merxem, and subsequent operations against the French fleet at Antwerp. Present in the actions at and near Waterloo on 16th, 17th, and 18th June.
62 Doctor Robertson served with the 13th Light Infantry throughout the campaigns in Affghanistan from 1838 to 1842 inclusive, and was present at the storm and capture of Ghuznée (Medal), assault and capture of the town and forts of Tootumdurrah, storm of Jhoolghur, night attack at Baboo Koosh Ghur, destruction of Khardurrah, assault of Perwandurrah, storming of the Khoord Cabool Pass, affair of Tezeen, forcing the Jugdulluck Pass, reduction of the fort of Mamoo Khail, heroic defence of Jellalabad and sorties on the 14th Nov. and 1st Dec. 1841, 11th March, 24th March, and 1st April, 1842; general action and defeat of Akbar Khan before Jellalabad, storming the heights of Jugdulluck, general action of Tezeen, and recapture of Cabool (Medal).
64 Mr. Rogers served in the Peninsula from January 1813 to the end of that war in 1814, including the action at Morales, battles of Vittoria, Pyrenees, Orthes, and Toulouse. He has received the War Medal with two Clasps.
66 Mr. Shekleton served in the Peninsula and has received the War Medal with seven Clasps for Albuhera, Vittoria, Pyrenees, Nivelle, Nive, Orthes, and Toulouse.
67 Mr. Shorland served the campaign of 1808-9, including the battle of Corunna. Campaign of 1810 and 11 in Portugal, including the battle of Busaco. Served also during the whole of the war with the United States of North America. He has received the War Medal with two Clasps.
70 Mr. Stephenson served in the Peninsula from March 1809 to the end of that war in 1814, and has received the War Medal with eight Clasps for Fuentes d'Onor, Ciudad Rodrigo, Badajoz, Salamanca, Vittoria, Pyrenees, Nivelle, and Nive.
71 Mr. J. Edmonstone Stewart served in the Peninsula from March 1811 to Feb. 1813, and was present in the retreat from Burgos.
73 Mr. Ward served in the Peninsula and has received the War Medal with one Clasp for Barrosa.
75 Mr. Wilkins served the campaign of 1814 in the Peninsula; was in the Kandian war in Ceylon during 1817 and 1818; and was Surgeon of a Light Battalion at the siege of Kolapore in 1827. Served with the 41st Regt. throughout the campaign of 1842 in Affghanistan (Medal), and was present in the engagements with the enemy on the 28th March and 28th April in the Pisheen Valley; in those of the 29th May near Candahar, 30th Aug. at Goaine, 5th Sept. before Ghuznee; at the occupation and destruction of that Fortress and of Cabool, the expedition into Kohistan, storm, capture and destruction of Istaliff, and the various minor affairs in and between the Bolan and the Khyber Passes.
76 Mr. Williams served at Walcheren in 1809, and in the Peninsula from 1810 to 1812.
77 Doctor Wilson served with the Guards the Eastern campaign of 1854-55, including the battles of Alma, Balaklava, and Inkerman, and siege of Sebastopol (Medal and Clasps): in a Dispatch referring to the battle of Inkerman, Lord Raglan writes, "The Duke of Cambridge speaks also in the highest terms of the spirited exertions of Assistant-Surgeon Wilson, of the 7th Hussars, who at a critical moment rallied a few men, which enabled them to hold the ground till reinforced."
79 Doctor Wood served with the 9th Lancers in the Gwalior campaign in 1843 (Medal); also the Sutlej campaign of 1846, including the battle of Sobraon (Medal).
80 Mr. Wyer served in the Peninsula and has received the War Medal with five clasps for Vittoria, Pyrenees, Nivelle, Orthes, and Toulouse.
81 Doctor James Young served in Africa from 1824 to 1827 inclusive, and was present at the battle of Doodwa against the Ashantees 7 August 1826.
82 Doctor W. H. Young served in the Peninsula from March 1812 to Jan. 1813. including the last siege of Badajoz, and battle of Salamanca. Served also the campaigns of 1813, 14, and 15, in Germany, Holland, and the Netherlands, including the attack on Bergen-op-Zoom, and battle of Waterloo. He has received the War Medal with two Clasps for Badajoz and Salamanca.

Assistant Surgeons.

1 Mr. Bremner joined the army in Portugal early in 1811, and being appointed to the Buffs in Sept. 1813 he was present with that Regt. at the battles of the Pyrenees, Nivelle, Nive, Orthes, and Toulouse, for which he has received the War Medal with five Clasps. Embarked at Bourdeaux for Canada in June 1814 and joined the Army of Occupation in France in 1815, with which he served until Nov. 1818.

2 Doctor Cannon served in the Peninsula and has received the War Medal with seven Clasps for Vittoria, Pyrenees, St. Sebastian, Nivelle, Nive, Orthes, and Toulouse.

3 Mr. Eddowes served in the Peninsula and has received the War Medal two with Clasps for Ciudad Rodrigo and Badajoz.

4 Mr. Evers served the Waterloo campaign.

5 Doctor Furnival served in the Peninsula and has received the War Medal with one Clasp for Badajoz.

6 Doctor Kenny served in the Peninsula and has received the War Medal with four Clasps for Vittoria, Pyrenees, Nivelle, and Nive. He served also the Waterloo campaign.

7 Doctor O'Beirne served in the Peninsula and has received the War Medal with eight Clasps for Ciudad Rodrigo, Badajoz, Vittoria, St. Sebastian, Nivelle, Nive, Orthes, and Toulouse.

8 Mr. Thompson served in the Peninsula and has received the War Medal with two Clasps for Albuhera and Badajoz.

9 Mr. Tobin served in the Peninsula and has received the War Medal with six Clasps for Vittoria, Pyrenees, Nivelle, Nive, Orthes, and Toulouse.

10 Doctor Venables served in the Peninsula and has received the War Medal with six Clasps for Vittoria, Pyrenees, Nivelle, Nive, Orthes, and Toulouse.

11 Mr. Verner served the Waterloo campaign.

Apothecaries.

1 Mr. Graham served in the Peninsula and has received the War Medal with one Clasp for Corunna.

Deputy Purveyors.

1 Mr. Findley served in the Peninsula and has received the War Medal with two Clasps for Pyrenees and Toulouse.

4 Mr. Newcombe served in the Peninsula and has received the War Medal with four Clasps for Pyrenees, Nivelle, Orthes, and Toulouse.

5 Mr. George Winter served in the Peninsula, and has received the War Medal with one Clasp for Vimiera.

VETERINARY SURGEONS.

Berington, James, Depôt ....16 Dec. 13
Burt, James, R. Art............. 1 June 07
🙰 🙰 Constant, John,¹ 5 Dr. Gds. ... 3 Mar. 14
Grellier, James, R. Waggon Train..21 Feb. 00
Hallen, Herbert, Cavalry Depot .. 3 Aug. 30
🙰 🙰 Hogreve, Henry,² 15 Drs. ..12 July 06
Lythe, John, R. Art............. 1 June 09
Percivall, Charles,⁴ R. Artillery ..23 April 18
Rainsford, James, 4 Dr. Gds. ....25 Dec. 28
Robertson, James, 10 Drs. ...... 2 Oct. 40
Smith, Opie, 2 Drs. ....20 Feb. 35
Steed, Edward Henry, Depot ....15 Mar. 98
Stockley, William, R. Artillery ...24 Apr. 05
Woodman, Wm., 2 Dr. Gds.......25 Feb. 13

1 Mr. Constant served the campaign of 1815 with the 13 Dragoons, and was present at Quatre Bras, the retreat on the following day, and battle of Waterloo.
2 Mr. Hogreve served in the Peninsula, France, and Flanders, from Dec. 1811 to the end of that war, including the third siege of Badajoz, and battles of Vittoria, Toulouse, and Waterloo.
4 Mr. Percivall served in the East Indies with the 11th Light Dragoons, and was present at the siege and capture of Bhurtpore in 1825-6 (Medal).

CHAPLAINS.

Rev. Carey, Nicholas ....19 Feb. 95
— Hudson, Joseph, MA.........25 Nov. 25
The Venerable Archdeacon, le Mesurier, J. T. H., AM. ...... } 16 April 12
Rev. Timbrell, John ....30 June 95

OFFICERS
ON THE
FOREIGN HALF-PAY.

GERMAN LEGION.

1st LIGHT DRAGOONS.

Rank	Name	Rank in the Army	When placed on half-pay
Captains	Bernard von Bothmer	28 Aug. 10	24 Feb. 16
	Henry George von Hattorf	25 Feb. 12	do
	Charles Elderhost	10 Mar. 13	do
	Morris de Cloudt	17 Sept.	do
Lieutenants	Augustus Fischer	13 Mar. 12	do
	Otto von Hammerstein	13 May 15	do
	Conrad Poten	6 July	do
Cornets	Charles von der Decken	18 April 14	25 Feb.
	Hannach Boguslaw Leschen	27 May	do
	Edward Trittau	14 May 15	24 Feb.

2nd LIGHT DRAGOONS.

Rank	Name	Rank in the Army	When placed on half-pay
Captains	George Braun	3 July 15	24 Feb. 16
	Augustus Poten	15 Oct.	do
Lieutenants	Ludolph de Hugo	24 Mar. 12	do
	Johannes Justinus von Fumetti	do	do
	Augustus Kuhls	28 May	do
	Herman Hen. Con. Ritter	18 Sept. 13	do
	Ern. Theo. Chr. Meier	15 Mar. 14	do
	Ferdinand Küster	21 Nov. 15	do
Cornets	Fred. Carl. Edmund Kuhls	10 April	do
	Ernest von Voss	4 July	do
	Ferdinand von Stolzenberg	21 Nov.	do
Surgeon	Frederick Detmer	13 July 13	do

1st HUSSARS.

Rank	Name	Rank in the Army	When placed on half-pay
Captains	Gustavus Schaumann	10 Oct.	24 Feb. 16
	Hieronimus von der Wisch	6 April 14	do
Lieutenants	Conrad Poten	14 July 11	do
	Henry Christoph. Behrens	19 Nov. 13	do
Cornets	Franz Geo. von Oldershausen	27 Jan. 14	do
	William Theodore Gebser	14 Feb.	do
	Frederick Jacob Rahlwes	26 April	do
	William de Hassell	13 Sept.	do

2nd HUSSARS.

Rank	Name	Rank in the Army	When placed on half-pay
Captain	Theodor von Stolzenberg	14 Nov. 12	24 Feb. 16
Lieutenant	Michael Löning	16 Nov.	do
Cornets	Ernest Soest	27 Nov. 13	do
	Victor, *Count* Alten	27 April 14	do
	Theodor von Marschalck	28 July 15	do

3rd HUSSARS.

Rank	Name	Rank in the Army	When placed on half-pay
Captains	Quintus, *Baron* Goebén	2 May 11	24 Feb. 16
	William von Schnehen	20 Sept.	do
	August. de Harling	8 Oct.	do
	George Meyer	27 Dec.	do
	Diede Wm. von der Hellen	17 Feb. 14	do
Lieutenants	John Henry D'Homboldt	14 Nov. 12	do
	Charles Augustus Reinecke	15 Nov.	do
	Christian Oehlkers	9 Oct. 13	do
	Frederick de Fresnoy	29 July 15	do
Cornets	Alex. *Baron* Hammerstein	9 Oct. 13	do
	Rudolph. Fredrichs	10 Oct.	do
	Hans. *Baron* Holdenberg	1 Dec.	do
	George Julius Meyer	5 May 14	do
Veter.-Surg.	Frederick Eidmann	12 July 06	do

1st LIGHT INFANTRY.

Rank	Name	Rank in the Army	When placed on half-pay
Captain	Augustus Wahrendorff	4 July 15	24 Feb. 16
Lieutenants	William de Heugel	20 Mar. 12	do
	Adolphus Koester	22 Oct. 13	do
	Nicholas de Miniussir	29 Jan. 14	do
	Harry Leonhart	25 Mar.	do
Ensigns	Gustavus George Best	26 Nov. 13	do
	Adolph. von Gentzkow	27 Nov.	do
Adjutant	John Fred. Wm. Bushe ....Ens.	29 May 15	do

Foreign Half-pay.

		Rank in the Army.	When placed on half-pay.
	2ND LIGHT INFANTRY.		
Captain	Charles Meyer	1 July 15	24 Feb. 16
Lieutenants	James Oliver Lindham, *KH*	8 July 11	do
	William Doring	10 April 14	do
Ensigns	Lewis Charles Baring	11 April	do
	Chr. Aug. Jacob Behne	26 June 15	do
Assist.-Surg.	Joseph Tholon	6 Oct.	do
	1ST BATTALION OF THE LINE.		
Captain	Leopold von Rettberg	18 Aug. 13	do
Lieutenants	Christian Hen. von Düring	17 Aug. 09	do
	Ludolph Kumme	18 Aug.	do
	Diederich de Einem	18 Mar. 12	do
	George Wichmann	30 Oct.	do
	Adolph. von Arentsschildt	18 Aug. 13	do
	Fred. Augustus Muller	22 Sept.	do
Ensigns	Augustus, *Baron* Le Fort	9 Sept.	do
	Arnold William Heise	7 Jan. 14	do
	Cha. Aug. von der Hellen	7 May	do
	2ND BATTALION OF THE LINE.		
Captain	Ferd. Adolphus *Baron* Holle	28 May 15	do
Lieutenants	Francis La Roche	27 Mar. 14	do
	George Fabricius	29 April	do
	Lewis Henry de Sichart	28 May 15	do
Ensigns	Gust. Fred. Wm. Hartmann	8 May	do
	Augustus Luning	17 June	do
Adjutant	Adolphus Hesse ......*Lieut.*	17 Mar. 12	do
	3RD BATTALION OF THE LINE.		
Captain	Frederick Erdmann	19 June 15	do
Lieutenants	Charles Brauns	14 Sept. 10	do
	Julius Brinkmann	11 May 12	do
	Henry Dehnel	20 Mar. 13	do
	Lewis de Bachellé, *Baron* von dem Brinck	20 Sept.	do
Ensigns	Frederick de Storren	18 Feb.	do
	Frederick von Schlutter	6 May	do
	Augustus William Kuckuck	8 Jun. 14	do
	Richard Hupeden	9 Jan.	do
Adjutant	Fred. Bern. Schneider ....*Lieut.*	18 Mar. 12	do
	4TH BATTALION OF THE LINE.		
Lieutenants	Caspar von Both	13 Dec. 08	do
	Adolphus Ludewig	19 Mar. 12	do
	Hen. Fred. Theo. de Witte	31 Oct.	do
	Ernest Brinckmann	4 Mar. 13	do
Ensigns	Augustus Schulze	15 June	do
	Frederick von Brandis	26 July	do
	Ferd. von Uslar Gleichen	30 May 14	do
	Arnold Appuhn	6 June 13	do
	5TH BATTALION OF THE LINE.		
Captains	Charles, *Baron* Linsingen	16 April 13	do
	Henry, *Baron* Dachenhausen	8 Dec.	do
	Charles Berger	21 Aug.	do
Lieutenants	Augustus Winckler	20 Mar. 12	do
	Joseph Korschann	25 Sept. 12	25 July 15
	George Klingsöhr	16 Dec.	do
	Lewis de Geissmann	16 April 13	24 Feb. 16
	George Wischmann	10 April 15	do
Ensigns	Ferdinand Scharnhorst	27 Mar. 13	do
	Charles Winckler	10 Jan. 14	do
	Lewis Klingsöhr	22 Mar.	do
	Ernest Baring	25 May	do
	Geo. Cha. Aug. von Loesecke	15 April 15	do
	Rudolph Carstens	15 May	do
Adjutant	William Walther......*Ensign*	22 Nov. 18	do

Foreign Half-pay.

6TH BATTALION OF THE LINE.

		Rank in the Army.	When placed on half-pay.
Lieutenants	Ernest, *Baron* Heimburg	16 Mar. 09	24 May 16
	Otto Schaumann	20 Sept. 10	do
	Frederick Hurtzig	21 Mar. 12	do
	Francis, *Baron* Acton	4 April 14	do
	🜚 Christ. Lewis von Ompteda	26 May	do
Ensigns	Alexander Autran	2 April	do
	🜚 Lew. Albrecht von Ompteda	15 April	do
	Herman Schwencke	8 June	do
	Edward von Brandis	9 June	do

7TH BATTALION OF THE LINE.

Lieutenants	🜚 Frederick von Diebitsch	23 July 11	24 May 16
	🜚 Theodore von Sebisch	23 Mar. 12	do
	🜚 Christian Frederick Eichhorn	3 April 14	do
	Augustus Steffen	27 May	do
Ensigns	🜚 Arnold Erich Backhaus	18 July	do
	🜚 Charles Ernest F. Neuschäffer	19 April	do
	🜚 Franz Frederick Backhaus	29 April	do
	Augustus von Hodenberg	2 June	do

8TH BATTALION OF THE LINE.

Lieutenant	🜚 Frederick Ziermann	27 Mar. 12	24 Feb. 16
Ensigns	Frederick Dorndorf	12 July 12	
	🜚 Godlove Künoth	13 July	do
	🜚 Frederick Henry Müller	13 April 14	do
	🜚 Geo. Fred. Godfrey Lunde	12 Sept.	do

ARTILLERY.

1st Lieuts.	Ferdinand de Brandis	28 Sept. 07	do
	William Rummel	14 Dec. 12	do
	🜚 William de Goeben	25 Nov. 13	do
	Frederick Drechsler	27 Nov.	do
	🜚 Augustus Pfannkuche	28 Nov.	do
	🜚 🜚 Henry Hartmann	26 Mar. 14	do
	Henry Bostlemann	16 May 15	do
2nd Lieuts.	🜚 Lewis Haardt	14 Dec. 12	do
	Lewis Scharnhorst	15 Nov. 13	do
	🜚 Charles Herman Ludowieg	16 Feb. 14	do
	John Fred. Schlichthorst	20 May	do
	Franz Rottiger	26 Nov.	do
	Adolphus Rechtern	24 July 15	do
	Lewis Hagemann	25 July	do
Paymaster	John Blundstone	9 April 05	do
Veter.-Surg.	John Frederick Hilmer	22 Aug. 06	do

ENGINEERS.

1st Lieut.	🜚 William Unger	14 Aug. 11	do

STAFF.

Brig.-Majors	🜚 Fr. Chr. *Baron* Heimburg ....*Capt.*	26 July 15	do
	🜚 🜚 George Baring ....*Capt.*	20 Nov.	do

MISCELLANEOUS CORPS.

BRUNSWICK CAVALRY.

Captains	*William de Wulffen	28 Sept. 09	14 June 16
	*Alexander von Erichsen	7 Mar. 11	do
	*Gustavus Conrad Alex.von Girsewald	4 Nov. 13	do
Lieutenant	William von Lubeck	1 Nov.	24 Feb.
Cornet	Frederick Moeller	10 Mar. 14	24 June
Adjutant	William Butze ....*Lieut.*	26 Sept. 09	do
Quar.-Master	Ferdinand de Bothmer	21 June 10	do

BRUNSWICK INFANTRY.

Lieutenants	Ernest von Patzinsky	27 Sept. 09	1814
	*Carl. Ernest Berner	do	do
	🜚 Frederick Hausler	27 June 11	do
	🜚 Albert von Greisheim	27 Aug.	24 June 15
	🜚 Charles Haberland	1 April 14	1814
Ensign	Johannes Cornelius Schot	1 April 13	do

Foreign Half-pay.

			Rank in the Army.	When placed on half-pay.
	CHASSEURS BRITANNIQUES.			
Captain	Nich. Philibert de Brem.	Major	4 June 14	24 June 14
Lieutenants	Etienne de Planta		3 Dec. 07	2 Nov. 15
	J— N— de Ponchalon		4 May 10	1814
	Jean Nepomucene Stoeber		28 June	do
	ƋP Armand Casimir G. Dufief		28 Oct.	do
	Jos. Ignace Gossencourt		22 July 13	do
	Frederick Wolf		21 April 14	do
Assist.-Surg.	Ignation Stumpa		12 Apr. 10	do
	ROYAL CORSICAN RANGERS.			
Captains	Joseph Panattieri		6 Jan. 07	1817
	Jacques Guanter		27 May 13	do
Lieutenants	Antonio D'Odiardi		10 Feb. 12	do
	Dominico Antonio Peretti		25 June	do
Ensign	Joseph Susini		19 May 14	do
	GREEK LIGHT INFANTRY.			
Lieutenants	Pietro Antonio Salvatorio		2 July 13	1814
	Pierre Astuto		25 June 14	do
	ROYAL MALTA REGIMENT.			
Lieutenant	Ern. Fer. Cha. Bern. Richter		20 Mar. 05	1811
	MEURON'S REGIMENT.			
Captain	George Alexander Dardel		24 Sept. 04	1808
Lieutenants	Charles de Gumoens		28 April 11	25 Sept. 16
	Antoine Fred. de Graffenried		30 April	do
	August. de Loriol		28 Sept. 14	do
	Jules Cæsar Saum		15 Jan. 16	do
	ROLL'S REGIMENT.			
Captain	Ferd. Compte de la Ville		21 Oct. 04	25 Dec. 17
Lieutenants	Jost Muller		5 Nov. 07	1816
	Charles Pannach		25 Jan. 10	do
	Edmund de Tugginer		26 Feb. 11	do
	Otto Henry Salinger		28 Feb.	do
	Henry d'Holbreuse		15 Oct. 12	do
	Joseph Gurtler		9 Dec.	do
	Edward de Tugginer		29 Sept. 13	do
	Jean Baptiste Phil. Stutzer		27 Oct. 14	do
Ensign	Charles de Bronner		22 June 15	do
Chaplain	William Peter Macdonald		1 July 12	1816
Assist.-Surg.	Charles Gemmellaro		25 Nov. 13	do
	SICILIAN REGIMENT.			
Lieutenants	Thomas de Fossi		6 April 09	25 Mar. 16
	Gustave de Roquefeuil		23 Aug. 10	do
	WATTEVILLE'S REGIMENT.			
Lieut.-Col.	Rudolphe de May		21 May 12	24 Oct. 16
Lieutenant	Albert Steiger		6 May 07	do
Ensign	Fra. Louis Con. Fischer		25 Jan. 14	do
Chaplain	Peter James de la Mothe		23 April 12	do
Assist.-Surg.	Jean Baptiste Boidin		1 May 01	25 July 16
	YORK LIGHT INFANTRY VOLUNTEERS.			
Captain	Arthur Leon de Tinseau		15 June 15	25 July 16
Lieutenants	Antoine Louis de Mendibus		8 July 11	19 Mar. 17
	John Ordon		10 July	do
Ensign	Louis Tholon		14 Sept. 13	25 July 16
	FOREIGN VETERAN BATTALION.			
Captain	Frederick Wyneken		8 July 11	24 Feb. 16
Lieutenants	George de Witte		20 Aug. 11	do
	ƋƉƇ Frederick von Finke		20 Mar. 12	do
	FOREIGN CORPS OF WAGGONERS.			
Cornet	John Albert Kropp		1 June 15	25 July 16

OFFICERS

TO WHOM

GOLD DECORATIONS

HAVE BEEN GRANTED

IN COMMEMORATION OF THEIR SERVICES IN THE FOLLOWING BATTLES OR ACTIONS.

Maida	4 July	1806
Roleia	17 Aug.	08
Vimiera	21 Aug.	
Sahagun, Benevente, &c. (actions of Cavalry)	Dec. 1808 & Jan.	09
Corunna	16 Jan.	
Martinique ....(attack and capture)	Feb.	
Talavera	27 & 28 July	
Guadaloupe .... (attack and capture)	Jan. & Feb.	10
Busaco	27 Sept.	
Barrosa	5 Mar.	11
Fuentes d'Onor	5 May	
Albuhera	16 May	
Java .... (attack and capture)	Aug. & Sept.	
Ciudad Rodrigo ...... (assault and capture)	Jan.	12
Badajoz .... (do. do.)	17 March & 6 April	
Salamanca	22 July	
Fort Detroit, America ...... (capture of)	Aug.	
Vittoria	21 June	13
Pyrenees	28 July to 2 Aug.	
St. Sebastian .... (assault and capture)	Aug. & Sept.	
Chateauguay, America	26 Oct.	
Nivelle	10 Nov.	
Chrystler's Farm, America	11 Nov.	
Nive	9 to 13 Dec.	
Orthes	27 Feb.	14
Toulouse	10 April	

OFFICERS WHO HAVE RECEIVED GOLD DECORATIONS.

NAMES AND PRESENT RANK.	DISTINCTIONS.	SIEGES, BATTLES, ETC.	RANK OR COMMAND AT THE TIME.
Auchmuty, Lieut.-Gen. Sir Samuel Benj., KCB. 7 F.	Medal and 1 Clasp	Orthes, Toulouse	Light Companies
Becktwith, Major-Gen. Charles, CB.	Medal	Toulouse	Assistant-Quar.-Mas.-Gen.
Bell, Lieut.-Gen. Sir John, KCB.	Cross	Pyrenees, Nivelle, Orthes, Toulouse	Assistant-Quar.-Mas.-Gen.
Bell, Lieut.-Col. Thomas, CB. ...... 4 F.	Cross	Salamanca, Pyrenees, Nivelle, Orthes	Major 48 Foot
Blake, Col. Wm. Williams, CB. .....late of 11 Dr.	Medal	Roleia and Vimiera	
Blakeney, General Rt. Hon. Sir E., GCB. GCH. 1 F.	Cross and 1 Clasp	Martinique, Albuhera, Badajoz, Vittoria, Pyrenees	Lieut.-Col. 7 Foot
Brisbane, Gen. Sir Thos. M., Bt., GCB. GCH. 34 F.	Cross and 1 Clasp	Vittoria, Pyrenees, Nivelle, Orthes, Toulouse	A Brigade
Browne, Lieut.-Col. Gustavus, CB. ...late of 95 F.	Cross	Salamanca, Pyrenees, Nivelle, Nive	9 Portuguese Caçadores
Browne, Col. Fielding, CB.	Medal	Badajoz	Capt. 40 Foot
Bunbury, Lieut.-Gen. Sir Henry Edward, Bt. KCB.	Medal	Maida	Deputy-Quar.-Mas.-Gen.
Burgoyne, Gen. Sir John F. Bart. GCB. Royal Eng.	Cross and 1 Clasp	Badajoz, Salamanca, Vittoria, *St. Sebastian, *Nive	*Comm. Royal Engineers
Clifton, General Sir Arthur B. KCB. KCH. 1 Dr.	Medal and 1 Clasp	Fuentes d'Onor, Vittoria	1 Dragoons
Combermere, Field Marshal Stapleton, Lord Vis- count, GCB. GCH. .... 1 Life Gds.	Medal and 1 Clasp	Talavera, Fuentes d'Onor, Salamanca, Orthes, Toulouse	Maj.-Gen. comm. Brig. Cavalry Lieut.-Gen. comm. Cavalry
Derinzy, Maj.-Gen. B. Vigors, KH. ret.f. p. Insp. F. O.	Medal	Toulouse	7 Caçadores
Dixon, Major Gen. Matthew Charles ... ret. f. p. R. Eng.	do	Detroit	Commanding Royal Engineers
Douglas, General Sir James, KCB .... 42 F.	Cross and 3 Clasps	Busaco, Salamanca, Pyrenees, Nivelle, Nive, Orthes, Toulouse	Colonel 8 Portuguese A Brigade
Douglas, General Robert, CB. ....late of R. Art.	Cross	Salamanca, Vittoria, Pyrenees, Nivelle	
Downes, General Ulysses, Lord, KCB. ...... 29 F.	Cross and 1 Clasp	Vittoria, Pyrenees, Nivelle, Nive, Toulouse	A. D. C. to the Duke of Wellington
Ellicombe, Lieut.-Gen. C. Grene, CB. ...... R. Eng.	Medal	St. Sebastian	
Fergusson, Lieut.-Gen. Sir James, KCB. ...... 43 F.	Medal	Badajoz	Captain 43 Foot
FitzGerald, General Sir John Foster, KCB. ...18 F.	Cross	Badajoz, Salamanca, Vittoria, Pyrenees.	A Light Battalion A Brigade
Fuller, Lieut.-Col. Francis, CB. ..late of 59 F. R. Art.	Medal	St. Sebastian	
Gardiner, General Sir Robert, GCB. KCH.	Cross and 2 Clasps	Barrosa, Badajoz, Salamanca, Vittoria, Orthes, Toulouse	
Gell, Major Thomas................late of 29 F.	Medal	Albuhera.	Captain 29 Foot
Goldie, Lieut.-Gen. George Leigh, CB. .... 77 F.	Medal	Albuhera	Captain 66 Foot
Gomm, General Sir W. M. GCB. .... 13 F.	Cross and 1 Clasp	Badajoz, Salamanca, Vittoria, St. Sebastian, Nive	Assistant-Quarter-Master-General
Gough, General Hugh, Vsc. KP. GCB. R. Horse Gds.	Cross	Talavera, Barrosa, Vittoria, Nivelle	87 Foot
Guise, General Sir John Wright, Bt., KCB ... 85 F.	Cross	Fuentes d'Onor, Salamanca, Vittoria, Nive	Col. comm. 3 Foot Guards
Halkett, Lt.-Col. Hugh, CB. KCH. late Ger. Leg.	Medal and 1 Clasp	Albuhera, Salamanca	2 Light Infantry German Legion
Harrison, Lt.-Col. John Bacon, CB. ..2 W. I. R.	Medal and 2 Clasps	Pyrenees, Nive, Orthes	50 Foot
Harvey, General Sir Robert John, CB. ...late of 50 F.	Medal	Orthes	Assist.-Quarter-Master-Gen. Port.
Hill, Col. Sir Robert C., CB. late of R. H. Gds.	Medal	Vittoria	A Brigade of Cavalry

Name	Medal/Clasps	Battles	Notes
Hope, General *Sir* James Archibald, *KCB.* ....9 F.	Cross and 1 Clasp	Vittoria, Nivelle, Nive, Orthes, Toulouse	Assist.-Adjutant-General
Kyle, Colonel *Alexander*	Medal	Vittoria	Captain 94 Foot
Lillie, Lieut.-Col. *Sir John Scott, CB.* late of Gr. Gds.	Cross	Pyrenees, Nivelle, Orthes, Toulouse	Lieut.-Col. 7 Caçadores
M'Donald, Lieut.-Gen. *Sir John, KCB.* .....92 F.	Medal and 1 Clasp	Vittoria, Pyrenees	A Portuguese Brigade
Macdonell, Lieut.-Col. *George, CB.* ...... late of 79 F.	Medal	Chateauguay	Glengarry Light Infantry
Mansel, Lieut.-Col. *John, CB.* .... late of 53 F.	Medal and 1 Clasp	Salamanca, Toulouse	A Provisional Battalion
Michell, Lieut.-Gen. *John, CB.* .... R. Art.	Medal and 1 Clasp	Orthes, Toulouse	
Napier, General *Sir* William P. P., *KCB.* ....22 F.	Medal and 2 Clasps	Salamanca, Nivelle, Nive	Major 43 Foot
Ross, General *Sir* Hew Dalrymple, *GCB.* .R. Art.	Cross and 2 Clasps	Busaco, Badajoz, Salamanca, Vittoria, Nivelle, Nive	
Schoedde, Maj.-Gen. *Sir* James Holmes, *KCB.*..55 F.	Cross and 1 Clasp	Nivelle	
Scovell, General *Sir* Geo., *KCB.* ....4 Drs.		Vittoria, Pyrenees, Nivelle, Nive, Toulouse	Staff Corps of Cavalry
GCH.		Corunna	Military Secretary
Seaton, General John, *Lord, GCB. GCMG.*	Cross and 3 Clasps	Albuhera	66 Foot, commanding a Brigade
GCH. ....2 Life Guards		Ciudad Rodrigo,* Nivelle,* Nive, Orthes, Toulouse	52 Foot, *a Brigade
Stewart, Maj.-Gen. *William* .... late of 3 F.	Medal	Albuhera	
Stovin, General *Sir* Frederick, *KCB. KCMG.*..83 F.	Cross and 2 Clasps	Salamanca, Vittoria, Pyrenees, Nivelle, Orthes, Toulouse	} Assistant-Adjutant-General
Strafford, Field Marshal John, *Earl of, GCB.*		Vittoria, Pyrenees, Nivelle, Nive, Orthes	
GCH. .... Coldstream Guards	Cross and 1 Clasp		A Brigade
Turner, Lieut.-Gen. George, *CB.* .... R. Art.	Medal and 1 Clasp	Orthes, Toulouse	
Tweeddale, General G., *Marq. of, KT. CB.* ...30 F.	Medal	Vittoria	Assist.-Quarter-Master-General
Vernon, General Henry Chas. Edw., *CB.*	Medal	Salamanca	Staff
Ward, Col. John Richard, *CB.* .... late of 2 Dr.	Medal and 2 Clasps	Badajoz, Salamanca, Pyrenees	{ 2nd Batt. 27 F. Light Inf. 4 Div. / 1 Battalion 36 Foot
Watson, General *Sir* James, *KCB.* ....14 F.	Medal	Java	Lieut.-Col. 14 Foot
Wilkins, Lt.-Col. *Geo., CB. KH.* late of Rifle Brig.	Medal	Salamanca	A Battalion of the Rifle Brigade
Wilson, Lieut.-Col. *Geo. Davis, CB.* late of 4 F.	Medal	Badajoz	
Woodford, General *Sir* Alex. *GCB.GCMG.*40 F.	Medal and 2 Clasps	Salamanca, Vittoria, Nive	
Woodford, Major-Gen. *Sir John Geo. KCB.KCH.*	Cross	Nivelle, Nive, Orthes, Toulouse	Assist.-Quarter-Master-General
Woodgate, Col. *William, CB.* .... late of 60 F.	Medal	Fuentes d'Onor	Battalion 60 Foot

OFFICERS

NOW HOLDING RANK IN THE ARMY

OF THE

MOST NOBLE ORDER OF THE GARTER.

(According to their Stalls.)

KNIGHTS. (KG.)

Colonel *His Royal Highness the Prince of* Wales.

Field Marshal *His Royal Highness The Prince Consort,* KT. KP. GCB. GCMG. Gren. Gds.

General *His Royal Highness the Duke of* Cambridge, GCB. KP. GCMG. *Commanding-in-Chief,* Scots Fus. Guards.

Field Marshal *His Majesty the King of the Belgians,* GCB. GCH.

Colonel Charles, *Duke of* Richmond, Aide-de-Camp to the Queen, Sussex Militia.

Colonel W. F. *Duke of* Buccluech, Edinburgh Militia.

Lieut.-General Henry, *Duke of* Cleveland.

Captain Richard, *Marquis of* Hertford, h. p. 22 Drs.

Major General Arthur, *Duke of* Wellington.

OFFICERS

NOW HOLDING RANK IN THE ARMY

OF THE

MOST ANCIENT AND MOST NOBLE ORDER OF THE THISTLE.

KNIGHTS. (KT.)

Field Marshal *His Royal Highness The Prince Consort,* KG. KP. GCB. GCMG. Gren. Gds.

General George, *Marq. of* Tweeddale, CB. ..30 F.

OFFICERS

NOW HOLDING RANK IN THE ARMY

OF THE

MOST ILLUSTRIOUS ORDER OF ST. PATRICK.

KNIGHTS. (KP.)

Field Marshal *His Royal Highness The Prince Consort,* KG. KT. GCB. GCMG. Gren. Gds.

General *His Royal Highness the Duke of* Cambridge, KG. GCB. GCMG. *Commanding-in-Chief* Scots Fus. Gds.

Major General Francis N. *Marq. of* Conyngham, GCH. Unatt.

General Hugh, *Visc.* Gough, GCB. R. Horse Guards.

OFFICERS

NOW HOLDING RANK IN THE ARMY

OF THE

MOST HONOURABLE ORDER OF THE BATH.

KNIGHTS, GRAND CROSS. (GCB.)

Field Marshal *His Royal Highness The Prince Consort, KG. KT. KP. GCMG.* Grenadier Guards (*Great Master of the Order.*)
Field Marshal *His Majesty the King of the Belgians, KG.* and *GCH.*
General *His Royal Highness,* George W. F. C. *Duke of* Cambridge, *KG. KP. GCMG. Commanding-in-Chief* Scots Fusilier Guards.

₿ Blakeney, General Rt. Hon. Sir E. *GCH*...1 F.
Bloomfield, Lieut. J. A. D. *Lord* (*Civil*) h. p. Coldst. Gds.
₿ Brisbane, Gen. Sir Thomas M. Bt. *GCH.* 34 F.
₿ Brown, General *Sir* George, *KH.* ....Rif. Br.
₿ Burgoyne, General *Sir* John F. *Bart...* R.Eng.
Caldwell, General *Sir* James L... Madras Engineers
₿ Clyde, General Colin, *Lord*...........93 F.
₿ Combermere, Field Marshal S., *Visc. GCH.* 1 Life Guards.
₿ Cotton, General *Sir* Willoughby, *KCH.* ..32 F.

₿ Douglas, Gen. *Sir* H. Bt. *GCMG.* (*Civil*) 15 F.
₿ England, Lt.General *Sir* Richard, *KH.* ..50 F.
₿ ⚜ Evans, Lt.Gen. *Sir* De Lacy ......21 F.
₿ ⚜ Gardiner, Gen. *Sir* Robert W. *KCH.* R. Art.
₿ ⚜ Gomm, General *Sir* W. Maynard ..13 F.
₿ Gough, Gen. Hugh, *Visc. KP.* R. Horse Guards.
Howard de Walden,Capt.C.A.*Lord*(*Civil*)h.p.8 F.
Howden, Maj.General J. H. *Lord, KH.* (*Civil*)
₿ M'Mahon, General *Sir* Thomas, Bt. ....10 F.
Outram, Lt. Gen. *Sir* James, *Bart*...Bombay Inf.
Pollock, General *Sir* George ....Bengal Artillery
Rose, Major General *Sir* Hugh H. ......45 F.
₿ ⚜ Ross, General *Sir* Hew D... Royal Artillery
₿ ⚜ Seaton, General John *Lord, GCMG. GCH.* 2 Life Guards
₿ ⚜ Simpson, General *Sir* James.........87 F.
₿ ⚜ Smith, Lieut.General *Sir* Harry George Wakelyn, *Bart.,* Rifle Brigade
₿ ⚜ Strafford, Field Marshal John, *Earl of, GCH.* Coldstream Guards
₿ ⚜ Woodford, General *Sir* Alex. *GCMG.* 40 F.

KNIGHTS COMMANDERS. (KCB.)

Airey, Major Gen. *Sir* Richard, Qr.Mr. General.
₿ Aitchison, Lt.General *Sir* John ....72 F.
₿ Auchmuty, Lt.Gen. *Sir* Sam. B. ....7 F.
Barker, Colonel *Sir* George Robert......R. Art.
₿ Bell, Lt.Gen. *Sir* John ....4 F.
Bentinck, Major General *Sir* Henry J. W. 28 F.
₿ ⚜ Bowles, Lt.Gen. *Sir* Geo. ....1 W. I. R.
Brotherton, Lt.Gen. *Sir* Thos. Wm. ..1 Dr. Gds.
Buller, Major Gen. *Sir* George .. from Rifle Br.
Bunbury, Lt.General *Sir* Henry Edw. Bart.
Cardigan, Major Gen. James Thos., *Earl of* 5 Drs.
Cautley, Colonel *Sir* Proby Thomas (*Civil*), late of Bengal Art.
Cheape, Lt.General *Sir* John .. Bengal Engineers
₿ ⚜ Clifton, General *Sir* A. B., *KCH.* ..1 Drs.
Codrington, Lt.General *Sir* William J.¼....54 F.
Cotton, Major General *Sir* Sydney J.
Cubbon, Lt.Gen. *Sir* Mark (*Civil*) .....Mad. Inf.
Dacres, Maj.Gen. *Sir* Richard J. ...from R. Art.
Denison, Colonel *Sir* Wm. Thos. (*Civil*) R. Eng.
₿ Douglas, Major General *Sir* James............42 F.
Douglas, Colonel *Sir* John ....79 F.
₿ Downes, General Ulysses, *Lord* ....29 F.
₿ Fergusson, Lieut.General *Sir* James ....43 F.
₿ Fitz Gerald, General *Sir* John Forster....18 F.
Franks, Major General *Sir* Thomas Harte
₿ Garrett, Major General *Sir* Robert, *KH.*
Grant, Major General *Sir* James Hope
Grant, Maj.General *Sir* Patrick..Bengal Infantry
₿ Guise, General *Sir* John Wright, Bt. ....85 F.
Hall, Insp.Gen..of Hospitals, *Sir* John, *MD.* h. p.
Hearsey, Maj.General *Sir* John B. ..Bengal Cav.
₿ Hope, General *Sir* James A. ....9 F.
Houstoun, General *Sir* Rob......Bengal Cavalry
Inglis, Major General *Sir* John Eardley Wilmot
₿ ⚜ Jackson, Lt.Gen. *Sir* James, *KH.* ..6 Drs.
Jebb, Colonel *Sir* Joshua (*Civil*)..r. f. p. R. Eng.

₿ Jones, Major Gen. *Sir* Harry D. from R. Eng.
Jones, Colonel *Sir* John ....60 F.
Leighton, General *Sir* David ....Bombay Infantry
₿ ⚜ Love, Lt.Gen. *Sir* James Fred. *KH.* 57 F.
₿ Lovell, Maj.Gen. *Sir* Lovell Benj., *KH.* 12 Drs.
Lucan, Lt.Gen. Geo. Chas., *Earl of* ..8 Hussars
Lugard, Major General *Sir* Edward
₿ McDonald, Lt.General *Sir* John..........92 F.
₿ McGregor, Lt.General *Sir* Duncan (*Civil*)
₿ MacAndrew, *Insp.Gen. of Hospitals, Sir* John *MD.* h. p.
₿ Maclean, Com.Gen. *Sir* George ....h. p.
₿ Maclaine, General *Sir* Archibald ......52 F.
Mansfield, Major General *Sir* Wm. Rose
Melville, Maj.General Henry *Viscount* from 60 F.
Michel, Major General *Sir* John
₿ ⚜ Moore, Lt.General *Sir* Wm. Geo. ..60 F.
Napier, Colonel *Sir* Robert ....Bengal Eng.
₿ Napier, General *Sir* William F. P. ......22 F.
Nicolls, General *Sir* Edward late of Royal Marines
₿ Pasley, Lt.General *Sir* Chas. Wm. ....R. Eng.
Pennefather, Major General *Sir* John L. ..46 F.
Phipps, Colonel Hon.Sir*Charles Beaumont* (*Civil*)
Rawlinson, Lt.Col. *Sir* H. C. (*Civil*) Bombay Inf.
Richards, General *Sir* Wm. .....Bengal Infantry
Roberts, Major General *Sir* Henry Gee, Bombay Army
⚜ Rokeby, Major General H. *Lord*
₿ ⚜ Rowan, Lt. General *Sir* William....19 F.
Scarlett, Major General *Hon. Sir* James Yorke
₿ Schoedde, Maj.General *Sir* James H.....55 F.
Scott, General *Sir* Hopton S. ....Madras Infantry
₿ ⚜ Scovell, General *Sir* George, 4 Dragoons
Seaton, General *Sir* Thomas, late of Bengal Inf.
Sheil, Major General Sir Justin (*Civil*) Bengal Infantry

Most Honourable Order of the Bath. 550

KNIGHTS COMMANDERS—continued.

𝕶 𝔓 Sleigh, General Sir James Wallace 9 Drs.
Smith, Sir Andrew, MD. (Civil) .. late Director General Army Medical Department
𝔓 𝕶 Somerset, Lt.Gen. Sir Henry, KH. 25 F.
Steel, Maj.Gen. Sir Scudamore W. Madras Army
𝔓 Stovin, General Sir Frederick, KCMG. ..83 F.
Straubenzee, Major General Sir Chas. T. Van
Stuart, Colonel Sir Charles S. ......Bombay Inf.
Tulloch, Major Gen. Sir Alex. Murray, (Civil)
  Military Superintendent of Out-Pensioners.
Walpole, Colonel Sir Robert..........Rifle Br.
Watson, General Sir James ....14 F.
Wetherall, Lieut.Gen. Sir Geo. Aug. KH. 84 F.
Whitlock, Major General Sir Geo. C. Madras Army
Williams, Maj.Gen. Sir Wm. F. Bt. from R. Art.
𝔓 Willshire, Lt.General Sir Thomas, Bt. ..51 F.
Wilson, MajorGen. Sir Archdale, Bart. Bengal Art.
𝔓 𝕶 Woodford, Maj.General Sir J. G., KCH.
Wood, Colonel Sir David E. ....R. Art.
Wymer, Lt.General Sir Geo. Petre....Bengal Inf.
𝔓 𝕶 Wyndham, General Sir Henry 11 Hussars
𝔓 𝕶 Yorke, Lieut.Gen. Sir Charles ...33 F.

COMPANIONS. (CB.)

Abbott, Colonel Augustus ......Bengal Artillery
Abbott, Maj.General Sir Fred. late of Bengal Eng.
Abbott, Major Henry Dyett ....Madras Inf.
Ba'Court Repington, Gen. Charles Ashe, KH. 41 F.
Adams, Colonel Frank ....28 F.
Adams, Com.Gen. George ....h. p.
Adye, Lt.Colonel John Miller........Royal Art.
Ainslie, Colonel Wm. B...............Unatt.
Airey, Lt.Colonel James T. ......Coldst. Grds.
Alexander, Lt.Colonel Geo. G. ....R. Mar.
Alexander, Major General James, Bengal Artillery
Alexander, Insp. Gen. of Hosp. Thos.
Anderson, Lt.Colonel John R..........R. Art.
𝔓 Anderson, Lt.Colonel Joseph, KH...late of 50 F.
Anderson, Colonel William late of Bengal Artillery
Anstruther, Major Gen. Philip late of Madras Artillery
Apthorp, Colonel East ....Madras Infantry
𝔓 Arbuthnott, General Hon. Hugh ....38 F.
Armstrong, Colonel James Wells ....Depot Batt.
Arnott, Surgeon Fras. S. MD. ....Bombay Army
Ashburnham, Maj.Gen. Hon. Thomas from 29 F.
Backhouse, Lt.Col. Julius B.... late Bengal Art.
𝔓 Bainbrigge, Lt.General Philip ....26 F.
Balders, Colonel Chas. Wm. Morley ....12 Drs.
Balfour, Lt.Colonel George (Civil)..Madras Art.
Barchard, Major Chas. Henry .....Bengal Inf.
Barrow, Lt.Colonel Lousada ...Madras Cavalry
Baumgartner, Lt.Colonel Robert J.........27 F.
Becher, Colonel Arthur M. ....Bengal Inf.
𝔓 𝕶 Beckwith, Maj. Gen. Charles
𝔓 Bell, Major General George
𝔓 Bell, Lt.Col. Thomas............late of 48 F.
Bent, Colonel George ....R. Eng.
Bingham, Lt.Colonel Geo. Wm. P. ......60 F.
Birch, Major General R. J. H. ..Bengal Infantry
Blair, Lt.Col. Charles Devaynes ..Bengal Army
Blake, Lt.Colonel Edw. S. ....Bombay Art.
𝔓 Blake, Col. William Williams....late of 11 Dr.
Blane, Lt.Colonel Robert ....Unatt.
Blundell, Maj.General Fred. ..Madras Artillery
Blunt, Lt.Colonel Chas. Harris .....Bengal Art.
𝔓 Booth, Dep. Commissary General William, h. p.
Borton, Colonel Arthur ....Depot Batt.
Bourchier, Lt.Colonel Eustace Fane ....R. Eng.
Bourchier, Lt.Colonel George ......Bengal Art.
Bradford, Maj.General John F. ..Bengal Lt. Cav.
Brandling, Lt.Colonel John James ......R. Art.
Brasyer, Lt.Colonel Jeremiah ......Bengal Army
𝔓 𝕶 Brereton, Maj.Gen. Wm. KH. from R. Art.
Brind, Colonel James..............Bengal Art.
Brooke, Maj.General George....Bengal Artillery
𝔓 Brown, Lt.Colonel Gustavus ......late of 95 F.
Brown, Superintending Surg. John C. Bengal Army
𝔓 𝕶 Browne, Colonel Fielding
Browne, Lt.Colonel James F. M. ......R. Eng.
Browne, Colonel Thomas Gore ....late of 41 F.
Browne, Maj.General Walter John ..Bombay Inf.
Brownrigg, Colonel John Studholme......Unatt.
Bruce, Lt.Colonel Herbert ....Bombay Inf.
Brydon, Surgeon William..........Bengal Army
Bunbury, Colonel Henry Wm. ......h. p. 23 F.
𝔓 Bunbury, Lt.Col. Thomas ....late of 80 F.
Bulwer, Lt.Colonel Edward............23 F.
Burton, Colonel William..late of Bengal Cavalry
Burton, Major Adolphus W. D.......7 Dr. Gds.
Byng, Lt.Colonel John ....Madras Cavalry
Cadogan, Colonel Hon. George ....h. p.
Cameron, Major General Duncan A.
Cameron, Lt.Col. Geo. Poulett ..Madras Infantry
Campbell, Colonel George ....52 F.
Campbell, Lt.Colonel Hugh A. B. ......R. Art.
Campbell, Maj.General John....Madras Infantry
Campbell, Surgeon John, MD. ....Bengal Army
Campbell, Colonel John F. G..............91 F.
Capon, Maj.General David ....Bombay Infantry
Carleton, Lt.Colonel Henry Alex.....Bengal Art.
Carmichael, Maj.Gen. Charles M. Bengal Cavalry
Carmichael, Lt.Colonel James D. ....32 F.
Carnegy, Maj.General Alex. ....Bengal Infantry
Carruthers, Lt.Colonel Richard ....late of 2 F.
𝔓 Cator, Lt.General Wm. ..from Royal Artillery
𝔓 𝕶 Chalmers, Lt.General Sir Wm. KCH.78 F.
Chamberlain, Colonel Neville Bowles Bengal Inf.
Chapman, Colonel Fred. E............R. Eng.
Christie, Colonel Samuel T..............80 F.
Church, Lt.Col. Sir R. GCH. ..late of Gr. Lt. In.
Claremont, Colonel Edward Stopford ....Unatt.
Cloete, Major General Sir A. J. KH. ....Unatt.
Coke, Colonel John ....Bengal Infantry
Colborne, Colonel Hon. Francis ....Unatt.
Cole, Colonel Arthur Lowry.............17 F.
Colebrooke, Lt.Gen. Sir Wm. M. G. KH. (Civil) Royal Artillery
Colvin, Colonel John........late of Bengal Army
Congreve, Colonel Geo.......... h. p. 29 F.
Conway, Colonel Thomas S. ....Gr. Gds.
Corbett, Major General Stuart ..Bengal Infantry
𝔓 Couper, Colonel Sir Geo. Bart. KH.
Cox, Lt.Colonel John Wm.............13 F.
Craigie, Maj.General P. Edmonstone ......31 F.
Crawford, Colonel Wm. Thomas ....R. Art.
Crommelin, Major Wm. Arden ....Bengal Eng.
Cuninghame, Colonel Arthur A. T. h. p.
Curtis, Colonel J. G. W. ..late of Bengal Infantry
Curzon, Colonel Hon. Rich. Wm. P.....Gr. Gds..
Custance, Lt.Colonel Wm. Neville....6 Dr. Gds.
D'Aguilar, Colonel Charles L. ....R. Art.

D D 2

Most Honourable Order of the Bath.

COMPANIONS—continued.

Daly, Lt.Colonel Henry ....Bombay Inf.
Dalzell, Lt.Colonel Hon. Robert A. G.
Daubeney, Colonel Henry C. Barnston..h. p. 71 F
Daubeny, Lt.Colonel James ....62 F.
Dawson, Colonel Robert K. (Civil) r. f. p. R. Eng.
Deacon, Lt.Colonel Charles Clement ......61 F.
Delamain, Colonel Cha. Hen. late of Bombay Cav.
De la Motte, Lt.General Peter .. Bombay Cavalry
Dennis, Colonel Maurice G............60 F.
De Rottenburg, Colonel George (Civil) ..100 F.
Dickson, Colonel Collingwood..........R. Art.
Digby, Major George S. ....R. Mar.
Dixon, Colonel George ....Depot. Batt.
Doherty, Colonel Henry Edward .....h. p. 9 F.
Douglas, Colonel John ....h. p.
𝔓 Douglas, General Robert... late of R. Artillery
Douglas-Monteath, Lt.General Tho. ..Bengal Inf.
Drake, Com. Gen. Wm. Henry
Drought, Lt.Colonel Richard ....Bengal Inf.
Drysdale, Lieut.Colonel William ....9 Drs.
Dumbreck, Insp. Gen. of Hosp. David, MD.
Dunlop, Colonel Franklin.............R. Art.
𝔓 Dunmore, Thomas ..Commissary-General h. p.
Dunsford, Lt.Colonel Henry Fred.....Bengal Inf.
Dupuis, Major General John Edw...from R. Art.
Durand, Colonel Henry Marion ....Bengal Eng.
𝔓 𝕸𝕸 Dyneley, Lt.General Tho..... R. Artillery
Eckford, Major-General James ..Bengal Infantry
Eden, Maj.General John
Edwardes, Lt.Colonel Herbert Benj. ..Bengal Inf.
Edwards, Colonel Clement Alex..........18 F.
Ellice, Colonel Charles Henry ....24 F.
𝔓 Ellicombe, Lt.General C. G., from R. Eng.
Elliot, Surgeon Major Richard Coffin ....R. Art.
Ellis, Lt.General Samuel Burdon ....R. Marines
English, Lt.Colonel Frederick ....53 F.
Evans, General Thomas ....81 F.
Evelegh, Colonel Fred. Chas. ....20 F.
Ewart, Colonel John Alex. ....78 F.
Eyre, Colonel Vincent ....Bengal Art.
Fair, General Alex. ....Madras Infantry
Farquhar, Colonel Robert ....Bombay Inf.
Farren, Colonel Richard T. ....Depot Batt.
Fenwick, Colonel William ....10 F.
Ferryman, Colonel Aug. H..............89 F.
𝔓 Filder, Commissary General William ....h. p.
𝔓 Finch, Lt.General Hon. John ....24 F.
Fisher, Lt.Colonel George .....Bombay Infantry
Fitzmayer, Colonel James Wm. ....R. Art.
𝔓 Fleming, Lt.General Edw. ....27 F.
Foley, Colonel Hon. St. Geo. Gerald ......Unatt.
Forbes, Lt.Colonel John ....Bombay Cavalry
Fordyce, Lieut.Colonel Chas. Fra........Unatt.
Forrest, Insp.Gen. of Hosp. John, MD.
Forster, Lt.Colonel Henry ....Bombay Artillery
Francklyn, Colonel John Henry ....R. Art.
Franklin, Major Chas. Trigance ....R. Art.
𝔓 Franklin, Insp.Gen. of Hospitals Henry ..h. p.
Franklyn, Colonel Charles ....84 F.
Fraser, Lt.Colonel James late of Bengal Cavalry.
Fraser, Dep.Insp.Gen. John, MD.
Frederick, Lt.General Edward ..Bombay Infantry
Freese, Colonel John Noble A...........R. Art.
𝔓 French, James, MD, h. p. Insp.Gen. of Hospitals
𝔓 𝕸𝕸 Fuller, Lt.Colonel Francis....late of 59 F.
Fyers, Lt.Colonel Wm. Aug...........Rifle Br.
Gairdner, Maj.General Wm. John, Bengal Infantry
Gaitskell, Lt.Colonel Fred. ....Bengal Art.
Gall, Lt.Colonel Richard Herbert .....14 Drs.
Galwey, Lt.Colonel Michael ....Madras Inf.
Gambier, Colonel Gloucester............R. Art.
Geddes, Colonel William ......Bengal Artillery

George, Colonel Frederick Darley ....Unatt.
Gibbon, Major James Robert ....R. Art.
Gibson, Insp.Gen. of Hospitals J. B., MD.
Glyn, Lt.Colonel Julius Richard ......Rifle Br.
Godby, Maj.General Christopher Bengal Infantry
𝔓 Goldie, Lt.General Geo. Leigh ....77 F.
Goodenough, Colonel Arthur Cyril....Depot Batt.
Goodwyn, Colonel Julius Edm. ....41 F.
Gordon, Col. Hon. Alex., Dep.Qr.Mas.Gen.Unatt.
Gordon, Dep. Insp. Gen. of Hosp. Arch. MD.
Gordon, Surgeon, Charles Alex., MD....10 F.
Gordon, Lt.Colonel Chas. Henry .....Depot Batt.
Gordon, Henry Wm. (Civil) Military Storekeeper
Gordon, Colonel John Wm............R. Eng.
𝔓 𝕸𝕸 Gore, Lt.General Hon. Charles, KH. 91 F.
Gough, Major General J. Bloomfield
Gowan, Maj.General Geo. Edw. Bengal Artillery
Graham, Major General Fortescue ....R. Marines
Graham, Colonel Henry Hope ....59 F.
Grant, Major General Charles ......Bengal Art.
Grant, Colonel John T................49 F.
𝕸𝕸 Grant, Insp. Gen. Sir J. R. MD, KH. h. p.
Grattan, Colonel John ....h. p. 18 F.
Groathed, Colonel Edw. Harris ....Unatt.
Green, Colonel Edward.... .. Bombay Infantry
Green, Lt.Colonel Geo. W. Guy.....Bengal Inf.
Green, Major Wm. H. R. (Civil) ..Bombay Inf.
Greenwood, Lt.Colonel Wm... late of R. Artillery
Griffith, Colonel Henry D. ....2 Dragoons
Gunning, John......h. p. Insp.-Gen. of Hospitals
Guy, Colonel Philip M. N. ....5 F.
Hagart, Colonel Charles ....Unatt.
Hagart, Lt.Colonel James M'Caul late of 7 Drs.
Hale, Colonel Edward B..............82 F.
𝔓 𝕸𝕸 Halkett, Lt.Col. Hugh, KCH. late of Ger.
Legion
Halkett, Lt.Colonel John Craigie..Bengal Infantry
Hall, Lt.General Henry ....Bengal Infantry
Haly, Colonel Wm. O'Grady ....38 F.
Hamilton, Maj.General Charles .. Bengal Artillery
Hamilton, Colonel Sir Chas. John J., Bart., late
of Scots Fusilier Guards
Hamilton, Colonel Fred. Wm. ......Gr. Guards
Hamilton, Lt.Colonel Henry ....78 F.
Hamilton, Colonel Walter .....Insp. F. Officer
𝔓 Harding, Lt.Gen. Geo. Judd ......Royal Eng.
Harding, Colonel Fra. Pym ....22 F.
Hardinge, Lt.Colonel Hon. Arthur E. Coldst. Gds.
Harness, Colonel Henry Drury ....R. Eng.
Harrington, Colonel Leicester, Earl of ....Unatt.
𝔓 Harrison, Lt.Colonel John Bacon ..late of 50 F.
𝔓 Harvey, General Sir Robert John ..2 W. I. R.
Hawkins, Maj. Gen. Francis Spencer, Bengal Inf.
Hay, Colonel Alex. S. Leith ....93 F.
Henderson, Lt.Colonel Robert Madras Engineers
Herbert, Colonel Charles ....54 F.
Herbert, Lt.General Charles ....Madras Infantry
Herbert, Colonel Hon. Percy E. ....82 F.
Hervey, Maj.General Andrew....Bengal Infantry
Heyland, Colonel Alfred Thos............56 F.
Hicks, Maj.-General George ....Bengal Infantry
Hicks, Colonel Thos. Wm...late of Bombay Art.
Hill, Colonel Percy ....Rifle Br.
𝔓 𝕸𝕸 Hill, Col. Sir Robert C. late of R. Horse Gds.
Hinde, Lt.Colonel John ....8 F.
Hocker, Lt.Colonel Edward ....R. Mar.
Hodge, Colonel Edw. C. ....Unatt.
𝔓 𝕸𝕸 Hodges, Capt. Geo. Lloyd (Civil) h. p.
Hoggan, Maj.General John.....Bengal Infantry
Hogge, Colonel Charles ....Bengal Art.
Holdich, Colonel Edw. Alan ....20 F.
Holloway, Colonel Thomas ....R. Mar.
Honner, Colonel Robert Wm. .....Bombay Inf.
Hope, Lt.Colonel William ....71 F.

Most Honourable Order of the Bath. 552

COMPANIONS—continued.

Hopkins, Colonel Wm. Friend ....R. Mar.
Hopkinson, Maj.Gen. *Sir* Chas. late of Mad. Army
Horn, Colonel Fred. ....h. p. 20 F.
Horsford, Colonel Alfred H. ....Rifle Br.
Huste, Major Dixon Edw...............R. Art.
Huish, Maj.General Geo. ....Bengal Infantry
Hume, Lt.Colonel Henry.............Gr. Gds.
Hungerford, Lt.Colonel T. J. W.....Bengal Art.
Hurdle, Major General Thomas ..r. f. p. R. Mar.
Huthwaite, Maj.General Edward Bengal Artillery
Hutt, Maj.Gen. George..late of Bombay Artillery
Ingall, Lt.Col. Wm. Lennox 62 F.
Inglis, Surgeon James Gordon, *MD*. ......64 F.
Innes, Dep. Insp.Gen. Fra. Wm. *MD*.
Innes, Dep. Insp.-Gen. John Harrie Ker.
Irving, Colonel Alex. ....R. Art.
Jackson, Colonel John ..late of Bombay Infantry
Jacob, Colonel Geo. Le Grand ......Bombay Inf.
Jee, Surgeon Joseph ....78 F.
Jeffreys, Colonel Edm. R. ....Depôt Batt.
Jenyns, Major Soame Gambier..........18 Drs.
Johnson, Lt.Colonel Edwin Beaumont Bengal Art.
Johnstone, Lieut.Colonel John D. ....33 F.
Jones, Colonel Henry R..............6 Dr. Gds.
Jones, Colonel Wm. ....61 F.
Kelly, Colonel Richard Denis ....34 F.
Kelly, Lt.Colonel Thomas C. ....47 F.
Kemball, Major Arnold B........Bombay Art.
P Kenah, Lt.General Thomas ....63 F.
P ᚎᚑ Kennedy, Maj.Gen. Alex. K. Clark, *KH*. 6 Dr. Gds.
P ᚎᚑ Kennedy, Lt.General Jas. Shaw ....47 F.
Kennedy, Colonel John Clark ....h. p. 18 F.
Kerr, Colonel *Lord* Mark..................13 F.
Kingscote, Lieut.Colonel *Robert N. F*....late of Scots Fusil. Guards
Lake, Colonel Noel Thomas ....R. Art.
Lake, Colonel Henry Atwell ....Unatt.
Lane, Maj.General C. R. W. ....Bengal Infantry
Lane, Maj.Gen. John Theophilus Bengal Artillery
Larcom, Maj.Gen. Thos. A. *(Civil)* r. f. p. R. Eng.
P ᚎᚑ Latour, Lt.General P. A. *KH*. ....3 Drs.
Lawrence, Colonel Arthur J. .....h. p. Rifle Br.
Le Mesurier, Lt.Colonel Wm. Geo. ......R. Art.
Lemon, Colonel Thomas ....R. Mar.
Leslie, Colonel John Thomas late Bombay Artillery
Liddell, Colonel John ....Bombay Inf.
Lightbody, Major John G. ....Bombay Art.
Lightfoot, Lt.Colonel Thomas ....84 F.
P Lillie, Lt.Colonel *Sir John Scott* late of Gr. Gds.
Lindsay, General Alex. ....Bengal Artillery
Linton, Insp.Gen. of Hosp. Wm. *MD*.
Little, Colonel Archibald ....9 Drs.
Lloyd, Colonel John ....late of Bombay Artillery
Lloyd, Maj.General Geo. Wm. A. Bengal Infantry
P ᚎᚑ Llewellyn, Lt.General Richard ......39 F.
Lockhart, Colonel Archer Inglis ....92 F.
Lockwood, Major General Geo. Henry
P Lockyer, Major General Henry Fred. *KH*.
Longden, Colonel Henry E. ....10 F.
Longfield, Colonel John ....8 F.
Lovell, Major John W. ....R. Eng.
Low, Lt.General John ......Madras Infantry
Lowe, Lt.Colonel Edward W. D. ....21 F.
Lowth, Colonel Robert Henry............86 F.
Luard, Maj.Gen. John Kynaston, Madras Infantry
Lumsden, Major Harry B. *(Civil)* ..Bengal Inf.
Lumsden, Colonel Thomas....late of Bengal Army
Lushington, Lt.Col. *Franklin*, late of Sco. Fus.Gds.
P ᚎᚑ Lygon, General *Hon*. E. P. ......13 Drs.
Lys, Lt.Colonel *Geo. Mowbray* ....late of 20 F.
Lysons, Colonel Daniel ....Unatt.

M'Causland, Colonel John K........Bengal Inf.
M'*Dowell*, Lt.Colonel G. J. M......late of 16 Drs.
M'Gregor, Maj.Gen. Geo. Hall late of Bengal Art.
M'Intyre, Lt.Colonel Colin C. ....78 F.
M'Mahon, Colonel Thos. W. ....5 Dr. Gds.
M'Murdo, Colonel Wm. M. S. ......Mil. Train
P M'Pherson, Major General Philip
Maberly, Lt.Colonel Evan ....R. Art.
P Macarthur, Major General Edward *(Civil)*
Macbeath, Colonel *George* ..late of Depot Batt.
Macdonald, Lieut.Colonel *Hon*. James ....Unatt.
P ᚎᚑ *Macdonald*, Lt.Colonel *Robert* late of 35 F.
Macdonell, Colonel Alex. ....Rifle Br.
Macdonell, Lt.Colonel *George* .....late of 79 F.
Macintire, Major Andrew Wm. ....Madras Art.
Mackenzie, Surgeon Wm., *MD*. ..Madras Army
Mackinnon, Maj.General Geo. Henry ....Unatt.
Mackinnon, Major Wm. Alex. .....Bengal Art.
Macpherson, Lt.Col. James Duncan ..Bengal Inf.
Malcolm, Lt.Colonel George ......Bombay Inf.
Malcolm, Major General Geo. Alex.
Mansel, Lt.Colonel *John* ....late of 53 F
Master, Lt.Colonel Robert Aug...Bengal Cavalry
Master, Lt.Colonel Wm. Chester ....5 F.
VC Maude, Lt.Colonel Fred. Fra. ....3 F.
Maude, Lieut.Colonel George Ashley ....R. Art.
Mauleverer, Colonel James Thos. ....30 F.
Maxwell, Colonel Alex................46 F.
Maxwell, Colonel Geo. V. ....88 F.
P Michell, Lieut.-Gen. John ....Royal Artillery
Middleton, Lt.Colonel Wm. Alex. .....R. Art.
P ᚎᚑ *Miller*, Lt.Colonel *F. Sanderson*..late of 6 Dr.
Moir, Major George ....Bengal Art.
Mollan, Lt.Colonel Wm. C. ....75 F.
Montgomerie, Maj.Gen. Patrick ..Madras Artillery
Montgomery, Colonel Alex. B. ....1 F.
Moore, Lt.Colonel Henry.........Bengal Infantry
Moore, Lt.Colonel R. Cornwallis Madras Artillery
Morgan, Lt.General John ......Madras Infantry
Morris, Lt.Colonel Charles Henry ..h. p. R. Art.
Morris, Maj.General Edmund Finucane 97 F.
Mouat, Dep.Insp.Gen. of Hosp. James
Mundy, Lieut.Colonel Geo. V..........19 F.
Munro, Colonel William ....39 F.
P ᚎᚑ Murray, General *Hon*. Henry ....14 Drs.
Napier, Colonel George T. C...........Unatt.
P Napier, Lt.General Thomas Erskine ....71 F.
Nash, Maj.General Joseph .....Bengal Infantry
Nicholson, Lt.Colonel Lothian........R. Eng.
Norman, Lt.Colonel Henry Wylie ....Bengal Art.
Norcott, Colonel Wm. S. R. ....Depot Batt.
O'Connor, Colonel L. S. ....1 W. I. Regt.
Ogilvie, Surgeon Geo. M. *MD*. ..Bombay Army
VC Olpherts, Lt.Colonel William ..Bengal Art.
Orr, Surgeon John Henry ....Madras Army
Orr, Lt.Colonel Wm. Adam.........Madras Art.
Ouvry, Lt.Colonel Henry Aime......h. p. 9 Drs.
Owen, Lt.Colonel Conrad John ....Bombay Cav.
Owen, Lieut.Colonel Henry Chas. C.....R. Eng.
Pack, Colonel Arthur J. Reynell- ....h. p. 7 F.
Paget, Colonel *Lord* Geo. A. F..........Unatt.
Pakenham, Colonel *Hon*. Wm. L........Unatt.
Palmer, Lt.Colonel Francis R...........60 F.
Parke, Colonel William ....72 F.
Parlby, General B. Brydges ....Madras Infantry
Parsons, Maj.General James ....Bengal Infantry
Pattle, Lt.General William ......Bengal Cavalry
P Paty, Lt.General Geo. Wm. *KH*. ......70 F.
Paulet, Colonel *Lord* Fred. ....Coldst. Gds.
Paulet, Maj.General *Lord* William
Payn, Lt.Colonel William ....53 F.
Paynter, Colonel David. Wm. ....R. Art.
Pears, Lt.Col. Tho. Townsend..Madras Engineers
Perceval, Colonel John Maxwell ....12 F.

Most Honourable Order of the Bath.

COMPANIONS—*continued.*

Petrie, Samuel (Civil) ......h.p. D.A.Com.Gen.
Poole, Colonel John ....late of 22 F.
P Power, General W. G. *KH*....Royal Artillery
Power, Deputy Commissary Gen. Wm. J. T.
Pratt, Lt.Colonel Robert ....23 F.
Pratt, Major General Thos. Simson
Price, Lt.Colonel Edward ....R. Art.
VC Probyn, Major Dighton M. ....Bengal Cav.
Purnell, Colonel William P...............90 F.
Purton, Lt.Colonel John ....late of Madras Army
Raines, Colonel Julius Aug. R. ....95 F.
P Rainey, Lt.General Henry, *KH*.........23 F.
KH Reed, Maj.General Thomas ....44 F.
Reid, Colonel Fra. Archibald ....Madras Infantry
Reid, Colonel Charles.................Bengal Inf.
Reignolds, Maj.General Tho. Scott.. r. f. p. 18 F.
Reilly, Major Wm. E. M..................R. Art.
Remmington, Lt.Colonel Fred. F.....Bengal Art.
Renny, Surg.-General Charles ...Bengal Army
Reynardson, Colonel *Edw. Birch* late of Gr. Gds.
Richardson, Major Joseph Fletcher ..Bengal Inf.
Richmond, Maj.Gen. Arch. F. ..Bengal Infantry
Riddell, Col. Chas. James ....R. Art.
Ridley, Major Gen. Chas. Wm.
Robe, Colonel Fred. Holt (*Civil*)....h. p. Unatt.
Roberts, Lt.General Abraham...Bengal Infantry
Robertson, Colonel Geo. Henry ....Bombay Inf.
Robertson, Lt.Colonel James Peter Military Train
Robertson, Major Gen. Robert Richardson
KH *Rooke,* Maj.General *Sir Henry W. KCH.*
Rowan, Colonel Henry S. ....R. Art.
Rowcroft, Colonel Francis..........Bengal Inf.
Russell, Colonel David........Insp. F. Officer
Russell, Lt.Colonel *Sir* Wm., *Bart.*......7 Drs.
St. George, Colonel John ....R. Artillery
Salter, Maj.General Henry Fisher ....Ben. Cav.
Sanders, Colonel Robert ....h. p. 19 F.
Saxe-Weimar, Col. *H. S. H. Prince of* Gr. Gds.
Scott, Dep.Insp.Gen. Charles, *MD.*
Scott, Major General John ....3 Dr. Gds.
Scudamore, Lt.Colonel Arthur ......14 Drs.
P Sewell, Lt.General Wm. Henry ....79 F.
Seymour, Colonel Francis ....Scots Fus. Gds.
Seymour, Lt.Colonel William Henry ..2 Dr. Gds.
Shirley, Colonel Horatio ....h. p. 88 F.
Showers, Colonel St. Geo. D........Bengal Inf.
P Simmons, Lt.Colonel *Joseph* .....late of 41 F.
Simmons, Colonel John L. A. ......R. Engineers
Simpson, Lt.Colonel John..............34 F.
Simpson, Major Wm. Henry late Madras Infantry
Smith, Colonel James W. ....Unatt.
Smith, Colonel John W. S. ....Depot Batt.
Smith, Dep. Com. Gen. John Wm.
Smith, Colonel Michael Wm. ......3 Dr. Gds.
Smith, Colonel Richard Baird ......Bengal Eng.
Smith, Colonel Robert ......late of Bengal Army
Smith, Lt.Colonel Thomas ....90 F.
Smyth, Colonel Henry ....76 F.
Smyth, Colonel John Rowland ..Insp. F. Officer
Somerset, Colonel Edward Arthur ....Unatt.
Somerset, Lt.Colonel Poulett G. H. ....7 F.
Sotheby, Lt.Colonel Fred. S., late of Bengal Army
Sparks, Colonel James P..................38 F.
Spence, Lt.Colonel *James* ....late of 31 F.
Spencer, Colonel *Hon.* Aug. A. ......h. p. 44 F.
Stack, Maj.General Maurice ....Bombay Cavalry
Stanton, Lt.Colonel Edward ....R. Eng.
Staveley, Colonel Chas. Wm. D.........44 F.
Steele, Lt.Colonel Edward ....83 F.
Steele, Colonel Thos. M. ....Coldst. Gds.
Stephenson, Colonel F. C. A. ......S. Fus. Gds.
Stepney, Colonel Arthur St. Geo. H...Colds. Gds
Sterling, Colonel Anthony C............Unatt.
Steuart, Colonel Charles ....14 Drs
Stevens, Lt.Colonel S. James..late of Bombay Inf.
Stisted, Colonel Henry Wm...............93 F.
Story, Maj.General Philip Francis Bengal Cavalry
Strange, Lt.Colonel Henry Fra.......R. Artillery
Street, Colonel John Alfred ....Depot Batt.
Stuart, Colonel John Ramsay ....21 F.
Sullivan, Colonel William .....Insp. F. Officer
Sutherland, Lt.General Wm. ....53 F.
Tapp, Colonel Thomas ....Bombay Inf.
Taylor, Lt.Colonel Alexander ......Bengal Eng.
Taylor, General Henry Geo. A. ..Madras Infantry
Taylor, Colonel Richard C. H. ....79 F.
Taylor, Insp. Gen. of Hosp. John Robert
Taylor, Major Robert Lewis (*Civil*) Bombay Inf.
VC Teesdale, Major Christopher Charles R. Art.
P Thackeray, General Fred. Rennell ....R. Eng.
Thelwall, Major John B................24 F.
Thompson, Col. John Armstrong, Bengal Infantry
Thomson, Lt.Colonel George late of Bengal Army
Thomson, Lt.Colonel Wm. B.........Bengal Inf.
Tice, Dep. Insp. Gen. John C., *MD.*
Timbrell, Lt.Colonel Thos. ..late of Bengal Army
VC Tombs, Colonel Henry ....Bengal Art.
Trevelyan, Lt.Colonel Henry W. ..Bombay Art.
Trollope, Colonel Charles ....h. p. 62 F.
Troubridge, Colonel *Sir* Thos. St. V. H. C. *Bt.*, h.p.
Tucker, Lt.Colonel Auchmuty ....Bengal Cavalry
Tucker, Maj.General H. T. late of Bengal Infantry
Tulloch, Maj.General Alex. ....Madras Infantry
Tulloch, Lt.General John........Bengal Infantry
Turner, Colonel Frank ....Bengal Art.
P Turner, Lieut.General George ..Royal Artillery
Turner, Lt.Colonel John ....R. Art.
Turner, Colonel Wm. West ....97 F.
P Tweeddale, General Geo. *Marq. of, KT.*..30 F.
Tytler, Colonel James M. B. F......Bengal Inf.
Upton, Major General *Hon.* Geo. Fred.
Van Cortlandt, Colonel Henry Chas.
P Vernon, General Henry C. E.
Waddy, Colonel Richard ....50 Foot
Wade, Colonel *Sir* C. Martine, late Bengal Infantry
Wade, Colonel Hamlet Coote....h. p. 1 Dr. Gds.
Walker, Colonel E. W. F. ......Scots F. Gds.
Walsh, Lt.Colonel Arthur S. S. ......R. Mar.
Walter, Lt.Colonel John McNeill ....35 F.
P Ward, Colonel *John Richard* ....late of 2 Drs.
Warde, Colonel Edward Charles ....R. Artillery
Warre, Colonel Henry J................57 F.
Warren, Major General Charles
Waters, Lt.Colonel Edmund Fred. Bengal Infantry
Welchman, Colonel John ....Bengal Inf.
Wells, Lt.Colonel Samuel...............23 F.
Wemyss, Lt.Colonel John M........R. Mar.
P Wemyss, Lt.General Thomas James ....17 F.
West, Colonel C. R. S. *Lord* ....h. p.
Westmorland, Lt.Col. F. W. H. *Earl of* Colds. Gds.
Wetherall, Colonel Edw. Robert.......Unatt.
P Whinyates, Lt.General Edw. C. *KH.* ..R. Art.
White, Maj.General Michael ....7 Dr. Gds.
White, Colonel Henry D. ....Unatt.
Whittingham, Colonel Ferdinand ....4 F.
Wilbraham, Colonel Richard ....Unatt.
Wilde, Lt.Colonel Alfred Thomas....Madras Inf.
P KH Wilkins, Lt.Colonel *George, KH.* late of
Rifle Brigade
Wilkinson, Maj.General Christ. Dixon Bengal Inf.
Wilkinson, Major *A. P. S.* ....late of 13 F.
Williams, Colonel Thomas............4 F.
Willis, Lt.Colonel Fred. Arthur ....84 F.
Willoughby, Colonel M. Franklin Bombay Artillery
P Wilson, Colonel *Sir* John M. *KH*......Unatt.

Wilson, Lt.Colonel Geo. Davis ....late of 4 F.
Wilson, Major Thomas F. ....Bengal Inf.
Wilton, Lt.Colonel John L. ....Unatt.
Windham, Maj.General Charles Ash
Wodehouse, Colonel Edwin ....R. Art.
Wood, Colonel John Stewart ....Unatt.
Wood, Colonel Robert Blucher ......h. p. 97 F.
Wood, General William, KH. ..3 West I. Regt.
Woodburn, Maj.General Alexander ..Bombay Inf.
Woodgate, Colonel William .....late of 60 F.
Woollcombe, Major John D........Bombay Art.
Wright, Maj.General Thomas
Wylde, Maj.General William from Royal Artillery
Wyllie, Maj.General William ..Bombay Infantry
Wynyard, Lt.General Edward ....58 F.
Wynyard, Major General Robert Henry
Yarborough, Colonel Charles Cooke ..h. p. 91 F.
Yorke, Colonel John ....Unatt.
Young, Lt.Colonel Cha. Wallace Madras Infantry
Young, Lt.Colonel Keith ....Bengal Inf.
Young, Commissary Wm. L. M.......Field Train

OFFICERS OF THE ORDER OF THE BATH.

Dean—Richard Chevenix Trench, *D.D.*
Bath King of Arms— Algernon F. Greville,[1] Esq.
Registrar and Secretary—Albert Wm. Woods, Esq., *Lancaster Herald, Heralds College.*
Gentleman Usher—*Hon.* Fredirick H. A. Chichester.

[1] Mr. Greville served the campaign of 1815 with the Grenadier Guards, and was present at the battles of Quatro Bras and Waterloo, as also at the attack and capture of Peronne; shortly after which he was appointed Aide-de-Camp to Sir John Lambert, with whom he served in the Army of Occupation in France until appointed Aide-de-Camp to the Duke of Wellington, on whose staff he served until the army came home in 1818. He was again nominated Aide-de-Camp to his Grace when the Duke was appointed Master-General of the Ordnance; was his Grace's private Secretary when Commander-in-Chief the first time, also when he was First Lord of the Treasury; when he was Secretary of State for Foreign Affairs, and when he was Commander-in-Chief the second time, in which capacity he served up to the day of the Duke's death.

OFFICERS
NOW HOLDING RANK IN THE ARMY OF THE MOST DISTINGUISHED ORDER OF
SAINT MICHAEL AND SAINT GEORGE.

GRAND MASTER AND FIRST AND PRINCIPAL KNIGHT GRAND CROSS,
General *His Royal Highness* the Duke of Cambridge, *KG. GCB. KP. Commanding-in-Chief*, Scots Fusilier Guards.

KNIGHTS, GRAND CROSS. (GCMG.)

Field Marshal *His Royal Highness The Prince Consort*, *KG. KT. KP. GCB.* Grenadier Guards
🅟 🎖 Gen. *Lord* Seaton, *GCB, GCH.* 2 Life Gds.
🅟 🎖 General *Sir* Alex. Woodford, *GCB*...40 F.
🅟 General *Sir* Howard Douglas, *Bt, GCB*...15 F.

KNIGHTS COMMANDERS. (KCMG.)

🅟 General *Sir* Frederick Stovin, *KCB*. ....83 F.
🅟 Lt.Col. *Sir* Joseph Rudsdell, late of Gr. Gds.

COMPANIONS. (CMG.)

Lt.Colonel *Marq.* Guiseppe de Piro,
        late of R. Malta Fencible Regt.
Dep. Com. Gen. James Woodhouse, h. p.

OFFICERS OF THE ORDER.
King of Arms ....*Sir* Charles Douglas, *CMG*.
Chancery of the Order..The Colonial Department, Downing-street.

FOREIGN ORDERS.

The Foreign Orders mentioned in the War Services belong to the following Countries, and the Dates are those of the Institution of the respective Orders:—

Affghanistan—Dooranée Empire (3 Classes) 1839.
Austria—Maria Theresa (3 Classes) 18 June, 1757.
  Leopold (3 Classes) 14 July, 1806.
Bavaria—Maximilian Joseph (3Classes) 1Jan. 1806.
Belgium—Leopold (3 Classes) 11 July, 1832.
France—Military Merit (3 Classes) Mar. 1759.
  Legion of Honour (5 Classes) 13 May, 1802.
Greece—Saviour (5 Classes) 1 June, 1833.
Hanover—Guelphs (3 Classes) 18 June, 1815.
Naples—St. Januarius (1 Class) July, 1738.
  St. Ferdinand and Merit, (3 Classes) 1 April, 1800.
  St. George and Reunion (3 Classes) 1 Jan. 1819.
Netherlands—Wilhelm (4 Classes) 30 April, 1815.
Persia—Lion and Sun (3 Classes) 1801.
Portugal—Tower and Sword (3 Clas.) 17 Apr. 1748.
  St. Bento d'Avis (2 Classes) 1789.
  Conception (3 Classes) 6 Feb. 1818.
Prussia—Black Eagle—18 Jan. 1701.

Prussia—Military Merit—1740.
  Red Eagle (3 Classes) 12 June, 1792.
Russia—St. Andrew—30 Nov. 1698.
  St. Alexander Newski—1722.
  St. Ann (2 Classes) 3 Feb. 1735.
  St. George (4 Classes) 26 Nov. 1769.
  St. Wladimir (5 Classes) 4 Oct. 1782.
Sardinia—St. Maurice and St. Lazarus (2 Clas.) 13 Nov. 1572.
  Military Order of Savoy.
Saxony—St. Henry (3 Classes) 7 Oct. 1736.
  Ernestine (4 Classes) 25 Dec. 1833.
Spain—Charles the Third (3 Clas.) 19 Sept. 1771.
  San Fernando (5 Classes) 31 Aug. 1811.
  St. Hermenigilde (2 Classes) 10 July, 1815.
  St. Isabella the Catholic (3 Classes) 1815.
Sweden—Sword (3 Classes) 17 April, 1748.
Turkey—Crescent (2 Classes) 6 July, 1804.
  Medjidie (5 Classes).
Tuscany—St. Joseph (3 Classes) 1807.
Wirtemburg—Military Merit (3 Classes) 1758

CASUALTIES SINCE THE LAST PUBLICATION.

RETIREMENTS BY SALE OF COMMISSIONS.

Colonels.

J. B. Riddlesden, 27 F.
E. W. W. Passy, 11 Drs.
H. Skipwith, 15 Drs.
C. R. Raitt, Unatt.
W. Cockell, 16 F.
G. W. Fordyce-Buchan, R. Horse Gds.
C. E. Doherty, 13 Drs.
J. D. Dyson, 3 Dr. Gds.
J. A. Robertson, 4 Dr. Gds.
F. C. Evelegh, 20 F.
T. Tulloch, 1 Dr. Gds.
J. M. Wood, 5 F.
T. R. P. Tempest, 23 F.

Lieutenant Colonels.

P. L. C. Paget, S. F. Gds.
Lord A. Vane Tempest, do.
F. W. Newdigate, Coldst. Gds.
Hon. J. L. Browne, Depot Batt.
J. M. Hogg, 1 Life Gds.
C. Holder, Scots Fus. Gds.
J. D. Astley, do.
Wm. Wheatley, do.
Hon. J. E. Fraser, do.
R. J. Loyd-Lindsay, do.
H. Blount, 68 F.
E. J. V. Brown, 60 F.
A. H. Russell, 58 F.
E. Hickey, 69 F.
J. Ward, Unatt.
Hon. A. F. Egerton, Gr. Gds.
J. R. H. Rose, 17 Drs.
T. P. Touzel, Unatt.
J. S. Naylor, 8 Drs.
T. H. Somerville, 3 F.
T. Lillie, Ceylon Rifles.
D. Stewart, Unatt.
A. Watson, Unatt.
F. J. Phillott, Unatt.
B. Blennerhasset, 71 F.
J. A. Digby, Gr. Gds.
J. Miller, 11 Hussars.
C. A. Baines, 16 F.
G. Black, 75 F.
R. Ficklin, 47 F.
J. Molloy, 9 F.
W. H. Sampson, Rifle Br.
J. C. Webster, 18 F.
C. R. Butler, 20 F.
R. A. Scott, 60 F.

Majors.

W. Codd, Unatt.
E. C. Giffard, do.
C. Murray, do.
D. G. A. Darroch, do.
W. Inglis, 5 Dr. Gds.
G. C. Miller, 77 F.
C. Sykes, 80 F.
A. J. B. Thellusson, Coldst. Gds.
R. Inglis, 7 F.
F. Yard, 17 F.
J. A. Bayley, 52 F.
Sir D. Baird, Bt. 98 F.
G. Paynter, 1 Dr. Gds.
J. Duff, 23 F.

W. Barnston, 55 F.
R. Bethune, 92 F.
C. F. G. Studdert, 80 F.
G. A. Currie, 75 F.
J. Massy, 2 Life Gds.
Sir H. S. Mildmay, Bt. 26 F.
G. Campsie, Ceylon Rifles.

Captains.

W. de Winton, 1 Life Gds.
A. S. Lumley, 2 Life Gds.
Hon. C. S. B. Hanbury, do.
Sir B. P. Henniker, Bt. R. Horse Gds.
J. C. Still, 3 Dr. Gds.
P. Pinckney, 6 Dr. Gds.
A. R. G. Costello, 7 Dr. Gds.
R. G. Glyn, 1 Drs.
T. K. Fitzgerald, do.
J. G. Sandeman, do.
H. Fawcett, 3 Drs.
T. W. Goodrich, 4 Drs.
H. Timson, 5 Drs.
W. S. Sleigh, 6 Drs.
M. D. Brisco, 7 Drs.
R. Hodgson, 8 Drs.
W. Mayne, 10 Drs.
Sir E. C. Cockburn, Bt. 11 Drs.
F. C. Shells, 11 Drs.
J. B. Miller, 15 Drs.
G. T. Macartney, 15 Drs.
E. T. Irvine, 16 Drs.
J. C. Hart, 16 Drs.
H. Baring, 17 Drs.
E. Stacey, 18 Drs.
Hon. W. F. Forbes, Gr. Gds.
St. V. B. H. Whitshed, Coldst. Gds.
T. F. S. Fothringham, Scots Fus. Gds.
T. J. Gregory, 1 F.
J. J. Symonds, 5 F.
D. D. Grahame, 5 F.
W. M. Mill, 6 F.
G. Dowglasse, 6 F.
J. A. M'Donald, 8 F.
J. W. Dimond, 8 F.
J. L. S. Aldersey, 10 F.
Hon. A. Bury, 10 F.
L. E. Knox, 11 F.
W. Dods, 14 F.
Hon. H. J. Liddell, 15 F.
C. A. Morshead, 15 F.
J. Smyth, 15 F.
H. Robinson, 15 F.
E. G. Mainwaring, 16 F.
W. L. F. Sheaffe, 19 F.
G. E. L. C. Bissett, 19 F.
T. Madden, 19 F.
C. Lutyens, 20 F.
J. Carden, 20 F.
V. H. Lee, 21 F.
C. S. Smelt, 21 F.
G. S. Nunn, 22 F.
R. K. Little, 22 F.
H. D. Radcliffe, 23 F.
H. Gillmore, 23 F.
R. B. T. Thelwall, 24 F.
W. B. C. Goodison, 24 F.

E. J. Disney, 24 F.
C. M. Layton, 25 F.
H. S. Brown, 25 F.
C. G. Harrison, 25 F.
P. A. L. Phipps, 29 F.
A. H. Williamson, 30 F.
E. Temple, 31 F.
J. Harris, 35 F.
W. R. Rainsford, 36 F.
W. H. A. Dashwood, 36 F.
T. Jackson, 37 F.
W. O'Hara, 40 F.
A. G. Lowry, 41 F.
J. A. Hamilton, 41 F.
B. S. Hoskins, 44 F.
R. W. Piper, 46 F.
H. G. E. Welby, 48 F.
T. Hebden, 50 F.
H. R. Mitford, 51 F.
W. H. Herrick, 51 F.
G. P. Heathcote, 52 F.
T. M. Roxby, 55 F.
J. P. Pye, 56 F.
A. L. Copland, 57 F.
M. Tighe, 58 F.
G. J. R. Wynyard, 58 F.
E. G. Byam, 59 F.
W. D. Phelips, 60 F.
H. Vaughan, 68 F.
C. N. Biggs, 69 F.
R. E. W. Cumberland, 70 F.
W. J. Denny, 71 F.
G. Campbell, 71 F.
R. D. Buchanan, 72 F.
B. G. D. Cooke, 73 F.
P. F. Shuldham, 73 F.
H. Morris, 80 F.
W. Barron, 96 F.
E. J. S. Ray, 91 F.
E. C. B. Elphinstone, 92 F.
J. Mason, 94 F.
J. Buchanan, 94 F.
P. S. Alcock, 95 F.
J. H. L. Bronke.
O. Lowry, 96 F.
J. D. Molson, 99 F.
P. G. B. Lake, 100 F.
J. Rowles, Rifle Brigade.
H. G. Lindsay, do.
H. J. Robertson, do.
J. M. Brown, 1 W. I. R.
A. Tunstall, do.
R. Scott, 2 W. I. R.
G. W. Hunt, Cape M. R.
W. A. M. Cunynghame, Canadian Rifles.
N. Chichester, 99 F.
H. J. Davies, 2 W. I. R.
T. M'Curdy, 31 F.
G. R. J. Marshall, 49 F.
W. G. Nugent, 3 W. I. R.
Sir W. Parker, Bt. do.
F. G. Steward, h. p. 50 F.
C. R. Storey, Unatt.

Lieutenants.

A. E. H. G. Visc. Grey de Wilton, 1 Life Gds.
A. T. Frederick, 5 Dr. Gds.

Casualties since the last Publication.

R. J. Grainger, 6 Dr. Gds.
F. Simpson, 4 Drs.
G. M. Bright, 5 Drs.
R. A. G. Cosby, 6 Drs.
W. J. S. Orde, 6 Drs.
W. H. Seymour, 7 Drs.
E. J. Howley, 10 Drs.
F. W. E. Savage, 13 Drs.
R. H. Bush, 13 Drs.
E. Buckley, 15 Drs.
N. A. Harris, Mil. Train.
Sir H. Fletcher, Gr. Gds.
J. Tymons, 1 F.
A. M. A. Page, 2 F.
T. Eman, 2 F.
F. E. Brace, 3 F.
F. Ball, 6 F.
H. E. W. Rumbold, 7 F.
E. T. Pinniger, 8 F.
H. E. Fitzgerald, 8 F.
O. D. W. Hunter, 10 F.
M. J. F. Kenny, 10 F.
R. F. Burrowes, 11 F.
A. F. B. Wither, 12 F.
S. V. Page, 12 F.
F. T. Elwood, 12 F.
W. A. Gibson, 15 F.
P. Malone, 16 F.
G. S. Butler, 17 F.
J. G. K. Houghton, 17 F.
C. W. Holworthy, 17 F.
R. W. Torre, 17 F.
C. Bunbury, 17 F.
W. T. Le Brun, 18 F.
T. H. Hoblyn, 20 F.
W. Blennerhasset, 21 F.
O. P. Leigh, 22 F.
T. Peach, 22 F.
G. Palliser, 22 F.
H. B. Chichester, 22 F.
G. R. Hassall, 22 F.
F. M. H. Dare, 23 F.

C. J. Hampton, 30 F.
J. W. Charlton, 32 F.
J. Evans, 38 F.
W. O. Smith, 39 F.
L. M. Fraser, 41 F.
H. D. J. Macleod, 41 F.
V. Benett, 43 F.
G. G. F. Pigott, 48 F.
F. P. Blackmore, 49 F.
C. Hudson, 50 F.
C. J. R. Troup, 52 F.
H. F. Curwen, 56 F.
J. H. R. Harrison, 58 F.
F. K. Statham, 59 F.
E. R. K. Harman, 60 F.
A. T. Ewens, 60 F.
J. Wigg, 60 F.
C. G. Jones, 60 F.
W. K. Murray, 60 F.
R. R. Daly, 61 F.
N. G. Elliott, 62 F.
C. T. C. Roberts, 71 F.
A. D. Bell, 74 F.
A. L'Estrange, 75 F.
D. T. Arnoldi, 76 F.
W. F. Field, 76 F.
R. B. Hill, 77 F.
R. A. Rising, 77 F.
N. J. Peach, 77 F.
W. W. Young, 78 F.
C. G. Durant, 79 F.
E. Gawne, 79 F.
G. Smith, 79 F.
H. G. Pattisson, 80 F.
J. Bennett, 80 F.
W. Humphreys, 81 F.
G. A. Conran, 86 F.
S. G. L. Fox, 87 F.
J. A. Browning, 96 F.
J. H. Thompson, 96 F.
H. L. Williams, 96 F.
M. J. Guest, Rifle Br.

J. B. Evans, do.
A. H. Hall, 2 W. I. R.
J. J. L. Duncan, 3 W. I. R.
J. R. Mather, do.
J. B. Scot, do.
J. H. H. Sandon, 3 W. I. R
J. Tucker, do.
G. S. Beet, do.
E. D. Crossman, Cape M. R.
J. S. Onion, Canadian Rifles.
J. C. Crawford, 57 F.
T. H. Holmes, 63 F.
T. Travenen, 9 F.
J. O. E. Tucker, 87 F.
R. Neville, Mil. Tr.

Cornets and Ensigns.
C. B. K. Alleyne, 7 Dr. Gds.
W. J. M'G. Dawn, 1 Drs.
R. A. Herbert, 2 Drs.
J. C. Swaine, 11 Drs.
J. White, 13 Drs.
T. Churcher, 15 Drs.
A. Hopper, 12 F.
R. Walker, 16 F.
B. B. Thompson, 38 F.
S. C. Mathew, 57 F.
H. S. Wakefield, 59 F.
J. A. Hudson, 60 F.
R. C. Musgrave, 71 F.
A. R. Mce Gwire, 79 F.
J. B. Campbell, 79 F.
H. P. Holford, 79 F.
W. J. Kerr, 79 F.
E. de Blaquiere, 88 F.
A. Bond, 92 F.
W. J. Pegus, 63 F.
R. Stuart, 1 Drs.

Received a Commuted Allowance.
Assist. Commissary General
J. W. Woodley, h. p.

RESIGNATIONS.

Captains.
J. Boulton, R. Art.
J. H. Blackburne, do.

Lieutenants.
L. B. Towne, 36 F.
A. P. Joy, R. Art.
J. H. Edgar, do.
D. H. Burnes, R. Eng.
H. P. L'E. St. George, do.
H. J. Jull, R. Mar.
D. G. Pitcher, do.

Cornets and Ensigns.
J. A. Beaumont, 4 Dr. Gds.
J. Russell, 9 Drs.
H. R. Eppes, 9 F.
F. J. Gosselin, 12 F.
H. Robinson, 13 F.
O. C. Weir, 17 F.
J. E. W. Hussey, 30 F.
T. J. Westby, 45 F.
A. S. Bell, 55 F.
W. C. Musters, 96 F.
R. A. Cumberlege, Cape M. R.

Pay-Masters.
J. R. H. Treeve, 4 F.

Assistant Surgeons.
J. Griffith, 15 Drs.
A. Spittall, Coldst. Gds.
E. P. Gamble, 25 F.
J. Greatorex, Staff.

Chaplain.
Rev. Dr. Sirr.

Dep. Assistant Commissaries General.
F. G. Woolrabe.
A. C. Colquhoun.

SUPERSEDED.

Lieutenant.
G. A. Hilton, 70 F.

Ensigns.
W. N. Franklyn, 8 Drs.
G. Houstoun, 10 Drs.
W. H. Mulloy, 2 F.
O. Robinson, 6 F.
J. T. U. Coxen, 60 F.
F. D. Walker, 11 F.

SERVICES DISPENSED WITH.

Paymaster.
J. Wilson, 3 W. I. R.

DISMISSED.

Lieutenant.
W. C. Goldie, 12 Drs.

CASHIERED.

Lieutenants.
G. W. Wigelsworth, 76 F.
W. M'D. Clarke, 76 F.
W. M. Ansell, Canadian Rifles.

Ensigns.
J. J. Scott, 47 F.

Assistant Surgeons.
T. J. O'Grady, 1 F.
A. M. Humphrey, 39 F.
W. Morris, R. Art.
M. C. Tonnere, Staff.

DEATHS.

Generals.
Sir J. Slade, Bt. 5 Dr. Gds.
F. C. White.
G. Gosselin.
J. Earl of Westmorland, 56F.
C.M. Earl Cathcart, 1 Dr.Gds.
Sir Alex. Leith, 31 F.
H. Evelegh, R. Art.
R. S. Brough, do.
Sir F. W. Trench.

Lieutenant Generals.
R. B. Macpherson, 88 F.
H. A. Proctor, 97 F.
J. C. Bourchier, 3 Dr. Gds.
G. Cardew, R. Eng.
Sir J. Thackwell, 16 Drs.
C. Gilmour, r. f. p. R. Art.
G. G. Lewis, R. Eng.
N. Hamilton, 82 F.

Major Generals.
H. Despard, from 99 F.
J. Reed.
Sir Wm. Eyre.
T. Blanshard, from R. Eng.
D. M'Adam, r. f. p. R. Mar.
T. Tothill, r. f. p. R. Mar.
R. C. Molesworth, r. f. p. R. Art.
F. Towers, Unatt.

Colonels.
E. J. Crabbe, r. f. p. 74 F.]
E. W. Bray, r. f. p. 39 F.
G. Hutchison, 80 F.
J. Macphail, h. p. 7 Drs.
J. Algeo, Unatt.
J. A. Udny, h. p. 62 F.
F. G. A. Pinckney, 73 F.
R. W. Bamford, Unatt. Staff Officer Pensioners.
F. W. Clements, r. f. p. 73 F.
J. Gray, Unatt.
J. M. B. Neill, h. p. 40 F.
A. Browne, late of 1 F.
E. Drummond, late of 86 F.
W. Fawcett, late of 34 F.
J. Fleming, late of 55 F.
E. G. W. Keppel, late of 48 F.
G. W. Prosser, late of 3 F.
H. Stisted, late of 57 F.
T. Warrington, late of 44 F.
T. Wildman, late of 5 Dr.Gds.
Geo. Baker, late of 16 Drs.

Lieutenant Colonels.
C. Purvis, h. p. Can. Fen.
C. H. Smith, h. p. 15 F.
J. Watson, Unatt.
W. Milne, r.f.p. 2 Vet. Batt.
G. Pinckney, r. f. p. 82 F.
W. Cox, r. f. p. 54 F.
J. Clarke, r. f. p. 66 F.
J. Smith, r. f. p. 14 F.
H. F. Stokes, r. f. p. 30 F.
T. C. Timins, 70 F.
E. C. Legh, 97 F.
R. D. Campbell, 71 F.
H. W. Montresor, R. Art.
C. W. Sibley, 64 F.
C. Holden, Unatt.
C. F. Seymour, 84 F.
T. Fenwick, R. Eng.

J. L. Black, late of 14 Drs.
P. Campbell, late of 95 F.
G. S. Deverill, late of 53 F.
A. Maclean, late of 3 W. I. R.
W. N. Orange, late of 67 F.
J. C. Peddie, late of 21 F.
P. Pratt, late of 12 F.
G. E. Raitt, late of 2 F.
W. B. Saunderson, late of 4 F.
N. F. Suckling, late of 67 F.
W. E. Sweny, late of 64 F.
Hon. J. Walpole, late of Colds. Gds.

Majors.
Hon. C. Murray, h. p. 17Drs.
O. H. Baynes, h. p. R. Art.
J. Crawfurd, Unatt.
F. W. Horne, 7 Hussars.
R. Gray, r. f. p. 6 Vet. Batt.
G. Pattoun, r. f. p. R. Mar.
D. Cooper, r. f. p. 17 F.
J. E. T. Quayle, 33 F.
H. H. A'C. Inglefield, Military Train.
L. H. Daniel, 38 F.
E. M. Davenport, 66 F.
J. Pratt, 1 W. I. R.
W. Middleton, 7 Dr. Gds.
O. H. St. G. Anson, 9 Drs.
W. Hamilton, 9 Drs.
R. Reynolds, 58 F.
Hon. B. R. Pellew, Rifle Br.
W. Anderson, 2 W. I. R.
W. W. Allen, late of 9 Drs.
J. Brine, late Unatt.
J. Chadwick, late of 79 F.
R. Ellis, late of 15 F.
G. Goodall, late of 1 F.
W. Gun, late of 36 F.
T. Kenyon, late of 8 F.
J. L. Nixon, late of W. I. R.
R. Warran, late of 6 Drs.

Captains.
O.F.C. Bridgeman, 2 Dr.Gds.
R. Blair, 2 Dr. Gds.
W. S. Sleigh, 6 Drs.
T. Barrett, 14 Drs.
T. Tayler, 17 Drs.
W. D. Seymour, 17 Drs.
J. Scott, Scots Fus. Gds.
T. M'Kenna, 1 F. (killed in action).
F. Clark, 4 F.
J. A. Fuller, 6 F.
H. E. Jones, 6 F.
W. V. Maskelyne, 7 F.
J. Cator, 10 F.
M. Ward, 10 F.
R. H. Fry, 15 F.
N. B. Walton, 17 F.
B. Davies, 20 F.
H. J. Palmer, 21 F.
F. A. Quartley, 26 F.
T. Rice, 36 F.
F. B. Dixon, 41 F.
W. Lawson, 42F. (of wounds).
Hon. H. Handcock, 44 F.
T. J. B. Connell, 46 F.
J. A. Dick, 52 F.
J. H. Ward, 58 F.

R. G. Brackenbury, 61 F.
W. S. Arnold, 67 F.
R. Whigham, 70 F.
J. B. Williams, 99 F
E. G. K. Ravenhill, 11 F.
J. O'Neill, Unatt.
H. N. Eden, R. Art.
F. Koe, R. Eng.
A. G. Goodall, R. Eng.
J. Inman, h. p. Unatt. Staff Officer of Pensioners.
R. M. Dickens, Adjutant, Staff College.
H. Timpson, R. Marines.
R. Beadon, h. p. 92 F.
W. Brett, Unatt.
Z. Fayerman, h. p. R. Mar.
C. Foss, h. p. 6 Gar. Batt.
D. Gordon, h. p. 5 W. I. R.
R. Gregory, h. p. R. Art.
W. Hardwick, h. p. 2 F.
S. Harrison, h. p. Unatt.
T. A. Kemmis, Unatt.
M. Lynch, h. p. 27 F.
A. M'Donald, h. p. 56 F.
A. M'Laine, Unatt.
J. W. Phillipps, Unatt.
W. H. Poole, h. p. R. Art.
H. Tench, h. p. 10 F.
G. Count Von der Decken, h. p. German Legion.
L. Krauchenberg, h. p. do.
C. Bacmeister, h. p. do.

Lieutenants.
R. Harding, Adj. 8 Drs. (of wounds).
A. C. Haymes, 8 Drs.
C. White, 12 Drs.
G. G. Cameron, Coldst. Gds.
R. B. Caton, 1 F.
B. D. Wright, 3 F.
A. A. James, 6 F.
G. Turville, 13 F.
A. Molony, 1 W. I. R.
T. Watts, 18 F.
E. Hales, 19 F.
T. S. Macdonogh, 20
A. W. Gilley, 20 F.
R. F. Melliar, 20 F.
L. Waring, 24 F.
C. B. Higman, 28 F.
J. W. MacCormack, 28 F. (killed in action).
K. A. E. P. Jones, 38 F.
S. R. R. Smith, 41 F.
F. Coucher, 46 F.
L. de M. Prior, 48 F.
J. T. Cooke, 49 F.
H. R. H. Wilson, 53 F.
T. Parr, 54 F.
F. Hoberdon, 55 F.
G. Sims, 56 F.
J. Steel, 60 F.
E. C. Allen, 60 F.
T. L. Twiston, 63 F.
M. Bell, 70 F.
T. R. Hawkins, 79 F.
W. Maclean, 80 F.
R. F. Harrison, 89 F.
J. Blagg, 91 F.
J. M. Allen, 91 F.

Deaths.

C. T. Paley, 94 F.
C. M'Kay, 97 F.
W. A. Bond, 99 F.
H. D. Baillie, Rif. Br.
H. E. Richards, Rif. Br.
J. Leggatt, 1 W. I. R.
E. Smith, 1 W. I. R.
W. P. Gilborne, do.
A. C. H. Light, R. Art.
H. P. Tillard, do.
W. T. Cathcart, do.
R. Thaine, R. Eng.
E. Walsh, do.
J. V. C. Reed, R. Mar.
H. L. T. Inglis, do.
H. Wolrige, do.
J. Allen, h. p. 38 F.
H. Boldero, h. p. 27 F.
T. C. Bonnor, h. p. Cor. Reg.
B. Brady, h. p. 97 F.
G. D. Bridge, h. p. 73 F.
S. Chambers, h. p. 54 F.
J. A. Collins, h.p. 3 W. I. R.
S. Cox, h. p. R. Mar.
W. Dawson, h. p. Ger. Leg.
J. Dusautoy, r. f. p. R. Mar.
T. G. Elrington, h. p. 62 F.
J. Fitchett, h.p. 7 Gar. Batt.
S. Forward, h. p. 27 Drs.
A. Geddes, h. p. 5 W. I. R.
H. Graham, h. p. 60 F.
A. Greer, h. p. 6 F.
G. Gunn, h. p. R. Mar.
J. Hojel, h.p. Caith. Fen. Inf.
W. Hole, h. p. 43 F.
W. Johnstone, h. p. 86 F.
P. Lockwood, h p. 30 F.
A. M'Donald, h. p. 26 F.
A. M'Intosh, r. f. p. 4 Vet. Batt.
J. M'Millan, h. p. 82 F.
J. Macdonald, h. p. 4 W.I.R.
J. MacGachen, h. p. 72 F.
L. Macpherson, h. p. 52 F.
G. Miller, h. p. 19 F.
W. Morton, h. p. 66 F.
J. O'Connor, h. p. 27 F.
A. O'Flyn, h. p. 87 F.
D. Ogilvie, h. p. 94 F.
R. T. Parsons, h. p. R. Mar.
E. L. E. C. De Pontcarré, R. Foreign Art.
J. Roberts, R. Art. Drivers.
W. Ryan, h. p. 63 F.
J. Saunders, h. p. 1 Gar. Batt.
T. Scott, h. p. 94 F.
J. Sleator, r. f. p. 5 Vet. Batt.
A. Smith, h. p. 42 F.
H. W. Smith, h. p. 67 F.
P. Smith, Junr.. h. p. R. Art. Drivers.
E. H. Steed, h. p. 25 Drs.
J. Tayloe, h. p. 77 F.
T. P. Taylor, h. p. R. Mar.
R. B. Walker, h. p. 48 F.
G. Wood, h. p. 95 F.
L. Kirchner, h. p. Ger. Leg.
J. Juliani, h. p. do.
M. Zujiani, h. p. do.

Cornets and Ensigns.

W. Agnew, 2 Dr. Gds.

A. J. B. Fellowes, 16 Drs.
T. H. Williams, 18 Drs.
G. G. Cameron, Coldst. Gds.
W. L. Butler, 6 F.
M. A. Scott, 9 F.
W. P. James, 10 F.
J. M. Tomlin, 12 F.
A. A. Fuller, 15 F.
J. F. O'Reilly, 18 F.
F. A. Campbell, 27 F.
M. H. Jones, 34 F.
A. L. Calcraft, 39 F.
C. W. Talmadge, 41 F.
J. Burton, 51 F.
W. Hamilton 73 F.
A. Whimpster, 74 F.
W. Blathwayt, 83 F.
G. H. Dickson, 89 F.
C. E. Woodward, 98 F.
P. Backhouse, h. p. 8 Drs.
W. Bernard, h. p. 60 F.
J. Cosnard, h. p. 88 F.
G. H. L. Crespin, h. p. R. Mar.
L. Daly, h. p. 75 F.
J. Haydon, h. p. R. Mar.
F. O. Hodgson, h. p. R. Wag. Tr.
W. F. Lum, h. p. 35 F.
C. Maclachlan, h. p. 72 F.
Sir M. C. Smith, Bt. h. p. 11 Drs.
H. Sunderland, h. p. 52 F.
H. A. Knop, h. p. Ger. Leg.
J. H. Wegener, h. p. do.

Paymasters.

J. R. L. Percy, 34 F.
A. E. Grant, 41 F.
J. H. Tuke, 74 F.
W. M. Pechell, 85 F.
C. Stokely, 1 W. I. R.
F. E. Leech, Invalid Depot.
H. H. Carmichael, h. p. 36 F.
V. Raymond, h. p. 27 F.
J. G. Whitaker, h. p. 9 Hussars.
J. Fagan, h. p. Depot. Batt.

Quarter Masters.

H. F. Lane, 8 Drs.
J. Hamilton, 8 F.
T. Lewis, 11 F.
J. Carden, h. p. 30 Drs.
J. Dixon, h. p. 104 F.
A. Harrison, h. p. 1 Gar. Batt.
W. Hill, h. p. Rifle Br.
J. Jones, h. p. R. Eng.
D. M'Cardy, h. p. 74 F.
W. Mew, h. p. 67 F.
W. North, r. f. p. 2 Life Gds.
J. Stubbs, h. p. 48 F.
H. Williams, h. p. 3 F.

Adjutants.

T. Trotter, h. p. 27 F.
F. M. Debs, h. p. Ger. Leg.
F. Brinckmann, h. p. do.

Chaplain's Department.

Rev. E. G. Parker.
—— N. R. Dennis, h. p.
—— C. J. Lyon, h. p.

COMMISSARIAT DEPARTMENT.

Deputy Commissary General.

E. A. F. Cowan, h. p.

Assist. Commissary General.

J. Lane, h. p.

Deputy Assist. Commissaries General.

G. S. Dwight.
S. B. Alder.
C. M. Seel.
T. P. Marter, h. p.

MEDICAL DEPARTMENT.

Inspector General.

Sir J. Pitcairn, h. p.

Assistant Inspector.

G. A. Morewood, h. p.

Surgeons Majors, &c,

R. R. Dowse.
J. Baird, h. p.
J. Leath, h. p.
M. Reynolds, h. p.
R. Sillery, h. p.
E. Salmon, h. p. S. F. Gds.

Surgeons.

D. Stewart, 92 F.
P. S. Warren, R. Art.
J. Trench, Staff.
R. R. Dowse, do.
F. Clarke, Staff.
J. H. Halahan, Staff.
C. Annesley, h. p. 2 Drs.
J. Carngie, h. p. 62 F.
A. Knox, h. p. Staff.
G. M'Culloch, h. p. Staff.
M. M'Dermott, h. p. 89 F.
J. Mackintosh, h. p. R. Art.
A. R. Ridgway, h. p. Staff.

Assistant Surgeons.

W. E. Lynch, 7 F.
A. M. Porteous, 18 F.
W. M. Mitton, 82 F.
J. Boutflower, Cape. M. R.
E. Bubb, R. Art.
J. Read, R. Art.
J. M'H. Gowan, Staff.
A. H. Taylor, do.
T. W. Bennett, do.
A. J. Griffith, do.
T. Bissett, h. p. 57 F.
T. Burke, h. p. 27 F.
J. Woodroff, h. p. Staff.
A. H. Taylor, Staff.

Acting Assistant Surgeon.

T. Lightfoot.

Purveyor.

G. Dalton.

Deputy Purveyors.

T. Smyth, h. p.
J. Moore, h. p.

Veterinary Surgeons.

T. Timm, h. p. 3 Dr. Gds.

INDEX.

Abadie, Henry Rich. 154	Adrien, John Joseph 224	Alexander, Claud 160	Altenstein, Hen. *Baron* 486
Abbot, *Rev.* Fred. J. 455	Adsetts, John 444	——Fred. Llewellyn 414	Alves, John 14
Abbott, Cha. Compton 459	Adye, John Miller, *CB.*	——George 540	Ambrose, Geo. Jas. 59, 175
——Cha. Thompson 442	52, 373	——Geo. Gardiner, *CB.*	Ames, Alfred 345
——Frederick Tydd 253	Adye, Mortimer 78, 374	54, 413	Ames, Frederick 344
Abell, Joseph 532	Affleck, Duncan C. 216	——Henry 104	Amey, William 445
Abercrombie, John 532	Agassiz, Lewis 511	——Henry 129	Amherst, *Hon.* Fred. 151
Abercromby, *Hon.* J. 345	——Roland Lewis 418	——James, *CB.* 121	Amiel, Charles Fred. 314
Ackland, Graves 465, 486	Agg, Thomas Francis 153	——*Sir* Jas. Edw. 42, 202	Amsinck, William 106
Acklom, George Evatt 258	——William 85, 269	——Robert 120	Amyott, Rich. Garrett 486
——J. E. 465	Aglen, Artemas Tho. 170	——Thomas, *CB.* 439	Anderson, Abraham 207
A'Court, Fred. Holmes 321	Agnew, Charles 145	——William 293	——Abraham Collis 74
Acton, Charles 269	——Charles 106	——William 443	——Alexander 37, 411
——Ed. Wm. Fred. 307	——Gerald Andrew 328	——Wm. Gordon 332	——Andrew, *MD.* 531
——Francis, *Baron* 543	——James 250	Algar, Jas. Sturg. H. 282	——Arthur 323
——Thomas 272	——Thos. R. 75, 464	Alison, Arch. 60	——Arthur, *MD.* 439
——Wm. M. Cole 470	Agnis, John Crown 138	——Fred. Montagu 86, 215	——David 59, 223
Adair, Alex. William 164	Ahmuty, James 120	Allaire, John Hillary 344	——David 386
——Allan Shafto 200	Ailesbury, G. W. F.,	Allan, Alex. *MD.* 211	——De Lancey R. 172
——Chas. William 413	*Marquis of* 125	——And. Timbrell 62, 231	——Edward Abbot 212
——Henry 413	Ainslie, Cha. Philip 29, 151	——Dudley North 382	——George 440
——Henry Atkinson 270	——Edw. Campbell 282	——John Younger 300	——George D. 283
——James 106	——Henry Francis 36	——Robert 532	——Henry 43, 359
——James W. D. 180	——James 136	——William 253	——Henry 380
——Richard Bratton 470	——Robert 511	Allanby, J. S. *MD.* 444	——James Alex. 202
——Rob. Alex. Shafto 125	——Wm. B. *CB.* 35	Allardice, John M'Dermid	——James Geo. 291
——Thomas James 31	Ainsworth, Oliver D. 33	307	——J. War. Hastings 298
Adam, W. 465	Airey, George John 418	Allardyce, James 532	——John 120
Adams, Allen Noble 217	——James Talbot, *CB.*	Allen, Chas. Davers 470	——John 215
——And. Leith, *MD.* 224	49, 163	——Charles J. Watson 148	——John, *MB.* 303
——Arthur Fulford 436	——*Sir* Richard, *KCB.*	——David Fred. 210	——John David 527
——Cadwallader 56, 266	12, 125	——George 167	——J. Hamil Pringle 379
——Edward 60	——Rob. Hen. Burrell 229	——George 486	——John Henry 361
——Frank, *CB.* 34, 234	——Thomas 229	——George 465	——John Rich. *CB.*60,373
——George, *CB.* 527	Aitchison, Alex. Allan 303	——George 520	——Joseph, *CB. KH.* 104
——George Forbes 444	——*Sir* John, *KCB.* 8, 302	——James 104	——Joseph Henry 129
——George Hewish 322	——William 55, 166	——Jas. W. Geo. 341	——Richard 81, 276
——Henry 157	Aitken, Alexander 515	——John Edward 312	——Robert 300
——Henry 212	Akerman, Hercules 170	——John Penn 470	——Robert 335
——Henry Balthazar 369	Akers, Charles Style 402	——R. Shuttleworth 470	——Rob. Carew, *MD.* 150
——John A. Phillips 376	Alban, Frederick 197	——Rt. Austin, *MD.* 444	——Samuel 404
——Jos. Hollingworth 527	Albemarle, G. T. *Earl of*	——Robert 470	——Thomas 310
——Michael Goold 62	17	——R. Austen, *MD.* 445	——Thomas 532
——Samuel 148	ALBERT, *His Royal*	——Robt. Calder 418	——Thomas 83, 291
——Thomas Edmund 234	*Highness The Prince*	——Robert Marshall 131	——Thomas E. 141
——William Edmund 239	*Consort, KG. KT.*	——Rodney Vansit. 413	——William 446
——William Henry 33	*KP. GCB. GCMG.*	——Wm. H. Craven 316	——*Rev.* William 455
Adamson, Joseph Sam. 52	5, 159, 343	Alley, Tottenham 486	——William 511
——Robt. Isaac 212	Alcock, Tho. St. Leger 106	Alleyne, Chas. B. K. 127	——W. Cochrane 18, 371
Adcock, Alfred Wm. 228	Alder, Sydney 288	——Douglas 312	——Wm. Forbes 318
——Herbert Burrows 182	——Walter K. 486	Allfrey, Good. Holms. 130	——Wm. H. H. 106
——John, *MD.* 444	Alderson, Henry Jas. 377	——Irving Stening 306	——William James 240
Addams, James 104	——Wm. M. Dixwell 308	Allhusen, F. H. Ehren. 205	Andrée, Rich. Collyer 120
Adderley, M. B. B. 128	Aldridge, John 217	Allinson, Edw. Dawson 442	Andrew, Charles 486
Addington, *Hon.* Charles	——John 81, 220	——John Hiram 499	Andrews, Charles 104
John 84, 248	——Robert Battelot 300	Allix, Charles 103	——Francis 106
——*Hon.* Leonard A. 375	——Thomas 217	Allman, Stephen Geo. 352	——Henry Smith 198
Addison, Alfred Chamberl.	Aldworth, Rich. Wm.	Allnutt, Wm. Winkw. 416	——Jas. Trevor White 358
294	58, 185	Alpe, Hamond 470	——John 443
——John 486	Alessi, M. de Marchesi 74	Alston, Arthur Rich. 291	——John 520
——Joseph Edward 56	Alexander, Archibald 139	——Sydney Vere 418	——Mottram 53
——Thomas 58, 172	——Boyd Francis 343	——W. Evelyn, *MD.* 444	——Robert 14
Addy, John 470		Alten, Victor, *Count* 541	——Robert Alex. 51

Andrews, Rob. Fleet. 130	Arden, G. Banks Hoy. 198	Ashmore, John 14	Austin, Edmund 307
——Wm. Gilly 80, 376	——William 151	——William 106	——Edw. Frederick 486
Andros, Edwyn Brent. 286	——William 486	Ashton, Arthur 186	——Frederick 282
——William 104	Arentesschildt, A. Von 542	——Henry 435	——Geoffrey Lewis 344
Angelo, Arthur 304	Argent, Samuel 444	——William, *MB.* 272	——Norton 520
——E. Anth. *KH.* 103,455	——Thomas 201	Askwith, Wm.Hur. 37, 372	——Thomas 463, 486
——Edward Fox 234	Arkwright, Henry 319	Aslett, John Thompson 81	——William, *MD.* 529
Angerstein, J. Jul. W. 12	Arnit,L.J.Amadée 79,402	——Wm. Stratton 77, 413	——William 106
Anglesey, H. *Marq. of* 103	Armitage, John 321	Astell, Charles Edward 452	Autran, Alexander 543
Anketell, Montray 470	Armstrong, Alexander 6	——Rich. Wm. 103	Awdry, John 175
Anley, Fred. Augustus 378	——Alex. Boswell 104	Astley, Edw. D'Oyly 190	Ayles, John Geo. Aug.
——Henry Thos. 175	——Alex. Moore 356	——Francis N. 134	*CB.* 56, 411
Annesley, A. Lyttleton 147	——Anth.W. S. F. 79, 212	——John Dugdale 104	Aylett, James 236
——*Hon.* Arthur 160	——Arch. C. Fall 303	——Ralph 540	Aylmer, Charles Wm. 294
——Chas.GasperDav. 212	——Arthur John 153	——Rich. Duckinfield 266	——Charles W. B. 211
——Fra, Chas. 188	——Carteret A. 192	Astuto, Pierre 544	——Fred. Cha. 54
——*Hon.* Hugh 166	——Charles 207	Atcherley, Fra. T.78, 237	——George Edw. 106
——James O. D. 296	——Charles 520	——Wm. Atcherley 151	——Henry 38, 372
——John George 147	——Daniel 529	Atchison, Geo. T. H. 295	——John Evans Freke 187
——Robert 192	——Edward 226	——Henry Alex. 470	Ayre, Wm. Gordon Jas. 420
——Steph. Fra. C. 64, 192	——Edward 120	——Thomas 470	Ayshford,Aaron Moore 486
——William Groves 182	——Edward Marcus 274	Atherley, Edw.G.Eliot 260	Ayton, Robinson 532
——*Hon.*W.Octav.B. 141	——Elliot 330	——Francis Henry 343	Aytoun, James 142
——William Richard 338	——Francis 195	——Mark Kerr 31, 331	——John Marriot 334
Ansell,Augustus E. H. 177	——Fran. Wheeler 486	Athorpe, John 321	——Marriott 337
——Augustus Francis 42	——Fred. Gerard 202	——Robert 404	Babington, Wm. 64, 142
——Rich. Turberville 414	——James 232	Atkin, John 486	Baby, Daniel Antoine 234
Anson, Alex. George 418	——Jas. St. Geo. 223	——William 51	Bace, Henry William 453
——Arch. E. Harbord 374	——Jas. W. *CB.* 42, 300	Atkinson, Aug. W. H. 341	Bachellé, Lewis de, *Baron*
——*Hon.* A. H. A. 86,142	——John 217	——Buddle 380	Von Dem Brinck 542
Anstruther, Phil. Rob. 334	——John 34, 354	——Charles 511	Backas, Conyngme J. 215
——Robert 160	——John 470	——Chas. Hercules 286	Backhaus,Arnold Erich 543
——R. Hamil. Lloyd 345	——John 486	——Edward D. 63, 247	——Franz Fred. 543
Anthony, Charles 153	——John 520	——Francis Forbes 202	Backhouse, John I. 511
——Paul 147	——John Cooper 486	——George 435	——Thos. Deering 299
Anton, Alexander 470	——John Fellows 356	——Humphry J. G. 443	Bacon, Anthony 106
——Henry 349	——Lancelot 150	——John 140	——Cæsar 106
Antrobus, E. Crawford 267	——Montgomery 486	——John 161	——Francis 418
Aplin, J. G. Rogers 78,264	——Richard 252	——John 85, 326	——John Joseph 335
——John 190	——Richard 486	——John 349	——Kenrick Verulam 236
——Phil. Hen. Prend. 175	——Rich, Say 18, 371	——John 486	——Robt. Cæsar 227
Appleby, Geo. Walton 232	——Robert Philip 226	——John Dickinson 246	Bacot, John 532
Appleton, Edward 76	——Robert Young 404	——Leonard Wilson 153	——Jno. Tho. Watson 441
Appleyard, F. Ern. 81,359	——Thomas 106	——Richard 197	Baddeley, Fred. Clinton
Applin, August. Oliver 296	——T. P. St. Geo. 266	——Robert 170	Herman Stuart 252
——Vincent 156	——William 383	——Thomas 290	——Fred. Henry 14
Appuhn, Arnold 542	——William 417	——Thomas, *MD.* 439	——John Fraser L. 77,374
Apreece, Thomas 534	——William 442	——Thos. Geo. B. 470	——Wm. H. Clinton 104
Arbuckle, B. H. Vaugh. 17	——William 444	——Thos. Johnston 239	Badgley, Alex. James 240
——Edm. KerrVaugh.175	——William 191	——Thos. Joseph 221	Bagenal, Walter P. 150
——Jas.Wm.Vaughan415	——William A. 79, 362	——William 150	Bagge, Rd. Salisbury 192
Arbuthnot,C. G. Jas. 9,326	——Wm. Andrew 203	Atthill, Robert C. T. 267	Bagnall, Charles 272
——Charles Geo. 78, 374	——William Bruce 135	——William 326	Bagnell, Frederick 197
——George 380	——Wm. Cairnes 205	Attwood, Fred. Rd. 233	Bagot, Charles 103
——Henry Thomas 378	Armytage, Edw. John 250	Atty, Charles 263	——Charles, *MB.* 350
——William 345	——Henry 103	Attyo, Fra. L. Octavius 172	——Edward 33
——W. Wedderburn 155	——Henry 62, 163	Aubin, Philip 50	——George 106
Arbuthnott, *Hon.* Hugh	Arnaud, John, *KH.* 17	Auchinleck, Grahame,	——George 298
CB. 6, 248	Arnoy, Chas. Aug. 32	*M.D.* 315	Bailey, Arthur 248
——*Hon.* John 470	Arnold, Wm. Graham 236	——John Claudius 380	——Charles 436
——John, *Visc.* 470	Arnott, Alexander 486	——Thomas 196	——Charles 470
——*Hon.* Wm. 15	——Archibald James 185	——Wm. Lowry 272	——Christopher Sam. 208
Archdall, Aud. Mervyn 470	Arrowsmith, Jas. P. 191	Auchmuty, *Sir* Sam.	——Frederick 145
——Henry 217	——John Williams 353	Benj. *KCB.* 8, 185	——Frederick 404
——Henry 470	Arthur, Alex. Miller 195	——Sam. ForbesFred. 234	——Hunt Johnson 444
Archer, Fran. Bisset 435	——David 457	Audain, John Willett P.	——Jas. Alderson 486
——J. H. Lawrence 282	——*Sir* Fred Leop. *Bt.* 58	65, 207	——John James 236
——Richard Hallilay 290	——Thomas 104	Austen, Cha. W. 62, 318	——William 403
——Samuel 340	Ashburnham, *Hon.* T.	——Henry Edmund 104	Bailie, Frederick 293
——Wm. Henry 106	*CB.* 11	——Hen. H. Godwin 228	——James 323
——Wm. M'Gregor 310	——Cromer 282	——John, *KH.* 103	——James 470
——Wm. Spearman 15	Ashe, Waller 321	Austin, Alfred 294	——William Alex. 316
Archibald, Rob. Wm. 279	——William Henry 291	——Alfred John 237	Baillie, Alex. Peter B. 312
Ardagh, John Charles 404	Ashmore, Charles 26	——Edgar Edw. 324	——Andrew 486

Index.

Baillie, Chas. Deyman	175
—— Charles H.	142
—— Duncan James	128
—— Geo. Clement	85, 401
—— Hugh	103
—— Hugh Smith	65, 128
—— James Baron	310
—— James William	129
—— Matthew John	302
—— Thomas	511
—— Wm. Hunter	330
Bain, D.S. Erskine, MD.	441
—— George	527
—— John	486
—— Wm., MD.	463, 532
—— William	486
Bainbridge, Edw. T.	220
—— Henry Sedley	170
—— Robert	154
Bainbrigge, Arthur	200
—— John Hankey	27
—— Philip, CB.	8, 232
—— Philip John	57, 400
—— Thomas Parker	486
Baines, Cuthbert A.	104
—— Henry Edward	381
Baird, Alexander	173
—— Sir David, Bt.	106
—— Frederick	274
—— James	253
—— John	540
—— William	255
Bake, S. G.	464
Baker, Chas. Osborn	414
—— Charles Stuart	280
—— Edw. Standish	223
—— Francis Bramley	167
—— George	295
—— George	486
—— Geo. Granville	470
—— J. B.	464
—— Jas. Bowyer	258
—— James Swayne	470
—— Reginald Phillips	418
—— Richard D.	470
—— Robert	436
—— Robert	470
—— Robert Broome	250
—— Thomas Durand	212
—— Thos. Rich.	106
—— Valentine	86, 146
—— William	470
—— Wm. Langworthy	193
—— William Thomas	321
Balck, Geo. Philip	470
Balcombe, James	156
Balders, Chas. Morley	133
—— Cha. Wm. Morley, CB.	26, 148, 359
Baldock, John	383
Baldwin, Fred. Chen.	353
—— George Walter	239
—— Godfrey	215
—— Robt. Bulkeley	326
—— Thos. Henry	342
Bale, William	486
Balfe, Walter	136
Balfour, Fra. Walter	106
—— Henry Lowther	376
—— Robert Wm.	106
—— Tho. Grah. MD.	439
—— Wm. Stewart	14
Balinhard, John Allan Carnegy de	486
Balinhard, W. Carnegy de	263
Ball, Francis A.	242
—— Howell	486
—— John	192
—— Joseph	383
—— Robert	486
—— Tertius	443
—— Thomas Gerrard	12
—— Thos. Shirley	146
—— William	486
—— William C.	436
Ballantyne, James G.	340
Ballingall, Wm. H.	245
Bally, Henry	299
—— St. John	264
—— William	242
Baly, George	346
Bamber, Hugh Wm.	417
Bamfield, Jno. Hichens	195
Bamford, Rob. Carter	470
Bampfield, Wm. John	170
Banbury, William	191
Bancroft, Wm. Chas.	207
Banks, William	156
Bannatine, Richard	532
Bannatyne, J. M.	82, 187
—— William	188
Banon, Rd. G. Davys	323
Banyard, John	520
Barber, Lionel Charles	402
Barbor, Rob. D.	106, 465
—— Robt. Wheatley	338
Barchard, George	207
Barclay, Alex. M.D.	257
—— David	153
—— Edward	470
—— Fred. Chas. D'E.	228
—— Pringle David	381
Barham, Fran. Foster	381
Baring, Charles	55, 163
—— Denzil Hugh	164
—— Ernest	542
—— Evelyn	382
—— Francis	61, 166
—— Frederick	486
—— George	543
—— Henry B.	106
—— Lewis Charles	542
Barker, Fra. Oliver MD	176
—— George Digby	310
—— Sir George Robert KCB.	37, 372
—— Henry	129
—— Henry Fred.	270
—— Henry John	283
—— John	142
—— John Barnett	180
—— Joseph	384
—— Walter Julius	417
—— Wm. Henry	267
Barlee, John Buckle	436
Barlow, Cuthbert	192
—— Cuthbert	515
—— Geo. Edw. Pratt	103
—— John Thomas	486
—— Maurice	17
—— Peter	202
—— Wm. Ruxton	380
Barnard, C. Loudon	413
—— Christopher John	354
—— Henry John	185
—— Markland	123
—— P. A.	465
Barnard, Robert Cary	106
—— Wm. A. M.	28, 160
—— Wm. Osborne	337
Barne, Fred. St. John	486
—— Newdegate	167
Barnes, Ardley H. F.	415
—— Caleb	76
—— C. Gabriel Alfred	130
—— Drury Richard	202
—— Edmund Charles	357
—— Edw. R. Bigsby	247
—— Ernest Fred.	176
—— Francis	252
—— George Adams	51
—— George West	253
—— James Whittaker	303
—— Rich. Knowles	470
—— Richard Moore	267
—— Samuel	520
—— William	51
Barnetson, Alexander	486
Barnett, C. FitzRoy	273
—— Chas. James	193
—— John	383
—— Oliver	141
—— Wm. Townsend	374
Barney, George	104
—— Richard	527
Barnham, H. Barry	463
Barnston, Francis	274
—— Roger	86, 299
—— William	106
Barnwell, Tobias	444
Barou, Richard John	50
Barr, David	120
—— William Lamb	272
Barrett, Chas. Carter	242
—— Knox	104
—— Richard	82
—— Richard Doyle	215
—— Samuel	138
—— Thomas	486
—— William, MB.	342
—— William Newman	511
Barrington, Henry	104
—— Joseph Tho.	380
Barron, Arthur Wm.	248
—— Fenwick B.	63, 131
—— Francis Joseph	153
—— Herbert	302
—— Luke, MD.	443
—— Netterville John	180
—— William	337
Barrow, John Edward	511
—— Rich. Wm.	356
—— Thomas	104
—— Thos. Waller	441
Barry, Charles	32
—— Chas. Francis	349
—— Charles William	402
—— Dan. Pat., MD.	157
—— G. W.	464
—— James, MD.	529
—— James	511
—— Hon. John Jas.	402
—— Philip	13
—— Philip J. S.	85, 401
—— Richard Edwyn	236
—— Robert	319
—— Robt. Fitzwilliam de Barry	283
—— St. Geo. Ryder	486
—— Thos. Stawell	322
—— William	279
Barry, William, MD.	530
—— William Henry	303
—— Wm. Wigram	59, 375
Barstow, George	77, 374
—— John Arthur	326
Barter, Richard	185
Bartholomew, Geo. C.	192
Barthorp, Arthur	146
Bartleet, Ern. Rogby	307
Bartlet, Alex. Edw.	444
—— Fred. George	486
Bartlett, Daniel	369
—— Henry	436
—— Henry Harrison	298
—— Rev. T. H.	455
Bartley, Alex. Fisher	260
—— George	515
—— John Cowell	77, 180
—— John Metge, MD.	532
—— Walter Tyler	182
Barton, Alexander	104
—— Christopher	135
—— Henry Augustus	232
—— Henry D. Chevers	277
—— Howard James	130
—— Hugh Saint Geo.	283
—— James	293
—— James	378
—— Montagu	321
—— Robert	404
—— W.	465
Barwell, Cha. Dawson	328
—— Fred. Leycester	267
—— Osborne	470
Bashford, Chas. Brome	145
Baskerville, Herbert Witherstone Minors	191
—— John	141
Bass, Emanuel Benj.	156
Bassano, Alfred	83, 240
—— Fra. Matthias	443
Basset, Arthur	470
—— Gustavus Lambert	302
Bassett, Wm. Watkin	276
Bastard, James Stokes	12
Batcheler, Edw. Beevor	341
—— Horatio Pettus	314
Batchellor, Sam. Geo.	470
Bate, Frederick	486
—— Henry Reginald	308
Bateman, Hugh Osb.	257
—— Robert	103
Bates, Henry	31, 340
—— Henry Stratton	293
—— John Victor	173
—— Robert	80, 215
Bateson, Richard	126
Bathe, Henry	185
—— Hen. Per. de	30, 166
—— Sir Wm. P., Bt.	104
Bathurst, Benjamin	470
—— Fredk. Thomas Arthur Hervey	160
—— Henry	104
Batley, George	130
Batt, Molyneux	340
Battersby, John Prevost	281
—— Robert	531
Battiscombe, H. Lum.	279
—— Wm. Benj.	330
Battley, D'Oyley Wm.	106
Battye, Montagu M'P.	192
Baugh, James	511
Baumgarten, Edw. P.	146

Baumgartner,R.Julian, CB.	51, 233	Beath, John H. *MD.*	176	Bell, William	276	Beresford, M. W. de la Poer	266
——Tho. Mowbray	318	Beaton, *Rev. Pat. AM.*	455	——William, *MD.*	529	——Mostyn de la Poer	302
Bawtree, Edw. Wm. *MD.*	442	Beatson, Geo S. *MD.*	439	——William	104, 465	Berger, Charles	542
		——Roger Stuart 53,	400	——William	470	——Ernest Arch.	193
Baxter, Fra. Hastings, *MD.*	141	Beattie, Henry Rich.	270	——William	15, 370	Berington, James	539
		Beatty, Andrew 56,	400	——William	63, 240	Berkeley, Edw. Stratton Fitz Hardinge	127
——James	520	——James M'Neill	340	——William Morrison	138	——Francis James	210
——James Fleming	276	Beauchamp, Cha. Eus.	486	Bellairs, Clement W.	382	——Fred. George	263
Bayfield, Samuel Jos.	443	——Fitzmaurice	185	——William	79	——Geo. Sackville	403
Baylay, Fred. George	378	——Henry B. *Earl* 6,	146	Bellamy, John	350	——*Hon.* G. C. Grant.	
Bayley, Daniel	463	Beauclerk, *Lord* George Aug.	106	——Percy Lytton	274	Fitz Hardinge	511
——Edw. Robt. Ward	215	Beaufort, Hen. *Duke of*	62	Belshes, John Murray	14	——Henry W.	131
——George	239	Beaufoy, Benjamin	52	Belson, George John	15	——Rich. Wm.	227
——Hen. Addington	527	——Charles	231	Beltz, Samuel	527	——Robert	236
——John	321	Beaumont, Dudley	314	Benbow, Edward	264	Bernard, Ludov. *MD.*	368
——John Arthur	106	——Fred. Edward B.	403	Bender, Benoit	51	——Luke FitzGerald	356
——Thomas	499	——G. Wentworth	167	Bengough, Har. M.	308	——Paolo	368
——William	303	——Rich. Henry B.	404	Benison, Alexander	291	——Peter	470
Bayliff, Rich. L. 218,	342	——Rich. Hen. John	43	——Jonathan	335	——Thomas	470
Bayly, Alexander Ross	187	Beazley, George Gant	318	——Samuel	250	——William	470
——Frederick	486	Beck, Richard Edw.	326	Benn, Anthony	39, 372	——*Hon.* W. Smyth	104
——George	85, 452	Beckham, Thomas	104	——Piercy	34, 371	——Wm. Tho. Philippe	356
——G.	464	Beckwith, Cha. *CB.*	103	Bennet, Philip	128	Berner, Carl Ernest	543
——Geo. Augustus	486	——Henry John	272	Bennett, Adrian	185	Berners, Herb. Johnes	257
——*Sir* Henry, *KH.*	104	——William, *KH.*	12	Bryan O'Donnell	486	Berry, Edward Ring	156
——Henry Elliott	356	Bedford, Rich. B. R.	312	——Francis Levett	280	——Geo. Fred.	228
——John	85, 401	——W. Fanshawe 34,	281	——George	65, 217	——Henry A.	234
——Neville Salt. K.	374	——Wm. Devaynes	515	——George B.	436	——James Parsons	470
——Paget	77	Bedingfield, John	264	——Henry Elkins	240	——Titus	531
——Rich. Kerr	255	——Philip	375	——James	470	Bertram, Chu. P. 81,	253
——Rich. Uniacke	178	Beech, William	527	——James	486	Best, George	382
——Thomas	486	Beechy, Fred. Robert	418	——Robert	290	——George Hollings	331
——Vere Temple	273	Beere, Daniel	187	——Thomas	2	——Gustavus George	541
——William	187	——Gerald Butler	205	——Thomas	151	——Mawdistly G. 84,	231
——Zachary Stanley	191	——William Henry	304	——Thos. Westropp	250	——Rd. Mordesley 62,	192
Baynes, Arthur S.	436	Beers, William	232	——William	104	——Thomas	296
——Chas. Dyneley	187	Beete, John Picton	106	——William	216	——Tho. Cha. Hard.	302
——Geo. Edward 82,	187	——Thos. Stirling	103	——Wm. Cha. Frind Burlton	182	Beswick, Frederick	363
——Geo. Macleod	470	Begbie, Francis Edm.	417	——Wm. Hen. Worthy	414	Bethune, Cha. Evers.	380
——Hen. J. Le Mar.	324	Behne, Chas. Aug. J.	542	Bennitt, Wm. Ward	173	——Dunc. Munro 63,	190
——John Lambert E.	281	Behrens, Hen. Chris.	541	Benson, Fra. N. B.		——Robert	106
——Robert Stuart	64	Belcher, Geo. B.	154	——Groves	211	Betson, William	192
——Simcoe	16	——William	247	——George Thomas	362	——William	155
Bayntun, Bath. Cha.	277	Beldham, John	299	——Hen. Roxby 44,	154	Bettesworth, Henry	470
——Charles	470	Belfield, Edward	402	——Tom	82, 294	Betts, George	315
Bazalgette, George	414	——William	515	——Wm. Welbore H.	466	——Wm. Thomas	232
——Jas. Arnold	255	Belford, William	486	Bent, George	231	Betty, Joshua Fred.	378
——John	103	BELGIANS, *His Majesty the King of the,*		——Geo. *CB.* 44, 125,	301	——Rowland Veitch	130
——Louis Howe	83, 228			——Hugh	375	——William Thomas	134
——Sidney Aug.	379	*KG. GCB. GCH.*	5	——John	384	Bevan, Charles D.	379
——Wm. Joseph	247	Bell, Arch. Hamilton	380	——Stephen Weston	178	Beverhoudt, Adam Von	75
Beachey, Rich. Wm.	307	——Arthur	442	——Thomas	415	——Adrian A. Von	323
Beadon, E. Musgrave	321	——Cha. Harland 81,	354	Benthall, John M.	157	Beveridge, Alex. Watt, *MD.*	443
——Reginald H.	283	——Charles William	152	Bentham, John	106		
——Valentine	76	——Edward Wells	11	Bentinck, Arth. C. 39,	132	Bewes, Wynd. Edm. 62,	303
Beale, Percy	192	——Edw. W. D. 57,	226	——Cha. Ant. Ferd. 9,	197	Bewley, George Wm.	133
——Robt. Henry	272	——George, *CB.*	18	——*Sir* Henry John		Bews, John Hamilton	266
——Thos. Chaytor	443	——James	208	——Wm. *KCB.* 11,	234	Bezant, John	486
——Wm. Gabbett	106	——James	120	——Walter T. Edw.	152	Bickersteth, Rob. 61,	134
Beales, William	51	——James Lancaster	381	Bentley, Alex. C. D.	470	Bicknell, Edw. Conduit	248
Beames, Pearson Tho.	298	——James N. *MD.*	332	——Frederic Stocks	123	——Herman	315
Beamish, Bernard	486	——*Sir* John, *KCB.* 8,	177	Benwell, Fred. Wm.	342	Biddle, John Matthew	144
——Caulfield Fra.	260	——John	511	——Thomas	486	——Thomas James	188
——Charles	62, 245	——John Charles	272	Benyon, Tho. Yate	133	——Waring Alex.	246
——David Gregory	181	——John Frederic	263	Bere, Edward Baker	106	Biddulph, Fra. Edw.	215
——Francis Potter	444	——Matthew John	201	Beresford, Edw. Mar.	166	——Michael Anthony	
——Geo. J. Newman	202	——Robert	106	——Francis Beresford	382	Shrapnel	56, 374
——Geo. Perceval	290	——Samuel	486	——George John	36	——Rich. Myddleton	126
——N. L.	106	——Sydney Wm.	315	——George Robert	470	——Robert	378
——Thos. Francis	352	——Thomas, *CB.*	104	——H. C. de la Poer	352	——Theophilus	470
——William Henry S.	151	——Thomas Lynden	363	——Henry Marcus	190	——Tho. Myddelton	32
Beasley, Geo. Tod.	181	——Whiteford John	332	——Marcus	10, 217	Bigge, Tho. Scovell	180
——Joseph Noble	323						

Index. 564

Biggs, John	132	Blackall, Robert	185	Bleazby, Fra. B.	486	Bolam, Chas. Godfrey	186
——Thomas	281	——Robert	120	Bleckley, T. M. *M.B.*	203	Bold, Walter Saxton	357
——Wm. Matthew	104	Blackburn, John	106	Blenkins, Geo. Eleazar	161	Bolden, Leonard	296
Bignell, Cha. Phillips	511	Blackburne, William	520	Blenkinsopp, Geo. Ant.		Boldero, G. Neeld 77,	220
Bigsby, George Gordon		——William	103	Leaton	56, 260	——Henry George	104
Chamberlin	404	Blacker, John Robert	470	——William	131	——Lonsdale	103
Bilham, David	520	——Lathan Wm.	436	Blennerhasset, Barry	104	Bolger, Edward	200
Billing, Arthur James	154	——William	148	——John Du B.	250	——George Edward	218
——Chas. Edward	177	Blackett, Charles Fra.	345	Blewitt, Charles	293	Bolland, Geo. Herbert	404
Billings, Francis Thos.	527	——Christopher Edw.	163	Bligh, Fred. C.	81, 253	Bolomey, Lewis W. Jas.	511
Billington, George M.	141	——Edward William	139	——George W.	83, 281	Bolton, Arth. Nassau	276
Bindon, Charles Hunt	328	——Edward William	343	Blinkhorn, Henry	135	——Augustus Samuel	123
——Henry Vereker	442	——Rob. Stewart	134	Blisset, Thomas	176	——Daniel	18, 399
Bingham, Alex. Baring	147	——William	340	Blissett, Henry	308	——Edw. Chichester	378
——Charles 38, 125,	372	Blackley, John Henry	380	Blois, William	29	——Francis John	358
——Geo. Lord 65,	163	Blacklin, Richard	43	——Wm. Thornhill	203	——John	51
——George Wm. Powlett, *CB.* 50,	291	Blackwell, Jas. Edw.	378	Blomefield, George	104	——John Haycroft	190
		Blackwood, John	534	Blood, Francis Gamble	298	——John Lawrence	375
——Henry 58,	181	Blair, Art. Kindersley	300	——John	296	——Philip	76
——Henry	328	——Cha. Thos. Fred.	188	Blomfield, Thos. Edwin	231	——Richard	182
——Tho. Rich. D.	340	——David Hunter	166	Bloomfield, Alfred	170	——Rich. G. Bomford	128
Binney, Chas. Richard	401	——Æneas Gordon	187	——Edwin	470	——Robt. Hen. *MD.*	532
Birch, Azim Salvator	258	——Jas. Bannatyne	183	——Hen. Keane 26,	195	——Samuel	486
——Alex. John Colvin	228	——Richard	260	——*Ld.J.A.D.KCB.*	486	——Theophilus	252
——Edward	195	——Thos. Newenham	486	——James Arthur	263	——William	279
——George	486	——Wm. Hen. Stopford	26	——John 18,	371	——Wm. John 79,	376
——James	470	Blake, Edward John	511	Closse, Edward Lynch	74	Bomford, Isaac Bomford	280
——James Francis	352	——Ethelbert H. *MD.*	274	——William C. L.	374	——John North	236
——Rich. J. Wyrley	140	——Frederick	173	Blount, Herbert 54,	296	Bonamy, John	50
——Robert Jones	207	——George Frederic	415	——Oscar Henry	308	Bonar, Alex. Macdonell	380
——Wyrley	260	——George Lascelles	414	——Robert	104	Bonavia, T. Emmanuel	368
Bird, Edward M.	106	——Geo. Pilkington	156	Bloxsome, Berkeley Ch.		Bonavita, Loreto	368
——George Beverley	269	——Henry Arthur	177	Wm. Chichester	353	Bond, Adolph. Fred. 61,	452
——Henry	277	——James Bunbury	486	——Wm. D.	226	——Clements Moffatt	246
——Henry 63,	358	——John	156	Bluett, Chas. Edw. L.	240	——David	240
——Henry Charles	106	——John	486	——Henry P.	193	——Edward	104
——Louis Saunders	121	——John Joseph	334	——W. H. P. Gordon	192	——Edward Staples	246
——Rob. Nicholas	218	——Lucius John	181	Blumberg, Fred. Wm.	154	——Frederic	156
——Shearman Godfrey	404	——Matthew Gregory	103	Blundell, Fred. *CB.*	120	——Henry	104
——Wm. Oliver	134	——Michael	148	——Hen. Blundell H.	344	——Henry	380
Birnie, Thomas Knox	170	——Richard, *RC.*	455	——Richard	136	——Henry	382
Biron, Edwin	180	——Robert Hoey Jex-	212	Blundstone, John	543	——Henry Auburey	330
Birrell, David	121	——Stephen	332	Blunt, Francis Chas.	436	——John	200
Birtwhistle, John	32	——Walter Francis	178	——Francis Theoph.	148	——Robert John	404
——John	240	——Wm. Greaves	134	——Grant	404	——Thomas Harman	356
Biscoe, George Grattan	51	——W. Williams, *CB.*	103	——Richard 6,	294	——Wadham Wynd.	470
——Robert	215	Blakely, Alex. Theo.	470	——Walter Frederick	202	——Wm. Dunn	279
Bishop, Arthur	240	Blakeney, Edw. Hugh	530	Blurton, George	250	——William Spittle	486
——Edgar Wain.	223	——*Rt. Hon. Sir Edw.*		Blyth, Augustus Fred.	43	Bone, Geo. Fred. *MD.*	441
——Henry	326	*GCB. GCH.* 6, 169,	463	——David	413	——Theo. Gord. *MD.*	442
——James	470	——Robert 80,	264	——D'Urban W. Farr.	257	Bonham, Francis	300
——Thomas	383	Blakiston, John 106,	123	——Frederick Samuel	252	——Jno. Brathwaite	104
——William	435	——Thomas Wright	377	——Matthew Smith	303	Bonney, Chas. Henry	272
——William	520	Blaksley, John	221	——Samuel Fritche	245	Bonnor, Benjamin John	380
Bishopp, Rich. Pret.	212	Blamire, Charles	341	——William D'Urban	151	——Thomas	106
Bisset, John Jarvis 34,	354	Blanchard, Arth. V. B.	190	Blythe, John David	260	Bonnyhare, Jas, *MD.*	326
Bissett, Richard S. A.	404	Blanckley, Ed. Jas. 80,	182	——Joseph Harry F.	486	Bontein, John Sims	416
Blachford, Aug. G. 31,	228	——Horatio N. Chas.	414	Boase, Geo. Clement	416	Booth, Edward	303
——Oswald Samuel	104	Bland, Edward Loftus	402	Bodkin, James	156	——H. J. Parkin 82,	257
Blachley, Henry	15	——Horatio	231	Bodle, George	362	——Jonathan	520
Black, Alfred Godfrey	236	——James	470	Boehmer, Frederick	177	——Robert	436
——George	104	——James Fox	307	Boevey, T. H. Crawley	298	——William, *CB.*	527
——G. Robt. Stewart	341	——John	527	Boghurst, Edward	486	——William	377
——James	383	——John L.	288	Bogle, Andrew Cathcart	192	——William	14
——James	511	——Robert John	486	——Robert	282	Boothby, Basil C. 465,	470
——James	520	Blane, Charles Collins	103	Boggie, John, *MD.*	531	——John George 77,	374
——John	486	——Charles G.	226	Boggis, James Edward	515	Borland, James, *MD.*	529
——Thomas	383	——Charles Garrow	436	Boiden, Jean Baptiste	544	Borrer, Cary Hampton	282
——Thomas	511	——*Sir Hugh S. Bart.*	104	Boileau, Chas. Hen.	286	Borrott, Herbert Chas.	178
——William Connel	137	——Robert, *CB.*	51	——Chas. Lestock	106	Berrow, John 82,	212
——William Thos.	196	——Seymour John 82,	270	——John Peter	486	Borrowes, Erasmus	314
——Wilsone	182	Blatherwick, Thomas	442	——Samuel Brandram	16	Borthwick, Alexander	283
Blackall, John	470	Blathwayt, Geo. Will.	104	——Wm. Simeon	403	——Michael Andrews	247
——John	76	Blay, Samuel Sutton	520	Boissier, John William	247	——Rt. MacGowan	312

E E

Index.

Borthwick, Walter 142	Bowlby, A. Picton 83,291	Braddell, Thomas 210	Brereton, Frank Sadlier 282
Borton, Arth., *CB.* 34, 362	——Harry Russell 217	Bradford, Edward 530	——Wm. *CB. KH.*
——Charles James 190	——Pulleney Edw. 264	——Francis R. 181	13, 370
——Edward Ellis 286	Bowler, John 106	——Geo. Nicholl J. 188	Breslin, Wm. I. *MD.* 532
——Henry Martin 380	Bowles, Edward 281	——Michael 404	Breton, Chas. E. B. 177
Bostlemann, Henry 543	——Sir G. *KCB.*8, 349,463	——Oliver John 250	——Henry Wm. 12
Bostock, Jas. William 207	——Humphrey 487	——Ralph 49, 159	——John 471
——John Ashton, *MD.* 167	——Vere Hunt 290	——Wilmot Hen. 52, 356	Brett, Chas. Curtis 359
Boswell-H., *Sir* G.A.F. 103	Bowling, John 534	Bradley, Henry 151	——Edward 234
Boswell, John 128	Bowman, Henry Samuel 471	——John Donaldson 202	——Edwin 131
Boteler, Robert 471	Bowness, John 106	Bradshaw, Alex. Fred. 346	——Harry Armstrong 257
Both, Caspar Von 542	——Joshua James 322	——Francis Green 487	——Henry 155
Bothmer, Bernard Von 541	Bowyer, George Henry 129	——James Edward 139	——John 344
——Ferdinand de 543	——Henry Atkins 146	——James Lewis 190	——John Davy 106
Bott, Thomas 84, 134	——Henry John 177	——John 444	——Kingston 340
Bottomley, Jos Drury 418	——Thomas James 227	——John Johnson 181	——Lionel Lowdham 350
Boucher, John Chas. 131	Boxer, Edw. Mounier 373	——Joseph John 282	——Rich. Rich W. 17
Boughey, John Fenton 173	Boyce, Abel Woodroffe 243	——Lawrence Aug. 376	——Wilford 307
Boulcott, John Wm. 322	——John 196	——Paris Wm. Aug. 57	——Wm. Freeland 59,273
Boulderson, John 300	——John Clarence 177	——William 240	Brettingham, Rich. W. 471
Boulnois, Stratton 300	——Octavius 237	Brady, H. Beauchamp 298	Brew, Charles 511
Boultbee, Edward J. 206	——Richard 177	——John Barrett 248	——Richard 349
Boulton, Chas. Arkoll 342	——Thomas 153	——Rupert George 172	Brewer, Thomas 416
——Richard 471	Boycott, Edw. E. D. 221	——Thomas Clark 443	Brewster, Hen. C. 62, 307
Bourbel, Aug. Alf. de 134	——William 236	——W. S. Richardson 106	Brice, Alex. Adair 487
Bourchier, Claud T. 78,343	Boyd, Alexander 515	Bragge, John Arthur 132	——George Tito 79, 210
——E. Fane, *CB.* 53,401	——Alex. Robt. A. 331	——William 103	——Wm. Henry 234
——George 444	——Charles 74	Braidley, Hen. Tring. 183	Brickdale, Matthew 420
——Henry Seton 416	——Edward 200	Braimer, James Louttit 487	Brickenden, R.T.W.L. 465
——Hugh Plunket 43	——Edward 50	Bramly, John Rob. J. 382	Bridge, Cyprian 42, 279
——James Johnes 270	——Fred. Wm. Arthur 415	Bramston, Thomas H. 160	——Edward 402
——John 315	——George Vachell 263	Bramwell, John 487	——George 123
——Legendre Ch. 61, 306	——Hen. Gillespie 242	Branch, Geo. Ferguson 511	——George 471
——Robt. Lennox 416	——James 87	Brancker, Wm. G. 380	——James 232
Bourke, Geo. Thomas 269	——Jas. Browne H. 210	Brand, Chas. Rowley 418	——Robert Onslow 471
——*Hon.* Edw. Roden 141	——Jas. Power 290	——Henry Robert 164	——William Albert 188
——*Hon.* J. Jocelyn 63,324	——Mossem 120	——James 106	Bridger, John 487
——Joseph 349	——Richard 515	Brander, Thos. Coven. 471	——John Huntingford 157
——Joseph 385	——Robert Tho. B. 363	——Wm. Maxwell 229	Bridges, Edward 186
——Oliver Paget 52	——William 240	Brandis, Edward Von 542	——Edw. Smith 160
——Paget John 195	——Wm. Cathcart 276	——Ferdinand de 543	——Henry Edward 132
——Thomas 86, 453	Boyes, Cha. R. *MD.* 531	——Frederick Von 542	Bridgett, Gregson 543
——Wm. Orme 212	——James Fischal 354	Brandling, John J. *CB.*	Bridgford, Sidney T. 417
Boustead, John 515	——Walter John 198	77, 373	Bridson, Wm. Paul 178
Bouverie, Ever. W. 11,152	Boyle, C. S. 463	Brandreth, Frederick 104	Brien, Edward Arthur 442
——Laur. Pleyd. 61, 310	——*Hon.* Edm. John 321	Branfill, Benj. Aylett 322	Briggs, George 106
Bovell, John Wm. 435	——Edward 298	Brannan, James 471	——James 337
Bovill, Edward 486	——Edw. Vicars 380	——John 520	——John 120
——James Owen 80, 350	——Gerald Edmund 345	Brathwaite, Frederick 527	——John 156
Bowater, Sir E. *KCH.* 7,266	——John Fred. C. 248	Brattle, Thomas 487	——John A. Julian 212
Bowden, George 511	——Robert 376	Braun, George 541	——John Pitts 296
——Henry George 167	——Robert 65, 413	Brauns, Charles 542	Bright, Rob. O. 57, 215
——Herbert G. 83, 223	——William 62, 326	Bravo, Alexander 349	Brigstocke, Augustus 269
——Wm. Carey 515	——William 515	Bray, Edward Wm. 318	Brinckman, Arthur 334
Bowdler, Geo. Andrew 486	——*Hon.* Wm, G. 77, 163	——Geo. Fred. C. 337	——Brinckman 103
——George Owen 252	Boylin, William 383	——William 142	Brinckmann, Ernest 542
Bowen, Charles 404	Boys, Edmund French 103	Braybrooke, Samuel 18	——Julius 542
——Edward 298	——Henry 106	——William 157	Brine, Andrew Gram 471
——Francis, *MD.* 463,534	Brabant, Edw. Yewd. 354	Breading, John Rem. 520	——Bruce 404
——Henry Griffith 324	Brabazon, Hugh 106	Brearey, Christ. Spen. 487	——Frederic 402
——H. St. John Cole 381	——Jas. Dupre 87, 210	Brebner, John 312	Bringhurst, John Hen. 106
——Hugh Thomas 51	——Jas. Henry 207	Bredin, Alexander 216	Brisac, Douglas P. 511
——John Watts 471	——Luke Brabazon 376	——Edgar G. 81, 376	Brisbane, *Sir* Thos.
——Robert 346	Brace, George Edw. 298	Breedon, Augustus 220	Makdougall, *Bart.*
——Robert 104	Bracken, Tho. P. A. 253	——Harry A. Arthur 175	*GCB. GCH.* 6, 243
——Thomas 182	Brackenbury, Cha. B. 377	Brem, Nich. Philibert de	Brisco, Hylton 104
——Thos. Frederick 253	——*Sir* Edward 104	74, 544	——Wastel
——William Rice 380	——Henry 172	Bremner, Alexander 534	Briscoe, Edward John 202
Bower, Geo. Cuthbert. 258	——Henry 380	Brenan, Gerald 243	——Henry, *MD.* 384
Bowers, Chs. D'Obree 350	Bradburne, Francis 487	——John 471	——Henry H. 315
——Chas. Robert 17	——Samuel 210	——Tho. Her. Alex. 415	——Henry Whitby 378
——Henry 435	Bradbury, Emanuel 129	Brendon, Algernon 81, 376	Brisley, Wm. Piers 383
——John Thomson 182	——John 129	Brennan, Richard 456	Bristow, Henry 103
Bowker, Henry Cowley 417	Bradby, Edward 304	Brereton, Charles 534	Broadbent, Corn. D. 345

Index.

Broadley, Edw. O.	62, 453
Broadrick, Edward	380
Brocas, Reginald	306
Brock, D. Cameron	169
——Edward	444
——James Athol	316
——Nichs. Mourant	316
Brockman, Chs. Fred.	178
——John Arthur	182
——Julius Drake	322
Brodhurst, John Edw.	131
Brodie, Francis	300
——Hugh, F. Ashley	381
Brodigan, Francis	234
Brodrick, Henry	285
Broke, Hor. Geo.	11, 324
Brome, Fr. H. Denny	181
——Fred.	463
Bromhead, Benj. P.	248
——Chas. James	229
——Edward	177
Bromley, Hen. Barrett	193
Bronner, Charles de	544
Brook, Rich. Crundel	252
Brook, Rd. Henry	353
——William John	237
Brooke, Arth. W. De Capell	139
——Chas. Clements	145
——Charles Francis	252
——Edw. Basil	28, 369
——Edw. Fra. Brown	253
——Edw. Thos.	403
——George, *CB*.	120
——Gustavus Holm.	403
——Henry	255
——Henry Francis	264
——Hen. Vaughan	335
——James Croft	58, 187
——Robert Wilmot	281
——Thomas	103
——Thomas	36, 197
Brookes, Joseph	246
——Joshua Rowland	416
——Richard Edw.	261
——William	82, 306
Brooks, Arthur	201
——George Benj.	120
——R. P.	362
Bros, Richard Follett	210
Brotherton, *Sir* Thos. William, *KCB*.	8, 129
Brough, Redmond W.	17
——Richard	515
Brougham, Wilfrid	146
Broughton, John D.	416
——Legh Delves	378
——Robt. Edwards	471
——Spencer D.	57, 373
——Wm. E. D.	37, 399
Broun, Montague C.	152
——Thomas	245
Brouncker, Hy. Fra.	229
Brown, Amyatt Ernlé	140
——Charles	487
——Charles Bradford	187
——Charles W.	288
——David Philip	142
——Edward	148
——Edward Cecil	264
——Ed. John Vesey	104
——Eugene	487
——Francis Carnac	487
——Frederick, *MD*.	532
Brown, Sir George, *GCB*. ——*KH*.	7, 343
——George	531
——George John	76, 139
——Gustavus, *CB*.	104
——Henry	463
——Henry James	314
——Hercules Edwin	302
——Hugh	75
——Jas. Montagu	85, 332
——John	247
——John	487
——John George	188
——John Henry	377
——John Tatton	16, 411
——John T. Butler	377
——Joseph	532
——Lancelot Chas.	280
——Nicholas R.	30
——Percival	43
——Richard Edward	277
——Robert	50
——Robert	272
——Robert	531
——Rob. B. Forsyth	151
——Robert Johnston	151
——Sidney Reynett	436
——Thomas	153
——Thomas	472
——Ths. Calderhead	157
——Th. Southwell	81, 274
——Walter Stewart	178
——William Edward	277
——William George	169
——Wm.Gustavus	31, 228
——Wm. Sampson	380
Browne, Alex., *M.D.*	532
——Andrew	56, 258
——Andrew Smythe Montague	137
——Arthur M. Peter	242
——Barton Parker	104
——Brotherton	104
——Aug. Ch. Gunter	139
——Chas. Edw. Gore	316
——Charles Fred.	245
——Charles Henry	182
——Charles Henry	338
——Charles Orde	379
——Cornwallis Wade	264
——Edward	260
——Edw. Pennefather Dalrymple	187
——Wade	300
——Edw. Stanley	64, 412
——Fielding,*CB*.	103,465
——Francis	534
——Francis Edw.	294
——*Hon.* Geo. Aug.	106
——George, *CB*.	104
——Geo. Richard	83, 324
——Henry	338
——Henry George	342
——Henry John	215
——Henry Ralph	60, 323
——Herbert Fr. Lewis	308
——James	220
——James	334
——James Frankfort Manners, *CB*.	57, 401
——*Hon.* Jas. Lyon	104
——John Fra., *RC*.	455
——*Hon.* John Howe Montague	312
——Mugens Jas. C.	205
Browne, Martin Jos.	341
——Melville	200
——Montague	228
——Peter Clifford	318
——P. Rutledge M.	471
——*Lord* Rich.Howe	185
——Rich. Th. Bookey	187
——Robert	318
——Rob. Fra. M.	103
——Rob. Wm., *AM*.	455
——St. John Thomas	38, 372
——Tho. Gore, *CB*.	163
——Valentine	471
——Walter John, *CB*.	120
——Wellington	314
——William	341
——William	363
——Wm. Benjamin	315
——Wm. Hen. S. M.	310
——Wm. Lloyd	148
——*Hon.* William	487
——William Pryce	185
——Wm. Sandys	151
Brownell, Joseph	358
Browning, Hugh Edm.	137
——Montague Chas.	326
——Wm. Henry	352
Brownlow, Edw. Fra.	300
——Francis	302
——Wm. Vesey	237
Brownrigg, Hy. John	436
——Henry Latham	319
——Latham, Col.	283
——J.Studholme,*C.B.*	35
Bruce, Alexander	534
——Alex.Cunningham	330
——*Lord* Charles William Bundenell	126
——Courtenay Wm.	134
——Edward Jackson	376
——Eyre Evans	120
——Geo. J. Brudenell	154
——James	383
——John	74, 453
——Michael	49, 159
——*Hon.* Robert	18
——Robert	60
——Robert	58, 172
——Robert	156
——Robert Cathcart	
——Robert Hervey	187
——Stewart Hervey	290
——Thomas	220
——William, *KH*.	104
——Wm. Tyrrell	106
——Wm. West James	334
Brumby, Charles	487
Brumell, William	231
Brune, Ernest A. P.	236
Brunker, James Robert	34
Brush, John Ramsay, *MD*.	532
Brutton, Edward	272
——Rob. Abernethie	415
Bruyeres, Hy. Pringle	516
Bryant, Jacob Francis	211
Bryce, George Leslie	202
Brydges, George	414
Brydon, Lewis Aug.	304
Brymer, James Edm.	318
Bryson, Allen, *MD*.	443
——Thomas	157
Bubb, Anthony	487
Buccleuch, W. F., Duke of	125
Buchan, Geo. Wm. F.	103
Buchanan, George	137
——Gilbert J. Lane	38, 372
——Henry James	82
——James	29
——Jas. John Neil	134
——Jas. Ross Gray	232
——John Grahame	471
——John L'E. L.	446
——Lewis Mans.	324
——Wm. Handasyde	186
——Wm. Theophilus	487
Buck, George	293
——Henry	84, 272
——Hugh Stukely	413
Buckeridge, Francis H.	487
Buckland, Francis T.	127
Buckle, Alfred John	306
——Geo. A. Bentley	252
——Rich. Nicholas	404
——Robt. Thos. *MD*.	442
——Sechwell Ray	416
Buckley, Chas. Edw.	344
——Edward Pery	10
——J.	465
——Wm. Henry	487
Budd, Frederick Edw.	413
——George	380
——Ralph	57, 202
——Richard	121
Budgen, Edward Hugo	316
——John	335
——Thomas	14
——Wm. Thomas	380
Bulger, George Ernest	192
Bulkeley, Charles	106
——Fra. Beaumaris	293
——Henry	135
Bulkeley, Richard Mostyn Lewis Williams	128
——Robert S. Wms.	145
——Tho. Jas. Williams	146
Bull, Fred. G.	61, 453
——John James	74, 276
Bullen, Henry	247
——Richard	403
Buller, Coote	81
——Edmund M.	85, 343
——Ernest Henry	344
——Fred. Charles	164
——Fred. Thos.	11
——*Sir* George,*KCB*.	13
——Henry George	58, 334
——James Hornby	156
——John	487
——John Edward	330
——Redvers Henry	283
——Reginald John	160
——Walter Gregory	334
Bulwer, E. G. *CB*.	64, 226
Bunbury, Charles Thos.	344
——Cha. Tho. V.	82, 316
——*Sir* Henry Edward, *Bt. KCB*.	103
——George William	267
——Henry Wm. *CB*.	41
——Stonehouse G.	80, 364
——Thomas, *CB*.	104
——William Reeves	316
Bunce, Julius	413
Bunn, Richard	247
Bunyon, Charles S.	487

E E 2

Burden, George 227	Burrell, Bryan 152	Butler, Rich. Pierce 310	Caldwell, Ralph Wm. 136
——Wm. 190	——Wm. Henry, MD. 531	——Robert Fowler 186	——Wm. B. 104
Burder, Wm. Howley 134	——Willoughby B. P. 270	——Thomas Pierce 228	Caley, Henry Francis 121
Burdett, Charles S. 104	Burridge, John Osborne 452	——Villars 293	Call, G. Fred. S. 56, 212
——Sir Chas. W. Bt. 273	——Thomas 177	——Lord Walter 106	Callander, G. Erskine 379
——Francis 104	Burroughes, Thos. D'E. 487	——Walter 471	——John A. Burn 128
——Sir Robert, Bart. 103	Burroughs, Fred. W.84, 332	——Webbe 61, 281	Callen, J. Chn. H. P. 300
Burdon, Robert 150	——Rich. Davies 270	——Whitwell 487	Calley, Henry 106
Burer, Gabriel 49	Burrowes, Peter 540	——Wm. F. 298	Callow, J. Woodyer 383
Burge, Benjamin Hen. 280	——Rob. Edw. KH. 103	——Wm. Theobald 187	Callwell, Robert J. 260
Burges, Somerville W. 471	——T. Aug. 260	Butt, John Wells 104	Calthorpe, Hon. Somerset
——Stapleton Dressing 302	Burrows, Arthur G. 53, 372	——John Thomas H. 306	John Gough 80, 133
Burgess, Chas. John 261	Burslem, J, Godolphin 487	——Robert Berkeley 382	Calvert, A. Motteux 375
——Henry Miles 380	——Nathaniel 295	——T. Bromhead 64, 312	——George 444
——Thos. Hen. MD. 446	——Rollo Gillespie 106	Butter, Archibald 206	——Reginald 147
Burgh, Francis de 147	Burt, James 539	——Henry Thomas 332	——Silvester 130
Burgmann, George 37, 400	——Charles Edw. 81, 376	Butterworth, Henry 487	Cambell, J. Goodrick 445
——George John 382	——George Henry 223	Butts, Aubrey Thos. 308	CAMBRIDGE, His
Burgoyne, Sir J. M. Bt. 160	Burton, Adolphus Wm.	——Fred. John 308	Royal Highnesss G.
——Sir John Fox,	Desart, CB. 77, 135	——William Pitt 176	W. F. C., KG. KP.
Bart. GCB. 7, 399	——A. Westbrooke 215	Butze, William 543	Duke of, GCB.,
——Rhodk. dhu G. H. 332	——Charles 341	Byam, Edward 11, 155	GCMG. 7, 125, 166
Burke, Bernard H. 156	——Charles William 326	——E. Willoughby G. 418	Cameron, Art. Wel. 331
——Henry 274	——Cuthbert Ward 415	——William 293	——Aylmer Spicer 231
——Hubert Plunkett 330	——Edward 531	Bygrave, Joseph 471	——Donald 487
——John 362	——Edw. John, MD. 440	Byng, A. Molyneux 160	——Donald Roderick 380
——Joseph 176	——E. J. Netterville 247	——George Stanley 345	——Duncan 487
——J. Hardman 77, 175	——Emanuel 511	——Hon. Gerald F. F. 487	——Dun, Alex. CB. 18
——Theobald 324	——Fowler 57, 338	——Henry Webb 253	——Eugene Hay 380
——Thomas 11	——Francis A. P. 104	——Hon. H. W. J.55, 163	——Geo. Simpson 181
——Walter Blake 212	——Gerard Septimus 201	Byrne, Francis Henry 520	——James 487
——William 106	——Hen. Aug. 202	——James Lambert 350	——James 511
Burkitt, Wm. Robert 304	——John Curson 471	——John 128	——John 487
Burlton, Geo. Le Hardy 487	——John Edward 330	——Luke 132	——John 59, 400
Burland, Benj. MB. 385	——John P. Mayers 290	——Thomas 62, 192	——John Cha. MD. 440
——Wm. Harris 190	——Robert Graves 141	——Thos. Edmund 376	——J. M'Leod, MB. 233
Burleigh, Godfrey W. 211	——William Penn 414	——Tyrrel Matthias 57	——Lachlan McL. 487
Burmester, A. F. 60, 280	Bury, George Butt 13	——Walo Rymer 272	——Nathaniel 104
Burn, Henry Wilson 487	——Phineas 152	Byron, Geo. Rochfort 290	——Patrick 120
——James 487	——Robert 145	——John 192	——Thos. Macknight 121
——James 515	Busfeild, William 223	——William Gerard 195	——Wm. Gordon 77, 177
——John Macvicar 379	Busfield, Currer F. 208	Bythell, Reginald 276	Campbell, Adam 453
——Robert 30, 371	Bush, H. Stratton 81, 253	Bythesea, Henry Fra. 169	——Adolphus Wm. 357
——Rob. David, MD. 384	——Robert 106	Cadell, Charles, KH. 104	——Alexander 50
Burnaby, Alex. Dickson 378	Bushe, C. Kendall 83, 280	Cadogan, Hon. G., CB. 29	——Alexander 487
——Charles Herrick 34	——John Fred. Wm. 541	Cafe, Haydon Lloyd 334	——Alexander 534
——Edwin 471	——Wm. Dascon 64, 142	Caffin, W. Geo. Chart 471	——Archibald 42, 452
——Edwyn Sherard 59, 159	Bushman, George 130	Cahill, Alexander 532	——Archibald 59, 217
——Fred. Gustavus 128	——Henry Augustus 142	——A. Peile, MD. 183	——Arch. Campbell 166
——Eust. Beaumont 269	Bussell, Edward 220	——Nicholas 487	——A. Colin Renton- 106
——Richard 87, 401	——Gust. Wm. H. 226	——Patrick 471	——Arch. Neil 59, 264
——Richard Beaumont 30	Bustard, William 298	Cain, Michael 540	——Arch. Wm. Fred. 382
Burnand, George Sapte 133	Busteed, John 487	Caine, H. Montcath 233	——Charles 487
——Norman 164	——Michael 487	——William 104	——Chas. Albert Lyon 404
Burne, Godfrey James 303	Butcher, Arthur 413	Caird, Alex. M'Neil 210	——Charles D. MD. 444
——Owen Tudor 217	——John Barlow 414	Cairncross, John 416	——Charles F. 85, 323
Burnell, Edw. S. P. 164	——John Lewis 511	Cairnes, George 106	——Charles William 487
——Hugh D'Arcy P. 153	Butler, Anthony 323	——Robt. James 377	——Colin 264
Burnet, John 487	——Charles 334	——William 220	——Colin 106
Burnett, Edm. Sidney 379	——C. Crawford Y. 213	——William Henry 264	——Colin 511
——Hamilton 210	——Chas. Richard 104	Cairns, William 383	——Colin Alex. 106
——John Philip 276	——Edmond, RC. 455	Calcott, Charles R. B. 232	——Colin Fred. 55, 261
——Richard Parry 471	——Edw. Chas. 81, 246	——George Berkeley 106	——Donald 13
——Thomas 382	——Edw. Kent S. 104	Caldecott, Henry 106	——Duncan 77
Burney, H. Somerville S. 360	——Edward Le Breton 307	Caldecott, Barnes J. 175	——Duncan Gordon 417
——William, KH. 29	——Fra. Le Breton 203	——Charles Thos. 307	——Sir Edw. FitzGer.
Burningham, Hen. G, C. 279	——Fra. Wm. H. D. 239	——Geo. Fowler 296	Bt. 82, 281
Burns, Hen. Macdonald 228	——George 534	——John Alex. 248	——E. S. Norman 106
——Samuel John Jas. 228	——Henry 81, 277	Calder, William 36	——Fielding Alex. 39, 411
Burnside, Fred. Rob. E. 220	——Henry 293	——William Menzies 266	——Francis W. G. 167
——Geo. Samuel 269	——James Arthur 15	Calderon, C. Matthew 139	——Fran. Pemberton 312
——Hen. E. H. 82, 286	——Percy Archer 56, 234	Caldwell, Sir Jas. Lily-	——Frederick 7, 370
Burr, John 157	——Pierce O'Brien 283	mon, GCB. 120	——Frederick 85, 354
Burrard, Sydney 63, 160	——Rd. Alexander 471	——John Fletcher 229	——Fred, Alex. 58, 373

Index.   568

Campbell, Fred. Augus 282
—— George 34, 370
—— Geo. H. Fred. 43, 452
—— Geo. Murray L. 379
—— Gilbert Edw. 331
—— Henry Dundas 104
—— Henry Francis 302
—— Hy. Geo. Lyon 223
—— Henry Jermyn M. 471
—— Hon. H. Walter 164
—— Henry W. 106, 463
—— Horatio Guy 416
—— Hugh Archibald B., CB. 57, 373
—— James 87, 367
—— James 103
—— James 104
—— James 487
—— James 511
—— James 532
—— James Hay 300
—— John, CB. 120
—— John, MD. 442
—— John 211
—— John 335
—— John 465, 471
—— John, MD. 463, 532
—— John 15
—— John 28
—— John 76
—— John Ball 233
—— John Cam. 106, 463
—— John C., MB. 139
—— J. Eneas Deans 332
—— J.F.Glen.CB.,26,330
—— John Henry 242
—— John M'C. 86, 376
—— John Pennock 237
—— John Thomas 185
—— Sir John W. Bt. 378
—— Morris Robinson 363
—— Neil 312
—— Patrick John 375
—— Patrick Scott 76
—— Patrick W. FitzR. 104
—— Robert 148
—— Robert 106
—— Robt. Chas. W. 379
—— Robt. Mitchell 404
—— Robt. Olphert 237
—— Rupert 487
—— Thomas Edmund 106
—— Walter 43, 452
—— Walter M. T. 403
—— William 172
—— William 471
Campion, Wm. H. 302
Campsie, Geo. R. 106
Canavan, John 212
Cane, Robert Emmett 380
—— Stopford 103
Cannon, Æneas, MD. 534
—— Rev. Francis 455
—— James 487
—— John Smith 337
—— Osborne Barwell 338
—— Ronquier John 471
Cant, David 312
Capadose, Henry 471
Capel, Arthur A. 321
—— Sydney Aug. 81, 452
Capon, David, CB. 120
Carbery, Andrew Tho. 203
—— John J. H. 202

Carbery, Wm. Declan 352
Carberry, D. Wm. 445
Cardell, George 444
Carden, Fred. Walter 140
—— George 180
—— Henry Robert 57
—— Paul Kyffin 511
—— William Joseph 308
Cardew, Ambrose M. 190
—— Geo. Masters 295
—— Henry 378
Cardiff, Rich. Wing. 195
Cardigan, Jas. T. Earl of KCB. 11, 133
Carew, H. W. S. 236
—— Robert 487
—— Walter Palk 128
Carey, Cha. LeMesurier 81, 290
—— Ernest Adolphus 223
—— Falkland 376
—— Francis 74, 232
—— Geo. Jackson 34, 354
—— James, RC. 455
—— John Westropp 511
—— Langer, MD. 385
—— Le Merchant Jas. 300
—— Michael 487
—— Rev. Nicholas 539
—— Robert 65
—— Thomas 224
—— Thomas Priaulx 377
—— Tupper 527
—— Walter Nowell 221
—— William 377
—— Wm. Dobree 379
Carfrae, John 120
Cargill, Wm. Walter 123
Carlaw, John 444
Carleton, D. W. 49, 163
—— Fred. Hone 328
—— William F. 282
—— William Henry 220
—— Wm. Naper 145
Carlisle, Anthony 282
—— John Robson 180
—— Thomas 306
Carloss, John Baxter 471
Carlow, Stewart Jas. 261
Carlyon, Clement W. 416
—— Thos. Tristrem S. 106
Carmichael, C. M. CB. 120
—— Geo. Lynedoch, 87, 335
—— James D. CB. 55, 240
—— Maurice Thomson 331
Carnaby, Alex. 487
Carnegie, W. F. L. 471
Carnegy, Alex., CB. 120
—— Jas. A. Ogilvy 220
—— Pat. Alex. W. 152
Carney, Thomas 213
Carolan, Geo. M'Gusty 302
Carpenter, Charles 376
—— Fredk. Stanley 435
—— G. W. W. 86, 185
—— Thos. David 121
Carr, George 440
—— John 192
—— John Ralph 177
—— Jonas King, MD. 231
—— Oswald 378
—— Ralph 471
—— Ralph 487
—— Ralph Edward 246

Carr, Samuel 527
Carrick, Somerset A.
Butler, Earl of 160
Carriere, Charles H. 342
Carrington, Charles W. 414
Carroll, James, MD. 191
—— James 520
—— John Thomas 248
—— Patrick 520
—— Walter 213
—— Wm. Joseph 404
Carruthers, Rd., CB. 104
—— Rich. James S. 331
—— William 64
Carson, John 520
—— Rd. Ber., MB. 173
—— William, MD. 440
Carstens, Rudolph 542
Cartan, William 58
Carte, John E., MB. 203
—— William 463
Carter, Arthur Shaen 269
—— Edward 328
—— Geo. Wm. 193
—— Harry Lee 157
—— Hugh Bonham 164
—— John Collis, MD. 529
—— John Henry 520
—— John Money 471
—— Rowland Winburn 316
—— Samuel George 288
—— Wm. George 164
—— Wm. Fred. 78, 290
—— William Henry 207
Carthew, Edm. John 79, 375
Cartmail, Joseph 300
Carwithen, Geo. Terry Lydor 231
Cartwright, Henry 103
—— John Theodore 354
—— Reginald 206
—— Stewart Davies 152
—— William 15
Cary, Annesley 226
—— Annesley 239
—— Lucius F. B. 345
—— Tho. Alphonso 349
—— Wm. Lucius 471
Casault, Louis Adolphe 342
Casement, Thomas 286
Casey, Thomas Page 471
Cashman, Richard Uniacke, MD. 384
Casolani, Frederick 436
Cass, Arthur Herbert 146
—— John 383
Cassan, A. W. 455
—— Edw. Sheffield 487
—— Matthew 77, 452
Cassidy, Arthur 156
—— Francis P. 83, 243
—— Fred. Young 239
—— John 296
—— Loftus 303
—— Thomas 328
Casson, John Taylor 202
Castieau, John Buckley 74
Castle, Frederick John 264
—— William 515
Castray, Luke R. 436
Cater, Thomas Orlando 15
—— Wm. Edmund 175
Cathcart, Hon. Adol. F. 471

Cathcart, Hon. Aug. Murray 56, 337
—— Hon. Frederick Macadam 26
—— Hugh Wm. Mort 240
—— Reginald Arch. E. 164
Cator, John Farnaby 471
—— Thomas William 307
—— William, CB. 10, 370
Cattell, Edward 436
—— William 133
Catton, Rich. Tho. G. 245
Catty, Charles P. 84, 182
Caulfield, Daniel 471
—— George 345
—— John 106
—— John 253
Cautley, Henry 404
Cavan, Philip Charles 104
Cavanagh, Wm. 357
Cavarra, Giuseppe 368
Cavaye, William 120
Cavendish, Lord Edw. 345
—— Hon. Henry Fred. Compton 8, 130
—— Henry George 296
—— James Chas. 379
Cay, Charles Vidler 164
—— Eustace 299
Cecil, Lord Adelbert P. 345
—— Lord Eustace H. Brownlow Gascoyne 163
—— Lord Thomas 103
Ceely, Arthur James 255
Cellem, Robert 527
Cetto, Louis Chas. Aug. Adrian de 380
Chabot, L. W. Visc. de, KCH. 103
Chads, John Henry 283
—— Wm. Catherwood 487
—— William John 77, 291
Chadwick, Edw. Fred. 280
—— Geo. Minchin 190
—— John 463, 487
—— Robert 151
—— Thos. Massey 188
—— William 463, 487
Chaffey, John 140
Chaine, William 135
—— William 139
Chalk, Frederic Murray 206
Challis, John Henry 487
Chalmer, F. D. 106
Chalmers, Andrew 527
—— Charles David 380
—— Fred. W. Marsh 344
—— John 172
—— Patrick 280
—— William 211
—— Sir William, CB. KCH. 8, 310
—— W. Kelman, MD. 216
Chaloner, John 471
Chamberlain, Sir Hen. Orlando Robert, Bt. 123
Chamberlin, Edw. H. 345
—— W. R. Bigsby 229
Chamberlayne, J. C. 487
—— Neville B, CB. 125
—— William 10
—— Wm. John 59, 352
Chambers, Chas. Hall 420
—— David Francis 306

Chambers, Evander 136	Chesney, Fra. R. 13, 370	Clark, James Edward 224	Clayton, FitzRoy A.T. 160
——Francis Hen. 250	——Francis Rawdon 401	——John, KH. 17	——Francis Henry 277
——George Fred. S. 380	Chesshire, Edward 471	——John, MD. 440	——George 341
——Henry 269	Chester, Arthur 304	——John Stephens 471	——James 227
——James W., MD. 245	——Heneage Charles 236	——Nassau 139	——Richard 296
——John 487	——John 86, 452	——Thomas 228	——Rich. Nugent 200
——Montagu 511	Chetwode, George 80, 143	——Thomas 242	——ValentineGardner 404
Chambre, William 32	——Richard 33	——Thomas 532	——William Clayton 319
Chambres, Wm. C. 487	Chetwynd, Hon. C. C. 267	Clarke, Alexander Ross 402	——Sir Wm. Rob. Bt. 10
Chamley, Braithwaite 318	Chevalier, Charles 487	——Andrew 401	Cleather, Edward John 104
Champion, Edw. Ken. 487	——George Robert 293	——Augustus 120	——Wm. Barclay Gor-
——Fred. Albert 270	Chichester, Adol.J.S.C.146	——Chas. Anthony 527	don 312
——Reginald Hen.80, 376	——Arthur 471	——Charles George 277	Cleaveland, Fred. Darby,
Chancellor, Fred. H. 374	——Arthur Charles 471	——Chas. Mansfield 277	39, 372
——John 471	——Hon. A.G.C. 60, 308	——Douglas Bennet 435	——James 383
Chandler, George Lee 374	——Cha. Raleigh 80, 363	——Fred.Geo. Nuttall 352	——Samuel 373
——John Thomas 263	——Cornwallis H. 200	——George Calvert 51,137	Cleeve, C. K. 464
Channer, Alfred W. 220	——Edmund P. 135	——George Ourry 263	——Stewart Alex. 269
Channon, John James 157	——Fra. Sherard 223	——Guy 33	Clegg, William 195
Chaplin, Arth. Lewis 436	——Henry Manners 321	——Henry 527	Cleghorn, George 137
——Frank 86, 131	——Hugh Arthur 315	——H. 157	Cleland, James Vance 135
——John Worthy 295	——John Octavius 207	——James 15	——Robt. Stewart 135
——Percy 269	——Newton Charles 135	——James 38	Clement, R. Alleyne 296
——Thomas 103	——Robert Bruce 315	——James Cumming 307	Clements, F. W. Rich. 404
Chapman, Alfred Aug.	Child, A. 465	——James George 261	——Henry 50
61, 212	——George 527	——J.StanhopePatrick 280	——Henry Topham 141
——Arthur Trevor L. 243	——George Richard 511	——John 139	——William Henry 415
——Chas. Samuel 273	——Smith Hill 132	——John 335	——William 269
——Fred. Barclay 141	——William 63, 453	——John 342	Clendon, Chas. Hope 415
——Frederick E. CB.	Childs, Joseph 15	——John, MD. 444	——William 35
37, 400	——Joseph Clarke 374	——John Cumming 200	Clephane, Rob. D. 104
——Geo. Henry Jas.	Chilton, Henry Haskett 132	——John Lardner 377	Clerihew, George, MD. 439
Mowbray 180	Chinn, Edward 177	——Joseph 16	Clerk, Alexander 436
——Hen. Parker 217	Chippindall, Edwd. 79, 215	——Joseph 540	——Godfrey 84, 344
——John James 417	——John Armitage 207	——Michael 144	——Henry 85, 373
——John Strange 530	Chisholm, Alex. Bain 231	——Montague de Sales	——John 344
——William D. 212	——Stewart 530	McKenzie G. Aug. 267	Clerke, Holt Waring 288
——Wm. Samuel 247	Chislett, Wm. Oakley 436	——Patrick Joseph 328	——Rich. Woll. 82, 232
Chapple, Edward 335	Chislette, Henry 534	——Paul Francis 277	——St. John Aug. KH.
——Robt. Augustus 384	Cholmeley, Hugh H. 160	——Robert 14	11, 306
Charleton, Fred. Hone 328	Christian, Samuel 239	——Robert 135	——Shadwell Henry 220
——Henry Wilmot 104	Christie, F.Gordon 82, 452	——Robert Boucher 298	——Sir Wm.Hen. Bt. 104
——Tho. Henry 298	——Henry Paget 56, 373	——Robert Brooks 252	Clery, Cornelius Fra. 240
Charlewood, John 106	——James Edm. 255	——Robert Stuart 201	——Daniel Geran 177
Charley, John 276	——John 511	——SeymourFitzJohn 253	——Geo. Carleton 154
Charlier, Charles Wm. 436	——John 125	——S. Molyneux 236	——James 342
Charlton, Edw. Spicer 335	——S.Tolfrey,CB. 35,314	——Stanley de Astel 150	Cleveland,Fred. D. 39, 372
——Rd. Granville 315	——W. B. Blayney 314	——Thomas 380	——Geo. D. Dickson 340
——Saint John 471	——William Harvie 106	——Walter 487	——H. Duke of, KG. 9
Charretie, Thomas 103	Chrystie, John Alex. 169	——William 55	——J. Wheeler 120
Charter, Ellis Jas. 68, 362	Church, H. Backhouse 228	——William 303	Cliffe, Edward 273
Charteris, Hon. Rich.	——Sir R., CB.GCH. 104	——William 487	Clifford, Hon. Hy.Hugh 60
49,166	Churchill, Cha. Henry	——William 520	——Henry 384
Charters, Robert 527	Spencer 79, 281	——Wm. HenryHardy	——JohnJames, MD. 145
——Samuel 74	——George Onslow 206	Forbes 59	——Miller 78, 373
Chartres, John Smith 443	——John Spencer 261	——Wm. Henry Jas. 272	——Richard Cormick 192
Chatfield, Cha. Kyrle 217	Chute, Arthur 334	——Wm. Hill Dawe 273	——Rob. Cav. Spen. 103
——Frederick 487	——James 273	——Wm. Palmer 342	Clifton, Sir Arthur Benj.
——George Kemp 266	——Richard 188	Clarkson, Cha. Jas. P. 237	KCB. KCH. 6, 136
Chatterton, Sir James	——Richard 232	——FrederickWilliam 250	——Chandos Fred. 148
Chas. Bart. KH. 10, 140	——Richard William 381	——T. Hollingworth 341	——Fred. Chandos 352
——Oliver Nicolls 453	——Trevor 31, 299	——Thomas Reeder 296	——Robt. Walter 384
Chauncy, Cha. Henry 264	Cinnamond, Joseph 487	——Walter 520	——Thomas Henry 57
Chawner, Edw. Hoare 471	Clancy, Richard 205	——William Henry 195	Clinton, Lord Edw.Wm.
Chaytor, John 36, 400	Clapcott, Charles 85, 240	Clavell, Richard King 412	Pelham 343
Cheape, Sir J. KCB. 120	Clapp, William Henry 446	Clavering, H.Mordaunt 103	——Frederick 103
Cheese, Joseph 471	Clapperton, John Wm. 418	Clay, Aiskew 233	——Henry 103
Cheesman, Edwin T. 445	Clare, Benjamin 487	——Albert Newby 312	——Henry Renebald 160
Cheetham, Charles 76	Claremont, Edw. Stop-	——George 215	——Michael 224
Chepmell, Charles 471	ford, CB. 42	——Richard 310	Clitherow, Jn. Christie 104
Chernside, H. L. 77, 374	Clark, Charles John 342	——Wm. Waldegrave	Clive, Edward 471
Cherry, Apsley 328	——Edw. Stevens 487	Pelham 487	——Hon. Geo. Herbert
——Cha. E. Le M. 240	——Geo. A. 520	Clayfield, Edw.Ireland 471	Windsor 270
Chesney, C. Cornwallis 402	——James Alston 152	Clayhills, Jas.Menzies 185	——Henry Edward 160

Clive, Henry Somerset	404	Codrington, Oliver 444	Collins, Francis, MD. 443	Connor, Frederick	172
Cloete, Sir Abra. Josias,		——Sir Wm. John,	——Francis 520	——John	316
CB. KH.	14	KCB. 9, 273	——Fras. Frederick 153	Conolly,Hen.Hamilton	376
Close, Arthur R.	257	Cody, William 352	——James 141	——James	57
——Frederick	376	Coen, William John 357	——James Joseph 282	——John Aug. 78,	163
——Geo. Champagne	260	Coëtlogon,H.W.R. de 205	——John, M.D. 323	——Patrick	520
——Maxwell	103	Coffey, Edward 206	——Rich. George 540	Conor, John Hornby	221
——William John	203	——Francis 233	——Samuel Travers 416	Conran, Edward 77,	352
Cloudt, Morris de	541	Coffin, Sir Edw. Pine 527	——Stephen Edward 511	——George	120
Clowes,Geo. Gooch 87,	144	——Isaac Campbell 121	Collinson, Tho. B. 85, 401	——Murrell	276
——Robert Langley	304	——Isaac Tristram 220	Collis, Gust. W. Berry 183	Conroy, Henry George	103
Clutterbuck, Geo. W.	290	Cogan, Francis 442	——Peter 471	Constable, James	177
——Jas. Edmund,MD.	211	Coghlan, Edward 362	——William 340	Constant, John	539
——William	276	——Hunter Alex. 213	——William 488	——Stephen Price	133
Clyde,Colin,Lord, GCB.		——John 532	Colliss, John 471	Conway, Tho. Sydenham,	
	7, 332	——Tho. RC. 455	Collum, John Deering 247	CB. 42,	159
Coast,MichaelW.Lade	345	——William Charles 172	——William 334	Conyers, Charles Edw.	78
Coates, Charles	341	Coke, John Talbot 221	Colls, Robert Stacy 86, 240	Conyngham, Fra. Marq.	
——Frederick	146	——Matthew 197	——William 488	of, KP. GCH.	17
——John, MD.	232	——Hon. Wenman Cla-	Colman, Geo. Butler T. 62	Cooch, Arthur Edw.	208
——William Henry	531	rence W. 60, 125, 166	——Thomas 104	——Charles	79
Coats, John	106	Colahan,John, MD. 229	——Wm. Fred. A. 272	——James Vaughan	180
Coathupe,H. Bentinck	302	Colborne, Hon. Fras.	——Wm. Thomas 471	Coode, Chas. Penrose	86
Cobb, John	415	CB. 40, 182	Colomb, Geo. Hatton 375	Cook, Abraham	356
——Robt. Norton	269	——Hon. James 58	——Geo. Thomas 17	——Alfred	252
Cobbe, Alex. Hugh 78,	323	——Hon. John 282	——John Chas. R. 416	——Arthur	188
——Chas. Power	200	Colby, Hen. Aug. 76	Colquhoun, F. C. 436	——Edwin Adolphus	106
——George 9,	370	Colchester, Thomas 532	——H. M. Lamont 308	——Henry	342
——George Power	233	Colclough, Anth. C. 531	——Isaac 210	——Jervis	75
Cobbold,Ernest St. George		——Beauchamp 215	——Wm. Campbell 205	——Robert	220
	382	——George 374	Cult, Charles Russell 276	——William Surtees	471
——Frederick	487	——M'Carty 488	——Geo. Fred.Russell 226	Cooke, Adolphus	488
Cobham, Alex. Wm.	258	Cole, A. L. CB. 39, 210	Colthurst, David L. 210	——Anthony Cha. 79,	401
——George Henry	200	——Francis Burton 185	——James Nicholas 318	——A. T. J.	463
——John Tho. Lyon	266	——George 520	——James Robert 104	——Edward Bowen	318
Cochran, James	106	——Harry Parnell 404	Colvile, Fiennes Mid. 257	——Jas. Robt. Davies	380
——John	383	——Henry 197	——Frederick 471	——John Henry 104,	123
Cochrane,BayardClark	404	——Hon. Hen. Arthur 471	——Henry 11	——Tho.Valentine 84,	413
——George Henry	187	——Jas. Tho. 386	Colvill, Hugh George 236	Cookes, George	471
——George	104	——John 218	Colville, Hon. Wm. Jas.	Cookesley, Aug. F.	436
——Hugh Stewart	185	——John A. 57, 205	78, 343	——Edw. Murray	223
——John Thomas	383	——John B. 464	Colvin, Wm. Butterw. 133	Cookney, Jas. W.	123
——Robert 75,	455	——John William 488	Colwell, Geo. H. T. 417	Cookson, Alf. Edw.	337
——R.	465	——Pennel 14	——John Blackwood 415	Cookworthy, Wm. S.	282
——Rupert Inglis	243	——Richard Sweet 364	Combe, Matt. M.D. 384	Coombe, Charles	532
——Thomas 86,	358	——Robert 104	Combermere, S. Visc.	——Joseph	488
——William	487	——RobertJohn,MD. 532	GCB. GCH. 5, 126, 462	Coope, Wm. Jesser	185
——Hon.Wm.Erskine	106	Colebrooke, Jas. Robt. 50	Comyn, John Sarsfield 384	Cooper, Arthur	134
——Wm. Montague	236	——Jas. Robt. A. 318	Comper, John Tho. 527	——Arthur Sisson	231
Cockburn, Alexander	471	——SirWm.Macb.Geo.	Condell, Cha. Edw. 332	——C. H.	464
——Chas. Fred.	376	CB. KH. 10, 370	Coney, Arthur Henry 295	——Charles Kelly	488
——Cha.Vansittart 38,	372	Coleman, Charles 511	——Rev. T. 455	——Edward Hen. 59,	159
——Sir Francis 8,	335	——Henry F. George 136	——Walter John 136	——Godfrey 83,	156
——Geo. Wm.	255	Coleridge, Fra. Geo. 231	Congdon, Geo. W. 44	——Henry 30,	260
——Jas.Balfour,MD.	384	Coles, Josias R. J. 65, 145	Congreve, George CB. 26	——Hen. Towry M.	416
——James 60,	452	——Richard George 169	——William 177	——Hen. Fallowfield	414
——James	126	——Robt. Bartlett 10,293	Coningham, Henry 120	——John	338
——James	520	——Wm. Cowper 11	——William 488	——John	540
——James Geo.	182	Collette, Henry 77, 295	Conington, John Codd 200	——John Coleberd	188
——Joseph Egerton	380	Colley, Geo. Pomeroy 172	Connel, Abr. Jas. Nisbett,	——Joshua Harry	185
——Phineas Charles	488	Collier, Charles, MD. 530	MD. 532	——Leonard Morse	32
——Thomas Hugh 84,	257	——Herbert Crom. 144	Connell, Adolp. Fred. 374	——Loftus L. Astley	321
——Wm. Horace	106	——James 511	——Francis John 237	——Richard Aug.	167
Cuckcraft,Wm.WildJos.	52	——Jas.SamuelCurrie 444	——Henry 435	——Robert	132
Cockell,Edw.Dampier	323	Colling, John 232	——James 530	——Samuel	488
——William	103	Collings, A. MD. 532	——Sept. Sherson 220	——Thomas	520
Cocker, Barnard Wm.	104	——George Mansell 404	——William 178	——William	299
Cockerill, T, Marshall	131	——John Edw. 56, 242	Conner, Daniel 416	——William John	188
Cockle, John Robert	286	Collington, John W. 377	Connolly, Edw. Jos. R. 414	Coote, Charles James	212
Cocks,Chas.Lygon 49,	163	Collingwood, Clennell 378	——Richard Geo. 412	——Charles Thomas	190
——Octavius Yorke	177	——Wm. Pole 81, 220	——Thos. Wm. John 404	——Chidley	104
——Philip Reginald	41	Collins, Edward Arch. 232	——Wm. Hallett 7	——George	196
Codd, William	106	——Edward 191	Connop, Henry 104	——Henry Joseph	82
Coddington,Arthur B.	404	——Esau 161	——Richard 17	——Richard	261

Index.

Coote, Rd. Gethin C. 488
—— Thomas Gethin 318
Cope, Geo. Harwood 202
Copeland, George 520
—— Thomas 520
Copinger, Henry 60
Coppin, Charles Fra. 415
Coppinger, Dudley B. 273
—— John Murray 488
Corballis, John Bart. 250
—— Wm. Richard 153
Corban, Wm. Watts 266
Corbet, Edwin And. 153
—— Rich. Arthur 173
Corbett, Aug. Patrick Meyers, MD. 296
—— Edmund 147
—— Stuart, CB. 121
—— William 85, 270
—— William 156
—— Wm.Hen., MD. 315
Corcoran, Alexis 364
Cordue, Samuel 280
Corfield, Alf. Downie 187
—— James Winsmore 272
Corham, William 488
Corlett, Thomas Art. 446
Cormick, John 63, 217
Cornes, John 213
—— John Edwin 403
Cornish, Cha. Orchard 213
Cornwall, Frederick 306
—— George 83, 332
—— W. H. Gardner 253
Cornwallis, Fiennes 139
Correll, Charles 315
Corrie, Samuel Tho. 213
—— Wm. Taylor 195
Corrigan, John Jos. 131
Corry, George 187
Coryton, Geo. Fred. 192
—— George Hunt 49
—— John Rawlins 7, 411
Cosby, Thomas Prittie 202
—— William 488
Cosens,Arth. Fred. P. 191
—— Geo. Weir 260
—— Robert 170
Cossar, Walter 420
Costin, Charles 202
Costley, J. W. W. 226
—— Theoph. Byers 472
—— Wm. R. C. 120
Costobadie, Clert. H. 136
Cotter, Arundel Hill 188
—— Duncan D. D. 183
—— John 175
Cotterell, Francis 383
Cottingham, Edw. R. 380
—— Thomas 488
Cotton,Adolph.Geo.F. 123
—— Corbet 30
—— Edw. Antonius 472
—— Geo.Wm. Vernon 341
—— James M.Vernon 233
—— Lynch Stapleton 338
—— Stapleton Charles 123
—— Sir Sydney John, KCB. 17
—— Thomas Forrest 531
—— Hon. Well. H. S. 58
—— Sir Willoughby GCB. KCH. 6, 240
Couch, William 223

Couche, Richard 511
Coulson, George Bell 342
—— John Byron B. 344
Coupe, Robert 205
Couper, Sir George, Bart. CB. KH. 103
—— Henry Edward 291
Court, John 515
Courtenay, Charles S. 185
—— Geo. Henry 488
—— Geo. Townsend 527
—— Wm. Allan 472
Couttis, John Chas. G. 37
Courtland,Arth.C.Van 131
Courtney, Edw. Hen. 403
—— Edward 436
Covenay, James 488
Coventry, Gilbert W. 312
—— John W. 205
Covey, Charles 296
Cowan, Alex.O. MD. 444
—— Charles 440
—— Joseph Henry 140
—— Patrick Joseph 314
Coward, Charles 446
—— Geo. Fletcher 350
Cowburn, Thos. Brett 270
Cowell, Henry 202
—— Henry Robert 175
—— James D. 84, 146
—— John 520
—— John Clayton 85, 402
—— John S. C. KH. 104
Cowen, Henry Lionel 353
Cowley, Charles 488
Cowper, Andrew John 205
—— Geo. Alex. MD. 532
—— Henry 515
Cowtan, Edwin 153
Cox, Charles 472
—— Charles 515
—— Charles 104
—— Charles James 123
—— Charles Henry 283
—— Charles Thomas 488
—— Douglas Leith 515
—— Edmund Henry 414
—— Easton John 175
—— Francis Edw. 86, 402
—— George Herbert 272
—— Henry C. M. 120
—— Howard Plestow 221
—— James Ponsonby 402
—— John, KH. 14
—— Jno.Hamilton 64, 306
—— John Ponsonby 296
—— Jno.Wm.CB.60, 200
—— Joseph Cooke 217
—— Ormsby 233
—— Reg.Albert Hoby 277
—— Rob. Wingfield 334
—— Samuel Symes 104
—— Talbot Ashley 175
—— Sir William 103
—— William 200
—— William Hamilton 373
—— Wm.Trevalyan H.294
Coxen, Edward 295
Coxon,George Stacpole 362
Coxworthy, F. T. H. 435
Crabtree, Abraham 520
—— George Longb. 488
Cracklow, Henry 120

Cracknell, Jas. Thos. 75
Cradock, Adam W. 472
—— Charles Bury 350
Cragg, Cecil Webb 344
Craig, Aylmer S. 472
—— Grahame 157
—— James 192
—— Robert Guthrie 296
Craigie, Peter Edmonstone, CB. 11, 239
—— Robt. Collins 369
Cramer, Chas. Pierson 283
—— Henry John 527
Crampton, Rob.Henry 172
Crane, Edw. Joseph 328
—— Henry Arthur 302
—— John Richard 295
Cranfield, Geo. Darley 472
Craster, Henry 300
—— James Thomas 248
Crauford, William 488
Craufurd, Fred. B. N. 314
—— J. Robertson 14
—— Robert E. F. 80, 374
Crause, Charles 488
—— John 519
Craven, Rev. C. A. Assheton, AM. 455
—— John Albert 128
Crawford, Adam Fife 12
—— Charles 404
—— Francis Haden 340
—— George 520
—— George Adam 379
—— James Robert 298
—— John Chesterton 416
—— Robt. Alex. 173
—— Rob. Fitzg. 35, 371
—— Thomas, MD. 213
—— William 515
—— Wm. T. CB. 40, 372
—— Crawfurd, W. J. M. 312
Crawhall, Wm. Henry 197
Crawley, Charles 205
—— Henry 53
—— Henry Owen 35, 399
—— Philip S. 77, 163
—— Thomas R. 65, 152
Creagh.C. Aug. Fitzg. 267
—— Denis 203
—— C. M. 465
—— Charles Osborne 322
—— Giles Vandeleur 103
—— James 169
—— James 32
—— James 322
—— James Henry 233
—— Jasper Byng . 43
—— John 180
—— Sir Michael, KH. 11
—— Tho. Miller 361
—— William 444
Crealock, Hen. H. 61, 328
Crean, John North 335
—— Robert Cardiff 385
Crease, Anth. R. V. 402
—— Chas. Blandford 188
—— John Fred. 416
Creasy, James Gideon 232
Creighton, Fitzmaurice 415
Cremer, James Smith 472
Crerar, James 283
Cresdee, William 150
Crespigny, G. B. C. 74, 358

Cresswell, Edw. John 266
—— George 472
—— Oswald 232
Crewe, Evelyn Harpur 129
—— Richard Harpur 129
Creyke, Alex. Stephen 402
—— Chas. William 295
Crichton,David M. M. 331
Crickitt, George Aug. 210
Crisp, Henry, MB. 290
—— Walter 280
Crispin, George 520
—— Hon. Champante 338
Crispo, Sydney Smith 488
Croasdaile, D. Richd. 286
Crocker, Alfred 441
Croft, Jas. Hen. H. 236
—— Jonathan 534
—— Thomas 352
Crofton, Edw. W. 38, 372
—— Fred. Robt. C. 145
—— Henry 295
—— Hugh Dennis 42, 361
—— John ffolliott 27, 452
—— Richard Hen. 60, 373
—— Walter Frederic 472
Crohan, Harry B. 319
Crokat, William 14
Croker, Arthur 444
—— Edward 107
—— Edward 263
—— John Charles 520
—— Ponsonby May C. 413
—— William 233
Croly, John 352
Cromartie, Fred. N. 377
—— F. M. 464
Crombie, Alexander 302
—— Thomas 30
Crompton, W. Joshua 37
—— Wm. Henry 195
Cronyn, George 273
Crooke, Rev. M. 455
Crooks, Wm. Smedley 520
Crookshank, Alex. C. 436
—— Arthur C. 245
—— Chichester G. 472
—— George 527
—— Richard 488
Croome, John 172
Crosbie, John Gustav. 283
—— Sir Wm. Bt. 472
Cross, James 532
—— Philip H. E. 442
—— Wm. Jennings 472
Crosse, Chas. K. 83, 270
—— Herbert Edw. G. 280
—— John B. St. Croix 147
—— John Hill 207
—— Joshua Grant 81, 324
Crossgrove, James 511
Crossman, Robert 231
—— William 402
Crosthwaite, Charles 382
Crow, William 488
Crowdy, John Henry 404
Crowe, Edm. Moresby 269
—— George Wm. 515
—— John, KH. 104
—— Joseph 488
—— Joseph P. H. 87, 192
—— Robert 282
—— Robert 448

Index. 572

Crowther, Rich. J. F. 75
—— Rd. W. B. 290
Crozier, Acheson 488
—— Arthur Wm. 299
—— Henry Darley 404
—— Rev. J. A. BA. 455
—— Stanley 257
—— William 212
Cruice, Edmund J. 77, 453
Cruikshank, Alex. R. 380
Cruise, Hy. J. Russell 148
Crump, Hammerton, MD. 218
Cruse, George 136
Crutchley, Chas. 31, 463
—— Robert J. L. 228
—— William 247
Cubbon, Sir M., KCB. 120
Cubitt, Cha. Campbell 286
—— Edward George 359
—— Edward George 488
—— Frank Astley 180
—— Lewis 335
Cuddy, Alex. Daniel 472
—— Stephen 532
Cuff, A. St. George 234
Cuffe, Sir Chas. Fred. Wheeler, Bart. 86, 294
—— Michael, RC. 455
—— Otway Wheeler 415
Cullen, Arthur John 382
—— David, MD. 346
—— William 120
—— Wm. Fleming 443
Cullinan, Hen. Vulent. 322
Cumberland, B. Harry 104
—— Bentinck L. 183
—— Charles Brownlow 14
—— Charles Edward 402
—— George Bentinck 337
—— George Burrell 106
Cuming, Edw. Wm. 312
—— Robert 280
—— Thomas 379
Cumming, Alexander 488
—— Hen. Wedderburn 104
—— John Archibald 169
—— John Hunt 190
—— Robert 435
—— Robert Gordon 276
—— William 264
—— W. James, MD. 384
Cummin, Isaac 156
Cuningham, John 129
Cuninghame, Alured F. 201
—— David 120
—— Rich. D. B. 127
—— William 147
—— Wm. Jas. M. 343
Cunliffe, Robt. Alfred 167
Cunningham, Alex. 532
—— Andrew Chas. 201
—— John P., MD. 442
—— Michael Jos. 324
Cunninghame, Jn. W. H. 127
—— W. Stroker 200
Cunyngham, Robt. K. A. Dick 332
Cunynghame, Arth. A. Thurlow, CB. 28
—— Edw. A. Thurlow 240
Cuppage, Alexander 479
—— Burke 30, 371

Cuppage, James Greer 211
—— John M. 81, 326
Cure, Alfred Capel 55, 159
Cureton, Edw. B. 81, 148
Curgenven, Samuel L. 247
Curll, Henry 435
Curran, John 173
—— William 444
Currer, Rich. R. 80, 337
Currie, Charles 354
—— Francis Gore 312
—— George Alfred 106
—— Henry 304
—— L. Douglas Hay 215
—— Rt. Hamilton 80, 250
—— Samuel, MD. 439
Curry, Michael 315
—— Rob. Murray 64, 412
Curteis, Edw. B. H. 337
Curtin, J. 463
Curtis, Charles 203
—— Fra. G. Savage 134
—— Henry 472
—— Philip Julian 282
—— Reginald 81, 375
Curtois, Rowland L. S. 169
Curzon, Hon. Ernest G. 270
—— Geo. Augustus 344
—— Hon. John Hen. R. 488
—— Hon. Leicester 53, 343
—— Hon. R. W. Penn 38, 159
—— Hon. Wm. Hen. 154
—— Wm. Southwell 380
Cusack, John 229
Cusine, John 488
Cust, Hon. Sir Edward, KCH. 10, 153
—— John Francis 57, 159
—— Hon. Peregrine F. 104
Custance, Neville 472
—— Wm. N., CB. 56, 134
Cutajar, Carlo 38
Cuthbert, Edm. Cha. 378
—— Robt. Alex. 37
—— Rob. Thos. P. 205
Cuthbertson, Tho. H. 324
Dachenhausen, Henry, Baron 542
D'Acosta, Louis 291
Dacre, Rev. Geo. 455
Dacres, Sir Richard Jas. KCB. 13, 370
Dadson, Jos. N. P. 379
—— Wm. Fred. P. S. 415
Dagg, Robert Alex. 369
D'Aguilar, C. Lawrence, CB. 40, 373
Daines, Charles 520
Dalby, Nic. Bennett 414
Dalgairns, William 486
Dalgetty, James W. 104
Dalgleish, James 300
—— Robert 488
Dallas, Geo. Fred. 81, 261
Dalrymple, Sir Adolphus John, Bart. 8
—— John H. E. 34, 166
—— Wm. Henry 527
D'Altera, Jas. J. 384
Dalton, Charles 13
—— Charles Jas. 37, 371
—— James Robert 215
—— Robt. Fitzgerald 274

D'Alton, Edward 57
—— Edward Rich. 488
Daly, C. Fetherstone 415
—— Daniel Edw. 357
—— Dennis 10
—— Edward 208
—— Edward Nugent 488
—— James M. 308
—— John 203
—— Robert 59
—— Vesey 261
Dalyell, John Tho. 77, 220
—— Melville 32
Dalzell, Hon. A. Alex. 16
—— John Alex. 86, 272
—— Hon. R.A.G. CB. 104
—— Robt. Augustus 16?
—— Wm. John 488
Dames, Mansell 488
—— Thos. Longworth 376
—— Wm. Longworth 17
Dampier, Stephen R. 123
Dana, Wm. Pulteney 515
Dandy, John 520
Dane, John 155
—— Richard 279
—— Richard, MD. 439
D'Anfossy, Le Chevalier 511
Dangan, William Hen. Visc. 86, 163
Danger, Thomas G. 358
Daniel, George Robt. 291
—— John Edgcumbe 527
—— Pet. Fane Edge 488
—— Rich. Hillman 212
—— Samuel 361
Daniell, C. Augustus 358
—— Cha. Fred. Torrens 77
—— Edwin G. 82, 187
—— Fred. Francis 306
—— Henry 103
—— John 106, 465
—— R. A. 465
—— Wm. Freeman MD, 441
Dann, George 383
Danyell, Arthur J. 239
Darby, Charles 84, 322
—— Joseph 12
D'Arcey, O'Connor, MD. 157
—— Oliver B. 81, 212
—— Oliver Geo. W. 252
D'Arcy, Geo. Abbas Kooli 103
—— Judge Thomas 75
Darcy, Is. Roboteau 488
Dardel, G. Alexander 544
Darell, Henry John 106
D'Arley, W. Wallace 32
Darker, James 193
Darley, Henry 133
Darling, Hon. Chas. 527
—— Montague Wm. 435
—— Sydney 190
—— W. Lindsay 8, 340
Darrah, Charles John 403
Darroch, Donald G. A. 106
Dartnell, G. Russell 530
—— John George 207
Darvell, Sydney 212
Darwall, Hen. Pounty. 380
Dashwood, Alex. W. 104
—— Barrington G. 217

Dashwood, Cha. B. 344
—— Cha. Lewes 180
—— Rich. Lewes 205
Dassauville, William Alston, MD. 384
Daubeney, Hon. Cha.
Bainston, CB. 38
—— Fred. Sykes 123
—— Geo. Rob. Hen. 224
Daubeny, Alfred G. 185
—— Edward 295
—— James, CB. 55, 288
—— James Francis 212
—— Redmond B. C. 298
—— Walt. Augustus 175
Daubuz, James Barill 488
—— John Theophilus 377
Daun, Robert, MD. 530
—— Phil. S. 308
Daunt, Robert 182
—— William 190
—— William, M.D. 532
Daveney, Burton 33, 169
—— Burton John 141
Davenport, Charles J. 134
—— John Salusb. 109, 435
—— Salusbury S. 350
—— Trevor 106
—— Wm. Bromley 288
—— Wm. Davenport 106
Davern, Avary J. 223
—— Geo. William 263
—— John 463, 472
Davey, Wm. Mauger 170
David, Fred. Lewis 415
Davidge, George A. 444
—— John 232
Davids, John Lenthal 308
Davidson, Barnard H. 283
—— Cha. Rich. T. 404
—— Fred. Augustus 210
—— G. Montgomerie 224
—— Henry Edward 342
—— James 520
—— James 532
—— Jas. Butchelor 488
—— Peter, MD. 443
—— Peter Fraser 527
—— W. Alex. MD. 129
Davie, G. Scott, MD. 312
—— Sir Henry Robert Ferguson, Bart. 11
Davies, Arthur 472
—— Augustus 304
—— David 488
—— Francis John 10, 295
—— Geo. Silvester 134
—— Henry 291
—— Henry, MD. 532
—— Hen. Fanshawe 160
—— H. G. Johnstone 413
—— Henry James 266
—— Jasper Gust. S. 404
—— John 440
—— John 462
—— John 472
—— John 472
—— Joseph 106
—— Owen 195
—— Richard 515
—— Robert 141
—— Robert 157
—— Robert Willock 192
—— Sydney Herbert 208

Davies, Thomas	195	Dearden, John	150	Derriman, Jas.Samuel	417	Dickinson, Frederick	318
—— Thomas Alfred	218	Deare, George	104	DeRobeck, Cha. Louis		—— Jos. Dan.	177
—— Thos. Owen S.	310	—— George Beresford	272	Constantine	283	—— Rob. Munro	193
—— Wm.Broug.*MD.*	444	—— Rob. Elphinstone	304	—— Rawdon C. Pat.	177	—— William Speke	341
Davis, Alfred	472	Death, William	157	de Ros, *Hon.* Dudley		Dickson, Alex. Geo.	134
—— Francis	215	De Beauvoir, *Sir* John		CharlesFitzgerald 65,126		—— Cha. Lennox	488
—— George Frederick	267	Edmund, *Bt.*	511	—— Wm. *Lord* 11, 463		—— Collingwood, *CB.*	
—— Grenow 82,	376	De Bellefeuille,L.C.A.		D'Erp,Balthazar,*Baron*472		36, 125,	372
—— Hen. T. Stanes	416	Lefebre	348	Derville, Adolphus	120	—— David	76
—— Howell	236	DeBossiere,J.V., *MD.*	264	Desain,FilippoGiacomo		—— David	488
—— James	207	De Butts, J.C. Black.	401	Cassar, *Marquis*	368	—— Edw. John	364
—— James	277	DeCarteret, Havill. J.	312	De Salis, Rodolph 39, 143		—— Francis	515
—— John	245	—— Edw. Charles M.	324	Desanges,R.W.Burd.	198	—— Graham Le Fevre	77
—— John Atkins	384	Decie, Richard	403	Desbarres,Hen.Wind.	488	—— John Henry 82,	269
—— John Henry	511	Decken, Cha. Von der	541	Desborough, John	374	—— Matthew Wm.	308
—— William	75	DeCourcy, N. Will.	413	—— Lawrence W.	233	—— Phillip 79,	375
—— William	350	Deedes, Granville	380	—— SamuelHolworthy*382*		Rob. Graham, *MD.*	
—— William	511	—— Herbert George	282	Deshon, Charles John	381		443
—— William Henry	233	—— William	237	—— Edward	296	—— Thos. Eccles	205
—— William Henry	488	—— William Henry	343	—— Fred. G. Thos. 78,360		—— William Thos. 62,	153
—— William Hone	139	Deeble, William	276	Desmond, John	362	Diddep, John	488
—— Wm. Sandom	413	Deering,Rup.Barb. 85,360		De Smidt, J.P.Larkins	527	Diebitsch, Fred. Von	543
Davison, *Sir* W., *KH.*	49	De Fauche, Charles	511	—— Johannes	527	Digby, Geo. Stephen,	
Davy, Daniel Bishop	344	Dehnel, Henry	542	Despard,Fred.William	341	*CB.* 83,	414
—— John, *MD.*	529	Delacombe,HenryEdw.	86	—— Philip Henry	472	—— Henry Robert	104
Davys, Edm. Soden	488	—— Henry Ivatt 13,	411	—— Wm. Edward	417	—— John Almcrus	104
—— James	349	—— William Addis	415	Des Voeux, B.	104	Digges, Chas.	488
Dawe, Charles	106	DeChaumont,F.S.B.F.,		—— *Sir* Wm. Henry	472	Diggle, Chas. *KH.*	14
Dawes, Wentworth	156	*MD.*	346	De Teissier, James Fitz		Dighton, Robert	488
Dawkins, Henry	103	De la Chaumette,H.L.383		Herbert 65,	359	Dilke, William	527
—— Wm. Gregory 49,163		De la Condamine,Thos.472		Detmer, Frederick	541	Dill, Marcus 56,	400
Dawson, Arthur Finch	141	De Lacy, John	33	DeVere,Fr.Horatio 80,402		Dillon, Edw. Langford 212	
—— Charles	213	Delamain, Edw. Smith 488		Deverell,W.Devon.51,362		—— Edw. Walter P.	468
—— Edward Finch	141	Delamere, P. Herbert 220		—— Thos.Josephus 43,308		—— Francis Wm.	104
—— Ersk.Scott F.G.83,332		De Lancey,O. Gaspard223		Deverill, Percy Julius	328	—— John	511
—— Francis	281	—— John	104	Devereux, Fred. Flood	323	—— Martin 84,	343
—— George Dudley	263	—— Peter	101	—— George Alfred	511	—— *Hon.* Robert Vil.	379
—— Harry Philip	306	Delancy, F.	129	—— *Hon.*G. Talbot 58,373		—— Robert 80,	237
—— Henry	151	De Lisle, Hirzel Fred.	472	Devine, John	156	—— Robert	106
—— John	192	—— Rich. Fr.Valpy	364	De Vismes, Francis	104	—— Robert Henry	223
—— Richard	82	Demain, H. Dickson	353	—— Henry A. D.	378	—— Theo. Augustus	511
—— Rich.W.Erskine	212	Delmé, Hen. Peter	488	Devlin, Henry William 444		—— Thomas	488
—— R. Kearsley, *CB.*	31	Delmege, Collis Chris-		Devon, Wm. Henry	75	—— Timothy John	245
—— Robert Edward	197	topher John, *MD.*	440	Dew, Fred. Napleton	324	Dinwiddie, Gil. Ham.	527
—— Robert Nicholl	403	De Moleyns, T. Aremb	379	—— George Meyrick	151	Dirom, Alexander	403
—— Thomas	131	Dempster, Chas. Car.	229	Dewar, John	331	Disbrowe, Geo., *KH.*	104
—— Thomas	295	—— Jas.Carroll,*MD.*	441	—— JamesWilliam 79,338		—— John George Ca-	
—— *Hon.* Vesey	164	—— John, *MD.*	529	Dewé, Henry	229	vendish 86,	257
—— William, *MD.*	529	—— William	50	Dewell,Chas.Goddard	330	Disney, Lambert John	
Day, Cyrus	203	Dempsy, Charles	530	De Winton, C. Lorenzo		Robert	298
—— Estcourt	232	Denford, Charles	488	86,	207	—— Robert	463
—— Fred. Hugh Irwin	294	Denison, C. Albt. 53,	270	—— Francis Walter	378	Dive, Hugh	515
—— Henry James 63,341		—— George	489	—— Parry	144	Divorty, Peter, *MB.*	196
—— Henry James	341	—— *Sir* Wm. T., *KCB.*		D'Eye, William Rust	330	Dixon, Albert	233
—— James Leslie	195		38,400	D'Holbreuse, Henry	544	—— Aug. Fred. De B.	195
—— John Godfrey	234	Denne, Lambert Hen.	376	D'Homboldt,JohnHen.541		—— Charles	13
—— Maurice	133	Dennie,HenryWm. 80,465		Dibben, George	520	—— Charles Frederick	382
Deacon,C.C., *CB.* 52,266		Dennis, Jas. Benj. 57,	373	Dick, Alexander	120	—— George	12
—— Daniel	196	—— John Fitz Thos.	77	—— Augustus Alex.	236	—— George, *CB,* 41,	361
—— Daniel	540	—— John Leslie 31,	270	—— Francis 37,	371	—— Henry	50
—— James	170	—— M.Griffin *CB.* 31,281		—— Hope	125	—— Henry	136
—— W. E. Durand 82,286		—— M.Strat.Tynte 74,307		—— *Rev.* John	455	—— Henry	416
Deakin, Jas.Fran,*MD.*299		Denny, Arthur M'G.	201	—— John Simeon Fra.	82	—— Jas. Alex.	138
Dealey, Charles	532	—— Robert Arthur	223	—— William, *MD.*	198	—— John	104
Deaman, Thomas	511	—— William	103	Dicken, Cha. Shortt	323	—— John Smart	511
Dean, Robert	488	—— William	440	—— Hen. Williams	380	—— Matthew Charles	12
Deane, Allen	130	Denton, Joseph Albert	353	Dickens,Rob.Vaughan195		—— Matthew Cha. 55,	373
—— Bonar Millett	223	Dent, Henry Francis	211	Dickenson, Edgar A.	216	—— Stewart Chas.	195
—— Edward Pope	123	—— Richard	208	Dickerson. Stephen H.	384	—— Thomas Fraser	250
—— George	169	—— William Seton	263	Dickin, Thomas Acherley		—— Wm. Manley Hall	
—— Hy.AllenMurray	488	Dorbishire, Philip	342	Massy	190	55,	372
—— Henry Charles	210	DeRenzy,G.Webb 106,465		Dickins, Compton Alwyne		Dobbin, Thomas	103
—— Hugh Pollexfen	239	Derinzy,Bar.Vigors,*KH.*14		Scrase	197	Dobbs, Percival Her.	340
Deans, James Alex.	315	—— G. A. F. 39,	372	—— Wm.D.Scrase 84, 217		Dobie, Wm. Alexander	349

Index. 574

Dobson, William 531
Dobyns, Robt. Wm. 488
Dobree, John Saumarez 527
Docker, Edw. Scott 155
Dodd, Chas. Wm. M. 511
Dodgin, John D. Gar. 324
—— Wm. Hen. Townsend Morris 416
Dodgson, Fra. Hume 380
—— Percy 151
D'Odiardi, Antonio 544
Dods, Henry Gleed 300
Dodwell, George 488
Doering, John Wm. 134
Doherty, Chas. Edm. 103
—— Daniel 520
—— Daniel Henry 138
—— Daniel John 173
—— Henry Edw., CB. 30
—— Sir Richard 10, 195
Dolan, Theophilus 176
Dolmage, Gideon 440
—— Jonas 223
Domenichetti, Rich., MD. 306
Domvile, William 123
Domville, Edm. Cha. 413
—— James Wm. 55, 372
Don, James 131
—— Wm. Gerard, MD. 234
Donald, Andrew 418
—— Henry Alex. 220
—— John 441
—— William 383
Donaldson, Jas. Y., MD. 444
—— Robert 106
—— Thomas 138
—— Vance Young 32
Doncaster, Harwick 123
Donegal, Marquis of, GCH. 125
Donelan, Anthony 58
—— Anthony Edmond 357
—— Edmd. Joseph B. 195
Donellan, Alexander 415
Donnall, Orlando Sawle 442
Donnelly, George 472
—— John 488
—— John F. Dykes 403
Donovan, Edw. Westby 57, 242
—— George 266
—— Henry Douglas 511
—— Thomas 52, 354
—— Tho. Henry S. 356
Dooley, Joseph 342
Doorly, Martin 352
Doran, James, MD. 284
—— Robt. H. Patrick 267
Dore, Fred. Nassau 452
—— Wm. Henry 472
Dorehill, George 472
—— Wm. John 257
Doring, William 542
Dormer, Hon. James Charlemagne 86, 200
—— Hon. John B. J. 304
Dorndorf, Frederick 543
Dorrofield, William 383
Doswell, Henry 488
Dougal, Tho. Ballard 312
Dougan, Geo. Aug. 527

Dougherty, Charles H. 304
—— William 520
Doughty, Chester 321
Douglas, Allen George 190
—— Arch. Alex. 86, 414
—— Arch. Philip 139
—— Frederick, MD. 193
—— Hen. Hamilton 472
—— Sir Howard, Bt.
GCB. GCMG. 6, 205
—— Sir Jas. KCB. 6, 255
—— Jas. Mainwaring 382
—— Sir John K., CB.
38, 312
—— John, CB. 37, 125
—— John 534
—— Joseph 455
—— Joseph 472
—— Rich. J. Hardy 414
—— Sir Robt. Bt. 277
—— Robert, CB. 7
—— Robert 226
—— Robert 472
—— R. 464
—— Rob. Percy 17
—— Rouse Douglas 337
—— Thomas Monteath CB. 120
—— William 10
—— William 78, 202
Doull, Alexander 380
Douthwaite, George 232
Dowbiggin, Montagu Hamilton 78, 341
—— Tho. Edward 135
Dowdall, Aylmer 75
Dowdeswell, Geo. Fra. 326
—— W. Fourbelle 135
Dowding, Wm. Mills 273
Dowell, George Dare 414
Dowker, Howard 120
—— Thomas 488
Dowland, John 472
Dowler, Francis Edw. 270
—— John 286
—— William 286
—— Reginald Blewitt 231
Dowling, Alf. Rich. B. 314
Dowman, James 76
—— John 472
—— William 252
Downer, George 511
—— Geo. P. Maxwell 488
Downes, Arthur Wm. 436
—— Henry, MD. 279
—— Major Francis 378
—— Ulysses, Lord, KCB. 6, 236
Downing, David 121
—— John David 197
Downman, J. T. 465
Dowse, Richard 529
Dowson, Charles S. 185
Doyle, Chas. Hastings 26
—— Michael Taylor 104
Doyne, Henry Archdall 377
—— Robert Stephen 488
Draffen, William Pitt 413
Drage, Frederick 280
—— William 326
—— William 363
—— William Henry 321
Drake, Edward Henry 181

Drake, Francis 181
—— John 527
—— John Alex. 135
—— John Cha. Tyrwhitt 172
—— John George 132
—— John Mervin C. 403
—— Sir Thos. T. F. E. Bt. 106
—— Wm. Henry 435
Draper, James 39
Drayson, Alf. Wilkes 375
Drechsler, Frederick 543
Dresing, Charles 472
Dreghorn, Allan H. 488
Drew, Browning 83, 306
—— Edwin 444
—— Francis Barry 360
—— John 464
Drewe, Edward Ward 106
—— Francis Edw. 81, 363
Driberg, William 106
—— William Charles 319
Drinan, Wm. Berry 350
Dring, William 288
Drinkwater, Thomas 511
Driver, Chas. Reed 463
Dromgoole, N. Flem. 472
Drouet, Lloyd R. C. 350
—— P. 464
Drought, Geo. P. 264
—— John Head 104
—— Thos. Arms. 26, 369
Drummond, Berk. 10, 175
—— Cecil Geo. Assh. 345
—— Geo. Duncan 488
—— G. 465
—— Hon. Jas. D. 147
—— John 10
—— William 103
Drury, George 413
—— Henry 488
Drysdale, And. Knox 312
—— John 84, 255
—— Robt. Carstairs 380
—— William, CB. 81, 146
Duberley, Geo. 104
Duberly, Henry 144
Ducat, Gordon Chas. S. 234
Du Bourdieu, John 472
Du Cane, Edm. Fredk. 402
—— Francis 80, 401
—— Percy Charles 137
—— Robert 472
Duchesnay, Henry Theodore 342
Ducie, Henry John, Earl of 122
Duckett, Sir G. F. Bt. 106
Ducrow, Peter And. John 261
Dudgeon, Edw. James 197
—— Frederick 252
—— James John 314
—— Peter 103
—— Robert Cecil 286
Dudley, Henry 353
Duesbury, C. J. Thorn. 294
—— Wm. Hen. T. 296
Du Jardin, Benj. Stephen 353
Duff, Arthur Meredith 304
—— Garden 312
—— James 106

Duff, John 31, 304
—— John, MD. 384
—— Robert William 364
—— Robert William 402
Duffield, Thomas 133
Duffin, Geo. Blair 217
Dufief, Armand C. G. 544
Dufresne, Louis Flavien 511
Dugdale, Hen. Cha. G. 344
Dugmore, Fred. Wm. John 352
Duke, Jones 520
—— Thomas Assheton 121
Dumaresq, Alex. Macl. 290
—— Wm. Henry H. D. 403
—— William Lovelace 375
Dumbreck, David, MD. CB. 439
Dumergue, George C. 246
Dun, Chas. Dennis 120
Dunbar, Arch. H. 294
—— Charles 520
—— James Brander 137
—— Penrose John 175
—— Thos. Clement 82, 306
—— William Matthew 243
Duncan, Alex. Wm. 380
—— Francis 379
—— James 154
—— James 464
—— J. Shand, MD. 444
—— Robert 284
—— William 472
—— William 511
Duncombe, Hon. Cecil 126
—— Chas. Wilmer 126
—— Fred. Wm. 345
Dundas, Jas. Durham 282
—— Lorenzo G. 288
—— Philip 29
—— Philip 103
—— Thomas 104
—— Thomas 197
Dundee, Frank Wm. 216
—— Robert Handley 436
Dunkellin, Ullick Canning Lord 49, 163
Dunlevie, Wm. S. Hen. 197
Dunlop, Alexander 352
—— Franklin, CB. 37, 371
—— James 345
—— John, MD. 442
—— John 306
—— Samuel 380
Dunmore, Thos. CB. 527
Dunn, Alex. R. 83, 342
—— Dennis 76
—— Edwin 436
—— Edw. Trevor 228
—— Francis Graham 352
—— Fred. John A. 356
—— George F. 463
—— Josias 326
—— Rich. Gadesden 191
—— Thomas 274
—— Thomas 352
—— William 15
—— William James 414
Dunne, Fran. Plunkett 33
—— John Hart 341
—— Richard 472
Dunnicliffe, Henry 488
Dunning, Samuel 361
Dunscombe, Nicholas 172

Index.

Dunsford, Henry	445	East, Cecil James	316
Dunsmure, Charles	104	Easton, Frederick	242
Duperier, Charles	76	Eaton, Charles	472
Du Plat, Chas. Taylor	374	——Deodatus Wm.	352
Dupuis, John Edward, CB.	14, 370	——Henry Pardoe	282
		——Richard	464
Durrant, Christ. Rawes	178	Eccles, Cuthbert	177
——Wm. Rob. E.	337	——Cuthbert	489
D'Urban, Wm. James	27	——Francis Edw.	190
Durie, Charles	83	——Hugh	276
——William, KH.	530	——William Hall	344
During, Christ. Henry Von	542	Echalaz, Henry	172
		——John George	274
Durnford, And. M. T.	511	Eckersall, Fred. S.	236
——Anthony Wm.	402	Eckford, James, CB.	120
——Arthur Geo.	404	——Robert	299
——Edward C. L.	415	Eddie, Wm. Cruick.	532
——Edward William	38, 400	Eddington, Adam	331
		Eddowes, James	534
——George	17	Ede, Denzil	489
——George	44	——John	489
——Geo. Augustus	515	Eden, George Morton	12
Durnfort, John	464	——Henry Horace	237
Dusautoy, Pet. John J.	76	——John, CB.	11
Dutton, Charles	472	——Morton Parker	378
——Wm. Holmes	17	——Morton Robert	276
Du Vernet, John Fras.	43, 452	——Tho. Millard B.	267
		——Wm. Hassall	16
Dwyer, Gage Hall	202	Edgar, Jas. H.	82, 298
——Henry	103	Edge, George	195
——John	78, 202	Edgeworth, William	140
——Lambart Francis Wilson	211	Edgcumbe, Hon. Cha. Ernest	160
——Patrick	324	Edgell, Henry James	328
——Robert	261	Edleston, Joshua	76
——Robert Hoare	418	Edlmann, Jos. Ernest	129
——Thos. Peard	18	Edmeades, Henry	379
Dyce, Arch. Brown	120	Edmonds, H.	104, 465
——John Robert	379	Edmonstoune, John	83, 240
——Thos. Rose	206	Edmunds, Thomas	349
Dyer, Fred. Carr S.	210	Edridge, Fred. L.	217
——Geo. Henry	444	Edwardes, B., KH.	106
——Henry Charles P.	413	——Hon. Cuthbert E.	345
——Henry C. S.	378	——David John	472
——John Akin	140	——Meyrick W. B.	350
——John Midlane	418	——Hon. William	164
——Robt. Turtliff	488	Edwards, Alexander	435
——Swinnerton H.	187	——Benj. Hutchins	369
Dyke, Fred. Hotham	298	——Charles	463, 489
Dymond, Robert	138	——Cha. Tollemache	350
Dyne, Musgrave Jas. Bradley	130	——Clement A. CB.	35, 212
Dyneley, Tho. CB.	9, 370	——Francis Drewe	200
Dynevor, R. Lord	125	——George	520
Dynon, John	140	——George	157
——Patrick	153	——Hugh Gore	104
Dyson, Edward	106	——James Bevan	403
——Jerry Francis	120	——Jas. Townsend	202
——John	75	——Lancelot Kerby	273
——John Daniel	103	——Peter	15
Eagar, Edw. H.	252	——S. Hy. Hutchins	340
——Rob. John	78, 239	——Thomas	489
Eager, Robert	492	——Thos. Willock	520
Eagle, Francis Blake	151	——Wright	489
Eagles, Edward B.	489	Egan, Edward	379
Eames, Leslie	294	——Edward	341
——Thos. Bunbury	349	——Rev. Hen. W. M. AM.	455
Earle, Arthur M.	81, 277	——Stephen	217
——Charles William	343	Egerton, Hon. Arthur Fred.	104
——William	160		
——William Henry	210	——Caledon Rich.	41, 363
Earlsfort, J. H. R. Lord	126	——Geo. Mark L.	344
Eason, Peter	75	——Philip le Belward	164

Egerton, Rowland	354	Ellis, Richard	519
——Hon. Seymr. J.G.	126	——Robt. Conway D.	223
Egginton, John Lloyd	131	——Robt. Richardson	267
Eichbauen, Cha. Wm.	436	——Robert Westropp	270
Eichhorn, Christian F.	543	——Samuel B., CB.	9, 411
Eidmann, Frederick	541	——Wilmot B. Edw.	378
Einem, Diederich de	642	——William	489
Ekin, James, MB.	178	Ellison, Andrew	455
Eld, Frederick	36	——Cuthbert Geo.	54, 159
Elderton, Edw. Halford		——Richard George	263
Pierce	232	Ellul, Carmelo, M.D.	368
Elderhost, Charles	541	Elmhirst, Charles	41, 190
Elgee, Charles	79, 360	——Harry	191
——CadwalladerWm.	375	——Wm. Augustus	190
——John Lindredge	374	——Thomas	257
Elgin, Edward Arthur	211	Elmley, Henry, Visc.	126
Eliot, Hon. Cha. Geo. Cornwallis	160	Elmsall, Wm. de Cardonnel	106
——Geo. Aug.	196	Elphinstone, Howard Craufurd	85, 402
——William Henry	205	——John Fred. Buller	167
Eliott, Geo. Aug.	231	Elrington, Fred. R.	57, 343
Elkington, Arthur	330	——Geo. Esdaile	50
——Arthur Guy	167	——Richard John	146
——John Harry F.	63, 182	——Thos. Gerard	330
Ellaby, Hugh Latimer	380	Elton, Fred. C.	79, 363
Ellerman, Edw. John	340	——Fred. Coulthurst	378
Elles, Wm. Kidston	248	——Isaac	106
Ellice, Cha. Hen.	32, 228	Elwes, Dudley G. C.	176
Ellicombe, Cha. Grene, CB.	8, 399	——John Emilius	185
Elliot, Alex. J. Hardy	78	——Wm. Chas. Cary	167
——Arthur Charles	334	Elwyn, Charles Edw.	382
——Fran. Hamilton	334	——Thomas	39, 372
——George	16	Ely, Henry Fred. W.	341
——George Augustus	212	Emerson, Alex. Lyon	234
——George Henry	416	——Edward	188
——Henry	489	——John	472
——Henry George	414	Elmes, Jonathan W.	211
——Henry Sheridan	377	Emly, Hen. Francis	277
——Hon. Gilbert	77, 343	Emmet, Rob. Alex.	331
——John McDowell	177	Emmett, Anthony	13
——Lempster R.	341	Emmott, William	520
——Philip Herbert	131	Enderby, Samuel	472
——Rich. Coffin, CB.	384	——William	180
——Riversdale	129	England, Edw. L.	200
——Wm. Hamilton	39, 372	——Poole Val.	16, 371
Elliott, Archibald	520	——SirRichard., GCB. KH.	9, 267
——Chas. Simeon	218	——Richard	87, 274
——C. S.	464	——Russell	139
——George	142	——Thomas	357
——John	413	Engledue, Wm. John	404
——John Fuizer	511	English, Fred., CB.	58, 272
——Richard	106	——William	148
——Richard Charles	472	Engstrom, Geo. Lloyd	380
——Robt. Arthur	335	Ennis, John	247
——William	74	Enriquez, Giovanni	368
——William	386	Ensor, James	512
——William	472	Entwisle, William	127
——Wm. Christ. Parkin	75, 412	Enys, Charles	218
——Wm. Henry, KH.	15	Erdmann, Frederick	542
Ellis, Arthur	414	Erichsen, Alex. von	543
——Arth. Edw. Aug.	242	Errington, A. Cha.	35, 269
——C.	464	Erroll, W. H. Earl of,	77
——C. David C.	281	Erskine, Hon. David	106
——Chas. Hen. F.	380	——George	52, 156
——Charles John	84, 413	——George Pott	147
——Hon. Fred. Geo.	139	——Henry David	167
——Frederick	145	——James Augustus	435
——Hen. Abigail	331	——John Low, MD.	178
——Henry Disney	79, 359	——Robert	489
——Hercules	472	——Wm. Macnaghton	135
——James Verling	318	Esmonde, Thomas	82
——Powrie	51	Espinasse, James	515

Index. 576

Espinasse, Jas. Wm.	197	Eyre, Robert	350	Farrant, Aug. Dover L.	412	Ferguson, Adam	255
Este, Michael Lambton	532	——Thomas Dowling	512	Farrants, James	520	——Austin Jonas	444
Estridge, Edward	436	Eyres, George Wm.	104	Farrell, Fras. Turnley	120	——Cha. John O'Neill	404
——Henry Whatley	261	Faber, Charles F.	274	——Fergus	170	——George Arthur	160
Ethelston, Edmund P.	296	——Wm. Raikes	30	——H. Chamberlayne	379	——Hector	208
Eteson, Francis	175	Fabricius, George	542	——James	520	——James	221
Eustace, Sir John R.		Faddy, Peter	14	——John Sidney	76	——John Stephenson	133
KH.	10	——Pet. Pickmore 41,	372	——Sidney Baynton	402	——Johnston	443
——Thomas Fox	266	Fagan, William	177	Farren, Rich.T.CB.38,363		——Robert	104
Evans, Aug. FitzGerald	427	——William John	436	Farrer, Henry	334	——William	277
——Augustine	417	Fahie, Conroy	217	——James	103	Fergusson, And. MD.	529
——Chu. Rich. Ogden	374	Fair, Alexander	362	——James S. H. 77,	248	——Sir Jas. KCB. 8,	257
——Daniel	512	——Alexander, CB.	120	Farrier, James	463	——James	489
——Dawson Kelly	182	Fairbairn,Wm.H.MD.	441	Farrington, Donald	177	——John O'Neill	360
——Sir De Lacy, GCB.		Faircloth, Hen. John	315	——Hast. D'Oyly	303	——William, KC.	9
	8, 220	Fairfax, Sir Hen., Bt.	103	——Lindsay 87,	236	Fern, Edwin Glass	266
——Edward	515	——Tho. Ferdinand	160	——Malcolm Cha.	269	Fernandez, F.	443
——Edward William	215	——Wm. Geo. H. T.	205	Fasken, Wm. MD.	420	Fernley, Thos. Henry	293
——Ernest Theodore	350	Fairfield, Charles	345	Fasson, Cha. Hamilton	442	Ferris, Geo. Augustus	338
——Francis Fosbery	418	Fairtlough, Cha. Edw.		——Stanhope H. MD.	384	——George Thomas	384
——Francis Herbert	216		55, 360	Fauchie, Martin	363	——John	154
——George	443	——Edw.D'Heillimer	202	Faught, John George	261	——John F.	453
——George Oliver	414	——James Wm.	29	Faulkner, Bolton W.	335	Ferryman, Aug. Halifax	
——Harry Dacres	382	——Samuel	197	——Henry Cole	452	CB.	30, 326
——Harry Lewis	414	——Wm. Haviland	472	Faunce, Thomas	43	Festing, Aug. Morten	436
——Henry Charles	248	Falcon, William H.	183	Faussett,GodfreyTreve	307	——Edw. Robt.	403
——Henry John	296	Falconar, Chesborough		——William 78,	258	——Francis Worgan	415
——Hugh	13	Grant, KH. 9,	303	Fawcett, Alfred	236	Fetherstonhaugh, Wm.	151
——John	145	Falconer, Alexander	164	——Anthony Molloy	145	Ffennell, Jas. Richard	208
——John	324	——Hon. Chas. Jas.		——Geo. Foyle	331	——Richard	489
——John	489	Keith	139	——Joseph Hodgson	169	Ffinney, S. Lee H. H.	280
——John Thomas	304	——James	304	——Morris James	166	ffolliott, Philip Homan	341
——Lloyd	170	Falkiner, Samuel	104	——Rowland Hill	242	Ffolliott, Frederick	213
——Matthew	324	Falkner, Edw. N.	237	Fawkes, Francis	300	——Nicholas	443
——Oliver, MD.	420	——Frederic	267	——Geo. Philip	232	Ffrench, Alfred Kirke	272
——Ralph	489	——James	211	——Richard	106	——Edward	106
——Richard John	233	Falls, John	108	Faxardo, Aug. Maria		——Thomas	58
——Robert Henry	344	Fane, Francis 86,	231	Guaxardo	527	——Thomas Charles	272
——Thomas, CB. 7,	315	——Frederick John	286	Fearnley, Fairfax	212	Ficklin, Robert	104
——Thomas	489	——Henry	104	Featherstonehaugh, A.	404	Fiddes, Edward	198
——Usher Wm., MD.	206	——Henry	106	——William Albany	197	——John M., MB.	385
——Warren, Edw.	273	——Henry John	315	Feilde, Fulford Bastard	527	——Thomas	120
Evelegh, Fred. C. CB.	103	——Mildmay 9,	337	Feilden, Henry Broome	182	Field, Geo.Thomas 78,	374
——Geo. Carter	472	Fanning, John	349	——Henry Wemyss	255	——Meyrick Beaufoy	276
——John Henry	472	——Matthew	291	——Oswald Barton	310	——Spencer	190
Everard, E. Pet. Hen.	236	Fanshawe, Basil	242	——Randle Joseph	281	——Thomas Samuel	
Evered, And. Rob. G.	273	——Charles 63,	400	——Robert	104	Poer 87,	376
——Cha. Edw. A.	247	——H. Dalrymple 65,	362	Feilding, Hon. Percy		Fielding, George A.	206
Everet, Wilton	196	Faris, William	31	Robert Basil 55,	163	——James Campbell	353
Everett, Edward	312	Farley, William	264	——Hon. Wm. H. A.	163	Fiennes, Hon. Ivo De	
——James	383	Farmar, Cha. Louis A.	414	Felix, Orlando	16	Vesci Twisleton	
——John Frederick	200	——Edw. Sterling 43,	452	Fellowes, Cha. Henry	229	Wykeham 84,	142
Everitt, Herbert	417	——Jasper	76	——Edward	77	——Hon. Nathaniel	226
Evers, George	534	——Richard	472	——James	404	Fife, John	146
Every, Oswald Wm.	328	——William Edward	413	——Peregrine Henry	412	Filder, William, CB.	527
Ewait, Cha. B. 79,	402	——Wm. Robarts 86,	316	Fellows, Francis Wm.	270	Filgate, Townley P.	
——Henry P.	127	Farmer, Reginald O.	375	Fendall, Geo. N. 83,	272	H. M.	155
——JohnAlex.CB.43,	310	——Wm. Langford	236	——William	104	Finch, Hon. Daniel	
——John W. Cheney	123	——Wm. Robt.Gamul	160	Feneran, Edward	264	Greville 79,	228
——Wm. Salisbury	160	Farnan, John	519	——Francis	360	——Hon. John,CB. 9,	228
Ewen, Arthur J. Allix	248	Farquhar, James	264	Fenn, John	146	Findlay, Alexander	104
Ewing, Alexander	140	——Robt. Townsend	381	Fennessy, Robt. Rich.	291	——James	540
——Alexander	314	Farquharson, Francis	120	Fenton, Edward Dyne	202	Findley, Thomas	534
——Alexander	436	——Francis	221	——Michael	224	Finey, Alen George	472
——John	441	——Francis Dundas	282	——Richard	191	Finke, Frederick Von	544
——Joseph	532	——Fran. Ed. H.	255	Fenwick, Bowes	228	Finlay, Geo. Hen.	274
Eyl, John George	527	——Henry	167	——Collingwood 62,	307	——Hamilton	276
Eynaud, Filippo	368	——Hen. Hubert	104	George Roe	332	——John	310
Eyre, Annesley	328	——James Ross 65,	166	——Henry King	201	Finnemore, Jas. H.	384
——Henry	18	——Mat. Hen.	417	——Horatio	106	Finnerty, Charles	453
——John	15	——Peter	103	——Percival 63,	298	——Charles	306
——Philip Homan	248	——Richard	229	——William, CB. 42,	192	Finnie, William	531
——Richard	264	——Robert	164	——Wm. Young	76	Finucane, Daniel	136
——Rich. Annesley	272	Farr, George	532	Fereday, Fred. Fran.	296	——George Thurles	38

Index.

Fischer, Augustus	541	FitzRoy, George Rob.	163
—— F. L. Constantine	544	—— Hugh	104
Fisher, Arthur A'Court, 85, 402		—— Philip	180
		—— William	290
—— Charles Edw.	335	—— Wriothesley A.	226
—— Edward Henry	373	Fitz Simon, Thos. J.	141
—— Edward Rowe	132	Fitz Simons, Arthur F.	252
—— *Rev.* Geo. R.	455	—— Edw. Jackson	310
—— Henry	442	Fitz Williams, Duncan	
—— Louis Walter	316	C. L.	354
—— Robert Roe	76	FitzWygram, Fred. Wellington John 61, 141	
—— Seth Nuttall	472		
—— W.	465	Flamank, John	104
Fishbourne, Fra. Rob.	205	Flamstead, George Ley	
Fisk, Wm. Hawley	472	Woolferstan D.	361
Fitz Gerald, Alfred J.	281	Flanagan, John B. 83, 315	
—— Augustine	321	Fleetwood, Thomas P.	188
—— Charles	266	Fleming, Arthur	75
—— Charles Lionel	104	—— A. de Montmorcy	258
—— Charles Lionel J.	349	—— Edward, *C B.* 8, 233	
—— Edward, *KH.*	104	—— George	157
—— Francis Aug.	197	—— Hamilton	44
—— Ferd. Ogilvy	213	—— James William	247
—— Geo. W. Yates	274	—— Joseph	237
—— Henry Lewis	200	—— Julius	50
—— James	183	—— William	335
—— John	512	Flemyng, Augustus	18
—— *Sir* John Forster, *KCB.* 6, 212		Fletcher, Alexander	148
		—— Edw. Cha.	33
—— Ormond	323	—— Francis Charteris	281
—— Richard	298	—— Henry Cha. 64, 166	
—— Richard Henry	489	—— John Fletcher	342
—— Thomas	520	—— R.	104
—— Thomas B. V.	472	—— Rich. D'Oyly 85, 349	
—— Thomas George	442	—— Thomas Hanmer	156
—— William Henry	369	—— Thos. Howard K.	206
—— Wm. Hervey	296	—— William 81, 258	
Fitzgerald, David	446	—— William	384
—— Francis Lewis	443	—— William	527
—— Gerald	231	Fleury, William, L.	267
—— Henry Chas. 81, 242		Flexman, James	512
—— John Gore	416	Flint, William Rich.	512
—— Joseph Wm.	131	Flood, Arthur Edw.	181
—— Maurice G. B.	338	—— Douglas	185
—— Wm. Hen. D.	79	—— Fred. Rich. Solly	272
Fitz Gibbon, Gerald	260	—— Henry	172
—— Luke	283	Floyd, Charles A.	145
—— Richard Ed.	350	—— *Sir* Henry, *Bt.*	103
—— William	489	—— Henry Ridout	273
Fitzgibbon, Charles P.	192	Flude, Thos. P. 33, 371	
Fitz Gibbons, James	455	Fluder, Alexander	210
Fitz Herbert, Rich. H.	106	Fludyer, Charles	160
Fitzherbert, John	472	—— William	12
Fitz Hugh, Henry T. 80, 375		Foaker, Frederick	440
		Fogo, Alex. Scott, *MD.*	227
FitzMaurice, *Hon.* Alex. Temple	302	—— James	15
		—— James M. S.	384
—— Arthur Wm.	228	—— Thos. Macmillan	350
—— *Hon.* Henry W.	302	Foley, *Hon.* Aug. F.	103
—— John, *KH.* 28, 122		—— Francis	221
Fitzmaurice, Geo. L.	534	—— *Hon.* St. George	
—— Maurice Henry	378	Gerald, *CB.*	40
Fitzmayer, James Wm. *CB.* 37, 371		—— Richard Yarde	258
		—— T. H. *Lord*	123
Fitz Patrick, Francis	283	Foll, Rich. N. C.	224
—— Joseph H. P.	133	Follett, Hardinge G.	185
Fitz Roy, *Lord* Aug. Cha.		Follows, William 81, 453	
—— Lennox	49	Folliott, John	269
—— *Lord* Charles	104	Fonblanque, Alfred	416
—— Cavendish Cha.	296	—— E. Barrington de	435
—— Charles Vane	344	—— John Samuel Mar de	
—— *Lord* Fred J. 52, 159		Grenier	489
—— Fred. Keppel	315	Foot, John	228
—— Fred. S. L'E.	205	—— Randall	489

Foot, William Yates	337	Fortescue, John Mill	489
Foote, John Hollis R.	489	—— Wm. M. Miller	282
—— Wm. Francis 83, 413		Fosbery, Henry William	512
Forbes, Chas. John	527	—— Wm. Tho. Exham	308
—— Cha. D'Oyley	436	Fosbroke, John Dudley	417
—— David	36	—— Thos. Dudley	173
—— David	120	—— Thos. Dudley 65, 412	
—— Edw. M'Mahon	350	Foskett, Joseph	472
—— Fran. Charteris	247	Foss, Henry Clinton	173
—— George	215	Fossi, Thomas de	544
—— George	106	Foster, Charles	436
—— Geo. H. Aun	375	—— Charles Edward	279
—— Geo. Wentworth	413	—— Chas. John 58, 153	
—— Henry Villiers	415	—— Charles M. 83, 240	
—— James	282	—— Edw. Cha. Colley	197
—— John	104	—— Edward H.	197
—— John	520	—— Edwin Fletcher	215
—— John	512	—— Fran. John	185
—— John 44, 452		—— Fred. Augustus	415
—— John	465	—— Henry 84, 335	
—— John Alex.	104	—— John, *MD.*	358
—— Jonathan	104	—— Thomas 18, 399	
—— Thos. John 7, 370		—— William John	215
—— William	77	—— Wm. Thomas	130
—— William	332	Fothergill, Chas. Wm.	417
Ford, Alfred John	245	—— William	106
—— Arthur	379	Fowke, Francis	401
—— Arthur White	489	—— John S. Ferguson	273
—— Charles	472	Fowler, Arthur Robert	253
—— Chas. Erskine 39, 400		—— Charles John	402
—— Edmund T. 39, 400		—— George	273
—— Frederick	318	—— Henry Day	316
—— George 106, 465		—— William	489
—— James Edw.	167	Fox, Aug.Hy.Lane 58, 159	
—— John 463, 489		—— Barry	106
—— John Randall M.	188	—— Charles Michael	243
—— T. S.	464	—— Chas. Richard	9
—— William	512	—— Frederick	217
Forde, Matthew Bligh	374	—— Henry Treffry	413
—— Thomas Douglas	261	—— James T. R. Lane	160
—— William	472	—— John J. Paterson	200
Fordyce, Alex. D.	266	—— Robt. Paterson	228
—— Chas. F. *CB.*	51	—— Samuel	520
Forester, Cecil Wm.	104	—— Thomas, *MD.*	530
—— *Hon.* Emelius J. W.	82	—— Thos. Wm. *MD.*	443
—— *Hon.* Geo. C. W.	30	Frampton,Heathfield J.	106
—— *Hon.* Hen. T.	104	—— Henry Wm.	417
—— Forlong, James	104	—— William John	185
Forrest, J. *M.D. CB.*	439	France, Richard	520
—— Wm. Charles 51, 135		Francis,Geo. Edmond	217
Forshall, Fras. Hyde	384	—— Henry 83, 291	
Forster, Bowes Lennox	380	—— Thos. John	131
—— Fra. Rowland 76,132		Francklyn, G. Wm. 33,210	
—— Frederick Blanco	181	—— John Hy. *CB.* 37, 372	
—— Henry Reginald	134	Frank, Philip, *MD.*	314
—— James Edward	176	Frankland, Wm. A.	403
—— John	84	Franklen, Chas. Rd.	378
—— John, *MD.*	532	Franklin, C. T. *CB.*77,374	
—— John Augustus	489	—— Henry	441
—— John Philip B.	177	—— Henry, *CB.*	529
—— Seaton Ralph	307	—— James	260
—— Thomas 28, 399		—— William	228
—— Thos. Bowes	120	Franklyn, C. *CB.* 26, 369	
—— Wm.Fred. *KH.*16,125		—— Edward Jas. *MD.*	135
—— William S.	464	—— Hy. Bowls, *MD.*	442
Forsyth, Burnet Bell	282	Franks, *Sir* T. H. *KCB.*	16
—— Fred. Arthur	181	Fraser, Alexander	519
—— Gerrard John	106	—— Alexander	193
Fort,Augustus, *Baron* le	542	—— *Hon.* Alex. Edw.	104
Forte, Nathaniel	191	—— Alex. George	224
Forteath, Alex. *MD.*	136	—— Alex. Maclean	15
Fortescue, Edmund	344	—— Andrew Simon	489
—— Hugh Granville	164	—— Arch. Campbell	531
—— John Chas. Wm.	54	—— Arch. Henry	324

Index.

Fraser, Charles	201	FremantleFitzRoy W. 344	Fyler, Lawrence 42, 148
——Charles	520	Fremantle, John C. S. 345	Fynmore, James 51
——Cha. Craufurd 84,147		French, Acheson 473	——Thomas 29
——Colin Alex.	444	——Arthur 417	Gabb, David Baker 195
——David	489	——Caulfield 334	Gabbett, Joseph 335
——Hon.David M. 63,374		——Geo. Hamilton 223	——Robert Poole 375
——Donald Maclean	226	——Henry John 27	Gage, Edward 106
——Duncan A.C.MD.307		——Hyacinth 489	——Hon. Edw. T. 54, 374
——Evan Baillie	473	——James, MD. CB. 529	——John Ogle 512
——George	134	——John Thomas 337	Gahan, Henry 62, 357
——George	255	——Richard 26	Gair, William 134
——Geo. Cruden	270	——William 376	Gairdner, Wm. John,
——Geo. Goodridge	247	——William 489	CB. 120
——Geo. Henry J. A. 375		Frend, George 106	Gaisford, John Wm. 104
——Hy.Martyn,MD. 346		——Wm. Causabon 246	Gaius, George Edwin 442
——Hon. Hen. Thos. 167		Fresnoy, Frederick de 541	Galbraith, Geo. Tho.
——Hugh	300	Fresson, Charles Hill 220	MD. 441
——Hugh	303	Frett, John 512	——James 294
——Hugh	463,532	Fretz, D. J. 464	——William 321
——James, MD.	267	Frings, Edw. Croker 170	——Wm. Arthur 273
——James	103	Frith, Edm. Bentley 150	Gale, Alex. Robinson 104
——James	106	——Fred. George 215	——Hen. R. Hoghton 156
——James	87, 281	——John Wharton 12	——William 489
——James	303	Frizell, John Bruck. 202	Galeani, Mich. MD. 532
——Jas. Alex. MD.	441	——Wm. Biston 465	Gall, Rd. Herbert, CB.
——James Alex.	349	Frobisher, Wm. Martin 274	60, 151
——James Francis	216	Frome, Edward 35, 399	Galletley, F. A. 464
——James Hardie	295	Fry, Charles Norris 187	Galliers, William 531
——James Keith	126	——John William 322	Galloway, David 75
——Jas. Stewart	120	——Oliver 75	——Thos. Jas. 30, 299
——John, MD. CB.	439	——Richard 75	Gallwey, John Blood 436
——John	10, 247	Fryer, Edw. John 344	——Melbourne Broke 384
——John	37, 411	——Henry Edmund 245	——Pat. Fitz Gerald 380
——John	42	Fugion, Edward 515	——Tho. Lionel J. 86, 401
——John Illidge	154	Fulford, Henry Grant. 338	Galton, Douglas 401
——Osborne Fre.Cha. 414		——William 76	Galwey, St. John D. 303
——Peter	532	Fullarton, Archibald 75	Gambell, Thomas 294
——Robert	218	——John 489	Gambier, Gloucester, CB.
——Robt.W.M'L. 59,182		——Wm. Fullarton 332	38, 372
——Robert W. MD.	532	Fuller, Francis, CB. 104	Gamble, Dominic Jacotin
——Simon	59, 412	——Francis Geo. Aug. 128	80, 177
——Thomas, MD.	146	——Fred. Hervey 104	——Geo. Francis 416
——Thomas	473	——Henry 418	——James 288
——William	16	——Henry Albert 318	——Richard, MD. 229
——William	103	——Samuel 145	Gamlen, Chas. Arthur 469
——William	286	——William 465	Gammell, Andrew 207
——William Thos.	255	——W. 489	——J. H. Houston 190
Frazer, Daniel	32	Fulton, William 78, 205	——William 250
——Donald Alex.	402	Fumetti, Joan. Just.	Gammie, Patrick 439
——Wynne Peyton	443	Von 541	Gandy, George 182
Frederick, Edw. CB.	120	Furlong, Charles John 369	——Henry 318
——Sir Richard	473	——Cha. Stuart Wms. 280	Gange, John 464
Fredrichs, Rudolph	541	——George William 220	Gannon, John 157
Freeborn, John	527	——John Shel., MD. 265	Gape, George Thos. 175
——William	169	Furnace, Norbury 473	Gapper, Edmund 473
Freeburn, James	520	Furneaux, Rich. Art.	——Peter 515
Freeling, Arth. Hy. 85,401		Lynd 202	Garden,John Campbell 489
——Sanford	375	——William 13	Gardiner, Benj. C. R. 138
Freeman,A.P.I.Walsh 489		Furnell, Geo. Stack. 357	——David 291
——John Watkins	207	Furnival, John James,	——Hen. Lyned. 61, 373
——Rich. Henry	207	MD. 534	——John Theod. A. 239
——Tho. Inego W.	104	Fursdon, Ellsworth 191	——Jno. Trevor Hall 295
——Wm. Thomas	178	——Geo. Edward 236	——Nathan Smith 55
Freer, Daniel Gardiner 106		Furse, Geo. Armand 255	——Richard 42, 307
——John, MD.	532	——Paul Geo. Fred. 436	——Sir Robert Wm.
——John Harbridge	17	Fyers, Amelius B. 402	GCB. KCH. 7, 370
——Richard	82, 233	——Henry Thos. 46	——Robert May 435
Freese,J.N.A. CB.39,372		——W. Aug., CB. 57,343	——Thomas 340
Freeth, James,KH. 10,291		Fyfe, William 473	——Thomas Geo. 334
——James Holt 63, 400		Fyffe, David 106	——William Alex. 208
——Richard King	374	——W. Johnstone,	——William Gregory 489
——Sampson	55, 400	MD. 133	Gardner, Andrew 489
Freke, Hon. F. J. E.	65	Fyler, Arthur Evelyn 267	——Anthony 223
Fremantle,ArthurJas. 163		——John Wm. T. 239	——George 150

Gardner, James	104
——James Anthony	185
——John	512
——Robert Ballard	416
——Rev. T.	455
——Tho. Thurville	444
——Wm. Bethell 42, 372	
Garforth, Frank	142
——John	240
Garlies, Lord Alan P.	128
Garland, George	257
——William	154
Garmston, Samuel	13
Garner, John Hutch.	104
Garnett, Albert Peel	147
——Fred. W.	321
Garnier, Brownlow N. 263	
——John	403
Garrard, Robert	133
Garnault, Benjamin	120
Garrett, Algernon Rob.	
	78, 207
——Francis Henry	206
——George, MD.	532
——Sir Robert, KCB.	
KH.	17
——Robt. John	141
Garsia, Christopher	299
——Michael Clare	349
Garstin, Edward	120
——James	489
——Robt. Longmore	30
——Wm.	74, 452
Garth, Thomas	473
Garvock, John	30
Gascoigne, Clifton	160
——Ernest Fred. 11, 298	
——John Hawkins 58, 411	
Gascoyen, Geo. Edw.	445
Gascoyne, Charles	16
——Geo. Edw.	444
——Thos. Bamber	473
Gash, Thomas	353
Gaskell, Robt. Bruce	220
——Wm. Plumer	228
Gatacre, Edw. Lloyd	186
Gatehouse, Edw.N.R.	358
Gates, William	521
Gatt, Arthur	540
——Frederick	368
——Salveiro 85, 368	
——William	368
Gatty, Edward	250
——Joseph	489
Gaudet, Jos. Maglovie	
Montague	436
Gaulter, Thos. Coke,	
MD.	440, 463
Gauntlett, George	103
Gavin, G. O'Halloran	106
——George Fred.	349
——William	352
Gawler, George, KH.	103
——John Cox 63, 303	
Gaye, Arthur Charles	444
Gaynor, B.	465
——Constant.W.Sept.248	
——Francis Seymour	341
Geary, Henry Le Guay 379	
Gebser, Wm. Theodore 541	
Geddes, Adam Gordon 515	
——Andrew David	233
——James	489
——John, KH.	11

578

Index.

Geddes, John	307	Gilbert, Philip Edw. V.	200	Glencross, William	217	Goode, John	473
—— Wm. Cameron	337	—— William	120	Glendinning, Thomas	489	—— Winter	83, 291
—— Wm. Loraine	186	Gilborne, Edward	384	Glentworth, Wm. Hale		Goodenough, Arthur	
Gee, Francis	473	—— Rev. J. H.	455	John Charles Visc.	345	Cyril, CB.	41, 363
—— Francis Horatio	210	—— Richard	326	Glinn, F. H.	464	—— Henry Philip	58, 373
Geissmann, Lewis de	542	Gilchrist, R. Muir, MD.	444	Gloag, John Wm.	445	—— Osborne Hall	379
Gell, Thomas	106	Gilby, Henry Mant	240	Gloster, Edw. Thos.	80, 248	—— Wm. Howley	84, 376
Gem, Henry	263	Gildea, George Fred.	220	—— Thomas	103	Goodeve, Henry Hills	381
—— Thomas	527	—— John Arthur	80, 315	Glover, Fred. Guy Eaton	257	Goodfellow, Samuel	120
Gemmellaro, Charles	544	—— Stanhope Mason	82	—— John	353	Goodlake, G. L.	65, 163
Gentzkow, Adolph. von	541	Gilder, Frederick	532	—— Robert Coke	257	Goodman, Edw. Barnes	369
George, Edw. Crossw.	177	—— Matthew Wm.	489	—— Sterling Freeman	104	Goodrich, Wm. Wynne	229
—— Edward Frederick	436	Giles, James	142	Glyn, Cair Smart	136	Goodricke, Hon. H.	328
—— Fred. Darley, CB.	34	—— Joseph	473	—— J. Plumptree Carr	344	Goodsman, David	15
—— Geo. Thorne	139	Gill, George	489	—— Jul. Rich., CB.	56, 343	Goodwin, Edward	123
—— James	331	—— Thos. M'Neille	200	—— Richard Thomas	228	—— John	443
—— John D'Olier	282	Gillam, George	135	—— Riversdale R.	84, 343	—— Rich. Henry	182
—— Owen William	126	Gillbee, James	512	—— Robert Carr	185	—— S. Osnaburgh	473
—— Rob. Villiers, MD.	441	Gilleland, John	473	—— Sidney Carr	344	Goodwyn, Henry Wm.	452
Geraghty, Patrick	217	Gillespie, Hen. James	13	Glynn, Henry	489	—— Julius Edmund,	
Gerard, Frederick	226	—— John	473	Goad, Wm. Trickett	240	CB.	39, 253
—— Sir Robert Tolver	106	—— J. Williams, MD.	181	Goate, Edward	50	Goold, Hugh Hamilton	413
Germon, Rich. Ch. H.	190	—— Robert, MD.	304	—— Wm. Ranby	245	—— James Knight	435
Gethin, George	217	—— Thomas Clark	132	Godber, Robert	473	Gordon, Abraham Hen.	13
Gibaut, Cliff. Gabourel	218	—— William John	266	Godby, Joseph	80, 375	—— Hon. Alex. CB.	
—— Philip	303	Gillett, Henry	200	Goddard, Cha. Edmund	323		30, 125
—— Walter Moses	211	Gilley, Thomas	106	—— F. Fitz Clarence	314	—— Alexander	202
Gibb, Alexander, MD.	363	Gillies, George James	380	—— Geo. Nugent R.	264	—— Alexander	33, 399
—— Charles John	78, 401	—— Mark M.	274	—— Norris	210	—— Alexander	489
—— Harry Wm. Scott	489	—— Walter	512	—— Samuel	521, 455	—— Alex. Wm.	82, 286
—— Reginald Kennett	318	Gilling, Thomas Gilling	223	Godfrey, Albert Henry	303	—— Archi. MD. CB.	439
—— Spencer Boyd	136	Gillman, Bennett Watk.	106	—— Cornelius	213	—— Arthur Helsham	103
Gibbes, J. G. Nathaniel	103	—— William Henry	36	—— James Alfred	417	—— Bertie Edward	
Gibbings, Thomas	55, 350	—— Wm. Howard	489	—— Wm. Fermer	334	Murray	53, 330
Gibbon, Edward Acton	186	Gillmor, William	357	Godley, Christoph, CB.	120	—— Charles	75
—— Jas. Robt., CB.	83, 373	Gillmore, John Parker	169	—— H. R. Crewe	80, 234	—— Chas. Alex., MD.	193
—— Stephen	489	—— Joseph Albert	489	—— Wm. Alex.	276	—— Chas. A. B.	80, 281
Gibbons, John	442	Gillum, Prideaux W.	62, 273	Godman, Rich. Temple	133	—— Charles E. P.	59, 306
—— Thomas	463, 489	—— Wm. James	81	Godwin, Cecil	207	—— Charles George	403
—— Thomas	489	Gilmour, C. Dalrymple	378	Goeben, Quintus, Baron	541	—— Charles Henry	
Gibbs, Charles	172	—— George	220	—— William de	543	CB.	56, 364
—— Edward	383	—— Wallace	379	Goff, Charles Talbot	138	—— Chas. S. S. E.	74, 226
—— George R.	218	Gilpin, Bradney Todd	288	—— Rob. Chas.	267	—— C. Van R. C.	263
—— John Matthews	218	—— Norcliffe	247	—— Trevor	223	—— Cosmo	6
—— Thomas	464	—— Rich. Thomas	104	Gogarty, Hen. Alex.	270	—— David Alex.	344
—— Alexander	207	Gilson, Alex. Daniel	223	Going, Richard	37	—— Duncan	106
—— Charles Edgar	266	Ginger, Joseph	473	Gold, Cha. Emilius	26, 293	—— Edward C. A.	79, 402
—— Charles Fred.	106	Gipps, Fred. Bowdler	245	—— Henry Yarburgh	473	—— Edward Smith	380
—— David	156	—— Henry	190	—— Wm. Geo.	18	—— George	489
—— Edgar	32	—— Reginald	59, 166	Goldby, William	360	—— George Grant	166
—— George	197	Girardot, Charles A.	104	Goldie, Geo. Leigh,		—— George Hamilton	402
—— Geo. Rawstorne	436	Giraud, Byng T., MD.	239	CB.	8, 308	—— Henry Wm.	12, 370
—— J. Brown, MD. CB.	439	—— Charles Hervé	239	—— James	145	—— Hen. Wm. CB.	464
—— Robert	323	Girdwood, Gilb. Prout	161	—— Thos. Wm.	435	—— Huntley Geo. MD.	298
—— Samuel, MB.	148	Girsewald, G.C.A. Von	543	Golding, Edward W.	335	—— James	14
—— William	252	Gist, Theophilus	139	—— Frederick Nassau	240	—— James	473
—— William Joseph	489	Givins, Hillier	191	Goldsmid, Albert	16	—— James	515
Gibsone, David And.	13	Gladstone, Edward	415	Goldsmith, Edward	135	—— James John	207
—— Hugh Fra. Hacket	303	Glancy, John	202	—— Oliver	229	—— John	104
—— John	154	Glanville, Francis	512	—— Oliver	527	—— John	16
—— John C. Hope	29, 359	—— Francis Robert	375	Goldsworthy, Roger T.	154	—— John Henry	178
Gichard, Wm. Robert	473	Glasco, John	531	—— Walter Tuckfield	144	—— John James Hood	236
Giddings, John	240	Glascott, William	237	Gomm, Sir W. M.		—— John Ponsonby	489
Giffard, Edward Carter	106	Glasgow, W. Macaulay	382	GCB.	7, 200	—— John Salmon	175
—— John	182	Glass, Archibald	540	Gonne, Thos.	154	—— John William, CB.	
Gifford, George St. John	75	—— Henry Edward	247	Gooch, Arthur	153		36, 125, 400, 404
—— Herbert Hale F.	129	Glasse, Francis	473	—— Geo. Cecil	332	—— Robt. Wm. Thew	332
—— John W. James	155	Gledstanes, Hugh B.	306	—— Henry	104	—— Rowland Hill	255
—— Walter Blachford	134	Glegg, Edward Holt	473	—— Percy Feilding	331	—— Sam. Enderby	54, 374
Gilbard, George James	153	—— Henry Vibart	463	Good, Henry Berkeley	299	—— Stephen Bilton	260
Gilbert, Arthur Strong	299	Gleichon, Fer. von Uslar	542	—— James	257	—— Theodore	
—— Francis Yarde	473	Gleig, Alex. Cameron	374	Goodall, George	404	—— Thomas Edward	151
—— James Anthony	473	—— Chas. Edw. Stuart	473	—— William	489	—— Thomas Edward	231
—— Joseph Mathers	196	—— Rev. G. Rob., AM.	455	—— William Robert	156	—— Webster Thos.	86, 294

Gordon, Sir Wm. Bt.	104	Graburn, John U.	136	Grant, John	489	Greathed, Edw. H. CB.	39
—Sir Wm. Bt. 85,	154	Grace, Morgan S.	444	—John	512	Greatorex, Frederick	130
—William 56,	210	—Sheffield	296	—John	531	Greatrex, Charles B.	489
—William	303	—Thomas	190	—John Charles	173	—Edward	531
—Wm. Aud. M.P.	382	Græme, Jas. D.	247	—John Gordon	264	—Edward Malcolm	155
—W. Fraser Forbes	217	Graffenried, Antoine F.		—John Henry	362	—Fred. Tichfield	303
Gore, Annes. Paul 82,	272	de	544	—John James 76,	357	—James	129
—Arthur	15	Graham, Allan	226	—John J. Forsyth	206	—Thomas Price	150
—Arthur Wm. K.	282	—Allan H. 58,	373	—John Marshall	401	Greaves, Charles	489
—Hon. Charles, CB.		—Birchall, Geo.	242	—John T. CB. 38,	266	—Geo. Richards	299
KH. 9,	330	—Charles C.	106	—Maximilian, MD.	155	—Richard	14
—Cha. Clitherow	318	—Frederick	527	—Murray D. V. T.	242	—Spencer Ley	243
—Chas. Jas. Knox	294	—Fortescue, CB.15,	411	—Sir Patrick,KCB.	120	Green, Andrew	106
—Edward Arthur	138	—George	106	—Patrick Jas. Jn.	337	—Andrew	344
—Fred. Wm. 87,	175	—George Wm.	192	—Robert	403	—Andrew Pellett S.	374
—George, KH.	104	—Gerald	402	—Rob. Alex. P.	444	—Rev.Charles,AM.	455
—Henry Pratt 83,	182	—Henry	104	—Robert Henry	382	—Charles M. 79,	237
—James Arthur 86,	300	—Henry Hope 34,	280	—Robt. J. Gordon	245	—Charles William	62
—Jas. Pollock 80,	169	—Humphrey	512	—Thomas Coote	290	—Edward Lister	308
—John	76	—Ivan, R. C. C.	436	—Thomas John	182	—Fran. John	352
—John	142	—James	37	—Thomas Linley	417	—James	299
—Ralph	377	—James	106	—WalterColquhoun	130	—John Hugh	314
—Thomas 81,	324	—James	190	—William	183	—J. M'Innes	446
—William	150	—James John 42,	452	—William	239	—J. S. N.	465
—Wm. Henry	242	—James Reg. T.	106	—William	330	—John William	237
—Wm. Rich. O.	106	—John	534	—Wm. Jas. E. 78,	374	—Owen	520
Goren, Ames	215	—John Gordon	136	—Wilmot	345	—Samuel	489
Gorges, Arth. Hamil.	380	—John Higgin 83,	223	Grantham, Charles C.	190	—Thomas Edward	156
—Rich. Archibald	417	—Lumley 56,	215	—Edward	340	—Thos. Hennis	220
Gorham, Cha. Alfred	380	—R.CuninghameC.	310	—Fred. Robert	260	—Thos. Littleton	120
Gorman, James	444	—Reginald Henry	343	—George	120	—William	255
—William Joseph	353	—Samuel James	415	—James	402	—W.	464
Gorringe, John, MD.	178	—Thomas	435	—Thomas	13	—William	527
Gorton, Edward	236	—William	103	Grantt, John	473	—Wm. Elmfreville	436
—Harry	257	—Wm. Henry	380	Granville, Bevil 86,	226	Greene, Dawson C. 78,	360
Gosling, Charles	283	—Wm. Wallace	134	—Fred.	106	—Dominick S. 83,	375
Gosselin, Nicholas	227	Grahame, J.	221	—R. Creighton	232	—Edward	489
—Thos. Reginald	250	—John	182	—Grape, Henry	489	—Joseph Alex.	307
Gossencourt,Jos.Ignace	544	Grain, Edw. Metcalfe	402	Gratrex, Thos. Price	150	—William	106
Gosset, Arthur	76	—Henry	401	Grattan, Albert O'D.	401	Greenhill, Charles	164
—Arthur Wellesley	172	Grange, Chas. W. 86,	356	—Henry	172	Greensill, J. S.	464
—Henry Allen	224	—Henry	263	—John, CB.	201	Greentree, Doveton D.	473
—James Wm. 85,	401	—Robert	123	Graves, Alex. Hope	270	Greenway, Theoph.	157
—Matth.Wm. Edw.	273	Granger, John	473	—Benjamin	49	Greenwood, George	103
Gossett, John N. 106,	465	Grant, Alex. G.	104	—Henry	381	—John James	242
—William Butler	403	—Charles, CB.	121	—Jas. William 76,	453	—J.	106
—Wm. Driscoll	401	—Charles	489	—John Stewart	530	—Joseph	473
Gostling, Charles 31,	371	—Charles	521	—Shapland	176	—William, CB.	50
—Fanshawe Wm.	266	—Charles Coote	207	—William	385	Greer, Arthur Jackson	221
Gouder, Giuseppe	368	—Charles Græme	210	—Wm. Grogan	290	—Henry Harpur 63,	296
Gough, Geo. Thomas	130	—Duncan	12	—William Henry	212	—William	489
—Hugh, Viscount,		—Edw. Fitzherbert	36	—William H.	473	Greetham, John Henry	489
KP. GCB. 6,128,	281	—Edward Charles	283	Gray, Alexander	341	—William Veall	152
—John Bloomfield,		—Fra. Rich. Chas.	140	—Arthur	252	Gregg, Charles Francis	515
CB.	13	—Frederick	207	—Basil	473	—George	328
—Thomas	345	—Fred. G. Forsyth	138	—Charles	444	—Henry William	330
—Tho. Armstrong	129	—George	342	—Charles Gordon	401	Gregor,GordonW.Fra.	473
Goulburn, Edward	103	—George	383	—Edw. Owen B.	417	Gregorie, Chas. Fred.	226
Gould, Arth. Rob. N.	338	—George Albert	220	—Elias Wm. D.	337	Gregory, Edw. Frank	340
—Francis Augustus	104	—George Arthur	385	—Fred. Warwick	418	—Fred. William	258
—Hen. Osborne	160	—Geo. Colquhoun	489	—Humphrey 80,	220	—George	414
—Robert Frcke	239	—George Fox	288	—James Clarke C.	121	—Hen. Jas. Michell	103
—John Stillman	473	—Herbert	291	—James Thomas	240	—Henry Patrickson	319
—Louis Philip	280	—James	453	—John	489	Gregson, Lancelot A.	232
—Nathaniel	131	—James	473	—Nicholas Loftus	201	Grehan, Peter	106
—Tho. Tyler	200	—James	489	—Owen Wynne	187	Greig, George	332
Govan,Chas.Maitland	375	—Sir Jas. H.,KCB.	16	—Robert	338	—John, MB.	227
Gow, Alex. Cunning	239	—Jas. M'Grigor	319	—St. George	170	—John James	106
—Wm. George	350	—James Murray	321	—Thomas Brown	420	—Robert	286
Gowan,Geo.Edw.CB.	120	—Sir Jas. Robert,		—Thomas Carstairs	413	—William	527
—Lawr. St. Patrick	151	MD. CB. KH.	529	—Thomas John	198	—William Isaac	527
Gower, Erasmus	148	—James S. MD.	272	—Wm. Ker	322	Greisheim, Albert Von	543
—Hugh B. B. L.	314	—John	440	—Wm. Robert	156	Grellier, James	539
—John Nathaniel	310	—John	473	Graydon, George 66,	372	Grenfell, Fra.Wallace	283

F F

Index.

Grenville,Thos.Lowrie 341	Grove, Jos. Cha. Ross 255	Hagart, Charles, *CB.* 32	Hall, Thomas 529
Gresson,William Hen. 233	——Robert 55	——Jas. M'Caul, *CB.* 104	——Tho. E. Arthur 330
Greville, Alg. Wm. F. 126	Grover, George Edw. 404	Hageman, Lewis 543	——William 520
——Arthur Chas. 77	Grubbe, Hon. Geo. H. 190	Hagger, T. O. 446	——Wm. Bruce R. 380
——Hen. Lambert F. 375	——John Heneage 13	Haggup, William 490	——William James 201
Grews, Robt. Alfred L. 129	——Thomas Hunt 106	Hague, Charles B. 74, 295	——William James 378
Grey, Alfred 205	Grueber, Daniel 490	——Harry Clayton 195	——William Sanford 515
——*Hon.* Charles 11	Grylls, Shadwell Mor-	Haig, Arthur Balfour 404	Hallen, Herbert 539
——Edward Simpson 144	ley 81, 376	——Jas. Felix 328	Hallett, Fra. Cha. H. 381
——Fra. Douglas 84, 290	Guanter, Jacques 544	——Robert Wolseley 376	——George Kerr 337
——Fra. Lennox Geo. 337	Guard, Morres 195	Hains,John McDonald 383	Hallewell, Cha. Jas. 354
——George Henry 160	Gubbins, Fra. Roche 172	Haines, Edw. E. 81,331	——Edm. Gilling 54
——John William 58, 321	——Geo. Stamer 276	——Fred. Paul 31, 187	Halliday, David 196
——Richard 260	——James 77,226	Hair, Archibald, *MD.* 532	——Fras. Aug. 78
Gribbon, Geo. Carson 444	——John Egerton 380	Haire, John 490	——Francis Edw. 415
Grier, Alex. Dixon 326	——Rich. Russell 283	Halahan, Henry Thos. 176	——Geo. Edm. 86, 316
——John C. Ferguson 191	——Stamer 237	——J. Wallon, *MD.* 529	Hallilay, Richard G. 490
——John Fred. 361	Gudgin, Tom Parinder 130	——Robert 228	Hallowes, Arth. C. 228
——John Joseph 50	Guernsey, Forbes Wm. 260	——Samuel Handy 258	——Brabazon M. 490
——John Joseph 206	Guest, Edward 490	——Samuel Handy 384	——George Skene 231
——Robert 490	Guille, Philip M'L. 379	Haldane, Alex. Hen. 172	——Henry Jardine 205
Grierson, Crighton 18	Guinness, Hen.Cramer 444	——Edw. Orlando V. 151	——John 323
——Henry 65, 205	Guise, *Sir* John Wright,	——Geo. Hen. John 291	——William 321
Grieve, Frank 261	*Bt., KCB.* 6, 321	Hale, Edw. Blagden, *CB.*	Hallum, James 512
——John 137	——John Chris. 60, 328	43, 316	Halpin, *Rev.* Robert 455
Griffin, Chas. Hen. 340	Gulland, Alex. D. 384	——John Rich. B. 42	——William 515
——Charles Lewis 260	Gulliver, George 532	——Lonsdale Aug. 403	Halton, Lancelot 153
——Francis John 65	Gumoens, Charles de 544	——Matthew Holford 232	Haly, Rich. Hebden
——Fred. Cockburn 376	Gun, A. 464	——Robert 142	O'Grady 319
——George 76	——George Allen 404	——Thos. E., *MD.* 186	——Wm. O'Grady, *CB.,*
——George 369	——Townsend Geo. 198	——Wm. Godfrey 416	31, 248
——George 532	Gunn, Fra. Leveson	Hules, William James 192	Hamer, Michael G. 490
——John 490	Gower. 444	Haliburton, A. L. 436	Hamilton, Alex. Chas. 404
——John Hungerford 15	——William 512	Haliday, Wm. R. 44, 246	——Andrew 239
——Michael James 277	Gunning, John, *CB.* 529	Halkett, Cha. H. C. 404	——Aug. H. Carr 378
——Thomas 319	——Matthew 104	——Hugh, *CB. GCH.*	——Charles, *CB.* 120
Griffith, Charles 490	Gunter, Edward 279	104	——Charles James 176
——Charles William 385	——James 129	——James 49, 153	——*Sir* Chas. John
——Edward Wynne 186	——Robert 132	Hall, Alex. Courtenay 183	Jas. *Bt.* 103
——Fra. Cha. Murhall 173	Gunthorpe, Joshua R. 512	——Angus William 279	——Chas. L. Baillie 269
——George 140	Gurney, Charles 185	——Archibald 232	——Chas. Henry 382
——Henry Darby, *CB.*	——John Gregory 354	——Arthur 354	——Charles Pratt 369
34, 125, 137	——William Prescod 330	——Charles 104	——Chas. William 120
——Henry Downe 74, 260	Gurtler, Joseph 544	——Charles 136	——Chris. M. 86, 331
——John 531	Guthrie, Alex., *MD.* 346	——Edmund 182	——Digby St. Vincent
——Julius George 120	——William 473	——Edward 212	85, 453
——Moses 532	Guy, Phillip M.N. 31, 180	——Frederick 324	——Francis Fisher 177
Griffiths,Arthur Geo.F. 290	——Thomas, *MD.* 218	——George 104	——Fra. Seymour 36
——Charles John 286	——William 353	——George 157	——Fra. Smith 50
——Edward St. John 215	Gwilt, John 56, 233	——George Hall 178	——Fra. Wm. 220
——Edwin 360	Gwyn, Hamond Weston 413	——Geo. Wm. Monk 304	——Fred. Gustavus 161
——Fred. Augustus 75	——Herbert Lionel 382	——Henry, *CB.* 120	——Fred. H. Anson 282
——John Thomas 51	——Reginald Thoresby 173	——Henry Edward 200	——Fred. Wm., *CB.,*
——Leonard 378	Gwynne,Cha. M. S. L. 288	——Henry John 145	26, 159
——Thos. Richardson 383	Hy. Lewis Edw. 473	——Henry Samuel 334	——George 490
Grigg, James Wm. 520	——Nadolig Ximenes 217	——Henry William 515	——George John 239
Grime, James 85	Gye, Lionel 382	——Jasper Taylor 104	——Henry 58, 310
Grimes, Geo. Dixwell 276	Gyll, Flomyng Geo. 382	——*Sir* John, *MD.*	——Henry 330
Grimes, John 473	Haardt, Lewis 543	*KCB.* 529	——Hen. Meade 56, 197
——Robert 490	Haberland, Charles 543	——John 12	——James, *R.C.* 455
Grimston,Rolland,V.S.190	Hackett, John 77, 258	——John 520	——James Banbury 369
——Walter John 375	——Patrick Wm. 190	——John Bolton 383	——Jas. Graham 286
——William Henry 200	——Robert Henry 215	——John Peter 363	——*Sir* James John 104
Grimwood, Thomas 520	——Samuel 79	——Julian Hamilton 164	——John 490
Grindlay, Robert 527	——Simpson 234	——Lewis Alex. 18, 399	——John G. Carter 127
Gritton, Fermor B. 413	——Thos. Bernard 226	——Lewis Fred. 376	——John Miller 416
——Henry 512	Hackman, Hen. Wm. 436	——Macdonald 288	——John Potter, *KH.* 103
Grogan, Charles Edw. 202	Hadaway, Sam. M. 439	——Richard Morgan 200	——Louis H. 78, 323
——John, *MB.* 532	Haden, Samuel 183	——Roger 203	——Richard 233
——J. E. K. 465	Hadden,Wm.Cha. 41, 400	——Samuel 197	——Richard 520
Grosvenor, *Hon.* Robt.	Hadfield, Cha. Jos. 65, 412	——Samuel M. F. 106	——*Rev.* Robert 455
Wellesley 126	——Henry Joseph 206	——S. W. 465	——*Hon.* Rob. B. 258
Grote, And. Macdonald 248	Hadley, Henry, *M.D.* 440	——Thomas 103	——Robert T. Fra. 338
Grove, Charles Thos. 490	Hadwen, Thomas 490	——Thomas 264	——Rob. G. 40, 400

Hamilton, Robt. Wm. 160
—Samuel B. 59, 231
—Thos. Bramston 380
—Tho. de Courcy 82
—Thomas Rice 286
—Walter, *CB.* 31, 369
—William 303
—William Digby 106
Hamley, Chas. Ogilvy 412
—Edward Bruce 54, 374
—Fran. Gilbert 74, 267
—J. O. 464
—Wm. George 56, 400
Hammersley, Fred. 106
—Frederick 80, 202
Hammerstein, A. *Baron* 541
—Otto Von 541
Hammill, Denzil 306
—Tho. Cochrane 104
Hammond, Chas. R. 178
—Frederick 103
—Henry 294
—John 170
—Lawrence N. D. 328
—William 512
Hamond, Hen. C. W. 261
Hampton, Thos. Lewis 133
Hanbury, Gurney 144
—*Sir* John, *KCH.* 6, 341
—Jas. Arthur, *MB.* 260
—William 242
Hancock, Henry 121
—Henry James B. 260
Hancocks, Wm. Fred. 321
Hand, Charles Aug. 290
—John Sidney 316
Handcock, Richard 50
—Richard 380
—Robert 188
—*Hon.* Rob. French 473
—Tobias 512
Handley, Aug. M. 216
Handy, Sam. Roden 328
Handyside, William 386
Hanham, John 361
Hannen, George Grote 379
Hankey, Aug. B. 86, 298
—Hen. Aitchison 15
Hanley, Dudley, *MD.* 442
—Malachi 473
—Roderick John 263
Hanly, Hugh 126
Hanmer, Henry, *KH.* 104
—William 323
Hannan, James 266
Hanning, James 123
Hanrahan, Thomas 357
Hansard, Arthur 353
Hanwell, Joseph 17
—Joseph 378
Harbord, Richard 185
—*Hon.* Walter 142
Harcourt, Albert J. 337
—Fra. Venables 103
—John S. Chandos 239
Harden, William 490
Hardie, G. K., *MD.* 442
Harding, Benjamin 104
—Edward 307
—Francis Pym, *CB.* 42, 223
—Geo. J. *CB.* 10, 399
—James 154
Harding, William 104
—William Tydd 443
Hardinge, *Hon.* Arthur Ed., *CB.* 41, 163
—Edward 86, 314
—Edward 384
—Edward Pelham 404
—Henry 77, 343
—Henry Charles 232
—Herbert Rich. 240
—Rich., *KH.* 17, 370
—William 267
—Wm. Sheffield 223
Hardman, Hy. Anthony 490
Hardy, Campbell 376
—Frederick 319
—Harmer 155
—John 141
—John Stewart 345
—Jonas Pasley 62
—Luke 520
—Robert Cope 156
—William 77, 362
Hare, Edward Henry 196
—*Rev.* George 463
—*Rev.* Henry 455
—James 282
—*Hon.* Ralph 380
—*Hon.* Richard 104
—Robert 252
—Robert Dillon 191
—Thomas 85, 354
—*Rev.* Wm., *AM.* 455
—William Henry 106
Harenc, Arch. Rich. 84, 338
Harford, Chas. Joseph 148
—Samuel Henry 197
Harger, John 350
Hargrove, Jn. Langford 490
Harington, Alex. S. 345
—Fred. Wm. 203
—Henry John 202
—Philip 415
—Rob. Ed. Stuart 344
Harkness, Jn. Granville 180
Harland, John 490
Harley, Robert Wm. 352
Harling, August. de 541
Harman, George Byng 80
—Ramsay 202
—Wentworth H. K. 380
Harmar, David James 123
—Edwin 240
—Morton Eagle 153
Harmer, Geo. Wm. M. 315
Harmond, Isaac 338
Harness, Arthur 380
—Henry D., *CB.* 39, 400
Harnett, Edward 147
—William Minchin 315
Harnette, Geo. Lidwill 354
Harold, John Casemir 16
Harper, Charles 527
—Thomas 334
Harpley, Matthew John 383
Harpur, John 77
Harran, Edward 132
Harrel, James Wharton 172
Harries, Thomas 56, 290
Harrington, Joseph 534
—Leicester, *Earl of*, *CB.* 26
—Sydney C. 446
—Anthony Chas. 527
Harris, *Hon.* Arthur E. 257
—Charles 490
—Chas. Harrington 354
—Edward Jackson 211
—Fred. Willoughby 246
—George Douglas 215
—Geo. Frederick 218
—George Harman 350
—Hamlyn Huntingd. 155
—Harry Bulteel, *KH.* 103
—John Robin 123
—Joseph 120
—Joseph 156
—Noel Hamlyn 378
—Philip 414
—*Rev.* J. B. 455
—Robt. Russell 62, 453
—*Sir* Thomas Noel 104
—William 473
—Wm. Fred. Vernon 300
—William Henry 240
Harrison, Albert Hy. 182
—Anth. Robinson 28
—Arthur John 186
—Broadley 62, 147
—Edward 307
—E. 465
—Edwin 383
—George Hyde 274
—Henry 176
—Henry 385
—Hen. Edw. 223
—Henry Laws 415
—Henry Wm. F. 154
—Horace Sibbald 185
—Hugh 473
—John 463, 473
—John 473
—John 531
—John Bacon, *CB.* 104
—John Christr. *KH.* 104
—Matt. Beachcroft 288
—Richard 403
—Robt. Prescott 85, 247
—Robt. Seppings 413
—Samuel 314
—Thomas A. John 377
Harrisson, Geo. Alex. 312
—Henry Albert 229
Harrow, Henry Edward 280
Hart, Geo. F. 236
—Henry George 56
—James 310
—John 490
—Richard 473
—Thornton 137
—William 258
Hartford, Augustus Hy. 246
Hartford, Hy. W. 220
Hatherly, N. C. 420
Harthill, Robert 532
Hartle, John F. A. 453
—Robert 530
Hartley, James 181
Hartman, Gust. A. 473
—Wm. Henry 74
Hartmann, Gust. F. W. 542
—Henry 543
Hartopp, Wm. Wray 128
Hartrick, William 185
Hartshorn, William 473
Hartwell, Francis H. 210
Harty, Joseph M., *KH.* 29
Harvest, Edward D. 338
Harvest, Hector 52
—Henry Lewis 326
Harvey, Charles Elwin 402
—Charles Lacon 330
—Charles Smith 382
—Edward 17
—George Lake 136
—Geo. Richards 341
—Geo. Sheppard 380
—Henry 346
—Henry B. 104
—Henry James 231
—John 76
—John 354
—John 473
—John Edmund 253
—John Richard 231
—Robert Charles 417
—*Sir* R. J., *CB.* 7, 350
—Thomas Peter 308
—William Crosbie 190
—Wm. Frederick 74, 453
Harward, Coningsby M. 196
—Geo. Sisson 377
Harwood, Edward 512
—John Arth. P. K. 201
Haselfoot, Charles 473
Hasleham, Wm. Gale 490
Hasler, Hy. Gratwicke 382
Haslett, Arthur Kyle 404
—William 200
Hassall, Chas. Vernon 326
—Thomas 383
Hassard, Alex. Jason 319
—Fairfax Charles 78, 401
—Henry Bolton 216
—Jason 79, 277
—Richard 490
Hassell, James William 169
—Wm. de 541
Hasted, Edw. Gould 277
Hastie, Charles 332
Hastings, Douglas 302
—Francis Wm. 78, 374
Hatchell, Christ. Hore 257
—Ebenezer John 284
—George 282
—John 172
Hatfield, William 324
Hatheway, Charles 490
Hathorn, John Fletcher 164
Hathway, Wm. H. 191
Hatton, Villiers La T. 104
—Walter Benson 224
Hattorf, Hen. G. Von 541
Haughton, Edward 340
—John 380
—William, *MB.* 384
Haultain, Fred. Wm. 373
Hausler, Fred. 543
Havelock, *Sir* Henry Marshman, *Bt.* 64, 212
Haverfield, John Tun. 413
Haverty, John Coghlan 270
Haviland, Francis 473
—John 520
Havilland, James de 81, 376
Haward, Wallace 243
Hawes, Geo. H. 78, 190
Hawke, *Hon.* Stanhope 473
Hawker, Charles 473
—Ernest Augustus 363
—Saml. W. H. 87, 220
Hawkes, Abraham 106

Index.

Hawkes, John Black. 465
—— Rich. Lloyd 246
—— Richard Parker 263
—— Robert 120
—— Robert 64, 314
—— Samuel 247
Hawkey, Hen.Cha. M. 473
—— John Frederick 414
Hawkins, Albert 384
—— Albert 443
—— Alex. Cæsar 78, 374
—— Fran. Spencer 120
—— George Palmer 473
—— Henry 104
—— John 473
—— John Summerf.61, 400
—— Samuel 15
—— Septimus M. 84, 338
—— Thos. Scott 52
—— Villiers Wm. C. 435
—— Walter Goodwin 205
Hawks, Hen. Wm. K. 205
Hawkshaw, John 32
Hawley, Robert B. 78, 281
—— Wm. Hanbury 202
Hawtayne, W. H. W. 250
Hawthorn, Robert 402
Hay, Alex. Murray 490
—— Alex. Sebast. Leith 41, 332
—— Sir And. Leith, KH. 104
—— Lord Arthur 49, 125, 159
—— Cha. Craufurd 17
—— Cha. Murray 12
—— Hon. Chas. R. 166
—— David 104
—— Dunlop 332
—— Edw. Drummond 357
—— Lord Edward 103
—— Graham 288
—— Henry Hird 133
—— Lord James 8, 322
—— James George 79
—— James Shaw 326
—— John Crosland 331
—— Rob. Albert E. 227
—— Robt. David D. 380
—— Robert John 375
—— Tho. H. V. Dal. 354
—— Thomas Rob. Drum. 82, 310
—— William 473
—— Wm. Drum. O. 302
—— W. Falconer 463
Haydon, Robert Owen 284
Haydock, Henry Jas. 212
—— Joseph Jas. B. 176
Haydon, Rob. L. 512
Hayes, Henry Horace 512
—— James 133
—— Patrick 318
—— Samuel Hercules 193
Haygarth, Francis 49, 166
Hayman, MatthewJones 79
Hayne, Geo. William 206
Haynes, Edw. Court 332
—— Jonathan W. 255
Hayter, Art. Divett 160
—— Charles James 186
—— George 512
—— Owen Edw. 436
Haythorne, Edm. 36, 169

Hayward, Edward 128
—— Geo. J. Whitaker 326
—— Hen. Blakeney 260
Hazen, Robt. Morris 282
Hazlerigg, Art. Grey 220
—— Thos. Maynard 382
Head, Sir Fran. Bond 106
—— Henry Bond 515
—— John 145
—— Samuel 200
Healey, John 318
Healy, John 473
—— John Denis 206
—— Rich. Calvert 207
Heane, Henry Wm. 258
Heard, Robert, MD. 295
—— William Hodder 473
Hearn, Chas. Bush 170
—— John Fleming 490
—— John Henry 384
—— Robert Charles 176
—— Robert Thomas 307
Hearne, Geo. Henry 490
Hearsey, Sir John Bennett, KCB. 120
Heartley, Andrew 455, 521
Heaslop, Colpoys P. 416
Heastey, Geo. Bayles 413
Heath, Edwin 515
—— Henry Gordon 213
—— Macclesfield Wm. 474
—— Thomas 490
Heathcote, Alfred S. 282
—— Bache Herpur 363
—— Chas. Graham 340
—— Cockshutt 474
Heatly, Chas. Fade 322
—— John 59, 318
Heaton, Arthur 205
—— Henry William 202
—— John Rich. 74, 247
Heuzle, Thomas 444
Hoberden, Henry 376
Hecker, Charles Higgin Teush 58, 359
Heddle, Alexander 490
Hedger, Walter 192
Hedley, George Luke 334
Heffernan, Nesbitt, MB. 196
Heigham, Charles Pell 231
—— Clement Hen. J. 210
—— G. Hen. John 86, 226
Heimburg, Ernest, Baron 543
—— F. C., Baron 543
Heise, Arnold William 542
Helden, Wm. Aug. T. 352
Hellen, C. A. von der 542
—— Diede. Wm. von der 541
Helmo, Arthur Thos. 335
—— Burchell 326
Helps, Rev. W. 455
Helsham, Henry 231
Hely, Egbert Chas. S. 319
—— Jas. Price, KH. 17
—— Joseph 515
Helyar, Edw. Hawker 261
—— Francis John 123
—— Frederick 183
—— John Welman 207
Hemmans, G. W. T. 415
—— Sam. Edw. W. 416

Hemmans, Tho. Hinton 50
Hemphill, And. T. 28, 232
—— William, MD. 294
Henderson, Rev. Alex.455
—— Bertram C. 316
—— Colin 444
—— David 474
—— Duncan, M.D. 532
—— Edmund Yeamans
Walcott 85, 401
—— Henry 192
—— James, KH. 28
—— James, MD. 529
—— James Allen 490
—— John 74, 207
—— John 220
—— Jn. K. Sheppard 226
—— Kennett Gregg 282
—— Robert Beatty 220
—— William 40, 372
—— William 490
—— Wm. Chipchase 321
—— Wm. Samuel 308
Hendley, John 442
—— Thomas 383
Hendry, Alexander 361
Heneage, Clem. W. 84,143
—— Edward 126
—— Mich. Walker 163
Henley, Arthur 270
—— James 81
—— James Frederick 344
Hennessy, Alex. C. 229
—— Frederick 337
Henning, James Edw. 191
—— Shurlock 324
Hennis, William How 31
Henry, Andrew 386
—— Chas. Stuart 55, 374
—— George Cecil 79, 375
—— Graham 104
—— John James 257
—— John 120
—— John 519
—— Richard 444
—— Richard Pentland 414
—— Robert Edward 322
—— Robert Emslie 266
—— Walter 529
—— William 175
—— William 386
Henshaw, Clinton F. 344
Henslowe, S. V. F. 303
Hensman, William 444
Henzell, Aubrey 200
—— William Henry 247
Hepburn, Fra. John S. 106
—— Henry Poole 49, 166
—— John 540
—— John Buchan 134
Hepworth, Alf. Jos. L. 384
Herbert, Arthur 106
—— Arthur James 52
—— Hon.A.Wm.E.M.142
—— Charles, CB. 42, 273
—— Charles, CB. 120
—— Dennis 6
—— George Flower 185
—— Henry Arthur 164
—— Henry Carden 321
—— Magnus Forbes
Morton 122
Herbert,Hon.PercyEgert.
CB. 34, 125, 316

Herbert, Hon. Wm. Henry 319
—— Wm. Henry 213
Herchmer, H. Turner 280
—— Lawrence W. 261
Hercy,EustaceLovelace 172
—— Francis John 172
Herd, Wm. Geo. R. 335
Hereford, Chas. 215
—— Richard James 303
Herford, Ivan S. And. 328
Heriot, John, MD. 532
—— Mackey, A. H. J. 416
Heron, John H. M. 169
—— Robert 300
Herrick, Benj. Bousf. 413
—— Edward 197
—— Edw. Henry 490
—— Gersham 180
—— Thomas 354
Herries, Fred. Stansf. 293
Herring, Henry L'E. 237
—— William 233
Herron, Samuel 490
Hertford, R. S. C.
Marquis of 474
Hervey, Andrew, CB. 120
—— Cha. Fred. 82, 452
—— Tho. Geo. O'D. 353
Heseltine, Gerald A. 418
Hesilrige, Arthur 280
Hesketh, J. 156
—— Wm. Crosbie 416
—— Wm. Pemberton 155
Hesse, Adolphus 542
—— John Valentine 279
Hessey, William 126
—— Wm. James 134
Hession, Thomas 444
Heugel, William de 541
Hewat, Richard 534
—— William 490
Hewetson, William 527
—— William 527
—— Charles 121
Hewett, Charles 358
—— Edward Osborne 403
—— Edwin 358
—— Frederick 512
—— Sir Geo. Hen. Bt. 26
—— Graham 417
—— Henry 414
—— James Waller 490
—— John 75
—— Thomas Meyrick 416
—— William 104
—— Wm. Vincent B. 416
Hewitt, Charles A. 228
—— H. H. 346
—— Hon. Jas. Wilfred 175
—— William Henry 120
Hewlett, Thomas 216
Hewson, Daniel Litton 172
—— George 512
—— John Lysaght 357
—— John Milliquet 75
—— John Mills 245
Heycock, Charles 326
Heygate, Edw. Nich. 402
Heyland, Alfred Thos.
CB. 39, 276
—— Arthur Rowley 276
—— John Rowley 104, 465
Heyman, Henry 375

Index. 584

Heywood, John James 169
—— Sidney Henry 340
—— William 202
Heyworth, Geo. Fred. 133
Hibbert, Edw.Geo. 77, 197
—— Francis Gordon 356
—— Hugh Robert 79, 185
Hichens, Richard 532
Hickes, Hen. J. F. E. 378
Hickey, Edward 104
Hickie, James Francis 185
Hickman, Robert John 282
—— Wm. Theodore 223
Hicks, Andrew John 263
—— George, *CB.* 121
—— James Clarke 155
—— William Grisdale 331
Hickson, Robert Atkin 323
Hiffernan, Chas. V. 215
—— Exham Long 216
Higgin, Walter 293
Higginbotham, Chas. 55
—— Henry 490
Higgins, Henry 138
—— Patrick 363
—— Thos. Gordon 15, 370
—— William 346
Higginson, Geo. P. 8, 334
—— Geo. W. Alex. 54, 159
—— Thomas C. 208
Higgon, John D. Geo. 377
Higman, Albert 415
Hignett, Cha. Harrison 260
Hilder, Jesse 490
Hill, Arthur 226
—— Arthur 416
—— Arthur B. G. S. 345
—— Aug. Fred. Arth. 337
—— Charles 137
—— Chas. Edw. 231
—— Charles John 104
—— Charles Rowland 375
—— Charles West 298
—— Dudley Clarges 252
—— Edward 106
—— Edward Ellice 417
—— Edward Nicholas 237
—— Edw. Rowley 29
—— Francis Charles 276
—— Fred. John Geo. 379
—— Fred.J.Ponsonby 169
—— Lord Geo. Aug. 106
—— *Hon.* Geoffrey
Rich. Clegg 128
—— Geo. Staveley 104
—— Henry 474
—— Henry Geary 380
—— Henry Seymour 253
—— Herbert John 299
—— Horace Fred. 343
—— James Dawson 290
—— James Morris 87, 156
—— John 521
—— John 34, 371
—— John Edwin D. 338
—— John Thomas 26
—— Kenrick 202
—— Octavius Wm. 279
—— Percy, *CB.* 38, 343
—— Peter Edward 378
—— Philip 103
—— Richard Fred. 104
—— Sir R. Chambre, *CB.* 103

Hill, Stephen John 35
—— Thomas 195
—— William 350
—— William C. 246
—— *Hon.* Wm. Noel 103
Hilliard, Christopher 490
—— George Edw. A. 322
—— Henry 515
Hillier, George E. 74, 140
Hilliker, Henry 474
Hillman, William 183
Hillyard, Geo. Anson 345
Hilmer, John Frederick 543
Hilton, Edwin Charles 274
—— James 521
—— William Legh 490
Hime, Frederick 404
Hinchingbrook, Chas.
Geo. Hen. *Visc.* 160
Hinchliff, C. Henry 291
Hincks, Thos. Cowper 266
Hind, Charles 42
Hinde, Edward 490
—— Geo. Langford 253
—— Henry Reynolds 474
—— John 59, 187
Hinds, Thos. Clowes 223
Hine, John 490
Hinge, Daniel 383
Hingeston, Henry 279
Hingston, Fran. B. 474
Hinton, James 206
—— Thos. Lambert 444
Hinxman, Rowley W. 282
Hipkin, Thomas 273
Hitchcock, Hen. Jas. 228
—— Rob. Bedford 418
—— William 229
Hitchins, Benj. R. 120
Hives, Thos. Walter 521
Hoare, Chas. Vyvyan 512
—— Edward 180
Hoban, Thomas 201
Hobart, Geo. Bertie B. 380
Hobbs, Fred. FitzWm.
Trench 274
—— George 252
—— George Lamont 260
—— Jas. Cavendish 237
—— Simpson Hackett 326
Hobson, Fred. Taylor 176
—— *Rev.* W. F. 455
Hocker, Edw., *CB.* 58, 412
Hockin, Hen. S. 131
Hockings, Robert 80
Hodder, Edward 490
Hodenberg, Aug. von 543
Hodge, DeBurghoEdw.206
—— Edw. C., *CB.* 30
Hodges, Geo. Lloyd 474
—— Henry Stephen 282
—— Thos. Eardley 474
—— Thos. Trophimus 307
Hodgetts, Thomas 453
Hodgkinson, Frank 139
—— William 247
Hodgson, Alderson 490
—— Christopher 197
—— Decim Filius de,
MD. 384
—— George Egerton 258
—— Studholme John 26
—— Wm. Chauval 78, 312

Hodnett, Wm. Patrick 273
Hodson, Robert 377
Hoffay, Ernest Albert 527
Hoffman, John, *MD.* 442
Hogan, Michael, *RC.* 455
Hogarth, Joseph 257
Hoge, David, William 383
Hogg, Edward 337
—— Fra. Robs., *MD.* 385
—— Jas. Macnaghten 104
—— John Roberts 404
Hoggan, John, *CB.* 120
Hogge, CameronN.63,159
—— Charles Wells 321
—— John, *KH.* 103
—— John Swaine 85, 180
—— Martin 417
—— SomervilleGeo. C.207
Hogreve, Henry 539
Hoile, David O., *MD.* 443
—— Edmond, *MD.* 444
Holbrook, Chas. Jas. 335
Holcombe, Alex. E. F.
52, 169
—— Francis 75
Holden, George C. 464
—— Henry 64, 150
—— Horatio Nelson 534
Holdenberg, Hans,
Baron 541
Holder, Cecil Frederic 136
—— Charles 104
Holdich, Edw. Alan,
CB. 34, 217
Holdsworth, Arthur H. 463
—— John Kelly 378
—— Samuel 515
—— Tho. W. E. 36
Hole, Lewis Blyth 182
Holford, Henry Price 146
Holgate, Bennett 74
—— Edward Milton 490
Holland, John 362
—— John 418
—— John Yate 414
—— Launcelot 103
—— Richard Henry 228
—— Rupert Charles 490
—— Thomas Edward 512
Holl, Charlton 121
Holle, Fred. A. *Baron* 542
Hollest, John Leigh 323
Hollier, Edward 534
Hollingsworth,Thos.S.229
Hollinsworth, Henry,
455, 474
Hollis, James 521
—— John Joseph 13
—— Wm. Henry 490
Hollist, Ed. Ommaney 380
Holloway, Benjamin 152
—— James Lewis 229
—— Thos. *CB.* 37,125,411
Hollway, Charles 330
—— Thos. Burchell 220
Holman, Charles 490
Holmes, Arthur L'F.
Ham. 148
—— Chas. W. S. D. 490
—— Christ. Francis 104
—— Fras. George 217
—— Geo. Chas. Hen. 295
—— George William 377
—— James 446

Holmes,Jas.Gus.Ham.148
—— James Nicol 106
—— John 266
—— Lionel 331
—— Ponsonby Ross 416
—— Richard Francis 326
—— Thos. Edmonds 257
—— William 444
Holmesdale, Wm. Archer, *Viscount* 163
Holroyd, Tyssen S. 243
Holt, Alfred 220
—— Christopher Fred. 349
—— Fran. Stirling B. 180
—— George 58
—— Rob. Wm. Fran. 418
—— William 521
—— William John 178
Holton, Francis, *MB.* 442
—— Thos. Noble 247
Holwell, W. A. 464
Holworthy, Edw.J. 80, 202
Holyoake, Fra. Edw. 223
—— Geo. Wm. Hen. 186
Home, Alex. G. *M.D.* 532
—— Anthony Dickson 442
—— Francis 104
—— Isaac Wm. 212
—— James Murray 106
—— John 120
—— John 490
—— John Home 10, 276
—— Richard 120
—— Richard Hare 201
—— Robert 404
—— William, *MD.* 440
—— William 490
Honyman, SirOrd, *Bt.* 103
Hood, *Hon.* Albert 345
—— *Hon.* Alex. N. 30
—— Ar. W.A. Nelson 231
—— Charles 79, 279
—— Chas. Clifton 296
—— Fra. W. *Visct.* 160
Hook, James 345
—— Lionel 353
Hooke, Henry Hudson 260
Hookey, George 420
Hooper, Alfred 255
—— Henry Filkes 307
—— Lucas George 146
Hope, Arch. White 17
—— Charles Errol 185
—— Frederick 28, 452
—— Fred. Harry 169
—— Henry Walter 160
—— Sir Jas. Arch. *KCB.*
7, 190
—— John Edward 79, 376
—— John Isaac 33, 399
—— William, *CB.* 59, 300
—— Wm. Astle, *MB.* 444
Hopkins, Edward 444
—— Francis Powell 205
—— George Rob. 83, 272
—— Henry 474
—— Jacob Biggs 183
—— John 266
—— J. P. *KH.* 106, 455
—— Patrick 361
—— Samuel 527
—— Wm. F. *CB.* 44, 411
—— Wm. Repton F. 417
—— Wm. Randolph 490

Hopper, Edward	106	Howorth,Patrick Albert	183	Humfrey, Benj. Geale	378	Hutchinson,Wm.F.M.	380
Hopson,F.Tho.Ongley	138	——Richard	51	——Benjamin Geale	104	——Wm. Nelson	16
——Wm. Hopson	107	——Rd. F. Armytage	261	——Charles Alex.	331	Hutchison, Fred. J.	291
Hopton, Edward	324	——Thomas Orton	258	——Fred. Thomas	269	——Henry M'Leod	203
Hopwood, Edwin Jas.	384	Hoyland, John	512	——John C. Taylor	216	——Joseph	342
——Hervey	103	Hoysted, Isaac	247	——Robert Blake	490	——Richard Cooper	298
Horan, Charles Thos.	319	——Thos. Norton	308	——Wm. Charles	439	Huthwaite, Edw. CB.	121
——Thomas	257	Hoyte, Alfred	286	Humphrey,Rob.Fraser	319	Hutton, Alfred	312
Hore, Fred. Standish	250	Hozier,Hen. Montague	380	Humphreys, C. Gard.	490	——Chas. Frederic	156
——John Christopher	416	——John Wallace	137	——Hen. Rose Morin	354	——Chas. Wollaston	280
——Thomas	32	Howison, Y. MD.	444	——John Goullin	474	——Fred. Wollaston	226
Horn, Frederick, CB.	26	Hubback, C. R. Kerr	129	——Windsor Henry	356	——George	121
——Fred. Gowland	217	Hubbard, James	490	Hungerford, Richard	272	——Geo. Allan	198
Hornbrook,T.Beckford	474	Hubbersty, R. Nathan	326	Hunt, Andrew	76	——Henry Francis	227
Hornby,Rob.Montague	156	Huddleston, Geo. Croft	150	——Arthur	156	——Henry Prim	82
——William	521	——G. Egerton	188	——Edm. D'Arcy 84,	141	——Robert	286
Horne, Arthur 34,	200	Huddlestone, Thomas	521	——Edward Joseph	290	——Thomas	104
——Charles James	207	Hudson, Alex. R,MD.	183	——George Evans 39,	411	——Thomas	107
——Edmund Garland	231	——Charles	474	——John	474	——Thomas Bruce	286
——George	148	——Edward	521	——John Dutton	123	——Wm.	490
——George	435	——Herbert Richard	274	——John Henry	444	Huxam, Reg. Edw.	239
——William Henry	130	——James	319	——Michael	490	Huyghue, Samuel	490
Horner, Gisborne	358	——John	257	——RobertWm.Bland	414	Huyshe, Alfred Geo.	175
——John	279	——Rev. Joseph, MA	539	——Thomas	137	——Geo. Lightfoot	318
Horniblow,Geo., M.D.	532	——Joseph Henry	104	——Thomas Rochfort	210	Hyde, George, MD.	183
——Thomas	234	——Thos. Wright 78,	250	——William Shapter	304	——Geo. Clarence	308
Hornsby, Geo. M.B.	381	——Wm. Henry	206	——Wm. Thomas	104	——Geo. Hooton	33
Horridge, Frank A.	240	Huey, Richard Wm.	30	Hunter, ArthurStewart	379	——John Martin	203
Horsey, Edw. Ralph	414	Huggins, John	534	——Charles	228	——Rich. Armstrong	213
——Wm.Hen.B.de 58,	159	Hughes, Charles	29	——Charles Fleming	302	Hyslop, Maxwell W.	332
Horsfall, Thos. Marsh	205	——Charles James	269	——Edward	515	Ibbetson, Chas. Parke	74
Horsford,Alf.H.CB.34,	343	——Edward	490	——Edward	288	——Edward	436
——George Fahie	474	——George William	178	——Fitz William Fred.	79	——Fred. Henry	435
Horsley, Nicholas	474	——Geo. Wm. B.	288	——George James	474	Iles, Wm. Robert	215
Hort, Rev. Charles J.	455	GordonStonhouse	331	——James	104	Illingworth, J. Alfred	444
——Fenton Josiah	353	——Henry Francis	490	——James	452	Image, John George	220
——John Josiah 54,	246	——J.	465	——James	474	Imlach, Alexander	474
Horton, George Wm.	103	——John Godfrey	224	——John	210	Impett, John 43,	304
——James	49	——John William	187	——OrbyMontgomery	353	Ince, Ralph Piggott	107
——J. A. Beale, MD.	444	——Joseph William	273	——Patrick	316	Ind, Fred. John Nash	247
Horwood, Geo. F. Fra.	172	——Pierce Wm.	201	——Robert Edward	436	Ingall, Frederick L.	107
Hoskins, Reginald	308	——Richard Thos.	294	——Rob. Hope Alston	531	——Wm. L., CB. 53,	288
Hoste,Dixon E. CB. 77,	375	——Robert	103	——Robert Scott	134	Inge, Augustus G. C.	132
Hotham, Augustus	474	——Robert 87,	349	——Thomas, MD.	530	——Charles	474
——Beaumont, Lord	9	——Robt. George	14	——Thomas	490	——Denison M. M.	141
——Charles	212	——Robert John	363	——William	283	——William	104
——George	474	——Spier 84,	319	——William, MD.	531	Ingham, Charles D.	234
——Richard	195	——Talbot de Bashall	354	——Wm. Dodsworth	490	——Chas. Thos.MD.	532
Houghton, Chas. Fred.	217	——William	316	Hunton, Rob.W.S. R.	381	——George	258
——Henry	337	Hugo, Ludolph de	541	Hupeden, Richard	542	——Joshua Cunliffe	246
——William	490	Huish, George, CB.	120	Hurdle, Thomas, CB.	18	——William James	442
Houlton, Sir Geo. 121,	474	——Henry, MD.	140	——Thomas	75	Ingilby, Charles H. 77,	375
House, Peter	145	Hulcett, Rev. Hugh	455	Hurford, Henry Payne	306	——William Bates 29,	371
Houson, Henry Basil	356	Hull,Arthur Hill	452	——Rich. John G.	131	Ingle, John	310
Houston, T. Blakiston	177	——Robert	181	——Thomas	445	Inglefield, S. H. Stovin	373
Houstoun, Alex. 33,	452	Hulme, John Lyon	75	Hurle, Arthur	164	Ingles, Henry A.	310
——Sir Robt. KCB.	120	Hulseberg, John Wild	170	Hurst, Charles Edw.	198	——Walter Lawrence	207
Howard,AlfredGordon	296	Hulton,FrancisThomas	290	Hurt, Charles	192	Inglis, Edward	490
——C. J. H.	300	Humbley,Wm.Welling-		Hurtzig, Fred.	543	——Frederick George	152
——Edward	210	ton Waterloo	474	Huskisson, John	413	——Jas. Gordon, MD.	291
——Hon. Fred. Chas.	164	Humby, John	75	——John William	276	——James Weir	417
——Thomas	123	Hume, Arthur	312	——Norman	299	——Sir John Eardley	
——Thomas	404	——Bliss John	314	——Samuel George	314	Wilmot, KCB.	15
——Walter	314	——Charles Wheler	264	Hussey, Chas. Edw.	218	——Raymond	107
——De Walden, C. A.		——Geo.Ponsonby 62,	205	——Henry	383	——Thomas	401
Lord, GCB.	474	——Gustavus	78	——Thomas	474	——William	107
Howden, James Adam	120	——Henry, CB. 52,	159	Hutchins, Wm.Jas.82,	197	——William 54,	277
——J. Hob. Lord KH.		——John Richard	274	Hutchinson, Alex. H.	377	Ingram, Geo. W. W.	436
GCB.	11	——Robert 62,	274	——Chas. Scrope	401	——Henry	290
Howell, Thomas	446	——Thos. David,M.D.	439	——Coote Synge 64,	130	——Robert Bethune	342
Howes, James	291	——Walter	248	——Edw. Hely	198	Inkson, James, MD.	314
Howett, Henry Hollis	211	——William 460,	521	——Frederick Jas. T.	474	Inman, James	418
Howlett, Frederick	380	Humfrey, Alexander	234	——Hon. Hen. Hely	103	——John	212
Howley, John	177	——Alexander	308	——John	490	——Tho. Withy	490

Index. 586

Innes, Alexander	490	Jackson, John Napper	17	Jeffreys, Edm. Richard,		Johnson, YorkeHobart	154
——Chas. Alex. MD.	270	——Jos. Dev.	148	CB.	40, 360	Johnston, Alfred W.	418
——Fra. W. MD. CB.	439	——Aïello Wm.	173	——Richard	465, 474	——Charles	376
——Francis	436	——Peter Nevil	201	——William Richard	414	——Christopher	354
——George Mignan	356	——Pilkington	378	Jeffreyson, George	491	——Edward	337
——Herbert M. Long	178	——Randle	308	Jeffries, Joseph	491	——Fowell Buxton	231
——John H. Ker, CB.	439	——Robert William	443	Jelf-Sharp, Henry	106	——Frederick	16
——Robert	490	——Standish Radley	151	Jellicoe, George Fred.	315	——George	416
——Thos. L. Mitchell	345	——Sydney Cosby	299	——Richard	515	——James	83, 187
——William	404	——William	314	Jemmett, Wm. Sugden	205	——James	316
Irby, Aug. Henry	58, 269	——William	491	Jenings, Geo. B.	81, 215	——James	104
——John Jas. Charles	463	——Wm. Hy. Munton	315	Jenkins, John	512	——James Crosse	191
——Leonard H. Lloyd	328	——Rev.Wm.W.AM.	455	——Lloyd Picton	201	——James W. MD.	420
Ireland, Edward	381	Jacob, Eustace W.	341	——Richard	59, 452	——James T. O. MD.	360
——Rich. Plunkett	352	——John, CB.	125	——Robert William	144	——John	62
Irvine, Alexander	298	Jagger, Joseph	512	——William Henry	319	——John	341
——Charles	51	Jago, Darroll Robert	380	Jenner, Aug. Fred. 77, 195		——John Tremenheer	253
——Duncan Malcolm	210	——John	304	——Kentish	446	——John Wm. MD.	321
——Hazlitt	81, 376	James, Benj. Rob.	157	Jennings, Alex. MD.	444	——Joseph, MD.	267
——John, MD.	442	——Charles	104	——Henry	139	——Joseph, S. MD.	229
——Matthew Bell	436	——Chas. Alf. Poyntz	299	——Peter Redmond	52	——Patrick	341
——Robert	491	——Chas. Butler	120	——Rich. Francis	282	——Richard	193
——Thos. Thompson	338	——Charles Dere	246	Jenyns, Soame Gambier, CB.	77, 156	——Robert	326
——William Henry	176	——Demetrius Grevis	474			——Thos. Henry	15
Irving, Alex., CB. 38, 372		——Demetrius W. G.	76, 172	Jephson, Henry	465	——Thomas Ormsby	252
——George	7			——Stanhope Wm. 34,172		——Walter Mowbray	188
——James	7	——Edward Renouard	403	——Wm. H. MD.	129	——Wm. Fred.	104
——Robert	491	——George	30	Jerome, Hen. Edw. 86, 215		——Wm. Walker W.	349
Irwin, Alexander	491	——George	157	——John	322	Johnstone, Chas. J. H.	378
——Chamney Graves	234	——Henry	75	——Joseph	521	——D. Baird Hope	331
——Fred. Chidley	234	——Henry	38, 400	Jervis, Edward	156	——Edm. John	436
——Fred.Chidley,KH.	103	——John	353	——Edward Lennox	150	——George	104
——John	324	——John Fencott	200	——Edwin	242	——Hamilton Trail	512
——John Robert	491	——Renouard Henry	217	——Henry	31, 359	——John	228
——Thomas	474	——Thos. Mansfield	255	——Henry Jervis W.	375	——John D. CB. 39, 342	
——William Arthur	196	——William	255	Jervois, Edwyn S.	474	——John Douglas	242
——William	33, 362	——William Hill	239	——John Gordon	401	——John Julius	160
——William Nelson	441	Jameson, David, MD.	532	Jesson, Thomas	381	——Montague Cholm.	16
Isaac, John Matcham	474	——Henry	304	——William, KH.	8, 307	——Robert Beckford	260
Isaacson, Eger. Ch. H.	491	——James, MD.	444	——Wm. Fra. D. 74, 401		——Samuel	217
——Henry Bevan	418	——John Lyster	442	Jervoise, Henry Clarke	164	——W. H. G.	464
Isacke, Hen. de Stut.	380	——Robert	364	——Jervoise C.	84, 226	Joice, William	132
——Hen. Wedderb.	380	——Thos. Ross, MD.	439	Jessop, Cha. Moore	443	Joiner, John	332
——Robt. Jas.	300	——William	491	Jevers, Henry Rogers	380	Jolliffe, Sir W.G.H.Bt.	474
Isdell, Chas. Wynn	207	Jamieson, James	337	Jex, Thomas	126	——Charles	414
Isherwood, John Henry Bradshaw	319	——Lachlan F.	143	Jeyes, Samuel, MD.	531	——Joseph Henry	413
		Jappie, William	491	Jocelyn, Hon. A. G. F.	107	——William	413
Ives, Cecil Rob. St. J.	128	Jardine, Alexander	18	——Hon. John S.	49, 166	Jones, Albert	247
Ivey, George James	350	——James	357	Joddrell, Henry Edm.	103	——Alexander Fair	139
——Wm.Fred.Torcato	441	——James Bell	444	John, Thomas	172	——Alfred Stowell	200
Ivimy, Wm. Henry	318	Jarrett, Chas. Berners	160	——Walter	236	——Arthur Trefusis	170
Izod, Wm. Henry	379	Jarvis, Geo. Eden	155	Johns, Charles E. 84, 210		——Benj. Orlando	14
Jacks, Walter	107	——Rob. Edw. C.	342	Johnes, Herbert Owen	142	——Chas. Hen. S.	279
Jackson, A.Tho. MD.	440	——Samuel Peters 86, 316		Johnson, Alured C. 86, 377		——Champion	218
——Andrew	176	——Sir Sam.Raymond	474	——Augustus Wm.	377	——Conyngham	86, 281
——Basil	104	——Wm. Dummer	197	——Benj. Oliver	195	——Dallas Gordon	404
——Charles Henry	322	Jary, Robt. Herber H.	148	——Chardin Philip 84, 145		——David J. Copeland	340
——David	328	Jauncey, John Knight	33	——Charles Gray	378	——Douglas	86
——Denis	252	Jauvrin, Herbert Small	291	——Clement Richard	267	——Ebenezer	105
——Frederick	491	Jay, William	188	——Edmund Geo.	544	——Ebenezer T. Thos.	413
——Fred. George	220	Jeames, Emanuel	344	——Sir Edward, MD.	532	——Edward Kent	338
——George	120	Jebb, Arthur	239	——Edward Colpoys	341	——Edward Monckton	217
——Geo. Edw. O. 83, 414		——Frederick Wm.	295	——Francis Dixon	260	——Felix Thos.	175
——Geo. Wm. Collins	107	——Sir Josh., KCB.		——George V.	374	——Fitzhardinge	148
——Gilbert Sidney	322		29, 463	——George William	404	——Francis Palmer	227
——Henry	74, 359	——Joshua Gladwyn	273	——Henry F. F.	55	——Sir Harry David, KCB.	12, 399, 462
——Henry	521	Jee, Joseph	310	——James Stephen	203		
——Henry B.	211	Jeeves, Wm. Younge	384	——Joseph Oliver	197	——Henry H. MD.	442
——Sir James, KH.		Jeffares, John Samuel	190	——Nicholas	121	——Henry Helsham	403
KCB.	10, 141	Jeffcoat, James Henry	191	——Ralph Boetler	615	——Henry Norris	382
——James	50	Jefferson, Frank	207	——Thos. George	150	——Henry R.	32, 134
——James	201	——Richard	515	——Wm. Augustus	103	——Henry Shawe	319
——James Bower	352	Jeffery, James	512	——Wm. N. Gibson	416	——Howard Sutton	415
——John Boddington	213	——John Morton	107	——Yurrall	474	——Hugh Maurice 84, 303	

Index.

Jones, Humphrey Stan. 435
——James 474
——Jeremy 464
——Jeremy 491
——Jeremy Peyton 188
——Inigo Wm. 105
——Sir J. KCB. 39, 281
——Jno. Chn. Hill 81, 273
——Joseph 247
——Joseph 521
——Lewis John Fillis 324
——Melville Geo. 384
——Michael 515
——Morgan Jones 302
——Nathaniel 121
——Owen Thomas 417
——Percy Malcolm 261
——Richard 9, 370
——Richard Paget C. 375
——Richard Roynon 377
——Robt. Owen 404
——Robt. Powell 330
——Rokeby Steele W. 350
——Samuel 534
——Stopford Thomas 512
——Theophilus 176
——Thomas 105
——Thomas 87, 132
——Thomas Edward 491
——Thos. Egerton 279
—— Thomas John 381
——Tho. Sheridan G. 247
——Vaughan 474
——William, CB. 30, 286
——William 474
——William MD. 531
——Wm. Prime 107
Jop, Robert 512
Jopp, James, MD. 246
Jordan, Edward 491
——John 308
——Joseph 79, 243
——Lutley 243
——Percival Walsh 195
Josselyn, Arthur Hen. 191
—— Fred. John 337
Joy, George 280
Joyce, Arthur Wellesley 175
——Edward 521
——Leonard Sumner 377
Joyner, Josh. Sumpner 444
Judd, William Henry 531
Judge, Arthur 107
Julian, Thomas Archer 270
Julius, Wm. Mavor 141
Julyan, Primrose G. 527
Justice, Philip William 274
——William 120
——Wm. Clive 306
Kains, Thomas 175
Kane, Charles George 191
——G. 464
——John Joseph 491
——Richard 300
Kantzow, Hen. Ives de 417
Karslake, Frederick 318
Kauntze, Edw. Hy. Ern. 135
——George E. F. 135
——Henry 147
Kay, Alfred Hervey 274
——Arthur 436
——Henry Monckton 417
——James 258
——William Algernon 296

Kaye, Arthur Lister 377
——Geo. Lister Lister 105
——Wilkinson Lister 474
Kayes, William 491
Kean, Henry 280
——Henry 107
——John Henry 491
Keane, Aug. Daniel 304
——Benj. Bloom. 85, 453
——Charles 322
——Edward 103
——Edw. A.W. Lord 107
——Geo. Michael 474
——Giles 59, 322
——Hon. Hussey F. 78, 401
Kearnes, John 491
Kearney, Charles 105
——Edward Barrett 178
——Patrick Barrett 349
Keate, Edward 377
Keating, James Singer 105
——John 188
——Richard 383
Keats, John Smith 474
——Wm. M'Geachy 319
Keen, Archibald Geo. 288
Keene, Arthur Ruck 345
——Edmund Ruck 106
——John Edw. Ruck 377
Keep, Wm. Thornton 491
Kehoe, Joseph Richard 208
Keir, Malcolm 157
Keith, William 404
Kekewich, Samuel B. 180
Kelaart, Edw. Fred. 441
Kellett, Edw. Young 443
Kellie, James, MD. 154
Kelly, Cha. Frederick 212
——Edward 383
——G. C. 282
——Henry Holdsw. 418
——James 349
——James William 139
——John 377
——John 75
——John Lovel 193
——Richard Dennis, CB. 39, 243
——Richd. Seym. 465, 521
——Thomas, KC. 28, 463
——Thomas 173
——Thomas 350
——Thos. Conyng. 52, 263
Kelsall, Gustavus N. 403
——Henry 207
——Henry 218
——John 41
——John R. 195
——Joseph 29
——Roger 104
Kelsey, Arth. Francis 246
——Charles 104
——Thomas Mortimer 182
Kemm, Henry Cæsar 330
Kemmis, George 201
——John Olpherts 205
——William 319
——William 380
Komp, George Rees 120
——John 359, 474
——William 212
Kempson, Cart. Houst. 185
——Edward 232
——Wm. John 341

Kempt, John Fra. 62, 197
Kenah, Thomas, CB. 8, 290
Kendall, Henry 142
——John Jennings 258
Kenmare, Thos. Earl of 474
Kennard, Edm. Hegan 142
Kennedy, Alex. Kennedy Clark, CB. KH. 11, 194
——F. Charlesworth 231
——Geo. Rob. Harry 38, 371
——Henry Friend 78, 281
——Hugh 78
——Irving Francis 253
——Jas. Shaw, CB. 8, 263
——John 139
——John Clark, CB. 41
——John Mackenzie 359
——John Pitt 491
——John Will. Alex. 413
——Patrick Henry 491
——Thomas 443
——Walter Craufurd 43
Kennett, Cha. Leighton 512
Kennicott, Benj. D. 416
Kenny, Court. W.A.T. 334
——Edward 50
——Matthias, MD. 534
——Stephen 474
——Tho. Nepean Edw. 303
——Wm. Henry 63, 453
Kenrick, Buxton M. 242
Kent, Edmund Watkin 228
——Henry 84, 308
Kentish, Allan Joshua 261
Keogh, Anthony Rob. 202
——Henry 156
——Lynch John 156
Keough, William 197
Keppel, Frederic Cha. 65, 159
Ker, Edward Stuart 270
——James 508
——Richard Hall 474
——William 175
——William Henry 220
Kerans, Thos. George 315
——William Robert 444
Korin, Frederick Geo. 128
Kerr, Benj. Cowan 183
——Claudius 352
——Francis Ernest 345
——Henry 185
——Henry Alex. 51
——Herbert 211
——John Henry 491
——John Manners 288
——Lord Mark 35, 200
——Lord Ralph D. 146
——Robert Dundas 474
——William 521
——William Fred. 176
——William Hen. 84, 200
Kerrick, Walter FitzG. 232
Kerridge, Charles Jas. 266
——William 232
Kershaw, William 260
Kersteman, Harry G. 491
Ketchen, James 120
Kettle, Robert 386
Kettilby, James 474
Kettle, William 532
Kettyles, Christopher 239
Key, Geo. William 29

Key, William Henry 279
Keysor, Fred. Charles 186
Keyworth, Charles 270
——John Walter 264
Kidd, John M'Mahon 105
——Leonard, M.B. 233
——Wm. Archibald 383
Kidston, Alex. Ferrier 255
Kildahl, James Robt. 302
Kilgour, Patrick 312
Killeen, Lord Arthur J. 107
——Chas. Preice 295
——Roger 220
Killery, St. John 444
Kilroy, Alex. Rob. 242
Kilvert, William 331
Kinahan, Chas. Hen. 290
——Chas. James 258
——Henry 176
——John 444
Kincaid, Sir John 122
Kindersley, Edw. N. 215
——Henry Wasey 236
King, Anth. Singleton 105
——Augustus Henry 377
——Chas. Edward 247
——Charles Richard 229
——E. C. 464
——Edward R. 38
——Francis George 220
——Francis James 150
——George 83, 363
——George 57, 200
——Geo. Smyth, MD. 203
——Gerald FitzGerald 200
——Gerald FitzGerald 263
——Henry John 82, 175
——Isaac 253
——James 474
——James Gerrard 350
——James Walker 282
——John 280
——John Duncan 455, 474
——John Henry 137
——John Hynde 54, 159
——John Robert 379
——Jos. Hen. Thos. 444
——Livins Sherwood 276
——Rich. Fitzgerald 201
——Sir R. Duckworth, Bt. 474
——Rich. Thomas 13
——Thomas 120
——Thomas 515
——Uriah Henry 420
——William 274
——William 464
——William 491
——William Affleck 210
——William James 28
——William John 76
——William Magrath 375
——W. M. 464
——William Ross 86
——Wm. Valentine 141
——William Wallace 148
Kingdom, Edw. Wm. Clemishaw, M.D. 532
Kingscote, Fitzhardinge 344
——Rob. Nigel Fitzhardinge, CB. 105
Kingsley, James Bell 474
——John 354
——Wm. Hen. Bell 295

Kingsmill, Parr Wm. 352	Knox, Francis Walters 443	Lambert, Montague 404	Latham, John 491
Kington, Wm. M. N. 133	—— George 105	—— Walt. M'Clellan 253	—— Matthew 475
Kinkee, Frederick 621	—— George 532	—— William 157	—— Oliver Matthew 264
Kinloch, Alex. Angus	—— George Uchter 379	—— William 324	Laughton, William 157
Airlie 345	—— George Williams 167	Lamborn, J. Sherrard 512	La Touche, D. Matthew 237
Kinneir, Joseph Hull 474	—— James 215	Lambrick, George 412	Latouche, T. Geo. D. 198
Kinsman, Charles Jas. 417	—— Jas. Dunlop 207	Lambton, Arthur 164	Laurent, John Mackie 173
—— Edward 417	—— John Hunter 319	—— Francis 65, 166	Laurie, John 120
—— William James 413	—— John Simpson 344	—— Fred. William 87,300	—— John Wimburn 177
Kippen, Horatio Nelson 197	—— Richard 59, 155	Lamert, George Fead 237	—— Julius Dyson 243
Kirby, Joshua Henry 322	—— Richard 74, 155	Lamont, W. R. Alex. 435	Lautour, Arthur 138
—— Michael 474	—— Rich. Annesley 178	Lamotte, C. Wyndham 475	—— P. Aug. CB, KH, 8, 138
—— Thomas H. 215	—— Robert Trotter 328	Lampen, Henry 243	Laver, Robert 198
—— William Hen. 63, 334	—— Thomas 63, 373	—— Robert 323	Law, Alfred Markland 226
Kirk, James 303	—— Thos. Edmond 61, 295	Lamprey, Jones, MB. 295	—— Cha. Edmund 41, 294
—— James Buchanan 337	—— Vesey Edmund 270	Lance, Wm. H. Joseph 340	—— Charles Fred. 107
—— Percy 308	—— William 105	Lancey, William 76	—— Fra. Towry Adeane 378
—— William John 452	—— Wm. Bevington 181	Land, James 444	—— James Horton 475
Kirke, John Henry 215	—— Hon. Wm. Stuart 106	—— John 36	—— James Smith 50
Kirkland, Sir John 527	Koester, Adolphus 541	Lander, Alfred 491	—— John 76
—— John Ag. Vesey 57, 180	Korschann, Joseph 542	—— James 444	—— John 176
Kirkman, J. 465	Kropp, John Albert 544	—— William Henry 491	—— Rich. Alexander 177
—— William Reuben 383	Kuckuck, Aug. William 542	Landers, James 521	—— Robert, KH. 18
Kirkpatrick, Thos. S. 234	Kuhls, Augustus 541	Landrey, John 354	—— Robert 239
Kirwan, And. Hyacinth 105	—— Ferdinand Carl E. 541	Lane, Alfred John 267	—— Wm. Henry, KH. 14
—— Chas. John 201	Kumme, Ludolph 542	—— Ambrose 491	Lawler, J. R. O'Meara 349
—— George 231	Kunoth, Godlove 543	—— Benjamin 443	Lawless, Hon. Edward 345
—— Henry 474	Kuster, Ferdinand 541	—— Chas. Hen. John 491	Lawless, Rev. G. AM. 465
Kirkwood, Jas. M. 337	Kyffin, Rob. Willington 515	—— C. Rich. W. CB. 120	—— Peter 338
Kitchener, Henry 182	Kyle, Alexander 103	—— George Dawkins 512	Lawlor, Digby Wm. 248
—— Henry Horatio 105	—— J. 519	—— Grenville Charles 344	—— Provo Wm. 475
Kittoe, George H. 177	—— Samuel Cotter 380	—— Henry 103	Lawrell, Digby Henry 107
Klingsöhr, George 542	Kyrle, J. Ernle Money 474	—— Henry Eyre Wyatt 415	—— Henry John 182
—— Lewis 542	Kysh, John Anthony 330	—— Henry James 156	—— Horatio William 342
Knaggs, Henry 354	Labalmondiere, Doug.	—— Henry John Bagot 164	Lawrence, A. J. CB. 29
Knapman, Wm. Stephens 75	W. P. 474	—— John 491	—— Edw. Daniel 436
Knapp, Chas. Barrett 446	La Cloche, Thomas 534	—— John 527	—— Henry 121
—— Francis Adam 350	La Coste, Charles Fred. 417	—— J. Theophilus, CB. 121	—— Hen. Jno. Hughes 161
—— George Henry 261	Lachlan, Robert 107	—— Joseph Vavasour 178	—— John 203
—— Geo. W. Wynford 290	Lacon, Edm. B. Knowles 227	—— Thomas Thornhill 330	—— John 226
Knatchbull, Francis 326	Lacy, Gilbert de Lacy 197	—— William 322	—— J. E. Wilson 79, 419
—— Norton 335	—— Henry Hearne 307	—— William Ralph 161	—— Samuel Hill 83, 231
Kneebone, Frederick 236	—— Richard 242, 358	Langdale, James, MD. 331	—— Thomas 269
Knight, Alfred 82	—— Rich. Walter 55, 276	—— Marmaduke R. 512	—— Wm. Hudson 475
—— Arnold More 354	—— Samuel Walter 491	Langdon, Colwell 491	Lawrenson, John 26
—— Brook John 474	—— Seymour de Lacy 381	Langford, Alexander 521	Lawrie, John 79, 363
—— Edward, MD. 530	—— Thomas E. 34	—— John Crawford 210	Laws, Edward 245
—— Frederic 298	—— William 82, 452	—— Wm. Bookey 16	Lawson, Barclay 374
—— Frederick Charles 491	Laffan, R. Michael 85, 401	Langham, Herbert Hay 126	—— James 286
—— Godfrey Lyon 291	LaGrange, J. Warring. 491	Langley, Geo. Colt 38, 412	—— John 453
—— Henry Sollers G. S. 215	Laidley, John 527	—— George Richard 475	—— J. Ambrose, MD. 441
—— J. T. 464	Laing, James M'Grigor 442	—— Oliver 63, 207	—— Robert, MD. 439
—— Lewis Edward 154	—— Joseph 202	—— Wm. Leslie, MD. 440	—— Stephen 363
—— Philip Henry 226	—— J. 465	Langmead, Rev. G. W. 455	—— Thos. Wm. 304
—— Thomas 363	—— Patrick Sinclair 227	Langrishe, Hugh Henry 475	Lawton, Hugh 344
—— William 328	Lake, Arthur 288	Langstaff, Theo. Fether. 193	Laxon, John 475
—— William 491	—— H. Atwell, CB. 37, 125	Langston, William 444	Layard, Bernard Gran. 63
—— W. 465	—— Noel T., CB. 34, 371	Langton, Edward 475	—— Brownlow Villiers 190
—— William Henry 264	Lakin, Edmund 240	Langtry, Robert 263	—— Charles Edmund 205
Knipe, Geo. Marshall 474	Lamb, George 153	Langworthy, V. Upton 186	—— Charles H. 231
—— John Copeland 324	—— James 342	Lanphier, J. P. Cosby 475	—— W. Twisleton 51, 353
—— Leonard 335	—— John Alex. 284	La Presle, Joseph Thos. 346	Laye, George 491
—— William 322	—— Samuel Burges 192	Laprimandaye, C. Hen. 291	—— F. F. 465
Knollys, Edward 59, 306	—— Wm. Wentworth 135	Lapsley, William 442	—— Joseph Henry 51, 360
—— Wm. Thos. 11, 288	Lambard, Henry 273	Larcom, George 345	Layton, Orlebar Fred. 382
—— Wm. Wallingford 332	Lambe, George Vautier 357	—— Thos. Aiskew, CB. 16	Lazenby, James 475
Knott, William 270	Lambert, Charles Henry 215	Lardner, George 435	Lazzarini, James 368
—— William 534	—— George 319	—— John 52	Lea, Fred. Percy 79, 465
Knowles, Charles B. 308	—— George Moore 239	Large, John Edward 345	—— Samuel Percy 475
—— Francis Edward 527	—— Sir Hy. John, Bt. 475	Lasalle, Aug. Bolle de 218	—— Wm. Percy 85, 223
—— William 76	—— James 383	Luscelles, Charles F. R. 103	—— Wm. Rob. Welch 507
—— Wm. Lancelot 290	—— John 491	—— Claude Geo. Wm. 376	Leach, Edmund 267
Knox, Brownlow Wm. 105	—— John Arthur 31, 159	—— Walter Richard 344	—— Geo. A. 85, 401
—— Francis 491	—— Louis James 231	Last, Edward 32	—— Henry 260

Index.

Leach, Henry	491	Le Grice, Fred. S.	380
—— Walter	300	Leibert, Edmund B.	155
—— William	180	Leigh, Henry	223
Leacock, C. Edm. B.	381	—— Henry	340
—— Joseph	464	Leighton, Sir D. KCB.	120
Leader, H. Peregrine	224	—— E. Wm. Forester	191
Leadbitter, John G.	323	—— Forrester O.	107
—— Matthew Edw.	322	Leir, Richard L.	250
Leahy, Arthur	85, 402	Leitch, James, MD.	253
Leake, Henry	299	Leith, Charles Forbes	211
—— Robert Martin	14	—— Sir Geo. H. Bt.	154
—— W. M.	105	—— James 84,	137
Lean, Francis	415	—— John Kenneth	519
Learmonth, Alex.	64, 154	—— John Macdonald	312
Leask, Jas. G. MB.	334	Leitrim, Wm. Earl of	105
Leatham, Alfred S.	306	Le Marchant, Edward	475
—— Francis	512	—— Sir John Gaspard	16
—— James	105	—— Thomas	42
—— James Birley	475	Le Mesurier, And. A.	202
—— Rich. Blackburn	175	—— Cecil Brooke	377
Leathes, Edward	491	—— Fred. Aug.	404
Leavach, John	491	—— Henry	527
Le Blanc, Francis	103	—— Rev. J. T. H. AM.	539
Le Blond, Jules Victor	288	—— Thomas Augustus	436
Leckie, William	80, 250	—— Thos. Maunsell	246
Lecky, James	418	—— William	435
—— John Gage	51	—— Wm. Abraham	28
Leconfield, Geo. Lord	103	—— Wm. G. CB.	61, 376
Le Cocq, Jas. H.	175	Lemoine, William	75
Le Couteur, John	104, 125	Lemon, Richard S.	202
—— John Halkett	57, 163	—— Thomas, CB.	41, 411
Ledgard, Nath. Polhill	236	Le Mottée, Osmond F.	380
Lee, David Ross	527	—— Wm. Albert	212
—— Frederick Rich.	512	Lempriere, Arthur R.	403
—— Henry	87, 152	—— George Reid	402
—— John	136	—— Henry	475
—— John	342	Lenon, Edmund Hen.	295
—— John	512	Lennard, John Barrett	403
—— Ranulph Charles	245	Lennox, Aug. F. F.	78, 374
—— Robert Newton	512	—— Lord Arthur	105
—— Thomas	362	—— Lord George	105
—— Thomas Denote	267	—— John Maitland	415
—— William	83, 182	—— Wilbraham O.	64, 402
—— William	475	Leonard, Falcon Peter	293
Leech, Jas. Wm.	512	—— Henry Bates	475
—— Rob. Stockham B.	228	Leonhart, Harry	541
Leeds, Joseph Robert	416	Lepper, Maxwell	84, 322
Lees, Charles Cameron	226	Le Quesne, John C.	148
—— Edward John	210	Leschen, Hannah B.	541
—— Harcourt James	283	Leslie, Angus	491
—— Wm. Munnings	226	—— Arthur	61, 252
Leeson, Aug. Johnnes	197	—— Charles, KH.	103
—— Charles Edward	243	—— Chas. Henry	80, 190
—— Henry	187	—— Chas. Robert	231
—— Ralph	239	—— George	374
—— Rich. John Philip	243	—— George	414
Leet, Charles Henry	181	—— John	181
—— George Knox	227	—— John, KH.	10, 245
—— John Knox	442	—— John Henry	300
—— Wm. Knox	200	—— John Thos. CB.	463
Le Febure, C. Edw.	291	—— Lewis Xavier	106
Le Feuvre, Lancelot	207	—— Thomas	128
Lefroy, John Hen.	42, 372	—— Wm. Henry, MB.	264
—— Robert	338	L'Estrange, Ant. Rob.	50
Legge, Hon. Arthur C.	32	—— Champagné	378
—— Hon. Edw. Hen.	164	—— Edward	18
—— Montagu A. H.	169	—— Edward, MD.	354
—— Wm. Douglas	181	—— Edw. Napoleon	223
Leggett, George Edw.	308	—— George	491
—— John	491	—— Guy Wm. Fred.	353
—— Robert Aufrère	298	—— Paget Walt.	80, 376
Legh, Hen. Martin C.	231	—— Toriano Francis	491
Le Grand, Fred. G.	415	Lethbridge, A. A. E.	150
Legrew, John	127	Letts, Alfred Benwell	175

Lever, Charles	130	Lindesay, Fred. J. S.	139
—— John Chas. Wm.	270	—— Joshua E. C. C.	237
Levett, Charles	129	—— Patrick	105
—— Edward	146	Lindham, Jas. O., KH.	542
Levinge, Cha. Hugh	332	Lindsay, Alex. CB.	120
Lewer, Alfred	385	—— Hon. Chas. Hugh	105
—— Robert	384	—— Hon. James	27, 150
Lewes, Henry C.	380	—— Martin Geo. Tho.	105
—— John	60	—— Robert, MB.	250
—— Wm. Langmead	340	—— Rob. J. Loyd	105
—— Wm. Price L.	269	—— Wallace	237
Lewin, Hen. Fred. C.	404	—— Wm. Bayford	203
—— Martin Budd	269	—— Wm. Chacon	105
Lewins, Robert, MD.	441	Lindsell, Robt. Henry	105
Lewis, Alexander	475	Lindsey, Henry John	491
—— Alfred	282	—— J. Mainwaring	436
—— Arthur Henry	293	—— Robert	527
—— Charles A.	26, 159	Linford, James	290
—— Chas. Bassett	258	Ling, John Theodore	130
—— Edw. Studley	180	Linsingen, Cha., Baron	542
—— Ernest	220	Linton, James Henry	307
—— Geo. Chas. Degen	.75	—— John	103
—— George William	227	—— Wm. MD. CB.	439
—— Gwynne Orton	185	Lipscomb, Fra. Wallis	213
—— Henry	491	Lisle, Benjamin de	491
—— Hen. Clutterbuck	436	Lister, Frederick D.	105
—— Henry Fra. Pe.	382	—— Frederick George	121
—— Henry Ralph	196	—— John	491
—— Henry Sturt	417	Litchfield, Edwin	436
—— James Henry	248	—— Richard	475
—— John	420	Lithgow, William	527
—— John Edward	57	—— Stewart Aaron	134
—— John Owen	60	Litle, Jas. Som., AB.	384
—— John Riggs Miller, MD.	384	Little, Arch., CB.	37, 145
—— Joseph William	293	—— Fra. Laurence	382
—— Leyson Edwin	175	—— Henry Alex.	185
—— Ralph FitzGibbon	322	—— John	190
—— Richard Hull	217	—— John William	491
—— Robert	300	—— Robert John	475
—— Robert	33	—— Simon Ridley	413
—— Stephen	512	—— William	362
—— Thomas, MD.	532	Littledale, Edward	107
—— Thomas	491	Livesay, William	257
—— William	491	Llewelyn, Jenkin H.	144
Ley, Edwin Granville, MD.	221	Lloyd, Caleb Coote	276
—— Frederick	415	—— Charles Fred.	228
Leyland, Thomas	127	—— Edward	82
Leyne, James	280	—— Edward Bell	491
Liddard, Thomas	342	—— Edward Fraser S.	404
Liddell, Hon. Atholl Cha.		—— Edw. Harf., MB.	444
—— John	281	—— Edward Thos.	38, 400
—— Hon. Geo. A. F.	27	—— Edw. W. Cadwall.	185
—— Gerald Geo.	227	—— Ernest Marsh	404
—— Robert Spencer	205	—— Evans Garnons	533
Ligertwood, Thos. MB.		—— Francis Thos.	380
—— Wm. MD.	442	—— G. W. Aylmer, CB.	120
—— Wm. MD.	444	—— Henry Olivier	227
Light, Hugo Shelley	296	—— Henry Vereker	512
Lightbody, John	531	—— Hugh Massy	202
Lightfoot, Thomas, CB.		—— Jacob Richards	414
	63, 319	—— John William	197
Lilley, John	161	—— L. Nesbitt	252
—— John Isaac	464	—— Mathew Pennef.	120
Lillicrap, Jas. Wm. Adams		—— Montfort H. Trant	326
Elliott	418	—— Mountford Stoughton	
—— Walter Welsford	84	Heyliger	43
Lillie, Sir John Scott, CB.	105	—— Richard	246
		—— Richard B.	246
—— Thomas	105	—— Robert	233
Lillingston, Edw. G.	300	—— Robt. Clifford	44, 296
Limbert, John	126	—— Samuel	512
Lindam, Chas. Jas.	123	—— Sandford M'Vittie, MD.	441

Index. 590

Lloyd, Thomas 245	Longmore, Charles 444	Luard, Rich. Geo. A. 60	Lyster, Septimus 80, 334
——Thomas Conway 215	——George 107	——Robert 76	——Thomas 404
——Thomas Francis 340	——Thomas 439	Lubeck, William Von 543	Lythe, John 539
——Tho. Wm. John 277	Löning, Michael 541	Lucan, George Charles,	M'Adam, Jas. Jno. L. 135
——William 383	Lonsdale, Alured 491	*Earl of, KCB.* 10, 143	——James Kennedy 185
——William, MD. 533	——Edgar 266	Lucas, De Neufville 252	M'Alester,Chas.Arch. 105
——William Digby 295	——Rich. Maitland 446	——Francis 64	——Chas. Somerville 261
Lluellyn, Rd., CB. 8, 250	——William 491	——Henry 260	M'Alpine, Robert 128
——William R. 378	Looker, William 527	——Jasper 263	M'Annally, Charles 491
Lock, Andrew Campbell	Lord, William Barry 383	——Jasper 491	M'Arthur, Alex. MD. 157
Knox 79, 267	——William C. 140	——Patrick Browne 192	——Charles 413
——Edward Seppings 316	Lorimer, William 533	——Richard 107	——Edward 414
——Frederick Edw. 205	Loriol, Augustus de 544	——Thomas Hill 182	——John 15
Locke, William 491	Losack,CharlesWarner332	——Thomas John 354	M'Auley, John 349
Lockhart, Allan Elliott 403	Lothian, John H. 272	——William 530	M'Barnet, Alex. C. 84,312
——Archibald Inglis,	Louis, Charles 412	Luck, George 206	——Cockburn 331
CB. 43, 331	——Marcus 75	Ludewig, Adolphus 542	——Donald Hay 190
——Græme Alex. 65, 310	Lougheed, Jas. W. 444	Ludowieg, Chas. H. 543	M'Bean, Fred. KH. 105
——L. W. Maxwell 331	——Joseph Fletcher 384	Lugard,*Sir* Edw.KCB. 16	——Thos. Hamilton 137
——Wm. Eliott 232	Loughnan,JosephT.M.382	Luke, Henry Francis 349	——William 223
Lockner, Aug. Meyer 402	Louth,R.P.O.P.,*Lord* 312	Lukin,Fred. Windham.130	——William 332
Lockwood,Aug.Purefoy137	Love,*Sir*Jas.Fred.KCB.	——William 527	M'Beath,George,CB. 105
——Geo. Henry, CB. 12	KH. 9, 125, 277	——WilliamW.A.79,376	M'Bride, Adam 157
——George Palmer 207	Lovekin,Jas. Magenis 187	Lukis,FrancisDuBois 291	M'Bryan, John 135
Lockyer, Edmund 107	Lovelace, Henry Philip 491	Lumley, Fred. Douglas 58	M'Call, James 105
——H. Frederick CB.,	Lovell,Charles Neville 374	Lumsden,Chas.George328	——William 157
KH. 16	——Esdaile Lovell 146	——Thomas 234	——William 54
Locock, Herbert 404	——John W. CB. 77, 401	Lunde, Geo. Fred.G. 543	M'Callum, Edw.Gough414
Lodder, Henry Call 83, 263	——Julius 283	Lundy, Edward Louis 291	——Henry Atkins 420
——Wm. Wynne 63, 280	——*Sir* Lovell Benj.	——James Bell 435	M'Cann, Pierce 208
Lodwick, Peter 120	KCB. KH. 11, 148	Luning, Augustus 542	M'Carthy, Florence T. 444
Loesecke,George C. A.	——Nich. De Jersey 141	Luscombe, Rand. R. 132	——Henry Hotham 420
Von 542	Loveridge, Chas. G. 273	Lushington, F. CB. 105	——Jas. Joseph,MD. 444
Loft, John Henry 512	——Henry Wm. 186	Lutman,JohnHenry83,228	——Justin Thadeus C. 492
Lofthouse, Dyas Ringrose	Lovett, John Henniker 127	——William Ivers 223	——Patrick 190
248	——John Richard 264	Luxmoore, Charles 247	M'Caskill, John 76
——Richard C., MD. 151	——Joseph Venables 491	——Tho. Coryndon 31	M'Causland, Con. 59, 400
Loftus, Arthur John 155	——Thomas 491	Lygon,*Hon.*EdwardPyn-	——F. H. 381
——Ferrars 105	——Thomas Heaton 107	dar, CB. 6, 150	——Marcus L. 195
——Frederick 475	Low, Alexander 38, 139	Lyle, Hugh Chetham 378	——Wm. Henry 312
——Henry 81, 300	——Alexander W. 169	——John Mackenzie 230	M'Clellan, Jas. C. 521
——William Jas. 55, 248	——Edw.Litton,MB. 444	Lynam, Charles 491	M'Clenahan, Thomas 521
Logan-Home, Geo. H. 475	——John, CB. 120	——Fred. Augustine 192	M'Cleverty, Wm. A. 26
Logan, Arch. Spiers 121	——John 205	Lynar, Edward Alex. 354	M'Clintock, Acheson 277
——Charles Atkinson 170	——John 76	Lynch, Arth. Hy. Fra. 198	——Theodore E. 436
——Geo. Eugene 130	——William 527	——Colmer 323	M'Cormick, T. C. 352
——Joseph 172	Lowder, Sam. N. 78, 413	——Edward Crean 401	M'Conechy, James 512
——Rob. Abraham 77,277	Lowe, Arthur Charles 103	——Henry Ern.G. C. 253	M'Court, John 83, 156
——Tho. Gal., MD. 439	——Drury Curzon 154	——Marcus 242	M'Coy, John 35, 371
——Walter Bernard. 228	——Edward W. D. CB.	——Martin 350	——Wm. Henry 350
Loggan, George 455	60, 220	——Martin Crean 50	M'Crae, Wm. Gordon 261
Logie, Cosmo G., MD. 128	——Rich.ButterHam. 338	——Robert Blake 13	M'Crea,Alex, William 279
Lomax, Richard 146	——Robt.Hy.C.D.83,160	——Wm. Joseph 216	——Fred. Bradford 187
Lombard, Graves C. S. 207	——Stanley John 315	——Wm. Wiltshire 172	——James 260, 358
London, Robt. Alex. 357	——Wm.D.Nath.125,138	Lynes, Sam. Parr 380	——Rob. Barlow 86, 374
Long, Charles Poore 200	Lowndes, James 123	Lynn, James 50	M'Creagh, Michael 132
——Edmund Slingsby 491	——John Henry 105	Lynne, Spencer 190	M'Crevey, Jas. MD. 294
——Fitz James 512	——Joseph 232	Lynott, Charles 353	M'Crohan, Denis Eug. 492
——James 436	——Wm. Seymour S. 183	Lyon, Francis 377	M'Crummen, W. Scal. 304
——Samuel 105	Lowrie,Wm.Frederick 369	——Fred. Lee Hopkn. 377	M'Dakin, Sam. Gordon255
——William 32	Lowry, Armar 491	——George 475	M'Dermott, James 492
Longbourne, Wm. F. 181	——Hen.L.Barnewell253	——Hen.DaltonWittit127	——Patrick 442
Longden, Cha. S. 83, 373	——Henry 350	——William 107	——Patrick Andrew 442
——Henry Errington,	——Hen. Macgregor 197	Lyons, Anth. Munton 512	——Thomas 455
CB. 43, 192	——James Corry J. 379	——Edward 380	——Thomas 492
——John Edward 236	——John 491	——James 377	M'Diarmid, J. Duncan 533
Longfield, Forster 187	——Robt. Wm. 57, 263	——Thomas Casey 86,217	M'Donald, Alastair
——John, CB. 26, 187	Lowth, Robt. Hy. 33, 322	——William 82, 180	M'Ian 77, 361
Longford, Edw. M. *Earl*	Lowther, *Hon.* Hen. C. 105	Lys, Geo. Mowb. CB. 105	——Allan 183
of 87, 127	Luard, Chas. Edward 404	Lysons,Daniel,CB. 36,125	——Alexander 157
Longhurst, Arthur Edwin	——Charles George 378	——Lorenzo George 226	——Alexander, MD. 533
Temple 201	——Henry Reynolds 402	Lyster, Arthur O'Neil 491	——Bernard 521
Longley, George 403	——John 105	——Frederick Torrens 195	——Colin 492
Longman, George 383	——John K. CB. 120	——Henry 491	——Donald 312

Index.

M'Donald, Donald 475
—— William 65, 232
—— Duncan D. M'Cay 441
—— Sir John, KCB. 8, 231
—— Christopher 132
M'Donnell, John 354
M'Donough, Bryan Patrick, MD. 446
—— Stephen 286
M'Douall, James 103
M'Dougall, Rev. H. 455
—— Thomas Wm. Jn. 452
M'Dowell, Edm. Gres. 258
—— G. J. Muat, CB. 105
M'Duff, Alexander 492
M'Ewen, Jas. Henry 178
—— Robert Bruce 331
M'Fall, D. Chambers 323
M'Farland, Fra. Edw. 444
M'Farlan, J. Warden 156
M'Gee, Hen. Edw. 52, 352
—— Joseph 170
M'Ghee, Rev. Rob. J. 455
M'Gill, Edward, MD. 135
—— John Shuter D. 356
—— Sydenham Clith. 303
—— William 312
M'Gillivray, James 386
M'Gilp, John 444
M'Gorrery, Henry 386
M'Goun, Thomas 257
M'Gowan, Alex. Thorburn, M.D. 270
M'Grath, Edward 334
—— James 276
M'Gregor, Alexander 363
—— Alex. Edgar 239
—— Sir Duncan, KCB. 9
—— James 530
—— John 492
—— Robert 442
M'Grigor, Robt. Lewis Grant 331
—— William Thomas 326
M'Haffie, James 13
M'Illree, John Drope 439
M'Innis, Peter 258
M'Inroy, William 107
M'Intosh, John 443
—— William 263
—— W. 492
M'Intyre, Angus 475
—— Colin Campbell 239
—— Colin Campbell, CB. 58, 310
—— Duncan 346
—— Peter 492
M'Iver, Ivor 202
M'Kay, George 302
—— John 253, 358
—— William 360
M'Kellar, Peter Martin 76
M'Kenzie, A. Webster 237
—— Alex. Wm. 264
—— Fergus 157
—— John 5
—— John 492
—— John M'Kay 242
M'Kerlie, J. Graham 56, 400
M'Killop, Rob. J. 58, 411
M'Kinnel, John, MD. 303
M'Kinnon, John 492
—— William 51
M'Kinstey, Walter T. 436

M'Kinstry, Alex. 80, 210
M'Lachlan, Neil 512
M'Laren, Alex. Donald 492
—— Peter 304
M'Laughlin, Edward 379
M'Lean, Arch. Donald 436
—— George Gordon 534
M'Leod, Alexander 197
—— John Chetham 83, 255
—— Martin 515
—— Norman 512
—— William Kelty 83, 304
M'Leroth, Thomas 492
M'Letchie, John 232
M'Loughlin, John 147
—— Michael 245
—— Patrick 492
M'Mahon, Cecil Thos. 203
—— Donat 157
—— Edmond John 435
—— Sir Thomas, Bt.
GCB. 6, 192
—— Thos. Westropp CB.
38, 133
—— William 84, 151
M'Master, Valentine
Mumbee 310
M'Meekan, Arthur Chas.
Joshua 415
M'Mullin, Edward 369
—— John 280
M'Munn, J. Alex. MD. 384
Robt. A. MD. 531
M'Murdo, Alured Chas. 107
—— Charles Edward 312
—— William Montagu
Scott, CB. 35, 125, 156
M'Murray, George 386
—— Joseph 206
M'Nab, Robert, MD. 442
M'Nair, Geo. August. 248
—— John Miller 312
—— Robert 452
M'Namara, Michael 492
M'Namee, John 357
M'Naughten, Duncan
Cameron 201
M'Neice, Henry 176
McNeill, Duncan 137
—— John 257
—— Malcolm 310
M'Nicol, Nicol 492
M'Niel, Donald 492
M'Niell, Christian Wm. 156
M'Niven, Thos. William
Ogilvy 105
M'Pherson, Alexander 492
—— Æneas 492
—— Cecil 210
—— Duncan 105
—— Ewan 50
—— FitzRoy 332
—— Philip, CB. 18
—— Philip 210
M'Queen, Donald 521
—— James 32
—— John 187
M'Rae, Farquhar 492
—— Theodore 492
M'Shane, Eugene 293
M'Sheehy, Edward
Louis, MD. 129
M'Sweeney, J., RC. 455

M'Tavish, Alexander
Camp. 284
M'Ternan, Constantine
Lemon H. 376
M'Wharrie, Rob. MD. 280
Maberly, E. CB. 55, 372
—— Wm. Leader 48
Macadam, Wm. KH. 103
Macalpine, James 492
Macan, Henry 121
Mac Andrew, J. Duncan 310
—— J. Sir, MD. KCB. 529
—— William, MD. 277
Macarthur, Edw. CB. 16
—— Peter 533
—— Thos. Alex. Clapperton 444
Macartney, Art. Suther. 380
—— Charles 492
—— George 342
—— James 284
—— John 154
—— John 307
—— James Nixon 107
—— Samuel Halliday 341
Macaulay, Hect. John 435
—— James Elmsley 148
—— Zachary 218
Macauley, Chu. Fitz-
Roy Somerset 350
—— James S. 349
Mac Bain, Giles 534
Macbean, Archibald 30
—— Forbes 331
—— Wm. Forbes 64, 357
—— Wm. Frederic 239
Macbeth, Alex. M. 157
—— Hugh Mackay 330
—— James, MD. 304
MacCarthy, Edw. D. J. 337
—— Edw. F. Aug. 229
—— Justin Edw. Dan. 252
—— Wm. Justin 60
MacDonald, Peter 361
—— R. D. 417
Macdonald, Alexander 105
—— Alex. Jas. John 81
—— Alfred 212
—— Charles Edward 416
—— Colin 512
—— George 14
—— George Fred. 207
—— Geo. Varnham 122
—— Henry Alfred 87, 308
—— Jas. Mitchell 64, 353
—— Hon. James Wm.
Bosville, CB. 51, 125
—— John 205
—— John 105
—— John James 216
—— Mortimer J. 356
—— Norman 180
—— Peter John 82
—— Ranald 475
—— Robert, CB. 105
—— R. D. 465
—— Robt. Geo. 338
—— Ronald 475
—— Stephen 492
—— William 74
—— William 521
—— Wm. Donald 81, 332
—— Wm. Peter 544
Macdonell, Alex. S. 530

Macdonell, Alex., CB. 40, 343
—— George, CB. 105
—— John Ignatius 300
MacDonnell, Arth. Rob. 403
—— Ewen 475
—— Henry J. 198
—— Robert John 315
Macdonnell, Jos. Wm.
MD. 446
—— William 203
—— William 446
MacDougall, Alex. J. 375
—— Sir Duncan 105
—— James 105
—— P. Leonard 41, 462
Macdowall, Day Hort 17
Mac Duff, John 34, 277
—— Robt. Scott 261
Macfadin, Fran. Hen. 196
Macfarlane, And. 475
—— Fran. John 131
—— R. 464
—— Robert Henry 180
MacGregor, Henry G. 211
—— John 475
—— John 492
—— Malcolm 64
—— Robert Henry 293
—— Robert Stuart 267
Macgregor, John Alex.
Paul 120
—— James 440
—— Malcolm J. R. 212
—— Rob. Donniston 154
Machell, Jas. Geo. 202
—— Robert Scott 288
Macintosh, Alex. F. KH. 9, 328
—— Archibald 416
Macintyre, Alex. MD. 196
Mac Kay, Lachlan 492
Mackay, Alex. 444
—— Alex. Forbes 331
—— Angus John, MD. 170
—— Angus Wm. 51
—— Angus William 349
—— Donald 521
—— Edward 266
—— Henry 76
—— Henry Fowler 475
—— Honeyman 74
—— Hugh Donald 492
—— James, MD. 444
—— James Duff 515
—— J. D. 465
—— Neil 492
—— Neil M'Innes 374
MacKenna, John B. 316
Mackenzie, Alex. 84, 310
—— Sir Alex. M. Bt. 310
—— Alexander 475
—— Alex. Wedder 475
—— Charles George 234
—— Colin 75
—— Geo. Henry 282
—— Hugh 205
—— Hugh Baillie 515
—— James Dixon 349
—— John, MD. 444
—— John 521
—— John 386
—— John Binnie 215
—— John Kenneth 74

Index. 592

Mackenzie, J. K. D.	322	Macneil, Roderick 8,	187	Mahony, John	294	Manning, John F.	436
——Kenneth Doug. 54,	331	Macneill, John M.	272	——Montague M. MD.	529	Mannock, Fra. Anthy.	
——Lawrence	151	——Robert	150	Maingay, Ferdinal B.	404	Strickland	131
——Rob. S. Muir	382	Macnish, Wm. MD.	533	Mainwaring, Chas. E.	375	Mansel, Arthur Edm.	138
——Roderick	80, 376	MacPherson, Wm. R.	221	——Chas. Walter Lee	164	——Frederick	217
——Thomas	310	Macpherson, Andrew		——George	76	——John, CB.	105
——Waller Scott	332	John	82, 228	——John Popham	221	——Rob.Chris.KH.	10,296
——William	492	——Donald	216	Mair, Arthur	107	Mansell, Wm. Mansell	413
——Wm. Ord, MD.	138	——Duncan	255	——Corn. Cuyler P.	105	——William	198
Mackesy, Wm. Henry	312	——Duncan	492	——John, MD.	531	Mansergh, Dan. Jas.	216
——Wm. Percy P.	444	——Eneas Macintosh	441	——W. Crosbie S.	197	——Henry Chas.	349
Mackey, Hugh Allen	382	——Evan	107	Mairis, Geoffrey	415	——John L. Otway	182
——John Alex.	105	——Ewen H. Davidson	332	——Valentine Hale	107	——Stepney P. E.	252
Mackie, William	173	——Herbert Taylor 84,	316	——Valentine Thos.	401	——Wilmsdorf Geo.	306
Mackinlay, John	334	——James	527	Maitland, Charles L.		Mansfield, Chas. Edw.	83
——Tho. D'Almaine	181	——James F.	187	Brownlow	49, 159	——John	521
MacKinnon, Dan. Hen.		——John	103	——Eardley	377	——William	521
	85, 452	——John Cameron	52	——Fred. Thos.	43	——Sir Wm. R, KCB.	16
——Edm. Vernon	515	——John Cosmo	404	——James M. H.	403	Manson, James	121
——Geo. Hy. CB.	16	——Lachlan	237	——John	264	Mant, Francis Arthur	380
Mackinnon, Charles	286	——Walter	233	——John, MD.	440	Mapleton, Hen. MD.	439
——David Reid	221	Macquarie, Geo. W.	157	——Keith Ramsay 84,	312	Maquay, John P.	403
——John Price	302	MacQueen, Donald J.		Majendie, Vivian D.	378	March, Chas. H. Gor-	
——Walter Carr	323	KH.	107, 465	Major, Fra. Wm. A. C.	527	don Lennox, Earl of	475
——William Alex.	255	——Geo. Bliss	281	——Robert Clement	435	——Leopold Geo. F.	492
Mackintosh, Robt.	465	——James	475	Malan, Charles H.	306	——Wm. Henry 60,	412
——William	521	Macqueen, Daniel, MD.		Malassez, Chas. Thos.	435	Marchant, Chas. Hen.	316
——Wm. Hen. MD.	384		442	——Maximilian	435	Marcon, Edward	197
Mackirdy, David E. 35,	298	——Mal. Potter	330	Malcolm, Edw. Donald	403	——Edward	475
Maclachlan, Alex. 12,	370	Macrae, Alex. MD.	338	——George	243	Mardon, James Howe	294
——Daniel, MD. 439,	463	Macreight, Fred. Arch.	210	——Geo. Alex. CB.	17	Margary, Alfred Rob.	107
Maclagan, David, MD.	530	Macy, Ernest Aug.	417	——John Dundas	475	Margesson, Philip D.	475
Maclaine, Sir Archi-		Madan, William	266	——Robert	231	——Wm. George	276
bald, KCB.	7, 270	Madden, Ambrose	350	Malcolmson, Alex.	140	Mariette, John Cha.	283
MacLaine, Lachlan	178	——C. D. MD.	257	——William	193	Marillier, Chas. Hen.	354
Maclaren, Bartie	279	——Chas. D. Ryder	188	Malet, Charles St. Lo	105	Marindin, Fra. Arthur	403
Maclauchlan, Jas. Aug.		——Francis	298	——Harold Esdale	155	——Hen. Rich.	107
	492	——Geo. Ernest P.	286	——Hen. Chas. Eden	160	Markey, Edw. Corrigan	232
Maclaurin, David Scott		——John	188	Malloy, James	157	Markham, Edwin	377
Kin.	515	——John William	177	Malone, Anthony	415	——Francis	345
Maclean, Alexander	255	——Samuel Alex.	269	——Joseph	141	Markland, George	51
——Alexander	453	——Wm. W.	188	Maloney, William	314	Marlow, Ben. Wm. MD.	234
——Alexander	512	Madox, Henry, KH.	103	Maltei, Antonio 63,	368	——Wm. B.	33, 399
——Allen Thomas	12	Magee, Henry	198	Malthus, Sydenham	334	Marr, Charles	465
——Andrew, M. D.	359	——William	492	Man, Garnet 80,	462	Marrett, J. F.	464
——Charles, M D.	529	Magens, Henry Cole	380	Mancor, Andrew	475	Marriner, George	279
——Sir Cha. F. Bt.	103	——Rich. Hen.	84, 240	——James	264	Marriott, H. Christ. 86,	316
——Donald	436	Magill, Henry	176	Manders, Thomas	515	——Hayes	77, 413
——Fitz Roy Donald	150	Jas. M'Gellicuddy	172	Mandeville, Edw. Wm.		——John Bosworth S.	132
——Sir George	527	——Robert	273	Thomas	186	——Thos. B. F.	39, 372
——George	36, 372	——William	229	Manera, Ajax Gowrie	337	——William	273
——Hampden Healy	183	Magin, Thomas,	413	Manjin, William	232	Marryat, George	105
——Henry Dundas	105	——William	492	Manico, Edward	512	——George Selwyn	134
——Henry John	343	Magnay, Chris. Jas.	207	Manifold, Michael F.	243	Marsack, Hen. Chas.	228
——James	475	Magor, Reuben Fred.	197	Manley, John	521	Marschalk, Theo. Von	541
——Lachlan H. Gil.	77	Magrath, Andr. Nich.	293	——Robert George	107	Marsden, George Wm.	323
——Peter	39, 372	——A. Wm. Chalmers	304	——Wm. Geo. Nich.	384	Marsh, Aug. Leacock	107
——Samuel	512	——Fred. Augustus	231	Manly, John Samuel	233	——Edward Herman	243
——S. B.	464	Maguire, Constantine	258	Mann, Gother Fred. 64,	400	——Fra. Hen. Digby	326
——William	107	——John	84, 281	——James	152	——Henry	82, 131
MacLeod, Nor. Mag.	304	——Thos. Collings	257	——Jas. Robert	401	——Henry Dyke	316
Macleod, Donald	120	Mahe, Rev. J. J.	455	——John Blaquiere	61	——Joseph	436
——Murdoch	255	Maher, Dan. Dud. Val.	144	Manners, Arthur C.	277	——Robert	107
Maclise, William	533	——Martin	492	——Charles	75	——Willoughby Digby	402
Mac Mahon, Wm. 54,	258	——Valentine	444	——Douglas Ernest	192	Marshall, Anthony	14
Macnaghten, Edm. Chas.		Mahon, Arthur P. V.	160	——Lord Geo. John		——Arthur Francis	296
	379	——Charles Geo.	246		85, 128	——Charles B.	354
——Fran. Edm. 87,	143	——Edmond	492	——Herbert R. 80,	362	——Edwin	381
Macnamara, Fr. R.	332	——James	492	——Richard	50	——Francis Glasse	322
——James Dillon	280	——John	245	——Rich. Abraham	169	——Frederick	127
——Michael John	350	——Maurice Hartland	145	——Robert	463	——Henry	154
——Nugent	414	——Thomas	37	——Wm. Norcott	282	——James	369
——William	132	——Thos. Davies	352	Manning, Cha. Downes	136	——John McLean	330
Macnee, Robert	335	Mahony, Henry	183	——Henry	176	——John Taylor	130

598 Index.

Marshall, John Wm. 283	Massey, *Hon.* L. Edw. 167	Maunsell, John M. 380	Meheux, Tho. Geo. S. 414
—— J. Williams 293	—— Nathaniel Wm. 237	—— Richard 105	Meik, Francis Tho. 85, 453
—— Pembr. O'M. H. 264	Massy, Augustine Wm. 276	—— Robert 82, 321	Meikleham, Geo. C. 299
—— Ralph 492	—— Godfrey William	—— Thomas 78, 234	Mein, Frederick R. 78,169
—— Stephen Henry 173	Hugh 80	—— Wm. Stopford 380	—— George 74, 363
—— Thomas 272	—— George Eyre 180	Maurice, Robert M. B.335	Meier, Ern. Theo. Chr.541
—— Thomas 492	—— Hamp. Hugh *MD*.130	Mawbey, Henry Way 413	Melburn, John Thos. 444
—— Thomas Sutton 436	—— Hugh 107	Mawby, Joseph 492	Meldrum, George 232
—— Thornton 533	—— Hugh Deane 352	Mawe, Thos. George 349	Mellish, Geo. W. 446
—— William 105	—— Hugh Francis 215	Maxse, Henry Fitz Har-	—— William 292
—— Wm. Fred. Thos. 215	—— John 107	dinge Berkeley 78	Melliss, Henry W. 345
—— Wm. Henry 120	—— Rich. Albert 283	Maxwell, Alexander,	Melville, Bruce Hull 404
—— Wm. Hen. Sutton 486	—— Wm. Godfrey D. 140	*CB.* 38, 261	—— *Rev.* Henry, *B.D.* 463
Marsland, Edw. Ash. 213	—— Wm. James 190	—— Chas. Francis 105	—— Henry, *Visct.*
—— Wm. Edward 129	Master, Richard Tho. 475	—— Edw. Herbert 55,324	*KCB.* 11, 342
Marson, Wm. Fleming 356	—— Wm. Chester, *CB.*	—— George 58, 294	—— Norman Leslie 160
—— Walter Sam. 290	60, 180	—— Geo. V. *CB.* 39, 324	—— Winnett Lockhart 356
Marston, Daniel 107	Masters, Robert 142	—— Henry 475	Melvin, Alexander 529
—— Henry Fletcher 190	—— William Godfrey	—— Henry De R. 464	Mendibus, Antoine L. de 344
—— Jeffery A. *MD.* 384	R. 413	—— James 78, 243	Mence, Martin 445
—— John Bates 193	Masterson, Edward 243	—— *Hon.* James Pierce 55	Meads, Herbert 34
Martelli, Tho. Chall. 380	Mather, Robert 140	—— John 492	—— Hugh Bowen 475
—— T. C. 464	Matheson, Roderick 456	—— John Rob. Heron 152	—— James D. 85, 350
Marten, Thos. *KH.* 12	—— Thomas 18	—— Robert James 314	—— William Fisher 435
—— Thomas Wright 185	Mathew, Cha. Barth. 273	—— Stuart John M. 376	Menteath, Chas. Geo. S. 299
Marter, R. Jas. Combe 129	—— E. Powell Lettice 243	—— *Sir* William Alex.	Menzies, Allan 475
Martin, Abraham 195	—— John James 358	*Bart.* 103	—— Charles, *KH.* 7, 411
—— Alexander 107	—— William Henry 321	—— William Robert 65,412	—— Charles Fred. 413
—— A. P. 338	Mathews, Fred. Ludw. 350	May, Allan 404	—— Duncan 530
—— Arthur Gonne Bell 146	Mathias, Rev. G. *MA.* 463	—— Rodolphe de 49, 544	—— Edward 441
—— Charles Henry 187	—— William 105	Maycock, Frederick 180	—— James 359
—— Charles Nassau 402	Mathison, Jas. Geo. S. 295	—— John Gittens 202	—— James Stewart 304
—— Curtiss 443	—— John Augustus 492	—— Joseph 83, 272	—— Robert 332
—— David William 248	Matson, Edward 14	Maydwell, Henry Law 61	—— Wm. Collier 65, 401
—— George 534	—— Henry 107	Mayer, Thomas Walton 404	Mercer, Alexander 492
—— Geo. Anne Green.418	Matthew, Tho. Patrick 440	Mayers, John P. 74, 322	—— Alex. Cavalie 9, 370
—— Henry Clinton 442	Matthews, John Henry 359	Maynard, Alex. G. S. 239	—— Arthur Hill Hasted 107
—— Henry Clinton 75	—— John Powell 492	—— Edmund G. 63, 324	—— Edw. Smyth 334
—— Henry Richmond 378	—— Hen. Garland 258	—— *Rev.* T. R. *MA.* 455	—— Henry 374
—— James 444	—— Mark 277	Mayne, Henry 521	—— Robert 13
—— James 534	—— Philip Wride 192	—— John 107	Meredith, Boyle 475
—— John James 177	—— Robert Lee 436	—— John T. Bolton 210	—— Henry Warter 77, 253
—— Robert Conolly 215	—— William 157	—— Taylor L. 84, 143	—— Rich. Martin 107
—— Robert Frederick 304	—— William 521	—— William 105	—— Thos. Boyle 213
—— Samuel Yorke 107	Matthey, Alphonso 499	—— William 78	Meredyth, Edw. Hen.
—— Thomas 82, 177	Maturin, Henry 315	Mayo, John 248	John 323
—— Walter Lawrence 206	—— Wm. Henry 435	Mayow, Geo. Wynell 43	Merrett, Thomas 356
—— William Geo. 378	Maud, Wm. Sherer 404	McCGwire, Edw. Tho.	Mesham, Charles 353
—— Wm. John Byde 192	Maude, Francis Corn-	St. Lawrence 169	Messenger, W. H. H. 252
—— Wm. Neufville 492	wallis, *CB.* 61, 375	Mead, Charles 512	Messiter, Arthur Henry 319
—— William Webber 172	—— Fred. Fra. *CB.* 55, 175	Meade, Frederick 16	—— Edward 121
Martindale, Ben Hay 401	—— Frederick Sidney 377	—— John Michael De	—— Edw. Moulton 418
—— Thomas 277	—— George Ashley, *CB.*	Courcy 414	—— Geo. Hughes 85, 298
Martley, John 362	55, 125, 372	—— Richard 283	—— John 105
Martyn, Cecil Edward 128	—— Robert Eustace 253	—— Richard Raphael 187	—— Sussex Lennox
—— Mountj. Fra. 42, 147	Maule, Geo. Edwin 379	—— Richard William 324	Aubrey Beauclerk 234
Marvin, George 383	—— Henry 436	—— Thomas Quin 419	Metcalf, Thomas Levet 75
—— Henry 183	—— Henry Barlow 379	Monden, James 353	—— Timothy 186
—— William 388, 404	—— Henry Budgen 177	Meadows, Robert W. 356	Metcalfe, Edward 142
Mascall, John Richard 415	—— John 107	Meane, John 261	—— Henry 382
—— John Richard 75	—— Robert 316	Meara, Wm. Hen. P. 83,180	—— Henry 203
Maskell, William Miles 196	Mauleverer, Benj. Ban-	Meares, Geo. Brooke 180	Motge, William Fred. 187
Maskery, Josh. Hamil. 414	bury 80, 324	—— John 492	Methold, Edward 107
Maskew, *Rev.* H. E. 455	—— Jas.Thos.*CB.*38, 237	—— John Hen. Goulds 218	Mourant, Edward 318
Mason, Geo. John Usil 247	—— William 74, 453	—— William Lewis D. 217	Meyer, Charles 542
—— Edward 210	Maunder, Edward 131	Meason, M. G. L. 465	—— George 541
—— Edward Montgm. 180	—— Wm. Morgan 146	Medewe, Dan. J. W. de 208	—— Geo. Julius 541
—— Edw. Snow 316	Maunsell, Charles S. 316	Medhurst, Fred. Edw. 257	—— Hen. Adolphus 263
—— Francis 492	—— Francis Edwin 178	—— John William 282	—— Lewis Chas. Aug. 56
—— John Monck 475	—— Frederick 12	Mee, Charles Henry 31	Meyrick, Augustus Wm.
—— Richardson 512	—— George 107	—— James 258	Henry 52, 166
—— Robert Gordon S. 269	—— George Joseph 205	Meech, Thos. Crosby 475	—— Wm. Henry 103
Massey, *Hon.* Eyre	—— James Kingsley 350	Meehan, Geo. W. 65, 453	Michael, Francis L. 150
Challoner Henry 60, 335	—— John Edmund 475	Meheux, Rich. William 77	—— John 443

Index. 594

Michel, Chas. Edw.	51, 273	Miller, Ormsby Bowen	147	Mitchell, John	9, 370	Montagu, Horace	147
——Sir John, KCB.	17	——Rowley	324	——John	41, 411	——Horace Wm.	53, 401
Michell, Francis	253	——Thomas	353	——John Wray	35, 371	——Jas. Van. Harthals	192
——George Dalton	294	——Thomas	105	——Parry	107	——Willoughby	74
——Henry Seymour	266	——Thomas Edmund	197	——Robert	492	Montanaro, B. J.	436
——John, CB.	9, 370	——William	359	——Thomas	519	——Henry	368
——John Edward	63, 375	——William	475	——Thomas John	129	Montford, Abr. Rich.	193
——Montagu, Tho. B.	253	——William Taylor	418	——Thomas Peter	475	Montgomerie, Alex.	475
——Thomas Ball	253	——William Uvedale	248	Mitford, Bertram Cha.	63	——Archibald Wm.	380
——Thos. Bernard	314	——William	492	——Henry	233	——Frederick	527
——Walter Taylor	475	——Zaccheus	492	——Henry George	36	——Patrick, CB.	120
——William Daniel	446	Millerd, Thomas	475	——John Philip	107	Montgomery, Alex.	431
Mickleburgh, John P.	270	Milles, Hon. Lewis Wat-		——William	303	——Alex. Barry, CB.	
Micklem, Edward	404	son	84, 343	Moberly, Alfred	170		39, 169
Middlemore, R. F.	82, 453	——Thomas	306	Mockler, Edward	440	——Alexander Geo.	354
Middleton, Empson Ed-		Millett, Rich. Tracey	381	——Robert	83, 291	——Alex. Nixon	185
ward	269	——Sydney Crohan	226	——Wm. Elliot	350	——Alexander Rich.	475
——Fred. Dobson	84, 236	Milligan, Charles	250	Moeller, Frederick	543	——Fr. Octavius	107
——H. Boucher Arth.	436	——Harry Robt.	282	Moffat, Bowland	57	——Hugh Parker	281
——John	515	——William	107	Moffatt, James W. S.	205	——Lambert Lyons	105
——Oswald Robert	178	——Wm. John Lane	303	——John Edward	442	——Nathaniel	253
——Thos. Falkner	492	Mills, Cha. Jas. Con-		——Kenneth M.	85, 356	——Robert	512
——Wm. Alex.	332	way	56, 334	——Wm. Henry	215	——Robert Blackall	200
——Wm. Alex. CB.	64, 373	——Edward	277	Moffett, William	201	——Robt. James	133
——Wm. Gustavus		——E.	436	Moffit, Andrew	444	Montmorency, Chas.	
Alex.	84, 332	——Fra. Vanderlure	123	Moffitt, James	349	Anne Law de	403
——Wm. Handcock	123	——John	445	Moggridge, John Y.	401	——H. John de	130
——Wm. Southby	295	——Nicholas	137	Mogridge, James Edw.	492	——Hon. R. H. de	242
Midgley, Benjamin	475	——Robert	145	Moir, William	521	——Joseph de	280
Midwinter, Thomas	521	——Thomas Arthur	170	Molesworth, Anthony		——Robert Geoffre	
Midwood, Thomas W.	435	——William Maxwell	105	Oliver	382	Aug. de	228
Miers, John Anthony	195	——William Wilson	290	——Edw. Nassau	86, 233	Montresor, Henry Edw.	
Mildmay, Sir Henry		Millward, Samuel	274	——Morgan Crofton	403		49, 159
St. John, Bt.	107	Milman, Egerton Cha.		——Richard	215	Moodie, Daniel	13
——Herbert Alex.		Wm. Miles	30, 247	——Robt. Sackville	512	Moody, Hampden Cle-	
St. John	344	——Geo. Alderson	81, 376	——Rev. T.	455	ment Blamire	85, 401
Miles, Chas. John	180	——George Bryan	60, 180	Moline, Jas. Prichard	441	——Rev. J. L.	455
——George	492	——Gustavus Hamilton		Mollan, Wm. Campbell,		——John Macdonald	416
——Herbert Chalmers	266	Lockwood	78, 374	CB.	60, 306	——Rich. Clement	41, 400
——Thomas George	195	——Wilbraham Digby	378	Moller, Arthur Mar-		Moon, John	237
——Thos. Wm. Shore	303	Milne, Geo. D. MD.	384	quhard Champion	252	Moonney, John D. E.	201
Mill, James	105	——James	156	Molloy, John	105	Moor, Hassell Rich.	14
Millar, Andrew, M.D.	420	——Jas. Miles	492	Moloney, Thomas, RC.	85	Moore, Alex. Geo. M.	139
——James, M.D.	533	Milner, Rev. E. W. MA.	455	——Jeremiah	364	——Arthur Hinton	123
——Rev. James	463	Milnes, Alfred Shore	492	——Patrick	349	——Rev. C.	455
——Joseph Allan	404	——Thomas M. S.	492	Molony, Chas. Mills	380	——Charles	455
——William	444	Milroy, David, MD.	237	——John Sharman	318	——Charles	107
Miller, Alex. Grant	379	Milsom, Thomas	288	——Trevor Charles	376	——Charles William	512
——A. P.	463	Milward, Thos. Walter	374	——William Mills	223	——Edward	62, 195
——Charles	255	Minchin, Chas. H.	492	Molyneux, A. Mitchell	227	——Edward	358
——Charles	76	——F.	465	——Hon. C. Craven	142	——Edward Henry	418
——Charles Paget	316	——George	492	——Edmund	135	——E. M.	464
——Charles Stuart	76	Mines, Thomas	252	Monck, Chas. Stanley	492	——Francis	6
——Colin Matheson		Minheer, William	318	——Hon. Richard	104	——Fred. Geo. F.	187
Milne, MD.	442	Minnett, John Christ. V.	203	Monckton, Hon. H.		——Fred. Wm.	443
——David	356	Minney, Charles John	446	Manners	81, 138	——George	515
——Dugald Stewart	295	Minnitt, Chas. Goring	213	Moncrieff, D. G. W.	403	——George	120
——Ebenezer, MD.	178	Minister, William	308	——George	16	——George Fred.	85, 453
——Fiennes, S. CB.	105	Miniussir, Nicholas de	541	——George Hay	166	——Geo. Thos. Carus	255
——Frederick	80, 376	Minter, George	107	Money, George	492	——Henry	435
——Frederick	81, 314	Minto, Jas. Clephane	338	Monins, Eaton	12	——Henry	105
——George	521	——James Clephane	533	Monk, Arthur Lloyd	223	——Henry Edward	335
——George Cumming	107	Mirehouse, Arth. W. L.	291	——Fred. Souter	436	——H. Garrett	324
——George Murray	86, 312	Missett, Joseph	521	——Henry George	276	——Isaac	55, 363
——George Robert	328	Mitchell, Alexander	239	Monkland, George	35	——James	170
——George Thomas	264	——Alexander R.	206	Monro, David Arthur	107	——James Adolphus	492
——Henry	156	——Arthur Bambrick	356	——James, MD.	164	——James Guy Piers	440
——James	105	——Charles B. H.	415	——Kenneth	379	——Jas. Stewart	475
——John	76	——Edward	403	——William	307	——John	352
——John	131	——Hamilton	337	Monsell, Charles	226	——John	513
——John	283	——Herbert Leonard	380	——Bolton Jas. Alfred	303	——John Croft	344
——John, MD.	529	——James A. F.	436	Monson, Hon. D. John	270	——John Leslie	243
——John	62	——J. H.	519	Montagu, Decimus	237	——John Wardrop	533
——John Jas. Cahill	353	——James Wm.	255	——George	74	——Joshua John	492

Index.

Moore, Mathias	404	Morphew, Augustus	443	Mould, John	142	Murphy, Jacob Camac	138
——Nicholas	81	Morphy, Martin	252	——Thomas R.	39, 400	——James	193
——Robert	180	——Richard	493	——Thos. Rawlings	318	——James	383
——Samuel	492	Morrah, James A.	282	Moule, John	121	——Jerome Richard	263
——Stephen	290	Morris, Arthur	283	——William	141	——John	493
——Thomas	360	——Campbell Tho.	198	Mounsey, Charles J.	300	——Joseph Wm. C.N.	198
——Thomas	475	——Chas. Fred.	227	Mounsteven, Hender	76	——Miah	286
——Tho. Chas. C. 41, 411		——Chas. Henry, CB.	54	——Wm. Tho. B. 43, 452		——Miah William	330
——Thomas Forsyth	436	——Clark	354	Mount, Charles George		——Michael	318
——Thomas Maitland	286	——Edm. F. CB. 11, 338		Henry, Earl of	126	——Thomas	186
——William	107	——Edward	446	Mount Edgcumbe, E.		——Thomas	261
——W. C.	464	——Frederick	342	Aug. Earl of	493	——Thomas John	284
——Sir William Geo.		——F. Bullen	306	Mountain, J. Kirby	141	——Stephen	270
KCB.	9, 281	——Sir George	105	——Robt. Frederick	373	——Wm. Lawrence	252
——Wm. W.	436	——Geo. Bentham	417	Mountford, Joseph	493	——William Lewis	198
——Wm. Yorke	14	——Henry Joseph 35, 371		Moynihan, Andrew	187	Murray, Adam	513
Moorhead, Alex. J.	463	——John	383	Moysey, Charles John	404	——Alexander 54, 323	
——Charles	492	——John Ignatius	418	Mudge, Henry Colton	414	——Alex. Bruce	312
——Edward, M.D.	236	——John W.H.C.G.	415	Muir, Wm. M. MD.	439	——Alex. Henry	376
——George Alex.	294	——Maxwell K.	335	Muirhead, Sam. P.	314	——Andrew	310
——James	331	——Montagu Cholm.	306	Mulhall, John	521	——Sir Arch. John	105
——Robt. Bradshaw	197	——Samuel	475	Mulrenan, Thomas	381	——Arthur	140
——Thomas, M.D.	186	——Thos. Rendall	331	Mullarky, Daniel	534	——Augustus Staveley	383
Moorsom, Chas. John	237	——Timothy	240	Mullan, Wm. James	315	——Augustus Wm. 74,349	
——Constantine M'D.	342	——Timothy	360	Mullen, John	8, 476	——Charles	107
——Henry Manvers	382	——Ussher Lee	415	——John F. Whitmore	322	——Charles	74
——Hen. Martin	344	——William	376	Muller, Edw. A. G. 43, 363		——Charles Balfour	300
——Robert	105	——William	521	——Fred. Augustus	542	——Charles Robert	476
Morant, George Fran.	148	——W.	464	——Frederick Henry	543	——Chas. Stewart	302
——Horatio H. 81, 296		Morrish, Henry Geo.	476	——Fred. Pritzler	169	——Daniel, MD.	342
Morehouse, George	513	Morrison, George P. E.	156	——Jost	544	——Hon. David Henry	107
Morel, Chas. Carew de		——Hans	476	Mulliner, Wm. Rice	352	——David Mortimer	291
77, 361		——John Chas. D. 84,413		Mullings, Arth. Rand.	152	——David Patterson	328
Moreton, Moses	492	——Rich. Fielding	153	Mullins, John	357	——Denis, MD.	531
Morewood, Henry F.	237	——Walter	191	——Wm. Hutchinson	404	——Duncan Forbes	352
Morgan, Alex. B.	533	——Wm. Lawtie	401	Mulock, Henry Hurd	172	——Francis	493
——Alex. Brooke	215	Morrogh, Alexander	145	——John Joseph	337	——Francis Pearson	353
——Arthur Edward	300	Morrow, Robert Bole	261	——Thomas Edm. 85,299		——Fred. Florence	279
——Augustus	282	Morse, Henry Browne	435	Munday, John	218	——Freeman	29
——Charles	227	Morshead, Pentyre A.	476	Mundell, Herbert V. 83,200		——George	476
——Chas. RC.	455	Mortashed, John	513	Mundy, Charles Fra.	242	——Geo. Freeman 62, 293	
——Charles Edward	295	Mortimer, Stanley	282	——Geo. V.E.CB. 51, 215		——Hon. David Hen.	106
——Edward	475	——Thomas B. 63, 307		——Godfrey Charles	26	——Hon. Hy. CB. 7, 151	
——Evan	75	——William Picton	314	——Pierrepont Hy. 40,372		——Henry	476
——George Anthony	274	Morton, Arthur	183	——Robert Miller	74	——James	521
——George Bernard	460	——James Francis	274	Munnings, Wm. Vesey	228	——Lord Jas. Cha. P.	103
——George Robert	202	——M. Villiers S.	245	Munn, Henry Oldman	150	——James Florence 85,318	
——Hen. Ross-Lewin	252	Moseley, Herbert H.	255	Munns, E. C.	465	——James Murray	382
——Hill Faulconer	234	——Wm. Henry	282	Munro, Alexander	55	——James Pulteney	415
——Horatio	257	Mosley, Edw. Nicholas	308	——Andrew	157	——James William	436
——Hugh	75	——Godfrey G.	493	——A. T.	465	——John	160
——Jas. Peattie	379	——Paget Peploe	147	——David	107	——John	334
——John, CB.	120	Mosse, Chas. Benj.	444	——Donald	302	——John	436
——John	513	——Henry Alexander	493	——Frederick	493	——John Digby	105
——John	521	——James Urquhart	210	——George 62, 452		——John Cha. D'Urban	
——John Mabbott	404	——John Forbes	213	——Geo. Granville G.	217		382
——Jonathan	338	——Lorenzo Nickson	295	——G. G.	464	——John Henry	250
——Monteford S.	280	——Philip Augustus	182	——George Traill	356	——Patrick Keith	160
——Palms Spread	274	——William	232	——Gustavus Francis	415	——Robert	277
——Thomas	493	Mostyn, John W. MD.	441	——Innes Colin	361	——Samuel Hood	105
——Wm. MD.	385	——Robert	493	——John St. John	107	——Tho. Andrew L.	401
Moriarty, David Barry	182	——Robert Algeo	205	——William, CB. 35, 250		——Tho. H. M'Dougal	243
Morice, David, M.D.	534	——Hon. Roger	166	——William	529	——William	107
——Jas. Anderson	417	——Hon. Savage	226	——William, MD.	332	——Wm. M'Carthy	350
Morison, James	533	——Thomas	530	Munsey, Tho. A. A.	121	——Wm. Robert	227
Morland, George	197	Mothe, P. J. de la	544	Murchison, Kenneth	76	——William Sim, MD.	294
——George Wm.	182	Motte, Peter de la, CB.	120	Murdoch, Wm. Walpole	476	Murrett, Thomas	120
Morle, John	475	Mottley, Thos. Martin	476	Mure, Chas. Reginald	257	Murtagh, John, MD.	533
Morley, Arthur G. E.	257	Mount, James, CB.	439	——George	493	——Thomas	444
——Edward Lacy	493	Moubray, Edward 78, 374		——John, MD.	440	Muschamp, Wm. Hy.	316
——Francis	175	——James	337	——William 65, 166		Musgrave, Benj. D'Urban	
——J. Evelyn K.	257	——Thomas 84, 272		Muriel, George William	306		323
——Wm. Geo. RC.	455	Mould, Frederick	403	Murphy, Adolphus	140	——Christopher Ed.	344
Morony, Robt. B.	175	——James Stirling	415	——Francis Eastwood	233	——Walter	315

Index. 596

Mush, John 211
Mussenden, William 144
Mutch, James 404
Muter, Dunbar D. 61, 281
—— Robert 105
Muttit, Hen. Moseley 293
Muttlebury, Geo. Alex. 132
Myers, Arthur B. R. 164
—— William 493
—— Wm. James 103
—— Wm. Jas. Kempt 345
Mylius, Fred. James 180
—— George F. 43, 463
—— Rodney 76
—— Wm. Colville R. 263
Mylne, Graham 316
Mylrea, Frederick Thos. 485
Mytton, Devereux H. 321

Naden, Greatrex 445
Nagel, John 465, 493
Nagle, Richard 237
Nally, John 319
Nangle, George 493
—— Henry 205
—— Walter Chidlock 376
Nantes, Richard 455, 493
—— William Henry 417
Naper, William Dutton 195
Napier, Hon. Charles 107
—— Chas. Jas. Dundas 415
—— Duncan Campbell 493
—— D. Campbell 436
—— Edward 141
—— Edward H. D. Elers 17
—— Geo. Thos. Conolly, CB. 28, 125
—— Joseph 227
—— Robt. Dunmore 143
—— Thos. E. CB. 8, 300
—— William Charles 196
—— Wm. C. E. 32, 462
—— Sir Wm. F. P. KCB. 7, 223
Nash, Chas. Widenham 107
—— George Stevens 418
—— John Tulloch 294
—— Joseph, CB. 121
—— T. Llewellyn, MD. 221
—— Wm. Adams 177
—— Wm. Russell 357
Nasmyth, Charles 75
Nason, Henry 493
—— John 78, 362
—— John Isaac 266
—— J. R. 465
Naylor, Charles Scarlin 364
—— George 415
—— James Sadler 105
Neal, William 246
Neale, Melville, MD. 441, 462
Neame, Albert 207
—— Charles Covell 493
Neave, Arundell 131
Nedham, Charles 243
—— William Robt. 35, 371
Need, Arthur 84, 151
Needham, John L. 418
Neild, Thomas Kent 183
Neill, Alexander 293
—— Matthew 533
—— William 521
—— Wm. Jas. Smith 379
Neilson, William 350

Nelson, Alex. A. 80
—— John Smyth 248
—— Michael 521
—— Richard J. 37, 399
—— Thomas L. K. 80, 252
—— William Francis 381
—— Wm. Frederick 533
Nepean, Alfred de Hochepied 413
—— Edmund 76
—— William 17
Nesbitt, Henry 197
Nesfield, Wm. Andrews 493
Nesham, Thomas W. 105
Ness, William Edward 286
Nestor, James 476
Nettles, Charles E. 138
Neuschäffer, Charles Ernest F. 543
Nevell, William 299
Nevile, Percy Sandford 224
Nevill, Henry D. 74, 223
—— William 271
Neville, Charles 316
—— Edward 57, 166
—— Richard 157
—— Robert 195
Nevinson, John B. L. 283
Newall, Tho. Prothero 415
—— William Edward 187
Newbatt, Charles H. 192
Newbigging, Robert G. 326
Newbolt, Edw. Dorrien 246
—— Francis 493
—— John Rice 180
—— Robert Henry 377
Newburg, Arth. A. C. 476
Newcombe, Joseph 534
Newcome, Wm. Henry 379
Newdigate, Edw. 79, 343
—— Fra. Wm. 105
—— Hen. Rd. L. 84, 343
Newenham, Richard 476
Newey, John 178
Newhouse, William 51
Newland, Peter Fred. 181
—— William 521
—— Wm. Henry 436
Newman, Cha. Rayner 50
—— Ernest Peake 263
—— Walter 379
Newport, Hen. Bolton 250
—— Simon George 312
Newsome, William 403
Newton, Geo. Glascott 197
—— George B. 420
—— Hibbert 493
—— Horace Parker 78, 374
—— John 493
—— Richard 243
—— Thomas Charles 493
—— Walter 493
—— Wm. Henry 105
—— William James 175
—— Wm. Saml. 30, 163
Neynoe, Cha. Fitz Roy 105
Nicholas, Albert 261
—— Griffin 81
—— James 476
—— John 335
Nicholetts, Gilb. Alf. 521
Nicholl, Christ. Rice H. 344
—— Hume 136
Nicholls, Henry 76

Nicholls, Henry Lionel 342
—— John 476
—— Samuel James 272
Nicholson, Brnsly. MD. 442
—— Christ. Hampden 476
—— Huntley 476
—— John 493
—— Lothian, CB. 61, 402
—— Richard 493
—— Stuart James 379
—— Thos. Wm. KH. 105
Nicolas, Paule Harris 493
Nicoll, Charles R. 161
—— James 521
—— Samuel James 493
—— Sam. John Luke 105
Nicolls, Augustus 476
—— Sir Edw. KCB. 7
—— Geo. Augustus 213
—— Geo. Greene 105
—— Gustavus 7, 399
—— Oliver 173
—— Oliver H. Atkins 378
Nicols, Adolphus 181
Nicolson, Patck. MD. 533
—— William 354
Nightingale, Arthur C. 332
—— Hen. Dickenson 415
Nisbet, Thomas 86, 129
Nisbett, Fra. Hen. Wm. 378
—— Henry 493
Niven, John 444
Nivison, Jas. Finlayson 533
Nixon, Arthur Jas. 84, 343
—— Murray Octav. 60, 373
—— William Frederick 315
—— Wm. Richmond 493
Noake, Maillard 152
Noble, Andrew 376
—— Samuel Black 240
—— William Henry 380
—— William Hatt 402
Noblett, Edw. Abbott 212
Nolan, Francis 349
—— John 268
—— John Philip 380
—— Richard Albert 260
—— Water Raymund 154
Nolloth, Peter Bramos 37
Nooth, Henry 49
—— Henry Stephen 476
Noott, Edward Gregg 353
—— Francis Harry 413
Norcliffe, Norcliffe, KH. 14
Norcott, Wm. Sherbrook Rmsy. CB. 36, 125, 361
Norman, Charles John 484, 302
—— John 51
—— Ralph 476
—— Robert 476
—— William 195
—— William 493
Norris, Charles George 314
—— Henry Albert 223
—— Henry Crawley 270
—— Nathaniel 321
—— Robert 493
—— William 343
North, Cha. N. 81, 281
—— Dudley 263
—— Joseph P. 138
—— Hon. Charles 345

North, Hon. Wm. H.
—— John 126
Northey, Aug. J. W. 107
—— Fran. Vernon 282
—— Geo. Wilbraham 232
—— William Brook 105
Norton, Chs. Grantley Campbell 226
—— James Roy 476
—— Rob. Tho. L. 160
—— Thomas Palmer 417
—— William 383
Norwood, Robert 131
Noseley, Geo. Roberts 345
Nott, Francis Percy 62, 452
—— Hollis Henry 415
—— John Henry 195
Nowlan, Art. W. C. 349
—— Henry James 253
—— John 267
—— John 521
Noyes, Geo. Augustus 381
—— K. Wm. Herbert 321
—— Lionel Herbert 382
Nugent, Andrew 137
—— Andrew 107
—— Cha. B. P. N. H. 79, 402
—— Cha. Lavallin 59, 361
—— Edmund Chas. 160
—— George 107
—— Sir Geo. Edmund 106
—— Geo. Stephens N. Hodges 527
—— St. Geo. Mervyn 87
—— James 74, 246
—— Jas. Thomas 182
—— John Vesey 269
—— Malachy 295
—— Morgan 534
—— William 190
—— William Sydney 286
Nunn, Jas. Loftus W. 314
—— Loftus 274
—— Loftus John 341
—— Wm. David 217
Nunnington William 279
Nurse, Chas. Bulkeley 415
Nuthall, Henry John 276
Oakes, C. Josa. Tuffnell 156
—— Frederick 443
—— Tho. Geo. A. 61, 148
Oakley, Geo. John A. 296
Oates, James Poole, KH. 49
—— William Coape 476
Obbard, Edward Kelly 330
O'Beirne, Francis 130
—— James, MD. 534
O'Brien, Aubrey Vere 283
—— Barthol. 62, 156
—— Cornelius George 185
—— David 83, 319
—— Edmund D. Collins 404
—— Francis 533
—— Henry 306
—— Hen. Higgins D. 76
—— Jerome 234
—— John Terence 493
—— John T. Nicolls 86, 217
—— Rich. Serrell 82, 452
—— Terence 27, 125
—— T. B. P. O'Brien 443
—— Thomas Michael 444
—— Wm. Creagh 303

G G

O'Brien W.E.Freeman 273	Oldham, John Field 50	Ormsby, John Wm.35, 371	Pagan, John Henry 288
O'Callaghan, Charles 444	——Riland W. 269	——Owen Lloyd 62, 453	——Samuel Alex. 493
——Cornelius 349	Oldright, John 76	——Sewell 493	Page, Geo. Curry 105
——Edward 207	O'Leary, Arthur 107	——William 349	——Geo. H. 78, 125, 253
——Patrick, MD. 583	——Eugene Francis 384	O'Rorke, Edw. Digby 283	——Philip Homer 188
O'Connell, Daniel 107	——John MacCarthy 243	——Marcus William 283	——Robert 476
——Edward 318	——Tho. Connor, MB. 260	Orpen, Arthur Herbert 444	——William 443
——George 220	Oliphant, George 521	——W. New. Morris 308	Paget, Lord Alfred 42
——Morgan James 169	Oliver, Cha. Valentine 294	Orr, Andrew 375	——Frederick 108
——Richard 373	——Edward Dudley 269	——James 493	——Lord Geo. Aug. .
O'Connor, Bernard R. 493	——George William 416	——John 107	Fred. CB. 28
——Charles Davis 436	——Henry James 224	——John 465, 493	——Leopold Grimston 374
——George 380	——Jas. Farquharson 195	——Spencer Edw. 192	——Patrick L. C. 105
——James Maurice 418	——John 493	——William 444	——Richard Horner 294
——John 183	——John Ryder 379	Orton, Rich. John W. 444	Paille, Peter Francis 527
——Luke 226	——Samuel Pasfield 382	——Thos. Jerram 384	Pain, George 442
——Luke E. 307	——Theophilus Henry 197	Osborn, Geo. Todding.195	Pakenham, Chas. W. 160
——L. Smyth, CB. 34, 349	——Thomas 120	——Henry John Robt. 126	——Edmund 270
——Maurice 494	——Wm. Silver, MD. 284	——Kean 436	——Hon. Fred. B. 86
——Rowland 218	Olivey, Walter Rice 198	——Thomas 527	——Hamilton Sandford 127
——Valentine 314	Olivier, Henry Stephen 105	Osborne, Osb.S. Delano 274	——Tho. Henry 56, 237
O'Conor, Frederick 444	O'Loughlin, Jos. Edw. 188	——Hen. St. George 136	——William 476
——Rich. J. Ross 81, 210	Ollerton, James 493	——Herbert Boyles 272	——Hon.W.Lygon,CB.36
O'Dell,Edm.Westropp 493	Olpherts, Robert 458	——Hon. D'Arcy G. 323	Palatiano, Geo. MD. 444
——Francis 290	O'Mahony, Redmond 229	——Francis 519	Paley, Raymond South 231
——Rev. M. C. 455	O'Malley, Austin P. 223	——Francis W. 195	Paliologus, Wm. Tho. 443
Odell, William, MD. 440	——Sir William 465	O'Shaughnessy, W. C. 350	Palling, Henry 513
O'Donnell, Sir C. R. 10	——William 300	O'Shea, Rodney Payne 217	Palliser, Arthur 123
——John 534	——Willem Boyd 316	——William Henry 155	——Edward M. 316
——John Vize 233	Ommanney, Fran.Mon.	Osmer, James John 298	——Henry 30, 371
——Michael 227	Maxwell 84, 374	Ostler, Wm. Grinfield 326	——Henry John 380
——P. 465	Omptedn,Christ.L.von 543	O'Toole, William 340	——John Augustine 307
O'Donoghue, Charles 307	——L. Albrecht von 543	Otter, Alfred Emanuel 417	——John Richard 170
O'Donovan, Dan., MD.443	O'Neal, John 442	Otway, Charles 14	——Richard Wm. 144
O'Dowd, Edward H. 135	O'Neill, Edward 260	——E. J. 465	——William 155
O'Dwyer,Joseph, RC. 455	——Francis 258	Oughton, James 493	Palmer, Archdale Robt.345
Oehlkers, Christian 541	——Henry 493	Ouseley, William 476	——Arthur Hare 303
O'Flaherty,John, RC.455	——Henry Arthur 28	Outram, Sir Jas. Bt.	——Charles 436
——Richard James 439	——John 141	GCB. 120	——Charles Edwards 200
O'Flanagan, John 476	——John James S. 217	——Joseph 328	——Chas. Quartley 531
Ogden, D. Anderson 274	——W. 464	Ouvry, Frederick 167	——Edmund 84, 374
Ogilvie, Alex., MD. 530	——William 64,452	——Henry Aime, CB. 59	——Edmund Thos. 385
——A. W. Armstrong 377	Onslow, Andrew Geo. 338	Ovens, John Coote 191	——Edward 344
Ogilvy, D. W. Balfour 228	——Arthur Edward 105	Overton, Wm. Henry 181	——Edward Despard 476
——John, MB. 242	——George 279	Owen, Arthur Allen 324	——Fra. R. CB. 60, 281
——Thomas 33, 127	Guild. Macleay 318	——Chas. Hen. 80, 376	——Frederick 167
——William 436	——Phipps Vansittart 493	——Charles Lanyon 416	——Henry Gordon 381
——Hon.W. H. Bruce 232	——Pitcairn 76	——Edw. Barry 107	——Henry Spencer 404
——W. Lewis Kinloch 282	Orange, F. X. de Coucy 246	——Fra. H. Edmund 418	——Henry Wellington 304
Ogle, Arthur 107	——John Edward 43, 452	——Henry Cha. Cun-	——Horrick Augustus 288
——Edmund 58, 400	Orchard, F. Simon A. 222	liffe, CB. 56, 401	——James 61
——Frederic Amelius 417	Ord, Alfred Robert 322	——Hugh 107	——James Q. 187
O'Grady, Carew L. A. 403	——Augustus William 217	——Sir John, Bart. 463	——John 105
——George Francis 352	——Fred. W. Craven 374	——John Fletcher 380	——John Reynolds 197
- ——John W. Waller 417	——Harry St. Geo.75, 401	——Loftus 103	——Nicholas 32
——John 50	——Wm. Redman 17, 399	——Robert 103	——Roger 127
——Stand. de Courcy 291	Orde, Hen. P. Shafto 205	——Stephen 435	——Thomas 216
——Hon. Thomas 7	Ordon, John 544	——William 270	——Thomas 263
O'Halloran, H. D. 34, 349	O'Reilly, Anth. Alex. 105	Owens, John 202	——William 435
——William 443	——Henry William 534	Owles, Alfred Job 134	——Wm. Henry 250
O'Hara, James 187	——John 493	Oxenden, Chas. V. 64, 343	Panattieri, Joseph 544
——Richard 378	——John 493	Ozanne, R. M. 464	Pannach, Charles 544
O'Hea, John 231	Orme, Herbert Lewis 513	Ozzard, Albert Henry 415	Pannell, Robert 493
O'Keefe, James 515	——William Henry 86,321	Pack, Arthur John Rey-	Panter, Herbert G. 349
O'Kelly, James 493	——Wm. Knox 64, 192	nell, CB. 42	Papillon, Alex. F. W. 76
Oldershausen,F.G.von 540	Ormerod, Oliver 145	——John Thomas 291	——John Ashton 403
Oldershaw, Charles 76	——Rich. W. 345	——Richard 253	Pardey, John Quin. 476
——Chas. Edward 79, 375	Ormond, Wm. Church 181	Packe, George 226	Pardoe, Edward W. 323
Oldfield, Aldred 205	Ormsby, Anthony 74	——Geo. Hussey 476	——Thomas Francis 302
——Copner Fran. 250	——Arthur 476	Packman, Frederick 218	Parish, Hy. W. 80, 260
——Edwin John 180	——Augustus Howard 476	Padwood, John 307	——Sir W. KCH. 527
- ——John, KH. 10, 399	——Geo. Fred. 130	Paddon, Hen. W. L. 186	Park, George, MD. 444
——Richard 376	——Henry Michael 493	Padfield, Francis 364	——Geo. Fortescue 274
Oldham, Francis George 404	——James 493	Pagan, Andrew 293	——Thomas 76

Park, Thomas	384	Pasley, Charles	401	Peach, James Peach	107	Pennant, *Hon.* Edw.G.	
——William Ker	153	——Clinton Hey. S.	380	——John Carroll	493	——Douglas	103
Parke, Charles	107	——George Malcolm	376	Peachey, Albert	175	Pennefather, George	293
——Charles Barker	414	——Hamilton Sabine	354	Peacocke, Geo. *MD.*	442	——Henry Vansittart	253
——Hy. Wm.	36,411	Passy, Edm. Wm. W.	103	——George	519	——John	207
——James Allan	224	Paterson, Edward Jas.	476	——George John 65,	207	——*Sir* John Lysaght,	
——Richard 83,	413	——F. T. Logan	290	——Henry	345	*KCB.*	11, 261
——Samuel	493	——Hen. Foljambe	384	——Steph. Ponsonby	107	——Nicholas	318
——William, *C.B.* 43,	302	——James, *MD.*	533	——Thos. Goodricke	334	——Richard	494
Parker, Arthur Cha.85,	300	——James	105	——Warren Wm. R.	493	Pennell, Croker Lovell	436
——Edward	105	——James	330	Peake,Geo.Wm.,*MD.*	213	——Reginald	264
——Edw. Augustus	16	——John Brand	404	Pearce, Charles Wm.	51	Pennington, *Hon.* Alan	
——Francis Geo. S.	273	——Joseph	9, 281	——T.	464	Jos.	344
——Fred. Saintbury	527	——William	462	——William, *KH.*	105	——Frederick	243
——Fred. Wyer	338	Patience, James 33,	293	Pearman, Edw. Wood	220	——Jas. Masterson	515
——George Hubert	331	Paton, Edward	521	Pears, Henry	231	——*Hon.* Jossylin F.	344
——Kenyon Stevens	493	——George	229	Pearse, Albert E.	307	——Rowland	494
——Richard 28,	126	——George	493	——A. T. Gratwicke	377	Penno, W. L.	464
——Robert Lesley	152	——James	177	——Edward Octavius	493	Pennycuick, Jas.F. 77,	375
——Wm. Henry	210	——Thomas	157	Pearson, Charles	105	Pennyman, James W.	476
Parkerson,Hen.Mount	316	Patrick, Robert	417	——Charles Knight	175	Penrice, Chas Walter	436
Parkin, John Bawden	476	Patrickson, Edw. Aug.	217	——David R. *MD.*	346	Penrose,Penrose C. 84,	412
Parkinson, C. Colvill	321	——Jas. Hen.	220	——Fra. Massey	229	Penruddocke, Thomas	476
——Chas. Fred.	43	Patten, Arthur Wilson	345	——Geo. John Hooke	152	Penson, Henry	383
——Charles Frederick	335	——Eustace J. Wilson	126	——Hugh Pearce	319	Pentingall, Edward	121
——Henry	182	——John Wilson	125	——Joseph	464	Penton, John	319
——John	277	Patterson, Chas.D. 82,	192	——Rd. Art. *M.D.*	533	——Thomas	144
Parks, Edw. Alex. H.	218	——Charles John	245	——Richard Lyons		Peploe, Daniel Peploe	476
Parlby, Brook B. *CB.*	120	——David Aikman	383	Otway 79, 125,	160	Pepper, George N.	239
——George	105	——Fred. Thos.	283	——Thos. Hooke	42	——Theobald	494
——William	26	——John Williams	493	——William	260	Peppin, Henry Cole	173
Parlour, William	519	——Leslie Ogilby	443	——William Charles	324	Pepyat, Geo. Bownell	75
Parnell, Arthur	404	——William	462	Pechell, Edward R. C.	356	Pepys, *Hon.* Walt. C.	283
——Henry	175	——Wm. Thos. L. 80,	330	Peck, Wm. Emmerson	404	Perceval, Ernest Aug.	324
——Wm. Henry	160	Pattison, Charles 86,	452	Pedder, Charles D.	250	——Frank F.	157
Parr, James	276	Pattle, Thomas 53,	129	——Rich. Newsham	146	——John James	210
——King John	444	——William, *CB.*	120	Peddie, Crofton	220	——John M. *CB.* 31,	197
——Thomas	441	Patton, Henry B.	233	——George	253	——Norman Spencer	382
——Thos. Chase	121	——Herbert Chas.	223	——William	453	——Spencer 30,	163
——Thos. Philip	137	——John	18	Peebles, Thomas 86,	195	Percival, Horace	378
——Thos. Roworth	345	——Walter D. P. 34,	304	Peel, Arthur Lennox	270	——Lewis	344
Parratt, Hillebrant M.	493	Paty, G.W.*CB.KH.* 8,	299	——Cecil Lennox	166	——Philip	312
——Jas. Edw. Thos.	439	——Geo. Wm. 77,	276	——Edmund Yates	52	Percivall, Charles	539
——Wm. Temple 82,	202	Patzinsky, Ernest von	543	——Edmund	493	Percy, Francis	494
Parry, Francis Joseph	416	Paul, Gregory	107	——Francis	243	——*Hon.* Hen. Hugh	
——Fred. Wm. Best	224	——James	293	——Jonathan	10	Manvers 32, 125,	159
——James	493	——Matthew Coombs	120	——John	78	——John William	190
——John Evans	521	——Thomas Henry	120	——Robert	200	——Jones Robt. L.	243
——John Horndon	414	——William Henry	246	——Spencer	169	Pereira, Wm. Duff	134
——Legh Richmond	197	Paulet, Charles Wm.	142	——William Henry	190	Peretti, Dominico A.	544
——Sidney	380	——LordFred., *CB.*26,	163	Peers, Hen. de Linné	493	Perham, John	494
——Thomas	493	——George	137	Pegley, Robert	521	——William	494
——William	530	——St. John Claud	133	Pegus, Wm. Jefferies	540	Perkin, William	522
——William Henry	242	——*Lord* William, *CB.*	18	Peile, John Henry	377	Perkins, Aug. Fred.	330
Parsley, *Rev.* L.	455	Pauli, Newton Jones	282	Peirse, Chas. Henry	369	——Edw. B. S.	416
Parsonage, Edw. *MD.*	444	Pavy, Francis	304	Pelham, T. Pelham	237	Pering, Geo. Harmer	220
Parsons, Clifford	175	Paxton, Archdall Fred.	493	Pellatt, Joseph	464	Perrin, Charles	294
——Gother Mann	353	——James, *MD.*	444	Pelley, Ernest Le	303	Perry, Adam	260
——Isaac	239	Payn, Thos. Geo. D.	158	Pelly, Henry Raymond	402	——Charles James	515
——James, *CB.*	120	——William, *CB.* 59,	272	——RaymondRichard	247	——Charles Smith	190
——*Rev.* J. L.	455	——Wm. Henry B.	245	Pemberton, Christ. P.	167	——George	167
——Lawrence H. H.	379	Payne, Charles Wil-		——G. Keating	476	——Henry	494
——Richard	245	liam Meadows	85	——George Rich	120	——James	120
——Robert Mann	402	——Gallway Byng 61,	412	——Wykeham Leigh	282	——Richard Lavite	494
Partridge, John	521	——Henry Lavington	130	Pender, Chas. Pressly	349	——Rich. Philip	380
——William	383	——John	521	——Francis Henry	180	——William	384
Paschal, George Fred.	105	——Pet. Trant Murray	37	Penfold, Edward	494	Perryn, George Edw.	279
Pascoe, Alfred Henry	416	——Wm. Aug. T.	107	——Robert	152	Persse, Dudley Tho.	201
——John	50	Paynter, David Wm.		Pengelley, E.	464	——Robert	356
——Richard Wm.	75	*CB.* 41,	372	——Wm. Jenny	87	——William Norton	379
——Robert James	417	——George	107	Penleaze, Henry	103	Perston, David, *MD.*	533
Paske, Hen. Gresham	335	——John	166	Penn, Lewis Wm. 80,	376	Pery, Wm. Cecil Geo.	326
Pasley, *Sir* Chas. Wm.		——Joshua	439	Pennant, Arch. Cha.		Pester, Henry 29,	371
KCB.	8, 399	Peach, Henry P. K.	128	Hen. Douglas	160	——John Constantine	344

G G 2

Index

Peter, Geo. F. C. 464
Peters, Edw. Nicolls 404
——James 123
Petit, Guglielmo 60
Petley, Pat. M'Leod 107
——Robert 476
Peto, James Fielder 123
——Wm. Lawes 83, 200
Petrie, Alfred Ernest 436
——Fra. Wm. Henry 195
——Martin 202
——Samuel, CB. 527
Pett, George 464
Pettigrew, James 157
Pettingal, Francis Wm. 76
Pettingall, Edward 122
Peyton, Algernon W. 126
——Francis 62, 340
——John 156
——John East Hunter 283
Pfannkuche, Augustus 543
Phelips, Hen. P. P. 377
——Richard 476
Phelps, John Shaw 202
Phibbs, John Ormsby 138
——Wm. Harloe 36
Philips, Edwin Wm. 246
——George 172
——George 402
——Henry 494
——James 242
——James Geo. 445
——John Alex. 15, 411
——Joseph 417
——Nathaniel Geo. 123
——William S. 80
Philpps, Sir Benj. T. 122
——Courtenay 107
——Edw. Berkeley 322
——George 513
Phillips, Charles 386
——Edward 144
——Fred. Hervey B. 476
——Geo. Hutchison 436
——Henry Long Wm. 192
——Henry Pearce 135
——Lewis Guy 160
——Rob. Newton 34, 360
——Thomas 155
Phillipson, John B. 142
Phillipps, Henry 105
——Charles Burch 182
——Henry Pye 172
——John James 282
——Paul Winslow 374
Phillott, Frederick J. 105
Phillpotts, Arthur Tho. 42, 372
——Hen. Francis 380
——William Coles 402
Philp, Francis Lamb 137
Philpot, Philip 195
Phipps, Hon. Sir Charles Beaumont, KCB. 103
——Ramsay Weston 379
——Richard Leckonby 43
Pickard, Arthur Fred. 382
——Henry William 494
——James 413
Pickering, Chas. Hart 380
——John, MD. 531
——Wm. Henry 33, 371
Pickford, Wm. Hen. 161
Pickles, Joseph Henry 155

Pickworth, John 144
Pictet, Armand Jaques 494
——Frederick 494
Pidsley, Sydenham L. 270
Pierce, Tho. Estwick 534
Piers, Henry W. 464
Pieters, Charles 476
Piffard, Reginald 138
Pigot, Richard 6, 132
Pigott, Arthur 74, 452
——Augustus 446
——Edw. Chas. P. 258
——Fran. Paynton 153
——George Edward G. F. 283
——Henry De Renzy 318
——John Pelling 80, 453
——Robert 476
——Stainsby Henry 246
——Wm. Hen. Sam. 303
Pigou, Arthur Comyn 374
——Lawrence 494
Pike, Francis 330
Pilcher, Jn. Montresor 13
Pilgrim, John Bunce 476
Pilkington, Jas. B. 334
——John Frederick 316
Pilleau, Henry 440
Pilling, Oswald 299
Pilsworth, William 85, 452
——William 224
Pinchard, Wm. B. 353
Pinder, George 37
Pinkerton, A. Wm. Pultney, MD. 385
——Claude Scott S. 173
Pinniger, Broome 494
Pinson, Albert Andrew 207
Pinwill, Wm. S. C. 233
Piper, Chas. Chris. 191
——Robt. Sloper 14
——S. Ayrault, MD. 533
Pipon, J. Kennard 37, 125
——Philip Gosset 77, 374
Piro, Marq. G. de, CMG. 49
——Giuseppe de 368
——Saverio de 368
Pitcairn, Andrew 79, 231
——Robert 44
Pitman, H. Bromley 224
——William 415
Pitt, Geo. Dean 314, 358
——Henry 513
——Henry D. 379
——Hon. Horace 105
——Philip Morton 258
——Thomas Henry 377
Pittendrigh, George 176
Pitts, Francis 476
Plant, Hen. W. W. 435
Planta, Etienne de 544
Plasket, Wm. A. H. 229
Platt, Arthur 207
——Charles 208
——Cha. Rowley 87, 261
——Henry Albert 350
Playfair, Andrew W. 494
——Jas. Octavius 404
Playne, Fred. Carl 344
Pleydell, Thos. Baker 82
Plowman, Thomas 494
Plummer, Heathcote 185
Plumridge, Jas. John 352
Plunket, Wm. C. 223

Plunkett, Arthur Jas. 349
——Hon. C. Dawson 54, 169
——Hon. Edw. S. 81, 335
——Hon. T. O. W. 169
——Thomas Richard 494
Pocklington, Evelyn H. Fred. 39
——Frederick 180
——George Henry 212
Pocock, Alf. Geo. D. 223
——G. F. Coventry 79
Pode, William 476
Podmore, Richard 120
Poe, Purefoy 494
Poett, Matthew 445
Pogson, Charles D. 231
Pohle, Mars Mourier 245
Pole, Arthur Cunliffe Van Notton 18
——Cha. Van Notten 354
——Edward 29, 148
——Edward Fred. 221
——Geo. Hen. Law 404
——Geo. Rob. 81, 452
——Mundy 107
——Samuel 107
Polhill, William 494
Pollard, George 294
——Henry Wm. 295
——William Henry 224
Pollock, Sir George, GCB. 120
——Samuel 107
——William Paul 476
Pollok-Morris, Wm. MD. 533
Polwhele, Thomas 121
Ponchalon, J. N. de 544
Ponsford, Henry 132
Ponsonby, Arth. E. V. 160
——Henry Fred. 52, 159
Poole, Arthur James 295
——Geo. Lawson H. 213
——Henry 33, 371
——Henry E. 193
——John H. CB. 29
——John Wm. 195
——Samuel Fred. 193
——Wellesley Wellington Waterloo 442
——Wm. John Evered 282
Poore, Fras. Harwood 417
——John 414
——Robert 84, 143
Pope, James 359
——Jas. Hughes 248
——John Andrew 295
——Richard Albert V. 250
Poppelwell, Geo. Bell 328
Portal, Robert 80, 140
Portelli, Michael 368
Porteous, Alexander 476
Porter, George 816
——Henry 494
——Henry Edward 12
——Henry Richard 377
——John 74, 295
——John Hall 513
——Joshua Henry 338
——Norton Lawrence 381
——Robert 494
——Whitworth 79, 402
——William 522

Portlock, Joseph Ellison 15
Poste, William 245
Posnett, Richard Jebb 322
Poten, Augustus 541
——Conrad 541
——Conrad 541
Potgieter, Conrad 435
Pott, James Gideon 147
——William 326
Potter, Thomas 476
Potterfield, W. 465
Pottinger, William 105
Potts, Cha. Highmore 32
——Charles Dennis 332
——Thomas 513
Poulden, Rich. Matt. 76
——Theodosius Wm. 183
Poulton, Cha. Walter 442
Poussin, Balthazard 513
Powell, Cha. Fred. 201
——E. O'Donovan 417
——Francis Graham 130
——Frederick 266
——George Henry 263
——Geo. Wm. 441
——Henry C. 65, 452
——Hen. Geo. Aug. 383
——James 156
——James Bruce 494
——Malachi 157
——Peter 476
——Ruben Hill 156
——Sam. Hopper 277
——Tho. Folliott 182
——Thomas H. 193
Power, John Dickson 192
——Richard 260
——Wm. Greenshields, CB. KH. 7, 370
——Wm. Jas. Tyrone, CB. 435
Powers, John 522
Powerscourt, Mervyn Wingfield, Visct. 126
Pownall, Cha. Ern. B. 296
——Walter 84, 175
Powney, Richard 120
Powys, Aubrey P. 207
——Hon. Charles 107
——Hon. Cha. J. Fox 246
——Hon. H. Littleton 107
——Hon. Leo. Wm. H. 237
——Littleton Albert 318
——Wm. Cunliffe 224
Poynter, Leonard B. A. 208
——Rentone Geo. F. 323
Poyntz, James 50
——William Henry 417
Pratt, Charles 103
——Charles Compton 13
——David 521
——Francis Edward 402
——George 446
——Henry Hamilton 334
——Robert, CB. 53, 226
——Roberts Torrens 298
——Thos. Simson, CB. 16
Prendergast, C.O.L.L. 270
——Chas. Middleton 270
——Jos. Sam. MD. 440
——Lenox 137
——Rob. Keating 440
Prenderville, John Hen. 357
Prescott, Albert S. K. 385

Index. 600

Prescott, Edw. Barker 242
—— William 121
Presgrave, W. F. A. E. 210
Preston, Cha. Edw. 213
—— Francis Henry 224
—— Hen. Evelyn W. 267
—— Jenico 282
—— Rev. J. D'Arcy W. 456
—— John Ingle 260
—— John Wm. 234
—— John William 521
—— Richard 79, 258
—— William R. 52, 260
Pretor, Sam. Ashton 145
Prettejohn, Rich. B. 84, 151
Pretyman, William 57, 281
Preussner, Victor 543
Prevost, Charles 239
—— George Phipps 226
—— Thomas Wm. 452
Priaulx, Henry 527
—— James 125
—— Osmond de Lancey 334
Price, Alfred Adams 295
—— Augustus Wm. 326
—— David 476
—— Edward, CB. 55, 372
—— George 132
—— George 196
—— Geo. Barrington 137
—— John Andrew 377
—— John Banner 435
—— Morgan Henry 416
—— Rice 476
—— Rich. Blackwood 58
—— Richard Charles 342
—— Richard Charles 404
—— Robert Henry 245
—— Robert Wynne 205
—— Rose Lambert 416
—— Thos. Charles 380
—— Wm. Henry 326
Prichard, Edm. Chas. 213
—— Octavius 533
Prickett, William 476
Prideaux, Sir Edm. Saunderson, Bt. 107
Pridham, William 494
Priest, John 494
Priestley, Edw. R. 61, 255
—— Francis Lloyd 261
—— Frederick J. B. 304
—— George 324
—— George 465
—— Horatio 240
—— J. Owen Jones 293
Primrose, Jas. M. 58, 257
Prince, Robert 279
Pringle, George 404
—— James 272
—— James 494
—— John 103
—— John Henry 103
—— John Watson 75
—— Norman 107
—— Norman Wm. D 248
—— Robert R. 464
Prior, Adrian de Mont. 382
—— Chas. Hamilton 299
—— Henry 121
—— J. De Mont. M. 64, 148
—— John Henry 335
—— Lodge Morres M. 515
—— Thomas Murray 43

Prissick, Thomas B. 436
Pritchard, Edw. Brace 415
—— Edw. Fitz-Gerald 414
—— Edw. Williams 151
—— Gordon D. 403
Pritchett, Wm. Morris 416
Prittie, Francis Wm. 236
Probart, Fra. Geo. C. 273
Probyn, John 494
Proctor, Henry 223
—— Wm. George 133
Protheroe, Dav. Garrick 182
—— Edward Schaw 384
Prust, Chas. Bateman 283
Pryce, Josiah 527
Pryor, John Basset 414
Pryor, Henry M. 283
Puddicombe, Rob. B. 494
Puget, Granville Wm. 243
—— John 144
Pugh, Walter Barnes 337
Pulleyne, Edward 144
Pulleine, Hen. Burm. 228
Pulliblank, Edw. Cooper 513
Pumfret, George 154
Purcell, E. T. Willoughby 377
—— John 267
—— Malcolm Brown 341
Purdon, Wm. Causabon 344
Purnell, Wm. P. 40, 328
Purves, John Home 61
Purvis, Herbt. Mark G. 376
Pusey, Henry Bouverie 307
Pye, Charles 272
—— Chas. Colquhoun 290
Pym, Chas. Melville 306
—— Edward Lawes 413
—— Frederick George 414
—— Sir William, M.D.
KCH. 529
Pyne, John 207
Quayle, Milren Tellet 253
Queade, Wm. Henry 197
Quealo, William 191
Quentin, George Augustus Frederick 107
—— Geo. Edw. 476
Quicke, Sidney Godol. 272
Quigley, Thos. Haswell 531
Quill, Arthur Saunders 357
—— Thomas Maurice 352
Quin, Charles William 299
—— Henry Evans 217
—— Peter Edward 223
Quincey, Paul Fred. de 299
Quinlan, Michael 186
Raban, William 50
Radcliffe, Emilius C. Delmé 86, 324
—— Geo. T. Delmé 261
—— Robt. Parker 63, 373
—— William 62, 306
—— Wm. Pollexfen 60, 217
Rae, Thomas 527
—— William 130
Rafferty, Geo. William 521
Ragueneau, Charles 527
Rahlwes, Fred. Jacob 541
Raiker, Joseph 151
Raikes, Edward Aug. 332
—— Geo. W. 85, 452
Raines, Joseph Robert 105

Raines, Julius Augustus
—— Robert, CB. 42, 335
Rainey, Hen. CB. KH.
9, 226
—— Henry Garner 56, 246
Rainforth, William 105
Rainier, Daniel 34, 340
—— John Baldwin H. 357
Rainsford, Hen. James 352
—— James 539
Rainsforth, Charles 494
Rait, Arthur John 382
Raitt, Charles Robert 103
Rulph, Joseph 476
Ralston, William C. 221
—— Wm. Henry 299
Ram, Stephen James 167
Ramadge, Henry Geo. 231
Rambaut, John, MD. 356
Ramsay, Balcarres Dalrymple Wardlaw 85, 125
—— Fox Maule 276
—— Francis 476
—— James 52
—— Nath. Crichlow 231
—— Thomas 444
—— Thomas Warton 527
—— William, M.D. 247
Ramsey, George 157
Ramsbottom, Frederick William 344
—— George Robert S. 321
—— John Richard 290
—— Walter B. MB. 280
Ramsden, George 494
—— Jno. Chas. Francis 378
Rance, Frederick 234
Rand, George 86,
Randall, A'fred 353
—— George 476
—— John Henry 436
Randell, Henry Lloyd 443
—— James Henry 354
Randolph, C. Wilson 58, 159
—— Francis 476
—— John Weech 105
Rankine, David 494
Rant, William 140
Raper, Aug. Frederic 250
Ratcliff, Thos. Hanson 515
—— William 494
Rathbone, Theodore William 141
Rattle, John Manley 436
Rattray, Adam Clerk 331
—— Alfred John J. 211
—— Charles, MD. 444
—— James Clerk 328
—— Jas. Clerk, MD. 231
Ravenhill, Fred. Geo. 377
—— Philip 79, 402
Rawdon, John Dawson 12
Rawlins, Arch. Macd. 335
—— Fra. Ironside 209
—— John 264
—— Sebastian White 144
—— Thos. Andrews 85, 359
Rawlinson, Geo. R. 131
—— Wm. Sawrey 141
Rawlison, George 107
Rawnsley, Rd. Burne 13
Rawstorne, John Geo.
57, 210

Ray, Sidney K. 444
Raye, Henry Robert 513
Rayment, George 129
Raymond, Elliott Arthur 258
—— Hy. Phipps 31, 361
Rea, Edward 37, 411
Read, Arth. W. Crewe 269
—— Constantine 476
—— Constantine Caridi 161
—— Constantine Hayward 353
—— Raphael Woolman 237
—— Robert 494
—— Thomas 513
—— William 216
Reade, Arthur Lloyd 288
—— Fran. Nevil 220
—— Geo. Wm. 350
—— Henry Cooper 440
—— Herbert Taylor 286
—— John By Cole 346
—— Jones Harper 175
Reader, Hen. Elmhirst 148
Ready, Charles 105
—— John Tobin 294
—— William 82, 452
Rechtern, Adolphus 543
Redman, Clavering 135
Redmond, J. Pat. 77, 286
Reece, John Deane 350
—— Bczsin 247
Reed, Fra. Jas. B. 269
—— James Wm. 527
—— Matthew Benj. Geo. 41
—— Robert Baynes 198
—— Thomas, CB. 11, 258
—— Thomas 105
Rees, John Vander H. 252
Reeve, Ellis Philip Fox 164
—— Frederick 303
—— John 7, 286
—— John 105
—— Maxwell 157
—— Wm. Henry 55, 163
Reeves, Boles 321
—— Conway Rich. 380
—— Conway Rd. D. 279
—— Edward Hoare 288
—— Geo. Marm. 33, 341
—— Lewis Buckle 494
—— Thomas 476
Reid, Alexander 273
—— David 226
—— Francis 337
—— Francis, MD. 181
—— Harry, MD. 306
—— Henry 107
—— Hugh William 345
—— John 127
—— Robert 340
—— Robert 127
—— Thomas Bussett 331
Reignolds, T. Scott, CB. 13
Reilly, John 247
—— William 534
—— W. E. M. CB. 79, 375
Reinecke, C. Augustus 541
Rendall, John King 140
Rendell, William Jasper 274
Renny, George 303
—— Henry 34, 315
—— Henry 376
—— Henry Laws 494

Index.

Rennick, H. de Parny 258	Richardson, John Hen. 10	Robbins, Nath. Eyre 383	Robinson, Cha. Walker 345
Rennie, C. Elphinstone 258	——John Soame 197	——Tho. Wm. 8, 314	——Douglas 302
——Dav. Field, MD. 442	——L. Andrews 133	Robe, Fred. Holt, CB. 29	——Frederic, MD. 167
——Dun. Robertson 442	——Mervyn 476	Roberts, Abraham, CB. 120	——Fred. John 123
——George 436	——Thomas 476	——Arthur J. 258	——George 494
——William 328	——Thomas 531	——Chas. Fyshe 379	——George Coke 147
Renouard, Hen. James 218	——Thomas Rumbold 126	——Charles John C. 266	——Sir Geo. Abercrom-
Renshaw, Rich. Wm. 150	——William 103	——Edm. Humphrey 443	bie, Bart. 82, 223
Renwick, W. Turn. 35, 399	——William, MD. 531	——Francis 331	——Rev. H. 455
Repington, C.A. A'Court,	——William Stewart 257	——F. Thomas 105	——Henry 436
CB. KCH. 7, 253	Richmond, Alexander 384	——Hy. Bradley 414	——Henry Edward 12
Retallack, Francis 290	——A. Fullerton, CB. 120	——Henry Gee 120	——Isaac Byrne 494
Rettberg, Leopold von 542	——C., Duke of, KG. 125	——John 521	——James 369
Reveley, G. Williamson 494	——Henry Fullerton 131	——John Cramer 105	——James 494
Revell, Albert John 246	——Henry Thos. 453	——Julius 476	——John 78, 258
——H. Albert Reade 141	——Matthew 107	——Peter 527	——John 494
Rew, Thos. Dennis 215	——Richard Olliffe 267	——Randal Howland 242	——John 385
Reynardson, E.B., CB. 103	——Sylvester 494	——Richard 190	——John George 105
Reyne, C. M. Rodney 207	Richter, Ern. Fer. C.B. 544	——Rich. Llewelyn 170	——John James 180
——James Frederick 247	Rickard, Martin 513	——Thomas Law 323	——Joseph 107
——Peter Bennet 37	Rickards, Andrew Knox 153	——William 79, 234	——Morris 232
Reynett, Sir Js. Henry,	——William 476	Robertson, Alexander 476	——Napier Douglas 185
KCH. 8, 264	Ricketts, Alfred 494	——Alex. Crawford 443	——Oliver 36
——Wm. Franco 494	——Charles 186	——Alex. Cunning. 61, 187	——G. Campobello 196
Reynolds, Francis 157	——Chas. Robert 417	——Archibald 105	——P. Vyvyan 515
——George Hewetson 216	——Charles Rodick 240	——Arthur Forbes 295	——Richard Harcourt 281
——John Williams 56, 125	——St. Vin. Wm. 28	——Arthur Masterton 132	——Rich. Rodd 196
——Thomas Matthew 494	Rickford, Tho. Parker 122	——Caleb 324	——Rich. Wood 208
Rhodes, Frederick 340	Rickman, Albert Divett 345	——Charles 107	——Stapylton 374
——Godfrey 85	——William 77, 360	——C. Duesberry 62, 400	——Thomas Auriol 379
——John William 283	Riddell, Archibald 527	——Rev. D. 455	——Wellesley, G. W. 436
Rhys, Thomas 308	——C. J. B., CB. 42, 372	——Frederick 193	——William 38, 400
Riach, John, MD. 533	——Geo. W. Hutton 151	——Frederick 477	——William 210
Riall, John Lewis 205	——Henry Jas. KH. 7,182	——George 335	——William 527
Ribton, Sir John, Bart. 494	Riddlesden, John Buck 103	——George Duncan 494	——William B. 83, 352
Ricardo, David 152	——Richard 477	——Geo. Forbes 332	——William Henry 42
Rice, Aug. Thomas 36	Rideout, A. Kennedy 378	——Geo. Francis 330	——William Henry 494
——Arthur 302	——Henry Wood 494	——George G. MD. 440	——William Henry 527
——Cecil 87, 302	Rider, W. Barnham T. 86	——George S. 269	Robley, Horatio G. 296
——Chas. Augustus 476	Ridge, James Stuart 513	——Gilbert Metcalfe 136	Robotham, John H. 130
——Herbert Henry 186	——Robert Stuart 76	——Henry, MD. 504	Robson, Henry 197
——Walter Brook 379	Ridgway, Poltimore 334	——Henry Fred. 252	Roch, Sampson 384
Rich, Charles David 145	——Samuel 476	——Henry Maxwell 382	Roche, Charles Boyse 361
——Sir Chas. H. John 123	Ridley, Chas. Wm. CB. 18	——James 380	——Edmund 57
——G. Whit. Talbot 80, 300	——Rich. Parnham 151	——James 494	——Francis La 542
——Frederick Henry 401	——William John 30, 166	——James 539	——John 44
——Henry 494	Ridout, John Gibbs 342	——Jas. Alex. 103	——Winship Percival 131
——John Sampson 476	——Joseph Bramley 314	——James Scott 446	Rochfort, Chas. Gust. 217
——Robert Jas. Evelyn 476	Ridsdale, W.H. Erring. 190	——J. Elphinston 59, 182	——Cowper 315
Richardes, W. Eardley 494	Riet, William Van der 494	——Jas. Hen. Craig 56,342	——Gerald 29
Richards, Albert 224	Rigaud, Gibbes 83, 281	——Jas. Jameson 404	——Henry Wollaston 186
——Arthur Oswald 190	Rigby, Samuel 494	——Jas. Macdonald 103	——John 494
——Fleetwood John 413	Riky, Benjamin 35, 264	——Jas. Peter, CB. 60,156	——John De Burgh 380
——George 476	Riley, Daniel 51	——John, MD. 533	Rocke, Henry B. H. 257
——Percival 334	——Fred. Arthur 344	——John 477	——Herbert 107
——Samuel 180	——H. Whewell Dan. 274	——John Leslie 436	——James Harwood 362
——Thomas 144	——John Edward 324	——Lewis Shuldham B. 50	——Richard 81, 302
——Thomas Bailey 252	——Philip Alfred 203	——Patrick 78, 364	——Richard Hill 172
——Sir Wm, KCB. 120	——Stephen Davis 120	——Peter, MD. 531	Roddy, Cha. Hamilton 353
——Wm. Hamilton 274	Rimington, Richard B. 403	——Robt. Henderson 382	——Thos. Fletcher 353
——Wm. Powell 81, 376	——Tho. Hosmer 36	——Robt. Jamieson E. 281	Rodgers, James 515
Richardson, Alfred Aug. 352	Rimmer, John Whittle 384	——Robert R. CB. 18	Rodney, Geo. B. 79, 412
——Chas. Clarke 299	Ring, James Tarrant 212	——Thos. Chevalier 200	——Lennox George 416
——Chris. Rowland 195	——Wm. Francis 81, 323	——William 513	Roe, Edward A. H. 193
——Edward 294	Rintoul, Robert 132	——Wm. Arthur 382	——Eugene Mervin 227
——Frederick 105	Riordon, John 521	——Wm. Buxton 312	——George Noble 175
——Frs. Moseley 527	Rippon, Geo. W. 445	——Wm. Donald 120	——John 195
——Isaac 50	Ritchie, James 494	Robeson, George 105	——Peter Burton 86, 281
——James 52	——Thomas 157	Robilliard, Chas. D.H. 416	——Peter Henry 531
——Jas. Thos. S. 310	Ritter, Herman H. Con. 541	Robin, Thos. Smith 223	——Robert Edward 148
——John 529	Rizzo, Felice 85, 368	Robins, Francis Wm. 283	——Sam. Black 331
——John Booth 379	——Vincenzo 368	Robinson, Augustus F. 527	——Wm. Carden 443
——John George 75	Robb, David 494	——Barnes Slyfield 326	Rofe, Samuel 515
——John G. 352	——David Elvy 446	——Charles Robert 232	Rogan, James 386

Index. 602

Roger, Charles 299
Rogers, Adam 494
—— Brumbead 216
—— *Rev.* Charles 463
—— Ebenezer 352
—— *Rev.* E. J. 455
—— Fred. James 207
—— George 215
—— George 346
—— Henry 78
—— Henry B. H. 44, 452
—— Henry Gordon 266
—— Henry James 299
—— Jacob Glynn 453
—— John 494
—— John Francis 436
—— John James Colin 444
—— John Thornton 242
—— Richard 464
—— Robert Montresor 258
—— S. O. 383
—— Thomas 315
—— William M. 436
—— William Reynolds 533
—— Wm. Stamford 446
Rokeby, Hen. Lord 12, 125
—— Langham 417
Rolland, James H. 534
Rolleston, Chas. John 304
—— Cornelius C. 83, 319
—— James Ffranck 267
—— Philip 436
—— Wm. Villett 211
Rollings, Gabriel Isles 383
Rollo, James 490
—— *Hon.* Robert 99
—— Robert A. 477
Rolls, Francis Tuach 272
—— Josiah Robert 331
Romer, Rob. C. 63, 373
—— Robt. Franck 15, 465
—— Robert William 83, 2.0
Romilly, Fred. 105
—— William 226
Roney, Richard 360
Rooke, Cresswell, K. C. 170
—— *Sir* Henry Willoughby, *CB, KCB* 103
—— Lewis 494
—— Lewis Stevens 207
—— William 379
—— Willoughby S. 167
Rooney, Bernard 494
Rooper, Wm. Trevor 344
Roper, Thomas 263
Roquefeuil, Gustave de 544
Rorke, Michael 521
—— Richard 354
Rose, Cowper 33, 399
—— Edward Lee 418
—— George Ernest 313
—— Hen. Joseph 173
—— Hugh 477
—— *Sir* Hugh Henry, *GCB.* 12, 260
—— H. M. St. Vincent 107
—— James 77, 172
—— John 494
—— John Rose Holden 105
—— William 477
Roseingrave, Matthew 494
Ross, Albert Ernest 180
—— Alexander 291
—— Alexander Aitken 210

Ross, Alex. Clrke. *MD.* 295
—— Archibald P. G. 57, 400
—— Emilius 494
—— Ewen 494
—— George 401
—— Geo. Campbell 144
—— Geo. Clarkson 228
—— Gillian Maclaine 477
—— Henry Paget Bayly 513
—— *Sir* Hew Dalrymple, *KCB.* 7, 370
—— Hugh 120
—— James Kerr, *KH.* 28
—— John 81, 343
—— John 513
—— John H. *MB.* 250
—— Pat. Wm. S. 81, 245
—— Richard 245
—— Robt. Dalrymple 436
—— Rob. Lockhart 57, 332
—— Robert Hill 245
—— Thomas 62, 303
—— William 198
—— Wm. Baillie, *MD.* 534
—— William James 349
Rosser, Chas. Potts 83, 134
—— George 154
—— George Frederick 153
Rosslyn, J. Alex. *Earl of* 11
Rotely, Lewis 494
Rothe, Geo. Walter C. 381
—— Lorenzo 105
Rothwell, William 494
Rottenburgh, Geo. de *CB.* 33, 342
Röttiger, Franz 543
Rotton, Chas. Paulett 376
—— Guy 83, 374
Rous, Geo. Grey 105
—— William John 166
—— *Hon* Wm. Rufus 477
Rouse, John R. 321
—— Richard 494
—— Robert Savery 206
Routh, Laurence 435
—— Randolph 435
Row, George Home 306
Rowan, Alexander M. 201
—— Henry S. *CB.* 38, 372
—— John Hill 495
—— John Joshua 288
—— Robert 465
—— Terence 243
—— *Sir* Wm. *KCB.* 8, 215
Rowland, Anthony 306
—— George 169
—— Henry 352
—— J. C. 464
—— Thomas 231
—— Wm. Hodnett 274
Rowlands, Hugh 79
Rowley, *Sir* Charles 105
—— Conwy G. H. 139
——— John Angerstine 200
—— Robert H. R. 376
Roworth, Cha. Edw. W. 182
Roxburgh, James 463
Royds, Clement Rob. N. 132
Royle, Arnold 444
Royston, C. P. *Visc.* 147
Ruck, Frederick Wm. 200
Rudall, Wm. Herbert 326
Rudd, John Trohear 280
—— Thomas, *MD.* 137

Rudd, Wm. Fred. John 169
Rudge, Arthur 384
—— John 192
Rudkin, Mark 477
Rudman, William 83, 240
Rudsdell, *Sir* Joseph 105
Ruel, Fred. Herbert 414
Runley, Randall 30
Rummell, William 543
Rumsey, Edw. Waugh 286
Rundle, Aldborough 279
Rundle, George Edw. 175
Runnacles, Anthony 477
Rushton, William 246
Russel, Hen. Cha. 12, 370
Russell, Lord A. G. 56, 343
—— Alex. Stevenson, *MD.* 233
—— Andrew Hamilton 105
—— Andrew H. 279
—— Baker Creed 185
—— Chas. Edward 350
—— *Lord* Cha. Jas. Fox 105
—— Christopher Jos. 404
—— *Lord* Cosmo Geo. 107
—— *Sir* Cha. *Bart.* 60, 159
—— David, *CB.* 30, 125, 369
—— D. G. N. Watts 282
—— Francis 328
—— Fred. Browne 74, 453
—— Henry Eyre 417
—— Henry James 495
—— Henshaw 63, 452
—— Hickman Rose 277
—— James 130
—— John J. Russell 266
—— John William 344
—— Richard 521
—— Thomas 207
—— *Sir* Wm. *Bt. CB.* 61, 142
—— William Russell 279
Russwurm, Wm. John 352
Ruston, William 521
Rutherfoord, Archibald 107
Rutherford, Alex. M. 353
—— Cornelius Clark 442
—— James 465, 496
—— James Hunter 75, 463
—— Wm. *MD.* 441
—— Rutherford, A. J. Oliver 299
Ruthven, Walter J. H. 344
Rutter, John 368
—— Theodore W. *MD.* 302
Rutledge, John Bruen 243
Ruttledge, T. Ormsby 77
Ruvignes, Cha. Hen.
Ruxton, Fred. Cha. 236
—— George 107
Ryall, Edward Cunny 322
Ryan, George A. 87, 299
—— John Dennis 495
—— Thomas 183
—— Valentine 291
Rybot, Henry Day 495
Rycroft, Thos. Christian 239
Rykert, Alfred Edwin 342
Ryland, Ashley Cowper 436
Rynd, Francis 177
—— M'Kay 78, 288
Sabin, J. E. 455

Sabine, Edward 14, 370
Sadleir, John Martley 416
—— Richard 380
—— Thomas John 286
—— William 37
Sadler, Ralph 253
—— Sam. Wm. Ralph 227
Safford, David Jn. D. 338
Sage, William 121
Sainsbury, Edwin T. 304
—— Walter Langford 283
St. Aubyn, Lionel 175
St. Clair, Chas. Wm. 81, 277
—— S. Graham Bower 220
St. Croix, Charles de 172
St. George, Hen. Cha. 298
—— James 464
—— John, *CB.* 35, 371
—— *Rev.* Leonard H. 455
—— Rich. Jas. M. 138
—— T. C. Belmore 310
St. Hill, Windle Hill 293
St. John, St. Andrew 418
—— Chas. Wm. 334
—— Edward George 173
—— Fred. Arthur 477
—— Fred. Edw. M. 416
—— Geo. F. Berkeley 107
—— John 495
—— John Henry 85, 331
—— John Hen. Herbert 217
—— Rich. Fleming 495
—— Rich. F. St. A. 283
—— Robert 302
—— St. Andrew B. 192
St. Leger, Hy. H. 314
St. Maur, Edward 105
St. Quintin, M. C. D. 103
Sainter, James Dow 444
Salamone, Paolo 521
Sale, Clement S. T. 246
—— John Henry 436
Salinger, Otto Henry 544
Salis, Henry Norman 140
—— Joseph 82, 156
—— Wm. Henry 354
Sall, Henry Mac. 85, 247
—— Wm. *KH.* 29, 455
—— William, *MD.* 440
Salmon, Charles 257
—— George Russell 380
Salmond, Francis Meik 221
—— William 404
Salter, Arthur 443
—— Edward Philip 153
—— Hen. Fisher, *CB.* 120
Saltmarshe, Arthur 299
Saltoun, Alex. *Lord* 107
Salvatorio, Pietro A. 544
Salwey, Alfred 435
—— Henry 103
—— William Henry 232
Sam, Seth 284
Sampson, John 60, 452
—— Wm. Henry 105
Sams, Chas. Hamilton 291
Samson, Alex. M. W. 349
Sandeman, Julian Fred. 382
Sanders, David Morison 495
—— Gilbert H. 465, 495
—— Henry Shearly 442
—— John Fred. 415
—— Robert, *CB.* 36
—— William 415.

Index.

Sanderson, Arthur	444	Savage, Henry	477
——Christopher	383	——Henry George	402
——George	261	——Henry John	26, 399
——Joseph	288	——Henry J.	74, 330
——Joseph Prosser	521	——John Morris	103
Sandes, Goodman	464	——Johnson, M.D.	530
——Hy. T. Thompson	381	——Philip Charles C.	356
Sandford, Rich. M. F.	403	——Rowland	513
Sandham, Chas. Freeman	74	Savary. Harry D. T.	266
——George	38	——William Tanzia	414
——Henry	30, 399, 404	Savile, Henry B. O.	477
——Robert	379	Saville, Henry	359
Sandilands, Erskine N.	187	Savory, Henry B.	310
——Philip	17	Sawbridge, E. Henry B.	229
——Philip Hen.	378	——Robt. Cooper	146
Sandwith, Fred. Browne	192	Sawkins, William	495
——Geo. Aug. Elliot	495	Sawrey, Hen. Beckwith	107
——Henry Fuller	261	Sawyer, Charles	61, 134
Sandys, A.W. M. Lord		——Chas. Rich. John	123
	8, 137	——Conrad	288
——Edwin William	380	——John Bland	212
——Francis Robt.	178	Sawyers, John	495
——Fred. Hervey	121	——Joseph, MD.	322
——George	120	SaxeWeimar, HisSerene	
Sanford, Geo. Edw.L.S.	404	Highness PrinceWm.	
Sankey, William	54, 190	Aug. Edw. CB.	
Sarel, Hen. Andrew 83, 154		37, 125, 159
Sargeant, Fra. O.	247	Sayce, Chs. Cartwright	178
Sargent, Edm. Wm. 83,212		——Henry Richmond	341
——Henry	120	Sayer, Frederic	125, 477
——John	383	——James Rob. S.	65,129
——John Neptune	65, 175	——Wm. L.	81
——John Payne	288	Scanlan, Fitzgerald E.	444
——Samuel	495	Scargill, James	33
——Samuel Tomyns	257	Scarlett, Hon. Sir Jas.	
Sarsfield, Bingham	495	Yorke, KCB.	12
Sartorius, Geo. Conrad	380	——Hon. Wm. F. 52, 166	
Satchwell, T. A. G.	464	——William James	133
Satterthwaite Jos. Hen.	404	Schack, Frederick	381
Saul, William John	324	Schalch, And. Archer W.	75
Saum, Julius Cæsar	544	Scharnhorst, Ferdinand	542
Saumarez, Hon.J.St.V.	103	——Lewis	543
Saunder Edw. Charles	436	Schaumann, Gustavus	541
——J. C.	464	——Otto	543
——Wm. Lawson	198	Schaw, Henry	402
Saunders, Andrew C.	495	Scheberras, Attilio	340
——Aubrey Wm. O.	182	Schembri, Joseph	443
——Charles Bertram	308	Schlichthorst, John F.	543
——Edw. William	202	Schlütter, Fred. Von	542
——George	441	Schnehen, William Von	541
——George Robert	344	Schneider, Fred. Bern.	542
——Henry Fred.	83, 352	——Robt. Wilmot	495
——John	150	Scobell, Henry Fred.	291
——Morley Caulfield	197	Schoedde, Sir James	
——Richard	52	Holmes, KCB.	11, 274
——Richard	165	Schomberg, Fred. S.	277
——Richard Westrop	188	——Geo. Aug.	61, 413
——Robt. Francis	495	Schooles, Hen. J. MD.	283
——Robt. John	495	Schot, Johannes Corn.	543
——Robt. Jos. Pratt	381	Schreiber, Arthur John	239
——Robt. Power	382	——Brymer Francis	378
——Thos. Greer	183	——George	105
——Thomas Harry	243	——Percy Bingham	170
——William	322	Schroeder, Hen. S. E.	444
——William Boyd	375	Schuler, Frederick	120
——William Henry	269	Schulze, Augustus	542
Saunderson, F. De L.	296	Schwencke, Herman	543
——John De Luttrell	375	Scobell, John	495
——Hardress Robt.	103	Scoltock, Samuel	521
——Somerset	147	Scoones, Henry Dalton	266
Savage, Edmund S.	211	Scot, T. Goldie, MD.	312
——Fred. Stuckley	80, 296	Scotland, David	135
——George William	247	Scott, Alex. de Courcy	403
——Harry Boscawen	415	——Arthur	87, 180

Scott, Chas. MD.CB.	439	Searle, Richard	76
——Charles	477	——William R.	412
——Hon. Cha. G.	103	Sears, John	521
——Chas. R. CB. 31, 462		Seaton, John, Lord, GCB.	
——Chas. E. S.	379	GCMG. GCH.	6, 127
——Courtenay H. S.	300	——Thomas	533
——Daniel, MD.	527	Sebisch, Theodore Von	543
——David	495	Seccombe, Thos. Strong	380
——Duncan Gordon	120	Seddall, John V. MD.	443
——Edward	107	Seddon, Henry Cooper	404
——Fra. Cunningham	255	Sedley, Anthony G.	105
——George	228	——Chas Herbert 80, 402	
——Geo. Fred. Cooper	39	——Frederick	129
——Henry	155	——John Somner 465, 495	
——Henry Alex.	12, 370	Sefton, Joseph	148
——Henry Boscawen	261	Segrave, O'Neil Stewart	200
——Hen. Young D.	401	——O'Neil	495
——Hopton Basset 81, 190		——William Francis	300
——Sir Hopt. S.KCB.	120	Seggie, Samuel	137
——Horatio	444	Selby, Robert	326
——James	121	——Robert Grey D.	436
——James	383	Semple, Andrew	443
——James	386	——Charles Wm.	306
——James	455, 521	——H.	107
——Jas. Edwd. MD.	346	——Henry	282
——James George	154	——John	107
——James Woodward	416	Senhouse, Wm. Wood	477
——John, CB.	11, 131	Senior, Henry	29
——John Alex.	444	——Thomas Palmer	188
——John James	443	——Warden	139
——John Mortimer	186	Serjeant, John	418
——Jonathan Gortly	303	Servante, Chas. Edw.	417
——Joseph O. Walter	246	Servanté, Henry	35, 399
——Luke, Frederic	170	Servantes, Wm. F. G.	436
——Lucas Clements	324	Sesino, Giuseppe	368
——Rev. Matthew R.	383	Seton, George	107
——Percy	495	——Miles Charles	295
——Ralph Robert	143	——William Carden	316
——Rich. Andrew	105	——William Carden	107
——Robert	326	Sevewright, Geo. V.	405
——Robert, MD.	531	Seward, Charles	346
——Robert Thomas	303	——Elliot	477
——Robert Thomas	307	——Thomas, MD.	444
——Theophilus Scott	192	Sewell, Alger. R. 85, 205	
——Hon. Tho. Cha.	345	——Charles	134
——William	136	——Herbert	139
——William	380	——John Aug.Geo. F.	156
——William	420	——Samuel F.	286
——Wm. Glendonwyn	105	——Stephen William	326
——Wm. Chas. Edw.	269	——Wm. Hen.CB. 8, 312	
——William Fortescue	308	Sexton, John	335
——William Henry 8, 246		——Michael John	380
——Wm. Henry H.	464	Seymour, David	197
——Wm. Lane R.	288	——Edward Adolphus	477
——Wm. Trelawny	382	——Francis, CB.	31, 166
——Scovell, Edmund John	337	——Fra. Hugh George	26
——Edward W.	56, 337	——Fred. Hor. Arthur	164
——Sir Geo. KCB. 6, 139		——John Busteed	414
——George Thomas	312	——J. Hobart Culme	296
——Thornton	290	——Edward Adolphus	
Scratchley, Horace Wm.	176	Ferdinand, Lord	132
——Peter Henry	403	——Leopold, Richard	160
Scrope, Arthur H.	142	——Wm. Fred. Ernest	164
Scudamore, A. CB. 60, 151		——Wm. Hen.CB. 60, 130
Seager, Edward	65, 143	Shackleton, William	156
Seagram, Charles	38	Shadforth, Henry	6
——Henry Fred.	227	——Henry J. Tudor	495
Seagrim, Albert	169	Shadwell, Josiah Fitz-	
Seale, Frederick S.	375	Thomas	226
Sealy, Francis	477	——Lancelot Amelius	236
——James	349	——Lawrence	54
——William	326	Shafto, William Henry	495
Seaman, Wm. C. MD.	302	Shairp, Alex. B. S.	416
Searle, Hy. Lindsay	414	Shakerley, Geoffrey Jos.	377

Index. 604

Shakerley, Hy. Webster	379	Sherlock, Fran. Geo.	302	Simmonds, Henry	105	Skoulding, John B. Wm.	383
Shakespear, Geo. B.	59, 373	——Henry	144	——H. Henry	340	Skues, Edw. W. MD.	443
——J. Davenport	77, 374	——Woodford Wright	245	Simmons, Edward Reg.	180	——Fred. McKenzie	349
Shanks, Joseph George	416	——Wright	213	——George LeBreton	404	——George	513
Shanly, Wm. John	170	Shervinton, Cha. R.	81, 156	——John Lintorn Arabin,		——Richard Alex.	298
Sharkey, Thomas	338	Sherwen, Peter	477	CB.	38, 401	——Wm. Mack. MB.	357
Sharp, Archibald H.	303	Sherwood, Tho. Hen.	220	——Joseph, CB.	105	Skurray, Francis Cha.	228
——Corn.	464	Shewell, George M.	416	——Richard	142	Skynner, Aug. Charles	107
——George	384	Shewen, Edw. T. P.	412	Simon, George	444	Skrine, Charles	310
——Henry C.	232	Shiffner, Bertie	279	Simpson, Alex. Duke	201	Skyring, Cha. Fra.	40, 400
——Henry Jelf	107	——Edward Thomas	273	——David	196	Slack, James	358
——Henry Jelf	166	Shinkwin, Robert S.	280	——Emanuel	146	Slacke, Owen R.	146
——John Edward 86,	453	Shipley, Reginald Yonge		——Sir Jas. GCB.	7, 323	——Wm. Randall	404
——Richard Palmer	105		55, 185	——James	495	Slade, Alf. Fred. A.	277
——William	318	——William Davies	279	——James	253	——Charles George	344
Sharpe, Henry E.	243	Shipton, James Maurice	242	——James M. Thos.	319	——Herbert D.	87, 129
——John	495	——John Noble	227	——James Woolley	534	——Marcus John	16
——John H.	274	Shirley, Arthur	29	——John, CB.	52, 243	——William Henry	13
——Martin Samuel	177	——George	266	——John	255	——William Hicks 84,	140
——Robt. Good	417	——Horatio, CB.	30	——John Bridgman	513	Sladen, Joseph	382
——Samuel	217	——John	521	——John Rawson	323	——William Dare	315
——William	335	Shirreff, Charles Æneas	121	——John W.	513	Slaney, Moreton	495
——Wm. Henry	356	——Robt. D. F.	187	——Patrick Browne	182	Slater, Henry Francis	477
Sharpin, Henry	495	Shone, Thos. Ackers	34	——Robt. Hamilton	173	——John James	105
Sharples, John	250	Shoolbred, Wm. Cha.	181	——Simon	381	——Stanley	316
Shaw, Archibald	190	Shore, Hon. Cha. John	167	——Thomas	270	——William	36
——Austin Cooper	155	——John	513	——Thos. Thomson	340	Slator, Nathaniel Rob.	234
——George	495	Shorland, James	533	——William, MD.	300	Slattery, Mathew	279
——George	78, 374	Short, Chas. Fred.	415	——Wm. Henry Randolph	81, 376	Slaughter, Charles	413
——George Gardine	76	Shortt, Charles Aug.	294			——Geo. Monlas	142
——George Kennedy	282	——Francis John	218	Sims, Vernon Wm.	416	Sleigh, Sir James Wallace, CB.	6, 145
——Henry John	62, 260	——John, MD.	530	Sinclair, Alex., MD.	531		
——Hugh	212	——John Baring	294	——Donald	521	Slessor, Edward Aug.	380
——John Wright	338	——Stuart James	195	——Edward M. MD.	338	Sloman, John	286
——Richard	145	——Wm. A. James	277	——George	452	Sly, William	208
——Samuel	120	Shoveller, William K.	477	——James	79, 376	Smail, James	416
——Samuel	495	Showers, Edw. M. G.	120	——James, MD.	173	Smales, Thomas	141
——Wilkinson	206	Shrapnel, J.	465	——John Hartley, MD.	533	Small, John	442
——Wm. Edward	148	Shubrick, Thomas	120	——William	332	——Robert	477
Shawe, Arthur George	243	Shuckburgh, Cha. Rob.	52	Singer, George Benj.	306	Smart, George Joseph	377
——Charles Aug.	9, 304	——George Tho. Fra.	107	——James	344	——Henry Dalton	74
——Chas. Fleetwood	252	Shute, Charles C.	4, 141	——Paulus Emilius	527	——Henry Hawley	210
——Laurence Paulett	418	——Henry Douglas M.	277	——Robert Burn	234	Smee, Walter N. Thos.	121
——L. R.	465	——James	414	Singleton, Henry Corbet	237	Smith, Alexander	496
——Wm. Lowe	540	——James	75	——John	42, 195	——Alexander, MD.	269
Shea, Henry John F.	380	——Neville Hill	60, 291	——John	77, 376	——Alex. Herbert A.	206
Shean, Robert	521	——Wm. Gordon	234	——Jonathan Felix	495	——Alf. Herbert Hugh	323
Shearman, Francis	352	Shuttleworth, A. A.	34, 371	——William, MD.	263	——Alfred John D.	177
——John	105	——Ashton John	382	Siree, Chas. Moore B.	175	——And. MD. KCB.	529
Sheehy, Roger	304	——Charles Ughtred	296	Sisson, Joseph	477	——Andrew Robertson	384
——Thomas, MD.	186	——Charles	255	——Marcus Jacob	527	——And. Wm. Douglas	416
Sheeran, Patrick	183	——Geo. Henry	269	Sitwell, Honorius S.	404	——Arthur George	134
Sheffield, John Charles	220	——Peter	298	——Rich. Staunton	74	——Arthur G.	350
——Robert	128	Sibbald, William	326	Sivewright, Geo. Viv.	404	——Astley Campbell	231
Shegog, George Alex.	180	Sibley, Henry William	261	Skeen, William	442	——Charles	32
Shekleton, Robert	533	Siborne, Herbert Taylor	402	Skelly, Francis	103	——Charles Bagot	436
Sheil, Charles H.	435	Sibthorp, Rich. Fra. W.	57	Skene, Alexander	75	——Chas. Edw. MD.	444
——Sir Justin, KCB.	121	Sichart, Lewis Hen. de	542	——John George	508	——Charles Francis	300
——Richard	182	Sidebottom, Leonard	359	Skerry, Cha. James	315	——Charles Hodgkinson	64, 375
Shelley, Charles	167	Sidey, James, MD.	533	Skey, Joseph, MD.	527		
Shelton, G.A.F. MB.	264	Sidley, Henry Edm. de		——Wm. Hen. Russell	248	——Chas. Jas. Forbes	215
Shephard, John	280	Burgh	34	Skinner, Cortlandt	216	——Corry Beverley	417
Shepheard, George	435	Sidney, Henry Marlow	129	——Cortlandt Geo. M.	245	——David	177
Shepherd, Geo. Alex.	383	Sievwright, Allan	375	——David Shorter	331	——David Rae	105
——John	464	——Andrew	191	——Frederick	446	——Donald Sinclair	134
——Robert	75	——Francis	531	——George Alex.	436	——Edm. Davidson	335
——Robert, RC.	455	Silver, Jacob M. W.	417	——George John	342	——Rev. E.	455
Sheppard, Hen. T.	243	——T. R.	513	——Rob. Fra. Hen. M.	316	——Edward Atkins	495
——Thomas	177	Sillery, Charles	53	——Samuel James	76	——Edward S. W.	223
——Thomas Winter	231	——Charles Jocelyn C.	197	——Theodore Henry	188	——Fitzroy George 86,	135
——Walter Cope	477	Sim, Charles	401	Skipper, Walter	341	——Fran. Montague	380
Sherer, Moyle	74	——Duncan	120	Skipton, Saml. S. MD.	310	——Fred. Augustus	169
Sheringham, C. T.	207	——Edw. Coysgarne	403	Skipwith, George	79, 361	——Fred. William	465
Sherlock, Charles W.	304	Simeon, Henry Scott	233	——Henry	103	——George	105

Index.

Smith, George	444	Smith, Thos. H.	83, 350	Somerset, Poulett G. H.		Spratt, Henry	477
—Geo. John Fitzroy	345	—Walter Caradoc	345	*CB.*	59, 185	—James	296
—Geo. Hankey	33, 303	—William	129	Somerville, *Rev.* D.	456	—Michael	413
—George Roche	533	—William	167	—*Hon.* Fred. Noel	345	—Robert Hall	266
—Geo.Wm.F.D.	236	—William	183	—Thos. Henderson	446	Spring, William	61
—Geo. Washington	340	—William	218	—Thos. Henry	105	Sproule, Edward	495
—Gerard	167	—William	379	—Wm. *MD.*	529	—Henry Masters	193
—HamiltonChas.87,314		—William	477	—Wm.Walton,*MD.*	442	—James	420
—Henry	76	—William	495	Soppitt, Matthew	120	Sprot, John	318
—Henry Bowyer	208	—William Charles	310	Sorell, Fred. Edward	328	Spry, Edward	414
—Henry Brown	463	—William Henry	417	Sotheby, Fred. Edward	344	—George Fred.	444
—Henry Hopewell	349	—William Honey	521	Souter, Richard	495	—James	203
—Harry Fowle	441	—Wm. John James	306	—Thomas George	187	Spurgeon, Christopher	246
—Sir Harry G. W.		—William Lea	201	South, Charles	515	Spurin, John	477
Bt. GCB.	8, 343	—Wm. Robt. B.	49	Southey, Arthur H.	234	Spurrier, John	527
—Henry Pascoe	495	—William Slayter	513	Southwell, Tho. Arthur	147	Spurway, John	80, 375
—Henry Porter	495	Smithett, Albert L. C.	312	Sowerby, T.	105	Squire, Charles Farran	444
—Hugh	54	Smithwick, Robert	518	Spaight, George	190	Squirl, Charles	172
—Hyde Serjison	237	Smyly, Philip	43, 341	—Henry	495	—Frederick	172
—James Berridge	495	Smyth, Chas. M.	190	Spalding, Richd. Carr	412	—William	330
—James Castor	216	—Edward Selby	39, 172	—Warner R.	461, 495	Stabb, Arthur Ewen	208
—James Ramsay	495	—Edw. St. Geo.	237	Spark, John	513	—Henry Sparke	240
—James Webber,		—Edm. Westropp	358	Sparke, John Francis	319	Stace, George Henry	321
CB.	34, 125	—Henry, *CB.*	35, 307	Sparkes, John Barnes	248	—Henry Coope	36
—John	135	—Henry Augustus	374	Sparks, Jas. P. *CB.*	33, 248	—Walter Samuel	401
—John	513	—Hen. Montagu	82, 452	—Mitchell George	44	—William	39, 400
—John Graydon	186	—Henry Shephard	123	—Robert Watson	186	—Wm. Gustavus T.	403
—John Lewis	17	—James	298	Sparrow, Geo. W. P.	283	Stacey, Edwin	495
—Sir John Mark		—James	218	—John	443	Stack, Edward	252
Fred. *KH.*	10, 399	—James Gibbons	250	—John Francis	227	—Fred. Rice	293
—John O. Gowan	140	—James Stewart	290	Sparshott, Edw. Chas.	416	—Thomas Lindsay	195
—John Stuart, *MD.*	441	—John Montresor	192	Spearman, *Sir* Alex-		—Maurice, *CB.*	120
—John Wm. *CB.*	435	—Jno. R. *CB.*	26, 369	ander Young, *Bt.*	527	—Nathaniel M.	18, 363
—John Wm. Sidney		—Robert	298	—Henry Charles	294	—Thomas	295
CB.	42, 362	—Robert Beresford,		— Horace Ralph	330	Stacpoole, Geo. Wm.	212
—John W. Simmons	136	*MD.*	442	Spedding, Carlisle	49	—Hub. C. Z. de	217
—Jones Julian	377	—Robt. Carmichael	107	Speedy, James	107	Stafford, Wm. Magenis	233
—Joseph	186	—Robert Dunkin	533	—James	444	Staines, John Augustus	182
—Joseph Alexander	349	—Thomas	495	—Robert	443	Stainforth, George	495
—Joshua Henry	402	—William	495	—Thos. Beckwith	80, 463	Stalford, J.	157
—Joshua Simmons	28	—William Adam	195	—Tristram, C. S.	315	Standbridge, Chas. H.	416
—Leonard Fleming	495	Smythe, Frederick	452	Speer, Wm. Henry	416	Stammers, Rob. T. F.	192
—Matthew	31, 315	—Joseph C.	272	Speirs, Archibald Alex.	167	Standen, David	436
—Matthew Skinner	258	—Terence W. W.	342	Speke, Chas. Benj. C.	261	Standish, Richard	513
—Michael Edward	452	—Wm. Dumville	444	Spence, Frederick	57, 239	Stanes, Robert	436
—Michael Wm. *CB.*		—Wm. James	40, 372	—James, *CB.*	105	Stanford, Joseph Arthur	341
	31, 131	Snell, Geo. Wm. Fred.	248	—John	369	Stanhope, *Hon. Sir* F.C.	74
—Noborne Gilpin	211	—William	443	—Robert	316	—Philip Spencer	12
—Opie	539	Sneyd, Clement John	221	Spencer, *Hon.* Aug.		Staniforth, John	295
—Opie	135	—Thos. Wm.	130	Almeric, *CB.*	26	Stanley, Chn. Geoffrey	240
—Percy, G. L.	403	Snodgrass, Archibald		—Charles	316	—*Hon.*Cha.Jas.Fox	105
—Peter	495	Campbell	78, 250	—*Hon.* Geo. Aug.	105	—Edward	461
—Philip	160	Snooke, Hargood Thomas		—Richard	533	—*Hon.* Fred. Arthur	160
—PhilipBroke,*MD.*	323		192	—*Hon.*Rob.Chas.H.	36	—Henry Edmund	226
—Ralph	495	Snow, Arthur Henry		—Wm. Francis	261	—*Hon.* John C.	160
—Richard Playne	146	Creswell	337, 358	—William Henry	172	—John	263
—Robert	248	—Edm. Brighouse	414	—William Isaac	213	—St. John	131
—Robert	338	—Walter C. E.	319	Speranza, Joseph	368	Stansfeld, John	170
—Robert	440	—Wm. Roger	436	Sperling, John	495	Stansfield, R. Johnson	248
—Robert	495	Soady, France Jas.	80, 375	Sperrin, John E. Monro	322	— Robert	495
—Robert Callwell	380	Soure, Charles	534	Spicer, William Fred.	105	Stanton, Edward, *CB.*	
—Rob. Carmichael	106	Soest, Ernest	541	Spiller, Augustus	276		53, 402, 404
—Robert George	131	Somers, Henry, *MD.*	441	—George	50	—William	527
—Robert Henry	436	—Richard John	147	Spink, John, *KH.*	10, 172	Staples, Fred. Blair	353
—Robert Murdoch	403	Somerset, Aylmer H.		Splaine, Abraham	51	Stapleton, FrancisGeo.	160
—Seton Lionel	107	T. H.	345	Spofforth, Rob.Jeffersn.	280	—Richard	495
—St. George Alex.	213	—Chas. Bruce H.	341	Spong, Ambrose	50	—William Bull	495
—Thomas, *MD.*	531	—Chas.Henry	34, 302	Spooner, Samuel	107	Stapley, W. B.	464
—Thomas	405	—Edward A. *CB.*	41	—Wm. Henry	265	Stapylton, G.G.C.	82, 340
—Thomas	338	—Fitz Roy, M. H.	401	Spoor, Nichlas. Appleby	231	—Henry Miles	85, 130
—Thomas	86, 452	—*Sir* Henry, *KCB.*		Spottiswood, Andrew	495	—Herman	65, 233
—Thomas	521	*KH.*	9, 231	Spottiswoode, Andrew	34	Stark, Charles	416
—Thomas, *CB.*	56, 328	—Hen.Chas.C.	74, 452	Sprague, JohnHanmer	534	Starke, William	205
—Thomas Charlton	30	—Hen. Geo. Edw.	175	Spratt, Fred. Horne R.	383	Starkey, Thos. Stanton	145

Index. 606

Starr, Edw. Henderson	414	Steward, Edw. A.T. 81,220	Stirling, Walter Geo. 380	Stott, Gibson 331
Statham, Richard	242	——Henry Holden 130	——William 378	Stotherd, Edward Aug. 282
Staunton, Cha. F. MD. 533		——Richard Oliver Fra.78	——William 416	——Richard Hugh 402
——George 31, 354		——William Alfred 234	Stisted, Henry Wil-	——Richard John
Staveley, Arthur Wm. 258		Stewart, Alexander 464	liam, CB. 31, 332	33, 399
——Charles Wm.Dun-		——Hon. Alexander 380	——Thomas H. 86, 142	Stourton, Hon. Everd. 144
bar, CB. 39, 258		——Alexander, MD. 529	Stobart, Henry 495	Stovin, Sir Fred. KCB.
——Edmund 379		——Alex. Charles 127	Stock, John Cassidy 55	KCMG. 7, 318
Staveley-Shirt, John 495		——Alex. Frederick 141	Stockenstrom, Sir An-	Stow, Harry 31
Stawell, William 495		——Alexander Fred. 246	drew, Bart. 477	Stracey, John Edw. 105
——Jonas 465		——Algernon, Aug. 379	Stocker, Ives 75	——Hardinge Rich. 246
Stayner, Thos. Allen 527		——Andrew 319	——Maurice E. Covey 377	——Henry Hardinge
Steade, Charles 496		——Archibald 439	Stockley, George Watts 403	Denne 167
Stebbing,Fred.Andrsn 117		——Arthur, MD. 529	——John S. 383	Strachan, Henry Aug. 54
Steed, Edward Henry 539		——Charles Edward 233	——William 539	——James 240
Steel, Charles 154		——Daniel Shaw 147	Stocks, Michael 82, 136	——W. H. P. Fitz M. 349
——Charles 148		——David 353	Stockwell, Charles M. 302	Strafford, John, Earl of,
——Chas. Dean 420		——Donald 105	——Clifton de N. Orr 193	GCB. GCH. 5, 163, 463
——Joseph 521		——Duncan 322	——John W. Inglis 335	Straghan, Abel 304
——Sir Scudamore		——Duncan 463	——William 443	——John 417
Winde, KCB. 120		——Duncan 477	Stoddard,Thomas Hen.212	Strahan, George C. 380
Steele, Alexander 521		——Edward Harding 403	Stoddart, George Ste-	——William 380
——Arthur Charles 495		——Fran. Archibald 353	phen Le Grice 134	Straith, Hector 107
——AugustusFred.64,145		——George Gilbert 169	——John Herbert R. 185	Strannghan,Dav.MD. 443
——Edward, CB. 60, 318		——Geo. Mackenzie 120	Stoeber, Jean Nepo. 544	Strange, Alexander 202
——Matthew Fred. 453		——Hopton Scott 195	Stokes, Alfred 248	——Charles 477
——Thomas Montagu		——Hugh 250	——Charles Patrick 177	——Charles John 78, 374
CB. 32, 125, 163		——James 153	——Edward John 250	——Henry Francis,
Steer, Charles Boyes 169		——James 228	——G. 464	CB. 53, 373
Steevens, Charles 105		——James 277	——Henry 216	——Henry Francis 37
——Nathaniel 79		——James 440	——Hen. Bowles Geo. 263	——James Douglas 379
Steffen, Augustus 543		——James Affleck 147	——John 80, 401	——Thomas Bland 377
Stehelin, Benj. S. 35, 399		——James Ainslie 413	——John Day 120	——Thomas George 293
——Edward Logan 334		——James Drummond 302	——Oliver Huldam 408	Strangways, Walter A.
——George Ffrench 282		——John Edmonds-	——Oliver Robert 375	Fox 377
——William Francis 295		toune, MD. 444	——Patrick Day 81, 453	Stransham, Anth. Blax-
Steiger, Albert 544		——John Edmonstone 533	——Rich. William 172	land 36, 411
Stephen, FitzRoy 344		——John Campbell 302	——Robert Barot 273	Stratford, Bryan 206
Stephens,A.Haggrstn. 343		——John Hamilton 18	——Robert Yallop 187	——James Campbell 173
——Edmund 404		——John Henry 413	——William John 75	——Robert 269
——Henry Sykes 32		——John Lorn 137	Stolzenberg, Ferd. Von 541	Straton, Francis 120
——John 521		——Ludovic Charles 441	——Theodor Von 541	——James Murray 263
——Wm. St. Leger 148		——Mervyn 495	Stone, Cecil Percival 308	Stratton, John H. 380
Stephenson, Fred.Chas.		——Mervyn 478	——Charles John 245	——Robert 531
Arthur, CB. 49, 166		——Neil Henry, MD. 340	——Edw. Wm. MD. 440	——Wm. Albert 60, 182
——George Alex. 533		——Peter Desbrisay 105	——Robt. Warner 157	Straubenzee, B. Van 190
——John 359		——Hon. Rand. Hen. 255	——Wm. Harry 178	——Charles 477
——Sussex Vane 167		——Richard Warren 404	Stoney, Andrew Acres 334	——Sir Charles T.
——William Walter 107		——Robert 312	——Francis Sadlier 380	Van, KCB. 18
Stepney, Arth. St. Geo.		——Robert 121	——George Butler 82, 453	——Fred. Van 86, 200
H., CB. 42, 163		——Robert Crosse 84,245	——Henry Butler 252	——Turner, Van 379
Sterling, Ant. C. CB. 38		——Robert John 352	——Richard Butler 380	Streatfeild, CharlesOgle 11
Steuart, Charles 31, 151		——William, MD. 443	——Robert Fannin 272	——Henry C. 29
——David 243		——William 175	Stoodley, Frederick 153	——Robert Champion 229
——Ramsay 334		——William 313	Stopford, George Mon-	Street, George 207
——Robt. Dalrymple 142		——William 417	tagu 85, 462	——Jas. Petrie, MD. 288
——William Ramsay 385		——William 103	——Henry Edward 246	——John Alf.CB. 42, 361
Stevens, John Harvey 13		——William 107	——John George 144	Streets, James 306
——S. J. CB. 463		——W. A. 465	——Walter James 270	Stretton,SeverusW. L. 105
——Thomas 13		——W. G. Drummond 86	Storer, Arthur Tillard 403	Stribling, Francis 240
——William 515		——Wm. Kipp. MD. 444	Storey, Edward James 294	Strickland, Edward 435
——William 527		——William Little 74,362	——George Robt. 323	——George 263
Stevenson, Chn. Henry 213		Stickney, Thomas 527	——John 346	——Walter Cecil 294
——Edward R. 107		Stiles, Bradford 252	——Robert 444	Stronach, William 495
——George Milne 105		Still, Nathaniel Tyron 477	Storks, Sir Henry	Strong,ClementW.49, 163
——Nathaniel 170		——Thomas Lloyd 378	Knight, KCB. 30	——Henry Harford 417
——Thomas 105		——Thomas Walter 129	——Henry N. Reeve 279	——Justinian Henry 337
——G. R. Thackery 379		Stillman, James 182	Storren, Frederick de 542	——Owen H. 192
——Henry Holford 84,312		Stirke, Julius Henry 197	Story, Charles William 229	Stroud,HenryWallace 340
——John 273		——Romain, Fleming 298	——Forbes Lugard 341	Strother, Anthony 138
——Montagu Dickin 237		——Wm. Reynolds 381	——Philip Conway 232	Strover, Henry 376
——William 266		Stirling, Charles Edw. 377	——Philip Fra. CB. 120	Stuart,Hon.Arch.Geo. 477
Steward, Christian B. 314		——Henry Luxmoore 418	——Robert Wm. 30	——Arthur John 414
——Eaton Stan. 283		——John Stirling 377	——Val. Fred. 78, 452	——Charles 26

607 Index.

Stuart, Charles Geo. 496	Suttie, Sir G. G. Bart. 496	Tanffe, George 169	Taylor, John 522
——Donald 107	——George Grant 175	Taberger, John, MD. 504	——John Barton 356
——Dudley Villiers 269	Sutton, Charles 180	Tabor, Charles Clifton 206	——John Robert, CB. 439
——Edward Andrew 169	——John 107	Tabuteau, Anth. O. 332	——John William 291
——George 28	——William 30, 239	Taddy, Edward 80, 376	——Joseph Henry 496
——George Evans 496	——Wm. Griffin 81, 359	——Augustus 293	——Joseph Marmadke. 384
——Hen. J.R. Villiers 296	Swaffield, Cha. J.O.85, 329	Tait, Greville Ewing 444	——Markham Le Fer 377
——Hugh Lindsay 533	——Robert Hassall 513	——T. Forsyth, CB. 125	——Monkhouse G. 360
——Hon. James 76, 343	Swain, Charles 436	Talbot, Fitzroy S. 379	——Nathaniel 436
——James 43, 453	——Charles 527	——George 39, 257	——Nathaniel 496
——James Fred. Dudley Crichton 52, 159	——Henry Thomas 496	——Henry Chas. 257	——Phillpotts Wright 103
	Swaine, Joseph 522	——John 307	——Pringle, KH. 15
——J. Glass Gordon 357	——Leopold Victor 345	——John Shrews 293	——Raynsford 247
——Hon. John 477	Swale, Henry 415	——Henry Lynch 84, 376	——Richard 522
——John 201	Swan, Fred. Geo. 436	——Hervey 213	——Richard Chambre
——John Patrick 453	——Graves Chamney 33	——Hon. R. A. J. 126	Hays, CB. 41, 312
——John R. CB. 39, 220	——Wm. Geo., MD. 208	——Robert .64, 373	——Rob. Kirkpatrick 321
——John Richardson 215	Swann, John Sackville 273	——William 496	——Thomas Matthew 120
——Peter 463, 496	Swanson, Henry 310	——Hon. Wm. Leopold 86	——William 414
——Robert 540	——Thomas 496	Tallan, Lawrence 477	——William 107
——Robt. Chas. Wm. 172	Sweeney, Francis B. 513	Tane, T. Jas, Waldgrave 496	——William 120
——Rob. Thomson 496	——James Fielding 197	Tanner, Albert 302	——Wm. O'Bryen 212
——Selkirk 446	Sweeny, John 386	——Edward 187	——Wm. Ryves Nash 477
——Thos. Evans 338	——Richard Thomas 318	——Kearns Deane 341	Taylour, Lord John H. 321
——William 516	Sweeting, George 496	——Thomas 177	Teale, Cha. Shipley 74, 452
——William 496	Sweny, George Aug. 178	——William 384	——Emanuel 170
——William Edington 152	——John Alfred 418	Tapp, W. H. 464	Tedlie, Edward 245
——William James 402	——John Charles 330	Tarby, J. 306	——James 65
——William Kier 60, 322	Swetenham, George 403	Tardrew, Thomas 127	——William 84, 281
——William Tyler 210	Swettenham, Thos. E. 239	Tarleton, Edw. Delaval 380	Teesdale, Charles P. 195
Stubbs, James Alex. 335	——W. Kilner, MD. 181	——James Hearn 273	——Christo C. CB.82, 377
——John 231	Swift, Benjamin, MD. 337	——Thomas 181	——Henry George 34, 371
Stucley, Wm. Lewis 160	——Richard 315	Tarrant, Thomas 384	Teevan, Alfred 183
Studd, Edward 103	——Richard 534	Tarte, Edmund Fred. 228	——Geo. James 334
Studdert, Ch. Fitz G. 107	——Wm. Alfred 6, 342	——Walter John 187	——Stephenson, MD.531
——George 178	Swinburn, John 28	Tasker, George 540	——Thomas 176
——George 477	Swinburne, James 131	Taswell, Edward 375	——Thos. Stephenson 445
——George Massey 350	——John 212	Tatam, John 383	Tegart, Fred. Thomas 353
——R. A. Fitzgerald 415	——Joseph 32	Tate, Francis Holt 274	Telfer, Buchan Fraser 527
Stumpa, Ignation 544	——John Dennis 318	——George R. MD. 385	——Geo. Home 527
Sturges, Rev. W. S. 455	——Paul 314	——Henry Carr 58, 412	——Jam. Drummond 477
Sturt, Charles Napier 160	——Tho. Rob. 15	——Robert, MD. 444	——John Thomson 440
——Henry Evelyn 417	Swindley, Frederick 148	Tatham, Walter John 382	——John Wm. G. 178
——Napier George 404	——John 359	Tatlock, Thomas 496	Telford, William 516
Stutzer, Jean B. P. 544	——John Edward 141	Tattersall, Geo. B. 107	Tempest, Lord A. F.
Suckling, F. Herbert 356	Swiney, George 120	Tatum, H. 464	C. W. Vane 105
Sulivan, Geo. A.F. 52, 140	Swinfen, Fred. Hay 153	Tayler, Alexander 82, 190	——Arthur Cecil 147
Sullivan, Augustus 349	Swinford, Thos. Fra. 340	——Henry 357	——Tho. Rich. P. 105
——Daniel 316	Swinhoe, Charles 276	——Robert Frederick 415	Temple, Augustus 349
——George 314	——Samuel 120	——Thomas 190	——Edwyn Fred. 274
——John 477	——William Geo. 344	Taylor, Alex. D. MD. 440	——Gustavus Hancock 513
——Thos. Durell 276	Swinny, Geo. Stoney 152	——Amelius 246	——John 105
——William, CB. 27, 369	Swinton, Wm. Murray 418	——Arth. Joseph 36, 371	——William, MB. 385
Summerfield, William 359	Swiny, Shapland Wm. 496	——Brook 28, 125	Templeman, Alfred 220
Summers, John, MD. 441	Swire, Roger 338	——Chauncy Arthur 250	Templeton, Rob. MD. 440
Sunter, T. Moore, MB. 441	Sykes, Aug. Joseph 177	——Duncan C. MD. 270	Tench, Donald Wm.81, 453
Surman, Wm. James 233	——Cam 107	——Duncan Norton 382	Tennant, Aralander 29
——Wm. Henry 356	——Rev. Wm. AM. 455	——Fra. Manby Shawe 477	——George 107
Surplice, Chas. Fred. 263	——William 193	——Francis Richard 477	——James Hett 260
——Rob. Napoleon 228	Sylvester, Hen. T. MD. 227	——George 439	Terrait, Daniel Fox 290
Susini, Joseph 544	Symonds, Jermyn C. 413	——Geo. John Malcm.332	Terrott, Chas. Ellison 290
Suther, Cuthbert C. 417	——William 496	——George Kepple 376	Terry, Astley Fellowes 283
——Melville 415	Symons, Chas. B. 31, 371	——George Lee Le M. 208	——Courtenay Forbes 283
——Wm. Grigor 412	——Cha. Edw. Hood 382	——George Wm. 383	——Fred. Stephen 231
Sutherland, Edward, 107, 123, 465	——George 156	——Graham 272	——Henry 516
	——Jelinger Henry 415	——Rev. H. A. 455	——John 477
——James S. C. 436	——John T. May, MD.385	——Hen. Geo. A. CB. 120	——Robert 29
——John Moira M. 436	Syms, Frederick Geo. 176	——Henry Hartley 180	——Stephen 477
——Robert 229	Synge, Fra. H. 82, 257	——James 477	——William Parker 190
——Robt. Macleod 63, 331	——Geo. Charles 82, 270	——James 414	Teulon, George 103
——Sutherland Hall 496	——Henry 303	——Jeremiah 10, 280	——Thomas 86, 245
——William, CB. 9, 272	——Millington Henry 401	——John 157	Teversham, Mark 208
——William James 107	——Rob. Follett 83, 349	——John 477	Tew, Cyril Blackburne 296
——Wm. John E. G. 258	Syret, James 496	——John 496	——George M'Leod 74

Index. 608

Tewart, John Edward	182
Teynham, G.H.R. *Lord*	513
Thacker, John	290
——William	152
——Wm. Fryer	213
Thackeray, Charles	234
——Fred. R. *CB.*	6, 399
——Fred. Rennell	304
——Joseph	496
Thackwell, Jos. Edwin	54
——Wm.de Wilton R.	248
Tharp, Horace Neville	436
——Wm. Montagu	288
Thellusson, Alx.D.	80, 302
——Arthur J. B.	107
Thelwall, Eubule D.	414
——John B. *CB.*	86, 228
Theobald, Cotton E.	274
——John Medows	288
——John Shadwell	212
Thesiger, *Hon.* Cha. W.	141
——*Hon.* Fred. A.	58, 335
Thiballier, Hubert	496
Thierry, Lewis de	513
Thiselton, Edward	245
Thistlethwayte, A. R.	
Wm.	240
Thobald, George	196
Tholon, Joseph	542
——Louis	544
Thomas, Barclay	86, 233
——Chas. Schomberg	344
——Fran. Arthur	321
——Francis William	415
——Henry	323
——Henry Arthur	418
——Henry John	55
——Henry St. John V.	
Le Marchant	380
——John David Cove	224
——John W.	63, 295
——Jonath. Christian	228
——Joseph H. Watkins	167
——Lloyd Henry	330
——Mark	513
——Morgan	529
——Wm. Hugh	212
——Wm. Jones	130
Thomlinson, Grant	331
Thompson, Alfred R.	436
——Arnold	65, 373
——Benjamin	496
——Charles	291
——Charles Wm.	74, 279
——Charles Wm.	58, 135
——Christopher, *MB.*	446
——Daniel	295, 358
——Edward	477
——Edwin Forbes	417
——*Rev.* F. F.	455
——George	321
——George	221
——George	463
——George Ashe	516
——George Irwin	337
——Geo. William	169
——H. Masterman	190
——Henry	215
——James	386
——James	444
——James	477
——James	527
——John	172
——John	242

Thompson, John	267
——John	359
——John	496
——John	534
——John Alexander	
William, *MD.*	314
——John Baylis	383
——John Wycliffe	77, 359
——Joseph John	353
——Justus Henry	436
——Leslie Jenkins	279
——Michael	299
——Pearson Scott	83, 151
——Ralph Keddey	496
——Richard	182
——Richard	76
——Richard	77
——Robert	272
——Robert	338
——Robert Thomas	276
——Thomas	215
——Thomas	519
——Thos. Hinde	310
——Thomas James	496
——Thos. Perronet	11
——Waldegrave Rock,	
MD.	442
——William	156
——William	337
——W. Dalrymple	210
——William Hamilton	280
——Wyndham A. R.	277
Thomsett, Rich. G.	258
Thomson, Alex. *MD.*	444
——Alex. Dingwall	207
——Arth. Sndrs. *MD.*	441
——Charles Alex.	273
——Colin Hugh	304
——Fran. Ringler	14
——George, *CB.*	453
——George	295
——George	513
——Geo. Latham	57, 177
——Henry	120
——Henry Geo.	170
——James	302
——James	358
——James Sinclair	272
——Joseph	496
——James Crooke	516
——R. Cunningham	172
——Robt. Thomas	107
——Sinclair William	427
——William	310
——William	349
——William	522
——Wm. Arthur, *MB.*	442
——Wm. Seaman	312
Thonger, Richard F.	145
Thorburn, William	221
——Wm. Stewart	170
Thoren, Oscar Wm. de	328
Thorndike, Daniel	31, 371
Thorne, George	349
Thornett, Thos. B.	356
Thornhill, Charles	380
——Henry	377
——Thomas A. *MB.*	142
Thornton, Cha. Edm.	185
——Edmund	452
——Geo. Stanislaus	296
——John	496
——Robert	442
——William	103

Thorold, Frederic	496
——George Edw.	39
——John Henry	211
——Reginald Gother	403
Thorp, Edward B.	83, 326
——John	516
——Robert	340
Thorpe, Robert Lestock	298
——Robert	121
Thring, John E.	84, 375
Throckmorton, Rich.	323
Thunder, Michael	221
Thurlow, Edw. Hovell	380
Thursby, James Legh	223
——Piers	145
——Ralph Lovel	354
——Richard Hasel	164
Thurston, H.N. Cotton	286
Thwaites, George S.	11
Thwaytes, William	180
Thynne, Alfred Walter	160
——*Lord* William	105
——Wm. Frederick	315
Tibbetts, William Edw.	239
Tibbits, James William	423
Tibbs, William Joseph	196
Tibeaudo, Anselm	185
Tice, John Charles	
Graham, *MD. CB.*	439
Tidy, Thos. Holmes	36
Tierney, *Sir* Matt. Edw.	
Bt.	105
Tighe, Daniel	496
——James Lowry	533
——John Aug.	279
——Michael Joseph	353
Tilford, Matthew	282
Tillbrook, Philip L.	267
Tilghman, Rich. M.	206
Tilly, Guavas Speedw.	401
——John	226
Timbrell, *Rev.* John	539
——Sydney James	516
——Thos. Richardson	516
Tingcombe, John Macl.	330
Tinley, Robert N.	41, 251
——Wm. Newport	250
Tinling, Chas. Hugh L.	74
——Geo. Vaughan	75
——Widdrington	436
——Wm. Pattison	64, 328
Tinmouth, Wingrove L.	415
Tinseau, Art. Leon de	544
Tippetts, Alfred M.	443
Tipping, Alfred	59, 159
Tireman, Henry Stephen	76
Tisdall, Archibald	245
——Charles Arthur	155
——James	496
——John Knox	403
——William St. Clair	205
Titterton, Henry	443
Tittle, John Moore	477
Tobin, John	477
——John	534
——John Richard	246
——Joseph Webbe	7, 370
Toby, Isaac	420
Tod, Edw. Henry M.	252
——Robt. Alex. B.	334
——Robt. Mercer	257
Todd, George	103
——Hen. Arthur Grey	177
——Jas. Arch. R.	323

Todd, John Aug.	151
——Mark Stanley	233
——Richard Cooper	341
——Suetonius Henry	120
——William	513
——William Egerton	315
Toke, John Leslie	337
Toker, Arth. Branth.	293
Tolcher, Christopher	496
——Henry John	276
Tollemache, Anastasius	
Eugene	224
Toller, Hugh Montil	196
Tollner, Wm. Michael	380
Tom, Wm. Hen. Vllck.	417
Tomes, John	527
Tomkinson, Edw.	77, 359
Tomkyns, George	120
Tompson, Hen. Steuart	269
Tongue, John Moore G.	28
——Vincent	281
Tonnochy, Augustus	144
——Valens	315
Toogood, Seymour H.	382
Toole, William	105
Topham, Richard	142
——*Sir* William	123
Topp, Henry	266
Toppin, James Morris	180
Topping, Henry	464
Torkington, Henry T.	496
Torrens, Alfred	294
——Hen. D'Oyley	64, 226
——Robt. Henry	130
Torriano, Chas. Edw.	377
——C. Strangways	477
Toseland, Edward	252
Tothill, John Henry H.	213
Tottenham, Arthur L.	344
——Charles George	166
——Frederick	233
——Julius	283
——Robert Loftus	378
Touch, Edward, *MD.*	261
Tour, Augustus de la	496
Touzel, Helier	6
——Tho. Percival	105
Tovey, Alexander	516
——Alex. Cha. H.	299
——Hamilton	404
——James Tennant	228
Tower, Conyers	131
——Francis	463
——Harvey	163
Towers, Thomas John	150
Town, Edward	496
Townley, Dawson	279
——Richard	340
——William	157
Townsend, Horace	341
——Christ. Wm.	381
——John	496
——Joseph	496
——Robert Lawrence	496
——T.	465
Townshend, Edward	261
——Hen. Dive	15
——Lee Porcher	107
——Thomas Henry	169
Tracey, Harry Adair	380
——Maurice	264
Tracy, *Hon.* S.C.G.H.	160
Trafford, Henry T.	257
Tragett, Thomas H.	277

Traherne, Anthony P. 210	Trotman, Geo. Hewitt 283	Tupper, Gasp. Le M.	Twyford, Albert Fred. 173
——Llewellyn Edm. 282	——P. P. 465	77, 375	——Henry Robert 246
Traill, John Murray 382	Trotter, Frederick 250	——James De Vic 226	——John 496
——Robert Gayer 216	——John Frederick 195	Turbervill, Gervas, KH.105	——William Jolliffe 226
Tranchell, Edw. Fred. 353	——John William 164	Turle, Wm. Greer 282	Twynam, Geddes S. 200
——Geo. Adolphus 353	——Robert Knox 105	Turnbull, Edward 436	——Philip Alex. A. 205
Trant, William 496	Troubridge, *Sir* T. St.	——Gavin Ainslie 148	Twyning, Wm. Edw. 213
Travers, Augustus W. 133	Vincent H.C.*Bt*. 36, 125	——John Robertsn.83, 200	Twysden, Edm. F. 274
——Francis Stewart 282	Troup, John Igglesden 181	——Wm. George 513	Tyacke, Thomas 223
——Fred. John 83, 373	——Robert Hon. W. 245	Turner, Alex. Wm. 436	Tydd, Benjamin 442
——Horace 436	Trousdell, W. G.*MD*.201	——Arthur St. Geo. 234	——Thomas 85, 307
——James 65, 352	Trower, Horace 152	——Arthur William 276	Tylden, John 32
——James Conway 415	Troy, Thomas 522	——Augustus Fred. 443	——*Sir* John Maxwell 105
——James Dalgairns 210	Troyer, Anthony 477	——Chas. Henry B. 295	Tylee, Alfred 36
——James Fra. Eaton 374	Truell, Robert Holt 272	——Edmund P. B. 377	Tyler, Charles 123
——John 57, 373	Trueman, C. Hamilton 240	——Francis Charles 250	——Charles James 377
——John Moore Clarke 210	Truscott, John 120	——Frederick Henry 103	——Cha. John Roper 175
——Joseph Oates 210	Trydell, Botet 17	——George 223	——Edw. James 180
——Joseph Oates 61, 412	——John Frederick 223	——George, CB. 9, 370	——Edw. Saumorez 403
——Joseph Oates 496	Tryon, John 250	——George Henry 267	——George Henry 64,200
——Julius Brockman 361	——Richard 344	——Henry 167	——Henry 522
——Lyon Conway 496	——Samuel 33	——Henry 299	——Henry Whatley 401
——Oates Joseph 299	——Thomas 81, 185	——Henry Ainslie A. 418	——Roper Dacre 196
——Richard Henry 228	Tubby, James Hardy 436	——Henry Austin 39, 372	——Trevor Bruce 382
——Wm. Hen. T. C. 151	Tucker, Aubrey H. 296	——Henry Ferdinand 293	——Wm. Robertson 205
——William Steward 344	——Charles 223	——Henry Fyers 404	Tyner, Charles 237
Treacher, Hen. Carver 328	——Heber Reeve 172	——Henry Scott 298	Tyrwhitt, Charles 31, 125
Treatrail, W. Michael 444	——Jervis 378	——Herbert 128	Uffington, Wm. Aug.
Trebeck, Thomas 496	——Martin 216	——James 76	Fred. *Visc*. 160
Tredcroft, Chas. L. 377	——Rich. Franklin 497	——James Alfred 443	Underwood, William 255
Treeve, Hen. Richard 285	——Thomas John 193	——James Graham 234	Unett, Henry Henzell 138
Trefusis,*Hon*.Rodolph 167	——Walter Sydney 150	——James Trench 303	——John 138
Tremenheere, G.H.W. 193	——William C. *MD*. 446	——John 267	——Walter 37, 138
Tremayne, Arthur 77, 150	——Wm. J. A. 446	——John, CB. 57, 373	Unger, William 543
Tremlett, Edmund J. 379	Tudor, Charles 496	——Michael 107	Uniacke, Charles Hill 137
Trench, Charles 380	——Frederick 51	——N.Oct.Simpsn.64,375	——Henry Turner 215
——*Hon*. F. Le Poer 190	——Henry 496	——Philip 435	——Norman Fitzgerald 282
——Power Le Poer 105	——Wm. Langley 36	——Robert 443	——Redmond 435
——Power D. Le Poer 379	——William Rapp 264	——Thomas 232	——Richard 7
——*Hon*.Wm.LePoer 403	Tuffnell, Arthur Jol-	——Thomas 496	Unsworth, *Rev*. T. 455
——W. Fitz J. LePoer 274	liffe 286	——Thos. M. 134	Unwin, Robert 182
Trenchard, Henry M. 269	——Arthur 282	——William 463	——William 217
Trenor, John 233	——Thos. Joliffe 443	——William 533	Upton, *Hon*. Arthur 13
Trent, Francis C. 264	——Vincent Fred. 380	——William Ross 175	——Edward James 302
——Geo. Edm. Phipps 232	Tugginer, Edmund de 544	——Wm. W. CB. 43, 338	——*Hon*.Geo.Fred.CB.16
——Harrison Walke J. 296	——Edward de 544	——Young 496	——Roger Dawson 145
——John 242	Tuite, Hugh Manley 18	Turnor, Christopher H. 345	——Urquhart,Cha. J. 293
Trevelyan, H. A. 86, 147	——Thomas Basil 195	——George 172	——Donald 496
——Jas. Harington 105	Tuke, Alfred John 291	——William 13	——Fra. Gregor 53, 169
Trevilian, John R. 176	Tullibardine, John J.	——William Weston 296	——John 233
Trevor, Ar. Hill, KH. 17	H. H. *Marq. of*, 167	Turton, Francis A. 444	——William Henry 306
——Edward 43, 452	Tulloch, Alex. CB. 120	——Robert Straker 350	——William Henry 321
——Fred. Anthony 177	——Alex. Bruce 170	Tuson, Edward Baily 442	Usher, Cha. Loftus T. 414
——John William 223	——*Sir* Alex. Murray,	——Henry Brasnell 415	——Edward Price 413
——William C. 80, 202	KCB. 18, 452	Tuyll, *Sir* Wm. KCH. 6,142	——William 534
——Wm. Gordon 314	——Jas. D. G. 52, 453	Tweddell, Fenwick M. 533	Usherwood, Charles 216
Trew, Thomas Eggar 527	——Jas.G. McDonald 220	Tweeddale, G. *Marq*.	Ussher, Edw. Pellew H. 80
Tribe, C. C. B. 216	——James T. *MD*. 444	*of*, KT. CB. 6, 237	——John 105
——Henry John 413	——John, CB, 120	Tweedie, Maurice 120	——John Theophilus 323
Trick, Thomas 516	——John 193	——Michael 378	Utterson, Arch. H. 210
Trigge, Alfred 294	——John Henry 227	——Michael 477	Utterton, Edwin 226
Trimen, Richard 245	——Thomas 103	Twemlow, George 121	Vacher,Fred.Smith 81,242
Trimmer,Augustus R. 258	Tulloh, Alexander 33, 371	——Geo. Hamilton 207	Valiant, Thomas Jas. 16
Tripp, John Henry 307	Tully, Ringrose Drew 418	——Walter Hamilton 233	Vallance,Thomas Wm. 140
Triscott, Wm. Robert 418	Tunbridge, John 464	Twentyman,Aug.Cha.177	Vallancey, Richard 496
Tristram, Barrington 496	Tunks, Thomas 296	——W. Lawrence 129	Vallange, Wm., *MD*. 533
Trittau, Edward 541	Tunstall, Gabriel 496	Twibill, James 248	Valpy, De Vic 326
Tritton,Edmund Spry 331	——William 496	Twigge, John Thomas 403	Vance, Horatio P. 84, 248
——Fred. Biscoe 84, 360	Tupman, George Lyon 416	Twining, George 436	Van Cortlandt, H. C. 105
Trocke, William 245	Tupper, Basil de B. 381	——*Rev*. J. T. *DD*. 455	——Henry Chas. *CB*. 102
Trollope, Charles, *CB*. 28	——Daniel Wm. 79, 267	——Rich. Radcliffe 242	Vandeleur, Arthur 81, 375
——*Right Hon. Sir*	——De Vic 187	Twiss, Arthur Wm. 375	——Boyle 140
John, *Bt*. 496	——Æmilius De Vic 378	——John 35, 399	——Crofton Toler 146
Tronson, Edward T. 29	——Frederic William 288	Twopeny, Edward 105	——David Roche 148

Index. 610

Vandeleur, Edward 130
——Hector Stewart 344
——John 103
——John Ormsby 245
——John Ormsby 345
——Robert 105
——Thomas Burton 185
——Wm. Richard 264
Vander Meulen, C. J. 105
——John H. 267
Vanderkiste, William 319
Vanderspar, W. C. 85, 353
Vane, Charles Birch 107
——Fred.Fletcher 83, 226
Van Homrigh, A. P. 173
Vanrenen, Edward 354
Vansittart, Francis 477
——Robert 105
Vardon, NoelHovenden Bryan 200
——Stafford Willard 340
Varley, William 135
Varlo, George 477
——Henry 477
Vassall, RawdonJ.Pop. 83
Vaughan, Hon. E. C. 345
——Edward Percival 234
——Ernest Courtenay 377
——Eugene James 64
——George Augustus 242
——Hect. Barlow 217
——Herbert 105
——Herbert Henry 477
——Jas. H. Bourdieu 148
——James Edward 344
——Louis Rich. G. 224
Vaughton, Theophilus 414
Vavasour, Mervin 477
Veale,H.R.Lobb,MD.384
Veitch, Thomas Geo. 477
——William 513
——Venables, C. 304
——Robt. MD. 534
——Thomas 338
Venour, William 261
Ventry, T.T.A. Lord 477
Vereker, Henry 496
——Hon.Adolph.E.P. 217
——Henry Thomas 496
——Hon. R. P. 282
——Thomas George 197
Verey, Charles 175
Vernede, Hen. T. 202
Verner, Edw. D. 534
——John Donovan 477
——Sir William, Bt. 105
Verney,SirHarry, Bt. 107
Vernon, Bowater Hen. 477
——Charles A. 218
——Geo. Aug. 105
——Henry Arthur 374
——Hen.Cha.Edw.CB. 7
——John Russell 496
——Leicester V. S. 477
Vernor, Robert 324
Verschoyle,HenryWm.160
——James Lorenzo 294
Versturme, Adph. H. 169
Vesey,Arthur Geo.61,261
——Charles C. W. 302
——George Francis 215
——George Henry 374
——George Waller 224
——John 496

Vetch, James 477
——Rob. Hamilton 404
Vialls, Geo. C. 80, 335
——Henry Thomas 107
——Otho 131
Vibart, Hen. C. 190
——Jas. Meredith C. 377
Vicars, Edward 31
——Edw. Rich. Fox 296
——Hy. Geo. Austin 212
——Robert Shafto 33
——Wm. Henry 103
——Victor, James C. 13
Vieth, Fred. Harris D. 290
——Russell Harris 205
——Fred. Wm. 496
Vigors, Hen. Rudkin 192
——HoratioNelson18,357
——Joshua Allen 42
——Philip Doyne 215
Ville, Ferdinand, Comte de la 544
Villiers,Charles C.78, 263
——Edw.Wildman B. 180
——Ernest 257
——James 52, 304
Vincent, Arthur Hare 135
——Edw. Marwood 298
——John 307
——Thomas 105
Virtu, Georgio 368
——John 455
Virtue, John 455
Vivian, Chas. C. Lord 107
——ErnestHenryPaul 231
——Geo. Majenble 417
——Harry H. Palmer 223
——John Augustus 176
——Richard Hussey 202
——R. 465
——Sir Robt. John ·
Hussey, KCB. 120
Vokes, Thomas 477
Voss, Ernest Von 541
——Howell Walters 384
Voules, Wm. James 291
Vousden, Thomas 360
Vowell, John Hooker 323
Vyner, Robt. Cha. de Grey 160
——William 383
Vyse, Edward 242
——Edward Howard 138
——George H. 59, 127
——Rich.Hen. Rich.
Howard 36, 128
Vyvyan, R. H. S. 123
Waddell-Boyd,Jas.85, 452
——William 522
Waddilove, Grainville 263
Waddington, Rich. P. 380
Waddy, Rich. CB. 35,267
Wade, Fred. William 284
——George 496
——Hamlet Coote, CB. 42
——James Herne 84, 328
——Mark Farley 234
——Thomas 513
——Walter Overbeck 330
——William Barton 232
Wadeson, Richard 306
Wadling, John C. 181
Wadman, Arthur Jas.
Phillips 129

Wahab, Charles 121
——Geo. Duncan 218
——Henry John 334
Wahrendorff, Aug. 541
Wake, Richard Wm. 477
Wakefield,HenryFurey 52
——Julian 318
——William 522
Walbridge, Hen. Wm. 496
Walcott,ChasEdm. 79, 376
Waldron, Fred. Wm. 435
——H. K. Johnstone 239
Waldy, Alfred Henry 261
——Edw.Garmonsway 307
——William Thomas 261
Wale, David 129
WALES, His Royal Highness ALBERT-EDWARD, Prince of, KG. 43
Walkem, John Walter 267
Walker, Albert L. 341
——Alexander 248
——Alexander 220
——Alexander 496
——Andrew George 243
——Andrew Murray 353
——Arthur 312
——Charles P. B. 55, 130
——Daniel Corrie 404
——Edwyn 152
——Edward 221
——Edw. James 380
——Edward Walter Forestier, CB. 26, 166
——Fitz William 62, 356
——George 240
——Geo. Alb. Aug. 378
——Geo. E. L. 402
——Geo. Frederick 415
——Geo. Fuller 223
——Henry 444
——Henry George 236
——HenryTorrens 87,231
——Hercules 80, 343
——James 496
——John 294
——John 464
——John Geddes 35
——Mark 81, 175
——Melville Aug. 310
——R. A. T. 464
——Samuel 107
——Samuel Cooper 340
——Smeeton 269
——Thomas 283
——William 127
——William 478
——Wm. Francis 377
Wall, George Parsons 291
——Michael 522
——Richard 496
——Thomas Frederick 248
Wallace, Alexander 484
——Cha. Jas. Stewart 231
——Chas. Tennant 294
——Hamilton John 198
——HenryRitchie302,331
——Hugh Ritchie 496
——SirJas. M., KH. 9,154
——John 334
——NesbitWilloughby283
——Peter M. 9, 370
——Robert, KH. 103

Wallace, Wm, MD. 533
——Wm. Edward 360
——Sir Wm. Thomas Francis A. Bt. 65, 160
Waller, Charles 374
——Edmund 185
——George Henry 185
——Jas.W.Samo,KH. 107
——Kilner 496
——Walter De Warrenne 277
——William Noel 377
Wallington,Chas. A.G.120
——J. C. 105
Wallis, Alex. Bruce 242
——Brown 342
——Samuel 522
——Wm. Beale 384
Walpole, Horatio 180
——Horatio 103
——John 35, 399
——Sir Robert, KCB. 29, 343
Walrond,CharlesWills 379
Walsh,Adolphus Fred. 288
——Arth. Huntly Hill 416
——Arth. Sandys Stawell 56, 411
——Charles Hussey 258
——Rev. E. L. 455
——Fred. Henry 310
——George 513
——John 156
——John 444
——John 478
——Lawrence de C. 496
——Lewis Edward 75
——Lewis Paxton 379
——Thomas 221
——Thomas 326
——Thomas 522
——William 340
——William 522
Walshe, Blayney T. 152
——Holwell Hely H. 350
——Hugh Crawford, MD. 384
Walter,FrederickArth. 272
——John M'Neill, CB. 57, 245
——Walter Philip 240
——Wm. Sanders 255
Walters, Fra.Dalrymp. 258
Walther, William 542
Walton, Bendyshe 83, 248
——Francis 414
——Wm. Morritt B. 380
——Wm. Lovelace 9, 180
Walwyn, Jas. Harford 226
Warburton, Aug. Fred.205
——Fred. Tynte 404
——Hen. Wm. Egerton 107, 465
——Robert Sandford 175
——Wm. White 50
Ward, Bernard Ed. 78,281
——Hon. Bernard Mathew 360
——Charles 253
——Edw. Cuthbert 206
——Edward John 378
——Edward L. 436
——Edward Wolstenholme 401

Index

Ward, Ellis Houlton 234
— Fra. Beckford 78, 373
— Henderson 478
— Henry 496
— James 51
— John 105
— John 522
— John 498
— John Rich. CB. 103
— John Richard 533
— Joseph 341
— Lambert Houlton 321
— *Hon.* Somerset Richard Hamilton 362
— William 478
— William Crofton 255
— Wm.Cuthbert 16, 399
— William Pearson 211
— William S. 223
Warde, Edward Charles, CB. 35, 371
— Francis 29, 371
— George 269
— J. Henry T. 462, 478
— Walter 74, 452
Wardell, Charles 516
— Geo. Wm. Henry 318
— George Vaughan 229
— John 496
— William Henry 379
— William Henry 516
Warden, Geo. Archib. 216
— Robert 54, 215
Wardlaw, Robert 38, 136
Wardrop, James John Majoribanks 161
Ware, George Hen. H. 269
— Robert 516
Waring, Edward 496
— Francis Robert 440
— Henry 172
— Henry 107
— Holt 324
— Lucas 228
— Samuel 288
Warlow, Thomas P. 375
Warne, John Cordeiro 228
Warner, Ashton Henry 253
— Richard 478
— W. Hucks Hard. 250
Warre, Henry J. CB. 39, 277
Warren, Arthur Frederick 79, 343
— Augustus Edmd. 310
— Aug. Rivers. 87, 217
— Charles, CB. 17
— Charles 233
— Dawson Stockley 202
— Falkland G. E. 378
— George 120
— George 404
— Henry Edward 281
— Jas. Low, MD. 533
— John 197
— John 300
— Lionel Smith 293
— Richard 402
— Robert 201
— Thos. Monsell 303
— William 107
— Wm. Henry 315
Warry, Edward Taylor 380
— William 79, 361

Wastie, William 182
Waterfall, John Henry 335
Waters, Edm. Fred. CB. 120
— Geo. Chas. Henry 281
— Marcus Antonius 308
— Marcus Antonius 13
— Thomas 75
— Wm. Henry 540
Watkins, Charles 223
— Westrop 120
— William Nowell 478
Watling, Cha. Wynt 444
Watson, Albert 105
— Alexander 243
— Andrew 496
— Andrew Vincent 478
— Atherton 513
— Cha. Edward 79, 185
— David 57, 316
— Frederic 196
— George 294
— George 304
— George 420
— George 497
— George Lewis 126
— Geo. Stretton 324
— Henry Charles 263
— Henry Edward 353
— Sir Jas. KCB. G, 202
— James 36
— James 444
— Jas. Kiero 282
— James Long 231
— John 37
— J. 157
— Musgrave 185
— Robert 330
— Robert 77
— Rupert Campbell 353
— Stephen 202
— Thos. Brereton 497
— Thos. Charles 203
— William 105
— William 361
— William Henry 378
— Wm. James 188
— *Sir* William Hy. 497
— Watt, Fitzjames Edw. 435
— James Duff 527
— James Landon 276
— William Godfrey 152
Watts, David John 513
— Joseph 299
— William Hill 321
— Wm. Newcomen 169
Wauch, David 497
Wauchope, Wm. John 153
Waugh, George 191
— Geo. Rowland 277
— William Petrie 105
Wavell, Arthur Henry 253
Way, Gregory Lewis 107
— Nowell Fitz Upton 417
Waymouth, Charles 154
— Samuel 32
Wayne, Herman 192
Weare, Henry Edwin 56, 267
Wearing, Thomas 9, 411
Weatherley, Fre. Aug. 134
Weaver, Edw. Francis 140
Webb, Chas. Hamilton 243
— Daniel Poploe 132

Webb, Edw.W.Henry 279
— Fran. Edw. 234
— George 413
— George Joseph 436
— Henry 78
— Henry Joseph 195
— Henry M. MB. 335
— John 138
— John Vere W. H. 187
— Randolph 384
— Robert 75
— Steph. M. MD. 246
— Theodosius 478
— Vere 441
— Vere 107
— William Henry 279
— Wm. Marshall 443
Webber, Chas. Edm. 403
— Fred, Wm. Swann 260
— Geo. Daniel 210
— Horace Hervey 380
— Wm. Geo. E. 255
Webster, Charles H. 218
— G. Murray, MD. 441
— George 129
— Guy 129
— Hen. Fra. Geo. 217
— James Carnegie 105
— Joseph 310
— Peter Chas. G. 144
— Richard 352
— Robert 181
— Robert 522
— Rowland 302
— Rowland Burdon 380
— William 522
— William 89
— William Francis 453
Wedderburn, H. S. 210
Wedderburne, George 185
Wedgwood, John D. 286
— Thomas 105
Weekes, Alfred W. P. 310
Wegg, John 44
Weguelin, T, M, L, 74, 342
Weigall, Hen. Stewart 308
Weir, Archibald 141
— Daniel 315
— John Charles 172
— Thos. C. B. 435
Westropp, M'Mahon 130
— William 497
Welch, Edward 332
— Robt. Preston L. 379
— Stephen J. W. F. 478
— Wm. Davis 417
Welchman, Geo. T. 75
Weld, William Walter 441
Weldon, William H. 155
Wellesley, Wm. H. C. 103
Wellings, George 478
Wellington, Arthur, *Duke of, KG.* 12
Wells, Fortescue 478
— Frederick 79, 169
— Horace Arthur 215
— John 322
— Samuel, CB. 55, 226
— Vincent 382
Welman, H. W. P. 83, 322
— Hercules A. 85, 360
— Wm. Hen. D. R. 341
Welsh, Astell Thomas 187
— James 120

Welstead, John Rich. 135
Wemyss, Charles 527
— James 478
— John M. CB. 64, 412
— John Otway 175
— Thomas J. CB.8, 210
— William 427
Wentworth, D'Arcy 107
— William Digby 135
Werge, Henry R. 79, 172
Wesley, Robert Butt 330
— Samuel Rob. 15, 411
West *Rev.* Alfred 455
— Arthur Thesiger 436
— *Sir* Aug. MD. 530
— Augustus George 307
— Charles Rich. Sackville, *Lord*, CB. 31
— Frederick 78, 361
— George Thomas 340
— James Alexander 59
— John H. MD. 221
— John Temple 105
— *Hon.* Wm. Edw. S. 160
— William Henry H. 414
— Westby, Ashley G. 187
— Basil Clifton 208
— Bernard Heyer 207
— Edward James 418
— John Wright 253
— Wm. Henry Jones 294
Westenra, Francis 32
Western, Maximilian J. 37
Westhead, G. E. B. 79, 361
Westmacott, S. 65, 400
Westmore, Richard 29
Westropp, Edw. H. 63, 236
— John Parson 33
— Rob. Gibbings 294
Wetherall, Charles 478
— Edw. Rob. CB. 37
— *Sir* George Aug. KCB. KH. 9, 125, 319
— Joseph Thomas 141
Wethered, Edwin R. 362
Wetherell, Rt. W. M. 208
Weyland, John 356
— John T. 107
Whaite, John Edmund 192
Whale, Thos. Martin 417
Whalley, Geo. Briscoe 478
— Palmer 344
— Percy Charles 382
Whannell, George 105
Wharry, Charles 383
— Thomas Candler 338
Wharton, T. Candler 338
Wheatley, Francis 123
— John 361
— Moreton John 403
— William 106
— Wm. Frank 319
Wheatstone, John B. 61
Wheeler, *Rev.* H. N. 455
— John Richard 170
— John Ross 62, 236
Wheeley, Jas. Seager 187
Whelan, John Thomas 49
— John Thomas 252
— Wm. Edward 187
Wheler, *Sir* Trevor, Bt. 74
Whichcote, George 15
Whigham, Robert 185
Whimper, Fred. A, 52, 463

Index. 612

Whimster, James	497	Whitmore, Edm. A. 55, 360		Wilkinson, Berdoe A.	402	Williams, Rh. Llewel.	169
Whinyates, Edw.		——Fran. Locker	78	——Charles	405	——Rich. Michael	138
——Charles, CB. KH. 9,	370	——Sir Geo. KCH. 6,	399	——Charles Edm. 35,	399	——Robert	107
——Francis Arthur	378	——Geo. Stoddart 80,	288	——Christopher	74	——Samuel	360
——Fran. Frankland	120	——Montagu Stopford	402	——Christ. D. CB.	120	——Sherburne	13
——Fred. Thomas	377	——Mortimer R.S. 59,	452	——Frederick G. 60,	255	——Sidney Watkin	350
——Fred. Wm.	13	——Thos. Chas. D.	128	——George Allix	376	——Thomas, MD.	531
Whipple, Arthur L.	198	Whitney, Benjamin	107	——George Anderson	534	——Thomas, CB. 33,	177
Whish, Claudius B.	151	Whittaker, John H.	298	——Geo. Faulkner	296	——Thomas	435
Whitty, Charles L.	294	Whitten, Andrew	261	——Henry	497	——Thomas John	383
Whitbread, Edmund J.	293	Whitton, Nicholas	193	——Henry Chandler	316	——Thos. M. KH.	17
White, Alfred H.	131	Whitting, John Everard	247	——Henry Clement	210	——Thos. Rob. MB.	324
——Aug. Barton	205	——Reginald	187	——Henry Green 49,	166	——Vyvyan	196
——Charles John	131	Whittingham, Ferdi-		——Henry John	190	——Watkin Lewis	120
——Chas. Wm.	167	nand, CB.	42, 177	——Henry J. William	264	——William	200
——Edward	161	——Paul Bernard 85,	401	——John	231	——William J.	527
——Edward Hillman	416	Whittington, Geo. Jno.		——John	445	——William	533
——Edward James	29	Chas.	356	——John Alexander	497	——Sir William Fen-	
——Edward Vernon	293	Whitty, Chas. Langley	294	——John Philip	436	wick, Bt. KCB. 14,	370
——Finch	321	——John	337	——Johnson	205	——Wm. Freke, KH.	15
——Francis Freeman	229	——Thos. Ravenscroft	181	——Joseph	52	——Wm. John 79,	375
——George	497	——William Nassau	192	——P.	464	Williamson, Alex. B.K.	310
——George	427	Whylock, James	13	——Wm. Edmund	273	——Charles	282
——Geo. Augustus	308	——Watkin S. MD.	443	Willan, James D.	435	——Chas. Cartwright	51
——George Francis	105	Whyte, Charles	182	——Stanhope L. D.	172	——Fred. Harcourt	237
——George Stewart	235	——Charles	439	——Wm. Moffat D.	478	——George, MD.	441
——Hans Robert	79	——Edward	356	Willans, Obé	157	——James	226
——Hans Thos. F. 87,	252	——John James	103	——St. John	156	——John	328
——Henry	150	Wichmann, George	542	——William R.	335	——John	478
——Henry	497	Wicke, John Henry	542	Willats, Peter John	50	——Thomas	522
——Henry Arthur 85,	401	Wickham, Edw. Tho.	286	Willcocks, R. Henry	350	——Usher	18
——Hen. D. CB.	36	——Edmund Hill	381	Willes, Geo. Shippen	138	——William 78,	321
——Henry Ellis	133	——Hen. Lamplugh	344	——Harry Charles	226	——Wm. Robert	264
——Henry George	169	——R. S.	465	——James Irwin 9,	411	Willington, Richard	29
——James	522	——Thomas	80, 242	Willett, Horace Edw.	246	——Rich. Butler	308
——John Lewis	516	Widmer, Christopher	531	Williams, Albert H. W.	376	Willis, Browne 17,	371
——Lancelot And.	444	Widdrington, Sidney		——Arthur	257	——Chas. Whateley	242
——Lawrence Luke E.	516	H. L. T.	172	——Arth. Wellesley	156	——Cuthbert	205
——Loraine	465	Wield, Robert	335	——Charles	157	——Edward	416
——Mathew L.	170	Wightman, George	105	——Charles	435	——Frederic A. CB. 64,	319
——Michael, CB. 11,	135	——James Tho.	497	——C. P.	497	——George Brander	497
——Moses, MD.	531	Wigley, Geo. James	497	——Chas. Richard	298	——Geo. Harry Smith	56
——Peter	533	Wigram, Ely D.	103	——Chas. Sidney	415	——Hen R. DeAnyers	269
——Raymond H. 65,	166	——Godfrey James	164	——Clement	296	——James L. N.	243
——Richard	444	Wigston, Francis	36	——Edward	298	——Sherlock Vignolles	169
——Robert 77,	154	Wigton, James	497	——Edward Arthur	374	——Wm. Jarvis	203
——Thomas	319	Wikeley, Chas. Edw.	216	——Francis	274	——Wm. W. Geo. B.	416
——Thomas 61,	266	Wilberforce, R G.	270	——George C.	455	Willoughby, Ch. C.	282
——Thomas E. MD.	293	Wilbraham, Hon. Edw.		——Henry	276	——Henry Safe	260
——Thomas Pilkington	404	Bootle	103	——Henry Augustus	203	Willox, James	522
——Thos. W. 78,	153	——Rich., CB.	33	——Henry Augustus	358	Wills, Charles Henry	232
——William	170	Wilby, William 63,	177	——Henry Francis 82,	281	——Thomas Lake	478
——William	497	Wild, Henry James	527	——Henry Llewelyn	381	Willshire, Sir Thomas,	
——William A. MD.	263	——Henry John	436	——Herbert John M.	178	Bart. KCB. 8,	269
——Wm. Richard	267	Wildes, George	227	——Herbert S.	181	Willson, Jas. K. 64,	452
Whiteford, Baldwin K.	218	Wildman, John	103	——Hugh	478	——Richard Kennett	414
——John	298	Wiles, Julius	444	——James	234	Wilmer, L. W.	328
——John	497	Wilford, Edm. Neal 32,	371	——James	478	——John Randall	382
Whitehead, Edmund	255	——Ernest C. 41,	358	——James Edmund	439	Wilmot, Eardley	28
——Robt. Children	279	——Ernest C.	356	——James Edwin	120	——Fre. M. E. 37,	371
——William	314	Wilkes, Edwin	444	——Sir Jas. Hamlyn	107	——Henry 84,	343
Whiteside, Fred. J. S.	195	Wilkie, Arthur Alex.	248	——John	383	——John Robert	277
——John	187	——Fletcher	105	——John Ignatius P.	346	Wilson, Sir Archdale,	
Whitfeild, H. Wase 35,	350	——Hales	236	——John Wm. C.	413	Bart. KCB.	121
Whitfield, Chas. T.	533	——John 35,	146	——Joseph	50	——Augus. Nicholas	322
Whiting Geo. Wm.	497	——John Lunan	197	——Lewis Duncan	26	——Benjamin F. D.	16
Whitla, George	341	Wilkieson, G. Hampden	288	——Lewis Vaughan	344	——Charles Stewart V.	380
——Jas. Buchanan	324	Wilkin, Henry John	142	——Montgom. 32,	399	——Chas. Thos.	177
——William	193	Wilkins, G. CB. KH.	105	——Montgomery	319	——Cha. Townsend	105
Whitlam, George	207	——G. H.	465	——Owen Lewis C.	128	——Charles Turville	157
Whitley, James	478	——Wm. Mortimer	533	——Philip Downes	215	——Charles Watson	378
Whitlock, Geo. Fred. T.	319	Wilkinson, A. Eastfield	142	——Reginald Stewart	332	——Charles William	403
——George Cornish	121	——Anthony Thos.	349	——Rich. Edmund	210	——Chas. Wm. Hen.	183
——Hubert Cornish	318	——Art. Phil. S., CB.	107	——Richard Harry	404	——Clifford	246

H H

Name	Page	Name	Page	Name	Page	Name	Page
Wilson, Dudley M.	382	Winter, James	208	Wood, John M. B.	239	Woolsey, O'Brien B.	375
——Edward	478	——Matthew	436	——John Stewart, CB.	38	Wordsworth, John	308
——Edw. Benjamin	356	Winterscale, J. F. M.	345	——Launcelot Edward	76	Workman, Thomas	478
——Edwin	300	Winthrop, Benjamin	152	——Peter Valentine	516	Worrall, Hen. Lechm.	120
——FitzRoy	345	——Stephen	223	——Robt. Blucher, CB.	26	Worsley, George	497
——Fra. Edw. E.	319	Wintle, Alfred	205	——Robert Hudson	295	——Pennyman White	283
——Fred. Edward	291	Wirgman, Theodore	144	——Samuel Edward	332	Wortley, Arch. Henry	
——Geo. Davis, CB.	105	Wisch, Hieronimus von		——Thomas	15	Plantagenet Stuart	77
——Geo. James	120	der	541	——Thomas	125	Wortham, Hale Young	16
——Henry	497	Wischmann, George	542	——Thomas, MD.	444	——Hale Young	379
——Henry	107	Wisdom, John	497	——Thomas Pattison	236	Worthington, Arthur	175
——Henry Brooke	300	Wise, Charles	32	——Wm. CB. KH. 7, 352		——Geo. Talbot	242
——Henry S. Lee	150	——Horatio James	350	——William	60	——Henry Clark	205
——James	527	——William	478	——William	255	——Richard Jukes	279
——James	478	Witchell, Thomas	156	——William	498	Worthy, Charles	316
——James, MB.	176	Withers, Edward	293	——William Arthur	258	Wragge, Alfred Rom.	373
——James Hamilton	403	——Hicks	383	——Wm. Mark 35, 163		Wray, Henry	401
——John	75	Withington, Peter	135	——Rev. W. Watson	455	——Hugh Boyd	497
——John	202	Witte, George de	544	Woodall, Frederick N.	304	——James	181
——John	255	——Hen. F. Theo. de	542	——Thomas Nind	277	——Tho. Charge	212
——John	540	Wodehouse, Alb. T.	380	Woodard, George H.	173	Wreford, Matthew	446
——John Gerald	319	——Hon. Berkeley	107	——Mortimer Neville	324	Wrench, Chas. James	226
——John Henry	497	——Edmund	59, 228	Woodburn, Alex. CB.	120	——Charles E.	446
——John J.	402	——Edwin, CB.		Woodcock, Frederick	513	——Edward Mason	148
——Sir John Morillyon,			43, 125, 372	Woodfall, Sam. Pratt	384	——E. Ommanney	106
CB. KH.	26, 463	Wodsworth, Dudley C.	198	Woodford, Sir Alex.		——Robert G. Wynne	210
——Joseph Fraser	478	Wohlman, George	224	GCB. GCMG.		Wrentmore, Geo. Josh.	436
——Richard	352	Wolf, Frederick	544		6, 252, 463	Wriford, George Hen.	414
——Rich. G. B.	13	Wolfe, Edward	107	——John	106	Wright, Alex. Boydell	299
——Robert, MD.	533	——George	172	——Sir John George,		——Alfred	315
——Samuel	123	——Wm. Clarges	62	KCB. KCH.	103	——Arth. F. Bingham	190
——Stephen Hen. K.	321	——W. S. Maynard	376	Woodforde, Rob. Reginald Augustus		——Augustus	464
——Sylvester, W.F.M.	274	Wolferstan, Henry P.	232		417	——B.	464
——Thomas	74	Wolff, Alexander Jos.	513	Woodgate, Ashley Hen.	282	——Charles	374
——Thomas	527	Wollaston, Fred.	107	——Francis	127	——Charles	29, 399
——T. Maitland 31, 187		Wolrige, Ambrose 414, 420		——John	516	——Charles Edward	337
——William Henry	267	——Ambrose A. R.	420	——William, CB.	103	——Charles James 39, 372	
——Wm. H. B. J.	497	——Henry Ridge	156	Woodhouse, James,		——Edward	497
——Willoughby James	376	Wolseley, Garnet Joseph		CMG.	527	——Edward W. C. 56, 363	
Wilton, John L. CB.	51		64, 328	Woodley, Jas. Wilknsn.	527	——Frederick	50
——John Robert 82, 281		——Geo. Benjamin	340	——Richard, MB.	534	——Frederick	217
Wiltshire, William	323	——Richard	443	Woodman, George Thomas, MD.		——Fred. Augustus	178
Wily, Henry William	452	——Wm. Charles	182		250	——George	478
——John	212	Wombwell, Adolphus U.	148	——William	539	——Henry Banks	152
Wimberley, Douglas	312	——Arthur	78, 361	Woodmass, Chas. Hen.	208	——Rev. Henry Press	455
Winchester, George	123	——Henry Herbert	142	Woodriff, Daniel Thos.	417	——Henry Richard	28
——John	106	Wood, Albert Charles	312	Woodroffe, Chas. Wm.		——James	516
Winckler, Augustus	542	——Arthur, MD.	533	MD.	170	——James, MD.	530
——Charles	542	——Sir David Edw.		Woodrooffe, Abel Hen.	250	——James Dennis	531
Winckworth, John	497	KCB.	37, 371	——Wm. Erskine	354	——John, KH.	9
Windham, Charles Ash	14	——Edw. Alex.	146	Woodruffe, Wm. John	338	——John	497
——George Smyth	343	——Edw. Negus	353	Woods, David	443	——John	513
——Jos. Chas. Smyth	380	——Edward Septimus	332	——Henry George	79	——John Hobson	357
——Stewart Smyth	344	——Francis	210	——James	315	——John Wm. Zorap.	130
Windle, John Shepard	497	——Frederick	497	——Richard	75	——J. G.	465
Windsor, Edwin A.	264	——Fred. Aug. Percy	478	——Richard Wm.	314	——Joseph C. H. MD.	384
——James	464	——George Horsley	497	——Robert	306	——Robert	76
——Rev. S. B.	455	——Henry	344	——William	497	——Robert	533
Wing, Vincent 107, 381		——Henry	330	——Wm. Fred.	211	——Robert James	132
Wingfield, Chas. Wm.		——Henry	478	——Wm. Henry MD.	420	——S.	464
	33, 371	——Henry	497	Woodward, Charles	404	——Thomas, CB.	15
——Digby H. R.	128	——Hen. Evelyn	154	——John	478	——Thomas	248
——Edw. Ffolliott	127	——Henry Owen	107	——George Paul Minchin, MD.		——Thomas	522
——Frederic Basset	436	——James	478		442	——Thomas Albert B.	291
——John Hope 59, 205		——James John	260	——Wm. Alex.	208	——Thomas Parker	318
——Richard	270	——Jas. Cha. R.	435	Wooldridge, De Lacy		——Rev. Walter M.	383
——Walter Clopton	129	——John	384	Rich. Fra.	354	——William	497
Winn, William	236	——John	540	Woolfreyes, John And.	157	——William Alfred G.	413
Winne, John James	497	——John Ayton	273	Woolhouse, And. M.	513	Wrighte, Wm.	497
Winniett, William	228	——John Gathorne	211	——Edward	207	Wrixon, Nicholas	107
Winnington, H. J.	478	——John Gillespie,		——George Rich.	444	——William Popham	293
Winsloe, Rich. Wm. C.	220	MD.	440	Woollard, Gilbert	107	Wrottesley, Hon. Chas.	
Winstanley, Arch. R.	226	——John Joseph	107	Woollcombe, Robert	415	Alex.	16
Winter, George	534	——John Manley	103	——Robert Wm. 463, 534		——Hon. George	402

Index.

Wroot, William Hen. 416	Wyndowe, Wm. F. 369	Yates, E. Waldegrave P. 136	Young, Hen. Harman 497
Wroughton, Hen. Alex. C. 200	Wyneken, Frederick 544	——Henry Peel 63, 375	——Henry William 154
Wulff, Henry P. 32, 399	Wynen, Alfred Gabriel 200	——John 478	——James 312
——Kenelm Chandler 478	Wynn, Herb. Wat. W. 106	——William Henry 188	——James 106
Wulffen, Wm. de 543	——*Hon.*Thomas John 345	Yelverton, *Hon.* Wil-	——*Rev.* James 455
Wyatt, Alexander H. L. 43, 195	Wynne, Arth. John H. 379	liam Charles 77, 374	——James, *MD.* 533
——Alfred Francis W. 42, 293	——Charles Robert 76	Yeoland, George 527	——James Robert 17
——Charles Edwin 151	——Charles B. 328	Yolland, William 39, 400	——John Eldon, *MD.* 443
——Francis Dalmahoy 350	——Edw. Cooper 328	Yonge, Fra. Arth. H. 229	——John George 497
——G. 464	——Edw. Toler 404	——G. N. K. A. 80, 362	——John Owen 282
——James Henry 86, 156	——Edw. Wm. Lloyd 160	——Henry John 286	——Plomer, *KH.* 15
——John 164	——George 39, 400	——Wm. James 65	——Plomer John 292
——*Sir* H. Robartes 103	——Hen. John Lloyd 127	——Wm. Lambert 377	——Richard 365
——Samuel 478	——John 478	Yorke, Fred. Aug. 40, 400	——Rich. Newton 380
——Walter J. 354	——Richard Miles 522	——*Sir* Charles, *KCB.* 10, 125, 242	——Robert 497
Wybault, Joseph Wm. 527	——William 164	——John, *CB.* 34	——Thomas 223
——Patrick Robert 527	Wynter, Robert 478	——Phillip James 103	——Thomas 263
Wybergh, Archibald 290	Wynyard, E. B. CB. 8, 279	Youell, George 273	——Tho. Newton 227
Wybrow, William 583	——Edward G. 49, 159	Youl, Henry 139	——William 266
Wyer, Geo. Goforth 534	——George Henry, 86, 279	Youle, David 404	——William 364
——John 533	——Henry Buckley J. 63	Young, Allen A. 276	——Wm. Henry, *MD.* 533
Wylde, Edw. Andrée 413	——Henry John 279	——Arthur Cotton 231	——William 383
——William, *CB.* 12, 370	——Robert Hen., *CB.* 17	——Chas. Frederick 267	——William 404
Wyllie, William, *CB.* 120	Wyse, Arthur George 264	——Charles Fred. 86, 375	——Wm. Baird 76
——Wm. Alex. P. 378	——John Francis 243	——Colin, *MD.* 533	——Wm. L. M. *CB.* 383
Wymer, *Sir* George Petre, *KCB.* 120	Wyvill, Richard R. 318	——Edwd. Wm., *MD.* 283	——Wm. Pym 74, 293
Wyndham, Alex. W. 478	Ximenes, Horace 207	——Frederick 120	Younger, John 381
——Charles 106	——Wm. Raymond 187	——George R. C. 375	Younghusband, Chas. Wright 63, 373
——Charles 103	Yaldwyn, John 120	——Geo. Samuel, 86, 314	——Edgar 253
——*Sir* Hen. *KCB.* 6, 147	Yale, Wm. Parry 106	——Gerald H. Baird 257	——William 417
——Henry 126	Yarborough, C.C. *CB.* 30	——Grahame 284	Yule, James Robert 381
	Yard, Frederick 107	——Henry 478	——Patrick 14
	Yardley, Thomas 322	——Henry 497	Ziermann, Frederick 543
	Yarnold, Benjamin 497		
	Yates, Edm. R. W. W. 55		

MILITIA
OF
ENGLAND AND WALES.

Inspector General of Militia—Major General Robert Percy Douglas.
Assistant Adjutant General—Colonel Brook Taylor, Unatt.

ROYAL ANGLESEY.
(*Light Infantry.*) [No. 61.]
Head Quarters, Beaumaris.
LIEUT.COLONEL COMMANDANT.
Thomas Peers Williams.........10 Mar. 53
CAPTAINS.
John Lewis Hampton Lewis,
  DL. JP. *late Capt* 5 *Dr.Gds.* 5 Oct. 52
Thomas Love D. Jones Parry 29 May 54
John Thomas Roberts, JP. ... 5 Oct. 55
LIEUTENANTS.
Henry Robert Poole ....22 Apr. 53
Chas. Robert Tennant, *late Lt.*
  35 *F.*................................ Aug. 55
William M'Kee ....21 Oct. 58
Henry Owen Williams ....26 Mar. 59
ENSIGNS.
Wm. Henry Copeland ....26 Mar. 59
Alfred Theodore Williams ...11 Apr. 59

Adjt. and Capt.—Edw. Oct.
  Pearse,[1] *Lt. h.p. R. Marine
  Artillery* ....21 July 58
Surg.—Walter Humphries, MD. 1 Nov. 55
Blue Facings.
Agents, Messrs. Cox & Co.

BEDFORD.
(*Light Infantry.*) [No. 18.]
[Embodied.]
Head Quarters, Weymouth.
COLONEL.
Rich. Thos. Gilpin, MP. DL. JP.
  Bt.Lt.Col. late of Rifle Br. .11 Sept. 48
LIEUT.COLONEL.
Robert Hindley Wilkinson ...24 Mar. 58
MAJOR.
William Stuart, MP. JP. ...... 9 June 58
CAPTAINS.
Wm. Copeland Redmond Judd 1 May 54
Edward Thornton .... 8 Nov. 54
George Cobb Ledger ....17 Mar. 55
Henry Meux Smith ....25 Mar. 56
George Sharpe .... 9 June 58
Fra. Fred. R. M. Morgan, *Instructor of Musketry*......25 Sept.58
LIEUTENANTS.
Welbore Ellis ....25 Mar. 56
Robert Macdonald Chambers 24 Mar. 58
Rich. Sambrook Crawley ....25 Mar. 58
Stephen Kent Winkworth ...26 Aug. 58
Consitt Wm. Fewson...........22 Sept.58
Geo. Robert Mascall ....10 Dec. 58
ENSIGNS.
Alfred Herbert Lucas .... 1 Sept. 58
Thomas Joseph Sunderland...19 Nov. 58
Frederick Luck ....27 Mar. 59
Edwin Robert Ives ....15 Apr. 59

Adjt. & Capt.—George Toseland(1), *late Adj.* 33 *F.*...... 9 Mar. 57
Paymaster.—John Robert Grayson, 14 May 58
Surg.—Michael Jas. MacCormack, M.D..........................21 Aug. 54
Assist.Surg.—Wm. Thomas
  Rawling ....23 Dec. 57
Qr.Master.—Adam Merrie ... 1 June 57
Dark Green Facings.
Agents, Messrs. Cox & Co.

ROYAL BERKS.
[No. 7.]
Head Quarters, Reading.
"Mediterranean."
COLONEL.
John Blagrave, DL. JP.......... 6 Sept.42
LIEUT.-COLONEL.
Charles Bacon....................31 Dec. 42
MAJOR.
Adam Blandy,*late Lieut.*15*Drs.*17Aug. 55
CAPTAINS.
Wm. Richard Mortimer Thoyts 9 Oct. 52
Charles Samuel Slocock........11 Oct. 52
Wm. Francis Wheble ....23 May 53
John Douglas ....12 Jan. 55
Christopher Deak Brickmann 22 Aug. 55
Thomas Fuller Maitland 26 Sept.57
Henry Hammer Leycester....10 Oct. 57
Edward Tew Thomson ....20 Jan. 58
LIEUTENANTS.
Richard Wm. Shackel ....27 May 54
Francis Rennel Cox ....11 Sept. 55
Chas. Stuart Vonles .... 2 Oct. 57
Ward Soane Braham ....14 Nov. 57
Henry Bayntun .... 5 Dec. 57
James Samuel Harrison......25 Feb. 58
A. B., *Lord* Norreys 12 Mar.58
Robert Tebbott ....19 May 59
ENSIGNS.
John Blandy Jenkins ....10 Oct. 57
Frederick Everett ....11 Oct. 57
Algernon Lewis Medley .....14 Nov. 57
John Janson Howard 8 June59

Adjt. & Capt.—Fred. Henry
  Lang, *late Capt.* 34 *F.* .....17 July 58
Paymaster.—
Quarter Master.—John Milne30 June 55
Surg.—Hy. Wilson Reed, MD.24 Feb. 55
Assist.Surg.—Henry Morris...15 July 59
Blue Facings.
Agents, Messrs. Hopkinson & Co.

ROYAL BRECKNOCK.
(*Rifles.*) [No. 132.]
Head Quarters, Brecon.
LIEUT.-COLONEL COMMANDANT.
Lloyd Vaughan Watkins, M.P.,
  *Lord Lieut. of Brecknockshire*15 Nov. 47
MAJOR.
Douglas John Dickinson(1),
  JP. *late Lieut.* 7 *Fusiliers* ...13 Nov.52
CAPTAINS.
William Bridgwater .... 3 May 53
Chris. Mackay Read, *late of*
  16 *F.*.............................16 July 54
John Forsyth Gregory .... 9 June 55
ArthurWilksLudlowGompertz 14Feb. 56
Moriscoe Lloyd Frederick ... 5 Sept. 57
LIEUTENANTS.
W. Dowding, *Act. Qr.Master* 26 June 55
Fred. Geo. Mogg ....14 Feb. 56
Loftus Neynoe ....16 April 58
Edward Tyrrell Lewis ....23 Aug. 59
ENSIGNS.

Adjt. & Capt.—Wm. Robert
  Brereton, *late Capt.* 70 *F.* 23 Jan. 56
Surg.—Arthur Sealy Lawrence26June20
Black Facings.
Agents, Messrs. C. R. and W. M'Grigor.

ROYAL BUCKS,
(KING'S OWN.)
[No. 35.]
Head Quarters, High Wycombe.
COLONEL.
R. J. *Lord* Carington, *Lord
  Lieutenant* .... 7 Mar. 39
LIEUT.COLONEL.
Walter Caulfield Pratt, JP. *late
  Capt.* 67 *F.* ....23 Apr. 55
MAJOR.
Henry Ayshford Sanford, *late
  Capt.* 43 *F.* ....31 May 59
CAPTAINS.
John Joseph Augustine Leonard Creaton,*late of Gr.Gds.*12 Sept.53
Lawrence Robert Hall .... 1 Oct. 55
Humbley Knapp, *late of* 5 *F.*...22 Feb. 56
Fred. Wm. Lane,(2) *late Capt.*
  67 *F.* .... June 59
Edw. Holden Steward, *late
  Capt.* 60 *F.* .... June 59
Edward Baldock................. June 59

LIEUTENANTS.
Randolph Henry Crewe........ 8 Feb. 56
John Wood 24 Sept.58
John Stratton Fuller .... do
ENSIGNS.
Fred. Pigott Hearn .... 8 Feb. 56
Geo. Aug. Leslie Wood ....22 Feb. 56
Paymaster.—C. T. Grove ....12 June 54
Adj. & Capt.—John M. M.
  Hewett (1), *late Capt.* 62 *F.*..28 Aug. 54
Qr.Master.—John Cross ......30 Sept. 59
Surgeon.—Edw. Dew, M.D. ...19 Dec. 54
Assist.Surg.—
Blue Facings.

CAMBRIDGE.
[No. 68.]
Head Quarters, Ely.
COLONEL.
Hon. Octavius Duncombe, MP.
  DL. *late Lieut.* 1 *Life Gds.* ... 2 Aug. 52
LIEUT.COLONEL.
Robert G. Wale, DL. JP. *late
  of* 33 *F.* ....31 Aug. 54
MAJOR.
C. Robert Pemberton,DL. JP. 11Sept.54
CAPTAINS.
John Bendyshe,[1] *late Lt.* 10 *F.* 30 Dec. 51
Edward Goodwin, *Gentleman-
  at-Arms* ....21 Mar. 53
Launcelot Reed .... 4 May 54
Wm. James Harrison .... 2 Apr. 57
Henry John Adeane, MP. *late
  Lt.* 62 *F.* ....26 Dec. 57
Philip Sidney Yorke .... 1 June 59
John Julius T. Haylock ....25 June 59
LIEUTENANTS.
Wm. H. Baldwin.................. 7 June 55

Militia of England and Wales.

Wm. Tilden Layton ....11 Sept. 55
Arthur Harris Rees ....26 Jan. 56
Edward Muriel Martin ...... 2 Apr. 57
William Fred. Dennis .... 3 July 59
Joshua Brereton................. 5 Nov. 59
George King .... 7 Nov. 59

Ensigns.

Paymr.—*Capt.* Geo. Copeland,
 h.p. Qr.M. S. F. Gds ....20 Oct. 55
Adjutant & Capt.—Michael
 Dickment, *late of Scots Fus.
 Gds.* ....30 June 53
Qr.Mast.—John Tibbles ... 10 Nov. 55
Surgeon.—John Masters ......28 June 59
Assist.Surg.—

Agents, Messrs. Cox & Co.

ROYAL CARDIGAN.

(*Rifles.*) [No. 64.]
Head Quarters, Aberystwith.
Lieut.Colonel Commandant.
Wm. Thomas Rowland Powell,
 DL. JP. *late Capt.* 87 F.....25 Mar. 54

Major.

Captains.

J. R. L. Phillips, DL. JP. *late
 Lieut.* 12 F....................... 2 Oct. 52
J. A. L. Philips, *late Capt.*
 83 F. .... 3 Aug. 55
Thomas Elliott, *late Lt.* 77 F...21 Sept. 55

Lieutenants.

Alexander Richards ....25 Oct. 52
Thos. John Hughes ....24 Feb. 55
Sylvanus Lewis ....27 Oct. 55

Ensigns.

Jenkin Jones Thomas .... 7 June 55
Edmund Lloyd ....28 Nov. 57

Adjt. & Capt.—P. F. Durham,
 DL. *late Captain* 37 F. ...26 Aug. 52
Surgeon--Thomas James......16 Sept. 52

Red Facings.

ROYAL CARMARTHEN.

(*Rifles.*) [No. 24.]
Head Quarters, Carmarthen.
Lieut.Colonel Commandant.
Lord Dynevor, DL. *Aide-de-
 Camp to the Queen* ....28 Jan. 31

Major.

Geo. Watkin Rice, DL. JP., *late
 Capt.* 23 F.......................26 Feb. 50

Captains.

David Davies, JP. *Lieut.* h. p.
 R. *Marines* ....26 Jan. 39
Rice Price Beynon, JP.........26 Feb. 50
Morgan Pryse Lloyd, JP. *late
 Ensign* 1 F......................26 Feb. 50
David Edward Jones, JP......15 May 56

Lieutenants.

R. G. Thomas ....10 Jan. 53
Arthur H. S. Davies .... Mar. 58
Lloyd Price........................15 Oct. 58

Ensigns.

Charles Lloyd....................15 May 56
Richard Hanbury Miers ..... 5 Mar. 58
Richard Richards Carver ... 5 Feb. 59

Adjutant.—Eugene James
 Vaughan, *Bt.Lt.Col. h.p.*
 57 F. ....27 July 46
Surg.—John Hughes............15 May 56

Red Facings.

ROYAL CARNARVON.

(*Rifles.*) [No. 56.]
Head Quarters, Carnarvon.

Honorary Colonel.

Hon. Edward Gordon Douglas-
 Pennant, *late of Gr. Gds. &
 Colonel in the Army* ....30 Aug. 52
Lieut.-Colonel Commandant.
John MacDonald, (1) DL. JP.,
 late Lieut.Col. 5 F. .... 24 Aug. 58

Major.

John Vincent Hawksley Wil-
 liams, JP. DL......................25 Aug. 58

Captains.

Geo. S. Douglas Pennant ....23 Nov. 58
John Bailey Williams ....24 Dec. 58
Owen Massey Jones ....30 July 59
Chas Abbott Delmar, *late Lt.*
 9 Drs. .... 4 Sept. 59

Lieutenants.

John Powell Allen ....23 Nov. 58

Ensigns.

Henry Kneeshaw .... 2 July 59
Adjt. & Capt.—Edward Deane
 Naves, *late Lt.* 97 F. ....20 July 59
Surgeon.—John Richards ......26 Nov. 52

Black Facings.

1ST ROYAL CHESHIRE.

[No. 6.]
Head Quarters, Chester.

Colonel.

Hugh, *Lord* Delamere, DL. JP.
 late of 1 *Life Gds.* ....28 Aug. 40

Lieut.Colonel.

Hon. T. Grenville Cholmon-
 deley, DL. JP. *late Capt.* 43 F. 1 Oct. 52

Majors.

W. Hosken Harper, JP. ......10 Jan. 53
Egerton Leigh, JP. *late Capt.
 2 Dr. Gds.* ....30 Aug. 53

Captains.

John Hurleston Leche, JP. ...15 Jan. 53
Wilbraham. Fred. Tollemache 25 Feb. 53
John Baskervyle Glegg, JP.
 late Lt. Scots Fus. Gds. ......20 Dec. 53
Thomas Henry Lyon ....16 Mar. 54
Wm. Ferguson Currie, *late
 Capt.* 81 F. ....15 Jan. 55
Fra. Elcocke Massey............20 July 55
Charles Hoskcn Franco, *late
 Lt.* 77 F. ....20 Oct. 55
Edward Jeffcock.................14 Oct. 58
John Colborne, *late of* 13 *Bom-
 bay N.I.* ....15 Oct. 58
John Hinton Daniell (2), *late
 Capt.* 43 F. .... 5 Apr. 59

Lieutenants.

Charles Eldon Clarke ....20 May 56
Edw. Wm. J. Nunn, *late Lt.*
 55 F. ....10 May 59

Ensigns.

Wm. Vigor Fox ....10 Mar. 55
Herbert Kelsall ....25 Aug. 55
Adjt. & Capt.—Charles Hen.
 White, *late Capt.* 14 F. .....12 Oct. 55
Qr.Mr.—E. C. Hicks........... 3 Jan. 55
Surgeon.—Thos. Frittain......20 Dec. 56
Assist.Surg.—Robert Plow-
 den Weston .... 1 Oct. 58

Blue Facings.

Agents, Messrs. Cox & Co.

2ND ROYAL CHESHIRE.

[No. 103.]
[Embodied.]
Head Quarters, Shorncliffe.
Lieut.Colonel Commandant.
William Davenport Davenport,
 DL. JP. *late Major* 26 F. ... 5 Apr. 53

Majors.

Geo. Francis Stuart, *late Capt.
 40 F.* ....25 July 53
Geo. Cornwall Legh, MP. DL.
 JP. ....30 July 53

Captains.

John FitzGerald, *late Capt.* 87
 F. ....25 Aug. 54
Henry Brougham Lock......... 6 Dec. 54
Nassau Wm. Stephens, *late
 Capt.* 94 F. ....30 Dec. 54
ÞCharles Poppleton(1), *late of
 Ordnance Field Train*......10 Jan. 55
James Golden Heap ....18 Jan. 55
Geo. Lewis Cuming ....25 Nov. 57
Francis Lloyd ....10 Dec. 57
Saint Vincent Tyler ....10 Feb. 58
Spence Derington Turner,
 Capt. h. p. Bengal Army ... 1 Feb. 59
Ralph Smyth, (3) *lateCapt.* 17F.15 July 59

Lieutenants.

Edward Reddish.................15 Jan. 55
James Taylor ....10 Apr. 55
Edw. Wm. Plowright ....26 Nov. 57
Wilks Hill ....20 Jan. 58
George Robert Willson......... 1 June 58
Fred. Henry Kelsall .... 5 June 58
Edgar Gardner ....10 June 58
Edw. Geo. M'Dougall Icke, *In-
 structor of Musketry* ....20 Dec. 58
Wm. Denn Hannagan ....20 June 59
John Fred. Wilkin...............15 July 59

Ensigns.

Wm. John St. Aubyn...........30 Aug. 58
Wm. Beunion Foulkes .... 1 Jan. 59
Henry John G. Harrison ... 5 Feb. 59
Fred. John Owen ....15 June 59
Geo. Ernest Emes Blunt ......20 July 59

Adjt. & Capt.—Trevor Daven-
 port, *Bt.Maj. late of* 12 F. 9 Apr. 53
Paymaster.—Wm. Ley Hunt ..10 Nov. 57
Qr.Master.—Thos. FitzGerald 21 Jan. 59
Surgeon.—Chas. John Sanford 5 Apr. 54
Assist.Surg.—Geo. D. Powell ..20 Jan. 58

Blue Facings.

Agents, Messrs. Cox & Co.

DUKE OF CORNWALL'S RANGERS.

(*Rifles.*) [No. 38.]
Head Quarters, Bodmin.
Lieut.Colonel Commandant.
Augustus Coryton, DL. *late
 Capt.* 85 F. .... 7 Feb. 57

Major.

J. B. Messenger, JP. DL.......25 Aug. 55

Captains.

Samuel Borlase, JP. DL. ......11 Sept. 20
Richard Johns, JP...............30 Aug. 25
Nicholas Kendall, MP. DL. JP.22 Oct. 26
John Whitehead Peard .... 4 June 53
Francis John Hext, DL. JP.
 late Lieut. 83 F. .... 6 June 53
James Rennell Rodd .... 3 June 54
J. F. Trist, (3) DL. JP. *late
 Lieut.* 41 *Madras Infantry* 24 Jan. 55
Viscount Valletort, *Equerry to
 H.R.H. the Prince of Wales* 2 June 55
Edward Carthew ....20 Oct. 55

Lieutenants.

Henry O'Neil .... 2 May 46
David Wm. H. Horndon ......27 Apr. 54
Wm. Rashleigh, DL. JP. ...... 4 Jan. 55
Edward Collins, DL. JP. .....24 Jan. 55
Edwin Charles Scobell......... 3 Apr. 56
Thos. Goodriche Wilson ..... 7 Feb. 57
Edward St. Aubin ....28 Aug. 58
Rich. Henry S. Vyvyan, JP.
 Gent. at Arms ....21 Jan. 59
Reginald Kelly .... 9 Aug. 59

Ensigns.

John Morris Prynne ....16 July 59

Militia of England and Wales.

Adjt. & Capt.—Thomas Fred.
Hill Alms,(2) *late Capt.* 54 F.28 Feb. 53
Qr.Master.—James Murray ... 7 Nov. 58
Surgeon.—John Ward, JP. ... 6 Jan. 23
Assist.Surg.—Frs. T. Nicholus 5 May 53
Black Facings.
Agents, Messrs. Cox & Co.

ROYAL CORNWALL AND DEVON MINERS ARTILLERY.
[No. 6.]
Head Quarters, Falmouth.
LIEUT.COLONEL COMMANDANT.
Sir Colman Rashleigh, Bart.
DW. DL. JP. .... 2 May 53
MAJOR.
Ralph Shuttleworth Allen, JP,
Capt. h. p. R. Artillery......20 May 53
CAPTAINS.
C. B. G. Sawle, MP, DL, JP. 12 July 44
N. Kendall, *late Lt.* 66 F.......26 Apr. 53
Hender John Molesworth St.
Aubyn, DL, JP................ 6 Nov. 55
Francis Howell, DL, JP. ......22 Apr. 56
LIEUTENANTS.
J. N. V. Willyams, JP,.........12 July 44
Robert Edyvean ....11 Jan. 54
John Borlase ....2 Sept. 58
Charles E. Treffry .... 8 June 59
SECOND LIEUTENANTS.
Henry Clark .... 2 June 55
Joseph Pomery ....10 Dec. 58
Reginald Kelly ....24 June 59
Adj. & Capt.—Wm. Ward,
Capt. on h. p. ....30 May 46
Surg.—W. H. Bullmore, M.D. 1 Mar. 45
Scarlet Facings.
Agents, Messrs. Cox & Co.

ROYAL CUMBERLAND.
[No. 9.]
Head Quarters, Whitehaven.
COLONEL.
Hon. H. C. Lowther(1), MP.
late Major 10 *Hussars and Lt. Col.* 12 F..................10 Sept. 30
LIEUT.-COLONEL.
Frederick Brandreth, JP, *late Lt.Col. Scots Fus. Gds.* ....24 May 54
MAJOR.
Wm. Godfrey Clerk Monins,
JP. *late Capt.* 23 F. ....26 Aug. 52
CAPTAINS.
Samuel Lacy Wm. Sanderson..10 May 53
Edward Beetham ....11 Dec. 54
Henry Spencer ....23 Dec. 54
Ralph Bromfield Fisher......28 Dec. 54
Wm. Henry Weston, *late Lt.*
77 F................................20 Mar. 55
Samuel A. Finnamore ....17 Dec. 55
John Skottowe ....31 Dec. 55
Thos. H. Rossall.............. 8 Apr. 58
LIEUTENANTS.
James Lumb ....18 Sept. 52
Alured Aug. D. L'Estrange...20 Mar. 55
Fielding Trimmer ....25 Sept. 55
Wm. Joseph Patrick Hamm...31 Dec. 55
John Walker .... 8 Apr. 58
Wm. Kinsey Dover............ 8 Apr. 58
William Gaitskill ....16 July 58
ENSIGNS.
Francis Fairtlough............12 Apr. 55
Thomas Ramsden Ashworth 14 Dec. 55
John Jameson..................28 Jan. 56
Wladimir B. J. O. Jackson ...31 Jan. 56
Edward Ogle Moore .... 1 Oct. 57

Adjt. & Captain.—William H.
S. Sharpe, *late Lient.* 1 F....14 Sept. 52
Acting Qr.Mast.—Wm. John
Robinson ....12 Oct. 59
Surgeon.—Thomas Delamain
Wheatley, M.D. ....31 Oct. 55
Assist.Surgeon.—John Dixon
Fidler, MD....................... 9 Nov. 55
Blue Facings.
Agents, Messrs. Hopkinson & Co.

ROYAL DENBIGH.
(*Rifles*.) [No. 46.]
Head Quarters, Wrexham.
COLONEL COMMANDANT.
Robert Myddelton Biddulph,
Lord Lieut. MP. JP. .... 3 Mar. 40
MAJOR.
John Jocelyn Ffoulkes, JP ...12 Mar. 57
CAPTAINS.
Robert William Wynne........ 9 Feb. 56
Boscawen Trevor Griffith, (1)
late Lieut. 23 F.............28 Sept. 58
Richard Austin Herbert, *late of* 2 *Drs.* ....23 July 59
Rowland Brodhurst Hill, *late Lieut.* 77 F. ....23 Dec. 59
LIEUTENANTS.
Thomas Lloyd .... 8 Dec. 59
ENSIGNS.
Geo. Henry Rose Briscoe ...20 Nov. 57
Wm. J. Geoghegan...........18 May 58
Hugh Robert Hughes ....16 Aug. 58
Adj. & Captain.—Dan. M'Coy,
DL. *late Capt.* 55 F. ....30 July 52
Surgeon.—Aug. Henry Churchill .... 2 May 55
Blue Facings.
Agents, Messrs. Barron and Smith.

1ST DERBY.
[No. 62.]
Head Quarters, Derby.
COLONEL.
H. M., *Lord* Waterpark, MP,
DL. JP. ....12 Apr. 31
LIEUT.COLONEL.
Edward Thomas Coke,(1) DL.
JP. *late Capt.* 69 F.........18 Nov. 53
MAJOR.
Ashton Mosley,(2) JP. *late Capt.* 60 *Rifles*.............21 Sept. 52
CAPTAINS.
Thomas Kemp Story ....16 Sept. 52
Thomas Edmund Marsland ..16 Mar. 54
George Newdigate,(3) JP, ...23 Mar. 54
Hodder Roberts, *late Lt.* 50 F.23 Oct. 54
John Wm. Thos. Locke, JP, *late Major Italian Legion* ...... 7 Dec. 54
Thomas Peach ....10 July 58
John Woolnough ....13 July 58
LIEUTENANTS.
Samuel Collinson *Act.Qr.Mr.* 13 Sept. 52
William Jessopp..............Sept. 55
Thomas Bateman ....19 Oct. 55
Charles Rodney Huxley ......17 Mar. 57
Robert Curzon................. 4 Oct. 58
Joseph Guliffe Robinson ......16 Aug. 59
Wm. Langton Coke ....16 Aug. 59
ENSIGNS.
Adjt. & Capt.—Chas. Yelverton Balguy, *late Capt.* 42 F. 28 Apr. 55
Paymaster & Captain.—John
Edwd. Loveson Gower, *late Captain* 50 F. .... 1 May 55
Surg.—Chas. Harwood, MD. 23 Dec. 54
Assist.Surg.—Chas. Edw. R.
Huxley .... 2 June 55
Yellow Facings.
Agents, Messrs. Cox & Co.

2ND DERBY.
[No. 34.]
(*The Chatsworth Rifles*.)
Head Quarters, Chesterfield.
LIEUT.COLONEL COMMANDANT.
Wm. Henry Fred. Cavendish, DL.
late of 52 F., *Groom in Waiting to the Queen* ....25 Jan. 55
MAJOR.
S. C. *Marq. of* Hartington, M.P.
DL..................................25 Jan. 55
CAPTAINS.
Francis Hurt, DL.............. 9 Feb. 55
Hon. Wm.Geo.Cavendish, MP.
late of 10 *Hussars* .... 1 May 55
Ferdinand Arkwright, *late of 4 Dr. Gds.* ....23 May 55
Edw. Lovett Darwin ....26 Feb. 56
Alfred James Milnes ....11 Mar. 56
Geo. L. R. Wilkinson ....18 Oct. 58
LIEUTENANTS.
Edward Smithers ....28 Feb. 55
Edward Ward Fox...........21 Apr. 55
Bernard Lucas ....25 June 55
Felix Garmston Goodwin.....26 Feb. 56
Fred. Halbrook Peat, *late of* 97 F........................11 Mar. 56
Tho. John Poyser ....18 Oct. 58
ENSIGNS.
Henry Moore Brownrigg, *late Capt.* 52 F. ....15 Aug. 56
John Bidwell ....15 Aug. 56
Adj. & Capt.—Geo. Elliott....26 Apr. 55
Surgeon.—Robt. Newbold ...19 July 59
Assist.Surg.—
Black Facings.

1ST DEVON.
[No. 41.]
Head Quarters, Exeter.
COLONEL.
Hugh, *Earl* Fortescue, K.G.,
Lord Lieut., late of 9 F......20 May 16
LIEUT.COLONEL COMMANDANT.
John Davie Ferguson Davie(1),
DL.JP. *late Capt.* Gren. Gds. 1 Nov. 58
MAJORS.
David Rattray (2), *late Capt.*
13 F........................... 6 Feb. 55
Samuel John Maclurcan, *late Capt.* 19 F. ....25 May 55
CAPTAINS.
Richard Hall Clarke, DL.......30 July 53
Charles Furston ....15 June 54
George Lane Dacie ....16 Jan. 55
George Henry Woods .... 6 Feb. 55
Halifax Wyatt.................. 6 July 55
William Arnold ....14 Aug. 55
John Tanner Davy .... 3 Nov. 55
Phillip Heatly Douglas ...... 8 Mar. 56
Thomas Dimond Hogg ...... 1 July 59
Alexander Ridgway ....21 July 59
LIEUTENANTS.
Henry A. Martyn Farrant....16 Jan. 55
George Byles ....24 Mar. 56
Falconer Cooke ....24 Mar. 56
John Innes Bathe ....24 Mar. 56
Edward Drewe .... 4 Apr. 56
Henry FitzWilliam Hallifax..11 Aug. 56
Richard Anson Brine ....28 June 59
Thos. Welby Northmore ....22 July 59
John Charles David Agar ...29 July 59
John Tyrrell ....13 Aug. 59
George Aug. Pollard ....13 Aug. 59
ENSIGNS.
John Hawkesworth ....11 Mar. 58
Albert Cecil Robert Drewe ...23 Oct. 58
Edward Cuthbert Ring........21 Dec. 58

Militia of England and Wales. 618

Adjt. & Capt.—Edmund Pitman, *late Capt.* 55 F. ....30 Dec. 54
Paymaster & Captain.—D ᚐᚐ Chas. Holman, (3) DL., *late of* 62 F. ....30 Dec. 54
Quarter Master.—John Macdonald, (4) *late of* 1 F. 1 Aug.56
Surgeon. — Henry Thomas Hartnoll ....12 Feb. 57
Assist.Surg.—Thomas Wilson Caird........................12 Feb. 57
White Facings.
Agent, Sir John Kirkland.

SOUTH DEVON.
[No. 25.]
Head Quarters, Plymouth.
LIEUT.COLONEL COMMANDANT.
John B. Y., *Lord* Churston, DL. JP. ....12 May 45
MAJORS.
John Line Templer, JP. ......15 Dec. 57
Hon. John B. Yarde Buller, JP.15 Dec. 57
CAPTAINS.
Henry Richard Roe, DL. JP..11 Apr. 46
Jno Newcombe Stevenson, JP..11 Apr. 46
Geo. Sidney Strode, JP..........25 June 53
John Camden Goodridge, JP...14 Aug. 52
Charles Aug. Coles................20 Nov. 54
Robert Trood ....13 Oct. 55
Wm. Rennell Coleridge, JP....19 Nov. 55
Charles Seale Hayne .... 1 Jan. 58
John Gore Hawkins ....12 Jan. 58
Henry Dimsdale Parr ....28 Jan. 58
LIEUTENANTS.
John Thomas Soltau ....19 Nov. 55
Robert Bent Farwell.............23 Jan. 56
Henry Swete Archer.............17 June 56
Edmund Lopes ....30 Nov. 56
Hugh C. Vaughan ....28 June 59
Berkeley Aug. M'D. Macpherson do
ENSIGNS.
Henry Smith ....13 Nov. 57
Clarence Hamilton Irvine......27 Nov. 57
Harry Elderton Whidborne...12 Jan. 58
George Marker ....28 June 59
Geo. Edmund Allen ....28 Oct. 59
Adj. & Capt.—Wm. Hawley Fisk, (5) *Capt. on h. p., formerly Capt.* 17 *Lancers*...22 Sept.36
Paymaster.—John Southwell Brown, JP. *late of* 10 *Hussars*31 Mar.55
Qr.Master.—William Jarvis, *late of* 77 F. .... 2 Aug. 56
Surgeon.—Frederick Vavason Sandford,(6) *late of R.N.* ... 1 Feb. 58
Assist.Surg.—Percy Leslie ... 1 Feb. 58
White Facings.
Agent, Sir John Kirkland.

DEVON ARTILLERY.
[No. 7.]
Head Quarters, Devonport.
LIEUT.COLONEL COMMANDANT.
Sir George Stucley, *Bart.*, DL. JP. *late of Royal Horse Gds*.30 July 49
MAJOR.
Richard Bury Russell, *late Lt.* 2 F. ....29 June 59
CAPTAINS.
John Norris Marshall ....10 May 54
Edward Barwell .... 1 May 55
John Cave New .... 4 July 59
Henry Charles Devon ....14 July 59
LIEUTENANTS.
Wm. Hammet Beadon 1 Apr.56

Thomas Reynolds Arscott .... 4 July 59
Reginald Guard Palmer......14 July 59
Wm. Arundell Yeo ....29 Oct. 59
George Lysaght .... 4 Nov. 59
SECOND LIEUTENANTS.
Frederic Lysaght .... 4 Nov. 59
Adj. & Capt.—John Lakin, *late of R. Art.*........................ 2 May 53
Surg.—Garland Foley Bayley Harrison ....18 Jan. 55
Scarlet Facings.
Agent, Sir John Kirkland.

DORSET.
[No. 42.]
Head Quarters, Dorchester.
COLONEL.
Richard Hippisley Bingham, (1) DL. JP. *late Capt. Madras Army* ....26 July 52
LIEUT.COLONEL.
D George C. Loftus, DL. JP. (3) *late Capt.* 3 F. *Guards* . 2 June55
MAJOR.
Edward Atkyns Wood ....12 Nov. 59
CAPTAINS.
George Gollop, *late Lt.* 2 F...23 Sept.52
Charles Littlehales, (4) *late Capt.* 78 F. .... 1 Feb. 53
John Davis .... 4 Apr. 53
Reginald Foot, *late of* 14 F. ...19 Mar. 55
John Gollop........................ 2 June 55
George Singer 23 June55
John Warry 26 Mar.56
LIEUTENANTS.
Wm. Henry Bragge ....26 Mar. 56
Grantham T. Fulwasser .....19 Mar. 58
Charles Herd...................... do
James Anderson, *late Lt.*4 F. do
Hubert C. Gould................. 7 Oct. 58
Robert Clayton Brown ....17 Nov. 58
ENSIGNS.
Freeman Aug. Padmore 2 June55
Percy Rollo Brett .... 5 Oct. 55
William Henry Bower .... 1 Mar. 56
Alex. Hammond Smith.......19 Mar.58
Fra. Henry Palmer Duncan... do
David Alex. Forbes .... 7 Oct. 58
Adj. & Capt.— Edw. H. Smith, *late Capt.* 76 F., *Actg. Paymaster* ....30 June 52
Surg.—George Curme 23 Sept.52
Assist.Surg.—Robert Clarke 30 May 55
Green Facings.
Agents, Messrs. Cox and Co.

1ST OR SOUTH DURHAM.
[No. 3.]
Head Quarters, Barnard Castle.
COLONEL.
Lieut.General *The Duke of Cleveland*, KG. ....16 May 42
LIEUT.COLONEL.
William Maude 15 Mar.58
MAJOR.
Arch. Hamilton Cochrane......15 Mar. 58
CAPTAINS.
John Haverfield, *late Capt.* 43 F. ....22 Jan. 55
Edward Kent Fairless .... 7 Mar. 55
John Russell Bowlby...........19 Mar. 55
William Ord.......................20 April55
John Fred. Gales 21 June55
Wm. Dale Trotter .... do
Geo. Henry Londridge Hawke12 Feb. 57
George Sowerby................15 Mar. 58

LIEUTENANTS.
William Atcheson ....22 Jan. 55
William Chaytor................21 June55
T. Kipling, *Act. Qr.-Master*... 1 Jan. 56
Robert Warner Stone.......... 1 Apr. 56
Henry James Fielding ....30 Mar. 57
Wm. Matthews Gales ....17 Aug. 57
Thomas Chas. J. Sowerby....15 Mar. 55
Charles James Briggs .... 2 Dec. 58
ENSIGNS.

Adjt. & Capt.—Edward Fred. Agnew, *late Capt.* 34 F. ...28 Feb. 56
Surg.—D Edward Nixon (4), *late of Coldstream Gds.* 24 Sept.21
Assist.Surg.—John Potts......22 Jan. 55
White Facings.
Agents, Messrs. Cox and Co.

2ND OR NORTH DURHAM.
[No. 43.]
Head Quarters, Durham.
LIEUT.COLONEL COMMANDANT.
Earl Vane, *late of* 1 L. *Gds.* ... 6 May 53
MAJORS.
Edward Johnson, JP............30Sept. 54
Alex. Cockburn, *late Capt.* 11 F. 1 Feb. 56
CAPTAINS.
Percival Spearman Wilkinson, JP................................14June 53
Tho. Wm. U. Robinson........12 Oct. 53
Albany Wm. Featherstonhaugh30 Sept.54
John Henry Lukis, *late of* 61 F. 1 Mar. 55
Robert John Burrell ....30 Apr. 55
James John Allison .... 6 June 57
Henry Drog Gaynor ....13 June 59
Francis Robert Burrowes, *late Lt.* 11 F. ....23 July 59

LIEUTENANTS.
James Robert Dalton Dewar...30 Apr. 55
Geo. Lewis Trotter............. 7 Sept.55
Augustus Rich .... 8 Feb. 56
Benjamin Eames ....20 Oct. 58
John Nicholas Garvey .... do
Edw. Temperley Gourley..... do
Joseph Baker ....15 July 59

ENSIGNS.

Adj. & Capt.—Thos. Scarman(*late Lieut. & Adj.* 31 Ft. ... 6 May 53
Surg.—Thomas Henry Wilkin 27 Sept. 58
Assist.Surg. — Francis Halloran Ffolliott ....15 July 59
Agents, Messrs. Cox and Co.

DURHAM ARTILLERY.
[No. 10.] [Embodied.]
Head Quarters, Gosport.
HONORARY COLONEL.
Henry Stobart, DL.,J.P. *Lieut. h. p. R. Art.*..................... 6Sept.59
LIEUT.COLONEL COMMANDANT.
George Hall, DL., *late Bt. Major Madras Art.*............... 6Sept.59
MAJOR.
W. Cookson (2), *late Capt.* 9 F. 4 Oct. 54

Militia of England and Wales.

CAPTAINS.
George Hodgson .... 22 Dec. 54
Edward Featherstonhaugh ...30 July 56
Hugh Stafford 17 Aug.57
Octavius Polly, *Capt. h. p. 7*
Madras Lt. Cavalry......... 31 Mar. 59

FIRST LIEUTENANTS.
John Charles Sandall .... 30 May 56
Chas. Spencer Malley 17 Aug.57
Richard Thomas Tidswell..... 17 Aug.57
Jas. E. Ainslie Mather .... 19 May 59

SECOND LIEUTENANTS.
Mark Quayle .... 24 Feb. 59
John James de la Taste......... 7 Mar. 59
Frederick Blacklin .... 31 Mar. 59
Arthur Munro .... 19 May 59

Adj. & Capt.—Robert William
Scott, *late of R. Art.* .... 2 June 53
Paymaster. — Cortlandt G.
M'Gregor Skinner .... 25 June 59
Surg.—James Trotter .... 11 Aug. 53

THE ESSEX RIFLES.
[No. 13.]
Head Quarters, Colchester.

HONORARY COLONEL.
Hon. C. H. Maynard, *late R. Horse Gds.* .... 30 Oct. 54
LIEUT.COLONEL COMMANDANT.
Edw. Henry Moore Kelly, *late Capt. 3 F.* .... 2 Feb. 58

MAJORS.
Fred. Geo. Whitehead, *late Capt. 42 F.* .... 6 June 57
Christopher Brice Wilkinson (3), *late Capt. 68 F.*...31 Aug. 58

CAPTAINS.
Frederic Wm. Kirby .... 2 Oct. 54
Samuel George Savill............ 1 Dec. 54
Capel Coape, *late Capt. 67 F.*.. 2 Dec. 54
Evelyn Philip Meadows ......15 June 55
John Savill .... 6 July 55
Marcus Wm. Davies .... 10 Aug. 55
Charles Andrew Irwin .... 10 Aug. 55
Griffin Curtis Galt .... 13 Oct. 58

LIEUTENANTS.
Francis Barrington Dickens... 9 June 54
Robert Swann...................... 6 July 55
William Gordon .... 10 Aug. 55
Edward Robinson .... 13 Oct. 58
Bertram A. J. Mitford .... do
Waldren Edw. R. Kelly ...... do
Wm. Roberts Knobel .... do
Fred. Oldham Yeo .... 21 Nov. 59

ENSIGNS.
Albert Robson Burkill......... 13 Oct. 58
Wm. Tate Philpott .... do
Lewis Dodgson .... 10 Dec. 58
Adj.&Capt.—StewartNorthey, *late Lieut.25 F*........ 22 Sept. 52
Paymaster.—
Qrmaster. — Stephen Orrell, *late 49 F.*..........................11 Sept. 55
Surg.— Edward Waylen 3 Nov.52
Assist.Surg.—Geo. Allat Edman .... 16 July 55
Agents, Messrs. Cox & Co.

WEST ESSEX.
[No. 19.]
Head Quarters, Chelmsford.

LIEUT.COLONEL COMMANDANT.
Samuel Brise Ruggles Brise, DL. J.P. *late of* 1 *Dr. Gds.*....25 Feb. 53

MAJORS.
Edward Jodrell (1) JP., *late Capt.* 18 *F.* .... 29 Dec. 54
Champion Russell, JP. ....17 May 55

CAPTAINS.
Horatio Edenborough (2) ......16 Mar. 53
Geo. Richard Layton............ 12 June 55
Humphrey Rich. Geo. Marriott22 Nov. 55
John Manners Tharpe .... 2 Jan. 56
Wm. James Lucas ....30 Oct. 58
Morrice H. H. Bird .... do
Myles Lonsdale Formby....... 31 Dec. 58
Wm. Maling Wynch 22 Sept.59

LIEUTENANTS.
Alfred M'Kenna .... 18 May 55
Henry Septimus Eicke .... 16 Oct. 58

ENSIGNS.
Adj. & Capt.—Robert Otho
Travers, *late Capt.1Dr.Gds* 27 Nov. 58
Qr.Master.—Charles Hyder...23 Sept.59
Surg. —Henry Bird............. 13 Oct. 52
Assist.Surg. — John Thomas
Gilson .... 5 Nov. 52
Yellow Facings.
Agents, Messrs. Cox and Co.

ROYAL FLINT.
(*Rifles.*) [No. 32.]
Head Quarters, Mold.

COLONEL.
Hon. Richard Thomas Rowley, DL. JP. *late Capt. Scots Fus. Gds.*.....................14 May 55

MAJOR.
Cowel Maddock Arthur Jones, DL. J.P. ....14 May 55

CAPTAINS.
Robert Wills, DL. JP. ....20 Oct. 52
Charles James Trevor Roper, DL. JP........................17 Feb. 53
Richard Pelham Warren, DL. JP. ....17 Feb. 53
Cecil Squire *late Capt.* 2 *F*...14 June 59

LIEUTENANTS.

ENSIGN.
Charles Wm. Shackle............11 Oct. 59

Adjt. & Capt.—Fred. Mathias,(1) *late Capt.* 54 *F.* ....27 Feb. 55
Surg.—William Williams, MD.20 Oct. 52

ROYAL GLAMORGAN.
(*Light Infantry.*) [No. 44.]
Head Quarters, Cardiff.

COLONEL.
C. J. Kemeys Tynte, MP. DL. 4 June 49
LIEUT.COLONEL.
Edward Robert Wood, DL. JP. *late of* 12 *Lancers* ....29 Oct. 58

MAJOR.
John Popkin Traherne, *late Ens.*39 *F.*.......................29 Oct. 58

CAPTAINS.
H. A. Goldfinch .... 15 Nov. 52
Charles Deacon, *late Captain* 9 *Lancers*.......................25 Apr. 53
Richard Mahony Hickson (2), *late Lt.* 73 *F.*....................19 May 55
Henry Ferth .... 11 Apr. 56
John Wm. N. B. Parry, *late Ens.* 29 *F.* .... 3 May 56
Wm. Brame Abbot............... 7 Feb. 59
George Rashleigh Gompertz... 2 Apr. 59
John Fred. Napier Hewett, JP., *late Lt.* 72 *F.* ....18 Aug. 59

LIEUTENANTS.
Tobias Fitzgerald .... 17 Feb. 46
Henry Burrowes................. 28 Dec. 55
Francis John Shortis............ 22 Mar. 56
Richard Fisher Evans 30 Sept.58
Henry Hammond Spencer ... do
John B. Kemeys Tynte (3) ...21 July 59
James Thorne George .... 10 Dec. 59

ENSIGNS.
Hon. Fred. Wm. de Moleyns...11 June 56

Adj. & Captain.—Wm. Henry Bennett, *late Capt.* 42 *F.*...15 May 56
Paymaster.—Martin Charles
Maher, *late Vet. Batt.* ....19 Dec. 54
Surgeon.—H. J. Paine .... 8 Nov. 52
Assist.Surg.—James Evans ... 8 Nov. 52
Blue Facings.
Agent, Edward S. Codd, *Esq,*

ROYAL GLAMORGAN ARTILLERY.
[No. 15.]
Head Quarters, Swansea.

LIEUT.COLONEL COMMANDANT.
Evan Morgan (1), DL. JP.
R. Art. Bt. Major ret. f. p. 2 Dec. 54

CAPTAINS.
John Crymes, *late Lt.* 46 *F*... 25 Apr. 55
Josiah Pryce .... 20 June 57
George Elliot Ranken ....14 Oct. 57

LIEUTENANTS.
Joseph Morley Dennis ....21 June 57
Robert Wm. Acheson Shortis .21 June 57
Thomas Bateman .... 18 May 59
James Simpson Ballard ...... 9 June 59

SECOND LIEUTENANTS.

Adj.—William Young .... 31 Jan. 55
Surg.—John Paddon, MB...... 9 Mar. 55

ROYAL SOUTH GLOUCESTER.
(*Light Infantry.*) [No. 23.]
Head Quarters, Gloucester.

HONORARY COLONEL.
Francis Wm. FitzHardinge
Berkeley, *late Capt. Royal Horse Guards* .... 22 Dec. 57
LIEUT.COLONEL COMMANDANT.
Henry W. Newman, DL. JP... 3 Apr. 54

MAJORS.
John Surman, DL. JP. *late Ens.* 58 *F.*........................ 3 Apr. 54
Henry Crawley, *Lt.Col. ret. f. p.* 20 *F.*....................29 Jan. 58

Militia of England and Wales.

CAPTAINS.
Montague John Merryweather 21 Apr. 36
Hamlet William Millett ......18 Sept. 52
Winchcombe Henry Howard
 Hartley, DL. JP.................. 3 Nov. 52
Arthur John Goldney .... 7 Dec. 52
Swinb. Fitzhardinge Berkeley 6 Apr. 53
William James Holt ....21 Oct. 54
Conway Whithorne Lovesey, JP.12 Oct. 55
Robert Heane ....18 Dec. 55
Thomas Morse ....22 Jan. 56
Geo. Henry Bengough ....21 Dec. 58

LIEUTENANTS.
Thomas Earle ....29 Dec. 38
Arthur Charles N. Goldney ...14 Feb. 55
William Robinson Partridge... 1 May 55
Henry Le Patourel ....18 Dec. 55
John Robert Fenn ....19 Feb. 56
John Pitt Bontein .... 4 July 56
Chas. Aug. Gibson...............13 Dec. 56
Edward Dangerfield ....29 Jan. 58
John Thomas Jackson .... 2 Nov. 58
John Wm. Berrington ....29 June 59

ENSIGNS.
John Powell.......................10 Mar. 58
Arthur Ryves 18 Mar.58
John Carrington 10 Sept.58
John Maurice Bernabo ....12 Mar. 59
Edward Daniel Gibson .... 6 Apr. 59
Robert Clayton Daubeny .....23 May 59
Adjt. & Capt.—James Robert-
 son, *late Lieut. 79 F* ....21 Nov. 53
Paymaster.—James Fallon ...27 Apr. 55
Qr.Master.—Jas. Cuningham 23 Apr. 55
Surg.—George A. Hepworth...10 Mar.55
Assist.Surg.—James Coles ...21 Mar.55

Blue Facings.

Agents, Messrs. Hopkinson and Co.

ROYAL NORTH GLOUCESTER.
[No. 69.]
Head Quarters, Cirencester.

COLONEL.
Thos. Henry Kingscote, DL.
 JP. *late of 2 Life Gds.* ......22 Feb. 40

LIEUT.COLONEL.
John Williams Wallington, JP.
 late Capt. 4 *Lt. Drs.* ....16 Dec. 54

MAJOR.
Henry Bold Williams...........30 June 59

CAPTAINS.
Leonard M. Strachey, DL. JP.
 late E. I. Co.'s Service......26 Sept. 51
Charles Castle, JP.............. 5 Oct. 52
Sir J. Maxwell Steele, *Bart.*JP.31 Dec. 52
E. W. A. Vaughan..............12 Apr. 53
John Jones, (1) *late Capt.* 46
 Bengal N. I. ....15 Apr. 53
Allen Alex. Bathurst, M.P. ...10 Nov. 54
William Brookes, JP. ....11 Dec. 55
Nathaniel Fred. Ellison........21 Dec. 57
Charles Hawkins Fisher.......4 Mar. 58
Robert Beckles Hunte, *late
 Lt.* 82 *F*. 30 June59

LIEUTENANTS.
H. C. *Viscount* Andover, JP.,26 Dec. 55
Charles Mansfield .... 7 Feb. 54
Nigel G. Rabbitts ....28 May 55
Arthur F. Howe Daniel ....28 May 55
Andrew Pepys Cockerell .....11 Dec. 55
Samuel Bomford, *late Lt.* 3
 Dr. Gds. .... 3 Feb. 56
John Averley Lathbury........ 7 Jan. 58
William Clarke ....23 Nov. 58
Wm. S. M. Goodenough ......23 May 59
William Robert Geo 30June59

ENSIGNS.
Wm. Wreford Brown...........23 May 59
David Henry Parry ....19 July 59

Adjt. & Capt.—John Tobin,
 Capt. h.p. Unatt. .... 9 Apr. 46
Paymaster.—Tho. Stevenson 5 Nov. 57
Qr.Mast.—John Gorman .....12 Dec. 55
Surgeon.—Sam.SwaineScriven15 Mar. 55
Assist.Surg.—Jno. Leete Eland 2 Apr. 55

Blue Facings.

Agents, Messrs. Cox and Co.

HAMPSHIRE.
[No. 122.]
Head Quarters, Winchester.

COLONEL.
The Marquis of Winchester,
 late Lt.Col. 10 *Hussars* ...... 7 June 43

LIEUT.COLONEL.
⑭ Severus Wm. Lynam Stret-
 ton,(3), *late Lt.Col.* 40 *F*. 9 Mar.55

MAJORS.
Eustace Heathcote, JP. *late
 Capt.*34 *F*. .... 1 Feb. 56
William Henry Digweed ...... 5 Apr. 59

CAPTAINS.
John Wickham .... 8 Sept. 53
Thomas Best .... 8 Sept. 53
Henry Barré Phipps, *late Capt.*
 31 *F*. .... 2 June 54
Wm. S. Greatheed, *late Lieut.*
 41 *F*............................30 Dec. 54
Hon. Oliver Geo. Lambert,
 late Lt. 12 *F*.................28 Aug. 58
Geo. Francis Birch .... do
Edmund Wm. Crofts, *late
 Capt.* 23 *F*. .... do
Peter Wright Breton (4), *late
 Capt.* 38 *F*. .... 9 Sept. 58
Fra. James Bampfylde, *late
 Capt.* 22 *F*. ....28 May 59
Henry Bathurst (5), *late Capt.*
 23 *F*............................23 July 59

LIEUTENANTS.
Tanfield Geo. Headley 10 June54
Seymour Horace Morgan......18 Sept. 55
Henry Cracroft Maine, *late Lt.*
 86 *F*...........................19 Nov. 55
Edw. Charles Forwood ....28 Apr. 56
Reginald Charles Riddell 30 June57
Henry Edwards 30 June57

ENSIGNS.
Charles James Brett ....5 April 58

Adjt.&Capt.—James Nicol, *late
 Capt.* 13 *F*. ....8 May 57
Qr.Master.—Capt. Tho. Wal-
 ter Hives, *h. p. Q.M.* 40 *F.*23 Apr. 58
Surg.—James Johnston, MD.
 late Surgeon 26 *F.* .... 3 Nov. 54
Assist.Surgeon.— Reginald
 Bayley Walters 23 Sept.54

Black Facings.

Agents, Messrs. Cox & Co.

HAMPSHIRE ARTILLERY.
[No. 16.]
[Embodied.]
Head Quarters, Pembroke.

COLONEL.
The Earl of Malmesbury 22 June54

LIEUT.COLONEL COMMANDANT.
⑭Rich. Beaumont Burnaby,(1)
 Col.ret.full pay R. Art....30 May 53

MAJOR.
⑭Claudius Shaw, (2) KSF. *late
 of R.Artil.& Col.of Artil.late
 British Auxiliary Legion of
 Spain* ....30 May 53

CAPTAINS.
John Beardmore, DL. JP...... 3 Dec. 52
Hugh Hamon John Massy, *late
 Capt.* 44 *F*. ....14 Jan. 53
William Bridges, *late Capt.*
 59 *F*........................... 7 Oct. 53
Robert Mansel, *late Capt.* 6
 Drs. ....30 Dec. 53
Arthur Robert Naghten ...... 3 Aug. 59

FIRST LIEUTENANTS.
John Robert Campbell ....24 May 55
James James ....26 Apr. 56
John Annesley Brownrigg ... 6 Oct. 58
Cecil Thomas Beeching....... 6 Nov. 58
George Mansel .... 3 Aug. 59

SECOND LIEUTENANTS.
Coventry Baynton............... 5 Apr. 59
George Staunton Lynch ......24 Aug. 59
James Winslowe Tighe.......21 Oct. 59
Fred. Ponsonby Cammilleri ...10 Dec. 59

Adj.& Capt.—James Frost,*late
 of Royal Artillery* ....11 May 59
Paymaster.—
Qr.Master.—Wm. Aslett ......24 Mar. 55
Surg.—Jas. Walkinshaw Bell
 Alder..........................26 Feb. 59
Assist.Surg. — Wm. Akers
 Harrison......................26 Feb. 59

Scarlet Facings.

Agents, Messrs. Cox and Co.

HEREFORD.
[No. 110.]
Head Quarters, Hereford.

COLONEL.

LIEUT.COLONEL COMMANDANT.
George, *Lord* Northwick, DL.
 JP. *late Capt.* 1*st Life Gds*.., 1 Mar. 53

MAJORS.
Thomas Powell Symonds, DL.
 JP. .... 5 July 59
J. Berington .... do

CAPTAINS.
W. Money Kyrle, DL. JP.......10 Sept. 50
Charles Ernest Turner, DL.
 late Capt. 44 *F*. ....24 Feb. 55
Thomas Griffith Peyton ....26 Feb. 55
Richard Sneyd Cox, DL.JP.... 1 May 56
John Harward Griffiths,DL.JP. 5 July 59
Edward Williams .... do

LIEUTENANTS.
Richard Fred. Webb 14 Mar.55
John Michael Browne ....15 Feb. 56
Thos. Millard Bennett ....5 July 59
Fred. Aldrich ....12 July 59
Edw. Napleton Cheese .... do
Henry Wood Willett .... do

ENSIGNS.
Wm. Christopher Seymour ...26 Feb. 56
Fra. Wm. Laing 3 Sept.58
Adjutant.—J. E. Money Kyrle,
 DL. *Capt. on h. p.* ....27 Apr. 46
Paymaster.—
Surg.—J. Morris ....17 July 46
Assist.Surg.—Rd. Thomason. 2 Jan. 55

Goslin Green Facings.

Agents, Messrs. Cox and Co.

Militia of England and Wales.

HERTFORD.
[No. 30.]
Head Quarters, Hatfield.

COLONEL.
The Marquis of Salisbury, KG. 9 May 51

LIEUT.COLONEL.
Robt. Algernon Smith Dorrien, JP. late Captain 3 Lt. Drs. 2 Dec. 54

MAJOR.
Joseph Foskett, JP., Capt. Unatt. late of 50 F. ....16 Dec. 54

CAPTAINS.
William Franks, JP. ....13 Apr. 52
Fred. Charles Gaussen ....30 Oct. 52
Adolphus Meetkerke........... 8 June 53
Octavius Frederic Tinitus, late Capt. 82 F. ....21 July 53
Bryan V. Douglas Vernon, late Lt. 60 F. .... 1 May 54
James John Gape ....16 Dec. 54
Henry Grimston Hale, late Lt. 11 Hussars ....16 Dec. 54
Thomas Byron Myers ....23 Oct. 58

LIEUTENANTS.
Robert Bruce Fellows ....30 Nov. 55
Alex. Geo. Bax .... 2 Dec. 58
Ernest Ibbotson .... 3 Dec. 58
Richard Cumberlege........... 8 Nov. 59
William Majoribanks .... 8 Nov. 59

ENSIGNS.
Stuart V. Fraser .... 2 Feb. 56
Humphrey Fred. H. B. Herne 10 Dec. 59
Adj. & Capt.—Edward Sims James (1), late Capt. 24 F.., 9 May 46
Surg.—Chas. R. Thompson ...22 Mar. 55
Assist.Surg.— Henry Fra. Coley............................ 1 June 55

Buff Facings.
Agent, Sir John Kirkland.

HUNTINGDON.
(Rifles). [No. 2.]
Head Quarters, Huntingdon.

COLONEL.
The Earl of Sandwich, Lord Lieut., and late of Gr. Gds. 4 Aug. 53

MAJOR.
The Duke of Manchester, DL. JP., late of Gr. Gds..........17 Aug. 52

CAPTAINS.
John Vise Kelly ....31 O t. 53
Frederic Nicholson Vane ... 29 A t. 55
Gilbert John Ansley .... 2 Oct 55
George John Rust .... 27 Ap. 57
Stephen Rowland Woulfe... 8 Ju y 59

LIEUTENANTS.
Herbert R. Mansel Jones.....29 Sept.57
Fred. James Rooper (1), late Lt. 38 F. ....18 Dec. 57
Wm. Whitter Goldicutt ......21 Mar. 59
Hon. Henry S. Blackwood.... 1 Aug. 59

ENSIGNS.
Morgan Vane ....12 July 59
Thomas Thornhill .... do
John E. D. Shafto .... 8 Oct. 59
Adj. & Capt.— Grenville G. Wells, late Capt. 41 F. ...23 Sept. 56
Surgeon.—Edmund Carver ... 8 Oct. 59

Black Facings.

ISLE OF WIGHT ARTILLERY.
[No. 17.]
Head Quarters, Fort Victoria.
LT.COLONEL COMMANDANT.
Percy Scott, JP. Lt. h. p. 98 F............................. 9 Dec. 59

MAJOR.
Robert Gordon, late of 66 F....14 Dec. 59

CAPTAINS.
Francis Worsley .... 7 Dec. 59
Benj. Whitmore Puckle........16 Dec. 59

LIEUTENANTS.
John Vicary .... 9 Dec. 59
William Puckle .... do.
Wm. Benett P. Brigstoke...... do.

SECOND LIEUTENANTS.
William Henry Pattinson..... 9 Dec. 59
Fra. Gordon Degge Watson ... do.

Adj. & Capt.—Thomas Alex. Robinson, late of Royal Art.20 Apr. 53
Surgeon.—Henry Waterworth.20 Apr. 53

Scarlet Facings.
Agents, Messrs. Cox and Co.

EAST KENT.
[No. 49.]
[Embodied.]
Head Quarters, Portsmouth.
The Motto "Invicta" under a White Horse. "Mediterranean."

COLONEL.
Geo. Brockman, late Capt. 85 F. ....15 Sept. 52

LIEUT.COLONEL.
Cholmeley Edward Dering, DL., late Capt. 85 F. ....10 Oct. 57

MAJOR.
Wm. Wray Maunsell, late Capt. 85 F. 14 Nov.57

CAPTAINS.
Richard D. Pennefather ......10 July 53
Henry Castle ....18 July 54
Wm. Henry Kebbel, late Lt. 66 F..........................22 July 54
Charles Castle ....22 Feb. 55
Duncan Inverarity .... 1 Oct. 55
Henry Thomas Howell ....19 Aug. 57
Stanislas Zaba ....14 May 58
Henry Gillett ....10 Nov. 58
John Edward Beales .... 2 Feb. 59
Hugesson Edw. Knatchbull.., 4 July 59

LIEUTENANTS.
Geo. Edw.Arthur Holdsworth 10 Apr. 58
William Tatham ....11 Apr. 58
Duncan Tylden Chisholm....26 Apr. 58
James Robert Monypenny ...14 May 58
Robert Owen Hordern .... 7 July 58
George Francis Simmons .....30 May 58
Corbet John Coventry ....18 Nov. 58
Samuel Lang ....10 Nov. 58
Aug. Fred Tanner .... 2 Feb. 59
Dominick Gore Daly .... 4 July 59

ENSIGNS.
Clement W.Featherstonhaugh 21 May 58
Cha. Callaway Ross .... 8 June 58
John A. C. Branfill ....10 Dec. 58
Geo. Ennis Vivian .... 2 Feb. 59
Edw. Hyde Hewett ....27 May 59
Philip Jas. Haydock ....31 May 59
Adj. & Capt. George Shirley Maxwell, late Lt. 20 F... 3 Feb. 59
Paymaster.— Robert Murphy Nicolls, late Capt. 65 F... 14 Mar. 59
Qr.Mast.—Robert Jones, late of 45 F.......................13 July 54
Surgeon.—Wm. Kaylet Curtis 27 Nov. 57
Assist.Surg.—Wm. T. Pater ...23 Dec. 57

Kentish Grey Facings.
Agents.—Messrs. Cox and Co.

WEST KENT.
(Light Infantry.) [No. 37.]
Head Quarters, Maidstone.

COLONEL.
Sir Thomas Maryon Wilson, Bart. DL. JP. ....21 Apr. 53

LIEUT.COLONEL.
Geo. Visct. Torrington, late Lt. 7 F. ....27 Feb 54

MAJOR.
George Robert Stevenson, JP. late Lieut. 7 Dr. Guards......13 May 53

CAPTAINS.
R. T. G. G. Monypenny, DL. JP., late Lieut. 86 F............20 Jan. 52
John Robinson, JP. late Lieut. 24 F..........................26 Sept.52
Thos. Montagu Martin Weller, JP..........................10 Nov. 52
Robert Sheffield Sorell ....21 Apr. 54
Robert Curteis Stileman ..... 6 Aug. 54
Alex. Val. Bond, late Lt. 85 F. 27 Nov. 54
Gordon Samuel Weld..........30 Jan. 55
John Jervis, DL. ....31 Jan. 55
Alex. Henry Ross .... 1 May 55
W. D. C. G. Monypenny ....28 June 59

LIEUTENANTS.
Thomas John Popplewell ....10 Dec. 54
Edw. H. Penfold................31 Jan. 55
Thomas Arthur Farrell .... 2 Aug. 55
Benj. Dawson Beales...........19 Jan. 58
Morgan Dalrymple Treherne 26 July 58
George A'Court Webb ....28 Mar. 59
Markland Barnard...............29 Mar. 59

ENSIGNS.
John Summons Ramsay ......20 Oct. 53
George Owen Ramsay .... 6 Sept. 54
George Robert Mascall........ 7 Apr. 55
Reginald Mortimer Kelson ...20 Feb. 56
John Joseph Tookie .... 7 Mar. 56
Wm. Waring Gwillim ....25 Feb. 57
Henry J. G. Robinson .... 2 Feb. 59
James Gordon Vinter...........28 June 59
Paymaster.—Denis Dunn, Bt. Major ret. f. p. 69 F......... 1 Jan. 55
Adj. & Capt.—Edw. Lynch, late Capt. 13 F. .... 8 Feb. 55
Qr.Master.—Henry Pratt. ...23 Aug. 56
Surg.—Rich. John Peckham... 6 Sept. 54
Assist.Surgeon.—Robert Vaile Skinner.......................17 May 53

Kentish Grey Facings.
Agent, Edward S. Codd, Esq.

KENT ARTILLERY.
[No. 18.]
Head Quarters, Dover.

COLONEL.
J. R. Viscount Sydney, DL. JP. 4 May 53

LIEUT.COLONEL.
John Farnaby Cator, DL. Capt. h. p. Royal Artillery 4 May 53

MAJOR.
Henry John Thomas, Lt.Col. h.p. R. Art. .... 8 June 59

CAPTAINS.
Robert Matthew Isacke........10 July 53
John Kirkpatrick................. 1 Dec. 55
Walter Thomas Waring........10 May 56
Chas. Nassau Girardot ....10 May 58
Charles Beauclerk .... 9 Oct. 58
William Bartram ....25 June 59

LIEUTENANTS.
Robert Alured Denne, late of Royal Navy ....22 Mar. 58
Leonard Strong .... 7 July 58
Wm. Stanley Ibilison.......... 2 Dec. 58
Francis Kegan Cox, late Capt. 25 F. .... 9 June 59
Thomas Farmer Bailey ....12 Aug. 59

SECOND LIEUTENANTS.
Stephen Matthew Crowe .....16 Aug. 59
John Curtois Adolphus Bones 20 Aug. 59
Henry Burham Scoones ..... 1 Dec. 59
Adj. & Capt.—John M'Cullum, late of R. Art. ....14 May 53
Qr.Mast.—George Parker, late of R. Art. .... 6 Jan. 55
Surgeon.—Octavius Frederic Heritage .... 1 July 55
Assist.Surgeon.—Henry Day 18 Oct. 55

Red Facings.
Agents, Messrs. Cox and Co.

1ST ROYAL LANCASHIRE.
(The Duke of Lancaster's Own.)
[No. 45.]
Head Quarters, Lancaster.
"*Mediterranean.*"

COLONEL.
John Talbot Clifton, DL. JP.
late Lieut. 1 Life Gds. ...... 8 Oct. 52

LIEUT.COLONEL.
Ed. Every Clayton, DL. JP.
late Capt. 80 F. ....25 Feb. 52

MAJORS.
George Orred ....10 Mar. 46
Wm. Asshcton Cross, DL. JP. 24 Nov. 55

CAPTAINS.
R. J. T. Williamson ....25 Nov. 51
Henry Master Feilden, DL. JP.15 Nov. 42
Richard Pudsey Dawson ... 1 Oct. 52
James Clarke, DL. JP. .... 3 Nov. 52
Robt. Whittle (8) late Lt. 91 F.19 Nov. 52
Clarence Horatio Cary, JP. ...21 Mar. 53
Luke Henry Hansard, DL. ... 6 Apr. 53
John Bayly ....11 Mar. 56
Edm. G. Stanley Hornby ...17 July 58
Wm Louis Robert J. Versturme
 (12), late Captain 27 F......6 Aug. 58
John Gould Noble..............16 Oct. 58
Evan Francis Anderton........29 Apr. 59

LIEUTENANTS.
George Parker.................14 May 55
Thos. H. Spence Campion......24 Nov. 55
John Scott ....24 Nov. 55
John Wood Younghusband ...24 Sept. 58
John Paris Bradshaw .... do

ENSIGNS.

Adj. & Capt.—Bryan Thornhill,
 late Capt. 2 Dr. Gds. ....25 Feb. 59
Paymaster.—William Francis Dick-
 son(11), h. p. 52 F. ....28 July 54
Qr.Master.— Robt. Knights,
 late of 12 Drs................1 Dec. 56
Surg.—Metcalfe Johnson......15 Aug. 59
Assist.Surg.—John Oldman... 1 Aug. 59
Blue Facings.

Agents, Messrs. Cox and Co.

2ND ROYAL LANCASHIRE.
(The Duke of Lancaster's Own Rifles.)
[No. 113.]
Head Quarters, Liverpool.

LIEUT.COLONEL COMMANDANT.
Sir T. G. Hesketh, Bt. DL. JP. 1 Mar. 52

MAJORS.
James Wardlaw(1) .... 4 Oct. 52
Nicholas Blundell, DL. JP. ... 3 Nov. 52

CAPTAINS.
Robert Johnson ....25 Apr. 46
Peter Slingsby Fitzgerald, late
 Capt. 60 Rifles .... 4 Oct. 52
Thomas Littledale, DL.JP. ... 7 Oct. 52
James Thomas Bourne, JP. ...14 Apr. 53
Alexander Thomas Knight ...15 Apr. 53
Thomas Richardson Lane ...15 Nov. 54
John Downes Rochfort........30 Aug. 55
Mathew Fordo ....15 Feb. 56
Frank Cavendish Ward ......24 Apr. 56
Charles S. Garraway 17 Sept.56
Le Gendre Starkie .... 4 Sept. 58
Charles Blundell..............26 Nov. 59

LIEUTENANTS.
Francis Howard Wright ......12 Jan. 55
Joseph Rowley.................25 Apr. 55
Robert William John Barlow...30 Aug. 55
Frederick Charles Cross ...... 7 Mar. 56
Astley Jephson .... 5 Nov. 58
Geo. Nathan Billam............. do
Henry Nichols................. do

Wm. Browning Gardner ...... 5 Nov. 58
Richard T. Irvine ....23 Nov. 58
Robert Highat.................13 May 59
Geo. T. Robert Preston .... 5 Nov. 59

ENSIGNS.
Geo. Mullifont Lane............ 2 Nov. 58
Henry Currey..................26 Oct. 59
Adj. & Capt.—Jas. Weir, late
 of Scots Fus. Gds. .... 7 Feb. 46
Paymaster.—
Qr.Master.— David Bilham,
 Hon. Capt. h. p. 20 F........21 Dec. 54
Surg. — William Hargreaves
 Manifold .... 5 Feb. 55
Assist.Surg.—Edw. Russell ...27 Feb. 55
Scarlet Facings.
Agent, Vesey W. Holt, *Esq.*

3RD ROYAL LANCASHIRE.
(The Duke of Lancaster's Own.) [No. 125.]
Head Quarters, Preston.
"*Mediterranean.*"

COLONEL.
John Wilson Patten, MP. DL.
 *Aide-de-Camp to the Queen*15 Nov. 42

LIEUT.COLONEL.
William Mathias,(14) late Lt.
 Col. 63 F. .... 3 Nov. 55

MAJORS.
Montague Joseph Feilden, MP.
DL. ....11 Mar. 53

CAPTAINS.
James German .... 1 Oct. 52
Thomas Richard Crosse........ 2 Oct. 52
William Nicholson ....12 Mar. 53
Wm. Thos. Harris, late Capt.
 35 F. ....25 May 54
John Edward Orrell ....13 Apr. 55
Frederick Silvester............14 Apr. 55
Frederick Townley Parker ...16 Apr. 55
Thos. Wilkinson Edwards, late
 Capt. 50 F. & Adj........... 4 June 55
Thomas Ealmes Withington... 8 June 55
John Robinson Pedder .... 7 Feb. 57
Robert Furey..................4 Sept. 58
James Ormsby.................20 July 59

LIEUTENANTS.
John Brophey,(16) late of 63 F.19 June 55
Frederick Beasley .... 3 Nov. 55
Peyton Sheals................. 8 Dec. 55
Thomas Conry Knox........... 8 Dec. 55
Henry Powys..................24 May 56
Robert Blackmore .... 7 Feb. 57
William Turner................ 4 Sept. 58
Thomas James Eccles .... do
Wm. Fitch Story............... do
William Henry White ....15 Oct. 58
Francis Law ....16 Oct. 58
John Leyland Feilden ....20 July 59

ENSIGNS.
Wm. Style Doria ....24 May 56
Fred. Aug. White ....16 Oct. 58
Charles Fred. Baldwin .... 3 June 59
Thomas Grimshaw .... 4 June 59
William Gardner Bird .... 4 July 59
Adj. & Capt. — W. Percival
 Kilgee, (15) late Capt. 50 F. 20 June 55
Paymaster.—Aylmer Lambert
 Bourke, late Capt. Unatt. ...22 Dec. 54
Qr.Master.—John Hewitt ... 8 Dec. 51
Surg.—Richard Allen .... 2 Feb. 58
Assist.Surg. — Henry Con-
 stantine Colgan, MD......... 5 Apr. 50
Blue Facings.
Agents, Messrs.Alex. F. Ridgway & Sons.

4TH ROYAL LANCASHIRE.
(The Duke of Lancaster's Own Light Infantry.)
[No. 84.]
Head Quarters, Warrington.

LIEUT.COLONEL COMMANDANT.
John Ireland Blackburne, late
 of 5 Dr. Gds. ....22 Mar. 53

MAJORS.
Richard Phibbs, DL. (9), late
 Capt. 48 F. ....28 Mar. 53
John Southcote Mansergh,
 late of 2 Dragoon Gds. .....31 Mar. 53

CAPTAINS.
David Ainsworth ....28 Mar. 53
Thomas Bourne, JP...........29 Mar. 53
William Walter Trafford ....29 Mar. 53
Henry Chas. Adolphus Clarke,
 late of 3 F. ....29 Mar. 53
Archd. Wm. Clarke ....29 Mar. 53
William Gray, MP. JP.......29 Mar. 53
Chas. Hoghton, late Capt. 1 Dr.
 Gds. ....25 Nov. 54
Lawrence Heyworth .... 8 May 55
George Arthur Crawford ....17 Apr. 58
George Barlow ....18 Apr. 59
William Gibton .... 4 Aug. 59
John J. Westenra Smith .....10 Oct. 59
Thomas Hargreaves ....19 Dec. 59

LIEUTENANTS.
Frederick Phillips 1Sept. 55
Bartholomew Lloyd O'Brien...11 Mar. 58
Wm. Selby F. Taunton.......24 Apr. 58
Cecil Wm. Betham...........16 June 58
Henry M. Howard...........18 Apr. 59
Henry Edward Butler ....30 May 59
Henry Wm. Coyne........... 5 Aug. 59
Wm. Sheffield Betham ....10 Oct. 59
Charles Gore Ring .... do

ENSIGNS.
Hugh Hilton Hornby ....25 Jan. 59
James Fred. Steiner ....14 Apr. 59

Adj. & Capt.—Thos. Robbins,
 late Lt. & Adj. 5 Dr. Gds....29 Mar. 53
Paymaster.— Sheffield Betham26 Feb. 56
Qr.Master.—Thomas Bestland
 Knott, late Lt. 4 F. .... 6 Oct. 56
Surg. — Thomas Birley Ec-
 cleston .... 7 Sept. 59
Assist.Surg.—Charles White . 7 Sept. 59
Blue Facings.
Agents, Messrs. Cox and Co.

5TH ROYAL LANCASHIRE.
[No. 135.]
Head Quarters, Burnley.

LIEUT.COLONEL COMMANDANT.
Charles Towneley, DL. JP. ...16 Mar. 53

MAJORS.
John Towneley, DL. ....14 Apr. 53
Alan Chambre (10), JP. late
 Capt. 17 Lancers............15 Aug. 54

CAPTAINS.
James Greenwood ....19 Apr. 53
John Joseph Middleton ......20 Apr. 53
Thomas Goulburne Parker,DL.21 Apr. 53
Edward Petre ....21 Apr. 53
George Decks Skingley.......22 Apr. 53
William Lister Sagar,JP......22 Apr. 53
John Pickup Lord ....23 Apr. 53
Frederic Broadbent ....23 Apr. 53
Daniel Grant Brereton ......16 Feb. 54
Antony Buck Creek ....16 June 54
Edward Dwyer ....23 July 55
Henry Kirwan Robinson (17) 19 Jan. 56

LIEUTENANTS.
Abraham Alfred Tweedale ...20 Feb. 54
Fred. A. C. Macdonald ....10 July 55
Henry Drury ....11 Feb. 56
SummerMitchell S.Brockhurst11 Feb. 56
Alfred Edmund Lawless ....19 Mar. 56
Richard Horley ....19 Mar. 56

Militia of England and Wales.

James Gunning Plunkett ......19 Mar. 56
Fra. Edw. Hassard..............28 May 56
Anthony Blake Lynch ....29 Dec. 57
Henry John Barker .... 1 Feb. 58
Edward Middleton 7 June59
Wm. Edmonstone Lendrick ... do

ENSIGNS.
George Fenton ....29 Dec. 57
Andrew Dillon Browne......... 2 Feb. 58
John Joseph Mills .... 1 July 59
Adj. & Capt.—Chas. Hamilton
  Fenton, (6) *late Capt* 9 F. 16 Mar. 53
  Captain ....18 Apr. 53
Qr.Mast.—William Flack ......12 Jan. 55
Surgeon.—Wm. Miller Coultate ....14 Nov. 57
Assist.Surg.— George Smirthwaite .... 8 July 58

Blue Facings.

Agents, Messrs. C. R. & W. McGrigor.

6TH ROYAL LANCASHIRE.
(*Rifles*.) [No. 82.]
Head Quarters, Ashton under Lyne.

COLONEL.
Hon. Edw. Bootle Wilbraham,
DL, JP. *Colonel, late of Coldst. Gds.* .... 8 Jan. 55
LIEUT.COLONEL COMMANDANT.
John Henry Pringle, *Colonel late of Coldst. Gds*..........9 Jan. 55

MAJORS.
Thos. Edw. Wilbraham, *late Capt. 30 F.* ....16 Feb. 55
John Hickinbotham Chambers, DL, JP. *late Capt. 46 F.*......................... 5 Dec. 55

CAPTAINS.
John Copley Wray ....23 Jan. 55
Wm. Henry Gillman, *Brevet Col. ret. f. p. 68 F.* ....16 Feb. 55
William Marshall ....19 Feb. 55
Richard Lambert, *late of R. Art.*..........................29 Mar. 55
Wm. Middleton Moore, *late Lt. 15 F.*....................15 June 55
Edw. Fleetwood Hesketh ..16 June 55
Henry Mawdsley .... 5 Dec. 55
Richard Whelan ....12 May 56
Roger Forrest ....30 Sept. 58
Wm. Fra. Smith .... do
Richard Lomax .... 1 July 59
William Singleton ....17 Aug. 59
Henry Richards ....12 Dec 59

LIEUTENANTS.
Joseph Rich. Hamilton ....29 Oct. 55
William Hicks ....29 Oct. 56
Richard Murray Thompson..15 Dec. 55
Wm. Bagot D'Arcy ....28 Jan. 56
John Clarke Swanton ......16 June 59
Matthew John Alfred Gosset 3 Dec. 59

ENSIGNS.
John Geo. D. Minchin .... 5 Apr. 56
Walter Miller Lambert.......29 Sept. 58
Meredith Thompson............13 Apr. 59
Edward Hewitt...............24 May 59

Adj. & Capt.—Wm. Hartshorn (13) *Capt. Unatt. late Capt. 24 F.*.................18 Jan. 55
Paymaster.—Christopher J. Hamilton ....16 May 55
Qr.Master.— Lovick Loftus Rendo ....23 Aug. 56
Surgeon,—John Gregson Harrison, M.D. .... 1 Sept. 56
Assist.Surg.— John Harkes Craig ....24 May 55

7TH ROYAL LANCASHIRE.
[No. 130.]
Head Quarters, Bury.
COLONEL.
Hon. *Charles James Fox Stanley, late Lt.Col. Gr. Gds.* ..21 Feb. 55
LIEUT.COLONEL COMMANDANT.
John Edward Madocks, *late Capt. 13 Drs.* ....22 Mar. 55

MAJORS.
John Hardy Thursby, *late of 90 F.* .... 5 Apr. 55
Robert Cumming, *late Capt. 52 F.* .... 3 Aug. 57

CAPTAINS.
Francis Lepper, *late Capt. 81 F.* ....12 Mar. 55
Charles Edward Leigh, *late of 90 F.* ....24 Mar. 55
Geo.John Stewart, *late Lt. 5 F.*26 Apr. 55
John Rowlandson Marshall,..12 May 55
Thomas Greenwood ....17 May 55
James Ashton ....18 May 55
Simeon Henry Stuart, *late Lt. Canadian Rifles* ....20 July 55
Edw. Chetham Strode, JP... 2 Feb. 58
Rich. Hackett, *late Ens. 24 F*. 2 Feb. 58
Thomas Ridgway Bridson ... 2 Feb. 58
John Hamilton .... 9 June 59

LIEUTENANTS.
Thos. Heywood................. 1 Aug. 55
Charles Wm. Fennel ....29 Oct. 55
Edmund Peck .... 8 June 57
Henry Smith................... 2 Feb. 58
Richard Cope ....17 June 58
Owen H. F. O'Malley ......16 Oct. 58
Geo. Edward Gorton .... 9 June 59
Henry William Mathews ... 1 July 59
Langford Rea................. 4 July 59

ENSIGNS.
Wm. Dunbar Quinlan .... 1 Aug. 55
Patrick John Tiernan .... 8 Jan. 58
George Hollings.............16 Oct. 58
John Rule Daniell............ do

Adjutant and Capt.—Bertie Mathew Roberts, *late Capt. 26 F.* ....11 Apr. 55
Qr.Master.— *Capt.* George Crispin, *h. p. 67 F.* ......14 Sept. 57
Surgeon.—R. T. Whitehead ..18 May 55
Assist.Surg.—Jn. Stubbs Wait 24 Aug. 57

ROYAL LANCASHIRE ARTILLERY.
[No. 19.]
[Embodied.]
Head Quarters, Kinsale.
LIEUT.COLONEL COMMANDANT.
Thomas Atchison, *Capt. ret. full pay, R. Art.* ....23 May 57

MAJORS.
James Bourne, DL, JP..........13 May 53
Henry Thomas Fyers, *Capt. h. p. R. Art.* .... 4 Oct. 59

CAPTAINS.
James Middleton ....23 Apr. 55
Benj. Remington Williams,(4) *late of Bengal Horse Art.*,..14 Jun. 57
William Graham Furnivall ..19 June 57
Hill Charley Moore .... 2 Feb. 58
William Walker 20 Sept.59
Henry Tuke Holmes .... 4 Oct. 59

FIRST LIEUTENANTS.
Alex. M'Caudie Campbell.....12 June 57
Daniel George Atchison 26 Mar.59
Fra. M. Drummond Davies ... 4 June59
Widenham Fra. Fosbery ......19 Aug. 59
Robert Hall ....20 Sept. 59
Thomas Christie,............. 4 Oct. 59

SECOND LIEUTENANTS.
Caleb Collins ....26 Apr. 59
John Fra. Henry Harrison... 4 June 59
George Wood ....10 Oct. 59
Richard Alison Johnson ......26 Oct. 59
Adj. & Capt.—Wm. Campbell, *late of R. Art.* ....13 Apr. 53
Paymaster.—Chris.M. Dawes.. 1 Oct. 57
Qr.Master.—John Blain .... 5 Oct. 57
Surg.—John Betham ....25 Jan. 59
Assist.Surg.—Chas. Calthrop Mitchinson.................... 4 June 59

Red Facings.

Agent, A. Lawrie, *Esq*.

LEICESTER.
[No. 26.]
Head Quarters,
HONORARY COLONEL.
The Duke of Rutland............21 Apr. 57
LIEUT.-COLONEL.
John King ....24 July 39

MAJORS.
Hon. Henry Lyttleton Powys, *late Major 60 F.* ....22 July 57
Robert Ralph Noel..............23 July 57

CAPTAINS.
Jonathan Wagstaff Bryan ...27 Apr. 31
Sir Fred. Thomas Fowke, *Bt.* June 46
Joseph Knight,*late Gentleman-at-Arms* ....27 Oct. 52
Edmund Arthur Paget ......15 Mar. 54
Geo. Thomas Mowbray ....11 Aug. 54
Wm. Henry Chapman 15 Sept.54
John Mathew ....12 Oct. 55
John Buckley ....31 Dec. 55
Wm. Edward Phelp ....23 July 57
Charles Henry Morris .... 6 Apr. 59

LIEUTENANTS.
Charles Maynard Heselrige... 6 Nov. 55
Percy Lionel Rawlins .... 3 May 56
Henry Bickley 30 Sept.57
John Henry Bryan............30 Sept.57
Godfrey P. Hallifax, *late of* 1 *Drs*. ....23 Nov. 57
Henry Moody................... 5 Dec. 57
Thos. Alex. Leigh Knipe ...28 June 59
Arthur Dixon Rawlins ......28 June 59
Thomas S. Harding, *late of Turkish Contingent*.........28 June 59
Thomas John S. Hotckin, *late of 3 F.* ....28 June 59

ENSIGNS.
Joseph Guy Knight ....28 June 59
Harby Barber ....14 July 59
Adj. & Capt.—James Palliser Costobadie, *late Capt. 70 F.* 1 July 53
Qr.Master.—Alfred Whitby ,..29 July 56
Surg.—Wm. Unwin .... 9 Nov. 57
Assistant Surg.—George Alex. Moorhead,..................13 Feb. 58

Yellow Facings.
Agents, Messrs. Cox & Co.

ROYAL NORTH LINCOLN
[No. 8.]
[Embodied.]
Head Quarters, Newry.
HONORARY COLONEL.
George Tomline, MP. *late of* 1 *Life Gds.* ....29 Mar. 51
LIEUT.COLONEL COMMANDANT.
Richard Ellison, DL, JP. ....19 July 53

MAJORS.
Hon. William John Monson MP, DL. .... 6 Aug.
John Golden ....26 Oct.

Militia of England and Wales. 624

CAPTAINS.
Henry Valentine Grantham...12 Sept. 53
Robert John Taylor ....13 June 54
Henry Lionel Dymoke, DL. ...12 Nov. 57
John Bell Brooking ....13 Nov. 57
William Longstaffe .... 6 Aug. 58
James Ward ....14 Aug. 58
Geo. Morland Hutton, DL.JP. 3 Feb. 59
Robert Henry Owston ....19 July 59

LIEUTENANTS.
James Sisson Cooper, *Instructor of Musketry*......... 1 May 56
Thomas Henry Whitaker .. 13 Nov. 57
William Cosby ....23 Feb. 58
Lambert Uniacke..............27 Feb. 58
Aug. Charles Short .... 6 Apr. 58
Robert Waller ....17 Aug. 58
Arthur Lousada............... 8 Nov. 58
Arthur Fred. Holdsworth...... do
John Woulfe Keogh ....25 Feb. 59
James Walter Tweed........... 7 Dec. 58
Lionel Wentworth Atkinson 11 Jan. 59
Chas. Wm. Joseph Taylor ...14 Jan. 59
John Cowell Helden .... 2 Mar. 59
Charles Fred. Sharp ....13 June 59
John Whitney..................27 June 59
Fra. Johnston Murray .... 6 July 59
John Mackenzie .... 8 Aug. 59
Redmond U. Somerville ..... 8 Aug. 59

Adj. & Capt.—John Mulhall,(3)
Q. M. h. p. 17 *F.* .... 2 May 53
*Paymaster.—*W. Telford,²
Capt. late Paym. 17 *F.* ......28 May 55
Qr.Master.—David Davis, *late of* 35 *F.*....................23 July 58
Surgeon.—Geo. Mitchinson ... 1 Mar. 58
Asst.Surg.— W.T.Girdlestone 17 Nov. 57

Blue Facings.
Agents, Messrs. Cox & Co.

ROYAL SOUTH LINCOLN.
[No. 29.]
Head Quarters, Grantham.
HONORARY COLONEL.
G. J. Lord Aveland ....31 Aug. 57
LIEUT.COLONEL COMMANDANT.
Henry Edw. Fane, *late Major* 4 *Lt. Drs.*......................20 Apr. 54
MAJORS.
Gervase T. Waldo Sibthorp, DL. JP. MP. ....20 Apr. 54
Chas. Thos. J. Moore, DL. JP. (*High Sheriff of the County*) 7 Jan. 56

CAPTAINS.
William Parker .... 6 Dec. 52
Struan Edward Robertson ...22 Apr. 53
Paul Mildmay Pell.............22 Apr. 53
Samuel Brailsford ....13 June 54
§Frederick Bowman(4).........13 June 54
Chas. John B. Parker ....29 July 54
Wm. Simpson Clarke..........18 Nov. 54
Charles Telford .... 8 Apr. 56
Arthur E. Tuke, *late Lt.* 21 *F.* 9 July 56

LIEUTENANTS.
P. de Franklin.................31 Oct. 54
John Mahon Williams .... 5 May 55
Charles Rothwell Norris ......15 May 55
Edward Davey Johnson ......16 Nov. 55
Robert Frudd..................18 Dec. 56
John Whitsed..................27 May 57
Edward Crockford ....15 July 59

ENSIGNS.
Charles Edm. H. Alpe ....29 Apr. 59
Adj. & Capt.—Charles Norris, *late Capt.* 64 *F.* ....30 June 52
p̶l̶a̶c̶e̶r̶.*—James Maxey Bu—n, late Capt.* 70 *F.* ... 9 Aug. 54

Qr.Master. — James Gannon 28 Oct. 54
Surg.—Chas. Ferneley .... 9 Aug. 54
Assist.Surg.—Tom Hewitt ... 7 July 58

Blue Facings.
Agents, Messrs. Cox & Co.

ROYAL LONDON.
[No. 106.]
Head Quarters, Artillery Place, Finsbury.
COLONEL.
Samuel Wilson, DL. JP. ......24 Mar. 54
LIEUT.-COLONEL.
George MacCall, *late of* 84 *F.*..31 Mar. 54
MAJOR.
Henry Boys Harvey, *late Lt.- Col.* 95 *F.*....................18 Dec. 57

CAPTAINS.
James Bunce Curling, *late Adj. of Gentlemen-at-Arms* ..... 8 Oct. 52
W. H. Brabazon Connor ..... 9 Oct. 52
John Harrison Allan ....12 July 53
George Barnes Hobson (2) *late Capt.* 72 *Bengal N. I.* .... 7 Dec. 55
John Britten .... 8 Feb. 56
Edward Vere Jones ....18 Dec. 57
Fred. Peto ....16 Sept. 58

LIEUTENANTS.
James Cunningham ....30 Mar. 57
Aug. Henry Garland...........31 Mar. 57
Miles Fisher Monckton, *late Capt. Osmanli Cavalry* ......18 Dec. 57
Rob. H. Hardy, *late Lt.* 5 *F.* 15 Sept. 58
Richard Lee Mayhew 16 Sept.58
James Johnston Brown 17 Sept.58
Augustus Newton .... 9 July 59
Fred. Richard F. Keats ......11 July 59
Thurlby Smith ....12 July 59
Geo. Coulson Childs ....12 July 59
John V. Monckton ....12 July 59

ENSIGNS.
Wm. Henry Howes .... 9 July 59

Adj. & Capt.—Wm. Thomas Hall, *late of* 6 *F.*............. 4 Feb. 46
Qr.Master.—John Birkin, *late of* 85 *F.*.....................18 Dec. 57
Surg.—Geo. Borlase Childs ... 6 Oct. 52
Assist.Surg.— Wm. Thomas Lewis .... 4 Nov. 59

Blue Facings.
Agents, Messrs. Bosanquet & Co.

ROYAL MERIONETH.
(*Rifles.*) [No. 60.]
Head Quarters, Bala.
LIEUT.COLONEL COMMANDANT.
₽Edw. Morgan, DL. JP. (1)
Capt. h. p. 75 *F.* ....20 Oct. 52

CAPTAINS.
Wm. Price Jones, JP. .... 9 Oct. 53
Charles Henry Lewis Lee ...11 July 59

LIEUTENANTS.
Edw. Gilliat Jones............11 July 59

ENSIGNS.
Wm. Downing Bruce..........27 Apr. 54

Adj. & Capt.—Robert Muscie Taylor, *late Lt.* 25 *F.*......... 4 Oct. 53
Surg.—Owen Richards ....15 Nov. 57

Black Facings.

1ST OR ROYAL EAST MIDDLESEX.
[No. 65.]
Head Quarters, Hampstead.
COLONEL.
Thomas Wood, *Aide de Camp to the Queen* ....12 Apr. 03
LIEUT.COLONEL.
Thomas St. Leger Alcock, *late Major* 95 *F.*..................30 Jan. 51
MAJOR.
William Reed, DL. JP. *late Capt.* 6 *F.*..................... 4 June 50

CAPTAINS.
James Prince ....17 Oct. 51
John Annah Ambrose, *late* 22 *F.* 8 Oct. 52
Wm. Fred. Northey ....28 July 54
William Robertson............10 Aug. 54
Frederick Gibbons ....20 Dec. 54
Edward Dunning Cole .... 8 Jan. 55
George Crozier Cole ....30 Mac. 57
Wm. Dakin Speer ....16 Oct. 57
Wm. Henry Mangles (2), *late Capt.* 50 *F.*................... 9 Aug. 58
William Henry Bent ....27 Oct. 58

LIEUTENANTS.
Alexander Noble, *Qr.Master* . 14 Apr. 13
William Plummer ....20 Mar. 57
William Vevers ....13 Oct. 57
Sussex Newton ....14 Oct. 57
Charles Francis Simms 20 Sept.58
William Croft .... do
Donald Noble ....13 Nov. 58
Charles W. B. Wells ....30 June 59
Robert James Blyth ....21 July 59

ENSIGNS.
Charles George Norris ....30 June 58
Wm. Albert Dixon ....22 Feb. 59
Edmund Parker...............22 June 59
Auch Dudingston Boyd ....28 July 59
Robert Burdett ....29 July 59
Fred. J. T. Nantes ....11 Oct. 59
Charles Dowell .... do
Adjt. and Capt.—Thos. R. John Geo. Thomson, *late of* 89 *F.* 30 July 55
Paymaster.—*Captain* Edward James Dyson .... 6 Jan. 55
Surgeon.—Francis Dalton .....25 Feb. 46
Assist.Surg.—Geo.Jas. S.Camden ....20 Jan. 55
John V. Monckton........... do

Blue Facings.
Agents, Messrs. Cox & Co.

2ND OR EDMONTON ROYAL MIDDLESEX.
(*Rifles.*) [No. 63.]
Head Quarters, Barnet.
COLONEL.
Geo., *Visct.* Enfield, *late Capt. Rifle Brig.*.....................29 Apr. 44
LIEUT.-COLONEL.
Hon. George H. C. Byng, MP..20 Oct. 5 3
MAJOR.
Charles Wm. H. Sotheby, *late Capt.* 60 *Rifles* ....12 Apr. 54

CAPTAINS.
Henry William Marriott 8 Aug.28
Charles William Grenfell, MP..18 Apr. 48
Henry Riversdale Grenfell,....24 Sept. 52
Theodore E. H. Platt, *late Lt.* 49 *F.*........................21 Feb. 53
Dottin Maycock, *late Lieut.* 6 *Drags.* ....21 Apr. 53
Edw. John Ottley .... 9 Aug. 53
Algernon Edward West.......17 Oct. 54
Jervoise Smith .... 9 Aug. 57
Constantine Hayward Read, *late Lt. Ceylon Rifles* ....24 June 59
Charles Ruddell Todd ....24 June 59

Militia of England and Wales.

LIEUTENANTS.
Robert Gervas Wylde ....31 Oct. 54
Fra. C. H. Russell, MP.........23 Dec. 54
Wm. Dawes Malton .... 9 Oct. 56
Fra. S. Maxwell Stephens ...25 Sept.57
Benj. Charles Stephenson ...24 Apr. 58
Francis Bynss.....................21 Oct. 58
Frederick Bridger................ do
Walter Stirling ....10 Jan. 59
Charles Lennox Peel, *late of 7 Hussars* ....23 June 59

ENSIGNS.
Charles Field Carr...............26 July 50

Adjt. & Captain.—Edw. Missenden Love, *late Capt.* COF.13 Apr. 59
Qr.Master.—Geo. Kettles ...18 Nov. 57
Surg.—Nicholas M'Cann, MD. 4 June 52
Assist.Surg.—Charles Godson 9 Oct. 56

Scarlet Facings.

3RD OR ROYAL WESTMINSTER MIDDLESEX.

(*Light Infantry.*) [No. 55.]
Head Quarters, Turnham Green.
"*Mediterranean.*"

COLONEL.
H. C. C. Viset. Chelsea, MP.
DL. JP........................... 6 Dec. 41
LIEUT.COLONEL.
John James Glossop, JP. ......10 Aug. 54
MAJOR.
Henry Penton, DL. ....18 Aug. 54
CAPTAINS.
Charles Ralfs .... 8 Feb. 14
Robert Monkhouse Piper ......23 Sept. 34
Edward Murray ....11 Jan. 53
Henry Joseph P. Woodhead...24 Dec. 53
William Henry Burgess......... 4 May 54
Fred. Thomas Parsons, JP. ...24 June 54
Joseph Percival Swan .... 3 Mar. 55
Lewis Hough .... 8 Jan. 58
Francis Nicholls ....25 Feb. 58
Nathaniel Taylor.................25 Oct. 58

LIEUTENANTS.
John Willcocks ....15 Dec. 56
Fred. Alfred Stone..............11 Jan. 58
Samuel John Unwin ....26 Nov. 58

ENSIGNS.

Adj. & Capt.—Wm. Thomas 27 May 59
Paymaster.—
Qr.Master.—James Lee ......27 May 59
Surgeon.—James M'Cann....27 Oct. 52
Assist.Surg.—Wm. Hurman.. 2 July 59

Blue Facings.

Agents, Messrs. Hopkinson & Co.

4TH OR ROYAL SOUTH MIDDLESEX.

[No. 128.]
Head Quarters, Hounslow.
LIEUT.COLONEL COMMANDANT.
John Scriven, DL. JP. *late Capt.* 51 F. 15 Sept.55
MAJORS.
Chas. Foveaux Kirby, (1) *late Major* 14 Madras N.I. ..... 4 Jan. 55
Arthur Chas. FitzJames, *late Lt.* 93 F. 12 Aug.59
CAPTAINS.
Geo. Barrington Godbold, *late 2d Lieut.* 87 F................26 Apr. 54

Edw. Hamilton Finney, *late of* 1 F. 20 Sept.54
Charles George Boulton ......19 Jan. 55
Charles Edw. Mortimer ......23 Sept. 55
Wm. Elias Taunton ....15 Oct. 55
Marmaduke Constable 26 Sept.57
Count William C. Rivarola,*late Capt.* 67 F. .... 6 July 59
Griffin Nicholas, *Bt. Major,* r. f. p. 5 F. .... 4 Nov. 59

LIEUTENANTS.
Charles Baynton ....1 Jan. 55
Charles Ferdinand Rutherford18 Aug. 56
Thos. Fitzgerald Wintour ......30 Oct. 55
Henry Edgerton King, *late Lieut.* 32 F. ....27 Oct. 57
Thos. Fitzmaurice Burke ......16 Dec. 57
Wm. Philip d'Allington Jones29 Oct. 58
Edward Bullock Jackson ...... do

ENSIGNS.
Preston Osborne Page ....19 Nov. 57
Thomas Allihone Norman......16 Dec. 57
George Rooke .... 6 June 58
Michael Angelo ....18 Apr. 59
Thomas Hunt ....19 May 59
Robert Fair Sproule .... 5 Aug. 59
Geo. Robert Harriott...........27 Oct. 59
Adj. & Capt.—Charles. Wm. Parker, *late Capt.* 60 F. ...22 Nov. 56
Paymaster.—Mathews Copplestone ....5 Apr. 58
Qr.Master.— Geo. Hope, *late of* 77 F. .... 3 Aug. 54
Surgeon.—John Berry Bryant 16 Oct. 51
Assist.Surg. —Edwin Adolphus, M.D. *late of* 75 F....16 Oct. 57

Blue Facings.

Agents, Messrs. Cox & Co.

5TH ROYAL ELTHORNE MIDDLESEX.

(*Light Infantry.*) [No. 28.]
[Embodied.]
Head Quarters, Aldershot.
LIEUT.COLONEL COMMANDANT.
Lodge Murray Prior, DL., m., *late of* 12 Lancers .... 4 May 55

MAJORS.
Edw. Deane Freeman, DL. JP.
late of 3 Dragoon Gds. ....21 July 55
Richard George Grange, *late Capt. Bengal Army* ....26 Jan. 58

CAPTAINS.
Edward Thomas King, *late of* 21 F. ....10 Oct. 53
Albert Wm. Murray, *late Capt. R. Trinidad Battalion* .... 9 Mar. 54
John Alex. Hunter, *late Capt.* 3 F. ....28 Dec. 54
Fred. William Woodall......... 3 Aug. 55
Joseph Deane Freeman........15 Oct. 55
Deane John Hoare..............12 Mar. 57
Arch. Cockrane Forster, *late of* 64 F. ....27 Oct. 57
George Lane ....17 Dec. 57
Wm. Henry Mordaunt..........26 Jan. 58
Henry Wilson, *lateCapt.*1 Dr. Gds. ....28 Jan. 58

LIEUTENANTS.
Henry Short ....11 Apr. 56
John Richd. Blake, *late of* 6 F.12 June 56
Roderick M'Donald Campbell.11 Jan. 58
William Thomas L. Lloyd......14 Apr. 58
Joseph Balderson ....12 Aug. 58
Wm. Robinson Truman ....27 Oct. 58
Wm. Griffin Stack, *Instructor of Musketry* ....31 Mar. 59
Wm. Alsey Turner ....20 Apr. 59
Arthur Horrex ....29 July 59
Octavius Weld ....30 Sept. 59

ENSIGNS.
D'Oyley Wm. Battley ....12 Aug. 58

Edward Chapman ....13 Nov. 58
Austin Heuston ....13 Dec. 58
Aubrey Howard James......... do.
Charles M. Hayes Newington 10 Jan. 59
Charles Randall ....25 Feb. 59
Frederick Barnes.................27 May 59
Fra. Geo. T. Cunynghame.....29 July 59
Arthur Bristow ....30 Sept. 59
Herbert Henry Duesbury...... 5 Oct. 59
Adj. and Captain.—Wm. Bell, *late Lt. and Adj.* 64 F......18 Mar. 56
Paymaster.—Richard Port, *late of Coldst.-Gds.* ....27 Feb. 56
Qr.Master. — John Coombes, *late of* 64 F...............31 Oct. 56
Surgeon.—S. W. M. Walker...30 Nov. 55
Assist.Surg. — Robert Henry Bolton 17 Sept.59

Blue Facings.

Agents, Messrs. Cox & Co.

ROYAL MONMOUTH.

(*Light Infantry.*) [No. 31.]
Head Quarters, Monmouth.
HONORARY COLONEL.
Henry MorganClifford,MP.DL. 5 Mar.58
LIEUT.COLONEL COMMANDANT.
John Francis Vaughan ....16 July 53
MAJORS.
John Selwyn Payne, *late Lieut.* 14 F................................. 9 Aug.58
Francis M'Donnell, *late Ensign* 71 F................................. 1 Mar. 59
CAPTAINS.
James Davies ....21 May 53
George Griffin Tyler............. 6 Jan. 55
Thomas Brook....................14 May 55
John Richard Russell .... 1 Jan. 56
Almericus Blakeney Savery ... 1 Aug. 57
John Griffith Wheeley 9 Aug.58
Bryan Sheehy 2 Nov.58
William Leigh..................... 1 Mar.59
LIEUTENANTS.
George Arthur Lloyd............ 2 Apr. 56
James Browne ....25 June 56
Robert Reddall Williamson ... 1 Aug. 57
John Samoiski 9 Aug.58
Rhys Brychan Powell .... 1 Mar, 59
William Bredin .... 4 Mar. 59
Arthur Edward Benson ....18 Nov. 59
ENSIGNS.
Fred. Charles Thynne ....13 July 55
Charles George Kane .... 8 Feb. 58
William Allanay 24Sept.58
Wm. Henry Wheeley .... 8 Aug. 59
Adjt.—John Money Carter, *Capt. h. p. Unatt.* ....19 Jan. 46
Paymaster. — Richard Jones, *late Capt. HanoverianHussars*26 June 54
Surg.—George Wilson ....10 Oct. 54
Assist.Surg. — James Eyres Coward. ....25 Jan, 56

Blue Facings.

Agent, E. S. Codd, *Esq.*

ROYAL MONTGOMERY.

(*Rifles.*) [No. 57.]
Head Quarters, Welchpool.
LIEUT.COLONEL COMMANDANT.
John Edward H. Pryce (1), *late Capt.* 2 F..................25June 55
MAJOR.
Geo. Bednell (2), *late Lieut. Bengal Army* 30June 55
CAPTAINS.
John H. Heyward ....22 May 54
J. P. Harrison ....11 July 55
Henry Nicholls ....18 Oct. 55
Richard Tanfield Vachell ......11 Oct. 55

Militia of England and Wales. 626

LIEUTENANTS.
Richard H. Sturkey .... 4 Aug. 55
James Sebastian Gill .... 24 Mar. 50
Alex. M. Sutherland............ 3 May 58
James Duncan Thomson ......11 Oct. 58

ENSIGNS.
Adj. & Capt.—Edw. Dwen, late
Ensign 43 F. ....29 June 46
Surg.—W. Slyman, M.D........10 Sept. 52
Scarlet Facings.
Agents, Messrs. Cox & Co.

1ST, OR WEST NORFOLK.
[No. 39.]
Head Quarters, Colchester.

LIEUT.COLONEL COMMANDANT.
Hambleton Francis Custance,
DL. ....16 May 54

MAJORS.
Charles Bedingfield ....16 May 54
Hon. Frederick Walpole(1), Lt.
R.N. ....17 May 59

CAPTAINS.
George Augustus Marsham ...26 May 52
Philip Bedingfield ....22 Apr. 53
Charles Edward Bignold .....30 May 53
Joseph Edwin Day............31 May 53
Thos. Wm. Fountaine, late of
70 F. ....27 Dec. 54
Henry Geo. Bedingfield ...... 8 Jan. 58
Robert Morris..................30 June 59

LIEUTENANTS.
Roseville Brackenbury .... 8 Jan. 56
James Menzies .... 3 Feb. 58
William Herring ....30 Mar. 58
George Hill....................14 June 59

ENSIGNS.
John Storer Brown .... 8 Jan. 58
John Henry Warnes ....30 June 59

Adj. & Capt.—Henry Peisley
L'Estrange, late Capt. 31 F. 17 Apr. 50
Paymaster.—Capt. Thos. Glee-
son, late Capt. 90 F. ......18 Dec. 55
Qr.Master.—Daniel Hampson 12 Jan. 55
Surg.—David Penrice ....10 Nov. 58
Assist.Surgeon.—Jas. Dalton
Peytherch......................20 May 58
White Facings.
Agents, Messrs. Cox & Co.

2ND, OR EAST NORFOLK.
[No. 40.]
Head Quarters, Yarmouth.

COLONEL.
Hon. Berkeley Wodehouse, DL.
late Major 8 Hussars......... 9 Sept. 42

LIEUT.COLONEL.
Sir Edmund Henry K. Lacon,
Bart. MP. DL. JP. ....31 Aug. 59

MAJOR.
John Marcon, JP. late Capt. 12
F. ....31 Aug. 59

CAPTAINS.
George Granville Glover, late
Capt. 7 Fusiliers ....23 Nov. 52
John Gay, DL. JP............10 Dec. 52
Wm. M. R. Haggard, DL. JP. 16 Dec. 54
Henry Coldham Mathew, JP...3 Nov. 56

Charles Applewhaite 25 Sept.57
Chas. P. S. Ensor, late Capt.
Madras Army ....18 Mar. 58
Charles Fred. Allen .... 7 Sept. 59
Robert Arthur Rising ....10 Dec. 59

LIEUTENANTS.
Wm. Wood Townshend........16 July 59
Wm. Danby Palmer ....22 July 59
Wm. Fred. Windham...........10 Oct. 59

ENSIGNS.

Adjt. & Capt.—Robert Charles
Holmes, late Capt. 10 Hussars 22 Mar. 58
Qr.Mr. — Wm. Hardiment ...10 Oct. 59
Surg.—Jn. Caporn Smith, JP. 18 Oct. 52
Assist.Surg.—Jas. Wm. Crow 30 Mar. 58
White Facings.
Agents, Messrs. Cox & Co.

NORFOLK ARTILLERY.
[No. 22.]
[Embodied.]
Head Quarters, Sheerness.

HONORARY COLONEL.
Jacob, Lord Hastings ....24 May 56
LIEUT.COLONEL COMMANDANT.
Fra. L'Estrange Astley, DL.JP. 1 June 55

MAJOR.
John Penrice, JP. .... 1 June 55

CAPTAINS.
Jas. Hay Wodehouse........... 2 June 55
Raoul Stephen Bedingfeld ... 4 June 55
Hon. Ralph Harbord[2], late
Capt. 71 F. ....30 May 59
Edw. Henry Rust D'Eye .....12 Sept. 59

LIEUTENANTS.
Robert Bacon Longe ....27 Aug. 55
Shovell Henry Brereton .....19 Oct. 57
Hon. Harbord Harbord........ 8 Apr. 59
Count Melchior G. de Wezell 12 Sept. 59

SECOND LIEUTENANTS.
Henry H. M. Seel ....26 Apr. 59
Fred. Henry Brice.............. 7 June 59
William Bedingfield .... 8 June 59
Adj. & Capt.—John Gilbertson 2 May 53
Qr.Master.—Arthur Russell...14 June 59
Surg.—Charles Cory Aldred,
JP.................................27 Aug. 53
Agents, Messrs. Cox & Co.

NORTHAMPTON.
[No. 48.]
Head Quarters, Northampton.
"Mediterranean."

COLONEL.
Thomas Philip Maunsell, MP.
DL. JP. .... 2 Apr. 45

LIEUT.COLONEL COMMANDANT.
Lord Burghley, MP. .... 7 Jan. 46

MAJORS.
Lord Brownlow Thos. Mon-
tague Cecil, late of Scots Fus.
Gds. ....10 July 54
Charles Hill, JP...............14 June 55

CAPTAINS.
Rich. Trevor Clarke, DL. JP. 4 Apr. 46
William Christie ....18 Apr. 46
Edward H. Finch Hatton.....25 Oct. 52
John Robinson
    ....25 Oct. 52

Herbert Staples Smith........31 Dec. 53
Thomas Robert Andrew ...... 6 May 54
Aldborough R. Rundle, late
Capt. 40 F. .... 2 Dec. 54
Henry Mincel Stockdale .....14 Nov. 57
Robert James D'Arcy.........19 Dec. 57
Wm. Kerr ....23 Feb. 58

LIEUTENANTS.
Frederick William Bowman ...14 Aug. 54
Hewitt Linton..................21 June 55
Wm. H. W. De Capel Brooke... 7 Jan. 56
Philip Wake ....15 Oct. 57
Wm. S. B. Whitworth ....16 Oct. 57
Thomas Henry Pares .... 7 Nov. 57
Charles Jennins ....26 Nov. 57
George Wm. Platt .... 9 Jan. 58
Philip Batty ....10 Jan. 58
Geo. Alfred Lawrence.........19 Apr. 58

ENSIGNS.
Henry Chas. Chaves Lucena 13 Nov. 57
Gerard Septimus Burton ....14 Nov. 57
Stuart Vivian Fraser ....10 Feb. 58
Grice Richard Smyth ....16 Feb. 58

Adjt. & Capt.—Thomas Rose,
late Capt. 15 F. .... 7 Feb. 46
Paymaster—James Ray Norton,
Capt. Unatt....................19 Apr. 55
Qr.Master.—Hiram Manfull ..20 Nov. 57
Surg.—Wm. Alex. Barr, M.D.24 Jun. 56
Assist.Surg.—Wm. Croome...22 Mar. 58
Yellow Facings.
Agents, Messrs. Cox & Co.

NORTHUMBERLAND.
(Light Infantry.) [No. 27.]
Head Quarters, Alnwick.

HONORARY COLONEL.
The Earl of Beverley, DL. JP.17 May 04
LIEUT.COLONEL COMMANDANT.
William Mathew Bigge, DL.
late Lt.Col. 70 F. .... 8 Sept. 52

MAJORS.
Lord Lovaine, DL. JP. late of
Gren. Gds. .... 8 Sept. 52
Lord Charles Beauclerk, late
Capt. 1 F. ....19 Feb. 57

CAPTAINS.
John Potts, JP. ....29 Apr. 31
George Burrell, late Lt. 45 F. 10 Oct. 52
James Crosby Anderson, late
Eus. 30 F. ....21 July 53
William Adamson ....21 July 53
John Jobling Weatherly ..... 2 Nov. 53
Ralph Henry Philipson........31 Jan. 55
Francis Blake ....14 May 55
Fenton John Aylmer (2), late
of 97 F. ....13 July 58
Wm. H. Shafto, late of 93 F. 19 Nov. 58
Fred. Stephen Steele, late Lt.
2 F. ....10 May 59

LIEUTENANTS.
John David Scott ....21 July 53
Knightley Holled Coxe ......29 Jan. 55
John Potts ....29 Jan. 55
Laurence Marlow Sidney ....31 Jan. 55
William Penrs ....20 Nov. 55
William Potts ....28 June 56
Geo. Pringle Hughes..........19 Nov. 58
Michael Dodd ....28 Dec. 58

ENSIGNS.
Adj. & Capt.—Herman Ernest
Galton (1), late Capt. 50 F. 12 Feb. 56
Paymaster.—
Qr.Master. — Joseph Jones,
late Qr.Mr. 33 F. .... 5 Nov. 58
Surgeon.—Edward Smiles...... 8 Sept. 52
Assist.Surg.—

Buff Facings.
Agents, Messrs. Cox and Co.

NORTHUMBERLAND ARTILLERY.
[No. 23.]
[Embodied.]
Head Quarters, Tynemouth.
Blue Facings.

LIEUT.COLONEL.
Charles Clementson .... 4 Feb. 58

MAJOR.
Charles John Reed .... 4 Feb. 58

CAPTAINS.
Henry Weston, *late of Indian Army* .... 3 Feb. 58
Robert Cairnes Bruce, *late Capt. 85 F.* ....12 Feb. 59
Henry St. George Priaulx, *late of 4 Drs.* ....15 Mar. 59
Percy Charles Stanhope ...... 7 June 59

LIEUTENANTS.
Thos. Forsyth Forrest ....13 July 58
John Wm. Finch 8 Sept.58
Alfred Joseph Macbay .... 6 Apr. 59
John Jameson .... 7 June 59

SECOND LIEUTENANTS.
William Barras ....24 Dec. 56
William Gethrin .... 3 June 59
Henry Spiller .... 8 June 59
Henry John Ryde ....17 Nov. 59

Adj. & Capt.—Wm. Macbay, *late of R. Art.* ....15 July 54
Surgeon.—Alex. Leslie Gracey, MD., *late of Turkish Contingent* ....21 Sept. 58

NOTTINGHAM, OR ROYAL SHERWOOD FORESTERS.
[No. 59.]
Head Quarters, Nottingham.

COLONEL.
Lancelot Rolleston..............11 Apr. 33

LIEUT.COLONEL.
William L. Mellish, *late Capt. Rifle Br.* .... 9 Nov. 52

MAJOR.
Alexander Boddam, *late Capt. 58 F.* ....13 Nov. 52

CAPTAINS.
Arthur Bromley 14 Sept.52
Arthur S. H. Lowe.............. 6 Nov. 52
Alfred Hurst Lowe.............. 9 Mar. 53
Godfrey G. G. C. Gardiner...... 5 May 54
Charles J. Barrow ....15 Dec. 54
Geo. Davis, *late Capt. E.I.C.S.* 8 Feb. 55
Anthony Henderson Fowke .... 6 Apr. 55
John Draper Hemsley .... 5 May 55
John Stephens ....10 Oct. 57
Aug. Mark Hammond ....16 Oct. 57
Wm. E. Smith, *Instructor of Musketry* ....28 Oct. 58
Wm. Francis Scully 30 Aug.59

LIEUTENANTS.
John Wm. Preston, *h. p. 76 F. Acting Qr.Master* ....23 Jan. 55
William Grant.................. 1 June 55
Anguish Honor Aug. Durant .18 Sept. 55
Thos. John Walsh, *late Ens. 73 F.* ....29 Sept. 55
Eyre Evans....................16 Dec. 55
Edward Alex. Sloane...........28 May 56
Loftus John Rolleston ....28 Oct. 58
Henry Peter Murphy ....31 Dec. 58
William Ainsworth ....29 Aug. 59
Jasper Burne....................... do

ENSIGNS.
Leonard Jaques ....26 May 58
Henry C. Ross Johnson ....27 Jan. 59
Arthur Hales .... do

Adj. & Capt.—John F. Girardot (1), *late Capt. 48 F.*....23 Oct. 56

Paymr.—Nicholas Wrixon(2) *late Brevet Major 21 F.*.....11 June 55
Surgeon.—James Anders.....28 Apr. 13
Assist. Surg.—Wm. Blucher Dolton M.D. ....12 Aug. 58
Blue Facings.
Agents, Messrs. Cox and Co.

OXFORDSHIRE.
[No, 51.]
[Embodied.]
Head Quarters, Dover.
"*Mediterranean.*"

COLONEL.
Chas. Oldfield Bowles, DL. JP. 3 Apr. 47

LIEUT.COLONEL.
John William Fane, DL. JP... 6 Apr. 47

MAJOR.
Anthony Morris Storer ....26 Mar. 53

CAPTAINS.
Andrew MarriottMathews,DL 23 Jan. 46
Hon. Algernon Sydney Arthur Annesley, *late Lt.* 16 *Drs*....18 Mar. 54
Nicholas Gifford ....20 Oct. 58
Thomas Frederick Bulkeley ... do
Edmund Wigley Severne ......11 Nov. 58
Fred. Walter Aston ....27 Nov. 58
Henry Moody ....17 Aug. 59
Thomas Mosley Crowder, *Instructor of Musketry* ...... 1 Nov. 59

LIEUTENANTS.
Edw. Trevor Arney ....21 Oct. 58
Samuel Perry .... do
Herbert Buchanan.............14 Dec. 58
Windham Fra. Phillips.........29 Dec. 58
Albert Maxwell Harte ....15 Jan. 59
Compton Legge ....16 Mar. 59
Edward Ramsay...............17 Aug. 59
Charles Rivers Bulkeley ...... 1 Nov. 59

ENSIGNS.
Henry Frank Otté Golding ...29 Dec. 58
Walter Hackett .... do
Henry Alan Clery .... 5 Jan. 59
Thomas Reid Brown ....18 Mar. 59
Geo. Manley Buckle .... 9 July 59
Charles Fred. King ....22 Sept. 59

Adj. & Capt.— G. Cuming, *late Capt.* 71 *F.* .... 3 Feb. 46
Paymast.—William Wykeham Holloway.................... 5 Sept. 58
Qr.Master.—John Mendows 3 Oct. 57
Surg.—Rich. James Hansard 5 May 55
Assist.Surg.—Robert George Watts .... 5 June 55
Yellow Facings.
Agents, Messrs. Cox and Co.

ROYAL PEMBROKE ARTILLERY.
[No. 24.]
Head Quarters, Pembroke.

LIEUT.COLONEL COMMANDANT.
Hugh Owen Owen, DL. JP...16 Sept.30

MAJOR.
Wm. Hen. Lewis, DL. JP. ...21 May 46

CAPTAINS.
Jas. Mark Child, DL. JP....... 6 Jan. 20
Geo. Bowen J. Jordan, DL. JP.21 May 46
Charles Cook Wells, DL. JP. *late Capt. H. E. I. C. S.*..... 3 June 54
Owen Tucker Edwards .... 1 May 57

LIEUTENANTS.
James James .... 7 Dec. 53
John Owen, *Qr. Master* ....17 June 54
William Green Hartley 28Sept.57
Henry Lyon Walcott...........11 Aug. 58
Henry Ackland .... 4 July 59

SECOND LIEUTENANTS.
John Delaware Lewis ....14 Aug. 57
Fred. William Hall.............10 Oct. 57
George Calvert ....15 Dec. 58
John Graham ....26 July 59
Adjt. & Capt. & Paym.—Wm. Moffat Douglas Willan, *Capt. h. p. R. Art.* ....14 Aug. 55
Surgeon.—Thos. Dumayne ...25 Mar. 11
Red Facings.
Agents, A. F. Ridgway & Son.

ROYAL RADNOR.
(*Rifles.*) [No. 50.]
Head Quarters, Prestign.

MAJOR COMMANDANT.
Lawrence Henry Peel,JP. *late of* 52 *F.*.................. 27 Mar. 54

CAPTAIN.
Hugh Powell Prickard ....25 June 59

LIEUTENANTS.
John F. Willis Kane .... 4 Oct. 58
Richard Winstanley Ormerod 25 June 59

ENSIGNS.

Adjt.& Capt.—Edw. Rawlings Hannam, *late Capt.* 60 *F.*...20 Dec. 56
Surg.—Edwd.MawthillTearne 8 Jan. 53
Scarlet Facings.
Agents, Messrs. Cox & Co.

RUTLAND.
(*Light Infantry.*) [No. 14.]
Head Quarters, Oakham.

CAPTAIN COMMANDING.
Hon. Henry Lewis Noel, JP. *late Lieut.* 68 *F.* .... 4 Oct. 52

LIEUTENANT.
Edward Costall .... 1 Jan. 55

Buff Facings.

SHROPSHIRE.
[No. 54.]
Head Quarters, Shrewsbury.

COLONEL.
Richard Frederick Hill, DL. *late Lieut.Col.* 53 *F.* ....21 Aug. 52

LIEUT.COLONEL.
Edward Corbett, *late Lt.* 72 *F.*16 Mar. 55

MAJOR.
Edward Ferrer Acton, DL. ...14 Dec. 52

CAPTAINS.
George Samuel Pechell, *late* 47 *Regt. Madras Army* ......28 Aug. 52
Rowland Whitchall Kenyon... 4 Nov. 55
Harry Calveley Cotton, *late Capt.* 21 *F.*.................31 Mar. 53
Godfrey Russell (2), *late R.N.* 14 June 53
Erasmus Salwey................14 June 53
Thomas Cholmondeley ....20 Feb. 55
Robert Phipps Dod ....26 Jan. 58
Thomas Meyrick............... 2 June 59
Thos. Kynnersley Gardner ... 7 June 59
Walter Thursby................22 July 59

LIEUTENANTS.
Thomas Matthews ....12 July 32

Militia of England and Wales. 628

Joseph Venables Lovett.......... 4 Nov. 57
Fred. Henry Mainwaring......10 Dec. 57
Robert Taylor Macsfield ......29 Jan. 58
Richard Altamont Smythe ... 7 June 59
Rowland Hill .... 7 June 59
Geo. Alex. Patten ....27 Aug. 59
Walter Boyce .... 8 July 59

ENSIGNS.
Robert Phillips ....20 Aug. 59
Adj. & Capt.—Spencer Cosby
Price, *late Lt. 72 F.*........24 Apr. 59
Paymaster.—F. Owen, *late
Capt. 44 F.* ....12 Dec. 54
Qr. Master.—James Armstrong 8 July 59
Surg.—John Nigel Heathcote 8 May 46
Assist. Surg.—James Walter
Cavanagh ....26 Dec. 57

Green Facings.
Agents, Messrs. Cox and Co.

1st SOMERSET.
[No. 16.]
Head Quarters, Taunton.

HONORARY COLONEL.
Charles K. Kemys Tynte, JP.
DL. *late Capt.* 11 *Hussars
and Gr. Gds.* ....20 Oct. 57

LIEUT. COLONEL COMMANDANT.
Richard Leckonby Phipps, DL.
JP. *Col. Unatt.* ....18 Oct. 25

MAJORS.
William Vaughan Jenkins, JP. 8 Sept. 55
John Mathew Quantock, JP.
late Lieut 4 Dr. Gds. ......14 Dec. 57

CAPTAINS.
Henry Godfrey Marsh, JP. ... 2 Mar. 31
Charles Warro Loveridge, JP. 19 June 35
Thomas Hussey, DL. JP. ...... 4 Apr. 46
Alfred Augustus Malet, *late
Capt. 8 F.* ....13 May 52
Isaac Elton, *late Brev. Major
45 F.* ....19 Oct. 52
Herbert Butler Batten, JP. ...20 Dec. 52
Gansel Jebb.......................16 Feb. 55
Robert Desmond Adair ...... 8 Sept. 55
George Deedes Warry, JP. ...14 Dec. 57
Henry Cornish Henley, JP. ... 9 Aug. 59

LIEUTENANTS.
Wm. G. V. Villiers ....23 Jan. 55
Richard Winsloe..................17 Feb. 55
Thomas Warry ....13 June 55
Arthur H. Nicholas Kemmis 8 Aug. 55
May Jenkins Freestun .... 9 Aug. 55
Schofield Patten ....24 Jan. 56
Coventry Carew ....21 Oct. 56
Mortimer Dettmar ....25 July 57
Robert Chaffey Chaffey ...... 2 Feb. 58
Septimus James Barrett ......10 Aug. 59

ENSIGNS.
Lionel Patton .... 2 Feb. 58
Fred. Arthur Holworthy ...... do
Aubrey De Lisle Patton ......29 June 59
Adjt. & Capt. and Paymaster
—Wm. Surtees Cook, *Capt.
h. p. Unatt.* ....21 Feb. 46
Surg.—Charles Hugo..........25 Dec. 17
Assist. Surg.— Henry Gully
Foy .... 4 Dec. 56

Black Velvet Facings.
Agents, Messrs. Cox and Co.

2ND SOMERSET.
[No. 47.]
Head Quarters, Bath.

COLONEL.
William Pinney, MP. DL. JP. 1 Jan. 50

LIEUT. COLONEL.
ዎ ልፀ Francis F. Luttrell (1),
DL. JP. *late of Gr. Gds.*... 4 June 30

MAJOR.
James Talbot Stanley, *late,
Capt.* 89*th F.* ....12 Apr. 56

CAPTAINS.
Robert J. Bisdee..................23 May 31
Edward Harwood ....21 Sept. 52
George Chamberlaine...........24 May 56
Chas. R. J. Sawyer, JP., *late
of Dutch Gr. Gds.* ....26 May 56
Wm. Henry Spurway............14 Dec. 57
William Barrett ....15 Dec. 57
Alfred Hudson Ricketts........16 Dec. 57
George Gyles .... 6 Oct. 58
Richard Marker ....20 Nov. 58
Robert Townley Woodman,
late Lieut. 14 *Drs.* ....25 July 59

LIEUTENANTS.
Robert Hetherington............20 May 54
Kilner Aug. Arthur B. Creagh 14 Dec. 57
Edward Fox.......................16 Dec. 57
John Hatton Brereton ....19 Apr. 59
Wm. Peard Jillard ....20 Apr. 59
Elliot Geo. Henry Salter, *late
Ens.* 73 *F.* ....25 June 59
Wm. Frederic Holt ....27 June 59
Wm. Fred. Gore Langton ... 28 June 59

ENSIGNS
George Henry Cook .... 2 Feb. 57
Christopher Lucas Salmon .. 17 Dec. 57
John A. P. K. Harwood ...... 6 Oct. 58
Wm. Vigne Andrews ....19 Apr. 59
Henry Master Sproule ....20 Apr. 59
Wm. Wilberforce Rawlins ....28 June 59
Adj. & Capt.—Alex. J. Mac-
pherson, *late of* 77 *F.*......18 June 46
Qr. Master.—Charles Fraser,
h. p. 49 *F.* ....29 Sept. 54
Surgeon.—John Grant Wilson,
MD. ....20 Apr. 59
Assist. Surg.—

Black Velvet Facings.
Agents, Messrs. C. R. and W. M'Grigor.

THE KING'S OWN 1st STAFFORD.
[No. 66.]
[Embodied.]
Head Quarters, Portsmouth,
"Mediterranean."

LIEUT. COLONEL COMMANDANT.
Hon. Wellington Pat. Manvers
Chetwynd Talbot, *late of*
7 *Fusiliers, Serjeant at Arms
in Ordinary to the Queen* ... 4 Mar. 53

MAJORS.
Charles Inge, *Capt.* h.p.53 F. 30 Sept. 52
Francis Chambers ....15 Jan. 59

CAPTAINS.
Hon. C. Wrottesley ....23 June 52
Sidney L. Lane ....25 Nov. 52
Thomas Wm. Fletcher, DL. ... 1 Feb. 53
Henry Jasper Willett............30 July 53
Charles Edw. Mousley, DL. JP. 30 July 53
Cecil Newton Lane...............27 July 54
Charles Eaton ....22 Nov. 54
John Philip Dyott ....14 Feb. 55
Pryce Ilbert Harrison ....15 Sept. 58
Carrington Jones, *Instructor of
Musketry* ....17 Sept. 58
Walter Richard Hickman......19 Apr. 59

LIEUTENANTS.
Askew James Hillcoat ....25 Dec. 11
John Taylor, *late Lt.* 10 *F.* ..14 Nov. 53
Francis Lambarde................23 Apr. 58
George Wm. Moore ....13 Sept. 58
John A. W. F. Wilson .... 1 Nov. 58
David Dowie .... 1 Dec. 58
Thos. John Gatehouse ....19 Apr. 59
Walter Ormerod Beales....... do.
Martin Blake .... 9 July 59
Robertson Gilchrist Marshall 12 Nov. 59

ENSIGNS.
Robert Hamilton Playfair ...22 June 59
William John Baldwin .... do
John Hampden Gledstanes ... 1 Aug. 59
Clement Moore ....15 Aug. 59
Wm. Henry Armitage ....10 Nov. 59

Henry Broomhead................17 Dec. 59
Godfrey John B. T. Dalton... do
Adj. & Capt.—Danl. Hillman 19 July 52
Paymaster.—Richard Mills ...23 Dec. 54
Surgeon.—John Ley Hichens 21 May 58
Assist. Surgeon.—William Alex.
Hearnden......................10 June 58

Blue Facings.
Agents, Messrs. Cox and Co.

THE KING'S OWN 2ND STAFFORD.
(*Light Infantry.*) [No. 58.]
[Embodied.]
Head Quarters, Dublin.

COLONEL.
Hon. E. R. Littleton, MP. DL. JP. 5 Jan. 53

LIEUT. COLONEL.
Richard Dyott, DL. JP., *late
Capt.* 53 *F.* ....29 Sept. 55

MAJOR.
Hon. Arthur Wrottesley ......13 Oct. 55

CAPTAINS.
Morton Edw. Buller, DL. JP. 4 Jan. 53
Robt. Thos. Kennedy Levett...22 Feb. 53
William Johnson..................22 Apr. 53
James Wemyss Anderson, *late*
92 *F.* ....16 Dec. 54
Thomas Salt......................23 Dec. 54
Archibald Iver....................28 Feb. 56
John Edward Knight............28 Sept. 57
Thos. Fletcher Boughey ......27 May 58
Isaac de Lianeour Wilson ...27 Sept. 58
Cecil Henry Crampton ....30 Sept. 58

LIEUTENANTS.
William Woodward ....15 Mar. 56
Robert Hanson Coldwell, *In-
structor of Musketry* ......22 May 56
Henry Hind.......................10 Oct. 57
Fred. Blackall Jervis ....10 Oct. 57
Augustus Pattison ....16 Oct. 57
William Henry Cooper ....23 Dec. 57
John Wm. Sneyd ....24 May 58
Fred. Clement Sneyd .... 9 Oct. 58
Rowland John Leuthall........27 Oct. 58
Henry Faulkener ....21 July 59

ENSIGNS.
John Wallace P. Lowe ....19 Feb. 58
Smith Hill Child..................19 Nov. 58
Thomas B. Shaw Hellier ......19 Nov. 58
Fra. B. Featherstonhaugh ... 6 Dec. 58
William Shaw .... 7 Dec. 58
Edw. Whitacre Davies ....21 Dec. 58
John Berkeley Michell ....25 Jan. 59
Wm. Beauclere Powell .... 1 Sept. 59
Robert Travers Atkins.......... do
Adj. & Capt.—Eyre Trench
John Richard Nugent, *late
Capt.* 59 *F.* ....24 May 56
Paymaster.—Lambert Disney 15 Oct. 57
Qr. Master.—Tho. W. Cudmore 14 Feb. 55
Surgeon.—Nich. C. Whyte ... 1 Mar. 56
Assist. Surg.— Cooper Hayes
Crawford .... 1 Mar. 56

Blue Facings.
Agents, Messrs. Cox and Co.

THE KING'S OWN 3RD STAFFORD.
(*Rifles.*) [No. 73.]
Head Quarters, Newcastle-under-Lyne.

HONORARY COLONEL.
Charles Bagot, *late of Gr. Gds.* 27 Mar. 58

LIEUT. COLONEL COMMANDANT.
Rich. Byrd Levett, *late Capt.*
60 *Rifles* ....13 Apr. 58

MAJORS.
Charles Coyney ....16 Apr. 53
Peter Broughton, *late Lieut.* 3
Dr. Gds. ....26 Apr. 58

I I

629 Militia of England and Wales.

CAPTAINS.
Henry Mayhew ....22 Aug. 53
John Wm. Crowe, *late Lieut.*
83 *F*..............................16 Dec. 54
John Maurice Foster...........18 Dec. 54
John F. F. Mytton, *late of* 89 *F*.12 Jan. 55
John Broughton ....30 Jan. 55
Clement T. Sneyd Kynnersley 11 Feb. 56
Edward Richard Adams......26 Apr. 58
Francis William Bott..........12 Aug. 58
Charles John Webb .... 7 Mar. 59
Wm. Lee Gresley.............. 1 Aug. 59

LIEUTENANTS.
Francis Vere Wright ....30 Jan. 55
Rowland Hugh Cotton ....13 Feb. 56
Walter Mainwaring Coyney... 8 Dec. 57
Edward John Jervis ....26 Apr. 58
Lord Alex. Victor Paget ......17 Aug. 58
Michael Arthur Bass ....17 Feb. 59
Thomas Donaldson .... 7 Mar. 59
Alex. Wm. Radford............23 July 59

ENSIGNS.
Dominick Herbert Traut...... 8 Dec. 58
Charles Donaldson............26 Mar. 59

Adj. & Capt.—Benj. Midgley,
Capt. Unatt. ....30 Mar. 53
Surg.—John Grant .... 1 May 57
Assist.Surg.— Alex. Wright,.12 May 57
Green Facings.
Agents, Messrs. Cox and Co.

1st or WEST SUFFOLK.
[No. 10.]
Head Quarters, Bury St. Edmunds.
HONORARY COLONEL.
Fred. *Marquis of* Bristol ......25 Mar. 46
LIEUT.COLONEL COMMANDANT.
Geo. Deare, *late Lt.Col.* 21 *F.* 18Sept. 55
MAJORS.
Windsor Parker, (2) DL. JP.,
late Capt. Bengal Army ... 9 Oct. 52
Fuller Maitland Wilson, JP.,..18 May 59

CAPTAINS.
Robert John Pettiward ....12 Aug. 52
John Thomas *Lord* Manners 31 May 53
Henry Maitland Wilson ...... 7 Dec. 54
Ninian Craig, *late Capt.*1*W.I.R.*17 Jan. 55
William Windsor Parker ......25 Aug. 55
Fred. Wm. John *Earl* Jermyn 17 Mar.56
Wm. Julius Marshall........... 7 Aug. 58
Edward Daubeney ....18 May 59
James Holmes..................19 May 59

LIEUTENANTS.
Charles Bidwell Edwardes ...24 Nov. 55
Alfred Robert Jennings........10 Apr. 56
Alfred Newbatt ....15 May 56
Lord Aug. Henry Chas. Hervey 15 June 59

ENSIGNS.
Edw. S. Osmond Clarke ...... 8 Oct. 55

Adj. & Capt.—John M'Gregor,
late of Scots. Fus. Gds. ...24 Jan. 46
Paymaster—Claude C. Lucas,
late Bt.Major Bomb. Army 27 Dec. 54
Qr.Master.—William Hall ...13 Jan. 57
Surgeon.—George Creed 22June 24
Assist.Surg.—John Kilner ...21 Sept. 53
Yellow Facings.
Agents, Messrs. Cox and Co.

SUFFOLK ARTILLERY.
[No. 25.]
[Embodied.]
Head Quarters, Gosport.
COLONEL.
Henry Bence Bence (1), *late
of* 16 *Drs.* .... 3 May 44

LIEUT.COLONEL COMMANDANT.
Rt. Alex. Shafto Adair, DL.,
Colonel 13 March 57, *and
Aide de Camp to the Queen* 30 Apr. 53
MAJOR.
James Mill Walker.............. 9 Nov. 55
CAPTAINS.
Hill Massenden Leathes ...... 1 May 52
Charles Gorton ....15 Sept. 54
Wm. Horsley H. Dakins ......19 Mar. 55
Wickham Talbot Harvey......14 Apr. 59
Howard Whitbread .... 1 July 59

FIRST LIEUTENANTS.
Edw. Griffith Austin, *late of
Bengal Art.*....................12 Apr. 59
Joshua Thelluson Rowley....13 Apr. 59
Robert Welch Coates..........14 Apr. 59
John Bryce Wilkinson ....15 Apr. 59
Fred. George Wilkinson ......28 June 59

SECOND LIEUTENANTS.
Gerard T. W. Ferrand ....12 Apr. 59
Charles Abercrombie Cooper 13 Apr. 59
Cooper Chas. R. Brooke......14 Apr. 59
Arthur H. Brittain ....13 May 59
Edw. Samuel Hamersley .....28 June 59

Adj. & Capt.—
Paymaster.—Fred. Barlow ...12 May 59
Qr.Master.—Pat. Fitzpatrick 8 Mar. 59
Surgeon,—Charles Sawer ...... 1 Oct. 52
Assist.Surg.—Geo. Hayward 23 Apr. 59
Scarlet Facings.
Agents, Messrs. Cox and Co.

1st ROYAL SURREY.
[No. 20.]
Head Quarters, Richmond.
COLONEL.

LIEUT.COLONEL.
George Palmer Evelyn (5), *late
Capt. Rifle Brigade* ....19 Mar. 56
MAJOR.
George Dennistoun Scott, DL.,
JP. *late Capt.* 1 *Dr. Gds.* ...19 Mar. 56
CAPTAINS.
Robert Grange, *Capt. h. p.,
Bengal Army* ....10 Oct. 52
Ed. Hugh Leycester Penrhyn,
JP..............................11 Oct. 32
Charles William Calvert, *late
Capt.* 2 *Dr. Gds.*..............14 Dec. 52
John Almon Boulcott..........14 Dec. 52
Charles Stephen Barron ......10 Feb. 53
William Platt .... 5 Oct. 53
Stewart Forbes .... 7 Jan. 56
Arthur Holme Sumner ....20 Mar. 56
Hon. Henry L. Pepys..........15 Jun. 58

LIEUTENANTS.
Joseph Whitmore ....19 Oct. 54
Henry Peters ....23 Apr. 55
Thomas Vivian Gurney........25 Oct. 55
Wm. Henry Medley ....17 Mar. 56
Perceval Aug. Carleton........11 Nov. 57
Simon Taylor, *late Capt. Madras
Army* ....12 Nov. 57
Henry Lahee Bayne ....18 Nov. 57
Geo. Clapperton Bayne........14 Nov. 57

ENSIGNS.
Henry Astley Harding ....12 Nov. 57
Geo. Papplewell Walker ......14 Nov. 57
Adam A. Pelham Bullock ....14 Nov. 57
Boyle Wm. Minchin ....14 Nov. 57
Wm. Edward Newbury........ 5 Feb. 58
Arthur de Vere Beauclerk ... 8 July 58

Adj. & Capt.—James Prosser,
late of Gr. Gds. 24Sept.58
Paymaster.—Frn.Jno.Bellew(6),
late E.I.C.S...................26 Mar. 55
Qr.Master.—George Rontree,
late 95 *F.* ....18 Dec. 54
Surg.—Richard Archer Warwick............................27 Oct. 55
Assist.Surg.—Henry Wm. Jackson.............................14 Nov. 57
Blue Facings.
Agents, Messrs. Cox and Co.

2ND ROYAL SURREY.
[No. 11.]
Head Quarters, Guildford.
COLONEL.
William, *Earl of* Lovelace, *Lord
Lieutenant* ....14 Aug. 52
LIEUT.COLONEL.
Hillebrant Meredith Purratt,
(1)DL. JP. *Lieut. h.p. R. Art.*29 Jan. 55
MAJOR.
John Henry Ellis Ridley, *late
of* 2 *Dr. Gds.* ....16 Oct. 54

CAPTAINS.
Samuel Nicholson, DL. JP. ... 5 Oct. 52
Walter Richard Barnes,(2)*late
Capt.* 27 *Bengal Inf.* .... 6 Oct. 52
Alexander Marshall .... 7 Oct. 52
Thomas Donoghue Wright,*late
of* 69 *F.* .... 5 Nov. 52
Wynn de Cerjat .... 8 Dec. 55
William James Sharpe ....29 Dec. 55
John C. Rees Weguelin ....22 July 59
William Pontifex ....23 July 59

LIEUTENANTS.
William De Norman .... 7 May 53
William St. James Ball .... 4 Apr. 54
Edward George Hartnell .....21 Apr. 54
John Richard Molineux.......27 June 54
Henry Marston ....11 Feb. 56
Louis Perre Goodchap ....18 Apr. 56
James Elyard...................29 Apr. 56
Charles Howard Chaplin, *late
Capt. Turkish Contingent* ... 7 July 56

ENSIGNS.
Fred. Henry Scott .... 2 Mar. 57
Adj. & Capt.—
Surg.—Henry Sharp Taylor... 6 May 54
Paymaster.—
Assist.Surg.—
Blue Facings.
Agents, Messrs. Cox and Co.

3RD ROYAL SURREY.
[No. 118.]
Head Quarters, Kingston on Thames.
LIEUT.COLONEL COMMANDANT.
T. Chaloner Bisse Challoner,
DL. JP. *late of* 1 *Dr. Gds.* 26 Mar. 53
MAJORS.
John Wm. Gooch Spicer, DL.
JP. *late Capt.* 3 *Dr. Gds.* ...24Sept.52
Thomas Henry Clarke Terry,
JP. *late Lieut.* 15 *Hussars*..11 Oct. 52

CAPTAINS.
Miles Stringer, *late Lt.* 6 *Dr.*17June 53
Hon. Geo. Charles Mostyn ...21June 53
Richard John Blunt, *Lt.* 25
Madras N.I. ....19 July 53
Hedworth David Barclay .....20 July 53
Charles Francis Evelyn.......22 July 53
James Legeyt Daniell..........19 Dec. 53
Fred. Lewis Austen ....20 Jan. 54
Charles Downes Manning....23 Feb. 58
Samuel Arthur Seawell........24 Feb. 58
Samuel Leo. Schuster 12 Sept.59

LIEUTENANTS.
Edward John Platt .... 2 Mar. 55
Lamorock Flower ....23 Feb. 58
Junius Eicke....................24 Feb. 58
Fred. Goulburn Walpole .....30 June 59
Henry Chandos Rivers........ 8 July 59

ENSIGNS.
Fred. Gilliott Smith .... 1 July 59
Frederick Brown .... 2 July 59
Wm. Fred. Rogers .... 9 July 59

Adj. & Capt.—Evelyn Latimer
Purratt, *late Capt.* 85 *F.* ...19 Apr. 53
Surg.—Matt.Trollope Coleman 2 July 53
Assist.Surg.—Herbert Chas.
Wilkin ....19 Oct. 57
Blue Facings.

Militia of England and Wales. 63

1st ROYAL SUSSEX.
(*Light Infantry.*) [No. 52.]
[Embodied.]
Head Quarters, Glasgow.

COLONEL.
ꝶ ꝶꝶ Charles, *Duke of Richmond*,(1)KG.*LordLieut.Aide-de-Camp to the Queen, late of 52 F.* .... 4 Dec. 19

LIEUT.COLONEL.
Lord Arthur Lennox, late Lt.-Col. 68 *F.* .... 14 Dec. 54

MAJOR.
Hon. Henry Gage, *late Lieut. Rifle Brigade* .... 10 Mar. 54

CAPTAINS.
Richard Bingham Newland ...12 Dec. 31
Thomas Eaton Swettenham ...20 Mar. 37
Rush Marten Cripps .... 21 Apr. 46
Edward John Bunny .... 18 Apr. 53
Henry Bethune .... 10 May 53
John Eldridge West,*late Capt.* 8 *F.* .... 24 Mar. 55
Joseph Fiennes Blake .... 8 June 55
John Kincaid Smith .... 21 July 58
Aug. Granville Morgan .... 15 Feb. 59
Frank Paul Mathews, *Instructor of Musketry* .... 23 Feb. 59

LIEUTENANTS.
Thos. Faulconer Wisden .... 23 May 55
Charles Bridger .... 31 Oct. 55
William Bridger .... 31 Oct. 55
Arthur Burton .... 31 Mar. 56
William Orme .... 21 July 58
Pargiter Malvoisie Dickenson do
Ormsby Vandeleur .... 18 Apr. 59
John Alex. Byrne .... do.
Samuel Septimus Hire .... do.
Charles Hamilton Bell .... do.

ENSIGNS.
Joseph Bonham Clay .... 31 May 58
Stewart Paxton Majoribanks ...26 June 58
Thos. Carr Foster .... 7 July 58
Thos. Jones Sherwood .... 31 Aug. 58
Charles Francis Browne .... 1 Dec. 59

Adj. & Capt.—William Fuller,
Lieut. on h.p. late Adj. 52*F.*23 July 52
Paymaster.—G. And. Coventry 12 May 59
Qr.Master.—John Foster, ... 9 Jan. 55
Surg.—Wm. Batley .... 14 Sept. 58
Assist.Surg.—C. H. T. Ewington .... 8 June 53

Blue Facings.
Agents, Messrs. Cox and Co.

ROYAL SUSSEX ARTILLERY.
[No. 26.]
Head Quarters, Glasgow.

COLONEL IN CHIEF.
ꝶ ꝶꝶ Charles, *Duke of Richmond*, (1) KG. *Lord Lieut.,* 4 Dec. 19

LIEUT.COLONEL COMMANDANT.
George Carr Lloyd, DL. JP.
late Capt.,Rifle Brig. .... 26 Apr. 53

MAJOR.
Charles Montague Chester, JP.
late Capt. 90 *F.* .... 18 Apr. 53

CAPTAINS.
Richard Wetherell, JP. .... 19 Sept. 26
Fred. Moor, JP., *late of* 2 *F* ..21 Apr. 46
Wm. Aug. St. Clair, (3) JP., *late Maj. Bombay Horse Art.*..10 May 53
Henry Davey Curteis Cole......22 Jan. 56
James Hayes Sadler .... 4 Oct. 58

LIEUTENANTS.
George Elliott Clarke.............. 9 Feb. 56
Jonathan Darby .... 1 Sept. 58

SECOND LIEUTENANTS.
Barton L. John Scobell ......30 Nov. 58
Wm. Rowe Lewis ....25 June 59
Edward Henniker ....16 Sept. 59
Donald Wyatt Frazer ....19 Nov. 59

Adj. & Capt.—Hen. Tho. Settle,
late of Royal Artillery .... 9 Apr. 53
Surg.—David James Hall,M.D. 1 July 59
Assist.Surg.—

Scarlet Facings.
Agents, Messrs. Cox and Co.

THE KING'S OWN.
(*Light Infantry.*) [No. 97.]
[Embodied.]
Head Quarters, Aldershot.

HONORARY COLONEL.
The Marquis of Dalhousie, KT. 8 Apr. 45

LIEUT.COLONEL COMMANDANT.
William Lewis Grant, DL. JP.,
late Capt. 7 *Fusiliers, and late Lt.-Col. Staff Italian Legion* ....25 Dec. 52

MAJORS.
Fred. John Sidney Parry, DL.
late of 17 *Lancers* .... 3 Feb. 57
Charles Adams, *late Major German Legion* .... Sept. 59

CAPTAINS.
Samuel James Remnant ......31 Dec. 55
Hewitt Massy Dillon .... 6 May 57
Cadwallader Edwards, *late of* 20 *F.* .... 21 Nov. 57
Armar Lowry, *late Capt.* 30 *F.* do
Wm. H. Heard, *Capt. h.p.* ..28 June 58
Wray Bury Palliser .... 2 July 58
Robert Augustus Warren......15 Oct. 58
Geo. Alex. Warburton ....11 Feb. 59
Charles Mackinnon Walmisley 1 June 59
Joseph Hamilton .... 3 Nov. 59

LIEUTENANTS.
Andrew Fred. Dunsterville ...10 Nov. 57
Elijah Littlewood, *Instructor of Musketry* .... 2 Dec. 57
John Fenwick Wilkinson......16 Dec. 57
Edward Vernon ....17 Apr. 58
Wm. Lewis Kulbach ....28 May 58
Henry John Hunter ....22 Nov. 58
Octavius Gibbon ....25 May 59
Charles Lawson Salis .... 8 June 59
Henry Marsden .... 7 Nov. 59

ENSIGNS.
Ernest Aug. Beaumont ....30 Oct. 58
James Henry Morrell ....22 Nov. 58
Alfred Dower Reynolds ...... 6 Jan. 59
Richard Wilton ....16 May 59
Edw. Corbett Strutt ....10 Aug. 59
Herbert George Hawkes ......19 Nov. 59

Adj. & Capt.— John Gray (1),
late of 89 *F.* and 7 *Dr. Gds.*23 Nov. 52
Paymaster.—James Little......18 Feb. 59
Qr.Mast.—Wellington White,
(2) *late of* 50 *F.* ....30 Mar. 57
Surgeon.— Morgan Culhane,
M.D. .... 21 Nov. 57
Assist.Surg.—Rob.O. Hayes (3),
M.D. .... 8 Dec. 57

Blue Facings.
Agents, Messrs. Cox & Co.

THE QUEEN'S OWN LIGHT INFANTRY.
[No. 83.]
Head Quarters, Bethnal Green.

COLONEL.
The Earl of Wilton, GCH. DL.
JP..............................7 Nov. 40

LIEUT.COLONEL.
Samuel Walker, *late Major* 65 *F* ....13 Dec. 58

MAJOR.
Henry Cooper ....13 Dec. 58

CAPTAINS.
Clarence Holcombe Judd .....15 July 54
Frederick Brash ....20 July 55
William Dixon ....20 July 55
Ardwick Burgess ....20 July 55
Charles Aug. North ....14 Sept. 55
Henry Jobling Wallack (4), *late Capt.* 77 *F.* ....14 Sept. 55
Robert Pipon ....31 Dec. 55
Edward E. Lawrence, *late of* 7 *Dr. Gds.* ....20 Jan. 58
Daniel Williams ....25 Oct. 58
Geo. Leslie, *late of* 77 *F.* ...., 22 Jan. 59

LIEUTENANTS.
Wm. Geo. Neilson ....30 July 55
William Hyland ....18 Sept. 55
James Henry Neilson .... 1 Nov. 55
James Wood ....12 Feb. 56
Edw. Lawson Thompson .....31 Mar. 56
Arthur John Thistlewayte ... 6 May 57
Robert Kirkwood ....25 Oct. 58

ENSIGNS.
John W. M. Van Heythuysen 24 Aug. 55
Geo. Stormont Murphy........22 Dec. 55
James Taylor Hyatt ....31 Jan. 56

Adj. & Captain.—Geo. Fred.
Weller Poley,*lateCapt.* 20 *F.* 6 Apr. 54
Paymaster.—Mark O'Shaughnessy ....28 Feb. 55
Qr.Mast.—James Davern......14 Mar. 55
Surg.—Geo. Alex. Falconer...
Assist.Surg.—

Blue Facings.
Agents, Messrs. C. R. and W. M'Grigor.

1st WARWICK.
[No. 36.]
Head Quarters, Warwick.
"The Bear and Ragged Staff."

COLONEL.

LIEUT.COLONEL.
Joseph M. Boultbee, DL. JP...27 May 47

MAJORS.
Charles Wise, *Brevet Lt.Col., late Major* 65 *F.* .... 2 Apr. 53
Thos.Barnard,(1)*lateCapt.*65*F.* 8 Aug. 55

CAPTAINS.
Marmion Edward Ferrers, JP. 2 Feb. 47
Richard R. Jee, JP. .... 9 Oct. 52
Stafford Squire Baxter .... 3 June 53
Fred. Manners Estwick, *late of* 47 *F.* .... 4 May 54
Gustavus Edw. Estwick ...... 8 Aug. 55
Wm.Hull, *late Lt. Coldst.Gds.* 26 Dec. 56
Henry Charles Palmer........ 7 Dec. 57
Geo. Wm. Featherstone ......28 Aug. 58
Spencer Geo. Aug. Thursby,
late Capt. 1 *F.* .... 15 Mar. 59
Henry S. Bowes-Watson .....10 Mar. 59

LIEUTENANTS.
Fred Wm. Strickland..........28 Dec. 54
John Joseph Coppinger........11 Sept. 56
Geo. Stowell Webb Ware......12 Feb. 57
Harry Hazlett Ramsdale ......30 Dec. 57
Henry John Yeatman .... 3 Apr. 58

ENSIGNS.
James Crosswell ....21 Feb. 59

Adj. & Capt.—Robert Dymock
Vaughton(3), *late Capt.* 90*F.* 7 Nov. 56
Qr.Master.—Thos. Bannister,
late of 37 *F.* ....8 Nov. 56
Surgeon.—Thos. Tranter......19 Dec. 54
Assist.Surg.—Fred. Goodchild 14 Feb. 55

Yellow Facings.
Agent, Vesey W. Holt, Esq.

I I 2

Militia of England and Wales.

2ND WARWICK.
[No. 53.]
[Embodied.]
Head Quarters, Newport.

LIEUT.COLONEL COMMANDANT.
Frederick Granville, DL. *late Major* 23 F. ...... 16 Feb. 58

MAJORS.
Erasmus Galton, DL. JP., *late of Royal Navy* ...... 16 Feb. 58
Wm. Reader, *late Capt.* 17 F. 6 Aug. 58

CAPTAINS.
William Richard Freer ...... 3 June 53
John Stratton, *late Lieut.* 38 F. 6 Jan. 54
Garnett Warburton, *late Capt.* 3 F. ...... 22 Apr. 54
John Hallewell Carew, *late Lt.* 9 F. ...... 9 Jan. 55
John Payn ...... 10 May 56
Geo. Digby Wingfield Digby .. 30 Jan. 57
Geo. Duncombe Perkins ...... 26 Feb. 58
Walter Furness ...... 25 June 58
Henry Loftwich Freer ...... 19 July 58
Henry Howkins ...... 14 Feb. 59

LIEUTENANTS.
Bowyer W. C. Browne Cave 10 Nov. 57
Arundell de P. O'Kelley ...... do.
Erasmus Harris Vaughton ... 26 Feb. 58
Malcolm Ronalds ...... 25 June 58
Richard James ...... 19 July 58
James Taylor Hyatt ...... 13 Aug. 58
Geo. Goodwin Norris ...... 16 Aug. 58
Henry Robert Grimes ...... 22 Nov. 58
Oct. Lewis Bland Ward ...... 25 May 59
James S. Rudd ...... 1 Sept. 59

ENSIGNS.
Harvey Charles Tryon ...... 14 Jan. 59
Edward Arnold Hill ...... 27 July 59
Charles Bunbury ...... 16 Sept. 59
John Jansor Howard ...... do
John Lyttleton Freeman ...... 10 Nov. 59

Adj. & Capt.—Rice Davies Knight, *late Capt.* 98 F. ... 18 Dec. 58
Qr. Mast.—Geo. J. Booker ... 12 Apr. 59
Surg.—Edw. Jackson, M.D. ... 14 Oct. 57
Assist. Surg.—Charles Rice Williams ...... 8 Nov. 57

White Facings.
Agents, Messrs. Cox & Co.

ROYAL WESTMORLAND.
Light Infantry.) [No. 17.]
Head Quarters, Appleby.

LIEUT.COLONEL COMMANDANT.
William, *Earl of Lonsdale* ...... 9 June 18

MAJOR.
James Fairtlough, *late Lieut.* 63 F. ...... 14 Aug. 54

CAPTAINS.
Benson Harrison, *late Ens.* 39 F. ...... 7 Sept. 52
Joseph Spencer ...... June 53
Henry Shawe Jones ...... 28 May 58

LIEUTENANTS.
John Thwaytes ...... 5 Nov. 58
Gilbert P. R. Jones ...... 12 Sept. 59
John Milner ...... 21 Nov. 59

ENSIGNS.

Adj. & Capt.—Hy. Thwaytes, *late Capt.* 17 F. ...... 27 Sept. 52
Surgeon.—Fred. Maxwell Dinwoodie ...... 30 Sept. 52

Blue Facings.

ROYAL WILTSHIRE.
[No. 33.]
[Embodied.]
Head Quarters, Dover.
"*Mediterranean.*"

HONORARY COLONEL.
Lord Broughton, GCB. DL. 8 Feb. 40

LIEUT.COLONEL COMMANDANT.
Lord Methuen, DL. *late of* 71 F. ...... 6 May 46

MAJORS.
Wm. Arthur Heathcote, J.P. *late Capt.* 59 F. ...... 19 Feb. 55
John Elton Mervin Prower, J.P. *late Capt.* 67 F. ...... 25 Jan. 59

CAPTAINS.
Frederick Breton ...... 19 Feb. 53
James Harvey Bathurst, *late Capt.* 75 F. ...... 24 May 53
Cha. K. Skeete, *late Capt.* 19 F. 24 June 54
John Leigh Reed ...... 8 Sept. 54
Wm. Fred. Foxcroft Jones, *late of* 52 F. ...... 5 Dec. 54
Nathaniel Whitchurch Sloper 20 Mar. 55
William Black ...... 5 Apr. 56
David Archer ...... 14 Oct. 56
Henry Leslie Hunt, *late* 67 F. 25 Jan. 59
Bartholomew Mahon ...... 17 May 59

LIEUTENANTS.
Robert Burrows Pilsworth ... 29 May 54
Fra. Fred. Pinkett, *Instructor of Musketry* ...... 22 Jan. 57
Thomas Edw. Pinkett ...... 9 Apr. 57
Hon. Henry Nelson ...... 1 Oct. 57
Fra. Woolryche Duhayne ...... 2 Oct. 57
Fra. Charteris Wemyss ...... 6 June 58
Samuel Master Davies ...... 25 Jan. 59
Henry Edwards ...... 17 May 59
Edw. John Hayward ...... 18 May 59
Thomas Holman ...... 19 May 59

ENSIGNS.
Edward Newnham ...... 10 Nov. 57
Edward Thomas Burr ...... 13 Aug. 58
Walter Long ...... 11 Sept. 58
Alfred Herbert Brooks ...... 27 Sept. 58
Wm. S. Perry Keene ...... 9 Oct. 58
Evan Thomas Williams ...... 12 Nov. 58
Edmund George Benson ...... 7 Feb. 59
Henry Marcy Clarkson ...... 9 June 59
Henry Aug. B. Bruce ...... 10 Aug. 59
Cavendish Charles Hurrell ... 11 Aug. 59

Adj. & Capt.—Walter Blakeney Persse, *late Capt.* 22 F. 8 July 59
Paymaster & Capt.—William Elston ...... 22 Mar. 55
Qr. Mast.—Michael M'Hugh ... 12 Apr. 59
Surg.—John Fred. Nicholls ... 8 Aug. 54
Assist. Surg. — Fra. Thomas Bayntun ...... 27 May 59

Blue Facings.
Agents, Messrs. Cox & Co.

WORCESTER.
[No. 67.]
Head Quarters, Worcester.

LIEUT.COLONEL COMMANDANT.
Thomas Webb, DL. JP. *late Capt.* 90 F. ...... 3 Feb. 57

MAJORS.
Thomas C. N. Norbury, *late Capt.* 6 Dr. Gds ...... 15 July 59
Charles Sidney Hawkins, DL. JP. ...... 15 July 59

CAPTAINS.
Edw. John Beckett Marriott, DL. JP. ...... 30 Jan. 46
Henry Handley Elrington ... 12 Oct. 52

Wm. Domvile, *late Capt.* 21 F. 20 Nov. 52
Thomas Clutton-Brock ...... 4 July 54
George William Coventry ...... 2 Aug. 55
Martin Edwin Vale ...... 16 Oct. 55
Edw. Lyttleton Francis ...... 2 July 58
Richard John Griffiths ...... 10 Aug. 58
William Taylor ...... 12 Apr. 59
Ernest Peel ...... 15 July 59
Wm. Parker Howell ...... 30 Aug. 59
Roland Davies ...... 30 Aug. 59

LIEUTENANTS.
George Williams ...... 26 Dec. 54
John Peel Durdin ...... 16 Oct. 55
Edward Hoste Hickman ...... 8 Dec. 57
Henry L'Estrange Saunders 9 Mar. 58
Edward James Passmore ...... 30 Mar. 58
Thomas Lyford Champion ... do
Christopher Henry Hooke ... 2 July 58
Frank Robert Paulet ...... 4 Mar. 58
John Lechmere ...... 12 Apr. 59
Thomas Rainforth ...... 2 Aug. 59

ENSIGNS.
Henry George Statham ...... 19 Mar. 58
Charles Broderick Garde ...... 28 Mar. 59

Adj. & Capt. — Ernest Lavie, *late Capt.* 8 F. ...... 10 June 46
Paymaster.—Captain Henry Mayne, *h. p.* 49 F. ...... 1 Dec. 57
Qr. Master.—Wm. Rainforth, *late of* 35 F. ...... 26 Nov. 56
Surgeon.—Edgar Lowe ...... 1 July 56
Assist. Surg.—Thos. O'Beirne 1 Dec. 57

Buff Facings.
Agents, Messrs. Cox & Co.

EAST YORK.
"*White Rose of York.*"
[No. 12.]
Head Quarters, Beverley.

LIEUT.COLONEL COMMANDANT.
George Hamilton Thompson, DL. *late Lt.* 1 Dr. Gds. ...... 15 Nov. 33

MAJORS.
Frederick Augustus Talbot Clifford Constable, DL. JP. ... 1 Feb. 53
Fred. Sidney Hutchinson, *late Capt.* 7 F. ...... 1 Feb. 55

CAPTAINS.
Samuel Standidge Walton ... 8 June 21
Field Uppleby ...... 15 May 46
Marmaduke Gerard Grimston, DL. JP. ...... 4 Dec. 46
Robt. Wharton Wilkinson, *late Lt.* 21 F. ...... 9 Sept. 52
Henry Janson ...... 18 Jan. 55
Henry Baines ...... 14 Feb. 55
Geo. Hibbert Marshall ...... 7 Mar. 55
John Daniel Ferguson ...... 2 June 55
Allen M. Beauchant ...... 27 May 58
Francis Garden Fraser, JP. ... 13 Jan. 59

LIEUTENANTS.
Geo. Fraser Smith ...... 7 Mar. 55
Donald Robert Ferguson ...... 17 Aug. 55
Major Dawson ...... 28 Aug. 55
William Richardson ...... 12 Sept. 55
Adjt. John Nicholson, (8) *Lt. h. p.* 14 F. *Act. Qr. Mast.* ... 13 Sept. 55
Charles Joseph Lynch ...... 7 May 58
Joseph Bolland ...... 27 May 58
Wm. Henry Deane ...... 13 Jan. 59
Wm. Handcock Middleton ... 4 Nov. 59

ENSIGNS.
Theodore Francis Haskoll ... 27 Nov. 55
James M'Creery ...... 28 Nov. 55
Amherst Henry Gage Morris, *late Brevet Major, 1 West India Regt.* ...... 8 Feb. 58
Robert Lister ...... 4 Nov. 59

Adj. & Capt.—Geo. Maunsell 12 Apr. 59

Militia of England and Wales.

Paymaster.—John William F. Sandwith, *late Capt. Bombay Army* .... 15 Nov. 55
Surg.—George Earle .... 2 June 55
Assist.Surg.—George Davenport Freeman .... 21 July 55

Buff Facings.

Agents, Messrs. Cox & Co.

THE NORTH YORK.
(*Rifles.*)
[No. 22.]
Head Quarters, Richmond.

COLONEL.

LIEUT.COLONEL COMMANDANT.
Hamlet Coote Wade, *CB.Brevet Colonel on h. p. late of* 13 *F.* 4 May 55

MAJORS.
Charles Henry Dowker,*a late Capt.* 1 *F.* .... 2 Aug. 59
John Wood Coates .... 2 Aug. 59

CAPTAINS.
John Jas. Robinson, *late Gent. at Arms* .... 2 July 46
George Smith .... 2 Mar. 53
Thomas Light Elwon .... 12 Jan. 55
John Woodall Woodall .... 26 June 55
Charles Sidney Bradley .... 17 Sept. 55
John Edward Buckle .... 19 Feb. 56
George Richard Withington ...11 Apr. 56
John Sherlock .... 13 Mar. 57
Robert Geo. Hopkinson .... 2 Aug. 59

LIEUTENANTS.
John Smurthwaite .... 30 Aug. 53
Edward Kemp .... 26 June 55
William Swire .... 19 July 55
Duncan Forbes .... 28 July 56
Eyre Ledgard .... 14 Aug. 57
Samuel Christian, *late of Bombay Army* .... 14 Nov. 57
Henry Cradock .... 7 Aug. 58
Wharton Watson .... 26 Aug. 59

ENSIGNS.

Adj. & Capt.—Dugald Stewart Miller, *late Capt.* 7 *F.* ...... 30 Mar. 55
Paymaster. —
Surgeon. — Edward Tweddell Atkinson .... 5 Jan. 56
Assist.Surg.—Charles James Devonshire .... 29 May 56
Quar. Mast.—Bryan Stapleton 26 Apr. 58

Black Facings.

Agents, Messrs. Cox & Co.

1ST WEST YORK.
(*Rifles.*) [No. 5.]
[Embodied.]
Head Quarters, Edinburgh.

LIEUT.COLONEL COMMANDANT.
Hon. Edw. G. Monckton, DL. JP., *late of Rifle Brigade* .... 2 Dec. 52

MAJORS.
Henry Fitzgerald, *late of* 1 *Life Guards* .... 12 May 51
Alex. Aitken, *late Capt.* 77 *F.*14 June 55

CAPTAINS.
Francis Salvin .... 3 Feb. 53
Thomas Nelson .... 27 Aug. 53
Wm. Lawes, *late of* 41 *F.* ...12 Jan. 55
Edward Muscroft .... 5 May 55

William Walker .... 19 Aug. 57
Thomas Joseph Herey .... 15 Feb. 58
James Lees Harwar .... 12 June 58
N. Edw. B. Kindersley, *late of Madras Army* .... 3 Nov. 58
Theodosius Stuart Russell ...30 June 59
Christopher John Lloyd, *Instructor of Musketry* .... 7 Nov. 59

LIEUTENANTS.
John Lambert Reid .... 19 Aug. 57
Fitzhugh B. Henderson .... 1 Apr. 58
John Arbuthnot Goldicutt ...   do
Richard Hewley Graham ......23 July 58
Charles Fox Oxley .... 6 Dec. 58
Calcraft Neeld Wyld ....28 Apr. 59
Charles Fred. Ledger ....   do.
Thurston Arch. Whittle .... 30 June 59
James Aug. Goldicutt .... 7 Nov. 59

ENSIGNS.
Wm. Lawrence Webb ....27 Sept. 58
Henry Cox Wilkin .... do
Samuel Backhouse .... 6 Dec. 58
Peter Hughes Hewitt ....14 Dec. 58
Thomas Atchin Andrus ....17 Dec. 58
Thornton Salvin .... 7 Feb. 59
John Bell Smyth .... 28 Apr. 59
Adj. & Capt.—Philip Gro. Hewett (11), *late Capt.* 20 *F.*13 Oct. 58
Paymaster.—John Simpson ...27 Sept. 58
Qr.Master.—William Cole ...... 1 Sept. 56
Surgeon.—Henry Muscroft ... 6 Nov. 55
Assist. Surg.—Wm. Fletcher Bowman .... 1 Sept. 58

Dark Green Facings.

Agents, Messrs. Cox & Co.

2ND WEST YORK.
(*Light Infantry.*) [No. 21.]
Head Quarters, York.

COLONEL.
John G. Smyth, MP. DL. ......23 July 52

LIEUT.COLONEL.
Joshua Crompton .... 16 Apr. 56

MAJORS.
Henry Van Straubenzee, DL. JP. *late of* 14 *Light Drags.* ...11 Oct. 52
Richard S. Carroll .... 16 Apr. 56

CAPTAINS.
Fred. William Thompson ......24 Mar. 52
John Sutton .... 12 Aug. 52
Rt. Greaves Walker .... 26 Apr. 55
Wm. Hall Wilkinson .... 5 Dec. 56
Henry Newton Brown ....30 May 56
John T. T. Duesbury .... 9 Jan. 57
Lloyd S. Baxendale .... 9 Jan. 57
George Henry Lamb (J), *late Capt.* 49 *F.* .... 20 Oct. 57
Richard Sterne Carrol .... 9 Nov. 57
Aug. R. G. de Vaux .... 1 June 58

LIEUTENANTS.
Thomas Studdart .... 30 May 56
James Bell H. Tate .... 20 Oct. 57
George Wm. Manley ....29 Oct. 57
Henry Chas. Chawner .... 9 Jan. 58
Foster Gray .... do
Oct. Ridley Lawson ....22 Dec. 58
Eugene T. C. Whittell .... 4 July 59
William Whitaker .... do
Albert Darley .... do
John Townsend Daniel .... do

ENSIGNS.
William Watts .... 1 Feb. 56

Adj. & Capt.—Charles John Ewen, *late Capt.* 65 *F.* ......21 Apr. 55
Paymaster.—Hy. Hollinsworth21 Apr. 55
Qr.Master.—Geo. Linford ...... 3 July 54
Surgeon. — Richard Savile Hanbury .... 24 Nov. 57
Assist.Surg.—Thos. Bigland... 9 Jan. 58

White Facings.

Agents, Messrs. Cox and Co.

3RD WEST YORK.
(*Light Infantry.*) [No. 1.]
[Embodied.]
Head Quarters, Newcastle-on-Tyne.

COLONEL.
Ferrars Loftus, DL. *late Lt. Col. of Gren. Gds.* ....18 Sept. 52

LIEUT.COLONEL.
Edw. Prothero, DL. *late Capt.* 14 *F.* .... 20 Mar. 55

MAJOR.
Thos.John Stannard MacAdam20 Mar. 55

CAPTAINS.
John Kendall .... 12 May 53
John Boham Chantrell .... 2 June 54
Frank Henry Endon Eudon ... 2 Sept. 54
Thomas Marshall .... 1 Feb. 55
John Henry Mainwaring ......20 Mar. 55
Frederick Durham .... 24 Nov. 55
Francke Mucklestone Allen ...13 Jan. 59
Thomas William Kinder ......11 Feb. 59
Douglas Loftus, *late Lt.Gr. Gds.* 9 July 59
Ferrars Compton Charges Loftus20 Oct. 59

LIEUTENANTS.
Henry Dickinson Wilkinson ... 2 Sept. 54
Gerald Rochfort .... 12 Jan. 55
Athelstan Owen Powell ......18 Mar. 56
John Geo. Smyth Willcocks, *Instructor of Musketry* ......17 Aug. 57
John Cadman .... 18 Jan. 58
Chamberlin Wm. J. Walker ...18 Jan. 58
Joseph Henry Palmer ....17 Mar. 59
Gordon James Douglas ....26 Apr. 59
Thomas Bolger .... 20 Oct. 59
Fred. Arthur Verner ....   do

ENSIGNS.
George Campbell .... 7 Apr. 58
Edw. Henry Saunders ....18 June 58
Wm. Parkin Brown ....27 Apr. 59
Robert Henry MacLoghlin ...31 Jan. 59
Thomas Walter Lambert ......17 Mar. 59
James Redfern Bottomley ...26 Apr. 59
Fred. A. Roberts .... 8 June 59
John Robert Clarke .... 19 June 59
Wm. Lisle B. Coulson ....20 Oct. 59
Adj. & Capt.—Alexander Hamilton Robson (7), *late Capt.* 3 *Buffs* .... 14 Feb. 55
Paymaster & Capt. —Edward Nicholson .... 11 Aug. 54
Qr.Master.—John Bull .... 4 Sept. 54
Surg.—Thom Guy, M.D. ......22 Aug. 54
Assist.Surg.—Rich. H. Perry 22 Aug. 54

Green Facings.

Agents, Messrs. Cox and Co.

4TH WEST YORK.
[No. 133.]
Head Quarters, Leeds.

LIEUT.COLONEL COMMANDANT.
Hon. Nathaniel Henry Charles Massey, *late Col. unatt.* ...18 May 53

MAJORS.
George Cairnes, *late Maj.* 36 *F.* 25 Apr. 54
Edward Wand, DL. JP. .... 9 Dec. 54

CAPTAINS.
Humphrey John Hare .... 1 Mar. 54
Matthew Wharton Wilson, *late of* 11 *Hussars* .... 4 May 54
Henry Blake .... 17 May 54
Thos. Sturges Walford .... 7 July 54
Thomas Bischoff .... 23 Jan. 55
John Douglas Willan, (1) *late Capt. E.I.C.S.* .... 8 Feb. 55
Arthur Mowbray Jones, *late of* 27 *F.* .... 20 Feb. 55
Henry Wins. Pemberton ...... 9 May 58
Joseph Hartley .... 28 May 58
Edw. Wilkes Waud .... 5 Dec. 58

LIEUTENANTS.
Henry Irwin .... 15 Aug. 54
Baker Bridge .... 27 Dec. 54

Arthur Cooper..................23 Aug. 55
Henry Barrow..................16 Oct. 55
Hon. Herman Stapleton........25 Jan. 56
Bryan Eyre Coote Comber ... 6 Feb. 56
George Shirley Terry............ 6 Dec. 58
Arthur Hay Maude .... do
William Mather .... do

ENSIGNS.

Eustace W. Roxby...............25 Jan. 56
Edw. Litton Holmes............16 Feb. 56
John Henry S. Harrison ....12 Mar. 56

Adj. & Capt.—Wm. Pollard,
DL. JP., *late Lieut.* 17 *F.* 5 Apr. 53
Paymaster.—Geo. Cairnes......13 June 55
Qr.Master.—John Kendall ... 1 Sept. 56
Surg.—Joshua Ingham Ikin 1 Mar. 54
Assist.Surg.—Alfred Beckett 12 Jan. 55
White Facings.
Agents, Messrs. Hopkinson & Co.

5TH WEST YORK.
[No. 4.]
Head Quarters, Knaresboro'.
LIEUT.COLONEL COMMANDANT.
Geo. L. Lister Kaye, *late Lt.Col.
unatt.* ....21 Feb. 54

MAJORS.
Wm. Drake Hague, *late Capt.*
15 *F.* ....26 Aug. 57

CAPTAINS.
Sir Charles Henry Ibbetson, Bt.31 Aug. 54
Duncan Littlejohn .... 7 Nov. 54

George Prickett ....21 Nov. 54
Henry Robert Markham ....27 Dec. 55
Wormley Edw. Richardson ...12 Jan. 55
Charles Craven '..................26 Jan. 55
Henry Wm. Solo..................17 Sept. 57
Godfrey Edw. A. Radcliffe ... 1 Oct. 57
Henry Sanderson ....28 Sept. 58
William Lynam ....14 Dec. 58

LIEUTENANTS.

John Whitacre Allen ....24 Nov. 55
Edward Dawson................... 1 Oct. 57
Lawrence Williams ....19 Oct. 57
Wm. Edwin Cadman............16 Oct. 58
Samuel Humby ....14 Dec. 58
William Waddington .... do
Robert Morrison ....24 June 59
Henry Broomhead .... do
Horace Kaye .... do

ENSIGNS.

Wm. S. Gilbert ....16 Mar. 59
Adj. & Capt.—Hen. Balguy (3),
late Capt. 4 *F.*................15 Apr. 56
Qr.Master. — *Capt.* John
Charles Croker,[10] h. p. 6 F.11 Oct. 57
Surgeon.—Thos. Mills Beaumont..........................17 Sept. 57
Assist.Surgeon.—Wm. Bulmer 1 Sept. 55
Buff Facings.

6TH WEST YORK.
[No. 134.]
Head Quarters, Halifax.
LIEUT.COLONEL COMMANDANT.
Charles Hind, (5) *Col. unatt.*...28 Dec. 53

MAJORS.
Robert Stansfield, *late of* 19 F.25 Apr. 54
Fred. J. Bayly, *late of* 91 *F.* 27 May 54

CAPTAINS.
Hylton de Cardonell Lawson,
late Lt. 3 *Dr. Gds.* ....23 Mar. 54
Charles Horton Rhys, *late of*
26 *F.* ....16 June 54
John Rodgers, *late Capt.* 26 *F.* 24 Oct. 54
John Sowden Scott, *late of* 31 *F.* 12 Dec. 54
William Alcock ....,23 Dec. 54
Chas. Tunstall Hyde ....18 Jan. 55
Edw. Francis Boultbee......... 6 Feb. 55
Fred. Bathurst Cooper ....20 Sept. 55
John Bradley Swann............12 Apr. 58
Rob. Macfarlane Hammond (12),
late Capt. 20 *Bombay Fusiliers* 1 July 59

LIEUTENANTS.

John Henry Cole Wynne ......16 June 54
Ion Fred. Aug. Stoddart ......23 Dec. 54
Henry James Noyes, *late Lt.*
26 *F.*............................. 6 Feb. 55
George Goodwin Norris.........27 Sept. 58
Henry Fox Davis .... 2 Oct. 58

ENSIGNS.

Charles King ....14 Oct. 58

Adj. & Capt.—Godfrey Armytage, DL.(4) *late Capt.* 6th *F.* 10 Oct. 53
Qr.Master.—Wm. Contes, *late
Capt.* 98 *F.* ....29 Dec. 57
Surgeon.—Lawrence Bramley 25 Apr. 54
Assist.Surg.—Henry Julian
Hunter............................24 June 59
Sky Blue Facings.

MILITIA OF SCOTLAND.

THE ROYAL ABERDEEN-SHIRE HIGHLANDERS.
[No. 89.]
Head Quarters, Aberdeen.

COLONEL.
Lieut.Colonel Commandant.
Henry Knight Erskine, JP.
late Capt. 33 *F.* .... 2 July 55

MAJORS.
Walter Boyd, *late Capt.* 87 *F.*18 Jan. 55
John Paton, DL. JP., *late Lt.*
91 *F.* .... 2 July 55

CAPTAINS.
Wm. Leith Hay, JP. ......19 Dec. 54
Thomas Innes, JP. ....27 Feb. 55
John Ramsay, JP. ....26 Mar. 55
John Turner .... 2 July 55
John C. Hunter .... 9 Nov. 55
Alexander Furquhar (3) ......21 Nov. 57
Stephen Ryder Dampier, JP.,
Gent. at Arms .... 8 Feb. 58
Robert Macfarlane ....28 Mar. 59

LIEUTENANTS.
Wm. Marshall Priest .... 2 July 55
James Morison ....31 Mny 55
Charles Leith Hay ....20 Dec. 58
Robert H. Playfair ....24 Feb. 59
Robertson Gilchrist Marshall   do
Daniel MacLeod Fullarton ...   do
Robert Campbell ....   do
Charles Fraser ....22 June 59

ENSIGNS.
Robert Hamilton Irvine ...... 6 Jan. 58

Adj. & Capt.—Edwd. Alleyne
Dawes, (1) *late Capt.* 97 *F.* 15 Apr. 58
Paymaster.—James Bland (2),
Capt. Unatt. late of 1 *F.*..26 Feb. 55
Qr.Mr. — Alex. Hutcheon,
late of 72 *F.* ....26 Feb. 55
Surgeon.—Geo. Morison, MD. 25 Feb. 58
Assist Surg.—Alex. Irvine ...10 Mar. 58

Blue Facings.

Agents, Messrs. Cox and Co.

ARGYLL & BUTE.
(*Rifles.*) [No. 117.]
Head Quarters, Campbelltown.

COLONEL.
The *Marquis of Breadalbane, KT.,*
Lord Lieutenant................

LIEUT.COLONEL COMMANDANT.
John Campbell, *Col. Unatt.*,
late 38 *F.*..............18 Dec. 54

MAJOR.
James Alex. Duncan Ferguss-
son,(1) *Lt.Col. E. I. C. S.* 27 Mar. 55

CAPTAINS.
Smollett M. Eddington, JP.,
late Lieut. 78 *F.* .... 9 Jan. 55
William Campbell .... 7 Dec. 55
Archibald Black ....25 Jan. 58
John Hoyle ....10 Sept. 59

LIEUTENANTS.

ENSIGNS.

Adj. & Capt.—Cokayne Frith,
late Capt. 38 *F.* ....13 Jan. 55
Surgeon.— Arch. Campbell,
M.D. ....15 Mar. 56

Black Velvet Facings.
Agents.—Messrs. Cox and Co.

PRINCE REGENT'S ROYAL AYRSHIRE RIFLES.
[No. 114.]
Head Quarters, Ayr.

HONORARY COLONEL.
Hon. F. Macadam Cathcart,
DL. JP., *late Capt.* 92 *F.* and
Bt.Col. .... 6 April 52

LIEUT.COLONEL COMMANDANT.
Sir James Fergusson (1), *Bt.*
late Captain Gr. Gds.........14 Sept. 58

MAJORS.
C. Somerville M'Alester, JP.12 April 50
Walter Ferrier Hamilton, JP.,
late Lieut. 83 *F.* ....

CAPTAINS.
Thomas Davidson, JP....... 8 April 46
Hugh Hamilton, *late Capt.*
1 *Dr. Gds.* ....14 Oct. 54
John Crichton ....21 Dec. 54
Fred. L. Fitzgerald, *late Lt.*
63 *F.* ....15 Sept. 55
William Arch. Hamilton.... 20 Mar. 57
William Wallace ....16 Oct. 58
William Cooper............12 Nov. 58
Alexander M'Lachlan .... 6 Aug. 59

LIEUTENANTS.
Blair Fullerton .... 7 Mar. 56
Robert Orr Crichton .... 6 Oct. 58
Thomas Alex. Riddell ......16 Dec. 58
Charles Dalrymple.............17 Feb. 59
Robert Meiklam................   do
Robert Sheddon Patrick .....20 Apr. 59
Robert Pattison..............30 June 59

ENSIGNS.
Fred. Campbell...............15 Sept. 55
Charles Birdwood.............. 2 Feb. 56
Arthur Prinsep................ 7 Mar. 56

Adj. & Capt.—James Miller,
late of S. F. Gds............ 3 Feb. 46
Paymaster.— Charles Henry
James ....12 Jan. 56
Qr.Master.—Wm. Weir, *late of R. Art.* ....
Surgeon, — James Montgo-
meric ....25 Mar. 59
Assist.Surg.—David Wield...24 Jan. 59

Scarlet Facings.

Agents, Messrs. Cox and Co.

BERWICK, HADDINGTON, LINLITHGOW, AND PEEBLES ARTILLERY.
[No. 3.]
Head Quarters, Dunse.

COLONEL.
William Hay, DL., *Capt. h.p.*
15 *F. Convener of the County of Berwick* .... 9 Feb. 42

MAJOR.
Geo. Home Logan-Home, *Capt.*
h.p. R. Marines ....21 May 55

CAPTAINS.
Joseph Hume ....30 April 46
Thomas Shairp ....25 Feb. 48
James Grant Suttie ....14 April 55
Thomas Alexander Hog ......29 Aug. 55

LIEUTENANTS.
Samuel Home Stirling...... 3 Mar. 55
John Dawson................22 Sept. 55
Richard C. A. Hamilton ......29 Dec. 55
Robert Haynes Lovell ....29 Dec. 56

SECOND LIEUTENANTS.
David Rutherford Greig .....30 Oct. 55
Alfred John Buckle ....10 Nov. 55
George Gordon Blair ....12 Feb. 56
Archibald Dickson ....13 Feb. 57

Adj. Capt. and Paymaster.—
James Cox, *late Capt.* 92 *F.*16 Feb. 46
Qr.Master, John Stewart,
late of 92 *F.* .... 3 Oct. 56
Surg.—Matthew Turnbull ...25 Nov. 21

Scarlet Facings.

Agent, Sir John Kirkland.

DUMFRIES, ROXBURGH, AND SELKIRK.
[No. 81.]
Head Quarters, Dumfries.

LIEUT.COLONEL COMMANDANT.
John James McMurdo, JP.
Bt.Lt.Col. Indian Army ... 1 Sept. 54

MAJORS.
The *Hon.* Henry Butler John-
stone, DL. ....30 Mar. 46
George Gustavus Walker .. 1 June 59

CAPTAINS.
William Alexander Oliver Ru-
therford, JP.............11 Feb. 46
Walter G. Farquhar John-
ston ....16 Jan. 55
George James Lennock, *late*
Ens. 33 *Regt.*............22 Jan. 55
Campbell Riland Bedford ...24 Sept. 55
James Connell ....21 July 59

LIEUTENANTS.
Gideon Curll .... 4 Mar. 46
David Cross Mitchell ...... 9 Sept. 57
William Mitchell ....13 July 59
Wm. Robert Thornhill.........19 Aug. 59

Militia of Scotland.

ENSIGNS.
Stuart Mitchell .... 5 Oct. 57
Lynch Bolingbroke .... do
Charles Fermoy Roche........30 Oct. 57
David Turnbull .... 1 Jan. 58
Robert Leacock Gledstanes...13 July 59
Adj., Capt. and Act. Paymast.
Robert Compton Noake,*late Lt. and Adj. R. Drs., and Lt. and Adj. 44 Foot* .... 5 Nov. 46
Qr.Mast.—Michael Moriarty 23 July 58
Surg.—Wm. Hastings Garner 28 June 59
Assist.Surg.— Charles Rattray, M.D. ....16 Nov. 57
• Yellow Facings.
Agents, Messrs. Cox and Co.

THE EDINBURGH, OR QUEEN'S REGIMENT OF LIGHT INFANTRY.
[No. 126.]
Head Quarters, Dalkeith.
COLONEL.
The *Duke* of Buccleuch, KG., *Aide de camp to the Queen* 6 Jan. 42
LIEUT.COLONEL.
Sir Archibald Hope, *Bart.* JP.28 Feb. 56
MAJOR.
John Fletcher, JP. ....28 Feb. 56
CAPTAINS.
John Alexander Mackay, JP. 25 June 31
Hector Archibald Macneil .. 6 Mar. 46
George Thomson, JP. ......25 April 46
John David Buchanan Hay...12 April 52
W. S. R. *Marquis of* Lothian,21 June 53
Archibald Scott..................23 June 59
LIEUTENANTS.
Charles William Cowan ...... 5 Jan. 55
John Fowler Kemp .... 9 Feb. 55
William Currie ....23 June 59
ENSIGNS.
Richard Cannon ....25 June 31
Edwin Aug. Windsor ....20 Dec. 55
John Dunbar................... 8 June 58
Adj. & Capt. & Paym.—Henry Samuel Bowman, *Captain Unatt. late Capt.* 35 F. ...30 July 55
Qr.Master. — Charles Mc Donald, *late of* 92 F. ......23 Jan. 55
Surg.—Wm. Bryce, M.D...... 1 May 55
Assist Surg.—Charles Dycer, M.D.........................23 June 59
Blue Facings.
Messrs. Cox and Co.

CITY OF EDINBURGH ARTILLERY.
[No. 11.]
[Embodied.]
Head Quarters, Dunbar.

LIEUT.COLONEL COMMANDANT.
Wm. Geddes,[1] CB., *late Lieut. Col. Indian Army* .... 6 Nov. 54
CAPTAINS.
Robert John Hughes .... 1 Mar. 59
Thomas Alexander Hill ...... 3 May 59
George Charles Finlay ...... 8 Sept. 59
FIRST LIEUTENANTS.
John Jekin Cockburn ....12 May 59
Geo. Charles Bowman......30 May 59
John Gordon Davidson ..... 8 Sept. 59

SECOND LIEUTENANTS.
Geo. Wm. Henry Knight ... 3 May 59
Ebenezer F. Macgeorge ... 9 June 59
William Pounsett .... 4 Nov. 59

Adj., Capt. & Paym.—John Boulton,[2] *late Capt.R. Art.* 6 Sept. 59

Qr.Master.—Fra. Murdoch ...28 July 59
Surg.—Tho. Smith Maccall, M.D. ....11 Nov. 57
Scarlet Facings.
Agents, Messrs. Cox and Co.

FIFE ARTILLERY.
[No. 12.]
[Embodied.]
Head Quarters, Pendennis.
COLONEL.
John Balfour, *Vice Lieut.* JP. *late of Gr. Gds.* ....23 Feb. 55
LIEUT.COLONEL COMMANDANT.
Chas. R.Wynne, *Brevet Major ret. f. p. R. Art.*...........23 Feb. 55
MAJORS.
James Wemyss, DL. JP. *Capt. Unatt.* .... 6 Oct. 45
F. J. T. Hutchinson, *Capt. Unatt.* ....23 Feb. 55
CAPTAINS.
William Forrest, *late of* 79 F.23 Feb. 55
Maconochie-Welwood(1), *Capt.* 2 *Bengal Lt.Cavalry* ......19 Mar. 55
George Hannay..............25 July 55
Richard Rennie..............10 Nov. 55
Henry J. G. Cowan .... 7 May 59
John Stewart Tulloch........10 June 59
1ST LIEUTENANTS.
John Redmond Nelligan......10 Nov. 55
Geo. James Williams .... 4 April 57
Thomas Jarvis .... 4 April 57
Henry Moore Johnstone ...... 7 May 59
Thomas Wm. Webb ....27 June 59
Stamford Robert Lumsdaine 2 Aug. 59

2ND LIEUTENANTS.
William Inglis .... 8 Apr. 59
Frederick Tweed .... 7 May 59
John Spenloe Waite ...... do
Albert K. Beveridge .... 9 June 59
Cecil Lyon ....27 June 59

Adj. & Capt.—Wm. Maxwell, *late of R. Art.* ....27 Feb. 55
Paymaster.—William Haig ..12 May 59
Qr.Master. — James Fenton, *late of R. Art.* .... 1 Mar. 55
Surgeon.—Wm. Bonthrone, MD. JP. ....18 Nov. 54
Assist.Surg.—Wm. H. Dewar27 Apr. 59
Scarlet Facings.
Agents, Messrs. Cox and Co.

FORFAR AND KINCARDINE ARTILLERY.
[No. 13.]
[Embodied.]
Head Quarters, Sheerness.
HONORARY COLONEL.

LIEUT.COLONEL COMMANDANT.
David Laird, *late Lieut.* 79 F. DL. JP. 16 Sept.57

MAJORS.
Robert Tod Boothby, *late of* 79 F. ....16 Sept. 57
Colin Campbell, *late of* 92 F. JP. ....25 Jan. 59
CAPTAINS.
James Fitzmaurice Scott, *late of* 5 *Dr. Gds.* DL. JP....17 Mar. 55
Hon. Wm. Arbuthnott, *late of E. I. C. S.* .... 8 May 55
Wm. T. Blair-Imrie, JP ...15 April 57
Alex. Moncrieff, JP........16 Sept. 57
Neil Wm. S. Kennedy .... 8 Jan. 58
Alan John Colquhoun ....11 Nov. 58
John Clervaux Chaytor ......25 Dec. 58
John Allen Allen, JP. ....18 Mar. 59
LIEUTENANTS.
Louis Tarlinski..................16 April 55
Wm. Wilson, *late of R. Art.* 8 Dec. 57
Edward Alfred Webster ......16 Jan. 58
James Whitton ....11 Nov. 58
Thomas M'Whannel............ do
Aug. Walter Cruikshanks ...25 Dec. 58
John Hay ....18 Mar. 59
Charles Basil Fisher ....12 May 59
2ND LIEUTENANTS.
Fra. Barclay Grahame.......30 Nov. 58
Geo. Duke Ormsby ....17 Mar. 59
Wm. C. B. Constable ...... do
John Allan Johnson............ do
Warham St. Leger Durdin... 4 May 59
Charles Edw. Ilderton.......20 June 59

Adj.andCapt.—Hon. Mackay, *Brev.Maj. ret.f.p.* 79 F. ..24 Jan. 55
Paymaster.—John Barclay ..21 Dec. 58
Qr.Mast. — James Graham, *late R. Art.* .... 3 Oct. 57
Surg.—Alex. Dickson, MD.,10 July 55
Assist.Surg.— Alex. Murray Officer, M.D.................10 July 55
Scarlet Facings.
Agent, Andrew Laurie, Esq.
Irish Agents, Sir E. R. Borough, *Bt.*, Armit & Co.

GALLOWAY.
(Rifles.) [No. 72.]
Head Quarters, Newtown Stewart.

HONORARY COLONEL.
Sir David Maxwell, *Bart., late Capt. Gren. Gds.* ....24 April 20
LIEUTENANT COLONEL.
Sir William Maxwell, *Bart., late Capt. Unatt* .... 1 Feb. 41
MAJOR.
Robert Duncan Fergusson, *late of Rifle Br.* ....20 Mar. 55
CAPTAINS.
Colvin Stewart ....25 June 55
W. C. Stewart Hamilton, *late of E. I. C. S.*...........11 July 55
W. F. B. G. Fergusson ......22 Aug. 55
*Hon.*Chas.MurrayHayForbes,[1] *late Lt.* 95 F................18 Sept. 57
LIEUTENANTS.
Arthur Graham Hay ....12 May 57
Wm. Robinson Lodge ....19 Dec. 57
Thos. H. P. Kennan..........17 Apr. 58
James Wm. Stuart ....18 Apr. 59
ENSIGNS.
Arthur James M'Queen ......21 Feb. 56
John White Heuston ....23 Dec. 58

Adj. & Capt.—Wm. Monro, *late Capt.* 79 F. .... 7 July 54
Qr.Master.—John Underwood16 Jan. 67
Surg.—Tho. Palothorpe, MD. 5 Nov. 57
Clothing, Grey; Facings, Dark Green.
Agents, Messrs. Charles R. and Walter M'Grigor.

Militia of Scotland. 636

INVERNESS, BANFF, ELGIN, AND NAIRN.
(*Highland Light Infantry.*) [No. 76.]

Head Quarters, Inverness.

LIEUT.COLONEL COMMANDANT.
Hon. Simon Fraser .... Dec. 55

MAJORS.
James Duff, *late Capt.* 74 F. 2 Jan. 55
Hon. James Grant, *late Lt.*
42 F. .... 3 Dec. 57

CAPTAINS.
Arthur J. Robertson .... 28 Apr. 25
Evan D. MacPherson, *late Capt.* 93 F. .... 17 July 55
Norman Alex. M'Leod .... 12 Jan. 56
Thomas Brown .... 16 Nov. 57
James Andrew Macra .... 24 Mar. 58
Wm. Fraser Tytler, *late Capt. Indian Army* .... 1 May 58
Walter G. J. McGrigor .... 8 Jan. 59
Donald Colin Cameron .... 13 Aug. 59

LIEUTENANTS.
Geo. Graham Ramsay .... 12 Jan. 56
John Saunders .... 9 Feb. 56
John Rose .... 23 Apr. 56
Arch. Hearne Mac Nab ...... 27 Aug. 59
John Grant .... 7 Sept. 59

ENSIGNS.
Duncan Dougal MacLeod......30 Nov. 58
Thomas Scott .... 7 Sept. 59

Capt. & Adj.—Wm. Donaldson, *late Scots Fus. Gds.* .... 24 Mar. 57
Paymaster.—Geo. Ferguson Maitland .... 11 Apr. 55
Qr.Master.—John Sharp, *late 96 F.* .... 23 Aug. 56
Surg.—Archibald M'Rae ...... 27 Jan. 55

Green Facings.

Agents, Messrs. C. R. and W. M'Grigor.

1ST ROYAL LANARK.
[No. 74.]
Head Quarters, Hamilton.

COLONEL.
The *Duke of* Hamilton ...... 23 Jan. 34

LIEUT.COLONEL.
Rt. Hon. *Lord* Belhaven, *late Capt. 2nd Life Gds.* .... 21 Nov. 33

MAJORS.
Sir Wyndham Carmichael Anstruther, *Bart. late of Coldst. Gds.* .... 23 Mar. 46
James Davidson, *late Capt.* 6 Drs. .... 9 Dec. 54

CAPTAINS.
Charles Horrocks, *late Capt.* 16 F. .... 21 Mar. 46
William Marshall Cochrane .24 Nov. 46
William Ramsay .... 9 Dec. 54
James Hunter, *late Brev. Maj. 53 Bengal N.I.* .... 8 Mar. 55
William Jolly .... 26 Mar. 55
James Coutts Crawford, *late Lieut. R.N.* .... 27 July 55
Sir Henry O. R. Chamberlain, *Bart. late Lt. 23 F.* .... 25 Feb. 56
Robert Hall McCasland .... 7 June 56
David Blair Lockhart .... 2 July 58

LIEUTENANTS.
John William Henderson ..... 9 Dec. 54
William Guntom .... 26 Mar. 55
David Wm. Mathie .... 2 May 55
Thomas Glennie .... 30 June 55
Edgeworth Horrocks .... 23 Aug. 55
James Hamilton Henderson 7 June 56
Geo. Johnson Gossling .... 1 Feb. 59

ENSIGNS.
Henry Dalglish .... 22 Aug. 55
James M'Gregor .... 26 Feb. 56
John Cameron Pender .... 27 Feb. 56
Alex. Martin Edmiston .... 28 Feb. 56
Arch. Wm. Ramsay Davidson 21 Sept. 57
Fred. Eccles Kinnier .... 26 Nov. 57
Geo. Paterson Lyon .... 30 Nov. 57

Adj. and Capt.—Arthur Aug. Longmore, *late Capt.* 26 F. 9 Aug. 55
Surg.—Walter Walker Lennox 25 Jan. 55
Assist.Surg.—John Holt ..... 1 Mar. 55
Paymaster.—William Ross ...27 Jan. 55
Qr.Mast.—Thos. Williamson, *late Qr.M.* 34 F. .... 15 Sept. 56

Blue Facings.

Agents, Messrs. Cox and Co.

2ND ROYAL LANARK.
[No. 78.]
[Embodied.]
Head Quarters, Aldershot.

LIEUT.COLONEL COMMANDANT.
David C. R. Carrick Buchanan, *late Cor. 2 Drs.* ...29 Nov. 54

MAJORS.
Arch. Hamilton Tattnall, *late Capt.* 92 F. .... 6 Dec. 54
Robert Harington, *late Capt.* 12 Lancers .... 12 Apr. 55

CAPTAINS.
Andrew Frazer, *Lt.Col. late H.E.I.C.S.* .... 5 Dec. 54
John Dickson .... 7 Dec. 54
John George Brown .... 8 Dec. 54
Walter Scott,[3] *late Capt. 43 Madras N.I.* .... 9 Dec. 54
Walter Brisbane Park,[2] *late Capt. 26 F.* .... 15 Feb. 55
George Aug. Alston .... 12 Mar. 55
Thomas Donald .... 14 Mar. 55
Walter Henry Gill,[1] *late Lt. Cape M. R.* .... 7 Nov. 55
William Wilson .... 30 Dec. 56
John Floyd .... 26 Aug. 58

LIEUTENANTS.
J. Carmichael Robertson ..... 6 Dec. 54
Geo. Binnie Wilkie .... 12 May 55
Andrew Smith .... 21 Aug. 55
Robert Pollock, *Instructor of Musketry* .... 25 Feb. 56
James Begg .... 26 Feb. 56
John David Campbell .... 5 April 58
Hector S. M'Neill .... 7 April 58
Wm. Benjamin Wilkin .... 21 May 58
Edward John Clifford .... 18 June 59
Wm. Henry Bower .... 20 June 59

ENSIGNS.
Albert Owen M'Dermotte ...15 Dec. 54
John Edw. Thompson .... 18 Sept. 58
Oliver Wm. S. Horner .... 21 May 58
Augustine Hugh H. Lefroy...15 Dec. 58
Douglas Standen Mason ...... 17 Dec. 58
Bernard Byrne .... 3 June 59
William Lefroy .... 18 June 59
Archibald Roger .... 26 Aug. 59
Thomas Acres Ogle .... 27 Aug. 59
William Porter .... 20 Sept. 59

Adj. & Capt.—Francis W. Johnstone, *late Capt.* 27 F. 12 Jan. 55
Paymaster.—James M'Gregor Hamilton .... 1 Apr. 55
Qr.Master.—Robt. Brown....10 Sept. 56
Surg.—Fred. Gourlay, M.D...28 Apr. 59
Assist.Surg.—John Gibson Smith .... 27 Nov. 57

Blue Facings.

Agents, Messrs. Cox and Co.

ROYAL PERTH.
(*Rifles.*)
[No. 86.]
Head Quarters, Perth.

HONORARY COLONEL.
Sir Thos. Moncrieffe, *Bart., late Lieut. Sco. Fus. Gds.*...30 Oct. 55

LIEUT.COLONEL COMMANDANT.
Henry M. Drummond, *late Capt.* 42 F. .... 5 Nov. 55

MAJOR.
John Walter Wedderburn, *late Capt.* 42 F. .... 5 Nov. 55

CAPTAINS.
Samuel Barrett .... 15 Feb. 34
Thomas Milles Riddell,[1] *late Lieut.* 7 *Dr. Gds.* .... 13 Dec. 54
Benj. H. B. Alston Stewart ... 2 Nov. 57
George Duncan Mercer .... 4 Dec. 58
Fra. MacNaghten Leslie ...... 28 June 5

LIEUTENANTS.
Oliver H. Minchin .... 20 May 57
Robert Henry Wilton .... 13 June 59

ENSIGNS.

Adj.—Lord Charles L. Kerr, *late Capt.* 43 F. .... 24 July 54
Paym.—
Qr.Master.—Alex. Geddes ...20 Dec. 56
Surg.—George Webster Absolon, M.D. .... 2 Nov. 54
Assist.Surg.

Scarlet Facings.

Agents, Messrs. Cox and Co.

RENFREW.
(*The Prince of Wales' Royal Regt.*)
[No. 129.]
Head Quarters, Paisley.

HONORARY COLONEL.
William Mure, DL. JP. .... 3 Feb. 31

LIEUT.COLONEL COMMANDANT.
Sir Robert J. Millicken Napier, *Bart.* DL. JP. *late Capt.* 79 F. .... 31 Mar. 54

MAJORS.
William Cunningham Bontine, *late Lieut.* 2 Drs .... 6 Jan. 55
Wm. Finlay Hamilton, *late Lieut.* 79 F. .... 27 June 55

CAPTAINS.
Alex. Sidney G. Jauncey, *late Lieut.* 11 F. .... 5 Jan. 55
James Lowndes, JP. *Gent. at Arms* .... 6 Jan. 55
John Simons .... 1 Apr. 56
James Anderson .... 2 Apr. 56
Rob. Walkinshaw Young ..... 31 Jan. 57
Chas. Bissett Thomson .....22 Sept. 59

LIEUTENANTS.
Frederick Debenham .... 1 Apr. 56
Abraham Thompson .... 3 Apr. 56
Henry Dunlop .... 31 Jan. 57
Alex. Boyd .... 18 June 59
Arthur Woolfrey Bridge ... 22 Sept. 59
Henry Barclay Dunlop........22 Sept. 59

Militia of Scotland.

ENSIGNS.
John May Somerville ....31 Jan. 57
George James Wilson ....28 Sept. 57

Adj. Capt. and Acting Paymaster.—Fred. Wm. Adam Parsons, *late Lt. 24 F.*... 24 Apr. 59
Qr.Master.—Littellus Birrell Barr .... 2 Oct. 56
Surg.—W. F. L. Gompertz ...11 July 57
Assist.Surg.—

Blue Facings.
Agent, V. W. Holt, *Esq.*

ROSS, CAITHNESS, SUTHERLAND, AND CROMARTY.
(*Rifles.*) [No. 96.]
Head Quarters, Dingwell.

HONORARY COLONEL.
Charles M'Kenzie Fraser (1), DL. JP. *late Capt. Cold. Gds.*..17 May 15

LIEUT.COLONEL COMMANDANT.
George Wm. Holmes Ross, DL. JP. *late Lieut. 92 F.* ....11 Feb. 56

MAJORS.
Fred. Fraser, JP. *late Ens.* 85 F. ....17 Mar. 56
Kenneth Macleay, DL. JP... 6 Oct. 57

CAPTAINS.
John Jos. Grove, JP. *late Capt. 25 F.* ....14 Sept. 53
Charles Munro, DL. JP. ..13 Aug. 55
Patrick M'Lean, JP..........26 Dec. 55
Duncan H. C. R. Davidson, JP. ....18 Feb. 56
Godfrey W. Davidson ......15 Apr. 56
Adrian Wm. Keith Falconer 7 Oct. 58

LIEUTENANTS.
George Sinclair Smith......13 Aug. 55
Hugh Lindsay M'Lennan ..29 Oct. 55
William Houstoun .... 8 Nov. 58
Robert Douglas ....17 Nov. 58
Geo. Sutherland Dunbar....17 Jan. 59

ENSIGNS.
Wm. D. B. Ketchen..........20 June 59
James Court Robertson ......29 July 59

Adj. & Capt.—JamesStewart, *late of 92 F.* ....28 July 56
Paymaster.—Alex. Mackenzie, JP., *late Capt. 25 F.* ..11 April 55
Qr.Master.—James Ewing, *late of 74 F.* ....27 July 57
Surg.—Alex. Thom .... 4 Dec. 55
Assist.Surg.—

Black Facings.
Agents, Messrs. C. R. and W. M'Grigor.

STIRLING, DUMBARTON, CLACKMANNAN, AND KINROSS.
(*The Highland Borderers Light Infantry.*)
[No. 90.]
[Embodied.]
Head Quarters, Shorncliffe.

HONORARY COLONEL.
James, *Duke of* Montrose, KT. 12 Oct. 27

LIEUT.COLONEL COMMANDANT.
Sir Alex. Cha. Gibson Maitland, *Bart. late of 79 F.* DL. JP. ....12 Mar. 55

MAJORS.
John Findlay, JP...........30 July 55
Joseph Dundas, JP........22 Jan. 58

CAPTAINS.
Thomas Graham ....22 Sept. 55
John C. Craigie Halkett, *late Lt. 45 F.*.................18 Oct. 55
James Colquhoun, *late of R. Art.*............................. 9 Feb. 58
John Crawford Tait........26 Feb. 58
James Frederic Bennett.... 9 Mar. 59
John Henderson .... June 59

LIEUTENANTS.
William McAlister Douglas ..29 Mar. 55
Matt. Chas. B. Macallister..27 Mar. 56
Edwin Grogan, *late Lt.* 6 F. 6 Nov. 56
David Murray Anderson, *late of Royal Navy* ....23 Mar. 58
Francis Pringle............18 June 59
Alex. Thomas Ewens .... 7 Nov. 59

ENSIGNS.
George Scott .... 1 Dec. 57
Arthur Fawkes................
Edgeworth Horrocks ....
John Dunbar ....17 Apr. 59
Waldron Edw. R. Kelly ......15 Nov. 59

Adj. and Capt.—Stephen Kenny (1), *late Capt.* 60 *Rifles*.19 Dec. 54
Paymaster. — Captain James Hollis, *Qr.Mast.* h. p.69 F. 8 April 57
Qr.Master.—David Hunter, *late of 35 F.* ....
Surg.—John Thomson.........27 Nov. 57
Assist.Surg.—John Mackenzie Pagan, M.D. ....17 Nov. 57

Yellow Facings.
Agents, C. R. and W. M'Grigor.

MILITIA OF IRELAND.

Inspector General of Militia in Ireland.—Colonel Charles Hastings Doyle, Unatt.

ANTRIM.
(*The Queen's Royal Rifles.*) [No. 79.]
[Embodied.]
Head Quarters, Bristol.

COLONEL.
The *Marq. of* Donegall, *G.C.H.,*
Aide-de-camp to the Queen,
late of 7 Hussars .... 3 Apr. 41

LIEUT.COLONEL.
George Ferguson ....22 Aug. 53

MAJOR.
W. J. Verner, *late Capt.* 21 *Fus.* 6 Mar. 54

CAPTAINS.
Jackson Wray, *late Capt.* 96 *F.* 28 June 46
Henry Stewart Beresford
Bruce, *late Lt. Rifle Brigade* 8 Nov. 54
Edmund Douglas Leslie ...... 8 Dec. 54
Richard Maunsell, *late Lieut.*
7 *Fus.* ....16 Dec. 54
Charles B. Hartwell............26 May 55
Alex. Whitla .... 9 July 56
Wm. Jackson Clarke............22 Dec. 56
John Ferguson Montgomery 12 Jan. 58
William J. Butson...............18 Mar. 58
Humphrey May ....21 Oct. 59
Alexander Murray .... do

LIEUTENANTS.
Fred. Gordon Thompson ......15 May 56
Lewis O'Berne Williams ......22 Dec. 56
Anthony, *Lord Ashley, late of*
Royal Navy .... 7 June 58
Hugh FitzGerald Mahony,
late Lt. 75 *F.* ....15 July 58
Charles Hill ....18 May 59
George G. Cuppage .... 2 Aug. 59
John Moutray Read 20 Sept.59
David Lewellyn .... do
Wm. Hoare Hume................21 Oct. 59

ENSIGNS.
Charles Marcus Lett ....21 June 58
George Gresham .... 9 Aug. 58
Thomas Lamont Hobbs ......11 Jan. 59
Malby Crofton .... 26 Feb. 59
Stewart Searles Mitchell..... 2 Mar. 59
John Wood ....18 May 59
Wm. Wallace Legge .... 2 Aug. 59
Cecil Robert Shepherd 20 Sept.59
William Mitchell ....25 Oct. 59

Adj. & Capt.—John Kenneth
Mackenzie(1), *late Brev.Maj.*
60 *Rifles, h. p.* ....12 Jan. 55

Paymaster.—*Captain* Donald
Sinclair, h. p. 93 *F.* 21 Sept.57

Qr.Master.—Alex. Markham 28 Jun. 46

Surg.—John L. Gaussen .... 5 Dec. 54

Assist.Surg.—Nathl. Hunter 7 Dec. 54
Red Facings.

Agents, Sir E. R. Borough, *Bt.* Armit & Co.

ROYAL ANTRIM ARTILLERY.
[No. 1.]
[Embodied.]
Head Quarters, Shorncliffe.

LIEUT.COLONEL COMMANDANT.
Viscount Massereene and Ferrard, *KP. DL*..................15 Nov. 54

MAJOR.
William Verner, JP. .... 9 July 59

CAPTAINS.
Stephen Richard Rice ....16 Dec. 54
George Gray, JP. ....23 Dec. 54
Edmond Alexander Hannay 4 Jan. 55
Benj. Clements Adair ....29 Mar. 55
Henry Alsager Pollock ....28 Mar. 59
Skiffington Thompson .... 1 Aug. 59

FIRST LIEUTENANTS.
Rich. Thomas Benson Russell 2 Jan. 56
Joseph William O'Donnell ... 2 Jan. 56
Horatio Sloane ....22 Dec. 56
Andrew O'Ryan .... 8 July 57
Henry Langtry ....28 Mar. 59
Alex. M'C. Markham..........20 Oct. 59

SECOND LIEUTENANTS.
Lambert M'Killop..............19 Mar. 59
James Craig .... do
Henry S. O'Brien Blake ......16 Apr. 59
Robert W. Goddard........... 14 May 59
Francis Green 7 Sept.59
F. C. Hamilton Parks ....11 Nov. 59

Adjutant.—Andrew Munro,
late of R. Art. .... 1 Dec. 54

Surgeon.—George Nixon, M.D. 9 Jan. 55

Assist.Surg.—Alex. Haldane
Cooke .... 8 Mar. 59

Paymaster.—William Houghton, *Paymaster h.p.* 11 *Huss.* 5 Jan. 55
Red Facings.
Irish Agents, Sir E. R. Borough, *Bt.,*
Armit & Co.

ARMAGH.
(*Light Infantry.*)   [No. 75.]
Head Quarters, Armagh.

COLONEL.
The Earl of Gosford, *KP.* ......19 Nov. 34

LIEUT.COLONEL.
William Cross, *late Capt.* 68 *F.* 25 July 59

MAJOR.
Henry William Caulfield ......25 July 59

CAPTAINS.
Edw. Stanley, *late Capt.* 62 *F.* 25 Nov. 54
Andrew Craig ....28 Nov. 54
Edward Wingfield Verner ...18 Jan. 55
Wm. Arbuthnot Hutchinson 18 Dec. 56
William Forbes Synnot ......12 July 59
John Smyth ....13 July 59
Wm. Paton, *late Lt. Indian*
Army ....14 July 59

LIEUTENANTS.
Wm. Walter Scott, *late Ens.* 17 *F.* 10 Apr. 55
Wm. Cross O'Brien Tenison,. 6 Aug. 55
Edw. Villiers Ryan............22 Sept.57
William Atkinson 22 Sept.57
John James La Touche........ 1 July 59
Thos. W. Stanley ....14 July 59

ENSIGNS.
Thomas Young ....23 Aug. 55
Alexander Cuppage.............. do.
William Brown .... do.
Geo. Grindall Atkinson........26 Jan. 58

Adjutant & Capt.—Wadham
Wyndham Bond, *Capt. Unattached, and late of* 4 *F.* ..24 Nov. 54

Paymaster.— James Atkinson
Vint .... 6 Mar. 55
Surg.—Joseph Marshall Lynn 8 Dec. 54
Assist.Surg.—Robt. Gillespie 24 Jan. 55
Qr.Master.—Wm. H. Barker 13 Jan. 55

Facings Grey.

Agents, Messrs. Cane & Sons.

ARMAGH ARTILLERY.
[No. 2.]
Head Quarters, Armagh.

CAPTAIN.
Richard Francis Kidd .... 7 Apr. 55

LIEUTENANT.
Thomas Leaver.................17 Apr. 55

SECOND LIEUTENANT.
Robert Tyndall Pope ....24 Jan. 56

Surgeon.—James King.........25 April 55

CARLOW.
(*Rifles.*)   [No. 70.]
Head Quarters, Carlow.

COLONEL.
Sir Thomas Butler, *Bt.* ..... 5 May 53

LIEUT.COLONEL.
John H. Keogh, *late Capt.* 30 *F.* 10 May 53

MAJOR.
D'Oyley, Wm. Battley, *late*
Brev. Maj. 77 *F.* .... 6 Mar. 55

CAPTAINS.
William Paul Butler.......... 41
John Cliffe Vigors............ 6 Mar. 55
Philip C. Newton ....25 Feb. 56
James Blackney ....21 Sept. 58

LIEUTENANTS.
Daniel Carey ....27 Mar. 55
Thomas Adam Browne......16 Oct. 55
Arthur FitzMaurice ....25 Feb. 56
Edward Butler ....21 Sept. 58

ENSIGNS.
John Fra. Humfrey ....22 Oct. 55
Richard Wilson Clarke ......12 Dec. 55
James Eustace ....28 Sept. 58

Militia of Ireland.

Adj. and Capt.—G. M. Knipe, *Capt. h. p. late of* 89 F. ..23 Dec. 54
Qr. Mr. & Act. Paym.—Wm. Beatty ....20 Jan. 55
Surgeon.—Thomas Bolton ... 5 Sept. 55

Yellow Facings.

Agents, Messrs. Cane and Sons.

CAVAN.
[No. 101.]
Head Quarters, Cavan.
COLONEL.

LIEUT.COL. COMMANDANT.
Thomas Taylor, *Earl of* Bective, JP. .... 5 Dec. 54

MAJORS.
Hardress L. Saunderson, *late Capt.* 66 F. ....29 Dec. 54
Samuel Moore ....6 Apr. 57

CAPTAINS.
Michael Phillips, JP. ......18 Feb. 48
Henry Dean Edwards ......16 Mar. 49
G. De Lapoer Beresford ...30 Dec. 54
Gerald Richard Dease ...... 1 Jan. 55
Charles P. Roche ....28 Dec. 55
John L. Nugent ....29 Jan. 56
Thomas Leslie ....24 Apr. 56
John Robert Gunning......15 Mar. 58

LIEUTENANTS.
James Berry .... 2 Jan. 55
Henry Michael Hearne ...... 2 Feb. 57
Thomas Henry Wilton......28 May 57
Henry Saunt Clemenger...... 5 Oct. 57
James Kerr ....12 July 58
John Bernard Laffere ...... 2 Aug. 58
Joseph Twigg .... 6 May 59
Fred. Betty ....15 Aug. 59

ENSIGNS.
William Frocke............10 Dec. 57

Adj. & Capt.—Nicholas Gosselin, *late Capt.* 46 F. .....21 Mar. 46
Paymast.—James Robinson, *late of* 32 F............. 6 Mar. 55
Surg.—W. Malcomson ......20 Jan. 56
Assist.Surg.—R. P. White ...17 May 59
Qr. Master.—Patrick Duff (1), *late of* 66 F. ....22 Feb. 55

Black Facings.

Agents, Messrs. Cane and Sons.

CLARE.
[No. 94.]
Head Quarters, Ennis.
COLONEL.
Crofton Moore Vandeleur, DL. JP. ....24 June 43

LIEUT.COLONEL.
Francis Macnamara, DL. JP. *late Capt.* 8 *Hussars* .... 4 Nov. 54

MAJOR.
Wm. E. Armstrong MacDonnell, DL. JP..........14 Dec. 54

CAPTAINS.
Augustine Butler, DL. JP... 3 Nov. 42
Marcus Paterson, JP. ......16 July 47
Robert A. Studdert, JP..... 5 Nov. 47
John O'Callaghan, JP. *late Capt.* 62 F. ....15 Nov. 54

Andrew Stacpoole, JP.........16 Nov. 54
George S. Studdert, JP. ......28 Nov. 54
William Stacpoole, JP. ......30 Jan. 55
John Smyth .... 1 May 55
John Westropp...............17 Sept. 55
William R. Mahon, JP. ......

LIEUTENANTS.
Richard Studdert ....25 Jan. 55
Crofton Fitzgerald1 ....25 Jan. 55
Charles Wm. Studdert........12 Mar. 55
Alexander Paterson............23 May 55
Geoffrey Davies...............19 Sept. 55
Alexander Bolton.............. 9 Apr. 56
Francis Westropp..............29 Sept. 57
Robert Branwell Walton......28 June 58

ENSIGNS.
Robert S. Lawler ....23 Apr. 55
Robert Blake.................. 7 Aug. 55
Chas. A. Wigelsworth ....17 Aug. 55
Richard Barclay ....15 Jan. 56
Thomas B. Gore ....12 Apr. 56
Hon. James F. Butler ....29 Sept. 57
John Martyn ....19 July 58
Adj. & Capt.—Chas. Wm. Gore, JP. *late Capt.* 72 F... 1 July 46
Paymaster.—Chas. M. Parkinson................... 6 Jan. 55
Surgeon.—Michael Healy, M.D. *late of the Royal Navy* 16 June 55
Assist.Surg.—John F. Macbeth.....................16 June 55
Qr. Master.—Hugh O'Loghlen, JP. ....25 Jan. 55

Yellow Facings.

Agents.—Sir E. R. Borough, *Bart.*, Armit, and Co.

NORTH CORK RIFLES.
[No. 116.]
[Embodied.]
Head Quarters, Hamilton.
COLONEL.

LIEUT.COLONEL.
William St. Leger Alcock
Stawell, JP. *late Capt.*23 F. 8 Nov. 54

MAJOR.
Robert Aldworth, JP.*late Capt.* 94 F....................30 June 55

CAPTAINS.
Fred. J. Rawlins, *late Lt.* 5 F. 1 Dec. 54
Edw. Braddell, *late Capt.* 70 F. 2 Dec. 54
Edward Hoare ....11 Jan. 55
Robert D. Perry, JP.......... 4 Apr. 55
Dominick R. Sarsfield .... 1 Dec. 55
Charles Frederick Knolles ...26 Mar. 56
Robert Aldworth ....12 Dec. 56
Eyre Massey Shaw ....12 Sept. 57
Crewe C. Townsend ....24 Nov. 53
William Lambert Howe ....19 Jan. 59

LIEUTENANTS.
Hubert Coghlan .... 1 Mar. 55
Charles Dudley Gabbett ..... 5 Apr. 56
Henry A. St. Clair Keogh ... 5 Apr. 56
John Quarry, *Instructor of Musketry* .... 1 Jan. 58
Richard Reynell Aylmer ...... do.
George Halbard .... 6 Apr. 58
Edmund Leahy ....19 June 58
Philip Sidney Dudley ....19 Jan. 59
Douglas Mercer .... 8 Apr. 59

ENSIGNS.
Thomas Richard Gabbett ....28 Sept. 57
Richard Connor ....24 Oct. 57
John Francis Bellis ....30 Oct. 57
James F. W. Cronin .... 1 Jan. 58
Samuel Townsend, JP........20 Apr. 58
Alexander Stuart............. do.
George Fra. Ormsby ....29 June 58

Capt. & Adj.—Frederick M. Callaghan, JP. *late Lt.* 60 *Rifles* .... 3 Nov. 54
Paymaster.—Richard Gethin Creagh ....23 Jan. 55
Qr. Master.—Foster Hewison, *late of Rifle Br.* ...... 6 Jan. 55
Surgeon.—James M'Dermott 23 July 50
Assistant Surgeon. — Thomas Henderson Somerville ...... 1 Oct. 59

Black Velvet Facings.
Irish Agents.—Sir E. R. Borough, *Bart.* Armit and Co.

87TH, OR SOUTH CORK.
(*Light Infantry.*)
Head Quarters, Bandon.
COLONEL.
Hon. H. B. Bernard............29 Mar. 54

LIEUT.COLONEL.
Henry Wallis, DL. JP. ......10 Jan. 55

MAJOR.
A. H. Lucas, JP., *late Capt.* 45 F. ....12 June 55

CAPTAINS.
Hewitt Poole, JP.............. 9 Aug. 34
George Bowles .... 2 Nov. 46
E. A. Shuldham, JP.......... 5 Apr. 52
Rd. T. Rye, JP...............22 Dec. 54
Sir Jas. L. Cotter, *Bart.* JP. *late of* 27 F. ....11 Oct. 52
Thomas Somerville ....22 Feb. 55
Robert Cole Bowen .... 5 Apr. 55
Michael Wall, *late of* 39 F..17 Oct. 55
Godfrey Baldwin .... 1 Oct. 59

LIEUTENANTS.
S. S. Tresilian ....16 Jan. 55
Jno. H. Cole ....19 Jan. 55
Richd. White, *late of* 66 F. ..19 Jan. 55
Fras. Heard ....19 Jan. 55
Thomas Geo. Walker, *late of* 75 F. ....15 Sept. 55
Chambre Baldwin ....18 Oct. 55
Robt. Holmes ....18 Oct. 55
Chas. Deane ....16 Feb. 56
Francis Rowland .... 1 Mar. 56

ENSIGNS.
W. P. Hosford ....19 Jan. 55
Wm. H. Bird ....19 Jan. 55
Richd. Ager ....27 Jan. 55
Thos. W. Markham ....27 Jan. 55
John Penrose Warren .... 1 Mar. 55
Mason Alcock ....12 Oct. 55
Lancelot John Kiggett ....17 Nov. 55
Samuel Medlicott ....16 Feb. 56
James H. F. Donegan ....19 July 58
Richard Nettles............... 9 Nov. 58

Adjutant & Capt.—Charles T. Tuckey, (4) *late Capt.* 41 F.12 June 55
Paymaster.—T. D. Perry, *late Capt.* 81 F..................12 Jan. 55
Qr. Master.—Denis Cummins ....10 Jan. 55
Surgeon.—J. G. Gregg, MD, 5 Mar. 46
Assist.Surg.—Hen. Storach 29 Nov. 55

White Facings.

Agents, Messrs. Cane and Sons.

ROYAL CORK CITY ARTILLERY.
[No. 5.]
Head Quarters, Ballincollig.
COLONEL.
The *Earl of* Bandon, DL. JP. 5 Sept. 4

Militia of Ireland. 640

LIEUT.COLONEL.
Andrew Jordaine Wood, DL.
JP. *late Capt.* 15*th Hussars* 4 Jan. 55
MAJOR.
Augustus Warren, JP. *late Capt.* 99 *F.* ....19 Jan. 55
CAPTAINS.
Richard Beare Tooker, JP. ...24 Dec. 50
John Longfield, JP................22 Dec. 54
Samuel Hodder, JP..............14 Feb. 55
1ST LIEUTENANTS.
Richard Boyle Robinson .....16 Jan. 27
Robert Tresilian Belcher ...14 Feb. 55
John Boles Gaggin .... 1 Aug. 55
John Michael Aylward Lewis 18 Jan. 56
2ND LIEUTENANTS.
David Fitzjames Barry........12 Feb. 55
John Tuckey......................14 Feb. 55
Edward Kelly .... 9 Aug. 58
Adj. & Capt. & Acting Paymaster.— Andrew Stevenson, *late of R. Art.* ....22 Jan. 55
Qr.Master.—Edwd. Webber Wigmore, *late of Madras Horse Art.* ....13 Jan. 55
Surgeon.—Thos. Waugh Belcher, MB. ....21 Feb. 55
Assist.Surgeon.—J. Johnson d'Altera.........................29 Aug. 57
Scarlet Facings.
Agents, Messrs. Cane and Sons.

WEST CORK ARTILLERY.
[No. 4.]
Head Quarters, Macroom.
HONORARY COLONEL.
The Earl of Shannon, DL. JP. 30 Nov. 54
LIEUT.COLONEL COMMANDANT.
Hon. W. H. White Hedges, DL. JP. ....30 Nov. 54
MAJOR.
William Henry Longfield, *late Capt.* 12 *F.*.................30 Nov. 54
CAPTAINS.
James Herrick .... 2 Dec. 54
Patrick Duncan .... 5 Dec. 54
George Thomas Evans, *late Capt.* 47 *F.*.................. 4 Jan. 55
William Fitzjames Barry, JP. 14 Feb. 55
Richard Pigott Beamish .....26 July 56
Edmond Scully, *late Capt. Br. German Legion* ....24 Oct. 57
LIEUTENANTS.
Robert John McClure .... 2 Dec. 54
F. M. Hutchinson Warren ...26 July 56
Victor Bodely Roche ....27 Sept. 57
Archibald Ormstron Hayes...24 July 58
2ND LIEUTENANTS.
George Horace Hayes........ 2 Jan. 56
Eyre Maunsell Eyre .... 7 Jan. 56
Michael Becher................14 Apr. 56
Edward Daly................... 9 Aug. 58
Paymaster.—William Hare Maunsell .... 7 Feb. 55
Adjutant & Capt.—Thomas Pudney, *late of Royal Art.* 1 Oct. 55
Qr.Master.—Alex. Fraser ... 4 Apr. 55
Surgeon.—Charles Creed ... 7 Mar. 56
Assist.Surg.—
Scarlet Facings.
Agents, Sir E. R. Borough, *Bart.*, Armit, and Co.

DONEGAL.
(102nd, *or Prince of Wales's.*)
[Embodied.]
Head Quarters, Colchester.
HONORARY COLONEL.
The Marquis of Abercorn, KG.GCH. *Lt. of County* ...13 Dec. 54

LIEUT.COLONEL COMMANDANT.
Lord Claud Hamilton........22 Sept. 55
MAJORS.
Jas. Henry Todd, (1) JP. *late Capt.* 40 *F.*................... 3 Apr. 55
James Hamilton, JP............13 Feb. 58
CAPTAINS.
Fras. Stewart Mansfield...... 8 Jan. 55
Soloman Darcus .... 8 Jan. 55
John Tredennick .... 6 Feb. 55
Charles Maturin ....12 Apr. 55
Robert Patterson Elliot, *Instructor of Musketry* ....21 May 58
John Alex. Donnelly .... 1 Nov. 58
Andrew Ferguson Knox, JP. 23 Dec. 58
Wm. d'Arcy, *late Capt.* 67 *F.* 23 Aug. 59
LIEUTENANTS.
Andrew Atkinson .... 8 Jan. 55
Valentine S. Griffith, *Instructor of Musketry* ....
Thos. Benison..................11 Oct. 57
Bennett Hume ....19 July 58
Alex. M'Causland Hamilton... do
Wm. Mackay Mackenzie...... do
Geo. C. M'L. Mason ....23 Aug. 59
ENSIGNS.
Robert Hay Maturin ....19 Aug. 58
John M'Causland Hamilton... do
Wm. Lancellot Baillie .... 1 Oct. 58
George Searle .... 4 Dec. 58
Joseph Lecky .... 8 July 59
George S. Murphy .... do
Thomas Richard Belton ....23 Aug. 59

Adjutant and Capt.—Joseph Hayes, *late Lt. St. Helena Regt.* .... 1 May 55
Paymaster.—Alex. Nesbitt Gillespie......................31 July 58
Qr.Master.—John R. C. Mason .... 3 June 58
Surg.—Rich. Hudson Courtenay ....30 Mar. 55
Assist.Surg.—Jas. V. M'Cormick ....18 Apr. 58
White Facings.
Agents.—Messrs. Cane & Sons.

DONEGAL ARTILLERY.
[No. 8.]
Head Quarters, Charlemont.
HONORARY COLONEL.
Sir James Stewart, *Bart.* ...26 Sept. 55
LIEUT.COLONEL COMMANDANT.
Robert Roe Fisher, *Bt.-Maj. R. Art. ret. f. p.* ....14 Mar. 55
MAJOR.
J. Harvey, *Capt. h. p. R. Art.* 30 Mar. 55
CAPTAINS.
Rob. Geo. Montgomery ......31 Jan. 55
Thomas Patterson ....19 Mar. 55
James Butler Staveley........28 Apr. 55
Mervyn Trevor Vesey........ 7 Mar. 58
LIEUTENANTS.
Nathaniel A. Baillie, *Act. Paymaster* ....10 Apr. 55
Thomas W. Lodge ....21 July 55
Wm. Geo. M'Cullagh ....21 July 55
Currel M. Hopkins ....16 Sept. 58
SECOND LIEUTENANTS.
Thomas Adams Hopkins... 1 Oct. 55
Hans Caulfield FitzGerald... 16 Sept. 58
Henry Arthur Herbert ...... 1 Oct. 58
Adj. & Capt.—Robert A. Robertson..................... 1 Sept. 55
Qr.Master.—John Kelly ..... 1 Sept. 55
Surg.—Robt. M. Tagart, MD. 4 Apr. 55
Agents.—Sir E. R. Borough, *Bart.*, Armit and Co.

ROYAL NORTH DOWN.
(*Rifles.*) [No. 77.]
Head Quarters, Newtown Ards.
COLONEL.
The Marquis of Londonderry, KP. *Lieut. of the County...* 1 Sept. 37
LIEUT.COLONEL.
Fras. Octavius Montgomery, *late Major* 45 *F.*, JP. ...... 2 Nov. 54
MAJOR.
Octavius La Touche, *late Capt.* 98 *F.*.................... 2 Nov. 57
CAPTAINS.
John Craig......................19 Dec. 54
Henry Keown, *late Capt.* 15 *Hussars* ....21 Dec. 55
Mathew William Forde ....30 Dec. 54
Gilbert Henry Howe ....16 Nov. 55
John Harrison .... 9 Sept. 56
Edw. Geo. Moore ....25 Feb. 58
LIEUTENANTS.
Alexander Allan Hunter......23 Dec. 54
John Amelius Massey Edmd. Stackpoole................... 5 Feb. 55
James Trail Hall .... 5 Feb. 55
James Brown ....15 Nov. 55
James Greer ....19 Aug. 56
Henry Lewis Mulock ....26 Sept. 57
Thos. Robert Johnston Logan... do
James Wentworth Ievers ... 4 May 58
ENSIGNS.
Thomas Henshaw ....21 Sept. 57
Wm. M'Clelland .... do
Wm. Shirley Cordner .... 8 Oct. 57
Adj. & Capt.—Geo. William Conyngham Stuart, *late Capt.* 75 *F.*...................25 Nov. 54
Paymaster.—
Qr.Mast.—Joseph Henshaw 22 May 55
Surgeon.—John Stream Armstrong.........................27 Jan. 55
Assist.Surg.—Richard Hamilton Cross .... 18 May 58
Agents, Sir E. R. Borough, *Bt.* Armit & Co.

ROYAL SOUTH DOWN.
(*Light Infantry.*) [No. 112.]
Head Quarters, Hillsborough.
COLONEL.
The Marq. of Downshire, KT. 30 July 45
LIEUT.COLONEL.
William Brownlow Forde, *late of* 67 *F.* JP. & DL ......14 Nov. 54
MAJOR.
U Peter Rutledge Montague Browne (2), DL. JP. *Capt. h.p.* 9 *F.* .... 30 Nov. 54
CAPTAINS.
Charles Arthur Forde .... 8 Jan. 55
Thomas Waring .... 8 Jan. 55
Wm. Fred. Norman, *late of* 91 *F.* ....21 May 55
Geo. Shuldham Peard (1), *late Capt.* 20 *F.*..................21 Sept. 57
John White ....10 Oct. 57
Douglas Hamilton ....19 Nov. 57
Henry Botel Hunt ....31 Mar. 58
Andrew Vesey Davoren .....13 Apr. 58
LIEUTENANTS.
Stapleton Hawker.............28 Apr. 56
John Declezeau ....23 Sept. 57
Robert M. Borthwick ....10 Mar. 58
Rich. Ravenscroft Nelson... do
Edward Lloyd Trevor .... do

Militia of Ireland.

ENSIGNS.
Desmond FitzGerald............20 Oct. 57
Craven Going..................23 Oct. 57
Cha. Alfred Kinahan ....10 Mar. 58
Joseph Baldwin .... do

Adj. & Capt.—Fred. Colborne
Curtis ....22 Dec. 54
Paymaster.—

Qr.Master.—John Macgroarty
12 Mar. 58

Surgeon.—George Croker..... 9 Jan. 55

Assist.Surgeon.—Rutherford
Kirkpatrick ....14 Oct. 57

Agents, Messrs. Cane & Son.

ROYAL DUBLIN CITY.

(*Queen's Own Royal Regiment.*) [100.]
[Embodied.]
Head Quarters, Plymouth.

COLONEL.
David Charles La Touche, DL,
JP. .... 8 Apr. 49

LIEUT.COLONEL.
Henry Musters, DL, JP. late
Capt. 2 Dr. Gds............11 Mar. 59

MAJOR.
Geo. Caleb Eyre Powell ...28 July 55

CAPTAINS.
Robt. Eglinton Seton, late
Lt. 93 F....................12 Feb. 55
J. Brenan,*Capt. h. p. late*22 F.28 Feb. 55
Robert Harkness M'Donnell,
late Lt. 56 F...............18 Apr. 55
Charles E. Bushe ....25 Mar. 56
Martin Fitzjohn Kirwan....30 Apr. 56
Owen M'Dermott, JP....... 1 Dec. 57
Hervey de M. Armstrong ... 23 June 58
Robert Bolton Smyth, *In-
structor of Musketry* ....27 July 59

LIEUTENANTS.
Thomas Bellew .... 7 July 56
William Hutchison ....19 July 56
Charles Taylor .... 1 Dec. 57
William Fleury ....23 June 58
Geo. Fearon Thorp ....13 May 59
Arthur Vowell ....22 Aug. 59
Francis Vowell ....29 Sept. 59
Charles Howard .... do

ENSIGNS.
William Wallace..............24 May 59
Alfred Handcock ....26 July 59
Henry Greene.................27 July 59
John Wall Radcliffe ....23 Aug. 59
Henry Vowell ....29 Sept. 59
John Henry Ryde ....20 Oct. 59
Robert Macintosh ....11 Nov. 59

Adjutant.—S. W. Russell(4),
Capt., late Capt 98 F......26 Jan. 46

Paymaster.—John D. Browne 17 Nov. 57

Qr.Master.—Captain Wm.
Holt, *Qr.Master h. p.* 95 F. 13 Jan. 58

Surg.—J. Leech, MD......... 6 Feb. 52

Assist.Surg.—Caleb S. Willis 19 Oct. 57

Blue.

Agents—Sir E. R. Borough, *Bt.*,
Armit and Co.

DUBLIN CITY ARTILLERY.

[No. 9.] [Embodied.]

Head Quarters, Colchester.

LIEUT.COLONEL. COMMANDANT.
Hon. Robert French Hand-
cock, *Capt. h. p. R. Art.*......17 Nov. 54

MAJOR.
Richard Wheatley Brettling-
ham, *Capt. h. p. R. Art.* ...17 Apr. 55

CAPTAINS.
Francis de Burgh ....21 Nov. 54
Henry Shaw .... 8 Dec. 54
Arthur Raymond Pelly......16 Nov. 58
William James Magill ....30 Apr. 59

LIEUTENANTS.
Thos. P. O'Meara .... 3 Apr. 56
Wm. B. Digby .... 8 Dec. 58
Henry P. Elrington, *late of
78 F.* ....18 Apr. 59
Allan G. W. Gardiner .... 2 May 59

SECOND LIEUTENANTS.
John Albert Vincent ....28 Feb. 59
John de M. Armstrong ......11 Mar. 59
R. Marmaduke Alloway......26 Mar. 59
Thomas Wm. Baker ....24 May 59

Adjutant.—Charles McCallum,
late of R. Art.................18 Dec. 54

Surgeon. — Edward Howell
Scriven ....30 Dec. 54

Qr.Master.—Wm. McAdam,
late of R. Art. ....20 Feb. 55

Scarlet Facings.

Agents, Sir E.R.Borough, *Bt.* Armit & Co.

DUBLIN COUNTY.

(*Light Infantry.*) [No. 109.]
Head Quarters, Lucan.

COLONEL.
William, *Earl of* Meath, DL, 10 May 47

LIEUT.COLONEL.
Wm. *Viscount* St. Lawrence,
late Capt. 7 *Hussars*......... 6 June 54

MAJOR.
Robert Bramston Smith ...... 3 Apr. 56

CAPTAINS.
C. Vesey Colthurst, JP, *late
of* 81 F.......................19 Apr. 48
William Westby Moore ..... 5 Oct. 56
James Hewitt Oliver .... 3 Apr. 56
John Hatchell ....16 Sept. 57
Thos. C. Baird, *late Capt.* 39
F. .... 1 July 58
Arthur P. Graves, *late of* 28 F. 1 July 58
Wilson Hartley, *late Capt.* 8
F. ....16 July 58
Edm. Alex. Mansfield ....29 June 59

LIEUTENANTS.
Charles Crosslett ....30 Apr. 56
James H. E. Butler...........26 Mar. 58
William Porter .... 1 July 58
Wm. Farran Darley .... 3 Mar. 59

ENSIGNS.
John French .... 8 July 59

Adjt. & Capt.—Montgomerie
Caulfeild, *late Capt.* 66 F.... 1 Dec. 54

Surg.—B. G. Guinness......... 1 Aug. 55

Assist.Surg.—Richard Newcombe Willis, M.D. .... 7 Jan. 56

Qr.Master.—William Hardic,
late of 90 F..................16 Mar. 55

Paymaster.—

FERMANAGH.

(*Light Infantry*). [No. 71.]
[Embodied.]
Head Quarters, Chester.

COLONEL.
W. Willoughby, *Earl of* En-
niskillen, DL. ....24 Oct. 34

LIEUT.COLONEL.
Hon. Samuel Crichton, DL....18 July 55

MAJOR.
Edw.Archdall,*late Capt.*14 F.18 July 55

CAPTAINS.
H A. Nixon(1), DL, *late Lt.*
27 F. ....10 Mar. 36
John Gerard Irvine, JP. ....10 Feb. 47
Thomas Nixon ....10 Mar. 47
Arthur D'Arcy ....15 Jan. 55
Charles Barton ....30 Oct. 57
John M. A. C. Richardson..24 Feb. 58

LIEUTENANTS.
A. W. Bailey ....28 Nov. 54
Henry Haire ....25 Mar. 58
Roderick Grey ....11 Nov. 58
B. T. Winslow ....16 Nov. 58
Samuel Y. Worthington .....14 June 59
Arthur St. George .... do

ENSIGNS.
John Oldham Ellis ....27 Apr. 58
Adam Loftus Tottenham ....11 Nov. 58
Sir Richard Gethin, *Bt.*......22 Dec. 58
Wm. P. M. W. Benson ...... 7 May 59
Thomas Gore Ormsby ....28 June 59
Thomas Chapman .... 8 July 59

Adj. & Capt.—Henry Beckwith Sawrey, *late Bt. Major*
88 F. ....18 July 55

Qr.Mast.—William Baker ...14 May 56

Paymaster.—Wm. Shegog ...24 Dec. 57

Surgeon.—G. D. Mansfield ...27 Mar. 55

Assist.Surg.—Fred. R. Wil-
son, MB. ....18 Dec. 57

Buff Facings.

Agents, Sir E. R. Borough, *Bart.*, Armit
and Co.

GALWAY.

[No. 91.]
Head Quarters, Loughrea.

COLONEL.
The *Marquis of* Clanricarde,
KP, *Lieut. of the County*... 1 Jan. 38

LIEUT.COLONEL.
The *Earl of* Clancarty ....20 Dec. 30

MAJOR.
Thomas Mahon, JP...........20 Nov. 11

CAPTAINS.
Thomas Seymour ....15 July 15
Henry J. Gascoyne, JP, *late
Capt.* 34 F................... 1 Nov. 36
Lord Dunlo .... 6 June 53
Francis Blake Foster, JP. ..21 Nov. 53
John Archer Daly .... 1 July 55
Oliver Martyn .... 2 Dec. 54
Butler Dunboyne Moore, *late
Capt.* 89 F..................22 Dec. 54
Walter Lawrence, *late Capt.*
41 F. ....25 Jan. 55
John Joseph Lapdell ....29 Jan. 56
John Wilson Lynch .... 7 July 59

LIEUTENANTS.
George William Maunsell .. 2 Dec. 54
Stephen John Cowan .... 2 Feb. 55
Dominick Bodkin ....27 Aug. 55
William Joseph Kirwan .....25 Mar. 56
J. William Comyn ....25 Mar. 56
John Joseph M'Dermott ..... 7 July 58
Valentine Blake .... do
John Skerrett .... do
Henry James Blake..........25 July 59
James Lopdell .... do

Militia of Ireland. 642

ENSIGNS.
Edward Collis ....10 Feb. 58
William Rogers .... 1 July 58
John D'Arcy .... 2 Aug. 58
David Rutledge .... do
Peter Herbert Daly ....15 July 59
Richard Daly Burke............ do

Adj.—John Blakeney, *late Lieut. R. W. Fus.*........ 1 Nov. 54
Paymaster.—S. S. Harrison... 1 July 23
Qr.Master.—Jas. Galbraith 5 Aug. 56
Surg.—J. Miller Davis........21 Sept. 55
Assist.Surg.—Andr. O'Kelly Nolan ....21 Sept. 55

Yellow Facings.

Agents, Messrs. Cane and Sons.

KERRY.
[No. 107.]
[Embodied.]
Head Quarters, The Curragh.

HONORARY COLONEL.
Right Hon. Henry Arthur Herbert, MP. *Lieut. of the County* .... 9 Jan.

LIEUT.COLONEL COMMANDANT.
Hon. Day Rolles B. De Moleyns, DL..................... 3 Aug. 54

MAJORS.
James Croslie .... 16 Apr. 59
Morris Chas. O'Connell (2), *late Capt.* 78 F...............17 Sept. 59

CAPTAINS.
Samuel Collis.................... Feb. 52
Daniel O'Connell, MP..........19 July 53
Edward Herbert .... 1 Nov. 54
Oliver D. Stokes, *late Capt. Madras N.I.* .... 5 Jan. 55
William Rowan .... 6 Jan. 55
Robert Leslie ....21 Aug. 55
Townsend Blennerhassett ... 7 Mar. 56
Henry Moore Sandes ....29 Oct. 57
Hon. Edw. Alured De Moleyns 20 Oct. 58
Richard Plummer.............17 Sept. 59

LIEUTENANTS.
Hugh Lawlor.................24 Jan. 55
Francis McGillicuddy ....14 Aug. 55
James McMahon Engar, *Instructor of Musketry* .....12 Mar. 56
Leslie Wren ....20 Aug. 57
John Robt. Day, *late of 96 F.* 28 Oct. 57
Francis Elliott Chute ....29 Oct. 57
Francis Chute ....16 Apr. 59
Charles Anthony Denny...... 9 Aug. 59
Alfred Godfrey...............17 Sept. 59

ENSIGNS.
John Langford Crumpe .....29 Oct. 57
Samuel Gun Raymond...... 6 Nov. 57
Michael Healy ....17 Dec. 57
Thomas Spring .... 4 Aug. 58
Rowland Purdon ....15 Oct. 58
William Crosbie..............30 Dec. 58
Maurice Thomas O'Connell...30 Apr. 59
John Yielding Engar.......... do
Thomas Arthur Walker .... 9 Aug. 59
Henry Taylor................10 Oct. 59

Adjt.—Capt. Thos. Spring (3), *late Capt.* 63 F...............25 Nov. 54
Paymaster.—R. D. Stokes ... 6 Mar. 24
Surgeon.—Thos. Maybury (4) 1 Jan. 55
Assist.Surg.—Clement Peat, MD. ....16 May. 55
Qr.Master.—Wm. Russell ...29 Jan. 56

Yellow Facings.

Agents Sir E. Borough, Bt., Armit & Co.

KILDARE.
(*Rifles.*) [No. 88.]
Head Quarters, Naas.

COLONEL.
Marquis of Kildare .... 6 June 49

LIEUT.COLONEL.
Robert Moore .... 1 Dec. 35

MAJOR.

CAPTAINS.
William Bruce, *late* 74 F. ..20 Mar. 55
Chas. Warburton ....23 Mar. 55
William Kirkpatrick ....27 April 55
Eustace Mansfield ....10 Apr. 56

LIEUTENANTS.
John S. Browne ....20 Mar. 55
Hugh Massey O'Grady .....25 May 55
Abraham Hutton King .....25 Nov. 55
Annesley Moekings ....10 Apr. 56
Richard Wm. Mansfield ....24 May 59

ENSIGNS.
Geo. Sutcliffe................. 8 July 13
Geo. Blacker Rawson ....10 Apr. 56

Paymaster.—
Adjt. & Capt.—Francis Kennedy(1), *late of* 77 F. ...... 5 June 55
Qr.Mast.—James Todd ...... 26 July 55
Surg.—Robert Huston...... 6 Mar. 55
Assist.Surg.—

Black Facings.

Agents, Sir E. R. Borough, Bt., Armit & Co.

KILKENNY.
(*Fusiliers.*) [No. 127.]
Head Quarters, Kilkenny.

HONORARY COLONEL.
Right Hon. W. F. Tighe, *Lt. and Custos Rotulorum* ...... 8 Jan. 55

LIEUT.COLONEL COMMANDANT.
Henry Wemyss, DL. JP.......20 Sept. 46

MAJOR.
Fred. Edward Tighe, *late Capt.* 82 F........................ 5 Nov. 54

CAPTAINS.
Thos. John B. O'Flahertie...29 Mar. 16
Pierce S. Butler, JP. .... 6 Nov. 38
Lord Walter Butler, JP. *late Brev.Maj. Scots Fus. Gds.* 2 Apr. 52
Hon. Leopold A. Ellis, JP. ...17 Nov. 54
James Langrishe, JP. .... 5 Dec. 54
Joseph Hobson, *late Lt.* 37 F. 5 Mar. 55
Thos. Power F. Bookey, JP. . 7 Sept. 55
Paul H. Hunt ....18 Sept. 58

LIEUTENANTS.
Thomas Jones ....24 Nov. 54
Henry Nixon .... 7 Feb. 55
Anthony Pack .... 8 Feb. 55
Louis Anderson ....12 Sept. 55
William Lyster ....28 Mar. 56
Christopher H. Prim ....27 June 56
Arthur Francis Tighe ....10 Apr. 58
J. S. Lane, JP. ....18 Sept. 58

ENSIGNS.
Meade Wright .... 8 Feb. 55
Albert H. B. O'Flahertie....12 Sept. 55
Robt. Wm. Hamilton Bolton.26 Mar. 56
John Shee .... 4 Nov. 57

Adjt. and Capt.—Jas. White Minchin, *late Captain* 62 F.12 Apr. 59
Qr.Master.—Wm. Hartford...24 May 56
Surgeon.—J. Symes, MD, ... 7 Mar. 56
Assist.Surg.—Rich. S. Magee 25 Nov. 57

Yellow Facings.

Agents.—Messrs. Cane and Sons.

KING'S COUNTY.
(*Royal Rifles.*) [No. 98.]
Head Quarters, Parsonstown.

COLONEL.
The *Earl of Rosse*, KP. *Lieut. and Custos Rotulorum*......19 June 34

LIEUT.COLONEL.
Thomas Bernard, DL. JP. *Capt. h. p. late of* 12 *Lancers.*6 Mar. 55

MAJOR.
Robert Warburton, *late Capt.* 48 F. .... 6 Mar. 55

CAPTAINS.
Wm. B. Buchanan, JP. *late of* 27 F. ....25 Nov. 44
Richard W. Bernard, *late of Austrian Service* ....27 Dec. 46
Montagu Blackett, JP........ 6 Mar. 55
George Beresford L'Estrange 6 Mar. 55
George W. F. Drought.......17 May 55
Thomas Acres Peirce, *late Ens.* 41 F. ....23 July 59

LIEUTENANTS.
Sandford Palmer ....17 May 55
Rowland Tarleton ....17 May 55
Somerville F. Baynton ..... 3 April 56
Charles Frank Rolleston...... 7 Aug. 58

ENSIGNS.
John Priaulx Armstrong .....25 May 58

Adjt. & Capt.—William Tyrrell Bruce, (1) *late Brev. Maj.* 18 F. ....16 Dec. 54
Paymaster.—Wm. L'Estrange, JP. *late Lieut.* 11 F....... 5 May 55
Qr.Master.—
Surg.—T. H. Baker ....26 Jan. 57
Assist.Surg.—Thomas Woods, MD. ....26 Jan. 57

Scarlet Facings.

Agents, Messrs. Cane & Sons.

LEITRIM.
(*Rifles.*) [No. 111.]
Head Quarters, Mohill.

COLONEL.
The *Earl of Leitrim*, JP. DL. *late Capt.* 43 F. & *Brevet Lt.Col* .... 2 Feb. 43

LIEUT.COLONEL.
Henry Theophilus Clements, JP. ....11 Jan. 42

MAJOR.
Hon. William Jas. Forbes (1), *late Lt. & Capt. Gren. Gds.*27 June 59

CAPTAINS.
Arthur J. V. L. Birchall, JP. 26 Dec. 54
George White ....28 Dec. 54
Forbes Johnston ....29 Dec. 54
John Alex. Wray ....12 Nov. 55
John Stratford Kirwan .....29 May 57
Robert O'Brian.............. 3 Apr. 58

LIEUTENANTS.
Andrew C. Johnston .... 7 Feb. 55
James Soden Cullen........ 8 Feb. 55
George N. R. Lambert...... 4 Jan. 56
Joshua Kell .... 3 Apr. 58
Daniel G. Grose ....30 Mar. 59
Hugh M'Ternan .... do

ENSIGNS.
James Morton ....10 Feb. 55
Wm. W. T. Hutchinson ....28 Dec. 55
Geo. Thomas Corscllis....... 4 Jan. 56
Wm. Phibbs ....14 Dec. 57
Edw. Fra. Waldron......... 8 Apr. 58
Michael O'Kelly .... 7 June 59

Adj. & Capt.—Malachi Hanley,
Capt. h. p. .... 20 Oct. 59
Paymaster. —

Surg.—Arth.Goff Thompson 2 Feb. 55
Assist.Surg.—SmithwickCarpenter .... 2 Mar. 55
Black Facings.
Agents, Sir E. R. Borough, *Bart.*,
Armit and Co.

ROYAL LIMERICK COUNTY.
[No. 123.]
[Embodied.]
Head Quarters, Portsmouth.

HONORARY COLONEL.
⚑ Rt. Hon. the *Earl of* Clare, (4)
late of Gr. Gds. .... 4 July 18

LIEUT.COLONEL COMMANDANT.
Samuel Auchmuty Dickson,
late Capt. 13 Drs. .... 11 May 54

MAJORS.
Sir Richard D.De Burgho, *Bt.* 13 Dec. 55
Thomas Wallnutt, *late Capt.*
74 *F.* .... 20 July 58

CAPTAINS.
Gibbon Fitzgibbon .... 10 Jan. 48
Jonathan W. Shelton, *late Lt.*
14 *F.* .... 5 Jan. 55
George E. Massy .... 5 Jan. 55
John Howley .... 5 Jan. 55
Michael J. Furnell .... 17 July 55
Arthur Lloyd .... 30 Sept. 57
William Browning .... 30 Sept. 57
George Stein .... 10 Nov. 58
George William Finch ..... 2 Dec. 58

LIEUTENANTS.
Charles Hayes O'Connor ....26 June 55
Bryan Edw. Sheehy .... 22 Sept. 57
John O'Leary .... 30 Sept. 57
Manley M.Palmer, *Instructor of Musketry* .... 30 Sept. 57
Bryan B. Sheehy .... 2 Jan. 58
Francis H. Walker .... 9 July 58
Daniel D. Power .... 2 Dec. 58
Charles Wm. Wyse .... 24 Mar. 59
John F. Egan, *late of* 48 *F.*... do

ENSIGNS.
Richard Croker .... 30 Sept. 57
Rochford Hunt .... 21 Oct. 57
Wm. W. Jevers .... 2 Jan. 58
Edward Sherman .... 9 July 58
Robert Rod ers .... 20 July 58
Luke G. T. M'Craith .... do
Robert Reeves .... 6 Nov. 58
Edward Burton .... 2 Dec. 58

Adjutant.—Capt. Rich. Butler
Low (1), *late Capt.* 53 *F.*... 6 Aug. 48
Paymaster.— Edw. C. D. Bell 25 Aug. 59

Qr.Master.—Eyre Powell ...12 Aug. 59
Surgeon.—ThomasWilkinson,
M.D. .... 1 Mar. 55
Assist.Surgeon.—Patrick Enwright, M.D. .... 26 Mar. 55
Blue Facings.
Agents, Messrs. Cane & Sons.

LIMERICK ARTILLERY.
[No. 20.]
Head Quarters, Limerick.
HONORARY COLONEL.
John *Viscount* Gort .... 7 Dec. 42
MAJOR COMMANDANT.
Hon. S. P. Vereker ....10 Sept. 42

CAPTAINS.
Ralph Westropp .... 30 June 37
Andrew Vincent Watson, (5)
late Capt. 27 *F.* .... 20 Nov. 55
Walker Mahony .... 12 July 59

FIRST LIEUTENANTS.
Charles F. Smyth .... 19 Feb. 56
Wm. Rumley Holland .... 12 July 59
Geo. Thomas MacFarlene ... do

SECOND LIEUTENANTS.
Fred. Furnell .... 12 July 59

Adj. & Capt.—William Phillips,
late R. Art. .... 8 Nov. 54
Qr.Master. — Christopher
Neary (2), *late of R. Art.*...14 April 55
Surg.—Wm. Daniel Murphy 6 Jan. 55
Blue—Facings Red.
Agents, Sir E. R. Borough, *Bt.*,
Armit & Co.

LONDONDERRY ARTILLERY COMPANY.
[No. 21.]
CAPTAIN.
Stewart Blacker .... 9 Jan. 55

LIEUTENANT.
Henry Scott Smith .... 9 Jan. 55

SECOND LIEUTENANT.

Surgeon.—Henry Carey Field 26 April 55

LONDONDERRY.
(*Light Infantry.*)
[No. 95.]
Head Quarters, Londonderry.

HONORARY COLONEL.
Sir Robt. Alex. Ferguson, *Bart.*
MP. JP .... 24 June 39

LIEUT.COLONEL COMMANDANT.
William Fitzwilliam Lenox
Conyngham, JP. *late* 88 *F.*25 Sept. 50

MAJORS.
Rowley Miller, JP. .... 25 Sept. 50
Stephen Henry Smith, *late*
64 *F.* .... 7 Feb. 55

CAPTAINS.
Stewart C. Bruce, JP. .... 26 Aug. 39
George Knox .... 8 Sept. 53
George Beresford Knox ..... 13 July 54
William E. Scott .... 10 Dec. 54
John Blackall, *Br.Maj. ret.*
f. p. 39 *F.* .... 10 Dec. 54
Alexander Shuldham, *late* 6 *F.* 4 Jan. 55
John George Smyly .... 22 Sept. 57
Robert Gage Richardson ....28 Aug. 58

LIEUTENANTS.
Conolly James Gage .... 5 Jan. 55
Conolly Skipton .... 5 Jan. 55
Stephen Crea Foster .... 5 Oct. 55
Armitage Loury Nicholson ... 5 Apr. 56
Henry Pilkington .... 13 July 58
Pechell Irvine .... 25 June 59
John Kinshela Miller .... 23 Aug. 59
Henry Rowley Miller .... do
Edmund S. Lecky .... 19 Sept. 59

ENSIGNS.
Samuel Maxwell Moore ..... 25 June 59
Adj. & Capt.—James David
Beresford, *late* 76 *F.*...... 8 Dec. 54
Paymaster.—Rowley Miller...20 Jan. 55
Qr.Master.—Thomas Lecky 13 July 58
Surgeon.—Hy. StaceySkipton 10 Dec. 54

Assist.Surgeon.—Wm. Miller 27 Nov. 57
Primrose Facings.
Agents, Sir E. R. Borough, *Bt.*
Armit & Co.

LONGFORD.
[No. 85.] (*Rifles.*)
Head Quarters, Longford.

COLONEL.
⚑ Hen.White(1), *lateLieut.*14
Drag. Lieut. of County...... 9 Jan. 37

LIEUT.COLONEL.
LukeWhite, *lateCapt.*13 Drs. 2 Mar. 59

MAJOR.
Hugh Massy, *late Major*
85 *F.* .... 26 May 56

CAPTAINS.
Ralph A. Dopping, JP. .... 30 Jan. 55
Robert Shuldham .... 18 Jan. 56
L. Loftus Bushe Fox, JP. .... 7 June 56
William Bond .... 18 July 59

LIEUTENANTS.
John Morrow .... 15 Aug. 55
John Shaw .... 18 Jan. 56
Henry O'Farrell Gregory ...10 July 58
James Bridgeman Edgeworth 18 July 59

ENSIGNS.
Fra. S. H. Dopping .... 17 Oct. 55
John Thomas Davys .... 18 Jan. 56
Aug. F. W. Gore,* *late Lt.* 7
Hussars .... 3 May 59

Adjt. & Capt. & Acty. Paymr.
—Henry Lees, J P. *late*
Capt. 28 *F.* .... 8 Dec. 54
Qr.Master.—
Surgeon.—David C. Peter ... 6 Feb. 55
Assist.Surg.—Robert Clarke
Gwydir .... 6 July 58
Scarlet Facings.
Agent, John Atkinson, Esq.

LOUTH.
[No. 108.] (*Rifles.*)
[Embodied.]
Head Quarters, Kinsale.

COLONEL.
Patrick, *Lord* Bellew, *Lieut. of the County* .... 17 Nov. 43

LIEUT.COLONEL.
Sir John S. Robinson, *Bart.*
JP. *late Lieut.* 60 *Rifles* ...23 Dec. 54

MAJOR.
John Taaffe, *Kt. of St. John of Jerusalem, K.M.,* late
Austrian Service .... 26 June 58

CAPTAINS.
Myles Wm. O'Reilly, DL. JP.13 June 55
Carleton Smith .... 8 Dec. 57
William Thomas Murray ... 2 Aug. 58
Henry M. Langton .... 5 Nov. 58
Clifford W. Chaplin (1), *late Lt.*
49 *F.* .... 11 Nov. 59
Robert Mathew Murphy ... 10 Mar. 59

LIEUTENANTS.
John M. J. Townley .... 10 Feb. 58
Wm. Thomas Cormick .... 2 Aug. 59
Edw. Thos. Lindsay .... 1 Sept. 58
Wm. John B. Standidge .....21 Sept. 58
Wm. Stares, *Instructor of Musketry* .... 11 Jan. 59
Wm. Joseph Power .... 30 Mar. 59

Militia of Ireland.

ENSIGNS.
William Mason.................. 6 July 58
Dudley H. S. Smith ....21 Sept. 58
Richard Burke ....10 Jan. 59
John Bellew Kelly ....14 Sept. 59
Hamilton Low ....17 Nov. 59
Adjt. & Capt.—William Johnstone Bellingham, *late Capt.* 50 F. .... 5 Jan. 55
Paymaster.—Francis Burke .23 Mar. 58
Surg.—E. D. Dickson, M.B. 17 Oct. 56
Qr.Mast. — Edward Burke, *late of* 50 F. ....19 Feb. 55
Black Facings.
Agents, Sir E. Borough, Bart., Armit & Co.

NORTH MAYO.
[No. 120.]
Head Quarters, Ballina.
COLONEL.
Charles Knox, DL. JP......25 Nov. 39
LIEUTENANT COLONEL.
G. G. Ouseley Higgins, MP.
DL. JP. .... 5 Feb. 55
MAJOR.
John Knox, JP..............25 Oct. 52
CAPTAINS.
Henry William Knox, DL.JP. 8 July 30
Earnest Knox, JP.......... 7 Feb. 48
Thomas Elwood, JP........28 Feb. 48
James Paget ....10 Feb. 55
James Vaughan Jackson ...19 Jan. 56
Fra. Lynch Blosse ....11 Feb. 59
LIEUTENANTS.
Alfred Knox, *Act. Q.M.*...... 1 Jan. 55
Thomas Palmer........... 3 Mar. 55
Thomas Gibbons ....16 May 55
Robert Thompson..........25 Jan. 56
Edw. J. Bolingbroke .... 3 Apr. 56
Dominick O'Donnell .... do
ENSIGNS.
Henry Garvey ....14 Feb. 55
Rob. Acton ....16 Feb. 55
Peter Lynch ....14 Sept. 55
David R. Fair ....19 Feb. 56
Fred. Aug. Browne .... 3 Apr. 56
Edmond H. Jordan ....16 May 56
Paymaster.—StanhopeKenny23 Feb. 55
Adj. & Capt.—Edward Leet (1), *late Capt.* 20 F. .....30 July 55
Surg.—Wm. H. Franklin...18 July 55
Assist.Surg.—
White Facings.
Agents.—Sir E. R. Borough, Bt. Armit & Co.

SOUTH MAYO.
(*Rifles.*) [No. 15.]
Head Quarters, Westport.
HONORARY COLONEL.
George, *Marq. of* Sligo,DL.JP.
LIEUT.COLONEL COMMANDANT.
MAJOR.
Samuel Percy Lea, *Capt. Unatt.* ....17 Apr. 56
CAPTAINS.
Hon. D. Bingham...........26 Dec. 54
J. H. Browne...............27 Dec. 54
P. Francis Blake, *late Capt.* 12 F. ....25 Jan. 55
Roger Palmer, JP..............25 Jan. 55
Walter Butler, *Capt. Unatt.* 1 May 55
D. E. Browne...............28 April 56
LIEUTENANTS.
C. H. Bingham ....27 Dec. 55

Henry F. Farrell ....23 Jan. 55
George W. Dillon ....24 Jan. 55
Annesley Knox ....31 Oct. 55
Henry T. Cuff...............12 Dec. 55
Francis Rutledge .... 1 July 56
ENSIGNS.
Henry John Buchanan ......31 Aug. 55
Richard Browne ....22 Nov. 55
John Stanley C. Larminie ...27 Mar. 58
Captain and Adjutant.—Wm. D. Butcher, *lateCapt.*12 F.23 Nov. 54
Paymaster.—John D. Browne14 Jan. 52
Qr.Master.—Michael Dodd 28 May 56
Surgeon.—J. H. Burke........ 9 Nov. 54
Assist.Surgeon.—Gerald Molloy ....19 Feb. 55
Black Facings.
Agents, Messrs. Cane and Sons.

ROYAL MEATH.
[No. 119.]
Head Quarters, Trim.
HONORARY COLONEL.
Tho. *Marq. of* Headfort, KP.
LIEUT.COL. COMMANDANT.
Thomas E. Taylor, *late Capt.* 6 *Dr. Gds.*..............12 Dec. 46
MAJORS.
Sir John Dillon, Bt. *late Capt.* 32 F.................13 Nov. 54
Hon. H. Langford Rowley ... 11 July 59
CAPTAINS.
J. Nicholas Coddington...... ..15 Nov. 54
John Farrell ....16 Dec. 54
Robert Fowler ....16 Dec. 54
Hon. Charles Bourke ....19 Dec. 55
Jas. Sanderson Winter ......29 Mar. 56
Edward Rotheram .... 6 Sept. 58
LIEUTENANTS.
Richard Donaldson ....15 Nov. 46
William Johnston...........29 Nov. 46
Charles Bethune Ewart .....19 Dec. 55
Thos. Taylour Clare......... 8 May 56
Henry S. Johnston ....12 July 58
ENSIGNS.
John P. Kearney .... 2 Sept. 58
Francis Rothwell ....15 Jan. 59
Adj. & Capt. — James Hay, *late Capt.* 15 F..............19 Dec. 54
Paymaster.— Edw. Wm. Williams, *late Lt.* 3 Bengal Cavalry ....10 Aug. 55
Surgeon.—J. Josh. O'Reilly, MD. ....12 Dec. 46
Assist.Surg.—David Trotter 2 Sept. 58
Blue.
Agents, Messrs. Cane and Sons.

MONAGHAN.
[No. 121.]
Head Quarters, Monaghan.
HONORARY COLONEL.
Charles Powell Leslie .... 6 Aug. 57
LIEUT.COLONEL COMMANDANT.
Thomas Oriel Forster, *late Capt.* 77 F...............29 June 55
MAJORS.
Thomas Coote ....17 Sept. 57
Charles Woodwright (2), *late Capt.* 18 F. .... 20 July 59

CAPTAINS.
Edw. Wm. Bond .... 4 May 46
Ralph Forster ....23 Nov. 55
Michael Edward Lewis...... 7 Apr. 56
Andrew H. Fuller...........30 Dec. 56
John Leslie .... 3 July 57
Jesse Lloyd, *late Capt.* 47 F. 9 Jan. 58
LIEUTENANTS.
Mathew Bleakley..........12 May 46
Richard Coote ....21 Feb. 55
George Smyth ....21 Feb. 55
John Cranston Dawson .... 8 Aug. 57
Frith Thompson .... do
John Crozier .... 7 Sept. 58
ENSIGNS.
Matthew B. Naghten ....21 Jan. 58
Henry S. Bird .... 8 July 58
Adj. & Capt. — Hugh Aug. Crofton (1), *late Lt.* 10 F...23 Dec. 57
Paymaster.—RobertThomson13 Jan. 55
Qr.Mast.—Wm. Watson .. 5 Feb. 55
Surg.— Wm. Nassau Irwin, MD.................... 7 Oct. 56
Assist.Surg.—Wm. Temple... 7 Sept. 58
White Facings.
Agents, Sir E. R. Borough, Bt., Armit & Co.

QUEEN'S COUNTY.
(*Royal Rifles.*) [No. 104.]
Head Quarters, Maryborough.
HONORARY COLONEL.
Sir Charles Henry Coote, Bart. MP. JP. DL. ....20 Nov. 24
LIEUT.COLONEL COMMANDANT.
Francis Plunkett Dunne, KSB. JP. DL. *Col. Unatt.*........15 Feb. 46
MAJORS.
Henry Daniel Carden, JP.*late of* 52 F. ....12 Jan. 55
Chidley Downes Coote, *late of* 52 F..................23 July 55
CAPTAINS.
Charles Hartpole Bowen, JP. 3 Apr. 41
Robert White .... 2 Sept. 46
Harman Fitzmaurice ....22 Nov. 54
George Carey, *late Capt.* 77 F. 4 Dec. 54
Hon. Robert Flower ....15 July 59
Percy Raymond Grace, JP. ... do
LIEUTENANTS.
Walter Joseph Borrowes....... 8 Feb. 58
ENSIGNS.
Wm. Maunsell ....11 Jan. 56
Joseph A. Lucas............ 7 Mar. 57
Adj.&Cpt.—Robt.Carr Coote, *late of* 11 F............24 Jan. 54
Paymaster.—
Qr.Master.—Wm. Ryan ...... 3 Nov. 59
Surg.—Geo. Pilkington,MD. 24 Aug. 55
Assist.Surg.—E. Carmichael. 11 Oct. 55
Scarlet Facings.
Agents, Sir E. R. Borough, Bart., Armit and Co.

ROSCOMMON.
[No. 93.]
Head Quarters, Boyle.
COLONEL.
Fitzstephen French, MP. DL.23 Dec. 54
LIEUT.COLONEL COMMANDANT.
P John Caulfield(1), *late Bt. Maj.* 6 *Dr. Gds.*.......... 7 May 40

K K

Militia of Ireland.

MAJORS.
John D'Arcy ....20 Jan. 55
Owen R. Nathaniel Lloyd ..15 July 56

CAPTAINS.
Robert H. French..........15 Jan. 55
William Curtis ....15 Jan. 54
Robert Roper ....20 Jan. 55
John Georges, *late of Bengal Army* ....24 Mar. 55
William Duckworth ....15 July 56
John W. Flanagan ....18 Dec. 57
Henry Caulfield, *Bengal Army* 1 Feb. 58
Richard Irwin ....17 Apr. 58

LIEUTENANTS.
Thomas McNaughten ...... 1 Feb. 55
Henry Crofton Lloyd ......15 July 56
William M'Dermott ....22 Oct. 57
James Bond ....28 Oct. 57
Wm. Watson Hackett......28 Oct. 57
Owen Edward Lynch ...... 1 Feb. 58
Oliver Corr................17 Apr. 58
Luke Leonard ....29 Mar. 59

ENSIGNS.
Daniel Kelly ....22 Sept. 56
Charles Fred. Mulloy ...... 3 Dec. 57
Coote Molloy Chambers ...14 Dec. 57
Rutledge Irwin Peyton ....12 Apr. 58
James Crofton ....22 Apr. 58
Thomas Wm. French ....29 Mar. 59
Christopher F. M'Dermott .. 2 June 59
Alexander Gunning .... do
Paymaster.—Edmund Corr..22 Oct. 57
Adj. & Capt.—Art. French Lloyd, *late Lt. 52 F.*......24 Mar. 55
Qr.Mast. — James Hendley, *ate of* 88 F............. 5 Feb. 55
Surg.—James Roche Nagle,..23 Oct. 57
Assist.Surg. — Thomas W. Brennan, MD,.......... 1 June 59
Buff Facings.
Agents, Messrs. Cane & Sons.
English Agent, Edw. S. Codd, Esq.

SLIGO.
(*Rifles.*) [No. 124.]
Head Quarters, Sligo.

COLONEL.
Francis Arthur Knox Gore, *Lieut. of the County* ......27 Jan. 47

LIEUT.COLONEL.
Geo. Aug. J. M'Clintock, JP, *late Capt. 52 F.*..........15 Mar. 56

MAJOR.
John ffolliott, JP ....15 Mar. 56

CAPTAINS.
James Jones, JP ....17 Dec. 41
Fredric Edgar Knox ...... 6 May 48
James Wood, JP ....12 Sept. 48
Henry Bliss Crofton .....,24 Feb. 55
Lewis George Jones, JP ...17 Sept. 55
John Gethin ....15 Mar. 56

LIEUTENANTS.
Ormsby Jones, JP..........15 Jan. 55
James Fitzroy Knox ......15 Jan. 55
Robert Seymour Ormsby ...27 Feb. 55
Roger Dodwell Robinson... 5 Nov. 55
Wm. Andrew Baker.........29 July 58
Richard B. Knott ....18 July 59

ENSIGNS.
John E. Knox ....31 Mar. 56
Henry Williams .... do
Thomas Little Robinson...... 2 Aug. 58
George D. Ormsly.........12 Jan. 59
Paymaster — Albert Henry Knox .... 2 Feb. 55
Capt. & Adj.—Maxwell Du Pre Strong, *late Capt.* 52 F,21 July 55
Quarter Master.—Wm. Savage................... 2 Feb. 55
Surg.—John Fawcett .....18 Jan. 55
Assist.Surg.—Richard Wood Fawcett .... 3 Feb. 55
Black Facings.
Agents, Messrs. Cane & Sons.

THE DUKE OF CLARENCE'S MUNSTER ARTILLERY, OR 1ST, OR SOUTH TIPPERARY MILITIA.
[No. 27.]
[Embodied.]
Head Quarters, Gosport.

LIEUT.COLONEL COMMANDANT.
Richard, *Earl of Donoughmore*, DL, JP, *late of* 98 F.24 July 49

MAJORS.
Henry William Massy, JP....17 Jan. 56
Wills Crofts Gason ....26 July 58

CAPTAINS.
Richard Orlando Kellett...... 1 Feb. 55
Henry Sargint ....13 Feb. 55
Hugh Gough, *late Capt.* 1 Drs.13 Feb. 55
Henry Sheppard ....28 July 55
William Quin................28 July 55
Edmond Southwell Mulcahy, JP........................17 Jan. 56
Richard Pennefather Going .15 May 56
Wm. Fitzwilliam Smithwick.30 Dec. 58

LIEUTENANTS.
Henry Pedder ....28 July 55
Edwin Thomas, *Instructor of Musketry* ....28 July 55
Thomas Carroll Dempster ...17 Jan. 56
John Sadlier Brereton ....28 Dec. 58
Marshall Robert Clarke, *late of* 30 F..................30 Dec. 58
John Chaytor................ 3 May 59
Richard Butler ....18 July 59

SECOND LIEUTENANTS.
Thomas Brereton............27 Mar. 56
Edward Austin Kenny...... 8 Oct. 58
Robert Prendergast..........28 Dec. 58
John Cooke................... do
George Langley .... do
Richard Moore Sadlier,...... 3 Feb. 59
Nicholas Herbert .... 3 May 59
Ambrose Going ....18 July 59
Adj. & Capt.—Benj. Grey Mackenzie, *late Capt.* 59 F.18 Jan. 56
Paymaster. — John Craven Mansergh, JP..............28 Dec. 58
Qr.Master.—John Carr, *late of* 10 F..................13 Feb. 55
Surg.—James Dempster, M.D, *late of* 94 F. ....30 Sept. 47
Assist.Surg.—Joseph Butler, M.D................... 5 April 58
Scarlet Facings.
Agents, Sir E. R. Borough, *Bart*., Armit, and Co.

2ND, OR NORTH TIPPERARY.
(*Light Infantry.*) [No. 105.]
Head Quarters, Cashel.

COLONEL.
G. Ponsonby, *Visc*. Lismore, *Lieut. of the County, late Cor.* 17 Lancers............11 Jan. 55

LIEUT.COLONEL COMMANDANT.
Cornwallis, *Visc*. Hawarden, DL, JP, *late Capt.* 2 Life Gds...................17 Nov. 54

MAJOR.
George Frend, *late Brev.-Maj.* 26 F. ....25 Jan. 54

CAPTAINS.
Bassett Holmes, JP. ......29 Nov 54

Robert Bell ....17 Aug. 55
George Francis Stoney.....30 May 56
Thomas M'Craith ....30 May 56
Samuel William Perry .....27 July 57
Francis Robert O'Donnell .. 22 July 59
Denis Duan Purcell .... do
John Graham .... 1 Aug. 59

LIEUTENANTS.
James Delany ....27 Mar. 56
Ralph Hall Bunbury ....30 May 56
Robert Ely................. 8 July 56
Wm. Alex. Garrett .... 3 Sept. 57
Thomas Vernon Sadleir ...25 July 58
Daniel Falkiner.............. do
Henry Foster .... do
John Jos. Scully .... do

ENSIGNS.
Fred. E. Bryan .... 15 July 59
James W. Sadier .... do
Paymaster. — Joseph Robinson, *late Maj.* 60 F......14 Mar. 55
Adj.—Thomas Andrews, JP., *late Capt.* 26 F. ....12 May 56
Qr.Mast.—Richd. Acres, *late of* 60 F...............17 Feb. 55
Surg. — Robert Armstrong Bugnell ....13 Jan. 55
Assist.Surg.— J. A. P. Colles 23 Jan. 55
Dark Green Facings.
Agents, Messrs. Cane and Sons.

ROYAL TYRONE.
(*Fusiliers.*) [No. 80.]
Head Quarters, Omagh.

COLONEL.
LIEUT.COLONEL COMMANDANT.
James Matthew Stronge, JP, DL., *late of* 5th Dr. Guards 20 Oct. 54

MAJORS.
David Robert Ross, *late Capt.* 66 F................... 4 July 55
James Alfred Caulfield (1), *late Lt. & Capt. Coldst. Gds.*23 June 59

CAPTAINS.
Burleigh Stuart............ 1 May 46
Francis Ellis, JP........... 1 Nov. 54
Robert Sandys Lindesay, *late of* 30 F. ....19 Mar. 55
Claud Houston ....23 June 55
John Herbert Armstrong, *late Lieut.* 95 F..............17 July 55
Wm. Hamilton Irwin ...... 6 Mar. 56
Edward Chaloner Knox ...12 April 56
Edward R. F. Strong ......16 Oct. 57
Charles King Colhoun.........23 Dec. 58
Deane Mann .... 19 July 59

LIEUTENANTS.
William Moore .... 1 May 46
Richard White .... 1 Sept. 54
John Maxwell ....21 Feb. 55
Thomas Andrew Young .... 6 Mar. 56
Joshua Pym .... 4 April 56
Daniel Wilson ....10 Feb. 57
George Perry M'Clintock ..10 Feb. 57
Robt. Saunderson Hamilton .29 Apr. 59
Robert Wm. Scott......... 10 July 59
John B. M'Crea...........15 Sept. 59

ENSIGNS.
Gisborne Knox Horner ....17 Nov. 57
John Robert Baillie........15 Jan. 58
Walter J. F. Quin..........29 Apr. 59
Adj. & Capt.—Wm. Laudie 5 Mar. 46
Surg.—Richard Ridgway ..16 Feb. 55
Assist.Surg.—John Moore ..16 Feb. 55
Quart.Mast.—John Core ..17 Jan. 55
Paymaster—William Maxwell Carpendale...............26 Feb. 55
Blue Facings.
Agents, Messrs. Cane & Sons.

Militia of Ireland.

TYRONE ARTILLERY.
[No. 28.]
Head Quarters, Moy.
MAJOR.
Joseph Greer, DL. JP.......24 Apr. 56
CAPTAINS.
Ynyr Henry Burges............11 Mar. 59
LIEUTENANTS.
Frederick Sam. Rogers .... 4 July 58
SECOND LIEUTENANTS.

Adj. & Capt.—Jos. Stanley
Wright, late of Roy. Art...19 April 55
Surg.—Robt. Crothers, M.D. 5 June 55
Agents, Messrs. Cane and Sons.

WATERFORD ARTILLERY.
[No. 29.]
[Embodied.]
Head Quarters, Gosport.
COLONEL.
Right Hon. Lord Stuart de
Decies ....30 Dec. 39
LIEUT.COLONEL.
Wray Palliser.............12 Oct. 10
MAJOR.
Gerard Noel Bolton, late Lt.
10 Bombay N. I. ....17 July 58
CAPTAINS.
John Palliser.................20 Sept. 39
John Esmonde, MP........ 1 Nov. 54
Leopold Geo. Fredk. Keane,
late Ens. 52 F. ....17 Nov. 54
Henry Meagher ....14 Dec. 54
Nicholas F. Gyles ....23 Feb. 55
Edward Lymberry .... 2 Dec. 57
Thomas Edward Power, JP... 26 July 58
George Meara ....26 Jan. 59
LIEUTENANTS.
John Russell Mulcahey .... 1 Feb. 55
John Snow.................30 Sept. 57
William Power .... 5 Dec. 57
Thomas O'Grady Ussher....17 June 58
Wm. Henry Greer, Instructor
of Musketry .... 8 Sept. 58
Fra. Aug. Blake ....29 Mar. 59
William Briscoe ....14 Apr. 59
Crofton Bernard Uniacke ... 6 Aug. 59
SECOND LIEUTENANTS.
Robert Brewster Montford...28 Dec. 58
Richard Charles Clarke ...... 4 Mar. 59
Arthur Lynch .... 5 Apr. 59
Michael Louis Luther........ 5 May 59
Edward Nunn ....31 May 59
Francis James Baker ....30 June 59
Thomas Wm. Harrison ......15 Oct. 59
George Lennox Swale ....26 Oct. 59
Adj. & Capt.—J. Warren
Glubb, late Capt. 44 F....17 Nov. 54
Paymaster.—Richard Elliott,
late Maj. 2 W. I. Regt..... 3 Feb. 55
Qr. Master.—James Ward ...30 Sept. 57
Surg.—Wm. Holland Gore,
MD. ....24 Dec. 57
Assist. Surg.—Richard Henry
Rogers..................12 Nov. 57
Scarlet Facings.
Agents, Messrs. Cane and Sons.

WESTMEATH.
(Rifles.) [No. 114.]
Head Quarters, Castleton-Delvin.
COLONEL.
Fulke S. Greville, KP. late 1
Life Gds..................22 Aug. 50
LIEUT.COLONEL.
Earl of Granard, KP,........26 Dec. 55
MAJOR.
John James Nugent, late Capt.
3 Dr. Gds................26 Dec. 55
CAPTAINS.
Ralph Thos. A. Smyth....... 7 Apr. 54
Arthur D. Chaigneau ......13 Nov. 54
Richard J. Connolly........30 July 55
Arthur Upton .... 1 Dec. 55
Thos. James Smyth..........26 Dec. 55
Sydney N. David Smyth ....31 Jan. 57
LIEUTENANTS.
Henry Fetherstonhaugh ...30 July 55
Wm. Maxwell Smyth ......26 Oct. 55
Hugh Morrow ....10 Aug. 58
Arthur Gamble............. do
Alfred de Blaquiere ....23 Nov. 58
Wm. Fred. Ebbs .... 1 Feb. 59
ENSIGNS.
Crofton T. B. Vandeleur.... 3 Dec. 58
John McLoughlin .... 20 Apr. 59
Anthony Adams Reilly ...... 27 May 59
Paymst.—Willoughby Boyd 16 Nov. 11
Adj. & Capt.— John Ballard
Gardiner (1), late Capt.
17 F. ....20 May 56
Quart. Mast.—Edw. Morris 26 Oct. 55
Surg.—John Wm. Williams..30 Nov. 58
Assist. Surg.—

Black Facings.
Agents, Sir E. R. Borough, Bt., Armit
& Co.

WEXFORD.
[No. 99.]
Head Quarters, Wexford.
COLONEL.
Robert Shapland, Lord Carew 5 Apr. 47
LIEUT.COLONEL.
Hon. Shapland Francis
Carew, late Lt. 8 Hussars..16 Mar. 54
MAJOR.
Charles H. Cliffe, late Lt. 50
F. ....12 Dec. 54
CAPTAINS.
Geo. Pemberton Pigott ......30 May 42
Augustus Kennedy ....30 May 42
Harry Alcock, JP..........12 Oct. 49
Lord Henry Loftus ....24 Nov. 54
William H. Farmar ......12 Dec. 54
John Daly Devereux ...... 6 Nov. 57
Narcissus Edmund Huson.. 6 Nov. 57
Philip John Doyne, late Capt.
Turkish Contingent ....20 Sept. 58

LIEUTENANTS.
Beauchamp Henry Colclough,
Instructor of Musketry ..25 Dec. 54
John Thomas Beatty ......27 July 55
Benjamin E. Ogle.......... 1 Mar. 56
James Gavan............. 9 April 56
Crosby Wm. Harvey ...... 9 Dec. 57
James Esmonde ....29 Dec. 57
Thomas R. Burrowes ......11 Nov. 58
ENSIGNS.
Charles James Harvey......27 July 55
George G. Richards........21 Jan. 56
Robert Roche ....26 Mar. 56
Geo. P. Pigott ....30 Nov. 57
Robert Neilson Goodall ...... 2 Feb. 59
Joshua Barker .... 3 Feb. 59

Adj. & Capt.—Capt. David
Beatty, late Lt. 28 & 99 F. 27 Feb. 46
Paymaster. — 33 Simon Newport (1), DL. JP., late Capt.
30 F. ....18 Jan. 55
Quart. Mast.—Wm. O'Brien,
late of 13 F. .... 9 Jan. 55
Surg.—Richard H. Verling,
late Surg. 44 reg. .... 4 Dec. 54
Assist. Surg. — Solomon Richard Biggs, M.D..........31 Jan. 56

Yellow Facings.
Agents, Sir E. R. Borough, Bt., Armit & Co.

WICKLOW.
(Rifles.) [No. 92.]
Head Quarters, Wicklow.
COLONEL.
Sir Ralph Howard, Bart. DL.
JP. .... 1 Oct. 34
LIEUT.COLONEL. COMMANDANT.
Edward Symes Bayly, DL. JP.
late Capt. 34 Regt. .... 9 Aug. 54
MAJOR.
Robert A.G. Cunninghame, JP.19 Feb. 53
CAPTAINS.
William Blachford .... 7 Sept. 29
Richard Hudson Hoey, late
Capt. 89 F................10 Mar. 43
William Grogan .... 3 Jan. 55
Robert Truell .... 3 Jan. 55
LIEUTENANTS.
Richard B. Hudson.......... 3 Jan. 55
Edw. Albert Dennis..........28 Jan. 56
John Franks ....24 June 59
Wm. Fisher ....15 July 59
ENSIGNS.
Robert N. Goodall........... 4 Feb. 56
George Arthur Scott..........11 Sept. 57
Richard Reynell Drought.... 7 Dec. 58
John Henry Leonard........ 6 Oct. 59
Adj. & Paymaster. — John
Stanley Howard, (1) late
Capt. 44 F. ....15 Sept. 57
Surg.—Allen K. Boyce, M.D, 12 Apr. 56

Black Facings.
Agents, Messrs. Cane and Sons.

CHANNEL ISLANDS MILITIA.

ROYAL JERSEY.

Adj. General.
Col. John Halkett Le Couteur, Aide-de-Camp to the Queen.

Militia Aides-de-Camp to the Lieut. Governor.
Col. James Robin
Col. Clement Hemery
Lt.-Col. Jas. J. Hammond
— C. W. Le Geyt
Major Edw. Lerrier Godfray
Major James H. Robin

Inspector of Militia.
Lt.-Col. Phil. Helleur

Artillery.
Col. John Hammond
Lt.-Col. Philip Le Feuvre
Assist. Insp. & Adj.
Capt. Philip Sorel

1st, or North West Regiment.
Lt. Col. Philip Helleur
Assist. Insp. & Adj.,
Capt. James Gibaut

2nd, or North Regiment.
Col P. R. Lempriere
Lt. Col. Philip De Carteret
Assist. Insp. & Adj.,
Capt. P. J. De Carteret

3rd, or East Regiment.
Col. Francis LeBreton
Lt. Col. John Touzel
Assist. Insp. & Adj.,
Capt. F. C. Lane.

4th, or South Regiment.
St. Lawrence Battalion.
Col. E. G. Le Couteur

Lt.-Col. F. J. Le Couteur
Assist. Insp. & Adj.,
Capt. C. Nicolle

St. Helier Battalion.
Col. John Le Couteur
Lt. Col. Cle. Hemery
Assist. Insp. & Adj.,
Capt. H. Bailhache

5th, or South West Regiment.
Col. James Kennard Pipon
Lt.Col. Ed. Sullivan
Assist. Insp. & Adj.,
Capt. Joshua Brayn

ROYAL GUERNSEY.

Aide-de-Camp to the Queen.
Col. Jas. Priaulx
Chief Inspector of Militia.
Col. Edw. Jas. White

Militia Aides-de-Camp to the Governor.
Lt.Col. W. J. Broun
Lt.Col. Josh. Priaulx
Chief Medical Officer.
S. E. Hoskins, M.D.
Artillery Regiment.
Col. Henry Giffard
Assist. Insp., Major P. Le Lievre

1st, or East Regiment.
(Light Infantry.)
Lt.Col.Comm. Joseph Collings.
Assist. Insp., Major Tho. P. Naftel.

2nd, or North Regiment.
(Light Infantry.)
Col. James Ozanne
Assist. Insp., Capt. A. D. Bell

3rd, or South Regiment.
(Light Infantry.)
Lt.Col.Com. R. MacCulloch
Assist. Insp., Capt. Joshua Le Pelley

4th, or West Regiment.
(Light Infantry.)
Major Commandant, Abraham Simon
Assist. Insp., Major

ROYAL ALDERNEY.

Artillery.
Capt. Comm. T. N. Robilliard
Infantry.
Maj. Comm. T. N. Barbenson

ROYAL SARK.

Lt.Col. Comm. Wm. T. Collings

War Services of the Officers of the Militia.

Aberdeen.—1 Captain Dawes served with the 97th Regt. in the Trenches at the siege of Sebastopol from 20th Nov. 1854 to 16th July 1855; assisted as Captain in command of a party of the 97th to repel a sortie on our right attack on 15th April, present also with the Regt. in the advanced trenches right attack during the assault on the Redan on the 18th June (Medal and Clasp.)
2 Captain Bland served in the Mahratta war, including the captures of Nagpore and Asseerghur; commanded two Companies of the Royals at the taking of the Hill Forts in Candeish; received a contusion on the head from a matchlock-ball at Nullyghaum, and was severely wounded in the leg at Asseerghur (Medal).
3 Captain Farquhar joined Omer Pasha's army at Eupatoria in Feb. 1855 as Deputy Inspector General of Hospitals but performed the higher duties of Inspector General during the greater portion of the war, and was afterwards present at the siege and fall of Sebastopol (Medal and Clasp, Turkish War Medal, 4th Class of the Medjidie, and the Ifdahar of Tunis; he is also a Bey in the Egyptian Army).

Anglesey.—1 Captain Pearse served with the Baltic Expedition of 1855 as Lieut. R. M. Artillery; was present in command of Artillery at the capture and destruction of the enemy's shipping at Koporia Bight and at the cutting out of 16 Russian Vessels in Verta Neva Bay. He afterwards served with the Turkish Contingent at Kertch as a Captain of Artillery from Nov. 1855 until that force was disbanded in June 1856, doing the duty of Adjutant to the Field Batteries. He has received the Baltic Medal, and 5th Class of the Medjidie.

Antrim.—1 Major Mackenzie served the Kaffir campaign of 1851-52, as Captain 2nd Batt. 60th Rifles (Medal), and was present at the forcing the passage of the Kei with Colonel Eyre's Division.

Argyll.—1 Lt.Colonel Fergusson was 24 years in the Bengal Cavalry: he served the Punjaub campaign of 1848-49, including the actions of Chillianwallah and Goojerat,—as Brigade Major of Cavalry at the former, and as Assistant Adjutant General to the 2nd Division of Infantry at the latter; he also acted as Deputy Adjutant General to the force detached under Sir Walter Gilbert in pursuit of the Sikhs and Affghans towards Peshawur (Medal and two Clasps, and Brevet Major).

Ayr.—1 Sir James Fergusson served with the Grenadier Guards the Eastern campaign of 1854 and up to 4th May 1855, including the battles of Alma and Inkerman (wounded), and siege of Sebastopol (Medal and Clasps).

Bedford.—1 Captain Toseland served with the 33rd Regt. at the siege and fall of Sebastopol from 19th Dec. 1854, including assaults of the Redan on the 18th June and 8th Sept. (Medal and Clasp.)

Brecknock.—1 Major Dickinson served with the Queen's Royals throughout the campaign of 1838-39 in Affghanistan and Beloochistan, and was present at the assault and capture of the fortresses of Ghuznee (Medal), and Khelat (leg broken by a musket shot).

Bucks.—1 Captain Hewett served the campaign on the Sutlej (Medal), including the battles of Ferozeshah (wounded) and Sobraon.
2 Captain Lane served with the 49th Regt. on the China expedition (Medal), and was present with the regiment at the attack and capture of Amoy, Chusan (2nd operation), Chinhae, and Ningpo; and he acted as Aide de Camp to Colonel Morris, who commanded the Brigade at Segoan, where he was dangerously wounded, and had his left arm amputated on the field. In 1846 he had the command of two companies of Infantry and a troop of Cavalry at Dungarvon during the riots, on which occasion he received the thanks of the Major General of the district, and also of the Commander in Chief in Ireland.

Cambridge.—1 Captain Bendyshe served with the 10th Regt. during the Sutlej campaign of 1845-6, and was present at the battle of Sobraon (Medal).

Carnarvon.—1 Lt.Colonel Mac Donald served with the 93rd Regt. during the campaigns of 1811 and 12, against the Caffres on the frontier of the Cape of Good Hope. Also the campaign of 1814 in Louisiana, and battle before New Orleans on the 8th Jan. 1815,—severely wounded in the head and leg.

Cavan.—1 Qr.Master Duff served with the 66th Regt. in suppressing the rebellion in Canada in 1837-38, and was present in the affairs at St. Denis and St. Charles.

Cheshire.—1 Capt. Poppleton served in the Field Train of the Ordnance, with the Division of the Army operating on the Eastern coast of Spain, in 1813-14. From Taragone he went to Genoa, and served two years in Italy and Sicily, and was present at the capture of Gaeta in 1815.
2 Captain Daniell served with the 49th Regt. in China (Medal),—at Amoy, Chusan, Chinhae, Ningpo, Segoan, Chapoo, Woosung, Chin Kiang Foo, and Nankin.
3 Captain Smyth served with the 17th Regt. in the Crimea from Dec. 1854, including the siege and fall of Sebastopol, and assault of the Redan on the 18th June and 8th Sept.; was also at the bombardment and surrender of Kinbourn (Medal and Clasp).

Clare.—1 Lieut. FitzGerald served as a Lieut. in Catty's Rifles and in the Hottentot Levies during the greater part of the Kaffir war of 1851-53, and was present at the operations in the Waterkloof and the Amatolas under Sir Harry Smith (Medal).

Cork.—4 Captain Tuckey served with the 41st throughout the campaign of 1842 in Affghanistan (Medal), and was present in the engagement with the enemy on the 28th April in the Pisheen Valley; in those of the 29th May near Candahar, 30th Aug. at Goaine, 5th Sept. before Ghuznee; at the occupation and destruction of that fortress and of Cabool, the expedition into Kohlstan, storm, capture and destruction of Istaliff, and the various minor affairs in and between the Bolan and the Khyber Passes.

War Services of the Officers of the Militia.

Cornwall.—2 Captain Alms served the campaign of 1843 in Scinde, under Sir Charles Napier, and was present with the expedition to Imaumghur, and battles of Meeanee and Hyderabad (Medal).

3 Capt. Trist served with the China expedition in 1842-43.

Cumberland.—1 Colonel the Hon. H. C. Lowther served in the 7th Hussars in the campaign of 1808-9 in Spain under Sir John Moore, and was present at the engagements of Mayorga, Sahagun, and Benevente, and in the retreat to Corunna. He served afterwards in the campaigns with the Duke of Wellington's army, from 1812 to the end of that war in 1814, and was at the investment of Pampeluna, and in several cavalry rencontres in the Pyrenees and South of France; also at the battles of Orthes and Toulouse. In 1815 he served in the 10th Hussars in the campaign of that year, and at the capture of Paris. Has received the Silver War Medal with three Clasps.

Denbigh.—1 Captain Griffith served with the 23rd Fusiliers at the siege and fall of Sebastopol in 1855, and at the assault of the Redan on the 8th Sept. (Medal and Clasp).

Derby.—1 Lieut.Col. Coke has received the Medal for Ava.

2 Major Mosley served with the 60th Rifles in Kaffirland in 1851-52, and was present in the operations in the Waterkloof in October, and passage of the Kei with Colonel Eyre's column on the 4th Dec. 1851 (Medal).

3 Captain Newdigate served as a Lieut. in the Native Levies at the Cape of Good Hope in 1851, and was present at the capture of Fort Armstrong.

Devon.—1 Lt.Colonel Ferguson Davie served with the Grenadier Guards at the siege and fall of Sebastopol from 29th Aug. 1855 (Medal and Clasp).

2 Major Rattray served with the 13th Light Infantry throughout the campaigns in Affghanistan of 1838 and 1842, and was present at the storm and capture of Ghuznee (Medal), assault and capture of the town and forts of Tootumdurrah, storm of Jhoolghur, night-attack at Baboo Khoosh Ghur, destruction of Khurdurrah, assault of Terwandurrah, storming of the Khoord Cabul Pass, affair of Tezeen, forcing the Jugdulluk Pass, reduction of the fort of Mamoo Khail, heroic defence of Jellalabad, and sorties on the 14th Nov. and 1st Dec. 1841, 11th March, 24th March, and 1st April 1842; general action and defeat of Akbar Khan before Jellalabad, 7th April 1842 (Medal), storming the heights of Jugdulluck, general action of Tezeen and recapture of Cabul (Medal). Was severely wounded whilst skirmishing on the Jugdulluck heights 29th Oct. 1841.

3 Captain Holman served in the Peninsula from Nov. 1811, attached to the Portuguese service, and was present with Lord Hill's corps covering the siege of Badajoz, advance on Llerena, siege and storm of the three fortified convents of Salamanca,—led the storming party to the gate of San Vincente at its capture, battle of Salamanca,—slightly wounded by a musket-shot in the leg; siege of Burgos, and storming the works and the White Church; several skirmishes on the retreat from thence near Torrequemada, and blowing up the bridge of Duenas; battles of the Pyrenees on the 28th, 29th, and 30th July; night-attack and defeat of a French battalion on the heights of Urdax, action near Zugarrimundi,—severe contused wound; battles of the Nivelle and the Nive, actions at Ustaritz and Villa Franque, battles of St. Pierre and Orthes, actions at Aire, Vic Bigorre, and Tarbes, and battle of Toulouse. Served the campaign of 1815, including the battle of Waterloo; also with the Army of Occupation in France. He has received the War Medal with six Clasps.

4 Lieut. Macdonald was engaged with the 1st Royals at the affairs of St. Charles and St. Eustache, and in disarming the rebels at Grand Brulé, during the Rebellion in Canada in 1837-38.

5 Captain Fisk served as Adjutant of the 17th Light Dragoons during the campaign of 1820 in Kutch.

6 Surgeon Sandford served in the Baltic Fleet and was at the capture of Bomarsund (Medal).

Donegal.—1 Major Todd served with the 40th Regt. throughout the operation in Candahar and Affghanistan in 1841-42 (Medal), also present in the action at Maharajpore 20th Dec. 1843 (Medal).

Dorset.—1 Colonel Bingham served 24 years in the Indian Army, and was with his Regiment in the Burmese war of 1824-5-6, for which he has the War Medal with one Clasp.

3 LieutCol. Loftus served in the Peninsula with the 3rd Foot Guards in 1809-10-11 and 12, and has received the War Medal with two Clasps for the battle of Busaco and siege of Ciudad Rodrigo.

4 Captain Littlehales served in the Kaffir war of 1846-47 (Medal).

Down.—1 Captain Peard served with the 20th Regt. the Eastern campaign of 1854, including the battles of Alma, Balaklava, and Inkerman, and siege of Sebastopol (Medal and Clasps).

2 Major Browne served at the defence of Cadiz in 1812; campaign of 1814 on the Canadian Frontier; with the Army of Occupation in France from 1815 to 1818. Has been instrumental on various occasions in saving the lives of 137 persons from shipwreck, for which he has been awarded the Gold and Silver Medals of the Royal Shipwreck Institution.

Dublin.—4 Captain Russell was a Captain in the 98th Regt. with the expedition to the North of China (Medal) in 1842, and was present at the storming of the city of Chin Kiang Foo, as also at the attack and capture of the Tartar entrenched camps on the heights outside the city; and he was also at the landing before Nankin.

Durham.—1 Lt.Col. Hall served as Staff Officer with the Madras Artillery, in the Light Field Force in the Southern Mahratta Country in 1841, and was present at the taking of the Fort of Nepaunee; served also with Lord Gough's expedition to China, commanding Troop of Horse Artillery (Medal, and Brevet Major). Joined Lord Raglan's force on 14th Nov. 1854, and served as an Assistant Engineer until after the storming of the Redan on the 18th June, on which day he was employed in the advanced parallel. Transferred to the Turkish Contingent with rank of Lt.Colonel, and succeeded to the command of the Field Artillery as Brigadier, which appointment he held until the peace (Medal with Clasp for Sebastopol, and 3rd Class of the Medjidie).

War Services of the Officers of the Militia. 650

2 Major Cookson served the Sutlej campaign of 1845-6 with the 80th Regt., and was present in the battles of Moodkee, Ferozeshah, and Sobraon (wounded), and has a Medal and two Clasps.

3 Capt. Scarman carried the colours of the 39th Regt. in the action of Maharajpore, and was wounded in the left leg by a grape-shot; shortly after which he received a severe wound in the left arm.

4 Surgeon Nixon served in the Peninsula with the Coldstream Guards, and has received the War Medal with two Clasps for the battles of Fuentes d'Onor and Salamanca.

Edinburgh.—1 Colonel Geddes served the Nepaul campaign of 1815-16, including the turning of the Cherich Ghat, surprise of Etounda, and surrender of Muckwanpore (Medal). Pindaree campaign of 1817-18. Action at Punniar, 29th Dec. 1843 (Medal and Brevet Lieut.Col.). In command of the Artillery for the suppression of the Belooch Robber Tribes, Jan. 1845. Served the Sutlej campaign of 1845-46; commanded the Horse Artillery at the battle of Moodkee; commanded two troops H. A. at Ferozeshah; commanded the Rocket Battery at Sobraon (Medal and Clasps, and C.B.).

2 Captain Boulton served at the siege of Sebastopol from March to July 1855 (Medal and Clasp).

Essex.—1 Major Jodrell served in the 18th Royal Irish through the whole of the operations in China (Medal), and was wounded at Chapoo.

2 Captain Edenborough served as a volunteer in New Zealand during the operations in 1845, and was present in several of the skirmishes; he also volunteered his services in the Mounted Police in New South Wales on several occasions, and was once slightly wounded.

3 Major Wilkinson served with the 68th Lt. Inf. throughout the Eastern campaign of 1854-55, including the battle of Alma, siege and fall of Sebastopol (Medal and Clasps).

Fermanagh.—1 Captain A. Nixon joined the 27th Regiment in the Peninsula, and was present at the battles of Vittoria, Pyrenees, Nivelle, Nive, Orthes (severely wounded) and Toulouse, siege of San Sebastian, and various minor affairs (War Medal and seven Clasps). Served in the American war in 1814-15, including the action at Platsburg; and was afterwards with the Army of Occupation in France after the Capitulation of Paris until 1818.

Fife.—1 Captain Maconochie-Welwood served under General Pollock in the campaign of 1842. Served in the Punjaub campaign of 1848-49, and was present during the whole siege operations leading to the storm of the town and surrender of the Fort of Mooltan; commanded a squadron of the 2nd Bengal Light Cavalry at the battle of Surujcoond, when on the 7th Nov. the Cavalry Brigade charged and took an entrenched battery, capturing the guns; afterwards proceeded in command of the detachment, including the siege guns, which were ordered to the Fort of Cheniote; was thanked in Division Orders for the expeditious way the party was brought up by forced marches, and was present at the surrender of the fort to General Whish (Medal and Clasp).

Flint.—1 Captain Mathias served with the 2nd Regt. in the Kaffir war of 1851-52 (Medal), and with the expedition north of the Orange River in 1852-53.

Galloway.—1 Captain Hon. C. M. H. Forbes served with the 95th Regt. at the siege and fall of Sebastopol from 30th May 1855 (Medal and Clasp).

Glamorgan.—1 Lieut.Colonel Morgan served in the Peninsula from Oct. 1813 to the end of that war, in the Racket Troop Royal Horse Artillery, and was at the passage of the Adour, investment of Bayonne, and battle of Toulouse (Medal); after which he embarked at Bourdeaux with the army for North America, serving on the Niagara frontier until the peace.

2 Captain Hickson served with the 73rd Regt. in the Kaffir war of 1850-53 (Medal).

3 Lieut. Tynte served in H. M. S. *Wellington* as Midshipman in the Baltic, and was present at the bombardment of Sweaborg (Medal).

Gloucester.—1 Captain Jones served as Assist.Quartermaster General of the Assam Field Force during the whole of the first Burmese war, and has received a Medal and two clasps for Ava and Assam. He is a F.R.A.S.

Hants.—1 Lieut.Col. Burnaby served the campaign of 1815, and was present at the battle of Waterloo.

2 Colonel Shaw served in the Peninsula with the Royal Artillery; joined the Army there on the retreat from Burgos, and was attached to the 18-pounder Brigade, or Battering Train. After the battle of Vittoria, formed a park of 172 pieces of artillery, captured in that action, Served during the whole of the Siege of St. Sebastian; was engaged at the crossing of the Bidassoa, the Nive, and the Adour. He served afterwards on the Niagara frontier during the American war; has received the War Medal, with two Clasps, for St. Sebastian and the Nive. In 1835 he joined the British Auxiliary Legion of Spain as Lieut.Colonel of Artillery; proceeded with the first battery to Vittoria, and was in the affair of Artaban; marched the artillery back to St. Ander, and at St. Sebastian was engaged in covering the passage of the troops across the Uremea on 28 May, 1836, when he got the decoration of 1st class of San Fernando; was also in the affairs of 1st, 4th, and 6th June following; also in the engagements on 1st Oct. following, when the Carlists attacked the lines around St. Sebastian, and were repulsed with great loss. In Nov. he took the chief command of the artillery of the Legion, and commanded it in the engagements from the 10th to the 15th March, 1837, when the strongly-fortified hill of Oramendi was taken by assault. On the 16th, when the left wing was driven in, covered the retreat of the remainder for about one mile, when the original position was taken up, for which service he was promoted to the rank of Colonel. In May following, was engaged on the 4th in covering the construction of a Pontoon bridge for the advance of the Spanish troops to take up a new position; on the 5th, with a strong redoubt occupied by the enemy; on the 6th, repulsed four vigorous attacks made for the purpose of capturing the guns of the Legion; on the 13th, was at the capture of Hernani; and on the 16th and 17th, directed the artillery in the capture of the Fort del Parque, and the strongly-fortified town of Yrun, which caused the capitulation of the important city of Fuente Arabia, and opened the communication between St. Sebastian

War Services of the Officers of the Militia.

and France: on this occasion he received a Gold Medal, and the decoration of the Laurelled, or 2nd Class of St. Fernando. On the 29th, same month, the Artillery was employed at Andoian to protect the advance of a Spanish Division, under General Espartero. Was frequently engaged in minor affairs, and occasionally acted as Engineer in the construction of the works thrown up for the defence of St. Sebastian.

3 Lieut.Colonel Stretton served the campaigns of 1812-13 in the Peninsula, with the 68th Light Infantry, and was severely wounded at the battle of Vittoria by two gun-shots lodged in the body, one of which has not been extracted. He has received the Silver War Medal with one Clasp for Vittoria.

4 Captain Breton served with the 38th Regt. in the Crimea from 13th Jan. 1855, including the siege and fall of Sebastopol (Medal and Clasp).

5 Captain Bathurst served with the 23rd Fusiliers in the Eastern campaign of 1854, and was severely wounded at the battle of Alma (Medal and Clasp).

Hertford.—1 Captain James served with the 24th Regiment, and was actively employed in Canada during the Rebellion in 1838-39.

Huntingdon.—1 Lieut. Rooper served with the 38th Regt. in the Crimea from 23rd Aug. 1855 (Medal and Clasp for Sebastopol).

Kerry.—2 Capt. O'Connell served with the 73rd in Canada during the Rebellion in 1838-39; at the siege of Monte Video from Sept. 1845 to Aug. 1846; and in the Kaffir war of 1846-47 (Medal).

3 Captain Spring served in the 24th Regt. in Canada during the Rebellion in 1838-39.

4 Doctor Maybury served with the late British Auxiliary Legion in Spain from July 1835 to Sept., 1837, first as Assist.Surgeon, and afterwards as Surgeon, of the 10th Munster Light Infantry; received two Medals, one for the 5th May 1836, and the other for the storming of Irun in June, 1837; was mentioned in General Orders for gallant conduct in dressing the wounded under the hottest fire in the actions of the 15th and 16th March 1837.

Kildare.—1 Captain Kennedy served with the 77th Regt. the Eastern campaign of 1854, and up to the 13th Jan. 1855, including the battles of Alma and Inkerman, and siege of Sebastopol (Medal and three Clasps).

King's County.—1 Major Bruce served in the 18th Royal Irish throughout the war in China of 1841, and was present at the storming and capture of Amoy, Woosung, Chappoo, Chin-Kiang-Foo, and operations before Nankin; likewise at the capture of the Bogue Forts, Boca Tigris, and barrier forts on the Canton river in 1847 (Medal). Served throughout the war in Burmah, and was present at the storm and capture of Martaban (as Major of Brigade), storming and capture of Rangoon (wounded). Served as Assistant Adjutant General of Division to the termination of the war, and present at the capture of Prome, and repulse of the enemy from that position; capture of the enemy's forts in the neighbourhood of Prome; occupation of Mecaday, storm and capture of the enemy's stockades in the vicinity of Donabew. Promoted to rank of Major for service in Burmah.

Lanark.—1 Captain Gill served in the Kaffir war of 1850-53 (Medal), and sustained an attack of the enemy at Fort Brown on the 9th April 1851, for which he was thanked in General Orders, and appointed Captain Commandant of the Fort; he also had a horse shot under him when carrying dispatches through the Ecca Pass, and out of his party of ten, three men were killed and five wounded.

2 Captain Park served with the 26th Regt. on the China expedition (Medal), and was present at Amoy, Golongso, Ningpo (defence of), Tscke, Chapoo, Woosung, Shanghae, Chinkiangfoo, and Nankin.

3 Captain Scott served in Ava during the campaigns of 1824-25; was badly wounded during the attack on Rangoon, and afterwards engaged at the taking of Tantabein and Donabew (Medal).

Lancashire.—1 Major Wardlaw served ten years in the Bengal Army, and was present at the battles of Moodkee, Ferozeshah, and Aliwal, and affair of Buddiwal (Medal and two Clasps).

4 Captain Williams served in the Punjaub campaign of 1848-49 (Medal).

6 Captain Fenton served with the 53rd Regt. in the Sutlej campaign in 1845-6, and was present at the affair of Buddiwal, and in the battles of Aliwal and Sobraon (Medal and one Clasp).

8 Captain Whittle served at the Cape of Good Hope with the 91st Regt., and was present under Sir Harry Smith at the attack and defeat of the emigrant Boers, on the 29th August 1848.

9 Major Phibbs served five years in India with the 48th Regt., including the campaign against the Rajah of Coorg in April 1834.

10 Major Chambre served in the 23rd Dragoons with the Army of Occupation in France; and in the 11th Dragoons, and on the Staff in India.

11 Major Dickson served with the 10th Regt. in Spain, from early in 1813 until the end of the war; was present at the attack of the pass Col de Balaguer, second siege of Tarragona, attack of the pass of Ordal, under Lord Wm. Bentinck, and the blockade of Barcelona. Proceeded to India in 1818, and served in the 41st throughout the Burmese war of 1824-26 (Medal), and was present in most of the actions in which the regt. was engaged. Was at the siege of Collapore in 1817. Also in Scinde and Affghanistan from Nov. 1840 to Feb. 1843 (Medal), and was with the force under General Nott during its march from Candahar, Ghuzneé, Cabul, Jellalabad, and Khyber Pass, to Ferozepore, in 1842-43.

12 Captain Versturme served in the 1st Hussars King's German Legion the campaigns of 1813, 14, and 15, in the Netherlands, France, and Germany, including the battle of Waterloo and capture of Paris.

13 Captain Hartshorn served with the 24th Regt. in Canada, during the rebellion of 1837-38, and was present at the bombardment of Navy Island; also the Punjaub campaign of 1848-49, as

War Services of the Officers of the Militia. 652

Adjutant of the 24th, including the passage of the Chenab, action of Sadoolapore, and battles of Chillianwallah (wounded), and Goojerat (Medal and Clasps).

14 Lt.Col. Mathias served in the Sutlej campaign of 1845-46 (Medal and one Clasp); commanded a strong detachment of H. M. Troops at the affair of Buddiwal; was in command at the battle of Aliwal, where he had charge of the howitzers (named in the Dispatches, and made Brevet Major); and commanded the Grenadier Company 62nd Regt. at the battle of Sobraon (wounded).

15 Captain Elgee served in the 50th Regt. the Sutlej campaign of 1845-46, including the battles of Moodkee, Ferozeshah, Aliwal (wounded), and Sobraon (Medal and three Clasps).

16 Lieut. Brophey served the Eastern campaign of 1854-55 in the 63rd Regt., including the battles of Alma (severely wounded), Balaklava, and Inkerman, and siege of Sebastopol (Medal and Clasps); he has the Medal for gallant conduct in the field, having distinguished himself while in charge of the colours, and also the French War Medal.

17 Captain Robinson served with the 4th Regt. the Eastern campaign of 1854 and up to 24th May 1855, including the battles of Alma and Inkerman and siege of Sebastopol (Medal and three Clasps).

Leitrim.—Major Hon. W. J. Forbes served with the Grenadier Guards in the Crimea from 20th Dec. 1854 and has the Medal with Clasp for Sebastopol.

Lincoln.—2 Captain Telford served in the Peninsula from March 1812 to the end of the war, including the battle of Salamanca, retreat from Burgos, action of Villa Muriel, affair at Osma, battle of Vittoria, carrying the outworks of San Sebastian 17th July, and first assault on the body of the fortress 25th July; also second assault and capture 31st Aug. 1813; battles of the Nivelle 10th Nov., and Nive 9th, 10th, and 11th Dec. 1813. Served subsequently in the American war. He has the War Medal with five Clasps for Salamanca, Vittoria, St. Sebastian, Nivelle, and Nive.

3 Captain Mulhall served twenty-seven years in the 17th Regt., and was present with it in the first Affghan campaign in 1839, including the capture of the fortresses of Ghuznee (Medal), and Khelat.

4 Captain Bowman served in the Commissariat Department in the Peninsula and south of France in 1812-13-14; and subsequently in the American war, and was present at New Orleans and Fort Bowyer in 1815; also in Belgium and France with the Army of Occupation in 1815-16.

Limerick.—1 Captain Low served with the 53rd Regt. in the campaign on the Sutlej in 1846, including the battles of Aliwal and Sobraon (Medal and Clasp).

2 Qr.Master Neary served the Eastern campaign of 1854-55, including the battles of Alma, Balaklava, and Inkerman (Medal and Clasps).

4 Lord Clare served on the Staff in the Peninsula, and was present at the battle of Busaco (Medal and Clasp).

5 Captain Watson served with the 27th in the Kaffir War (Medal).

London.—2 Captain Hobson served with the 72nd Bengal N.I. throughout the 1st and 2nd siege operations before Mooltan in 1848-49, including the storm and capture of the city and surrender of the fortress and garrison, affair of the 9th Sept., assault of the Suburbs on 27th Dec. 1848; also present at the surrender of the fort and garrison of Cheniote, and at the battle of Goojerat (Medal and two Clasps).

Longford.—1 Colonel White served in the Peninsula with the 14th Light Dragoons, and has received the War Medal with two Clasps for Badajoz and Salamanca.

2 Lieut. Gore served as a Lieutenant in the 7th Hussars in the Indian Campaign in 1858, including the affair of Meangunge, siege and capture of Lucknow, as orderly officer to Brigadier C. Hagart, also present at the operations across the Goomtee, attack on fort Ruyaghur, action of Allygunge, capture of Bareilly, relief of Shahjehanpore (Medal and Clasp).

Louth.—1 Captain Chaplin served with the 49th Regt. in the Crimea from 15th June to 8th Aug. 1855, including the siege of Sebastopol and assault of the Redan on the 18th June (Medal and Clasp).

Mayo.—1 Captain Leet served in the Eastern campaign of 1854 in the 20th Regt., including the battle of Alma (Medal and Clasp).

Merioneth.—1 Lieut.Col. Morgan embarked with the 7th Fusiliers for Portugal, in March 1810, and was present at the battles of Talavera, Busaco, and Albuhera, where he was severely wounded in the knee, and disabled for nearly twelve months. In April 1813 he rejoined the regiment in the Peninsula, and was present at the battles of Vittoria, the Pyrenees, Nivelle, Nive, Orthes, and Toulouse; after which he accompanied the Fusiliers to America, and was present at the attack on New Orleans, in January 1815. He has received the War Medal with eight Clasps.

Middlesex.—1 Major Kirby served for 23 years in the Madras Army, ten of which on the Regimental Staff, and seven in political employment in the Mysore Commission. Was present in the Goomsoor campaign of 1836, where a chief was taken prisoner by him, and his company (the light) took many prisoners and arms. He held command of four companies at the advance post of Durgapersaud, for a short time. Served in the China expedition (Medal), and was present at the storming of Chin Kiang Foo, and at the investment of Nankin.

2 Captain Mangles served with the 50th Regt. in the Eastern campaign of 1854, including the battles of Alma and Inkerman, and siege of Sebastopol (Medal and Clasps).

Monaghan.—1 Captain Crofton served with the 6th Regt. during the Kaffir war in 1850-51, and was engaged with the Kaffirs in the Bomah Pass in the Amatola Mountains on the 24th Dec. 1850 on which occasion his horse was shot under him; was also present in the combined attack on the Amatolas on the 28th June 1851 (Medal).

2 Major Woodwright served with the 18th Royal Irish throughout the war in China (Medal) and was present at the taking of Amoy, Chapoo, Shanghai, and Chinkiangfoo. He also served with the 18th in the Burmah war of 1852-53 to the conclusion (Medal) and was present at the naval action and destruction of the enemy's stockades on the Rangoon river, landed in command

L L

of a company of the Royal Irish and with the Marines of the *Fox* frigate stormed and destroyed the Dalla stockades; served during the three succeeding days' operations in the vicinity and at the storm and capture of Rangoon, and on the 14th April was with the storming party at the Great Dagon Pagoda, also present at the capture of Prome and repulse of the night attack on the heights of Prome in Jan. 1853; commanded a company of the 18th during the whole of the successful operations in the Donubew district including the 17th March 1853 (wounded) when the 18th stormed and carried the first stockade, also the 19th March when the stronghold of the Burmese Chief Mea Toon was stormed and after considerable loss captured.

Montgomery.—1 Lt.Col. Pryce served with the 2nd Queen's Royals in the campaign in the Southern Mahratta Country and the Concan in 1844-45, and was in the storming party at the capture of the Fortress of Panulla; and commanded an outpost at the capture of Munohur and Munsuntosh.

2 Major Beadnell served the campaign of 1840-41-42, and was present in the actions of Killa Azider, Goaine, Ghuznee, occupation of Cabool, and all the affairs in which the Candahar Division under General Nott was engaged in its progress through the Khoord Cabool, Tezeen, Jugdulluck, and Khybcr Passes (Medal).

Norfolk.—1 Captain Hon. Fred. Walpole was engaged in the operations in China (Medal), while serving as Flag Lieutenant to the Naval Commander in Chief, Sir G. H. Seymour.

2 Captain Hon. R. Harbord served with the 71st Highlanders in the Crimea from 20 Dec. 1854 to Feb. 1855, and has the Medal and Clasp for Sebastopol.

Northumberland.—1 Captain Galton served the Eastern campaign of 1854-55 with the 50th Regt., including the battles of Alma and Inkerman, and siege of Sebastopol (Medal and three Clasps).

2 Captain Aylmer served with the 97th Regt. at the siege of Sebastopol from 20th Nov. 1854 (Medal and Clasp, and 5th Class of the Medjidie).

Nottingham.—1 Captain Girardot commanded a detachment on board the *Birkenhead*, when wrecked off Danger Point, Cape of Good Hope, on the night of the 26th Feb. 1852. He served with the 43rd in the Kaffir war of 1852-53 (Medal).

2 Major Wrixon served in Spain from April 1812 to the end of the campaign, including the first siege of Tarragona, retreat therefrom, actions before Alcoy, battle of Castalla, second siege of Tarragona, action at Ordal, investment of Barcelona, besides various other affairs. Served also at the siege and capture of Genoa, and with the expedition to Naples.

Perth.—1 Captain Riddell served with the 7th Dragoon Guards in the Kaffir war of 1846-47 (Medal).

Roscommon.—1 Lieut.Colonel Caulfield served as a Lieut. in the 4th Regt. from 1809 to 1813, in the Mediterranean and on the coast of Africa, and in the Peninsular war; was present in the advance to Madrid, battle of Salamanca, siege of Burgos, and several affairs on the retreat from Burgos. He has received the War Medal with one Clasp.

Ross.—1 Colonel Fraser served in the Peninsula as a Captain in the Coldstream Guards, and was wounded at the attack on Burgos: right leg amputated. He has received the War Medal with one Clasp for Salamanca.

Shropshire.—2 Captain Russell served in the Royal Navy, and was on board H. M. S. *Albion*, with Admiral Sir F. A. Ommanney, at Navarino (Medal).

Somerset.—1 Lieut.Col. Luttrell served with the Grenadier Guards in the Peninsula, and has received the War Medal with two Clasps for the battles of the Nivelle and Nive. He served also the campaign of 1815, and was present at the battle of Waterloo.

Stirling.—1 Captain S. Kenny served in the Caffre war of 1851-52 and 53 (Medal).

Suffolk.—1 Colonel Bence served the campaigns of 1809-10-11, in the Peninsula, with the 16th Light Dragoons, and was in fourteen actions, including Oporto, Talavera (wounded), passage of the Coa, and Busaco. Has received the War Medal with two Clasps for Talavera and Busaco.

2 Major Parker served seventeen years with the Army of India, and was present at the siege and capture of Bhurtpore and its dependencies in 1825-26 (Medal).

Surrey.—1 Lieut.Colonel Parratt served at Walcheren in 1809; and in the Peninsula from 1811 to the end of that war in 1814, including the defence of Cadiz, siege of San Sebastian, battles of Nivelle and Nive, actions at Vic Bigorre and Tarbes, and battles of Orthes and Toulouse. He has received the War Medal with five Clasps.

2 Captain Barnes served with the troops under General England in Southern Affghanistan. Accompanied Colonel Wymer's expedition from Candahar for the destruction of the enemy's forts in the Urghundab Valley. Served with General Nott's force at Candahar (Medal), advance and re-capture of Ghuznee (Medal), Cabool (Medal).

5 Lieut.Colonel Evelyn was present at the defence of Kulafat in 1854. He was appointed by the British Government to serve under General Cannon with the Staff of the Turkish Army, in which he received the rank of Keimahan. He accompanied the Allied expedition to the Crimea, and was present in the battles of Alma, Balaklava, and Inkerman; in the trenches before Sebastopol, and at the defence of Eupatoria. Received the honorary rank of Lieut.Colonel in the British Army, 23rd Oct. 1857 (Medal and four Clasps for the Crimea, Turkish Medal).

6 Captain Bellew served in the Pindarree war, and was present at the surrender of Ajmeer and Kunmulnair, storming the town, bombardment and surrender of the fort of Madpoorajpore, attack and capture of the fort of Lamba Rajesthan; was employed against the Hill Tribes of the Lurka Kholes; served during the first Burmese war (Medal) as Military Secretary to Brigadier General Morrison, and was present at the affairs of Padirah and Mahatee, and storm and capture of the fortified heights of Arracan.

Sussex.—1 The Duke of Richmond joined the army in Portugal, on the 24th July 1810, as Aide de Camp and Assistant Military Secretary to the Duke of Wellington, with whom he remained until

War Services of the Officers of the Militia. 654

the close of the war in 1814, and was present in all the skirmishes, affairs, general actions, and sieges, which took place during that period, amongst which were the battles of Busaco and Fuentes d'Onor, storming of Ciudad Rodrigo, storming of Badajoz, battles of Salamanca, Vittoria, and the Pyrenees, the first storming of San Sebastian, action at Vera, and battle of Orthes. He was sent home with duplicate Dispatches of the battle of Salamanca, and the capture of Astorga by the Spaniards; and with the Dispatches of Vera and the entrance of the army into France. In Jan. 1814, being desirous of obtaining a practical knowledge of Regimental duty in the field, he left the Duke of Wellington's Staff to join the first battalion of his Regt., the 52nd Light Infantry, and was present with it in the battle of Orthes, where he was severely wounded in the chest by a musket-ball, which has never been extracted. At the end of 1814, he was appointed Aide de Camp to the Prince of Orange, and was with him in the battles of Quatre Bras and Waterloo;—after the Prince of Orange was wounded, the Duke of Richmond joined the Duke of Wellington as Aide de Camp, and remained with his Grace during the remaining part of that campaign. His Grace has received the War Medal with eight Clasps.

2 Captain St. Clair served with the Bombay Horse Artillery in the campaign of 1839-40, in Affghanistan, and was present at the storm and capture of Ghuznee (Medal), and occupation of Cabool; also at the storming of Khujjuck.

Tyrone.—1 Major Caulfield served with the Coldstream Guards in the trenches before Sebastopol from Jan. 1855 until a few days before the fall of the town, and was present at the attack on the enemy's works on the 18th June (Medal and Clasp).

The King's Own.—1 Captain Gray served in the 7th Dragoon Guards with the expedition against the insurgent Boers beyond the Orange River, and was present in an affair on the 20th April 1845. Served also throughout the Kaffir war of 1846-7 (Medal).

2 Quartermaster White served with the 50th Regt. the Gwalior campaign, and was present at the battle of Punniar (Bronze Star). Served also the Sutlej campaign of 1845-46, including the battles of Moodkee, Ferozeshah, Aliwal, and Sobraon—at Sobraon he carried the Queen's colour (Medal and three Clasps). Has also a Medal for Meritorious Services.

3 Assist.Surgeon Hayes served in the Crimea during the siege and fall of Sebastopol (Medal and Clasp).

The Queen's Own.—4 Captain Wallack served the Sutlej campaigns 1845-46 in the 9th Regt., including the battles of Moodkee, Ferozeshah, and Sobraon (Medal and two Clasps).

Warwick.—1 Major Barnard was wounded in the head on the 19th July 1847, when engaged in action with the rebel natives at Wanganui, in New Zealand.

3 Captain Vaughton served with the 90th Light Infantry at the siege of Sebastopol from 2nd Dec. 1854 to 19th July 1855, and was present at the repulse of the Russian sortie on the night of the 22nd March, in which he commanded a detachment of the 90th; was also at the taking of the Quarries on the 7th June, and attack of the Redan on the 18th June (Medal and Clasp).

Westmeath.—1 Captain Gardiner served on the Staff of Colonel Outram, and in command of a detachment of the 17th Regt. in the Southern Mahratta campaign of 1844-5, and was present at all the operations of the Light Field Force, including the capture of Gotea, 21st, and of Munohur Stockades and Fort, 25th Jan. 1845; at the latter he led the Forlorn Hope, and was severely wounded. Of his party of sixteen men, four were killed and nine wounded. Received the thanks of the Governor in Council of Bombay, and those of the Commander in Chief in India, in General Orders, for his services.

Wexford.—1 Captain Newport served with the 39th Regt. upwards of 20 years, and in the Peninsula was employed as Adjutant to the Light Brigade under Major Gen. Crawfurd in all its movements, opposed to the Corps of Marshal Regnier on the memorable junction of Lord Hill's Division with the Main Army on the Sierra of Busaco: he was present at the battle of Busaco, retreat to the Lines of Torres Vedras, expulsion of Marshal Massena and his army from Portugal, capture of the fortresses of Campo Mayor and Olivença, first siege of Badajoz, battle of Albuhera, surprise and capture of Marshal Gerard's Division at Aroyo de Molino; and the second siege of Badajoz (War Medal with two Clasps for Busaco and Albuhera).

Wicklow.—1 Captain Howard served the Eastern campaign of 1854-55 with the 44th Regiment, including the battles of Alma and Balaklava, and siege of Sebastopol (Medal and Clasps).

Wiltshire.—1 Captain Persse served with the 90th Lt. Infantry in the Crimea from 4th Dec. 1854 to 25th Feb. 1855 and has the Medal with Clasp for Sebastopol.

York.—1 Captain Willan served throughout the Sutlej campaign of 1845-46, and was present at the battle of Ferozeshah (Medal).

3 Captain Balguy served as a Lieutenant in the 6th Regt. in the Kaffir war of 1846-47 (Medal), the latter part of which he was selected to organize and command a mounted force of 80 men of the regiment. Served as Captain of the Light Company of the 4th Regt. in the Eastern campaign of 1854 (Medal and three Clasps for Alma, Inkerman, and Sebastopol).

4 Captain Armytage served with the 6th Regt. in the Kaffir war of 1846-7, at the close of which he was appointed Superintendent of the military village of Woburn, on the immediate frontier of the colony. He served also through the Kaffir war of 1850-51-52, and was severely wounded on the 28th Jan. 1852.

5 Colonel Hind served with the 45th Regt. in the Kaffir war of 1846-7 (Medal).

6 Major Dowker served as Adjutant of the 6th Regt. in the Kaffir war of 1846-47 (Medal).

7 Captain Robson was present with the Buffs at the battle of Punniar, 29th Dec. 1843, and has received the Bronze Star.

8 Lieut. Nicholson served the Waterloo campaign with the 14th Regt., including the taking of Cambray.

9 Captain Lamb served in the Eastern campaign of 1854-55, including the battle of Inkerman,

siege of Sebastopol, sortie on 26th Oct., and capture of the Rifle Pits on 19th April, and assaults of the Redan on 18th June and 8th Sept. (Medal and two Clasps, Knight of the Legion of Honor, and 5th Class of the Medjidie).

10 Captain Croker served with a detachment of the 6th Regt. sent from Bombay in 1837 against the rebels in Canara. Served in the Kaffir war of 1846-47 (was acting Adjutant in the Trans Kei Expedition); also in that of 1850-52 (Medal),—at the commencement of which he was appointed Field Adjutant,—in July 1851 acting Brigade Major, and in Feb. 1852 D.A.Q.M.G. of the 1st Brigade: was engaged in all the principal affairs of the war; five times noticed in General Orders, and repeatedly in Dispatches.

11 Captain Hewett served with the 20th Regt. in the Crimea from 20th May 1855, including the siege and fall of Sebastopol, and affair of the 18th June; was also at the capture of Kinbourn (Medal and Clasp).

12 Captain Hammond served in Affghanistan in 1842-3. The Persian Campaign of 1856-7, accompanied the expedition to Borazjoon, and present during the night attack and battle of Kooshab where he commanded an escort to one of the advanced batteries (Medal and Clasp).

www.ingramcontent.com/pod-product-compliance
Lightning Source LLC
Chambersburg PA
CBHW021821220426
43663CB00005B/97